CSf	San Francisco Public Library	CStb	Santa Barbara Public Library
CSfCP	The Society of California Pioneers Library, San Francisco	CStbS	University of California, Santa Barbara, Library
CSfCSM	State Division of Mines and Geology Library, San Francisco	CStcl	Santa Clara Public Library
CSfCW	San Francisco College for Women Library, San Francisco	CStclU	University of Santa Clara Library, Santa Clara
CSfGG	Golden Gate College Library, San Francisco	CSterCL	Santa Cruz County Public Library, Santa Cruz
CSfMI	Mechanics' Institute Library, San Francisco	CStmo	Santa Monica Public Library
CSfP	Pacific-Union Club Library, San Francisco	CSto	Stockton-San Joaquin County Library, Stockton
CSfSC	Sierra Club Library, San Francisco	CStoC	University of the Pacific Library, Stockton (formerly College of the Pacific)
CSfSO	Standard Oil Company of California Library, San Francisco	CStr	Santa Rosa Public Library
		CStrCL	Sonoma County Free Library, Santa Rosa
CSfSt	San Francisco State College Library, San Francisco	CStrJC	Santa Rosa Junior College Library, Santa Rosa
CSfU	University of San Francisco Library, San Francisco	CSuLas	Lassen County Free Library, Susanville
		CTur	Turlock Public Library
CSfWF-H	Wells Fargo Bank, History Room, Library, San Francisco	CTurS	Stanislaus State College Library, Turlock
		CU	University of California Library, Berkeley
CSj	San Jose Public Library	CU-A	—— University of California Library, Davis
CSjC	San Jose State College Library, San Jose		
CSjCL	Santa Clara County Free Library, San Jose	CU-B	—— Bancroft Library, Berkeley
		CU-Law	—— Law Library, Berkeley
CSlu	San Luis Obispo Public Library	CUk	Ukiah Public Library
CSluCL	San Luis Obispo County Free Library, San Luis Obispo	CUpl	Upland Public Library
		CV	Vallejo Public Library
CSmH	Henry E. Huntington Library, San Marino	CViCL	Tulare County Free Library, Visalia
CSmat	San Mateo Public Library	CVtCL	Ventura County Free Library, Ventura
CSmatC	College of San Mateo Library, San Mateo	CVtP	Ventura County Pioneer Museum, Ventura
CSmyS	St. Mary's College Library, St. Mary's		
CSoCL	Tuolumne County Free Library, Sonora	CVtV	Ventura College Library, Ventura
CSr	San Rafael Public Library	CWeT	Trinity County Free Library, Weaverville
CSrCL	Marin County Free Library, San Rafael	CWh	Whittier Public Library
CSrD	Dominican College Library, San Rafael	CWhC	Whittier College Library, Whittier
CSt	Stanford University Libraries, Stanford	CWiwCL	Glenn County Free Library, Willows
CSta	Santa Ana Public Library	CWoY	Yolo County Free Library, Woodland
CStaC	Santa Ana College Library, Santa Ana	CYcCL	Sutter County Free Library, Yuba City
CStaCL	Orange County Free Library, Orange (formerly in Santa Ana)	CYrS	Siskiyou County Free Library, Yreka

OUT-OF-STATE

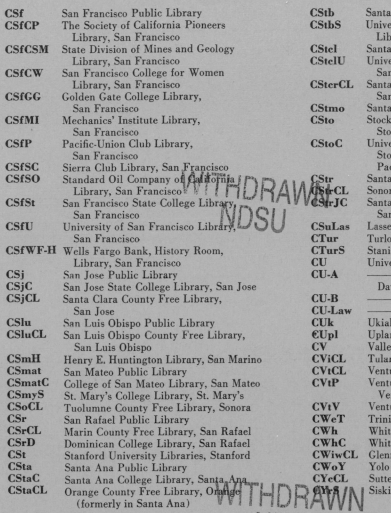

AU	University of Alabama, University	NHi	New York Historical Society, New York
CaBViPA	Provincial Archives, Victoria, British Columbia	NIC	Cornell University, Ithaca
		NN	New York Public Library
Co	Colorado State Library, Denver	NbHi	Nebraska State Historical Society, Lincoln
CoD	Denver Public Library		
CoU	University of Colorado, Boulder	NcU	University of North Carolina, Chapel Hill
CtY	Yale University, New Haven	NdU	University of North Dakota, Grand Forks
GEU	Emory University, Atlanta	NjN	Newark Public Library
GU	University of Georgia, Athens	NjR	Rutgers University, New Brunswick
HHi	Hawaiian Historical Society, Honolulu	NvHi	Nevada State Historical Society, Reno
IC	Chicago Public Library	NvU	University of Nevada, Reno
ICN	Newberry Library, Chicago	ODa	Dayton Public Library and Museum and Montgomery County Library
IHi	Illinois State Historical Library, Springfield		
		OHi	Ohio State Historical Society, Columbus
In	Indiana State Library, Indianapolis	OU	Ohio State University, Columbus
InI	Indianapolis Public Library	OrU	University of Oregon, Eugene
KHi	Kansas State Historical Society, Topeka	PHi	Historical Society of Pennsylvania, Philadelphia
KU	University of Kansas, Lawrence		
KyU	University of Kentucky, Lexington	T	Tennessee State Library, Nashville
MHi	Massachusetts Historical Society, Boston	TMC	Cossitt Reference Library, Memphis
MWA	American Antiquarian Society, Worcester	TxU	University of Texas, Austin
MdHi	Maryland Historical Society, Baltimore	UHi	Utah State Historical Society, Salt Lake City
MiD	Detroit Public Library		
MiD-B	—— Burton Historical Collection	UPB	Brigham Young University, Provo
MoHi	Missouri State Historical Society, Columbia	UU	University of Utah, Salt Lake City
		ViU	University of Virginia, Charlottesville
MoKU	University of Kansas City, Kansas City	ViW	College of William and Mary, Williamsburg
MoS	St. Louis Public Library		
MoSHi	Missouri Historical Society, St. Louis	WHi	State Historical Society of Wisconsin, Madison
MoSU	St. Louis University, St. Louis		
N	New York State Library, Albany	WM	Milwaukee Public Library

CALIFORNIA LOCAL HISTORY

CALIFORNIA LOCAL HISTORY

A Bibliography and
Union List of Library Holdings

SECOND EDITION
REVISED AND ENLARGED

Edited by
MARGARET MILLER ROCQ
for the
California Library Association

STANFORD UNIVERSITY PRESS
STANFORD, CALIFORNIA
1970

An earlier edition was published in 1950 under the title
California Local History: A Centennial Bibliography,
edited by Ethel Blumann and Mabel W. Thomas.

Stanford University Press
Stanford, California
Copyright © 1950 and 1970 by the Board of Trustees of the
Leland Stanford Junior University
Printed in the United States of America
ISBN 0-8047-0716-2
LC 70-97912

Dedicated to
the late
Helen Harding Bretnor
whose quiet resourcefulness was the
final authority for the answers to the
historical and bibliographical
quandaries

Contents

Introductory Remarks

In an enlightened growing society, whether services are given or received, there is the desire that services undergo continuous progress. With *California Local History: A Bibliography*, Second Edition, the accomplishments, on behalf of research, not only have provided leadership but have stimulated the confidence that, with knowledge and determination, progress results in excellence. The realization of this confidence is largely due to the vision and the initiative of the Regional Resources Coordinating Committee, now the Research Resources Coordinating Committee, of the California Library Association. High praise must be given to the committee members who gave most generously of their time and effort to ensure that this bibliography became a reality. Sincere gratitude and congratulations for work well done have been earned by the committee members.

We have in California a diversity of life ranging from big-city urbanity to the rural life of areas far removed from the city; we have vast natural resources and advanced educational facilities. Contributions such as this bibliography are of inestimable value in providing us with the materials relating to the history of our state.

There is nothing stronger than the force of conviction. It was conviction that this bibliography would be of value that resulted in its successful completion. The publication *California Local History: A Bibliography* is an outstanding accomplishment of the California Library Association, culminating in 1969. All is not complete, however, as local history is never final, but continues and must be recorded in bibliographical form. Thus the Research Resources Coordinating Committee continues its work to provide the next chapter in California local history.

PHYLLIS I. DALTON, *President*
California Library Association, 1969

Preface

The year 1950 witnessed the centennial celebration of California's entry into the Union and, at the same time, it also saw the publication of a unique reference tool designed for the writers, booksellers, historians, and librarians of the state —*California Local History: A Centennial Bibliography*, compiled by the California Library Association Committee on Local History. The idea for such a work originated with the Reference Librarians Council of the San Francisco Bay Region, which initially planned to develop, in preparation for the Centennial years, a checklist of county and local histories held by member libraries. Later the scope of the project was enlarged, making it statewide, and ninety-eight California libraries contributed their holdings to this endeavor. Soon after its publication the first edition, despite its many limitations, became what is probably the most widely used bibliographical reference work for the study of California local history.

It was in the spring of 1957 that the Northern Division of the California Library Association's Regional Resources Coordinating Committee first considered the possibility of compiling a supplement to the original edition. A small subcommittee was appointed to explore the idea. After studying its report, the parent Committee determined that sufficient new material was available to make the preparation of a ten-year supplement desirable. (Later this decision was to be changed because of the quantity of new items received, and a second edition was authorized.) By 1958, Margaret Miller Rocq, the just-retired chief librarian of the Standard Oil Company of California, had agreed to be the Chairman of the Subcommittee which would prepare the supplement. Subsequently she was also appointed the editor. In 1959 the first of several letters was sent to the ninety-eight original contributors plus an additional two hundred and ninety other California librarians, asking them to participate in the project. They were requested to list their holdings of materials included in the first edition as well as to indicate any new titles they had acquired in the field. At the same time, some two hundred letters were sent to selected out-of-state libraries likely to have holdings in the field of California local history, asking them to participate in the project by indicating their holdings of California county and regional histories. Thus the supplement could indicate locations throughout the nation for these works.

The first edition apparently had proved to be a most valuable tool, since the response from the various libraries was rather overwhelming. The cards started pouring into the California Historical Society headquarters, the Society earlier having generously offered the project a permanent home. As the cards arrived, it became obvious that volunteer labor would not be sufficient to see the project through to completion. Therefore in mid-1961 the California Library Association underwrote the employment of a paid assistant to aid Mrs. Rocq. And, as the project neared its final completion, a second assistant was temporarily hired. These two are the only persons who received any financial remuneration. At about this same time, the first of a series of "volunteer" work parties was initiated (composed of members of Mrs. Rocq's Local History Subcommittee along with some of the members of the Regional Resources Coordinating Committee) to help in the checking involved in such a compilation. As the work progressed, a pattern of monthly Saturday afternoon work parties evolved, where a small group of librarians met regularly for more than five years to work on this monumental undertaking.

Though it has become a cliché in some library circles to say that all bibliographies and/or union lists such as this are obsolete before they are published, we feel this is an invalid criticism when the object is to compile and readily make available to the public a listing, with locations, of such a rich store of historical materials as does this bibliography. For, regardless of the fact that some libraries in the state were unable to participate in the project, the second edition of this Bibliography does contain some 17,000 items, published before 1961, concerned with California local history, as opposed to the 5,342 items appearing in the first edition. In its own way, it appears to be a landmark in the field of local history bibliography, since apparently no other state's local history has been the subject of such a comprehensive work in a first edition, let alone a second.

As those who are familiar with the first edition will recognize, the format and style of this edition are much the same. Though it might have been preferable to have made some major changes in compiling the second edition, it seemed logical to follow the original pattern, since the project originally started as a supplement. By the time it was realized that a second edition rather than just a supplement was in order, the committee had made the basic decisions which committed the editor to the present format. Because the project was made possible through the voluntary efforts of so many, it did not seem feasible to redo much of the work that had already been done, thus further delaying the publication date. However, it should be pointed out to all users of the Bibliography that an early decision by the committee to prepare a more comprehensive index did considerably delay the completion date of the project.

The list of those who have worked on the Bibliography at one time or another is too long to enumerate here. However, the Subcommittee, as listed in the Editor's Foreword, includes those who have made a substantial contribution. As the Bibliography neared completion, the committee was saddened by the death of one of its most cherished and hardworking members, Helen Harding Bretnor, and it is with great affection that the Bibliography is dedicated to her memory.

Obviously a bibliography such as this one would not have seen the light of day without the herculean effort of its editor. Margaret Rocq has unstintingly given of herself and has worked far harder than anyone should expect of someone who is supposedly retired. All those who have any interest whatsoever in California history will forever be in her debt. As the long-time chairman of the Northern Division of the Regional Resources Coordinating Committee, I personally am in a position to have observed her incredible devotion to the project. Happily, Mrs. Rocq was fortunate to have the assistance of two specialists in the field: Helen Bruner, former librarian of the Sutro Library and a member of the Committee that compiled the first edition; and James Abajian, Librarian of the California Historical Society. Without their knowledge of California history, and that of Helen Bretnor, this Bibliography would not be as accurate or as complete.

Hopefully, the cooperative efforts of so many libraries and librarians again will have produced a work that will prove indispensable to the historians, writers, booksellers, and librarians concerned with California history both within the state and throughout the world.

JANE WILSON, *Chairman, 1960–66*
Northern Division,
Regional Resources
Coordinating Committee,
California Library Association

Editor's Foreword

The second, revised, edition of this Bibliography, like the first edition, is a "composite and co-operative work built up by California librarians." One hundred and seventy-seven California libraries and fifty-three out-of-state libraries contributed a listing of their California local history holdings. The cooperating libraries include state, county, public, university and college, historical society, museum, and a few special libraries. The majority of the libraries represented in the first edition also contributed new material to the second edition. Among the large libraries that increased their contributions substantially are the California Historical Society Library, the Henry E. Huntington Library, and the Library of the University of California, Los Angeles. Users should note that a few of the nonpublic libraries represented have restrictions on the use of their library materials.

The second edition has been expanded to include books, pamphlets, and other publications issued since 1949 and, equally important, publications omitted from the first edition. Local history materials comprise not only city and county histories ("mug books"), city and county directories, and Great Registers, but also histories of social movements, of industry and business; biographies of prominent and notorious men and women; journals of pioneers; and records of fraternal societies, clubs, schools, Chambers of Commerce, and other organizations.

In an effort to keep the Bibliography to a manageable size, the following categories are omitted: fiction; poetry; cookbooks; books in the field of natural science; journeys or voyages to California, with the exception of some of local interest and of a few early explorers; almanacs; broadsides; psalters; juvenile books; single maps and pictures; school and college catalogs issued after 1942; newspapers and periodicals, except special numbers; periodical articles, except reprints from journals other than those of historical societies; federal and state publications, with some exceptions; and purely administrative reports of local governmental bodies. Manuscripts, except those held by the smaller libraries, are omitted because listings are more appropriately found in other sources, some of which are listed in the BIBLIOGRAPHICAL REFERENCES.

Works dealing with a number of individual localities, and serial publications like *California Bluebook*, are listed only in the division CALIFORNIA STATEWIDE, and should be considered as supplementary to the county lists.

All the entries in the second edition were submitted by the contributing libraries, with the exception of some titles and holdings from Greenwood's *California Imprints, 1832–1862: a Bibliography*. Most of the entries in the first edition appear also in the second. Those omitted are either outside the scope of the second edition or were not reported by any library. New publications added were limited to imprint dates between 1949 and 1960, with the exception of a few outstanding titles published subsequently.

The expanded divisions are: Directories, General References, and Bibliographical References. The GENERAL REFERENCES divisions show the greatest expansion and contain a wealth of new material. Many of the added publications are pamphlets and leaflets issued by associations, societies, fraternal organizations, and business firms. The INDEX also was expanded to include personal and place names appearing in the titles, and some subject entries. A new feature is the list of COLLECTIONS, which represents a sampling of this type of resource available in libraries of the state. This section includes special indexes, historical collections of telephone directories, collections of pamphlets, clippings, pictures, and maps on special subjects. Because public libraries usually hold maps, pictures, and clippings concerning their own localities, collections of this type are omitted.

Since the second edition is a revision of the first, and since most of the titles of the first are included in the second, the bibliographical style of the second edition, including punctuation and capitalization, follows that of the first.

The cooperative and composite nature of the work has resulted in unavoidable bibliographical variations and undoubtedly some omissions and errors. One of the editorial problems was assignment of equivocal titles to a county or other locality, which often had to be arbitrary; an example of this is the Pious Fund of the Californias, which is listed under San Francisco. Probably one of the most common omissions is that some titles will fail to show all possible library symbols because the final list could not be checked by every library. Although we examined a majority of the Bibliography's titles in the Library of the California Historical Society and other San Francisco Bay Area libraries, time and distance did not allow personal checking of all the items listed. We agree with the EDITORS' FOREWORD of the first edition, which states: "Few bibliographies are ever complete ... Moreover, it should not be forgotten that

each library's contributions are but selections from its holdings. The local library should still be the richest source for the history of its own region."

Members of the Subcommittee on California Local History wish to thank the former chairmen, Elmer Grieder and Jane Wilson, of the Regional Resources Coordinating Committee, for their support and encouragement. Special thanks go to Jane Wilson for her continuing devotion and hours of work over the years of her chairmanship. We also acknowledge with gratitude the assistance of James Abajian and the staff of the California Historical Society, and the Society's courtesy in providing a convenient working space. Our thanks are due also to Robert Greenwood (Talisman Press) for permission to use some supplementary titles and library symbols from his *California Imprints*. I personally thank the members of the Subcommittee and the working members of the Regional Resources Coordinating Committee, who assisted in the compilation and the endless checking of the Bibliography and its Index, and Vera Plescia, who was my right-hand assistant throughout its preparation.

MARGARET MILLER ROCQ

CALIFORNIA LOCAL HISTORY SUBCOMMITTEE MEMBERS

James de T. Abajian   Ralph W. Johnson
Richard F. Bernard   Dorothy Jones
Helen H. Bretnor   Allan R. Ottley
Helen M. Bruner   Mary Helen Peterson
Dolores Cadell   Margaret D. Uridge
Herbert W. Drummond   Margo W. Westgaard
Robert D. Harlan   Jane Wilson
Eugenia E. Ironside   Lyle H. Wright

Margaret M. Rocq, *Chairman*

Explanatory Notes

I. Arrangement.
  A. COUNTIES.
     The basic arrangement is by counties in al-
     phabetical order, subdivided as follows:
     1. COUNTY HISTORIES.
        Multi-county histories are listed only
        under the first county named in the title,
        but each of the counties included is
        indexed.
     2. GREAT REGISTERS.
     3. DIRECTORIES.
        City and county directories only. Cham-
        ber of Commerce, newspaper, govern-
        ment, and special business directories
        are listed with GENERAL REFERENCES.
        Multi-city and multi-county directories
        are listed only under the first city or
        county named in the title, but each city
        or county included is indexed.
        Subdivisions are:
        a. County. (Arrangement by dates cov-
           ered.)
        b. Principal cities. (Arrangement by
           dates covered.)
        c. OTHER CITIES AND TOWNS. (Alpha-
           betical arrangement by name of city
           or town.)
     4. GENERAL REFERENCES.
        All materials about that county not spe-
        cifically designated as belonging to one
        of the above categories.
        Subdivisions are:
        a. County in general, including towns
           not separately listed.
        b. Principal cities, by name.
  B. REGIONAL WORKS.
     Publications dealing with several individ-
     ual localities within a group of counties.
     Subdivisions are:
     1. Northern and Central California.
     2. Southern California.
     3. The Central Valley.
     4. The Sierra Nevada.

  C. CALIFORNIA STATEWIDE.
     Publications dealing with a group of indi-
     vidual localities in more than one region,
     as well as with the state as a whole.

  D. COLLECTIONS. (For arrangement see expla-
     nation at beginning of that section.)
     The section has a separate index immedi-
     ately following it, as the items are not in-
     cluded in the general INDEX.

  E. BIBLIOGRAPHICAL REFERENCES.
     Selected reference books, the titles of which
     are not included in the INDEX.

  F. INDEX.
     Editors; translators; illustrators; Califor-
     nia printers and publishers before 1900;
     other personal names; place names and a
     few subjects. All entries are indexed except
     those in COLLECTIONS and BIBLIOGRAPHICAL
     REFERENCES. A separate index to COLLEC-
     TIONS follows that section. Special char-
     acteristics are:

     1. City and county departments and bu-
        reaus, except public libraries and
        schools, are grouped under a subheading
        "Government." For example: Berkeley.
        City planning commission is indexed
        under "Berkeley. Government."

     2. California missions and ranchos are
        listed alphabetically under the heading
        "Missions" and "Ranchos," respectively.

II. Form of Entry.

    A. The form of author and title entry is based on library usage and generally follows the American Library Association, *Cataloging Rules*. Foreign personal names are therefore entered and indexed according to ALA rules. Exceptions are:

        1. Law cases are entered under name of contestants (i.e., Jones, Edwin vs. Miller, James) unless the title is an opinion of the judge or decision of the court, in which cases they are entered under the name of the judge or the court.

        2. Great Registers are entered under the name of each county, with the title: *Index to the Great Register of ——— County*.

        3. After the name of a city the word "California" is omitted in author entries and imprints, to save space.

    B. In cases of inconsistency in entries for titles contributed, the form of entry selected was that used by the Bancroft Library, or if the title was not in Bancroft, the entry used by the California State Library or the University of California, Los Angeles.

III. Symbols of Contributing Libraries.

    A. The location symbols following the titles are those used in the Library of Congress National Union Catalog.

    B. Location symbols are used under all entries, with the following exceptions:

        1. CALIFORNIA STATEWIDE, locations listed for only a few rare items.

        2. BIBLIOGRAPHICAL REFERENCES, no locations shown.

        3. Widely held items: instead of locations, one of the following phrases, "Available in many California libraries," or "Available in many libraries." (However, all location symbols, regardless of number, are given for county histories and directories.)

    C. Directories, reports, etc. covering a number of years: a library symbol with no specific dates following indicates that the library holds the complete set.

IV. Abbreviations and Signs.

    Abbreviations are used chiefly in the imprints of the titles listed and in the INDEX. Standard abbreviations are used for months, regions, states, and cities, and do not appear in the following list.

[ ] = information supplied from sources other than the title page.

? = unverified information.

( ) = When enclosing first names or initials in author entries, indicates the name of a firm other than that of architects, engineers, printers, or publishers.

(!) or *sic* = quotation literally given though it appears to be a misstatement.

Abp.	Archbishop
acad.	academy
admin.	administration
agric.	agriculture
Am.	American
assoc.	association
bd.	board
bind.	binding
bk.	book
Bp.	Bishop
bro., bros.	brother, brothers
bul.	bulletin
bur.	bureau
c.	copyright
co., cos.	company, companies
col.	colored
comp.	compiled, compiler
Cong.	Congress
corp.	corporation
dept.	department
diagrs.	diagrams
div.	division
doc.	document
ed., eds.	edition, editor, editors
educ.	education
eng.	engineering
enl.	enlarged
facsim.	facsimile
fold.	folded
front.	frontispiece
geol.	geological
govt.	government
hist.	historical
illus.	illustrations, illustrator
imp.	imperfect
inc.	incorporated
incl.	including
inst.	institute
internat.	international
introd.	introduction
jl.	journal
jr.	junior
l.	leaf, leaves
lib.	library
litho.	lithograph, lithographed, lithographer
ltd.	limited

mag.	magazine
mimeo.	mimeographed
misc.	miscellaneous
mo.	month, monthly
ms., mss.	manuscript, manuscripts
n.d.	no date of publication
no., nos.	number, numbers
n.p.	no place of publication
off.	office
p.	page, pages
photo. copy	photographic copy
photos.	photographs
pl.	plates
port., ports.	portrait, portraits
pref.	preface
print.	printed, printer, printing
priv. print.	privately printed
priv. pub.	privately published
pseud.	pseudonym

pub.	public, published, publisher, publication
q.	quarterly
reprint.	reprinted
rev.	revised
ser.	series
sess.	session
soc.	society
sr.	senior
suppl.	supplement
supt.	superintendent
tr.	translated, translator
trans.	transactions
typew.	typewritten
univ.	university
unp.	unpaged
v.	volume, volumes
v.d.	various dates
v.p.	various paging

CALIFORNIA LOCAL HISTORY

A Bibliography and
Union List of Library Holdings

ALAMEDA COUNTY

(Created in 1853 from portions of Contra Costa and Santa Clara counties)

COUNTY HISTORIES

1. Baker, Joseph Eugene, ed. Past and present of Alameda county, California... Chicago, Clarke, 1914. 2 v. illus., ports., map. v.2 contains biographical sketches.
C CAla CAlaC CB CBb CFS CHi CL CLU CLob CO COMC CRic CSf CSfCP CSfCSM CSfMI CSmH CStoC CU-B CtY MoSHi MWA NN NHi WHi

2. Guinn, James Miller. History of the state of California and biographical record of Oakland and en-virons... L.A., Historic record co. [c1907] 2 v. ports.
C CAla CAlaC CB CBu CHi CL CLCM CLCo CLO CLU CMartC CMont CNa CO (v.2 only) COMC CSf CSfCP CSfCSM CSfCW CSfU CSj CSmH CSmat CStclU CStoC CU-B CoD MWA

3. Halley, William. The centennial year book of Alameda county, California...to which are added bio-graphical sketches of prominent pioneers and public men ... Oakland, Author, 1876. 586 p. illus., ports. "Bio-graphical": p. 529–571.
C CAla CAlaC CB CBb CCH CFS CHi CL CLCo CLSM CLSU CLU CLiv CLod CMartC CO COMC CSf CSfCP CSfCSM CSfCW CSfWF-H CSmH CSt CStclU CStoC CU-B CoD CtY IC ICN MWA MiD-B N NIC NN NHi NvHi UPB

4. —— Index...comp. by Mabel W. Thomas and Ethel Blumann. Oakland pub. lib., 1947. 140 l. Typew.
CO CStclU

5. Historical records survey. California. ...Ala-meda county (Oakland)... S.F., Northern Calif. hist. records survey, 1942. v.2. (Inventory of the county ar-chives of Calif. no. 1) Mimeo. v.1 not published.
C CB CBb CHi CLCM CLCo CLSU CLU CO COMC CSf CSfCP CSmH CSrCL CSt CStclU CU-B CWhC ICN MoS N NN WHi

6. Merritt, Frank Clinton. History of Alameda county, California. Chicago, Clarke, 1928. 2 v. illus., ports. v.2: Biographical.
C CAla CAlaC CB CHi CL CLU CMartC CN CO CSf CSfCSM (v.2 only) CSfU CSj CSmH CSrD CStoC CU-B CtY MWA NN WHi

7. —— Index to volume I, comp. by Marguerite E. Cooley. Produced on a Works progress administration project, sponsored by the Oakland public library. Oak-land, 1939. 223 l. Typew.
C CO

8. [Munro-Fraser, J. P.] History of Alameda county, California...and biographical sketches of early and prominent citizens and representative men... Oak-land, Myron W. Wood, 1883. 1001 p. ports. Preface signed by M. W. Wood and J. P. Munro-Fraser, historian. "Biographical sketches": p. 836–999.
C CAla CAlaC CB CBb CCH CChiS CH CHi CL CLO CLSM CLSU CLgA CLiv CMartC CN CO COMC CP CPa CRic CSf CSfCP CSfCW CSfMI CSfU CSjC CSmH CSt CStclU CSto CStoC CU-B CaBViPA CoD CoU CtY ICN IHi In KHi KU MiD-B MoSHi MWA N NN NHi NvHi

9. Oakland tribune. Alameda county, the Eden of the Pacific...a history of Alameda county from its for-mation to the present... Citizens who have aided the march of progress. [Oakland] 1898. 233 p. illus., ports., map.
C CAlaC CHi CL COHN CSf CSfCP CSfCW CSj CSjC CStoC CU-B Co NN

10. Tays, George, ed. Historical sites and land-marks of Alameda county, California... pub. by Ala-meda county library under the auspices of the Works progress administration, official project number 165-03-6364. Oakland, 1938. 349 l. Mimeo. "Footnotes": p. 308–337. "Authorities": p. 338–349.
C CAla CAlaC CB CHi CLU CMartC CO COMC CRc CRcS CRic CSf CSfCP CSfMI CSjCL CSto CU-B

11. Thompson and West, pub. Official and histori-cal atlas map of Alameda county, California... Oakland, 1878. 170 p. illus., maps. History of Alameda county, California: p. 13–28–1/2.
C CAla CAlaC CB CHi CL CLU CO COMC CSf CSfCP CSmH CU-B CtY NN

12. U.S. Works progress administration. History of rural Alameda county... Produced on a Works pro-gress administration project, official project—165–03–6504...sponsored by Alameda county, California, for the Alameda county library. Prepared under the direction of William E. McCann...[and] Edgar J. Hinkel... Oak-land, 1937. 2 v. Typew. Bibliography: v.2, p. 91–807.
C CAla CAlaC CO CSfU CSmH CU-B

GREAT REGISTER

13. Alameda county. Index to the Great register of the county of Alameda. 1866– Place of publication and title vary.

C has 1867, 1872–80, 1882 (biennially to)–1962. CHi has 1877, 1878 (biennially to)–1896. CL has 1873, 1875–77, 1879, 1882 (biennially to)–1892. CO has 1867, 1876, 1884 (biennially to)–1890, 1894. CSmH has 1880, 1882, 1884, 1886, 1894. CU-B has 1872–73, 1878–79, 1884 (biennially to)–1894, 1904.

DIRECTORIES

14. 1870. Cook & Miller, comp. and pub. Directory of the city of Oakland and county of Alameda, for the year 1870... Oakland, 1870. 200 p.
C CCH CHi CO CU-B

15. 1871/72. County directory publishing co., pub. Alameda and Contra Costa counties... Sacramento, Crocker, 1871. 413 p.   C CHi CO CSf

16. 1876. Paulson, L. L., pub. Hand-book and directory of Alameda county... S.F., Francis & Valentine, 1876. 184 p.   C CHi CLU CSf

17. 1879. McKenney, L. M., & co., pub. McKenney's district directory of Alameda, Contra Costa, San Mateo, Santa Clara, Santa Cruz, San Benito and Monterey counties. 1879. [S.F.? 1879] 510 p.
C CHi CLU CO CSmH CU-B

18. 1889. Oakland city and Alameda county business directory for 1889. A complete business directory of Oakland, California, and all towns in Alameda county... Alameda county directory co. [1889?] 280 p.
CHi CO CSfCP CStrJC

Oakland

19. 1869. Directory of the township and city of Oakland, together with the townships of Brooklyn and Alameda, for the year 1869... Comp. and pub. by B. F. Stilwell. [Oakland, Oakland news off.] 1869 [c1868] 272 p. This is the first Oakland directory.
C CHi CO CSmH CU-B

20. 1872/73–1878/79. Langley, Henry G., comp. and pub. A directory of the city of Oakland and its environs... Oakland, 1872–78. Subtitle varies. Beginning in 1874 include Alameda. 1878/79, include Berkeley and Temescal.

C has 1875/76, 1878/79. CAla has 1878/79. CHi has 1872/73, 1875/76, 1878/79. CLU has 1874/75. CO has 1872/73–1875/76. CSfCP has 1872/73–1875/76. CSfCW has 1872/73, 1875/76. CSmH has 1872/73, 1875/76. CU-B has 1872/73–1875/76.

21. 1876/77–1881/82. D. M. Bishop & co., comp. and pub. Bishop's Oakland directory... Oakland, 1876–81. Include Alameda. Beginning in 1878/79 include Berkeley. Publisher varies: 1881/82, Directory pub. co.

C has 1876/77–1881/82. CAla has 1877/78, 1879/80–1881/82. CHi has 1876/77–1877/78, 1881/82. CLU has 1876/77–1881/82. CO has 1876/77–1881/82. CSmH has 1876/77–1879/80. CU-B has 1876/77–1881/82. NHi has 1877/78. WHi has 1877/78.

22. 1877. Bynon & Sherman, pub. Business directory of Oakland, Alameda and Berkeley. Oakland, Arcade print. house [1877] 91 p.   C CLU

23. 1883/84–1888/89. McKenney directory co., pub. Oakland, Alameda and Berkeley city directory. S.F., 1883–89. None published 1885/86. Title varies. Publisher varies: 1883/84–1886/87, L. M. McKenney & co.
C (1884/85–89) CAla CHi CMartC (1887/88) CO CStrJC CU-B

24. 1889/90– Polk, R. L., & co., pub. Polk's Oakland city directory including Alameda and Berkeley ... Oakland, 1890– None published 1919, 1920, 1929, 1931, 1932, 1936, 1942. Publisher varies: 1890–1906, F. M. Husted; 1907–24, Polk-Husted. Content varies: 1892, 1894, 1900, 1905 include Alameda county. Beginning 1928, include Emeryville and Piedmont.

C has 1891–1918, 1921–28, 1930, 1933–35, 1937–41, 1943. C-S has 1907–08, 1910–11, 1913, 1916. CAla has 1889/90, 1891, 1892, 1894–1918, 1921–28, 1930, 1933–35, 1937–41, 1943. CHi has 1889/90, 1891–1918, 1921–28, 1930, 1933–35, 1937–41, 1943. CL has 1913–14, 1916–18, 1921–28, 1930, 1933–35, 1937–41, 1943. CO has 1891–1918, 1921–28, 1930, 1933–35, 1937–41, 1943. CSfCP has 1891–1918, 1921–28, 1930, 1933–35, 1937–41, 1943. CSfCW has 1922. CSmH has 1892–93, 1896, 1907, 1911. CU-B has 1891–1918, 1921–28, 1930, 1933–35, 1937–41, 1943. MoS has 1899, 1913–18, 1921–25, 1928, 1930, 1933–35, 1937–41. MoSHi has 1908. NHi has 1891–1901. WHi has 1892–93, 1895–96, 1899, 1911, 1917, 1924, 1938, 1943.

25. 1899/1900. Oakland modern directory co. Oakland, Alameda and Berkeley city directory. Oakland, 1899.   CU-B

Other Cities and Towns

26. 1888. Bean's directory of the city of Alameda, Alameda county, Calif. [n.p., 1888?] illus.
CAla CHi CU-B

27. 1893–1904. Husted, F. M., pub. Husted's Alameda and Berkeley directory... Oakland, 1893–1904. Title varies.

C has 1900, 1903. CAla has 1893, 1900, 1903. CHi has 1904. CU-B has 1903.

28. 1923. Berkeley gazette. Berkeley directory, 1923... [Berkeley, 1923] unp. illus., map.   CU-B

29. 1934. Directory publishing co., pub., Berkeley business and professional directory...1934. [Berkeley, 1934]   CU-B

30. 1946. Midwest publishing co., comp. and pub. Eden township directory. S.F., 1946. 156 p.
CHi CO

31. 1950–1951. Sandness, Ina, comp. and pub. Directory of Emeryville, California, 1950–1951. [Berkeley, East bay trade press, 1951?] 113 p.   CB CHi

32. 1925/26– Polk, R. L., & co., pub. Polk's Hayward city directory... S.F., 1925– Title varies: 1925/26, Polk's Hayward directory, embracing San Lorenzo, Mt. Eden and Ashland; 1927/28–1951(?) Polk's Hayward and San Leandro city directory.

C has 1925/26. CH has 1925/26, 1931/32, 1934, 1940, 1946, 1948, 1953, 1956/57, 1959. CHi has 1927/28, 1938, 1940, 1946, 1948, 1951, 1953, 1955, 1956/57, 1959. CL has 1938, 1940, 1946, 1951, 1953, 1955. CO has 1940. CSmat has 1958, 1959.

33. 1946. Midwest publishing co., comp. and pub. Piedmont city directory. S.F., 1946. 84 p.
CHi CU-B

34. 1924. Coast directory co., pub. San Leandro city directory, 1924. Sacramento, 1924. 119 p.   C

35. 1953/54– Polk, R. L. and co., pub. Polk's

San Leandro city directory... S.F., 1954– Preceded by Polk's Hayward and San Leandro city directory.

CH has 1953/54, 1956, 1959. CHi has 1953/54–56, 1959. CL has 1953/54–55. CSmat has 1958–59.

GENERAL REFERENCES

36. Alameda-Contra Costa transit district. A pictorial history of public transportation in the East Bay, commemorating the achievements of the past century and the commencement of operations by the Alameda-Contra Costa transit district. Oakland, 1960. [32] p. illus. (A.C. Transit-times, special issue)   CHi CU-B

37. —— Public transit plan for Alameda-Contra Costa transit district. S.F., De Leuw, Cather & co., 1958. v.p. maps.   CAla

38. Alameda county. Board of education. Course of study in the public schools of the county of Alameda ... 1880– Oakland, Tribune pub. co., 1880–
C has 1897, 1904, 1907–08, 1912, 1915–16, 1918, 1927/28, 1933. CU-B has 1880.

39. —— —— Local history, geography and civics. Alameda county, Cal. [Oakland, Enquirer press, 1902] 18 p. map.   CO

40. —— **Board of public welfare.** Survey of social agencies of Alameda county, California, prepared by Jean Howard McDuffie... ed. by Porter Garnett. Oakland, 1917. 56 p. maps.   CU-B TxU

41. —— **Board of supervisors.** Alameda county, California; farms, orchards, vineyards...by Daniel H. Bradley. [Oakland, c1915] [64] p. illus.
    C CHi CL CLU CSj CU-B

42. —— —— Alameda county, California, U.S.A. ...where industrial opportunity offers a challenge to creative genius...by Mark M. Jones. [Oakland, c1915] 64 p. illus., maps.
    C CAla CHi CL CLU CSfCP CSmH

43. —— —— Alameda county; center of scenic California. [Oakland, c1929] 13 p. illus., col. map.
    CHi CRcS
Other editions followed. C (1950?) CRcS (1950?) CU-B (193–?)

44. —— —— Alameda county fact book, Oakland, Berkeley, Alameda; the East Bay district and its relation to the Panama-Pacific international exposition... [Oakland, Kelley-Davis co. print., 1914?] [24] p. illus.
    CO CU-B OrU

45. —— —— Alameda county government. [Oakland? Inter city print. 1948] 46 p. map.   CHi
Other editions followed. C (1954) CAla (1955?) CHi (1954) COHN (1953, 1958)

46. —— —— Alameda county, the ideal place for your California home... by Henry Anderson Lafler. [Oakland, c1915] [64] p. illus., map.
    C CAla CHi CL CLO CLU CO CRic CSf CSfU CSmH CStmo CU-B CWhC

47. —— —— Directory of manufacturers and wholesalers of metropolitan Oakland area, which includes all of Alameda county, California, 1951– [Oakland] 1951–
C has 1951–52, 1955, 1958. CB has 1955, 1958. CHi has 1958.

48. —— —— Industrial development study of Alameda county, California. Report. Recommendations and findings by a panel of the Urban land institute, Jan. 21–25, 1957. [n.p.] 1957. 59 p.   CAla CH

49. —— —— Name and boundaries of election precincts of the county of Alameda as adopted by the Board of supervisors of said county, July 25, 1892... [Oakland, 1894] 35 p.   CU-B

50. —— —— New supervisorial districts and names and boundaries of the election precincts of the county of Alameda...1896. [Oakland, 1896] 43 p.
    CU-B

51. —— —— **Investigating committee.** Highland-Alameda county hospital investigation report... [Oakland?] 1951. 22 p. Mimeo.   CHi

52. —— **Charters.** Charter of the county of Alameda; adopted November 2, 1926—ratified January 18, 1927. [n.p.] Board of fifteen freeholders, 1927. 14 p.
    CRcS

53. —— —— Same. [with amendments] Oakland, 1954. 16 p.   CAla

54. —— **Commission to the Lewis and Clark centennial exposition.** Alameda county, its industries and environs. [Oakland, R.S. Kitchener, 1905] [32] p. illus., map.   CSmH CU-B

55. —— **Commission to the Louisiana purchase exposition.** Alameda county, its industries and environs. [n.p., c1904] [64] p. illus.   CAla CU-B

56. —— **County clerk.** Instructions to election boards, Alameda co., Cal., 1896. Prepared by Frank C. Jordan, county clerk. [Oakland, Oakland tribune print., 1896] 28 p.   CU-B

57. —— **County planning commission.** Master plan, county of Alameda, state of California. [Alameda, 1958]   CSt

58. —— **Development commission.** Alameda county [a brief outline] Oakland, Tribune press [1941] [24] p. illus., map.   C

59. —— —— Alameda county California "Where every prospect pleases" Where rail and water meet. [Oakland, Curtis-Baum advertising service, 1922] [16] p. illus.   CHi

60. —— **Exposition commission.** Alameda county, a county of progress and prosperity. [n.p., 1915?] [16] p.   NN

61. —— **General exposition commissioners.** Alameda county; its industries and environs. [Oakland, R.S. Kitchener press, c1909] [48] p. illus., map.   CHi

62. —— **Juvenile court and probation dept.** Survey of services to children and youth in southern Alameda county. [n.p., n.d.] 2 v. Processed.   CH

63. —— **Ordinances, etc.** Road law of Alameda county, approved March 30, 1874. [n.p., 1874?] 25 p.
    CU-B

64. —— **Superintendent of schools.** Boundaries of townships and school districts of the county of Alameda. May 1890. Oakland, Journal steam bk. and job print., 1890. 49 p.   CU-B

65. —— —— Railroads in Alameda county. Hayward, 1959. 47 p.   CAla

66. —— **World's fair assoc.** Columbian exposition souvenir of Alameda county, California... Oakland, Tribune pub. co. [1893] 48 p. illus., ports.
    CLU CSmH

67. Alameda county agricultural society. Alameda county agricultural society's annual exhibition...1860... [Alameda] Alameda herald print. [1860] 24 p.   CU-B

68. —— Same. 1861... S.F., Agnew & Deffebach, print., 1861. 24 p.   CU-B

69. Alameda county banking and building asso-

ciation. Prospectus, constitution and by-laws... Brooklyn (East Oakland), Cal. Incorporated January 25, 1877. S.F., W. Johnstone & co., print., 1877. 28 p.   CU-B

70. Alameda county, California... [Oakland, Tribune press, 1940?] [16] p.   CHi

71. Alameda county homeopathic medical society. Constitution and by-laws...as revised at the regular meeting held December 13, 1897. [Oakland, Artistic life print., 1897] 11 p.   CHi

72. Alameda county law suits. [n.p., 1880?–99] 6 v.
                                                              CU-B

73. Alameda county planing mill owners' association. Price list...June 1, 1906... [Oakland, R.S. Kitchener print., 1906?] 8 p.   CU-B

74. Alameda county poultry association. Official catalogue eighth annual exhibition of the...and sixth annual exhibition of the California pigeon club, Oakland, Calif., November 21st–27th, 1911. [Oakland, W. J. McCamman, n.d.] [52] p. illus., ports.   C

75. Alameda county society of architects. Yearbook [of the architectural exhibitions] 1916. [S.F., Print. by Taylor & Taylor, 1916] illus., pl.   CHi CU-B

76. Alameda county taxpayers' association, inc. Alameda county government, an administrative and financial survey... Oakland [1947] 165 l. Mimeo. Louis J. Kroeger, Director of survey.   C CLSU CMont

77. Alancraig, Henel Smith. Codornices village: a study of non-segregated public housing in the San Francisco bay area. [Berkeley, 1953] Thesis (M.A.)—Univ. of Calif., 1953.   CU

78. Albany. Chamber of commerce. Albany, California; the northern gateway to Alameda county. [1937?] 34 p. illus., ports., map.   CO

79. Albany police and fire employees civil service club. The story of the city of Albany, California... [Albany] 1947. 97 p. illus., ports.   CHi CL CU-B

80. Alviso, Valentine et al. vs. Vallestero, Jesus, et al. In the Supreme court of the state of California. Valentine Alviso, et al., plaintiffs and appellants, vs. Jesus Vallestero et al., defendants and respondents. Appellants' points. J. W. Harding, appellants' attorney. [n.p., 1877?] 15 p. Las Pozitas rancho.   CLU

81. Anderson, Kenneth Roderick. An analytical comparison of land used and land zoned for industrial purposes in Alameda county, California. [Berkeley, 1953] Thesis (M.A.)—Univ. of Calif., 1953.   CU

82. Anderson academy, Irvington. Catalogue. 1899/1900– S.F., L. Roesch co., 1900–
CHi has 1899/1900, 1903/04, 1912/13.

83. Baggley, Fanny Elizabeth. The financial development of the East bay district, 1900–1927. [Berkeley, 1934] Thesis (M.A.)—Univ. of Calif., 1934.   CU

84. Bartels, Ronald Earl. The incorporation of the city of Fremont, California: an experiment in municipal government. [Berkeley, 1959] Thesis (M.A.)—Univ. of Calif., 1959.   CU

85. Bartlett, William P. The Livermore valley. Its resources, soil...early history... Livermore, Livermore herald print. off., 1878. 26 p.
                                          CHi CLiv CSmH CU-B

86. Bell, Mary Sloan. Naturalization procedures in California with special reference to Alameda county. [Berkeley, 1923] Thesis (M.A.)—Univ. of Calif., 1923.
                                                              CU

87. Berger, Philip Raymond. A reorganization plan for the government of Alameda county, California. [Berkeley, 1942] Thesis (M.A.)—Univ. of Calif., 1942.
                                                              CU

88. Bernal, Augustine, and Bernal, Huana Higuera vs. Bernal, Juan Pablo, et al. Rancho el Valle de San Jose. Referees' report in the case of Augustine Bernal and Huana Higuera Bernal, his wife, plaintiffs, vs. Juan Pablo Bernal et al., defendants. S.F., Towne & Bacon bk. and job print, 1868.   CSmH

89. Bonfils, Winifred Black. The life and personality of Phoebe Apperson Hearst... S.F., John Henry Nash, 1928. 155 p. port.   CHi CSd CSjC CSlu

90. Bowman, Jacob N. The early Peraltas and Rancho San Antonio. [Berkeley, 1951] 19 l. Typew.
                                                              CU-B

91. —— New Haven and the two Alvarados. [Berkeley, 19–?] 17 l. Typew.   CU-B

92. —— The Peraltas and their houses. S.F., Calif. hist. soc., 1951. 19 p. plans. (Calif. hist. soc. Pam. no. 18)   C CHi CL CLU CSf CSmat CStclU

93. Bunje, E. T. H., Schmitz, F. J., and Penn, H. "Journals of the Bay cities"...1854–1936... Berkeley. Works progress administration, 1936. 90 l. (Cultural contributions of Calif. Bay cities ser.) East bay cities only.   C CSf CSmH CU-B

94. Burgess, R. N., co., San Francisco. Oakland and Antioch railway. [S.F., 19—] [32] p. illus.
                                                      C-S CLU

95. Caine, Glen George. Political action by organized labor in Alameda county, California with special reference to the 1956 election. [Berkeley, 1957] Thesis (M.A.)—Univ. of Calif., 1957.   CU

96. California. Joint highway district no. 13. Broadway low level tunnel; dedication ceremonies, Sunday, December 5th, 1937. [n.p., 1937] [4] p. illus., map.
                                                              CHi

97. —— **University. Bureau of public administration.** Report on proposed park reservations for East bay cities (California), prepared for the Bur. of pub. admin., Univ. of Calif., by Olmsted brothers, landscape architects, and Ansel F. Hall. December, 1930. 40 p. illus.   CAla CHi CLSU CMartC CU-B

98. —— —— **Heller committee for research in social economics.** Cost of living studies. IV. Spending ways of a semi-skilled group. A study of the incomes and expenditures of ninety-eight street-car men's families in the San Francisco east bay region... Berkeley, Univ. of Calif. press, 1931. [295]–366 p. incl. tables. (Univ. of Calif. publications in economics. v.5, no. 5)
                                                  CSf CU CU-B

99. California infantry. 2d brigade. Regulations for Camp Allen: first arrival encampment of the second brigade, California militia. October 6, 1863. Sacramento, Benj. P. Avery, state print., 1863. 26 p.   CSmH

100. California jockey club. Souvenir program, Bay district track, spring meet, 1896. Oakland, 1896. 14 p. illus.   CHi

101. California nursery co., Niles. [Descriptive catalogs] 1886/87– [n.p.] 1887–
CHi has 1886/87, 1890–91, 1893/94, 1906/07–1907/08, 1911/12–1915/16, 1917/19, 1919, 1926, 1928–29.

102. California taxpayers' association. The government of Alameda county, California... [L.A.] 1933. 4 v. (Its Assoc. study no. 257) Mimeo.

C CLSM CLSU CLU CU-B

103. —— Report on personnel administration, Alameda county... [Oakland] 1933. 73 l. CU-B

104. Candrian, Herman Anton. Candrian's A to Z street guide, Oakland... Alameda, Berkeley, Emeryville, Piedmont, Richmond, San Leandro... S.F., Kohnke print. co., c1935. 118 p. CHi

105. —— Candrian's street number guide. [1924, 1926] S.F. [1924–26] 1 v. CU-B

106. —— Same, with title: Candrian's double indexed street number guide ... Berkeley, Sather Gate bk. shop [n.d.] 96 p. C C-S CHi

107. Carleton, Mary Tennent. A sketch of Alameda county with special reference to Berkeley, dating from 1859 as seen through a study of the life and family of Napoleon Byrne. 10 l. Typew. CHi

108. Carlson, Toma Elizabeth (Akers). Mexican ranchos in the vicinity of Mission San José [Berkeley, 1931] 198 l. maps. Thesis (M.A.)—Univ. of Calif., May 1931. "The fortunes of three rancheros, Agustín Alviso and Tomás Pacheco, owners of El Potrero de los Cerritos rancho and José de Jesús Vallejo, the owner of El Arroyo de la Alameda rancho, have been traced through the court records in this thesis." C CU-B

109. Carpentier, Reuben S., vs. Montgomery, Z. et al. In the Supreme court of the United States. Brief for appellees. Henry P. Irving of counsel. [n.p., 18—] 32 p. Rancho San Antonio suit. CHi

110. Castlewood country club, Pleasanton. Castlewood country club; former estate of the late Mrs. Phoebe A. Hearst. [S.F., 1926] [42] p. illus., map.

CHi CU-B

111. Chickering, Martha Alexander. Public provisions for the care of the dependent sick in Alameda county, California. [Berkeley, 1936] Thesis (M.A.)—Univ. of Calif., 1936. CU

112. Circulars for auction sales concerning real estate in early Alameda. 6 l. Ms. CAla

113. City and county government association, Alameda county. Centralized government for Alameda county and its cities, under a system of boroughs... [Oakland, Oakland enquirer, 1916] 10 p. CU-B

114. —— ...Some of the benefits that would accrue under a city and county charter... [Oakland, 1916?] [4] p. CU-B

115. Colquhoun, Joseph Alexander. Illustrated album of Alameda county, Calif.; its early history and progress...illus. by E. S. Moore. Oakland, Pac. press, c1893. 62 p. illus. CSf CSmH CU-B

116. —— Same. (*Calif. review*, v.1, no. 4, Mar., 1894) C CLU CU-B

117. [Committee for the Alameda county association of social workers] Community resources in Alameda, Berkeley and Oakland; a reference book of local social and health agencies... [Oakland? 1939?] 163 p. CU-B

118. Community chest of Oakland. Council of social agencies. Social service index committee. Social service index of Alameda county charities commission... [Oakland] 1941. 18 p. CU-B

119. —— —— Directory, health and medical agencies available to residents of Alameda county... Oakland [1944?] 53 p. CHi

120. Conners, Mollie. Pioneer women of Alameda county. (Oakland enquirer, Apr. 12, 1921–May 13, 1921). CO has scrapbook of clippings.

121. The Cost Estate ... concluding portion of an opinion upon the matter of the Cost Title...of that certain tract of land in Alameda county known as the Encinal of Temescal. S.F. [n.d.] [2] l. CHi

122. Country club, Washington township. History of Washington township, Alameda county, California... [Niles, "Washington press," 1904] 133 p. illus. "Pioneers of Washington township": p. 123–24.

C CAla CFS CHi CLU CO CRic CSS CSfCP CSfP CSmH CSmat CSto CStrJC CU-B

123. —— Same. 2d ed. [Niles?] 1950. 190 p. illus., maps. C CNF CO CSf CSjC CSmat

124. Crosby, Sarah Baxter. Studies of Alameda county delinquent boys... [Berkeley, 1928] Thesis (M.A.)—Univ. of Calif., 1928. CU

125. Cummings, Alton Root. Washington township, Alameda county, California. [Berkeley, 1937] 8 v. in 1. CU-B

126. Curtis, Grace Holden. The Abbott case: a fair trial and a free press. [Berkeley, 1957] Thesis (M.A.)—Univ. of Calif., 1957. CU

127. Darling, Ira John. The East bay municipal utility district. [Berkeley, 1935] Thesis (M.A.)—Univ. of Calif., 1935. CU

128. Daughters of the American revolution. California. Edmund Randolph chapter, comp. Alameda county records. 1948. 1 v. Typew.

C C-S CL

129. —— —— **Genealogical records committee.** Records from California courthouses: Alameda county. [n.p.] 1957. v.2. Publication begins with v.2.

C CHi

130. Davis, William Rude. [Scrapbooks containing letters from W. R. Davis to J. C. Rowell, with newspaper clippings concerning Davis' activities in behalf of the University of California, and as a candidate for governor of the state of California. 1896–1901] 22 l. ports.

CU-B

131. —— [Scrapbooks of William R. Davis, containing newspaper clippings, letters, etc., dealing with Davis' political, social and business activities in Alameda county during the period 1869–1912] 12 v. CU-B

132. Davoust, Martial, comp. Illustrated souvenir showing a few Alameda county homes. Pub. under the auspices of the Oakland board of trade... [Oakland] 1903. 13 p. 57 pl.

C CHi CLU CO CSmH CU-B

133. Decoto land company. Articles of association ...Incorporated June 11, 1870. S.F., E. Bosqui & co., print., 1870. 20 p. CSmH

134. DeNier, Flora Loretta. Robert Livermore and the development of Livermore valley to 1860. [Berkeley, 1927] 221 l. illus., port., maps. Typew. Thesis (M.A.)—Univ. of Calif., 1927. CU CU-B

135. De Rojas, Lauro Antonio. ...Spanish trails of the Contra Costa of the San Francisco bay...for Alameda county library and the Board of supervisors... Berkeley, 1937. 31 l. pl., maps. Reproduced from typew. copy. Bibliography. C CU-B

136. De Veer, Daisy Williamson. The story of Rancho San Antonio; a brief history of the east San

Francisco bay district... Oakland, Author, 1924. 93 p. illus., maps.   C CHi CLSU CLU CMartC CRic CSalCL CSmH CU-B NN

137. Diablo's complete guidebook to the East bay and the University of California. Berkeley, Diablo press [c1962] 185 p.   CAla

138. Doble steam motor corp. The Doble steam car. [n.p., 192–?] 15 p. illus.   CHi

139. —— Report. 1923/24. Emeryville, 1923.
                                              CU-B

140. Doe, Bartlett & Doe, John S., vs. Vallejo, José Jesus, et al. In the Supreme court of the state of California. Bartlett Doe & John S. Doe, appellants, vs. José Jesus Vallejo et al, respondents. Brief for respondent Clark, Jas. C. Cary [and] E. B. Mastick, for respondent Clark. S.F., Mining and scientific press, 1866. 17 p. A land suit. Rancho Arroyo de Alameda.   CLU

141. Dominican congregation of the Queen of the Holy Rosary, Mission San Jose, California. Historical sketch of the...by a member of the Order. [n.p., 1926] 59 p. illus.   CSfU

142. East bay cities sewage disposal survey. Board of consulting engineers. Report upon the collection, treatment and disposal of sewage and industrial wastes of the East bay cities, California... [Oakland?] 1941. 549 p. illus., maps.
                  CHi CLSU CLU CO CStclU

143. —— —— Abridgment. 60 p.   CHi

144. East bay country club. East bay country club, Oakland. [n.p., n.d.] 8 p. illus., map.   CHi

145. East bay municipal utility district. Additional water supply of East bay municipal utility district. A report...by Arthur Powell Davis. [1924] 64 p.
                              C CL CU-B

146. —— The Mokelumne river water supply project. [1927] 12 p. map. Mimeo.   CU-B

147. —— The story of water; a brief history of the East bay municipal utility district... Oakland [1932?] 31 p. illus., map.   C CU-B

148. —— Same. 1936. 36 p. illus., map.   CU-B

149. —— Water and tax rate reduction for East bay municipal utility district. [n.p., 1936] [12] p.   CHi

150. —— Same. [1938] 36 p. illus.   CHi

151. East bay regional library committee. A regional library service for the East bay area; report of a survey by Joseph L. Wheeler... Oakland, Nov., 1948. 68 p. maps. Mimeo.
              C CH CLSU CMartC CMont

152. East bay regional park district. East bay regional park opening celebration October 18, 1936. Oakland, 1936. 8 p.   CAla

153. —— Graphic report of proposed recreational facilities for the East bay regional park district, comprising the cities of Oakland, Berkeley, Alameda, Piedmont, Albany, San Leandro, Emeryville, California. [n.p., 1936?] 1 v. maps, photos.   CU-B

154. East bay supporters for the southern crossing. The case for a southern crossing of San Francisco bay. [Presented to California toll bridge authority, Dec. 12, 1956?]. 1 v. unp.   C

155. East bay transit co., Oakland. Annual report ...1937–1939. [S.F., 1938–40] 3 v.   CU-B

156. Edwards transcript of records. Alameda county. No. 2000–2152, 2302–7477, 7611, 7914. Deeds recorded Jan.–June 1884, 1885–1901, June 9, 1902, June 9, 1903. S.F., Edwards pub. co., 1884–1903. 30 v.   CU-B

157. Emeryville industries association. Emeryville and what makes it the home of industry. [1924?] unp. illus., map.   CO

158. —— A roster of Emeryville industries. [1936?, 1942?] 1948, 1954, 1957. [Emeryville? 1936?–57] 5 v.
                                              CU-B

159. Emeryville golden jubilee rodeo, August 17 and 18, 1946... [Berkeley, Lederer, Street and Zeus co.] 1946. 32 p. illus.   CHi

160. Emeryville herald. ...33rd anniversary of the city of Emeryville; commemorating 33 years of progress in the Emeryville and Golden Gate communities... 26 p. illus., ports. (Emeryville herald. Suppl., Friday, Dec. 6, 1929) "Alanson Sessions, editor."   CO

161. Evangelista, Lucrecio Sahagun. A study of certain phases of the general property tax in the East bay region. [Berkeley, 1933] Thesis (M.S.)—Univ. of Calif., 1933.   CU

162. Faulkner, William B. Faulkner's handbook and directory of Murray township, Alameda county... Livermore, Herald print., 1886. 124 p.   CLiv CU-B

163. Freeman, Leslie J. Alameda county, past and present... San Leandro, San Leandro reporter, 1946. 159 p. illus., ports.
   C CHi CL CLod CMartC CRic CSf CSfP CSfU CSfWF-H CSmH CStclU CU-B CtY NN

164. Frickstad, Walter Nettleton. Post offices in Alameda, Contra Costa, and Madera counties, California, 1850–1951. Oakland, 1953. 13 l.
   C (Reproduced from typew. copy) CU-B

165. Gilberg, Richard Latter. Constructing a case-judging device for a family agency. [Traveler's aid society of Alameda county] [Berkeley, 1957] Thesis (M.A.)—Univ. of Calif., 1957.   CU

166. Gilman, Trustum C. Petition of T. C. Gilman to the Legislature. S.F., Francis & Valentine, print. [1865?] 6 p. Petition for compensation for bridge built across San Antonio creek, 1852–53.   C CU-B

167. Golden Gate sanitary district. Ordinances of the...Alameda county, State of California. [n.p., 1895?] 23 p.   CU-B

168. Gutleben, Dan. The first successful beet sugar factory in the United States, at Alvarado, California. Walnut Creek, 1959. 56 p. plans, diagrs.   CHi CU-B

169. Hall, Wilbur. The romance of Obapesla... [Oakland, Pub. by the Kennedy co. for the Dons of Peralta, 1923. 16 p. illus., map. "Obapesla? What? Oakland, Berkeley, Alameda, Piedmont, Emeryville, San Leandro, and Albany."
                  CAla CLU CO CSmH CU-B

170. Harroun, Philip E. Report to the Water commission of the East bay cities on water supply, for the cities of Oakland, Berkeley, Alameda and Richmond... S.F. [1920] 62 p. illus., map.   CU-B

171. The Hayward journal. ...Alameda county... Hayward, 1925. 112 p. illus., ports.   C

172. Hearne bros., Detroit. Official Hearne brothers polyconic projection maps of all of Alameda county. Constantly revised and kept up to date. [Detroit, 195–?] 1 v. maps.   C

173. Heininger, Charles P., pub. Souvenir of Alameda county, Cal. [n.p., 188–?] folder (16 l.)
                                           CHi NN

174. Higgins, F. Hal. John M. Horner and the development of the combined harvester. Reprinted from *Agricultural history*, v.32, no. 1, 1958.   CHi

175. Historic homes of the East bay section. [*Oakland Post-enquirer*, Feb. 25–July 1, 1922] illus.
CO has scrapbook of clippings.

176. Historical records survey. California. Directory of churches and religious organizations in Alameda co., Calif., 1940...Prepared by the...Work projects administration. S.F., Northern Calif. hist. records survey project, 1940. 79 l. Reproduced from typew. copy.
C CHi CL CLU COHN CSf CSfCW CSmH CStclU CU-B

177. Holden, Erastus W., comp. Historic California: clippings. Alameda, Alameda free lib., 1937. 5 v.
v.5: Alameda county.   CAla

178. Hunter, Muriel Bigelow. A study of the function of medical social service in the Alameda-Contra Costa medical association. [Berkeley, 1957] Thesis (M.A.)—Univ. of Calif., 1957.   CU

179. Industrial growth 1915–1919; Oakland and Alameda county, California. [n.p., n.d.] 57 p. illus.
C CL

180. Inskeep, L. D. Taxation in Alameda county. A paper read...June 24, 1904. [Oakland?] Pub. by the Alameda county assoc., 1904. 4 l.   CSmH

181. International institute. A directory of the foreign communities of Alameda county... [Oakland] 1936. 27 p.   CO

182. Ivens, Charles Philip. The office of Public defender with special reference to Alameda, Los Angeles, and San Francisco counties. [Berkeley, 1940] Thesis (M.A.)—Univ. of Calif., 1940.   CU

183. Jay, Richard Edgar. A case study of retail unionism: the retail clerks in the San Francisco East bay area (Alameda county). [Berkeley, 1953] Thesis (M.A.)—Univ. of Calif., 1953.   CU

184. Johnson, Dorothy Caroline. Unemployment work relief in Alameda county, California. [Berkeley, 1933] Thesis (M.A.)—Univ. of Calif., 1933.   CU

185. Johnson, Marc William. The organization of state emergency relief in Alameda county, California. [Berkeley, 1937] Thesis (M.A.)—Univ. of Calif., 1937.
CU

186. Johnston, Nathan Robinson. Looking back from the sunset land; or, People worth knowing... Oakland, 1898. 624 p.   CHi CSmH

187. Kennedy, Helen Weber, comp. Vignettes of the gardens of San Jose de Guadalupe... S.F., S.F. garden club, 1938. 51 p.
C CHi CO CRcS CSf CSj CSjC CSjCL CSmH CU-B

188. Kenny, Robert Walker. An analysis of the 1921 proposed charter for the city and county of Alameda... [Alameda, 1935?] 20 l.   CU-B

189. Kimber, John E. The Southern Alameda county musical association. [Niles, Township register print., 1938] 23 p. Includes by-laws.   CHi

190. King, Clinton S. In memoriam: Clinton S. King, including addresses at the memorial services held at San Lorenzo... [San Lorenzo, 1899] 19 p.   CHi

191. Knights of Columbus. Oakland council no. 784. Catholic historical review of Alameda county. Oakland [c1930] [104] p. illus.   CO CSfCW CU-B

192. Knowland, Joseph Russell. Alameda county's interest in Hetch Hetchy grant. Speech of...in the House of representatives, Aug. 29, 1913. Wash., D.C., 1913. 14 p.   CSmH

193. Kruckeberg, Henry W. George Christian Roeding, 1868–1928, the story of California's leading nursery man and fruit grower. L.A., Calif. assoc. of nurserymen, 1930. 109 p. illus.   CBb CHi CRic

194. Lauer, Lillian Williamson. The community press in Livermore, California: a case study. [Berkeley, 1959] 96 p. tables, diagrs.   CU CU-B

195. Laymance (M. J.) & co., Oakland. Special credit sale of 13 small farms...in the Meyers tract, adjoining the town of Decoto, Alameda county, California ...at auction, Saturday Sept. 13, 1890... Oakland, Oakland daily tribune print. [1890] [4] p. map.   CHi

196. League of California municipalities, East bay division. Intergovernmental relations committee. City-county fiscal relations in Alameda and Contra Costa counties; a summary report. [Berkeley] 1951. 6 l.
CU-B

197. Leavenworth, Martha. The financial picture of Alameda county, California, 1915–1940. [Berkeley, 1941] Thesis (M.A.)—Univ. of Calif., 1941.   CU

198. Leona Heights, Alameda county. Leona Heights hotel and family resort (formerly Laundry farm). [S.F., 1897?] 50 p. illus.   CHi

199. Life at Parks air force base. San Mateo [c1955] unp. illus.   CAla

200. Livermore. Board of trade. Semi-tropical Livermore, Alameda county, California, published quarterly... Livermore, Livermore herald power print. house, 1887. 62 p. illus., map.   CLU CLiv CSmH CU-B

201. Livermore sanitarium. The Livermore sanitarium, Livermore, California... [S.F., Barnhart & Swasey, 1904?] 43 p. illus.   CU-B

202. Mabrey, Eli Nelson. An educational survey of the rural schools of Alameda county, California. [Berkeley, 1918] Thesis (M.A.)—Univ. of Calif., 1918.   CU

203. McCarthy, Francis Florence. The history of Mission San Jose, California, 1797–1835. With an epilogue covering the period from 1835 to 1855, by Raymund F. Wood. Fresno, Acad. lib. guild, 1958. 285 p. illus. Includes bibliography.
Available in many California libraries and N

204. McIver, C. C. Linda Vista vineyards, Mission San Jose, Alameda county, California. [S.F., H.S. Crocker co., 189–?] [60] p. illus.   CU-B

205. McKeand, G. W., comp. Abstract of title to land on Sausal creek and Fruit Vale avenue, county of Alameda, state of California. Oakland [1888–1900] 244 p. 2 maps (1 fold.) Part ms., part reproduced from ms.
C

206. McKeany, Maurine. History of the care of the dependent child in Alameda county, 1853–1934. [Berkeley, 1936] Thesis (M.A.)—Univ. of Calif., 1936.   CU

207. Martinez, Tyrrell Woodward. ...Rancho San Antonio: outstanding illustration of the Spanish land policy in California... Berkeley, 1936. 149 l. (Calif. historic sites and landmarks. Alameda county ser.) Reproduced from typew. copy. "Written under the auspices of Works progress administration."   CHi CU-B

208. Masters, Romney S., Smith, R. C., and Winter, W. E. An historical review of the East bay ex-

change; Oakland, Berkeley, Alameda, Piedmont, Albany, Emeryville, San Leandro, El Cerrito... [S.F.] Pac. telephone & telegraph co., 1927. 119 p. illus., ports., maps.
 C CHi CLU CMartC CO CSfCW CSfP CSfU CSmH CStrJC CU-B

209. Maverick, Lewis Adams. Activity in real estate in Alameda county, California, 1853 to 1930. [Berkeley, 1932] Thesis (Ph.D.)—Univ. of Calif., 1932.   CU

210. Mendenhall, Wm., vs. Paris, Florentine et al. In the Supreme court of the state of California. Wm. M. Mendenhall, plaintiff and appellant vs. Florentine Paris et al., defendants and respondents. Respondents' brief. J. W. Harding, attorney for respondents. [n.p., 187–?] 6 p. map. Rancho Valle de San Jose suit.
                                                                                                CLU

211. Methodist Episcopal church. Metropolitan district. Directory of Methodist churches and institutions. [n.p., 1952] 79 p. illus. Issued at the General conference...San Francisco, April 22–May 6, 1952.
                                                                                                CHi

212. Moitoret, Anthony F. An analysis of costs of government in Oakland and Alameda county, California. [Oakland, 1927] 43 p.   CU-B

213. Mountin, Joseph Walter. Study of health and hospital service, Alameda county, California... [Oakland, Print. by C. R. Mulgrew] for Alameda county bd. of supervisors & Alameda county tuberculosis assoc., 1930. 92 p.   CO

214. Moussette, Edna Camille. Methods of financing social work in Alameda county. [Berkeley, 1930] Thesis (M.A.)—Univ. of Calif., 1930.   CU

215. Mullan, John. In the matter of the final survey and location of the private land claim rancho "El Sobrante," said to be situate in the counties of Alameda and Contra Costa, California, reply to... Wash., D.C., Thomas McGill & co., 1880. 6 p.   CHi

216. Murdoch, Norman. A suggested procedure for developing a transit plan for the East bay. [Berkeley, 1951] Thesis (M.A.)—Univ. of Calif., 1951.   CU

217. Native sons of the golden West. Livermore. Las Positas parlor, no. 96. The history of the Livermore valley, by Elmer Rowley, ed. [and others] Livermore, 1931. 45 l. photos., map. Typew. "Compiled from a group of contest essays, written...by the students of Mrs. Mason's United States history class of the Livermore union high school, and from additional sources."—Pref.
                                                                                            CO CSf

218. Nehrbas, H. F., vs. Central Pacific railroad co. In the Superior court of the state of California in and for the county of Alameda...H. F. Nehrbas, plaintiff, vs. the Central Pacific railroad co., defendant... argument of W. H. L. Barnes... S.F., Crocker [1882] 65 p.   CHi

219. Niles. Chamber of commerce. Niles, Alameda county, California, an industrial center. Niles, Washington press [1910?] 16 p. illus.   CHi

220. Nye, Stephen Girard. Addresses and letters of travel. With a biographical sketch. S.F., Priv. print., 1908. 353 p. illus., ports. Prominent judge in Alameda county.
 C CHi CL CLSU CLU CO CSf CSmH CU-B

221. Oakland. Board of trade. Alameda county and city of Oakland, California. Oakland, Tribune print., 1902. 15 p. map.   CSmH CU-B

222. —— Chamber of commerce. Alameda county, California. 1926. 32 p. illus.   CAla CRcS CU-B

223. —— —— Directory of firms employing 100 or more persons in Alameda county. Oakland, 1959. 27 p.   CAla

224. —— —— Directory of personnel managers, purchasing agents and traffic managers of major firms in Alameda county. Oakland, 1956. 30 p.   CAla

225. —— —— Handbook of comparative data Bay area counties: two metropolitan areas. Oakland, 1958. 15 p.   CAla

226. —— —— Industrial facts about Oakland and Alameda county, California... Oakland, Alameda county Bd. of supervisors [1931] 31 p. illus., maps.   CU-B

227. —— —— Same; new ed. 1935. 28 p.   CAla

228. Oakland and Alameda county; industrial growth, 1915–1919. [n.p., 1919?] 57 p. illus., ports.   C

229. The Oakland land and improvement co. Description of the Santa Rita ranch and the surrounding country of Pleasanton, Alameda county, California. [n.d.] 16 p.   CU-B

230. Oakland tribune. The birth of Fremont, Alameda county's 12th city, 1956. [4] p. mounted clippings. illus.   CU-B

231. O'Conner, Rita Catherine. The care of crippled children in Alameda county. [Berkeley, 1941] Thesis (M.A.)— Univ. of Calif., 1941.   CU

232. Olmsted bros. Report on proposed park reservations for East bay cities... [Berkeley, 1930] 40 p. illus.   CHi CLSU CLU CU-B

233. Pacific coast merchants' protective association, Alameda county....A complete list and ratings of the residents of Oakland, Alameda, Berkeley, and the farmers of Alameda county. S.F., 1886. 1 v.   CHi

234. The People's coal mining co. [Prospectus] ...S.F., Towne & Bacon, 1867. 6 p.   C CU-B

235. Peralta, Antonio, Wm. W. Chipman and Gideon Aughinbaugh, a copy of the original agreement. 3 l.   CAla

236. A plea for justice. The people of Alameda, Berkeley and Oakland versus the political ring of Alameda county. A complete refutation of all the misrepresentations made by the Oakland chamber of commerce against the constitutional amendment for the consolidation of cities. [n.p., 1913?] 16 p.   CU-B

237. Raeburn, Albert. The East bay regional park district. [Berkeley, 1943] Thesis (M.A.)—Univ. of Calif., 1943.   CU

238. Rand, Augustus C. In the Superior court of the state of California, in and for the county of Alameda. In the matter of the estate of Augustus C. Rand, deceased. Points and authorities of Mrs. Babcock, devisee under the will. Pillsbury & Titus, attorneys for executor. J. B. Crockett, of counsel. Gray & Haven, attorneys for contestant... S.F., Bacon & co., 1882. 14 p.   CHi

239. —— In the Supreme court of the state of California. In the matter of the estate of Augustus C. Rand, deceased. Cyrus A. Pomeroy, contestant, vs. George Babcock, executor, et al., contra. Petition to have case heard in bank. Pillsbury & Titus, att'ys. for George Babcock and Mary Ann Babcock. Joseph B. Crockett, of counsel. Gray & Haven, att'ys. for contestant. Filed...1882. [S.F.] Law journal print, W. T. Baggett & co. [1882] 12 p.   CHi

240. Reller, Theodore and Coney, Robert C. Mt. Eden; a projection. [Mt. Eden? 1957?] 61 p. Mimeo.
CH

241. Rhodehamel, Josephine (DeWitt) Printed maps of Alameda county and its larger cities...Special study submitted...for the degree of Master of arts in librarianship, University of California, May, 1939. 122 p. maps. Typew.
CO

242. Ricks, Clayne Johnson. The development of the planning agency in Alameda county, California. [Berkeley, 1958] Thesis (M.A.)— Univ. of Calif., 1958.
CU

243. Robbins, Robert Lash. Postamp history of Rancho Peralta; a stirring narrative of the east bay empire... [n.p., Postamp pub. co., c1940] 40 p. col. illus. (mounted postamps)
CHi CO

244. Rolle, Andrew F. An American in California; the biography of William Heath Davis, 1822–1909. San Marino, Huntington lib., 1956. 155 p. illus. (Huntington lib. publications) "Descriptive bibliography of manuscripts": p. 144–149.
Available in many California libraries and
HHi MoSU N

245. Rosenson, Alexander Moses. Origin and nature of the C.I.O. movement in Alameda county, California. [Berkeley, 1939] Thesis (M.A.)— Univ. of Calif., 1939.
CU

246. San Francisco, Oakland and San Jose railway and the Oakland traction consolidated. Alameda county: the facts concerning its growth and development, its advantages and possibilities. S.F., Edward Hilton, pub., c1905. unp. illus.
CAla

247. San Lorenzo. St. Felicitas parish. Opening of new church and parish hall, March 22, 1953. [n.p.] 1953. 32 p. illus.
CHi

248. Sappers, Vernon J., ed. From shore to shore —the Key route. Oakland, Peralta associates, 1948. 20 p. illus., map.
C CHi CO

249. Scharringhausen, Charles Thomas. A century of journalism in Alameda county, 1854–1954. [Berkeley, 1955] Thesis (M.A.)— Univ. of Calif., 1955.
CU

250. Shinn, Charles Howard. Graphic description of Pacific coast outlaws. Thrilling exploits of their archenemy, Sheriff Harry N. Morse... [S.F., R. R. Patterson, n.d.] 32 p. port. Reprinted from *New York sun*.
C CBaB CHi CL CLSM CLU COr CRic CSf CSfCP CSfWF-H CSmH CStmo CU-B

251. —— Same. Including a biographical sketch of Harry N. Morse from the Bancroft library. Intro. and notes by J. E. Reynolds. L.A., Westernlore press, 1958. 107 p. illus.
CBb CChiS CCoron CLO CLSM CMartC CP CSd CSf CStmo CSto

252. Shutes, Milton Henry. A history of the Alameda county medical association... [Oakland] Alameda county medical assoc., 1946 [i.e. c1947] 137 p.
C CHi CLM CO CSmH CU-B

253. Smith, Esther Mary. Characteristics of the population of Alameda county, California, 1940–1947. [Berkeley, 1949] Thesis (M.A.)— Univ. of Calif., 1949.
CU

254. Smith, Wilbur, & associates. Report on a proposed Alameda county highway master plan. Prepared in cooperation with the California state division of highways, and the cities within the county. S.F., 1959. 131 p. maps.
CAla

255. Smythe, Dallas Walker. An economic history of local and interurban transportation in the East bay cities with particular reference to the properties developed by F. M. Smith. [Berkeley, 1937] Thesis (M.A.)— Univ. of Calif., 1937.
CU

256. [Social agencies in Alameda county, 1927–1936] [Oakland, 1927–36] v.p.
CO

257. Society of Mayflower descendants in the state of California. Alameda county colony. ... Directory, 1960–61. [1960] 11 l. Mimeo.
CHi

258. Soito, Patricia. A hundred years of Pleasanton, "the most desperate town of the West"... S.F., Print. by Phillips & Van Orden co., c1949. 30 p. illus., ports., map.
C CAla CHi CO CRic CSf CSmH

259. Solovsky, Ruth Mary (McGinty) Spanish and Mexican ranchos in the San Francisco bay region: San Antonio, San Pablo, and San Leandro, by Ruth Mary McGinty. [Berkeley, 1921] 94 l. Thesis (M.A.)— Univ. of Calif., 1921.
CU CU-B

260. Studt, Ray N. ...Historic sites and landmarks of old San Antonio... Berkeley, 1937. 115 l. (Calif. historic sites and landmarks. Alameda county ser.) Typew. "Written under the auspices of Works progress administration."
CU-B

261. Tax association of Alameda county, Oakland. ...A digest or summary of the provisions of the charter proposed by the Board of freeholders for consolidated city and county government... [Oakland, 1921] 15 p.
CO CU-B

262. —— Report on emergency hospital, detention home and care of indigents. Oakland [Press of Carruth & Carruth] 1912. 15 p.
CSmH

263. Taylor, Charles William. Bench and bar of Alameda county, 1953. [Angwin] C. W. Taylor and Theodore N. Chapin [c1953] 207 p. ports.
C CHi CO

264. Thomas bros., comp. Popular atlas of Alameda county, showing all streets, address block numbers...and other useful information. S.F., c1957. 112 p.
CAla

265. Thompson, E. B. E. ...Washington press... Irvington [Press print. off.] 1898. 44 p. illus., ports. Contains short biographical sketches.
CAlaC CFS

266. Transcript of records. Alameda county. no. 707–1009 (old no. 5474–5778) Jan. 4, 1909–Jan. 3, 1910. Oakland, F. Boegle, 1909–10.
CU-B

267. Troth, Isaac, vs. Frakes, Louis. Brief. James C. Zabriskie, attorney for Troth. S.F., Towne & Bacon, 1867. 7 p. At head of cover-title: United States land office.
CHi

268. U.S. Circuit court (9th circuit) Clement Boyreau vs. R. Campbell, and others...Opinion by Justice McAllister. S.F., Eureka print. [1856] 14 p.
C CLU CSmH CU-B

269. —— General land office. Copy of the official translation of the papers on file in the United States land office, Washington, D.C., relating to the Spanish grant issued to Don Luis María Peralta in 1820. 11 p. map. Typew. Includes text of Luis Peralta's will and of his correspondence with various officials regarding the grant to him of Rancho San Antonio.
CO

270. —— Works progress administration. Visulore; a practical volume of educative resources of Alameda county, 1936–1937; prepared by personnel from Works progress administration, Teresa G. Earnshaw—supervisor, project 1952; sponsored by Alameda county library. [Oakland, 1937?] 2 v.   C CO CU-B

271. Ward, John B. vs. Mulford, Thomas W., and Smith, E. Minor. In the Supreme court of the state of California. Brief for appellant [in the case of] John B. Ward vs. Thomas W. Mulford and E. Minor Smith. S.F., Turnbull & Smith print., 1868. 11 p.   CHi

272. —— Brief for respondents... S.F., M. D. Carr & co., print., 1868. 11 p.   CHi

273. —— ... Transcript on appeal... S.F., Wade & co., print. [1867] 26 p.   CHi

274. Washington college, Irvington. Catalogue ...1873/74– S.F., A. L. Bancroft & co., 1874–
CU-B has 1873/74, 1876/77, 1878/79, 1887/88.

275. Washington news, Centerville. Sesquicentennial, Mission San Jose; 150th anniversary, May 30–31–June 1, 1947... [Centerville, 1947] [52] p. illus.
CHi

276. [Waterman, Edgar R.] comp. "Vade mecum" manual of Oakland, Berkeley and Alameda... [Oakland, United States industrial co., c1904] 128 p. illus. (Waterman's "Vade mecum" manuals; a ser. of elegant guide books for all Am. cities)
CO CU-B ViU

277. Wells, Evelyn. A hundred years of Alameda county. 1921. illus., ports. Published serially in *San Francisco call post*, beginning Jan. 24, 1921.   CO

278. Wente bros., Livermore. The story of Wente wines... [n.p., 1960?] [6] p. col. illus.   CHi

279. Weymouth, Almon, vs. the Western Pacific railroad co. In the United States land office. Almon Weymouth, claimant, vs. the Western Pacific railroad company, contestant. J. W. Harding, of counsel for claimant. [S.F., 1872] 29 p. Rancho Las Pocitas suit.   CLU

280. Wood, Raymund Francis. A brief history of Mission San Jose. Fresno, Acad. lib. guild, 1957. 58 p. illus.   CFS CLSM

281. Wren, A.C. Resources of Pleasanton and surrounding country, 1893–1894. Pleasanton, Pleasanton times, 1893. 34 p.   CHi

282. Yockey, Paul Milton. Administrative agreements among local government agencies in the Oakland-Berkeley region. [Berkeley, 1942] Thesis (M.A.)—Univ. of Calif., 1942.   CU

283. Zugg, Maxine Melba. A history of the care of the blind in Alameda county, California. [Berkeley, 1935] Thesis (M.A.)— Univ. of Calif., 1935.   CU

Alameda

284. Abstract of title to all those certain pieces or parcels of land situate in the encinal of San Antonio, township of Alameda...the same being a portion of what is known as the "James J. Foley tract" of land... S.F., J. Winterburn & co., print., 1873. 45 p.   CLU CU-B

285. Adelphian club, Alameda. Year book, 1908/09. [Alameda? 1908?] 52 p.   C

286. Alameda. Board of health. First annual report of the Board of health of the city of Alameda, California, 1888. Alameda, Argus steam news, bk. & job print., 1889. 45 p.   CU-B

287. —— **Board of trade.** Alameda...city of homes... [Alameda] Press of the Alameda daily encinal [1903?] [32] p. illus.
CHi CL CLU CSmH CU-B

288. —— **Chamber of commerce.** Alameda, California, industrial development; industrial sites in Alameda, California. Alameda, [1948?] folder. illus., map.
C

289. —— —— Alameda manufacturers and industries. July 28, 1950. 4 p.   CAla

290. —— —— Alameda...standard industrial survey summary report outlined by the Industrial plant location committee... Alameda, 1955. 4 p. Typew.   CAla

291. —— **Charters, ordinances, etc.** Charter and general ordinances of the city of Alameda in force March 1, 1903... Comp. by Howard K. James. Alameda [Argus pub. co.] 1903. 252 p.   CHi

292. —— —— Charter of the city of Alameda... voted for and ratified...on the 18th of July, 1906. 76 p.
CSfMI

293. —— **Christ Episcopal church.** Diamond jubilee, 1872–1947. [n.p., 1947] 24 p. illus., port.
CHi CO

294. —— **First Presbyterian church.** ...Seventy-fifth anniversary, 1865-1940... [Alameda, 1940] 18 p. illus.   CU-B

295. —— **Free library.** E. K. Taylor eucalyptus tree. 3 p. Typew.   CAla

296. —— —— Frémont oak of Alameda. 2 p. Typew.   CAla

297. —— —— History of Alameda free library. 25 p. Typew.   CAla

298. —— —— The Indian mound of Alameda. unp. Typew.   CAla

299. —— —— Kohlmoos hotel, Alameda, California. 5 p. illus. Typew.   CAla

300. —— —— A public library grows, Alameda, California, 1879–1953. Alameda, 1953. 16 p.   CAla

301. —— **High school.** Commencement programmes. [1st?, 1878?– [n.p., 1878?–
CHi has 4th–6th, [27th], 1881–83, 1908.

302. —— **Junior chamber of commerce.** Community survey. A study of the public's opinion of Alameda as a community. [Alameda?] 1959. 32 p.   CAla

303. —— **Planning board.** Alameda outline master plan adopted April 30, 1956. Alameda, 1956. 23 l.
CAla

304. —— **Planning department.** Economic and industrial survey, city of Alameda, California. Prepared as a unit of the master plan project. Prepared by James M. Campbell. [n.p.] 1957. 20 p. maps.   CAla

305. —— **St. Joseph's parish.** History of St. Joseph's parish, on the occasion of its diamond jubilee. [n.p., n.d.]   CAla

306. Alameda building and loan association. Prospectus of the Alameda loan and building association, of Alameda county, Cal. S.F., Winterburn & co., print. & electrotypers, 1876. 16 p.   CU-B

307. Anderson, A. J. Meet the Governor of California...Earl Warren. Burbank, Author, c1947. 72 p.
CSdU

308. Bartholomew, Harland, and associates, St. Louis. A report of street and off-street parking; prepared for the city council of the city of Alameda, California. St. Louis, 1947. 33 p. illus.   CAla

309. —— A report of transit facilities and mass transportation... St. Louis, 1947. 57 p. maps. CAla

310. —— A report on major street and freeway improvements... St. Louis, 1947. 16 p. maps. CAla

311. Board of fire underwriters of the Pacific. Specific rates for Alameda, Cal. ... [S.F., 1924] 101 l. CU-B

312. California. University. Department of city and regional planning. A community orientation survey of the city of Alameda. [Berkeley? n.d.] 35 p. map. CAla

313. Chipman, William Farragut. Alameda city early history...with biography of W. W. Chipman presented to the Society of California pioneers... S.F., 1933. 23 l. CAla

314. —— ...In memoriam. Presented to the members of the Eulexian lodge by W. C. Sharpsteen. [n.p., n.d.] 10 p. Mimeo. CHi

315. —— Information taken from blueprint showing amount of land sold by Wm. W. Chipman and G. Aughinbaugh between October 6, 1851 and August 5, 1853. 2 l. Typew. CAla

316. Citizen hook and ladder co., no. 1, of Alameda. Constitution and by-laws...Adopted October 2, 1876. Amended May 5, 1887. Alameda, Encinal bk. & job print., 1887. 20 p. CU-B

317. Cohen, Alfred A., vs. Gray, James M., et al. In the District court of the fifteenth judicial district of the state of California in and for the city and county of San Francisco. Argument of Alfred A. Cohen, plaintiff on motion for injunction. [S.F.?, 1877?] 44 p. CHi CLU

318. Collins, Arthur P. Chabot ranch—its program and philosophy. [1953?] 7 p. Alameda county Boys camp. C

319. Curtis, Jane Isobel. [Alameda history highlights. 1935?] 7 l. Typew. CAla

320. Elks, Benevolent and protective order of. Alameda lodge no. 1015. 50 grand years, 1916–1956... [n.p.] 1956. 20 p. illus. CAla

321. Federal writers' project. California. Alameda: the Island city... City of Alameda, co-sponsor. [n.p.] 1941. 200 p. CAla

322. Fox, Charles J. Old remembrances of Alameda. [n.p.] 1952. 7 p. Typew. CAla

323. Frazier, Mrs. R. Mosaic gleanings: a souvenir for 1881–83 and recollections of treatment in Alameda. Oakland, Daily evening tribune print. co., 1883. CBb

324. Government Island, Alameda. [1931?] 18 p. Typew. map. CAla

325. Hawes, Harry G. History of Government Island, Alameda, California. 1954. 9 l. Typew. CAla

326. Hibberd, James F., and Piper, William A., vs. Smith, John, et al. In the Supreme court of the state of California. James F. Hibberd, and William A. Piper, respondents, vs. John Smith, Charles Shore, H. C. Tappan, Russel M. Rogers and Elisha H. Rogers, appellants. Transcript on appeal. Theodore H. Hittell, S. F. & L. Reynolds, and M. G. Cobb, att'ys. for appellants. A. M. Crane, att'y. for respondents. S. F., M. D. Carr & co., 1869. 87 p. CHi

327. —— ...Brief for appellants. Theodore H. Hittell, attorney for appellants. S.F., Women's print., 1882. 18 p. CHi

328. Holden, E. D. History of Alameda railroads. 8 p. Typew. CAla

329. Irvine Leigh Hadley. Alameda, California. S.F., Sunset mag. homeseekers' bur. [1911?] 57 p. illus., maps. CHi CO CSfCP MWA

330. [James, Howard Kellogg] Order of the First Crusade. [Alameda] 1934. 31 p. CHi

331. Justin, Mrs. Jerry. History of Lincoln school, Alameda, California, 1855–1950. 3 p. Typew. CAla

332. Lane, Thomas M. History of the development of Alameda fire department. [n.p.] 1956. 27 p. Typew. CAla

333. McNutt, Susie L. Brief history of Christian church of Alameda. Alameda, 1906. 24 p. NN

334. Miller Rose Baldramos. Alameda in the '80's. [n.p.] 1956. 26 l. Typew. CAla

335. Musical center of Alameda associated studios. [Brochure] Mrs. William B. Kollmyer, director. Alameda [191–?] [9] p. CHi

336. Oak Grove institute, Alameda, California. 3 l. Typew. CAla

337. Public administration service. Revenue structure and fiscal trends, city of Alameda, California, 1951. Chicago, 1951. 57 p. CAla

338. Scoggins, Verne. It happened in California (the story of a state, its governor, Earl Warren, and 11 years of history-making growth and expansion) [n.p.] A group of friends of Earl Warren, 1953. 13 p. CRcS

339. Shakespeare club of Alameda. ...[History and membership] by F. B. Graves. [n.p., 1901] [10] p. CHi

340. —— [Scrapbook, including programmes, menus and greeting cards, 1889–1914] 1 v. CHi

341. Stone, Irving. Earl Warren, a great American story. N.Y., Prentice-Hall [1948] 176 p. port. CLO CNa COnC CRedCL CSjC

342. Tabor, Rodney L. Address delivered by... pastor of First Presbyterian church in Alameda at the funeral of Henry Huntley [!] Haight, Sept. 4th, 1878. S.F., Francis & Valentine print. [1878] 22 p. CHi

343. Taylor, E. K. Early Alameda. 6 p. Typew. CAla

344. Trenor, Susan Eliza. In memoriam. S.F., Priv. print. for the family, 1876. 30 p. illus. CHi

345. Vigness, Paul Gerhardt. Alameda community book. Alameda, Cawston, 1952. 239 p. illus., ports. "Biographical": p. [133]–235. C CAla CL CO CU-B

346. —— History of Alameda...(Narrative and biographical) Alameda, Cawston, 1939. 241 p. illus., ports. C CHi CL CLU CO CRic CSf CU-B NN

347. Warren, Earl. The public papers of Chief Justice Earl Warren. N.Y., Simon and Schuster, c1959. 237 p. Ed. by Henry M. Christman. CSalCL

348. Wendte, Charles W. In memoriam. Mrs. Maria L. Varney, wife of Thos. Varney, a service...at Hamilton church, Oakland... [Oakland, 1888] [8] p. CHi

349. West end engine co. no. 1, Alameda. Constitution and by-laws... S.F., J. Winterburn & co., print., 1878. 13 p. illus. CU-B

350. Wilcox, I. A. Alameda, California. 25 p.

Typew. From *Alameda semi-weekly encinal*, Sept. 16, 1890.   CAla

351. Wooley, H. M. History of Alameda (city). unp. Typew.   CAla

Berkeley

352. Alameda county. Board of supervisors. Berkeley and the University of California, some aspects of city-university relationship. [Oakland, 195–?] 18 p. illus.   C

353. —— —— Directory of manufacturers, Berkeley, California, 1952–1953, at the hub of Pacific coast industrial expansion... [Oakland? 1953] 24 p.   C CU-B

354. Alameda county abstract co. Abstracts of title, relating to all that lot of land situated in the town of Berkeley, county of Alameda, state of California, described as follows to-wit: Lot no. 8 in Block no. 1...so designated on a certain map entitled "Amended map of a portion of La Loma Park and the Wheeler tract..." filed October 15, 1902, in the County recorder's office of said Alameda county. Also a strip of land along the north line of said lot no. 8... [Oakland, 1907] 85 p.   CSfCW

355. Albertype co., New York, pub. Berkeley and the University of California. Brooklyn, N.Y. [1915] [18] pl.   CU-B

356. Anna Head school, Berkeley. [Catalog] 1893/94– Berkeley, 1894–
CHi has 1914/15. CU-B has 1893/94–1899/1900, 1903/04–1904/05, 1909/10–1910/11, 1919/20, 1925/26, 1930/31–1931/32.

357. Ashby nursery, Berkeley. Price list... [Berkeley, n.d.] 11 p.   CHi

358. [Ashdown, A.] Persistent unlawful appropriation of private property and invasion of private rights by the board of regents of the University of California... [S.F., 1881] 8 p.   CU-B

359. Bacon, Henry Douglas. An address on the occasion of the dedication of the Bacon art gallery and library building, Berkeley, Calif., August 23rd, 1881. [n.p., 1881?] 8 l.   CHi CU-B

360. [Bancroft, Hubert Howe] Analysis and valuation of the Bancroft library. [n.p., 1902?] 9 p.   C COHN CU-B

361. Bancroft, Philip. Hubert Howe Bancroft; an address by his son...September fifth, 1948. [S.F., Priv. print., 1948] 22 p.   CHi CRcS CSfP

362. Barrows, David Prescott. Are Berkeley socialists bolshevists?...On the recognition of the Russian soviet government...[Berkeley? 1919] 8 p.   CU-B

363. Barry, E. F. Beautiful Berkeley... Berkeley, Youngs & Barry, c1904. 24 p. illus., ports.   CHi CSmH CU-B

364. Bartlett, William Chauncey. Address...at the graduating exercises [University of California at Berkeley] June 9, 1891. Berkeley, Print. at the Deaf and dumb, and the blind institution, 1891. 6 p.   CHi

365. —— Quarter centennial of the Berkeley club ... [Berkeley, 1898] 11 p.   CLU CSmH CU-B

366. Bath, Gerald Horton. Only tomorrow; an article emphasizing the usefulness of a private school, written...for the Anna Head school. Berkeley [Anna Head school, c1934] [16] p.   CHi

367. Benton, Joseph Augustine. Sermons, addresses, poems, and miscellaneous notations and records, 1845–1881. Includes material valuable to the history of California, the Pacific school of religion and College of California.   CBPac

368. Berkeley. Directory of manufacturers, Berkeley, California. Compiled and published as a public service by the city of Berkeley. [1958/59] Distributed by the Berkeley chamber of commerce.   CB

369. —— **Board of education.** Rules and regulations and course of study of the public schools of the town of Berkeley, 1883. [Berkeley, Advocate print., 1883] 22 p.   CU-B

370. —— **Board of trade.** Berkeley, California, illustrated. [Berkeley, Berkeley daily gazette, c1903?] 32 p. illus.   CHi CU-B

371. —— —— Same. [1904?] [20] p. illus.   CU-B

372. —— **Chamber of commerce.** Berkeley, California. [Berkeley, Lederer, Street & Zeus co., 1914?] 16 p. illus., map.   CHi CO CU-B

373. —— —— Berkeley, California, "the city of finer living." [1940?] [28] p. illus., map.   C CL

374. —— —— Berkeley tourist and business survey... Berkeley, H. B. Knowles, 1924. 147 p.   CU-B

375. —— —— The book of Berkeley, 1931... [Berkeley, 1931] 36 p. illus. "Prepared jointly by the Berkeley chamber of commerce and the Berkeley daily gazette."   CHi CO

376. —— —— Constitution and by-laws...and original list of directors and members. [Berkeley? 1906?] [16] p.   CU-B

377. —— —— Greater Berkeley, California, year book, 1930. Berkeley, 1930. 64 p. illus., maps.   CHi CO CU-B

378. —— —— Industrial Berkeley, California. [Berkeley, 1944] 18 p. illus.   CO

379. —— —— Industrial directory of Berkeley, California... [Berkeley, 1946] 1 v.   CU-B

380. —— —— Same. [1948] 48 p.   CU-B

381. —— —— Industrial facts about Berkeley and Alameda county, California. [Berkeley, 1934?] 28 p. illus., maps.   CU-B

382. —— —— Old China hands, a roster. 3d ed., rev. and enl. Berkeley, 1945. 70 p. illus., map.   CSf

383. —— —— The story of Berkeley... Berkeley [1908] 38 p. illus.   CHi CSmH CU-B

384. —— **Charters, ordinances, etc.** Charter of the town of Berkeley, adopted March 5, 1895, and ordinances...from organization of the town, April 1, 1878. Berkeley, Daily gazette, 1902. 154 p.   CHi

385. —— —— Charter...prepared and proposed by the Board of freeholders, elected November 21, 1908 ... Compiled, annotated and indexed by Hon. L. Ernest Phillips... [Berkeley?] 1909. 154 p. port.
          CSfCP CSfMI CStclU (61 p.) MoS

386. —— —— Ordinances of the town of Berkeley... Berkeley, Advocate print., 1882. 24 p.   CHi

387. —— **City planning commission.** Berkeley master plan, 1955. [Berkeley, 1955] 111 p.   CSt

388. —— **First Congregational church.** Manual of the First Congregational church of Berkeley, Cal. S.F., Bacon & co., bk. & job print., 1878. 15 p.   CU-B

389. —— —— Same. [Berkeley] Print. by Berkeley press, 1886. 48 p. CU-B

390. —— —— Same. January, 1902. [Berkeley, 1902] 74 p. CU-B

391. —— First Presbyterian church. Manual... S.F., Oakland [etc., 1885–96].
CLU has 1888, 1894. CU-B has 1885–86, 1888, 1890–91, 1895–96.

392. —— —— Sixty-fifth anniversary committee. Sixty-five years of history...First Presbyterian church, Berkeley, California, 1878–1943. [Berkeley, 1943] 30 p. illus., ports. C CHi CSmH CU-B

393. —— —— Year book and directory. 3d, Oct. 1939. Berkeley, [1939?] CU-B

394. —— Pacific school of religion. Religious progress on the Pacific slope. Addresses and papers at the celebration of the semi-centennial anniversary of the Pacific school of religion, Berkeley, California. Bost., Chicago, Pilgrim press [c1917] 326 p. ports.
C CHi CLO CLU CSfCW CU-B

395. —— —— Rev. Joseph Augustine Benton; in memorial. S.F., printed for the trustees of the Pac. theological seminary by Bacon & co., 1892. 83 p. illus., port. Pastor, Sacramento, 1849–1863; San Francisco, 1863–1869. Senior professor in the Pac. theological seminary, 1869–1892. CHi CSfCW

396. —— —— Same. S.F., Pac. press & pub. co., 1899. 83 p. illus., port.
CHi COHN CSfP CSmH CU-B

397. —— Public schools. Office of elementary education. Source book on the history of Berkeley; comp. under the direction of Ruby Minor. [Berkeley, Author, c1939] 152 l. Mimeo. CB CO

398. —— Third Church of Christ, Scientist. Constitution and by-laws. [Berkeley, 1950] 29 p. CU-B

399. —— Trinity Methodist Episcopal church. Historical record [Verbatim copy from the records...by Maude Alfreda Martin, Sierra chapter, D.A.R. S.F., 1948] 4 l. CL

400. —— —— Year book... Berkeley, California ...[S.F.] Economist pub. co. [1894?] [48] p. illus. CU-B

401. Berkeley; a journal of a city's progress. Berkeley, Chamber of commerce, 1911–12. v.1–3, 1911–12. No more published. C

402. Berkeley advocate. Holiday edition, Dec. 1892. 36 p. illus. Special souvenir edition. CU-B

403. Berkeley, California, illustrated and described. Oakland, Elliott [1885?] 50 p. illus.
C CHi CLU CSmH CU-B

404. Berkeley civic bulletin. v.1–5, no. 3, v.6, no. 1, 3–8, v.7, no. 2–5, v.8, no. 1–4, v.9, no. 1–2, v.10, no. 1. Aug. 15, 1912–Apr. 24, 1923. Berkeley, City club of Berkeley, 1912–23. 10 v. CU-B

405. The Berkeley club. Anniversary of the Berkeley club, 1873–1909... [n.p., 1909?] 31 p.
CHi CU-B

406. —— Historical sketch of the Berkeley club for its first quarter century [1909] 29 p.
CHi CLU CSmH CU-B

407. —— A memorial of Edward Rowland Sill who died February 27th, 1887...Together with extracts from his correspondence. [n.p., n.d.] CHi CSd CSfWF-H

408. —— Roster, 1873–1923, together with the titles of papers read before the club. [n.p.] 1923. 36 p. CHi

409. —— Twentieth anniversary of the Berkeley club, Thursday, February 16, 1893. [n.p., 1893?] [15] p. C

410. Berkeley evening world. Berkeley, California. A portrayal of the beautiful college town around California's state university... Berkeley, 1898. [16] p. illus.
C CO CU-B

411. [Berkeley fire] Miscellaneous Berkeley and San Francisco newspapers issued at the time of the Berkeley fire of September 17, 1923. [Berkeley, etc. 1923] 1 portfolio. illus. CU-B

412. Berkeley garden club. Roster. 1951. Berkeley [1951?] 1 v. CU-B

413. Berkeley gazette. Anniversary edition. 1947– Berkeley, 1947– illus., ports.
CHi has May, 1947. CU-B has May 21, 1952, May 23, 1957, May 22, 1958.

414. —— Berkeley daily gazette national publicity edition, 1916. [Berkeley, 1916] [56] p. illus., ports. CU-B

415. —— [Berkeley diamond jubilee supplement] [Berkeley, 1941] 20 p. illus., ports. CU-B

416. Berkeley guarantee savings and loan association. The Berkeley scene, 1922–1947. [Berkeley, 1947] [16] p. illus., ports. CHi CU-B

417. Berkeley gymnasium. Catalogue...1879/80– S.F., 1880–
C has 1884/85, 1886/87. CHi has 1879/80. CLU has 1887/88. CU-B has 1880/81–1882/83, 1886/87–1887/88.

418. —— Prospectus of the Berkeley gymnasium, a preparatory school to the University. June, 1877. Oakland, Pac. press [1877] 9 p. CHi CU-B

419. Berkeley land and town improvement association. By-laws... S.F., A. L. Bancroft & co., print. & lithographers, 1873. 15 p. CU-B

420. Berkeley league of fine arts. Annual exhibition. 1st, 1923/24– Berkeley, 1924–
CHi has 2nd 1924/25.

421. Block, Eugene B. The wizard of Berkeley. N.Y., Coward, c1958. 254 p. Biography of Edward O. Heinrich. CHi CSd CSf CRedCL CStmo

422. Boone's university school, Berkeley. Prospectus...1912/13. Oakland [1912] CU-B

423. [Bowman, Jacob N.] The population of early Berkeley. [Berkeley, 193–?] 5 l. Typew. CU-B

424. Brodie, S. Dan. 66 years on the California gridiron, 1882–1948; the history of football at the University of California. [Oakland, Olympic pub. co., print. by Fontes print. co., Oakland, c1949] 477 p. illus., ports.
C CHi CL CLSU CLU CMartC CO CSalCL CSf CU-B

425. Browne, John Ross. Letter in relation to the proposed town site of Lower Berkeley & the value of property & growth of population in & around Oakland. S.F., Excelsior press, 1870. 52 p. C CHi CU-B

426. Bunker, Frank Forest. ...The reorganization of the schools of Berkeley—a plan... Berkeley, 1909. [22] p. CSf CU-B

427. Burnes, Caroline Hyman, and Ranger, Catherine Marshall. A history of the California school for the deaf at Berkeley... [S.F., State college] 1957. 176 l. illus. CSfSt

428. —— Same. 1860–1960. Berkeley [1960?] 157 p. illus.   CChiS CHi

429. Butterfield (H. M.) dahlia garden. Dahlias, 1923 catalogue... [Berkeley, 1923] 12 p. illus.   CHi

430. California. Legislature. The act passed by the legislature of California, at the session of 1877–8, incorporating the town of Berkeley, Alameda county. Approved, April 1, 1878... Berkeley, Wm. Henry Chapman, 1878. 44 p.   CHi

431. —— **Assembly. Committee on public buildings and grounds.** Report...in relation to the construction of the College of letters. [Sacramento] State print. [1874] 464 p.   CSmH CU-B

432. —— **Joint committee on management of state university.** Report of the joint committee...appointed to examine into the management of the University of California, including the administration of the trusts confided to the regents thereof. [Sacramento] State print., 1874. 109 p.   CU-B

433. —— **Senate. Committee on state university.** Report of the Committee on state university to whom was referred Memorial of the Mechanics' institute of San Francisco. Sacramento, State print., 1870. 6 p.   CSmH CU-B

434. —— **University.** Addresses at the inauguration of Horace Davis as president of the University of California, Berkeley, March 23, 1888. Sacramento, State print., 1888. 31 p.   CHi CLU CO CSmH CU-B

435. —— —— Addresses at the inauguration of Martin Kellogg, LL.D., as president of the University of California, Berkeley, March 23, 1893. Berkeley, 1893. 63 p.   CLU CSmH CU-B

436. —— —— Addresses at the inauguration of W. T. Reid as president of the University of California, and the dedication of the Bacon art and library building, Berkeley, August 23, 1881. Sacramento, State off., 1881. 100 p.   CLU CO CSmH CU-B

437. —— —— Addresses delivered at the memorial service for Bernard Moses, April thirteenth, nineteen hundred and thirty, University of California, Berkeley. [Print. under the direction of the Univ. of Calif. print., 1931] 31 p.   CHi CU-B

438. —— —— Addresses of Hon. John S. Hager, LL.D., and of President Edward S. Holden, LL.D., on the occasion of the inauguration of the president of the University of California at the annual commencement at Berkeley, June 30, 1886. Sacramento, State print., 1886. 11 p.   CU-B

439. —— —— [Announcements issued...in connection with the San Francisco earthquake and fire... Berkeley, 1906] 15 pieces in portfolio.   CU-B

440. —— —— California's memorial stadium. [n.p., n.d.] 24 p.   C CO

441. —— —— Same. [Prospectus] [Berkeley, 1921] 20 p. illus., ports.   CHi CU-B

442. —— —— "Charter day." Programme... Berkeley, [1869?–]
CHi has 1884, 1890, 1897, 1902–05, 1920.

443. —— —— Class day and commencement exercises... Berkeley, 1874–
C (1874) CHi (1874, 1877) CU-B (1886, 1913)

444. —— —— [Commencement programmes]
C has 1912. CHi has 1886, 1891, 1899, 1916, 1918, 1930.

445. —— —— ...Endowed chairs of learning.

[Berkeley and Los Angeles, Univ. of Calif. press, 1947] 56 p. illus., ports.   CU-B

446. —— —— ...Endowed scholarships and fellowships; a record of contributions... [Berkeley, Univ. of Calif. press, 1951] 110 p.   CU-B

447. —— —— ...Formal recognition of the transfer of the Lick observatory to the board of regents of the University... Berkeley, Wednesday, June 27, 1888. Sacramento, State print. off., 1888. 24 p.   CHi CU-B

448. —— —— ...Gifts received 1922/23– Berkeley, 1923–
CHi has 1922/23–1955. CU-B has 1924/25–1925/26, 1927/28–1957.

449. —— —— ...Graduates, 1864–1905. November, 1905. Berkeley, Univ. of Calif., 1905. 261 p.
            CHi CL CPom CSd CStoC CU-B CV

450. —— —— ...Graduates, 1864–1910. May 1911. Berkeley, Univ. of Calif., 1911. 268 p. (Univ. of Calif. bul., 3d ser., v.4, no. 9)   CHi CL CU-B

451. —— —— ...Graduates, 1864–1916. Berkeley, 1916. 560 p.   CHi CL CSdS CU-B

452. —— —— ...Graduates of the colleges of letters, social sciences, natural sciences...1864–1899. Berkeley, Univ. press, 1899. 71 p. tables. (Univ. of Calif. bul. n.s. v.1, no. 2)   CHi CL

453. —— —— Guide to the campus. Berkeley, Univ. of Calif. press, 1926. 31 p. illus., map.
                                                    CLO CU-B

454. —— —— Honoring Robert Gordon Sproul on the occasion of his twenty-fifth year as president of the University. 88th charter anniversary...March 22–23, 1956. [Berkeley, 1956] [20] p. illus., ports.   CU-B

455. —— —— In memoriam. Berkeley, Univ. of Calif. press [1886]– Brief obituaries of the faculty and administrative officers.
CHi has 1928–57. CU has 1886–1930 with title, Memorials of persons connected with the University; 1931, 1935–date.

456. —— —— ...The inauguration of Benjamin Ide Wheeler as president of the University... Berkeley, Univ. press, 1899. 30 p.   CSmH CU-B

457. —— —— Inauguration of David Prescott Barrows as president of the University, Wednesday, March 17, to Tuesday, March 23, 1920. Berkeley, 1920. 162 p.
C CHi CL CLSU CLU CO COHN CSf CSfCW CSmH CStcl CStmo CU-B

458. —— —— The inauguration of Robert Gordon Sproul as president of the University of California, Greek theater, October twenty-second, nineteen thirty. Berkeley, 1930. [5] p.   CU-B

459. —— —— Mr. H. D. Bacon's proposed gift to the University. Memorial of the Regents and correspondence. [S.F., 1877?] 8 p.   CHi

460. —— —— The 1939 Nobel prize award in physics to Ernest Orlando Lawrence, February 29, 1940. Berkeley, Univ. of Calif., 1940. 36 p. port.   CHi

461. —— —— Officers and assistants. 1894– Berkeley, 1894– Title varies: 1894–Fall 1945, Officers and students.
CHi has 1896–1915. CU-B

462. —— —— Prospectus of the University of California at Berkeley [!] Alameda county, California. S.F., Excelsior press, Bacon & co., print., 1868. 67 p.
                                          CHi CSfCW CU-B

463. —— —— Same. 1869/70. S.F., Turnbull & Smith [1869] 27 p. CHi

464. —— —— Prospectus of the University of California. Opening of the exercises of the University in the buildings of the College of California, in the city of Oakland, on the 23d of September, 1869. [n.p., 1869] 21 p. CHi

465. —— —— Register... 1870– Berkeley, 1870/71–
CHi has 1870/71–1879/80, 1882/83–1906/07. CSfCW has 1877/78–1888/89. CU-B has 1870/71–1872/73, 1874/75, 1876/77–1881/82, 1886/87–1905/06, 1908/09, 1910/11–1926/27, 1932/33–1933/34, 1942/43–1943/44.

466. —— —— The semicentenary celebration of the founding of the University of California... Berkeley [Univ. of Calif. press] 1919. 563 p. illus.
C CL CLSU CO CSf CSfCW CSmH CStoC CU-B

467. —— —— Several questions answered for those who seek admission. [Oakland, 1873] 4 p. CHi

468. —— —— Statutes of the University of California. Rules of order and general regulations...December 13, 1869. Sacramento, State print., 1869. 10 p. CHi CU-B

469. —— —— Same. 1872. 11 p. CHi

470. —— —— The university; an introduction to the Berkeley campus. [Berkeley, Univ. of Calif. press, 1936] 62 p. CHi CO CSmH CU-B

471. —— —— University of California; a glimpse of its military activities, 1917–1918. [Berkeley, 1919?] [24] p. illus. CHi CU-B

472. —— —— **Academic council.** Standing rules of the Academic council. Berkeley, 1893. 10 p. CHi

473. —— —— **Academic senate.** By-laws and rules of order of the Academic senate... Berkeley, 1885. 8 p. CHi

474. —— —— **Alumni association.** Constitution...Adopted, June 27th, 1888. [S.F.? 1888] 8 p. CHi CU-B

475. —— —— —— Same. Adopted December 15, 1894. S.F., W.A. Woodward & co. print. [1894] 8 p. CU-B

476. —— —— —— The golden book of California, ed. by Robert Sibley... [Berkeley, 1937] 1294 p.
C CBev CHi CL CLO CLU CNF CO CRcS CSd CSdS CSf CSmH CSto CU-B

477. —— —— —— ...Jubilee announcement and programme, 1860–1910... [Berkeley, Univ. press, 1910] 16 p. illus. (Univ. of Calif. bul. 3d ser., v.3 no. 6) CU-B

478. —— —— —— Proceedings at the banquet given to Professor Joseph Le Conte by the Alumni association of the University of California, September 24, 1892. [n.p., 1892?] 16 p. C CHi CLU CU-B

479. —— —— —— Proceedings at the banquet of the Alumni association of the University of California, in honor of the president of the University, and in celebration of the twenty-fifth anniversary of the founding of the University... Held at the Palace hotel, San Francisco, March 23d, 1893. [S.F., 1893] 27 p.
CHi CSmH CU-B

480. —— —— —— Proceedings of the ...annual meeting...7th, 1879. Berkeley, Univ. press, 1879. 1 v. CU-B

481. —— —— —— Report of a committee from the University alumni association on the University of California. [Oakland, Daily evening tribune bk. & job print. house, 1878] 16 p. CU-B

482. —— —— —— The University of California honor roll June 4, 1919... [Berkeley, 1919] 54 p. illus., ports. Honor roll of faculty, alumni and students in the World war. CU-B

483. —— —— **Alumni commissioned officers association.** Constitution ... S.F., Brunt press, 1900. 8 p. CU-B

484. —— —— **Architectural association.** Year book. [S.F., 1912–] illus., plans.
CHi (1912) CU-B (1912, 1914)

485. —— —— **Associated students.** Constitution and by-laws...1901. Berkeley, Univ. press, 1901. 1 v. CU-B

486. —— —— —— The first annual California homecoming celebration... [Berkeley, 1941] unp. illus., col. diagrs. CU-B

487. —— —— —— On the campus. [Berkeley, Associated students store, 1924?] 1 v. illus., port. CU-B

488. —— —— **Bacon art gallery.** Catalog... Sacramento, State print., 1882. 14 p. (Univ. of Calif. lib. bul. no. 4) CHi

489. —— —— **College of pharmacy.** ... Constitution, by-laws... S.F., Alta Calif. print. house, 1873. 10 p. CHi CU-B

490. —— —— **Committee on grounds and buildings.** Report...relative to the boundaries of the University site at Berkeley. [S.F., 1882] 6 p. CU-B

491. —— —— —— To the Board of Regents of the University. [Report] [Oakland, 1869?] 8 p. CHi

492. —— —— **Faculty club.** ...Officers and committees; constitution, by-laws... Berkeley, 1909. 31 p. CU-B

493. —— —— —— Same. [Berkeley, 1921] 36 p. CHi

494. —— —— **Junior day.** Junior exercises '78 ...University of California, Friday, May 4th, 1877 [program] [Berkeley, 1877] [4] p. CU-B

495. —— —— **Library.** Library of French thought. The dedication...exercises conducted by the Friends of France...on September 6 (Lafayette day), 1917... Berkeley, Univ. of Calif., 1918. 36 p. illus., ports. CL CU-B

496. —— —— **Mining and agricultural college, S.F.** Announcement of the mining and agricultural college, San Francisco, 1863–4. S.F., Print. by Towne & Bacon...1864. 8 p. C CHi CU-B

497. —— —— —— Memorial. To the...legislature of the state of California... [n.p., 1863] 10 p. C CHi

498. —— —— **Office of the registrar.** Berkeley fire papers now in the Registrar's office, Berkeley campus (7-23-43), some of which are duplicated herein. [Berkeley, 1943] 30 l. Typew. CU-B

499. —— —— **President.** ...Report of the President... [1868/69]– Berkeley, 1869–
CHi has 1881/82–1925/26, 1930/32–1938/40. CU-B has [1868/69]–1902/04, 1906/08–1938/40.

500. —— —— **Regents.** By-laws...July, 1874. [Berkeley, 1874] 4 p. CHi

501. California. University. Regents (*cont'd*)
Same. ...Adopted May 18th, 1880. [Berkeley, 1880] 8 p.
CHi CU-B

502. —— —— —— Memorial...on the wants
of the University. [n.p., 1880?] 14 p.   CU-B
Other editions followed.
CHi has [1881?], [1884?]

503. —— —— —— Preamble and resolutions of
the joint committee from the State grange, Mechanics'
state council, and Mechanics' deliberative assembly, and
reply of the Board of Regents of the University of California. [S.F., 1874] 8 p.   CHi

504. —— —— —— Report and resolutions of
the special committee on the organization of the colleges... [Oakland, 1868] 10 p.   CHi

505. —— —— —— Report to the secretary.
1868/69– Berkeley, 1869–
CHi has 1868/69 (typed copy), 1872/73, 1874/75,
1879/80–1900/01, 1904/05–1909/10. CU-B has 1874/75–
1877/78, 1879/80–1900/01, 1904/05–1909/10.

506. —— —— —— The state university. Memorial by the Board of Regents. Disastrous effects of the
passage of the Carpenter bill—its unconstitutionality.
[n.p., n.d.] [4] p.   CHi

507. —— —— —— Statements of...to the joint
committee of the Legislature, March 3, 1874. S.F., Excelsior press, Bacon & co., print., 1874. 70 p.
CHi CSmH CU-B

508. —— —— —— War memorial. Agreement
between the Regents...and Walter S. Martin, Charles
Templeton Crocker, John D. McKee [and others] trustees.
[S.F., 1921] 24 p.   CU-B

509. —— —— **School of Librarianship. Alumni association.** Alumni directory, 1902–1956;...library
students from the University of California summer
schools, 1902–1907; California State library school, 1914–
1920; U.C. school of librarianship, 1920–1956. Berkeley,
1956. 95 p.   C

510. —— —— **School of optometry.** Directory
of Optometry alumni, 1925–1953. [12th ed.] Berkeley,
[1953?] 61 p.   CHi

511. —— —— **Science association.** Constitution and by-laws. [n.p., n.d.] 8 p.   CHi

512. —— —— **Special committee on the Morrill college aid act.** ...Report... [Berkeley? 1891]
6 p.   CU-B

513. —— —— **Veterinary dept.** ...California
veterinary college, first annual announcement, 1895. S.F.,
Calif. turf, 1895. 15 p.   CHi

514. California taxpayers' association. Report on
University of California, an analysis of the growth of the
University from 1918 to 1929... 1931. 52 p. (Assoc.
report no. 38, pt. 2)   CSdS

515. Chung Mei home, Berkeley. [Invitation to
opening exercises of the new Chung Mei home for Chinese boys] [Berkeley, 19—?] [3] p.   CU-B

516. City argus, San Francisco. Berkeley water
supply. What the Alameda water company has done for
the beautiful university town... [S.F., 1889] [8] p.
illus.   CU-B

517. City commons club, Berkeley. The City commons club and its precursors. Berkeley, 1946. (In its *Bul.*
v.22, no. 1, p. [5–7]   CU-B

518. College women's club, Berkeley. By-laws.
[Berkeley?] 1931. [16] p.   CHi

519. —— Directory and calendar, 1930–1931. Berkeley, 1930. 47 p.   CHi

520. Conmy, Peter Thomas. History of the en-
trance requirements of the liberal arts colleges of the
University of California, 1860–1927. [Berkeley, 1928]
Thesis (M.A.)—Univ. of Calif., 1928.   CU

**521. Cragmont improvement association, Berke-
ley.** Constitution, by-laws, activities, membership, June
1927. [Berkeley, 1927] 18 p.   CU-B

522. Crampton, Charles Gregory. The Bancroft library... Berkeley, 1938. 25 l.   CU-B

523. Cutter laboratories, Berkeley. Annual report. [n.p., 1951–]
CHi has 1951. CL has 1954–60.

**524. Daughters of the American revolution. Cali-
fornia. John Rutledge chapter, Berkeley.** History
of...from June 13, 1913, to December 1, 1919, and by-
laws as revised and amended March 8, 1920. [Berkeley?
1922?] 16 p.   C

525. Deutsch, Monroe E., ed. The abundant life;
Benjamin Ide Wheeler... Berkeley, Univ. of Calif. press,
1926. 385 p. illus.   CHi CRic

526. Dietrich, Margaret Keyes. History and development of the crime prevention division of the Berkeley
police department. [Berkeley, 1950] Thesis (M.A.)—
Univ. of Calif., 1950.   CU

527. Dodge, ver Mehr co., Berkeley. Kensington
park. [Oakland, R. S. Kitchener print., 191–?] [14] p.
illus., pl.   CU-B

528. Draper, Benjamin. "A great university." [S.F.]
Calif. Acad. of sciences, c1956. 39 l. illus.   CU-B

529. Drury, Wells. Berkeley, California. S.F., Sunset mag. homeseekers' bur.; for the Berkeley chamber of
commerce [n.d.] 63 p. illus.
C C-S CHi CSfMI CSmH CU-B

530. Dyer, Ephraim. The Dyer genealogy. [Berke-
ley, 1959] 98 p. ports., maps, facsims., tables.
CHi CU-B

531. Ehlers, Richard H. Narration of story of
Berkeley, California...at Auditorium dedication, Monday, June 5, 1950. [n.p., n.d.]   CB

532. [Eyster, Nellie Blessing] A beautiful life;
memoir of Mrs. Eliza Nelson Fryer, 1847–1910... Berkeley [Press of Lack bros.] 1912. 107 p. pl. ports.
CHi CSfCW CU-B

533. Ferrier, Francis. North Cragmont, Berkeley.
Berkeley [1910?] [32] p.   CHi

534. Ferrier, William Warren. Berkeley, California; the story of the evolution of a hamlet into a city of
culture and commerce... Berkeley, Author, 1933. 406 p.
illus.
C CHi CL CLSU CLU CLod CMartC CO CSd
CSf CSfMI CSfU CSmH CU-B NN

535. —— ...Berkeley street nomenclature...
[Berkeley, 1923] 43 p. of mounted clippings. C CU-B

536. —— The first fifty years of the First Congregational church of Berkeley, California: an address...
1925. [Berkeley? 1925?] 35 p.   C CHi CU-B

537. —— Origin and development of the University
of California. Berkeley, Sather gate bk. shop, 1930. 710
p. front., map.
C CBu CHi CL CLSU CLU CLgA CMartC CRedl
CSd CSdS CSf CSfCW CSmH CStcl CStclU CU-B
CViCL

538. —— Our church in social thinking and action; an address...given at...the First Congregational church of Berkeley...1936. Berkeley, 1936. 28 p. C CU-B

539. —— The story of the naming of Berkeley. [Berkeley, Daily gazette, 1929] 22 p.
C CAla CHi CO CRic CSmH CU-B

540. Fletcher, John Dundas. An account of the work of relief organized in Berkeley in April and May, 1906. [Berkeley] 1909. Thesis (M.A.)—Univ. of Calif., 1909. CU

541. Franklin, Fabian. The life of Daniel Coit Gilman...N.Y., Dodd, 1910. 446 p. ports.
C CBu CL CLSU CLU CRedl CSf CSmH CU-B

542. Gilman, Daniel Coit. The building of the University. An inaugural address delivered at Oakland, Nov. 7th, 1872...S.F., J.H. Carmany & co., 1872. 29 p.
C CHi CLU CO CU-B

543. —— Statement of the progress and condition of the University of California... Berkeley, 1875. 56 p.
CHi CSmH CU-B

544. Good government club, Berkeley. Constitution and by-laws. [Berkeley? 1894?] 5 p. CHi

545. —— Same. S.F., F.G. Wood co. print. [n.d.] 8 p. CHi

546. Goss, Helen (Rocca) Council-manager government in Berkeley, California, 1923–35. [Berkeley, James J. Gillick co.] 1935. 63 p. charts. CHi

547. Greene, Charles Samuel. The University of California... [S.F., Press of Brown, Meese & Craddock] 1898. 16 p. illus., ports. Reprinted from the *Overland Mo.*, 2d ser., v.31, no. 185, May, 1898.
C CO CSmH CU-B

548. Hall-Scott motor car co., inc., Berkeley. [Care and operation book for] Hall-Scott airplane engines... [S.F., Pernau pub. co., 1917?] 42 p. illus.
CHi

549. —— Hall-Scott "big four" type A-7a 100 h.p. airplane engine. Care and operation book. [S.F., Pernau pub. co., 1917?] 42 p. illus., diagrs. CHi CU-B

550. —— Price list of parts, Hall Scott type A-5 aviation motor. [n.p., 1916] 16 p. illus. CHi

551. —— Supplement [1916] [n.p., n.d.] [8] p. illus. Text in English and Russian. CHi

552. Harmon seminary, Berkeley. Catalogue... a boarding and day school for young ladies...1884/85. S.F., A. L. Bancroft & co., 1884. CU-B

553. Harris, Arthur. City manager government in Berkeley (California)...for the Committee on public administration of the Social science research council. Chicago, Public administration service, 1940. 70 p. CSfSt

554. Harte, Francis Bret. Berkeley, Xanadu of the San Francisco bay. [Berkeley] Hart press, 1951. [4] p. illus. CU-B

555. Haven, Erastus Otis. The function of universities; an address delivered at the commencement exercises of the University of California, June 1, 1881. S.F., Cubery & co., Steam bk. and job print., 1881. 15 p. C

556. Havens, Harold. North Cragmont, Berkeley, California... Oakland, R. S. Kitchener [n.d.] [16] p. illus., maps. CU-B

557. Henderson and Tapscott, Oakland. North Berkeley terrace an unequaled opportunity for successful speculation... [n.p., n.d.] [4] p. illus., map. CHi

558. Hilgard, Eugene W. Biographical memoir of Joseph Le Conte, 1823–1901... Wash., D.C., Judd & Detweiler, inc., print., 1907. [71] p. port. "Read before the National academy of sciences, Apr. 18, 1907." CHi

559. —— Report...to the president of the University. Sacramento, State off., print., 1877. 80 p. CHi

560. ...Hitchcock foundation lecturers [and professors. 1909–November 16, 1946. Berkeley, 1946] 3 l.
CU-B

561. Hodghead, Beverly L. The general features of the Berkeley charter; an address by Beverly L. Hodghead, mayor. Delivered at convention of League of California municipalities at Santa Cruz, on September 21, 1909. [Berkeley? 1909?] 7 p. CU-B

562. Holcomb, Breed & Bancroft. Elm terrace, Berkeley. Oakland [1905] [8] p. illus., map. CU-B

563. Holmes public library, Berkeley. ...Address to the public and constitution... [Berkeley, 1893] unp.
CSmH

564. Homestead loan association of Berkeley. Introducing the Homestead loan association of Berkeley. [Berkeley? 1902?] [23] p. illus. CU-B

565. Houston, Mary Ruth. The early history of Berkeley, California. [Berkeley, 1925] 110 l. illus., maps. Thesis (M.A.)—Univ. of Calif., Aug. 1925.
CU CU-B

566. [Hutchinson, Frederic Clarence] Report on the municipal voting system of the city of Berkeley. [Berkeley, 1945] 56 l. CU-B

567. Improvement clubs of Berkeley. Conference committee. Berkeley, California, a city of homes. [Berkeley, 1906] [46] p. illus. CHi CoU

568. [Jackson, Abraham Wendell] ...To the mine owners, mining engineers, and mining superintendents of the Pacific coast. [Berkeley? 1878?] 4 p. CHi

569. Jamison, Jacob Harry. The city-manager form of government in Berkeley. [Berkeley, 1924] Thesis (M.A.)—Univ. of Calif., 1924. CU

570. Johnson, Mary. The city of Berkeley; a history from the first American settlers to the present date, April, 1942. 127 p. Typew. CB

571. Jones, William Carey. Illustrated history of the University of California...1868–1895. S.F., Frank H. Dukesmith, 1895. 413 p. ports.
Available in many California libraries and CaBViPA

572. —— Same. Rev. ed. Berkeley, Students' cooperative soc. [c1901] 430 p. illus., ports.
C CHi CLU CLod CRcS CRic CSalCL CStrJC CU-B

573. Kantorowicz, Ernst. The fundamental issue; documents and marginal notes of the University of California loyalty oath. [S.F., 1950] 40 p. CU-B

574. Kurtz, Benjamin Putnam. Charles Mills Gayley... Berkeley, Univ. of Calif. press, 1943. 289 p. port. CHi CRic

575. Lathrop, Elizabeth. The story of a Berkeley home. [Berkeley? 1910] [16] p. illus., maps. CHi

576. Lee, Robert Greeley. The Berkeley municipal election of 1947; a study in voting behavior. [Berkeley, 1948] Thesis (M.A.)—Univ. of Calif., 1948. CU

577. Linsley, Earle Garfield. Some phases of stream development in the Oakland and Berkeley hills. [Berkeley, 1908] Thesis (M.S.)—Univ. of Calif., 1908. CU

578. McWilliams, Carey. Witch hunt. Bost., Little, 1950. 361 p. CSd CU-B

579. Mason-McDuffie co., Berkeley. Claremont, a private residence park at Berkeley. Oakland, Pr. by R. S. Kitchener [n.d.] 16 p. illus. CHi

580. —— Over fifty years in Berkeley. [Berkeley, 1938?] 15 p. illus. CHi

581. Mehnert, Klaus. Ein Deutscher Austauschstudent in Kalifornien. Stuttgart, Deutsche Verlags-Anstalt, 1930. 175 p. CU-B

582. Meikle, Brock, and Skidmore, Berkeley. [Photograph album of real estate in Berkeley Highlands, Kensington and Thousand Oaks. Berkeley, 1914?] 22 mounted illus., 22 mounted photos. CU-B

583. Mitchell, Edward H., pub. University of California, Berkeley. [S.F., 190–?] 15 photos. CU-B

584. Mobilized women's organizations of Berkeley. Berkeley's war work, 1917. [Berkeley] 1918. 23 p. CU-B

585. Morse, Clinton Ralza. California football history, a history of football at the University of California from its inception in 1882 to 1923. Berkeley, Berkeley gazette [c1924] 175 p. illus., ports. C CHi CSf CStmo CU-B

586. —— Same. Berkeley, Gillick press [c1937] 223, [36] p. illus., ports. CU-B

587. National board of fire underwriters. Committee on fire prevention and engineering standards. Report on the Berkeley, California conflagration of September 17, 1923. [N.Y.? 1923] 9 p. illus. CHi

588. Newell-Murdoch company. Thousand Oaks, Berkeley. [S.F., Honig advertising service, 1915?] 24 p. illus. CU-B

589. Newman club, Berkeley. The Catholic chapel and lecture hall at the University of California. Berkeley [Merchants press] 1909. 16 p. illus. CHi CSfCW

590. —— Constitution and by-laws, revised 1915. Berkeley [n.d.] 8 p. CHi

591. —— Historical sketch of Newman hall and the work carried on in the interest of the Catholic students at the University of California. Berkeley [1911] 22 p. mounted illus. CHi CU-B

592. —— Newman hall Catholic chapel and library at the University of California. From August 1, 1916, to August 1, 1917... [Berkeley? 1916?] 56 p. illus. CHi

593. Niehaus bros. & co., West Berkeley. Manufacturers of and dealers in moulding, brackets, door and window frames...catalogue. [S.F., McNeil bros., n.d.] 108 p. illus. Also called: West Berkeley planing mills. CHi

594. "Occident" publishing co. An account of the Greek-letter fraternities in the University of California... Berkeley, 1883. 44 p. CLSU CU-B

595. Official scorebook of the football game between Leland Stanford jr. university and University of California, Thanksgiving day, Thursday, November thirtieth, 1893. [n.p., 1893] 35 p. illus., ports. CU-B

596. [Olney, Warren] Sixty years [a paper read before the Berkeley club, October 16, 1902] [Berkeley, 1902] 28 p. CHi

597. Olneys & Middleton, auctioneers. Map-catalogue...great credit sale of Berkeley real estate...Friday, 9th and Saturday, 10th October 1874... S.F., Calif. reporter print., 1874. 7 p. maps. CHi

598. Olympic club, San Francisco. Fall games of the Olympic athletic club held at Berkeley campus, Thanksgiving day... [S.F., Francis, Valentine & co., print., 1889] [8] p. illus. CU-B

599. O'Neill, Edmond. An account of the birth and growth of the Faculty club of the University of California. Berkeley, 1933. 10 p. port. CU-B

600. Overstreet, Harry Allen. University of California, a monograph. S.F., Dept. of educ., Calif. Louisiana purchase exposition commission, 1904. 20 p. illus., pl. CChiS CSfCW

601. Parker, William Belmont. Edward Rowland Sill; his life and work. Bost., Houghton, 1915. 307 p. illus. COnC

602. Patrons of husbandry. California state grange. Memorial of California state grange and Mechanics deliberative assembly on the state University. [Sacramento, State print., 1874] 9 p. CSmH CU-B

603. [Peatfield, J. J.] A mine of musty manuscript; the Bancroft library. [S.F., 1895] [11] p. illus., port. CU-B

604. Peralta building and loan association. By-laws. S.F., Henderson & Crane, print., 1889. 31 p. CSmH CU-B

605. Peralta Hall (Girls' school) Berkeley. ... Announcement...2d. 1891/92— [n.p.] 1891— CU-B has 1891/92.

606. Phi Beta Kappa. California alpha, University of California. ...Constitution, by-laws, list of public addresses, list of members. Berkeley, 1910. 16 p. CU-B

607. —— —— Same. 1917. 29 p. CU-B

608. Pheobe Hearst architectural plan for the University of California. The international competition... [S.F., Crocker, 1899] 152 p. illus. CHi CU-B

609. —— The Phoebe A. Hearst architectural plan for the University of California. S.F., J. B. Reinstein [1899?] [12] p. CHi CU-B

610. —— Programme for an international competition for the Phoebe Hearst architectural plan of the University of California. Berkeley, 1897. 39 l. CLU CO CSmH CU-B

611. —— The visit of the jurors in the Phebe [!] A. Hearst architectural competition... Reprinted from the *University chronicle*, v.24, no.3 June, 1899. CHi

612. [Photographs of men prominent in the history of the University of California. n.p., n.d.] 45 p. CU-B

613. Plehn, Carl Copping. ...Berkeley should own its water works. An address...Jan. 14, 1899... [Berkeley, 1899] [6] p. of mounted clippings. CU-B

614. Pond, William Chauncey. Founders' day address...Delivered at the Pacific theological seminary, Berkeley, California, October 11, 1913, on the forty-seventh anniversary of the founding of the institution. [Berkeley? 1913?] 19 p. CSmH CU-B

615. Priestley, Herbert Ingram. The Bancroft library, University of California. [Berkeley, 1938] 12 l. Typew. CU-B

616. Red cross. U.S. American national Red cross. ...Red cross relief work in the Berkeley fire disaster... [Berkeley? 1924] 15 p. illus. CU-B

617. Reinstein, Jacob Bert. Address..."for the purpose of suggesting and discussing matters necessary to the prosperity of the university," Jan. 15, 1898. [S.F., Woodward & co., print., 1898?] 41 p. CHi CU-B

618. Ritter, Mary (Bennett) More than gold in California, 1849–1933. Berkeley, Professional press, 1933. 451 p.

Available in many California libraries and CaBViPA.

619. [Robbins, Robert Lash] Westward the course of empire; Berkeley, California, year 1950 in stamp and story. [n.p., c1950] 16 p. illus.   CHi

620. Salbach, Carl. Iris. [Catalogs] Berkeley [193–?—]

CHi has 1931, 1934, 1937, 1941, 1943, 1946–47, 1950.

621. San Francisco call. Beautiful Berkeley and some of its progressive features. [S.F.] 1896. [12] p. of mounted clippings. illus., ports.   CU-B

622. Sather gate studio, Berkeley. S.A.T.C.-N.U. Souvenir booklet. Pictures of officers, companies, barracks, drills and ceremonies. S.F., Sunset pub. house [n.d.] unp. illus. Students' army training corps—Naval unit established, Oct. 1918.   CHi

623. Savage, Michael Thomas. A study of the Democratic party in the city of Berkeley. [Berkeley, 1959] Thesis (M.A.)—Univ. of Calif., 1959.   CU

624. School of the art of the theatre, Berkeley. School of the art of the theatre, Berkeley, California, June 19th, 1922, to July 29th, 1922. Under the direction of Samuel J. Hume & Irving Pichel. [Berkeley, 1922] [2] p.   CHi

625. [Schulte, Gustavus] Columbia's wrath, not sparing the regents of the state University of California ... [Oakland? 1874?] 25 p.   CU-B

626. —— A glance from a German standpoint at the State University of California, particularly, and the educational systems of America and Germany, comparatively. S.F., Bacon & co., print., 1871. 57 p.   C CHi CU-B

627. —— Our state university and the aspirant to the presidency. [Booklyn, 1872] 10 p.   CHi

628. —— The resignation of the Board of regents ... [Oakland, 1874] 25 p.   CU-B

629. Sears, Jesse Brundage. Berkeley school properties survey... [Berkeley] Berkeley bd. of education, 1926. 195 p.   CLSU CLU CU-B

630. Sheehan, Jack F. The games of California and Stanford...football...baseball...track...tennis...since the inaugural football match in March, 1892... S.F., Press of Commercial pub. co., 1900. 104 p. ports.
      C CHi CSf CSfCW CSmH CU-B

631. Shepherd, Charles Reginald. The story of Chung Mei; being the authentic history of the Chung Mei home for Chinese boys up to its fifteenth anniversary, October, 1938... Phila., Bost., [etc.] Judson press [c1938] 264 p.   C CHi CO CU-B

632. —— The story of Chung Mei... N.Y., Am. Baptist home mission soc. [1948] 64 p.   CU-B

633. —— The ways of Ah Sin: a composite narrative of things as they are. N.Y., Revell, c1923. 223 p.
                                                            CRedCL

634. Sibley, Robert, ed. The romance of the University of California. S.F., Pub. by H. S. Crocker for the Univ. of Calif. alumni assoc., 1928. 59 p. illus.
                          CL CSdS CSfCW CU-B

635. —— Same. 2d ed. Berkeley, Calif. alumni assoc., 1932. 62 p. illus., ports.   CChiS CHi

636. —— University of California pilgrimage; a treasury of tradition, lore and laughter. [1st ed. Berkeley, Lederer, Street and Zeus, c1952] 201 p. illus. (part col.)   C CHi CSd CU-B

637. Sigma Xi. ...Report of the committee of the society of Sigma Xi on the plague conditions in Berkeley, San Francisco, and Oakland. [Berkeley? 1908?] 8 p.
                                                            CU-B

638. Sill, Edward Rowland. Sill memorial number. (*Univ. of Calif. mag.* v.2, no. 4, May 1896)   CHi

639. Smith, Dora. History of the University of California library to 1900. [Berkeley, 1930] Thesis (M.A.)— Univ. of Calif., 1930.

C (microfilm) CL (microfilm) CU

640. Snell seminary, Berkeley. Catalogue. 1887/ 88— Oakland, Carruth & Carruth print., 1888—

CHi has 1887/88, 1889/90. CU-B has 1895/96, 1901, 1902/03, 1904/05, 1908/09–1909/10, 1913/14.

641. —— Commencement, 1889, at the First Congregational church, Oakland, California. Thursday, May 23d, 1889, 7:45 p.m. [Oakland? Carruth & Carruth?] 1889. 4 p.
                                                            CHi

642. Sproul, Robert Gordon. Inaugural address... October 22, 1930. Berkeley, Univ. of Calif., 1930. 29 p.
                                                            CStmo

643. Starr King school for the ministry, Berkeley. President's and treasurer's report. 1914/15— Berkeley, 1915–

CU-B has 1914/15–1915/16.

644. —— Register. 1904/06— Berkeley, 1906–
CU-B has 1904/06–1907/08, 1916/17, 1928/29.

645. Stewart, George Rippey. The year of the oath; the fight for academic freedom at the University of California... N.Y., Doubleday, 1950. 156 p.
CChiS CHi CLU CNa CRb CSd CSdS CStmo
CU-B CV

646. The story of the Berkeley fire [of September 17, 1923. Berkeley? 1924] [15] p. illus., map.
                                    CB CHi CU-B

647. Suggestions for the better direction of the University of California. S.F., W.M. Hinton & co., 1881. 14 p.
                                                      C CLU

648. Sunset mausoleum association. Sunset mausoleum, Berkeley hills, California. [Berkeley? 1928?] 12 p. illus., map.   CHi CU-B

649. Sutcliffe, George, comp. Who's who in Berkeley, 1917. [Berkeley? 1917] 80 p. illus.   CU-B

650. [Sutliffe, Albert] comp. A description of the town of Berkeley, with a history of the University of California... S.F., Bacon & co., 1881. 24 p.
                                          CHi CSmH CU-B

651. Swift, John Franklin. The present and future of the university. An address delivered on commencement day, June 29, 1887. Sacramento, State print., 1887. 16 p.   CLU

652. Thwaites, Reuben Gold. The Bancroft library. A report submitted to the president and regents of the University of California... Berkeley, 1905. 18 p.
                                          CHi CL CLU

653. Toll, Marilyn Poest. Political activities of the University of California and the state colleges of California. [Berkeley, 1961] Thesis (M.A.)—Univ. of Calif., 1961.   CU

654. Town and gown club, Berkeley. Constitution and by-laws, adopted, 1897, rev., 1902, rev., 1904. [Berkeley] 1904. 19 p.   CHi

655. The University of California and its relations to industrial education as shown by Prof. Carr's reply to grangers and mechanics... S.F., B. Dore & co., print., 1874. 112 p.   C CHi CSmH CU-B

656. Veteran volunteer firemen's association of Berkeley. ...Annual oldtimers' affair...[1st]–15th, 1934–1948. [Berkeley, 1934–48] 15 v. illus., ports.
CHi (14th)   CU-B

657. —— Golden anniversary, 1904–1954. Berkeley, 1954. 56 p. illus.   CHi

658. Watson, James Earl. A history of political science at the University of California, 1875–1960. [Berkeley, 1961] Thesis (Ph.D.)—Univ. of Calif., 1961.
CU

659. Waterman, Syvanus D. History of the Berkeley schools... Berkeley, Professional press, 1918. 181 p.
C CHi CLU CO CSfCP CSfCW CSmH CU-B

660. Wayave, Marian Antoinette. A study of data indicative of employment in Berkeley, California, 1925–1931. [Berkeley, 1931] Thesis (M.A.)—Univ. of Calif., 1931.   CU

661. Wedertz, Gilbert Clarence. History of the origin and administration of public endowments of the University of California. [Berkeley, 1929] Thesis (M.A.)— Univ. of Calif., 1929.   CU

662. West Berkeley college settlement. ...Annual report for 1900–1901... West Berkeley [1901] 33 p.
CU-B

663. Wheat, Carl Irving. The Bancroft library, whence, what, whither; an address delivered...on May 22, 1955...in commemoration of the 50th anniversary of its acquisition by the University of California. Berkeley [Friends of the Bancroft library] 1955.
CHi CSfWF-H

664. Wheeler, Benjamin Ide. ...Inaugural address of Benjamin Ide Wheeler as president of the University ... Berkeley, Univ. press, 1899. 12 p.   CU-B

665. Wilkinson, Warring. The earliest residents and houses in Berkeley. Oct. 30, 1908. 2 l.   CU-B

666. Wilson, Jackson Stitt. How I became a socialist...Berkeley, The Author, 1912. v.p.   CHi
667. —— J. Stitt Wilson to the people of Berkeley. [Berkeley? 1917?] [4] p. illus., port.   CU-B

668. Worden, Willard E. [Scenes at the University of California, 1904–191–?...in the Worden collection in the Wells Fargo history room, San Francisco] [S.F., 1946] 26 photos.   CU-B

669. Writers' program. California. Berkeley, the first seventy-five years...Co-sponsors: city of Berkeley. Berkeley festival association. Berkeley, Gillick press, 1941. 159 p. illus., ports. Bibliography: p. 149–154.
C CBb CHi CL CLO CLU CNa CO CRc CRedl
CSfCP CSfSt CSj CSluCL CSmH CStclU CU-B
CV N NN

Hayward

670. Emerson, W. O. Biographical sketch of the late James G. Cooper, M.D., of Hayward [n.p.] 1902. 32 p.   CHi

671. Hayward. Chamber of commerce. Book of the year. Hayward, 1948. 64 p.   CH
672. —— —— Information directory of the Hayward area... Hayward, 1949–
CH has 1949–59. CHi has 1950.

673. —— **Planning commission.** Hayward prepares a master plan for future development. Hayward, 1953. 95 p. maps.   CH CSt

674. —— —— Report of survey to supplement the Hayward master plan report. [n.p., 1956] 57 p.   CH

675. —— **Public school. Laurel district.** Commencement programmes.
CHi has 1891.

676. —— **Trinity Episcopal church.** Golden jubilee anniversary; fifty years in the life of Trinity Episcopal church Hayward, California, 1886–1936. [Hayward, 1936?] 32 p. illus., ports.   CHi

677. Hayward pioneer days fiesta, Hayward, Calif., 1946. ...Souvenir program. [Hayward? 1946] [24] p.   CH CU-B

678. Hayward review. Classified booster directory ... Hayward, 1946. 48 p.   CH

679. —— Hayward diamond jubilee, 1926. [Hayward, 1926] [36] p. illus., maps.   CH

680. —— Hayward review special, 1908. [Hayward, 1908] [20] p. illus., ports., maps.   CO

681. Haywards park homestead union. Prospectus, articles of association...of the Haywards park homestead union, incorporated, June 1869. S.F., Cubery & co., print., 1869. 20 p.   CU-B

682. Haywood fire company no. 1. Constitution, by-laws, and list of members of Haywood fire company no. 1, Haywood, Cal. Approved, May 11th, 1872. S.F., Winterburn & co., print., 1873. 15 p.   CU-B

683. Laymance real estate co. California: Hayward. Hayward home farm tract. [1913?] unp. illus.   CO

684. Richert, Robert B. Government in unincorporated sectors of the greater Hayward area. [Berkeley, 1948] 111 p. Thesis (M.A.)—Univ. of Calif., 1948.
CH (photocopy) CU

685. Rotary club, Hayward. Silver anniversary year book, July 1, 1947–June 30, 1948. [n.p., 1948?]
CH

686. Seramur, Paul Lawrence. Subdivision control in the Hayward area; a case study of the growth of residential areas in a selected urban area of California. [Berkeley, 1949] Thesis (M.A.)—Univ. of Calif., 1949.
CU

687. Wight, Edward Allen, and Merritt, LeRoy Charles. The Hayward public library; a survey of its resources, services... Berkeley, 1955. 68 p.   C CH

Oakland

688. Adams, Arthur Lincoln. How shall Oakland secure public ownership of waterworks... [Oakland, 1904?] 14 p.   CSmH CU-B

689. Adams, Edson Francis. Oakland's early history. [Oakland, Tribune pub. co., 1932] 22 p.
Available in many libraries.

690. Alameda county. Board of supervisors. Oakland, Alameda county, California... [Oakland, c1929] 13 p. illus., ports., map.   CU-B

691. Allardt, G. F. A plan for supplying the cities of Oakland and San Francisco with water. S.F., 1880. 25 p. map.   CSmH

692. Allen, Merritt Parmelee. Joaquin Miller, frontier poet. N.Y., Harper, 1932. 162 p. port.   CHi

693. Altruria co-operative union of Oakland. By-laws... [Oakland] Howe print. co., 1895. 16 p.
CU-B

694. Andersen, Arthur R. How sturdy an oak; a centennial history of Live Oak Lodge no. 61, Free and accepted Masons in California. Oakland, Greenwood print., ltd., 1954. 181 p. illus.   CHi

695. Annexation; facts and figures, comparative tax rates, map showing tax districts and polling places, effects of annexation on outlying districts. Oakland [1909] unp. Pub. by the City of Oakland, Oakland chamber of commerce and the Oakland merchants' exchange.   CO

696. Arbor villa, the home of Mr. and Mrs. Francis Marion Smith, East Oakland, 1902. 55 pl., ports. Ms. notes.   CO CU-B

697. —— Same. E. T. Dooley, photographer. 47 pl.
                                                              CU-B

698. Archibald, Robert A. The Oakland veterinary hospital for horses & dogs, 1722–1724 Webster street, Oakland, California. Oakland [1910?] 16 p. illus.   CHi

699. Arlett, Arthur M. A history of Plymouth church, Oakland, California... [Oakland, Plymouth church council, 1933. [21] p. illus.   CO CSmH

700. Associated alumni of the Pacific coast. Oration, poem, and speeches, delivered at the second annual meeting...held at Oakland, California, June 6th, 1865. S.F., Towne and Bacon, 1865. 108 p. The Associated alumni was composed of graduates of all American colleges and universities who had emigrated to California; contains list of 500 or more members, with their colleges, occupations, and California residences.
                                                         CHi CSfP

701. —— Same. Third annual meeting, Oakland, Calif., June 6, 1866... S.F., A. Roman and co., 1866. 93 p.
                                                              CHi

702. Athenian-Nile club, Oakland. Three score and ten; a commemoration of the life of the Athenian-Nile club. Oakland, 1953. 16 p. illus., ports.   CHi CU-B

703. Athens athletic club, Oakland. Twenty-fifth anniversary souvenir edition. Oakland, 1950. 96 p. illus.
                                                              CHi

704. Auxiliary liberal league, Oakland. Preamble, constitution and by-laws of Auxiliary liberal league no. 256. Oakland, W. P. Truesdell, print., 1883. 10 p.   CSmH

705. Baird, Adam. Autobiography. Oakland, Scofield print. [1926?] 20 p.   CBb CHi CU-B

706. Bamford, Georgia (Loring) The mystery of Jack London; some of his friends, also a few letters... Oakland, Author, 1931. 252 p. illus., ports. "The intellectual and social life of Oakland in the '90's is pictured in this book, which has been withdrawn from publication."
C CBaB CChiS CHi CL CLSU CLU CO CRedl CSdS CSf CSmH CStclU CStrJC CU-B

707. Barnard, W. E. & co., auctioneers. Special credit sale: of Oakland property..."The Gaskill tract" on Saturday, June 8th '78... Oakland, Butler & Bowman, print. [1878] folder. map.   CHi

708. Barnes, Mrs. David. A history of Piedmont avenue school; 1891–1932... [Oakland] Piedmont press [1932] [7] p.   CO

709. Bartholomew, Harland, and associates, St. Louis. A report on freeways and major streets in Oakland, California... St. Louis, 1947. 41 p. illus., pl. Mimeo. (Unit of the Oakland master plan)   CHi

710. —— A report on off-street parking and traffic control in the central business district and three outlying centers... St. Louis, 1947. 67 p. illus. Mimeo. (Unit of the Oakland master plan)   CHi

711. —— A report on transit facilities and mass transportation in the Oakland metropolitan area... St. Louis, 1947. 57 p. illus., maps. Mimeo. (Unit of the Oakland master plan)   CHi CO

712. Beckman, Roy C. The romance of Oakland; a story of the growth and development of Oakland and Alameda county... [Oakland, Landis & Kelsey, c1932] 32 p. illus.   CHi COHN CU-B

713. Bell, Howard Holman. George C. Pardee and the Oakland water supply, 1889–1890. [Berkeley, 1947] 124 l. Thesis (M.A.)—Univ. of Calif., Feb. 1947.   CU-B

714. Bennett, John E. Shall we have a municipal water supply? What Spring valley has done and is doing to defeat it. Address...at Hamilton hall, Nov. 2, 1906. [n.p., n.d.] 31 p.   C

715. Benton, Joseph Augustine. Some of the problems of empire; oration delivered at the commencement of the College of California, Wednesday, June 3d, 1868... S.F., Excelsior press, Bacon & co., print., 1868. 19 p.
                                      C CHi CLU CSmH CU-B

716. Bisbee's (Miss) school for young ladies, Oakland. Boarding and day school for young ladies. Miss S. B. Bisbee, principal... [Announcement] [Oakland 18–?] [4] p.   CU-B

717. Bishop, Harris, comp. Souvenir and résumé of Oakland relief work to San Francisco refugees, 1906; supervised by the Finance committee. [Oakland, Oakland tribune, 1906] 96 p.   C CHi CO CSfWF-II CU-B

718. [Blake, Evarts I.] ed. Greater Oakland, 1911 ... Oakland, Pac. pub. co. [1911?] 455 p. illus., ports., map.
C CChiS CHi CL CLU CO COHN CSf CSfCP CSfCW CSmH CU-B NN

719. The Blue book, 1902/3; Oakland, Alameda, Berkeley. Oakland, Hicks-Judd co. [1903?] 157 p. illus., ports.   C CO CU-B

720. Bowhill, Thomas. The Alvarado artesian water of the Oakland water company compared with the surface waters of Lake Temescal and Lake Chabot of the Contra Costa water company. A bacteriological analysis of the two waters... [n.p., 1895?] 45 p. illus., tables.
                                                          CLU CU-B

721. Bradford, Ward. Biographical sketches of the life of Major Ward Bradford. [n.p., Pub. for the author 189–?] 95 p. illus., port.   CLgA CU-B

722. Brown, Charles Reynolds. Fifty years: an anniversary sermon; delivered Sunday morning, Nov. 20, 1910, at the First Congregational church, Oakland, Cal. [Oakland, Wood, 1910] 19 p. ports.   CHi CLU CO

723. —— The higher life of Oakland. [Sermon preached in the First Congregational church, Oakland, California...November 22d, 1903] Oakland, Enquirer pub. co., 1903. 18 p.   CLU

724. —— My own yesterdays. N.Y., Century [c1931] 332 p. port. "Reminiscences of his Oakland pastorate": p. 87–133.   CL CLSU CO CSf

725. Brown, Elmer Ellsworth. ...The school... [Oakland, 1896] 12 p. About the Tompkins school, Oakland.   C CU-B

726. Buckham, John Wright. John Knox McLean, a biography. Oakland, Smith bros., 1914. 122 p. ports.
                            CHi CL CLU CSf CSfCW CSmH

727. Buckingham, Fisher A. Origins and early economic developments of Oakland... [Berkeley, 1947] v.p. Thesis (M.A.)—Univ. of Calif., in economics.
                                                       CO CU-B

728. Buckley, Homer W. A chronology of legislation specifically naming the municipality of Oakland from 1849 to and including 1933... [Oakland] 1934. 18 l. Mimeo.   CO

729. —— **comp.** Court house site; use to which property was put, 1820 on. [Oakland, 1930] 20 l. Typew.
                                                                    CO

730. Builders' exchange, Oakland. Official directory...Issued 1895... Oakland, McCombs & Vaughn, print., 1895. 120 p.   CU-B

731. Business and professional women's club, Oakland. History of Business and professional women's club of Oakland. [Oakland, 1940] 8 l. Typew.   CU-B

732. California vs. Southern Pacific co. Supreme court of the United States, no. 9, original. The state of California, complainant, vs. Southern Pacific company, defendant. In equity. Brief on behalf of the city of Oakland. [n.p., 189–?] 229 p.   CU-B

733. California. Laws, statutes, etc. An act to authorize the city of Oakland to obtain a supply of water. [n.p., 1874] 7 p.   C CSmH

734. —— **University. Heller committee for research in social economics.** Cost of living studies. Estimated annual family expenditures, by Committee on living costs, Oakland forum. Berkeley, Univ. of Calif., 1927. 13 l. illus.   CU

735. California military academy, Oakland ... Annual catalogue of the Oakland academy... 1st- 1865– CHi has 7th, 9th, 1871, 1873. CU-B has 3d, 1867.

736. California pioneer society of Alameda, Contra Costa and adjacent counties. Constitution and by-laws. Oakland, Pac. press pub. house, 1887. 45 p.
                                                                    CHi

737. California pottery co. Manufacturers of clay products. Founded 1873. Price list revised April 1, 1927. [n.p., 1927] 13 p. illus.   CHi

738. Campbell, Fred M. The public schools of Oakland, California. Oakland, Bd. of educ., 1887. 39 p. illus.   C

739. Central bank, Oakland. The gay nineties in Oakland. [Oakland? 1941] [32] p. illus.   CHi CO

740. Central national bank, Oakland. Oakland, California; the city of diversified industry. Oakland [c1920] illus.   CU-B

741. —— **Report.** [Oakland, 19—?–] CHi has 1909–12, 1918, 1922–24, 1926.

742. [Chabot observatory; copies of papers found in corner stone at razing of building in 1929, including address of Mayor Martin at laying of corner stone, May 21, 1883]   CO

743. [Chamberlain, Arthur Henry] Complimentary souvenir book, fifty-third annual convention, National education association and International congress of education. Oakland, August 16–28, 1915. [Oakland? 1915] 190 p. illus., map.
                                        CHi CSdS CSfCW CU-B

744. Chickering, William H. The Bay cities scheme costly and chimerical; an open letter to the citizens of Oakland...Detailed reasons why it should be rejected. [Oakland, 1904?] 15 p.   CSmH CU-B

745. Claremont country club. By-laws, etc., officers and members. Oakland, 1903– CHi has 1908, 1911.

746. Claremont pines corp., comp. Claremont pines progress...former Bowles estate. Oakland [1927?] 16 p. mounted pl.   CHi

747. Clark, Max A. X. Social service organizations of Oakland, California. Oakland, 1939. 85 [i.e. 86] l.
                                                            CO CSdS

748. Clarke, Thomas Brownell. The Oakland ghost and ancient phenomena, with a review of the Oakland committee. S.F., 1877. 39 p.
                                            CLU CSmH CU-B

749. Club notes; music, art, drama, v.1, no. 1–v.8, no. 26, March 14, 1904–Feb. 8, 1909 [Oakland, 1904–10] 10 v. illus., ports. Organ of Ye Liberty playhouse, Oakland.   CU-B

750. College homestead association. ...Articles of agreement of the Homestead association: together with water report and map...And a series of college papers, by S. H. Willey, College of California. January 16, 1865. S.F., print. by Towne & Bacon, 1865. 29 p.
                                            CLU CSmH CU-B

751. Committee of one hundred and one, Oakland. [Brochure. Oakland, 1952?] [4] p.   CHi

752. Committee on church, Seminary Park, Alameda county. Specifications of materials to be furnished...in the erection and completion of a church and vestry buildings, at Seminary Park, Alameda county. [Seminary Park, 18–?] 14 p.   CU-B

753. Conmy, Peter Thomas. The beginnings of Oakland, California, A.U.C. Oakland, Oakland public lib., 1961. 66 p.   CAla CHi

754. Contra Costa water co. ...Water rates, rules and regulations, adopted by the directors, July 1, 1867. Oakland, 1867. 12 p.   CU-B

755. Contra Costa water co. vs. Breed, A. H. ... Contra Costa water co. (a corporation), plaintiff and respondent, vs. A. H. Breed, auditor of the city of Oakland, defendant and appellant. Re-argument before the court in banc by Guy C. Earl in behalf of appellant... [S.F.] Pernau [1903] 165 p.   CU-B

756. Contra Costa water co. vs. Oakland et al. ...Contra Costa water company, a corporation, plaintiff and respondent, vs. the city of Oakland et al., defendants and appellants... [Oakland, 1909] 2 v. in 1.   CU-B

757. Coyle, Robert Francis. Making memories. By Rev. R. F. Coyle, pastor First Presbyterian church, Oakland, Cal. [Oakland, Jordan print. co., 189–?] 24 p.
                                                                    CU-B

758. Crabtree's travel hotel and shopping guide of Oakland, Alameda and Berkeley... v.1, no. 1, March 1920– [Oakland, Tribune press, 1920–] illus. CU-B has March 1920, March 1921.

759. Crocker, Florence B. [Who made Oakland?] ... Oakland, Clyde Dalton, c1925. 158 p. illus., ports., map.
C CHi CO COHN CSf CSfU CSjC CSmH NN

760. Crombie nursery, Oakland. [Catalogs] CHi has 1932, 1940 and [n.d.]

761. Cubberley, Ellwood Patterson. Report of a survey of the organization, scope and finances of the public school system of Oakland, California... [Oakland?] Bd. of educ., 1915. 48 p.   CL CO CU-B

762. Cummings, George Alfred, and Pladwell, E. S. Oakland, a history... [Oakland, Tribune press, c1942] 119 p. illus., ports., maps.
C CAla CBb CHi CLU CLod CMartC CO CRic
CSjC CSmH CStrJC CWhC NN

763. Cunningham, Curtiss & Welch, pub. Oakland, California. [S.F., 1905]   CSmH

764. Daniels, Paul I. Collecting and distributing a domestic water supply... [Oakland] East bay water co., 1921. 24 p. illus.   C CHi CLO CO CU-B

765. Daughters of the American revolution. California. Oakland chapter. History of Oakland chapter, 1897 to 1922. [Oakland, 1922] 21 p.   C

766. Davie, John L. My own story, by John L. Davie, Mayor emeritus of Oakland. Oakland, Post-enquirer pub. co., 1931. 174 p. illus., ports. First published in *Post-enquirer*, July 6–Sept. 19, 1931.   C CHi CL CLU CO CSdS CSf CSmH CV

767. de Kruif, Paul. Kaiser wakes the doctors. N.Y., Harcourt, Brace and co. [c1943] 158 p.   CHi

768. De Witt & Snelling booksellers, Oakland. Catalogue. no. 1, 1904?– [Oakland? 1904?–] CHi has no. 5, Nov. 1908, no. 6, March 1909.

769. Diggins, John Anthony. Reverend William Gleeson (1827–1903) historiographer of the Catholic church in California. [S.F., 1951] Thesis (M.A.)—Univ. of San Francisco, 1951.   CSfU

770. Dille, Elbert Riley. ...Rome's assault on our public schools...Two discourses by Rev. E. R. Dille, D.D., delivered in the First M.E. church, Oakland...1889; being replies to an address by Rev. Father Gleeson (printed herewith) delivered at the inauguration of St. Mary's... college, Aug. 11, 1889. [Oakland] Carruth & Carruth, print. [1889] 34 p.   CLU CO CU-B

771. —— Then and now; sixty years reviewed; some personal and pastoral reminiscences... Oakland, Kennedy co., 1923. 22 p. port.   CHi CSfCW

772. Dingee, William J. Catalogue and price list of Oakland real estate. Oakland, Pac. press, 1887. 29 p.   CSmH

773. Dolsen, James H. The defense of a revolutionist, by himself; the story of the trial of James H. Dolsen... Oakland, Author, 1920. 128 p.   CHi

774. Dupré, Josephine A. Defense of J. A. Dupré, M.D., in her relations with A. F. Evans as his physician ... [Oakland, 1889?] 48 p.   CHi

775. East Oakland improvement association. East Oakland and Fruit Vale, Alameda county, California; a land of health and homes. [S.F., Crocker, 1888] [32] p. illus.   CLU CO CSmH CU-B

776. Ebell society, Oakland. ...Yearbook. 1893/ 94– Oakland, 1893–
CHi has 1929/30. CU-B has 1893/94, 1897/98–1898/99.

777. Edwards, Ben F. 100 years of achievement and challenge; a brief history of the First Presbyterian church of Oakland, California. Oakland, Centennial committee of the First Presbyterian church, 1953. 72 p. illus.
C CCSC CHi CMartC CSfU CStoC CU-B

778. Elks, Benevolent and protective order of. Oakland lodge no. 171. Oakland 171 primer...comp. by the Los Angeles reunion committee of Oakland lodge no. 171, B.P.O.E. [Oakland] 1909. [55] p. illus., ports.   CHi CSmH CU-B

779. —— —— ...Official guide of the Elks' street fair and carnival, Oakland, June 14–21, 1902. [Oakland, 1902] [96] p. illus., ports.   CHi CU-B

780. Emerson, David L. Speech...on Oakland judged from an eastern standpoint, delivered in Dietz hall (Oakland) Nov. 30, 1875...Oakland, Butler & Bowman [1875] 24 p.   CHi CLU CSmH CU-B NHi

781. —— Valedictory address, delivered at Oakland college, June 1, 1864. Subject: The scholar. Also: The Rev. T. Starr King—lessons of his life and death, delivered in the college chapel, March 10, 1864. [n.p., 1864?] 3 p.   C CHi

782. Eugenia Poston club. In memoriam. Eugenia C. Murrell Poston. S.F., Author, 1908. 61 p. illus. By pupils of Mrs. Poston's school of Marysville and, later, of Oakland.   C CHi CLU CMary CSmH

783. Fabiola hospital, Oakland. Nineteenth annual report...for 1897. [n.p., 1897] 63 p.   CHi

784. —— Souvenir programme, Fabiola May fete, Oakland trotting park, May 1, 1895. [Oakland? 1895] 56 p. illus., ports.   CHi

785. —— Same, May 1, 1896. Oakland, Oakland enquirer pub. co., 1896. 98 p. illus.   CHi

786. Farnsworth, J. A., jr., comp. The California door company, Oakland. [n.p., United sash and door dealers, c1923] 262 p. illus.   CHi

787. [Felton, John Brooks] The railroad system of California. Oakland and vicinity. State univ., etc. S.F., J.H. Carmany & co., 1871. 48 p. maps.
C CLU CSmH CU-B

788. Ferrier, William Warren. Henry Durant, first president, University of California... Berkeley, Author, 1942. 165 p. port. Bibliography: p. 159–161.
C CHi CL CLSU CLU COHN CSf CSmH CStclU CStrJC CU-B

789. Field seminary, Oakland. Catalogue, Field seminary, school for girls and young ladies. 15th year, 1886/87. Oakland, Enquirer steam print. [1886?] 7 p.   CHi

790. Flynn, J. T. Report and recommendations covering the legal status and physical features of the Oakland water front...June 15, 1909. Oakland, Calif. river & harbor league [1909?]   CHi CLU CSmH CU-B

791. Freemasons. Oakland. Gethsemane chapter, no. 5, Rose Croix. Reception of the heart of our martyred brother, Ex-Gov. Ygnacio Herrera y Cairo, at the hands of our sister Señora Rosalia L. de Coney... Masonic temple, Oakland, April 24, 1893. [n.p., 1893?] 12 p.   CHi

792. —— —— Live Oak lodge, no. 61. Souvenir; fortieth anniversary...[1854–1894] [n.p., 1894] 93 p. (lacks p. 18–30) illus.   CHi

793. —— —— Oakland lodge, no. 188. Seventy-fifth anniversary, 1868–1943. [Oakland? 1943] 120 p. illus., ports.   CHi CO

794. —— —— Sequoia lodge no. 349. 1902– 1952; fifty year history of Sequoia lodge no. 349 F. & A. M. Oakland, The Lodge [1952?] 50 p. illus., ports.   CHi

795. Fruitvale. Board of trade. Beautiful Fruitvale. S.F., William T. Grubb, 1905. unp. illus.   CO

796. Gilmore, W. A., comp. Souvenir. Oakland fire department. Published in the interest of the Firemen's relief fund—March, 1901. [Oakland Tribune, 1901] 126 p.   CHi CSmH

797. Gladding, Richard S., comp. and pub. Pocket business directory of Oakland, Cal....also...sketch of Oakland... Oakland [1881?] 164 p.
CSmH CU-B

798. Grand army of the Republic. Dept. of California. Official souvenir of the twenty-seventh annual encampment, G.A.R., Department of California. Held at Oakland, California, April 23–28, 1894, including views of Oakland and a description of the city. Oakland, Pac. press, 1894. [30] p. illus.
CMartC CO CSmH CU-B

799. Green, Buddy, and Murdock, Steve. The Jerry Newson story. [Berkeley, East Bay Civil rights congress, 1950] 48 p. illus.   CHi

800. Guillou, Helen Rogers (Blasdale). Bibliography of the Eucalyptus press, 1932–1950. Oakland, Mills college, 1950. 41 p. front.   CHi   CRcS

801. Harlow, James. Land of the Oaks. 1st ed. Oakland, Bd. of educ. of the Oakland unified school district, c1953. 141 l. illus.   CLU

802. —— Same. rev., 1955. [Oakland? 1956, c1955] 248 p. illus., maps.   CO

803. Hegemann, Werner. Report on a city plan for the municipalities of Oakland and Berkeley... Prepared and published under the auspices of the municipal governments of Oakland and Berkeley, the Supervisors of Alameda county [etc., etc.] 1915. 156 p. illus., maps.
C   CH   CHi   CL   CLU   CO   CSd   CSf   CSfCW   CSmH   CU-B   ViU

804. [Heinold, George] John Heinold and his First and last chance. [Oakland, International press, 1936] 16 p. illus., port.   CU-B

805. Hering, Rudolph. Report...to the council of the city of Oakland on a proper system of sewerage for Oakland, California...December 31, 1889. Oakland, Enquirer pub. co., 1890. 23 p.   CSmH

806. Herrick, Don Henry. The yesterday of the waterfront: being a dialogue on its historic sites and landmarks. For Alameda county library and the Board of Supervisors. Berkeley, 1937. 96 l.   CU-B

807. Holcomb, Breed & Bancroft. Santa Fe tract, Oakland... [S.F., L.A., Norman Pierce co., 1904?] [12] p. illus.   CU-B

808. —— The Santa Fe tracts; a new city of homes on the Key route, Oakland, Berkeley... [1905?] 24 p. illus., fold. maps.   CU-B

809. Home club, East Oakland. Constitution and by-laws. [Oakland? 1910] 22 p.   CHi

810. Home club, Oakland. Pure milk commission. A sketch of the origin and work of the Home club milk commission in Oakland, California. [Oakland, 190–?] 31 p. illus.   CU-B

811. Hopkins academy, Oakland. Catalogue... 1873/74–1891/92. [S.F., Cubery & co., print., 1873–93] CU-B has 1873/74, 1875/76, 1888/89, 1891/92.

812. Horton school, Oakland. Catalogue. 1889/90– Oakland, 1890–
CU-B has 1889/90, 1892/93, 1894/95–1895/96, 1899/1900–1902/03, 1904/05–1905/06.

813. Hotel promotion committee. The bankers' hotel must be built. Prolonged delay in completing project is greatly impairing the city's reputation... [Oakland, 1908] 129 p.   CSmH

814. Howard, John B. Brief of examination of the title of Theodore Le Roy, to the tract of land heretofore occupied by the Patten brothers, in East Oakland... [S.F.] Bonnard & Daly, print. [1876] 13 p.   CSmH

815. Hubbard, Elbert. ...Journey to the home of Joaquin Miller... Also a study of his work by George Wharton James. N.Y., The Roycrofters, 1903. 106 p. ports.   CSd   CSf

816. Huntington, Collis Potter, vs. Oakland. ... C. P. Huntington, vs. the city of Oakland et al.... [n.p., 1880?] 20 p.   CO   CSmH   CU-B

817. The illustrated directory of Oakland, California. Comprising views of business blocks, with reference to owners, occupants, professions and trades, and brief history of the city. Oakland, Illustrated directory co., 1896. 104 p. illus.   CHi   CLU   CO   CSmH

818. Industrial survey associates. Oakland to 1980; a population and economic analysis prepared for the Oakland city planning commission...1956. 70 p. map, tables, diagrs.   CChiS   CO

819. International institute, Oakland. For the building of international understanding in Oakland. [Oakland? 1931?] [8] p.   CU-B

820. International typographical union of North America. Union no. 36, Oakland. Official yearbook and souvenir, ninety-first annual convention...August 13 thru 19, 1949. [Berkeley, Lederer, Street & Zeus co., 1949] [94] p. illus. (part col.), ports.
C   CHi   CRic   CSf

821. [Irish, John P.] Oakland... Oakland, E. A. Heron, agent for the purchase, sale and care of real estate, 1887. 14 p.   CSmH   CU-B

822. James, Elias Olan. The story of Cyrus and Susan Mills. Stanford [1953] 27 p. illus.
C   COMC   CRedl   CSd   CStmo

823. Jewett, Henry Erastus. Israel Edson Dwinell, D.D. A memoir with sermons. Oakland, W.B. Hardy [1892] 320 p. port.
C   CBb   CHi   CLU   COHN   CSfCW   CSmH   CU-B

824. Joaquin Miller foundation. The Board of trustees extends a cordial invitation to become a member of the Joaquin Miller foundation, inc. [Oakland, Tooley-Towne press, 1953] [12] p. illus.   CHi

825. Johnson, Roosevelt. Oakland, California... Its industries and environs. [S.F., Gensler-Pierce co., c1903] [35] p. illus.   CHi   CU-B

826. —— Same. 1904. 62 p.   CHi

827. Johnson homestead association. Articles of association, certificate of incorporation and map, etc. S.F., Towne & Bacon, print., 1865. 23 p.   CSmH

828. Jones, DeWitt, ed. Oakland parks and playgrounds; supervising editor, DeWitt Jones... Sponsored by the Oakland parks and recreation departments. [Oakland, 1935] 321 l. (Project no. 3-F2-163) Typew.   CO

829. —— Port of Oakland... Sponsored by the Oakland Board of port commissioners. The State emergency relief administration project no. 3-F2-85. [Oakland] 1934. 388 l. Typew.   CHi   CO   CU-B

830. Judson Pacific–Murphy manufacturing corp. By-laws of the Judson manufacturing comp'y of Oakland, California. Incorporated July 3, 1882. S.F. Crocker, 1882. 10 p.   CSmH

831. Kaiser aluminum and chemical corp. Annual report. Oakland [194–?–]
CL has 1949–50, 1952–60.

832. —— Prospectus; 700,000 shares...4¾ cumulative preferred stock... [n.p.] 1955. 35 p.   CHi

833. Kaiser–Frazer corp. Prospectus, 1,700,000 shares...common stock... [n.p.] 1945. 15 p.   CHi

834. Kaiser industries. Annual report. 19– Oakland, 19–
CL has 1948–1950, 1952–1961.

835. —— [Descriptive folder, 1950] Oakland [1950?]   CL

836. —— Facts in brief about Henry J. Kaiser... [Oakland? 1946?] 52 p.   CHi

837. —— Kaiser today: 40 years of progress. Oakland [n.d.]   CL

838. Kaiser steel corporation. ...Annual report...
19– Oakland? 19–
CHi has 1951–53, 1957. CL has 1952–58.

839. Close-ups, some of the men in Kaiser steel. [n.p., 1956] 38 p. ports.   CHi

840. Keep, Rosalind Amelia. Fourscore years; a history of Mills College... Mills College 1931. 142 p. illus., ports   CBaB CHi CSmH

841. —— Same. Rev. ed. 1946. 203 p. illus., ports.
C CChiS CHi CL CLSU CLU CMont CSf CSfCW CSrD CStclU CU-B

842. [Keller, Michael J.] Album of Oakland, California...and a description of Oakland, by the president of the Board of trade. Oakland, Pac. press, 1893. [20] p. illus.   C CHi CO CSmH CU-B

843. Kelly, E. S. Condensed sketch of the early history of California, San Francisco and Oakland. By...one of the earliest pioneers of Oakland. Oakland, Pac. press, 1879. 46 p.   C CO CSmH CU-B

844. Kelsey's nurseries. Catalogue and price list for fall and winter, 1874...of trees, and plants... Oakland, Butler & Stilwell, steam bk. & job print., 1874. 16 p.   CU-B

845. Kent, Regina. Oakland; a story for children. Oakland, Oakland bd. of educ. [c1930] 113 p. illus.
CU-B OrU

846. Key system transit lines. Annual report. [Oakland? 192–?–]
CHi (1924, 1935)   CL (1950–59)

847. —— Plan for readjustment, dated July 20, 1929. [S.F., 1929] 21 p.   CU-B

848. Killip & co., auctioneers, San Francisco. Catalogue of choicely bred trotting stock...1892...at Oakland trotting park. [S.F.? 1892] 40 p .   CU-B

849. —— ...Catalogue of high-bred trotting brood mares, stallions, fillies...the property of the estate of the late Daniel Cook, February 28th, 1883, at the Oakland trotting park... S.F., A. Carlisle & co. [1883] 28 p.   CHi

850. Knapp, Henry R., firm, pub. Picturesque Oakland. S.F., 1889. 47 pl.   CHi CLU CO CSmH

851. Koford, Henning, ed. Dr. Samuel Merritt, his life and achievements; the Samuel Merritt hospital, its history and trustees. Oakland [Kennedy co., print.] 1938. 79 p. illus., ports.   CHi CSf CU-B

852. Ladies' relief society, Oakland. Annual report... 1st– 1870– Oakland, 1870–
C has 36th, 38th, 40th, 55th–56th, 58th–59th, 1906–08, 1910, 1926–27, 1929–30. CHi has 10th–12th, 1883. CU-B has 14th, 15th, 30th, 31st, 34th–39th, 40th–60th, 63d–66th, 1884/86–1937.

853. —— By-laws and rules...[Oakland, Carruth & Carruth co., print., n.d.] 8 p.   CU-B

854. —— Old ladies' home; ceremonies of laying the corner-stone at Temescal, the crowning work of the Ladies' relief society... [Oakland? n.d.] 11 p.   CU-B

855. —— Register...1884/85–1940. Oakland, [1884?–1939?] 43 v.   CU-B

856. —— Rules for the government of the Home for aged women...of Oakland, California. [Oakland, 1882?] 11 p.   CU-B

857. Lake Merritt breakfast club. 1960 roster... Oakland, 1960. 73 p. ports.   CHi

858. Laymance real estate co. The protection Rockridge affords. [Oakland, n.d.] [12] p.   CU-B

859. —— Rock Ridge properties... Oakland [191–?] [6] p. illus., map.   CU-B

860. Leon, Wilmer Joseph. The Negro contractor in Oakland, California, and adjacent cities. [Berkeley] 1954. Thesis (M.A.)—Univ. of Calif., 1954.   CU

861. Lewis, Dio. Oakland (California). Its climate, etc. An address...March 31st, 1877. S.F., Cubery & co., print., 1877. 10 p.   CSmH

862. London, Charmian (Kittredge). The book of Jack London. N.Y., Century, 1921. 2 v. illus., ports.
CHi

863. London, Jack. Jack London, American rebel. N.Y., Citadel, 1947. 533 p.   CSd

864. London, Joan. Jack London and his times; an unconventional biography. N.Y., Doubleday, 1939. 387 p. port.   CSf

865. Loofbourow, G. T., & co., pub. Oakland: "Athens of the Pacific"...also facts and figures of Alameda county. [comp. by George W. Calderwood and G. T. Loofbourow] Oakland, 1896. 128 p.   CHi CSmH

866. —— Same. Published under the joint auspices of the Merchants' exchange and Board of supervisors of Alameda county. Oakland, 1897. 97 p. illus.
CO CSmH CU-B MoSHi

867. —— Same. 1902. unp. illus.   CU-B

868. Lowry, Russell. History of the First national bank of Oakland, California. 1874–1908... [Oakland, c1908] 16 p. illus.   C CHi CO CSmH CU-B

869. Lucky stores, inc. Prospectus...40,000 5½% cumulative preferred shares...and 50,000 common shares ... [n.p.] 1947. 27 p.   CHi

870. Macarthur, Walter. San Francisco bay; sailing ships in Oakland creek, shipyards and docks... Sketched ...1928. 54 col. sketches.   CSmH CU-B

871. McDevitt, William. Jack London as poet and as platform man. Did Jack London commit suicide? S.F., Recorder-Sunset press, 1947. 32 p.   CSf

872. —— Jack London's first... S.F., Recorder-Sunset press, 1946. 32 p.   CHi

873. McDonnell nursery. Flowering and bedding plants. [Oakland, 1939] [8] p.   CHi

874. McLean, John Knox. The understanding of the holy, the highest end of culture; commencement sermon, on occasion of the annual closing of the Home school, Oakland...May, 1877. Oakland, Butler & Bowman, bk. & job print., 1877. 19 p.   CU-B

875. MacMullan, C. S. Say, you dons! Call it "Lake Peralta," "Lake Peralta" is its fit and old designation... Oakland [n.d.] 4 p.   CO

876. Malcolm, J. S. The most beautiful philanthropy of modern times. East Oakland, Josephine Cottage pub. co., 1904. 11 p. Describes orphanage established by Mrs. Francis Marion Smith.   CHi

877. Marberry, M. Marion. Splendid poseur; Joaquin Miller—American poet. N.Y., Crowell, 1953. 310 p.
CBb CMon CRedCL CSalCL CSd CSf CViCL

878. Marsh, Henry M., and Hirschler, Horace. Hy-pres manufacturing company, Oakland, California; a statement of affairs, management, future... [S.F., Taylor & Taylor, 1917] [26] p.   CHi

879. —— Marchant calculating machine company, Oakland, California; a statement of affairs, management, future... Oakland, Gross & Miller, inc., 1919. 33 p. illus.   CHi

880. Masonic relief bureau, Oakland. How Oakland's Masonic relief bureau gave aid to distressed worthy brethren and other refugees. Oakland, 1906. 36 p. ports.
C

881. Meads, Simeon P. In my own lot and place; an autobiography. Oakland [Author, 19–?] 102 p. illus., ports. Author settled in Oakland in 1876.
C CHi CL CLU CSf CSmH CU-B

882. Merriman school for girls, Oakland. ...The school that is different, 1915–1916. [S.F., 1915] [20] p. illus.
CHi

883. Metropolitan Oakland area committee, pub. Buyers' guide; a directory of manufacturers, distributors, wholesalers, jobbers of metropolitan Oakland area which includes all of Alameda county...1940–1941. [Oakland, 1940?] 325 p.
CHi

884. —— It's an amazing new west and metropolitan Oakland area, California, is at its very heart! Oakland [1945?] 48 p. illus., maps.
CU-B

885. —— The metropolitan Oakland area; Alameda, Albany, Berkeley, Emeryville, Hayward, Oakland, Piedmont, San Leandro and the country communities of Alameda county, California, U.S.A.; Treasure Island's mainland. [Oakland, 1939?] [32] p. illus. "Edited by Harvey C. Scott."
CHi CSmH CU-B

886. —— Same. [Oakland, 194–?] [36] p. illus., map.
CU-B

887. Miller, Joaquin, i.e., Cincinnatus Hiner. My own story. Chicago, Belford-Clarke co., 1890. 253 p. illus.
CHi

888. —— Overland in a covered wagon; an autobiography. N.Y., Appleton, 1930.
CBb

889. Miller, Juanita Joaquina. My father, C. H. Joaquin Miller, poet. Oakland, Tooley-Towne, 1941. 218 p. illus.
CBb CHi

890. Mills, Benjamin Fay. Inaugural address of Benjamin Fay Mills as minister of the First Unitarian church of Oakland, California, March eighteenth, 1900. [Oakland] The Society [1900] 7 p. port.
CU-B

891. Mills, Cyrus Taggart. In memoriam: Rev. Cyrus Taggart Mills, May 4th, 1819...April 20th, 1884. [Oakland, 1884?] 84 p.
CHi

892. Mills, Susan Lincoln (Tolman) To the friends and patrons of Mills college. Oakland, Priv. pub., 1886. 7 p.
CHi CU-B

893. Mills college. Addresses at the inauguration of Rev. C. C. Stratton, D.D., as president of Mills college, California, Friday, May 4, 1888. [S.F., C. A. Murdock & co., print., 1888?] 29 p.
CU-B

894. —— Alumnae of Mills college and seminary. [Oakland? 1907] 26 p.
CU-B

895. —— Alumnae of Mills seminary, 1866 to 1884. S.F., Dodge bros. steam print. [1884?] 8 p.
CU-B

896. —— Catalogue...1872/73– S.F., F. Eastman, print., 1873–
CHi has 1879/80, 1885/86. CL has 1911/12–to date. CU-B has 1872/73–1877/78, 1879/80–1884/85, 1886/87–1917/18, 1922/23, 1928/29–1941/42, 1946–1957.

897. —— Commencement exercises of Mills seminary, Thursday, June 1st, 1876... [n.p., 1876] [4] p.
CU-B

898. —— Same. Thursday, May 27, 1880. S.F., Bacon & co. print., 1880. 4 p.
CHi

899. —— Dedication of El Campanil and its chimes

of bells at Mills college, April the fourteenth, Nineteen hundred and four. [S.F., N. Pierce co., 1904?] 27 p. illus.
CU-B

900. —— Exercises of class night and commencement day, Mills college, May 1890. [Oakland, Enquirer steam print, 1890?] 27 p.
C

901. —— Exercises of inauguration of Homer Baxter Sprague, president of Mills college, Alameda co., California October 24th, 1885. [Mills college? 1885?] 35 p.
CHi CU-B

902. —— Golden jubilee celebration of the granting of a college charter by the state of California in 1885. [Commencement program] Mills college, 1935. [8] p.
CHi

903. —— Mills alumnae, 1857–1903. [Register] [S.F., Print. by the Gensler-Pierce co., 1903?] 21 p.
CU-B

904. —— Mills college, a residence college for women. "Education is environment." Oakland [Mills college] 1937. unp. illus.
CHi

905. —— Mills college 1852–1937; a statement covering the history, present position, plans, and needs of the pioneer college for women on the Pacific coast. [n.p., n.d.] 48 p. illus.
CHi

906. —— Mills college for young ladies; its attractions, home and school life. [S.F., Mysell Rollins co., 190–?] 18 p. illus.
CU-B

907. —— Mills college for young women, California. [n.p., 1903?] [16] l. illus.
CU-B

908. —— Mills college, Oakland, California; commemorating eighty-five years of distinguished service... [Oakland, Mills college, 1937] 32 p.   CHi CSf CU-B

909. —— Mills seminary and college: new course of study approved by the Board of trustees, May 1885. [Oakland? 1885?] 13 p.
CU-B

910. —— The Mills seminary for young ladies; its location, surroundings, and a description of the building. S.F., Franklin print. house, 1871. 16 p.   CU-B
Other editions followed.   CHi (1877, 1885) CU-B (1871, 1873, 1877, 1885)

911. —— "One of America's most interesting colleges"... Oakland, Mills college, c1935. unp. illus.
CHi

912. —— President Stratton and Mills college. [n.p., 1890?] 8 p.
CU-B

913. —— Prospectus of the Mills seminary, Seminary park, Brooklyn, Alameda county, California. S.F., Franklin print. house, 1871. 16 p. illus.
CU-B

914. —— Souvenir of Mills college and seminary illustrating principal points of interest... Seminary Park, 1893. [48] p. illus.
CU-B

915. —— A voice of the future; a century of educational pioneering, 1852–1952. S.F., Recorder-Sunset press, 1952. 31 p. illus.
CHi

916. —— "What's past is prologue;" a century of education, 1852–1952... [Oakland, 1952] 47 p.   CHi

917. —— **Alumnae association.** By-laws. [n.p., 1921] 15 p.
CU-B

918. —— —— Mills alumnae association, 1879. [S.F.] Bacon & co., print. [1879] 31 p.
CU-B

919. —— —— Same, 1879–1912. [n.p., 1912?] 21 p.
CU-B

920. —— **President.** Report...1931/32–1938/39. Oakland, 1932–39. 8 v. in 1.
CU-B

921. Minton, H. C. The genius of art; an address delivered at the commencement of Mills college...May 28, 1890. San Jose, Smith & Wilcox, 1890. 16 p.   CHi

922. Mitchell, Edward H., pub. Souvenir of Oakland, California. [S.F., 190–?] 15 mounted photos.
CU-B

923. Montgomery, Zachariah. The Schroder trial. Bottom facts and leading incidents connected with the killing of Dr. Alfred LeFevre, and the trial and disgraceful acquittal of the slayer... [Oakland, c1881] 21 p. port.   C CHi CLU CO CSmII CU-B

924. Moore, Albert Alfonzo. Genealogy and recollections... S.F., Priv. print. by Blair-Murdock co., 1915. 170 p. illus., ports.   C CLU CSfCP

925. Moore shipbuilding company, Oakland. Cargo ships of war; the tale of the shipbuilder of Oakland... S.F., 1923. 87 p.   CHi

926. Mott, Frank K. The creation, history and development of Lake Merritt. [Oakland, 1936] 13 l. Mimeo.   CO

927. —— Grand avenue heights at the head of Lake Merritt ... [Oakland, R. S. Kitchener print., 1907] [12] p. illus., map.   CU-B

928. Mott, Gertrude. The story of Woodminster. 1936. 10 l. Typew.   CO

929. Mountain view cemetery association, Oakland. By-laws and rules... Oakland, 1873. 24 p.
CHi CU-B

930. —— Same. Oakland, Evening Tribune print., 1880. 33 p.   C CHi

931. —— Organization of Mountain view cemetery association, Oakland, California... S.F., print. by M.D. Carr & co., 1865. 80 p.   CLU CO CU-B

932. National education association. Official program, fifty-third annual convention... Oakland, California, August 16 to 28, 1915. [Oakland, Kelley-Davis co., print., 1915] 46 p.   CHi

933. Native sons of the golden West. Alameda county parlors. Oakland souvenir, Admission day celebration, Oakland, California, September 6, 7, 8 & 9, 1913. [Oakland, The International press, 1913] 48 p. illus., port.   C C-S CLU

934. —— **Athens parlor, no. 195.** By-laws of Athens parlor no. 195, N.S.G.W. Instituted at Oakland, California, September 28, 1895. Oakland, Enquirer job print. [1895?] 25 p.   CHi

935. Newhall, H. M., & co., auctioneers, San Francisco. Great auction sale of Oakland and Alameda real estate, improved and unimproved, Tuesday, April 11, 1876... Oakland, Butler & Bowman, print. [1876] 18 p. maps, diagrs.   CHi

936. Noel, Joseph. Footloose in Arcadia; a personal record of Jack London, George Sterling, Ambrose Bierce. N.Y., Carrick & Evans, 1940. 330 p.   CChiS CRcS

937. Norman, Albert E. A steeple among the oaks. A centennial history of the First Methodist church, Oakland, California. Oakland, 1962. 73 p. illus.   CHi

938. [Notices of the sale of lots in four real estate tracts in Oakland: the McKee tract, Wakefield tract, Piedmont cable tract, Warner tract] [n.p., 1891–1905] 4 pieces in portfolio. illus., maps.   CU-B

939. Oakland vs. Carpentier, Horace W., et al. In the Supreme court... The city of Oakland, respondent, vs. Horace W. Carpentier et al., appellants. Brief and argument of respondent, Eugene Casserly, counsel... S.F., Robbins & co., 1863. 66 p.   CLU CSmH

940. —— ...Respondent's brief by David P. Barstow ... S.F., Towne & Bacon, print. [1863?] 50 p.   CU-B

941. —— ...Statement of case. Thompson, Irving & Pate, attorneys. [S.F., 1863] 15 p.   CSmH

942. Oakland vs. Oakland waterfront co. ...The city of Oakland (a municipal corporation) plaintiff and appellant, vs. the Oakland waterfront company (a corporation) defendant and respondent. Transcript on appeal... Oakland, Enquirer, 1909. 4 v. Paged continuously (3478 p.)   CSfCW

943. —— ...The city of Oakland (a municipal corporation) plaintiff and respondent vs. the Oakland water front company (a corporation) defendant and appellant ... Transcript on appeal... [Oakland] Oakland tribune print., 1896. 2 v. Paged continuously (2010 p.)
CLU CSfCW CSmH

944. —— ...Brief on behalf of plaintiff by William Rude Davis. [Oakland] Oakland enquirer pub. co. [1899?] 89 p.   CSfCW CSmH CU-B

945. Oakland vs. Wheeler, Peter L., et al., as trustees of the Samuel Merritt hospital. In the Supreme court of the state of California...Transcript on appeal from judgment of the Superior court... S.F., 1915. 707 p.   CHi

946. Oakland. Board of engineers. Report...on the grades, streets and sewerage, of the city of Oakland, 1869. [Oakland] Oakland news steam bk. & job presses, 1870. 15 p.   CU-B

947. —— **Board of fund commissioners.** [Minutes...and record of bonds issued, June 8, 1855–Sept. 1, 1897] [117] p.   CU-B

948. —— **Board of health.** ...Report...1873–74, 1885–86, 1892/93, 1896/97, 1901/02–1902/03. Oakland, 1875–1903. 8 v.   CU-B

949. —— **Board of port commissioners.** Port of Oakland, Oakland, California... Oakland, 1930. 35 p. illus., map.   CHi CU-B
Other editions followed.   C (1950?, 1953?, 1957?) CHi (1952?) CU-B (1951?, 1958?)

950. —— —— Statement of Port of Oakland to Senate fact finding committee on establishing a Port authority for San Francisco bay. [Oakland? 1949] 1 v. v.p. illus., maps, diagrs.   CU-B

951. —— —— ...Why do we have a port commission? [Report covering the first seven years of the Oakland port commission] Oakland, 1934. 8 l. Typew.
CU-B

952. —— **Board of public works.** ...[Blue prints of waterfront leases] Oakland, 1919–21. 32 pl.   CO

953. —— —— Report...relating to water front, and memorandum of proposed agreement with Southern Pacific company and Western Pacific railway. September 28th 1908. [Oakland? 1908] 10 p.   CSmH

954. —— **Board of trade.** Oakland, California... [Oakland, 1887] folder (16 p.) illus., map, tables.
CU-B

955. —— **Brooklyn Presbyterian church.** 1861–1911; jubilee anniversary history... [Oakland, Progress press, 1911?] 20 p. illus.   CHi

956. —— **California college.** Annual catalogue. 188–?– Oakland, 188–?–
CHi has 1889/90–1897/98, 1899/1900–1900/01, 1903/04.

957. —— —— Articles of incorporation and by-laws ...R. H. Cross [secretary] [Oakland?] 1908. 18 p.
                         CHi   CU-B

958. —— —— By-laws, board of trustees... [Oakland?] 1892. 10 p.   CHi

959. —— —— ...Reports of the president and faculty. 1892. [Oakland, 1892] 22 p.   CHi CU-B

960. —— **California college of arts and crafts.** ...Announcement of courses, 1909–1932. Oakland, 1909–1932. illus., pl.   CU-B

961. —— —— Announcement of the...annual Summer session, 1921–1935. Oakland, 1921–35. 15 v. in 1. illus., ports.   CU-B

962. —— —— Portfolio of pictures of California college of arts and crafts, Oakland, California. [S.F., Taylor & Taylor, 1936] [16] l. illus.   CHi

963. —— **California medical college.** Annual announcement... [S.F., 1879–1891] 7 v. in 1. illus.
                         CU-B

964. —— **Chamber of commerce.** Articles of association and by-laws of the Oakland chamber of commerce together with list of officers, standing committees and members for 1892–93. Oakland, Tribune pub. co., 1892. 27 p.   CSmH

965. —— —— Executive directory of firms employing twenty-five or more persons in the metropolitan Oakland area. Oakland, 1959. 95 p.   CAla

966. —— —— Handbook of comparative data bay area counties, two metropolitan areas. Oakland, 1957. unp.   CRic

967. —— —— Industrial Oakland, California. [1925] 47 p. illus.   CU-B

968. —— —— It's an amazing new West, and metropolitan Oakland area, California, is at its very heart! [Oakland, 1944] 48 p. illus.   C CU-B

969. —— —— Metropolitan Oakland area, Alameda county, California; the natural industrial center of the new West. Oakland, 1945. 39 p. illus. Illustrated brochure with text in English, Spanish, Portuguese, French and Russian.   CHi

970. —— —— Oakland achievement. v.1, no. 2 (Mar. 1915)–v.4, no. 2 (Dec. 1920)   CO

971. —— —— Oakland, California... [1909] [60] p. illus., map. "Issued by the Sunset mag. homeseekers' bur."   CL CSmH

972. —— —— Same; revised [1911?] 61 p. illus., maps.   C CHi CL CU-B NN

973. —— —— Oakland, California, the coming commercial city of the Pacific coast... [Oakland, 1908?] [16] p. illus., tables.   CU-B
Other editions followed.   CO (1909) CU-B (1924, 1926, n.d.)

974. —— —— Oakland in the early days, 1852–1952. Prepared by Catherine Penprase. [1952?] 5 p. Mimeo.   CHi

975. —— —— Oakland outlook. v.1. Mar. 1, 1922– Called *Metropolitan*, Jan. 13, 1937–Aug. 1946.
C has 1947–1958. CO has 1922–date.

976. —— —— **Special transportation committee.** The jitney from the community standpoint...April 22, 1915. [Oakland, 1915?] [8] p.   CU-B

977. —— **Charters, Ordinances, etc.** Amended Oakland city charter as adopted by the City council in committee of the whole. [Oakland, 1874?] 42 p.   CU-B

978. —— —— Charter for the city of Oakland, prepared and proposed by the Board of fifteen Freeholders, elected December 10, 1887... Oakland, Tribune, 1888. 98 p.   CLU

979. —— —— Same. ...July sixth, 1910. Oakland, Borland-Nilson press, 1910. 112 p.
             CHi CSfMI CSmH

980. —— —— General municipal ordinances... in effect January 1, 1892. Compiled by authority of the city council by Fred L. Button... Also city charter (annotated) and list of officers. Oakland, Tribune pub. co., 1892. 280 p.   CHi CSmH

981. —— **Citizens.** Affidavit of citizens of Oakland. [Sacramento, State print., 1878]   CSmH

982. —— —— Communication to Senator John W. Barnes. [Sacramento, State print., 1878]   CSmH

983. —— —— Home reception by the citizens of Oakland, California, to Hon. Victor H. Metcalf...at Macdonough theatre, Oakland, California... September twenty-second, nineteen hundred and four. [Oakland, 1904] [8] p. port.   CU-B

984. —— —— Oakland: A city of great commercial promise. Issued...February 17, 1894. Oakland, Enquirer pub. co., [1894] 13 p.   CSmH

985. —— —— The railroad system of California. Oakland and vicinity... S.F., J. H. Carmany & co., 1871. 48 p. maps.   CLU

986. —— **Citizens' committee.** ...Municipal ownership of water and available sources of supply for Oakland, California. Report of Citizens' committee, January 10, 1903... [Oakland] Oakland enquirer [1903] 50 p.   C CU-B

987. —— **City attorney.** Report of the City attorney on the legal principles and method of procedure applicable to the issuance of bonds for certain purposes by the city of Oakland... [Oakland] Oakland enquirer print. [1899] 63 p.   CU-B

988. —— **City engineer.** Oakland water-front: plan of improvements for immediate construction. Oakland, 1909–12. 23 sheets.   CO

989. —— **City planning commission.** The Oakland civic center and Lake Merritt improvement; a unit of the Oakland master plan. [1947] 74 l. maps. Mimeo.   CHi CU-B

990. —— —— Report of East bay mass transportation survey...SERA project no. 3–E5–548, WPA project no. 65–3-3466... Oakland, 1936–37. 2 v. illus., maps. v.1 planographed, v.2 blueprinted. I. S. Shattuck, director.   CHi CL

991. —— —— Shoreline development, a part of the master plan. Oakland, 1951. 89 p. maps, charts.   CHi

992. —— **College of California.** Anniversary of the collegiate school at Oakland, in the Presbyterian church, Thursday, June 14th, 1860, at 9 o'clock, A.M. [Oakland?] 1860. [4]p. Lists names of all students and instructors.   CHi

993. —— —— Catalogue of the College of California, and College school: Oakland, Cal. 1855/56–1867/68.
C has 1860/61, 1863/64–1867/68. CHi has 1861/62–1865/66. CLU has 1855/56, 1861/62–1863/64, 1865/66–1867/68. CSmH has 1862/63–1863/64. CStrJC has 1867/68. CU-B has 1861/62–1863/64, 1865/66–1867/68.

994. —— —— Circular. To the friends of education in California. The college of California is now prepared to come before the public and ask for funds to establish

and endow it... [S. F., Towne & Bacon, print., 1859] [4] p.   CU-B

995. —— —— The incorporation, organic basis, and laws of College of California, at Oakland, California... S.F., Towne & Bacon, 1862. 15 p.   C CSmH CU

996. —— —— Laws of the College of California. [Oakland, 1860] 7 p.   CHi CSmH CU

997. —— —— Movement for a university in California. A statement to the public, by the trustees of the College of California, and an Appeal, by Dr. Bushnell. S.F., Print. at the off. of the Pac. pub. co., 1857. 23 p.
          C CHi CLU CSmH CU-B CtY NN

998. —— —— Oration and poem delivered at the commencement of the College of California, Oakland, California, Wednesday, June 1st, 1864. S.F., Print. by Towne & Bacon, 1864. 16 p.   CU-B

999. —— —— Oration and poem, delivered at the commencement of the College of California, Wednesday, June 7th, 1865. Together with the annual report of the Vice president of the College. S.F., Print. by Towne & Bacon, 1865. 30 p.   CHi CLU CSmH CU-B

1000. —— —— Oration at the commencement of the College of California, Wednesday, June 5, 1867. The truly practical man...by Benjamin Silliman. S.F., Towne & Bacon, 1867. 22 p.   C CHi

1001. —— —— Oration delivered at the fourth anniversary of the College of California, Friday, October 1, 1858... S.F., Towne & Bacon, 1858. 24 p.
                    CHi CLU CSmH CU-B

1002. —— —— Oration of the Rev. William A. Scott, D.D., delivered on the occasion of the first anniversary of the College of California, and of the Seminary for young ladies, at Oakland, Cal. Oct. 31, 1855, and catalogues of the officers and students of these institutions... S.F., Steam presses of Monson & Valentine, 1856. 26 p.
     CBPac CHi CLU CSaT CSmH CU CU-B NN

1003. —— —— Oration, poem and speeches, delivered at the general alumni meeting, held at the College of California, Oakland, Cal., Tuesday, May 31st, 1864. 96 p.   CHi CLU CU-B

1004. —— —— Order of exercises at the commencement of the College of California, at Oakland, in the Presbyterian church, Wednesday, June 1, 1864. [n.p., 1864?] [4] p.   C

1005. —— —— Same. ...June 1865, June 1867. [Oakland? 1865–67. 2 v. in 1.   CU-B

1006. —— —— Roll of students registered in the College of California, 1860/61–1868/69. Comp. by Edward Ryce. Berkeley, 1934. 38 l. photostat.   CHi

1007. —— —— ...Rules of the Board of trustees. Adopted, December 7th, 1858... [Oakland? 1858] broadside.   CU-B

1008. —— —— A statement in behalf of the College of California. 1860. [n.p., 1860] 16 p.
                          CLU CSmH CU-B

1009. —— —— Oakland college school. Preparatory department of the College of California...Oakland, California. [Catalogue of students and announcement of courses] 1866/67–1868/69. S.F., Print. by Towne & Bacon, 1867–68. 3 v. illus.   CU-B

1010. —— —— Oakland college school. [Prospectus and announcement for term commencing July 22, 1868] [S.F., Bacon & co., print., 1868?] [4] p. illus.
                          CLU CU-B

1011. —— —— Prospectus of the Oakland college school, 1865. [S.F.] Print. by Towne & Bacon, 1865. 12 p.
                  CHi CLU CSmH CU-B

1012. —— —— State university school, late Oakland college school, preparatory to the University of California...Oakland, Calif. [Catalogue of students and announcement of courses] 1869/70. S.F., Excelsior press, 1870. 25 p. illus.   CHi CU-B

1013. —— **College of the Holy Names.** ...Bulletin [announcement of courses] 1937/38– Lake Merritt, Oakland, 1937–   CU-B

1014. —— **Convent of Our Lady of the Sacred Heart.** Prospectus... [Oakland, Press of Harrington & McInnis, 189–?] 31 p.   CSmH

1015. —— —— ...Silver jubilee memorial, Convent of Our Lady of the Sacred Heart, Oakland, Cal., 1868–1893. [S.F.] S.F. print. co., 1893. 172 p. illus.
              CHi COHN CSfU CSmH CU-B

1016. —— **Council.** The quality of the water furnished by the Contra Costa water company compared with that supplied eastern cities. [1881] 11 p.   C

1017. —— —— Smelting works. The objections to certain smelting works in populous localities. [Oakland? 1872] 38 p.   C CSmH CU-B

1018. —— **Elmhurst Christian church.** The beginnings of the Elmhurst Christian church, Oakland, California, with a biography of the Reverend J. A. Shoptaugh, by Laura A. Davis Shoptaugh. Oakland, Piedmont press, 1949. [15] p.   C CU-B

1019. —— **Female college of the Pacific.** Catalogue...1867/68–1868/69. S.F., Print. by Towne & Bacon, 1867–68. 2 v.   CU-B

1020. —— **Fire department. Relief fund association.** ...Constitution and by-laws and list of charter members. [n.p., 1898?] 17 p.   CHi

1021. —— **First Baptist church.** A history of the life and activities of the First Baptist church...Oakland, California, 1854–1954. [Redwood City, Myers yearbook, inc., 1954] 56 p. illus., ports.   C CHi

1022. —— —— A jubilee reception given to Rev. E. H. Gray, D.D. on the occasion of his fiftieth anniversary as minister of the gospel... S.F., Leader pub. co., 1890. 55 p. ports.   CLU CSmH CU-B

1023. —— **First Christian church.** Year book and directory. 1931/32. Oakland, 1932.   CU-B

1024. —— **First Congregational church.** The church manual...February, 1873. S.F., Cubery & co., print., 1873. 39 p.   CU-B

1025. —— —— Same. no. 3. 1881.   NN

1026. —— —— Commemorative exercises on occasion of the twenty-fifth anniversary of the First Congregational church, Oakland, California. December 9, 1885. Oakland, Oakland tribune pub. co., 1886. 89 p. illus.
              C CHi CLU CSmH CU-B

1027. —— —— ...Diamond jubilee, 1860–1935. [1935] [5] p.   CO

1028. —— —— A directory giving names and residences of members of the First Congregational church of Oakland...1876. [Oakland, Butler & Bowman, steam bk. & job print., 1876] 19 p.   CU-B

1029. —— —— Directory... Herbert Atchinson Jump, pastor... Oakland, 1912. 95 p. "By-laws. (As amended to May 1, 1912)" p. 81–94.   CHi

1030. —— —— Souvenir of carnival fair given by First Congregational cadet corps, April 7, 8 and 9, 1904, containing history of church and cadet corps compiled by Henry B. Mowbray. [Oakland?] Baker print. co., 1904. [34] p. illus., ports.   CHi   CO   CU-B

1031. Oakland. First Congregational church (cont'd) Centennial history committee. A century closes, the church continues...1860–1960...[Oakland, 1960?] 91 p. illus., ports.   CHi   CU-B

1032. —— First Methodist Episcopal church. Souvenir year book...Dec. 1902. 72 p. illus., ports.   CO

1033. —— First Presbyterian church. Manual... 1874. S.F., Winterburn & co., print. & electrotypers, 1874. 28 p.   CU-B

1034. —— —— Manual and directory... Oakland, 1896– front.
C has 1907, 1910.

1035. —— —— ...90th anniversary... (*Temple tidings.* Mar. 28, 1943. p. 3–14)   CO   CU-B

1036. —— —— Same; 91st birthday of Oakland's first church, 1944.   CO   CU-B

1037. —— —— Year book...of Christian activities for the year ending April 11, 1883. S.F., Print. by Torras & Freeman [1883] 62 p.   CU-B

1038. —— First Unitarian church. Annual report and directory 1st, 1887–1888. Oakland, Press of H. D. W. Gibson, 1888. 10 p.   CLU   CO

1039. —— —— Same. [7th] 1893–4... [S.F., Print. at off. of "Pacific coast wood and iron," 1893] 72 p.   CU-B

1040. —— —— Dedication of the new religious home ...founded Oct. 3, 1886. Sunday... September 6, 1891. Together with discourse preached by Rev. Minot J. Savage of Boston. [Oakland? 1891] 39 p.   CSmH

1041. —— —— Parish directory...1896–7. [n.p., 1897?] 56 p.   CO

1042. —— —— Ladies. Borrowings, compiled by ladies of the First Unitarian church... S.F., C. A. Murdock & co., 1889. 78 p.   CHi   CU-B

1043. —— Fred Finch children's home. The Fred Finch orphanage. [Oakland? 1895] [4] p. illus.   CU-B

1044. —— Free library. Reference dept. Inventory of Coolbrith material purchased from Mrs. Ina Craig ... Oakland, 1947. 9 l.   CO

1045. —— —— —— Oakland, a reading list on its history... [Oakland] 1932. 13 p.   CO   CU-B

1046. —— —— —— An Oakland chronology...to commemorate the anniversary of the incorporation of the town of Oakland, May 4, 1852... [Oakland] 1930. [9] p.
CHi   CL   CO   CRic   CU-B

1047. —— —— —— Same, 2d ed. revised. Comp. by the...History division during the Centennial celebration of the incorporation of the town of Oakland, May 4, 1852... Oakland, 1952. 17 p.
CHi   CL   CRcS   CU-B   N

1048. —— —— —— An Oakland miscellany... 1947. 2 v. maps. Typew. Comp. by Mabel W. Thomas. Collection of articles, extracts, copies of pioneers' papers and reminiscences, etc., dealing with Oakland's early days.   CO

1049. —— —— —— The Oakland public library; a bibliography of its history and activities from 1868 to 1946. Comp. ...by Mabel W. Thomas. Oakland, 1947. 51 l.   CO

1050. —— —— Survey committee, 1927. Sum-mary report on a survey of the Oakland public library, including the Oakland art gallery, the Oakland public museum, the Snow African collection. 1927. 15 p.   CO

1051. —— Hamilton church. Manual and historical sketch of the first independent church of Oakland, Cal. Oakland, Butler & Bowman, 1878. 18 p.   CSmH

1052. —— King's daughters' home. Information about the King's daughters of California home for incurables and the campaign to secure $100,000 for a new building... [Oakland, 1910] 24 p. illus.   CU-B

1053. —— Lakeshore avenue Baptist church. Twenty-five years of radio ministry. [Oakland? 1950?] 16 p. illus., ports.   CHi

1054. —— Mary R. Smith's cottages. Annual report... 1st– 1903– [East Oakland?] 1903–
CHi has 5th, 1907. CU-B has 2d, 1904.

1055. —— Mayor (Davie) A message from Mayor Davie to the taxpayers and citizens of the city of Oakland. Oakland, C. Leidecker [1915] 16 p.   CSmH

1056. —— —— (Mott) A review of municipal activities in the city of Oakland, California, 1905–1915, Frank K. Mott, Mayor. 1915. 46 p.   CHi   CU-B

1057. —— —— Third inaugural message of Frank K. Mott, mayor; presented to the city council of the city of Oakland...April 5th, 1909. [Oakland, 1909] [14] p.   CHi

1058. —— Municipal art museum. Early paintings of California in the Robert B. Honeyman, Jr., collection... Oakland, 1956. 47 p. illus. Edited by Paul Mills.
C CHi CL CRcS CSd CSf CSfCSM CSfCW CStmo

1059. —— —— William Keith memorial gallery. An introduction to the art of William Keith. [St. Mary's College, 1956?] 8 p. illus.   C   CHi

1060. —— Park commission. The park system of Oakland, California... [Oakland, Press of Carruth & Carruth, 1910] 156 p. illus., ports., maps.
CHi   CO   CSfCW   CSmH   CU-B

1061. —— Plymouth avenue church. The church manual...With roll of members, November, 1875. Berkeley, Print. at the Univ. press off., 1875. 24 p. Congregational church, corner Plymouth Ave. and Elm St.   CU-B

1062. —— —— Membership list...1915– [Oakland? 1915–] Title varies: Directory of Plymouth church.
C has 1915–17, 1920, 1928.

1063. —— Public schools. Anthony Chabot school. Life of Anthony Chabot, by children of the sixth grade, Gertrude Smith, teacher, of Anthony Chabot school. Oakland, 1930. 57 p. illus., maps. Mimeo.   CHi   CO

1064. —— —— Oakland high school. Twelfth commencement...Camron [sic] hall, Friday, May 20, 1881. [Oakland] "Tribune" print. [1881] [4] p.   CU-B

1065. —— Radio station KGO. Scrap book, KGO, General electric co., Oakland, California. [v.p., 1924] 1 v. of mounted clippings. illus., ports.   CU-B

1066. —— Real estate dealers. Bay cities water scheme opposed by real estate dealers... [Oakland? 1905] 11 p.   CSmH

1067. —— Relief committee. Finance committee, 1906. Final statement...with the exception of the reserve fund up to and including April 6, 1907. [n.p.]   CO

1068. —— **Sacred Heart church.** Golden jubilee souvenir...1876–1926. [Oakland, 1926?] 68 p. illus.
CHi

1069. —— **St. Joseph's Portuguese church.** Chapel in honor of Our Lady, Help of Christians, and St. John Bosco... Artistic work by Rev. Luigi Sciocchetti. [Oakland? 19—] [8] p. of illus.
CU-B

1070. —— **St. Paul's church.** [Notice of opening, December 8, 1912] [n.p., 1912?] 4 p. pl.
C

1071. —— **Street dept.** Report of Oakland traffic survey; WPA project no. 5577... Oakland, 1937. 2 v. I. S. Shattuck, director.
CL CLSU CSf CU-B

1072. —— —— Same. 1938–1939... [Oakland, 1939?] 8 l.
CU-B

1073. —— **Taxpayers.** Proceedings of a meeting of the taxpayers of Oakland, held at Dietz hall, April 1st, 1876. S.F., J. Winterburn & co., print., 1876. 26 p. CU-B

1074. —— **Woman's sheltering and protection home.** ...Its officers and committees. Anthony Chabot's deed of trust creating the home. Constitution and by-laws. Oakland, 1895. 19 p. port.
CU-B

1075. Oakland academy, Oakland. Third annual catalogue of the academy, from January to December, 1867. S.F., Edward Bosqui & co., 1868. 13 p. front.
C CHi

1076. Oakland and Alameda water co. Prospectus of the Oakland and Alameda water co. to furnish the cities of Oakland and Alameda with pure water. Oakland, 1877. 8 p.
CU-B

1077. Oakland and surroundings, illustrated and described... Oakland, Elliott, 1885. 157 p. illus., maps.
C CL CLU CO CSmH CU-B NHi NN

1078. Oakland bank for savings. President's report. [Oakland, 1920] [3] p.
CHi

1079. Oakland, Cal. in photo-gravure from recent negatives. N.Y., A Wittemann, c1892. 16 pl. Loose-leaf.
CO

1080. Oakland citizens' union. Constitution... Oakland, J. S. Butler & co., 1873. 8 p.
CU-B

1081. Oakland civic auditorium and opera house, Oakland, California; a California million dollar amusement and recreation palace. [n.p. c1916] [16] p. illus.
C

1082. Oakland daily transcript. Information concerning the terminus of the railroad system of the Pacific coast. Oakland, 1871. 46 p. maps.
CHi CLU CSjC CU-B

1083. Oakland enquirer. Special edition illustrated Oakland enquirer Jan. 1888. Descriptive of Oakland and vicinity. Oakland, 1888. 76 p. illus.
CHi

1084. —— Same. For the National educational association [July, 1888] [Oakland, 1888] 40 p. illus., plates.
CLU CU-B

1085. —— Same. Published under the auspices of the Board of trade. Oakland, Jan. 1887. 36 p. illus.
CHi CU-B

1086. Oakland forum, Oakland. [Annual and directory of membership] 1924/25– [Oakland, 1925–] CU-B has 1924/25, 1927/28, 1929/30.

1087. Oakland hotel co. Hotel Oakland, Oakland. [Oakland? 191–?] [16] p. illus., map.
CU-B

1088. —— Same. [1912?] [40] p. illus.
CU-B

1089. —— Hotel Oakland. Guest book. Oakland [1915] 104 p.
CO

1090. Oakland iron works. Descriptive catalogue of the refrigerating and ice machinery... [Oakland? 1893] 111 p. illus.
CHi

1091. —— ...Manufacturers of Tutthill water wheels and contractors for the development of water powers. n.p. [ca. 1900] 14 p. illus.
CHi

1092. Oakland league of women voters. Report on Oakland's government. [Oakland] Oakland public schools, 1953. 36 l. Bibliography: p. 36.
C

1093. Oakland new century club. Annual greeting ...1910. Oakland, 1910. 40 p. pl.
C

1094. [Oakland pamphlets on city-county consolidation] [1910?–22]
CO

1095. Oakland Philomathean library. Constitution and by-laws. [n.p., n.d.] Ms.
C

1096. Oakland poultry yards. Manufactory of the Pacific incubator and brooder, price list of fowls and eggs... [Oakland, Pac. press print] 1885. 41, 25 p. illus.
CHi

1097. Oakland real estate association. Constitution and by-laws...adopted 1908. [n.p., n.d.] [14] p.
CHi

1098. Oakland real estate gazette. v.1:1–10, 12–14. Nov. 7, 1868–Aug. 16, 1869. S.F., 1868–69.
CU-B

1099. Oakland seminary for young ladies. Announcement; re-opening Oakland seminary for young ladies... [Oakland, 1899] 23 p. illus.
CU-B

1100. —— Catalogue...1862– S.F., 1862– CHi has 1864/65, 1897/98. CU-B has 1862–1866/67, 1868/69.

1101. —— Commencement and graduating exercises of the Oakland seminary for young ladies at the new hall of the College of California, June 7th, 1867... [S.F., Sterett & Cubery, print., 1867] [3] p.
CU-B

1102. —— Oakland seminary for young ladies. Mrs. M. K. Blake, principal... [n.p., n.d.] 4 p.
CHi

1103. Oakland society for the prevention of cruelty to animals of Alameda county. ...The Oakland society for the prevention of cruelty to animals of Alameda county, Cal., incorporated 1874... [Oakland, Print. by Oakland enquirer, 1897?] 24 p.
CU-B

1104. Oakland times. [History of the Oakland water front. Oakland, 1879] Scrapbook of clippings from the *Oakland daily times*, September to December, 1879.
CO

1105. The Oakland times annual...1885. Oakland, Times pub. co. [1884?] 1 v. illus.
CU-B

1106. Oakland tribune. Bright spot; 1959 progress report on Metropolitan Oakland area. [Oakland, 1959] v.p. illus., maps, tables.
CB CU-B

1107. —— A general historical, statistical and descriptive review of Oakland, California; her resources, advantages... Oakland, 1890. 66 p. illus., ports. Contains 225 portraits of "prominent residents."
CHi CL CSmH

1108. —— Illustrated special edition Oakland tribune...January, 1888. Oakland, 1888. 106 p. illus., ports., map.
CHi CLU CO CSmH

1109. —— Kaiser center. Oakland, 1960. 47 p. illus., ports., map.
CU-B

1110. —— Oakland centennial, 1852–1952. [Oakland, 1952] v.p. illus., ports.
CU-B

1111. —— ...Special edition of fifty thousand copies! Containing matter historical, descriptive and expository of the resources, industries and possibilities of Oakland and Alameda county... Oakland, 1887. 46 p. illus., maps.   CU-B

1112. —— Yearbook. Oakland, 1888–1949. Title varies slightly.
C has 1890, 1912–13, 1916–17, 1919–28, 1930–39, 1942, 1944, 1947, 1949. CHi has 1919, 1921–23, 1925, 1932–33, 1937–49. CL has 1890, 1909–20, 1921–24. CLU has 1933, 1946. CSmH has 1936–37, 1941, 1944. CU-B has 1888, 1890, 1912–49. MiD has 1939.

1113. Oakland woman's christian temperance union. [Report] 1886–87. [Oakland, Pac. press, 1887] 34 p.   CHi

1114. Odd fellows, Independent order of. Oakland. Fountain lodge, no. 198. Constitution, by-laws, rules of order and order of business... Instituted at Oakland, Alameda co., January 10th, 1872. S.F., J. Winterburn & co., print., 1875. 68 p.   CSmH

1115. Odd fellows' library association, Oakland. By-laws... [Oakland, n.d.] 12 p.   CRcS CU-B

1116. Ye olden Oakland days; a series of ninety-one articles published in the Oakland tribune from July 4, 1920, to October 22, 1922; contributed by Oakland pioneers. Typewritten and indexed by SERA and WPA workers under the direction of the Reference department of the Oakland free library. 1937. 128, 73 l. Typew.   CO

1117. Olney & co., auctioneers. 200 splendid lots in the Watts tract, Oakland, at auction... Saturday, December 16, '76... Oakland, Butler & Bowman, print. [1876] 15 p.   CSmH

1118. Orpheus society, Oakland. Oakland Orpheus, fiftieth anniversary concert, 1893–1943... Sunday, March 21, 1943, Oakland auditorium theatre. Oakland, 1943. 11 p. Contains history of the Society.   CHi

1119. Pacific female college. Circular... 1864/65–1866/67. S.F., Towne and Bacon, 1864–66.   C (1864/65) CLU (1864/65) CU-B (1864/65–1866/67)

1120. Pacific intermountain express co. Annual report. 1st, 1941– [n.p., 1941–]
CHi has 10th, 1950. CL has 1954–60.

1121. —— Offering circular, 15,552 shares... common stock... [n.p.] 1947. 18 p.   CHi

1122. Pacific press publishing house. Album of Oakland, California... Oakland, 1893. 18 pl.
                                     C CSf CSmH CU-B NN

1123. —— ... Our picture book of illustrated sketches. Oakland [n.d.] [24] p. illus.   CU-B

1124. Pardee, Enoch H. Undeceived. Mayor Martin loses his temper, and unfortunately unmasks himself just in time. [Oakland? 1884] 3 p.   CU-B

1125. Peoples water co. Compilation of deeds and various conveyances relating to lands, water rights, rights of way, etc., of the Oakland division of Peoples water company, as of date January 1st, 1906, by J. H. Dockweiler, consulting engineer. [Oakland] 1909. v.p. Typew.   CO

1126. Permanente cement co. Prospectus... 150,-000 shares, common stock... [n.p.] 1947. 56 p.   CHi

1127. Peterson, Martin Severin. Joaquin Miller, literary frontiersman. Stanford, c1937. 198 p. port. Bibliography: p. 179–91.   CBaB CRcS CRedCL CRic

1128. The Pocket exchange guide of San Francisco ... complete descriptions of Oakland, Petaluma, Salinas ... S.F., Tiffany & MacDonald, pub. [1875] 197 p.
                            C CSfCW CSfU CSmH CU-B NN

1129. Porter, F. R. ... Oakland's early days and her many hardy pioneers... [n.p., 1909] [2] p. illus., port. Mounted newspaper clippings.   CU-B

1130. Poston's (Mrs.) seminary, Oakland. Catalogue... 1862/63. Marysville, Daily appeal power press print., 1863.   CU-B

1131. Public administration service, Chicago. The city government of Oakland, California; a survey report. Chicago, 1948. 211 p. Mimeo.   CO

1132. Real estate union, Oakland. By-laws... Incorporated Nov. 12, 1874. Oakland, 1874. 20 p.   CU-B

1133. Realty syndicate, Oakland. Oakland and the Realty syndicate... Oakland [1915?] [16] p. illus.
                                                               CHi

1134. —— Picturesque Oakland—a century ago and now. [Oakland, MacGibbon advertising service, 1922] [12] p. illus., map.   CHi CO CU-B

1135. —— Smith reserve; the princely estate of F. M. "Borax" Smith. [Oakland, 1926?] folder. illus., map.
                                                               CHi

1136. —— Views on the line of the San Francisco, Oakland and San Jose railway. [S.F., Norman Pierce co., 191–?] [23] p. illus.   CHi

1137. Reception and banquet tendered by the citizens of the city of Oakland to Rev. Chas. R. Brown at the Home club, November twenty-fourth, 1908. [Oakland?, Enquirer pub. co., 1908] 32 p.   CHi

1138. Reinhardt, Aurelia Henry. In memoriam... 1877–1948. Mills college, Eucalyptus press, 1948. 25 p.
                                                               CHi

1139. Robinson, Charles Mulford. A plan of civic improvement for the city of Oakland... Oakland, Oakland enquirer pub. co., 1906. 20 p.
                                             C CHi CO CU-B

1140. Rock Ridge park. [S.F., n.d.] [24] p. illus., map.   CU-B

1141. Rotary club of Oakland. Golden anniversary, Rotary club of Oakland, February 1959. [Oakland, 1959] 20 p. illus., ports.   CU-B

1142. Sackett school, Oakland. ...Annual catalogue... 2nd, Jan. 1882. Oakland, 1882–   CU-B

1143. —— ...Closing exercises at First Congregational church parlors, Tuesday evening, Nov. 23d, at 7:30 o'clock, p.m. 1880. S.F., A. L. Bancroft & co., print., 1880. 4 p.   CHi

1144. Safeway stores, inc. Annual report. 1949– Oakland, 1949–
CHi has 1954. CL has 1949–60.

1145. St. Andrew's society of Oakland. Constitution and by-laws... Oakland, Tribune pub. co., 1888. 15 p.   C CSmH

1146. St. Mary's college, Oakland. Dedication of ... on Sunday, August 11th, 1869... S.F., Monitor pub. co., 1869. 24 p. illus., ports.   CU-B

1147. Schaufler, Elsie, comp. Trustees and directors of the Oakland free library, 1868–1949... Oakland, 1949. [17] l. Typew.   CO

1148. Schuyler, James Dix. Report of J. D. Schuyler, C. E., on the probable cost of the construction of the Contra Costa water works. [n.p., 187–?] 20 p. tables.
                                                                 C

1149. Sequoyah country club. By-laws and roster of members. [Oakland? 1926] 37 p.   CHi

1150. Sessions, E. C., & co. Regents' sale of University of California property, Oakland...Sept. 19, 1874 ... S.F., Winterburn & co., print. [1874] Broadside. illus.   CU-B

1151. [Shinn, Charles Howard] Adams point property, Oakland, Cal., Lake shore land co. ... [S.F., Crocker, 189–?] 35 p. illus., map.   CO

1152. Society of newspaper artists. "Smiles" in black and white, by members... Oakland, 1911. 2 l. pl.
                                                              CU-B

1153. Souvenir album; fire and earthquake views of Oakland. Worrall [n.d.]   CStclU

1154. The Spectator, a journal of civic progress, v.1, no. 1–v.2, no. 23; Dec. 16, 1909–Nov. 25, 1911. Oakland, Santa Fe improvement assoc. of Oakland, 1909–11. 2 v. illus. No more published?   CO

1155. Sprague, Homer Baxter. Inauguration address of Homer Baxter Sprague, president of Mills college...October 24th, 1885. [n.p., 1885] 23 p.   CU-B

1156. —— To my friends. [S.F., 1886] 34 p.
                                                       CHi CU-B

1157. State of Maine association, Oakland. ... Annual reunion... [1st 1878?– Oakland, 1878?–] CHi has 6th, 21st, May 19, 1883, June 4, 1898.

1158. Stone, Irving. ...Sailor on horseback, the biography of Jack London. Boston, Houghton, 1938. 338 p. illus.
Available in many libraries.

1159. Straub manufacturing co., Oakland. The Straub mill, construction, metallurgical features, application. [n.p., n.d.] 20 p. illus.   CHi

1160. Strong, Joseph Dwight. A plea against dueling. A discourse delivered in the First Presbyterian church, at Oakland, California, Sunday, September 25th 1859. S.F., Towne & Bacon, print., 1859. 16 p.
                               C CHi CLU CSmH CU-B

1161. Stuart, Reginald Ray. A history of the Fred Finch children's home...1891–1955. Oakland, Printed by Lawton Kennedy for Fred Finch children's home [c1955] 94 p. illus., ports.   C CHi CSf CU-B

1162. Taylor, Samuel W. Line haul; the story of the Pacific intermountain express. S.F., Filmer pub. co., 1959.   CHi CRcS CSd

1163. Tennyson nursery co. Retail price list... Oakland, 1927. 15 p. illus.   CHi

1164. Tevis, William S. The water question; reply of President Tevis of Bay cites [!] water co., to Mr. Chickering. [Oakland, 1905] 24 p.   CSmH CU-B

1165. Todd, Emma G. Pinxit; or, Portraits of modern politics. S.F., Hicks-Judd co., [c1894] 296 p.   C

1166. Truman, Charles H. J., pub. Growth of Oakland. 1927. 16 p. illus.   CO

1167. Union club of the city of Oakland. By-laws. Oakland, Butler & Bowman, print., 1877. 25 p.   CO

1168. Union gas engine co., Oakland. ...Catalogue no. 20 of "Union" marine engines made by Union gas engine company, Kennedy and Canal streets, East Oakland... [S.F.] c1907. 52 p. illus.   CHi

1169. Union veteran's union. California dept. Abe Lincoln command no. 2, Oakland, Cal. ...By-laws. [Oakland? 1888–?] 8 p.   CSmH

1170. United auto supply co., Oakland. Catalogue no. 26. Accessories for the Ford automobile... [n.p., n.d.] 79 p. illus.   CHi

1171. U.S. Federal works agency. Recent migration into Oakland, California, and environs. [Wash.,

D.C.? 1942] 6 l. Mimeo. With this is bound its *Recent migration into San Francisco, California*... [1942]   CO

1172. —— Post-office, Oakland. Oakland official postal guide...1892–1895. [Oakland, 1892–95] 4 v.
                                                              CU-B

1173. —— Works progress administration. California. Oakland, 1852–1938; some phases of the social, political and economic history of Oakland, California... Editors, Edgar J. Hinkel, William E. McCann. Pub. by the Oakland public library as a report of official project no. 465-03-3-337, conducted under the auspices of the Works progress administration. Oakland, 1939. 2 v. Paged continuously (945 l.) Mimeo. Bibliography: v.2, l. 912–945.
C CH CHi CMartC CO CRc CRic CSS CSf CSfSt CSmH CU-B NN

1174. Wagner, Harr. Joaquin Miller and his other self. S.F., Harr Wagner, 1929. 312 p. illus., ports.
                                              CBb CHi CRcS

1175. War camp community service. ...How Oakland served the defenders... [Oakland, Horwinski, 1920] 36 p. illus.   CO

1176. Ward, David Henshaw. "Rosebank" Oakland, California, April 1883. Compliments of D. Henshaw Ward to Allen H. Babcock. August 12, 1883. 10 photos. Views of Henry Douglas Bacon home.   C

1177. Water or bondage? Which is it? Business men's reasons for opposing bonds... [Oakland, 1905?] 16 p.   CSmH

1178. Weinstock-Nichols co. Catalog no. 6. [Oakland, 1914] 192 p. illus.   CHi

1179. Wendte, Charles William. The wider fellowship...1824–1927. Bost., Beacon press, 1927. 2 v. illus., ports. Many reminiscences of his pastorate in Oakland, 1893–1897.   CHi CLU CO CU-B

1180. Western department stores. Report to stockholders, January 31, 1949–January 31, 1952. [Oakland] 1949–52.   CHi

1181. Western electro-mechanical co. Commercial testing devices, electrical tests and measurements... [n.p., n.d.] 35 p. illus.   CHi

1182. Whitney, Josiah Dwight. An address delivered at the celebration of the sixth anniversary of the College of California, held in Oakland, June 6, 1861... S.F., Whitton, Waters & co., 1861. 56 p.
                                       CLU CO CSmH CU-B

1183. [Wickham Havens, inc.] Oak park tract, Oakland, California. [Oakland, R. J. Kitchener, 1905?] 16 p. illus., map.   CHi

1184. —— [Oakland, album] Oakland [191–?] 90 pl. on 45 l.   CO

1185. Wight, Edward Allen. A survey of the administrative organization of the library department of the City of Oakland. Berkeley, 1955. 86 p.   C

1186. Willey, Samuel Hopkins. A history of the College of California...S.F., S. Carson & co., 1887. 432 p.
C CHi CLU CMont CO CSfCW CSfU CU-B CaBViPA

1187. —— Same. (Calif. hist. soc. Papers, v.1, pt. 2, p. 1–424, 443–440)
Available in many libraries.

1188. —— The plans of the College of California for an abundant water supply at Berkeley... [n.p., 18–?] 8 p.   CU-B

1189. —— Statement in regard to the College of California. N.Y., J. F. Trow, print., 1855. 15 p.   CLU

1190. Withers, Zachary. Our inheritance. Oakland, Tribune pub. co., 1909. 104 p. port.   CHi

1191. Woman's Baptist missionary society of the Pacific coast. Annual reports. [1st?, 1876?– Oakland, 1876?–]
CHi has 6th, 1881.

1192. Women's athletic club of Alameda county. Brief history of Women's athletic club of Alameda county from 1926-1949. Oakland, 1949. 76 p. illus., ports.
CO CU-B

1193. —— [Calendar of events] Dec. 1935–Dec. 1948. [Oakland, 1935–48]   CU-B

1194. —— [Description of the Club, 1929. Oakland, 1929] [30] p. illus.   CHi

1195. Woodward & Taggart. Credit sale of Oakland business property at auction, Thursday, April 11th, 1878, at 2 p.m. ... S.F., Harrison, 1878. [6] p. maps.
CHi

1196. Wulzen, Albert H. Panorama of Oakland, Cal. [Oakland, 1879?] 7 fold. p.   CU-B

1197. Young women's Christian associations. Oakland. ...Report. 1878, 1900, 1939. Oakland, 1878–1939. 3 v.   CU-B

Piedmont

1198. [Brigman, Annie W.] Plain tales from the Piedmont hills. Oakland, Wickham Havens [n.d.] [4] p. pl.   CLU

1199. Goodrich, Mary. Piedmont gardens. Oakland, The Piedmont press, 1928. 15 p. illus.   CHi

1200. Havens, Frank C. Frank C. Havens' world famed collection of valuable paintings by great ancient and modern masters...will be sold at public auction... Oct. 23 [1917] [n.p., 1917] 17 p.   CHi

1201. Pattiani, Evelyn (Craig) Queen of the hills; the story of Piedmont, a California city. Fresno, Academy library guild, 1954. 179 p. illus.
Available in many California libraries and NN UPB

1202. Piedmont land co., San Francisco. Description of property at Piedmont Park, Oakland heights, offered for sale by the Piedmont land company. S.F., Crocker, 1877. 15 p.   CHi

1203. Plath, Henry W. The extensive and notable collection of western Americana formed by Dr. Henry W. Plath, Piedmont, California. Sold by his order. Public auction sale... N.Y., Parke-Bernet galleries, inc., 1959. 219 p. illus., facsims.   CHi CLgA

1204. Ransom (Miss) and Miss Bridges' school for girls, Piedmont. [Catalogue] [Piedmont?] 19—
CHi has 1912–14, 1916, 1924.

1205. —— [Illustrated brochure. S.F., John Henry Nash] 1926. 61 p.   CHi

1206. [Wickham Havens, inc., Oakland] Beautiful Piedmont residences; a picture book of the most attractive community of homes in all California. [Oakland, 1913] [8] p. illus.   CHi CO

San Leandro

1207. Best manufacturing co., San Leandro. [Descriptive catalogs of steam freighting]
CHi has 1905, and [n.d.]

1208. Caterpillar tractor co. Fifty years on tracks. Peoria, Ill., 1954. 102 p.   CHi

1209. —— Selling the caterpillar. [n.p., c1926] 302 p. illus.   CHi

1210. Cunningham, Ross A. A master plan for recreation facilities for San Leandro. Stanford, 1952. Thesis (Ph.D.)—Stanford, 1952.   CSt

1211. Davis (Charles G.) [Ghageda gardens], San Leandro. [Catalog] [n.p., n.d.] [4] p.   CHi

1212. First national bank. Our bank's first decade, June 28, 1928 to June 28, 1938... [n.p., 1938?] 16] p. illus., port.   CHi

1213. Freeman, Leslie J., comp. The Estudillo's of San Leandro... [n.p., 193–?] [15] p.
CHi CO CU-B

1214. —— Historic San Leandro, California... [San Leandro, San Leandro news, 1940] 44 p. illus., ports.
C CHi CL CO CSf CSmH CU-B

1215. —— The Peralta's of San Leandro... [n.p., 1939?] [16] p.   CHi CO CU-B

1216. Riordan, LeRoy Edward. Organised groups and the legislative process in municipal government. [San Leandro] 1961. Thesis (M.A.)—Univ. of Calif., 1961.   CU

1217. San Leandro, vs. Le Breton, Edward J. In the Supreme court of the state of California. The town of San Leandro, plaintiff and respondent vs. Edward J. Le Breton, adm'r, etc., et al., defendants and appellants. Transcript on appeal (from Superior court, Alameda county)... S.F., Torras & Freeman, print., 1884. 56 p. Land suit over part of the Rancho de San Leandro.
CLU

1218. San Leandro. Board of trade. San Leandro, Alameda county, California. San Leandro, 1906. 16 p. illus.   CHi

1219. —— **Chamber of commerce.** Builders of San Leandro; building today for a better tomorrow. ... Annual report, 1957; program of work, 1958; membership roster... [San Leandro, 1958] 40 p.   CHi

1220. —— —— Business directory... [San Leandro? 1942] [84] p.   CHi

1221. —— —— San Leandro presents its first annual blue book, an informational and buyers guide. San Leandro [News-observer] 1948. 74 p. fold. map. CHi

1222. —— **Charters, ordinances, etc.** An act to incorporate the town of San Leandro... San Leandro, Alameda county gazette bk. & job print., 1872. 35 p.
CHi

1223. —— —— ...Town of San Leandro, 1872–3. Haywood [!] Alameda county Advocate print., 1873. 38 p.
CHi

1224. —— **First Presbyterian church.** First Presbyterian church... San Leandro, Calif., 1866–1941, seventy-fifth anniversary. [1941] 19 p. illus., ports. CO

1225. —— **St. Leander's church.** St. Leander's dedication and spring festival. Souvenir program. [San Leandro, 1957?] 84 p. illus., ports.   CU-B

1226. San Leandro, Alameda county, California. [n.p., 19–?] 32 p. illus.   CHi CU-B

1227. The second Souther farm sale will take place Wednesday, April 20, 1892, at 12 noon, prompt. The sale includes the entire collection of brood mares, colts, and fillies which will be sold without limit or reserve. Lunch at 11. Catalogues and any further information of Killip & co., 22 Montgomery street, San Francisco, Cal., or of Gilbert Tompkins, Souther farm, San Leandro, Cal. [S.F.? 1892] 121 p. illus.   CHi

1228. Shaffer, Harry E. The story of our home town, San Leandro, Calif., 1956. 23 l.   C

1229. Stuart, Reginald Ray. How firm a foundation; a centennial history of the First Methodist church, San Leandro. San Leandro, 1953. 112 p. illus.   CHi
CL CMartC CPa CSf CSfU CStcrCL CStoc

1230. —— San Leandro, a history. San Leandro, First Methodist church, 1951. 287 p. illus.
Available in many California libraries and NN

1231. Sweepstake plow co. Illustrated price list of spring wagons. Feb., 1878. San Leandro [1878] illus.
CU-B

ALPINE COUNTY
(Created in 1864 from portions of Amador, Calaveras, Mono and El Dorado counties)

GREAT REGISTER

1232. Alpine county. Index to the Great register of the county of Alpine. 1866– Place of publication and title vary.
C has 1873, 1875–77, 1879, 1886 (biennially to date). CHi has 1948. CL has 1867, (suppls. 1868–69), 1872–73, 1875–77, 1879, 1882 (suppl.), 1884, 1888, 1890. CSmH has 1873. CU-B has 1873, 1875, 1879–80, 1892, 1916.

GENERAL REFERENCES

1233. Alpine county, Calif. Official tax list of Alpine co., 1916.   CU-B

1234. The Banner, Sonora. The forest...the recreational and other features of the Stanislaus national forest in Alpine... [Sonora, 1923?] 76 p. illus., map.
C CU-B

1235. Globe gold and silver mining co., Alpine county. Some facts about gold and silver mines and mining; also the prospectus of... N.Y., 1872. 24 p.   C

1236. Maule, William M. A contribution to the geographic and economic history of the Carson, Walker and Mono basins in Nevada and California... S.F., Forest service, U.S. Dept. of agric., 1938. 46 p. illus., pl., maps, facsims.   CHi

AMADOR COUNTY
(Created in 1854 from portion of Calaveras county; annexed sections of El Dorado county in 1855, 1857, and 1863)

COUNTY HISTORIES

1237. [Mason, Jesse D.] History of Amador county, California, with...biographical sketches of its prominent men and pioneers. Oakland, Thompson & West, 1881. 344 p. illus., ports.
C CCH CHi CJ CL CLSM CLU CO CS CSd CSf CSfCP CSfCW CSfMI CSmH CSt CSto CU-B CoD ICN MWA N NN NcU NHi WHi

1238. Sargent, Elizabeth Ann (Quinn) "Mrs. J. L. Sargent," ed. Amador county history... [Jackson] Amador county federation of women's clubs, 1927. 127 p. illus., ports.
C CHi CJ CL CLU CLod CO CS CSS CSf CSfCP CSfCW CSmH CSt CStclU CSto CU-B CYcCL ICN MWA MiD-B NHi WHi

GREAT REGISTER

1239. Amador county. Index to the Great register of the county of Amador. 1866– Place of publication and title vary.
C has 1867–68, 1871–73, 1875–77, 1879–80, 1884 (biennially to)– 1962. CHi has 1871 (suppl.), 1872, 1875.

CL has 1872–73, 1875, 1876 (suppl.), 1877, 1879 (suppl.), 1882, 1884, 1886 (suppl.), 1888, 1890. CSmH has 1867, 1880, 1882, 1894. CU-B has 1867, 1868 (suppl.), 1872–73, 1879–80.

GENERAL REFERENCES

1240. Alta California, inc., comp. & pub. Amador county, California, "heart of the Mother Lode"... Sacramento [1938?] 9 l. Reproduced from typew. copy.
CSfCP CU-B

1241. Amador canal mining co. Documents and reports relating to Amador canal and mining company, Amador, Calif. [S.F., Women's union print., 1873] 43 p.
CLU CU-B

1242. Amador county. Board of supervisors. Resources of Amador county, California... Jackson, A. B. Sanborn, comp. & pub., 1887. 32 p.
CHi CSfCP CSmH

1243. —— **Chamber of commerce.** Amador county... Jackson [192–?] 12 p. illus., map.   CRcS

1244. —— —— Same. [1940] 14 p. illus., map.
CRcS

1245. —— —— Same. [1948?] 10 p. illus., map.
CHi

1246. —— **Ordinances.** The ordinances of the Board of supervisors of the county of Amador... Jackson, Amador sentinel job off., 1887. 34 p.   CHi

1247. —— **Public schools.** Complete roster of the public schools of Amador county...beginning July 1, 1915. [n.p., n.d.] 4 p.   CHi

1248. —— **Township 3. Justice's court.** Justices docket...1854–1901. 9 v. receipts, clippings, calendars. Ms.   C

1249. Amador county agricultural society. Constitution... Organized April 1862. Jackson. T. A. Springer, print., 1862. 14 p.   C

1250. Amador mining co. Annual report. 1867/68– 1871/72. S.F., 1869–72. 4 v.
CLU has 1867/68–1871/72. CSmH has 1867/68, 1869/70. CU-B has 1867/68–1871/72.

1251. —— By-laws... S.F., F. Eastman, print., 1867. 8 p.   CU-B

1252. Amador progress-news. Souvenir of Amador's 100th birthday, 1854–1954. [Jackson? 1954] 23 p. illus., ports.   C CHi CSfCSM

1253. Amador record, Sutter Creek. Special mining edition, April 1897. 38 p. illus., maps.   C CSjC

1254. Ashburner, William. Report upon the property of the Amador mining company, Amador county, California, February 28th, 1868. S.F., Towne & Bacon, 1868. 21 p.   CLU

1255. Bell-Wether gold mining co. [Statement and a report on Bell-Wether mine by M. A. Delano] Chicago, 1896. 28 p.   CHi

1256. Brown, Pearl Emma. The history of early mining in Amador county. [Berkeley, 1909] Thesis (M.A.)—Univ. of Calif., 1909.   CU

1257. Consolidated Amador, Volcano hydraulic gold mining and land company of California. By-laws... Incorporated April 27, 1877. S.F., A. L. Bancroft & co., 1878. 8 p.   CU-B

1258. Crosley, Mary Edith. Volcano, California, most picturesque of the Mother Lode towns. [North Hollywood, March productions, 1957] 30 p. illus.
C CHi CL CO CSto CU-B

1259. Doble, John. Journal and letters from the mines: Mokelumne Hill, Jackson, Volcano and San Francisco, 1851–1865. Ed. by Charles L. Camp. Denver, Old West pub. co. [1962] 304 p. illus., maps. "1000 copies designed and printed by Lawton Kennedy."

CHi CTurS

1260. Empire gold mining co. The Empire gold mining company, Plymouth, Amador county... Phila., McLaughlin bros. bk. & job print. establishment, 1878. 19 p.   C CSalCL CU-B

1261. —— Prospectus capital, $2,000,000. 200,000 shares-par $10. Self-sustaining and dividend-paying. Phila., McLaughlin bros., 1879. 23 p. Report of William Ashburner, mining engineer: p. 5–17.   CHi CSmH

1262. Freemasons. Volcano lodge no. 56. A centennial souvenir...1854–1954... [Volcano? 1954] 32 p. illus., ports.   CHi

1263. Gregory, U. S. Autobiographical experiences ... [S.F., Pernau-Walsh print. co., 1928?] 47 p. port.
CLU CO CSmH

1264. Immigration association of California. [County scrapbooks] [S.F., 188–?]   C

1265. Ione. Board of trade. Resources surrounding Ione, Amador county, Calif. [Ione, Ione echo print., 1901] 9 p. illus.   CU-B

1266. —— **Community Methodist church.** Celebration of the 93rd year, a history of the church, 1852–1945. Ione [1945] 50 p. illus., ports.   C

1267. [Kip, Leonard] The Volcano diggings; a tale of California law. By a member of the bar. N.Y., J. S. Redfield, 1851. 131 p.   CHi CLU CSmH

1268. Knights of the Assyrian cross. Sutter Creek legion, no. 1. Constitution, by-laws, and rules of order. S.F., A. L. Bancroft & co., 1874. 20 p.   CHi

1269. Lane, Stuart C. A history of Volcano, Amador county, from the gold rush to the seventies. Sacramento, 1959. 116 p. Thesis (M.A.)—Sacramento State college.
CSS

1270. Potter, Frank M., vs. Randolph, Clark, et al. In the Supreme court of the state of California, Frank M. Potter, plaintiff and respondent, vs. Clark Randolph, et al., defendants and appellants. Points and authorities for respondent, filed Sept. 1898. Sacramento, 1898. 21 p.
CHi

1271. Preston school of industry, Ione. Seventh biennial report of the Board of trustees...July 1, 1904 to June 30, 1906. Ione, 1906. 129 p. illus., ports. CHi

1272. Schacht, Frances. Camera history of Amador county: a collection of old pictures with descriptive text. [S.F.] Foster & Futernick bindery, 1937.   CJ

1273. Sutter Creek boosters' club, Sutter Creek. 2nd annual Sutters gold rush and round up...August 13–14 souvenir program. [n.p.] 1938.   CSmH

1274. Swenson, Stella Spillner. One hundred years at Silver Lake, Amador county California... A report presented to Doctor Rockwell D. Hunt, director of California history foundation, College of the Pacific, April, 1948. [Stockton? 1956] 67 p.   CHi CSto

1275. U.S. Land office. John W. Lawton and the state of California vs. Eldridge G. Hiner, Charles Ostrum, Henry Wallace, John W. Mullis, Spencer C. Way, and Merritt W. Walker. Brief. S.F., Towne & Bacon, 1867. 8 p.   CHi

1276. Whittle, John C., vs. Doty, I. J. In the Supreme court of the state of California, John C. Whittle,

plaintiff and respondent, vs. I. J. Doty, defendant and appellant. Transcript on appeal. Jackson, Amador sentinel newspaper and job off., 1885. 20 p.   CHi

1277. Woman's improvement club, Plymouth. Constitution and by-laws. [Jackson, n.d.] 11 p.   CHi

Jackson

1278. Argonaut relief fund. Report [of the fund's charitable relief to victims of the Argonaut mine disaster, at Jackson, California, on August 27, 1922] [Jackson? 1924] [6] p.   CU-B

1279. Execution of Rafael Escobar. [on Aug. 10, 1855, at Jackson, Amador county, California] S.F., Fishbourne lithographic soc. [1855] 2 l.   CSmH

1280. Jackson. Congregation B'nai Israel. ... Constitution and by-laws of congregation B'nai Israel, located at Jackson, Amador county, California... S.F., M. Weiss, Oriental print. & pub. house, 1873. 19 p.   CU-B

1281. Journeyman barbers international union of America. Local 533, Jackson. By-laws, April 1, 1920. Stockton, 1920. [3] p.   CHi

1282. Kirkwood gold mining co. Prospectus... Jackson, Ledger print. [1900] 12 p. map.   CHi

1283. Murder of M. V. B. Griswold, by five Chinese assassins; together with the life of Griswold, and the statements of Fou Sin, Chou Yee and Coon You... Also a history of the murder... Illus. with correct likenesses of the murderers. Jackson, T. S. Springer & co., print., 1858. 32 p. illus., ports.
C CHi CLU CSfCP CSmH CU-B ICN

1284. Native daughters of the Golden West. Jackson. Ursula parlor, no. 1. Observance of the seventy-fifth anniversary of the mother parlor, 1886–1961 ...September 23, 1961. Jackson, 1961. 8 p. ports. CHi

1285. Native sons of the golden West. Jackson. Excelsior parlor, no. 31. By-laws...approved, September 1st, 1898. Jackson, Amador dispatch print., 1898. 34 p.   CHi

1286. Odd fellows, Independent order of. Jackson. Jackson Rebekah degree lodge no. 50. Constitution, by-laws and rules of order... Jackson, Amador dispatch print., 1888. 32 p.   CHi

BUTTE COUNTY
(Created in 1850)

COUNTY HISTORIES

1287. McGie, Joseph F. A history of Butte county; a source book for teachers. [rev. ed.] Oroville, Butte county off. of educ., 1958. 333 p. illus.   C COroB

1288. —— Same. [3d rev. ed.] [Orville? 1960] 336 p. illus.   CHi

1289. Mansfield, George Campbell. History of Butte county, Calif., with biographical sketches... L.A., Historic record co., 1918. 1331 p. illus., ports.
C CBb CCH CChi CChiS CHi CL CLSU CLU CO COroB CRb CSS CSf CSj CSmH CSt CStoC CU-B NN WHi

1290. National league of American pen women, inc. Butte county branch. Here is my land; sketches of Butte county, California... [Chico, Print. by Hurst & Moore] 1940. 86 p. illus., ports., map.
C CAla CB CChi CChiS CCorn CHi CL CO COroB CRbCL CSf CSjC CSmH

1291. Wells, Harry Laurenz, and Chambers, W.

L. History of Butte county, California... S.F., H.L. Wells, 1882. 2 v. in 1. illus., ports., maps. 305 p.
C CChi CChiS CHi CL CO COroB CSf CSfCP CSmH CU-B NHi NN NvHi

GREAT REGISTER

1292. Butte county. Index to the Great register of the county of Butte. 1866– Place of publication and title vary.
C has 1872–73, 1875, 1879–80, 1882, 1886 (biennially to) – 1962. CChiS has 1908, 1918, "Copy of uncancelled entries"...1884, 1888. CHi has "Copy of uncancelled entries"...1886. CL has 1872–73, 1875 (suppl.), 1877 (suppl.), 1879, 1882, 1884 (addendum), 1886, 1888, 1890. CLU has 1867. CSmH has "Copy of uncancelled entries" ...1880–82. CU-B has "Copy of uncancelled entries"... 1872–73, 1879–80, 1890.

DIRECTORIES

1293. 1878. McKenney, L. M., comp. Marysville appeal directory of northern California for 1878...a complete directory of residents in the counties of Butte, Colusa, Nevada, Placer, Sutter, Tehama, and Yuba, including the cities and towns, with historical and statistical sketch of each. Marysville, Lockwood & Dawson, 1878. 428 p. CHi (facsim.) CMary CU-B

Chico

1294. [1911?–1958?] Polk, R. L. & co., pub. Polk's Chico–Oroville city directory. S.F., L.A. [1911?– 58?] Title varies: 1913, Chico, Oroville, Biggs, Durham, Gridley, Hamilton City, Palermo, Paradise, Stirling City and Wyandotte directory. Continued as Polk's Chico city directory and Polk's Oroville city directory.
CHi has 1913–14, 1927/28, 1937/38, 1948, 1950, 1952–1958.

1295. 1961– Polk, R. L. & co., pub. Polk's Chico city directory. L.A., 1961– Preceded by Polk's Chico–Oroville city directory.
CHi has 1961.

Oroville

1296. 1960– Polk, R. L. & co., pub. Polk's Oroville city directory. L.A., 1960– Title varies: 1960, Polk's Oroville–Paradise city directory. Preceded by Polk's Chico–Oroville city directory.
CHi has 1960–61.

GENERAL REFERENCES

1297. Alta California, inc., comp. & pub. Butte county, California, "land of golden opportunities"... Sacramento [1938?] 16 p. CU-B

1298. Associated chambers of commerce of Butte county. [Brochure] [n.p., 1925?] 16 p. illus.
CHi CRcS

1299. Barry, John D. Report on the proposed eocene tunnel at Big Bend on the north fork of the Feather river, Butte county... S.F., B.H. Daly, 1880. 17 p. fold. maps. CHi

1300. Baum, Milton S. Economic impact of the construction of Oroville dam and power plant upon the Oroville area. Prepared for California Department of water resources. Sacramento, 1956. 45 l. map.
C CChiS CSdS

1301. Big Bend tunnel and mining company, Butte county. A river turned out of bed for nearly fourteen miles and made to flow through a mountain...completed September 1887... 16 p. map. C

1302. Biggs. Community church. ...A souvenir of the diamond jubilee, sixty-third anniversary, 1872 [to] 1935. [Biggs, Biggs news commercial print. and pub., 1935] 50 p. illus. C

1303. Biggs argus. Biggs in picture and story; special photographic edition. Biggs, 1907. 12 p. illus.
COroB

1304. Bleyhl, Norris Arthur, and Skelly, Grant T. A survey of public library service in Butte county, California. Chico, 1956. 38 p. C

1305. Boyle, Florence Danforth. It was told to me, a novel with historical background. [Oroville? 1950] 22 p. illus., ports. CHi CRcS CSd CSdS CStcrCL

1306. Breese, Frances Juliet. I live for Paradise. Chico, Chico record, 1946. 78 p. CChiS

1307. Brouillette, Joseph F. A history of Stirling city, Butte county, California. Chico, 1959. 166 l. illus., maps. Thesis (M.A.) – Chico state college, 1959.
CChiS

1308. Butte county. Memorial exercises for General John Bidwell... [Oroville, Oroville register, 1900] [29] p. port. C CLU CO CSmH CU-B

1309. —— Board of supervisors. Butte county, where northern California oranges grow... A plain unvarnished story of the resources of Butte county... Oroville, Oroville Mercury print., 1901. 46 p. illus., map.
CHi CU-B

1310. —— —— Same. 1903. 48 p. illus., map.
CSmH CU-B

1311. Butte county, California; illustrations descriptive of its scenery, residences, public buildings, manufactories, fine blocks, mines, mills, etc. from original drawings by artists of the highest ability. With historical sketch of the county. Oakland, Smith & Elliott, 1877. 18 print. p. [80] p. of pl., maps. C gives 168 p. "The Historical matter is mainly selected from an article furnished by Judge W. T. Sexton entitled 'A Brief Glance at the Past and Present of Butte County,' and first published in the *Oroville Mercury* in 1875."– Pref.
C CChi CHi CSf CSmH CU-B

1312. Butte county in the Sacramento valley, California. [Oroville] Oroville register print. [n.d.] [8] p.
CHi

1313. Butte county railroad co. Pine chips. A brief preachment on sights and scenes along the line of the Butte county railroad... Chico, B. C. R. R. co., c1904. [64] p. C CChiS CHi CU-B

1314. California. Laws, statutes, etc. Road laws in force in Butte county, California. Published by order of the Board of supervisors. Oroville, Gray & De Mott, print., 1876. 18 p. CLU

1315. —— Supreme court. Opinion of the Supreme court of California in Moore et al. vs. Wilkinson delivered by Justice Field, of that court, at its April term, 1859. [n.p., 186–?] 9 p. (In U.S. Supreme court. *Some opinions and papers of Stephen J. Field*...[189–?] v.6) CSmH

1316. California irrigated land co. The Gridley colonies, Butte county, California...3,000 acres which have been subdivided into ten and twenty acre tracts... S.F. [1905?] 24 p. illus., maps. CU-B

1317. California northern railroad. Engineer's report of the preliminary surveys, business and connections of the California northern railroad, made to the president and directors, July 30th, 1859. By W. S. Watson, chief engineer and commissioner...Oroville, Butte county. Sacramento, James Anthony & co., 1859. 20 p. fold. map.
C CSmH CU-B

1318. Carson, Arenia Thankful (Lewis) Captured by the Mill Creek Indians; a true story of the capture of the Sam Lewis children in the year 1863; incidents in the early history of Butte county by the sole survivor. [n.p.] c1915. 16 p.   CHi

1319. Chapman's magazine, Berkeley. Butte county. (In v.1, no. 2, p. 45–58 [1941?])   CChiS CO

1320. Cherokee Flat blue gravel co., California. By-laws... S.F., Edward Bosqui & co., 1866. 15 p.
                                                        CHi

1321. —— Report of the general superintendent... 1871. S.F., 1871. 1 v.   CLU CU-B

1322. Cummings, George W. Report on the Davis ditch and mining property, situate in Butte county, California. Oroville, Mercury print. [1879] [17] p.   CLU

1323. Daughters of the American revolution. California. Genealogical records committee. ... Butte county, California, wills from 1850 to 1900...notes taken and compiled by Laura Cline Patterson... Chico, 1951. 157 l. Bound with Tehema county, California, wills from 1850 to 1900...   C CL

1324. Downer and Garlow vs. Ford, J. B. In the Supreme court state of California. Downer and Garlow, respondents, vs. J. B. Ford, appellant. Burt & Rhodes, attorneys for respondents. [n.p., 18—] 8 p. A brief in a suit involving Oroville town lots.   CLU

1325. Drobish, Mrs. Harry E. The story of Curry Bidwell Bar State park and of W. T. (Bill) Curry. Oroville, Bidwell Bar park assoc., 1957. 9 p. illus.
                                        CChiS CU-B CViCL

1326. Ekman, A. Mineral resources of Butte county, California. Oroville, Oroville Mercury print., 1898. 15 p. illus.   CLU

1327. Feather river territorial. Special edition, 1959. Oroville, Am. west pub. house, 1959. 26 p. illus.
                                                        CRb

1328. Gerdts, Genevieve McGee. An economic and historical survey of Butte county from 1848–1890. [Berkeley, 1933] Thesis (M.A.)– Univ. of Calif., 1933.   CU

1329. Glassford, William Alexander. Butte county, California, at the base of the Sierras... Denver, News print., c1896. 7 p.   CU-B

1330. Goodner, Ivan E. Reports upon irrigation project for the Paradise irrigation district, Butte county, California. [n.p., n.d.] 41 p. maps.   C

1331. Great West (periodical) Oroville number Sacramento, 1911. 24 p. (v.11, no. 3, July 1911)
                                                        COroB

1332. —— What Butte county offers the homeseeker. [Sacramento? 1918] 22 p. illus.   CChiS

1333. Hall, William Hammond. Butte water supply and land project: the physical, engineering and business problems and conditions... S.F., Bacon & co., 1891. 44 p.   C CHi CLU CSfCP CSmH CU-B

1334. Handbook of Butte county... [1905?] [48] p.
                                                        CU-B

1335. Hill, Roderic Lee. Relationships between types and sizes of rural land ownerships in the Oroville area, California. [Berkeley, 1942] Thesis (M.S.)—Univ. of Calif., 1942.   CU

1336. Immigration association of California. [County scrapbooks] [S.F., 188–?]   C

1337. League of women voters of Chico. A profile of Butte county, published through the cooperation of the Butte county Board of supervisors...1958. 49 p.
                                                        COroB

1338. Lucas, Kenneth. Study of the water problems and land use of the Oroville–Wyandotte irrigation district. Chico, 1959. 134 l. maps. Thesis (M.A.)—Chico state college, 1959.   CChiS

1339. McAfee & Baldwin. Descriptive circular of the Palermo colony, Palermo, Butte county, Calif. ... S.F., Crocker [1888?] 64 p.   CU-B

1340. Mansfield, George C. Butte county, Sacramento valley, California. What Butte county offers the homeseeker... [n.p., 1917?] 40 p.
                          CHi CL CLU CSmH CU-B

1341. —— Butte, the story of a California county. [Oroville, Oroville register print.] c1919. 40 p.
                                                   C CChiS

1342. —— The Feather river in '49 and the fifties. Oroville, Author, c1924. 42 p. illus.
    C CHi CLSU CLU CMary CO CSfCP CSmH
CU-B

1343. —— Same. Reprinted by Margaret Mansfield. Burlingame, 1948. 40 p. illus.   C

1344. Monday club of Oroville. Yearbook. 1931/1932. [n.p., 1932]   CHi

1345. Native sons of the golden West. Argonaut parlor, no. 8, and Native daughters of the Golden West. Gold of Ophir parlor, no. 190. Souvenir book, California's fourth railroad, February, 1864, Oroville, February 11, 1950. [Oroville] 1950. 16 p. Issued to commemorate marker.   CHi

1346. Odd fellows, Independent order of. Bidwell. Constitution, by-laws and rules of order, of Bidwell lodge no. 47, I.O. of O.F. Instituted at Bidwell, October 25, 1856. Approved by Grand lodge. Oroville, Printed at "Daily Butte record" office, 1856. 24 p.   CHi

1347. Oroville. Chamber of commerce. Oroville, district incomparable. [S.F., Village press, 1912] 16 p. illus.   CHi COroB

1348. —— —— A survey of facts—The Oroville district: educational, agricultural, industrial... [n.p., 1926?] Mimeo.   COroB

1349. Oroville mercury. Homeseekers and development number, 1912... Oroville, Mercury print., 1912. 48 p. illus.   C COroB

1350. Osborn, Arthur D. A history of the Biggs, Butte area. Chico, 1953. 104 p. map. Thesis (M.A.)— Chico state college, 1953.   CChiS

1351. [Palermo land and water co.] From wilderness to town. [S.F., Crocker] 31 p. illus.   CU-B

1352. Paradise and allied communities. Chamber of commerce. The land of Paradise... [Chico, Hurst & Moore, print., 194–?] [12] p. illus., map.   CHi

1353. Paradise irrigation district. Reports upon irrigation project for the Paradise irrigation district, Butte county, California... [Paradise? 1917?] 41 p. maps.   CHi

1354. Reclamation district no. 542 vs. Turner, R. M. In the Supreme court of the state of California. Reclamation district no. 542, appellant, vs. R. M. Turner, respondent. Appellant's points and authorities. H. V. Reardan, attorney for appellant... Oroville, Oroville mercury print. [1893] 12 p.   CHi

1355. —— ...Brief for Respondent... [n.p., 1893]
                                                        CHi

1356. —— Reclamation district no. 542, plaintiff and appellant, vs. R. M. Turner, defendant and respondent. Appellant's reply brief... Oroville, Oroville mercury print. [1893] 34 p.   CHi

1357. —— ...Transcript on appeal. H. V. Reardan, attorney for appellant, Oroville, Cal. Freeman & Bates, attorney for respondent, San Francisco, Cal. ... Oroville, Oroville mercury print. [1893] 29 p.   CHi

1358. Rice culture at Biggs & Richvale, Butte county, California. [n.p., n.d.] [4] p.   CHi

1359. Smith, Roy James. An economic analysis of the California state land settlements at Durham and Delhi ... [Berkeley, 1937] 424 l. maps. Thesis (Ph.D.)—Univ. of Calif., 1937.   CU

1360. Spring valley hydraulic gold mining co. [Prospectus]. [N.Y., 1882] [3] p.   CSmH

1361. —— Reports of the Spring valley hydraulic gold company, comprising the Cherokee Flat blue gravel and Spring valley mining and irrigating company's property... [N.Y., J. J. Caulon, 1880] 36 p.   CSmH

1362. Thermalito colony co., Oroville. Thermalito catechism; questions and answers relating to resources, progress and prospects of the beautiful colony of Butte county, California. [n.p., 1891?] 14 p.   CHi

1363. —— Thermalito colony, The Pasadena of central California. [S.F., 1888?] illus., maps.   CLU

1364. Wangelin, George. [Three articles about early Butte county newspapers, written in 1934, and reproduced in the Oroville mercury-herald of July 2, 3, and 5, 1948] Oroville, 1948.   CU-B

1365. Wood, Jesse. Butte county, California. Its resources and advantages for home seekers... A pamphlet endorsed by the county Board of supervisors... Sacramento, A. J. Johnston & co., 1886. 92 p.
CHi CSmH CU-B

1366. —— Same. [Chico? 1888] 80 p. illus.
C CHi CLU CU-B

1367. —— Resources of Butte county; an address delivered before Butte county teachers' institute, November 13, 1882. [Oroville, Weekly Mercury, 1882] [n.p., n.d.]   C

Chico

1368. Albertype co., New York, pub. Souvenir of Chico, California. Photo-gravures. Brooklyn [n.d.] unp. illus.   C

1369. Beals, Frank Lee. The rush for gold... Chicago, Wheeler pub. co., 1946. 252 p. illus. (Am. adventure ser.)   CChiS CHi

1370. Benjamin, Marcus. John Bidwell, pioneer; a sketch of his career. Wash., D.C., 1907. 52 p. illus.
CChi CHi CSfWF-H CStoC

1371. Bidwell, John. Echoes of the past... Chico, Chico advertiser [1914] 91 p. port.
C CChi CChiS CHi CL CLO CLSU CLU CLgA CRedl CSS CSbr CSf CSfCW CSfP CSjC CSmH CStmo CU-B CaBViPA OrU UHi

1372. —— Same. Chicago, R. R. Donnelley & sons, 1928. 377 p. map. (Lakeside classics)
C CBb CBev CHi CLO CLU CLgA CMont CSd CSfCW CSmH CStbS CU-B IHi MiD TMC UHi ViU ViW

1373. —— In California before the gold rush. With a foreword by Lindley Bynum. L.A., print. by Ward Ritchie, 1948. 111 p. ports. "Articles...[which] appeared first in...the *Century magazine* for Nov. and Dec. 1890 and Feb. 1891...later issued, with an additional chapter of reminiscences, by the *Chico advertiser*, about 1914, with the title *Echoes of the past*."
Available in many libraries.

1374. —— [Manuscript maps and drawings of the Chico ranch and other property of John Bidwell] [Chico, 1859–19–?] 4 folders. 9 loose maps.   C

1375. —— Memorial. Chico, Normal school, 1900. 18 p. (*Normal record.* v.5, no. 2, April 1900)   CHi

1376. California. State college, Chico. Annual catalogue and circular... Sacramento [1890?–
CHi has 7th, 1896. CL has 1924 to date.

1377. —— —— Information catalog. Chico, 19–
CL has 1928 to date.

1378. Chico. Chamber of commerce. Chico, Butte county, California. [Chico, Record print., 1903?] [44] p. illus., map.   CHi CLU

1379. —— —— Same. [Chico, Briscoe-Nash pub. co., 1903?] 36 p. illus.   CHi

1380. —— **Charters, ordinances, etc.** Charter and codified ordinances of the town of Chico... Chico, Chronicle-record print., 1890. 57 p.   CHi

1381. —— —— The code of the city of Chico, California, 1958. The charter and general ordinances of the city. Published by order of the Council. L.A., Michie city pub., 1959. Loose-leaf.   CChiS

1382. —— —— The ordinances of the city of Chico, a municipal corporation of the fifth class [revised and codified] Compiled by Rich'd White, city clerk, and published by order of the Board of trustees. Chico, Enterprise print., 1897.   CChi

1383. —— **First Presbyterian church.** Minutes of a meeting... [In memoriam...John Bidwell] [1900] 6 l. Ms   C

1384. —— **Trinity Methodist church.** Our heritage, 1858–1958. One hundreth anniversary celebration, December, 1958. Chico, 1958. 38 p. illus.   C CHi

1385. —— **Union Congregational church.** Church manual... Chico, Courant job press, 1867. 11 p. CU-B

1386. Cody, Cora Edith. John Bidwell: his early career in California. [Berkeley, 1927] 192 l. illus., ports., maps. Thesis (M.A.)—Univ. of Calif., 1927.
CChiS (microfilm) CU CU-B

1387. Compton, Henria Packer. Mary Murdock Compton. [Chico? 1953] 27 p. illus., port.
CChi CHi

1388. Diamond match co. Apiary department, Chico. [Catalog of] bee keepers supplies. [n.p., 1919] 74 p. illus.   CHi

1389. Freemasons. Chico. Chico lodge no. 111. In observance of the centennial anniversary... Dispensation issued December 31, 1856, first meeting January 10, 1857. [Chico, Hurst & Yount, 1957] [17] p.   CHi

1390. Gulick, Robert Lee. Chico state college; historical sketch. [n.p., n.d.]   CChiS

1391. Hunt, Rockwell Dennis. John Bidwell, prince of California pioneers...Caldwell, Ida., Caxton [c1942] 463 p. illus., ports. "Bibliographical notes": p. [437]–439.
Available in many libraries.

1392. Hutchinson, William Henry. The California investment; a history of the Diamond match company in California. Chico, Diamond match co., 1957. 399 p. tables.   CChiS CHi

1393. Moore, Gail Everett. History of Chico state college. [Corvallis, Ore., 1939] 141 p. illus., charts, maps. Planographed.
Thesis (M.A.)—Oregon state college, 1939.   CChiS

1394. Parry, C. C. Rancho Chico. S.F., Overland

monthly pub. co. [Bacon & co., print., n.d.] 16 p. illus. Reprinted from *Overland monthly* for June 1888.

C CChiS CU-B NN

1395. Rancho Chico nursery. Descriptive catalogue of fruit, shade and ornamental trees...for sale at the Rancho Chico nursery, Chico, John Bidwell, Proprietor. [Chico Enterprise print.] 1851–

C has 1887–92. CChiS has 1851–89.

1396. Royce, Charles C. John Bidwell, pioneer, statesman, philanthropist... Chico, Priv. pub., 1906. 66 [224] p. illus., ports.

C CChi CChiS CHi CL CLU CMont CSdS CSfCP CSmH CU-B

1397. Rumble, G. W. Resentment; the worse than bandit gang... [S.F.] c1913. His own story of trial and imprisonment.

CHi

1398. Starmer, Garrett, ed. Let's look at Chico... Chico, Chico state college, 1951. unp.

CChiS

1399. U.S. General land office. [Deeds to Arroyo Chico and Farwell grants, confirming land to John Bidwell. Wash., D.C., 1860, 1863] 2 v. map. Manuscript copies on vellum of original deeds. Seals of the U.S. General land office attached. Arroyo Chico deed has also seal of the Butte county, California, District court attached.

C

1400. Wallace, G. Gale. A survey of selected aspects of social organizations, groups, and agencies in Chico, California. Chico, Chico state college, 1954. 122 p. tables.

CChiS

1401. Waterland, John S. [Scrapbook] "Old timer" series from the Chico record August 9, 1934–September 8, 1940.

CChi

1402. Woodland, John E. The location of the Chico freeway: a study of community dynamics. Chico, 1958. 111 l. map, tables, diagrs.

Thesis (M.A.)—Chico state college, 1958. CChiS

CALAVERAS COUNTY
(*Created in 1850*)

GREAT REGISTER

1403. Calaveras county. Index to the Great register of the county of Calaveras. 1866– Place of publication and title vary.

C has 1867, 1871–73, 1875–77, 1879–80, 1882 (biennially to) –1962. CHi has 1876. CL has 1873, 1875, 1876 (suppl.), 1877 (suppl.), 1879, 1882 (suppl.), 1884, 1886, 1888 (suppl.), 1890. CU-B has 1867, 1872–73, 1879, 1898.

GENERAL REFERENCES

1404. Agricultural association of Calaveras county. 39th district. Premium list and speed program of the fair. San Andreas, 1894. unp. CU-B

1405. Alta California, inc., comp. & pub. Calaveras county, California, "where the big trees grow"; a general and historical summary... Sacramento [1938?] 10 l. CU-B

1406. Argonaut mining company vs. Kennedy mining and milling company. In the Superior court of the county of Calaveras and state of California [nos. 1408 and 1179] Argonaut mining company, plaintiff, vs. Kennedy mining and milling company, defendant. Two actions...Before Hon. G. W. Nicol, judge... S.F., Crocker [1898] 2 v. in 1. plans, diagrs. CLU

1407. Beasley, Thomas Dykes. A tramp through

the Bret Harte country... S.F., Elder, 1914. 96 p. illus., map.

Available in many libraries.

1408. Buckbee, Edna Bryan. Pioneer days of Angel's Camp. Angels Camp, Calaveras Californian [c1932] 80 p. illus., ports.

Available in many libraries.

1409. Calaveras Californian. Jumping frog jubilee. Souvenir edition, Calaveras Californian. Angels Camp, May 18–19, 1929, official program... [1929] [24] p.

CHi CLSU CU-B

1410. Calaveras county. Chamber of commerce. Calaveras county, mining, farming, agricultural and stock lands. [San Andreas, Calaveras prospect, n.d.] [34] p.

C

1411. —— —— Same. [1927?] 18 p. illus., map.

CHi CRcS

1412. —— —— Historic Calaveras county of California; scenic grandeur, healthful climate, nature's playground. [San Andreas, 1948?] 10 p. illus. CHi

1413. —— Mining laws. [Old record book of mining laws and claims of Calaveras county, Oct. 1854. 1857] [126] p. Ms. C

1414. —— Sheriff's office. [Claim of B. K. Thorn, sheriff, for expenses incurred in the arrest of C. E. Bolton, alias Black Bart, 1883] 2 l. Typew. CU-B

1415. Calaveras county historical society. Old Calaveras; winning essays [in annual essay contest] San Andreas, 1957– illus.

C has 3d, 1959. CHi has 1st, 1957. CL has 1st–2d, 1957–58.

1416. Calaveras county: illustrated and described; showing its advantages for homes. Oakland, Elliott, 1885. 104 p. illus., map.

CAla CLCM CLCo CLU CSfCP CSmH CU-B

1417. Calaveras county Jumping frog jubilee, Angels Camp. Century of gold, Jumping frog jubilee [1949] official souvenir review. [Angels Camp, Calaveras county fair, 1949?] 20 p. illus. CHi

1418. California. Legislature. Assembly. Articles of impeachment exhibited by the Assembly of the state of California, against James H. Hardy, district judge of the sixteenth judicial district of said state. [Sacramento, Benjamin P. Avery, state print., 1862] 9 p. The sixteenth judicial district encompassed Calaveras county. CU-B

1419. —— —— —— Official report of the proceedings, testimony, and arguments, in the trial of James H. Hardy...before the Senate of the state of California, sitting as a high court of impeachment. Sumner & Cutter, official reporters. Sacramento, Benj. P. Avery state print., 1862. 711 p.

C CHi CLSM CLU CSmH CSt CU CU-B CU-Law NIC NN WHi

1420. California exploration limited. The Thorpe gold mining syndicate. S.F. [1898] 16 p. CU-B

1421. California infantry. San Andreas Light infantry company (Militia) By-laws... San Andreas, W. M. Denig & co., print., 1865. 8 p. CU-B

1422. Cataract and wide west hydraulic gravel mining company. Eho mining district, Calaveras county. Prospectus... S.F., Floto & co., 1876. 12 p.

CSmH

1423. Copperopolis community center. Official souvenir booklet celebrating the 100th anniversary of the discovery of copper at Copperopolis, Calaveras county, California. [Copperopolis, 1960] 36 p. illus., ports.

CHi CU-B

1424. Demarest, D. C. A bit of Mother Lode history. Oakland, 1951. 36 p.
        CBb CHi CRic CSfWF-H CSto CU-B

1425. —— Has the Mother Lode seen its finish? Oakland, 1951. 16 p.   CHi CSfWF-H CU-B

1426. Ellsworth, Rodney Sydes. Discovery of the big trees of California, 1833–1852. [Berkeley, 1934] Thesis (M.A.)–Univ. of Calif., 1934.   CU CU-B

1427. Freemasons. California. Knights Templars. Calaveras and Tuolumne counties, their resources, industries and advantages...1904. 159 p. illus.   C

1428. Goodrich, Mary. On the old Calaveras road ... [n.p., 1929] 17 p. illus., port.
C CBu CHi CLSU CLU CLob CSd CSf CSmH CU-B

1429. Hogan dam, first flood control reservoir in central California. Ed. by Mrs. Joanna London. Articles written by Mrs. K. L. Parker, Lyle Payton, and William Post. Stockton, 1941. [32] p. Ms.   CSto

1430. Houseworth (Thomas) & co., San Francisco. Views of the big trees of Calaveras county, California... S.F., [n.d.] [3] p. illus.   CHi

1431. Immigration association of California. [County scrapbooks] [S.F., 188–?]   C

1432. Kaler, Elizabeth. Memories of Murphys. [Murphys? 1959] 16 p. illus. "Reprinted in part from Mother Lode magazine."   CHi CSto

1433. [Kerr, Mark B.] ed. Mining resources of Calaveras county, California... For distribution at the Mining fair on Calaveras county day, February 21, 1898. [n.p.] Pub. by Calaveras county exhibit [Print. by Byron Ring, S.F.] 1898. 72 p. illus.
        C CHi CLU CSmH CU-B

1434. Marshall mining co., Angels Camp. Prospectus... St. John, N.B., J. & A. McMillan, 1892. 34 p. map, diagrs.   CHi

1435. Matteson, Thomas Jefferson. The diary of Thomas Jefferson Matteson. [San Andreas] Calaveras co. hist. soc. [1954] 30 p. illus., ports.
        C CHi CL CSmH CSto

1436. Mercer's cave: California's greatest natural wonder, located at Murphys... [n.p., n.d.] [4] p. illus., map.   CHi

1437. Murphys. St. Patrick's church. St. Patrick's centennial year, 1858–1958. Murphys, 1959. [7] p. ports.   CHi

1438. The new Calaveras cave, Murphys, Calaveras county, California. W. J. Mercer, proprietor. Description and guide. S.F., Bacon & co., print., c1887. 26 p.   C CHi CU-B

1439. Petherick, William. Report on the Keystone copper mine... Stockton, O. M. Clayes & co., 1865. 5 p.   CU-B

1440. Schwarz, Theodore E. Report of Theodore E. Schwarz, mining engineer, to the Oro plate mining and milling company. Bost., A. Mudge & sons, print., 1881. 19 p. map.   CHi

1441. Seel, E. M. The story of the Mokelumne river ... S.F., P.G.&E. publicity dept. [1930?] 30 p. illus.   CHi CLSU CO CSf

1442. Silliman, Benjamin. Reports on the gold and silver deposits at Quail Hill, Calaveras co., Calif. ... S.F., Print. at off. of Mercantile gazette, 1867. 14 p.   C CSmH CU-B

1443. Storms, William H. Ancient channel system of Calaveras county. Sacramento, State print. off., 1894. 13 p. (Calif. state mining bur. pub.)   C

1444. U.S. 59th Congress. 2d session. Creation of the Calaveras big tree national forest, California... Wash., D.C., 1907. 8 p. maps.   C

1445. Veiller, J. Statement in relation to the Rich Gulch gold & silver mine, Calaveras county, California... N.Y., Baker & Godwin, print., 1865. 23 p.   CU-B

1446. Vischer, Edward. ...The mammoth tree grove, Calaveras county, California, and its avenues. Consisting of title page and 12 plates with 25 engravings... S.F., Author, 1862. (Vischer's views of Calif.) Other editions followed.
C CLO CLSU CLU CMartC CSfCP CSfSC CSmH CU-B

1447. Wells, Andrew Jackson. Calaveras county, California. S.F., Sunset mag. homeseeker's bur. [1908?] 31 p.   CL CU-B

1448. Williams, J. Otis. Mammoth trees of California... With a handbook in brief for a trip to the Calaveras groves and Yosemite valley... Bost., Alfred Mudge & sons, 1871. 55 p.   C CHi CLU CU-B

1449. Wood, Ethelyn E. Special phases of the early history of Calaveras county, California... Stockton, 1947. 138 l. maps. Typew. Thesis (M.A.)–College of the Pacific, 1947.   CStoC

1450. Wood, Harvey. Personal recollections of Harvey Wood, with an introduction and notes by John B. Goodman. Pasadena, Priv. print., 1955. 27 p. illus., ports., map, facsims. (Scraps of Californiana, no. 1) Printed for members of the Zamorano club of Los Angeles.
        CHi CL CTurS N

1451. Wood, Richard Coke. Calaveras, the land of skulls (The Calaveras country) [Sonora, The Mother Lode press, 1955] 158 p. illus., ports. Bibliography: p. 150–153.
Available in many California libraries and CoD NN

1452. —— Murphys, queen of the Sierra. Angels Camp, Calaveras Californian, 1948. 88 p. illus., ports., map.
Available in many libraries.

1453. —— Tales of old Calaveras. [n.p., 1949?] 94 p. illus., ports., map.
C CHi CL CLS CLU CLod CMerCL CRedCL CRic CSf CSfSC CSfWF-H CSjC CU-B

COLUSA COUNTY

(Created in 1850 but attached to Butte county until 1851)

COUNTY HISTORIES

1454. [Green, Will Semple] Colusa county, California. Illustrations descriptive of its scenery, fine residences, public buildings... etc... With historical sketch of the county [by Will Semple Green] S.F., Elliott & Moore, 1880. 196 p. illus., ports., maps.
C CHi CColu CLU CSf CSj CSmat CU-B CaBViPA NN

1455. —— Same. Including specialized articles by others. Pref. by Lucille La Bourdette. Supplement. Sacramento, Reproduced for E. Eubank by the Sacramento lithograph co. [1950] facsim. 196 p. illus., ports., maps.
C CChiS CFS CHi CL CLO CLU CLod CN CO CRb CRedCL CSS CSf CSfCSM CSt CStcrCL CSto CStoc CU-A CU-B CaBViPA CtY ICN MiD-B NN

1456. McComish, Charles Davis, and Lambert,

Rebecca T. History of Colusa and Glenn counties, California, with biographical sketches... L.A., Historic record co., 1918. 1074 p. illus., ports.
C CChiS CColu CHi CL CLO CLU CO CSf CSmH CU-B CWiwCL

1457. Rogers, Justus H. Colusa county: its history ...with a description of its resources... Also biographical sketches of pioneers and prominent residents... Orland, 1891. 473 p. illus., ports., map.
C CAla CB CCH CChiS CColu CHi CL CLCM CLCo CLSU CLU CO CSf CSfCP CSfCW CSmH CSt CStoC CU-B CoD CtY ICN MoSHi MWA NHi WHi

GREAT REGISTER

1458. Colusa county. Index to the Great register of the county of Colusa. 1866– Place of publication and title vary.
C has 1871–73, 1875–76, 1880, 1886, 1890 (biennially to)–1962. CHi has 1873. CL has 1867, 1873, 1875–77, 1879, 1882 (suppl.), 1886 (suppl.), 1888, 1890 (suppl.). CSmH has "General list of citizens"... for 1880 only. CU-B has July 1867, Oct. 1872, Aug. 1873, Apr. 1879, 1879 (suppl.), 1940.

DIRECTORIES

1459. 1907/08. Directory publishing co., pub. Colusa city directory, 1907/08. S.F., 1907. 72 p. C

GENERAL REFERENCES

1460. Blanding, William, and Louis A. Garnett. Swamp and overflowed lands of William Blanding and Louis A. Garnett in Colusa county. [n.p., n.d.] 558 p. Ms. C

1461. Catlin and Blanchard, firm. Register of actions, Catlin and Blanchard, kept by George A. Blanchard beginning January 11, 1888. 1888–[1891] 299 p. Ms. C

1462. Chapman's magazine, Berkeley. Colusa county. [1941?] 16 p. CO

1463. Colusa county. Board of supervisors. Colusa county. [Colusa, Colusa sun print., 1904?] 12 p. illus. CU-B

1464. —— Board of trade. Colusa county. [Colusa? 1894] 12 p. illus. CU-B

1465. —— Chamber of commerce. Little would one think on passing through the county by railroad that it contains such beautiful scenes and fertile soil as the following photographs indicate... [Colusa? 1907?] 52 p. illus., maps. CHi

1466. Colusa county and the Sacramento valley, California. S.F., 1909. 32 p. CHi

1467. Colusa county, California. [n.p., 1931?] 16 p. illus., maps. CHi

1468. Colusa county teachers' association. Colusa county... [Oakland, Pac. press, 1888] 48 p. illus.
C CLU CSmH CU-B

1469. Colusa sun. Colusa county annual and directory, being a holiday supplement... Historical and descriptive sketches of Colusa and all towns, etc., in the county. Names and addresses of taxpayers, local sketches ...Jan. 1, 1876–1893. Colusa, 1876–[1893?]
C CHi (1878, 1893) CSmH (1876) CU-B (1878)

1470. Colusa sun-herald. Colusa, the county of opportunity, California. [Colusa, 1913?] 16 p. illus., map.
CHi CU-B

1471. Colusi county historical society. With Brough (i.e. Bruff) through Colusi county in 1850; being a descriptive account of the region during California's first year of statehood. Orland, Unit press [n.d.] unp.
CHi CRb

1472. Conmy, Peter Thomas. Will Semple Green, Colusa pioneer and prophet of the Sacramento valley, 1832–1905. [Oakland?] 1955. 6 p. Mimeo. C CRcS

1473. Crane, Ellis T. Examination of books and accounts of reclamation district no. 108 from January 28, 1884, to October 1, 1894. [n.p., 1895?] 39 p. CLU

1474. DeJarnatt & Crane. Colusa county, California. Oakland, Pac. press, 1886. 126 p. illus., map.
CHi

1475. —— Same. 2d ed. ... Oakland, Pac. press, 1887. 104 p. illus. C CSmH

1476. Hartog, John H., comp. Album of the "County of Good Luck" in California. [Colusa, 1906?] 52 p. illus., map. CU-B

1477. Immigration association of California. [County scrapbooks] [S.F., 188–?] C

1478. Kimball, Adolphus Wellington. Record of births at which Dr. Adolpus Wellington Kimball was the attending physician in Williams, Colusa county during the years 1884–1921. Also an incomplete record of marriages for the years, 1887–1898 and deaths, 1888–1898... 1940. [11] l. Typew. C

1479. Lefebvre, Leon. History of Swift's stone corral. [1938] 26 l. Typew. (Carbon copy) C CHi

1480. Montgomery, A., vs. Merrill, N. S., et al. In the Supreme court of the state of California. A. Montgomery, appellant, vs. N. S. Merrill, et al. Transcript on appeal. John T. Harrington, attorney for respondent, H. M. Albery, attorney for appellant. Colusa, Colusa sun print. [1883] 75 p. CHi

1481. Reclamation district no. 124 vs. Gray, R. A. In the Supreme court of the state of California. Reclamation district no. 124, plaintiff and respondent, vs. R. A. Gray, defendant and appellant. Brief for W. C. Dyas, as Amicus curiae. Colusa, 1891. 35 p. CHi

1482. Spect, Jonas, vs. Hagar, George. In the Supreme court of the state of California. Lou G. Spect, executrix, and W. G. Dyas, executor of the last will and testament of Jonas Spect...vs. George Hagar... Transcript on appeal. H. M. Albery, attorney for appellants ... [Colusa] Colusa sun print. [188–?] 139 p. map. Colusa town lot suit. CHi

1483. "Truth wears no mask." Facts, figures and comments on the division of Colusa county and the proposed creation of the county of Glenn... S.F., Crocker, 1889. 57 p. maps. CHi

1484. Wood, Elizabeth (Lambert) Pete French, cattle king. Portland, Ore., Binfords, c1951. 230 p.
CRb

CONTRA COSTA COUNTY
(Created in 1850)

COUNTY HISTORIES

1485. History of Contra Costa county. With illustrations descriptive of its scenery, residences, [etc.] From original sketches by artists of the highest ability. Oakland, Thompson & West, 1882. illus., map, pls.
CSfU NN

1486. History of Contra Costa county, California, with

biographical sketches... L.A., Historic record co., 1926. 1102 p. illus., ports.

C C-S CCH CHi CL CLO CLS CLU CMartC CO CRic CSf CSjC CSmat MiD-B MWA NN WHi

1487. Hulaniski, Frederick J., ed. The history of Contra Costa county, California... Berkeley, Elms pub. co., 1917. 635 p. illus., ports.

C CB CHi CL CLU CMartC CO CPa CRic CSS CSf CSfCP CSfMI CSjC CSmH CSt CU-B CYcCL MWA NN WHi

1488. Illustrations of Contra Costa county, California, with historical sketches. Oakland, Smith & Elliott, 1878. 54 p. illus., maps.

CL CMartC CRic CSf CSfCP CSjC CSmH CStclU CU-B NHi NN

1489. —— Same. A facsimile reproduction of the original ed. ...1878. Under the auspices of the Contra Costa county historical society. [Sacramento, Sacramento lithograph co., 1952] 54 p. illus., ports., maps.

C CBb CChiS CHi CLU CO CSS CSf CSto CStoC CU-B MoSHi NIC

1490. [Munro-Fraser, J. P.] History of Contra Costa county, California... and biographical sketches... S.F., W. A. Slocum & co., 1882. 710 p. ports.

C C-S CAla CHi CL CLCM CLU CMartC CO CP CRic CRiv CSf CSfCP CSfCW CSfMI CSfSt CSmH CSmyS (microfilm) CStclU CSto CStoC CU-B MWA N NHi TxU

1491. Purcell, Mae (Fisher) History of Contra Costa county... 1st ed. Berkeley, Gillick press, 1940. 742 p. illus., ports., maps. "Bibliography—references": p. 740–741.

C CAla CB CF CHi CL CLCo CLU CLob CLod CMa CMartC CN CO CP CPa CRic CS CSd CSf CSfMI CSfSt CSj CSjC CSjCL CSmH CSmat CSt CStmo CSto CU-B CV CVtCL CWoY CYcCL NN WHi

GREAT REGISTER

1492. Contra Costa county. Index to the Great register of the county of Contra Costa. 1866– Place of publication and title vary.

C has 1867, 1871–73, 1875, 1877, 1879–80, 1884, 1886, 1890 (biennially to)– 1962. CHi has 1873. CL has 1873, 1875 (suppl. 1 & 2), 1876 (suppl.), 1877 (suppl.), 1879, 1882, 1886, 1888, 1890. CMartC has 1898. CRic has 1918, 1924. CSmH has 1868, 1871, 1880, 1882. CU-B has 1867–68, 1871–73, 1879.

DIRECTORIES

1493. 1908. Directory publishing co., pub. Contra Costa county directory... S.F., 1908. 319 p.   C

Richmond

1494. 1909. Directory publishing co., pub. Richmond, California, directory... S.F., 1909. 152 p.
                                                        C

1495. 1909– Polk, R. L., & co., pub. Polk's Richmond city directory including Martinez and El Cerrito. S.F., 1909– Title varies: 1911/12, Polk's Richmond, Pullman, San Pablo and Stege directory; 1912/13, Polk's Richmond, San Pablo and Martinez directory; 1914/15, Polk's Richmond and Contra Costa county directory; 1916/17, Polk's Richmond, Martinez and Contra Costa county directory; 1918–1922/23, Polk's Richmond and Martinez directory, includes Pullman, San Pablo, El Cerrito (Rust) and Stege; 1923/24–27, Polk's Richmond and

Martinez directory; 1928–37, 1939, Polk's Richmond city directory including Martinez.

C has 1911/12–1914/15, 1916/17, 1918–30, 1932, 1934, 1937, 1939–40. CHi has 1929, 1942, 1947/48, 1950, 1953–58, 1960. CL has 1922/23, 1927, 1937, 1940, 1950, 1953–57. CMartC has 1909–18, 1921–30, 1932, 1934, 1937, 1939–40, 1942, 1950, 1954/55–56, 1958. CO has 1914/15–57. CRic has 1909–59. CSmat has 1958–59.

1496. 1920. Western directory co., pub. Richmond including Pullman and Stege and Martinez city directory... Long Beach, 1920. 2 v.

                                        C CMartC CRic

Other Cities and Towns

1497. 1947. Midwest publishing co. Concord city directory, 1947. S.F., 1947. 61 p.   CMartC

1498. 1961– Polk, R. L., & co., pub. Polk's Concord city directory. L.A., 1961–   CHi

1499. 1947. Midwest publishing co. Lafayette city directory. Walnut Creek city directory. S.F., 1947. 103 p.   CMartC

1500. 1931– Polk, R. L., & co., pub. Polk's Pittsburg and Antioch city directory. L.A., 1931–

CHi has 1931, 1947, 1949/50, 1952/53–55, 1957, 1959–60. CL has 1931, 1937, 1949/50, 1952/53–54, 1957. CMartC has 1931, 1947, 1949/50, 1952/53–57, 1959. CSmat has 1958, 1959. CU-B has 1959.

1501. 1950. Spectator press, pub. Walnut Creek, Lafayette city directory. Carmel [1950] unp. illus.
                                                        CMartC

GENERAL REFERENCES

1502. Abstract of the title of the tract of land situate in the county of Contra Costa, state of California, and known as "Los Meganos." [n.p., 1873] 66 l.   CU-B

1503. Abstract of title of what is known as the "river property" fronting the Marsh ranch, Contra Costa county, California... [Martinez, 1887] 187 l.   CU-B

1504. Adams, Edson F., et al. vs. Hopkins, Emily B., et al. ...Edson F. Adams, et al., plaintiffs and appellants, vs. Emily B. Hopkins, et al. ...Bernardo Fernandez, counsel. Martinez, T. S. Davenport, print., 1898. 851 p.   CU-B

1505. —— In the Supreme court of the state of California. [S.F. no. 1757] Edson F. Adams et al., plaintiffs and respondents, Joseph Wohlfrom et al., defendants and appellants. Closing brief of appellants, Joseph Wohlfrom et al. R. H. Countryman... attorney for appellants, Joseph Wohlfrom et al. ... S.F., C. A. Murdock & co. [1901] 55 p.   CHi

1506. —— ...Opening points and authorities of appellants, Joseph Wohlfrom et al. R. H. Countryman... attorney for appellants, Joseph Wohlfrom et al. ... [S.F.] C. A. Murdock & co. [1899] 24 p.   CHi

1507. Antioch vs. Williams irrigation district et al. ...Town of Antioch, a municipal organization, plaintiff, vs. Williams irrigation district et al., defendants... Albert Edward Chandler... [n.p., 192–?] 155 p.
                                                        CU-B

1508. —— ...Oral argument of Albert Raymond on behalf of respondents. S.F., Pernau-Walsh print. co. [192–?] 364 p.   CU-B

1509. The Antioch ledger. ...Bridge opening supplement. Industrial–agricultural–progress edition. [Antioch, 1926] unp. illus.   C

1510. —— The Golden link, June 1924. Antioch,

1924. 51 p. illus., maps. "Presented in commemoration of the granting of the permit to bridge the San Joaquin river at Antioch." C CSf

1511. Bank of Martinez. Seventy-fifth anniversary 1873–1948. Martinez, 1949. 20 p.
CHi CLO CLU CU-B

1512. Blum, Simon. Contra Costa county lands... located from 12 to 25 miles of the city of Oakland... Apply to Simon Blum... [Martinez, 1890] 16 p.
CSmH CU-B

1513. Bowers rubber co. Building a rubber factory. S.F., Schmidt litho. co. [1906?] [24] p. illus. CU-B

1514. Brady, Doris W. Family fun in the Diablo area; a where-to-go, what-to-do recreation guide for east Contra Costa county dwellers. Walnut Creek, Brady, 1958. 52 p. illus., maps. CMartC

1515. Brown, Carrie L. (Smith), comp. Orinda roads of Spanish or historic origin. Orinda, 1948. illus., map. "Compiled for the Women's guild of Orinda community church." CHi

1516. Bruce, Donald. The public lands of Alameda & Contra Costa counties, survey of Rancho del Sobrante ... S.F., Bruce's print. & pub. house, 1878. 8 p.
C CHi CU-B

1517. Burgess, R. N., co. Scenic trips and lands in the Mount Diablo country, Contra Costa county, California. [S.F., Print. by Crocker, 19–?] [18] p. illus.
CU-B NN

1518. Bush, David & Don. Land circular, Contra Costa county, Martinez, February, 1887... [S.F., Bancroft co., print., 1887] 14 p. CU-B

1519. Byron Hot Springs, California. [S.F., 1903?] [3] p. CU-B

1520. Byron Hot Springs hotel. Automobile guide to Byron Hot Springs with map... [n.p., n.d.] folder. illus., map. CHi

1521. The Byron times. Byron times development edition... Special number. 3d–17th, 1912–1937. S.F., Byron, 1912–37. illus., maps.
C has 3d–12th, 14th–16th, 1912–1930/31, 1932/33–1936/37. CMartC has 11th–12th, 14th, 16th, 1928/31, 1932/33, 1936/37. CO has 10th–12th, 14th, 1926/27–1930/31, 1932/33. CSmH has 6th–10th, 12th–16th, 1918–27, 1930–37. CU-B has 6th–10th, 12th–16th, 1918–27, 1930–37.

1522. California. Laws, statutes, etc. Road laws of Contra Costa county. Approved March 23d, 1868. S.F., W. B. Cooke & co., print., 1868. 20 p. CU-B

1523. —— Superior court (Alameda county) ... Town of Antioch (a municipal corporation), plaintiff, vs. Williams irrigation district, et al., defendants. W. H. Metson, as executor of the last will and testament of Josephine K. Metson, deceased, and Mary Helen Curtis, intervenors. Opinion of the court on the demurrers to the complaint, and also on the application for a preliminary injunction. Oakland, Tribune press [1921] 44 p.
CU-B

1524. —— Superior court (Contra Costa county) Edson F. Adams et al., plaintiffs, vs. Emily B. Hopkins et al., defendants. Final report of the referees in the partition of the Rancho El Sobrante. Filed this [3d] day of August, 1909. [Martinez, 1909] 208 p. map.
C CLU CRic

1525. —— Superior court (San Francisco) ... Henry F. Emeric, plaintiff, vs. Henry V. Alvarado, ad-

ministrator, etc., et al., defendants. Final decree of partition of San Pablo ranch. S.F., Crocker [1894] 493 p.
CHi CLU CRic CU-B

1526. —— University. Department of city and regional planning. Concord: a study of the decision-making process as it has affected physical development, 1947–1957. Berkeley, Univ. of Calif., 1957. 9 p.
CMartC

1527. Carlson, Ruth Elizabeth (Kearney) Rodeo corral, 1954. [Rodeo? 1955?] 49 l. illus.
CMartC CU-B

1528. [Carquinez bridge co.] Carquinez strait bridge. [S.F., 1932] [12] p. fold. illus., plan. CU-B

1529. Castro, Victor, vs. Adams, Edson, et als. ...In the Supreme court of the state of California, Victor Castro, plaintiff and appellant, vs. Edson Adams, et als., defendants and respondents. Clinton C. Tripp, cross complainant, defendant and appellant. Transcript on appeal from the Superior court of Contra Costa county... Martinez, Contra Costa gazette press, 1906. 236 p. Land titles in Alameda and Contra Costa counties. CLU

1530. [Central business development, inc.] Brochure offering for sale the historical adobe of early California at Concord, California. [Concord, 1948] 7 l. mounted photos. CU-B

1531. Collier, George C. Rancho Laguna de los Palos Colorados; a history of the Moraga ranch. [n.p.] 1956. 26 p. CMartC

1532. Concord. Chamber of commerce. Concord, Contra Costa county, California. Concord [1921?] [12] p. illus., maps. CHi

1533. Concord civic league. Report on parks and recreation... Concord, 1957. 46 p. diagrs., maps.
CMartC

1534. Contra Costa coal mine. Prospectus of the Contra Costa coal mine... [Berkeley? 1900?] 8 p.
CSmH

1535. Contra Costa county. Contra Costa county government; approved by the Board of education, 1956... Martinez, Contra Costa co. schools, 1956. 122 p.
CMartC

1536. —— Board of publicity. County of Contra Costa, an empire rich in industry and agriculture. [Walnut Creek, 193–?] 32 p. illus. CHi CU-B

1537. —— Board of supervisors. Contra Costa county, California... Martinez [1907] 53 p. illus., maps.
CU-B

1538. —— —— Same. [Martinez, Gazette print., 1915?] [20] p. illus. CU-B

1539. —— —— Contra Costa county's water requirements. [Martinez, 1959?] unp. maps. CMartC

1540. —— Board of trade. Contra Costa county, California; its climate, its soil, productions and location ... S.F., W. B. Bancroft & co., print., 1887. 31 p. illus., ports. CLU CU-B NHi NN WHi

1541. —— —— Contra Costa county, California: its situation, topography, bays and rivers, soil, climate, resources and productions... Martinez, Contra Costa gazette press, 1887. 16 p. CSmH CU-B NN

1542. —— Central Contra Costa sanitary district. The collection, treatment and disposal of the sewage of central Contra Costa county, California. S.F., Brown and Caldwell, 1956. 215 p. illus., maps. CMartC

1543. —— Flood control and water conservation district. Walnut Creek watershed program for soil conservation and flood control, prepared...in cooperation with Soil conservation service, United States department of agriculture. Wash., D.C., 1952. 183 p. CMartC

1544. —— **Housing authority.** A survey of housing in Contra Costa county, June 1950. Conducted in selected areas of: Antioch, Crockett, Martinez, North Richmond, Pittsburg, Port Chicago, Rodeo, San Pablo, West Pittsburg. S.F., Clark, 1950. 239 p. maps, tables. CMartC

1545. —— —— A survey of housing Contra Costa county, June 1950. Supplemental tables. S.F., Contra Costa co. housing survey, 1950. unp. tables. CMartC

1546. —— **Planning commission.** A general plan for Clayton valley. Martinez, 1956. illus., maps. CMartC

1547. —— —— A general plan for Lafayette. Martinez, 1957. unp. illus. CMartC

1548. —— —— A general plan for Orinda. Martinez [1955?] 30 p. map. CMartC

1549. —— —— The general plan for the Moraga area, April, 1955. Martinez, 1955. 33 p. maps, tables. CMartC

1550. —— —— A general plan for the San Ramon valley. Martinez, 1955. 10 p. maps. CMartC

1551. —— —— A general plan for the Vine Hill-Pacheco planning area. Martinez, 1957. 29 p. illus., maps. CMartC

1552. —— —— General plan for Ygnacio valley, November, 1954. Martinez, 1954. 4 p. map. CMartC

1553. —— —— Lafayette general plan. Martinez, 1955. 30 p. maps. CMartC

1554. —— **Recorder's office.** [Cattle brands registered in Contra Costa county 1845–1868. Berkeley, 1939] 148 l. Photographic copy of original ms. "List of marks and brands recorded in Alameda co.": l. 142–48. CU-B

1555. Contra Costa, California; combining agriculture and industry. [n.p., 1924] 13 p. illus., map. CRcS

1556. Contra Costa county development association. Contra Costa county, California, as a factory location; a preliminary report. Richmond [n.d.] 8 p. illus., maps. CRic

1557. —— Contra Costa county, California; industrial, commercial, agricultural, recreational, residential ... Richmond, 1936. 38 l. maps.
  C CLSU CMartC CRic CSfMI CWhC

1558. —— Directory of manufacturers, Contra Costa county, California... Martinez, 1939–
CMartC has 1950, 1952, 1958–60. CRic has 1939–date (broken file)

1559. —— History of New York Landing; Nortonville; Pittsburg Landing; Somersville; Empire Mine. Martinez [n.d.] 5 p. CHi CMartC CRic

1560. —— Live in Contra Costa county, California. Richmond [1939?] 7 p. illus., map. CRcS

1561. —— Play in scenic Contra Costa. Richmond [n.d.] 5 p. map. CRcS

1562. —— Remarks, by Loren J. Westhaver... [and others] at the Contra Costa county business-industry outlook conference at Diablo country club, April 29, 1959. [n.p., 1959] unp. CMartC

1563. —— **Committee on history and landmarks.** Rambling bits on the history and landmarks of San Ramon and adjacent valleys... Danville, 1928. 10 p. CMartC CRic

1564. Contra Costa county development league, Martinez. Contra Costa county, California, the county of homes... [Martinez? 19–?] 45 [3] p. illus. CU-B

1565. Contra Costa county water district. Financial feasibility of domestic water system acquisition. Board of directors, Ralph Bollman [and others] S.F., Stone & Youngberg, 1959. 65 p. map, tables. CMartC

1566. Contra Costa gazette. ...Supplement... 1916. Martinez, 1916. 1 v. illus. CRic CU-B

1567. Contra Costa news. Special edition, July 1, 1897. Martinez, 1897. 24 p. illus., tables.
  CHi CMartC

1568. Contra Costa water co. Appeal of the Contra Costa water company. In the matter of the survey of the rancho El Sobrante... [S.F., 1881] 12 p. CSmH

1569. Coro foundation, San Francisco. Orinda survey; an incorporation study of the Orinda area, Contra Costa county, California. S.F., 1954. 11 l. maps.
  C CMartC

1570. Currey, John, vs. Alvarado, Juan Bautista, et al. In the Supreme court of the state of California. John Currey, appellant, vs. Juan B. Alvarado, et al., respondents... S.F., C. W. Gordon, bk. and job print., 1871. 3 v. in l. San Pablo rancho suit. CLU CU-B

1571. —— ...John Currey, plaintiff and appellant, vs. Juan B. Alvarado, et al, defendants and respondents. Transcript on appeal from the fifteenth district [!] court in and for the county of Contra Costa. S. F. & L. Reynolds, attorneys for defendants and respondents Emeric and Rockfellow... S.F., Women's co-operative print. union, 1876. 140 p. CLU

1572. Daily independent, Pittsburg. The romantic history of Contra costa county... Pittsburg, 1938. 48 p. illus., ports., map. CSf

1573. de Laveaga, Delight. History of Santa Maria church, Orinda, California. [n.p., 1939] [8] p. CU-B

1574. Description of the "Morago rancho." 12,605 acres of the choicest land in California, situated in Contra Costa and Alameda counties, Cal. ... [S.F., 1889?] 16 p. map. CU-B

1575. Early, H. Eugene. The Moragas in California: father and son. [Berkeley, 1937] 105 l. maps. Thesis (M.A.)—Univ. of Calif., 1937.
CFS (Micro-film copy) CU CU-B

1576. Easton, Wendell. Contra Costa co., California, and its offerings for settlement. Geography, climate, soil and productions. Catalogue of Contra Costa lands. Folding maps of Gwin estate and of Contra Costa county. S.F., 1884. 18 p. CSmH CU-B NN WHi

1577. Edwards, Hugh P. [Diaries of Hugh P. Edwards, written at the Edwards' ranch, Crockett, California. 1872–1909] 35 v. Ms. CU-B

1578. Emeric, Henry F., vs. Alvarado, Henry V. In the Superior court in and for the city and county of San Francisco...Henry F. Emeric, plaintiff, vs. Henry V. Alvarado, admr., etc., et al., defendants. Partial report of referees in partition of San Pablo rancho. S.F. [1892] 143 p. San Pablo rancho suit. CHi

1579. Emeric, Joseph, vs. Alvarado, Juan Bautista, et al. San Pablo rancho suit. Briefs and other records in this case, including those after Henry V. Alvarado, administrator, became defendant, 1874–1894. [S.F., 1874–1894] CU-B

1580. —— In the Superior court...Joseph Emeric, plaintiff, vs. Henry V. Alvarado, administrator of the estate of Juan B. Alvarado, deceased, et al., defendants. Additional findings and conclusions of law and interlocutory decree... S.F., G. Spaulding & co., print. [1889] 613, 64 p. CMartC CRic CU-B

1581. —— ...In the Supreme court of the state of California. Joseph Emeric, plaintiff and respondent, vs. Juan B. Alvarado, et al., defendants and respondents, Emily S. Tewksbury, et al., defendants and appellants. Third supplement to transcript... [S.F., 1882] 161 p.
CHi

1582. —— ...Joseph Emeric, respondent, vs. Juan B. Alvarado, et al., respondents, Emily S. Tewksbury, et al., appellants. Points and authorities of respondents, Theodore H. Hittell, attorney... S.F., Frank Eastman, 1881. 75 p.
CHi

1583. —— ...Joseph Emeric, plaintiff and respondent, vs. Henry V. Alvarado, admr., etc., et al., defendants and respondents, A. Maraschi et al., appellants. Transcript on appeals of A. Maraschi et al., from Superior court—Department 4, San Francisco... S.F., W. C. Brown, print. [1889] xxxi, 1198 p.
CLU

1584. Esser, Harold J. The Ellis Landing shell-mound. 10 p. Typew.
CRic

1585. "First landmarks caravan." [Martinez? 1932] 5 l. Description of tour sponsored by the Contra Costa county federation of women's clubs.
CU-B

1586. Freemasons. Martinez lodge, no. 41. Centennial celebration souvenir commemorating the 100th anniversary...July 26, 1952. [n.p.] 1952. [14] p. illus.
CHi

1587. Goold, Mrs. Charles, and Wood, Charlotte. Rambling bits on the history & landmarks of the San Ramon & adjacent valleys... [n.p., 1928] 11 p. Mimeo.
CHi

1588. Gregory, Platt, vs. McPherson, Daniel R. In the Supreme court of the state of California. Platt Gregory, plaintiff and appellant, vs. Daniel R. McPherson, defendant and respondent. Brief for respondent. John Currey, for respondent. S.F., Sterett print. [185–?] 25 p. "An action to recover...a part of the Rancho Las Nueces, or San Miguel, in Contra Costa county."
CLU

1589. Gunderson, Gilfred Leroy. The abandonment of traditional council-manager government in Antioch, California. [Berkeley, 1961] Thesis (M.A.)— Univ. of Calif., 1961.
CU

1590. Hammond, George P. Romance of the California ranchos; an address...at the dedication of the Salvio Pacheco adobe in Concord...by the officers of the Contra Costa hist. soc., Aug. 22, 1954. [n.p., 1956?] 12 p.
CHi

1591. Hearne bros., Detroit. Official Hearne brothers polyconic projection maps of all of Contra Costa county. Constantly revised and kept up to date. [Detroit, 195–?] 1 v. maps.
C

1592. Herman, Fred George. Press access to information in Contra Costa county; a case study. [Berkeley, 1956] Thesis (M.A.)—Univ. of Calif., 1956.
CU

1593. Hoff, A., and Nieto, A. R., comps. El Sobrante civic survey; a study of the feasibility of incorporation or annexation for the community of El Sobrante. S.F., Coro foundation, 1955. 29 p. map, tables.
CMartC

1594. Homan, A. Gerlof, and Robison, H. E. Economic and financial aspects of public ownership of the Concord water system. Prepared for city of Concord, California. [Menlo Park, Stanford research inst.] 1956. 78 p. diagrs., tables, plans. (Project no. I-1522)
CMartC

1595. Immigration association of California. [County scrapbooks] [S.F., 188–?]
C

1596. Jennings, James B. The Richmond-San Rafael bridge, a photographic story. A representative selection of construction photographs illustrating progress during the first two years... Richmond, Pub. by J. B. Jennings [etc.] c1955. 1 v. (chiefly illus., ports., map, diagrs.)
CU-B

1597. Jones, William Franklin. Nortonville, Calif. [n.p., 1950?] 11 l. Original photographs, taken in Nortonville about 1876...with brief descriptive notes.
C

1598. Keith, James Dunbar. The story of Crockett. [Richmond, Contra Costa development assoc.] Sept. 1930. [33] l. Mimeo.
C

1599. —— Same. 1931. 25 p.
CHi CMartC CRic CU-B

1600. —— Same, revised May 1939.
CHi CMartC CRic

1601. Knox, Newton Booth. The geology of the Mount Diablo mine. [Berkeley, 1938] Thesis (M.A.)— Univ. of Calif., 1938.
CU

1602. Lau, Leung-Ku. An estimate of stream flow through Carquinez strait at Martinez, California. [Berkeley, 1955] Thesis (M.S.)—Univ. of Calif., 1955.
CU

1603. Lawrence, E. A. Romero ranch... [S.F., 1860] 12 p.
CSmH CU-B

1604. Lord, Russell F. Reports of Russell F. Lord, civil and mining engineer, on the Rancho de los Meganos and his coal field, in Contra Costa county. N.Y., John Polhemus, 1881. 39 p.
CHi

1605. Loucks, Annie. Early history of Pacheco, Contra Costa county, California. [Richmond, Contra Costa development assoc.] 1939. 10 p.   CHi CRic CU-B

1606. Lyman, George Dunlap. John Marsh, pioneer... N.Y., Scribner, 1930. 394 p. illus., ports. Bibliography: p. 343–384.
Available in many libraries.

1607. Macomber, Nancy. Contra Costa county, rainbow's end. Richmond, Contra Costa county development assoc., 1948. 10 p.
CRic

1608. Mallett, Fowler. Genealogical notes and anecdotes. [Berkeley?] Priv. print., 1953. 208 p.
CHi CNF

1609. Martinez, Carmel Grace. Don Ignacio Martinez...1774–1848. In *Pony express courier*, Placerville, 1943–44.   CMartC CSmH CU-B

1610. Martinez. Chamber of commerce. Acquaint yourself with facts and statistical information about Martinez, California. [1939?] 19 p.
CHi

1611. Metcalfe, William L., comp. Souvenir; Contra Costa county, California, as reviewed under the vitascope; a pen picture of its wonderfully productive valleys, superbly illustrated... [Richmond] Richmond record, c1902. 118 p. illus.
CHi CMartC CO CRic CU-B

1612. Moraga land association, San Francisco. Description of the "Moraga Rancho"; 12,605 acres of the choicest lands in California. Situated in Contra Costa and Alameda counties, Cal. In close proximity to Oakland and San Francisco... S.F., M'Neil bros. [1889?] 16 p. map.
CHi

1613. Native daughters of the Golden West. Donner parlor, no. 193. Doctor Marsh. [n.p.] 1932. Typew.
CSd

1614. Oakland dock and warehouse co. A photographic story of the Richmond–San Rafael bridge. Oakland [195–?] 1 v. unp. illus., diagrs.
C

1615. Orinda country club. Report 1932. [Orinda] 1933. 1 v. illus., ports., maps, tables.   CU-B

1616. Outdoor art shows inc., Walnut Creek. The 4th annual art fair. [Walnut Creek] 1952. 16 p.   CHi

1617. Petersen, Emily June (Ulsh) Doctor John Marsh, California pioneer, 1836–1856. [Berkeley] 1924. 202 l. illus., port. Thesis (M.A.)—Univ. of Calif., 1924.   CU   CU-B

1618. Pillsbury, Evans Searle. ...In the matter of the estate of Josephine L. Sanford, deceased. Brief for respondents Mary Sanford and Huntington Sanford and the executors and trustees. E. S. Pillsbury, Horace D. Pillsbury, attorneys for Mary Sanford and Huntington Sanford, Garret W. McEnerney, attorney for the executors and trustees... S.F., Crocker [1901] 39 p.   CU-B

1619. Pittman, Tarea Hall. The operation of state and county residence requirements under the California indigent aid law in Contra Costa county. Berkeley, 1946. Thesis (M. Social welfare)—Univ. of Calif., 1946.   CU

1620. Pivernetz, Joseph Albert. An economic survey of the industrial development of Crockett, California. [Berkeley, 1931] Thesis (M.A.)—Univ. of Calif., 1931.   CU

1621. Public administration service, Chicago. Organization and administration of the Contra Costa county flood control and water conservation district, Contra Costa county, California; a survey report. Chicago, 1958. 62 p. map, tables.   CMartC

1622. —— Organization and administration of the public works department, Contra Costa county, California; a survey report. Chicago, 1958. 157 p. map, tables.   CMartC

1623. Public affairs research, inc. Pleasant Hill government study. Oakland, 1958. 45 p.   CMartC

1624. Purcell, Mae (Fisher) Landmarks of Contra Costa county... [n.p., 1941?] 25 l. Mimeo. Includes bibliographies.   CHi   CMartC   CO   CRic   CSf

1625. Remond, Auguste. Report of an exploration and survey of the coal mines, Mount Diablo district, Contra Costa county. S.F., L. Albin, print., 1861. 24 p.   CLU

1626. Rigdon, Vera Esta. The geography of the Carquinez strait. [Berkeley, 1924] Thesis (M.A) — Univ. of Calif., 1924.   CU

1627. Rodeo. Garretson heights elementary school. Rodeo round up club. Round up of Rodeo history; and historical booklet... [Rodeo] 1954. 42 l. illus., maps.   CMartC   CU-B

1628. Saint Mary's college. Catalog. CL has 1923- to date.

1629. Saint Mary's collegian. ...Diamond jubilee commemorative edition, being a survey of events in the history of St. Mary's college from 1863 to 1938. Saint Mary's college, 1938. 24 p. illus., ports.   CU-B

1630. [Sanford, James T.] [Deed relating to the Marsh ranch, Contra Costa county, California, made by James T. Sanford and Spencer W. Richardson, William H. Hill and Edward D. Adams, co-partners under the name of Richardson, Hill and company] [Bost., 1876] 41 p.   CU-B

1631. Sanford, Josephine L., vs. Savings and loan society, et al. ...Josephine L. Sanford, administratrix, etc., vs. Savings and loan society, et al. In equity... [S.F., 1890–95] 8 v. in 2.   CU-B

1632. San Francisco bulletin. California home (John Marsh) Contra Costa county, California, from San Francisco evening bulletin, July 19, 1856. [Richmond] Contra Costa county development assoc. [193–?] 4 l. Mimeo.   CMartC   CRic

1633. San Francisco sulphur co. vs. Contra Costa county. ...San Francisco sulphur company (a corporation) substituted in the place and stead of the Pacific sulphur and chemical company (a corporation), plaintiff and appellant, vs. county of Contra Costa, defendant and respondent... S.F., 1927–28. 4 v. in 1.   CU-B

1634. San Pablo and Oakland artesian water company. ...Incorporated April 11th, 1903. Prospectus [S.F.?, 1903?] 8 p.   CSmH

1635. Teese, Edith. Water front development in the San Pablo and Richmond, California region, to 1917. [Berkeley, 1947] Thesis (M.A.)—Univ. of Calif., 1947.   CU

1636. Thompson, Margaret (Ballard) History of coal mining in the Mount Diablo region, 1859–1885. [Berkeley, 1931] 96 l. illus., maps. Thesis (M.A.)— Univ. of Calif., 1931.   CU   CU-B

1637. Tudor engineering co. A report of freeways, expressways and major streets for Contra Costa county, California. Prepared for Board of supervisors. [S.F., 1958] 99 p. maps.   CMartC

1638. —— Report on county roads and highways, Contra Costa county, Calif. Prepared for Board of supervisors. S.F., 1952. 51 p. maps.   CMartC

1639. —— Supplement to the report on county roads and highways... S.F., 1954. 21 p. maps.   CMartC

1640. U.S. General land office. ...In the matter of the survey of the Rancho "El Sobrante." [S.F., 1880?– 81] 3 pamphlets in 1 v. Contents: no. 1 Argument of Edson Adams in reply to the brief of J. W. Shanklin, filed in behalf of Henry Peirce.- no. 2 H. P. Irving's reply to John Mullan's brief.- no. 3 Before the Secretary of the interior...Notice of appeal and specifications of error for the state of California and owners of certain indemnity, swamp and overflowed and salt marsh and tide lands. Concerning claim of Juan José and Victor Castro to Rancho "El Sobrante."   CHi (no. 1)   CLU

1641. —— —— Decision of the commissioner of the General land office [James A. Williamson]...Juan José and Victor Castro, confirmees, situated in the counties of Contra Costa and Alameda, in California. Wash., D.C., Govt. print. off., 1881. 24 p.   C

1642. —— Navy pre-flight school, St. Mary's college. The history of U.S. Navy pre-flight school, St. Mary's. St. Mary's college. [Print. by Lederer, Street and Zeus co., inc., 1946] 215 p. illus., ports.   CU-B

1643. —— Secretary of the interior. Decision of the Secretary of the interior in the matter of the survey of the Rancho El Sobrante, Juan José and Victor Castro, confirmees, situated in the county of Contra Costa, in California. Wash., D.C., Govt. print. off., 1882. 24 p.   CHi

1644. —— Work projects administration. California. Martinez waterfront... Martinez, 1940. 2 v. illus.   C   CMartC   CU-B

1645. —— —— —— Mt. Diablo pictorial history. Sponsored by state Division of parks. S.F., Works progress admin., area no. 7 [1939?] v.p. mounted pl. (part col.) ports. Typew.   CMartC   CSmat

1646. Valley pioneer. Centennial edition. Danville, 1958. 32 p. illus., ports.   CMartC

1647. Veale, R. R. Contra Costa county landmarks ... [Martinez? 1932?] 10 l. Part mimeo., part typew.   CMartC   CO   CRic   CU-B

1648. Walnut kernel, Walnut Creek. 25th anniversary historical & progress edition, August, 1957. [Walnut Creek, 1957] 1A-40A, 88 p. illus., ports.
CMartC CU-B

1649. Wells, Andrew Jackson. Contra Costa county, California... [S.F.] Sunset homeseekers' bur., 1909?] 64 p. illus.
CHi CL CU-B

1650. Whitnah, Joseph C., comp. Capital of the United nations in the Moraga valley on San Francisco bay, state of California. Martinez, Contra Costa county board of supervisors [1945?] unp. illus., map.
CMartC CSmyS

1651. —— The story of Contra Costa county, California. [Richmond, Contra Costa county development assoc., 1936?] 40 p. illus., maps.
CHi CSfMI CU-B

1652. Winkley, John W. Dr. John Marsh: wilderness scout. Martinez, Contra Costa co. hist. soc. [c1962] 95 p.
CHi

1653. Wittenmyer, Lewis Cass. Abstract of title to lands in the Rancho San Ramon... S.F., A. L. Bancroft & co., 1874. 105 p. map.
CU-B

1654. —— Complete search and abstract of the title to the Rancho de San Pablo, in Contra Costa county, Cal., down to the commencement of the action for the partition thereof: with official survey, maps, etc.: carefully compiled from the official records of said county, and the files and records of the state and federal courts... S.F., Carr, 1867. 701 p. maps.   C CL CSmH CU-B

Richmond

1655. Alvarez, Arthur C. Port of Richmond, city of Richmond. Analysis of the financial experience of the city of Richmond from 1926 to 1948 under its leases to the Parr-Richmond terminal company and outline of course of action open to the city of Richmond...March, Sept. 1950. Berkeley, 1950. 3 v.
CRic

1656. Aronovici, Carol, and Neutra, Richard. Civic center design for Richmond, California... Richmond, City planning commission, 1930. 7 p. illus.
CRic

1657. Barbour, W. Miller. An exploratory study of socio-economic problems affecting the Negro-white relationship in Richmond, California; a project of unity community defense services incorporated. N.Y., National urban league, 1952. 73 p. tables. Mimeo.
CRic

1658. Burg bros., inc. Richmond's new sky line, 1918. Nicholl-Macdonald civic center tract... [S.F., Jay D. Cassatt co., 1918] [12] p. illus., map.   CHi CU-B

1659. California. Reconstruction and reemployment commission. Richmond, California; a city earns the purple heart. [n.p.] 1944. 24 p. illus., maps, tables.
CBev CRic

1660. Civic center club. The history of Richmond, California. Richmond [n.d.] 6 p.   CMartC

1661. Contra Costa county labor journal. ...Labor day number...1922–1923. [Richmond, 1922–23] 2 v. illus., ports.
CU-B

1662. Coolidge, Coit. History of the Richmond public library. Richmond, 1940. 11 p. Ms.   CRic

1663. De Romanetti, Raymond Paul. Public action and community planning: a study in the redevelopment of Richmond, California. [Berkeley, 1956] Thesis (M.A.)—Univ. of Calif., 1956.
CU

1664. Fogg, George Everett. Recreation space in urban industrial areas. Richmond, California. [Berkeley, 1959] Thesis (M.S.)—Univ. of Calif., 1959.
CU

1665. Fridell, Lee D. The story of Richmond. [Richmond] Richmond public schools, 1951. 66 p. illus.
CMartC

1666. —— The story of Richmond, El Cerrito, San Pablo, Pinole, Hercules. Richmond, Richmond union high school district, c1954. 165 p. illus., ports.
CAla CB CHi CO CRic CStclU CU-B

1667. Griffins, Evan. Early history of Richmond, Contra Costa county, California... Richmond, 1938. 11 p. Mimeo.   C CHi CMartC CRic CSf CU-B

1668. —— —— Supplement, 1939. 8 l.
CHi CMartC CRic CU-B

1669. Hanson, Erle C. Street cars in Richmond, California; chronological history. San Mateo, 1957. 14 p. illus., maps. (Western railroader, v.21, no. 1, Nov. 1957)
CHi CRic

1670. Haviland, Dozier & Tibbetts, San Francisco. Report on proposed water supply for the Richmond municipal water district... S.F., Oakland, 1913. 211 p.
CHi CU-B

1671. —— Report on Richmond harbor project... [Richmond, Daily independent press] 1912. 229 p.
C-S CHi CL CRic CU-B

1672. Homan, A. Gerlof. An evaluation of further economic growth possibilities of Richmond, California. Prepared for the Planning commission, city of Richmond. Menlo Park, Stanford research inst., 1957. 109 p. maps, tables. (SRI project no. I-1918)   C CRic CSfSt

1673. Independent printing co. Richmond: the early years. [Richmond, 1960] 20 p. illus., ports., maps, facsims.
CHi CU-B

1674. International brotherhood of boilermakers, iron shipbuilders and helpers of America. Local 513. Richmond, "arsenal of democracy." Berkeley, Tam Gibbs co., print. [1947?] 103 p. illus., ports., tables, diagrs.
CU-B

1675. Kenny, Robert W. Police and minority groups; an experiment. [Address...1946] [n.p., 1946?] 19 l. Typew.
CRic

1676. Kerley, A. C. Arlington terrace, a residence park of exceptional beauty. A. C. Kerley, sole owner, Richmond, California. [S.F., Taylor, Nash & Taylor, 191–?] [11] p. illus., map.   CHi

1677. Luke, Sherrill David. The problem of annexing north Richmond to the city of Richmond. [Berkeley, 1954] 14 p. maps. Thesis (M.A.)—Univ. of Calif., 1954.
CRic (also 2 cop. on microfilm) CU-B

1678. Macdonald, Augustin Sylvester. The beginning of the city of Richmond. [n.p., n.d.] 4 p.
CMartC

1679. —— San Francisco bay: Richmond harbor, California. Oakland, 1928. 7 p.   C CHi CSf CU-B

1680. Metcalfe, William L., comp. Souvenir Contra Costa county. Photostats of selected pages dealing with the city of Richmond, California... Richmond, Richmond record, 1902. [27] p. illus., ports.
CMartC CRic

1681. New Richmond land co., San Francisco. Wall's second addition to the city of Richmond. [S.F., 1914?] [4] p. illus., maps.   CHi

1682. Parsons, Joan. The mountain speaks. Richmond, Contra Costa development assoc., 1948. 8 p.
CRic

1683. Permanente metals corp., Richmond. Construction record of the prefabricated ship, Robert E. Perry, hull 440. Richmond [1942] 58 p. illus., diagrs.
CHi

1684. —— Official sea trial of Permanente's first victory ship the S.S. Australia Victory... Richmond [1944] 17 l. illus.
CHi

1685. —— Prospectus. 600,000 shares...capital stock... [n.p.] 1948. 36 p.
CHi

1686. Realty bonds and finance co., inc. The heart of Richmond, where investment today means fortunes tomorrow. [S.F., Print. by Bolte & Braden co., 1907?] 23 p. illus.
CU-B

1687. Richmond. Chamber of commerce. Handbook of Richmond, California. 1939– illus., maps.

C has 1946, 1949. CHi has 1940–41, 1951/52. CLU has 1947. CO has 1939, 1942, 1946. CRic has 1939–date. CU-B has 1940, 1944–45.

1688. —— —— Richmond, the Pittsburg of the west. S.F., Hicks-Judd, 1907. 64 p.
CHi CSf CSmH

1689. —— —— Richmond, then and now. Pictures tell the story of the remarkable growth of this great industrial community. Dec. 12, 1945. unp. illus.
C CO

1690. —— —— Richmond, California, where industry serves; an industrial survey of the Pacific coast's fourth largest port... [Richmond? 1926?] 31 p. illus.
CHi

1691. —— —— Richmond united. 1926–1934. 7 v. illus., ports.
CRic

1692. —— —— Richmond wins the peace. Richmond [n.d.] 35 p. illus., maps.
CRic

1693. —— **Charters.** Charter of the city of Richmond. [Richmond? 1909] 30 p.
CHi

1694. —— **City council.** Postwar Richmond, California; a pictorial summary of postwar accomplishments, 1945–1949. Richmond, 1949. 48 p. illus., ports., maps.
C CRic CU-B

1695. —— **City manager.** An avalanche hits Richmond. 1944. 141 p. maps. The impact of war production.
CBaB CHi CLSU CO CRic

1696. —— **City planning commission.** Commercial development in Richmond; its problems and prospects. Richmond, 1958. 24 p. illus.
CMartC

1697. —— —— The Hensley industrial center... Richmond, 1954. 10 p.
CSt

1698. —— —— A report on housing and redevelopment. Richmond, 1950. 66 p.
CSt

1699. —— —— Residential redevelopment; a progress report. Richmond, 1958. 41 p. illus., charts.
CMartC

1700. —— —— The Richmond general plan; an interim guide to community development. Adopted Jan. 20, 1955... Richmond, 1955. 62 p. maps.
CMartC

1701. —— **Mayor.** Richmond, California, "the industrial city." [Richmond, 192–?] [24] p. illus.
CU-B

1702. Richmond daily news. First anniversary edition, Richmond daily news...December 20, 1914. 42 p. illus., maps.
C CRic

1703. Richmond independent. ...Anniversary edition...30th. 1940. Richmond, 1940. illus., ports.
CU-B

1704. —— Greater industry edition...July 31, 1931. Richmond, 1931. 40 p. illus. (Twenty-second year, no. 45)
C

1705. —— 100th anniversary, Contra Costa county, 1850–1950. [Richmond, 1950] 24 p. illus., ports., map. (Issue of Feb. 17, 1950)
CU-B

1706. —— Special souvenir magazine edition... Ed. and comp. by the Woman's improvement club of Richmond, California. Richmond, 1910. 42 p. illus.
C

1707. Richmond industrial commission. Richmond, California. [S.F.] Sunset mag. [n.d.] 62 p. illus., maps.
C

1708. Richmond police relief fund association. Souvenir booklet. [Richmond] 1947. 93 p. ports.
CU-B

1709. Smoyer, Winston R. City manager government in Richmond, Calif. [Berkeley, 1939] Thesis (M.A.)—Univ. of Calif., 1939.
CU

1710. [Thollaug, Kenneth Frederick] Discovering our Richmond public library. [n.p.] 1951. 10 l. Typew.
CRic

1711. Whitnah, Joseph C. A history of Richmond, California... Pub. by Richmond chamber of commerce. Richmond, Independent print. co., 1944. 128 p. illus., ports.

C CAla CHi CLU CLgA CMartC CNF CO CRic CSd CSf CSjC CSmH CStrJC CU-B NN

1712. Wise, Harold F., associates. Report to the redevelopment agency of the city of Richmond on retail trade in the Richmond area; the situation of 1955; the prospects for 1980. Palo Alto, Author, 1955. 26 p. tables.
CRic

1713. Wulzen realty co., San Francisco. The Robert Seaver addition; the key to the city of Richmond. [S.F., 1920?] [16] p. illus., map.
CHi

DEL NORTE COUNTY
(Created in 1857 from a portion of Klamath county which had originally been in Trinity county)

COUNTY HISTORIES

1714. [Bledsoe, Anthony Jennings] History of Del Norte county, California, with a business directory and traveler's guide. Eureka, Wyman & co., 1881. 175 p.
CLU CSf CU-B NHi

1715. [Childs, John N.] pub. Del Norte county as it is, giving its history, growth, wealth and attractions... a political, physical, social and financial history since its settlement to the year 1894. Crescent City, Print. in "Crescent City news" job off. by J. N. Bowie, 1894. 144 p. illus., ports., map.
C CHi CLU CSf CSmH CU-B

1716. Smith, Esther Ruth. The history of Del Norte county, California; including the story of its pioneers with many of their personal narratives. Introd. by Oscar Lewis. Oakland, Holmes bk. co., 1953. 224 p. illus. Bibliography: p. 219–224.

C CAla CArcHT CBb CChiS CHi CL CLU CLgA CO CP CRedCL CSd CSf CSfCP CSjC CSt CStclU CSto CStoC CU-B CaBViPA ICN MiD-B MoSHi N NHi NIC NN OrU

GREAT REGISTER

1717. Del Norte county. Index to the Great register of the county of Del Norte. 1866– Place of publication and title vary.

C has 1872, 1875, 1876, 1890 (biennially to)–1896, 1902 (biennially to)–1908, 1912 (biennially to)–1962. CL has 1872–73, 1875, 1886. CSmH has 1880, 1882. CU-B has 1872–73, 1879.

GENERAL REFERENCES

1718. Bledsoe, Anthony Jennings. Indian wars of the northwest... S.F., Bacon, 1885. 505 p. Overland expedition of Gregg party in 1849; first settlement of Del Norte; Redding expedition and events of Klamath war; Eel river valley; etc.
Available in many libraries.

1719. —— Same. Oakland, Biobooks, 1956. 292 p. map. (Calif. relations, no. 43).
Available in many libraries.

1720. Browder and Munn. Del Norte county, Calif. and adjacent territory. [n.p., 1915?] [40] p. illus., maps. "This pamphlet is made possible by the...Board of supervisors of Del Norte county and the Board of city trustees of Crescent City, Calif."—Foreword.
C CHi CL CSfCP CSmH CU-B

1721. Campbell, James M. Industrial data and report on industrial development, Del Norte county, California. Presented by the Del Norte county Chamber of commerce. [Crescent City?] 1951. 85 p. illus., maps.
CArcHT CHi

1722. Chaffee, Everett Barker. Jedediah Smith in California. [Berkeley, 1930] Thesis (M.A.)—Univ. of Calif., 1930.
CU CU-B

1723. Chase, Don Marquis. A century of life and faith in Del Norte county. Crescent City [1954] 54 p. illus.
C CArcHT CChiS CHi CL CO CRedCL CSd CSdS CSf CStclU CU-B KyU MWA OrU

1724. —— He opened the West, and led the first white explorers through northwest California, May–June 1828. Crescent City, Del Norte triplicate press, c1958. 36 p. illus., maps. "Sponsored by the Del Norte county historical society."
C CArcHT CB CChiS CHi CL CLO CLU CRedCL CSdS CSf CSfCSM CSmH CU-B CaBViPA MoHi UPB

1725. —— and Helms, Marjorie Neill. Pack saddles and rolling wheels; the story of travel and transportation in southern Oregon and northwestern California from 1852. Crescent City, c1959. 64 p. illus.
C CArcHT CHi CRedCL CSd CSdS

1726. Chase, Doris Harter. Crossing the plains, an account of the George Harter family's trip from Cass county, Michigan, to Marysville, California, in 1864; taken from the diary of George Harter. Sacramento, Author, c1957. 23 p.
CSdS

1727. —— They pushed back the forest. Sacramento, c1959. 78 p. illus., ports., maps. The story of the pioneers of the 1850's.
C CArcHT CChiS CHi CO CSd CSdS CU-B

1728. Coan, Ernie. The Del Norte Indian. Presented to the California section, California state library, Sacramento, California. Colfax, c1953. 54 l. map. Typew.
C

1729. Crescent City. Chamber of commerce. Frontier with a future; forests, factories, farms and fishing, Del Norte county, California. [Crescent City, 1948?] 13 p.
CHi

1730. Del Norte county. Board of supervisors. Del Norte county, California and adjacent territory. [n.p., 1915] [40] p.
CSmH

1731. —— Board of trade. Memorial to the Congress of the United States...setting forth the claims of the harbor of Crescent City, Del Norte county, California, and praying for an appropriation for harbor improvements. [n.p., n.d.] 27 p.
CSmH

1732. —— Citizens' committee on statistics. An appeal to Congress for the improvement of Crescent harbor! Report of the Citizens' committee on statistics. Crescent City, 1873. 6 p.
CU-B

1733. Del Norte triplicate, Crescent City. 100 years of progress [1854–1954. Centennial ed.] Aug. 5, 1954. Crescent City, 1954. v.p. illus., maps.
CU-B OrU

1734. Dodds, Gordon Barlow. R. D. Hume: Rogue River monopolist. Madison, Wis., 1958. 372 l. Thesis (Ph.D.)—Univ. of Wisconsin. Chapter 9, l. 265–288, contains material on Del Norte county, the Klamath and Smith rivers.
CArcHT

1735. Dornin, May. The emigrant trails into California. [Berkeley, 1922] 195 l. Typew. Thesis (M.A.)—Univ. of Calif., 1922.
CU CU-B

1736. Hahn, Campbell and associates, Burlingame. Industrial survey of Del Norte county, California. [Burlingame] 1949. 93 l. maps, diagrs.
CArcHT

1737. Hight, Grace. Early days of Smith river. [n.p., 1948?] [15] p. "A paper read at the Smith river woman's club, Sept. 3, 1948."
CHi

1738. Howell, Floyd K. A tax study of the California counties of Del Norte, Humboldt, Mendocino and Sonoma. [Berkeley, 1951] Thesis (M.A.)—Univ. of Calif., 1951.
CU

1739. [Jenkins, Robert James] Del Norte county as it is...from its settlement to the present year, 1894... Crescent City, Print. by J. N. Bowie, 1894. 144 p. illus.
CSmH

1740. [Johnson, J. Freelen] Seventy-five years of Methodism in Del Norte county, California. Crescent City, 1930. [22] p. illus., ports.
CSmH CU-B

1741. McBeth, Frances Turner. Lower Klamath country. Berkeley, Anchor press, 1950. 76 p. maps.
C CAla CArcHT CChiS CHi CL CLU CMS CO CP CSd CSfCP CSfCSM CSfU CSjC CStoC CStrCL CStrJC CaBViPA MiD

1742. —— Pioneers of Elk Valley, Del Norte county, California; fifty years in the history of Elk Valley from 1850 to the turn of the century. Angwin, Pac. union college press, 1960. 60 p. illus., ports.
CAla CHi CU-B

1743. McFadden, William S. Reminiscence of a journey from Corvallis, Oregon to Crescent City, California, March to April, 1874. [Portland, Ore.?] 1937. 43 l. (Mimeo. bul. of the Historical records survey of Oregon, no. 6)
CHi

1744. Metsker, Chas. Frederick. ...Atlas of Del Norte county, California, November 1949. Tacoma, Wash., 1949. 34 l. maps.
CSf

1745. Parker, J. Carlyle, comp. An annotated bibliography of the history of Del Norte and Humboldt counties. Based on a preliminary study by R. Dean Galloway. [Arcata] Humboldt state college library, 1960. 88 p.
CArcHT CHi CU-B

1746. Public administration service, Chicago. Local government in Del Norte county, California; a survey report. Chicago [1957] 204 p. diagrs.
C

1747. Rogers, Fred B. Early military posts of Del Norte county. [S.F., 1947] 11 p.
CU-B

1748. Scotton, Steve W., ed. Del Norte county,

California; its industries, resources... [Crescent City] Crescent City news job print., 1909. 41 p. illus., ports.
C CLU CSf CSmH CU-B OrU

1749. Smith, Jedediah Strong. The travels of Jedediah Smith; a documentary outline including the journal ...by Maurice S. Sullivan. Santa Ana, Fine arts press, 1934. 195 p. illus., ports., map.
Available in many libraries.

1750. Southern Pacific co. Passenger dept. The Klamath country... [S.F., 1908?] illus., maps.
CSf OrU

1751. Tarbell, Alan T., organization, Los Angeles. The building of an empire; Crescent City, California. [L.A.? c1929] [15] p. illus.   CHi

1752. Wiley, Francis A. Jedediah Smith in the west. [Berkeley, 1941] 415 l. Thesis (Ph.D.)—Univ. of Calif., 1941.   CArcHT CU

1753. Woolley, H. S. Woolleyport harbor; its advantages and possibilities as the principal port of entry between San Francisco and the Columbia river; an address... [Crescent City, News job press, 1911] 12 p.
CHi

EL DORADO COUNTY
(Created in 1850)

COUNTY HISTORIES

1754. Historical souvenir of El Dorado county, California, with illustrations and biographical sketches... Oakland, Paolo Sioli, 1883. 227 p. illus., ports.
C CCH CHi CL CLU CPla CSf CSfCP CSmH CU-B NHi NN NvHi

1755. Jerrett, Herman Daniel. California's El Dorado yesterday and today... Sacramento, J. Anderson, 1915. 141 p. illus., ports.
C CBb CCH CFS CHi CL CLCo CLO CLSM CLSU CLU CMartC CO CS CSf CSfWF-H CSj CSmH CStoC CU-B CtY MiD MoSHi NN WHi

1756. Upton, Charles Elmer. Pioneers of El Dorado... Placerville, Author, 1906. 201 p. illus.
C CFS CHi CL CLSM CLU CO CP CPla CS CSfCP CSmH CStoC CU-B CaBViPA CtY MoSHi NN

GREAT REGISTER

1757. El Dorado county. Index to the Great register of the county of El Dorado. 1866– Place of publication and title vary.
C has 1867-69, 1872-73, 1875-80, 1882, 1886 (biennially to)– 1896, 1898 (suppl.), 1900 (biennially to)– 1912, 1914 (July and Oct.), 1916 (biennially to)– 1912, 1914. CHi has 1872, 1875, 1879-80, 1882, 1894, 1896, 1900, 1902, 1926. CL has 1867, 1868-69 (suppls.), 1873, 1875-76, 1879 (suppl.), 1882, 1884 (suppl.), 1886, 1888, 1890. CLU has 1867. CSmH has 1879, 1880. CU-B has 1867, 1868 (suppl.), 1872-73, 1875-76, 1879-80.

DIRECTORIES

1758. El Dorado district. Church of Jesus Christ of latter-day saints, comp. Directory of residents and businesses of the city of Placerville, 1947. Placerville, 1947. 100 p.   CHi

GENERAL REFERENCES

1759. Bell, John C. Obituary addresses on the occasion of the death of Hon. John C. Bell, assemblyman from El Dorado county; delivered in the Assembly and Senate of California, seventeenth and eighteenth of April, 1860. Sacramento, Charles T. Botts print., 1860. 29 p.
C CU-B

1760. Bowman, Amos. Report on the properties and domain of the Calif. water company, situated on Georgetown divide: embracing the mining, water and landed resources of the country between the south and middle forks of the American river in El Dorado county, Calif. ... S.F., A. L. Bancroft & co., 1874. 225 p. illus., maps.
C C-S CHi CL CLU CSfCW CSmH CU-B

1761. California vs. Bowker, Chester C. In the Supreme court of the state of California. The people of the state of California, respondent vs. Chester C. Bowker, appellant. Appeal from the district court of the eleventh judicial district, El Dorado county. S.F., Wade & Nixon [1860?] 20 p.   CHi

1762. California. Dept. of natural resources. Division of beaches and parks. Emerald Bay. Sacramento, State print. off., 1955.   CRcS

1763. California water co., New York. [Report of the] California water company...for property purchased in El Dorado county, California... N.Y., Baker & Godwin, print., 1880. [47] p. illus., fold. map.   CHi CLU

1764. Camp Agassiz, Glen Alpine. [Descriptive brochure. S.F., Norman Pierce co., c1904] 22 p. illus., map.   CHi

1765. Cedar Spring gold mining co. Prospectus of the Cedar Spring gold mining company, of El Dorado county, California. June 1, 1881. Salem, Mass., Salem press, 1881. 14 p. map.   CU-B

1766. Cederberg gold mining co. By-laws of the Cederberg gold mining company, located, El Dorado county, California. S.F., "Voice of Israel" pub. co., 1872. 12 p.   CU-B

1767. Central star gold mining co. Prospectus of the Central star gold mining company, El Dorado county, California. [n.p., 1881?] 4 p.   CHi

1768. Church union gold co., New York. ...A description of its resources and the report of Professor Silliman, on its advantages. N.Y., Francis & Loutrel, 1865. 16 p. map.   CHi CSmH

1769. Collyer, Gilbert Abram. Early history of El Dorado county. [Berkeley, 1932] 166 l. illus., ports., maps. Thesis (M.A.)—Univ. of Calif., 1932.
CU CU-B

1770. El Dorado county. Board of trade. El Dorado county, California; its resources, opportunities... [Placerville, Republican print., 1911?] 31 p.
CL CU-B

1771. —— Chamber of commerce. El Dorado county, California; history, industry, recreation. Placerville, 1939–
CHi has 1939, 1946-47, 1949, 1951.

1772. —— —— Mines and mining in El Dorado county. Placerville [1933?] 7 p. illus.   CRcS

1773. —— —— Nuggets from El Dorado county, California. Placerville, 1907. 62 p.   CSS

1774. —— District court. Syllabus, Jan. 1853-1857. (J. M. Hovell, district judge) 100 p. [12 l. Ms.] Contains also Rules of the Placerville Union club, minutes...1860.   C

1775. —— Expositions commission. El Dorado county, California. [Sacramento, News print., 1915] [28] p. illus.   CHi CU-B

1776. —— **Superior court.** Rules of the Superior court of the county of El Dorado. [n.p., 1901] [14] p.
CHi

1777. El Dorado county invites you to a vacation in the high Sierras. Placerville, Old Hangtown press [n.d.] 4 p. illus., map.   CRcS

1778. El Dorado gold mining and milling co., inc. N.Y., John B. Watkins, print., 1887.   CSmH

1779. Freemasons. Placerville. Palmyra lodge, no. 26. By-laws...with a history of El Dorado lodge, no. 26, F. & A. M. and Palmyra lodge no. 151, F. & A. M. and their consolidation as Palmyra lodge no. 26, F. & A. M. [n.p., 1907?] 47 p.   CHi

1780. Glenwood mill and mining co. Prospectus of the Glenwood mill and mining company, Greenwood, El Dorado county, California... [S.F., Spaulding & Barto, 18–?] 12 p.   CU-B

1781. Immigration association of California. [County scrapbooks] [S.F., 188–?]   C

1782. James W. Marshall pioneer museum, Kelsey, California. Catalogue... [Sacramento, 1928] 247 l.   CU-B

1783. Lawrence (M.) & co., Tallac. Souvenir of Tallac, Lake Tahoe... [n.p., 1900?] unp. illus. CHi

1784. Marks, Bernard. A California pioneer, the letters of Bernard Marks to Jacob Solis-Cohen, 1853–1857. N.Y., American Jewish hist. soc., 1954. 57 p. "Reprinted from *Pub. of the Am. Jewish hist. soc.*, v.14, no. 1."   CHi

1785. Michigan-California lumber co. California's El Dorado. This little brochure brings you a few notes on the history of the El Dorado...and the history of lumbering... Camino, 1940. 16 p.   CSmH

1786. Mountain democrat, Placerville. Centennial edition of gold discovery, January 22, 1948.   CHi

1787. —— El Dorado county; the open door to California. Placerville [1927] 6 p. illus., map.   CRcS

1788. —— Seventy-fifth anniversary souvenir review edition... Placerville [1928] 32 p. illus., ports. (v.76, no. 1, Jan. 6, 1928)   C CHi CO CU-B

1789. Naper, Joy H., vs. Skinner, J. D. ...Joy H. Naper, contestant, vs. J. D. Skinner, appellant. Petition for rehearing. George E. Williams, att'y for appellant. Sacramento, H. A. Weaver & co.'s law print. off. [187–?] 9 p.   CU-B

1790. —— ...Joy H. Naper, contestant, vs. J. D. Skinner, respondent. Transcript on appeal. Williams & Carpenter, att'ys for respondent. Geo. G. Blanchard, att'y for contestant. Sacramento, H. A. Weaver & co.'s law print. off. [1874] 71 p.   CU-B

1791. Odd fellows, Independent order of. Cosumnes lodge, no. 63, Latrobe. Constitution, by-laws and rules of order...Instituted December 4, 1856. S.F., J. Winterburn & co., 1881. 56 p.   CHi

1792. Orr, Thomas. Life history of Thomas Orr, jr. Pioneer stories of California and Utah. 1930. 51 p. illus.
CHi

1793. Pilot Creek water co. vs. Mansfield, Nathan E. ...Pilot Creek water co., appellant, vs. Nathan E. Mansfield, respondent. Respondent's brief. Geo. G. Blanchard, Chas. F. Irwin, and G. H. Ingham, for respondent. Sacramento, G. E. Jefferis' law print. off. [18–?] 8 p.   CU-B

1794. Resources of El Dorado county... Placerville, Fellows & Selkirk, 1887. 208 p. illus.
C CLU CSS CU-B

1795. Roberts, W. G., vs. Ball, A. E. In the Supreme court of the state of California. W. G. Roberts, plaintiff and appellant, vs. A. E. Ball, as administrator of the estate of Edwin S. Chester, deceased, and Anglo-Californian bank, limited (a corporation), defendants and respondents. Transcript on appeal. Maxwell, Dorsey & Soto, attorneys for plaintiff and appellant. H. I. Kowalsky, attorney for defendants and respondents. Filed... 1893... S. F., Crocker [1893?] 65 p.   CHi

1796. [Roche, Carl] Mines and mining in El Dorado county... S.F., Francis, Valentine & co., 1882. 14 p.
CU-B

1797. Rocky-Bar mining co. Circular, articles of association, resolutions...1850. [N.Y.?] 1850. 12 p. Signed: Jas. Delavan, secretary.   CHi CLU

1798. —— Same. Bound with: Carl I. Wheat. The Rocky-Bar mining company. Printed for members of the Roxburghe club of San Francisco, and the Zamorano club of Los Angeles. S.F., 1934. 12 p. facsim.
CHi CLU CSf CStrJC

1799. Upton, Will Oscar. Churches of El Dorado county, Calif., their history covering a period of ninety years from 1850 to 1940... Placerville. Old Hangtown press, 1940. 59 p. illus., ports.
C CHi CLU CSf CSmH CU-B

1800. Voiles, Jane. El Dorado county pictures of pioneer homes and landmarks of Gold rush days... [Oakland? 1940?] 5 l.   CU-B

1801. Volcano quartz mining co. Volcano quartz mining company, located at Volcanoville, El Dorado county... [N.Y.? 1852?] 32 p.   CSmH CU-B

1802. Wagon train caravan. [Program] 1951– [n.p.] 1951–
CHi has 1951–52, 1955.

1803. Weeks, David [and others] ...Utilization of El Dorado county land... Berkeley [1934] 115 p. illus., maps. (Calif. Agric. experiment station, Bul. 572, May 1934) "Results of a cooperative investigation conducted by the Calif. forest and range experiment station of the U.S. Forest service, U.S. Dept. of agric., and the Calif. agric. experiment station."
CLO CLSU CLU CStmo CU-B

1804. Wheat, Carl I. The Rocky-Bar mining company. An episode of early western promotion and finance. Printed for members of the Roxburghe club of San Francisco, and the Zamorano club of Los Angeles. S.F., 1934. 12 p. Insert. Facsim.: Circular, articles of association, resolutions...1850.   CHi CLU CSf CStrJC

Coloma

1805. Allen, William Wallace, and Avery, Richard Benjamin. California gold book; first nugget, its discovery and discoverers, and some of the results proceeding therefrom. S.F. and Chicago, Donohue & Henneberry, 1893. 441 p. illus.
CBb CHi CLgA CLSM CMartC CPom CRcS CRedl CSbr CSd CSf CSfCW CSfP CStmo CU-B UHi

1806. Allhoff, Martin J. [A history of the Coloma vineyard winery and Coloma vineyard house. Sacramento, 1933] 14 ms. sheets. mounted photos.   C

1807. Bekeart, Philip B. The first flake of gold discovered by James Wilson Marshall, January 24, 1848, Sutter's saw mill, Coloma, El Dorado county, California. 11 p. Reprinted from the *Mountain democrat*, Placerville, Apr. 27, 1934.   CHi CSfP CStoC

1808. —— James Wilson Marshall, discoverer of gold

...with personal reminiscences and correspondence relating to the discovery of gold. S.F., Soc. of Calif. pioneers, 1924. 97 p. illus., ports.
C CLSU CO CSfCP CSfCSM CSmH

1809. Brown, James Stephens. California gold. An authentic history of the first find... Published by the author, Salt Lake City, Utah. Oakland, Pac. press, 1894. 20 p. port.
C CLU CSf CSfCP CSmH CU-B CaBViPA

1810. —— A compilation of authentic information regarding the first discovery of gold in California, January 24, 1848; by Arthur Prestley Tregeagle and Louetta Brown Tanner, compilers. [Salt Lake City, Pyramid press, 1953] 31 p. illus.   C UHi

1811. —— Life of a pioneer; being the autobiography of James S. Brown. Salt Lake City, G. Q. Cannon & sons co., 1900. 520 p. illus.   CHi CLgA

1812. California historical society. California gold discovery; centennial papers on the time, the site, and artifacts. S.F., 1947. 56 p. illus., ports. (Special pub. no. 21) Reprinted from *Calif. hist. soc. Q.*, v.26, no. 2. Print. by Westgate press, Oakland.
CBb CBev CIIi CLSU CLgA CRic CSS CSalCL CSd CSj CSjC CSmH CSmat CStrJC CU-B CaBViPA

1813. Coloma. Church of Jesus Christ of latter-day saints. Gold in '48; sidelights on the historic discovery. Mormon historical exhibit, Gold discovery park. [n.p., 1948?] [10] p. illus., map.   CHi

1814. [Cress-Ley] 100th anniversary gold discovery celebration; what to see, where to go, what to do...Coloma... [Placerville, Old Hangtown press, c1948] 24 p.   CHi

1815. Crosley, Mary Edith. Coloma. Universal City, Crosley bks. [1958] 30 p. illus., ports., map.
C CHi CL CO CU-B

1816. Fitch Thomas. Souvenir of the unveiling of Marshall monument, May 3rd, 1890. Historical sketches of Placerville and Coloma from Tom Fitch's directory of El Dorado county, 1862... [n.p., 1890] 8 l. port. Cover title.   CLU

1817. —— Same, Reproduced... [n.p., 1947?] 10 p. illus.   CSmH CU-B

1818. Hittell, John Shertzer. Marshall's gold discovery. A lecture...delivered...on the 24th of January, 1893, the 45th anniversary of the discovery. S.F., B.F. Sterett print., 1893. 20 p.   CS CHi

1819. Macdonald, David F. Moral law; a series of practical sermons on the decalogue, or the ten commandments; preached in Emmanuel church, Coloma, California. Sacramento, James Anthony & co., 1858. 152 p.
C CBPac CHi CL CLU CSaT CSmH CSfCP CSfP CU

1820. McMurtrie, Douglas Crawford, ed. A report in April, 1848, on the discovery of gold and other minerals in California, and on the people, commerce, agriculture, customs, religion, press, etc., of the new Pacific coast territory; here reproduced from the New York herald, morning edition, of August 19, 1848. Evanston, Ill., 1943. 7 l. Reproduced from typew. copy.
CSto MoS

1821. Parsons, George Frederic. The life and adventures of James W. Marshall, the discoverer of gold in California. Sacramento, James W. Marshall & W. Burke, 1870. 188 p. front. Reprinted in 1935 by Grabhorn press for George Fields, S.F.
Available in many libraries.

Placerville

1822. Directory of the city of Placerville, and towns of Upper Placerville, El Dorado, Georgetown, and Coloma, containing a history of these places... By Thomas Fitch and co. [Placerville] Placerville republican print., 1862. 128 p.   C CHi CLU CSmH CU-B

1823. Drury, Wells. To old Hangtown or bust. Pilgrimage of J. M. Studebaker... Placerville, priv. print., 1912. 48 p.   C CHi CLU CLob CSmH CU-B

1824. E clampus vitus, Placerville. Roster, January 24, 1954, commemorating 106th anniversary of the discovery of gold at Coloma. [Placerville] Mountain democrat print. [1954] 40 p.   CHi

1825. Freemasons. Placerville. El Dorado commandery no. 4. Souvenir of the 29th conclave at San Francisco, 1904. Containing a short history of El Dorado commandery and brief illustrated sketches of El Dorado and Amador counties, California. Placerville, Nugget press, 1904. 108 p. illus., ports.   CStrJC

1826. [Myers, Jackson R.] "Placerville saved." To the honorable the Senate and Assembly of the state of California. [n.p., 1881?] 5 p.   C CU-B

1827. Placerville. Confidence engine co., no. 1. Code of laws and order of business... Organized, May 22, 1857. Placerville, Print. at the Democrat off., 1882. 10 p.   CHi

1828. —— Neptune engine company, no. 2. Constitution and by-laws...together with the rules of order; adopted April 7, 1859. Placerville, T. Fitch, 1862. [10] l. Photostat negative.   C

1829. —— Volunteer fire dept. 100th anniversary ...1853–1953; program [n.p.] 1953. [8] p. illus.   CHi

1830. Placerville academy. Catalogue...1877/1878. [S.F., Bacon & co., 1877?] 16 p.   CHi CU-B

1831. The Placerville times. ...1938, the big year ... [Placerville, 1937] 24 p. illus., ports. (Issue of Dec. 29, 1937) Life and activities in and historical data about Placerville and El Dorado county.   C CHi

1832. Placerville union club. Rules...minutes, and 3 pages of club accounts. 1860. Ms. Bound with: El Dorado county. District court. Syllabus, Jan. 1853–1957.   C

1833. Quirot & co., pub. Placerville. S.F., [185–?] illus. No. 41 [A collection of views and broadsides... relating to California of the '50's]   CSmH

1834. Shufelt, S. A letter from a gold miner, Placerville, California, October 1850. San Marino, Friends of the Huntington lib., 1944. 28 p.
CBb CHi CLSM CLgA CRedl CSdS CSf CSmH CStbS CStoC CVtV CWhC ViU

1835. Upton, Charles Elmer. Down Wild Goose canyon. Placerville, Author, 1910. 42 p. illus.
C CL CLU CSfCW CSmH CU-B

1836. —— The life and work of the Reverend C. C. Peirce... Placerville, Author, 1903. 141 p. ports.
C CHi CLU CSmH CU-B

FRESNO COUNTY
(Created in 1856 from portions of Mariposa, Merced, and Tulare counties)

COUNTY HISTORIES

1837. Historical records survey. California. ... Fresno county (Fresno)... Co-sponsored by the county of Fresno. S.F., Northern Calif. hist. records survey project, 1940. 624 p. illus., maps. (Inventory of the county archives of Calif. ...no. 10) Mimeo.

C CBb CF CFS CHanK CHi CLCM CLCo CLO CLSM CLSU CLU CMary CMont CO COMC CPa CSS CSf CSfCP CSfCSM CSjC CSjCL CSluCL CSmH CSrCL CSt CStclU CU-B ICN WHi

1838. History of Fresno county, California, with illustrations descriptive of its scenery, farms, residences, public buildings... with biographical sketches. S.F., Elliott, 1881. 246 p. illus., ports., maps.

C CF CFS CHi (1882) CSt CU-B CYcCL CoD (1882) NN (1882) NvHi

1839. A memorial and biographical history of the counties of Fresno, Tulare, and Kern, California... Chicago, Lewis [1892?] 822 p. illus., ports.

C CAla CBaK CCH CF CFs CHan CHanK CHi CLSM CLSU CLU CMa CO COMC CSf CSfCP CSj CSjC CSmH CStoC CU-B CViCL CoD CtY IC MoShi N NN NHi UPB WHi

1840. Thompson, Thomas Hinckley. Official historical atlas map of Fresno county, California... Tulare, 1891. 122 p. illus., maps.

C CF CFS CHi CO CSmH CSt CYcCL NvHi

1841. Vandor, Paul E. History of Fresno county, California, with biographical sketches... L.A., Historic record co., 1919. 2 v. illus., ports.

C CBaK CCH CF CFS CHi CL CLCM (v.1 only) CLO CLU CMa CO CSf CSfCW CSmH CSto CU-B MWA NN WHi

1842. Walker, Ben Randal, ed. Fresno community book... Fresno, Cawston, 1946. 392 p. 75 pl., ports., maps.

C CFS CLU CO CSf CSmH CU-B CViCL

1842a. —— The Fresno county blue book...with biographies of representative Fresno county people. Fresno, Cawston, 1941. 555 p. illus., ports., maps.

CBaK CF CFS CHanK CL CLU CLob CMa CO CU-B CViCL NN

1843. Winchell, Lilbourne Alsip. History of Fresno county and the San Joaquin valley, narrative and biographical...under the editorial supervision of Ben R. Walker... Fresno, Cawston [c1933] 323 p. illus., ports., map.

C CBaK CF CFS CHi CL CLCo CLob CMa CO CSf CSmH CU-B NN

1844. —— Same, with title: History of Fresno and Madera counties... Joseph Bancroft, editor for Madera county. Fresno, Cawston [c1933] 344 p. illus., ports., map.　　　　　　　　　　　　　　　　　　　　　CFS

GREAT REGISTER

1845. Fresno county. Index to the Great register of the county of Fresno. 1867– Place of publication and title vary.

C has 1867, 1871–73, 1875–77, 1879–80, 1884, 1886, 1890 (biennially to)–1962. CFS has 1879–80, 1906–12. CHi has 1872. CL has 1873, 1875, 1876 (suppl.), 1877, 1879, 1882 (biennially to)–1890. CU-B has 1872–73, 1875, 1879–80.

DIRECTORIES

1846. 1881. Fresno republican, comp. & pub. General directory of Fresno county, Calif. for 1881; containing a description of the county, its topography, resources, history, &c.; sketches of its towns, settlement, industries, & business houses... Fresno, 1881. 183 p.

C CFS CHi CViCL

1847. 1894–1907. Husted, F. M., pub. Directory of Fresno city and business directory of Fresno county, 1894–1907... S.F., 1894–1907. Title varies. Publisher varies: 1898, C. T. Cearley; 1900, C. Hedges; 1905, Fresno directory co.; 1906, A. Kingsbury & co.

C has 1894, 1898, 1900, 1904, 1907. CFS has 1894/95, 1898, 1900, 1901/02, 1904–07. CHi has 1894.

1848. 1908–1949. Polk, R. L. & co., pub. Polk's Fresno city directory including Fresno county. S.F., 1908–49. Publisher varies: 1908–1925, Polk-Husted directory co. Continued as Polk's Fresno city directory.

C has 1908/09–11, 1913–14, 1917, 1920, 1922–25, 1927–28, 1932–36, 1940–41, 1944, 1947, 1949. C-S has 1908/09, 1911–13. CFS has 1908/09–37, 1939, 1941–49. CHi has 1915, 1924–27, 1929, 1931, 1949. CL has 1921, 1925–29, 1931, 1933–34, 1937, 1940–42, 1944, 1947. CO has 1937. CU-B has 1920.

1849. 1941/42– A. B. C. directory, pub. Greater Fresno. [Fresno] 1941– illus., maps.

CFS has 1941/42, 1955/56, 1958/59.

Fresno

1850. 1887. Reuck & Hodge, comp. The Fresno city directory...containing the names, occupations and locations of residents. Fresno, 1887. 64 p. illus.　　CHi

1851. 1892/93–1896. Dunbar, A. R., & co., pub. Fresno city directory and gazeteer of Fresno county. Fresno, 1892–96.

CFS has 1896. CU-B has 1892/93.

1852. 1951/52– Polk, R. L., & co., pub. Polk's Fresno city directory... L.A., 1951– Content varies: 1951/52–56 includes Kingsburg, Reedley, Sanger, and Selma. Preceded by Polk's Fresno city directory including Fresno county.

C has 1953. CFS has 1951/52–61. CHi has 1951/52–61. CL has 1951/52–60. CSmat has 1958–59.

Other Cities and Towns

1853. 1958. Clovis. Chamber of commerce. Clovis business directory. [2d ed.] Clovis [1958] 44 p. illus.　　　　　　　　　　　　　　　　　　　　　CFS

GENERAL REFERENCES

1854. Atlas of Fresno county, California. Fresno, Harvey, 1907. 75 l. of maps, 2 fold. maps.　CHi CSf

1855. Bagley, F. S., vs. Cohen, Edgar A., & Cohen, J. B. In the Supreme court of the state of California... Points and authorities for appellants... S.F., Jos. M. Torres, 1896.　　　　　　　　　　　CHi

1856. Barcus, Wallace F. A controlled study of Indian and white children in the Sierra joint union high school district, Tollhouse, Fresno county. Fresno, 1956. 44 l. graphs, tables. Thesis (M.S.) – Fresno state college, 1956.　　　　　　　　　　　　　　　　　　　　CFS

1857. Beatty, William C. A preliminary report on a study of farm laborers in Fresno county from January 1, 1959 to July 1, 1959, for the Fresno county rural health and education committee. [Fresno?] 1959. 145 p. tables, maps. "A Rosenberg foundation project."　　　　C

1858. Bedrosian, Sarah G. Mortgage lending in Fresno county, California, 1946–1957. Fresno, 1958. 188 l. Thesis (M.A.) – Fresno state college, 1958.

CFS

1859. Bennett, Stanley M. Collective bargaining in the wine industry of the central San Joaquin valley: 1937–1953. Fresno, 1953. 139 l. tables. Thesis (M.A.) — Fresno state college, 1953.　　　　　　　　CFS

1860. The Bishop Kip—Fort Miller centennial, Oct. 21–30, 1955, 100th anniversary of the first recorded religious service in the Fresno area. [Program] Fresno, 1955. 5 p.   CViCL

1861. Bostwick, R. F. L. A. Nares, as I knew him. [Fresno?] 1948. 15 l. Typew.   CFS

1862. —— Laton and Western railroad company and the Hanford and Summit Lake railway company. [Fresno?] 1946. 15 l. Typew.   CFS

1863. Briggs, Fergusson & co. ...Subdivision of the Fruit Vale estate... S.F., Crocker, litho. [1889?] 47 p.   CU-B

1864. Burns, Walter Noble. The Robin Hood of El Dorado; the saga of Joaquin Murrieta... N.Y., Coward, 1932. 304 p.
Available in many libraries.

1865. California. Committee to survey the agricultural labor resources of the San Joaquin valley. Transcript of public hearing, June 20 and 21, 1950, Fresno, California. [Sacramento, State print. off., 1950] 131 l. Mimeo.   CViCL

1866. California homes and industries and representative citizens; Fresno county. S.F., Elliot, 1891. 96 p. illus.   C CFS CHi

1867. California immigrant union, S.F. Vineland, Fresno county... S.F., Jos. Winterburn & co., print., 1873. 35 p.   CHi CU-B NN

1868. California taxpayers' association. ... Report of the Fresno county schools... L.A., 1931. 104 p. maps, tables, diagrs. Reproduced from typew. copy. (Assoc. report, no. 151)   CL

1869. Cearley, Charles T., comp. Fresno county California scenes. Fresno, 1904. unp.   CHi CSmH

1870. Chaddock, E. LeRoy. Fifty years as a raisin packer. Fresno, 1943. 256 l. Typew.   CFS

1871. Clausen, Walter B. Fresno county, California... S.F., Sunset mag. homeseekers bur. for the bd. of supervisors... [1914?] 64 p.   CHi CU-B

1872. Coleman, Earl H. The Diamond D saga. [n.p.] 1959. [8] p. illus. History of Blayney meadow.   CFS

1873. Cory, Braly & Harvey, Fresno. Fresno county, California, where can be found climate, soil, and water. Fresno [1886?] 88 p. illus.   CFS

1874. Creme petroleum co. Coalinga, California, the world's greatest oil field; past, present, future. [S.F.] 1910. 16 p. illus.   CFS

1875. Cunningham, James Charles. The truth about Murietta; anecdotes & facts related by those who knew him and disbelieved his capture. L.A., Wetzel pub. co., inc. [c1938] 286 p. illus., ports.   CLO

1876. De Koning, Richard M. Occupational survey: a study of durable goods manufacturers in Fresno county. Fresno, 1958. 77 l. illus. Thesis (M.A.)–Fresno state college, 1958.   CFS

1877. Description of central California; Fresno, Tulare, & Kern counties... S.F., Hicks-Judd, 1891. 108 p.   CViCL

1878. Dionisio, William P. Martin Theodore Kearney: his influence on the organization of the raisin industry in Fresno county. [Davis, 1956] 24 l. Typew. "Senior history paper at the University of California, Davis, in Dr. C. B. O'Brien's class, 1956."   C

1879. Dixon & Faymonville. Abstract of title to lands in Fresno co., Calif. ...to the 16th day of March, A.D., 1874... [Millerton, 1874] 47 l.   CU-B

1880. Edgerly, Asa Sanborn. He did it; or, The life of a New England boy written in his adopted state, California. S.F., H. S. Crocker co., 1909. 139 p. illus.   C

1881. Facts about Fresno county, California's marvel. [Fresno, Franklin print., 1896?] 24 p. illus., map.   CFS

1882. For whom was Selma named? Mystery of long standing cleared up. [n.p., n.d.] [6] p. port.   CFS

1883. Fowler. First Armenian Congregational church. Fortieth anniversary of the dedication, October, 1903–March 10–12, 1944. [Fowler, 1944] 6 p. illus., port.   CU-B

1884. Freemasons. Kingsburg. Traver lodge, no. 294. Golden jubilee souvenir book published by the Traver lodge, no. 294...chartered, October 10, 1889. [Kingsburg, 1939] 34 p. illus., ports.   CHi

1885. Fresno. Railroad consolidation plan of the county of Fresno and the city of Fresno. Fresno, 1953. 24 p.   CFS

1886. —— **Chamber of commerce.** Fresno city and county illustrated and described... Fresno, Trade-immigration pub. co., 1896. 119 p. illus.   CU-B

1887. —— —— Fresno county, California... [Fresno] Fresno republican print. [189–?] [16] p. illus.   CU-B

1888. —— —— Souvenir, Fresno county...16th international C. E. convention. [Fresno, 1897] [22] p. illus.   CFS CHi CU-B

1889. Fresno bee. Fresno county centennial edition, 1856–1956, April 18, 1956. Fresno, 1956. v.p. illus., ports., map.   CU-B

1890. Fresno canal and irrigation co., Kings river. ...Findings and decree of the district court of the thirteenth judicial district, engineers' report, and form of contracts for water rights granted by the company. S.F., Women's co-operative print., 1875. 27 p.   CLU

1891. Fresno-Clovis area planning commission. Existing conditions; a look at the Fresno-Clovis metropolitan area. Fresno [1957] 55 p. illus.   CFS

1892. Fresno, Coalinga and Monterey railroad. Fresno, Coalinga and Monterey railroad. [Fresno, 1911] 62 p. illus.   CFS

1893. Fresno community council. Fresno county recreational inventory: indoor facilities, outdoor facilities, group activities and Sierra mountains. [Fresno, 1959] 141 l. illus. Mimeo.   CFS

1894. —— Social resources of Fresno county. [Fresno, 1952] 113 p.   CF

1895. Fresno county. Centennial committee. Fresno county centennial almanac; a compendium of interesting and useful historical facts & old tales gathered to mark the 100th anniversary of the founding of Fresno county. Fresno, 1959. 184 p. illus., ports.
Available in many California libraries and NIC.

1896. —— **Chamber of commerce.** Fresno county, California. [Fresno, Evening democrat print., 19–?] 46 p. illus.   CSmH CU-B

1897. —— —— Fresno county facts. 1921–
CFS has 1921, 1924, 1934, 1944–45, 1947, 1950, 1953. CU-B has 1936.

1898. —— —— Fresno's back yard. [32] p. photos.   C

1899. —— —— The products of California and Fresno county. [Fresno, Franklin print., 1903?] [14] p.   CU-B

1900. —— —— The wonders of Fresno county, California. Fresno, Franklin print. house [1906?] [48] p. illus., map.   CHi

1901. Fresno county abstract co., inc. Abstract of title to Rancho Laguna de Tache... [Fresno? 1908?] 235 p.   C CHi CLU CSmH CU-B CViCL

1902. Fresno county agricultural association. Premium list and rules and regulations of the seventh annual fair of the Fresno county agricultural association... Sept. 30 to Oct. 4, 1913. [Fresno, 1913?] 180 p. illus.   CU-B

1903. Fresno county and city Chamber of commerce. Fresno county, California, the nation's agricultural leader. [Fresno, 1952] [21] p. illus.   CFS

1904. —— Who's who in Fresno, buyer's guide and membership directory. Fresno [1958] 65 p.   CF

1905. Fresno county farmers' club, Fresno. ... Annual report of president...[1st, 1897–98] Fresno, Fresno republican print. [1898?] [8] p.   CU-B

1906. Fresno county historical society. Publications. v.1, no. 1–3, 5, 1929–1937. no. 4 not published.
C has v.1, no. 1. CFS has v.1, no. 1–3, 5. CHi has v.1, no. 5. CSf has v.1, no. 2. CSmH has v.1, no. 2. NN has v.1.

1907. Fresno county taxpayer's association. Fresno county free library study. Fresno, 1955. 3v. in 1.   CF

1908. Fresno herald. Classified directory of business concerns, institutions, and professional people. Fresno, 1920. 48 p.   CViCL

1909. Frodsham, Noel. A study of the Russian-Germans in Fresno county, Calif. Redlands, 1949. 98 l. illus. Thesis (M.A.)– Univ. of Redlands, 1949.
CFS (microfilm copy)

1910. Fuller, Varden, and Viles, George L. Labor-management relationships and personnel practices, market milk dairies... [Fresno?] 1953. 44 l. illus. (Calif. Univ. College of agric. Giannini foundation of agric. economics. Mimeo. report, no. 140)   CLU

1911. Grosse, Marion A. A century of lumbering in Fresno county. [Fresno, 1956] v.p. illus. A series of articles which appeared in the *Fresnopolitan*, v.1, nos. 6, 7, 8, August-September, 1956.   C

1912. Hearne bros., Detroit. Official Hearne brothers polyconic projection maps of all of Fresno county. Constantly revised and kept up to date. [Detroit, 195–?] 1 v. maps.   C

1913. Hogue, Murray & Sesnon. Fresno county, California, where can be found...the only sure combination for the "vineyardist," the fruit grower, cattle raiser, and farmer... Oakland, Pac. press, print. [1887?] 103 p.   CL CLU CU-B

1914. Hollingsworth (W. I.) & co., Los Angeles. Dos Palos rancho...cream of the San Joaquin... L.A. [1913?] [8] p. illus., map.   CHi

1915. Howard, Fred K. History of the Sun-Maid raisin growers. [Fresno, 1922] 44 p. illus.   CFS

1916. Jackson, Joseph Henry. The creation of Joaquin Murieta. [Stanford, 1948] 6 p. Reprinted from *"The Pacific Spectator,"* v.2, no. 2, Spring 1948.   CHi

1917. James, George Wharton. Winter sports at Huntington Lake lodge in the high Sierras; the story of the first annual ice and snow carnival of the Commercial club of Fresno, Calif. Pasadena, Radiant life press, 1916. 50 p. pl.   C CFS CLO CLU CSmH NN

1918. Joaquin Murieta, the brigand chief of California... S.F., Grabhorn, 1932. 116 p. illus. (Americana reprints, no. 1)
C CBb CChiS CHi CL CLU CLgA CMartC CSf CSfCW CSmH CStclU CSto CU-B CYcCL

1919. Joaquin Murrieta, el bandido Chileno en California. Segundo edicion. San Antonio, Tex., "Editorial Martinez" [c1926] 264 p. pl.   CLO

1920. Joaquin, (the Claude Duval of California) ; or, The marauder of the mines. A romance founded on fact. N.Y., R. M. DeWitt [c1865] 160 p.
CL CLU CSmH CU-B

1921. Kadishay, Yair. Adjustment possibilities on cotton farms in western Fresno county, California. [Berkeley, 1957] Thesis (Ph.D.)– Univ. of Calif., 1957.   CU

1922. Kaupke, Charles L. Forty years on Kings river, 1917–1957. Prepared for Kings river water association, Fresno, California. [Fresno, Hume print. and litho. co., 1957] 81 p. map.
C CFS CHan CHi CViCL

1923. Kearney, Martin Theodore, comp. & pub. Fresno county, California, and the evolution of the Fruitvale estate... [Fresno, 1899?] unp. illus.
CFS CHi CP CSmH

1924. —— Same. Rev. ed. 1903. 179 p. illus.
C CHi CU-B

1925. —— Fresno county, a wonderfully prosperous district in California. [Chicago, 1893] 29 p. illus.
CFS

1926. —— How to make money in California... Fresno [1893?] 38 p.   CU-B

1927. Kerman. Chamber of commerce. Kerman, the land of opportunity. Kerman [1928?] 13 p. illus.
CFS

1928. Kings river–Pine Flat association. The Kings river–Pine Flat project... [n.p.] 1941. 15 p.
CFS

1929. —— Report on the Kings river project. Fresno, 1943. 143 p.   CFS

1930. Kings river water association. Kings river—facts and falsehoods. Fresno, 1950. 28 p.   C

1931. Kingsburg cotton oil co. Annual report. CHi has 1952.

1932. Laferrier, Albert Alphonse. Civil service in Fresno county, California, 1943–1957: a fight against patronage. Fresno, 1958. 120 l. Thesis (M.A.)– Fresno state college, 1958.   CFS

1933. Lethent water and land co. Prospectus. Location works: Fresno and Tulare counties, California. [S.F., Crocker, 1893] 15 p. map.   CU-B

1934. Levick, M. B. Fresno county, California. Issued by Sunset mag. for Supervisors of Fresno co. [1912] 64 p. illus., map.   CU-B

1935. —— Same. 1915. 65 p.
CL CSfCP CU-B NN

1936. Levy, Louis C. History of the cooperative raisin industry of California. Fresno, 1928. 46 p.   CFS

1937. [McGroarty, John Steven] Fresno county, the geographical hub of the state of California. [Fresno county expositions commission, 1915] [50] p. illus., map.
C CHi CLU CSmH CU-B

1938. Mahakian, Charles. History of the Armenians in California. [Berkeley, 1935] Thesis (M.A.)— Univ. of Calif., 1935.   CU CU-B

1939. Martin, George. Fresno county, California, and its offering for settlement. S.F., Pac. coast land bur. [1884?] 31 p. map.   C CHi CViCL

1940. Meyer, Edith Catharine. The development of the raisin industry in Fresno county, California. [Berkeley, 1931] 115 l. illus., maps. Thesis (M.A.)– Univ. of Calif., 1931.   CU CU-B

1941. Mitchell, Richard Gerald. Joaquin Murieta: a study of social conditions in early California. [Berkeley, 1927] 119 l. Thesis (M.A.)– Univ. of Calif., May 1927.   CU CU-B

1942. Muench, Joyce Rockwood. Along Sierra trails; Kings canyon national park... N.Y., Hastings house [1947] 101 p. illus.
Available in many libraries.

1943. Nielson, Ernest J. [Biography of Frank Dusy, 1837–1898. Fresno, 1949] [10] l. Typew.   CFS

1944. Nolte, G. S. The collection and disposal of storm and flood waters in the Fresno metropolitan area. Palo Alto, c1957. 83 p. maps, tables, diagrs.   CF

1945. Otis, George B. Reminiscences of early days ...the pioneer days of Selma and surrounding country. [Selma, Press of the Selma irrigator, 1911] 54 p.
                                        C CL CU-B

1946. Paz, Ireneo. Vida y aventuras del mas celebre bandido sonorense Joaquin Murrieta, sus grandes proezas en California. 4a. edicion. Mexico, El autor, 1908. 281 p.
                                                     CSmH

1947. —— Same. 5a. edicion. L.A., O. Paz y Cia, 1919. 128 p.   C CL CLU

1948. —— Same. 6a. edicion. L.A., C. G. Vincent & co., 1923. 110 p.   CHi CSf

1949. —— Same, with title: Life and adventures of the celebrated bandit, Joaquin Murrieta, his exploits in the state of California, trans. by Frances P. Belle. Chicago, Regan pub. corp., 1925. 174 p.
Available in many libraries.

1950. —— Same. 2d ed. Chicago, Charles T. Powner, 1937. 174 p.
   CBb CLO CLU CLgA CMartC CMon CRic
CSdS CSfWF-H

1951. Phillips, George. History of the "76 brand" in Fresno and Tulare counties, California. Fresno, 1958. 23 l. Student paper, Fresno state college.   CFS

1952. —— The upper Kings river, a background for the cities of Sanger, Centerville, and Minkler... Fresno, 1957. 23 l. Typew. Student paper, Fresno state college.
                                                     CFS

1953. Producers cotton oil co., Fresno. Annual report.
   CL has 1955–60.

1954. Progressive map service, Fresno. Key map of Fresno county, and a portion of Kings & Tulare county; ownership atlases. [Fresno, 1942–43] 103 maps.
                                                     CFS

1955. Redinger, David H. The story of Big Creek. L.A., Angelus press, 1949. 182 p. illus. Hydro-electric development in the Sierras.
                        C CFS CHi CMon CP

1956. Reedley. Chamber of commerce. Reedley —in pictures... [Reedley, 1923?] folder (18 p.) illus.
                                                     CHi

1957. Ridge, John Rollin. The life and adventures of Joaquin Murieta...3d ed. S.F., MacCrellish & co. [1871] 98 p.
   C CCorn CL CLS CSmH CStclU CU-B

1958. —— Same, revised, with title: The history of Joaquin Murieta... Hollister, Evening free lance, 1927. 84 p. (With Hoyle, M. F.) *Crimes and career of Tiburcio Vasquez.* Hollister, 1927)
   C CBb CHi CL CLO CLU CLgA CSS CSfCP
CSfCW CSmH CU-B

1959. —— Same. [new ed.] with an introduction by Joseph Henry Jackson. Norman, Okla., Univ. press, 1955. 159 p. illus., ports., facsim.
Available in many California libraries and UHi

1960. Rohrbacher, C. A. Fresno county, California, descriptive, statistical and biographical... [Fresno] 1891. 164 p.   CLU CU-B

1961. St. George vineyard, Maltermoro. Westward leads the golden star of empires. Maltermoro, Keystone pub. co. [1897?] 29 p. illus.   CU-B

1962. San Francisco & Fresno land co. A home in California. How to get it. Words of wisdom. [Fresno, 1901] 10 p. illus.   CSmH

1963. Sanger. Chamber of commerce. Sanger, Fresno county, California. [Sanger, 1922] 26 p.
                                              CHi CU-B

1964. Sanger herald. History of Sanger, California, 1888–1938. [Sanger] 1938. 56 p. illus., ports. (Issued as suppl. to Sanger herald, v.49, no. 29, April 29, 1938)
                                                     CFS

1965. Scrapbook of clippings about Fresno and Fresno county, California, from the Fresno morning republican and the Fresno bee, 1929–30. 1 v. of newsp. clippings. illus., ports.   CU-B

1966. 76 land and water co. The 76 land and water co's lands. Geography, topography, soil, climate, productions of Fresno and Tulare counties, California. Traver, Kitchener & Baker [1884?] 29 p. map.   C CU-B

1967. Southern Pacific co. Colonists tickets will be sold to California via the Southern Pacific every Tuesday, February 12 to April 30, 1901...do not overlook the advantages of Fresno... [n.p., 1901] [3] p. illus.   CU-B

1968. Teilman, Ingvart, and Shafer, W. H. The historical story of irrigation in Fresno and Kings counties in Central California. [Fresno, Williams and son, print., 1953] 63 p. illus.   C CFS

1969. Thickens, Virginia Emily. Pioneer colonies of Fresno county. [Berkeley, 1942] 117 l. maps. Thesis (M.A.)– Univ. of Calif., 1942.   CU

1970. Tucker & Hogue. Fresno county, California... Fresno, Daily evening expositor print. [18–?] 31 p .   CU-B

1971. Walker, Ben Randal. [Biography of M. Theo. Kearney] Fresno, 1949. [6] l. Typew.   CFS

1972. Wells, Andrew Jackson. Fresno county, California... S.F., Sunset mag. homeseekers' bur. [1910?] 32 p. illus.   CHi CSmH CU-B

1973. —— Same. 1911. 62 p.   CU-B

1974. Wohlgemuth, Carl D. A study of residential mobility. Fresno, 1958. 54 l. illus. Thesis (M.A.)– Fresno state college, 1958.   CFS

1975. Wootten, Clarence B. Kerman, once part of vast waste area...brief history, discovery and development. Kerman [n.d.] 12 p. illus.   CFS

Fresno

1976. Bell, A.D. Fresno, California. Great progress of the town and county. Description of the colonies, the fruit orchards, the raisin vineyards, the wine vineyards. S.F., Merchant pub. co., 1884. 24 p.   CHi CU-B

1977. California. Commission of immigration and housing. Report on Fresno's immigration problem, with particular reference to educational facilities and requirements...March, 1918. Sacramento, State print. off., 1918. 28 p.   CL CSf

1978. —— **State college, Fresno. Dedication committee.** Brief history of Fresno state college. Fresno, 1958. 36 l. Typew.   CFS

1979. —— —— General catalog. Fresno.
CL has 1940 to date.

1980. California home for the aged, Fresno. Souvenir program of the California home for Armenian aged on Ventura Avenue, Fresno, California. Formal grand opening, Sunday, June 22, 1952. [Fresno, 1952] illus., ports.   CU-B

1981. Cheney, Charles Henry. General report on progress of a city plan for Fresno, to the Fresno city planning commission, June 1, 1918. [Fresno] Reprint. by Fresno-Clovis area planning commission, 1957. 63 p. illus.   CFS

1982. Eckenrod, Gervase Andrew. A distributive occupations survey of Fresno, California, 1956. [Fresno?] Fresno junior college and Bur. of business educ., Calif. state dept. of educ., 1956. 47 l. tables.   CFS

1983. Fresno. Armenian Holy Trinity church. History...1900–39. Fresno, Asbarez pub. co. [1939?] 41 p. In Armenian.   CHi

1984. —— **Charters, ordinances, etc.** Charter and ordinances, issued under charter provisions by authority of the Board of trustees; codified by W. A. Sutherland and H. E. Barbour. [Fresno?] 1906. 478 p.   C

1985. —— **First Baptist church.** History and directory of the First Baptist church...commemorating twenty-five years of service, March 18, 1882–March 18, 1907: Arthur Polk Brown, Pastor. [Fresno? 1907] 49 p. illus.   CFS

1986. —— **St. Paul's Armenian cathedral.** [The Armenian Apostolic church in California and St. Paul's Armenian cathedral of Fresno. Fresno, 1953] 156 p. illus., ports. Title page and text in Armenian, with a section in English.   C CHi

1987. Fresno bee. Fresno state college new campus dedication May 4th through May 10th. Fresno, 1958. 2E-48E p. illus., ports.   CU-B

1988. Fresno city unified school district. Directory. Fresno [1940?–]
CFS has 1939/40, 1945/46, 1948/49–

1989. —— A history of Fresno; the story of Ash Tree. Fresno, 1955. 65 p. illus., ports., maps.   CFS

1990. The Fresno clarion; a family magazine for civic betterment. v.1–23, Sept. 1, 1933–1956. Fresno, 1933–48. 15 v. illus., ports. Title varies.   CFS CU-B

1991. Fresno county. Chamber of commerce. Fresno, California, where irrigation is king...[Fresno, 1908?] 32 p.   CU-B

1992. Fresno daily evening expositor. ...Holiday edition, Daily evening expositor...[January 1, 1890] [Fresno, 1890] 32 p. illus.   CU-B

1993. Fresno free kindergarten association. Annual statement for the year ending December 31, 1893– Fresno, 1894–
CFS has 1893–94.

1994. Fresno police relief association. Fresno police annual. [Fresno] 1954– Local criminal history.
CFS has 1912 of a prior series (?); 1954–

1995. Fresno republican. Imperial Fresno. Resources, industries and scenery, illustrated and described ... Fresno, 1897. 144 p. illus., ports., map.
CHi CL CLU CO CSd CSfCP CSfCW CSmH CU-B NN

1996. —— A modern newspaper building; souvenir of the Fresno republican. Fresno, 1904. 35 p. illus.
CFS

1997. Golden jubilee, Fresno, 1885–1935. Official program... [Fresno republican print., 1935] unp. illus., ports. Contains "Story of the City of Fresno," by Ben R. Walker.   CHi

1998. Graff, Hans, 1863–1918, in memoriam. [Fresno? n.d.] 27 p. port.   CFS

1999. Hogan, Fred P. The history of Fresno state teacher's college... [n.p.] 1929. 149 l. Thesis (M.A.)— Stanford Univ., 1929.   CFS

2000. Klette, Charles Herman Bruno. Band leaders of Fresno. [n.p., 1940?] [5] l. Typew.   CFS

2001. McLane, Charles Lourie. The growth and development of the Fresno state college for the first twenty-five years, 1911–1936. [Fresno, 1937] 276 l. illus., pl. Typew.   CFS

2002. Manoogian, Richard Jacob. A civic center for the city of Fresno. [Berkeley, 1955] Thesis (M.A.) —Univ. of Calif., 1955.   CU

2003. Morrow house, Fresno. [Pages from the Morrow house register, 1877] 16 l. Ms.   CFS

2004. Outland, George E. Study of casework and relief services in city of Fresno. Fresno, Community chest, 1947. 109 [24] l. Mimeo.   CFS

2005. Roeding park, Fresno. Memorial dedication of the Lisenby bandstand [April 22, 1923. Fresno, 1923] [6] p. illus.   CHi

2006. Rowell, Chester, born 1844—died 1912. [Fresno, 1912] 36 p. port. Dr. Rowell was a State Senator and Mayor of Fresno.   CFS

2007. Rowland, Eugenia. Origin and development of Fresno state college. [Berkeley, 1949] 289 l. Thesis (M.A.)—Univ. of Calif., 1949.
CFS (microfilm copy)

2008. Sarafian, Krikor A. History of the Armenian general benevolent union in the California district, 1910– 1953... [Fresno?] 1954. 210 p. illus., ports. In Armenian.   CHi

2009. Saroyan, William. The bicycle rider in Beverly Hills. [autobiography] N.Y., Scribner, 1952. 178 p.   CSd

2010. Short, Frank Hamilton. Selected papers... addresses, civic studies & public letters. Printed for private distribution. S.F. [Grabhorn] 1923. 219 p.
CSfCW CU-B

2011. Singleton, Francis X. Cathedral in the valley [jubilee history of St. John's cathedral, Fresno, California, 1902–1952] Fresno, 1952. 98 p. illus., ports. Includes portraits and brief biographies of the parish priests since 1882.
C CFS CHi CLgA CSf CSfCW CSfU CViCL CU-B

2012. Smith, F. F. Report of a survey of child welfare agencies in the city of Fresno. 1936. 168 p. maps, charts, tables.   CF

2013. Tyler, William B. Picturesque Fresno; a series of twenty photogravure plates. World's fair ed.— Vol. I. S.F., W. B. Tyler, c1890. 20 pl.   CSmH CU-B

2014. Walker, Ben Randal. Fresno: 1872–1885...
Fresno, 1912. 64 p.   CU-B

2015. —— Same. [c1934] 15 p. illus., ports., map.
(Fresno county hist. soc. Pub., v.1, no. 2)
                              C CHi CLU CSf CSmH

2016. Whitney, Joel Parker. California and colonization... [The Washington irrigated colony, Fresno,
California] Buffalo, N.Y., Haas, Nauert & Klein, 1879.
50 p. maps.   CHi CSf

GLENN COUNTY
(Organized in 1891 from portion of Colusa county)

GREAT REGISTER

2017. Glenn county. Index to the Great register of
the county of Glenn. 1891– Place of publication and
title vary.
  C has 1892 (biennially to)– 1932, 1932–34, 1936 (biennially to)– date. CU-B has 1896, 1906.

GENERAL REFERENCES

2018. Alfalfa farms co., San Francisco. Relics of
'49 Glenn ranch. [S.F.? 1908?]   CSmH

2019. Alta California, inc., comp. & pub. Glenn
county, California, "where water is king"; a general and
historical summary... Sacramento, 1939. 5 l.
                                         CRcS CU-B

2020. Bank of Orland vs. Stanton, H. C. et al. In
the Supreme court of the state of California. The Bank
or Orland, a corporation, appellant vs. H. C. Stanton,
sheriff of the county of Glenn et al, respondents. Appellant's reply brief. Orland, Orland register, 1901. 10 p.
                                               CHi

2021. —— ...Respondents' points and authorities.
[Sacramento?] 1901. 6 p.   CHi

2022. Dunn, Arthur. Glenn county, Calif. ... Issued by the Sunset mag. homeseekers' bur. for the Bd. of
supervisors of Glenn county. [S.F., 1915?] 32 p. illus.
         CChiS CHi CL CLU CSmH CU-B

2023. Eubank, Elizabeth, comp. Glenn county di-
rectory; a handbook of ready reference, 1947–48. Wil-
lows, Sacramento lithograph co., 1948. 217 p. illus., map.
Includes about 100 pages of historical and economic
data.
  C C-S CChiS CHi CLO CLSU CLU CMartC
CO CRedCL CSdS CSf CSfCP CSfCW CSfSt
CSfU CSjC CSmat CStaC CStclU CStrJC CU-B
CV CViCL

2024. Glenn county. Board of supervisors.
Glenn county, California, offers the west's greatest opportunities in diversified farming. Willows [1934?]
11 p. illus., map.   CRcS

2025. Glenn county, California, as she is... [Wil-
lows] Willows review print. [1897?] [24] p. illus.   C

2026. Orland unit water users' association. U.S.
government irrigation. Come and see the land where you
are sure to have water the year round. Orland, Glenn
county, California. [Orland, 1915] [12] p. illus.   CHi

2027. Sacramento valley irrigation co. California,
now or never. Chicago, J.S. & W.S. Kuhn [1909?] 47 p.
col. illus. The Kuhn irrigation project, Glenn and Colusa
counties.   CS CSCL

2028. —— California now or never; question and
answers, Kuhn irrigation project, 250,000 acres, Sacramento valley, California. Willows, H. L. Hollister & co.
[1909?] 17 p. illus.   CHi

2029. U.S. Bureau of reclamation. Opportunities
for farm ownership. Orland irrigation project, California.
[Wash., D.C., Govt. print. off., 1927] 19 p. illus., map.
                                               CU-B

2030. West, Raymond H. The story of St. John,
the ghost city of Glenn county, on the old wagon road
to the gold mines of Shasta. [Orland? n.d.] 24 p. Reprinted from the *Orland Register*.
                        C CChiS CHi CSmH

2031. Wigmore, L. W. The story of the land of
Orland; a century of facts, legend and folklore. Orland,
Orland register, 1955. 113 p.   CChiS CStrJC

2032. Willows. Chamber of commerce. Glenn
county, California, where water is king. [Willows, 1930?]
[8] p.   CHi

2033. Wilson, Bourdon. Glenn county, California.
S.F., Sunset mag. homeseekers' bur. [1910] 32 p. illus.,
maps.   CHi CU-B

HUMBOLDT COUNTY
*(Created in 1853 from portion of Trinity county; in
1875 annexed a portion of Klamath county)*

COUNTY HISTORIES

2034. [Coy, Owen Cochran] The Humboldt bay
region, 1850–1875... L.A., Calif. state hist. assoc., 1929
[c1930] 346 p.
  C CAla CAna CArcHT CB CChiS CEH CF
CFS CHi CL CLAC CLCM CLCo CLO CLSM
CLSU CLU CLgA CMartC CMerCL CO CP CPa
CRedl CSS CSd CSdS CSf CSfCP CSfCW CSfP
CSfU CSjC CSjCL CSmH CStb CStclU CStmo
CStoC CU-B CWeT CWhC CYcCL ICN WHi
CaBViPA GEU ICN IHi KHi MdHi Mid-B MoHi
MoSHi OHi TxU UHi WHi

2035. Fountain, Susie (Baker). History of Hum-
boldt county. [Blue Lake, 1954–58] 1 v. illus., ports.
Volume made up of issues and clippings from the *Blue
Lake advocate*.   CLU

2036. History and business directory of Humboldt
county. Descriptive of the natural resources... Lillie E.
Hamm, publisher. Eureka, Daily Humboldt standard,
1890. 224 p. map.
  C CCH CEH CHi CL CLAC CLU CSmH
CU-B MiD-B N NN

2037. History of Humboldt county, California, with
illustrations, descriptive of its scenery, farms...with biographical sketches. S.F., Print. for W. W. Elliott, 1881.
218 p. illus., ports., maps.   CHi CSf

2038. Same. S.F., Elliott, 1882. 218 p. illus., ports.,
maps.   C CArcHT CEH CHi CLU CSd CU-B

2039. Irvine, Leigh Hadley. History of Humboldt
county, California, with biographical sketches... L.A.,
Historic record co., 1915. 1290 p. illus., ports.
  C C-S CArcHT CEH CF CHi CL CLAC CO
CS CSf CSmH CSrCL CU-B NN

2040. Souvenir of Humboldt county... Issued by the
Humboldt times, under the auspices and direction of the
Supervisors of Humboldt county and the Humboldt cham-
ber of commerce... Eureka, Times pub. co., 1902. 192 p.
illus., port., map.
  CArcHT CEH CHi CL CLU CSf CSmH CStrCL

2041. Same, 2d ed., with title: Humboldt county
souvenir... Eureka, Times pub. co., 1904. 210 p. illus.,
map.
  C CArcHT CEH CHi CLO CSf CSfCP CSmH
CStrCL CU-B NHi NN

GREAT REGISTER

2042. Humboldt county. Index to the Great register of the county of Humboldt. 1866– Place of publication and title vary.

C has 1871–73, 1875, 1879–80, 1882, 1890 (biennially to)– 1914, 1918 (biennially to)– 1932, 1933, 1934, 1935, 1936 (biennially to)– 1962. CHi has 1872. CL has 1873, 1875 (suppl.), 1877, 1879, 1882, 1886, 1888 (suppl.), 1890. CSmH has "List...copied from the Great register" 1872. CU-B has 1948, also "List...copied from the Great register" Aug. 1871, Oct. 1872, Aug. 1873, Aug. 1879, Oct. 1880, Oct. 1884.

DIRECTORIES

2043. 1885. McKenney, L. M. & co., pub. 8-county directory of Humboldt, Napa, Marin, Yolo, Lake, Solano, Mendocino and Sonoma counties. S.F., 1885. 671 p.   C CHi CSf CSfCP

2044. 1895. Spencer, Ed. B., pub. Business directory of Humboldt county, 1895–6. A complete register of the citizens of Eureka and Humboldt county, California, with classified directory; description of Humboldt county mail routes... Eureka, Standard print. [1895] 152 p.
          C CArcHT CHi CSmH CU-B

2045. 1902–1950. Polk, R. L., & co., pub. Polk's Eureka city directory including Arcata and Humboldt county... S.F., 1902–50. Title varies: 1902–194–? Eureka city and Humboldt county directory. Publisher varies: 1902, F. M. Husted; 1907/08–1926? Polk-Husted. Continued as Polk's Eureka city directory.

C has 1910, 1933. C-S has 1907/08. CArcHT has 1926–27, 1932, 1935–36, 1940, 1942, 1946–48. CHi has 1902, 1914/15, 1916, 1927, 1948, 1949/50. CL has 1932, 1939–42, 1946/47, 1949/50. CU-B has 1939–40.

2046. 1903. Lampson & Buckley, pub. Humboldt county directory, year 1903. [n.p., 1903?] 259 p.   CHi

Eureka

2047. 1893/94. Eureka business directory. A complete register of the citizens of the city of Eureka, Humboldt county, California. Eureka, Standard pub. co., 1893. 97 p.   CSmH CStrJC

2048. 1901. Husted, F. M., pub. Directory of Eureka City, giving names, occupations and addresses of all adults, also a classified business directory of the county. Eureka, 1901.   CArcHT

2049. 1952/53– Polk, R. L., & co., pub. Polk's Eureka city directory including Arcata, Fortuna, Samoa and Scotia. L.A., 1953– Preceded by Polk's Eureka city and Humboldt county directory.

CArcHT has 1952/53 to date. CHi has 1952/53, 1954–60. CL has 1952/53, 1955, 1957–58.

GENERAL REFERENCES

2050. Anderson, George Esborne. The Hoopa valley Indian reservation in north-western California: a study of its origins. [Berkeley, 1956] Thesis (M.A.)– Univ. of Calif., 1956.   CU

2051. Arcata. Ordinances, etc. Charter and ordinances of the city of Arcata. Also some legislative acts relating to municipalities... Eureka, Pub. by the Board of trustees, 1904. 104 p.   CSmH

2052. Blue Lake advocate. Commentary edition on Arcata and Mad river railroad centennial, 1854–1954. Blue Lake, 1954. 8 p. illus. (v.66, no. 4)   CRcS

2053. —— Special Christmas edition, Dec. 23, 1954. Blue Lake, 1954. 12 p. (v.66, no. 34)   CSt

2054. Borden, Stanley T. Arcata and Mad river, 100 years of railroading in the redwood empire. San Mateo, 1954. 39 p. illus., map. "Reprinted from *Western railroader*, v.17, no. 8, 1954, issue 176."   CArcHT CHi

2055. —— Oregon & Eureka railroad. (*Western railroader*, v.22, no. 1, issue no. 229, November 1958, p. 1–18) illus., map.   CArcHT CHi

2056. [Brizard, A., inc.] Fifty years of progress. A memorial of the fiftieth anniversary of the establishment of the business at Arcata, Humboldt county, California, June 1913. 24 p. illus.
          C CArcHT CSfCP CStrJC CU-B

2057. California. Dept. of natural resources. Division of beaches and parks. An archeological investigation of Fort Humboldt state historical monument by John S. Clemmer. [Sacramento? 1960] 36 p. illus., maps.
                                                        C

2058. —— —— —— A report on the archeological findings at Fort Humboldt state monument, California, by Donald P. Jewell and John S. Clemmer. [Sacramento? 1960] 23 p. illus., map.   C

2059. —— **State college (Humboldt) Arcata.** Arcata community survey. Arcata, 1947. 79 p. Mimeo.
                                                   CArcHT

2060. —— —— Same, with title: Survey of a community; "The pageant of Humboldt."... unp.   CArcHT

2061. —— —— **Division of health and physical education.** An intercollegiate athletic history of Humboldt state college, 1914–1952. [Arcata, 1953] 41 l. Foreword signed: J. M. Forbes.   CArcHT

2062. The Californian, Eureka. Humboldt county supplement, August 22, 1914. Eureka, 1914. 54 p. illus.
                                              CArcHT CU-B

2063. Campbell, James M. Humboldt county revised economic survey, 1954; report prepared for the Humboldt county Planning commission. [n.p., 1954?] 80 l. maps.   CArcHT

2064. —— Proposed master plan of beaches, parks and recreation, Humboldt county, California. Prepared for the Humboldt county Planning commission. [Eureka?] 1951. 37 l. maps.   CArcHT

2065. Carr, John. Pioneer days in California...Historical and personal sketches. Eureka, Times pub. co., 1891. 452 p. port. Biographical sketches of pioneers of Humboldt and Trinity counties, California: p. 420–452.
          C CArcHT CBu CEH CHi CL CLU CLgA
CO CSf CSfCP CSfCW CSj CSjC CSmH CSmat
CU-B IHi

2066. —— A vulcan among the Argonauts; being vivid excerpts from those most original & amusing memoirs of John Carr, blacksmith; ed. with a preface & postscript by Robin Lampson... S.F., George Fields, 1936. 73 p. illus.
          CBb CHi CLO CRcS CRedl CSd CSf CSfCW
CSfP CSjC CStbS CSto CStoC CYcCL

2067. Colivas, Jerome J. A history of water transportation in Humboldt county; a brief history of shipping, shipbuilding, ship disasters, and harbor improvements. Eureka, 1955. unp. Ms.   CArcHT

2068. Coy, Owen Cochran. The settlement and development of the Humboldt bay region, 1850–1875. [Berkeley, 1918] 500 l. illus., map. Thesis (Ph.D.)– Univ. of Calif., 1918.   CU

2069. Crocker, H. S., co., pub. Humboldt county. Where it is, how to get there and what you can do in Humboldt. Fortuna, 1915. 128 p. illus. (part. col.) maps.
                                              CArcHT CL

2070. —— Humboldt county, the land of unrivaled underdeveloped natural resources on the westernmost rim of the American continent. Eureka, 1915. 127 p. illus., ports., map.   CHi CStrJC

2071. Cutten, Charles Pryde. The discovery of Humboldt bay. [S.F.? 192–?] 47 l. Typew. Notes, with manuscript additions, on the Gregg party and other explorers and settlers of the Humboldt bay region. Part of this material was published in the *Soc. of Calif. Pioneers Q.,* v.9, no. 1, March 1932.   CArcHT

2072. Davidson, George. Discovery of Humboldt bay, California... Geographical society of the Pacific publication. S.F., 1891. 16 p. 5 fold. maps.
C CHi CLU CLgA CP CSfCM CSmH CU-B CaBViPA

2073. Davies, Sarah M. A history of Humboldt state college. Stanford, 1947. 200 p. Thesis (M.A.)—Stanford univ., 1947.   CArcHT CSt

2074. Eddy, John Mathewson. In the redwood's realm; by-ways of wild nature and highways of industry as found...in Humboldt county, California. Comp. ...under the direction of the Humboldt chamber of commerce...S.F., Print. by D. S. Stanley & co., 1893. 112 p. illus., maps.
C CArcHT CEH CHi CL CLU CSf CSfCP CSfCW CSmH UPB

2075. Eel river and Eureka railroad co. Freight tariff and classification of Eel river and Eureka railroad co. ... Eureka, Nerve print. co., 1894. 54 p.   CU-B

2076. Eureka. Chamber of commerce. Economic survey of Humboldt county, California...1947– Eureka, 1947– Publisher varies: 1947– Humboldt county chamber of commerce; 1957– Eureka chamber of commerce. CArcHT has 1947, 1952, 1959–60. CEH has 1960.

2077. Eureka and Humboldt county; a compilation of facts for the information of business men, tourists and the world at large. (*Thompson's illus. Q.* Holiday ed., 1895?) 111 p. illus.   CArcHT

2078. Federated commercial bodies of Humboldt county. Humboldt county, California. [Eureka? 1921?] 32 p. illus.   CHi CU-B

2079. Fritz, William G. A history of Humboldt county sheriff's department, 1853–1960. [Eureka, Humboldt county sheriff's dept., 1960] 45 l.   CArcHT

2080. Geer, Knyphausen. Captain Knyphausen Geer; his life and memories. (37 pages typed from captain Geer's diary) Ms.   CArcHT

2081. Genzoli, Andrew M. Fortuna; a growing city reflects...Diamond jubilee edition, 1878–1953... [Fortuna, Humboldt beacon, 1953] [48] p. illus., map, port.   CArcHT CHi

2082. —— Humboldt county's century, a chronology of discovery, exploration and settlement. Eureka, Humboldt county chamber of commerce, 1953. 7 p. illus. Reprinted from the *Humboldt times,* Sunday, April 12, 1953.   CRcS OrU

2083. —— and Martin, Wallace E. Redwood frontier, wilderness defiant: tales out of the conquest of America's great forest land, Humboldt, Del Norte, Trinity, Mendocino. Eureka, Schooner features, c1961. 56 p.   CAla

2084. Grant, Joseph Donahoe. Saving California's redwoods...excerpts from three addresses... Berkeley, Save the redwoods league [1922] 16 p. illus.
CHi CLO CSfCW CU-B

2085. Hawley, A. T. The climate, resources and advantages of Humboldt county, Calif., described in a series of letters to the San Francisco daily evening bulletin...March, A.D., 1879... J. E. Wyman & son, 1879. 42 p.   CLU CSmH CU-B NHi

2086. Heizer, Robert Fleming, ed. The four ages of Tsurai; a documentary history of the Indian village on Trinidad bay by Robert F. Heizer and John E. Mills. Translations of Spanish documents by Donald C. Cutter. Berkeley, Univ. of Calif. press, 1952. 207 p. illus., maps. Bibliography included in "Notes" p. 191–207.
CArcHT CEH CSS CSf CSfCSM CSfSt CUk

2087. Hines, Joseph Wilkinson. Touching incidents in the life and labors of a pioneer on the Pacific coast since 1853. San Jose, Eaton & co., print., 1911. 198 p. port.   CArcHT CBb CHi CSf OrU

2088. Homes for a million people!...southern Humboldt... Ferndale, Enterprise off., 1888. 29 p.
CLU CU-B

2089. Humboldt canal co. Prospectus, certificate of incorporation and by-laws... S.F., L. Albin, print., 1863. 16 p. map.   CLU CU-B

2090. Humboldt county. Board of education. Course of study for the public schools of Humboldt county, California. Eureka, Democratic standard, 1881. 16 p.   CHi

2091. —— **Board of trade.** Humboldt county, the redwood wonderland. [Eureka, 1937?] 24 p. illus.
CEH CL CRcS CU-B

2092. —— —— List of historical places in Humboldt county. Also early history of Humboldt county. [1933] [9] l. Mimeo.   CHi

2093. —— —— Prosperity in Humboldt county, California. Eureka [1925] 15 p. illus., maps.   CRcS

2094. —— —— Recreation along Humboldt highways. Eureka [n.d.] 11 p. illus., map.   CRcS

2095. —— **Chamber of commerce.** Harbor improvement... Eureka, Humboldt times print. [1892?] 8 p.   CU-B

2096. —— —— Humboldt county, California. [Eureka, Press of Jewett bros., 1908] 60 p. illus., map.
CArcHT CU-B

2097. —— —— Humboldt county's century... Eureka, 1953.   OrU

2098. —— —— Resources of Humboldt county, California. Eureka [1950?] 5 p. illus.   CRcS

2099. —— **Commission to the State and Mechanics' institute fairs, 1887.** A remarkable country! ...pub. under the joint direction of the Commissioners of Humboldt county, Calif., to the State and Mechanics institute fairs, 1887... Eureka, 1887. 12 p. illus.
CU-B

2100. —— —— 1888. Humboldt county, California ... S.F., A. J. Leary [1888] 15 p.   CU-B

2101. Humboldt county, California. Eureka, Eureka print. co. [1915] 31 p. illus.   CArcHT

2102. Humboldt county, California, redwood, nature's timber masterpiece. [n.p., 1917] unp. illus. Illus. with over 80 photographic reproductions.   CArcHT

2103. Humboldt county historical society, Eureka. [The history of the Humboldt county historical society, constitution and membership, and papers presented to the society. Ed. by Hyman Palais. Eureka, 1954] 81 p. illus.   CEH CHi

2104. —— The Humboldt county historical society. Ed. by Hyman Palais. Eureka [1949?] 60 p.
CLU CU-B

2105. Humboldt times. Centennial edition. Northwestern California celebrates a century of progress, 1854–1954. Eureka, Eureka newspapers [1954] unp. illus., ports.   CHi CU-B

2106. —— Humboldt county, California, wants your factory. Eureka, c1917. [48] p. illus. On cover: Industrial edition.   C CArcHT CEH

2107. —— Transportation and exposition number... Supplement to the Humboldt times. Eureka, 1904. 310 p. illus., ports.   C

2108. —— Same. ...November 19, 1914. Eureka, 1914. 48 p. illus.   CArcHT

2109. Humboldt view book. [Eureka, Eureka print co., 1914?] 16 p. illus.   CArcHT

2110. Immigration association of California. [County scrapbooks] [S.F., 188–?]   C

2111. Irvine, Leigh Hadley. The playground of the west... [Eureka, Daily standard press, 191–?] 23 p.
                                                             CU-B

2112. —— What Humboldt offers you. Eureka, Reissued by the Humboldt chamber of commerce [1913?] 36 p. illus.   CHi CU-B NN

2113. Kelly, Isabel Truesdell. A study of the carver's art of the Indians of northwestern California. [Berkeley, 1927] Thesis (M.A.)—Univ. of Calif., 1927.
                                                             CU

2114. Kendal, Henry A. Trinity river diversion? ... Eureka, 1942. 31 p.   C

2115. Lambert & McKeehan, printers. Humboldt county, California. [Eureka, 1914?] 31 p. illus.   CU-B

2116. [Lewis, Oscar] ed. The quest for Qual-a-wa-loo (Humboldt bay) a collection of diaries and historical notes pertaining to the early discoveries of the area now known as Humboldt county, California. Ed. and pub. from manuscripts furnished by Clarence E. Pearsall, George D. Murray, A. C. Tibbetts and Harry L. Neall. [S.F., 1943] 190 p. illus., ports., map.
C CArcHT CBb CChiS CEH CHi CL CLU CO CRcS CRic CSS CSbr CSf CSfSt CSj CU-B CaBViPA NN UHi

2117. Martin, Wallace E. Marine disasters of the Humboldt–Del Norte coast, northern California, USA. Eureka, c1956. chart. illus., map. Includes alphabetical list of vessels lost on the Humboldt–Del Norte coast, 1850–1942.   CArcHT

2118. Melendy, Howard B. The construction of Humboldt county court house at Eureka, California, 1883–1889. [Eureka? 1953] 14 p. illus.
                                        C CArcHT CHi CLU CU-B

2119. —— One hundred years of redwood lumber industry, 1850–1950. [Stanford] 1952. 377 l. map. Thesis (Ph.D.)—Stanford univ., 1952.   CArcHT CSt

2120. Merriam, John Campbell. The highest uses of the redwoods... [Berkeley] Save-the-redwoods league [1941] 47 p. illus., port., map.   CArcHT

2121. Morgan, Dale L. The Humboldt, highroad of the west. N.Y., Farrar & Rinehart, 1943. 374 p. illus. (Rivers of Am.) Bibliography: p. 355–365.
                                                     CHi CSluCL

2122. Murdock, Charles Albert. A backward glance at eighty, recollections & comment... Massachusetts 1841, Humboldt bay 1855, San Francisco 1864. S.F., Elder, 1921. 275 p. illus., ports.
Available in many California libraries and CaBViPA

2123. O'Neale, Lila Morris. Yurok-Karok basket

weavers. [Berkeley, 1930] Thesis (Ph.D.)—Univ. of Calif., 1930.   CU

2124. Pacific lumber co., comp. Scotia, home of the redwood... Scotia, 1929. 16 p. illus.   CHi

2125. Phelps, N. S. Boundaries and descriptions of the school districts of Humboldt county, as they appear on the county assessor's map, up to the month of October, 1885... Eureka, Times-Telephone print., 1886. 76 p. chart.   CSf

2126. Pine, William D. Humboldt's timber, a present and future problem. [Eureka, Humboldt county board of supervisors, 1952] 24 p. illus.   CArcHT

2127. Puter, Stephen A. Douglas. Looters of the public domain, by S. A. D. Puter, king of the Oregon land fraud ring, in collaboration with Horace Stevens... embracing a complete exposure of the fraudulent system of acquiring titles to the public lands of the United States ... Portland, Ore., Portland print. house, 1908. 494 p. illus., ports. Describes C. A. Smith land frauds and many others.   CArcHT CRcS

2128. Save the redwoods league. Dedication of the Humboldt pioneer memorial redwood grove. [Berkeley, 1923] [16] p. illus.   C

2129. [Scotia theatre association] Wi-ne-ma theatre, Scotia, California in the redwoods. [S.F., Taylor & Taylor, 1920] [8] p. illus.   CHi CU-B

2130. Swinehart, Durward Bruce. A study of Prairie creek redwoods state park. Sacramento, 1953. 94 p. Thesis (M.A.)—Sacramento state college.   CSS

2131. Thornbury, Delmar L. California's redwood wonderland, Humboldt county... [S.F., Print. by Sunset press, c1923] 167 p. illus., maps.
C CArcHT CEH CHi CL CLU CLgA CMartC CNF CO CRcS CRic CSf CSfSC CStrCL CU-B CUk MiD NN OrU

2132. United Americans, Order of. California. Eureka chapter. By-laws of Eureka chapter, no. 1, O.U.A. of the state of California. Instituted March 8th, 1850. S.F., R. B. Quayle, print., 1855. 23 p.   CLU

2133. Vaux, Henry James, and Hofsted, Eugene A. An economic appraisal of forest resources and industries in Humboldt county. Prepared for the Humboldt county forestry committee by [the] school of forestry, University of California and [the] Humboldt county dept. of forestry in cooperation with [the] California agricultural extension service. Berkeley, 1954. 108 l. diagrs., maps, tables.   CArcHT

2134. —— Timber in Humboldt county. [Berkeley] Div. of agric. sciences, Univ. of Calif. [1955] 55 p. illus., maps, diagrs., tables. (Calif. agric. experiment station, Bul. 748)   CArcHT

2135. Wade, Kathleen Camilla. ...The redwood state parks of Humboldt county... Berkeley, 1937. 9 l.
                                                             CU-B

2136. Wallace, William James. Hupa education: a study in primitive socialization and personality development. [Berkeley, 1946] Thesis (Ph.D.)—Univ. of Calif., 1946.   CU

2137. Ward, Charles Willis. Humboldt county, California... [Eureka, Ward-Perkins-Gill co.] 1915. 128 p. illus.
           CArcHT CEH CHi CL CRic CSmH CU-B

2138. Washington. State university, Pullman, Wash. Dept. of oceanography. Humboldt bay, California: a literature survey. Seattle, 1955. 144 l. table.
                                                             CArcHT

2139. Wattenburger, Ralph Thomas. The redwood lumbering industry on the northern California coast, 1850–1900. [Berkeley, 1931] 87 l. Thesis (M.A.) —Univ. of Calif., 1931.   CArcHT CU

2140. Wheelock, Harrison. Guide and map of Reese river and Humboldt... S.F., Towne and Bacon, 1864. 52 p. map.   NHi

2141. Wood, L. K. The discovery of Humboldt bay ... [S.F., 1932] 22 p. "Originally published in the *Humboldt times,* beginning on April 26, 1856..."
C   CArcHT   CEH   CHi   CL   CLU   CO   CSfU
CSmH   CStrJC   CU-B   CaBViPA   MoKU

Eureka

2142. Bliven,   . Bliven's pocket guide, Eureka, Cal. ... [Eureka] Lambert & McKeehan [19–?] [48] p. illus.   CU-B

2143. Cottage gardens nurseries, inc. [Catalogs] CHi has 1917.

2144. Eureka. Charters. Eureka city charter, 1895. [n.p., 1895?] 57 p.   CHi

2145. —— First Presbyterian church. History ...1890–1960. [Eureka, 1960] 40 p. illus.   CEH CHi

2146. —— Volunteer fire department. Souvenir, Eureka volunteer fire department. Fifty years, 1864–1914. Eureka, Eureka print. co. [1914] 97 p. ports.
CArcHT CHi CSmH

2147. Eureka newspapers, inc. Classified directory and guidebook, 1949– Eureka, c1948– Title varies: 1949 Business and professional directory.
CArcHT has 1949, 1951/52, 1955/56. CEH has 1949. CHi has 1949.

2148. Humboldt county. Chamber of commerce. City of Eureka, Humboldt county, California. [Eureka, Eureka print. co., 1917] 15 p. illus.   CL CU-B

2149. Melendy, Howard B. One hundred years of masonry in Humboldt lodge no. 79 F. & A. M., 1854– 1954. Ann Arbor, Mich., [Edwards bros., inc., c1954] 107 p. illus.   CHi

2150. Miller, Thomas. Dedicatory souvenir; eighty-one years of Methodism in Eureka, California, 1850 [to] 1931. [n.p., n.d.] 36 p. illus., ports.   C

2151. Noe, A. C., pub. Eureka, Humboldt county, California. Eureka, 1902. col. map. Pictorial map, in perspective, showing individual buildings. Marginal insets of business houses, residences, etc.   CArcHT

2152. U.S. Work projects administration. Survey of federal archives. Ship registries and enrollments, port of Eureka, California, 1859–1920. 1941. 167 p. Mimeo.
C   CArcHT   CEH   CHi   CLSM   CLSU   CMartC
CMont   CSd   CSf   CSfCW   CSmH   CStmo   CSto

IMPERIAL COUNTY
(Created in 1907 from a portion of San Diego county)

COUNTY HISTORIES

2153. Farr, Finis C., ed. The history of Imperial county, California... Berkeley, Elms & Franks, 1918. 526 p. illus., ports.
C   CAla   CB   CCH   CEc   CEcI   CHi   CL   CLO
CLSU   CLU   CLob   CRedl   CSd   CSdS   CSf   CSfCP
CSfMI   CSjC   CSmH   CU-B   MWA   NN   WHi

2154. Tout, Otis Burgess. ...The first thirty years, being an account of the principal events in the history of Imperial valley, southern California, U.S.A. ... San Diego, Author [1931] 429 p. illus., ports., maps. Bibliography: p. 9–12.
C   CCoron   CEc   CEcI   CHi   CL   CLAC   CLCM
CLCo   CLU   CLob   CSd   CSdCL   CSdS   CSf   CSjC
CSmH   CU-B   MWA   NN

GREAT REGISTER

2155. Imperial county. Index to the Great register of the county of Imperial. 1908– Place of publication and title vary.
C has 1908 (biennially to) – 1962.

DIRECTORIES

2156. 1910/11–1920/21. Thurston, Albert G., comp. and pub. Thurston's Imperial valley resident directory... L.A., 1910–20.
C has 1912/13, 1917/18. CHi has 1910/11, 1912/13, 1914/15. CL has 1914/15, 1917/18. CLU has 1917/18. CU-B has 1920/21.

2157. 1924–1949. Los Angeles directory co., pub. Imperial valley directory, including Brawley, Calexico, Calipatria, El Centro, Heber, Holtville, Imperial, Niland and Westmorland... L.A., 1924–49. Title varies.
C has 1926, 1928. CHi has 1928, 1936, 1947, 1949. CL has 1924, 1926, 1928, 1930, 1937, 1939, 1942, 1947, 1949.

2158. 1952– Polk, R. L., & co., pub. Polk's Imperial Valley directory. L.A., 1952–
CHi has 1952, 1957, 1959. CL has 1952. CU-B has 1957.

GENERAL REFERENCES

2159. All-American canal board. Report...Dr. Elwood Mead, W. W. Schlecht, C. E. Grunsky on a canal located entirely within the United States from the Colorado river at Laguna dam into the Imperial valley, California, July 22, 1919, together with the report of the engineer in charge of surveys and examinations, Porter J. Preston, June 17, 1919. Wash., D.C., Govt. print. off., 1920. 98 p. tables, maps.   CLU

2160. Automobile club of southern California. Imperial county; general information for the resident and visitor within the county. El Centro [n.d.] 24 p. map.   CHi

2161. Bitler, Don V., ed. The Imperial valley, California. El Centro, Bd. of supervisors of Imperial county, 1920. 34 p. illus., map.   CAla CHi

2162. Brawley news. ...Inland empire edition... Mar. 15, 1947. Brawley, 1947. 1 v. illus.   CU-B

2163. —— Salton sea, unique playground in the desert. [Brawley, 1959] [18] p. illus., ports., map.   CU-B

2164. Burgess, Charles P. Imperial irrigation district, California. Prepared for Blyth and co., inc. and Kaiser and co. [S.F.?] Kaiser & co., 1943. 60 p. illus., map.   C CHi

2165. Burns, Helen. Salton sea story... Palm Desert, Desert mag. press, c1952. 30 p. illus., maps.
CHi CL CP CPs CStmo

2166. —— Same. [6th rev. ed.] Palm Desert, Desert mag. press, 1958. 34 p. illus., maps.   C CSd

2167. Caine, Ralph Lawrence. Legendary and geological history of lost desert gold. Palm Desert, Desert mag. press, c1951. 71 p. illus.
C   CL   CLSM   CLob   CNa   CSd   MiD

2168. Calexico. International desert cavalcade of Im-

perial valley. International desert cavalcade of Imperial valley. 1st– 1940– Calexico, 1940–
C (3d, 1942) CL (1st– , 1940–) CLO (3d, 1942) CLU (2d, 3d, 7th, 1941–42, 1946)

2169. Calexico chronicle. Imperial valley...Annual magazine edition. 1st–3d, 1908–1910. Calexico, 1908–10.
C (2d–3d) CHi (1st–2d) CLU (2d) CSmH (2d)

2170. Cory, Harry Thomas. The Imperial valley and the Salton sink, with introductory monograph by W. P. Blake. 1st ed. S.F., J. J. Newbegin, 1915. 61[1204]–1581 p. illus., ports., maps. "Part IV is the author's paper: 'Irrigation and river control in the Colorado river delta.' "—Pref.
C CEc CL CLSU CLU CO COnC CRedl CSd CSdS CSf CU-B CViCL MiD NvU

2171. Darnell, William Irvin. The Imperial valley, its physical and cultural geography. [San Diego, 1959] illus., tables. Thesis (M.A.)—San Diego state college, 1959. CEc

2172. Dowd, M. J. The Colorado river flood-production works of Imperial irrigation district, history and cost. [n.p.] 1951. 70 p. illus., maps. Includes bibliography. CLU

2173. Edgar, Mrs. W. A. Reminiscences of Imperial's (Imperial county) early days...1927. Typew. CEcI

2174. El Centro progress. San Diego and Arizona railway edition. El Centro progress... El Centro, Dec. 5, 1919. 144 p. illus.
C CLSU CLU CSd CSmH CU-B

2175. Gifford, Edward Winslow. The Kamia of Imperial valley... Wash., D.C., Govt. print. off., 1931. 94 p. illus., map. (U.S. Bur. of Am. ethnology. Bul. 97)
CBb CL CLSU CLU CO CRedl CSdS CSf CSfCW CSmH CStclU CStmo CU-B

2176. Griswold, Mrs. A. H. History and landmarks of El Centro (Imperial co.) California... 1926. Typew. CEcI

2177. Grunsky, Carl Ewald. ...The Colorado river in its relation to its Imperial valley, California... Wash., D.C., Govt. print. off., 1917. 39 p. map. (65th Cong., 1st sess. S. doc. no. 103) CSf CU-B

2178. Harrigan, B. A., ed. and comp. Imperial county, California. [n.p., Imperial county bd. of supervisors, 1925] 16 p. CRcS

2179. Hays, Robert. An epitome of the history of Imperial valley. [n.p., n.d.] 5 l. CU-B

2180. Heber, Anthony H. Address of Hon. A. H. Helse, president of the California development company to the settlers of Imperial valley in support of water and property rights owned by the company in the valley at Imperial, California, July 25, 1904... [L.A., So. Calif. print. co., 1904?] 61 p. illus., ports., plan.
C CHi CLU CSmH

2181. Heffernan, W. T. Personal recollections of the early history of Imperial valley. Written in 1928 for the Imperial Valley pioneer assn. Rev. for publication in 1930. Calexico, Calexico chronicle, c1930. port. 22 p. Bound with: Rockwood, Charles R. Born of the desert.
C CEc CHi CLU CSmH CU-B

2182. Holt, Leroy M. Imperial valley scrapbook. [n.p.] 1953. CEc

2183. Holt, Luther Myrick, comp. The unfriendly attitude of the United States government towards the Imperial valley... Imperial, Imperial daily standard print., 1907. 45 p. C CSmH CU-B NN

2184. Holt, Marguerite. History of Calexico, Imperial county, California...1927. Typew. CEcI

2185. Holt, William Franklin. Biography. [n.d.] Typew. CEc

2186. Hotel Barbara Worth, El Centro, California; monument to those who conquered "La Palma de la mano de Dios." [n.p., n.d.] 21 p. C

2187. Howe, Edgar F., and Hall, Wilbur Jay. The story of the first decade in Imperial valley, California... Imperial, E. F. Howe & sons, 1910. 291 p. illus.
C CEc CHi CL CLO CLSU CLU CO CPom CRedl CSd CSf CSfCP CSmH CU-B N NN UPB

2188. Hutchison, Ann. Adventuring on desert roads ... S.F., Harr Wagner [c1934] 153 p.
CBev CL CLU CO CRcS CRedl CU-B NN

2189. Imperial county. Board of supervisors. Imperial valley, 1901–1915. Comp. by Mrs. Wiley M. Weaver under direction of Board of supervisors. [L.A., Kingsley, Mason & Collins co., 1915] [30] p. illus. CHi CU-B

2190. ——— Board of trade. Imperial county, California; dairying for profit. El Centro [1930?] 10 p. illus. CRcS

2191. Imperial irrigation district. The Boulder dam, All-American canal project. [El Centro] 1924. 30 p. CLU

2192. ——— The Boulder dam, All-American canal project. Facts. Imperial, 1924. 21 p. CLU

2193. ——— Boulder dam, All-American canal project and Imperial valley pictorially. [L.A., 1926] 40 p. illus. CLU

2194. ——— Official statement of the Board of directors; facts regarding the proposed All-American canal contract. El Centro, 1931. 24 p. CHi

2195. Imperial land co. From desert to garden... as illustrated in the Imperial settlements... L.A., Times mirror print. & bind. house [1902] [16] p. illus.
CLO CSmH CU-B

2196. ——— Imperial catechism; questions and answers regarding the Imperial valley, August, 1903. 10th rev. ed. [L.A.?] 1903. 23 p. illus. CHi

2197. Imperial water co., no. 1. [Report] [Imperial, 19—?–]
CU-B has 1912, 1915.

2198. James, George Wharton. Wonders of the Colorado desert... Bost., Little, 1906. 2 v. paged continuously (547 p.) illus., map. Other editions followed. Available in many libraries.

2199. Kelly, Allen. Calexico, king cotton's capital. [Calexico, Farmers and merchants club in conjunction with the Board of city trustees, 1914?] 12 p. illus., map. CSf CU-B

2200. Kennan, George. The Salton sea; an account of Harriman's fight with the Colorado river. N.Y., Macmillan, 1917. 106 p. illus., maps.
Available in many California libraries and UPB.

2201. Kinsey, Don Jackson. The river of destiny; the story of the Colorado river. L.A., Dept. of water and power, c1928. 63 p. illus., ports., maps. Includes material on Imperial valley, the All-American canal, the Colorado river aqueduct, and Hoover dam. CLU

2202. MacDougal, T. [and others] The Salton sea, a study of the geography, the geology, the floristics, and

the ecology of a desert basin... Wash., D.C., 1914. (Carnegie inst. of Wash. Pub. no. 193)
C CEc CHi CL CLSU CLU CRedl CSd CSfCSM CSmH CU-B

2203. Moody, Burdett. The Colorado river Boulder canyon project and the All-American canal. L.A., Boulder dam assoc., 1925. 20 p. map.   CLU

2204. Moore, Frank W. Of the Salton sea. Redlands, Fortnightly club, 1957. 9 p. Typew.   CRedl

2205. Mott, Orra Anna Nathalie. The history of Imperial valley. [Berkeley] 1922. 145 p. illus., maps. Thesis (M.A.)—Univ. of Calif., 1922.   CU CU-B

2206. ——, comp. Imperial valley scrapbook... August, 1922. 41 p. illus. Ms.   CU-B

2207. National agricultural workers union. The use of Mexican contract nationals and its effects on the employment of domestic agricultural workers in the Imperial valley of California. [n.p.] 1953. 33 l. Mimeo.
CLO

2208. Nicholas, B. C. Some educational problems of Imperial valley... El Centro [Imperial valley press print.] 1910. 31 p.   CU-B

2209. Peterson, Frederick William. Desert pioneer doctor... [Calexico] Calexico chronicle, 1947. 130, 85 p. illus., ports.
C CBb CEc CHi CL CLSU CLU CMon CO CSd CSmH CStmo

2210. Pettitt, George Albert. So Boulder dam was built. Oakland, The Six cos., 1935.   CRcS

2211. Rockwood, Charles Robinson. Born of the desert. Calexico, Calexico chronicle, 1930. port. 44 p. Contains also: Personal recollections of the early history of the Imperial valley, by W. T. Heffernan.
C CEc CHi CLU CSmH CU-B

2212. Romer, Margaret. History of the city of Calexico. L.A., 1923. Thesis (M.A.)—Univ. of So. Calif., 1923.   CEc CLSU

2213. —— Same. Reprinted from the annual publication of the *Hist. soc. of So. Calif.,* 1922. 45 p. illus., map.   CLO CLSM CSd

2214. Southern Pacific co. Imperial valley, California. [S.F.? 1908?] 37 p. illus.
CHi CL CSmH CU-B

2215. Steere, Collis Huntington. Imperial and Coachella valleys. Stanford [1952] 85 p. illus., maps. Bibliography: p. [86]
Available in many California libraries and MiD NvU ODa

2216. Tait, Clarence Everett. Irrigation in Imperial valley, California; its problems and possibilities... [Wash., D.C., Govt. print. off., 1908] 56 p. map. (60th Cong. 1st sess. S. Doc. 246)
C CL CLU CO CSf CSmH

2217. U.S. Bureau of reclamation. The Colorado river...a comprehensive report on the development of the water resources of the Colorado river basin for irrigation, power production, and other beneficial uses in Arizona, California, Colorado, Nevada, New Mexico, Utah, and Wyoming... [Wash., D.C., Govt. print. off.] 1946. 295 p. illus., maps.   CL CLSU CLU CO

2218. —— —— Development of the Imperial valley...A report on problems of Imperial valley and vicinity with respect to irrigation from the Colorado river. Wash., D.C., Govt. print. off., 1922. 233 p.
CBb CSmH

2219. —— —— Problems of Imperial valley and vicinity...A report...with respect to irrigation from the Colorado river... Wash., D.C., Govt. print. off., 1922. 326 p. maps, plans, diagrs. (67th Cong. 2d sess. S. Doc. no. 142)   CLO CLSM CLU

2220. —— Congress. House. Committee on claims. Southern Pacific Imperial valley claim... Wash., D.C., Govt. print. off., 1910. 192 p. illus.   CSmH

2221. —— Special commission on agricultural disturbances in Imperial valley. ...Report to the National labor board... [Wash., D.C.? 1934] 14 l. CU-B

2222. The Valley Imperial. v.1, 1956– Holtville, Imperial valley pioneers, 1956– illus. annual.
C (v.1–2, 1956–1958) CEc (v.1) CHi (v.2) CL (v.1) CO (v.1) CP (v.1)

2223. West side imperial irrigation co. An all American canal for Imperial valley. Why it should be built, some facts not generally known. L.A., [n.d.] 12 p.
C

2224. Wilson, Bourdon. Imperial county, California. S.F., Sunset mag. homeseekers' bur. 29 p. illus.
CHi CU-B

2225. Woodbury, David Oakes. The Colorado conquest... N.Y., Dodd, 1941. 367 p. illus., maps.
Available in many California libraries and N ODa UPB

2226. Woodward, Arthur. Journal of Lt. Thomas W. Sweeny, 1849–1853. L.A., Westernlore press [c1956] 278 p. illus.   CHi

INYO COUNTY

(Created in 1864 from portions of Mono and Tulare counties and first named Coso county; name changed to Inyo when county was organized in 1866; annexed section of San Bernardino county in 1872)

COUNTY HISTORIES

2227. Chalfant, Willie Arthur. The story of Inyo ... [Chicago] Author, 1922. 358 p. map.
C CAla CAlaC CAltu CAna CB CBaB CBaK CBev CBu CCH CChiS CCoron CEcI CF CFA CFS CGl CHanK CHi CInI CJ CL CLCM CLCo CLO CLSM CLSU CLU CLgA CLob CMS CMa CMartC CMary CMerCL CO CP CPa CPom CRb CRcS CRedCL CRedl CRic CRiv CS CSalCL CSbCL CSdCL CSdS CSf CSfCP CSfMI CSfP CSfSC CSfU CSj CSjC CSjCL CSlu CSluCL CSmH CSoCL CSrCL CStaCL CStb CStmo CSto CStoC CStrJC CSuLas CU-B CViCL CVtCL CWiwCL CYrS CtY N NvU

2228. —— Same. Rev. ed. [L.A., Citizens print shop] 1933. 430 p. map.
C CAln CBaK CBb CBev CL CLCo CLO CLS CLU CLgA CO COMC CPom CQCL CRiv CSbCL CSd CSdU CSf CSfCSM CSfMI CSfSt CSfU CSjCL CSmH CSt CStmo CStoC CU-B CWhC MWA NIC NN NvU TxU UPB WHi

GREAT REGISTER

2229. Inyo county. Index to the Great register of the county of Inyo. 1871– Place of publication and title vary.
C has 1871–72, 1875, 1877, 1879–80, 1882, 1884, 1886, 1890 (biennially to)– 1908, 1916 (biennially to)–1932, 1933, 1934, 1935, 1936 (biennially to) 1962. CHi has 1910. CInI has 1916–59 (few missing issues). CL has 1873 (biennially to)–1879, 1882 (suppl.), 1886, 1888 (suppl.), 1890. CLU has May 1916. CSmH has 1873,

1882. CU-B has 1872–73, 1875, 1879–80, Aug., Nov. 1938, Aug., Nov. 1940.

GENERAL REFERENCES

2230. Adams, Ansel Easton. Born free and equal, photographs of the loyal Japanese-Americans at Manzanar relocation center, Inyo county, California. N.Y., U.S. camera, 1944. 112 p. illus., ports.
                                        CHi CInI CLU CSd

2231. Austin, Mary (Hunter) Earth horizon; autobiography. Bost., Houghton, 1932. 381 p. illus.
                                        CHi CInI CRcS CRedCL

2232. —— The land of little rain. Bost. & N.Y., Houghton, 1903. 280 p. illus.
Available in many libraries.

2233. —— Same. Photos. by Ansel Adams. introd. by Carl Van Doren. Boston, Houghton, 1950. 133 p. 48 pl., map. Bibliography: p. 131–32.
Available in many libraries.

2234. Brady, James. Report of the Wonder, Zacatecas, Canton, Colopaxi, and Tingahoki mines, comprising a part of the Waucoba m. & s. co., in Inyo county... S.F., A. L. Bancroft & co., 1873. 14 p.   CU-B

2235. California. Legislature. Senate. Special investigating committee on water situation in Inyo and Mono counties. Report. 1931. 10 p. Reprinted from Senate jl. of May 7, 1931.   CInI

2236. California development board. Agricultural and industrial survey of Inyo county, California, June–July, 1917. [n.p.] 1917. unp.   CInI

2237. California interstate telephone co. Romantic heritage of Inyo-Mono, a saga of the old west...and the new. [Victorville, 1961] [12] p. illus.   CHi

2238. Doyle, Helen (MacKnight) A child went forth; the autobiography of Dr. Helen MacKnight Doyle; with a foreword by Mary Austin. N.Y., Gotham house, 1934. 364 p.
Available in many libraries.

2239. —— Mary Austin, woman of genius. N.Y., Gotham house [1939] 302 p.   CInI CRcS

2240. Eastern California museum. Handbook... [Independence? 1930?–]
CHi has [no. 1, 1930?] CInI has [no. 2, 3, 1950?, 1957?]

2241. Eaton, Allen Hendershott. Beauty behind barbed wire; the arts of the Japanese in our war relocation camps. N.Y., Harper [1952] 208 p. illus.   CInI

2242. Fox, Rollin Clay. The secondary school program at the Manzanar war relocation center. L.A., 1946. Thesis (Ed.D.)– U.C.L.A., 1946.   CLU

2243. Guide to Inyo, Mono counties, the eastern slope of the "Scenic high sierras"... [n.p., Direct-mail press, 1925?] [24] p. illus., map.   CHi

2244. Harrington, Mark Raymond. A Pinto site at Little lake, California. L.A., Southwest museum, 1957. 91 p. illus., maps. (Southwest museum papers, no. 17)
C CInI CLO CSd CSfCSM CSt KU TxU

2245. Hart, Alan S. The story of District IX. Bishop, Author, 1952. 203 p. illus., ports., maps.   CInI

2246. Homes for settlers. Government land...resources of Inyo county... Independence, Inyo independent print., 1886. 32 p.   CU-B

2247. Hungerford, John B. The Slim princess; the story of the Southern Pacific narrow gauge. Reseda, Hungerford press, 1956. 32 p. illus.   CInI CRcS CSdCL

2248. —— Same. 2d ed. [c1958]   C

2249. Immigration association of California. [County scrapbooks] [S.F., 188–?]   C

2250. Inyo county. Board of supervisors. Inyo county and the famous Owens river valley, source of the Los Angeles aqueduct. [n.p., 1910?] [24] p.   CSmH

2251. —— **Superintendent of schools.** A brief history of the schools of Inyo county... Independence, 1954.   CInI

2252. Inyo register. Inyo county, California, anno Domini 1912. Beautiful Owens valley. Bishop, 1912. 46 p. illus., ports., map.   C CHi CInI CSmH CU-B

2253. Inyo-Mono association. Inyo-Mono; America's range of recreation. Bishop, Inyo-Mono assoc. [n.d.] folder (11 p.) map.   CRcS

2254. Krautter, Frances Corey. The story of Keeler, southern terminus of the Carson and Colorado railroad. [Acoma Acres? Owens Inyo co., 1959] [32] p. illus.   C CInI

2255. Lingenfelter, Richard E., and Dwyer, Richard A. The 'Nonpareil' press of T. S. Harris. L.A., Dawson, 1957. 59 p. illus. (Early Calif. travels ser., 39) 250 copies printed on a Kelly, the later Nonpareil of Clyde Browne.
CHi CInI CL CLO CLSM CLgA CP CRedl
CSd CSf CSto CU-B

2256. Manzanar commercial club. Manzanar, Owens river valley, Inyo county. [Manzanar, 1916?]
                                                      CInI

2257. Margrave, Anne. An Inyo chronology, 1825–1931... Independence, Inyo independent [1937] folder (6 p.)   CHi

2258. Nash, Ray. Manzanar from the inside; text of an address delivered before the Commonwealth club of California, San Francisco, California, July 31, 1942. 13 p.   CInI

2259. New Coso mining co. Annual report to the stockholders... S.F., 1877. 31 p.   CSfCSM

2260. —— Report of L. L. Robinson... on the properties of the company at Darwin, Inyo co., Calif., Dec. 1875. S.F., B.F. Sterett, 1875. 25 p.   CU-B

2261. Owen's river canal co. Prospectus...containing a short geographical and historical account of the Owen's river country, with valuable statistical information. N.Y., Chapin, Bromell & Scott, 1864. 13 p.
                                              CHi CLU

2262. Owens valley. Chamber of commerce. Inyo county, California, endowed with a greater variety of natural resources than any other county. Bishop [Owens valley herald print shop, 1909?] [52] p. illus., maps.
                                        C CHi CLU CU-B

2263. Parcher, Frank M. Owens valley, California. Boise, Ida., Author, 1948. 14 p. (Parcher guides)
                                                      CInI

2264. Parcher, Marie Louise. Bishop, California ... Boise, Ida., F.M. Parcher, c1946. [16] p. illus.
                                              CInI CU-B

2265. —— **and Parcher, Will C.** Dry ditches. Bishop, Authors, 1934. 41 p. The sketches in this volume were written during the period of the evacuation of the Owens valley and originally appeared in the Inyo independent, Independence, Calif.   CInI

2266. Parcher, Ward. High Sierra of Inyo and Mono counties. L.A., Author [n.d.] 15 p. illus., maps.
                                                      CRcS

2267. Pearce, Thomas Matthews. The beloved house. Caldwell, Ida., Caxton print., 1940. CRcS

2268. Potosi mining and smelting co. Prospectus of the Potosi mining and smelting company, Cerro Gordo, Inyo county, California. [S.F.? 1874?] 8 p.
CHi CSfCSM CU-B

2269. —— Same. S.F., A.L. Bancroft & co. [1876?] 29 p. CU-B

2270. Putnam, George Palmer. Up in our country. Illus. by Joe Donat. N.Y., Duell, Sloan and Pearce [1950] 224 p. illus. C CInI CO

2271. Ray, Lorin, comp. Mementos of Bishop, California. [100 years of real living] Bishop, Bishop chamber of commerce, 1961. 92 p. illus. CHi CLSM

2272. Richmond mining and milling co. ...Prospectus. [N.Y., The Spectator co., print., 1882] 8 p. map, pl. NHi

2273. Schumacher, Genny, ed. Deepest valley; guide to Owens valley and its mountain lakes, roadsides, and trails, by Paul C. Bateman [and others] S.F., Sierra club, c1962. 206 p. illus., maps. CL

2274. Silliman, Benjamin. Reports upon the Potosi mine. S.F., Towne and Bacon, 1864. 12 p. C CHi

2275. Swansea mining co. Prospectus...Mines situated at Cerro Gordo, reduction works at Swansea, Inyo county, Calif. ... S.F., J. Winterburn & co., 1876. 17 p.
CU-B

2276. Thoroughgood, Inez Tingley. Mary Hunter Austin. [L.A., 1952] Thesis (M.A.)—U.C.L.A., 1952.
CLU

2277. Underhill, Ruth Murray. The northern Paiute Indians of California and Nevada. [Lawrence, Kansas] U.S. Bur. of Indian affairs, branch of educ., 1941. 71 p. illus. CAla CRcS

2278. U.S. War relocation authority. Bibliography of war relocation authority: Japanese and Japanese Americans. [Wash., D.C., 1945?] CInI

2279. —— —— Manzanar libraries (and visual aid program); a report prepared by Ruth Budd, director of school and community libraries... [1945] unp. CInI

2280. —— —— Manzanar high school. Our world, 1943–1944. [1944?] unp. CInI

2281. Wasson, Joseph. An account of San Ygnacio and the leading mines of Cerro Gordo district, Inyo county, California. N.Y., 1880. CSfCSM CSmH

DEATH VALLEY

2282. Adams, Ansel Easton. Death valley. Story by Nancy Newhall, guide by Ruth Kirk, maps drawn by Edith Hamlin. S.F., 5 Associates, 1954. 55 p. illus.
C CArcHT CHi CInI CL CLSM CLgA CO CSf CSfCSM CSfSt CSjC CSluCL CSto

2283. Belden, L. Burr, ed. Death Valley heroine, and source accounts of the 1849 travelers. San Bernardino, Inland print. & engraving co. [c1954] 78 p.
C CHi CInI CL CLO CLU CSd CSf CSfU CSjC CStoC CU-B NN

2284. —— Goodbye, Death valley! The 1849 Jayhawker escape. Illus. by Orpha Klinker, cover sculpture by Cyria Henderson. [Palm Desert, Desert mag. press, c1956] 61 p. ports. (Death valley '49ers, inc. Pub. no. 4) C CHi CInI CL CLSM CLU CLob CO CSfU CSluCL CStoC CU-B

2285. —— The Wade story; "In and out of Death Valley." San Bernardino, Inland print. and engraving co., 1957. 15 p. illus. CHi

2286. Brier, Mrs. Julia. [Story of a trip through Death valley in 1849, printed in *Carson, Nevada, news,* May 27, 1913] 2 p. CU-B

2287. Caruthers, William. Loafing along Death valley trails; a personal narrative of people and places. Palm Desert, Desert mag. press, c1951. 186 p. illus., ports.
Available in many California libraries and NN

2288. Castle publishing co., Goldfield, Nev. Death valley Scotty's castle. Goldfield, Nev., c1941. 74 p. illus., port. CL CLU CStmo

2289. Chalfant, Willie Arthur. Death valley; the facts... Stanford, London, Milford, Oxford, 1930. 155 p. illus.
Available in many California libraries and IHi MiD MoS NN ODa

2290. —— Same. 2d ed. Stanford, c1936. 160 p. illus.
Available in many California libraries and NN. Other reprints followed: 1939, 1947, 1951, 1953.

2291. Clements, Lydia (Brooks) Indians of Death valley. [Hollywood, Hollycrofters, c1953] 23 p. illus. Bibliography: p. 22–23. C CInI CLO

2292. Coolidge, Dane. Death valley prospectors... N.Y., Dutton, 1937. 178 p. illus., ports.
Available in many libraries.

2293. Corle, Edwin. Death valley and the creek called Furnace. With photographs by Ansel Adams. L.A., Ward Ritchie [c1941, c1962] 60 p. 60 pl.
CAla CHi CSfMI

2294. Crampton, Frank A. Deep enough; a working stiff in the western mine camps. Denver, Swallow [c1956] 275 p. illus., ports. (Sage books)
CHi CSalCL CSd CU-B

2295. —— Legend of John Lamoigne and song of the desert-rats. Denver [Swallow] c1956. 32 p. illus., ports., map. (Sage books) CHi CL CLU

2296. The Death valley chuck-walla v.1–2, Jan. 1– June 1, 1907. Greenwater, Chuck-walla co., 1907. 2 v.
CL CSmH (v.1 no. 6, Apr. 1907 only) CU-B

2297. Death valley '49ers, inc. The story of Death valley, its museum and visitor center. [n.p., 1960] 30 p. illus., ports. CHi CU-B

2298. Edwards, Elza Ivan. Desert treasure, a catalog-bibliography. L.A., Edwards and Williams, 1948. cl-c30, 42 p. The 2d part, 42 p. at end, has title: Desert treasure, a bibliography. It was also issued separately in the same year. CHi CLU CSjC

2299. —— "Into an alkali valley"; the first written account of Death valley. L.A., Edwards & Williams, 1948. 8 p. "An extract from the 'Log' of Sheldon Young... reproduced by permission of the Huntington library, San Marino, California": p. 7–8.
C CHi CL CLO CLU CO CRedl CSmH CU-B

2300. —— The valley whose name is Death... Pasadena, San Pasqual press, 1940. 122 p. map. "Bibliographies": p. 71–122.
C CBb CHi CInI CL CLSU CLU CLod CMerCL CO CRic CSalCL CSbr CSd CSfSC CSj CSjC CSmH CU-B CViCL MoS NN

2301. Ellenbecker, John G. The Jayhawkers of Death valley... Marysville, Kan., 1938. 130 p. illus., ports.
C CHi CInI CL CLU CO CRedl CSmH CStbS CU-B NN

2302. —— —— Supplement... [n.p., 1942?] 5 p. inserted at end. CL CO CSmH CU-B

2303. Evans, Charles Benjamin Shaffer. "The Death valley story of '49", outline no. 1. [1950?] 60 l. Reproduced from typew. copy.   C

2304. Federal writers' project. California. ... Death valley; a guide... Bost., Houghton, 1939. 75 p. illus., map. (Am. guide ser.) Bibliography: p. [71]
Available in many California libraries and CoU MiD NN OrU UPB

2305. Gilbert, Edward M. Panamint legend. L.A., Hesperus press, [c1957] 16 p. illus.   C CP

2306. Glasscock, Carl Burgess. Here's Death Valley ... Indianapolis, Bobbs [c1940] 329 p. illus., ports.
Available in many California libraries and MiD MoS NN NjN

2307. Goff, Francis Willis. Death valley bibliography. Sacramento, June 1934. 20 l. Typew.   C

2308. Hanna, Phil Townsend. Death valley tales ... [Palm Desert, Desert mag. press, 1955] 59 p. (Death valley '49ers, inc. Pub. no. 3)
                    C CInI CL CLU CU-B

2309. Houston, Eleanor Jordan. Death valley Scotty told me— With drawings by Margaret M. Bridwell. [Louisville, Ky.? 1954] 106 p. illus.
C CInI CL CO CRedCL CSS CSd CSjC CSluCL CStmo CViCL KyU

2310. —— Same. 2d ed. [1955] 106 p. illus., ports.
                                        CU-B CViCL

2311. Hufford, David Andrew. Death valley; Swamper Ike's traditional lore: why, when, how?... L.A., Author, 1902. 43 p. illus., ports.
C CBb CCoron CHi CInI CL CLSU CLU CO CSf CSfMI CU-B

2312. Jaeger, Edmund Carroll. Naturalist's Death valley. Pen sketches by Edmund C. Jaeger, Morris Van Dame; photographs by M. Curtis Armstrong. Palm Desert [1957] 68 p. illus. (Death valley '49ers, inc. Pub. no. 5)   C CHi CU-B

2313. Kern county. Superintendent of schools. Death valley, 1941. Hand set and printed by Jay and Elizabeth Dresser. [Bakersfield? 1941]   CBaK

2314. Kirk, Ruth. Exploring Death valley, a guide for tourists. Photographs by Louie Kirk. Stanford [1956] 82 p. illus., ports., maps.
Available in many California libraries and MiD NN UPB

2315. Lee, Bourke. Death valley... N.Y., Macmillan, 1930. 210 p. illus. Bibliography: p. 209–210.
Available in many libraries.

2316. —— Death valley men... N.Y., Macmillan, 1932. 319 p.
Available in many libraries.

2317. Long, Margaret. The shadow of the arrow... Caldwell, Ida., Caxton, 1941. 310 p. illus., maps. Bibliography: p. [303]–306.
Available in many California libraries and MoS NN

2318. —— Same. Rev. and enl. ed. 1950. 354 p. illus., ports., maps. Bibliography: p. [340]–345.
Available in many California libraries and IHi MiD OU UHi UPB

2319. Lorton, William B. Over the Salt Lake trail in the fall of '49; introduction by John B. Goodman III. L.A., Priv. print., 1957. [13] p. illus. (Scraps of Californiana, no. 3)   CHi CL CP

2320. MacKellar, Christine Poole. The history of Death valley, 1849–1933. [Berkeley, 1941] Thesis (M.A.) – Univ. of Calif., 1941.   CU

2321. Manly, William Lewis. Death valley in '49 ... San Jose, Pac. tree & vine co., 1894. 498 p. illus., port.
Available in many libraries.

2322. —— Same. Ed. by Milo Milton Quaife. Chicago, R. R. Donnelley & sons co., 1927. 307 p. front., map. (Lakeside classics)
Available in many libraries.

2323. —— Same. N.Y., Santa Barbara, W. Hebberd, c1929. 523 p. illus.
Available in many libraries.

2324. —— Same. Centennial ed. with introduction by Carl I. Wheat. L.A., Borden pub. co., 1949. 540 p. illus., maps.
CInI CL CLS CLSU CLU CLob CMon CO CRcS CSal CSdS CSfCSM CStrCL CU-B

2325. —— The Jayhawkers' oath and other sketches. Selected and ed. by Arthur Woodward. L.A., Warren F. Lewis, 1949. 170 p. illus., maps.
Available in many libraries.

2326. Merrill, Orin S. "Mysterious Scott," the Monte Cristo of Death valley, and tracks of a tenderfoot ... Chicago, Merrill, c1906. 210 p. illus., map.
C CL CLS CLSU CLU CP CSmH CU-B

2327. Milligan, Clarence P. Death valley and Scotty... L.A., Ward Ritchie, 1942. 194 p.
C CBb CHi CL CLO CLSU CNa CO CRedl CRic CSd CSdS CSf CSmH NN

2328. Norman, Sidney. Chasing rainbows in Death valley... L.A., L.A. mining review, 1909. 32 p. illus., ports.   CLSM

2329. Palmer, Theodore Sherman. Chronology of the Death valley region in California; 1849–1949; an index of events, persons and publications connected with its history. [Wash., D.C., B.S. Adams, print.] 1952. 25 p.
C CBaB CInI CL CLO CLSM CLU CLob CO CSd CSf CU-B

2330. —— Place names of the Death valley region in California and Nevada... [n.p.] 1948. 80 p.
C CHi CInI CL CLO CLU CSd CSfCSM CSmH CU-B

2331. Panamint mining and concentration works. Prospectus. Tinted lithograph view of the Panamint range mountains, 30 by 14 inches, folded in original printed wrappers with 7 pages of text. S.F., 1875.
                                            CL CU-B

2332. Parsons, George Whitwell. A thousand mile desert trip and story of the "Desert sign post"... L.A. [Times mirror] 1918. 16 p. illus.
                            CL CLU CSmH CStmo

2333. Perkins, Edna (Brush) The white heart of Mojave; an adventure with the outdoors of the desert... N.Y., Boni & Liveright [c1922] 229 p. illus.
Available in many libraries.

2334. Powers, Professor. "Death valley" land of mystery. Millions in sight. Suggestions to prospectors. [L.A., Efficiency print. co.] 1919. 11 p. illus.
                                        CSmH CU-B

2335. Putnam, George Palmer. Death valley and its country... N.Y., Duell [1946] 231 p.
Available in many libraries.

2336. —— Death valley handbook. N.Y., Duell [c1947] 84 p. map.
Available in many libraries.

2337. Scott, Walter. Death valley Scotty rides again;

tales told by Death valley Scotty, winter of 1952–1953, at Scotty's castle. [2d ed. Death Valley, 1955] 59 p. illus.

    C CInI CL CLO CLU CSd CSf

2338. Shannon, Thomas. Thomas Shannon's journey of peril. With the Jayhawkers in Death valley fifty-three years ago... San Jose, 1903. 2 l.   CU-B

2339. Spears, John Randolph. Illustrated sketches of Death valley and other borax deserts of the Pacific coast... Chicago & N.Y., Rand McNally, 1892. 226 p. illus., map.

    C C-S CBb CHi CInI CL CLO CLSU CLU CP CPom CSd CSf CSfCSM CSfP CSfWF-H CSj CSmH CU-B IHi MiD MoS NN

2340. Stephens, Lorenzo Dow. Life sketches of a Jayhawker of '49... [San Jose, Nolta bros.] 1916. 68 p. illus., ports.

    C CBb CHi CL CLO CLSU CLU CSfWF-H CSmH CU-B CaBViPA

2341. U.S. National park service. ... Death valley national monument, California... Wash., D.C., Govt. print. off., 1934–[38?] 2 v. illus.

    CLSU CStmo CU-B

2342. Walker, Ardis M. Freeman junction...the escape route of the Mississippians and Georgians from Death valley in 1849... published for the dedication of the Freeman junction monument on November 9, 1961, by the Death valley '49ers, inc. San Bernardino, Inland print. and engraving co., 1961. 16 p. illus.   CHi

2343. —— The Manly map and the Manly story. Palm Desert, Desert mag. press, 1954. 24 p. fold. map, facsim. (Death valley '49ers, inc. Pub. no. 2)

    C CBaB CHi CInI CL CLSM CLU CLob CP CSd CSfCSM CU-B

2344. Wallace, William James, and Taylor, Edith S. The surface archaeology of Butte Valley, Death Valley national monument. L.A., Archaeological research associates, 1956. 15 l. illus.   CLU

2345. Weeks, Ernest Albert. Death valley...a brief history of early passage to goldfields. Morrill, Neb., J. W. Snyder [1941] 68 p.   NN

2346. Weight, Harold. Lost mines of Death valley. Map by Norton Allen. 1st ed. Twenty nine Palms, Calico press [1953] 72 p. illus. (Southwest panorama no. 2)

Available in many California libraries and MiD MoS UPB

2347. —— Twenty mule team days in Death valley. With some observations on the natural history of mules and muleskinners, and the mining of desert borax, and a reprint of Henry G. Hanks' report on Death valley, 1883. Twentynine Palms, Calico press [1955] 44 p. illus., ports., map. (Southwest panorama, no. 3)

    C CBaB CHi CL CLU CLob CO CRcS CSbCL CSd CSdS CSfCSM CSto CViCL CU-B KyU MoS UPB

2348. —— William B. Rood, Death valley 49er, Arizona pioneer, Apache fighter, river ranchero and the treasure of ruined "Los Yumas." Twentynine Palms, Calico press [1959] [32] p. illus., ports., map. Reprinted from *Calico print*, Aug.-Sept., 1952 with additional material.   CHi CL CSbCL

2349. Wilson, Neill Compton. Silver stampede; the career of Death valley's hell-camp, Old Panamint... N.Y., Macmillan, 1937. 319 p. illus., ports.

Available in many libraries.

2350. Wolff, John Eliot. Route of the Manly party

of 1849–50 in leaving Death valley for the coast... [Pasadena? 1931] 29 p. illus.

    C CHi CL CLO CLU CO CSfSC CSmH CStmo CU-B MoS

KERN COUNTY
(Organized in 1866 from portions of Los Angeles and Tulare counties)

COUNTY HISTORIES

2351. Comfort, Herbert G. Where rolls the Kern; a history of Kern county, California... Moorpark, Enterprise press, 1934. 241 p.

    C CB CBaK CHi CL CLSU CLU CP CPom CSmH CStb CU-B CVtCL ICN NN

2352. Historical records survey. California. ... Kern county (Bakersfield) ... S.F., Northern Calif. hist. records survey, 1941. 2 v. illus. (Inventory of the county archives of Calif. no. 15) Mimeo.

    C CBaK CBb CF CFS (v.2) CHi CLCM CLCo (v.2) CLO CLSM CLU CMary CMont (v.2) CO (v.2) COMC CPa CSS (v.2) CSf (v.2) CSfCP CSfCSM (v.2) CSjCL CSluCL CSmH (v.2) CSrCL CStclU CU-B (v.2) ICN WHi

2353. History of Kern county, California, with illustrations descriptive of its scenery, farms, residences, public buildings...with biographical sketches. S.F., Elliott, 1883. 226 p. illus., map.   C CBaK CHi CU-B

2354. Miller, Thelma (Bernard) History of Kern county, California, with personal sketches... Chicago, Clarke, 1929. 2 v. illus., ports. v.2, biographical.

    C CBaB CBaK CFS CHi CSf CU-B NN

2355. Morgan, Wallace Melvin. History of Kern county, California, with biographical sketches... L.A., Historic record co., 1914. 1556 p. illus., ports.

    C CBaB CBaK CCH CFS CGl CHi CL CLAC CLCM CLSU CLU CLob CO CPg CRic CSdS CSf CSmH CSto CU-B CViCL CVtCL CtY In MWA MiD-B WHi

GREAT REGISTER

2356. Kern county. Index to the Great register of the county of Kern. 1866– Place of publication and title vary.

    C has 1867, 1872–73, 1875, 1877, 1879, 1880 (biennially to)– 1962. CHi has 1879–80, 1882. CL has 1873 (suppl.), 1875–76, 1877 (suppl.), 1879, 1882 (biennially to)– 1890. CLU has 1880. CSmH has [1867], 1872–73, 1879–80, 1882. CU-B has 1867, 1868 (suppl.), 1872, Jan., Aug. 1873, Apr., Aug. 1879, 1880, Nov. 1940.

DIRECTORIES

2357. Bensel, Maitland & co.'s Bakersfield and Kern county directory for the years 1891/2. Bakersfield, 1891.   CU-B

2358. Kern county. Chamber of commerce. Industrial directory [of Kern county] 1947 [with 1948 supplement] Bakersfield.   CFS

Bakersfield

2359. 1902– Bakersfield and Kern City directory, 1902–1905; 1907–1908.   CBaK

2360. 1906– Kingsbury's...directory of Bakersfield and Kern City... 1906–07– [Bakersfield] A. Kingsbury & co., c1906– 1 v.   CU-B

2361. 1910– Polk-Husted directory co., pub. Bakersfield city directory, 1910–
    C-S has 1911.

2362. 1915– Polk, R. L., & co., pub. Polk's Bakersfield city directory... L.A., 1915–
CHi has 1915, 1919–26, 1928–30, 1932–36, 1938, 1940, 1948–49, 1951–52, 1954– CSmat has 1958–59. CU–B has 1925, 1937.

2363. 1942. A.B.C. directory, pub. Greater Bakersfield directory. [Bakersfield] 1942.   CBaK

2364. Bakersfield. Church of Jesus Christ of latter-day saints, comp. Directory of Bakersfield stake of the Church of latter-day saints. Bakersfield, 1956.
CFS

Other Cities and Towns

2365. 1950– Clark, John H., comp. and pub. Delano city directory. Arcadia, 1950–   CBaK

2366. 1958– Delano-McFarland city directory. Arcadia, 1958–   CBaK

2367. 1958– Polk, R. L., & co., pub. Polk's Delano-McFarland city directory including Earlimart, Pond and Richgrove. L.A., 1958–
CHi has 1958, 1960.

2368. 1939– Penner, J., comp. and pub. Directory of Shafter and vicinity. 1939–   CBaK

2369. 1926– Polk, R. L., & co., pub. Taft city directory, including Fellows and Maricopa. L.A., 1926–
Publisher and title vary: 1926–48, Polk-Husted directory co., Taft, Ford City, Fellows and Maricopa directory.
CBaK has 1926, 1949, 1952–60. CHi has 1949, 1952–55, 1956–58. CL has 1952–55.

2370. 1957– City directory service company, pub. Taft, Oildorado city of opportunity...1957–
CBaK has 1957–58.

2371. 1940– Wasco news, comp. Directory of the city of Wasco. Shafter pub. co., 1940– Title varies: 1940, Directory of Wasco and vicinity including Lost Hills. Publisher varies.
CBaK has 1940, 1957.

GENERAL REFERENCES

2372. American association of university women. Inyokern–China Lake branch. Indian Wells valley, a handbook. China Lake, 1948. illus.
C CBaK CHi CLSU CU-B

2373. —— —— Same. [1953] 89 p. illus., map.
CLU CStmo

2374. —— —— 3d ed. 1960. 87 p. illus.   CHi

2375. Apperson, Byron Hays. A study of delinquency trends in Kern county, California, 1934 to 1954. Fresno, 1956. 69 l. tables. Thesis (M.A.)– Fresno state college, 1956.   CFS

2376. Armstrong, H. K. Estimate of Kern county land company future royalty oil, income, and earnings as of November 1, 1939. L.A., 1939. 80 l. map.   CLU

2377. Automobile club of southern California. Touring bureau. Kern county... [L.A.,? 191–?] 32 p. illus.   CU-B

2378. Bailey, Richard C. Historic chronology of Kern county. 3d ed. [Bakersfield? 1960] 11 p.   CU-B

2379. Bakersfield Californian. Bakersfield and Kern county; the financial and commercial center of the greatest oil and agricultural region in the west... Bakersfield, 1912? 136 p.   C CBaK

2380. —— Special railroad edition, March 1895. Bakersfield [Kern pub. co.] 1895. 28 p. illus., ports., map.   C

2381. Barlow & Hill, Bakersfield. California oil fields; up-to-date indexed maps. Kern river, Coalinga, Sunset, Midway and McKittrick, the world's largest oil fields. Bakersfield [1908] 31 p. maps.
CHi CSfSO CU-B CViCL

2382. —— Same. c1910. 33 p. fold. maps.
CSfSO CU-B

2383. Blythin, Margaret Allewelt. The Kern diaries, 1848–1849; a contribution to western history. [Berkeley, 1940] Thesis (M.A.)– Univ. of Calif., 1940.
CU

2384. Bonsal, Stephen. Edward Fitzgerald Beale, a pioneer in the path of empire, 1822–1903. N.Y., Putnam, 1912. 312 p. illus., ports.
C CBaB CBaK CHi CL CLO CLSU CLU CO CRic CSS CSalCL CSd CSf CSfP CSmH CSmat CStbS CU-B OrU

2385. Burola, Nathan, vs. Kern county land co. In the Superior court of the state of California, in and for the county of Kern. Nathan Burola, administrator of the estate of Jose Antonio Dominguez, deceased, plaintiff, vs. Kern county land company...defendants. Santa Barbara, 1939. 5 v. of depositions. Typew.   CHi

2386. California. Committee to survey the agricultural labor resources of the San Joaquin valley. Transcript of public hearing, August 1, 1950, Bakersfield, California. [Sacramento, State print. off., 1950] 153 l. Mimeo.   CLU CViCL

2387. —— Superior court (Kern county) In the Superior court, county of Kern, State of California. Charles Lux, et al., plaintiffs, vs. James B. Haggin, et al., defendants. Decision of Hon. B. Brundage, judge. Delivered in open court, Nov. 3, 1881. [n.p., 1881] 33 p. Suit over riparian rights.   CLU

2388. —— Supreme court. In the Supreme court of the state of California, in bank. Charles Lux, et al., vs. James B. Haggin, et al. Opinion filed April 26, 1886. Stetson & Houghton, plaintiffs' attorneys. McAllister & Bergin, of counsel. Louis T. Haggin defendant's attorney. Garber, Thornton & Bishop, Flournoy & Mhoon of counsel. [S.F.? 1886] 139 p. Majority opinion written by Judge McKinstry.   CLU

2389. —— —— Same. [Including decision] in bank of October 27, 1884. Sacramento, State print., 1886. 181 p.   CHi CLU

2390. Camp (S. A.) companies. The history and development of the S. A. Camp companies of the San Joaquin valley. [Bakersfield, 1958?] 1 v.   C

2391. Columbian oil co. Wells in Kern river district, Kern county, California... [Oakland, Baker print. co., 1900] 51 p. mounted photos.   CFS

2392. Conner, Robert L. Kern county, California ... S.F., Sunset mag. homeseekers' bur. [1910?] 32 p. illus.   C CL CU-B

2393. Cooper, Margaret Aseman. Land, water, and settlement in Kern county, California: 1850–1890. [Berkeley, 1954] Thesis (M.A.)– Univ. of Calif., 1954.
CU

2394. Crites, Arthur S. Pioneer days in Kern county. L.A., Ward Ritchie, 1951. 279 p. illus.
C C-S CBaB CFS CHi CL CLO CLSM CLU CLob CP CPom CSmH CU-B CViCL

2395. Crowe, Earle. Men of El Tejon; empire in the Tehachapis. L.A., Ward Ritchie, 1957. 165 p. illus. Includes bibliography.
Available in many California libraries and NN

2396. Daughters of the American revolution.

California genealogical records committee. Abstract of wills, probate court, Kern county, California. Early marriage records...Copied by Bakersfield chapter... [Bakersfield] 1952. 63 l. Typew. The wills are of the period 1876 to 1899; the marriage licenses are of the period 1850–1900.   C CL

2397. Deadrich, E. Report on the organization review of the county of Kern... S.F., 1956.   CBaK

2398. The Delano record. Souvenir war album, dedicated to the service men and women of Delano, Earlimart, Pixley and McFarland. Delano, 1945. [76] p. ports.   CU-B

2399. Dunn, Arthur. Kern county, California. [S.F., Sunset pub. house, 1912?] 30 p. illus., map.
                                                      CHi

2400. —— Same. [S.F., 1914?] 64 p. illus., maps.
        CBaK CHi CL CLU CU-B NN

2401. Dunn, Cecil Letts, and Neff, Philip. The Arvin area of Kern county, an economic survey of the southeastern San Joaquin valley in relation to land use and the size and distribution of income. Prepared for the Board of supervisors of Kern county... [n.p.] 1947. 59, [78] l.   CLO

2402. Etcheverry, Bernard Alfred. Water supply from Central valley project required for lands in the Kern county. Dec. 31, 1938.   CBaK

2403. Evans, Kristiane Skjerve. An educational survey of Kern county, California. [Berkeley, 1918] Thesis (M.A.) – Univ. of Calif., 1918.   CU

2404. Ferguson, Jack E. Camp Arvin; a short description of the camp, its founding, people, and its social and administrative organization from 1935 through 1939. [Sacramento] 1958. 26 l. tables, diagrs. Typew. "A paper submitted... in the Division of social sciences at Sacramento state college." Bibliography.   C

2405. Fowler, Harlan Davey. Camels to California; a chapter in western transportation. Stanford [1950] 93 p. illus., port., map. (Stanford transportation ser., 7)
    CBea CHi CLO CLSM CLU CLgA CNF CNa COnC CP CRcS CSd CSf CSjC CSmH CSt CVtV

2406. [Fox, Charles P.] Kern county, California ... [S.F., Sunset press, 1905?] [16] p. illus.   CU-B

2407. Giffen, Helen S., and Woodward, Arthur. The story of El Tejon... L.A., Dawson's bk. shop, 1942. 146 p. illus., port., maps.
    C CBaB CBaK CHi CL CLSU CLU CO CSf CSfCP CSfCW CSmH CU-B CViCL NN

2408. Goldschmidt, Walter Rochs. As you sow. N.Y., Harcourt [c1947] 288 p. illus. Comparative study of three agricultural communities in Kern and Tulare counties.
Available in many libraries.

2409. —— Large farms or small: The social side. Paper prepared for the annual meeting of the Western farm economics association, 1944. Mimeo. Comparison of Arvin and Dinuba.   CBaK

2410. —— Small business and the community, a study in central valley of California on effects of scale of farm operations. Report of the Special committee to study problems of American small business, United States Senate...1946. 139 p. illus., maps. (79th Cong., 2d sess. S. committee print no. 13) Comparative study of Arvin and Dinuba.
    CBaK CChiS CL CLU CSdS CSfSt CU-B

2411. —— Social structure of a California rural com-

munity... [Berkeley, 1942] 271 l. Typew. Thesis (Ph.D.) – Univ. of Calif., 1942. Community of Wasco.
                                                      CBaK

2412. [Haggin, James Ben Ali] comp. The desert lands of Kern County, Cal. Affidavits of various residents of said county. Also report of General G. S. Alexander, Col. Geo. H. Mendell and Prof. Geo. Davidson. S.F., C. H. Street, 1877. 306 p. maps.
                        C CSmH CU-B NHi

2413. —— Kern valley lands...for sale by Land department of J. B. Haggin... [Bakersfield, 189–?] folded sheet. maps.   CU-B

2414. Hart, Leo B. [Our conquest]. A report on the development of Kern county rural schools, 1939–1946. Bakersfield [1947?] unp. illus., ports., maps.
                                          CBaK CLSU

2415. Henderson, John Dale, comp. Bibliography of Kern county; a preliminary list. [n.p.] 1937. 52 l. Typew. "Appendix, regarding Fort Tejon and vicinity, bibliography, by Arthur Woodward."   C

2416. Historic Kern. Kern county historical society, Kern county museum, Fairgrounds, Bakersfield. v.1, 1949–
CBaB has v.1– CBaK has v.1– CHi has v.1– CU-B has v.1–11. NbHi has v.4 no. 3, Jan. 1953.

2417. Immigration association of California. [County scrapbooks] [S.F., 188–?]   C

2418. Irvine, Leigh Hadley. Kern, land of the sun. Bakersfield [Coats print. co.] 1925. 24 p.
                                        C CBaK CSf

2419. Kern county. Agricultural commissioner. Agriculture in the golden empire of Kern; Kern county agriculture crops report, 1939. Bakersfield, 1939. 31 p. illus., map.   CRcS

2420. —— **Board of supervisors.** New issue of Kern county bonds, bids to be received by the county treasurer of Kern county, until 12 o'clock, Sept. 9, 1889... Bakersfield, 1889. 18 p.   C-S

2421. —— **Board of trade.** Cities and towns of Kern county. Bakersfield, 1958.   CBaK

2422. —— —— Kern county, California. Bakersfield, Echo print. [1905?] 30 p. illus.   CU-B

2423. —— —— Kern county, California views. Bakersfield [1912] 134 p. illus.   CBaB

2424. —— —— The spirit of Bakersfield and Kern, Kern county, California. [By A. W. MacRae and others] [Bakersfield, Kern valley print. works, 1908]   CBaB

2425. —— **Chamber of commerce.** The golden empire of Kern. Bakersfield [1939] 21 p. illus., maps. Other editions followed.
            CFS (1941, 1953?) CHi (1941) CRcS

2426. —— —— Joseph Di Giorgio: a tribute... sponsored by the Kern county Chamber of commerce and the Kern county Board of Supervisors. [Bakersfield, Bakersfield Californian, 1937] 42 p. illus., ports.
                                          C CSmH

2427. —— —— Kern county, California; a presentation of its resources and attractions...written by John L. Gill... Bakersfield, Stewart print. co. [1920?] 96 p. illus.   CBaK CHi

2428. —— —— Kern county, California, the market basket of southern California. Bakersfield [1930?] folder (12 p.) illus., map.   CRcS

2429. —— —— Kern county cotton. Bakersfield, 1934. folder (4 p.) illus.   CRcS

2430. —— —— Kern county pictorial... [Bakersfield? 1937?] [60] p. illus., map.   C   CBak   CHi   CLU   CSf   CSmH   CU-B

2431. —— —— Kern county welcomes home seekers. Bakersfield [1922?] folder (10 p.) illus., map.   CRcS

2432. —— Towns of Kern county. Bakersfield, 1927.   CBaK

2433. —— Citizens. A community aroused. [Bakersfield? 1947?] [40] p. illus., ports., facsims. "Kern county's answer to one portion...of a syndicated column written by Harold L. Ickes...on Thursday, November 27, 1947;" submitted by a special citizens' committee investigating Di Giorgio farms; Walter Kane, chairman.   C   CLU   CU-B

2434. —— Committee on county exhibit, Mechanics institute fair. ...A short descriptive sketch of Kern county. [Bakersfield, 1887] 8 p.   C-S   CU-B

2435. —— Grand jury. [Report of findings and recommendations regarding the government of Kern county] Bakersfield, 1951. 14 p.   CU-B

2436. —— —— ...Reports of the grand jury and expert Edgar Moore, made to the Superior court of Kern county on the thirty-first day of October, 1895. Bakersfield, A. C. Maude, 1895. 144 p.   CLU   CSmH

2437. —— Planning commission. Boron plan project, 1959. Bakersfield, 1959.   CBaK

2438. —— —— Shafter plan project, 1959. Bakersfield, 1959.   CBaK

2439. —— —— Tehachapi plan project, 1959. Bakersfield, 1959.   CBaK

2440. —— Superintendent of schools. Desert trek. Bakersfield, 1959.   CBaK

2441. —— —— Kern county; a resource guide for teachers. Bakersfield, 1955. illus., maps. Loose-leaf.   CBaK   CFS

2442. —— —— A report on the development of Kern county rural schools, 1939–1946. Bakersfield [1946?] unp. illus. Reproduced from typew. copy.   CFS

2443. —— —— ...Source materials for use in the study of the unit, Kern county Indians. Bakersfield, 1944. 38 p. illus. (Social studies bul., no. 1, Aug. 1944)   CBaK

2444. —— Superior court. Oil lands case. [Bakersfield, Bakersfield Californian] 1901.   CBaK

2445. Kern county, California, in the delta of Kern river... S.F., Sunset press [1905] 16 p. illus.   CHi   CU-B

2446. Kern county employee's association. Kern county government: districts and departments. 1948.   CBaK

2447. Kern county historical society. Annual publication. no. 1–1935– Bakersfield, 1935– Contents: 1. In the south San Joaquin ahead of Garcés...by Herbert Eugene Bolton.—2. El camino viejo á Los Angeles...by Frank Forrest Latta.—3. History of Kern county newspapers, by Alfred Harrell.—Early days in Kern county, by S. A. Woody.—4. Sierra prologue: recollections of the Kern frontier, by Ardis Manly Walker.—5. Notes on the life of Edward M. Kern, by H. A. Spindt.—Alexis Godey in Kern county, by F. F. Latta.—6. Old adobes of forgotten Fort Tejon, by Clarence C. Cullimore.—7. Story of Colonel Thomas Baker and the founding of Bakersfield, by Naomi E. Bain.—8. Francisco Garcés, pioneer padre of Kern, by Ardis Manly Walker.—9. Excavation of a Yokuts Indian cemetery, Elk Hills, Kern county, by Edwin Francis Walker.—10. Historic county of Kern, by Glendon J. Rodgers. —11. Old adobes of forgotten Fort Tejon. Rev. and enl., by Clarence C. Cullimore.—12. Upper San Joaquin valley, by Genevieve (Kratka) Magruder. — 13. Collector's choice; the McLeod basket collection, by Richard C. Bailey.—14. Land of Havilah, 1854–1874, by William Harland Boyd.—15. Edward M. Kern, the travels of an artist-explorer, by William J. Heffernan. — 16. A California martyr's bones, by Clarence C. Cullimore.—17. San Joaquin vignettes, by John Barker.—18. Kern's desert, by Erma Peirson.—19. Spanish trailblazers in the south San Joaquin, 1772–1816, by Jesse D. Stockton.—20. Heritage of Kern, by Richard C. Bailey.—21. The McKittrick ranch, by Calhoun Collins.—22. Explorations in Kern, by Richard C. Bailey.—23. A journey into the past, by John B. Dowty.—24. General Beale's sheep odyssey, by Earle Crowe.—24a. Garlock memories, by Paul B. Hubbard.— 25. Kern panorama...1866–1900, by Ralph F. Kreiser and Thomas Hunt.—26. Explorations in Kern, by Richard C. Bailey. [2d ed.]

CBaK has complete file. Other California libraries have scattered numbers. CoD (no. 6, 11) MWA (no. 7, 13–14, 18, 20) MiD (no. 18) N (no. 6) NN (no. 3–5)

2448. Kern county land company. The cost of making a settler's home in the famous Kern delta... [Bakersfield, Californian print., 1894] 13 p. illus.   CL   CU-B

2449. —— Greatest irrigated farm in the world. S.F., Crocker [1893?] 24 p. illus.   CBaK   CU-B

2450. —— The Kern county land company (incorporated)... [S.F., Crocker] c1892. 3 v. illus., maps. (Kern county ser., no. 1–3)   CHi   CL   CLU   CSmH

2451. —— ...The peach in Kern county. S.F., Britton & Rey, litho., c1890?] [4] p. illus.   CU-B

2452. —— Report...1938– [S.F., 1938–
CHi has 1945, 1948–51, 1953, 1955–56. CL has 1954–60. CSmH has 1938–date. CU-B has 1938–47.

2453. Kern herald. Kern county industrial and black gold edition. Bakersfield, 1940. 32 p. illus.   CBaK

2454. Kern valley colony. Homes in Kern county ...plan of a colony... S.F., Joseph Winterburn & co., print. & electrotypers, 1878. 32 p. maps.   CHi   CLU   CU-B

2455. Kern valley oil company. Prospectus of the Kern valley oil company, San Francisco, California, incorporated under laws of South Dakota, March 5, 1901. [Oakland, Baker print. co., 1901] 12 p. fold. map.   CU-B

2456. Kroeger, Louis J., and associates. Administrative organization and practices, Kern county, California; a report. S.F., 1952. 12 v.   CBaK

2457. Laton. Chamber of commerce. Where would you like to live? If you live where you like, it is likely you would like to live in Laton. [Laton, 19—?] folder ([24] p.) illus., map.   CU-B

2458. Levick, M. B. Kern county, California. S.F., Sunset mag. homeseekers' bur. [1911?] 48 p.   CHi

2459. Lux, Charles, et al., vs. Haggin, James B., et al. ...In the Superior court for Kern county, state of California. Charles Lux et al. vs. J. B. Haggin et al. ... [S.F.? 1881?] 4 v. illus.   CSfCP   CU-B

2460. —— Same. [S.F.? 1882–85] 10 v.   CU-B

2461. —— In the Superior court for Kern county,

state of California [no. 214] Charles Lux, et al., vs. J. B. Haggin, et al. Argument of Hall McAllister, esq., counsel for plaintiffs. [n.p., 1881?] 159 p.   CLU CViCL

2462. —— Water rights no. 214: Charles Lux vs. J. B. Haggin, et al., in equity, before Hon. B. Brundage, judge, etc. [n.p., n.d.] 76 p.   C-S

2463. McCoy, Ray S., jr. History and economics of the California cotton industry. Claremont, 1954. Thesis (M.A.)—Claremont men's college, 1954.   CBaK

2464. Miller, Henry. Contract and agreement between Henry Miller and other of the first part, and James B. Haggin and others of the second part. [n.p., 1888] [24] p.   CBaK CLU CU-B

2465. Miramonte colony association, San Francisco. Miramonte colony association in the heart of the great artesian belt, Kern county, California. [n.p., 1887?] [4] p.   CHi

2466. Molander, Ruth Emilia. A study of 101 migrant families receiving assistance under the regulations of the California aid-to-needy-children law, in Kern county in June, 1940. [Berkeley, 1943] Thesis (M.A.)—Univ. of Calif., 1943.   CU

2467. Morning echo, Bakersfield. Progress edition and review of the oil industry. Bakersfield, 1911. [112] p. illus., ports.   C CBaK

2468. Oildale news. Bakersfield earthquake. Souvenir edition. Oildale, Oildale print. co., 1952. illus.   CBaK

2469. Oriental mining co., New York. [Prospectus ...of the company at Havilah, Kern county, California. N.Y., 1880] [2] p.   CHi

2470. Petersdorf, C. F., von. The mineral resources of Kern county, California. Bakersfield, Californian print, 1895. 51 p. illus.   CSfCSM

2471. Petroleum reporter, Taft. Souvenir number, the California oilfields in pictures "as was" and "as is." Taft, 1926. 56 p. illus., ports.   CHi

2472. Porter, David Dixon. Daily journal kept on the camel deck of the U.S. ship *Supply*. 1936. 19 p. Typew.   CSd CU-B

2473. Poso irrigation district. Mortgage of the Poso irrigation district to the California safe deposit and trust company of San Francisco. Executed September 16th, 1893. [S.F.? 1893] 39 p.   CSmH

2474. —— Poso irrigation district: location, Kern county, California, on the line of the Southern Pacific railroad, near Delano. Organized September, 1888. [Prospectus] [n.p., 1892?] 27 p.   CLU

2475. Randall & Denne, pub. Index atlas of Kern county, California; containing over five million acres of land...showing the boundary and ownership of each piece of land separately... [San Jose? c1901] 70 p. illus., maps.   CHi

2476. Robinson, William Wilcox. The story of Kern county. Bakersfield, Title insurance & trust co., 1961. 64 p. illus., map.   CHi CLSM CLU CSmH CU-B

2477. Rodgers, Glendon J. Exploring Kern county. S.F., Fearon pub., inc., 1960. 59 p. illus.   CHi

2478. —— Kern is our home. [Bakersfield?, 1950] 125 p. illus., ports. Bibliography: p. 123–125.
CBaB CBaK CFS CHi CLO CLU CO CSmH NN

2479. —— Same. [3d rev. print.] [1953] 132 p. illus., ports., maps. Bibliography: p. 130–132.   CL

2480. —— Know your Kern county. S.F., Fearon pub., inc. [c1961] 72 p. illus.   CHi

2481. —— Stories along the Kern. [S.F., Fearon pub., 1958] 103 p. illus.   CFS CHi CSluCL CViCL

2482. Settle, Glen A. Tropico: Red Hill with a glamorous history of gold. Also, chronological review of the Antelope valley. Rosamond, Priv. print., 1959. 16 p.
CHi CLSM CLU CSmH CU-B

2483. Settlers' experience in Kern county, California, as related by themselves, with advice to newcomers. Bakersfield, Californian print., 1894. 58 p. Reprinted from prize letters appearing in the *Californian*.   CSmH

2484. Sierra club, San Francisco. The Kings river region should be a national park. S.F., 1939. 15 p. illus., map.   CSmH CU-B

2485. Spindt, Herman A. The Butterfield stage route in Kern county, 1858–1861. Presented to the Kern county hist. soc., May 29, 1934. 32 p. Typew.   CBaK

2486. The spirit of Bakersfield and Kern, Kern county, California. [Bakersfield, Kern valley print. works] 1908. [88] p. illus. (part col.) port.   C CBaK

2487. Stacey, May Humphreys. Uncle Sam's camels ...ed. by Lewis Burt Lesley... Cambridge, Mass., Harvard, 1929. 298 p. illus., ports., map.
Available in many California libraries and CaBViPA

2488. Stockton, Jesse D. History of Kern county. In: Those who serve. Comp. by Frank S. Reynolds post no. 26, American legion of Bakersfield... p. 13–55.
CBaB CBaK

2489. Stone, Leila O. Old Bull road over Greenhorn mountains, 1856–1948. [McCloud, 1948] 14 l. 24 pl. map. Reproduced from typew. copy. The plates are mounted photos. with manuscript annotations.   C

2490. Stretch, Richard H. [Report on Erskine creek mines] Havilah, 1876. 10 p. maps, diagr. Ms.   C

2491. Success gold mining and reduction co. [Prospectus. L.A., n.d.] [12] p. illus., fold. map. Cover title: Randsburg mines of the Success gold mining and reduction company.   CLU

2492. Taft. Chamber of commerce. Taft, the heart of black gold. 1920. 96 p. illus., ports.   CSfCSM

2493. Tejon ranch co., Bakersfield. Annual report.
CL has 1950–60. CSmH has 1950– date.

2494. —— Story of ranch. Bakersfield [n.d.]   CL

2495. Tracy, Fannie C. (Rowlee). The Tracy saga. By Fannie C. Tracy and Glendon J. Rodgers. [Kern county] Cardon house, 1962. 410 p. illus.
CHi CSmH CU-B

2496. United States vs. Haggin, James B. Testimony taken before the register and receiver of the United States land office. At Visalia, Cal. ...commencing December 3, 1877. 2 v.   CSmH

2497. United States vs. Southern Pacific co., et al. Investigation of well drilling, Kern trading and oil company, Coalinga and Midway-Sunset oil fields, California. United States of America, plaintiff, vs. Southern Pacific company, et al, defendants. In equity no. 46 and in suits A-16, A-24, A-25, A-26, and A-28. S.F., 1916. 70, 32 p. map.   CSfSO

2498. U.S. District court. California. (Southern district, Northern division) Opinion of Judge Benjamin F. Bledsoe. United States of America, plaintiff, vs. Southern Pacific company, et al., defendants. In equity 46 civil A-16, A-24, A-25, A-28. [L.A.?] 1919. 22 p.   CHi

2499. Voegelin, Charles Frederick. A characterization of the Kern river Shoshonean language. [Berkeley, 1933] Thesis (Ph.D.)—Univ. of Calif., 1933.   CU

2500. Walker, David H. Kern county, California. [S.F.,Sunset mag. homeseekers' bur., 1909?] 32 p. illus.   CU-B

2501. Watkins, Carleton E. Photographic views of Kern county, California. S.F. [1889?] 39 pl.   CSmH

2502. Wedel, Waldo Rudolph. ...Archaeological investigations at Buena Vista lake, Kern county, California... Wash., D.C., Govt. print. off., 1941. 194 p. illus., maps. (U.S. Bur. of Am. ethnology. Bul. 130) "Literature cited": p. 169–71, 187–88.
CBaB CBaK CHi CL CLSU CLU CO CRedl CSdS CSfU CSmH CU-B IHi TxU ViU

2503. Weldon. Methodist church. Celebrating the 50th anniversary of the dedication of the original church buildings of Weldon and Kernville community Methodist churches, November 28, 1948... [n.p., 1948?] 21 p. illus., port.   CHi

2504. —— —— In the Master's service at Weldon Methodist church; the story of sixty years of Christian leadership...1886–1946. [n.p.] 1947. [26] p. illus., ports.   CHi

2505. Wells, Andrew Jackson. Kern county, California... Sunset mag. homeseekers' bur. ... [S.F., 1915] 60 p. illus.   CU-B

2506. Whitmore, W. K. Mojave gold mining district [and The Whitmore brothers gold mine. Mojave, 1925] 5 l. Typew.   CU-B

2507. Whitney, Caspar. Charles Adelbert Canfield. N.Y. [Merrymount press] 1930. 217 p. illus., ports.   CBb CLU CSmH CU-B

2508. Who's who in Kern county. 1st–2d, 1940–1941. Bakersfield, Wilson and Peterson, comp. and pub., 1940–41.
CBaK CHi (1940) CLU (1940) CSmH (1940) CU-B (1940)

2509. Williamson, Mary Helen. Unemployment relief administration in Kern county, 1935–1940. [Berkeley, 1941] Thesis (M.A.)—Univ. of Calif., 1941.   CU

2510. Witter, Dean, & co. Kern county land company; a story of science and finance... S.F. [1939] 31 p. illus.   CU-B

2511. —— ...Special report...Kern county land company. [S.F.? 1946] 6 l.   CU-B

2512. Wood, Raymund Francis. The life and death of Peter Lebec. Fresno, Academy lib. guild, 1954. 78 p. illus. Bibliography: p. 76–78.
CBaB CBaK CFS CHi CLO CLU CP CRic CSS CSd CSf CSmH CStmo CSto CStoC CU-B CWhC

2513. Wynn, Marcia Rittenhouse. Desert bonanza; story of early Randsburg, Mojave desert mining camp. Culver City, M.W. Samuelson, 1949. 263 p. illus., map.
Available in many California libraries and MiD NN

2514. —— Pioneer family of Whiskey Flat.... [L.A., Print. by Haynes corp., 1945] 130 p. illus., port.
Available in many California libraries and CoD, MoSHi N NN UPB

Bakersfield

2515. Bakersfield. Charters. Charter of the city of Bakersfield...ratified and approved January 23, 1915... Bakersfield, Bakersfield Californian print. With supplements through 1959.   CBaK

2516. —— **City highway committee.** Thoroughfares report. [Bakersfield, 1956]   CBaK

2517. Bakersfield Californian. Bakersfield story: then and now. Special issue of Saturday, Sept. 12, 1953 showing earthquake damage and rebuilding. Bakersfield, 1953.   CBaK

2518. —— ...Homeseekers' and development number... Bakersfield, 1910. 53 p. illus.   CBaK CU-B

2519. —— Oil serves you...Special oil issue. Bakersfield, 1956.   CBaK

2520. Blodget, Rush Maxwell. Little dramas of old Bakersfield, as seen by a boy and told in after years. L.A., Print. by Carl A. Bundy, 1931. 222 p. illus., map.
C CBaB CBaK CBb CHi CL CLO CLSU CLU CLob CSfP CSmH CStmo CU-B NN

2521. California oil world, Bakersfield. Supplement: Conditions today. Bakersfield, 1910. 80 p. illus., ports.   CBaK

2522. Crites, Arthur S. History of the Rotary club of Bakersfield, no. 717, chartered May 1, 1920. Bakersfield, 1954. 265 p. illus.   CBak CLU

2523. Doctor, Joseph E. Shotguns on Sunday. L.A., Westernlore press [1958] 230 p. illus. (Great west and Indian ser., 14)
CBaB CBaK CBb CFS CHi CLU CRb CRcS CSalCL CSd CSdU CSmH CSto CU-B CViCL

2524. Hopson mortuary. Down memory lane... Bakersfield, Bakersfield Californian, 1946.   CBaK

2525. Kern county museum, Bakersfield. Statement and report of the Board of trustees... [Bakersfield, 1951?] 21, [33] l.   CU-B

2526. Said, B. K. Bakersfield in its pioneer days, 1870–1875. [Bakersfield?] Society of Kern county pioneers [n.p., n.d.] unp. illus.   CBaB

2527. Sanborn map co. Insurance maps of Bakersfield, California. N.Y., c1912. 98 p.   CSmH

2528. Wear, George W. Pioneer days and Kebo club nights. Bost., Meador pub. co., 1932. 156 p.
C CBaB CBaK CFS CHi CSmH CU-B NN

KINGS COUNTY

(Created in 1893 from portion of Tulare county; annexed a portion of Fresno county in 1909)

COUNTY HISTORIES

2529. Brown, James Lorin. History of Kings county...Comp. for use in the elementary schools of the county. [n.p., Corcoran journal print., 1936?] 37 p.
C CFS CHan CLU CO CViCL

2530. —— The story of Kings county, California... Berkeley, Print. by Lederer, Street & Zeus co., in cooperation with the Art print shop, Hanford [1942] 126 p. illus., map.
C CBaK CChiS CF CFS CHan CHanK CL CLCo CLSU CMS CMa CMerCL CO CS CSto CStoC CU-B CViCL

2531. Brown, Robert R., and Richmond, J. E. History of Kings county...Hanford, Cawston, 1940. 385 p. illus., ports. "Biographical": p. 215–385.
C CHan CHanK CHi CL CLCo CLU CO CSf CU-B NN

2532. Small, Kathleen Edward, and Smith, J. Larry. History of Kings county, California. Chicago, Clarke, 1926. 2 v. illus., ports.
C CCH CHan CHanK CSf CSmH

GREAT REGISTER

2533. Kings county. Index to the Great register of the county of Kings. 1896– Place of publication and title vary.

C has 1900 (biennially to)– 1916, 1918 (index and suppl.), 1920 (biennially to)– 1930, 1930 (suppl.), 1932 (biennially to)– 1962.

DIRECTORIES

2534. 1901. Hanford daily journal, pub. Kings county directory. Hanford, 1901. 144 p.   CViCL

2535. 1948– Polk, R. L., & co., pub. Polk's Kings county city directory...L.A., 1948– Content varies: 1952–1955 includes Avenal, Corcoran, Hanford and Lemoore; 1956–1958(?) includes Armona, Avenal, Corcoran, Hanford, Kettleman city, Lemoore and Stratford.

CHan has 1948, 1952–53, 1955–56, 1958. CHanK has 1948, 1952–53, 1958. CHi has 1948, 1952–53, 1955–56, 1958. CL has 1952–53, 1955.

Hanford

2536. 1906– Hanford daily sentinel, pub. Hanford city directory... [Hanford, 1906–] Publisher varies: 1906 Hanford sentinel.

C has 1906. CHan has 1930, 1939.

2537. 1943. Hanford publishing co. Hanford city directory. Hanford, c1943. unp. illus.   CHan

2538. 1949. Hanford. Church of Jesus Christ of latter day saints, comp. & pub. Directory of residents & businesses of Hanford... [Hanford, 1949?] 167 p. fold. map.   CHan

2539. 1959/60– Polk, R. L., & co., pub. Polk's Hanford-Corcoran-Lemoore directory including Armona. L.A., 1960–

CHanK has 1959/60. CHi has 1959/60. CL has 1961.

GENERAL REFERENCES

2540. Armstrong, Ervin S., et al. vs. Kettleman North Dome association et al. ...Ervin S. Armstrong, et al., plaintiffs, vs. Kettleman North Dome association, et al., defendants. Shell oil company, Union oil company of California, Belmont investment company, Petroleum securities company, Pioneer Kettleman company, L. D. Helm, cross-complainants. [L.A., 1936–38] 99 [i.e. 101] v.   CLU

2541. —— ...Brief of Kettleman oil corporation, ltd., and Kettleman and Inglewood corporation in reply to opening brief of certain cross complainants. Herbert W. Clark, Morrison, Hohfeld, Foerster, Shuman & Clark... attorneys for Kettleman oil corporation, ltd., and Kettleman and Inglewood corporation. Boyce Gross...of counsel. S.F., Pernau-Walsh print. co. [1938] 63 p.   CLU

2542. —— ...Shell oil company, a corporation, one of the defendants herein, and cross-complainant, vs. Kettleman North Dome association, a corporation, et al., cross-defendants. Reply brief of Kettleman North Dome association. L. R. Martineau, Jr., George W. Nilsson, Warren Stratton...Attorneys for Kettleman North Dome association. L. A., Parker & Baird co., law print. [1938] 398 p. fold. map.   CLU

2543. Beebe, James Wilbur. Kettleman hills and Dudley ridge gas area; a story of their development from the year 1900 to September 1932... [Fresno, c1932] 46 p. illus., maps.   C CHan CL CU-B

2544. Brown, James Lorin. The Mussel Slough tragedy. [n.p., 1958] 153 p. illus. Includes bibliography. Available in many libraries.

2545. Buckner, Leona Kreyenhagen. Lemoore story. [Lemoore] Chamber of commerce [1962] 18 p. Typew.   CHi

2546. California. Superior court (Los Angeles county) ...Ervin S. Armstrong, et al., plaintiffs, vs. Kettleman North Dome association, a corporation, et al., defendants. Shell oil company a corporation, et al., cross-complainants, vs. Kettleman North Dome association, a corporation, et al., cross defendants. Opinion of the court, Minor Moore, judge. L.A., Daily journal [1938?] 328 p.   CLU

2547. Featherstone, M. S. The Mussel Slough tragedy. [n.p., n.d.] 2 l. Typew. "Written shortly after the tragedy."   CFS

2548. A few letters of pioneers gathered together by the members of the Nineteenth century round table, in 1927–8. 32 p. Typew.   CHanK

2549. [Fowler, Velma] History of Kings county, 1773–1939. [Berkeley? 1939] 9 l.   CU-B

2550. Hanford. Chamber of commerce. Health and wealth in Hanford, Kings county, California. Hanford, Brannen and Bennett [1947?] 22 p.   CRcS

2551. —— **First Methodist church.** Seventy-fifth anniversary, December 20 and 21, 1952. [n.p.] 1952. [8] p. illus. Contains Hanford's pioneer church by W. C. Williams.   CHan CHi

2552. —— **First Presbyterian church.** Seventy-fifth anniversary, October 21, 1954. 2 p.   CHan

2553. Hanford daily journal. Greater Kings county edition. May 23, 1909. [Hanford, 1909] [22] p. illus.   CU-B

2554. Hanford morning journal. Classified booster directory... [Hanford] 1931. 16 p.   CHan

2555. Hanford sentinel. ...Progress edition. History of Kings county, 1893–1953. [Hanford, 1953] 74 p. illus., ports.   CHi CU-B

2556. Heermans, Edward McGrew. Kings county, California, "the little kingdom of kings."... L.A., Print. by Neuner co., c1915. [46] p. illus. Imprint varies.

C CHan CL CLU CSmH CU-B

2557. Holt, Moton B., ed. A history of the church of the Savior, Hanford, California, 1880–1950; pioneer Episcopal church of the San Joaquin. Riverdale, Riverdale press, 1951. 63 p. illus.   C CHan

2558. Jacobs, Julius L. Story of Kings county. April 30, 1955. [Hanford, Kings county schools, 1955] 91 p. Mimeo.   CHan CHanK

2559. Kettleman Hills historical association, Avenal. Kettleman gusherado, program, Avenal, October 10, 11, 12, 1958. Avenal, 1958. [24] p. illus. Contains "History of the Kettleman hills" by Mrs. Carl Peters.   CFS

2560. Kings county. Chamber of commerce. The facts about Kings county. [Hanford, 1929?] 73 l.   CHan CU-B

2561. —— —— Kings county, California. Hanford [1928?] 22 p.   CRcS

2562. Kings county, California, for diversified products and successful agriculture, viticulture and horticulture. [1901] 31 p.   NN

2563. Kings county centennials commission. Dedication ceremonies by Kings county centennials commission and California centennials commission at the unveiling of permanent historical markers, February 4th, 1950... [Lemoore, Lemoore advance] 1950. 6 p.   CHan

2564. Kings county centennials committee. 100 golden years. Kings county celebrates California centennials. 1948–1949–1950. Hanford, Art print shop, 1948. unp. illus.　　　　　　CAla CHan CRcS CSf

2565. Kings county fair. Official souvenir program and guide, September 12th thru 15th, 1957. Hanford, 1957. unp. Contains history of the Kings county fair.
　　　　　　　　　　　　　　　　　　　　　　CHan

2566. Kings county homecoming committee, inc. Golden days, Kings county homecoming magazine. Fresno, 1959. 28 p. illus.　　　　　　　　　　CHan

2567. Kings county peace officers association. Kings county peace officer 1955... Hanford [1955?] 71 p. photos. Contains historical and biographical material.
　　　　　　　　　　　　　　　　　　　　　　CHan

2568. Kings county promotion association. Kings county, California, the home of health, wealth and happiness. Hanford [1905?] 47 p. illus.　　CHi CU-B

2569. Kings county resources illustrated...Daily Democrat souvenir. Hanford, W. W. Barnes [1897–98?] 148 p. illus., ports.　　　　CHan CSjC CSmH

2570. Kings county war album. [Hanford, Hanford sentinel-journal, 1949] 177 p. ports. Photographs and brief biographical sketches of men who served in World war II.　　　　　　　　　　　　　　　　　CHan

2571. Latta, Frank Forrest. Little journeys in the San Joaquin. [Shafter] Author, c1937. [19] p. illus., map. Nineteen articles appeared originally in the *Hanford daily sentinel.*　　　C CHan CU-B CViCL

2572. Lemoore commercial club. Just a glimpse of Lemoore, in Kings county, California, "the keystone nugget of the Golden state." Lemoore [1922?] 16 p. illus.
　　　　　　　　　　　　　　　　　　　　　　CU-B

2573. McKinney, William Clyde. The Mussel Slough episode; a chapter in the settlement of the San Joaquin valley, 1865–1880... [Berkeley, 1948] 121 l. mounted photos., maps. Thesis (M.A.)—Univ. of Calif., 1948.　　　　　　　　　　　　　　　CU-B

2574. Muñoz, Pedro. Diary of Fray Pedro Muñoz. Translated by the third year Spanish class of East Bakersfield high school, under the direction of James G. Esneault. 1947. unp. Mimeo.　　　　　　CBaB

2575. Oil royalty exchange, Los Angeles. The romance of Kettleman Hills. L.A. [1932] 16 l. illus., map.
　　　　　　　　　　　　　　　　　　　　　　CFS

2576. Packard, Walter Eugene. The development and present status of irrigation in Kings and Tulare counties. [Berkeley, 1910] Thesis (M.S.) — Univ. of Calif., 1910.　　　　　　　　　　　　　　　CU

2577. Pardee, George C. Revenue and taxation; an address delivered before the thirty-second fruit growers' convention, at Hanford, Cal., December 4, 1906. [n.p., n.d.] 16 p.　　　　　　　　　　　　　　CHi

2578. Settlers' committee of the Mussel Slough country. An appeal to the people. History of the land troubles in Tulare and Fresno counties... Visalia, Visalia delta bk. & job print., 1880. 12 p. The battle of May, 1880, took place in what was then Tulare county.
　　　　　　　　　　　　　　　　　　　　　　CU-B

2579. —— The struggle of the Mussel Slough settlers for their homes...History of land troubles in Tulare and Fresno counties... Visalia, Delta print. establishment, 1880. 32 p.　　　　　C CHi CLU CU-B

2580. Smith, Anthony H. "The Portuguese"; early settlers and builders of Kings county. 1948. 5 p. Typew.　　　　　　　　　　　　　　　　CHan

KLAMATH COUNTY

(Organized in 1851; dissolved in 1874. Comprised the present county of Del Norte and portions of Siskiyou and Humboldt counties)

GREAT REGISTER

2581. Klamath county. Index to the Great register of the county of Klamath. 1866–73. Place of publication and title vary.

C has 1869, 1872, 1873. CL has 1869 (suppl.), 1873. CU-B has 1872, 1873. 3 v.

LAKE COUNTY

(Organized in 1861 from portion of Napa county; annexed section of Mendocino county in 1864)

COUNTY HISTORIES

2582. Mauldin, Henry K. Your lakes, valleys and mountains, history of Lake county. Ed. by Ben Shannon Allen. S.F., East wind print. c.1960– Contents: v.1. Clear Lake and Mt. Knocti.　　　　　　　CHi

GREAT REGISTER

2583. Lake county. Index to the Great register of the county of Lake. 1867– Place of publication and title vary.

C has 1872–73, 1875, 1879, 1880, 1884, 1888 (biennially to)– 1906, 1910 (biennially to)– 1962. CHi has Nov. 1918, June, Nov. 1933. CL has 1875, 1877, 1879, 1882 (suppl.), 1886, 1888 (suppl.), 1890. CSmH has 1879–80. CU-B has 186–?, July 1867, [July] 1871, Oct. 1872, Aug. 1873, Aug. 1879. [Oct.] 1898, Nov. 1934, Aug. 1936, Nov. 1938, Nov. 1940.

GENERAL REFERENCES

2584. Ashburner, William. Report of William Ashburner...James D. Hague...Thomas Price...M. C. Vincent...on the properties of the Sulphur bank quicksilver mining co., Lake county, Calif. S.F., E. Bosqui & co., print., 1876. 32 p.　　　　　　CSmH CU-B

2585. Bartlett Springs, Lake county, California. [S.F., D. S. Stanley & co., print, 190–?] 33 p. illus.　　CSmH

2586. Bartlett Springs: where they are, what they are and how to get there. S.F., 1880. unp.　　　CU-B

2587. Beakbane & Hertslet, ed. Lake county, California. "The Switzerland of America." Climate, attractions and resources... Lower Lake, Clear Lake press, 1887. 68 p. illus.　　　　　　　　　　CU-B

2588. Clear Lake collegiate institute, Lakeport. ...Catalogue of the officers and students...1st–2d, 1876/77–1877/78. Lakeport, 1876–78.　　　CU-B

2589. Crawford, C. M. Pioneer recollections of Lake county. Personal reminiscences of the man who claimed to be the first white child born in Lake county, completed in June, 1946. [n.p., 1946] 19 p. Mimeo.
　　　　　　　　　　　　C CHi CLp CSmH CU-B

2590. Deacon, Alice Wray. Scottslandia; a romantic history of Scotts valley. Lower Lake, Observer press, 1948. 61 p. illus.　　　　　　　　　　　CHi MWA

2591. [Dow, Wallace H.] Souvenir of Blue lakes, Lake co., Calif. [n.p., 189–?] 39 mounted photos.
　　　　　　　　　　　　　　　　　　　　　　CU-B

2592. Floyd, Cora (Lyons). In the matter of the

estate of Cora Lyons Floyd. Oral closing argument...
S.F. [1905] 100 p.   CHi

2593. Goss, Helen (Rocca) The life and death of
a quicksilver mine. L.A., Hist. soc. of So. Calif., 1958.
150 p. illus. (Its Special book pub. no. 3) Includes
bibliography.
Available in many California libraries and CoD

2594. Hanson, Nicholas Wilson. As I remember.
[Chico] Chico enterprise, 1942. 191 p. illus., ports. An
old man's story of his early life in Lake county and Colusa county.   CChiS CHi CSmH CU-B

2595. Harrington, Mark Raymond. An ancient
site at Borax Lake, California. L.A., Southwest museum,
1948. 131 p. illus. (Southwest museum papers, no. 16)
Bibliographical footnotes.
              C CHi CLLoy CSdS CSfCSM

2596. [Hertslet, Evelyn M.] Ranch life in California. Extracted from the home correspondence of E. M. H.
London, W. H. Allen & co., 1886. 171 p. illus.
          C CLO CLU CSd CSmH CU-B UHi

2597. Immigration association of California.
[County scrapbooks] [S.F., 188–?]   C

2598. [Kelseyville sun] Lake county, California.
Its present and future. [Kelseyville] 1908. 10 p.   CHi

2599. Lake county. Board of supervisors. A description of Lake county, California... [Lakeport] Clear
Lake press, 1888. 80 p. illus.   CLSU CU-B

2600. —— —— Lake county, California. Lakeport
[1939] 16 p. illus., map.   CRcS

2601. —— **County clerk.** Report...for the year
ending February 1, 1876. S.F., Spaulding & Barto, 1876.
77 p.   CHi

2602. Lake county, Cal., illustrated and described...
Oakland, Elliott, 1885. 94 p. illus.   C CSmH NN

2603. Lake county, California; "the Switzerland of
America." [S.F., Village press, 1920?] 6 p. illus., map.
                                                    CRcS

2604. Lewis, Ruth [and others] comp. Stories and
legends of Lake county...2d ed. Print. by students of
Kelseyville high school, c1936. 130 p.
                        CHi CLp CU-B

2605. Lower Lake improvement association. Lake
county, California, the Switzerland of America... [Lake-
port? 1907?] 24 p. map.   CHi

2606. Middletown independent. Lake county,
"The Switzerland of America." [Middletown, n.d.] 26 p.
illus.   CHi

2607. Nobles, William M. Memories of pioneer life
in Lake county, related by William M. Nobles and his
wife, Mary Ellen (Reeves) Nobles, to Linnie Marsh
Wolfe. [n.p., 1935] 41 l.   CU-B

2608. Redington quicksilver co....Report...1867/
69–75. S.F., 1870–76. 3 v.
CLU has 1867/69. CSmH has 1867/69–1870. CU-B has
1867/69–1875.

2609. Simoons, Frederick John. The settlement of
the Clear Lake upland of California. [Berkeley, 1952]
Thesis (M.A.)—Univ. of Calif., 1952.   CU

2610. Walter, Carrie (Stevens) A letter about
Lake county, California... [S.F.?] 1888. [8] p. illus.
                        C C-S CU-B

2611. Witter medical springs, San Francisco.
The story of Witter springs. [S.F., 1922] [14] p. illus.
                                                    CHi

LASSEN COUNTY
*(Created in 1864 from portions of Plumas
and Shasta counties)*

COUNTY HISTORIES

2612. Fairfield, Asa Merrill. Fairfield's pioneer history of Lassen county, California; containing everything
that can be learned about it from the beginning of the
world to the year of our Lord 1870...also...the biogra-
phies of Governor Isaac N. Roop and Peter Lassen...and
many stories of Indian warfare never before published...
S.F., Pub. for the author by Crocker [c1916] 506 p.
illus., ports., map.
   C C-S CAla CAlaC CAltu CB CBaK CBb
CCH CChiS CF CFS CGl CHi CL CLSM
CLSU CLU CLgA CMartC CMary CMont CO
CP CQCL CRb CRedCL CRiv CS CSS CSalCL
CSd CSf CSfCP CSfCSM CSfCW CSfMI CSfP
CSmH CSt CSto CStoC CStrJC CSuLas CU-B
CV CYrS CtY MWA MiD-B MoSHi NN NvHi
NvU WHi

2613. —— —— Index...comp. by Lassen county
free library, January 1923. Lenala A. Martin, librarian.
[Susanville, 1923] 62 l. Autographed from typew. copy.
   C C-S CChiS CCH CIIi CMary CSmH CSuLas

GREAT REGISTER

2614. Lassen county. Index to the Great register of
the county of Lassen. 1866– Place of publication and
title vary.
   C has 1868, 1873, 1877, 1886, 1890, 1898, 1900 (biennially to)– 1962. CL has 1868 (suppl.), 1872, 1873 (biennially to)–1879, 1882 (suppl.), 1884, 1886, 1888
(suppl.) 1890. CSmH has 1880, 1882. CU-B has 1868,
1872, 1879, 1879 (suppl.), 1880. 6 v.

DIRECTORIES

2615. McKenney, L. M., & co., pub. County directory of Lassen, Plumas, Del Norte, Siskiyou, Tehama
counties, giving name, occupation and residence of all
adult persons in the cities and towns... S.F., 1885.   C

GENERAL REFERENCES

2616. Butler, James Thomas. Isaac Roop, pioneer
and political leader of northeastern California. [Berkeley,
1958] Thesis (M.A.)—Univ. of Calif., 1958.   CU

2617. Chapman's magazine, Berkeley. Lassen
county. (In v.1, no. 1, p. 125–38 [1941?])
                        CO CRb CU-B

2618. Cox, Ronald Woodworth. Westwood, Lassen
county: its growth and management. [Berkeley, 1935]
Thesis (M.A.)—Univ. of Calif., 1935.   CU

2619. Davis, William Newell, jr. Days gone by.
Bieber, 1939–40. (In Big Valley gazette)   C CU-B

2620. Haueter, Lowell Jack. Westwood, California:
the life and death of a lumber town. [Berkeley, 1956]
179 l. illus., maps. Thesis (M.A.)—Univ. of Calif., 1956.
                                                    CU-B

2621. Honey Lake valley farmer... v.1, no. 1,
April 1892. Honey Lake City, Farmer's pub. co., 1892.
1 v. illus.   C

**2622. Honey Lake valley land and water co., San
Francisco.** Engineers reports on its irrigation system
in Honey Lake valley, Lassen county, Cal. S.F., 1891.
13 p. maps.   CSfCSM

2623. —— Prospectus. [S.F., Valley & Peterson print., 1891?] 32 p. fold. map.   CU-B

2624. Immigration association of California. [County scrapbooks] [S.F., 188–?]   C

2625. Kirov, George. Peter Lassen, highlights on his life and achievements. Pub. by the Senate of the state of California... Sacramento, State print. off., 1940. 35 p. illus., port.
C CBb CHi CLSU CO CRb CRedCL CSS CSf CU-B

2626. Lassen county. v.1, no. 1, June 30, 1888. Susanville, 1888. 4 p. illus., port.
C CHi CU-B

2627. —— **Chamber of commerce.** "Lucky Lassen"... [Westwood, 1930?] folder (11 p.) illus., map.
CHi CRcS

2628. Lassen county historical society. Lucky land of Lassen; dedicated to preserve the history of Lassen county—past-present-and future. Susanville, 1959– 3 v. Contents: v.1. Brief history of Lassen co. hist. soc.—Issac Roop goes west.—v.2. Biographies of early pioneers.—Early locations in Lassen county.—History of Susanville post office.—v.3. Hayden Hill, Lassen county's mining district, the productive years, mines, biographies.
CSuLas

2629. Lassen county land and cattle company. Prospectus...Incorporated July 12th, 1884... S.F., Wm. C. Brown...print., 1884. 32 p.   CU-B

2630. Parkhurst, Genevieve Yoell. Lassen county, California... S.F., Sunset mag. homeseekers' bur. [1909] 31 p. illus.   CHi CL CU-B

2631. Perry, George W. Buckskin Mose; or, Life from the lakes to the Pacific, as actor, circus-rider, detective, ranger, gold-digger, Indian scout, and guide... N.Y., 1873. Fairfield quoted this book but did not consider it authentic.   CU-B

2632. —— Same. N.Y., Worthington co., 1890, c1889. 285 p. illus.   C CHi CO

2633. Roop, Wendell. Isaac Roop goes west; compiled from family papers, public and published records. Sewell, N.J., Author [n.d.] 10 p.   CRedCL

2634. Sifford, Alexander. Fort Defiance. Susanville, Author [n.d.] unp.   CChiS

2635. Smith, Reuben William, III. The Fort Kearney, South pass and Honey Lake wagon road. [Berkeley, 1952] Thesis (M.A.)—Univ. of Calif., 1952.   CU

2636. Smythe, William Ellsworth. ...The irrigation problems of Honey Lake basin, California... [Wash., D.C., 1902?] 113 p.   CSmH

2637. The Standish colony...in the highlands of California. [n.p., 189–?] 34 p. illus., map.   CHi

2638. Swartzlow, Ruby Johnson. Peter Lassen, northern California's trail-blazer. S.F., Calif. hist. soc., 1940. 24 p. illus., port.
C CAna CChiS CHi CL CLSU CO CPom CRb CSf CStrJC CaBViPA OrU

2639. Vogel-Jørgensen, T. Peter Lassen of California, en Dansk pioners skaebne og aeventyr i wild west. København, Berlingske forlag, 1937. 216 p. illus., maps, ports.   CHi

2640. Wilson, Bourdon. Lassen county, California. S.F., Sunset mag. homeseekers' bur. [1910] 32 p. illus., maps.   CSf CU-B

LOS ANGELES COUNTY
(Created in 1850; annexed portion of San Diego county in 1851)

COUNTY HISTORIES

2641. Burdette, Robert Jones, ed. Greater Los Angeles and southern California, their portraits and chronological record of their careers... Chicago, L.A. [etc.] Lewis, 1906. 240 p. illus., ports.
C CCH CHi CL CLLoy CLO CLU CSmH MiD-B WHi

2642. —— Greater Los Angeles and southern California, portraits and personal memoranda. Chicago, 1910. 295 p. illus., ports.
CBev CCH CHi CL CLCM CLCo CLSM CLSU CLod CSd CSf CSmH NHi NN UPB WHi

2643. Guinn, James Miller. Historical and biographical record of Los Angeles and vicinity... Chicago, Chapman pub. co., 1901. 940 p. illus., ports.
C CCH CF CFS CHi CL CLCM CLCo CLO CLSU CO CP CSdS CSf CSfCP CSmH CStmo CU-B CWhC CoD MWA NHi NN NvHi

2644. —— A history of California and an extended history of Los Angeles and environs... L.A., Historic record co., 1915. 3 v. illus.
C CBb CCH CF CGl CHi CL CLCM CLCo CLO CLS CLSM CLU CP CSf CSfCP CSfU CSmH CSta CStmo CU-B CoD CtY MWA NN WHi

2645. Hawley, A. T. The present condition, growth, progress and advantages, of Los Angeles city and county, southern California...By authority of the Los Angeles chamber of commerce, and published by that body for free distribution. July, 1876. L.A., Mirror print. house, 1876. 144 p. maps.
CCH CL CLCM CLSU CLU CP CS CSmH CU-B NHi WHi

2646. Historical records survey. California. Inventory of the county archives of California. no. 20. Los Angeles county (Los Angeles) Tax collectors office. L.A., So. Calif. hist. records survey project [194–?] 172 p.
C CHi CLO CLSU CLU CRedl CSmH CU-B ICN MoS N NN

2647. —— —— Same. Assessors office. 1941. 228 p.
C CBb CHi CLO CLSU CLU CSdS CSf CSmH CU-B ICN

2648. —— —— Same. County clerk's office. 1943. 215 p.   CLO CLSU CSmH CU-B

2649. —— —— Same. County and municipal special districts. 1943. 141 p.
CLO CLSU CSmH CU-B ICN

2650. An illustrated history of Los Angeles county, California...and biographical mention of many of its pioneers, and also of prominent citizens of to-day. Chicago, Lewis, 1889. 835 p. illus., ports.
C CBb CCH CHi CL CLCM CLCo CLO CLSM CLSU CLU CLob CMary CO COr CP CPom CRiv CSf CSfCP CSjC CSmH CStb CStmo CU-B CYcCL CoD CtY ICN MWA NHi NN WHi

2651. Ingersoll, Luther A. Ingersoll's century history, Santa Monica bay cities...prefaced with...a condensed history of Los Angeles county, 1542–1908; supplemented with an encyclopedia of local biography... L.A., Author, 1908. 512 p. illus., ports. (Ingersoll's century ser. of Calif. local history annals. [v.2])
C CCH CHi CL CLCM CLCo CLO CLSM

CLU CO CSf CSmH CStmo CU-B CoD CoU
N NHi NN WHi

2652. [**Los Angeles. Centennial celebration, 1876. Literary committee**] An historical sketch of Los Angeles county, California. From the Spanish occupancy ...September 9, 1771, to July 4, 1876. L.A., L. Lewin & co., 1876. 88 p. Prepared by a committee (Juan José Warner, Benjamin Hayes and J. P. Widney)
C CCH CHi CL CLCM CLM CLO CLSM CLSU COMC COr CP CPom CRedl CSf CSfCSM CSmH CSt CU-B CoD KHi MWA NHi PHi WHi

2653. —— —— —— Same. A reprint of the original ed....1876, to which is added an invaluable intro. written by Dr. J. P. Widney... L.A., O. W. Smith, 1936. 159 p. ports.
C CAla CAlh CB CBaK CBb CBev CCH CHi CL CLCO CLLoy CLO CLS CLSM CLSU CLU CLgA CLob CMa CO CP CPom CRiv CSd CSdS CSfCW CSfU CSmH CStaC CStaCL CStclU CStmo CStoC CU-B CWhC CtY NHi NN ODa WHi

2654. McGroarty, John Steven. The county of Los Angeles... Chicago, Am. hist. soc., 1923. 183 p. ports.
C CHi ICN NN

2655. —— History of Los Angeles county...with selected biography of actors and witnesses in the period of the county's greatest growth and achievement... Chicago, Am. hist. soc., 1923. 3 v. illus., ports. v.2–3 contain bibliographical material.
C CAla CB CBaK CBb CCH CGl CHi CL CLCM CLCo CLLoy CLM CLO CLU CLob CMartC CMon CO COMC COnC CP CPa CRiv CSS CSd CSf CSfCSM CSjC CSmH CSta CStaCL CStbS CStclU CStmo CStoC CU-B CWhC CtY MWA MiD-B MoSHi NIC WHi

2656. Spalding, William Andrew, comp. History and reminiscences, Los Angeles city and county, California... L.A., J. R. Finnell & sons [1931] 3 v. illus., ports. v.2–3 have title: History of Los Angeles city and county ...biographical...1931.
C CBev CCH CGl CHi CL CLLoy CLO CLU CLob CNF CSjC CSmH CSta CStmo CU-B MWA WHi

2657. [**Wilson, John Albert**] History of Los Angeles county, California... Oakland, Thompson & West, 1880. 192 p. illus., map.
C CAna CArcHT CChiS CL CLAC CLCM CLCo CLM CLSM CLU CLob CLom CNa COr CP CPom CSf CSfCP CSmH CSt CStaCL CStclU CStmo CU-B CoD ICN NHi NN WHi

2658. —— Same. With intro. by W. W. Robinson. Berkeley, Howell-North, 1959. reprint: 192 p. plates, col. map.
C CAla CAlaC CB CBb CBev CChiS CFS CHi CL CLM CLO CLS CLSU CLU CLgA CMartC CMon CNF CNa CRcS CRic CSd CSdS CSmat CStaC CSto CU-B CoD MWA NIC NN UU

GREAT REGISTER

2659. Los Angeles county. Index to the Great register of the county of Los Angeles. 1866– Place of publication and title vary.
C has 1873, 1875–76, 1879–80, 1882, 1884, 1888 (biennially to)– 1896, 1902 (biennially to)– 1962. CL has 1873, 1875, 1876 (suppl.), 1877 (suppl.), 1879 (suppl.), 1880, 1882 (suppl.), 1884, 1886, 1888 (Appendix), 1890 (Appendix), 1892, 1896. Also Great register for the city and county of Los Angeles, 1882, 1888. CLSM has 1890

and (suppl.). CLU has 1877, 1879, 1884, 1886, 1888, 1890. CSmH has 1875, 1882, 1888, 1890. CU-B has 1872–73, 1879–80, 1940.

DIRECTORIES

2660. 1872. Los Angeles city and county directory for the year 1872. [n.p., n.d.] lvii, 35 l. T.p. wanting in all known copies. Publication is variously ascribed to A. J. King and A. Waite, A. J. King and Alonzo Stratton, A. Waite and Charles Beane. Date of publication is in doubt, 1871/72, 1872 or 1873?
CLCM CU-B CL and CLU have photostatic copies.

2661. —— Same, with title: The first Los Angeles city and county directory, 1872. Reproduced in facsim. with an introd. by Ward Ritchie and early commentaries by J. M. Guinn. [L.A.] Ward Ritchie, 1963. 131 p. illus., facsims. Caption title: Los Angeles city and county directory.
CHi CSmH CU-B

2662. 1881/82. Southern California directory co., pub. Los Angeles city and county directory. S.F. [1881?]
C CL CU-B

2663. 1883/84. Southern California publishing co., pub. Los Angeles city and county directory... S.F., A. J. Leary [1884] 526 p. [Historical sketch of Los Angeles city]: p. 25–31.
C CL CSmH CStrJC

2664. 1883/84–1884/85. Atwood & Ernst, pub. Los Angeles city and county directory. Publisher varies: 1883/84 Atwood & Ferguson.
C (1883/84) CL CLU (1883/84) CSmH (1884/85) CU-B (1884/85)

2665. 1886/87. Bynon, A. A. & co., pub. Los Angeles city and county directory... L.A., Times-mirror co., print., 1886.
C CHi CL CLSU CLU CPom CSmH CU-B

2666. 1887/88. Maxwell, George W., pub. Maxwell's directory of Los Angeles city and county.
CL CLU CStmo CU-B

2667. 1890/91. Pearsall, W. M., pub. Los Angeles and Orange county business directory. L.A., 1890. Los Angeles city charter: p. 38–86. Los Angeles city municipal laws: p. 87–124.
CHi CL CLU

2668. 1894. Pattee, F. A., & co. Directory of the farmers and fruit growers of Los Angeles county... L.A. [1894] 125 p. illus.
CU-B

2669. 1898/99–1914. Bards & co., comp. Business and professional directory of Los Angeles, California, including the surrounding towns. [N.Y., Bards & co., 1898, 1914]
CHi has 1914 CLU has 1898/99, 1914.

2670. 1910– Western directory association, pub. Los Angeles business directory, including surrounding towns. L.A. [1910]–
CL has Apr. 1910, 1911/12, 1914, 1918, 1927, 1939, 1941–42, 1944, 1947–60. CLSU has 1918.

2671. 1911/12– Foster directory co., pub. Southern California business directory. L.A., [1912–] Title varies; 1911/12, Business directory of Los Angeles, Pasadena, Long Beach, San Pedro, Santa Monica, Venice, Santa Ana and neighboring towns.
CL has 1915. CLU has 1911/12, 1913/14. CSdS has 1915.

2672. 1915?– City business directory association. City business directory of greater Los Angeles... Annual ed. [L.A., 1915?–] Publisher varies.
C has 1958. CBb has 1956. CBev has 1958. CL has

1927–42, 1944, 1947–60. CLLoy has 1952, 1954. CLU has 33d, 35th, 1948, 1950.

2673. 1948. Southern California publishing co., pub. Greater Los Angeles county directory. L.A. [1948]
CL

2674. 1957. Los Angeles. Chamber of commerce. Western industrial directories. Los Angeles county. L.A., 1957.   CL

Los Angeles

2675. 1875–1942. Los Angeles directory co., pub. Los Angeles city directory. L.A., 1875–1942. None published 1889, 1919.

Title varies: 1875, Directory of Los Angeles. 1878–1879/80, 1887/88, 1890–91, 1900/01, 1907–13, 1916, Los Angeles city directory. 1892, Los Angeles city directory and gazetteer of southern California. 1893, Corran's Los Angeles directory. 1894, 1896–98, Maxwell's Los Angeles city directory and gazetteer of southern California. 1899, Maxwell's Los Angeles city directory. 1901–04, 1924–42, Los Angeles directory co.'s Los Angeles city directory. 1905–06, Dana Burk's Los Angeles city directory. 1914–15, 1918, Los Angeles city directory...including San Pedro and Wilmington. 1920–21, Los Angeles directory co.'s Los Angeles city directory, including San Pedro, Wilmington, Palms, Van Nuys and Owensmouth. 1922, Los Angeles directory co.'s Los Angeles city directory, including San Pedro, Wilmington and the San Fernando valley. 1923, Los Angeles directory co.'s Los Angeles city directory, including San Pedro, Wilmington, Sawtelle, Palms, Westgate and San Fernando valley.

Publisher varies: 1875, Mirror bk. and job print. off. 1878, Mirror print., ruling & bind. house. 1879–80, Morris & Wright. 1887/88, 1888, 1890–91, 1893, W. H. L. Corran. 1892, 1894, George W. Maxwell. 1895–99, 1913–42, Los Angeles directory co. 1900–01, Los Angeles modern directory co. 1901–12, Los Angeles city directory co.

[Historical sketch of Los Angeles] in 1875, 1878, 1879–80, 1894, 1895, 1897, 1898.

C has 1875, 1888, 1893, 1897, 1899, 1902–18, 1920–42. CBev has 1942. CHi has 1878, 1888, 1891–94, 1897–99, 1900/01, 1901, 1903–18, 1920–38, 1940–42. CL has 1875, 1878–1879/80, 1887/88, 1890–1918, 1920–42. CLSU has 1878, 1888, 1890–94, 1899, 1901, 1904–18, 1920–42. CLU has 1878, 1887/88, 1890–1918, 1920–42. COr has 1923. CP has 1879/80, 1881/82, 1884/85, 1886/87, 1887/88, 1892, 1896. CPom has 1887/88. CSfCP has 1875, 1891, 1898, 1911–13, 1916–17. CSfCW has 1914–15. CSmH has 1875, 1878, 1887/88, 1892, 1894–99, 1900/01, 1901, 1903–18, 1920–34, 1936–38. CStmo has 1896, 1898. CU-B has 1875, 1879/80, 1887/88, 1890, 1918, 1922, 1924, 1926–33, 1935–42. MoS has 1898, 1900, 1903, 1906–07, 1910–18, 1920, 1922–30, 1933, 1935, 1937–38, 1941. NHi has 1887/88, 1890–91, 1893, 1897, 1899, 1916.

2676. 1883–1884. Los Angeles directory publishing co., pub. Los Angeles city and Santa Ana valley directory...containing a history of Los Angeles...also containing a brief history and business directory of Santa Ana. [L.A.] "Non-pareil press" of T. S. Harris, 1883. 220 p.   CHi CL CU-B

2677. 1887–1888. Smith & McPhee, pub. Los Angeles city directory, containing...Los Angeles, East Los Angeles, Boyle Heights, Brooklyn Heights and West Los Angeles... L.A. [1887?]   CL

2678. 1896–1906/07. Mercantile directory company, pub. Business directory and mercantile register of Los Angeles, Pasadena, Long Beach, San Pedro, San Bernardino, Redlands, Riverside, Santa Monica, Ocean Park,

Venice and neighboring towns. L.A. [1896–1906] 1896 compiled by A. Marks.
C (1906/07)   CHi (1906/07)   CL (1896)   CLU (1906/07)   CSmH (1896)   CU-B (1896, 1906/07)

2679. 1903. Howes & Le Berthon, pub. Souvenir office buildings directory of Los Angeles, California, 1903 ...Also directory of the business section by streets... L.A. [1903?] [47] p.   CU-B

2680. 1906–1907. International publishing co., pub. International directory of Los Angeles...and complete business directories of the French, German, Italian and Spanish colonies... [L.A., 1906]   CL

2681. 1932– Westwood Hills news publishing co., pub. Westwood Hills directory. Westwood Hills, 1932–
CL has 1932–33.

2682. 1940. New age publishing co., pub. The official Central Avenue district directory: a business and professional guide. L.A., 1940.   CL

2683. 1953– Directory publishing co., pub. East Los Angeles, Montebello, Pico and portion of Rivera city directory, 1953. Thousand Oaks, 1953–
CL has Jan. 1953.

2684. 1955/56– City directory co., pub. Westwood, Brentwood, Bel-Air city directory. L.A., 1955–
CBev has 1956/57. CL has 1955/56, 1956/57, 1958/59. CStmo has 1958/59.

2685. 1961. S & K publications, inc., pub. Western Los Angeles city directory covering West Los Angeles, Brentwood, Westwood, Cheviot Hills, and Rancho Park. Santa Monica, 1961.   CL

Other Cities and Towns

2686. 1920– Polk, R. L., & co., pub. Polk's Alhambra city directory. L.A., 1920– Publisher varies: 19——1952 Los Angeles directory co. Content varies: 1923–25 includes Alhambra, El Monte, Monterey Park and Wilmar; 1926–28 add Rosemead; 1931–32 add Temple city; 1941 add Garvey; 1943, 1952 includes Alhambra, Monterey Park and San Gabriel; 1954–56 includes Alhambra and San Gabriel.
C has 1923, 1925–28, 1930–32, 1935. CHi has 1928, 1932, 1935, 1937, 1941, 1943, 1946, 1949, 1952, 1954, 1956, 1962. CL has 1920, 1922–28, 1930–32, 1935, 1937, 1941, 1943, 1946, 1949, 1952, 1956.

2687. 1959– Polk, R. L., & co., pub. Polk's Arcadia city directory. L.A., 1959–
CHi has 1959–60. CL has 1959–60.

2688. 1960– Luskey bros., pub. Luskey's Artesia criss cross city directory, including Hawaiian Gardens and Dairy Valley. Anaheim, 1960–
CL has 1960.

2689. 1923/24– Coulson directory co., pub. Azusa, Baldwin Park, Covina, Glendora, Puente and suburban directory. Baldwin Park [1923–
CCH has 1923/24. CL has 1923/24, 1940, 1952, 1956/57, 1960. CU-B has 1923/24.

2690. 1931– Pacific directory co., pub. Baldwin Park and Covina city directory... South Pasadena, 1931– Title varies. Publisher varies: 1931–194–? Los Angeles directory co.
C has 1931. CHi has 1947, 1950. CL has 1931, 1949–50, 1954, 1956–57, 1959–60. CPom has 1955–

2691. 1940– Pacific directory co. Bellflower city directory. South Pasadena, 1940– Publisher and title vary.

C has 1940. CHi has 1946. CL has 1940–41, 1943, 1948, 1950, 1952, 1959–60.

2692. 1949– Lester, E. O., & sons, pub. Bell-Maywood, Cudahy, Bell Gardens city directory. L.A., 1949– Publisher varies: 1949 American directory co.
CL has 1949, 1951–52.

2693. 1925– Beverly Hills. Chamber of commerce and Civic association. Beverly Hills city directory. Beverly Hills, 1925–
CBev has 1925–1959/60.

2694. 1927– Beverly Hills city directory. 1927–
Publisher and title vary.
CL has 1927, 1930–31, 1937, 1941, 1943, 1946, 1948–49, 1955–58.

2695. 1940. City business directory association.
City business directory of Beverly Hills. L.A., 1940.
100 p.   CBev

2696. 1937– Polk, R. L., & co., pub. Polk's Burbank city directory. L.A., 1937– Publisher varies: 1937–52 Los Angeles directory co.
C has 1939. CHi has 1937, 1946, 1949, 1952, 1953/54.
CL has 1937, 1940, 1942, 1946, 1949. CU-B has 1953/54.

2697. 1931– Pacific directory co., pub. Compton city directory. South Pasadena, 1931– None published 1941–45. Publisher and title vary.
CHi has 1940, 1946/47, 1949. CL has 1931, 1940, 1946/47, 1949, 1951.

2698. 1939– Covina city directory. 1939– Publisher and title vary.
CL has 1939–41, 1943, 1947.

2699. 1933– Crescenta-Canada valley directory.
1933– Publisher and title vary.
CL has 1933, 1951.

2700. 1924– S and K publications, pub. Culver City and adjacent areas of Palms, Mar Vista, Venice city directory. Santa Monica, 1924– Publisher and title vary.
C has 1931. CBev has 1959–60. CHi has 1937, 1949. CL has 1924–25, 1927, 1931, 1937, 1949, 1959–60.

2701. 1948– Los Angeles directory co., pub.
Downey city directory... L.A., 1948– Publisher and title vary.
CHi has 1948, 1950. CL has 1948, 1950–51, 1955, 1957–58, 1961.

2702. 1946– Pacific directory co., pub. El Monte community directory... South Pasadena, 1946– Publisher and title vary.
CHi has 1946, 1948, 1950. CL has 1946, 1948, 1950, 1953, 1958.

2703. 1953– Directory publishing co., pub. Encino, Sherman Oaks, Van Nuys directory. Thousand Oaks, 1953–
CL has Aug. 1953.

2704. 1957/58– Polley, Fred F., comp. Gardena Valley city directory. Norwalk, 1957–
CL has 1957/58.

2705. 1915/16–1921. Cowan, A. T., pub. Directory...Glendale and Casa Verdugo... Glendale, 1915–1921. Publisher varies. Title varies: 1915/16–1917, Resident and business directory of Glendale, Tropico and Casa Verdugo.
CHi has 1917. CL has 1915/16, 1917, 1919, 1921.

2706. 1922– Polk, R. L., & co., pub. Glendale city directory. L.A., 1922– Publisher varies: 1922–48 Glendale directory co.
C has 1930–34, 1936, 1939–40. CHi has 1928, 1947–48,

1951, 1953–55, 1957–58, 1960. CL has 1924-39, 1941–45, 1947–49, 1951, 1954–55, 1957–58, 1960.

2707. 1927— Western directory co., pub. Glendale city directory. Long Beach, 1927–
CLU has 1927.

2708. 1961– B & G pub. Granada Hills including portions of Mission Hills, Northridge, San Fernando, Sepulveda city directory. San Fernando, 1961–
CL has 1961.

2709. 1959/60– S & K publications, inc., pub.
Hawthorne, Lawndale and Lennox area city directory.
Santa Monica, 1959–
CL has 1959/60.

2710. 1906. George, Mrs. Charles J., comp. Directory of the city of Hollywood, Los Angeles county, California, for the year 1906. L.A., Baumgardt pub. co., 1905.
                                                    CHi

2711. 1923– Huntington Park and Walnut Park city directory. 1923– Publisher and title vary.
C has 1946. CHi has 1946, 1948. CL has 1923, 1925, 1928–29, 1931, 1937, 1942, 1944, 1946, 1948, 1950, 1952, 1956, 1959.

2712. 1928. Haynes printing co., pub. City and telephone directory of Huntington Park and Walnut Park.
Huntington Park [1928?] 254, 58 p.   C

2713. 1923– Los Angeles directory co., pub.
Inglewood, Lennox city directory. L.A., 1923– Publisher varies: 1923–27, Kaasen directory company. Content varies: 1923–42, includes Hawthorne.
C has 1927, 1931. CHi has 1925, 1927, 1931, 1942, 1947, 1950. CL has 1925, 1927, 1929, 1931, 1933, 1935, 1938, 1940, 1942, 1947, 1960. CU-B has 1929, 1931.

2714. 1952– Luskey bros., pub. Lakewood, Los Altos, East Long Beach criss cross city directory. Anaheim [1952]–
CL has 1952, 1959.

2715. 1952– Polk, R. L., & co., pub. Polk's Lakewood city directory including Bellflower, Lakewood Plaza and Paramount. L.A., 1952–
CHi has 1952.

2716. 1960– La Mirada directory co., pub. La Mirada city directory. 1960–
CL has 1960.

2717. 1925– Polk, R. L., & co., pub. Polk's Lancaster city directory. 1925– Publisher and title vary.
CL has 1925–26, 1961.

2718. 1957– Pacific directory co., pub. La Puente city directory. Arcadia, 1957–
CL has 1957, 1959–60.

2719. 1899– Polk, R. L., & co., pub. Polk's Long Beach city directory. Long Beach, 1899–
C has 1931–33, 1935–41. CHi has 1932–33, 1935, 1938, 1943/44, 1948, 1951/52, 1953–55, 1957–58, 1960. CL has 1909-10, 1913–18, 1921–45, 1948, 1951–55, 1957, 1959–61.
CLob has 1899-1962. CU-B has 1930–33, 1935–37, 1954–55, 1957. MoS has 1943/44.

2720. 1899. Directory of Long Beach, Terminal and San Pedro, 1899–1900... [Long Beach? 1900?] 57, 5, 31 p. illus.   CLU CSmH

2721. 1919– Western directory co., pub. Long Beach city directory... 1919–
C has 1919, 1927–30.

2722. 1952– Lynwood city directory. 1952– Publisher and title vary.
CL has 1952, 1961.

2723. 1960– Luskey bros., pub. Luskey's Manhattan Beach criss cross city directory. Anaheim, 1960–
CL has 1960.

2724. 1953– Directory publishing co., pub. Mar Vista, Venice and vicinity city directory. Thousand Oaks, 1953–
CL has Oct. 1953.

2725. 1916– Polk, R. L., & co., pub. Polk's Monrovia city directory, including Duarte. L.A., 1916– Publisher varies: 1916?–52, Los Angeles directory co. Content varies: 1916?–58, Monrovia, Arcadia, Duarte.
C has 1923–25, 1927, 1930, 1931/32, 1935. CHi has 1928, 1931/32, 1935, 1944, 1948, 1950, 1952, 1953/54, 1955, 1958–59, 1961. CL has 1916–17, 1922–25, 1927–28, 1930, 1931/32, 1937, 1948, 1950, 1953/54, 1958–59, 1961. CMon has 1944, 1948, 1950, 1953/54, 1955, 1958–59. CU-B has 1925, 1935.

2726. 1939– Montebello city directory. 1939– Publisher and title vary.
CL has 1939–40, 1950, 1952–53.

2727. 1957/58– Lester, E. O., pub. Monterey Park and South San Gabriel city directory. L.A. [1957–]
CL has 1957/58.

2728. 1960– Community directory co., pub. Montrose community directory. Montrose, 1960–
CL has 1960–61.

2729. 1944– Glendale directory co., pub. North Hollywood and Studio City directory. Glendale, 1944–
CHi has 1946/47. CL has 1944, 1946/47.

2730. 1956– Norwalk, La Mirada city directory. Publisher and title vary.
CL has 1956–57, 1960.

2731. 1933/34. Palisadian, pub. Directory of Pacific Palisades and the North Santa Monica bay area...
[Pacific Palisades, 1933] 32 p. map.   C CL

2732. 1953– Directory pub. co. Palms and vicinity city directory. Thousand Oaks, 1953–
CL has Sept. 1953.

2733. 1952– Polley, Fred F., comp. Paramount-Hollydale community directory. Norwalk, T.L.M. pub. co., 1952–
CL has 1952, 1960.

2734. 1893/94– Polk, R. L., & co., pub. Polk's Pasadena city directory including Altadena. Pasadena, L.A. [1893?]– Title varies: 1895 Maxwell's Pasadena city directory and gazetteer of southern California; 1906/07–1926 Thurston's residence and business directory of Pasadena; 1927–51 Thurston's Pasadena city directory. Publisher varies: 1895, 1925–51 Los Angeles directory co.; 1902/03 Leroy Leonard and Albert G. Thurston; 1914/15–192–? Albert G. Thurston. Content varies: 1902/03 North and South Pasadena and Altadena; 1906/07–1912 Pasadena, South Pasadena, Altadena and Lamanda Park; 1914/15-1930, 1955–58 Pasadena, Altadena and Lamanda Park; 1931 Pasadena, Altadena, Lamanda Park and Flintridge; 1932–54 Pasadena, Altadena, Lamanda Park and San Marino.
C has 1923, 1925, 1927–33, 1935–39, 1941–42. CHi has 1895, 1902/03, 1909/10, 1912, 1914/15, 1925–35, 1938, 1941, 1949, 1951, 1953–62. CL has 1900, 1902/03, 1904, 1906/07–1931, 1932–37, 1939–43, 1947, 1949, 1951, 1953–56, 1958, 1960. CLU has 1893/94, 1895, 1906/07, 1908/09, 1912. CP has 1895, 1897, 1900, 1902/03–1943, 1947, 1949, 1951. CSmH has 1893/94, 1895, 1897, 1900, 1902/03–1922, 1924–34, 1938, 1940–43, 1947. CU-B has 1911, 1921/22, 1928–29, 1931–33, 1935–39, 1958.

2735. 1953– Lester, E. O., pub. Pico-Rivera, Los Nietos, and vicinity city directory. L.A., 1953–
CL has 1953–54, 1960.

2736. 1896/97. Milliken, James, comp. Milliken's city directory of Pomona... L.A., California directory co. [1896] 130 p.   C CHi

2737. 1898–1900/01. Norton, W. A., comp....
Pomona city directory, including Claremont, Covina, San Dimas, Lordsburg, Spadra and Lemon... [Ontario, 1898–1900] Publisher varies: 1898 Saturday beacon. Content varies: 1898 Pomona, North Pomona, Claremont, Chino, Lordsburg, Spadra, San Bernardino, Ontario, North Ontario, Azusa, Covina.
C has 1898. CPom has 1898. CSmH has 1900/01.

2738. 1905–1907. Pomona business men's association. Directory of Pomona, Chino, Claremont, Cucamonga, Lordsburg, North Pomona, Ontario, San Dimas and Upland... [Pomona] Daily progress [1905–1907]
C has 1905. CCH has 1905, 1907. CPom has 1905–07. CSmH has 1905–07.

2739. 1911–[1951?] Los Angeles directory co., pub. Pomona city directory, including Chino, Claremont, La Verne, San Dimas, and West Covina... L.A. [1911?–1951?] Content varies: 1931–40? includes Ontario, Upland, Chino, Claremont, La Verne, San Dimas, Alta Loma, Cucamonga, Etiwanda; 1945–48 includes Claremont, La Verne and San Dimas.
C has 1926, 1928, 1931, 1934. CHi has 1911, 1931, 1945, 1948, 1951. CL has 1911, 1914, 1919–20, 1922–24, 1926, 1928, 1931, 1934, 1937–38, 1940, 1945, 1948. CPom has 1911?- CU-B has 1934. CUpl has 1934.

2740. 1914. Doyle, T. M., pub. Doyle's valley directory... of Pomona, Ontario, Upland, San Dimas, Chino, Claremont, Lordsburg–La Verne and a resident directory of Cucamonga, North Pomona, Etiwanda, Narod, Ioamosa, Spadra, Walnut (Lemon)... Pomona [1914]   CSmH

2741. 1956– Luskey bros., pub. Luskey's official Pomona, Claremont, La Verne, San Dimas and Walnut criss cross city directory... Anaheim, 1956–
CL has 1961. CPom has 1956, 1959.

2742. 1921/22–1952. Los Angeles directory co., comp. Redondo Beach city directory, including Hermosa Beach and Manhattan Beach. L.A., 1921–1952. Publisher varies: 1921/22–1927? Kaasen directory co.
C has 1931. CHi has 1936, 1947, 1952. CL has 1921/22, 1923/24, 1925–27, 1931, 1936, 1947, 1952.

2743. 1960– Luskey bros., pub. Redondo Beach (Blue book) criss cross city directory.   CL

2744. 1953– Pacific directory co. Rosemead area city directory. Arcadia, 1953–
CL has 1953–54.

2745. 1921– L.A. directory co., pub. San Fernando valley directory. ...San Fernando, Burbank, Van Nuys, Lankershim and Owensmouth and all other towns in San Fernando valley. L.A., 1921–
C has 1923–24, 1928, 1930. CCH has 1922. CL has 1921–24, 1926, 1928, 1930, 1937–40. CSmH has 1923. CU-B has 1928, 1930.

2746. 1951– Pacific directory co. San Marino city directory. San Marino, 1951–
CL has 1951–52.

2747. 1908– Polk, R. L., & co., pub. San Pedro city directory. L.A., 1908– Publisher varies: 1932–49, Los Angeles directory co. Content varies: 1932–52, San Pedro and Wilmington.
C has 1923–24, 1928, 1932. CHi has 1932, 1946, 1949,

1952, 1956–57, 1959. CL has 1908, 1923–24, 1926, 1928, 1930, 1932, 1935, 1937, 1940, 1946, 1949, 1952, 1956–57, 1959. CU–B has 1932, 1934, 1957.

2748. 1899. Santa Monica directory co., pub. Santa Monica official business and residence directory and telephone guide. [n.p., 1899]   CStmo

2749. 1905. Santa Monica city and Ocean Park directory.   CStmo

2750. 1907. King, L. H., pub. Directory of the Santa Monica bay district of the permanent residents of Santa Monica, Ocean Park, Sawtelle and Palms. 1907.
                                                          CStmo

2751. 1908/09–1960/61. S & K publications, inc., pub. Santa Monica city directory...including Brentwood Heights and Ocean Park... L.A., 1908–1960. No directories were issued for 1926, 1929, 1932, 1934, 1935, 1937, 1939, 1941, 1942, 1943, 1944, 1945, 1946, 1949, 1950, 1951, 1955, 1956, 1957. Title varies. Publisher varies: 1908/09–1952/53, Los Angeles directory co., 1954, R. L. Polk & co.
C has 1913/14, 1923/24–1936. CCH has 1908/09, 1923/24. CHi has 1913/14, 1930/31, 1933, 1940, 1947/48, 1952/53, 1954. CL has 1913/14, 1915/16, 1917, 1919/20, 1921/22, 1923/24–1940, 1947/48, 1958/59. CLU has 1912, 1913/14. CSmH has 1911. CStmo has 1912–40, 1952/53, 1954, 1960/61. CU–B has 1928–1930/31, 1947/48, 1952/53.

2752. 1953– Pacific directory co. Sierra Madre area city directory. Arcadia, 1953–
CL has 1953, 1956, 1959.

2753. 1926– South Gate city directory. Publisher and title vary.
CHi has 1947, 1949. CL has 1926, 1928, 1930, 1945/46, 1947, 1949, 1951, 1961.

2754. 1920– South Pasadena city directory. [L.A., 1920– Publisher and title vary.
C has 1930, 1937–38. CL has 1920, 1926, 1927/28, 1929–34, 1936–38, 1940, 1952/53.

2755. 1948– Polk, R. L., & co., pub. Temple City city directory. L.A., 1948 Publisher varies: 1948–51, Los Angeles directory co.
CHi has 1948, 1951, 1953, 1959. CL has 1948, 1951, 1953, 1959. CU-B has 1951.

2756. 1946– Western directory co., pub. Torrance city directory. Santa Ana, 1946– Publisher and title vary.
CHi has 1946. CL has 1946, 1949, 1956, 1959.

2757. 1948– Tujunga-Sunland, Shadow Hills-Hanson Heights directory. Publisher and title vary.
CL has 1948–1950.

2758. 1945– Glendale directory co., pub. Van Nuys, Sherman Oaks and Encino directory. Glendale, 1945–
CL has 1945–46, 1961/62.

2759. 1914/15– Watts-Compton city directory. Publisher and title vary.
CL has 1914/15, 1919, 1921, 1922/23, 1925, 1927/28, 1932.

2760. 1916– Polk, R. L., & co., pub. Whittier city directory. L.A., 1916– Publisher varies: 19— –1926? Kaasen directory co.; 1928–51, Los Angeles directory co. Content varies: 1924–34, Whittier City and Rivera; 1938–39, Whittier, Los Nietos, Rivera & Santa Fe district; 1947–49, Whittier, Los Nietos, Rivera & Santa Fe Springs; 1951–52, Whittier & Los Nietos.
C has 1924, 1928–32, 1934. CHi has 1928, 1932, 1936,

1938–39, 1947, 1949, 1951–57, 1959, 1961. CL has 1916, 1920–24, 1926, 1928–32, 1934, 1939, 1942, 1947, 1949, 1952–56, 1959, 1961. CU-B has 1929–1930/31, 1956. CWhC has 1951.

GENERAL REFERENCES

2761. Adams, Emma Hildreth. To and fro in southern California with sketches in Arizona and New Mexico. Cincinnati, W.M.B.C. press, 1887. 288 p.
C CBaB CBb CHi CLO CLSU CLU CRedl CSd CSdS CSfCP CSmH CStmo CU-B CaBViPA MiD TxU ViW

2762. —— To and fro, up and down in southern California, Oregon, and Washington territory... Cincinnati, Cranston & Stowe, c1888. 608 p. illus. Includes chapters on the city of Los Angeles, native Californians, schools of Los Angeles, colonization schemes, vineyards and orange groves, biographical sketches of H. H. Bancroft, J. J. Warner, the Picos.
C CL CLO CLU CPom CSalCL CSf CSfCW CSfWF-H CU-B CaBViPA

2763. —— Same. S.F., Hunt & Eaton, c1888. 608 p. illus.   CHi CP CRic

2764. Aitken, Melbourne F. Benjamin D. Wilson, southern California pioneer. [L.A.] 1946. Thesis (M.A.) —U.C.L.A., 1946.   CLU

2765. Allen, Velta Myrle. Within adobe walls. Sunland, Cecil L. Anderson, 1948. 45 p. illus.   CHi CPom

2766. The almond colonies of southern California. Antelope valley. Manzana, 1893. 40 p. illus., maps.
                                                           CSmH

2767. Altadena. Chamber of commerce. Altadena "the beautiful." "The paradise of the foothills." Comp. under the direction of Charles E. Decker. [Altadena, 1926] 48 p. illus.   CLU

2768. [Altadena] Pasadena's highland suburb. Altadena [n.d.] 6 l. illus.   CHi

2769. American association of advertising agencies. Los Angeles newspaper reader survey [conducted by Daniel Starch] N.Y, [c1939] 93 p. illus., maps.   CLU

2770. American pipe and construction co., Monterey Park. Annual report.
CL has 1954–60.

2771. American society of appraisers. Los Angeles chapter. Membership roster. L.A.
CL has 1956/57, 1958/59.

2772. Anderson, Homer G. Sunland-La Crescenta area, Los Angeles county. [L.A.] 1947. Thesis (M.A.)— U.C.L.A., 1947.   CLU

2773. Antelope valley ledger gazette. 50th anniversary edition...December, 1936. Lancaster, 1936. 36 p. illus.   CSmH CU-B

2774. Armitage, Merle. Success is no accident; the biography of William Paul Whitsett. [Yucca valley] Manzanita press [1959] 326 p. illus., ports.
                                                     C CLO CP

2775. Arnold, Bion Joseph. ...Report on the transportation problem of Los Angeles; with an introduction by Thos. E. Gibbon. [n.p.] 1911. 20 p. illus., ports., maps. (The California outlook, v.11, no. 19, Nov. 4, 1911. Supplement)   CL

2776. Arnold, Ralph. California petroleum corporation; report on the properties of the American petroleum company and the American oilfields company of California. [L.A.?] 1912. 58 p.   CHi

2777. Arrow research institute. Cults, sects, philosophical groups, and small denominations in Los Angeles and southern California. L.A., 1958. 16 p.

C CAla CStmo

2778. Automobile club of Southern California. Engineering dept. An appraisal of freeways vs. surface streets in the Los Angeles metropolitan area. [L.A.?] 1954. 28 p. illus., map.   C

2779. Avakian, John Caspar. The property republic, being an outgrowth of a plan for the development of the metropolitan district of Los Angeles... L.A., 1925. 221 p. illus., maps.   CLU

2780. Bailey, Harry P. Physical geography of the San Gabriel mountains, California. [L.A.] 1950. Thesis (Ph.D.)—U.C.L.A., 1950.   CLU

2781. Baker, Donald M. Report on a rapid transit system for Los Angeles, California [to Central business district association, Los Angeles, California] November 15, 1933. [n.p.] 1933. 90 l. maps, tables, diagrs.   CL

2782. Baldwin, Anita M. Santa Anita rancho, Los Angeles county, California. [n.p., 1918?] 23 p. illus.

CLU CSmH

2783. [Baldwin, Elias Jackson] E. J. Baldwin's pure grape brandy and California wines. [S.F., Schmidt label & litho. co., 1883?] 16 p.   CHi

2784. Baldwin Park bulletin. Christmas number, December 24, 1915. Baldwin Park, 1915. unp. illus.   C

2785. Banning, William. Six horses. N.Y., Century, c1930. 410 p. ports., maps. Bibliography: p. 377–387.

CAna CHi CLgA CSd CStmo

2786. Barber, Farrell. History of Aircraft accessories corporation. [Kansas City, Mo., 1943] 51 p.

CHi

2787. Beaudry, Prudent. Prospectus for the sale of Los Angeles lands with a schedule of the same. The property of Prudent Beaudry. S.F., Bacon & co., bk. and job print., 1869. 8 p.   CSmH

2788. Bell, Horace. Reminiscences of a ranger; or, Early times in southern California. L.A., Yarnell, Caystile & Mathes, print., 1881. 457 p. The city of the Angels and surrounding countryside as seen by a pioneer (1852–1881) —politics, bandits, ranchero life, including reminiscences of San Francisco and Sacramento.
Available in many libraries.

2789. —— Same. Santa Barbara, Hebberd, 1927. 499 p. illus.
Available in many libraries.

2790. —— Same. L.A. Primavera press, 1933. 499 p.

CHi CV

2791. —— On the old west coast; being further reminiscences of a ranger...Ed. by Lanier Bartlett. N.Y., Morrow, 1930. 336 p. illus., ports.
Available in many libraries.

2792. Bemis, George W. From rural to urban, the municipalized county of Los Angeles... L.A., Haynes foundation, 1947. 33 p.

C CBev CLO CLS CLSU CLU CU-B

2793. —— Intergovernmental coordination of public works programs in the Los Angeles metropolitan area. L.A., Haynes foundation, 1945. 24 p. (Pub. of the John Randolph Haynes & Dora Haynes foundation: Pamphlet ser. 10)   CLU

2794. —— Los Angeles county as an agency of municipal government. L.A., Haynes foundation, 1947. 105 p. maps. (Pub. of the John Randolph Haynes & Dora Haynes foundation: Monograph ser. no. 10)

CL CLS CLU CSfSt CWhC

2795. Bigger, William Richard. Flood control in metropolitan Los Angeles. [L.A.] 1954. Thesis (Ph.D.) —U.C.L.A., 1954.   CLU

2796. Bixby, Fred Hathaway. Bixbyana, this house and the Hathaway-Bixby story... Long Beach, 1962. 22 p. "250 copies designed and printed by Lawton Kennedy."   CHi

2797. Blumer, J. G., ed. A dictionary of Sierra Madre and a guide, philosopher and friend for tourists, travellers and investors. L.A., Out West co., 1906. 66 p.

CL CLU

2798. Boal, John M., ed. The home land, Los Angeles and southern California; containing historical and descriptive statements of certain sections of this land of sunshine and flowers. L.A., 1884. 74 p. illus.   C NHi

2799. Board of commissioners in partition. Report of the Board of commissioners to adjust the liabilities between the counties of Los Angeles and Orange, showing the indebtedness of Orange county to Los Angeles county on March 11th, 1889 and other matters pertinent to a final adjudication and settlement of the business affairs between the two counties. Presented to the Board of supervisors of Los Angeles and Orange counties, May 1890. [n.p., n.d.] 96 p.   CL

2800. Boundaries of the school districts of Los Angeles county, California. [L.A.] Daily news print., 1870. 12 p.   CSmH

2801. —— Same. March 1st, 1890. L.A., Evening express, 1890. 46 p.   CPom

2802. Bowen, Edith Blumer, comp. Annals of early Sierra Madre... [Sierra Madre] Sierra Madre hist. soc., 1950. 206 p. illus., ports.   C CHi CL
CLU CP CSf CSjC CU-B

2803. Brennan, Arcadia Bandini, vs. the Title insurance and trust company, et al. In the Superior court of the state of California, in and for the county of Los Angeles. Arcadia Bandini, plaintiff, vs. the Title insurance and trust company, a corporation, et al., defendants. [L.A., 1913] 3 pts. in 1.   CSmH

2804. Bridge, Norman. The marching years... N.Y., Duffield and co., 1920. 292 p. port. "A partial list of papers and publications by Dr. Bridge": p. 291–92.

C CHi

2805. Brigham, Robert Leslie. Land ownership and occupancy by Negroes in Manhattan Beach, California. Fresno, 1956. 124 l. illus., map. Thesis (M.A.)—Fresno state college, 1956.   CFS

2806. Broderick, W. J., vs. Valdez, Ynocente, et al. In the Circuit court of the United States for the state of California. W. J. Broderick vs. Ynocente Valdez, et al. Plaintiff's brief. J. W. Harding, plaintiff's att'y. [n.p., 187–] 5 p. Suit over part of the Rancho La Puente.

CLU

2807. Brook, Harry Ellington. The city and county of Los Angeles in southern California... L.A., Kingsley-Barnes & Neuner co., 1898. 63 p. illus., maps.
CCH CL CLU CPom CSfCSM CStoC CU-B NN
Other editions followed.
C (1909) CHi (1904–05, 1913, 1915) CLSU (1908, 1910, 1924) CSmH (1902, 1905–07, 1919) CU-B (1902, 1904, 1906, 1908, 1915) MiD-B (1907) NHi (1901) NN (1901–20) OrU (1909)

2808. —— The county and city of Los Angeles in southern California, issued for distribution at the World's Columbian exposition by the County board of supervisors ... [L.A.] Times-mirror co., 1893. 32 p. illus., map.

C-S CL CLU CP CSfCP CSmH CU-B NHi

2809. —— The county and city of Los Angeles in southern California, July 1897... L.A., Kingsley-Barnes & Neuner co. [1897?] 32 p. illus., map.
CL CLO CLU CStmo CU-B NHi

2810. —— Same. October, 1897. 63 p.   CStmo

2811. Brooks, Thomas. Notes on Los Angeles water supply. L.A., 1938. [9] p. illus., maps.   CLU

2812. Browning, J. W. Hand book on Los Angeles, city and county property, giving resources, climate, progress, outlook, etc. [L.A., Times-mirror print., 1885?] 20 p.
CSmH

2813. Brunner, Francis. Southern California's prettiest drive; a tour along the crescent shore of Santa Monica bay and up into the picturesque canyons of the Santa Monica mountains. Santa Monica, Outlook print. [1925?] 32 p. illus.   CLU CStmo

2814. Brunner, Mary Frances, comp. Newhall: a history and description of Newhall, California; comp. by Mary F. Brunner, branch librarian, ed. by Lois Goddard and Catherine Greening. L.A., L.A. county pub. lib., 1940. 7 v. illus., maps. Loose-leaf scrap books, with typew. text, containing clippings, mounted photographs, letters, etc.   CLCo

2815. Bureau of Jewish social research, New York (City) [Report. n.d.] v.p. tables. A report on the Jewish population in Los Angeles.   CL

2816. Burnight, Ralph F. The Japanese in rural Los Angeles county. L.A., So. Calif. sociol. soc., Univ. of So. Calif., 1920. 16 p. (Studies in sociol. Sociol. monograph no. 16)   C CL CLSU CLU CO CU-B

2817. [Buschlen, John Preston] Señor Plummer; the life and laughter of an Old-Californian, by Don Juan [pseud.] L.A., Times-mirror, 1942. 242 p. illus., ports.
C CBb CBev CBu CL CLO CLSU CLU CO CRedl CSalCL CSf CSmH CStmo CU-B CV

2818. —— Same. 2d ed. Hollywood, Murray & McGee, 1943. 242 p. illus., plates.   CHi

2819. Bynum, Lindley, and Jones, Idwal. Biscailuz, sheriff of the new west; with introduction by Erle Stanley Gardner. N.Y., Morrow, 1950. 208 p. illus., ports.
CCoron CHi CLO CLU CMon CMont CNa CRedl CRic CSd CSdS CSf CStmo CViCL CWhC

2820. California. Dept. of natural resources. Division of beaches and parks. Pio Pico. Sacramento, State print. off., 1958.   CRcS

2821. —— **Railroad commission. Engineering dept.** ...Report on service, operating and financial conditions of the Los Angeles railway corporation...Nov. 10th, 1919. Richard Sachse, chief engineer. L.A. [1919] 41, 180 l. tables, maps, diagr. Reproduced from typew. copy. At head of title: Application 4238.   CL

2822. Not in use.

2823. —— **Superior court. Los Angeles county juvenile dept.** Report on conditions and progress of the juvenile court, 1930, 1931, 1932, 1933. L.A. [1934] 83 l. tables, diagrs.   CL

2824. —— **Supreme court.** In the Supreme court of the state of California. In the matter of the application of Horace Bell for a writ of habeas corpus. [1886] 40 p.
CLSM

2825. California federation of business and professional women's clubs. Los Angeles district. Club directory, constitution and by-laws. 1933/34– [L.A., 1934– Annual.

CL has 1933/34–1936/37, 1938/39–1940/41, 1943/44–1944/45, 1946/47.

2826. California federation of women's clubs. Los Angeles district. Yearbook 19–?/ – L.A., 19–?– illus., ports. Title varies: 19 / –1932/33, Directory.

CL has 1917/18, 1923/24, 1925/26–1933/34, 1935/36–1936/37, 1939/40, 1941/42–1942/43, 1946/47–1948/49, 1950/51.

2827. California history and landmarks club. [Report] 1931–32. 23 p.   CHi

2828. California homes and industries; a serial showing the improvements and progress of the state...This number is devoted exclusively to Los Angeles county... S.F., Elliott, 1891. 87 p. illus.   C CL CLSU

2829. California immigrant union, San Francisco. ...The Centinela colony, near the city of Los Angeles. L.A., Herald steam bk. and job print., 1874. 12 p. (Supplement to *All about California*)   CSmH

2830. California institute of technology, Pasadena. Industrial relations section. Survey of selected personnel practices in Los Angeles county as of April 1, 1949, compiled by Robert D. Gray and staff. Pasadena [1949?] 74 p. (Its Bul. no. 17)   CL

2831. California taxpayers' association, inc. ... Centralization of public health services in Los Angeles county... L.A., 1932. 37 l. Typew.   CU-B

2832. —— City and county consolidation for Los Angeles. [L.A., 1917] 194 p. tables, maps, charts.
C CLU

2833. Campbell (Thomas D.) & co., Los Angeles. Chino ranch, for alfalfa, hogs, dairying, deciduous fruits, sugar beets... L.A. [1910?] [7] p. illus., map.   CHi

2834. Carpenter, Bruce R. Rancho Encino: its historical geography. [L.A.] 1948. Thesis (M.A.) — U.C.L.A., 1948.   CLU

2835. Carpenter, E. R. "Sausal Redondo" argument in favor of survey made in July 1868. S.F., Edward Bosqui & co., 1069. 24 p.   CHi CLU

2836. Carpenter, Ford Ashman. The land of the beckoning climate... [L.A.] Pub. by the Supervisors of L.A. county and distributed through the L.A. county chamber of commerce, 1932– illus.
CLO (1938) CLU (1932) CU-B (1936)

2837. Carroll, June Starr. The Elizabeth lake — Leonis valley area. [L.A.] 1948. Thesis (M.A.) — U.C.L.A., 1948.   CLU

2838. Case, Frederick E. The housing status of minority families, Los Angeles, 1956. L.A., Los Angeles urban league, 1958. 78 p. maps. A joint project of the Los Angeles urban league and Univ. of Calif., Los Angeles.

2839. Cecil, George Henry. Conservation in Los Angeles county...Los Angeles city school district, division of curriculum and instruction, vocational and practical arts section... [L.A.] 1935. 82 p.   CLU

2840. —— Same. [L.A.] 1937. 95 p. (L.A. city school district school pub. no. 275)   CLU

2841. Central business district association, Los Angeles. Transit study. Los Angeles metropolitan area. L.A., 1944. 39 p.   NN

2842. Chaffee, Mary. ...Social work as a profession in Los Angeles. L.A., So. Calif. sociol. soc., Univ. of So. Calif. [1918] 10 p.   CL CLU

2843. Chang, Stella Lynn. A descriptive study of the curriculum, personnel and facilities of commercial

and professional institutions in the greater Los Angeles area offering training to students in television performance. [L.A.] 1958. Thesis (M.A.)—U.C.L.A., 1958.
CLU

2844. [**Chapin, Lou V.**] Art work on southern California. S.F., Calif. photogravure co., 1900. 12 parts in 2 v. illus. Text signed by Lou V. Chapin.
CL CLSU CSmH

2845. Citizens adoption committee, Los Angeles county. Children without homes of their own; a study of children needing adoption and other foster care in Los Angeles county. 1953. 60 p. illus.
CL

2846. —— ...Gleanings from twenty-two months of activity by Mary Stanton. L.A., 1952. 21 p.
CL

2847. Citizens committee on governmental reorganization, Los Angeles. [First] report, submitted May 14, 1936. [L.A., 1936] 7 p.
CL

2848. Citizens committee on local taxation, Los Angeles county. Report...on local taxation. L.A., 1941. 37 l.
CL

2849. Citizens' committee on parks, beaches, and recreational facilities, Los Angeles. Parks, beaches and recreational facilities for Los Angeles county. [L.A.] Haynes foundation, 1945. 18 p. map.
C

2850. Citizens traffic and transportation committee for the extended Los Angeles area. Transportation in the Los Angeles area; the final report, 1957. 53 p. illus., maps, diagrs.
CLS

2851. The city and county of Los Angeles; commercial and manufacturing interests; representative business enterprises and professional men. Seaside and mountain resorts. [L.A., Times-mirror press] 1894. 178 p. illus., ports.
C CL CSmH

2852. Civic bureau of music and art of Los Angeles, pub. Los Angeles county culture and the community... [L.A., 1926?] [67] p. illus.
CHi CL

2853. —— Same. [L.A., Geo. Rice and sons, 192–?] [79] p. illus., map.
CHi CU-B

2854. Clodius, Albert Howard. The quest for good government in Los Angeles 1890–1900. [Claremont, 1953] 567 l. Thesis (Ph.D.)—Claremont college, 1953.
CCH

2855. Close, Lorenzo C., comp. Interesting views of Ocean Park and vicinity and the Pickering pleasure pier. Ocean Park, 1927. 20 p. illus.
CStmo

2856. Cohn (K.) & co. The Montebello tract... L.A. [n.d.] illus., maps.
CLU

2857. Committee on governmental simplification. Municipal and county studies. L.A., 1934–36. 4 v. tables, charts, diagrs.
CL-MR

2858. The Community relations conference of southern California. Annual report. 1st– [1947?]– L.A. [1947?–]
CL has v.7–13, 1953–59.

2859. Complete visitors guide of Los Angeles, Hollywood, Pasadena, Beverly Hills, Long Beach, Santa Monica, the beaches and southern California... [L.A., 1948] illus., maps. 50 pages on Los Angeles; 3–4 pages on each of the other cities mentioned in title.
C CL CLU CSf CU-B MiD

2860. Condon, James Edward. Condon's blue book of wealth; a list of 8,500 people who possess wealth aggregating more than $1,000,000,000, compiled from the tax records of Los Angeles city and county and Ventura county, California, separately classified and alphabetically arranged. L.A., 1917. 197 p.
CLU

2861. —— Same. 1920. 189 p.
CSd

2862. —— Southern California blue book of money. Taxpayers assessed on $5,000 and upwards in Los Angeles, Pasadena, South Pasadena, Long Beach, Pomona, Monrovia, Arcadia, Santa Monica, Venice, etc., also San Diego. L.A., 1913. 137 p.
CLU

2863. Conference on childhood and youth in war time. Today's children in tomorrow's world, a report. 2d. [L.A., 1944] 73 p.
CL

2864. Conmy, Peter Thomas. Stephen Mallory White, California statesman. S.F., Native sons of the Golden west, 1956. 15 p.
CHi CP CRcS CStrCL

2865. Conner, Edward Palmer. The romance of the ranchos... L.A., Title insurance & trust co. [1929] 40 p. illus., map. "Reprinted...from the *Los Angeles times.*"
C CBev CHi CL CLLoy CLU CLob CMS CO CPom CSfU CSmH CSmat CStmo CU-B

2866. —— Same. c1939. 44 p. illus., map. Brief historical sketches of California ranchos, forerunners of towns, then cities. "In Los Angeles county, ranchos Santa Monica, San Fernando, Azusa, La Cañada, Puente and Tujunga, all gave their names to the towns founded within their borders."
C CBev CHi CLSU CLU CLob CRcS CSS CU-B CWhC

2867. —— Same. 1941. 44 p. illus., map.
CHi CStmo

2868. Connor, J. Torrey. Saunterings in summerland... L.A., E. K. Foster, 1902. 80 p. illus.
C CL CLU CSmH CU-B

2869. Coronel, Manuel F. Report on the bill to divide the county of Los Angeles and create the new county of Anaheim. [Sacramento, Gelwicks, state print., 1870]
CSmH

2870. Council of labor and building trades council, Los Angeles. Official trades and labor souvenir directory of Los Angeles and vicinity... L.A., Kingsley-Barnes & Neuner co. [1896] 96 p.
CLO

2871. Council of social agencies of Los Angeles. Personnel practices in member agencies of the Los Angeles community welfare federation, 1937. L.A. [1937] 71 l. diagrs.
CL

2872. —— **Division of social studies.** The bill for social welfare in Los Angeles, 1938. How much is it? Who pays it? How is it spent? [L.A., 1939] 23 p. tables, diagrs.
CL

2873. Coverdale and Colpitts, New York. Report to the Los Angeles metropolitan transit authority on a monorail rapid transit line for Los Angeles. N.Y., 1954. v.p. illus., diagrs., maps.
C CL

2874. Covina argus-citizen. Special historical edition, Sept. 26, 1952.
CHi

2875. Covina women's club, comp. Historical sketches of Covina & Azusa valley.
CCov

2876. Crebs, Clara (Wells) History of the Los Angeles federation, tenth district California congress of mothers and parent-teacher associations from May 1, 1911 to May 1, 1922... [n.p., n.d.] 178 p. port.
CL

2877. Croker, Richard S. Historical account of the Los Angeles mackerel fishery. Terminal island, Calif. state fisheries laboratory. 1938. 62 p. (Div. of fish & game. Fish bul. no. 52)
CLSU CLU CO CSdS CSf CStmo CViCL

2878. Crumly, Charles W. ...Geography; Los Angeles and vicinity, preparatory for federal-state-county-city examinations... [L.A., Calif. educational pub., 1940] unp. Reproduced from typew. copy.
CL

2879. Cumming, Gordon Robertson. A plan for metropolitan county police in Los Angeles county. [Berkeley, 1935] Thesis (M.A.)—Univ. of Calif., 1935.
CU

2880. Cunningham, William Glenn. The aircraft industry. L.A., L. Morrison, 1951.   CSd

2881. Curtis, Freddie. Arroyo Sequit... L.A., Archaeological survey assoc. of So. Calif., 1959.   CSd

2882. Daily tribune, Covina. Covina diamond jubilee history. (Issue of June 2, 1959)   CCov

2883. Dakin, Susanna (Bryant) A Scotch paisano; Hugo Reid's life in California, 1832–1852, derived from his correspondence... Berkeley, Univ. of Calif. press, 1939. 312 p. illus., map.
Available in many libraries.

2884. Daniel, Mann, Johnson & Mendenhall. Los Angeles metropolitan transit authority rapid transit program. Report relating to: transit system equipment, transit facilities, alignments and station locations [and] cost estimates. [L.A.] 1960. 22 p. illus., maps.   CL

2885. Daughters of Charity. One hundred years of service...1856–1956, dedicated to the people of Southern California... [L.A.? 1956?] 3 6 p. illus., ports.   CLU

2886. Daughters of the American revolution. California. El camino real chapter, Los Angeles. Newspaper clippings about pioneers, southern California, Los Angeles community and county, January 1st, 1892 to September 1st, 1892, January 1st, 1942 to September 1st, 1942... [1942] 220 p. illus., ports.   CL

2887. —— —— —— Newspaper clippings of the activities of pioneer residents of Los Angeles and southern California, October 1st, 1892–March 26th, 1943... (incomplete) [1943]   CL

2888. —— —— —— Newspaper clippings of the activities of pioneer residences of Los Angeles and southern California. 192 p. illus., ports.   CL

2889. —— —— **Genealogical records committee, comp.** ...Baptismal records of Los Angeles county, 1771–1873. [n.p.] 1945. 413 l., 115 l. Typew.
C C-S CL CLO

2890. —— —— —— Court house and church records from California... [n.p.] 1936– 3 v. Title varies. v.2 and 3: Los Angeles county marriages, 1876–1888.
C C-S CL

2891. —— —— —— Early California wills, Los Angeles county, 1850–1890. [L.A.? 1952] 2 v. in 1. Typew.
C CL

2892. —— —— —— [Veterans' grave registration, Los Angeles county, to 1940]... [n.p.] Author [1943] 2 v. Typew.   C C-S CL

2893. Davies, John M., comp. Los Angeles city and county, resources, climate, progress and outlook; pub. by the Los Angeles board of trade... L.A., Gilchrist print. house, 1885. 68 p. map.   CHi CP CSmH

2894. Dean, Helen C. Unmarried parenthood, an analysis of 1839 unmarried parenthood cases active with health and welfare agencies in Los Angeles county during April, 1944... 1946. 133 p. illus. (Welfare planning council of Los Angeles region. Research dept. Pub. no. 3)
CL

2895. Dean iris gardens, Moneta. Catalogs. CHi has 1914, 1915/16.

2896. De Guyer et al. vs. Banning, William. In the Supreme court of the state of California. De Guyer, et al., plaintiffs and appellants, vs. William Banning, defendant and respondent. Reply to respondent's brief.

Bicknell & White, attorneys for defendant. Smith, Winder, & Smith, of counsell... [L.A.] Freeman, print. [1889] "Ejectment for a tract of land in the inner bay of San Pedro, called Mormon Island."—p. [3]   CLU

2897. DeLong, James. Southern California, for climate, soil, productions, and health. Lawrence, Kansas, Journal steam print., co., 1875. 43 p.   NHi

2898. —— Same. Kansas City, Mo., Ramsay, Millet & Hudson, print., 1877. 130 p. illus., maps.
CL CSmH

2899. Donoghue, James R. Intergovernmental cooperation in fire protection in the Los Angeles area. L.A., 1943. 126 p. (Bur. of governmental research, Univ. of Calif. at L.A., Studies in local govt., no. 7) Bibliography: p. 121–26.   CStmo

2900. Drescher, Thomas B. The electric power supply for the Los Angeles–San Bernardino lowland. [L.A.] 1951. Thesis (M.A.)—U.C.L.A., 1951.   CLU

2901. Duarte. Chamber of commerce. Andreas Duarte and the community that bears his name, 1841–1941. [Duarte? 1914?] 12 p. illus.   CLU

2902. Duke, Donald, comp. Pacific electric railway; a pictorial album of electric railroading. San Marino [c1958] 62 p. illus., map. (Pac. railway jl., v.2, no. 7, Sept., 1958)   C CBb CBev CHi CLO CLSM CP CStmo

2903. Eagle Rock. Chamber of commerce. Eagle Rock, California... [1935?] [41] p. illus., map, plan. Includes a history of Eagle Rock by Mrs. C. W. Young.
CLO

2904. Eberly, Gordon Saul. Arcadia, city of the Santa Anita. Claremont, Saunders press, 1953. 239 p. illus., ports.   C CHi CL CLO CLSM CLU CLob CMon CO CP CStmo NN

2905. Electronic representatives association. Southern California chapter. E R A...directory. CL has 1960/61.

2906. Eliot, Charles William. Waterlines, key to development of metropolitan Los Angeles... L.A., Haynes foundation, 1946. 39 p. illus. (Pub. of the John Randolph Haynes & Dora Haynes foundation: Monograph ser. no. 9)   C CBev

2907. El Monte. Ramona freeway; city of El Monte presentation to joint committee on streets and highways, presented July 21, 1952. [El Monte? 1952] v.p. maps.
CU-B

2908. Emerson, Folger. Report of survey of administration of justice in Los Angeles county, California to Edmund G. Brown, attorney general. [S.F., 1956?] 42 l.   CL

2909. Evens, Evan Lewis. A history of Antelope valley. [1926?] 5 l. Typew.   CLCo

2910. Federal art project. Southern California. Historical murals in the Los Angeles county hall of records, Board of supervisors' hearing room. [n.p., 1939] unp. illus. "Accepted and dedicated May 20, 1939."
C CL CLSU CSd CSmH

2911. Feichert, Mary St. Joseph, Sister. The history of *The Tidings*, official organ of the Archdiocese of Los Angeles, 1895–1945. Wash., D.C., 1951. 149 p. Thesis (M.A.)—Catholic univ. of America, 1951.   CSrD

2912. Feldman, Frances (Lomas) History of the committee on mental health, health division, Welfare planning council, Los Angeles region, 1936–1953. [L.A.] 1955. 42 p.   C

2913. Ferguson, Charles Kasreal. Political problems and activities of Oriental residents in Los Angeles and vicinity. [L.A.] 1942. Thesis (M.A.) — U.C.L.A., 1942.   CLU

2914. Ferguson, Jenniellen Wesley. City council organization and procedures in Los Angeles county. L.A., Bur. of governmental research, Univ. of Calif., L.A., 1955. 77 p.   CL

2915. Firman, David. Montebello, California. [L.A.] 1949. Thesis (M.A.)—U.C.L.A., 1949.   CLU

2916. Fisher, Robert. The work of the Committee on the revision of the civil service provisions of the Los Angeles county charter... [L.A.? 1939. [8] 158 l. Thesis (M.A.)—Occidental college, 1939.   CLO

2917. Fletcher, Lehman Blanton. Growth and adjustment of the Los Angeles milkshed: a study in the economics of location. [Berkeley, 1960] Thesis (Ph.D.) —Univ. of Calif., 1960.   CU

2918. Forbes, Harrie Rebecca Piper (Smith) "Mrs. A. S. C. Forbes," comp. Then and now; 100 landmarks within 50 miles of Los Angeles civic center... [L.A., Bd. of supervisors of L.A. county] c1939. [63] p. illus.
C CHi CL CLO CLSU CLU CO CSf CSfCW CSfWF-H CU-B

2919. Forbes, James B. The story of Michillinda, a city surburban... L.A., So. Calif. land and securities co. [1912] 36 p.   MiD-B

2920. Force, Mary Elizabeth (Harris) John Rowland and William Workman, pioneers of southern California. [Berkeley, 1932] 134 l. illus., maps. Thesis (M.A.)—Univ. of Calif., 1932.   CU CU-B

2921. Ford, John Anson. Thirty explosive years in Los Angeles county. San Marino, Huntington lib., 1961. 231 p.   CAla CHi CSfU CSmH

2922. Forest and water associations of Los Angeles county. [Newspaper clippings, letters and documents pertaining to the associations. Incorporated May 2, 1899]   CL

2923. Frank, Elisabeth R. Background for planning. [L.A.] Welfare planning council, L.A. region [1949?] 125 p. maps, diagrs.   CL

2924. —— Same. 1955. 105 p. maps, charts. (Welfare planning council, L.A. region. Pub. no. 15)
C CL CLLoy CLU

2925. —— Differentiating communities in Los Angeles county. L.A., 1957. 2 v. maps. (Welfare planning council, L.A. region. Special report ser., no. 50)   C

2926. Fry, George, and associates, inc., Chicago. Survey of organization and operations, Chief administrative office, the county of Los Angeles. [L.A.] 1960. v.p. illus.   CL

2927. Gardena, California... [Brochure. n.p., n.d.]
C-S

2928. Giddings, B. F., pub. The Guide board to southern California; a business and tourist hand book. Revised and published monthly... L.A. [1892?]–93.
CL has Dec. 1892, Dec. 1893. CSmH has Mar. 1893.

2929. Gillespie's guide; street and car directory of Los Angeles and eighty-eight surrounding towns. Comp. by Gordon F. Gillespie. L.A., c1921. maps.   CHi
Other editions followed.
1934, 1937, comp. by R. L. Gillespie. Publisher varies: 1925, 1931, 1934, 1937 Gillespie guide co.   CHi (1934, 1937) CStmo (1931) CU-B (1925)

2930. Gillingham, Robert Cameron. The Rancho San Pedro; the story of a famous rancho in Los Angeles

county and of its owners the Dominguez family. L.A., The Dominguez estate co., c1961. 473 p. illus., ports., maps, facsims.   CHi CLSM

2931. Given, John New. The attitudes and opinions of selected community groups toward junior college education in Los Angeles. [L.A.] 1957. Thesis (Ed.D.) — U.C.L.A., 1957.   CLU

2932. Glassell, Andrew, et al., and Scherer, J. C., et al. vs. Verdugo, Teodoro, et al. In the Supreme court of the state of California. From the Superior court of Los Angeles county. Andrew Glassell, et al., plaintiffs and respondents, and J. C. Scherer, et al., intervenors and respondents, vs. Teodoro Verdugo, et al., defendants and appellants. Transcript on appeal. [n.p.] 1894. 323 p. Water rights suit.   CLU

2933. Gleason, George. The fifth migration...California migratory agricultural worker situation. Prepared for the Los Angeles committee for church and community cooperation. [L.A., 1940] 29 p.   CO CStoC CU-B

2934. Glendora citrus association. By-laws. Azusa, Pomotropic press, 1896.   CSmH

2935. —— Glendora citrus association, 1895–1945... Glendora [1945?] [24] p. illus.   CLU

2936. Glendora foot-hills school, Glendora. The Glendora foot-hills school upon the George D. Whitcomb foundation. [Glendora? 1921] 56 p.   CSmH

2937. Goedhard Neil. Basic statistics of the Los Angeles area. [L.A.] 1955. 74 p. maps, diagrs., tables. (Air pollution foundation. Report no. 6)   C

2938. Golter, Samuel Harry. The City of Hope. N.Y., Putnam [1954] 177 p. illus., ports.
C CHi CNa CSd CStmo CU-B

2939. Gotchy, L. T. Dawn mine and Millard canyon area. 1958.   CP

2940. Gray, Blanche. Ruffled petticoat days. [1st ed.] Culver City, Murray and Gee [1953] 147 p. illus. Autobiographical.   C CLSM

2941. Greater Los Angeles citizens committee. Shoreline development study, Playa del Rey to Palos Verdes, a portion of a proposed master recreation plan for the greater Los Angeles region. [L.A.] 1944. 39 p. illus., maps, plans.   C CL-MR

2942. Greater Los Angeles illustrated. [L.A.? 1907?] 192 p. illus., ports.   CLU

2943. Greer, Scott Allen. The participation of ethnic minorities in the labor unions of Los Angeles county. [L.A.] 1952. Thesis (Ph.D.)—U.C.L.A., 1952.   CLU

2944. —— and Kube, Ella. Urban worlds: a comparative study of four Los Angeles areas. [L.A.] Occidental college. Laboratory in urban culture, 1955. 224 l.   CLO

2945. Griffith, Griffith Jenkins. Parks, boulevards and playgrounds. L.A., Prison reform league pub. co. [c1910] 80 p. illus., port.   C

2946. Not in use.

2947. Groeling, John Carman. A historical study of the early development of Bellflower, California. [Whittier] 1954. 111 l. plates, mounted photos. Thesis (M.A.) —Whittier college, 1954.   CWhC

2948. Guenther, Dorothy Barbara, comp. Material on Antelope valley... [n.d.] v.p. Typew. Abstracts from papers by early settlers, letters, etc.   CLCo

2949. Halberg, June Elizabeth. The Fitts-Palmer campaign for district attorney in Los Angeles county, 1936. [L.A.] 1940. Thesis (M.A.)—U.C.L.A., 1940.
CLU

2950. Hallock, E. G., et al. vs. Markham, H. H.
In the Superior court of Los Angeles county. ...E. G.
Hallock, et al., plaintiffs, vs. H. H. Markham, defendant.
Brief and argument on behalf of plaintiffs... [L.A.,
188–?] 42 p.   CHi

2951. Hamilton, James Alexander. A hospital
plan for Los Angeles county, California. [L.A., Los Angeles county-wide hospital survey, 1947?] 51 p. illus.,
maps, tables.   C

2952. Hanson, Earl. Los Angeles county population
and housing data; statistical data from the 1940 census...
L.A., Haynes foundation, 1944. 30 p. illus., maps. Re-
produced from typew. copy.
C CL CLO CLS CLSU CLU CO CSdS CSf
CWhC

2953. Harris, Nicholas Boilvin. Famous crimes by
Nick Harris, famous Pacific coast criminologist... L.A.,
Arthur Vernon agency, 1933. 95 p. ports.   CBb CHi

2954. —— In the shadows. L.A., Times-mirror press,
1923.   CSd

2955. Harrison, Benjamin Samuel. Fortune fav-
ors the brave; the life and times of Horace Bell, pioneer
Californian. L.A., Ward Ritchie, 1953. 307 p. illus. Bib-
liography: p. 291–294.
C CBb CHi CLSM CLU CP CRc CSd CSdS
CSf CSjC CStbS CStmo CU-B CViCL

2956. Harvil corporation, Compton. Annual report.
CL has 1951–52, 1954–60.

2957. Hatfield, D. D., and Jones, Linnea. Los Angeles public service guide...to the city, county, state and
federal offices and departments... L.A., O. W. Smith
[1946] 235 p. illus., maps.
C CBb CL CLS CLSU CLU CU-B

2958. Hathcock, Donald Lee. The history of Bald-
win Park, California (a resource unit for teachers of
Baldwin Park schools). [Whittier] 1954. 126 l. Thesis
(M.A.)—Whittier college, 1954.   CWhC

2959. Hayes, Benjamin Ignatius. Pioneer notes
from the diaries of Judge Benjamin Hayes, 1849–1875.
L.A., Priv. print., 1929. 307 p. illus., ports., map. "Edited
and published by Marjorie Tisdale Wolcott."
Available in many libraries.

2960. Hearne bros., Detroit. Official Hearne brothers polyconic projection cloth maps of all Los Angeles
county. Constantly revised and kept up to date. [De-
troit, 195–?]   C

2961. Heininger, Charles P., pub. Album of Los
Angeles, Cal. and vicinity. S.F., c1888. 10 p. illus.
                                                          CL CSmH NN

2962. Hill, Robert Thomas. Southern California
geology and Los Angeles earthquakes... L.A., So. Calif.
acad. of sciences, 1928. 232 p. illus., maps.
Available in many libraries.

2963. Hinrichsen, Kenneth Conrad. Pioneers in
southern California hydroelectric water power: Chaffey
and Baldwin. [Berkeley, 1949] Thesis (M.A.)—Univ. of
Calif., 1949.   CU CU-B

2964. Historical records survey. California. Directory of churches and religious organizations in Los
Angeles county. Prepared by the So. Calif. hist. records
survey project...Work projects admin. L.A., 1940. 329
(i.e. 332) l. Reproduced from typew. copy. v.1: Los Angeles county.
C CBb CL CLO CLSU CLU CSd CSdS CSf
CSmH CU-B N NN TxU

2965. The Hollenbeck, Los Angeles. Vistas in
southern California... [S.F., S.F. print. co., c1893] 46 p.
illus.   CL CO CU-B

2966. Holtzman, Abraham. Los Angeles county
chief administrative officer: ten years' experience. L.A.,
1948. 77 l. (Bur. of governmental research, Univ. of
Calif. at L.A., Studies in local govt., no. 10)   CL

2967. —— The office of the chief administrative officer: Los Angeles county. [L.A.] 1947. Thesis (M.A.)—
U.C.L.A., 1947.   CLU

2968. Hooker, Phyllis Ann. Voting behavior in sixteen cities in Los Angeles county, 1920–1940. [L.A.]
1946. Thesis (M.A.)—U.C.L.A., 1946.   CLU

2969. Hotchkis, Katharine (Bixby) Christmas at
Rancho Los Alamitos. Illus. by Clement Hurd. S.F.,
Calif. hist. soc., 1957. 30 p. illus.
CHi CL CLSM CLU CP CRcS CSal CSalCL
CSd CSf CStmo

**2970. Housing research council of Southern Cal-
ifornia.** Public housing, Los Angeles area; analysis and
report. [L.A.] 1950. 116 p. maps, plans.   CL

2971. Howell, William E. Wm. E. Howell's real
estate tract directory and land purchasers' guide of Los
Angeles county... L.A., Times-mirror print. house, 1888.
279 p. illus.
C CHi CL CLO CLSU CLU CPom CSmH

2972. Hubbard, Carson Bernard, ed. History of
Huntington Park...In two parts, narrative and biographical. Huntington Park, Cawston, 1935. 257 p. illus.,
ports., map.   CBb CL CLU CU-B NN

2973. Hussey, John Adam. The Wolfskill party in
California. [Berkeley, 1935] Thesis (M.A.)– Univ. of
Calif., 1935.   CU CU-B

2974. Immigration association of California.
[County scrapbooks] [S.F., 188–?]   C

2975. Index of names found in three volumes of Mexican documents from 1823 to 1850 in the County recorder's
office of Los Angeles county, State of California. [n.p.,
n.d.] 35 l.   CL

2976. Ives, Sarah Noble. Altadena, comp. for the
Altadena historical and beautification society... Pasa-
dena, Starr-news pub. co. [c1938] 351 p. illus., ports.
C CBb CHi CL CLO CLSU CLU CLob CSmH
CU-B NN

2977. Jackson, William Henry. Diaries of William
Henry Jackson, frontier photographer, to California and
return, 1866–67...Ed. by LeRoy R. Hafen and Ann W.
Hafen. Glendale, Arthur H. Clark, 1959. 345 p. illus.
(The Far West and the Rockies hist. ser., 1820–1875,
v.10)   CSdS CStclU CSto CU-B

2978. James, George Wharton. Scenes on the line
of the Pasadena mountain railway and From orange
groves to snow. Pasadena, Pasadena mountain railway
co. [1893] unp. illus.   CLU

2979. —— Same, with title: Mount Lowe railway.
Mount Lowe hotels and From orange groves and roses to
snow. Pasadena [1895?] 28 p.   CLSU

2980. —— Same, with title: Mount Lowe and its
wonderful railway. 2d ed. comp. by John Sharp. Mt.
Lowe, Echo pub. co., 1896. 151 p.
                                             C-S CLU CP CSmH

2981. —— Same, with title:...Scenic Mount Lowe
and its wonderful railway...4th ed. ... L.A., Pac. electric
railway, 1904. 126 p. illus., ports.
                                    C CHi CL CLU CP CU-B

2982. —— Same. 5th ed. ... 1905. 126 p. illus., ports.
                         CL COHN

2983. Jamison, Judith Norvell. Coordinated public planning in the Los Angeles region. L.A., 1948. 198 p. map. (Bur. of governmental research, Univ. of Calif. at L.A., Studies in local govt., no. 9) Mimeo.
    CL CLO CLS CLSU CLU CSmH CStmo

2984. —— Intergovernmental cooperation in public personnel administration in Los Angeles area. L.A., 1944. 107 p. (Bur. of governmental research, Univ. of Calif. at L.A., Studies in local govt., no. 8)   CL

2985. Jennings, David Laurence. Cahuenga Pass: a significant gateway through an intra regional barrier in the Los Angeles metropolitan area. [L.A.] 1944. Thesis (M.A.)– U.C.L.A., 1944.   CLU

2986. Johnson, Milo Perry. The trade and industrial education of Negroes in the Los Angeles area. [L.A.] 1945. Thesis (M.A.)– U.C.L.A., 1945.   CLU

2987. Johnson water gardens, Hynes. Catalogs. CHi has 1929, 1930.

2988. Joint committee of the welfare federation and welfare council on job classification and salary study. Job classification and pay plan. [L.A.?] 1946. 102 p.   CL

2989. Jones, Dana H. L. J. Rose and the founding of Rosemead. [Rosemead] First state bank of Rosemead, 1953. 36 p. port.   C CHi CLO CWhC

2990. Jones, Harold T. Administration of elections in Los Angeles city, county and state of California. L.A., Office of the City clerk, 1955. 214 p.
                     C CL-MR CLU

2991. Jones, Helen L. Metropolitan Los Angeles: its governments [by] Helen L. Jones [and] Robert F. Wilcox, under the direction of Edwin A. Cottrell. L.A., Haynes foundation, 1949. 224 p. illus., maps.
    C CBaB CBev CChiS CL CLO CLS CLU CP CRedl CSd CSdS CSfCW CSfSt CSt CStbS CU-B CWhC NjR ODa TxU ViU

2992. Kasun, Jacqueline (Rorabeck) Some social aspects of business cycles in the Los Angeles area, 1920–1950. L.A., Haynes foundation, 1954. 155 p. illus. (Pub. of the John Randolph Haynes & Dora Haynes foundation: Monograph ser. no. 36) Includes bibliographies.
    C CL CLS CLU CSS CSd CSdS CSt

2993. Kelker, De Leuw & co., Chicago. Report and recommendation on a comprehensive transit plan for the city and county of Los Angeles... [L.A., Neuner corp., print.] 1925. 202 p. illus.
    C CHi CL CLO CLS CLSU CLU CO CSfCW CSmH CU-B

2994. Kennedy, Harold W. The history, legal and administrative aspects of air pollution control in the county of Los Angeles. Report submitted to the Board of supervisors of the county of Los Angeles. [L.A.] 1953. 83 p.   CLS CStbS

2995. —— Los Angeles county narcotic law program. [L.A.] 1960. v.p.   CL

2996. —— Los Angeles county narcotics legislation program—1960. Presented to President's interdepartmental committee on narcotics, March 21, 1960, Los Angeles hearing. [L.A.] 1960. v.p.   CL

2997. Ketcham, Ronald M. Integration of public library services in the Los Angeles area. L.A., 1942. 185 p. tables, maps. (Bur. of governmental research, Univ. of Calif. at L.A., Studies in local govt., no. 6)   CL

2998. —— ...Intergovernmental cooperation in the Los Angeles area... L.A., 1940. 61 p. (Bur. of governmental research, Univ. of Calif. at L.A., Studies in local govt., no. 4) Reproduced from typew. copy.
    CL CLO CLSU CLU CO CStmo CWhC

2999. Kiakis, Harry. The Watts towers. [S.F.?] Bern Porter, 1959. 11 plates.   CLU

3000. Kidner, Frank Le Roy, and Neff, Philip. An economic survey of the Los Angeles area... L.A., Haynes foundation, 1945. 151 p. (Pub. of the John Randolph Haynes & Dora Haynes foundation: Monograph ser. no. 7) Reproduced from typew. copy.
    CBb CBev CL CLO CLS CLSU CLU CO CSdS CSf CSmH CStmo CU-B CWhC ViU

3001. —— Statistical appendix... L.A., 1945. 827 p.
    C CL CLO CLS CLSU CLU CO CSdS CSf CSmH CStmo CU-B

3002. —— Los Angeles, the economic outlook. L.A., Haynes foundation, 1946. 24 p. A condensation prepared by Molly Lewin of *"An economic survey of the Los Angeles area"* by the same authors.
    C CLO CLS CLSU CLU CStmo CU-B

3003. Kimball, Ruth Pratt. Glendora, California, 1887–1937. History and souvenir program of the golden get-together celebration, May 29, 1937. [Glendora, Glendora press-gleaner, 1937?] 28 p. illus.
                 CHi CLU CPom

3004. King, Veronica. Problems of modern crime ... London, Heath, 1924. 284 p. Practically all of this group of American murder cases took place in Los Angeles county.   CL CLSU

3005. Kraus, Phillip. The office of public defender in Los Angeles county. [L.A.] 1937. Thesis (M.A.)– U.C.L.A., 1937.   CLU

3006. Krythe, Maymie Richardson. Port admiral Phineas Banning, 1830–1885. S.F., 1957. 251 p. illus., ports. (Calif. hist. soc. Special pub. no. 28) Bibliography: p. 237–245.
    C CBaB CBb CHi CLSM CLgA CNa CO CP CSS CSd CSf CSalCL CSjC CSluCL CSmH CStcl CStmo CStoC CaBViPA

3007. Lake vineyard land and water association. Description of orange and vine lands in Los Angeles county, California. For sale by the Lake vineyard land and water association... [S.F., Hall's illustrated land jl. print., 1876?]   CSmH

3008. [Lanterman, Frank] La Cañada, California. [La Cañada, J. H. Button, 1948] 24 p. illus.   CHi

3009. Lemert, Edwin M., and Rosberg, Judy. The administration of justice to minority groups in Los Angeles county. Berkeley, Univ. of Calif. press, 1948. 27 p. (Univ. of Calif. publications in culture & soc., v.2, no. 1)
    CL CLSU CLU CSdS CSf CU-B

3010. The Llano colonist, 1916–19. Llano, Job Harriman, 1916–19. weekly. "Devoted to the cause of cooperation, socialism and unionism." Photostat copies, Apr. 21–28, May 26, 1917.   CL

3011. Los Angeles (Archdiocese) Catholic directory. L.A., The Tidings, 1951–
    C has 1952. CHi has 1955, 1961. CLLoy has 1951–52, 1959–60.

3012. —— The centennial, 1840–1940. L.A., 1940. 200 p. illus., ports.   CSf CSfCW CSfU

3013. Los Angeles. Board of city planning commissioners. Conference on the rapid transit question... [L.A., n.d.] 64 p.   CL

3014. —— —— Second conference on the mass transportation question... [L.A., n.d.] 31 l.   CL

3015. —— **Bureau of budget and efficiency.** A study of local government in the metropolitan area within the county of Los Angeles... 1935. 298 l. maps. Reproduced from typew. copy. Bibliography: 1. 289–297.
CL CL-MR CLO CLSU

3016. —— —— A study of proposed city and county government of Los Angeles within the present city limits. L.A. [1932?] 11 p. tables.   CL CL-MR

3017. —— **Bureau of municipal research.** Merchandising in the El Monte district and problems of a freeway through El Monte. [L.A.] 1952. 12 p. illus., map, table.   CU-B

3018. —— —— Unified local government and tax reform for Los Angeles county, California; a report to the Citizens committee for the city county unification, February, 1934. [L.A., 1934] 132 l. Mimeo.
CL CLU ViU

3019. —— **Chamber of commerce.** ...Alphabetical and classified directory of members. L.A., 1923. 332 p.   NHi

3020. —— —— The city and county of Los Angeles in southern California. L.A., 1898. 63 p. illus.   CHi

3021. —— —— Directory of exporters and importers of Los Angeles county. L.A.
CL has 1953.

3022. —— —— Directory of farm associations in Los Angeles county and California. L.A.
CL has 1957.

3023. —— —— Directory of radio and TV stations in Los Angeles county. L.A.
CL has 1960.

3024. —— —— Directory of trade associations in Los Angeles county. L.A., 19— Title varies.
CL has 1934, 1936–37, 1939–40, 1949.

3025. —— —— Educational facts about education costs, a study of expenditures, revenues, tax rates, tax yields, average daily attendance and related matters of the Los Angeles consolidated school district, 1928–29, 1937–38. [L.A.] 1938. 117 l. Reproduced from typew. copy.
CLU

3026. —— —— Electronics industry directory: Los Angeles metropolitan area. [L.A.] 1958–
C has 1958. CL has 1958.

3027. —— —— Facts and figures concerning southern California and Los Angeles city and county. L.A., Evening express co., print., 1888. 36 p. map.
CL CLU (lacks maps) CSmH CU-B PHi

3028. —— —— Information sources on business permits, licenses, etc. L.A.
CL has 1959.

3029. —— —— Land of promise, Los Angeles and southern California. L.A. [1898?] 28 p. illus., maps.
C

3030. —— —— Los Angeles city and county. Resources, growth and prospects. 1890. 54 p.
C CL CLSU CSmH CU-B NN

3031. —— —— Los Angeles county, some facts and figures...including a list of the membership of the Los Angeles chamber of commerce. L.A., 1925–
(CL 1925, 1926) CLSU (1926) CSmH (1925) CU-B (1925)

3032. —— —— Los Angeles county spreads her wings. History of National air races. [L.A., c1929] 30 p. illus., map, tables, diagrs.   CU-B

3033. —— —— Los Angeles to-day, city and county. [L.A., 1925?] 48 p. illus.   CLU

3034. —— —— New facts and figures concerning southern California... L.A., Evening express co., print., 1891. 33 p. map.   CL CLU CSmH CU-B

3035. —— —— Report on the electronics industry, Los Angeles metropolitan area. L.A. [c1955] 47 p. illus.
CL CLU

3036. —— —— Two years of progress in Los Angeles city and county, 1894–1895. 1895. 36 p. illus., map.
CL CLSU CU-B

3037. —— —— Visitors' guide to Los Angeles county industry. L.A., 19—
CL has 1954.

3038. —— —— **Industrial dept.** General industrial report of Los Angeles county, California, and surrounding communities... [1919]–33.
CL has 1918/19–1924, 1927, 1929–30, 1932–33. CLO has 1927. CLSU has 1927. CSmH has 1927.

3039. —— —— Industrial firms employing 50 or more persons in the Los Angeles district. L.A., 1939. 25 l.   CU-B

3040. —— —— Manufacturer's directory and commodity index. [8th ed.] [L.A., 1923]   C CL

3041. —— —— **Mining dept.** Mining directory-catalog and engineers' handbook of machinery, equipment and supplies for mines... L.A. [c1932] 156 p. illus., table, diagrs.   C

3042. —— —— **Research dept.** Los Angeles marketing atlas...showing: shopping centers, industrial areas, census tract boundaries, communities and cities, marketing facts, population... L.A. [1953?] illus. loose-leaf.   CL CLS

3043. —— **Citizens' committee on parks, playgrounds and beaches.** Parks, playgrounds and beaches for the Los Angeles region; a report submitted...by Olmsted brothers and Bartholomew and associates, consultants... 1930. 178 p. illus., maps.
C CL CLSU CLU

3044. —— **City planning commission.** Development plan for the Santa Monica bay shoreline, Topanga canyon to El Segundo. L.A., 1945. 12 l. illus., map.
CL CL-MR

3045. —— —— Mass transit facilities and the master plan of parkways [by Milton Breivogel and Stuart M. Bate. L.A.] 1942. 26 p. maps, diagrs.   CL CL-MR

3046. —— —— Master plan of shoreline development... L.A., 1941. 33 l. illus., map, tables.   CL-MR

3047. —— —— A parkway plan for the city of Los Angeles and the metropolitan area... L.A., 1941. 51 p. maps, table.   CL-MR

3048. —— **Joint survey committee.** Wage survey in Los Angeles county, March 1, 1957. [L.A., 1957] 15 p.   CLU

3049. —— **Junior chamber of commerce.** Los Angeles county sport land. [L.A.] 1929. 47 p. illus.   CLU CU-B

3050. —— **Transportation engineering board.** Factual survey, presenting summaries of field, office and derived data relating to transportation... 1938–39. [n.p., n.d.] 100 p. maps, tables, diagrs. (WPA O.P. no. 665–07–3–11)   CL-MR

3051. —— —— A transit program for the Los Angeles metropolitan area... L.A. [1939] 67 p. illus., maps, diagrs.   CL-MR CLU

3052. Los Angeles and Pasadena railway co. Prospectus...Inc. June 1884... [L.A., 1884?] 4 p.
CSmH

3053. Los Angeles and southern California guide book and room, board and hotel directory...Also describing all points of interest in and around Los Angeles... [L.A.] L.A. home co. [1907?] 240 p. illus. CLU

3054. Los Angeles bar association. Year book of the Los Angeles bar association (city and county). L.A., 1913–18. No more published?
CHi (1918) CL (1913, 1918)

3055. Los Angeles city and county consolidation commission. Report. [n.p.] 1916. Bound with: Los Angeles realty board, inc. Report... on the subject of city and county consolidation. [12] p. CL

3056. Los Angeles city and county guide book for tourists and strangers... [L.A., Kingsley Barnes & co., 1885] 82 p. CSmH

3057. Los Angeles clearing house association. Scrip prepared during the bank holiday of 1933... but never issued... [n.p.] 1934. 3 l. CL

3058. Los Angeles consolidation committee. ... What consolidation means for San Pedro and Wilmington ... [n.p.] 1909. unp. CL

3059. Los Angeles county vs. Hardy, Carlos S. The Senate of the state of California sitting as a high court of impeachment in the matter of the impeachment of Carlos S. Hardy, a judge of the Superior court of the state of California, in and for the county of Los Angeles ... Sacramento, State print., 1930. 1378 p.
CHi CRcS

3060. Los Angeles county. Air pollution control district. Basic data on air pollution control in Los Angeles county. Martin A. Brower, editor. L.A., 1956. 22 l. CLU

3061. —— —— Crossing the smog barrier: a factual account of southern California's fight against air pollution. L.A. [1957] 22 p. illus. CLU CSt

3062. —— —— Smog. Los Angeles fights back! [L.A., 1956] 12 p. CLU

3063. —— **Board of education.** Official list of teachers of Los Angeles county...1892/93– [L.A., 1892–1900]
CSmH has 1895, 1898–1900. CU-B has 1892/93.

3064. —— **Board of engineers, flood control.** Provisional report... to the Board of supervisors, Los Angeles county. June 3, 1914. [L.A., 1914] 6 p.
CSmH

3065. —— —— Report on San Gabriel river control...to the county Board of supervisors... [L.A., 1913]
CSmH

3066. —— —— Reports...to the Board of supervisors, Los Angeles county, California. [L.A., 1915] 399 p. illus., maps. CLU

3067. —— **Board of supervisors.** Authority and scope of Los Angeles county government. L.A., 1958. folder. illus., map. CL-MR

3068. —— —— Boundaries of judicial townships, road districts and supervisoral districts in Los Angeles California, as established...April 9th, 1888. L.A., Evening express co., 1888. 23 p. CSmH

3069. —— —— Boundaries of the public school districts and municipal corporations of Los Angeles county, California, March 15th, 1889. L.A., Evening express co., 1889. 85 p. CL

3070. —— —— Dynamic Los Angeles county. A local market of four million people with huge and diversified resources. 1938. 48 p. illus. CSmH

3071. —— —— Los Angeles county, California. L.A. [1936] folder. illus. CRcS

3072. —— —— Same. [L.A., Ford, Ellis and co., 1940?] 32 p. illus. CU-B

3073. —— —— Official boundaries of political subdivisions of the county of Los Angeles... [L.A.]
CL has 1889–90, 1896, 1902, 1908–20. CSmH has 1914, 1916. CU-B has Jan. 1916. NN has 1912.

3074. —— —— Official boundaries of the sixth congressional district...state senatorial assembly and assembly districts within the county of Los Angeles...June 1900. L.A., F. Blech & co., 1900. 102 p. CLO CSmH

3075. —— —— Petition ...for an appropriation for the support of the nonresident indigent sick of Los Angeles county. [Sacramento, Gelwicks, state print., 1870]
CSmH

3076. —— **Bureau of efficiency.** ...Charts...[of] the plan of governmental organization in the county of Los Angeles, the city of Los Angeles, the other nine chartered cities within the county and the thirty-four remaining cities of the county... [n.p., 1934] 46 charts.
CL

3077. —— —— Comparison study of salaries and wages, maintenance and operation, number of employees of Los Angeles county, 1922–23 to 1933–34. [L.A., 1935] 128 p. tables, diagrs. Mimeo. CL CLU

3078. —— —— Growth of county functions, Los Angeles county, Calif., 1852–1934... [L.A., 1936] 136 l. Mimeo. CL CLSU CLU CO

3079. —— —— An investigation of outdoor relief of the Los Angeles county charities office. [n.p., 1915] 30 l. Reproduced from typew. copy. CL

3080. —— —— A presentation of problems involved in the proposal that Los Angeles city separate from the county of Los Angeles and form a city and county government with the present city limits. [L.A.? 1932] 65 l. map, tables. CL CL-MR CLU CU-B

3081. —— —— Survey of judicial townships of Los Angeles county, California. [n.p., 1933] 17 l. CL

3082. —— **Chamber of commerce.** Directory of manufacturing, Los Angeles county and district. 1st– , 1924/25– [L.A., Board of supervisors of L.A. county]
C has 21st (1940?) CLU has 15th, 16th, 22d, 23d, 1931, 1933, 1946/47, 1950.

3083. —— —— Dollars and census; a record of balanced community development. [L.A., 1932] 23 p. tables, diagrs. CU-B

3084. —— —— Know Los Angeles county; communities, wealth, history, features, economic trends... [1938] 81 l. map. Reproduced from typew. copy.
CBev CL CLO CLSU CO NN

3085. —— —— Same, by Wm. J. Dunkerley, under the direction of Leonard E. Read... L.A. county Bd. of supervisors [c1939] 76 p. map.
C CBev CL CLO CLSU CLU CSmH CU-B CWhC

3086. —— —— Los Angeles, city and county; a few facts for the visitor, for the homeseeker, for the investor. L.A., L.A. county Bd. of supervisors [1954?] CStmo

3087. —— —— Los Angeles county, California... [L.A., c1925] 52 p. illus. CLSU CLU CU-B
Other editions followed.

CHi (1929, 1933, 1935) CRcS ([1931?], 1935, 1936)
CSmH (1929) CU-B (1940)

3088. —— —— Same. Eagle Rock edition. 64 p.
illus., map.   CLO

3089. —— —— Manufacturing and foreign trade
directory of Los Angeles county and district... L.A.,
19—
CL has 1912, 1916–20, 1922, 1925, 1946–47. CSmH has
13th, 1928. CU-B has 3d, 5th–6th, 9th, 13th, [c1918?]
1920–21, 1924, 1928.

3090. —— —— A summer tourist in southern California. [L.A.] Author, 1910. 20 p. illus.   CU-B

3091. —— —— Same. Huntington Park ed. [L.A.,
Lithographed by Sterling press, 1931] [48] p. illus.
                                                       CU-B

3092. —— —— Same. Long Beach ed. [L.A., Lithographed by Sterling press, 1931] [52] p. illus. CU-B

3093. —— **Domestic trade dept.** Industrial
minerals, non-metallics; production, marketing, aid to
miners. L.A., Bd. of supervisors of L.A. county [1944]
42 p.   CL

3094. —— —— **Industrial dept.** Collection of
eight studies on the industrial development of Los Angeles county. L.A. [n.d.] 8 v. in 1.   CLU

3095. —— —— —— An industrial development
plan for Los Angeles county. [L.A., Bd. of supervisors
of L.A. county, 194–?] 22 l.   CLU

3096. —— —— —— Industrial establishments in
Los Angeles county employing more than 25 or more
persons. L.A. [n.d.] 75 p.   CLU

3097. —— —— —— Same. Rev. ed. 1952. 70 p.
                                                        CLU

3098. —— —— Statistical record of Los Angeles county industrial development. L.A. [1945?] [11]
l.   CLU

3099. —— —— **World trade dept.** Directory [of]
Los Angeles county exporters. L.A., Bd. of supervisors
of L.A. county.
CL has 1958.

3100. —— **Charter revision committee.** ...Re-
port. L.A., 1938. 33 p.   CL-MR

3101. —— **Charter study committee.** Recommendations...presented to the Board of supervisors. L.A.,
1958. v.p.   CL-MR

3102. —— **Charters.** Charter of the county of Los
Angeles, annotated. 1912– L.A., 1912–
CL has 1912, 1919, 1926, 1930, 1939, 1949, 1958–59.
CStmo has 1926, 1949.

3103. —— —— [Los Angeles county charter. The
final draft...with corrections and notations as originally
pencilled by Lewis R. Works... L.A., Bd. of freeholders,
1912] unp.   CL

3104. —— **Chief administrative officer.** Guide to
departmental organization and functions. [L.A.] 1957.
103 p. illus.   CL

3105. —— —— Same. L.A., 1961. 105 p. charts.
                                                      CL-MR

3106. —— —— Summary of transit surveys. L.A.
[1949] 44 l.   CL

3107. —— **Civic bureau of music and art.** Los
Angeles county culture and the community... L.A.,
Pub. for the county Bd. of supervisors, 1927. 68 p. illus.
                                                C CO CSmH

3108. —— —— Same. L.A. [1929?] 80 p. illus.
                                            C CHi CSmH NN

3109. —— **Civilian defense organization.** ...Re-
port of civilian war services by the Citizens service corps
for the period of 1941 to Dec. 31, 1944... [L.A.] Citizens service corps[1945] 47 l.   CL CLO

3110. —— **Commission on human relations.** A
comparative statistical analysis of minority group population for Los Angeles county from April, 1950 to July 1,
1959. L.A. [1960] unp. tables.   CL-MR

3111. —— **Committee for church and community cooperation.** The Japanese on the Pacific coast;
a factual study of events, December 7, 1941 to September
1, 1942, with suggestions for the future. Statement for
the Los Angeles county committee for church and community cooperation, prepared by Dr. George Gleason.
[L.A.] 1942. 20 p. Bibliography: p. 18.   CL

3112. —— **Committee on governmental simplifi-
cation.** Report... L.A., 1935. 219 p. illus., maps.
C CL CLLoy CL-MR CLSU CSdS CSmH
CWhC

3113. —— **Committee on opportunities and
needs of the aging.** A study of housing needs of the
aging in Los Angeles county, June, 1950. L.A., 1950. 4 l.
                                                        CL

3114. —— **Coordinating councils.** Report of proceedings of the conference, 1933–1935. L.A., 1933–35.
                                                        CL

3115. —— —— **Information division.** Juvenile delinquency and poor housing in the Los Angeles metropolitan area. [L.A.] 1937. v.p. illus., maps (fold.)
                                                        CL

3116. —— —— **Juvenile research committee.**
Youth's new day, the juvenile problem in Los Angeles
and tools for its solution... L.A., Lions club, c1935. 95
p. map.
                                            C CL CLSU

3117. —— **County clerk's office.** Comparative statistics, 1880–90, [pub. by authority of T. H. Ward, county
clerk, comp. by D. S. Alexander] [L.A., 1890?] 8 p.
                                                       CHi

3118. —— **Dept. of recreation and parks.** Plummer park; its history and objectives. L.A., 1950. 9 p.
                                                      CL-MR

3119. —— **Dept. of the County surveyor.** History
of the boundary of the county of Los Angeles... [L.A.,
1938?] 38 l. maps. Typew.   CLU CSmH CU-B

3120. —— **Emergency relief committee. Subcommittee on relief standards and procedure. Survey committee.** The administration of funds for unemployment relief by the Los Angeles county Department of
charities, prior to November 24, 1933. A report submitted
by Helen R. Jeter...December 5, 1933... [n.p., n.d.]
139 l.   CL CLSU

3121. —— **Flood control district.** ...Flood of
March 2, 1938, by M. F. Burke, hydraulic engineer. May
20, 1938. [L.A., 1938] 52 l.   CLU

3122. —— —— Floods of January 15–18, 1952.
[L.A.] 1952. 1 v. maps.   CLU

3123. —— **Historical landmarks committee.** Historical landmarks in Los Angeles county. L.A. [1944]
1948, 1950.
CBev (1944) CHi (1950) CL (1948) CL-MR (1948)

3124. —— **Housing authority.** Real property sur-
vey and low income housing area survey of a portion of
Los Angeles county. L.A., 1939–40. 2 v. maps, tables.
(WPA project no. 665–073–269)   CL CL-MR

3125. —— **Library** ...History of the Los Angeles

county free library, 1912–1927. L.A., 1927. 40 p. illus., map.   CBev CLU CSmH

3126. Los Angeles county. Library (*cont'd*) ... Twenty-five years of growth, 1912–1937. [1937] 76 p. illus., maps.   CL CLSU

3127. —— **Los Angeles county war services.** ... Final report of the war service corps, Jan. 1st, 1945 to Sept. 2nd, 1945... L.A., 1945. 55 l.   CL CLSU

3128. —— **Regional planning commission.** A comprehensive report on the master plan of airports for the Los Angeles county regional planning district. L.A., 1940. 165 p. illus.   CL-MR CLU

3129. —— —— A comprehensive report on the master plan of highways... v.1. [L.A.] 1941. illus., map. No more published?   CL CL-MR

3130. —— —— A comprehensive report on the regional plan of highways; section 2–E, San Gabriel valley. L.A., 1929. 139 p. illus., maps.
CHi CL CL-MR CLSU CLU CU-B CWhC

3131. —— —— A comprehensive report on the regional planning of highways; section 4, Long Beach–Redondo area. 1931. 206 p. illus., maps.
CHi CL CLLoy CLO CLSU CLU CSalCL CStmo CU-B CWhC

3132. —— —— The East San Gabriel valley; an area use plan. L.A., 1956. 26 p. illus., maps.
CL CL-MR CLS CSt

3133. —— —— Freeways for the region... [L.A., 1943] 47 p. illus., maps.   CFS CHi CL CLU

3134. —— —— Land use survey, county of Los Angeles; a report of Work projects administration project 665–07–3–65. [L.A.] 1940. unp. maps, diagrs.
CL CL-MR

3135. —— —— Master plan of land use inventory and classification. [L.A.] 1941. 110 p. illus., maps.
CHi CL CL-MR

3136. —— —— Planning for people in north Los Angeles county. [L.A., 1959–61] 3 v. illus., maps.
CL CL-MR

3137. —— —— The regional planning commission, county of Los Angeles. [L.A., Southwest litho. co.] 1929. 31 p. illus., plans, diagrs.   CHi CL

3138. —— —— Regional recreation areas plan... Comp. by Don A. Philipp. L.A. [1959] 90 p. illus., maps.
CL-MR CLU

3139. —— —— Report of a highway traffic survey in the county of Los Angeles. 1934. 32 p. illus.
CL CLSU CLU

3140. —— —— Same. L.A., 1937. 62 p. illus., maps.   CLU

3141. —— —— Report on master plan of parks, county of Los Angeles (unincorporated area)... [L.A., 1948] 179 p. map, tables, diagrs.   CL-MR

3142. —— —— Shoreline development, county of Los Angeles, 1944; report in the revised master plan... L.A., 1946. 31 p. illus., maps.   CL CL-MR CLU

3143. —— —— Shoreline development [master plan] for the Los Angeles regional planning district. L.A., 1940. 47 p. maps, tables, plan.   CL-MR

3144. —— —— The southeast area, an area land use plan. L.A., 1959. 34 p. illus., maps. (Its Subregional area studies)   CL CL-MR

3145. —— —— Same. L.A., 1961. 61 p.
CL CL-MR

3146. —— —— Where now, brown cow. A general survey of the Los Angeles county dairy industry... [Text by R. James Fairman] [n.p.] 1951. 24 l. illus., maps.
CL

3147. —— **Superintendent of schools.** Addresses delivered at the annual session of the county teachers' institute. March 28, 29 and 30, 1898. L.A., Times-mirror print. [1898]   CSmH

3148. —— —— Boundaries of the public school districts of Los Angeles county, California. L.A., McBride print., 1880.   CSmH

3149. —— —— Financial and educational data concerning Los Angeles county school districts... L.A., 1936. 58 l.   CLU

3150. —— —— Handbook of community resources ... [L.A.] 1954. 180 p. illus.   CWhC

3151. —— —— Historic landmarks in Los Angeles county, a descriptive guide for teachers [prepared by Marie B. Dickinson]... [rev. ed.] L.A., 1956. 97 p. illus., maps. (Curriculum supplement. Social studies. no. 5) Bibliography: p. 87–94.
CL CL-MR CStbS CStmo CWhC

3152. —— —— Los Angeles county; a handbook of its government and service. Ed. by Harold T. Shafer and Frances Hall Adams. L. A., L.A. county Bd. of supervisors [1950] 322 p. illus. (Social studies curriculum monograph. no. 57)   CBev CL CLO CLS CLU

3153. —— —— ...Los Angeles county government ... L.A., 1940– 3 pts. in 1 v. illus., maps. Comp. and ed. by J. Holmes Ford. Contents: pt. 1. Administration and education.—pt. 2. Protection of life, health, and property.–pt. 3. Engineering and fiscal admin.   CL

3154. Los Angeles county agricultural association. ...List of premiums and rules and regulations of the ... annual fair...to be held at Downey city, California...2d, 1885. L.A., Gilchrist print. house [1885] 33 p. illus.   CU-B

3155. Los Angeles county committee for interracial progress. Minutes of the committee meeting.
CL has May 1944–April 1946.

3156. Los Angeles county conference on employment, University of California at Los Angeles, 1950. Proceedings... [n.p., State print. off.] 1950. 188 p. charts.   CL

3157. Los Angeles county employees' association. Historical synopsis of Los Angeles county. [1922] 54 p.   CSmH

3158. —— Los Angeles county government: departmental services, 1934. [L.A., 1934] 121 p. illus., ports.
CL CLO CLSU CWhC

3159. Los Angeles county fair association. Bulletin. v.1– , Feb. 15, 1950– Pomona, 1950– illus., ports.
CU-B has v.1, no. 1–2, Feb. 15, 1950–June 1950, July 1952–July 1, 1953.

3160. —— ...Los Angeles county fair...1st– , 19— Pomona, 19—
C has 19th, 21st, 1940, 1948. CU-B has 19th, 21st, 23d, 28th–33d, 1940, 1948–50, 1955–60.

3161. Los Angeles county illustrated. Commercial review. L.A., Calif. advertising co., 1899. 110 p. illus.
CLU

3162. Los Angeles county medical association. Directory of members...1885– L.A., 1885–
C has 1933, 1938, 1950. CLM has 1885, 1911–12, 1914, 1927–

3163. —— The story of the Los Angeles county medical association. [L.A., 1946] 202 p. illus. (Its Bul., v.79, no. 3, Jan. 31, 1946, 75th anniversary number)
CLM CLU

3164. Los Angeles county pioneer society. Annual report. L.A., 1905– Title varies.
C has 1905, 1906, 1908/9–1914/15. CHi has 1905, 1909/10, 1912/13–1914/15. CL has 1905, 1909/10, 1911/12–1914/15. CU-B has 1908/9–1909/10, 1912/13–1913/14. NN has 1909/10–1914/15.

3165. —— ...Historical record and souvenir. L.A., Times-mirror press, 1923. 283 p. illus., ports.
CHi CLSU CLU CLob CSalCL CSfCW CSmH CU-B CWhC In MiD-B NN

3166. Los Angeles daily journal. The bench and bar of Los Angeles county. L.A., 1922. 44 p. ports.
C CHi CSmH

3167. —— An historical review of bench and bar. L.A., 1907. 14 p. illus., ports.
CL

3168. [Los Angeles herald] The Herald pamphlet for 1876. Containing a complete description of Los Angeles county, California... L.A., Herald pub. co., 1876. 65 p.
CL CP NHi

3169. Los Angeles metropolitan parkway engineering committee. Interregional, regional, metropolitan parkways. [L.A., 1946] 29 p. illus., maps.
CL CL-MR

3170. Los Angeles metropolitan traffic association. Express busses in subways; 1954 supplemental study of mass transportation. [L.A., 1955] 23 l. illus., maps.
CL

3171. —— Express busses on elevated roadways; 1957 supplemental study of mass transportation. L.A., 1957. 13 l. illus.
CL CLU

3172. —— Express busses on freeways; transit study, 1953, Los Angeles metropolitan area. [L.A., 1953] 41 p. illus., maps.
CL CLU

3173. —— Freeways, Los Angeles metropolitan area. L.A. [1956] 14 l. maps, tables.
CL

3174. —— Operating taxes levied on typical private transit lines, Los Angeles metropolitan area. 1955 supplemental study of mass transportation. L.A. [1955] 6 l. illus.
CL

3175. Los Angeles morning herald. ...Land of heart's desire, southern California, its people, homes and pleasures, art and architecture... L.A., L.A. morning herald, 1911. 117 p. illus., ports.
CHi CL CLSU CLU CPom CSmH MiD NN

3176. Los Angeles olive growers' association. Sylmar brand olive oil and ripe olives. [L.A., Cook Dearborn print. co., 1915?] 32 p.
CHi

3177. Los Angeles Pacific railroad. ...Balloon route. Scenes from an electric car. [L.A., 1897?] unp. illus.
CU-B

3178. —— Deed of trust...securing a bonded indebtedness of $5,000,000. [L.A.? 1904] 51 p.
CLU

3179. Los Angeles racing association. Second season...Santa Anita Park, Arcadia... L.A., J. C. Effinger [1908] [98] p. illus.
CHi

3180. Los Angeles railway corp. Fare and service of the Los Angeles railway, containing orders of the Railroad commission of the state of California... [L.A.] 1921. [9] p.
CL

3181. Los Angeles realty board, inc. Report...on the subject of city and county consolidation. [12] p.

Contains also: Los Angeles city and county consolidation commission. Report. [n.p.] 1916.
CL

3182. Los Angeles research jury. Economic and population characteristics of Los Angeles county, first quarter, 1944. A pilot study. First report. [L.A.] L.A. times, 1944. 15 p. illus., map.
CL

3183. Los Angeles Saturday night. 150th birthday of Los Angeles city and county; a pre-Olympiad feature. 1781–1931. [1931] unp. illus. Suppl. to v.11, no. 8, Aug. 29, 1931.
CL CLSU CStmo

3184. Los Angeles times. Annual blue book register ... L.A., 19–
CL has 1934.

3185. —— The county of Los Angeles, America's 3rd market. A. The source of sales. B. The point of sales. C. Sales timing. [L.A.] 1948. 4 v. illus., maps. loose-leaf.
CL CLU (v.1)

3186. —— The march of progress. Historic highlights from southern California's romantic past. [L.A., c1935] 15 l. illus., ports.
C

3187. —— Men of achievement in the great southwest...a story of pioneer struggles during early days in Los Angeles and southern California... 1904. 149 p. illus., ports., map.
C CL CLO CLU CSmH CStmo CU-B

3188. —— A new survey! 23 market areas of Los Angeles county. [L.A.] 1935. unp. col. illus., maps. CL

3189. —— **Merchandising service.** Los Angeles county grocery stores. L.A., 19–
CL has 1952, 1955, 1957–60.

3190. —— **Research dept.** Los Angeles county market data. [L.A.] 1939. [22] l. maps.
CLU

3191. [Ludwig Salvator, archduke of Austria] Eine blume aus dem goldenen lande; oder, Los Angeles. Prag, H. Mercy, 1878. 257 p. illus., port.
CHi CL CLSU CLU CPom CSmH CU-B NHi

3192. —— Same. 2. verb. aufl. Würzburg, Wien, L. Woerl [1885] 240 p. illus., port., maps.
C CL CLO CLU CSfCW CSmH CU-B NN

3193. —— Los Angeles in the sunny seventies. A flower from the golden land, by Ludwig Louis Salvator; translated by Marguerite Eyer Wilbur... L.A., B. McCallister, J. Zeitlin, 1929. 188 p. illus.
Available in many California libraries and MiD-B

3194. Lummis, Charles Fletcher. Letters and diary of Charles Fletcher Lummis to Maurice M [!] Newmark, 1911–1927. [n.p., n.d.] 3 v. Copied by Violet Barker, Works progress administration, Statewide pub. lib. project no. 12287.
CL

3195. McCune, Ellis. Intergovernmental co-operation in recreation administration in the Los Angeles area. L.A., Bur. of governmental research, Univ. of Calif., 1954. 73 p. maps, diagrs., tables.
CL

3196. McPherson, William. Homes in Los Angeles city and county, and description thereof, with sketches of the four adjacent counties... L.A., Mirror bk. & job print. establishment, 1873. 74 p.
C CL CLU CSfCSM CSmH CU-B MHi NHi

3197. —— Same. [Los Angeles], Southern California chapter, Antiquarian booksellers assoc. of America, 1961. 70 p. facsim.
CHi CLSM CP

3198. Marblehead land co. Rancho Malibu, an historic real estate offering. [L.A., n.d.] 27 p. illus. CLU

3199. Marshall, Jessie, vs. Taylor, Jacob S. In the Superior court of the county of Los Angeles, state of California. Dept. no. 5. [People vs. J. S. Taylor] J. W.

McKinley, judge, Jessie Marshall, plaintiff, vs. Jacob S. Taylor, defendant. L.A., 1890. 2 v. in 3.

CL has v.2, pt. 1–2.

3200. Marshall, Thomas Chalmers. Into the streets and lanes; the beginnings and growth of the social work of the Episcopal church in the diocese of Los Angeles, 1887–1947. Claremont, Pub. for the Diocesan dept. of social relations by Saunders press, 1948. 178 p. illus., ports.

C CHi CL CLM CLO CLS CLU CO CSdS CSf CSmH CU-B

3201. Maulsby, F. R. Antelope valley, California. [S.F., Sunset mag. homeseeker's bur. for the Lancaster chamber of commerce, 1913] 14 p. illus., map.   CHi

3202. Maxwell, H. M., comp. & pub. Los Angeles county tract directory; an alphabetical list of all tracts or subdivisions and grants of land in Los Angeles county, giving technical description and general location, with book and page of record of corresponding maps, including all entries to July 15th, 1894, also boundaries of incorporated cities and irrigation districts... 1894. 200 p.

CL CPom CSmH

3203. Maynard, Glyde. History of the development of San Antonio canyon, California... [L.A.] 1935. 65 p. Typew. Thesis (M.A.)—U.C.L.A., 1935.   CPom

3204. Medical directory of practitioners of medicine and dentistry in the city and county of Los Angeles. 1– , 1912– L.A., 1912– Annual.

CLM has 1–2, 6, 11, 1912–13, 1917, 1923.

3205. Meehan, Francis. Triunfo. Lake Sherwood, 1948. 6 p. mounted pl. "Done into type by hand and privately printed by Dorothy and Frank Shields, San Francisco, 1948."   CHi

3206. Mendell, George Henry. Southern California seaboard commercial points. Natural advantages of Redondo Beach for the accommodation of deep-sea commerce... S.F., Crocker, 1888. 52 p. maps.   CU-B

3207. Merchants and manufacturers association of Los Angeles. Survey analysis. L.A.

CL has v.1, 3–13, 15–45.

3208. Merritt, Le Roy Charles, and Wight, Edward Allen. The Arcadia public library; a survey of its administrative organization and services to adults and children. Berkeley, 1955. 80 p.   C

3209. Miguel Leonis association. History and preservation of Miguel Leonis adobe, Calabasas, California. L.A., 1962. 5 l. plates.   CHi

3210. Miller box manufacturing co. Bee keepers' supplies... L.A., 1919. 32 p. illus., map.   CHi

3211. Miradero, the country home of L. C. Brand, Los Angeles county, California. [L.A., Kingsley, n.d.] 28 p. illus.   CLU

3212. Morris, Lucie. History of the town of Lancaster, center of Antelope valley, California. 1934. 86 l. Typew. Thesis (M.A.)—Univ. of So. Calif., 1934.

CLCo CLSU

3213. —— comp. Personal interviews with early residents of Antelope valley. [1939] v.p. Typew. CLCo

3214. National Negro congress. Los Angeles council. Jim Crow in national defense. [L.A., 1940?] 27 p.   CHi

3215. National probation association. The juvenile court of Los Angeles county, Calif. Report of a survey by Francis H. Hiller... [L.A., Rotary club of L.A., c1928] 58 p.   CL CLSU

3216. National recreation association. Leisure time

resources in greater Los Angeles and adjacent areas; directory of community activities, organizations...[Comp. by Harold W. Lathrop] N.Y., 1955. 224 p.   CL

3217. Newhall, Ruth Waldo. The Newhall Ranch; the story of the Newhall land & farming company. San Marino, Huntington lib., 1958. 120 p. illus., ports., maps.

Available in many California libraries and MoS

3218. Newman's directory and guide of Los Angeles and vicinity. A handbook for strangers and residents... L.A., T. Newman, 1903. 107 p. illus., map.   C CSmH

3219. Newman's directory and guide of Los Angeles and southern California... L.A., Times-mirror [1906?] 98 p. map.   CLU CP

3220. Newman's tract directory of Los Angeles county; an alphabetical list of all recorded subdivisions in Los Angeles county. Comp. by William D. Reyburn. [L.A.] T. Newman, 1903. 307 p.   CLU CSmH

3221. Newmark, Harris. Sixty years in southern California, 1853–1913... N.Y., Knickerbocker press, 1916. 688 p. illus., ports.

Available in many California libraries and CaBViPA IC MiD MoS NjR OU TxU

3222. —— Same. 2d ed., rev. and augm. ... N.Y., Knickerbocker press, 1926. 732 p. illus., ports.

C CHi CL CLO CLU CLob COr CPom CRcS CSalCL CSf CSfCP CSfU CSlu CSmH CSrD CU-B

3223. —— Same. 3d ed., rev. and augm. ... Bost., Houghton, 1930. 744 p. illus., ports.

Available in many California libraries and GEU GU ODa WM

3224. Newport (F. P.) & co. Pacific terminal. [L.A., 1914?] [7] p. illus., map.   CHi

3225. Nikolitch, Milan. Sewerage systems of Los Angeles and sewage irrigation in southern California. [Berkeley, 1906] Thesis (M.S.)—Univ. of Calif., 1906.   CU

3226. Norman, Emmett B. Early citrus industry: picking, packing and marketing. [n.d.] 45 p. illus. Ms. A personal history of the citrus industry in Duarte.   COnC

3227. Norman-Wilcox, Gregor. The furnishings of the Hugo Reid Adobe. [5] p. Reprinted from *Lasca leaves*, v.1, no. 2, April, 1961.   CHi

3228. North American aviation, inc. In the matter of arbitration between North American aviation, inc. and United automobile, aircraft and agricultural implement workers of America, locals 887, 972 and 1151...before special arbitration panel...David L. Cole, chairman, Benjamin Aaron...Santa Monica, California, August 15–19, 1952. L.A., Horace E. Snyders & associates, Court reporters and notaries, 1951. 4 v.   CLU

3229. Norton, Edwin Clarence. The dean speaks again; giving hitherto unpublished excerpts from personal papers, diaries, and letters...[1st ed.] Claremont, Creative press, 1955. 125 p. illus.   CO CRedl CStoC

3230. Oberbeck, Grace Johnson (Smith) History of La Crescenta–La Cañada valleys... Montrose, Ledger, 1938. 93 p.

C CBb CHi CL CLO CLSU CLU CSmH CU-B MWA NN

3231. O'Connor, M. J., vs. Good, B. F. et al. In the District court of the seventeenth judicial district, of the state of California in and for the county of Los Angeles. M. J. O'Connor, plaintiff, against B. F. Good, et al., defendants. Pleadings, findings and judgement. Gould & Blanchard, attorneys for defendants. [L.A., 1877?] 20 p. Relates to rancho Sausal Redondo.   CHi CLU

3232. O'Day, Edward Francis. Bel-Air Bay; a country place by the sea... [L.A., Young & McCallister] 1927. 30 p. illus., maps.
CBb CHi CL CLO CLSU CLU CO CSf CSmH CStclU CStmo

3233. Odd fellows, Independent order of. El Monte. Lodge no. 424. A history of El Monte, "The end of the Santa Fe Trail." [El Monte] 1923. 88 p. illus., ports.　　　　　　　　　　　　CU-B

3234. [Olden, William R.] Lands in Los Angeles county, California; important letter from the U.S. General land office. S.F., E. Bosqui & co. [1869?] [4] p. Includes letter from Joseph S. Wilson on Resources of California, reprinted from *San Francisco bulletin*, May 25, 1869; and map of part of Los Angeles county showing the "Abel Stearns ranchos."　　　　C CLU

3235. Olmsted, Frederick Law. A major traffic street plan for Los Angeles; prepared for the committee on Los Angeles plan of major highways of the Traffic commission of the city and county of Los Angeles... L.A., 1924. 69 p. maps.　　　　CL CLU

3236. Oppenheim, Ramsey. Los Angeles, land of destiny, a narrative of a market. [L.A.] Pacific markets section, Western advertising, 1941. 32 p. illus.　CLU

3237. Pacific electric railway co. [Scrapbook of 20 mounted diagrams depicting the growth of the Pacific electric railway from 1895–1916. L.A., 19–?] 1 v.　CSmH

3238. The Palisadian. Community progress edition, 1922–1953. Pacific Palisades, 1953. v.p. illus., map. (25th anniversary ed., v.26, no. 5, May 29, 1953)　　C

3239. —— 100 years observance of our community's background. Pacific Palisades, 1949. 34 p. illus. (Centennial edition, 1849–1949, v.22, no. 7, June 17, 1949)
CLU

3240. Palm, Charles W. Political statistician of Los Angeles county...from the treaty of Guadalupe Hidalgo to date; containing the vote polled for each candidate at every election held since 1850... L.A., 1892. 80 p.
C CLU CSmH

3241. Parks, Marion. In pursuit of vanished days; visits to the extant historic adobe houses of Los Angeles county. L.A., McBride, 1928–1929. 2 v. illus., ports., maps. (Hist. soc. of So. Calif. Annual publications. v.14, pt. 1–2. (1928–1929)　　CHi CL CLSU CLU

3242. Pasadena. Public library. Fine arts and Californiana department, comp. Who was who in southern California. [1936–] 7 v. Loose-leaf. ports. Compiled from newspaper clippings.　　　　CP

3243. Peck, Stuart L. An archaeological report on the excavation of a prehistoric site at Zuma creek, Los Angeles county, California. [L.A.] Archaeological survey assoc. of So. Calif., 1955. 83 p. illus., maps, diagrs. (Its Paper, no. 2)　　　　　　　CSd CSfSt

3244. Pegrum, Dudley Frank. The Los Angeles metropolitan transportation problem, a preliminary analysis. [n.p.] 1957. 63 l.　　　　　　　　CL

3245. Petchner, William C. Romance and drama in the valley of the sunshine; being a story of old Palmdale. L.A., Palmdale fruitland co., c1914. [19] p.　C

3246. Pflueger, Donald. Glendora, the annals of a southern California community. Pen drawings by Arthur Camargo. [1st ed.] Claremont, Saunders press, 1951. 262 p. illus., port. Bibliography: p. 255–56.
C CHi CL CLO CLS CLU CLob CMon CO COr CP CPom CRcS CSd CSdS CStclU CU-B CWhC NN

3247. Picturesque Los Angeles county, California. Illustrative and descriptive. Pub. by the Am. photogravure co. ... Chicago, Fred'k Weston print. co., 1887. 21 p. 65 pl.
C CBb CL CLO CLSU CLU CP CSd CSfCW CSmH MiD-B NN

3248. Place, George E., & co., pub. Los Angeles city and county guide book...1885. [L.A., 1885] 84 p. illus., map.　　　　　　　　　　　　CL

3249. Place, John L. The Pacific face of the Santa Monica mountains, southern California: a geographic interpretation. Berkeley, 1952. Thesis (M.A.)—U.C.L.A., 1952.　　　　　　　　　　　　　　CLU

3250. Poly industries, inc., Pacoima. History. [n.p., n.d.] Reprinted from *Burbank daily review*.　CL

3251. Pottenger, Francis Marion. The fight against tuberculosis; an autobiography. N.Y. [c1952] 276 p.
CHi

3252. Pratt, L. M., & co. Altadena... L.A. [1905?] [40] p. illus.　　　　　　　CLO CU-B

3253. Pridham's Los Angeles county medical and pharmaceutical directory; a list of physicians and druggists in the county, arranged alphabetically by post offices; Los Angeles physicians and druggists...to which is added a list of nurses...1895. 1st ed. L.A., R. W. Pridham [1895] 71 p.　　　　　　　　　　CLU

3254. Public employment bureau. Los Angeles district. ...Annual report, 1st–5th, 1913/14–1917/18. L.A., 1914–1918. 4 v. tables.　　　　　CL

3255. Rancho Santa Anita, inc. The romance of Rancho Santa Anita. Arcadia [n.d.] unp. illus. Consists chiefly of biography of "Lucky" Baldwin. Another edition, with identical text and varying illustrations, was issued by Eaton's restaurants, 1940.
CLO (1940) CLU (both editions)

3256. Rand McNally guide to Los Angeles and environs... N.Y., Rand McNally, c1925. 237 p. illus., maps.
C CL CPom CRedl CSd CSdS CU-B NN

3257. Ransom (J. B.) organization. Montebello Park; the model community of the new east side. L.A., c1925. 24 p. illus., maps.　　　　　　CL

3258. Reagan, J. W. ...Report of J. W. Reagan... upon the control of flood waters...Filed with the Board of supervisors of the Los Angeles county flood area district and adopted January 2, 1917... [L.A., Citizen print shop, 1917] 35 p.　　CL CLSU CLU CSmH CU-B

3259. —— A report on floods, river phenomena and rainfall in the Los Angeles region, California. [L.A., L.A. county Bd. of engineers, flood control, 1939] 434 l. Typew.　　　　　　　　　　　　CLU

3260. Record-Ledger of the Verdugo Hills. The green Verdugo Hills. [Tujunga, n.d.] unp. illus., ports.
CL

3261. Registered historical landmarks, county of Los Angeles. [L.A., Di Palma, 1958] [36] p. illus., map.
C CBev CL CLU CMon CP CPom CStmo CU-B

3262. Reid, Hugo. Hugo Reid's account of the Indians of Los Angeles co., Cal. ... Salem, Mass., Print. at the Salem press, 1885. 33 p. illus.
C CHi CL CLU CRedl CSmH CU-B

3263. —— The Indians of Los Angeles county... L.A., Priv. print., 1926. 70 p. "This reprint is from the scrap-book collection of clippings from the *Los Angeles star* in the Bancroft library at the University of California..."—Foreword.

C CBb CHi CL CLO CLSU CLU CSd CSf
CSfCP CSmH CStmo CU-B

3264. Renié map service. New Renié commercial
atlas of Los Angeles city and county...G. M. Barthold
editor. L.A., E.A. Westberg [c1945] illus., maps. Loose-
leaf.　　　　　　　　　　　　　　CL CLS CLU

3265. —— The new Renié pocket atlas of Los Angeles...city and county...and, The new Renié pocket
atlas of Orange county and cities. L.A., Calif. blueprint
& map co., 1943. 111 maps. Revised and pub. annually.
C (1944) CLU (1949, 1958) CRedl (1950, 1956)
CSd (1950) CStaC (1943) CStmo (2 latest eds.)
CWhC (1954) ODa (1949)

3266. Rhoades, William Lauren. The history of
the famous Sierra Madre villa. [Sierra Madre, 1939]
25 l. Typew.　　　　　　　　　　　　　　　　C

3267. Robinson, Duane Morris. Chance to belong;
story of the Los Angeles youth project, 1943–1949. Foreword by C. Whit Pfeiffer. N.Y., Woman's press [1949]
173 p. illus., maps.
C CArcHT CBb CChiS CL CLS CLU CP CSS
CSfSt CSfU

3268. Robinson, William Wilcox. The forest and
the people; the story of the Angeles national forest...
L.A., Title insurance & trust co., 1946. 44 p. illus.
C CBev CHi CL CLO CLSU CLU CO CPom
CSf CSmH CStmo CU-B CoD

3269. —— [History of local cities] L.A., Title guarantee and trust co. [1936] 2 v.　　　　　　CLLoy

3270. —— Lawyers of Los Angeles; a history of Los
Angeles bar association and of the Bar of Los Angeles
county. [L.A.] L.A. bar assoc., 1959. 370 p. illus., ports.,
map.
C CBev CHi CL CLO CLU CO CSd CSdS
CSfU CU-B CViCL

3271. —— The Malibu: Rancho Topanga Malibu
Sequit, an historical approach. Personal considerations,
essays by Lawrence Clark Powell. Illus. by Irene Robin-
son. L.A., Dawson, 1959. 86 p. illus., map.
C CBb CChiS CHi CL CLLoy CLO CLSM
CLU CLob CO CP CRedl CSd CSdS CSf CStmo
CStoC CU-B CoD

3272. —— Ranchos become cities... Pasadena, San
Pasqual press, 1939. 243 p. illus. Development of the
following cities from ranchos: San Pedro-Wilmington,
Glendale, Long Beach, Whittier, San Fernando, Culver
City, Inglewood, Santa Monica, Beverly Hills, Pasadena,
Monrovia, Pomona.
Available in many California libraries and CoD NIC
NN ODa TxU UPB

3273. [Rodd, Marcel] Souvenir-album. Los Angeles, Hollywood, and the southland at a glance... Hollywood [c1942] 96 p. illus.　　　　　　　　CHi

3274. Root, Virginia V. Following the pot of gold
at the rainbow's end in the days of 1850. Ed. Leonore
Rowland... Downey, Print. by Elena Quinn [1960] 31
p. illus., ports.　　　　　　　　　　　　　CHi

3275. Rose, Leonard John, jr. Catalogue of Rose-
meade stock farm; highly-bred trotting stock, property of
L. J. Rose, Los Angeles, Cal. ... S.F., Britton & Rey,
1888. 108 p. illus.　　　　　　　　　　　CHi

3276. —— L. J. Rose of Sunny Slope, 1827–1899,
California pioneer, fruit grower, wine maker, horse breed-
er. San Marino, Huntington lib., 1959. 235 p. plates.
(Huntington lib. publications)
C CChiS CHi CLO CLU CMon CP CSalCL
CSd CSdS CSmH CStclU CWhC

3277. Rotholtz, Benjamin. Wilson's illustrated and
descriptive souvenir and guide to Los Angeles and near-
by towns. L.A., Wilson pub. co. [1901] 157 p. illus., map.
　　　　　　　　　　　　　　　　　　　　　　C

3278. Rowland, Leonore. The romance of La
Puente rancho. [Puente, 1948] 23 p.　　CL CPom

3279. —— Same. Including excerpts from "La Puente
valley, past and present" by Janet and Dan N. Powell
(W.P.A. Writers project) [Covina, Neilson press, 1958]
68 p. illus., ports.
C CBb CHi CL CLO CLU CLob CO CP CPom

**3280. Sabichi, Francisco, vs. Aguilar, Merejildo
et al.** ...Transcript from the district court of the 17th
judicial district of the state of California, in and for Los
Angeles county. Francisco Sabichi, plaintiff, vs. Merejildo Aguilar, Jose La Luz Valenzuela, Vicenta Ruiz...
[et al.] defendants. Glassell, Chapman & Smith, plaintiff's att'ys. Howard & Sepulveda, att'ys for defendants.
L.A., Republican print., 1869. 14 p.　　　　CU-B

3281. San Dimas press. Chamber of commerce edition; midwinter, 1929. San Dimas, 1929. [56] p. illus.,
ports.　　　　　　　　　　　　　　　　　　C

3282. Santa Anita rancho. Private catalogue 1916
...collection of imported purebred, and homebred, registered thoroughbred, Arabian, and Percheron horses...
[L.A., Geo. Rice & sons] 1916. 122 p. illus.　　CHi

3283. Saunders, Howard Raymond. Mapfax of
Los Angeles county. Sherman Oaks, Metropolitan surveys, c1943. 76 p.　　　　　　　　　　　　ViU

3284. Sayers, Charles Leroy. The development of
the community orchestra in selected cities of Los Angeles county. [L.A., 1948] 197 l. tables. Thesis (M.A.)
—Occidental college, 1948.　　　　　　　　CLO

3285. Scott, Mellier Goodin. Cities are for people;
the Los Angeles region plans for living... L.A. [Litho-
graphed by Homer Boelter co.] 1942. 109 p. illus., maps.
(Pac. southwest acad. Pub. 21) Industrial history of Los
Angeles with suggestions for the future.
C CBev CChiS CL CLO CLSU CLU CSfMI
CU-B CViCL CWhC ViU

3286. —— Metropolitan Los Angeles: one community. L.A., Haynes foundation, 1949. 192 p. illus., ports.,
maps. "Primarily...intended as a supplementary text-
book for senior high schools in Los Angeles and Orange
counties."
Available in many California libraries and NN ODa
ViU

**3287. Scudder, Kenyon Judson, and Beam, Ken-
neth S.** Who is delinquent?...The Los Angeles county
plan of coordinating councils including a study of fourteen thousand Juvenile court cases, administered by the
Juvenile court and Probation department... [L.A.] Rotary club of L.A., 1934. 56 p. illus.　C CL CLSU

3288. —— —— Why have delinquents?...The Los
Angeles county plan of coordinating councils adminis-
tered by the Juvenile court and Probation department...
[L.A., Rotary club of L.A.] c1933. 48 p. illus.
　　　　　　　　　　　　　　　CL CLO CLSU

**3289. "Seeing California" traffic and informa-
tion bureau, Los Angeles.** Seeing California, '49–04.
72 p. (v.2, no. 1, Nov., 1904)　　　　　　CHi

3290. Sepulveda land case. [In the Supreme court
of the state of California. [n.p., 1869?] 2 v. Binder's
title. Collection of documents.　　　　　　CLU

3291. Shippey, Lee. Folks ushud know, interspersed
with songs of courage... Sierra Madre, Sierra Madre

press, 1930. 96 p. ports. The second of a series which began with "Personal glimpses," the four books of which will form a sort of Who's who of southern California's more famous residents.

CBb   CL   CLSU   CLU   CSmH

3292. —— Personal glimpses of famous folks and other selections from the Lee side o' L.A. ... Sierra Madre, Sierra Madre press, 1929. 96 p. ports.

CBb   CHi   CL   CLLoy   CLO   CLSU   CLU   CSd   CU-B

3293. Shrode, Ida May. The sequent occupance of the Rancho Azusa de Duarte, a segment of the upper San Gabriel valley of California. Chicago, 1948. 165 p. illus., maps. Thesis—Univ. of Chicago, 1948.

C   CL   CLU   CLob   CMon   NN   NcU   OU

3294. Sierra Madre. Board of trade. Vistas of Sierra Madre, California. [Sierra Madre news, 1908] [32] p. illus., map.   C

3295. Sierra Madre water co. Amended by-laws... adopted August 17, 1885... L.A., Times-mirror co., 1886. 12 p.   CHi

3296. Smith, Marian Elizabeth. Pío Pico, ranchero and politician. [Berkeley, 1928] 218 l. port. Thesis (M.A.)—Univ. of Calif., 1928.   CU   CU-B

3297. Smith, Valene L. Canoga Park; a study of water problems as related to land use. [L.A.] 1950. Thesis (M.A.)—U.C.L.A., 1950.   CLU

3298. Sons of the revolution. California society. Roster...24th year, January, 1916. [L.A., 1916] 12 p.   CHi

3299. Southern California research council. Report, no. 1– [L.A. 1953– Sponsored jointly by Occidental college and Pomona college. Contents: no. 1. The effect of a reduction in defense expenditures upon the Los Angeles area.—no. 2. The Los Angeles economy; its strengths and weaknesses.—no. 3. The next 15 years, 1955–70; the Los Angeles metropolitan area.—no. 4. Guides to prosperity in the Los Angeles economy.—no. 5. Manpower outlook for the Los Angeles area in the 1960s. —no. 6. The cost of metropolitan growth, 1958–70.

CL has no. 1–3. CLO has no. 1–6. CLU has no. 1, 3, 4, 6. CP has no. 1.

3300. Sprague engineering corp., Gardena. Annual report.

CL has 1954–60.

3301. —— Prospectus.

CL has 1954.

3302. Stanford research institute. The smog problem in Los Angeles county; a report on studies to determine the nature and sources of smog. L.A., Committee on smoke and fumes, Western oil and gas assoc., c1948–1954. 4 v.   CLO   CLS

3303. Staniford, Edward F. Business decentralization in metropolitan Los Angeles. [L.A., Bur. of governmental research, Univ. of Calif., 1960] 57 p.   CL

3304. [Stephens, Bascom A.] ed. Resources of Los Angeles county, California. L.A., Sprague & Rodehaver, print., 1887. 95 p.   CL   CSmH

3305. Stevenson, James O. Tax equalization survey, Los Angeles county municipalities. [L.A.] L.A. Bur. of municipal research, 1943. 106 [26] p. illus., maps, plans.   CL

3306. Stewart, Marie. History of Los Encinos state historical monument. [Prepared by Marie Stewart, president, Encino history committee, inc. Encino, 1958?] 14 p.   CU-B

3307. Stuart, James Ferguson. Further argument against the survey made in July 1868 of the Rancho Sausal Redondo... S.F., Excelsior press, 1869. 35 p.   CU-B

3308. —— Objections to the survey of the Rancho Sausal Redondo, as made by George H. Thompson, Deputy United States surveyor, in July, 1868. Argument against the survey, James F. Stuart, counsel for objectors. S.F., Excelsior press, 1868. 34 p.   CLU   CSfCW

3309. Sunkist growers, Los Angeles. [Annual report]

CHi has 1953, 1960–61.

3310. Sunny California from the mountains to the sea: Los Angeles and vicinity. [L.A., Calif. postcard co., n.d.] [42] p. illus.   CLU

3311. Swanson, John E. Cooperative administration of property taxes in Los Angeles county. L.A., Bur. of governmental research, Univ. of Calif. at L.A., 1949. 63 p. (Studies in local govt., no. 12)   CL

3312. Swett, Ira L., ed. Los Angeles Pacific. [L.A.? 1955]   CP

3313. Taxpayers association of California. City and county consolidation for Los Angeles. L.A., 1917. 197 p.   CHi   CL   CLSU   CLU

3314. Tays, George. Transcriptions and translations of original documents relating to ranchos in Los Angeles county, and particularly to Rancho San Pedro and Rancho Los Nietos with its principal subdivision, Rancho Los Cerritos... L.A., 1939. 3 v. Typew.   CL   CU-B

3315. Terry, R. A. History of the Harbor branch, Los Angeles county medical society, 1905–1942. Long Beach, 1942. 15 p.   CLM

3316. Thomas, Evan William. An analysis of proposals to provide rapid and adequate mass transportation for the Los Angeles area. [L.A.] 1939. Thesis (M.A.) —U.C.L.A., 1939.   CLU

3317. Thomas bros. Complete commercial street atlas of Los Angeles county. 1954 ed. L.A., 1953. 151 p. maps.   CLU

3318. —— Popular atlas, Los Angeles county...and postal delivery zone maps. L.A., c1951. 169 p. maps (part col.)

CLU also has 1955, 1959–60 eds.

3319. Times-mirror co. List of tax-payers, farmers, producers, etc., in Los Angeles county, Calif. With post-office addresses, and statistics of land under cultivation, trees, vines, grain and hay; also amounts taxable (above debts) to each person. Comp. from the official records. L.A., 1894. 128 p.   CLU

3320. Tipton, Gene B. The labor movement in the Los Angeles area during the nineteen-forties. [L.A.] 1953. Thesis (Ph.D.)—U.C.L.A., 1953.   CLU

3321. Title guarantee and trust co. The story of your land. L.A., c1938. unp.   CAla

3322. —— Tract index, Los Angeles county. [L.A.? n.d.] "Supplement, Tract index, 1949" laid in at end.

CLU

3323. Treganza, Adan Eduardo. The Topanga culture and southern California pre-history. [Berkeley, 1950] Thesis (Ph.D.)—Univ. of Calif., 1950.   CU

3324. Truman, Benjamin Cummings. Semi-tropical California: its climate, healthfulness, productiveness, and scenery... S.F., A. L. Bancroft, 1874. 204 p.

Available in many California libraries and GEU MiD T ViW

3325. Trump, James K. The administration of five

districts in the Los Angeles metropolitan area. [L.A.] 1950. Thesis (M.A.)—U.C.L.A., 1950.   CLU

3326. —— County administered fire protection, a case study in a metropolitan area. L.A., Bur. of governmental research, Univ. of Calif. at L.A., 1951. 86 p. illus. (Studies in local govt., no. 13)   CLU CStmo

3327. **Union Bank, Los Angeles.** Growth pattern: the dynamic Los Angeles metropolitan area. [L.A., 1958] 30 p. illus., graphs.   C

3328. **United States vs. Garcia, M. de J.** District court of the United States for the district of California. The United States vs. M. de J. Garcia. Brief for the United States. Signed: J. W. Harding, of counsel for the United States. [S.F., 1871] 18 p. Rancho Los Nogales.   CLU

3329. **U.S. Army. Corps of engineers.** ...Los Angeles drainage area flood control. Prepared under the direction of Lieutenant Colonel Edwin C. Kelton, district engineer. [L.A., 1939] 177 l.   CLU

3330. —— **Census office. 7th census, 1850.** Census of the city and county of Los Angeles, California, for the year 1850 together with an analysis and an appendix... L.A., Times-mirror press, 1929. 139 p. illus., ports., map.
Available in many libraries.

3331. —— —— —— Census of the city and county of Los Angeles, California, for the year 1850. Comp. by John R. Evertsen. Map no. 1 of the city of Los Angeles, known as Ord's survey. Appendix: Los Angeles county boundaries in 1850. Founding and naming of Los Angeles. John R. Evertsen—A sketch. The story of Pierre Lebecque.
C CL CLLoy CLSM (Original draft...schedules 1, 3–6) CLU CSmH

3332. —— **Congress. Senate. Committee on commerce.** Deep-sea harbor in southern California. Report of a hearing... Wash., D.C., Govt. print. off., 1896. 95 p. tables.   CL

3333. —— **General land office.** Decision of the Commissioner of the General land office, in Sausal Redondo and other cases, involving the question as to survey of the ranchos Tajauta, Aguage del Centinela, Cienega ó Paso de la Tijera, and Sausal Redondo, in California. Dated June 22, 1870. Wash., D.C., Govt. print. off., 1870. 17 p.   CLU

3334. —— **Works progress administration.** El Monte from the pioneer days; history and biographical sketches compiled and written for the city of El Monte by the Works progress administration, project N–5740. [n.p., 194–?] 2 v. Mimeo.   CHi

3335. **Venice evening vanguard.** Special edition, 1919. [Venice, 1919] 36 p. illus.   C

3336. **Verdugo Hills realty company.** Walnut gardens, Tujunga; the fast growing community in the green Verdugo Hills...[Prospectus] Tujunga [192–?] [4] p. map.   CU-B

3337. **Vernon, Arthur, and Keppen, Charles, ed.** California tintypes, Los Angeles ed. ...[n.p., n.d.] 152 p. ports.   CL CLU CSmH

3338. **Vernon, Charles Clark.** A history of the San Gabriel mountains. [L.A., 1952] 216 l. Thesis (M.A.)– Occidental college, 1952.   CLO

3339. **Veysey, Lawrence R.** A history of the rail passenger service operated by the Pacific electric railway company. [L.A.] Interurbans, 1958.   CP

3340. —— The Pacific electric railway company since 1910; a study in the operations of economic social and political forces upon American local transportation. [n.p.] 1953. 484 p. illus., ports., maps, diagrs., tables. On film (positive)   CU-B

3341. **Voorhis, H. Jerry.** The story of the Voorhis school for boys... San Dimas, Viking print shop, 1932. 20 p. illus.   CHi

3342. **Wagg, Peter A. [pseud.?]** Southern California exposed...ed. by Homer Fort... [L.A., 1915] 24 p.   CSmH

3343. **Waite, Charles F.** Incorporation fever: hysteria or salvation? An excerpt from a report on incorporation and annexation in Los Angeles county, prepared for the Falk foundation. L.A. [L.A. daily jl.] 1957. 7 p.   CL

3344. **Walker, Edwin Francis.** Five prehistoric archaeological sites in Los Angeles county, California. L.A., Southwest museum, Administrator of the fund, 1952. 116 p. illus. (Pub. of the Frederick Webb Hodge anniversary pub. fund, v.6)
C CL CLO CLU CPom CSfCSM CSfSt

3345. **Wallace, William James.** The house of the Scotch paisano; archaeological investigations at the Hugo Reid adobe, Arcadia, California. [n.p.] 1957. 26 l. 2 plans. Mimeo.   CLU

3346. **Warner, Francis D.** Elias J. Baldwin, not anybody's hostler... 4 p. Typew.   CL

3347. **Webber, L. P.** Prospectus of Westminister colony, Los Angeles county, Cal. [n.p., 187–?] [2] l. map.   CU-B

3348. **Welfare council of Metropolitan Los Angeles.** Report of the subcommittee on housing for aged. [L.A.] 1950. 12 l. illus.   CL

3349. —— **Research dept.** Camps and campers in the Los Angeles area...Prepared by the Research dept. staff and Camping survey committee. [L.A.] 1950. 140 p. charts, tables, maps. (Its Report no. 9)   C

3350. —— —— Child care program survey; facts concerning day care and nursery centers in Los Angeles county... [L.A.,] 1945. 8 l. tables. (Special report ser. no. 2)   CL

3351. —— —— Facts concerning child care centers in Los Angeles county, January 1946... [L.A., 1946] 9 l. tables. (Special report ser. no. 3)   CL

3352. —— —— Los Angeles county population— census tracts by study areas, 1950 census. [L.A.] 1952. [25] p.   CLU

3353. —— —— Public health nursing in Los Angeles county... [L.A.?] 1949–51. 2 v. maps, tables.   C

3354. **Welfare planning council, Los Angeles region. Research dept.** A community study of El Monte area, 1956, by Herbert R. Larsen... [L.A.?] 1956. 24 l. maps. (Information ser., no. 11)   C

3355. **Wendt, Wilhelmine.** Smog over Los Angeles. [L.A., Wendt pub., c1959] 53 p.   C CLU CSd

3356. **White, Leslie Turner.** Me, detective... N.Y., Harcourt, c1936. 302 p. illus., ports. Los Angeles crimes.
C CBb CBev CBu CL CLSU CLU CRcS CSalCL CSdU CSf CSmH CStmo CU-B CViCL

3357. **Whiteman, Luther, and Lewis, Samuel L.** Glory roads: the psychological state of California... N.Y., Crowell, 1936. 267 p. This book includes such movements as Dr. Townsend's plan, bartering "Tradex" and "Epic," which more or less centered in L.A. county. Available in many California libraries and ViW

3358. Who's who in Los Angeles county... L.A., Lang, 1924–[1933] illus., ports. Title varies: 1924–1926/27 issued under title: Who's who in Los Angeles; 1926/27–contains The women of Los Angeles, by Florence Collins Porter; 1927/28– Womens who's who in Los Angeles county.

CBb has 1930/31. CBev has 1928/29. CHi has 1925/26–1928/29. CL has 1924–1932/33. CLLoy has 1924–1925/26. CLSU has 1924–1925/26. CLU has 1925/26–1932/33. CSdS has 1927/28. CSmH has 1925/26, 1927/28, 1930/31. CStmo has 1928/29, 1930/31. MoS has 1928/29.

3359. Who's who in Los Angeles county. 1950/51– L.A., Who's who hist. soc., 1950– Editor: 1950/51– Alice Catt Armstrong.

C has 1950/51, 1952/53. CBea has 1950/51. CHi has 1950/51. CLM has 1950/51. CRic has 1950/51. CStmo has 1950/51, 1952/53. CU-B has 1950/51.

3360. Why taxes are high in Los Angeles county. [n.p., 1930?]   CSmH

3361. [Wicks, M. L., and Jones, John J.] Palmdale. (Das Palmen-thal.)... [L.A., 1885] [3] p. Text in German.   CL

3362. Wilson, Agnes E. The facilities for the care of dependent, semi-delinquent and delinquent Negro children in Los Angeles, a study made at the request of the Budget committee of the Community welfare federation, Feb.-Mar., 1925. [L.A.] n.d. 44 p.   CL

3363. Winjum, Orel Raymond. Classification in the Los Angeles county civil service. L.A., 1938. Thesis (M.A.)– U.C.L.A., 1938.   CLU

Alhambra

3364. Alhambra. Board of trade. Alhambra, the gateway to the San Gabriel valley... [Alhambra? 1909] [16] p. illus.   CU-B NN

3365. —— **Chamber of commerce.** Descriptive booklet of the city of Alhambra... [L.A., Western litho. co.] 1915. 31 p. illus.   CL CU-B

3366. Crossman, Carl Dunbar. Alhambra booster book; a guide for newcomers. [Alhambra, c1932] 20 p. illus.   CU-B

3367. Hull, Osman Ransom. ...Survey of the Alhambra public schools... L.A., Univ. of So. Calif., 1929. 107 p. (Studies, 24 ser., no. 5)   CSmH

3368. Northrup, William Moulton, ed. Alhambra (San Gabriel-Monterey Park) community book...In two parts, narrative and biographical. Alhambra, Cawston, 1944. 249 p. illus., ports.   C CL CLU NN

3369. —— Same. 1949. 179 p. illus., ports.
                                                       CL CLU

3370. .... ed. History of Alhambra... In two parts, narrative and biographical. Alhambra, Cawston, 1936. 219 p. illus., ports.   C CL CU-B MWA NN

3371. Scharer, Norman B. The development of public secondary education in Alhambra, California. Thesis (Ph.D.)– U.C.L.A., 1947.   CLU

Azusa

3372. Aerojet-General corp., Azusa. Annual report.
CL has 1950, 1960.

3373. Azusa herald & pomotropic. 50 years of progress, October 20th 1887—October 20th 1937...

Golden anniversary, October 20, 1937. Azusa, 1937. 48 p. illus., ports., maps.
                        C CHi CLO CLU CSmH CU-B

3374. Azusa irrigating co. By-laws...adopted September 7, 1886. L.A., Hellman, Stassforth & co. [1886?] 14 p.   CHi

3375. Azusa old and new; being a true recital of the founding and development of a California community. Azusa, Azusa foot-hills citrus co., 1921. 28 p.
                                                  CHi CSfCP

3376. Azusa water development and irrigation co. Contract between the Azusa water development and irrigating company and the old users. June 1, 1888. [Azusa, Pomotropic print., 1889] 12 p.   CSmH

3377. Baker, Charles Chaney. The birthday of Rancho Azusa. [2] p. Reprinted from the *Pomotropic*, Nov. 5, 1915.   C

3378. Goold, Edmond L. In the matter of the survey of the ranchos San Jose, Addition, and Azusa. Before Hon. Sherman Day, U.S. surveyor general. Brief for the claimants. [S.F.] Cosmopolitan print. co. [n.d.] 47 p.
                                                        CU-B

3379. Hutchinson, Louisa Williamson. Azusa; the blessed miracle. From an Indian legend. Published at the time of the 50th anniversary of the founding of the city of Azusa, May 1, 1937. Azusa, Pomotropic press [1937] 11 p.   CHi CPom

3380. Larrabee, Charles Hathaway. In the matter of the survey of the ranchos San Jose, Addition & Azusa, before Hon. Sherman Day, U.S. surveyor general. Brief for the settlers. S.F., Women's co-operative union print., 1869. 50 p.   CU-B

3381. [Moody, Charles Amadon] Azusa, California. [n.p., n.d.] 163–177 p. illus.   CLU CU-B

Beverly Hills

3382. Allen-Pinchon, Mary. Beverly Hills. Southern California. [L.A., Segnogram press, 191–?]
                                                        CSmH

3383. Anderson, Clinton H. Beverly Hills is my beat. Englewood Cliffs, N.J., Prentice-Hall [1960] 218 p. illus.   C CHi CU-B

3384. Bartholomew, Harland, and associates, St. Louis. Report upon streets, parking, zoning, city of Beverly Hills, California. Prepared for the City council. St. Louis, 1948. 66,20 p.   CBev

3385. Benedict, Pierce Edson, ed. History of Beverly Hills...In two parts, narrative and biographical. Beverly Hills, Cawston—H. M. Meier, 1934. 235 p. illus., ports., maps.
             CBev CL CLSU CLU CLob CSmH CU-B NN

3386. Beverly Hills. Chamber of commerce. Beverly Hills, California, midway between Los Angeles and the sea. [Beverly Hills, 192–?] [24] p. illus.
                                                   CBev CU-B

3387. —— **City council.** 1952–1958: five years of municipal progress in Beverly Hills. Beverly Hills [1958] 16 p.   CBev

3388. —— **Community Presbyterian church.** The story of the Beverly Hills Community Presbyterian church; the first twenty-five years, 1921–1946. 32 p.
                                                       CBev

3389. —— **Junior chamber of commerce.** Second annual year book, 1939. Beverly Hills, Chancey-Citizen co. [1939?] 32 p.   CBev

3390. —— **Temple Emanuel.** Dedication services, November, 1944. 1 v. illus., ports.   C

3391. Beverly Hills hotel and bungalows. The hotel and bungalows at Beverly Hills, California, midway between Los Angeles and the sea. [n.p., 1920?] [9] p. illus., map.   CHi

3392. Cold water literary society, Beverly Hills. Minutes. Jan. 5, 1887–Dec. 1, 1894. Ms.   CBev

3393. Litton industries, Beverly Hills. Annual report.
CL has 1959–60.

3394. Maddox, C. Richard. Beverly Hills justice. 1959. 70 p.   CBev

3395. Northrop corp. Annual report.
CL has 1947–48, 1950–54.

3396. Robinson, William Wilcox. Beverly Hills; a calendar of events in the making of a city. L.A., Title guarantee & trust co., 1938. 23 p. illus., map.
C CBev CHi CL CLO CLU CO CSmH CStmo CU-B CWhC

3397. —— Same. c1942. [23] p.   CHi NN

3398. Rodeo land and water co. Beverly Hills. Exclusive residence district in the foothills, between Los Angeles and the sea. L.A. [n.d.] 12 l.   CSmH

3399. Security–first national bank of Los Angeles. The ranch of the gathering of the waters [Rancho rodeo de las aguas]... L.A., 1934. 18 p. illus. The site of Beverly Hills.   C CBev CL CLU CSmH

3400. —— The story of the murals in the Beverly Hills branch... [L.A.] c1934. 18 p.   CSmH

3401. [Whitelaw, Frank J.] On the road to Beverly Hills. [n.p., Clason map co., n.d.] [16] p.   CHi

Burbank

3402. Flying tiger line, inc. Annual report.
CL has 1950–60.

3403. Lockheed aircraft corp. Annual report.
CL has 1948–58, 1960.

3404. Magnolia Park. Chamber of commerce. The story of Burbank from her eventful pioneer days... Burbank, 1954. 46 p. illus.   CHi

3405. Menasco manufacturing corp. Annual report.
CL has 1958–59 (25th anniversary).

3406. Monroe, George Lynn, ed. Burbank community book...In two parts, narrative and biographical. Burbank, Cawston, 1944. 216 p. illus., ports.
C CBb CL CLU NN

3407. Pacific airmotive corp. Annual report.
CL has 1957–60.

3408. Security first national bank, Los Angeles. Ranchos de los Santos, the story of Burbank. L.A., 1927. illus.   C CHi CL CLSU CLU CSmH

3409. Walt Disney productions. Annual report.
CL has 1948–60.

3410. —— Report by Sutro and co., Burbank. Burbank, 1960.   CL

Claremont

3411. Arnold, Frank R. Getting to know your Claremont. [n.p., 1936] [19] p.   CSmH

3412. Blaisdell, James Arnold. Addresses presented on the occasion of a memorial service honoring James Arnold Blaisdell. Claremont, Bd. of Fellows of Claremont college [1957] 22 p.   CHi

3413. Brackett, Frank Parkhurst. Granite and sagebrush; reminiscences of the first fifty years of Pomona college. L.A., Ward Ritchie [1944] 251 p. port., col. plates.
C CBb CChiS CHi CLU CSd CStoC

3414. Citizens national bank of Claremont. Claremont...then and now. Claremont, c1954. unp. illus.
C CHi CL CO CPom

3415. Claremont. Girls collegiate school of Claremont. [Brochure] Claremont [1940] 10 p. illus.
CHi

3416. —— —— Meadowlark, the Girls collegiate junior school. [Claremont, n.d.] [4] p. map.   CHi

3417. Claremont college. Claremont, an educational ideal. [Pomona? 192–?] 24 p.   CU-B

3418. Claremont colleges. Dedication of the Honnold library, serving Pomona college, Scripps college, Claremont college, Claremont men's college. [Claremont, Ward Ritchie, 1952?] 23 p. port.   C CU-B

3419. —— **Graduate school.** [Catalog]
CL has 1938– to date.

3420. Claremont men's college. [Catalog]
CL has 1929– to date.

3421. Davis, Harold H., ed. This is Claremont... Claremont, Saunders press, 1941. 147 p. Bibliography: p. 147.
Available in many California libraries and NHi NN OrU

3422. Douglass, Enid Hart. The Claremont planning commission: a study of social backgrounds, attitudes, and opinions. [Claremont, 1959] 73 l. map. Thesis (M.A.)– Claremont college, 1959.   CCH

3423. Edmunds, Charles Keyser. In memoriam. [L.A., Ward Ritchie, 1949?] 20 p. port.   CLO

3424. Indian Hill, Claremont... [n.p., n.d.]   C-S

3425. [Kerr, Willis Holmes] Willis Holmes Kerr, librarian emeritus, Claremont college... Claremont college, 1952. 19 p.   CHi

3426. Marston, George White. Over the years, recollections of George White Marston, trustee since 1887, Pomona college, October 14, 1937. [Claremont, 1937] [26] p. port.   CHi CLO CU-B

3427. Padua Hills, inc. Padua Hills; a residential community of distinction... [n.p., 1935?] [5] p. illus., map.   CHi

3428. Pomona college. Alumni directory. 1948. Claremont, 1948.   CSdS CU-B

3429. —— Annual catalog. 1895/96– Claremont [etc.] 1895–
CU-B has 1895/96–1897/98, 1930/31, 1932/33, 1935/36–1940/41, 1945/46, 1957/58–1958/59.

3430. —— Fiftieth founders' day, October 14, 1937. Claremont, Pomona college, 1937. 49 p.   CHi

3431. —— The inauguration of Elijah Wilson Lyon as the sixth president of Pomona college, October 18, 1941. [Claremont, 1941] 56 p.   CU-B

3432. —— [Pamphlets] 3 v. Contents: v.1. The twentieth anniversary of Pomona college, the dedication of the Frank P. Brackett observatory.—In recognition of scholarship.— Pomona college directory, 1912–13, first semester.— Needs and resources of Pomona college.— Pomona college alumni bulletin, 1915.— Pomona college bulletin, art number, 1906.— Pomona college bulletin, 1904.— Bulletin of Pomona college campus. v.2. In recognition of scholarship, Pomona college, 2d semester

1913-14.— Claremont and Pomona college.— Pomona college bulletin, 1908, 1910, 1912-14.— v.3. Pomona college bulletin March 1916.   **C**

3433. —— Pomona college who's who, 1894-1930. Claremont, 1930.   **CSd**

3434. —— Report of the president. Claremont. CU-B has 1933/34, 1935/36-1943/44.

3435. —— Shaping human powers is the supreme art. [L.A., Ward Ritchie, 1937?] 15 p. illus., map.   **CHi**

3436. —— **Alumni association.** To honor those who served, a war memorial at Pomona college. [Claremont, 1946?] [24] p. illus., ports., plans.   **CU-B**

3437. Scripps college. [Catalog]
CL has 1929- to date.

3438. —— The humanities at Scripps college. L.A., Ward Ritchie [c1952]   **CP**

3439. —— The inauguration of Frederick Hard as president...March 25, 1944. [L.A., 1944] 49 p. illus., ports.   **CHi**

3440. Stephenson, Nathaniel Wright. In memoriam. Claremont, Scripps college, 1935. 31 p. port.
                                                              CLO

3441. Sumner, Charles Burt. The story of Pomona college. Bost., N.Y. [etc.] Pilgrim press [c1914] 417 p. illus., ports.
C CBev CHi CL CLO CLS CLSU CLU CPom CRedl CSd CSdS CSf CSmH

3442. Watson, Jane Werner. The Seaver story... Foreword by R. J. Wig, president, board of trustees, Pomona college. Claremont, Pomona college, 1960. 30 p. illus., ports. A biography of Frank Roger Seaver. Claremont.   **CHi**

Glendale

3443. Forest lawn memorial park association, inc. Art guide of Forest Lawn, with interpretations. Intro. by Bruce Barton. Glendale, c1936. 90 p. illus.   **CHi**

3444. —— Same. c1941. 130 p. illus.   **CU-B**

3445. —— Same. c1949. 309 p. illus.   **CLO CLU**

3446. —— Pictorial Forest Lawn... [Glendale] c1932. [32] p. illus., map.   **C CU-B**
Other editions followed. CHi (c1944) CLO (c1953) CLU (c1952) CSmH (1939)

3447. Glendale. Charter. Charter of city of Glendale (as amended January 14, 1947). [n.p., n.d.] 46 p.
                                                              CLO

3448. Glendale merchants association. Glendale, your home. [1928] 52 p. illus.   **CU-B**

3449. Glendale realty board. Why Glendale, California, is the fastest growing city in America. Glendale [1922?] 14 p. illus.   **CLU**

3450. Hancock, Ralph. The Forest Lawn story. L.A., Academy pub. [1955] 160 p. illus.
                                        C CLU CO CSd NN

3451. Klett, Gordon A. Glendale, California: a geographic analysis of use variances (1947-1949). [L.A.] 1951. Thesis (M.A.)— U.C.L.A., 1951.   **CLU**

3452. Lawson, Melvin. ...Administrative phases of city manager government in Glendale, California... [L.A.] 1940. 90, 12 l. Thesis (M.A.)—U.C.L.A., 1940.
                                                              CLU

3453. Los Angeles herald. Glendale number; Sunday magazine pictorial section, October 17, 1909.
                                                              CBaB

3454. Lynch, Chester Baker. A history of the Glen-

dale public schools from 1879 to 1957 with emphasis on school organization and administration. [L.A., 1957] 196 l. plates, map, tables. Thesis (M.A.)— Occidental college, 1957.   **CLO**

3455. Parcher, Carroll W., ed. Glendale community book. Carroll W. Parcher, editor-in-chief. George S. Goshorn, associate editor. Glendale, J. W. Akers, 1957. 1039 p. illus., ports.   **C CHi CL CLU**

3456. Robinson, William Wilcox. Glendale, a calendar of events in the making of a city. L.A., Title guarantee & trust co. [c1936] [23] p. map.
C CBev CHi CL CLSU CLU CSmH CStrJC CU-B CWhC

3457. —— Same. [c.1942] [23] p. map.
                                        CHi CStmo NN

3458. St. Johns, Adela Rogers. First step up toward heaven: Hubert Eaton and Forest Lawn. Englewood Cliffs, N.J., Prentice-Hall [1959] 293 p. illus.
                                              C CLO CU-B

3459. Security trust and savings bank. Glendale branch. Publicity dept. First of the ranchos; the story of Glendale...2nd ed. c1924. 48 p. illus., ports.
                                                          CL CLO

3460. —— —— —— Same. 3d ed. c1927.
                                              C CLU CU-B

3461. Sherer, Caroline Shaw. How much he remembered; the life of John Calvin Sherer, 1852-1949. [n.p.] 1952. 64 p. illus., ports.
                                C CBb CChiS CHi CStbS CU-B

3462. Sherer, John Calvin. History of Glendale and vicinity... [Glendale] Glendale history pub. co., 1922. 476 p. illus., ports. Biographies: p. [301]-476.
                                CHi CL CLO CLU CSmH NN

3463. [Stamats and McClure] pub., Glendale. Glendale, California, the jewel city. [1912?] [44] p. illus., ports. Includes "Beautiful city of Tropico."   **CLU**

3464. Starbuck, Margaret. So this is Glendale: welcome to a new neighbor; a sketch of the city's colorful history, where to find schools... Glendale [c1939] [30] p. maps.   **CL**

3465. Who's who in Glendale, a biographical dictionary of notable men and women of Glendale, California, 1936-1937, ed. by Dorothy Thies. Glendale, Hist. pub. co. [n.d.] 116 p.   **C CL**

Hollywood

3466. Benton, Frank Weber. Hollywood, California, all the year. [L.A., Benton pub. co., c1922] [48] p. (chiefly illus., part col.)   **CU-B**

3467. Brookwell, George. Saturdays in the Hollywood Bowl. Hollywood, Suttonhouse [c1940] 93 p. illus., ports.   **C**

3468. Browne, Michael. Survey of the Hollywood entertainment film during the war years 1941-1943. [L.A.] 1951. Thesis (M.A.)— U.C.L.A., 1951.   **CLU**

3469. [Cannom, Robert C.] Van Dyke and the mythical city, Hollywood. [Culver City, Murray & Gee, c1948] 424 p. illus., ports. A biography of Woodbridge Strong Van Dyke II.   **CHi**

3470. Carter, Emily Barker, comp. Hollywood, the story of the Cahuengas... [Hollywood, c1926] 86 p. illus. A bulletin of the Hollywood high school.
                                CL CLO CLSU CSmH OrU

3471. Connell, Will. In pictures; a Hollywood satire ... N.Y., T.J. Maloney, inc. [c1937] 104 p. illus.
                                CL CLO CLSU CLU CSmH

3472. Cowing, George Cecil. This side of Hollywood; together with The private life of Goldilocks and other bedtime stories for grown ups. Pasadena, Shaw print., c1938. 152 p. CL CLSU CLU CSmH

3473. Croswell, Mary E. Story of Hollywood, issued by the Hollywood board of trade... [Hollywood, c1905] 34 p. illus., ports. CHi CLU CU-B

3474. Crowther, Bosley. Hollwood rajah; the life and times of Louis B. Mayer. N.Y., Holt [c1960] 339 p. illus. C CL

3475. —— The lion's share; the story of an entertainment empire. N.Y., Dutton, 1957. 320 p. illus, ports CL

3476. Day, Beth (Feagles) This was Hollywood; an affectionate history of filmland's golden years. [1st ed.] Garden City, N.Y., Doubleday, 1960. 287 p. illus., ports. CL CU-B

3477. Day, George Martin. The Russians in Hollywood; a study in culture conflict... L.A., Univ. of So. Calif press, 1934. 101 p. Bibliography: p. [103]
C CBev CLO CLSU CLU CSdS CSfCW CSmH CU-B

3478. De Mille, Agnes George. Dance to the piper. Bost., Little, 1952. 342 p. ports. CSd

3479. De Mille, Cecil Blount. The autobiography of Cecil B. De Mille. [Edited by Donald Hayne] N.Y., Prentice-Hall, 1959. 465 p. illus., ports. CHi CL

3480. De Mille, William Churchill. Hollywood saga... N.Y., Dutton [1939] 319 p. illus., ports.
C CBb CBu CHi CL CLO CLSU CLU CLgA CO CSf CStmo ODa

3481. Dunne, George Harold. Hollywood labor dispute; a study in immorality. L.A., Conference pub. co. [1950?] 44 p. illus. CLU

3482. Fellig, Arthur. Naked Hollywood by Weegee [pseud.] and Mel Harris. N.Y., Pellegrini & Cudahy, 1953. unp. illus. CChiS

3483. Field, Alice Evans. Hollywood, U.S.A.: from script to screen. Introd. by Will Hays. N.Y., Vantage press, 1952. 256 p. illus., ports. CL CLO ODa

3484. Florey, Robert. Hollywood d'hier et d'aujourd'hui. Preface by René Clair. Paris, Éditions Prisma [1948] 381 p. illus., ports. CStmo

3485. Fowler, Gene. Father Goose, the story of Mack Sennett. N.Y., Covici, Friede, 1934. CHi CSd

3486. Fox, Charles Donald. Mirrors of Hollywood, with brief biographies of favorite film folk... N.Y., Charles Renard corp., 1925. 143 p. illus., ports.
C CL CLSU CLU CSmH

3487. Goldwyn, Samuel. Behind the screen. N.Y., Doran, 1923. CBb

3488. Goodman, Ezra. The fifty-year decline and fall of Hollywood. N.Y., Simon, c1961. 465 p.
CHi CL CU-B

3489. Griffith, Richard. The movies; the sixty year story of the world of Hollywood and its effect on America. N.Y., Simon, 1957. 442 p. illus., ports.
CBb CL CSd

3490. Halliday, Ruth Staff. Stars on the crosswalks; an intimate guide to Hollywood... Sherman Oaks, Mitock, 1958. 100 p. illus.
C CHi CL CLO CLU CP CSd

3491. Hampton, Benjamin Bowles. A history of the movies... N.Y., Covici, 1931. 456 p. illus.
C CBaB CL CLSU CLU CStmo

3492. —— Same. London, N. Douglas, 1932. 456 p.
CU-B

3493. Hancock, Ralph. Douglas Fairbanks: the fourth Musketeer. N.Y., Holt, 1953. 276 p. illus. CSd

3494. —— Fabulous boulevard. N.Y., Funk & Wagnalls [c1949] 322 p. Story of Wilshire Boulevard. Available in many libraries.

3495. Heydemann, Lillian P. Hollywood on your budget (a novel guide) by Lily Carthew [pseud.] L.A., Research pub. co., 1942. 219 p. NN

3496. Hill, Laurance Landreth and Snyder, Silas E. Can anything good come out of Hollywood?... L.A., Times-mirror press, 1923. 64 p. illus., ports.
CL CLO CLSU CLU CSmH

3497. Hollywood. Blessed Sacrament church. The Blessed Sacrament church (a sketch) [Hollywood, 1927?] [29] p. illus., ports. CU-B

3498. —— —— History of Blessed Sacrament parish, 1904–1954. Golden jubilee souvenir, October 15–16–17, 1954. Hollywood [1954?] 51 p. illus., ports., facsims.
CHi CLgA CStclU

3499. Hollywood news publishing co., comp. Hollywood business and professional directory. 1924– [28?] Hollywood. C (1928) CHi (1928) CU-B (1924)

3500. Hollywood play house... [L.A.] Hollywood playhouse realty corp. [n.d.] 32 p. illus., ports. CHi

3501. Holstius, Edward Nils. Hollywood through the back door... N.Y., Longmans, 1937. 316 p.
C CL CLSU CLU

3502. Hopper, Hedda. From under my hat. Garden City, Doubleday, 1952. 311 p. CSd

3503. International motion picture almanac, 19— N.Y., Quigley, 19— v. illus., ports. Title varies: 19 – 1935/36, The motion picture almanac. Imprint varies.
CBev has [1934/35–1962] CLLoy has 1939/40. CLSU has 1929, 1932–1941/42, 1943/44–1959, 1961. CStmo has 1956, 1958/59.

3504. Irwin, William Henry. The house that shadows built. Garden City, N.Y., Doubleday, 1928. 293 p. pl. The story of Adolph Zukor and the rise of the motion picture industry. CHi CSdS

3505. Jacobs, Lewis. The rise of the American film; a critical history... N.Y., Harcourt, c1939. 585 p. illus., ports. Bibliography: p. 541–564.
CBaB CBev CBu CL CLO CLS CLSU CLU CO CRedl CSdS CSf CSmH CStmo

3506. Jones, Isabel Morse. Hollywood bowl... N.Y., L.A., G. Schirmer, 1936. 203 p. illus., ports., map.
C CBb CBev CChiS CHi CL CLO CLSU CLU COnC CPom CRedl CSd CSdS CSmH CStmo CViCL

3507. Kahn, Gordon. Hollywood on trial; the story of the 10 who were indicted. Foreword by Thomas Mann. N.Y., Boni and Gaer, 1948. 229 p.
CChiS CLO CStmo

3508. Kimbrough, Emily. We followed our hearts to Hollywood. N.Y., Dodd, 1943. 210 p. illus.
CChiS CRic

3509. [Knepper, Max] Sodom and Gomorrah; the story of Hollywood. L.A., Author [c1935] 236 p. "Preface by Upton Sinclair." CLU

3510. Koury, Phil A. Yes, Mr. De Mille. N.Y., Putnam, 1959. CBb

3511. Lambert, Gavin. The slide area; scenes of Hollywood life. N.Y., Viking press [1959] 223 p.
CU-B

3512. Lasky, Jesse Louis. I blow my own horn. Garden City, N.Y., Doubleday, 1957. CSd

3513. Look. Movie lot to beachhead, the motion picture goes to war and prepares for the future, by the editors of Look, with a preface by Robert St. John. Garden City, N.Y., Doubleday, 1945. 291 p. illus., ports. CHi

3514. Major, Henry. Hollywood with "Bugs" Baer and Henry Major. [n.p.] Lithographed by Daniel Murphy and co., inc. [c1938] illus., 248 pl. (ports.) on 124 l. CLO

3515. Max Factor & co. Annual report. CL has 1948–55.

3516. Miller, Diane Disney. The story of Walt Disney. N.Y., Henry Holt, 1957. 247 p. illus., ports. CL CSd

3517. Miller, Max Carlton. For the sake of shadows. N.Y., Dutton, 1936. 200 p. CU ODa

3518. Moses, Walter Irwin. Adventures of a writer in movieland... [L.A.? c1924] 63 p. CHi

3519. Newman, Ben Allah. Rudolph Valentino. Hollywood, Ben-Allah, 1926. CSd

3520. Northcutt, John Orlando. The Hollywood bowl story. Hollywood, Hollywood bowl assoc., 1962. 30 p. photos. CL

3521. Palmer, Edwin Obadiah. History of Hollywood... Hollywood, Cawston, 1937. 2 v. illus., ports., map. "References": v.1, p. 267–68. v.1. Narrative.—v.2. Biographical.
C CBev CHi CL CLLoy CLO CLSU CLU CO CSmH CStmo MoS NN ODa

3522. —— Same...rev. and extended ed. Hollywood, Author, 1938. 294 p. illus., ports., maps.
C CBb CHi CL CLLoy CLU CSmH

3523. Parsons, Louella (Oettinger) The gay illiterate. Garden City, N.Y., Doubleday, 1944. 194 p. CRedCL CSd

3524. Partridge, Helen. A lady goes to Hollywood... N.Y., Macmillan, 1941. 259 p. NN

3525. Powdermaker, Hortense. Hollywood, the dream factory; an anthropologist looks at the movie makers. [1st ed.] Bost., Little, 1950. 342 p.
CBb CHi CL CLO CLob CRic CSd ODa

3526. Raborn, George. How Hollywood rates. Los Altos, Bert Nelson, c1955. 74 p. C

3527. Ramsaye, Terry. A million and one nights; a history of the motion picture... N.Y., Simon, 1926. 2 v. illus., ports.
C CBb CBev CL CLSU CLU CSf

3528. Ray, Charles. Hollywood shorts, compiled from incidents in the everyday life of men and women who entertain in pictures... L.A., Calif. graphic press, 1935. 177 p. CSmH

3529. Rivkin, Allen. ...The Rivkin-Kerr production of Hello, Hollywood! a book about the movies by the people who make them. N.Y., Doubleday, c1962. 571 p. CL

3530. Rosten, Leo Calvin. Hollywood; the movie colony, the movie makers... N.Y., Harcourt [c1941] 436 p.
C CBaB CBb CBev CBu CChiS CHi CL CLO CLS CLSU CLU CO CRcS CSS CSd CSlu CStmo CU-B CViCL ODa

3531. Royal homes of the picture stars. v.1 of a series. [Oakland, Ralph A. Grover] c1926. 32 p. illus. C

3532. Security trust & savings bank, Los Angeles. Hollywood branch. In the valley of the Cahuengas; the story of Hollywood...by Laurance L. Hill. [Hollywood] c1922. 48 p. illus., ports., maps.
C CHi CLLoy CSmH CU-B

3533. —— —— Same. 5th ed. c1924. 48 p. illus., ports., maps. CHi CL CLSU CLU CO CSmH

3534. Sennett, Mack. King of comedy, by Mack Sennett, as told to Cameron Shipp. Garden City, N.Y., Doubleday, c1954. 284 p. illus., ports. CL

3535. Sheehan, P. P. Hollywood as a world center ... [Hollywood, Hollywood citizen press, c1924] 115 p.
C CHi CL CLSU CLU CSmH CU-B

3536. [Stricker, Thomas Perry] Hollywood bowl. L.A., Pepper tree press [c1939] 16 p. illus., ports.
CBev CLO CLU CSmH CU-B

3537. Swope, John. Camera over Hollywood...with an appendix containing photographic data. N.Y., Random house [c1939] 96 pl. CU-B ODa

3538. Tyler, Parker. Hollywood hallucination... N.Y., Creative age press [1944] 246 p.
C CBev CL CLSU CLU CSalCL CStmo NN

3539. [Ullback, Sylvia] Hollywood undressed, observations of Sylvia as noted by her secretary. N.Y., Brentano's, 1931. 250 p. CLSU CLU

3540. Wagenknecht, Edward Charles. The movies in the age of innocence. Norman, Okla., Univ. of Okla. press, c1962. 280 p. illus., ports. CL

3541. Wagner, Rob, and Hughes, Robert. Two decades; the story of a man of God, Hollywood's own padre. L.A., Young and McCallister, 1936. unp. illus. C

3542. Warner bros. pictures, inc. A financial review and brief history, 1923–1945. [n.p., 1946?] 39 p. illus., ports. CHi

3543. Wing, Ruth, ed. The blue book of the screen. Hollywood, Blue book of the screen, inc. [c1923] 415 p. illus. CHi

3544. Woon, Basil Dillon. Incredible land; a jaunty Baedeker to Hollywood and the great Southwest ... N.Y., Liveright [c1933] 374 p. illus., map.
C CHi CL CLU CMartC CMont CO CRcS CSf CSlu CStmo CU-B MiD

3545. Zukor, Adolph. The public is never wrong; the autobiography of Adolph Zukor, with Dale Kramer. N.Y., Putnam, 1953. 309 p. illus., ports. CBb CL

Inglewood

3546. American MARC, inc. Annual report. CL has 1957–59.

3547. Hamilton, Lloyd Parke, ed. Inglewood community book. Inglewood, Cawston, 1949. 443 p. illus., ports. CL CLU

3548. Inglewood Chamber of commerce. Annual report...1936/37–1938/39. [Inglewood, 1937–39] CU-B

3549. Inglewood land co. Inglewood bungalow park; every lot a bargain! [n.p., 1911?] [8] p. illus., map. CHi

3550. Kingsbury, Josephine. The establishment of Inglewood, 1887–1890. 1941. 50, 4 l. Typew. "History 274B, Dr. J. W. Caughey, May 21, 1941." "Sources of information": 4 l. CLCo

3551. Robinson, William Wilcox. Inglewood; a calendar of events in the making of a city. L.A., Title guarantee & trust co., c1935. 20 p. illus., map. CLSU

3552. —— Same. c1937. 23 p. illus., map.   C
CAla CBev CHi CL CLO CLU CO CSd CSmH
CWhC

Other editions followed.   CHi (1955)   CLU (c1947)
CSluCL (1955)   CStmo (c1947)   CU-B (c1947)   NN
(c1942)   NbHi (c1955)

3553. Rosenberg, Roy. History of Inglewood...
narrative and biographical. Inglewood, Cawston, 1938.
215 p. illus., ports.   CHi CL CLU CSmH NN

3554. Smoot-Holman company, Inglewood. ...
Catalog no. 3 [of] kitchen enameled ware... [Ingle-
wood? 193–?] 15 p. illus.   CHi

Long Beach

3555. Case, Walter Hodgin. History of Long Beach
and vicinity...In which is incorporated the early history
written by the late Jane Elizabeth Harnett... Chicago,
Clarke, 1927. 2 v. illus., ports. v.2: Biographical.
  C CBb CHi CL CLob CSf CSmH CSta NN

3556. —— History of Long Beach...In two parts,
narrative and biographical... Long Beach, Press-telegram pub. co., 1935. 336 p. illus., ports.
              CHi CLO CLob CU-B NN

3557. —— Long Beach blue book...(Narrative and
biographical) Long Beach, Cawston, 1942. 434 p. illus.,
ports.   C CHi CL CLU CLob

3558. —— Long Beach community book...In two
parts, narrative and biographical. Long Beach, Cawston,
1948. 431 p. illus., ports.
              CBev CHi CL CLob CSf

**3559. Chafor, George, and Chafor, Edward, vs.
city of Long Beach.** Argument by William Atkinson
Alderson in behalf of the plaintiffs in the case of George
Chafor and Edward Chafor, infant, against the city of
Long Beach... L.A., Empire day assoc. of L.A. [1914?]
              CSmH

3560. Church and fraternal directory... Long Beach,
F. C. Foote, c1904. 96 p.   CLob

3561. Crandall, Mary R. Early legends of Long
Beach. [n.p., n.d.] 30 l. Typew.   CLob

3562. The Daily telegram, Long Beach. Industrial
and development number, April 1922. Long Beach [1922]
35 p. illus.   CU-B

3563. Draine, Edwin Hilary. The geographic implications of land subsidence in the Long Beach, California,
harbor area. [L.A.] 1958. Thesis (M.A.)—U.C.L.A.,
1958.   CLU

3564. Galbreath, Vera L. The story of the Long
Beach oil field, a seminar paper in Pacific slope history...
May 25, 1926. 30 l. Typew.   CLob

3565. Gee, Denson W., ed. Long Beach in the world
war... Long Beach, Arthur L. Peterson post, no. 27, Am.
legion, c1921. 156 p. illus., ports.   C CL CSmH

3566. Hancock oil co. Annual report.
CL has 1948, 1955–56.

3567. Hanson, Conrad A. Study of selected aspects
of the social and cultural history of Long Beach, California, for the period 1920–1929; a research paper, 1955.
20 l. Typew. Bibliography: l. 21.   CLob

3568. Harnett, Jane Elizabeth. Notes on the story
of Long Beach. 1914. 15 p.   CLob

3569. —— Same. 1941. 11 l.   CLob

3570. Hartmann, Sidney A. History of the Long
Beach Jewish community. Long Beach, Jewish community council, 1957. 64 p. illus.   CHi CLob

3571. Hoffman, Hortense. Long Beach, from sand
to city. [Long Beach?] 1953. 46 p. illus.
              CL CLob CPom

3572. —— Same. Rev. and enl. [Long Beach, Book-
mark] 1957. 73 p.   C CHi CL CLob CO COr
CP CSd CStmo CSluCL CU-B

3573. The Indians of Pubugna. [Long Beach, Jefferson junior high school print shop, 1929] 31 p. With this
is bound a brief history of Long Beach.   CLob

3574. Kendall, Sidney C. Long Beach; the city by
the sea. [L.A., 1903] 59 p. illus., map. "Reprinted from
Out West mag., June, 1903."   CLU CU-B

3575. Kroeger, Louis J., and associates. Toward
better city government; final report of an administrative
survey of the city of Long Beach, California. 1949. 78 l.
              CChiS

**3576. Long Beach. Board of harbor commission-
ers.** History of Rancho Los Cerritos. Long Beach, Long
Beach litho., inc. [n.d.] unp. illus.   CLob

3577. —— —— The port of Long Beach, California.
Long Beach, 1947. 16 p.   CBev

3578. —— **Board of trade.** Souvenir of Long
Beach. Long Beach, L.A., A. Stert, 1900. unp. illus.,
maps.   CU-B

3579. —— **Board of trustees.** A certified copy of
the records and proceedings of the Board of trustees. ...
in the matter of creating a bonded indebtedness for the
construction of double-decked cylinder pier. Long Beach,
The Tribune [1903?]   CSmH

3580. —— **Chamber of commerce.** Long Beach,
California. S.F., Sunset mag. homeseekers' bur. [1915]
[8] p. illus., map.   CHi

3581. —— **Citizens monumental association.** Souvenir of the unveiling, dedication and presentation of
the Abraham Lincoln G.A.R. memorial monument dedicated to the veterans of the civil war, 1861–65, at Long
Beach, California, July 3rd, 1915. Long Beach, Geo. W.
Moyle pub. co. [1915] 86 p. incl. illus., ports.
              C CSmH

3582. —— **Museum of art.** Arts of Southern California... [Long Beach, 1957–61] illus. CL has pt. 1,
architecture, pt. 10, collage.

3583. —— **Public library, comp.** Earthquake clippings. [n.p.] 1933. 8 v. From various newspapers.
              CLob

3584. —— —— Long Beach local history. Clippings.
24 v.   CLob

3585. Long Beach independent-press telegram.
Consumer analysis of the Long Beach, California market.
Long Beach, 1953–
  CLU has 1953–59.

3586. Long Beach press-telegram. Classified booster directory...1917–40. Long Beach, 1917–40. Publisher
varies: 1917–20 Long Beach telegram; 1922–23 Long
Beach press.
  CLob has 1917, 1920, 1922–23, 1928–29, 1935–36, 1939–
40.

3587. Long Beach sun. ...Business men's numerical
telephone directory and guide book. 1928–29. Long Beach
[1928–29?]   CLob

3588. Long Beach telegram. ...Industrial and
tourist edition...1917. [Long Beach, 1917] 38 p. illus.,
ports.   CU-B

3589. McCann, Charles W. Long Beach senior citizens survey; a community study of the living conditions
and needs of the persons 65 and over in Long Beach.

Long Beach, Community welfare council, 1955. 59 p. map, tables.   CLO CLU

3590. Mangold, George Benjamin. Life—in Long Beach; a survey of community welfare services and needs ... Long Beach, Community chest, 1939. 108 p.
C CL CLSU CSdS

3591. Miller, Andrew George. City manager government in Long Beach (California)... Chicago, Pub. admin. service, 1940. 47 p.   C CLSU CLU ViU

3592. Municipal convention and publicity bureau, comp. Long Beach, California...50th anniversary, Xth Olympiad souvenir. [Long Beach, Print. Press-telegram job print. dept., 193–?] 23 p. illus.   CSf CU-B

3593. —— Long Beach, past and present. [Long Beach, 1932] Mimeo.   MoS

3594. Pacific coast club. ...Inaugural volume, MCMXXVI. [Long Beach? c1926]   CSmH

3595. Robinson, William Wilcox. Land titles in Long Beach. L.A., Title guarantee & trust co. [c1935] [10] p. map.   C CHi CLO CLU CLob CSmH CStrJC CU-B CWhC

3596. —— Long Beach, a calendar of events in the making of a city. L.A., Title guarantee & trust co., c1935.
CLU
Other editions followed.
CAla (1954)   CHi (c1942, 1948, 1954)   CLU (c1942, 1948, 1954)   CSlu (1954)   CP (1954)   CSluCL (1954) CStmo (1948)   CWhC (1948)   MoHi (1954)   NN (c1942)

3597. Ryckman, John W., ed. Story of an epochal event in the history of California: the Pacific southwest exposition...1928. [Long Beach] Long Beach chamber of commerce [1929] 292 p. illus.   CMerCL CRedl CSd CSdS CStmo CViCL MoS ODa

3598. Security trust and savings bank. Publicity dept. Ranchos of the sunset; the story of Long Beach... [n.p.] c1925. 48 p. illus., ports.   C CHi CL CLO CLSU CLob CPom CSmH CU-B

3599. Southern California tuna club. Year book. [Long Beach] 19–
CHi has 1934–36, 1939–47, 1949, 1952–54.

3600. Steinbrugge, Karl V. Subsidence in Long Beach, Terminal island, Wilmington, California. [n.p.] Pacific fire rating bur., 1958. 38 p. illus., maps.   CLU

3601. Stert, A., comp. Picturesque Long Beach and other seaside resorts... L.A., Passenger dept., L.A. terminal railway [189–?]   CSmH

3602. Thompson, I. Owen. Long Beach to Portland. Long Beach, 1914. 76 p. illus.
CLU CSmH CU-B

3603. Van Camp sea food, inc. Annual report. CL has 1952–61.

3604. Wride, Rosalie Reine. A history of the Long Beach oil fields. [L.A., 1949] 139 l. incl. maps, tables. Thesis (M.A.)—Occidental college, 1949.   CLO

3605. Young, Hugh A. Furlough den. Long Beach, Seaside print. co., 1949. 103 p.   CLob

Los Angeles

3606. Abbe, Patience, Richard, and Johnny. Of all places! N.Y., Stokes, 1937. 233 p. ports.
Available in many libraries.

3607. [Abbott, James Whitin] Among cities Los Angeles is the world's greatest wonder—Why?... [L.A., c1914] 32 p.   CSmH

3608. Adair, Charles Henry. Los Angeles, the miracle city. L.A., Adair pub. co., 1931. 33 p. illus., map.
CHi CO CStmo

3609. Adamic, Louis. The truth about Los Angeles. Girard, Kan., Haldeman-Julius, c1927. 64 p. (Little blue book no. 647)   CLU

3610. Adams, Howard. Report on the Los Angeles city planning department, November 1956 [prepared for] Samuel Leask, city administrative officer, city of Los Angeles. Cambridge, Mass. [1956] 175 p.   CL

3611. Ainsworth, Edward Maddin. Enchanted pueblo. Illustrated by Orpha Klinker. [L.A., Bank of America, 1959] 48 p. illus., ports.
Available in many libraries.

3612. —— History of the Los Angeles times. [L.A., 1941?] 42 p. illus.   CSmH

3613. —— Same. [L.A., 1952?] 64 p. illus., ports.
CHi CL CP

3614. —— Memories in the city of dreams: recuerdos de la calle Olvera; a tribute to Harry Chandler, gran benefactor de la ciudad; foreword by Christine Sterling. L.A., Christine Sterling, 1959. 40 p. illus.   CMon

3615. Alderman, Frances L., and Wilson, Amber M. About Los Angeles. Bost., Heath, 1948. 313 p. illus.
CBev CL CLO CLU CMont CNa CSdS CUk NN ODa

3616. Alexander, Robert E. Rebuilding a city; a study of redevelopment problems in Los Angeles. L.A., Haynes foundation, 1951. 69 p. illus. (Pub. of the John Randolph Haynes & Dora Haynes foundation: Monograph ser. no. 16)
CChiS CSfSt CSt CStmo ODa

3617. Alexandria hotel. The Alexandria. [L.A., 1915?] folder (4 p.) illus.   CHi

3618. Allen, Robert Sharon, ed. Our fair city... N.Y., Vanguard, c1947. 387 p.
Available in many libraries.

3619. Allen's water gardens. [Catalogs] CHi has [1919?]

3620. Allied artists pictures corp. Annual report. CL has 1954–59.

3621. The Ambassador. The guest at the Ambassador. [n.p., n.d.] [13] p. illus., map.   CHi

3622. American cement corp. Annual report. CL has 1951, 1957–60.

3623. American historical revue and motion picture exposition. ...First annual American historical revue and motion picture exposition commemorating one hundredth anniversary of the Monroe doctrine, 1823–1923, directed and supervised by the motion picture industry, Los Angeles, July 2nd to August 4th, 1923. L.A. [1923?] [24] p. illus.   CHi

3624. American institute of banking. Los Angeles chapter. First annual minstrel show...souvenir program, October 3, 1907. L.A. [1907] 147 p. illus. Includes articles on banking and portraits of bankers of Los Angeles.   C

3625. American mutual fund, inc. Annual report. CL has 1955–57, 1959.

3626. —— Prospectus. CL has Jan. 6, 1958.

3627. American potash and chemical corp. Annual report. CL has 1952–60.

3628. [American sight seeing car and coach co.]

Seeing Los Angeles. L.A., W. E. Bridgman, c1902. [27] p.   CL   CSmH

3629. Ancient Arabic Order of the Nobles of the Mystic Shrine for North America. Los Angeles. Al Malaikah Temple. Official souvenir program [76th Imperial council session] June 19–23, 1950. L.A., 1950. 64 p. illus., ports., map.   CL

3630. [Anderson, Gregg] To remember Gregg Anderson; tributes by members of the Columbiad club, the Rounce and Coffin club, the Roxburghe club, the Zamorano club. [L.A.] Print. for priv. circulation, 1949. [98] p. illus.   CHi

3631. Anderson, Herbert C. A brief history of the printing department of Los Angeles trade-technical junior college...including biographical sketches of the printing instructors and the Bruce McCallister memorial award. 1924–1925. [L.A.] Press of L.A. trade-technical junior college, 1952. 69 p. illus., ports.   CL   CLU

3632. Andrae, Elsbeth. The dear old boys in blue; memories of the early days of the Veterans administration center, Los Angeles... S.F., Reynard press, 1948. 25 p.   CHi   CStmo

3633. Andrews, Roger M. Los Angeles in the industrial mirror; an address before the Los Angeles Optimists club, March 27, 1924. L.A., L.A. Chamber of commerce [1924] [11] p.   CHi

3634. Angelus temple pictorial review. Beautiful Angelus temple at Echo park, Los Angeles, California. Aimee Semple McPherson, pastor-evangelist. [L.A.? 1931?] (chiefly illus.)   CLU

3635. Archaeological institute of America. Southwest society. Catching our archaeology alive; beginning the Southwest museum. L.A., 1905. 31 p. illus., ports. "From *Out West*, January 1905."   C

3636. —— —— ...The Southwest museum; three years of success. L.A., 1907. 82 p. illus., ports.
                                                    CSmH   CU-B

3637. —— —— The Southwest society...Something about its aims and its first year's work. [L.A., 1904] 30 p. illus.   C   CSmH   CU-B

3638. —— —— ...Two great gifts: the Lummis library and collections [and] Munk library. L.A., 1910. 34 p. illus., ports.   C   CO   CSf   CSmH   CU-B

3639. Archer (Fred) school of photography. [Brochure] [L.A., 194–?] unp. illus. (part col.)   C

3640. [Archer, H. Richard] The private press of Thomas Perry Stricker. [L.A., 1947] 12 p. Printed by Fred Anthoenson for the Zamorano club.   CHi

3641. Arden farms. Annual report.
CHi has 1939–41. CL has 1948–60.

3642. —— Prospectus.
CL has 1954.

3643. Armenian center, Los Angeles. Armenian center. [commemoration book] L.A., 1949. unp. illus., ports. Text chiefly in Armenian.   C

3644. Army-Navy conference of industry, labor and other leaders, Los Angeles, 1944. War report; edited minutes...January 7–8, 1944. [1944] 133 l. illus., maps.   CL   CLU

3645. The Arroyo Seco parkway. Dedication ceremonies, Monday, Dec. 30, 1940. [L.A.?] 1940. [16] p. illus.   C

3646. "As we see 'em," a volume of cartoons and caricatures of Los Angeles citizens. [L.A., E. A. Thomson, 190–?] 316 p. of ports.   CHi   CLO   CLU

3647. Atchison & Eshelman. Los Angeles then and now... L.A., Geo. Rice & sons, 1897. 200 p. illus., ports.
                    C   CL   CLLoy   CLO   CLU   CSjC   CSmH

3648. Augsburg, Paul Deresco. Advertising did it! The story of Los Angeles...published in The Dearborn independent of November 25, 1922. 4th ed. L.A., W. P. Jeffries co. [n.d.] 11 p.   CL

3649. Babcock, Henry Andrews. Report on the feasibility of redeveloping the Bunker Hill area, Los Angeles, for the Community redevelopment agency of the city of Los Angeles. L.A., 1951. 55 p. illus., map.
                                                    CL   CLU

3650. Babcock, Wm. H., & sons, Chicago. Report on the economic and engineering feasibility of regrading the Bunker Hill area, Los Angeles, to the City council of the city of Los Angeles and the Board of supervisors of Los Angeles county. [Chicago] 1931. 96 p. illus., maps, diagrs.   CL   CLU

3651. Baist, George William. Baist's real estate atlas of surveys of Los Angeles, California. Complete in one volume. Comp. and pub. from official records, private plans [and] actual surveys. Phila., c1921. 50 col. maps.
                                                        CLU

3652. —— Same. 1923.   CLU

3653. Baker, Lorin Lynn. That imperiled freedom ... L.A., Graphic press pub. co., 1932. 448 p. History of the Julian oil scandal and corruption in Los Angeles politics.   CL   CLU   CSmH   CU-B

3654. Baker, Robert Munson. Why the McNamaras pleaded guilty to the bombing of the *Los Angeles Times*. [Berkeley, 1949] Thesis (M.A.)—Univ. of Calif., 1949.   CU

3655. [Banning, Pierson Worrall] comp. Los Angeles facts [scrapbook]...[1911– Contains clippings and pamphlets concerning the history and development of Los Angeles. v.4–6 have subtitle: Draft data.
CL has v.1, 4–8, 11.

3656. Barker bros., Los Angeles. Barker brothers, 1880–1955. [75th anniversary] L.A., [Geo. Rice & sons, print.] 9 p.   CLO

3657. Bartlett, Dana Webster. The better city; a sociological study of a modern city... L.A., Neuner co. press, 1907. 248 p. illus.
   C   CBb   CHi   CL   CLO   CLSU   CLU   CLob   COHN
CRedl   CSf   CSmH   CStmo   CU-B

3658. Bartlett, Lanier, and Bartlett, Virginia Stivers. Los Angeles in 7 days, including southern California... N.Y., McBride, 1932. 298 p. map.
   C   CBu   CL   CLO   CLU   CMartC   COr   CSd   CSf
CSmH   CStmo   CU-B   NN

3659. Baruch, Dorothy (Walter) ...Glass house of prejudice. N.Y., Morrow, 1946. 205 p. Race problems as seen in Los Angeles.
   C   CBb   CBev   CBu   CChiS   CL   CLLoy   CLO   CLS
CLSU   CO   CRedl   CSdS   CSf   CStmo   CViCL

3660. Bass, Charlotta A. Forty years; memoirs from the pages of a newspaper. L.A., c1960. 198 p. illus., ports., map.   CHi   CL

3661. Beck, Frederick K. Second carrot from the end. N.Y., Morrow, 1946. 160 p. "The story of Roger Dahlhjelm and...[the author's] Farmers market years."
   C   CLU   CSfMI   CSluCL   CViCL   MoS   ODa   OrU

3662. Bernard, J. P. Non-tourist Los Angeles. [S.F., Unicorn pub. co., 1959] 60 p. illus., maps.
                                              C   CL   CU-B

3663. Berry, Alice Edna (Bush) The Bushes and

the Berrys. L.A. [Ward Ritchie] 1941. [ltd. ed. of 100 copies]   CBb CHi

3664. Bicknell, Edmund, comp. Ralph's scrap book; illustrated by his own camera and collection of photographs... Lawrence, Mass. [Andover press] 1905. 453 p. illus., ports.   CHi

3665. Bingham, Edwin Ralph. Charles F. Lummis and his magazine. [L.A.] 1950. Thesis (Ph.D.)— U.C.L.A., 1950.   CLU

3666. —— Charles F. Lummis, editor of the Southwest. San Marino, Huntington lib., 1955. 218 p. plates, ports. (Huntington lib. pub.) Bibliography: p. 192–201.
C CHi CLO CP CRcS CRedl CSd CSmH CStmo

3667. —— The saga of the Los Angeles Chinese. [L.A., 1942] 185 l. illus. Thesis (M.A.)—Occidental college, 1942.   CLO

3668. Blake, Aldrich. You wear the big shoe...An inquiry into the politics and government of the American city, with a case study of the Los Angeles metropolitan area. [L.A., c1945] 111 p. Names the important city bosses in Los Angeles; discusses the city's lack of civic consciousness.   CBev CL CLU CO CSf

3669. Blue diamond corp. Annual report. CL has 1950–58.

3670. Bogardus, Emory Stephen. The city boy and his problem; a survey of boy life in Los Angeles, sponsored and financed by the Rotary club of Los Angeles... [L.A., House of Ralston, print.] c1926. 148 p.
C CL CLSU CLU CO CSmH

3671. Bolsa Chica oil corp. Annual report. CL has 1958–60.

3672. Bonelli, William G. Billion dollar blackjack. Beverly Hills, Civic research press [1954] 230 p. illus.
C CHi CL CLU CSS CSd CSfSt CStmo CU-B NN

3673. Bowen, William M. Vicious attack on men who saved Exposition park. The issue: Bowen's "activities" which recovered and improved Park or Neylan's vicious political thrust. [L.A.? 1915] 19 p.   C CSmH

3674. Bradley bungalow co. The bungalow de luxe. [L.A., c1912] [30] p. illus., plans.   CU-B

3675. Brent, Joseph Lancaster. The Lugo case, a personal experience. New Orleans, Searcy & Pfaff, 1926. 69 p. With, as issued, the author's Capture of the ironclad, *Indianola*. [New Orleans, 1926]
CHi CLU CU-B IHi

3676. Broadway-Hale stores, inc. Annual report. CL has 1954–60.

3677. —— Report on its history and prospects 1950. L.A. [1950?]   CL

3678. [Brook, Harry Ellington] Los Angeles, the Chicago of the southwest. [L.A.] L.A. Chamber of commerce, 1904. [16] p. illus.   CLU

3679. Brown, Forman George. Olvera street and the Avila adobe... L.A., Dobe dollar bk. store, c1930. 20 p. illus.
C CHi CL CLO CLSU CLU CRedl CSmH CStmo CU-B

3680. —— Same. L.A., Times-mirror press, c1932. 20 p. illus.   CU-B

3681. Brown, Seth. Seth Brown and the I.T.U. in Los Angeles; a tape recorded interview [conducted by Corine L. Gilb]. L.A., Inst. of industrial relations, Univ. of Calif., 1957. 150 l. port.   CLU

3682. Brown, William E. California dry; an address delivered before the Women's city club of Los Angeles... [L.A.?] Out West mag., 1914. 16 p.   CHi

3683. Browne, Clyde. Abbey San Encino Garvanza, Oldtown, Los Angeles... [L.A., 1932] [7] p. illus.   CSmH

3684. —— Abbey San Encino (Holy Oak) L.A., 1922. 19 p. illus., ports., pl.   CLO

3685. Brunswig drug company. Annual report. CL has 1954–60.

3686. Budget finance plan. Annual report. CL has 1954–60.

3687. Bullock's, inc. Annual report. CL has 1950–61.

3688. Bungalowcraft company. ...California bungalow homes, third edition... L.A., c1911. 128 p. illus., plans.   CHi

3689. —— Model and modern bungalow plans, outside and inside. L.A. [191–?] 15 p. illus., plans.   CU-B

3690. Burdette, Clara (Bradley) The rainbow and the pot of gold... Pasadena, Clara vista press, 1908. 147 p. illus., ports. "Story of the life of Temple Baptist church [of Los Angeles]"—Foreword.
C CHi CL CLSU CLU CSmH CU-B

3691. Burdette, Robert Jones. Robert J. Burdette; his message, ed. from his writings by his wife, Clara B. Burdette. Pasadena, Clara Vista press [c1922] 460 p. illus., ports.   CStmo

3692. Bureau of Jewish social research, New York. Health work, Jewish organizations, Los Angeles, California. [N.Y., n.d.] unp.   CL

3693. Burns, William John. The masked war; the story of a peril that threatened the United States, by the man who uncovered the dynamite conspirators and sent them to jail... N.Y., Doran [c1913] 328 p. port. The dynamiting of the Los Angeles times.
C CHi CL CLSU CLU CRedl CSf CSmH CStmo CViCL

3694. Business men's association of Los Angeles. [Los Angeles railway terminal pamphlets. 1920–1926] 4 v. in 1. plans.   CL

3695. Bymers, Gwendolyn June. A study of employment in women's and misses' outwear manufacturing Los Angeles metropolitan area, 1946–1954. [L.A.] 1958. Thesis (Ph.D.)—U.C.L.A., 1958.   CLU

3696. [Bynon, A. Bert] San Pedro; its history. [L.A., Boyle heights press, 1899] 52 p. illus., map.
C CLSU CLU CSmH NN

3697. Byron Jackson co. ...Annual statement: 1951. [n.p., 1952?] 15 p. illus., port., map.   CHi

3698. —— [Catalog irrigating and harvesting machinery] S.F. [1887?]   C-S

3699. —— Horizons, 1872–1945; a study in transition, a future perspective. L.A. [c1945] 72 p. illus.   CHi

3700. Bystrom, Shirley Caroline. Los Angeles, 1846–1860. [Berkeley, 1951] Thesis (M.A.)—Univ. of Calif., 1951.   CU CU-B

3701. California vs. Broadhead, Thomas H. ... The people of the state of California, plaintiff, vs. Thomas H. Broadhead, defendant [no. 5869, bribery] Reporters' transcript... L.A., Girvin [1909] 27 v. in 6.   CL

3702. California. Commission of immigration and housing. A community survey made in Los Angeles city... S.F. [1919?] 74 p.
CL CLO CLSU CSf CSmH CU-B

3703. —— **Laws, statutes, etc.** Senate concurrent resolution relative to the erection of a breakwater at Wilmington harbor, to which is appended a report and map, prepared by Gen. B. S. Alexander, U.S.A. Sacramento, D. W. Gelwicks, state print., 1870. 11 p. chart, diagrs.   CLU

3704. —— **Legislature. Senate. Committee on local governmental agencies.** Minority report concerning application of city of Los Angeles for purchase of federal lands in Mono county. [Sacramento] 1945. 10 p.   CInI CL

3705. —— —— —— —— Report concerning application of city of Los Angeles for purchase of federal lands in Mono county. [Sacramento, 1945] 12 p.   CL

3706. —— **State college, Los Angeles.** An occupational study of the Los Angeles business and industrial community. Sponsored by the Sears-Roebuck foundation. [L.A.] 1957. 222 p. graphs.   CLS

3707. —— —— A state college looks at the business and industrial community it serves; an account of a community occupational study of the metropolitan Los Angeles area. Sponsored by the Sears-Roebuck foundation. 1956. 76 p. illus.   CL CLS

3708. —— **University.** The University: an introduction to the Los Angeles campus. [Berkeley, Univ. of Calif. press, 1936] 52 p. illus.   CHi

3709. —— —— **Los Angeles.** Addresses delivered at the dedication of the new campus and new buildings, March 27 and 28, 1930. Berkeley, Univ. of Calif. press, 1930. 87 p.   CHi CU-B

3710. —— —— —— [Dedication, March 27–28, 1930] 2 v. A collection of contemporary local newspaper accounts.   CLU

3711. —— —— —— Dedication of the campus of the University of California at Los Angeles, October twenty-fifth, nineteen hundred and twenty-six. Berkeley, 1927. [45] p. illus.   CHi

3712. —— —— —— Gifts to the University of California Los Angeles, 1919–1954. L.A., 1955. 105 p. illus., ports.   CL CU-B

3713. —— —— —— Memorial addresses at a service honoring Ernest Carroll Moore, 1871–1955. Held in Royce Hall auditorium on the Los Angeles campus of the University of California, February 15, 1955. [17] p.   CHi CLO

3714. —— —— —— Memorial addresses honoring Edward Augustus Dickson, 1880–1956. [Berkeley? 1956?] 22 p.   CHi

3715. —— —— —— **Alumni association.** California of the southland, a history of the University of California at Los Angeles... [L.A.] 1937. 95 p. illus., port. C CBaB CHi CL CLO CLSU CLU CSmH CStmo

3716. —— —— —— **Institute for social science research.** Social science research in the Los Angeles area... L.A., 1936. 210 l.   CLU CU-B

3717. —— —— —— **William Andrews Clark memorial library.** ...William Andrews Clark memorial library; report of the first decade, 1934–1944. Berkeley & L.A., Univ. of Calif. press, 1946. 78 p. port.   CBev CHi CL CLO CLSU CLU CSf CSmH CStmo

3718. —— —— —— Same. Report of the second decade, 1945–1955. L.A., 1956.   CHi CLO CStmo

3719. California club of Los Angeles. Officers, members, articles of incorporation, by-laws and house rules. L.A., 18– Title varies slightly.

CHi has 1889, 1920, 1947, 1949, 1955. CL has 1894–96, 1899, 1901–20, 1923, 1926, 1937, 1949. CLU has 1896, 1910, 1920. CU-B has 1937.

3720. California shipbuilding corp. Calship, an industrial achievement. [L.A., 1946] 197 p. illus.

CHi

3721. California Spanish missionary society. Foreign work at home for our Spanish neighbor, June 1897. 16 p. illus.   CHi

3722. Cameron, Marguerite. El pueblo; a general history of one of America's largest cities... L.A., N.Y. [etc.] Suttonhouse [c1936] 153 p. illus., maps. Juvenile history.   C CHi CL CO CSf CSmH IC

3723. Caplan, Jerry Saul. The CIVIC committee in the recall of Mayor Frank Shaw. [L.A.] 1947. Thesis (M.A.)—U.C.L.A., 1947.   CLU

3724. Carnation company. Annual report. CL has 1956–60.

3725. Carr, Harry. Los Angeles, city of dreams... illustrations by E. H. Suydam. N.Y., Appleton-Century, 1935. 403 p. illus. Available in many California libraries and MiD N NN ODa OU UU

3726. Carr, O. O. Tribute to the memory of Josiah Hopkins... Hollywood, Pioneer press [c1937] 30 p.

CHi

3727. Carthay circle theatre. California, 1826–1926. [Catalog of paintings hung in the Tower room of the Carthay circle theatre; issued by the Historical committee of the Carthay center] [L.A., Printed by Guy W. Finney co., inc., c1926] 32 p. illus. (part col.), ports.

CHi CU-B

3728. Case, Frederick E. Cash outlays and economic costs of homeownership. L.A., Real estate research program, Bur. of business and economic research, Univ. of Calif. L.A., c1957. 58 p. tables.   CL

3729. —— Los Angeles real estate; a study of investment experience. L.A., Real estate research program, Graduate school of business admin., Univ. of Calif. L.A., c1960. 103 p. illus., map.   CL

3730. Catholic directory of census of Los Angeles city, and parish gazetteer of the diocese of Monterey and Los Angeles. L.A., Reardon, 1899. 365 p. illus., ports.

CHi CL CLLoy CLSU CLU CSmH

3731. Central business district assoc. Los Angeles parkway and transit system. L.A., 1946. 40 p. illus., maps.   CL CLU

3732. —— Parkway transit lines in the central business district... L.A. [1944?] 26 p. illus., maps.   CL

3733. —— A quarter century of activities, 1924–1949. [L.A., 1949?] 33 l. illus.   C

3734. —— Report on transportation survey of Hill street and rerouting of Asbury rapid transit system... [L.A., 1940] 54 l. maps, tables, diagrs.   CL

3735. —— Report on transportation survey of Main street and rerouting of Pacific electric railway coach and rail lines. [L.A., 1942] 38 l. maps, tables.   CL

3736. Chamber of mines and oil. Year book... report, by-laws, list of members, regulations, statistics, special articles... L.A., 1910. unp.   C CSfSO

3737. Cheney, William Murray. A natural history of the typestickers of Los Angeles, comp. from the letters of Wm. M. Cheney, by Edwin H. Carpenter. L.A., Rounce & Coffin club, 1960. 62 p. ports.   CHi CU-B

3738. Childs & co. Price list, 1872–73, Los Angeles

nursery and fruit garden... S.F., Cubery & co. [1872?] 7 p.   CHi

3739. Christian science publishing society. The Los Angeles case; the People vs. Merrill Reed et al. Reprinted from the *Christian science jl. and Christian science sentinel.* Bost. [c1909] 81 p.   CLU

3740. Citizen's committee on governmental reorganization. [Reports] to the...committee. [L.A.] 1935–
CL has v.1–6.

3741. Citizens' manpower committee. History of the Los Angeles citizens' manpower committee, 1943–1945. [L.A., 1945] 31 p. illus., ports.
C CL-MR CWhC

3742. Citizens national trust and savings bank of Los Angeles. Annual report.
CL has 1949–60.

3743. Citizens' tax committee. Report...submitted to the Honorable Mayor and City council, Mar. 17, 1944. [L.A., Jeffries banknote co.] 95 p. tables.   CL

3744. City club of Los Angeles. Year book. v.1– , 1907–
CL has v.1–10, 1907–17.

3745. Clapp, Edwin Jones. Los Angeles should be the home of aircraft industries... L.A., Chamber of commerce, 1926. 11 p. illus., map.   CLU

3746. Clark, Donavon Lee. A history of the Southwest museum, 1905–1955. [Claremont, 1956] 221 l. illus., ports. Thesis (M.A.)—Claremont college, 1956.   CCH

3747. Clark, Stephen C. The diocese of Los Angeles, a brief history... [Pasadena] Committee on diocesan anniversaries, 1945. 92 p. ports.
CHi CL CLO CLSU CLU CSmH CWhC

3748. Cleland, Robert Glass. History of Occidental college, 1887–1937... L.A., [Print. by Ward Ritchie] 1937. 115 p.
C CBb CHi CL CLLoy CLO CLSU CLU CSmH CU-B

3749. [Cline, William Hamilton] ...Twelve pioneers of Los Angeles, 1928. L.A., Times-mirror print. house [n.d.] unp. illus., ports.
CL CLO CLU CSmH

3750. Clover, Samuel Travers. A pioneer heritage. L.A., Saturday night pub. co., 1932. 291 p. illus., ports. A biography of Allan Hancock, a descendant of two distinguished California pioneers, Count Agostin Haraszthy and Major Henry Hancock.
CBb CHi CSdU CSfCW CU-B

3751. Cohn, Alfred Abraham, and Chisholm, Joseph. "Take the witness!"... N.Y., Stokes, 1934. 315 p. port.
C CBb CBev CBu CL CLO CLSU CLU CMartC CMerCL CO CRcS CSalCL CSd CSdS CSmH CSmat CStmo

3752. Cole, George Llewellyn. Medical associates of my early days in Los Angeles... L.A. [Phillips print. co.] 1930. [134] p. illus., ports. "Reprint from 1930 *Los Angeles county medical assoc. bulletins.*"
CHi CLM CLU

3753. Community coordination...v.1–11, no. 2... L.A., Coordinating councils [1933–1943] 11 v. illus., ports. Work of the coordinating council system in its fight against juvenile delinquency in Los Angeles.
CL CLSU has v.1–10, 1933–42.

3754. Community surveys associated. Recreation for everybody; a community plan for recreation and

youth service for Los Angeles. A report of a survey conducted...for the Welfare council of metropolitan Los Angeles, a department of the Los Angeles community welfare federation... L.A., 1946. 2 v. illus., maps, tables, diagrs.
C CL CLO CLS CLSU CLU CO CSfSt CWhC

3755. Congress of industrial organization. Industrial union council. Los Angeles. Unions mean higher wages; the story of the LaFollette committee hearings in Los Angeles. [L.A., 1940] 31 p. illus.   CLU

3756. Consolidated rock products co. Annual report.
CL has 1948, 1954–60.

3757. Consolidation committee of Los Angeles. Report...what consolidation means for San Pedro and Wilmington. [L.A.] n.p., 1909. unp.   CL-MR

3758. Contract for unified operator of railroad facilities at Los Angeles harbor. Agreement between Board of harbor commissioners of the city of Los Angeles, Southern Pacific railroad company, Southern Pacific company, Pacific electric railway company, Los Angeles & Salt Lake railroad company, the Atchison, Topeka and Santa Fe railway company. n.p. [1928] 37 p. map.   CL

3759. Cooley, Laura Clarissa. The Los Angeles public library. [n.p.,1941] 23 p. illus., ports.   CL

3760. Coons, Arthur Gardiner, and Miller, Arjay R. An economic and industrial survey of the Los Angeles and San Diego areas...Sacramento, State planning bd., 1941 [i.e. 1942] 411 p. map. Prepared in cooperation with the Berkeley office of the National resources planning board.
CBev CChiS CL CLO CLSU CO CSdS CSfSt CSfU CSmH CStmo CWhC IC

3761. —— Same. (Summary)... Sacramento, State planning bd., 1942. 40 p.
CLO CLSU CSdS CSfSt CSmH

3762. Copeland, Clem A. Population of the city of Los Angeles from 1890 to 1932... [L.A.] Western statistical assoc., c1926. [19] p.   CL CU-B

3763. Cory, Clarence Linus. Report on the annual and accrued depreciation of the gas and electric properties of the Los Angeles gas and electric corporation as of October 1, 1913. S.F. [1914] unp. Typew.   CLU

3764. —— Valuation of the electric plant and system of the Los Angeles gas and electric corporation, Los Angeles, California, July 1, 1910. [L.A., 1910] 357 l. Typew.   CU-B

3765. —— Valuation of the gas properties of the Los Angeles gas and electric corporation based on cost to reproduce new... S.F., 1911–15. maps. Typew.
CLU has 1911, 1914, 1915.

3766. Craggs, Mary Eleanor, Sister. The career of John Steven McGroarty. Wash., D.C., 1958. 89 p. Thesis (M.A.)—Catholic univ. of America, 1958.   CSrD

3767. Crawford, Fred G. Organizational and administrative development of the government of the city of Los Angeles during the thirty-year period, July 1, 1925, to September 30, 1955. [L.A.] School of public administration, Univ. of So. Calif., 1955. 281 p. illus.
C CL CLS CLU CSd CSfSt

3768. Critic of critics. ...v.1–3, no. 2, June 2, 1930–Sept. 1931. L.A., Critic of critics pub. co., 1930–31. 3 v. in 1. illus., ports. Issued twice monthly, June–Nov. 1930; monthly, Dec. 1930–Sept. 1931, except July and August. No more pub. A short-lived magazine which attempted to bring to light corruption in the City of the Angels.
CL

3769. Crockett & Conklin, comp. Souvenir: Los Angeles fire department. Published in the interest of the firemen's relief fund. [L.A.?] 1900. 116 p. illus., ports.
CLU

3770. Crowther, Mrs. Henry Christian. High lights, the Friday morning club, Los Angeles, California, April 1891–1938... [L.A., Mrs. Cecil Frankel, 1939] 62 p. port.
CHi

3771. Cunningham, Curtiss & Welch. Souvenir of Los Angeles. Photo-gravures. S.F., c1899. [17] l.
CHi

3772. Cunningham, Frank. Sky master, the story of Donald Douglas. Phila., Dorrance and co. [1943] 321 p. illus., ports.
CStmo

3773. Darrow, Clarence Seward. The Darrow bribery trial, with background facts of McNamara case and including Darrow's address to the jury, edited by Patrick H. Ford. Whittier, Western print. co., c1956. 61 p. illus.
CLU

3774. —— Plea of Clarence Darrow in his own defense to the jury at Los Angeles, August, 1912. L.A., Golden press, 1912. [62] p. port.
CLU

3775. Daughters of Charity of St. Vincent de Paul. One hundred years of service...1856–1956... [L.A., 1956] 36 p. illus.
CHi

3776. Daughters of the American revolution. California. Cabrillo chapter, Los Angeles. History of Cabrillo chapter of the Daughters of the American revolution, Los Angeles, California, for the fifteen years from 1913–1928... [n.p., 1928] 286 l. illus., ports. Typew.
CL

3777. David, Leon Thomas. Law and lawyers; one hundred twenty-eight years in the history of Los Angeles as seen from the city attorney's office. [L.A., 1950] 35 p. ports.
CHi CSf CStmo

3778. Davis, C. M., comp. Los Angeles illustrated, showing homes, public buildings, business blocks, parks and general views... Issued by Kingsley-Barnes & Neuner co. through the courtesy of the Chamber of commerce... [189–?] unp.
CHi CSmH NN

3779. Davison, Frank Bush. ...Commemorative of the official opening, the Los Angeles aqueduct and Exposition park, November fifth and sixth, nineteen hundred thirteen. Compliments of the Los Angeles celebration commission... [L.A., Print. by Kingsley, Mason & Collins co., c1913] [32] p. illus., ports.
C CLSU CLU CSmH CU-B MoS NN

3780. Dawson, Ernest. Los Angeles booksellers of 1897... Claremont, Saunders press, 1947. 12 p. illus., port.
CBb CHi CLO CLSU CLU CLob CU-B

3781. Dawson, Glenn, comp. The Plantin press, Los Angeles; catalogue of an exhibition of the work of Saul & Lillian Marks: a selection from the printing produced at the Plantin press since 1931. Shown at the University of California library, Los Angeles, March, 1955. [L.A., Plantin press, 1955] 10 p. illus.
CLO

3782. Deep water harbor in southern California; Port Los Angeles vs. San Pedro. Full report of oral testimony at public hearings in Los Angeles, December, 1896. L.A., Evening express co., 1897. 237 p.
C CL CLO CLSM CLU CSmH CStmo CU-B

3783. De Leuw, Cather & co., Chicago. City of Los Angeles; recommended program for improvement of transportation and traffic facilities. Submitted to the Mayor and City council...Harold M. Lewis...and Joe Ong... [L.A.] 1945. 38 p., 15 l. illus., maps.
CL

3784. Dickinson, R. B. Los Angeles of today archi-

tecturally... [L.A.] Morgan & Walls, Eisen & Hunt [etc.] 1896. 71 pl.
CL CLU CSmH

3785. Dickson, Edward Augustus. University of California at Los Angeles; its origin and formative years. L.A., Friends of the UCLA library, 1955. 61 p. illus.
CLO CLU CStoC

3786. Dixon, Marion. The history of the Los Angeles central labor council. [Berkeley, 1929] Thesis (M.A.) — Univ. of Calif., 1929.
CU

3787. Dobie, Edith. The political career of Stephen Mallory White; a study of party activities under the convention system. Stanford, 1927. 266 p. port. (Stanford univ. pub., Univ. ser., History, economics, and political science. v.2, no. 1)
CHi CSfCW CStoC

3788. Dolley, Helen. Meyer Lissner prize for "The best charter for Los Angeles"... University of southern California, May 1, 1914. [n.p., 1914] [28] l.
CL

3789. Domer, Marilyn. The zoot-suit riot; a culmination of social tensions in Los Angeles. [Claremont, 1955] 193 l. maps. Thesis (M.A.) — Claremont college, 1955.
CCH

3790. Dorsey, Susan Almira (Miller) History of schools and education in Los Angeles: our schools from pueblo to metropolis. [n.p., n.d.] 19 l.
CL

3791. Douglas, J. R. The bank and community; a history of the Security trust and savings bank of Los Angeles, 1889–1929. L.A. [Security trust and savings bank] 1929. 61 p. illus., ports.
CSmH CU-B

3792. Douglas oil co. of California. Annual report.
CL has 1955–60.

3793. Dow, Lorenzo I., jr. The general cargo ocean trade of the port of Los Angeles, California. [L.A.] 1952. Thesis (M.A.) — U.C.L.A., 1952.
CLU

3794. Ducommun metals and supply company. Annual report.
CL has 1954–59.

3795. Duke, Donald. Two angels on a string; the story of Angels flight, Los Angeles' funicular railway. [San Marino, 1958] 12 p. illus. (Pacific railway jl., v.2, no. 5, Feb. 1958)
C CL CSf CStmo

3796. Duncan, Blanton, vs. Times-mirror co. In the Supreme court of the state of California, Blanton Duncan, plaintiff and appellant, vs. The Times-mirror company, appellant's brief. L.A., Mackin & Mosteller, 1897. 89 p.
CHi

3797. —— Same. ...Appellant's reply brief. L.A., Law print. house, 1897. 26 p.
CHi

3798. [Dustin, C. Mial] Milestones in history. The Citizens national bank of Los Angeles... [L.A., Birely & Elson print. co. inc., 1913?] [20] p. illus.
CLU CU-B

3799. Eales, John Ray. A brief, general history of the Los Angeles city school system. [L.A.] 1956. Thesis (Ed.D.) — U.C.L.A., 1956.
CLU

3800. Eberle economic service, ltd. Eberle economic service. v.1–1924– Weekly letters and supplements. L.A., 1924– illus. Economic conditions in Los Angeles during the depression period 1930–1935.
CL has v.1–6 (incomplete), v.7–12, 1930–35. CLSU has v.1–9, 1924–32. CLU has v.1–12, 1924–35.

3801. Edson, Charles Farwell. Los Angeles from the Sierras to the sea. Etchings and drawings by Marion Holden Pope. L.A., Potter, c1916. unp. illus.
C CBb CHi CL CLO CLU CPom CSmH CStmo CU-B NN

3802. Eggert, Jerry, ed. Proclamacion de la natividad, el pueblo de Nuestra Señora la Reina de Los Angeles de California, 1781–1956... Historical sketch [of Los Angeles] L.A., Holmes & Narver, c1956. unp. illus. (part col.) Here & now, v.3, no. 26) CL

3803. Electrical products corp. Annual report. CL has 1955–58, 1960.

3804. Eliot, Charles William. Citizen support for Los Angeles development. [L.A., Haynes foundation, 1945] 12 p. (Pub. of the John Randolph Haynes & Dora Haynes foundation. Pamphlet ser. 9) C CLU

3805. Ellis, Arthur M., comp. Historical review, seventy-fifth anniversary, May 5, 1929, Los Angeles lodge no. 42, F. & A. M. ... [L.A., Ralston] c1929. 129 p. illus., ports. C CHi CL CLSU CLU CSmH

3806. Endore, S. Guy. "Justice for Salcido." Introd. by Carey McWilliams. L.A., Civil rights congress of L.A., 1948. 31 p. CLU

3807. —— The Sleepy lagoon mystery. L.A., Sleepy lagoon defense committee, 1944. 48 p. illus. A famous Los Angeles murder mystery involving some Mexican youths. CL CLU CU-B

3808. Ervin, Frank. Traffic study and report of traffic conditions of the cities of Los Angeles, San Francisco and Oakland, made and compiled by Capt. Frank Ervin, commanding traffic department, Portland police department to Chief of police L. V. Jenkins, July 30, 1925. [Portland, Ore., 1925] 8 l. CU-B

3809. Fairview land and water co. By-laws... adopted March 1st, 1886. L.A., Kingsley, Barnes & co., 1886. 16 p. CHi

3810. Farmer brothers co. Annual report. CL has 1954–58.

3811. Farmers and merchants national bank of Los Angeles. The Farmers and merchants national bank of Los Angeles, April 10, 1871–April 10, 1921... [L.A., 1921] 34 p. illus., ports. C CHi CLU CSmH CU-B

3812. Fashion group, inc. California fashion explorers, by the Fashion group of Los Angeles. L.A., Ward Ritchie, 1945. 114 p. illus. C CLU CStmo

3813. Field & Peacock associates. Los Angeles residents appraise the public library system; a survey for the city of Los Angeles, June 10, 1948. [n.p.] 1948. v.p. CL CLU (Film copy)

3814. La Fiesta de Los Angeles. Official program. 1894– [L.A.] R.W. Pridham, 1894– C (1895, 1931) CHi (1896, 1931) CLU (1894–95, 1931) CSmH (1894–97)

3815. Filtrol corp. Annual report. CL has 1948–1950.

3816. Finney, Guy Woodward. Angel city in turmoil...A story of the Minute men of Los Angeles in their war on civic corruption, graft and privilege. L.A., Am. press [c1945] 211 p. illus. Available in many California libraries and NN

3817. —— Death watch on *The Gazette*... L.A., Press pub. co., c1933. 62 p. CHi

3818. —— The great Los Angeles bubble. A present-day story of colossal financial jugglery and of penalties paid. [L.A., Milton Forbes co., c1929] 203 p. Story of the financial misadventures which led to the crash of the Julian petroleum corporation. C CBb CHi CL CLLoy CLO CLS CLSU CLU CSdS CSf CSfCW CSmH CStmo CU-B CWhC MoS OrU

3819. First national bank of Los Angeles. Research dept. Commerce through Los Angeles harbor. Prepared in co-operation with the College of commerce and business administration, Univ. of So. Calif. [L.A.] 1923. 64 p. maps, diagrs. CL CLU

3820. Fisher, Lloyd H. The problem of violence; observations on race conflict in Los Angeles. Based on material collected by Joseph Weckler for the American council on race relations. [L.A.?] Am. council on race relations [n.d.] 20 p. maps. CLU

3821. Flandreau, John Howard. The Los Angeles aqueduct. L.A., 1947. 116 l. Thesis (M.A.) — Occidental college, 1947. CLO

3822. Flannery, Helen Ida. The labor movement in Los Angeles, 1880–1903. [Berkeley, 1929] Thesis (M.A.) — Univ. of Calif., 1929. CU

3823. Fluor corp. Annual report. CL has 1954–60.

3824. —— Tenth anniversary supplement. L.A. [n.d.] CL

3825. [Forbes, Harrie Rebecca Piper (Smith)] Battalla de la mesa "The Battle of the mesa" 1847–1926. [L.A., East side print. & pub. co., 1926] 22 p. illus. C CHi CL CU-B

3826. Foster, Gerard J. Tidewater industrial sites at Los Angeles-Long Beach harbor, California. [L.A.] 1953. Thesis (M.A.) — U.C.L.A., 1953. CLU

3827. Frank, Herman Washington. Scrapbook of a western pioneer... L.A., Times-mirror press [c1934] 256 p. illus., ports. C CBb CBev CHi CLSU CLU CO CRcS CSdS CSfCW CSmH CStmo CU-B

3828. Freemasons. Los Angeles. Holland lodge no. 20. 10th anniversary number...Jurisdiction of M.W. Sovereign grand lodge of California...Sept., A.D. 1921 ... [L.A.? 1921] folder (6 p.) Gives a short history of the lodge. CHi

3829. Frick, Mary E. Histories of the Metropolitan high school and the Huntington Park opportunity school ... [L.A.?] 1931. 116 l. tables, forms, diagrs. Thesis (M.A.) — Univ. of So. Calif., 1931. C

3830. The Friday morning club. By-laws (revised July, 1893, April, 1896) [n.p., n.d.] 10 p. CHi

3831. The Fröbel institute. The Fröbel institute, Casa de rosas. L.A. [n.p., 1894?] 18 p. illus. CHi

3832. From pueblo to city [Los Angeles, Cal.] 1849–1910. [L.A., Le Berthon, 1910?] 79 p. illus., ports. CL CLU CSmH

3833. Fuller, Elizabeth. ...The Mexican housing problem in Los Angeles... L.A., So. Calif. sociol. soc., Univ.. of So. Calif. [1920] 11 p. CSmH

3834. Garden city company of California. California garden city homes, MCMXV; a book of stock plans designed by Walter S. Davis. L.A., 1915. 78 p. illus. (incl. plans) CHi CSfCW

3835. Garrett corp. Annual report. CL has 1949, 1951–56, 1958–60.

3836. Gaw, Allison. A sketch of the development of graduate work in the University of southern California, 1910–1935. L.A., Univ. of So. Calif., 1935. 64 p. illus., ports., tables. CL CSfCW

3837. General campaign strike committee for the unionizing of Los Angeles. California labor's greatest victory; final report...June 1, 1910–April 1, 1912... O. A. Tveitmoe, president, Andrew J. Gallagher, secretary. [L.A., 1912] CSf

3838. German American trust and savings bank. Twenty-five years of growth; a quarter century of achievement. L.A. [1915] [20] p. illus., ports.   CU-B

3839. Getty museum. The J. Paul Getty museum guidebook. [Prepared by W. R. Valentiner and Paul Wescher] 2d ed. [L.A.] 1956. 35 p. illus.   CL

3840. Gibbon, Thomas E. Argument of T. E. Gibbon, vice president of the Los Angeles terminal r'y co., in behalf of San Pedro before the Board for locating a deep water harbor in southern California sitting at Los Angeles, Calif. L.A., Times-mirror print., 1897. 36 p.
CL CU-B

3841. Gibson, Mary S. Caroline M. Severance, pioneer, 1820–1914. L.A., 1925. 15 p.   CHi CLU

3842. Gin Chow's first...annual almanac... L.A., Wetzel pub. co., 1932. illus.   CSf

3843. Gladding McBean & co. Annual report.
CL has 1953–60.

3844. —— [Catalogs and price lists of clay products, pottery and tiles] 1905–1932. S.F., 1905–32.
CHi has 1905, 1915, 1920, 1923 (clay products) 1932 (pottery) 1919, 1923 (tiles).

3845. A glimpse of institutional Japanese First Presbyterian church. L.A., 1905. [10] p. ports.   CLU

3846. The Gold crown mining and milling co. [Prospectus] L.A., Lang-Chappel co. [n.d.] [12] p.
CHi

3847. Goldberg, Gloria. ...Budget for moderate income families: Prices for Los Angeles, Sept. 1948. L.A., John Randolph Haynes & Dora Haynes foundation, 1949. 51 p.   CStmo

3848. Golden state mutual life insurance co. Historical murals portray the contribution of the Negro to the growth of California from exploration and colonization through settlement and development. [L.A., 1952?] 15 p. illus.   CHi

3849. Goodman, T. William. Culbert L. Olson and California politics, 1933–1943. [L.A.] 1948. Thesis (M.A.) — U.C.L.A., 1948.   CLU

3850. Goodrich, Ernest Payson. Report to Harbor commission of Los Angeles, concerning the development and construction of an ocean harbor... [L.A.] L.A. examiner [1922] 81 p. illus., map.   CL CSmH

3851. Gordon, Dudley Chadwick. An entertaining guidebook to the cultural assets of metropolitan Los Angeles... [L.A., Ward Ritchie, c1940] 64 p. illus., map.
CHi CL CLO CLSU CLU

3852. Gourley, Gerald Douglas. Public relations and the police; with a foreword by August Vollmer. Springfield, Ill., Thomas, 1953. 123 p. illus.   CL CLU

3853. Grand army of the Republic. Official souvenir program, 46th national encampment, G.A.R. ...Los Angeles, Calif., September 9th to 14th, 1912. [n.p., 1912] 63 p.   CSmH

3854. Graphic, Los Angeles. Los Angeles, the old and the new. Christmas supplement, 1906. [L.A.] 1906. 50 p. illus., ports.   CL

3855. Graves, Jackson Alpheus. California memories, 1857–1930... L.A., Times-mirror press, 1930. 330 p. illus., ports.
Available in many California libraries and CaBViPA

3856. —— Celts who have helped build up Los Angeles; an address delivered before the Celtic club of Los Angeles...April 11th, 1916, at the Sierra Madre club, Los Angeles, California. [L.A.? 1916?] 26 p. port.
CHi CLU

3857. —— My seventy years in California 1857–1927 ... L.A., Times-mirror press, 1927. 478 p. illus. Biography of a noted California lawyer which contains chapters on Los Angeles in 1875, political bosses in Los Angeles, brief banking history of Los Angeles.
Available in many California libraries and CaBViPA ViU

3858. Great Britain. Foreign office. Southern California. Vice Consul Mortimer's report, with press comments...Reprinted from the British Foreign off. edition no. 718. [n.p.] 1890. 24 p.   CU-B

3859. Great Western financial corp. Annual report.
CL has 1957–59.

3860. Griffin, Donald F. Plans and action for the development of the Los Angeles metropolitan coastline... L.A., Haynes foundation, 1944. 28 p. illus., maps.
C CBev CLO CLS CLSU CLU CO CSmH CU-B

3861. [Griffin, George Butler] Pocket guide of Los Angeles, California...August 1886... L.A., Place & co. [1886] 94 p.   CU-B

3862. Griffin, John Strother. Los Angeles in 1849, a letter from John S. Griffin, M.D., to Col. J. D. Stevenson, March 11, 1849. L.A., Priv. print., 1949. 19 p. "One hundred copies printed for Glen Dawson by Wm. M. Cheney."   CHi CL CLM CLO CLSM CLU CU-B CoD

3863. Griffith, Beatrice Winston. American me. Bost., Houghton, 1948. 341 p. illus.   CMont CStmo

3864. Guthrie, Chester Lyle. ...The Pico house... Berkeley, 1936. 10 p. Typew.   CU-B

3865. —— ...Site of Misión Vieja... Berkeley, 1936. 16 p. Typew.   CU-B

3866. Gwynn, Alfred E., co., Los Angeles, pub. A book of California bungalows. L.A. [n.d.] [80] p. illus., plans.   CHi

3867. —— Same. 3d ed., new and enl. 97 p. illus.
CHi

3868. Hales, George P. Los Angeles city hall. L.A., Bd. of pub. works, c1928. 63 p. illus.
CL CLO CLSU CLU CPom CRcS CSfCW CSmH CStmo CoU NN

3869. Hanson, Earl, and Beckett, Paul. Los Angeles: its people and its homes... L.A., Haynes foundation, 1944. 206 p. illus., maps. Reproduced from typew. copy.
C CBev CL CLO CLSU CLU CO CSmH CStmo CU-B CWhC

3870. Hart, Lincoln. "Our town." [L.A., Boulevard press] c1942. 55 p.   CL

3871. Hartt (W. A.) firm. Description of Hartt's gravity elevator and tramway combined. [L.A.? 1896?] 16 p. diagrs.   CHi

3872. Harvard school. [Catalog] 1889/90– L.A., 1889– illus., ports.
CSmH has 1902/03–1903/04. CU-B has 1889/90, 1900/01, 1902/03–1903/04, 1907/08.

3873. Haverlin, Carl. Romance of transportation and the story of the Packard building. L.A., E. C. Anthony, inc., 1929. 32 p. illus.   CLU

3874. Hayes, Mary Agnes Imelda, Sister. A history of Griffith Park in Los Angeles. [Berkeley, 1951] Thesis (M.A.)—Univ. of Calif., 1951.   CU

3875. Hebrew benevolent society. Constitution and by-laws... L.A., Print. at the So. Californian off., 1855. 12 p.   CU-B

3876. —— Same. Issued by the Southern California

Jewish historical society, Los Angeles, as a souvenir program, Feb. 4, 1954. facsim.   CHi CU-B

3877. Hellman (Isaias W.) building, 4th and Main Sts., Los Angeles, Cal. ... [L.A., Kruckeberg press, 1909] [15] p. illus., plans.   CHi

3878. Henry, Helga Bender. Mission on Main street. Bost., W. A. Wilde co. [1955] 200 p. illus., ports. A history of the Union rescue mission.
          CBb CHi CL CLU CStmo CU-B

3879. Herrick, Elisabeth Webb. Curious California customs... L.A., Pac. carbon & print. co. [c1934] 110 p. illus.   C CHi CLLoy CLSU CLU CRedl CSd CSf CStmo CU-B

3880. —— Same. [c1935] 225 p. illus.
          CLO CSmH

3881. Hewett, Edgar Lee. ...Lummis the inimitable... Santa Fe, N.M., 1944. 14 p. port. At head of title: Archaeological institute of America. Papers of the School of American research.   CL

3882. Hill, Laurance Landreth. La reina, Los Angeles in three centuries; a volume commemorating the fortieth anniversary of the founding of the Security trust & savings bank of Los Angeles, February 11, 1889... [L.A.] Security trust & savings bank, 1929. 208 p. illus., ports.
Available in many California libraries and NN ViU

3883. —— Same. 4th ed. 1931. 208 p. illus., ports.
          CCoron CLob CMont CSdU KHi OrU

3884. Historical records survey. California. Calendar of the Francis Bret Harte letters in the William Andrews Clark memorial library (University of California at Los Angeles)... L.A., Southern Calif. Hist. records survey project, 1942. 36 l.   CHi COnC CSdS

3885. Historical society of southern California, Los Angeles. ...Centennial year roster, 1950. [n.p., n.d.] [19] p. illus.   CHi

3886. —— Constitution, standing rules, and list of officers and members...together with the inaugural address of the president. L.A., News and recreation print., 1884. 13 p.   CHi CP

3887. Hoffman electronics corp. Annual report. CL has 1948–60.

3888. Hollenbeck home. Hollenbeck home for the aged... L.A., [1930?] 42 p. illus.   CLU

3889. —— Manual...with by-laws and house rules. [L.A., 1908?] [26] p.   CHi

3890. Hotel Clark. The new Hotel Clark. [L.A.? 1917?] [7] p. illus., maps.   CHi

3891. Houston, Robert d'Auria. This is Los Angeles; a complete guide book. L.A., D. D. Houston [1950] 176 p. illus., maps. Bibliography: p. 169.
          C CLO CLU CSf NN ODa

3892. Howard & Smith, nurserymen. [Illustrated catalog] L.A., c1917. 31 p.   CHi

3893. Howland & Chadwick. ...Catalogue of photographic apparatus... [Rochester, N.Y., Rochester optical co., 1895] 68 p. illus.   CHi

3894. Hubbell oil company vs. Morrison, Charles J. ...Hubbell oil company (a corporation) plaintiff, vs. Charles J. Morrison, administrator of the estate of James Orwin, deceased... [n.p., 1906?] 98 p. Los Angeles land title.   CLU

3895. Hull, Osman Ransom. Survey of the Los Angeles city schools. [L.A.] L.A. city school district, 1934. 395 p. illus., maps, tables, diagrs.
          CL CLS CLU CSfSt

3896. Hunt, Rockwell Dennis. 1850, a year of destiny... [L.A., Univ. of So. Calif. press, 1947] [20] p. (Fourteenth annual research lecture of the Div. of research of the graduate school, Univ. of So. Calif.)   CHi

3897. —— The first half century. L.A., Univ. of So. Calif., 1930. 109 p. illus., ports. [Semicentennial pub. from the Univ. of So. Calif. press] Also issued as: Los Angeles. Univ. of So. Calif. Publications: Univ. chronicle.
Available in many libraries.

3898. —— "Mr. California"; autobiography. S.F., Fearon, 1956. 380 p. illus., ports.
          CBb CHi CLO CLS CNa CP CRedCL CSalCL CSd CSf CStmo CSto

3899. Hunter, Burton Leath. The evolution of municipal organization and administrative practice in the city of Los Angeles... L.A., Parker, Stone & Baird co., 1933. 283 p. Bibliography: p. [245]–246.
          C CL CLSU CLU CO CSdS CSf CSmH CU-B ViU

3900. Hunter, Sherley. Why Los Angeles will become the world's greatest city...Photography by Philip Du Bois, typography by Wendell W. Fish. [L.A., H. J. Mallen & co., inc., 1923] 42 p. illus.   CL CSmH

3901. Hunter, Dulin & co. Statistical department. Los Angeles from a business commercial and industrial standpoint. [L.A., 1923] 20 p. illus., map.   CL

3902. Huntley, Robert Joseph. History of administrative research, city of Los Angeles. L.A., 1952. 45 l.
          CL ViU

3903. Hutton (E. F.) & co. ...Byron Jackson company... [n.p., 1954?] 7 p.   CHi

3904. [Huyck, Charles L.] "Die Walküre," a classic feat of broadcasting, October 18, 1926. L.A.? 1926] 13 p. illus. Transmission from Los Angeles to San Francisco of the first opera broadcast by telephone.   CHi

3905. Illustrated daily news. Prospectus...Cornelius Vanderbilt, jr., publisher... [L.A., 1923] [18] p. illus.   CLU

3906. Inside facts about Los Angeles street railroad financiering. L.A., 1891. 8 p. "From the *Los Angeles Times,* July 22, 1891."   CSmH

3907. Interchurch world movement of North America. ...The Mexican in Los Angeles. Los Angeles city survey, G. Bromley Oxnam, director. [n.p.] 1920. 28 p. maps.   CL

3908. International association of printing house craftsmen, Los Angeles club. The story of printing in Los Angeles. L.A., 1949. 54 p. illus.   C CHi CLO

3909. International typographical union of North America. Union no. 174, Los Angeles. Mr. Otis and the Los Angeles "Times." L.A., 1915. 24 p.
          CL CLU

3910. International union, united automobile, aircraft and agricultural implement workers of America. Los Angeles local 887. Strike home; a report on the 54-day strike of 33,000 North American workers. [L.A., 1953] 42 p. illus.   CLU

3911. Interurbans special. no. 1–20 [194–?] L.A. Title varies: no. 1–10, Interurbans. Special number; no. 11– Interurbans special. Editor and publisher: Ira L. Swett.
C has no. 11, 13, 16, 18, 20. CBev has no. 18. CL has no. 11–13, 16, 18, 20. CLO has no. 11. CLS has no. 20. CLU has no. 5, 7, 10–20. CStmo has no. 16, pt. 3, 18, 20. CU-B has 5–9, 11–13.

3912. Investment and real estate blue book of Los Angeles. L.A., Foreman [1924?] 72 p. illus.   CLU

3913. Investment company of America. Annual report.
CL has 1949–58, 1960.

3914. —— Prospectus.
CL has 1955–56.

3915. Jackson, George Alden. A history of the adult education program in the Los Angeles public schools. [L.A.] 1957. Thesis (Ed.D.) —U.C.L.A., 1957.
CLU

3916. Jacobs (J. L.) & co., Chicago. Administrative coordination and simplification of Los Angeles municipal governmental machinery, July, 1945. [Chicago, 1945] 13 l.
CL

3917. Jacques, Janice. The political reform movement in Los Angeles, 1900–1909. [Claremont, 1948] 125 l. Thesis (M.A.)—Claremont college, 1948.
CCH

3918. Jamison, Judith Norvell. Administration of city planning in Los Angeles. [L.A.] 1947. Thesis (M.A.)—U.C.L.A., 1947.
CLU

3919. Janss investment co. Short history of Los Angeles. [L.A.? 1935?] [16] p. illus., ports., map.
CLU

3920. Jeffress, Mary H. A historical study of the Community health association of Los Angeles. [L.A.] 1949. Thesis (M.A.)—U.C.L.A., 1949.
CLU

3921. Jensen, Mary Grace. The rise and expansion of public secondary education in the Los Angeles city high school district... [Berkeley, 1941] 461 l. Thesis (Ed.D.)—Univ. of Calif., 1941.
CU

3922. Jewel manufacturing co. Jewel gas-making machinery, the acme of perfection. L.A. [191–?] 15 p. illus.
CU-B

3923. John Randolph Haynes and Dora Haynes foundation, Los Angeles. Metropolitan Los Angeles, a study in integration. L.A., 1952–55. 16 v. illus., maps (part col., part fold.) (Its publications. Monograph series, no. 18–33) Includes bibliographies.
Contents: v.1. Characteristics of the metropolis, by E. A. Cottrell and H. L. Jones.—v.2. How the cities grew, by R. Bigger and J. D. Kitchen.—v.3. Regional planning, by J. N. Jamison.—v.4. Law enforcement, by R. F. Wilcox.—v.5. Sanitation and health, by W. W. Crouch, W. Maccoby, M. G. Morden and R. Bigger.—v.6. Fire protection, by J. Trump, J. R. Donoghue and M. Kroll.—v.7. Highways, by R. F. Wilcox.—v.8. Water supply by V. Ostrom.—v.9. Recreation and parks, by E. McCune.—v.10. Personnel management, by H. L. Jones.—v.11. Governmental purchasing, by P. Beckett, M. Plotkin and G. Pollak.—v.12. Schools, by H. L. Jones.—v.13. Public libraries, by H. L. Jones.—v.14. Finance and taxation, by W. W. Crouch, J. E. Swanson, R. Bigger, and J. A. Algie.
v.15. Intergovernmental relations, by W. W. Crouch.—v.16. The metropolis: is integration possible? by E. A. Cottrell and H. L. Jones.
Available in many libraries.

3924. Johns, Dorothy. Victims of the system; how crime grows in jail and city hall. [L.A., Lino print. co., 1908] 20 p.
CU-B

3925. Johnson, Jeremiah, auctioneer. Grand auction sale...Thursday, January 6th, 1887...Robert Turner, esq., owner. L.A., Day [1887] [2] p. illus. "Real property—Los Angeles."
CLU

3926. Jonathan club. Jonathan club of Los Angeles, 1909–1910. [L.A., 1910?] 62 p.
CLU

3927. —— Roster. 1949. L.A., 1949.
CU-B

3928. Kassel, Lola Idelle. A history of the govern-

ment of Los Angeles, 1781–1925... 1929. 63, 5 l. Thesis (M.A.)—Occidental college, 1929.
CLO

3929. Keim, Thomas Beverley. ...The recall of superior court judges in Los Angeles in 1932... [L.A.] 1936. Thesis (M.A.)—U.C.L.A., 1936.
CLU

3930. Kelly, Allen. Historical sketch of the Los Angeles aqueduct, with map, profile and illustrations... L.A., Times-mirror print. co., 1913. 37 p., 48 l. illus., map.
C CChiS CHi CL CLO CLS CLSU CLU CPom CSmH CU-B

3931. Kewen, Perrie. The battle of Los Angeles. 1890. From the *Pacific national guardsman*, Sept. 1890, p. 29–34.
CL

3932. Kiersted, Wynkoop. Report of Wynkoop Kiersted, appointed by the Los Angeles city water company, to submit evidence before the Board of arbitrators ...in the matter of the valuation of the water works property of the Los Angeles city water company, Los Angeles, California, January and February, 1899. [L.A., 1899] 12 p.
CSmH

3933. Kilner, William H. B. Arthur Letts, 1862–1923, man and merchant, steadfast friend, loyal employer. [L.A., Priv. print, by Young & McCallister, inc., 1927] 273 p. illus., ports., facsims.
CBb CHi CLU

3934. King, Lenora H. Society's yearbook; a current history of Los Angeles' epoch year, with glimpses of the days that were. By Angeles Ayers [pseud.]... [L.A.] Author, 1926. 304 p.
CLU

3935. Kinsey, Don J. The water trail; the story of Owens valley and the controversy surrounding the efforts of a great city to secure the water required to meet the needs of an ever-growing population... L.A., Dept. of water & power, c1928. 39 p. illus.
CLO CLSU CLU CSmH

3936. Knight, John B., co. A study of public knowledge and attitudes made expressly for the city of Los Angeles, July 1955. [n.p.] 1955. 28 l.
CL

3937. Kraus, Henry. In the city was a garden; a housing project chronicle. N.Y., Renaissance press, 1951. 255 p.
C CArcHT CHi CLU CMont CO CPa NN

3938. Krenkel, John H. History of the port of Los Angeles. [Claremont, 1935] 151 l. charts, maps. Thesis (M.A.)—Claremont college, 1935.
CCH

3939. Kuhrts, Jacob. Reminiscences of a pioneer. [L.A., 1907] 1 v.
CSmH

3940. Lane-Wells co. ... Annual report. [L.A.] illus., charts.
CHi has 1951, 1953.

3941. Latham, H. W., vs. Los Angeles et al. [Documents in the case of H. W. Latham, vs. the city of Los Angeles and L. M. Bigelow relating to the contested title to certain lands around the Plaza. L.A., 1888?] 4 v. maps.
CLU

3942. Layne, Joseph Gregg. Annals of Los Angeles, from the arrival of the first white men to the civil war, 1769–1861... S.F., Calif. hist. soc., 1935. 97 p. illus. ([Calif. hist. soc.] Special pub. no. 9)
CBb CHi CL CLLoy CLO CLSU CLU CLgA CO CSf CSfCP CSfU CSjC CSmat CSmH CU-B

3943. League for better city government. The new charter. A series of questions and answers designed to explain to the voters of Los Angeles the scope and purpose of the amendments... [L.A.?] 1897. 16 p.
CSmH

3944. Le Berthon, J. L., pub. Architecture of R. B. Young. L.A., 1905. unp.   CSmH

3945. Lee, Laurie. City of the sun. L.A., 1952. 13 p.   CHi

3946. Leeming, Arthur Thomas. Los Angeles as a wholesale center. [Berkeley, 1938] Thesis (M.A.)—Univ. of Calif., 1938.   CU

3947. Leonard, Ethel. ...Report of sanitary investigation of the tributaries and mountain streams emptying into Owens river from the upper end of Long Valley via Owens river gorge... Including the chemical sanitary analysis of the water by A. F. Wagner... [L.A.? 1914] 28 p.   CSmH

3948. Lesser, Robert Charles. Man and music; a civic music center for the city of Los Angeles. [Berkeley, 1954] Thesis (M.A.)—Univ. of Calif., 1954.   CU

3949. Lewis, Edwin L. [Street railway development in Los Angeles and environs, 1873–1938] [n.p.] 1921. 21 l.   CL

3950. Lewis, James Gordon. An historical survey of radical sectarianism in Los Angeles. [L.A., 1951] 283 l. Thesis (M.A.)—Occidental college, 1950.   CLO

3951. Lewis, William Stanley. A partial history of the Los Angeles public library, comp. from original sources from the beginning of the library idea in Los Angeles to 1899. [L.A.] 1936. v.p. illus., ports.   CL

3952. Liggett, Hazel Mary. ...The relation of wages to the cost of living in Los Angeles 1915 to 1920... L.A., So. Calif. sociol. soc., Univ. of So. Calif. [1921] 10 p.   CSmH

3953. Lincoln, Nebraska luncheon club of Los Angeles. By-laws, objects, membership list. [Organized October 7th, 1935] [L.A.] 1938. [12] p.   CHi

3954. Lissner, Meyer. Reform in Los Angeles; retrospective,—prospective; an address...before the City club of Los Angeles, Saturday, April 10, 1909. [L.A., City club of L.A., 1909] 15 p.   C

3955. Litle, Selma Elizabeth Louisa. The Padua Hills project introduces Mexican folk lore into California culture. [L.A.] 1943. Thesis (M.A.)—U.C.L.A., 1943.   CLU

3956. Livingstone, David. New commerce with ancient markets. Pub. by the Los Angeles chamber of commerce under its greater harbor program. L.A., 1939. 73 l. diagrs. Reproduced from typew. copy.   CL CLU

3957. Locke, Charles Edward. White slavery in Los Angeles... [L.A., Times-mirror print., c1913] 68 p.   CSmH

3958. Los Angeles vs. Baldwin, Leon McL., et al. ...The city of Los Angeles vs. Leon McL. Baldwin, et al. Argument of John F. Godfrey, city attorney and attorney for plaintiff... [L.A.? 1877] 114 p.   CU-B

3959. Los Angeles vs. Hunter, Jesse D., et al. In the Supreme court of the state of California. The city of Los Angeles, plaintiff and respondent, vs. Jesse D. Hunter, et als., defendants and appellants. The city of Los Angeles, plaintiff and respondent, vs. Thomas D. Buffington, et als., defendants and appellants. Appeal from the Superior court of Los Angeles county. Hon. G. A. Gibbs, judge. Transcript on appeal... L.A., Parker & Stone co. [1907] 1284 p.   CSmH

3960. Los Angeles vs. Pfahler, Andrew. In the Supreme court of the state of California. Ex parte Andrew Pfahler; application for discharge under writ of habeas corpus, points and authorities for respondent. Constitutionality of the provisions of the charter of Los Angeles for the passage of local ordinances by vote of the electors

of the city. W. B. Mathews, city attorney, Herbert J. Goudge...and Hunsaker & Britt, attorneys for respondent ... L.A., Parker & Stone, 1906. 153 p.   CL

3961. Los Angeles vs. Southern California telephone company. Before the Railroad commission of the state of California. The city of Los Angeles, complainant, vs. Southern California telephone company, defendant...Opening brief in behalf of the city of Los Angeles. Reply brief on behalf of the city of Los Angeles. Ray L. Chesebro...Carl I. Wheat. L.A., Parker, Stone & Baird co. [1935] 2 v.   CHi

3962. Los Angeles. Annual all city art exhibition. Seventh annual city of Los Angeles art exhibition [at the] Greek theatre and city parks. [Oct. 12 through Oct. 28] 1951. [L.A., 1951] [16] p. illus., ports.   CL

3963. —— Board of civil service commissioners. Forward through a half century, 1903–1953; Los Angeles city civil service. [n.p., n.d.] 20 p. illus., ports.   CL

3964. —— Board of consulting engineers. Report...to the Board of water and power commissioners of the city of Los Angeles on the storage and distribution of water... [L.A., 1928] 3 pts.   CSmH

3965. —— Board of economic survey of the port of Los Angeles. ...Economic survey of the port of Los Angeles, July 15, 1933... [L.A., Bur. of print., 1933] 231 l. illus., maps. Reproduced from typew. copy.
                                                        CL CLU

3966. —— Board of education. Los Angeles city schools and the war. 2d ed. Report of the war organization of Los Angeles city schools from the beginning of the war to February 1, 1918. [L.A., 1918] 84 p. illus.
                                                            CLU

3967. —— —— Los Angeles city schools, prepared for teachers and visitors, National education association convention. L.A., 1931. 60 p. illus.   CL

3968. —— —— The progress of Los Angeles. [L.A., L.A. trade-technical junior college, n.d.] unp.   CL

3969. —— —— The reconstruction program of the Los Angeles city schools, 1933–35 inclusive. [L.A., n.d.] 19 p. illus.   CL

3970. —— Board of harbor commissioners. Annual report of commerce... 19– L.A., Bd. of harbor commissioners [19 – v. tables. Title varies.
CL has 1915/16–1940/41. CLSU has 1921/22, 1925/26, 1932/33. CLU has 1913/14–1919/20, 1922/23–1939/40, [suspended 1941–46], 1946/47, 1950/51–1957/58. CSmH has [1912/13], [1915/16], 1923/24–1940/41, 1947/48. CStmo has 1913, 1953/54, 1957/58. CU-B has 1927/28, 1934/35–1939/40.

3971. —— —— Los Angeles, the great seaport of the Southwest. [L.A., 1921?] illus.   CSmH

3972. —— —— Same. 1923. illus.   C CLSU

3973. —— —— The port of Los Angeles: its history, development, tributary territory, present and prospective commerce, and relation to the Panama canal... [L.A.? 1913] 158 p. illus., maps.   CL CLO CO CSmH

3974. —— —— The port of Los Angeles... L.A., 1917. 272 p. illus.   CL CSmH CU-B

3975. —— —— Port of Los Angeles shipping directory. L.A., 19–
CLU has 1954–56.

3976. —— Board of public service commissioners. Complete report on construction of the Los Angeles aqueduct; with introductory historical sketch... L.A., 1916. 319 p. illus., port., maps.

CHi CInI CL CLO CLSU CLU COnC CRedl CSd CSfCW CSfMI CSmH CU-B

3977. Los Angeles. Board of public commissioners (*cont'd*) Owens Valley and the Los Angeles water supply. ...Issued for the information of the Governor and members of the California legislature... [L.A., 1925] 29 p. CSmH

3978. —— —— Reply to the proposal and accompanying documents dated Nov. 29, 1924 submitted by W. W. Watterson. [L.A., 1925] 129 p. Deals with water supply. CInI

3979. —— **Board of public utilities and transportation.** A study of the feasibility and desirability of a city wide motor coach system to replace existing local transportation systems in the city of Los Angeles. Comp. by S. M. Lanham... [L.A., 1935] 39 p. maps, diagrs. CL

3980. —— **Board of trade.** Annual report... [188–?–
C has 1886. CL has 1886, 1888, 1894–1904. CSmH has 1884–86. CU-B has 1885–88.

3981. —— —— Constitution and by-laws. L.A. [Gibson co., print.] 1883. 22 p. CL CSmH

3982. —— —— Same. L.A., Commercial print. house, 1884. CL

3983. —— **Boynton normal.** Boynton normal; a school for teachers. L.A. [1908] [5] p. folder. CHi

3984. —— **Bureau of budget and efficiency.** Organization, administration, and management of the Los Angeles public library. L.A., 1948–51. 12 v.
C CBev CL CLO CLSU CLU CO CSf CSmH CStmo CViCL ViU

3985. [—— **Bureau of engineering. Federal coordination division**] Survey of unemployment relief activities in the city of Los Angeles, California, 1932–1938. [L.A., 1938] 48 p. CL

3986. —— **Cathedral of Saint Sophia (Orthodox Eastern church, Greek)** The Cathedral of Saint Sophia in Los Angeles, and the Greek Orthodox church: its history and its faith by A. P. D. Valakis. [n.p.] 1955. 52 p. illus., ports. CHi

3987. —— **Chamber of commerce.** An account of the first annual banquet of the Los Angeles Chamber of commerce. Fifth year. Redondo, February 25, 1893. [L.A., Kingsley and Barnes] 1893. 57 p. illus., fold. plan. CLO

3988. —— —— The Antonio F. Coronel collection ...Chamber of commerce building, Los Angeles, California, 1906. L.A., Baumgardt pub. co., 1906. 28 p. port. CLU CSmH CU-B

3989. —— —— Exhibit and work of the Los Angeles Chamber of commerce... [L.A.] 1910. 8 p. illus. CU-B

3990. —— —— Facts about industrial Los Angeles ...published by the Industrial department of the Los Angeles Chamber of commerce... L.A., c1921–
C has 1929. CL has 1921/22, 1924–27, 1929. CLSU has 1924. CSmH has 1921/22. CU-B has 1921/22.

3991. —— —— From ciudad to metropolis; research reveals the 60 year progress of Los Angeles in 21 aspects. L.A., 1948. CLU CSmH CU-B

3992. —— —— General industrial report of Los Angeles... c1926. 47 l. CL CLO CLSU CU-B

3993. —— —— Los Angeles and vicinity... L.A. [1904] 100 pl.
C CL CLU CP CSmH CU-B CoD CoU NN

3994. —— —— Los Angeles business directory. 1st–

1956– L.A., 1956– Title varies: 1st, 1956, Los Angeles metropolitan area business directory.
C (1956) CL (1956, 1958, 1961) CLO (1958) CLU (1956, 1958)

3995. —— —— Los Angeles, the center of an agricultural empire... L.A., Agricultural dept. of the L.A. Chamber of commerce, 1928. 31 p. illus., maps. C

3996. —— —— Los Angeles today, December 1, 1909... L.A., Neuner corp., 1909– illus.
CHi has 1924, 1929. CL has 1919–20, 1922–24. CLSU has 1913. CLU has 1913, 1924. CSf has 1911. CSmH has 1909–10, 1919–20, 1922–24. CU-B has 1910, 1912–13, 1917, 1919–23.

3997. —— —— The members' annual. v.1, 1888– L.A., 1888–
C has v.10–12, 22–23, 26–28, 1898–1900, 1910–11, 1914–16. CHi has v.11, 1899. CL has v.6–7, 13, 16, 18–21, 24–41, 1894–95, 1901–04, 1906–09, 1912–29.

3998. —— —— The port of Los Angeles, its history development and commerce... L.A., 1922. 95 p.
CL CLO CLSU

3999. —— —— Schools and colleges of Los Angeles. [L.A.] 1919–22. 72 p. illus. Also published in Spanish.
C has 1920. CLSU has 1919–21. CSmH has 1922. CU-B has 1920 and Spanish ed.

4000. —— —— The twin harbors of Los Angeles and Long Beach; being a history of the beginning and development of...a great world port... 1938. 21, xv l. Reproduced from typew. copy. CL

4001. —— —— **Citizens' relief committee.** Report...of receipts and disbursements of funds and work for the relief of sufferers from the earthquake and fire which occurred at San Francisco, April 18, 1906. [L.A.?] 1908. 47 p. C CHi CL CSf CSfMI CU-B

4002. —— —— **Dept. of foreign commerce and shipping.** The story of Los Angeles harbor; its history, development, and growth of its commerce...National foreign trade week, May 19–25, 1935. [1935] 22 l.
CL CLO CLSU CLU

4003. —— —— **Domestic trade dept.** Chain and multiple-outlet stores in Los Angeles, California. [L.A.] 1934. 32 l. CL

4004. —— —— —— Same. [L.A.] 1940. 24 l. CL

4005. —— —— **Research committee.** Research reveals the 60 year progress of Los Angeles in twenty-one aspects. [L.A., 1948] [43] p. CHi

4006. —— —— **Women's community service auxiliary.** Southern California competitive festival of the allied arts...1934...Los Angeles... [L.A., 1934] 32 p. CU-B

4007. —— **Charter revision committee.** Report of the Los Angeles charter revision committee, October 1, 1941. L.A. [1941] 51 p. forms. CL

4008. —— **Charters.** Charter. 1873– L.A., 1873–
CL has 1873, 1889, 1903, 1905, 1909, 1911, 1913, 1919, 1921, 1923, 1925, 1927, 1929, 1931, 1933, 1935, 1937, 1939, 1941, 1946, 1948, 1957. CLLoy has 1948. CLSM has 1878, 1889, 1903, 1905, 1913, 1923. CLU has 1873, 1878, 1889, 1905, 1909, 1911, 1919, 1925. CSd has 1889. CSmH has 1878, 1903, 1911, 1923. ViU has 1937.

4009. —— **Christ church.** Christ church of Los Angeles, 1907. 83 p. illus. (Includes a directory of members) C

4010. —— **City administrative officer.** Metropolitan government for Los Angeles: a workable solution, by Samuel Leask and George A. Terhune. L.A., 1961. v.p. map.   CL

4011. —— —— Outline of departments and activities, 1925/26 [and chronological growth of municipal activities, Los Angeles, 1925/26–1957/58. n.p., 1958?] [22] l.   CL

4012. —— City clerk. Facts about the city of Los Angeles... L.A. [1944–] Title varies.
CL-MR (1944–) CSt (1951)

4013. —— —— Your government at a glance. L.A., 1955. 38 p.   CSt

4014. —— City college. The need for a 4-year college in Los Angeles. L.A. [n.d.] 22 p. illus., diagrs., graphs.   CLS

4015. —— —— A study of the needs of higher education in Los Angeles. [L.A., 1949] 106 p. illus., diagrs., graphs.   CLS

4016. —— —— Twenty-five years of community service; a history of Los Angeles city college. L.A. [Associated students of L.A. city college] 1954. 26 p. illus., ports.   C CL

4017. —— City council. Official atlas, district zoning maps, 1924–25, of the city of Los Angeles... [n.p., 1924–25?] 2 v. in 1. maps.   CL

4018. —— —— City planning commission. Blight; the problem [and] the remedy. L.A., 1948. 31 l.   CL-MR

4019. —— —— Comparison of blighted and good areas in Los Angeles. [L.A.] 1945. [15] l.   CLU

4020. —— —— Los Angeles civic center, master plan, buildings & ownerships... L.A., 19–   CL-MR

4021. —— —— [Maps showing distribution of racial and national groups in the Los Angeles area, according to the 1940 census. L.A., 1943] 14 pieces in portfolio.   CLU

4022. —— —— Master plan of public works facilities. L.A., 1953. 26 p. illus., maps.   CL-MR

4023. —— —— Master plan of the Exposition park area. L.A., 1957. [8] p. illus.   CL-MR

4024. —— Civil service commission. Forward through a half century, 1903–1953. L.A. [1954] 20 p. illus. (Annual report, 1953)   CL-MR

4025. —— Commission for reorganization of the city government. Final report to the mayor and city council... L.A., 1953. 21 p. chart.   CL-MR

4026. —— —— Comments and recommendations on municipal art department... L.A., 1952. 5 p.   CL-MR

4027. —— —— Comments and recommendations on real property control in the city of Los Angeles. L.A., 1952. 15 p.   CL-MR

4028. —— —— Comments and recommendations on recreation and parks department. L.A., 1952. 11 p.
CL-MR

4029. —— —— Recommendations for reorganization of receiving hospital and ambulance services... L.A., 1952. 10 p.   CL-MR

4030. —— —— Recommendations for reorganization of the Department of public works. L.A., 1952. 15 p.
CL-MR

4031. —— —— [Reports] to the mayor and city council. [L.A., 1950–53]
CL CL-MR (Dec. 1950–Jan. 1951)

4032. —— —— Task force on library and recreation and parks. Recommendations for reorganization of the Los Angeles public library... L.A., 1952. 11 p.   CL-MR

4033. —— Congregation B'nai B'rith. B'nai B'rith temple, Los Angeles. Dedication...1929... [L.A., Mayers co., inc., 1929] [36] p. illus.   CU-B

4034. —— Consolidation committee. Report of the consolidation committee of Los Angeles. Filed... June 8, 1909... [L.A., 1909] 10 l.   CSmH

4035. —— Coordinating board. Annexation policy and program. L.A., 1960. v.p. maps, tables.
CL-MR

4036. —— Curb exchange. Report of the president. 193–?– L.A., 193–?–
CL (1931–33) CU-B (1931)

4037. —— Dept. of building and safety. Conservation, a new concept in building law enforcement [by Gilbert E. Morris. Rev. Nov., 1958. L.A.] 1958. 247 p.   CL

4038. —— Dept. of city planning. Civic beauty in Los Angeles. L.A., 1947. 12 p.   CL-MR

4039. —— —— The redevelopment of the Los Angeles plaza area. L.A., 1949. 20 l. illus.   CL-MR

4040. —— Dept. of playgrounds and recreation. Recreation, a post-war plan for the city of Los Angeles. L.A., 1946. [12] p. illus., diagrs.   CL-MR

4041. —— Dept. of public service. Municipal hydro-electric power system... [L.A., 1921] 16 p.
CSmH

4042. —— —— Owens Valley and the Los Angeles aqueduct. 1925. 6 p.   CInI

4043. —— Dept. of recreation and parks. Recreation and parks in Los Angeles. L.A., 1957. 37 p. illus.
CL-MR

4044. —— Dept. of water and power. A brief summary of important historical data and current facts concerning the municipally owned Department of water and power, city of Los Angeles. [1st]– 1945–
CLU has 1945–51.

4045. —— —— The romance of water and power. L.A., 1926. 39 p. illus. The history of Los Angeles water supply from Spanish times to 1926.   CLU

4046. —— —— Water and power 1902–1952: five decades that transformed Los Angeles. L.A. [1953?] 8 p. illus., tables.   CL-MR

4047. —— Efficiency commission. The city government of Los Angeles, California. Organization charts. L.A., 1914. [2] p. charts.   CL

4048. —— Fire dept. ...Official call book...Street directory... [L.A.] G. Rice & sons, 1894. 96 p.
CSmH

4049. —— First Christian reformed church. Silver anniversary...1914–1939, Los Angeles... [L.A.? 1939?] 23 p. illus., ports.   CU-B

4050. —— First church of the Nazarene. Directory and yearbook. 1934/35. L.A. [1934?] illus., ports.
CU-B

4051. —— First English Lutheran church. ... Golden jubilee and dedication service... [L.A.? 1937?] [11] p. illus., ports.   CU-B

4052. —— First Methodist Episcopal church. Pages' club. The horizon. L.A., 1938. 95 p. illus., ports.
CL CLSU CLU CU-B

4053. —— First Unitarian church. A history of the First Unitarian church of Los Angeles, California, 1877–1937. [By John D. K. Perry] Published on the occasion of the celebration of the sixtieth anniversary of the founding of the church. L.A. [1937?] 31 p. illus., port.   CLU CSmH

4054. Los Angeles (*cont'd*) **Griffith observatory.**
Griffith observatory and planetarium Los Angeles. [L.A.,
Southland pub. co.] 1935. [48] p. illus.   CHi   CU-B

4055. —— —— The story of Griffith observatory and
planetarium... L.A. [1952] 49 p. illus.   CL-MR

4056. —— **Harbor committee.** [Form letter dated
January 1895, relating to the Southern Pacific railway
company's lines in Los Angeles harbor area] [L.A.?
1895] [2] p.   CSmH

4057. —— **Highland Park Presbyterian church.**
Marching along, a history of the Highland Park Presby-
terian church, 1898–1948. [n.p.] 1948. 34 p. illus., ports.
C. Henry Harrington, ed.   CLO

4058. —— **Housing authority.** Housing survey
covering portions of the city of Los Angeles, California,
conducted under the supervision of the Housing authority
of the city of Los Angeles, California and published by
them as a report of Work projects administration project
no. 65-1-07-70, A. E. Williamson, survey supervisor. L.A.,
1940. 3 v. illus., maps (part col., part fold.) tables,
diagrs., forms. Mimeo.   CL   CLU

4059. —— **International church of the four-
square gospel.** Constitution and by-laws...Aimee
Semple McPherson, president. L.A. [1939] 62 p.
                                                 CU-B

4060. —— —— ...Yearbook...1937, 1939–40. L.A.
[1937–40]   CU-B

4061. —— **Junior chamber of commerce.** Membership manual. [194–?– L.A., [194–?– Title varies.
CL has 1948, 1958/59–1960/61.

4062. —— **Los Angeles high school.** Dedication.
Memorial library and memorial window 1930. L.A.
[1930?] 31 p. illus.   CHi

4063. —— —— High school. [Curriculum] [L.A.,
189–?] 10 p.   CU-B

4064. —— **Mission covenant church.** A half century...1889–1939... [L.A.?] 1939. [56] p. illus., ports.
                                                 CU-B

4065. —— **Municipal art commission.** Annual
reports. 1921–1929. L.A., Bur. of print., 1930. 100 p.
incl. 42 pl.   CSf

4066. —— —— Facts book of the Municipal art
commission [including the] Bureau of music... L.A.,
1945. 25 p.   CL-MR

4067. —— —— 1961 progress report. 50th anniversary. [L.A., 1961] [14] p. illus., ports.   CL

4068. —— —— Report...for the city of Los Angeles
... L.A., W.J. Porter, 1909. [41] p. illus.
                                                 C   CHi   CL

4069. —— —— Roots of California contemporary
architecture, by Esther McCoy. [An exhibition of the
work of Irving Gill, Greene & Greene, Bernard Maybeck,
Richard Neutra, R. M. Schindler, Frank Lloyd Wright]
Sept., 1956. [L.A., 1956] [20] p. illus.   CL

4070. —— **Occidental college.** Inauguration of
Arthur Gardiner Coons as president...October 3, 1946.
L.A. [Ward Ritchie] 1946. 53 p. illus., ports.
                                                 CL   ViU

4071. —— —— Occidental college founders' day
exhibition, 1936. Showing the works of Gordon Newell
'28 and Ward Ritchie '28. [L.A., Ward Ritchie, 1936]
19 p.   C

4072. —— **Ordinances, etc.** [Building code] 1889,
1899, 1906, 1950. L.A. Publisher varies.
CLLoy has 1950. CLU has 1889, 1899. CSmH has 1906.

4073. —— —— Compiled ordinances and resolutions
of the city of Los Angeles...1884– L.A., Marley & Freeman, 1884–
CLLoy has 1885–87. CLU has 1884, 1887. CSmH has
1884.

4074. —— —— ...The mayor and common council
of the city of Los Angeles do ordain as follows... [L.A.,
1860] 4 p. (L.A. Star, June 23, 1860)   CU-B

4075. —— —— Same, printed in Spanish. 4 p.
(L.A. Star, Junio 30, 1860)   CU-B

4076. —— —— Municipal code of the city of Los
Angeles. Ordinance no. 77,000 codifying all of the penal
and regulatory ordinances... L.A., Parker, Stone and
Baird co., 1936. 970 p.   CLLoy

4077. —— —— Ordenanzas de la ciudad de Los An-
geles, traducidas al Español por J. H. Van Rhyn. L.A.,
Imprenta del "Los Angeles Star," 1860. 40 p.
CHi   CSmH (photostatic copy)   CU-B

4078. —— —— The ordinances and resolutions of
the city of Los Angeles...1872–75. L.A., Herald pub. co.,
1875. 166 p.   CSmH

4079. —— —— Penal ordinances...1900, 1904, 1910.
L.A. Publisher varies.   CLU

4080. —— —— Revised ordinances of the city of
Los Angeles... L.A., Print. at the "So. Californian" off.,
1855. 26 p.   CLCM   CU-B

4081. —— —— Same, printed in Spanish. L.A.,
Imp. del "California Meridional," 1855. 19 p.
                                                 CLCM   CSmH

4082. —— —— Same, revised...passed and approved May 29, 1860. L.A., L.A. Star, 1860. 39 p.
                                                 CLCM   CU-B

4083. —— **Park commission.** Silver Lake Parkway, a brief discussion of the proposed Silver Lake Parkway and its relation to a park and boulevard system for
Los Angeles. L.A., 1912. 11 p. illus.   CHi

4084. —— **Public library.** Biggest lender in the
west. L.A., 1956. 12 p. illus., map.   CL-MR

4085. —— —— Board of directors, 1872–1925; librarians, 1872–1925. [n.p., n.d.] 15 l.   CL

4086. —— —— Dedicatory exercises of the central
library building, Los Angeles, 15 July 1926. [L.A., 1926]
30 p. illus.   CL   CL-MR   CLU   CU-B

4087. —— —— Public library, Los Angeles, California at World's fair, Chicago, 1893. Exhibit A, B, C, D.
[n.p., n.d.] 4 v. illus.   CL

4088. —— —— **Library school.** *Los Angeles times*
index to Los Angeles' participation in the European war,
1917–1918... [n.p., n.d.] 339 p. Typew.   CL

4089. —— —— —— **Alumni association.** Library
school and training classes, Los Angeles public library.
Directory of graduates. [n.p.] 1934. 45 p.   CL

4090. —— —— **Municipal reference dept.** Chronological record of Los Angeles city officials, 1850–
1938. Comp. from the Minutes of the City council...Pre-
pared by the Municipal reference department of the Los
Angeles public library as a report on project no. SA 3132-
5703-6077-8121-9900 conducted under the auspices of the
Works progress administration. [n.p.] 1938. v.p. Reproduced from typew. copy.   CL

4091. —— —— —— In and around the Civic Center of Los Angeles; guide to places of historical interest,
public buildings... L.A., 1930. folder (6 p.)   CRcS

4092. —— **Queen of Angels hospital.** Silver jubilee, 1926–1951. [L.A.? 1951?] unp. illus.   C

4093. —— **Roman Catholic orphan asylum.** Report of trustees. [Sacramento, Charles T. Botts, state print., 1861] 2 p.   CSmH

4094. —— **Simpson Methodist Episcopal church.** Yearbook.
CHi has 1891–93.

4095. —— **Social service commission.** Social service directory... [L.A., 1920–1935]
CBev has 1935. CLSU has 1920, 1927. CLU has 1927.

4096. —— **Southwest museum.** Casa de adobe handbook. [L.A., 1938] 23 p. illus.   CU-B
Other editions followed.   CHi (1955) CLO (1954)

4097. —— —— The Southwest museum. [L.A., Frank E. Garbutt co., n.d.] 36 p. illus., port.   CL

4098. —— **Stock exchange.** Constitution; adopted and effective August 19, 1946. [L.A., 1946–] 1 v. Loose leaf.   CLU

4099. —— **Trinity evangelical Lutheran church.** ...Golden anniversary... [L.A.? 1932?] [31] p. illus., ports.   CU-B

4100. —— **Trinity Methodist church.** Yearbook ...   ViU

4101. —— **University of southern California.** ...Catalogue, 1886–87. L.A., Times-mirror print., 1887. 89 p. illus.   CU-B

4102. —— —— Exercises in dedication of George Finley Bovard administration auditorium, Hoose hall of philosophy and Stowell hall of education... June 19 to 23, 1921. [L.A., J. R. Miller, Univ. of So. Calif. press, 1921?] 239 p. illus., port.   CL CU-B

4103. —— —— Inauguration ceremonies of Rufus Bernhard von Kleinsmid...as president of the University of southern California and exercises of the Pan-American educational conference, April twenty-seven to twenty-nine, nineteen twenty-two. L.A., Univ. of So. Calif., 1922. 230 p. illus.   CL CSfCW

4104. —— —— Inauguration of Fred D. Fagg, jr. as president of the University of southern California, on June 11, 1948. 105 p. illus., port.   CL

4105. —— —— Now they belong to the ages. L.A., Univ. of So. Calif., 1927. 23 p. illus., ports.   CL

4106. —— —— Proceedings, twenty-fifth anniversary celebration of the inauguration of graduate studies, the University of southern California; edited by Herbert Wynford Hill. 1910–1935. L.A. [Univ. of So. Calif. press] 1936. 255 p. diagrs.   CL

4107. —— —— The second fifty years. L.A., Univ. of So. Calif. press, 1927. 28 p.
CHi CL CLLoy CLO CLSU CLU CSdS CSfCW CSmH CU-B

4108. —— —— The semicentennial celebration of the founding of the University of southern California... 1880–1930. L.A., 1930. 211 p.
CCSC CL CLLoy CLO CLSU CLU CSdS CSfCW

4109. —— —— **Bureau of business research.** An economic survey of Hollywood...directed by Thurston H. Ross... [n.p., 1938] unp. illus., maps.   CL CLSU

4110. —— —— **General Alumni association.** Cardinal and gold; a pictorial and factual record of the highlights of sixty years of progress on the southern California campus...1880–1940; edited by W. Ballentine Henley, [and] Arthur E. Neelly. [L.A., 1939] 151 p. illus.   C CHi CLM CCSC

4111. —— —— **Graduate school.** Graduate studies in a world reborn; the proceedings of the twenty-

fifth anniversary of the founding of the Graduate school of the University of southern California, January 25–28, 1945, ed. by Emory S. Bogardus. 1920–1945. L.A., 1945. 216 p.   CL

4112. —— —— **School of library science. Alumni association.** Directory of graduates, 1892–1950 [of the] Library school, Los Angeles public library, and School of library science, University of southern California. L.A., 1951. 39 p.   CL

4113. Los Angeles advertising club. Victory committee. How you can help solve Los Angeles' manpower problem. [L.A.] 1944. 19 p. illus.   CU-B

4114. Los Angeles architectural club. Yearbook. 1912– L.A., 1912–
CHi (1912) CStmo (1912) CU-B (1913)

4115. Los Angeles athletic club. Annual letter of the Board of directors to members...1914. [L.A., 1914] 1 v. illus.   CU-B

4116. —— Pictorial tour of the Los Angeles athletic club and allied institutions: Los Angeles athletic club, Pacific coast club, Long Beach, Hollywood athletic club, Santa Monica athletic club, Surf and sand club, Hermosa. [L.A., 1930?] 40 p. illus., ports., map.   CU-B

4117. Los Angeles Baptist city mission society. Twenty-fifth anniversary, 1906–31. [L.A.] Twenty-fifth anniversary committee [1931?] 46 p. illus., ports. CLU

4118. Los Angeles bench and bar. Centennial edition, 1949–50. [L.A., Wilson and sons, 1950] 315 p. illus., ports.   C CHi CLO

4119. The Los Angeles blue book of land values. 1932– L.A., Investors appraisal service, 1932–
CLU has 1937.

4120. Los Angeles blue book, society register of Southern California...William Hord Richardson, editor and publisher. Season of 1894–95– v.1– Beverly Hills [c1894]– illus. Sub-title varies. Publisher varies.
C has 1944, 1952. CHi has 1938, 1943, 1945–47, 1949, 1951–52, 1954. CL has 1920–22, 1927, 1929, 1931–32, 1934, 1938–43, 1945–61. CLO has 1941–42, 1945–46, 1950–53, 1956. CLSU has 1920–21, 1923–30, 1939–40, 1943–44, 1952, 1957–62. CRedl has 1940. CSd has 1950. CSmH has 1894–95, 1926–27, 1929, 1931, 1938–46, 1948–49, 1950–55, 1957–58, 1960. CU-B has 1944.

4121. Los Angeles camellia council. Program [of the] ...annual camellia show and festival. 19– [L.A.?] 19–
C has 1956–58.

4122. Los Angeles central city committee. Economic survey: a joint report by [the author] and the Los Angeles city planning department. L.A., 1960. 44 p. illus. (L.A. centropolis, 1980, study no. 1)
CL CL-MR

4123. Los Angeles central labor council. Golden anniversary, 1901–51. L.A., 1951. illus.   CLU

4124. ...Los Angeles Chinese directory 1951. S.F., Chinese directory service [1951] 1 v. illus.   CU-B

4125. Los Angeles city government conference, 1932–34. History, duties, organization of the municipal departments, city of Los Angeles. Part 1–2 1932–34. A series of papers prepared for the Los Angeles city government conference in cooperation with the School of government, University of southern California. [n.p., 1932–34]   CL CLSU CU-B

4126. Los Angeles city school district. Curriculum division. California yesterday, today, and tomorrow. L.A., 1949. 233 p. illus., maps. (Its school pub.

no. 468) For use in the observance of the California centennial years 1948, 1949 and 1950.

CP CSdS CSf CStmo CSto

4127. —— —— Pioneer and early public schools of California and of Los Angeles. L.A., 1948. 49 l. illus. (Its Bul. no. 25) CL

4128. Los Angeles city teachers club. Year book. 19– [n.p., 19–]

CL has 1914/15–1915/16, 1920/23–1923/25.

4129. Los Angeles civic light opera association. Highlights on 20 years of civic light opera. [Ed. and pub. by a committee of past presidents, William C. Hartshorn, chairman...Written by Franklin Lacey. L.A.? Eureka press, 1957] [20] p. illus., ports. CL

4130. Los Angeles country club. Constitution, by-laws, rules, officers and members; 19– Beverly Hills, 19– CLU has 1911.

4131. —— History. Beverly Hills, 1936. 40 p. illus., ports. Introduction signed: Anne Trabue.

CLU CSmH

4132. Los Angeles county. Board of supervisors. Fort Moore pioneer memorial, dedication ceremonies, July 3, 1958. L.A., 1958. unp. illus. CL-MR

4133. —— **Chamber of commerce.** Industrial survey, Los Angeles–Long Beach harbor district. [L.A., 1936] 37 p. illus., maps. CLSU CLU

4134. —— **Dept. of parks and recreation.** Plummer park, its history and objectives. [L.A.] 1950. 9 l. CL

4135. —— **Grand jury.** ...The people vs. N. D. Oswald. Testimony taken before the grand jury... L.A., Peterson [1909] 2 v. in 1. CL

4136. —— **Youth committee.** The Echo park study, a social analysis of an urban area, with a description of the study method. [L.A., 1950] 70 l. maps, tables. CL

4137. Los Angeles county museum. Annual exhibition: artists of Los Angeles and vicinity...1950– L.A., 1950–

CLU has 1950, 1952–57.

4138. —— California centennials exhibition of art. Section I: "Historic California." Section II: "Artists of California, 1949." September 30, through November 13, 1949. L.A., 1949. 148 p. illus., ports.

CHi CL CSdS CSf CStmo

4139. —— Early prints and drawings of California from the Robert B. Honeyman, jr., collection. Loan exhibition December 10, 1954–January 16, 1955. L.A. [1955] 44 p. illus. C CHi CL

4140. —— Irving Gill, 1870–1936...in collaboration with the Art center in La Jolla. L.A., 1958. 58 p. illus., port. CHi CSd

4141. —— List of collections and exhibits to be assembled in the Los Angeles museum of history, science, and art... [L.A., 1928] 23 p. C

4142. —— Los Angeles, 1850–1900; an exhibit, September 1958 to January 1959. L.A., 1959. 56 p. illus.

CHi CLM

4143. —— Los Angeles, 1900–1961. L.A., 1961. 60 p. illus., map. CHi

4144. —— Los Angeles, September 1781, to September 9, 1850; an exhibition of paintings, documents and realia selected from private collections and those of the Museum. September 11 through October 6, 1957. [Catalog] L.A. [1957] 31 p. illus., ports., facsims.

CHi CL CU-B

4145. "Los Angeles en la mano"; unica guia en español que impulsa, fortalece y afianza la amistad y el comercio. 1947. L.A., Casa editora Crespi, 1947. illus., ports. CL

4146. Los Angeles evening express. Anniversary number. L.A., 1923–1931. illus., ports.

C (1923–24, 1929) CStmo (1931)

4147. —— Yearbook, 1928; Los Angeles and the wonderful southland of California. L.A., 1928. 80 p. illus. CHi

4148. Los Angeles examiner. Los Angeles reports to its citizens. (Los Angeles Examiner, Tuesday, September 4, 1956) [L.A.] 1956. 20 p. illus. CRcS

4149. —— What is Los Angeles? S.F. [1920] 25 p. CU-B

4150. Los Angeles gas and electric corp. From Indians to moderns. [L.A., 1928] 19 p. CHi

4151. Los Angeles gas and electric corp. vs. Western gas construction co. U.S. Circuit court of appeals for the ninth circuit, no. 2159. Transcript of record... Los Angeles gas and electric corporation...plaintiff in error...upon writ of error in the United States district court of the southern district of California, southern division. S.F., Filmer [1907] 2v. CL

4152. The Los Angeles girls' council, Los Angeles, California, 1927–1935... [L.A., 1935] 59 p. CL

4153. Los Angeles herald. Happy-land edition... Sunday, December 19, 1909. [L.A., 1909] 162 p. illus. C

4154. Los Angeles, illustrated. In albertype. L.A., Stoll & Thayer, 1889. 24 pl.

C CHi CLU CSmH CU-B

4155. Los Angeles, illustrated and descriptive sketch of early California. L.A., Payne, Baird and Stanton, 1897. 61 p. illus. CHi

4156. Los Angeles investment co. Annual report. CL has 1950–60.

4157. —— Inexpensive bungalows... [L.A., 1914?] 95 p. illus., plans. CHi

4158. —— Modern homes of California. Ed. by W. Francis Gates. [L.A.] 1913. 95 p. illus., plans. (12th bungalow book ed.) CHi

4159. —— Practical bungalows, typical California homes, with plans...Ed. by W. Francis Gates. [L.A., 1912] 95 p. illus., plans. (7th bungalow book ed.) CHi

4160. Los Angeles Jewish community council. Judge Harry A. Hollzer, 1880–1946. [L.A., n.d.] 17 p. port. CL CLU

4161. Los Angeles jockey club. Second season. Ascot Park... [L.A., J. L. LeBerthon, 1904] [94] p. CHi

4162. Los Angeles map and address co. Atlas of Los Angeles. [L.A., 19–] 239 double maps. CLU

4163. Los Angeles memorial coliseum commission. Los Angeles memorial coliseum. [L.A., Sterling press, 1938?] [17] p. illus., plan. C

4164. Los Angeles orphans home society. Constitution & by-laws...organized July, 1880. L.A., Mirror print., 1880. 12 p. CLU

4165. Los Angeles police relief association. Annual souvenir...1911. Ed. and comp. by Frank C. Jenness. [L.A., 1911] unp. illus., ports. CLU

4166. Los Angeles real estate advertiser. v.1– 1871– L.A., Real estate & law off. of Slauson & Widney, 1871–

CLU has v.1, no. 5, July 1871.

4167. Los Angeles settlement association. The College settlement. L.A. [1905] 29 p. illus.   CL CLU

4168. —— ...Report of instructive district nursing for the city of Los Angeles under the supervision of the College settlement. L.A. [1898–1912]   CL

4169. Los Angeles star. The first issue of the Los Angeles star; Los Angeles' first newspaper, with a note by Henry R. Wagner. L.A., Bruce McCallister, 1932. [6] p. facsim. (v.1, no. 1, May 17, 1851)
C CHi CLO

4170. Los Angeles street and business directory... [L.A., N.A. Wolcott, 1893] 96 p. "Compliments of Natick house, H. A. Hart & sons, props."   CL CLU

4171. Los Angeles taxpayers auxiliary committee. Tax report. no. 1–5 [1935] L.A. [1935]   CL

4172. Los Angeles, the great seaport of the southwest. [L.A., 1923?] [89] p. illus., tables.   CL

4173. Los Angeles, the metropolis of the south. Her manufactures, trade, commerce, railroads and transportation facilities. [L.A.?] 1888. 128 p. illus.   CLU

4174. Los Angeles, the old and the new... [L.A., Times-mirror print. & bind. house, 1911] 96 p. illus. Supplement to *Western insurance news*, v.8, no. 12.
CLSU CSmH CU-B

4175. Los Angeles, the wonder city; a pictorial representation... [L.A., C. P. Grossman, c1931] [96] p. illus., ports.
C CL CLO CLSU CRcS CSf CSmH CStmo CU-B CoU

4176. Los Angeles times. Annual midwinter number. L.A.
C has 1915–34, 1950–52, 1955– to date. CSjC has 1956–59.

4177. —— Fiftieth anniversary edition, December 4, 1931. [L.A., 1931] 6 pts. in 1 v. illus., ports., maps. (Its 47th annual midwinter number)
C CHi CL CLO CSmH

4178. —— ...The forty-year war for a free city, a history of the open shop in Los Angeles... [L.A.] 1929. 28 p. illus., ports.   CL CLU CSmH

4179. —— Los Angeles reports to its citizens. Title varies.
CStmo has 1958, 1959.

4180. —— 75th anniversary. Part V, Jan. 3, 1956. [L.A., 1956] 216 p. illus.   CHi

4181. Los Angeles type founders, inc. Type specimens and price list. No. 14, Feb. 1956. L.A., 1956. [108] p. illus.   CHi

4182. —— Same. No. 15, April 1959. 1959. [156] p. illus.   CHi

4183. Los Angeles urban league. Minority housing in metropolitan Los Angeles; a summary report. [n.p.] 1959. [54] p. tables, maps.   CL

4184. Los Angeles year book, 1945– L.A., 1946– 1945: Your city in war work and peace plans, 1941–1945; 1948: Know your city; 1949: The first hundred years, 1850–1950.
CBev (1945) CHi (1948, 1949) CL-MR (1948, 1949) CLSM (1949) CRcS (1948) CSfCW (1948) CSjC (1949) CStmo (1945) CU-B (1949) ViU (1949)

4185. Lucey (J. F.) co. ...Oil well supplies, gas, water well and mining supplies... [n.p., 1910?] 332 p. illus. (Catalog no. 6)   CHi

4186. Ludwig, Ella A. History of the Harbor district of Los Angeles...Containing also...personal sketches of many men and women... [L.A.] Historic record co. [192–?] 358 p., 329–938 p. illus., ports., map.
C CBb CHi CL CLO CLS CLU CLob CO CPom CSd CSf CSmH CStclU CU-B NN

4187. Lui, Garding. Inside Los Angeles Chinatown. [L.A.? 1948] 207 p. illus., ports., maps.
C CBb CHi CL CLLoy CLO CLSU CLU COr CRedl CSd CSf CSmH CStmo CU-B

4188. Lummis, Charles Fletcher. ...Out West: Los Angeles and her makers, a record; a historical résumé of the making of the city of the Angels...followed by biographical studies... L.A., Out West mag. co., 1909. [225]–420 p. illus., ports. (Out West, v.30, no. 4, Apr. 1909) Makers of Los Angeles: p. [311]–340 ed. by Charles Amadon Moody.
C CHi CL CLM CLU CSmH CU-B

4189. Lunden, Samuel. Community development through an exposition for Los Angeles. L.A., Haynes foundation, 1944. 42 p. illus., maps, diagr. (Pub. of the John Randolph Haynes & Dora Haynes foundation. no. 7)
C

4190. Lybrand, Ross bros. and Montgomery. Organizing for tomorrow's educational needs; a survey of administration and supervision within the Los Angeles city school system. L.A. [L.A. bd. of educ.] 1960. v.p. illus., map.   CL

4191. [McCarthy, John Russell] Joseph Francis Sartori, 1858–1946. L.A., Ward Ritchie [c1948] 120 p. ports. "The story of Mr. Sartori's life is also the story of the growth and development of Los Angeles..."
C CBb CHi CL CLO CLSU CLU CSmH

4192. McClenahan, Bessie Averne. The changing urban neighborhood, from neighbor to nighdweller; a sociological study... L.A., Univ. of So. Calif. [c1929] 140 p. illus., map. "Selected bibliography": p. [117]–128. A detailed investigation of a selected middle class urban area in Los Angeles.
C CL CLSU CLU CSS CSmH

4193. [McFie, Maynard] The gay nineties. [L.A., Sunset club, 1945] 25 p. Reminiscences of Los Angeles in the nineties, its industrial magnates and business enterprises, mainly the oil industry.
C CHi CL CLO CLSU CLU CLob CMont COr CPom CSd CSf CSj CStmo

4194. McGroarty, John Steven. Los Angeles from the mountains to the sea...with selected biography of actors and witnesses of the period of growth and achievement... Chicago, Am. hist. soc., 1921. 3 v. illus., ports.
C CBev CCSC CHi CL CLLoy CLO CLSU CLU CLob CPom CPs CSd CSf CSfCW CSjC CSmH CStclU CU-B MoS NN

4195. —— Same, Special limited edition. Chicago [n.d.] 2 v. illus., ports.
CHi CL CLU CLob CSmH

4196. —— The pioneer; a fascinating chapter from the pages of California's history. [L.A., Hellman commercial trust and savings bank] 1925. 19 p. port.   C

4197. —— A year and a day; Westwood Village, Westwood Hills. [L.A., Westwood Hills press, 193–] 16 p. illus., map.   CLU

4198. The Machinery and electrical co. The M. and E. company catalogue of ore buckets, ore cars, hoisting engines, whims... L.A., Ford Smith & Little [n.d.] [9] p. illus.   CHi

4199. Mackey, Margaret Gilbert. Cities in the sun... L.A., Goodwin press [c1938] 181 p. illus. Also published under title: Los Angeles proper and improper.

Brief historical sketches of Los Angeles and other cities, i.e. Long Beach, Pomona, San Bernardino, Pasadena, etc., including historical spots, industry, educational institutions.
Available in many libraries.

4200. McKim, Paul N. A survey of the Federal theater project of Los Angeles 1936–1938—as observed in the *Los Angeles examiner* and the *Los Angeles times.* [L.A.] 1953. Thesis (M.A.)—U.C.L.A., 1953.   CLU

4201. McKinnon, Mary Concepta, Sister. The educational work of the California institute of the Sisters of the Immaculate Heart of Mary. [L.A., 1937] Thesis (M.A.)—U.C.L.A., 1937.   CLU

4202. Macmillan petroleum corp. Annual report. CL has 1954–59.

4203. McOuat, H. W. Case history of Los Angeles harbor. Long Beach, 1950. 26 p. maps.   CHi

4204. McPherson, Aimee Semple. In the service of the King; the story of my life. N.Y., Boni, 1927. Autobiography of the evangelist and founder of the Angelus temple in Los Angeles.   CL CLU

4205. —— The story of my life. [Ed. by Raymond W. Becker] In memoriam, Echo park evangelistic association, Los Angeles. Hollywood [International correspondents] c1951. 246 p. illus., ports.   CL

4206. —— This is that; personal experiences, sermons and writings. L.A., Bridal call pub. house, c1921. 672 p. illus., ports.   CL CStmo

4207. Malibu business guide and directory. [1949?–1958?] Malibu, Chamber of commerce [1949–58?] illus. C (1954) CHi (c1957) CL (1951) CLU (1949–58)

4208. Marengo water co. By-laws... L.A. [Gilchrist print.] 1886. 12 p.   CHi

4209. [**Marlborough school.** Golden jubilee] Leaves from a Marlborough diary, 1888–1939, dedicated to the memory of Mary E. Caswell. [Hollywood, Hollycrofters, 1939] 95 p. illus., ports.   CL

4210. Marquis, Neeta. Immanuel and the fifty years, 1888–1938... L.A., Immanuel Presbyterian church, 1938. 75 p. illus., ports.   C CCSC CHi CL CLO CLSU CLU CSmH CU-B

4211. Martin, George R. The Clarke story; Chauncey Dwight Clarke, Mary Rankin Clarke. Claremont, Claremont college, 1956.   CHi CP

4212. Martin, James R. The University of California (in Los Angeles) a resume of the selection and acquisition of the Westwood site. L.A., 1925. 317 p. illus., ports.
          CBb CHi CL CLS CLU CSfCW CStmo

4213. Matson, Clarence Henry. Building a world gateway; the story of Los Angeles harbor... L.A., Pac. era pub. [1945] 255 p. illus., port., maps.
C CBev CHi CL CLO CLSU CLU CLgA CLob CO CSd CSmH CStmo CU-B CoD

4214. Mavity, Mrs. Nancy (Barr) Sister Aimee. Garden City, N.Y., Doubleday, 1931. 360 p. illus., ports.   CL CStmo

4215. Mayo, Morrow. Los Angeles... N.Y., Knopf, 1933. 337 p. illus., maps.
Available in many libraries.

4216. Meline, F. L., inc. Los Angeles, the metropolis of the West. [L.A.] Author, c1929. 32 p. illus., maps.   CL CLSU CSf

4217. Memorial to Congress by the citizens of San Pedro and Wilmington, Los Angeles county, California for an additional appropriation for Wilmington harbor and San Pedro bay, March 13, 1890. L.A., Times-mirror, 1890. 7 p.   CLU

4218. Menzies, Austin Francis Mills. The office of city attorney of Los Angeles. [L.A.] 1935. Thesis (M.A.)—U.C.L.A., 1935.   CLU

4219. Mercantile consolidated co., comp. Los Angeles of today; a glance at her history, a review of her commerce... [L.A.] George Rice & sons [n.d.] 150 p. illus., ports.   CLO

4220. Metropolitan surveys, Los Angeles. An industrial survey of the city of Los Angeles, and the contiguous territory. Compiled from official city, county, federal governmental and personal records, and based with mathematical precision upon a development of the original U.S. C & G survey system of triangulation, with rectangular grid coordinates... L.A. [c1935] 26 p. 10 maps.   CLU CSmH CStmo

4221. Metropolitan trust company of California. Amendment of trust 108, October 15, 1931. Muscoy ranch. Metropolitan trust company of California, trustee. [L.A.? 1931?] 49 p.   CSmH

4222. Metropolitan water district of southern California. ...Report on effect of world depression on future population growth of Los Angeles metropolitan area, [by] A. L. Sonderegger, January 30, 1933. [n.p., 1933?] 33 l.   CU-B

4223. Mexico. Primera secretaria de estado. Departamento del interior. ...Se erige en ciudad el pueblo de los Angeles de la Alta California, y será para lo sucesivo la capital de este Territorio... Mexico, 1835. Broadside. Decree establishing Los Angeles as capital of the territory of Alta California.   CU-B

4224. Michelson, Arthur U. From Judaism and law to Christ and grace. L.A., Jewish hope pub. house, c1943. 144 p. illus., ports.   CL

4225. Miller, Richard Connelly. Otis and his Times: the career of Harrison Gray Otis of Los Angeles. [Berkeley, 1961] Thesis (Ph.D.)—Univ. of Calif., 1961.   CU

4226. Mink, James V. The papers of General William Starke Rosecrans and the Rosecrans family; a guide to collection 603. L.A., Univ. of Calif., 1961. 39 p. illus.   CHi CLU

4227. Mixon, Mrs. John L. The Presbyterian church, U.S.A., in the inner city of Los Angeles, California. 3 pts.   CCSC

4228. Mobilization for democracy. Los Angeles against Gerald L. K. Smith; how a city organized to combat native fascism! [L.A., 1945] [36] p. illus.   CLU

4229. Monnette, Orra Eugene. A short account of Don Felipe de Neva, Spanish governor of California and founder of the city of Los Angeles, 1781... [L.A., L.A. pub. lib., 1930] 11 p. illus.
CHi CL CLO CLSU CLU CO CSmH CU-B

4230. —— The universality of education, dedicatory address...new central library building, July 15, 1926. [L.A., Fletcher Ford co., 1926] 16 p.   CSmH

4231. Monolith Portland cement co. Annual report.
CL has 1954–58, 1960.

4232. Monterey oil co. Annual report.
CL has 1953–56, 1958–59.

4233. Moore, Charles Irwin Douglas. The Pacific mutual life insurance company of California; a history of the company and the development of its organization, the sixtieth anniversary 1868–1928. [L.A., Times-mirror, 1928] 304 p. illus., ports., facsims.   CHi CSfCW

4234. Moore, Ernest Carroll. I helped make a university. L.A., Dawson, 1952. 175 p. History of the University of California, Los Angeles.

CHi CL CLO CLU CP CSdS CSf CU-B

4235. Moore, Marianne. Idiosyncrasy & technique. Inaugurating the Ewing lectures of the University of California Los Angeles, October 3 and 5, 1956. Berkeley and L.A., Univ. of Calif. press, 1958. 27 p.   CHi

4236. Morris, Samuel B. The water problem of Los Angeles. L.A., Dept. of water and power, 1949. [10] p. illus. Reprinted from *Western city*, May 1949.   CLU

4237. Morris & Snow seed co. [Catalogs] [L.A.? 1920?]   CHi

4238. Mosher, Henry M., pub. Views of Los Angeles and vicinity. L.A. [1905?] 30 pl.

C CBb CHi CL CLU

4239. Mosher, Leroy E. Stephen M. White, Californian, citizen, lawyer, senator, his life and his work... together with his principal public addresses, comp. by Robert Woodland Gates. L.A., Times-mirror, 1903. 2 v. port.   CHi CSfCW

4240. Mount Saint Mary's college. The new Mount Saint Mary's college now being erected on Mount Saint Mary in the Santa Monica hills in Los Angeles, with a foreword by the Right Reverend J. J. Cantwell... [L.A., Young & McCallister, 1930] [6] p. 5 pl.

CSmH CU-B

4241. Municipal league of Los Angeles. Report of the executive committee of the Municipal league on the Los Angeles city school department, October 13, 1914... L.A., 1914. 6 p.   CU-B

4242. Munk, Joseph Amasa. Activities of a lifetime. L.A., Times-mirror press, 1924. 221 p. illus., ports.   CHi

4243. Murphy, Bill. Los Angeles, wonder city of the west; a pictorial guide and souvenir. S.F., Fearon pub., c1959. 64 p. illus., ports., map.

C CBev CL CLO CSd CSfU CU-B

4244. Nadeau, Remi A. City-makers; the men who transformed Los Angeles from village to metropolis during the first great boom, 1868–76. Garden City, N.Y., Doubleday, 1948. 270 p. Bibliography: p. 254–61.

Available in many libraries.

4245. —— Los Angeles from mission to modern city. N.Y., Longmans, 1960. 302 p. illus., ports.

CLSM CLom CSdU CSf CSfMI CSfU CSmH CU-B

4246. —— The water seekers. [1st ed.] Garden City, N.Y., Doubleday, 1950. 309 p. illus. Bibliography: p. 296–301.

C CBb CInI CLgA CP CSd CStmo

4247. National Catholic war council. The Santa Rita settlement... L.A., [1921?] 38 p. illus., ports.

CL

4248. National education association. Official pocket hotel guide of Los Angeles, California. Convention July 11 to 14, 1899. [L.A., 1899] 56 p. illus.   CLU

4249. —— Official program and guide...thirty-eighth annual meeting...Los Angeles, California July 11 to 14, 1899. L.A., L.A. Educational pub. co. [1899] 1 v.

CSmH

4250. —— ...Souvenir of southern California... L.A., Times-mirror, 1899. [86] p. illus., ports.   CHi

4251. National home for disabled volunteer soldiers, Pacific branch. Pacific branch, National home for disabled volunteer soldiers, 1861–1865. [L.A., Kingsley, Barnes & Neuner co., print., 1894] [2] p.

CSmH

4252. Neal, Thomas Atwill. Saint Vibiana's cathedral, 1876–1950...Photographs by Arnold Gustav Hylen. L.A., Dawson, 1950. 11 p. mounted photos. Fifty copies printed by Wm. M. Cheney.

CLLoy CLO CLU CSmH CU-B

4253. Neblo, Sandro. Sacred earth. [1st ed.] Hollywood, 1948. 126 p. Russians in Los Angeles.   CLU

4254. Neff, Philip. Business cycles in Los Angeles [by] Philip Neff [and] Annette Weifenbach; a condensation prepared by Molly Lewin of business cycles in selected industrial areas by the same authors. L.A., Haynes foundation, 1949. 25 p. diagr. (Pub. of the John Randolph Haynes & Dora Haynes foundation. Pamphlet ser. 15)   C CLU CU-B

4255. —— Favored industries in Los Angeles, an analysis of production costs. L.A., Haynes foundation, 1948. 25 p. (Pub. of the John Randolph Haynes & Dora Haynes foundation. Pamphlet ser. 13)   C CLU

4256. Nelson, Lawrence Emerson. Los Angeles: mother and stepmother of colleges. Redlands, Fortnightly club, 1957. 18 p. Typew.   CRedl

4257. Nesbitt, Florence. Study of a minimum standard of living for dependent families in Los Angeles, made...for the Los Angeles community welfare federation. November 1927. L.A., L.A. community welfare federation, 1927. 36 p.   CL

4258. Netz, Joseph. ...The great Los Angeles real estate boom of 1887. [n.p., n.d.] 23 l. Reproduced from typew. copy.   C CL

4259. Nevins, John A. The Puente area; a study of changing agricultural land use. [L.A.] 1951. Thesis (M.A.)—U.C.L.A., 1951.   CLU

4260. Night in Los Angeles. N.Y., Newcomb pub. co., c1912. [16] p. of illus.   CHi CU-B

4261. North American aviation, inc. Annual report.

CL has 1948–60.

4262. —— Inside North American aviation. L.A. [n.d.]   CL

4263. North American press association, San Francisco. Standard guide Los Angeles, San Diego and the Panama-California exposition... S.F., c1914. 143 p. illus.   C CPom CU-B MoS NN OrU

4264. Northwestern national bank vs. Alvord, Wm., et al. ...Northwestern national bank vs. Wm. Alvord, et al. No. 14871. Edward Russell vs. Pacific railway company, et al. No. 14491. Brief filed on behalf of defendants, I. W. Hellman, E. F. Spence, J. F. Crank... [by John D. Bicknell] L.A., Wm. E. Ward, print., 1893. 162 p.   CSmH

4265. Norton, Richard Henry. Reminiscences of an agitator; with a diagnosis and a remedy for present economic conditions. L.A., Glass bk. binding co., 1912. 91 p.   CHi CL

4266. Nuestra Señora la Reina de Los Angeles mission, pub. The King's highway, El Camino real y Nuestra Señora la Reina de Los Angeles de Porciuncula [mission] [4th ed.] L.A. [c1934] [42] p. illus. CStmo

4267. —— Same. 5th ed. [c1939] [24] p.   CHi

4268. Oates, Robert M. The Los Angeles rams. [Culver City, Murray & Gee, 1955] 96 p. illus., ports., tables.   CU-B

4269. O'Day, Edward Francis. A city home set in a country garden; being an attempt to appraise certain higher values of urban life which are notably expressed in Beverly Park. L.A., 1927. 18 p. illus., maps. Printed for Western states properties, inc., by Young & McAllister.
CLU CSfU

4270. O'Donnell, Mary Patricita, Sister. The effect of John J. Cantwell's episcopate on Catholic education in California (1917–1947) [Wash., D.C.] 1952. 119 l. Thesis (M.A.)—Catholic Univ. of Am., 1952.   CSrD

4271. Olympic games, Los Angeles, 1932. Compendium of the Olympic games...Tenth Olympiad. L.A., Olympiad pub. co. [1932?] 32 p. illus.   CSf

4272. —— ...Official pictorial souvenir, prepared and issued by the Organizing committee. L.A., 1932. 60 p. illus.   CHi

4273. —— ...Official report. L.A., Xth Olympiad committee of the games of Los Angeles, 1933.   CSd

4274. O'Melveny, Henry William. William G. Kerckhoff; a memorial. L.A., Priv. print., 1935. 75 p. port. "100 copies printed by the Adcraft press, Los Angeles, November, 1935."   CBb CLU

4275. [Oppenheim, James] Talk. [L.A., c1921] 11 p.   CU-B

4276. Orcutt, William Warren. Memorabilia of William Warren Orcutt, 1869–1942. L.A., Fred S. Lang press, 1945. 93 p.   CHi

4277. Organized labor movement, Los Angeles. ...Official year book and reference manual... 19– L.A., 19– illus., ports.
CL has 1922–35. CLU has 1934. CU-B has 1923.

4278. Orme, Henry Sayer. Smallpox in Los Angeles in 1887. [L.A., n.d.] 17 p.   CLM

4279. O'Rourke, Lawrence W. The office of mayor in Los Angeles; an administrative analysis. [L.A.] 1954. Thesis (M.A.)—U.C.L.A., 1954.   CLU

4280. Ostrom, Vincent. Water & politics; a study of water policies and administration in the development of Los Angeles. L.A., Haynes foundation, 1953. 297 p. maps. (Pub. of the John Randolph Haynes & Dora Haynes foundation: Monograph ser. 35)
C CChiS CL CLS CMerCL CSd CSdS CSt CU-B CWhC ViU

4281. Otis, Harrison Gray. "What the course of *The Times* shall be;" letter of Gen. Otis to Mr. and Mrs. Chandler—their statement. [L.A., 1917?] 15 p. facsim., port. Cover title: A letter from Harrison Gray Otis.
CHi CL CSmH

4282. Otis art institute. Work by members of the faculty. (Exhibition) L.A. [n.d.] [24] p. illus.   CL

4283. Pacific clay products. Annual report.
CL has 1953–60.

4284. Pacific coast blue book co. Los Angeles—Pasadena blue book...
CL has 1903.

4285. Pacific electric railway co. Statistical data.
CL has 1948.

4286. Pacific finance corp. Annual report.
CL has 1951–60.

4287. —— Prospectus.
CL has 1955.

4288. Pacific lighting corp. Pacific lighting corporation; a description... [L.A., 1932] 47 p. illus., map.   CHi

4289. Pacific mill and mine supply co. Manufac-

turers, distributors belting, hose, packings, mechanical rubber goods... [Chicago, Cuneo press, 1931] 159 p. illus.   CHi

4290. Pacific mutual life insurance co. Annual report.
CL has 1948–55.

4291. Pacific outdoor advertising co. Annual report.
CL has 1948, 1954, 1956–57.

4292. Pacific portable construction co. Pacific factory-built houses. L.A. [192–?] 32 p. illus., plans.   CU-B

4293. Pacific southwest academy of political and social science. Los Angeles; preface to a master plan, ed. by George W. Robbens [and] L. Deming Tilton... L.A., Pac. southwest acad., 1941. 303 p. illus., maps.
Available in many libraries.

4294. Packman, Mrs. Ana Begue. Leather dollars; short stories of pueblo Los Angeles... L.A., Times-mirror press [c1932] 79 p. illus. "Folk-tales, legends, songs, customs and the intimacies of a Hispano-California household, handed down through the generations."—p. [5]
C CL CLLoy CLO CLS CLSU CLU CO COnC CPom CRedl CSmat CSmH CStmo CU-B CViCL

4295. [Page, James Rathwell] I. N. Van Nuys, 1835–1912. L.A. [Ward Ritchie] 1944. 34 p. illus., port.
C CBb CHi CL CLO CLSU CLU CSmH

4296. Parker, William Henry. Parker on police, ed. by O. W. Wilson. Springfield, Ill., Thomas, 1957. 235 p. illus., port.   CL CLU ViU

4297. [Parkinson, John] Incidents by the way... [L.A., c1935] 342 p. illus. Limited ed. of 150 copies. The author was the architect for Los Angeles city hall, and other buildings.   CHi

4298. Parks, Marion. Doors to yesterday; a guide to old Los Angeles...pub. by Los fiesteros de la calle Olvera (The fiesta-makers of Olvera street) and History-landmarks hostesses of the Tenth Olympiad, Los Angeles. c1932. 16 p. illus.
CHi CL CLO CLU CP CSmH CU-B

4299. Pauley petroleum, inc. Annual report.
CL has 1959–60.

4300. Payne (Theodore), nursery. Catalogs.
CHi has 1914, 1918–20, 1922–24, 1926–30.

4301. Pen sketches of Los Angeles. [L.A., Times-mirror print. house, 1896] 51 pl.
C CL CLU CSmH NN

4302. Perry, Louis Barnes. A survey of the labor movement in Los Angeles. [L.A.] 1950. Thesis (Ph.D.) —U.C.L.A., 1950.   CLU

4303. Petrolia asphaltum and oil co. [Prospectus] [n.p., 1887] [3] p.   CSmH

4304. Pettingell, Frank Hervey. A chronological history of the stock exchanges of Los Angeles. 4 l. Typew.   C

4305. Peyton, Thomas Roy. Quest for dignity, an autobiography of a Negro doctor. L.A., Warren F. Lewis [c1950] 156 p.   CHi

4306. Phillips, Alice Mary. Los Angeles, a guide book comp. ...for the National educational association. L.A., Neuner co., 1907. 151 p. illus.
C CHi CL CLO CLSU CLU CPom CSd CSf CSfCP CSmH CSta CStmo CU-B NjR UPB ViU

4307. Pictorial American, pub. Greater Los Angeles illustrated, the most progressive metropolis of the twentieth century. L.A. [1907?] 224 p. illus., ports.
C CStmo

4308. [Pierce & McConnell] [Los Angeles views] [n.p., n.d.] unp. illus. A collection of mounted photographs of landmarks and commercial establishments in Los Angeles, taken about 1893.   CL

4309. Pig 'n' whistle corp. Annual report. CL has 1951–54.

4310. Pirtle, John A. The views herein are from photos, and represent some of the beauty spots on Verdugo canyon tract... L.A., Topogravure print. co. [190–?]
CSmH

4311. Police relief association. Annual souvenir... [L.A.] 1911.   CSmH

4312. Porter, Florence Collins, ed. The story of the McKinley home for boys. The Woman's auxiliary of the McKinley home for boys, publishers... L.A., Times-mirror, 1921. 76 p. illus., ports.   CL CSmH

4313. Potter, Bernard. Los Angeles, yesterday and today. L.A., Wetzel pub. co. [1950] 201 p.
CBb CBev CLU CO CStmo NN OU

4314. Powell, Lawrence Clark. Islands of books. L.A., Ward Ritchie, 1951.   CRcS

4315. —— Recollections of an ex-bookseller. L.A., Zeitlin & Ver Brugge, 1950. 17 p.   CLU

4316. —— Ten years (almost) of Rounce & coffinism. L.A., The Rounce & coffin club, 1941. 15 p.   CLU

4317. Powell, William J. Black wings. L.A., Ivan Deach, jr., 1934. 218 p. illus., ports., map.   CHi

4318. Power, Ralph Lester. Libraries of Los Angeles and vicinity... L.A., Univ. of So. Calif. press [c1921] 63 p.   C CL CLO CLSU CLU

4319. Powers, Luther M. ...Reports on the sanitary investigation of Owens river and the Los Angeles aqueduct by health commissioner Luther M. Powers and city chemist E. H. Miller, as shown by their depositions taken in the action of Hart vs. the city, et al., together with annotations as to scientific authorities upon the technical questions referred to... [L.A.? 1914?] 29 p.
CSmH

4320. Precipice cañon water co. Articles of incorporation and by-laws... L.A., E. H. Freeman, 1887. 15 p.
CHi

4321. Protestant Episcopal church in the U.S.A. Los Angeles (Diocese) Journal of the fifth annual convention...held in St. Paul's Pro-cathedral, Los Angeles, Cal., May 16 and 17th, A. D., 1900. L.A., Norman V. Lewis, print., 1900. 111 p.   C

4322. Public school teachers' alliance of Los Angeles. Constitution... [L.A.] H. M. Lee & bros. print., 1898. 16 p.   CSmH

4323. Purdy, Mary. The governorship of John Gately Downey of California, 1860–62. Stanford, Author, 1933.
CStclU

4324. Purex corporation, ltd., Lakewood. Annual report.
CL has 1950–60.

4325. Putnam, Frank B. First bank in El Pueblo. [L.A., 1956–57] [9] l. of mounted clippings.   CU-B

4326. Quinton, John Henry. Report upon the distribution of the surplus waters of the Los Angeles aqueduct by J. H. Quinton, W. H. Code, Homer Hamlin, advisory engineers. L.A., 1911. 25 p.   CSmH

4327. Raulston, Marion (Churchill) Memories of Owen Humphrey Churchill and his family. [L.A.] 1950. [97] p. illus., ports.   CHi CLU

4328. Real estate and building association of Los

Angeles. Constitution and by-laws... L.A., Mirror bk. and job print., 1875. 16 p.   CSmH

4329. Real estate circular. Large sale of valuable real estate!! in the city of Los Angeles...at public auction...the 24th of April, 1872... [L.A.] News job print. [1872] 10 p.   CSmH

4330. Redondo Beach co. ...Natural advantages of Redondo Beach for the accommodation of deep sea commerce. S.F., Crocker, 1888. 52 p.   CSmH

4331. —— Redondo Beach, the summer and winter resort of southern California. [n.p., 189–?] 8 p. illus.
CHi

4332. Redondo hotel, Redondo Beach. [n.p., 1895?] [20] p. illus.   CHi

4333. Reeves, Cuthbert Edward. ...The valuation of business lots in downtown Los Angeles, by Cuthbert E. Reeves and the Los Angeles Bureau of municipal research, Los Angeles, California. L.A., L.A. Bur. of municipal research, c1932. 38 p. plans, tables, diagrs. (Studies in land valuation, L.A. county, Calif. no. 1)
CLU CU-B

4334. Republic supply company of California. Annual report.
CL has 1956 60.

4335. Rice, Craig, ed. Los Angeles murders... N.Y., Duell, c1947. 249 p.
C CBb CBev CBu CHi CL CLO CLSU CLU CMerCL CMont CO CRcS CSf CSfMI CSluCL CStmo CViCL MoS

4336. Rice, Hallie Evelyn. Pio Pico, the last Mexican governor of California. [Berkeley, 1933] Thesis (M.A.)— Univ. of Calif., 1933.   CU CU-B

4337. Rice, William Broadhead. An account of an eccentric Angeleno; and example of early Los Angeles dialect humor. [n.p., n.d.] [5] p. Biography of Paul R. Hunt, died 1860.   CLU

4338. —— The Los Angeles star, 1851–1864; the beginnings of journalism in southern California... Berkeley, Univ. of Calif. press, 1947. 315 p.
Available in many libraries.

4339. —— Southern California's first newspaper; the founding of the Los Angeles star. L.A., G. Dawson, 1941. 54 p. Printed by Anderson & Ritchie.
C CHi CL CLO CLU CSd CSfCP CSfCW CSmH CU-B

4340. —— William Money, a southern California savant... L.A., Priv. print., 1943. 61 p.
C CBb CHi CL CLO CLSU CLU CO CSmH CU-B

4341. Richardson, James Hugh. For the life of me; memoirs of a city editor. N.Y., Putnam, c1954. 312 p.
CMont CP CSd CStmo

4342. Richardson, T. A. The industries of Los Angeles, California: her resources, advantages and facilities in trade, commerce and manufactures... L.A., Industrial pub. co., 1888. 179 p. illus.
C CL CLO CPom CSfCSM CU-B

4343. Richfield oil corp. Annual report.
CL has 1948–60.

4344. Rider, Arthur W. Historical address on the occasion of the 50th anniversary of the organization of the Southern California Baptist convention... L.A., So. Calif. Baptist convention [1941] 27 p.   CSmH

4345. Rieder, Michael. Los Angeles, California. [L.A., 1910?] [31] p. of illus.   CU-B

4346. Rineer, James Snyder. A study of the organization and management of the Los Angeles public library; a term report presented to the School of government, University of Southern California, in partial fulfillment of course requirements in 205ab. [n.p.] 1938. 96 l. diagrs. CL

4347. Ritchie, Ward. The Ward Ritchie press, and Anderson, Ritchie & Simon. [L.A.] 1961. 156 p. illus. "1000 copies of the trade edition." CHi

4348. Roberts, Belle McCord. A word in appreciation of Charles Heston Peirson... L.A., So. Calif. Edison co. [1926] 27 p. CHi

4349. Robinson, Madeleine J. The pulpit under the palm; story of the Pancake mission and its ministry and service to the unemployed during the dark days of the depression. [Riverside, 1944] 206 p. illus. CL

4350. Robinson, William Wilcox. Culver City, a calendar of events in which is included, also, the story of Palms and Playa del Rey together with Rancho de los Bueyes. L.A., Title guarantee & trust co. [c1939] [28] p. illus., map.
C CBev CHi CLO CLU CSmH CStmo CU-B

4351. —— Same. c1942. [28] p. illus., map.
CHi NN

4352. —— The Indians of Los Angeles; story of the liquidation of a people. L.A., Dawson, 1952. 42 p. (Early Calif. travels ser., 8) 200 copies printed by Muir Dawson.
C CLO CLSM CLgA CO CSS CSf CSjC CStmo CU-B

4353. —— Los Angeles from the days of the pueblo; together with a guide to the historic old Plaza area including the Pueblo de Los Angeles, state historical monument. S.F., Calif. hist. soc. [1959] 96 p. illus.
Available in many California libraraies and CoD MiD MoSU NN

4354. —— Profile of Los Angeles. [L.A., 1954] 16 p. illus. (L.A. county museum. Q., v.11, no. 4, Winter 1954) CLU

4355. —— San Pedro and Wilmington; a calendar of events in the making of the two cities and the Los Angeles harbor... L.A., Title guarantee & trust co., c1937. [24] p. illus., map.
C CHi CLSU CLU CSd

4356. —— Same. c1942. [24] p. illus., map.
CBev CLU CO CSmH CStmo CStrJC CU-B NN

4357. —— The story of Pershing square... L.A., Title guarantee & trust co., 1931. 37 p. illus.
C CBb CBev CHi CL CLO CLSU CLU CLob CO CP CSfU CSmH CStrJC CU-B

4358. —— The story of the Southwest museum. L.A., Ward Ritchie, 1960. 50 p. illus., ports.
CAla CHi CLSM CU-B

4359. —— What they say about the Angels... Pasadena, Val Trefz press [1942] 88 p. illus.
C CBev CHi CL CLO CLU CLgA CO CRic CSmH CU-B CViCL NN

4360. Rogers, Warren S. Mesa to metropolis; the Crenshaw area, Los Angeles. [L.A.? 1959] 20 p. illus. "Reprinted from a serialization in the *Angeles Mesa News-Advertiser*, September-October, 1959."
C CHi CL CLU CU-B

4361. Rotary club of Los Angeles. History of the Rotary club of Los Angeles, organized June 25, 1909, club no. 5, Rotary international. L.A., 1955. 311 p. illus., ports., map. CL

4362. Rueger, Henry, comp. and pub. Rueger's atlas of the city of Los Angeles. L.A. [n.d.] 75 l. maps.
CLU

4363. Ruess, Stella (Knight) Los Angeles in block print. [Hollywood, Bryant press, c1932] 23 l. illus.
C CSmH

4364. St. Denis (Ruth) school of dancing and its related arts, Los Angeles. [Catalog] Second season, 1916. CHi

4365. San Pedro. Board of trade. San Pedro; the harbor city. [L.A., Commercial print. house, 1903] 16 p. illus. CLU CU-B

4366. San Pedro merchants association. Your San Pedro home. [Anchor press, 1932?] 44 p. CHi

4367. Schwartz, Ellen Louisa. Some aspects of the Los Angeles city school districts' retirement system for the certified employee. [L.A.] 1943. Thesis (M.A.)— U.C.L.A., 1943. CLU

4368. Science research associates. What Los Angeles educators think of their school system; summary of results of educators opinion inventory conducted on March 17, 1953, by Lyle M. Spencer, president. L.A., L.A. city bd. of education [1953] 31 p. illus. CL

4369. Scigliano, Robert G. Democratic political organization in Los Angeles. [L.A.] 1952. Thesis (M.A.)— U.C.L.A., 1952. CLU

4370. Scott, Joseph. ...Joe Scott story; how a poor boy grew with great men to build a great city...as told to Edward Prendergast. [L.A., 1952] v.p. ports. CU-B

4371. Scratches; a volume of cartoons and caricatures of Los Angeles citizens and newspaper artists. [L.A., 1911] unp. CLU

4372. Scruggs, Baxter S. A man in our community; the biography of L. G. Robinson of Los Angeles, California. Gardena, Institute press, 1937. 134 p. illus., ports. CHi

4373. Seaboard finance co. Prospectus, 200,000 shares...common stock... [n.p.] 1946. 63 p. CHi

4374. Searing, Richard Cole. The McNamara case: its causes and results. [Berkeley, 1952] Thesis (M.A.)— Univ. of Calif., 1952. CU CU-B

4375. Security first national bank of Los Angeles. Annual report.
CL has 1947–60.

4376. —— [The California community foundation; four pamphlets on its aims and purposes] n.p. [1915–1935] 4 v. in 1. The foundation was originally named the Los Angeles community foundation. CL

4377. Security title insurance co. Annual report.
CL has 1954–60.

4378. Security trust & savings bank. El pueblo, Los Angeles before the railroads... [L.A.] Equitable branch of Security trust & savings bank, c1928. 80 p. illus., ports.
C CArcHT CBb CBev CHi CL CLLoy CLO CLSU CLU CLob CPom CSfP CSluCL CSmH CStmo CU-B MoHi NN

4379. —— Dept. of research and service. Industrial summary of Los Angeles for the year 1923–1928... L.A., 1924–1929. Annual.
C has 1923–27. CL has 1923–28. CLSU has 1923–28. CLU has 1927. CU-B has 1923–28.

4380. —— Highland Park branch. The five friendly valleys; the story of greater Highland Park... 2d ed. [L.A.] c1923. 48 p. illus., ports.
C CHi CL CLO CLSU CLU CSmH CU-B

4381. —— Research and publicity depts. "Since you were here before"; a story of the changes that have come to Los Angeles since it was host to the American bankers association in 1910 and 1921... L.A., c1926. [80] p. illus.

CL CLO CLSU CLU CLob CSmH

4382. Seewerker, Joseph. Nuestro pueblo; Los Angeles, city of romance... Bost., Houghton, 1940. 184 p. illus. Illus. by Charles Hamilton Owens.

Available in many libraries.

4383. Severance, Caroline M. (Seymour) Mother of clubs...Ed. Ella Giles Ruddy... L.A., Baumgardt, 1906. CHi CSd

4384. Sherwood, Frank P. The mayor and the fire chief; the fight over integrating the Los Angeles fire department. University, Ala., Univ. of Alabama press [c1959] 24 p. illus. (The Inter-university case program. Case ser. no. 43) CSfSt

4385. Shevky, Eshref, and Williams, Marilyn. Social areas of Los Angeles; analysis and typology. Berkeley, & L.A., Univ. of Calif. press, 1949. 172 p. maps.

Available in many California libraries and ViU

4386. ——, and Lewin, Molly. Your neighborhood: a social profile of Los Angeles. L.A., Haynes foundation, 1950. 35 p. (Pub. of the John Randolph & Dora Haynes foundation: Pamphlet ser., no. 14)

C CChiS CL CLO CLS CLSU CLU CO COHN CSS CSfSt CStmo CWhC ViU

4387. Shippey, Lee. The Los Angeles book. Photos. by Max Yavno. Bost., Houghton, 1950. 117 p. illus., map.

Available in many California libraries and NN ODa

4388. Shochat, Fern Dawson. The fiftieth anniversary of Dawson's book shop, 1905–1955. [L.A.? 1955] 23 p. illus., ports. CHi CLO CP CSfCW

4389. Shuler, Robert P. Julian thieves in politics ... L.A. [n.d.] 64 p. CHi

4390. —— "McPhersonism"; a study of healing cults and modern day "tongues" movements, containing summary of facts as to disappearances and reappearances of Aimee Semple McPherson. [L.A., 1924?] 128 p. illus. C CHi

4391. —— "Miss X"...[Aimee Semple McPherson] L.A. [192-?] 96 p. ports. CHi

4392. —— The strange death of Charlie Crawford. L.A., Author [1931] 64 p. CFS CLU

4393. Siegler corp. Annual report. CL has 1957, 1959.

4394. Simmons, Matty. On the house. Decorations by Fabrès. N.Y., Coward [1955] 259 p. illus. Los Angeles and San Francisco restaurants. CSfMI

**4395. Sketches of the Los Angeles fair; held by the Southern California horticultural society... [L.A.? 1878] [15] p. illus. CSmH CU-B

4396. Slater, E. O. Sanitary features of the Los Angeles aqueduct... [Easton, Pa., 1915] 10 p. CSmH

4397. Sleepy Lagoon defense committee. The Sleepy Lagoon case, prepared by the Citizens' committee for the defense of Mexican-American youth. L.A., [1943] 24 p. CLU CSmH

4398. Smart, William David. [Letter of William David Smart to H. I. Priestley, giving the history of the Mexican evangelical church of Los Angeles. L.A., Aug. 27, 1940] 2 l. Typew. CU-B

4399. Smith, Caroline Estes. The Philharmonic orchestra of Los Angeles; the first decade, 1919–1929. [L.A.], United print. co., 1930] 283 p. illus., port.

C CBb CHi CLU CRedl CSd CStmo ODa

4400. Smith, F. Leslie. A study of the distribution of character-building facilities in the immediate city district of Los Angeles. Prepared by F. Leslie Smith, research division, Community welfare federation. [L.A.] 1928. 48 l. CL

4401. Smith, Sarah Hathaway (Bixby) Adobe days; being the truthful narrative of the events in the life of a California girl on a sheep ranch and in El Pueblo de Nuestra Señora de Los Angeles... Cedar Rapids, Iowa, Torch press, 1925. 208 p.

C CAna CBu CHi CL CLLoy CLSU CLU CLgA COnC CPom CRedl CSalCL CSmH CStmo CU-B

4402. —— Same. Rev. ed. Cedar Rapids, Iowa, Torch press, 1926. 217 p.

CBb CCSC CChiS CHi CLO CLSU CLU CMartC CO CSd CSjC CVtCL

4403. —— Same. 3d ed. rev. L.A., J. Zeitlin, 1931. 148 p. illus., ports.

Available in many libraries.

4404. Society of colonial wars in the state of California. Officers and members, 1913. [L.A.? 1913?] [9] p. CHi

4405. —— Register. L.A. [189-?–
CHi has 1905, 1907, 1911, 1928, 1957. CSfCW has 1910.

4406. Sojourner truth industrial club, inc. Golden anniversary 1905–1954, October 17–21, 1954. [L.A., 1954] [16] p. illus., ports. CL

4407. Sokoloff, Lillian. ...The Russians in Los Angeles... L.A., 1918. 16 p. (So. Calif. sociol. soc. Sociol. monograph, no. 11)

C CBu CL CLSU CLU CSmH

4408. Somerville, J. Alexander. Man of color, an autobiography by Dr. J. Alexander Somerville; a factual report on the status of the American Negro today. L.A., Lorrin L. Morrison, print. and pub. [c1949] 170 p. port. CHi

4409. Southern California Baptist convention. We the Baptists of southern California. L.A. [n.d] 89 p. illus. CL

4410. Southern California business. v.1–18, no. 2; Feb. 1922–Feb. 1939. [L.A., 1922–39] illus., ports. Published by the Los Angeles chamber of commerce. Supersedes the *Los Angeles chamber of commerce bulletin.* No more pub.

CL has v.1–17. CLSU has [v.10–17] CLU has v.1, 4–18. CSmH CU-B has v.2–9.

4411. Southern California Edison co. Annual reports.

CHi has 1939, 1948–50, 1959. CL has 1950–60.

4412. —— Prospectus...December 9, 1947. [L.A., Parker & co.] 1947. 51 p. map. CHi

4413. Southern California gas co. Annual report. CL has 1937, 1940–46, 1948–59.

4414. —— Operating and financial statistics 1946–1956. [n.p., 1957] 47 p. map. CHi

4415. Southern California investment co. The Southern California investment company... L.A., F. A. Garbutt's print. house, 1886. 12 p. CSmH

4416. [Southern California symphony assoc.] Symphonies under the stars. Hollywood bowl mag. v.1–, 1922– [L.A.] 1922–

CL has 1923–56, 1958– CLSU has 1926, 1929–32, 1934–38, 1940, 1942, 1944–45, 1947–49, 1958– CLU has 1927–39, 1941, 1943–44, 1947–48, 1950, 1952–53. CSmH has 1922–23, 1925–47.

4417. Southern California water co. Prospectus...

36,000 preferred shares, 5½ convertible series... [L.A., Jeffries banknote co.] 1948. 45 p. map. CHi

4418. Southern counties gas company of California. Annual report.
CL has 1957–60.

4419. Spalding, William Andrew. William Andrew Spalding, Los Angeles newspaperman; an autobiographical account edited with an introduction by Robert V. Hine. San Marino, Huntington lib., 1961. 156 p. illus.
CHi CLSM CSmH

4420. Spilman, W.T. The conspiracy: an exposure of the Owens river water and San Fernando land frauds. L.A., The Alembic club [1912] 71 p. illus.
CLSM CSmH

4421. Spriggs, Elisabeth Mathieu. The history of the domestic water supply of Los Angeles. [n.p.] 1931. 80 l. port. CL

4422. Standard federal savings and loan association, Los Angeles. California here I come! [L.A., 1954?] [10] p. illus., map. CL

4423. Stanley, Norman S. No little plans, the story of the Los Angeles chamber of commerce. [L.A.? 1956?] 32 p. illus. Reprinted from *Southern California business,* Sept. 1956. C CL

4424. Steele, William Riggs. My early life... [L.A.? 1939] 18 p. port. CHi

4425. [Stephens, Bascom A.] ...Los Angeles; a succinct history of the city... L.A., Evening express, 1885. 10 l. Photostat copy of sheets from *Evening express* Oct. 20, 21, 24, 27–30, and Nov. 2, 1885. CL

4426. Sterling, Christine. Olvera street, its history and restoration... [L.A., Old mission print. shop] c1933. 26 p. illus. CHi CL CLSU CLU CStmo CU-B

4427. —— Same. Los Angeles, Mario Valdez, c1947. 23 p. C CHi CLO

4428. Stevenson, Jonathan Drake. Selected letters from the J. D. Stevenson letter book June 1846–May 1847. N.Y., N.Y. hist. soc. [n.d.] 31 p. Mimeo. CSto

4429. Stewart, Pearl Pauline (Stamps) Abel Stearns: California pioneer, 1798–1871. [Berkeley,] 1925. 474 l. illus., ports., map. Thesis (M.A.)— Univ. of Calif., 1925. CU CU-B

4430. Stimson, Grace Heilman. Rise of the labor movement in Los Angeles. Berkeley, Univ. of Calif. press, 1955. 529 p. tables. (Pub. of the Inst. of industrial relations, Univ. of Calif.) Bibliography: p. 501–513.
C CHi CL CLO CLS CLU CP CSd CSf CStmo

4431. Stirdivant, Clarence Edwin. Recruitment, examination and assignment of certificated personnel in the Los Angeles city school districts. [L.A.] 1949. Thesis (M.A.)— U.C.L.A., 1949. CLU

4432. Stock, Chester. ...Rancho La Brea; a record of Pleistocene life in California... L.A. [Phillips print. co. 1930] 82 p. illus., map. Bibliography: p. 75–79.
C CChiS CL CLO CLS CMartC CSf CSmH CStmo CStrJC CU-B
Other editions followed. CHi (1942) CL (1942) CLSU (1949) CLgA (1956) CO (1942) CP (1956) CSfCSM (1949) CU-B (1942) CViCL (1953)

4433. Stoker, Charles. Thicker 'n thieves. Santa Monica, Sidereal co. [c1951] 415 p.
CBb CHi CL CLU CStclU CStmo CU-B

4434. Sturtevant, Edmund D. Catalogue of rare water lilies and other choice aquatic plants, 1907–'08. Established 1876... [L.A., Kruckberg press, 1907] 16 p. illus. CHi

4435. Sumner, Ann. Pioneer families of Los Angeles... [L.A., 1935] illus., ports. Loose-leaf, typew. "Articles written for the late *Los Angeles evening express* ...from August through December, 1926." CLU

4436. Sumner, C. A., & co. Los Angeles: the paradise of America... L.A. [1888] CL

4437. Sunset club, Los Angeles. Annals...v.1– , 1905– L.A. [Young & McCallister] 1905–
CHi has 1927. CL has 1905, 1916, 1927, 1957.

4438. —— Final meeting of our first forty years, June 28, 1895–May 31, 1935. [L.A., G. Rice & sons, 1935?] 32 p. port. CHi CLU

4439. Sunset press, pub. A picture tour of Los Angeles... L.A., S.F. [n.d.] [45] p. of illus. CSd CU-B

4440. Superior oil co. Annual report.
CL has 1951–60.

4441. Swigart, William Russell. Biography of Spring street in Los Angeles... [L.A., Author, 1945] 190 p. C CBb CL CO CSmH NN

4442. Taber, G. Major. Evidences of prehistoric inhabitants... L.A., Humanitarian review off. [1897?] 11 p. CSmH

4443. Tarakanoff, Vassili Petrovitch. Statement of my captivity among the Californians. Written down by Ivan Shiskin, and translated from the Russian by Ivan Petroff, with notes by Arthur Woodward. L.A., Dawson, 1953. 50 p. illus. (Early Calif. travels ser., 16) 200 copies printed by Plantin press.
Available in many libraries.

4444. Taylor, Katherine Ames. The Los Angeles tripbook... N.Y., Putnam [c1928] 94 p. illus.
C CL CLSU CPom CSmH CU-B MiD NN

4445. Technical glass company, inc. Catalogue 336, popular priced glassware. [n.p., 192–?] [21] p. illus. CHi

4446. Telautograph corp. Annual report.
CL has 1950, 1954–60.

4447. Thomas, Lately [pseud.] Vanishing evangelist [the Aimee Semple McPherson kidnapping affair] N.Y., Viking press, 1959. 334 p. illus., ports.
C CHi CL CStmo

4448. Thompson and co., comp. & pub. Historical and descriptive review of the industries of Los Angeles, 1886–7... [L.A., 1887] 154 p. illus. CU-B

4449. Thompson manufacturing co. [Catalog of lawn sprinklers and hardware specialties]
CHi has 1923, 1925.

4450. Thriftimart, inc. Annual report.
CL has 1957–61.

4451. Thrifty drug stores co., inc. Annual report.
CL has 1954–60.

4452. Tichenor, Henry Mulford. A wave of horror; a comparative picture of the Los Angeles tragedy. St. Louis, National Rip-Saw pub. co., 1912. 31 p. CLU

4453. Tidewater oil co. Annual report.
CL has 1956–60.

4454. Tilton, George F., comp. ...Tilton's trolley trip. L.A., c1909. CSmH

4455. Times-mirror co. Annual report.
CL has 1954–59, 1960.

4456. Title guarantee and trust co. Mural paintings in the Title guarantee building. L.A. [c1931] [16] p. illus. CHi

4457. Title insurance and trust co. Annual report.
CHi has 1957–59. CL has 1954–60.

4458. Toro, Juan de. Brief sketch of the colonization of California and foundation of the pueblo of Our Lady of Los Angeles... L.A., Daily commercial job print. house, 1882. 13 p. CU-B NHi

4459. Townsend, Francis Everett. New horizons (an autobiography) Chicago, J. L. Stewart, 1943. The proponent of the "Townsend plan." CSd

4460. Traid corp., Encino. Annual report. CL has 1958.

4461. Treanor, Thomas Coghill. John Treanor, a sketch of his life... L.A., Zamorano club, 1937. 85 p. CBb CHi CL CLO CLSU CLU CSmH CU-B

4462. The true history of the McNamara case; speeches of Anton Johannsen, Clarence Darrow and Mother Jones given at the Labor Temple, August 7, 1915, under the auspices of the Industrial council. Kansas City, Mo., Carpenter Local no. 61 [1915?] 32 p. CLU

4463. Truman, Benjamin Cummings. Los Angeles, the queen city of the angels. L.A., M. Rieder, c1904. [63] p. illus. CHi CL

4464. [Turner, Burnett C.] Proposed Los Angeles civic center. [n.p., 1947] v.p. illus., maps. CL

4465. Underwood, Agness. Newspaperwoman. N.Y., Harper [c1949] 297 p. CHi

4466. Union labor temple association. By-laws... as amended January 21, 1920. [L.A., 1920] 8 p. CHi

4467. Union league club. By-laws. L.A., Kingsley and Barnes print., 1891. C

4468. —— Twenty-fifth anniversary. [L.A., H. T. Watson, 1914] [154] p. illus., ports. CL CLU NN

4469. Union oil company of California. Annual report. CHi has 1944, 1948–49, 1953–54, 1959. CL has 1920–52, 1954, 1956–60.

4470. —— 50 years of progress, the story of Union oil company. [n.p., 1940] 31 p. illus. Reprinted from *Petroleum world*, May, 1940. CHi

4471. —— This is Union oil center. L.A. [n.d.] CL

4472. Union Pacific railway co. The solution of the Los Angeles station problem offered by the Union Pacific system... [L.A., 1925] 1 v. CSmH

4473. United California bank. Annual report. CL has 1955–61.

4474. U.S. Board appointed to locate a deep-water harbor...at Port Los Angeles or at San Pedro, Cal. Deep-water harbor at Port Los Angeles or at San Pedro, Cal. ... [Wash., D.C., Govt. print. off., 1897] 330 p. maps. (55th Cong. 1st sess. S. Doc. 18) Report made to U.S. Secretary of war by J. G. Walker, Rear-admiral U.S.N., chairman. C CHi CL CLO CLSU CLU CSmH CStmo (reprint) CU-B

4475. —— **Bureau of reclamation.** Copies of contracts between United States Department of interior, Bureau of reclamation, and Metropolitan water district, city of Los Angeles, Southern California Edison co., ltd., for water and power from Boulder dam. [L.A.] Reprinted by Los Angeles Examiner [1930] 18 p. CSmH

4476. —— **Citizens service corps., Los Angeles.** A report on civilian war services, June 30, 1943. H. F. Whittle, volunteer director. [L.A.] 1943. 16 l. CL

4477. —— **Engineer department.** ...Deep-water harbor at San Pedro bay. The report of a board of engineer officers of the U.S. Army as to the proposed deep-water harbor at San Pedro or Santa Monica bays. [Wash., D.C., Govt. print. off., 1892] 120 p. fold. maps. (52d Cong. 2d sess. H. Ex. Doc. no. 41) CL CLSM

4478. —— Report of the Board of U.S. engineers of 1892 locating the deep-water harbor for Los Angeles at San Pedro or Santa Monica bays. L.A., Times-mirror, 1894. 25 p. CSmH

4479. —— **Public health service.** Report of a survey of the city Health department of Los Angeles... April-August, 1939. [Sacramento, State print. off., 1940] 461 p. illus. CL CLO CLSU CLU CO CSf CU-B

4480. U.S. Borax and chemical corp. Annual report. CL has 1957–60.

4481. University club of Los Angeles. The Toreador, 1898–1948, fiftieth anniversary number. L.A. [Ward Ritchie, 1948?] 63 p. illus., ports. CHi CLO

4482. —— Twenty-fifth anniversary year book. L.A., 1924. 95 p. illus., ports. List of members included. CLU CSfP

4483. Utility appliance corp. Annual report. CL has 1950–59.

4484. Valdivia, Antonio de, Father. Sagrada trecena al thaumaturgo seraphico, á el Chrisostomo Franciscano San Antonio de Padua. Dispuesta por el P. Fr. Antonio de Valdivia, predicador iubilado, y actual predicador mayor del Convento de las Llageas de N.P. S. Francisco de la ciudad de Los Angeles... Con licencia, en la puebla por Diego Fernandez de Leon, y por su original en Mexico por la viuda de Miguel de Ribera Calderon [17—] [16] p. CSmH

4485. [Van Norden, Rudolph Warner] Pacific electric railway company. [L.A., 1912] [109] p. CSmH

4486. Van Tuyle, Bert, comp. Know your Los Angeles; an unusual guide book. L.A., c1938. 44 p. illus., map. CSmH CStmo

4487. —— Same. L.A., E. P. Wallace press. 68 p. CLSU

4488. —— Same. 3d ed. L.A., Ahlrich, c1941. 44 p. illus., map. CBev

4489. Vidor, King Wallis. A tree is a tree. N.Y., Harcourt, c1953. 315 p. illus., ports. CL CSd CU CU-B

4490. Volunteers of America, Los Angeles. ... Annual report. 1939/40– L.A., 1940– CU-B has 1939/40.

4491. Wagenseller-Durst, inc. Bullocks inc. L.A., 1950. CL

4492. Wagner, Anton. Los Angeles; werden, leben und gestalt der zweimillionenstadt in Südkalifornien... Leipzig, Bibliographisches institut, ag., 1935. 295 p. illus. maps. C CBb CL CLO CLSU CLU CSmH CU-B CWhC NHi NN

4493. [Wagner, Henry Raup] The earliest documents of El Pueblo de Nuestra Señora, la Reina de los Angeles. [L.A., 1931] 5 p. facsims. "65 copies printed for Henry R. Wagner for members of the Zamorano Club and a few other friends by Bruce McCallister." CHi CL CLSM CSmH MWA

4494. [Ward bros., Columbus, Ohio] pub. Souvenir of Los Angeles and vicinity. c1886. 8 p. illus. CLU

Other editions followed.　C (1888)　CHi (c1898)
CL (1887)　CP (1887)　CSfCP (1887)　CSmH (1888)
CU-B (1887)

4495. —— Winter scenes in Los Angeles... c1889.
8 p.　　　　　　　　　　　　　CLU　CSmH　CU-B

**4496. Warren & Bailey company, Los Angeles,
San Francisco & Fresno.** Catalog C...mine, mill and
industrial supplies, valves, boiler fittings, steam specialties, belting, hose, packing, insulating materials, roofing,
1937. [n.p., R. R. Donnelly & sons co., c1938]　186 p.
illus., part. col.　　　　　　　　　　　　　CHi

4497. Water and power problems of the Los Angeles
metropolitan area and its industrial and commercial activity. Issued by Los Angeles Chamber of commerce, the
Metropolitan water district of southern California, Southern California Edison company, ltd., Los Angeles gas and
electric corporation, Department of water and power,
city of Los Angeles. [L.A., 1931]　32 p. illus., map.
　　　　　　　　　　　　　　　　　　CLU

4498. Webb, Jack. The badge. Englewood Cliffs,
N.J., Prentice-Hall, 1958.　310 p. illus. Los Angeles police
department.
　C　CL　CLLoy　CLU　CMont　CSd　CSluCL　CViCL

4499. Weber show case & fixture co. Catalogue
no. 2 of display cases...　[L.A., 1909?]　16 p. illus.
　　　　　　　　　　　　　　　　　　CHi

4500. Weinstock, Matt. Muscatel at noon. N.Y.,
Morrow, 1951.　215 p.　　　　　CHi　CStmo　CViCL

4501. —— My L.A. ...　N.Y., Current bks., 1947.
239 p. illus.
Available in many libraries.

**4502. Welfare council of metropolitan Los An-
geles. Research department.** Report of the Midnight
mission study; a study of the clients served by the Midnight mission, brief history of such services in Los Angeles, service statistics of the agency...　1947.　36 l.
tables, diagrs. (Special report ser. no. 8)　　　CL

4503. [West, Henry Hebard] comp. The Western
union telegraph; photographs and letters, etc. of the old
timers, 1885–1900...　[n.p.] 1939.　4 v. illus., ports.
Typew. Contains documents and letters (part manuscript
and photostat) mounted autographs, photographs and
newspaper clippings.　　　　　　　　　　　CL

4504. West, Jessamyn. To see the dream. N.Y.,
Harcourt, c1957.　314 p.　　CRedCL　CU　CU-B

4505. Westates petroleum co. Annual report.
CL has 1952–60.

4506. Western air lines inc. Annual report.
CL has 1946, 1948–50.

4507. —— Wings over the West; the story of America's oldest airline. [L.A., 1951?]　48 p. illus.
　　　　　　　　　　　　　　　　CHi　CL

4508. The Westerners. Los Angeles posse. The
Westerners brand book, Los Angeles corral. v.1– , 1947–
S.F., 1948– illus., ports., fold. maps, facsims. Books for
1952–1955 never issued.
Available in many libraries.

4509. Westwood Hills press. Westwood Hills pictorial. L.A. [1946]　54 p. illus.　　　　　　CLU

4510. —— Westwood Hills, Westwood Village, Los
Angeles, California, America's most unique shopping
center. "A village within a city." [Westwood? 193–?]　37
p. illus., ports., map.　　　　　　　CLU　CU-B

4511. Wheelock, Walter. Angels flight... Glendale, La Siesta press, 1961.　36 p. illus. Funicular railway
in downtown Los Angeles.　　　　　　　　CHi

4512. White, Douglas. Los Angeles from an "auto."
An illustrated description of the world's most beautiful
"auto" ride on board the electric automobiles of the California Auto-Despatch co. L.A., Home print. co., 1906.
　　　　　　　　　　　　　　　　　　CSmH

4513. White, Stephen M. Deep sea harbor; San
Pedro–Santa Monica; speech of Hon. Stephen M. White,
of California in the Senate of the United States, May 8,
9, & 12, 1896. Wash., D.C., 1896.　61 p.　　C　CHi

4514. Whiting, Perry. Autobiography of Perry
Whiting, pioneer building material merchant of Los An-
geles... L.A., Smith-Barnes corp. [c1930]　334 p. illus.,
ports.
　C　CBb　CHi　CL　CLO　CLSU　CLU　CSd　CSmH
CU-B

4515. Widney, Joseph Pomeroy. The greater city
of Los Angeles...　[L.A., 1938]　[8] p.
　　　　　　　CLO　CLSU　CLU　CSmH　CU-B

4516. —— Joseph Pomeroy Widney...founder of the
Los Angeles county medical association and the College
of medicine of the University of Southern California...
S.F., 1936.　10 p. illus., ports. Reprint from *California
and Western medicine*, April, May and June, 1936.
　　　　　　　　　　　　　　　　　CStmo

4517. Wielus, Isabel Christina. Las fiestas de Los
Angeles. [L.A.] 1946. Thesis (M.A.)—U.C.L.A., 1946.
　　　　　　　　　　　　　　　　　　CLU

4518. Willard, Charles Dwight. The free harbor
contest at Los Angeles... L.A., Kingsley-Barnes &
Neuner co., 1899.　211 p. illus., ports., maps.
　C　CHi　CLO　CLSU　CLU　CPom　CSd　CSdS
CSfCP　CSmH　CStmo　IC

4519. —— The Herald's history of Los Angeles city
... L.A., Kingsley-Barnes & Neuner co., 1901.　365 p.
illus., port., maps.
Available in many libraries.

4520. —— A history of the Chamber of commerce
of Los Angeles, California; from its foundation, September 1888, to the year 1900... L.A., Kingsley-Barnes &
Neuner co. [c1899]　322 p. illus., ports. Lists members
with brief biographies.
　C　CBb　CHi　CL　CLO　CLSU　CLU　CLob　CSdS
CSfP　CSjC　CSmH　CStmo　CU-B　MoS　NHi　NN

4521. Williams, Charles. Story of Aimee McPherson, was she kidnapped?...2d ed. L.A., Williams &
Williams, c1926.　36 p. Los Angeles evangelist and
founder of Four-Square Gospel church.　　　CLU

**4522. Williamson, Martha Burton (Woodhead),
ed.** Ladies' clubs and societies in Los Angeles in 1892,
reported for the Historical society of southern California
... L.A., Elmer R. King, c1925.　85 p. illus.
　　　　　　　　　CHi　CL　CSmH　CStmo

4523. Willy, J. Knight. The story of the Los Angeles Statler. Evanston, Ill., Hotel monthly press, 1953.
　　　　　　　　　　　　　　　　　　CSd

4524. Wilshire boulevard hotel co. Trust indenture. Wilshire boulevard hotel company to Security trust
& savings bank, trustee... L.A., Flint & MacKay [1919]
78 p.　　　　　　　　　　　　　　　CSmH

4525. [Wilshire country club] 25th anniversary
issue, 1919–1944. L.A., 1944.　19 p. (Wilshire club news,
v.11, no. 9, Sept. 1944)　　　　　　　　　CHi

4526. Wilson, Henry L. The bungalow book. 2d ed.
L.A., Author [c1907]　[112] p. illus., plans.　　CHi

4527. Wilson, James Q. A report on politics in Los
Angeles. Cambridge, Joint center for urban studies of the

Massachusetts inst. of technology and Harvard univ., 1959. v.p. illus.   CL

4528. Wittemann, Adolph, pub. Souvenir of Los Angeles; photogravures. N.Y., Albertype co., 1894. 16 pl.   C-S CL

4529. Wittemann bros., pub. Los Angeles and vicinity. [N.Y., c1886] 12 pl.   CL CLU

4530. Women's athletic club of Los Angeles. [Program] Nov. 1935–Nov. 1939, 1940–Sept. 1941, Nov. 1941, Jan.-Apr. 1942. L.A. [1935–1942] 1 v. illus., ports.   CU-B

4531. Wood, Berthelot. Why "The Times" is first ... [L.A., Times-mirror, 1924] 31 p.   CSmH

4532. Wood, Harvey. Personal recollections of Harvey Wood, with an introduction and notes by John B. Goodman III. Pasadena, 1955. 27 p. illus., ports., maps, facsims. (Scraps of Californiana, no. 1) Printed for members of the Zamorano club.
CBb CHi CLO CLSM CSjC

4533. Wood, Richard Coke. The history of the Owens Valley and the Los Angeles water controversy. Stockton, 1923 (i.e. 1934). 91 p. mounted illus. Thesis (M.A.) — College of the Pacific, 1934.   CStoC

4534. Woodbury business college. Annual catalogue... [L.A.? 1895?] 36 p. illus.   CHi

4535. Woodman, Ruth C., comp. Story of the Pacific coast borax company, division of Borax consolidated, limited. [L.A., Ward Ritchie, 1951] 58 p. illus., ports., map.   C CBaK CHi CLO CLU CSfCP

4536. Woodward, Lois Ann. ...Brand park or Memory garden... Berkeley, 1936. 8, 2 l. Typew.   CU-B

4537. —— ...Los Angeles plaza... Berkeley, 1936. 27 p.   CU-B

4538. —— ...Merced theater... Berkeley, 1936. 8 l. Typew.   CU-B

4539. —— ...Nuestra Señora la Reina de los Angeles... Berkeley, 1936. 21 p.   CU-B

4540. Woollacott, H. J. Fair Oaks ranch Lamanda Park, California... [L.A., C.E. Bireley co., 189–?] 3 l.   CSmH

4541. Workman, Boyle. Boyle Workman's The city that grew, as told to Caroline Walker... L.A., Southland pub. co., 1935 [i.e. 1936] 430 p. illus., port.
C CBb CCSC CHi CL CLLoy CLM CLO CLS CLSU CLU CLgA CLob CPom CSd CSmH CStmo CU-B NN UPB

4542. Writers' program. California. Los Angeles; a guide to the city and its environs...Sponsored by the Los Angeles county Board of supervisors. N.Y., Hastings house, 1941. 433 p. illus., maps. (Am. guide ser.) "Selective bibliography": p. 413–419.
Available in many California libraries and CoU MiD NHi NN ODa T UPB WM

4543. —— —— Same. Completely revised. 2d ed. N.Y., Hastings house, 1951. 441 p. illus., maps. (American guide ser.) "Sponsored by the Los Angeles County Board of Supervisors." Bibliography: p. 421–427.
Available in many California libraries and MiD MoS NN ODa OrU

4544. Yeatman, Walter C., and Jones, Allen. A study of population trends in Los Angeles and the nation ...Prepared for the Citizens committee for city and county consolidation. L.A., 1933. 45 l. (L.A. Bur. of municipal research. General study no. 5)
CL CLO CLSU CLU

4545. Yoshioka, Ben Tsutomu. In-service training of the police officers in the Los Angeles police department and the Los Angeles Sheriff's department. [Berkeley, 1941] Thesis (M.A.)—Univ. of Calif., 1941.   CU

4546. Young, John Parke, ed. Los Angeles: its economic and financial position. Specially prepared for Dulin & co. by Young & Koenig, inc. ... L.A., Dulin & co. [c1936] 31 p. illus.   C CLO CLU

4547. Young, Pauline Vislick. The pilgrims of Russian-town... Chicago, Univ. of Chicago press [c1932] [296] p. illus.   CBb CU

4548. Young, William Stewart. A history of Hollenbeck home... L.A. [Print. Jeffries banknote co.] 1934. 270 p. illus., ports. A famous "old folks home" in Los Angeles.   C CHi CL CLO CLU CSmH

4549. Young men's Christian association, Los Angeles. [Brochure] [L.A.] 1908. [96] p.   CHi

4550. Young's Los Angeles, California; city railway directory and street number guide. Accurately locating any given number on any street or avenue... L.A., L.W. Young, c1904. 180 p. fold. map.   C

4551. Zamorano club. A bookman's view of Los Angeles. Published for members of the Grolier club, by members of the Zamorano club. L.A., 1961. 107 p. illus., facsims.   CHi CLSM

4552. —— The roster. Zamorano club, Los Angeles & Roxburghe club, of San Francisco. S.F., Grabhorn, 1955. 32 p.   CHi CLU CSf

4553. —— The Zamorano 80; a selection of distinguished California books made by members of the Zamorano club. L.A. [Castle press] 1945. 66 p. illus., facsims.   CBb CHi CLgA CSf

4554. Zimmerman, Paul. The Los Angeles Dodgers. N.Y., Coward [1960] 221 p. illus.   CSfMI

Monrovia

4555. Davis, Charles F., ed. History of Monrovia and Duarte...Mr. and Mrs. E. B. Norman, authors of Duarte history. Narrative and biographical. Monrovia, Cawston, 1938. 229 p. illus., ports.
CHi CL CLU NN

4556. —— The Monrovia blue book, a historical and biographical record of Monrovia and Duarte... A.H. Cawston, managing editor and pub. Monrovia, 1943. 147 p. illus., ports. Based in part upon the author's: *History of Monrovia and Duarte*, 1938.
C CHi CL CLU CMon CSmH

4557. —— Monrovia–Duarte community book... Monrovia, Cawston, 1957. 384 p. illus., ports., facsims.   C CHi CL CLU CMon CU-B

4558. ——, pub. Picturesque Monrovia. [Monrovia 1929] 64 p. pl.   CLO CSmH

4559. Monrovia. City planning commission. Master plan: research analysis proposals, 1954; Simon Eisner, city planning consultant. Rev. 1955. Monrovia, [1955] 184 p.   CMon

4560. —— **City school district.** Report of the survey, April 1957. [Irving R. Melbo, director] [Monrovia?] Bd. of trustees, 1957. 379 p.   CMon

4561. —— **First Presbyterian church.** Golden jubilee, 1888–1938. [Monrovia, Commercial print. dept., Monrovia newspost, 1938?] [24] p. illus., ports.   CU-B

4562. —— **Ordinances, etc.** Municipal code: general ordinances of the city, adopted, November 5, 1957, effective, December 5, 1957, operative, January 1, 1958;

published by order of the City council. Tallahassee, Municipal code corp., 1957. 589 p.   CMon

4563. Monrovia–Duarte union high school. Report of the survey, April, 1951. [Irving R. Melbo, director] [Monrovia?] Bd. of trustees, 1951. 359 p.   CMon

4564. Robinson, William Wilcox. Monrovia; a calendar of events in the making of a city. L.A., Title guarantee & trust co. [c1936] [16] p. map.
C CBev CHi CLO CLU CStmo CStrJC CU-B CWhC

4565. —— Same. c1942.   CHi NN

4566. Wiley, John L. History of Monrovia... Pasadena, Pasadena star-news, 1927. 291 p. illus., ports.
C CBb CHi CL CLO CLU CLob COr CPom CSf CSmH CU-B MWA NN

Palos Verdes

4567. Historical records survey. California. Inventory of the Bixby collection in the Palos Verdes library and art gallery. ... L.A., Southern Calif. Hist. records survey project, 1940. 41 l.
CBb CLob CRedl CSd CSdS N ViW

4568. Hunt, Myron. Palos Verdes—where bad architecture is eliminated. [L.A.? 1927?] 15 p. illus. "Reprinted from *Pacific coast architect*, April 1927."
C

4569. Lewis, Edward Gardner. Palos Verdes, Los Angeles. [Atascadero, Atascadero press, 1922?] 31 p. illus., ports., maps.   CU-B

4570. —— Trust indenture Palos Verdes project between E.G. Lewis and Title insurance and trust company, trustee... L.A., 1921. 122 p.
C CL CLSU CLU CU-B

4571. Palos Verdes, Los Angeles. [Atascadero, Atascadero press, n.d.] 46 p. illus., ports., maps, plans.
C

4572. Palos Verdes bulletin, v.1–8, no. 8; Nov. 1924–May/June 1933. Palos Verdes Estates, 1924–33. illus., ports. mo. Publication suspended Nov. 1931–Sept. 1932, inclusive.
C has v.1–8, Nov. 1924–May/June 1933. CL has v.1–7, Nov. 1924–Oct. 1931. CSf has v.5–7 no. 2, Jan. 1929–Feb. 1931. CSmH has v.1 no. 1–13, v.2 no. 1–12, v.3 no. 1–11, v.4 no. 1, 7–11, v.5 no. 1–7, 9–10, v.6 no. 4, 8, 11–12, v.7 no. 1–5. CU-B has v.1–4.

4573. Palos Verdes Estates. Building regulations of Palos Verdes Estates, Los Angeles county. L.A., Giles pub. co., c1924. 162 p.   C

4574. —— Palos Verdes Estates; prominent among the world's famous residential communities. [L.A., n.d.] [24] p. illus.   C

4575. —— The Palos Verdes of today, 1926. [L.A.? 1926] 20 p. illus., map.   C CU-B

4576. Palos Verdes homes association. ...Protective restrictions, Palos Verdes Estates, Los Angeles, California. Articles of incorporation and by-laws... L.A. [1923] 64 p.   C CLSU CLU

4577. Palos Verdes project. ...Meetings of underwriting subscribers of Palos Verdes project, Trinity auditorium, Los Angeles, 1922 [a report of proceedings and addresses] [L.A., 1922] 39 p. illus., ports., map.
C CLU CSmH NHi

4578. —— The protective restrictions for Palos Verdes Estates. [Prepared under the direction of Mr. Jay Lawyer, general manager of the Palos Verdes project.] 13 p. illus.   C

4579. Raup, Hallock Floyd. Rancho Los Palos Verdes. L.A., 1937. 17 p. illus., map.   CHi

4580. Sepulveda, José Loreto. [Invitation to a "Reunion de amigos" at Rancho Palos Verdes. L.A., 1853] 1 l.   CSmH

4581. La Venta. [n.p., n.d.] [11] p. pl.   C

Pasadena

4582. Ainsworth, Edward Maddin. Pot luck; episodes in the life of E. Parker Lyon. Foreword by Irvin S. Cobb. Hollywood, Putnam, 1940. 201 p. illus., ports.
CHi CMon CSd CStmo

4583. Allen, Mary Louise. Education or indoctrination. Caldwell, Ida., Caxton, 1956. 216 p. Bibliography: p. [207]–211. The Pasadena public school controversy, 1950–51.   C CChiS CLS CStmo CViCL

4584. Annual register of organizations of Pasadena and vicinity...Comp. & pub. by Turner & Stevens co. ... 1st, 1935– Pasadena, 1935–
CHi (1938) CLSU (1947–48) CU-B (1939)

4585. Arroyo Seco water co. Rules and regulations for the distribution and sale of water... Pasadena, N. N. Farey & co., 1887. 8 p.   CHi

4586. Ashton, George Franklin. Upton Sinclair. [Berkeley, 1951] Thesis (M.A.) — Univ. of Calif., 1951.
CU CU-B

4587. Beard, William. City manager plan in Pasadena, California... [L.A.] 1938. 119 l. Thesis (M.A.) — U.C.L.A., 1938.   CLU

4588. Blair, William L., ed. Pasadena community book; in two parts, narrative and biographical. Pasadena, Cawston [c1943] 789 p. illus., ports.
CHi CLSU CLU CO NN
Other editions edited by Clarence Fred Shoop and William L. Blair.
C (1947) CHi (1947) CL (1951, 1955)

4589. Boy Scouts of America, Southern California area, Troop 40. Guide to the San Rafael area, Pasadena. Pasadena, San Rafael P.T.A., 1955. [34] p. illus., map.   C CL CLO CP

4590. Branson, Helen Kitchen. Let there be life; the contemporary account of Edna L. Griffin, M.D. Pasadena, M.S. Sen [c1947] 135 p. port.   CHi

4591. Bryan, Paul G. Pasadena pioneer pictorial. [Mountain View mausoleum assoc., 1954]   CP

4592. Busch gardens. Busch gardens...private estate of Mrs. Lillie Busch. Photo-gravures. Brooklyn, Albertype co. [n.d.] [12] pl.   CLU

4593. California institute of technology. ...Annual catalogue. 1st– 189–
CL has 1920– to date. CU-B has 4th, 1895/96.

4594. —— The inauguration of President Lee A. DuBridge. Pasadena, 1946. 55 p. port. (Bul. of the Calif. inst. of tech., v.55, no. 4)   CLU

4595. California taxpayers' association, inc. ... Report on city of Pasadena, California...for fiscal year ending June 30, 1928... L.A., 1929. 196 p.   CU-B

4596. —— Survey of the Pasadena city schools... L.A., 1931. 331 p.   CL CLS CLSU CO CU-B

4597. Carew, Harold David. History of Pasadena and the San Gabriel valley, California. With personal sketches of...men and women, past and present... [Chicago] Clarke, 1930. 3 v. illus., ports., maps.
C CBb CBev CHi CL CLO CLSU CLU CPom CSf CSmH CSta CU-B CaBViPA MWA NN UPB

4598. Chapin, Alonzo Franklin. A book of the

crown city and its tournament of roses, Pasadena, California. [Pasadena, Pasadena daily news, 1907?] unp. illus., ports.   CL

4599. —— Thirty years in Pasadena, with an historical sketch of previous eras... [L.A.] 1929. 323 p. illus., ports. v.1 only published.
C CHi CL CLO CLSU CLU CLob CSmH CWhC NN

4600. Coleman chamber music association, Pasadena. ...Concerts 1904–1954. Pasadena, 1953. 19 p. illus., port.   CHi

4601. Consolidated electrodynamics corp. Annual report.
CL has 1948–58.

4602. Coolidge rare plant gardens, inc. [Catalog. n.p., n.d.] 23 p. illus.   CHi

4603. Cottrell, Edwin Angell [and others] Pasadena social agencies survey... Pasadena, 1940. 378 p. maps. Photoprinted.   C CL CLSU CLU

4604. Daggett, C. D. Pasadena, the city of homes. Compliments of Los Angeles & Pasadena electric railway. 16 p.   NN

4605. [Damon, George Alfred] Picturesque Pasadena. [Chamber of commerce & civic assoc. of Pasadena, 19—?] 55 p. illus.
C CHi CL CLSU CSmH CU-B CViCL NN

4606. DeLanty, B.F. Municipal ownership of electric light and power in Pasadena, California; an address ...at the Public ownership league conference, Seattle, Wash. [Pasadena, Municipal print. dept.] 1928. 22 p. illus., tables, diagrs.   CLU

4607. Earley, T., comp. Pasadena, San Marino, and vicinity. [L.A., Western empire pub. co., 1894?] 30 p. illus., map.   CHi

4608. Las Encinas sanitarium. [Brochure] [n.p., 1935?] 30 p. illus., map.   CHi

4609. English classical school for girls. Annual announcement...
CHi has 1897/98.

4610. [Farnsworth, R. W. C.] comp. and pub. A southern California paradise (in the suburbs of Los Angeles). Being a historic and descriptive account of Pasadena, San Gabriel, Sierra Madre, and La Cañada; with important reference to Los Angeles and all southern California... Pasadena, 1883. 132 p. illus. "Pasadena directory": p. [127]–132.
C CHi CL CLO CLSU CLU CSd CSfWF-H CSjC CSmH CU-B KHi NHi

4611. Gibbs, Jeanie W. Memoirs of the Pasadena children's training society. Pasadena, 1930. 44 p. illus.   C

4612. Giddings, Jennie (Hollingsworth) I can remember early Pasadena. L.A., Priv. print. by L. L. Morrison [c1949] 141 p. col. port., maps.
C CBaB CBev CHi CL CLO CLU CO CP CSfU CSmH CStmo CU-B NN

4613. Gordon, Robert Matteson. The epic movement and the California election of 1934. Stockton, 1957. 225 p. maps, tables. Thesis (M.A.)— College of the Pacific, 1957.   CStoC

4614. Graham photo co. The Busch gardens, Pasadena, California. [L.A., n.d.] [16] p. of col. illus.
CHi CU-B

4615. Green, Adam Treadwell. Seventy years in California. [S.F.] Priv. print. [Taylor & Taylor] 1923. 42 p. port.   CHi CSf CSfP

4616. Green, Harriet L. Gilmor Brown, portrait of a man—and an idea... Pasadena, 1933. [21] p.
CSmH

4617. Happy thoughts from home thinkers. Pasadena, 1888. 35 p. Pub. by the Unitarian church? Contents: Pasadena animals.—The public schools.—The library.—Society.—Antiquities of Pasadena.—Business directory.
CP

4618. Hayden, Dorothea (Hoaglin) These pioneers. L.A., Ward Ritchie, 1938. 287 p. port.
C CBb CHi CSd

4619. [Heininger, Charles P.] pub. Album of Pasadena, Cal. and vicinity, containing forty-nine photographic views and interesting descriptive reading matter. S.F. [188–?] 18 p. illus.   CLO CP CSmH

4620. Hill, Clyde Milton. Report of the survey of the Pasadena city schools; a cooperative study, 1951–1952 [by] Clyde M. Hill and Lloyd N. Morrisett, directors of the study. Pasadena [1952?] 939 p. illus., maps.
CLO CLS CLU CSdS CSfSt

4621. —— Same. Abridged report... [Pasadena, Geddes press, print., 1952] 203 p. illus.
CLO CLU CSdS CSfSt

4622. Holder, Charles Frederick. All about Pasadena and its vicinity; its climate, missions, trails and cañons, friuts, flowers and game... Bost., Lee & Shepard; N.Y., C. T. Dillingham, 1889. 141 p. illus.
C CL CLO CLSU CLU CP CSd CSmH CU-B CoD MiD-B NHi NN

4623. —— The highlands of Pasadena (North Pasadena)... S.F., Crocker, 1889. 65 p. illus.
CL CP CSmH NN

4624. —— Pasadena; its climate, homes, resources, etc., etc. Issued under the auspices of the Pasadena, Cal., board of trade. Buffalo, N.Y., Matthews Northrup & co., 1888. 40 p. illus.   CL CLU CP CSmH

4625. Hopkins-Smith, pub. Pasadena and Pasadenans in honor of Pasadena's fiftieth birthday. [Pasadena, 1924]. 56 p. illus.   CHi

4626. Hotel Green. [L.A., Kingsley-Barnes & Neuner co., 19—?] [48] p. illus.   CU-B

4627. Same... [S.F., Norman Pierce co., print., c1905] 16 p. illus.   CU-B

4628. Hulburd, David. This happened in Pasadena. N.Y., Macmillan, 1951. 166 p. The Pasadena public school controversy, 1950–1951.
C CChiS CHi CLO CLS CLU CMerCL CSd CSdS CSfSt CStmo CViCL ViU

4629. Huntington hotel. The Huntington, Pasadena, California. [Pasadena? 19—] [24] p. illus., map.
CU-B

4630. —— The picture bridge, paintings by Frank M. Moore, word pictures by Don Blanding... [n.p., 1933?] 41 p. illus., map.   CHi

4631. In its fifty-fifth year, the Tournament of roses, present—memories of the past—a challenge for the future. [n.p., 1944] [36] p. illus.   CHi

4632. Jannoch nurseries. Descriptive price list of perennials. Pasadena [n.d.] 14 p.   CHi

4633. Knight, William H. Pasadena, gem city of southern California... Pasadena, Bd. of trade, 1893.
C-S

4634. Koiner, Carl Wellington. History of Pasadena's municipal light and power plant... [Pasadena, Municipal print. dept.] 1925. 36 p. illus.   CL CLU

4635. Lee, Glynn B. A study of the zenith of evolutionary socialism in California: Upton Sinclair and his crusade of EPIC. Chico, August, 1951. 125 l. Thesis (M.A.)— Chico state college, 1951.			CChiS

4636. Lukens, Theodore Parker. Pasadena, California, illustrated and described...Pub. by T. P. Lukens, Pasadena, Cal. Oakland, Elliott, 1886. 45 p. illus., map.
CHi CL CLU CP CSmH

4637. Lyman, Edward D. Homer P. Earle. L.A. [Ward Ritchie] 1946. 20 p.			CLO

4638. McCunn, Drummond J. A study of Pasadena and its public schools. [L.A.] 1950. Thesis (Ed.D.) — U.C.L.A., 1950.			CLU

4639. Macdonnell, James S. From a bank pulpit ... Pasadena, Castle press [1937] 103 p. port.
CL CSmH CU-B

4640. Miller, Eleanor. When memory calls...with pen drawings by Lewis D. Johnson... Gardena, Institute press, 1936. 225 p.			CHi

4641. Millikan, Robert Andrews. The autobiography of Robert A. Millikan. N.Y., Prentice–Hall, c1950. 311 p. illus.			CRedCL

4642. Milliken (C. S.) firm. [Catalog] Southern California iris gardens.
CHi has 1931.

4643. Montgomery, James M. ...Report on water system... Pasadena, 1958. 178 p. illus.			CS

4644. Moss, Edwin. Sixty years, the Church of the Angels, the Bishop's chapel... [Pasadena, 1951] 51 p. illus., ports.			C CHi CP CSmH CU-B

4645. Munro, J. S., & co., Oakland. Catalogue, auction sale of fine paintings from the Pasadena gallery of fine arts...commencing Thursday, November 13, 1919 ... [Oakland, J. W. McCombs, print.] 1919. [8] p.
CHi

4646. National commission for the defense of democracy through education. The Pasadena story; an analysis of some forces and factors that injured a superior school system. [Wash., D.C.] National educ. assoc. of the U.S., 1951. 39 p.			CChiS CLU CSdS

4647. North Pasadena land and water co. Articles of incorporation and by-laws... Pasadena, Pasadena and valley union print., 1885. 10 p.			CHi

4648. Oneonta club, South Pasadena. Oneonta club, organized April 1923... Constitution, by-laws, and roster. [South Pasadena, 1927] 3 v.			CSmH

4649. Orton school. Annual announcement...1897/ 98. [Pasadena, 1897?]			CSmH

4650. Pasadena. Board of trade. Illustrated souvenir book, showing a few Pasadena homes, with short descriptive data. [n.p.] 1897. 61 pl.
CHi CSmH

4651. —— —— Same. L.A., Kingsley-Barnes & Neuner co., press, 1898. 72 pl.			CSmH

4652. —— —— Same. L.A., Print. by Out West co., 1903. 96 p. illus.
C CLU CP CSfCW CSmH CU-B CoU MiD NHi

4653. —— Pasadena, crown of the valley... [Pasadena] 1892. 39 p. illus.			CLU CU-B
Other editions followed. Title varies. Publisher varies: 1894, E. Norman Baker. 1908, Van Ornum, Drake & Melville.			CL (1894) CLO (1894) CLU (1894, 191–?) CSmH (1894, 1908, 191–?) CU-B (1900, 1917) NHi (1908)

4654. —— Chamber of commerce and civic association. Pasadena, summer and winter... [Pasa-

dena] 1922. [32] p. illus.			CL CLO CSmH CU-B
Other editions followed: CHi (1951) CLO (1929) CSmH (193–?)

4655. —— Charters, ordinances, etc. Charter... adopted January 24, 1901. Amended February 16, 1905, March 3, 1909, January 21, 1913, April 29, 1919, May 16, 1921, May 18, 1923, January 17, 1927 and January, 1931. Also municipal ordinances affecting administrative affairs of the city. [Pasadena, Municipal print., dept.] 1931. 64 p.			CSmH

4656. —— —— Charter and ordinances of the city of Pasadena...prepared in accordance with an action of the city council at its meeting held the first day of August 1905. Pasadena, Morris-Thurston co., 1905.
CSmH

4657. —— —— Ordinances of the city of Pasadena, comp. and indexed by the city attorney, N. P. Conrey. Pasadena, Pasadena star, 1887. 160 p.			CHi CSmH

4658. —— Citrus fair. ...Annual citrus fair of the San Gabriel valley, to be held at Pasadena...[2d] 1885. [L.A., Print. Times-mirror co., 1885] 90 p. illus.
CLU CU-B

4659. —— City school district. Dept. of vocational education. Survey of occupations, Pasadena, California, June 1934... Pasadena, 1935. 11 p. Mimeo.
CP

4660. —— Classical school for boys. ...Classical school for boys. Pasadena [1897?] [4] p.			CHi

4661. —— First Congregational church. ...Seventy-five years of service, 1885–1960 [by Dr. Leonard W. Collins] [Pasadena? 1960?] 23 p. illus., ports.
CHi

4662. —— Mayor (Waterhouse) To the voters of the city of Pasadena [in regard to the purchase of the water plants] [Pasadena? 1906] [7] p.			CSmH

4663. —— Music festival. ...Annual Pasadena music festival...2d, 1937. [Pasadena, 1937] [4] p.
CU-B

4664. —— Presbyterian church. ...Fifty years, 1875–1925. [Pasadena, 1925] 19 p. illus.
CHi CSmH

4665. —— —— The story of the Pasadena Presbyterian church. Pasadena, 1945. 24 p. illus.			CHi

4666. —— Public library. Fine arts and Californiana dept., comp. Interesting women of Pasadena. [1931–] 2 v. Loose-leaf. Clippings from *Pasadena post* and *Pasadena star news*, 1931–			CP

4667. —— —— —— Men of Pasadena. [1938–] 4 v. Loose-leaf.			CP

4668. —— —— —— Pasadena history; miscellaneous collection of newspaper clippings from the *Pasadena star-news.* 1935–			CP

4669. —— —— —— Pasadena pamphlets...1892– 1908. illus., maps. Contents: Dr. Reid's Pasadena handbook, by H. A. Reid.—Pasadena, California, issued by Pasadena Board of trade.—Inside facts concerning the Pasadena and Mt. Wilson railway company.—Some interesting and picturesque drives in and about Pasadena, by Charles A. Day.—Pasadena and Sierra Madre mountain railway with references to other mountain railways.
CLO CP

4670. —— Throop memorial Universalist church. ... 1886–1936 by William Wallace Wilcox. Pasadena, Walter Ward, 1936. 48 p.			CHi CSmH

4671. Pasadena academy. Catalogue, 1887–1888, and prospectus of the California college of music... Pasadena, Star job print. co., 1888. 32 p.			C

4672. Pasadena art institute. Early prints of California from the Robert B. Honeyman collection, Pasadena art institute, 11 May to 29 June, 1952. [Pasadena, 1952] 15 p. Mimeo.   CHi

4673. Pasadena community book. v.1– 1943– Pasadena, A.H. Cawston, 1943– Editor, 1951– C.F. Shoop.
C (1951, 1955) CHi (1951, 1955) CLO CLU (v.1, 2, 4) CMon (1955) CSfCSM (1955)

4674. Pasadena community playhouse. Chronological list of productions... [Pasadena, 1917–38] Title varies.
CP has Nov. 1917 to July 1934. CSmH has Nov. 1917–[Aug. 13, 1938]

4675. —— Historical and organization outline of the Pasadena playhouse. [Pasadena?] 1938. 19 l.   CSmH

4676. —— Plays produced originally at the Pasadena playhouse. [Pasadena? n.d.] 12 p.   CSmH

4677. —— ...Midsummer drama festival, 1st–7th annual...1935–1941. [Pasadena, Login print. co., 1935–41] 7 v. illus.   CHi (3d 1937) CSmH

4678. Pasadena community playhouse association. The Community playhouse association of Pasadena; the Pasadena community guild. An outline of their organization with accompanying documents. [Pasadena] Pasadena playhouse press, 1933. 23 l.   CLU

4679. —— Yearbook. 1925/26. Pasadena [1925?]
CU-B

4680. Pasadena daily news. New Year's number... 1909–1911. Pasadena, 1909–1911. illus., ports.
C (1909) CU-B (1911) CoD (1909)

4681. —— Pasadena beautiful. Crown of the San Gabriel valley. The ideal city of homes. Pasadena [1904?] [71] p. illus.   CLU

4682. Pasadena evening post. Tournament of roses, New Year's number. Pasadena, 19—
C has 1921, 1923, 1925, 1927, 1929, 1931. CL has 1923, 1931. CLU has 1921.

4683. Pasadena lake vineyard land and water co. By-laws... Pasadena, Pasadena and valley union print, 1884. 8 p.   CHi

4684. Pasadena land and water co. Articles of incorporation and by-laws...L.A., Mirror-print, 1883. 14 p. Folded sheet: Water rules (inside cover)   CHi

4685. Pasadena orange growers' association. Annual report.
CHi has 1918/19–1927/28, 1929/30–1930/31.

4686. Pasadena savings and loan association. Valley of the Hahamog-na; Pasadena through two centuries. [Pasadena? 1952] [50] p. illus., map, ports.
CHi CL CLO CP

4687. Pasadena star, Pasadena. G.A.R. edition, Pasadena daily star; description of the climate, etc... Pasadena, 1877.   CU-B

4688. —— Pasadena, California, the city beautiful. Edition de luxe of the Pasadena evening star. [Pasadena] Star pub. co. [1902?] unp. illus.   CLU CSmH

4689. —— Same. [1904?] 64 l.   NN

4690. —— The fiftieth anniversary, 1886–1936. Pasadena, 1936. illus.   MoS

4691. —— Tournament of roses number. 1903–[Pasadena, Calif., 1903– illus., ports. Title varies: 1903, 1906 Souvenir of the Tournament of roses. Publisher varies.
C has 1906, 1920, 1922, 1926, 1930, 1941. CHi has 1928, 1940. CL has 1914, 1922, 1924, 1930. CLO has 1906, 1925.

CLSU has 1923–34. CLU has 1910, 1920, 1922, 1924, 1926, 1928, 1930, 1932. CRcS has 1938. CSf has 1906. CSmH has 1903, 1906, 1942, 1947. CU-B has 1906, 1910, 1928, 1933, 1940. NN has 1906.

4692. Pasadena star-news and the Pasadena post. Classified booster directory...1941. Pasadena, 1941. 24 p.
CHi

4693. [Pasadena] tournament of roses golden jubilee, 1889–1939. Pasadena, Login print. co., c1938. unp. illus. (part col.)   CL

4694. Pasadena tournament of roses pictorial. v.1–[1934– Pasadena, Login print. & bind. co. [c1934– illus. Annual.
C has 1934–35, 1949. CL has 1951–57, 1960–61. CLO has 1937–42, 1946–47, 1949–

4695. Pasadena tournament of roses review. 19—L.A., 19— illus. (part col.) Annual.
CL has 1948, 1950, 1952, 1956.

4696. Pasadena transfer & storage co. A thumbnail history of Pasadena. L.A., George Rice & sons [n.d.] [16] p. illus., ports.   CLO

4697. Pfeiffer, Clyde Emmett. A history of the Pasadena junior college. [L.A., 1941] 218 l. Thesis (M.A.) — Occidental college, 1941.   CLO

4698. Powell, Lawrence Clark. Vroman's of Pasadena. Pasadena, 1953. 14 p. 50 copies printed by Anderson, Ritchie & Simon, Los Angeles.
CLU CP CSd CU-B

4699. —— Same. [Garden City, N.Y., Doubleday] 1953. 14 p.   CLO

4700. The Raymond. East Pasadena, Los Angeles county, California. [Bost., Amer. print. co., 1886?] [32] p. illus.   CHi CSmH

4701. —— Same. [S.F., Norman Pierce co., c1904] [16] p. illus.   CU-B

4702. Raymond improvement co. Division no. 1. Raymond improvement company tract, adjoining Raymond hotel grounds, South Pasadena. L.A., L.A. Litho. co. [188–?] map.   CSmH

4703. Reid, Hiram Alvin. History of Pasadena, comprising an account of the native Indian, the early Spanish, the Mexican, the American, the colony and the incorporated city... Pasadena, Pasadena history co., 1895. 675 p. illus., ports. "Flora of Pasadena and vicinity. By Alfred James McClatchie": p. 605–649. "List of works consulted": p. 5–7.
C CHi CL CLO CLSU CLU CLob CSf CSmH CU-B N NN NHi

4704. —— Pasadena handbook; giving name and location of over two hundred natural objects, historic sights and structures, places of interest, mountain features, etc. in and around Pasadena. Pasadena, Glasscock's, 1905. 19 p. illus., port., map.   CLSU

4705. Rieder, Michael, pub. Pasadena, the crown of the valley. L.A., c1905. [64] p. (chiefly illus.)   C

4706. Riley, Richard James. Upton Sinclair and the 1934 California gubernatorial elections. [Chico] 1952. 111 l. Thesis (M.A.) — Chico state college, 1952.
CChiS

4707. Ritter, Lloyd E. The Chronicle, Pasadena's first newspaper, and its participation in the growth of the community. [L.A., 1950] 161 l. Thesis (M.A.) — Occidental college, 1950.   CLO

4708. Robinson, William Wilcox. Pasadena... L.A., Title guarantee & trust co., c1935. illus., map.
C CHi CLU CSd CU-B CWhC

Other editions followed. CAla (1955) CBev (c1942) CHi (1949, 1955) CLU (1949, 1955) CO (1942, 1955) CSluCL (1955) CSmH (c1942) CStmo (1949) CStrJC (c1942) NN (c1942) NbHi (1955)

4709. Rust (Edward H.) Palm nurseries, South Pasadena. Catalog. [L.A., Geo. Rice & sons, print., 1917?] 45 p. illus.   CHi

4710. Samuelsen, Rube. The Rose Bowl game. [1st ed.] Garden City, N.Y., Doubleday, 1951. 299 p. ports.
CHi CLO CStmo

4711. Saunders, Charles Francis. The story of Carmelita... Pasadena, A. C. Vroman, inc. [c1928] 54 p. illus.
C CBb CHi CL CLO CLSU CLU CLob CP CPom CRic CSd CSmH CU-B

4712. Security trust and savings bank. Pasadena and Maryland branches. Publicity dept. The story of Pasadena...3d ed. c1924. 48 p. illus., ports.
CL CLO CLU CSmH

4713. —— Same. 4th ed. 1927. 48 p. illus., ports.
C CHi CLob CU-B

4714. —— **South Pasadena branch.** On old Rancho San Pascual; the story of South Pasadena. South Pasadena, c1922. 48 p. illus.   CU-B

4715. —— Same. 1924. 48 p. illus.
C CHi CL CLO CLSU CLU

4716. Sinclair, Upton. Epic answers; how to end poverty in California. L.A., End poverty league [1934?] 32 p. Published also in *The epic plan for California.*
CHi

4717. —— The epic plan for California. N.Y., Farrar & Rinehart, inc., 1934. Contents: I, governor of California. — EPIC answers. — The lie factory starts. — Immediate EPIC.   CL CSd

4718. —— I, candidate for governor, and how I got licked... L.A., End poverty league, inc. [1935] 215 p. Published also in *The epic plan for California.*
CHi CRedCL CStoC

4719. —— I, governor of California and how I ended poverty; a true story of the future... L.A., End poverty league [1933?] 64 p. Published also in *The epic plan for California.*   CHi CMartC CRcS CSdS

4720. —— Immediate EPIC; the final statement of the plan. L.A., End poverty league [1934?] 38 p. Published also in *The epic plan for California.*   CSdS

4721. Social register association. ...South Pasadena and San Marino register... South Pasadena [1928] 96 p.   CSmH

4722. Sower, Edwin R. Tournament of roses, the Rose Bowl game; our first 70 years. [1959]   CP

4723. [Spalding, Graydon Edward] The Spalding collection. Pasadena playhouse, 1927–1935. [Pasadena, 1953] 2 v. in 1. Typew. Compiled in memory of the photographer, Charles Gordon Spalding.   CSmH

4724. Stanford research institute. Southern California laboratories. An economic survey of the city of Pasadena. South Pasadena [1959]   CP

4725. Stiles, Maxwell. The Rose bowl; a complete action and pictorial exposition of Rose bowl football... Ed. by Ward B. Nash... L.A., Sportsmaster publications [1946?] 128 p. illus.
CChiS CL CLSU CO CSf CU-B

4726. Stone, Irving. Rose Bowl town. [Printer's copy, n.d.]   CP

4727. Suesserott, H. H., pub. Souvenir of Pasadena, Calif. [Pasadena, c1887?] 12 pl.   C

4728. Throop polytechnic institute and manual training school. ...Annual catalogue...1st– , 189–?– Pasadena, 189–?–
CHi has 3d, 6th, 7th, 9th, 1894/95, 1897/98, 1898/99, 1900/01.

4729. Thurston, Albert G., pub. Illustrated souvenir book. [Pasadena? 1909?]   CP

4730. —— Thurston's strangers' guide to Pasadena ... Pasadena, c1920. 47 p.   CHi

4731. Union national bank of Pasadena. Builders of Pasadena. [1951]   CP

4732. United for California league. [Pamphlets against Upton Sinclair's EPIC] L.A. [1934]
CHi CRcS

4733. U.S. National youth administration. A survey of community resources. Pasadena. Sponsored by Pasadena employment bureau, 1936. 40 p. illus., maps. (Research project 3162-Y-3) Mimeo.   CLO CP

4734. Vroman, Adam Clark. [Collection of photographs, 1895–1904] 18 v. Volume 1: Pasadena and vicinity, 1900.—Volume 2: Pasadena and vicinity, 1895–96.
CP

4735. —— Photographer of the Southwest, Adam Clark Vroman, 1856–1916. Ed. by Ruth I. Mahood, introd. by Beaumont Newhall. L.A., Ward Ritchie, 1961. 127 p. (chiefly illus., plates, ports.)   CL CU-B

4736. The Whiskey war in Pasadena. "The battle is not yours, but God's." This document is published so that the friends of ordinance 45 may have at command a body of facts...and thus be able to defend it. [Pasadena? 1888] [4] p.   CSmH

4737. Wilson, Benjamin Davis. Benjamin Davis Wilson, 1811–1878. [Pasadena, A. C. Vroman, 19—] [39] p. port. "Narrative...dictated...at the request of Hubert Howe Bancroft...and a copy...retained by Mr. Wilson for himself and family—from which this copy is taken."   CHi CLU

4738. Wilson, Carol (Green) California Yankee: William R. Staats, business pioneer... Claremont, Saunders press, 1946. 184 p. illus., ports. "Sources": p. [169]–175.
Available in many libraries.

4739. Wood, John Windell. Pasadena, California, historical and personal; a complete history of the organization of the Indiana colony, its establishment on the Rancho San Pascual and its evolution into the city of Pasadena. Including a brief story of San Gabriel mission, the story of the boom and its aftermath... [Pasadena] Author, 1917. 565 p. illus.
Available in many libraries.

Pomona

4740. Beloian, Charles M. Street names of Pomona: their origins and trends. Claremont, 1955. 11 p. Typew. A paper written for an English class at Pomona college.   CPom

4741. Brackett, Frank Parkhurst. Brief early history of the San José rancho and its subsequent cities, Pomona, San Dimas, Claremont, La Verne and Spadra. L.A., Historic record co., 1920. 203 p. illus., ports. History of Pomona valley with biographical sketches.
CHi CLSU CPom CSf

4742. California. State park commission. Pomona water power plant, state historical landmark. Dedicatory ceremonies...Pomona college, Claremont, Calif., May 7, 1955. [Marked by the California state park commission in cooperation with the Historical society of Pomona valley, inc. [n.p.] 1955. [18] p. illus., ports.   CHi

4743. Description of the advantages which Pomona offers tourists, invalids and speculators... Oakland, Pac. press, 1887. [S.F., Reprint. Easton, Eldridge & co., 1887?] CSmH CU-B

4744. Dienes, Kalman I. Problems of transition in Pomona valley. Claremont, Foundation for regional economic studies, Claremont men's college, c1949. 88 p.
C CBev CHi CL CLS CLSU CLU CSdS CSf CSmH CU-B

4745. Driscoll, Roy L., ed. Pomona valley community book. Pomona, Cawston, 1950. 445 p. illus., ports.
C CL CPom

4746. Faull, Harry A. From pathways to freeways; a study of the origin of street names in the city of Pomona. Presented at Historical society of Pomona valley, April 1, 1952. 17 p. Typew. CPom

4747. Fryer, Roy M. Early educational institutions of Pomona valley. Address given at the Historical society of Pomona, April 24, 1945. 14 l. Typew. CPom

4748. —— A few facts in the history of Pomona valley. Address...at a meeting of Pioneers of Pomona valley, September 8, 1934. 11 l. Ms. CCH

4749. Garner, Bess (Adams) Story of the Adobe de Palomares in Pomona, California... Claremont, Saunders press, 1940. 28 p. illus.
C CHi CLO CLSU CLU CO CPom CSmH

4750. —— Windows in an old adobe... Pomona, Print. by Progress-bulletin in collaboration with Saunders press, Claremont, 1939. 245 p. illus., ports. Bibliography: p. 235–36.
Available in many libraries.

4751. Hickson, A. L. A short history of the Pomona valley bar association, 1917–1954. [n.p.] 1954. 82 p. port. CPom

4752. History of Pomona valley, Calif., with biographical sketches... L.A., Historic record co., 1920. 818 p. illus., ports. "Also contains history of part of San Bernardino county."—Gudde.
C CBb CCH CHi CL CLCM CLO CLSU CLU CPom CSf CSmH CU-B MWA MiD-B NN

4753. Holt, Raymond. A library with a built-in-future; a plan for meeting the problems of Pomona's public library. [n.p.] 1955. 31 l. illus. C

4754. Kellogg (W. K.) Arabian horse ranch, Pomona. The romance of Pomona ranch. [n.p., n.d.] 32 p. illus., ports., map. C CHi CPom CU-B

4755. Los Angeles county. Bureau of public relations. Unemployment survey of Pomona valley, 1928. Conducted in cooperation with the sheriff's office by members of Dr. William Kirk's sociology classes at Pomona college, directed by Robert O'Brien-Willis Lyman. Claremont, Lawson-Roberts pub. co. [1928] 4 l. CCH

4756. Mangold, George Benjamin. A social survey of Pomona, California welfare and character building agencies under the auspices of the Pomona community chest. Chino, Print. by the boys of the Calif. junior republic, 1934. 68 p. CLSU

4757. Morgan, F. P. The origin and history of Convair Pomona. Convair division of General dynamics corporation. [n.d.] 31 p. illus. CPom

4758. Palomares, José Francisco. Memoirs... Translated from the manuscript in the Bancroft library by Thomas Workman Temple II. L.A., Dawson, 1955. 69 p. illus., maps. (Early Calif. travels ser., 33) 205 copies printed by George Yamada.
CL CLO CLSM CLgA CSS CSjC CStclU CSto CStoC CU-B CVtV

4759. Pomona. Board of trade. Pomona... [Pomona] Oct., 1891. 12 p. illus. CLSU

4760. —— —— Same. [L.A., Kingsley-Barnes & Neuner co., 1894?] 16 p. illus. CHi CLU

4761. —— —— Same, by F. Llewellyn. [Pomona? 1903?] 16 p. illus. Reprinted from *Out West*, Mar., 1903. CU-B

4762. —— —— Same. [L.A., Out West co., 191–?] [24] p. illus. CHi CLU

4763. —— —— Pomona souvenir. 1902. Greeting. [L.A., Kingsley, Moles & Collins, 1902] [22] p. illus. CLU

4764. —— **Chamber of commerce.** Pomona, California, an official outline survey... Pomona [1924] 24 p. illus. CSmH

4765. —— **Charters.** Charter of the city of Pomona, 1911. [Pomona? 1911?] 50 p. CSmH

4766. —— **City administrative officer.** Three years of municipal progress in the city of Pomona, 1950 to 1953. 1953. 64 p. C

4767. —— **Fire dept.** Souvenir, Pomona fire department. Portraits and views of homes and business buildings and interiors. L.A., Tigner & Brooks, 1903. 86 p. CHi CLU CU-B

4768. —— **First Christian church. Historical committee.** History of the First Christian church of Pomona, California, 1883–1943, by Pearl K. Baughman and Donald F. West, for the sixtieth anniversary of the church, October 31—November 7, 1943... [Pomona, c1943] 94 p. illus., ports. CSmH NN

4769. Pomona land and water co. Southern California Pomona, illustrated and described... [L.A., Bacon & co., 1882] 8 p. CLU

4770. —— Same. Pomona, 1885. 42 p. illus. CHi CLU CSmH CU-B

4771. —— Same. 1888 ed. 36 p. illus., map. CSmH

4772. Pomona times-courier. The Pomona times-courier pictorial annual for 1886... Pomona, Lee & Sumner, 1886. [104] p. illus. CU-B

4773. Pomona valley directory guide book. Pomona, The Bulletin, 1924–25. CCH CU-B

4774. Reese, Herbert Harshman. The Kellogg Arabians; their background and influence...In collaboration with Gladys Brown Edwards. L.A., Borden pub. co., 1958. 222 p. illus., ports. C CStmo

4775. Robinson, William Wilcox. Pomona, a calendar of events in the making of a city. L.A., Title guarantee & trust co. [c1936] [24] p. ports., map.
C CBev CHi CLO CLSU CLU CPom CSmH CStmo CStrJC CU-B CWhC

4776. —— Same. c1942. [24] ports., map. CHi NN

San Fernando Valley

4777. Albertype company, New York, pub. Mission San Fernando Rey de España. [Brooklyn, N.Y., n.d.] 12 pl. CU-B

4778. California immigrant union, San Francisco. Land for sale. 1,000 acres in the town of San Fernando. 36,000 acres in Maclay's San Fernando ranch. S.F. [187–?] [4] p. map. CHi CLU

4779. [Daughters of the American revolution. California. San Fernando valley chapter] The valley of San Fernando. [n.p., c1924] 120 p. illus., ports.
C CHi CL CLSU CLU CO CSdS CSmH CU-B

4780. Engelhardt, Zephyrin, Father. ...San Fernando Rey, the mission of the valley... Chicago, Franciscan herald press, 1927. 160 p. illus. Bibliographical foot-notes.
Available in many libraries.

4781. Harrington, Mary Raymond. The story of San Fernando mission. [San Fernando?] San Fernando mission curio shop, c1954. 22 p. illus.
C CHi CL CLS CO

4782. Height, Lewis H., jr. Settlement patterns of the San Fernando valley, southern California. [L.A.] 1953. Thesis (M.A.) — U.C.L.A., 1953.   CLU

4783. Keffer, Frank McCleunan. History of San Fernando valley...in two parts, narrative and biographical; managing editors, Harold McLean Meier [and] Arthur Hamilton Cawston. Glendale, Stillman print. co., 1934. 329 p. illus., ports.
CBb CBev CCH CHi CL CLCM CLCo CLO CLU CLob CP CSf CSmH CU-B MWA NN

4784. Leaming petroleum co. Prospectus of the Leaming petroleum company, San Fernando district. Los Angeles county, Cal. ... S.F., Spaulding & Barto, print., 1872. 12 p.   CLU

4785. Los Angeles. City planning commission. Planning for the San Fernando valley...By Charles B. Bennett and Milton Breivogel. [L.A., 1945] 12 p. illus., maps.   CLO

4786. —— —— ...Restudy of the zoning pattern in the San Fernando valley. L.A., 1955. unp. map, tables.
CL-MR

4787. Padick, Clement. Control and conservation of natural runoff water in the San Fernando valley. [L.A.] 1956. Thesis (M.A.) — U.C.L.A., 1956.   CLU

4788. Roure, Joseph B. History of the mission San Fernando, Rey de España. San Fernando, 1922. 13 p. illus., ports.   CHi CLU

4789. Robinson, William Wilcox. San Fernando valley, a calendar of events. L.A., Title guarantee & trust co. [c1938] [28] p. map.
C CBev CHi CL CLO CLSU CLU CO CSmH CStmo CU-B CWhC

4790. —— Same. c1951. 36 p. map.
CHi CL CLO CLU CStmo CU-B NN NbHi

4791. —— The story of San Fernando valley. L.A., Title insurance and trust co., 1961. 63 p. illus., ports., maps.   CHi CLSM

4792. San Fernando Presbyterian church. Presbyterian church, San Fernando, California, 1889–1939... [S.F.? 1939] [16] p. ports.   CU-B

4793. Security trust and savings bank. Lankershim branch. Publicity dept. A daughter of the snows. The story of the great San Fernando valley... c1923. 56 p. illus., ports., map.
C CHi CL CLO CLSU CLU CLob CSfCP CSmH CU-B

San Gabriel

4794. Bodkin, John J. San Gabriel mission. [2d ed.] L.A., Tidings co., 1900. 32 p. illus.   CLob

4795. —— Same. 6th ed. L.A., 1907. 34 p. illus., ports.   CHi

4796. Bowling, William C. A curriculum analysis of the school district of San Gabriel, California. June, 1955. [Chico] 1955. 392 p. charts, diagrs. Thesis (M.A.) — Chico state college, 1955.   CChiS

4797. Buschman, J. C. E. Die sprachen Kizh und Netela von Neu-Californien. Berlin, Akademie der Wis-

senschaften, 1856. p. 501–531. Concerning the language of the Indians of missions San Gabriel and San Juan Capistrano.   C

4798. Clary corp. Annual report.
CL has 1955–60.

4799. Cleland, Robert Glass. El molino viejo. [L.A.] Ward Ritchie, 1950. 57 p. illus.
C CBb CHi CL CLO CLSM CLU CLob CO CP CPom CRedl CSf CSlu CStoC CU-B

4800. Conkling, Harold. ...San Gabriel investigation. Report for the period July 1, 1923 to September 30 [1928]... [Sacramento, State print. off., 1927–29] 2 v.
CL CLSU CSdS CSmH CU-B

4801. Engelhardt, Zephyrin, Father. ...San Gabriel mission and the beginnings of Los Angeles... San Gabriel, Mission San Gabriel, 1927. 369 p. illus. Bibliographical foot-notes.
Available in many libraries.

4802. Guthrie, Chester Lyle. ...Misión San Gabriel Arcángel... Berkeley, 1936. 39 l. Typew.   CU-B

4803. Hotel San Gabriel, East San Gabriel, California ... [Chicago, Donohue & Henneberry, print., 1888–?] 11 l. pl.   CSmH

4804. Houghton, Frank B., comp. History of San Gabriel mission, founded 1771, situated in a picturesque setting of romance with the historic background of early Spanish traditions. [n.p., c1939] 18 p. illus.   CLU

4805. Krug, Mary Benigna, Sister. Relations of Mission San Gabriel to the beginning of diocesan organization in southern California. Wash., D.C., 1942. 66 p. Thesis (M.A.) — Catholic univ. of Am., 1942.   CSrD

4806. Lasuén, Fermín Francisco de. Memorandum of Father Fermín Francisco de Lasuén concerning his administration of the holy sacrament of confirmation at Mission San Gabriel Arcángel, written January 18, 1791, with a list of persons confirmed January 15, 1791. 3 l. Typew.   CU-B

4807. McGroarty, John Steven. The valley of Our Lady; the romantic history of Los Angeles and the San Gabriel valley... [n.p., n.d.] 14 p. illus. Reprinted from *West coast mag.* for July, 1909. v.6, no. 4.
CSmH CU-B

4808. McLean, Mildred. San Gabriel mission and the mission play. Chicago, American autochrome co. [n.d.] 88 p. Bound with: A. J. Nolan. *The old missions of California.*   CStmo

4809. O'Melveny, Stuart. It's best to divide with our friends. L.A. [Anderson, Ritchie & Simon] 1955. 33 p. illus., ports.   C CHi CLO CLU

4810. Ott, Susana Clayton. The good night at San Gabriel. N.Y., Harper [1947] 63 p.   CHi

4811. San Gabriel. Women's chamber of commerce. ...San Gabriel. [1915?] 26 p. illus.   CU-B

4812. San Gabriel elementary school district. Report of the survey of the public schools of the San Gabriel elementary school district. 1949. 238 p.   C

4813. Southern California orange carnival, Chicago, 1891. San Gabriel valley, the heart of southern California; souvenir...April 17, 1891. L.A., W. A. Vandercook, print. [1891] 7 p.   CHi

4814. Steiner, Rodney. Recreation and watershed problems in the southwestern San Gabriel mountains, California. [L.A.] 1951. Thesis (M.A.) — U.C.L.A., 1951.
CLU

4815. Sugranes, Eugene Joseph. Glory of San Gabriel...with mention of other California Franciscan

missions and their founders. San Gabriel, 1917. 90 p.
illus., ports.   CHi CLU CSd CSmH

4816. —— The old San Gabriel mission; historical
notes taken from old manuscripts and records... San
Gabriel, 1909. 104 p. illus., ports.
CHi CL CLLoy CLSU CLU CLob CO COHN
CPom CSd CSf CSfU CSmH CStrJC CU-B
CaBViPA MiD

4817. —— Same. 1921. 89 p. illus.   CLU CLob

4818. Temple, Thomas Workman. [Collection of
baptismal records from the San Gabriel mission, and the
Plaza church in Los Angeles] Genealogical records committee of the California state society, Daughters of the
American revolution. 1945. 413 l. Typew. Baptismal
records, Los Angeles county, 1771–1873.   CLU

San Marino

**4819. Friends of the Huntington library, San
Marino.** Membership list. San Marino.
CHi has Dec. 31, 1946, Dec. 31, 1949.

4820. [Gabriel, O. Nicholas] The story of Gains-
borough Heath and the old adobe. [L.A., Stowell & Sinsa-
baugh, 1928] 23 p.   CSmH

4821. Harris, Alice A. The Huntington art gallery
and library at San Marino, California. 4 l. Typew.
                                                 CStmo

**4822. Henry E. Huntington library and art gal-
lery, San Marino.** California in maps, 1541–1851, notes
on an exhibition... [San Marino, 1949] 8 p. map.
Exhibition and notes prepared by Willard O. Waters.
                                                  CHi

4823. —— A century of California literature; an
exhibition prepared for the California literary centennial.
San Marino, Anderson and Ritchie, 1951. 27 p. illus.
                                              CHi CLO

4824. —— Handbook of the art collections... San
Marino, 1941– illus.
CHi (1941) CCSC (1948) CStmo (1955)

4825. —— Los Angeles: the transition decades, 1850–
70; an exhibition at the Huntington library. San Marino,
1937. 25 p. illus., map. This hand list has been written
by Robert Glass Cleland.
CHi CL CLO CLSU CLU CO CSfSt CSjC
CSmH IHi MoS OU ViU

4826. —— Visitor's guide to the exhibitions and gardens of the Henry E. Huntington library and art gallery.
San Marino, 1945. 48 p. illus., port.   CHi CLU

4827. —— Will Bradley, his work; an exhibition.
[Exhibition and handlist prepared by Carey S. Bliss]
San Marino, 1951. 25 p. illus., facsims., port.
                                             CHi CU-B

4828. Hertrich, William. Early San Marino... San
Marino, 1945. 24 p.   CHi CSmH

4829. —— The Huntington botanical gardens, 1905–
1949; personal recollections of William Hertrich, Curator
Emeritus. San Marino, Huntington lib., 1949. 167 p.
C CHi CL CLLoy CLO CLU CO CSdS CSf
CSmH CU-B

4830. Marcosson, Isaac F. A little known master of
millions, the story of Henry E. Huntington, constructive
capitalist... Bost., Print. for E. H. Rollins & sons, 1914.
[30] p. port.   CLSU CSmH

4831. Nelson, Elmer S. Treasures of the past. L.A.,
1929. This article, descriptive of the Huntington library
and art gallery, appeared in three parts in the *Pacific
mutual news* and is reprinted.   CRb

4832. San Marino garden club. Year book, 1946/
47– San Marino, 1946– Founded in 1935.
CHi has 1946/47–1947/48, 1949/50–1951/52.

4833. Schad, Robert O. Henry Edwards Huntington, the founder and the library. San Marino, Huntington
lib., c1931. 32 p. illus., port. (Reprinted from Huntington lib. bul., May 1931)   CHi CStmo

4834. —— A quarter century at the Huntington library. [S.F.] Priv. print., 1952. 8 p.   CSmH

4835. Wagner, Henry Raup. Bullion to books;
fifty years of business and pleasure... L.A., Zamorano
club, 1942. 370 p.   CBb CHi CSfCW CSmH

4836. —— In memoriam; tributes paid at the bier
of Henry Raup Wagner... [L.A., Zamorano club, 1957]
14 p.   CHi

4837. —— Sixty years of book collecting. [S.F.]
Roxburghe club, 1952. 51 p. illus.   CHi

4838. Watkins, Louise Ward. Henry Edwards
Huntington; a character sketch of a great man. [Gar-
dena, Priv. print. at the Spanish Am. inst. press, 1928]
27 p.   CSmH

4839. Wright, Louis B. The Huntington library and
the cultural heritage of America. [n.p.] 1946. 11 p.
                                                  CHi

4840. Zamorano club. The published writings of
Henry R. Wagner. Issued at the first far western meeting
of the Bibliographical society of America, held at the
Henry E. Huntington library on August 27, 1955, in
honor of Henry R. Wagner... L.A., Ward Ritchie, 1955.
30 p. port.   CBb CHi

Santa Catalina Island

4841. Brown, Charlotte Maud. Catalina island,
limited bibliography. [L.A., Author, 1927] 4 l.   CLSU

4842. Catalina's yesterdays... L.A., Print. by Mayers
co., c1926 by Santa Catalina island co. 21 p. illus., maps.
                               CLSU CLU CLob CSd

4843. Holder, Charles Frederick. An isle of summer, Santa Catalina; its history, climate, sports and antiquities. L.A., McBride, [1892?] 14 p. illus., map.
"Compliments of Wilmington transportation co." From
the *Californian*, Dec. 1892, p. 64–73.
                                       C CP CU-B NHi

4844. —— Same, with title: Santa Catalina; an isle
of summer... S.F., C. A. Murdock & co., 1895. 126 p.
illus.   C CL CLO CLU CStrJC CU-B

4845. —— Same. L.A., McBride, 1897. 121 p. illus.,
map.   CHi CSmH

4846. —— Same. L.A., McBride, 1901. 91 p. illus.
                        CBb CLSU CLU CSfP CSmH

4847. [Marcrate, Arthur N.] The history of the
Tuna club, founded 1898, incorporated 1901, Avalon,
Santa Catalina island, Calif. 1st ed. [n.p., c1948] 197 p.
illus., ports. Includes bibliography.   CHi CLU

4848. Ocampo, Estevan de. Relacion del estado
qvetenia la isla de Santa Catalina, de lo que iba obrando
el capitan de cauallos don Esteuan de Ocampo, en orden
à mejorar su defensa, y la forma en que la ocupò el
enemigo. [Madrid? 1667?] [4] p.   CU-B

4849. Reynolds, Ann Cloud. Wild goat trails of
Catalina... Avalon, Author, 1941. 40 p. port., map.
                                    C CHi CLU CU-B

4850. Robinson, William Wilcox. The island of
Santa Catalina... L.A., Title guarantee & trust co., 1941.
[48] p. illus., map.
C CBev CHi CL CLLoy CLO CLSU CLU
CLob CO CPom CSf CSmH CStmo CU-B NN

4851. Tuna club, Avalon. Annual tournament. [L.A.] 19—
CHi has 1930, 1936.

4852. Vaughan, Ruben V. Doc's Catalina diary, ed. by Betta Rebal Tigge. [n.p., Limb pub. co., 1956] 74 p. illus., map.   C CL CLU

4853. Williams, Iza. Santa Catalina island. L.A., Rieder, c1904. [48] p. illus., map.   CHi CLU

4854. —— Same. c1905.
CHi CLSU CLU CSmH CU-B MiD-B

4855. Williamson, Martha Burton (Woodhead) History of Santa Catalina island. [17] p. (Reprint from Hist. soc. of so. Calif. Annual pub., v.6, 1903)   C

4856. Wilson, Harry William. Wilson's guide to Avalon the beautiful, and the island of Santa Catalina ...2d and condensed ed. ... Avalon and L.A., Wilson map & guide co., 1914. [26] p. illus.   C

4857. Windle, Ernest. History of Santa Catalina island (& guide)... Avalon, Catalina islander, c1931. 159 p. illus., ports., maps. Bibliography: p. 157.
CL CLSU CSd CSf CSmH CU-B

4858. —— Windle's history of Santa Catalina island ...2d ed. Avalon, Catalina islander, c1940. 159 p. illus., ports., map.   C CHi CL CLSU CSf CU-B

4859. Wrigley (Wm., jr.) enterprises. Catalina, California's magic ile. [Heintz & Robertson direct mail press, n.d.] unp.   CLSU

Santa Monica

4860. Armour, Richard. Drug store days; my youth among the pills and potions. N.Y., McGraw-Hill, c1959. 184 p. illus.   CStmo

4861. Associated telephone co. Prospectus. 280,312 shares cumulative preferred stock... [n.p.] 1945. 27 p. Supplement attached to p. 1.   CHi

4862. Beautiful Santa Monica, by-the-sea... [L.A., W. P. Bolton, 1905–06] [30] p. illus.   CU-B

4863. California state chamber of commerce. Standard industrial survey summary report: Santa Monica. S.F., 1959. [4] p.   CStmo

4864. Cleland, Donald Milton. A historical study of the Santa Monica city schools. [L.A.] 1952. Thesis (Ed.D.)— U.C.L.A., 1952.   CLU

4865. The coming city. S.F., Harrison, print. [1875?] 12 p.   CU-B

4866. Cowick, Kate L. The Outlook's story of Santa Monica. [Santa Monica, Outlook, 1932] 40 p. illus.
C CL CSmH CStmo

4867. Daniell, John Bampfylde. The bay area pageant; the story of the Santa Monica bay area, 1542–1957. [Santa Monica, 1957] 23 p. illus., ports., map. Reprinted from the *Santa Monica evening outlook.*
CHi CL CStmo

4868. Douglas aircraft co., inc. Annual report. CHi has 1958–59, 1961–62. CL has 1946–60.

4869. Dowsing & Proctor, real estate agents. Santa Monica by the sea, the greatest summer and winter resort on the Pacific coast. A paradise for the home-seeker. [L.A., B. R. Baumgardt & co., 189–?] 14 p. illus.
CLU

4870. Dvorin, Eugene P. Tax exemptions and local self government; a case study of Santa Monica, California... L.A., Bur. of governmental research, Univ. of Calif., 1958. 47 p. illus., map.   CSfSt CStmo

4871. Eisner, Simon, and associates. [Facts about Santa Monica] Santa Monica, City planning commission,

1956–57. Contents: [v.1] Trading area...central business district.—[v.2] Land use inventory.—[v.3] Community surveys of resident population and income.—[v.4] Public facilities.   CStmo

4872. —— The master plan report, Santa Monica, California. Santa Monica, City planning commission, 1957. 80 p. charts, tables.   CStmo

4873. Furstman, J.M. A health survey of the city of Santa Monica, Calif. ...Surveyed...for the Santa Monica council of social welfare, August 1927... Monrovia [1927] 26 p. Typew.   CStmo

4874. Glines, Carroll V. Grand old lady; story of the DC-3. Cleveland, Pennington press, c1959. 250 p. illus., ports. Contains material about Douglas aircraft company of Santa Monica.   CStmo

4875. Hultquist, Warren E. The city planning movement in Santa Monica, California. [L.A.] 1953. Thesis (M.A.)— U.C.L.A., 1953.   CLU

4876. McCarthy, John Russell. These waiting hills, the Santa Monicas... [L.A., Times-mirror press, c1925] 73 p. front.
C CHi CL CLO CLSU CLU CO CSmH CStmo NN

4877. Macdonald-Wright, Stanton. Santa Monica library murals. L.A., Angelus press [1935] unp. illus.
CStmo

4878. Mangold, George Benjamin. Social service in Santa Monica... [n.p., n.d.] 81 p. Mimeo.   CStmo

4879. Michel, Marcella. Early riser. [n.p., 1954?] 34 l. port. Reminiscences of Herman Michel, former mayor and business man of Santa Monica.   CStmo

4880. Robinson, William Wilcox. Santa Monica. L.A., Title guarantee & trust co., c1935. [15] p. map.
C CBev CHi CL CLO CLSU CLU CSd CSmH CStmo CStrJC CU-B CWhC

4881. —— Same. c1950. 16 p. map.
CHi CL CLO CLU CStmo NbHi NN

4882. —— Same. 1955. 16 p. map.
CAla CHi CL CLU CSluCL

4883. Santa Monica. Charters.
CStmo has 1907, with amendments through 1940, and 1946, with amendments to date.

4884. Santa Monica; a protected harbor. Santa Monica's and San Pedro's claims fully considered...Review of the reports of engineers... Santa Monica, Press of the Outlook, 1894. 22 p. illus.   CL

4885. Santa Monica community book. [1st]–5th editions, 1934–1953. Santa Monica, A. H. Cawston, 1934–53. Title varies. Editor varies: 1st–4th ed., Charles Sumner Warren.—5th ed., Carl Frederick White.
C (1st, 3d, 5th) CBev (2d, 3d) CHi (1st, 4th) CL (1st–5th) CLO (1st) CLSU (2d) CLU (2d, 4th) CSf (1st, 5th) CStmo (1st–5th) CU-B (1st, 3d) NN (3d)

4886. Santa Monica evening outlook. Diamond jubilee edition, 1875–1950. v.75, no. 162, July 8, 1950. Santa Monica, 1950.   CStmo CU-B

4887. —— Santa Monica, illustrated. [1890?] 56 p. illus.   CHi CStmo NN

4888. Santa Monica land co. Santa Monica canyon. [Santa Monica, 1914?] [6] p. illus., map.   CHi

4889. Santa Monica–Ocean Park chamber of commerce. Santa Monica, California, industrial directory. Sept. 1953–Feb. 1960.
CStmo has 1960.

4890. Santa Monica topics. ...Classified booster

directory, containing the names, addresses and telephone numbers of representative manufacturing, business and professional interests and institutions of Santa Monica, Ocean Park, Venice and the Bay district. 1928/29–1936/ 37. Santa Monica [1928?–36?] Publisher varies: 1928/29 Santa Monica evening outlook.
CStmo has 1928/29, 1936/37.

4891. Siffert, Donald E. A comparative survey of city governments in Santa Monica, California. [L.A.] 1956. Thesis (M.A.)—U.C.L.A., 1956.　　CLU CStmo

4892. Souvenir, Santa Monica. [L.A., Times-mirror print. & bind. house, 1901] [20] p. illus.　　CU-B

4893. —— Same. [1902] 71 p.　　CLSU

4894. Stapleton, Charles R. Recreation and its problems on the Santa Monica-Venice shoreline, southern California. [L.A.] 1952. Thesis (M.A.)— U.C.L.A., 1952.　　CLU

4895. Stier, Julius H. Survey of land utilization in the city of Santa Monica with forecasts of elementary school population and school housing needs. Santa Monica, 1950. 132 l. maps, charts.　　CLU

4896. System development corp. System development corporation. [Santa Monica? 195–?] [20] p. illus., ports.　　CU-B

4897. Trecker, Harleigh Bradley. Report of Santa Monica social service survey, conducted by the Council of social agencies... [n.p.] 1942. 58 p. Mimeo.
CStmo

4898. Ward, Ben E. Santa Monica! the Long Branch of the Pacific. Grand excursion and liberal credit sale at auction of 54 choice sea-side lots, Wednesday, June 9th, 1886... [L.A.] Gilchrist print., 1886. [4] p. illus., map.　　CLU

4899. Woodward, Lois Ann. ...Santa Monica beach state park... Berkeley, 1937. 20 p. Typew.　　CU-B

Whittier

4900. Arnold, Benjamin F., and Clark, Artilissa Dorland. History of Whittier... Whittier, Western print. corp., 1933. 393 p. illus., ports.
C CHi CL CLO CLU CPom CSmH CWhC NN

4901. Cooper, Charles W. The A. Wardman story. Whittier, Whittier college, 1961. 96 p.　　CHi

4902. Finney, Guy Woodward. Mericos H. Whittier, his career; the story of a California oil pioneer, civic leader and humanitarian... [L.A., Stationers corp., print., c1940] 115 p. ports.　　CLO

4903. Harris, Herbert Eugene. The Quaker and the west; the first sixty years of Whittier college. [n.p., c1948] 175 p. illus., ports.　　C CBaB COnC

4904. —— Whittier, California. [Whittier, Calif., W. A. Smith, 1909] 16 p. illus.　　CU-B

4905. Maulsby, Orlando W. Rolling stone, the autobiography of O. W. Maulsby. L.A., Priv. print., 1931. 130 p. port.　　CHi

4906. Osborne, Sherrill B. Whittier, California. [Whittier, Whittier Bd. of trade, 1904?] [16] p.　　CLU

4907. Robinson, William Wilcox. Whittier; a calendar of events in the making of a city. L.A., Title guarantee & trust co. [c1935] [15] p. ports., map.
C CAla CBev CHi CL CLO CLSU CLU CSmH CStrJC CU-B CWhC

4908. —— Same. [c1947] 15 p. map.
CHi CLO CLU CStmo

4909. —— Same. [c1955] 15 p. illus., map.
CHi CSluCL NbHi

4910. Whittier. Chamber of commerce. Whittier, Los Angeles co., California... [Whittier, Print. Whittier news] 1917. [16] p. illus.　　CL CU-B

4911. —— —— Same. [1923] 35 p. illus.　　CU-B

4912. —— **Fire department.** Souvenir Whittier fire department, published in the interest of the relief fund of the Whittier fire department. L.A., 1904. unp. illus., ports.　　CLU

4913. Whittier college. [Catalog]
CL has 1913–to date.

4914. The Whittier news. Annual edition, 1915– Whittier [1914]– illus., ports.
C has 1915–18, 1921–23. CU-B has 1925. CWhC has 1925.

4915. —— Before the town began; short stories published in the Whittier news during Whittier's celebration of the California centennial. [Whittier? 1950?] [20] p.
CLU

4916. Williams, Beverly Clara (Parsons) A history of the Whittier city school district. [Whittier] 1959. 42 l. Thesis (M.A.)— Whittier college, 1959.　　CWhC

MADERA COUNTY
(Created in 1893 from portion of Fresno county)

COUNTY HISTORIES

4917. Madera county. Board of education. History of Madera county to accompany a course of study for the Madera county schools. Madera, 1939. 95 p. Mimeo.
CHi CMa

GREAT REGISTER

4918. Madera county. Index to the Great register of the county of Madera. 1893– Place of publication and title vary.
C has 1898 (biennially to)– 1918; 1918 (suppl.), 1920, 1922, 1924, 1926, 1930 (biennially to)– 1962. CU-B has 1940.

DIRECTORIES

4919. 1914– Polk, R. L., & co., pub. Polk's Madera city directory, including Chowchilla... L.A., 1914– Title and content vary.
C has 1914. CHi has 1958.

GENERAL REFERENCES

4920. Butin, Mary Ryerson. Life's story [an autobiography of Madera county's health officer. Madera, 1932] 18 l. Mimeo.　　CFS

4921. Fisher, C. E. Madera county (California) S.F., Sunset pub. house [1920] folder (30 p.) illus., maps.　　CU-B

4922. Levick, M. B. Madera county, California. S.F., Sunset homeseekers' bur. [1911] 31 p. illus., maps.
CHi CU-B

4923. Madera. Board of trade. Madera county, California. [Madera, 1905?] 24 p.　　CHi

4924. Madera county. Board of supervisors. Madera county, California, offers, invites you... [Madera, Daily tribune print, 1926] [12] p.　　CHi

4925. —— **Chamber of commerce.** Along the Madera route to Yosemite. Madera [n.d.] folder (30 p.) illus., map.　　CRcS

4926. —— —— Madera county, California. Madera, 1920. 15 p. illus., maps.　　CFS CHi

4927. —— —— Madera; scenery, recreation. Madera [1933?] folder (11 p.) illus., map.　　CHi CRcS

4928. —— —— Presenting Madera county magic. Madera [1953] 30 p.   CHi

4929. Nutting, W. R., ed. The Howard and Wilson colony company of Madera, Fresno co., California... [S.F., Calif. view co., 1891] 32 p.   CU-B

4930. Oakhurst. Chamber of commerce. Oakhurst welcomes you; a fast-growing and progressive community ... [Oakhurst, 1960] 96 p. illus., ports., map.   CU-B

4931. Osborn, Thomas W., comp. Madera county; 1955 classified map directory. [Madera, Madera county chamber of commerce, c1955] [20] p. illus., maps.
                                                                        CU-B

4932. People's protective association, Oakhurst. Constitution and by-laws of the People's protective association of Fresno Flats, California. Madera, Mercury bk. and job print., 1897. 18 p.   CU-B

4933. Shay, John C. Twenty years in the backwoods of California. Being the actual experiences and observations of a native son of California, covering a period of twenty years in one locality, while engaged in prospecting, gold mining, homesteading, stock raising and the roadside smithy. Bost., Roxburgh [c1923] 142 p.
CAna CBb CHi CLSM CSd CSf CSfCW CSfP CSmH CStmo CYcCL

4934. Spence, Alice. Iron mining and deposits in Madera county. [Fresno, 1958] 18 l. Typew. Student paper at Fresno state college.   CFS

4935. Woman's improvement club, Madera. Yearbook. 1906–
CHi has 1914/15.

MARIN COUNTY
(*Created in 1850*)

COUNTY HISTORIES

4936. Historical records survey. California. ... Marin county (San Rafael) ... S.F., 1937. 136 l. illus. (Inventory of the county archives of Calif., no. 22) Reproduced from typew. copy.
C CBb CHi CL CLCo CLO CLSM CLSU CLU CMary CMont CO COMC CSalCL CSf CSfCP CSmH CSr CSrCL CSt CU-B CYcCL ICN TxU

4937. [Munro-Fraser, J. P.] History of Marin county, California and biographical sketches... also an historical sketch of the state of California... S.F., Alley, Bowen & co., 1880. 516 p. ports.
C CCH CHi CL CLU CO CSf CSfCP CSfCSM CSfCW CSfU CSj CSmH CSrCL CU-B CoD MWA NHi NN

GREAT REGISTER

4938. Marin county. Index to the Great register of the county of Marin. 1866– Place of publication and title vary.
C has 1867, 1873, 1875–76, 1879–80; 1886 (biennially to)– 1930, 1934 (biennially to)– 1962. CL has 1873 (biennially to)–1879, 1882, 1886 (biennially to)– 1890. CSmH has 1872–73, 1877 (suppl.), 1877, 1880, 1886, 1888–89. CU-B has 1868, 1872–73. 1875, 1879–80, 1896, 1898, 1908, 1910, 1912, 1914, 1918 (biennially to)–1938.

DIRECTORIES

4939. 1887/88. American directory publishing co., pub. San Rafael and Marin county directory. [S.F., 1887?] 115 p.   CLU

4940. 1890. Directory of Marin county, with descriptive sketches of the county and town of San Rafael. S.F., J. J. Ibbotson & co., 1890.   CSf

4941. 1905/06. Kingsbury, A., & co., pub. Kingsbury's...directory of San Rafael city and Marin county ...including Crocker-Langley business directory of San Francisco. [San Rafael] c1905.   C CSr CU-B

4942. 1909/10. Marin county directory co., pub. Directory of Marin county, San Rafael city and San Anselmo; also Mill Valley, Sausalito, Tiburon, Belvedere, Ross, Kentfield and Fairfax... 1909–10.   CSr

4943. 1925. Polk, R. L., & co., pub. The independent's Marin county directory. San Rafael, Sausalito, San Anselmo, Mill Valley, Fairfax, Novato... Oakland, 1925.   CHi

4944. 1931/32. A.B.C. publishing co., pub. Marin county A.B.C. directory. [Glendale, 1931] v.p.   CHi

4945. 1939/40– A to Z directory publishers, pub. Marin county directory, embracing San Rafael, San Anselmo, Fairfax... San Rafael, 1939–
CHi has 1939/40, 1949/50, 1952/53. CSr has 1942/43, 1946/47, 1949/50, 1952/53, 1954/55.

4946. 1957/58. Marin directory publishers, pub. Marin county directory, embracing San Rafael... San Rafael, 1958.   CSr

San Rafael

4947. 1904. Directory publishing co., pub. San Rafael city directory, containing complete directory of all residents... S.F., 1904. 72 p. illus., map.   CLU

4948. 1911/12. Polk-Husted directory co., pub. San Rafael, San Anselmo, Mill Valley, Sausalito and Marin county directory... Oakland, 1911.   C-S CSr

4949. 1960– Polk, R. L., & co., pub. Polk's San Rafael city directory, including Fairfax, Kentfield, Ross and San Anselmo... L.A., 1960–
CHi has 1960. CSr has 1960.

GENERAL REFERENCES

4950. Associated chambers of commerce of Marin county. Marin county, California... [San Rafael] 1949. 15 p. illus.   CHi CRcS

4951. Austin, Miriam M. Out of doors in Marin. rev. ed. San Rafael, Author, 1958. 74 p. illus.   CSrCL

4952. Belvedere. Reed school. Shark Point and High Point, a history of the Tiburon-Belvedere area. [Belvedere, 1954] unp. illus., maps. Reproduced from typew. copy. "The research for this history was done by the students of the eighth grade of Reed school."
C CHi CL CLU CRic CSr CU-B

4953. Belvedere land co. Souvenir of Belvedere. [S.F., 1895?] unp.   C-S CHi

4954. Bingham, Helen. In Tamal land... S.F., Calkins pub. house [c1906] 141 p. illus.
Available in many California libraries and CaBViPA NN

4955. Blanding, Gordon. Richardson's bay as a site for a naval base. [S.F., Author, 1921] [8] p.   CHi

4956. Bowlen, Frederick J. ...Their hills afire; the story of the Mill Valley conflagration, July 2, 1929. S.F., 1935. 22 p. Typew. 6 mounted photos. At head of title: Presented...through the joint cooperation of Fred J. Bowlen, Society of Calif. pioneers, and the SERA of San Francisco. Project 2-F7-218. Jan. 14, 1935.   CHi CSf

4957. Boyd, Margaret Kittle. Reminiscences of early Marin county gardens... [S.F.? 1934] [21] p. At head of title: The San Francisco garden club.
C CHi CSf CSfCP CSmH CSr CU-B

4958. Branson (Katharine) school, Ross. The Katharine Branson school, 1936–37. [S.F., Kennedy-Ten Bosch co., print., 1936] 37 p. illus.   CHi

4959. —— Same. 2d ed. [n.p., 1954] [32] p.   CHi

4960. California. Dept. of social welfare. A study of Marin county, California; building services into a public assistance program can pay off. [Sacramento, State print. off.] 1958. 52 p. illus.   C CL CRcS

4961. California historical society. Drake's plate of brass; evidence of his visit to California in 1579. S.F., 1937. 57 p. illus., port., maps. (Calif. hist. soc. Special pub. no. 13) Bibliography: p. 49–57. The plate was found at the Laguna ranch, near Drake's bay, close to Point Reyes.
C CBu CHi CL CLSU CLU CMartC CMont CO CRc CRedCL CRedl CSf CSfCW CSmH CSr CStrJC CU-B CaBViPA HHi MoS OrU

4962. —— Same. S.F., 1953. 102 p. illus., maps. (Calif. hist. soc. Special pub. no. 25) Bibliography: p. 85–93.
CBb CHi CLSM CRcS CRic CSalCL CSbr CSfSt CSluCL CStclU CSto CStrCL CV CVtV

4963. Country club of Marin county. By-laws, list of members, rules.
CHi has 1909.

4964. Davidson, George. Francis Drake on the northwest coast of America in the year 1579. The Golden Hinde did not anchor in the bay of San Francisco. [S.F., F. F. Partridge print.] 1908. 114 p. (Geographical soc. of the Pac. Transactions and proceedings, v.5, ser. 2)
C-S CHi CLgA CMont CP CSfP OrU

4965. —— Identification of Sir Francis Drake's anchorage on the coast of California in the year 1579. S.F., 1890. 58 p. maps.
C CHi CL CLU CLgA CSS CSd CSf CSfCP CSfCSM CSfCW CSfWF-H CSmH CStclU CU-B CaBViPA HHi

4966. Denver, James William. Before the committee on public lands. In the matter of the survey of the Rancho Corte de Madera del Presidio. Brief on the laws of Mexico in relation to the salt marsh and tide lands, applicable to private land grants, by J. W. Denver and A. St. C. Denver... [S.F.] Judd & Detweiler [188–?] 8 p.   C CHi CLU

4967. Dickinson, A. Bray. North Pacific coast railroad company, the history of a railroad into the redwoods; a series of articles from the San Rafael independent-journal. [Sacramento, 1959] unp.   C

4968. Donnelly, Florence G. Early days in Marin; a picture review. San Rafael, Marin county savings and loan assoc., 1960. 62 p. photos.   CHi CSr CSrCL

4969. [Drake, Sir Francis] Sir Francis Drake, description of his landing at Drake's bay, Marin county, Calif., June 17, 1579. Being an exact copy of parts of the original report of this voyage... [S.F., 1915] 22 p. illus. Official publication of the Marin county, Calif., exhibit, Panama-Pacific international exposition.   CLU

4970. Duffy, Clinton T. The San Quentin story, as told to Dean Jennings. [1st ed.] Garden City, N.Y., Doubleday, 1950. 253 p.
CArcHT CLU CLgA CNa CP CPa CSS CSal CSd CSf CSfP CSrCL CStmo CViCL CWhC ODa

4971. Duffy, Gladys (Carpenter) Warden's wife, by Gladys Duffy with Blaise Whitehead Lane. N.Y., Appleton-Century, 1959. 346 p.   CArcHT CMon CNa CSd CSf CStmo CUk CViCL

4972. F[arquhar], F[rancis] P. Nova Albion. [S.F., Silverado squatters, 195–?] [7] p. illus., map.
CHi

4973. Fink, Colin G. Drake's plate of brass authenticated; the report on the plate of brass... S.F., Calif. hist. soc., 1938. 28 p.
C CHi CL CLS CLSU CO CRcS CSS CSf CSfCP CSfP CSj CSmH CStrJC CU-B CaBViPA

4974. Finnie, Richard, ed. Marinship; the history of a wartime shipyard, told by some of the people who helped build the ships. Sausalito, California, 1942–45. S.F., 1947. 403 p. illus., ports., maps.
C CHi CL CLSU CMartC CO CRcS CSdS CSf CSfCP CSfP CSmH CSr CSrD CU-B

4975. Gardner, Peter. Before the Secretary of the Interior, in the matter of the survey of the Rancho Corte de Madera del Presidio. Petition for Peter Gardner et al. for re-hearing. J. W. Denver, A. St. C. Denver... S.F., Judd & Detweiler [1882] 27 p.   C CLU

4976. —— To the committee on public lands of the Senate of the United States. In the matter of the Rancho Corte de Madera del Presidio in Marin county, California. The statement of Peter Gardner in reference to the survey of the Rancho Corte de Madera del Presidio, in Marin county, California. Also, petition of settlers. J. W. Denver, A. St. C. Denver, attorneys. [n.p., 1883?] 7 p.
C CLU

4977. —— ...The statement of Peter Gardner et al. for re-hearing. J. W. Denver, A. St. C. Denver... [S.F.], Judd & Detweiler [1882] 27 p.   C

4978. Gift, George W. Something about California ...Marin county... San Rafael, San Rafael herald, 1875. 32 p.   C CLU CSmH CU-B

4979. Gilmer, Jeremy F., vs. A tract of land called "Lime Point," S. R. Throckmorton, owner. Supreme court of California. Jeremy F. Gilmer, Captain, etc. in the army of the United States, vs. a tract of land called "Lime Point." Brief for the intervenors, John Parrott and A. G. Dallas. S.F., Painter & co., 1861. 14 p.   CU-B

4980. Harlan, George H. Historic spots in Marin county, California. El Marinero chapter, Daughters of the American Revolution, Historic spots committee...in collaboration with the Marin county historical society. [Sausalito] 1955. 1 v. Loose-leaf. Mounted photos. Typew.
C

4981. Heizer, Robert Fleming. Archaeological evidence of Sebastian Rodríguez Cermeño's California visit in 1595...with an introduction by Alfred Louis Kroeber and a report by Colin Garfield Fink and Eugene Paul Polushkin on the examination of ten iron spikes recently found at Drake's bay. S.F., Calif. hist. soc., 1942. 32 p. illus., map.
CHi CLO CMartC CMont CRic CSS CSd CSf CSjC CStbS CStclU CStoC TxU

4982. Herschler, John Barton. Muir woods national monument: A monument of California redwood trees ...With photographs by the author. [Estes Park, Colo., Author, 1939] 40 p. illus., map.   C

4983. Immigration association of California. [County scrapbooks] [S.F., 188–?]   C

4984. Inverness heights company, comp. Inverness, the beautiful, on Tomales bay and Inverness river... [S.F., Janssen litho. and label co., 1908?] [20] p. illus., maps.   CHi CSf

4985. Kent, Elizabeth (Thacher). William Kent, Independent; a biography. Kentfield, Author, 1950. 421 p. port. Typew.   CHi CSrCL

4986. Kent, William. Reminiscences of outdoor life. With a foreword by Stewart Edward White... S.F., A. M. Robertson, 1929. 305 p. CHi

4987. Lowrie, Donald. My life in prison. N.Y., Mitchell Kennerley, 1912. 422 p. CSd ViU

4988. [Lyford, B. F.] Lyford's Hygeia (or goddess of health) ; Tiburon Point tract, Marin county, Cal. ... [S.F.] Hicks Judd co. [1895] 32 p. illus., maps. Includes articles of Jared C. Hoag. CHi

4989. McAdie, Alexander G. Nova Albion—1579 ...Worcester, Mass., American antiquarian soc., 1918. 12 p. illus. Reprinted from *Proceedings*, October, 1918. CHi

4990. McCue's plain talk. v.1. no. 1, Jan. 1907. Corte Madera, 1907. C CLU CU-B

4991. McNear, George W., vs. Towne, Asa P. In the Supreme court of the state of California. Geo. W. McNear, respondent, vs. Asa P. Towne, appellant. Transcript on appeal... San Rafael, "Marin county journal," 1871– [73] 2 v. in 1. Includes two different actions in the suit over that part of the Rancho San Pedro, Santa Margarita y las gallinas, known as the Simpton lot. CLU

4992. Mahon, Timothy, vs. Richardson, Esteban. ...Timothy Mahon, respondent, vs. Esteban Richardson, et al., appellants; and Timothy Mahon, vs. S. Sepulveda, et al. Appellants' brief in reply. T. J. Bowers, S. F. Reynolds, of counsel for appellants. S.F., C. W. Gordon, print., 1874. 29 p. Regarding swamp land in Marin county. CLU

4993. Marin art and garden center, Ross. Souvenir programs, Marin art and garden fair. 1st– , 1946– CHi has 5th–6th, 8th–9th, 1950–51, 1953–54.

4994. Marin county. Planning commission. Bolinas-Stinson Beach master plan; a section of the Marin county master plan. [San Rafael] 1961. 46 p., A-1-5. map. CHi

4995. —— —— Marin county streets and highways plan. San Rafael, 1952. 145 p. maps. CHi CSt

4996. Marin county conservation league. Exploring Marin. San Anselmo and Ross, 1941– no. 1– illus., maps. Contents: 1. Sir Francis Drake highway, by Sally Carrighar.–2. Coast highway, Manzanita to Tomales, by Sally Carrighar.–3. Southern Marin, by Mrs. Henry Rideout. C CHi CSfCP CU-B

4997. Marin county journal, San Rafael. Illustrated edition... October, 1887. 35 p. illus., map. C CLU CSfCP CSmH

4998. Marin county promotion league. Marin county, the garden spot of California. S.F., Commercial art co. [n.d.] 10 p., 14 l. of illus. CHi CL CSfCP

4999. Marin county society for the prevention of cruelty to animals, Sausalito. By-laws...adopted Nov. 12, 1897... Sausalito, News print, 1897. 14 p. CHi

5000. Marin journal, San Rafael. New era ed. San Rafael, 1909. [30] p. illus., ports. CHi CU-B

5001. Marin municipal water district vs. Marin water and power company and Mercantile trust company of San Francisco. ...Marin municipal water district (a public corporation) plaintiff and respondent, vs. Marin water and power company (a corporation) and Mercantile trust company of San Francisco (a corporation) defendants and appellants... Lilienthal, McKinstry & Raymond...attorneys for appellants. Curtis H. Lindley ...George H. Harlan... attorneys for respondent... [S.F., 1916–1917] 4 v. in 1. CU-B

5002. Marin water and power company vs. town of Sausalito. ...Marin water and power company, a corporation, plaintiff, vs. town of Sausalito, a municipal corporation, defendant...Lilienthal, McKinstry & Raymond, attorneys for plaintiff, O. F. Meldon, Thomas Beedy & Lanagan, attorneys for defendant... [S.F., 1912–20] 3 v. in 1. CU-B

5003. Marinship corporation. The first two years... [S.F., Taylor & Taylor, 1943] [26] p. illus., ports. CHi

5004. Martin, Charles, vs. Hill, William, et al. In the Supreme court of the state of California. Charles Martin, plaintiff and appellant, vs. William Hill, trustee, et al., defendants and respondents...Transcript on appeal, points and authorities of appellant and respondent etc. S.F., 1883–84. 9 v. in 1. A suit involving the Rancho Laguna de San Antonio. CLU

5005. Marvellous Marin county; San Francisco's most unique suburb. San Rafael, Marvellous Marin inc. [1936?] folder (90 p.) illus., map. CRcS

5006. Matthews, Herbert Hill. A self-survey of the Mill Valley elementary schools. [Berkeley, 1921] Thesis (M.A.)—Univ. of Calif., 1921. CU

5007. Mendell, George Henry. Report upon the blasting operations at Lime Point, California, in 1868 and 1869. Wash., D.C., Govt. print. off., 1880. 12 p. incl. diagr. fold. map. CLU

5008. Mill Valley and Mt. Tamalpais scenic railway. [Descriptive folder] [n.p., n.d.] [16] p. illus., map. CHi

5009. Mt. Tamalpais & Muir Woods railway. [Descriptive folder] [n.p.] 1917. illus., map. CHi

5010. —— Mt. Tamalpais and Muir Woods, "the crookedest railroad in the world." Tickets and general information... S.F. [n.d.] [12] p. illus., fold. map. CU-B

5011. —— Muir Woods guide. [n.p., 1915?] folder (6 p.) illus. CHi

5012. Mount Tamalpais, Marin county, California. [n.p., n.d.] folder (4 p.) illus., map. CRcS

5013. Nichols, William Ford. Why a Sir Francis Drake association in California?... [n.p., 1922] 15 p. (Sir Francis Drake assoc. Leaflet, no. 1) CHi

5014. Nimitz, Chester W. Drake's cove. [Point Reyes, Drake navigators guild, 1954?] 10 p. illus., ports., maps. Re-published from *Pacific discovery*, v.11, no. 2, 1958. CHi CRb CRcS CSf CSmat

5015. North Pacific coast railroad company of California. Prospectus. [n.p.] 1879. 13 p. CSmH CU-B

5016. Northwestern Pacific railroad. Marin county—where you should make your home... [n.d.] 15 p. illus. CSf

5017. Northwestern realty co., San Francisco. A trip to Marin heights and the famous Lithia springs. [S.F., 19–?] [18] p. illus., map. CHi

5018. Pope, John Keith. ...Launching the Lehi; the story of the Lehi expeditions. S.F., Academy phototype service, 1954. unp. illus. CSf

5019. Raymond, Lee, and Rice, Ann. Marin Indians. Illus. by Geraldine Von Hanssen. [San Rafael, Author, 1957] 15 p. illus. Includes bibliography. C CAla CHi CNa CO CSfWF-H CSrCL

5020. Ricketson, Barton, vs. Richardson, William A., et al. In the Supreme court of the state of California, October term, 1861. Barton Ricketson, plaintiff and appellant, vs. William A. Richardson, dec'd, Manuel Torres, executor, Samuel R. Throckmorton, J. Mora Moss, et al., defendants and respondents. Appeal from the Seventh judicial district, county of Marin, in an action to foreclose a mortgage. Argument of Gregory Yale, for the appellant. [S.F.] Towne & Bacon, print., 1861. 96 p. Sausalito rancho.   CLU

5021. —— In the Supreme court, state of California, April term, 1862. Barton Ricketson, plaintiff and respondent, vs. Richardson, Throckmorton, Davidson, Torres, executor and other. Brief of respondent on Janes' intervention and appeal. By Gregory Yale. 15th May, 1862. S.F., Towne & Bacon, print. [1862] 35 p.   CLU

5022. Robertson, John Wooster. Francis Drake & other early explorers along the Pacific coast. S.F., Grabhorn, 1927. 290 p. front. (col. map) illus., maps (1 fold.)
CBb CEH CHi CMont CSf CSfCW CSjC CV

5023. —— The harbor of St. Francis; Francis Drake lands in a fair and good bay near north latitude 38°; also a narration of the arguments advanced by certain historians in their selection of "The harbor of St. Francis" together with a relation of the Spanish discovery of the Bay of San Francisco... S.F. [Grabhorn] 1926. 119p. maps.
CHi CLU CMont CRedl CSS CSf CSfCP CSfCW CSfP CSfWF-H CSjC CSmH CU-B OrU UHi

5024. Rogers, R. Naylor, comp. Souvenir of Marin county... [Sausalito, The News, 1907] unp. illus.   CHi

5025. Ross. St. John's parish. ...Thirtieth anniversary of the incorporation of St. John's parish, in the town of Ross. April 18, 1938. [n.p., n.d.] 32 p. illus.
CHi

5026. Rothwell, Bertha (Stedman) Pioneering in Marin county, a historical recording. S.F., Author, 1959. 290 p. Typew.   CSrCL

5027. Roxburghe club of San Francisco. Tamalpais, enchanted mountain. [S.F.] 1946. 63 p. front. Ed. by Edgar M. Kahn.
C CAla CHi CLU CO CSf CSmH CSr CU-B

5028. Sausalito land ferry co. To the stockholders of the Sausalito land and ferry company. January 20, 1874. S.F., Alta Calif. print., 1874. 4 p.   CLU

5029. Sausalito; the Geneva of America, Marin county, California. [S.F., Commercial art co., c1911] [30] p.
CHi

5030. Schlemmer, Ruth H. A fifty year look at Mill Valley's library (as furnished to the MV RECORD) August 15, 1960. 7 l. Mimeo.   CHi

5031. Shell, Elton Eugene. Marin's historic Tomales and Presbyterian Church. Tomales, 1949. 32 p. illus., ports., map.
C CCSC CHi CL CLSU CU-B

5032. Souvenir of Mount Tamalpais. [S.F.?, Golden era co., 1885?] [16] p. illus.   CHi CLU

5033. Spector, Herman K. San Quentiniana; books published by officials and inmates of San Quentin. San Quentin, 1953. 24 l.   C

5034. Stanley, Leo Leonidas. Men at their worst ...with the collaboration of Evelyn Wells. N.Y., Appleton-Century, 1940. 322 p. illus., ports.
CHi CSrCL CU-B CUk

5035. —— Twenty years at San Quentin...resident physician. [n.p., 1933] 15 p. illus., port.   CU-B

5036. [Swain, Charles H.] Report of the San Rafael and Coast range mines, Marin county, Calif. S.F., F. W. Croudace & co., 1879. 5 p.   CU-B

5037. —— Report on the property of the Hite mine. S.F., Francis & Valentine, 1878. 12 p.   CSmH

5038. Tasker, Robert Joyce. Grimhaven. N.Y., Knopf, 1928. 241 p. Experiences in San Quentin prison.
CMartC CViCL ViU

5039. Thompson, James Alden. The scenes of my childhood, introd. by Kathleen Norris. Garden City, N.Y., Doubleday, 1948. 128 p.   CHi

5040. Town talk pub. co. ... Souvenir, edition de luxe, Marin county. S.F. [190–?] [44] p. illus., port.
CU-B

5041. Treganza, Adan Eduardo. The examination of Indian shellmounds within San Francisco bay with reference to the possible 1579 land fall of Sir Francis Drake. [Vacaville, Reporter pub. co., 1957] 15 p. illus., maps.
CSfSt

5042. Wagner, H. Howe. Mount Tamalpais state park, Marin county...written under auspices of Work projects administration, official project 665–08–3–147. Sponsored by state of California, Department of natural resources... [Sacramento, State print. off., 1941] 78 p. illus., maps. (Calif. hist. survey ser. Historic landmarks, monuments & state parks, ed. by Clark Wing. [1]) Bibliography: p. 66–68.
C CBev CBu CChiS CLSU CLU CMartC CO CSfSC CSjC CU-B

5043. West Point club, Mt. Tamalpais. West Point inn, maintained by West Point club, Mt. Tamalpais. [n.p., 1957?] 6 p. Mimeo.   CHi

5044. White, Winifred Mary, Sister. Eugene Casserly, his political and legal career, San Rafael, California. Wash., D.C., 1952. 98 p. Thesis (M.A.)—Catholic univ. of America.   CSrD

5045. Wilkins, James H. The evolution of a state prison. Historical narrative of the ten years from 1851–1861...printed in the Bulletin, a San Francisco newspaper, extending from June 13, 1918 through July 10, 1918. 96 p. Mimeo.   CSrCL

5046. Winn, W. B., ed. Souvenir of Marin county, California. Published by the Marin county journal. San Rafael, 1893. 116 p. illus.   CSfCP CSr CU-B

5047. Wurm, Theodore G. The crookedest railroad in the world; a history of the Mt. Tamalpais and Muir Woods railroad of California, by Theodore G. Wurm and Alvin C. Graves. Fresno, Acad. library guild, 1954. 121 p. illus., ports., maps, facsims. (Acad. transportation ser. 1) Bibliography: p. 113–115.
C CHi CLgA CMont CO CRedCL CSd CSf CSrCL CSrD CU-B CV

San Anselmo

5048. Curry, James. History of the San Francisco theological seminary of the Presbyterian church in the U.S.A. and its alumni association. Vacaville, Reporter pub. co., 1907. 206 p. illus., ports. Includes "biographical sketches of the founders and principal supporters."
C CCSC CHi CL CLU CLgA CO CSf CSfCW CSmH CU-B

5049. San Anselmo. First Presbyterian church. The golden jubilee, 1897–1947. [Souvenir and a brief history] [San Anselmo, 1947] 15 p. illus.   CHi

5050. San Francisco Presbyterian orphanage and farm, San Anselmo. Annual report... S.F. [189–?–]
C (1904) CHi (1902) CU-B (1900)

5051. —— ...Organized and incorporated in 1895, founded by Mrs. P.D. Browne, Claire H. O'Neill, superintendent. San Anselmo, 1938. 22 p. illus., ports. CHi

5052. San Francisco theological seminary. Diamond jubilee, 1871–1946... [n.p., 1946?] 16 p. illus., ports., maps.   CHi

5053. —— Our teachers of the Christian faith. [n.p., 1951?] 19 p. illus., ports.   CHi

5054. —— The San Francisco theological seminary of the Presbyterian church, organized...1871... S.F., G. W. Stevens, print., 1872. 8 p.   CU-B

5055. —— Souvenir program San Francisco theological seminary diamond jubilee celebration, May 12, 13, 14 and 15, 1947. [San Anselmo? 1947] 36 p. illus., ports.   CU-B

5056. —— Vicennial record of the students... 1871–1891. S.F., Occident print. house, 1891. 81 p.
CSfCW   CU-B

5057. Wicher, Edward Arthur. A summary of the history of the San Francisco theological seminary. [S.F., 1921] 25 p.   C   CL   CO

San Rafael

5058. Dominican college, San Rafael. Commencement programs.
CHi has May 28, 1896.

5059. —— Dominican college, conducted by Sisters of the order of Saint Dominic. Chartered August, 1890... San Rafael, 1916. [22] p. illus.   CHi

5060. —— Same. [1936] [62] p. illus.
CSmH   CU-B

5061. —— [Prospectus] San Rafael, Sunset press [1904] 15 p. illus.   CHi

5062. —— Student list of Dominican college and Dominican convent, 1923–1924. [S.F., 1923] 13 p.
CHi

5063. Dominican convent. ...A school for girls conducted by the Sisters of Saint Dominic... [S.F., 1923] 27 p. illus.   CHi

5064. Dwyer, John T. One hundred years an orphan; St. Vincent's, San Francisco's home for boys at San Rafael, 1855–1955. [Fresno, Acad. library guild, 1955] 159 p. illus.
C   CHi   CLgA   CSfCW   CStclU

5065. Elliott, W. W., pub. San Rafael illustrated and described. S.F., 1884. 58 p. illus.
C   CLU   CSmH   CU-B

5066. Hitchcock military academy. [Catalog] San Rafael.
CHi has 1910/11, 1914/15–1925. CU-B has 1903/04, 1905/06.

5067. —— ...Life & environment. Founded 1878. [S.F., Taylor & Taylor, c1919] 11 p.   CHi

5068. —— Same. San Rafael [c1922] 14 p. 12 pl. in folder.   CHi

5069. Hussey, John Adam. ...Misión San Rafael Arcángel... Berkeley, 1936. 48 p. Typew.   CU-B

5070. Miller, Edith Dillard. The historical development of San Rafael high school (1887–1958). San Rafael, 1958. 61 p. Thesis (M.A.)– Dominican college, 1958.
CSrD

5071. Mount Tamalpais military academy. [Catalog] San Rafael, 189–?–
CHi has 1907/08. CU-B has 1891/92, 1893/94–1901/02, 1903/04–05, 1909/10, 1914/15, 1916/17–18.

5072. —— [Descriptive brochure and calendar, 1908–1909] San Rafael, 1908. 24 p.   CHi

5073. —— Mount Tamalpais military academy, San Rafael, California. [Peck-Judah co., inc., n.d.] 16 p. of illus.   CHi

5074. Pratt, Frederick H. F. H. Pratt, general merchandise...San Rafael, California. Accts. from 1872 ...[to 1879] [San Rafael, 1872–79] 4 v. Original ms.
CU-B

5075. San Rafael. Mount Tamalpais cemetery and mausoleum. The Mount Tamalpais cemetery, a rural burying-place for San Francisco. Begun June 2d, 1878, consecrated August 10th, 1879, incorporated June 2d, 1880... S.F., E. Denny & co., 1880.
C   CLU   CU-B

5076. —— Roman Catholic orphan asylum. Report of the superintendent... [Sacramento, O. M. Clayes, state printer, 1864] 4 p.   CSmH

5077. San Rafael military academy. Catalog, no. F, I, N. San Rafael.
CU-B has 1932/33, 1936/37, 1941/42.

5078. Sisters of the Order of St. Dominic, San Rafael. The Dominicans of San Rafael; first chapters in the story of the Dominican congregation of the Holy Name of Jesus in California... [San Rafael] Dominican convent of San Rafael, 1941. 108 p. illus., ports.
CBb   CHi   CLU   CO   CSfCW   CSmH   CSrD   CU-B

5079. Views of San Rafael, Calif. [San Rafael, 1906?] 19 pl.   NN

5080. Young ladies' seminary, San Rafael. Closing exercises of the Young ladies' seminary, to be held at the Tamalpais hotel, San Rafael, Friday afternoon, December 17th, 1875. [San Rafael? 1875] [3] p.
CU-B

MARIPOSA COUNTY
(Created in 1850)

GREAT REGISTER

5081. Mariposa county. Index to the Great register of the county of Mariposa. 1866– Place of publication and title vary.
C has 1872–73, 1875–77, 1879–80, 1882 (biennially to)– 1926, 1926–28, 1930 (biennially to)– 1962. CL has 1872–73, 1875, 1877, 1879 (suppl.), 1882, 1884, 1886 (suppl.), 1888, 1890 (suppl.) CU-B has July-Aug. 1867, Oct. 1872, Aug. 1873, Aug. 1873 (suppl.), Sept. 1873 (suppl.), Aug. 1875, Apr. 1879, 1879 (suppl.), Oct. 1880, Index: 1926, 1934.

GENERAL REFERENCES

5082. Alexander, Henry Eugene, vs. Donohoe, Joseph A. ...Joseph A. Donohoe impleaded with Eugene Kelly and others, ads. Henry Eugene Alexander, answer of Joseph A. Donohoe. Martin & Smith, attorneys for Joseph A. Donohoe. [n.p., 1884?] 103 p.   CU-B

5083. Allen, John. John Allen's letters from California. Edited, with an introduction by Russell E. Bidlack. 32 p. Mimeo. Reprinted from *Washtenaw impressions*, May, 1961.   CHi

5084. Allyn, Timothy C. The Mariposa estate. Report. N.Y., 1862. 24 p.   CHi   NN

5085. Alta California, inc., comp. & pub. Mariposa county, California. "Since 1849—a land of recreation and opportunity—on the Mother Lode." A general and historical summary. Sacramento [1938] 11 l. Reproduced from typew. copy.   CU-B

5086. Alta California, San Francisco. [Clippings from Daily Alta California, August 1850–April 1851] Photocopies. Items dealing with Mariposa battalion.
CFS

5087. Barrett, Ila (Goss) Memories of Coulterville. [Sonora, Mother lode press, 1954] 77 p. illus.
C   CMerCL

5088. Boggs, Biddle, vs. Merced mining company. In the Supreme court of the state of California. Biddle Boggs vs. Merced mining company. Appellant's brief in reply. [n.p., 186–?] 8 p. Signed: Cook & Fenner, of counsel for appellant. CLU

5089. —— ...Biddle Boggs, respondent, v. the Merced mining company, appellant. Argument on rehearing of the case. Brief for appellant. Halleck, Peachey & Billings, and Gregory Yale, of counsel. [n.p., n.d.] 42 p. CSmH CU–B

5090. —— ...Biddle Boggs vs. Merced mining company. [Arguments on behalf of the respondent, by Joseph G. Baldwin and S. Heydenfeldt, of counsel] [S.F.? 1859?] CSmH

5091. —— [Briefs & other records in land claim. Merced mining company, appellant. Biddle Boggs, appellee. S.F.? 1857] 6 v. CSmH

5092. —— Speech of S. W. Inge in defence of miners' rights. Argument...in the case of Biddle Boggs against the Merced mining company. Delivered in the Supreme court of California on the 29th of October, 1859. [Sacramento? 1859?] CSmH

5093. Browne, John Ross. The Mariposa estate: its past, present and future. Comprising the official report of J. Ross Browne (U.S. commissioner) upon its mineral resources... N.Y., Russell's Am. steam print. house, 1868. 62 p. map.
C CHi CLU CSfCSM CSfCW CSmH CU–B NHi

5094. Burns Ranche gold mining co. An account of its location, title, mineral riches, etc., with its charter and proceedings, letters, certificates and other matters relating to it, etc. December, 1851. N.Y., 1851. 20 p. CHi

5095. California. Supreme court. Decision of the Supreme court, in the suit of Merced mining co. vs. John C. Frémont, et al. [n.p., n.d.] 12 p. CHi

5096. —— —— Decisions of the Supreme court of the state of California,...Biddle Boggs v. The Merced mining company, Moore v. Shaw, and Fremont v. Fowler. S.F., Print. by Towne & Bacon [1859–61] 47 p. CSmH CU–B

5097. —— —— The Frémont decision. Decision of the supreme court of the state of California, in the case of Biddle Boggs, vs. Merced mining company, together with the findings and judgment of the thirteenth judicial district, and remarks by the press. S.F., Print. by Royal P. Locke, 1859. 45 p. C CLU CSmH CU–B

5098. —— —— Opinion of the Supreme court of California in Biddle Boggs vs. the Merced mining company, delivered by Chief Justice Field... [n.p., 186–?] CSmH

5099. Chamberlain, Newell D. The call of gold; true tales on the gold road to Yosemite... [Mariposa, Gazette press, c1936] 183 p. illus., ports., maps.
Available in many California libraries and NN TxU

5100. Crampton, Charles Gregory. The opening of the Mariposa mining region, 1849–1859, with particular reference to the Mexican land grant of John Charles Frémont. [Berkeley, 1941] 327 l. illus., maps. Thesis (Ph.D.)—Univ. of Calif., 1941. CFS (micro-film copy) CU CU-B

5101. Crosley, Mary Edith. Hornitos. [Universal City? Crosley books, c1959] 25 p. illus.
C CHi CO CTurS CU-B

5102. Duncan, John. Frémont gold mines and property, California. An answer to the pamphlet of Mr. David Hoffman... London, John Nichols, print., 1852. 22 p. CSmH

5103. Eccleston, Robert. Mariposa Indian war, 1850–51; diaries of Robert Eccleston: the California gold rush, Yosemite and the High Sierra. Edited by C. Gregory Crampton. Salt Lake City, Univ. of Utah press, 1957. 168 p. port., map. (Bancroft lib. pub. no. 6)
Available in many California libraries and KU UHi UU

5104. Farmers loan and trust co. vs. Donohoe, Joseph A., et al. In the Circuit court of the United States, Ninth circuit, district of California. The Farmers loan and trust company, vs. Joseph A. Donohoe, and the Mariposa land and mining company of California. [S.F., 1878] 41 l. CU-B

5105. Frémont, Jessie (Benton) Far-West sketches. Bost., D. Lothrop co. [c1890] 206 p.
C CBb CL CLO CLU CO CP CPom CRic CSal CSmH

5106. The Frémont grant, California. [S.F.] O'Meara & Painter, print., [1885] 31 p. illus., map. CSmH

5107. Gazette-Mariposan. Mariposa county... Mariposa, W. N. Brunt co., 1904. 48 p. illus.
C CHi CSfCP CSmH CU-B

5108. Hatcher, Arthur. A brief history of Mariposa courthouse and airport. [Mariposa, 1937] 16 p. CHi

5109. Hodgskin, James B. Suggestions for the formation of the Mariposa trust fund. Submitted to the holders of stocks & bonds of the Mariposa company... N.Y., 1868. 13 p. CSmH

5110. Hughson, L. E. The Indian troubles in Mariposa county in 1850–51 and the acts of the Legislature regarding them... [n.p., n.d.] 22 l. Autographed from typew. copy. CL

5111. Leitch, B. M. Mariposa grove of Big trees, California. [Wawona? c1910] [32] p. illus. "Designed by H. C. Tibbitts." C CRic CSf

5112. Levick, M. B. Mariposa county, California. S.F., Sunset mag. homeseekers' bur. [1912] 31 p. illus., map. CHi CU-B

5113. McLean, John T. Statement concerning Senate bill no. 2708 and House bill no. 7712, authorizing the purchase by the United States, and the making free, of the toll-roads passing over the Yosemite national park. [n.p., 189–?] 19 p. CU-B

5114. Mariposa centennials. Souvenir program, Mariposa centennials, 1854–1954, commemorating the 100th anniversary of the Mariposa county courthouse... and of the Mariposa gazette... Mariposa, 1954. 32 p. illus., ports., maps. C CFS CHi CU-B

5115. Mariposa company vs. Garrison, Cornelius K. In the United States Supreme court. Appeal book... Dudley Field, plaintiff's attorney. B. F. Dunning, defendant's attorney. N.Y., M. B. Brown & co., 1864. 142 p. CHi

5116. —— Papers read on motion to dissolve injunction. Dudley Field, plaintiff's attorney. B. F. Dunning, defendant's attorney. N.Y., M.B. Brown & co., 1864. 40 p. CSmH

5117. The Mariposa co. The Mariposa company, 34 Wall street, New York ... organized 25th June, 1863. N.Y., Wm. C. Bryant & co., 1863. 81 p. map.
C CFS CHi CL CLU CSmH CU-B NHi

5118. —— Proceedings of the meeting of the bondholders of the Mariposa company, May 20th, 1868, and the report of the committee of investigation, read at the bondholders' meeting of May 27th, 1868, with the proposed plan for the purchase of the Garrison title by the bondholders. N.Y., N.Y. print. co., 1868. 15 p. CSmH CU-B

5119. —— **Committee of the bondholders.** Final report...Accepted and adopted June 4th, 1868. N.Y., N.Y. print. co., 1868. 9 p. Signed: Benj. M. Stilwell, Wm. Aufermann [and] Geo. E. King.   CSmH

5120. Mariposa county. Chamber of commerce. Mariposa county; history, industries, scenic attractions. 1939. folder (10 p.) illus.   CRcS

5121. Mariposa county Panama-Pacific exposition commission. Mariposa county, California. [1914] 16 p. illus.   CAla

5122. The Mariposa estate. "Las Mariposas." Trust for developing... S.F., Wm. P. Harrison, print., 1874. 34 p.   CSmH CU-B

5123. Mariposa gazette. Centennial edition, 1854–1954... [Mariposa, 1954] A-H, 64 p. illus., ports., maps.
CBaB CFS CHi CL CLgA CO CPom CSt CSto CTurS CU-B

5124. —— Gold; 86th anniversary souvenir edition ... [Mariposa, 1940] 20 p. illus.   CU-B

5125. Mariposa grant, inc. The tragedy of Mariposa grant, a human interest story of the rise, fall and dawning rehabilitation of an empire of marvelous riches. S.F. [190–?] [12] p.   CSmH

5126. The Mariposa land and mining co. of California. By-laws...Incorporated November 4th, 1874. S.F., 1875. 16 p.   CHi CU-B

5127. —— The Mariposas estate; its mineral wealth and resources...comprising the official reports of Professors J. Adelberg...B. Silliman jr. ...and others. Also, that of J. Ross Browne, U.S. commissioner, upon its mineral resources. Transmitted to Congress on the 5th of March, 1868, by the Hon. Hugh McCulloch, secretary of the treasury of the United States, and other documents laid before the trustees of the Mariposa land and mining company... N.Y., Russells' American steam print., 1873. 191 p. diagrs.   CHi NHi

5128. —— Mortgage upon the Mariposa estate held by the Farmer's loan and trust co. of New York, trustee, to secure the convertible bonds of the Mariposa land and mining company of California, dated December 15, 1875. N.Y., National print. co., 1876. 12 p.   C

5129. —— [Officers, statements, by-laws, etc.] N.Y., Evening post steam presses, 1875. [26] p.   C

5130. —— Proceedings of the annual meeting of stockholders... October 25, 1875. [N.Y., 1875?] 8 p.   CU-B

5131. —— Statement... N.Y., 1872–77.
C has Mar. 31, 1876. CHi has 1872. CU-B has 1876–77.

5132. —— ...To the trustees of the Mariposa land and mining company. [Report made by the president, Mark Brumagim, Feb. 15, 1873] [N.Y., 1873] 18 l.   CHi CU-B

5133. Mariposa quartz convention. Quartzburg mining laws, 1851. [n.p.] 1851. 2 l. The Mariposa quartz convention was held in the mining camp of Quartzburg.   CHi CSfCSM

5134. The Mariposas estate. London [Chiswick press: print. by Whittingham and Wilkins] 1861. 63 p. fold. map.   CHi CLU CU-B

5135. Maxwell Creek gold mining co. Report, February 11, 1864. S.F., L. Albin, print., 1864. 8 p.   C

5136. Merced mining co. Annual report of the trustees of the Merced mining company. Organized March 4, 1851. S.F., Alta Calif. steam presses, 1852. 16 p.   CU-B

5137. Mountain view house, Mariposa. Mountain view house. [Register] Chas. E. Peregoy. [1870–78] [213] p. Photostat (negative) of ms. The entries are dated principally between June 1870 and October 1874, with one entry at the end for June 1878.   C

5138. Odd fellows, Independent order of. Mariposa co. Hornitos lodge, no. 99. Constitution, by-laws, rules of order and order of business of Hornitos lodge, no. 99...Instituted September 13th, 1860. S.F., Jos. Winterburn & co., 1875. 96 p. illus.   C

5139. —— —— Same. 1885. 55 p. illus.   C

5140. Phillips, Catherine (Coffin) Coulterville chronicle, the annals of a mother lode mining town... S.F., Grabhorn, 1942. 275 p. illus., ports. Bibliography: p. 262–268.
C CAla CBb CHi CL CLO CLSU CLU CLgA CO CSS CSf CSfP CSfSC CSjC CSmH CStclU CU-B CV CoD MiD

5141. Silliman, Benjamin. A report of an examination of the Mariposa estate in California, made in May 1864. N.Y., Wm. C. Bryant & co., 1864. 33 p.   C

5142. —— Review of the nature, resources and plan (now in progress) of the northern division of the Mariposa estate... N.Y., September 1873. 95 p.
C CHi CSfCW CSmH CU-B

5143. Simonin, Louis Laurent. ...Mineur des placers du comté de Mariposa (California—États-Unis) (Ouvier chef de métier dans le système du travail sans engagements) d'après les renseignements recueillis sur les lieux de juin à décembre 1859... [Paris? 1861?] p. 145–206. tables. At head of title: no. 22.
CLU CSfCW

5144. La Victoire copper mining co. ...Reports ...1865/66. S.F., 1866.   CU-B

5145. —— **Committee of investigation.** ...Report to stockholders...Aug. 19th, 1865. S.F., 1865. 10 p.   CU-B

5146. Wood, Raymund F. California's Agua Fria; the early history of Mariposa county. Fresno, Acad. lib. guild, 1954. 112 p. illus., maps.
Available in many California libraries and CtY MWA MoSHi NIC NN UPB

Yosemite

5147. Adams, Ansel Easton. The four seasons in Yosemite national park; a photographic story of Yosemite's spectacular scenery. Ed. by Stanley Plumb. [L.A., Times-mirror print., 1936] [46] p. of illus. double map.
C CFS CHi CLU CLgA CO CSfCW CSfSC

5148. —— My camera in Yosemite valley; 24 photographs and an essay on mountain photography. Yosemite national park, V. Adams; Boston, Houghton, 1949. 69 p. Bibliography: p. 70.
C CArcHT CL CLU CLgA CSfCW CSrD CStmo CU-B OrU

5149. —— Yosemite valley. Ed. by Nancy Newhall. S.F., Five associates, 1959. unp. illus.
C CAla CChiS CL CLU CSluCL

5150. Adams, Virginia, and Adams, Ansel Easton. Illustrated guide to Yosemite valley... S.F., Crocker, 1940. 127 p. illus., maps. "A brief bibliography, by Francis P. Farquhar": p. 127.
C CBu CHi CLU CMerCL CNa CO CSalCL CSfCW CSfSC CSjC CSluCL

5151. —— Same. [5th ed.] Stanford [1952] 128 p. illus.
C CArcHT CChiS CL CLO CLSU CLU CO

CRedl CRic CSalCL CSf CSfCSM CStmo CSto CU-B CViCL ODa

5152. Ahwahnee hotel. Yosemite national park... L.A., John B. Browne, jr. [193–?] 23 p. illus.
CHi CU-B

5153. Bailey, Charles A. A trip to Yosemite 1884. 429 p. Bound ms. illus.
CSfSC

5154. Barrett, Samuel Alfred, and Gifford, E.W. Miwok material culture. Yosemite national park, Yosemite natural history assoc. [1959?] [119]–376 p. illus., pl. (Bul. of Milwaukee public museum, v.2, no. 4, March 1933)
C

5155. Bickmore, Albert Smith. California and the Yosemite valley. [no. 195] Stenographer's notes of a lecture by Prof. Albert S. Bickmore... Given under the auspices of the State department of public instruction, American museum of natural history, 1896. 27 p.
C

5156. Big Oak Flat and Yosemite stage co. Yosemite Valley via Big Oak Flat, only 32 hours from San Francisco... [S.F.? 1901?] 23 p.
CSmH

5157. Bingaman, John W. Guardians of the Yosemite, a story of the first rangers. c1961. illus., ports., map. 123 p.
CHi

5158. Bruce, Wallace. The Yosemite. Bost., Lee & Shephard; N.Y., Charles T. Dillingham, 1880. 19 l. illus.
C CHi CL CLO CLSU CLU CMont COHN CSf CSfCP CSmH CU-B

5159. Buckley, James Monroe. ...Two weeks in the Yosemite and vicinity... N.Y., Phillips & Hunt; Cincinnati, Ohio, Walden & Stowe, 1883. 36 p.
C CHi CLU CSfSC CSmH CU-B

5160. Bunnell, Lafayette Houghton. Discovery of the Yosemite and the Indian war of 1851, which led to that event... Chicago, Fleming H. Revell [c1880] 331 p. illus., port., map. Farquhar notes 2d edition (no date) and 3d edition, revised and corrected, 1892.
C CBu CChiS CHi CL CLU CP CSfU CSfWF-H CSj CSjC CSmat CSmH CU-B MoKU N

5161. —— Same. 3d ed. 1892.
CPom NjN

5162. —— Same... 4th ed., reprinted from third ed. L.A., G.W. Gerlicher, 1911. 355 p. illus., port., map. Available in many California libraries and MoS UPB

5163. Butler, Sir William Francis. Far out; rovings retold... London, W. Isbister, ltd., 1880. 386 p.
C CLU CO CSf CU-B

5164. California. Commissioners to manage the Yosemite valley and Mariposa big tree grove. Information for the use of Yosemite visitors... Sacramento, State print., 1886. 27 p. illus., map.
CHi CSfU

5165. —— Same. 1887. 24 p. illus.
CHi CU-B

5166. —— —— Report. 1866/67–1902/04. Sacramento, Supt. state print., 1867–1904. 19 v. Complete list in Farquhar.
CHi has 1866/67. CLU has 1887/88, 1891/92, 1895/96. CSmH has 1868–1904. CU-B has 1866/67–1877/79, 1882/84–1884/86, 1888/90–1902/04.

5167. —— —— Rules, regulations, and by-laws... 1866, 1885. S.F., 1866–85.
C (1866) CHi (1885) CU-B (1866, 1885)

5168. —— Office of State engineer. To preserve from defacement and promote the use of the Yosemite valley, by W. H. Hall, state engineer. Sacramento, J. D. Young, state print., 1882.
C CLU

5169. —— State board of trade. Yosemite valley, history, description and statement of conditions relative to the proposed recession to the national government. [S.F.? 1904?] 33 p. fold. map. (Calif. state board of trade circular, no. 13)
C CHi CSfCW CU-B

5170. —— State geologist (Josiah Dwight Whitney) The Yosemite book, a description of the Yosemite valley and the adjacent region of the Sierra Nevada and the big trees. N.Y., Julius Bien, 1868. 116 p. illus., maps. Only 250 copies issued of this special edition with actual photographs.
C CLU CLgA CP CSd CSfSC CSmH CU-B

5171. —— —— ...The Yosemite guide-book: a description of the Yosemite valley and the adjacent region of the Sierra Nevada, and of the big trees of California... Published by authority of the Legislature. [Cambridge, Mass., Univ. press, Welch, Bigelow, & co.] 1869. 155 p. illus., maps. Other editions followed in 1870, 1871, and 1874.
Available in many California libraries and UPB ViU

5172. Chase, Joseph Smeaton. Yosemite trails; camp and pack-train in the Yosemite region of the Sierra Nevada... Bost. & N.Y., Houghton, 1911. 354 p. illus., map.
Available in many California libraries and CaBViPA MiD ODa

5173. Cheney, Warren. Yosemite illustrated in colors ... S.F., Crocker [1890] 38 l. illus.
C CLU CSfCW CSfSC CSmH CU-B

5174. Churchill, Caroline M. Over the purple hills; or sketches of travel in California... Denver, Author, c1876. 252 p. Publisher varies.
CUk
Other editions followed in 1877, 1878, 1883, 1884.
CFS (1884) CHi (1884) CSd (1883) CSf (1877) CSfCW (1878)

5175. Clark, Galen. Indians of the Yosemite valley and vicinity... Yosemite valley, Author, 1904. 110 p. port.
Available in many California libraries and IC

5176. —— Same. 1907. 112 p.
CHi CV

5177. —— The Yosemite valley, its history, characteristic features, and theories regarding its origins... Yosemite valley, Nelson S. Salter, 1910. 108 p. illus., port.
C CL CLO CLSU CLU CMerCL CO CSf CSfSC CSj CSjC CSmH CStmo MoS OrU

5178. Clark, Lewis Wilber. Trail guide to the high Sierra camp areas of Yosemite national park. Stanford [1953] 47 p. illus., maps (part col.)
—— Pocket guide to the high Sierra camp areas, Yosemite national park. [Stanford, c1953] col. map (fold.)
C CArcHT CL CLO CRic CSS CSfCSM CU-B MiD

5179. —— Trail guide to the North country, Yosemite national park. Stanford [1954] 47 p. illus., maps (part col.)
—— Pocket guide to the North country, Yosemite national park. [Stanford, c1954] col. map (fold.)
C CFS CL CLU CSfCSM CSluCL MiD

5180. —— Trail guide to the South boundary country, Yosemite national park. Stanford [1955] 47 p. illus., maps (part col.)
—— Pocket guide to the South boundary country, Yosemite national park. [Stanford, 1955] col. map (fold.)
C CFS CL CLU CO CRic CSd CSfCSM MiD

5181. [Crane, Marcia D.] Arcadia and the lion's den. Camping party to Yo Semite, June 1886. 64 p.
CHi CU-B

5182. Degnan, Laurence. The old stagedriver's

Yosemite yarns [by] Laurence Degnan [and] Douglass Hubbard. [Illustrated by] Ed Vella. [Fresno? 1961] 24 p. illus. Includes bibliography.   C CTurS

5183. [Denison, E. S.] Yosemite and the big trees of California... [S.F.] Litho. Crocker [1881] [103] p. of illus.   CL CLSU CSmH CU-B

5184. Ellis, Dorothy. Ahwahnee: Yosemite national park, California. [Printed for the Yosemite Park and Curry company, by Johnck and Seeger. S.F., 1935]   C

5185. Farquhar, Francis Peloubet. Yosemite, the big trees and the high Sierra, a selective bibliography. Berkeley, Univ. press, c1948. 104 p. illus., ports.
          CHi CRedCL CSfSt CSto

5186. Fiske, George. [Photographs of Yosemite. n.p., n.d.] 25 mounted photos.   CFS

5187. Foley, D. J. Yosemite souvenir & guide... Yosemite, "Tourist" studio, 1902. 110 p. illus., maps.
          CHi CU-B NN
Other editions followed in 1903, 1904, 1906, 1907, 1908, 1909, 1911, 1915.
          C (1903, 1908) CHi (1906, 1907) CLSU (1909) CO (1907) CSf (1907) CSfCP (1909) CSfCW (1909) CSmH (1904) CU-B (1903–1915)

5188. Foster, Samuel Lynde. In the canyons of Yosemite national park of California. Bost., Humphries [c1949] 121 p. illus., ports.
          C CArcHT CL CLU CMerCL CSd CSf CU-B CV

5189. Fryxell, Fritiof, ed. Thomas Moran, explorer in search of beauty; a biographical sketch... East Hampton, N.Y., East Hampton free library, 1958. 84 p. illus., ports.   CHi CU-B

5190. Gordon-Cummings, Constance Frederica. Granite crags... Edinburgh & London, William Blackwood & sons, 1884. 384 p. illus., map.
          CBu CL CLU CO CSfCW CSfSC CSmH CU-B

5191. —— Same. 1886.
          C CLSU CP CU-B MiD

5192. —— Same. 1901.   CU-B

5193. Gusto, Leo. Hiking in the Yosemite. S.F., Priv. print., 1926. 31 p.   CSf

5194. Hall, Ansel Franklin. Guide to Yosemite; a handbook of the trails and roads of Yosemite valley and the adjacent region. S.F., Sunset pub. house, 1920. 98 p. maps.   C CFS CHi CLO CLSU CLU CSf

5195. —— Handbook of Yosemite national park... N.Y. & London, Putnam, 1921. 347 p. illus., map. "References" at end of most chapters.
Available in many California libraries and MiD ODa

5196. —— Yosemite valley, an intimate guide. Berkeley, National parks pub., c1929. 80 p. illus.
          CLU CSf CU-B

5197. Hastings, Cristel. Here and there in the Yosemite. S.F., Cloister press, 1923. 64 p.   CHi

5198. Heininger, Charles P., pub. Pacific coast album; with views of Yosemite, Big tree grove, and various points of interest. S.F. [1888] 22 p. fold. pl.
          CSf CSfSC

5199. Historic American buildings survey. Historical data to accompany Historic American buildings survey drawings of Cedar cottage, Yosemite national park. S.F., 1940. 10 l. 14 mounted photos. Typew.
          CU-B

5200. Hittell, John Shertzer. Yosemite; its wonders and its beauties... S.F., H. H. Bancroft & co., 1868. 59 p. illus., map.   C CHi CLU CSmH CU-B

5201. Houseworth (Thomas) & co., pub. ... Large views of Yo Semite valley and the big trees... S.F. [n.d.] [5] p. fold. leaflet. (Catalogue no. 1)   CHi

5202. —— Tourists' guide and correct map of routes to Yo-Semite valley and big trees. S.F. [n.d.] fold. leaflet. map.   CHi

5203. —— Views of the Yo-Semite valley for the stereoscope... S.F. [n.d.] [6] p. fold. leaflet.   CHi

5204. —— Yosemite views [sketches by T. E. R.] [S.F., 1879?] 10 mounted pl. in portfolio.   CU-B

5205. Hubbard, Douglass. Ghost mines of Yosemite, with photographs by the author. [Fresno? Awani press, 1958] [38] p. illus., ports., map, facsims.
          C CAla CBaB CFS CL CLSM CLU CMerCL CNa CP CRb CRic CSalCL CSd CSfCSM CStcl CSto CTurS CU-B

5206. Hutchings, James Mason. In the heart of the Sierras: the Yo Semite valley, both historical and descriptive... Yo Semite valley, Pub. at the Old cabin; Oakland, Pac. press, 1886. 496 p. illus., port., maps. Farquhar notes other printings in 1886, 1887, and 1888, together with a Tourists' edition, n.d.
Available in many California libraries and CoU MiD-B OU

5207. —— Memorial of J. M. Hutchings and J. C. Lamon, settlers in Yosemite valley, Mariposa county, California. [S.F.? 1868]   CSmH

5208. —— Scenes of wonder and curiosity in California... S.F., Hutchings & Rosenfeld [c1860] 236 p. illus. Other editions followed in 1861, 1862, and 1865.
Available in many California libraries and CaBViPA ViU

5209. —— Same. ...A tourist's guide to the Yo Semite valley... N.Y. & S.F., A. Roman & co., 1870. 292 p. illus. Farquhar notes other printings in 1871, 1872, 1875, and 1876.
          C C-S CHi CL CLSU CMerCL CSalCL CSf CSfCSM CSfU CSfWF-H CSmH CU-B NN ViW

5210. —— Same ...Tourist's guide to the Yo Semite valley and the big tree groves for the spring and summer of 1877. S.F., A. Roman & co. [1877] 102 p.
          C C-S CHi CLU CSfCP CSfCW CSfSC CU-B

5211. —— Souvenir of California Yo Semite valley and the big trees... S.F. [1894] 101 p. illus., map.
          C C-S CHi CLU CSf CSfCW

5212. Johnston, Hank. Short line to Paradise, the story of the Yosemite valley railroad. Long Beach, c1962. 96 p. illus.   C CAla CTurS CU-B

5213. Jump, Herbert Atchinson. The Yosemite; a spiritual interpretation... Bost. [etc.] Pilgrim press [c1916] 35 p. illus.
          C CL CLU CRedl CSmH CU-B NN

5214. Kettlewell, Edith Germain. Yosemite; the discovery of Yosemite valley... [Berkeley] 1931. Thesis (M.A.)—Univ. of Calif., 1931.   CU CU-B

5215. King, Thomas Starr. A vacation among the Sierras: Yosemite in 1860. Ed. ...by John A. Hussey. S.F., Bk. club of Calif., 1962.   CAla

5216. Kneeland, Samuel. The wonders of the Yosemite valley, and of California...with original photographic illustrations by John P. Soule. Bost., Alexander Moore, 1871. 71 p. illus.
          CArcHT CHi CL CO CSd CSfCP CSfCW CSmH CU-B

5217. —— Same. Bost., Alexander Moore; N.Y., Lee, Shepard & Dillingham, 1872. 79 p. illus., maps.

C CHi CLO CLSU CP CSjC CSmH CU-B OrU UPB

5218. —— Same. 3d ed. rev. & enl. [Same imprint as above] 98 p. illus., maps.
CSf CSjC CSmH CU-B

5219. Kuykendall, Ralph Simpson. Early history of Yosemite valley... Wash., D.C., Govt. print. off., 1919. 12 p. Reprinted from *Grizzly bear*, July, 1919.
C CHi CO OrU

5220. Kyle, Charles Wesley. Yosemite, the world's wonderland. [S.F., Printed by Chase and Rae, c1915] 31 p. illus. C C-S

5221. Laws of Congress and California, relating to the Yosemite valley, place the management of that valley in the hands of the governor & Yosemite commissioners. A plea for justice to the Coulterville and Yosemite turnpike company. S.F., Alta Calif. print., 1878. 24 p. CHi

5222. Laws relating to the Yosemite valley and Mariposa big tree grove. [n.p., 1874?] 35 p. CLU

5223. Le Conte, Caroline Eaton. [Holograph journal of a trip to the Yosemite valley in 1878] [Berkeley? 1880] 2 v. illus. CU-B

5224. Le Conte, Joseph. Autobiography... N.Y., Appleton, 1903. 337 p.
C CBb CBu CHi CL CLU CMartC CMerCL CO CRedl CSf CSfCP CSfCW CSfSC CSmat CSmH CStmo CU-B CViCL

5225. Lehmer, O. W. Yosemite national park. [Chicago] Poole bros., print., c1912. [32] p. illus. (part. col.)
C CFS CU-B

5226. Leonard, Zenas. Narrative of the adventures of Zenas Leonard... Print. & pub. by D. W. Moore, Clearfield, Pa., 1839. 87 p.
CHi CLU CSmH CU-B CaBViPA

5227. —— Same, with title: Leonard's narrative... Cleveland, Burrows bros. co., 1904. 317 p. illus., ports., maps.
C CHi CL CLSU CLU CLgA CSalCL CSd CSmH CU-B CViCL CaBViPA

5228. —— Same, with title: Narrative of the adventures of Zenas Leonard... [Clearfield, Pa.] Raftsman's journal, 1908. 106 p. CLU CSmH

5229. —— Same, ed. by Milo Milton Quaife. Chicago, Lakeside press, Christmas, 1934. 278 p. map (Lakeside classics)
C CHi CO CSdS CSfSC CSmH CSto CU-B CViCL CaBViPA

5230. —— Same, ed. by John C. Ewers, with title: Adventures of Zenas Leonard, fur trader. Norman, Univ. of Okla. press, [1959] 172 p. illus. (The Am. exploration and travel ser., 28) C CSto

5231. Lester, John Erastus. The Yo-semite. Its history, its scenery, its development. Providence, Author, 1873. 40 p.
C CHi CL CLU CSfCP CSmH CU-B MiD-B NN

5232. [Mackenzie, George G.] The Yosemite despoilers; a reply to Gov. Waterman's statements... [N.Y., 1890] CU-B

5233. —— Yosemite: where to go and what to do... S.F., C. A. Murdock & co., 1888. 98 p. illus.
C CLO CSf CSfCW CSmH CU-B

5234. [McLean, John T.] Yosemite... The Coulterville route to Yosemite... [S.F.? 1877?] [16] p. illus. CU-B

5235. Magill, Harry Brown. Motoring thru the Yosemite. S.F., Yosemite pub. co. [c1922] [44] p. illus., map. CO CU-B

5236. —— Same. [c1926] unp. illus.
CAla CFS

5237. Matthes, François Emile. Sketch of Yosemite national park and an account of the origin of the Yosemite and Hetch Hetchy valleys... [Wash., D.C., Govt. print. off.] 1912. CU-B OrU

5238. —— Same. 1920. 45 p. illus., map.
CHi CO CSfSC CSj

5239. —— The story of Yosemite valley... N.Y., 1924. 21 p. illus. C CL CLU CU-B

5240. Minner, Bessie. Voice of Yosemite. [Bakersfield, Bakersfield Californian, c1925] 12 p. port.
CU-B

5241. Morhange, Salvador. Les arbes géants de Californie et la vallée de la Yosemite... Bruxelles, Merzbach & Falk, 1880. 44 p. CU-B

5242. Morse, Cora A. Yosemite as I saw it. Oakland, The Outlook, 1896. 23 p. illus., port. C-S

5243. —— Same. 3d ed. [Oakland, Kitchener print.] c1896. [48] p. illus. CHi

5244. Muench, Josef. Along Yosemite trails. N.Y., Hastings house [1948] 101 p. (chiefly illus.) map (on lining paper).
C CCoron CFS CLO CLU CLgA CMon CNa COr CRic CSS CSd CSf CSluCL CU-B MiD UPB

5245. Muir, John. Letters to a friend. Written to Mrs. Ezra S. Carr. 1866–1879. Bost., Houghton, 1915. 194 p. "Between 1868 and 1879, Yosemite is almost constantly the theme."—Farquhar.
CL CLSU CMartC CP CRedl CSfSC CSmH CU-B

5246. —— The Yosemite... N.Y., Century, 1912. 284 p. illus., maps.
Available in many California libraries and MiD NN ODa

5247. —— Same. 1920. 284 p. illus., fold. maps.
CHi CSluCL

5248. —— and Adams, Ansel. Yosemite and the Sierra Nevada... Bost., Houghton, 1948. 132 p. illus. Excerpts from Muir with photographs by Adams.
Available in many California libraries and MiD ODa

5249. Murphy, Thomas Dowler. Three wonderlands of the American west: being the notes of a traveler concerning the Yellowstone park, Yosemite national park, and the Grand canyon of the Colorado river... Bost., L.C. Page and co., 1912. 180 p. plates (part col.), maps.
CSluCL

5250. [Muybridge, Eadweard J.] Views in Yosemite valley. [n.p., n.d.] 32 mounted photos. CU-B

5251. —— Yosemite views. [S.F., A. J. Leary, n.d.] 40 mounted photos. C

5252. Nelson, Thomas, and sons, pub. ...The Yosemite valley, and the mammoth trees and geysers of California... N.Y. [187–?] 40 p.
CHi CLU CRedl CSfSC CU-B

5253. [Olmsted, Frederick Law] Governmental preservation of natural scenery. [Brookline, Mass., 1890] [3] p. CU-B

5254. Orr, J. B. An interpretation of Yosemite valley. S.F., Sunset press, 1901. [16] p. illus. C CLU

5255. Osborne-Stallinger, Frances. Facets of Yosemite. San Jose, Victor Hills, 1938. 16 p. CRcS

5256. Pacific novelty co., pub. The Yosemite national park, California. Photo-gravures. S.F. [n.d.] [12] pl.   CLO

5257. Paden, Irene (Dakin) The Big Oak Flat road; an account of freighting from Stockton to Yosemite Valley [by] Irene D. Paden and Margaret E. Schlichtmann. S.F., 1955. 356 p. illus., ports., maps (2 fold.) Bibliography: p. 325–343.
Available in many libraries.

5258. Pillsbury, Aetheline B. The real Yosemite ... Oakland, Pillsbury picture co., 1906. [41] p. illus.
                                                                    C   CU-B

5259. Popham, William Lee. Yosemite valley romance. Louisville, Mayes print. co., c1911. 119 p.
                                                                         CHi

5260. Proctor, Alexander Phimister. An ascent of Half dome in 1884. S.F. [Grabhorn press] 1945. [20] p.
                                        CHi   CLU   CLgA   CSfSC

5261. [Reynolds, Mattie V.] John Bowling. Discoverer of Yosemite valley. [Santa Cruz, 1939] 6 l. Typew.   CU-B

5262. Robinson, Charles D. The Wawona hotel... around the Mariposa big trees... [S.F.? 1882?] 11 p.
                                                                        CU-B

5263. R[obinson], L[ilias] N[apier] R[ose] Our trip to the Yo-semite valley and Sierra Nevada range, by L.N.R.R. [London, J. Martin & son, print.] 1883. 37 p.   C

5264. Russell, Carl Parcher. One hundred years in Yosemite... Stanford, 1931. 242 p. "Documents, chronology and bibliography": p. 169–230.
Available in many California libraries and NN   NjN

5265. —— Same, with subtitle: The story of a great park and its friends. Berkeley, Univ. of Calif. press, 1947. 226 p. illus., ports., map. Bibliography: p. [195]–213.
Available in many California libraries and IC   MiD MoS   NdU   ODa   OrU

5266. —— Same. Yosemite, Yosemite natural history association, 1957. 195 p. illus.
                C   CBaB   CLO   CMon   CP   CSalCL   CSfU   CSjC CStcl   NN   UPB

5267. —— "What one knows best one loves best." Yosemite's educational work outlines U.S.N.P.S. superintendents' conference. Mesa Verde national park, October 1925. [n.p., 1925] 12 p. mounted illus.   CU-B

5268. San Francisco and San Joaquin valley railway. The Yosemite and big trees of California. New route... [S.F., Payot, Upham & co.'s print., 18–?] [8] p. illus.   CU-B

5269. Scott, Ferris Huntington. The Yosemite story. Santa Ana, 1954. 64 p. illus.
          C   CFS   CHi   CL   CLgA   CO   CSfCW   CStcl   CU-B MoS

5270. Sierra club, S.F. The Sierra club cordially welcomes Warren G. Harding, president of the United States...[to] Yosemite national park, July 29 and 30, 1923. [n.p., 1923] [4] p. port.   CU-B

5271. Smith, Bertha H. Yosemite legends... S.F., Elder, c1904. 64 p. illus.
Available in many California libraries and IC

5272. Smith, Elinor Shane. Po-ho-no, and the legends of Yosemite...2d ed. Monterey, Peninsula print. co., c1917. 39 p. illus.
                  C   CLU   CMerCL   CMont   CRcS

5273. —— Same. [1927] 39 p. illus.   CHi   CU-B

5274. Southern Pacific co. Tioga pass tour. [S.F.] c1928. 7 p. illus.   CSf

5275. —— Yosemite national park, California. S.F., 1901. [34] p. illus.   CHi   CU-B

5276. —— Same. 1905. 32 p. illus.   CSf   CU-B

5277. Souvenir of Yosemite. [n.p., 1886?] 28 p. illus. (part. col.) mounted group ports.   CLU

5278. Sussman, Emilie (Wormser). My trip to Yosemite. From the journal of Emilie Sussman, 1872. S.F. [Grabhorn press] 1939. 7 p.   CHi

5279. Taber, Isaiah West. [Photographs of the Yosemite national park; also one of Mt. Shasta, Calif. and of Cape Horn, Columbia river, Ore. [n.p., n.d.] 15 mounted photos.   CU-B

5280. Taylor, Katherine Ames. Lights and shadows of Yosemite; being a collection of favorite Yosemite views, together with a brief account of its history and legends... S.F., Crocker [c1926] 87 p. illus.
                        C   CBb   CHi   CLO   CLU   CViCL

5281. —— Yosemite tales and trails. S.F., Crocker, 1934. 78 p. illus.
           C   CBu   CMon   CMont   CSf   CSfSC   CStcrCL

5282. —— Same. Stanford, 1948. 95 p. illus., maps.
Available in many California libraries and MiD

5283. Taylor, Rose (Schuster) The cemetery in Yosemite valley. 5 cameragraph sheets. Reproduction from original in possession of Mrs. King Becker.   C

5284. —— The last survivor. S.F., Jonck & Seeger, 1932. 20 p. illus., ports. Biography of Maria Lebrado Yerdies, a Yosemite Indian.   CHi   CSd

5285. —— Yosemite Indians and other sketches... S.F., Johnck & Seeger, 1936. 103 p. illus., ports.
         C   CHi   CLSU   CLgA   CMartC   CMerCL   CO   CRb CRic   CSS   CSfSC   CSfU   CStrJC   CViCL   NN

5286. Tompkins, Sarah (Haight) Diary of Miss Sarah Haight [Mrs. Edward Tompkins] describing a wedding journey into the Yosemite valley, 1858. [1858] 18, 2 typew. sheets. Contains copies of excerpts from the Daily Alta California, May 21, 1858, and the Daily Examiner, Sept. 30, 1888.   C

5287. —— The Ralston-Fry wedding and the wedding journey to Yosemite, May 20, 1858. From the diary of Miss Sarah Haight [Mrs. Edward Tompkins] Ed. by Francis P. Farquhar. Berkeley, Friends of the Bancroft library, 1961. 23 p. ports. (col.)   CHi   CLSM

5288. Treasures of Yosemite national park. [n.p., n.d.] 22 p. col. pl.   CLU

5289. Turner, Charles Quincey. Yosemite valley through the stereoscope... [1902] 86 p.   CSmH

5290. —— Same. N.Y., S.F. [etc., c1908] 70 p.
                                                                    CL   CU-B

5291. U.S. Superintendent of Yosemite national park. Report...to the Secretary of the interior...1891–1915. Wash., D.C., Govt. print. off., 1891–1915. maps.
CHi has 1915. CLU has 1896/97, 1900. CO has 1912–14. CSdS has 1890/91, 1893/94, 1896/97, 1907/08, 1908/09. CSmH has 1890/91–1915?

5292. U.S. camera magazine. The U.S. camera Yosemite photographic forum... June 16th–30th, September 1st–15th [1940] 59 p. illus., ports. Reprint.   CU-B

5293. Van Name, Willard Gibbs. A new raid on the Yosemite national park. [n.p., 1927?] 16 p. illus., maps.   CU-B

5294. Voigt, Eduard. Yosemite... Berlin, D. Reimer (E. Vohsen) 1909. 112 p.   CHi   CU-B

5295. Watkins, Carleton Emmons. [Photographs of scenes in California; chiefly Yosemite national park and Mendocino county] [187–?] 15 mounted photos.
CU-B

5296. —— Same. [and of scenes in Oregon] [18—] 31 mounted photos in 2 portfolios.
CU-B

5297. —— Yo-Semite Valley. [Photographs] San Francisco, 1863.
CSmH

5298. —— Same. [c1867] 34 mounted photos. (incl. map) in portfolio.
CLU

5299. Wells, Andrew Jackson. The Yosemite valley of California... S.F., 1905. 45 p. illus.
CHi CL CU-B

5300. —— Same. 1907.   CHi CSf CSmH OrU

5301. Wiley, William Halstead. The Yosemite, Alaska, and the Yellowstone...Reprinted from "Engineering." London offices of "Engineering"; N.Y., J. Wiley & sons [1893] 230 p. illus., port.
CBb CLSU CLU CSmH CU-B CaBViPA

5302. Williams, John Harvey. Yosemite and its high Sierra. Tacoma, Wash., & S.F., 1914. 150 p. illus.
C C-S CBaB CHi CL CLO CLU CMartC CMerCL CMont CRedCL CSd CSfCP CSfCW CSfSC CStcl CViCL ODa OrU

5303. —— Same. 2d ed., rev. and greatly enl. ...S.F., Author, 1921. 193 p. illus., map.
C CArcHT CBu CChiS CCoron CHi CL CLU CMerCL CO COnC CRic CSS CSf CSjC CSluCL CSmH CU-B

5304. Wilson, Herbert Earl. The lore and the lure of Yosemite... S.F., Robertson, 1922. 132 p. illus.
Available in many libraries.
Other editions followed. CChiS (1925) CLO (1923, 1925) CLU (1925) COHN (1926) CSS (1925) CSd (1928) MiD (1925) MoS (1928) OrU (1928)

5305. Wonders of Yosemite, Calif.; a descriptive view book in colors. S.F., Souvenir pub. co. [c1913] [28] p. illus. (25 col.)
C

5306. The "Yosemite," by M.I.W. 1866. Being the journal, at present in the possession of Mr. Norman B. Livermore, of a trip on horseback to the Yosemite valley in June, 1866... [S.F., 1942] 26 l. Mimeo. from the original.
CL CSfSC CU-B

5307. Yosemite, Sept. 23–Oct. 9, 1891. [Photograph album] [n.p., 1891?] 31 l. of mounted photos.
CU-B

5308. Yosemite boys' camp. Season, 1921. [S.F., Taylor & Taylor, 1921] [11] p. illus.
CHi

5309. Yosemite national park company. Yosemite national park, California. [n.p., 1920?] 30 p. illus.
CHi

5310. Yosemite national park; a word and picture journal through the world-famous Yosemite national park. Yosemite, J. B. Browne, jr. [1928?] 50 p. illus., maps.
CFS CLU

5311. Yosemite national park, California. Natural color reproductions, reproduced from kodachrome originals by Curt Teich & co., inc. [L.A., Distributed by Western pub. & novelty co., n.d.] 18 col. pl.
CSfCW

5312. Yosemite park & Curry company. Ahwahnee. [n.p., n.d.] 16 p. illus.
CSf

5313. —— Yosemite lodge. 1927. 15 p. illus. CSf

5314. —— Yosemite national park, California. [1928] 16 p. illus.
CSf

5315. —— Same. 1939. folder (14 p.) illus., map.
CRcS

5316. The Yosemite trip book. S.F., Crocker, c1926. 61 p. illus.
CSjC CU-B
Other editions followed.   CFS (c1927) CLO (c1938)

5317. Yo Semite valley and the Big trees via the Big Oak Flat direct route... S.F., Alta Calif. print, 1881. [16] p. illus., map (fold.)
C CLU

5318. "Yosemite valley" and the "Mariposa big tree grove" in the statutes of California... National park service, Field div. of education, Berkeley [1934] 46 l. Typcw.
CU-B

5319. Yosemite valley, Calif. S.F., Hartwell & Mitchell, pub., 1893. 6 l.
CU-B

5320. Yo-Semite valley, California. Cosmopolitan saloon, John C. Smith, proprietor... S.F., Brown & Mahanny, print. [n.d.] folder (6 p.)
CHi

5321. Young, John F. Views in Yosemite valley... [n.p.] 1888. 32 photos. on 24 l.
CU-B

MENDOCINO COUNTY
(Created in 1850, but united with Sonoma county up to 1859)

COUNTY HISTORIES

5322. Carpenter, Aurelius O., and Millberry, Percy H. History of Mendocino and Lake counties, California, with biographical sketches... L.A., Historic record co., 1914. 1045 p. illus., ports.
C CCH CF CHi CL CLO CLU CLp CO CRic CSf CSfU CSmH CU-B CUk MWA

5323. Mendocino county. Public schools. The history of Mendocino county for boys and girls. Ukiah, 1957–58. v. p. illus. Reprinted from the *Newsletter* Sept.-Dec., 1957 and Jan.-May, 1958.
CHi CUk

5324. [Palmer, Lyman L.] History of Mendocino county, California. Comprising its geography, geology, topography, climatography, springs and timber. Also, extended sketches of its mills and milling, mines and mining interests... S.F., Alley, Bowen & co., 1880. 676 p. front., port. Includes biographical sketches.
C CChiS CCH CHi CL CLAC CLSU CLU CO CSf CSfCP CSfCW CSmH CStoC CU-B CUk CYoCL IC ICN MoSHi MWA NHi NN UPB WHi

GREAT REGISTER

5325. Mendocino county. Index to the Great register of the county of Mendocino. 1866– Place of publication and title vary.
C has 1867, 1871, 1873, 1875–77, 1879, 1880 (biennially to)– 1898, 1902 (biennially to)– 1926, 1930 (biennially to)– 1962. CL has 1872–73, 1875–77, 1879, 1882 (biennially to)– 1890. CO has 1880. CSmH has 1875, 1880. CU-B has 1867, 1868 (suppl.), 1872, 1873, 1875, 1879, 1880, 1882, 1904, 1914, 1916, 1920 (biennially to)–1938, 1939 (special), 1940.

DIRECTORIES

5326. 1900. Keller, John J. A complete business directory of Mendocino and Lake counties. Ukiah, 1900. 108 p.
CU-B

GENERAL REFERENCES

5327. Anderson valley community Methodist church. 90th anniversary celebration, April 17, 1955. [n.p., 1955] [15] p.
CHi

5328. Ashburner, William. The Mount Vernon coal

mine, Mendocino county, Cal. ...June 8th, 1872. S.F., E. Bosqui & co., print. [1872] 13 p.   CU-B

5329. Baechtel, Samuel Simon. Pioneer notes... Berkeley, 1941. 20 l. "Photographic copy of manuscripts in the possession of Mr. William H. Baechtel."
                                                    CU-B CUk

5330. Brinzing, M. The early history of the Mendocino coast. [Berkeley, 1950] Thesis (M.A.)—Univ. of Calif., 1950.   CU

5331. California vs. Hastings, S. C., et al. ... The people of the state of California plaintiffs and respondents, vs. S. C. Hastings and John Currey, defendants and appellants. Transcript on appeal, from the seventh judicial district, Mendocino county. R. McGarvey, attorney for appellants. Thos. B. Bond, attorney for respondents. S.F., Truesdell, Dewey & co., 1867. 28 p.   CU-B

5332. —— ...The people vs. S. C. Hastings and John Currey and certain real estate described in the complaint. Robert McGarvey, attorney for defendants. S.F., B. F. Sterett, print., 1867.   CU-B

5333. California. Legislature. Special joint committee on the Mendocino war. Majority and minority reports... [Sacramento, C. T. Botts, 1860] 75 p.
                                                CHi CSmH CUk

5334. —— —— —— Correspondence relative to Indian affairs in Mendocino. [Sacramento, C. T. Botts, 1860] 10 p.   CSmH

5335. Central Mendocino county power co. Trust indenture, Central Mendocino county power company (a corporation) to Mercantile trust company of California (trustee) securing an authorized issue of $150,000 first mortgage six and one-half percent thirty year gold bonds, dated June 1, 1923, interest payable June 1, and December 1. [S.F., 1923] 71 p.   CU-B

5336. Cleland, Lucy (Gibson) Aunt Lucy's book about the Gibson family in Mendocino county, California, 1849–1949. [n.p.] National press [1950?] 87 p.   C

5337. Crump, Spencer. Redwoods, iron horses and the Pacific. The story of the California Western "Skunk" railroad. L.A., Trans-Anglo [c1963] 160 p. illus.
                                                    CAla

5338. Fort Bragg. Chamber of commerce. Fort Bragg and surrounding country. Fort Bragg [n.d.] [8] p. illus.   CU-B

5339. The Hopland oil co., San Francisco. ... Prospectus... S.F. [1901?] 15 p. illus.   CHi

5340. Immigration association of California. [County scrapbooks] [S.F., 188–?]   C

5341. Industrial survey associates. Mendocino county; its economic assets, needs and prospects. A report prepared for the Mendocino county Chamber of commerce. S.F., 1951. [96] l. illus., map. Bibliography: l. 93–96.   C CUk

5342. —— Noyo harbor, California: its present and future development; a report to the Noyo harbor district commission. S.F., 1952. 25 l. illus., map. Bibliography: l. 24–25.   C

5343. Karinen, Arthur Eli. The historical geography of the Mendocino coast. [Berkeley, 1948] Thesis (M.A.)—Univ. of Calif., 1948.   CU

5344. Levick, M. B. Mendocino county, California ... S.F., Sunset mag. homeseekers' bur. [1911?] 31 p. illus.   CL CU-B

5345. Martin, Wallace E. Marine disasters of the Mendocino coast, northern California, USA. Eureka,

c1957. Chart. illus., map. Includes alphabetical list of vessels lost on the Mendocino coast from 1850 to 1957.
                                                    CArcHT

5346. Mendocino county. Chamber of commerce. Magnificent Mendocino county "in the Redwood empire." [Ukiah, 1929] 7 p. illus., map.   CHi CRcS

5347. —— —— Same. [193–?] folder (16 p.)
                                                CHi CRcS

5348. Mendocino county centennial celebration. 1949. Pageant, horse show, fair, Ukiah, California, August 19, 20, 21, 1949. Souvenir program. Includes history of Mendocino county. [Ukiah, 1949] 40 p. illus., map.
                                        CHi CU-B CUk

5349. Mendocino county fair association. The Yokaya pow-wow and harvest festival at Ukiah, California, September 18–25, 1922... [Ukiah, Chamber of commerce, 1922] [4] p.   CU-B

5350. Mendocino county historical essay contest: Anderson valley district, Fort Bragg district, Hopland district, Little Lake district, Mendocino district, Point Arena district, Potter valley district, Round valley district, Ukiah district. Typew.   CUk

5351. Mendocino herald. Martial law in Round valley, Mendocino county, California, the causes which led to that measure, the evidence... Ukiah, 1863. 24 p.
                                                    CSmH

5352. Miller, Curtis A., co. Mendocino county, California... [Ukiah? 1920?] [20] p. illus.
                                                CL CU-B

5353. Murphey, Edith Van Allen. Indian uses of native plants. [n.p.] 1959. 72 p. illus.   CAla

5354. Noyo river apple co. The Noyo river apple company. Northspur, Mendocino county... S.F. [n.d.] [30] p. illus.   CU-B

5355. Parsell, Alfred P. A home of their own; the story of the Ukiah Indian rancheria. Typew.   CUk

5356. —— The story of the Ukiah valley and its Indian population. Typew.   CUk

5357. Picturesque Mendocino. Illustrated... [Ukiah] Ukiah Republican print. [n.d.] [96] p. illus.   CU-B

5358. Poage, W. G. Mendocino county, California ... Ukiah [190–?] [16] p. illus., map.   CHi CSmH

5359. Poli, Adon. Forest land ownership in northern Mendocino county, California... Berkeley, Calif. forest & range experiment station [1948] 49 p.
                                            CHi CO CU-B

5360. Purdy (Carl) Nurseryman, Ukiah. [Catalogs] CHi has 1903–05, 1911–13, 1916, 1919–22, 1925–32.

5361. Redwood journal, Ukiah. 1948 in pictures. Ukiah, c1949. unp.   CUk

5362. Ryder, David Warren. Memories of the Mendocino coast; being a brief account of the discovery, settlement and development of the Mendocino coast, together with the correlated history of the Union lumber company and how coast and company grew up together. S.F., Priv. print. by Taylor & Taylor, 1948. 81 p. illus. Available in many libraries.

5363. Sanford, John Bunyan. Picturesque and industrial Mendocino. Comp. ...at request of the Board of supervisors of Mendocino county... Ukiah, Dispatch-democrat print., 1908. [39] p. illus.   CHi CLU

5364. Ukiah dispatch-democrat. Souvenir edition. Picturesque and industrial Mendocino, January 1900. [Ukiah, 1900] 16 p. illus., map.   CU-B

5365. Union lumber co. Fort Bragg by the sea, California. [Fort Bragg, 190–?] [21] p. illus.   CHi

5366. —— Photographs taken for the Union lumber company about 1921 [i.e. 1921–1924] showing cutting, second-growth, and reforestation. Redwood region. [Fort Bragg, 1924?] 42 mounted photos.   CU-B

5367. Waldteufel, J. A. Mendocino county information. Ukiah [1910?] 32 p. map.   CU-B

5368. Watkins, Carleton Emmons. Mendocino coast. [n.p., n.d.] 53 mounted photos. in 2 portfolios.   CU-B

5369. Willits. Chamber of commerce. Willits and vicinity. 1905. [20] p.   NN

MERCED COUNTY

(Created in 1855 from portion of Mariposa county)

COUNTY HISTORIES

5370. History of Merced county, California, with illustrations descriptive of its scenery, farms, residences, public buildings...With biographical sketches of prominent citizens. S.F., Elliott & Moore [Print. Pac. press, Oakland] 1881. 232 p. illus., map.
C CHi CL CMerCL CSf CSfCP CSmH CU-B NHi NN

5371. A memorial and biographical history of the counties of Merced, Stanislaus, Calaveras, Tuolumne and Mariposa, California... Chicago, Lewis pub. co., 1892. 408 p. illus., ports.
C CAla CHi CL CLU CMS CMerCL CO CSadC CSf CSfWF-H CSmH CU-B NHi

5372. Merced county. Office of Superintendent of schools. History of Merced county. Centennial edition. Merced, 1955. 48 p. illus., map.
C CFS CHi CLU CMerCL CO MWA

5373. Outcalt, John. History of Merced county, Calif., with a biographical review of the leading men and women of the county... L.A., Historic record co., 1925. 913 p. illus., ports.
C CCH CHi CL CLO CLU CMerCL CO CSf CSmH CSto CStrJC CU-B MWA

5374. Radcliffe, Corwin. History of Merced county ...(narrative and biographical) Merced, Cawston, 1940. 414 p. illus., ports., map.
C CFS CHi CL CLCo CLU CMerCL CO CSf NN

GREAT REGISTER

5375. Merced county. Index to the Great register of the county of Merced. 1866– Place of publication and title vary.
C has 1867, 1869, 1871–72, 1875–77, 1879–80, 1888 (biennially to)– 1962. CHi has 1944, 1946. CL has 1867, 1869 (suppl.), 1873, 1875–76, 1879, 1882 (biennially to)– 1888. CMerCL has 1918, 1932, 1936, 1938, 1940, 1950. CSmH has 1880. CU-B has 1867–69 (suppl.), 1872–73, 1879–80.

DIRECTORIES

5376. 1914– Polk, R. L., & co., pub. Polk's Merced city directory. L.A., 1914– Title varies: 1926/27– 1955, Polk's Merced-Madera directory.
C has 1914, 1926/27, 1952/53. CHi has 1930/31, 1946, 1948, 1952/53, 1954–55, 1958. CL has 1935, 1941, 1946, 1952/53, 1954–55. CMerCL has 1914, 1917, 1922, 1924, 1926/27, 1928/29, 1930/31, 1935, 1938, 1946, 1948, 1952/ 53, 1954–55, 1958.

5377. 1961– Polk, R. L., & co., pub. Los Banos and Dos Palos city directory. L.A., 1962–
CHi has 1961.

GENERAL REFERENCES

5378. California pastoral and agricultural company, Merced. Chowchilla herd of shorthorns. [n.p., 1903?] 20 p. illus.   CHi

5379. Crocker-Huffman land and water co. Merced county, California. [S.F., Murdock press, 1902] [32] p. illus., fold. map.   CHi CU-B

5380. Daughters of the American revolution. California. Genealogical records committee. Early marriages, Merced county, 1855–1905. Comp. by Myrtle Dix... [n.p., n.d.] [200] p. Typew.   CHi

5381. Farmers' canal company of Merced county. An important scheme. Are the waters of the Merced to be used for irrigation? Professor Davidson reports in favor of a proposed plan. [S.F., Bacon & co., 1877] 14 p.   CHi

5382. Farquhar, Franklin Smith. History of Livingston, California, narrative and biography... Livingston, Chronicle, 1945. 168 p. ports.
C CHi CMS CMcrCL CSf CSmII CU-B NN

5383. Graham, John Charles. The settlement of Merced county, California. [L.A.] 1957. Thesis (M.A.)— U.C.L.A., 1957.   CLU

5384. Los Banos. May day celebration, 1949. Its May day in Los Banos, fiftieth year, 1949; official souvenir program. Los Banos, 1949. 50 p. illus., ports.   CHi

5385. Los Banos enterprise. Golden anniversary section. City of Los Banos celebrates its fiftieth year as an incorporated city May 8, 1907. Los Banos, 1957. 12 p. illus., ports.   CHi CU-B

5386. Men who entered the service from Merced county, California—European war, 1914–1918. [n.p., n.d.] 34 l. Reproduced from typew. copy.   CU-B

5387. Merced. The next twenty years; report on the general plan, Merced city-county urban area. 1959. 148 p.   CMerCL

5388. —— Workable program; codes and ordinances, administrative organization, finance, comprehensive plan, neighborhood analysis, rehousing, citizen participation. 1959. [26] p. Mimeo.   CMerCL

5389. —— **Chamber of commerce.** Merced, a friendly city... Merced, 1939. 4 p. Mimeo.   CRcS

5390. —— —— Merced county, California. [n.p., 1911] [24] p. illus.   CL CU-B

5391. —— —— Water; key to wealth — health in Merced county, California. [Merced, 1951?] [14] p.   CHi

5392. —— **City planning department.** 1944–1959, 58–59, the next twenty years; annual report. [1959] 16 p. Mimeo.   CMerCL

5393. —— **Redevelopment agency.** Merced's fifteenth street urban renewal project. 1959. 23 p. Mimeo.   CMerCL

5394. Merced county. Statistical report... 1915/ 16, 1928/29–1933/34, 1935/36–1940/41. Merced [1916– 41] illus.   CU-B

5395. —— **Board of trade.** Rare opportunity for home seekers to purchase valuable lands in the county of Merced, California. 1887.   CLCo

5396. —— **Chamber of commerce.** Merced county; the natural gateway to Yosemite. Merced, 1929. folder (8 p.)   CRcS

5397. —— **Panama-Pacific exposition commission.** Merced county where location and soil make for prosperity and contentment. [Merced, 1915] [32] p. illus.   CHi CL CLU CU-B

5398. Merced irrigation district. Report... S.F., 1920. [904] p. illus., maps, designs, tables. Typew.
                                                           CFS

5399. Merced sun. Merced county in picture and story; climate, soil irrigation. Merced, 1902. 20 p. illus.
                                               CMerCL CSf
Other editions followed.   CHi (1913) CMerCL (1903) CO (1913) CU-B (1904, 1913) NN (1903)

5400. Merced sun-star. Fair and centennial edition. Aug. 22, 1955.   CHi

5401. Milliken, Ralph LeRoy. Henry Miller slept here. [Los Banos, Los Banos enterprise, c1955] [10] p. illus., port.   C CHi CO CTurS

5402. —— The Los Banos farm center; its history. [n.p., 1959?] 2 p.   CHi

5403. —— The Los Banos Henry Miller May day celebrations... Los Banos, Speedprint letter shop, 1950. 14 p.   CHi CU-B

5404. —— The plains over; the reminiscences of William Jasper Stockton. Los Banos, Los Banos enterprise, 1939. 55 p. port.   CHi CTurS

5405. —— Then we came to California; a biography of Sarah Summers Clarke, written in the first person by Ralph LeRoy Milliken. Merced, Merced express, 1938. 95 p. port.   CFS CHi CTurS

5406. —— West side centennials of 1958. Los Banos, Speedprint advertising [c1957] 12 p. illus., port.
                        CFS CHi CL CTurS CU-B

5407. Planada development co. Planada, the cream of California. [L.A.? Segnogram press, 1911] 62 p. illus. (part col.)   CU-B

5408. Rice, Inez. Valley over the hill. San Antonio, Naylor co. [1959] 266 p. illus.   CSd CU-B

5409. Stanfield, Mary E. Brief history of Atwater and communities, including Castle air force base. [n.p.] Atwater history club, 1958. 229 p. illus.
                        C CFS CMerCL CTurS

5410. United States farm land co. Chowchilla ranch. 108,000 acres. The homeseeker's opportunity located in Merced and Madera counties, California. [S.F., Sunset pub. house, 1913?] 16 p. illus., map.   CU-B

MODOC COUNTY
(*Created in 1874 from portion of Siskiyou county*)

COUNTY HISTORIES

5411. Brown, William Samuel. California northeast, the bloody ground. Foreword by Joseph A. Sullivan. [1st Calif. ed.] Oakland, Biobooks, 1951. 207 p. illus., port., fold. map. (Calif. relations, no. 28) On cover: Annals of Modoc.
Available in many California libraries and CaBViPA CoD N NIC NN NvU OrU

GREAT REGISTER

5412. Modoc county. Index to the Great register of the county of Modoc. 1875– Place of publication and title vary.
C has 1875, 1876, 1879, 1880, 1888 (biennially to)–

1926, 1930 (biennially to)– 1962. CL has 1875–76, 1877 (suppl.), 1879, 1886 (suppl.), 1888, 1890. CU-B has 1879.

DIRECTORIES

5413. 1950. Alturas. Church of Jesus Christ of latter-day saints. Missionaries and the Alturas branch, comp. Alturas city directory of residents and businesses. Alturas, Alturas plaindealer, 1950. 69 p.
                                                           CHi

GENERAL REFERENCES

5414. Alturas. Chamber of commerce. Alturas; in the Shasta cascade wonderland of California. Alturas [1937] 7 p. illus., map.   CRcS

5415. —— **Modoc county high school.** [Commencement programmes]
CHi has 1909.

5416. Auble, C. C. Historical description of Modoc county and northeastern California, giving its industrial resources. S.F., 1899. 32 p. illus.   C CU-B

5417. Biddle, Ellen McGowan. Reminiscences of a soldier's wife. Phila., Lippincott, c1907.   CAltu CU-B

5418. Brady, Cyrus Townsend. Northwestern fights and fighters. Illustrated with original drawings, maps, and photographs. Garden City, N.Y., Doubleday, 1923. 373 p. illus., ports., maps.   CAltu CRbCL

5419. Brown, William Samuel. History of the Modoc national forest service, California region. S.F., 1945. 87 l. Mimeo.   CHi

5420. Chapman's magazine, Berkeley. Modoc county. (In v.1, no. 1, p. 113–23 [1941?])
                        CChiS CO CRb CU-B

5421. Davis, William Newell, jr. California east of the Sierra: a study in economic sectionalism. [Berkeley, 1942] 272 l. illus., maps. Thesis (Ph.D.)—Univ. of Calif., 1942. C (microfilm) CSuLas (microfilm) CU-B

5422. Duke, Vetelene (Williams) The South fork valley and other stories... Monterey, Press of W. T. Lee, 1946. 71 p. illus.   C CHi CLU

5423. [French, Gertrude Payne] comp. Early history stories of Modoc county. [Alturas] Alturas plaindealer [193–?] [42] p.   C

5424. French, R. A., comp. A historical, biographical and pictorial magazine devoted to Modoc county. Pub. by the Alturas plaindealer, 1912... [Alturas, 1912] 79 p. illus., ports.   C CHi CSfCP CU-B

5425. Glassley, Ray Howard. Pacific northwest Indian wars. Portland, Ore., Binfords, c1953.   CAltu

5426. Gloster, Dorothy V. A brief history of Alturas. 24 p. Typew.   CHi

5427. —— A brief history of the Catholic church of the Sacred Heart of Jesus, at Alturas, Modoc county, California. 13 p. illus. Typew.   CHi

5428. King, Murray E. The last of the bandit riders, by Matt Warner as told to Murray E. King. Caldwell, Ida., Caxton, c1940.   CAltu

5429. Levick, M. B. Modoc county, California. S.F., Sunset mag. homeseekers' bur. [1912] 32 p. illus., map.
                                                    CHi CU-B

5430. Memories of Corporation ranch, Modoc county, California. [n.p., 19–?] 2 p. l., 10 mounted pl.   CU-B

5431. Modoc county. Board of education. Modoc county, past and present. Alturas, Modoc county schools, 1946. [145] l. Reproduced from typew. copy. Bibliography: 10 l. at end.   C CAltu

5432. —— **Development board.** Modoc county California; the sportsman's paradise. Alturas [192–?] 6 p.   CHi CRcS

5433. Modoc county cattlemen's association. Modoc county brand book. [n.p., 1951?] unp. illus.
CChiS CSf CSmH

5434. Odd fellows, Independent order of. Modoc county. Alturas lodge no. 80. Constitution, by laws and rules of order... S.F., Jos. Winterburn & co., 1886. 50 p.   C

5435. Thompson, William. Reminiscences of a pioneer... S.F., 1912. 197 p. illus., ports. Author editor of Alturas newspaper around 1900; also early day Indian fighter. Participated in Modoc wars.
Available in many California libraries and OrU

5436. Vassar, Rena Lee. The Fort Bidwell, California, Indian school: a study of federal Indian education policy. [Berkeley, 1953] Thesis (M.A.)—Univ. of Calif., 1953.   CU

5437. Wilson, Bourdon. Modoc county, California. S.F., Sunset mag. homeseekers' bur. [1910] 31 p. illus., map.   CU-B

MONO COUNTY

(*Created in 1861 from portions of Calaveras, Mariposa, and Fresno counties*)

COUNTY HISTORIES

5438. Cain, Ella M. (Cody) The story of early Mono county; its settlers, gold rushes, Indians, ghost towns. S.F., Fearon pub., 1961. 166 p. illus., ports.
CHi CLSM CSfMI

5439. Historical records survey, California. ... Mono county (Bridgeport) S.F., Northern Calif. hist. records survey project, 1940. 139 l. map. (Inventory of the county archives of Calif. ...no. 27)
C CBb CF CHanK CHi CL CLCM CLCo CLO CLSM CLSU CLU CMont CO COMC CSS CSf CSfCP CSfCSM CSjC CSjCL CSmH CSt CU-B CYcCL ICN MoS N NN WHi

GREAT REGISTER

5440. Mono county. Index to the Great register of the county of Mono. 1866– Place of publication and title vary.
C has 1872, 1875, 1876, 1879, 1880 (biennially to)– 1932, 1933, 1934, 1935, 1936 (biennially to)– 1962. CHi has 1875. CL has 1873, 1875, 1879 (suppl.), 1882 (biennially to)– 1890. CU-B has 1872–73, 1875, 1877, 1879–80, Nov. 1920, Nov. 1922, May 1924, Nov. 1926, May, Aug., Nov. 1928, Aug., Nov. 1930, May, Aug., Nov. 1932, Aug. 1934, Aug. 1936, Aug. 1938, May, Aug., Nov. 1940.

GENERAL REFERENCES

5441. Bailey, Stanley. Statement of Mr. Stanley Bailey of the San Francisco chronicle and Mr. E. A. Johnson of Mono county. February 27, 1939. [Berkeley, 1939] 2 l. Typew. On the discovery of a cave in Mono county.
CU-B

5442. Browne, John Ross. The Bodie Bluff mines located in Mono county, California, belonging to the Empire gold and silver mining company of New York. With pen and pencil. N.Y., Clark & Maynard, 1865. 15 p. illus., map.   CLU

5443. Bulwer consolidated mining co., San Francisco. ...Annual report...1877/81. S.F., 1880–81. 2 v. in 1. map.   CSmH CU-B

5444. Chalfant, Willie Arthur. Gold, guns and ghost towns. Stanford [c1947] 175 p. Stories from the author's *Outposts of civilizations and Tales of the pioneers.*
Available in many California libraries and CaBViPA GU MiD ODa

5445. —— Tales of the pioneers. Stanford [c1942] 129 p. port. Tales of Mono county and neighboring mining communities in Nevada.
Available in many libraries.

5446. Hamblet, Millie (Hunewill) Saga of the Circle H; commemorating the first hundred years of the Hunewills, 1861–1961. Bridgeport, Priv. pub. [1961] 54 p.   CHi

5447. McIntosh, F. W., comp. Mono county, California... [Reno, Nev., Presses of Gazette pub. co., 1908] 95 p. illus.   C CHi CO CSmH
Other editions followed, 1875, 1896, 1906.   CSmH

5448. Petition of inhabitants of Antelope and Slinkard valleys, relative to division of Mono county. [Sacramento, D. W. Gelwicks, state print., 1868] 4 p.   CSmH CU-B

5449. Russell, Carl Parcher. Early mining excitements east of Yosemite... S.F., 1928. [16] p. illus., map. Reprinted from *Sierra club bul.*, 1928.
CHi CLSU CSfCSM CSfSC CU-B

5450. Schumacher, Genny. The Mammoth lakes Sierra; a handbook for roadside and trail, by Genny Schumacher [and others] S.F., Sierra club [1959] 145 p. illus.   C CAla CInI CL CO CSfCSM CSfSt

5451. Wasson, Joseph. ...Complete guide to the Mono county mines. Description of Bodie, Esmeralda, Indian, Lake, Laurel Hill, Prescott, and other mining districts...new ed. S.F. [1879?] 60 p. illus., maps.
C CBb CLU CSfCSM CU-B

5452. Willard, Bettie, and Crow, Owena. Mammoth lakes, California. Boise, Ida., Frank M. Parcher, 1948. 17 p.   CInI

Bodie

5453. Attwood, Melville. ...Rough notes on the geology of Bodie, illustrating the two ages of gold. S.F., Alta Calif. steam print. house, 1881. 12 p.
CBb CSmH CU-B

5454. Bodie consolidated mining co. ...Annual report...1879/80– S.F., 1880–
CHi has 2d rept. Feb. 1881. CLU has 1881/82. CSmH has 1879/80–1880/81. CU-B has 1879/80–1880/81.

5455. Cain, Ella M. (Cody) The story of Bodie; with introd. by Donald I. Segerstrom. S.F., Fearon pub. in cooperation with the Mother Lode press, Sonora [1956] 196 p. illus.
Available in many California libraries and CoD N NN UPB

5456. Chappell, Maxine. Bodie and the bad man; historical roots of a legend. [Berkeley, 1947] Thesis (M.A.)—Univ. of Calif., 1947.   CU

5457. Goodson, D. V. Mining laws of Bodie mining district, comp. from the original records. Bodie, Bodie standard print. house, 1878. 23 p.   CHi

5458. Hakes, O. F. Mining laws of Bodie mining district. Bodie, Miner-index office, 1902.   C

5459. International union of mine, mill and smelter workers. Bodie fraternal burial association. Statements, reports, accounts, etc., 1898–1908. Bodie, 1898–1908. Ms.   CU-B

5460. —— **Bodie miners' union.** [Correspondence, reports, etc., 1890–1930] In portfolio. Ms. CU-B

5461. Knights of Pythias. Bodie. Mono Lodge, no. 59. By-laws, order of business and rules of order... S.F., C. W. Nevin, 1891. 13 p. CHi

5462. Odd fellows, Independent order of. Bodie. Mila Rebekah Lodge, no. 240. Constitution... S.F., Grand lodge, 1900. 41 p. CHi

5463. Smith, Grant Horace. Bodie; the last of the old-time mining camps... S.F., Calif. hist. soc., 1925. 19 p. illus. CHi CU-B

5464. Smith, Herbert Lee, comp. The Bodie area; the chronicles of the last old time mining camp excitement. v.1–8, no. 1. 1877–83. 160 l. Typew. C CU-B

5465. Standard consolidated mining co. Annual reports, 1880–1884. S.F., Bunker & Hiester [1880–82], W. T. Galloway [1883–84] 5 v. CHi

5466. —— Superintendent's second annual report... February 1st, 1881. S.F., 1881. 19 p. CHi

5467. Standard gold mining co. Report of the Standard gold mining co., of Bodie, Mono county, Califronia [!] [S.F., 1879] 11 p. CLU

5468. Union consolidated mining co. Location of property, Bodie, Mono county, California. N.Y. [1880?] 23 p. fold. chart. CHi

5469. U.S. Circuit court of appeals (9th circuit) In the Circuit court of the United States for the ninth circuit, district of California. Jupiter mining company vs. Bodie consolidated mining company. Charge to the jury delivered March 12th, 1881, by the Honorable Lorenzo Sawyer, circuit judge. [n.p., 1881?] 29 p. CHi

5470. Wasson, Joseph. Bodie and Esmeralda, being an account of the revival of affairs in two singularly interesting and important mining districts, including something of their past history, and the gist of the reports of Profs. Benj. Silliman and Wm. P. Blake [and others]... S.F., Spaulding, Barto & co., 1878. 60 p. illus., map. C CHi CLSU CLU CO CSf CSfCP CSfCSM CSmH CU-B

5471. —— The mines of Bodie... N.Y., 1879. 46 p. map. CSfCSM CSmH

MONTEREY COUNTY
(*Created in 1850*)

COUNTY HISTORIES

5472. Barrows, Henry D., and Ingersoll, Luther A., eds. A memorial and biographical history of the coast counties of central California...Henry D. Barrows, editor of the historical department and Luther A. Ingersoll, editor of the biographical department... Chicago, Lewis, 1893. 446 p. illus., ports. Includes Monterey, San Benito, Santa Cruz, and San Mateo counties.
CHi CL CMont CO CPg CRc CSalCL CSf CSfWF-H CSjC CSmH CStoC CU-B IC NHi NN WHi

5473. Guinn, James Miller. History and biographical record of Monterey and San Benito counties and history of the state of California, containing biographies of well-known citizens... L.A., Historic record co., 1910. 2 v.
C CHi CL CMont CPa CPg CSal CSalCL CSf CSfCP CSfU CSt CU-B CYcCL WHi

5474. —— History of Monterey county, California, with illustrations descriptive of its scenery, farms, residences [etc.]...With biographical sketches of prominent citizens. [S.F.] Elliott & Moore, 1881. 188 p. illus., maps. "Personal and historical reminiscences of San Benito county, by a pioneer." [etc.] p. [131]–166.
C CO CSalCL CSf CSfCP CSmH CU-B NHi

5475. Watkins, Rolin G., ed. History of Monterey and Santa Cruz counties, California... Chicago, Clarke, 1925. 2 v. illus., ports. v.2 biographical.
C CAla CCH CChiS CHi CL CMont COMC CSal CSalCL CSf CSfCSM CSmH CStcrCL CStoC CU-B CtY MWA NN WHi

5476. —— **and Hoyle, M. F., eds.** History of Monterey, Santa Cruz and San Benito counties... Chicago, Clarke, 1925. 2 v. illus., ports. Major Rolin G. Watkins, editor Monterey and Santa Cruz counties; M. F. Hoyle, editor San Benito county. v.2 biographical.
C CLCM CLCo CLU CO CPg CSalCL CSf CSmH CStcrCL CU-B

GREAT REGISTER

5477. Monterey county. Index to the Great register of the county of Monterey. 1866– Place of publication and title vary.
C has 1867, 1869, 1872, 1875, 1876, 1879, 1880, 1884 (biennially to) – 1902, 1906 (biennially to) – 1914, 1918 (biennially to) – 1962. CHi has 1876. CL has 1869, 1873, 1876–77, 1879, 1882 (suppl.), 1884 (biennially to) – 1888, 1890 (suppl.) CLU has 1875. CSmH has 1880, 1882. CU-B has 1867–68, 1872–73, 1873 (suppl.), 1879, 1916 (primary), 1922, 1926, 1932, 1936, 1938, 1940.

DIRECTORIES

5478. 1913. Sinclair, R. D., comp. Monterey county, California. [Monterey? 1913] 4 v. in 1. illus. CU-B

Monterey

5479. 1907. Perry, T. F., pub. Directory of Monterey, Pacific Grove, Seaside, Del Monte Grove and Vista Del Rey... Pacific Grove [1907] 164 p. illus.
C CMont

5480. 1947– Polk, R. L., & co., pub. Polk's Monterey-Pacific Grove city directory, including Carmel, Seaside and Del Rey Oaks... L.A., 1947– Preceded by Polk's Salinas, Monterey and Pacific Grove directory. Content varies: 1947, Monterey, Pacific Grove and Carmel; 1949–56, Monterey, Pacific Grove, Carmel and Seaside.
CHi has 1947, 1949, 1951, 1953–61. CL has 1953, 1954/55, 1956–58. CMont has 1947, 1949, 1951, 1953–58. CSal has 1947, 1951, 1953–57. CSalCL has 1954/55, 1959. CSmat has 1958–59. CU-B has 1947, 1949, 1954/55, 1959.

Salinas

5481. 1926– Polk, R. L., & co., pub. Polk's Salinas city directory... L.A., 1926– Content varies: 1926–33? Salinas, Monterey, Pacific Grove, Carmel, Del Monte, King City, etc.; 1937?–41, Salinas, Monterey, Pacific Grove and Carmel.
C has 1939. CHi has 1926–28, 1941, 1946, 1949, 1952–61. CL has 1939, 1941, 1953/54–1957/58. CMont has 1926, 1930, 1937, 1939, 1941. CSal has 1930, 1933, 1937, 1939, 1941, 1946, 1949, 1952–55, 1957/58–1959. CSalCL has 1946–59. CSfU has 1933. CSmat has 1958–59. CU-B has 1930, 1939, 1949, 1953/54–1955, 1959–60.

GENERAL REFERENCES

5482. Allen, Rutillus Harrison. Economic history of agriculture in Monterey county, California, during the

American period. [Berkeley, 1934] Thesis (Ph.D.)—Univ. of Calif., 1934. CSalCL CU

5483. Bedell, Clyde O. Fulfilment...with an acknowledgment to John Northern Hilliard for much of part two. Monterey, Monterey peninsula communities [1923?] 46 p. illus. "Part one of this booklet is designed to create for you...the atmosphere of the Monterey Peninsula of old—and of today...Part two is a miniature cyclopedia of information and fact..." C CHi CLU CMont CRcS CSalCL CSfCP CU-B

5484. Big Sur guide to the circle of enchantment... from Monterey to Morro Bay. 1st– [Big Sur, 1954– illus. Title varies: v.1, The Big Sur, yesterday, today, tomorrow; a guide to Highway One from Monterey to Morro Bay.—v.2, Monterey peninsula and Big Sur; a guide to state Highway 1 from Monterey to Morro Bay.—v.3, Big Sur guide to the circle of enchantment, featuring the Hearst castle; from Monterey to Morro Bay.—v.4, Big Sur guide to the Hearst castle. Editor: v.1—Emil White. Available in many libraries.

5485. Butler, A. W., comp. Resources of Monterey county, Calif., including the great Salinas valley...Pub. by the Mayor and Common council of Salinas City, for free distribution. S.F., Cubery & co., print., 1875. 32 p. C CL CLU CU-B MWA NHi NN

5486. California. Dept. of natural resources. Division of beaches and parks. Point Lobos reserve; report of the Point Lobos advisory committee to the California state park commission, March 1, 1936. Berkeley, Issued by Save-the-redwoods league, Univ. of Calif. 756 p. illus., maps. Typew. CMont CSf CU-B

5487. ——— ——— ——— Point Lobos reserve state park ...interpretation of a primitive landscape, ed. by Aubrey Drury. Sacramento [1954?] 96 p. illus., map. CHi CL CLU CRcS CSdS CStmo CU-B MiD UPB

5488. ——— **District court. 3d judicial district.** Court calendar. Monterey county. July term, 1875. [Monterey, 1875] CSmH

5489. Carmel Pacific spectator-journal. Spectator's guide and omnibook. Carmel, 1955. 120 p. illus., ports., maps. (Its Special no. v.12, no. 15, Dec. 2, 1955) CLU CO

5490. Casey, Beatrice (Tid) Padres and people of old mission San Antonio [de Padua] King City, Rustler herald, 1957. 59 p. illus. CHi CU-B

5491. Cooper, Martha M. (Brawley) Cooper and allied families; a genealogical study with biographical notes... N.Y., Am. hist. co., 1940. 57 p. illus. CMont

5492. Correia, Delia Richards. Lasuén in California. [Berkeley, 1935] Thesis (M.A.)—Univ. of Calif., 1935. CU CU-B

5493. Coulter, John Wesley. The geography of the Santa Lucia mountains with special consideration of the isolated coast region. [Berkeley, 1922] Thesis (M.A.)—Univ. of Calif., 1922. CU

5494. Cutter, Donald C. Malaspina in California. S.F., John Howell, 1960. 96 p. illus. (part. col.) map. "1000 copies designed and printed by Lawton Kennedy." CHi CL CLSM CSfSt CSfU CU-B

5495. Douglas school for girls, Pebble Beach. The Douglas school for girls. [Carmel, Carmel press, 193–?] [26] p. illus. CHi

5496. Dunn, Arthur. Monterey county, California ...Souvenir edition...Issued by Sunset mag. homeseekers' bur. ...for the Bd. of supervisors of Monterey county. S.F. [1915] 63 p. illus., map. CHi CL CLU CSal CSalCL CSfU CU-B

5497. Dunning, Duncan. A working plan for the Del Monte forest of the Pacific improvement co. [Berkeley, 1916] Thesis (M.S.)—Univ. of Calif., 1916. CU

5498. Earley, Thomas J. Padres and people of Salinas...history of the Catholic clergy, layfolk and institutions in and about Salinas, California, 1877–1952. Fresno, Acad. lib. guild, 1953. 89 p. illus., ports. C CHi CL CLgA CRcS CSfCW CStclU

5499. Engelhardt, Zephyrin, Father. Mission Nuestra Señora de la Soledad. Santa Barbara, Mission Santa Barbara, 1929. 88 p. illus., port., map. C CBb CBu CChiS CHi CL CLU CO CSS CSalCL CSf CSfCW CSj CSmH CStclU CU-B CVtV CaBViPA

5500. ——— Same, bound with *San Miguel Arcangel.* 1929. C CBu CLSU CLU CLgA CO CSbr CSmH CStclU CStmo CStrJC CU-B

5501. ——— ... San Antonio de Padua, the mission in the Sierras... Santa Barbara, Mission Santa Barbara, 1929. 140 p. illus. C CBu CChiS CHi CL CLU CO CSalCL CSbr CSfU CSmH CStclU CStmo CU-B CaBViPA

5502. ——— Same, bound with *San Miguel Arcangel.* 1929. C CBu CLSU CLU CLgA CO CSbr CSf CSfSt CSmH CStclU CStrJC CU-B

5503. Feldheym, Leonard. The California sardine industry in world trade. [Berkeley, 1940] Thesis (M.A.) —Univ. of Calif., 1940. CU

5504. Fernández, Justino. Thomás de Suría y su viaje con Malaspina 1791. Mexico, Libreria de Porrua Hermanos y Cia., 1939. 134 p. CHi CU-B

5505. Fisher, Anne (Benson) The Salinas, upside-down river... N.Y., Toronto, Farrar & Rinehart [1945] 316 p. illus., ports., map. (Rivers of Am.) Bibliography: p. 305–08. Available in many libraries.

5506. Ford & Sanborn co. The house of Ford & Sanborn co., Salinas, Kings City, Spreckels, from 1868 to 1907. [n.p., 1907] [15] p. illus. CSmH

5507. Gahagan, G. William. Key to the Monterey peninsula. Illus. by C. Whitman. Burlingame, Welcome house pub., c1956. 127 p. illus., maps. CHi CL CMont CRic CSf

5508. Gaylord, Florence H. Views in and around Asilomar. [S.F., Sunset press, c1929] unp. illus. C

5509. Gerbrandt, Geraldine Frances C. Historical study of the community of Soledad and its schools. [San Jose, 1958] Thesis (M.A.)—San Jose state college, 1958. CSal

5510. Gonzales tribune. Resources of Monterey county. And midwinter fair edition of the Gonzales tribune. Gonzales, Renison & Farley, 1894. 42 p. illus., ports. CLU CSal CSalCL

5511. Hahn, Campbell and associates, Burlingame. The master street and highway plan; Monterey, Pacific Grove and adjacent area, Monterey county, California, 1949. [1949] 35 p. illus., maps. Processed. CMont

5512. The hand book to Monterey and vicinity: containing brief resumé of the history of Monterey since its discovery; ...descriptive sketches of the town...and other places of interest in the county. A complete guide book, for tourists, campers and visitors. Monterey, Walton & Curtis, 1875. 152 p. C CHi CLU CMont CP CSalCL CSmH CU-B

5513. Hare, Lou G. Work of the Surveyor's office, Monterey county, California... Salinas, Salinas daily jl., 1914. 8 p. illus. (Bul. no. 14). Relates in part to excavations at the mission San Antonio de Padua.   CHi

5514. Harrison, Edward Sanford, pub. Monterey county souvenir edition, illustrated, resources, history, biography... S.F., Oakland, Pac. press [n.d.] 88 p. illus., map.   C CHi
CLSU CLU CMont CSalCL CSfCP CSfCW NN

5515. Hills, Miles vs. Sherwood, Frederick and Winterburn, George H. In the Supreme court of the state of California. Transcript on appeal. Amended complaint. In the district court of the third judicial district of the state of California, in and for the county of San Francisco. Miles Hills, plaintiff, vs. Frederick Sherwood and George H. Winterburn, as executors of the last will and testament of James Stokes, deceased... [n.p., 1871?] 272 p. About the ownership of Rancho los Vergeles near Salinas.   CU-B

5516. Historical records survey. California. Biographies; data compiled by the WPA historical survey of the Monterey peninsula, 1937. 2 v. Typew.   CMont

5517. —— —— Chronological digest of Monterey county records, 1850– January 1939; compiled by the WPA. [1939] 33 p. Typew.   CMont

5518. Historical survey of the Monterey peninsula. Spanish and Mexican land grants. Monterey, 1937. 94 p.   CMont

5519. Hoadley, Walter Evans. Agricultural labor in the Salinas valley... [Berkeley, 1938] 92 l. Typew.   CU-B

5520. —— A study of one hundred seventy self-resettled agricultural families, Monterey county, California, 1939. [Berkeley, 1939] Thesis (M.A.)—Univ. of Calif., 1940.   CU

5521. Hollister division committee of Monterey county. Reasons for the division of Monterey County. S.F., Winterburn & co. [1871] 12 p.   C

5522. Ingels, Elizabeth. Monterey peninsula: legends, history, business directory; Monterey, Pacific Grove, Carmel. [Monterey, Author, c1931] unp. illus., map.   CHi CMont

5523. Jochmus, Augustus Carlos. ["The circle of enchantment."] [Pacific Grove, Chamber of commerce, 1931] 64 p. illus.   CMont

5524. Jones, William O. The Salinas valley: its agricultural development, 1920–40. Thesis (Ph.D.)—Stanford university, 1947.   CSt

5525. King City. Chamber of commerce. Southern Monterey county. [King City, 1914?] [16] p. illus.   CHi

5526. Levick, M. B. Monterey county, California. S.F., Issued by Sunset mag., homeseekers' bur. for the Monterey county Bd. of supervisors [n.d.] 64 p. illus.
      C CHi CMont CSal CSalCL CU-B PHi

5527. Lowenstein, Norman. ...Salinas lettuce strike, 1936. [Berkeley, 1939] 73 l. Typew.   CU-B

5528. McDougall, John. Looking back down an age old trail... [Salinas, 1930–31] Appeared in 35 nos. of the Salinas index-journal, June 13, 1930–Feb. 21, 1931. A narrative of a trip across the plains in 1852, and early times in Salinas and Monterey county.   CSmH

5529. McNamee, Andrew, vs. McCusker, Daniel, et al. In the Supreme court of the state of California. Andrew McNamee, respondent, vs. Daniel McCusker et al., appellants. Transcript on appeal. B. S. Brooks, for appellants. A. Craig, for respondent. S.F., Women's union print., 1874. 65 p. Monterey county land suit.   CLU

5530. Marx, Charles David. ...Report of irrigation problems in the Salinas valley... [Wash., D.C., Govt. print. off., 1902?] 213 p.   CSalCL CSmH

5531. Mason, John Alden. The ethnology of the Salinan Indians. [Berkeley, 1911] Thesis (M.A.)—Univ. of Calif., 1911.   CU

5532. Monterey & Salinas valley R.R. co. [Shipping record, Oct. 29, 1874–Aug. 6, 1877?] unp.   CMont

5533. Monterey county. Board of supervisors. Monterey county. [This brochure prepared and produced by Herbert Cerwin and staff for the Monterey county publicity committee... n.d.] unp. illus. Largely illustrations.   CHi CL CMont CSal CSalCL

5534. —— —— Monterey county, California. Mineral, and timber wealth, varied industries. [Monterey, n.d.] 17 p.   CHi

5535. —— **Chamber of commerce.** Here are suggestions for your enjoyment of the Monterey peninsula. Monterey [193–?] 4 p. map.   CRcS

5536. —— —— Souvenir of Monterey county, the premier county of California... [S.F., Print. by Sunset press, 1902?] 27 p. illus.
      CL CMont CSalCL CSmH CU-B

5537. —— **Dept. of Administrative management.** County government in Monterey county. Salinas, 1959. 35 p. Mimeo.   CMont

5538. —— **Housing authority.** Characteristics of the low rent housing market in Salinas-Alisal and Seaside, California; based on housing surveys conducted during July, 1950... 1950. 56 p. illus. Processed.   CMont

5539. —— **Planning commission.** Park and recreation plan, Monterey county, California. 1944. 43 p. illus., maps.   CMont

5540. —— —— Streets and highways master plan; Salinas and vicinity. [1950] 30 p. illus., maps. Processed.   CMont

5541. —— —— Zoning ordinance, county of Monterey state of California. 1945. 24 p.   CMont

5542. —— —— Same. 1955. 53 p. Zoning ordinance no. 911, amending ordinance no. 568 in its entirety.   CMont

5543. Monterey county trust & savings bank. Fifty years of service... [Watsonville, 1940?] 27 p. illus., map.   CHi

5544. Monterey, Fresno & eastern railway co., San Francisco. This is a projected 140 mile standard gauge, standard equipment, high grade railroad from Monterey bay to the city of Fresno... proposed capitalization... $5,000,000... [S.F., Noland Davis co., 1906?] [15] p. illus., map.   CHi

5545. [Monterey peninsula country club. n.d.] 29 p. illus.   CHi CMont CSalCL

5546. —— By-laws... Pebble Beach, 1959. 36 p.   CHi

5547. Monterey peninsula crime study committee. Crime and delinquency on the Monterey peninsula. 1955. unp. illus.   CMont

5548. Native sons of the golden West. Santa Lucia parlor, no. 97. Souvenir... Salinas city, Cal. [Salinas, 1899?] 71 p. illus., ports.   C

5549. Neasham, Vernon Aubrey. ...The historical background of Point Lobos reserve... Berkeley, 1937. 17 l. Typew.   CU-B

5550. O'Donnell, Mayo Hayes. Peninsula diary. [Monterey, 1949?–52?] 1 v. of mounted clippings. CU-B

5551. Pacific improvement co. Photographs of the Seventeen mile drive, scenic boulevards, Pacific Grove, Pebble Beach lodge, property of the Pacific improvement company, San Francisco. comp. by A. D. Shepard, general manager. [S.F.?] 1910. [1] l., 84 photos. CU-B

5552. Park, Shirley Harriet (Hannah) The early development of the Salinas valley. [Berkeley, 1936] 162 l. illus., map. Thesis (M.A.)—Univ. of Calif., 1936. CU CU-B

5553. Parker, Paul. Paul Parker writes of old days in Monterey county. [Salinas, 1935] 4 p. of mounted clippings. CU-B

5554. Perles, Alfred. My friend Henry Miller; an intimate biography; with a preface by Henry Miller. N.Y., Day, c1956. 255 p. port. CMont CSalCL

5555. Phegley, James W., comp. and ed. List of important documents contained in the Archives of Monterey county at the Court house in Salinas, 1770–1846. Bancroft library, August 8, 1935. 39 l. Typew. CU-B

5556. [Photograph album of Hotel Del Monte, the Seventeen mile drive, Pebble Beach, Pacific Grove and vicinity] [n.p., 191–?] 27 photos. CU-B

5557. The preservation of Point Lobos, California and its grove of Monterey cypress. [Monterey? 193–?] 23 pl. NN

5558. Queen, William M. Sanctuary lights on the Monterey peninsula. Fresno, Acad. lib. guild, 1954. 55 p. illus. C CHi CL CLgA CMont CRedCL CSf CStcl CU-B

5559. A ramble through Monterey county, California. [S.F., Schwabacher-Frey stationery co., 1920?] 22 p. illus. CL CMont CRcS CSal CSalCL CU-B

5560. Rideout, Lionel Utley. Fermín Francisco de Lasuén and the economic development of the California missions. [Berkeley, 1940] Thesis (M.A.)—Univ. of Calif., 1940. CU

5561. The Rustler, King City. Monterey, the mission county. 1915 colonists' and homeseekers' ed., the Salinas valley rustler, magazine section. October first. King City, 1915. 64 p. illus., ports. CU-B

5562. The Rustler-Herald, King City. Salt of the earth. [King City, c1951] 76 p. illus., ports. CMont CU-B

5563. [Salinas. Board of trade] Monterey county, its general features, resources... S.F., Lith. Dickman-Jones co. [n.d.] 88 p. illus. CHi CL CU-B

5564. —— **St. Paul's Episcopal church.** St. Paul's Episcopal church, 1071 Pajaro street, Salinas, California. [1960] 7 p. Reproduced from typew. copy. CHi

5565. Salinas daily journal. The Monterey county progress edition, December, nineteen-fifteen... [Salinas, 1915] [36] p. illus., ports. CSal CU-B

5566. Shepard, A. D. Pebble Beach, Monterey county, California. [S.F., Steele, c1909] unp. illus. CMont CO CSmH CU-B

5567. Smith, Frances Norris (Rand) The mission of San Antonio de Padua. Stanford, 1932. 108 p. illus., maps.
Available in many California libraries and UPB

5568. Smith, Francis James. The impact of technological change on the marketing of Salinas lettuce. [Berkeley, 1961] Thesis (Ph.D.)– Univ. of Calif., 1961. CU

5569. Stone Cañon consolidated coal co., Oakland. Bondholders' agreement, dated September 22, 1909. [n.p., 1909] 17 p. CHi

5570. —— [Brochure] [n.p., 1906] [12] p. CHi

5571. [Stuart, James F.] Open letter to the President of the United States... S.F., Bacon & company [1878?] 7 p. Pertains to the Milpitas rancho. Stuart was attorney for the settlers. CHi CU-B

5572. Taylor, Eva (Stevens), comp. Oxcart, chuckwagon and jeep; memoirs [of] mission San Antonio, Milpitas rancho, Military reservation. San Lucas, Author, 1945. 58 p. illus., ports. C CHi

5573. Tays, George. Ignacio Vallejo adobe at Bolsa de San Cayetano... Berkeley, 1937. 4 l. Typew. CU-B

5574. The Traveler. Paraiso hot springs, Monterey county, California. [S.F., Hicks-Judd co., 1893] 6 p. CSmH

5575. —— Same. ...W. W. and Mary A. Ford, owners... [S.F., 189–?] 16 p. illus., map. CHi

5576. Walter, Arthur. School finances of Monterey county, California, and the crisis in education... [Salinas, Index print, 1921] 30 p. CSmH CU-B

5577. Weston, Edward. My camera on Point Lobos; 30 photographs and excerpts from E. W.'s daybook. Yosemite national park, V. Adams; Bost., Houghton, 1950. 79, [2] p. 30 pl. Bibliography: p. [81] CL CLO CLU CMont CRcS CSalCL CSfCSM CStmo CSto CV

5578. Wickson, Gladys Clare. The integration of geographic forms in the Salinas valley. [Berkeley, 1929] Thesis (M.A.)– Univ. of Calif., 1929. CU

5579. Writers' program. California. Monterey peninsula... Stanford Univ., Delkin [c1941] 207 p. illus., maps. (Am. guide ser.) Bibliography: p. 194–198.
Available in many California libraries and CoU MiD MoS NHi NN ODa TxU UPB

5580. —— —— Same...American centennial edition. Stanford Univ., Delkin [1946] 200 p. illus., maps. (Am. guide ser.) "Second revised edition." CAla CBev CBu CL CLSU CLU CMont CRc CSal CSluCL CStmo

5581. —— —— **Division of recreation.** Historical episodes in Monterey county, 1542–1905. Monterey, 1939. 186 p. Typew. CMont

Carmel

5582. Adamic, Louis. Robinson Jeffers; a portrait. Seattle, Univ. of Wash., 1929. 35 p. CHi

5583. Bostick, Daisy F., and Castelhun, Dorothea. Carmel—at work and play... Carmel, Seven arts, c1925. 109 p. illus. C CHi CL CLSU CLU CMont CO CRcS CSd CSf CSfCW CSluCL CSmH CStclU CStcrCL CStmo CU-B N NN OrU

5584. —— Carmel—today and yesterday. Carmel, Seven arts, c1945. 123 p. illus. C CCoron CHi CLO CLU CMont CPom CSd CSj CSjC CSmat CSmH CU-B KyU NN

5585. Brooks, Charles Stephen. A western wind ... N.Y., Harcourt, c1935. 158 p. illus.
Available in many California libraries and MiD OrU

5586. Carmel. All Saints' Episcopal church. Guide book. [Monterey, c1951] [15] p. illus. CHi CU-B

5587. —— **Presbyterian church. Women's association.** Year book...1957– [n.p., 1957–] CHi has 1957-58.

5588. Carmel business association. Carmel-by-the sea... [Carmel, Carmel press, n.d.] unp. illus.
CHi CL CMont

5589. Carmel development co. Carmel-by-the-sea ...a town in a pine forest... Carmel [n.d.] [24] p. illus., maps.   CHi

5590. Engelhardt, Zephyrin, *Father.* ...Mission San Carlos Borromeo (Carmelo). The father of the missions... Santa Barbara, Mission Santa Barbara, 1934. 264 p. illus., port.
Available in many California libraries and CaBViPA

5591. Gilbert, Rudolph. Shine, perishing republic; Robinson Jeffers and the tragic sense in modern poetry. Bost., Humphries, c1936. 197 p.   CMont

5592. Gray, Eunice T. Cross trails and chaparral. Carmel, Seven arts, c1925. 88 p.
C CHi CLO CLSU CLU CMont CO CSalCL CSmH

5593. Kent manor project, Carmel. The Kent manor project in Carmel highlands. [1952?] 4 p.   CHi

5594. Muir, Denis. Carmel & Monterey; the pictures by George Mathis. San Anselmo, Kingfisher press, c1946. unp. illus., map.   CO

5595. El Paseo: the passage way where new California meets old Spain. [Carmel] Lewis Charles Merrell and the Press in the forest, 1928. [11] l. illus.   CHi

5596. Peninsula pictorial. Carmel, Carmel work center [1955?] [32] p. illus. Photographs by Steve Crouch.   CLO

5597. Powell, Lawrence Clark. An introduction to Robinson Jeffers. Dijon, Bernigaud & Privat, 1932. port., map.   CRcS

5598. —— Robinson Jeffers; a lecture to Professor James L. Wortham's class in narrative poetry given on May 22, 1949. [L.A.?] L.A. city college press, 1951. 20 p.
CMont

5599. —— Robinson Jeffers; the man and his work; a foreword by Robinson Jeffers; decorations by James Hawkins. Rev. ed. Pasadena, San Pasqual press, c1940. 222 p. illus., ports., map.   CHi CMont CU-B

5600. R[eynolds], S[tephen] A[llen]. Carmel; its poets and peasants; a peninsula pot-pourri of pleasantry and philosophy. [by "Sar."] Carmel [c1927] 32 p. illus.   C CHi CLU CMont CSalCL CU-B

5601. Slevin, L. S. Guide book to the mission San Carlos at Carmel and Monterey, California... Carmel, 1912. 34 p. illus.
CBb CHi CLSU CLgA CSalCL CSf CU-B

5602. Smith, Frances Norris (Rand) The architectural history of Mission San Carlos Borromeo, California...Pub. by the California Historical survey commission, Berkeley. [Sacramento, State print. off.] 1921. 81 p. illus.
Available in many California libraries and MoHi NN T

5603. Smith, Joseph. Carmel-by-the-sea. Echoes of its early history its traditions and its designs. Story and illustration by Joseph Smith. Carmel-by-the-sea, Author, 1938. [37] p. illus., maps.   CSf CSfCW

5604. Squires, James Radcliffe. The loyalties of Robinson Jeffers. Ann Arbor, Univ. of Mich. press, c1956. 202 p.   CMont CU-B

5605. Stanton, Robert. The Church of the way-farer and its biblical garden, by Robert Stanton...and Butler Sturtevant... Carmel-by-the-sea, The Community church [1940] 22 p. illus., maps.   CHi

5606. Sterling, George. Robinson Jeffers; the man and the artist. N.Y., Boni & Liveright, c1926. 40 p.
CHi CMont CU-B

5607. Western woman. Celebrated artists of the Carmel-Monterey colony. Rev. ed. [n.d.] (v.13, no. 2–3)
CSal

5608. White, Emil, ed. Carmel by-the-sea, in story and picture. [Big Sur? 1958] 40 p. illus.
C CAla CL CLO CLU CMont CO CRic CSd CSjC CStmo NN

5609. White, Richard Edward. Padre Junipero Serra and the mission church of San Carlos del Carmelo. S.F., P. E. Dougherty & co., 1884. 32 p.
C CHi CL CLU CMont CSalCL CSmH CU-B

5610. Wiese, Kenneth William. Craftsmen of Carmel, California. Fresno, 1958. 132 l. photos. Thesis (M.A.)– Fresno state college, 1958.   CFS

Monterey

5611. Abstract of title to a lot of land in the city of Monterey, being a portion of lot 4 in Block "B"...Dated April 3rd, A.D., 1912. 46 p. Typew.   CMont

5612. Abstract of title to Oak Grove. Formerly a part of the tract of land known as the "Durr tract," lying next to and west of the Hotel Del Monte grounds... [n.d.] unp.   CMont CSmH

5613. Amat, Thaddeus, Bp.. Exhortacion pastoral que el ilmo. S.r D. Tadeo Amat, Obispo de Monterey, dirige a los fieles de su diocesis... L.A., Impreso en la oficina del "So. Californian," 1856. [6] p.
CLCM CSmH

5614. Andresen, Anna Geil. Historic landmarks of Monterey, California...with a resumé of the history of Monterey since its discovery, and a sketch of the old social life... [Salinas, Salinas index press, c1917] 93 p. illus.
C CHi CMont CSal CSalCL CSfCP CSmH CU-B

5615. —— Story of La Granja; the Field residence, on Munras Avenue, Monterey, California; written for the centenary of the home, 1824–1924. [Priv. print., n.d.] 14 p. illus.   C CMont

5616. Associated veterans of the Mexican war. History of the celebration of the fiftieth anniversary of the taking possession of California and raising of the American flag at Monterey, Cal. by Commodore John Drake Sloat, U.S.N., July 7th, 1846...Held at Monterey, California, July 7th, 1896. Also of the fiftieth anniversary of the raising of the American flag at San Francisco, California, July 9th, 1846, by Captain James B. Montgomery, U.S.N. ...Held July 9th, 1896. Preceded by an account of the celebration of the fiftieth anniversary of the raising of the bear flag at Sonoma, California, June 14th, 1846, held Saturday, June 13th, 1896... Oakland, Carruth & Carruth, 1896. 55 p. illus.
C CHi CL CLSU CLU CMont CP CSalCL CSf CSfU CSmH

5617. —— History of the joint anniversary celebration at Monterey, Cal. of the 110th anniversary of American independence and 40th anniversary of the taking possession of California and the raising of American flag at Monterey by Commodore John D. Sloat of the U.S.N., July 7, 1846, the celebration being held Monday, July 5, 1886. [S.F., Fraternal pub. co., 1886?] 29 p. illus., ports.
CHi CL CLU CMont CSalCL CSf CSfCP CSmH CU-B MiD-B NN NHi

5618. —— Report of the committee of arrangements ...of the celebration of the fiftieth anniversary of the raising of the American flag by Commodore John D. Sloat, U.S.N., at Monterey, California, July 7, 1846, held at Monterey, July 7, 1896. [n.p., 1896] 10 p. (With Sloat monument assoc. of California. The Sloat monument... [1896]) CU-B

5619. Bancroft, H. H., & co. Monterey and Hotel del Monte. S.F., 1890. 6 l. 12 pl. CU-B

5620. Bechtel, Kenneth K. Commodore Jones' war, 1842. S.F., Grabhorn, 1948. 4 p. Includes letter by William H. Meyers written ten days after the Monterey incident. CMont CU-B (also original Meyers journal & letters)

5621. Beechey, Frederick William. Narrative of a voyage to the Pacific and Beering's strait... in the years 1825, 26, 27, 28... London, Henry Colburn & Richard Bentley...1831. 2 v. illus., port., maps. Ch. I & II of v.2: California. C CBb CHi CL CLO CLSU CLU CLgA CMont CO CP CSdS CSfCP CSfWF-H CSmH CU-B

5622. —— Same. Phila., Carey & Lea, 1832. 493 p. Other editions were published in English and other languages. CHi CLO CSmH CU-B

5623. —— An account of a visit to California, 1826–'27; reprinted from a narrative of a voyage to the Pacific and Beering's strait performed in His Majesty's Ship Blossom under the command of Captain F. W. Beechey, in 1825, '26, '27, '28. Introduction by Edith M. Coulter. Printed at the Grabhorn press for the Book club of California [1941] 74 p. illus., map. C CHi CL CLO CLU CSj CSjC CSmH CStclU CStmo CU-B

5624. Beilharz, Edwin Alanson. Felipe de Neve: governor of California and commandant general of the interior provinces. [Berkeley, 1950] Thesis (Ph.D.)– Univ. of Calif., 1950. CStclU (microfilm) CU

5625. Bennett, Robert. The wrath of John Steinbeck; or, St. John goes to church; with a foreword by Lawrence Clark Powell; illustrated by Artemis. L.A., Albertson press, c1939. [11] p. illus. CMont

5626. Bestor, Arthur Eugene, jr. David Jacks of Monterey, and Lee L. Jacks, his daughter. With a foreword by Donald Bertrand Tresidder. Stanford, c1945. 44 p. CHi CMont CSalCL CSfWF-H CU-B (on film)

5627. Blanch, Josephine Mildred. The story of a friendship. Robert Louis Stevenson, Jules Simoneau; a California reminiscence of Stevenson. 1st ed. [n.p.] 1921. [15] p. CHi CU-B

5628. —— Same. 2d ed. [N.Y.? Scribner?] 1927. [15] p. illus., ports. CHi CU-B

5629. Bland, Henry Meade. Stevenson's California. San Jose, Pac. short story club, 1924. 34 p. illus. C CHi CL CLSU CLU CMont CO CSalCL CSd CSf CSmH CU-B

5630. [Brown, A. A.] A friendship; Robert Louis Stevenson, Jules Simoneau. [S.F., Taylor, Nash & Taylor, 1911] 8 p. illus. CHi CU-B

5631. Brown, Wallace Clarence, comp. Historic Monterey and surroundings. Special souvenir ed. Monterey cypress. Monterey, 1899. 47 p. illus. C CHi CMont CSalCL CSf CSmH CU-B

5632. Browne, John Ross. Muleback to the convention; letters of J. Ross Browne, reporter to the constitutional convention, Monterey, September-October, 1849.

S.F., Bk. club of Calif., 1950. 42 p. col. illus., port., facsim. CBb CHi CL CLO CLSM CLod CRedl CSf CSfWF-H CSjC CSto CStoC CU-B CaBViPA

5633. —— Report of the debates in the convention of California, on the formation of the state constitution in September and October, 1849. Wash., D.C., John T. Towers, 1850. 479 p. CChiS CHi CLgA CMont CRedl CRic CSd CSf CSfP CStmo CStoC CU-B ViU ViW

5634. —— Same, translated into Spanish. N.Y., S. W. Benedict, 1851. 439 p. C-S CHi CLgA CSfCSM CStoC CU-B

5635. California. Constitution. Constitution of the state of California. S.F., Print. at off. of the Alta Calif., 1849. 19 p. "The first appearance of the constitution in book form, and one of the earliest works printed in San Francisco. In an official report dated Monterey, October 12, 1849, Henry W. Halleck, Secretary of state, announces that 8000 copies were printed."—Cowan. C CHi CLCM CLSU CLU CSfCP CSmH CU CU-B CtY ICN NN

5636. —— —— Same, with an introduction by Robert Glass Cleland. San Marino, Huntington lib., 1949. 19 p. facsim. (Friends of the Huntington lib. Occasional pub.) CChiS CHi CLS CLSM CLgA CSd CSdU CSfWF-H CU-B

5637. —— **Dept. of natural resources. Division of beaches and parks.** Material dealing with the planning progress toward the preservation of historic Monterey, California; progress report on research and planning undertaken by the city of Monterey with cooperation of the California state park commission and support from the Carnegie institution of Washington, D.C. Oct., 1938. v.p. Typew. C CMont

5638. —— —— —— Monterey. Sacramento, State print. off., 1958. unp. CRcS

5639. Chorley, Lloyd Kenneth. Thomas Oliver Larkin, early California business man. [Berkeley, 1931] Thesis (M.A.)– Univ. of Calif., 1931. CU CU-B

5640. Chrisman, G. H. Beautiful Monterey by the sea. Monterey, Monterey daily cypress [1906] unp. illus. CMont CSal

5641. Civil enrollment committee, San Francisco. U.S. army military training camp, Monterey, California, July 10th to August 5th, 1916. [S.F., 1916] [64] p. illus., map. CU-B

5642. Colton, Walter. Glances into California, introduction by Edwin Corle. L.A., Dawson, 1955. 43 p. illus. (Early Calif. travels ser., 29) Chapter fourteen of Colton's Deck and port. First pub. 1850. 250 copies printed by Grabhorn press. CHi CLSM CLgA CSjC CU-B CaBViPA

5643. —— The land of gold; or, Three years in California. N.Y., D. W. Evans & co., 1850. 456 p. front. (port.) CL CMont CSfWF-H CU-B CaBViPA

5644. —— Three years in California [1846–1849] N.Y., Barnes; Cincinnati, Ohio, H. W. Derby & co., 1850. 456 p. illus., ports., map. Other editions, 1854, 1859, 1860. Available in many California libraries and CaBViPA ViU

5645. —— —— Index ... Joseph Gaer, editor ... [S.F., 1935] 21 l. (Index no. 11, SERA project 2–F2–132 ⟨3–F2–197⟩ Calif. literary research) Mimeo. C C-S CHi CLSU CLU CMont CO CP CRic CSdS CSfP CSmH CStmo

5646. —— Same, with title: The California diary; foreword by Joseph A. Sullivan. Oakland, Biobooks, 1948. 261 p. illus., map. (Calif. centennial ed. 16)
Available in many California libraries and CaBViPA

5647. —— Three years in California, together with excerpts from the author's *Deck and port*, covering his arrival in California, and a selection of his letters from Monterey. Introd. and notes by Marguerite Eyer Wilbur. [Stanford, 1949] 376 p. ports., map. With reproduction of title-page of original ed., 1850.
Available in many California libraries and CaBViPA MoS OrU UHi

5648. Conmy, Peter Thomas. The centenary of the American consulate in California: Thomas Oliver Larkin, consul, 1843–1848. [S.F.] 1943. A report submitted by the Grand historian, Native sons of the golden west, San Francisco, Oct. 15, 1943.   CHi CU-B

5649. —— The constitutional beginnings of California. S.F., Native sons of the golden West, 1959. 28 p.
C CAla CHi CLO CP CRcS CSd CSf CSmat CSt CStbS CSto CStclU CStmo CU-B CViCL

5650. Cook, Sherburne Friend. ...The Monterey surgeons during the Spanish period in California... [Baltimore, Md., Johns Hopkins press, 1937] p. 43–72. "Reprinted from *Bul. of the Institute of the history of medicine*, vol.V, no. 1, Jan. 1937."   CU-B

5651. [Costansó, Miguel] Diario historico de los viages de mar, y tierra hechos al norte de la California... [México] Impr. del Superior Gobierno [1770] 56 p.
CHi (facsim.) TxU

5652. —— Same, reprinted. Mexico, Chimalistac, c1950. 71 p. facsim.   CL CU-B

5653. —— An historical journal of the expeditions by sea and land to the north of California; in 1768, 1769, and 1770; when Spanish establishments were first made at San Diego and Monte-Rey. From a Spanish MS. Translated by William Reveley, Esq. London, A. Dalrymple, 1790. 76 p. maps.
C CHi CSmH CU-B (typew. transcript) CaBViPA

5654. —— ...The narrative of the Portolá expedition of 1769–1770...ed. by Adolph van Hemert-Engert ...and Frederick J. Teggart... Berkeley, Univ. of Calif., 1910. 69 p. front. (facsim.) (Pub. of the Acad. of Pac. coast history, v.1, no. 4) Spanish and English text. Translated by R. C. Hopkins.
Available in many California libraries and CaBViPA MoS N TxU

5655. —— The Portolá expedition of 1769–1770; dairy of Miguel Constansó. Ed. by Frederick J. Teggart ... Berkeley, University of Calif., 1911. 167 p. map. (Pub. of the Acad. of Pac. coast hist. v.2, no. 4, p. [161]–327) "It is entirely distinct from the *Diario Histórico* of the same author and has not hitherto been printed."—Introduction.
C CBev CBu CChiS CHi CL CLSU CLU CLgA CSS CSf CSfCW CSmH CStrJC CU-B CViCL CaBViPA

5656. Cowan, Robert Ernest. The Spanish press of California, 1833–1844. [S.F., 1902] [11] p. Reprinted from the California historic-genealogical soc. pub. no. III.
CHi CLO CLgA CPom CSd CSf CU-B

5657. —— Same. 1833–1845. S.F., J. H. Nash, 1931. 21 p.   CHi CSfCW

5658. —— Same. [Anaheim] The Orange county club of printing house craftsmen, 1949. 62 p.
CHi CLO

5659. Culleton, James. Indians and pioneers of old Monterey; being a chronicle of the religious history of Carmel mission considered in connection with Monterey's other local events and California's general history; also a sketch of aboriginal Monterey. Fresno, Acad. of Calif. church history, 1950. 286 p. illus. (Acad. of Calif. church history Pub. no. 2)
Available in many California libraries and KyU UPB

5660. Dakin, Susanna (Bryant) The lives of William Hartnell. Stanford [1949] 308 p. illus., ports., maps. Bibliography: p. 295–302.
CBb CHi CLSM CLgA CMont CP CRedCL CSd CSf CSjC CStmo CStoC CU-B CV CoD

5661. Data on Colton hall [1850–1903] [n.p., 19—?] 11 l. Reproduced from typew. copy.   CU-B

5662. Del Monte golf and country club. [Descriptive brochure. S.F., Crocker, 1913?] [31] p. illus
CHi

5663. —— Golf and other sports at Del Monte. [S.F., Crocker, 1912?] [32] p. illus.   CHi CMont

5664. —— Views of the golf course and surroundings, Del Monte golf and country club. Del Monte [190-?] 24 pl.   CU-B

5665. Del Monte properties co. Annual report. CL has 1949-60.

5666. —— [Brochure. n.p., 1949] [20] p.   CHi

5667. —— Del Monte and Pebble Beach. On the Monterey peninsula... [n.p., 1924?] 18 p. Reprinted from *Pacific gold and motor* of Dec. 1923.   CSmH

5668. —— Pebble Beach on the Monterey peninsula. Del Monte [1929] 2 p. maps.   CRcS

5669. Downey, Joseph T. The cruise of the *Portsmouth*, 1845–1847; a sailor's view of the naval conquest of California. Ed. by Howard Lamar. New Haven, Yale univ. lib., 1958. 246 p. illus., maps. (Western hist. ser., no. 4)
CAla CBb CHi CLO CLSM CNF CRcS CSdS CStclU CStmo CU-B CaBViPA ViU

5670. Downing, Margaret Mary. Juan Bautista Alvarado, politician. [Berkeley, 1938] Thesis (M.A.)—Univ. of Calif., 1938.   CU CU-B

5671. Drewes, Rudolph Herman. Pedro Fages, California pioneer. [Berkeley, 1928] Thesis (M.A.)—Univ. of Calif., 1928.   CU CU-B

5672. Dupetit-Thouars, Abel Aubert. Voyage of the *Venus*: sojourn in California. Tr. by Charles N. Rudkin. L.A., Dawson, 1956. 113 p. illus. (part col.), map. (Early Calif. travels ser., 35) Excerpt from Voyage autour du monde sur la frégate *Venus* pendant les années 1836–1839... 200 copies printed by Plantin press.
C CLLoy CLO CLSM CLgA CMont CSS CSd CSjC CSto CU-B CVtV

5673. Duvall, Marius. A navy surgeon in California, 1846–1847. The journal of Marius Duvall. Edited by Fred Blackburn Rogers. S.F., John Howell, 1957. 114 p. illus., port., 3 fold. facsims.
CHi CL CLM CLO CLSM CRcS CSS CSal CSalCL CSd CSf CSfSt CSjC CSto CStoC CU-B CaBViPA

5674. Eitel, Edward E. Picturesque Del Monte... Monterey, Pac. improvement co., 1888. [17] p. illus.
CSmH CU-B

5675. Eldredge, Zoeth Skinner. The march of Portolá and the discovery of the bay of San Francisco... The log of the *San Carlos* and original documents tr. and annotated by E. J. Molera... S.F., Calif. promotion committee, 1909. 71 p. illus., map.

Available in many California libraries and CaBViPA MiD MoS N NHi NN OrU

5676. Estracto de noticias del puerto de Monterrey, de la mission, y presidio que se han establecido en el con la denominacion de San Carlos, y del suceso de las dos expediciones de mar y tierra que a este fin se despacharon en el año proximo anterior de 1769. [Mexico, Impr. del Superior Govierno, 1770] [5] p. 1st ed. The Portolá expedition.   CSmH CU-B

5677. —— Same. [Mexico, Impr. del Superior Govierno, 1770] [8] p. Same text with a few slight typographical changes.—Cowan.

CHi (facsim.) CU-B TxU

5678. —— Same, reprinted. Madrid, J. Porrúa Turanzas, 1959. 13 p.   CU-B

5679. —— Same, with title: Noticias de California, first report of the occupation by the Portolá expedition, 1770, with facsimiles of the original printings, a new translation, contemporary maps, and a narrative of how it all came to pass by George Peter Hammond. S.F., Bk. club of Calif., 1958. 53 p. illus., fold. maps, facsims. Reprints 1st and 2d eds. of 1770.

CHi CL CLS CLSM CLgA CP CSS CSalCL CSf CSfCSM CSjC CStclU CSto CU-B CaBViPA

5680. Fages, Pedro. ...Expedition to San Francisco bay in 1770, diary of Pedro Fages; ed. by Herbert Eugene Bolton... Berkeley, Univ. of Calif., 1911. 19 p. (Pub. of the Acad. of Pac. coast history. v.2, no. 3) Spanish and English on opposite pages.

CHi CSmH CU-B MoS TxU

5681. —— A historical, political, and natural description of California, by Pedro Fages, soldier of Spain, newly translated into English from the original Spanish by Herbert Ingram Priestley... Berkeley, Univ. of Calif. press, 1937. 83 p. fold. map. Continues and supplements Extracto de noticias del puerto de Monterrey, 1770, and Miguel Costansó's Diario histórico de los viajes de mar y tierra hechos al norte de la California, 1770.

Available in many California libraries and ViU.

5682. Field, Isobel (Osbourne) This life I've loved. N.Y., Longmans, c1937. 353 p. illus.

CHi CMont CU-B

5683. Field, Maria Antonia. Copa de oro, festival days in old California. S.F., Cloister press, 1948. [32] p.

CHi CMont CStclU

5684. —— Monterey zephyrs, by Maria Antonia [pseud.] Illus. by the author. Privately printed ed. S.F., A. M. Robertson, 1912. 32 p. illus.   CU-B

5685. —— Where Castilian roses bloom; memoirs... S.F., Grabhorn, 1954. 142 p. illus., ports., facsims.

CHi CLgA CMartC CMont CRedCL CSal CSalCL CSf CSfCW CU-B

5686. Figueroa, José. Manifiesto [!] a la republica Mejicana que hace el general de brigada Jose Figueroa, comandante general y gefe politico de la Alta California, sobre su conducta y la de los Señores D. Jose Maria de Hijar y D. Jose Maria Padres, como directores de colonizacion en 1834 y 1835. Monterrey, 1835. C. Augustin V. Zamorano. 184 p.

C CHi CLCM CSmH CU-B CtY

5687. —— Same, trans. into English. [S.F.] Herald off., 1855. 104 p.

C CHi CL CP CSf CSfCW CSmH CSmyS CSrD CU-B CViCL NN

5688. —— Same. Foreword by Jos. A. Sullivan. Oakland, Biobooks, 1952. 103 p. (Calif. relations, 32)

Available in many California libraries and N ViU

5689. Fisher Anne (Benson) Cathedral in the sun. N.Y., Carlyle house, 1940. 408 p. illus. San Carlos Borromeo mission.   CHi CSalCL CSfCW CU-B

5690. —— Same. Palo Alto, Pac. bks. [1951] 408 p. illus., map.   CSfU

5691. No more a stranger. Stanford, c1946. 265 p. illus., ports. Robert L. Stevenson in Monterey.

Available in many libraries.

5692. Forbes, Margaret Beresford. Monterey sanctuary... Pacific Grove, c1940. 75 p. illus.

C CMont CO CRic CSalCL CSf CU-B

5693. Ford, Tirey Lafayette. Dawn and the dons; the romance of Monterey... S.F., Robertson, 1926. 236 p. illus.

Available in many California libraries and CaBViPA MoHi NN NvU TxU UPB

5694. Foster, Stephen Clark. El Quacheno, how I want to help make the constitution of California—stirring historical incidents... L.A., Dawson, 1949. 35 p. "One hundred copies printed...by William M. Cheney."

CHi CL CLO CU-B

5695. Franklin, Viola Price. Stevenson in Monterey or an afternoon with Jules Simoneau... Salem, Ore., Statesman pub. co., 1925. 18 p.   CHi CSmH

5696. Gannett, Lewis Stiles. John Steinbeck; personal and bibliographical notes. N.Y., Viking [c1939] 14 p.   CMont CU-B

5697. Gay, Antoinette (Guernsey) Calle de Alvarado. Monterey, Monterey trader press, c1936. 91 p. illus. "Memories and legends... told the writer by old timers and descendants of Monterey pioneers."—Foreword.

C CHi CMont CSalCL CSbr CSmH CU-B

5698. —— Presidio of Monterey, 1770–1940. Monterey, Trader press [n.d.] 20 p.   CMont

5699. Goodwin, Cardinal Leonidas. The establishment of state government in California, 1846–1850. N.Y., Macmillan, 1914. 359 p.

CHi CLgA CRcdl CSd CSf CSfCW CSfP CSjC CStbS CU (Thesis) CU-B OrU

5700. Gross, Harold William. The influence of Thomas O. Larkin toward the acquisition of California. [Berkeley, 1938] Thesis (M.A.)— Univ. of Calif., 1938.

CU CU-B

5701. Halleck, J., and Hartnell, W. E. P. Translation and digest of such portions of the Mexican laws of March 20th and May 23d, 1837, as are supposed to be still in force and adapted to the present condition of California; with an introduction and notes... S.F., Alta Calif. press, 1849. 26 p.

CSfCP CSmH CU-B ICN

5702. Hammond, George Peter, ed. The Larkin papers; personal, business, and official correspondence of Thomas Oliver Larkin, merchant and United States consul in California. [1822–58] Berkeley, Pub. for the Bancroft lib. by the Univ. of Calif. press, 1951–64. 10 v. ports.

Available in many California libraries and CoD MoS MoSU N TxU

5703. Hansen, Woodrow James. Men of the constitutional convention of 1849. Reprinted from the *Proceedings* of the second annual meeting of the *Conference of California historical societies.* San Jose, June 21–23, 1956. 36 p.   CNC

5704. Harding, George Laban. Don Augustin V. Zamorano, statesman, soldier, craftsman, and California's first printer. L. A., Zamorano club, 1934. 308 p. illus., port., map.
C CBev CBu CHi CL CLO CLSU CLU CMartC CRc CRedl CSf CSfCP CSjC CSmat CSmH CStrJC CU-B

5705. [Heininger, Charles P.], pub. Souvenir of Monterey, California. [S.F., n.d.] 14 p. 12 pl.   C-S

5706. Hellum, Bertha. Signers of the first state constitution. [n.p., n.d.] v.p. illus.   CMartC

5707. Historical survey of the Monterey peninsula. Adobes and old buildings in Monterey; data compiled by the WPA Hist. survey of the Monterey peninsula. 1937. 164, 38 p. Typew.   C CMont CU-B

5708. —— Monterey historical survey book review ...Compiled by the Recreation division, Works progress admin. 1937. 407 p. Typew. A bibliography on...historical events in Monterey.   CMont

5709. Holden, Erastus D. California's first piano ...[1931] 11 p. Ms. Source material on Monterey history and José Abrego.   CMont CSd

5710. Hotel Del Monte. Art gallery, Hotel Del Monte, California. [Monterey? n.d.] 17 pl.   CU-B

5711. —— Same. July to November 1912. [n.p.] 1912. 14 p.   CHi

5712. —— Monterey, California; the most charming winter resort in the world... [n.p., 1880] 16 p.
                                            CSmH NN

5713. —— Souvenir guide...to Monterey and its environments. [Monterey, 1885?] 24 p. illus., maps.
                                         CHi CMont NN

5714. Hotel Del Monte. [S.F., Denison news co.] [18—?] 23 pl.   CU-B

5715. Hotel Del Monte, Monterey, California... [S.F., Sunset press, n.d.] [24] p. illus.
                                      CSfCP CSmH CU-B

5716. —— Same. S.F., Sunset press [1897] 16 p. illus., map.   CSf CU-B
Other editions followed   CHi (1899, 1908)

5717. Hunt, Rockwell Dennis. ...The genesis of California's first constitution (1846–49)... Baltimore, Johns Hopkins press, 1895. 59 p. (Johns Hopkins univ. studies in hist. and political science...13th ser., viii)
CChiS CHi CLgA CPom CSd CSdS CSf CStbS CStmo CSto CStoC CU-B N ViW

5718. Illustrated guide to the scenery and attractions of the Pacific coast...and especially to Monterey... [Del Monte, 1881] 24 p. illus.   CMont

5719. Jackson, Alonzo C. The conquest of California; Alonzo C. Jackson's letter in detail of the seizure of Monterey in 1842 and his letter on the final conquest of 1846. [Priv. print. from the original unpublished manuscripts, 1842–1846 for the friends of Edward Eberstadt and sons, 1953] 31 p. illus., facsims.
C CHi CL CLU CMont CU-B CaBViPA IHi KyU N TxU UHi

5720. Jarvis, Chester Edward. The capitals of California, 1849–1854. [Berkeley, 1942] Thesis (M.A.) — Univ. of Calif., 1942.   CU CU-B

5721. Jeans, Raymond William. Architectural remains of old Monterey. [Berkeley, 1917] 91 l. illus., map. Thesis (M.A.)—Univ. of Calif., 1917.   C CMont

5722. Jochmus, Augustus Carlos. The city of Monterey; its people—anecdotes—legends—romances—

achievements, 1542–1924... Pacific Grove [Author] c1925. [34] p. illus., ports.
  C CLSU CLU CMont CSalCL CSfP CSmH CU-B

5723. —— Monterey...1542–1930... Pacific Grove [1930?] 75 p. illus., ports.
C CHi CLU CMont CO CSal CSalCL CSfCP CSfWF-H CSmH CStmo CU-B NN

5724. Jones, James McHall. Two letters of James McHall Jones, delegate to the California constitutional convention, 1849. From the collection of Thomas W. Norris. [S.F., Grabhorn, 1948]   CHi CRcS CU-B

5725. Jones, Thomas ap Catesby. ...Correspondencia sobre las Californias e invasiòn del puerto de Monterrey por el comodoro norte americana Thomas ape [sic] Jones, 1843... México, D.F., Vargas Rea, 1944. 27 p. (Papeles ed las Californias, 6)   CHi TxU

5726. Kelsey, Raynor Wickersham. The United States consulate in California. [Berkeley, 1909] Thesis (Ph.D.)—Univ. of Calif., 1909.   CU-B

5727. —— Same. Berkeley, Univ. of Calif., 1910. 107 p. (Pub. of the Acad. of Pac. coast history, v.1, no. 5)   CHi CStrJC CU CU-B CViCL CWhC

5728. King, Mary Wilma, Sister. William E. P. Hartnell; a California patriarch, 1820–1854. Wash., D.C., 1958. 87 p. Thesis (M.A.)—Catholic univ. of Amer., 1958.   CSrD

5729. Larkin, Thomas Oliver. Chapters in the early life of Thomas Oliver Larkin...from his original manuscripts, edited...by Robert J. Parker... S.F., Calif. hist. soc., 1939. 77 p. illus., map.
C CBb CHi CLSU CLU CMont CO CSalCL CSf CSjC CSmH CStrJC CU-B CaBViPA

5730. —— First and last consul: Thomas Oliver Larkin and the Americanization of California. A selection of letters, ed. by John A. Hawgood. San Marino, Huntington lib., 1962. 123 p. port.   CAla CHi CSmH CU-B

5731. —— Tomas Oliverio Larkin, tiene el honor de noticiar á V. que el Ecsmo. Sor. Presidente de los Estados-Unidos del norte; se ha dignado conferirle el nombramiento de consul de dicha república para esta puerto; y habiendo tomado hoy poseción de su nuevo empleo, se ofrece respetuosamente á la disposición de V. Monterrey. Abril 2 de 1844. [n.p., n.d.] folder (4 p.)
                                     CHi CSfCP CU-B

5732. Larsen, Walter Stanley. Walter Colton: Yankee alcalde. [L.A.] 1950. Thesis (M.A.)—U.C.L.A., 1950.   CLU

5733. Latin American village studio. The golden journey, illustrating certain passages from the diary of Gaspar de Portolá, and covering his march through California, May 11, 1769 to June 3, 1770. Santa Barbara, c1947. 11 col. pl.   CRcS

5734. Lisca, Peter. The wide world of John Steinbeck. New Brunswick, N.Y., Rutgers univ. press, c1958. 326 p.   CMont CU-B

5735. MacFarland, Grace. Monterey, cradle of California's romance... Monterey, Press of Weybret-Lee co., 1914. 95 p. illus.
C CHi CL CLO CLSU CLU CMerCL CMont CO CSalCL CSf CSfCP CSfP CSmH CU-B

5736. McMurtrie, Douglas C. The ultimate fate of California's first press. Stockton, Stockton high school, 1935. 13 p. illus.   CHi CL CSto CU-B

5737. Mason, R. B., Military governor, Alta California. Extract from the regulations for collecting the tariff of duties on imports and tonnage. Published for the information of shipmasters and merchants... [S.F., 1847] 4 p. tables. CHi CSmH

5738. —— Laws for the better government of California, "The preservation of order, and the protection of the rights of the inhabitants," during the military occupation of the country by the forces of the United States. ... S.F., S. Brannan, pub., 1848. 68 p.
C CSmH CSt

5739. Maxwell, Richard T. Visit to Monterey in 1842. Ed. by John Haskell Kemble. L.A., Dawson, 1955. 40 p. (Early Calif. travels ser., 25) 200 copies printed by Joseph Simon.
Available in many California libraries and CoD

5740. Meyers, William H. Naval sketches of the war in California. Reproducing twenty-eight drawings made in 1846–47, by William H. Meyers...descriptive text by Capt. Dudley W. Knox...introduction by Franklin D. Roosevelt. N.Y., Random house, 1939. 39 p. col. pl., maps. CBb CHi CMont CSalCL CSd CStbS CStmo CU-B TxU

5741. Micheltorena, Manuel. ...Correspondencia entre el general Michiltorena [sic] y el comodoro Thomas Apc. [!] Jones sobre las Californias... Mexico, Vargas Rea, 1944. 38 p. map. (Papeles de las Californias. 8)
CU-B

5742. Miron, George Thomas. The truth about John Steinbeck and the migrants... L.A. [Haynes corp.] c1939. 26 p. CL

5743. Monterey. Ayuntamiento. Sesiones del Ayuntamiento, 1844. Consists of 7 photostat sheets, in Spanish, and their typewritten translation, of extracts from meetings of the municipal government in 1844, found in a record book. CMont

5744. —— **Chamber of commerce.** Old Monterey. "The city of history and romance." Monterey [n.d.] [4] p. illus., map. CHi CRcS

5745. —— **General committee selected to secure the new soldiers' home.** Claims of Monterey, California, for the new soldiers' home. [S.F., Women's print, 1887?] 15 p. illus. CHi CMont CSmH

5746. —— **Library association.** Constitution and rules...together with a catalogue of books. Organized, 1849. S.F., O'Meara & Painter, print., 1854. 17 p.
CLU CU-B

5747. —— **Ordinances, etc.** The ordinances of the city of Monterey...with appendix containing the charter of said city. February 1913. [n.p., n.d.] 279 p. CU-B

5748. —— —— Zoning ordinance... Monterey, 1940. 19 p. map. CMont

5749. —— **Planning commission.** Master plan of the city of Monterey...May 24, 1939. [Monterey, Commercial print. co., 1939] 31 p. illus.
CHi CLSU CMont CO CSf CSfCP

5750. —— **Public school.** Old Monterey, sketches of leading places of interest. Monterey, Monterey New era off., 1896. 20 p. CSalCL CSmH

5751. Monterey constitutional convention centenial celebration. 100th anniversary...August 20–September 5, 1949. [Souvenir program] [S.F., Monette & Gordon, c1949] 32 p. illus., ports. CHi

5752. Monterey foundation. Old Monterey, doorway to history. [S.F.? Printed for Monterey foundation by Crocker, 1951] 28 p. illus., map.
C CB CHi CL CLSM CLU CMont CRic CU-B

5753. Monterey history and art association, ltd. Officers and directors, articles of incorporation, constitution, by laws, members. [Monterey, 1960?] 20 p.
CHi CU-B

5754. —— Welcome to Monterey! Special session, state Supreme court, honoring 110th anniversary of the drafting and signing of the California constitution in Colton hall, Monterey, September 1–15, 1849. [Monterey, 1959] [15] p. illus., ports. CHi CU-B

5755. Monterey peninsula herald. ...California constitutional convention centennial edition... [Monterey, 1949] [136] p. illus., ports., maps. (Special issue, v.60, no. 202, Aug. 27, 1949) C CHi CMont CU-B

5756. —— Souvenir building edition. [History of the Herald and dedication of its new building] Monterey, 1954. 16 p. illus., ports. CU-B

5757. —— United States flag raising centennial at Monterey, July 4–7, 1946...Centennial ed. [Monterey, 1946] [60] p. illus. C CHi CU-B

5758. Monterey state capital committee. ...Report on the advantages of Monterey as the site for the state capital of California. April 14, 1938... [Chicago? 1938] 84 l. Mimeo. C CMont CSmH CU-B

5759. Morgan, Christine A. Reminiscences of Mrs. Thomas W. Morgan (1847–1922). 80 p. Typew. CMont

5760. Morrow, William Chambers. Souvenir of the Hotel Del Monte, Monterey, California... [S.F., Crocker, 189–?] 33 p. illus., map.
C CHi CL CLU CSf CSmH CU-B

5761. Munras family...various papers concerning the affairs of the Munras family of California... Typew.
CSf

5762. [Neasham, Vernon Aubrey] Historic Monterey to be preserved. Berkeley, 1938. 12 l. Typew. CU-B

5763. —— ...The raising of the United States flag at Monterey, July 7, 1846. [Berkeley, 1946] 2 l. Photostat of typew. report. CU-B

5764. O'Day, Edward F. The friendship of Robert Louis Stevenson and Jules Simoneau. S.F., Print for Howard F. Griffith by John Henry Nash, 1927. CMont

5765. Officers club. Constitution and by-laws of the Officers club. Presidio of Monterey, California. [n.p., 1908] [15] p. CSmH

5766. Oliver, J. K. Monterey and its environs; with a brief history, legends...maps, etc. 2d ed. Monterey, c1913. unp. illus. CHi CMont CSalCL CSf

5767. —— Same. 3d ed. Monterey, Author, 1913. 44 p. illus. CHi CLSU CU-B

5768. —— Views and legends of Monterey and surroundings. S.F., Murdock press, c1907.
C CHi CMont CSalCL CSmH CU-B

5769. Osbourne, Katharine (Durham) Robert Louis Stevenson in California... Chicago, McClurg, 1911. 112 p. illus., ports.
Available in many libraries.

5770. Oyster, Mary Agnes. Gwin in the California constitutional convention of 1849. [Berkeley, 1929] Thesis (M.A.)—Univ. of Calif., 1929. C CU-B

5771. Pacific planning and research. General plan for future development, Monterey, California. Palo Alto, 1959. [86] p. maps. CMont

5772. Portolá, Gaspar de. Diary of Gaspar de Portolá during the California expedition of 1769–1770; edited by Donald Eugene Smith and Frederick J. Teggart.

Berkeley, Univ. of Calif., 1909. 59 p. front. (*Pub. of the Acad. of Pac. coast history*, v.1, no. 3)

Available in many California libraries and MoS N TxU

5773. —— The official account of the Portolá expedition of 1769–1770; edited by Frederick J. Teggart. Berkeley, Univ. of Calif., 1909. 29 p. front. (Pub. of the Acad. of Pac. coast history, v.1, no. 2)

CHi CP CRedl CSalCL CU-B

5774. Powers, Laura Bride. Monterey; capital of old California; a tour of the historic points of interest. Monterey, Old customs house hist. museum [n.d.] folder (8) p. illus.

CRcS

5775. —— Old Monterey; California's adobe capital ... S.F., Print. for the San Carlos press, 1934. 299 p. illus., ports. Bibliography: p. 289–90.

Available in many California libraries and CaBViPA InI NN TxU

5776. Promovido por el Sor. Toserero departmental en averiguación de los efectos del Sor. Limantour QE. recibó D. Tomás O. Larkin, por orden del G'ral. Micheltorena. Monterey, Agosto 12 de 1845. [16] p.   CU-B

5777. Pyle, John William. Thomas O. Larkin: California's business man, 1832–1844. [Berkeley, 1938] Thesis (M.A.)—Univ. of Calif., 1938.   CU CU-B

5778. Reglamento para el govierno de la provincia de Californias. Aprobado por S. M. en real orden de 24, de octubre de 1781. En Mexico: Por D. Felipe de Zuniga y Ontiveros, calle del Espiritu Santo, ano de 1784. 38 p.

CSf (photostat) CSmH

5779. —— Same. [California historical society's publication] Reimpreso en la imprenta del Colegio de Santa Clara [Calif.] 1874. 68 p.   CStclU CU-B

5780. —— Same, reprinted. S.F., Grabhorn, 1929. 55 p.   CL CLLoy CLgA CSfCW CStcl CU-B

5781. —— Same, translated into English by John Everett Johnson. S.F., Grabhorn, 1929. [60] p.   CL CLLoy CLgA CP CSf CSfCW CStcl CU-B ViU

5782. Reglamento provicional para el gobierno interior de la ecma. diputación territorial de la Alta California. Aprobado por la misma corporación en sesión de 31° de julio del presente año. Monterrey, A. V. Zamorano y ca., 1834. 16 p. "First book printed in California."— Cowan.   CLCM CU-B

5783. —— Same. A facsimile edition...Translation by Ramon Ruiz & Theresa Vigil. A note on the printing by George L. Harding. An historical note by George P. Hammond. S.F., Bk. club of Calif., 1954. 16 p.

CHi CLSM CLgA CMartC CMont CRedl CSalCL CSd CSf CU-B

5784. Rinn, Ida Louise. The voyages of Vizcaino. [Berkeley, 1926] Thesis (M.A.)—Univ. of Calif., 1926.   CU CU-B

5785. Ritchie, Ward. Job printing in California, with four original examples of early California printing. L.A., Dawson, 1955. 31 p. typog. specimens. (Early Calif. travels ser., 26) 200 copies printed by Wm. M. Cheney.   CHi

CL CLO CLSM CLgA CSjC CSto CU-B CVtV

5786. Ritterband, Robert M. The well-educated Ramage; a brief account of the first printing press in California. L.A., Author, 1953. 25 p.   CHi CL

5787. Rose (Lester) Gardens. [Catalogs] CHi has 1934?, 1947.

5788. Rudolph's (restaurant). Historic Mariposa hall, founded 1891; Rudolph's since 1906. [Monterey, Cypress press, n.d.] [5] p. illus.   CHi

5789. Ruschenberger, William Samuel Waithman. Sketches in California, 1836. Introd. by John Haskell Kemble. L.A., Dawson, 1953. 25 p. (Early Calif. travels ser., 13) 210 copies printed by Plantin press.

C CHi CL CLM CLO CLSM CLgA CMont CSS CSf CSjC CStoC CU-B CVtV MoS

5790. Not in use.

5791. Sanchez, Louis A. Notes by Louis Sanchez on adobes and old buildings in Monterey [a work compiled by the WPA historical survey of the Monterey peninsula in 1937] [1952] 5 l.   CU-B

5792. Scott, Irene. Life and work of Sebastian Vizcaino. [Berkeley, 1946] Thesis (M.A.)—Univ. of Calif., 1946.   CU

5793. Seawell, Emmet. Address of Judge Emmet Seawell, Associate justice of the state supreme court, delivered October 11, 1929 from the portico of Colton hall, Monterey... [S.F., Walter N. Brunt press, 1929?] [8] p.

CHi

5794. Shepardson, Lucia. Monterey adobes. Monterey, Monterey press, c1935. 30 p. illus.   CMont

5795. —— Monterey roads. Monterey, Monterey press, 1935. 35 p.   CMont CSmH

5796. —— Monterey trails. Monterey, Monterey press, 1935. 38 p. illus.   CFS

5797. Shubert, Helen Victoria. California's defense against United States military occupation, 1846. [Berkeley, 1933] Thesis (M.A.)—Univ. of Calif., 1933.   CU CU-B

5798. Sloat monument association of California. The Sloat monument "to commemorate the taking possession of California by Commodore John Drake Sloat, United States navy, July 7, 1846." Dedicated June 14, 1910 by the United States government, with the aid of the M. W. Grand lodge of Free and accepted masons of the state of California... [Oakland, Carruth & Carruth co., 1910] 19 p. illus., ports.   CMont CU-B

5799. Smith, Nelson Croford. An introduction to the translation of the Costansó diary of the *California expedition* of 1769–1771. [29] l. Thesis (Ph.D.)—Univ. of Calif., 1910.   CU-B

5800. Southern Pacific co. Road of a thousand wonders. Del Monte, Monterey. Pacific Grove, one wonder ... [n.p., 1909?] [4] p. illus.

C CRedCL CSalCL CSf CSfCW CSjC CU-B

5801. Stevenson, Robert Louis. Robert Louis Stevenson's story of Monterey: the old Pacific capital. S.F., Colt press [1944] 55 p. illus. (Calif. classics, no. 1) "In 1880, *The Old Pacific capital* appeared in...*Fraser's magazine*. It was later reprinted in *Across the plains*."—Foreword.

C CBaB CBb CChiS CHi CLU CMont Co CSd CSfSt CSjC CSmat CSmH CStmo CU-B CViCL

5802. Stone, George E. [Historic Monterey; 12 hand colored stereographs] Carmel, Author [n.d.] 12 pl.

C

5803. Tays, George. ...Old custom-house at Monterey... Berkeley, 1936. 44 l. Typew.   CU-B

5804. —— ...Royal presidio chapel of San Carlos de Borromeo... Berkeley, 1936. 27 l. Typew.   CU-B

5805. Tedlock, Ernest Warnock. Steinbeck and his critics; a record of twenty-five years; an anthology with introduction and notes by E. W. Tedlock, jr. and C. V. Wicker. Albuquerque, Univ. of New Mexico press, c1957. 309 p.   CMont CU-B

5806. [**Torquemada, Juan de**] ...The voyage of Sebastian Vizcaino to the coast of California, together with a map & Sebastian Vizcaino's letter written at Monterey, December 28, 1602. S.F., Bk. club of Calif., 1933. 50 p. fold. map. An extract from the account of the expedition in Juan de Torquemada's Monarchia indiana, which was based on the narrative written by Father Antonio de la Ascensión, who accompanied Vizcaino.—Bancroft.   CHi CMont CSfP CU-B

5807. Truman, Benjamin Cummings. Hotel Del Monte A.B.C. primer...Artist and designer, E. McD. Johnstone. [N.Y., Liberty print. co., 1885] [32] p. illus., plans.   C

5808. Under three flags; a collection of views of Monterey...under Spain, Mexico and the United States. S.F., W. K. Vickery, 1894. 32 photographs in portfolio.
C CHi CLO CMont CP CSalCL CSf CSmH CU-B

5809. Underhill, Reuben Lukens. From cowhides to golden fleece; a narrative of California, 1832–1858, based upon unpublished correspondence of Thomas Oliver Larkin [of Monterey]... Stanford, 1939. 273 p. illus., port., map. Bibliography: p. 257–59.
CBaB CBev CHi CMont CRedl CRic CSal CSdS CSfP CSlu CStbS CStmo CU-B CaBViPA HHi MoS ODa OrU TxU

5810. —— Same. [c1946] 289 p.
Available in many California libraries and CaBViPA MiD MoSU N

5811. U.S. Board of land commissioners for California. Transcript of the proceedings in case no. 714; city of Monterey, claimant vs. the United States, defendant, for the place named "Pueblo lands." 119 p. Photostatic copy.   CMont

5812. —— **Laws, statutes, etc.** Modifications of the Mexican military contribution tariff. [U.S.] Treasury department. [S.F., 1848] 3 p.   CHi CSmH

5813. —— **President, 1841–1845 (Tyler)** ... Taking possession of Monterey. Message from the President of the U.S. ...in relation to the taking possession of Monterey by Commodore Thomas ap Catesby Jones... 117 p. (27th Cong., 3d sess., II. Doc. no. 166)
CHi CL CLSU (micro-print ed.) CLU CSf CSmH CU-B CaBViPA

5814. United States flag raising centennial, 1946. Souvenir program, July 4–7, 1946. Monterey, 1946. [34] p.   CHi

5815. Vila, Vicente. The Portolá expedition of 1769–1770; diary of Vincente Vila, ed by Robert Selden Rose. Berkeley, Univ. of Calif., 1911. 119 p. (Pub. of the Acad. of Pac. coast history, v.2, no. 1)
CBb CHi CU-B

5816. Vizcaino, Sebastian. Letter [to Count de Monte-Rey]...written from Monterey on December 28, 1602 and sent to New Spain by the Almiranta. [S.F., Grabhorn] 1949. 9 p. Issued by Thomas W. Norris, Christmas, 1949.   CHi CU-B

5817. Wagner, Henry Raup. The first American vessel in California; Monterey in 1796. L.A., Dawson, 1954. 33 p. illus., port. (Early Calif. travels ser., 20) Includes a translation of a portion of Mémoires du Capitaine Peron, Paris, 1824. 325 copies printed by Caroline Anderson.
Available in many California libraries and MiD-B TxU

5818. Waldron, D. G., ed. Biographical sketches of the delegates to the convention to frame a new constitution for the state of California, 1878. Together with a suc-

cinct review of the facts leading to the formation of the Monterey convention of 1849, a list of its members, and the constitutional act of 1878. Waldron & Vivian, pub. and ed. S.F., Francis & Valentine, 1878. 176 p.
CHi CLgA CP CSf CU-B

5819. Watson, Douglas Sloane. The Spanish occupation of California: Plan for the establishment of a government. Junta or council held at San Blas, May 16, 1768. Diario of the expeditions made to California. Assembled for this book...The "Plan" and "Junta" have been translated from the Spanish documents by Douglas S. Watson & Thomas Workman Temple II, & the "Diario" of Miguel Costansó follows the translation of Frederick J. Teggart. S.F., Grabhorn, 1934. 62 p. illus., ports., fold. map. (Rare Americana ser. 2, no. 2)
CBb CHi CLO CLgA CP CRedl CSf CSfCW CSfP CSjC CStcl CStmo CSto CU-B ViU

5820. Wentz, Roby. Eleven Western presses; an account of how the first printing press came to each of the eleven Western states. Printed for members at the 37th annual convention of the International association of printing house craftsmen. L.A., 1956. 57 p.
CHi CLO CSd CSf CSto CU-B

5821. Wheat, Carl Irving. The pioneer press of California. Woodcuts by M. Dean. Oakland, Biobooks, 1948. 31 p. illus., facsims.
CBb CChiS CHi CL CLLoy CLO CLgA CRedCL CRedl CRic CSdS CSf CSmat CSto CV

5822. —— Pioneers: the engaging tale of three early California printing presses and their strange adventures. L.A., Priv. print., 1934. 29 p. illus.   CBb CHi CL

5823. Wittemann, Adolph, pub. Monterey and the Hotel Del Monte in photogravure from recent negatives... N.Y., 1892. 31 photos.   CSf

5824. —— Same. N.Y., Albertype co., 1894. 18 pl.   NN

5825. Wright, Agnes Elodie. The beginnings of Monterey, 1542–1785. [Berkeley, 1931] 76 l. illus., map. Thesis (M.A.)—Univ. of Calif., 1931.   CU CU-B

5826. Wright, Benjamin Franklin. Memoirs... [Monterey, Palace stationery co., c1936] 51 p. illus. About Hotel Del Monte and famous people who were guests.   CHi CMont CU-B

5827. Wright, Flora Alice. Richard Barnes Mason, governor of California. [Berkeley, 1919] Thesis (M.A.) —Univ. of Calif., 1919.   CU CU-B

5828. Zamorano, Augustín Vicente. The hand of Zamorano. A facsimile reproduction of a manuscript on the Californias in 1829, written by Don Agustín Vicente Zamorano, as secretary to Governor José María de Echeandia, translated by Arnulfo D. Trejo and Roland D. Hussey, with a preface by George L. Harding. L.A., Zamorano club, 1956. 2 p.l., 6 p., and 7 p. facsim. of the manuscript.   CLSM

Pacific Grove

5829. Barry & Austin, auctioneers. Map of 300 home sites in Pacific Grove which will be sold separately at absolute unreserved auction sale... [Pacific Grove, 1919?] [5] p. illus., maps.   CHi

5830. Chautauqua literary and scientific circle. Pacific coast branch. By-laws, adopted August 1st, 1894, Pacific Grove assembly. S.F., Bk. room print., 1895. 12 p.   CHi

5831. —— —— Chautauqua assembly; a summer

school of science, Pacific Grove, Monterey, Calif., session 1888–94. S.F., Bancroft co., 1888–94. illus., ports.

    CHi (1888)   CMont (1890)   CU-B (1888–94)

5832. Grand army of the Republic. Official souvenir, 34th annual encampment, dept. California & Nevada; Pacific Grove, Calif., May 8th to 11th, 1901. Salinas, Daily index print. [1901] 38 p. illus.

    CMont CSalCL CSmH

5833. Grimes, W. V., ed. Souvenir of the tenth anniversary of the founding of the Pacific Grove museum, 1899–1909. Pacific Grove, Daily review print. [n.d.] 30 p.

    C

5834. History of Pacific Grove. [n.p., n.d.] Pamphlet.

    CSal

5835. Jochmus, Augustus Carlos. Pacific Grove, California, and the Monterey peninsula. Pacific Grove, Author, 1928. 48 p. illus.   CMont

5836. McLane, Lucy Neely. A piney paradise by Monterey bay, Pacific Grove; the documentary history of her first twenty-five years, and a glimpse of her adulthood. S.F., Lawton Kennedy, 1952. 231 p. illus.

Available in many California libraries and N NN

5837. —— A piney paradise by Monterey bay; Monterey peninsula tradition. 2d ed. Fresno, Acad. lib. guild, 1958. 387 p. illus.

    CChiS CHi CL CLSM CLU CMont CNa CSjC CSluCL CStmo CoD N NN

5838. Pacific Grove. Board of city trustees. Beautiful Pacific Grove, Monterey county, California... [S.F., Sunset press, 1902?] [32] p. illus.

    CHi CMont CU-B

5839. —— —— Pacific Grove, Monterey county, California. [Pacific Grove, Pacific Grove review print, n.d.] [32] p. illus., map.   CHi CU-B

5840. —— **First Methodist church.** Unveiling of plaque honoring Methodist founders of Pacific Grove, California, February 22, 1953... [Pacific Grove, 1953] [4] p.   CU-B

5841. Pacific Grove review. ...Pacific Grove... Special souvenir ed. ... Pacific Grove, n.d.] 34 p. illus.

    CU-B

5842. Southern Pacific co. Pacific Grove, near Monterey, leading family resort. Summer, 1893. S.F., Crocker, 1893.   CSmH

5843. —— Summertime at Pacific Grove, California. [1903] 20 p. illus.   CMont

5844. Wight, Edward Allen, and Merritt, LeRoy Charles. Public library service in Pacific Grove; a report of a study of the organization, services and collections in a residential city on Monterey peninsula, California. Berkeley, 1957. 79 p.   C

NAPA COUNTY

(Created in 1850; annexed section of Lake county in 1872)

COUNTY HISTORIES

5845. Historical records survey. California. ... Napa county (Napa)... S.F., Northern Calif. hist. records survey, 1941. 619 p. illus., maps. (Inventory of the county archives of Calif. ...no. 29)

    C CBb CF CFS CHi CL CLCM CLCo CLO CLSM CLSU CLU CMartC CMary CMont CNF CO COMC CPa CSS CSf CSfCP CSfCSM CSjC CSjCL CSluCL CSmH CSt CStclU CU-B CYcCL ICN MoS N NN WHi

5846. Kanaga, Tillie, comp. History of Napa county, California. Oakland, Enquirer, 1901. 372 p. illus. Ed. by W. F. Wallace. Includes biographical sketches.

    C CAla CHi CL CLU CN CNF CO CSf CSfCP CSt CStclU CU-B CYcCL MWA

5847. Menefee, Campbell Augustus. Historical and descriptive sketch book of Napa, Sonoma, Lake and Mendocino... Napa City, Reporter pub. house, 1873. 356 p. illus., ports. Includes biographical sketches.

    C CAla CB CChiS CCH CHi CL CLAC CLCM CLCo CLSM CLSU CLU CN CNF CO COMC CP CPa CS CSS CSf CSfCP CSfCSM CSfCW CSfMI CSfP CSfU CSfWF-H CSj CSmH CSmat CSrD CSt CSto CStoC CStr CStrJC CU-B CUk CtY ICN N NN NHi WHi

5848. [Palmer, Lyman L.] History of Napa and Lake counties, California...and biographical sketches... S.F., Slocum, Bowen, & co., 1881. 600, 291 p. ports.

    C C-S CAla CBb CCH CHi CL CLAC CLSM CLU CLp CMary CN CNF CO COMC CPe CRb CSd CSf CSfCP CSfCSM CSfCW CSfMI CSfU CSmat CSmH CSrD CSt CStb CSto CStoC CU-B CYcCL CoD CtY ICN MiD-B MWA N NHi NIC NN WHi

GREAT REGISTER

5849. Napa county. Index to the Great register of the county of Napa. 1867– Place of publication and title vary.

    C has 1867, 1872, 1875, 1880, 1888 (biennially to)– 1900, 1904 (biennially to)– 1962. CL has 1873, 1876–77, 1879, 1882, 1886 (biennially to)– 1890. CNF has 1890. CSmH has 1879–80, 1879 (suppl.). CU-B has 1867–68, 1872–73, 1879–80, 1898.

DIRECTORIES

5850. 1874. Paulson, L. L., comp. & pub. Handbook and directory of Napa, Lake, Sonoma and Mendocino counties... S.F., 1874. 296 p. maps.

    C CSS CSmH CU-B

5851. 1889/90. Uhlhorn, John F., pub. The Napa and Sonoma counties directory. S.F. [1889?]   C CU-B

5852. 1908/09–1958/59. Polk, R. L., & co., pub. Polk's Napa city directory including Calistoga, St. Helena and Napa county. Publisher varies: 1908/09?–192–? Polk-Husted directory co. Content varies: 1908/09 Napa city, St. Helena, and Calistoga; 1910/11 Napa city, St. Helena, Calistoga, Oakville and Rutherford. Continued as Polk's Napa city directory.

    C has 1928/29, 1937. C-S has 1908/09, 1910/11, 1912/ 13. CHi has 1910/11, 1926/27, 1935, 1947, 1948/49, 1950, 1953–54, 1956–1958/59. CL has 1935, 1939, 1942, 1950, 1953–54, 1956–57. CO has 1926/27. CSmat has 1958/59.

Napa

5853. 1960– Polk, R. L., & co., pub. Polk's Napa city directory including Calistoga, St. Helena, Oakville, Rutherford, and Yountville. Title varies: 1960 Polk's Napa city directory including Calistoga and St. Helena. Preceded by Polk's Napa city directory...including Napa county.

CHi has 1960–61.

GENERAL REFERENCES

5854. Adams, I. C. Memoirs and anecdotes of early days in Calistoga. [Calistoga, Author] 1946. [62] l. illus., ports.   CBb CHi CN CU-B

5855. [Anderson, Winslow] Napa soda springs...
[Napa soda springs, 1890?] 8 p. illus.   CU-B

5856. Bank of America. Napa county branches.
Map of Napa county and a short history of Napa county.
[St. Helena, 1938] folder (4 p.)   CRcS

5857. Baptists, California. Pacific Baptist association. Minutes of the second anniversary...held with
the St. Helena church, St. Helena, California, September
3d, 4th, and 5th, 1859. S.F., B.F. Sterett print., 1859. 16 p.
          CU-B

5858. Beard, James E. The story of the electric.
[n.p., n.d.] [52] p. illus. Reprinted from *St. Helena
Star.*   CHi

5859. Beaulieu vineyard, San Francisco. Beaulieu family of wines. Beaulieu vineyard, a family estate...
founded and owned continuously by the de Latour family
since 1900. Vineyards and winery at Rutherford, Napa
county, California. [n.p., 1950?] 24 p. illus.   CHi

5860. Bothe's Paradise park; largest in beautiful
Napa valley. [Berkeley, Gillick press, n.d.] 11 p. illus.,
map.   CRcS

5861. Bucknall, Mary Eliza (Davis) Early days.
[n.p., Priv. print., n.d.] 9 p. illus.   C CHi CSmH

5862. California. Board of state viticultural commissioners. The vineyards in Napa county; being the
report of E. C. Priber, commissioner for the Napa district
... Sacramento, State print. off., 1893. 47 p.   CU-B

5863. Calistoga. Chamber of commerce. Calistoga, California, in the land of the geysers. Calistoga
[1937?] 2 p. illus., map.   CRcS

5864. Calistoga centennial, 1959, honoring the founding of Calistoga by Sam Brannan in 1859. [Napa, Don
Crawford associates, 1959] 100 p. illus., port. Cover
title: Complete Napa valley history.
          CHi CN CO CStrJC

5865. Calistoga real estate co. Garden spot of California, Napa valley... Calistoga [1927?] 63 p. illus.
          CU-B

5866. Christian Brothers. Prospectus of the Novitiate, Mount La Salle... [n.p., 1936] 32 p. illus.
          CHi

5867. Clyman, James. James Clyman, American
frontiersman, 1792–1881; the adventures of a trapper and
covered wagon emigrant...ed. by Charles L. Camp. S.F.,
Calif. hist. soc., 1928. 247 p. illus., ports., facsims., maps.
(Calif. hist. soc. Special pub. no. 3)
          CHi CLgA COnC CRcS CSf

5868. —— Same, with title: James Clyman frontiersman...2d ed. Portland, Ore., Champoeg press [c1960]
352 p. 1450 copies designed and printed by Lawton Kennedy.
Available in many libraries.

5869. Coombs, Nathan. Executors' sale. Public
auction of the Yount estate, at Yountville, Napa county
...1870... S.F., Alta Calif. bk. & job print. house, 1870.
8 p.   CSfCP CU-B

5870. Davis, Dee T. Brief sketches of Napa county
history. Pub. and distributed by office of Napa county
Superintendent of schools, 1956.   CN

5871. —— History of Napa county... [Napa?]
1940. 14 l.   CSmH CU-B

5872. —— Stories of Napa county. Napa [1940?]
[39] l.   C

5873. [Davis, Hensley S.] Napa county, California.
[Napa, Napa chamber of commerce, 1905] 35 p.
          CN CU-B

5874. [Edwords, Clarence Edgar] A Virginian's
view of Napa valley... [Napa, Napa register press,
1906?] 15 p.   CU-B

5875. Gift, George W. Something about California
...Napa county: its agricultural resources, vineyards...
Napa, Reporter bk. press, 1876. 62 p. map.
          CSmH CU-B

5876. Handbook of Calistoga springs...Its mineral
waters, climate [etc.] The celebrated great geysers and
petrified forest, and the Clear lake country. S.F., Alta
Calif. bk. & job print. house, 1871. 30 p. illus., map.
          CL CLU CSmH CStrJC CU-B

5877. Hanrahan, Virginia. Historical Napa valley.
[Napa, 1948–49] [29] l. of mounted clippings.   CU-B

5878. —— Napa county history, 1823–1948... Produced and distributed by Napa chamber of commerce.
[Napa, 1948] 18 l. Mimeo.
          CHi CO CSfCW CU-B

5879. Hunt & Wood. Napa county land register...
S.F., Bacon & co., print. [1884] 72 p. illus.
          CSfCP CU-B

5880. —— Same... [Oakland, Pac. press, 1885?]
92 p. illus.   C CSmH CU-B

5881. —— Napa county land register and Napa city
business directory...Napa, Napa register print., 1884.
75 p. illus.   CU-B

5882. Illustrated guide. White Sulphur springs near
St. Helena, Napa county, Cal. [n.p., 187–?] 11 p. illus.
          CHi CU-B

5883. Illustrations of Napa county, California, with
historical sketch. Oakland, Smith & Elliott, 1878. 28 p.
illus., maps.   C CSfCP CSmH CU-B NHi NN

5884. Immigration association of California.
[County scrapbooks] [S.F., 188–]   C

5885. Issler, Anne (Roller) Our mountain hermitage; Silverado and Robert Louis Stevenson. Stanford [1950] 138 p. illus., ports., map. "Based upon...
[the author's] Stevenson at Silverado." Bibliography:
p. 121–27.
Available in many California libraries and MoS NN
UU ViU

5886. —— Stevenson at Silverado. Caldwell, Ida.,
Caxton, 1939. 247 p. illus., ports.
Available in many California libraries and CoD MoS
          OrU TxU UU

5887. Jackson, F. L., pub. Napa county, and its
many great resources... Napa [1886] 51 p.
          CHi CU-B

5888. Jenkins, James Gilbert. Life and confessions
of James Gilbert Jenkins: the murderer of eighteen men
...as narrated by himself to Col. C. H. Allen, sheriff of
Napa county...Phonographically reported and arranged
for the press by R. E. Wood... S.F., William P. Harrison
& co., 1864. 56 p.
          CHi CLO (facsim. ed.) CSmH CU-B

5889. Kerr, Farnum Woodward. A case study of
planning public relations in southeastern Napa county,
California. [Berkeley, 1956] Thesis (M.A.)—Univ. of
Calif., 1956.   CU

5890. Kettlewell, B. F. Napa county land register
... St. Helena [n.d.] 12 p.   CU-B

5891. Kingsbury, Ralph. The Napa valley to 1850
... [L.A.] 1939. 130 p. illus. Thesis (M.A.)—Univ. of
So. Calif., 1939.   CN

5892. Krug (Charles) Winery, St. Helena. State
historical landmark 563...dedication by the California

historical society...October 5, 1957. [n.p.] 1957. [14] p. illus., port. CHi CRcS

5893. Lange, Dorothea, and Jones, Pirkle. Death of a valley [Berryessa valley] N.Y., 1960. [38] p. illus. (aperture, Nov., 1960) CHi

5894. Levick, M. B. Napa county, California... Sunset mag. homeseekers' bur. ... [S.F., 1911?] 29 p. illus. CU-B

5895. Lidstone & Penn, St. Helena. Seven springs, Howell mountain. St. Helena [191–?] [7] p. illus. CHi

5896. McKittrick, Myrtle Mason. Salvador Vallejo, last of the conquistadores. Arcata [1949?] 58 p.
CArcHT CChiS CHi CLU CSd CSdS CSjC
CSrD CSto CStoC

5897. Melone co., Napa. California's Oak-knoll ranch in the redwood empire. [n.p., n.d.] [4] p. CHi

5898. Muller, Herman, vs. Boggs, Angus L., et al. In the Supreme court, state of California. Herman Muller, plaintiff and respondent, vs. Angus L. Boggs et al., defendants and appellants. Brief for appellants. Hoge & Wilson, of counsel for appellants. S.F., Towne & Bacon, 1864. 38 p. CLU

5899. Napa—areal view with description and 2 maps. [n.p.] Algea and Nenus print shop [n.d.] 2 p. CRcS

5900. Napa city and county portfolio and directory; photographic reproductions of picturesque Napa county views... Napa, H. A. Darms [c1908] 126 p. illus.
C CHi CL CLU CN CO CSfCP CSmH CU-B

5901. Napa county. Board of supervisors. Napa county booklet. Issued by boards of trade under authority of the supervisors... [Napa] 1902. 31 p. illus.
CL CSmH CU-B

5902. —— —— Napa county, California. [Napa? 1907?] 48 p. illus. CL CN CSmH CU-B

5903. —— —— Same. Napa, Francis & Francis [1915?] [24] p. CHi

5904. —— —— The resources of Napa county, California... Napa, 1887. 34, 14 p. illus., map.
C CHi CLU CN CSfCP CSmH CU-B NHi

5905. —— **Chamber of commerce.** Napa county —agricultural—industrial—and scenic. Napa [n.d.] 20 p. illus., map. CRcS

5906. Napa county abstract co. ...Abstract of title of property belonging to Minnie Ellis...1915. Description: Lot 17, block "E" Caymus rancho... Napa [1915] l. 3233–3284. CU-B

5907. The Napa county abstract, with supplements. Giving every real-estate owner of the county, value of real estate and improvements...v.1, no. 1. S.F., Abstract pub. co., 1878. 107 p. CHi

5908. Napa county historical society. Annual report. 1st– 1949– Napa, 1949–
C (1949, 1950, 1955) CHi (1951) CN (1949) CNF (1949–51)

5909. —— Stories, 1952. [12] p. Mimeo.
CHi CN

5910. Napa county immigration association. Napa county... Napa, Napa daily & weekly reporter print., 1885. 16 p. CU-B

5911. Napa register. Col. Nelson M. Holderman Day. [Napa, 1952] [1-A]–24-A p. illus., ports. (Special section of the *Napa register*, June 5, 1954) C

5912. Napa soda springs; California's famous mountain spa. [S.F., E.D. Taylor co., n.d.] unp. illus. C

5913. O'Brien, John Joseph. The history of electric railroad transportation in the Napa valley, California, 1905–1953. [S.F.] 1953. 264 p. illus., map, diagrs., facsims. Thesis (M.A.)—Univ. of S.F., 1953. CSfU

5914. St. Gothard inn, St. Helena. [Descriptive leaflet. n.p., 1911?] [12] p. illus., fold. map. CHi

5915. St. Helena. Chamber of commerce. St. Helena, the heart of the beautiful Napa valley... St. Helena [n.d.] folder (7 p.) illus., map. CRcS

5916. St. Helena sanitarium, Sanitarium. A brief account of the St. Helena sanitarium, formerly Rural health retreat, near St. Helena, California. [St. Helena, 1896] 24 p. illus. CU-B

5917. —— St. Helena-California sanitarium... Sanitarium [n.d.] 30 p. illus. CHi

5918. —— St. Helena sanitarium and hospital, established 1878. Sixty years of service. ... [Sanitarium, 1930] 24 p. illus. CHi

5919. St. Helena star. Fiftieth anniversary edition. Sept. 26, 1924. St. Helena, 1924. 24 p. illus., ports. Contains also *San Francisco Chronicle*. Progressive California number. Napa county section. March 14, 1923. C

5920. —— Grand army edition...July 16th, 1886... St. Helena, 1886. 34 p. illus. CU-B

5921. —— St. Helena centennial edition, 1854–1954. Issue of Sept. 30, 1954. CHi

5922. Searls, May Lavinia. The geography of the Wooden, Gordon, Capelle area of Napa county, California. [Berkeley, 1927] Thesis (M.A.)—Univ. of Calif., 1927. CU

5923. Stevenson, Robert Louis. The sea fogs, by Robert Louis Stevenson, with an introduction by Thomas Rutherford Bacon... S.F., Elder [c1907] 24 p. (Half-title: Western classics, no. 1) A chapter from his Silverado squatters. CBb CHi CSfCW

5924. —— Same. Bohemian Grove [Grabhorn, 1942] 13 p. CHi

5925. —— Silverado journal [edited by] John E. Jordan. S.F., Bk. club of Calif., 1954. 95 p. facsims. "Four hundred copies printed." The journal is the early version of the author's *The Silverado squatters*.
C CBb CL CLU CO CSalCL CSf CSjC CStoC
CaBViPA CoD MiD

5926. —— The Silverado squatters. London, Chatto & Windus, 1883. 254 p. front.
CLSU CLU CMont COr CRedCL CSd CSjC
CSmH CU-B ViU

5927. —— Same. Bost., Roberts bros., 1884. 287 p.
CSfCP CoD ODa
Other editions followed.
CRedl (1899) CSdS (1899) CSf (1900) CSjC
(1888) CStaC (1905) CStmo (1904)

5928. —— Same. N.Y., Scribner, 1895. 208 p. front.
C CBu CHi CL CO CSrD MiD

5929. —— Same. 380 copies printed by John Henry Nash of San Francisco. 1923. 99 p. illus., port.
C CL CSmH CStrJC MiD ViU

5930. —— Same. S.F., Grabhorn press, 1952. 181 p. illus. (Biobooks, 31). "Reprinted from the first edition published by Chatto & Windus, London, 1883."
Available in many California libraries and CoD

5931. U.S. vs. Yount, George C. Supreme court of the United States, no. 242; appeal from the district court of the United States for the northern district of California. [n.d.] 37 p. Transcript of the proceedings in case no. 243; George C. Yount vs. the United States, for the place named Caymas. C

5932. U.S. Circuit court (9th circuit) ...Charlotte Hayner, plaintiff, vs. John A. Stanly et al., defendants. Opinion of the court delivered by the Hon. Lorenzo Sawyer, July 31st, 1882. B. S. Brooks, and Wm. Leviston, plaintiff's attorneys. Stanly, Stoney & Hayes, Delos Lake, and John Garber, defendants' attorneys. [S.F., 1882?] 16 p. A Napa valley land suit. CLU

5933. Ver Mehr, Jean Leonhard Henri Corneille. Checkered life: in the old and new world. S.F., Bancroft, 1877. 476 p. CBb CHi CSfCW

5934. Veterans' home association of California. Annual report of the president and other officers...1888– S.F., 1888– Yountville veteran's home. CHi

5935. Veterans' home of California [Yountville], a sketch of its origin, progress, etc. S.F., Shannon-Conmy co., 1911. 51 p. CHi

5936. Watson, Elizabeth Ann. Sketch of the life of George C. Yount. [n.p., 192–?] [16] p. illus., port. C CHi CLU CSfCP CSmH CU-B

5937. Wells, Andrew Jackson. Napa county, California. S.F., Sunset mag. homeseekers' bur. [1909?] 31 p. illus., maps. CU-B

5938. Wood, Ellen (Lamont) George Yount, the kindly host of Caymus rancho. S.F., Grabhorn, 1941. 125 p. illus. C CBev CHi CL CLU CN CRedCL CRic CSS CSfCP CSjC CSmH CU-B

5939. Wright, Elizabeth Cyrus. Early upper Napa valley. [Calistoga, 193–] 113 p. CU-B

Napa

5940. Basalt rock co. Annual report. CL has 1954, 1959.

5941. California. Napa state asylum for the insane. By-laws of the trustees and rules and regulations of the resident physician... Napa, Reporter bk. press, 1876. 31 p. CHi

5942. Elks, Benevolent and protective order of. Napa lodge no. 832. Golden anniversary. 50 years [1903–1953] Napa [1953] [28] p. illus., ports. CU-B

5943. Hutchinson, Frederic Clarence. T. B. Hutchinson of Napa. [Berkeley? 1950?] 168 p. Mimeo. CHi

5944. King, Percy S., comp. Historical data concerning Yount lodge no. 12, F. & A. M. Published in Dec. 1926 by courtesy of Harry L. Johnston, P. M. [Napa?] 1926. 28 p. CHi

5945. Napa. Chamber of commerce. Beautiful Napa, a pictorial journey. [Napa, 191?] [24] p. illus., maps. C CU-B

5946. —— —— Napa, California. Napa [1938] 12 p. CHi

5947. —— Charters, ordinances, etc. Charter and municipal code of the city of Napa... [Napa] Napa register, 1897. 199 p. CHi

5948. —— —— Charter and ordinances of the city of Napa... Napa, Reporter pub. house, 1874. 84 p. CSmH

5949. —— First Baptist church. Centennial, 1860– 1960... [Napa, 1960] 25 p. illus., ports. CHi CU-B

5950. —— Public schools. [Commencement programmes] CHi has 1888.

5951. Napa city fire company 2. Constitution and by-laws... Napa, Print. by Francis & Gardner, 1873. 16 p. CU-B

5952. Napa ladies' seminary. Catalogue...1878/ 79–1879/80. Napa, Register bk. and job print. house, 1879–80. 2 v. in 1. CU-B

5953. Oak Mound school for boys and young men, Napa. [Descriptive notes] [n.p., 1891] 1 l. CHi

5954. Odd fellows, Independent order of. Napa lodge, no. 18. The constitution and by-laws...Instituted November 26th, 1853. Napa City, Montgomery & Brownson print., Reporter off., 1859. 64 p. CHi

5955. Yerger, Donald Price. A study of the drop out student of the Napa union high school district, Napa, California. Fresno, 1957. Thesis (M.A.)—Fresno state college, August 1957. CFS

NEVADA COUNTY
(Created in 1851 from portion of Yuba county)

COUNTY HISTORIES

5956. Bean, Edwin F., comp. Bean's history and directory of Nevada county, California. Containing a complete history of the county, with sketches of the various towns and mining camps...also, full statistics of mining and all other industrial resources... Nevada, Print. at the Daily gazette bk. & job off., 1867. 424 p. C CGr CHi CL CLCM CLU CSf CSfU CSmH CStclU CU-B CtY MWA NHi

5957. [Wells, Harry Laurenz] History of Nevada county, California; with illustrations descriptive of its scenery, residences [etc.]... Oakland, Thompson & West, 1880. 234 p. illus., map. C CGr CHi CL CLSU CLU CLgA CO CRiv CSf CSfCP CSfWF-H CSmH CSt CU-B NHi NN

GREAT REGISTER

5958. Nevada county. Index to the Great register of the county of Nevada. 1866 Place of publication and title vary. C has 1867–68, 1871, 1873, 1875–77, 1879 (May and Sept.), 1880 (biennially to)– 1898, 1902 (biennially to)– 1962. CHi has 1876. CL has 1868, 1869 (suppl.), 1872– 73, 1876–77, 1879 (April, Aug.), 1882 (suppl.), 1884 (biennially to)– 1890. CLU has 1890, 1898. CSmH has 1872, 1875, 1879 (May, Sept.), 1880 (Nov.), 1882 (Nov.), 1884 (biennially to)– 1890, 1892 (Nov.), 1898 (Nov.). CU-B has 1867 (July, Aug. suppl.), 1868 (suppl.), 1872– 73, 1878.

DIRECTORIES

5959. 1856. Brown, Nat P., and Dallison, John K., pub. Brown & Dallison's Nevada, Grass Valley, and Rough and Ready directory...With an historical sketch of Nevada county...An almanac for 1856... S.F., Print. at the Town talk off., 1856. 133 p. Historical sketch by Aaron Augustus Sargent. C CHi CLU CSfCP CSmH CU-B NbHi NvHi

5960. 1871–72. County directory pub. co. Nevada county directory, for 1871–72... Sacramento, Crocker, 1871. C CHi CSfCP CSfWF-H CSmH CU-B

5961. 1895. Poingdestre, John Edmund. Nevada county mining and business directory, 1895... Oakland, Pac. press. illus., maps. C CHi CSmH CU-B

5962. 1933/34. A to Z directory and guide book, Grass Valley– Nevada City. Nevada City [1933?] maps. CU-B

GENERAL REFERENCES

5963. Alta California, inc., comp. & pub. Nevada county, California; a general and historical summary. Sacramento [1938] 17 l. Reproduced from typew. copy.
CU-B

5964. Altrocchi, Julia (Cooley) Snow covered wagons; a pioneer epic; the Donner party expedition, 1846–47. N.Y., Macmillan, 1936. 202 p. Poem.
Available in many California libraries and CaBViPA IHi

5965. Bear river tunnel co. ...[Prospectus] Location of property, Nevada and Placer counties, state of California. Bost., A. Mudge and son, print., 1881. 58 p.
CLU

5966. Belden, David. Speech...against the repeal of the specific contract act, in reply to Hon. F. M. Smith ...February 9, 1866. Sacramento, Crocker, 1866. 23 p.
CHi

5967. Berry, John J., ed. Life of David Belden. N.Y., Belden bros., 1891. 472 p. port.
C CBb CHi CSf CSfCW CSjC

5968. Bishop, Isabella Lucy (Bird) Journey to Truckee. Berkeley, Elkus press, 1945. 13 p. Reprinted from *A lady's life in the Rocky mountains*, a series of letters written by Isabella L. Bird to her sister in England, and pub. in 1879 by John Murray, London.
CSmH

5969. Black, George. Report on the middle Yuba canal and Eureka lake canal, Nevada county, California. S.F., Towne & Bacon, 1864. 32 p.   C CHi

5970. Breen, Patrick. Diary of Patrick Breen, one of the Donner party. Ed. by Frederick J. Teggart. Berkeley, Univ. of Calif., 1910. 16 p. (Pub. of the Acad. of Pac. coast history, v.1, no. 6)
CHi CLSM CSalCL CSdS CU-B

5971. —— Same...with introduction & notes by George R. Stewart. S.F., Bk. club of Calif., 1946. [39] p. illus., port.   CBb CHi CRic CSjC

5972. California. Dept. of natural resources. Division of beaches and parks. The Donner party tragedy... Sacramento [1946] 15 p. "References": p. 15.
CO CRcS CRic CSdS IHi

5973. —— **Superior court (Nevada county)** Rules for the government of practice in the Superior court of the county of Nevada, state of California. Adopted October 16, 1893. Grass Valley, Daily morning union, 1894.   CSmH

5974. California water co. ltd., London. Prospectus... [London, Nassau steam press, 1857?] 24 p. fold. maps.   CHi

5975. Canfield, Chauncey de Leon. The diary of a forty-niner. N.Y., S.F., M. Shepard co., 1906. 231 p. Fictional form, but based on recollections of an old miner, Lewis Hanchett.
CHi CRic CSfP CSmH CStbS MiD ViU

5976. —— Same. Bost., Houghton, 1920. 353 p.
Available in many California libraries and CaBViPA ODa ViU

5977. —— Same. ...introduction to California centennial edition by Oscar Lewis. Stanford, J. L. Delkin, c1947. 192 p.   CBev
CChiS CLO CMerCL CMont CRic CSS CStmo

5978. Casserly, Eugene. The issue in California; letter of Eugene Casserly to T. T. Davenport...August 27, 1861. S.F., Charles F. Robbins, 1861. 15 p.
CHi CSmH CU CU-B

5979. Croy, Homer. Wheels west. N.Y., Hastings house [1955] 242 p. "An attempt to simplify the Donner story...Told...through the eyes of James Frazier Reed."
C CBea CChiS CL CLSM CLU CMon CNF CP CRcS CRic CSS CSf CSlu CStcl CStmo CStoC CaBViPA

5980. De Groot, Henry. Report of the gold bearing gravel lands, timber tracts & hydraulic works of the Chalk bluff ditch and mining company... S.F., Alta Calif. print. house, 1873. 35 p.   CLU

5981. Donnelly, Florence. The paper mill at Floriston in the heart of the Sierras [sic] [Wilmington, Del., 1952] 13 p. illus., port. Reprinted from the *Paper maker*, v.21, no. 1, 1952.   CHi

5982. Dwyer, John T. Pioneer priest in Nevada county; Reverend John Shanahan, 1792–1870. Fresno, Acad. lib. guild [1954] 11 p.   CHi CSfCW

5983. Edwards, W. F., pub. W. F. Edwards' tourist guide and directory of the Truckee basin...Chas. D. Irons, editor and compiler. Truckee, "Republican" job print., 1883. 137, 81 p. "Contains directories of Boca, Clinton, Truckee and Lake Tahoe, a history of Truckee, with sketches of the press, the '601' vigilance committee, the industries, deserted villages, etc."—Norris.
C CHi CLU CMartC CSfSC CSmH CU-B MoSHi

5984. Eureka consolidated Blue gravel mining co. Prospectus...of Moore's Flat, Nevada county, August 24th, 1878. S.F., Edward Bosqui & co., 1878. 15 p.
CHi

5985. Fairview gold mining co. Annual reports. CHi has 1906/07–08.

5986. Ferguson, Charles D. Experiences of a forty-niner during thirty-four years' residence in California and Australia. Ed. by Frederick T. Wallace. Cleveland, Williams pub. co., 1888. 507 p. illus., port. Cover title: A third of a century in the gold fields.
CBb CChi CHi CLO CLgA CP CRcS CRedl CSf CSfCP CSfCW IHi

5987. —— Same. Chico, H. A. Carson, 1924. 154 p. illus.   CBb CChiS CHi

5988. —— Same, with title: California gold fields; foreword by Joseph A. Sullivan. Oakland, Biobooks, 1948. 163 p. illus., map. Print. at Times-star press, Alameda.
Available in many libraries.

5989. Fletcher, Daniel Cooledge. Reminiscences of California and the Civil war. Ayer, Mass., Press of Huntley S. Turner, 1894. 196 p. port.
CBb CHi CLO CSd CSf CSfCW CSjC CStbS ViU

5990. Fryer Noble metal mining co., New York. The Meadow lake mining district. [N.Y., Sears & Cole, 1875] 23 p.   CHi

5991. Gold mines of Nevada county. Record for fifty years... [n.p., n.d.] 19 p. illus.   CSmH CU-B

5992. Grass Valley. Chamber of commerce. The little town of Rough and Ready... [1938?] 2 l. Mimeo.
CU-B

5993. —— **Evening school.** Nevada county trails, by the English class... 1940. 24 l. illus., maps.   CO

5994. Grass Valley morning union. Nevada county mining review. Grass Valley, 1895. 144 p. illus., ports.
C CHi CLU CO CSfCP CSmH CU-B

5995. Hague, James D. The water and gravel mining properties belonging to the Eureka lake and Yuba

canal company and to M. Zellerbach, Esq. [S.F., 1876] 73 p. Folding map of San Juan Ridge, Nevada county.
CHi

5996. Hall, Carroll Douglas. Donner miscellany; 41 diaries and documents. S.F., Bk. club of Calif., 1947. 97 p. illus., port.
C CBb CHi CL CLO CLU CLgA CO CRedl CSf CSfWF-H CSj CSmH CaBViPA IHi

5997. Hartwell, J. G. Map of Nevada county, California...showing towns, villages, roads, streams, mining ditches, and U.S. land surveys, quartz and placer mining claims... S.F., W. T. Galloway, 1880.   C CSmH

5998. Houghton, Eliza P. (Donner) The expedition of the Donner party and its tragic fate. Chicago, McClurg, 1911. 374 p. illus., ports.
Available in many California libraries and CaBViPA IHi

5999. —— Same. L.A., Grafton pub. corp., 1920. 374 p. illus., ports.
C CBb CChiS CEH CHi CL CLS CLU CLod CO COnC CRcS CSf CSmH CU-B CViCL CaBViPA

6000. Huerne, Prosper. Examination of the grand channel of auriferous gravel in the mining districts of North Bloomfield, Nevada county, California. S.F., Edward Bosqui & co., 1877. 15 p. Also published in French.
CL CLU

6001. Lawrence, George Alfred. Silverland... London, Chapman and Hall, 1873. 259 p.   C-S CU-B

6002. Leete, Harley M., jr. Sketches of the gold country. Illus. by Clifford L. Warner. 1st ed. Nevada City, Nevada City nugget press, 1938. 30 p. illus. Light sketches of present-day Nevada City, Grass Valley, Dutch Flat, Washington, Bloomfield, French Corral, You Bet, Red Dog, Rough and Ready and North San Juan.
CHi CLSM

Other editions followed: 2d ed. 1939, 3d ed. 1943, 4th ed. 1947. C (1939) CLO (1939) CLS (1947) CLU (1947) CMont (1939) CO (1947) CRcS (1939) CSS (1943) CSfWF-H (1939) CSmH (1943) CU-B (1943)

6003. Levick, M. B. Nevada county, California. S.F., Sunset mag. homeseekers' bur. [1911] 31 p. illus., maps.
CHi CSf CU-B

6004. McGlashan, Charles Fayette. History of the Donner party... Truckee, Crowley & McGlashan, 1879. 193 p. Many editions followed.
Available in many libraries.

6005. —— Same. ...with foreword, notes, and a bibliography by George H. Hinkle and Bliss McGlashan Hinkle. Stanford [c1940] 261 p. illus., ports., maps. Bibliography: p. xxxix-xlvi.
Available in many California libraries and IHi OU

6006. —— Same... Stanford [c1947] 261 p. illus., ports., maps, facsim. Bibliography: p. xli-xlviii. The facsimile is a photolithographic reproduction of the 4th edition, with imprint: S.F., A. L. Bancroft & co., 1881.
Available in many California libraries and OU

6007. Nevada City nugget. 100 years of Nevada county, 1851–1951. [Nevada City] 1951. 136 p. illus. (Special ed. v.26, no. 20, May 18, 1951)
C CHi CO CSd MoS

6008. —— Special mining number, May 10, 1929. Nevada City, Willoughby & Willoughby, 1929. 32 p. illus., map.
C CHi

6009. —— Same, May 16, 1930. [Nevada City, 1930] 32 p.
CHi

6010. Nevada county. Board of supervisors. Nevada county, gold capitol of California! [Grass Valley, Grass Valley-Nevada City union print, 1952?] 32 p. illus.
CHi

6011. —— —— Nevada county, state of Calif. ... Grass Valley, Press of Union pub. co. [191–?] 32 p. illus.
CHi CLU CSj

6012. Nevada county development association. Nevada county, California. [Grass Valley, 1918?] [40] p. illus., map.
CHi

6013. —— Same. By Edward G. Kinyon. [Nevada City] 1938. folder (4 p.) illus., map.
CRcS

6014. Nevada county promotion committee. Nevada county, California... [n.p., 19—?] [36] p. illus.
CHi CL CLU CO CSmH CU-B

6015. Preston, E. M., comp. Nevada county, the famous Bartlett pear belt of California...Pub. by the Nevada county land & improvement association. Nevada City, Brown & Calkins, print., 1886. 93 p. illus., map.
C C-S CLU CSmH CU-B NHi

6016. Reed, Virginia Elizabeth B. A happy issue; the hitherto unpublished letter of a child... [written May 16, 1847] survivor of the Donner party. Stanford, 1935. 13 p.
CLSM

6017. Ritchie, Robert Welles. The hell-roarin' forty-niners. N.Y., J. H. Sears & co. [1928] 298 p. illus. CGr has autographed ms. with title: *Across the plains.*
Available in many California libraries and ViU

6018. Rogers, Andy. A hundred years of rip and roarin' Rough and Ready. [Rough and Ready?] c1952. 119 p. illus.
C CChiS CHi CL CLU CRedCL CSS CSto CStoC CU-B

6019. Royce, Sarah. A frontier lady; recollections of the gold rush and early California. New Haven, Conn., Yale, 1932. 144 p. map.
Available in many California libraries and IHi ODa OrU ViW

6020. Sargent, Aaron Augustus. Sketch of Nevada county... [S.F., 1856] 45 p. Extract from *Brown and Dallison's Nevada, Grass Valley and Rough and Ready directory.*
C CU-B

6021. Schaeffer, Luther Melancthon. Sketches of travel in South America, Mexico and California. N.Y., James Egbert, print., 1860. 247 p. Includes "the 'Gold lake' expedition and diggings of the Nevada City-Grass Valley region."—Wheat.
Available in many California libraries and CaBViPA

6022. [A scrapbook of mounted newspaper clippings relating to Nevada county, California. Grass Valley, etc. 1882?–1887?]
CSmH

6023. Silliman, Benjamin. Report on the deep placers of the South and Middle Yuba, Nevada county, California, in connection with the Middle Yuba and Eureka lake canal companies. New Haven, Priv. print., 1865. 43 p.
C CHi CLU

6024. South Yuba water co. ...South Yuba water company. History and resource. N.Y. [A. B. King print.] 1894. illus., port., fold. map. Nevada and Placer counties.
CLU

6025. Stewart, George Rippey. Donner Pass and those who crossed it... S.F., Calif. hist. soc. [1960] 96 p. illus., ports., maps, facsims.
C CAla CHi CLSM CLU CSf CStcl CU-B

6026. —— Ordeal by hunger; the story of the Donner party... N.Y., Holt [c1936] 328 p. illus., maps. Same. (Centennial edition) 1946.
Available in many California libraries and CaBViPA IHi

6027. —— Same. New ed., with a supplement and 3 accounts by survivors. Boston, Houghton, c1960. 394 p. illus., maps.   CL CU-B

6028. Stookey, Walter M. Fatal decision; the tragic story of the Donner party. Salt Lake City, Deseret bk. co., 1950. 209 p. illus., ports., map.   CL CRcS

6029. Thornton, J. Quinn. ...The California tragedy. [Oakland, Biobooks, c1945] 161 p. illus. Reprinted from author's account of the Donner party in his *Oregon and California in 1848*, N.Y., Harper, 1849.
Available in many California libraries and CaBViPA

6030. Truckee. Chamber of commerce. Truckee, California; "recreational center of the Sierra." Truckee, 1939. 8 p. illus., map.   CRcS

6031. White, Edith. Memories of pioneer childhood and youth in French Corral and North San Juan, Nevada county, California...told by Edith White, emigrant of 1859... [n.p., 1936] 29 l. Typew.   CHi CU-B

6032. Wisker, A. L. Meadow Lake mining district, Nevada county, California, and properties of Meadow Lake gold, a California corporation. [S.F., 1947] 25 p. illus.   C

6033. Wolfe, J. L. Yuba river canyon country bulletin. Number 1–56. Grass Valley, Grass Valley chamber of commerce, 1932–1933. Mimeo.
C (nos. 48–54, photostatic copy)   CO

Grass Valley

6034. Burr, Charles Chauncey, ed. Lectures of Lola Montez (Countess of Landsfield) including her autobiography. N.Y., Rudd & Carleton, 1858. 292 p. port.   CHi CSfCW

6035. Byrne, William S. Directory of Grass Valley township for 1865; containing a historical sketch of Grass Valley, of Allison ranch, and Forest Springs; also, a description of the principal mines... S.F., Print. by Charles F. Robbins & co., 1865. 144 p.
C CHi CLU CSfCP CSmH CU-B NHi

6036. Condy, H. Richard, firm. ...Catalogue J [watches and jewelry] [n.p., n.d.] 36 p. illus.   CHi

6037. Curtis, Edward. Two California sketches; William Watt, representative miner, a tribute to his memory. Leland Stanford...a biography; also an essay on viticulture. S.F., Thomas' steam print. house, 1880. 44 p.   CHi

6038. D'Auvergne, Edmund B. Lola Montez; an adventuress of the 'forties. N.Y., Lane, 1909. 375 p.
C CU-B

6039. —— Same. 2d ed. London, T. W. Laurie; N.Y., Brentano's, 1925. port.
CBev CL CLSU CLU CO CRcS CSS CSalCL CSd CSf CSfCP CSfWF-H CViCL

6040. Delano, Alonzo. Alonzo Delano's California correspondence: being letters hitherto uncollected from the Ottawa (Illinois) free trader and the New Orleans true delta, 1849–1852; ed. with an introd. and notes by Irving McKee. Sacramento, Sacramento bk. collectors club, 1952. 155 p. illus., maps. (Sacramento bk. collectors club. Pub. no. 5)
Available in many California libraries and MoHi N

6041. —— Life on the plains and among the diggings ... Auburn, Buffalo, N.Y., Miller, Orton & Mulligan, 1854. 384 p. illus.
C CHi CL CLSU CLU CO CP CSbr CSd CSf CSfCP CSfCW CSfWF-H CSjC CSmH CU-B CaBViPA GU ViU

6042. —— Across the plains and among the diggings ...a reprint of the original edition... N.Y., Wilson-Erickson, 1936. 192 p. illus.
Available in many California libraries and OrU UHi

6043. —— The miner's progress; or, Scenes in the life of a California miner. Being a series of humorous illustrations of the "ups and downs" of a gold digger in pursuit of his "pile." Sacramento, Daily union off., 1853. 13 p. illus. Verses by A. Delano and sketches by C. Nahl.
CO CSmH CU-B ICN MH ViU

6044. —— Same. Reprinted. [S.F., Grabhorn, 1943] [1] l., facsim.: 13 p. illus.   CLgA

6045. —— Old Block's sketch book...illus. ... by Nahl... Sacramento, James Anthony & co., 1856. 78 p. illus.
C CHi CLU CRedl CSmat CSmH CU-B CtY NN

6046. —— Same. Santa Ana, Fine arts press, 1947. 89 p. illus.
Available in many California libraries and CaBViPA

6047. —— Pen knife sketches; or, Chips of the Old Block. A series of original illustrated letters, written by one of California's pioneer miners, and dedicated to that class of her citizens by the author. Sacramento, Pub. at Union off., 1853. 112 p. Illustrations by Charles Nahl.
C CHi CLU CO CRedl CSmH CStcl CStclU CU-B CtY ICN ViU

6048. —— Same. 1854. 112 p. illus., plates.
CHi WHi

6049. —— Alonzo Delano's Pen-knife sketches; or, Chips of the Old Block... S.F., Grabhorn, 1934. 79 p. illus.
Available in many California libraries and ViU

6050. —— A sojourn with royalty and other sketches by Old Block. Collected and ed. by G. Ezra Dane... S.F., Geo. Fields, 1936. 96 p. illus.
C CArcHT CBb CHi CLS CLU CLgA CLod CO CRcS CRedl CRic CSCL CSf CSfCW CSmH CStrJC CU-B

6051. Eureka gold mining co., Grass Valley. Annual report.
CHi has 1871–73.

6052. Evans, M. Discourse pronounced by Rev. M. Evans, at the funeral obsequies of James King of William, in Grass Valley, Cal., May 22, 1856. "Fiat justutua, ruat coelum." Published at the request of the citizens of Grass Valley. Grass Valley, Print. at the Telegraph off., 1856. 10 p.   CLU

6053. —— Masonic address delivered before Madison lodge, no. 23, F. & A. M. on the anniversary festival of St. John the Baptist, June 24, A.L., 5856, A.D. 1856. In Grass Valley, Nevada co., California... Grass Valley, Print. at the Telegraph off., 1856. 19 p.   CLU

6054. Goldberg, Isaac. Queen of hearts; the passionate pilgrimage of Lola Montez. N.Y., John Day, 1936.   CRcS

6055. Grass Valley. Chamber of commerce. The city of Grass Valley; where the days of '49 are linked with the progress of today. Grass Valley [192–?] folder (6 p.)   CHi CRcS

6056. —— —— The home of Lotta Crabtree... Grass Valley. [1938?] broadside. Mimeo. CU-B

6057. —— —— Lola Montez. The only home Lola ever owned... Grass Valley, California... [1938?] 2 l. Mimeo. CU-B

6058. —— **Charters.** Charter and code of ordinances of the city of Grass Valley adopted July 7th, 1893, with amendments and ordinances in force to date. October 19th, 1912... [Grass Valley, 1912?] 164 p. CHi

6059. —— **Church of Jesus Christ of latter day saints.** Program of dedication of Grass Valley Ward chapel... [Grass Valley, 1949] [8] p. illus. CHi

6060. —— **First Methodist church.** Centennial celebration... December 8th, 1952... Program. Grass Valley, 1952. 14 p. CHi

6061. Grass Valley fire association. Constitution and by-laws... adopted Nov. 16, 1868. Organized June 7th, 1858. Re-organized June 19th, 1861. Grass Valley, Byrne & Mitchell, print., 1868. 31 p. C

6062. Grass Valley gold mining co. Charter of the ...company, organized July 25, 1851... N.Y., E. Winchester, 1851. 40 p. CLU CSmH

6063. —— First annual report... August 3, 1852. Proceedings of the trustees, and other documents. N.Y., 1852. 34 p. CSmH

6064. —— Same, revised. 1852. 47 p. C CHi CLU

6065. Grass Valley mining district. Mining laws ...Adopted in convention at Hamilton hall, July 27th, 1872. [n.p., 1872] CSmH

6066. [Heydenfeldt, Solomon] Opinion in the matter of the contract between the Grass Valley silver mining co., and the Chollar silver mining co. S.F., F. Eastman, 1867. 20 p. CU-B

6067. Holdredge, Helen (O'Donnell) Woman in black; life of Lola Montez. N.Y., Putnam [1955] 309 p. illus. Includes bibliographies.
C CBb CHi CRedCL CSS CSd CSf CSfSt

6068. Idaho Maryland mines corp., Grass Valley. Annual report.
CL has 1954, 1959.

6069. Latham, Milton Slocum. Speech... delivered at Nevada, on Monday evening, August 1st, 1859. Sacramento, "Daily Standard steam presses" [1859] 14 p. A political speech with references to Broderick, Gwin, Terry, etc. C CU-B

6070. Lewis, Oscar. Lola Montez; the mid-Victorian bad girl in California... S.F., Colt press [c1938] 70 p. illus.
C CBb CHi CLU CMartC CO CRcS CSf CSfP CSfWF-H CSmH CU-B CV

6071. Life of Rev. Father Dalton, 1826–1891. Typew. CGr

6072. Lopes, Frank Albert, jr. A history of Grass Valley, California, 1849–1855. Sacramento, 1956. 88 l. Typew. Thesis (M.A.) — Sacramento state college, 1956. C CSS

6073. Miner's union of the town of Grass Valley. Constitution, by-laws, order of business and rules of order... Organized May 1869. Grass Valley, Daily national print., 1869. 20 p. C

6074. Mount St. Mary's academy, Grass Valley. ...Graduating exercises... Wednesday, June 25, 1888... [n.p., n.d.] 1 fold. l. CHi

6075. Nevada irrigation district, Grass Valley. By-laws, rules and regulations and rates of tolls and charges. [Grass Valley, Eagle print. co., 1936] 15 p. CHi

6076. Odd-fellows, Independent order of. Grass Valley lodge, no. 12. Constitution and by-laws... Instituted at Grass Valley, July 28, 1853. Sacramento, Crocker, 1868. 84 p. C

6077. —— —— 100th anniversary... 1853–1953 [a brief history] [n.p., n.d.] 4 p. CHi

6078. Pennsylvania consolidated mining co. vs. Grass Valley exploration co. In the circuit court of the United States, ninth circuit, northern district of California. Hon. W. W. Morrow, judge, Pennsylvania consolidated mining company, plaintiff, vs. Grass Valley exploration company, defendant... S.F., C. A. Murdock & co. [1901] 111 p. illus., maps. C

6079. Poingdestre, John Edmund, comp. "The quartz crowned empress of the Sierras": Grass Valley and vicinity. Oakland, Pac. press [1894] 54 p. illus.
C CHi CLU CSmH CU-B

6080. —— Same. [1895] 54, [16] p. illus. (incl. ports.) A historical sketch of Grass Valley, by Samuel Butler: p. 3–9. Principal gold producing mines of Grass Valley and vicinity: p. 12–27. CoD

6081. Rourke, Constance. Troupers of the gold coast; or, The rise of Lotta Crabtree. N.Y., Harcourt, 1928. 262 p. illus., ports.
Available in many California libraries and CaBViPA ODa

6082. Silliman, Benjamin. Notes on the quartz mines of the Grass Valley district... Nevada City, Daily gazette bk. & job off., 1867. 14 p. CU-B

6083. Union quartz mountain mining and crushing co., Grass Valley. Organized April 5th, 1851, incorporated June 27, 1851, located on Wolf Creek, between Grass Valley and Nevada City... [N.Y.? 1851] 23 p. CSmH

6084. —— [Prospectus] California gold mining stock. [N.Y.? 1852] [3] p. CHi

6085. U.S. Circuit court of appeals (9th circuit) ...Pennsylvania consolidated mining company, plaintiff, vs. Grass Valley exploration company, defendant. Opinion by Hon. W. W. Morrow... rendered July 28, 1902. S.F., Murdock press, 1902. 36 p. diagrs. C

6086. Wisconsin hotel, Grass Valley. Register. W. H. Mitchell proprietor. [Grass Valley, 1869–91] 4 v. C

6087. Woodworth mines, Grass Valley. Statement ... N.Y., W. J. Read, print., 1865. 16 p. CHi

6088. Wright and Potter, comp. Facts and statistics relating to the Edmonton gold mine, Grass Valley, Nevada county, California. Bost., 1866. 55 p. diagrs., map. C CLU

6089. Wyndham, Horace. The magnificent Montez; from courtesan to convert. London, Hutchinson & co., 1935. 288 p. illus., ports.
C CChiS CHi CL CO CRcS CSdS CSf CSfCW CSfWF-H CSmH

6090. —— Same. N.Y., Hillman Curl, 1936.
C CBb CL CLSU CSS CSmH CU-B CViCL

Nevada City

6091. Campbell, Rembrance Hughes. "Carry on," edited by Emma Louise Campbell. [Shanghai? 1930] 53 p. Contains extracts of articles written for the *Nevada*

City morning union and his narrative "A brief history of our trip across the plains with ox teams in 1853."   C

6092. Chace, George Ide. Report...on the Flack Lode, Nevada City. Providence, R.I., Providence press co., 1865. 7 p.   CSmH

6093. Cosmopolitan benevolent society, Nevada City. Official list of the grand award premiums to the holders of season tickets in the Cosmopolitan benevolent society's fair! Nevada, California... [S.F., Winterburn & co.'s print., 1871] 41 p.   CU-B

6094. Davis, H. P. Gold rush days in Nevada City. Nevada City, Berliner & McGinnis, 1948. 64 p. illus., map.
C CBu CHi CL CLS CLU CLgA CO CRic CSS CSf CSfCP CSfCSM CSfWF-H CSmat CSmH CU-B

6095. Douglass, Belle. The last of the Oustomahs. Nevada City [December 1921] unp.   C

6096. Native sons of the Golden West. Grand parlor. Twenty-second session, official souvenir program, April 25, 1898, Hydraulic parlor no. 56, Nevada City, Cal. [Nevada City? 1898] 56 p. illus.   CHi

6097. Nevada City. Nevada City poll list. Election Nov. 2d, 1868. [Nevada City? 1868] 31 l.   CU-B

6098. —— Chamber of commerce. Come to Nevada City, California, treasure chest of the west. Nevada City [19—?] [8] p. illus., map.   CHi CRcS

6099. —— —— Nevada City, Nevada county, California... [Nevada City, 1915?] [11] p. illus., map.
CHi

6100. [Poingdestre, John Edmund] comp. Nevada City and its resources, mining interests and business firms. [Nevada City, Daily herald print.] 1893. unp.
CSmH

6101. Thompson, Hugh B. Directory of the city of Nevada and Grass Valley containing a history of the city. S.F., Charles F. Robbins, 1861.
C CHi CSmH CU-B

ORANGE COUNTY
(Created in 1889 from portion of Los Angeles county)
COUNTY HISTORIES

6102. Armor, Samuel, ed. History of Orange county, California, with biographical sketches...Contributors ...William Loftus, G. W. Moore, Chas. C. Chapman, Linn L. Shaw and others. L.A., Historic record co., 1911. 705 p. illus., port.
C CAna CBev CF CHi CL CLCM CLCo CLO CLS COr CPom CSfCP CSmH CSta CU-B

6103. —— Same, revised. History by Samuel Armor. L.A., Historic record co., 1921. 1669 p. illus., ports.
C CAla CHi CL CLAC CLO CLSU CLU CO COr CSf CSmH CSta CStaC CStaCL CU-B MiD-B MWA NN NIC WHi

6104. Pleasants, Adalina (Brown) History of Orange county, California... L.A., J. R. Finnell & sons pub. co.; Phoenix, Ariz., Record pub. co., 1931. 3 v. illus., ports. v.2–3 biographical.
C CAna CL CLO CLU CO COr CPom CSmH CSta CStaC (v.1 only) CStaCL MWA NN WHi

GREAT REGISTER

6105. Orange county. Index to the Great register of the county of Orange. 1890– Place of publication and title vary.
C has 1892, 1894, 1896, 1900 (biennially to)– 1930,
1934 (biennially to)– 1962. CL has 1890. CSmH has 1908. CU-B has 1940.

DIRECTORIES

6106. 1901. Southern California directory co., pub. Orange county directory... Santa Ana, 1901.
CSta

6107. 1903. Orange county directory co., pub. Orange county directory. A complete and reliable edition, containing the names and addresses of all residents of the county over sixteen years of age. A complete business directory of Santa Ana. Santa Ana, 1903. 256 p.
CHi CLU CSmH

6108. 1903. Gaskell, Charles Arthur, pub. What's what and who's who; a handbook and directory of Orange county... L.A., 1903.
CLU COr CSmH CSta CU-B

6109. 1911–1922. Kaasen directory co., pub. Anaheim, Fullerton, and northern Orange county directory... Anaheim, 1911–1922. Publisher varies: 1911, 1913–14 Albert G. Thurston.
CL has 1911, 1913–14, 1919–20, 1922. CSta has 1919–20, 1922. CStaCL has 1922.

6110. 1918. Santa Ana directory co., pub. Orange county coast cities directory...Huntington Beach, Newport Beach, Balboa, Laguna Beach, Seal Beach, San Juan Capistrano, and the districts of Delhi, El Toro, Harper, Irvine, Talbert, Trabuco, Westminster and Wintersburg. [Santa Ana? 1918?] 123 p.   C

6111. 1924– Western directory co., pub. North Orange county directory... Long Beach, 1924– 1924–41 published as *Orange county directory, section 1.*
C has 1924, 1927, 1930–37, 1940. CHi has 1941, 1948. CL has 1924, 1926–27, 1929, 1931, 1937, 1941, 1948, 1952. COr has 1924–37. CSta has 1924–41, 1945, 1948, 1951. CStaC has 1941, 1945. CStaCL has 1924–37, 1945. CU-B has 1924, 1937.

6112. —— South Orange county directory... Long Beach, 1924– 1924–41 published as *Orange county directory, section 2.*
C has 1924, 1927, 1930–37, 1940. CHi has 1945, 1947. CL has 1924, 1926–27, 1929, 1931, 1937, 1941, 1947, 1951, 1952. COr has 1924–37. CSta has 1924–41, 1945, 1947, 1951. CStaC has 1941, 1945. CStaCL has 1924–37, 1945, 1947. CU-B has 1924, 1937.

6113. 1950– Directory service co., pub. Luskey's official north Orange county criss cross city directory: including Anaheim, Fullerton, Buena Park, Brea, La Habra, Placentia, Yorba Linda, Olive, Stanton, Cypress, Los Alamitos, Atwood and contiguous rural areas... Santa Ana, 1950– Title varies.
COr has 1950, 1953. CSta has 1953. CStaCL has 1950-51, 1953.

6114. 1951. Directory service co., pub. Luskey's southern Orange county city directory...for the cities of Santa Ana, Orange, Tustin, Huntington Beach, Laguna Beach, Newport Beach, San Clemente, Seal Beach... Santa Ana, 1951.   CL COr CStaCL

6115. 1952. Luskey bros. and co., pub. Luskey's beach cities official criss cross directory. Santa Ana, 1952.
CSta CStaCL

Orange

6116. 1907. Orange county directory co., pub. Orange city directory...Orange, El Modena, Olive, Villa Park, West Orange and Yorba...   COr

6117. 1907. Santa Ana directory co., pub. Orange city directory... Santa Ana, 1907.   CSta

6118. 1919. Hansen directory co., pub. Hansen's Orange residence and business city directory, including Olive, El Modena, Villa Park, McPherson and West Orange. 1919.   COr

6119. 1922– Luskey bros. and co., pub. Luskey's official Orange criss cross city directory; including Olive, El Modena, and Silverado... Publisher varies: 1922–50 Western directory co. Content varies: 1922–50 Orange, Olive, El Modena, Villa Park, Santa Ana, Tustin and Garden Grove; 1958/59 Orange, Olive, El Modena, Orange Park Acres, Villa Park, and Silverado.
CL has 1961. COr has 1922–50, 1958/59. CSta has 1958/59. CStaCL has 1958/59.

Santa Ana

6120. 1905. Orange county directory and advertising co., pub. Santa Ana city directory. 1905.   COr

6121. 1905– Directory service co., pub. Luskey's official Santa Ana and Tustin criss cross city directory. Anaheim, 1905– Title varies. Publisher varies: 1905–20 Santa Ana directory co.; 1923–1949/50 Western directory co. Content varies: 1916–23 Santa Ana, Tustin and Garden Grove; 1949/50 Santa Ana, Orange and Tustin; 1951–54 Santa Ana, Orange, Tustin and central Orange county towns and rural areas; 1956 Santa Ana, Tustin and Lemon Heights.
C has 1923–1949/50. CHi has 1916, 1954. CL has 1916, 1918, 1921, 1949/50, 1956, 1960. CLU has 1916. COr has 1952, 1954, 1956. CSta has 1905, 1908–09, 1910-11, 1913–14, 1915, 1916, 1918, 1920, 1923, 1949–50, 1952, 1954, 1956, 1960. CStaCL has 1949–50, 1952, 1954, 1956. CU-B has 1951.

6122. 1915. Santa Ana. Chamber of commerce. Santa Ana city directory. Santa Ana, 1915. 306 p.   C

Other Cities and Towns

6123. Luskey bros. and co., pub. Luskey's Anaheim criss cross city directory... Anaheim, 1955–
CL has 1961. COr has 1955. CSta has 1955–57, 1959. CStaCL has 1959.

6124. 1956– Luskey bros. and co., pub. Luskey's Buena Park criss cross city directory. Anaheim, 1956–
CL has 1960. CSta has 1960. CStaCL has 1956, 1960.

6125. 1955– Luskey bros. and co., pub. Luskey's Fullerton criss cross city directory... Anaheim, 1955–
CL has 1960. CSta has 1955–56, 1958–59. CStaCL has 1958–59.

6126. 1958. Luskey bros. and co., pub. Luskey's ...Garden Grove criss cross city directory. Anaheim, 1958.   CL

6127. 1951– Luskey bros. and co., pub. Luskey's Huntington Beach...criss cross directory including Fountain Valley. Anaheim, 1955–
CL has 1959–60. CStaCL has 1951, 1960.

6128. 1940?–Dawson, Sam, pub. Laguna Beach city directory...
CStaCL has 7th, July 1947.

6129. 1951. Laguna Beach and San Clemente city directory.   CStaCL

6130. 1956– Luskey bros. and co., pub. Luskey's Laguna Beach criss cross directory... Anaheim, 1956–
CHi has 1959. CL has 1959–61. CSta has 1957–58, 1960. CStaCL has 1956, 1958–59.

6131. 1957/58– Luskey's La Habra...criss cross directory. Anaheim, 1957–
CL has 1959. CStaCL has 1957/58.

6132. 1955– Luskey bros. and co., pub. Luskey's Newport Beach, Costa Mesa criss cross city directory. Anaheim, 1954–
CL has 1962. CSta has 1955, 1960. CStaCL has 1955.

6133. 1961. San Clemente. Chamber of commerce. San Clemente, Capistrano Beach, Dana Point, San Juan Capistrano city directory. San Clemente, 1961.   CL

GENERAL REFERENCES

6134. Alpha Beta food markets, La Habra. Annual report.
CL has 1955–59.

6135. Arcadia metal products, Fullerton. Annual report.
CL has 1959–60.

6136. Ashby, Gladys E., and Winterbourne, J.W. A study of primitive man in Orange county and some of its coastal areas... Santa Ana, 1939. 91 l. illus. "This book represents the findings of Works progress administration anthropological projects No. 4465–No. 7680, sponsored by Board of education, Santa Ana."
CStaCL   CU-B

6137. Ball, Charles Dexter. Orange county medical history... Santa Ana, Print. & bind. by A. G. Flagg, 1926. 205 p. ports. "Orange county medical assoc.": p. 82–205.
C CLM CLU COr CSmH CSta CStaCL CU-B

6138. Banks, Homer. The story of San Clemente; the Spanish village... San Clemente, c1930. 80 p. illus.
C CBb CHi CL CLO CLU CLob CRcS CSd CSf CSmH CSta CStaCL CU-B NN

6139. Bay Island club, Balboa. Bay Island club, 1903–1960. [Corona del Mar, 1960] 7 p. illus.   CHi

6140. Beckman instruments, inc., Fullerton. Annual report.
CL has 1955–60.

6141. Beek, Joseph Allan. Balboa Island yarns. [n.p., 1950] 61 p. illus.   CL

6142. Bolsa Chica gun club, Bolsa. Rules and regulations...1902/03– L.A., Out West co., print. [1902/1911]
CSmH has 1902/03–1903/04, 1910/11.

6143. Brunner, Edmund de Schweinitz, and Brunner, Mary V. ...Irrigation and religion; a study of religious and social conditions in two California counties... N.Y., Doran [c1922] 128 p. illus., maps. (Committee on social and religious surveys. Unique studies of rural Am., town & country ser., no. 8) The two counties are Orange and Stanislaus. Bibliography: p. 128.
C CBev CL CLO CLU CMS CO CRedCL CSd CSf CSfCW CSmH CU-B IC

6144. Carthew, Arthur Williams. The lower basin of the Santa Ana river. [Berkeley, 1931] Thesis (M.A.) —Univ. of Calif., 1931.   CU

6145. Cleland, Robert Glass. The Irvine ranch of Orange county, 1810–1950. San Marino, Huntington lib., 1952. 163 p. illus., ports., map.
Available in many California libraries and MiD N NHi NN NcU OrU TxU UHi UU ViU

6146. Dawson, Raymond E. A history of Tustin, California, with special emphasis upon its citrus development. [L.A.] 1938. Thesis (M.A.)—Univ. of So. Calif., 1938.   CLSU CStaCL

6147. **Fox, Clara Mason.** A history of El Toro; comp. for the El Toro woman's club... Santa Ana, Public steno. shop, 1939. 63 l. Mimeo.
CLU CSmH CSta CStaCL

6148. **Fullerton. Chamber of commerce.** Fullerton, California, home of the Valencia orange. [Fullerton, 1912?] [29] p. illus.
CLU

6149. **Grimshaw, Mary Alice.** The history of Orange county, 1769–1889. 1937.
CAna

6150. **Harding, Purl W.** History of Brea to 1950 ... Brea, Brea progress, 1950. 67 p. illus., ports.
CL CStaCL CU-B

6151. **Head, H. C.** The history of Garden Grove. Written in conjunction with the celebration of the first annual "Grovers day," held on September 30, 1939. Garden Grove, Garden Grove news [1939] 19 p.
CLU

6152. **Hebert, Ray.** Fabulous Irvine ranch. An exclusive series of articles from the *Los Angeles times*. L.A., 1959. 1 v.
CLob

6153. **Hill, Merton E.** One hundred years of public education in Orange county. Orange county supt. schools, 1957. 370 p. illus.
CStaC CStaCL

6154. **Holmes, Roger.** Fabulous farmer; the story of Walter Knott and his berry farm...Illus. from the sketches of Paul van Klieben and Clarence Ellsworth. L.A., Westernlore pub. [1956] 184 p. illus.
CHi CLO CNa CP CRcS CSd CStmo CoD

6155. **Hufford, David Andrew.** ...A rambling sketch in and about Laguna and Arch beaches, Orange county, California. L.A., Author [c1922] 15 l. illus.
CLU CU-B

6156. **Hunt food and industries, inc., Fullerton.** Annual report.
CL has 1954–55, 1957.

6157. **Jensen, James Maurice.** The Mexican American in an Orange county community... Claremont, 1948. Thesis (M.A.)—Claremont college, 1948.
CAna

6158. **Knowlton, Charles S.** Post offices of Orange county, California, past and present. Fullerton, Author, print. by Placentia courier, 1947. 16 p.
CL CLU CO CPom CSta CU-B

6159. **Lund, William S.** Orange county; its economic growth, 1940–80. SRI project no. I-2768 prepared for Orange county Board of supervisors. Stanford research institute. So. Calif. laboratories, 1959. 188 p. illus., maps.
COr CStaCL

6160. **McDannald, D. W.** Spring eternal. Orange county, California... [Santa Ana, Bd. of supervisors, 1915] 16 p. illus.
CHi CL CLU CU-B

6161. —— Same. [1917?] 31 p. illus., map, port.
CHi

6162. **Meyer, Samuel A., comp.** 50 golden years; a history of the city of Newport Beach, 1906–56. [Newport Beach, Newport harbor pub. co., 1957] 292 p. illus.
C CHi CL CLO CLU CO COr CP CSd CStaC CStaCL CU-B NN

6163. **Moeller, Earne W., and Weimer, George N., comp.** A guide for industrial locators [in Orange city] [n.p.] Author, 1957.
COr

6164. **Nenno, Faustina.** Placentia round table club; the first thirty-five years, January 1902–December, 1937. "no. 102." Placentia, Placentia courier, 1938. 215 p.
CBb CHi CRcS CV

6165. **Norris, Frank R.** A live ghost town. [n.p., c1950] 84 p. illus., port., map. Knott's berry farm.
CO CSd CU-B

6166. **Orange. Chamber of commerce.** Orange, California, the heart of the Valencia orange district. [1922?] [12] p. illus.
CU-B

6167. —— **Union high school.** The orange and white; golden anniversary story of Orange high, 1903–53. Orange, 1953.
C

6168. **Orange county. Associated chambers of commerce.** Spring eternal in Orange county, California. [L.A., Press of West coast mag., 1907] [32] p. illus.
CL CU-B

6169. —— **Board of supervisors.** The majestic empire of Orange county, California. [Santa Ana, 1960] 28 p. illus., map.
CHi

6170. —— —— Orange county, California; nature's prolific wonderland. F. W. Slabaugh, ed. [Santa Ana? 1926] [24] p. illus., map.
CHi

6171. —— —— Same. [1938?] 22 p.
CRcS

6172. —— —— Orange county progress report. 1955.
COr has v.1, no. 1–10, v.2, no. 1–2.

6173. —— —— Our Orange county life. [Santa Ana? 193–?] [24] p. illus.
CU-B

6174. —— **Chamber of commerce.** Orange county in southern California. [Santa Ana, 189–?] folder (8 p.) map.
CU-B

6175. —— —— Orange county, southern California ...a plain statement of resources and attractions to homeseekers. Orange, Orange news print., 1897. [20] p. illus.
CLU CU-B

6176. —— **Planning commission.** The master plan of shoreline development for Orange county... Adopted by Orange county Planning commission, October 17, 1941. Adopted by Board of supervisors, November 12, 1941. [Santa Ana, Dennis print., 1941] 83 p. maps.
CO CSta CStaCL

6177. **Orange county herald, Santa Ana.** Orange county through the camera... Santa Ana [190–?] 8 l. ports.
CLU CU-B

6178. **Orange county historical society.** Orange county histories series v.1–3. Santa Ana, Press of the Santa Ana high school & junior college, 1931–39. 3 v. illus.
Available in many California libraries and MWA NHi (v.2) NN

6179. Orange county, "the biggest little county on earth." Orange county quarter centennial edition. Santa Ana, Santa Ana daily register, 1913. illus., maps. "An elaborate history and description much of which was written by T. E. Stephenson."—Dawson, *West & Pacific*.
CoD

6180. **Orange post.** Progress edition, August 27, 1915. 32 p. illus., ports.
C

6181. Orange, "you'll like it." [L.A., Calif. rotogravure corp., 192?] 13 p. illus.
CRcS

6182. **Patterson, R. L.** Report to Orange county Board of supervisors and Orange county harbor commission on the improvement of upper Newport bay, Newport bay harbor, Orange county, California. [Newport Beach] 1950. 100 l. illus., maps (part fold., part col.)
C

6183. **Plummer, Louis E.** History of the Fullerton union high school and Fullerton junior college 1893–1943. Fullerton, Fullerton J.C. press, 1949. 243 p. illus.
CStaC

6184. **Post, William S.** ...Santa Ana investigation.

Flood control and conservation... [Sacramento, State print. off., 1929] 357 p. illus.
CL CLSU CO CSf CStaCL CU-B

6185. Robinson, William Wilcox. The old Spanish and Mexican ranchos of Orange county. [L.A., Title insurance and trust co., 1950] 18 p. fold. map.

C CHi CL CLO CLSM CLU CO CP CSd Other editions followed.

CAla (1955) CHi (1955) CLO (1952) CSluCL (1955) CStmo (1952) CViCL (1955) MoS (1954)

6186. Santa Ana. Board of trade. Orange county. History, soil, climate, resources, advantages. Santa Ana, 1891. 64 p.
CLO CSmH CSta

6187. —— Chamber of commerce. Orange county and the Santa Ana valley... [Santa Ana, 1898?] [48] p. illus.
CLU CSmH CU-B

6188. —— —— Orange county, California, the most celebrated celery district in the world. [Santa Ana, 1905?] [64] p. illus., map.
CU-B

6189. Santa Ana valley immigration association. The Santa Ana valley of southern California, its resources, climate, growth, and future. Santa Ana, Print. by Burton-Taney steam print. house, 1885. 36 p.
CHi CL CLU CSmH

6190. Sherman, H. L., comp. History of Newport Beach... Pub. by the city of Newport Beach, California, in cooperation with the Newport Harbor chamber of commerce. L.A., Times-mirror, c1931. 215 p.

C CAna CHi CL CLO CLU COr CPom CSd CSmH CSta CStaCL CU-B NN

6191. Sherwood, Frank P. Decisions ahead; a long-term development program for the city of La Habra, California... [L.A.] The Mangore corp. [1958] 218 l. illus.
CLU

6192. Smiley, Frances Catherine. An educational survey of Orange county, California. [Berkeley, 1921] Thesis (M.A.)—Univ. of Calif., 1921.
CU

6193. Soiland, Albert. The saga of Newport bay and Newport harbor yacht club... L.A. [1936] 66 p. illus., ports., map, facsim.
CSmH CU-B

6194. Stephenson, Terry Elmo. Caminos viejos; tales found in the history of California of especial interest to those who love the valleys, the hills and the canyons of Orange county... Santa Ana, Pub. on the press of the Santa Ana high school & junior college by its director, T. E. Williams, 1930. 110 p. illus., ports., maps. Contents: On Portolá's trail. — The first settlers. — The march to conquest.—The Flores uprising.—Stage coach days.—Buried treasure.

Available in many California libraries and NN

6195. —— Don Bernardo Yorba. Santa Ana, Pub. at Fine arts press by T. E. Williams, 1941. 115 p. illus., port., map. "...gives the story of each of the Santa Ana grants, and Don Bernardo's connection with each, as well as a history of the Yorba Family in California."—J. Gregg Layne.

C CAna CBb CHi CL CLSU CLU CO COr CSf CSfCW CSmH CSta CStaC CStaCL

6196. —— Shadows of Old Saddleback; tales of the Santa Ana mountains...Santa Ana, Pub. on the press of the Santa Ana high school & junior college by its director, T. E. Williams, c1931. 209 p. illus., map.

Available in many libraries.

6197. —— Same. Foreword by Phil Townsend Hanna. [Santa Ana] Fine arts press, 1948. 207 p. illus., port.

C CHi CL CLSU COr CSmH CStaC CStaCL CU-B

6198. Thurston, Joseph Smith. Laguna Beach of early days. [Laguna Beach? 1947] 198 p. illus., ports.

C CBb CHi CL CLO CLU CO COr CRedl CSd CSmH CSta CStaCL CSterCL CStmo NN

6199. Tri-college survey committee. Occupational survey of Orange County...for Fullerton junior college, Orange Coast junior college, Santa Ana junior college. Office of County supt. of schools, 1958. 322 p. charts. Mimeo.
CStaC

6200. U.S. General land office. In the General land office. Survey of the Rancho Santiago de Santa Ana. Brief of Montgomery Blair for Bolsa claimants. [n.p., 1881?] 25 p.
CLU

6201. —— Work projects administration. California. Orange county historical project... [n.p., 1936?] 32 v. illus. Typew. Partial contents: 2. Cities and towns.—3-4. Pioneer tales.—7. Biography.
CSta CStaC CU-B

6202. Westerberg, B. K. Dana Point and Capistrano Beach. [1948–53] 6 p. Mimeo.
CStaCL

6203. Westminster plaza association. Cash book; including list of shareholders, treasurer's accounts and miscellaneous receipts. Westminster, 1908–12. 18 p.
CStaCL

6204. —— Certificates of the capital stock of the Westminster plaza assn.; receipts, etc. Westminster, 1908–09. unp.
CStaCL

6205. Wieman, William Wallace. The separation and organization of Orange county. [n.p.] 1938. 64 l. map. Thesis (M.A.)—Univ. of So. Calif.
CLSU CStaCL

6206. Wilson, Nichols Field, comp. Adventures in business, a tribute to business...Knott's berry place. Buena Park, Ghost town press, 1944–46. 3 v. illus.
CRic CSta

6207. Wolf, H. Comer. Trabuco cañon mine, a report and recommendations... 9 l. illus. Typew. CLO

Anaheim

6208. Anaheim. Board of trade. The frostless belt ... Anaheim [1915] 12 p.
CSmH

6209. —— Ordinances, etc. Ordinances... Anaheim, Anaheim gazette job print., 1877. 14 p. CSmH

6210. Anaheim bulletin. Centennial edition. Anaheim, 1957. 1 v. (v.p.) illus., ports. (v.35, no. 32, Sept. 6, 1957)
C

6211. Anaheim gazette. 69th anniversary and historical edition...1870–1939. Anaheim, 1939. 12 p. illus., ports.
CSmH CU-B

6212. Anaheim immigration association. Anaheim, southern California, its history, climate, soil and advantages for home seekers and settlers. Anaheim, Anaheim gazette job print., 1885. 32 p. illus. CU-B

6213. Anaheim union water co. Articles of incorporation and by-laws... Anaheim, Anaheim gazette job print., 1884. 16 p. CHi

6214. Carosso, Vincent. Anaheim, California: a nineteenth century experiment in commercial viniculture. 11 p. Reprinted from *Bul. of the Business hist. soc.*, June 1949. CHi

6215. Carr, John F., & co., N.Y., pub. Anaheim: its people and its products. N.Y., 1869. 16 p. CU-B

6216. Gronowicz, Antoni. Modjeska, her life and loves. N.Y., T. Yoseloff [1956] 254 p. illus., ports.
CStaCL CU-B

6217. Interstate engineering corp. Annual report. CL has 1955–60.

6218. MacArthur, Mildred Yorba. Anaheim, "the Mother colony." Comp. and written in honor of the original colonists. L.A., Ward Ritchie [1959] 260 p. illus., ports., maps (on lining-papers) Includes bibliography.
C CAna CBev CHi CLO CLSM CLU COr CP CSdS CStaCL CStmo CU-B NN

6219. Melrose, Richard, ed. Anaheim. The garden spot of southern California... Anaheim, Anaheim gazette job print., 1879. 23 p.
CU-B

6220. Modjeska, Helena. Memories and impressions of Helena Modjeska; an autobiograhy... N.Y., Macmillan, 1910. 571 p. illus.
CHi CStaCL

6221. Munz, Philip Alexander. A short history of the Rancho Santa Ana Botanic garden. Anaheim, Rancho Santa Ana Botanic garden, 1947. 31 p. illus.
C CHi CLSU CLU CO CSdS CSf CSmH CSta CU-B CWhC

6222. Parker, Elenora Alice. Development and growth of Anaheim public schools, 1859–1928. [Anaheim, Colonist press, Anaheim-union high school, 1929] 98 p.
C

6223. Raup, Hallock Floy. The German colonization of Anaheim, California... Berkeley, Univ. of Calif. press, 1932. 146 p. illus.
CChiS CHi CLSU CLU CSdS CSf CSmH CU-B OrU

San Juan Capistrano

6224. Bedford-Jones, Henry. The story of mission San Juan Capistrano. Santa Barbara, 1918. 51 p. port. "Thirty copies hand printed by the author."
CLM CLU

6225. —— Same, with title: The mission and the man; the story of San Juan Capistrano... Pasadena, San Pasqual press, 1939. 50 p. port.
Available in many California libraries and UPB

6226. Boscana, Geronimo. Chinigchinich, a historical account of the origin, customs, and traditions of the Indians at the missionary establishment of St. Juan Capistrano, Alta California; called the Acagchemen nation. Together with *Life in California*, by Alfred Robinson. N.Y., 1846. p. [227]–341. illus., port.
C CL CLSU CLU CSf CSfCW CSmH CStaCL CStrJC CU-B

6227. —— Same. Oakland, Biobooks, 1947. 72 p. (With Robinson, Alfred. *Life in California*. Oakland, 1947)
C CHi CL CLO CLS CLSU CLU CLgA CMon CO CRedCL CSS CSbr CSmH CStmo CU-B CV

6228. —— Chinigchinich (Chi-ni'ch-nich). A revised and annotated version of Alfred Robinson's translation of Father Geronimo Boscana's historical account of the belief, usages, customs and extravagencies [!] of the Indians of this mission of San Juan Capistrano, called the Acagchemem tribe. Santa Ana, Fine arts press, 1933. 249 p. port., maps. "Edited by Phil Townsend Hanna... annotations by John P. Harrington...foreword by Frederick Webb Hodge...illustrations by Jean Goodwin... published by Thomas E. Williams." "Bibliography, by John P. Harrington": p. [229]–244.
Available in many libraries.

6229. —— A new original version of Boscana's historical account of the San Juan Capistrano Indians of southern California, by John P. Harrington. Wash., D.C., Govt. print. off., 1934. 62 p. port. (Smithsonian misc. collections, v.92, no. 4)
CLSU CLU CO CRcS CSd CSf CSmH CU-B

6230. Bruton, Lydian. The swallows of Capistrano. L.A., Wetzel [c1948] [18] p. illus.
CHi

6231. Byers, Samuel H. M. Bells of Capistrano. L.A., Potter bros. co., 1916. 176 p. illus.
CStaCL

6232. Engelhardt, Zephyrin, *Father*. San Juan Capistrano mission. L.A., Standard print. co., 1922. 259 p. illus., ports., maps.
Available in many California libraries and CaBViPA

6233. Fox, John Samuel. ...San Juan Capistrano... Berkeley, 1936. 281 p. Typew.
CU-B

6234. O'Sullivan, St. John. Little chapters about San Juan Capistrano. [L.A., G. Rice & sons press] c1912. 30 p. illus.
CHi CLU

6235. —— Same. Rev. ed. 1929. 40 p.
C CLU CSd MoKU

6236. San Juan Capistrano. Community Presbyterian church. San Juan Capistrano community Presbyterian church, 1919–1959. [San Juan Capistrano, 1959] 23 p. illus., ports.
C CHi CU-B

6237. Saunders, Charles Francis. Capistrano nights; tales of a California mission town by Charles Francis Saunders and Father St. John O'Sullivan... N.Y., McBride, 1930. 202 p. illus. (incl. map) pl.
CBb CBea CLLoy CLU COr CRic CSal CSd CSf CSfCW CSfU CSjC CSluCL CSmat CStaCL CStmo CViCL ODa WM

6238. Walder, Margaret Frederick. The historical geography of mission San Juan Capistrano. [L.A.] 1957. Thesis (M.A.)—U.C.L.A., 1957.
CLU

Santa Ana

6239. Benton, Frank Weber. Santa Ana and vicinity; California the wonderland. [L.A., Benton pub. co., c1923] [28] p. col. illus.
CU-B

6240. Hull, Osman Ransom. ...Santa Ana school housing survey... L.A., Univ. of So. Calif., 1928. 88 p. illus., maps.
CLU CSmH

6241. Kroeger, Louis J., and associates. Library services and facilities, city of Santa Ana, California. S.F., 1953. 19 p.
C

6242. Leecing, Walden A. The Santa Ana community players, 1920–27. [Stanford, 1956] Thesis (M.A.)—Stanford univ., 1956.
CSt

6243. Orange county title co., Santa Ana. From the days of the Dons. [Santa Ana, A. G. Flagg print. bookbinding] 1931. 15 p. illus.
CLO

6244. Santa Ana. Chamber of commerce. Community survey of Santa Ana, California. 1952. 56 p. illus.
CStaC

6245. —— —— Santa Ana, California. [Santa Ana, 193–?] 30 p.
CRcS

6246. —— —— Santa Ana, the county seat and commercial center, Orange county. [Santa Ana, 1911?] [22] p. illus.
CHi

6247. —— **First Baptist church.** Diamond anniversary...First Baptist church...Santa Ana, 1871. [1946?] 24 p. illus., ports.
CSta CU-B

6248. —— **First Methodist church.** History... Nov. 29, 1873–Nov. 29, 1948. [by Helen S. McArthur] [Santa Ana, 1949] 72 p. illus., ports.
CSta CStaCL

6249. —— **Publicity dept.** Map of Orange county,

California, where you will like to live. Santa Ana [1937?] folder (2 p.) illus., map.   CRcS

6250. Santa Ana valley irrigation company, Santa Ana. By-laws... (as amended November 10th, 1882) Santa Ana, Stamps bros. print., 1883. 14 p.   CHi

6251. Southern California paradise. History of Santa Ana city and valley... Santa Ana, 1887. 40 p. illus.
CSmH NHi

6252. Stephenson, Terry Elmo. Epitome of the history of Santa Ana... [Santa Ana, 1942] [4] p. port. Reproduced from typew. copy.   CLU CSmH

6253. Swanner, Charles Douglas. Santa Ana, a narrative of yesterday, 1870–1910. [1st ed.] Claremont, Saunders press [1953] 157 p. illus.
C CBb CHi CL CLO CLSM CLU CLob CNa CO COr CP CPom CSd CSta CStaC CStaCL CU-B N NN

6254. —— The story of Company L, "Santa Ana's own." Claremont, Fraser press [c1958] 90 p. illus.
CSlu CSta CStaC CStaCL

PLACER COUNTY
(Organized in 1851 from portions of Sutter and Yuba counties)

COUNTY HISTORIES

6255. Angel, Myron, and Fairchild, M. D. History of Placer county, with illustrations and biographical sketches... Oakland, Thompson & West, 1882. 416 p. illus., ports. Literary work under charge of Myron Angel, assisted by M. D. Fairchild.
C CAuP CHi CL CLSM CLSU CLU CLgA CO CSf CSfCP CSfCW CSfMI CSmH CSt CU-B CoD IC ICN KHi N NHi NN WHi

6256. Lardner, William Branson, and Brock, M. J. History of Placer and Nevada counties, California, with biographical sketches... L.A., Historic record co., 1924. 1255 p. illus., ports.
C CAuP CGr CHi CL CLAC CLU CLod CMS CO CSS CSf CSfCP CSmH CStoC CU-B ICN MWA

GREAT REGISTER

6257. Placer county. Index to the Great register of the county of Placer. 1866– Place of publication and title vary.
C has 1867–68, 1871–73, 1876–77, 1879, 1880 (biennially to)– 1962. CAuP has 1902, 1908, 1918, 1932, 1934, 1946, 1950, 1952, 1954, 1956, 1960. CHi has 1872, 1920, 1944, 1948. CL has 1867–68 (suppl.), 1873 (suppl.), 1877 (suppl.), 1879–80, 1882 (biennially to)– 1890. CLU has 1900, 1912, 1914. CSmH has 1871 (suppl.), 1880, 1898 (suppl.), 1904. CU-B has 1867, 1868 (suppl. 1–3), 1872, 1875, 1879–80, 1882, 1884, 1892, 1894, 1896, 1900, 1902, 1908, 1910, 1912, 1914, 1918 (biennially to)– 1930, 1934 (biennially to)– 1942.

DIRECTORIES

6258. 1861. Steele, R. J.; Bull, James P.; and Houston, F. I., pub. Directory of the county of Placer for the year 1861; containing a history of the county, and of the different towns in the county... S.F., C. F. Robbins print., 1861. 208 p.
C CHi CLU CSfCP CSmH CtY

6259. 1875. Placer weekly argus, pub. Placer county business and official directory. Auburn, 1875. 136 p.   C CSmH PHi

6260. 1884/85. Truckee basin and Lake Tahoe directory for 1884–85 giving name, business of the adult population on the line of the C.P.R.R., from Truckee to Wadsworth...Reno. Reno, Reno evening gazette [1884?] 163 p.   C

6261. 1892/94. Rentschler, G. W., comp. A directory of Placer, Nevada, Yuba, Sutter, Butte, Colusa, Glenn, Tehama, and Shasta counties...for 1892–94. S.F., San Francisco directory co. [1892?] 629 p.
C CHi (facsim.) CMary

6262. 1899/1900. Predom, J. A., and Rush, T. H., pub. Auburn city directory, 1899/1900, containing a list of the residents of Auburn, principal business firms, hotels, and other information. ... Auburn, 1899. 46 p.
C CU-B

GENERAL REFERENCES

6263. Alpine meadows of Tahoe, inc. Prospectus. L.A., 1960. [24] p. illus., maps.   CHi

6264. Applegate. Applegate school. Applegate; its story. Compiled and written by the children...1933–35. [Applegate, 1935?] 8 p. Mimeo.   CHi

6265. [Baker, Edward Dickinson] Speech of Hon. E. D. Baker. Delivered at Forest Hill, August 19, 1859. From the phonographic report of the Sacramento Union; made by Charles A. Sumner. [n.p., 1859] 13 p.
CHi CSfCW

6266. Brandi, C. F. "High in the Sierra" '52. [Reno?] A. Carlisle & co. of Nevada print., c1952. 96 p. illus.   CHi

6267. Butler, Henry Everett. Citrus colony at Penryn, Placer county, California. 1924. 3 p. Typew.   C

6268. California. Dept. of employment. Classified business and industrial directory of Placer county, supplied to the Placer county Chamber of commerce by the Division of development and stabilization of employment, state of California. [Sacramento? 195–?] 22 p.
CO

6269. —— Legislature. Assembly. Investigating committee on the boundary line between Placer and Nevada counties. Report...in Assembly, March 16th, 1866. [Sacramento, 1866]   CSmH

6270. Carpenter, Jerry E. California winter sports and the VIIIth Winter Olympic games, 1960, at Squaw Valley. S.F., Fearon, 1958. 84 p. illus., maps.
C CChiS CNa CO CSd CSf CStmo CU-B

6271. Dardanelles consolidated gravel mining co. [Statement] Bost., James S. Adams print., 1881. 31 p. illus.   CHi

6272. Daughters of the American revolution. California. Genealogical records committee. Early California wills, Placer, Shasta and Yuba counties, 1849–1900. Vital statistics, Placer and Shasta counties. Copied by the following chapters: Major Pearson B. Reading, Sacramento [and] San Francisco... Sacramento, 1952. 29 l. Typew.   C CL

6273. Davis, Leonard M. A history of Roseville, 1864–1909. [n.p.] 1958. 141 p. map. Typew. Bibliographical footnotes.   C

6274. Dutch Flat. Methodist church. Centennial of the Dutch Flat Methodist church...August 30, 1959. [n.p., 1959] [8] p. Includes historical sketch.   CHi

6275. The early citrus fruits of Placer county... [Newcastle? 1887] 8 p.   CU-B

6276. Gilchrist, Adeline Howard. Virginia town. [n.p., Placer co. hist. soc., 1953] folder (8 p.)   CHi

6277. Gittings, Samuel Evans. The foundations of Placer county agriculture, 1850–1900. Sacramento, 1959. 248 p. Thesis (M.A.)—Sacramento state college, 1959.   CSS

6278. Goulden & Jacobs. Summit soda springs. [S.F., Railway pub. co., n.d.] 14 p. illus.   CHi

6279. Greenbie, Sydney. Gold of Ophir; or, the lure that made America. Garden City, N.Y., Doubleday, 1925. 330 p. illus.   CHi

6280. Griffith, Enid S. A small town reaches out; the origin and early history of Penryn, Placer co., California. [n.p., n.d.] 38 p. illus.   CHi

6281. Hansen, Charles. Bits of Todds Valley history. [Todds Valley] Todds Valley school, 1933. 93 p. illus., map. Mimeo.   CHi

6282. [Immigration association of California] [County scrapbooks] [S.F., 188–?]   C

6283. Industrial survey associates. Placer county, its present and potential economic development; a report prepared for the Placer county chamber of commerce. S.F., 1951. 77 [15] l. diagrs., tables.   C   CO   CSfCSM

6284. Katzenstein, George B. Historical sketch of Newcastle lodge, no. 339, I.O.G.T. (Independent order of good templars)... [n.p., 1878?] 10 p.   CHi

6285. Lawrence, J. T., et als vs. Neff, J. H., et als. In the Supreme court of the state of California. J. T. Lawrence et als., appellants, vs. J. H. Neff et als., respondents. Appellants' brief and points [altered in ms. to read "Transcript on appeal"] Fellows & Norton, attorneys for appellants. Sacramento, E. G. Jefferis' law print. off. [1870] 25 p.   CHi

6286. Lewis, Harriet Jane, and Lewis, Francis A. Stories of Placer county-Tahoe in golden California for children... [Sacramento, Chas. N. Fleming co., c1932] 61 p. illus.   C   CSS   CU-B   NN

6287. Madden, Joseph Francis. The resources of the Newcastle fruit district. Newcastle [1887?] 96 p. map.   CHi   CU-B

6288. Micoleau, Tyler. The story of Squaw Valley. N.Y., A. S. Barnes [1953] 95 p. illus.
      C   CAuP   CSalCL   CSf   ODa

6289. Newcastle building and loan association. Annual report...April 30, 1919. [n.p.] 1919. [1] l.
      CHi

6290. —— By-laws...adopted May 15th, 1889. [n.p., 1889?] folder (6 p.)   CHi

6291. —— Same, as amended 1908. [n.p., 1908?] 4 p.   CHi

6292. —— Constitution and by-laws... Newcastle, Newcastle pub. co., 1903. 9 p.   CHi

6293. Olympic games (Winter), Squaw Valley, 1960. 8 pamphlets in 1 v. illus., maps.   CSf

6294. —— **Organizing committee.** Fact sheet. S.F., 1959. 16 l. diagr.   C

6295. —— —— Official souvenir program of the VIII Olympic winter games; Squaw Valley, Lake Tahoe, California, February 18–28, 1960; ed. Lee Klein. S.F., 1960. 122 p. illus.   CRcS

6296. The Pacific railroad. A defense against its enemies, with report of the Supervisors of Placer county, and report of Mr. Montanya, made to the Supervisors of the city and county of San Francisco. [S.F.?] 1864. 35 p.
      CHi   CLU   CSmH   CU-B

6297. Parkhurst, G. Yoell. Placer county, Califor-

nia. S.F., Sunset mag. homeseekers' bur. [1909] 31 p. illus.   CHi

6298. Perry, Albert H. A general history of the Placer county citrus colony. [n.p.] 1958. 33 p. illus., facsim. Typew. Bibliography: p. [32–33]   C

6299. Placer county. Board of supervisors. Placer county, Calif.; a continent within a county...Comp. by a comm. selected by the Auburn chamber of commerce. Lincoln, Print. by F. L. Sanders [191–?] 32 p. illus., maps.   CL   CLU   CRcS   CU-B

6300. —— —— Placer county, California, the gateway county of the golden state. S.F., Sunset mag. community development div. [1920?] 15 p. illus., map.
      CRcS

6301. —— **Board of trade.** Placer county, California... Auburn, Placer county republican [n.d.] [24] p.   C   CU-B

6302. —— —— Same. [n.p., 1887?] 16 p. map.
      CHi   CSmH   CU-B

6303. —— **Chamber of commerce.** A brief history of the efforts of the residents of Placer county... in their continued fight for an adequate trans-Sierra route into northern California, 1844 to...1952. [n.p., 1952] [4] p. illus.   CHi

6304. —— —— By-laws and constitution. [n.p., n.d.] [4] p.   CHi

6305. —— **Ordinances, etc.** License ordinances of Placer county passed by the Board of supervisors, January 11, 1905... Auburn, Herald print., 1905. [23] p.
      CHi

6306. —— **Superintendent of schools.** Centennial handbook, 1848–1950, Placer county and California. [1948] 105 p.   CHi

6307. —— —— Second annual report. S.F., Waters bros. & co., 1863. 48 p. Includes proceedings of the county teachers' convention and a history of each school district in Placer county, ed. by A. H. Goodrich.   C

6308. Placer county agricultural training college, Penryn. Prospectus and letters from distinguished Californians and English members of the Placer county citrus colony and miscellanea. [Lond., T. Pettitt & co., print., 1894?] 24, 35 p. illus., map.   CU-B

6309. Placer county citrus colony. Placer county citrus colony in the lower foothills of Placer county, California. S.F., Crocker, 1889. 24 p. illus.
      CHi   CSf   CU-B

6310. Placer county historical society. Placer nuggets. [Auburn, 1956–] 1 v. irregular (unnumbered and undated)   C   CHi

6311. [Placer county immigration society] Placer county, Calif. Its resources and advantages... [Auburn? 1886?] 38 p. map.
      C   CLU   CSmH   CU-B

6312. The Placer herald. Centennial edition. Auburn, Sept. 12, 1952. 1 v. illus., ports., maps, facsims.
      CHi   CO

6313. Placer-Nevada-Sierra county medical society. Constitution and by-laws...amended and re-adopted, Feb. 14, 1903. Scrapbook 91.   C

6314. —— Records...1889–1927. Scrapbook 90.   C

6315. Power, Bertha (Knight) comp. William Henry Knight, California pioneer. [N.Y.] Priv. print., 1932. 252 p. illus., ports., map.
      C   CBb   CHi   CL   CLSU   CLU   CO   CSf   CSfCW CSmH   CU-B

6316. Robie, Wendell T. The history of Placer county and the Auburn area. Auburn, 1958. 8 p.   CHi

6317. Sacramento, Placer and Nevada railroad co. To the voters of Placer county. [n.p., n.d.] 16 p. At end of p. 16: Approved April 30th, 1860.   CU

6318. Scott, Edward B. Squaw Valley. A photographic historical of the Squaw Valley-Sierra Nevada region. Crystal Bay, Lake Tahoe, Nevada, Sierra-Tahoe pub. co., 1960. 88 p. illus., ports., maps.
  CAla CLgA CRedCL CSf CSfSC

6319. Shepard, W. A., comp. and pub. Resources of Placer county, California. Issued upon the authority of the Placer county improvement and development association and the Board of supervisors. Auburn, 1904. [24] p.
  CHi CSmH CU-B

6320. Stretch, Richard Harper. Report of Prof. R. H. Stretch on Iowa Hill canal and gravel mines, Placer county, Calif. N.Y., 1879. 34 p.   C

6321. Taylor, Isaac M. Report on the Dutch Flat blue gravel mining co's property. [S.F., Waters & co., print., 187–?] 14 p. illus., (fold. map)   CLU

6322. Williams, Emma. Main street, Dutch Flat. [Dutch Flat?] 1953. 3 l.   CU-B

Auburn

6323. Auburn. Auburn school. Third annual graduating exercises...at the Auburn opera house, Friday, June 23, 1893. [n.p., Argus print., 1893] [4] p.   CHi

6324. —— Chamber of commerce. Classified business and professional Auburn area directory. [Auburn, 1949] 32 p. illus.   CHi

6325. —— —— Official souvenir program, the gold rush revival June 6–8, 1947. Auburn, c1947. [35] p. illus.   CHi

6326. —— Pioneer Methodist church. The centennial of the Pioneer Methodist church, Auburn, California, June 6, 1852 to June 1, 1952... [Auburn, D. S. Loughlin, 1952] [36] p. illus., ports.   C

6327. —— —— Pioneer Methodist church, Auburn, California, 1955. [Auburn, 1955] 12 p. illus.   CHi

6328. —— Sierra normal college. Commencement exercises... [n.p., 1895] [3] l.   CHi

6329. Auburn blue book. Comp. by Mrs. P. T. Smith, Mrs. Earl Lukens [and] Mrs. D. W. Lubeck. [Auburn, Republican press, 1913] 141 p. illus.
  C CAuP CHi CSf

6330. Auburn '49er association. Auburn California centennial; [the story of the gold discovery centennial] Auburn, 1948. [26] p. illus.   CHi

6331. Auburn Saturday club. Season of 1906 [officers, program, membership list] [Auburn, Placer county Republican, 1906] 16 p. Organized 1904.   CHi

6332. Davis, Leonard M. A story of an early California mining camp—Auburn, 1848–51. [Sacramento, 1953] 171 p. Thesis (M.A.)—Sacramento state college, 1953.   C CSS

6333. Placer county leader, pub. Picturesque Auburn. Special souvenir edition, Tuesday, May 8, 1900. Auburn, 1900. [12] p. illus., ports.   CHi CSmH

Lake Tahoe

6334. Bowe, Richard J., ed. Historical album: Lake Tahoe region. [n.p., n.d.] unp. (chiefly illus.), map.   CL

6335. James, George Wharton. The lake of the sky, Lake Tahoe...its history, Indians [etc., etc.] with a full account of the Tahoe national forest, the public use of the water of Lake Tahoe and much other interesting matter. Pasadena, Author, c1915. 395 p. illus. Other editions followed.
  Available in many libraries.

6336. MacDonald, Claire. Lake Tahoe, California. [Mount Vernon, N.Y.] Priv. print. for Claire MacDonald [by W. E. Rudge, c1929] 30 p. illus.   C CHi CSfCW

6337. McKeon, Owen F. The railroads and steamers of Lake Tahoe. San Mateo [1946] 22 p. (*Western railroader* v.9, no. 5, March, 1946)   CHi CRcS

6338. Price, Bertha de L., comp. Legends of Tahoe. [n.p., n.d.] unp.   CHi CSd CU-B

6339. Scott, Edward B. The saga of Lake Tahoe; a complete documentation of Lake Tahoe's development over the last one hundred years. [1st ed. Crystal Bay, Nev., Sierra-Tahoe pub. co., 1957] 515 p. illus. Includes bibliography.
  Available in many libraries.

6340. Southern Pacific co. Lake Tahoe, California. S.F. [n.d.]   C
  Other editions followed.   CHi (1912) CRcS (1930)

6341. Tahoe tattler (newspaper). The story of Lake Tahoe. [Tahoe City, 1941] 15 p. illus.   C CHi

6342. Warriner, John. Lake Tahoe; an illustrated guide and history. S.F., Fearon, c1958. 60 p. illus.
  C CAla CAuP CLU CNa CO COr CP CRic CSd CSfSt CStmo

6343. Waymire, James A. Lake Tahoe and Truckee river water supply, distribution of interstate waters. Oakland, Jordan print. co., 1908. 21 p.   C

PLUMAS COUNTY
(Created in 1854 from portion of Butte county)

COUNTY HISTORIES

6344. Fariss & Smith, pub. Illustrated history of Plumas, Lassen & Sierra counties... S.F., 1882. 507 p. illus., ports., map.
  C CAltu CCH CChi CHi CL CLU CO CP CQCL CSS CSf CSfCP CSfCSM CSmH CStoC CSuLas CU-B CoD CtY NN NvHi

GREAT REGISTER

6345. Plumas county. Index to the Great register of the county of Plumas. 1866– Place of publication and title vary.
  C has 1867, 1868, 1871, 1872, 1875–77, 1879–80, 1884 (biennially to) – 1962. CHi has 1871, 1898, 1902. CL has 1867, 1868 (suppl.), 1872–73, 1876–77, 1879, 1880 (biennially to) – 1888. CSmH has 1882. CU-B has July 1867, Sept. 26, 1868 (suppl.), 1871–73, 1879–80, 1882.

GENERAL REFERENCES

6346. Alta California, inc., comp. & pub. Plumas county...a general and historical summary... Sacramento [1938?] 13 l. Reproduced from typew. copy.
  CU-B

6347. Beckwourth, James P. The life and adventures of James P. Beckwourth, mountaineer, scout, and pioneer...Written from his own dictation, by T. D. Bonner. N.Y., Harper, 1856. 537 p. illus., port.
  C CBb CBu CChiS CHi CL CLU CSdU CSf CSfCW CSfWF-H CSmH CStrJC CU-B CaBViPA

6348. —— Same. 1858. Other editions followed.
CHi CLSU

6349. Blake, William Phipps. Report on the Green mountain gold mine...with a letter to the stockholders ...by H. C. Bidwell, president, New York, March 1st, 1880. [N.Y., Dennison & Brown, print., 1880] 11 p. front., plan.   CHi CLU

6350. [Carlisle, A., and co., S.F.] Plumas, the recreation county... [S.F., 1927?] [32] p. illus.
CHi CL CRcS CSmH CU-B

6351. Chapman's magazine, Berkeley. Plumas county. (In v. 1, no. 2, p. 26–44 [1941?])   CChiS CO

6352. Cherokee gold mining co. The Cherokee gold mining company of California. Incorporated under the general laws of the state of New York. Mines and mills of the company located in Plumas county, California. N.Y., Dennison & Brown, print., 1880. 14 p.   CHi

6353. Clappe, Louise Amelia Knapp (Smith) The Shirley letters from California mines in 1851–52; being a series of twenty-three letters from Dame Shirley [pseud.]...now reprinted from the *Pioneer magazine* of 1854–55... S.F., Thomas C. Russell, 1922. 350 p. illus.
C CAna CHi CL CLSU CLU CLgA CMont CP CRic CSfCP CSfP CSmH CStmo CStrJC CU-B CaBViPA

6354. —— California in 1851–[1852]; the letters of Dame Shirley [pseud.]; introduction and notes by Carl I. Wheat. S.F., Grabhorn, 1933. 2 v. (Rare Americana series. no. 5–6)
Available in many California libraries and ViU

6355. —— The Shirley letters from the California mines, 1851–52; with an introd. and notes by Carl I. Wheat. N.Y., Knopf, 1949. 216 p. illus., map (on lining-papers) (Western Americana...)
Available in many California libraries and MiD MoS OrU UHi ViU WM

6356. Dressler, Albert. California's pioneer mountaineer of Rabbit Creek; John Thomas Mason's meanderings in the out of the way places of the western wilds... S.F., Author, 1930. 72 p. illus., map.
C CBb CHi CL CLSU CLU CMont CO CRcS CRedCL CSS CSd CSfP CSfWF-H CSmH CStrJC CU-B CoD IHi

6357. Feather river inn, Blairsden. [Brochure. N.Y., Munro & Harford co., 1927?] [20] p.   CHi

6358. Gold stripe mining co. of California. [Statement to the stockholders] [N.Y., Dennison & Brown, print., 1880] 11 p. illus., map.   CHi

6359. Hahn, Campbell & associates, Burlingame. A survey of resources, Plumas county, California, prepared for the Board of supervisors and County planning commission. Burlingame [1949] 69 l. illus., maps.   CO

6360. Hutchinson, William Henry. Tales of pioneer Plumas county. Centennial edition. Quincy, Plumas county fair [1954] 32 p.   C CQCL

6361. Jackson, William Turrentine. A history of mining in the Plumas Eureka state park area, 1851–90. Prepared for the Division of beaches and parks, state of California, Oct. 1960. 56 p. processed.   C CHi

6362. —— Same, 1890–1943. Prepared...February, 1961. 48 p. Mimeo.   CHi

6363. Odd fellows, Independent order of. Plumas co. Constitution and by-laws of Olive branch encampment, no. 9, I. O. of O. F., La Porte, Plumas co., Cal. ... S.F., Joseph Winterburn & co., 1868. 35 p.   C

6364. Pacific planning and research. General plan

Plumas county, California. [Sacramento] 1959. 75 p. col. maps, tables.   C

6365. Plumas county. Board of supervisors. Plumas county, Calif. [Sacramento, News pub. co., 1914?] 22 p. illus., map.   CLU

6366. —— —— Same. Quincy [1937?] 3 p. illus., map.   CRcS

6367. —— —— Plumas; the recreation county. [S.F., 1927?] [30] p. illus.   CHi

6368. —— —— Scenic Plumas county, California, the Feather river county. [Quincy, 194–?] 7 p. maps.
CRcS

6369. —— **Chamber of commerce.** Plumas facts. [Quincy?] The Feather river bul., 1938. 13 p. map.
CRcS

6370. Plumas county historical society. Publications. no. 1– 1960– Mimeo. Contents: no. 1. Pioneering ranching, Early doctor, Place names, Brief review of Plumas beginnings.—no. 2. General history of Sierra valley.—no. 3. Over the snow on the long boards! Early days in the Johnsville mining area. Eureka mills vs. Jamison city. —no. 4. The ranches of Indian valley, Some early schoolmarms, The Round valley dams.—no. 5. Plumas national forest, Early days in Humbug valley and Yellow creek, Meadow valley's past. — no. 6. $93 million in bullion shipped. The life and times of La Porte. The naming of Whiskey creek. La Porte school. Gibsonville.   CStrJC

6371. Plumas county publishing co. Plumas county, California; its mineral, forest, agricultural & other resources, an ideal summer resort. [Quincy? 1902] 50 p. illus., map.   CHi

6372. Plumas-Sierra historical association. Annual report. 1st– 1941– Reproduced from typew. copy.
C

6373. Smith, Gerald Grogan. The Feather river highway, 1851–1937... [Berkeley, 1937] 81 l. map. Typew. Thesis (M.A.)—Univ. of Calif., 1947.   CU-B

6374. Stanford research institute. Industrial development possibilities in the Feather river area of California; final report prepared for Western Pacific railroad company. [Menlo Park] 1956. 94 p. maps, tabs., diagrs. (SRI project, 1-1743)   CSfSt

6375. Stretch, R. H. The Laporte gold gravel mines, limited, Plumas county, California. Report...estimate of profits. Glasgow, McCorquodale & co., ltd., 1882. 31 p. illus., fold. maps.   CHi

6376. Torrey, Harriet (Ford) Just between ourselves; a book of recollections of my father, James Ford, written for the family... [n.p., 1947?] 60 l. Reproduced from typew. copy. Account of pioneer life in Plumas county.   C

6377. Ward, Harriet (Sherrill) Prairie schooner lady; the journal of Harriet Sherrill Ward, 1853, as presented by Ward G. DeWitt and Florence Stark DeWitt. L.A., Westernlore press, c1959. 180 p. illus. (Great west and Indian ser. 16)
CBb (also typew. copy of original diary) CHi CQCL CSalCL CSd CSdS

RIVERSIDE COUNTY

(Created in 1893 from portions of San Diego and San Bernardino counties)

COUNTY HISTORIES

6378. Gabbert, John Raymond. History of Riverside city and county... Phoenix, Ariz., Riverside record pub. co., 1935. 615 p. illus., ports.

C CHi CL CLAC CLCM CLCo CLob CPs CRiv CSmH CSta CU-B NN WHi

6379. Holmes, Elmer Wallace, and others. History of Riverside county, California, with biographical sketches... L.A., Historic record co., 1912. 783 p. illus., ports.

C CBea CCH CF CHi CL CLCo CLO CLSU CLU CRiv CSd CSf CSjC CSmH CStoC CU-B CaBViPA MWA NN WHi

6380. Paul, Arthur G., ed. Riverside community book. Riverside, Cawston, 1954. 496 p. illus., ports., maps.   C CHi CL CLU CO CPom CPs CU-B

GREAT REGISTER

6381. Riverside county. Index to the Great register of the county of Riverside. 1894–

C has 1900 (biennially to)– 1962. CSmH has [1896], 1900, 1910–12. CU-B has 1906, 1912 (primary), 1916–18, 1922, 1930–34, 1938–44, 1948.

DIRECTORIES

6382. 1893. Cornell, D. A., pub. Riverside directory...A full and complete general and business directory... Riverside, Daily press print., 1893.   CSmH

6383. 1897/98. Bushnell, A. M., & co., pub. Riverside city and county directory, 1897/98. Riverside, 1897. illus.   CSmH

Riverside

6384. 1905–1951. Los Angeles directory co., pub. Riverside city directory... L.A., 1905–51. Publisher varies: 1905–21 Riverside directory co. Content varies: 1908–14 Riverside city and county, Corona, Hemet and San Jacinto; 1915–17 Riverside city and county, Corona, Elsinore, Hemet, Perris and San Jacinto; 1918/19 Riverside directory including San Jacinto and Hemet.

C has 1912, 1913, 1923, 1927, 1929–34, 1937. CHi has 1930, 1933–34, 1937, 1939, 1941, 1947, 1949, 1951. CL has 1912–13, 1915–16, 1918–19, 1921, 1923, 1925, 1927, 1929, 1931–32, 1933–34, 1936–37, 1941–42, 1947, 1951, 1960. CU-B has 1927, 1941.

6385. 1952– Luskey bros., pub. Riverside criss cross city directory, including Anza Village, Arlington, Glen Avon, Highgrove, La Sierra, La Sierra heights, Pedley, Sunnyslope, West Riverside. Santa Ana, 1952– CHi has 1952. CL has 1960.

Other Cities and Towns

6386. 1959– Luskey bros., pub. Luskey's official Coachella valley criss cross directory... Anaheim, 1959– CL has 1959, 1961.

6387. 1924– Corona city directory. Publisher and title vary.
CL has 1924, 1927, 1939, 1944, 1961.

6388. 1938/39– Palm Springs city directory. Publisher and title vary.
CL has 1946/47, 1948/49, 1950–51, 1954. CPs has 1938/39, 1939/40, 1941/42, 1944/45, 1946/47, 1948/49, 1950–51, 1953, 1955–60.

6389. 1956– Luskey bros., pub. Luskey's San Gorgonio pass criss cross city directory. Santa Ana, 1956– CL has 1956, 1959.

GENERAL REFERENCES

6390. Agua Caliente band of mission Indians. Annual progress report. v.1, 1952– Palm Springs [1953– illus., maps.
CU-B has v.1, no. 1, 1952.

6391. Ainsworth, Edward Maddin. Five acres of heaven; presented by Col. E. B. Moore and Mrs. Marion U. Moore of Joshua Tree, California, to all those who love the desert. [L.A., Boelter lithography] c1955. 30 p. illus. (part col.)
    CHi CL CMon CO CSf CStmo TMC

6392. —— Painters of the desert... Palm Desert, Desert mag. press, 1960 [i.e. 1961] 111 p. illus. (part col.) ports.   CLSM

6393. American association of university women. China Lake branch. Indian Wells valley handbook. [Ridgecrest, Hubbard print., c1953] 89 p. illus., map. Bibliography: p. 87–89.   CO

6394. —— —— Same. 3d ed. 1960. 87 p. illus. CHi

6395. Banning herald. Banning, Calif. [Banning, 1889?] cover title. 23 p.   CoD

6396. Beaumont. Chamber of commerce. Beaumont, Riverside county, California. [Beaumont, Beaumont gazette, 1939?] [7] p. illus., map.   CHi

6397. [Blair, Montgomery] Sobrante San Jacinto viego [!] and nuevo survey. Argument for setting aside this survey on behalf of John Greenwade, Abel Stearns, Madame Serrano, and other citizens of San Bernardino county, California. [Wash., D.C., 1867?] 36 p. Signed: M. Blair, F. A. Dick, of counsel for the contestants. Land in Riverside county.   CLU

6398. Blossom, Herbert Henry. The agricultural development of the Coachella valley, California. [Berkeley, 1959] Thesis (M.A.)— Univ. of Calif., 1959.   CU

6399. Bowers, Stephen. A remarkable valley and an interesting tribe of Indians. San Buena Ventura, 1888. 7 p. On cover: The Conchilla valley and the Cahuilla Indians. Deals with the Coachella valley.   CLU

6400. Bridge, Norman. California's Alps, the Idyllwild sanatorium (Strawberry valley)... [n.p., 1901?] 20 p. illus.   CHi CU-B

6401. California teachers' association. Addresses delivered before the California teachers' association, at Riverside, December 28–31, 1891, by professors in the University of California. Berkeley, 1892. 74 p. (Univ. bul. no. 37)   CHi

6402. Clark, Miles. The original Desert almanac. 2d ed. Containing useful information and interesting facts of the desert of America, especially the Colorado desert of southern California with particular attention to the Coachella valley. Northridge, Northridge press, c1957. 72 p. illus.   C CLU

6403. Coachella valley county water district. Official statement on water problems of the Coachella valley. [n.p.] 1932. 14 p.   CHi

6404. Collier, William, and Graham, D.M. Elsinore, a home in southern California. L.A., Times-mirror print., 1885. 16 p. map.   CSmH CU-B

6405. The Corona independent. Progress achievement number. [June 1915] Corona [1915] [28] p. illus., ports.   CU-B

6406. Corona publishing co. Corona, California, the queen colony, illustrated. Corona, 1902. unp. illus.   CSf

6407. Desert bank, Indio. Coachella valley where water is king. [n.p., 1950?] [12] p.   CHi

6408. Development company of Riverside. Co-operative ranching with irrigated crops in southern California: oranges, lemons [and] cotton. [Riverside, 19—?] [24] p. illus.   CU-B

6409. Graham, Donald M. Elsinore, a new colony in southern California. Its history, location, climate... L.A., Times-mirror print., 1884. 26 p.   CSmH

6410. Hall, William Hammond. Alessandro irrigation district, California; its physical, engineering and business problems and conditions... S.F., Bacon & co., 1891. 72 p. illus., maps.   C CHi CLU

6411. —— Perris irrigation district, California: its physical, engineering and business problems and conditions... S.F., Bacon & co., 1891. 75 p. maps, illus.
                                        C CHi CLU NHi

6412. Hemet, California. City of Hemet, Riverside county, state of California, golden anniversary year, 1910-1960. [Hemet, 1960] [28] p. illus., ports., map, facsims.   CHi CU-B

6413. Hemet news. 50th anniversary supplement. Sept. 15, 1960. Hemet, 1960.   CHi

6414. —— Ramona play edition, April 19, 1940. Hemet, 1940. 50 p. illus., ports. Includes information about Hemet and San Jacinto.   C

6415. Hill, Robert T. Report on oil prospects at Beaumont, California...Dec., 1929. 9 p. map. Typew.
                                                       CBea

6416. Hoyt, Franklyn. The Bradshaw road (Riverside county) Reprinted from *Pac. hist. review*, v.XXI, no. 3, Aug. 1952.   CPs

6417. —— A history of the desert region of Riverside county from 1540 to the completion of the railroad to Yuma in 1877. [L.A.] 1948. 93 p. map. Typew. Thesis (M.A.)— Univ. of So. Calif., 1948
CBea (microfilm) CPs

6418. Hughes, Tom. History of Banning and San Gorgonio pass... [Banning] Banning record print. [1938?] 213 p. illus., ports.   C CBea CLU CPs

6419. Indio; its climate and resources. [n.p., 1888?] 26 p. illus.   CU-B

6420. Industrial survey associates. Riverside county, its present and future economic development; prepared for the Riverside county Board of trade. S.F., 1952. 87 l. illus., maps.   C

6421. James, Harry C. The Cahuilla Indians. L.A., Westernlore press, 1960. 185 p. illus. (Great west and Indian ser., 18)   CBea CSf

6422. Lakeview land co., Pasadena. [Profitable homes, Riverside county. S.F., Kingsley-Barnes & Neuner co., 1895] [31] p. fold. map.   CHi

6423. Legends and history of the San Jacinto mountains. Long Beach, c1926. 21 p. illus.   CLU

6424. McAdams, Henry E. Early history of the San Gorgonio pass gateway to California. L.A., 1955. 327 p. maps. Typew. Thesis (M.A.)—Univ. of So. Calif., 1955.
                                                      CBea

6425. McCown, B. E. Temeku; a page from the history of the Luiseno Indians. [n.p.] Archaelogical survey assoc. of So. Calif., 1955. 97 p. 27 pl.   CHi CSd

6426. McEuen, Virgil. The beginnings and organization of Riverside county... [L.A.] 1919. 71 p. Mimeo. Thesis, Univ. of So. California, 1919.   CL CLSU

6427. McMullen, Leon Russell. Two gateways of southern California: San Carlos pass and Cajón pass, 1772-1883. [Berkeley, 1932] 111 l. illus., maps. Thesis (M.A.)— Univ. of Calif., 1932.   CU CU-B

6428. Mahud, Tawfik Hassan. Processing and marketing aspects of the date industry in the Coachella valley, California. [L.A.] 1958. Thesis (M.A.)— U.C.L.A., 1958.   CLU

6429. [Maulsby, F. R.] Beaumont, Riverside county, California; issued by Sunset mag. homeseekers' bur. for the Beaumont Board of trade... [S.F., 1918?] 12 p. illus.   CBea CHi CU-B

6430. Mecca land co. Mecca, California. [L.A., Baumgardt pub. co., 1904?] 48 p. illus.
                                        CHi CL CU-B NN

6431. Palo Verde valley chamber of commerce, Blythe. Palo Verde valley. [Blythe, 1943] 16 p. illus., ports.   CU-B

6432. —— Palo Verde valley, California, fastest growing farming community... [Blythe, 194-?] [20] p. illus.   CU-B

6433. Pease, Robert W. Problems of recreational land use of the Elsinore basin of southern California. [L.A.] 1946. Thesis (M.A.)— U.C.L.A., 1946.   CLU

6434. Perris. Chamber of commerce. Perris valley, a homeland... Perris [1912?] 16 p. illus., map.
                                                       CHi

6435. Renié, Jack Joseph. New Renié pocket atlas of Riverside and San Bernardino counties and cities, and maps of Hoover dam and Las Vegas, Nevada; also Imperial valley and cities. [Premier, 1st ed.] L.A., Calif. map co. [1947] 152 p.   CHi CRedl

6436. Riverside, California, the home of the orange; a general historical, statistical and descriptive review of Riverside county... L.A., Ledger pub. co. [n.d.] 74 p. illus., map.   C

6437. Riverside county. Board of supervisors. Riverside county, California. [Issued by the Board of supervisors and the Chamber of commerce.] [Riverside, Mission print shop, n.d.] [29] p. illus.   CHi CU-B

6438. —— —— Same. Riverside, Press print. co. [1913?] 31 p.   CLU

6439. —— —— Same. Riverside, Chamber of commerce, 1930. 11 p. illus., map.   CRcS

6440. —— **Board of trade.** Riverside county, California. Its productions, resources and advantages as a place of residence and of profitable investment... Riverside, Daily press print. house, 1894. 47 p.   CSmH

6441. —— **Chamber of commerce.** Riverside county, California, an agricultural empire... [Riverside, Rubidoux print. co., 1946?] [32] p.   CHi

6442. —— **Planning commission.** Planning, Riverside county California, 1930-1960. Riverside [1960] 52 p.   CL

6443. Riverside county, California. [Riverside, Cloister print shop, M. J. Westerfield, 1914?] [32] p. illus.
                                        CHi CSmH CU-B

6444. Riverside daily press. Golden anniversary; 50 years of Riverside county, California. [Riverside, 1943] [166] p. illus., ports.   CU-B

6445. Riverside reflex. v.1-2. May 7, 1892–Apr. 29, 1893. Riverside, 1892–93. 2 v. illus., ports.
                                                  CL CU-B

6446. Robinson, William Wilcox. The story of Riverside county. Riverside, Riverside title co., c1957. 52 p. illus., ports., fold. map.
C CAla CHi CL CLO CLSM CLU CO CP CSd CSluCL CU-B

6447. Shumway, Nina (Paul) Your desert and

mine, with an introduction by Harold O. Weight. L.A., Westernlore press, 1960. 322 p. illus.   CSf CU-B

6448. The Temecula valley and its surroundings, including Murrietta, Linda Rosa, Rosita and the Pauba valley, San Diego county, California. [San Diego? 1887?] 16 p.   CLU

6449. Thompson, John. Settlement geography of San Gorgonio pass, southern California. [Berkeley, 1951] Thesis (M.A.)— Univ. of Calif., 1951.   CU

6450. Varcoe, (Wm.) & co., comp. Elsinore, San Diego co., Cal. [S.F., W. W. Elliott, lith., 1887] illus.
                                                        CSmH

6451. Walker, David H. Palo Verde valley, California... S. F., Sunset mag. homeseekers' bur. [1911?] 31 p. illus.   CU-B

6452. Whittington, Roberta E. Hemet-San Jacinto. [L.A.] 1951. Thesis (M.A.)— U.C.L.A., 1951.   CLU

6453. Woodward, Lois Ann. ...Mount San Jacinto ... Berkeley, 1937. 36 l. Typew.   CU-B

Palm Springs

6454. Admiral, Don. Palm Springs desert area and vicinity. Palm Springs, Desert Sun [n.d.] 31 p. illus., maps.   CLU

6455. Bourne, Arthur Ross. Some major aspects of the historical development of Palm Springs between 1880 and 1938, and in addition a continuation of the historical changes in the Indian land problem and four cultural institutions until 1948. [L.A.] 1953. 135 l. Typew. Thesis (M.A.)— Occidental college, 1953.   CLO

6456. Chase, Joseph Smeaton. Our Araby: Palm Springs and the Garden of the sun... Pasadena, Print. for J. S. Chase by Star-news pub. co., 1920. 83 p. illus., map.
C CBea CHi CL CLO CLU COnC CPom CRedl CSd CSf CSmH CStmo CU-B NN

6457. —— Same. New ed., rev. and enl. N.Y., J. J. Little & Ives co., 1923. 112 p. illus.
C CBb CL CPs CRedl CSdS CSf NN

6458. Desert inn. Palm Springs, California. [n.p., 1933] 34 p. illus., maps.   CSf

6459. —— Sands of time. [Palm Springs, 193–?] [32] p. illus., map.   CU-B

6460. Jensen, Thomas A. Palm Springs, California: its evolution and functions. [L.A.] 1954. 221 p. illus., maps. Thesis (M.A.)—U.C.L.A., 1953.   CLU CPs

6461. Jewish community center. ...Dedication book, 1951. [n.p., 1951] 92 p. illus.   CHi

6462. Lloyd, Elwood. Enchanted sands. The early history of Palm Springs... [L.A., Arthur H. Steake, c1939] 58 p. illus.   C CSd

6463. Nelson, Jack. History of Palm Springs. From *Palm Springs villager*, Feb.–May/June 1948. Loose-leaf.
                                                        CPs

6464. Palm Springs area; yearbook. 1953. Palm Springs, F. H. Scott, c1953. illus. (part col.), ports., maps. (Western resort pub.)   C CL

6465. Palm Springs life. Palm Springs, Chaffey co., inc. [1936?] 79 p. illus.   CHi

6466. Patencio, Francisco. Stories and legends of the Palm Springs Indians, by chief Francisco Patencio, as told to Margaret Boynton. L.A., Times-mirror [1943] 132 p.   CLU CPs

6467. Richards, Elizabeth W. A look into Palm

Springs' past. Palm Springs, Santa Fe federal savings and loan assoc. [1961?] 39 p. illus.   CHi

6468. Romero, Jose. (The letter of Captain Jose Romero dated January 16, 1824 at Los Veranitos de los Cahahagullas [believed to be what is now Palm Springs]) Typew. Transcription of the letter in Spanish and translation in English; description of events concerning the writing of the letter; several letters bearing on the authenticity of Romero's letter.   CPs

6469. U.S. Congress. Senate. Committee on Indian affairs. Palm Springs band of mission Indians. Hearing[s]...on S. 1424...and S. 2589... October 24, 1935, April 6, 1936, July 6, 29, and August 16, 1937... Wash., D.C., Govt. print. off., 1937. 279 p. maps.
                                                        CU-B

6470. Wheeler, George O., comp. The story of Palm Springs tramway, eighth wonder of the world! An informative authentic summary of 10 years planning and an investment to date of $200,000. Palm Springs, Village pub. co. [n.d.] 30 p. illus., ports., map.   CL

Riverside

6471. Benton, Arthur Burnett. The Mission inn ...the sketches by Wm. Alexander Sharp. [L.A., Segnogram pub. co.] c1907. 29 l.
                    C CHi CSdS CSfCW CSmH

6472. Bliven, Bruce O. Riverside, California... [S.F., Sunset homeseekers' bur., 1912?] 32 p. illus.
                                              CSmH CU-B

6473. [Chase, Ethan Allen] Celebration in honor of the eightieth birthday of Ethan Allen Chase of Riverside, California, at the Chase plantation, Corona, January the eighteenth, nineteen hundred and twelve. Riverside, Press print. co. [1912] 98 p. illus.   CHi

6474. Cottrell, Dorothy. A little chapel of memory. [Riverside, 1933?] [32] p. illus.   CHi

6475. Cundiff, Willard. Who's who in Riverside, California; a portfolio of proofs of men of affairs, from the original cartoons; comp. by L. G. Coop. L.A., Thorpe eng. co. [1908] 20 l. illus.   CHi CL CRiv CSmH

6476. The days of peace and rest at the Glenwood mission inn by those who know. East Aurora, N.Y., Roycrofters, 1907. 18 p.   CHi NN

6477. Easter sunrise pilgrimage to Father Serra cross Mount Rubidoux, Riverside, California, 1917– [Riverside, 1917–]
CHi has 1917, 1936. CSmH has 1919.

6478. Fiftieth anniversary of Riverside, California. Fairmount Park, Sept. 14th, 1920. Riverside daily press [1920?] 2 l.   CU-B

6479. Gale, Zona. Frank Miller of Mission inn. N.Y., London, Appleton-Century, 1938. 188 p. illus., ports.
Available in many libraries.

6480. Green, Earle M. Getting acquainted with your community; history and government of the city of Riverside. [Riverside?] Author, c1953. 107 p.
                                                    C CPs

6481. Hornbeck, Robert. Roubidoux's ranch in the 70's... Riverside, Riverside press print. co., 1913. 230 p. illus., ports. Founding of Riverside by "a colony for California"; biography of Judge J. W. North, instigator; early settlers and events.
C CHi CL CLO CLSU CLU CLob CPom CPs CRedl CRic CSd CSf CSmH CU-B CaBViPA KU MoHi MoSHi NN NjR UU

6482. Hutchings, DeWitt V. The story of Mount Rubidoux, Riverside, California... [Riverside, 1926?] 48 p. illus.   CHi CL CU-B

6483. Jordan, David Starr. California's Mission hotel, the Glenwood... [1905] [16] p.   NN

6484. Mission inn. The bells and crosses of the Glenwood mission inn, Riverside, California. [n.p., 1915] 63 p. illus.
CHi CL CLO CRcS CSd CSdS CSmH CU-B

6485. —— Same [and the Henry Chapman Ford paintings of the California missions], Riverside, California. [n.p., n.d.] 78 p. illus.   CHi

6486. —— Descriptive list of paintings and objects of art in the Spanish gallery of the Mission inn [by Francis S. Borton] [Riverside, 1920?] 30 p. illus.
CHi

6487. —— Handbook of the Glenwood mission inn. [Riverside, 1920?] 62 p. illus.   CHi
Other editions followed. 1926, 1929 edited by Francis S. Borton and DeWitt V. Hutchings. 1936, 1940, 1944 edited by DeWitt V. Hutchings.
C (n.d.) CHi (1926, 1929, 1940, 1944) CRcS (1936) CSmH (1940)

6488. Monterey and Los Angeles (Diocese). Ceremony of the blessing of the cross on Mount Rubidoux, Riverside, Cal., Friday, April 26, 1907. [Riverside, 1907] [7] p.   CSmH

6489. North, John G. Riverside, the fulfillment of a prophecy. [L.A., n.d.] [14] p. illus.
CLU CU-B NN

6490. Patterson, Tom. The beginnings of Riverside. [Riverside, Press-enterprise co., 1960] 12 p. illus., map.
CHi

6491. Picturesque Riverside, California. [Riverside, Press print. co., n.d.] 2 l., 35 pl.   CU-B

6492. Riverside. Chamber of commerce. Greeting and invitation from Riverside. The greatest orange growing district on earth. [Riverside, Press print. co., 19—] illus.   CSmH

6493. —— —— Riverside, California. [Riverside, Enterprise co., print., 1904?] 19 p. illus.   CHi CU-B

6494. —— **Charters.** Charter. [Riverside, 1929?] 81 p.   CLU

6495. Riverside daily press. Annual, New Year's 1890– Riverside, 1890–
CHi has 2nd, 1891. NHi has 9th, 1898.

6496. —— ... Prosperous Riverside edition... [Riverside, Press print. co.] 1907. 48 p. illus., ports. CU-B

6497. —— [Special number commemorating the 65th anniversary of the Mission inn, November 22, 1941] Riverside, 1941. 6, 8 p.   CCH CSmH

6498. Roe, James H. Notes on early history of Riverside, California...Copy made from the original notes in the local history collection of the Riverside public library. 1932. 95, 24 l. Typew.   CRiv

6499. Rudisill, H. J., comp. Riverside illustrated; a city among the orange groves. Its history, resources... [S.F., Crocker] 1889. 56 p. illus.   CHi CU-B

6500. San Pedro, Los Angeles and Salt Lake railroad. Riverside, the city beautiful. A brief description ...[3d ed.] L.A., 1908. [24] p. illus.   CU-B

6501. South Riverside land and water co. "Gem of the orange belt."...future prospects of South Riverside... Sioux City, Iowa, Sioux City engraving co. [1887] [24] p.   CSmH CU-B

6502. —— South Riverside and Auburndale... South Riverside, South Riverside bee job print [1890] [12] p.   CU-B

6503. Southern California colony association. Riverside colony. [Riverside, 1871] [4] p. Prefatory material signed by J. W. North, president and general agent...June 20th 1871.   CSmH

6504. [Taylor, R. B.] South Riverside, southern California. Sioux City, Iowa, Palmer, Naire & co. litho. [1887?] 10 l.   CSmH

6505. Tigner, J. H. Souvenir of the city of Riverside. L.A., 1906. illus. Published in the interest of the Riverside Fire department.   CLU CSmH

6506. Wallace, William Swilling. Antoine Robidoux, 1794–1860; a biography of a western venturer. L.A., Dawson, 1953. 59 p. (Early Calif. travels ser., 14) 450 copies printed by the Castle press.
CBb CLSM CLgA CP CRcS CSd CSjC CSto CU-B CVtV

6507. Ward bros., pub. Riverside and vicinity. Columbus, Ohio, c1887. [7] p. 15 pl.   CSmH CU-B

6508. West Riverside, California; facts and figures... [n.p., 1905?] [16] p. illus.   CU-B

SACRAMENTO COUNTY
(*Created in 1850*)

COUNTY HISTORIES

6509. Davis, Winfield J. An illustrated history of Sacramento county, California. Containing...biographical mention of many of its pioneers and also of prominent citizens of today... Chicago, Lewis, 1890. 808 p. illus., ports.
C C-S CAlaC CCH CHi CL CLSU CLU CLod CMont CO CS CSCL CSS CSf CSfCP CSfCW CSfMI CSmH CStoC CU-B CoD MiD-B MWA N NHi NN NvHi WHi

6510. Reed, G. Walter, ed. History of Sacramento county, California, with biographical sketches... L.A., Historic record co., 1923. 1004 p. illus., ports.
C CCH CHi CL CLAC CLCo CLO CLU CO CS CSCL CSS CSd CSf CSmH CSto CStrJC CU-B ICN MWA NN WHi

6511. Willis, William Ladd. History of Sacramento county, California, with biographical sketches... L.A., Historic record co., 1913. 1056 p. illus., ports. "Biographical": p. [427]–1056.
C CBb CF CHi CL CLCo CLO CLU CO CRic CS CSCL CSS CSd CSf CSmH CU-B CoD CtY MWA NN WHi

6512. [Wright, George F.] ed. History of Sacramento county, California... Oakland, Thompson & West, 1880. 294 p. illus., maps.
C CAla CBb CCH CHi CL CLAC CLU CMartC CN CS CSCL CSS CSf CSfCP CSfCW CSfWF-H CSmH CSt CSto CYcCL CoD NHi NN WHi

6513. —— Same. Reproduction...with introduction by Allan R. Ottley. Berkeley, Howell-North, 1960. [6] p., facsim., 294 p. illus., maps.
C CAla CAlaC CHi CLgA CMartC CNF CO CU-B

GREAT REGISTER

6514. Sacramento county. Index to the Great register of the county of Sacramento. 1866– Place of publication and title vary.

C has 1867–68, 1872–73, 1875–77, 1879–80, 1882, 1886 (biennially to)– 1892, 1896 (biennially to)– 1902, 1906 (biennially to)– 1936, 1940 (biennially to)– 1962. CL has 1873, 1876–77, 1879–80, 1882 (suppl.), 1884, 1886 (Addenda), 1888, 1890 (Addenda). CS has 1868, 1874–77, 1879–80, 1882, 1886, 1888, 1890, 1912 (2 vols.) CSmH has 1872, 1880, 1882. CU-B has 1867, 1868 (suppl.), 1871–73, 1879, 1880, 1898.

DIRECTORIES

6515. 1868–1869. Draper, R. E., comp. Sacramento city and county directory...1868, 1869. Sacramento, Crocker, print., 1868–69.

C C-S (1869) CHi CLU CS CSmH CU-B NHi (1868)

6516. 1879/80–1888/89. McKenney directory co., pub. Sacramento city and county directory. S.F., 1879–88. Content varies: 1879/80 includes Amador, Eldorado, Placer and Yolo counties. 1884/85 includes Amador, Eldorado and Placer counties.

C has 1879/80, 1884/85. C-S has 1879/80. CHi has 1884/85, 1888/89. CS has 1879/80, 1884/85, 1888/89. CSS has 1888/89. CSf has 1879/80. CSfCP has 1879/80, 1884/85. CSmH has 1879/80. CU-B has 1879/80, 1884/85.

6517. 1889/90–1911. Sacramento directory co., pub. ...Sacramento city and county directory. Sacramento, 1889–1911. Publisher varies: 1889/90–1899 F. M. Husted; 1900–02 Home directory co.; 1903–06 H. S. Crocker; 1907 Mrs. F. M. Husted.

C has 1889/90–1911. C-S has 1907–11. CHi has 1889/90, 1893, 1895, 1897–98, 1904, 1907–11. CS has 1889/90–1911. CSCL has 1889/90–1911. CSS has 1889/90, 1893, 1903, 1905–06, 1909–11. CSfCP has 1889/90–1911. CSfMI has 1908. CU-B has 1889/90–1911. MoS has 1898, 1907. MoSHi has 1907. NHi has 1898.

6518. 1891/92. Crocker, H. S., pub. Directory for Sacramento city and county... Sacramento, 1891. 664 p. C CS CSfU

6519. 1922– McNeel directory co. Sacramento county rural directory. Sacramento, Independent print. co., 1922– Title varies.

C has 1934, 1939, 1941. CS has 1932, 1934, 1939, 1941. CSCL has 1922.

6520. 1957– Sacramento directory co., pub. Sacramento suburban directory including Arden, Broderick, Carmichael, Del Paso Heights, Fair Oaks, Foothill Farms, North Highlands, North Sacramento, Town and Country, West Sacramento. L.A., 1957–

C has 1957, 1959. CHi has 1957, 1960–61. CL has 1957, 1959.

Citrus Heights

6521. 1933– Citrus Heights community club. Directory of residents in the Citrus Heights community. [Roseville, Tribune print., 1933]–

CHi has 1933, 1941.

Sacramento

6522. [185–?]–1856/57. Colville, Samuel, pub. Colville's Sacramento directory. Sacramento [185–?]– 1856. Title varies: 1853–54, The Sacramento directory, for the year 1853–54...together with a history of Sacramento, written by Dr. John F. Morse...

C has 1853/54–1855/56. C-S has 1854/55. CCH has 1855/56. CHi has 1854/55 (facsim.), 1855/56 (facsim.), 1856/57. CLU has 1854/55–1856/57. CS has 1853/54–1855/56. CSfCP has 1855/56–1856/57. CSmH has 1853/

54–1856/57. CU-B has 1854/55–1856/57. ICN has 1856/57. MWA has 1854/55, 1856/57. NHi has 1853/54, 1856/57. NN has 1856/57. WHi has 1856/57.

6523. 1851. Culver, J. Horace. The Sacramento city directory...January 1, 1851. Sacramento city, Transcript press, K st., between Second and Third, 1851. 96 p.

C CHi (facsim.) CS CSf CSmH

6524. 1857/58. Irwin, I. N., comp. Sacramento directory and gazetteer for the years 1857 and 1858... S.F., Print. by S. D. Valentine & son, 1857. 106 p.

C CHi CLU CS CSfCP CSmH CU-B ICN MWA NHi

6525. 1858/59. Taylor, L. S., comp. Taylor's Sacramento directory...1858–[59] Sacramento, Crocker, 1858. 78 p. C CLU CS ICN

6526. 1860. Cutter, D. S., & co., comp. & pub. Sacramento city directory, for the year A.D. 1860; being a complete general and business directory of the entire city, embracing an account of the city government...also, containing correct statistics of all the churches, Sunday schools, societies, courts, schools, fire departments; telegraph, express, rail road, stage and steamboat co's; also, the agricultural resources of the county... Sacramento, Crocker, 1859. 128 p.

C CHi (facsim.) CS CSmH CU-B MWA NHi NN

6527. 1861/62. Bidleman, H. J. The Sacramento directory... Sacramento, Crocker, 1861. 168 p.

C CS CU-B

6528. 1863/64. Mears, Leonard, comp. Mears' Sacramento directory... Sacramento, Print. by A. Badlam, 1863. 142 p. C CLU CS CSmH CU-B

6529. 1866. Draper, Robert E., comp., & pub. Sacramento directory for 1866... Sacramento, Crocker, 1866. 201 p. C CHi CS CSmH CU-B

6530. 1870. McKenney, L. M., comp. & pub. McKenney's Sacramento directory, for the year 1870... together with statistics, historical references and a large amount of general information appertaining to the city... Sacramento, Russell & Winterburn, steam bk. & job print. [n.d.] 332 p. C CHi CL CS CU-B

6531. 1871. Crocker, Henry Smith, pub. The Sacramento directory, for the year commencing January, 1871... together with the municipal government, societies and organizations, and a general variety of useful and statistical information... Sacramento, 1871. 432 p. map. "History of Sacramento," p. [9]–110. Note on page 4 states that it was compiled by Daniel J. Thomas.

C CHi CLU CS CSmH CU-B

6532. 1872–1887/88. —— Same [for the years 1872, 1873, 1874, 1875, 1876, 1878, 1880, 1881, 1883/84, 1885/86, 1887/88. Sacramento, 1872–87] Compiler varies: 1873–76 by John F. Uhlhorn; 1878 by Harry R. Lewis; 1881 and 1883/84 by L. M. McKenney.

C has 1872–1887/88. CHi has 1880, 1887/88. CS has 1872–1887/88. CU-B has 1873, 1876, 1883/84.

6533. 1880/81. Maxwell, J. J. Maxwell's directory of Sacramento, containing a complete directory of residents, including Washington, Yolo county... Comp. and pub. by Maxwell bros., Sacramento, 1880. 351 p. map. C

6534. 1882. Sacramento city directory...Also, a buyer's guide to the leading business houses of San Francisco. Oakland, Pac. press, 1882. 329 p. C CHi CS

6535. 1929/30. A to Z directory publishing co., pub. Sacramento business men's directory. Sacramento, 19—? CS

6536. 1949/50– News publishing co., pub. Sacramento and vicinity A.B.C. directory. Sacramento, 1949–
CS has 1949/50, 1951.

6537. 1912– Sacramento directory co., pub. Sacramento city directory...including Broderick and West Sacramento...Monterey Park, 1912– None published 1944, 1946, 1948, 1950, 1951, 1954.

C has 1912 to date.

C-S has 1912, 1914, 1918. CHi has 1912–18, 1920–22, 1925, 1927, 1930–31, 1938, 1941–58, 1960. CL has 1914, 1918, 1922, 1926–27, 1931, 1933, 1935, 1937, 1940–59, 1961. CO has 1954. CS has 1912 to date. CSCL has 1912 to date. CSS has 1912, 1925–27, 1929–49, 1955 to date. CSfCP has 1912 to date. CSfMI has 1915. CSmat has 1958–59. CU-B has 1912 to date. MoS has 1927.

General References

6538. Ackley, Mary E. Crossing the plains, and early days in California; memories of girlhood days in California's golden age. S.F., Priv. print., 1928. 68 p. illus.   CHi CS CSf CU-B

6539. Alviso, Blas P., vs. The United States. In the court of claims. no. 560...Brief of U.S. solicitor. Claim for property taken by Lt. Col. J. C. Frémont of the U.S. Army.   CHi

6540. —— ...Report in the case of Blas P. Alviso vs. the United States... [Wash., D.C., U.S. Govt. print. off.] 1860. 43 p. (U.S. 36th Cong., 1st sess. H. R. no. 229)   CSfCW

6541. American library association of California. Sacramento county in the heart of California. [1918?] unp. illus.   CS

6542. Better farming. Colony dept. Sunset colonies: Fair Oaks and Olive Park, in the heart of California. [issued by] Farm, field and fireside and western rural colony department. Chico [1894?] 49 p. illus., ports.   CU-B

6543. Black, Jack. The big break at Folsom, a story of the revolt of prison tyranny...with a sequel by the same author [entitled] Out of prison. [S.F., The Bulletin, n.d.] 71 p.   CHi

6544. Blenkle, Joe A. The story of Folsom Dam, Folsom, California; official souvenir program, Folsom Dam dedication. [Folsom, 1956] 31 p. illus.   C

6545. Book club of California, San Francisco. Pioneers of the Sacramento; a group of letters by & about Johann Augustus Sutter, James W. Marshall & John Bidwell. Introd. by Jane Grabhorn. S.F., 1953. 34 p. fold. col. map, facsim. "Limited to four hundred copies printed by Edwin & Robert Grabhorn for the Colt press, San Francisco."
CHi CL CLU CSCL CSalCL CSf CSfCSM CSfU CSjC CSto CStoC CaBViPA CoD KyU NHi

6546. Bovee, Toy & co., San Francisco. ...Grand special excursion to, and credit auction sale at, Natoma, Sacramento county, Saturday, Apr. 6, 1889... S.F., Crocker [1889] fold. map. Descriptive material printed on back of map.   CHi

6547. Bowman, Jacob N. Sutterville two years older than Sacramento, by J. M. [i.e. N.] Bowman, historian, California state archives. [Sacramento, 1952] (In *Sutterville* star. v.1, no. 1, Nov. 13, 1952, p. [1], 7)   CU-B

6548. Brainard, Sara Louise. A true and accurate account of the early transportation on the Sacramento river... [n.d.] 13 l. Typew.   C

6549. Bryan, W. H., ed. Souvenir of the capital of California; Sacramento city and county as seen through the camera... S.F., Stanley-Taylor co., 1901. 15 p. pl.
C CS CU-B NN

6550. —— Same. Sacramento, Record-Union and Weekly union, 1901. 15 p.   CSS CSmH

6551. Buckley and Taylor (firm). Abstract of title to the San Juan tract, Sacramento county, California, on which is located the Farm, field and fireside's Sunset colonies, Fair Oaks and Olive Park. [Sacramento, 1895] 45 p.   C

6552. Buckley-Gerger abstract and title co. Abstract of the title of Rancho del Paso...subdivided by Sacramento valley colonization co., Sacramento California. [Sacramento, 1910] 71 p. map.   C

6553. Carmichael co., Sacramento. Carmichael colony, in the heart of California. [1909?] [28] p. illus.
C

6554. —— Same. [Sacramento, n.d.] [28] p. illus.
C

6555. Catholic herald. Catholic directory of the diocese of Sacramento. Sacramento, 19–
CS has 1950, 1953–54, 1958–60.

6556. Central Pacific railroad co. The general railroad laws of California, the Pacific railroad act of Congress and the by-laws of the Central Pacific railroad company of California. Sacramento, H. S. Crocker & co., print., 1862. 104 p.   C CU-B

6557. —— Report of the chief engineer on the preliminary survey and cost of construction of the Central Pacific railroad of California across the Sierra Nevada mountains from Sacramento to the eastern boundary of California. Sacramento, October 1, 1861. [n.p., n.d.] 36 p. tables.   C CSmH CU CU-B WM

6558. —— Same, dated October 22, 1862. Sacramento, H. S. Crocker & co., print., 1862. 56 p. fold. map. "Estimated revenue" included in title.
C CLU CSfCW CSmH CU CU-B NvHi

6559. Codman, Winnifred R. [Miscellaneous papers] [Fair Oaks, 1950–] 1 v. v.p. Contains articles on wide variety of issues and subjects affecting the Fair Oaks area.   C

6560. Cole, Nellie May Henderson. Consolidation of Sacramento city and county government, 1853–63. Sacramento, 1958. 114 p. Typew. Thesis (M.A.)—Sacramento state college, 1958.   C CSS

6561. Cross, Lilian A. Sylvan recollections, a history of the Sylvan district, Sacramento county, California ... [Sacramento? c1943] 27 l. Mimeo.
C CHi CSmH CU-B

6562. Dana, Julian. The Sacramento, river of gold ... N.Y., Farrar & Rinehart, 1939. 294 p. illus. (Rivers of Am., ed. by Hervey Allen)
Available in many libraries.

6563. Davis, Winfield J. Sacramento county, California, its resources... Sacramento, Woodman & Hoey, print., 1905. 28 p. illus.
CSf CSfCSM CSmH CU-B

6564. Espinosa, Humberto José. Implications of the Folsom dam on the future development of the adjacent areas. [Berkeley, 1953] Thesis (M.A.)—Univ. of Calif., 1953.   CU

6565. Fair Oaks, California; the paradise of the fruit grower, health seeker and tourist. In the valley of the celebrated gold-bearing American river, fourteen miles from Sacramento. Sacramento, Fair Oaks development co., 1900. 41 p. illus., fold. maps.   C NN

6566. Fair Oaks Episcopal seminary. Circular...
3rd, 1869/70. [S.F., H. H. Bancroft & co., 1869] CU-B

6567. French, H. A., comp. Needs and commerce
of the Sacramento river; a memorial submitted to the
committee on rivers and harbors, House of representatives; U.S.; prepared by H. A. French under the authority
of the Chamber of commerce, Sacramento, Cal. Sacramento, J. M. Anderson, 1901. C

6568. Goethe, Charles Mathias. Indian tribes of
Sacramento county. [Sacramento, 1910] [10] p. Typew. C

6569. Goodman, John B. The Sacramento Placer
times, 1849–51. [L. A., 1950] [20] p. illus., facsim. "125
copies...printed...as a keepsake for the members of the
Zamorano club, Los Angeles." C CHi

6570. Greater north area chamber of commerce.
Who's who in the Greater north area, serving all of Sacramento county north of the American river. Classified
business-professional directory and alphabetical membership directory. North Sacramento, 1957–
CS has 1957.

6571. Guernsey, Frank A., comp. Chronological
history of state prison at Folsom. [Represa? Folsom state
prison] 1940. unp. Title-page: Calendar of highlights in
Folsom prison history. C

6572. Haub, C. W. Sacramento city and county,
California; the capital and the garden of an empire. [prepared for Sacramento county Board of supervisors] Sacramento, The News pub. co., 1907. 47 p. illus. CS

6573. Hearne bros., Detroit. Official Hearne
brothers polyconic projection maps of all of Sacramento
county. Constantly revised and kept up to date. [Detroit,
195–?] 1 v. (chiefly maps) C

6574. Immigration association of California. ...
Sacramento county. [S.F., 188–?] C CU-B

6575. Industrial survey associates. The economy
of the Sacramento area...and its potentials for industrial development. [S.F., 1951] 53 p. illus.
CO CS CSS

6576. Interurbans. ...Sacramento northern...
[L.A., 1951?] 47 p. illus., plans, facsims., diagrs. (Special no. 9) C CLO CS CSCL CYcCL

6577. League of woman voters of Sacramento.
Sacramento county government. Sacramento, 1955. 20 p.
CS

6578. Levick, M. B. Sacramento county, California.
S.F., Sunset mag. homeseekers' bur. [1911] 62 p. illus.,
map. CHi

6579. —— Same. 1915. 64 p.
CS CSCL CSfCP CU-B

6580. Lillard, Jeremiah Beverly. The archaeology
of the Deer Creek-Consumnes area, Sacramento co., California... Sacramento, Sacramento junior college, Bd.
of educ., 1936. 36 p. (Sacramento junior college. Dept.
of anthropology, bul. 1) C CSS

6581. Low, George P. The Folsom-Sacramento electric transmission plant. S.F., 1896. 14 p. illus. Photostat
(negative) "A revised reprint" from the *Jl. of electricity*,
v.1, no. 3, 1896. C

6582. Lyon & Hoag, pub. By the Sacramento's
waters... S.F. [1902?] [24] p. illus. CU-B

6583. McClatchy, Charles Kenny. Private thinks,
by C. K. N.Y., Scribner, 1936. Foreword by Senator
Hiram W. Johnson. CRcS

6584. Morse, John F., and Colville, Samuel. Illustrated historical sketches of California...together with
a more ample history of Sacramento valley and city, and
biographical references to prominent individuals... Sacramento, Print. at Democratic journal off., 1854. 46, 8 p.
illus. C CHi CL CLU CS CSmH CSt CU-B
ICN NN

6585. Natoma water and mining co., Folsom. Memorial of the Natoma water and mining company, to the
committees on state prison of the Senate and Assembly of
the state of California. [Sacramento, T. A. Springer, state
print., 1870] CSmH

6586. Peterson, Harry C. List of historic spots in
Sacramento county, 1930. [11] l. Mimeo. C

**6587. Protestant Episcopal church in the U.S.A.
Sacramento (Diocese)** Diocese of Sacramento. Constitution and canons, together with articles of incorporation and by-laws of the diocesans corporation and Trinity
cathedral church, etc. [Woodland, Mail of Woodland
print] 1930. 56 p. C

6588. Rancho Del Paso. Catalogue of thoroughbreds; stallions and brood mares. Property of J. B. Haggin
... [S.F., Hicks-Judd, 1891] 231 p. CHi

6589. Roberts, Wayne William. A history of early
Folsom California, from 1842–62. [Sacramento, 1954?]
104 l. Typew. Thesis (M.A.)—Sacramento state college,
1954. C CSS

6590. Sacramento bee. Sacramento county and its
resources... [Sacramento, J. McClatchy & co., 1894]
200 p. illus., ports., map. C CHi
CLU CS CSCL CSS CSfCW CSmH CU-B ICN

6591. —— Same. 2d ed. [Sacramento, J. McClatchy
& co., 1895] 198 p. illus., ports.
CHi CS CSmH CU-B NHi

6592. Sacramento county. Board of supervisors.
Resources of Sacramento county, California. [Sacramento, 1899] 23 p. illus. CU-B

6593. —— —— Sacramento county... [Sacramento? 1902?] 12 p. illus. CU-B

6594. —— —— Sacramento county...issued under
direction of the Board of supervisors and Exposition commissioners of Sacramento county... [Sacramento? Alvord & Young, 1915] 64 p. illus. Publisher varies.
CChiS CHi CLU CS CSS CU-B NN

6595. —— **Chamber of commerce.** Resources of
Sacramento county, California. 1901. 16 p. CU-B

6596. —— **City and county commissioner.** ...
Final report of...N. A. H. Ball, closing up affairs of the
city and county of Sacramento to date of consolidation
act. Sacramento, James Anthony & co., print., 1858. 16 p.
CSmH

6597. —— **Exposition commission.** Report...on
Sacramento county's participation in the Panama-Pacific
international exposition, held in San Francisco, and the
Panama-California exposition held in San Diego with
report of Sacramento valley exposition commissioners
appended and filed with the Board of supervisors of
Sacramento county. [Sacramento, 1916] 56 p. illus. C

6598. Sacramento abstract and title co. Abstract
of title to Aiken land in sections 4 and 5, township 8
north range 5 east Mount Diablo base and meridian
(Sutter grant) in the county of Sacramento state of California. [Sacramento] 1919. [300] l. maps. Typew. (part
in ms.) C

6599. Sacramento and Placerville railroad co.
Rules, regulations, classification and freight tariff, to take
effect July 1, 1880. [n.p., 1880?] 31 p. C

6600. Sacramento farm homestead association. Officers, certificate of incorporation, articles of association, and by-laws. Incorporated April 9th 1869. S.F., M. D. Carr & co., 1869. 15 p. fold. map.   CU-B

6601. Sacramento suburban fruit lands co. Romance and history of Rancho Del Paso, Sacramento, Calif. Minneapolis, Minn. [n.d.] 8 fold. p.   C

6602. Sacramento valley farms co. Live Oak and Sunset colonies. S.F. [n.d.] unp. illus., maps.   CSf

6603. Spaeth, Reuben Louis. Heinrich Lienhard in California, 1846–50. [Berkeley, 1933] 363 l. Thesis (M.A.)—Univ. of Calif., Dec. 1933.   CU CU-B

6604. Stanford research institute. Industrial potential of lands adjacent to the Sacramento-Yolo port and deep water channel, by Keith E. Duke. Menlo Park, 1959. 139 p. illus. (part fold.)   CS

6605. Stillman, Jacob David Babcock. Observations on the medical topography and diseases of the Sacramento valley, California, in the years 1849–50... N.Y., Print. by J. F. Trow, 1851. [19] p.   CU-B

6606. Thorpe, W. B. Sacramento city and county, California... Prepared by authority of the Board of supervisors of Sacramento county. Sacramento, News pub. co., 1906. 46 p.   CU-B

6607. U.S. District court. California (Northern district) ...The United States v. Henry Cambuston. No. 349. "Eleven leagues on the Sacramento river." Opinion of his honor Ogden Hoffman, district judge, rejecting the claim. S.F., Print. for the U.S., Daily national print., 1859. 32 p.   CLU CSmH CU-B

6608. Winter, Carl George, and Weber, J. Martin. Heart of California; Sacramento county then and now. Illustrations by Margaret C. Winter. S.F., Fearon, 1959. 106 p.   CSS

Sacramento

6609. Adams, McNeill & co. [Catalog of] Adams, McNeill & co., importers and wholesale grocers. Sacramento, 1879. 1 v. illus.   CU-B

6610. Agassiz institute. Proceedings...with the constitution and by-laws, and the names of the officers and members. Incorporated Nov. 12, 1872. Sacramento, E. G. Jeffries & co., 1872. 84 p. illus., fold. diagr.   C CSmH

6611. Agresti, Olivia Rossetti. David Lubin, a study in practical idealism. Bost., Little, 1922. 372 p.   CHi

6612. Arcade park co. By-laws. Sacramento [1910?] 13 p.   CHi

6613. Baker, Edward Dickinson. Speech...Delivered at Forest Hill, August 19, 1859. From the phonographic report of the Sacramento union made by Charles A. Sumner. Sacramento, Daily union off., 1859. 13 p.   CHi CSfCW

6614. Baker, Frank Kline. ...Souvenir history of the First Methodist Episcopal church, Sacramento, California. Written for the sixtieth anniversary...Sacramento, Press of J. M. Anderson, 1909. 112 p. illus., ports.   C CLU CS CSf CSmH CU-B

6615. Ball, Donald Clyde. A history of the E. B. Crocker art gallery and its founders. [Stockton] 1955. 135 p. Thesis (M.A.)—College of the Pacific, 1955.   C CS

6616. Baptists. California. Sacramento valley Baptist association. Minutes of the organization and first meeting of the Sacramento valley Baptist association, held with the First Baptist church, Sacramento, September 12–14, 1857. Rev. J. B. Saxton...moderator, Rev. H.

H. Rhees...clerk, Gordon Backus...treasurer. Sacramento, Crocker & Edwards, 1857. 16 p.   CBPac

6617. Barber and Baker (firm). Sacramento illustrated. S.F., Monson & Valentine, 1855. 36 p. illus.   C CLSM CS CSmH CU-B NHi

6618. —— Same. With an introductory note by Caroline Wenzel. Sacramento, Sacramento book collectors club, 1950. 135 p. illus., map, facsims. (Sacramento book collectors club. Pub. no. 4)   C CB CBb CChiS CHi CL CLgA CMerCL CO CRedCL CRic CS CSCL CSS CSf CSmH CU-B CV CViCL

6619. Beckman, Nellie Sims. History of the Tuesday club of Sacramento. [n.d.] 3 p. ports. Typew.   C

6620. Beer (S.) gold mill and extraction co. Catalogue number 2. [Sacramento? n.d.] 21 p. illus., diagrs.   CHi

6621. Benton, Joseph Augustine. California as she was: as she is: as she is to be. A discourse delivered at the First Church of Christ, in Sixth street, Sacramento City; on the occasion of the annual Thanksgiving. November 30, 1850. Sacramento City, Placer times press, 1850. 16 p.   C CSfCW CSmH CtY WHi

6622. —— The California pilgrim: a series of lectures... Sacramento, S. Alter; S.F., Marvin & Hitchcock, 1853. 261 p. illus. In allegorical language.
Available in many California libraries and CaBViPA OrU UPB

6623. Berry, Richard N., auctioneers. Catalogue of real estate to be sold on Friday, June 18th, 1852...at the Orleans Hotel... Sacramento, Democratic jl. off., 1852. 11 p.   CU-B

6624. Blackmon, R. E. Castine, the *Sacramento Union*, and Lincoln. [Berkeley, 1954] Thesis (M.A.)—Univ. of Calif., 1954.   CU

6625. Blinn, Henry. "I saw hard old times"; colorful highlights on the great California gold rush in a letter, written at Sacramento city, December 23, 1849. Stockton, San Joaquin pioneer & hist. soc., 1950. 8 p.   C CHi CSto CStoC

6626. B'nai B'rith. Sacramento. David Lubin lodge no. 37. Ten decades of service. Centennial program...Founded May 16, 1858, as Etham lodge no. 37, name changed January, 1922 in memory of David Lubin ... [Sacramento, 1958] [40] p. illus.   C CHi

6627. [Booth, Newton] In memoriam. Newton Booth, born in Salem, Indiana, Dec. 30, 1825. Died in Sacramento, California, July 14, 1892. [n.p., 1892?] [14] p.   CHi

6628. —— Newton Booth of California, his speeches and addresses; ed. with introd. and notes by Lauren E. Crane. N.Y., Putnam, 1894. 521 p. port.   CHi CL CLO CSd CSfCW CSjC OrU

6629. Booth & co. Journal. Entries covering Apr. 2, 1860– Dec. 31, 1863. [Sacramento, 1860–63] 655 p. Ms.   C

6630. Bowman, Jacob N. Date of the beginning and the completion of the state capitol. [Berkeley, 1954] 5 l. Typew.   CU-B

6631. —— The discovery of the cornerstone of the capitol building in Sacramento, October 15, 1952. [Berkeley, 1952] 9 l. Typew.   CU-B

6632. —— Location of the cornerstone of the capitol building, Sacramento, laid by the Grand lodge of Masons of California, May 15, 1861. [1952] 10 l. Typew.   CU-B

6633. —— The plans of the capitol building of 1860. [Berkeley, 1952] 5 l. Typew.					CU-B

6634. Breuner (John) & co. Catalog. Sacramento, 1904. 160 p. illus.					CHi

6635. Briggs, Robert O. The Sacramento valley railroad, 1853–65. [Sacramento, 1954?] 100 l. illus. Typew. Thesis (M.A.)—Sacramento state college, 1954.					C CSS

6636. Bruner, Claude B. History of the Sacramento northern electric railway. [Sacramento, 1945] 10 l. Typew.					C

6637. Butler, Mattie E. Richards. Woman's forum, 1925–50. [Sacramento, Olmsted & Wood, 1951?] 60 l. ports.					C

6638. California. Constitutional convention, 1878–79. Debates and proceedings of the Constitutional convention of the state of California, convened at the city of Sacramento, Saturday, September 28, 1878. E. B. Willis and P. K. Stockton, official stenographers. Sacramento, State office: J. D. Young, supt., 1880–81. 3 v.					CHi

6639. —— **Laws, statutes, etc.** An act to establish a paid fire department for the city of Sacramento, also, an act for an exempt firemen's association in the city and county of Sacramento. Pub. by J. F. Crawford. Sacramento, Crocker, 1872. 18 p. illus.					C

6640. —— **Legislature.** ...Resolutions of the Legislature of California, recommending the payment of a debt incurred by the city of Sacramento, in providing for the sick and the burial of deceased emigrants to that city... [Wash., D.C., Hamilton print., 1852] 1 p. (32d Cong., 1st sess. S. Misc. doc., no. 23)					CU-B

6641. —— —— **Assembly. Committee on claims.** Report of the Committee on claims, on the claim of the city of Sacramento ag'st the state of California. Submitted, March 14, 1855. [Sacramento] B. B. Redding, state print. [1855] 7 p.					CHi CSmH

6642. —— **State agricultural society.** Constitutional laws, rules, and regulations...instituted May, 1854. Sacramento, S. Aspell & co., 1859. 16 p.					C CHi

6643. —— **State college, Sacramento. Library.** Library program for Sacramento state college; a critical appraisal of library holdings and services. Ed. by Alan D. Covey. 1956. 217 p. Processed.					C

6644. —— **State library.** Centennial, 1850–1950. Sacramento, State print. off., 1950. [7] p.					C CHi CRcS

6645. California artillery. Sacramento light artillery. 1864– (Militia) Constitution and by-laws of the Sacramento light artillery, organized October 7, 1864. Sacramento, Badlam's job print., 1864. 12 p.					CU-B

6646. —— —— —— Instructions for field artillery; extracts collected for the use of the Sacramento light artillery, November, 1864. Sacramento, J. Anthony & co., print., 1864. 32 p.					CU-B

6647. California central railroad. Report of the chief engineer on the progress of construction and future revenue of the road. January 1st, 1859. Sacramento, James Anthony & co., print., Union job off., [1859] 18 p. Report by chief engineer, Theodore Judah. This railroad later known as the Central Pacific. CLU (imp.) CSmH

6648. California development association. Sacramento industrial survey. [n.p., 1925?] 121 l. Reproduced from typew. copy.					CU-B

6649. California eastern extension railroad co. ...its present condition, future business and estimated revenue when completed. Sacramento, Daily bee presses, 1859. 8 p. fold. map.					CSmH CU-B

6650. California facts. Sacramento. [n.p., n.d.] 16 p. illus.					C

6651. California fruit exchange. Annual report. 1st– [1900?]– [Sacramento? 1900?–
CHi has 47th–51st, 58th, 60th–61st, 1947–51, 1958, 1960–61.

6652. —— Proceedings...fruitgrowers' convention of the state of California...1st– [187–?]– Sacramento, State print. [187–?]–
CHi has 28th, 34th, 36th, 38th–39th, 1903, 1907, 1909, 1911–12.

6653. California national bank. Seventy-eight years of service. Sacramento, 1927. [56] p. illus., ports. "The California national bank and the California trust and savings bank, amalgamated with the National bank of D. O. Mills & co." "This booklet is compiled as a souvenir of the opening of the new banking house at seventh and J streets on the fourth of April, 1927."					C CHi CS CSmH

6654. California state convention of olive growers. ...Proceedings...2d–3d; 1892–93. Sacramento, State off., 1892–93. 2 nos. in 1 v.					C

6655. California–Western states life insurance co. Annual report. CL has 1954–60.

6656. Capital concert series. Artists engaged for popular musical evenings. 4th season, 1899/1900. [Sacramento? 1899] 1 v. ports.					CU-B

6657. Capital homestead association of Sacramento. One hundred and ten and one-fourth acres of land. Two hundred and ten shares. Shares one hundred and fifty dollars each. The title to this land is a United States patent. Only two conveyances from government... C. H. Haswell, pres't; J. D. Garland, sec'y. ... Sacramento, Russell & Winterburn, 1869. 28 p. fold. plan.					C

6658. Capital savings bank. By-laws...Incorporated February 8th 1869. Sacramento, Crocker, 1869. 12 p. illus.					C
Other editions followed.					CHi (1873, 1878)

6659. Capital woolen mills. By-laws...Incorporated April 30, 1868... Sacramento, Crocker, 1868. 11 p.					C

6660. Cendrars, Blaise. L'or; la merveilleuse histoire du général Johann August Suter. Paris, B. Grasset, 1924. 277 p.					CSdS

6661. —— Same, with title Sutter's gold, tr. into English by Henry Longan Stuart. N.Y. & London, Harper, 1926. 179 p. illus., port.
Available in many California libraries and CaBViPA ODa OrU UHi UU ViU

6662. Chambers, John S. California pioneers: John A. Sutter, James W. Marshall. (Speech delivered before the Cherry tree club, Sacramento, Feb. 22, 1918). [Sacramento, News pub. co., 1918] 9 p.					CHi

6663. City hotel. [Register of City hotel, nos. 69–77 K Street, Sacramento; P. Conlan, proprietor, April 8, 1876–Mar. 27, 1877] 1 v. front. Ms.					C

6664. Clairmonte, Glenn. John Sutter of California, decorations by L. Vosburgh. N.Y., Nelson, c1954. 185 p.					CRedCL CSS

6665. Cluness, W. R. Annual address to the Sacramento society for mutual improvement, by W. R. Cluness, retiring president. S.F., A. L. Bancroft & co. [18–?] 8 p.					CU-B

6666. Caggins, Caroline (Leonard) Growing up with Sacramento [articles published in the *Sacramento Union* and other clippings about the gold rush and early Sacramento] [Sacramento, 1939] illus., ports., map. Collection of newspaper clippings.   C CU-B

6667. Collins, Laura T. Sutter's fort...Sacramento, Larkin print. co., c1939. 40 p. map.
          C CHi CMont CS CSfWF-H CaBViPA

6668. Colored citizens of the state of California. Proceedings of the first State convention...held at Sacramento, Nov. 20th, 21st, and 22nd, in the Colored Methodist church. Sacramento, Democratic state jl. print., 1855. 27 p.   CHi (facsim.) NN

6669. —— ...Second annual convention...Dec. 9th, 10th, 11th and 12th. S.F., J. H. Udell and W. Randall, print., 1856. 44 p.   C CHi (facsim.) CSmH CU-B

6670. Conwill, Sarah June. Regulation of lobbying in California. [Berkeley, 1959] Thesis (M.A.)—Univ. of Calif., 1959.   CU

6671. Council of federated trades. Official programme of the annual picnic. Together with brief reviews of the unions affiliated with the council. Labor day, September 7, 1892. Sacramento, Day & Joy print., 1892. 43 p.
          C

6672. Crocker art gallery. Catalogue of paintings ...Comp. by Mrs. A. L. Doyle. Sacramento, A. N. Bullock press [n.d.] 55 p.   CHi

6673. —— Same. Sacramento, Crocker, 1876. 125 p.
          CSfCW

6674. —— Same. Comp. by W. F. Jackson. Sacramento, Jos. M. Anderson, print., 1910. 87 p.   CHi

6675. —— The Crockers, their home and gallery. [Sacramento? n.d.] 5 l. Contains also: Free list of the paintings hanging in the 1870 gallery.   CU-B

6676. —— The E. B. Crocker art gallery, Sacramento, California... Sacramento, 1937. 75 p.   C CS CSmH

6677. —— Free list of the paintings hanging in the 1870 gallery. [Sacramento? n.d.] 4 l. Bound with: The Crockers, their home and gallery.   CU-B

6678. —— ...Three centuries of landscape drawing [exhibition held] August and September 1940... [Sacramento, 1940] 12 p.   CSmH

6679. —— Same. Exhibition held in August through October 1940. Catalogue by N. S. Trivas... Sacramento, 1941. 23 p.   CSmH

6680. Dana, Julian. Sutter of California... N.Y., Press of the pioneers, 1934. 423 p. illus., ports., map. Bibliography: p. 397–401.
Available in many California libraries and CaBViPA MoS OrU T UHi

6681. —— Same. N.Y., Halcyon house [1938]
          CSfCSM

6682. Daughters of the American revolution. California. Sacramento chapter. Deaths & interments, 1849–1885. [n.p., 193–?] [242] l. Typew.   CHi

6683. —— —— **Sequoia chapter, San Francisco.** Annual compilation of births, marriages, deaths in the *Sacramento union*, 1859–86. S.F., 1956. 2 v. Typew.
          C CHi CL

6684. [Davis, Winfield J.] Some unwritten history. Sacramento in embryo—how government was established from chaos. Illustrations, including plans, by Carl Ewald Grunsky. [1889–92] [17] p. illus. Reproduced by cameragraph from *Themis*. May 5, 1889–June 11, 1892.
          C

6685. Day, Ella (Perry) Stockton. Sacramento recollections. [Sacramento, 1930] 10 l. Typew.   C

6686. Day, Rowena. Electric light and power in Sacramento, 1879 to 1895. [Sacramento, 1956] 38 l. Typew. Originally prepared for the course Historical method and bibliography at Sacramento state college. Bibliography: p. 37–38.   C CS

6687. —— Same, with title: Carnival of lights; the story of electric light and power in Sacramento, 1879–95. Sacramento, Sacramento state college alumni assoc., 1957. 44 p.   C CS CSS

6688. [Delano, Alonzo] The Central Pacific railroad; or, '49 and '69. By Old Block. S.F., White & Bauer, 1868. 23 p.   CHi

6689. De Leuw, Cather & co. Report on a plan for trafficways and modifications to railroad operations and facilities, Sacramento metropolitan area. S.F., 1958. 2 v. maps.   CS

6690. Democratic party. California. Convention. Proceedings...held in Sacramento city, the 23d of February, 1852. Sacramento, Democratic jl. off., 1852. 22 p.
          C CSmH CU-B NN

6691. —— —— —— Same. ...July 18–20, 1854. S.F., Times and transcript off., 1854. 8 p.   C

6692. Devlin, William. [Scrapbook of clippings from the Sacramento record union on the constitutional convention, 1878–79, on corporations. 1878–79] 100 p. Record of the convention, as printed in the newspaper from the 56th day, Nov. 22, 1878, to the 124th day, Jan. 29, 1879.   C

6693. DuFour, Clarence John. John A. Sutter, his career in California before the American conquest. [Berkeley, 1927] 335 l. Typew. Thesis (Ph.D.)—Univ. of Calif., 1927.   CU CU-B

6694. Dwinell, Israel Edson. Manual of the "First church of Christ" (Congregational), in Sacramento, California. Sacramento, Russell & Winterburn, 1871. 29 p.   C

6695. Edgerton, Henry. Speech...delivered before the taxpayers' mass meeting, in Sacramento city, Saturday night, August 16th, 1873. [Sacramento, 1873]   CSmH

6696. Elks, Benevolent and protective order of. Sacramento lodge no. 6. Elks building; dedication number. Sacramento [News pub. co.] 1926. 126 p. illus., ports.   C CS

6697. —— —— ...Golden anniversary (1895–1945) Sacramento, 1945. 103 p. illus., ports.   CS

6698. —— —— Sacramento SIX lodge, California state Elks association reunion, Sacramento, the heart of California, October 8th & 9th, 1920. Souvenir edition *B.P.O.E. SIX*, v.8, no. 19, Oct. 1920. Sacramento, 1920. 82 p. illus.   CS

6699. Elliott, Janet. The history of the seat of government of California... Stockton, 1942. 138 p. 4 mounted pl. Thesis (M.A.)—College of the Pacific, 1942.
          CStoC

6700. Exempt Firemen's association. Constitution and by-laws of the Exempt Firemen's association of Sacramento. Organized August 14, 1866. Sacramento, Russell & Winterburn, print., 1866. 24 p.   C

6701. —— Same. Sacramento, 1893. 52 p.   CHi

6702. A faithful translation of the papers respecting the grant made by Governor Alvarado to Mr. J. A. Sutter. [Sacramento city, 1850] 12 p. Signed at end by officers of the Association. The translation was made by Hartnell for the Squatters association, and is the first known pamphlet published in Sacramento, having been printed by J. Plumbe in April, 1850.—Cowan. CHi ICN

6703. —— Same, with an introduction by Neal Harlow. Sacramento, Sacramento bk. collectors club, 1942. 13 p. map.
C CHi CL CLU CS CSCL CSf CSmH CU-B

6704. Federation of the women's improvement clubs, Sacramento valley. By-laws... Woodland, Home alliance, 1902. unp. C

6705. Feldhusen's Sacramento. Sacramento's largest and only exclusive mail-order provision house. Sacramento, 1920. 32 p. illus. CHi

6706. Festival of flowers given in honor of Margaret E. Crocker, by the citizens of Sacramento, Cal., May 6, 1885, with notice of the Art gallery, Marguerite home, Sutter's fort, State capitol, and a concise history of Sacramento. Sacramento, Crocker, 1885. 75 p. illus.
C CHi CS

6707. Fisher, Leigh & associates. ...Air trade analysis and area airport development program for the city and county of Sacramento. South Bend, Ind., 1959. [135] p. illus. CS

6708. Fong, Allen Don. A new California state fair. [Berkeley, 1955] Thesis (M.A.)—Univ. of Calif., 1955.
CU

6709. Freye, Paul. A history of the First Congregational church of Sacramento, California... [Sacramento] The Pioneer Congregational church [1949] 62 p. ports.
C CS CSCL

6710. Fruit growers of California [association] Memorial by the convention of fruit-growers of California to the Congress of the United States, respecting the duties upon foreign-grown fruits... Sacramento, 1896. 12 p.
CHi

6711. Galloway, John Debo. The first transcontinental railroad: Central Pacific, Union Pacific. N.Y., Simmons-Boardman [1950] 319 p. illus., ports.
CHi CLgA CRedCL

6712. Gallucci, Mary McLennon, and Gallucci, Alfred D. James E. Birch; a Sacramento chapter in the history of pioneer California transportation. Sacramento, Sacramento county hist. soc., 1958. 37 p. ports. (Pub. no. 1) "Notes": p. 35–37. C CChiS CHi CLSM CO CP CS CSalCL CSf CSfSt CSto

6713. Gardiner, Phyllis (Hyatt) The Hyatt legacy; the saga of a courageous educator and his family in California. N.Y., Exposition press [1959] 301 p.
C CPs

6714. Gebhardt, Charles L. Sutter's fort; a study in historical archeology with emphasis on stratigraphy. Sacramento, Div. of beaches and parks, 1958. 26 p. illus., maps. Processed. C

6715. Gerrish, Samuel Howard. Samuel Howard Gerrish, 1834–1912; excerpts from autobiography and family history. 1932. 36 l. Typew. C

6716. Givan, Albert. Historical report of the water supply of the city of Sacramento and the filtration plant. [n.p., 192–?] 307, 76 l. tables (1 fold.) fold. profile.
CU-B

6717. Goethe, Charles Matthias. Seeking to serve ... Sacramento, Keystone press, 1949. 212 p. illus., maps. CRic CU-B

6718. Gostick, Oda M. History and service record of the Sacramento chapter of the American red cross, 1898–1958. [Sacramento?, 1958] 1 v. illus., facsim. Loose-leaf. C

6719. Greene, Charles L. History of the First Christian church of Sacramento, California, from October 13, 1855, to October 13, 1930, and continued to January 1, 1936. [Sacramento, 1936] 25 l. Typew. C

6720. Grunsky, Carl Ewald. Report on the economic aspects of a deep water ship canal with a terminal port at Sacramento. S.F., Crocker, 1925. 198 p. illus.
CS CSmH

6721. —— Report...on water supply for city of Sacramento. [Sacramento] Retail merchants assoc. [1919] 19 p. C CS

6722. —— The restoration of Sutter's fort, the Native sons' committee and the first board of Sutter's fort trustees. May 1956. 13 p. plan. Typew. C

6723. —— The site of Sutter's fort from surveys. [Original plans and blueprint] [n.p., n.d.] 2 fold. sheet (plans) in pocket. C

6724. Gwinn, Herbert D. The history of Sutter's fort, 1839–1931. Stockton, 1931. 95 p. pl., maps, plans. Thesis (M.A.)—College of the Pacific, 1931. CStoC

6725. Hale bros. & co. [Descriptive catalogs] CHi has 1893, 1905.

6726. Hall, Carroll Douglas. Heraldry of New Helvetia, with thirty-two [i.e. 33] cattle brands and ear marks reproduced from the original certificates issued at Sutter's fort, 1845 to 1848... S.F., Bk. club of Calif., 1945. 91 p. Includes biographical sketches of brand owners. "Printed...at the L. D. Allen press..." C CBb CHi CL CLO CLU CLgA CO CSf CSmH CU-B

6727. —— Old Sacramento; a report on its significance to the city, state and nation, with recommendations for the preservation and use of its principal historical structures and sites. Sacramento, Div. of beaches and parks., 1958. 2 v. illus.
C CAla CHi CL CLSM CLU CLob (v.2) CRcS CRic (v.2) CS CSS CSd CSmat CU-B CaBViPA

6728. Hatch, Frederick Winslow. Sixth anniversary address before the Sacramento society for medical improvement, March 1874. S.F., Winterburn & co., 1874. 10 p. C CU-B

6729. [Heininger, Charles P.] Souvenir of Sacramento, California. [S.F., Author, c1887] 30 p. illus.
C CS CSmH CU-B

6730. Heisch, Edward Joseph. California's capitol park at Sacramento... Author, c1936. 31 p. illus. CS

6731. Heiser, Harvey Michael. "Memories of the fire service"... Fresno, Fresno litho. co., c1941. 177 p. illus., ports. Sacramento fire department. C
CBb CLU CS CSCL CSS CSd CSf CSmH CU-B

6732. Henry, Henry A. Form of service at the consecration of the new synagogue, Benai Israel, Sacramento, Cal., on Sunday, May 22, 5624 (1864) the consecration sermon by the Rev. H. A. Henry, Rabbi preacher of the congregation Sherith Israel, San Francisco. S.F., "The Hebrew," 1864. 12 p. C

6733. Hoagland, John, vs. Sacramento. ...John Hoagland, appellant, vs. city of Sacramento, respondent. Argument of Creed Haymond, of counsel for respondent. Sacramento, H. A. Weaver's law print. off. [18—] 79 p.
CU-B

6734. Hoit, C. W. Fraudulent Mexican land claims in California, and the false location of the Sutter grant. A lecture...repeated at the State house assembly chamber, July 28, 1869... Sacramento, Crocker, 1869. 26 p.
C CS CU-B

6735. Hotel Senator. Sacramento [n.d.] 24 p. illus., col. pl., ports., plan.   C

6736. Hume, Charles V. The Sacramento theatre, 1849–85. Stanford, 1955. Thesis (Ph.D.) — Stanford univ., 1955.   CSt

6737. Hyde, Charles Gilman. A report upon possible sources of water supply for the city of Sacramento, California...April 15, 1916... [S.F., Rincon pub. co., 1916] 660 p.   CL CO
CS CSd CSf CSfCP CSfSC CSfMI CSmH CU-B

6738. —— Report upon proposed filtered water supply for the city of Sacramento... [n.p., 1910?] 248 l. Typew.   CU-B

6739. —— Summary of a report upon the disposal of the sewage of the city of Sacramento, in collaboration with the Division of water and sewers. Sacramento, 1939. [16] p. charts, tables (part fold.)   CS

6740. Illustrated review of Sacramento... v.1, July 1924. Sacramento, News pub. co., 1924. 1 v. illus.   C

6741. Independent-Leader. 40th anniversary number, October 1927: Greater Sacramento. [Sacramento, Larkin print. co.] 1927. 24 p. illus.   C

6742. Jensen, Jane L. The development of the Sacramento public schools, 1853 to 1900. Sacramento, 1954. 173 p. Thesis (M.A.)—Sacramento state college, 1954.   CSS

6743. Johnson, Joseph Willmott. The "Forty thieves" and the seventy million "suckers"... Sacramento, Yeggy & Johnson, c1937. 111 p.   CSmH

6744. Jones, Florence A. Peterson. A study of changes in educational policies and administration in the public elementary schools of Sacramento from 1875 to 1950. Sacramento, 1952. 59 p. Thesis (M.A.)—Sacramento state college, 1952.   CSS

6745. Jones, J. Roy. Memories, men and medicine; a history of medicine in Sacramento, California, with biographies of the founders of the Sacramento society for medical improvement and a few contemporaries...Illustrated with views of Sacramento and some important characters. [Sacramento] Sacramento society for medical improvement, 1950. 505 p. illus., ports.   C CHi
CL CO CS CSCL CSS CSf CU-B CaBViPA

6746. —— The old Central Pacific hospital... Sacramento, Western assoc. of railway surgeons [19—?] 29 p.   CHi

6747. Jones, William Anwyl. Sutter of California and Sutter's fort. Fair Oaks, 1944. 11 p. Mimeo.   CRcS

6748. Joslyn, David L. The romance of the railroads entering Sacramento. Bost., 1939. 42 p. illus. (The Railway and locomotive hist. soc., bul. no. 48, March 1939)   CS

6749. —— Through the years; 1854–1954; a historic background of Union lodge. Sacramento, 1954. 31 p. illus. A report on the centennial observance of Union lodge no. 58, F. & A. M.   CS

6750. Kaplan, Bernard M. The Jews of Sacramento, an historical outline from 1849 to 1903. [n.p., 1903?] 4 p. ports.   C

6751. Kern, Edward Meyer. A transcript of the Fort Sutter papers. Together with the historical commentaries accompanying them. Brought together in one volume for purposes of reference. [n.p., Pub. by Edward Eberstadt, 1922] 38 v. in 1. Contains transcripts of the original documents, now in the Huntington library, and historical introductions. Edition limited to 20 copies.   CU-B ViU

6752. Kimball, J. N. Sacramento and the trail of '49. [c1928] 25 p. illus.   C CHi

6753. Kimball-Upson co. [Descriptive catalogs] Sacramento, 19—
CHi has 1913–14, no. 26, 27, 30 [1917–20]

6754. Kingsley art club. [Scrapbook] [Sacramento, n.d.] Chiefly newspaper clippings, 1941–52.   C

6755. Kirk, Geary & co. Fifth annual catalog of cameras and photographic supplies. [Sacramento, n.d.] 84 p. illus.   CHi

6756. Knights of Pythias. Sacramento lodge, no. 11. Constitution, by-laws, rules of order, etc., ...Organized December 2d, 1869. Sacramento, Russell & Winterburn, 1870. 42 p.   CHi

6757. Kubler, E. A. Johann August Sutter in der deutschen literatur... 9 p. Reprinted from *Monatshefte für deutschen unterricht*, v.XXVII, no. 4, April, 1935.   CHi

6758. Laufkotter, John A. John A. Sutter, Sr. and his grants. Sacramento, Russell & Winterburn, 1867. 45 p.   C CHi

6759. Lavenson's firm. California's great mail-order shoe house, fall and winter, 1901–1902, catalogue 28. Sacramento, 1901. 62 p. illus.   CHi

6760. Lawson, William A. The Crocker art gallery of Sacramento. [4] p. illus. "Reprint from the *Sacramento Bee*, Oct. 19, 1929."   C

6761. League of women voters of Sacramento. A Sacramento dilemma. Sacramento, 1959. 8 l.   C

6762. Lee, Sooky. Redevelopment of the west end of Sacramento, California. [Berkeley, 1954] Thesis (M.A.)—Univ. of Calif., 1954.   CU

6763. Lehr, Ernest. Sutterville; the unsuccessful attempt to establish a town safe from floods. Sacramento, 1958. 102 p. Thesis (M.A.)—Sacramento state college, 1958.   C CSS

6764. Lewis (L. L.) & co. Our annual catalogue and price list of leaf stoves & ranges. Sacramento, Crocker, 1896. 96 p. illus.   CHi

6765. Lienhard, Heinrich. Californien unmittelbar vor und nach der Entdeckung des Goldes... Zürich, Fäsi & Beer, 1898. 318 p.
CHi CLSU CSfP CStoC MoKU UHi

6766. —— I knew Sutter...tr. from the original German by students...at C. K. McClatchy senior high school. Sacramento, Nugget press, 1939. 25 p. port. A translation of chapter X of the author's *Californien unmittelbar vor und nach der Entdeckung des Goldes* pub. at Zurich in 1898.—Pref.   C CHi CS CSS CSjC

6767. —— A pioneer at Sutter's fort, 1846–50; the adventures of Heinrich Lienhard...tr., ed., and annotated by Marguerite Eyer Wilbur from the original German manuscript. L.A., Calafía soc., 1941. 291 p. illus., ports. (Calafía ser., no. 3) Bibliography: p. 276–77.
Available in many California libraries and MoS N UHi

6768. Lindsell, Harold. The land problems of John Sutter. [Berkeley, 1939] 137 l. maps. Thesis (M.A.)— Univ. of Calif., 1939.   CU CU-B

6769. Links, Fred. California's state capitol. [Sacramento] State dept. of finance, 1956. 95 p.
CHi CLom CS CStmo

6770. Lord, Myrtle Shaw. A Sacramento saga; fifty years of achievement—Chamber of commerce leadership ... Sacramento, Sacramento chamber of commerce [1946] 414 p. illus.
Available in many California libraries and MoSHi NN ODa

6771. Low, Frederick Ferdinand. Some reflections of an early California governor contained in a short dictated memoir...and notes from an interview between Governor Low and Hubert Howe Bancroft in 1883. Ed. with preface and notes by Robert H. Becker. [Sacramento] 1959. 77 p. col. port. (Sacramento bk. collectors club. Pub. no. 7)   CBb CChiS CHi CL CLO CLSM CRedCL CRic CSCL CSjC CSto

6772. McClellan air force base. McClellan directory and guide to Sacramento air materiel area and McClellan air force base. McClellan, 1957– 2 v. illus., ports. CS has 1957-58.

6773. MacCurdy, Rahno Mabel. The history of the California fruit growers exchange... L.A., Calif. fruit growers exchange [G. Rice & sons, print.] 1925. 106 p. illus.   C CBb CHi CL CLO CLSU CLU CO COnC CSd CSf CSjC CSmH

6774. Mier, Frederick H. Sacramento, California. [Sacramento, n.d.] 2 v. Scrapbook consisting chiefly of photographs of residents of and buildings in Sacramento, taken between 1870 and 1952.   C

6775. Miller, John Franklin. Speech [of] Gen'l John F. Miller on the Chinese question. In the constitutional convention at the state capitol, Sacramento, December 9, 1878. [Sacramento? 1878?] 16 p.   CHi

6776. Miller, John H. Sacramento, the city beautiful. Sacramento [Bening advertising co.] 1925. 30 p. illus.   C

6777. Mills (D. O.) bank. [Signature book, 1849?–1864?] 72 l. Ms.   C

6778. Milne, D. B., and co. Catalogue of real estate to be sold on Wednesday, May 26th, 1852...R. N. Berry, auctioneer... Sacramento, Times and transcript off., 1852. 16 p.   CU-B

6779. Miners' depot. Book of records...J. C. Kinkead, recorder. Miners depot, 1855-56. 57 p. Ms.   C

6780. Mitchell, E. H., pub. Views of Sacramento, California. [1895?] folder.   CS

6781. Mitchell, Stewart. Early Sacramento. Sacramento, Sacramento historic landmarks commission, 1959. 3 p. Mimeo.   CP CRcS

6782. Mohan, Hugh J. Pen pictures of our representative men, by Hugh J. Mohan, E. H. Clough, John P. Cosgrave. Sacramento, H. A. Weaver's valley press print. house, 1880.   CHi

6783. Moreland, William Hall, Bp. Eighth annual address of the Bishop of Sacramento. [n.p., 1906] 16 p.   C

6784. —— Reply of Right Reverend, the Bishop of the Diocese, to the request of petitioners asking permission to organize a parish, to be known as Trinity Parish of Sacramento. 4 p. Mimeo.   C

6785. Morgan, Mary Evangelist, Sister. Mercy, generation to generation; history of the first century of the Sisters of Mercy, Diocese of Sacramento, California. Foreword by Joseph T. McGucken. S.F., Fearon [1957]   C CS

6786. Morse, John Frederick. Eulogistic tribute to the character and memory of P. G. R. Matthew Purdin.

...Delivered Saturday evening, April 9, 1859. Sacramento, H. S. Crocker & co., 1859. 10 p.
          C CLU CSfP CSmH CU-B CtY

6787. —— The first history of Sacramento city, written in 1853...with a historical note on the life of Dr. Morse, by Caroline Wenzel. Sacramento, Sacramento bk. collectors club, 1945. 127 p. illus., port. First appeared in Colville's Sacramento city directory of October, 1853, under title: *History of Sacramento*. cf. Pref. Bibliographical foot-notes.
          C CHi CL CLU CMerCL CRcS CS CSCL CSS CSf CSfCP CSfWF-H CSjC CSmH CU-B N

6788. Morton, Mrs. Merren Gillis. "Achievements," a history of the Tuesday club of Sacramento, California... Sacramento, 1933. 136 l. Typew.   C

6789. Moulton, Mrs. D. A. Notes on the Kingsley art club. [1930?] 5 l. Typew.   C

6790. Muse, Edward M. Splendid memorial arch proposed for erection in Sacramento to honor the pioneers of California. [1927] 4 cameragraph sheets. front. (mount. photo.)   C

6791. Nagel, Charles E. Sacramento's cholera epidemic of 1850. [Sacramento, 1956] 1 v. v.p. Typew. Originally prepared for the course Historical method and bibliography at Sacramento state college. Includes bibliography.   C

6792. Native sons' hall association of Sacramento. Receipt book, [Constitution and by-laws, adopted Nov. 9, 1906] [n.p., 1914?] 20 p.   CHi

6793. [Native sons of the golden West] ...The new Sacramento... Sacramento, Sept. 9, 1895. 32 p. illus.   C CS

6794. —— Souvenir and official program, Admission day celebration, September 4th-9th, 1905, Sacramento, California. Sacramento, Crocker [1905?] [104] p. illus., ports.   CHi CS

6795. —— Sutter's fort committee. Memorandum book used at Sacramento by Eugene J. Gregory and Frank D. Ryan for the listing of subscriptions to the fund for the purchase of the Sutter fort property, etc. [1890] unp. Ms.   C

6796. Natomas co. Annual report to stockholders for year ended December 31, 1937. [Sacramento, 1938] [12] p.   CHi

6797. Odd fellows bank of savings. By-laws... Sacramento, Crocker, 1870. 16 p.   CSmH

6798. Olsen, William H. Archeological investigations at Sutter's fort state historical monument, July and August, 1959. Sacramento, Dept. natural resources, Div. beaches and parks, May 1961. [56] p. illus., fold. maps, tables.   C CHi

6799. Orleans hotel. [Register of Orleans hotel, Sacramento, Aug. 22, 1859-Sept. 4, 1861] [275] p. Ms.   C

6800. Parkinson, R. R., comp. Pen portraits; autobiographies of state officers, legislators, [etc.] Comp... during the session of the Legislature of 1877-78. S.F., Alta California print., 1878. 142 p.
          C CBb CBu CHi CL CLSU CLU CO CS CSbr CSfCW CSfU CSjC CU-B

6801. Patterson, John A. The development of public recreation in the city of Sacramento. Sacramento, 1957. 107 p. Thesis (M.A.)—Sacramento state college, 1957.   CSS

6802. Paul, Prince of Wurttemberg. Early Sacramento glimpses of John Augustus Sutter, the Hok Farm and the neighboring Indian tribes. From the journals H. R. H. Duke Paul Wilhelm of Wurttemberg; translated by Louis C. Butscher, University of Wyoming. 26 p. Typew.   CS

6803. Perry, Laura Dray. [Reminiscences. S.F., 1934–38?] 4 pts. in 1 v. illus. Contents: [pt. 1] Sacramento—Once upon a time.—[pt. 2 & 4] When Sacramento was younger.—[pt. 3] Memories of old Sacramento.   C

6804. Pickett, Charles Edward. Oration delivered in the Congregational church, Sacramento, California, July 4, 1857. S.F., Whitton, Towne & co., 1857. 32 p.
C CHi CLU CSmH CU-B NN PHi

6805. Pictorial union. A holiday sheet for Christmas and the New Year. Sacramento, James Anthony & co., January 1, 1854. 4 p.   CS

6806. Placerville and Sacramento valley railroad co. Report of the chief engineer...June, 1860. S.F., Commercial steam presses, 1860. 31 p. fold. map. Report by William J. Lewis.   C CSmH CU CU-B NN

6807. Placerville and Sacramento valley railroad of California...and statute acts of state of California, authorizing the issue of bonds and mortgage bonds. N.Y., Slote and Janes, 1864. 64 p. map.   C

6808. Plumbe, John. The settlers and land speculators of Sacramento. To James Gordon Bennett, esq., editor and proprietor of the New York Herald. N.Y., 1851. 32 p.   C CSmH NHi

6809. Price, Sophie. The Sacramento story. [1st ed.] N.Y., Vantage press [1955] 80 p. illus.
C CHi CL CLU CMerCL CMont CNa CO CP CPa CRedCL CRic CS CSCL CSd CSf CSluCL CU-B CoD NN

6810. Public administration service. The government of metropolitan Sacramento. Chicago, 1957. 261 p. illus., maps, diagrs. A report prepared at the request of the Sacramento metropolitan area advisory committee.
CChiS CS CSCL CSS CSfSt CSt ViU

6811. Reinhart, Harold F. Temple B'nai Israel and the Sacramento Jewish community...Souvenir of the celebration of the seventy-fifth anniversary of the consecration of September 3, 1852, of the first building of Congregation B'nai Israel, of Sacramento, the first synagogue building in western America. [Sacramento? 1927? Berkeley, 1940?] 32 l. illus., ports., facsim.
C CS CU-B

6812. Republican party. California. Convention. Proceedings of the Republican ratification meeting held in Platt's music hall, San Francisco, Saturday evening, June 29th, 1861; also proceedings of the Republican state convention held at Sacramento June 18th, 19th and 20th, 1861. S.F., Towne & Bacon, 1861. 32 p.
C CHi CLU CSmH CU-B IHi

6813. —— —— Proceedings of the Republican state convention, held at Sacramento, June 20th, 1860. [n.p., 1860] 12 p.   CSfCW CU-B

6814. —— —— —— Proceedings of the Union state convention, held at Sacramento, on the 17th and 18th days of June, 1862. S.F., Eastman & Godfrey, print., 1862. 20 p.   C CLCM CSmH CU-B

6815. Robinson, Donald. Hoboken and this is no jokin'; or Tents and past tense. [Sacramento?] 1956. 23 l. Typew. Originally prepared for the Historical method and bibliography course at Sacramento state college.   C

6816. Rusco, Elmer Ritter. Machine politics, California model: Arthur H. Samish and the alcoholic bev-

erage industry. [Berkeley, 1960] Thesis (Ph.D.)—Univ. of Calif., 1960.   CU

6817. Sacramento (City) Poll list... [n.p.] 1868.
C

6818. Sacramento. Board of education. History and progress of the Public school department of the city of Sacramento, 1849–93, by Winfield J. Davis; also annual report of the Board of education, 1894. Sacramento, D. Johnston & co., print., 1895. 174 p. illus., port.
C CLU CSmH

6819. —— **Board of trade.** Annual report, 1880. Sacramento, Crocker [n.d.] 64 p.   C CHi CU-B

6820. —— **Board of trustees.** Messages and reports of the meetings of the Board of trustees, Jan. 1, 1898, to Jan. 3, 1900. Clippings from the *Sacramento Bee and Union.*   C

6821. —— —— An ordinance granting to the Western Pacific railway company...the right...and franchise for the term of fifty (50) years to construct...and operate, in and across the city of Sacramento... [Sacramento, 1907] [3] p.   C

6822. —— **Central Pacific railroad hospital.** Condensed history and statement of the workings... Sacramento, Crocker, 1880. [21] p.   CSmH

6823. —— **C. K. McClatchy senior high school.** The beginnings of drama in Sacramento 1849 and 1949, compiled and written by [the] students... Sacramento, Nugget press, 1955. 25 p. illus. Bibliography: p. 22–23.
C CS CSS CStoC CU-B

6824. —— —— Capitals of California, compiled and written by the students... Sacramento, Nugget press, 1950. 33 p.   C CSS CStoC

6825. —— —— Early Sacramentans, compiled and written by [the] students... Sacramento, Nuggett press, 1949. 37 p. illus., mounted ports.
C CS CSCL CSS CStoC CU-B

6826. —— —— Park grants of John A. Sutter, junior, by [the] students. Sacramento, Nuggett press, 1948. [34] p. illus.   C CS CSS CU-B

6827. —— —— Sacramento water supply, compiled and written by [the] students... Sacramento, Nugget press, 1952. 21 p. illus. Includes bibliography.
C CS CSCL CStoC CU-B

6828. —— —— Nugget editions club. Early day romances, Sutter's fort, 1847–48. Sacramento, Nugget press [c1943] 61 p. illus.
C CLSU CS CSS CSmH CU-B

6829. —— **Chamber of commerce.** Greater Sacramento, her achievements, resources and possibilities. Sacramento, Keltman & co., c1912. 48 p. illus.   CU-B

6830. —— —— Hub of western industry; Sacramento, California. 1944. 30 p. illus., maps.   CS CSCL

6831. —— —— Industrial facts, source of raw materials, extent of market, vital concentration center, hub of transportation, Sacramento, California. Sacramento, 1932. unp.   CS

6832. —— —— Industrial survey of Sacramento. Sacramento, 1925. v.p. Mimeo. Loose-leaf.   CS

6833. —— —— Sacramento, California. Sacramento [192–?] folder (6 p.)   CRcS

6834. —— —— Sacramento, capital of California; the land of promise and recreation. Sacramento [n.d.] 4 p. 2 col. maps.   CRcS

6835. —— —— Sacramento, the gateway to California. Sacramento, 1922. 24 p. illus.   CS

6836. —— —— Same. [Sacramento, A. N. Bullock, 1926] 64 p. illus.   C CS

6837. —— —— Who's who in Sacramento; buyers' guide and membership directory of the greater Sacramento chamber of commerce. Sacramento, 1952–
C (1952)   CS (1952, 1954–1958/59)   CU-B (1952)

6838. —— —— Citizens' committee. Report of the Citizens' committee appointed by the Chamber of commerce...to investigate all sources of pure water supply. Rendered June 28, 1913. 30 p.   C

6839. —— —— Industrial dept. Directory of manufacturers and wholesale distributors, Sacramento, California.
C has 1936–37. CHi has 1921. CS has 1921, 1936–37, 1939, 1941, 1948, 1959.

6840. —— Charters, ordinances, etc. Charter and ordinances of the city of Sacramento... Sacramento, 1850–
C has 1853, 1856, 1881, 1893, 1896. CS has 1850, The first charter of Sacramento. Reproduced by cameragraph from: *Laws of California*, 1850, and later revisions to date. CSS has 1955. CSmH has 1853, 1893.

6841. —— Citizens' water investigation committee. Report... Sacramento, D. Johnston & co., 1901. 127 p.   C CS CU-B

6842. —— City library. Directory of community resources for program planners. Sacramento, 1953. 25 l.
C

6843. —— —— Same. [Sacramento] 1954. 30 p.
C

6844. —— —— History of the Sacramento city free library. [Sacramento, 1935] 7 p. Typew.   CS

6845. —— City planning commission. An appraisal of planning in the Sacramento area past, present and future. Sacramento, 1952. 39 p.   CS

6846. —— —— A general plan for Sacramento. Sacramento, 1959. 12 p. illus.   CS

6847. —— —— Land use today in Sacramento. Sacramento, 1953. 33 p. illus.   CS CSt

6848. —— —— Population growth of the city and county of Sacramento, 1850–1980. Sacramento, 1953. 37 p. maps, charts.   CS

6849. —— —— Sacramento urban redevelopment; existing conditions in blighted areas. Sacramento, 1950. 53 p.   CS CSt

6850. —— Committee of citizens. ...Grand railroad celebration in honor of the completion of the great national railway across the continent...celebrated in Sacramento...May 1869... Sacramento, Crocker [1869] [2] p.   CU-B

6851. —— Common council. Proceedings...during the fiscal year of 1855–56. [Sacramento, 1855–56]
CSmH

6852. —— Congregation B'nai Israel. Minutes of annual meeting, October 30, 1906. [Sacramento, 1906] 9 l. Photostat copy (negative)   C

6853. —— Fire department. Souvenir, Sacramento fire department, illustrated. [Sacramento] 1913. 119 p. illus., ports.   C CS CSmH

6854. —— —— Same. October, 1928. [1928] 103 p. illus., ports.   CHi

6855. —— —— Knickerbocker engine company. Minutes...Organized July 21st 1854. Sacramento, 474 p. Ms. and clippings.   C

6856. —— First Baptist church. Diamond jubilee, 1850–1925. [1925] 19 p. illus., ports.   C

6857. —— —— ...Historical data of the First Baptist church of Sacramento, California...comp. by Edgar A. Stickney... [Sacramento]1950. 52 p. illus., ports.
C CS

6858. —— First Congregational church. Directory, alphabetical and district and handbook. Sacramento, 1908. 29 p. illus., port.   C

6859. —— Historic landmarks commission. Sidewalk history; pioneer sites of old Sacramento. [Sacramento] City of Sacramento, 1958. 43 p. illus. "Sacramento: its earliest years, 1808–1849," by Allan R. Ottley.
C CAla CHi CL CLU CLob CO CP CS CSS CU-B CViCL

6860. —— Municipal utility district. Report of the Board of consulting engineers of the Sacramento municipal utility district of the proposed Silver Creek project. Sacramento, 1927. 36 p. maps.   C

6861. —— Protestant orphan asylum. Petition of the managers...for state aid. [Sacramento, Gelwicks, state print., 1870] 6 p.   CSmH

6862. —— Redevelopment agency. Population and employment survey of Sacramento's west end, by Davis McEntire. Sacramento, 1951. 45 p. (Its report no. 2)   CS

6863. —— —— Survey of business in Sacramento's west end, by Harold F. Wise. Sacramento, 1951. 11 p. (Its report no. 1)   CS

6864. —— St. Paul's church (Episcopal) Manual and directory, St. Paul's church (Episcopal) ...Sacramento... Sacramento, Pac. print. house, 1896. 65 p.
CS CSCL

6865. —— Superintendent of schools. Sacramento city schools then and now (1912–1941) 29 years of progress... Sacramento, Unified schools district, 1942. 84 p. illus.   CHi CRcS CS

6866. Sacramento athletic club. Official programme. The circus maximus of Caesar Augustus, reproduced by the Sacramento athletic club at the California state fair, Sept. 4th to Sept. 16th, 1893.   Sacramento, 1893. 1 v. unp. illus.   C

6867. Sacramento bee. The Bee's centennial album. February 4, 1957. Sacramento, 1957. 9 pts. in 2 v. illus., ports., facsims.
C CAla CHi CLU CO COHN CRedCL CSjC CSmH CU-B MoS

6868. —— 85th anniversary number, Feb. 3, 1942. illus.   C MoS

6869. —— Gold rush centennial edition. Tuesday, September 6, 1949. [Sacramento, 1949] 2 pts. in 1. illus., ports.   C CO

6870. —— Landmarks. Sacramento, March 13, 1960. 12 p. illus. Pictures of west end's historical landmarks.
CHi CS

6871. —— Progress edition... [Sacramento, 1948] 1 v. v.p. illus., ports.   CU-B

6872. —— Sacramento, a crisis of growth. [Sacramento, 1956] 46 p. illus., maps (part. fold., part. col.)
C CS

6873. —— ...Sacramento golden empire centennial, 1839–1939... [Sacramento, 1939] [60] p. illus., ports.   CMerCL CS CSmH CU-B MoS WM

6874. —— Sacramento guide book... [Sacramento, c1939] 220 p. illus., ports., maps.
Available in many California libraries and CoD NN

6875. —— Seventy-fifth anniversary number, Feb. 3, 1932.   C CHi CRb CS

6876. The Sacramento blue book—containing the addresses, telephone numbers and at home days of the ladies of Sacramento, also the lists of members of the Tuesday club, Saturday club [etc.]... Sacramento, D. Johnston & co., 1902. 87 p.   C CS

6877. Sacramento business barometer. 1927– Sacramento, Chamber of commerce. illus. Called *Capital business* 1927–1937.

CS has Jan. 1927-Feb., 1928, Sept.-Nov., 1932, June-Aug., Dec., 1933, Feb.-Dec., 1934, Jan.-July, 1935, Nov.-Dec., 1936, Jan.-Aug., Oct.-Nov., 1937. CU-B has Jan.-Nov. 1937.

6878. Sacramento city central homestead association. Act of incorporation, articles of association, by-laws, etc.,... containing sectional maps showing location, etc. Incorporated August 12, 1869... Sacramento, Crocker, 1869. 20 p. maps.   C

6879. Sacramento city extension homestead association. Articles of association, act of incorporation, by-laws, etc. ...Sacramento, Crocker, 1869. 34 p.
                                                      C CU-B

6880. Sacramento city mission association. Social problems and efforts, an annual review of the work, the plans and the principles. [n.p., n.d.] 15 p.   C

6881. Sacramento composition co. Sacramento 1947 business and professional directory. Sacramento, 1947. 48 p.   CS

6882. Sacramento French and international mutual life insurance association. Rules and regulations ...founded by F. Chevalier, of Sacramento. Sacramento, Russell & Winterburn, print., 1869. 13 p.   CU-B

6883. Sacramento genealogical society. Sexton's record, St. Joseph's cemetery, 1864–1946; St. Mary's cemetery, 1929–1954; Sacramento memorial cemetery; Citrus Heights cemetery, Sacramento county. [Sacramento, 195–?]   C

6884. Sacramento Hussars. Constitution and by-laws... Adopted December 9, 1881. Sacramento, E. & H. Rivett, print., 1882. 15 p. illus.   C

6885. Sacramento industrial improvement association. First annual report... Sacramento, Crocker, 1895. 64 p.   C CS

6886. Sacramento medical society. Constitution, by-laws, rules of order and code of ethics, adopted... on the 25th of April, 1855; together with the act of enrollment, the names of original members... Sacramento, Print. State tribune off., 1855. 45 p.   C CU-B

6887. Sacramento memorial auditorium, dedicated to those who made the supreme sacrifice in the service of the United States, February 22, 1927. [Sacramento, Keystone press] 1927. unp.   C

6888. Sacramento metropolitan planning committee. Model zoning ordinance for use in Sacramento metropolitan area. Sacramento, City planning commission, 1948. 71 l.   C

6889. Sacramento retail merchants' association. Constitution and by-laws, 1915. Sacramento, 1915. 13 p.
                                                      CHi

6890. [Sacramento river floods of 1878 and 1881] [Newspaper clippings from the daily issues of the Sacramento daily bee. Appended: Report of the Board of commissioners of the Sacramento river drainage district to the Governor of California] [Sacramento, 1879] 1 v.
                                                      CU-B

6891. Sacramento savings bank. By-laws of the Sacramento savings bank. Incorporated March 19, 1867. 2d ed. Sacramento, Russell & Winterburn, print., 1867. 16 p.   C

6892. —— Same. 3d ed. 1868. 15 p.   CU-B

6893. —— Same. 4th ed. 1869. 15 p.   C

6894. —— ...Fiftieth anniversary, March 19, 1917. [Sacramento, 1917] [55] p. illus., ports.
                                                      C CHi CS

6895. Sacramento society for medical improvement. [Constitution and minutes. 1868–1924] 5 v.   C

6896. Sacramento souvenir guide, devoted to the interest of the tourist, the commercial traveler and all visitors to our city and vicinity... Sacramento, William E. Terwilliger [1911] 40 p. illus.   C CHi

6897. Sacramento street fair and trades carnival, 1900. Souvenir of Sacramento street carnival, May 1, 1900. 2 v. mounted photos.   C

6898. —— [Souvenir program] Sacramento, News pub. co., 1900. [48] p. illus., ports.   C CS

6899. Sacramento, the commercial metropolis of northern and central California... Sacramento, A. J. Johnston & co., 1888. 72 p.   C CS CU-B

6900. —— Same. 1889. 61 p.   CSmH

6901. Sacramento Turn-Verein. Fest-schrift. Souvenir album, 1854–1954... May 15–May 23, 1954. [Sacramento, 1954] illus., ports., facsims.   C

6902. —— Gedenkblatt zum goldenen jubilaüm, am 2, Juni 1904... Souvenir of the golden jubilee June 2, 1904, 1854–1904. Sacramento, 1904. 76 p. illus.   C

6903. The Sacramento union. Anniversary edition. Sacramento, 1921–51. illus., ports.
C (70th, 90th, 100th) CS (90th) CU-B (90th)

6904. —— California state fair annual...Supplement to the Sacramento Union... Sacramento, 1920. 128 p. illus.   C

6905. —— Classified business and professional directory, 1920– Sacramento, 1920–
C has 1939/40. CS has 1919/20, 1922, 1924, 1929.

6906. —— Suburban sketches. no. 1–57 [Sacramento, 1872–73] [47] p. Mounted photostats (positive) of articles published at irregular intervals in the *Sacramento union* between June 1, 1872, and April 12, 1873.   C

6907. Sacramento valley beet sugar co. By-laws ...Incorporated April 24th 1868... Sacramento, Crocker, 1869. 11 p.   C

6908. Sacramento valley railroad co. First mortgage: 10 per cent bonds... [S.F.] O'Meara & Painter, print. [1855] 8 p.   CLU CSmH CU-B

6909. —— Report of committee of board of directors ...made August 7th, 1855. S.F., O'Meara and Painter, print., 1855. 12 p.
                               C CHi CLU CSmH CSt CU-B

6910. —— ...Report of the chief engineer on the preliminary surveys, and future business of the Sacramento valley railroad. Sacramento, Democratic state journal off., 1854. 24 p. Signed: Theodore D. Judah.
                                          CLU CSmH CU-B

6911. —— Reports of the president, trustee and superintendent of the Sacramento valley R. R. co. for the five years terminating December 31st, 1860, with the proceedings of the fifth annual meeting of stockholders. S.F., Painter & co., 1861. 24 p.   C CLU CSmH CU-B

6912. Sacramento woman's council. A silhouette of service. [Sacramento, 1955] 127 p. ports.   C CS

6913. —— The scrapbook of Nellie Story Dunlap, first recording secretary of the Women's council. [Sacramento, n.d.] 1 v. Consists almost entirely of newspaper clippings pertaining to the Sacramento Woman's council, 1904–1910.   C

6914. —— Record of relief afforded since April 18th, 1906 [to persons who escaped from the San Francisco earthquake and fire] [Sacramento, 1906?] 301 p.   C

6915. Sargent, Aaron Augustus. Agricultural college; address of Hon. A. A. Sargent, delivered before the state agricultural society, September 21, 1865. Sacramento, O. M. Clayes, state print., 1866. 15 p.   CHi

6916. Saturday club. Constitution and by-laws, list of members, study outlines, yearbooks, etc. [Sacramento, J. M. Anderson, 189–?–

C has 1893–1906/07, 1908/09–13, 1915/16, 1930, 1938/39, 1944.

6917. Savage, Margot Hoppe. The history of Sacramento community forum (Sacramento town hall). Sacramento, 1957. 174 p. Thesis (M.A.)—Sacramento state college, 1957.   CSS

6918. Schaw, Ingram, Batcher & co. Manufacturers of sheet steel and iron pipe, dealers in hardware... Sacramento, Crocker [1894] [24] p. illus.   CHi

6919. Schoendorf, A.J. Beginnings of cooperation in the marketing of California fresh deciduous fruits and history of the California fruit exchange. [Sacramento, Inland press] 1947. 65 p. illus., ports.   CHi

6920. Schoonover, Thomas J. The life and times of Gen.'l John A. Sutter. Illustrated pocket ed. Sacramento, D. Johnston & co., print., 1895. 136 p. illus., ports.
C CHi CL CLSU CLU CMartC CP CSf CSfCW CSjC CSmH CU-B CaBViPA

6921. —— Same; rev. and enl. ed. Sacramento, Carpenter print. co., 1907. 312 p. illus., ports.
Available in many California libraries and MoS N TxU

6922. Sears, Jesse Brundage. The administrative organization of Sacramento's school system. Sacramento, Bd. of educ., 1940. 116 p.   CSS

6923. —— Sacramento school survey. Sacramento, Bd. of educ., c1928. 2 v.   CSS

6924. Sheetz, Carson Park. History of labor unions in Sacramento, 1849–1899. [Berkeley, 1934] Thesis (M.A.)—Univ. of Calif., 1934.   CU

6925. Sheppard, Eli T. Frederick Ferdinand Low, ninth governor of California. 47 p. Reprint from the *Univ. of California chronicle,* v.19, no. 2.   CHi CU

6926. Society of California pioneers, Sacramento. Constitution, by-laws and list of officers and members of the Sacramento pioneers association. Sacramento, Russell & Winterburn, 1866. 34 p.   CSmH
Other editions followed.   C (1872, 1891) C-S (1891) CHi (1872, 1877, 1910) CPom (1912) CSf (1891) CSfCW (1891) CSmH (1872, 1891)

6927. Sons and daughters of the Sacramento society of California pioneers. Constitution and by-laws... Sacramento, D. Johnston & co., 1891. 25 p.
C CHi CU-B

6928. Southern Pacific co. Public relations department. First in the west; Sacramento valley railroad, of 100 years ago, is oldest link in SP's western lines. [S.F., 1955] 16 p. illus., map.   C

6929. —— —— Memorandum about the Sacramento valley railroad company, first of Southern Pacific's lines in the west. [n.p., 1955] 15 l.   C

6930. Stanbery, Henry Van Beuren. Forecasting a city's future; Sacramento, California, by Van Beuren Stanbery...and Miriam Roher... Sacramento, State reconstruction and reemployment commission, 1946. 64 p. illus., charts.   CHi CRcS CS

6931. [Stanford, Leland] To the directors of the C.P.R.R. co. of California... [n.p., 1855] 8 p. Office C.P.R.R. co., Sacramento, November 25th, 1855. Printed signature: Leland Stanford, president Central Pacific railroad co.   NN

6932. Staniford, Edward Fawsitt. Governor in the middle; administration of George C. Pardee, governor of California, 1903–1907. [Berkeley, 1955] Thesis (Ph.D.) — Univ. of Calif., 1955.   CU

6933. Stanly, Edward. Speech of the Hon. Edward Stanly, delivered at Sacramento, July 17th, 1857, at a public meeting held in the Forest theatre. [Sacramento, 1857] 16 p.   CHi CU-B CtY

6934. Starr, J. B., auctioneers. Real estate to be sold...July 12, 1852 [etc.]: at the Orleans Hotel [Sacramento] Sacramento, Union job off., 1852. 8 p.   CU-B

6935. Stoddard, Walter Eugene. The first 100 years of Sacramento lodge no. 40, F. & A. M. [Sacramento, Sacramento news pub. co., c1953] 159 p. illus., ports.
C CHi CS

6936. Stokes, Darius. A lecture upon the moral and religious elevation of the people of California, delivered before the congregation of the African Methodist Episcopal church, Sacramento City, June, 1853. ... S.F., Evening jl., 1853. 18 p.   CHi (facsim.) CSmH

6937. Sutter, John Augustus. The diary of Johann August Sutter... S.F., Grabhorn, 1932. 56 p. illus., ports. (Rare Americana ser., no. 2)
C CBb CHi CL CLO CLU CLgA CMartC CO CSf CSfP CSjC CSmH CSmat CStcl CU-B CV CYcCL

6938. —— Neu-Helvetien;...nach den handschriften erzählt von Erwin Gustav Gudde. Frauenfeld und Leipzig, Huber & co. [1934] 122 p. illus., ports., maps.
C CChiS CHi CL CLSU CLU CSS CSf CSmH CU-B UU

6939. —— New Helvetia diary; a record of events kept by John A. Sutter and his clerks at New Helvetia, California, from Sept. 9, 1845, to May 25, 1848. S.F., Grabhorn, in arrangement with the Soc. of Calif. pioneers, 1939. 138 p. illus., map.
Available in many California libraries and CaBViPA MoS N NHi NvU TxU UHi UU ViU ViW

6940. —— Six French letters, Captain John Augustus Sutter to Jean Jacques Vioget, 1842–1843, together with translations in English by the Nugget editions club of C. K. McClatchy senior high school. Sacramento, Nugget press, 1942. 40 p. illus., map.
C CHi CLSU CLU CS CU-B

6941. —— Sutter's own story; the life of General John Augustus Sutter and the history of New Helvetia in the Sacramento valley...by Erwin G. Gudde. N.Y., Putnam, 1936. 244 p. illus., ports., maps.
Available in many California libraries and CaBViPA KHi MoHi NvU ODa TxU UHi

6942. Sutter, John Augustus, jr. ...Statement regarding early California experiences, edited, with a biography, by Allan R. Ottley. Sacramento, Sacramento bk.

collectors club, 1943. 160 p. illus., port. Bibliography: p. [143]–150.
C CBb CHi CL CLSU CLU CMerCL CO CRcS CRedCL CS CSjC CSmH CU-B OrU TxU

6943. Sutter club. Constitution and by-laws [and list of members] Sacramento, 1943. 27 p. [10] l.   CHi

6944. —— List of members. Sacramento [1913] 28 p.   CHi

6945. Sutter's fort historical museum, Sacramento. ...Sutter's fort historical museum... Sacramento, Bur. of printing, Documents div. [1944] 48 p. illus., ports., maps. Later editions issued by California. Dept. of natural resources. Div. of beaches and parks. Title varies. 1948, 1950 comp. by Carroll Douglas Hall.
Available in many California libraries.

6946. Sweetser, A. C. History of the First Congregational church in Sacramento, California... [Sacramento, J. M. Anderson, 190–?] 27 p. port.
C CSmH CU-B

6947. Swisher, Carl Brent. Motivation and political technique in the California constitutional convention, 1878–79. Claremont, Pomona college, 1930. 132 p. (Political science monograph ser.)
CBb CChiS CHi CSfCW CStbS

6948. Tenney, Jack Breckinridge. The Tenney committee; the American record. Tujunga, Standard publications, 1952. 96 p.   CSto

6949. [Thompson and co.] Historical and descriptive review of the industries of Sacramento, 1886... Sacramento, Priv. print., 1886. 163 p. illus.   CLU CU-B

6950. The Thompson-Diggs co. [Catalogue 15]... Mechanics' tools, farming tools, builders' hardware... Sacramento [Crocker, n.d.] 1339 p. illus.   CHi

6951. —— [Catalogue 16] Sacramento, News pub. co. [1917] 1082 p. illus.   CHi

6952. Thunen, Frances. The Sacramento civic theater: a study of its origins, development, and functions as a community service. [L.A.] 1959. Thesis (M.A.)— U.C.L.A., 1959.   CLU

6953. Tolles, James R. The future of Sacramento. A lecture delivered ...at Pioneer hall, October 18, 1874, and...repeated at Central hall, January 6th, 1875. Sacramento, 1875. 19 p.   CS CU-B

6954. Trice, Andrew H. Present and future requirements for agricultural labor from the Sacramento labor market area. Prepared for Redevelopment agency of the city of Sacramento. Sacramento, 1959. 50 p. illus.
CS

6955. Tuesday club. History of the Tuesday club of Sacramento; being a continuing history, and a sequel to "Achievements"... [1934/35–1959/60] [Sacramento, 1952–1959?] Typew.   C

6956. —— [Scrapbook of constitution and by-laws, Tuesday clubhouse association, convention programs, yearbooks and reports]   C

6957. —— [Scrapbook of newspaper clippings, photographs, etc.] Sacramento, 1900– 1 v. illus., mounted photos.   C

6958. Union party. California. Proceedings of the Union state convention, held at Sacramento, on the 17th and 18th days of June, 1862. S.F., Eastman & Godfrey, print., 1862. 20 p.   C CU-B

6959. —— —— Same, on the 17th, 18th and 19th days of June, 1863. S.F., F. Eastman, print., 1863. 28 p.
CU-B

6960. United States vs. Sutter, John A. In the United States district court, Northern district of California. The United States vs. John A. Sutter. No. 319 "New Helvetia." Testimony taken in behalf of the claimant, in support of the official survey of the land finally confirmed. Volney E. Howard and Crockett and Crittenden, attorneys for the claimant. S.F., Print. for the claimant, 1861. [96] p.   CSmH CU CU-Law

6961. —— ...Testimony taken in behalf of the United States, in support of their exceptions to the official survey of the land finally confirmed. Calhoun Benham, U.S. attorney. S.F., Print. for the United States, 1861. 170 p.   CSmH CU CU-B

6962. United States. Board of land commissioners for California. The Sutter claim, the evidence taken in case 192 before the Board of U.S. land commissioners, together with the brief of the U.S. land agent [John H. McKune] Sacramento, State journal off., 1854. 27 p.
C

6963. —— Commission for ascertaining and settling private land claims in California. Opinion of the Board of U.S. land commissioners in case no. 92, John A. Sutter, claimant, for the place called "New Helvetia", containing 33 square leagues of land, delivered by Commissioner R. A. Thompson, Tuesday, May 15, 1855. [S.F.? 1855?] 8 p. Caption title: The Sutter claim. Settlement of titles in Sacramento.   CLU

6964. Van Voorhies-Phinney co. Threescore years and ten; a brief history outlining the development of the Van Voorhies-Phinney co. from its small beginning in 1850 to the present time. Sacramento [192–?] [12] p. illus., ports.   CHi CU-B

6965. Walsh-Richardson co. [Catalog] no. 20, 1910. Sacramento [1910] illus.   CU-B

6966. Warren & son's garden and nurseries. 1853–54. A descriptive catalogue of fruit and ornamental trees, grape vines, shrubs... [n.p., 1853?] 62 p.   CHi

6967. Way, Frederick. Saga of the *Delta Queen*. Cincinnati, The Picture marine pub. co., 1951. 218 p. illus.   CS CSto

6968. Weinstock, Lubin and co. [Catalogs] Sacramento [189–?–
CHi has Spring & summer, 1905, Fall & winter, 1913–14, 1917–18. CU-B has [189–?]

6969. —— Living a principle through half a century ... Sacramento, 1924. 16 p. illus.   CS

6970. Weller, John B. Speech...delivered in Sacramento, at a mass meeting of the Democracy, held on Saturday night, July 25th, 1857. Phonographically reported by Charles A. Sumner. Sacramento, James Anthony & co., print., Union bk. and job off., 1857. 15 p.   CU-B

6971. Wenzel, Caroline. Sacramento city free library; paper read before Business woman's club, October, 1923. 5 p. Typew.   C CS

6972. Western hotel. [Descriptive leaflet] [Sacramento, 1900?] [4] p. illus.   CHi

6973. Western real estate research corp. Analysis of the Sacramento labor market area, prepared for Redevelopment agency of the city of Sacramento, California. [L.A., 1958?] 1 v. tables.   CS

6974. —— Economic feasibility of relocation, Sacramento labor market area. Prepared for Redevelopment agency of the city of Sacramento, California. L.A., 1958. 25 p. tables.   CS

6975. Wheeler, Mayo Elizabeth. John A. Sutter, a California pioneer: an historical sketch and a collection of correspondence. [Berkeley,] 1924. 528 l. Thesis (M.A.) — Univ. of Calif., 1925.   CU-B

6976. Wheeler, Osgood Church. A funeral discourse on the death of Mr. Zebulun Gardner, delivered in the First Baptist church, Sacramento, California, September 1, 1861... Sacramento, Crocker, 1861. 8 p.
                                              C   CHi

6977. —— Human charity; an address, delivered before the Order of ancient Freemasons, in Sacramento, California, June 24, 1852. Bost., Print. at the off. of the Freemason's mag., 1852. 15 p. Advocates the establishment of a public library in Sacramento.   C

6978. White, William E. An outline of the labor market problem in Sacramento redevelopment. [Sacramento] 1957. [15] l. map.   C

6979. Whittier, Fuller and co. [Price list of] doors, windows, blinds & glass. Sacramento [187–?]   CU-B

6980. Wilbur, Marguerite Eyer. John Sutter, rascal and adventurer. Based on source material, manuscripts and letters pertaining to Captain John Augustus Sutter... N.Y., Liveright, 1949. 371 p. illus., ports., map.
Avaliable in many California libraries and CaBviPA MiD   MoS   UHi

6981. Wilson, Evon L. A history of the founders and early organization of Scottish Rite freemasonry in Sacramento. Sacramento, Sacramento Scottish Rite bodies, 1956. 116 p. illus., ports.   CHi   CS

6982. Wittemann, Adolph. Souvenir of Sacramento, Cal. In photogravure from recent negatives... N.Y., Albertype co., c1892. 16 pl.
                        C   CHi   CLU   CSmH   CU-B

6983. —— Same. N.Y., c1897. 19 pl.
                             C   CHi   CSfU   CU-B

6984. —— Same. Brooklyn, c1901. 19 pl.   NN

6985. Wood, Forrest Glen. A frontier newspaper and the Civil war period; the Sacramento Union, 1851–65. Sacramento, 1958. Thesis (M.A.) — Sacramento state college, 1958.   CSS

6986. Writers' program, Calif. California's state capitol...Sponsor: California state department of education. [Sacramento, State print. off., 1942] 94 p. illus.
C   CL   CLO   CLSU   CLU   CMont   CO   CRcS   CRic CS   CSCL   CSS   CSalCL   CSd   CSf   CSj   CSmH CU-B   CViCL   T

6987. —— Theatrical annals of Sacramento...Comp. by the northern California writers' project, Works project administration from newspapers in the California state library. [Sacramento?] 1939–40.   C

6988. Young, Clement Calhoun. The legislature of California; its membership, procedure, and work... S.F., Parker print. co., 1943. 350 p.   CChiS

6989. Young men's Christian associations, Sacramento. ...Organized October 23, 1866... Sacramento, Crocker, 1866. 15 p.   C

6990. Young men's republican club. Constitution ...Organized July 17, 1860... Sacramento, Crocker, 1860. 10 p.   CSmH

6991. Yuba vineyards co., Sacramento. How you can make more money ["Buy a Yuba vineyard"] Sacramento [Anderson print. co., 1920?] [16] p. illus., map.
                                              CHi

6992. Zabriskie, James C. Reply of James C. Zabriskie, to a committee of citizens of Sacramento, in reference to the Vigilance committee and democracy. Sacramento, "Calif. am." job print., 1856. 8 p.   CSmH

6993. Zollinger, James Peter. Johann August Sutter; der könig von Neu-Helvetien. Zürich, Schweizer spiegel verlag, 1938. 336 p. col. front., plates, ports., facsim.   CLgA

6994. —— Sutter, the man and his empire. N.Y., Oxford, 1939. 374 p.
Available in many California libraries and MoS   OrU UHi

SAN BENITO COUNTY
(Created in 1874 from portion of Monterey county; annexed small sections of Fresno and Merced counties in 1887)

COUNTY HISTORIES

6995. Historical records survey. California. ... San Benito county (Hollister) S.F., Northern Calif. hist. records survey project, 1940. 585 p. illus., maps. (Inventory of the county archives of California.... no. 36) Mimeo.
C   CB   CBb   CF   CHank   CHi   CL   CLCM   CLCo   CLO CLSM   CLSU   CLU   CMary   CMont   CO   COMC   CPa CPg   CSS   CSalCL   CSf   CSfCP   CSfCSM   CSjC   CSjCL CSmH   CSrCL   CSt   CStclU   CU-B   CViCL   ICN   MoS N   NN   WHi

6996. History of San Benito county. With illustrations descriptive of its scenery, farms [etc.]... S.F., Elliott & Moore, 1881. 188 p. illus.
C   CHi   CHoCL   CO   CSf   CSmH   NN

GREAT REGISTER

6997. San Benito county. Index to the Great register of the county of San Benito. 1867– Place of publication and title vary.
C has 1875–77, 1879, 1880 (biennially to) – 1886, 1890 (biennially to) – 1906, 1910 (biennially to) – 1962. CHi has 1880. CL has 1876–77, 1879, 1882 (suppl.), 1884 (biennially to) – 1890. CLU has 1875. CSmH has Oct. 9, 1880. CU-B has 1879–80, 1880 (suppl.)

GENERAL REFERENCES

6998. Beers, George A. Vasquez: or, The hunted bandits of the San Joaquin... N.Y., Robert M. DeWitt [1875] 141 p. port.   C   CL   CLO   CSmH   CU-B

6999. California. State library. Sacramento. A study of the libraries of the city of Hollister and the county of San Benito, California. Sacramento, 1954. 21 l.
                                              CL

7000. California development board, San Francisco. Agricultural survey of San Benito county, California. Made for the San Benito county Chamber of commerce and the Board of supervisors. S.F. [n.d.] 92 p. illus.   CHi

7001. Coffey, Titian J. Argument of...before the Senate committee on private land claims against the passage of House bill no. 65, to grant to William McGarrahan the tract of land in California called "Panoche Grande." Wash., D.C. [1866?] 24 p. Claim contested by the New Idria mining co.   CHi

7002. Flint, Thomas. Diary: California to Maine and return, 1851–1855. The adventure that ended with the purchase of the Rancho San Justo... by the Flint-Bixby company, and Col. W. W. Hollister. Hollister, Free lance [1926] 49 p.
CBb   CHi   CL   CLU   CSalCL   CSf   CSfCP   CSfWF-H CU-B

7003. Greenwood, Robert, comp. The California outlaw: Tiburcio Vasquez; including the rare contemporary account by George Beers. Los Gatos, Talisman press, 1960. 296 p. ports., facsims.   CSf CSfSt CStcl

7004. Hammack, David. A climber's guide to Pinnacles national monument. S.F., Sierra club [c1955] 13 p. illus.   CAla

7005. Hawkins, Thomas S. Some recollections of a busy life. S.F. Priv. print. for the author by Elder [1913] 161 p. illus.
C CHi CLU CSalCL CSf CSmH (1924)

7006. Hollister free lance. Grand army edition of the Hollister free lance, San Benito co., Cal. ...June, 1886. [Hollister, 1886] 16 p. illus.   CU-B

7007. —— Resources of San Benito county, California... Hollister, Free lance job print., 1887. 10 p.
CU-B

7008. —— ...San Benito county, de luxe edition, May, 1916. illus., ports. 68 p.   NN

7009. Hoyle, M. F. Crimes and career of Tiburcio Vasquez, the bandit of San Benito county... Hollister, Evening free lance, 1927. 26 p. port. Cover title: California's age of terror. With: Ridge, John Rollin. *Life and adventures of Joaquin Murieta*...Hollister, 1927.
CBb CHi CL CLO CLU CLgA CMartC CMont CO CSalCL CSd CSf CSfCP CSfWF-H CSjC CSmH CU-B CViCL

7010. Immigration association of California. [County scrapbooks] [S.F., 188–?]   C

7011. Jones, William Carey, Sr. Land titles in California; argument before the commission on private land claims in California, in the case of Cruz Cervantes, claiming the Rancho of Rosa Morada, delivered on Friday and Saturday, 4th and 5th June, 1852. S.F., Monson, Whitton & co., print., 1852. 55 p.
C CLU CSfCW CSmH CU-B

7012. [Leigh, John Wyckham] San Benito county. Memorial of opponents. [n.p., 187–?] 8 p. Signed by J. W. Leigh, editor Monterey democrat. Opposed formation of San Benito county.   CLU

7013. McGarrahan, William, vs. Maxwell, J. W. C. ...William McGarrahan, respondent vs. J. W. C. Maxwell and others, appellants. Transcript on appeal. Hoge & Wilson, for appellants. Patterson & Wallace, Sharp & Lloyd, for respondent. Sacramento, State print. off., 1864. 156 p. The names of John W. Dwinelle and Edmond L. Goold have been added in manuscript to the list of appellants' attorneys on cover. Panoche Grande claim litigation.   CLU

7014. —— ... Brief of appellants... S.F., Francis, Valentine & co. [1864?] 51 p.   CLU

7015. McGarrahan, William, vs. New Idria mining co. ...William McGarrahan, appellant, vs. the New Idria mining company, respondent. Abstract of authorities. B. S. Brooks, attorney for appellant. J. P. Hoge, S. A. Sharp, Wm. H. Patterson, of counsel. S.F., Francis & Valentine print., etc. [1874?] 111 p. Panoche Grande claim litigation.   CLU

7016. McGarrahan, William. The history of the McGarrahan claim, as written by himself. [n.p., 187–?] 411 p. 2 fold. maps. "This is the most complete history of this claim [Panoche Grande] literature of which is very extensive."—Cowan.   CHi CLU CSf CSfCW

7017. —— The McGarrahan memorial. Correspondence between President Grant and secretary Cox; Testimony vs. Memorial; Return of Judge Ogier; Statement of Hon. Jeremiah S. Black; Briefs of Hon. Wm. M. Evarts and Col. D. S. Wilson; Report of Messrs. Williams and Ferry, of Senate committee. S.F., Smyth & Shoaff, 1870. v.p. fold. maps.   CHi CU-B

7018. [McGarrahan claim] [A collection of congressional documents presenting the claim for title to the Rancho Panoche Grande, California] Wash., D.C., 1870–[1893] 6 pt. in 1 v.   CLU

7019. —— [A collection of pamphlets] [v.p., v.d.] 9 v. in 1.   CU-B

7020. New Idria mining and chemical co., Idria. Annual report... [S.F., Schwabacher-Frey co.] illus. CHi has 1953/54.   CHi

7021. Pinnacles, national monument; San Benito county, California. Hollister, Cook's studio [n.d.] folder (6 p.) illus., map.   CRcS

7022. Ridge, John Rollin. Career of Tiburcio Vasquez, the bandit of Soledad, Salinas, and Tres Pinos ... S.F., Fred'k MacCrellish & co., 1874. p. 83–98. With his *Life and adventures of Joaquin Murieta*.   CSmH

7023. San Benito county. Board of supervisors. San Benito county, where "blest with nature's best a little effort does the rest." [Hollister, Evening free lance press, 1915] [13] p. illus., map.   CHi

7024. —— **Chamber of commerce.** Hollister classified directory. [Hollister] 1949.   CU-B

7025. —— —— San Benito county; cradle of early California history. Hollister [n.d.] folder (4 p.) illus., maps.   CRcS

7026. San Benito county... A brief statement of its advantages... [Hollister] Hollister bee print. [1902?] 32 p. illus.   CU-B

7027. San Benito county, California, on the highway between Yosemite and the sea. [S.F.] Schwabacher-Frey [1922] 11 p. illus., map.   CRcS

7028. Sawyer, Eugene Taylor. The life and career of Tiburcio Vasquez...to which is appended Judge Collins' address to the jury in behalf of the prisoner... [San José, 1875] 48 p. ports.
C CL CLU CMont CSfCP CSjC CSmH CU-B

7029. —— Same, reprinted with foreword by Joseph A. Sullivan. Oakland, Biobooks, 1944. 91 p. ports. (Calif. centennial editions, no. 2)
C CBb CHi CL CLO CLU CLgA CO CRcS CSalCL CSd CSdS CSf CSfWF-H CSjC CSmH CStrJC CU-B

7030. Shaw, Charles P. Argument...before the judiciary committee of the House of representatives, forty-first congress, in the matter of the application of William McGarrahan, for the Rancho Panoche Grande, California. Wash., D.C., M'Gill & Witherow, 1870. 190 p.
CHi CSfCW

7031. Truman, Benjamin Cummings. Life, adventures and capture of Tiburcio Vasquez... [L.A.] Los Angeles star, 1874. 44 p.   C CLO CSmH CU-B

7032. —— Same. L.A., Abbey San Encino press, 1941. 43 p. front. (port.)   CLO CLU CMont

7033. United States vs. Gomez, Vicente P. ... The United States vs. Vicente P. Gomez, claiming "Panoche Grande." Brief for the United States, on claimant's motion to vacate the order restoring the cause to the docket to be tried...Edmond L. Goold, counsel. S.F., Valentine & co. [1861?] 24 p.   CSmH

7034. U.S. Board of commissioners of California land claims. ...Opinion of the board delivered by Harry I. Thornton on the claim of Cruz Cervantes. Opinion delivered by Hiland Hall, on the claim of Pearson B. Reading. Opinion delivered by James Wilson, on the claim of Carmen Sibrian de Bernal. S.F., Monson, Haswell & co., 1852. 63 p.

                     C CHi CSfCW CSmH CU-B

7035. Wagner, Harr, ed. The year-book of San Benito county, for the year 1882... Hollister, "Democrat" off., 1882. 40 p.   CLU CU-B

7036. Wells, Andrew Jackson. San Benito county, California... S.F., Sunset mag. homeseekers' bur. [n.d.] 32 p. illus., ports., map.   CSf

7037. Wilson, Bourdon. San Benito county California. S.F., Sunset mag. homeseekers' bur. [1910] 31 p. illus., maps.   CHi CSf CU-B

7038. Yazdanmehr, Djahanguir. Investigation of water supply from San Benito river. [Stanford, 1950] 116 l.   CSt

San Juan Bautista

7039. [Abbe, Frank B.] San Juan Bautista. Souvenir, Centennial celebration, June 24, 1897. [n.p.] 1897. 45 p. illus., ports.

                   C CHi CLU CSmH CU-B

7040. Engelhardt, Zephyrin, *Father.* Mission San Juan Bautista, a school of church music... Santa Barbara, Mission Santa Barbara, 1931. 148 p. illus., ports., maps. Includes music.

Available in many libraries.

7041. Martin, John M. A brief sketch of Mission San Juan Bautista, California. [n.p.] Scher, c1931. 16 p. illus.   CStmo

7042. Milliken, Ralph LeRoy. "The city of history," San Juan Bautista, California. [Los Banos, Los Banos enterprise, 1950] [11] p.   CHi

7043. —— Same, with title: San Juan Bautista, California, the city of history. [2d ed.] [Los Banos, Los Banos enterprise, c1951] [16] p. illus.

        C CHi CL CLU CO CSfWF-H

7044. —— Mission San Juan Bautista. [San Juan Bautista] c1939. [4] p.   CHi

7045. Mylar, Isaac L. Early days at the Mission San Juan Bautista... Watsonville, Evening Pajaronian, c1929. 195 p. illus.

    C CHi CL CLO CLSU CLU CLgA CMont CSf CSfCW CSjC CSmH CU-B NN

7046. San Juan. Board of trustees. Memorial of the Board of trustees of the town of San Juan, requesting the legalizing of the act of incorporation of said town. [Sacramento, Gelwicks, state print., 1870]   CSmH

7047. San Juan mission news. Brief history of the Mission San Juan Bautista, San Juan, California. San Juan, 1919. 19 p.   CHi

7048. San Juan valley improvement club. San Juan Bautista and San Juan valley. [1906]

                       CU-B NN

SAN BERNARDINO COUNTY

(Created in 1853 from portions of Los Angeles and San Diego counties)

COUNTY HISTORIES

7049. Beattie, George William, and **Beattie, Helen Pruitt.** Heritage of the valley; San Bernardino's first century... Pasadena, San Pasqual press, 1939. 459 p. illus., ports., maps. "List of references": p. 427–439.

C CBaB CBea CBev CBu CCH CCoron CF CFS CGl CHi CL CLCM CLCo CLO CLSM CLSU CLU CLgA CLob CO COr CP CPom CPs CRcS CRedl CRiv CSbCL CSdS CSf CSfCP CSjC CSmH CSmat CStaCL CStb CStmo CU-B CViCL CYcCL ICN MiD MoSHi N NN UPB UU WHi

7050. —— Same. Oakland, Biobooks, 1951. 459 p. illus., ports., maps.

C CHi CLU CRcS CRedCL CSd CSmat CStcrCL CSto CoD N UHi

7051. Brown, John, jr., and **Boyd, James.** History of San Bernardino and Riverside counties...with selected biography... [Madison, Wis.] Western hist. assoc., 1922. 3 v. illus., ports. v.2–3 include biographical material.

C C-S CBb CBea CHi CL CLAC CLCM CLU CLob CO CRedl CRiv CSbCL CSd CSmH CU-B MWA NN UPB WHi

7052. Caballeria y Collell, Juan. History of San Bernardino valley from the padres to the pioneers, 1810–1851... San Bernardino, Times-index press, 1902. 130 p. illus., port.

C C-S CAla CB CBaK CBb CCH CHi CHoCL CL CLCM CLCo CLO CLSM CLSU CLU CLgA CLob CO COnC CPom CRedl CRiv CSbCL CSd CSf CSfCP CSfCW CSfP CSjC CSmH CStmo CStoC CStrJC CU-B MiD-B N UHi

7053. Historical records survey. California. Inventory of the county archives of California. San Bernardino county (San Bernardino) v.1. L.A., So. Calif. hist. records survey, 1940.   C

7054. History of San Bernardino county, California, with illustrations descriptive of its scenery, farms [etc.] ... S.F., Elliott, 1883. 204 p. illus., ports., maps.

C CHi CL CLCM CLSU CLob CRedl CSbCL CSmH CStcl CU-B NHi

7055. Ingersoll, Luther A. Ingersoll's century annals of San Bernardino county, 1769 to 1904...with an encyclopedia of local biography ... L.A., Author, 1904. 887 p. illus., ports.

C C-S CBb CCH CF CHi CL CLAC CLCM CLCo CLO CLSM CLSU CLU CLob CMont CO COnC CP CPom CRedl CRiv CSbCL CSd CSf CSfCP CSfCSM CSfCW CSmH CSmat CStaCL CStmo CU-B CoD CtY MiD-B MoS N NHi NN UHi UPB WHi

GREAT REGISTER

7056. San Bernardino county. Index to the Great register of the county of San Bernardino. 1866– Place of publication and title vary.

C has 1872, 1876, 1879–80, 1882, 1884, 1888 (biennially to)– 1898, 1902 (biennially to)– 1962. CHi has 1876, 1880. CL has 1873, 1876, 1877 (suppl.), 1882 (biennially to)– 1890. CRedl has 1888, 1892, 1894, 1896 (suppl.), 1898. CSbCL has 1894. CSmH has 1880, 1882. CU-B has 1867–68 (suppl. to 1867), 1872–73, 1879–80, 1940.

DIRECTORIES

7057. 1887. Morrill, F. L., & co., pub. San Bernardino city and county directory... L.A., 1887. 225 p.

                      C CSbCL

7058. 1889. Flagg & Wallsen, pub. San Bernardino city and county directory. San Bernardino, 1889.   CRedl

7059. 1891. Bagot, George, pub. San Bernardino county directory for 1891. Riverside [n.d.]   CRedl

7060. 1898. Bushnell, Arthur M., comp. San

Bernardino county directory. L.A., Kingsley-Barnes & Neuner co., 1898. **CRedl**

7061. 1893–1895. Milliken, James, pub. ... Milliken's San Bernardino county directory. A complete compilation of...all the adult population of San Bernardino city and county. A classified business directory of San Bernardino, Redlands, Ontario, Colton...

CL has 1893–95. CRedl has 1893–95.

7062. 1951– Luskey bros., pub. Luskey's San Bernardino criss cross city directory... containing an alphabetical directory of business concerns and residents, and a classified business directory... Title varies.

CHi has 1951. CSbCL has 1958.

San Bernardino

7063. 1902. Perry, T. F., comp. and pub. ... Directory of the city of San Bernardino...Compiled and published... in connection with the Los Angeles city directory co. L.A., 1902. **CCH**

7064. 1904– San Bernardino directory co., pub. San Bernardino city directory, including Colton and Rialto. San Bernardino, 1904– Title varies: 1904–28 San Bernardino and Colton. Publisher varies: 1904–13? Los Angeles directory co.

C has 1920, 1922, 1926, 1928, 1930, 1933, 1939. CCH has 1924. CHi has 1914/15, 1933, 1937, 1939, 1942, 1944, 1949. CL has 1911–13, 1915–17, 1919, 1922, 1924, 1926, 1928, 1930, 1933, 1937, 1940, 1942, 1949, 1958, 1961. CMont has 1939. CU-B has 1926, 1928.

Other Cities and Towns

7065. 1952– Directory service co., pub. Luskey's ...greater Chino criss cross city directory... Santa Ana, 1952–

CL has 1952.

7066. 1955/56– Luskey bros., pub. Luskey's Colton criss cross city directory. Anaheim, 1955–

CL has 1959. CSbCL has 1955/56.

7067. 1960– Luskey bros., pub. Luskey's... desert empire...including Joshua Tree, Morongo Valley, Twenty-Nine Palms, and Yucca Valley criss cross city directory. Anaheim, 1960–

CL has 1960.

7068. 1960– Luskey bros., pub. Luskey's Fontana-Bloomington... criss cross city directory. Anaheim, 1960–

CL has 1960.

7069. 1900/01. Norton, W. A., pub. ...Ontario city directory, including North Ontario, Chino, North Cucamonga...1900 and 1901... [Ontario] 71 p. **CSmH**

7070. 1940–1951. Los Angeles directory co., pub. Ontario City directory including Upland, Chino, Alta Loma, Cucamonga, Etiwanda. L.A., 1940–1951. Publisher varies. Content varies: 1940 includes Pomona, Claremont, La Verne, San Dimas also.

CHi has 1948/49, 1951. CL has 1945/46, 1951. CUpl has 1940, 1945/46, 1948/49, 1951.

7071. 1954– Directory service co., pub. Luskey's Ontario-Upland criss cross directory. Santa Ana, 1954–

CUpl has 1954.

7072. 1896– Arthur commercial press, pub. Redlands city directory including Loma Linda and Yucaipa Valley. Redlands, 1896– Publisher varies: 1896–1902/03 W. M. Newton; 1905–17 Paul W. Moore; 1919–36 Los Angeles directory co. Content varies.

C has 1902/03, 1915/16, 1921, 1927, 1929. CCH has

1923. CHi has 1900, 1912/13, 1929, 1933, 1936, 1952. CL has 1896, 1902/03, 1911–13, 1915/16, 1919, 1921, 1923, 1925, 1927, 1929, 1931, 1936, 1950. CLU has 1907/08. CRedl has 1896, 1900, 1902/03, 1905, 1907/08, 1909/10, 1911/12, 1912/13, 1914/15, 1915/16, 1917, 1919, 1921, 1923, 1925, 1927, 1929, 1931, 1933, 1936, 1939, 1941, 1947, 1950, 1952. CSmH has 1900. CU-B has 1907/08.

GENERAL REFERENCES

7073. Alexander, J. A. The life of George Chaffey; a story of irrigation beginnings in California and Australia...with... a chapter on the Imperial valley, by H. T. Cory... Melbourne, London, Macmillan, 1928. 382 p. illus., ports., maps. George Chaffey, a Canadian engineer, came to southern California in 1880 and became interested in the problem of irrigating the arid regions of that section. Mr. Chaffey was also one of the founders of the Chaffey college of agriculture, now the Chaffey junior college.

Available in many libraries.

7074. Altergott, Alexander. Economic history of the valley of the Mohaves; a thesis presented to the department of economics, University of Southern California...for the degree of Master of arts. 1930. 132 p. Typew. A history of the Colorado river basin from the time of the aboriginal inhabitants to the present day. Included is an account of the origin and development of the town of Needles. **CLSU CSbCL**

7075. American potash & chemical corp. The story of the American potash & chemical corporation, Trona on Searles lake, California. N.Y. [c1933] 25 p. illus. **CHi**

7076. —— Same, with title: Trona, at Searles Lake, California. [n.p., 1934] 45 p. illus., maps, diagrs. **CHi CU-B**

7077. Arrowhead hot springs company. Arrowhead hot springs, Cal. [n.p., 1909?] 23 p. illus. **CHi**

7078. —— Same. [L.A., Arrowhead press [n.d.] [32] p. illus., map, plans. **CHi CU-B**

7079. Bailey, Gilbert Ellis. Arrowhead springs, California's ideal spa. [L.A., Union litho. co., 1917] 70 p. illus. Includes sections on history and legends of the area as well as geology, etc. **C CL CLO CLSU CSmH**

7080. Banks, John L., jr. The upper Santa Ana river watershed. [L.A.] 1949. Thesis (M.A.) — U.C.L.A., 1949. **CLU**

7081. Barstow printer-review. ...Centennial edition. Special number of the Barstow printer-review, January 5, 1950. Barstow, 1950. 1 v. v.p. **C**

7082. Barstow woman's club. Colorful history of Barstow and vicinity. **CSbCL**

7083. Battye, Charles, comp. True tales of Needles, the Colorado river and the desert. Author, 1945. 76 p. illus. Scrapbook of newspaper clippings. **CSbCL**

7084. —— Origin and early development of water rights in the east San Bernardino valley. Redlands, San Bernardino valley water conservation district. Bul. no. 4, Nov. 1951. 70 p. illus. **CSbCL**

7085. Beattie, George William. Historic crossing places in the San Bernardino mountains. 1931. 14 p. Typew. **CSbCL**

7086. —— San Bernardino county landmarks and historical points of interest. 8 v. Typew. **CSbCL**

7087. Belden, L. Burr. [Collection of newspaper articles on the history of San Bernardino and the surrounding area] **CSbCL**

7088. Benton, Frank Weber. San Bernardino county, California, in the golden west. [L.A., Author, 1930] [28] p. col. illus.   C

7089. Bloomington fruit association. [Articles of incorporation and by-laws as amended October 6, 1916. n.p., 1916?] 14 p.   CLU

7090. Cadwell, Ernest. History of Fontana. [Bloomington] San Bernardino county hist. soc. and the Fontana chamber of commerce [1955] 54 p. illus.
                                        CLU COnC

7091. California electric power co., San Bernardino. Annual report.
CL has 1954–60.

7092. —— Prospectus.
CL has 1955.

7093. California interstate telephone co., Victorville. Annual report.
CL has 1955–61.

7094. —— Prospectus.
CL has 1954.

7095. —— Romantic heritage of Mojave river valley, a saga of transportation and desert frontiers. [Victorville, 1961] [8] p. illus.   CHi

7096. —— Romantic heritage of upper Mojave desert, a saga of pioneer discoveries and modern achievements. [Victorville, c1961] 19 p. illus., maps.   CHi

7097. —— Romantic heritage of Victor valley, a saga of desert exploration and expansion. [Victorville] 1961. [16] p. illus.   CHi

7098. [Chaffey brothers, proprietors] Etiwanda. Riverside, Press & horticulturist print. [n.d.] 12 p.
                                        CSmH CU-B

7099. Citizens national bank, Yucaipa. Into the green valley; a story of Yucaipa valley. [Yucaipa, 1957] [12] p. illus., map.   CHi CL CU-B

7100. Coke, Larry. Calico. [Barstow, Barstow printer-review, c1941] 57 p. illus., ports.
                    C CHi CL CSd CSmH

7101. Cole, Frank R. Gold around our valley. Redlands, Fortnightly club, 1953. 11 p. Typew.   CRedl

7102. Colton. Board of trustees. Colton, the hub city. [Colton, 19—?] 20 p. illus.   CU-B

7103. Cox, Silas, vs. Clough, F. S. et als. No. 9990 in the Supreme court of the state of California. Silas Cox, et als., plaintiffs and respondents, vs. F. S. Clough, et als., defendants and appellants. Transcript on appeal. Byron Waters, and Satterwhite & Curtis, attorneys for appellant... San Bernardino, Times bk. and job print., 1885. [3]–161 p. Clippings giving judgment in case, attached to verso of p. 161. A San Bernardino county water rights suit.   CLU

7104. Crafts, Eliza Persis (Russell) Robbins, and McGehee, Mrs. Fannie P. Pioneer days in the San Bernardino valley... Redlands, 1906. 214 p. illus., ports.
    C CHi CL CLO CLSU CLU CLob CO CRedl CSf CSj CSjC CSmH CU-B CaBViPA NN

7105. Croy, Hazel Miller. A history of education in San Bernardino during the Mormon period. [L.A.] 1935. Thesis (Ed.D.)— U.C.L.A., 1935.   CLU

7106. Crozer, Elizabeth (Warder) ...Archeological survey of the Twenty Nine Palms region; with an introduction by Edwin F. Walker. L.A., Southwest museum, 1931. 93 p. illus. (Southwest museum papers, no. 7)
    C CBea CL CLO CLSU CLU CSS CSd CSfCSM CSjC CSmH CStmo CU-B TxU

7107. —— The archeology of Pleistocene Lake Mohave. A symposium. L.A., Southwest museum, 1937. 118 p. illus., maps. (Southwest museum papers, no. 11)
                    CBea CHi CSfCSM CU-B

7108. —— The Pinto basin site, an ancient aboriginal camping ground in the California desert. L.A., Southwest museum, 1935. 51 p. illus., fold. map. (Southwest museum papers no. 9)   CBea CLob

7109. Cucamonga homestead association, Los Angeles. By-laws... [L.A., 1874] 4 p.   CSmH

7110. —— Cucamonga homestead association... [L.A., 1874] 6 p. Description of property.
                                        CHi CSmH

7111. Curtis, Jesse William. The bench and bar of the county of San Bernardino, state of California. [San Bernardino, 1957] 40 p.   C CHi

7112. Daughters of the American revolution. California. Genealogical records committee. [San Bernardino county scrapbook. San Bernardino, 1950] 32 p. illus.   C

7113. Desert–mountain–valley club, San Bernardino. San Bernardino county, California. [San Bernardino? 192–?] [16] p. illus.   CU-B

7114. Diamond jubilee committee. The Pinkos (Jewish chronicle) published under the supervision of the Diamond jubilee committee commemorating seventy-five years of Jewish activities in San Bernardino and Riverside counties, 1860–1935. San Bernardino, The Sun print. house [1935] 75 p. illus., ports.   C

7115. Drake, Austin. Big Bear valley; its history, legends and tales. Big Bear lake, The Grizzly [c1949] 79 p. illus., ports., maps.
    C CBb CHi CL CLO CLSM CLU CP CSd CSmH

7116. Etiwanda water co. By-laws... Riverside, Press and horticulturist print., 1884. 8 p.   CHi

7117. Federal writers' project. San Bernardino; a guide to the nation's largest county... (Am. guide ser.) Typew.   CSbCL

7118. Finkenbinder, Charles E. Mojave desert trails; Mojave desert, Death valley, Boulder dam. [L.A., c1940] 72 p. illus., maps. "Maps by Jack Renié, Los Angeles"   C CLO

7119. Fox, Maude A. Both sides of the mountain. Palm Desert, Desert mag. press [1954] 132 p. illus., ports.   C CBb CHi CO CP CPs CRedl CSd

7120. Frazee, William D. San Bernardino county, its climate and resources... San Bernardino, San Bernardino daily & weekly argus, 1876. 97 p.
                    CU-B MWA NHi

7121. Garrison, Jural Jeanne. Barstow, California. [L.A.] 1950. Thesis (M.A.)— U.C.L.A., 1950.   CLU

7122. [Gird, Richard], comp. Information about lands, productions, climate and water in semi-tropic or southern California. What home-seekers and investors need to know. Brief description of title, situation, soil, water, climate, and productive capacity of the famously rich Chino ranch with map showing its location in San Bernardino county, California. [Chino] Chino valley champion print. [1888] [4] p. map.   CU-B

7123. Hale, Edson D. The county of San Bernardino, California, and its principal city. A descriptive and historical sketch. San Bernardino, Bd. of trade, 1888. 70 p. illus., map.   CL CRedl CU-B

7124. Heffernan, Helen. Desert treasure, a story of adventure, and the Mohave desert, its people, plants

and animals... S.F., Harr Wagner, 1939. 298 p. illus.,
map.   C

7125. Hentschke, Max. A California dream come
true. [n.p., 1936?] [8] p. About a half century in San
Bernardino valley.   CHi

7126. Hill, Merton Earle. A decade of rural education, 1911–1920. [n.p., 1920] 1 p.   CSmH

7127. Hinckley, Edith Barrett (Parker) Frank
Hinckley, California engineer and rancher... together
with genealogical tables of the Hinckley and Meek families... Claremont, Saunders press, 1946. 149 p. illus.,
ports.
C CHi CL CLSU CO CPom CRedl CSdS
CSmH CU-B

7128. Histories of school districts of San Bernardino
county. Handmade booklets.   CSbCL

7129. Holcomb, William F. History of Holcomb
valley, San Bernardino county, California. 14 p. Typew.
                                                          CSbCL

7130. Holmes, Bernese Gay. Letters of the early
pioneers of Big Bear lake prior to 1930. Reseda, Valley
business service, 1955. 118 p. illus.
                        C CL CLU CSbCL

7131. —— Tales of the pioneers of Big Bear lake,
California... Chatsworth, West valley settlers, 1956. 54
p. illus.   CHi CP CSbCL

7132. Holt, L. M. ...The great interior fruit belt
and sanitarium, southern California, San Bernardino
county... San Bernardino, Times bk. & job print., 1885.
69 p.   CL CLU CSmH CU-B

7133. —— ...Further information. A large edition
of the "Pointer" is issued by the Immigration association
of San Bernardino county, calling attention to the great
interior fruit belt and sanitarium. [Riverside, 1885] 12 p.
                                                          CU-B

7134. Iaeger, Louis John Frederick. Diary of
L. J. F. Yager, ferryman of the Colorado river... from
Dec. 11, 1855 to June 28, 1857. Ms.   CSbCL CU-B

7135. Immigration association of California.
[County scrapbooks] [S.F., 188–?]   C

7136. Industrial survey associates. The future of
industry in the San Bernardino valley. A report prepared
for the San Bernardino valley industrial committee. 1951.
[78] l. Bibliography. l. [75]–[78]   C CO

7137. Jones, Clark Harding. A history of the development and progress of Colton, Calif., 1873–1900.
[Claremont, 1951] 141 l. Thesis (M.A.) — Claremont
college, 1951.   CCH CSbCL

7138. Kepley, William Neal, jr. ...Voting behavior in a California city. [L.A.] 1941. Thesis (M.A.)—
U.C.L.A., 1941. About Needles.   CLU

7139. Knott's berry farm, Buena Park. Calico,
ghost town, 1881; S. California's greatest silver camp.
[Buena Park, c1952] 56 p. illus., ports., maps.
                                             CLU CU-B

7140. [Kriebel, Fred L.] The Arrowhead book...
Arrowhead hot springs, Arrowhead hot springs co.
[c1914] [40] p. illus.   C CU-B

7141. Lade, Charles G., jr. Lucerne valley, California. Agricultural land use as related to the physical setting. [L.A.] 1953. Thesis (M.A.) — U.C.L.A., 1953.
                                                          CLU

7142. LaFuze, Mrs. C. E., comp. History of Lake
Arrowhead country; compiled for the Women's club of
Lake Arrowhead, 1955. 8 l. Typew. Illus. with news-
paper photos.   CSbCL

7143. Lake Arrowhead golf & country club. The
Lake Arrowhead golf & country club, Lake Arrowhead in
Arrowhead woods... [Prospectus] [n.p.] c1924. [28]
p. illus., maps, plan.   CU-B

7144. Lawton, Harry. Willie boy, desert man hunt.
Balboa Island, Paisano press, 1960. 233 p. illus., maps.
                                           CBea CU-B

7145. Lindgren, Waldemar. The silver mines of
Calico, California. Author's ed. [N.Y.?] 1887. 18 p.
illus., map. (Am. inst. of mining engineers. Trans. Scran-
ton meeting, Feb., 1887)   CLU

7146. Loehr, Helen. [Pioneers] San Bernardino
county historical society, 1949. [n.p., 1949] 29 p. Mimeo.
                                                          CHi

7147. Loma Linda sanitarium, Loma Linda. [De-
scriptive brochure. L.A., n.d.] [13] p. illus.   CHi

7148. Lucerne valley. Chamber of commerce.
Lucerne valley tells the world. [Pasadena, Post print. co.
for Victor valley news-herald, 192–?] 11 p. illus.   CHi

7149. Lugo, José del Carmen. Vida de un ranchero
...Se incluye una narración de la Batalla llamada del
"Rancho del Chino," acción de guerra en que tuvó parte
autor. Escrita por D. Tomás Savage para la Bancroft
library, año de 1877. 68 p. Typew. "The original of this
manuscript is in the Bancroft library."
                             CRedl CSbCL CU-B

7150. —— [Vida de un ranchero, tr. into English
by Helen Pruitt Beattie from the original narrative as
told to Thomas Savage. East Highlands, 1950?] 6 l.
                                                          CLU

7151. McDaniel, Bruce William. Dune and desert
folk. With original illustrations. L.A., Swetland pub. co.
of Calif. [c1926] 31 p. illus.   CU-B

7152. Macedonian silver ledge co., California.
[Descriptive brochure] Buffalo, N.Y., Rockwell, Baker
& Hill, print., 1865. 20 p.   CHi

7153. Morrill, Frank L. Southern California. A
description of San Bernardino county... L.A., Express
print. co., 1886. 64 p. illus.   C CU-B

7154. O'Neal, Lulu Rasmussen. A peculiar piece
of desert; the story of California's Morongo basin. L.A.,
Westernlore press, 1957. 208 p. illus. Includes bibliography.
  Available in many California libraries and CoD MiD

7155. Paxton, June Le Mert. My life on the Mojave. [1st ed.] N.Y., Vantage press [1958, c1957] 168 p.
illus.   CAla CL CMon CU-B

**7156. Pedder, Beatrice; Bouck, Kenneth; and
Warfield, Robert, eds.** Big Bear panorama... Big Bear
lake, Big Bear high school [c1934] 111 p. illus. A history
of Big Bear valley, ed. and pub. by pupils of the Big Bear
high school.   CLO

7157. Peter Pan woodland club: a word-picture im-
pressionism depicting present features, projects, personnel. Big Bear city [Peter Pan woodland club, 1927?]
[16] p. illus.   CHi

**7158. The Piute company of California and
Nevada.** The Piute company of California and Nevada.
Organized April 13th, 1869; incorporated June 30th, 1870.
S.F., E. Bosqui & co., print., 1870. 23 p. illus., maps.
Mining company—includes Clarke district, San Bernar-
dino co.   CLU CSfCSM CU-B

**7159. Pope, Emily F., et als. vs. Kinman, N. et
als.** ...Emily F. Pope, et als., representatives of Andrew
J. Pope, deceased, plaintiffs and appellants, vs. N. Kinman, et als., defendants and respondents. Transcript on

appeal. From 18th district court, San Bernardino Co. H. C. Rolfe, attorney for plaintiffs. Waters & Swing and C. W. C. Rowell, attorneys for defendants... San Bernardino, "Index" bk. and job print., 1879. 72 p. Suit over the water rights of Rancho Muscupiabe in San Bernardino county. CLU

7160. Redlands orange grove and water company. Some facts relating to orange culture in southern California, San Bernardino county. Comp. for the Redlands Orange Grove and water co. May 1, 1889. Redlands, Citrograph steam print., 1889. 24 p. CSmH CU-B

7161. Rice, L. J. Tightening a noose to acquire a title; a true story involving the San Bernardino county court house property... [L.A., Business print., inc., c1938] 11 p. illus. CHi CL CLU CSmH CU-B

7162. Robinson, William Wilcox. The story of San Bernardino county. [San Bernardino, Pioneer title insurance co., c1958] 70 p. illus., fold. map, ports.
Available in many California libraries and UHi UPB

7163. Rolfe, Horace C., comp. [Scrapbook containing newspaper articles and pictures on the history of San Bernardino city and valley] 2 v. CSbCL

7164. Rumble, Josephine R. History old government road across the Mojave desert to the Colorado river ... 35, 61 p. 65 pl. Mimeo. Works progress administration project, number 3428. C CHi CSbCL

7165. —— History the Mill creek zanja, San Bernardino...1819–1937. 82 p. 18 pl. Mimeo. "Research work was begun by Josephine R. Rumble under SERA project number 36-F8-386, and compiled, edited, and rewritten under WPA project number 3428."—Foreword. C CHi CRedl CSbCL

7166. The San Bernardino asistencia, Barton road, west of Redlands... [n.p., 193–?] [4] p. CHi

7167. San Bernardino county. Your county government; 100 years of progress, comp. by the elective and appointive officials of the county of San Bernardino. [San Bernardino, 1953?] 40 p. illus., facsim. CU-B

7168. —— **Board of supervisors.** San Bernardino county, California. A brief historical review. Topography and scenery... Redlands, Citrograph bk. press, 1903. 32 p. illus. CHi CLU CSmH CU-B

7169. —— —— San Bernardino county... [San Bernardino? Sun press, 1915?] [32] p. illus. CHi

7170. —— **Chamber of commerce.** San Bernardino county... San Bernardino, 1894. 12 p. CL

7171. —— **Flood control district.** Hydrologic and climatic data, by Lloyd Martin. San Bernardino, 1951–54. 3 v. in 2. CLU

7172. —— **Free library.** [Photostats of manuscript records of cases involving titles to ranchos in county] 12 v. CSbCL

7173. —— **Sheriff's office. Employees benefit association.** Century of progress: 1853–1953. [San Bernardino, 1953?] 240 p. illus. CHi

7174. San Bernardino county bar association. Proceedings..."John Marshall day," February 4th, 1901. [n.p.] 1901. 37 p. C

7175. San Bernardino county, California. [L.A., Out west co., 1904?] [64] p. illus. CHi CSbCL

7176. San Bernardino county, California. [San Bernardino? Sun print. and pub. house, 1925?] [28] p. illus., map. CHi

7177. San Bernardino county; for home life, for pleasure. [n.p., n.d.] folder (2 p.) illus., maps. CRcS

7178. San Bernardino county immigration association. San Bernardino county and valleys tributary thereto. San Bernardino, Times bk. and job print., 1885. 69 p. CHi

7179. San Bernardino daily sun. San Bernardino ...the imperial county. (souvenir number) San Bernardino, 1898. 30 p. NN

7180. San Bernardino rancho. Deed of sale of the Rancho of San Bernardino to Conn, Tucker & Allen by Lyman Rich, Ebenezer Hanks, and Jane, his wife...Dated 15th of February, 1858. [10] l. Ms. CSbCL

7181. San Bernardino valley index. Illustrated description of San Bernardino county... San Bernardino, 1881. 34 p. illus. C

7182. Sanders, Francis Charles Scott. ...The Arrowhead hot springs... S.F., Bolte & Braden co., c1915. 48 p. illus. CU-B

7183. San Jacinto tin co. vs. Baker, R. S., et al. In the Supreme court of the state of California. The San Jacinto tin company, plaintiff and respondent, vs. R. S. Baker, et al., defendants and appellants. Respondent's points and authorities. B. S. Brooks, attorney for respondents... [S.F.] W. C. Brown, print. [1883] 6 p. San Bernardino county land suit. CLU

7184. San Pedro, Los Angeles & Salt Lake railroad. Passenger dept. Legends of the Arrowhead (mountain). L.A. [n.d.] [32] p. CLU

7185. Scott, Ferris Huntington. Rim of the world guide. Santa Ana, 1952. 38 p. illus. CL

7186. Seely, David Randolph. Seely Flats, San Bernardino county—early history. 2 l. Typew. CSbCL

7187. Seven Oaks, a mountain resort, Charles C. Le Bas & J. B. Proctor, proprietors. S.F., Hicks-Judd co. [n.d.] [14] p. illus. CRedl

7188. Smith, Erie Aurora. Progress to a centennial; a history of the Warm springs school district. San Bernardino, San Bernardino county hist. soc., 1957. 102 p. illus. C CU-B

7189. Smith, Gerald Arthur. A history of the county school administration of San Bernardino county, Calif. [San Bernardino] San Bernardino county hist. soc., 1954. 438 p. illus., ports., facsims. C CHi

7190. —— Indians of San Bernardino valley. Redlands, Valley fine arts press, 1940. 13 p. illus., map. CChiS CRedl CSbCL CStmo

7191. —— Prehistoric man of San Bernardino valley. Redlands, San Bernardino county hist. soc., 1950. 32 p. illus. C CHi CLU CRedl CSbCL

7192. Southern California colonization bureau. California's model colony, Yucaipa valley. [L.A., A. H. Gaarder print., 19–?] [16] p. illus. CU-B

7193. Southern California improvement co. Minneola valley in southern California. Government lands at government prices; railroad lands at very low prices. All under the Minneola canal from which a first-class water right can be obtained... [L.A., Commercial print. house, 1894?] [16] p. illus., map. CLU CSmH

7194. Spell, Hazel M. The Twentynine Palms story. [2d ed.] Twentynine Palms [The Little church of the desert] 1954. 40 p. CHi

7195. —— Same. [3d ed.] [Twenty-nine Palms] 1959. 44 p. illus. C CAla CL CLU CLob CP CSd

7196. [Stuart, James Ferguson] ...To the owners of the Rancho Muscupiabe, lying in San Bernardino county, California. S.F., 1890. 11 p. Presentation of a claim for attorney's fees, signed James F. Stuart.   CLU

7197. Tyler, Joseph B. ...Diary, comp. by Mrs. C. E. LaFuze. 1955–1956. 133 p. photos, map. Typew.
CSbCL

7198. Ward bros., pub. Souvenir of San Bernardino, Cal. [Columbus, Ohio, 1887] 8 p.   CU-B

7199. Welch, S. L. San Bernardino county, southern California. L.A., 1887. 84 p. illus.   CU-B

7200. Wells, Andrew Jackson. San Bernardino county, California... S.F., Sunset mag. homeseekers' bur. [1909] 48 p. illus.   CL CU-B

7201. Wheeler, R. B. ...San Bernardino county, California... S.F., Sunset mag. homeseekers' bur. [1912?] 32 p. illus.   CLU CU-B

7202. Writers' program. California. The old West. Pioneer tales of San Bernardino county...Sponsored by Arrowhead parlor no. 110, Native sons of the golden west. San Bernardino, Sun co. [1940] 53 p. illus.
CBev CHi CLO CLSU CLU CSmH CoD CoU MoSHi TxU

7203. Yucaipa valley residential and business guide. Nov. 1947– Yucaipa, A. H. Earle, 1947–
CRedl has 1948, 1950, 1952–57.

Chino

7204. Bynum, Lindley, ed. The record book of the Rancho Santa Ana del Chino. L.A., John C. Frémont high school, 1935. 55 p. illus. "The record book transcribed here covers the period 1849 to 1853."
CHi CL CLO CLU CLob CPom CSf CSfCP CSmH CStrJC CU-B NN

7205. Duffy, Homer L. The romance of Rancho Santa Ana del Chino. Address before the Chino rotary club, September 27, 1944. 7 p. Processed.   CPom

7206. Gird, Richard, pub. Town of Chino, San Bernardino county, California. [Chino, 1887] map.
CSmH

7207. Gray, John Alexander. History of El Rancho Santa Ana del Chino. [L.A., Printed by Cadmus press, 1916] [27] double l. mounted illus., mounted ports.
CU-B

7208. Rhodes, Edwin, comp. and ed. Break of day in Chino; a collection of incidents and impressions marking the early life of Chino, as recorded by various reliable authors. Chino, 1944. 96, 10, 7 l. photos. Typew.
CHi

7209. —— Same. Chino, 1951. 95 p. illus.
C CLSM CPom CSmH NN

7210. Scudder, Kenyon Judson. Prisoners are people. Garden city, Doubleday, 1952. 286 p. California institution for men, Chino.
CAla CChiS CLS CNa CSd CStmo CU-B ViU

Ontario

7211. Armstrong nurseries. [Catalogs]
CHi has 1917, 1922–23, 1926–29, 1931–33, 1936–39.

7212. [Blackburn, R. E.] A choice bit of the land of sunshine, fruit and flowers, Ontario, southern California. [Ontario? 1896?] [32] p.   CLU CU-B

7213. Bolton, Mabel Moore. The Chaffey experiment; the history of a unique community project in Ontario, California. 1933. 161 p. Typew. Thesis (M.S.) 1933.   COnC

7214. The Daily report. ...Centennial edition,

1774 to [1950] [Ontario-Upland, 1950] 5 pts. in 1 v. illus., ports., maps.   CU-B

7215. Hart, F. W. Ontario colony. The model colony of southern California. The fruit growers' paradise... [Ontario] Ontario record print. house [1895?] 10 p. folder. illus.   CSmH

7216. Hill, Merton Earle. Building a community high school, Chaffey, 1911–20 a decade of rural education. [n.p., 1920?] 33 p.   CHi

7217. —— The development of an Americanization program. [Ontario] Board of trustees of the Chaffey union high school and the Chaffey junior college, 1928. 119 p. illus.   CLU

7218. —— ...History of Chaffey junior college. [n.p., 1946] unp.   COnC

7219. Lee, Beatrice Paxson. The history and development of the Ontario colony. [L.A.] 1929. 141 p. Thesis (M.A.)—Univ. of So. Calif., 1929.   CHi

7220. Ontario. Chamber of commerce. Life and a living. Ontario, the city that charms; southern California. [Ontario, Report job rooms, 1914?] [16] p. illus.
CU-B

7221. —— —— Ontario colony, California, comprising Ontario, Upland, San Antonio Heights. [Ontario? 1904] [4] p. illus.   CU-B

7222. Ontario diamond jubilee. Official program ...April 20–May 5, 1957. Ontario, 1957. unp. illus.   C

7223. Ontario land & improvement co. The gem of the foothills of southern California: Ontario... Ontario [c1887] folder (5 p.)   CSmH

7224. —— Same, with title: Ontario, California... 3d ed. [Ontario] Press of Ontario pub. co., 1908. [31] p.
CSmH

7225. Ontario, located in San Bernardino county, California, on the Southern Pacific railroad... Riverside, Press & horticulturist steam print., 1883. 48 p. illus., maps.   C CLU CSmH CU-B NHi

7226. Ontario observer. Souvenir edition...February 15, 1896. 48 p. illus., ports.   CHi

7227. Ontario real estate exchange. 20 facts concerning Ontario the model colony. S.F., Schmidt label & litho. co. [1882?] [4] p. illus., maps.   CHi

7228. Smith, W. W. Early history of Ontario, emphasizing the development of educational facilities in the community... [n.p., 1929?] The establishment of Chaffey college of agriculture.   CSmH

7229. Walker, David H. Ontario, California... S.F., Sunset mag. homeseekers' bur. [1912?] 32 p. illus.
CU-B

7230. Widney, Robert Maclay. Ontario. Its history, description, and resources... Riverside, Press & horticulturist steam print. house, 1884. 49 p. illus.
CHi CL CLU CSmH CU-B

Redlands

7231. Allen, Paul F. Boom, boomed, booming (land in southern California, especially in San Bernardino county in the 1880's) Redlands, Fortnightly club, 1957. 18 p. Typew.   CRedl

7232. Bear valley mutual water co. Articles of incorporation and by-laws... [Redlands, David Kerr, 1903?] 22 p.   CHi

7233. Cañon Crest park. Winter homes of Alfred H. and Albert K. Smiley. [L.A., Out West, n.d.] 16 p. illus. "Reprinted from *Out West mag.*, March, 1903"
CLU CRedl

7234. Casa Loma, Redlands. ...Opening, Feb. 25th, 1896. J. T. Ritchey, owner and proprietor.   CRedl

7235. The Citrograph (newspaper) Smiley memorial edition. February 28, 1903. [Redlands, 1903] [8] p.   CHi

7236. Clement, Henry G. History of the Redlands public schools. Redlands, Fortnightly club, 1935. 39 p. Typew.   CRedl

7237. Cole, Frank R. Cottonwood row in the morning. Redlands, Fortnightly club, 1947. 8 p. Typew.   CRedl

7238. —— Schools of Redlands and vicinity. Redlands, Fortnightly club, 1949. 16 p. Typew.   CRedl

7239. Description of Redlands... [S.F., Pac. press print., 1882] 26 p. illus.   CLU CRedl CSmH

7240. Dike brothers & company, pub. Redlands, California. Redlands [1904?] 18 p. illus.
                                         CRedl CU-B

7241. Fisk, John P. Some facts about Redlands and vicinity. 2d ed. ... Redlands, Citrograph print. co., 1898. 16 p. folder.   CHi

7242. Folkins, Hugh M. Government of the city of Redlands and the county of San Bernardino. 1949. 67 p. charts, tables. Mimeo.   CRedl

7243. [Graham, Henry L.] Redlands... L.A., Engraving and printing by Out West co. [19—?] [40] p. illus.   CU-B

7244. Hinckley, Edith Barrett (Parker) On the banks of the Zanja; the story of Redlands. [1st ed.] Claremont, Saunders press, 1951. 151 p. illus. Includes bibliography.
C CChiS CL CLO CLSM CLU CO CP CPom CRedl CSd CSdS CSjC CStoC CViCL N NN

7245. —— Redlands yesterdays to 1956. Redlands, Citrograph print. co., 1956. 64 p.   CRedl

7246. Hornbeck, Robert, pub. Redlands. [Views by Chase Thorn] [Redlands?] 1913. [14] p. illus.   C

7247. Illustrated guide to Redlands, points of interest, how to reach them, railroad timetable, electric timetable. Redlands, Citrograph, 1905. [16] p. illus.   CRedl

7248. Information about Redlands. Redlands, Review press, 1903. [16] p. illus.   CRedl

7249. Jump, Herbert A., comp. Redlands, California. Description of Smiley heights, the most famous park in southern California... Redlands, Chamber of commerce, 1915. 21 p.   CRedl

7250. The Lincoln shrine, Redlands, California: an account of its conception...Dedicated February 12, 1932. [L.A., Printed by Bruce McCallister, 1932] [16] p.   CSmH

7251. Nelson, Lawrence Emerson. Redlands: biography of a college; the first fifty years of the University of Redlands. Redlands, Univ. of Redlands [c1958] 310 p. illus., ports.
                C CLO CLS CP CPom CRedl CU-B OrU

7252. Redlands. Board of trade. Picturesque Redlands. [Photographs by Everett of Redlands. S.F., Union litho. co.] 1899. [33] p. illus.   CLU
Other editions followed.   CLU (1901, 1903) CRedl (1901, 1902, 1903) CSmH (1901)

7253. —— Redlands, California, a perfect climate, the finest orange groves in the state, beautiful parks and fine residences. L.A., Out West co., 1904. 16 p. illus.   CRedl

Other editions followed.   CHi (1906, 1909) CSmH (1905?, 1906)

7254. —— —— Redlands, California, sixty six miles east of Los Angeles; ten trains each way daily. Redlands, Citrograph print. co. [1904] [16] p.   CRedl

7255. —— **Chamber of commerce.** Redlands, California. Redlands, Citrograph print. house [1912] 15 p. illus.   CRedl

7256. —— —— Redlands, California, Big Bear valley and the resorts in the San Bernardino mountains. Redlands, 1917. 24 p. illus.   CL CRedl CU-B

7257. —— —— The unfolding of the facts about Redlands, California... Carl A. Bundy, Quill and press, 1923. 14 p. illus.   CRedl

7258. —— **First Congregational church.** The First Congregational church of Redlands, California, 1880–1955. By Edith Parker Hinckley. [Redlands? 1955?] 54 p.   CHi CU-B

7259. —— **Union high school.** ...Manual... 1897 approved by the board. Redlands, Citrograph print. co., 1897. 31 p. illus. Alumni register, p. 27–28.   CHi

7260. —— **University.** Catalog.
CRedl has 1916– to date.

7261. Redlands daily facts, pub. Illustrated Redlands. Incorporation edition... Redlands, 1897. 96 p. illus., ports.   C CRedl CSmH CU-B NN

7262. —— Same. 1912.   CSbCL

7263. Redlands golden jubilee, 1888–1938. [Redlands, Citrograph print. co., 1938] 215 p. illus., ports., maps.   CRedl

7264. Redlands orange grove and water co. Prospectus. Redlands, Citrograph print. co., 1890. 32 p.   CRedl

7265. Redlands, situated in the finest part of the celebrated San Bernardino valley, San Bernardino county, California... [n.p., n.d.] 13 p. fold. map.   CHi

7266. Redlands, the radiant garden spot of California and a busy business centre. [Detroit pub. co., n.d.] [32] p.   CRedl

7267. Redlands university club. [Book of dues, etc.] constitution and by-laws, secretary's book. Ms.   CRedl

7268. Redlands water co. Articles of incorporation and by-laws...adopted November 24, 1885. San Bernardino, San Bernardino times book and job print., 1886. 16 p.   CHi

7269. Security first national bank, Los Angeles. The growth and economic stature of San Bernardino and Riverside counties, 1960. [L.A.] 1960. 104 p.   CHi

7270. Sloane house, Redlands. Register November 15, 1891 to April 15, 1892. Ms.   CRedl

7271. Southern California power co. Prospectus ...a statement of the plans of the company for development and use of electric power for lighting, heating and manufacturing purposes. Redlands [Citrograph print. co.] 1897. 16 p. illus.   CHi CRedl

7272. Souvenir of Redlands, California. [Redlands?] F. C. Hoogstraat [189–?] 63 pl.   CLU CSmH

7273. —— Same. [2d ed.] [1902] 28 l. illus.
                CHi CL CLO CLU CRedl CU-B

7274. Tisdale, William M. Redlands, California. [Redlands, c1897] 32 p. illus.   CHi CRedl

7275. Tresdail, Roger W. Redlands... Redlands, Citrograph print. co., 1927. 57 p. illus.   CRedl CU-B

7276. Twentieth century Redlands, the city of homes and flowers. [Redlands?] Print. by the Citrograph [19–?] [32] p. illus., ports. CSmH CU-B

7277. "Uncle Abe." Souvenir tribute to beautiful Redlands! in the twentieth century morning dawn. Redlands, Redlands daily review press [n.d.] 11 p. illus. CRedl

7278. Windsor hotel. Journal of accounts, December 20, 1892 to December 30, 1893. Ms. CRedl

San Bernardino

7279. Covered wagon days; San Bernardino, Calif. San Bernardino, Sun co., Nov. 13, 1938. 36 p. illus. CSbCL

7280. Evans, John Henry. Charles Coulson Rich; pioneer builder of the West. N.Y., Macmillan, 1936. 400 p. illus., ports., map. One of the founders of the city of San Bernardino.
C CBb CBu CHi CL CLS CLSU CLU CO COHN CRedl CSdS CSf CSmH CStmo CU-B

7281. Evening index, San Bernardino. ...Souvenir number. San Bernardino festival of the Arrowhead, May 19–20–21–22–23, 1908. San Bernardino, 1908. 58 p. illus. CSmH CU-B

7282. Miller, George. A Mormon bishop and his son; fragments of a diary kept by G. Miller, sr., bishop in the Mormon church, and some records of incidents in the life of G. Miller, jr., hunter and pathfinder [ed.] by H. W. Mills. London, England, M.R.C.S., L.R.C.P [n.d.] 91 p. ports. Contains a copy of George Miller's letter to Byron Waters in reference to "Indian troubles at San Bernardino, California from 1863 onward." CRedl

7283. —— Same. L.A., 1917. 92 p. CSmH CU-B

7284. Mormon politics and policy. Political and judicial acts of the Mormon authorities in San Bernardino, California... L.A., print. at off. of El Clamor publico, 1856. 8 p. CSmH CU-B

7285. Poulsen, Anton B. The Mormon outpost of San Bernardino, California. [Salt Lake City] 1947. Thesis (M.S.)—Univ. of Utah, 1947. UU

7286. Raup, Hallock Floy. San Bernardino, California; settlement and growth of a pass-site city. Berkeley, Univ. of Calif. press, 1940. 52 p. illus., maps. (Univ. of Calif. Publications in geography, v.8, no. 1)
CChiS CHi CLO CLSU CLU CO CRedl CSdS CSfSt CSmH CStrJC CU-B KU OrU TxU UHi

7287. Richards, Elizabeth W. Circa 1890; being a sentimental collection of moments of life and times in San Bernardino, California, in celebration of the 70th anniversary year of the Santa Fe federal savings and loan association. [San Bernardino? 1959] [28] p. (chiefly illus., ports., map) C CLO CLU CU-B

7288. Rolfe, Horace C. Centennial history of San Bernardino. [San Bernardino, Security title insurance and guarantee co., 1907?] [4] p. CSmH

7289. San Bernardino. Chamber of commerce. San Bernardino, California. San Bernardino, 1929. 29 p. illus. CRcS

7290. —— **City planning commission.** Your city's planning program. San Bernardino, 1950. 28 p. CSt

7291. —— **Congregation Emanuel.** Dedication book. Temple and community center. San Bernardino, Inland print., 1953. [105] p. illus. CHi

7292. —— **National orange show.** Official souvenir program. 12th, Feb. 1922. [San Bernardino, 1922] 1 v. illus. CU-B

7293. —— —— ...Pictorial folder, 1928. fold. pl. C

7294. San Bernardino association of Congregational churches and ministers. Records... [n.p., 1887–1934] 296 p. Ms. CCH

7295. San Bernardino, California; the home of the National orange show...Reprints from prize-winning articles, 1914–22. [San Bernardino? 1922?] [38] p. illus., ports. CU-B

7296. San Bernardino [county] bar association. Tribute...to the memory of William Jesse Curtis. San Bernardino [1927] unp. port. CLU CSmH

7297. Sturges academy. Register...from 1883–88. CSbCL

7298. Tuck, Ruth D. Not with the fist, Mexican-Americans in a southwest city. N.Y., Harcourt, 1946. 234 p. CSd CStmo CStoC CU-B

SAN DIEGO COUNTY
(Created in 1850)

County Histories

7299. Black, Samuel T., ed. San Diego and Imperial counties, California, a record of settlement, organization, progress and achievement, by Samuel F. [!] Black... Chicago, Clarke, 1913. 2 v. illus., ports. v.2 includes biographies. "This work is a compilation of data...much of which appears in Smythe's *History of San Diego*."—Foreword.
CEc CHi CLU CSdS CU-B MWA NHi NN

7300. ——, ed. San Diego county, California; a record of settlement, organization, progress and achievement... Chicago, Clarke, 1913. 2 v. illus., ports. v.1: History.—v.2: Biography.
C CAlaC CCoron CL CLCo (v.2) CNa CO CSd CSdCL CSf CSfP CSmH CStclU WHi

7301. Heilbron, Carl H., ed. History of San Diego county...Winifred Davidson, historian; A. H. Cawston, managing editor; Robert F. Heilbron, Barbara Biewener, assistant editors. In collaboration with the Advisory board and a selected group of contributors. San Diego, San Diego press club, 1936. 479, 314 p. illus., ports., maps. Contents: pt. 1. Narrative.—pt. 2. Biographical.
C CBb CBev CCoron CF CFS CHi CL CLSU CLU CLob CNa CO CPa CSd CSdCL CSdS CSdU CSfCP CSmH CU-B NN WHi

7302. Historical records survey. California. Inventory of the county archives of California. no. 38. San Diego county (San Diego) v.1 & 3. San Diego, So. Calif. hist. records survey, 1941. v.1. Administrative offices. May, 1943. 357 p. v.3. Tax and financial offices. Jan., 1941. 238 p. v.2 was not published.
C CHi CLO (v.3) CLSU CLU CSd (v.1) CSdS CSf (v.3) CSmH CU-B ICN (v.3) WHi (v.3)

7303. History of San Diego county. With illustrations ... S.F., Elliott, 1883. 204 p. illus., ports., maps. "History of San Bernardino county, California. By Warren Wilson": p. [141]–204.
C CCH CHi CL CNa CSd CSmH NHi

7304. An illustrated history of southern California. Embracing the counties of San Diego, San Bernardino, Los Angeles and Orange, and the peninsula of Lower California...also, full-page portraits of some of their eminent men, and biographical mention of many of their pioneers and of prominent citizens of to-day. Chicago, Lewis, 1890. 898 p. illus., ports.

    C CCoron CHi CL CLAC CLCM CLCo CLO CLS CLSM CLSU CLU CLob CPa CRiv CSS CSbCL CSd CSf CSmH CSta CStaCL CStmo CStoC CU-B CoD CoU CtY IC MWA NHi WHi

7305. McGrew, Clarence Alan. City of San Diego and San Diego county...with selected biography... Chicago, Am. hist. soc., 1922. 2 v. illus., ports.

    C CCoron (v.2 only) CHi CL CLO (v.1 only) CLU CNa CO CSd CSdCL CSdS CSdU (v.1 only) CSf CSmH CU-B MWA NN WHi

7306. [Van Dyke, Theodore Strong] The city and county of San Diego...containing biographical sketches... San Diego, Leberthon & Taylor, 1888. 218 p. illus., ports. Edited and published by T. T. Leberthon and A. Taylor.

    C CCH CHi CL CLCM CLCo CLO CLSM CLSU CLU CNa CO CP CRic CRiv CSd CSdCL CSdS CSf CSfCW CSmH CSta CU-B CoD CtY MiD-B MoSHi N NHi NN TxU UPB WHi

7307. Waite, F. D. San Diego. The city and the county...Compiled under the auspices of the executive committee of the San Diego chamber of commerce and citizens. Containing an article on climate by R. B. Davy, M.D. San Diego, Gould & Hutton, 1888. 72 p. illus.

    CLCM CSd CSmH CU-B MHi

GREAT REGISTER

7308. San Diego. Index to the Great register of the county of San Diego. 1866– Place of publication and title vary.

    C has 1867, 1871–73, 1875–77, 1879–80, 1884, 1886, 1890 (biennially to)– 1898 (suppl.), 1902, 1904, 1906, 1910 (biennially to)– 1962. CHi has 1876. CL has 1873, 1876–77, 1879–80, 1882, 1886, 1888, 1890. CLU has 1875. CSmH has 1890, 1894, 1896. CU-B has July 1867, Oct. 1872, 1872 (suppl.), Aug. 1873, Aug. 1879, Oct. 1880, Oct. 1894, 1940.

DIRECTORIES

7309. 1886/87–1897. Olmsted co., pub. San Diego city and county directory. San Diego, 1886–97. Title varies: 1889–1892/93 San Diego, Coronado and National City. Publisher varies: 1886/87 A. A. Bynon & co.; 1887/88 Geo. W. Maxwell; 1889 Bynon & Hildreth; 1892/93–95 S. H. Olmsted and A. A. Bynon.

    C has 1886/87, 1887/88, 1889, 1892/93, 1895, 1897. CHi has 1887/88, 1889, 1892/93, 1895. CLU has 1889, 1897. CNa has 1897. CSd has 1887/88. CSdS has 1886/87, 1889, 1892/93, 1895, 1897. CSmH has 1887/88. CU-B has 1887/88.

7310. 1899/1900. Fisher, Ward & Pomeroy, comp. San Diego city and county directory... San Diego, Baker bros., print., 1899.

    C CHi CNa CSdS

7311. 1901–1938. San Diego directory co., pub. San Diego city directory...including Carlsbad, Chula Vista, Coronado, El Cajon, Escondido, La Jolla, La Mesa, National City, Oceanside, and all other towns and post offices throughout the county. San Diego, 1901–38. Continued as Polk's San Diego city directory.

    C has 1901, 1906–30, 1932–38. CCoron has 1907, 1910, 1913–15, 1917–18, 1922–24, 1926–34, 1939–40, 1943. CHi has 1901–35, 1937–38. CL has 1911, 1913–27, 1928–34, 1936. CLU has 1905. CNa has 1901, 1903, 1905, 1907–08, 1911–18, 1920–24, 1927–38. CSd has 1901, 1903–38. CSdS

has 1901, 1903–38. CSmH has 1901, 1903–05, 1907, 1909, 1914, 1921, 1924, 1927. CU-B has 1907, 1910, 1913–15, 1917–18, 1922–24, 1926–34, 1939–40, 1943. MoS has 1935.

7312. 1953/54– Polk, R. L., & co., pub. San Diego suburban directory...including Chula Vista, Coronado, El Cajon, La Mesa, Lemon Grove and National City. L.A., 19—

    CCoron has 1953/54, 1955–57. CHi has 1953/54, 1956–60, 1961/62. CL has 1953/54–1957, 1959. CLU has 1953/54, 1955. CNa has 1955–58.

San Diego

7313. 1889/90. Monteith, John C., pub. Monteith's directory of San Diego and vicinity... San Diego, 1889. 472 p.   C CHi CNa

7314. 1925– Colored people's business directory, v.1– 1925– San Diego [City print. co., 1925?–]

    CHi has v.2, 1926.

7315. 1939– Polk, R. L., & co., pub. Polk's San Diego city directory, including La Jolla. Publisher varies: 1939–50 San Diego directory co. Content varies: 1939–50 includes Chula Vista, Coronado, La Jolla, La Mesa and National city. Preceded by San Diego directory co.'s San Diego City directory including towns and post offices throughout the county.

    C has 1939, 1941, 1944/45, 1957–58. CCoron has 1941, 1952–56. CHi has 1939–43, 1944/45, 1947/48, 1950, 1952–61. CL has 1940–1944/45, 1947/48, 1950, 1952–56, 1958, 1960. CLU has 1952, 1953/54, 1955–56. CNa has 1939–43, 1944/45, 1947/48, 1952–58. CSd has 1939–50, 1952–55. CSdS has 1939–41, 1943 to date. CSmat has 1958–59. CU-B has 1958.

Other Cities and Towns

7316. 1954. Crow, pub. El Cajon Valley directory. El Cajon, c1954.   CSd

7317. 1950– Escondido city and rural directory. Publisher and title vary.

    CL has 1950, 1953–56. CSd has 1952.

7318. 1939– La Jolla city directory. Publisher and title vary.

    CL has 1939, 1951, 1953. CSd has 1951–58/59, 1962.

7319. 1962. Luskey bros., pub. Luskey's Oceanside-Carlsbad criss cross city directory. Anaheim [1962]   CL

GENERAL REFERENCES

7320. Adair, Etta Florence. The name San Diego. 10 p. Typew.   CSd

7321. Alexander, W. E., comp. Plat book of San Diego county, California... L.A., S.F., Pac. plat bk. co. [19–?] 152 p. illus.

    CLU CSd CSdS CSmH CU-B NN

7322. Allen, Margaret V. Ramona's homeland... Chula Vista, Denrich press [c1914] [43] p. illus.

    CLO CLSU CLU CSfCW CSmH

7323. American public health association. Public health in San Diego county and city; the report of a study...April–June 1946. N.Y., 1946. 111 p. Mimeo.

    CSd

7324. Arnold, Henry Harley. The history of Rockwell field. [n.p., 1923] Typew.   CSd

7325. Bailey, Philip A. Golden mirages...The story of the lost Pegleg mine, the legendary three gold buttes and yarns of and by those who know the desert. N.Y., Macmillan, 1940. 353 p. illus., ports., maps. Bibliography: p. 339–41. Contains information on mines and legends of San Diego county.

Available in many libraries.

7326. Bellon, Walter, and Lane, Fred T., comp. Condensed history of San Diego county park system, with map showing locations of all parks and a short description and map showing location of Spanish and Mexican ranchos, government watering places, Washingtonia palm groups rediscovered by Supervisor Walter Bellon and party, and other points of historical interest...4th ed. San Diego county bd. of supervisors, 1944. unp. illus., maps. Mimeo. C

7327. Bigger, Richard. Metropolitan coast: San Diego and Orange counties, California... L.A., Bur. of governmental research, Univ. of Calif., 1958. 95 p. maps (part fold.) tables. Bibliographical footnotes.
CL CLSM CLU CSd CSdS CSfSt CSfU CStaCL CoD TxU

7328. Binney, Fred A. From San Diego to Linda Rosa in a wagonette, 1889. Linda Rosa, 1889. unp. Typew. "A memory of by-gone California days and of Grandpa and Grandma Binney...by Hildegard Binney-Norberg." CSd

7329. Bliss, Robert. Journal... 33 p. Typew. Journal of a private in the Mormon battalion. CSd

7330. Brackett, Robert W. A history of the ranchos; the Spanish, Mexican, and American occupation of San Diego county and the story of the ownership of the land grants therein...With research and editorial supervision by the Federal writers' project of the Works progress administration, Southern California...Sponsored by the San Diego historical society. San Diego, Union title insurance & trust co., 1939. 86 p. illus., map. Bibliography: p. 85–86.
C CCoron CHi CL CLO CLS CLSU CLU CLob CNa CO CSdS CSf CSmH CU-B CoD MWA N TxU UPB

7331. —— Same. 3d ed. 1947. 65 p. illus., map.
CCoron CLO

7332. —— Same. 4th ed. 1951. 65 p. illus.
CHi CNa CSdCL CSdU CSfU

7333. Buck, E. L. ...The great San Jacinto valley, San Diego county, California... San Jacinto, Register bk. and job print, 1885. 10 p. CLU

7334. Bynum, Lindley. An early California Christmas in the year 1775 taken from the manuscript diaries of J'n Bautista de Anza and Father Pedro Font through the courtesy of the Bancroft library. Decoration by Don Louis Perceval. L.A., H. H. Boelter litho. [1956?] [32] p. illus., map (on lining papers). "Translation from Herbert Eugene Bolton's 'Anza's California expeditions,' v.3 and 4." C CL CLO CLSM CO

7335. California. Commissioner to investigate disturbances in San Diego. Report of Harris Weinstock, commissioner to investigate recent disturbances in the city of San Diego and the county of San Diego, to His Excellency Hiram W. Johnson, governor of California. Sacramento, Supt. state print., 1912. 22 p.
CHi CL CO

7336. —— **Development board.** Agricultural and soil survey of San Diego county, California... [San Diego, Press of Frye and Smith, 1918] 93 p. C CU-B

7337. California taxpayers' association, inc. The government of San Diego county... L.A., 1931. 313 p. (Assoc. report no. 150) CSd CSfSt TxU

7338. California water and telephone co. The water story of the Sweetwater district. National city, 1955. 25 p. illus., maps, charts. CNa CSd

7339. Carillo, Januarius M., Father. Story of Mission San Antonio de Pala. Balboa Island, Paisano press [1959] 39 p. illus., ports., map.
C CHi CL CLSM CO CSd CStclU CU-B

7340. Carlsbad. Friends of the library. History of Carlsbad... Carlsbad [1960?] 82 p. illus., port., map. CHi

7341. Chula Vista. Community Congregational church. A history of the Community Congregational church, Chula Vista...1890–1950. Comp. by Ruth Chase. [Chula Vista? 1950?] 13 l. illus. CHi

7342. Clarke, James Mitchell. Tuna clippers... research by John Floyd. Prepared under direction of City schools curriculum project. [2d ed.] San Diego [1937?] illus. Mimeo. CSd

7343. —— Same. 3d ed. 1939. 51 l. pl. Mimeo.
CU-B

7344. —— Water at the missions...from research by Lorraine Van Lowe...prepared under direction of City schools curriculum project. San Diego, 1936. 2d ed. Mimeo. Bibliography: p. 26–27. CSd CSdS

7345. Collier, D. C., & co. There's only one Point Loma, the cream of San Diego the beautiful, on the harbor of the sun... [San Diego, Frye & Smith, 1913?] [28] p. illus., map. CHi

7346. Couts, Cave Johnson. From San Diego to the Colorado in 1849; the journal and maps of Cave Couts, ed. by William McPherson. L.A., Arthur M. Ellis, 1932. 78 p. illus., ports., maps.
CEc CHi CLLoy CLO CLSM CSd CSdS CStmo

7347. Coy, Owen Cochran. Battle of San Pasqual; a report of the California Historical survey commission with special reference to its location... Sacramento, State print. off., 1921. 18 p. illus., maps. Bibliography: p. 18.

Available in many California libraries and IHi UHi

7348. Crouch, Herbert. Reminiscences...1915. 150 p. Typew. Memoirs of experiences and life in San Diego county, beginning 1869. CSd

7349. Curti, G. Philip. The Borrego valley: the birth of a desert community. [L.A.] 1955. Thesis (M.A.) — U.C.L.A., 1955. CLU

7350. Daughters of the American revolution. California. Abstract of wills, 1848 to 1900, San Diego county, California, on file, office of the county clerk... [San Diego, 1952] 398 l. map. Typew. C CL

7351. Davidson, John. Place names: San Diego county...1934–1936. Typew. Collection of articles for San Diego evening tribune using the card file "Place names of San Diego city and county" compiled by Miss L. B. Hunzicker. Contains source material collected through interviews and from unpublished records.
CSd

7352. Davidson, Winifred. Baptisms administered by Father Fernando Parron and Father Francisco Gomez. 1935. 240 p. Typew. Baptisms from number 1–2704 tr. from the Spanish. CSd

7353. —— Index of baptisms registered at Mission San Diego. 33 p. Typew. CSd

7354. —— Loma lore. Point Loma [n.d.] 12 l. Typew. C

7355. —— Old tales of the Southwest... [San Diego, 1935–1937] 50 p. of mounted clippings. illus., ports. Clippings from the *San Diego union*, April 14, 1935–Dec. 19, 1937.   CU-B

7356. —— San Diego county landmarks. 2 v. Typew.   CSd

7357. Davis, Abel M. Valley center, California; from the memoirs of Abel Davis. [n.p., 1955?] 72 p. illus.   CSd CSdCL

7358. Davis, Carlyle Channing. The true story of "Ramona"... N.Y., Dodge [c1914] 265 p. illus., ports.
CHi CLO CLgA CLod CSf CStmo

7359. Davis, Edward H. Diégueño ceremony of the death images. [n.p.] 1919.   CSd

7360. —— Early cremation ceremonies of the Luiseno and Diégueño Indians. N.Y., Museum of the Am. Indian, 1921.   CSd

7361. Day & Zimmermann, inc., Philadelphia, Pa. Day & Zimmermann report (no. 4072). Commercial and industrial survey, city and county of San Diego; prepared for San Diego chamber of commerce, 1945. 11 v. illus., maps.
C CHi CL CLSU CLU CSd CSdS CSf

7362. —— San Diego as others see us! Digest of the Day and Zimmermann report... Prepared for the San Diego chamber of commerce, San Diego [1945] 106 p. illus., maps.   CNa CO

7363. Derby, George Horatio. Biographical notes of George Horatio Derby. Original copy. Letters written to John Vance Cheney from Wm. C. Bartlett, Oakland, California, 1896, and others, relative to history of G. H. Derby ("John Phoenix").   CSd

7364. Dixon, Benjamin Franklin. Don Diego's old school days; the story of the beginnings of public education, San Diego, city and county, California. [Donor's ed.] San Diego, San Diego county hist. days assoc., 1956. 32 p. illus.   CHi CSd CSdS

7365. —— Palm Springs oasis; old Butterfield station midway between Carrizo and Vallecito. 1958. Typew.   CSd

7366. Edwards, Elza Ivan. Lost oases along the Carrizo...with photographs and foreword by Harold O. Weight. L.A., Westernlore press, 1961. 126 p. A descriptive bibliography of the Colorado desert, p. 53–85.
CHi CLSM

7367. Eidenmiller, D. I. Economic geography of avocado growing in San Diego county. [Berkeley, 1949] Thesis (M.A.)— Univ. of Calif., 1949.   CU

7368. El Cajon valley. Chamber of commerce. El Cajon, California, valley of opportunity. [El Cajon, 1952?] [7] p. illus., map.   CHi

7369. Elliott, James Wilkinson. Adventures of a horticulturist. Point Loma, Author, 1935.   CSd

7370. Engelhardt, Zephyrin, Father. San Diego mission... S.F., J. H. Barry co., 1920. 358 p. illus., ports., maps.
Available in many California libraries and CaBViPA UHi

7371. —— San Luis Rey mission. S.F., J. H. Barry co., 1921. 265 p. illus., ports., maps.
Available in many California libraries and CaBViPA

7372. Escondido. Chamber of commerce. Escondido, the sunkist vale in picture and paragraph. Escondido, Times-advocate print. [1910?] [9] p. illus. CHi

7373. —— —— Same. [1914?] [20] p. illus.
CU-B

7374. Escondido land & town co., San Diego.

Escondido, San Diego county, California. A descriptive pamphlet of climate, resources, topography and inducements to settlers. Also a description of San Marcos. San Diego, Gould & Hutton [1887] 48 p. illus., map.
CSmH NHi

7375. Esterbloom, Gloria L. This, our beloved valley. [National city] c1954. 54 p. illus. Sweetwater valley, San Diego county.   CLU CNa CSdCL

7376. Fenton, Laura. Henry Fenton; typical American. [San Diego? 1953?] 160 p. illus., ports.
CHi CSd

7377. Fletcher, Edward. An auto trip through San Diego's back country. San Diego [1906] 31 p. illus., map.   CLU CSd CSmH

7378. Frazee, William D. Oceanside, the gate-way city of all San Diego county...its resources, climate and attractions... San Diego, Gould & Hutton, print., 1888. 98 p. illus.   CLU CSd CSmH CU-B MiD NN

7379. Geiger, Maynard J., Father. Mission San Luis Rey de Francia, the king of the missions, an historical sketch. Re-edited by the Rev. Bonaventure Oblasser. [n.p., 1939] [32] p. illus., port., map.   CLU

7380. Giddings, George H. Memoirs. 37 p. port. Typew. G. H. Giddings was connected with the San Antonio-San Diego mail line.   CSd

7381. Gilbert, Anna M. La Mesa, yesterday and today. San Diego, Press of the City print. co., c1924. 63 p. illus. Appendix: Emory's notes, p. 53–62. "Some southern California names and their meanings": p. 63.
CHi CL CLO CLU CSd CSmH

7382. Goodwin, Percy H. Brand book of San Diego county. San Diego, Author [n.d.]   CSd

7383. Green, F. E. San Diego old mission dam and irrigation system. 1935. Typew. Contains also description of the modern water system.   CSd

7384. Greenwalt, Emmett Alwyn. The Point Loma community in California, 1897–1942. [Berkeley, 1949] Thesis (Ph.D.)— U.C.L.A., 1949.   CLU

7385. Hanbury & Garvey, firm, San Diego. Tierra perfecta, the perfect land of the Mission fathers... [S.F., Francis, Valentine & co., print., 1887] 22 p.   CSmH

7386. Hazzard, George H. Saga of San Diego. San Diego, Neyenesch print., inc., 1941. 60 p. illus. In verse form.   CLU CSmH

7387. Hearne bros., Detroit. Official Hearne brothers polyconic projection cloth maps of all San Diego county. Constantly revised and kept up to date. Detroit [195-?] 1 v. (chiefly maps)   C CSd

7388. Hegland, Edwina Kenney, and Hegland, Sheridan. USO, "the heart of San Diego"; a history of USO in San Diego city and county, 1941–1946... San Diego, USO council, 1946. illus.   CSd

7389. Hensley, Herbert C. The Little Landers of San Ysidro. [n.d.]   CSd

7390. —— Campo, and other tales. [n.p., n.d.] Typew. Tales of the San Diego county—Baja California border.   CSd

7391. Hildreth, Ada Waite. A short story of the work of Dr. H. L. Hildreth, physician in the United States Indian service, among the Indians of San Diego county ... San Diego, 1939. Typew.   CSd

7392. Hill, Joseph John. The history of Warner's ranch and its environs... L.A., Priv. print., 1927. 221 p. illus., ports., maps. "...Printed for John Treanor... by Young and McCallister, of Los Angeles..."

Available in many California libraries and MoSHi TxU UHi

7393. Hilliard, J. L. A few chronicles of Point Loma. [n.d.] Typew. CSd

7394. Historical records survey. California. Directory of churches and religious organizations...Prepared by the...Historical records survey project...Work projects administration. L.A., 1940. Reproduced from typew. copy. v.2: San Diego county.
C CL CLO CLSU CLU CSd CSdS CSf CU-B N NN TxU

7395. History of Cabrillo rifles (1917–1918) written for [San Diego county war history committee] [n.p., n.d.] unp. illus. Typew. CSd

7396. Hunzicker, Lena B., comp. Place names of San Diego city and county. [1915–1926] CSd

7397. Immigration association of California. [County scrapbooks] [S.F., 188–?] C

7398. James, George Wharton. Picturesque Pala; the story of the mission chapel of San Antonio de Padua connected with Mission San Luis Rey. Pasadena, Radiant life press, 1916. 82 p. illus., port.
C CBb CHi CL CLO CLU CP CSd CSf CSfCW CSfU CSj CSluCL CSmH CU-B

7399. Johnson, Mary Elizabeth. Indian legends of the Cuyamaca mountains. [San Diego, Print. by Frye & Smith, c1914] 27 p. illus. CLU CSd CSmH

7400. Jones, Ollie Jo. Rancho Santa Margarita y las Flores. San Diego, 1957. 97 p. illus. Thesis (M.A.)— San Diego state college, 1957. CSdS

7401. Junipero land and water co. Grantville! San Diego county, California...descriptive pamphlet of the climate, resources, topography... San Diego [1888] CSd

7402. Kaplan, Oscar. A housing report on the San Diego metropolitan area. San Diego, San Diego chamber of commerce, 1952. 38 l. CSdS

7403. Kelly, Charles, comp. History of the Christian churches of San Diego county, California. [n.p.] 1937. CSd

7404. —— Reminiscences (written 1900–1924). Typew. Life on a California cattle ranch, covering a period of fifty years beginning in the late seventies. History, legends, personal adventures, character sketches and stories of animals. CSd

7405. Kelly, John. Life on a San Diego county ranch. [n.p.] 194 p. Typew. CSd

7406. Kimball, Laura Frances. Records of death, Rancho de la Nación and Vista cemetery. [1956] Typew. CSd

7407. Kirkpatrick, James D., comp. Poway, California, a historical scrapbook. 1957. 20 p. CSd CSdCL

7408. Knowlton, Murray. The cruise of a tuna clipper. A narrative of San Diego's fishing industry... San Diego, City schools, 1937. 177 p. illus. Prepared under the direction of the San Diego city schools curriculum project, WPA. CSd

7409. La Force, Beatrice. Alpine history; a brief account of early days. [Alpine] c1952. 32 p. illus.
C CHi CLU CNa CSd CSdCL CSdS CSto

7410. La Mesa. Chamber of commerce. La Mesa, jewel of the hills. La Mesa, So. Calif. pub. co. [1950?] [10] p. illus., map. CHi

7411. Lareau, Richard John. A recreational de-velopment of Mission bay in the San Diego area. [Berkeley, 1955] Thesis (M.A.)— Univ. of Calif., 1955. CU

7412. Lee, Melicent Humason. Indians of the oaks ... Bost., Ginn, c1937. 244 p. illus. Contents: Indians of the oaks.—Secrets of the trail. Published separately in 1931 under title: *The Indians and I.*
CBev CL CO CSd (1931) CSdS CSf

7413. Leffer, Don B. La Mesa, a study of its future... San Diego, San Diego state college. Public affairs research inst., 1959. 113 p. illus., maps. CL

7414. —— Report on Del Mar...San Diego, San Diego state college. Public affairs research inst., 1959. 44 p. illus. CL

7415. —— Solana Beach, 1959... San Diego, San Diego state college. Public affairs research inst., 1959. 60 p. illus. CL

7416. —— Spring valley, today and tomorrow... San Diego, San Diego state college. Public affairs research inst., 1958. 54 p. illus. CL

7417. Little Landers, inc., San Ysidro. [Account books, 1911–1914] Utopian colony in San Diego county. CSd

7418. —— By-laws...as finally adopted. CSd

7419. —— Land property held and sold by the Little Landers, inc. ... CSd

7420. —— [Prospectus. 1912–13] CSd

7421. —— The true Arcadia. CSd

7422. —— [Views of the Little Landers colony] CSd

7423. Loma homestead, Point Loma. Loma-land, a favored spot for rest & residence... San Diego, Theosophical pub. co., 1901. 19 l. illus. CHi CSmH

7424. Lummis, Charles Fletcher. Preliminary report of Warner's ranch Indian commission. [L.A.] The Commission [1902] CSd

7425. McCain, Ella (Williams) Memories of the early settlements: Dulzura, Potrero, and Campo. [Potrero?] c1955. 146 l. C CL CSd CSdCL CSdS

7426. McGroarty, John Steven. The endless miracle of California. [Chula Vista, Denrich press, n.d.] [29] p. illus. Deals with Rancho Santa Fe. CHi CSd
Other editions followed. CHi (192–?) CLU (192–?) CNa (1928)

7427. McKenney, J. Wilson. On the trail of Peg Leg Smith's lost gold. Palm Desert, Desert press, c1957. 50 p. illus. CLSM CNa CPs

7428. [Marsden, Griffis] The field glass. [by] G.M. ... Chula Vista, Denrich press [1917] illus. CSd

7429. The Master Mason. Souvenir edition, 75th anniversary, San Diego lodge no. 35, F[ree] & A[ccepted] M[asons], v.6, no. 4, May, 1928. 48 p. illus., ports. CHi

7430. —— Same. 100th anniversary, 1851–1951, v.39, no. 8, Aug. 1951. 11 p. illus., ports. CHi

7431. Memphis, El Paso and Pacific railroad. Levels: trail line, Jamul to Dos Potreros; no. 4, October, 1869. [San Diego, 1869] CSd

7432. Menzel, Spencer Lewis. The development of the Sweetwater area (California). [L.A.] 1942. Thesis (M.A.)— Univ. of So. Calif., 1942. CNa

7433. Metropolitan life insurance co., New York. A review of health conditions and needs in San Diego county, California (including San Diego city) N.Y., Print. for the General federation of Women's clubs, Dept. of public welfare [1932] 44 p. map.   CLU

7434. Milliken's souvenir guide to the resources of San Diego County; illustrations by the Los Angeles photo engraving co. Calif. directory co. [1897] 44 p.
CSd

7435. [**Mills, John S.**] San Diego, California, city and county. [San Diego, Bd. of supervisors & Chamber of commerce of San Diego county, 1907] 48 p. illus.
CHi   CU-B
Other editions followed.   CHi (1909) CL (1913?) CSd (1913?) CSf (1909) CSmH (1915) CU-B (1909, 1913?)

7436. Moaning cave, Vallecito, California... [n.p., n.d.] [6] p. illus., map.   CHi

7437. Mohr Adams Plourde co. The integrated master plan for industrial development south bay region. San Diego, 1957.   CSd

7438. Moore, Bertram B. Early history of San Diego county; the story of San Diego's roads. Prepared for the County surveyors office. San Diego [1951] 24 p.
CSdCL

7439. Moore, H. E. Old mission dam of Mission San Diego de Alcalá... [San Diego? 1935] 12 l.
CU-B

7440. Morrison, Lorrin L. Warner, the man and the ranch. L.A., 1962. 87 p. illus., maps.   CAla

7441. Nelson, Ruth R. Rancho Santa Fe, yesterday and today... [Encinitas, Coast dispatch] 1947. 83 p. Bibliography: p. 83.   C CHi CSd CSdCL

7442. Nida, Richard Hale. The Escondido-San Pasqual-San Bernardo area: a study in the historical geography of San Diego county, California. [Berkeley, 1935] Thesis (M.A.)—Univ. of Calif., 1935.   CU

7443. Oceanside. Chamber of commerce. Oceanside, "where life is worth living." Oceanside, 1931. 30 p. illus.   CHi

7444. —— —— Oceanside; thriving coastal city. San Diego, c1954. 12 p. illus., map.   CHi CNa CU-B

7445. —— —— Same. c1958. 20 p. illus.   CNa

7446. Oliver, Harry. Desert rough cuts; a haywire history of the Borego desert... L.A., Ward Ritchie [c1938] 64 p. illus.   CHi CLO CLU COr CSd

7447. —— The old mirage salesman; a whimscal[!] desert digest of refreshing nonsense, heralding the life of the southwest's foremost story-telling desert rat Harry Oliver... Palm Springs, Print. by the Printery, c1952. 111 p. illus.   CU-B NN

7448. Oneonta! by the sea. San Diego [1888?] 4 p. illus.   CSd

7449. Orman, George, comp. Population trends and projections of the San Diego metropolitan area... San Diego, City planning commission, 1958. 85 p. maps, tables.   CSdU

7450. Palm valley land co. Views of Palm valley, San Diego county, Cal.; the earliest fruit region in the state... S.F. [n.d.] 16 p. mounted views.   C

7451. Parker, Horace. Anza-Borrego desert guide book; southern California's last frontier. Maps by Jack P. Welch. Balboa island, Paisano press [1957] 108 p. illus. Includes bibliography.
Available in many libraries.

7452. Parsons, Theron. Extracts from his diaries (1868-1892) 1925. Ms. copied from originals.   CSd

7453. Peet, Mary Rockwood. San Pasqual, a crack in the hills. Culver City, Highland press, 1949. 227 p. illus., map.
C CL CLO CLSU CLU CNa CO CRedl CSd CSdS CSjC CSmH

7454. Peirce, Rollin. History of Ramona, a San Diego county village. [n.p., n.d.] 56 l. illus.
CSd CSdCL

7455. [**Phillips, Irene (Ladd)**] Around the Bay in thirty minutes; historical sketch. [National City, South bay press, 1960] 20 p. illus., maps.   CNa CU-B

7456. —— Development of the mission olive industry and other South bay stories. [National City, South bay press, 1960] 100 p. illus.   CU-B

7457. —— El Rancho de la Nación, embracing the towns of National City, Chula Vista, and the flourishing communities of Sunnyside, Harborside, Lincoln Acres, Bonita, Castle Park. National City, South bay press, 1959. 99 p. illus., ports., map. "Compiled from the periodicals of the day and from the diaries and private letters of Frank Augustus Kimball, California pioneer."
C CL CLSM CLU CNa CSd CSdS CSf CU-B

7458. —— The railroad story of San Diego county. Fiesta del Pacifico ed. National City, South bay press, c1956. 76 p. maps. "Quotes from the periodicals of the day and from the diaries and private letters of Frank Augustus Kimball."
CLU CNa CSd CSdCL CSdS CU-B

7459. —— San Diego land and town co., 1880-1927. National City, South bay press, c1959. 112 p. illus. The story of El Rancho de la Nación.   C CSd CU-B

7460. Picacho mill and mining co. Prospectus... Mines and mill located at the foot of Chimney peak, twenty miles north of Fort Yuma, in San Diego county, Cal. ... S.F., Cuddy & Hughes, print., 1874. 12 p.
CSmH CU-B

7461. Porter, R. S., comp. Highways and byways of San Diego county. Chula Vista, 1914.   CSd

7462. Porter, Rufus K. Correspondence of Rufus K. Porter of San Diego. Typew. Published in the *San Francisco bulletin*, 1865-1883. A history of the early days of San Diego city and county. Mr. Porter was San Diego correspondent for the *Bulletin*.   CSd

7463. Powers, Grant. Camp Joseph H. Pendleton, formerly Rancho Santa Margarita [y Las Flores] [n.p.] 1943. [8] p.   CHi

7464. Rainford, Alice. Memoirs of Del Mar. 8 p. Typew. Concerning Del Mar life from 1885 to 1899.
CSd

7465. Renié, Jack Joseph. The new Renié atlas of San Diego city and county. L.A., Renié map service, c1956.   CSd

7466. —— Renié pocket atlas of San Diego... county and cities; also Imperial valley and cities. L.A., Renié map service [n.d.]   CSd

7467. Rensch, Hero Eugene. The Indian place names of Rancho Cuyamaca. Cuyamaca rancho state park, Calif. Dept. of natural resources. Div. of beaches and parks, 1950. 40 p. Mimeo.   CHi

7468. Resources of San Diego county, v.1, no. 1, January 1897. Special edition. 15 p.   C

7469. Rohr aircraft corp., Chula Vista. Annual report.
CL has 1955-60.

7470. Rush, Philip S., comp. Beautiful San Diego county, a book of pictures. [San Diego, 1961] 64 p.
CHi CSfU

7471. San Diego. Bureau of information. San Diego county... L.A. [1887] [8] p.   CU-B

7472. —— Chamber of commerce. Classified directory, manufacturers and wholesale distributors, in the city and county of San Diego.
CSdS has 1952–54, 1957/58.

7473. —— —— Climate, resources, commerce, etc., of the city and county of San Diego...September, 1887. [San Diego, 1887] 28 p.   CLU CU-B NHi

7474. —— —— San Diego, the city and county ... San Diego, Gould & Hutton, 1888. 44 p.
CLU CSmH CU-B

7475. San Diego, California and state highway to Imperial valley: Photogravures. San Diego, I. L. Eno [n.d.]
CSd

7476. San Diego-California club, comp. Agriculture in San Diego county, California. 1st– [193–?]– San Diego, Pub. by San Diego-California club for the Board of supervisors of San Diego county, 193–?–
CNa (1953) CRcS (7th, 1940)

7477. San Diego college of letters. First annual announcement, the San Diego college of letters, Pacific Beach, San Diego, California... [Pacific Beach, Pac. print. co., n.d.] 8 p.   C

7478. San Diego county. District boundaries, San Diego county, no. 1. Transcribed by Historical records survey, San Diego, California. [San Diego, 1938] 337, 7 l. "Transcription of the original *Record of district boundaries*, San Diego county, no. 1."   CLU

7479. San Diego county. ...Fact-finding study of social and economic conditions of Indians of San Diego county, California, and reports from specialists in allied fields. [San Diego? 1932?] 126 p. Study sponsored by San Diego county, and carried on jointly by selected workers from the San Diego county welfare commission, the state Department of social welfare, and the Office of Indian affairs. "Authoritative books on the Mission Indians": p. 4.   CLSU CLU CSmH

7480. —— List of all property assessed in the county of San Diego, for the year 1854, with taxes chargeable on the same. [1854?] Ms.   C

7481. —— Board of supervisors. Citrus fruit growing, apple, and poultry industry in San Diego county, California... [1914?] 31 p. illus.   CU-B

7482. —— —— San Diego, California, city and county. Published by the Board of supervisors and the Chamber of commerce of San Diego county... [San Diego, 1913?] 56 p. illus.   CL CSd CU-B NN

7483. —— Same. [1920] 72 p. illus.
CO CSmH CU-B

7484. —— —— San Diego; the place of opportunity. First Pacific U.S. port north of Panama invites the world to her Panama California exposition, 1915—. San Diego, 1915. 32 p. illus., ports., maps.   CSd

7485. —— Chamber of commerce. For the want of a nail... [San Diego, 1951] Deals with San Diego water problem.   CSd

7486. —— —— Wholesale buyer's guide. San Diego, 1950–
CSd has 1950.

7487. —— Charters, ordinances, etc. Charter and administrative code. [San Diego, 1942]   CSd

7488. —— Office of the Superintendent of schools. Report of the survey of La Mesa-Spring Valley school district, La Mesa, California, 1945. San Diego, 1945. 149 l. illus.   CLU

7489. —— Planning commission. A decade of county planning, San Diego county, California, 1930–1940... [San Diego, 1940] 22 p. illus.   CU-B

7490. —— —— Master plan major highways, adopted by the San Diego county Board of supervisors on April 1, 1952. [San Diego] 1952. 30 p. maps.
CSdS

7491. —— Public schools. Annual report, educational department, San Diego, California, January 1891.
C

7492. —— —— The San Diego schools, 1893–95.   C

7493. —— Treasurer. Cash book of the Treasurer of San Diego county. [1853–59] Ms.   C

7494. San Diego county district agricultural association. Annual fair, premium list. 1st, 1880– [n.p.] 1880–
C has 2d, 1890. CSd has 1st, 1880.

7495. San Diego county historical days, 1949. [Program] Old San Diego, Oct. 1st and 2nd, 1949. [San Diego] 1949. 26 p. illus.   CHi

7496. San Diego county, land register and business directory. 1885–1886. San Diego, Union steam print. house, 1885–86.
C has Oct. 1885. CU-B has Jan. and Apr. 1886.

7497. San Diego county, semi-tropic California; health, profit, pleasure. San Diego, Easton, Eldridge and co. [1890?] 35 p. illus.   CSd

7498. San Diego mail line, A. L. Seeley & co., proprietors. [Passenger and freight record book, 1880–1886] 2 v. Ms.   CSd

7499. San Diego mission. Plat of three tracts of land of the Ex-mission San Diego finally confirmed to J. S. Alemany, bishop, etc.; surveyed...by Henry Hancock, dep. sur. September, 1860... Shows location of mission buildings, garden and olive orchard. Traced from blueprint, Oct. 1920.   CSd

7500. San Diego southern railway co. Excursions to Tia Juana, Mexico and Sweetwater dam. [n.d.]
CSd

7501. Schubert, Mary Agathonia, *Sister*. San Luis Rey, the king of the missions... [L.A.] 1939. 87 l. Thesis (M.A.)—Loyola univ., Los Angeles, 1939.   C CSd

7502. Security first national bank, Los Angeles. Research dept. The growth and economic stature of San Diego county, 1960. [San Diego] 1960. 88 p.   CHi

7503. Sessions, Kate Olive. Horticulture in San Diego county. 1933. 9 p. Typew.   CSd

7504. South coast land co., Los Angeles. Del Mar, California. [L.A.] c1912. [28] p. illus., map.   CLU

7505. —— Stratford Inn, Del Mar; "the spot beautiful," southern California. San Diego, Frye & Smith, print. [n.d.]   CSd

7506. Southern California blue book co., pub. Southern California blue book for San Diego and adjoining towns... [L.A.?] 1904–1909.
CL CSd (1905–06)

7507. Southern California rancher. San Diego county's historic ranchos. [San Diego, 1943–1946?] unp. illus. A series of articles prepared at the direction of Guard D. Gunn.   CSdS

7508. Stanford, Rolland Clinton. Seeing San Diego, county and city; what to see and do; where to go in southermost California. San Diego, c1949. 104 p. illus., maps. CSd

7509. Stephenson, Terry Elmo. Forster vs. Pico, a California cause célèbre; a court battle in 1873 for the great Rancho Santa Margarita, Pio Pico's escape from California, the recapture of San Diego in 1846, cattle days lived again... Santa Ana, Fine arts press, 1936. 40 p. illus., ports. CHi CL CLU CU-B

7510. Stewart, George Rippey. John Phoenix, esq., the veritable Squibob, a life of Captain George H. Derby, U.S.A. N.Y., Holt [c1937] 242 p. illus., ports. Includes bibliographies. CHi CRcS CSd CStmo

7511. Sweetman, J. W. Diamond deposits of California. San Diego, Author [n.d.] Typew. CSd

7512. Tac, Pablo. Indian life and customs at Mission San Luis Rey; a record of California mission life by Pablo Tac, an Indian neophyte. Written about 1835. Ed. and tr. by Minna and Gordon Hewes. San Luis Rey, Old Mission, 1958. 33 p. illus. C CHi CL CLob CNa CO CSd

7513. Taggart, George Washington. Narrative of George Washington Taggart, member of the Mormon battalion. [1846-47] 11 p. Typew. CSd

7514. Tays, George. ...Misión de San Diego de Alcalá... Berkeley, 1937. 70 l. Typew. CU-B

7515. Tebor, Irving B., and Larrabee, Helen L. Background for planning for social welfare in San Diego county...Publication no. 1, Research dept. San Diego, Community welfare council, 1958. 58 p. maps, tables. CSdU

7516. Telfer, William Booth. Early transportation arteries of San Diego county. San Diego, 1951. 156 p. maps. Thesis (M.A.)— San Diego state college, 1951. CSdS

7517. Thelen, Mrs. E. War history of San Diego county woman's committee of the councils of state and national defense. [San Diego, n.d.] Typew. CSd

7518. Thomas bros. Popular atlas, San Diego county... L.A., c1951. 95 p. col. maps. C CSdS (1958)

7519. —— Street guide, San Diego county, showing streets, address block numbers, bus lines, parks, schools, points of interest... L.A., c1951. 191 p. maps. CSdS

7520. Tilton, L. Deming. The appearance of the coast highway, San Diego county. [n.p., n.d.] CSd

7521. Tingley, Katherine A. (Westcott) Life at Point Loma. Point Loma, Aryan theosophical press, 1909. CSd

7522. Todd, Charles Burr. The battles of San Pasqual; a study, with map, itinerary and guide to the battle fields... Pomona, Author, 1925. 23 p. illus., map. C C-S CHi CL CLSU CLob CO CPom CSd CSmH CU-B

7523. Tyler, Daniel. A concise history of the Mormon battalion in the Mexican war, 1846-1847. Salt Lake City, 1881. 376 p. CHi CLgA

7524. Union title insurance and trust co., San Diego. Borrego Springs, desert playground. San Diego, c1951. 12 p. illus., map. CHi CNa CU-B

7525. —— Carlsbad, resort and ranch community. c1952. 12 p. illus., map. CHi CU-B

7526. —— Catalog of recorded plats in San Diego county, California. 1948 ed. San Diego [1949?] 80 p.

illus. "Includes all maps filed up to and including November 1, 1948." CLU

7527. —— Chula Vista. c1958. 18 p. illus. CNa

7528. —— El Cajon, busy valley community. c1953. 12 p. illus., map. CHi CU-B

7529. —— El Cajon, city in the news. c1956. 18 p. illus. CNa

7530. —— Encinitas, colorful garden spot. c1953. 12 p. CHi

7531. —— Escondido, gateway to the stars. c1951. 12 p. illus., maps. CHi CNa CU-B

7532. —— Fallbrook, the friendly village. c1953. 12 p. CHi CNa

7533. —— Lakeside, ranch and home community. c1954. 12 p. illus. CHi

7534. —— La Mesa, growing suburb and city. c1953. 12 p. illus., map. CHi CNa CU-B

7535. —— Rancho Santa Fe, heritage of the dons. c1951. 12 p. illus., map. CHi CNa

7536. —— San Diego county historical scrapbook; a picture history of San Diego county. Issued on the 50th anniversary... San Diego [1953] [32] p. illus. CHi CNa CU-B

7537. —— [San Diego county history, 1542-1953] 34 p. illus. (Its Topics 50th anniversary ed., v.7, no.5, Sept.-Oct., 1953) CHi

7538. —— Vista, center of "Avocado land." c1954. 16 p. illus., map. CHi

7539. United States vs. Jones, William Carey. In the District court of the United States, Southern district of California. Mission lands of [San Luis Rey] The United States, appellants, vs. [W. Carey Jones] appellee. no. [339] Land commission, no. [348] Exhibits, from 1 to 42, inclusive, filed in behalf of appellants. [S.F.] Daily herald print [185-?] 127 p. CU-B

7540. —— ...United States vs. Wm. Carey Jones, same vs. William Workman, et al. Brief. V. E. Howard, for appellees. [S.F.] Agnew & Deffebach [185-?] 13 p. Concerning lands of Mission San Gabriel and Mission San Luis Rey. CHi

7541. United States vs. Ybarra, Andres. Supreme court of the United States no. 121; appeal from the district court, U.S., from the Southern district of California. [n.d.] 19 p. Transcript of the proceedings in case no. 395, Andres Ybarra vs. the United States, for the place named Los Encenitos. C

7542. Van der Veer, Judy. Brown hills. N.Y., Longmans, c1938. 273 p. illus. CCoron CU

7543. —— A few happy ones. N.Y., Appleton, c1943. 247 p. CCoron CU-B

7544. —— My valley in the sky. N.Y., Messner [c1959] 256 p. CCoron CRcS CU-B

7545. —— November grass. N.Y., Longmans, 1940. 246 p. CSdS

7546. —— River pasture. N.Y., Longmans, 1936. 213 p. illus. CCoron CSdS

7547. [Van Dyke, Theodore Strong] The advantages of the colony of El Cajon, San Diego county, California. The superiority of its fruit lands. San Diego, Daily Union, 1883. 32 p. CLU CSmH NHi

7548. —— County of San Diego. The Italy of southern California. San Diego, San Diego union co., 1886. 72 p. CLO CLU CSd CSmH CU-B NHi NN

7549. —— Same. San Diego, Gould, Hutton and co., 1890. 69 p.   CSd

7550. Vogler, William Herman. Silk, iron, and oil in San Diego county from 1900 to 1910. San Diego, 1953. 121 p. maps. Thesis (M.A.)—San Diego state college, 1953.   CSdS

7551. Vroman, Adam Clark, and Barnes, T. F. The genesis of the story of Ramona; why the book was written, explanatory text of points of interest mentioned in the story with thirty illustrations from original photographs. L.A., Kingsley-Barnes & Neuner co., 1899. [137] p. illus.   C   CLU   CU-B

7552. Wade, Bob. San Diego scrapbook. [n.p.] 1946. unp. Radio scripts about San Diego county.   CSd

7553. Wade, Kathleen Camilla. ...Cuyamaca rancho state park... Berkeley, 1937. 51 l. Typew.   CU-B

7554. Welch, S. L., comp. Southern California illustrated. Edition for San Diego county. Containing a description of its principal cities, towns, ranches... L.A., Warner bros. [1887] 68 p. illus., maps.   CSd   CU-B   NN

7555. Why not San Diego county, California. [S.F., Sunset pub. house, 1915?] 48 p.   NN

7556. Wilkinson, J. A. Across the plains in 1859. 28 p. Typew.   CSd

7557. Woman's national Indian association. The Ramona mission and the mission Indians. 1889. 18 p.   CLO

7558. Wood, Henry Patton. Home-land...city and county of San Diego, California... [San Diego, Frye, Garrett & Smith] c1901. 36 p. illus.   CU-B
Other editions followed.   C (1902)   CHi (1904) CSd (1904)   CSmH (1904)   CU-B (1904)

7559. Wood, J. C. Report to Hon. A. V. Brown, postmaster general, on the opening and present condition of the United States overland mail route between San Antonio, Texas, and San Diego, California... [Wash., D.C.? 1858?] 43 p.   CSmH

7560. Wood, Nahum Trask. Diaries, reminiscences and recollections of a California pioneer. Ms.   CSd

7561. Woodward, Arthur. Lances at San Pascual. S.F., Calif. hist. soc., 1948. 84 p. illus. (Calif. hist. soc. Special pub. no. 22) "Bibliographical references:" [67]–84.
Available in many libraries.

7562. Woodward, Lois Ann. ...Carlsbad beach state park ... Berkeley, 1937. 11 l. Typew.   CU-B

7563. Wright, William Lawton. The Warner's ranch Butterfield station puzzle... L.A., Westerners, 1961. 37 p. illus. (The Westerners brand book, no. 9)   CHi

Coronado

7564. Come to Coronado; for health, for fun, to make a home. Coronado [n.d.] folder (16 p.) illus.   CRcS

7565. Coronado. Sixty three years... [n.p., 1953] [16] p. illus.   CHi

7566. —— City council. City of Coronado, California, December 19th, 1957. [Coronado] 1957. [40] p. illus., facsims.   CHi

7567. Coronado beach co. Coronado beach, San Diego county, California... Chicago, Rand McNally, print., 1887. 32 p. illus., map.   CHi   CSmH   CU-B
Other editions followed.   CL (1888)   CLU (1888) CSmH (1888)   CU-B (1888, 1890)   NN (1890)

7568. —— The greatest seaside resort of the Pacific coast... S.F., Frank Eastman & co. [n.d.] [28] p. illus., map.   CHi

7569. Coronado tent city, Coronado Beach. Opens June 1st... [n.p., 1903] [32] p.   CHi

7570. Hotel del Coronado. Concerning Hotel del Coronado and Coronado Beach, California. Chicago, R. R. Donnelley & sons, 1889. 44 p. illus., fold. map, tables.   CHi

7571. —— Same. [Chicago, Press of the H. O. Shepard co., 190–?] 44 p. illus., tables.   CU-B

7572. —— Coronado Beach, San Diego county, California. Its attractions as a health and pleasure resort ...its luxurious hotel, the Hotel del Coronado... Portland, Me., Pub. for E. S. Babcock by Lakeside press [1890] illus. maps, tables.   CU-B
Other editions followed. Place and publisher vary: 1894–1901, Oakland, Pac. press pub. co.   C (1891) CHi (1894?)   CLU (1891, 1897?)   CSmH (1894, 1896? 1899?)   CU-B (1896, 1898, 1900, 1901)

7573. —— Leaves from our scrapbook. [n.p., 1938] 24 p.   CHi

7574. Matsui, Haruyo, Count. Coronado, and some California missions, as seen thro Japanese eyes... [L.A.?] Santa Fe [1903?] 48 p. illus.   CU-B

7575. Peterson, J. Harold. The Coronado story. Coronado, 1954. 233 p. illus.
      C   CCoron   CHi   CNa   CSd   CSdCL   CSdU

7576. —— Same. 2d ed. 1959. 256 p. illus., port.   CHi

7577. Reid, James W. The building of Hotel del Coronado. [Coronado, 1937] [8] p.
      CCoron (1957 reprint)   CHi

7578. Union title insurance and trust co., San Diego. Coronado, celebrated crown city. San Diego, c1951. 12 p. illus., maps.   CHi   CNa   CU-B

7579. —— The story of the Hotel del Coronado. San Diego, 1948. 15 p. illus., ports., maps.   CHi   CNa

Julian

7580. Julian mines; exceptions to the survey of the Cuyamaca grant, before the Surveyor-general of the United States for California. S.F., A. L. Bancroft & co., 1873. 170 p. maps.   C   CSmH

7581. Julian women's club. Julian, California. [1954] 4 p.   CHi

7582. Moody, Dan W. The life of a rover. 1865–1926... [Chicago] 1926. 116 p. illus., map.
      CSd   CU-B

7583. The Mountain stage, Julian. There's gold in Julian. [Julian, 1950?] [12] p. illus., map.   CHi

7584. Sheldon, Gale W. Julian gold mining days. San Diego, 1959. 283 p. illus. Thesis (M.A.)—San Diego state college, 1959.   CSdS

7585. Taylor, Dan Forrest. Julian gold. [n.p., 1939–57?] Typew.   CSd

7586. Thomas, Sadie M. Story of Julian district. [San Diego, Julian Chamber of commerce and Board of supervisors of San Diego county, 193–?] 30 p. illus.   CHi   CLU

La Jolla

7587. California. University. Scripps institute of oceanography, La Jolla. Catalog.
CL has 1935– to date.

7588. —— —— —— ...History and organization... 1951. v.p. CAla

7589. [Chapman, John] La Jolla; its probable meaning and origin. [n.p., 1936] 6 l. Typew. CU-B

7590. Clarkson, Edward Dessau. Ellen Browning Scripps, a biography. La Jolla, The author, c1958. 123 p. illus., ports. Mimeo. CHi CSd

7591. La Jolla. Art center. Annual painting and sculpture exhibit, 1st, 1960– La Jolla, 1960–
CHi has 1st, 1960.

7592. Miller, Max Carlton. The town with the funny name. N.Y., Dutton, 1948. 224 p.
Available in many California libraries and MiD NN

7593. Randolph, Howard Stelle Fitz. La Jolla, year by year. La Jolla [San Diego, Neyenesch printers, inc.] 1946. 150 p. illus., ports.
C CCoron CHi CLO CLU CNa CSd CSmH CoD

7594. —— Same. Rev. ed. La Jolla, Lib. assoc. of La Jolla, 1955. 177 p. illus.
CSdCL CSdS CSdU NN

7595. Scripps, Ellen Browning. Ellen Browning Scripps, 1836–1936. La Jolla, 1936. 60 p. illus., port.
CLO CSd

7596. —— Ellen Browning Scripps; a collection of clippings pertaining to her life. Assembled by the San Diego public library, 1959. CSd

7597. —— Last will and testament. Curtis Hillyer [and] J. C. Harper...attorneys for Robert P. Scripps, executor. San Diego [1932] CSd

7598. Smith, Katharine J. Ellen Browning Scripps "Our fairy godmother." [n.d.] 12 p. Typew. CSd

7599. Thorpe, Rose Hartwick. The white lady of La Jolla... San Diego, Grandier & co., print. [c1904] 45 p. illus. C CLO CSmH MiD

7600. Union title insurance and trust co., San Diego. La Jolla, the jewel city. San Diego, c1953. 15 p. illus., map. CHi CNa CU-B

National City

7601. Freemasons, National City. South West lodge, no. 283. The fiftieth anniversary of South West lodge, no. 283, F. & A. M. National City [1937] [10] p. port. CHi

7602. —— —— Historical sketch of South West lodge no. 283, F. & A. M. 1957. CSd

7603. —— —— The seventy-fifth anniversary... [1962] [23] p. port. CHi

7604. Kimball, Frank Augustus. Diaries of Frank A. Kimball, founder of National City, and Augustus B. Kimball. The diaries begin with the year 1855 and end with the year 1934. Diaries are missing for the years 1859, 1871–73 and 1875. Ms. CNa

7605. —— [Excerpts from the diaries of Frank A. Kimball, 1868 to 1912. 1956] 113 l. Typew.
CSd CSdS

7606. —— Letters written from July 1879 to November 1907. They cover every phase of local history, industry and social life of their period. Partially indexed by Paul T. Mizony. 29 v. Ms. CNa

7607. King, Francis Xavier. Frank A. Kimball, pioneer of National City. [San Diego] 1950. 275 p. illus. Thesis (M.A.)—San Diego state college, 1950.
CNa CSdS

7608. Mizony, Paul T. Church bell in the belfry of First Methodist church, National City, California. 1958. Typew. CSd

7609. —— A few of the highlights of early day history of National City, California. [n.p., n.d.] CSd

7610. —— Postmasters of National City. 1957. 3 p. Typew. CSd

7611. —— Reference data on early day churches of National City, California. 1957. 6 p. Typew. CSd

7612. National City. Board of trade. National City, California. [n.p., 190–?] [24] p. illus., map. CHi

7613. Union title insurance and trust co., San Diego. National City, active south bay city. San Diego, c1954. 16 p. illus., map. CHi CNa

Palomar Mountain

7614. Beckler, Marion Floyd. Palomar mountain, past and present. Palm Desert, Desert mag. press [1958] 47 p. illus. CLU CNa CSd CSdCL CSdS

7615. California. Dept. of natural resources. Division of beaches and parks. Mt. Palomar. Sacramento, State print. off., 1955. CRcS

7616. California institute of technology, Pasadena. Dedication of the Palomar observatory and the Hale telescope, June 3, 1948. [S.F., Grabhorn, 1948] 33 p. CHi CLO CLU CStclU CU-B

7617. Clower, Hardigain. Mount Palomar... [San Diego] 1940. 49 l. CSdS CU-B

7618. Collins, Archie Frederick. The greatest eye in the world. N.Y., Appleton-Century, 1942. CSd

7619. Fassero, James Sebastian. Photographic giants of Palomar. L.A., Print. by Westernlore press [c1947] 60 p. illus., port.
C CL CLSU CNa CO CSalCL CSdS CSluCL CSmH CU-B

7620. —— Same. [Rev. and enl. ed.] [L.A., 1952] 72 p. illus. C CSd

7621. Fletcher, Edward. Azalea park, an ideal place for your summer vacation; a descriptive article of San Luis Rey valley and Palomar mountain, San Diego county, Cal. [San Diego, Frye & Smith, print., n.d.] 16 p. CHi

7622. Tays, George. ...Palomar mountain state park... Berkeley, 1937. 9 l. Typew. CU-B

7623. Watterson, T. V. Palomar observatory... San Diego, Frye & Smith, c1941. unp. photos.
C CO COr CSluCL CViCL

7624. Wood, Catherine M. Palomar from tepee to telescope... San Diego, Frye & Smith, c1937. 149 p. 135 illus.
C CCoron CHi CL CLU CLob CMont CNa CO CSd CSdS CSdU CSf CSfCW CSfSt CSmH CStmo CU-B

7625. Woodbury, David Oakes. The glass giant of Palomar... N.Y., Dodd, 1939. 368 p. illus., ports. Bibliography: p. 365–368.
Available in many California libraries.
Other editions followed. C (1948) CSd (1953) CSf (1953) CStmo (1948)

7626. Wright, Helen. Palomar, the world's largest telescope... N.Y., Macmillan [1952] 188 p. illus.
C CNa CP CSd CSluCL CStmo CViCL

San Diego

7627. ...A B C guide and business directory of San Diego, National City, Coronado and Old Town... March 1889. San Diego, C. J. Stilwell, 1889. 80 p. CU-B

7628. Adams, H. Austin. The man, John D. Spreckels... San Diego, Press of Frye & Smith, c1924. 315 p. illus.
Available in many libraries.

7629. —— The story of water in San Diego... Chula Vista, Denrich press [n.d.] unp. illus.
        CHi CLU CPom CSd CSmH CU-B

7630. Allen, Dorothea White. Miss Isabel Frazee, "the girl who makes the thing." 1952. Typew. CSd

7631. American council on race relations. Intergroup relations in San Diego; some aspects of community life in San Diego which particularly affect minority groups... S.F. [1946] 35 p.   C

7632. Ames, George Walcott. ...San Diego presidio site... Berkeley, 1936. 31 l. Typew.   CU-B

7633. The Amphion club. Scrapbooks, 1910–1948. 5 v. of clippings, programs, photographs.   CSd

7634. Arnold, Charles Elmo, comp. The Arnold family in California since 1853, in San Diego since 1869 ... [San Diego, 1948?] 127 l. including coat of arms, ports., facsims, charts.   C CHi

7635. Atherton, Lucien C. The early history of the San Diego presidial district, 1542–1782... [Berkeley, 1930] 133 l. mounted photos, maps, Typew. Thesis (M.A.)— Univ. of Calif., 1930.   CU CU-B

7636. Atkinson, Fred William. The Argonauts of 1769; a narrative of the occupation of San Diego and Monterey by Don Gaspar de Portolá... Watsonville, Pajaronian press, 1936. 166 p. illus., port., map.
C CHi CL CLO CMont CO CRcS CSal CSalCL CSd CSf CSfP CSfU CSjC CSmH CSmat CStrJC CU-B

7637. Bar association of San Diego. ...Its history, constitution, by-laws and membership. San Diego [Transcript press] 1915. 34 p.   CHi

7638. Barnes, Calvin Rankin. History of St. Paul's church, San Diego... [San Diego] The Parish, 1944. 46 p. illus., ports.   C CHi CLU CSd

7639. Benchley, Belle (Jennings) My animal babies. Bost., Little, 1945. 264 p. illus. Stories about the San Diego zoo by its director.
CBev CBu CChiS CL CLSU CLU CMerCL CMont CO CRcS CRedCL CRedl CSalCL CSdS CSf CStmo CViCL

7640. —— ...My friends, the apes... Bost., Little, 1942. 296 p. illus.
CBb CBev CBu CL CLU CMerCL CMont CO CRcS CRedCL CRedl CSalCL CSd CSdS CSf CStmo

7641. —— ...My life in a man-made jungle... Bost,. Little, 1940. 293 p. illus.
Available in many libraries.

7642. Blaisdell, James A. Address at the dedication of the Junipero Serra museum, July 16, 1929. San Diego, San Diego hist. soc. [1929] 13 p.   CHi

7643. B'nai B'rith. San Diego. Lasker lodge no. 370. The Yoval. San Diego, 1937.   CSd

7644. Book of the dead of the vicinity of San Diego, 1849–1880. [n.p., n.d.] 54 p.   CSd

7645. Bowers, W. W. The building of the Horton house. 3 p. Typew.   CSd

7646. —— San Diego, California, as a summer and winter resort for pleasure seekers and invalids. [San Diego, 1885?] 8 p.   CU-B

7647. Boyce, Ruth. Guide to San Diego libraries... Prepared under direction of City schools curriculum project, Work projects admin. O.P.N. 665–07–3–96. San Diego, 1940. 61 l. Reproduced from typew. copy.
    CLU CSd

7648. Brown, Elton T. The exposition in black and white...pencil drawings of the Panama–California international exposition, 1916. Coronado, Coronado strand, 1916. 24 p. illus.   CHi CNa

7649. Bryan, Roger Bates. An average American army officer... San Diego, Buck-Molina, 1914. 166 p. illus., ports.   CSd CU-B

7650. Cabrillo quadricentennial committee. [Quadricentennial celebration, Sept. 28, 1942]   CSd

7651. California. Centennials commission. Exhibition of historic art, California centennial celebration, San Diego, August 1 through September 9, 1950. Sacramento, Calif. state print. off., 1950. [48] p. illus.
    CHi CRcS CSd CStmo

7652. —— **State college, San Diego.** Catalog. Sacramento, State print off., 1905–
CHi has 1904/05. CL has 1906– to date.

7653. —— —— **Campus laboratory school.** Bits from early history of San Diego, by 7A boys. San Diego, 1916. v.p. Typew.   CSdS

7654. —— —— **Institute of public opinion.** Metropolitan San Diego housing survey, June 1948. [San Diego, 1948] 200 p. map, tables.   C CSdS

7655. —— **State reconstruction and reemployment commission.** Planning pays profits, the story of San Diego. 1945. 31 p. (Pamphlet, no. 8)
    CHi CSdS

7656. —— **University. Heller committee for research in social economics.** Cost of living studies. V. How Mexicans earn and live. A study of the incomes and expenditures of one hundred Mexican families in San Diego, California... Berkeley, Univ. of Calif. press, 1933. 114 p. incl. tables. (Univ. of Calif. pub. in economics. v.13)
    CL CLSU CO CSdS CSf CSfCW CU CU-B

7657. Cameron, John. Dams and reservoirs of San Diego... [San Diego, San Diego city schools, 1939] 103 p. illus.   CSdS CU-B

7658. —— Same. 3d ed. 1940.   CLSU

7659. Carter, George Francis. Pleistocene man at San Diego. Baltimore, Johns Hopkins press, 1957. 400 p. illus., maps. Bibliography: p. 380–387.
C CChiS CNa CP CSS CSd CSdS CSdU CSf CSfSt CSluCL O TxU ViU

7660. Carteri, B. J. Carteri center. San Diego, Author, 1932. 26 p. History of early real estate development in the Adams avenue area.   CSd

7661. Chapman, Edna E. An historical study of the health education department of the San Diego city schools. [L.A.] 1951. Thesis (M.A.)— U.C.L.A., 1951.   CLU

7662. Chenkin, Gary. The port of San Diego, California. Stanford, 1959. Thesis (M.A.)— Stanford univ., 1959.   CSt

7663. Choate, Rufus. Interview of Rufus Choate by Edgar Hastings, June 1957. [San Diego] Typew.
    CSd

7664. Citizens aqueduct celebration committee. San Diego's quest for water. [San Diego, 1947] [48] p. illus.   CLU CSd

7665. Clark, George H. The life of John Stone

Stone, mathematician, physicist, electrical engineer and great inventor. [San Diego, Frye & Smith, ltd., 1946]
CSd

7666. Clarke, James Mitchell. San Diego has five beaches... San Diego [San Diego city schools] 1937. 39 l. illus. CU-B

7667. Cleather, Alice Leighton. H. P. Blavatsky, a great betrayal. Calcutta, Thacker, Spink & co., 1922. Biography of a prominent theosophist. CSd

7668. Cleveland, Daniel. San Diego pueblo lands. [n.d.] 6 p. Typew. CSd

7669. —— San Diego sixty years ago. [n.d.] 10 l. Typew. C

7670. Clough, Edwin Howard. "Ramona's marriage place," the house of Estudillo...Chula Vista, Denrich press [c1910] [35] p. illus. C CLO

7671. Clower, Hardigain. City planning in San Diego... [San Diego, San Diego city schools, 1940] 53 l. CLU CSdS CU-B

7672. College hill land association. Facts concerning the city of San Diego...with a map showing the city and its surroundings. San Diego, San Diego print co. [1888?] 14 p. map. CHi

7673. College woman's club. Pathfinder social survey of San Diego. San Diego, Labor temple press, 1914. CSd

7674. Committee of six hundred. [Scrapbook] [n.d.] San Diego women banded together to stop crimes. CSd

7675. Community chest of San Diego. Ten years after. San Diego, 1939. CSd

7676. Cosgrove, Terence B. An opinion on the rights of the city of San Diego to the waters of the San Diego river. San Diego, 1941. CSd CSmH

7677. Cundiff, Willard. A San Diego cartoon book, depicting in jocund vein a few gentlemen therefrom. Illustrated by Willard Cundiff. [San Diego, Thorpe engraving co., 1909] 263 l. (chiefly illus.)
C CLU CU-B

7678. Cuyamaca club. Articles of incorporation, constitution, by-laws, officers and members. [n.p.] 1907. CSd

7679. Daughters of the American revolution. California. San Diego chapter. San Diego yesterdays, being sketches of incidents in the Indian, Spanish, Mexican, and American history of the city of San Diego... [San Diego, c1921] 73 p.
CHi CL CLU CO CSd CSmH CU-B NN TxU UPB

7680. Davidson, Edward, and Orcutt, Eddy, comp. "The country of joyous aspect." San Diego, a brief history, 1542–1888... [San Diego, Arts & crafts press, c1929] [75] p. illus. "Published on the 40th anniversary of the San Diego trust and savings bank." Third edition.
C CBev CCoron CHi CL CLSU CLU CLob CNa COr CSd CSdU CSf CSmH CStrJC

7681. —— Same. 3d ed. [1935?] 80 p. illus.
CU-B

7682. Davidson, Winifred. San Diego's "Firsts." 2 v. 312 p. Typew. 78 "firsts" appeared in *San Diego union* beginning Aug. 27, 1933. CSd

7683. —— Where California began... San Diego, McIntyre pub. co., c1929. 170 p. illus.
Available in many libraries.

7684. Davis, Edward J. P. Historical San Diego, the birthplace of California; a history of its discovery, settlement and development. 1st ed. [San Diego] 1953. 120 p. illus., maps.
Available in many libraries.

7685. —— The United States navy and U.S. marine corps at San Diego; an authentic record of the establishment of the U.S. navy and marine corps facilities in and adjacent to San Diego, California. 1st ed. San Diego, Pioneer print., 1955. 104 p. illus.
C CCoron CSd CSdCL CSdS CSdU

7686. Davis, William Heath, vs. U.S. In the matter of the claim of William H. Davis vs. the United States, for destruction of his wharf & warehouse at New San Diego, California, by United States troops, during the war of rebellion. Petition of claimant, affidavits for and against claimant, testimony taken before commission of investigation, map showing the location of wharf and warehouse, and argument of claimant's attorney. S.F., 1881. 152 p. CHi

7687. Diamond carriage and livery co. San Diego, a momento. San Diego [n.d.] unp. CSd

7688. Dickson, Ray Clark. San Diego suite; impressions in prose of a city. San Diego, Neyenesch print., c1947. unp. illus. CNa CSd

7689. Diffendorf, Grace B. The long lane. N.Y., Vantage press, 1959. CSd

7690. Dixon, Benjamin Franklin. Beginnings of public education in San Diego. [San Diego, 1950] 23 l.
CHi CU-B

7691. —— Don Diego's "California background"; handbook: class in San Diego history. Preliminary ed. for the use of San Diego schools, libraries, press class in San Diego history. San Diego, 1956. unp. illus., maps.
C CSd CSdS CU-B

7692. —— A history of school district number one, San Diego, California, 1850–1870. [San Diego] 1949. illus. Typew. CSd

7693. —— The overland mail centennial. [San Diego, San Diego hist. soc., 1957] [8] p. CHi

7694. Dodge, John Mason. "Jack" Dodge (John Mason Dodge), the friend of every man; his life and times... L.A., Sherman Danby, 1937. 179 p. illus.
CHi

7695. Donley, Ward Thomas. Alonzo Horton, founder of modern San Diego. San Diego, 1952. 167 p. Thesis (M.A.)—San Diego state college, 1952. CSdS

7696. Donnelly, John Eugene. The Old Globe theater at San Diego, California: an historical survey of its origin and development. [L.A.] 1957. 122 p. Thesis (M.A.)— U.C.L.A., 1957. CLU CSd

7697. Drama league of America. San Diego center. Historians note book. [Scrapbook] CSd

7698. —— —— The San Diego center, 1917–1918.
CSd

7699. Dunbar, Horace. Marcy's mill and the men who winnowed the facts... San Diego, F. E. Marcy, 1944. 92 p. illus. CSd

7700. [Edmunds, Charles K.] George White Marston. [Claremont, Pomona college, 1934] [19] p. CHi

7701. Edwards, William Aloysius. San Diego, California; an historical sketch... [San Diego, n.d.] 5 p. illus. CLU CSmH

7702. —— Same. [1892] [49] p. (chiefly illus.)
CU-B

7703. —— San Diego, California. Private hospital. [San Diego, 1891?] [11] p. illus.   CU-B

7704. —— Souvenir of San Diego; 350th anniversary of the discovery of the bay of San Diego, September 28, 1892. San Diego, Stenhouse & co., 1892. [47] p. CHi

7705. Ernest, Sue. The golden pueblo. [San Diego?] 1950. [96] l. Reproduced from typew. copy.   C

7706. Fages, Pedro. Letters of Captain Don Pedro Fages & the Reverend President Fr. Junipero Serra at San Diego, California, in October, 1772. Translated into English with an introduction by Henry R. Wagner. S.F. [Grabhorn] 1939. 9 p. 2 l. of facsims.   CHi CSjC

7707. Federal art project. Southern California. San Diego civic center fountain and Donal Hord, sculptor. [San Diego? 1940?] 23 l. illus. Reproduced from typew. copy.   CLU CSd

7708. Federal writers' project. San Diego. ...San Diego, a California city...sponsored and published by the San Diego historical society. [San Diego, c1937] 138 p. illus., maps. (Am. guide ser.) Bibliography: p. 127–130.
Available in many California libraries and MiD MoSHi OrU UHi

7709. Fiesta del Pacifico, San Diego. Official program. San Diego [Yale print co.] 19—
CSd has 1956–58.

7710. Fletcher, Edward. Memoirs of Ed. Fletcher. [San Diego, Pioneer press, c1952] 751 p. illus., ports.
C CHi CNa CSd CSdU CU-B

7711. [Fox, Joseph S.] The old house speaks. [San Diego, Arts & crafts press, 1943] [16] p. illus., ports. Story of the Machado house.   CU-B

7712. Frate, Julia Flinn de. This was yesterday. San Diego, East San Diego press, c1951–53. 3 v. in 2.
C CHi CNa CSd CSdCL

7713. [Frazier, S. R.] Shall the city of San Diego acquire the system of water-works of the Southern California mountain water company? 46 p. illus., maps. Reprinted from *San Diego sun*, 1912.   CHi

7714. Gaskell, Charles Arthur, pub. San Diego year book and classified business directory. San Diego [1903?] 19 p.   CLU

7715. Getz, T. P. The story of Ramona's marriage place; Old San Diego, California... North San Diego [The author, 1912] 13 p. illus.
C CHi CLU CU-B

7716. Goodhue, Bertram Grosvenor. The architecture and the gardens of the San Diego exposition; a pictorial survey of the aesthetic features of the Panama California international exposition; described by Carleton Monroe Winslow; together with an essay by Clarence S. Stein... S.F., Elder, c1916. 154 p. illus.
C CBu CCoron CHi CL CLSU CLU CMont CNa CO CRedl CSd CSdS CSfU CSj CSmat CSmH CViCL

7717. Goss, Mary Lathrop. American national Red Cross, San Diego, California chapter, March 1917 to December 1918: a history of the general activities and organization. 1922. v.p. Typew.   CSd

7718. Green, Joseph L., pub. San Diego street guide. 1943.   CSd

7719. Grugal, Donald Morris. Military movements into San Diego from the Mexican war to statehood, 1846–1850. San Diego, 1950. 123 p. illus. Thesis (M.A.)— San Diego state college, 1950.   CSdS

7720. Gunn, Douglas. A historical sketch of San Diego, San Diego county, California. [n.p., 1876] 16 p.
CHi CSmH CU-B TxU

7721. —— Picturesque San Diego, with historical and descriptive notes... Chicago, Knight & Leonard co., 1887. 98 p. illus.
C CHi CL CLO CLSU CLU CNa CO CPom CRedl CSd CSdS CSf CSfCP CSfCSM CSmH CU-B NHi NN UPB

7722. —— San Diego. Climate, productions, resources, topography. San Diego, Union steam bk. & job print. off., 1886. 78 p. map. 4th ed., revised.
CHi CLO CLU CSd CSmH CU-B NN

7723. —— San Diego. Climate, resources, topography, productions, etc. San Diego, San Diego print. co., 1887. 132 p. illus.
CBb CHi CLSU CLU CSd CSmH CU-B CoD NN

7724. Hebert, Edgar Weldon. The San Diego naval militia, 1891–1920. San Diego, 1956. 161 p. Thesis (M.A.)— San Diego state college, 1956.   CSdS

7725. Hensley, Herbert C. Early San Diego; reminiscences of early days and people. [n.d.] 3 v. Typew.
CSd

7726. —— Reminiscence. [n.p., n.d.] 98 p. Typew.
CSd

7727. Herring, Hubert. The education of George W. Marston... Claremont, Pomona college, c1946. 29 p. front.
C CL CLO CLSU CLU CPom CSd CSdS CSf CSmH CU-B

7728. Herrold, George H. San Diego California, 1887–1888. 1956. Typew.   CSd

7729. Hevener, Harold Guy, jr. The pueblo lands of the city of San Diego, 1769–1950. San Diego, 1950. 144 p. illus. Thesis (M.A.)— San Diego state college, 1950.   CSdS

7730. Hewes, Laurence Ilsley. Intergroup relations in San Diego. S.F., American council on race relations, 1946.   CSd

7731. Hewett, Edgar Lee. Ancient America at the Panama-California exposition. 1915. [8] p. pl. Reprinted from the *Theosophical path*, Feb. 1915.
CSd CSdS

7732. —— **and Johnson, William Templeton.** ...Architecture of the Exposition... [Wash., D.C.] 1916. [40] p. illus. (Archaeological inst. of Am. Papers of the School of Am. archaeology, no. 32)
CL CSdS CSmH

7733. Higgins, Shelley J. This fantastic city, San Diego, by Shelley J. Higgins as told to Richard Mansfield. San Diego, 1956. 352 p. illus., port., maps.
C CL CLU CNa CP CSd CSdS CSdU CSluCL CU-B NN

7734. Hill, Earl W. ...The Panama extravaganza ... East San Diego, Moyer print. co. [1916] 18 p., 3 l.
CSmH

7735. Hill, Louis C. Report on program of water development, the city of San Diego and the San Diego metropolitan area [to the San Diego Board of engineers] San Diego, Municipal employees' assoc., 1937. 31, 16 p. illus. (In *Municipal employee*, section 1 & 2, May 1937)
CSd CSdS

7736. Historical shrine foundation of San Diego county. The Thomas Whaley house, San Diego, California. [San Diego, 1960] [39] p. illus., port., facsims.
CU-B

7737. Hobby, Carl F. Sketches of San Diego; written and illustrated by C. F. Hobby. San Diego, Elite print. co., 1919.   CSd

7738. Hopkins, Harry C. History of San Diego, its pueblo lands & water... San Diego, City print. co. [c1929] 358 p. illus.
CCoron CHi CL CLSU CLU CO CRcS CSS CSd CSf CSfCW CSmH CU-B CWhC MWA NN

7739. Hunzicker, Lena B. Dr. C. C. Parry of the U.S. and Mexican boundary commission. [n.d.] Typew.
                                                                CSd

7740. Industrial survey associates. San Diego's transportation needs land, sea, and air, and industrial site requirements; a report prepared for the City council and Harbor commission of San Diego, California. S.F., 1953. 1 v. v.p. illus., map.   C

7741. James, George Wharton. Exposition memories, Panama–California exposition, San Diego, 1916... and the prose and poetic writings of San Diego writers read at the exposition. Pasadena, Radiant life press, 1917. 216 p. illus., ports.
C CCoron CHi CL CLO CLSU CLU CSd CSdU CSf CSmH CU-B

7742. —— Rose Hartwick Thorpe and the story of "Curfew must not ring tonight." Pasadena, Radiant life press, 1916.   CSd

7743. Jenkins, Malinda (Plunkett) Gambler's wife; the life of Malinda Jenkins as told in conversations to Jesse Lilienthal. Bost., Houghton, 1933. 296 p.
                                                            CHi CSd

7744. Jones, L. E., pub. Your San Diego. San Diego, c1941.   CSd

7745. Kearny, Stephen W. A letter from Brigadier general Stephen W. Kearny, San Diego, Upper California, January thirtieth, 1847. Carmel, Thomas W. Norris, 1950. 8 p.   CHi CRcS CSd

7746. Kerley, Jay L. California and the navy; commemorating the California Pacific international exposition, San Diego, 1935. San Diego, 1935. unp. illus.
                                                    C CSd CSdU

7747. Kettner, William. Why it was done and how, comp. by Mary B. Steyle. San Diego, Frye & Smith, 1923. 173 p. ports. A record of political events occurring during the author's eight years in Congress (1913–1921)
                                            CSd CSdS CSfCW

7748. Killion, P. Errett, comp. The growth of San Diego from 1900 to 1931... San Diego [n.d.] 11 p. Mimeo.   CSd

7749. Kingdom of the sun (periodical) San Diego, the birthplace of California. Special issues. [Oro Grande, L. D. Gregory, 1915–35] illus.
CHi (1915, 1916)   CLU (1916, 1917)   CSd (1915)
CU-B (1916)   NN (1935)

7750. Klauber, Wangenheim co. Ninetieth anniversary, 1869–1959... [San Diego, 1959] 32 p. illus., ports.   CHi

7751. Knowlton, Murray. San Diego harbor, a survey of San Diego harbor, its ships, piers, dredges, planes and people...prepared under the direction of the San Diego City schools curriculum project, Works progress administration. San Diego, 1938.
                                        CLU CSd CSdS CU-B

7752. —— Waterfront... City schools curriculum project, Works progress administration. San Diego, 1937. Mimeo.   CSd

7753. Lathrop, Harold W., comp. Directory of community activities, organizations, resource persons, recreational areas and facilities. [San Diego, U.S.O. advisory council, 1953] 126 p.   CSdS

7754. Lawyers institute of San Diego. Article of incorporation... [San Diego? 1920?] 16 p.   CHi

7755. Lee, Dwight Van Deusen. The counseling resources of San Diego, California. [L.A.] 1948. Thesis (M.A.) — U.C.L.A., 1948.   CLU

7756. Lesley, Lewis Burt, ed. San Diego state college, the first fifty years, 1897–1947. San Diego state college, 1947. 93 p. illus.   CSd CSdS

7757. —— The struggle of San Diego for a southern trans-continental railroad connection, 1854–1891. [Berkeley, 1933] 392 l. maps. Typew. Thesis (Ph.D.) — Univ. of Calif., 1933.   CU-B

7758. —— Same. Reprinted from *Greater America*: essays in honor of Herbert Eugene Bolton, p. 499–518. Berkeley, Univ. of Calif. press, 1945.   CSdS

7759. Lewis, T. L. Brief summary of the organization and activities of the San Diego division of the State council of defense of the state of California. Typew.
                                                                CSd

7760. Lloyd, Mary. The birthplace of California; old San Diego, founded 1769...Originated and produced by Maryloyd. [San Diego, Neyenesch print., c1950] [44] p. illus.   C CHi CSd

7761. Luco, Juan M., et als vs. Commercial bank of San Diego. In the Superior court of the city and county of San Diego, state of California. Juan M. Luco, et als, plaintiffs, vs. Commercial bank of San Diego, et als., defendants, final decree. San Diego, Union steam print. house, 1886. 60 p.   CHi CLU

7762. Lyle, Eugene P., III, and Diffin, Charles W. The city of wings; a narrative of aviation and its swift development as seen in San Diego from the earliest days of flying to the present... San Diego, City schools, 1938.   CSd

7763. McGhee, Earl Samuel. E. W. Morse, pioneer merchant and co-founder of San Diego. San Diego, 1950. 260 p. illus. Thesis (M.A.) — San Diego state college, 1950.   CSdS

7764. McLean, Thomas David. Is Old San Diego historical?... [San Diego? 1946] 7 p.   CU-B

7765. McRae, Milton Alexander. Forty years in newspaperdom... N.Y., Brentano's [c1924] 496 p. illus., ports., map, facsims.   CSd CU

7766. Mandeville, Frank H., pub. ...Tourists' guide to San Diego and vicinity...Historical...information...August 16th, 1888. San Diego, Gould & Hutton, steam print., 1888. 80 p. illus.   CSmH CU-B

7767. Mangold, George Benjamin. Comunity welfare in San Diego... a survey conducted under the joint auspices of the Community welfare council of San Diego, San Diego county welfare commission and city of San Diego. [San Diego, Dove and Robinson, 1930] 205 p. tabs., diagrs.   C CLU CSd CSdS

7768. Maritime research society of San Diego. Sailing vessels in the San Diego trade... [San Diego] 1940. [8] p. (Its Bul. no. 1, May, 1940)   CO CU-B

7769. Marston, Anna Lee, ed. Records of a California family; journals and letters of Lewis C. Gunn and Elizabeth LeBreton Gunn... San Diego, Priv. print. by Johnck & Seeger, S.F., 1928. 279 p. San Diego pioneer family which first settled in Sonora, Tuolumne county.

C CBb CHi CL CLSU CLgA CO CSd CSdS CSf CSmH CU-B

7770. Marston, Mary Gilman. George White Marston, a family chronicle. [L.A.] Ward Ritchie, 1956. 2 v. illus.
C CHi CLO CLU CNa CSd CSdS CStoC CU-B

7771. Mayer, Pearl LaForce. Historic landmarks of San Diego. [San Diego, Priv. print.] 1930. 26 p.
CHi CSd CSmH

7772. Midwinter carnival; given in honor of Admiral L. A. Beardslee, U.S.N., San Diego, Cal., Feb. 20–22, 1897... [San Diego, Garrett & Smith, 1897] [64] p. illus.
C

7773. Miller, Max Carlton. Harbor of the sun; the story of the port of San Diego... N.Y., Doubleday, Doran & co., 1940. 329 p. illus.
Available in many California libraries and CoU MiD MoS NN ODa OrU OU TxU UPB

7774. ——— I cover the waterfront. N.Y., Dutton, 1932. 204 p. Stories of the San Diego waterfront collected when author was reporter on the *San Diego sun.*
Available in many California libraries.

7775. Morgan, Neil Bowen. Crosstown. [Foreword by Bennett Cerf] [San Diego, Crosstown, c1953] 56 p. illus.
C CLU CNa CSd CSdS

7776. ——— My San Diego. Forewords [by] Max Miller, Art Linkletter [and] Gregory Peck. [1st ed. San Diego? 1951] 56 p. illus.   C CL CO CSd CSdS

7777. Morning choral club. History of the Morning choral club. 2 scrapbooks.
CSd

7778. Morse, Ephriam Weed. Letters from Ephriam W. Morse of San Diego to R. W. Laine, 1878–79. [San Diego, 1938] 11 l. Typew.
CU-B

7779. Mott, George Fox, jr. "San Diego—politically speaking"... San Diego, 1932. 250 p. Bibliography: p. [139]–151.
CBb
CL CLSU CLU CSd CSdS CSmH CU-B ViU

7780. National probation association. The juvenile delinquency problem in San Diego; a report of a survey. N.Y., S.F., 1943. 75 p.
CStmo

7781. Nelson, Herbert Joseph. The port of San Diego: development of terminal facilities for water-borne commerce by federal and municipal agencies. San Diego, 1956. 162 p. illus., pl., maps. Thesis (M.A.)—San Diego state college, 1956.
CSdS

7782. Neuhaus, Eugen. The San Diego garden fair, personal impressions of...the Panama California international exposition... S.F., Elder, 1916. 76 p. 31 pl.
Available in many California libraries and MoS ODa ViU

7783. Nolen, John. San Diego, a comprehensive plan for its improvement. Bost., G. H. Ellis co., print., 1908. 109 p. illus. (incl. plans)
C CHi CLO CLU CRedl CSd CSfCW CU-B

7784. Nolen, John, and associates. A comprehensive city plan for San Diego, California; prepared for the City planning commission, the Harbor commission, the Park commission of San Diego... [Watson-Jones, print.] 1926. 36 p. illus., maps.
C CLSU CSd CSdS CSmH CU-B

7785. Old San Diego; old town, its origin and points of historic interest. San Diego, Dove & Robinson [n.d.] 16 p. illus., map.
CHi

7786. Orange blossom mining and milling co. [Prospectus. San Diego, Neyenesch & Reed, 1906?] [20] p. illus., ports., map.
CHi

7787. Outcalt, Irving E. On becoming a Californian. 1941. 35 p. Typew. "Reminiscences of San Diego in 1891 and later."
CSd

7788. Packard, J. C. Photographs of San Diego. [n.p., n.d.] 24 mounted photos.
CSf

7789. Palmer, Lillian Pray, ed. Book of memory for the ages. San Diego, L.D. Gregory, 1925.
CSd

7790. Piburn, John Logan. So this is California! [San Diego, City print. co., c1933] 252, [9] p.   NN

7791. Picturesque San Diego and Coronado. San Diego [Press of Stenhouse & co.] 1898. 18 p. illus.   C

7792. Pourade, Richard F. The history of San Diego; a planned series on the historic birthplace of California. Commissioned by James S. Copley. [1st ed.] San Diego, Union-Tribune pub. co. [1960–] illus., ports., maps, facsims. Contents: v.1. The explorers.—v.2. Time of the bells.—v.3. The silver dons.
CAla (v.2) CHi CLSM (v.1) CLom (v.1) CSdU (v.1) CSf (v.1) CSfU (v.2) CU-B (v.1)

7793. Pratt, Alice. Neighborhood house, its history and activities. 1927. 11 p. Typew.
CSd

7794. Pratt, Janette. Our drink of water; the San Diego water system...prepared under direction of San Diego city schools curriculum project... San Diego, 1936. illus. Bibliography: p. 177–78.
CSd

7795. Presidio Hill guide book; a short story of its history and park development. San Diego [Frye & Smith, 1937] 20 p. illus.
CHi

7796. Pumphrey, Margaret Blanche. Highways and byways of San Diego...prepared under direction of San Diego City schools curriculum project, Works progress administration. San Diego, 1936. Mimeo.
CSd CSdS CU-B

7797. ——— Under three flags... Caldwell, Ida., Caxton, 1939. 293 p. illus. Stories for children about the history of San Diego.
C CL CMerCL CMont CNa CO COnC CRcS CSal CSd CSdS CSf CSfCW CSlu CSluCL CStmo NN T

7798. ——— Same. 1943. 293 p.   CHi

7799. Pyle, Fred D. Feature history city's portion El Capitan—Lakeside pipe line... San Diego, Bur. of water development, 1937. 2 v.
CSdS

7800. ——— Feature history college reservoir and pipe line. San Diego, Bur. of water development, 1939. 500 p. illus.
CSdS

7801. ——— Feature history Hodges reservoir dam strengthening, P.W.A. docket California 1223-R. San Diego, Bur. of water development, 1937. 448 p. illus., diagrs.
CSdS

7802. ——— Outline of municipal water supply. San Diego, Div. of development and conservation, 1935. 33 p. illus. Mimeo.
CSdS

7803. Register publishing co. San Diego business register and shopper's guide. [San Diego]
CSd has 1947–59. CSdS has 1946, 1953, 1959.

7804. Requa, Richard S. Inside lights on the building of San Diego's exposition, 1935.... [San Diego, 1937] 151 p.   C CCoron CHi
CL CLO CLU CSd CSdS CSmH CStoC CU-B

7805. Rhodes, May (Davison) The hired man on horseback, my story of Eugene Manlove Rhodes. Bost., Houghton, 1938. 263 p.   CHi CSd

7806. Rieder, M. San Diego and vicinity; photographic views. L.A., c1906.   CSd

7807. Rimbach, Fred Jay. A history of the cemeteries in the city of San Diego, California. San Diego, 1949. [32] l. Typew.   C CSd

7808. Roberts, Rose. Providing for social security in San Diego...Prepared under direction of City schools curriculum project, Works progress administration... San Diego, 1939. 44 p. Mimeo.   CSdS

7809. —— Social service agencies in San Diego... Prepared under direction of City schools curriculum project, Work projects administration... San Diego, 1940. 68 p. Mimeo.   CLU CSdS

7810. Rolle, Andrew F. William Heath Davis and the founding of American San Diego. San Diego, Union title insurance trust co. [1952?] [20] p. illus., ports., map.   C CHi CNa CO CP CSd CStmo

7811. Rowan, Loleta Levete. Sixty, fifty and twenty-five years ago in San Diego. 1940. 7 p. Typew.   CSd

7812. Rury, Maude M. Tuna: some notes on the tuna industry of San Diego...Compiled under the supervision of Cornelia D. Plaister, San Diego city librarian... the City library extension project, no. 3978, Works progress administration. [San Diego] 1936. 131 p. illus. Mimeo.   CSd

7813. Ryan, Frederick L. The labor movement in San Diego. San Diego, San Diego state college, 1959.
                                                        CSd

7814. Ryan aeronautical co. Annual report. CHi has 1951. CL has 1948–60.

7815. Rynning, Thomas Harbo. Gun notches... N.Y., Stokes, 1931.   CSd

7816. San Diego et als vs. Allison, Robert, et als. In the Supreme court of the state of California. The President and trustees of the city of San Diego, et als, respondents, vs. Robert Allison, et als, appellants. Brief of respondents. Volney E. Howard & C. P. Taggart, for respondents. I. Hartman, for appellants. San Diego, Bushyhead & Gunn, 1873. 12 p.   CHi

7817. —— ...Brief of appellants in reply. J. Hartmann, S. Heydenfeldt. S.F., Law print. house of Woman's pub. co., 1873. 4 p.   CHi

7818. —— ...Statement of case [by I. Hartman, atty., for appellants. n.p., 1870?] 7 p.   CU-B

7819. San Diego. Board of park commissioners. Balboa park, souvenir guide, San Diego. 1925. 48 p. illus.   CSd CSdS

7820. —— **California Pacific international exposition, 1935.** Illustrated catalogue [of the] official art exhibition, the Palace of fine arts, Balboa park, San Diego...May 29th to November 11th, 1935. [San Diego, Frye & Smith, 1935] 44 p. illus.   C CHi CSd CU-B

7821. —— Official daily program... San Diego, George Hoffman, jr., 1936. 4 p.   CRcS

7822. —— —— Same. 2d ed. c1935. 76 p.   CHi

7823. —— —— Official guide. [San Diego, G. F. Wolcott, c1935] 84 p. illus.   CMont CSf CU-B

7824. —— **Chamber of commerce.** By-laws. San Diego, 1887. 19 p.   CHi

7825. —— —— Classified business directory of members. July 1, 1918. San Diego [1918?]   CU-B

7826. —— —— Descriptive, historical, commercial, agricultural, and other important information relative to the city of San Diego...Containing also a business directory of the city... [San Diego] Print. at off. of "San Diego daily union," 1874. 50 p. illus.
       C CHi CLU CSd CSmH CU-B MoKU NHi

7827. —— —— Historical San Diego; here California began. San Diego, The San Diegans [n.d.] folder (14 p.) illus., maps.   CRcS

7828. —— —— Metropolitan San Diego housing report. 1952–
CSdS has 1952–53; 1956 summary.

7829. —— —— The rising city of the west. San Diego, southern California. The Pacific terminus of the Texas Pacific railroad. N.Y., Wm. Moore steam bk. job print., 1872. 8 p. map.   NHi

7830. —— —— San Diego and southern California...[San Diego, San Diego bulletin print., 1870] 8 p.
                                                       CU-B

7831. —— —— San Diego "our Italy"... San Diego, Gould, Hutton & co., print., 1895. 62 p. illus.
                           CLO CLU CSmH CU-B

7832. —— **Charters.** Charter of the city of San Diego, adopted March 16, 1889. [with subsequent amendments] Publisher varies.
CHi (1910) CLU (1915) CSd (various eds.)

7833. —— **City attorney.** Report upon the legal status of the Plaza. Dec. 19, 1892.   CSd

7834. —— **City manager.** City of San Diego yearbook. 19— [San Diego, 19— Title varies.
CRcS has 1936/37, 1939/40.

7835. —— **City planning commission.** A major street plan for San Diego, California. [San Diego, Dove & Robinson] 1930.   CSd

7836. —— —— Planning San Diego, a program for the development of a post-war plan... San Diego, 1943. 25 p. illus., maps. Bibliography: p. 25.   CLO

7837. —— **Congregation Beth Israel.** The anniversary story. Souvenir history and program commemorating the 75th anniversary. San Diego, 1952. 50 p. illus.
                                                   CHi CSd

7838. —— **Dept. of social welfare.** Juvenile delinquency in San Diego. San Diego, 1949.   CSd

7839. —— **Fire dept.** San Diego fire fighters. San Diego, Frye & Smith, 1956.   CSd

7840. —— —— Souvenir, San Diego fire department. [San Diego, Frye & Smith] 1906.   CSd

7841. —— **First Methodist church.** History of the First Methodist church, 1869–1957. Comp. by Samuel D. Erwine. [San Diego, 1957] 62 p.   CCSC CSd

7842. —— **First Presbyterian church.** Annual report of the trustees... [San Diego]
C has 1907–08, 1910.

7843. —— **First Unitarian church.** First Unitarian church [by Eunice H. Pierce] [1959] Typew.   CSd

7844. —— **Harbor dept.** Port director's annual tonnage report.
CSdS has 1950/51–1953/54.

7845. —— —— The port of San Diego...industrial and harbor data for fiscal year... San Diego, 19—
CSdS has 1928/29, 1930/31–1931/32, 1934/35–1936/37, 1938/39, 1940/41, 1946/47–1947/48, 1951/52–1952/53, 1954/55–1957/58.

7846. —— —— The port of San Diego, the southwest terminal for navigation, transportation and aviation. San Diego [1930?] illus., maps.   CLU
Other editions followed.   CLU (1932?) CNa (1948)

7847. —— **High school.** [Commencement programmes] 1st, 1889–
CHi has 3d, 1891.

7848. San Diego. High school (*cont'd*) A history of San Diego high school, 1882–1932. Sponsored by the Porterfield chapter of Quill and scroll [1932] 64 p. illus., ports.   C CSd

7849. —— Japanese Congregational church. 50th anniversary dedication 1907–57. San Diego [1957] 38 p. illus., ports. Text in Japanese and English.
CCSC CHi

7850. —— Panama-California exposition, 1915–16. Digests of the Argentine republic, Chile, Latin America in general, comp. by A. J. Mende... [n.p., n.d.] unp. Typew.   CSdS

7851. —— —— Digests of the republics of Brazil, Uruguay and Paraguay, comp. by A. J. Mende. [n.p., n.d.] unp. Typew.   CSdS

7852. —— —— Ground breaking...1911. [San Diego, Frye & Smith] 1911.   CSd

7853. —— —— Makers of [the] exposition, 1915. [n.p., n.d.]   CSd

7854. —— —— 1916 San Diego California exposition. [L.A., Union litho. co., 1916] [12] p. illus.   CHi

7855. —— —— Official banquet, Cafe Cristobal. [Jan. 1, 1915]   CSd

7856. —— —— The official guide and descriptive book of the Panama-California international exposition, giving in detail, location and description of buildings, exhibits...Ed. by Esther Hansen. San Diego, National views co. [1916?] 56 p. illus., port., fold. map.
CHi CSd CSf CU-B

7857. —— —— Same. San Diego [Pac. photoengraving co., 1914?] 79 p. illus., maps, plans.   CHi

7858. —— —— Official publication... San Diego [I. L. Eno] 1916. unp. pl.   C

7859. —— —— Same. Brooklyn, Albertype co., 1916.   CSd

7860. —— —— Official views. San Diego, 1915. unp. illus. (part. color)   CSd

7861. —— —— [Picture album] San Diego, Pictorial pub. co. [n.d.] unp. illus.   CAla

7862. —— —— Report, April 30, 1916. L.A., W. J. Palethorpe, 1916.   CSd

7863. —— —— San Diego all the year, 1915. San Diego, c1915. [16] p. illus.   CU-B

7864. —— —— San Diego and vicinity. Chicago, Reilly & Britton co. [c1915] [48] p. pl.   CHi CLO

7865. —— —— ...The San Diego exposition; Panama-California exposition, San Diego, California. [San Diego, 1914?] [12] p. illus.   CSf CSfCW CU-B

7866. —— —— Souvenir book. San Diego, I. L. Eno [1915] [64] p. chiefly col. pl.   CHi

7867. —— Planning dept. Master plan for University of California community. San Diego, 1959. 58 p. illus.   CSdS

7868. —— Playgrounds and recreational dept. A brief guide to San Diego, your new home. 1941. Mimeo. Cover title: Trips of interest in San Diego.   CSd

7869. Not in use.

7870. —— Theodore Roosevelt junior high school. Block print history of San Diego. San Diego, 1927. unp. illus.   C

7871. —— Unified school district. 100 [i.e. one hundred] years of public education in San Diego, July 1, 1854 to June 30, 1954. San Diego [1954] 24 p. illus. (Its report to the community, 1954)   C CHi CLU

7872. —— University Christian church. History ...by 50th anniversary book committee. San Diego [1956] 84 p. illus., ports.   CHi CSd

7873. —— Water dept. Feature history, El Capitan dam. [n.p., n.d.] 6 v.   CSdS

7874. —— Woodrow Wilson junior high school. San Diego in block print; a series of block prints and descriptions picturing historic and scenic places in and around San Diego... [San Diego] Print. by boys of the Woodrow Wilson print shop [19—] [53] p. illus.
CU-B

7875. San Diego building, loan and life association. The plan and by-laws... San Diego, Telegram print. co. [1888?] 15 p.   CLU

7876. San Diego–California club. A glimpse at San Diego county; southern California at its best. [San Diego, 1950] [24] p. illus.   CHi

7877. —— Presenting with pictures an impression of San Diego, where California began and is its best. San Diego, [1935] 32 p. illus.   CWhC

7878. —— San Diego California; cool in summer, warm in winter. San Diego [n.d.] folder (6 p.)   CRcS

7879. —— San Diego's historical landmarks. San Diego, San Diego county Bd. of supervisors [n.d.] 16 p.
CRcS

7880. —— This is San Diego. [San Diego, Neyenesch print., 1949] 52 p. illus., map.   CHi

7881. —— What life will mean to you. [San Diego, Frye & Smith, c1920] [35] p. illus.   C

7882. San Diego county. Board of supervisors. San Diego facts. San Diego, Watson-Jones, inc. [1929?] 31 p. map.   CHi

7883. —— Chamber of commerce. For greater San Diego, the new metropolis of the Pacific coast... San Diego [1914] 48 p. illus.   CU-B

7884. —— —— The port of San Diego (El puerto de San Diego), the southwestern gateway of the United States; a pamphlet...Printed in English and Spanish languages. [n.p.] The Tribune co. [1901]   CSd

7885. —— —— San Diego today. San Diego, c1953. 51 p. illus.   CHi CSd

7886. —— —— Souvenir of San Diego for the sovereign grand lodge, I.O.O.F. September 1888... [San Diego] The California print. co., 1888. 24 p.   CU-B

7887. —— —— [Souvenir pamphlet describing San Diego as a naval base for the light forces of the U.S. fleet...Navy day, Oct. 27, 1933] San Diego, Frye & Smith, 1933. 19 p. illus.   CLU CSd

7888. San Diego county immigration association. San Diego, California. Lands and agricultural products, minerals, etc. The city of San Diego, commerce, manufactures, resources, statistics, etc. From Morse Whaley & Dalton, San Diego, Cal., real estate dealers. [San Diego, 1885] [32] p.   CU-B

7889. San Diego daily transcript. Directory of San Diego attorneys. San Diego, 1950.   CSd

7890. San Diego gas & electric co. Annual report ... [n.p.] illus. (part. col.), maps.
CHi has 1949, 1953. CL has 1953–60.

7891. —— Prospectus...common stock... [n.p., 19—]
CHi has 1941, 1953–54.

7892. —— Prospectus ... first mortgage bonds, series C due 1978... [n.p.] 1948. 39 p.   CHi

7893. San Diego historical society. *Lelia Byrd* sesquicentennial. San Diego, 1952. 3 p. illus., ports., maps. Commemorative material regarding the *Lelia Byrd* and the battle of San Diego bay. CSdS

7894. San Diego land & town co. Guide to San Diego bay region, California... Chicago, Rand McNally [1888?] 27 p. illus. CLU CSmH CU-B

7895. —— Report of Benjamin Kimball to the Board of directors on the condition of the company's affairs in California. Boston, July 1888. Bost., G. H. Ellis, print., 1888. 44 p. CU-B

7896. —— San Diego: Southern California. The Italy of America... Bost. [1892?] 32 p. illus., fold. map. C CLU

7897. —— Same. Ed. by Dwight Braman. [San Diego? 1894?] 32 p. illus., map. C CLU

7898. San Diego magazine. San Diego magazine; a journal of community development and activities. 160th anniversary number. [San Diego, Chamber of commerce, 1929] 24 p. illus. (July 1959, v.5, no. 7) C

7899. —— Souvenir number commemorating restoration of old mission. 1931. 20 p. (Sept. 1931, v.7, no. 9) C

7900. —— "We" in San Diego—official program and Lindberg number. San Diego, Commercial press, 1927. 16 p. illus., ports. (Sept. 1927) CCoron

7901. San Diego museum. The San Diego museum, 1926. [San Diego, Berneker bros., print., 1926] 8 p. CHi

7902. San Diego society of natural history. The San Diego society of natural history, 1874–1924. A brief history prepared upon the occasion of the fiftieth anniversary of its incorporation... San Diego, Print. for the Society, 1924. 24 p. ports. C CLSU CU-B

7903. ...The San Diego tourist... [v.1, 1907?] — [San Diego, 1907?—
C has v.6, no. 8, v.7, no. 6, v.9, no. 8, 10–12, v.10–13; 1912–20. CU-B has Feb. 1917.

7904. San Diego union. Exposition edition, April 28, 1935. San Diego, 1935. CSd

7905. —— ...San Diego in 1886. [San Diego, 1887?] [4] p. CU-B

7906. —— San Diego: the California terminus of the Texas and Pacific railway. An account of the arrival and reception at San Diego, August 26, 1872, of Col. Thomas A. Scott and party... [San Diego, 1872] 34 p. C CSmH CU-B

7907. San Diego water co. vs. City of San Diego. ...The San Diego water co., respondent, vs. the city of San Diego et al, appellant. Brief for respondent. John Garber, amicus curiae... [n.p., 1896] 64 p. CU-B

7908. San Diego water co. Report, with comparative statements issued Oct. 1, 1889 for the information of consumers and the general public. San Diego, 1889. 21 p. CSd

7909. Savage, Hiram N. Barrett dam construction; feature history. H. N. Savage, hydraulic engineer, 1919–22. 3 v. photos., maps. Typew. v.2 and 3: History of construction. CSd

7910. —— El Capitan dam; feature history...1931–35. 6 v. photos., maps. Typew. CSd CSdS

7911. —— Lower Otay masonry dam construction; feature history. 1917–1919. 4 v. photos., maps. Typew. CSd

7912. —— Morena reservoir dam and spillway... feature history. 2 v. photos. Typew. CSd

7913. —— Otay reservoir, San Diego second main pipe line: feature history...1930. 2 v. photos. Typew. CSd

7914. —— San Dieguito project. Sutherland reservoir dam: feature history. 3 v. photos., maps. Typew. CSd

7915. Schoor, Gene. The Ted Williams story. N.Y., Messner, 1954. 188 p. Biography of a big-league ball player. CSd

7916. Schroeder, Theodore Albert. Free speech for radicals. Enlarged ed. ... N.Y., Free speech league, 1916. 206 p. "The history of the San Diego free speech fight": p. 116–190. CU-B

7917. [Scrap book of advertisements of business establishments in San Diego, Calif., including pictures of California, chiefly of San Diego. n.p., n.d.] 1 v. mounted illus. (part. col.) CU-B

7918. Scripps, Edward Wyllis. Damned old crank. N.Y., Harper, 1951. CSd

7919. Sequoya league. Los Angeles council. Relief of Campo. 1905. Indian settlement. CP CSd

7920. Sessions, Kate Olive. [A collection of clippings pertaining to her life. Assembled by the San Diego public library, 1959] CSd

7921. Shippey, Lee. Luckiest man alive; being the author's own story. L.A., Westernlore press, 1959. 203 p. CHi CRedl CSalCL CSd CStmo

7922. Smith, Walter Gifford. The story of San Diego... San Diego, City print. co., 1892. 163 p. illus. C CCoron CHi CL CLSU CLU CLob CSd CSf CSjC CSmH CU-B NN ViW

7923. Smythe, William Ellsworth. History of San Diego, 1542–1907... San Diego, History co., 1907. 736 p. illus., ports. "List of publications consulted in the preparation of this work": p. [7]–10. C CCoron CHi CL CLO CLSU CLU CLob CNa CO CRedl CSS CSd CSdS CSf CSfCP CSfCSM CSfP CSjC CSta CU-B CaBViPA CoU IC In KU TxU

7924. —— Same. 1908. 2 v. in 1. illus., ports. C CAna CHi CLSU (v.1) CLob CSd CSdS CSmH CStmo CU-B MiD-B MoSHi NHi (v.1) NN UPB

7925. Sorenson, E. John D. Spreckels and San Diego. [Berkeley, 1948] Thesis (M.A.)— Univ. of Calif., 1948. CU

7926. Southwest institute. Southwest institute, for girls and boys. [Catalog] 18—?–
CU-B has 1887/88–1889/90, 1891/92, 1894/95–1895/96, 1898/99.

7927. Stone, Harold Alfred, and others. City manager government in San Diego... Chicago, Pub. admin. service, 1939. 72 p. C CChiS CLSU CLU CO CPom CSd CSdS CSf

7928. Stone, Joe. [Scrapbook on William E. Smythe. Articles which appeared in the *San Diego tribune*, May 27–June 1, 1959] CSd

7929. Suhl, Alvena Marie. Historical geography of San Diego. [Berkeley, 1928] Thesis (M.A.)—Univ. of Calif., 1928. CU

7930. Taylor, Robert Bartley. Memorial. [n.p., n.d.] CSd

7931. Tays, George. ...The adobe chapel of the Immaculate Conception... Berkeley, 1936. 11 l. Typew.
CU-B

7932. —— ...Plaza in old San Diego... Berkeley, 1937. 30 l. Typew.
CU-B

7933. Turpin, Vicki. San Diego; this is how it was ...so they say!! [San Diego, Land title insurance co., 1956?] 30 p. illus., port., maps.
CStmo

7934. Union title insurance and trust co. The San Diego story. San Diego, c1954. 20 p. illus., ports. Reprinted from *Union-title-trust, Topics* published in commemoration of its 50th corporate anniversary, Sept.–Oct., 1954.
CHi

7935. —— Same. c1955. 28 p. illus.
CNa

7936. United States vs. Arguello, Santiago. In the District court of the United States, Southern district of California. Mission lands of Mission San Diego. no. 347. Land commission, no. 175. Exhibits from 1–42, inclusive, filed in behalf of appellants. S.F., Commercial steam presses [1858] 127 p.
CU-B

7937. United States vs. President and trustees of the city of San Diego. ...Brief on behalf of contestants Luco and the estate of Arguello. [n.p., 1869?] 34 p.
CU-B

7938. U.S. General land office. Pueblo lands of San Diego. Exceptions to surveys made by John C. Hays, July 1858. Filed in the office of United States Surveyor general for California, May 19, 1868. S.F., Print. by Mullin, Mahon & co., 1869. 44 p. Cover title.
C CLU (30 p.) CSd CSmH CU-B

7939. Van Dyke, Theodore Strong. The advantages of San Diego for residence or business. Issued by the Chamber of commerce, San Diego. S.F., W. W. Elliott & co., 1883. 32 p. illus.
CHi CSd CU-B

7940. Van Winkle, Eleanor (Ewing) Eleanor Wheeler Ewing; a biography. San Diego, Torrey pines press, 1934.
CSd

7941. Vincenz, Jean Lacey. San Diego metropolitan government. San Diego, 1958. 119 p. illus. Thesis (M.A.) — San Diego state college, 1958.
CSdS

7942. Vizcaíno, Juan. The sea diary of Fr. Juan Vizcaíno to Alta California, 1769. Tr. and with introd. by Arthur Woodward. L.A., Dawson, 1959. 27 p. illus., maps. (Early Calif. travels ser., 49) 225 copies printed by Mallette Dean.
CAla CL CLLoy CLSM CLgA CSd CSdS CSf CU-B

7943. Ward bros., Columbus, Ohio. Album of San Diego and Coronado beach, Cal. [Columbus, Ohio, 1883] 11 p.
C-S CL CSd CU-B

7944. —— Same. [c1887] 15 p. fold. pl.
CLU CSmH

7945. —— Same. [1889] 12 pl.
NN

7946. —— Souvenir of San Diego, Cal. Columbus, Ohio, c1886. unp. illus.
CHi CL CLU CSd CSmH CU-B

7947. Water data. [A collection of pamphlets relating to the water supply of San Diego and vicinity. San Diego? 1909?–12] 10 pamphlets in 1 v. illus., ports., maps.
CLU

7948. Wegeforth, Harry Milton, and Morgan, Neil. It began with a roar; the story of San Diego's world-famed zoo. 1st ed. San Diego, Pioneer print., 1953. 196 p. illus., port., facsims.
C CCoron CNa CSd CSdS CSdU CStmo

7949. Werner, Willis. Factographs. Typewritten copies of radio broadcasts January 1–June 19, 1940. Interviews, biographies, histories of industries and business firms constitute a cross section of life in San Diego just prior to World War II.
CSd

7950. Whaley, Corrine Lillian. California's oldest town, 1769–1893. c1893. v.p. Typew.
CSd

7951. Who's who in San Diego. San Diego, S. Gabriel, c1936.
CSd

7952. Widger, Charles Alonzo. Descriptive views in colors of the Panama California exposition, 1915... [Chicago, Publishers' press] c1914. 14 col. pl.
C CHi

7953. Wilson, Harlan Leffingwell. A history of the San Diego city schools from 1542 to 1942, with emphasis upon the curriculum; a thesis presented to the faculty of the School of education, the University of Southern California... for the degree of Master of science in education. Illus. [1942] Typew. Thesis (M.S.) — Univ. of So. Calif., 1941.
CLSU CSd CSdS

7954. Writers' program. California. Balboa park, San Diego, California; a comprehensive guide to the city's cultural and recreational center...Sponsored and published by the Association of Balboa park institutions. [San Diego, Neyenesch print.] 1941. 83 p. illus. (Am. guide ser.)
C CLSU CO NN

7955. Young, Otis E. The west of Philip St. George Cooke, 1809–1895. Glendale, Arthur H. Clark co., 1955. 393 p.
CSalCL

7956. Zoological society of San Diego. Official guide book of the San Diego zoo, Balboa park, San Diego, California. San Diego, c1944.
CSd CSf

Other editions followed.   C (1956) CBev (1956) CU-B (1957)

SAN FRANCISCO CITY AND COUNTY
(*Created in 1850*)

COUNTY HISTORIES

7957. The bay of San Francisco, the metropolis of the Pacific coast, and its suburban cities. A history... Chicago, Lewis, 1892. 2 v. illus., ports.
C C-S CAla CB CCH CHi CL CLO CLSM CLSU CLU CLgA CMary CMl CO COMC CPg CRcS CRic CS CSS CSf CSfCP CSfCW CSfMI CSfP CSfU CSfWF-H CSjC CSmH CSmat CSrD CSt CStb CStcl CStclU CSto CStoC CU-B CV CoD CoU CtY IC ICN MiD-B MoSHi N NHi NN WHi

7958. Byington, Lewis Francis, ed. The history of San Francisco... Chicago, Clarke, 1931. 3 v. illus., ports., maps. v.2 and 3 contain biographical material.
C CB CBb CCH CHi CL CLCM CLgA CO CSbr CSf CSfMI CSfSt CSfU CSfWF-H CSmH CStcrCL CStmo CStoC CU-B CtY MWA NN WHi

7959. Dwinelle, John Whipple. The colonial history of the city of San Francisco: being a synthetic argument in the District court of the United States for the Northern district of California, for four square leagues of land claimed by that city. S.F., Print. by Towne & Bacon, 1863. 102, 115 p. map.
CAlaC CCH CHi CL CLSM CLU CMartC CPom CSalCL CSf CSfU CSmH CSmat CSt CStmo CU-B CViCL NHi

7960. —— Same. Reprinted under the direction of

the city attorney of San Diego. San Diego, Frye & Smith, 1924. 115 p. map.
C CChiS CCH CF CHi CL CLO CLSU CLU CMartC CO CP CSd CSf CStb CStmo CU-B CViCL NN

7961. —— Same. 3d ed. ...S.F., Print. by Towne & Bacon, 1866. 106,391 p. illus., maps.
C CBaK CL CLSM CLU CLgA CSalCL CSf CSfCP CSfCW CSfMI CSfP CSfU CSfWF-H CSmH CSt CStaCL CU-B

7962. —— Same. 4th ed., 1867. 34,106,365,391 p. illus., map.
C CHi CLSM CLU CPa CSf CSmH CU-B CtY

7963. Eldredge, Zoeth Skinner. The beginnings of San Francisco from the expedition of Anza, 1774, to the city charter of April 15, 1850... S.F., Author, 1912. 2 v. illus., ports., maps.
C CAla CAlaC CAltu CAna CArcHT CB CBaB CBaK CBev CBu CCH CF CFA CFS CHi CHoCL CL CLCM CLCo CLS CLSM CLSU CLU CLgA CLob CLod CMS CMartC CMont CO COHN COMC CP CPa CPom CRb CRcS CRcdl CRic CRiv CS CSS CSalCL CSbr CSd CSdS CSf CSfCP CSfCW CSfMI CSfP CSfSt CSfU CSfWF-H CSj CSjC CSjCL CSlu CSmH CSmat CSrCL CSrD CSt CStaCL CStb CStcl CStclU CStcrCL CStmo CSto CStoC CStrJC CU-B CV CViCL CYcCL CYrS CaBViPA CoD CtY IC ICN MiD-B N NHi NN OrU UPB WHi

7964. Harding, Dorothy H. (Huggins), comp. Continuation of *The annals of San Francisco*...compiled from the files of contemporary magazines and newspapers. S.F., Calif. hist. soc., 1939– illus., port. v.1 (Calif. hist. soc. Special pub. no. 15) "Takes up the thread of the city's intimate history where the work of Soule, Gihon and Nisbet left it...in 1855."—Introd., v.1.
C CAla CBb CChiS CCH CF CFS CHi CL CLCM CLCo CLSM CLSU CLU CLgA CLod CMary CP CPa CS CSaT CSf CSfCP CSfCW CSfSt CSfU CSfWF-H CSjC CSmH CSmat CSt CStb CStbS CStcrCL CSto CStrJC CU-B CtY ICN MoSHi MoSU NHi

7965. Historical records survey. California. ... The city and county of San Francisco (San Francisco) ...co-sponsored by the city and county of San Francisco. S.F., Northern Calif. Hist. records survey project, 1940. 2 v. (Inventory of the county archives of Calif. ...no. 39) Mimeo.
C CBb CF CHanK CHi CLCM CLCo CLO CLSM CLSU (v.1 only) CLU CMary CMont (v.2 only) CO (v.2 only) COMC CSS (v.2 only) CSf CSfCSM (v.2 only) CSjC CSjCL CSluCL CSmH CSrCL (v.2 only) CSt (v.2 only) CU-B (v.2 only) ICN WHi (v.2 only)

7966. Hittell, John Shertzer. A history of the city of San Francisco and incidentally of the state of California... S.F., A. L. Bancroft & co., 1878. 498 p.
C CAla CAltu CAna CB CBaK CCH CF CHi CL CLCM CLCo CLSM CLSU CLU CLgA CO CP CSalCL CSbCL CSd CSf CSfCP CSfCW CSfMI CSfP CSfU CSfWF-H CSmH CSoCL CSrD CSt CStb CStoC CU-B CYcCL CaBViPA CtY ICN KHi MiD-B NHi NN WHi

7967. Millard, Bailey. History of the San Francisco bay region...; history and biography... S.F., Am. hist. soc., 1924. 3 v. illus., ports., map.
C CBu CHi CL CLgA CMartC CO CPs (v.1

only) CRcS CSf CSfMI CSfWF-H CSjC CSmH CSrCL CU-B CaBViPA CtY MiD-B NN WHi

7968. [Murray, William H.] The builders of a great city; San Francisco's representative men; the city, its history and commerce... S.F., San Francisco jl. of commerce pub. co., 1891. v.1, 356 p. ports. No more published.
C C-S CBaK CHi CL CLU CO CSf CSmH CSt CStb CU-B CYcCL

7969. San Francisco: its builders past and present, pictorial and biographical. Chicago, S.F., Clarke, 1913. 2 v. ports.
C CBu CCH CHi CLU CLgA CO CSf CSfCW CSfMI CSjC CSmH CStoC CU-B

7970. Soulé, Frank; Gihon, John H.; and Nisbet, James. The annals of San Francisco; containing a summary of the history of the first discovery, settlement, progress, and present condition of California, complete history of all the important events connected with its great city; to which are added, biographical memoirs of some prominent citizens... N.Y., D. Appleton & co., 1855. 824 p. illus., ports., maps.
C C-S CAla CAlaC CB CBaB CBaK CBb CBu CChiS CCH CFA CFS CHi CL CLCM CLCo CLM CLO CLSM CLSU CLU CLgA CLod CMartC CMary CMl CMont CO COMC CP CPa CRcS CRedl CRic CRiv CS CSS CSaT CSalCL CSd CSdS CSf CSfCSM CSfCW CSfMI CSfP CSfSt CSfU CSfWF-H CSjC CSmH CSmat CSt CStbS CStclU CStcrCL CStmo CSto CStoC CStrJC CU-B CV CViCL CWoY CYcCL CYrS CaBViPA CoU CtY IC ICN In KHi KyU MHi MiD MiD-B MoS MoSHi N NHi NN OrU T TxU UU ViU ViW WHi WM

7971. —— —— Index...Joseph Gaer, editor. ... [S.F., 1935] 96 l. (Index 19. SERA project 2–F2–132 (3–F2–197) Calif. literary research) Reproduced from typew. copy.
C C-S CChiS CFS CHi CLCo CLO CLSM CLSU CLU CLgA CLob CMary CO CRic CSalCL CSdS CSf CSfCP CSfMI CSfP CSfU CSjC CSmH CStclU CStmo CStoC CU-B

7972. —— —— Index...Compiled under the direction of Charles Francis Griffin... S.F., Calif. hist. soc., 1935. 22 p. (Special pub. no. 10)
C C-S CHi CL CLCM CLCo CLSU CLgA CMary CO COMC CP CRic CRiv CS CSf CSfCW CSfMI CSfU CSfWF-H CSjC CSmH CSmat CStclU CU-B ICN NHi

7973. Young, John Philip. San Francisco, a history of the Pacific coast metropolis. S.F., Chicago, Clarke [1912] 2 v. illus., ports., maps.
C C-S CAla CAlaC CB CCH CHi CL CLCo CLU CLgA CLod CMartC CO COHN CP CPa CPs CRcS CRic CRiv CS CSalCL CSf CSfCP CSfCW CSfMI CSfP CSfSt CSfU CSfWF-H CSjC CSmH CSmat CSrD CSt CStb CStclU CSto CU-B CaBViPA CoD CtY IC ICN N NHi NN

GREAT REGISTER

7974. San Francisco. Index to the Great register of the city and county of San Francisco. 1866– Place of publication and title vary.
C has 1866–67, 1869, 1871–73, 1875 (suppl.), 1876–78, 1880, 1882, 1886 (biennially to)– 1892, 1896 (biennially to)– 1904, 1907, 1908, 1910, 1912, 1913, 1914, 1916 (suppl. index to Oct. 4, 1919), 1920 (and suppl.), 1921,

1922 (and suppl.), 1923 (suppl.), 1924 (and suppl.), 1925 (suppl.), 1927 (suppl.), 1928 (suppl.), 1930, 1932 (and suppl.), 1933, 1934 (suppl.), 1934 (second suppl.), 1935, 1936 (biennially to)– 1962. C-S has 1866. CHi has 1867, 1872, 1877, 1879, 1908. CL has 1866. CLU has 1867, 1873, 1882. CSf has 1867–69, 1872–73, 1876–77, 1905, 1908, 1910–1919, 1921, 1923–26, 1928. CSmH has 1866–1873, 1905. CU-B has 1866–67, Aug. 1868 (suppl. to 1867), Nov. 1868, 1869 (suppl. to 1868), 1871–73, 1873 (suppl.), 1875, 1877–78, Apr. 1879 (suppl. to 1878), 1879–80, 1882, 1905, v.3.

7975. —— Same. The names comprising the two volumes of registered voters of San Francisco for 1866 are copied from the file in California state library by General John A. Sutter chapter, Sacramento, D.A.R. [Roseville? 1948] 2 v.   C

DIRECTORIES

7976. 1850. Bogardus, John P. Bogardus' San Francisco, Sacramento city and Marysville business directory for May, July, 1850. [S.F.] Pub. monthly at William B. Cook & co.'s bookstore [1850] 2 v.
    CHi (May, facsim., July) CSf CSmH CU-B

7977. 1850. Campbell and Hoogs, pub. Campbell & Hoogs' San Francisco and Sacramento city directory, for March, 1850. [S.F.] Pub. monthly at the office of the proprietors in Clay street [1850] 8 p.
    CHi CSf CSmH CU-B NN

7978. 1850. Kimball, Charles Proctor, pub. San Francisco city directory. Sept. 1, 1850. S.F., Jl. of commerce press, 1850. 136 p.
    C-S CHi CLU CMartC CSalCL CSfCP CSfCSM CSfP CSmH CStcrCL

7979. —— Same. [S.F., 186–?] 139 p. "First reprint, made in the late 1860's, of the first known San Francisco general directory. Kimball's original directory, published in 1850, had 136 pages. The reprint has 'Omitted names' (p. 136–139) cf. Wagner, H. R., *California imprints*, p. 42–43."
    C CHi CLU (with ms. note "Reprint 1870") CSfCP CSfCW CSfMI CSfU CSmH CU-B IHi MoSHi WHi

7980. —— Same. [S.F., 189–?] 139 p. "Second reprint, made about 1897 or 1898...'The second reprint is distinguishable from the first by the fact that in the list of "Omitted names" two Donahoes have been inserted.'— Wagner, H. R., *California imprints*, p. 43."
    C CHi CLU CO CSfU CSfWF-H CSmH CStrJC CU-B NHi

7981. 1852. Bonnard, F. A., pub. Register of first-class business houses in San Francisco, October, 1852. S.F., 1852. 95 l. illus.
    C CHi CSfCW CSfWF-H CSmH CU-B NHi

7982. 1852. Morgan, A. W., and co., pub. A. W. Morgan and co.'s San Francisco city directory, September, 1852... S.F., F. A. Bonnard, print., 1852. 125 p. Pagination varies among copies.
    C CHi CLU CSfCP CSfWF-H CSmH CU-B CtY NHi

7983. 1852. Parker, James M., pub. The San Francisco directory, for the year 1852–53...First publication. S.F., Monson, Haswell & co., print., 1852. 145 p. map.
    C CCH CHi CLU CS CSfCP CSfP CSfWF-H CSmH CU-B

7984. 1854. Le Count and Strong, pub. Le Count and Strong's San Francisco directory for the year 1854... comp. by Frank Rivers. S.F., S.F. herald off., print., 1854 [c1853]
    C CHi CLU CSfCP CSfP CSfU CSfWF-H CSmH CU-B MWA NHi NN

7985. 1856. Baggett, Joseph, & co., pub. San Francisco business directory, for the year commencing January 1, 1856. Containing the name and location of every business house in the city...together with the name of each individual composing the same... S.F., Steam presses of Monson & Valentine [print.] 1856. 222 p.
    C CHi CLU CSf CSfCP CSmH CU-B

7986. 1856. Colville, Samuel, pub. Colville's San Francisco directory, vol. 1. For the year commencing October, 1856; being a gazetteer of the city...Prefaced by a history of San Francisco, and reviews of industrial enterprises, associations, etc. S.F., 1856. 307 p. map.
    C CHi CLU CSfCP CSfWF-H CSmH CU-B MWA NHi WHi

7987. 1856. Harris, Bogardus and Labatt, comp. and pub. San Francisco city directory, for the year commencing October, 1856. Containing a general directory of citizens, a street directory, and an appendix of all useful and general information pertaining to the city ... S.F., Whitton, Towne & co., print., 1856. 138 p.
    C CHi (lacks p. 105–38) CSfCP CSmH CU-A CU-B (lacks p. 121–22) MWA NHi

7988. 1858– Polk, R. L., & co., pub. Polk's San Francisco city directory [v.1]– 1858– L.A., 1858– Title varies: 1858–95 Langley's San Francisco directory; 1896–1929 Crocker-Langley's San Francisco city directory. Publisher varies: 1858–89, S. D. Valentine & son; 1890–94, Painter & co., receivers; 1895, J. B. Painter; 1896–1929, H. S. Crocker.
    C has 1858 to date. C-S has 1860, 1871–72, 1882, 1885, 1886–99, 1902–16. CAla has 1889–90, 1892–1905, 1907–46, 1948/49, 1951, 1953–59. CB has 1951, 1953 to date. CHi has 1858–1946, 1948–51, 1953 to date. CL has 1859–65, 1867–69, 1871-74, 1897, 1900, 1903, 1905, 1911–21, 1923–25, 1927–34, 1936–37, 1939–1945/46, 1948/49, 1951, 1953–56, 1959–60. CLO has 1858–95. CLU has v.1–5, 7–14, 16–38 and 1897–1900, 1904–05, 1908–09, 1911–12, 1915–16. CO has v.3–38 and 1896 to date. CRcS has 1930 to date. CSalCL has 1957. CSfCP has 1895–1929. CSfCW has 1860, 1872–74, 1879, 1884, 1886, 1888–90, 1908–26, 1928, 1931–33, 1936, 1941, 1943, 1945/46, 1948/ 49. CSfMI has 1859 to date. CSfP has 1858–65, 1867–69. CSfU has 1858–95. CSfWF-H has v.2–6, 7–10, 12–13, 19–21, 23, 27–36 and 1894, 1896–98, 1900–07. CSmat has 1863, 1869, 1944, 1953–57, 1959. CSmH has 1858–1916, 1924, 1939. CU-B has 1858–65, 1867–69, 1871–1905, 1907–46, 1948/49, 1951, 1953–54, 1957–61. CViCL has 1889. CaBViPA has 1858, 1865, 1870. MoS has 1897–1903, 1909–11, 1924–25, 1928–32, 1935–44. NHi has 1859–60, 1864, 1868, 1872, 1878, 1881–82, 1891–93, 1896, 1902–03. NN has 1872. OrU has 1869. WHi has 1865, 1867–69, 1875–90, 1892–1903, 1907, 1912, 1919, 1923, 1928, 1932, 1937, 1942, 1948/49, 1953.

7989. 1861–1865. Gazlay, David M., pub. Gazlay's business directory of the five great cities of California and Oregon, San Francisco, Sacramento, Stockton, & Marysville, Cal.; and Portland, Oregon, combined in one. S.F., 1861–64. Title varies: 1861, 1863, Gazlay's San Francisco business directory.
    C (1861) CHi (1861, 1863) CMary (1864–65) CSf (1861, 1863) CSfCP (1861, 1863) CSmH (1863–64) CU-B (1861)

7990. 1864. Stilwell, B. F., & co., pub. San Francisco business directory and mercantile guide, for 1864–65. A general business directory for all persons throughout this state; also Oregon, Nevada territory and Mexico. S.F., 1864. 384 p. map. "Valuable because of the sketch of the history of many of the business houses."—Norris.
C CHi CLU CSf CSfMI CSfWF-H CSmH CSto CU-B CoD NHi

7991. 1865. Rood, A. N., & co., pub. San Francisco pocket guide and business directory: including the fire alarm telegraph and table of stamp duties. Monthly ed., June 1865. S.F. CU-B

7992. 1872/73. Gilbert & Swanick, pub. San Francisco business directory... S.F. 350 p. CLU

7993. 1875–1879. Bishop, D. M., & co., comp. Bishop's directory of the city and county of San Francisco... Stockton, B. C. Vandall [1876]–79.
C has 1875–78. C-S has 1879. CHi has 1875–78. CL has 1875. CLU has 1875, 1878–79. CO has 1877, 1879. CSfCP has 1875, 1877–79. CSfWF-H has 1875–79. CSmH has 1875–79. CU-B has 1875–79; also suppl. to the 1877 annual directory, March 1877, 46 p.

7994. 1877. Heugh, pub. San Francisco business directory for 1877. CLU CSf CSfU CSmH NHi

7995. 1877. McKenney, L. M., pub. Business directory of San Francisco and principal towns of California and Nevada, 1877... S.F., c1877. 593 p.
C C-S CFa CHi CL CLU CMont CS CSfCP CSfWF-H CSmH CSto NHi

7996. 1877/78. Langley, Henry G., pub. Langley's San Francisco business directory and metropolitan guide. S.F., 1877. fold. maps. CSfCP CSmH CU-B

7997. 1880. Dalton & co., pub. The San Francisco, Oakland, and Alameda directory: containing a complete alphabetical list of names, location and business of every merchant...a classified business directory...also a general register of U.S., state, and city officers... together with new and reliable street directories. S.F., c1880. 485 p.
CHi CL CLU CSf CSfCP CSfU CSfWF-H CSmH CU-B

7998. 1883. Harrington pub. co., pub. Harrington's pocket business directory of the Western addition, Hayes valley, and Mission containing complete list... firms doing business in that portion of San Francisco, situated west of Larkin and southwest of Ninth streets... S.F., c1883. CU-B

7999. 1885. Bowser, George, pub. Business directory of the city and county of San Francisco, Cal. ... S.F., 1885. C CHi CP CSfU CU-B

8000. 1887– Uhlhorn & McKenney, pub. San Francisco business directory, including Alameda, Berkeley and Oakland. S.F. [1887?]
CHi CLU CSfMI CSfU CSfWF-H CSmH NHi

8001. 1888/89–1891/92. Niles-Rentschler directory co., comp. San Francisco business directory, including Oakland, Alameda, Berkeley, Arcata, Blue Lake, Eureka, Ferndale, Hydesville, Rohnerville, Alton, Singley's, Port Kenyon, etc. S.F., San Francisco directory co., 1888–91. Title varies: 1888/89, Northern Pacific coast directory including the following towns: San Francisco, Oakland, Alameda and Berkeley.
CHi (1891/92) CLU (1891/92) CSmH

8002. 1889. [California publishing co., pub.] Merchantile directory of the city of San Francisco... S.F. [c1888] CU-B

8003. 1889. Secundino Apac., comp. Directorio comercial de Mexico, Centro America y San Francisco, Cal. [S.F., 1889] illus. CLU

8004. 1889/90. Thomson & Orebaugh, pub. The Thomson & Orebaugh wholesale and manufacturers' pocket business directory of San Francisco, Cal. For the use and convenience of out of town buyers. [S.F., 1888?] 55 p. CU-B

8005. 1898. California state directory co., pub. Rensselaer's San Francisco wholesale, manufacturers, business directory...including a general directory of towns listed... S.F. [1898?] 198,568 p. CHi

8006. 1898/99. Bards and co., pub. Classified business directory of San Francisco, Sacramento, Oakland, Stockton, San Jose, etc. ...containing a classified list of the representative men engaged in professional and commercial pursuits...Comp. by M. M. Pruden. N.Y. [1898?] 346 p. C

8007. 1900. San Francisco street directory publishing co., pub. San Francisco street and avenue directory, giving over 1,700 streets, avenues [etc.] as they appear in the "Crocker-Langley directory,"...also containing an official list of all the street railways of San Francisco...besides block maps of the city...together with classified index to various business houses of San Francisco... S.F., 1900. 176 p. illus., maps. CLU

8008. 1904. Ideal publishing co., pub. San Francisco office building and business directory, 1904... S.F., 1904. C-S CHi

8009. 1905/06. Mercantile directory co., comp. and pub. Business directory and mercantile register of San Francisco, Oakland, Sacramento, Stockton, Alameda, San Jose, Vallejo, Benicia, Berkeley, Elmhurst, Fruitvale, San Rafael, San Leandro, and neighboring towns... S.F.
CHi CLU CO CSmH

8010. 1905/06. Spaulding-Bonestell co., pub. San Francisco classified business directory with telephone numbers, 1905–1906, containing a complete classified business directory, giving names of all business houses and professional people...; also a revised street and avenue cuide [!] of San Francisco. S.F., c1905. 370 p.
C-S CHi CSf CSfCP CSmH

8011. 1906. Beecher and Pike, pub. Relief business directory, May, 1906, giving names, business and address of San Francisco firms and business men who were compelled to change their location by the disaster of April 18, and who have since located in San Francisco, Oakland, Berkeley, Alameda and Emeryville... [Berkeley?] c1906. [55] p.
C CHi CO CSfCP CSfU CSfWF-H CSmH CU-B

8012. 1906. Crocker, H. S., & co., pub. Crocker-Langley San Francisco business directory for the year ending June 1, 1906– [v.1–] S.F., 1906–
CHi has v.2 for year ending Sept. 1, 1906. CSfMI has v.1–3, from June 1, 1906–Dec. 31, 1906.

8013. 1906. Greater San Francisco directory. Business edition...Containing an alphabetical list of all business and professional residents of the city...Comp. and pub. by Greater San Francisco assoc. v.1, 1906–
S.F., 1906– C-S CHi CSf CSfCP CSmH CU-B

8014. 1906. San Francisco examiner, pub. San Francisco–Oakland business directory...May 15, 1906. S.F., 1906. [38] p. CSfMI

8015. 1906. Temporary directory co., pub. Temporary directory of San Francisco business and professional men together with directory of municipal and

state officers, and other useful information gathered from latest announcements. S.F. [1906?] 60 p.
C-S CHi CU-B

8016. 1906–1907. Fry, Walter S., co., comp. & pub. San Francisco–Oakland directory; business edition, July 1906...Rev. quarterly. Oakland, 1906–07.
CHi (no. 3, 1907) CO (1906) CSfCP (1906) CSfMI (no. 3, 1907) CSmH

8017. 1949. Lum, Jimmy, advertising service, pub. San Francisco Chinese directory including Oakland-East Bay section. S.F., 1949. 72 p. In English and Chinese.
CHi

8018. 1961. San Francisco. Chinese chamber of commerce, pub. San Francisco Chinatown business directory... S.F., 1961. 57 p. In English and Chinese.
CHi

GENERAL REFERENCES

8019. Abbey homestead association. Articles of association, certificate of incorporation, rules of order, map, officers, remarks, etc. ...Incorporated February 20th, 1869. S.F., Alta Calif. print. house, 1869. 20 p.
CHi CLU

8020. Abrahamsen, Helen Mary. What to do, see, eat in San Francisco. Maps and drawings by Robert J. McFadden. Palo Alto, Pac. bks. [1952] 80 p. illus.
C CL CO CSf CSluCL MiD

8021. —— Same. 2d ed., with title: A complete guide to San Francisco and the bay area. Maps and drawings by Robert J. McFadden. Palo Alto [1954] 80 p. illus.
C CL CO COr CSluCL MiD ODa

8022. —— Same. 3d ed. [c1955] 80 p. illus.
CPa CRic CSjC

8023. Abrahamson co., inc., Oakland. Welcome to our California midwinter international exposition. Souvenir. Compliments of the Abrahamson co., incorporated, at the opening of their new store...March 5th, 1894. [Oakland, 1894] 30 pl.
CU-B

8024. Accidents on street cable railroads. [n.p., 1887?] 6 p.
C

8025. Ackerman bros. ...Rules for governing clerks. S.F., A.L. Bancroft & co., print., 1874. 12 p.
CU-B

8026. Adam, George. Earthquakes; an astronomical question... S.F., C.A. Murdock & co., print., 1906. 15 p. illus.
CSmH

8027. Adams, Edgar Holmes. Private gold coinage of California, 1849–1955. Its history and its issues. Brooklyn, Author, 1913. 110 p. pl. Reprint. from the *Am. jl. of numismatics*, 1912.
CSf CSfWF-H CStclU

8028. Adams, George Crawford. Memorial of George Crawford Adams. [S.F., 1910] 67 p. port.
CU-B

8029. Adams, Theodore, vs. the United States. To the honorable the Senate and House of representatives of the United States in Congress assembled; the Court of claims respectfully presents the following documents as the report in the case of Theodore Adams vs. the United States. Wash., D.C., U.S. govt. print. off., 1861. 91 p. (36th cong. 2d sess. H. R. report of C. C. no. 256) Concerns the U.S. appraiser's building.
CHi

8030. Adams & co. vs. Cohen, Alfred A. Arguments of the Hon. Edward Stanly, of counsel for the receiver, and T. W. Park, esq., of counsel for Alvin Adams, with the charge of the court, at the trial of Alfred A. Cohen on a charge of embezzlement, in the case of Adams & co., by H. M. Naglee, receiver, versus Alfred A. Cohen ... S.F., Whitton, Towne & co., 1856. 88 p.
C CHi CSmH CU-B

8031. Adelphi debating club. Constitution and by-laws... S.F., B.F. Sterett, bk. & job print., 1868. 23 p.
CU-B

8032. Aerial steam navigation co. Report... [S.F.? 187–?] 4 p. illus.
CHi

8033. Afro-American league [of San Francisco] Souvenir programme for the emancipation celebration [S.F., 1902] 16 p. illus., ports. Includes "A brief history of the Afro-American league of San Francisco, with some reference to its objects and what it has accomplished."
CHi

8034. Agricultural convention. Proceedings of the Agricultural convention held at San Francisco, Feb. 24, 1860. S.F., Towne & Bacon, 1860. 8 p.
CU

8035. Aguirre, Miguel, et al vs. Riordan, Patrick William, *Abp.* In the Superior court in and for the county of Los Angeles, California. Miguel Aguirre, et al, plaintiffs vs. Patrick William Riordan, the Roman Catholic Archbishop of San Francisco, as a corporation sole, et al, defendants. Memorandum of authorities for use on argument of demurrer and motion to strike out portions of the complaint. [L.A., n.d.] 206 p.
CSf

8036. Aiken, Charles Sedgwick, comp. California today, San Francisco, its metropolis; a concise statement concerning the state that faces the Orient, and the city by the Golden Gate. S.F., Calif. promotion committee of S.F., 1903. 192 p. illus.
C-S CLU CPom CSfCW

8037. —— San Francisco, California's metropolis. [S.F., S.F. Commissioners to the Louisiana purchase exposition, 1904] [8] p. illus.
CU-B

8038. Aitken, Frank W., and Hilton, Edward. A history of the earthquake and fire in San Francisco; an account of the disaster of April 18, 1906 and its immediate results... S.F., Edward Hilton co., 1906. 285 p. illus., maps.
Available in many California libraries and CaBViPA MiD MiD-B NN

8039. Aked, Charles F. The city beautiful! A vision of San Francisco in 1915. A sermon preached in the First Congregational church of San Francisco, Sunday morning, April 14, 1912. [S.F., Thos. J. Davis & son, 1912] 12 p.
CHi

8040. —— Hero souls filled with new wine!...A sermon preached in the First Congregational church of San Francisco. S.F., 1912. 12 p.
CHi

8041. Alameda coal mining co. By-laws... S.F., L. Albin, print., 1862. 10 p.
C

8042. [Alaska commercial co.] 310 Sansome St. [S.F., 1927?] 38 [6] l. illus. (mounted photos.) Reproduced from typew. copy.
CHi

8043. Albertson, Dean Howard. Jacob P. Leese, Californio. [Berkeley, 1947] Thesis (M.A.)— Univ. of Calif., 1947.
CU

8044. [Album of portraits of noted persons, including Joaquin Miller, also actors and actresses who appeared in the early San Francisco theatre. [n.p., 1872?] 1 v. (35 mounted ports.)
CU-B

8045. Album of Sutro Heights, San Francisco, California. [n.p., 1890] [4] p. fold. illus., map.
C C-S CSf CSmH CU-B

8046. Alexander, Barton Stone. The proposed canal through Mission creek and Channel street in Mission bay, for navigation and drainage. Opinions of General S. B. [i.e. B. S.] Alexander, and Professor George Davidson. [S.F., 1872] 42 p.   CHi CU-B

8047. Alexander & Baldwin, ltd. Annual report. CL has 1954–60.

8048. Alexander-Yost co. Catalogue of tools and supplies for machinists and metal workers. S.F. [1903] 1 v. illus.   CHi CU-B

8049. Allen (E. T.) firm. [Catalog]...fire arms, sportsman's sundries... S.F., 1890. 76 p. illus. (no. 38, 1890)   CHi

8050. Allen & co. Two .2000. thousand. Van Ness avenue. [n.p., n.d.] [12] p. illus., plans. Descriptive brochure of medical building at 2000 Van Ness avenue.
                                                        CHi

8051. Allen & Higgins lumber co. [Catalogue of] hardwood lumber. S.F. [189–?] 1 v.   CU-B

8052. Allgemeine deutsche unterstüzungs-gesellschaft. Allgemeine deutsche unterstüzungs-gesellschaft zu San Francisco. [S.F., 1865] [2] p. illus.   CU-B

8053. —— Jahres-bericht...[18—?– S.F., Drucke de L. Roesch co. [18—?–
CHi has 1910. CSfCW has 1904, 1914. CU-B has 1887, 1899.

8054. Allison, Tempe Elizabeth. Shakespeare on the San Francisco stage (1850–1906) [Berkeley, 1922] Thesis (M.A.)—Univ. of Calif., 1922.   CU

8055. Almanach français pour 1859—Ire année—A l'usage de la population française de Californie. S.F., H. Payot [1858?–] 1859 includes "Guide commercial," (chiefly San Francisco).
CLU (1859)   CSmH (1860)   CU-B (1859)

8056. Alta California. The Alta California almanac and book of facts...Edited by John S. Hittell. v.1–16, 1868–1883. S.F., 1868–1883.
C has 1868, 1873, 1874–83. CHi has 1868, 1872–73, 1877–81, 1883. CLU has 1874–76, 1878–83. CSf has 1871, 1881. CSmH has 1868–69, 1871, 1873–74, 1876, 1878, 1881–82. CU-B has 1868–83. CViCL has 1878–79, 1881.

8057. —— The Alta California commercial edition. 1889. Railroads, manufacturing, financial, commercial and professional representative firms of San Francisco, Cal. [S.F., 1889] 32 p.   C   CLU   CSmH

8058. —— Memorial of William C. Ralston. Born at Wellsville, Ohio, January 12, 1826. Died in San Francisco, August 27, 1875. [S.F., 1875] 42 p. port.   C
CHi CLU CSf CSfCW CSfP CStclU CStrJC CU-B

8059. Altrocchi, Julia Cooley. The spectacular San Franciscans. N.Y., Dutton, 1949. 398 p. ports.
Available in many California libraries and CaBViPA CoD IC MiD MoSHi N NN ODa OU T TxU UPB

8060. Alvord, William. In memoriam. William Alvord, born January 3, 1833; died December 21, 1904. By Theodore Henry Hittell. S.F., Calif. Acad. of sciences, 1905. 8 p. port.   CHi

8061. Amalgamated association of street railway employees of America, Division no. 205. ...In the matter of the arbitration of certain differences between the Amalgamated association of street railway employees of America, division no. 205, and United railroads of San Francisco. Argument of Tirey L. Ford, general counsel, United railroads of San Francisco. [S.F., 1903?] 64 p.
                                                        CU-B

8062. Amalgamated sheet metal workers' international alliance. Local no. 104. Souvenir pictorial history of local union no. 104... [S.F., 1910] 129 p. illus.   CHi

8063. American alliance. Constitution... S.F., J.R. Brodie & co., 1887. 12 p.   CHi

8064. American association of university women. San Francisco bay branch. Outline of history of San Francisco bay branch...1886–1930. [S.F.? 1930?] xvi p.
                                                        CHi

8065. American bankers' association. "American banker" guide to the twenty-ninth annual convention... to be held at San Francisco, Cal. ...October 20th, 21st, 22d, 1903... N.Y., Stumpf & Steurer [1903] 136 p. ports.   CU-B

8066. —— To guide your footsteps. [Twenty-ninth convention American Bankers association, San Francisco, California, October twentieth to October twenty-fourth, nineteen hundred and three] [S.F., Sunset press, 1903] 39 p. illus., map.   CHi

8067. American bar association. Exhibit of old law books and manuscripts on the occasion of the sixty-second annual meeting...at San Francisco, California in the central court of the Veterans war memorial building, July 5–15, 1939. S.F., Bar assoc. of S.F., 1939. 20 p.
                                                        CHi

8068. —— Same. ...On the occasion of the seventy-fifth annual meeting...in San Francisco California, September 15–19, 1952. [S.F., Parker print. co., 1952] 24 p. illus.   CHi

8069. American citizen. The specific contract law. A reply to the pamphlet issued by the San Francisco chamber of commerce, against its repeal. Written and published by order of an American citizen, and intended for circulation among the members of the Senate and Assembly of the sixteenth session of the legislature of the state of California, and the people of the state generally. Sacramento, Crocker, 1865. 21 p.   CHi

8070. American district telegraph co. American district telegraph company. [S.F., Crocker, 1883?] [40] p. illus.   CU-B

8071. American institute of architects. San Francisco chapter. Constitution and by-laws... S.F., Calif. architectural pub. co., 1890. 15 p.   CU-B

8072. American institute of graphic arts, New York. Catalogue of an exhibition of the work of Edwin and Robert Grabhorn of San Francisco... [N.Y., 1942] 30 p. ports.   CHi

8073. American institute of mining and metallurgical engineers. San Francisco section. Roster. S.F., 1937. 1 v.   CU-B

8074. American legion. Dept. of California. Sixteenth annual convention... San Francisco, California, August 11 to 15, 1934. [n.p., n.d.] 55 p. illus., ports., plans.   CHi

8075. American mercantile union. Confidential reference book, city and county of San Francisco and vicinity, 1886. [S.F.? 1886?] Credit rating book.   CHi

8076. American northland oil co. Annual report. CL has 1954–60.

8077. American pipe co. [Catalog] S.F. [187–?] 60 p.   CHi

8078. American president lines, ltd. Annual report.
CL has 1949–1960.

8079. American Russian commercial co. By-laws ...S.F., O'Meara & Painter, print., 1855. 15 p.
CSmH CU-B

8080. American smelting and refining co. ... Catalog no. 25, Selby smelting works, San Francisco. [n.p., c1925] 208 p. illus.   CHi

8081. American speaking telephone co. List of subscribers June 1, 1878. [S.F.? 1878?] 1 l. fold.   CHi

8082. Ames Harris Neville co. [Catalog] Wood printing presses, box brands, skeletons, type holders... [S.F., Taylor, Nash & Taylor, 1912?] 16 p. illus.   CHi

8083. ——— Catalogue. 1907– [S.F., Pernau pub. co.] 1907– illus.   CHi (1907) CU-B (1907, 1925)

8084. Amos, B. E. Snap shots of scenes at the Panama-Pacific exposition, San Francisco, 1915. 115 late views ... S.F., Amos pub. co., 1915. [64 p. of illus.]
CHi CU-B

8085. Anderson, David. The enchanted galleon. [S.F.] Priv. print. [Windsor press] 1930. 18 p. illus. About Robert Louis Stevenson and the Stevenson memorial in San Francisco.   CLU CMont CSmH

8086. Anderson, Garland. The how's and why's of your success... [S.F.? 192–?] 30 p. port. Cover title: From newsboy and bellhop to playwright.   CHi

8087. Anderson, Gregg. Recollections of the Grabhorn press. Meriden, Conn., Priv. print., 1935. 16 p. illus.   CHi

8088. Anderson, Walker, vs. McCord, Sylvester, and Etique, Peter. ...Walker Anderson, respondent, vs. Sylvester McCord & Peter Etique, appellants. [S.F., 18—?] 49 l. Signed: Jas. B. Townsend, of counsel for appellants. A San Francisco pueblo land case.   CLU

8089. Anderson, William C. The national crisis. An address delivered before the Young men's christian association of San Francisco, Cal., at their eighth anniversary, August 12th, 1861. S.F., Towne & Bacon, print., 1861. 10 p.   C CBPac CU

8090. ——— The substance of four discourses, on the Bible in common schools, delivered in the First Presbyterian church, San Francisco... S.F., Print. and pub. by Towne & Bacon, Excelsior bk. and job off., 1859. 31 p.
CLU CSmH CU CU-B KHi NN PHi

8091. Anderson and Elias teredo-proof pile co. ...Capital stock, $1,000,000. 100,000 shares, $10 per share. S.F., Bacon & co., print. [1889?] 8 p. illus.
CU-B

8092. [Andreen, Philip] Minnesskrift, illustreradt album, utgifvet af Svenska evangeliskt Lutherska Ebenezer-församlingen i San Francisco, Cal., med anledning at des tjugufem-ars jubileum, den 8–12 Augusti 1907. Rock Island, Ill., Augustana bk. concerns tryckeri, 1907. 280 p. illus., ports.   CHi

8093. Andrews, Bunyan Hadley. Charles Crocker. [Berkeley, 1941] Thesis (M.A.)—Univ. of Calif., 1941.
CU

8094. Andrews, Elton Randolph. Mass transportation facilities between the city of San Francisco and the cities of the East bay: a study of mass transportation within a metropolitan area. [Berkeley, 1949] Thesis (M.A.)—Univ. of Calif., 1949.   CU

8095. Andrews, Hannah S. In memoriam. S.F., Joseph Winterburn & co., print., 1867. 64 p. illus.   CHi

8096. Angel Island foundation. Angel Island foundation, a non-profit corporation, enlists your support ... [S.F., 195–?] [4] p. illus.   CHi

8097. Ansichten von Californien und der California midwinter international exhibition. [S.F.? 1894?] 120 p.
CU-B

8098. Antisell (T. M.) piano co. [Catalog] S.F. [1885?] 1 v. illus.   CU-B

8099. El Anuario de San Francisco, California. S.F., L. Gregoire & co., 1888. 1 v. illus.   CU-B

8100. Appert, Richard. San Francisco. S.F. [n.d.] 50 p. illus.   CStoC

8101. Appleby, William. Descriptive catalogue of plants cultivated and for sale by William Appleby European nursery... S.F., Bruce's print. house, 1875. 9 p.
CHi

8102. Archambault, John Joseph. Evolution of the Crocker first national bank of San Francisco. [Berkeley, 1950] Thesis (M.A.)—Univ. of Calif., 1950.   CU

8103. Archibald, Katherine. Wartime shipyard, a study in social disunity. Berkeley, Univ. of Calif. press, 1947. 237 p. illus.   CHi

8104. Archibald, Katherine (Mullen) Vignettes of San Francisco by Almira Bailey [pseud.] S.F., S.F. jl. [c1921] 97 p.
C CHi CL CLSU CLU CMerCL CSf CSfCS
CSjC CSmH CU-B NjR

8105. The architecture and landscape gardening of the exposition; a pictorial survey...with an introduction by Louis Christian Mullgardt. S.F., Elder, c1915. 202 p. illus.
Available in many California libraries and ViU

8106. Argenti, Felix, vs. City of San Francisco. State of California, district court of the Fourth judicial district, city and county of San Francisco. Felix Argenti, respondent, vs. the city of San Francisco, appellant. Transcript on appeal to the Supreme court of the state of California. McDougall & Sharp, for respondent. F. M. Haight, for appellant. Filed April 24, 1859. S.F., Francis, Valentine & co., 1859. 37 p.   CHi

8107. ——— ...Transcript of amended complaint. S.F., S.H. Wade & co. [1864] 99 p.   CHi

8108. Argenti, Magdaline, vs. City of San Francisco. State of California in the district court of the Fourth judicial district, in and for the city and county of San Francisco. Magdaline Argenti, executrix, appellant, vs. the city of San Francisco, respondent. Transcript on appeal to the Supreme court of the state of California. McDougall & Sharp, for appellant, John H. Saunders, for respondent. S.F. [Francis, Valentine & co.] 1862. 49 p.
CHi

8109. ——— In the Supreme court of the state of California. M. Argenti, executrix, &c., of Felix Argenti, deceased, appellant, vs. the city of San Francisco, respondent. Brief for appellant... S.F., Agnew & Deffebach, print., 1862. 24 p.   CHi

8110. ——— ...Second brief and argument for appellant. Sol. A. Sharp, counsel for appellant. S.F., Agnew & Deffebach [1864] 18 p.   CHi

8111. Argenti, M., vs. Sawyer, E. D. In the Supreme court of the state of California. M. Argenti, executrix, &c., vs. E. D. Sawyer, judge of the fourth judicial district court. Petition for mandamus. John B. Felton, attorney for petitioner. Horace M. Hastings, attorney for defendant. S.F., Edward Bosqui and co., print., 1867. 4 p.
CHi

8112. Argentine republic. Comisión, Exposición internacional Panamá-Pacífico, 1915. The Argen-

tine republic, Panama-Pacific exposition, San Francisco, 1915. N.Y., Press of J. J. Little & Ives co., 1915. 88 p. pl.
CHi CSfU CStoC

8113. Argonaut. ...Sketch book. [Cartoons of San Francisco stock exchanges and brokers] S.F., Argonaut pub. co., 1878. 8 sheets. CHi

8114. —— ...Sketch book. Mechanic's fair, 1877. S.F., 1877. [16] p. illus. CHi

8115. Armsby, Leonora (Wood) We shall have music. S.F., Priv. print. [c1960] 126 p. illus.
CHi CSfMI

8116. Armstrong, George S., & co., inc., New York. Crown Zellerbach corporation; a survey. S.F. [Recorder print. and pub. co.] 1937. 146 p. illus. CHi

8117. —— Crown Zellerbach corporation; 1952 report. S.F. [Recorder print. and pub. co.] 1953. 125 p. illus., maps. CHi

8118. Army & navy club of San Francisco. Constitution and by-laws, house rules and list of members... [S.F., 1909?] [31] p. CHi

8119. ...Army directory, San Francisco bay area... Presidio of San Francisco and Bay cities. Jan.-Mar., July-Sept. 1941. [S.F., Army directory, 1941] CU-B

8120. Army relief society. Army relief society and Army welfare military tournament. Presidio of San Francisco, May 18 and 19, 1928. [n.p., 1928] 86 p. CHi

8121. Arnold, Bion Joseph. Report on the improvement and development of the transportation facilities of San Francisco, submitted to the Mayor and the Board of supervisors... S.F., 1913. 475 p. illus.
C CHi CL CO COHN CSf CSfCW CSfMI CSfP CSmH CU-B

8122. Art photo-engraving co. Art photo-engraving. [S.F., Cubery & co., print., n.d.] [12] p. illus.
CU-B

8123. Asbury, Herbert. The Barbary Coast; an informal history of the San Francisco underworld. N.Y., Knopf, 1933. 319 p. illus., ports. Bibliography: p. [315]–319.
Available in many California libraries and KU MoS NbHi ODa OU OrU T TxU UPB ViU

8124. —— Same. Long Beach, Brown and Nourse, 1949. 319 p. pl., port.
Available in many libraries.

8125. Ashton, Charles, vs. Dashaway association et al. In the Supreme court of the state of California. Ashton (Charles), in his own behalf, etc., plaintiff and appellant, vs. the Dashaway association, et al, defendants and respondents. Plaintiff's points and authorities. S. Heydenfeldt, jr., Jos. P. Kelly, attorneys for plaintiff and appellant. S.F., W.M. Hinton & co. [1884?] 44 p. CHi

8126. Associated charities of San Francisco. ... Report...1891–1914. S.F., C.A. Murdock & co., print. [etc.] 1892–[1919] illus.
C has 1901/03. CHi has 1904–10, 1918. CL has 1891–? CU-B has 1891, 1894, 1909–10; July 1912–Dec. 31, 1914.

8127. Associated oil co. Bridging the bay, San Francisco–Oakland bay bridge. [n.p., c1934] 14 p. CHi

8128. —— Spinning the cables, San Francisco–Oakland bay bridge. [S.F., c1935] 16 p. illus. CHi

8129. Association for the improvement and adornment of San Francisco. ...Annual report...1st, 1904–05. [S.F., 1905]
C C-S CLU CSmH CU-B

8130. Association of Christian science students of Eugenia M. Fosbery, C.S.B., San Francisco. Constitution and by-laws...adopted July 16, 1960. [S.F.? 1960?] [6] p. CHi

8131. Association of collegiate alumnae. California branch. [List of officers and members; reports... S.F.? 1908?] 46 p. CHi

8132. —— —— Sketch of the history of the association... S.F., Paul Elder, 1911. 38 p. CHi

8133. Association of junior leagues of America. Annual exhibition...1935– N.Y., 1935– 1 v. 1935 exhibition held at San Francisco museum of art. CHi

8134. Association of master plumbers of San Francisco. ...Schedule of prices and charges for material and labor adopted July 23, 1896. S.F., R. Munk, print. [1896?] 24 p. CHi

8135. Association of pioneer women of California. Year book.
CHi has 1916, 1920, 1922, 1926.

8136. Association of San Francisco distributors. Articles of incorporation and by-laws...November 20, 1937. [S.F., 1937?] 27 p. CHi

8137. Atchison, Topeka & Santa Fe railway co. Reasons why Santa Fe railway seeks to acquire control of Western Pacific railroad company. [n.p., 1960] [6] p. CHi

8138. —— San Francisco. Chicago, Passenger department, Santa Fe route, 1901. 114 p. illus., maps.
CHi CSf CSfCW CSmH CU-B

8139. —— Same. 1902. 114 p. illus., maps.
CHi CU-B

8140. Aten, Harold Deane. The premium on gold in New York and the discount on greenbacks in San Francisco, 1863–1871. [Berkeley, 1929] Thesis (M.A.)—Univ. of Calif., 1929. CU

8141. Athearn, Chandler, Hoffman & Angell. A history of the law firm now known as Athearn, Chandler, Hoffman & Angell. S.F., 1950. 38 p. CHi CU-B

8142. [Atherton, Edwin N., & associates] Legislative investigative reports. Submitted by H. R. Philbrick. December 28, 1938. [Sacramento? 1938?] [188] p. incl. tables. Reproduced from typew. copy. CLU

8143. Atherton, Edwin Newton. ...Full text of Atherton's graft report! S.F., 1937. 8 p. ports. (San Francisco Chronicle, March 17, 1937. Special section)
CO CSf CU-B

8144. Atherton, Gertrude Franklin (Horn) Adventures of a novelist. N.Y., Liveright, 1932. 598 p. illus., ports.
Available in many libraries.

8145. —— ...Golden Gate country. N.Y., Duell [1945] 256 p. (Am. folkways, ed. by Erskine Caldwell)
Available in many California libraries and CoU IC MiD MoHi MoS N NvU ODa OU OrU TxU UHi ViU

8146. —— My San Francisco, a wayward biography. Indianapolis, N.Y., Bobbs [1946] 334 p. illus.
Available in many California libraries and CoD IC MiD MoS N NN NjR ODa OU OrU TxU ViU

8147. Atmospheric gas co. of San Francisco. The portable atmospheric gas machine. Described. S.F., M. Weiss, Oriental print and pub. house, 1872. 9 p. illus.
CHi

8148. Austin, Florence Olive. The history of the curriculum of the University of California medical school. [Berkeley, 1930] Thesis (M.A.)—Univ. of Calif., 1930.   CU

8149. Austin, Leonard. Around the world in San Francisco. Stanford Univ., Delkin, 1940. 111 p. illus. "Five hundred copies printed at the Grabhorn press."
C CH CHi CL CLU CLod CMerCL CRcS CSalCL CSf CSfWF-H CSjC CSmH CSmat CU-B

8150. —— Same, with subtitle: A guide book to racial and ethnic minorities of the San Francisco–Oakland district. S.F., Abbey press [1955] 113 p.
C CAla CHi CO CRic CSf CSto CU-B

8151. —— Same, with subtitle: Where San Franciscans from all nations meet, eat, dance, and get to know one another. S.F., Fearon pub. [c1959] 96 p. illus.
CAla CSfSt CU-B

8152. Austin, Mary (Hunter) California earthquake of 1906. S.F., A.M. Robertson, 1907. 371 p.
CStclU

8153. Automobile club of California. First annual auto show, Coliseum, San Francisco, February 18th to 25th, 1907; given by the Automobile dealers' association of San Francisco under the auspices of the Automobile club of California. [S.F., 1907] 132 p. incl. illus., advertisements.   CHi

8154. Babow, Irving Paul. A civil rights inventory of San Francisco...by Irving Babow and Edward Howden. A study conducted under the auspices of the Council for civic unity of San Francisco with the assistance of a grant from the Columbia foundation... S.F., 1958–
Contents: pt. 1. Employment.
CLO CSd CSf CStclU

8155. Backus, Joseph Moorhead. Gelett Burgess: a biography of the man who wrote "The purple cow." [Berkeley, 1961] Thesis (Ph.D.)—Univ. of Calif., 1961.
CU CU-B

8156. Backus, Joyce. A history of the San Francisco Mercantile library association. [Berkeley, 1931] Thesis (M.A.)—Univ. of Calif., 1931.   CU

8157. Badger, G. Washington. An address delivered before the Dashaway association, Sunday, March 23d, 1862. S.F., Towne & Bacon, print., 1862. 16 p.   CU-B

8158. Badlam bros. Catalogue of gas heating stoves ... [S.F., Cubery & co., n.d.] [4] p.   CHi

8159. —— Peerless automatic gas machine for heating, lighting and cooking... [S.F., n.d.] 32 p. illus. Contains illus. of California residences.   CHi

8160. Baer, Warren. The Duke of Sacramento; a comedy in four acts...to which is added a sketch of the early San Francisco stage... S.F., Grabhorn, 1934. 77 p. illus.
Available in many libraries.

8161. Bahrs, George Ohrt. The San Francisco employers' council. Phila., Pub. for Labor relations council of Wharton school of finance and commerce by the Univ. of Pa. press, 1948. 39 p. (Industry-wide collective bargaining ser.)
C CL CLSU CLU CO CSfU CU-B ViU

8162. Bailey, Hiram Percy. Shanghaied out of 'Frisco in the 'nineties. Bost., C.E. Lauriat co. [1925] [187] p. illus., map.   CSfCW

8163. Bailey, Vernon Howe. San Francisco a month ago; drawings in pencil... [N.Y., 1906] [8] p. illus.
CU-B

8164. Baird, John H., et als vs. Duane, Charles P., et als. In the Supreme court of the state of California. John H. Baird et als, respondents, vs. Charles P.

Duane et als, appellants. Reply to respondent's brief... S.F., Edward Bosqui and co., print., 1869. 22 p.
CHi CU-B

8165. Baird, Joseph Armstrong. Time's wondrous changes: San Francisco architecture, 1776–1915. With foreword by Susanna Bryant Dakin. S.F., Calif. hist. soc., 1962. 67 p. illus., maps. (Calif. hist. soc. Special pub. no. 36) Bibliography: p. 64–67.   CHi

8166. Baizley, Bessie M. Story and poem of Valencia's wreck and description of the earthquake of the California coast and fire of San Francisco... [San Jose?] 1906. 32 p. port., pl. Cover-title: Souvenir sketches of 1906.   CLU

8167. [Baker, Edward Dickinson] Baker memorials, consisting of a memoir, funeral sermon, and dirge ...Compiled and published by the California regiment... Phila., Collins, print., 1862. 33 p. port.   CHi

8168. —— Masterpieces of E. D. Baker. Ed. by Oscar T. Shuck. S.F., 1899. 366 p. port. (Eloquence of the Far west, no. 1)   CHi CSf

8169. —— Oration...[over the remains of Senator David C. Broderick, Sept. 18, 1859] [S.F., 1859] 10 p.
CSmH

8170. —— Same. [S.F.? 1859?] [4] p.   CHi

8171. Baker, Ray Stannard. ...A test of men; the San Francisco disaster as a barometer of human nature ... [N.Y., 1906] [16] p. illus., ports.   CU-B

8172. Baker & Hamilton. [Catalogue] no. 1–, 186–?– S.F. [186–?]–
C-S has no. 14, 1877. CHi has no. 7, 11, 15, 17, 48, 75, [1871] 1877, 1879, 1883, 1906. CU-B has 11, 14–15, 1875, 1877–[1879, 1910].

8173. —— Catalogue of baling presses and excavating machinery manufactured and sold by the Price press company. 1876. S.F. [1876] 1 v. illus.   CU-B

8174. —— [Catalogue of] cultivators [and] seed drills for hand and horse. [189–?] S.F. [189–?] 1 v. illus.
CU-B

8175. —— [Catalogue of] horse powers, saw mills, bells. [189–?] S.F. [189–?] 1 v. illus.   CU-B

8176. —— Circular [of] popular styles of vehicles. S.F. [1896?] 1 v. illus.   CU-B

8177. —— Illustrated catalogue of plows, agricultural machinery and wagons [of] Sweepstake plow co., San Leandro, Cal. S.F. [1880] 1 v.   CU-B

8178. —— Special circular of single and gang plows. 1897/98. S.F. [1897] 1 v. illus.   CU-B

8179. Baker, Hamilton and Pacific co. Catalogue no. 11. [S.F., 1933?] v.p. illus.   CHi

8180. Baker's (Mrs. Colgate) young ladies' seminary. Mrs. Colgate Baker's English, French and German boarding and day school for young ladies, and kindergarten for children...San Francisco. [Prospectus] [S.F.] C.A. Murdock & co., 1879. [12] p.   CU-B

8181. Bakewell, John, jr. The San Francisco city hall competition; how the successful architects arrived at their solution. S.F., 1912.   CSf

8182. [Baldwin, Elias Jackson, firm, pub.] The Baldwin, Tallac, Oakwood [hotels]. E. J. Baldwin, proprietor, photos by Taber, half-tones by Bolton & Strong. S.F., S.F. print. co. [1892?] 71 p. illus.   CHi

8183. Baldwin, Janet M. Memorial and petition of Janet M. Baldwin to Hon. Thomas F. Bayard, secretary of state. Henry N. Clement, attorney and counselor for petitioner. S.F. [1887] 15 p. Widow seeks $100,000

indemnity of the Mexican government for the murder of her husband, Leon McLeod Baldwin, by Mexican outlaws. CHi

8184. Baldwin, Rosa Lee (Marcum) The bells shall ring; an account of the chime bells of Grace cathedral, San Francisco... S.F., 1940. 96 p. illus., ports.
C CL CLU CO CSf CSfSt CSmH CU-B MoS

8185. Baldwin & Howell. Attractive bungalows of moderate cost for Westwood park in Sutro forest, San Francisco. [S.F., 191–?] [19] p. illus., plans. CHi

8186. —— Same. [S.F., 1916?] 24 p. plans. CHi

8187. —— The beauties of elsewhere; a story of what San Francisco has not. [S.F.? 1910?] [16] p. illus. CU-B

8188. —— Ocean boulevard lots. [S.F., n.d.] [8] p. illus., map. CHi

8189. —— Presidio terrace [San Francisco] exclusively for homes. [S.F.? 190–?] 6 l. incl. maps. CHi

8190. —— Proposed site of the zoological garden at the Mission, from the plans presented by Baldwin and Howell... [S.F., 1897] 2 pl. CHi

8191. —— Receivers' sale. At auction, Tuesday, May 28th, 1912...California safe deposit & trust co. properties... [S.F., 1912] 6 p. illus. CHi

8192. Baldwin hotel. Souvenir of the Baldwin hotel, San Francisco. [S.F., Crocker, 1887?] unp. illus. (1 fold.) CU-B

8193. Baldwin-Lima-Hamilton corp. Exhibit at the Panama-Pacific international exposition, San Francisco, Cal., 1915. [n.p., 1915?] 31 p. illus., tables. CU-B

8194. Ball, John. Spirits, and the destruction of San Francisco... S.F. [c1905, i.e. 1906?] 19 p. CHi CLU

8195. Bamford, Mary. Angel island, the Ellis island of the west. Chicago, Woman's Am. Baptist home mission soc., 1917. 104 p. illus. CHi CSf

8196. Banco El Hogar Argentino. El Banco El Hogar Argentino en la exposición universal de San Francisco de California, E.U. de N.A. [Buenos Aires, P.F. Rotger, 1915?] 15 p. illus. CU-B

8197. Bancroft, A. L., & co. Account of stock of A. L. Bancroft & company, 1879. 620 p. Ms. CU-B

8198. —— Author's carnival album. S.F., 1880. 60 p. illus. CHi

8199. —— Specimens of type, cuts, etc., in use in the steam printing house of A. L. Bancroft & co. [S.F., n.d.] 176 p. illus. CHi

8200. ——, pub. Bancroft's tourist's guide. The Geysers. San Francisco and around the bay (north)... S.F., 1871. 228 p.
C CHi CL CLO CLU CSmH CU-B NN

8201. —— Bancroft's tourist's guide. Yosemite. San Francisco and around the bay (south) S.F., 1871. 256 p.
C C-S CL CLU CO CP CSf CSfCP CSfSC CSmH CU-B

8202. —— ...Catalogue of school library books and school apparatus, March, 1887. S.F., 1887. 17 [23] p. illus. CHi

8203. Bancroft, Anne. Memorable lives of Bummer & Lazarus (citizens of San Francisco) 185?–1865... L.A., Ward Ritchie, 1939. 26 p. illus.
C CBb CHi CL CLO CLU CMartC CO CRcS CSf CSfWF-H CSmat CU-B

8204. Bancroft, George. George Bancroft and his services to California. Memorial address delivered May 12,

1891...by Theodore H. Hittell. S.F., Calif. hist. soc., 1893. 20 p.
CHi CLgA CP CRedl CSS CSjC CStclU

8205. Bancroft, H. H., & co. Abstract of the ejectment suits in the district courts of the city and county of San Franicsco and in the U.S. Circuit court. Compiled from the original complaints on file in the Clerk's office and carefully compared. S.F., 1868. 24 p. CHi

8206. —— Catalogue of religious books for sale by ... [S.F.?, n.d.] [3] p. CHi

8207. —— Useful information for travelers. S.F. [1887?] [24] p. illus. CU-B

8208. Bancroft, Hubert Howe. Literary industries. A memoir. S.F., The History co., 1890. 808 p. port. (His Works, v.39) CChiS CHi CStmo

8209. —— Popular tribunals. S.F., History co., 1887. 2 v. map (v.1) (His History of the Pac. states of North Am., v.31 and 32)
Available in many libraries.

8210. —— Same. N.Y., Harper, 1891. 446 p. port.
CIIi CSd CSfCW CStmo

8211. —— [Scrap-book of materials about Hubert Howe Bancroft, his works, and the Bancroft library] [n.p., 188–?–90] 73 l. illus., ports. CU-B

8212. —— Some cities and San Francisco, and Resurgam. N.Y., Bancroft co., 1907. 64 p.
Available in many California libraries and CaBViPA CoU IHi N NN ViU

8213. —— Spreckels's broom in San Francisco. How one man was found to save the city from the looters ... [N.Y., 1902] 1 fold. l. CU-B

8214. —— Why a world centre of industry at San Francisco bay? N.Y., Bancroft co., 1916. 47 p.
C CHi CLU CO CSfCP CSmH CU-B

8215. The Bancroft company...cordially inviting yourself and friends to visit our new piano and organ warerooms... S.F. [1887?] C-S

8216. [Bancroft library, San Francisco] Evolution of a library. [N.Y., Bancroft co. of New York, 1898] 28 p. illus. CHi

8217. Bandmann, Nielsen & co. Nobel's patent blasting oil (nitro-glycerine)... S.F., Mining and scientific press bk. and job print. off., 1865. 33 p. diagrs. Contains also: Supplement to first edition. S.F., Dewey & co., print., 1866. 8 p. CHi

8218. Bank of America. Annual report.
CHi has 1939, 1941–45, 1947–49, 1951, 1956–57. CL has 1952–53, 1956–60.

8219. —— Circular [Prospectus] Oct. 19, 1949. 22 p. CHi

8220. —— Special report and analysis. S.F. CL

8221. Bank of California vs. United land association and Tripp, Clinton C. In the Circuit court of the United States, Ninth circuit, Northern district of California. The Bank of California, complainant, vs. United land association and Clinton C. Tripp, defendants. Bill of complaint. Filed August 8, 1891. Newlands, Allen & Herrin, of counsel. [S.F.? 1891] 65 p. San Francisco land suit. CLU

8222. Bank of California. Annual report.
CHi has 1950–59, 1961–62. CL has 1956–60.

8223. —— [Notice of incorporation and announcement of commencement of operations, etc.] S.F., 1864. 1 l. CHi

8224. —— A series of historical advertisements commemorating the founding of the Bank of California national association, in its seventy-fifth year. [S.F., 1939] [11] pl.   C CHi CO CSfCW CSmH CU-B

8225. —— [Statement, officers] S.F. [19—?–] 5 v.
CHi has July 1, 1905, Nov. 20, 1917, Mar. 4, Nov. 1, 1918, June 30, 1919.

8226. The Bank of California against the Sutro tunnel: argument and statement of facts showing why the amendments to Senate bill 16, adopted by the House of representatives, should be concurred in by the Senate ... Wash., D.C., Gill & Witherow, 1874. 100 p.   C-S

8227. Banks, Charles Eugene, and Read, Opie. The history of the San Francisco disaster and Mount Vesuvius horror...illustrated with photographic scenes of the great disasters and stricken districts. [Chicago? c1906] 464 p. illus., maps.
Available in many California libraries and MiD-B MoS TxU UPB

8228. Banquet tendered to his excellency, Governor R. W. Waterman, and friends, by his staff, at the Palace hotel, San Francisco, Cal., twenty-second of February, 1889. [S.F., Brunt & co., 1889] 59 p. illus.   CU-B

8229. Baptists. California. San Francisco Baptist association. Minutes... [1851]– 1851–1852 were published in New York. 1853–1880, Minutes of the anniversaries, held at various places in California, were printed within the state.
CBPac has 11th, 1861. CSaT has 11th, 1861. CSmH has 11th, 1861. CU-B has 6th–7th, 9th–10th, 1856–57, 1859–60.

8230. —— —— **State convention.** Minutes of a Baptist convention held with the First Baptist church, San Francisco. Feb. 2d, 3d, and 4th, 1860. S.F., Towne & Bacon, 1860. 24 p.   CU-B

8231. Bar association of San Francisco. Constitution and by-laws... S.F., Women's co-operative print. off., 1884. 20 p.   CSmH

8232. —— Same. S.F., Rincon pub. co., 1912. 28 p.   CHi

8233. —— Directory of members, 1952. S.F. [1952] 60 p.   CHi CU-B

8234. Bardell, James C. San Francisco-Oakland bay bridge. S.F., Author [1937?] 6 pictures with description in folder.   CRcS

8235. [Bardell art printing co.] Views of the PPIE exposition, San Francisco 1915. [S.F., 1915?] [24] mounted col. pl.   CU-B

8236. Barkan, Hans. Cooper medical college, founded by Levi Cooper Lane; an historical sketch. [n.p., 1954] p. 145–84. illus., ports. Reprinted from the *Stanford medical bul.*, v.12, no. 3, August 1954.   CHi

8237. Barker, Charles Albro. ...Henry George... N.Y., Oxford univ. press, 1955. 696 p. port.
          CHi CSf

8238. Barlow, Chester. The story of the Farallones arranged and published by H. R. Taylor... Alameda [Press of Pac. town talk, S.F.] 1897. [32] p. illus.
          C CHi CLU CO CSf CSmH CU-B

8239. Barnes (J. D.) co. A maritime necessity. [S.F., I. Upham co., 191–?] 15 p. illus., facsim.   CU-B

8240. Barnes, William Henry Linnow. An address delivered...at the Metropolitan theater, San Francisco, Cal., on the fourth of July, 1870. S.F., Edward Bosqui & co., print., 1870. 19 p.   CHi

8241. Barron, William E., vs. Kennedy, George. In the Supreme court, state of California. William E. Barron, vs. George Kennedy. Appeal from the district court of the twelfth judicial district, in and for the city and county of San Francisco. S.F., Commercial steam bk. and job print., 1860. 7 p.   CLSM

8242. Barrows, Charles Dana. The expulsion of the Chinese; what is reasonable policy for the times? A sermon delivered by Rev. Charles D. Barrows, D.D., pastor, First Congregational church, San Francisco. S.F., Samuel Carson & co., 1886. 19 p.   CHi

8243. Barrows, Stephen S. San Francisco bay ports. A paper for honors in economics... 1917. 70 p. maps. Typew.   CU-B

8244. Barry, James H. Biographical and historical sketch of Philip A. Roach. [S.F.?] 1889. 43 p.
          CHi CLU

8245. Barry, John Daniel. The city of domes; a walk with an architect about the courts and palaces of the Panama–Pacific international exposition... S.F., J.J. Newbegin, 1915. 142 p. illus.
Available in many California libraries and NHi ViU

8246. —— The meaning of the exposition. S.F., Crocker, 1915. 25 p.   CHi CRedl

8247. —— Palace of fine arts and the French and Italian pavilions; a walk with a painter, with a discussion of painting and sculpture... S.F., Crocker, 1915. 71 p.
          CHi CMartC CSfCW

8248. Barry, Theodore Augustus, and Patten, Benjamin Adam. Men and memories of San Francisco, in the "spring of '50."... S.F., A.L. Bancroft & co., 1873. 296 p.
Available in many California libraries and CaBViPA CoD N NHi NN ViW

8249. —— Same with title: San Francisco, California, 1850, foreword by Jos. A. Sullivan. Oakland, Biobooks, 1947. 178 p. ports., map. (Calif. centennial ed. No. 8) "A fire-defying landmark [by] Pauline Jacobson, from the *San Francisco bul.*, May 4, 1912": 12 p. inserted in pocket at end.
Available in many California libraries and CaBViPA CoD MiD OrU

8250. —— The Barry and Patten index, by Guy J. Giffen. Oakland, Biobooks, 1949. [8] p. port. Mimeo.
          CHi

8251. Barstow, George, vs. City railroad co. In the California Supreme court. George Barstow, respondent, vs. City railroad company, appellant. Transcript on appeal, with points and authorities for appellant. E. J. & J. H. Moore, attorneys for appellant. Barstow, Stetson & Houghton, attorneys for respondent. S.F., E. Bosqui and co., print., 1871. 146 p.   CHi

8252. Barstow, George. Introductory address delivered at the opening of the medical department of the University of the Pacific at San Francisco, California, May 5th, 1859. S.F., Towne & Bacon, print., Excelsior bk. & job. off., 1859. 20 p.   C CLU CSmH CU-B

8253. Bartell, M. J. Report on the underground water supply of San Francisco county; present yield, probable additional yield... S.F., Phillips & Van Orden co., 1913. 173 p. illus., charts.   CHi

8254. Bartholomew, Harland. The San Francisco bay region...importance of a plan for further growth... [S.F., 1925?] 30 p.   CO CU-B

8255. Bartlett, Alfred. The story of my life. [S.F.] Overland pub. co., 1922. [15] p. ports.   CHi

8256. Bartlett, C. Julian. A great cathedral rises in the west. S.F., Protestant Episcopal church, 1960. 36 p. illus. (*Cathedral news*, Golden anniversary issue, Epiphany, 1960) Deals with Grace Episcopal church, San Francisco.　　　　　　　　　　　　　　　　　　　　CHi

8257. Bartlett, Washington. Memorial of the life and services of Washington Bartlett (late governor of California), adopted by the Society of California pioneers ... [S.F., 1888] 45 p.
　　　　CHi CMartC CP CSf CSfCW CStoC

8258. Bash, Bertha. The San Francisco quartermaster depot, 1847–1928. [n.p., 1928] 10 l. Typew.
　　　　　　　　　　　　　　　　　　　　CU-B

8259. Baumann, H. C., architect. The Baumann brochure. [n.p., n.d.] 14 p. illus.　　　　CHi

8260. Bay area planning director's committee. A regional planning agency for the San Francisco bay area; a report and statutory proposal. Prepared for the Bay area planning commissioners' study committee at the request of a conference of city and county planning commissioners of the San Francisco bay area. [Berkeley? 1956] vi p., 34 pl.　　　　　　　　　　　CSfSt

8261. Bay bridges educational bureau. Facts about the San Francisco-Oakland bay bridge. S.F., c1935. 36 p. illus.　　　　　　　　　　CHi CRcS
Other editions followed. Title varies. CHi (4th, c1936) CRcS (3d, 1936) CU-B (2d, c1936) CV (3d, 1936) MoS (2d, c1936)

8262. Bay cities home building co., inc. A statement concerning California home building companies with particular reference to bay cities home building company. [S.F., 191–?] [8] p. illus.　　　　　　CHi

8263. Bay cities naval affairs committee. National security and naval base facilities on San Francisco bay. [S.F.?] 1923. 16 p.　　　　　　　　CU-B

8264. Bay cities water co. Irrigation versus San Francisco; the difficulties which the farmers interpose to a mountain water supply. [n.p., n.d.] 16 p. illus. (Water paper, no. 5)　　　　　　　　　　　　　CHi

8265. —— [Pamphlets on San Francisco watersupply. S.F., 19—?–05] 4 v. in 1. illus., fold. map. Contents: [no. 1] Is San Francisco in danger of water famine?–[no. 2] The waters and watersheds of the American-Cosumnes region.–[no. 3] What is and what is to be, the cost of water in San Francisco?–[no. 4] Mountain water for San Francisco.
CHi (no. 4 only)　CU-B

8266. Bay city publishing co. San Francisco, an illustrated review of its progress and importance. S.F., Geo. Spaulding & co. print., 1887. 156 p. illus.
　　　　　　　　　　　　　　　　CHi CSf

8267. Bay city wheelmen. Programme [of] the Bay city wheelmen...May 30th, 1895... S.F., Hicks-Judd co., print. [1895] [40] p. illus., ports.　　CHi CU-B

8268. Bay district association. Races! Races! Races! 1883. August 11, 15, 18, 22 and 24 and Sept. 1. N. T. Smith, president, T. W. Hinchman secretary. [S.F.] Breeder and sportsman print. [1883] [4] p. illus.
　　　　　　　　　　　　　　　　　　　　CU-B

8269. Bay region business. Pub. by the San Francisco Chamber of commerce. S.F., 1944–
　　　　　　　　　　　C CO CSf CU

8270. Bean, Walton E. Boss Ruef's San Francisco, the story of the Union labor party, big business, and the graft prosecution. Berkeley and L.A., Univ. of Calif.

press, 1952. 345 p. illus., ports. Bibliography: p. [327]–335.
Available in many California libraries and MoS ODa TxU ViU

8271. Beans, Rowena. "Inasmuch..." the one hundred-year history of the San Francisco ladies' protection and relief society, 1853–1953, ed. by Carol Green Wilson. S.F., 1953. 83 p. illus., ports.　C CHi CU-B

8272. [Beard, Henry] ...In the matter of the survey of the outboundaries of the Pueblo lands of San Francisco, made by James T. Stratton, deputy, and approved by L. Upson, Surveyor general for California, August 13, 1868. [n.p., 188–?] 24 p. At head of title: before the Hon. Secretary of the interior. Signed: Henry Beard, for himself and his associates, D. K. Tripp and Chas. F. Peck, att'ys for the state of California.　CLU

8273. Beaux arts gallery. Loan exhibition of paintings by modern masters, Mar. 10–Mar. 25, 1930. [S.F., Taylor and Taylor, 1930] [8] p. illus.　　　CHi

8274. Bechtel corp. Engineers and builders for industry; an evaluation of engineering and construction services. [n.p., 1959] 63 p. illus.　　　　CHi

8275. Beckett, Welton, and associates. The development of the Golden Gateway; prepared for the Redevelopment agency of San Francisco, March 1960, Embarcadero–lower Market approved redevelopment project area E-1. Welton Beckett and associates... Lawrence Lackey...Stacey & Skinner...Kern county land company, Del E. Webb construction company. [S.F.? 1960?] 34 p.
　　　　　　　　　　　　　　　　　　　　CHi

8276. Bedlam & Berry's real estate advertiser. v.1:1–3, 5–12. Sept., 1870–Aug. 1871. S.F., 1870–71.
　　　　　　　　　　　　　　　　　　　　CU-B

8277. Beebe, Lucius Morris. Cable car carnival [by] Lucius Beebe and Charles Clegg. Decoration by E. S. Hammack. [1st ed.] Oakland, G. Hardy, 1951. 130 [5] p. illus., ports., map.
Available in many libraries.

8278. —— Same. 2d ed. 1951.
Available in many libraries.

8279. —— San Francisco's golden era; a picture story of San Francisco before the fire, by Lucius Beebe & Charles Clegg. Berkeley, Howell-North, 1960. 255 p. illus. (part. col.) ports.
CAla CChiS CHi CLSM CSf CSfMI CSfU CSmH CU-B CaBViPA CoD MoS ODa TxU UHi

8280. —— U.S. west; the saga of Wells Fargo. N.Y., Dutton, 1949. 320 p. illus., ports., maps.
Available in many libraries.

8281. Behr, Hans Herman. In memoriam. S.F., Calif. acad. of sciences, 1905. 7 p.　　　　　CHi

8282. Bekeart, Philip K. Three generations, 1837–1949, Jules François Bekeart, a gunsmith; Philip Baldwin Bekeart, his son; Philip Kendall Bekeart, his grandson; 100th anniversary of the establishment in the firearms business in California, April 1, 1949. [Oakland, Westgate press, 1949] [26] p. illus.
C CHi CLSU CLU CSf CSfCSM CSfWF-H CSmH CU-B

8283. Belcher silver mining co. Annual report... December 31st, 1873. S.F., Women's co-operative print. union [n.d.] 19 p.　　　　　　　　　CHi

8284. Bell, James, et al vs. Ellis, John S. In the Supreme court of the state of California. James Bell et al, respondents, vs. John S. Ellis, sheriff, etc., appellant.

Reply to respondents' brief... S.F., Edward Bosqui and co., 1867. 6 p.   CHi

8285. Bell, Wendell. People of the city, a sociological study of urban life in San Francisco... Stanford, 1954. 251 p.   CSt

8286. Bellevue hotel...San Francisco. [n.p., n.d.] [8] p. illus. "Opened August, 1910."   CHi

8287. Bellingall, Peter W. [Autobiography. n.p., n.d.] 162 p. port.   CHi

8288. Bellingham bay coal co. By-laws... S.F., Agnew & Deffebach, 1859. 15 p.   CSmH (imp.) CU

8289. Benard de Russailh, Albert. Last adventure, San Francisco in 1851; translated from the original journal of Albert Benard de Russailh by Clarkson Crane. S.F., Westgate press, 1931. 94 p. illus. "475 copies printed in May, 1931, at the Grabhorn press, San Francisco." A pamphlet (11 p., 13cm.) with title: *A prologue, The spirit of California*, by M. Albert Benard... is inserted between p. 56 and 57.
Available in many California libraries and CaBViPA CoD NjR

8290. [Bender, Albert M.] Caroline Walter, 1858–1935. [S.F., Grabhorn, 1935] 5 p. port.   CHi

8291. Benedict. The coming horse show, an article ...on the first annual horse show to be held in the Mechanics pavilion, San Francisco, Nov. 28, 29, 30, and Dec. 1, 1894. [S.F., Overland monthly pub. co., 1894] 15 p. illus. Reprint. from *Overland monthly*, Oct., 1894.
                                                        CHi

8292. Benedict, William F. The Anza expedition of 1775–76, to colonize San Francisco used as a theme for the naming of thoroughfares in the metropolitan housing project at Parkmerced, San Francisco. S.F., Author, 1941. 9 l. Mimeo.   CHi

8293. Bennett, H. C. The affairs of the California labor exchange. [S.F.? 1872?] 8 p.   CHi

8294. Bennett, John Edward. Rebuilding of San Francisco... [S.F.? 1906] [8] p.   CU-B

8295. Bennett, Nathaniel. The queue case. [S.F., n.d.] 12 p. History of the "pigtail ordinance."   CU-B

8296. Bennett, Raine. An open letter to the citizens of San Francisco, from Raine Bennett. [1st ed. S.F., Am. arts foundation, c1926] 50 p.   CHi CSmH

8297. Bergenroth, Gustav. The first vigilance committee in California. Tarrytown, N.Y., W. Abbatt, 1929. Reprint. from *Mag. of history*. Extra no. 151, v.38, no. 3, p. 141–49.   CStoC

8298. ——— Same, in *Gustave Bergenroth, a memorial sketch* by William Cornwallis Cartwright. Edinburgh, Edmonston and Douglas, 1870. p. 22–44, reprint. from *Household words*, Nov. 15, 1856.   CHi CSfP CU-B

8299. Berger & Carter co. ...Tools and supplies for machine shops and factories; iron and steel. Catalog F-G 18. [S.F., Sunset pub. house] c1918. 1239 p. illus. (part color)   CHi

8300. Bernthal, G. A. Kurzgefasste geschichte der Evangelisch-Lutherischen St. Paulusgemeinde zu San Francisco... [S.F., Eureka press, 1917] 83 p. illus.
                                                        CHi

8301. Berr, Jules. Hotel rooms business directory of the leading wholesale and retail business houses of San Francisco, for 1871–72... S.F., A. Roman & co. [c1871] 150 p.   CLU CSmH CU-B

8302. Berry, John Francis. Student demonstrations

in San Francisco, May 12–14, 1960. [Berkeley, 1961] Thesis (M.A.)—Univ. of Calif., 1961.   CU

8303. Berry, Rose Virginia (Stewart) The dream city; its art in story and symbolism. [S.F., W.N. Brunt, c1915] 335 p. illus., plan. The Panama–Pacific international exposition.   CHi CO COHN CSfP CSmH

8304. Berthold, Victor Maximilian. Handbook of the Wells, Fargo & co.'s handstamps and franks used in the United States...Canada... N.Y., Scott stamp & coin co., 1926. 83 p. illus.   CHi

8305. ——— The pioneer steamer *California*, 1848–1849. Bost., N.Y., Houghton, 1932. 106 p. illus., maps, facsims. "The first of the U.S. Pacific steamships." "Revised De Lancy passenger list of the *California*."
CAna CBb CChiS CCoron CHi CRcS CRic CSd CSf CSfCW CSjC CStbS CStclU CStmo CSto

8306. Best, Alfred M. Best's special report upon the San Francisco losses and settlements of the 243 institutions involved in the conflagration of April 18-21, 1906. N.Y., Alfred M. Best co., inc., 1907. 63 p.
                                          CHi CLU CSmH CU-B

8307. Bethlehem steel co. The Golden Gate bridge. [Bethlehem, Pa., c1937] 20 p. illus.
                                          CAla CHi CLO CU-B

8308. ——— **Shipbuilding division.** A century of progress, 1849–1949; San Francisco yard.... [S.F., 1949] [32] p. illus., ports., maps, tables.   CHi CU-B

8309. Billings, Frederick. An address delivered at the fifth anniversary of the Orphan asylum society of San Francisco at Musical hall, Tuesday evening, Feb. 5th, 1856. S.F., Whitton, Towne & co., print., Excelsior job off., 1856. 22 p.
                          C CBPac CHi CLU CSmH CU-B NN

8310. Bird, Philip Smead. Child dependency with particular reference to conditions in San Francisco. [Berkeley, 1910] Thesis (M.A.)—Univ. of Calif., 1910.
                                                        CU

8311. Bisagno, Joseph. In memory of "Joe" read as a eulogy to the late Mr. Joseph Bisagno at his funeral services at San Francisco, on November sixth, nineteen hundred & nineteen. [by Asa V. Mendenhall] S.F., Priv. print., 1919. [3] p.   CHi

8312. Bisbee, Frederick Adelbert. A California pilgrimage...A souvenir of the United universalist conventions, California, 1915. Bost., Murray press, 1915. 124 p. illus.   CHi CSf CSjC CU-B

8313. Bishop oil co. Annual report... [S.F.? 195-?–
CHi has 1956–58. CL has 1954–60.

8314. ——— Report to shareholders.
CL has 1957–60.

8315. Black, Charles William. Analysis of the wholesale automobile accessory, supply, and parts business in San Francisco, 1903–May 1932. [Berkeley, 1933] Thesis (M.S.)—Univ. of Calif., 1933.   CU

8316. [Black, Chauncey Forward] ed. Some account of the work of Stephen J. Field as a legislator, state judge, and judge of the Supreme court of the United States, with an introductory sketch by John Norton Pomeroy... N.Y., Samuel B. Smith, 1881, c1882. 63,464 p.   CBb CHi CSf CSfCW CSfP CYcCL

8317. ——— Same. 1895. 522,198 p. Contains also: The story of the attempted assassination of Justice Field, by George C. Gorham.   CHi

8318. Blackmar & co. Descriptive catalogue of select music published by... [S.F., 1890?] 30 p.   CHi

8319. Blair, Fred, and Hon, Billy. Prominent clubmen in caricature. S.F., Author, 1928. 143 p. illus. CHi

8320. Blair, Hosea. Monuments and memories of San Francisco [by] Hosea and Nellie A. Blair. [S.F., 1955– (chiefly illus.) Contents: [1] Golden Gate park.–[2] Japanese tea garden.–[3] The Presidio. C CB CHi CL (v.1) CNF (v.1) CO CP CRic (v.1) CSf CSfU CSto

8321. Blake, Evarts I., comp. San Francisco, a brief biographical sketch of some of the most prominent men who will preside over her destiny for at least two years... S.F., Pac. pub. co., c1902. 223 p. illus., ports. C CHi CLU CO CSf CSfMI CSfU CSmH CU-B

8322. Blake, Moffitt & Towne. The brochure, one of a series of direct mail advertising guides published by the pioneers in quality printing papers. S.F. [1923] 26 p. CHi

8323. —— The catalog; one of a series of direct mail advertising guides. S.F., c1922. 27 p. illus. CHi

8324. —— Catalogue [of papers] 1875. S.F. [1875] 1 v. illus. CU-B

8325. —— Pioneers in paper; the story of Blake, Moffitt & Towne. Published in commemoration of the organization's seventy-fifth anniversary. [S.F., 1930] 49 p. illus. CHi

8326. —— Samples [from Whiting paper co., Holyoke, Mass., manufacturers of all kinds of first class papers] S.F., Blake, Robbins & co. [188–?] [28] l. CU-B

8327. Blanchard's (Miss) school for girls. Announcement. [S.F., 19—?– CHi has 1912/13–1913/14.

8328. Blanquie, Raoul. [The French hospital... San Francisco. S.F.] Author, 1951. [9] l. Mimeo. CHi

8329. Blattner, Helen Harland. The political career of William McKendree Gwin. [Berkeley, 1914] Thesis (M.A.)—Univ. of Calif., 1914. CU

8330. Bloch, Louis. The years of paper; in memory of Louis Bloch. [S.F., Crown Zellerbach corp., 1951] [12] p. illus., port. CHi

8331. Bloomfield, Arthur J. The San Francisco opera, 1923–1961. N.Y., Appleton-Century-Crofts [c1961] 251 p. illus. CAla CSfMI CSfU

8332. Blum, Eva Lereta (Dill) The early explorations of the San Francisco bay region. [Berkeley, 1930] 125 l. maps. Thesis (M.A.)—Univ. of Calif., 1930. CU CU-B

8333. Blumenthal, Louis H. Three generations of service to the community, 1877–1954; the story of the San Francisco Jewish community center and the YM-YWHA. Foreword by Lloyd W. Dinkelspiel. S.F., 1954. 44 p. illus., ports. C CHi CO

8334. Blyth & co., inc., comp. Blyth & co., inc., a profile [1914–1954] [S.F., 1954] 56 p. ports. CHi

8335. Blythe, Thomas H., deceased. In the Supreme court of the state of California. In the matter of the estate of Thomas H. Blythe, deceased. Florence Blythe, respondent vs. Abbie Ayres, et al., the Blythe company, appellants. Argument [of Delphin Michael Delmas] on behalf of the Blythe company. [S.F., James H. Barry, print., n.d.] 46 p. CHi

8336. —— ...Argument of Geo. W. Towle and D. M. Delmas, on behalf of the Blythe company, filed December 13, 1893, in the Supreme court of California, in the estate of Thomas H. Blythe, deceased. [n.p., 1893] 218 p. With this is bound: Argument of D. M. Delmas in the Blythe case. 46 p. CU-B

8337. B'nai B'rith. San Francisco. District grand lodge, no. 4. Constitution...and general laws... I.O.B.B. S.F., W.A. Woodward & co., 1894. 98 p. CHi

8338. Board of marine underwriters of San Francisco. Constitution, rates of premium, and rules of marine insurance...adopted August 28, 1865. S.F., Turnbull & Smith bk. card and job print., 1866. 19 p. illus. CLU

8339. —— Same. S.F., 1867. 21 p. illus. CHi CLU

8340. Bode, William Walter. Lights and shadows of Chinatown... [S.F., Crocker] c1896. [23] p. illus. C CHi CL CLU CLod CO CSf CSfU CSmH CU-B

8341. Boden, Charles R. David Terry's justification. [S.F., c1933] 23 p. illus. CSmH

8342. Bohemian club. The annals of the Bohemian club, from its beginnings...v. [1]–4, 1872/80–1905/06. [S.F., 1898–1930] illus. ports. Editor: 1872/80–1887/95, R. H. Fletcher, 1895/1906, Clay M. Greene. Available in many California libraries and NHi (v.1–2, 1872/80, 1880/87)

8343. —— Bohemian grove. [Photographs, 1906–1909. S.F.? 1909?] 54 photos. (incl. ports.) CU-B

8344. —— Bohemia's proposed new clubhouse; report of the Board of directors of the Bohemian club to the members of the club. January 9, 1933. [S.F., 1933] 24 p. tables. CHi CU-B

8345. —— A brief catalog of the published works of Bohemian club authors. S.F., Grabhorn, 1937. 50 p. CHi CLO CStclU CU-B

8346. —— Catalogue, figure-composition exhibition of contemporary paintings in oil by California artists... [S.F., 1928] [6] p. CHi

8347. —— [Catalogue of] annual exhibition of paintings and sculpture by members. 1st– , 1891–?– S.F., [189–?– CHi has 1900, 1902, 1904, 1909, 1911–12, 1922–23.

8348. —— A chronicle of our years, commemorating the seventy-fifth anniversary of the founding of the Bohemian club of San Francisco, 1872–1947. [S.F., Grabhorn, c1947] 106 p. CHi CStclU CU-B

8349. —— ...Constitution, by-laws and rules, officers and committees, members...1873– S.F., 1873– Publisher and title vary. C has 1914, 1936, 1939, 1947, 1960. CHi has 1884, 1892, 1901, 1904, 1907, 1917, 1928, 1931, 1935–36, 1939, 1941, 1947, 1949, 1951, 1960. CL has 1911. CLSU has 1907, 1931, 1939. CLU has 1911. CRedl has 1901. CSd has 1947. CSf has 1901, 1904, 1936, 1939. CSfCW has 1895, 1901, 1907. CSfU has 1911, 1939. CSmH has 1873, 1887, 1895. CStclU has 1955. CU-B has 1873, 1875, 1885, 1887, 1892, 1901, 1904, 1907, 1911, 1914, 1917, 1922, 1928, 1931, 1935–36, 1939, 1941, 1943, 1945, 1947, 1949, 1952, 1955, 1960.

8350. —— Early Bohemia. [S.F.? 1881?] 51 p. CU-B

8351. —— Midsummer encampment. Grove guide, information for members, program. 1930–1937, 1940–1942, 1952–1953. [S.F.] 3 v. fold. maps. CU-B

8352. —— [Miscellaneous publications] 1882–1958. S.F., 1882–1958. 12 v. illus., ports. CU-B

8353. —— Place names for Bohemians—clubhouse to grove. Bohemian grove. [Monte Rio] Silverado squatters, 1957. 16 p. "Written by Francis P. Farquhar and printed by Edwin Grabhorn..."   CStr

8354. —— Report of the president and treasurer... 1903/04– S.F., 1904–

CHi has 1914/15, 1927/28, 1929/30, 1931/32, 1933/34–1940/41, 1942/43–1945/46. CU-B has 1903/04–1909/10, 1912/13–1915/16, 1918/19, 1920/21–1922/23, 1924/25–1939/40.

8355. —— Souvenir catalogue of the annual exhibition of works by the artist members of the Bohemian club, marking seventy-five years of Bohemian art, 1872–1947. May 2 to May 17, 1947. [n.p., n.d.] 8 p.   CHi

8356. —— Treasures from the libraries of Bohemians; book exhibit in the art gallery, March 1st to 15th, 1950. [S.F., Grabhorn, 1950] 10 p.   CHi

8357. Bollens, John Constantinus. The problem of government in the San Francisco bay region. Berkeley, Bur. of pub. admin., Univ. of Calif., 1948. 162 p. map.
CBu CChiS CL CLSU CLU CLgA CMartC CMont CO CRcS CSf CSfSt CSj CSmH CU-B

8358. Bolton, Herbert Eugene. Fray Juan Crespi, missionary explorer on the Pacific coast, 1769–1774. Berkeley, Univ. of Calif. press, 1927. 402 p. illus., maps. "Crespi's diaries are printed here as the principal part of this book."—Preface.
Available in many libraries.

8359. —— Outpost of empire; the story of the founding of San Francisco. N.Y., Knopf, 1931. 334 p. illus., port., maps. Published in 1930 as v.1 of his *Anza's California expeditions.*
Available in many libraries.

8360. Bolton, James R., vs. the United States. ...Title papers, briefs of counsel, opinion of the board, and decree of confirmation, in case no. 81, J. R. Bolton vs. the United States, for the lands of the ex Mission of Dolores. S.F., J.A. Lewis, 1855. 124 p.
CSfCW CSfP CSmH CU-B PHi

8361. Bonanza kings. Their splendor throned on human misery. Rolling in wealth wrung from ruined thousands. California and Nevada impoverished to enrich four men. A plain history of swindles perpetrated on a gigantic scale. The colossal moneyed power that menaces Pacific coast prosperity. [n.p., n.d.] 38 p.   CHi

8362. Bonestell & co. Centennial, Bonestell & co., paper merchants since 1852. [S.F., 1952] unp. illus., ports.   CHi CU-B

8363. [Bonfils, Winifred (Black)] John Irby's passing creates a void—he lives on in friends' memory—stands close to door "up yonder." By Annie Laurie [pseud.] S.F., Priv. print., 1925. 15 p. port.   CHi

8364. Bonnet, Theodore F. The regenerators; a study of the graft prosecution of San Francisco... S.F., Pac. print co., 1911. 261 p. illus., ports.
C CHi CL CLSU CLU CLgA CO CSf CSfCW CSfP CSfU CSmat CSmH CStrJC CU-B

8365. Book club of California. The Book club of California, founded 1912. Board of directors, committees, constitution and by-laws, list of charter members. S.F., 1913.   CHi CSf

8366. —— The Book club of California: its purposes, membership and list of publications. S.F., 1928. [11] p.   CHi

8367. Bookbinders and blank book manufacturers of San Francisco. Trade price list. Adopted August 15th, 1873. S.F. [1873] 8 p. tables (1 fold.)   CU-B

8368. Bookbinders guild of California. First annual exhibition...[1902. S.F., The Twentieth century press, n.d.] 15 p.   CHi

8369. Boone's inc. [Sale catalogue of Boone's, inc., successors to Manufacturers' supply co., San Francisco. S.F., Phillips & Van Orden co., n.d.] 32 p. illus.   CHi

8370. Booth, H. J. Address of H. J. Booth, esq., retiring president of the Mechanics' institute, delivered at their rooms, March 7th, 1867. S.F., Towne and Bacon, 1867. 8 p.   CHi

8371. Booth, Newton. Address delivered by Hon. Newton Booth, at the opening of the sixth industrial exhibition of the Mechanics' intitute, of the city of San Francisco, in the pavilion, August 8th, 1868. S.F., Dewey & co., print., 1868. 8 p.   CU-B

8372. Boruck, Marcus Derckheim. Lecture delivered...in the Assembly chamber of the state capitol at Sacramento, on Thursday evening, Feb. 28, 1895, on the press, as it was—as it is—as it should be. S.F., Francis & Valentine, print. [1895] 23 p. San Francisco history.
C CHi CLU CSmH CU-B

8373. Bosqui, Edward. Memoirs. [S.F., 1904] 281 p.
CBu CL CSf CSfP CSfU CSmH CU-B TxU

8374. —— Same. Foreword by Harold C. Holmes. Introd. by Henry R. Wagner. Oakland, Holmes Book co., 1952. 180 p. illus., port., facsims. 350 copies printed by Grabhorn press. "Edward Bosqui imprints": p. 175–[181]
Available in many California libraries and N OU

8375. Bottome, Phyllis. Stella Benson. Written by Phyllis Bottome and printed for Albert M. Bender. [S.F., Grabhorn] 1934. [13] p.   CHi

8376. Bours, William M. Turning points in the evolution of Grace cathedral, diocese of California... S.F. [Recorder print. & pub. co.] 1939. 15 p.   CU-B

8377. Bower, John C., and Farrington, Joseph W., vs. Coon, H. P. et als. In the Supreme court of the state of California. John C. Bower and Joseph W. Farrington, plaintiff and appellants vs. H. P. Coon et als., defendants and respondents. Appellants brief on appeal. S.F., M.D. Carr, 1869. 47 p.   CHi

8378. —— ...Brief of appellants. S.F., M.D. Carr, 1869. 23 p.   CHi

8379. Bowers (W. F.) and co. ...Pacific coast agents for the Gutta percha & rubber manufacturing company. [S.F., 18—?] 54 p. illus.   CHi

8380. Bowers rubber co. [Catalogue] S.F. [188–?–1892]   C-S (n.d.) CHi (1892) CU-B (189–?)

8381. —— Scenes in the San Francisco factory of the Bowers rubber co. [S.F.] 1891. 1 v.   CU-B

8382. Bowie, Augustus J. In memoriam, Dr. Augustus J. Bowie by Levi Cooper Lane. [S.F.?] 6 p. Reprinted from *Pacific medical and surgical jl. and Western lancet* [1887?]   CHi

8383. [Bowlen, Frederick J.] comp. Bancroft building fire, San Francisco. April 30, 1886. [S.F., 1940] 7 l. mounted photos. Typew.   C CSf CU-B

8384. —— Fire horses: Farewell, good and faithful servant! [S.F.?] 1938. 155 l. Typew.
C CSf CSfCP CU-B

8385. —— Firefighters of the past. A history of the

old Volunteer fire department of San Francisco from 1849–1866... [S.F.] 1939. 168 l. Typew.
C CSf CSfCP CU-B

8386. —— Fires we have fought... [S.F.?] 1944. 105 l. Typew. CU-B

8387. —— Roster of Exempt firemen. Also roster of the Exempt fire company of San Francisco. [S.F.] 1940. 125 l. Typew. C CSf CSfCP CU-B

8388. —— San Francisco fire department history. 43 p. Mounted newspaper clippings. CSf CSfCP

8389. Boyd, James Thomas. History of the title of the San Francisco homestead union, to a tract of land in the city and county of San Francisco: being a portion of the San Miguel rancho, distributed to the shareholders, February 15th, 1864... S.F., Towne & Bacon, 1864. 19 p. fold. map. CHi CSf CSmH

8390. Boyes, Marcia Edwards. The legend of Yerba Buena island, known originally as Sea Bird island, later as Wood island, and quite commonly as Goat island ... [Berkeley, Print. by Professional press, c1936] 46 p.
C CBu CHi CO COHN CSfCP CSfCW CSfWF-H CU-B

8391. Boys aid society of California. ...Annual report... [1st–50th, 187–?–1924] [S.F., 187–?–1924] illus.
CHi has 17th, 1890/91. CU-B has 2d, 5th–8th, 10th, 13th–14th, 25th–30th, 32d–50th, 1874/76, 1878/79–1881/82, 1883/84, 1886/87–1887/88, 1898/99–1903/04, 1905/06–1924.

8392. —— Constitution and by-laws... [S.F., 1905] 20 p. CU-B

8393. Bradford, James B., pub. The strangers' guide to the city of San Francisco... S.F., Bacon & co., 1875. 66 p. CU-B

8394. Bradstreet, J. M., and sons. ...Daily reports. Local 777–2017. Nov. 13, 1869–Aug. 28, 1873. S.F., 1869–73. 2 v. CU-B

8395. Branaman, Marybeth. Growth of the San Francisco bay area urban core. [Berkeley] Real estate research program, Bur. of business and economic research, Univ. of Calif. [c1956] 57 p. illus., maps (part fold.) (Its Research report, no. 8) CSfSt CU TxU

8396. Brandon, J[oseph] R. A reply to the Rev. Mr. Hemphill's discourse on "Our public schools," "Shall the Lord's prayer be recited in them?" S.F., M. Weiss, 1875. 21 p. CHi

8397. [Brandt, Fred, and Wood, Andrew Y.] Fascinating San Francisco... S.F. [Independent pressroom] 1924. 63 p. illus. "This booklet... produced by Horne and Livingston for the San Francisco Chamber of commerce."—1 p. at end.
Available in many California libraries and MiD T

8398. Brandt, Rudolph. Ocean shore, "reaches the beaches". San Mateo, Western railroader [n.d.] 32 p. illus. (*Western railroader*, v.15, no. 7, issue 151)
CHi CSf

8399. Brannan's bank. Samuel Brannan's bank, n.e. corner Montgomery and California streets, San Francisco. Deposits secured by $450,000 productive real estate in trust for their redemption. S.F., Alta job off., 1857. 20 p. C CU-B

8400. Braun (C. F.) & co. A catalog of the products of C. F. Braun & co., manufacturing mechanical engineers...Catalog-A-1919. [S.F., John Kitchen, jr. co., n.d.] 89 p. illus. CHi

8401. Braun-Knecht-Heimann co. The history of the Braun-Knecht-Heimann company. Seventy-fifth anniversary, 1852–1927. S.F. [1928] [22] p. illus., ports.
CHi CStclU CU-B

8402. —— ...Illustrated catalogue and price-list of assayers' materials, mine and mill supplies... S.F. [1883–1910] illus. Established 1852; incorporated Oct. 1895. 1883–99 issued by the company under its earlier name: John Taylor & co.
CHi (n.d., 1886, 1889, 1910) CU-B (1883, 1886, 1892, 1899)

8403. Bremervörde verein. Constitution des Bremervoerde vereins, gegrundet zu San Francisco, den 2 Oktober 1872. S.F., Fischer & Walter, Abendpost-Accidenz-Druckerei, 1879. 19 p. CU-B

8404. Brick construction association, Los Angeles. Burnt clay products in fire and earthquake; "The truth hurts no sound, reliable material." L.A., c1907. [100] p. illus. CHi

8405. Bridge and beach manufacturing co. Pacific coast price list. July, 1907. S.F. [etc.] [1907] 1 v. illus. CU-B

8406. Bridges-Robertson-Schmidt defense committee. The law and Harry Bridges. [S.F., 1952] [28] p. CHi

8407. Brierly, B. Thoughts for the crisis: a discourse delivered in the Washington St. Baptist church, San Francisco, Cal., on the Sabbath following the assassination of James King of Wm. by James P. Casey. S.F., print. at Eureka bk. & job off., 1856. 20 p. Second edition, 1856, is identical.
C CHi CLU CSmH CU-B PHi

8408. Briggs, Arthur R. Destruction of San Francisco; how it was accomplished and the present outlook. [S.F., 190–?] [4] p. (Calif. State board of trade bul., no. 16) CU-B

8409. Brignardello, Santiago, et al vs. Gray, Franklin C. In the Supreme court of the United States. Santiago Brignardello, et al, plaintiffs in error, against Franklin C. Gray, defendant in error. Brief for defendant. Philip G. Galpin, of counsel. N.Y., Bloom & Smith, 1862. 14 p. CHi

8410. Bringham (J. C.) co. Catalogue no. 8... canvas and leather specialties...leather novelties. [S.F.? 192–?] 27 p. illus. CHi

8411. Brinton, Christian. Impressions of the art at the Panama-Pacific exposition; with a chapter on the San Diego exposition... N.Y., John Lane, c1916. 203 p. illus.
C CL CLU CMartC CMont CO CSalCL CSbr CSd CSf CSfCW CSfP CSmat CSmH CU-B CViCL

8412. Brittain & co., inc. Fishing tackle... [S.F., Associated print. and supply co., 1907?] 68 p. illus. CHi

8413. Brittan, Holbrook & co. Catalogue of stamped and Japanned ware, house furnishing goods, tinners' machines, tools &c. San Francisco and Sacramento, Cal. August, 1871. N.Y., H.P. Lowry, stationer, 1871. 329 p. illus. CHi

8414. Broderick, David Colbreth. Speech of Hon. D. C. Broderick...on the Pacific railroad bill delivered ...January 13th, 1859. S.F., Pub. by J.W. Sullivan [1859] 14 p. C CSmH

8415. Bromley, George Tisdale. Long ago and the

later on; or, Recollections of eighty years. S.F., A.M. Robertson, 1904. 289 p. port.   CBb
CHi CRic CSd CSfCW CSfP CStbS CYcCL

8416. Bronson, William Knox. The earth shook, the sky burned. [1st ed.] Garden City, N.Y., Doubleday, 1959. 192 p. illus., ports., maps.
Available in many California libraries and CoD MiD ODa

8417. Bronstrup, G. A. Club men in caricature... S.F. [The Hicks-Judd co.] 1918. [163] p. of illus., pl., ports.   CHi CSfCW CSfP CSfU

8418. Brooks, Benjamin S. Petition of Benj. S. Brooks, John Center, and Egbert Judson to the Senate and House of representatives. David S. Turner, attorney in fact. Analysis of title to the Yerba Buena island, bay of San Francisco. Wash., D.C., McGill & Witherow, 1870. 6 p.   CHi

8419. Brooks, George W. The spirit of 1906. S.F., Calif. insurance co., 1921. 79 p. illus.
CHi CL CLU CSf CSfCP CSfCW CSmH CU-B

8420. Brooks, Thaddeus R. Report...and table of soundings along the water front of the city of San Francisco... March, 1866. S.F., Towne & Bacon, 1866. 8 p.
CSmH CU-B

8421. Brothers, Hal. J. San Francisco, serene, indifferent and beautiful, sketched in pencil and crayon... with a brief description of the city by Frank Morton Todd. S.F., Robertson, 1924. 14 p. 20 pl.
C CBu CHi CLO CSalCL CSd CSf CSfCW CSfU CSmH NN

8422. Brotherton, T. W. Address...before the Church Union, on March 11th, 1872. S.F., Cubery & co. [1872] 15 p.   CHi CSmH

8423. Brown, Donald Mackenzie, ed. China trade days in California; selected letters from the Thompson papers, 1832–1863. With a foreword by Robert Glass Cleland. Berkeley, Univ. of Calif. press, 1947. 94 p. ports. The letters of A. B. Thompson constitute the larger part of this volume. Bibliography: p. 89–92.
Available in many California libraries and HHi MoS

8424. Brown, Edgar O., vs. City and county of San Francisco. In the Supreme court of the state of California, October term, 1860. Edgar O. Brown, plaintiff and respondent, vs. the city and county of San Francisco, defendants and appellants. Brief of William Carey Jones, of counsel for respondent. [n.p., 1860] 36 p.
CHi CU-B

8425. —— ...Brief on behalf of respondent. Eugene Lies, of counsel for respondent. S.F., J.B. Painter, bk. and job print., 1860. 35 l.   C CSmH CU-B

8426. Brown (Edward W.) co. Bakers' and confectioners' supplies and utensils. S.F. [191–?] 96 p.
CHi

8427. Brown, Elizabeth Anne. The enforcement of prohibition in San Francisco, California. [Berkeley, 1948] 60 l. Thesis (M.A.)—Univ. of Calif., 1948.
CU CU-B

8428. Brown, Helen (Hillyer) The great San Francisco fire; an account of the San Francisco earthquake and fire of April 1906 written shortly after the event by Helen Hillyer Brown (Mrs. Philip King Brown) in reply to many inquiries received from friends throughout the country. S.F., Leo Holub, 1956. 14 p. illus.
C CHi CU-B

8429. Brown, John Henry. Reminiscences and incidents of "the early days" of San Francisco...actual ex-

perience of an eye-witness, from 1845 to 1850. S.F., Mission jl. pub. co. [1886] [106] p.   C CHi
CL CLU CSf CSfCW CSmH CU-B NHi NN

8430. —— Same. With an introduction & reader's guide by Douglas Sloane Watson. S.F., Grabhorn [c1933] 138 p. illus., map. (Rare Americana ser. no. 10)
Available in many California libraries and UHi

8431. —— Yerba Buena, 1846, a description of the town with an account of its early inhabitants...Prepared for the Am. lib. assoc. by Gelber, Lilienthal. S.F., Grabhorn press, 1939. 7 p. fold. col. plate.
CL CLU CRcS CSfCW CSmH CStrJC CU-B MoS ODa

8432. —— Same, with title: Early days of San Francisco, California... Oakland, Biobooks, 1949. 147 p. map. (Calif. centennial ed. no. 20) With index compiled by Alameda public library.
Available in many California libraries and CaBViPA CoD ICN N

8433. Brown, Marion Agnes, and Williamson, Jean. San Francisco, old and new. S.F., Grabhorn, 1939. 104 p. illus.   C CHi CL
CMerCL CMont CRcS CSf CSfWF-H CSmH CViCL

8434. Brown, Rita Marie, Sister. The history of Immaculate conception academy, San Francisco, California, 1883–1953. S.F., 1953. Thesis (M.A.)—Univ. of San Francisco, 1953.   CSfU

8435. Brown, Thomas Pollok. Spanning the bay with the world's greatest bridges. Little stories of the Western Pacific, issued by Western Pacific news service. [S.F., n.d.] fold. sheets.   CHi

8436. —— U.S.S. *San Francisco* memorial at Land's end, overlooking the Pacific ocean and Golden Gate straits. [S.F.? 1950] 7 p.   CU-B

8437. Browne, Martha Fay Rambo. The Golden gate and its old fort, prepared for The National society of colonial dames of America in the state of California. S.F., 1933. 12 p. front. Bibliography: p. [13]
C CHi CLU CO CRic CSf CU-B

8438. Brownell (Jas. S.) firm. Instructions for setting up the Frue ore concentrator or vanning machine. [S.F.? 1888] 6 p. fold. pl. Jas. S. Brownell, successor to H. J. Summerhayes, successor to Adams & Carter, San Francisco.   CHi

8439. Broyles, Owen Milton. The financial history of the Pacific gas and electric company. [Berkeley, 1930] Thesis (M.A.)—Univ. of Calif., 1930.   CU

8440. Brucato, John G. The farmer goes to town; the story of San Francisco's Farmer's market. S.F., Burke pub. co., 1948. 143 p. illus., ports.   C CBu CHi
CL CLSU CLU CMartC CO CSf CSfMI CSfSt

8441. Bruce, John Roberts. Gaudy century; the story of San Francisco's hundred years of robust journalism. N.Y., Random house, c1948. 302 p.
Available in many California libraries and CaBViPA MoS TxU ViU

8442. —— Skylines... [S.F., 1931–36] 129 p. of mounted clippings.   CSf CU-B

8443. Bruguiere, Francis. San Francisco. S.F., Crocker, 1918. [61] p. illus. Photographs, with brief introductory text.
C CBb CHi CLU CMerCL CO CSd CSf CSfCW CSfMI CSfP CSfU CSj CSlu CSmat CSmH CU-B CViCL NN

8444. Brumagim, John S., vs. Bradshaw, Turell

T., et als. In the Supreme court of the state of California. ...J. W. Brumagim, administrator of the estate of Robert Dyson, deceased, plaintiff and respondent, vs. T. T. Bradshaw et als., defendants and appellants... S.F., 1867–70. 9 v. in 1. CU-B

8445. [Bryan, William H.] Review of the tide land swindle. [n.p., 1866] 2 pt. in 1 v. Each part signed: W.H. Bryan. A defense of the validity of the purchase of marsh and tide land in the vicinity of San Francisco and Oakland. CLU

8446. Buchanan, Albert Russell. David S. Terry of California, dueling judge. San Marino, Huntington lib., 1956. 238 p. (Huntington lib. pub.)
Available in many libraries.

8447. Buchanan, Ralph Earle. Chinatown [Gung Hei Fat Choi; or, Happy Year in San Francisco's Chinatown. S.F., c1956] [11] l. illus., mounted port. Typew. CSf CSfMI CU-B

8448. Buel, James William. Metropolitan life unveiled; or, The mysteries and miseries of America's great cities, embracing...San Francisco... St. Louis, Hist. pub. co., 1882. 606 p. illus. CHi CSluCL

8449. Buena Vista homestead association. Map, prospectus, articles of association and certificate of incorporation... S.F., Truesdell, Dewey & co., 1869. 20 p. fold. map. CHi

8450. Builders' association of California. Official directory, constitution and by-laws...also a complete list of architects. S.F., 1905. 136 p. illus., ports. The Association was founded May 6, 1885. CHi

8451. Builders' exchange of San Francisco. By-laws of the Builders' exchange. Adopted July 23, 1890. S.F., Crocker, 1890. 26 p. CU-B

8452. —— Handbook...1895/96– S.F., 1895– illus. C (1895/96) CHi (1895/96, 1904) CSf (1908) CSmH (1895/96) CU-B (1895/96, 1913)

8453. Bullard (E. D.) co. Bullard safety equipment, catalog no. 40. [S.F.?] 84 p. illus. CHi

8454. Bunje, E. T. H.; Schmitz, F. J.; and Penn, II. "Journals of the Golden Gate," 1846–1936...California cultural research sponsored by the University of California, Berkeley. Berkeley, Works progress admin., 1936. 134 l. Mimeo. C C-S CO CSf CSmH CU-B

8455. Bunker, William Mitchell. The commercial prospects of California. Address of William M. Bunker, Washington, D.C., representative of Chamber of commerce of San Francisco, at the quarterly meeting of the Chamber July 31, 1903. S.F., Commercial pub. co., 1903. 12 p. CU-B

8456. Bunten, Laurie. In loving memory of Laurie Bunten. [S.F., Bohemian club, 1910] [7] p. illus. CHi

8457. Bureau of municipal research, New York. Report on a survey of the government of the city and county of San Francisco... S.F., Rincon pub. co., print. [1916] 681 p. CHi CSf CSfMI CSfP CSfSt CSmH CU-B

8458. Burgess, Charles P. San Francisco-Oakland bay toll bridge revenue bonds. S.F., Kaiser & co. [1938] 32 p. illus., map. CHi

8459. Burgess, Gelett. Bayside Bohemia; fin de siècle San Francisco & its little magazines. Introd. by James D. Hart. S.F., Bk. club of Calif., 1954. 42 p. illus., facsims. (part. col.) CL CLO CLU CSalCL CSf CSmH CStclU CStmo CSto

8460. —— Gelett Burgess & the Hyde street grip. Introduction by Joseph M. Backus. [S.F., Grabhorn] 1959. 18 [3] p. illus. CHi CU-B

8461. Burgoyne, William M., vs. Supervisors of the county of San Francisco. In the Supreme court of California. William M. Burgoyne vs. Supervisors of the county of San Francisco. Plaintiff's brief. [S.F., 1854] 23 p. Signed: J. B. Crockett, referee. CSmH CU-B

8462. Burke, Andrew F. The Pious fund, California's first trust fund. [S.F., 1950] 8 p. CSfCW

8463. [Burke, Earl V.] "400 California street," a banking institution known around the world for 83 years. [S.F., Bank of Calif., 1946] 23 p. illus., ports. Reprint. from Bay area business, Fall ed., 1946. CHi

8464. Burke, John H., vs. Flood, James C., et al. In the Superior court of the city and county of San Francisco, state of California, Department no. 2, Hon. J. F. Sullivan, judge. John H. Burke (on behalf of himself and all others the stockholders of the Consolidated Virginia mining company), plaintiffs, vs. James C. Flood, the Consolidated Virginia mining company, and James C. Flood and James V. Coleman, as executors of the will of W. S. O'Brien, deceased, defendants. ...Opening argument of John Trehane, esq., on behalf of the stockholders, on the seventh day of the trial, Monday, December 20th, 1880. S.F., A.J. Leary, print. [1880?] 67 p. CHi

8465. —— ...Oral argument of Hall McAllister, esq., of counsel for defendants. [S.F.] Bacon & co. [1880] 124 p. CHi

8466. —— In the twenty-third district court of the state of California. John H. Burke, (for himself and all the other stockholders of the Consolidated Virginia mining company), plaintiff, vs. James C. Flood, John W. Mackay, James G. Fair, Pacific mill and mining company, and the Consolidated Virginia mining company, defendants. Cases cited by plaintiff's counsel in the argument on demurrer, Feb. 21, 1879. S. W. Holladay and John Trehane, plaintiff's attorneys. [S.F.? 1879?] 23 p. CHi

8467. Burke, Katherine Delmar. Storied walls of the exposition. [n.p.] c1915. 84 p. illus. C CHi CMerCL CMont CO CSf CSfP CSmH CU-B

8468. Burke, William G. Japanese school question. William G. Burke, city attorney (incumbent). S.F., Rincon pub. co. [1907] 15 p. Regarding segregation of Japanese in San Francisco public schools. CHi

8469. Burke's (Miss) school. Miss Burke's outdoor kindergarten and nursery school. S.F. [1940?] [5] p. illus. CHi

8470. —— Works and days...1915–1916. [S.F., Taylor & Taylor, 1915] [45] p. illus., ports. CHi

8471. Burnett, Peter Hardeman. Recollections and opinions of an old pioneer... N.Y., Appleton, 1880. 448 p. CHi CLSM CLgA CP CSf CSfCW CSfP CSjC CU-B T

8472. —— Index...Joseph Gaer, editor. ... S.F. [1935?] 44 l. (Index no. 2, SERA project 2-F2-132 (3-F2-197) Calif. literary research) Reproduced from typew. copy. CHi CLSM CP CSdS CSf CStmo CU-B

8473. —— Same, with title: An old California pioneer, by Peter H. Burnett, first governor of the state; with maps and index; foreword by Joseph A. Sullivan.

Oakland, Biobooks, 1946. 287 p. illus., maps, facsims. (The Calif. centennials, no. 5)

Available in many libraries.

8474. Burnham, Daniel Hudson, and Bennett, Edward H. Report on a plan for San Francisco...Presented to the Mayor and Board of supervisors by the Assoc. for the improvement and adornment of San Francisco. Ed. by Edward F. O'Day. Sept. MCMV. [S.F., Sunset press, 1905] 211 p. illus., maps. Pub. by the city.

C CBu CChiS CHi CLSU CLU CLgA CO CSf CSfCW CSfP CSfU CSmH CSrD CU-B CV MoS

8475. Burns, B. .J The Stetefeldt furnace: its results and advantages. S.F., B.J. Burns, agent, 1871. 16 p. illus.
CU-B

8476. [Burrows, George] Impressions of Dr. Wadsworth as a preacher. By a clergyman. S.F., Towne & Bacon, 1863. 24 p. Inscribed by author. Relates to Charles Wadsworth.   CHi

8477. Burton, Jean. Katharine Felton and her social work in San Francisco. Stanford Univ., Delkin, 1947. 274 p. illus., ports.

C CHi CL CLU CMartC CO CRcS CSS CSf CSfCW CSfU CSmat CSmH CSrD CViCL

8478. Burton, W. G. Views of points of interest on the street railroads in and about San Francisco. S.F., Street railway employees' hospital assoc. of S.F. [1904?] 176 p. illus., ports.   C CHi CSf CU-B

8479. Bush and Mallett. Catalog [of] wholesale gas fixtures. no. 1. [S.F., 18—?] illus.   CU-B

8480. Bushnell, Horace. California: its characteristics and prospects. Written by...and published originally in the "New Englander." S.F., Whitton, Towne & co., print., 1858. 32 p. Valuable for its report on the Vigilance committee and the squatter situation.

C CHi CLCM CLSU CSmH CU-B NN NjR PHi

8481. —— Society and religion: a sermon for California, delivered...1856...at the installation of Rev. E. S. Lacy, as pastor of the First Congregational church, San Francisco. S.F., Print. Sterett & co., 1856. 31 p.

C CBPac CHi CSaT CSmH CU CU-B CtY MWA NN PHi WHi

8482. Butchers' board of trade. San Francisco & Alameda counties. Yearly celebration of butcher's day, 8th, at Shell Mound park, Oakland race track, May 22, 1901. Souvenir album and program. S.F., Phillips, Smyth & Van Orden print., 1901. 44 p. pl., ports. Contains some biographical notes.   CHi

8483. Butler, Mary F. Mary F. Butler, 1864–1929 [by Edward J. Whelan] [S.F., Taylor & Taylor, 1929] [8] p.   CHi

8484. Butler, Vincent Kingwell. Tributes to the memory of Vincent Butler, 1892–1935. S.F. [Taylor & Taylor] 1936. 71 p. port.   CHi CLgA CSf CSfCW

8485. [Butler-Huff & co. of California] "The people's bank" [i.e., Bank of California national trust & savings association. S.F., 1945] 28 p.   CHi

8486. Butterfield (William) art auctioneer. Auctioneer William Butterfield will sell by auction the large varied collection of books contained in this catalogue, being the fourth consignment to him direct from Great Britain... [S.F., 18—?] 62 p.   CU-B

8487. Butterfield & Butterfield, auctioneers. Art objects; property of M. H. deYoung memorial museum sold by order of the Board of trustees... S.F. [194–?] 36 p.   CHi

8488. —— Contents of the San Francisco residence of the late Mary K. Hopkins (Mrs. Timothy Hopkins)... Auctions Monday through Friday, October 19th to 23rd. S.F. [1942] 83 p.   C

8489. —— Important continental and English furnishings...from the estates of the late Sen. Hiram W. Johnson...the late Marie Beck, and other owners... [S.F., 1957] 16 p.   CHi

8490. —— Sherwood hall, the estate of the late Mary K. Hopkins (Mrs. Timothy Hopkins)...auction Monday, October 5 [1942] S.F. [1942] 24 p.   CU-B

8491. Buyers' guide to San Francisco for 1887-8 for the use of merchants throughout the Pacific coast... Distributed by the wholesale trade. Pub. annually by the Rippey pub. co. 128 p.   CU-B

8492. Byrne, James W. The protection of San Francisco; the military value of the Farallones. S.F. [Bruce Brough press, print.] 1928. 14 p.   C

8493. —— Recollections of the fire. S.F., Priv. print., 1927. 55 p. illus. "Reprint. from the *Argonaut*, issues of November 27, December 4, and December 11, 1926."   CSfP CSfU CSmH CU-B

8494. [Byrns, Ray W.] Souvenir of the United States naval training station, San Francisco... [S.F., Blair-Murdock co., 1913?] 52 p. illus.   CHi

8495. The cable cars of San Francisco. Municipal railway of San Francisco. [S.F., n.p., n.d.] [12] p. illus.   CHi

8496. Cable railway co. Cable railway company in reply to the pamphlet issued by the Market street cable company. [S.F., 1884] 20 p.   CU-B

8497. [Cade and Franz] Official guide and maps of San Francisco street railways... [S.F., c1894] 140 p. maps.   CHi

8498. Caen, Herbert Eugene. Baghdad-by-the-bay. Garden City, N.Y., Doubleday, 1949. 276 p. illus. Illus. by Howard Brodie.

Available in many California libraries and MiD NN ODa TxU

8499. —— Bagdad, 1951. [1st ed.] Garden City, N.Y., Doubleday, 1950. 120 p.

Available in many California libraries and NN

8500. —— Don't call it Frisco. [1st ed.] Garden City, N.Y., Doubleday, 1953. 287 p.

Available in many California libraries and MiD NN ODa UPB

8501. —— Guide to San Francisco. With drawings by Earl Thollander. [1st ed.] Garden City, N.Y., Doubleday, 1957. 224 p. illus.

Available in many California libraries and NjR ODa UPB

8502. —— New guide to San Francisco and the Bay area. With drawings by Earl Thollander. Garden City, N.Y., Doubleday [1958] 224 p. illus.

CBb CChiS CCoron CHi CLO CMont CO CPa CSalCL CSbr CSf CSfSt CSluCL CStmo CStoC CV CViCL MiD TxU

8503. —— Only in San Francisco [1st ed.] Garden City, N.Y., Doubleday, 1960. 286 p.
CAla CHi CSf CU-B

8504. —— The San Francisco book; photos. by Max Yavno. Boston, Houghton, 1948. 119 p. illus., ports.

Available in many California libraries and MiD NN ODa UPB

8505. —— This is San Francisco. [S.F., S.F. Chronicle, 1941] 18 p. illus. CHi

8506. Cafe Zinkand. Cafe Zinkand, San Francisco ... [S.F., 1896?] 96 p. illus., ports. CLU

8507. Cahen, Blanche. Interesting talks on the Gobelins, Sèvres and tapis of the French building, Panama-Pacific international exposition. [S.F., 1915] 20 p. CU-B

8508. Cahen, Louis H., and Fitzpatrick, Edward L. The empire of the Golden Gate, 1858-1928, prepared for Sutro & co. at the moment of their seventieth year of activity... S.F., Crocker, 1928. 53 p. illus., port.
C CAla CHi CL CLU CLgA CO CSf CSfCW CSfP CSfU CSmH CU-B CaBViPA

8509. Cahn, Leni. Community integration of foreign groups through foreign war relief agencies in San Francisco. [Berkeley, 1946] Thesis (M.A.)—Univ. of Calif., 1946. CU

8510. Caire (Justinian) co. ...Illustrated catalogue and price list... no. 1-, 18—?- S.F., 18—?- CHi has no. 3, 4?, 7, 9, 1889, 1896, 1911, 1924.

8511. —— Silver and gold tables... S.F., A. Chaigneau [18—?] [40] p. Prepared by Falkenau and Reese. CHi

8512. Cairns, Patricia A. Regional planning in the Bay area. [Stanford, 1952] Thesis (M.A.)—Stanford univ., 1952. CSt

8513. Caldwell, George Walter. Legends of San Francisco... S.F., Phillips & Van Orden co. [c1919] 91 p. port. In verse form.
C C-S CHi CLSU CLU CMartC CO COHN CSf CSmH CV

8514. Caldwell college of oratory and acting. Annual catalogue, 1902? S.F., Press of Monarch print. co. [1902?] pl. CHi

8515. Caledonian club of San Francisco. Constitution and by-laws... S.F., Cunningham, Curtiss & Welch, print., 1878. 72 p. CHi CSmH CU-B

8516. —— Same. S.F., Geo. M. Wood & co., print., 1890. 65 p. CHi

8517. —— Eighty-third annual gathering and games, Labor day, September 6, 1948. Sigmund Stern Grove, San Francisco. [n.p., 1948] 16 p. CHi

8518. [Calhoun, Patrick] Some facts regarding Francis J. Heney, esq., acting as assistant district attorney of the city and county of San Francisco... [n.p.] 1909. 90 p. CHi CLU CO CSmH CU-B NN

8519. Calhoun, Wendell T. ...Improving the San Francisco wholesale fruit and vegetable market, by W.T. Calhoun, H.E. Erdman, and G.L. Mehren. Berkeley, 1943. 72 l. incl. map, tables, diagrs. CL

8520. California vs. Botkin, Cordelia Adelaide. The people of the state of California, plaintiff and respondent, vs. Cordelia Botkin, defendant and appellant. [S.F., 1899?] 947 p. CO

8521. California vs. the Broadway wharf co. In the Supreme court of the state of California. The people, ex rel. The Board of harbor commissioners, respondents, vs. the Broadway wharf company, appellants. Brief for appellants. H[enry] H. Haight, for the commissioners of the funded debt. S.F., T.B. Deffebach & co., print., 1866. 43 p. CHi

8522. California vs. Calhoun, Patrick. ...The people of the state of California vs. Patrick Calhoun, defendant...Reporter's transcript of excuses of jurors and examination of jurors on their voir dire. v.VII. [n.p., 1909] CU-B

8523. California vs. Carey, James. ...The people of the state of California, plaintiff and respondent, vs. James Carey, defendant and appellant. Appellant's opening brief. William F. Herron, attorney for appellant. [S.F] Pernau-Walsh print. co. [1921] 85 p. CU-B

8524. California vs. de la Guerra, Pablo. In the Supreme court of the state of California. The people of the state of California, ex rel. M. M. Kimberley, vs. Pablo de la Guerra. A. Packard, attorney for appellants. Eugene Liés, of counsel. S.F., Women's co-operative union print., 1870. 22 p. Contested election of Pablo de la Guerra... District judge of the First judicial district. CHi

8525. California vs. Holladay, Samuel W. ...The people ex rel. Bryant, appellants, vs. Samuel W. Holladay, et al., respondents. Respondents' petition for rehearing. Mastick, Belcher & Mastick, attorneys for petitioners. R. H. Lloyd, attorney for R. G. Davisson. Jarboe, Harrison & Goodfellow, of counsel... [S.F.? 1886] 28 p. San Francisco pueblo lands. CU-B

8526. California v. McGlynn, John A., et al. In the Supreme court of the state of California. The state of California, respondents, vs. John A. McGlynn, et al., appellants. April term, 1862. Appellants' points and authorities. Hoge & Wilson, counsel for appellants. S.F., Towne & Bacon, print. [1862] 48 p. CSfCW

8527. California vs. Mt. Shasta manufacturing company. In the Supreme court of the state of California. People of the state of California upon the relation of M. V. Loy, appellant, vs. Mt. Shasta manufacturing company, respondent. Transcript on appeal. P. O. Chilstrom, attorney for appellant. James Alva Watt, attorney for respondent. T. V. Cator, of counsel... [n.p., 1894] 16 p. CHi

8528. California vs. Randall, Charles W. ...The people of the state of California, ex relatione John G. McCullough, attorney general, plaintiffs, v. Charles W. Randall, et als, defendants. Separate answer and disclaimer of Charles W. Randall. Selden S. Wright, Gregory Yale, Patterson, Wallace & Stow, attorneys for defendant. [n.p., 1865] 6 l. CU-B

8529. California vs. Reed, E. P., et al. ...The people, plaintiffs and respondents, vs. E. P. Reed, et al., defendants and appellants. Brief of appellants on rehearing. William Matthews, attorney for appellants... [S.F.? 1889] 10 p. San Francisco land titles. CU-B

8530. California vs. Ruef, Abraham. The affidavit of Abraham Ruef filed in the Superior court for San Francisco on Friday, March 20, 1908, in the case of the People vs. Abraham Ruef showing the persistent efforts made by the prosecution and their agents to induce Abraham Ruef to commit perjury by bearing false witness against Patrick Calhoun and Tirey L. Ford of the United railroads... [Oakland, Allied print. trades council, 1908] 14 p. CHi CSf CSmH CU-B NN

8531. —— In the District court of appeal of the state of California, First appellate district....Brief of amici curiae upon petition for rehearing... [S.F., 1910] 101 p. CHi

8532. —— In the Supreme court of the state of California. Appellant's petition for a rehearing of the motion of the Attorney-general to dismiss the order of this court of January 22, 1911, transferring the above entitled cause to this court, after decision by the district court of appeal for the first appellate district. [S.F.] James H. Barry co. [1911] 93 p. CHi

8533. California vs. San Francisco. In the Supreme court of the state of California. The people, etc., ex rel. Cornelius Mooney, appellant, vs. the Board of supervisors, etc., respondents. Reply to respondents' brief. John B. Felton, Theodore H. Hittell, Wm. H. Culver, attorneys for appellant. S.F., E. Bosqui & co. print., 1867. 6 p.   CHi CU-B

8534. —— In the Supreme court of the state of California. The people, ex rel. Harpending, vs. the county court of San Francisco. The people, ex rel. Grogan, vs. the same. Brief in reply. Doyle & Barber, Delos Lake, for appellant and relator. S.F., B.F. Sterett, print., 1869. 5 p. In the matter of the extension of Montgomery and Connecticut streets.   CHi

8535. —— ...The people, ex rel. Grogan, vs. the county court of San Francisco... [S.F., 1868] 838 p. fold. map.   CU-B

8536. —— ...The people of the state, etc., vs. the city and county of San Francisco. Petition by appellant for rehearing. Philip G. Galpin, of counsel... S.F., Law jl. print. [1888] 42 p.   CU-B

8537. —— ...The people of the state of California, upon the relation of Alexander W. Macpherson, vs. the Board of supervisors of the city and county of San Francisco. Petition and notice of application for peremptory writ of mandamus. Jo Hamilton, attorney general. McAllisters & Bergin and W. H. Patterson, attorneys and counsel for relator and applicant. S.F., Steam print. house of A.L. Bancroft & co., 1870. 108 p. fold. map.   CU-B

8538. California vs. Santa Fe land improvement company. ...The people of the state of California, ex rel. Board of state harbor commissioners, plaintiff, vs. Santa Fe land improvement company, a corporation, et al., defendants. Defendants' brief on demurrer. Charles E. Wilson, attorney for defendants... S.F., The Blair-Murdock co. [1912] 43 p.   CU-B

8539. California vs. Schmitz, Eugene E. In the District court of appeal of the state of California. The people of the state of California vs. Eugene E. Schmitz, appellant. In the Superior court of the state of California, in and for the city and county of San Francisco. The people of the state of California vs. Eugene E. Schmitz and Abraham Ruef, defendants. (Crim. no. 305. Dept. no. 6) Transcript on appeal. Indictment for extortion. [n.p., n.d.] 672 p.   CHi

8540. —— ...The people of the state of California, plaintiff and respondent, vs. Eugene E. Schmitz, defendant and appellant...Brief of appellant to show that the indictment is fatally defective, and that the decision of the Court of appeal was clearly right... [S.F.] Press of James H. Barry co. [1908] 80 p.   CHi CU-B

8541. —— ...Points and authorities on the sufficiency of the indictment... [S.F.] Press of James H. Barry co. [1907] 130 p.   CU-B

8542. California vs. Southern Pacific railroad co. In the Supreme court of the state of California. The people of the state of California...vs. Southern Pacific railway company...San Pedro lumber company...Kerckhoff-Cuzner mill and lumber company and others. Appeal from the Superior court of Los Angeles co., Hon. Walter Bordwell, judge. Joint transcript of appeal; J. W. McKinley, Frank Karr [and others] attorneys for defendants, appellants and respondents... L.A., Parker & Stone [1911] 390 p. Relating to titles to tide lands in California.   CL

8543. California. Attorney general's office. ...

Communication from the Attorney general and copies of leases of the government reservation in San Francisco. [Sacramento] G. Kerr, State print., 1853. 8 p.
                                                CSmH CU-B

8544. —— **Board of state harbor commissioners.** The port of San Francisco; one of the world's great maritime centers. [1951] 22 p.   CO

8545. —— —— San Francisco subway; double traffic paved vehicular driveway below the tidewater level, planned and constructed by California harbor commission in 1924... Sacramento, State print. off., 1925. 32 p. illus., ports.   CHi

8546. —— **Board of state viticultural commissioners.** Report of the sixth annual state viticultural convention, held at Pioneer hall, San Francisco, March 7, 8, 9, 10, 1888. Sacramento, State off., J.D. Young, state print., 1888. 218 p.   CHi

8547. —— **Centennial commission, San Francisco.** Official souvenir program. San Francisco centennial celebration, 1850–1950. September 2–9, 1950. S.F., Centennial committee, inc., 1950. 36 p. illus., ports.
                                                          CSf

8548. —— **Commission, Golden Gate international exposition.** California at the Golden Gate international exposition located on Treasure island, San Francisco bay... [Sacramento? 1941] 130 p. illus., ports.
                               CBu CLO CO CRcS CSf CU-B

8549. —— **Dept. of finance. Budget division.** Management survey [for the] Board of state harbor commissioners for San Francisco harbor. [Sacramento] 1955. 123 p. illus.   CL

8550. —— **Dept. of natural resources. Division of mines.** Geologic guide book of the San Francisco bay counties; history, landscape, geology, fossils, minerals, industry, and routes to travel, prepared under the direction of Olaf P. Jenkins, Charles V. Averill [and others] contributing authors. S.F., 1951. 392 p. illus., maps, diagrs., profiles. (Its Bul. 154)
Available in many libraries.

8551. —— **Dept. of public works.** ...Annual progress report, San Francisco-Oakland bay bridge. v.1-6, July 1, 1933–June 30, 1939. Sacramento [1935–39] 6 v. illus., ports., plans (part fold.), tables, diagrs.
                                     CHi CSfU CStmo (v.4)

8552. —— —— **Division of San Francisco bay toll crossing.** A report...on additional toll crossings of San Francisco bay. 1948. 144 p. illus., maps.
    CHi CL CLSU CMartC CO CSdS CSf CU-B

8553. —— —— Same, Summary...1948. 13 p. fold. maps.   CLSU CP CSdS

8554. —— —— Same. 1949. v.p. illus., maps.   CHi CL CU-B

8555. —— —— —— A report on the southern crossing of San Francisco bay. [Berkeley?] 1954-57. v.p. fold. maps. Title varies: Dec. 1954, A progress report ...Dec. 1957, Southern crossing.
    CRcS (1957) CSdS (1954–56) CSluCL (1954)

8556. —— —— —— Studies of southern crossings of San Francisco bay, January, 1959. Sacramento, State print. off., 1959.   CRcS

8557. —— **District court. (4th district)** In the District court fourth judicial district, San Francisco, California. State of California v. Andrew J. Butler & John A. McGlynn. Opinion of Judge Hager ordering an injunction, to restrain the sale of real estate by the executors of the late David C. Broderick, on the alleged grounds that the will is a forgery and the estate an escheat. S.F., Valentine & co. [1862] 16 p. CU-B

8558. —— —— **(12th district)** Decision of Judge Pratt in the Pueblo land case delivered at the January term, 1868. W. W. Johnson and others, vs. the Board of supervisors of the city and county of San Francisco. S.F., B.F. Sterett, print., 1867. 21 p.
CHi CU-B

8559. —— —— —— ...J. B. Felton et al., vs. L. L. Robinson. Opinion of the court. S.F. [Daily stock exchange print.] 1876. CSmH

8560. —— —— **(15th district)** ...Joseph M. Wood, plaintiffs [sic] vs. the City and county of San Francisco, defendants. Findings and decision of the court. S. W. Holladay of counsel. S.F., Frank Eastman, print., 1877. 7 p. CHi

8561. —— —— —— Official report of the trial of Laura D. Fair for the murder of Alex P. Crittenden, including the testimony, the arguments of counsel, and the charge of the court, reported verbatim, and the entire correspondence of the parties...from the short-hand notes of Marsh & Osbourne... S.F., Sumner Whitney & co., 1871. 325 p. CHi CSfCW CSmH

8562. —— —— **(23d district)** ...City and county of San Francisco, plaintiff, vs. the Spring Valley water works, defendant. Opinion of Hon. James D. Thornton, judge. W. C. Burnett, attorney for plaintiff. Hon. John F. Swift, of counsel. Chas. N. Fox, esq., attorney for defendant. Filed [187–?]... [S.F.] W.M. Hinton co., print. [187–?] 53 p. CHi

8563. —— **Governor (Riley)** Governor Bennett [!] Riley's proclamation to the people of San Francisco June 4, 1849 [with explanatory comments by John B. Goodman III] L.A., Priv. print., 1956. 15 p. 2 fold. mounted facsims. C CHi CL CLO CLU CSmH CU-B

8564. —— —— **(Bigler)** ...Governor's message in answer to a resolution of the Assembly requesting information in relation to water lots in the city of San Francisco, sold in 1850. [Sacramento] G. Kerr, State print. [1853?] 28 p. CHi CSmH CU-B

8565. —— —— **(Rolph)** In the matter of the application made on behalf of Thomas J. Mooney for a pardon. Decision of Hon. James Rolph, jr., governor of the state of California, together with the report of Hon. Matt I. Sullivan... Sacramento, State print. off., 1932. 93 p. illus.
CL CLU CRcS CSf CSfCW CSj CSmH CU-B

8566. —— —— **(Olson)** ...Full and unconditional pardon for Thomas J. Mooney...received at San Quentin penitentiary on July 17, 1918, and given no. 31921 ... Sacramento, G.H. Moore, State print. [1939] Broadside.
CU (original document) CU-B

8567. —— **Laws, statutes, etc.** An act to open and establish a public street in the city and county of San Francisco, to be called "Potrero avenue," and to take private lands therefor. [Sacramento? 1879?] 23 p.
CLU

8568. —— —— An act to provide for funding the legal and equitable debt of the city of San Francisco, and for the final redemption of the same. Approved May 7, 1855. [S.F.? 1855?] 6 p. CLU

8569. —— —— Quarantine laws for the bay and harbor of San Francisco, California, approved, April 2d, 1866, and sanitary regulations of the Board of health pursuant thereto. S.F., Turnbull & Smith, print., 1866. 8 p. CSmH

8570. —— —— The San Francisco and San Jose railroad act. Approved April 19, 1861... S.F., Print. at off. of the "Evening mirror," 1861. 4 p.
CHi CSmH CU-B

8571. —— **Legislature.** The bulkhead question completely reviewed. The law and the testimony. Speeches of the Hons. Henry Edgerton, R. C. Clark, E. D. Wheeler, J. A. Watson, John Conness and F. A. Sawyer delivered in the Senate and Assembly of the state of California, April, 1860...together with the bill providing for the construction of a bulkhead, or sea-wall, as it passed the Legislature. Sacramento, Daily standard off., 1860. 67 p.
C CHi CL CLU CSmH CU-B

8572. —— —— **Assembly.** The entire official testimony and the report of the committee as to the necessity of a "Bulkhead or sea-wall" on the waterfront of the city of San Francisco, taken before a special Assembly committee of 1859... Sacramento, Print. at Daily standard off., 1860. 60 p. CU-B

8573. —— —— —— Majority report of special committee on Mr. McMullin's bill for the repeal of the confirmation act in relation to the beach and water lots of San Francisco, etc.; passed May 1, 1851... [Sacramento] Eugene Casserly, State print. [n.d.] 46 p.
CU-B

8574. —— —— —— Testimony against the necessity of a bulkhead or seawall in the harbor of San Francisco, by Major Hartmen Bach, Prof. George Davidson, Capt. J. L. Gilmer, and Capt. Jas. Alden, taken before the Assembly committee of 1859. [Sacramento? 1859] 15 p. CU-B

8575. —— —— —— **Committee on commerce & navigation.** Report...in relation to extending the city front of San Francisco. Sacramento, State print., 1853. 5 p. (Doc. no. 27. In the Assembly, Sess. 1853) Signed J. Cardozo. CHi

8576. —— —— —— **Committee to investigate the affairs of the San Francisco City hall commission.** Report. [Sacramento, State print., 1874] 7,289 p. CSmH CU-B

8577. —— —— —— **Interim fact-finding committee on tideland reclamation & development.** Relief of congestion on transbay crossings. 1949. 109 p.
CSmat

8578. —— —— —— —— Report on San Francisco bay project—the Reber plan. 1951. CSmat

8579. —— —— —— —— Report on tideland reclamation & development in northern California. 1951.
CSmat

8580. —— —— —— **Select committee upon the extension of the water front of the city of San Francisco.** ...Report of a portion of the Select committee... [Sacramento] State print. [1853?] 22 p.
CSmH CU-B

8581. —— —— —— **Special committee on sales of water lots property [in San Francisco].** Report... [Sacramento] H.B. Redding, State print. [n.d.] 27 p. (Doc. no. 9 In the Assembly, Sess. 1854) CSmH

8582. —— —— —— **Joint budget committee.** Financial history of the San Francisco-Oakland bay bridge; report... [Sacramento] Pub. by the Senate of the state of Calif., 1953. 121 p. illus. CL

8583. —— —— **Senate. Fact-finding committee on San Francisco bay ports.** Ports of the San Francisco bay area, their commerce, facilities, problems, and progress. [Sacramento, 1951] 598 p. illus., maps, tables. CSfU

8584. California. Legislature. Senate. Fact-finding committee on San Francisco bay ports (*cont'd*) Report on San Francisco bay ports. [Sacramento, 1951] 3 v. illus., maps.   CSfSt CSt

8585. —— —— —— Interim committee on San Francisco bay area metropolitan rapid transit problems. Final report. John F. McCarthy, chairman. 1957. 29 p.   C

8586. —— —— —— Special committee on the bulkhead. Majority report...on the bulkhead... Sacramento, State print. [n.d.] 6 p.   CHi

8587. —— —— —— —— Minority report... on the bulkhead. Testimony taken before a select committee of the Senate, March 14th, 1860 in relation to Senate bill no. 167. Sacramento, State print. [1860] 37 p.   CHi

8588. —— Railroad commission. Report and recommendation of the Railroad commission of the state of California. In the matter of the valuation of the Spring valley water company's properties desired by the city and county of San Francisco for a municipal water supply. S.F., 1920. 11 p.   CHi CU-B

8589. —— San Francisco bay area rapid transit commission. Report on organization and financial aspects of a proposed rapid transit system for the San Francisco bay area. Menlo Park, Stanford research institute, 1956. 75 p. (S.R.I. project no. I-1247)
                                                 CChiS CPa

**8590. —— —— Report to the Legislature of the state of California, December, 1957. [Sacramento, State print. off.] 1957. 184 p. illus., tables, diagrs.
                                            CO CRcS CSbr CSt

8591. —— San Francisco bay ports commission. A report on intercoastal shipping with special reference to the San Francisco bay ports area, prepared by J.A. Stumpf. [n.p.] 1953. 38 p. (Its report pt. 2)   C

**8592. —— —— A report on Pacific coastwise shipping with special reference to the San Francisco bay ports area, prepared by Ramond Foss Burley. [n.p.] 1953. 39 p. (Its report pt. 3)   C CL

8593. —— San Francisco port authority. Frontiers on the sea (Port of San Francisco). S.F., 1958.
                                                     CRcS

8594. —— San Francisco world trade center authority. Prospectus. S.F., [1951] 55 p. illus.
                            CHi CSfMI CSfSt CSfU CStclU

8595. —— State board of trade. The city of San Francisco. Prepared for the State board of trade... S.F., Mysell-Rollins co., 1900. 82 p.
                             CSj CSmH CU-B NHi NN

**8596. —— —— San Francisco; its commercial, climatic and physical features... [n.p., 1902?] folder (2 l.)   CSmH

8597. —— State college, San Francisco. Bulletin. S.F., 1922– Title varies.   CSfSt

8598. —— —— Cosmopolitan San Francisco; answers to questions of former summer session students at San Francisco state college... S.F., 1935. 61 l. Mimeo.
                                                 CHi CSf

**8599. —— —— San Francisco state college, its second half century. S.F., Priv. print., 1954. 32 p. illus.
                                                     CHi

8600. —— —— Women's faculty club. Yearbook. S.F., 19—?–
CHi has 1951/52„ 1957/58–59, 1960/61.

8601. —— State earthquake investigation commission. The California earthquake of April 18, 1906. Report of the...commission... Wash., D.C., Carnegie inst. of Wash., 1908–10. 2 v. illus., maps.
Available in many California libraries and CaBViPA MiD MoS NN OrU TxU UU ViU

8602. —— —— Preliminary report of... [Berkeley, 1906] 19 p.   CAla CHi OrU

8603. —— State Library. Sutro branch. The Sutro branch of the California state library, by Milton J. Ferguson. [n.p., 19—?] 8 p.   C C-S

8604. —— —— —— The Sutro library, a branch of the California state library. S.F. [195–?] [5] p. Mimeo.   C C-S CHi

8605. —— Superior court (San Francisco) The Bainbridge will contest. Superior court, department nine. Probate. San Francisco, California. James V. Coffey, judge...Opinion of court granting motion for new trial after verdict. S.F., Recorder print. and pub. co., 1914. 18 p. "The will of Caroline H. Bainbridge."   CHi

8606. —— —— Charles L. Fair, plaintiff vs. James S. Angus et al., defendants. Opinion of Hon. Charles W. Slack, judge. [S.F., S.F. law jl., 1896] 34 p.   CHi

**8607. —— —— Maguel Noe, Vincente Noe, Catalina Noe and Catalina Splivalo, plaintiffs, vs. Sigmund Augustine, et als., defendants. No. 52, 756. Decision by A. A. Sanderson, judge. Sept. 8th, 1896. [S.F., Calloway, Gibbings & co., 1896?] [12] p. Compliments of San Miguel defense association. An action to quiet title to an undivided one-half of "something over four thousand acres of land...known as the San Miguel rancho."   CHi

8608. —— —— W. H. Robinson, plaintiff, vs. the Southern Pacific company, defendant... Opinion of the court. Hon. John Hunt, judge...Filed...1892... S.F., W.L. Mitchell, print. [1892] 26 p.   CHi

8609. —— Supreme court. Land titles in San Francisco. Decisions of the Supreme court of the state of California, in the cases of Hart vs. Burnett et al., and Holliday vs. Frisbie... S.F., H.H. Bancroft & co., 1860. 188 p.   C CHi CSfP CSmH CU-B NN

8610. —— —— Tide lands in the pueblo of San Francisco, Cal. Opinions in the cases of United land association et al., vs. Thomas Knight. Rendered January 2d and September 4th, 1890. [S.F.? 1890?] 38 p
                                                 CLU CSf

8611. —— University. Hastings college of the law, San Francisco. Address by Samuel Mountford Wilson delivered at the first commencement...May 30, 1881. S.F., Edward Bosqui & co., print., 1881. 19 p.
                                                     CHi

8612. —— —— —— Catalogue of the officers and students...with a statement of the course of study, etc. 1878/79– S.F., 1878–
CL has 1921–to date? CU-B has 1878/79.

8613. —— —— —— Circular of information... 1891–1892. Sacramento, State print. off., 1892. 15 p.
                                                     CHi

8614. —— —— Heller committee for research in social economics. Cost of living studies. II. How workers spend a living wage. A study of the incomes and expenditures of eighty-two typographer's families in San Francisco, by Jessica B. Peixotto. ... Berkeley, Univ. of Calif. press, 1949. [161]–245 p. incl. tables. (Univ. of Calif. pub. in economics. v.5, no. 3)
                    CL CLSU CLU CO CSf CStmo CU CU-B

8615. —— —— —— Cost of living studies.

Prices for San Francisco, November 1925. Berkeley, Univ. of Calif. press, 1925. 18 l. of tables.   CU

8616. —— —— —— Cost of medical care; the expenditures for medical care of 455 families in the San Francisco bay area, 1947–1948 by Emily Harriett Huntington. Berkeley, Univ. of Calif. press, 1951. 146 p. tables, forms.   CHi CU

8617. —— —— —— The dependent aged in San Francisco. Prepared under the Heller committee... in collaboration with the Coordination committee of the San Francisco community chest... Berkeley, Univ. of Calif. press, 1929. 127 p. tables. (Univ. of Calif. pub. in economics. v.5, no. 1)   CU CU-B

8618. —— —— —— Food for four income levels. Prices for San Francisco 1943–1949. Berkeley, Univ. of Calif. press, 1943–49. 7 v. tables.   CU

8619. —— —— —— Living on a moderate income; the incomes and expenditures of street-car men's and clerks' families in the San Francisco bay region, by Emily H. Huntington and Mary Gorringe Luck, with an introduction by Bruno Lasker... Berkeley, Univ. of Calif. press, 1937. 206 p. incl. tables.   CU

8620. —— —— —— Quantity and cost budget for dependent families or children. Prices for San Francisco, October, 1936–37, March, 1939–45... Berkeley, Univ. of Calif. press, 1936–45. 9 v. in 1. Mimeo. None issued in 1938. Title varies: 1936, Budget for dependent families or children; 1937–1943, Quantity and cost budget for dependent families or children; 1944–1945, Restricted quantity and cost budget for maintenance of families or children; 1946– Quantity and cost budget for dependent families or children.   CU

8621. —— —— —— Quantity and cost budgets for three income levels. Prices for San Francisco. Nov. 1932–1949. Berkeley, Univ. of Calif. press, 1932–49. 1932–1942 include supplements: Clothing budget. Title varies: 1933–1936, Quantity and cost budgets for 1. Family of an executive, 2. Family of a clerk, 3. Family of a wage earner, 4. Dependent families or children; 1937–1941, Quantity and cost budgets for four income levels... 1942, 1946–1949, Quantity and cost budgets for three income levels... 1943–1945, Wartime budgets for three income levels...   CU

8622. —— —— —— Quantity and cost budgets for two income levels: family of a salaried junior professional and executive worker; family of a wage earner. Prices for the San Francisco bay area. 1954–1958, 1961. [Berkeley] 1954–61. diagrs., tables. No more published after Sept. 1961.   CSf CU

8623. —— —— —— Unemployment relief and the unemployed in the San Francisco bay region, 1929, 1934, by Emily H. Huntington... Berkeley, Univ. of Calif. press, 1939. 106 p. incl. tables, form.   CU

8624. —— —— —— Wartime and postwar earnings, San Francisco, 1944–1946. A joint publication of the Heller Committee for research in social economics and the Bureau of business and economic research of the University of California. Berkeley, Univ. of Calif. press, 1948. 129 p.   CU

8625. —— —— **Medical school.** Announcement for the academic year 1864–65, 1871. S.F., 1864–71. 2 v.   CU-B

8626. —— —— —— Plan and announcement of Toland medical college... S.F., Towne and Bacon, print., 1865. 16 p.   CU-B

8627. —— —— —— Valedictory address delivered by Thomas M. Logan, M.D. professor of hygiene; at the commencement exercises... held in Pacific hall, San Francisco, October 29th, 1874. [S.F., 1874] 15 p.   CHi

8628. —— —— —— Same... Delivered in Calvary church, San Francisco, November 4th, 1873. By Edward R. Taylor, and Prof. John F. Morse. S.F., Winterburn & co., print., 1873. 31 p.   CHi

8629. California academy of sciences vs. City and county of San Francisco. ...California academy of sciences, appellant vs. the city and county of San Francisco, et al., respondents. Appellant's points and authorities. S. W. Holladay, attorney for appellant... [S.F.] Bacon print. co. [1894] 44 p.   CU-B

8630. California academy of sciences. [Annual report] 18—?– S.F., 18—?–
CHi has 1917, 1930, 1946–49, 1958, 1960–61.

8631. —— The California academy of sciences. S.F., [n.d.] 12 p. illus.   CHi

8632. —— A century of progress in the natural sciences, 1853–1953. S.F., 1955. 807 p. illus., ports., maps. Includes bibliographies.   C

8633. —— ...Circular. S.F., Print. by F.A. Bonnard, Dispatch off., 1853. 8 p.   CHi CSmH CU

8634. —— Constitution and by-laws... founded April 4, 1853. S.F., 1860. 12 p. Title and printer vary.
CHi (1871, 1876, 1881, 1892, 1904, 1930) CLU (1860) CSmH (1860) CU-B (1860)

8635. —— ...An historical sketch and list of the officers and members, January, 1913. S.F., 1913. 20 p.   CHi

8636. —— Laying the corner-stone of the building of the California academy of sciences. S.F., 1889. 29 p. front.   CHi

8637. —— The North American hall of the California academy of sciences, dedicated September 22, 1916. S.F., 1939. 24 p. illus.   CHi

8638. —— The Simson African hall of the California academy of sciences, dedicated December 14, 1934. S.F., 1937. 31 p.   CHi

8639. California Alpine club. Schedules. no. 1, 1910/11– S.F., 1910–
CHi has no. 6, 1915/16 to date.

8640. California and Hawaiian sugar refining corporation, San Francisco. Twentieth anniversary souvenir... March tenth, nineteen twenty-six. [n.p., 1926] 7 l. illus.   CHi

8641. [California and Nevada newspapers issued at the time of the San Francisco earthquake and fire. S.F., etc., 1906] 1 portfolio.   CU-B

8642. California and New York steamship co. Prospectus... S.F., A. Hamilton, 1857. [8] p. plan.
C CHi CSmH CU-B

8643. California anti-slavery society. Principles and constitution adopted May 20, 1912. S.F. [Marnell & co., 1912] 12 p.   CHi

8644. California art union. Catalogue... S.F., Wade & co., steam bk. & job print. [18—?] 8 p.   CU-B

8645. —— A classified catalogue of the paintings on exhibition at the room of the California art union, no. 312 Montgomery street, with the constitution and by-laws, and list of officers. S.F., 1865. 26 p.   CHi CU-B

8645a. California artillery. 1st California guard, 1849– (Militia) Constitution and by-laws... instituted July, 1849, as revised, April, 1850. S.F., Print. at Alta Calif. off., 1850. 16 p.   CSmH

8646. —— —— Same. By-laws ... instituted July, 1849. Revised May 25th, 1852. S.F., Alta Calif. steam presses, 1852. 16 p.   CU-B

8646a. —— —— Same. Revised May 25, 1862 [!], Feb. 1, 1855, July 27, 1860, July 7, 1864. S.F., Agnew & Deffebach, 1864. 21 p.   CHi

8647. —— —— First California guard. Sir, a court of appeal will be held at the new armory of this corps on the corner of Dupont Street and Broadway, on Saturday, the 28th inst. ... All members having excuses to offer for non-payment of fines and dues will have an opportunity of offering them. Per order, John E. Durivage, acting secretary, San Francisco, Sept. 26th 1850. [S.F., 1850] 1 fold. l.   CU-B

8648. California association of stationary engineers, San Francisco, no. 1. Constitution, by-laws and rules of order ... S.F., Wm. G. Layng, 1884. [26] p.   CHi

8649. California avenue homestead association. Prospectus, articles of association and certificate of incorporation ... S.F., Waters, Newhoff and co., print., 1860. 23 p. illus., table.   CU-B

8650. California Bible society. ... Annual report ... [1st– , 1850?– S.F. [1850?]– CHi has 24th, 27th, 49th, 1874, 1877, 1897/98.

8651. California brass works. Price list ... All kinds of plumbers' brass goods and steam work, manufactured by Weed & Kingwell. S.F., 1872. 1 v. illus.   CU-B

8652. California building, loan and savings society. Seventh annual report ... October 31st, 1867. S.F., Alta Calif. general print. house, 1868. 30 p.   CHi

8653. California camera club. Constitution and by-laws ... S.F., 1896. 24 p.   CHi

8654. California canning peach growers. ... Annual report ... S.F., 1922.   CHi

8655. California casualty indemnity exchange. "California casualty." S.F. [1944] 31 p. ports.   CHi

8656. California chemical paint co. Averill's chemical paint, manufactured by the California chemical paint co., of the purest white and any desired shade of color ... S.F. [1871] 32 p.   CU-B

8657. California Chinese exclusion convention. Proceedings and list of delegates, California Chinese exclusion convention, called by the Board of supervisors ... and commercial organizations. S.F., Star press–James H. Barry, 1901.   CStclU

8658. California cloak co. Telegraph cipher of fall & winter styles, 1883, Charles Mayer, California cloak company. S.F. [1883] [5] p.   CU-B

8659. California club of California. State and national legislation, international legislation, municipal work accomplished and under way by the California club since its organization December 27, 1897 ... S.F., 1916. 16 p.   CHi

8660. —— **Outdoor art league dept.** San Francisco the beautiful. [n.p., n.d.] [5] p.   CHi

8661. California dramatic association. The constitution and by-laws ... S.F. [J.P. Tracy & co.] 1878. 16 p.   CHi CSf

8662. California electric supply co. ... Distributors and manufacturers of high grade radio apparatus ... Bulletin 100, August 1920. [S.F.? 1920?] [16] p. illus.   CHi

8663. California electrical works. California electrical works ... [n.p.] 1905. [9] p. illus., ports. Reprint. from the *Jl. of electricity, power and gas*, June 1905.   CHi

8664. —— Catalogue ... all kinds of electrical apparatus made to order & repaired; contractors for the construction of telegraph lines ... S.F., 1878. 36 p.   C-S

8665. —— Same. 3d. ed. [S.F., Crocker] 1880. 44 p. illus.   CHi CU-B

8666. —— [Catalogue] Condulets ... S.F., 1906. 48 p. illus. (Bul. no. 10)   CHi

8667. —— [Catalogue] Electro medical supplies. Oakland [189–?] 1 v. illus.   CU-B

8668. California Froebel society. Sixteenth year, 1896–1897. [S.F.? 1896?] 15 p.   CHi

8669. California fruit canners association. California fruit canners association ... S.F. [1915?] 40 p.   CHi

8670. California furniture co. ... (N. P. Cole & co.) [Catalogue] S.F. [1900?] 158 p. illus.   CU-B

8671. —— Their homes and how we have furnished them. [S.F., 189–?] [16] p. illus.   CU-B

8672. California genealogical society. ... Organized February 12, 1898, incorporated, January 19, 1921. [S.F.? 1921] 7 p.   CHi

8673. —— International congress of genealogy in San Francisco, California, July 26th to 31st, 1915. [S.F.? 1915?] [3] p.   CHi

8674. —— ... Officers and members. S.F., 1912– CHi has 1912–13, 1915, 1918.

8675. California guide book co. Traveler's guide to San Francisco. S.F., c1928. 128 p. illus., fold. map.   CU-B

8676. California historic landmarks league. Constitution and by-laws ... S.F., 1902. 14 p.   CHi

8677. California historical society. [Annual report] S.F. [1922?– Includes list of members. CHi has 1922, 1924, 1926–27, 1931, 1947, 1949, 1951, 1956.

8678. —— By-laws adopted April 7, 1922. [S.F., 1922] 7 p.   CHi

8679. —— Same, adopted September 11, 1957, effective January 1, 1958, amended April 15, 1959. [S.F., 1960] 4 l.   CHi

8680. —— [Descriptive brochure] S.F., 1923– CHi has 1923–24, 1926–27, 1933.

8681. —— Early San Francisco in colored prints. [S.F., 1932] 14 col. pl.   CO CU-B

8682. —— Official opening, Pioneer hall, San Francisco, 1938. [S.F., 1938] 3 p. Contributed for the official opening by Lawton Kennedy.   CHi

8683. —— Papers. S.F., 1887. 1 v. in 2 pts. Partial contents: v.1, pt. 1, p. 41–60, History of the Pious fund, by J. T. Doyle.—p. 61–94. The first phase of the conquest of California, by William Carey Jones.—v.1, pt. 2, History of the College of California, by S. H. Willey. CHi CLgA CSS CSd CSjC CStbS CStclU CU-B

8684. —— Pictorial treasures, opening exhibition, Nov. 30 and Dec. 1, 1956. S.F. [1956?] 4 p.   CHi

8685. —— Schubert hall. [S.F., 1962] 12 p. illus.   CHi

8686. —— Secretary's report, 1890/91. [S.F., 1891] [4] p.   CHi

8687. —— 2090 Jackson Street, 1894–1956. [S.F., 1956?] 4 p. illus.   CHi

8688. California horticultural society. Report of the second annual fair of the ... society, held in the city of San Francisco, from the 2d to the 26th September, 1858. S.F., Towne & Bacon, 1858. 44 p.   CLU CU

8689. California hotel. For tourists: facts worth knowing. [S.F., 1893] 32 p.   CHi

8690. California ice manufacturing co. California ice manufacturing company (limited) to be incorporated under the laws of the state of California. [S.F.] Cuddy & Hughes, print, 1871. 33 p.   CU-B

8691. California infantry. 1st regt. Co. B. By-laws of the City guard, Co. B, 1st infantry regiment, 2d brigade, N.G.C. Adopted by the company, March 24th, 1887. Approved by the commander-in-chief, March 29th, 1887. S.F., J. Winterburn & co., print., 1887. 14 p.   CHi CU-B

8692. —— —— The "City guard". A history of company "B", 1st regiment infantry, N.G.C. During the Sacramento campaign... Including a brief history of the company... March 31, 1854, to July 3, 1894. S.F., Filmer-Rollins electrotype co. [1895] 263 p. illus., ports. Reviews the railroad strike in California.
          CHi CLU CSf CSfCW CSfP CSfU CSjC

8693. —— —— **Co. C.** Souvenir National guard. [Historical review of the National guard of California and description of new armory dedicated October 9, 1893] [S.F.? 1893] 32 p. illus., ports.   CU-B

8694. —— —— **Co. F.** By-laws of the Light guard, Company F, 1st infantry, 2d brigade, N.G.C. ... Adopted, August 6th, 1878... S.F., Women's cooperative print. union, 1878. 18 p.   CU-B

8695. —— —— **Co. I.** Rules and regulations of the Sumner light guard, Co. I, 1st regiment, 2d brigade, California militia... S.F., Towne & Bacon, print., 1863. 15 p.   CSf CU-B

8696. —— **2d regt. Co. F.** History of "F" co., 2d inf'ty, N.G.C. and annual report of Col. Wm. R. Smedberg, president, April 1st, 1879. [S.F.] Alta Calif. print. house, 1879. 44 p.   CU-B

8697. —— —— —— Souvenir, "F" Company veterans, San Francisco, Cal., November 21, 1891. [Comp. and arranged by Colonel W. B. Burtis, president. S.F., 1891] [19] l. illus., port.   CU-B

8698. California ink co. ...Annual report. S.F., 1960–
CHi has 1960–62.

8699. —— Inks. S.F. [19—?] 1 v. of illus. (part col.)   CU-B

8700. California insurance company of San Francisco. San Francisco conflagration losses. [S.F., 1907?] 31 p. illus.   CHi

8701. California kindergarten training school. [Brochure] Organized 1880. S.F., 1889. 11 p.   CHi

8702. —— Chips from a kindergarten workshop. [S.F., C.A. Murdock & co., print., 1892] 48 p.   CHi CU-B

8703. —— [Commencement] programme. S.F., 1888–
CHi has 1888, 1894–95, 1897.

8704. California labor exchange. Report of the transactions of the California labor & employment from April 27th, 1868, to November 30th, 1869. [Sacramento, Gelwicks, state print., 1870]   CSmH

8705. California midwinter exposition hotel directory. v.1, no. 2– 1894– S.F., 1894– 1 v. illus., maps.   CU-B

8706. California mill co. ...Mill work in all its branches. [S.F., Edw. S. Knowles, 1904] 211 p. illus., diagrs.   CHi

8707. California mining bureau association. Constitution, by-laws, rules of order and order of business... S.F., M.D. Carr & co., print., 1865. 24 p.   CHi

8708. California mining co. Annual report. S.F., 1877–
CHi has 1877–80.

8709. The California monopolists against the Sutro tunnel... [S.F.? 1874] 6 p. Contents: Agreement, signed by Adolph Sutro.–Report of a meeting of the Board of trustees of the Ophir gold and silver mining company, signed by Jos. Marks.   CHi CLO

8710. California mutual life insurance co. S.F. [1868?]   CSmH

8711. California, New York and European steamship co. Prospectus... N.Y., 1858. 20 p.   CHi

8712. California Northwestern railway. All aboard ... the picturesque route of California [Marin, Sonoma, Mendocino, Humboldt and Lake counties] [S.F., 1899?] 32 p. illus.   CHi CStrCL

8713. —— San Francisco to Ukiah, Cal., with all connections; also a general description of places of importance... S.F., 1899. 40 p. illus. (Its Official bul. v.11, no. 11, July, 1899)   CSf

8714. California Pacific title insurance co. Plan and agreement December 11, 1924. D. L. Randolph [and others] committee... [S.F.? 1924] 16 p.   CU-B

8715. —— Plan and agreement for the reorganization of California Pacific title insurance company. John S. Drum, A. Crawford Greene, committee ... [S.F.? 1924] 13 p.   CU-B

8716. California Pacific utilities co. Annual report.
CL has 1954–60.

8717. —— Prospectus. 33,610 shares... common stock... [n.p.] 1946. 55 p. map.   CHi

8718. California packing corp. Annual report...
CHi has [1917–19], 1934, 1937–50, 1952–57, 1959–60.
CL has 1949–61.

8719. —— Certificate of incorporation; certificate of increase of number of directors; certificate of alterations of provisions of certificate of incorporation... [S.F., Taylor & Taylor, 1936] 89 p.   CHi

8720. —— ...A study of impressive progress. S.F., Dean Witter & co. [n.d.]   CHi CL

8721. California paint co. Price list. S.F. [1881] 1 v.   CU-B

8722. California pharmaceutical society and college of pharmacy. Proceedings... annual meeting. [1st– , 187–?– S.F. [187–?–
CHi has 10th, 1879.

8723. California polo and pony racing association. By-laws adopted... [S.F.] 1903. 10 p.   CHi

8724. California powder works. By-laws ... S.F., Edward Bosqui & co., 1865. 18 p.   CHi

8725. —— Santa Cruz gunpowder....Mills at Santa Cruz; office 314 Cal. street, San Francisco. S.F., E. Bosqui & co., print. [n.d.] [15] l.   CHi

8726. California promotion committee. Around San Francisco bay. S.F., 1908. 27 p. map, tables.   CU-B

8727. —— Official program. California's welcome to

the fleet, San Francisco, May, 1908. [S.F., 1908] 40 p. map.   CHi CU-B

8728. —— San Francisco and its environs. S.F., 1903. 112 p. map.
      C CHi CL CSf CSfCW CSmH CU-B NN

8729. **California psychical research society.** Announcement... [S.F., 1921] 10 p. "Founded September 13, 1912."   CHi

8730. **California redwood association.** California redwood for the engineer. [S.F.] c1917. 19 p. illus.
                                                               CHi

8731. —— The home of redwood erected in the south gardens of the Panama-Pacific international exposition, San Francisco, 1915, by the California redwood association with the cooperation of Humboldt, Mendocino and Sonoma counties. Louis Christian Mullgardt, architect. [S.F., Taylor & Taylor, 1915] [34] p. illus.
                                                               CHi

8732. —— Specialty uses of California redwood. S.F. [c1917] 24 p. illus.   CHi

8733. **California safe deposit and trust co.** [Directors, officers, statement of condition...] S.F., Crocker, 1893. 8 p. illus., map.   CHi
      Other editions followed.   CHi (1894, 1897)

8734. **California savings and loan society.** Report. 2d, 1874. S.F., 1874 [i.e. 1875] 1 v.   CU-B

8735. —— Semi-annual statement for term ending June 30, Dec. 31, 1882. [S.F., 1882?] 2 v.   CHi

8736. **California saw works.** Price list and catalogue. [S.F., Martin & Martin, etc., n.d.] illus.
      CHi has 1900, 1903. CU-B has 1909.

8737. **California seed co.** ...1913 catalogue of seeds, trees, plants. [S.F., 1913?] 71 p. illus.   CHi

8738. **California silk manufacturing co.** Act of incorporation and by-laws... S.F., A.L. Bancroft & co., 1871. 12 p.   CHi

8739. **California society for the prevention of cruelty to children.** Annual report [S.F.? 18–?–] Society founded 1857.
      CHi has 1904, 1911, 1917.

8740. —— Everyday episodes of our forty years' work. [S.F.] 1917. 45 p. illus.   CU-B

8741. **California state chamber of commerce.** Golden Gate bridge opening March of progress program, Tuesday, February 9, 1937. S.F., Station KGO, 1937. 4 p. Mimeo.   CRcS

8742. **California state sunday school convention.** Proceedings and address...held in San Francisco, Calif., May 29th, 30th and 31st, 1860. S.F., Towne & Bacon, 1860. 24 p.   C CBPac CU-B

8743. **California state teachers institute.** Proceedings of the California state institute and educational convention at San Francisco. May 27–June 1, 1861. Sacramento, Charles T. Botts, State print., 1861. 166 p.
                                                         C CU-B

8744. **California state vinicultural society.** Report of the annual meeting...San Francisco, August 27, 1879. S.F., S.F. merchant, 1879. 14 p. Reprint from the *San Francisco merchant*, September 12, 1879.   CHi

8745. **California sugar & white pine co.** ... Wholesalers of California sugar pine, California white pine, Arizona white pine, doors, sash, mouldings, lath, incense cedar pencil slats. [S.F., Union litho. co., 1912?] [52] p. of illus.   CHi

8746. California sugar refinery. [n.p., 1951?] 16 [i.e. 30] l. illus., mounted photos.   C

8747. **California teachers' association. Bay section.** Constitution... [Oakland, McCombs print., 1918?] 8 p.   CHi

8748. —— —— Educational exhibits, Panama-Pacific international exposition, April 5–10, 1915... S.F., Hansen co., 1915. 15 p.   CHi

8749. **California tennis club.** Constitution and by-laws [and] membership roll to which is added a brief account of the origin and development of the club. S.F., 1930. 32 p. illus., ports.   CHi

8750. **California trust co.** [Circular] S.F. [1870?]
                                                               CSmH

8751. **California type foundry.** Price list specimens. S.F. [1947?] 8 p. illus.   CHi

8752. —— Specimens of roman and display letter manufactured by the California type foundry...Wm. Faulkner & sons, agents. S.F. [1868?] [20] p.   CHi

8753. **California water and telephone co.** Annual report.
      CHi has 1953. CL has 1954–60.

8754. —— Prospectus.
      CL has 1955.

8755. **California wine association.** ...Capital ten million dollars...Principal cellars: "Winehaven" on San Francisco bay. [S.F., Stanley-Taylor co., 1910?] [62] p. illus.   CHi

8756. **California wire cloth co.** [Catalog] [S.F.? 1916?] 58 p. illus.   CHi

8757. **California wire works.** [Catalogue. no. 1– , 187–?–] S.F. [187–?–19—?]
      CHi 1892 and no. 12, 16–17, 3d ed., 21, pt. 1, [188–?], [189–?], 1894, 1900. CU-B has [1879] and no. 12, 16, 17, 3d ed., 20, pt. 1, [188–?], [189–?], 1894, 1898.

8758. **Californians, inc., pub.** The chapter in your life entitled San Francisco. Some notes of introduction together with 81 photographs. S.F., 1936. [62] p. illus., map.
      Other editions followed: 1936, 1937, 1939, 1940, 1941, 1946, 1947, 1948.
      Available in many California libraries and CaBViPA CoD CoU MiD NHi NN OU

8759. —— San Francisco, center of the California vacationland; a guide book for visitors. S.F., 1933. 63 p. illus.   CHi CU-B

8760. —— Same. 1934. 63 p. illus.
                                    C CLSU CO CSf CU-B

8761. —— 254 days that made California tourist history; a report on the tourist in this state during the 1939 exposition. [S.F.] 1939. [8] p. (Its bul. Dec. 1939)
                                                               CSfU

8762. **[California's diamond jubilee committee]** California's diamond jubilee, celebrated at San Francisco, September 5 to 12, 1925. S.F., E.C. Brown [c1927] 107 p. illus.
      C CHi CL CLO CLSU CLU CO CSfCW CSfU CSfWF-H CSjC CSmH CU-B MoS N

8763. —— Official program, California's diamond jubilee, San Francisco, Sept. 5th to 12th... [S.F., Sunset press, 1925] 47 p. illus., ports.
                                          CHi CLU CSf CU-B

8764. —— 65 views of diamond jubilee celebration, San Francisco, September 5–12, 1925. 1850–1925. Admission day parade and night parade. [S.F., 1925] [32] p. illus.   CHi CLU

8765. **[California's golden jubilee committee]** Official souvenir of California's jubilee held at San Francisco, Calif., beginning January 24, 1898 and ending January 29, 1898, containing the programme of each day's events. ...Comp. and published under the supervision of the Jubilee committee. [S.F.] Crocker [1898] 88 p. illus., ports.   CHi CLO CSf CSmH

8766. Calkins, Robert De Blois, and Hoadley, Walter E., jr. An economic and industrial survey of the San Francisco bay area... Sacramento, State planning bd., 1941. 298 p. maps. Reproduced from typew. copy.
CLSU CO CSdS CSf CSfSt CSfU

8767. —— Same ... (summary... Sacramento, State planning bd., 1942. 28 p.
CLSU CO CSdS

8768. Calling and address list of San Francisco, Oakland and Alameda and San Rafael...1889-90. S.F., Crocker [1889?]   CLU CU-B

8769. Cambrian mutual aid society of San Francisco. Constitution, by-laws and rules of order... established September 3d, 1869, incorporated July 23d, 1870. S.F., Winterburn & co., 1873. 48 p.   CU-B

8770. Camera de commercio Italiana di San Francisco. Relazione riassuntiva dell'opera... S.F., Dempster bros., 1894. 24 p.   CHi

8771. Cameron, Roy Schooling. An examination of residential exclusion provisions in zoning districts permitting heavy industry in the San Francisco bay area. [Berkeley, 1951] Thesis (M.A.)—Univ. of Calif., 1951.
CU

8772. Camp, William Martin. San Francisco, port of gold. Garden City, N.Y., Doubleday, 1947. 518 p. illus., ports.
Available in many California libraries and CaBViPA IC MiD MoS N NjR ODa TxU UPB

8773. Campbell, Maury Barrett. Pay dirt! San Francisco; the romance of a great city. [S.F., Vigilante publications, 1949] 66 p. illus. (part col.) ports., col. maps.
C CBev CHi CL CLU CO CSjC CU-B

8774. Campbell, Metson & Drew. ...In the matter of the application of Eugene E. Schmitz for a writ of habeas corpus... [S.F.? 1907] 199 p.   CU-B

8775. Candrian, Herman Anton. Candrian's double indexed street number guide with car-o-grams and new maps of San Francisco and northern California, showing auto roads... S.F. [n.d.] 96 p. plans.   C CHi

8776. —— Candrian's new San Francisco street guide including Daly City, Colma, Bay Shore City, Brisbane, South San Francisco, San Bruno, San Bruno Park, San Mateo, Lomita Park, Burlingame, Millbrae, Belle Air Park, Hillsborough, with the latest map of city and county of San Francisco...Comp. by G. E. Owens. S.F., Kohnke print co., c1936. 248 p. map.   CHi

8777. —— Same. Latest certified ed. S.F. [1938?] 96 p. map.   CHi

8778. Canessa, Ercole. Catalogue, Canessa's collection, Panama-Pacific international exposition, 1915. [S.F., Canessa print. co., 1915] [59] p. pl., coat of arms.
CU-B

8779. Cannon, George Quayle. Writings from the "Western standard," pub. in San Francisco, California. By Elder George Quayle Cannon. Liverpool, G.Q. Cannon, 1864. 512 p.   CHi CLO

8780. Cannon, J. B., & co. Catalogue of valuable city property, to be sold by J. B. Cannon & co. ...Friday, August 9, 1850... S.F., Alta Calif. steam presses, 1850. 8 p.   CU-B

8781. Canon Kip community house. [Report] [n.p., 1942] [4] p. Originally Cathedral mission of the good samaritan.   CHi

8782. Cardinell-Vincent co., pub. San Francisco, the city loved around the world. [S.F., c1915] [48] p. illus.   C CHi CStmo

8783. —— San Francisco two years after the great fire of April 18, 19, 20, 1906. S.F. [1908] [54] p. illus.
CHi CSmH CU-B

8784. The Cardoza co. Type faces. [S.F.] 1952. [6] p.   CHi

8785. Carey, Joseph. By the Golden Gate; or, San Francisco, the queen city of the Pacific coast; with scenes and incidents characteristic of its life... Albany, N.Y., Albany diocesan press, 1902. 291 p. port.
C CHi CL CLU CO CSf CSfCW CSfMI CSfP CSmH CU-B NHi UHi

8786. Carlisle (A.) & co. First hundred years; printers, lithographers, stationers. [S.F., 1952] [44] p. illus., ports.   C CHi CU-B

8787. —— Printers, lithographers, stationers... [S.F., 1949?] [10] p. illus. Illustrations of new building.   CHi

8788. Carlisle, Henry C. Outline of the pioneer period 1846-1849 in reference to San Francisco street names. [S.F., 1958] tables.   CU-B

8789. —— San Francisco street names; sketches of the lives of pioneers for whom San Francisco streets are named. [S.F., Am. trust co., 1954] [53] p. illus., map.
C CB CHi CL CLO CLU CLgA CO CSalCL CSf CSfCW CSfU CSfWF-H CStclU CU-B CoU

8790. Carlson, Wallin John. A history of the San Francisco mining exchange. [Berkeley, 1941] Thesis (M.A.)—Univ. of Calif., 1941.   CU

8791. Carmelite monastery of Cristo Rey. S.F., 1958. p. 274-324. illus. (*St. Ignatius church bul.*, v.44, no. 9)
CSf

8792. Carmick, Edward H., et al vs. the United States. In the United States court of claims. Edward H. Carmick, Albert C. Ramsay vs. the United States. [Wash., D.C., 1853-66] v.p. 18 pamphlets bound together on the subject of the contract for transportation of mails from Vera Cruz, Mexico, via Acapulco, Mexico, to San Francisco.   CSfCW

8793. [Carnahan, Melissa Stewart McKee] Personal experiences of the San Francisco earthquake of April 1906. [Pittsburgh, Pa., Pittsburgh print. co., 1909] 62 p. illus.   CSf CSmH CU-B

8794. Carr, John R. Catalogue and price list. [1891] S.F. [1891] 1 v. illus.   CU-B

8795. Carr, William George. John Swett; the biography of an educational pioneer... Santa Ana, Fine arts press, 1933. 173 p. illus., ports.
CBb CHi CLgA CMartC COnC CRcS CSf CSfCW CStmo

8796. Carrasco, H. C. A San Franciscan tells the story of the Mooney case... [S.F.?] Railroad employes' committee for the release of Thomas J. Mooney [193-?] 30 p. illus., ports.   CU-B

8797. Carrillo, Carlos Antonio. Exposicion dirigada á la Camara de diputados del congreso de la Union por el Sr. D. Carlos Carrillo, diputado por la Alta California. Sobre arreglo y administracion del fondo Piadoso. Mexico, setiembre 15 de 1831. Mexico, Imprenta del C. Alejandro Valdés, 1831. 16 p. Concerns the regulation and administration of the Pious fund.   C-S CHi CU-B

8798. —— Same. Translated and edited by Herbert Ingram Priestley. S.F., J.H. Nash, 1938. xx [16] p.
Available in many California libraries and N

8799. Carroll, Luke Michael. Holy Cross parish and Lone Mountain district of San Francisco...published in honor of golden jubilee, October, 1937. [S.F.] 1937. 64 p. illus., ports., map.
C CHi CL CLgA CSf CSfCW CSfU CSmH CSrD CU-B

8800. Carter, John Denton. Before the telegraph: the news service of the San Francisco bulletin, 1855–1861 ... [Glendale, 1942] p. 301–317. "Reprint. from *Pac. hist. review*, v.XI, no. 3, Sept., 1942." CSf CU-B

8801. —— The San Francisco bulletin, 1855–1865: a study in the beginnings of Pacific coast journalism... [Berkeley, 1941] 250 l. Thesis (Ph.D.)—Univ. of Calif., 1941. CU CU-B

8802. Cary, Thomas G. The first San Francisco vigilance committee. [1881] 78–88 p. Excerpt from *Internat. review*, July 1881. C

8803. Casserly, Eugene. In memoriam... [S.F., Bar of S.F., 1883] 9 p. CHi

8804. Castle, Michael, et al., vs. Siegfried, John C., et al. In the Supreme court of the state of California. Michael Castle, James A. Robinson and Elena A. Selby, partners under the firm name of Macondray & co., plaintiffs and appellants, vs. John C. Siegfried and Max Brandenstein, partners under the firm name of Siegfried & Brandenstein, defendants and respondents. Transcript on appeal. Galpin & Ziegler, attorneys for plaintiffs and appellants. Mastick, Belcher & Mastick, attorneys for defendants and respondents... S.F., Mysell & Rollins [1892] 150 p. illus. CHi

8805. Castro y Rossi, Adolfo de. Portrait of Ambrose Bierce. N.Y., Century, 1949. 351 p. illus.
CHi CU-B

8806. Catalogne, Gérard de. Les nostalgies de San Francisco. [Haiti, Deschamps, 1945?] 85 p. illus. CL

8807. Cathedral mission of the good samaritan. ...Year book, 1903. [S.F., The Church press, n.d.] 49 p. pl. CHi

8808. Cather, Helen Virginia. The history of San Francisco's Chinatown. [Berkeley, 1932] Thesis (M.A.) —Univ. of Calif., 1932. CU

8809. Caughey, John Walton. Hubert Howe Bancroft, historian of the West... Berkeley & L.A., Univ. of Calif. press, 1946. 422 p.
Available in many California libraries and IHi

8810. Celebration of the eighty-eighth anniversary of the national independence of the United States, July 4th, 1864. S.F., Painter & co., 1864. 20 p. CHi

8811. Celebration of the sixtieth anniversary of the capture of the city of Mexico...at the Presidio of San Francisco, Cal., Saturday, September 14, 1907. [S.F.] 1907. 16 p. illus., port. C CU-B

8812. Celtic union. The Irish fair to be held at Mechanics' pavilion, San Francisco, Saturday, August 20th, to Saturday, September 10th, 1898. S.F., Crocker, 1898. 70 p. illus., ports. CLU CU-B

8813. Cemetery beautifying and anti-removal association. [Constitution. n.p., 1921?] [4] p. CHi

8814. [Cemetery defense league] Argument against the Calvary cemetery ordinance and why it should be repealed. [n.p., 1924?] [3] p. CHi

8815. Central anti-coolie club of the eleventh ward of San Francisco. Constitution and by-laws. S.F., 1876. [10] p. CLU

8816. Central bureau of San Francisco organizations. Memorial on Hunter's point naval base site submitted to Joint congressional committee on naval base... November 16, 1920. [S.F., 1920?] 35 l. maps.
C CU-B

8817. Central Pacific railroad. Rules, regulations and instructions for the use of agents, conductors, etc. S.F., 1882. 224 p. CHi

8818. Central Pacific railroad company vs. the State Board of equalization. In the Supreme court of the state of California. The Central Pacific company, petitioner, vs. the State Board of equalization, respondent. Argument of Creed Haymond. S.F., Crocker [1881?] 54 p. CHi

8819. Central park homestead association. Abstract of title of lands of the Central park homestead association...William Hollis, president, Edward Barry, secretary. S.F., J. Winterburn & co., 1867. 80 p. fold. map. CHi

8820. Central railroad co. Articles of association and by-laws... S.F., Waters bros. & co., 1862. 17 p.
CHi CSmH (imp.)

8821. Century club of California. Constitution, by-laws and regulations, adopted March 30, 1904. [S.F.] Woodward press, 1904. 29 p. CHi

8822. —— Historical sketch list of officers, list of members, four years' work, constitution, by-laws. S.F., 1893. 29 p. illus. CHi

8823. Le Cercle commercial français de San Francisco. Guide franco-californien, 1931–1932. Édité par le Cercle commercial français de San Francisco, 1932. 222 p. illus., ports. CLSU CSf

8824. Chadwick guide systems. All about San Francisco. Know and visit unique places located on keyed map of principal streets. New map of Golden Gate park. S.F., 1939. illus., map. CAla

8825. —— San Francisco guide. [1930?–1945?] Title varies. 1943? copyright by James L. Delkin.
C (1943?) CAla (1939) CHi (1937, 1943? 1945) CLU (1943?) CU-B (1930?)

8826. Chamber of commerce journal. Issued by the Chamber of commerce of San Francisco. v.1, Apr.-Oct. 1911. S.F., 1911. illus. With October 1911 the *Merchants' association review* is incorporated with this under the title: *San Francisco chamber of commerce journal.*
CSf

8827. Chambliss, William H. Chambliss' diary; or, Society as it really is... N.Y., Chambliss & co., 1895. 408 p. illus., ports.
C CBb CHi CLSU CLU CO CSf CSfCW CSfP CSfWF-H CSmH CU-B

8828. Chamisso, Adelbert von. Bemerkungen und Ansichten von dem Naturforscher der expedition... (In Kotzebue, *Entdeckungs-reise*...Weimar, Gebrüdern Hoffman, 1821. v.3. illus., map) "For German and English texts of the portions relating to California, see August C. Mahr's *The visit of the "Rurik" to San Francisco in 1816,* Stanford University, Calif., 1932, the English translation of the *Tagebuch* being reprinted from *Overland monthly,* 1873, v.10. This translation was again reprinted, San Francisco, 1936, under title: *A sojourn at San Francisco Bay, 1816*...illustrated by a series of drawings...by the Rurik's artist, Louis Choris."—Waters.
CL CSmH CU-B

8829. —— Same, with title: Reise um die welt... auf der brigg *Rurik*, kapitain Otto v. Kotzebue (In v.1–2 of his *Werke.* Leipzig, 1836)   CHi CU-B (1852)

8830. —— Same (In v.4–5 of *Werke.* Berlin, Bong & co.)   CSdS

8831. —— Remarks and opinions...(In v.2–3 of Kotzebue, *Voyage of discovery...* London, 1821)   CU-B

8832. —— A sojourn at San Francisco bay, 1816, by ...the Russian exploring ship *Rurik*... S.F., Bk. club of Calif., 1936. 16 p. illus. "250 copies printed by the Grabhorn press for the Book club of California in December 1936."
C CHi CL CLO CLU CLgA CMerCL CO CSf CSfU CSmH CStmo CU-B CaBViPA

8833. Chapel, Charles Edward. Levi's gallery of long guns and western riflemen. [S.F., Levi, Strauss & co., 1950?] [12] p. fold.] illus., ports.   CHi

8834. Charities endorsement committee of San Francisco. ...Handbook of endorsed charities, 1904. S.F., Merchants' assoc. of S.F. [1904]   CU-B

8835. —— Same, 1909. S.F., Merchants' assoc. of S.F. [1909]   CU-B

8836. Charlton, E. P., & co., pub. San Francisco and California... Portland, Me., L. H. Nelson co., c1905. [48] p. illus.   C CHi

8837. —— Views of San Francisco and vicinity. [S.F., 1903?] [32] p. illus.   CHi

8838. Chart, Obed. Memorial of Obed Chart and others of relinquishment of the interest of the United States in certain lands at the Presidio of San Francisco to holders of deeds thereto from the city and county of San Francisco. S.F., Women's union print., 1874. 16 p. fold. maps.   CU-B

8839. —— Same. S.F., Upton bros., steam print., 1886. 15 p.   CHi CU-B

8840. [Charter association] New charter catechism; plain questions and honest answers. [S.F., 1897?] 13 p. (Pub. no. 7)   CHi

8841. Charter convention of one hundred, San Francisco, 1897. ...Reports of committees considered and amended in committee of the whole... [S.F., 1897?] 147 p.   CU-B

8842. Chatom, Paul, jr. Industrial relations in the brewery, metal and teaming trades in San Francisco. [Berkeley, 1915] Thesis (M.S.)—Univ. of Calif., 1915.   CU

8843. Cheney, D. B. The Baptists; their history, faith, and polity, a lecture delivered before the Addisonian society, San Francisco. S.F., Towne & Bacon, 1866. 60 p.   CHi

8844. Cheney, Sheldon. An art-lover's guide to the Exposition; explanations of the architecture, sculpture and mural paintings... Berkeley, At the sign of the Berkeley oak, 1915. 100 p. illus., plans.
CHi CMartC CO CRedl CSfP CSfWF-H CU-B

8845. Chevalier, August, pub. "The Chevalier" illustrated map guide of San Francisco, "the exposition city"... S.F., c1913. 96 p. fold. map.   CHi CSf

8846. —— 'Up to date' San Francisco and vicinity (also 7 views of California missions). S.F. [1913?] [3] p. 29 pl.   CU-B

8847. Chi Alpha, San Francisco. Constitution, by-laws, original members and present members. [S.F., Cubery & co.] 1873. [10] p.   CHi

8848. Chinatown, San Francisco, Cal. S.F., Bancroft co., 1890. 5–8 l. 12 pl.   CBb

8849. Chinatown declared a nuisance!... [S.F.? 1880] 16 p.   CHi CLU CSmH

8850. Chinatown; San Francisco's bit of old China. [S.F.] Ching Wah Lee studio [1960?] [16] p.   CHi

8851. Chinese consolidated benevolent association. Financial report of relief fund, 1920/22. [S.F., Thing Wan, print., 1922?] 216 p. illus., map. In Chinese.   CHi

8852. —— Memorial of the Six Chinese companies; an address to the Senate and House of Representatives of the United States. Testimony of California's leading citizens before the joint special congressional committee. Read and judge us. San Francisco, Dec. 8th, 1877. S.F., Alta print. [1877?] 53 p.   CHi

8853. Chinese hospital. The Chinese hospital of San Francisco... Oakland, Carruth & Carruth, print., 1899. 15 p.   CU-B

8854. The Chinese in California; description of Chinese life in San Francisco, their habits, morals and manners. illus. by Voegtlin. S.F., Pettit & Russ, 1880. 122 p. illus.   CHi

8855. Chit chat club. ...Annual meeting...1st–1875?– S.F., 1875?–
CHi has 12th, 17th, 19th, 36th, 1886, 1891, 1893 (copy), 1910. CSfSt has 5th, 1879. CU-B has 3d–6th, 16th, 36th, 1877–80, 1890, 1910.

8856. —— ...The Chit chat club of San Francisco, 1948–1954. Organized November 1874. [S.F., 1955?] [14] p.   CHi CSmH CU-B

8857. Chittenden, Hiram Martin, and Powell, A. O. Report on the water supply system of the Spring Valley water company, San Francisco, Cal. ... [n.p., 1912] 44 p. illus., map.
C CBu CHi CL CLU CSf CSfCSM CSfCW CSmH CStoC CU-B

8858. Chivers, Herbert C., co., architects, San Francisco. Bungalows. [n.p., n.d.] 32 p. illus., plans. (Bungalow book no. 1)   CHi

8859. Chollar Potosi mining co. Annual report... June 10, 1873. S.F., A.J. Leary, print., 1873. 18 p.   CHi

8860. Choris, Ludovik. Port San Francisco et ses habitants... (In his Voyage pittoresque autour du monde. Paris, 1822. pt. 1.) 10, 3 p. illus. Photostatic reproduction, on 28 l. Choris was the artist of the first von Kotzebue expedition, which visited San Francisco in 1816 on the ship Rurik.   CLU CSfCP CSmH

8861. —— San Francisco one hundred years ago, tr. from the French of Louis Choris by Porter Garnett; with illustrations from drawings made by Choris in the year 1816... S.F., A. M. Robertson, 1913. 20 p. illus. "The description of San Francisco here presented for the first time in an English translation constitutes one chapter of a work entitled *Voyage pittoresque autour du monde...* Paris, 1822."—Translator's note.
Available in many California libraries and CaBViPA MiD MoS NN ViU

8862. —— Voyage pittoresque autour du monde, avec des portraits de sauvages d'Amerique... Paris, Firmin Didot, 1822. col. pl.   CHi CU-B

8863. Christian Science benevolent association on Pacific coast, San Francisco. Sanatorium... 400 West Portal avenue, San Francisco... [Bost., Christian Science pub. soc., 1951] 15 p. illus.   CHi

8864. Christie machine works. On the job half a century; being the story of Christie machine works, 1893–1943. S.F., 1944. 28 p. illus., ports.   CHi

8865. Chu, Peter. Chinese theatres in America... Bureau of research, Federal theatre project (Division of W.P.A.) region of the West... [n.p., pref. 1936] 303 l. Typew.   CU-B

8866. Church union of San Francisco. Constitution and by-laws... S.F., Print. at the Churchman off., 1870. 11 p.   CU-B

8867. —— Same. S.F., Cubery & co., 1874. 14 p.
                                                  CHi CSmH

8868. Cioffi, Ralph Walter. Mark Hopkins, inside man of the big four. [Berkeley, 1950] Thesis (M.A.)—Univ. of Calif., 1950.   CU

8869. Citizen, *pseud.* Letters to the Hon. Wm. M. Gwin, by "Citizen." S.F., 1854. 22 p.   C CSmH CU-B

8870. Citizens' alliance of San Francisco. A few of the things done by the Citizens' alliance of San Francisco. [S.F., 190–?] 22 p.   CU-B

8871. City and county federation of women's clubs. Yearbook. v.1– , 1918–20– S.F., 1920–
  C (v.1) CHi v.1, 1918–20, 1923/25–1925/27) CSf (v.1)

8872. City of San Francisco and a glimpse of California. S.F., Enterprise pub. co., 1889. 137 p. illus., ports.   C CHi CLU CU-B

8873. City of San Francisco and the state of California. [S.F., Metropolitan pub. co., 1892] 171 p. illus. Commercial directory.
                        C C-S CHi CLU CSf CSmH

8874. City street improvement co. ...Incorporated May 11, 1891, general contractors. Streets, sewers, wharves, bridges... S.F., 1898. [39] p. illus., tables.
                                                  CU-B

8875. Civic league of improvement clubs and associations of San Francisco. Constitution and by-laws. [S.F.] Arrow print. co., 1907. 14 p. Organized May 1906 as Civic league of San Francisco.   CHi

8876. —— Same. [S.F.] A. Carlisle & co., 1912. 15 p.   CHi

8877. —— Report on Hunter's point naval base submitted to joint congressional committee on naval base... November, 1920. [n.p., n.d.] 43 p. illus.   CSf

8878. —— **Tunnel committee.** Tunnels: their effect on traffic conditions, business development and real estate values; gateways to the greater San Francisco. [S.F., 1912?] 32 p. illus., map.   CHi

8879. Clabrough, Golcher & co. Catalogue of arms, ammunition, fishing tackle and sporting goods. [S.F., 18—?–]
CHi has no. 15, 17, 21–22, [1890], 1892/93, 1902/03–1903/04.

8880. Clark, Arthur H. The clipper ship era; an epitome of famous American and British clipper ships, their owners, builders, commanders, and crews. N.Y., Putnam, 1910. 404 p.   C-S CHi CSfCW CSto

8881. Clark, Jacob, vs. Shaffner, Taliaferro P. Argument of William P. Chambers [in the case of] Jacob Clark...against Taliaferro P. Shaffner, impleaded with the Atlantic giant powder company, of California...in the Superior court of New York. N.Y., Russell bros., print., 1875. 130 p.   CHi

8882. Clark (N.) & sons. [Catalogue. Manufacturers of clay products] [S.F., 191–?–] illus.
CHi has no. 25, no. 30, rev. Jan. 1, 1921.

8883. Clark, William Squire. Letters of ...edited by Grace Clark Strohn. [n.p., n.d.] 14 p. illus.   CHi

8884. Clarke, William Carey. The vegetation cover of the San Francisco bay region in the early Spanish period. [Berkeley, 1959] Thesis (M.A.)—Univ of Calif., 1959.   CU

8885. Clay products institute of California. Earthquakes and building construction; a review of authoritative engineering data and records of experience ... L.A., c1929. 110 p. illus., fold. pl.   CU-B

8886. Clear light oil co. Prospectus... [Oakland, Tribune, 1900?] 16 p. illus., map.   CHi

8887. Cleaveland, Alice Mae. The North bay shore during the Spanish and Mexican regimes. [Berkeley, 1933] Thesis (M.A.)—Univ. of Calif., 1933.
                                                  CU CU-B

8888. Clemens, Samuel Langhorne. Mark Twain: San Francisco Virginia City territorial enterprise correspondent; selections from his letters to the Territorial enterprise: 1865–1866. Ed. by Henry Nash Smith & Frederick Anderson. S.F., Bk. club of Calif., 1957. 117 p. illus., ports.
CHi CLO CLSM CSalCL CSfU CStclU CSto CaBViPA

8889. —— Washoe giant in San Francisco being heretofore uncollected sketches by Mark Twain [pseud.] published in the *Golden era* in the sixties...Collected and edited, with an introduction, by Franklin Walker. S.F., G. Fields, 1938. 143 p. illus. "The complete list of Mark Twain material in '*The Golden era*'": p. 141–142. "Printed by the Ward Ritchie press."
Available in many libraries.

8890. Clement, Ada. A few reminiscences by Ada Clement for her family and friends. [S.F., 1952] 42 p. port.   CHi

8891. Cloman, Flora (Smith) Clement. I'd live it over. N.Y., Farrar & Rinehart [c1941] 380 p. illus., ports., pl.   CRedCL CU-B

8892. Cloud, Archibald Jeter. Lowell high school, San Francisco, 1856–1956; a centennial history of the oldest public high school in California. Palo Alto, Pac. bks. [c1956] 52 p. illus.   C CHi CSf

8893. Coast counties gas and electric co. Annual report [191–?–] [n.p. 191–?–]
CHi has 1939–40, 1942, 1945–47.

8894. —— Prospectus. 75,000 shares ... Series A, 4% preferred stocks... [n.p.] 1947. 39 p.   CHi

8895. Cobb, H. A. Catalogue of valuable property, situated in San Francisco, for sale at auction on Wednesday, April 15, 1857... S.F. [1857] 8 p. illus. (plan) (Auctioneer's suppl., to the *Calif. advertiser, and guide to business*...v.1, no. 8, April 15, 1857)   CLU CSmH

8896. Cobb, H. A., and Sinton, R. H. ...Executor's sale. Public auction of the Broderick estate, in the city of San Francisco...on Saturday, Nov. 30, 1861... [S.F.] Alta job off. [1861] 48 l. John A. McGlynn, executor of the estate.   CLU CU-B

8897. —— Same, on Saturday, Sept. 13, '62, at 11 o'clock, A.M., at Platt's music hall, Montgomery street ... [S.F.] Alta job print. [1862] 52 p.
                                          CHi CLU CSmH

8898. —— Same, on Thursday, Feb. 5, 1863, at 12 o'clock M., at salesroom, 406 Montgomery St. ... S.F., Alta job print. [1863] 18 p.   CLU

8899. —— ...Great peremptory sale of fifty vara lots in Precita valley, and 4, 5, 6 & 7 acre lots on the

Bernal heights, and other valuable real estate in the city of San Francisco...on Saturday, July 14, 1860... [S.F.] Alta Calif. job print. [1860] 15 p. illus., fold. plan.
CLU

8900. —— ...Great peremptory sale of 500 fifty vara lots, in the Precita valley tract, city of San Francisco ...on Monday, September 26th, 1859... [S.F.] B. F. Sterett, print. [1859] [3]–26 p.   CLU   CU-B

8901. —— ...Great peremptory sale of 1000 homestead lots! In the Hayes valley tract, city of San Francisco...on Saturday, June 11th, 1859... [S.F.] Sterett, print. [1859] 12 p.   CHi   CLU   CSmH

8902. —— ...Public auction of 550 homestead lots, in the city of San Francisco...on April 27, 1861. [S.F.] Print. at Alta job off. [1861] 24 p.
CHi   CLU   CSmH   CU-B

8903. —— ...Public auction of 400 homestead lots in the city of San Francisco...on Saturday, Oct. 26, 1861... [S.F., 1861] 15 p.   CLU

8904. —— ...Public auction of real estate in the city of San Francisco...on Monday, Oct. 10, 1859... [S.F.] B. F. Sterett, print. [1859] 49 p. illus.
CHi   CLU   CSmH   CU-B

8905. —— ...Public auction of real estate in the city of San Francisco...on Tuesday, Nov. 15, 1859... [S.F.] B. F. Sterett print. [1859] [47] p. illus., map.
CLU   CSmH   CU-B

8906. —— ...Public auction of real estate, in the city of San Francisco...on Saturday, July 28, 1860... [S.F.] Alta job off. print. [1860] 16 p. illus.   CLU

8907. **Cobbledick (Frank M.) co.** Ball & roller bearings... [n.p., 1926] 40 p. illus.   CHi

8908. **Coblentz, Stanton Arthur.** Villains and vigilantes; the story of James King, of William, and pioneer justice in California... N.Y., Wilson-Erickson, 1936. 261 p. illus., ports. "Principal authorities consulted": p. 255–256.
Available in many California libraries and CaBViPA MiD   N   NN   NjR   ODa   OU   T   UPB

8909. —— Same. N.Y., T. Yoseloff [1957] 261 p. illus.
C   CBev   CChiS   CLSU   CMerCL   CMon   CNf   CRb CSS   CSdS   CSfSt   CSfU   CSlu   CStoC   CStrCL   MiD NN

8910. **Cody, Alexander John, Father.** Lt. Albert J. Hogan, A.A.F. S. F., Univ. of S.F. press, 1945. 41 p. port. Biographical sketch of a young San Franciscan.
CLgA

8911. —— A memoir, Richard A. Gleeson, S.J., 1861–1945. S.F., Univ. of S.F. press, 1950. 215 p. ports.
CHi   CLgA   CSfU

8912. **Coffey, James V., vs. Edmonds, M. A.** ... James V. Coffey, contestant vs. M. A. Edmonds, respondent. No. 7800. Contestant's reply brief. Jno. C. Burch, Geo. Flournoy, of counsel for Coffey. Thos. F. Barry, Crittenden Thornton, attorneys... [S.F.] W.M. Hinton & co., print. [1881] 17 p.   CU-B

8913. **Coffman, William Milo.** American in the rough; the autobiography W. M. (Bill) Coffman. N.Y., Simon, c1955. 309 p. illus.   CHi   CMont   CSf

8914. **Cogswell polytechnical college.** Announcement. 1888/89– S.F., 1889–
CU-B has 1888/89, 1893/94, 1900/01, 1902/03–1903/04.

8915. —— Prospectus. S.F., W.A. Woodward & co., print., 1888. 12 p. illus., port.   CU-B

8916. **Cohen, Alfred Andrew.** An address on the railroad evil and its remedy delivered...at Platt's hall, San Francisco, on Saturday, Aug. 2, 1879. S.F., Francis, Valentine & co., 1879. 23 p.   CHi

8917. **Cohen, Presley W., vs. Sharp, George F.** In the Supreme court of the state of California. Presley W. Cohen (by his guardian, Mary G. Cohen), plaintiff and appellant, v. George F. Sharp, defendant and respondent. Points and authorities for appellant. Morgan & Heydenfeldt, atty's. for appellant. S.F., Swett & Bumm's steam print. establishment, 1872. 4 p.   CHi

8918. **Cohen, Sandford H.** Cohen's legal, professional and commercial guide for 1881. S.F., S.W. Raveley, 1881. 284 p.   C-S   CSfWF-H

8919. **Coit, Daniel Wadsworth.** Drawings and letters...An artist in El Dorado, ed., with a biographical sketch, by Edith M. Coulter. [S.F.] Print. for Bk. club of Calif. by Grabhorn, 1937. 31 p. illus.
C   CBb   CHi   CL   CLU   CLgA   CO   CRic   CSf   CSfCW CSfSt   CSfWF-H   CSmH   CU-B

8920. —— A memoir of Daniel Wadsworth Coit of Norwich, Connecticut, 1786–1876. Cambridge, Univ. press, 1909. 178 p. port.   CBb   CHi

8921. **Colasanti, Arduino, comp.** [Catalog] Italian fine art section [Panama-Pacific exposition, San Francisco]... [Roma, E. Calzone, 1915] 62 p. pl.
CStoC   CU-B

8922. —— Same. In Italian. 60 p. pl.   CU-B

8923. **Cole, Cornelius.** Memoirs of Cornelius Cole, ex-senator of the United States from California. N.Y., McLoughlin bros., 1908. 354 p. front. (port.)
Available in many California libraries and AU   N   T ViU

8924. **Cole, Peter.** Cole's war with ignorance and deceit, and his lecture on education, delivered in the St. Cyprian church, Tues. eve., Aug. 11, 1857. S.F., Print. by J.H. Udell and R.P. Locke, 1857. 81 p.
C   CHi   CSmH   CU-B

8925. **Coleman, Charles M.** P.G.& E. of California, the centennial story of Pacific gas and electric company, 1852–1952. N.Y., McGraw-Hill, 1952. 385 p. illus.
CChiS   CHi   CLO   CLgA   CNa   CSd   CSf   CSfCW CSfP   CStmo   CV   CaBViPA

8926. **Coleman, Harry J.** Give us a little smile, baby. N.Y., Dutton, 1943. 258 p. illus., ports., facsims. Autobiography...newspaperman, cartoonist and photographer.   CHi   CSd   CU-B

8927. **[Coleman, William Tell]** San Francisco vigilance committees. By the chairman of the committees of 1851, 1856 and 1877. [N.Y., 1891] illus., ports. (Century mag., Nov. 1891, p. 133–50)
C   CHi   CL   CU-B

8928. **Collier, Charles W.** The story of the Limited editions group of San Francisco. [S.F.] Print. by the members, 1955. 21 p. illus., ports.   CHi

8929. **Collin, Francis Eric.** Collin's guide of San Francisco... [S.F., c1913] 160 p. illus., map.   CO

8930. **Collins, Arthur Llewellyn.** A history of the boot and shoe industry of San Francisco. [Berkeley, 1934] Thesis (M.A.)—Univ. of Calif., 1934.   CU

8931. **Collins, Asa Weston.** Doctor Asa; illus. by Paul Landacre. L.A., Ward Ritchie, c1941. 172 p.
CBb   CHi

8932. **Colmar, Mary.** A trip through Golden Gate park...dedicated to the California state floral societies. 8th ed. [S.F.] St. Francis press, c1927. [12] p. illus., map.   CHi

8933. Colton, Ellen M., vs. Stanford, Leland, et al. In the Superior court of Sonoma county. Ellen M. Colton, plaintiff, vs. Leland Stanford, et al., defendants. Argument of Hall McAllister, counsel for defendants. [n.p., n.d.] 2 v.   CHi

8934. —— ...Argument of L. D. McKisick, of counsel for defendants. S.F., Crocker, 1885. 871 p.
                                                          CHi

8935. —— In the Superior court of the city and county of San Francisco, state of California. Ellen M. Colton, plaintiff vs. Leland Stanford, et al., defendants. (Re-engrossed copy) Amended complaint...G. Frank Smith, attorney for plaintiff. Stanly, Stoney & Hayes, D. M. Delmas and W. T. Wallace, of counsel. [n.p., 1883] 67 p. Contains also: Answer of defendants Stanford, Huntington and Crocker.   CHi CU-B

8936. —— ...Answer of defendants Stanford, Huntington and Crocker. S.F., Crocker [1882] 65 p. Bound with Colton vs. Stanford et al. Amended complaint...   CHi CU-B

8937. [Columbia park boys' club of San Francisco] [S.F., etc., 1898–1908] 9 v.   CSf CU-B

8938. Columbia steel co. San Francisco-Oakland bay bridge. [S.F., 1935] [20] p. illus.   CHi CU-B

8939. Coman, Edwin T., jr., and Gibbs, Helen M. Time, tide and timber; a century of Pope & Talbot. Stanford, 1949. 496 p. illus.
Available in many libraries.

8940. Commercial soap co. Price list...[S.F.? 1885?] 15 p.   CHi

8941. Committee of forty-three. The state of the city; a report to the people of San Francisco on industrial relations...delivered by Mr. A. Crawford Greene at a luncheon[!] meeting in the Palace hotel, on Monday 9th, 1938. [S.F., 1938] [15] p.   CU-B

8942. Committees on pilotage. Report of the Committees on pilotage appointed January, 1883, by the California ship owners' association, the Board of trade of San Francisco, and the Chamber of commerce of San Francisco, for the purpose of endeavoring to reduce the pilotage and towage charges at San Francisco by legislative enactment. S.F., G. Spaulding & co., print., 1883. 21 p.   CU-B

8943. Commonwealth club of California. ... Half century observance...1903–1953... [S.F., 1953] [20] p. Anniversary issue of *The commonwealth.*   CHi

8944. —— Transactions. v.1– 1903–
C CL CLSU (v.3–) CLU (1906/07, 1925–26) CO CSdS CSf CSjC CSmH CU-B MoS (v.2–5, 1906/07– 1910)

8945. Commonwealth investment co. Annual report. 1st– 1933?– [S.F.? 1933?–
CHi has 1st?–3d, 1933–1935.

8946. Community chest of San Francisco. Directory of social and health agencies, San Francisco... S.F., 1924– 1st directory issued in 1924, 2d in 1927.
CHi has 1938. CSf has 1938, 1944, 1946/47–1950/51, 1953/54–1958/59. CSfCW has 1955. CU-B has 1936, 1938, 1944, 1946/47.

8947. —— List of contributors of ten dollars and over... [S.F., 1928] 140 p.   CHi

8948. —— List of contributors of twenty-five dollars and over... 1927, 1929. [S.F., 1927–29]   CHi

8949. —— Our common heritage...silver anniversary report, 1947. [22] p.   CHi

8950. —— **Committee on the aged.** One in ten;

facts about San Francisco's older people... S.F., 1955. 36 p. charts.   CSf

8951. Compressed air and general machinery co. General catalogue 10A... [Chicago, R.R. Donnelley & sons co., 1912?] 687 p. illus.   CHi

8952. —— Giant air compressors, giant drills, mining machinery. S.F. [Press of Hicks-Judd co., 189–?] 68 p. illus.   CU-B

8953. Concordia club. Constitution and by-laws... S.F., 1881. 20 p.   CLU

8954. Conference on labor relations and arbitration, San Francisco, 1956. Proceedings for a Conference on labor relations and arbitration at Fairmont hotel, San Francisco, May 23, 1956. Presented by Institute of industrial relations, Graduate school of business administration, School of law, University extension of the University of California, in cooperation with American arbitration association [and others] Conference coordinator, Virginia B. Smith. Berkeley [1956?] 65 l.   CL

8955. Conkling, Roscoe, and Shipman, William D. Central Pacific railroad company in equitable account with the United States...a review of the testimony and exhibits presented before the Pacific railway commission ... N.Y., Henry Bessey, print., 1887. 134 p.   CHi

8956. Conmy, Peter Thomas. The date of the founding of San Francisco. Oakland, Oakland pub. lib., 1947. 23 l. Mimeo.
Available in many libraries.

8957. —— The friar Joseph Sadoc Alemany, bishop of Monterey, Alta California, 1850–53, archbishop of San Francisco, 1853–1885. [n.p.] 1943. 6 p. Mimeo.
                                                        CLgA

8958. —— The history of St. Francis church in San Francisco, 1849–1949. 130 p. Typew.   CO

8959. —— Philip Augustine Roach, 1820–1889, California pioneer. S.F., Grand parlor, Native sons of the golden west, 1958. 29 p. port.
CBaB CCoron CHi CLU CP CRcS CRic CSS CSd CSf CSfSt CStmo CSto

8960. —— San Francisco city and county consolidation, 1856. [S.F.] Grand parlor, Native sons of the golden west [1955?] 7 p. Mimeo.
         CHi CLU CO CRcS CSmat CU-B MoS

8961. —— 60 years of the past presidents association of the Native sons of the golden west, 1900–1960. S.F., General assembly, Past presidents' assoc., 1959. 64 p. ports.   CHi

8962. —— The vigilance committee of 1856. [S.F. 1938] 5 p.   CO

8963. Connelly (James A.) co., auctioneers. Prior properties will be sold at public auction by referees, by order of Superior court, city and county of San Francisco, state of California. Time of sale: Thursday, October 13th, 1927 at 12 o'clock noon... [S.F., 1927] [11] p.
                                                       CU-B

8964. Connolly, John F. X., Father. The University of San Francisco "a credo—and a commitment to excellence"... N.Y., Newcomen soc. in No. Am., 1960. 24 p.   CHi

8965. Conrad, Barnaby. San Francisco; a profile with pictures. N.Y., Viking press [1959] 228 p. illus. (part col.) ports. (A studio book)
Available in many California libraries and CaBViPA NN ODa

8966. Conroy & O'Connor. Catalogue...hardware, metals and miscellaneous goods. S.F. [1866?] 132 p.
                                                        CHi

8967. Conservative rubber production co. Bulletin no. 2 to the shareholders...November 1st, 1902... [n.p., 1902?] [12] p. illus.   CHi

8968. Consolidated Virginia mining co. Annual report... S.F., Stock report off., 1877–79. 3 v.   CHi

8969. [Contemporary periodical and newspaper accounts of the San Francisco earthquake and fire. 1906] 1 v. illus.   CU-B

8970. Continental building and loan association. By-laws. [S.F., 1894] 30 p.   CHi

8971. Cook, Morton L., comp. Tivoli opera house souvenir containing a complete record of performances from July 3, 1879 to July 3, 1896, accurately compiled from our files. The only theatre in the United States devoted exclusively to opera... [S.F., 1896] [46] p. illus., ports.   CHi

8972. Coolidge, J. A., vs. Kalloch, I. S., mayor. J. A. Coolidge, plaintiff, vs. I. S. Kalloch, mayor, defendant, argument of W. T. Baggett upon defendant's demurrer. W. T. Baggett and H. E. Highton, attorneys for defendant. (May 27, 1880) S.F., Pac. coast law print. and pub. co., 1880. 22 p.   CU-B

8973. Coon, Henry Irving. Life of Henry P. Coon. S.F., Priv. print. [n.d.] 14 p. Life of an early mayor of San Francisco.   CSfCW

8974. Cooper medical college. Annual announcement...1883–1908. S.F., 1883–1908. fronts. (plans) (*Its* Miscellany. no. 3–16)
CHi has 1902/03. CU-B has 1883–91, 1893, 1895, 1900/ 01, 1904/05, 1908/09.

8975. —— Clinics. Annual report for 1894 of the clinics conducted under the auspices of Cooper medical college... S.F., Woodward [1894] 42 p.   CHi

8976. —— Morse dispensary. Annual report... 1883/84–93. S.F., 1885–93. (*Its* Miscellany. no. 17–25)
CHi has 1885/86, 1892/93. CU-B has 1883/84–1887/88, 1889/90.

8977. The Co-operato. ...The Co-operato no. 2, 645 Folsom street, San Francisco. [S.F., Town talk print, n.d.] 7 p. Home opened Dec. 22, 1898.   CHi

8978. Corbett, Francis J. Report on the Presidio of San Francisco. [S.F., 1954] 32 l.   CU-B

8979. Corcoran, Frank P., comp. Origin and development of San Francisco high schools. [n.p., n.d.] 9 p. Mimeo.   CHi

8980. Corinthian yacht club. By-laws and rules. S.F. [Cooper & co.] 1897. [66] p.   CHi

8981. Cornelius, Fidelis, Brother. Keith, old master of California. N.Y., Putnams [1942–1957] 2 v. illus. (part. col.), ports., facsims. v.2, Supplement. [Fresno, Acad. lib. guild]
CChiS CHi CLgA CRedlCL (v.1) CSfCW CSfWF-H (v.1) CYcCL

8982. Cornwall, Bruce. Life sketch of Pierre Barlow Cornwall. S.F., A.M. Robertson, 1906. 87 p. illus.
CBb CHi CP CSd CSfCW CSfP CU-B

8983. Coro foundation. A study of the effect of land acquisition for the Bayshore freeway on San Francisco industry. S.F., 1954. 1 v. unp. tables.   C

8984. Cory, Clarence Linus. [Official correspondence, 1907–1910. S.F., C.L. Cory, 1910?] 24 l. Binder's title. Facsimile reproductions of correspondence and newspaper clippings relating to the charge brought by the Public ownership association of San Francisco that Professor Cory was soliciting the opportunity at Pasadena to make a report against publicly owned utilities.

Correspondence relates to his first Pasadena report in 1907 and to the proposed report in 1910.   CLU

8985. Cory, Harry Thomas. ...Water supply of the San Francisco-Oakland metropolitan district... [N.Y., 1916?] 199 p.   CLU CU-B

8986. Cosmopolitan publishing co. The industries of San Francisco, California...together with a historical sketch of her rise and progress. S.F. [1889] 196 p. illus.
C CSf CU-B

8987. Cosmos club. Constitution, by-laws, house rules and list of members...April, 1907. [S.F., 1907] 44 p. front.   CU-B

8988. Costansó, Miguel. Noticias of the port of San Francisco in letters of Miguel Costansó, Fray Juan Crespi and Fray Francisco Palou in the year 1772. [S.F., Windsor press, 1940] 22 p. Translated by Mrs. Edward E. Ayer.
C CHi CL CLSU CLU CO CSf CSmH CU-B NHi

8989. Cote, Reynold Frederick B. The history of the San Francisco stock and bond exchange. [Berkeley, 1922] Thesis (M.A.)—Univ. of Calif., 1922.   CU

8990. Courtney, William J. San Francisco's anti-Chinese ordinances, 1850–1900. [S.F.] 1956. 88 l. Typew. Thesis (M.A.)—Univ. of San Francisco, 1900.   CSfU

8991. Coverdale and Colpitts, New York. Report on the Bridge railway of the San Francisco-Oakland bay bridge, May 15, 1953. N.Y., 1953. 68 l. map, diagrs. (fold.), tables. Reproduced from typew. copy.   C

8992. Cowan, Robert Ernest. Booksellers of early San Francisco. L.A., Ward Ritchie, 1953. 111 p. ports. Bibliography: p. 102–111.
C CBb CHi CLO CO CP CSS CSd CSf CSfSt CSfU CSt CU-B CaBViPA ViU

8993. —— ... Forgotten characters of old San Francisco. [L.A.] Ward Ritchie, 1938. 65 p. illus., ports. At head of title: 1850–1870.
Available in many California libraries and MoS

8994. Cowan, Sam K., ed. Gold book; official guide and directory, Golden Gate bridge fiesta. [Franklin Johnson, publisher] S.F., W.L.Mackey & co., c1937] 128 p. illus., maps.   C

8995. Cox, Jerome B., vs. Delmas, D.M. In the Supreme court of the state of California. Jerome B. Cox, plaintiff and respondent, vs. D. M. Delmas, defendant and appellant. Brief for respondent. Galpin & Ziegler, attorneys for respondent... S.F., W.A. Woodward & co. [1892?] 86 p.   CHi

8996. Cox (Thos. A.) & co. Cox's seed annual. Oakland & S.F., 1884–
CHi has 1884, 1889, 1893, 1905.

8997. Crafts, James F. A romance of insurance: Fireman's fund insurance company, 1863–1951...[Address delivered at a meeting of the Newcomen society, San Francisco, June 4, 1951] N.Y., S.F. [etc] Newcomen soc. in No. Am., 1951. 24 p. illus.   CU-B

8998. —— Same, with title: Fireman's fund, a character sketch... [S.F., Kennedy-Ten Bosch, print., 1951] 24 p. illus.   CHi

8999. Cram, Charles S., vs. Grady, John H. Charles S. Cram, plaintiff, vs. John H. Grady, tax collector of the city and county of San Francisco, defendant. Transcript on appeal. [S.F.] Barry, Baird & co., General print. [1884?] 15 p.   CU-B

9000. Crane, James M. The past, the present and

the future of the Pacific. S.F., Print. by Sterett & co., 1856. 79 p.
C CHi CLSM CLU COMC CP CSfP CSmH CSt CU-B CtY

9001. **Crespi, Cesare.** San Francisco e la sua catastrofe. S.F., Tipografia internazionale, 1906. 66 p. 27 pl. CSf CSmH CU-B

9002. **Crocker, Aimée.** And I'd do it again. N.Y., Coward, 1936. 291 p. illus., ports. At head of title: Aimée Crocker (Princess Gallitzine) CSfCW CU-B

9003. **Crocker, H. S., co., pub.** Catalogue and price list of drawing materials and surveyor's instruments, 1900. [S.F.?, 1900] 312 p. illus. CHi

9004. —— Catalogue of legal, official and miscellaneous blanks, revised March 1892... S.F., Crocker, 1892. 62 p. illus. CHi

9005. —— Same. Catalog 5, rev. 1920. CHi

9006. —— Descriptive catalogue of blank books, memorandums...1877. S.F., 1877. 1 v. illus. CU-B

9007. —— Descriptive catalogue of ruled and flat papers, envelopes, cards and card board, shipping tags ...1878. S.F., 1878. 1 v. illus. CU-B

9008. —— Midwinter fair and the Golden State. Art views. S.F., 1894. 2 pts. in 1 v. (Colored art views, nos. 1-2) CHi CLU CLgA CSf CU-B (no. 1)

9009. —— Souvenir of San Francisco. S.F., 1915. [46] p. 23 p. of illus. CHi CSf

9010. —— ...Stationery catalog. [S.F., 1930?] 545 p. illus. (part col.) CHi

9011. **Crocker, William H.** In memoriam. S.F., Calif. acad. of sciences, 1938. 6 p. port. CHi

9012. —— William H. Crocker, 1861-1937. [S.F., Print. for Californians, inc., by Taylor & Taylor, 1938] [3] l. CHi

9013. **Crocker-Citizens national bank.** Annual report.
CHi has 1944, 1946-54, 1956-57. CL has 1957-60.

9014. —— The Crocker national bank of San Francisco, successors September 1st, 1906 to the Crocker-Woolworth national bank of San Francisco... [S.F., 1906?] [21] p. illus. CHi

9015. —— Episodes in the industrial progress of the west. Portfolio number 1. [S.F., 1934] [12] l. illus. CHi

9016. —— Growing and building with the west; a brief history of the Anglo California national bank of San Francisco. [S.F., 1937?] [12] p. illus. CHi CU-B

9017. —— A map of the city and county of San Francisco; being a brief review of the peoples, personalities and places that help make our town the fabulous city by the Golden Gate. S.F., 1949. 8 p. illus., map. CRcS

9018. —— San Francisco, a credit study of its municipal bonds. [S.F., c1936] [30] p. illus., map., tables. CU-B

9019. —— San Francisco—world city. [S.F.] 1957. [28] p. illus. "First printing, June, 1955... Third revised printing, October, 1957." COHN

9020. **Crocker-Woolworth national bank of San Francisco vs. the Nevada bank of San Francisco.** In the Supreme court of the state of California. The Crocker-Woolworth national bank of San Francisco plaintiff and respondent, vs. the Nevada bank of San Francisco, defendant and appellant. Argument of Mr. D. M. Delmas for the appellant, before the court in bank. [S.F.] The Star press [1895?] 135 p. CHi

9021. **Crockett, Peter Campbell.** Trans-Pacific shipping since 1914. [Berkeley, 1922] Thesis (Ph.D.)— Univ. of Calif., 1922. CU

9022. **Croke, James, Father.** In memoriam of the Very Rev. James Croke, D.D., formerly Vicar-general of the archdiocese of San Francisco, Cal. Westchester, N.Y., Boys N.Y. Catholic protectory print., 1889. 19 p. CSfCW

9023. **Crompton, Arnold.** Apostle of liberty: Starr King in California. Bost., Beacon press, 1950. 74 p. port. CBb CHi CL CLSM CP CSd CSdU CSf CSfP CSjC CStmo CSto

9024. **Cronin, Bernard Cornelius.** ...Father Yorke and the labor movement in San Francisco, 1900-1910... Wash., D.C., Catholic univ. of Am. press, 1943. 239 p. (Catholic univ. of Am. Studies in economics, v. 12) CHi CL CLU CLgA CO COHN CSf CSmH CSrD

9025. **Cross, Ira Brown.** ...Collective bargaining and trade agreements in the brewery, metal, teaming and building trades of San Francisco... Berkeley, Univ. of Calif. press, 1918. 364 p.
CL CLSU CLU CSf CU-B

9026. [**Crowe, Frederick E.**] Seeing San Francisco by kodak the fourth day after the clock stopped, 5:16 A.M. April 18, 1906... [L.A., Chamber of commerce relief fund, 1906] [60] p. illus. CLU CSf CU-B

9027. **Crown point gold and silver mining co.** Report...May, 1874. S.F., Stock report print., 1874. 25 p. CHi

9028. **Crown Zellerbach corp.** ...Annual report. [n.p., 19—?—] col. illus., map. CHi has 1952, 1955, 1957, 1959, 1961-62.

9029. **Cubery, William M.** Fifty years a printer. [S.F., Cubery & co., 1900?] 26 p. illus. CHi

9030. **Culinary workers, bartenders, and hotel service workers, San Francisco.** Wage scale and working conditions...effective September 1, 1950. [n.p., 1950] 42 p. CHi

9031. **Cummings, Carlos Emmons.** East is East and West is West; some observations on the world's fairs of 1939 by one whose main interest is in museums. [East Aurora, N.Y., Roycrofters, 1940] 382 p. illus. CL

9032. **Cunningham, Curtiss & Welch.** Glimpses of San Francisco: photogravures. S.F., c1899. 32 pl. C CHi CLU CU-B NN

9033. —— San Francisco illustrated. Photo-gravures. S.F., Author; Brooklyn, N.Y., Albertype co. [c1899] 27 pl. C NN

9034. —— Same. c1900. CSf CSmH

9035. —— San Francisco [views] [S.F., 1901] 30 mounted pl. CHi CSfCW CU-B

9036. —— Select San Francisco; photo-gravures. S.F., 1898. [66] pl. CU-B

9037. **Curley, John E.** Civilian defense in San Francisco. S.F., 1942. 67 p. clippings, diagr. Thesis (M.A.)—Univ. of San Francisco, 1942. CSfU

9038. **Curro, Evelyn.** First annual Americana calendar. San Francisco cable car edition; with twelve historic cars in full color, dated from 1873 to 1951. S.F., Curro co., 1950. 24 p. col. illus. CHi CSf

9039. **Curtis, George M.** The Fair case in California. By George M. Curtis, of the New York bar. Freeport, N.Y., E. Bartlette Helland, 1899. 20 p. CHi

9040. Curtis, H. Taylor, auctioneer. Administrator's sale [of] valuable and historical paintings to close the estate of the late Thomas Hill, the great American painter. Descriptions by Katherine Hilliker. [S.F., International print. co., 1913] [32] p. illus.   CHi

9041. Curtis, Hal. Starr King, patriot and mason. Limited ed. [written for the 1951 golden jubilee celebration of Starr King lodge no. 344, F. & A. M.] S.F., Crane print. co., c1951. 43 p.   CHi CSf CSfP

9042. Curtis studios, inc. The Wickham Havens collection...paintings...furniture...unrestricted public sale April 5, 6, 7, 1933. Exhibition and sale at the Curtis studios. S.F., 1933. 49 p. illus.   CHi

9043. Cushing, John E. Captain William Matson (1849–1917) ; from a handy boy to shipowner. S.F., Newcomen soc., 1951. 28 p. illus.   CHi

9044. Custom house regulations at San Francisco, California. February, 1864. S.F., Edward Bosqui & co., 1864. 54 p.   CHi

9045. Cutler, Leland W. America is good to a country boy. Stanford, 1954. 271 p.
                              C CHi CPa CSd CSf

9046. Cypress lawn cemetery association. Cypress lawn cemetery. S.F., Sunset press, 1905. 46 p. illus.
                                                      CHi

9047. —— Same. S.F., 1922. [65] p. illus.   CHi

9048. Daggett, Stuart. Chapters on the history of the Southern Pacific. N.Y., Ronald, 1922. 470 p. illus., maps.   CChiS CLgA CSf CSto

9049. Daily commercial news. ...Centennial of gold discovery. Special edition, January 21, 1948. S.F., 1948.   CHi

9050. —— The Raker bill and the Hetch Hetchy controversy...Reprint. S.F., 1920. 28 p.
                              CL CSf CSt CU-B

9051. Dairy delivery co. ...Organized June 1, 1906. [S.F., Stanley-Taylor co., n.d.] [24] p. illus.
                                                      CHi

9052. Dakin, Susanna (Bryant) The perennial adventure; a tribute to Alice Eastwood, 1859–1953. S.F., Calif. acad. of sciences, 1954. [51] p. illus., ports.
                              CHi CRcS CSf CU-B

9053. Dalziel-Moller co., San Francisco. ...Catalog D 1915...plumbing supplies and fixtures... [N.Y., Force pub. co., inc., n.d.] 319 p. illus.   CHi

9054. Dames Françaises. Grand promenade-concert patriotique donné par les Dames Françaises pour la bénéfice des familles des morts et blessés de l'Armée Française, à Mechanics' pavilion, les 22, 23, et 24 Septembre, 1870; catalogue général des objets présentés au comité des Dames Françaises... S.F., Mahon, Rapp, Thomas & co., 1870. 23 p.   CHi

9055. Dana, Julian. A.P. Giannini giant in the west ... N.Y., Prentice-Hall, 1947. 345 p. port.
CHi CNa CRcS CRic CSd CSfP CStclU CU-B CViCL

9056. —— The man who built San Francisco; a study of Ralston's journey with banners... N.Y., Macmillan, 1936. 397 p. illus., ports.
Available in many libraries.

9057. Danielson, Melvin David. Origin and development of teacher training in San Francisco state college. [Berkeley, 1960] Thesis (Ed.D.)—Univ. of Calif., 1960.   CU

9058. Danilevitch, Eugene Boris. United States trade with Siberia, with special reference to San Fran-

cisco. [Berkeley, 1926] Thesis (M.A.)—Univ. of Calif., 1926.   CU

9059. Danis, George Hearst. The marketing of men's clothing in San Francisco. [Berkeley, 1934] Thesis (M.A.)—Univ. of Calif., 1934.   CU

9060. Dare, Helen. Tributes to Anne Bremer, by Helen Dare, Charles Erskine Scott Wood [and others] S.F., Print. for Albert M. Bender by John Henry Nash, 1927. 31 p.   CHi

9061. Dare, Richard Kock. The economic and social adjustment of the San Francisco Chinese for the past fifty years. [Berkeley, 1959] Thesis (M.A.)—Univ. of Calif., 1959.   CU

9062. Dashaway association. Constitution and by-laws...Adopted May 3d, 1862. S.F., Print by Waters bros & co., 1862. 20 p.   CU-B

9063. Daughters of the American colonists. San Francisco chapter. Historic spots in California. [n.p., n.d.] [22] l. illus. Typew.   C-S

9064. Daughters of the American revolution. California. Ceremonies at the planting of the Liberty tree in Golden Gate park by Sequoia chapter...April 19, 1894... [S.F., 1894] 39 p. 7 pl.   C CU-B

9065. —— Pioneer obituaries from the San Francisco chronicle, 1911–1928. The loss of the steamer "Central America", from the Daily Alta California, 1857. Copy of the first telephone directory issued in San Francisco, 1878. [S.F.] 1952. 124 l. Typew.   C CL CSf

9066. —— [Register, Golden Gate international exposition] [S.F., 1939–1940] 1 v. unp. Contains signatures of members of the D.A.R. visiting the exposition.   C

9067. —— **California chapter.** By-laws. [S.F., 1915?] 7 p.   CHi

9068. —— —— Same.... [and list of members, September, 1909, and July 1918] [n.p., 1918] 25 p.
                                                      CHi

9069. —— —— **Genealogical records committee.** Epitaphs. Mission San Francisco de Asis cemetery (Mission Dolores). Collected by Charles Francis Griffin. S.F., S.F. chapter, D.A.R., 1950. 79 l. diagrs., facsims.
                                                  C CSf

9070. —— —— Records from tombstones in Laurel Hill cemetery, 1853–1937, San Francisco, California... 1935. 152 l. Typew.   C C-S CL CSf

9071. —— —— Vital records from Masonic cemetery, San Francisco, Calif. 1934. [98] l. Typew.
                              C C-S CL CSf

9072. —— —— Vital records from the Daily Alta California, including records from the Golden era and the Wide west, 1854. Comp. by El Palo Alto, San Francisco, Tamalpais and California chapters... [S.F.] 1955. unp.
                              C C-S CHi CL

9073. —— —— Vital records from the *Daily evening bulletin*, San Francisco. 1856– Typew. Covers years 1856–57, 1858–59, 1864, 1866–68, 1871–72.
                              C C-S CHi CL CSf

9074. —— —— [Vital records from the] *San Francisco bulletin*, October-December 1855, *Alta California & Wide west*, 1855. Births, marriages, deaths. [S.F.] 1956. unp.   CHi CL

9075. —— —— **La Puerta de oro chapter.** La Puerto de oro chapter, Daughters of the American revolution, San Francisco, California, 1946–1947. [n.p., n.d.] [8] p. List of members.   CHi

9076. **Daughters of the American revolution.**
California (*cont'd*). **San Francisco chapter.** Year
book.
CHi has 1934/35, 1937/38–1961/62. CU-B has 1926/27,
1937/38–1939/40, 1941/42, 1946/47, 1948/49, 1958/59.

9077. —— —— **Sequoia chapter.** By-laws...
[S.F.? n.d.] 12 p.   CHi

9078. —— —— **State officers club.** Yearbook.
CHi has 1931, 1935, 1937–38, 1941, 1946–47.

9079. —— —— **Tamalpais chapter.** San Francisco cemetery records, 1848–1863. 1938. unp. Typew.
C C-S CL CSf

9080. **Davidson, George.** The discovery of San
Francisco bay; the rediscovery of the port of Monterey;
the establishment of the Presidio, and the founding of
the Mission of San Francisco... S.F. [F.F. Partridge
print.] 1907. 153 p. (Geographical soc. of the Pac. Transactions and proceedings. v.4, ser. 2)
Available in many California libraries and CoU

9081. —— Report...upon a system of sewerage for
the city of San Francisco. S.F., Frank Eastman & co.,
print., 1886. 20 p.   CLU CSmH CU-B

9082. **Davis, Alfred E.** In memoriam. [S.F.] Soc. of
Calif. pioneers, 1907. 7 p. Typew.   CRcS

9083. **Davis (George A.) firm.** [Catalog of har-
rows and plows] S.F. [188–?] 1 v. illus.   CU-B

9084. [**Davis, Horace**] Appeal from the Garfield
monument association of the Pacific. [S.F., The Assoc.,
1881] [2] p.   CHi

9085. —— The patriotic services of Thomas Starr
King; an address. S.F., 1899. 9 p.   CHi CU-B

9086. **Davis, Isaac Elphinstone, et al vs. Spring**
Valley water works co. et al. ...Isaac E. Davis, et al,
appellants, vs. the Spring Valley water works co., et al,
respondents. Transcript on appeal. G. F. & W. H. Sharp,
attorneys for appellants. Sharp & Lloyd and Campbell,
Fox & Campbell, attorneys for respondents. S.F., Kane
& Cook, print., 1877. 112 p.   CU-B

9087. **Davis, John Francis.** Founding of San Fran-
cisco, Presidio and Mission. Sesquicentennial address...
S.F., Pernau-Walsh print. co., 1926. 18 p.
C CHi CL CLSU CLU CSf CSfCW CU-B

9088. **Davis, Margaret B.** The woman who battled
for the boys in blue, Mother Bickerdyke, her life and
labor for the relief of our soldiers, sketches of battle
scenes and incidents of the sanitary service. S.F., A.T.
Dewey, 1886. 166 p. port. "Published for the benefit of
M[ary] A[nn Ball] Bickerdyke."   CHi CU-B

9089. **Davis, Melvin Keith.** Water pollution control
in the San Francisco bay region. [Berkeley, 1959] Thesis
(M.A.)—Univ. of Calif., 1959.   CU

9090. **Davis (W.) & sons.** Catalogue no. 27, May 1,
1915...wholesale manufacturers of harness, saddles,
horse collars... [n.p., 1915] 72 p. illus.   CHi

9091. **Davis, William Heath.** Seventy-five years in
California; a history of events and life in California...
under the Mexican regime...a reissue and enlarged illu-
strated edition of "Sixty years in California." S.F., John
Howell, 1929. 422 p. illus., ports., maps.
Available in many libraries.

9092. —— Sixty years in California... S.F., A.J.
Leary, 1889. 639 p.
Available in many libraries.

9093. **Davis bros., Toklas and co.** Book of suggestions. S.F. [188–?] 1 v. illus.   CU-B

9094. —— Catalogue and retail price list of clocks.
S.F. [188–?] 1 v. illus.   CU-B

9095. —— Catalogue of lawn tennis and sporting
goods. S.F. [188–?] 1 v. illus.   CU-B

9096. —— Retail catalogue condensed. S.F.
[188–?] 1 v. illus.   CU-B

9097. —— Views of San Francisco, Yosemite valley
and Pacific coast. [S.F., 188–?] folder (58 illus. on
29 l.)   CHi CU-B

9098. **Davison, Berlinda.** Educational status of the
Negro in San Francisco bay region. [Berkeley, 1922]
Thesis (M.A.)—Univ. of Calif., 1922.   CU

9099. **Day, J., and Day, J. L.** An illustrated and
descriptive souvenir and guide to Golden Gate park...
S.F., Authors, 1914. 61 p. illus.   CHi

9100. **Day (Thomas) & co.** A catalogue of combination [light] fixtures... [S.F., n.d.] 20 pl.   CHi

9101. —— ...Steam catalogue... [S.F.? 1885?]
715–1070 p. illus. Running title: The United brass co.'s
illustrated catalogue.   CHi

9102. —— The Walworth gas machine... S.F.
[n.d.] 24 p. fold. pl.   CHi

9103. [**Dearing, Octavius A.**] Printing for profit
illustrating the "Dearing" specialties in printing office
furniture. S.F., Palmer & Rey, 1885. 35 p. illus.   CHi

9104. **Deckelman bros.** Catalogue no. 9...barbers'
chairs, furniture and supplies. S.F. [190–?] 144 p. illus.
CHi

9105. **Deering, Margaret (Perkins) "Mrs. James**
Henry Deering." The hills of San Francisco, prepared
for the National society of colonial dames of America in
the state of California...1936. 24 p. illus.
C CHi CLO CSf CSmH CU-B

9106. **DeFord, Miriam Allen, "Mrs. Maynard**
Shipley." California's disgrace; how and why Tom
Mooney was framed, including a complete history of the
world-famous Mooney case from 1916 to 1933... 1938.
187 l. Typew. Bibliography: 1. 186–187.
CLU CU CU-B

9107. —— They were San Franciscans... Cald-
well, Ida., Caxton, 1941. 321 p. illus., ports.
Available in many California libraries and CaBViPA
CoD MoS NHi NN OU TxU UHi

9108. **De Forest (Lee) inc.** De Forest radio telephone and telegraph equipments. Catalogue no. 101. S.F.
[n.d.] 31 p. illus., port.   CHi

9109. **De Fremery, James, and De Fremery, W.**
C. B., vs. Austin, Alexander. ...James De Fremery
and W. C. B. de Fremery, respondents, vs. Alexander
Austin, tax collector of the city and county of San Francisco, appellant. Transcript on appeal. W. C. Burnett,
attorney for appellant. Campbell, Fox & Campbell, attorneys for respondents... S.F., Spaulding & Barto,
steam bk. and job print., 1877. 249 p.   CU-B

9110. **Deimel, Henry Lito, jr.** The Mexican market
for San Francisco exporters. [Berkeley, 1923] Thesis
(Ph.D.)—Univ. of Calif., 1923.   CU

9111. **Deitrick, Elizabeth Platt.** Best bits of the
Panama-Pacific international exposition and San Fran-
cisco. S.F., Galen pub. co. [c1915] 82 p. illus.
CHi CSfU CStclU

9112. **DeLeuw, Cather & co.** A report to the city
planning commission on a transportation plan for San
Francisco... [S.F., 1948] [100] p. maps, charts.
CHi

9113. **Delkin, James Ladd, ed. and pub.** Flavor
of San Francisco, a guide to "the city"...Stanford [1943]
130 p. illus., maps.

C CBu CHi CL CLU CO CRcS CRic CSf
CSfWF-H CSmat CStmo (1946)

9114. —— Same. [5th rev. ed.] [1952] 128 p.
illus., maps. C CO

9115. —— War effort information manual for San
Francisco, compiled from official sources... Stanford
[1942] 142 p. illus. C CL CRcS CSf

9116. Delmas, Delphin Michael. Speeches and addresses... S.F., A.M. Robertson, 1901. 363 p. port.
CHi CSf CSjC CU-B

9117. Del Monte milling co. Price list no. 77, April
13, 1896. [S.F., 1896?] folder ([8] p.) illus. CHi

9118. De Mille, Anna Angela (George) Henry
George, citizen of the world. Chapel Hill, Univ. of North
Carolina press [c1950] 276 p. illus. CHi CU-B

9119. Democratic party. San Francisco. Brief record of the regular democratic general committee of San
Francisco and the "Junta" self-constituted and so-called
general committee of the same city and county... [n.p.,
1896?] 16 p. CHi

9120. —— Plan for the reorganization of
the democracy of the city and county of San Francisco
adopted by the committee of fifty and approved by the
democratic state central and county committees, Apr. 6,
1882. [n.p., n.d.] 28 p. CU-B

9121. —— —— **Committee of fifty.** Address
by the Committee of fifty to the people. [S.F.? 1882]
[4] p. CHi CU-B

**9122. Democratic state convention, San Fran-
cisco. 1886.** Platform and resolutions adopted by the
Democratic state convention held in Odd Fellows' hall,
San Francisco, September 2, 1886. [S.F., Thomas' print.,
1886] 16 p. ports. Bound with: Ingersoll, Robert G. A
vindication of Thomas Paine... 1877. CHi

9123. Denny, J. O., ed. The Bar association of San
Francisco, an illustrated history, from 1872 to 1924...
S.F., A. Wheeler, 1923 [c1924] 116 p. illus., ports.
C CHi CO CSf CSmH CU-B

9124. Derleth, Charles. The destructive extent of
the California earthquake; its effect upon structures and
structural materials within the earthquake belt... S.F.,
A.M. Robertson, 1907. 132 p. illus., maps.
CHi CLSM CSf CSfP CU-B

9125. De Rupert, A. E. D. Californians and Mor-
mons... N.Y., J.W. Lovell, 1881. 166 p.
C CBb CHi CL CLO CLSU CLU CO CSd
CSf CSfCP CSfCW CSmH CSmat CU-B CoD IHi
MoS UHi

**9126. Desert water, oil and irrigation company
(a corporation) plaintiff and respondent vs. the
state of California, defendant and appellant.** Petition for modification of language of the court's decision.
Percy V. Long, city attorney, city and county of San Francisco, J. F. English, assistant city attorney, amici curiae.
S.F., Rincon pub. co., print. [1914] 23 p. CU-B

9127. Desmond, Felix P. Rare photographs of old
San Francisco. [1906-1920] [98] p. illus., ports. C-S

9128. Deutsch, Arthur K. The romance of life insurance; my 25 most interesting cases. Edited by Jack
Piver. [S.F.?] c1944. 48 p. port. CU-B

9129. Deutsch, Monroe E. Albert M. Bender. S.F.,
Grabhorn, 1941. 4 l. CHi CU-B

9130. —— Saint Albert of San Francisco... S.F.
[Grabhorn] 1956. 17 p. "The foregoing article appeared
in the Spring-Summer, 1955 issue of the *Menorah journal* ..." CHi CU-B

9131. —— The status of the American Jew; address...at the dinner in honor of the 95th anniversary
of the founding of Temple Emanu-El, San Francisco...
December nineteenth, 1945. [S.F., Schwabacher-Frey,
1946] [9] p. CHi

**9132. Deutsche sängerfest in Californien. 2d, San
Francisco, 1861.** Text-buch und program für das zweite
Deutsche sängerfest in Californien. Abgehalten in San
Francisco, vom 22, bis 27. august 1861. [S.F., Druck
California demokrat, 1861] 11 p. CU-B

9133. Devine, Preston. The adoption of the 1932
charter of San Francisco. [Berkeley, 1933] Thesis
(M.A.)—Univ. of Calif., 1933. CU

9134. Devlin, Madison. San Francisco panorama.
S.F., Fearon, c1958. [64] p. (Chiefly illus.)
Available in many California libraries and CoD NN

9135. Devol, Carroll Augustine. The army in the
San Francisco disaster... [Wash., D.C., 1907] [29] p.
illus. From Jl. of the U.S. infantry assoc., July 1907.
CU-B

9136. Dewey (S. P.) & son, auctioneers. ...Auc-
tion sale of real estate in the city of San Francisco... on
Saturday, June 20, '60... [S.F.] Alta Calif. job print
[1860] 17 p. CU-B

9137. Dewey, Squire Pierce. The bonanza mines
and the bonanza kings of California. Their 5 years reign:
1875-1879. "When the wicked rule the people mourn."
[n.p., 1879] 87 p. maps. CHi CU-B

9138. Dewey & co. United States and foreign patent
solicitors. S.F. [n.d.] 47 p. illus., diagr. CHi

9139. De Witt, Frederic M., pub. An illustrated
and descriptive souvenir and guide to San Francisco. A
new handbook for strangers and tourists...With a short
historical sketch and a bird's-eye view of the business
center of the city... S.F. [c1897] 144 p. illus. On
cover: Published annually with revisions.
C (1897) CL (1899-1900, 1902) CLU (1897) CO
(1897, 1899-1900, 1902) CSf (1897) CSfCP (1900)
CSfWF-H (1897) CSmH (1899-1900, 1902-03) CU-B
(1899-1900, 1902-03) CaBViPA (1897) NN (1900)

9140. —— San Francisco, a selection of thirty-seven
engravings of representative views. S.F. [189-?] [16] p.
CHi

9141. —— Same. ...a selection of sixty-four engravings of representative views. S.F. [190-?] 31 pl.
CO

**9142. de Young memorial museum, Golden Gate
park.** ...Program...Sept. 1940-1957. [S.F., 1940-57]
2 v. illus. CU-B

9143. —— Second exhibition of painting and sculpture by California artists, 1916. S.F., 1916. 6 p. CHi

9144. —— Story of its foundation and the objects
of its founder. Description of its various galleries...
[S.F.] Pub. under the auspices of the Park commission
[1921?] 178 p. port.
C CHi CLSU CO CSf CSfCP CU-B

9145. Diamond, Goddard E. D. The secret of a
much longer life and more pleasure in living it. [S.F.?
1906?] 127 p. port. CHi CU-B

9146. The Diamond palace...The most beautiful
jewelry establishment in the world...The palace and its
designer...A feature of San Francisco...S.F., G. Spaulding & co., 1882. 24 p. CU-B

9147. Dick, Adelaide Clara. Personnel work in the
San Francisco bay region. [Berkeley, 1927] Thesis
(M.A.)—Univ. of Calif. CU

9148. Dickie, George W. The commerce of San Francisco... [S.F.] Industrial pub. co., 1891. 16 p.
C CHi CU-B

9149. Dickieson, Marjory Helen. A survey of the applied arts in industry and commerce in San Francisco. [Berkeley, 1927] Thesis (M.A.)—Univ. of Calif.   CU

9150. Dickson, Samuel. "Grand old man of the Pacific," the life story of Captain Robert Dollar, presented by W. & J. Sloane on their radio program...KNBC-San Francisco...March 20, 1949.... [S.F., Pac. shipper, 1959] 17 p.   CU-B

9151. —— San Francisco harbor, yesterday and to-day... S.F., S.F. junior chamber of commerce, 1946. [14] p. illus.   CiH

9152. —— San Francisco is your home. Stanford [c1947] 262 p. illus.
Available in many California libraries and CoD IC MiD N ODa

9153. —— San Francisco kaleidoscope. Stanford [c1949] 293 p. illus.
Available in many California libraries and CoD IC MiD N NN UPB

9154. —— The streets of San Francisco. Stanford [1955] 186 p. illus.
Available in many California libraries and CoD MiD MoS NN NjR ODa TxU

9155. —— Tales of San Francisco; comprising San Francisco is your home, San Francisco kaleidoscope, and The streets of San Francisco. Stanford, 1957. 711 p. illus.
Available in many California libraries and MoS N ODa OU TxU UHi UPB UU ViU

9156. Diekelmann, William. ...San Francisco earthquake and fire, April 18, 1906. [S.F., 1906] 1 v. of photos.   NN

9157. Di Giorgio fruit corp. ...Annual report... S.F., 19—?– illus.
CHi has 33d, 1953. CL has 1952–60.

9158. Dillon, Richard Hugh. The Bay area bookman. Berkeley, Calif. library assoc., 1961. 39 p. illus. Issued by the Regional resources coordinating committee as a souvenir of the Calif. lib. assoc. conference, San Francisco, 1961.   CHi CU-B

9159. —— Books and browsing in San Francisco. [S.F., 1958] 20 p. illus. Issued by the Committee as a souvenir of the Am. lib. assoc. conference, San Francisco, 1958.   C CHi CSf CU-B

9160. —— Bully Waterman, & the voyage of the clipper *Challenge*, New York to San Francisco, 1851. S.F., The Roxburghe club, 1956. 22 p. wood-engravings 125 copies printed by Adrian Wilson for the Albert Bender memorial fund.   CBb CHi CLO CU-B

9161. —— Embarcadero. N.Y., Coward [1959] 313 p. illus.
Available in many libraries.

9162. —— The hatchet men: the story of the tong wars in San Francisco's Chinatown. N.Y., Coward [c1962] 375 p. illus.   CAla CU-B

9163. —— Shanghaiing days. N.Y., Coward-McCann [1961] 351 p.
Available in many libraries.

9164. —— Sutro library through the centuries. [Sacramento, State print. off., 1958] 18 p. illus., ports., facsims.
C C-S CHi CLO CP CRcS CSf CSmat CU-B

9165. —— Same, with title: The anatomy of a library.   C C-S CHi CU-B

9166. Disturnell's San Francisco street directory and guide, containing the names and location of all streets, avenues, courts, alleys and squares in the city and county of San Francisco... S.F., W.C. Disturnell, 1885. 128 p. map.   CHi CSf CSmH CU-B

9167. —— Same. 1892. 132 p.   CU-B

9168. Disturnell's strangers' guide to San Francisco and vicinity... S.F., W.C. Disturnell, 1883. 162 p. map.
C CHi CL CLU CPom CSf CSfCP CSfCW CSmH CU-B NN

9169. Dixon, James, comp. Dixon's marine guide to the port of San Francisco... N.Y. & S.F., Dixon & co. [1889] 162 p.   CLU CSf CSmH CU-B

9170. Dixon (Joseph) crucible co., Jersey City, N.J. Through Frisco's furnace. [S.F., 1906] [24] p. illus.
CSmH CU-B MiD-B

9171. Dobbin, Hamilton H. [Scrapbook of photographs of prominent persons, places, and events in and about San Francisco, 1890–1927]   C

9172. Dobie, Charles Caldwell. Dear dead delights ... [Del Monte, 1927] 52 p. illus.   CU-B

9173. —— Onward; the postamp pageant of San Francisco, a fascinating history of the city told in stamp and story...Supplemented by a brief outline of the history of San Francisco's Fire department, as compiled by Battalion chief Frederick J. Bowlen... [S.F., O. Casperson & sons, c 1940] [32] p. illus., ports.
C CHi CU-B

9174. —— The owl takes flight. [S.F.? Bohemian club, 1933] [16] p. illus. Deals with Bohemian club quarters.   CHi

9175. —— San Francisco; a pageant... N.Y., London, Appleton-Century, 1933. 351 p. illus.
Available in many California libraries and MiD N ODa OU TxU ViU

9176. —— Same. 1939. 440 p. illus.
C CBb CHi CL CLSU CLU CLgA CO CSf CSmH CU-B IC NN UPB

9177. —— San Francisco's Chinatown... N.Y., London, Appelton-Century, 1936. 336 p. illus.
Available in many California libraries and NjR NN ODa

9178. Doble (Abner) co. Bulletin...Tools. [S.F., 1889?–] illus.
CHi has no. 4, 1901.

9179. [Dodd, Jack L.] Bohemian eats of San Francisco. [S.F., 1925] [53] p. illus.
CHi CLU CSf CU-B

9180. Dodge and Pierce. Catalogue & price list [of] amateur printing presses, printing materials, fancy cards, etc. S.F. [189–?] 1 v. illus.   CU-B

9181. Doe (B. & J. S.) firm. Price current... manufacturers of and dealers in doors, windows and blinds... S.F., Brodie & co., 1880–1896. 2 v. illus.
CHi CU-B

9182. Doe, Stephen. Narrative, life and trials of professor Stephen Doe... S.F., 1873. 57 p. port.   CHi

9183. Dohrmann, Frederick W., jr. Three years on a board; being the experiences of the San Francisco Board of education, 1922–1923–1924...Written and published for private circulation by F. Dohrmann, jr. S.F., 1924. 118 p.   C CHi CSfCP CSmH CU-B

9184. Dollar, Robert. Memoirs of Robert Dollar. S.F., Priv. pub. for the author by W.S. Van Cott & co., 1917.   CHi CRcS CU-B

9185. —— Same. Rev. ed. S.F., Priv. pub., 1918. 353 p. illus., ports. Other editions followed: 1921, 1922, 1925, 1928. CBb CHi CSfCW CU-B

9186. —— Private diary of Robert Dollar on his recent visits to China. S.F., Robert Dollar co., 1912. 210 p. illus., ports. CHi CRcS CU-B

9187. Dolliver & bro. Dealers in improved shoe machinery, boot and shoe uppers, leathers and findings... [Catalog] [N.Y., E.B.Stimpson & son, pubs., n.d.] 48 p. illus. CHi

9188. Donahue, Peter. A sketch of the life of Peter Donahue of San Francisco 1822-1888. S.F., Crocker, 1888. 16 p. illus., port. CHi CSfCW

9189. Donaldson, Robert S. The church in greater San Francisco. N.Y., Bd. of home missions of the Presbyterian church in the U.S.A., Education dept., 1921. 24 p. illus. CO

9190. Dondero, Raymond Stevenson. The Italian settlement of San Francisco. [Berkeley, 1953] Thesis (M.A.)—Univ. of Calif., 1953. CU

9191. Doran, Beverly Ann. S[erranus] Clinton Hastings. [Berkeley, 1952] Thesis (M.A.)—Univ. of Calif., 1952. CU

9192. Dore (Maurice) & co. ...Administrator's sale. Public auction of the Beideman estate in the city of San Francisco...Wednesday, July 24th, 1867... S.F., Alta Calif. print., 1867. 63 p. CHi CU-B

9193. —— ...At auction. Important credit sale of valuable city real estate, improved and unimproved. By order of the Directors of the Odd fellows' savings bank. H. A. Cobb, auctioneer...Tuesday, March 26, 1878... S.F., Winterburn & co., print. [1878] 22 p. CU-B

9194. —— ...Catalogue of an extraordinary sale at auction at Platt's hall of over 300 central, healthful & beautiful large city lots! On Tuesday, November 5th, 1878, at 12 o'clock, noon... S.F., Winterburn & co., print. [1878] 32 p. CU-B

9195. —— Catalogue of rare plants, trees, shrubs, &c. to be sold at auction...May 17, 1878...H. A. Cobb, auctioneer. S.F., Winterburn & co., print. [1878] 13 p. CU-B

9196. —— ...Catalogue of real estate situated in San Francisco, Santa Clara county, Los Angeles county, and Virginia City, Nev., and the Island de Santa Catalina, to be sold...November 17, 1874...per order of trustees, James Lick trust. S.F., Winterburn & co., print., 1874. 50 p. diagrs. CLU CU-B

9197. —— Catalogue of valuable business and residence property, to be sold on a liberal credit on Thursday, April 20, 1876... S.F., Winterburn & co., print., 1876. 26 p. illus., maps. CHi CU-B

9198. —— Special and peremptory sale of valuable business property...Aug. 11th, 1886... S.F., Winterburn & co., print., 1886. 12 p. maps. CHi

9199. —— Special auction sale by order of Benjamin Richardson, of centrally located, improved and unimproved business property and outside lands south of the park, Wednesday, October 20th, 1886... S.F., Commercial pub. co. [1886] 10 p. plats. CHi

9200. —— Special auction sale of valuable improved and unimproved properties in the city of San Francisco, Alameda, Marin and San Mateo counties...by order of Albert Gansl...to be held Thursday, May 2d, 1878 ...H.A. Cobb, auctioneer. S.F., Winterburn & co., print. [1878] 13 p. CU-B

9201. —— ...Third annual peremptory sale of the

Real estate associates, to be held at Platt's hall on Tuesday, April 10, 1877, at 12 o'clock, noon... S.F., Winterburn & co., 1877. 40 p. CU-B

9202. Dore, Walter H. History of the Dore family by Benjamin Dore and Walter H. Dore. [Berkeley, 1908] 27 p. CHi CU-B

9203. The Double cross street guide of the city and county of San Francisco, California... S.F., Polito & Plummer, 1910. 191 p. C-S

9204. Douglas, W. S. San Francisco bay area rapid transit and the economics of transportation... [n.p., 1954?] 16 l. CSt

9205. Douglas, William J., vs. Hunt, John, jr., et al. ...William J. Douglas, appellant, vs. John Hunt, jr., the city and county of San Francisco, and Christopher Hutchinson, respondents... S.F., 1874. 4 v. in 1. CU-B

9206. Douglass, Harlan Paul. ...The San Francisco bay area church study... S.F., Northern Calif.-western Nevada council of churches, 1945. 113 p. illus., diagrs. CSf

9207. Dow (George E.) pumping engine co. General catalogue... S.F., Stanley-Taylor co., 1900. 113 p. illus. CHi CU-B

9208. —— Illustrated catalogue... S.F., 1895. 86 p. illus. CHi

9209. Dowling, Thomas H. Memorial of Thomas H. Dowling, and accompanying papers in regard to his claim to the island of Yerba Buena, in the harbor of San Francisco, California. Wash., D.C., Print. by W.H. Moore [1869?] 34, 24 p. CHi CU-B

9210. Downey, Joseph T. Filings from an old saw; reminiscences of San Francisco and California's conquest, by "Filings"—Joseph T. Downey. Ed. by Fred Blackburn Rogers. S.F., J. Howell, 1956. 170 p. illus. "Republished in this present volume is a series of eighteen...articles printed in the [Golden] era...January 9 to July 3, 1853... Available in many California libraries and CaBViPA CoD KU KyU MoS N OU UHi UPB

9211. Doxey, William, pub. Doxey's guide to San Francisco and vicinity... S.F. [1881] 176 p. CHi CSalCL CSfCP CSmH CU-B

9212. —— Doxey's guide to San Francisco and the pleasure resorts of California... S.F., 1897. 208 p. illus., map. C CHi CL CLU CP CSf CSfCP CSfCW CSmH CU-B MoS NN

9213. Doyle, John Thomas. As to the division of the fees in the Pious fund case. [n.p., n.d.] 52 p. C-S

9214. —— Brief history of the Pious fund of California. [n.p., 1870?] 20 p. CLSM CStclU CU-B

9215. —— The Central Pacific R. R. debt; California's remonstrance against refunding it. [n.p., 1881] 29 p. CHi CU-B

9216. —— [A collection of pamphlets by and about John Thomas Doyle, his affairs, his family, his neighbors, his associates. 1854-1898] CSfCW

9217. —— In the International arbitral court of the Hague. The case of the Pious fund of California. Statement of the proceedings and letters to the most Reverend P. W. Riordan, archbishop of San Francisco, Cal. By John T. Doyle, for forty-five years chief counsel for the claimants. S.F., G. Spaulding & co., print., 1906. 106 p. Contains also: The Pious fund case. In the matter of the distribution of the award. C-S CHi CLgA

9218. —— Memorandum as to the discovery of the bay of San Francisco. With introductory remarks by John D. Washburn...before the American antiquarian society, at their annual meeting, October 21, 1873. Worcester, Mass., Print. Charles Hamilton, 1874. 14 p.
C CHi CLU CSf CSfCW CSmH CU-B

9219. —— Same. S.F., Bacon & co., 1889. 18 p. map. (Reprint from *Proceedings of the Am. antiquarian soc.,* 1874)
CHi CLU CSfCW CSmH CU-B NHi

9220. —— The Pious fund case. In the matter of the distribution of the award. Fees of counsel. 67 p. Bound with: In the International court of the Hague. The case of the Pious fund.   CHi CLgA CU-B

9221. —— Some account of the Pious fund of California and the litigation to recover it. S.F., E. Bosqui & co., print., 1880. 11 [i.e. 12] pamphlets in 1 v.
CSfCW CU-B

9222. —— To his Excellency, Romualdo Pacheco, governor, etc... [S.F., 1875] 6, 6 p. Two letters to Governor Pacheco of California opposing the grant of patents applied for by the Southern Pacific and Central railway companies for sixty acres of land in Mission bay.
CLU

9223. Doyle, Marie Alfred, *Sister.* The political career of Cornelius Cole, 1863–1873. San Rafael [Catholic univ. of Am., Pac. coast branch] 1955. 61 p. front. (port.) Thesis (M.A.)—Catholic univ. of Am., 1955.
CSrD

9224. Dreiser, Theodore. Tom Mooney. [S.F., Free Tom Mooney United front conference, n.d.] [10] p. illus.   CSto

9225. [Dressler, Albert] ed. and pub. Emperor Norton, life and experiences of a notable character in San Francisco, 1849–1880... 2d ed. S.F., 1927. 30 p. illus., ports.
Available in many libraries.

9226. —— [San Francisco and vicinity...1906–07] 3 v. [345, 153, 117] mount. photos. Contents: v.1 [First views of earthquake ruins and fire]—v.2. Ruins.—Refugees.—Removing debris.—Early reconstruction.—Pioneer banks.—Six months after fire.—v.3. Reconstruction.—Six months after fire.—One year after fire.   C

9227. —— ...Marine views, Sutro park, chutes, Golden Gate park. 1895–1900. 186 mount. photos.   C

9228. Druids' hall society of the city and county of San Francisco. Certificate of incorporation and by-laws...Incorporated Nov. 7th, 1868... S.F., Excelsior press, Bacon & co., print., 1868. 14 p. A society composed of members of the United ancient order of druids organized to provide a building for the Druids of San Francisco.   CU-B

9229. Druids, United ancient order of. San Francisco. General relief committee. Constitution and rules of order...Organized August 4th, 1867. S.F., Winterburn & co., 1875. 15 p.   CU-B

9230. Drummond, Herbert William, jr. Squatter activity in San Francisco, 1847–1854. [Berkeley, 1952] Thesis (M.A.)—Univ. of Calif., 1952.   CU

9231. Drury, Aubrey. John A. Hooper and California's robust youth. Together with a foreword by Arthur W. Hooper. S.F., 1952. 85 p. illus.
CBb CHi CO CRcS CRic CSf CSfP CSjC CStclU CStoC CStrCL CU-B N

9232. Drury, Clifford M. San Francisco YMCA; 100 years by the Golden Gate, 1853–1953. Glendale, Arthur H. Clark co., 1963. 256 p. illus.
CAla CHi CU-B

9233. Drury, P. Shelden, ed. The startling and thrilling narrative of the dark and terrible deeds of Henry Madison, and his associate and accomplice, Miss Ellen Stevens, who was executed by the Vigilance committee of San Francisco, on the 20th September last. Cincinnati, Barclay & co. [c1857] [9]–36 p. illus., pl.
CHi CLU CSmH CU-B

9234. Due, John F. The San Francisco and Alameda railroad. [San Marino, Southern Calif. chapter, Railway and locomotive hist. soc. and the Pacific railroad soc., 1956] 8 p.   CSt

9235. Duffus, Robert Luther. The tower of jewels; memories of San Francisco. [1st ed.] N.Y., W.W. Norton & co. [1960] 250 p. "The story of Fremont Older and the *San Francisco bulletin."*
CSf CSfMI CSfU CU-B

9236. Dumas, Alexandre. The journal of Madame Giovanni...tr. from the French ed. (1856) by Marguerite E. Wilbur... N.Y., Liveright [c1944] 404 p. Has been attributed to Vicomtesse de Saint Mars. cf. *Bibliothèque nationale, Catalogue général,* and Quérard, J.M., *Les supercheries littéraires dévoilées.* French ed., 1856, has Title: *Taïti-Marquises-Californie; journal de madame Giovanni, rédigé et publié par Alexandre Dumas.*
C CAna CBev CChiS CL CLSU CLU CMary CO CRcS CSalCL CSf CSmH CStmo CViCL CaBViPA

9237. Dunann, Charles Richard. The adequacy of provisions regarding residential land use in areas zoned for light industry in the San Francisco bay area. [Berkeley, 1951] Thesis (M.A.)—Univ. of Calif., 1951.
CU-B

9238. Dunham, Carrigan and Hayden co. Catalogue...Electrical supplies... S.F., 19—?– illus.
CHi (no. 32) CU-B (no. 32–33)

9239. —— Fierro en paz, iron in peace. S.F. [1916] 21 p. illus. "A souvenir, commemorating sixty-seven years of progress."   CU-B

9240. —— [Various catalogues and price lists. S.F., etc., 1879–1920?] 7 v. illus. Wholesale dealers in tools, pipe, builders' and plumbers' hardware, electrical supplies, guns, automobile and garage accessories...
CHi

9241. Dunlap, Florence McClure. Samuel Brannan. [Berkeley, 1928] 160 l. Thesis (M.A.)—Univ. of Calif., 1928.   CU CU-B

9242. Dunlap, Marjorie Elise. Personnel policies and practices in five San Francisco department stores. [Berkeley, 1936] Thesis (M.S.)—Univ. of Calif., 1936.
CU

9243. Dunn, Joseph Allan Elphinstone. Care-free San Francisco. S. F., Robertson, 1913. 83 p. illus.
C CBu CHi CL CRic CSalCL CSf CSfMI CSfP CSfWF-H CSmH CU-B MoSHi NN

9244. Dunne, William F. The great San Francisco general strike; the story of the West coast strike—the bay counties' general strike and the maritime workers' strike... N.Y., Workers lib. pub. [1934] 79 p.
CHi CL CLU CSmH TxU

9245. Dupont, Samuel Francis, vs. Wertheman et als. In the Supreme court. Transcript of record on appeal. Samuel F. Dupont, plaintiff and appellant, vs. Rudolph Wertheman, et als., defendant and respondent. Hall McAllister, Delos Lake, counsel for respondent.

Baldwin & Bowman, counsel for appellant. S.F., Print. by Towne & Bacon, 1858. 60 p. Suit involving San Francisco pueblo lands. CLU

9246. Durtain, Luc. ...Crime à San Francisco; récit orné de huit lithographies originales de George Annenkoff. Paris, Au Sans pareil, 1927. 88 p. illus. CU-B

9247. Duryea, Edwin, jr. The facts about the Bay cities water company's water supply for San Francisco... [n.p., 1907] 32 p. fold. maps. "An address before the Commonwealth club on March 13, 1907." C CU-B

9248. Dyson, Robert, vs. Bradshaw, T. T., et als. ...Robert Dyson, appellants, vs. T. T. Bradshaw et als., respondents. Appellant's reply to respondents' brief. Cook & Hittell, attorneys for plaintiff. [S.F.? 1863?] 14 p. CU-B

9249. E clampus vitus. Clamperegrination in old San Francisco, ceremony of initiation. Annual banquet, 1940. S.F., Windsor press, 1940. [5] p. illus., map. CHi

9250. —— Ritual and ceremony of initiation of the ancient and honorable order of E. clampus vitus. [S.F.] the Grand lodge of California [1960?] 23 p. CHi

9251. Eagles, Fraternal order of. San Francisco. Constitution and laws of the Grand aerie and constitution for subordinate aeries... Milwaukee, S.E. Tate print. co. [1908?] 46 p. CHi

9252. [Earthquake album. S.F., 1906] [89] l. photos. CU-B

9253. Easterday (C. M.) firm. [Catalogue of] automobile and garage supplies. S.F. [192–?] 1 v. illus. CU-B

9254. [Easton, Adeline (Mills)] The story of our wedding journey, "as it was written down by one who heard," by Nellie Olmsted Lincoln. S.F., Priv. print., 1911. 39 p. illus., ports. Coypright by A.M. Easton. CHi

9255. Easton, Eldridge & co. Catalogue of blooded stock and thoroughbreds, brood mares and colts, belonging to Henry W. Seale, esq. [S.F., 19—?] 11 p. CU-B

9256. —— ...Catalogue of oil paintings & sketches, by J. B. Wandesforde, to be sold at auction... March 29th, 1883... [S.F.] C.A. Murdock & co. [1883] 16 p. CU-B

9257. —— Catalogue of the art collection of the late Mrs. Kate Johnson...sold...at auction, in the Golden Gate hall...1894... S.F., Bosqui print. co., 1894] 60, 11 p. CHi

9258. —— Catalogue of the elaborate parlor, drawing-room, dining-room, music-room, library, and chamber furniture of the residence of Miss Mary Lake...at auction ...June 23 and 24, 1896... [S.F., 1896] 28 p. CU-B

9259. —— On account of departure, P. A. Finigan offers for sale at auction...his entire stock of finely bred horses, also his carriages, country wagons, road carts, buggies, harness, saddles, etc. ...Tuesday, May 17th 1892... [S.F., 1892] 10 p. illus. CU-B

9260. Eaves, Edward Paul. A history of cooks and waiters' union of San Francisco. [Berkeley, 1931] Thesis (M.A.)—Univ. of Calif., 1931. CU

9261. Eaves, Lucile. ...A history of California labor legislation, with an introductory sketch of the San Francisco labor movement. Berkeley [1910] 461 p. (Univ. of Calif. pub. in economics. v.2) C CHi CL CLSU CLU CO CRedl CSf CSmH CU CU-B

9262. Economical gas machine co. ...Incorporated May 11th, 1872. S.F., M. Wiess, print., 1872. 6 p. illus., diagr. CU-B

9263. [Eddy, Elford] The log of a cabin boy. S.F. [Schmidt litho. co.] 1922. 40 p. illus. CHi CStclU CU-B

9264. Edwards (E. H.) co. Edwards wire rope, the rope to choose. You can bet your life on Edwards wire rope. [n.p., n.d.] 24 p. illus. CHi

9265. —— Same. 32 p. CHi

9266. Edwards (James W.) dental depot. ... Catalogue of dental instruments and materials. [n.p., 1893] 558 p. illus. CHi

9267. Edwards, Vina Howland. The story of the San Francisco Presbyterial society; with thumb-nail histories of societies. Oakland, A. Newman, 1933. 80 p. C CHi CO CU-B

9268. Edwards, William Grimm. The hardwood-using industries of the San Francisco bay region. [Berkeley, 1926] Thesis (M.S.)—Univ. of Calif., 1926. CU

9269. Edwards Abstract from records. San Francisco. no. 1–16657. Documents recorded May 29, 1891–Dec. 31, 1930. [S.F.] Edwards pub. co., 1891–1930.
CHi has no. 10040–10944, 13650–16657, Dec. 31, 1908–Dec. 29, 1911, Dec. 31, 1920–Dec. 31, 1930. CU-B has no. 1–10586, May 29, 1891–June 1926 (incomplete)

9270. Edwords, Clarence Edgar. Bohemian San Francisco, its restaurants and their most famous recipes; the elegant art of dining. S.F., Elder [c1914] 138 p.
Available in many California libraries and NN ViU ViW

9271. Egl, Anthony, et al vs. Central Pacific railroad co. In the District court of the fourth judicial district. Anthony Egl et als, plaintiffs, vs. the Central Pacific railroad company, defendants. Complaint. Alfred A. Cohen, Delos Lake, attorneys for plaintiffs. [S.F.? 1876] 8 p. CHi CU-B

9272. Eisen vineyard co. By-laws...and prospectus ... S.F., LeCount Bros., 1885. 16 p. CHi CU-B

9273. Eldredge, Zoeth Skinner. The key to the Pacific. S.F., National bank of the Pac. [1906] [8] p. fold. map. CHi CU-B

9274. Electrical engineering co. ...Electric dynamos and motors... S.F. [Dewey eng. co., n.d.] 8 p. front. CHi

9275. Eliel, Paul. The waterfront and general strikes, San Francisco, 1934... [S.F., Hooper print. co., c1934] 256 p.
CBaB CHi CL CLU CSS CSf CSfMI CSfP CSfU CU-B OU

9276. Élite directory for San Francisco and Oakland ...containing the names of over six thousand society people... S.F., Argonaut pub. co., 1879. 288 p. map. "Points of etiquette": p. [219]–263.
C CHi CLU CSf CSfCW CSfP CSmH CStoC CU-B

9277. Elks, Benevolent and protective order of. San Francisco edition of reunion bulletin, San Francisco's invitation to the B.P.O.E. The convention paper...welcome to San Francisco and Oakland. [n.p., 1909?] 16, A-P p. illus. CHi

9278. Ellery arms co. ...Outing goods catalog. 3d ed. ... S.F., 1917. 96 p. illus. CHi

9279. Ellinwood, Charles N. San Francisco's water

supply and sewerage. [n.p., 1900?] 29 p. illus. "Lecture at Cooper medical college, February 16, 1900."
C CHi CSmH CU-B

9280. Elliot, George H. The presidio of San Francisco [1870] (In *Mag. of history* Extra number—no. 182. 1933. p. [13]–31) Cameragraph.   C CSf CSmH

9281. —— Same. 9 p. (Reproduced from *Overland monthly* v.4, p. 336–44, Apr. 1870)   C CSf

9282. —— Same. [with] Concepcion de Arguello [poem by Bret Harte] [Wash., D.C.? 1874?] 30 p.
CU-B N NN

9283. Elliott library institute. Petition of the officers and directors... [Sacramento, Thompson, state print., 1878]   CSmH

9284. Ellis, Henry Hiram. From the Kennebec to California; reminiscences of a California pioneer. Selected and arranged by Lucy Ellis Riddell. Introd. by Robert Glass Cleland. Ed. by Lawrence R. Cook. L.A., W.F. Lewis [c1959] 88 p. illus. (Western heritage ser., 1)   CHi CSf CU-B

9285. Ellis, Moses, vs. City and county of San Francisco. ...Moses Ellis, appellant, vs. the city and county of San Francisco, et als., respondents. Transcript on appeal. E. B. Mastick, attorney for appellant. Wm. H. Patterson, of counsel. Haight & Temple, attorneys for respondents. S.F., Excelsior press, Bacon and co., 1869. 50 p.   CU-B

9286. Eloesser-Heynemann co. "Seventy-five years," 1851–1926. S.F., Press of Ingram-Rutledge co. [n.d.] [6] p. illus., port.   CHi

9287. Emerson manufacturing co. [Catalog of] flags, burgees, pennants, banners, etc. S.F. [Colonial press, 1915?] 45 p. illus.   CHi

9288. Emge, Ludwig Augustus. San Francisco's first successful Cesarean section performed by Elias Cooper, founder of California's first medical school. Presidential address [by] Ludwig A. Emge. [S.F., Pac. coast soc. of obstetrics and gynecology, 1938] 18 p. illus., port., facsims. Reprint from *The Western jl. of surgery, obstetrics and gynecology*, Feb., 1938.   CHi

9289. Emmet, Boris. California and Hawaiian sugar refining corporation of San Francisco, California. ...Stanford, 1928. 293 p. illus., tables. (Stanford business ser. no. II)   CChiS CHi CSfCW CU-B

9290. Empire publishing co. The San Francisco blue book; a society directory of the northern counties of California... Riverside [1952] 66 p.   CHi

9291. Employers' association. Declaration of principles and by-laws... [S.F.? 1901?] 11 p.   CU-B

9292. The Emporium economist. Fall/Winter 1900/01, Spring/Summer 1905. S.F., 1901–1905. 2 v. illus.   CHi (1905) CU-B

9293. Emrich, Duncan, ed. Comstock bonanza; western Americana of J. Ross Browne, Mark Twain, Sam Davis, Bret Harte, James W. Gally, Dan de Quille, Joseph T. Goodman, Fred Hart... N.Y., Vanguard [1950] 363 p.   CBb CSf CU-B

9294. Engelhardt, Nickolaus Louis. San Francisco school building, survey... [S.F.? 1948–] 12 v. illus., maps, graphs, charts.   CSfSt

9295. Engelhardt, Zephyrin, *Father.* ...San Francisco or Mission Dolores... Chicago, Franciscan herald press, 1924. 432 p. illus. Bibliographical foot-notes. Available in many libraries.

9296. —— Mission Dolores (San Francisco de Asis) San Francisco, being extracts from Fr. Zephyrin Engel-hardt's book "Mission Dolores." S.F., Priv. print. by F.J. Angell & H. Fahey, 1928. 103 p. illus., maps.
CHi CLU CSfU CStrJC CU-B

9297. Engineers' club of San Francisco. Roster of members. 1929– S.F., 1929–
CHi has 1929, 1931, 1950. CU-B has 1929, 1931, 1935, 1938, 1945.

9298. Enos, John Summerfield. Report of John Summerfield Enos, commissioner of labor statistics of the state of California, to his excellency Hon. George Stoneman, governor of California, upon an inquiry as to "The condition of the laborers employed by contractors on the seawall at San Francisco," etc. Under Senate resolution of Mrach 3, 1885. Sacramento, J. J. Ayers, supt. state print., 1886. 140 p.   CSfCW

9299. Esberg, Milton Herman. ...A man and his friends; the life story of Milton H. Esberg, good citizen, successful business man and warm hearted loyal friend... S.F., Recorder-Sunset press, 1953. 163 p. illus.
CHi CSf CU-B

9300. Esperanto association of California. Illustrita gvidlibro tra San Francisko, Kalifornio. S.F., 1915. 48 p. illus.   CU-B CViCL

9301. Estee, Morris M. Address delivered at the opening of the 22d industrial exhibition of the Mechanics' institute, September 1st, 1887. [S.F.? 1887?] 12 p.
CU-B

9302. —— Republican speech of Hon. Morris M. Estee, delivered at Odd fellows hall, San Francisco, September 24th, 1898. [S.F., 1898?] 22 p.   CHi CU-B

9303. —— Speech of Hon. Morris M. Estee, Republican nominee for governor, delivered at San Francisco... August 1st, 1894. S.F., Frank Eastman & co. [1894] 24 p.
CHi CU-B

9304. Estell, James M. Speech of Gen. James M. Estell, delivered in the Hall of Representatives, Sacramento city, Cal., to a question of privilege, in connection with the Vigilance committee. [Sacramento, 1857] 13 p.
CHi CSmH CU-B

9305. Eureka benevolent association. ...Annual report...1878/79. [S.F., 1879] 1 v.   CU-B

9306. Eureka benevolent society. ...Annual report... [1st, 1906/07] and list of members of the society. [S.F., Jal-Um-Stein print. co., 1907] 32 p.   CU-B

9307. Eureka endowment association of California. Constitution and laws... S.F., W.A. Bushnell, 1891. 23 p.   CHi

9308. Evans, Cerinda W. Arabella Duval Huntington, 1851–1924. Newport News, Va. [Whittet & Shepperson, Richmond, Va.] 1959. 16 p.   CSmH CU-B

9309. —— Collis Potter Huntington. Newport News, Va., Mariners' museum [c1954] 2 v. illus., ports.
CHi CP CU-B

9310. Evans, Elliot A. P., comp. A catalog of the picture collections of the Society of California pioneers. S.F., The Society [1956] 45 p. illus.   CHi CL CSjC

9311. Evans, Henry Herman. Bohemian San Francisco. With illus. from old woodcuts. S.F., Porpoise bookshop, 1955. 32 p. illus.
C CAla CHi CL CLO CLU CO CSfU CSt CSto CU-B UHi

9312. —— Curious lore of San Francisco's Chinatown. S.F., Porpoise bookshop, 1955. 30 p. illus.
C CAla CHi CLO CLU CO CSt CSto CU-B

9313. —— San Francisco's Fisherman's wharf. With illus. from old woodcuts. S.F., Porpoise bookshop [c1957] 31 p. illus.

C CAla CArcHT CB CHi CL CLU CSt CSto CU-B UPB

9314. Evans, Taliesin. ...All about the Midwinter fair, San Francisco, and interesting facts concerning California... S.F., W.B. Bancroft & co., 1894. 111 p. illus., ports.   C CHi CO CSfCW CU-B

9315. —— Same. 2d ed. c1894. 195 p.   CLSU

9316. Evidence of the amount of lands held in San Francisco against "Peter Smith deeds"; and explanations of the "Peter Smith map."... S.F., Towne & Bacon, print. [1859] 10 p. Relates to the San Francisco pueblo land claim.   CSf CSmH CU-B

9317. Ewan, Joseph. San Francisco as a mecca for nineteenth century naturalists with a roster of biographical references to visitors and residents. 63 p. Bibliography: p. 42–63. Reprint. from *A century of progress in the natural sciences—1853–1953.*" [c1955]   CHi

9318. Ewell, Raymond Henry. San Francisco's dining out guide...of San Francisco and the bay area. S.F., Epicurean press [c1947] 104 p.   CO

9319. —— Same. 2d ed. Berkeley, 1948. 96 p.   CHi CSf

9320. Ewing, Russell Charles. ...The founding of the Presidio of San Francisco... Berkeley, 1936. 24 l. Typew.   CU-B

9321. Excelsior co. Illustrated catalogue and price list Excelsior windmill, horse power and pump works... S.F. [n.d.] 23 p.   C-S

9322. L'Exposition de San Francisco. no. 1, July 1915. S.F., 1915. 1 v. illus., ports.   CU-B

9323. Exposition press union. The world's greatest exposition and those who built it. In picture and prose. S.F., 1916. 128 p. illus. (part col. mounted)   CU-B

9324. Factful and colorful guide to San Francisco. S.F., Smith news co. [1958?] 32 p. map.   CHi

9325. [Fair, James Graham] In the Supreme court of the state of California. In the matter of the estate of James G. Fair, deceased. Points and authorities for respondent. Franklin K. Lane, City and county attorney, attorney for respondent... S.F., Star press–James H. Barry [1899] 99 p.   CHi

9326. Fair, Laura D. Wolves in the fold; a lecture ...also a statement of facts and defence of her cause with letters from prominent citizens to her... S.F., 1873.   CHi CSmH

9327. Fairbanks & Hutchison. Pacific coast dept. Fairbanks' scales; price list. 1877. S.F. [1877] 1 v. illus.   CU-B

9328. Fairmont hotel. The Fairmont, the most superbly situated hotel in the world, offering every convenience and luxury of the twentieth century. S.F. [19—] [16] p. illus.   CU-B

9329. "The Family," San Francisco. Constitution and by-laws and list of members. July, 1907. S.F., 1907. 36 p.   CSf

9330. Fang, John T. C., ed. Chinatown handy guide. S.F., Chinese pub. house, 1959. 128 p. illus.   CAla CHi

9331. Fardon, G. R. San Francisco album, photographs of the most beautiful views and public buildings of San Francisco; photographed by G. R. Fardon. S.F., Herre & Bauer [1856] [33] p. 30 photos.
CHi (facsim.)   CSmH   OrU (facsim.)

9332. Fargo, Frank F. A full and authentic account of the murder of James King, of William, editor of the *San Francisco evening bulletin,* by James P. Casey, and the execution of James P. Casey and Charles Cora, by the Vigilance committee, compiled from the columns of the *Alta California* and originally written for that paper. S.F., 1856. 24 p. port.
C CL CLU COMC CSf CU-B NN WHi

9333. —— A true and minute history of the assassination of James King of Wm. at San Francisco, Cal. ... S.F., Whitton, Towne & co., print., 1856. 26 p.
C CHi CLU CSfP CSmH CU-B CtY N

9334. Farley, Charles A. The moral aspect of California: a Thanksgiving sermon, preached to the First Unitarian church of San Francisco, California. Sunday, December 1, 1850... N.Y. [1850?] 16 p.   CHi

9335. Farmers and mechanics bank of savings. By-laws and agreement...1870, 1877. S.F., 1870–77. 2 v.   CU-B

9336. Farquhar, Francis Peloubet. Edward Vischer & his "Pictorial of California." S.F., Grabhorn, 1932. 8 p. illus., port. A biographical sketch as told by Hubert Vischer to Francis P. Farquhar. 100 copies priv. print. for the author.   CBb CHi

9337. Farwell, Willard Brigham. The Chinese at home and abroad. Together with the report of the Special committee of the Board of supervisors of San Francisco, on the condition of the Chinese quarter of that city... S.F., A.L. Bancroft co., 1885. 2 v. in 1. map.
C CHi CL CLSU CLU CO CSf CSfCW CSfP CSmH CU-B ViU

9338. The fate of the San Francisco grafters. Benedict Arnold of his native city... S.F., Cubery & co., 1908. 47 p.   C CHi CO CSf CSfP CSmH CU-B N

9339. Fatout, Paul. Ambrose Bierce, the Devil's lexicographer. [1st ed.] Norman, Okla., Univ. of Okla. press [1951] 349 p.   CLO CStcl

9340. Fauber, Richard Earl. The reformer without a cause: Hiram Johnson, 1919–1929. [Berkeley, 1960] Thesis (M.A.)—Univ. of Calif., 1960.   CU

9341. Faulkner, William. San Francisco. Artist: William Faulkner; photographer: Kem Lee; publisher: Bern Porter. S.F., 1954. 11 pl. (in portfolio) Of fifteen copies, this is copy no. 1.   CLU

9342. Fauntleroy, Joseph. John Henry Nash, printer; legend and fact in the development of a fine press; intimately reviewed. Oakland, Westgate press, 1948. 69 p. ports.   CHi CStclU

9343. Faust's pocket guide and complete street directory of San Francisco... S.F., H.W. Faust, c1890. map.   CU-B

Other editions followed. Title varies.
CHi (c1890, 11th ed., c1898, 1903) CSf (c1898) CSfCP (c1898) CSmH (c1890, 11th ed.) CU-B (c1898)

9344. Fawcett, Helen. The San Francisco vigilance committee of 1856. [Berkeley, 1929] 148 l. Thesis (M.A.)—Univ. of Calif., 1929.   CU

9345. Federal writers' project. California. Festivals in San Francisco...sponsored by International institute. Stanford, Delkin, 1939. 67 p. illus. (Am. guide ser.) "1000 copies printed at the Grabhorn press, 1939." Bibliography: p. 66–67.
Available in many California libraries and NN TxU UPB

9346. —— San Francisco. Almanac for thirty-niners...Sponsored by the Bret Harte associates of California. Stanford, Delkin [c1938] 127 p. illus. Bibliography: p. 124.
C CBb CBu CChiS CHi CL CLU CLgA CMont

CO CRcS CSal CSf CSfP CSfWF-H CSj CSluCL CSmH CU-B CViCL TxU

9347. Federation of Jewish charities, San Francisco. ...Annual report...1910–22– S.F., 1910?-23? 13 v.   C CHi (1912) CSf CU-B

9348. Feigenbaum & co. Catalogue of Feigenbaum & co. Importers of fancy goods, notions, cutlery, pipes, etc. S.F. [n.d.] 400 p. illus.   CHi

9349. —— Illustrated catalogue of children's carriages, bird cages, velocipedes, baskets, brushes, etc. S.F. [187–?] 1 v. illus.   CU-B

9350. Feldhaus, Joseph Anthony. The Moragas: soldiers, explorers, founders. S.F., Univ. of S.F., 1950. Thesis (M.A.)—Univ. of San Francisco, 1950.   CSfU

9351. Fell, James. British merchant seamen in San Francisco 1892–1898... London, Edward Arnold, 1899. 206 p.
C CHi CLU CO CSfCW CSfP CSmH CU-B NHi

9352. Ferina, Bessie Mae. The politics of San Francisco's Chinatown. [Berkeley, 1949] Thesis (M.A.)— Univ. of Calif., 1949.   CU

9353. Fibreboard paper products corp. Annual report.
CL has 1955–60.

9354. Fickert, Charles M. The bomb cases; a personal statement from district attorney Charles M. Fickert. [S.F., 1917?] [4] p.   CU-B

9355. Field, Charles Kellogg. In memoriam, 1873–1948. [n.p., n.d.] [3] p.   CHi

9356. Field, Henry M., comp. Biographical notice of Stephen J. Field. Taken partly from the record of the family of the late Rev. David D. Field, of Stockbridge, Mass., compiled by his youngest son, Henry M. Field, and partly from documents in the possession of different members of the family. Not published, but printed for the use of the family. [n.p., n.d.] 112 p.   CHi

9357. Field, Stephen Johnson. Personal reminiscences of early days in California with other sketches. Printed for a few friends. [n.p., c1880] 248 p.
CHi CMartC CMary CStclU

9358. —— Same. To which is added the story of his attempted assassination by a former associate on the Supreme bench of the state, by Hon. George C. Gorham. Printed for a few friends. [Wash., D.C., c1893] 406 p.
CHi CP CSfCW CSfP CSto

9359. —— Same. Edition with larger type on larger paper. 472 p.
C CBb CHi CLgA CStbS CStclU CStmo MoS

9360. —— Same, with title: California alcalde. Foreword by Joseph A. Sullivan. Oakland, Biobooks, 1950. 174 p. port., fold. col. map. (Calif. centennial ed. no. 21)
Available in many libraries.

9361. —— Sketch of [his] life. Published in the *New York sun*, April 25, 1880. 36 p.   CHi

9362. —— Some opinions and papers of Stephen J. Field, associate justice and chief justice of the Supreme court of California, U.S. circuit judge for the ninth and tenth circuits, and associate justice of the Supreme court of the United States. [n.p., n.d.] 6 v.   CHi

9363. Fields (George) bookseller, pub. Catalogue number two... S.F. [n.d.] 22 p.   CHi

9364. Finch, Lorna M. Hazel. The history of the chain marketing of gasoline in San Francisco. [Berkeley, 1933] Thesis (M.A.)—Univ. of Calif., 1933.   CU

9365. Fireman's fund insurance co. Annual report.
CHi has 1957, 1962. CL has 1950–60.

9366. —— A log of the Fireman's fund cruise around San Francisco bay, April 20, 1941. [S.F.? 1941] 27 l. Reproduced from typew. copy.   CO

9367. —— Prospectus. August 25, 1948 and March 10, 1954.   CHi

9368. —— Record of the Fireman's fund insurance company in the San Francisco disaster of April 18–21st, 1906. [S.F., Britton & Rey print., 1907] 8 p.   CU-B

9369. —— Welcome to the Fund... [S.F., n.d.] [28] p. illus.   CHi

9370. Fireman's fund record. Seventy-five eventful years, 1863–1938. S.F., 1938. (v.60, no. 5, May, 1938)
CHi

9371. —— Storied San Francisco. A special edition of *Fireman's fund record*...commemorating the United nations conference on international organization, San Francisco. [S.F., 1945] [54] p. illus. (v.67, no. 5, May, 1945)
C CChiS CHi CLO CLU CLgA CO CSdS CSf CSfWF-H CSmat OU

9372. The first grand celebration of the admission of California into the Union, in San Francisco, October 29, 1850. Program. [n.p., n.d.] 7 l.   CU-B

9373. First national bank of San Francisco. Annual statements. S.F., 19—?–
CHi has 1912, 1914.

9374. First steamship pioneers. Festival in celebration of the twenty-fifth anniversary of the arrival of the steamer *California* at San Francisco, February 28th, 1849, given by the society of "First steamship pioneers," February 28, 1874. S.F., Crocker, 1874. 62 p.
C CMont CSf CSfCP CSfCW CSmH CU-B

9375. —— First steamship pioneers. Ed. by a committee of the association. [S.F., H.S. Crocker, 1874] 393 p. Biographies of some of the better known passengers of the steamer *California* on her first trip to California, arriving February 28th, 1849.   CHi

9376. Fischer, Arthur H. David Belasco in San Francisco. Stanford, 1957. Thesis (M.A.)—Stanford univ., 1957.   CSt

9377. Fisher, Robert L. Mobility patterns of the San Francisco elementary school population, by Robert L. Fisher and John Gianopoulos. [S.F., S.F. state college] 1956. 45 l. illus.   CSfSt

9378. [Fisher's theatre] Souvenir program benefit California eye and ear hospital, October 22, 1902. [S.F.] Francis, Valentine & co., print. [1902] [32] p.   CHi

9379. Fitch, Guillermo, and Piña, Blas. Narrative of Guillermo Fitch and Blas Piña, taken on board of steamer *M.S. Latham* on her voyage from San Francisco to Donahue. April 16th, 1874. Translated by members of Los Hispanistas, Spanish club of the C. K. McClatchy senior high school, from the original Spanish of California Ms. E 67, no. 3, in Bancroft library, Berkeley, California. Sacramento, C. K. McClatchy senior high school, 1941. x, 34 p. front.   CHi

9380. Fitzhamon, E. G. The streets of San Francisco... [S.F., 1928–29] [162] p. of mounted clippings. illus., ports. Clippings from the *S.F. chronicle* Aug. 26, 1928–April 7? 1929.
CHi CO CSf CSfCP CSmH CU-B

9381. Fitzpatrick, F. W. The San Francisco calamity. Report of investigations made by F. W. Fitzpatrick, executive officer of the international society of building commissioners, on behalf of that society, the United States government, many technical journals, etc. [Chicago, 1906] [17] p. illus. CU-B

9382. Flammer, Charles. The philosophy of quality; a way of life...50 years in the service of A. Schilling & company, San Francisco, April 23, 1897 to April 22, 1947. S.F., Grabhorn, 1947. 92 p. ports. CHi CStclU

9383. Flavin, M. J. Catalogue and price list of M. J. Flavin's great IXL. S.F. [1883] 1 v. illus. CU-B

9384. Flayderman, Harry. Henry Raschen, painter of the American west. [n.p., c1958] 26 l. Mimeo. CHi

9385. [Fleet at San Francisco. 1908] C CL CSmH CU-B

9386. Fleming, Sandford. The history of the First Baptist church of San Francisco, California, 1849–1944 ... [S.F.? 1944] [37] p. illus., ports. CHi CO CSmH CU-B

9387. Fletcher, Robert Howe. Pen drawings in Chinatown, by Ernest C. Peixotto. With certain observations by Robert Howe Fletcher. S.F., Robertson [c1898] 18 l. illus. C CHi CLU CSmH CU-B MoS

9388. Floating sea-bath co. Prospectus... S.F., Calif. demokrat print., 1878. 6 p. C

9389. Flood building. A building new as tomorrow ... S.F., [1950?] [16] p. illus. (part col.), plans. CHi

9390. Florence Crittenton home of San Francisco. The sixty-fifth year; story of the Florence Crittenton home, 1889–1954... [n.p., 1954] [12] p. illus. CHi

9391. Flowers for genius, gathered on the shores of the Pacific. S.F., Whitton, Towne & co., print., 1854. 64 p. Reprint of newspaper reviews of the appearances of Matilda Heron on the San Francisco stage. CLU

9392. Flynn, William. Men, money, and mud; the story of San Francisco international airport. [S.F., William Flynn publications, 1954] 63 p. illus., port. C CHi CRcS CRic CSd CSf CSt CStclU CU-B

9393. Foley, Donald L. The suburbanization of administrative offices in the San Francisco bay area. Berkeley, Univ. of Calif. [c1957] 48 p. tables, maps, diagrs. (Calif. Univ. Bur. of business and economic research. Real estate research program. Research report, no. 10) CSfSt CU

9394. Folkers (J.H.A.) and bro., firm. Catalogue and price list, and description of electrical apparatus for medical use. S.F. [188–?] 1 v. illus. CU-B

9395. —— Catalogue of dental goods... S.F., Winterburn & co., 1878. 196 p. CHi CU-B

9396. —— Catalogue of surgical instruments, appliances... S.F. [1884] 1 v. illus. CU-B

9397. Font, Pedro. ...The Anza expedition of 1775–1776; diary of Pedro Font, ed. by Frederick J. Teggart... Berkeley, Univ. of Calif., 1913. 131 p. front., facsim. (Pub. of the Acad. of Pac. coast history. v.3, no. 1) CU-B CViCL MoS

9398. —— Font's complete diary, a chronicle of the founding of San Francisco; translated from the original Spanish manuscript and edited by Herbert Eugene Bolton ... Berkeley, Univ. of Calif. press, 1931. 552 p. illus., maps. "First published as Volume IV in Bolton, *Anza's California expeditions,* of which this volume is a reprint." —Footnote, p. x. Available in many California libraries and CaBViPA KU KyU MoS MoSU OU TxU UHi UU WM

9399. —— ...San Francisco bay and California in 1776; three maps, with outline sketches reproduced in facsimile from the original manuscript...with an explanation by Irving Berdine Richman. Providence, R.I. [Bost., Merrymount press] 1911. 7 p. maps. C CHi CL CLU CO CSd CSf CSfCP CSfMI CSmH CU-B CaBViPA ViU

9400. Foreman, Grant. The adventures of James Collier, first collector of the port of San Francisco. Chicago, Black cat press, 1937. C CBb CHi CL CLU CLgA CO COHN CRedCL CSS CSd CSf CSfCW CSmat CSmH CStrJC CU-B CaBViPA

9401. Forester, Cecil Scott. One hundred years of consular correspondence. [n.p., 1949?] 21 l. Mimeo. CU-B

9402. Foresters of America. San Francisco. Court Golden Gate no. 5. By-laws... S.F., Sanders print. co., 1916. 40 p. CHi

9403. —— —— Same. [S.F.] Levison print. co., 1937. 32 p. CHi

9404. Formes, Karl. My memoirs; autobiography ...published in his memory... S.F., James H. Barry, 1891. 240 p. port. CHi

9405. Foster, Jonathan Douglass. Organized "boys' work" in San Francisco. [Berkeley, 1922] Thesis (M.A.)—Univ. of Calif., 1922. CU

9406. Foster and Kleiser co., San Francisco. Catalogue of painted bulletins, wall displays...issued January 1, 1921. [S.F., Taylor & Taylor, 1920] 62 p. illus. CHi

9407. —— Facts about Foster and Kleiser company. [S.F., 1945] 11 p. illus., maps. CHi

9408. —— Fifty years of outdoor advertising, 1901–1951. S.F. [1951?] 26 p. CHi

9409. —— Forty years of advertising, 1901–1941. [S.F., 1941] 29 p. CHi

9410. —— ...Outdoor advertising. Painted display service on the Pacific coast. [S.F., Taylor & Taylor, 1923] [35] l. illus. CHi

9411. —— ...Poster advertising, 1921. S.F. [Taylor & Taylor, c1920] 13 p. CHi

9412. —— A presentation of poster advertising on the Pacific coast together with important statistical information and specifications...in the cities and towns in California...Dated July 1, 1923. [S.F., Taylor & Taylor, 1923] 71 p. illus. CHi

9413. [Foster lunch system, ltd.] Fosters restaurants and bakeries, San Francisco, Oakland, Berkeley. A story of 25 eventful years, 1922–1947. [n.p., n.d.] [32] p. illus. CHi

9414. [Fourgeaud, Victor John] The first Californiac, being a reprint of Prospects of California written by Dr. Victor H. [!] Fourgeaud for the April 1, 1848 issue of the California star, San Francisco's first newspaper, of which Samuel Brannan was the publisher... S.F., Press of Lewis and Dorothy Allen, 1942. [xv] 44 p. illus., port. CHi CSf

9415. Fowler, Charles Evan. The San Francisco-Oakland cantilever bridge. N.Y., Seattle, 1915. 18 l. illus. CSfMI

9416. Fragley, Martin F., vs. Phelan, James D. ...M. F. Fragley, plaintiff and appellant, vs. James D. Phelan, et al., defendants and respondents. Respondents' points and authorities. Franklin K. Lane...attorney for respondents... S.F., Star press [1899] 79 p. CU-B

9417. France. Commission, Panama-Pacific international exposition, 1915. Catalogue officiel de la section Française. [Paris, 1915?] 510 p. fold. plans.
CHi CSfMI CSfU CU-B

9418. —— —— Fine-arts, French section; catalogue of works in painting, drawings, sculpture, medals-engravings and lithographs. [Paris, Librairie centrale des beaux-arts, 1915?] 351 p.
CHi CSd CSfMI CU-B

9419. —— —— ...La science Francaise. Paris, Ministere de l'instruction publique et des beaux-arts, 1915. 2 v. ports. At head of title: Exposition universelle de San Francisco.
CStoC

9420. —— **Consulat. San Francisco.** Unis-Stats. Exportations et importations de San-Francisco en 1909. [Paris, 1910?] 23 p.
CU-B

9421. —— —— —— Etats-Unis. Situation économique de San-Francisco et en général de la région de cette circonscription consulaire en 1907–1908. [Paris, 1909?] 29 p.
CU-B

9422. Francesca relief society. By-laws... S.F. [n.d.] 7 p.
CHi

9423. Francis, Robert Coleman. A history of labor on the San Francisco waterfront... [Berkeley, 1934] 230 l. Thesis (Ph.D.)—Univ. of Calif., 1934.
CU

9424. —— A survey of Negro business in the San Francisco bay region. [Berkeley, 1929] Thesis (M.A.)—Univ. of Calif., 1929.
CU

9425. Francisca club. Annual reports.
CHi has 1914–15.

9426. —— Constitution, by-laws and house rules... S.F. [Pernau pub. co., n.d.] 23 p.
CHi

9427. —— Constitution, by-laws, list of members and annual report... 1906–1908. S.F. [Pernau pub. co.] 1908. 48 p.
CHi

9428. Franco-American commercial co. ...Catalogue of costly oil paintings of great value and merit! Comprising the works of eminent artists of England, France, Italy, Dusseldorf and New York. To be sold... December 14th and 15th, 1865... [S.F.? 1865] 21 p.
CU-B

9429. Franco-American tallow and fertilizing co. ...All kinds of organic and chemical fertilizers... [S.F., M.V. Lacaze, n.d.] 6 p.
CHi

9430. Frangini, A. Italiani in San Francisco e Oakland, Cal. Cenni biografici. S.F., Tipografia Lanson-Lauray & co., 1914. 135 p. illus., ports.
CHi CLU

9431. Frankenthal and co. Catalogue...direct importers of American, English, German and French fancy goods... S.F. [187–?] 1 v.
CU-B

9432. Franklin, Sid, comp. Market street railway company, a history... S.F., 1941. 14 l. Typew.
CSf

9433. Franklin hospital. ...Franklin hospital, founded 1852... [S.F., Schwabacher-Frey] 1948. 48 p. illus.
CHi CSf

9434. [Franklin printing trades association] Organized felony; the picket and the wrecking crew weapons of San Francisco's labor monopoly... [S.F., 1914] 20 p. Signed: Executive committee F.P.T.A. ... J. D. Roantree, secretary.
CHi CLU

9435. Frear stone co. [Prospectus] [S.F.? 1872?] [4] p.
CU-B

9436. Freeman, John Ripley. On the proposed use of a portion of the Hetch Hetchy, Eleanor and Cherry valleys...for impounding Tuolumne river flood waters and appurtenant works for the water supply of San Fran-

cisco, California... S.F., Rincon pub. co., 1912. 401 p.
C CHi CL CLSU CLU CO CSS CSf CSfCSM CSfCW CSfP CSfSC CSfSt CSfU CSfWF-H CSmH CStoC CU-B ViU

9437. Freemasons. California. Report of the General Masonic relief fund incident to earthquake and fire of April 18, 1906... [L.A., W.P. Jeffries co., print.] 1906. 112 p.
CLU CO CSf CSfWF-H CU-B

9438. —— —— The Masonic widows' and orphans' home of California. Official program of the festivities at Mechanics' pavilion, San Francisco, May 9–14, 1898. 216 p. illus., ports.
C CSf CU-B

9439. —— —— **Grand lodge.** California Masonic centennial, 1850–1950, Oct. 9–13, 1950, San Francisco, California. [S.F., 1950] [32] p. illus., ports.
CHi

9440. —— —— —— A Masonic burial service, as arranged by Alex. G. Abell, R. W. Grand secretary of the...Grand lodge...of the state of California. S.F., F. Eastman, print., 1856. 14 p.
C CHi CSmH CU-B

9441. —— —— —— Masonic ceremonial at laying the corner-stone of the City hall and Law courts of the city of San Francisco, February 22d, 1872. With full list of articles deposited in the corner-stone. S.F., 1872. [2] p. illus.
CU-B

9442. —— —— **Royal Arch Masons. Grand chapter.** Report of the committee on earthquake and fire, history of the second day's session of the Grand chapter of Royal arch Masons of the state of California at its fifty-second annual convocation, Masonic temple, Montgomery & Post Streets, San Francisco... L.A., Neuner co. press, 1910. 77 p. illus., facsims.
C CHi CLU

9443. —— —— **Scottish rite. Grand consistory.** Proceedings of the M. P. Grand consistory...in and for the state of California, held in San Francisco, Oct. 13th, 1870, Dec. 27th, 1870, and Jan. 11th, 1871... S.F., 1871.
CHi

9444. —— —— **San Francisco. California lodge no. 1.** The centennials...California lodge no. 1, F. & A. M. by Ralph Ernest Mott. [S.F., 1949] 29 p. illus.
CHi

9445. —— —— —— List of members...from its organization, October, A.L., 5849, to January 5th, A.L., 5860. [S.F.? 1860] p. 49–54.
CHi

9446. —— —— **Fidelity lodge no. 120.** One hundred years of freemasonry, 1857–1957... S.F., 1957. [25] p. illus., ports.
CHi

9447. —— —— **Islam temple.** Shrine golden jubilee, June, 1933. [S.F.? Walter N. Brunt, print., 1922] [36] p. illus.
CHi

9448. —— —— **Knights templar. Golden Gate commandery no. 16.** Templar drill and reception tendered to the Grand Commandery Knights templar of California...April 23, 1893. [S.F.] 1893. 36 p. illus., ports.
CHi

9449. —— —— **Mission lodge no. 169.** History of Mission lodge no. 169...1863 diamond jubilee 1938. S.F., 1938. 143 p. illus., ports.
CHi

9450. —— —— **Mount Moriah lodge no. 44.** A history...by R[aymond] T[homas] Nixon. [S.F., 1928?] 56 p.
CHi

9451. —— —— **Occidental lodge no. 22.** By-laws... S.F., Franklin off., 1852. 12 p.
CHi

9452. —— —— —— Same. Rev. January 15, 1900. S.F., Joseph Winterburn co. print., 1900. 65 p.
CHi

9453. —— —— —— Centennial, 1852–1952... [S.F., 1952] 48 p. illus., ports.
CHi

9454. —— —— —— Roster of Occidental lodge no. 22, F. & A. M. Compiled by William Penn Humphreys. [S.F., Hansen co., 1925?] 132 p. CHi

9455. —— —— Oriental lodge. By-laws... S.F., F. Eastman print., Franklin off., 1856. 13 p. NN

9456. —— —— Pacific lodge no. 136. By laws. S.F., Gazlay's bk. and job off., 1861. CSmH

9457. —— —— Scottish rite. [Brochure, Scottish rite temple] S.F., Walter N. Brunt co., press, n.d.] [16] p. illus., plans. CHi

9458. —— —— Starr King lodge no. 344. ... Fiftieth anniversary... [1901–1951] [n.p., 1951] 36 p. illus., ports. Includes reprint of *Starr King, patriot and mason*, by Hal Curtis, 1951. 43 p. CHi

9459. —— —— —— Grand reception honoring most worshipful Alfred Fisher Breslauer, grand master of Masons in California, October 8, 1960. S.F., 1960. [6] p. port. CHi

9460. —— U.S. Knights templars. Grand encampment. ...Official souvenir and guide... of the twenty-ninth triennial conclave held at San Francisco, California, 1904. S.F., 1904. [222] p. illus., ports. CLU

9461. French, Fern Edwards. An analysis of the population in the nine littoral counties of San Francisco bay, 1910–30. [Berkeley, 1939] Thesis (M.A.)—Univ. of Calif., 1939. CU

9462. French, Wheeler N., vs. Teschemacher, Henry F., et al. In the Supreme court of the state of California. Wheeler N. French, appellant, vs. Henry F. Teschemacher, the Board of supervisors of the city and county of San Francisco, et al., respondents. Brief of appellant's counsel. H. & C. McAllister, and Hoge & Wilson, of the counsel for appellant. S.F., Towne & Bacon, 1864. 45 p. The brief contests the constitutionality of a subscription by San Francisco to the capital stock of the Western Pacific railroad company and the Central Pacific railroad company of California. CLU

9463. French mutual beneficial association. Annual report. 1872–73. [S.F.?] 1873. 1 v. Founded November 30, 1867. CHi

9464. French mutual benevolent society. By-laws ...S.F., L. Lacaze print., 1899. 16 p. Incorporated as La société française de bienfaisance mutuelle. CHi

9465. —— Souvenir programme, published on the occasion of the grand festival, carnival, kermesse and concert, for the benefit of the new French hospital held at Mechanics' pavilion, San Francisco... S.F., 1895. unp. illus. CSf CSmH

9466. Friedman (M.) and co. [Furniture catalog] S.F. [191–?] 1 v. illus. CU-B

9467. Friends of France, San Francisco. .. Origin and purposes of the society... [S.F., 1917] 8 p. CHi

9468. Frisch, Jerome. Unemployment compensation for long-shoremen in San Francisco. [Berkeley, 1941] Thesis (M.A.)—Univ. of Calif., 1941. CU

9469. Frost prevention co. The Bolton orchard heater known also as the "Fresno pot" and the "California oil pot," the pioneer without a peer. S.F. [1911] 32 p. illus., facsims., tables. CU-B

9470. Frothingham, Richard. A tribute to Thomas Starr King. Bost., Ticknor and Fields, 1865. 247 p. front. CHi CL CP CSf CSfCW CStmo

9471. Fuller (W. P.) and co. Catalogue and descriptive price list of brushes. S.F. [18—?] 1 v. illus. CU-B

9472. —— Same, Catalog 31. Brushes. [n.p., 193–?] 35 p. illus. CHi

9473. —— Catalog of lubricating oils. S.F. [19—?] 1 v. illus. (part col.) tables. CU-B

9474. —— Ninety years; the story of William Parmer Fuller. S.F., Priv. print. [Grabhorn] 1939. 144 p. front. (port.) illus. CBb CHi CLO CSf

9475. —— Price lists of French window glass and car, picture, photographic, colored and ornamental glass ... S.F., Crocker, 1901. [18] p. illus. CHi

9476. —— W. P. Fuller & co., San Francisco... views illustrating our facilities for the manufacture and distribution of goods. S.F., Sunset press [1902] [61] p. pl. CHi CU-B

9477. Furman, Edwin H. [Photograph album of San Francisco scenes, chiefly of the 1850's and 1860's] 48 p. of mounted illus., ports. CU-B

9478. [Furuseth, Andrew] A symposium on Andrew Furuseth. New Bedford, Mass., Darwin press [n.d.] 233 p. illus. CHi

9479. Gaddis, Thomas E. Birdman of Alcatraz; the story of Robert Stroud. N.Y., Random house [1955] 334 p. CU-B

9480. Gaer, Joseph, ed. ...The theatre of the gold rush decade in San Francisco... [n.p., 1935] 99 l. (Monograph no. 5, SERA project 2–F2–132 [3–F2–197] Calif. literary research) C CL CLSU CSd CSdS CSf CSfP CSfWF-H CSmH CU-B

9481. Gagey, Edmond McAdoo. The San Francisco stage: a history. N.Y., Columbia univ. press, 1950. 264 p. illus. Available in many California libraries and KU OU

9482. Gamble, James, vs. Tripp, Dwight K., et al. In the Supreme court of the state of California. James Gamble, plaintiff and respondent, vs. Dwight K. Tripp and Western savings and trust company, defendants and appellants. Transcript on appeal. Galpin & Zeigler, attorneys for defendants and appellants. W. H. L. Barnes, attorney for plaintiff and respondent... [S.F.] Dempster Bros., print. [1892] 62 p. CHi

9483. Gantner & Mattern co., knit goods. [Catalogs] CHi has no. 8, 10, 1906, 1910.

9484. Garden club of St. Francis wood. Constitution and by-laws. [S.F., Taylor & Taylor, 1929] 16 p. CHi

9485. Gardner, Roy. Hellcatraz, by Roy Gardner (once America's most notorious mail robber and escape artist, who served two years on Alcatraz) [n.p., 193–?] 109 p. illus., ports. C CHi CU-B

9486. Garfield monument association of the Pacific coast. History of the monument with the address [by Horace Davis] at the unveiling. [S.F., 1885?] 15 p. CHi CU-B

9487. Garlock packing co. Catalogue R. 1914. S.F. [1914] 1 v. CU-B

9488. Garnett, Porter. The Bohemian jinks. A treatise. S.F., Bohemian club, 1908. 137 p. illus., ports., map. An account of the woodland mid-summer dramatic and musical performances given by the Bohemian club of San Francisco. C CHi CL CLU CSf CSfCW CSmH CStmo CU-B

9489. —— The inscriptions at the Panama-Pacific

international exposition... S.F. [Taylor, Nash & Taylor, print.] 1915. 35 p.

C CHi CO CRedl CSf CSmH CStoC CU-B

9490. Garnier, Paul. Voyage médical en Californie (1851). With an introduction by Gilbert Chinard. Wash., D.C., Institut Français de Washington [n.d.] 47 p. cover title. Reprint. from the *French American review*, July-Sept., 1949. The original edition of this work was published under the same title in Paris, 1854.   CHi

9491. Garratt (W. T.) & co. Catalogue and price list of pumping and hydraulic machinery... S.F. [1887-1902]   CHi (1887) CU-B (1902)

9492. —— [Catalogue of bells and gongs] S.F. [1875?] 1 v. illus.   CU-B

9493. —— [Catalogue of]...brass and bell foundry, machine and hydraulic works... S.F., 1883. 241 p. illus.   CHi

9494. —— Catalogue of the Hall duplex steam pumps. S.F., Bancroft, 1889. 32 p. illus.   C-S

9495. —— Revised price list of iron pipe and fittings... S.F., Eastman & Thomas, 1896–97. 2 nos. illus.

CHi has n. 2, 4 for 1896, 1897.

9496. —— Richards' patent machinery for irrigation and reclamation. S.F., Geo. Spaulding & co., 1887. 34 p.   CHi

9497. —— W.D. Hooker's patent steam pump... S.F., Spaulding & Barto [n.d.] 18 p.   C-S

9498. Garrett, Lula May. A social history of the city of San Francisco for the year 1851. [Stanford] 1939. Thesis (Ph.D.)—Stanford univ., 1938/39.   CSt

9499. Garwood, Henrietta M., vs. Wood, Joseph M., et al. ...Henrietta M. Garwood, respondent, vs. Joseph M. Wood, Michael Higgins, et al., appellants. Transcript on appeal from the fourth judicial district, San Francisco county. Samuel L. Cutter, jr., for respondent. Jos. M. Wood, appellant, in person. Sacramento, Crocker, 1866. 66 p.   CU-B

9500. Gavin, Constance May, vs. The Protestant Episcopal Bishop of California et al. In the Supreme court of the state of California. Probate S.F. no. 14,581. In the matter of the estate of James L. Flood, deceased. Petition of Constance May Gavin for partial distribution. Constance May Gavin, petitioner and appellant, the Protestant Episcopal Bishop of California, et al., respondents. Appellant's opening brief... S.F., Pernau-Walsh print. co. [1932] 554, 64 p.   CHi CRcS

9501. —— ...Brief for respondents. S.F., Pernau-Walsh print. co. [1932] 522 p.   CHi CRcS

9502. —— ...Respondents' petition for a rehearing. S.F., Pernau-Walsh printing co. [1933] 1–128, 455–469 p. At head of cover-title: An appendix hereto contains a copy of the opinion in the case...   CHi

9503. Gazlay, David M., comp. Gazlay's American biography for 1861...Distributed gratuitously...throughout California, Oregon, etc. S.F., Gazlay's steam book & job print., 1861. 240 p. Illus. advertisements of San Francisco.   C CHi CLU CSfCP CU-B

9504. Geary street extension homestead association. Articles of association... S.F., Excelsior press, Bacon & co., 1869. 18 p.   CHi

9505. Géauque, Hélène. Adventuring in San Francisco with Hélène and Edwin Géauque. S.F., Benham press [c1931] [18] p. illus.

CHi CLU CSfCW CU-B

9506. Geiser (W. B.) and co. Catalogue. no. 14, 1900/01. S.F. [1901?] illus.   CU-B

9507. General electric co. The General electric company at the Panama-Pacific exposition. [n.p., 1915?] 11 p. illus.   CHi CU-B

9508. Genthe, Arnold. As I remember, with one hundred and twelve photographic illustrations by the author. N.Y., Reynal & Hitchcock [1936] 290 p. illus., ports.   CHi CRcS CSfCW CU-B

9509. —— Old Chinatown. A book of pictures by Arnold Genthe. With text by Will Irwin. N.Y., M. Kennerley, 1913. 208 p. illus.

C CBu CChiS CHi CL CLSU CLU CMartC CO CRcS CRedl CSf CSfCW CSfP CSmH CU-B CWhC CoD MiD MoS

9510. —— Old Chinatown; a photographic calendar for the year 1946. Oakland, Mills college, 1946. 26 p. illus., ports.   CHi

9511. —— Pictures of old Chinatown, by Arnold Genthe; with text by Will Irwin. N.Y., Moffat, Yard & co., 1908. 57 p. 46 pl.

Available in many California libraries and MiD MoS

9512. Gentles, Frederick Ray. The San Francisco press, 1887–1895: the fight for circulation. [Berkeley, 1939] Thesis (M.A.)—Univ. of Calif., 1939.   CU

9513. Geographical society of the Pacific, San Francisco. Constitution and by-laws... [S.F., A.J. Leary, 1881?] 21 p.   CHi

9514. Georgas, Demitra. Greek settlement of the San Francisco bay area. [Berkeley, 1951] Thesis (M.A.) —Univ. of Calif., 1951.   CU

9515. George, Henry, jr. The life of Henry George ... Garden City, N.Y., Doubleday, 1930. 634 p. illus., port.   CSf

9516. Germain, Dwight. [Specimens of printing done in the printing office of Dwight Germain. [S.F., 1870–85] 177 p. of mounted specimens.   CU-B

9517. German-American publishing co. San Francisco. Wie es war, wie es ist, wie es sein wird. Oakland [1906?] 75 p. illus., ports.   C CHi CU-B

9518. German general benevolent society. ... Annual report of the German general benevolent society and Franklin hospital, owned and operated by the society ...77th, 1931. [S.F., 1932] 8 p. incl. tables.   CU-B

9519. —— ...Constitution and by-laws... S.F., 1883. 73 p. illus. Title and text in German and English.   CHi

9520. —— Sixty years...by Heinrich Kaufmann... S.F., 1914. 92 p. illus., ports.

CHi (in English and German) CSfSt (in German)

9521. German relief bazaar "For humanity's sake," Civic auditorium, May 19th to May 24th, 1916. S.F., Louis Roesch co., 1916. [50] p. illus., port.   CHi

9522. German savings and loan society. By-laws. ...Incorporated February 10th, 1868; re-incorporated June 29th, 1886. [S.F.] 1911. [12] p.   CHi

9523. —— Half yearly report... S.F., 1896–1900. 4 v.

CHi has June 20, Dec., 1896, Dec. 30, 1899, June 30, 1900, (in German)

9524. —— Prospectus and extract from the by-laws ... S.F., Democrat job off., 1868. 15 p. tables.   CHi

9525. —— Prospectus and extract from the by-laws ...[passbook] S.F., 1903. 15 p.   CHi

9526. Germania trust co. vs. San Francisco. In the Supreme court of the state of California. [S.F., no.

2031] Germania trust company, plaintiff and respondent, vs. City and county of San Francisco, defendant and appellant. Appellant's reply brief. Garber, Creswell & Garber, Smith & Pringle, attorneys for appellant... S.F., Crocker [1899] 59 p. CHi

9527. Gerould, Katharine (Fullerton) The aristocratic west. N.Y., Harper, 1925. 220 p. front., pl.
CRcS CU-B

9528. Gerstle, Mark L. Historical report of the San Francisco depot, Fort Mason, general supply depot, zone 13, for period April 1, 1917 to April 30, 1919. Major-general C. A. Devol, U.S. army, commanding. Prepared by Major Mark L. Gerstle, Q. M. corps, U.S. army, historical officer. [n.p., n.d.] 72 p. ports. charts. Typew. CHi

9529. Giant powder co. Giant powder, manufactured exclusively by the Giant powder company... S.F., Women's cooperative union print, 1869. 25 p. CU-B

9530. Gibbons, Henry. Annual address before the San Francisco county medical society, delivered pursuant to appointment January 27, 1857... S.F., Whitton, Towne & co's Excelsior steam presses, 1857. 24 p.
C CSmH CSt CU-B

9531. —— Fifty years ago; an address to the graduating class of the medical college of the Pacific for 1878. [S.F.] Bancroft & co. [1878] 21 p. CHi

9532. —— In memoriam. First of the "Lane lectures" of 1885 by Dr. Levi Cooper Lane. S.F., Howard & Pariser, 1885. 22 p. CHi

9533. —— Valedictory address to the graduating class of the medical department of the University of the Pacific, delivered at the public commencement, held March 15th, 1862. S.F., Towne & Bacon, print., 1862. 21 p. C CSmH CU-B

9534. [Gibbons, Henry, jr.] Exercises held at Lane hall of Cooper medical college in memory of Doctor Henry Gibbons, junior, on Sunday the eighth day of December, 1911. [S.F., Printed by order of the directors and faculty of Cooper medical college, 1911?] 18 p. port.
CHi

9535. Gibson, Robert W. Military news in San Francisco daily newspapers. [Stanford] 1956. Thesis (M.A.)—Stanford univ., 1956. CSt

9536. Giffen, Guy James, and Giffen, Helen. The story of Golden Gate park. S.F., 1949. 71 p. illus., map.
C CHi CLO CMartC CO CSf CSfCP CSfCW CSmH CU-B UPB

9537. Gilbert, Benjamin Franklin. Naval operations in the Pacific, 1861–1866. [Berkeley, 1951] Thesis (Ph.D.)—Univ. of Calif., 1951. CU

9538. Gilbert, Grove Karl. ...The San Francisco earthquake and fire of April 18, 1906, and their effects on structures and structural materials; reports by Grove Karl Gilbert, Richard Lewis Humphrey, John Stephen Sewell and Frank Soulé, with preface by Joseph Austin Holmes... Wash., D.C., Govt. print. off., 1907. 170 p. illus., maps. (U.S. Geol. survey. Bul. no. 324) Partial contents: List of papers relating to the earthquake and fire: p. 159–161.
Available in many California libraries and OrU

9539. Gillespie, Charles V. Abstract of title to the lands of the Park Hill homestead association. S.F., A.L. Bancroft & co., 1878. 147 p. CHi

9540. Gilliam, Harold. The face of San Francisco. Text by Harold Gilliam, photographs by Phil Palmer. [1st ed.] Garden City, N.Y., Doubleday [1960] 256 p. illus., maps. CHi CRic CSf CSfU CU-B

9541. —— San Francisco bay. [1st ed.] Garden City, N.Y., Doubleday, 1957. 336 p.
Available in many California libraries and CaBViPA CoD MiD ODa TxU

9542. —— San Francisco, city at the Golden Gate by Harold Gilliam and Ann Gilliam. Sketches by Fritz Busse. N.Y., Arts, inc. c1959. unp. illus.
CAla CStcrCL

9543. Ginty, John, comp. Perfection block and street guide of the city and county of San Francisco... S.F., James H. Barry co., 1914. 192 p. fold. map.
CHi CU-B

9544. Girard water wheel co. [Catalog] 1895. S.F., 1895. 44 p. illus. CHi

9545. Givens, James David. San Francisco in ruins; a pictorial history... Denver, Colo., Smith-Brooks co., c1906. 112 p. Text by A. M. Allison.
C CHi CMont CO CSd CSf CSfCW CSfU CSmH CU-B

9546. Glasscock, Carl Burgess. Lucky Baldwin... Indianapolis, Bobbs, 1933. 308 p. illus., ports.
Available in many libraries.

9547. Gleason, Joseph M., Monsignor. Scrapbooks of clippings...concerning San Francisco [n.d.] 4 v. CSfCW

9548. Gleeson, Richard A., Father. Dominic Giacobbi; a noble Corsican... N.Y., America press [c1938] 285 p. illus., port. Life of a celebrated priest in California; one of the Italian pioneers. CHi CLgA CSfCW

9549. —— My golden jubilee thoughts... [S.F., 1927] 24 p. port. CHi

9550. Glesener (A.J.) co. Catalogue B. Heavy hardware... [Chicago, R.R. Donnelley & sons co., 1930] 232 p. illus. CHi

9551. Glimpses of the San Francisco disaster, graphically depicting the great California earthquake and fire; original photographs of the world's greatest conflagration ... Chicago, Laird & Lee, c1906. [114] p. of illus., map.
CHi CL CLgA CLob CO CSd CSf CSfU CSmH CStclU CU-B NHi OrU

9552. Globe hotel school and woman's union mission of San Francisco to Chinese women and children, San Francisco. Twentieth annual report... 1889. [S.F., R.R. Patterson, 1890] 16 p. CHi

9553. Godchaux, Edmond. [Views of housing conditions in San Francisco, 1894. S.F., 1921] 146 [145] photos. C

9554. Goddard & co. The Pacific iron works, embracing foundry machine, boiler, forging and smithing... S.F., Winterburn & co., 1867. 96 p. illus., tables. CHi

9555. Godoy, José Francisco. San Francisco, California. Su historia, recursos, situation actual, industria y comercio. Mexico, "El Ferrocarrilero," 1890. 93 p. illus., map. CLU CU-B

9556. Goelzer, Edward Sherman. Marketing of coffee in the San Francisco bay region. [Berkeley, 1929] Thesis (M.S.)—Univ. of Calif., 1929. CU

9557. Goethe-Schiller denkmal gesellschaft. Gedenkblätter zur Goethe-Schiller feier; veranstaltet von den Deutschen Californiens, San Francisco, November 5–9, 1895. S.F., L. Roesch co., 1895. 100 p. illus., ports.
CHi CSf

9558. —— Das Goethe-Schiller denkmal in San Francisco, California. Erinnerungen an den "Deutschen Tag" der California midwinter international exposition, 1894, und das "Goethe-Schiller Fest" 1895 und an die

"Enthüllung des Denkmals" im Golden Gate park, 1901. S.F. [1901] 113 p. illus.   CHi CSdS

9559. Goldbeck, Herman Gilbert. The political career of James Rolph, jr.: a preliminary study... Berkeley, 1936. 4 p.l., 168, xiii l. Typew. Thesis (M.A.)—Univ. of Calif., 1936.   CU CU-B

9560. Goldberg, Bowen and co. [Catalog] S.F. [185–?–
CHi has 1895, 1896, 1906, 1924. CU-B has 1891, 1900, 1925.

9561. Golden Gate bridge and highway district. The Golden Gate bridge at San Francisco. v.1, Report of the chief engineer with architectural studies to the Board of directors, Golden Gate bridge and highway district, August 27, 1930. v.2...Traffic analysis and report of the traffic engineer, to accompany report of chief engineer, August 27, 1930. [S.F., 193–?] 2 v. illus.
        CLSU (v.1) CO (v.1) CU-B (v.2)

9562. ——— The Golden Gate bridge; report of the chief engineer to the board of directors... [S.F., c1938] 246 p.
CBu CChiS CHi CLSU CMartC CO CRcS CRedl CSS CSj CSmat CSmH CSrCL CUk MoS MoSHi NHi ODa T TxU ViU

9563. ——— Same. Synopsis of the report of the chief engineer with summary sheets and addenda. S.F. [1938?] 16 p.   CO

9564. ——— The Golden gate bridge, history and principal characteristics. [S.F.] Knight, Counihan, 1933. [20] p. illus., map.   CHi

9565. Golden Gate kindergarten association. ...Report...1st, 1879/80–1908. S.F., Dodge bros., print. [1880]–1908.
CHi has 8th, 10th, 80th, 1886/87, 1888/89, 1959. CU-B has 1879/80, 1880/95, 1896/1900, 1901/02, 1906–08.

9566. The Golden Gate park, in Albertype. S.F., Jos. A. Hofmann, 1889. [2] p. 16 pl.   C

9567. Golden Gate park news. Souvenir of Golden Gate park, rehabilitation edition. [S.F.] Phillips & Van Orden co. [1908] 50 p. illus., ports.   CU-B

9568. Golden Gate park, San Francisco, Cal., July 4, 1888. [S.F.? 1888] [12] p. illus. (incl. ports., music)
                                              CU-B

9569. Golden Gate pocket guide and city map...v.1, no. 1, Jan., 1904– S.F., James P. Chadwick, pub., 1904– illus., maps.
C has v.1, no. 10, Oct. 1904. v.2, no. 7, July 1905. v.3, no. 2, Feb. 1906. C-S has v.3, no. 3, Mar. 1906. CHi has v.2, no. 9, Sept. 1905. CU-B has v.3, no. 1, Jan. 1906.

9570. Golden state and miners' iron works. Circular... S.F., B. Dore & co., 1881. 109 p. fold. table.
                                              CHi

9571. Golden state co., ltd. Annual report.
CHi has 1939–44, 1946–51.

9572. ——— [Brochure. S.F.? c1929] 23 p.   CHi

9573. ——— Prospectus. 50,000 shares Golden state company, ltd., 4% cumulative preferred stock... [n.p., 1946] 37 p.   CHi

9574. Goldsmith, Babette G. Municipal employee organizations in the San Francisco bay area. [Berkeley, 1940] Thesis (M.A.)—Univ. of Calif., 1940.   CU

9575. Goldthwaite, Elmire. The opera, nineteen hundred and thirty-two; commemorating the formal opening of San Francisco's war memorial opera house, a temple of music. S.F., Knight-Counihan print., 1932. 32 p. ports., pl.   CHi

9576. Gong, Eng Ying. Tong war! The first complete history of the Tongs in America; details of the Tong wars and their causes; lives of famous hatchetmen and gunmen; and inside information as to the workings of the Tongs, their aims and achievements... N.Y., Nicholas L. Brown, 1930. 287 p. illus.   CSto

9577. Goodrich, Mary, and Sharon, Mrs. William E. The Palace hotel. S.F., Crandall press, 1930. 37 p. illus., ports.
C CBu CHi CL CLSU CLU CMartC CO CSf CSfP CSfWF-H CSmH CU-B CoD

9578. Goodrich, W. S. A study of the homeless man problem in San Francisco, made for the joint committee on single men and unemployment of the Council of social and health agencies and the Community chest of San Francisco, March-May, 1924. [S.F., 1924?] 110 p. charts. Mimeo.   CHi

9579. Goodwill industries of San Francisco. A living memorial to human service. S.F., 1951. [20] l. Multilith.   CHi

9580. Goold, Edmond Louis. In the matter of the "Rancho Cañada de Guadalupe la visitacion y rodeo viego [!]" Argument of Mr. Edmond L. Goold, in resistance of the application to institute proceedings in chancery to cancel patent. Wash., J.L. Ginck, print., 1876. 25 p. Located in San Francisco and San Mateo counties at the county boundaries on the bay.   CLU

9581. [Gordon, George] Prospectus of South park; offering building lots fronting on ornamental grounds and brick residences to private families. S.F., Whitton, Towne & co., print., 1854. plan. 8 p. Signed: Geo. Gordon.   CHi (facsim.) CLU

9582. Gordon (James E.) firm. Price-list of American and foreign hardware. 1877. S.F. [1877] 1 v. tables.   CU-B

9583. Gorham, George C. The story of the attempted assassination of Justice Field... [n.p., n.d.] 198 p. Also bound with: Pomeroy, John Norton. Some account of the work of Stephen J. Field.   CHi

9584. Gorham-Revere rubber co. [Catalog] 1912. S.F. [1912] 1 v. illus.   CU-B

9585. Gould & Curry silver mining co. Annual reports... [S.F.? 1860?–
CHi has 4th-6th, 8th, 10th, 12th, 14th, 1863–65, 1867, 1869, 1871, 1873. CU-B has 3d, 1862.

9586. ——— By-laws. Incorporated June 27th, 1860. S.F., F. Eastman, print., 1861. 15 p.   CU-B

9587. Grabhorn press. Nineteenth century type displayed in 18 fonts, cast by United States founders now in cases of the Grabhorn press. S.F., Sold by D. Magee, 1959. [48] p. illus.   CHi

9588. Grady, Henry F., and Carr, Robert M. The port of San Francisco, a study of traffic competition, 1921–1933. Berkeley, Univ. of Calif. press, 1934. 501 p. illus., map.
C CBu CHi CL CLSU CLU CO CSf CSfU CU-B

9589. Graham, C. Water color sketches of the white city and the sunset city, by C. Graham, director of color of the California midwinter fair. [S.F., S.F. Examiner, n.d.] pt.1. 12 col. pl. Views and buildings at the Chicago world's Columbian exposition, 1893, and the San Francisco California midwinter fair, 1894.   CLgA

9590. Graham, Howard Jay. A study of the registration and voting behavior of certain professional classes in the San Francisco bay region. [Berkeley, 1930] Thesis (M.A.)—Univ. of Calif., 1930. CU

9591. —— When the bay bridge was a joke... [S.F., 1934] [36] p. illus., ports. Mounted clippings. C CSfP CU-B

9592. Graham (James) manufacturing co. [Catalog of] stoves, ranges. Established 1882. [S.F.? 1913] [118] p. illus. CHi

9593. Graham, Jerry B. Handset reminiscences; recollections of an old-time printer and journalist. Salt Lake City, Century print. co., 1915. 307 p. port. CBb CHi

9594. Graham, Mary, ed. Historical reminiscences of one hundred years ago. The Mission San Francisco de Assis. (Mission Dolores) Maria de la Concepción Argüello. S.F., P.J. Thomas, print., 1876. iv, [5]–39 p. illus. CHi CLU CSfCW ViU

9595. Grand army of the Republic. Dept. of California. By-laws and rules of order of Lincoln post, no. 1 ... S.F., Frank Eastman & co., print., 1882. 21 p. CHi

9596. —— —— Proceedings of the eighteenth annual encampment... held at San Francisco, February 18th, 20th and 21st, 1885. S.F., Geo. Spaulding & co., print., 1885. 168 p. CHi

9597. —— —— Roster of Gen'l Geo. G. Meade post... S.F., C.W. Gordon, print., 1902. 14 p. CHi

9598. Granstaff, Viola. Harr Wagner, California educational publicist. [L.A.] 1956. Thesis (M.A.)—U.C.L.A., 1956. CLU

9599. Grant from the Mexican nation to Fernando Marchina, with a history of his choice and occupancy of land under said grant, to make the same his legitimate property, to nearly all of San Francisco, etc. [translation] S.F., Mining and scientific press print. off., 1865. 4 p. CLU

9600. Graphic research service. City and county of San Francisco; precinct maps. S.F. [1952?] 19 col. maps. CSf

9601. Graves, Samuel. Memoirs and Masonic history of the late Samuel Graves. S.F., Frank Eastman & co., print., 1882. 173 p. port. CHi

9602. [Gray, George D.] Laurel Hill cemetery, San Francisco, 1915. [S.F., 1915] 15 p. illus., plans. C CHi CLU CU-B

9603. Gray, Gertrude Mary, Sister. A preliminary survey of the life of the most Reverend Joseph Sadoc Alemany, O.P., first archbishop of San Francisco... San Rafael, Catholic univ. of Am., Pac. coast branch, 1942. 125 l. Reproduced from typew. copy. Thesis (M.A.)—Catholic univ. of America, 1942. COHN CSfCW CSrD

9604. Great American importing tea co. ... Wholesale price list. [n.p., n.d.] 16 p. CHi

9605. The great Dutch Flat swindle!! The city of San Francisco demands justice!!...An address to the Board of supervisors, officers and people of San Francisco. [n.p., 1864] 131 p. and appendix, 15 p. C CLU (lacks appendix) CSf CSmH CU-B (lacks appendix)

9606. Great earthquake, April 18, 1906. Views of its calamitous results in San Francisco and vicinity. Mountain View, Pac. press pub. co., c1906. [40] p. illus. CHi OrU

9607. The great earthquake in San Francisco, Oct. 8, 1865. [S.F., 1865] CSmH

9608. The Great monopoly; objections to the Parsons' bulkhead bill (Senate bill no. 167), by those who will suffer by it. S.F., Alta Calif. job print., 1860. 14 p. C CLU CU-B

9609. Great western smelting and refining co. [Brochure] S.F. [1905] 34 p. illus., facsims. CU-B

9610. Greater San Francisco association. Greater San Francisco, the clearing house of California for her commerce with the world. S.F., c1912. 16 p. illus., fold. map. CHi

9611. Greaves, Jessie Hooper. I remember, I remember; an account of the life of a little girl in San Francisco over fifty years ago. S.F., Priv. print., 1939. 42 p. port. CHi

9612. Greely, Adolphus Washington. Earthquake in California, April 18, 1906. Special report...on the relief operations conducted by the military authorities of the United States at San Francisco and other points, with accompanying documents. Wash., D.C., Govt. print. off., 1906. 167 p. illus. (U.S. Army. Pacific division) C CL CLU CO CSf CSfCP CSfU CSmH CU-B MiD-B OrU T

9613. Green, Anna Walda. The Musicians' union of San Francisco. [Berkeley, 1930] Thesis (M.S.)—Univ. of Calif., 1930. CU-B

9614. Green, Floride. Some personal recollections of Lillie Hitchcock Coit–5... S.F., Grabhorn, 1935. 47 p. illus., ports. C CBb CHi CMont CO CRcS CSf CSfCP CSfP CSfU CSfWF-H CSmat CSmH CStmo CU-B CV

9615. Green, Jonathan S. Journal of a tour on the northwest coast of America in the year 1829. Containing a description of a part of Oregon, California and the northwest coast... One hundred sixty copies reprinted for Chas. Fred. Heartman, New York City, 1915. 104 p. illus. (Heartman's hist. ser. no. 10) Reprint. from *Missionary herald*, Boston, Nov. 1830, with extracts from the same periodical, 1821–30...Ship put in at San Francisco and Monterey, and author visited Dolores and San Carlos missions. C CHi CL CLU CSf CSmH CU-B

9616. Greenberg's (M.) sons. M. Greenberg's sons 90th anniversary. [Program, Sept. 18, 1943] [S.F., 1943] [8] p. illus., ports., facsim. CU-B

9617. —— Manufacturers of fire hydrants and fire protection brass goods plumbing...machine works... Catalog 'S' issued 1937... S.F., 1937. 115 p. illus. CHi

9618. —— 100th anniversary program, 1854–1954. [S.F., 1954] [12] p. illus. CHi

9619. Greene, Clay M. Park development in San Francisco, past, present and future. S.F., J.H. Barry [n.d.] 16 p. illus. CHi CSf

9620. Greene, Laurence. The filibuster; the career of William Walker... Indianapolis, N.Y., Bobbs [c1937] 350 p. illus., ports., maps, plan. CSd CU-B

9621. Greenebaum (Alfred) & co. Catalogue and price list...importers and commission merchants. S.F., Howard & Pariser [n.d.] C-S

9622. Greenhood, Clarence David. P.G.: the Green knight [1871–1951]; in memory of Porter Garnett. S.F., Bk. club of Calif. [1951] 17 p. CHi CMont

9623. The Greeters guide of San Francisco ... v.1, no. 1, 1917– S.F., Calif. information bureaus, inc., 1917– illus., maps. C has v.7, no. 4, 1924. CSfCP CU-B has v.4, no. 9, v.5, no. 6, v.6, no. 4, Sept. 1921, June 1922, Apr. 1923.

9624. Gregory (H. P.) & co. ...Catalogue of machinery for sale by H. P. Gregory & co., sole agents for Pacific coast for J. A. Fay & co.'s wood-working machinery, Blake's patent steam pumps, Tanite co.'s emery wheels and machinery... [S.F., W.P. Harrison, print., 187–?] 103 p. illus.   CU-B

9625. Grey, Arthur Leslie. Financial aspects of the development of urban passenger transportation, with special reference to San Francisco, California. [Berkeley, 1954] Thesis (Ph.D.)—Univ. of Calif., 1954.   CU

9626. Griffin, George Butler. Documents from the Sutro collection, translated, annotated and edited by Geo. Butler Griffin. L.A., Franklin print. co., 1891. 213 p. (Pub. of the Hist. soc. of so. Calif., v.2, pt. 1)
                                          C-S CHi CMartC CSalCL

9627. Griffin, William H. ...San Francisco official street and house number directory... [S.F.] c1906. 135 p.   CHi

9628. Griffin bros., inc. Catalog of printing machinery equipment and supplies for the composing room, pressroom, bindery. S.F. [n.d.] 76 p. illus.   CHi

9629. Griffiths, Philip R. A history of the Emerson minstrels on the San Francisco stage, 1870–89. [Stanford] 1955. Thesis (M.A.)—Stanford univ., 1955.   CSt

9630. [Griswold, Wolcott N.] Answer to an anonymous pamphlet entitled, Report of committee on charges against E. J. Fraser, M.D. [by W. N. Griswold and C. W. Breyfogle] S.F. [J.F. Brown, bk. and job print.] 1875. 24 p.   CHi

9631. Groh, R. S. The relationship between the San Francisco city planning commission and the San Francisco redevelopment agency. [Berkeley, 1952] Thesis (M.A.)—Univ. of Calif., 1952.   CU

9632. Gross, Alexander, ed. Famous guide to San Francisco and the world's fair, pictorial and descriptive, with 9 maps and 78 illustrations... N.Y., "Geographia" map co., 1939. 144 p. illus., maps.
        CO CSf CSfCP CSfCW CSluCL CSmat CSmH MiD

9633. Grunsky, Carl Ewald. Appraisement of the properties of the Spring Valley water works for the Board of public works. S.F., J. Thomas print. house, 1901. 62 p.
                                                          C

9634. Gruskin, Alan D. The water colors of Dong Kingman; and how the artist works. N.Y., The Studio publications, 1958.   CRcS

9635. Guardia Lerdo, San Francisco. Estatutos y leyes organicas de la compañia indipendiente mexicana Guardia Lerdo, organizada en San Francisco el 2 de febrero de 1873. S.F., J. Ocaranza, 1873. 16 p.   CHi

9636. Guide monthly and San Francisco business directory. S.F., Guide pub. co., 1865–
    C has 1867–68. CLU has v.6, no. 1, 3. CU-B has v.1, no. 1–10, v.2, no. 4, v.5, no. 5, Nov. 1866–Aug. 1867, Feb. 1868, Oct. 1868. NHi has v.1, no. 2, Dec. 1866.

9637. Guild of arts and crafts, San Francisco. ...Exhibition of sketches by members. 219 Sutter St. May 9th to 17th, 1896. [S.F., 1896] 15 p.   CU-B

9638. Guilford, Adrian P. Brother Justin and the foundation of the San Francisco district of the Christian schools. [Berkeley, 1947] 123 l. Thesis (M.A.)—Univ. of Calif., 1947.   CU CU-B

9639. Guilfoyle, Merlin Joseph, Bp. San Francisco, "no mean city." Fresno, Acad. library guild, 1954. 154 p. illus.
    C CAla CHi CL CLU CO COHN CSalCL CSd
    CSf CSfCW CSfMI CSfU CSluCL CU-B UPB

9640. Gump, S. & G., co. Catalogue, the Gump collection of valuable paintings to be sold at auction at Irving hall...commencing Wednesday evening, April 16th. Louderback & bro., auctioneers. [S.F., 189–?] 28 p. front., pl.   CU-B

9641. Gump's. This is Gump's. [S.F.? 1950?] folder (12 p.) illus.   CHi

9642. Gunnison, Charles A. [In memoriam] Charles A. Gunnison, secretary, Commercial publishing company, died at San Francisco, Cal., October 27th, 1897. [S.F., 1897]   CSmH

9643. Gunst, M. A., pub. The house of staples and the men who built it. [S.F.] 1918. [76] p. illus., ports. A history of M. A. Gunst & co., branch of General cigar co., San Francisco.   CHi

9644. Gwin, William McKendree. An address... to the people of the state of California, on the Senatorial election of 1857, giving a history thereof, and exposing the duplicity of Broderick. Also extracts from speeches delivered at various places upon the political issues of the day. S.F., Off. of the Daily national, 1859. 13 p.
                                                    C CSmH

9645. —— Speech of Mr. Gwin, of California, on land claims in California, delivered in the Senate of the United States, August 2, 1852. [Wash., D.C., Print. at the Congressional globe off., n.d.] 8 p.   CHi

9646. Hackett, Frederick H., ed. Industries of San Francisco. Her rank, resources, advantages, trade, commerce, and manufactures. Conditions of the past, present and future... S.F., Payot, Upham & co., 1884. 203 p. illus., ports.   C CHi CLU CSf CSfWF-H

9647. Hagerty, Josephine. Memoir of Rev. Mother Teresa Comerford, foundress of the convents of the Presentation order on the Pacific coast... S.F., P.J. Thomas, 1882. 120 p. illus.   C CHi CSfCW

9648. Hagopian, Blanche Noble. Manufacturing and wholesaling millinery in San Francisco. [Berkeley, 1933] Thesis (M.A.)—Univ. of Calif., 1933.   CU

9649. Hague. Permanent court of arbitration. Recueil des actes et protocoles concernant le litige du "Fonds pieux des Californies", soumis au tribunal d'arbitrage, constitué en vertu du traité conclu à Washington le 22 mai 1902 entre les États-Unis d'Amérique et les États-Unis mexicains. La Haye, septembre-octobre 1902. La Haye, Van Langenhuysen frères, 1902. 110 p.   CSfP

9650. Hahnemann medical college of the Pacific. Annual announcement. 1st– , [1884?–] S.F. [1884?–]
    CHi has 1892, 1902–03, 1915/16. CU-B has 4th–6th, 8th–15th, 17th–21st, 1887–89, 1891–1897/98, 1899/1900–03.

9651. Haight, H[enry] H., vs. Green, A. In the Supreme court of the state of California. H[enry] H. Haight, ex'r, vs. A. Green. Brief of plaintiff and respondent. H. H. Haight, respondent in person. [n.p., n.d.] 6 p.   CHi

9652. Haight, Mrs. W. A. Some reminiscences of the San Francisco Protestant orphan asylum. [S.F., 1900] [16] p.   CU-B

9653. Hakurankwai Kyokwai, Tokyo. Japan and her exhibits at the Panama-Pacific international exhibition, 1915. Prepared by Hakurankwai Kyokwai (société des expositions). Tokyo, Japan. [Printed by the Japan mag. co., 1915] xxviii, 373, 76 p. illus., ports., fold. map, plans.   CHi CU-B

9654. Haldeman-Julius, Anna Marcet (Haldeman) The amazing frameup of Mooney and Billings... Girard, Kan., Haldeman-Julius publications [c1931]

113 p. "The contents of this book were published as a series of articles in the *American freeman*."
CO CSfCW CU-B

9655. Hale and Norcross silver mining co. Annual report. [S.F.? 186–?–
CHi has 6th–13th, 1867–1874.

9656. —— By-laws...Incorporated March 19th, 1861. S.F., Print. at Commercial herald off., 1868. 11 p.
CHi

9657. Hale bros., inc. [Catalog] no. 25, 32, Fall and winter, 1906–07, Spring and summer, 1910. S.F., 1906– illus.
CHi

9658. Hall (A. I.) & son. Annual illustrated catalogue. no. 9, 1901–02. S.F. [1901] 1 v. illus. CU-B

9659. Hall, Carroll Douglas. Bierce and the Poe hoax. S.F., Bk. club of Calif., 1934. 24 p. ports. 250 copies printed. CHi CRcS

9660. —— The Terry-Broderick duel...woodcuts by Mallette Dean. S.F., Colt press, 1939. 89 p. pl.
CBb CHi CLS CRcS CRedCL CRic CSf CSfCW CSfP CSfWF-H CSjC CStmo

9661. Hall, E. J., vs. Dowling, T. H., and Jennings, J. C. In the Supreme court of the state of California. E. J. Hall, appellant, vs. T. H. Dowling, and J. C. Jennings, respondents. Brief of appellant. S.F., Wade & Nixon, print. [1860?] 41 p. Signed: E. L. B. Brooks, attorney for plaintiff. Suit for possession of the island of Yerba Buena. CLU

9662. Hall, Kate Montague. Paintings of the exposition...Artists proof edition...limited to one thousand sets... S.F., John E.D. Trask, 1915. [24] l. pl. CHi

9663. Hall (R.) and co. Hall's family receipt book for 1866... [S.F.] Sterett print. [1866] 30 p. CHi

9664. Hallawell seed co. Annual catalog.
CHi has 1916–19, 1922, 1924, 1927, 1932, 1952–53.

9665. Halleck et al vs. Guy, Abel. In the Supreme court, October term, 1857. Halleck, et al., respondents, executors for Folsom, vs. Abel Guy, appellant. Brief for respondents. Frederick Billings, attorney for respondents. Gregory Yale, of counsel. [S.F.] O'Meara & Painter, print. [1857] 30 p. CHi CSmH CU-B

9666. [Hallidie, Andrew Smith] A. S. Hallidie's wire rope traction street railway. [S.F.? 1875] 9 p. illus., diagrs. CHi

9667. —— Same, with title: The traction railway company's system of wire rope street railways, A. S. Hallidie, patentee. S.F., C.A. Murdock, print., 1880. 9 p. illus., pl., diagrs. CSfCW

9668. —— Address by A. S. Hallidie, president of the Mechanics' institute, San Francisco, Cal. Delivered at the annual meeting, March 10th, 1894. [S.F., 1894?] 12 p. CSmH

9669. —— Address of A. S. Hallidie in response to an invitation from the North end protective league, San Francisco, (Monday, October 1, 1888) [S.F., 1888?] 15 p. CU-B

9670. —— A brief history of the cable railway system, its origin and progress, and papers in connection therewith. From the report of the Mechanics' institute exposition, 1890. S.F., 1891. 20 p. incl. tables, pl. (1 fold.)
C CLU CU-B

9671. —— Drinking and high license; an address ...before the Century club of San Francisco (by invitation) Wednesday, September 10, 1890. [S.F.] C.A. Murdock & co. [1890?] 15 p. CHi

9672. —— The duty of San Francisco. Address of A. S. Hallidie, September 23d, 1896. [S.F.? 1896?] 11 p.
CU-B

9673. —— The invention of the cable railway system. [S.F., 1885] CHi CSfCP CSmH

9674. —— Same. [1895] 8 p.
CLU CSf CU-B

9675. —— The mechanical miners' guide, issued by A. S. Hallidie, wire, and wire rope works... S.F., C.A. Murdock & co., print., 1873. 52 p. illus. (part fold.), tables, diagrs. CU-B

9676. —— Transportation of ore and other material by means of endless travelling wire ropes. Hallidie's patent endless wire ropeway (wire tramway) with suggestions as to its erection. S.F., Alta Calif. print. house, 1882. 24 p. CHi

9677. Hamilton, James William, and Bolce, William J., jr. ...Gateway to victory. Foreword by General Douglas MacArthur. Stanford [c1946] 220 p. illus., ports., map. At head of title: The wartime story of the San Francisco Army port of embarkation.
Available in many California libraries and NN ODa

9678. Hamilton, Robert LeRoy. A convention and exhibition center for San Francisco, California. [Berkeley, 1955] Thesis (M.A.)—Univ. of Calif., 1955. CU

9679. Hamlin (Sarah Dix) school. Annual circular... [S.F., 189–?– illus.
CHi has 1911/12, 1915/16, 1919/20–1920/21, 1929/30.
CU-B has 1892/93, 1897/98, 1899/1900–1900/01, 1909/10, 1920/21, 1929/30, 1938/39.

9680. —— The Sarah Dix Hamlin School. [S.F., Taylor & Taylor, 193–?] [12] p. CHi

9681. —— Same. [S.F., Taylor & Taylor, 1940?] [16] p. illus. CHi

9682. Hammond (C. S.) & co., inc. The San Francisco disaster photographed; fifty glimpses of havoc by earthquake and fire. N.Y., 1906. [35] p. of illus.
C CHi CU-B

9683. Hammontree, Marie. A. P. Giannini, boy of San Francisco. Illustrated by Raymond Burns. Indianapolis, Bobbs-Merrill [1956] 192 p. (The childhood of famous Am. ser., 99) C CHi CSf

9684. Hampton, Mary. Your introduction to San Francisco. [S.F., Author, 1938] 30 p. map. CHi

9685. Hanlon, John, ed. Visitacion valley and the Reis tract. [S.F.?] 1926. 16 p. CSf

9686. Hanscom, William Wallace. Cable railway propulsion. S.F. [Technical soc. of the Pac. coast, 1884] 30 p. illus. C

9687. Hanson, Erle C. San Francisco & East bay pictures of trolley cars of days gone by, from the collection of Erle Hanson. [Oakland, 19—] [37] p. of mounted photos. CO

9688. Harbor day news. Special edition, Aug. 16, 1935. S.F., 1935. illus., maps. CU-B

9689. Harbor Hill school. Harbor Hill school, a school for the "between age." [S.F., 193–?] [4] p.
CHi

9690. [Harding, George Laban] George Prescott Vance, 1851–1936. S.F., Priv. print., 1937. 26 p. port.
CHi

9691. Hardy, Caroline M. Twenty-five years of the Society for christian work, First Unitarian church, San Francisco... [S.F., 1898] 22 p. CHi

9692. Hare, Lloyd C. M. Salted Tories: the story of

the whaling fleets of San Francisco. Mystic, Conn., Marine hist. assoc., 1960. 114 p.   CAla CHi CSfU

9693. Harker, Mifflin. The churches of San Francisco... S.F., Towne & Bacon, print., 1866. 24 p.
CU-B

9694. Harkness, Harvey Willson. [In memoriam] ...Born May 25, 1821, died July 10, 1901 by Theodore Henry Hittell. S.F., Calif. Acad. of sciences, 1905. 6 p. port.   CHi

9695. Harlan, George H. Of walking beams and paddle wheels; a chronicle of San Francisco bay ferryboats...[1st ed.] S.F., Bay books ltd. [1951] 157 p. illus., ports., map, tables.
Available in many libraries.

9696. Harlan, Joel, and Huff, Lucien B., vs. Peck, Lewis, et als. ...Joel Harlan and Lucien B. Huff, administrators of George Harlan, deceased, respondents, vs. Lewis Peck, et als., appellants. Points and brief for respondents [Clarke & Carpentier] [n.p., 18—?] 53 p.
CU-B

9697. Harland, Hester. Reminiscences. S.F., 1941. 164 p. Mimeo.   CHi

9698. Harlow, Alvin Fay. Bret Harte of the old West. Illus. by Hamilton Green. N.Y., Messner [c1943, 1945] 307 p. illus.   CBb CRic

9699. Harlow, Neal Roten. The maps of San Francisco bay from the Spanish discovery in 1769 to the American occupation. [S.F.] Bk. club of Calif., 1950. 140 p. 39 maps (part fold.)
C CHi CLO CLSM CLU CLgA CRedl CSS CSf CSfSt CSfU CSjC CSt CSto CStoC CU-B CaBViPA

9700. Harmon (S. H.) lumber co. [Catalog] S.F. [Edw. S. Knowles, print., 1904] 210 p. illus.   CHi

9701. Haro, Josefa de, et al vs. the United States. In the Supreme court of the United States. December term, 1865. Josefa de Haro, et als., appellants, vs. the United States. Appeal from the Northern district of California. Brief for appellants. Patterson, Wallace & Stow, Wm. Carey Jones, J. S. Black, of counsel. S.F., Wade & co., print., 1865. 84 p. A suit involving San Francisco pueblo lands, specifically the Potrero tract.   CLU

9702. —— ...Argument for appellants. M. Blair, F. A. Dick, of counsel. [Wash., D.C.?] J. L. Pearson, print. [1866?] 87 p. map.   CLU

9703. —— ...Josefa de Haro, et al, appellants, versus the United States, appellee. Argument. Harvey S. Brown, for appellee. [n.p., 1866?] 36 p.   CLU

9704. Harpending, Asbury. The great diamond hoax and other stirring incidents in the life of Asbury Harpending. Ed. by James H. Wilkins... S.F., J.H. Barry co., 1913. 283 p. ports.
Available in many California libraries and TxU

9705. —— Same. [New ed.] Norman, Univ. of Okla. press [1958] 211 p. illus.
CBaK CBb CChiS CHi CLSM CRb CRcS CSdS CSf CSmH CStmo CViCL MiD MoS N ODa TxU ViU

9706. Harper's weekly. [The San Francisco earthquake and fire] v.50, no. 2576–2577, May 5–12, 1906. N.Y., 1906. illus.   CU-B

9707. Harriman, Edward Henry. [Report to Board of directors Southern Pacific company on assistance rendered by that company in San Francisco earthquake, 1906] [N.Y.? 1906] [3] p.   CSmH

9708. Harrington, W. D. S., comp. and pub. ...Pocket business directory of the Western addition, Hayes Valley and Mission... S.F., c1883. 77 p.   CU-B

9709. Harris, Jeannette Claire. The insufficient earnings cases of the San Francisco county emergency relief administration. [Berkeley, 1937] Thesis (M.A.)— Univ. of Calif., 1937.   CU

9710. Harris, Lawrence W. A point of view and an occasional other vagrant vignette or two. S.F., 1953. 96 p. illus.   CHi CLU

9711. Harrison, Ralph Chandler. In memoriam, by Edward Robeson Taylor. [S.F., Taylor & Taylor, 1918] [5] p.   CHi

9712. Harrison street boys club. Annual report of the President. 1st– 1892– S.F., S.F. boys club assoc. [1893–] illus.   CU-B

9713. Harron, Rickard and McCone. Bulletin. no. 100, Aug. 1904. S.F. [1904] 1 no. illus.   CU-B

9714. —— Catalog. no. 2, 4. S.F., 1902–13. 2 no. illus.   CU-B

9715. Hart, Ann (Clark) comp. and ed. Clark's point, a narrative of the conquest of California and of the beginning of San Francisco... S.F., Pioneer press, 1937. 56, 76 p. illus., ports. Part II, "Lone mountain, the most revered of San Francisco's hills..." has special title-page. "Inscriptions copied from headstones... of Laurel Hill, dedicated in 1854 as Lone Mountain cemetery": p. [65]–76.
Available in many California libraries and CaBViPA NN

9716. Hart, Jerome Alfred. In our second century, from an editor's notebook... S.F., Pioneer press, 1931. 454 p. port.
C CHi CLSU CLU CLgA CMerCL CO COnC CRcS CRedl CSf CSfCP CSfCW CSfP CSfU CSmH CU-B CUk CWhC IHi MoS

9717. Hart, William, vs. Beidemann, J.C., et al. In the Supreme court, state of California. William Hart, respondent, v. J. C. Beidemann, et al., appellants. Abstract of record and brief of points and authorities for respondent. S.F., Commercial steam presses [1858] 28 p.   CHi

9718. Hart [William] vs. Burnett, Beidemann, et al. ...Argument made by William J. Shaw, before the Supreme court of the state of California...in the case of Hart (Jesse D. Carr) vs. Burnett et al., (involving the validity of Peter Smith titles, and the question of titles in the old missions and villages of California), delivered at Sacramento, on the 8th, 9th, 10th and 12th of December, 1859. Reported by Charles A. Sumner. S.F., Pub. by appellants, 1859. [3]–167 p. Ejectment for a number of lots in San Francisco.
CHi CLU CP CSf CSfCW CSfP CSmH CU-B NN

9719. —— Same. S.F., Commercial bk. and job print. off., 1860. 167 p.   CLCM CLSM CSmH NN

9720. —— ...Reply to second part of petition for rehearing. Wm. J. Shaw, of counsel for appellants. [S.F.] Towne & Bacon, print. [1860?] 8 p.
CHi CLU CSmH

9721. —— Titles to land in the city of San Francisco, Supreme court of California, December, 1859. Wm. Hart, respondent, vs. Burnett et als, [!] appellants. Ejectment. Argument of Edmund Randolph, for appellants. [Reported by Charles A. Sumner] Sacramento, J. Anthony & co., 1860. 33 p.
CHi CLU CSmH CSt CU-B NN

9722. Harte, Francis Bret. San Francisco in 1866; being letters to the Springfield Republican, ed. by George R. Stewart and Edwin S. Fussell. S.F., Bk. club of Calif., 1951. 88 p. fold. pl. "Four hundred copies printed..."

Available in many California libraries and CaBViPA KyU

9723. —— Sketches of the sixties by Bret Harte and Mark Twain. Being forgotten material now collected for the first time from the Californian, 1864–67. S.F., John Howell, 1927. 228 p. illus., facsims.

CChiS CHi CL CRcS CRedl CSal CSf CStcl CStoC CU-B CYcCL

9724. Harter, Charlotte M. San Francisco's business elite, 1849–60. [Stanford] 1958. Thesis (M.A.) — Stanford univ., 1958.   CSt

9725. Harvard club, San Francisco. Constitution, by-laws, and list of members. [S.F., 187–?–
CHi has 1896, 1898, 1909, 1933. CU-B has 1886.

9726. —— Proceedings of the twentieth anniversary. [S.F.] 1893. 43 p.   CHi

9727. Harvey, C. D., vs. Duffey bros. In the Supreme court of the state of California. C. D. Harvey, appellant, vs. Duffey bros., respondents. Transcript on appeal. [From Superior court, City and county of San Francisco.] Olney, Chickering & Thomas, attorneys for appellant. Warren Gregory, of counsel. E. R. Taylor, attorney for respondent... [n.p., 1892] 181 p.   CHi

9728. Harvey (C. D.) firm. [Catalog of] hot water and steam heating radiators and boilers. 1886. S.F. [1886] 1 v. illus.   CU-B

9729. Haskell, Leonidas, vs. Cornish, Henry C. In the Supreme court, January term, 1858. In the appeal by H. C. Cornish, the defendant, from the judgment in the twelfth district court. Leonidas Haskell, respondent, vs. Henry C. Cornish, appellant. Abstract of facts disclosed by the records... [n.p., 1858] [3] p.   CHi

9730. Hassler, William Charles. The milk supply of the city of San Francisco and the plan proposed for its supervision. [n.p., n.d.] [5] p.   C

9731. Hastings, John, vs. Halleck, Peachy, Billings & Park. Action in the twelfth judicial district for professional negligence of attorneys. Argument of Gregory Yale... S.F., Daily herald print., 1858. 42 p.   CU-B

9732. —— Same, with the three decisions of the Supreme court in the case. S.F., O'Meara & Painter, 1859. 84 p.   CU-B

9733. Hastings, Serranus Clinton, vs. Cunningham, James, et al. ...S. Clinton Hastings, appellant, vs. James Cunningham, et als., respondents... S.F., 1868. 2 v. in 1.   CU-B

9734. Hastings clothing co. [Catalog. Organized in 1854 as Heuston & Hastings] S.F. [1898] 1 v. illus.
CU-B

9735. —— Same. [S.F., 1903] 22 p.   CHi

9736. Hatteroth (William) firm. Illustrated catalogue of surgical instruments and appliances, Caswell, Hazard & co., New York. S.F. [187–?] 1 v. illus. Firm formerly Hatteroth and Russ.   CU-B

9737. —— Same. 2d ed. [Phila., John T. Palmer, print.] 1895. 381 p. illus.   CHi

9738. Haviside (J. J.) & son, ship riggers. Epitome of useful information for ship masters and owners, 1902. [S.F., 1902] 196 p. illus.   CHi

9739. Hawaiian construction co. Extracts from articles of incorporation and by-laws... S.F., Jos. Winterburn co., 1892. 16 p.   CHi

9740. [Hawes, Horace] Report of the proceedings and arguments in the probate court of the city and county of San Francisco, state of California, on the trial to admit to probate the "last will and testament" of Horace

Hawes, (deceased). By J. C. Bates, one of the counsel for contestant. S.F., A. L. Bancroft & co., 1872. 600 p. port.   CHi CSmH

9741. Hawkins, Edward Russell. The history of grocery chain stores in the San Francisco region. [Berkeley, 1932] Thesis (M.A.) — Univ. of Calif., 1932.   CU

9742. Hawks & Shattuck. New specimen book and price list of types, rules, borders and other printing material. S.F., 1889. [268] p. illus.   CHi

9743. Hawley (Marcus C.) & co. Catalogue of hardware and agricultural implements...1875. S.F., Francis & Valentine, 1875.   C-S

9744. Hax, John E. Experiences of a systematizer. S.F., 1941. 76 p. tables.   CU-B

9745. Hay, Emily P. B. William Keith as prophet painter. S.F., Paul Elder [c1916] 41 p.   C-S CHi

9746. Haymond, Creed. Argument of Creed Haymond, before the Circuit court of the United States, at San Francisco, August, 1882, in the railroad tax cases. S.F., Crocker, 1882.   CStclU

9747. —— California railroad tax cases. Argument of Creed Haymond in the Supreme court of the United States, January 12th & 13th, 1888. Wash., D.C., Judd & Detweiler print., 1888. 205 p.   CLO

9748. —— The Central Pacific railroad co. Its relations to the government. It has performed every obligation. Oral argument of Creed Haymond, its general solicitor made before the Select committee of the U.S. Senate ...March 17th and 26th and April 7th, 1888; reported by James L. Andem. S.F., Crocker, 1888. 256 p.
CHi CMartC

9749. —— Pacific railroads. Argument of Creed Haymond, before Senate committee March 17th. The Central Pacific railroad company has performed every obligation. [n.p., n.d.] 181 p.   CSf

9750. —— To the people. The railroad tax cases. History of the litigation. An open letter from... [n.p., n.d.] 22 p.   CHi

9751. Haynie, Robert M. A construction chronicle; the history of Haas and Haynie corporation... N.Y., The Newcomen soc. in No. Am., 1961. 24 p. illus.   CHi

9752. Head, Frances Catherine. Trade unionism in the clothing industries of San Francisco. [Berkeley, 1935] Thesis (M.A.) — Univ. of Calif., 1935.   CU

9753. Heald's business college. Circular and catalogue. 1868, 1896. S. F., 1868–96. 2 v. illus.
CHi (1896) CU-B

9754. [Healy, Clyde E.] San Francisco improved ...October 10, 1935 to August 31, 1939. [S.F., 1939] 74 l. Typew.   CU-B

9755. Healy-Tibbitts construction co. Souvenir dedication of the Twin Peaks reservoir, Sunday, May 12, 1912. [S.F., 1912] [11] p. illus.   CHi CU-B

9756. [Hearst, George] Memorial addresses on the life and character of George Hearst (a senator from California) delivered in the Senate and House of representatives, March 25, 1892, and February 24, 1894... Wash., D.C., Govt. print. off., 1894.   CHi CSjC

9757. Hearst, William Randolph. Selections from the writings and speeches of William Randolph Hearst. [E. F. Tompkins, editor] S.F., Priv. pub., 1948. 765 p.
CHi

9758. —— William Randolph Hearst, a portrait in his own words, ed. by Edmond D. Coblentz. N.Y., Simon, 1952. 309 p.   CSd CSlu

9759. Heath, Erle. Seventy-five years of progress; historical sketch of the Southern Pacific... [S.F., So. Pac. bur. of news, 1945] 51 p. illus., ports., maps. "Revision of the '75 years of progress' articles which first appeared in the *Southern Pacific Bul.* during 1944."
C CHi CRcS

9760. [Heco, Joseph] Hyoryu ki. Floating on the Pacific ocean, by Hikozo. Translated from the 1863 ed. by Tosh Motofuji. L.A., G. Dawson, 1955. 89 p. illus. (Early Calif. travels ser., 30) "[Original] printed...in Japan in 1863...This is a complete translation of the 1863 edition with all illustrations reproduced."—Publisher's note.
CLgA CSd CSto CU-B CVtV

9761. —— The narrative of a Japanese; what he has seen and the people he has met in the course of the last forty years. Ed. by James Murdoch... [Yokohama? Yokohama print. & pub. co., 189–?] 2 v. illus., map. "A more extensive but not identical autobiography" than the 1863 edition.—Publisher's note in 1955 edition.
CHi CU-B (v.1)

9762. Heidelberg inn. Speisenkarte [containing "What you see at the Heidelberg"] S.F., Louis Roesch, c1912. [20] p. illus.   CHi

9763. Heininger, C. P., pub. Historical souvenir of San Francisco, Cal., with views of prominent buildings, the bay, islands, etc. S.F. [c1886] 30 p.   CHi
Other editions followed. Title varies.
CAla (1892–3?) CHi (c1887, 1889) CLU (1889) CO (1888) CSf (1888) CSfCW (1888) CSmH (1888) CU-B (1888, 1889) CViCL (1887?) MoSHi (1889) NN (1887)

9764. Helbing, August. He led the way; words spoken at the obsequies of August Helbing, August 19, 1896 by Jacob Voorsanger. [S.F., Cubery & co., 1896] 12 p. port.   CHi

9765. Helbing hat co. [Catalog] Hats—caps... Seasons, 1916, 1922. [S.F., Taylor & Taylor, 189–?–] illus.   CHi

9766. Heller, Elinor Raas. Bibliography of the Grabhorn press, 1915–1940, by Elinor Raas Heller & David Magee. S.F., Grabhorn, 1940. 193 p. illus., facsims.
CBb CHi CLgA CSfCW

9767. Hellman, Isaias W. Wells Fargo bank & union trust co., a century at the Golden Gate, 1852–1952. N.Y., Newcomen soc. in No. Am., 1952. 32 p. illus.
CHi CSfCW

9768. Hendry (C. J.) co. Catalogue no. 38, anvil brand tackle blocks... [n.p., n.d.] [24] p. illus.   CHi

9769. Hendry, George Whiting. The Spanish and Mexican adobe and other buildings in the nine San Francisco bay counties, 1776 to about 1850 by G. W. Hendry...[and] J. N. Bowman...[Berkeley, 1940–45?] 7 v. maps (part fold.), plans, fold. tables, and portfolio of 17 maps. Typew.   C CU-B

9770. Hendy (Joshua) iron works. Bulletin. no. 105, 108, 110, 113–114. S.F. [190–?] 5 no. in 1 v. illus.
CU-B

9771. —— Catalogue of boilers, engines, pumps, etc. ... S.F., John W. Howard, print. [n.d.] 114 p. illus.
CHi

9772. —— Catalogue of hydraulic mining machinery. S.F., 1885–96.
CHi has 1885 [1896] CU-B has [188–?]–87.

9773. —— Gold and silver quartz mining and milling machinery. Catalogue. no. 2 (3d ed.) S.F. [n.d.] 1 v. and suppl. illus.   CU-B

9774. —— This is Hendy, a pictorial presentation of its story from gold rush days through World War II— and a glimpse into its plans for the future. Sunnyvale [1946?] 65 p. illus. (part. col.)   CHi

9775. —— ...Vertical, horizontal, marine and hoisting engines and boilers, smelting, mining...machinery. [Catalogue "K", issued in 12th year of manufacturing.] S.F. [n.d.] 64 p. illus., diagr.   CHi

9776. Hennings, Robert Edward. James D. Phelan and the Wilson progressives of California. [Berkeley, 1961] Thesis (Ph.D.)—Univ. of Calif., 1961
CU CU-B

9777. Henshaw, Bulkley & co. The Kinkead mill, "The mill that saves the values." [S.F., Commercial pub. co., n.d.] 19 p. illus.   CHi

9778. Hercules gas engine works. Instructions for installing and operating Hercules engines. S.F., c1908. 16 p. illus.   CU-B

9779. Hermann safe co. Safe service...since 1889. S.F., 1949. 19 p. illus., ports.   CHi

9780. Hernandez Cornejo, Roberto. Chilenos en San Francisco de California (recuerdos historicos de la emigración por los descubrimientos del oro, iniciada en 1848)...Valparaiso, Imp. San Rafael, 1930. 2 v.
CLO CLU CSmH CU-B

9781. Herrmann, the hatter. Catalogue for 1882. S.F., 1882. 64 p. illus.   CHi

9782. Hesseltine, Lee Frazelle. The foreign trade of San Francisco with China, 1910–1921 inclusive. [Berkeley, 1923] Thesis (M.S.)— Univ. of Calif., 1923.   CU

9783. Hetch Hetchy water bond campaign committee. Speakers' manual. $10,000,000 Hetch Hetchy water bond campaign. Election October 7, 1924... S.F., J.H. Barry co. [1924] [8] p.   CU-B

9784. Hettrich, A. L., co., pub. Catalogue of sea shells, corals and natural history specimens... S.F. [n.d.] 23 p. illus.   CHi

9785. —— San Francisco and California. S.F., c1906. 60 p. illus.   C CAla CHi CRic CU-B

9786. —— San Francisco of yesterday and to-day. Oakland, Press of Harrington-McInnis co. [1906] folder (8 l.)   CHi

9787. Hewitt, A. Josephine, comp. Story of Laurel Hill cemetery. [S.F.] 1952. 23 l. Mimeo.   CHi

9788. Hewitt, Ronald. ...From earthquake, fire and flood... N.Y., Scribner, 1957. 215 p. illus.   CSf

9789. Heyman co., inc. [Catalog] For over forty years in California the name Heyman has been synonymous with household hardware. [S.F.? n.d.] 568 p. illus.
CHi

9790. Heyman-Weil co. General catalog no. S22. Jobbers, importers, exporters and manufacturers. S.F. [1932?] 468 p. illus.   CHi

9791. —— Same. No. S26. [192–?] 489 p. illus.
CHi

9792. Heyneman, Julie Helen. Arthur Putnam, sculptor. S.F., Johnck & Seeger, 1932. 190 p. illus., ports.
CHi CSd

9793. Hibernia savings and land association. By-laws and certificate of incorporation... S.F., Mullin, Mahon & co., 1867. 20 p.   CHi

9794. Hibernia savings and loan society. By-laws ...S.F., Mullin, Mahon & co., 1869. 28 p. tables.   CHi

9795. —— Real estate for sale. Catalogue. Apr., 1883. S.F., 1883.   CU-B

9796. Hibernians, Ancient order of, San Fran-

cisco. Constitution and by-laws... S.F., Cosmopolitan print. co., 1874. 24 p. CHi

9797. Hichborn, Franklin. "The system," as uncovered by the San Francisco graft prosecution... S.F., Press of the James H. Barry co., 1915. 464 p.
Available in many California libraries and MoS N NHi NN

9798. Hicks-Judd co. Catalogue of Eureka loose leaf ledgers, binders and time-saving devices. [190–?] S.F. [190–?] 1 v. illus. CU-B

9799. Hiester, W. A. Attorneys' directory. [S.F.] Brief and transcript print. co. [1900?] 36 p. CSmH

9800. Highton, E. R. Address upon the philosophy of the Dashaway association...February 19th, 1860. S.F., J.B. Painter, print., 1860. 14 p. CU-B

9801. —— Some general observations on matters of public interest with special reference to the municipal government of San Francisco... S.F., H.H. Bancroft & co., 1866. 76 p. C CHi CLU CSf CSfU CU-B

9802. Hill, John H., vs. Haskin, J.W. In the Supreme court of the state of California. John H. Hill, plaintiff and appellant, vs. J. W. Haskin, defendant and respondent. Transcript on appeal. C. H. Sawyer, att'y. for appellant. H. F. Crane, Wm. F. Wells, att'ys. for respondent. S.F., A.L.Bancroft & co., 1870. 18 p. CHi

9803. Hill, Robert R., administrator. Catalogue of the paintings and sketches of the late Thomas Hill the great American artist. The entire collection now on exhibition and sale... [S.F., Stanley-Taylor co., print. c1910] [36] p. illus. CHi

9804. [Hill, Thomas] "The last spike," a painting by Thomas Hill illustrating the last scene in the building of the overland railroad, with a history of the enterprise. S.F., E. Bosqui & co., 1881. 40 p. illus. CHi

9805. Hillcrest club. Hillcrest club. [n.p., n.d.] 11 p. illus. CHi

9806. Hills bros. Behind the cup; the story of Hills bros. coffee. [S.F., 1930] 39 p. illus. (incl. map) CU-B

9807. Hilp (Henry) firm. A new departure! Clothing direct from the manufacturer to the consumer... [S.F., n.d.] [8] p. illus. CHi

9808. Himmelwright, Abraham Lincoln Artman. The San Francisco earthquake and fire; a brief history of the disaster; a presentation of facts and resulting phenomena, with special reference to the efficiency of building materials. Lessons of the disaster... N.Y., Roebling construction co. [c1906] 270 p. illus.
C CHi CL CLSU CLU CLgA CO CSf CSfCW CSfU CSfWF-H CSmH CStmo CU-B CoU MiD-B NHi OU OrU UU ViU

9809. Hinckley & co. ...Circular and pattern list of the Fulton foundry and iron works... S.F., Waters, Newhoff & co., 1869. 62 p. illus. CHi

9810. Hinckley, Spiers and Hays, firm. Catalogue of mining machinery, section II, gold mills and hydraulic appliances. 1889. S.F. [1889] 1 v. Successor to Fulton iron works, Hinckley & co. CU-B

9811. Hirsch & Kaiser, firm. Catalog of cameras, photographic apparatus, plates and papers. [n.p., n.d.] CHi has 2d, 4th, 5th, 9th ed.

9812. Hiscock, Ira V. An appraisal of the public health program, San Francisco...for the fiscal year 1929–1930... [S.F., 1930] 115 p. CLSU CO CU-B

9813. Historical records survey. California. Calendar of the Major Jacob Rink Snyder collection of the Society of California pioneers...Sponsored by the department of state of California. Co-sponsored by the Society of California pioneers. S.F., Northern Calif. hist. records survey, 1940. 107 l. Reproduced from typew. copy. CHi CPa CSjC MoS N

9814. —— —— A directory of churches and religious organizations in San Francisco, California, 1941 ... S.F., Northern Calif. hist. records survey, 1941. 116 l. maps.
C CHi CL CLO CLSU CLU CO COHN CPa CSf CSfCW CSfU CSmH CU-B N NHi NN TxU

9815. —— —— Guide to church vital statistics records in California. San Francisco and Alameda counties: six denominations... S.F., Northern Calif. hist. records survey project, 1942. 63 l. Reproduced from typew. copy. "Pub. of the Northern Calif. hist. records survey project": leaves 61–63.
C CHi CLU COHN CSS CSf CSmH CU-B MoS N OrU TxU ViU

9816. [The History company, San Francisco] The Bancroft historical library. [S.F., W.B. Bancroft & co.'s print., 1887] 38 p. CU-B

9817. History of the "Mint" saloon and restaurant, 605 Commercial street, San Francisco, California. The oldest establishment in the city. [S.F., Murdock press, 1904?] 19 p. CSmH

9818. Histrionic memoir of the Misses Adelaide and Joey Goughenheim: with opinions of the press. S.F., Steam presses of Monson, Valentine & co., 1856. 32 p. CU-B

9819. Hittell, John Shertzer. A brief statement of the moral and legal merits of the claim made by José Y. Limantour to 15,000 acres of land, in the city and county of San Francisco. S.F., Whitton, Towne & co., 1857. 40 p. map. C CHi CLU CSmH CU-B

9820. —— A guide book to San Francisco. S.F., Bancroft co., 1888. 60 p. maps.
C CHi CSd CSf CSfCP CSmH CU-B CaBViPA MoS

9821. —— In the Supreme court of the state of California. In the matter of the estate of John S. Hittell, deceased. Transcript on appeal. Theodore H. Hittell attorney for Mary H. Kingsbury and himself, appellants. Smith & Pringle, attorneys for Anne P. Greer, respondent. W. B. Kohlmeyer, attorney for executor. [S.F., 1903] 27 p. CHi

9822. Hittell, Theodore Henry. In memoriam: Theodore Henry Hittell; born April 5, 1830—died February 23, 1917. G. W. Dickie, Leverett Mills Loomis, Ransom Pratt, committee. S.F., Calif. acad. of sciences, 1918. 25 p. port. CHi

9823. —— Memorial of S. M. Tibbits, A. M. Simpson and others, grantees of city and county of San Francisco, for establishment of southern line of Presidio reservation, in accordance with survey of U.S. Surveyor-general, with reasons therefor &c., &c. S.F., Women's union print, 1874. 18 p. fold. maps. CHi CU-B

9824. Hoadley, Milo, vs. San Francisco. ...Milo Hoadley, respondent, vs. the city and county of San Francisco, appellant... S.F., 1871–73. 4 v. in 1. CU-B

9825. —— In the Supreme court of the state of California...Brief for respondent... S.F., Women's union print, 1873. 14 p. CHi

9826. —— ...Final brief for respondent. S. W. Holladay, attorney for respondent. W. C. Burnett, attorney for appellant. S. F., Bonnard & Webb, legal print., 1872. 26 p. CHi

9827. Hobby, Carl F. Chinatown of San Francisco ... [S.F.] c1936. [20] p. illus., map.　　　CHi

9828. Hockwald chemical co. Catalog no. 46. Manufacturers [of] soaps, cleansers, deodorants, insecticides... [S.F., Western catalog service, n.d.] 32 p. illus.　　　CHi

9829. Hodson, Burt, and Walsh, F. M. San Francisco destroyed. Milwaukee, C.N. Casper co., c1906. 2 p. 42 pl.　　　CHi

9830. Hoelscher (William) & co. I. De Turk (vineyardist since 1859), California wines and brandies ... [price list] S.F. [Louis Roesch co., n.d.] [30] p. illus.　　　CHi

9831. Hoitt, Ira G., comp. Pacific coast guide and programme of the Knights Templar triennial conclave at San Francisco, August, 1883, as prepared by the triennial committee. S.F., Hoitt, 1883. 230 p. illus., ports., map.
　　　C-S　CHi　CLU　CSf　CSfCP　CSfU　CSfWF-H　CSmH　CU-B

9832. —— Pacific coast guide and programme of the twentieth national encampment Grand Army of the Republic, at San Francisco, August, 1886. S.F., A.J. Leary, 1886. 155 p. illus., map.
　　　CLCM　CSf　CSfWF-H　CSmH

9833. —— Purchasers' index to San Francisco... S.F. [1882] 128 p. illus.　　　CHi

9834. Holbrook, Samuel F. Threescore years: an autobiography, containing...two years in California... Bost., J. French and co., 1857. 504 p. illus.
　　　CHi　CP　CStoC

9835. Holbrook, Merrill & Stetson. Catalogue and price list, plumbers' sanitary apparatus, brass goods, fixtures, tools and supplies. S.F. [187–?–1910] illus.
CHi has 1883 and no. 35, 69, 105, 129, 134, 138, 142, 146, 148, 150, 155, 160. CU-B has no. 69, 83, 129.

9836. Holden, Erastus W., comp. Historic California: clippings. Alameda, Alameda free lib., 1937. 5 v. v.3–4: Early San Francisco.　　　CAla

9837. Holdredge, Helen (O'Donnell) The house of the strange woman. San Carlos, Nourse pub. co., c1961. 244 p.　　　CHi　CSdU

9838. —— Mammy Pleasant. N.Y., Putnam [c1953] 311 p. illus., ports.
Available in many libraries.

9839. —— —— Index...compiled by San Francisco public library. Reference department. S.F., 1954. unp.　　　CSf

9840. —— Mammy Pleasant's partner. N.Y., Putnam [1954] 300 p. illus., ports.
CBb　CHi　CLU　CLgA　CMont　CRedCL　CSd　CSf　CSfSt　CSjC　CSlu　CStmo　CStoC　CU-B　CViCL

9841. Holmes, Eugenia Kellogg. Adolph Sutro, a brief story of a brilliant life... S.F., Press of S.F. photoengraving co., 1895. 56 p. port.
Available in many libraries.

9842. Holmes (H. C.) bookseller. ...A catalogue of some choice books...no. 1, 1905. [n.p., 1905?] 64 p.　　　CHi

9843. Holmes (H. T.) lime co. Catalogue... Sacramento, Crocker [1875?] 19 p. illus.　　　CHi

9844. —— Same. S.F., Hicks-Judd co., print. [189–?] 14 p.　　　CHi

9845. Holway, Ruliff Stephen. ...Physiographically unfinished entrances to San Francisco bay. Berkeley, Univ. of Calif. press, 1914. [81]– 126 p. illus., maps. (Univ. of Calif. pub. in geography, v.1, no. 3)
　　　C　CLSU　CLU　CSdS　CSf

9846. Home insurance co., New York. Sixty miles around San Francisco, with driving instructions. N.Y. [1918] [24] p. fold. map, forms.　　　CU-B

9847. Home mutual building and loan association of San Francisco. By-laws... S.F., E.C. Hughes, steam bk. and job print., 1885. 16 p.　　　CU-B

9848. Home mutual insurance co. [Company's pocket manual] S.F., 1865.　　　CSmH

9849. Homestake mining co. Annual report. CL has 1952–59.

9850. Hooper (C. A.) and co. [Catalog. 1888?] S.F. [1888?] 1 v. illus.　　　CU-B

9851. Hooper printing & lithograph co. Type selections, linotype display. S.F. [n.d.] [46] p.　　　CHi

9852. Hoover, Mildred (Brooke) The Farallon islands, California; a paper read before the National society of colonial dames of America in the state of California, San Francisco, California, April 5, 1932... Stanford; London, H. Milford, Oxford univ. press [c1932] 17 p. illus., map.
Available in many libraries.

9853. Hoover school of physical culture. Annual catalogue... S.F., 1901. 66 p. illus.　　　CHi

9854. Hoover-Young San Francisco bay bridge commission. San Francisco bay bridge; report of the Hoover-Young San Francisco bay bridge commission... [Sacramento, State print. off., 1930] 234 p. 26 illus.
CHi　CL　CLO　CLSU　CLU　CMartC　CO　CSf　CSfCW　CSfP　CSfU　CSj　CSmH　CU-B　T

9855. Hopkins, Caspar Thomas. Common sense applied to the immigrant question: showing why the "California immigrant union" was founded, and what it expects to do... [S.F., Turnbull & Smith, 1869] 64 p.
　　　CHi　CL

9856. —— An examination into the conditions and prospects of the insurance business in San Francisco. S.F., Turnbull & Smith, 1867. 22 p.　　　C

9857. —— Ship building on the Pacific coast... A report to the Board of marine underwriters of San Francisco...December 16th, 1867. S.F., Print at Commercial herald off. [1867] 84 p.　　　CSf　CU-B

9858. —— Ship building on the Pacific coast (no. 2). Published by the Board of marine underwriters. S.F., Alta Calif. print. house, 1874. 31 p.
　　　CHi　CLU　CSmH　CU-B

9859. —— [and others] Report on port charges, shipping and shipbuilding to the Manufacturers' association, the Board of trade, and the Chamber of commerce, of San Francisco... S.F., Crocker print., 1884. 106 p.
　　　CSmH (1885 ed.)　CU-B

9860. Hopkins, Ernest Jerome. Fortitude. Hugh Walpole stumbles upon priceless literary treasure in a San Francisco book shop; pays a big sum for long-lost letters of Sir Walter Scott... S.F., Print. for John Howell by John Henry Nash, 1920. 8 p. port.　　　CHi

9861. —— What happened in the Mooney case... N.Y., Brewer, Warren & Putnam, 1932. 258 p. illus., ports.
CBev　CBu　CHi　CL　CLSU　CLU　CMartC　CO　CSf　CSfCW　CSmH　CStrJC　CU-B　CViCL

9862. Hopkins, Lois Scott. Interest rates paid for automobile credit by San Francisco bay area families. [Berkeley, 1958] Thesis (M.S.)— Univ. of Calif., 1958.　　　CU

9863. Hornblower, William B., et al vs. Masonic cemetery association. William B. Hornblower, plaintiff and respondent, F. E. Edwards, intervenor and appellant,

Martin Kelly, intervenor and appellant vs. Masonic cemetery association of the city and county of San Francisco (a corporation), defendant and respondent. Brief of Francis J. Sullivan, one of the amici curiae... S.F., Pernau-Walsh print. co. [1923] 9 p. CHi

9864. **Horse show association of the Pacific coast.** Official catalog...annual exhibition of horses, 1894–1896. S.F., 1894–96. 3 v. illus. CHi

9865. —— ... Prize list, 1896... S.F., Crocker [1896] 48 p. CHi

9866. **Horst (E. Clemens) co.** Scenes from E. Clemens Horst company's hop ranches during harvesting time... [S.F., Janssen press, 1920?] [32] p. illus. CHi

9867. Hospitality hikes. 1922, hike 1–9, 12, 14, 1923, hike 1–7, 9–10, May 28–July 23, Aug. 13, Aug. 22, 1922–July 29, Aug. 12–19, 1923. S.F., 1922–23. 1 v. illus., maps. CU-B

9868. **Hotchkis, Preston.** The Lost Angels camp, Bohemia; the first fifty years, 1908–1958. [L.A., Ward Ritchie, 1958] 30 p. illus., ports., facsims. CLO CU-B

9869. **Hotel Argonaut.** San Francisco city and state maps... [S.F., n.d.] folder. illus., maps. CHi

9870. **Hotel Mark Hopkins.** Hotel Mark Hopkins atop Nob Hill, San Francisco. [S.F., 192–?] [16] p. illus. CU-B

9871. —— The 30th Christmas... [S.F., 1956] [16] p. illus. CHi

9872. **Hotel St. Francis.** [Brochure] [S.F., 1905?] [32] p. illus. CU-B

9873. —— Guide and shopping list; where to go, what to see and where to shop. [S.F., 1913] 63 p. illus. C-S

9874. —— Hotel St. Francis information book. S.F. [19–?] 23 p. illus., maps. CHi

9875. **Houghton, Sherman O., vs. Steele, John, et al.** ...Sherman O. Houghton, plaintiff and appellant, vs. John Steele and J. G. Eastland, executor of the will of P. B. [i.e. C] Lander, deceased, defendants and respondents. Points and authorities for respondents. Taylor & Haight, att'ys for respondents... [S.F.? 1881] 39 p. CU-B

9876. **House and street directory co., pub.** San Francisco house and street directory, 1940. S.F. [1940] unp. CHi

9877. **House carpenters' eight hour league, no. 1, San Francisco.** Constitution, by-laws and rules of order... S.F., Winterburn & co., 1867. CHi has 1867, 1869.

9878. —— Resolutions passed by the House carpenters' eight-hour league, requesting the passage of a bill to provide for the erection of a city hall in San Francisco. [Sacramento, Gelwicks, state print. [1870] CSmH

9879. **Household furnishing co.** Descriptive catalogue of housekeeping articles, consisting of tinned, planished, japanned, wooden, rattan, brass, copper, fire gilt and plated ware. [187–?] S.F. [187–?] 1 v. CU-B

9880. **Houseworth, Thomas, & co.** Catalogue of photographic views of scenery on the Pacific coast, and views in China and Japan, for the stereoscope... S.F., Wade & co., print. [1870] 70 p. CHi

9881. **Howard, Oliver Otis.** Unparalleled suffering and destitution. [N.Y., 1906] [4] p. Published for California relief fund. NN

9882. **Howe scale co.** Descriptive catalogue of butchers' and packers' tools, fixtures, supplies... S.F., Upton bros. & Delzelle [n.d.] 287 p. illus. CHi

9883. **Howes (E. K.) & co.** ...Catalogue of wood and willow ware, brushes... [187–?] 1872. [S.F., 187–?–72] 2 v. illus. CU-B

9884. **Hoy, William.** The Chinese six companies; a short general, historical resume of its origin, function, and importance in the life of the California Chinese... S.F., Pub. by the Chinese consolidated benevolent assoc. (Chinese six companies) [c1942] 35 p. illus.
C CHi CLSU CLU CLgA CMont CO CRcS CRic CSf CSlu CSmat CSmH CStmo CU-B CV

9885. —— King Chow temple. [S.F., 1939?] 16 p. illus. CHi CU-B

9886. **Hoyt, Josephine.** A proposal for a representative council and controlled executive form of government for the city and county of San Francisco. [Berkeley, 1920] Thesis (M.A.)— Univ. of Calif., 1920. CU

9887. **Hubbard, A. T., ed.** The port of San Francisco and its recent progress...Distributed by the Board of state harbor commissioners. S.F., 1926. 16 p. illus. C CRcS CSmH CU-B

9888. **Hubbard, Anita Day.** ..."Cities within the cities." Published in the San Francisco bulletin, August-November, 1924. 2 v. Typew. CSf

9889. **Hubbard, Elbert.** The Panama exposition. [S.F., Panama-Pacific internat. exposition, 1915] [16] p. CU-B

9890. **Hueter bros., and co.** ...San Francisco pioneer varnish works... S.F., 1889. 8 p. CSf

9891. **Huff, Boyd Francis.** The maritime history of San Francisco bay. [Berkeley, 1955] Thesis (Ph.D.) — Univ. of Calif., 1955. CU

9892. —— El Puerto de los balleneros; annals of the Sausalito whaling anchorage. L.A., Dawson, 1957. 47 p. illus., map (on lining paper) (Early Calif. travels ser. 42) 200 copies printed by George Yamada. C CL CLO CLSM CLgA CSS CSto CStoC CU-B CoD N

9893. **Hughes, Lillian Gobar.** Housing in San Francisco 1835–1938. [Berkeley, 1940] Thesis (M.A.)— Univ. of Calif., 1940. CU

9894. **Hughes & co.** Office of Hughes & co., brokers in stock privileges. S.F., Francis & Valentine, 1876. 16 p. CU-B

9895. **Humboldt association.** [Pamphlet in celebration of the twenty-fifth anniversary of the arrival of the ship *Humboldt* at San Francisco. S.F., 1874?] 24 l. CLU CSmH

9896. **Hume, M., pub.** San Francisco architecturally. [S.F., Geo. Spaulding & co.] 1903. [62] l. illus. CHi

9897. **Humphreys, William P., & co., comp. and pub.** Atlas of the city and county of San Francisco from actual surveys and official records... [Phila.] Print. by F. Bourquin, 1876. 215 p. of maps. "For many years this was the standard authority."—Cowan. C CHi CLU CO CSf CSfU CSmH CU-B

9898. **Humphreys, William Penn.** Report on a system of sewerage for the city of San Francisco. S.F., Spaulding & Barto, print., 1876. 31 p. diagrs. C CHi

9899. **Hungerford, Edward.** Wells Fargo, advancing the American frontier. N.Y., Random house [1949] 274 p. illus., ports. CHi CLgA CSf CSmat CStmo CSto

9900. Hunt, Andrew Murray. Report on the cost of an electric plant for lighting the street and municipal buildings of San Francisco and the approximate cost of operating the same... [n.p., 1899] 8 p. map.   C

9901. [Hunt, Haywood] The first quarter century of craftsmanship in San Francisco. A brief sketch of highlights in the "Share your knowledge" movement by the Golden Gate. S.F., S.F. club of print. house craftsmen, 1946. 20 p. illus., fold. pl.   CHi

9902. Hunt, Henry T. The case of Thomas J. Mooney and Warren K. Billings. Abstract and analysis of record before Governor Young of California. Pub. by National Mooney-Billings committee...[1929] 444 p. map.   C CLO CSmH CU-B

9903. Hunt, R. O. Pulp, paper and pioneers; the story of Crown Zellerbach corporation... N.Y., Newcomen soc. in No. Am., 1961. 32 p. illus.   CHi

9904. Hunt, Timothy Dwight. Address delivered before the New England society of San Francisco, at the American theatre, on the twenty-second day of December, A.D. 1852, by Rev. T. Dwight Hunt, pastor of the New England church. S.F., Cooke, Kenny & co., 1853. 20 p.
            C CHi CSmH CU-B MWA NN

9905. —— Sermon suggested by the execution of Jenkins, on the Plaza, by "the people" of San Francisco during the night of the 10th of June, 1851... S.F., Marvin & Hitchcock, 1851. 26 p.   CO CSmH CU-B

9906. Hunt brothers co. Hunt's California canned fruit. [S.F.? Schmidt litho. co., 1915?] [8] p. illus. (part col., incl. maps)   CHi

9907. Hunt filter co. Hunt continuous filter. S.F. [1910?] [8] p. illus.   CU-B

9908. Hunter, Stanley Armstrong. Temple of religion and Tower of peace at the Golden Gate international exposition... [Berkeley, Print. by Univ. of Calif. press] 1940. 96 p. illus., ports.
            C CHi CLSU CLU CMartC CO CRcS CSf CSfCW CSfSt CSj CSluCL CSmH CU-B CViCL

9909. [Huntington, Collis Potter] Memorial service...held at the First Presbyterian church, San Francisco, California, at eleven o'clock on the morning of Friday, August seventeenth, nineteen hundred. [S.F., 1900] 8 l.   CHi CLU CSmH

9910. —— Preamble and resolutions in memory of Collis P. Huntington adopted by the Board of directors of Central Pacific railroad company. S.F., 1900. [4] p.   CHi

9911. Huntington, Hopkins & co. San Francisco and Sacramento. Descriptive circular and price-list of Rider compression engines. 1877. S.F., 1877. 1 v. illus.   CU-B

9912. —— Illustrated catalogue and price list of hardware, iron, steel, coal, etc. ... Sacramento, Crocker, 1879– illus.
CHi has 1879, 1884. CSmH has 1879.

9913. Huret, Jules. ...En Amérique. De San Francisco au Canada... Paris, E. Fasquelle, 1905. 564 p.   CU-B

Other editions followed: CBaB (1907)   CL (1907) CLO (1907) CLU (1907) CSfCW (1907) CSfP (1907) CSmH (1908) CU-B (1907, 1909, 1911) CaBViPA (1907)

9914. Hurt, Peyton. Interrelationships of the agencies controlling San Francisco bay. [Berkeley, 1932] Thesis (Ph.D.)—Univ. of Calif., 1932.   CU

9915. Hutchinson, William E. Byways around San Francisco bay. N.Y., Cincinnati, Abingdon press, 1915. 184 p. illus.
            C C-S CHi CL CLO CLU CMartC CMerCL CNF CO CPom CRic CSd CSf CSfCW CSfMI CSmH CStclU CU-B NN WM

9916. Ideal stamp mill co. The Ideal stamp mill. [S.F., n.d.] 15 p. illus.   CU-B

9917. Illustrated directory; a magazine of American cities, comprising views of business blocks, with reference to owners, occupants, professions and trades, public buildings and private residences. v.1, San Francisco. S.F., Illustrated directory co., 1894–5. 11 pts. in 1 v. 292 p. Beginning with no. 4 pub. by the Hicks-Judd co.   C CHi CO CSfWF-H CU-B

9918. Illustrated fraternal directory. 1889, 1891. S.F., Fraternal soc. pub. co., 1889–1891. illus., ports.   CHi

9919. Imperishable pavement co. Office...64 Merchants exchange. San Francisco, Sept. 20th, 1874. Sir: The Directors...desire to inform you that the delinquent day of the assessment of $22.50 per share... [S.F., 1874] [3] p.   CU-B

9920. The Improver, official organ of Civic league of improvement clubs and associations of San Francisco. v.1–[4?] 1912–[15?] S.F., 1912–[15?]
            C has v.2, no. 11, v.3, no. 1, 3, 5, 8, v.4, no. 1–2, 1913–15. CU-B has v.1, no. 8, v.3, no. 8, Aug. 1912, Aug. 1914.

9921. Incandescent supply co. ...Dealers' confidential discount schedule and net prices applying to catalogue no. 20. [S.F.? 1934] 27 p.   CHi

9922. —— Illustrated price list, catalog no. 20, August 1934... [S.F.? 1934] 48 p. illus.   CHi

9923. Industrial and immigration association of California. ...Address and by-laws. S.F., Edward Bosqui & co., 1867. 32 p.   CHi

9924. Industrial association of San Francisco. An analysis of San Francisco's present economic condition. [S.F., 1925] 11 p. diagrs.   CU-B

9925. —— Graphic proof. S.F., Taylor and Taylor print., 1926. [32] p.   CHi

9926. —— San Francisco, a city that achieved freedom. 1931. [16] p.   CHi CSf CStclU

9927. Industrial indemnity co. Annual report of the president.
CHi has 1947–55.

9928. Industrial league of California. San Francisco division no. 2. Constitution and by-laws... S.F., Francis & Valentine, 1867. 20 p.   CHi

9929. Industrial survey associates. The San Francisco bay area, its people, prospects, and problems; a report prepared for the San Francisco bay area council, March 1, 1948... S.F., 1948. 48 p. illus., maps.
            C CO CSfSt CStrJC

9930. Ingram, Robert Lockwood. A builder and his family, 1898–1948; being the historical account of the contracting, engineering & construction career of W. A. Bechtel, and of how his sons and their associates have carried forward his principles in their many activities; comp. in the fiftieth anniversary year of Dad Bechtel's start in construction. S.F., Priv. print., 1949. 112 p. illus., ports.
            C CHi CLU CO CSfP CSfWF-H CSmH CU-B

9931. Innis, Kenneth Frederick, jr. A report on San Francisco bay shrimp studies. [S.F.] 1956. 141 p. illus., diagrs., map. Thesis (M.S.) — Univ. of San Francisco, 1956.   CSfU

9932. Installment home association of San Francisco. S.F., A.S. De Guerre, 1890. CSmH

9933. Interior, *pseud.* Letters addressed to the Hon. Wm. M. Gwin, by "Interior." As they originally appeared in the "Marysville herald"...of September 26 [Oct. 31, 1854]... [Marysville? 1854?] 8 p. CHi

9934. International aviation meet, San Francisco, 1911. Official souvenir program, January 7th to 16th, inclusive, Tanforan aviation park, San Francisco. S.F., L. Friedman [1911] 15 p. illus., ports. CHi CU-B

9935. International congress of viticulture. Official report of the session...held in Recital hall at Festival hall, Panama-Pacific international exposition, San Francisco, Cal., July 12 and 13, 1915. [S.F., Dettner print. co., 1915?] 324 p. illus. CHi

9936. International institute of San Francisco. Lives make America's destiny. So the pattern is woven. [S.F., c1942] 2 v. in 1. CHi CU-B

9937. International longshoremen's association. Local 38–79. The maritime crisis: what it is and what it isn't... [S.F., 1936?] 19 p. illus. CHi

9938. —— —— The truth about the waterfront; the I.L.A. states its case to the public. [S.F., 1934?] 19 p. CHi

9939. International science foundation. Scientific resources of the San Francisco bay area. S.F., 1956–57. 2 v. C CRcS CSfSt

9940. International typographical union of North America. Official souvenir fifty-seventh convention...San Francisco. S.F., Williams print. co., 1911. [156] p. illus. CHi

9941. —— The 100th annual convention in San Francisco. S.F., Internat. typographical union, 1958. CRcS

9942. —— **Union no. 21, San Francisco.** The Printers' appeal. San Francisco, April 18, 1880. To the people of San Francisco...[S.F., 1880] 4 p. CU-B

9943. [Inwood, George] Evidence of George Inwood's loan of $5,700, in 1849, to the First Baptist church, and of the various means used by said organization to evade payment. S.F., Commercial bk. and job. steam presses, 1861. 26 p.
  C CHi CSmH CU-B NN NvHi

9944. Iroquois club. Constitution, by-laws, and order of business and rules of order... [S.F.] P. E. Dougherty & co., 1887. 24 p. CHi

9945. Irvine, James. Last will and testament of James Irvine. [S.F., 1886?] 11 p. CU-B

9946. Irving institute. [Announcements] 1884/85–1885/86, 1888/89–1889/90, 1894/95, 1897/98. S.F. illus. CU-B

9947. Irwin, Charlotte Martin. Unions of white collar WPA workers in the bay region, November 1935 to May 1937. [Berkeley, 1939] Thesis (M.A.)— Univ. of Calif., 1939. CU

9948. Irwin, Inez Haynes. The Californiacs. S.F., A.M. Robertson, 1916. 63 p. col. front. Reprint from *Sunset*, Feb. 1916.
  CBb CChiS CCoron CHi CLO CLSM CPs CRcS CRic CSalCL CSd CSfCW CSjC CStcl CStoC

9949. —— The native son. S.F., A.M. Robertson, 1919. 69 p. col. front.
  CHi CRic CSfCW CSjC CStclU CStoC CV CWhC

9950. Irwin, William Henry. The city that was; a requiem of old San Francisco... N.Y., B.W. Huebsch, 1906. 47 p. "This is a recast of a newspaper article of the same title published in the *Sun*, April 21, 1906."
Available in many libraries.

9951. —— Same. 1908. CU-B

9952. Issler, Anne (Roller) Happier for his presence; San Francisco and Robert Louis Stevenson. Stanford [1949] 178 p. illus., ports. Bibliography: p. 165–172.
Available in many libraries.

9953. [Italian centennial committee of San Francisco] 100th anniversary of the unification of Italy, October, 1861–October, 1961. 26 p. CHi

9954. Ito, Sotomi, and co. Partial catalogue and net wholesale price list. Oct. 1895. S.F. [1895] 1 v. CU-B

9955. Iverson, Willa Okker. The strange case of Constance Flood; a documentary account. N.Y., Putnam, 1956. 382 p. illus., ports.
  CHi CP CRcS CSd CSf CSlu CStmo CU-B

9956. Jackson, Charlotte E. (Cobden) The story of San Francisco; illustrated by Kurt Werth. N.Y., Random house [1955] 182 p. illus. (Landmark bks. 59)
  C CMont CPa CSalCL CSdS CSluCL

9957. —— Same, in German. Wien, Bergland verlag [c1957] 179 p. illus. CU-B

9958. Jackson, Hartley Everett. In memoriam. Goleta, Internat. graphics arts educ. assoc., 1956. [8] p. CSjC

9959. Jackson, Herbert Edward. Peanuts and peanut oil; with special reference to the trade of San Francisco. [Berkeley, 1924] Thesis (M.S.)— Univ. of Calif., 1924. CU

9960. Jackson, Joseph Henry. Christmas by the Golden Gate... Bost. & N.Y., Houghton, 1928. 14 p. illus.
  C CBu CHi CLSU CO CSmH CU-B

9961. —— Gertrude Atherton. [N.Y.? 1940?] [20] p. port. CHi

9962. —— The girl in the belfry; by Joseph Henry Jackson and Lenore Glen Offord. Greenwich, Conn., Fawcett pub., 1957. CRcS

9963. —— My San Francisco. N.Y., Crowell [1953] 42 p.
Available in many California libraries and CoU MiD NN ODa TxU UPB

9964. —— ed. San Francisco murders... N.Y., Duell [c1947] 314 p. (Regional murder ser., ed. by Marie F. Rodell. IV)
Available in many libraries.

9965. —— The Western Gate, a San Francisco reader. [N.Y.] Farrar, Straus and Young [1952] 542 p. (City & country readers ser. [4])
Available in many California libraries and CaBViPA IC MiD MoS N NN ODa

9966. Jackson, Phyllis Wynn. Golden footlights; the merry-making career of Lotta Crabtree; portraits by Lloyd Lózes Goff. N.Y., Holiday, c1949. 310 p. illus. CMont

9967. Jackson street free kindergarten association. Annual report. 1st– , 1880– S.F., Dodge bros., 1880–
CHi has 1st–2d, 5th–7th, 1880–81, 1884–86.

9968. Jacobs, Alger Jay. An analysis of the wholesale drug business in San Francisco, 1900–1930. [Berkeley, 1931] Thesis (M.A.)—Univ. of Calif., 1931.   CU

9969. Jacobson, Pauline. City of the golden 'fifties. Berkeley and L.A., Univ. of Calif. press, 1941. 290 p. "These sketches first appeared as a weekly Saturday feature of the *San Francisco bulletin* from March, 1916, to August, 1917."—Author's pref.

Available in many California libraries and CaBViPA CoD MiD NHi NN ODa

9970. —— A fire-defying landmark. Reprint from the *San Francisco bulletin*, May 4, 1912. 15 p. port.

C C-S CHi CLU CSf CSfWF-H CSmH CU-B

9971. —— Manager Woods' happy burnt district home. S.F., Priv. print., 1912. 16 p. pl. "This article was originally printed in the *San Francisco bulletin* of October 28th, 1906; and is descriptive of the temporary Hotel St. Francis, erected on the lawns of Union square ..."   C-S CHi

9972. James, Jack, and Weller, Earle. Treasure island; "the magic city," 1939–1940. The story of the Golden Gate international exposition... S.F., Pisani print. & pub., c1941. 309 p. illus.

Available in many California libraries and NHi

9973. James, Juliet Helena (Lumbard) A foreword to the Panama-Pacific international exposition... S.F., Ricardo J. Orozco press, 1915. 9 p.   CHi

9974. —— The meaning of the courts of the Golden Gate international exposition, 1939. Berkeley [The Professional press, c1939] 40 p.   CRcS CU-B

9975. —— Palaces and courts of the exposition; a handbook of the architecture, sculpture and mural paintings with special reference to the symbolism. S.F., Calif. bk. co., 1915. 156 p. illus.

Available in many California libraries and ViU

9976. —— Sculpture of the exposition palaces and courts; descriptive notes on the art of the statuary at the Panama-Pacific international exposition. S.F., Crocker [c1915] 96 p.   CHi CMartC CRcS CRedl CSfP

9977. James, Marquis. Biography of a bank; the story of Bank of America N. T. & S. A. N.Y., Harper, 1954. 566 p. illus., ports. Notes giving sources: p. 523–554.

Available in many California libraries.

9978. Japan society of America. Catalogue of the first exhibition... S.F., 1906. 29 p. pl.   CHi

9979. —— Constitution and by-laws...organized October 7th, 1905. S.F., Taylor, Nash & Taylor, print., 1913. 31 p.   CHi

9980. [Jarboe, John R.] Memorial...adopted and ordered printed by the Bar association of San Francisco, January 15, 1894. S.F., C.A. Murdock & co., 1894. 15 p.   CSmH

9981. Jean, Wong Koon. Facilities for financing foreign trade between San Francisco and China. [Berkeley, 1924] Thesis (M.A.) — Univ. of Calif., 1924.   CU

9982. Jeffersonian society. Celebration of Thomas Jefferson's birthday by the Jeffersonian society of San Francisco, April 13, 1869, as published in the *Weekly Examiner* of April 24th. 16 p.   C

9983. —— Constitution, by-laws and standing rules ... S.F., M.D. Carr & co., 1869. 12 p.   CHi

9984. Jenness, Charles Kelley. The charities of San Francisco: a directory of the benevolent and correctional agencies... S.F., Bk. room print., 1894. 93 p.

C CSf CU-B MoS

9985. Jensen, George Charles. The city front federation of San Francisco; a study in labor organization... [Berkeley] 1912. 65 l.   CU CU-B

9986. Jesuit mothers of San Francisco. History of the Jesuit mothers, 1932–1950. [S.F., 1951] 121 p.   CSfCW

9987. Johnson, Bascom. Moral conditions in San Francisco and at the Panama-Pacific exposition. N.Y., Am. social hygiene assoc., 1915. 21 p.   CU-B

9988. Johnson, Charles Spurgeon. The Negro war worker in San Francisco, a local self-survey...a project, financed by a San Francisco citizen, administered by the Y.W.C.A., and carried out in connection with the race relations program of the American missionary association ...and the Julius Rosenwald fund. [n.p.] 1944. 98 p.   CHi

9989. Johnson (F. S.) co. Catalogue no. 24... wholesale manufacturers and dealers in harness, saddles ... S.F. [n.d.] 280 p. illus.   CHi

9990. Johnson, Kenneth M. José Yves Limantour v. the United States. L.A., Dawson, 1961. 81 p. map. (Famous Calif. trials, v.1)   CHi CLSM

9991. Johnson, Otis Russell. In memoriam... 1887–1957. [S.F., Taylor & Taylor, 1957] [5] l.   CHi

9992. Johnson, Peter. Memoirs of Captain Peter Johnson. [S.F., Priv. print., 1938] 76 p.   CHi

9993. Johnson, Robert Barbour. The magic park ... S.F., Century press; A & A printers [1940] 53 p. illus.   C CHi CSf

9994. Johnson, Robert Samuel. Senator Hiram Johnson and American foreign affairs. [Berkeley, 1945] Thesis (M.A.) — Univ. of Calif., 1945.   CU

9995. Johnson, Simeon M. A letter to the President about the title of Yerba-Buena island, bay of San Francisco, with an analysis of the report of the Senate Pacific railroad committee upon the same. Wash., D.C., M'Gill & Witherow print., 1870. [14] p.   CSf

9996. Johnson & Joseph co. Catalog...ship chandlers, yacht and motor boat equipment... S.F. [188–?– CHi has no. 36, 44 [1930?, 1940?]

9997. Johnston, James A. Alcatraz island prison, and the men who live there. N.Y., Scribner, 1949. 276 p. illus., port.

Available in many libraries.

9998. —— Prison life is different by [the] warden of Alcatraz prison. Bost., Houghton, 1937. 337 p. illus.   CHi CRcS CSd CSdS CStmo

9999. Johnston, Samuel P., ed. Alaska commercial company, 1868–1940. [S.F.? Edwin E. Wachter, print., 1940?] 65 p. illus.   CHi

10000. Joint committee from the Chamber of commerce and the San Francisco produce exchange on sea wall and warehousing. Report...with the views of the members... S.F., C.A. Murdock & co., print., 1886. 20 p.   CHi CLU CSmH

10001. Jones, Hank. "A few more left!" the story of Isaac Hillman. San Leandro, 1958. 43 l.   CHi N

10002. Jones, Idwal. Ark of empire; San Francisco's Montgomery block. Illus. by A. J. Camille. [1st ed.] Garden City, N.Y., Doubleday, 1951. 253 p. illus., ports.

Available in many California libraries and CaBViPA CoD CoU MiD MoS N NN ODa UHi

10003. Jones, Melvin Richard. Public management of defense production in the San Francisco bay area. [Berkeley, 1954] Thesis (M.A.) — Univ. of Calif., 1954.   CU

10004. Jones, R. C. Prominent San Franciscans (in caricature). S.F., Press of C.A. Murdock & co. [1908?] 167 p. ports. Pages 7–167 are caricatures.
CHi CLU CSmH CU-B

10005. [Jones, W. A.] Plan for the cultivation of trees upon the Presidio reservation. [S.F.? 1883?] 8 p.
CU-B

10006. Jones, William Carey. The "Pueblo question" solved in a plain statement of facts and law... S.F., Commercial steam bk. & job print. establishment, 1860. 36 p.
C CHi CLCM CSfP CSmH CU-B CtY

10007. Jones, William Cockrell. An analysis of the trade agreements of organized labor in San Francisco, California. [Berkeley, 1921] Thesis (M.A.)— Univ. of Calif., 1921.
CU

10008. Jones & Bendixen, auctioneers. Catalogue of stock of wines, liquors, cigars, teas, hams, etc., etc. to be sold this day! Friday, December 27, 1867, at the store of F. C. Belden, 612 Sacramento Street... S.F., Alta print. house, 1867. 6 p.
CHi

10009. Jordan, David Starr, ed. The California earthquake of 1906... S.F., A.M. Robertson, 1907. 371 p. illus., maps. Partly reprint. from various periodicals.
Available in many California libraries and MiD N TxU

10010. Jordan, Lois. The work of the White angel of San Francisco waterfront... S.F. [n.d.] 54 p. illus., ports.
CSf

10011. Josselyn (G. M.) and co. G. M. Josselyn & co., importers and wholesale dealers in ship chandlery, agents for the Taunton sheathing metal manufacturing co. S.F., Winterburn & co., print., 1880. 64 p.
CU-B

10012. Journal of progress; a bulletin of events telling of the rebuilding of San Francisco. Issued by the Passenger department, Southern Pacific company... v.1, no. [1–2] [4]–42; May 19, 1906–Mar. 2, 1907. S.F., 1906–07.
CU-B

10013. Journeymen bricklayer's protective association. Code of laws... rev. ed. S.F., Turnbull & Smith, 1867. 24 p.
CHi

10014. Judges and criminals: shadows of the past. History of the Vigilance committee of San Francisco, Cal., with the names of its officers. S.F., Print. for the author, 1858. 100 p. A history of the Vigilance committee of 1856. Ascribed to Dr. Henry M. Gray.—Cowan.
C CHi CLU CLgA CSfCP CSfWF-H CSmH CSt CStclU CU-B

10015. [Judson Pacific-Murphy corp. A romance of steel in California. [S.F., Clavering press, 1946] [72] p. illus., facsims. "Seventy-eighth anniversary souvenir book... The narrative was written by Marsh Maslin."
CHi CSfP CSfSt

10016. Jue, George K. Chinatown—its history, its people, its importance... S.F., Chamber of commerce, 1951. 11 l.
CSf CU-B

10017. Jungblut (August) and co. Catalogue and reduced price list. [187–?] S.F. [187–?] illus.
CU-B

10018. Junior league of San Francisco, inc. A family guide to the San Francisco bay area. San Carlos, Nourse [c1962] 120 p.
CAla

10019. Kadelburg, Heinrich. Fünfzehn jahre des deutschen theaters in San Francisco... S.F., Druck von Rosenthal & Roesch, 1883. 32 p.
C CHi CLU CSf CSfCW CSmH CU-B

10020. Kahn, Edgar Myron. Andrew Smith Hallidie; a tribute to a pioneer California industrialist. Fore-word by Carl I. Wheat. S.F. [Lawton Kennedy, print.] 1953. 33 p. port.
C CHi CSf CU-B

10021. —— Bret Harte in California; a character study. With an introduction by Carl I. Wheat. S.F., Priv. print. by Haywood H. Hunt, 1951. 25 p. port.
CHi CLgA

10022. —— Cable car days in San Francisco... Stanford [c1940] 124 p. front., illus.
CHi CRedl CSdS CSfSt CSfU CSlu CStmo CU-B CV CoD MoS NHi ODa OrU OU UPB

10023. —— Same. rev. ed. Stanford [c1944] 134 p. front., illus.
Available in many California libraries and MoSU N TxU

10024. —— Early San Francisco Jewry. [S.F.? 1955] 27 l.
CU-B

10025. —— ...From Land's end to the ferry [by] Edgar M. Kahn, Francis P. Farquhar, Lee L. Stopple... S.F., Black vine press [1942] [61] p. At head of title: Charles L. Camp, George D. Lyman... [and others] "These word pictures on the various phases of the Embarcadero of yesterday were originally written at the request of Richard Wagner of the Harbor day comm. of the San Francisco jr. chamber of commerce."
C CHi CLU CSf CSmH TxU

10026. Kahn (Henry) and co. Illustrated catalogue of microscopes, objectives and accessories. [1892?] S.F. [1892?] 1 v. illus.
CU-B

10027. Kahn, Jules. Histoire de San Francisco, 1776–1906. Paris, Editions Sansot, L.–H. Alexandre, 1927. 192 p.
C CO CSmH CU-B MoS NN

10028. Kahn, Julius. Memorial addresses delivered in the House of representatives of the United States in memory of Julius Kahn, late a representative from California... Sixty-eighth congress, February 22, 1925. Wash., D.C., Govt. print. off., 1925. 73 p. illus., port.
CHi CSfCW

10029. —— The San Francisco disaster—honest and dishonest insurance. Speech of Hon. Julius Kahn, of California, in the House of representatives... June 28, 1906. Wash., D.C., 1906. 8 p.
C CU-B

10030. Kahn, Brod and co. Illustrated price list of optical, mathematical and scientific instruments. Ed. 1. S.F., 1882. 1 v. illus.
CU-B

10031. Kalkhorst, Anton B. C. The house of Berendsen. Thirty years of history of an enthusiastic youth and energetic man & leading wholesale firm of San Francisco. S.F., Priv. print. by J.H. Nash, 1919. 36 p. ports., chart.
CHi

10032. Kalloch, Isaac S. In the Superior court of the city and county of San Francisco, department no. 5. In the matter of Isaac S. Kalloch... S.F., Frank Eastman & co., print. [1874] 50 p.
CSmH

10033. —— [Kalloch trials; a collection of pamphlets, 1857–1880] 1 v.
CU-B

10034. Kavanagh, Dennis John, Father. The golden jubilee of Rev. William H. Culligan, S.J., 1887–1927. [n.p., n.d.] 15 p. illus.
CStclU

10035. —— The Holy Family sisters of San Francisco. A sketch of their first fifty years 1872–1922. S.F., Gilmartin co., 1922. 328 p. illus., ports.
C CBb CHi CLU CLgA CO COHN CSd CSf CSfCW CSrD CU-B

10036. Keane bros. Illustrated circular. Spring/summer 1881. S.F., 1881. 1 v. illus., music.
CU-B

10037. Keast, Frederick E., comp. Since 1856, a brief chronology of H. S. Crocker co., the Union lithograph company, and the H. S. Crocker company, inc. ... [S.F., Crocker, 1944] unp.   CHi CSmH

10038. Keeler, Charles Augustus. San Francisco and thereabout... S.F., Calif. promotion committee, 1902. 97 p. illus.
Available in many California libraries and CoU MHi MoS NHi NjR TxU UHi UPB ViW

10039. —— Same. 1903. 97 p. illus.
                                    C CHi CSdU CU-B ViU

10040. —— Same. S.F., A.M. Robertson, 1906. 97 p. illus.
                    C CHi CRedl CRic CSto CU-B MoSHi NN OrU TMC

10041. —— San Francisco through earthquake and fire... S.F., Elder [c1906] 55 p. 14 pl.
C CHi CLO CLSU CLU CO CP CRedl CRic CSd CSf CSfCSM CSfCW CSfU CSfWF-H CSluCL CU-B CoU MiD MoS NN OrU

10042. Keesling, Francis V. Golden Gate bridge, dedication address, Redwood theatre, Crissy field, San Francisco, May 28, 1937. [S.F.] 1937. [14] p. front.
                                                            CHi

10043. —— San Francisco charter of 1931. S.F., Author, 1933. 88 p. chart.   CHi CSfMI

10044. Keith (N. S.) firm. Keith's apparatus for electric power. S.F., 1887. [14] p.   CU-B

10045. Keith, William. Catalog, the John Zeile collection of Wm. Keith paintings sold by order of the American trust company... S.F., Joseph Basch galleries [1931] 7 p.   CHi

10046. —— Catalog, twenty-four landscape paintings...to be sold at auction in the Sutter street salesrooms...Jan. 16, 1913. [S.F.] H. Taylor Curtis, 1913. 24 l. illus., port.   CHi

10047. Keller, Marvel. Decasualization of longshore work in San Francisco; methods and results of the control of dispatching and hours worked, 1935–37... Phila., 1939. 157 p.   CO

10048. Kellersberger, Getulius. The Vigilantes committee in California, 1851–1856 and 1877. [n.p., Austin? 1953] 12 l.   CO

10049. Kelly, Mary. Shame on the relief; being an exposé of the disgraceful methods of the Relief committee during the dark days following San Francisco's great disaster. [S.F., 1908?] 15 p.   CU-B

10050. Kemble, Edward Cleveland. Yerba Buena —1846 (Sketched through a loophole)...Reproduced from the *Sacramento daily union* of Aug. 26, Sept. 16 and Oct. 17, 1871, with a biographical foreword by Douglas S. Watson. S.F., Johnck & Seeger, 1935. 17 p. illus.
C CHi CLO CLU CMont CSf CSfCW CSfU CSfWF-H CSmat CSmH CU-B CaBViPA

10051. Kemble, John Haskell. The genesis of the Pacific mail steamship company. [Berkeley, 1934] Thesis (M.A.)— Univ. of Calif., 1934.   CU CU-B

10052. —— San Francisco bay, a pictorial maritime history. Cambridge, Md., Cornell maritime press, 1957. 195 p. illus., maps.
Available in many California libraries and CaBViPA ODa UU

10053. —— Side-wheelers across the Pacific. [S.F] S.F. museum of science and industry, 1942. 38 p. illus.
                                                CStclU CU-B

10054. Kemper, Lucrezia. The story of Keyston bros., seventy-five years' history of a business and a family, 1868–1943. [S.F.] 1944. 52 l. illus., ports., facsims.
                                                CHi CSmH

10055. Kendig, Wainright and co. Catalogue of second great sale of valuable city property to be sold... on Tuesday, August 13, 1850... S.F., Alta Calif. steam presses, 1850. 16 p.   CU-B

10056. Kendrick, Charles. Can we have peace? S.F., Off night club, 1945. 19 p.   CHi

10057. Kennedy, Elijah R. The contest for California in 1861; how Colonel E. D. Baker saved the Pacific states to the Union...With illustrations. Bost., Houghton, 1912. 361 p. illus., ports.
Available in many California libraries and MoS OrU ViU

10058. Kennedy, Laurence Joseph. The progress of the fire in San Francisco, April 18th to 21st, 1906, as shown by an analysis of original documents. [Berkeley, 1908] Thesis (M.A.)— Univ. of Calif., 1908.   CU

10059. Kennedy, Van Dusen. Arbitration in the San Francisco hotel and restaurant industries. Phila., Pub. for Labor relations council of Wharton school of finance and commerce by the Univ. of Pa. press, 1952. 113 p.   CLU CU-B

10060. Ker, Minette Augusta. The history of the theatre in California in the nineteenth century. [Berkeley, 1924] Thesis (M.A.)— Univ. of Calif., 1924.
                                                    CU CU-B

10061. Kessel, Joseph. ...Dames de Californie... Un chapitre de ma vie. Paris, E. Hazan [1928] 120 p. port.   CU-B MoS

10062. Kewell (Chas. H.) co. Anglers' specialties catalogue... [n.p.] 1917. 32 p. illus.   CHi

10063. Keyes, Erasmus Darwin. Fifty years' observation of men and events civil and military. N.Y., Scribner, 1884. 515 p.
C CBb CHi CLS CLSU CLU CO CPom CSf CSfCP CSfP CSmH CU-B CaBViPA

10064. Keyston bros. Catalog of harness, saddlery, leather goods...[since 1868] [S.F., 1868?–]
CHi has no. 61 [1928], no. 85 [n.d.], accompanied by 1952 price list.

10065. Keystone type foundry. Abridged specimen book... [n.p.] September 1906. 623 p. illus.   CHi

10066. Kibbe, Wallace, & son. A specimen book of type faces. S.F. [n.d.] [22] p.   CHi

10067. Kilcline, William F. ...Legal aid society ... [S.F., 1961] [8] p. Reprint. from *The Recorder*, February 15 and 16, 1961.   CHi

10068. Killinger, Emily Tibbey. The islands of San Francisco bay, prepared for the Colonial dames of America in the state of California... S.F., Dec. 1, 1934. 12 p. illus.   C CHi CLU CO CRic CSf CU-B

10069. King, Joe. San Francisco giants. Introd. by George Christopher. Pref. by Ford C. Frick. Englewood Cliffs, N.Y., Prentice-Hall [1958] 177 p.
C CChiS CMont CPa CSf CSfMI CStmo CUk CViCL

10070. King, Joseph L. History of the San Francisco stock and exchange board... S.F., Author, 1910. 373 p. illus., ports.
Available in many libraries.

10071. King, Margaret Goddard. The growth of San Francisco as illustrated by shifts in densities of population. [Berkeley, 1928] Thesis (M.A.)— Univ. of Calif., 1928.   CU

10072. King, Thomas Butler. Letter from the Hon. T. Butler King to the Hon. Wm. C. Dawson. N.Y., Holman & Gray, print., 1855. 19 p. "...account of the difficulties, labor, risks, and responsibilities... in San Francisco."
C

10073. King, Thomas Starr. Address before the First Unitarian society of San Francisco, in memory of their late pastor...March 15, 1864 by Robert B. Swain. S.F., Frank Eastman, print., 1864. 28 p.   CHi

10074. —— Funeral service of the Free and accepted Masons of the state of California, as read at the burial of the Rev. and W.˙. Brother Thomas Starr King ...March 6, A.L. 5864, A.D. 1864. [n.p., n.d.] 15 p.
CHi

10075. —— "He was a good man." A discourse in memory of William Macondray. Preached in the First Unitarian church, San Francisco, Sunday morning, August 31, 1862. S.F., Towne & Bacon, 1862. 33 p.
CLU CSmH CU-B

10076. —— In memory... a discourse given to his flock in San Francisco, May 1, 1864 by Henry W. Bellows. S.F., 1864. 47 p.   CHi CP

10077. —— Peace: what it would cost us. Address ...August 29, 1861. [S.F., 1861] Broadside.   CHi

10078. Kingsbury, Kenneth R. [In memoriam] 1876–1937. [S.F., Print. for Californians, inc., by Taylor & Taylor, 1938] [5] p.   CHi

10079. Kinney (R. W.) co. Price list [of] malleable, wrought and cast iron, soil, brass...pipe and fittings. no. 4, Nov. 22, 1906. S.F., 1906. illus.   CU-B

10080. Kip, Leonard. California sketches, with recollections of the gold mines. Albany, N.Y., Erastus H. Pease & co., 1850. 57 p. "Narrative of San Francisco, Stockton and the mining camps."
C CLU CP CSj CSmH CU-B

10081. —— Same. With introduction by Lyle H. Wright. L.A., N.A. Kovach, 1946. 58 p. illus., map. (Half-title: Calif. centennial ser.)
Available in many California libraries and MiD MoHi ViU ViW

10082. Kip (Maria) orphanage ... Annual report ...S.F., Woodward & co. [1902]–
CHi has 1896, 1902, 1905–06.

10083. [Kip, William Ingraham, Bp.] Celebration of the twenty-fifth anniversary of the consecration of the Bishop of California. S.F., Pac. churchman print., 1878. 8 p.   CHi

10084. Kipling, Rudyard. Rudyard Kipling in San Francisco: being an excerpt from his "American notes" as originally published in "The Pioneer" of Allahabad, India in 1889. S.F., Priv. print. by Haywood H. Hunt, 1926. 51 p. front.   C CLgA CRedCL

10085. —— ...Rudyard Kipling's Letters from San Francisco... S.F., Colt press [Grabhorn, print.] 1949. 76 p. "These letters are part of the correspondence and articles written by Rudyard Kipling in 1887–1889 for the Indian *Civil and military gazette* in Lahore; and the Allahabad *Pioneer*."—Foreword.
C CAla CBev CChiS CL CLU CO CPom CRcS CRedl CRic CSd CSf CSjC CSluCL CSmat CSmH CStclU CU-B CV

10086. Kirchner, Stewart Wayne. Union security and the Taft-Hartley act in the San Francisco area. [Berkeley, 1949] Thesis (M.A.)— Univ. of Calif., 1949.   CU

10087. Kittredge (Jonathan) firm. Price list of fire and burglar-proof safes. 1871. S.F. [1871] 1 v. illus.   CU-B

10088. Klarenmeyer (S.) firm. Catalogue of the leading underwear house... [S.F., 188–?] 15 p. illus.   CHi

10089. Klauber, Laurence Monroe. Two days in San Francisco, 1906. [n.p., 1958] 26 l.
C CHi CSd CSf CSt CU-B

10090. Klein (John M.) electrical works. [Catalogue no. 17. S.F., 1897] 95 p. illus.   CHi

10091. Klein, Julius. The development of the manufacturing industry in California up to 1870. [Berkeley, 1908] Thesis (M.L.)— Univ. of Calif., 1908.   CU-B

10092. Klinkner (Charles A.) and co. Catalogue. Ed. 3. 1890. S.F. [1890] 1 v. illus.   CHi CU-B

10093. —— ...Illustrated catalogue of red rubber stamps... [3d ed. S.F., 1896] 250 p. illus.   CHi

10094. Klumpke, Anna Elizabeth. Memoirs of an artist. Ed. by Lilian Whiting. Bost., Wright & Potter print. co., 1940. 91 p. port.   CHi

10095. [Knapp, Eloise (Mabury)] A biographical sketch of Sue Ella Bradshaw, C.S.D. S.F., Priv. print. for Calif. students' Christian scientist assoc., by J.H. Nash, 1929. 30 p.   CSmH

10096. Knapp, Henry R., pub. Chinatown. S.F., 1889. 12 pl.   CSmH

10097. Knies, Donald A. Labor conflict on the San Francisco waterfront, 1934–1938. [Stanford] 1952. Thesis (M.A.)— Stanford univ., 1952.   CSt

10098. Knight, Robert Edward Lee. Industrial relations in the San Francisco bay area, 1900–1918. Berkeley, Univ. of Calif. press, 1960. 463 p. (Pub. of the Inst. of industrial relations, Univ. of Calif.)
CAla CSf CU (also Ph.D. thesis, 1958) CU-B

10099. Knight, Thomas, vs. the United land association et al. In the Supreme court of the United States. October term, 1891. Thomas Knight, plaintiff in error, v. The United land association and Clinton C. Tripp, defendants in error. Brief on behalf of plaintiff in error. Samuel M. Wilson [and] Edward R. Taylor, counsel for plaintiff in error. S.F., W.A. Woodward & co., print., 1891. 121 p.   CLU

10100. Knight-Counihan co. Rhyme and reason in bank stock school stationery... [n.p., 1920?] [20] p. illus.   CHi

10101. Knights of honor, San Francisco. Eureka lodge, no. 1756. Constitution, by-laws, rules of order, etc. ...instituted at San Francisco, Sept. 4, 1879. S.F., Barry and Baird, 1880. 56 p.   C

10102. —— **Germania loge no. 1718.** Nebengesetze der Germania loge no. 1718 der Ehren-ritter (Knights of honor) S.F., Eureka press, 1910. 20 p.
CHi

10103. Knower, Daniel. The adventures of a fortyniner. An historic description of California, with events and ideas of San Francisco and its people in those early days. Albany, N.Y., Weed-Parsons print. co., 1894. 200 p. illus., port.
C CHi CL CLSU CLU CO CP CSbr CSd CSf CSfCP CSfCW CSfP CSj CSjC CSmH CU-B CaBViPA IHi TxU

10104. Knowles, Barton Harvey. The early history of San Francisco's water supply, 1776–1858. [Berkeley, 1948] Thesis (M.A.)— Univ. of Calif., 1948.   CU

10105. Kohler, Chase and co. Illustrated catalogue of piano fortes, manufactured by Chickering & sons. 1871. S.F. [1871]   CU-B

10106. Kollmann, Max, comp. San Francisco Chronicle classified business directory and street guide of San Francisco. [S.F., The Hansen co., 1909—] Title varies.   C-S (1919)   CHi (1909, 1924)   CSf (1909)

10107. Köneke and co. Price list and descriptive catalogue of the Coventry bicycles. 1877. S.F. [1877] 1 v. illus.   CU-B

10108. Koster, Frederick J. Law and order and the San Francisco chamber of commerce; an address... S.F., Chamber of commerce, 1918. 16 p. illus.
                CHi CLU CSf CSfCW CSmH CU-B

10109. Kothé, Leonore. [Original pencil sketches of San Francisco's Chinatown] 31 mounted pl.   CSf

10110. Kramer-Ewing construction co. Stop paying rent. The Kramer-Ewing construction company will build you a home. [S.F., 1955?] 16 p. illus.   CU-B

10111. Krogh manufacturing co. Bulletin. no. 78–80, 82–83, 85, 92. S.F. [1915?] 7 nos. illus., tables.
                                                            CU-B

10112. —— Catalog...of pumps and pumping machinery. [S.F., 1882–1900] illus. Publisher varies.
C-S has [1883, 1891] CHi has 1882, 1899–1900. CU-B has 1900.

10113. Krumm, Walter Courtney. The San Francisco stage, 1869–1879. Stanford, 1961. Thesis (Ph.D.)— Stanford univ., 1961.   CHi (microfilm) CSt

10114. Kuykendall, Ralph Simpson. History of early California journalism. [Berkeley, 1919] Thesis (M.A.)— Univ. of Calif., 1919.   CU CU-B

10115. Kwang, Chang Ling. Letters of...the Chinese side of the Chinese question...communicated to the San Francisco Argonaut of the dates August 7th, 10th, 17th, and September 7th, 1878. 16 p.   CHi

10116. Labor defense league, S.F. Citizens of California! Especially of the Bay cities. Do you wish to be known as approving the arrest and conviction of such an eminent and public-spirited citizen as Miss Charlotte Anita Whitney on the absurd charge of criminal syndicalism?... [S.F., Labor defense league, 1920?] [7] p.
                                                            CU-B

10117. Laborer, pseud. To the old line democrats! Friends and neighbors... [S.F., 1856] 8 p. "Albert Miller?" penciled as author.—cf. p. 8.   CHi

10118. Lachman, Arthur & co. [Catalog] Lachman quality wines...famous since 1860... [S.F., 191–?] [13] p.   CHi

10119. Lacombe, George. Roster of the 347th field artillery, A.E.F., 1918–1919. [S.F., n.d.] 43 p. illus.
                                                            CHi

10120. Lacy, Edward Silas. The schools demanded by the present age. A sermon delivered in the First Congregational church, San Francisco, on Sunday, May 11, 1856. S.F., Whitton, Towne & co., print., Excelsior bk. and job off., 1856. 15 p. A plan for establishing a college for California.
                C CBPac CLU CSaT CSmH CU-B NN

10121. Ladies' aid and protection society, for the benefit of seamen of the port of San Francisco. Constitution and by-laws... S.F., C.A. Calhoun, print., 1856. 10 p.   CSmH

10122. Ladies' depository. The first annual report of the Board of directors...for 1867. S.F., E. Bosqui & co., 1867. 12 p.   CHi

10123. Ladies' seamen's friend society of the port of San Francisco. ...Annual report... S.F., Geo. Spaulding & co., 1857—
CHi has 9th, 11th–12th, 13th–14th, 18th–20th, 23d–24th, 28th, 39th, 41st, 1865, 1867–68, 1869–70, 1874–76, 1879–80, 1884, 1895, 1897. CSmH has 1st, 3d, 4th, 6th, 1857, 1859, 1860, 1862. CU has 6th, 1862.

10124. Ladies union beneficial society. Constitution, by-laws, and act of incorporation. Organized September, 1860. Incorporated Feb. 1861. [S.F.] B.F. Sterett, print., 1861. 12 p.   CHi (photocopy) CU-B

10125. Laffan, Edmund, vs. Naglee, Henry M. In the Supreme court of the state of California. Edmund Laffan, respondent, vs. Henry M. Naglee, appellant. Brief for respondent. Hoge & Wilson, attorneys for respondent. S.F., Fireman's jl. print. off., 1857. xvi, 56 p. San Francisco property suit.   CLU CSmH

10126. Lafler, Henry Anderson. How the army worked to save San Francisco. Being of a supplementary nature to "...personal narrative of...Frederick Funston, brig.-gen., U.S.A." in the *Cosmopolitan magazine* for July. S.F., Calkins newspaper syndicate, 1906. 20 p.
            C CHi CLU CSfWF-H CSmH CU-B NN

10127. Lahey, Edward C. California's miser philanthropist: a biography of James Lick. [Berkeley, 1949] Thesis (M.A.)— Univ. of Calif., 1949.   CU

10128. Lake, Delos. Speech of Delos Lake on the trial of Hogg and others before a military commission at San Francisco, June, 1865. S.F., Towne & Bacon, 1865. 17 p.   CHi

10129. Lambert, Richard. Civic federation: report on the assessor's office. [S.F., 1896] 32 p.   C

10130. Lampson, Robin. San Francisco souvenir; a series of ten California historical sketches in cadence written for original publication on the radio. S.F., Print. by Windsor press for...Wells Fargo bank & union trust co., 1938. 36 p.
C CAla CChiS CHi CL CLU CO CSf CSfSt CSfU CSfWF-H CSmH CStrJC CU-B

10131. Lamson, George F., auctioneer. Catalogue [household furnishings] Dec. 15–16, 1879. S.F., 1879.
                                                            CU-B

10132. —— [Catalogue of contents of R. E. Doyle residence] Sept. 1–2, 1886. S.F., 1886.   CU-B

10133. Land, Ruth Entelman. Use of advertising media by certain men's clothing retailers in San Francisco and Los Angeles. [Berkeley, 1940] Thesis (M.A.) — Univ. of Calif., 1940.   CU

10134. Land mortgage union of California. By-laws... S.F., Frank Eastman, 1871. 29 p. tables.   CHi

10135. Landaeta, Martín de. Noticias acerca del puerto de San Francisco (Alto California). Anotaciones de José C. Valades. Mexico, Antiqua librería Robredo, 1949. 78 p. (Biblioteca Mexicana de obras ineditas) Twenty-six letters written in 1800–1807.
C CHi CL CLU CLgA CO COHN CSfU CSmH CSt CStrJC CU-B CaBViPA NHi OU TxU

10136. Lande, C. J., vs. Jurisich, George. Brief of San Francisco legal aid society as amicus curiae. S.F., Recorder print. and pub. co. [1942] 31 p.   CHi

10137. Landers shoes for men and women. [Catalog] S.F. [1901?–1905?] illus., ports.
CHi has [1905?] CU-B has [1901?]

10138. Landis, J. T. Portsmouth square speaks. San Francisco history as it happened around the Square. [n.p., 1950] 10 p.   CSmat

10139. Lane, Allen Stanley. Emperor Norton, the mad monarch of America. Caldwell, Ida., Caxton, 1939. 286 p. illus., ports. Bibliography: p.[283–286]
Available in many California libraries and CaBViPA
IC

10140. Lane, Charles Milton. James King of William and the San Francisco bulletin, 1855–1856. [Berkeley, 1958] Thesis (M.A.)— Univ. of Calif., 1958.   CU

10141. Lane, Franklin Knight. ...Joseph Britton, appellant, vs. the Board of election commissioners of the city and county of San Francisco, et al., respondents. Respondents points and authorities... S.F., Star press— J.H. Barry, 1899. 37 p.   CU-B

10142. Lane, Levi Cooper. An address delivered at the opening of Lane hospital, January 2, 1895. Sacramento, 1895. Reprint. from the *Occidental medical times,* January 1895. 11 p.   CHi

10143. —— Address delivered before the Celsian society; or, Students' association of the Medical college of the Pacific, September 6, 1879. S.F., W.M. Hinton & co., print. [1879?] 7 p.   CHi

10144. —— Address, delivered by Dr. L. C. Lane, professor of surgery, at the commencement exercises of the Medical college of the Pacific, November 2d, 1876. S.F., Bonnard & Daly [1877?] p. 289–308. Reprint. from *Pacific medical and surgical journal,* December 1876.
CHi

10145. —— An address delivered to the graduating class of Cooper medical college, Nov. 13, 1890... and an address...by Edward Robeson Taylor... Sacramento, 1891. 27 p. Reprint. from the *Occidental medical times,* 1891.   CHi

10146. —— Same. By Levi C. Lane and Edward R. Taylor. S.F., Goodwin & Taylor [n.d.] 45 p.
CHi CLM

10147. —— Exercises in memory of Levi Cooper Lane held at Lane hall of Cooper medical college on Sunday afternoon the ninth day of March in the year nineteen hundred and two. S.F., Print. for the faculty of Cooper medical college by the Stanley-Taylor co., 1902. 49 p. port.   CHi

10148. —— Opening address, delivered by Dr. L. C. Lane, at Toland medical college, San Francisco, June 4th, 1866. S.F., T.G. Spear, print., Pioneer press, 1866. 15 p.
CHi

10149. —— Shadows in the ethics of the International medical congress. S.F., A.L. Bancroft & co., 1885. 12 p.   CHi

10150. —— Valedictory address, delivered at the closing exercises of Toland medical college, November 4th, 1869... S.F., Spear & co., print., 1869. 18 p.   CHi

10151. —— Valedictory delivered at the ninth annual commencement of the Medical department of the University of the Pacific, at Mercantile library hall, December 7th, 1871... S.F., Print. by J.F. Brown, 1871. 18 p.   CHi

10152. Langendorf united bakeries, inc. Annual report... [n.p., 19—?—]
CHi has 1945/46–1946/47. CL has 1951–60.

10153. Langley, Henry G., pub. A map and street directory of San Francisco... S.F., 1870. 84 p.   C

10154. —— Street and avenue guide of San Francisco. Containing a new map of San Francisco, and many items of valuable information... S.F., 1875. 106 p. map.
C CHi CLU (lacks map) CSf CSfCP CSfWF-H CU-B

10155. Langley and Michaels co. New price list of Solon Palmer's perfumery, toilet soaps, cosmetics, etc. [187–?] S.F. [187–?] 1 v.   CU-B

10156. —— Prices current of drugs, chemicals, proprietary medicines... S.F. [Hicks-Judd co., 1897] 567 p. illus.   CHi

10157. Langton's pioneer express. Special and general instructions for the use and reference of agents and employees. S.F., Towne and Bacon, 1860. 12 p.
CHi

10158. Lanson, Georges, ed. Les Français en Californie, San Francisco, Oakland, etc. Almanach de la colonie pour 1923... [S.F., 1923] 176 p. illus., ports.
CHi

10159. —— Guide des Français en Californie, 1916–1917. S.F., 1916. 272, xxxi p. illus., ports. Contains "Le 'directory' de le colonie de langue française de San Francisco" and "Le 'directory' commercial français d'Oakland, Berkeley, Alameda, San Jose, Stockton, etc."
CBb CHi

10160. Lapparent, Albert Auguste Cochon de. Le désastre de San-Francisco... Paris, L. de Soye et fils, 1906. 15 p.   CU-B

10161. Larcher school of languages. The Larcher school of languages (established July, 1887) permanently connected with Barnard's business college. S.F., Francis Valentine & co. [1888?] 14 p.   CU-B

10162. [La Reintrie, Henry Roy de] "The other side." "Bird's-eye view" of the claim of José Y. Limantour, number 548, "in 1857." S.F., Frank Eastman, print., 1858. 24 p. Concerns the claim of José Y. Limantour "to four leagues of land, in the county adjoining and near the City of San Francisco."—p. 3.
CLU CMont CSfP CSt CSmH CU-B NN

10163. Larson, George. "Worth looking into." S.F. [n.d.] 22 p. illus.   CU-B

10164. Latta, Estelle Cothran. Controversial Mark Hopkins. N.Y., Greenberg, 1953. 195 p. illus.
CHi CP CRcS CRedCL CSd CSf CSfP CV

10165. Laurel hall club. Year book. 1907/08— S.F. [1908?–]
CHi has 1916/17. CU-B has 1907/08.

10166. Laurenti, Luigi Mario. Effects of nonwhite purchase and occupancy on market prices of residences in San Francisco, Oakland and Philadelphia. [Berkeley, 1957] Thesis (Ph.D.)— Univ. of Calif., 1957.   CU

10167. Law, Herbert E., vs. City and county of San Francisco. Transcript on appeal, Herbert E. Law, plaintiff and appellant, vs. city and county of San Francisco, defendant and respondents... S.F., 1904. 345 p.
C-S

10168. Lawless stellar compass co. The Lawless stellar compass and great circle course projector and how to use it. S.F. [190–?] 26 p.   CHi

10169. Lawson, Will. Pacific steamers. Glasgow, Brown, Son & Ferguson, ltd., 1927. 244 p. illus.
CSf CSfP

10170. Leale, John. Recollections of a tule sailor ...(1850–1932) master mariner, San Francisco bay; with interpolations by Marion Leale. S.F., George Fields, 1939. 311 p.
Available in many libraries.

10171. Lebenbaum (L.) and co. Catalogue and price list. [1879, 188–?] S.F., [1879–188–?] 2 v.
CU-B

10172. Lebenbaum bros., importers. ...Wholesale and retail grocers... S.F., 1890. 40 p. illus.   CHi

10173. Le Berthon, J. L., pub. San Francisco. Earthquake edition. L.A., Home print. co. [1906] 32 p. of views.   C CHi CLU CSmH CU-B

10174. Le Conte, Helen Marion (Gompertz) Helen Marion Gompertz Le Conte, April 11, 1865–August 26, 1924, by J. S. Hutchinson. [S.F., Taylor & Taylor, 1925] [8] p. port. Reprint. from *Sierra club bul.*, v.12, no. 2, 1925.   CHi

10175. Lecouvreur, Frank. From East Prussia to the Golden Gate. Letters and diary of the California pioneer, ed. ...by Mrs. Josephine Rosana Lecouvreur. Tr. and comp. by Julius C. Behnke. N.Y. and L.A., Angelina bk. concern, 1906. xiii, 15–355 p. illus., ports., maps.   CHi CLLoy CLSM CSd CSfCW

10176. Lee, Jun M. A civic project in the Chinatown redevelopment area. [Berkeley, 1955] Thesis (M.A.)— Univ. of Calif., 1955.   CU

10177. Lee, Mary Bo-Tze. Problems of the segregated school for Asiatics in San Francisco. [Berkeley, 1922] Thesis (M.A.)— Univ. of Calif., 1922.   CU

10178. Lee, Richard B. Synopsis of the proceedings of a general court martial, convened on the 19th January, 1857, for the trial of Major R. B. Lee, U.S.A. [n.p.] 1857. 46 p.   CU-B

10179. [Lee, Samuel D.] comp. San Francisco's Chinatown; history, function and importance of social organizations. [S.F., Central district coordinating council, 1940] [23] l.   CRic CSf

10180. —— Same. 1953. 10 l. Reproduced from typew. copy.   CU-B

10181. Lee and Praszker, firm. Foundation conditions, Golden Gateway, Embarcadero lower Market street, approved redevelopment agency of the city and county of San Francisco, California. S.F., 1960. 23 l. diagrs. (part fold.)   C

10182. Lees, Isaiah W. Full and complete statement of the forgeries and frauds of H. S. Tibbey, late secretary of the Dupont street commission and Board of public works for widening Dupont street and opening Montgomery avenue. ...Published by order of the Dupont street commission and Board of public works. S.F., Bunker & Hiester, print., 1879. 162 p.
                          CHi CLU CSmH CU-B NHi

10183. —— Petition for relief [and] statement of facts concerning a fraud on the United States government, committed at and near San Francisco, Cal., in June and July 1867. [n.p., 186–?] 11 p.   CU-B

10184. Leese, Jacob P., vs. Clark, William S., et als. In the Supreme court of the state of California. Jacob P. Leese, appellant, vs. William S. Clark, et als., respondents. no. 2822. Appeal from the Fourth district court. Brief of O. C. Pratt, of counsel for respondents. S.F., Wade & Nixon, print., 1860. 54 p. A San Francisco pueblo land case.   CLSM CLU CSmH

10185. —— ...Brief for respondents, showing that the decision on the former appeal is not the "law of the case" on the second appeal. Thompson Campbell and O. C. Pratt, counsel for respondents. S.F., Alta job print. [1862?] 90 p.   CLU

10186. —— ...Petition for rehearing in behalf of respondents. O. C. Pratt, counsel for respondents. [S.F.] Towne & Bacon print. [186–?] 45 p.   CLU

10187. The legacy of the exposition; interpretation of the intellectual and moral heritage left to mankind by

the world celebration at San Francisco in 1915. S.F. [Print. for the Exposition by J.H. Nash] 1916. 187 p. Letters of appreciation. "Prepared by James A. Barr and Joseph M. Cumming, and edited by Oscar H. Fernbach, of the Exposition staff, under the personal direction of Charles C. Moore."
    C CBb CBu CHi CL CLO CLSU CLU CMerCL CO CRedl CSd CSf CSfCW CSfP CSmH CSrD CU-B ViU

10188. The Legal aid society of San Francisco. Annual report. [n.p., 19—?–
    CHi has 1956–58, 1960–61.

10189. Leib, Keyston & company. Kolster radio corporation [formerly Federal-Brandes, inc.]; the strategic exploitation of a new science. S.F., 1928. [45] p. illus.   CHi

10190. —— Pacific gas and electric and the men who made it... [S.F.] c1926. [44] p.   CHi CSfP

10191. —— Paraffine companies, inc.; a story of paint. S.F., 1926. [52] p.   CHi

10192. —— Zellerbach, the house of paper... [S.F., S.V. Cagley, print.] 1927. [50] p. illus., port.
                                           CHi CU-B

10193. Leman, Walter M. Memories of an old actor. S.F., A. Roman co., 1886. 406 p. port.
                                        CHi CP CSf

10194. Lent, William Mandeville. In memory of William Mandeville Lent, born at New York City, March 15, 1818, died at San Francisco, October 17, 1904. From a series of articles by Judge C. C. Goodwin of Salt Lake City entitled "As I knew them" and published in "Goodwin's weekly," November, 1911. S.F., Priv. print. by Taylor, Nash and Taylor [1912] 10 p.   CHi

10195. Leong, Gor Yun. Chinatown inside out... N.Y., B. Mussey [c1936] 256 p. illus.
    CBev CHi CL CLSU CLU CMartC CO CRcS CRedl CSf CU-B

10196. Lerman, John. Oration...California's Admission day, Sept. 9, 1915. S.F., 1915. 14 p. port.
                                        C-S CHi CU-B

10197. Leslie salt co. Salt by Leslie. [S.F., c1947] [36] p. illus., chart.   CHi

10198. Lethin, Agnes E. Personal experiences during the catastrophe at San Francisco. Elgin, Ill., 1906. 22 p. pl.   CLU

10199. Leupp, Harold Lewis. The library at the exposition. A survey of the Panama-Pacific international exposition in the interest of the American library association and affiliated organizations. S.F., 1915. 14 p.
                                           CU-B

10200. Levi, Strauss and co. [Catalog] fall/winter 1902/03, spring/summer 1905, fall/winter 1907/08— spring/summer 1908, 1908/09. S.F., 1902–08. 3 v. illus.
                                           CU-B

10201. Levison, Jacob B. Memories for my family. S.F., John Henry Nash, 1933. 282 p. illus., ports.
                                          CBb CHi

10202. Levy, Harriet Lane. ...920 O'Farrell street ... Garden City, N.Y., Doubleday, 1947. 273 p. illus.
    Available in many California libraries and NN ODa TxU

10203. [Levy, S.] San Francisco, a city of ruins. [Alameda, T.P.S. pub. co., c1906] 46 p. (chiefly illus.)
                                           CO

10204. Lewis, Oscar. A[lbert] M[aurice] Bender some aspects of his life and times begun in playful mood for his entertainment on his 75th birthday and now completed for his sorrowing friends as a token of remembrance and affection. S.F., Grabhorn, 1941. [14] p. illus.   CHi CSf

10205. —— Bay window Bohemia; an account of the brilliant artistic world of gaslit San Francisco. [1st ed.] Garden City, N.Y., Doubleday, 1956. 248 p. illus.
Available in many California libraries and CaBViPA CoD CoU MiD NN NjR ODa TxU

10206. —— A family of builders; the story of the Haases and Thompsons, California pioneers since gold rush days. S.F., Priv. print., 1961. 72 p. illus.   CHi

10207. —— George Davidson, pioneer west coast scientist. Berkeley, Univ. of Calif. press, 1954. 146 p. illus., ports., maps.
CChiS CHi CLgA CP CRb CRcS CRedCL CRic CSd CSdS CSf CSfCSM CSfP CSalCL CStclU CStmo

10208. —— One fifty-five Sansome; being the story of the land on which the Industrial indemnity building stands today. S.F., 1956. 26 p.
CHi CSfWF-H CU-B

10209. —— Partners in progress, 1864–1950; a brief history of the Bank of California, N. A., and the region it has served for 85 years [address made by] James J. Hunter... N.Y., S.F., etc., The Newcomen soc. in No. Am., 1950. 76 p. illus. (part mounted)
CHi CL CLU CSfP CU-B

10210. —— San Francisco since 1872, a pictorial history of seven decades, with photographs and poems from the collection of Milton S. Ray... S.F., 1946. 101 p. illus., ports.
Available in many California libraries and NN OrU

10211. —— Silver kings, the lives and times of Mackay, Fair, Flood, and O'Brien, lords of the Nevada comstock lode. [1st ed.] N.Y., Knopf, 1947. 286 p. illus., ports.   CHi

10212. —— ed. This was San Francisco: being first-hand accounts of the evolution of one of America's favorite cities. N.Y., McKay [c1962] 291 p. illus.
CAla CHi CSfU

10213. —— Within the Golden Gate, a survey of the history, resources, and points of interest of the bay region prepared for delegates to the United nations conference on international organization. [S.F.] S.F. bay area council, c1945. 48 p. illus.
C CHi CLU CO CRic CSmat CU-B

10214. —— Same. c1947. [48] p.
CHi CSfWF-H

10215. —— and Hall, Carroll D. Bonanza inn; America's first luxury hotel. N.Y., London, Knopf [c1939] 346 p. illus., ports.
Available in many California libraries and CaBViPA MHi MiD MoS ODa TxU ViU

10216. Lewis, Richard. Poor Richard's guide to non-tourist San Francisco. S.F., Unicorn pub. co., 1958. 48 p. illus.   CAla CHi CL CRic CSS CSd CSf

10217. Lewis homestead association. Prospectus, articles of association, certificate of incorporation, and maps of the property... S.F., Waters, Newhoff & co., 1870. [35] p. illus., maps.   CHi

10218. —— [Prospectus] Improved homestead lots ... [S.F., n.d.] [4] p. illus.   CHi

10219. Library association of California, San Francisco. [Constitution, lists of members and officers. S.F.? 1903?] [8] p.   CHi

10220. Lichtenstein, Joy. "Kelly, Burke and Shea"; a romance of the fire insurance business in the "horse and buggy days" of San Francisco by Joy Lichtenstein and A. W. Paynter. [S.F., Kennedy-ten Bosch co., print., 1945] 29 p.   CHi

10221. Lichtenstein bros. [Catalog] 1906. S.F. [1906?] 76 p. illus.   CHi

10222. Lick, James, vs. Faulkner, William. The currency question. In the Supreme court of the state of California. James Lick, appellant, vs. William Faulkner, et al, respondents. Argument for appellant [by Henry Huntly Haight]... [n.d., n.p.] 101 p. Cover-title.
CHi CSmH

10223. Lick, James, vs. Mesa, Antonia. ...Argument for plaintiff. James Lick, plaintiff, vs. Antonia Mesa, et al., defendants. Henry Huntly Haight, attorney... [n.p., 18—] 25 p.   CU-B

10224. Lick, James. The deed of James Lick [to Thomas H. Selby et al] a certified copy of the original, executed June 2d, 1874 and recorded June 3d, 1874. S.F., Print. by Sterett for the Soc. of Calif. pioneers, 1874. 19 p.
CHi CSmH

10225. —— Deed of trust. James Lick to Thomas H. Selby, D. O. Mills, H. M. Newhall, Wm. Alvord, George H. Howard, James Otis, and John O. Earl. Dated July 16th, A.D. 1874... [S.F.? 1874] 10 l.   CHi CSmH

10226. —— Deed of trust of James Lick, esq., of San Francisco, California, dated September 21, 1875, and recorded in the office of the recorder of the county of San Francisco, state of California... [S.F., H. E. Mathews & co., print.] 1875. 24 p.   CSmH

10227. Lick (James) trust. Ceremonies and literary exercises at the unveiling of the Lick bronze statuary by the Lick trustees, assisted by the Society of Calif. pioneers, 1894. S.F., Sterett print. co., 1894. 48 p.
CHi CSmH

10228. Liebes (H.) & co. [Catalogs] S.F. [188–?– CHi has 1886/87, 1890/91–1891/92, 1893/94, 1896/97, 1911/12, 1913/14.

10229. Liebes, Richard Alan. Longshore labor relations on the Pacific coast, 1934–1942. [Berkeley, 1942] 391 l. map. Thesis (Ph.D.)—Univ. of Calif., 1942.
CU

10230. Liebman, Carl, vs. the City and county of San Francisco. ...Carl Liebman, plaintiff, vs. the city and county of San Francisco, defendant... [n.p., n.d.] 2 v. in 1.   CU-B

10231. Lietz (A.) co. [Catalog] Engineering, surveying, mining and nautical instruments... [S.F., Crocker, 1919] 612 p. illus.   CHi

10232. —— ...Manual of modern surveying instruments and their uses... S.F., 1899. 200 p. illus.   CHi

10233. Life insurance premium investment company of California. Tontine investment policy... [S.F., James H. Barry, n.d.] 17 p.   CHi

10234. Lightner air amalgamator and concentrator co. ...Mining yesterday and today... [S.F.? 1907?] [12] p. illus.   CHi

10235. Lilienthal, Jesse Warren. In memoriam, by Lillie Bernheimer Lilienthal. S.F., John Henry Nash, 1921. 218 p. ports.   CHi

10236. Lincoln grammar school association. Constitution and by-laws...as adopted...Feb. 20, 1913. [n.p., n.d.] 6 p.   CHi

10237. —— Same, with list of members... [S.F., Phillips & Van Orden co., 1932] 21 p. illus.   CHi

10238. —— Lincoln grammar school, a record compiled for the boys. S.F. [Recorder press] 1938. 97 p. illus., ports.   CHi CO CSf CU-B

10239. —— Tenth banquet, February 12, 1898... Lincoln school boys, 1865–1880. Menu, programme, roll of honor, songs, historical...comp. by Charles B. Turrill] [S.F., Francis-Valentine co., 1918] [18] p.   CHi

10240. Lincoln monument league. Officers, advisory board and committees... [S.F., 1897] 16 p. ports.   CHi

10241. Link-belt co. Pacific division, San Francisco. ...General catalog 36... [S.F., Borden print. co., c1936] 320 p. illus.   CHi

10242. Linthicum, Richard. Complete story of the San Francisco horror...comprising also a vivid portrayal of the recent death-dealing eruption of Mt. Vesuvius... profusely illus. with photographic scenes of the great disasters... [Chicago? c1906] 408 p. illus., ports., map. Available in many California libraries and MiD MoS NHi NN UPB ViU

10243. Lipman, Frederick L. Interest rates in relation to the cost of capital for public utilities...March 21, 1916. Submitted in testimony taken before Honorable H. M. Wright, standing master in chancery for the district court of the United States, in the proceeding entitled Spring Valley water company vs. the city and county of San Francisco, et al., in equity nos. 14735, 14892, 15131, 15344, 15569, Circuit court of U.S., ninth judicial circuit, northern district of California, and 26 and 96 district court of U.S., northern district of California, second division. [n.p., 1916] 9 p.   CU-B

10244. Lippmann, C. R. A trip through Golden Gate park; an outstanding achievement in landscape architecture. S.F., Print. corp., 1937. 32 p. illus.   CSf

10245. [Little, William C.] Arraignment, demands and resolutions adopted by mass meeting of citizens of San Francisco, in Metropolitan temple...June 19th, 1894. [S.F., 1894] 12 p.   CHi

10246. Little children's aid society. Auxilliary. Golden age of volunteer service, 1907–1957. S.F., Canessa print co., 1957. 16 p. Founded August 1907 as The Catholic settlement and humane bureau.   CHi

10247. Livingston, Edward. A personal history of the San Francisco earthquake and fire in 1906. S.F. [Print. Windsor press] 1941. 45 p. illus., port.
                                        CHi CL CSf CSfU

10248. Livingstone, Alexander P., comp. Complete story of San Francisco's terrible calamity of earthquake and fire; the most appalling disaster of modern times; immense loss of life and hundreds of millions of property destroyed; compiled from stories told by eyewitnesses... [S.F.?] Continental pub. house [1907] 272 p. illus., ports.   NN

10249. Lloyd, Benjamin E. Lights and shades in San Francisco... S.F., Print. A.L. Bancroft & co., 1876. 523 p. illus. Available in many California libraries and CaBViPA CoU NHi NN UPB

10250. Lockwood, Rufus A. Vigilance committee of San Francisco; Metcalf vs. Argenti et al.; speeches of Rufus A. Lockwood, Esq. S.F., 1852. 47 p.
                                C CHi CLU CSmH CU-B WHi

10251. The London & San Francisco bank, ltd. Memorandum of association, special resolutions, and amended articles of association. London, Metchim & son [1875] 47 p. "Formed in the year 1865": p. 10.   CHi

10252. Long, Percy V. The consolidated city and county government of San Francisco. S.F., 1912. 30 p.
        C CHi CLSU CLU CSf CSmH CStclU CU-B

10253. —— ...The Hetch-Hetchy grant. Brief of the city and county of San Francisco...before the Senate public lands committee...1913. S.F., James H. Barry, 1913. 32 p.   CHi

10254. Longley's American restaurant, New York City. Longley's American restaurant... [n.p., 1951?] folder ([10] p.) illus. Contains description of Samuel Longley's experiences in San Francisco, 1849.   CHi

10255. Loo, Florence S. Women police in the San Francisco bay region. [Berkeley, 1931] Thesis (M.A.) —Univ. of Calif., 1931.   CU

10256. Loomis, Charles Grant. The German theater in San Francisco, 1861–1864. Berkeley, Univ. of Calif. press, 1952. (Univ. of Calif. pub. in modern philology, v.36, no. 8, p. 193–242)   CHi CL CSf CU-B

10257. Loomis, Richard T. The history of the building of the Golden Gate bridge. [Stanford] 1958. Thesis (Ph.D.)—Stanford univ., 1958.   CSt

10258. Lord, Jack, and Jenn Shaw. Where to sin in San Francisco. Many drawings by Lloyd Hoff. Preface by Beniamino Bufano. [S.F., The Book cellar] c1945. 191 p. illus.   C CU-B

10259. —— Same. S.F., Richard Guggenheim, 1953. 186 p. illus.   CHi UPB

10260. Lorentzen, Eden Christian. Entrance requirement to craft organizations in San Francisco. [Berkeley, 1923] Thesis (M.A.)— Univ. of Calif., 1923.
                                                    CU

10261. Lothers & Young studios. [Photographs of houses in Sea Cliff, San Francisco. S.F., 192–?] 60 mounted photos. in 1 v.   CU-B

10262. [Loucks, W. E., comp.] Sun-kist brand, California products. The value of Sun-kist as a trade builder. [S.F., Printed for J. K. Armsby co. by Taylor, Nash & Taylor, 1913] 31 p. illus.   CHi

10263. Louisiana. Panama-Pacific exposition commission. Louisiana at the Panama-Pacific international exposition, San Francisco, Cal., nineteen-sixteen [i.e., 1915] Report of the Louisiana commission. New Orleans, 1915. 114 p. illus.   CU-B

10264. Lowe, Pardee. Father and glorious descendant. Bost., Little, 1943. 322 p.   CHi CSd CU-B

10265. Lowe bros., contractors. Contract for soap ...Dated 10th December, 1867. S.F., Cubery & co., print., 1868. 10 p.   CU-B

10266. Lubin, Jerome Walter. The possible future contribution of state highways to metropolitan transit within the San Francisco bay area. [Berkeley, 1951] Thesis (M.A.)— Univ. of Calif., 1951.   CU

10267. Luca, Mark C. A history of the educational practices of San Francisco art museums. [Berkeley, 1958] Thesis (Ph.D.)— Univ. of Calif.   CU

10268. Lumbermen's timber co., San Francisco. ...Standing timber is the most attractive basis for intelligent and conservative investment now available. [S.F., 1913?] 16 p.   CHi

10269. Lundberg, Ferdinand. Imperial Hearst; a social biography...with a preface by Dr. Charles A. Beard. N.Y., Equinox cooperative press, 1939. 406 p.
                                        CRcS CSd CSfU CSlu

10270. Lux, Miranda (Wilmarth) Last will of Miranda W. Lux. [S.F.? 1894?] 45 p.   CHi

10271. Lux college. Lux college, a technical school for women. Thirtieth year, March 1943. S.F. [1943] 36 p.
CU-B

10272. —— [Materials on Lux college, San Francisco, founded by Mrs. Miranda Lux. S.F., 1945–53] 11 pieces in portfolio. illus., ports.   CU-B

10273. Lux school of industrial training. ... Dedication exercises, Friday, May twenty-second, nineteen fourteen. [n.p. 1914] [31] p. illus., ports.   CHi

10274. Lyman, George Dunlap. Ralston's ring; California plunders the Comstock lode... N.Y., London, Scribner, 1937. 368 p. ports.
Available in many California libraries and KyU MiD MoS N NHi ODa TxU ViU

10275. Lynch, Jeremiah. Buckleyism. The government of a state. S.F., 1889. 33 p. Being an account of Chris. Buckley, a political boss of San Francisco.
C CHi CL CLU CO CSf CSmH CU-B NHi

10276. —— Same. Ed. and rev. by Louis E. Phillips, with the consent of Mr. Lynch. S.F., 1890. 14 p.
CHi

10277. —— The lady Isis in Bohemia. [S.F., Print. for J. Lynch by Taylor, Nash and Taylor, 1914] [28] p. illus. Presentation of an Egyptian mummy to the Bohemian club.   CHi CSf CU-B

10278. —— A senator of the fifties; David C. Broderick of California... S.F., A.M. Robertson, 1911. 246 p. pl., ports., facsim.
Available in many California libraries and ODa OrU ViU

10279. Lynch, Laurence Soulé. In memoriam... S.F., Priv. print., John Henry Nash, 1919. 10 p. illus., port.   CHi

10280. Lyon & Hoag, firm, comp. Ashbury terrace, "for those who love the beautiful, who care where they live." S.F. [1912?] 12 p. fold. map.   CHi

10281. Lyon mill and mining co. By-laws... S.F., Stock report off., 1874. 12 p.   CHi

10282. MacAdam, Madelene Victoria (Brocklebank) Fortune in my own hands... Bost., Christopher pub. [1940] 382 p. S.F. real estate.
CHi CL CSf   CU-B

10283. McAdie, Alexander George. Ephebic oath, and other essays... S.F., Robertson, 1912. 62 p. illus. (Philopolis ser.) San Francisco.
C CHi CLO CLU CMont COHN CSf CSfCW CSfMI CSfP CSmH CSrD CU-B

10284. —— Infra nubem; the lights outside; La Bocana. S.F., Robertson, 1909. 42 p. illus. (Philopolis ser.)   CHi CLU

10285. McAfee, Baldwin & Hammond. [Auction catalogue and maps of 47 lots facing Golden Gate park] S.F., 1890. [4] p. 2 maps (1 col.)   CHi

10286. McAllister, Cutler. A memorial. S.F., Priv. print. for the family and friends, 1879. 64 p. port.
CHi CSmH

10287. McAlpine, William J. A memoir on the water supply of the city of San Francisco. [S.F.] C.A. Murdock & co., 1879. 18 p.   C CLU

10288. McAlpine's (Mrs.) boarding and day school for young ladies, San Francisco. Prospectus ...Conducted by Mrs. McAlpine and daughter, no. 608 Sutter street...S.F., Towne & Bacon, 1864. 12 p.
CU-B

10289. McArdle, Mary Aurelia, *Sister*. California's pioneer Sister of mercy, Mother Mary Baptist Russell (1829–1898) Fresno, Acad. lib. guild, 1954. 204 p. illus.
CHi CLU CLgA CSd CSdU CSf CSfCW CSfU (has Thesis, 1953) CSfWF-H

10290. MacArthur, Walter. Last days of sail on the West coast, San Francisco harbor. [S.F., James H. Barry co., c1929] 138 p. pl. (1 col.) fold. map.
CHi CL CLU CSd CSfMI CSfP CU-B

10291. McAstocker, David Plante. "Once upon a time", being the life of Adrian Ignatius McCormick of the Society of Jesus. Bost., Stratford, 1926. 238 p. ports. Life of a young San Franciscan.   CLgA

10292. McCarthy, Francis Florence. Hunter's point... S.F., Flores Paramount press [1942] 43 p. illus., ports.
C CHi CLgA CSf CSfCW CSfU CSrD CU-B

10293. McCarthy, Mary Eunice. Meet Kitty. N.Y., Crowell [1957] 186 p. illus. Biography of Catherine McCarthy.   C CSd

10294. McClintock, Miller. Report on San Francisco citywide traffic survey... S.F. [Print. by Pisani print. & pub. co.] 1937. 460 p.
CL CLSU CLU CO CSf CU-B

10295. —— A report on the street traffic control problem of San Francisco prepared for the San Francisco traffic survey committee. S.F., 1927. 356 p. maps, charts.
CHi

10296. McCoppin, Frank. Address on the new charter for the city and county of San Francisco...Aug. 11, 1896. 13 p.   NN

10297. McCurdy, Evelyn M. The history of the Adelphi theatre, San Francisco, California, 1850–58. [Stanford] 1953. Thesis (M.A.)— Stanford univ., 1953.
CSt

10298. McCurtain, Marilyn Esther. Political ecology of three metropolitan areas of California: San Francisco, Los Angeles, San Diego, 1850–1950. [Berkeley, 1955] Thesis (M.A.)— Univ. of Calif., 1955.   CU

10299. McDevitt, V. Edmund, Brother. The First California's chaplain; the story of the heroic chaplain of the First California volunteers during the Spanish-American war. Fresno, Acad. lib. guild, 1956. 259 p. illus.
CHi CLgA CSalCL CSf CSfCW

10300. Macdonald (D. A.) and co. [Catalog of] doors, sashes, blinds and mouldings. 1876. S.F., 1876. 1 v. illus.   CU-B

10301. McDonald, Frank Virgil. Notes preparatory to a biography of Richard Hayes McDonald of San Francisco, California. Vol. 1. Cambridge, Mass., Univ. press: John Wilson and son, 1881. [214] p. illus., ports. No more published.   CHi

10302. McDonald, Henry M. Argument against the selection of Hetch Hetchy as a source of water supply for San Francisco, based upon the report of George S. Nickerson, consulting engineer, respecting the availability of the South Eel river and Putah Creek water-sheds, as a source of supply, submitted by Henry McDonald to the members of the United States senate November 25, 1913. [n.p., 1913?] 20 p.   CU-B

10303. MacDonald truck and tractor co. MacDonald; the answer to the short haul heavy duty problem. [S.F., Johnck, Beran & Kibbee, n.d.] [8] p. illus.
CHi

10304. McDowell, Irvin. Speech delivered by Major-General McDowell...at Platt's hall, San Francisco... Friday, October 21st, 1864...Speech of Hon. John Conness, delivered at Platt's hall, San Francisco... October 18, 1864. [S.F.? 1864] 16 p.   CHi

10305. McEnerney, Garrett W. Case of the Pious fund of the Californias [before the Permanent court of arbitration under the Hague convention 1899]. United States of America vs. The Republic of Mexico. Supplemental brief upon behalf of the United States. Hague, Mouton, 1902. 68 p. Appendix (10 p.) CHi CRic

10306. McGilvary, John D. The Shriners' finest hour. S.F., Shriners' hospital for crippled children, 1955. 32 p. port. CHi CSf

10307. McGinnis, Felix Signoret. In memoriam, 1883-1945. [S.F., Printed for Californians, inc., by Taylor & Taylor, 1945. [4] l. CHi

10308. McGloin, John Bernard, Father. Eloquent Indian; the life of James Bouchard, California Jesuit. Stanford, 1949. 380 p. illus., ports.
CBb CHi CLgA CNa COnC CRcS CRedCL CSd CSfCW CSfWF-H CV

10309. —— History of San Francisco: class notes. University of San Francisco. [S.F., 195-?] 101 l. Reproduced from typew. copy. CLgA

10310. McGowan, Edward. Narrative of Edward McGowan, including a full account of the author's adventures and perils while persecuted by the San Francisco vigilance committee of 1856... S.F., Author, 1857. 240 p. illus.
C CHi CLU CSfCP CSfU CSmH CU-B MiD-B NN NvHi

10311. —— Same. Print. by T.C. Russell, at his private press, 1917. 240 p. illus., port. "Reprinted line for line and page for page, from the original edition, published by the author in 1857, complete, with reproductions, in facsimile, of the original illustrations, cover-page title, and title-page."
C CHi CL CLSU CLU CLgA CP CSf CSfP CStcrCL CStmo CU-B CaBViPA

10312. —— Same, reprinted with title: McGowan vs. California vigilantes; foreword by Joseph A. Sullivan. Oakland, Biobooks, 1946. 205 p. 3 fold. facsim. (Calif. centennials, no. 7)
Available in many California libraries and CaBViPA

10313. McGowan, Joseph Aloysius. San Francisco-Sacramento shipping, 1839-1854. [Berkeley, 1939] Thesis (M.A.)— Univ. of Calif., 1939. CU CU-B

10314. Macgregor, William Laird. Hotels and hotel life, at San Francisco, California in 1876. S.F., S.F. news co. [1877] 45 p. illus.
CHi CU-B CaBViPA

10315. —— San Francisco, California, in 1876... For private circulation only. Edinburgh, T. Laurie, 1876. 71 p. Author's name spelled "MacGregor" in this book.
C CHi CP CSmH CU-B NHi NN

10316. McGuire, Dan. San Francisco 49ers. All about the thirteen wild and woolly years of the 49ers. N.Y., Coward [c1960] 189 p. illus., ports. CHi CSf

10317. [Mack, Gerstle] Lewis and Hannah Gerstle. [N.Y.] Author, 1953. 131 p. illus., ports., charts. CHi

10318. McKee (Samuel) & co. Office of Samuel McKee & co., brokers in "stock privileges", no. 319 California street. S. F., W.P. Harrison bk. and job print., 1875. 8 p. CU-B

10319. McKenzie, William, vs. Dickinson, Harvey. In the Supreme court of the state of California. William McKenzie, respondent, vs. Harvey Dickinson, appellant. Transcript on appeal. G. F. & W. H. Sharp, counsel for appellant. Collins & Clement, counsel for respondent. S.F., Wade & co., print., 1870. 233 p. CHi

10320. Mackenzie & Harris, inc. M & H type specimens and price lists. S.F., 1948–
CHi has 1948-49, 1957.

10321. McKinney, Mary Frances. Denis Kearney, organizer of the Workingmen's party of California. [Berkeley, 1940] Thesis (M.A.)— Univ. of Calif., 1940. CU

10322. McLaren, John. In memoriam by John L. McNab. [S.F.? 1939?] [4] p. CHi

10323. McLeod, Alexander. ...Pigtails and gold dust in California. Caldwell, Ida., Caxton, 1947. 326 p. illus. At head of title: A panorama of Chinese life in early California.
Available in many California libraries and CaBViPA

10324. McLeran, Thomas G., vs. Benton, J. E., et al. In the Supreme court of the state of California. T. G. McLeran, appellant, vs. J. E. Benton et al., respondents. Transcript on appeal from fourth district court. B. S. Brooks, att'y for appellant. Winans & Belknap, W. H. Brooks, att'y for appellant. Winans & Belknap, W. H. Patterson, att'ys for respondents... S.F., Women's cooperative print. union, 1875. 128 p. A San Francisco property suit. CLU

10325. McLeran, Thomas G., vs. McNamara, John, et al. In the Supreme court of the state of California. Thomas G. McLeran, plaintiff and appellant, vs. John McNamara et als., J. and D. Callaghan, defendants and respondents. Transcript on appeal, San Francisco county. B. S. Brooks, att'y for appellant. W. H. L. Barnes, att'y for respondent... [S.F.] B. H. Daly, print. [1878?] 37 p. San Francisco land suit. CLU

10326. McMiller, Harold Armin. A study of regional recreation planning in the San Francisco bay region. [Berkeley, 1953] Thesis (M.A.)— Univ. of Calif., 1953. CU

10327. MacMullen, Jerry. Paddle-wheel days in California... Stanford [1944] 157 p. illus.
Available in many libraries.

10328. McMullen, Mary Justine, Sister. The career of Peter Hardeman Burnett, California's first governor. Wash., D.C., Catholic univ. of Am., 1950. 148 p. Thesis (M.A.)— Catholic univ. of America, 1950 CSrD

10329. McMurtrie, Douglas Crawford. The Pacific typographical society and the California gold rush of 1849, a forgotten chapter in the history of typographical unionism in America... Chicago, Ludlow typograph co., 1928. 20 p. Reprint of article on "The Pacific typographical society and the Alta California" pub. in *Alta Calif.*, Oct. 28, 1851.
C CBb CHi CL CLO CLSU CLU CO CSd CSf CSmH CU-B

10330. Macomber, Benjamin. ...The jewel city: its planning and achievement; its architecture, sculpture, symbolism, and music; its gardens, palaces, and exhibits ... S.F. & Tacoma, J.H. Williams, 1915. 204 p. illus.
Available in many California libraries and NN ViU

10331. Macondray & co., inc. A chronicle of one hundred years, 1848-1948. [L.A., 1948] 37 p. illus., ports., facsims. C CHi

10332. McPhee, Douglas G. San Francisco's six years of achievement under the new charter; the story of a city whose people decided to have a better government. [S.F., Recorder print. & pub. co., 1938] 64 p.
CHi CO CSf CSmH CU-B

10333. —— The story of Standard oil company of

California. [n.p., 1937] 31 p. illus. "Reprint. from a series of articles in the *California oil world*..."
CHi CSfSO

10334. McPheeters, Julian C. The life story of Lizzie H. Glide. S.F., Eagle print. co. [c1936] 110 p. illus., ports.
CHi

10335. McPherson, Hallie Mae. William McKendree Gwin, expansionist. [Berkeley, 1931] Thesis (Ph.D.)— Univ. of Calif., 1931.
CU CU-B

10336. McRuer, D. C. Summary of objections to the "Goat island bill." Presented to the Senate committee on military affairs in behalf of the citizens of San Francisco. [n.p., 1873] 46 p.
CSmH

10337. McWilliams, Carey. Ambrose Bierce, a biography. N.Y., Albert & Charles Boni, 1929. 358 p.
CHi CSd

10338. Maddux air lines. Maddux air lines. [L.A., L.A. litho. co., inc., 1928] folder (63 p.) illus., map.
CHi

10339. Magee, David Bickersteth. Bibliography of the Grabhorn press, 1940–1956, by David & Dorothy Magee [with a check-list, 1916–1940] S.F., Grabhorn, 1957. 119 p. illus. (col.), facsims.
CBb CLO

10340. —— The hundredth book; a bibliography of the publications of the Book club of California & a history of the club. [S.F.] Printed at the Grabhorn press for the Book club of Calif., 1958. xxiii, 79 p. facsims. (part col.)
CLU

10341. Mahan, Terrance Leon. The fifth St. Ignatius church in San Francisco, California 1910–1950. [S.F.] 1951. 186 p. illus. Thesis (M.A.)— Univ. of San Francisco, 1951.
CSfU

10342. Mahoney, David, and Sharp, Solomon A., vs. Middleton, John, et al. David Mahoney, and Solomon A. Sharp, plaintiffs and respondents, vs. John Middleton, et al., defendants and appellants. Transcript on appeal. Wilson & Crittenden, att'ys for appellants. Sharp & Lloyd, John B. Felton, Wm. H. Patterson, att'ys for respondents. S.F., Print. by Turnbull & Smith, 1870. 273 p. One of a series of actions to settle title to the Laguna de la Merced rancho.
CLU

10343. Mahr, August Carl, ed. ...The visit of the "Rurik" to San Francisco in 1816... Stanford; London, H. Milford, Oxford univ. press, 1932. 194 p. illus. (Stanford univ. pub. Univ. ser. History, economics, and political science. vol. II, no. 2) Original texts and English translation on opposite pages. Bibliography: p. 187–188.
Available in many California libraries and CaBViPA KU NHi OU OrU TxU ViU

10344. Main & Winchester. Descriptive catalogue and price list of horse boots [and other equipment]... S.F. [1878?–89] illus.
C-S has 1880, 1889. CHi has [1880?] 1889. CU-B has [1878?]

10345. The Main sheet, pub. in the interest of goodfellowship. Official organ Indoor yacht club. Wm. J. Lynch, pub. S.F., 1911–1917. Monthly.
CSf

10346. Maine, Charles, et al vs. Central Pacific R. R. co. et al. In the Superior court of the city and county of San Francisco, state of California. Dept. 5. Before Hon. John Hunt. Charles Maine, et al., vs. Central Pacific R. R. co., et al. Argument of Samuel M. Wilson for the defendants. S.F., Bacon & co., print., 1886. 344 p.
CHi

10347. Maisel, Sherman J. Housebuilding in transition, based on studies in San Francisco bay area. Berke-

ley, Univ. of Calif. press, 1953. 390 p. illus. (Univ. of Calif. Bur. of business and economic research. Pub.)
CLU CU

10348. Majors, Alexander. Seventy years on the frontier; Alexander Majors' memoirs of a lifetime on the border. With a preface by "Buffalo Bill," (General W. F. Cody). Ed. by Colonel Prentiss Ingraham. Chicago, N.Y., Rand, McNally, 1893. 325 p. illus., ports.
CHi CSd

10349. Manning, James Francis. William A. Leidesdorff's career in California. [Berkeley, 1941] Thesis (M.A.)— Univ. of Calif., 1941.
CU

10350. Mansbach (E.) & co. Catalog. [1885?] S.F., J. Winterburn & co. [1885?] 48 p. illus.
CHi

10351. Manson, Marsden. In the matter of the application of San Francisco for reservoir rights of way in Hetch Hetchy valley. [S.F.] James H. Barry co. [1907] 5 p.
CHi

10352. —— ...In the matter of the application of the city and county of San Francisco for reservoir rights of way in Hetch Hetchy valley and Lake Eleanor, within the Yosemite national park... [S.F.?] 1905. 30 p.
CHi CSfSC CSmH CU-B

10353. —— ...Reply to the statement and argument of counsel on behalf of Modesto irrigation district. [S.F.] James H. Barry co. [190–?] 17 p. chart.
CHi

10354. —— Petition...to the Secretary of the interior department...to re-open the matter of the application of Jas. D. Phelan, for reservoir rights of way in the Hetch-Hetchy valley and Lake Eleanor sites...[and] Decision of the Secretary of the interior department... granting the city and county of San Francisco... reservoir rights of way... [S.F., Recorder print. co., 1908] 8 p.
CSmH

10355. —— Report...to the Mayor and Committee of reconstruction on the improvements now necessary to execute and the cost of the same. Fire avenues... lowering Rincon hill...waterfront improvements. [S.F.] 1906. 37 p. maps.
C CHi

10356. —— Report...to the Mayor and Committee on reconstruction on those portions of the Burnham plans which meet our commercial necessities and an estimate of the cost of the same... [S.F.] 1906. 37 p.
C-S CLU CU-B

10357. —— A statement of San Francisco's side of the Hetch Hetchy reservoir matter December 30, 1909. [S.F., 1910?] 8 p.
C CU-B

10358. Manufacturers association of California. Proceedings. [S.F.? 1885?] 11 p.
CHi

10359. —— Report on shipping and ship-building to the Manufacturers' association, the Board of trade and the Chamber of commerce... S.F., 1885. 62 p.
CU

10360. Manufacturer's shoe and supply co. [Catalog] [n.d., n.p.] 99 p. illus.
CHi

10361. —— Same. 1904. S.F., Murdock press, 1904. 96 p. illus.
CHi

10362. Marberry, M. Marion. The golden voice; a biography of Isaac Kalloch... N.Y., Farrar, Straus & co., 1947. 376 p. illus.
C CBb CBev CHi CL CLO CLSU CLU CO CSf CSfP CSfU CSmH CStrJC CU-B CViCL

10363. Marcus, William A. The day before—the days to come...commemorating the 53rd anniversary of the San Francisco conflagration, April 18, 1906. S.F., Chamber of commerce, 1959. 12 p. Mimeo.
CHi

10364. Marder, Luse and co. How printing types are made. [S.F., 187–?] 6 p. illus.   CU-B

10365. —— Price list of the Pacific type foundry, Marder, Luse & co. June 1880. S.F. [1880] 1 v. illus.   CU-B

10366. —— Progress of American typefounding! Marder, Luse & company's emancipation proclamation to the printers of the world, of the abolition of irregular type bodies!... [Berkeley] Tamalpais press, 1958. [4] p. mounted facsim.   CU-B

10367. Mardikian, George Magar. Song of America. N.Y., McGraw, c1956. 312 p.
                    CHi CMont CRcS CRedCL CSf

10368. Marengo, Mary Ellen, *Sister.* The history of Saint Rose academy, San Francisco, California (1862–1906). San Rafael [Catholic univ. of Am., Pac. coast branch] 1955. 120 p. Thesis (M.A.)— Catholic univ. of America.   CSrD

10369. Marine engineer's beneficial association no. 35. ...Souvenir manual. [n.p., n.d.]   CU-B

10370. Maritime federation of the Pacific coast. Bay area district council no. 2. Men and ships; maritime strike pictorial, 1936–1937. [S.F., 1936–37] 33 l. illus.   CHi

10371. Mark-Lally co. Catalogue. 1913. N.Y. [1913?] 1 v. illus.   CU-B

10372. Market and Fourteenth streets homestead association. Abstract to title to the lands of the... association, as shown on the accompanying diagram, and situated in the city and county of San Francisco, state of California. John Landers, president; Josiah H. Applegate, secretary. S.F., J.H. Carmany & co., 1876. 81 p. 2 fold. plans.   CHi CLU

10373. Market street railway. Rules and regulations for drivers of fare box cars. [S.F., 1878] [5] p.
                    CHi

10374. —— Rules—conductors and drivers. S.F. [1881] 38 p.   CHi

10375. Marks, Isaac D., vs. Mahoney, David, et al. U.S. District court, district of California. Isaac D. Marks, plaintiff, vs. David Mahoney, Josefa de Haro, Natividad de Haro, Prudencia de Haro, Candelaria de Haro, Alonzo de Haro, Carlotta de Haro, Rosalia de Haro, et al., defendants. [n.p., 1867?] 4 l. Suit over the Rancho Laguna de la Merced.   CLU

10376. Mars, Amaury. Pyrénées et la Californie... S.F., J. Tauzy et cie, 1898. 299 p. illus., ports. Includes "Notes biographiques et commerciales sur nos compatriotes de San Francisco."
                    C CLU CSf CSfCW CSmH CU-B

10377. [Marsh, Clifford Wanzer] ...Facts concerning the great fire of San Francisco. Bridgeport, Conn., Marigold-Foster print. co. [1907] 14 p.   CU-B

10378. Marshall, Max Skidmore. Crusader undaunted: Dr. J. C. Geiger, private physician to the public. N.Y., Macmillan, 1958. 246 p. illus.   CSd CSf

10379. Marshall-Newell supply co. Catalogue A. ... S.F. [c1914] 583 p. illus.   CHi

10380. Marshall square building. ...S.F. [1926?] [4] p. illus.   CHi

10381. Martin, [Genevieve (Frisette)] Louis Sloss, jr. collection of California paintings. S.F., Calif. hist. soc., 1958. 18 p. port.   CHi

10382. Martin, Mildred Purnell. City government

in San Francisco: a half century of charter development. [Berkeley, 1911] Thesis (M.A.)— Univ. of Calif., 1911.
                    CU

10383. Marwedel (C. F.) firm. Catalogue and price list of...importer of and dealer in fine tools and supplies for machinists, engineers, molders...[6th ed.] S.F. [Jennie E. Patrick, print. co.] 1888. 140 p. illus.
                    CHi

10384. Marwedel (C. W.) firm. Illustrated catalogue no. 11. Tools, metals, shop supplies, automotive equipment... [S.F., Phillips & Van Orden co., 1922?] 1068 p. illus.   CHi

10385. Marye, George Thomas. From '49 to '83 in California and Nevada chapters from the life of George Thomas Marye, a pioneer of '49, by George Thomas Marye, jr. S.F., Robertson, 1923. 212 p. illus., ports. "Republished from various numbers of the *Overland monthly,* issued...from 1914 to 1918." Marye lived in San Francisco from 1849 to 1869.
Available in many California libraries and MoS ViU

10386. Maslin, Marshall, ed. A camera tour in color: San Francisco and bay cities. S.F., The Printing corp., c1938. [28] p. (chiefly col. illus., map)
                    CHi CU-B

10387. [Mason-McDuffie co.] St. Francis wood, San Francisco's residence park. [S.F., 191–?] [6] p. illus.   CHi

10388. —— Twelve reasons why you should buy now in St. Francis wood. [S.F., Print. by Taylor, Nash & Taylor, 191–?] 15 p. illus.   CHi

10389. Masonic savings and loan bank. Prospectus and extract from the by-laws of the Masonic savings and loan bank. Incorporated November 4th, 1869. S.F. [F. Eastman, print., 1869] 15 p.   CU-B

10390. —— [Prospectus and] ordinary deposit book. [S.F.? 1878] [20] p.   CHi

10391. Masonic veteran association of the Pacific coast. Proceedings of all meetings... S.F. [187–?–] CHi has Oct. 15, 1891, 28th annual meeting, 1906.

10392. Massachusetts. Board of Panama–Pacific managers. The industries and foreign trade of Massachusetts. Massachusetts exposition ed. [Bost.? 1915] 182 p. diagr.   CU-B

10393. —— —— Massachusetts at the Panama–Pacific international exposition, San Francisco, California, 1915. Report of... Bost., Wright & Potter print. co. [1916?] 234 p. illus., ports., plans (fold.)   CHi

10394. Massey, Ernest de. A Frenchman in the gold rush; the journal of Ernest de Massey, argonaut of 1849, translated by Marguerite Eyer Wilbur. S.F., Calif. hist. soc., 1927. 183 p. illus., maps. (Calif. hist. soc. Special pub. no. 2) Tr. from the manuscript now the property of the Los Angeles public library.
Available in many California libraries and CaBViPA MoS TxU

10395. —— Relation du voyage d'Ernest de Massey de Passavant, Hte Saone, en Californie, 1849–1850. [n.p., n.d.] 411 p. Ms.   CL

10396. Master bakers' protective association. Revised constitution and by-laws...San Francisco and Alameda counties. S.F., E.D. Taylor print. shop, 1897. 73 p. ports.   CU-B

10397. Masters, R. S.; Smith, R. C.; and Winter, W.E. Historical review of the San Francisco exchange. [S.F.] Pac. telephone & telegraph co., 1927. 113 p. illus., ports., maps. Bibliography: p. [114–115]

C CHi CLU CO CSf CSfCW CSfP CSj CSmH
(1926?) CStrJC CU-B

10398. Mather, Stephen Tyng. National memorial broadcast in honor of Stephen Tyng Mather, as sponsored by the Bohemian club of San Francisco through the courtesy of the National broadcasting company, July 10, 1932. [S.F.?] 1932. 19 p. CHi

10399. Matson, William. Address of William Matson, president of the Chamber of commerce of San Francisco, at the last meeting of the trustees prior to the amalgamation of the Chamber of commerce of San Francisco, the Merchants' association and the Downtown association, San Francisco, October 25, 1911. [S.F., 1911?] 11 p. CHi

10400. Matson lines. Annual reports.
CHi has 1910–12, 1916, 1951, 1954–55, 1958.

10401. —— In commemoration, special historical number dedicated to the founder of the Matson line, *Matsonews*, December, 1943. [S.F., 1943] 23 p. illus., ports. CHi

10402. —— Ships in gray; the story of Matson in World War II. [S.F., c1946] 49 p. illus., ports. CHi

10403. Matthews, Lillian Ruth. Women in trade unions in San Francisco. Berkeley, Univ. of Calif. [1913] 100 p.
C CLSU CLU CO CSS CSf CSmH CU (Thesis–Ph.D., 1912)

10404. Mauzy (Byron) firm. New era catalog no. 14: musical instruments... S.F. [Blair-Murdock co., 1913?] 63 p. illus. CHi

10405. Maxim gas company of California. The Maxim gas machine described and compared. S.F., Excelsior press, print., 1871. 31 p. CU-B

10406. —— Same. S.F., Bacon & co., 1872. 20 p. illus. CHi

10407. May, Ernest R. The Overland monthly under Bret Harte. [L.A.] 1949. Thesis (M.A.)— U.C.L.A., 1949. CLU

10408. Maybeck, Bernard Ralph. Palace of fine arts and lagoon, Panama–Pacific international exposition, 1915. With an introduction by Frank Morton Todd. S.F., Elder [c1915] 13 p. illus.
CHi CLO CMartC CMont CO CRedl CSf CSfP ViU

10409. Maybell, Stephen. Greenbacks and prosperity. Hon. Stephen Maybell's letter of acceptance of the candidacy for Congress of the W.P.C. Greenback national labor party for the first congressional district; also his great financial drama in four acts... [S.F., S.F. daily graphic, 1880] 8 p. CHi

10410. Meadow valley mining co. Report...July 31, 1871– S.F., Cosmopolitan print. co., 1871–
CHi has 1871 (biennial), 1872–73 (annual)

10411. Mechanics' state council. Constitution and by-laws... S.F., J. Winterburn, 1868. 36 p. CHi

10412. Meddaugh & Chapman, pub. Ruins of San Francisco, California, April 18, 1906... Wastonville [Register press] c1906. [21] l. of illus. map. CHi

10413. Medical news. Guide to San Francisco. [n.p., 1958?] 36 p. illus., maps. Compliments of CIBA pharmaceutical products, inc. CHi

10414. Medico-dental building corp. The house the doctors built. [S.F., Taylor & Taylor, 1935] [12] p. illus. CHi

10415. Meese & Gottfried co. [General catalog] Section no. 9. 1st ed. S.F., c1908. 15 p. illus. CHi

10416. —— Same. No. 10. Modern machinery for elevating, conveying and screening and the mechanical transmission of power... S.F., c1922. 532 p. illus., tables, diagrs. CHi

10417. Megquier, Mary Jane (Cole) Apron full of gold; the letters of Mary Jane Megquier from San Francisco, 1849–1856. Ed. by Robert Glass Cleland. San Marino, Huntinton lib., 1949. 99 p. illus., port. (Huntington lib. pub.) "From manuscripts in the Huntington library."
Available in many California libraries and MiD OrU ViU ViW

10418. Meherin (Thos.) firm. ...Price list of trees, seeds and plants for 1886 ...agent for the nurseries of R. D. Fox... S.F., E.C. Hughes, print. [1886] 27 p. CHi

10419. Meiggs wharf co. Articles of incorporation and by-laws... S.F., Alta Calif. job print. house, 1874. 13 p. CU-B

10420. Men who made San Francisco. [S.F., Press of Brown & Power stationery co., 191–?] 274 p. illus., ports.
C CHi CO CSf CSfCW CSfMI CSfWF-H CSmH CSrD CU-B

10421. —— Same [volume 2] [S.F., Press of Brown & Power stationery co., 1912?] 310 p. illus., ports. CLU

10422. Mensch, Ernest Cromwell. Alcatraz... S.F., c1937. 32 p. illus., map.
C CBu CHi CL CO CSf CU-B

10423. —— The Golden Gate bridge; a technical description in ordinary language. S.F., 1935. 64 p. illus., maps.
C CBu CHi CL CLgA CO CSal CSd CSf CSmat CSmH CSrCL CU-B CViCL MHi ODa

10424. —— The San Francisco Oakland bay bridge ... S.F., c1936. 64 p. illus.
C CHi CL CLgA CSd CSf CSmat CSmH CU-B CV CViCL

10425. —— Same, with title: A technical description of the San Francisco Oakland bay bridge in non-technical language. [S.F.] c1935. 64 p. illus.
C CBu CHi CL CLgA CO CSf CSfU CSmH CStmo

10426. Mercantile illustrating co. San Francisco, the metropolis of western America; her phenomenal progress, incomparable industries and remarkable resources... S.F. [1899?] 212 p. illus.
CSf CSfWF-H CStclU CU-B

10427. Mercantile trust co. of San Francisco. ... Directors, officers, etc. [n.p., 1900?] [8] p. CHi

10428. Merchant marine league of California. The Pacific coast congress, San Francisco, California, Nov. 17, 18, 19, 1910... S.F., Sunset pub. house, 1910. 16 l. C-S

10429. Merchants' association of New York. Committee for the relief of the San Francisco sufferers. Report... [N.Y.] 1906. 32 p.
C CHi CU-B NN

10430. Merchants' association of San Francisco. ...Annual report... [189–?]– [S.F., 189–?]
CHi has 1905/06–1906/07, 1911/12. CU-B has 1909/10–1910/11.

10431. —— Handbook of manufacturers in and about San Francisco... S.F. [C. A. Murdock & co., c1910] 168 p. illus., maps. CHi

10432. —— Merchants' association...Brief history ...List of members...1896... S.F., 1896. 44 p.
C CU-B

10433. —— Report on the operation of the street railroad lines of San Francisco. A report to the Committee ...[by Warren Manley] [S.F.] 1909. 36 p. plan. CLU

10434. Merchants' club. Constitution and by-laws ... S.F., Commercial pub. co. [1886?] 22 p. List of charter members, p. [21] CHi

10435. Merchants' exchange. Annual report... 1901/1902– S.F., Commercial news pub. co., 1902–
CHi has 1905/06–1908/09.

10436. Merchants' exchange bank. By-laws. S.F., 1870. CSmH

10437. —— Proceedings of the stockholders' meeting...held at its office on July 25th, 1882. [Stenographic report] With appendix. S.F., Bacon & co., 1882. [103] p.
CHi

10438. Merle, Benoit V., et al vs. Dixey, Francis, et al. ...Benoit V. Merle, and Susana Martinez de Merle, plaintiffs and appellants, vs. Francis Dixey, et als., defendants and respondents. Transcript on appeal from the district court of the fourth judicial district, state of California, in and for the city and county of San Francisco. Gregory Yale, attorney for respondents. John B. Felton, attorney for appellants. S.F., S.H. Wade & co., print. [1863] 25 p. San Francisco land suit. CLU

10439. Merrill, George Arthur. José Francisco de Ortega; the landsman who discovered the Golden Gate which navigators had failed to find. [Redwood City, Hedge print. co., n.d.] [6] p. CHi

10440. —— The story of Lake Dolores and Mission San Francisco de Asis. Redwood City, Hedge print. co., 1942. [4] p. map.
C CHi CLU CSf CSfWF-H CU-B

10441. Merrill, Mollie Slater. Gullible's travels to the Panama-Pacific international exposition. [S.F.] c1915. 27 p. illus. CHi CU-B

10442. Merritt, Warren Chase. Fisherman's wharf, San Francisco; drawings by Warren Chase Merritt; recipes by Aline Merritt. S.F., Fearon, c1958. [28] p. illus. CU-B

10443. Messing, Aron J. ...Catechism for instruction in the Mosaic religion for the Hebrew free school of San Francisco...2d ed. S.F., M. Weiss, 1887. 47 p.
CHi

10444. Metropolitan improvement co. San Francisco as a field for investment. S.F., 1914. 15 p. illus. C

10445. Metropolitan life insurance co. Fiftieth anniversary of Metropolitan's Pacific coast head office. S.F. [1951?] 32 p. illus. CHi

10446. Mexican phosphate and sulphur co. Nitrogeneous superphosphate fertilizers, manufactured...from genuine imported guano or phosphates. [S.F., 1889] 12 p. CU-B

10447. Meyer, Carl, of Basel. Prospectus to form a society for emigration to California; trans. from the German ed. of 1852, by Ruth Frey Axe. Claremont, Sanders studio press, 1938. 26 p. CBb CHi CStoC

10448. Michaelis publishing co. Ruins of San Francisco. Kansas City, Mo., c1906. [24] p. of illus.
CHi CU-B

10449. Michel & Pfeffer iron works. A master thinks in iron. [Hotel Mark Hopkins, San Francisco. Weeks & Day, architects & engineers] [S.F.? 1926?] 40 p. illus. CHi

10450. Middleton (John) auctioneers. Auction sale of real estate in the city of San Francisco...on Monday, Nov. 28, 1859... [S.F.] Alta Calif. job print. [1859] 33 p. CHi CLU

10451. —— Catalogue. Auction sale of salt marsh and tide lands belonging to the state of California, at Platt's hall. Commencing Tuesday, February 28th, 1871 ... [S.F., 1871] 7 p. CHi

10452. —— Catalogue...One hundred 50-vara lots at auction! [Known as the Hayes tract] on Monday, the 1st day of September, 1856... [S.F., 1856] 11 p. CLU

10453. —— Catalogue...Sale of the entire tract of land known as the Potrero nuevo...on the 4th day of August, 1856... [S.F.] Franklin off. print [1856] 23 p.
CLU

10454. Mighels, Ella Sterling (Clark) Cummins. San Francisco redi-vivus! An open letter to all San Franciscans and all Californians... [Oakland, Press of Harrington-McInnis co., n.d.] 27 p.
CHi CLU CSmH CU-B

10455. Mighels, Henry R. Sage brush leaves. S.F., Edward Bosqui & co., 1879. 335 p. port. "Letters from the Palace Hotel" and "Letters from the French hospital" give impressions of scenes during the year 1878.
C CBb CHi CL CLSU CLU CO CRedl CSf
CSfCP CSfCW CSfP CSmH CU-B

10456. Military order of the loyal legion of the United States. [Proceedings at the meeting of Oct. 15, 1896, Headquarters commandery of the state of California, San Francisco. [n.p.], 1896] [20] p. CHi

10457. Miller, Albert. In memoriam... N.Y., James T. White & co., 1922. 8 p. CHi

10458. [Miller, B. P.] Opera in the west. [S.F., Taylor & Taylor, 191–?] [3] p. CHi

10459. Miller, Clement H. Address by Clement H. Miller, C. E., before the San Francisco center of the California civic league on the wisdom of the proposed grant by Congress of the use of Hetch Hetchy valley as a reservoir site for storing flood waters for municipal purposes among the cities bordering San Francisco bay. [n.p., 1913] 11 p. CU-B

10460. Miller (F. A.) & co. Exotic gardens and conservatories...general and descriptive catalogue of new and rare plants, trees and shrubs, seeds and bulbs, 1879 ... S.F., Winterburn & co., 1878. 24 p. CHi

10461. Miller, Geraldine, *Sister*. The public career of Joseph McKenna. San Rafael, Catholic univ. of Am. Pac. coast branch, 1941. 51 p. Thesis (M.A.)—Catholic univ. of America. CSrD

10462. Miller, Henry Commercial. The possibilities of San Francisco as an export center for paints and varnishes. [Berkeley, 1924] Thesis (M.S.)—Univ. of Calif., 1924. CU

10463. Miller, John Franklin. Memorial addresses on the life and character of John Franklin Miller, a senator from California, delivered in the Senate and House of representatives, forty-ninth congress, first session, May 28, and June 19, 1886. Wash., D.C., Govt. print. off., 1887. 90 p. port. CHi CSfCW

10464. Miller, Sievers & co. Exotic gardens and conservatories...general and descriptive catalogue of new and rare plants, trees and shrubs, seeds and bulbs... S.F., John H. Carmany print., 1876. 32 p. illus. CHi

10465. Miller, Sloss & Scott, jobbers, importers and exporters of hardware. Catalogue no. 7. S.F., Hicks-Judd co. [1898?] 1236 p. illus. CHi

10466. Miller typographic service, inc. Catalogue of type faces, part II. S.F. [n.d.] 73 p. CHi

10467. Mills, Marmion D. Report on the rehabilitation of the San Francisco municipal railway from 1947 to 1951... [S.F.] 1951. 50 p. maps (fold.), tables. CHi CSfU

10468. Mills, William N. History and restoration of the ship *Balclutha*. S.F. [1955?] 16 p. illus. Paper presented at Northern California section, Society of naval architects and marine engineers. CHi

10469. Mills tower. [Brochure. S.F., 1930?] [14] p. illus., plans. CHi

10470. Miners' association, San Francisco. Articles of agreement, by-laws, and list of members... [S.F.] Daily exchange print. [1879?] 16 p. CHi

10471. Miners' foundry and machine works. The Hicks steam engine... [S.F.] Winterburn & co., print. [1868?] 23 p. illus. CU-B

10472. Mining and scientific press. After earthquake and fire, a reprint of the articles and editorial comment appearing in the *Mining and scientific press* immediately after the disaster at San Francisco, April 18, 1906. S.F., 1906. 194 p. illus.
C C-S CHi CL CLSU CLgA CO CP CSf CSfCW CSfU CSmH CU-B OrU

10473. Mintie (A. E.) and co. Pocket memorandum and medical receipt book. [1878] S.F. [1878] 1 v. illus. CU-B

10474. Mission bank. [Report to the state superintendent of banks... S.F., 1911] [4] p. CHi

10475. Mission foundry and stove works. [Catalog] [S.F.? 192–?] [4] p. illus. CHi

10476. Mission promotion association. Constitution and by-laws [adopted February 15th, 1909] S.F. [1909?] 21 p. CHi

10477. Mission street railroad homestead association. Articles of association, certificate of incorporation, and by-laws...Incorporated June 16, 1869. S.F., C. Dondero & co., print., 1869. 16 p. CU-B

10478. Mississippi wire glass co. New York. Earthquake & fire, 1906, San Francisco. Concerning the fire resistance of building materials tested in San Francisco, 1906... [N.Y., Press of J.E. Hetsch, 1907] 90 p. illus. CSfCW CU-B

10479. Mitchell, Edward H., pub. Greater San Francisco as seen today. S.F., c1908. folder (18 p. of illus.) CU-B

10480. —— San Francisco view book. [S.F., 1899] 32 pl. C CHi
Other editions followed. CSmH (1905?) NN (1905? 1906?)

10481. Mobley, Lawrence E. San Francisco's "Golden Era": 1852 to 1860, its contents and significance plus representative selections and an index of contributors. [East Lansing, Mich.] 1961. 352 p. illus. Reproduced from typew. copy. Thesis (Ph.D.)—Michigan state univ., 1961. CHi

10482. Modern San Francisco and the men of today, 1905–1906. [S.F.] Western press assoc. [1906] [112] p. illus., ports.
C CLU CSfCW CSfMI CSfWF-H CU-B

10483. Modern San Francisco, 1907–1908. [S.F.] Western press assoc. [1908] [128] p. illus., ports.
C CBu CHi CL CLSU CLU CO CRedl CSdS CSf CSfMI CSfU CSjC CU-B NN

10484. Moerenhout, Jacob A., vs. Brown, Harvey S. In the Supreme court, state of California. Jacob A. Moerenhout, appellant, vs. Harvey S. Brown, respondent. Brief of respondent on rehearing. Hoge & Wilson, of counsel for respondent. S.F., Towne & Bacon, print., 1864. 18 p. Suit arising from the appellant's purchase of a part of the Bernal grant. Bernal grant was the Rancho Rincon de las Salinas y Potrero viejo in San Francisco. CLU

10485. Moerenhout, Jacob A., vs. Williams, Henry F. In the Supreme court of the state of California. Jacob A. Moerenhout, appellant, vs. Henry F. Williams, et al., respondents. Transcript on appeal. B. S. Brooks, for appellants, J. B. Harmon, for respondents. [S.F.] Women's co-operative print [1870?] 131 p. San Francisco land suit. CLU

10486. Mohr (R.) & sons. Optical catalogue. no. 2, 3 [1911?, 1912] [n.p., 1911?–12] CHi

10487. Moise (L. H.) firm. Catalogue [of] leading manufacturers of red rubber stamps, stencils, badges ... S.F., 1894. 192 p. illus. CHi CU-B

10488. Moise, Klinkner co. Catalog, red rubber stamps, stencils, metal, glass and electric signs... S.F. [n.d.] illus. CHi has no. 25, 50.

10489. The Monadnock; the newest, the finest, the leader among San Francisco's office buildings... [S.F., Designed and print. by F. J. Cooper, 1906?] [20] p. illus. CHi

10490. Moncrief, Frank M. Recreation in San Francisco; a study of the distribution of public and voluntary agency services in San Francisco in April, 1949, as measured by attendance at public recreation department units and constituency of voluntary agencies. S.F., Social planning dept., Community Chest of S.F., 1950. 25 p. maps, charts, tables. CSfSt

10491. The Monitor. Archdiocese of San Francisco, 1853–1953. S.F., 1953. 136 p. illus., ports., map, facsim. (*Its* commemorative issue, v.96, no. 23, Sept. 4, 1953) CHi CO

10492. —— ...Eightieth anniversary and exposition number... S.F., 1938. 40 p. illus., ports. CO CU-B

10493. —— Golden jubilee of the archdiocese of San Francisco, 1853–1903. S.F., 1904. unp. illus., ports. (*Its* jubilee edition, v.57, no. 16, Jan. 23, 1904) COHN

10494. —— A history of the Monitor, in two parts ... S.F. [n.d.] 33 p. CSf

10495. Monotype composition co. A catalogue of type faces with an explanation of the products and service ... S.F. [Mackenzie & Harris, inc., 1915?] 55 p. illus. CHi

10496. —— ...Specimens of new and exclusive and of ordinary type faces... S.F. [c1925] 114 p. CHi

10497. Monroy, Florence Riley. Water and power in San Francisco since 1900: a study in municipal government. [Berkeley] 1944. Thesis (M.A.)—Univ. of Calif., 1944. CU

10498. Montague (W. W.) and co. [Catalogs and price lists of hardware, mantels and grates, pumps, etc.] 1877–1899/1900. S.F., 1877–1900. illus.
CU-B has 1877, 1881, 1883–84, 1890, 1894/95, 1899/ 1900.

10499. —— A few representative buildings heated by our Palace Queen, Palace Duke, Palace King, Commander warm air furnaces. S.F., 1895. 36 p. illus., tables. CU-B

10500. —— Illustrated catalogue and price-list of Alaska refrigerators and ice chests. 1904. S.F., 1904. 84 p. illus.   CHi

10501. Montgomery, Zachariah. Letter addressed to Maj.-Gen. McDowell, touching the assassination of the President, the riotous destruction of printing offices in San Francisco... S.F., 1865. 16 p.   CLU CU-B

10502. —— A relic of war times. Meeting August 3, 1864...Democratic indignation meeting at Hayes' Park, San Francisco, Cal. The arrest of Col. Weller and Bishop Kavanaugh denounced. Resolutions protesting against arbitrary arrests unanimously adopted. Speech of Hon. Z. Montgomery. Reproduced in pamphlet form at request of old California friends in 1897... [n.p.] 1897. 22 p.   CHi

10503. —— Remarks...before the Roman Catholic Sunday-school teachers, July 6th, 1873. S.F., 1873. 7 p.   CHi

10504. —— Speeches of Zach. Montgomery. [S.F., 18–?] 12 l. of mounted clippings.   CU-B

10505. Monthly guide book...v.1, no. 2, Feb. 1877. S.F., Robertson & co., 1877. fold. plan.   CU-B

10506. Mooar, George. The prominent characteristics of the Congregational churches... S.F., Towne & Bacon, print., 1866. 60 p.
                      CHi CLU CSfCP CSmH CU-B

10507. Mood, Fulmer. Andrew S. Hallidie and librarianship in San Francisco, 1868–79. [N.Y.] 1946. p. 202–210. "Reprint. for private circulation from *Library Q.*, v.16, no. 3, July 1946."   CHi

10508. Mooney, Thomas J. [Correspondence and papers, 1906–1942] 50 cartons, 84 v., 37 scrapbooks, 15 bundles and portfolio. Trial records; correspondence while in prison and of the various defense organizations (particularly the Tom Mooney Molders Defense Committee); correspondence of Gov. Olson concerning the pardon; financial records; scrapbooks and bundles of newspaper clippings; script and film of motion picture; pamphlets and propaganda material.   CU-B

10509. —— [Pamphlets; gift of estate of Thomas J. Mooney. v.p., 190–?–42] 130 pamphlets in 7 v. illus. Contents: v.1–3. Pamphlets on labor. v.4. Pamphlets on the Mooney case. v.5. Pamphlets on the race question, communism, and social change. v.6. Pamphlets on socialism. v.7. Pamphlets on Upton Sinclair.   CU-B

10510. —— ...Thomas J. Mooney, petitioner, against Court Smith, warden of San Quentin penitentiary, state of California, et al., respondents. Brief in support of petition for certiorari... N.Y., Ballou press [1938] 188 p. At head of title: In the Supreme court of the United States, October term, 1937, no. 738.   CU-Law

10511. —— ...Thomas J. Mooney petitioner, vs. James B. Holohan, warden of San Quentin penitentiary, respondent... [1934?] 2 v. in 1.   CU-B CU-Law

10512. —— ...Tom Mooney's message to organized labor...on the 1938 California elections. S.F., Tom Mooney molders defense committee [1938] [32] p. illus., ports.   CO CU-B

10513. Moore, Albert Alfonzo. ...In the matter of Patrick Calhoun on habeas corpus... [S.F.? 1910?] 103 p.   CSfCW CU-B

10514. Moore, Avery C. Destiny's soldiers. S.F., Fearon pub. [c1958] 197 p. port. Biography of Gen. Albert S. Johnston.   CHi CSd

10515. Moore, Bertram Bradt. Garrett Garreon Bradt, 1827–1902, pioneer and builder of San Francisco

and San Diego. [San Diego?] San Diego hist. soc. [1951?] 30 p. illus.   CHi CNa CSd CSf

10516. Moore (Charles C.) and co., engineers, inc. Gas machines; general catalogue of Alamo and National gas and gasoline engines. 1905. S.F., 1905. 1 v. illus.   CU-B

10517. Moore (George P.) co. [Catalog of] automobile supplies. [1912?] S.F. [1912?] 1 v.   CU-B

10518. Moore, John K., vs. Beideman, J. C. Twelfth district court, Twelfth judicial district, in and for the city and county of San Francisco, state of California. Before Hon. O. C. Pratt, J. Wednesday, Feb. 28th, 1866. John K. Moore, vs. J. C. Beideman. Counsel for plaintiff—Geo. F. Sharp, esq., and J. H. Moore, esq. Counsel for defense—J. B. Felton, esq., Wm. Hayes, esq., E. J. Pringle, esq., and James M. Taylor, esq. [S.F.? 1866?] 1,832 p. fold. pl.   CHi

10519. Moore, John K. Examination of John K. Moore. [n.p., n.d.] 28 p. Examination lasted from August 30 to September 13, 1864. S.F. land case.
                                              CHi CU-B

10520. Moore, Thomas Morrell. Panama-Pacific international exposition. S.F., Remington typewriter co., inc., 1915. 30 p.   UHi

10521. Moose, Loyal order of. San Francisco lodge no. 26. ...By-laws... [S.F., Mercury press, 1925] 47 p.   CHi

10522. Morbio, Patricia. Patricia Morbio, 1889–1937. [S.F., Print. for Albert M. Bender by Grabhorn, 1937] [4] l. port.   CHi

10523. Morgen, Millard Robert. The administration of Patrick H. McCarthy, mayor of San Francisco, 1910–1912. [Berkeley, 1949] Thesis (M.A.)—Univ. of Calif., 1949.   CU

10524. Morphy, Edward. The port of San Francisco ... Sacramento, State print. off., 1923. 57 p. illus.
CBb CHi CL CMartC CO CSf CSfCP CSfMI CSfP CSmH CU-B CViCL

10525. —— San Francisco's thoroughfares...Published in the San Francisco chronicle, January, 1919–July, 1920. Typew.   CSf

10526. Morris, Charles, ed. The San Francisco calamity by earthquake and fire...told by eye witnesses... [Phila., Chicago [etc.] J.C. Winston co. c1906] 446 p. illus. ports. Publisher varies.
C CBu CHi CL CLSU CLgA CSd CSf CSfCP CSfCW CSfU CSlu CSmH CStmo CU-B MiD-B MoS N NbHi NjR OU

10527. Morris iron co. [Catalog of] fixtures for street, park lighting and electric railways. Bul. no. 21. S.F., 1912. illus.   CU-B

10528. Morrow, Robert F., vs. Lehn, Charles. In the Supreme court of the state of California. Robert F. Morrow and A. E. Head, plaintiffs and respondents, vs. Charles Lehn, defendant and appellant. Transcript on appeal from the Twelfth district court city and county of San Francisco. Saffold & Meux, attorneys for appellant. Wilson & Wilson, att'ys for respondents... S.F., B.H. Daly, bk. and job print., 1880. 174 p. A tide land suit.   CLU

10529. Morrow, William W. An address delivered ...on the opening of the sixteenth industrial exhibition held under the auspices of the Mechanics' institute of San Francisco, August 2d, 1881. S.F., E. Bosqui & co., print., 1881. 22 p.   CHi

10530. —— The earthquake of April 18, 1906, and

the great fire in San Francisco on that and succeeding days... S.F., 1906. 29 p.   CHi CSf CU-B

10531. —— Remarks of Judge W. W. Morrow at opening of the United States post office and court house, August 29, 1905. [S.F., 1905?] 16 p. pl. A history of the U.S. post office in San Francisco.   CLU

10532. Morse (C. C.) & co. [Catalogs—plants, seeds, trees]
CHi has [1905?], 1907, 1910–11, 1914–15, 1917.

10533. Morse, Harry N. Report...on Dupont-street frauds etc. [S.F.] 1879. 43 p.   CLU CU-B

10534. Morse's (Harry N.) night patrol. Rules for the guidance of Harry N. Morse's...night patrol... S.F., Crocker [18—?] 21 p.   CU-B

10535. Mortensen, Clara Estelle. Organized labor in San Francisco from 1892 to 1902. [Berkeley, 1916] Thesis (M.S.)—Univ. of Calif., 1916.   CU

10536. Morton, Theophilus B. Vindication of Hon. M. M. Estee; address delivered by T. B. Morton, president of the Afro-American league of San Francisco, at its regular monthly meeting, Monday, July 2, 1894. [S.F., Valleau & Oliver, n.d.] 11 p.   CHi

10537. Moses, Bernard. ...The establishment of municipal government in San Francisco... Baltimore, Md., Pub. agency of Johns Hopkins univ., 1889. 83 p. (Johns Hopkins univ. studies in hist. & political science. 7th ser., II–III)
C CHi CL CLS CLSU CLU CLgA CO CRedl CSS CSf CSfCW CSfU CSmH CStclU CU-B MoS N OrU TxU ViU

10538. —— Old regime of San Francisco. [n.p., 1885?] 11 p. Bibliographical foot-notes.   CLU

10539. —— Prejudices against the Jews, a paper read before the Emanuel association, San Francisco, January 25, 1887. S.F., 1887. 39 p.   CHi

10540. [Mosgrove, S., agent] Nob Hill of University heights, the handsomest block in the city and county of San Francisco. S.F., Cubery & co. [1892?] [4] p. map.   CHi

10541. Moss, Franklin et al vs. Southern Pacific railroad co. In the Supreme court of California. Franklin Moss et al., plaintiffs and respondents, vs. the Southern Pacific railroad company, defendant and appellant. Points of respondents. Wm. Matthews attorney for respondents... [S.F., Cubery & co., print., 1876. 9 p. CHi

10542. Mount Gregory water and mining co. Water supply for San Francisco, Oakland...Oakland, Butler & Stilwell's steam print., 1874. 15 p.   CU-B

10543. Mount Zion hospital and medical center. ...75th anniversary, 1887–1962. S.F., 1962. 31 p. illus.   CHi

10544. Mountain lake water co. Mountain lake water company, of San Francisco. Capital stock $500,000, divided into 10,000 shares of $50 each. S.F., Print. at Courier off., 1851. 14 p.   C CU-B

10545. —— Mountain lake water co. of San Francisco. Organized August 14, 1851, under the general incorporation act of California. Capital stock, $500,000, divided into 10,000 shares of $50 each. N.Y., 1852. 43 p.   CHi

10546. Mountin, William J. History of the Rotary club of San Francisco, founded November 12, 1908, Club no. 2 ... S.F., [Print. by Recorder press] 1940. 196 p. illus., ports.   CHi CL CSf CSfU CU-B

10547. Mourelle, Francisco Antonio. Voyage of the *Sonora* in the second Bucareli expedition to explore the Northwest coast, survey the port of San Francisco, and found Franciscan missions and a presidio and pueblo at that port... S.F., T.C. Russell, 1920. 120 p. maps.
Available in many libraries.

10548. Muench, Josef. San Francisco bay cities; around the Golden Gate in pictures; with an introd. by Joseph Henry Jackson. N.Y., Hastings house [c1947] 101 p. illus.
Available in many California libraries and NN ODa

10549. Mui, Mook-lan Moline. Social welfare services for children in San Francisco's Chinatown. [Berkeley, 1949] Thesis (M.A.)—Univ. of Calif., 1949.   CU

10550. Mullan, John. Fridolin Grim et al. vs. Additional homestead entries and purchasers from the Central Pacific railroad company. Arising in the U.S. Land office, San Francisco land district, California. Involving lands in townships 1 and 2 south, range 2 west, and townships 1 and 2 south, range 3 west, Mount Diablo base and meridian. Argument on the jurisdiction of the Interior department in the above entitled cases... Wash., D.C., T. McGill & co., law print., 1885 [i.e. 1886] 16 p. At head of title: Before the Hon. Secretary of the Interior.   CLU

10551. Mulligan, Alexander O. vs. Smith, Andrew D. In the Supreme court of the state of California. A. O. Mulligan, plaintiff and appellant, vs. A. D. Smith, defendant and respondent. Opening brief of appellant. J. H. Brewer, attorney for plaintiff. Nathaniel Bennett [and] Delos Lake, counsel for appellant. S.F., Bacon, 1880–81.   CLU (1880) CU-B (1880–81)

10552. Munder (Norman T. A.) & co. Descriptive catalogue of a printing exhibit at the Panama-Pacific international exposition, San Francisco, 1915. Baltimore [1915] 28 p.   CHi

10553. Municipal blue book of San Francisco, 1915. Comp. and ed. by George Homer Meyer, D. Wooster Taylor and Arthur M. Johnson. [S.F., Calif. press, 1915] 253 p. illus., ports.
C CHi CLU CO CSf CSfU CU-B

10554. Municipal reform league. ...Why the proposed new charter should not be adopted. Caution. Do not be misled by the "Synopsis of the new charter" prepared by Mr. J. Richard Freud, secretary of the Mechanics' association. Read the charter itself. August, 1896. [S.F., 1896] 15 p.   CSmH

10555. Municipal reform party. Declaration of principles, const. and by-laws. S.F. [1878?] 16 p.   CU-B

10556. Murdock, Charles Albert. Horatio Stebbins, his ministry and his personality. Bost., Houghton, 1921. 269 p. port.   CHi CRcS CRic CSd CSfCW

10557. [Murphy, Anna L.] In the Superior court of the county of Alameda, state of California. Before Hon. F. W. Henshaw, judge. In the matter of the estate of Anna L. Murphy, deceased. Anna T. Wolseley, Daniel T. Murphy and Samuel J. Murphy, plaintiffs, vs. Mary H. Murphy, Frances J. Murphy, et als., defendants. Contest of will after probate. Plaintiff's brief. [S.F.? 189–?] 137 p.   CHi

10558. —— Same. Plaintiff's brief in reply. S.F., Geo. Spaulding & co., print. [189–?] 131 p.   CHi

10559. Murphy, Leontina. Public care of the dependent sick in San Francisco, 1847–1936. [Berkeley, 1938] Thesis (M.A.)—Univ. of Calif., 1938.   CU

10560. Murray, Eugene vs. Green, Alfred A. et al. In the Supreme court of the state of California. Eugene Murray, plaintiff and respondent, vs. Alfred A.

Green, et al., defendants and appellants. Transcript on appeal from Fourth district court. B. S. Brooks, att'y for appellants. E. A. Lawrence [and] J. F. Sullivan, att'ys for respd't. [n.p., 1877] 43 p. San Francisco land suit.
CLU

10561. Murray, Justin. Cable car daze in San Francisco. Stanford, James Ladd Delkin [c1947] [89] p. illus.
C CLU CStmo

10562. Murray, Philip. "...a burden on the conscience of the American people." The Harry Bridges case ... [S.F., Harry Bridges victory committee, 1945] 16 p.
CHi

10563. Mutual aid and benevolent society of the employees of the San Francisco gas-light co. Constitution, by-laws, and rules of order...organized May, 1877. S.F., 1877. 26 p.
CHi

10564. Muybridge, Eadweard J. Panorama of San Francisco, from California street hill. S.F., c1877. Folded panoramic photo.
C CHi CMont CSf CSfCW CSfSt CSfU CSfWF-H CSjC CSmH CU-B NN

10565. Myers, James Edward. The educational work of Andrew Jackson Moulder in the development of public education in California, 1850–1895. [Berkeley, 1961] Thesis (PhD)—Univ. of Calif., 1961.
CU

10566. [Myrick, Thomas S.] Twelve years of teaching the public schools of San Francisco, October, 1867. S.F., F. Eastman, print., 1867. 8 p.
CU-B

10567. Mysell-Rollins bank note co. Catalog. no. 35, suppl. S.F. [n.d.] illus.
CU-B

10568. The mysteries and miseries of San Francisco. By a Californian. Showing up all the various characters and notabilities, (both in high and low life) that have figured in San Francisco since its settlement. N.Y., Garrett & co. [c1853] 208 p.
CHi

10569. A mystery of Twin Peaks... [S.F.? 1925?] 21 p. illus.
CHi

10570. Naber, Alfs and Brune. Catalogue and bartenders' guide. S.F., Schmidt label & litho. co., 1884. 32 p. illus. (part col.) ports., fold. map.
CU-B

10571. Naglee, Henry Morris. Correspondence between Henry M. Naglee, receiver, Palmer, Cook & co., and Edward Stanly. Submitted by the former to the creditors of Adams and co. S.F., Whitton Towne & co., print., Excelsior bk. and job off., 1856. 31 p.
C CHi CLU CSmH CU-B

10572. —— The love life of Brig. Gen. Henry M. Naglee, consisting of a correspondence on love, war and politics. [n.p.] 1867. 182 p. illus., port.
CHi

10573. [Nahl, Perham Wilhelm] ed. and pub. Souvenir, early days in California. [S.F.] c1894. [30] p. illus.
C C-S CLSU CLU CMont CSmH CU-B

10574. Nast, Greenzweig y ca., San Francisco. Setiembre, 1880. Lista de precios del suplemento no. 1 al catalogo ilustrado de... fabricantes é importadores de relojes, diamantes, joyeria y novedades... S.F., A.L. Bancroft y ca., 1880. 20 p.
CHi

10575. Nathan, Dohrmann and co. Lamp department catalogue. no. 8, 1895/96. S.F. [1895?] illus.
CU-B

10576. National association of credit men. ...Report of Special committee on settlements made by fire insurance companies in connection with the San Francisco disaster. [N.Y., 1907] 15 p.
CHi CU-B

10577. National association of power engineers. California, no. 3. Report of California, no. 3, National association of stationary engineers, on the San Francisco calamity, April 18–19–20, 1906. [S.F., Crocker, 1906] [159] p. illus.
C CHi CLU CO CSf CSfCW CSfU CSmH N

10578. National association of stationary engineers. San Francisco, no. 1. Constitution and by-laws ...Adopted February 13, 1896. S.F., G.W. Gordon, 1896. 66 p.
CHi

10579. National association of stationers & manufacturers. ...Souvenir of the eleventh convention... held at the Fairmont hotel, San Francisco, California, September 27–30, 1915. [n.p., n.d.] [14] col. illus.
CSfU

10580. The National bank of the Pacific, San Francisco. [Letter from the president listing the status of insurance companies following the earthquake and fire. S.F., 1906?] 11 p.
CU-B

10581. —— [Letter from the president correcting November letter regarding status of insurance companies and giving information relating to business and real estate following the earthquake and fire. S.F., 1906] [8] p.
CU-B

10582. National democratic association of San Francisco. Constitution... S.F., M.D. Carr & co., print., 1865. 12 p.
CU-B

10583. National education association. Golden Gate park, San Francisco, California; souvenir, July 20, 1888. [S.F., 1888] [12] p. illus., ports.
C-S

10584. —— Official...convention guide book and program...San Francisco, Cal., July, 1911. S.F., Bd. of education, 1911. 202 p. illus.
C-S CSfCW CU-B

10585. —— Official program; sixty-first annual meeting...Oakland–San Francisco, June 28–July 6, 1923. [S.F.? 1923] 79 p. maps.
CHi

10586. —— Souvenir of the California kindergartens. N. E. A., July, 1888... [S.F., 1888] [4] p.
CU-B

10587. National fire proofing co., pub. Trial by fire at San Francisco, the evidence of the camera. Chicago, Franklin co., print. [1907?] [61] p. illus.
C C-S CHi CO CSd CSfWF-H MiD-B NHi ViU

10588. National guard officers' association of California. Proceedings of the seventh annual convention of...held at San Francisco, December 1st, 1890. S.F., E.H. Hughes, 1891. 24 p.
CHi

10589. National meter co., New York. National meter company of New York at the Panama-Pacific international exposition, manufacturers of Crown, Empire, Nash, Gem, Empire-compound and premium water meters. [S.F., 1915] [16] p. illus. (part col.)
CHi CU-B

10590. National Mooney-Billings committee, New York. The scandal of Mooney and Billings; the decisions of the California supreme court, the Advisory pardon board, Gov. Young denying pardons to Mooney and Billings. N.Y., 1931. 62 p.
MoS

10591. National probation association. The juvenile court, city and county of San Francisco, California. Report of a survey by Francis H. Hiller... N.Y., 1941. 121 l. Mimeo.
C CHi CL CLSU CO CSf

10592. National sales managers' association of America. San Francisco division. [Constitution and by-laws; members] 1912–1913. [S.F., Taylor, Nash & Taylor, 1912?] [15] p.
CHi

10593. National shooting bund of the United States. Third festival, July fourteenth until July twenty-third, nineteen hundred and one, Shellmound park, San Francisco, Cal. [S.F., E.C. Hughes, 1901] 68 p. illus.
CHi

10594. National society for sanity in art, inc. San Francisco branch. Exhibition by members of the San Francisco branch...Palace of the Legion of honor, the month of August, 1939. [S.F.? 1939?] [7] p.　CHi

10595. National society of Colonial dames of America resident in the state of California. Octagon house...2645 Gough Street, San Francisco. [S.F.? 195–?] [4] p.　CHi

10596. Native sons of the golden West. Constitution and by-laws of the Grand parlor...and constitution for subordinate parlors. S.F., Valleau & Peterson, 1890. 173 p.　CHi

10597. —— Same, as amended...Grass Valley, 1933. S.F., Walter N. Brunt press [1933] 116 p.　CHi

10598. [——, pub.] Golden jubilee celebration, 1850–1900, San Francisco, September 8–9–10. [S.F., Stanley-Taylor co., print., 1900] [79] l. illus., ports. Biographical sketches of prominent Californians.
C CHi CLU CSf CSfCW

10599. —— Official program and souvenir...Admission day. Ninth September meeting. S.F., Crocker [1890] 62 p. illus.　CHi CSfWF-H

10600. —— Same. 1910 festival in celebration of the sixtieth anniversary...San Francisco, Sept. 8, 9, 10. S.F., Town talk press, 1910. 128 p. illus., ports.
CHi CSf

10601. —— Souvenir program launching of the armored cruiser "California" under the auspices of the Native sons of the golden West, April 28, 1904, at the Union iron works. S.F., Phillips, Smyth & Van Orden, 1904. 36 p. illus.　C-S CHi

10602. —— **San Francisco. Mission parlor no. 38.** By-laws...Organized August 28th, 1884. Adopted March, 1897; approved April, 1897. S.F., Brunt press, 1898. [42] p.　CSmH

10603. —— —— —— Same, approved December 14, 1907. S.F., 1908. 28 p.　CSmH

10604. —— —— **Presidio parlor, no. 194.** By-laws...March 7, 1939, San Francisco, California. [S.F.] Norton print. co. [1939] 16 p.　CSmH

10605. —— —— **San Francisco parlor, no. 49.** By-laws... S.F., North Beach press, 1932. 24 p. CSmH

10606. —— —— Same. S.F., Pac. states print. co. [1947] 28 p.　CHi

10607. —— —— **Yerba Buena parlor, no. 84.** By-laws... S.F., Hicks-Judd co., 1890. 24 p.　CHi

10608. Native sons of Vermont. Pacific coast association, San Francisco. ... Report for the years 1879–80 and 1880–81. S.F., Crocker, 1881. 53 p.　CHi

10609. Natomas co. Annual report. CL has 1950–60.

10610. Nature's herb co. Herbs and spices for home use ... S.F. [1958] 36 p.　CHi

10611. Neale, Walter. Life of Ambrose Bierce... N.Y., Author, 1929. 489 p. illus., ports.　CHi

10612. [Neil, Henry] ...Complete story of the San Francisco earthquake...embracing a full account in pictures and story of the awful disaster that befell the city of San Francisco and all the other towns and cities shocked by the fatal earthquake, April 18, 1906 with a full account of the generous aid supplied to the sufferers by the people of the United States... By Marshall Everett [pseud.]... Chicago, Bible house, c1906. 304 [32] p. illus.
C CHi CL CLSU CLgA CMont CRcS CSf CSfCW CStclU CStcrCL MoKU NN

10613. [Neilson, William McCann] A faint idea of a terrible life! The Rev. I. S. Kalloch (mayor of San Francisco) from his expulsion from college until now... [S.F.] J.K. Cooper [1881] 123 p.　CHi CLU CP

10614. Nelson (A.E.) co. The story of Barrett & Hilp. [S.F., c1945] [36] p. illus., ports.　CHi

10615. [Nerac, Ellen] In the Supreme court of the state of California. In the matter of the estate of Ellen Nerac, deceased. (D. S. Clark, appellant.) Brief for respondent. John B. Felton, Theodore H. Hittell, attorneys for respondent. S.F., Deffebach & co., print., 1868. 6 p.
CHi

10616. Neuhaus, Eugen. The art of the exposition ... S.F., Elder, c1915. 91 p. illus. Other editions followed.
Available in many California libraries and CaBViPA ODa ViU

10617. —— The art of Treasure island...artistic aspects of the Golden Gate international exposition of 1939. Berkeley, Univ. of Calif. press, 1939. 185 p. illus.
Available in many California libraries and ODa

10618. —— The galleries of the exposition; a critical review of the paintings, statuary and the graphic arts in the Palace of fine arts at the Panama–Pacific international exposition. S.F., Elder, c1915. 96 p. illus.
Available in many libraries.

10619. —— Same. 2d ed. c1915. 98 p. illus.　CHi

10620. —— William Keith; the man and the artist. Berkeley, Univ. of Calif. press, 1938. 95 p. illus.
CHi COnC CRcS CRedCL CSd CSfCW CStmo CU CYcCL

10621. Neustadter bros. Catalogue of standard white shirts and gent's furnishing goods. Spring 1877, 1916. S.F., 1877–1916. 2 v. illus.　CU-B

10622. Neville, Amelia (Ransome) The fantastic city; memoirs of the social and romantic life of old San Francisco...; edited and revised by Virginia Brastow. Bost. & N.Y., Houghton, 1932. 285 p. illus., ports.
Available in many California libraries and MoS ODa

10623. Neville & co. [Price list] Bags, twines, nets, burlaps, hop cloth, tents...no. 1– 189–?– S.F., 189–?– illus.
CHi has 8, 11, 189–?, 1901. CU-B has 12, 14, Apr. 1902, Apr. 1905.

10624. New California tourists' guide to San Francisco and vicinity, Monterey, Santa Cruz, Yosemite, Big trees, the Geysers...containing also an historical sketch of California, and San Francisco... S.F., S. Carson & co., 1886. 169 p. illus., maps.　CSfCW CSmH CU-B

10625. New Fillmore hotel. New Fillmore hotel, the house of comfort... [S.F.? 1932?] folder (4 p.) illus.　CHi

10626. New Silver street kindergarten society. Superintendent's report of the work...since January 1st, 1882, and a history of the free kindergarten movement... Mrs. Kate Smith Wiggin, superintendent. S.F., C.A. Murdock & co., print. [1882?] 53 p.　CHi

10627. The new society blue book; San Francisco, Oakland, Piedmont, Alameda, Berkeley, Hillsborough, Burlingame, San Mateo, Redwood, Woodside, Atherton, Menlo Park, San Rafael, Ross, Belvedere, Sausalito, Mill Valley, etc. S.F., M.M. Pinchard [1912]–
C has 1919, 1922–23, 1925–26, 1928–29. C-S has 1912–13. CHi has 1912–13, 1917–18, 1931. CO has 1912–13, 1915–16, 1922–26. CRcS has 1932. CSf has 1926–27. CStrJC has 1928. CU-B has 1912–19, 1921–30.

10628. New York times. San Francisco 1906–1956. April 15, 1956. Section 10. N.Y., 1956. 16 p. illus.
CRcS

10629. New York world. California ed. Supplement to the N.Y. world, Sunday, March 20, 1904. N.Y., c1904. 12 p. illus., ports.
CU-B

10630. Newell (E. E.) co. pub. Our bridges. [S.F., 1936] [24] p. chiefly illus.
CSmat CU-B

10631. Newell Murdoch co. Forest Hill, San Francisco, a 230 acre natural park in the geographical residence center of town... S.F. [Janssen L & L co., 1912?] [9] p. map.
CHi

10632. —— Same. [21] p. illus., map.
CHi

10633. Newhall, G. A. Argument made before the Senate and Assembly, San Francisco delegation, Feb. 4th, 1897. [n.p., 1897] 3 p.
CU-B

10634. Newhall (H. M.) & co., auctioneers. ... Catalogue of elegant bronze fountains statuary, bronze vases and figures...to be sold at auction...Nov. 12, 1873... [S.F.] F. Eastman, print. [1873] 8 p.
CU-B

10635. —— Catalogue of elegant oil paintings, large, medium and cabinet pictures..."Samson and Delilah" by Jacobs...also portraits... to be sold at auction ...Wednesday, March 4, 1874... S.F., Frank Eastman, print., 1874. 12 p.
CHi

10636. —— Catalogue of regular sale to be held this day, Thursday, Nov. 22, 1866... San Francisco, Cal. S.F., Frank Eastman, print., 1866. 14 p.
CHi

10637. —— Catalogue, special and peremptory sale of champagne wine, red and white wine, vermouth, etc., to be sold Tuesday morning, July 10, 1866...by order of C. W. Rand, U.S. Marshal. Terms—cash in U.S. gold coin. ... S.F., Frank Eastman, print., 1866. 4 p.
CHi

10638. Newhall, Ruth Waldo. The Folger way, coffee pioneering since 1850. S.F., J. A. Folger & co. [1961?] 72 p. illus., ports.
CHi

10639. Newman, Bartell B. vs. San Francisco, et al. ...B. B. Newman plaintiff and appellant, vs. the city and county of San Francisco, et als., defendants and respondents... B. B. Newman, plaintiff in person for appellant. Messrs. Geo. Flournoy, jr., Newlands, Allen & Herrin, Haggin & Dibble, Olney, Chickering & Thomas, and Theodore H. Hittell, attorneys for respondents... S.F., Winterburn & co., print. [1889] 2 v. in 1.
CU-B

10640. [Newman, Bartell B.] San Francisco land titles as affected by Senate bill no. 109. [Wash., D.C.] H. Polkinhorn, print. [1864] 14 p.
CSmH

10641. Newman and Levinson, firm. Catalogue... and price lists... 1885–1905. S.F., 1885–1905. illus. CHi has 1885, 1905. CU-B has 1885–86, 1892–93.

10642. [Newman's Richelieu cafe. Descriptive brochure...] [S.F., E.C. Hughes, 1900?] [35] p. illus., ports.
CHi

10643. —— Same. [1901?] [54] p. illus., ports.
CHi

10644. Newspaper artists league. First annual exhibition, 1903. [S.F., 1903?] [31] p. ports.
CHi

10645. Nichols, Ward M., and Williams, W. Morris. A survey of employment by occupation and industry for San Francisco. S.F., S.F. Unified school district [1949] 191 p. Bibliography: p. 186–188.
CHi CO CSf

10646. Nichols, William Ford, Bp. Days of my age. Chimney corner chats for the home circle. S.F., Priv. print., 1923. 381 p. illus., ports.
CHi

10647. —— A father's story of the earthquake in San Francisco, April 18, 19, 20, 1906. [S.F., Foster & ten Bosch, 1906] 42 p. illus.
C CHi CLU CSmH CU-B

10648. Ning Kue Kung Wul [district association] Constitution and by-laws. S.F., Chung Sai Yat Po, 1929. 24 p. illus. In Chinese.
CHi

10649. Noble, John Wesley. Never plead guilty; the story of Jake Ehrlich [by] John Wesley Noble [and] Bernard Averbuch. N.Y., Farrar, Straus [1955] 306 p.
CMont CSalCL CSd CSf CStmo CU-B

10650. Noe, José de Jesús vs. Card, Stephen. In the Supreme court of the state of California. José de Jesús Noe, et al., appellants, vs. Stephen Card, et al., respondents. Brief for the appellants. Tully R. Wise, attorney. [S.F., 1859] 41 p. San Francisco lot case.
CSmH

10651. —— ...Brief of Hoge & Wilson, of counsel for Stephen Card and other respondents. [n.p., 1859] 93 p.
CLU

10652. Noe ranch association. Articles of association and agreement of the Noe ranch association, with by-laws of the board of directors. Phila., Print. by M.P. Williams, 1856. 30 p.
CHi

10653. Noe's college of osteopathy. Catalogue ... session of 1898–99... [S.F.? 1898?] 20 p.
CU-B

10654. Nolan, Edward D. The preparedness day tragedy, July 22, 1916... Oakland, "The World" [n.d.] 15 p.
CLU CU-B

10655. Norman, Robert T. The planning of an intercity rapid transit system for the San Francisco bay area: some theoretical considerations. [Stanford] 1957. Thesis (M.A.)—Stanford univ., 1957.
CSt

10656. Norris, Frank. The letters of Frank Norris. Ed. by Franklin Walker. S.F., Bk. club of Calif., c1956. 99 p.
CHi CSalCL

10657. Norris, Kathleen (Thompson) Family gathering. [1st ed.] Garden City, N.Y., Doubleday, 1959. 327 p. illus. Memoirs.
CHi CLgA CRcS CSf CSfP

10658. —— My San Francisco. Garden City, N.Y., Doubleday, Doran & co., 1932. 23 p. illus.
C CBu CHi CL CLod CMartC CO CPom CRedCL CSS CSf CSfCP CSfCW CSlu CSmH CStcl CStmo CU-B NN

10659. —— Noon; an autobiographical sketch. N.Y., Doubleday, 1925.
CHi CRcS

10660. North American investment corp. Annual report. 3d–7th, 9th–12th, 15th–17th, 1928–1932, 1934–1937, 1940–1942. S.F., 1928–1942. 11 v.
CHi

10661. North American press association. Standard guide to San Francisco and the Panama-Pacific international exposition... Includes many progressive cities of central California... S.F., c1913. [114] p. illus., ports., maps.
C C-S CHi CO CSfU CSjC CU-B CaBViPA MoS NN

10662. North Beach and Mission railroad co. ... Certificate of abandonment of portions of their routes... 1868. 1 p.
C

10663. Nunan, Thomas. Diary of an old Bohemian ... S.F., Harr Wagner [c1927] 177 p.
CChiS CHi CRic CSluCL CStmo

10664. Nurses' settlement (incorporated) ... San Francisco, California... S.F., C.A. Murdock & co. [1908?] 19 p. illus., front.
CU-B

10665. Oakes, Charlotte. The Vischer family papers: a descriptive catalogue. [Berkeley, 1950] Thesis (M.A.)— Univ. of Calif., 1950. CU

10666. Oakeshott, Gordon B., ed. San Francisco earthquakes of March, 1957. S.F., Calif. div. of mines, 1959. 127 p. illus., maps, plans, facsims., tables. (*Its* special report, 57) CHi CLgA

10667. Oakey, Alexander F. My home is my castle. S.F., Pac. states savings, loan and building co., 1891. 102 p. illus., plans. CHi

10668. [Oakland. Free library. Reference dept.] San Francisco–Oakland bay bridge. Newspaper clippings, 1925–June 1946. [Oakland, 1925–46] 19 v. of mounted clippings. illus., ports., maps. CO

10669. O'Brien (J. J.) & co., San Francisco. [Catalogue of drygoods] 1888, 1889. S.F., Bancroft co. [1888–89] CHi (1888) CU-B (1889)

10670. O'Brien, Mary Louise. Pioneering with Fuller; a hundred years 1849–1949. [S.F., Print. for W.P. Fuller and co., by Grabhorn, 1949] 125 p. col. pl., fold. geneal. tables.
C CHi CLU CSS CSf CStclU

10671. O'Brien, Robert. This is San Francisco. N.Y., Whittlesey house [c1948] 351 p. illus. Taken largely from the author's column "Riptides" in the *San Francisco chronicle.*
Available in many California libraries and IC MiD MoS N NN NjR ODa OU OrU UHi UU ViU

10672. —— Two young men from Bremen [August Schilling and George F. Volkmann] [S.F., Grabhorn] 1947. 12 p. Reprint. from the *San Francisco chronicle*, May 7, 1947. CHi

10673. —— Written in bronze and courage; the story of M. Greenberg's sons. [S.F.?] 1953. 13 l. CU-B

10674. O'Brien co., inc. ...Collections and legal business handled throughout the world... [Pocket ed. of the regular O'Brien co. directory] [S.F.?] 1902. 22 p. CHi

10675. Ocean shore railroad co. Annual report, 1st, 1912. S.F., 1913. CHi

10676. —— [Prospectus] July, 1906. [S.F.? 1906] 8 p. map. CHi

10677. Oceanic steamship co. Articles of incorporation and by-laws. [S.F.? 1906?] [23] p. CU-B

10678. Ockey, William Cecil. San Francisco dry goods wholesaling. [Berkeley, 1931] Thesis (Ph.D.)— Univ. of Calif., 1931. CU

10679. O'Connell, Anna. Assassination of the Constitution in the house of its guardians, "The Daniel O'Connell case." By Mrs. Daniel O'Connell. S.F., Author, 1921. 82 p. pl. CHi

10680. O'Connell, Daniel. The inner man. Good things to eat and drink and where to get them... S.F., Bancroft co., 1891. 160 p. CHi CSf CSmH CU-B

10681. O'Connor, Grover. The story behind St. Francis wood...commemorating the 25th anniversary of the establishment of St. Francis wood. S.F. [St. Francis home assoc.] 1937. 13 p. CHi CU-B

10682. O'Connor, Mary Gabriel, *Sister*. Denis Kearney, sand-lot orator; a chronicle of California. Wash., D.C., 1937. 220 p. Thesis (M.A.)—Catholic univ. of America, 1937. CSrD

10683. O'Connor, Moffatt & co. Through the years to a greater O'Connor-Moffatt & co. [1866–1929] [S.F., 1929] [46] p. illus. CHi CU-B

10684. O'Day, Edward Francis. John Henry Nash, the Aldus of San Francisco. S.F., S.F. bay cities club of print. house craftsmen, 1928. [16] p. port. CHi CStclU

10685. —— Old San Francisco; a series of twenty-six articles on the famous and historic spots of old San Francisco reprinted from the *San Francisco news...* [S.F., 193–?] [28] p. illus.
CHi CLU CO COHN CSf CSfWF-H CSmH CU-B

10686. —— San Francisco, past and present. With a foreword by Harry Leon Wilson. S.F., Adobe press, 1935. 23 p. C CHi CSalCL CSfU CStclU

10687. —— The soul hunter, for the Reverend Richard A. Gleeson, S.J., on the occasion of his sixtieth year as a hunter. S.F., Recorder print. & pub. co., 1937. [3] p. folded. CSfCW CStclU

10688. —— Varied types... S.F., Town talk press, 1915. 329 p. ports. C CLU CSf CSfU

10689. O'Day, Nell. A catalogue of books printed by John Henry Nash, compiled and annotated, including a biographical note. S.F. [John Henry Nash] 1937. 100 p. port. CHi CLgA

10690. Odd fellows' cemetery association. Annual reports of the officers...1880/81. S.F., 1881. 1 v. CU-B

10691. —— By-laws and rules and regulations... 1877, 1879. S.F., 1877–1879. 2 v.
CHi (1877) CU-B (1877, 1879)

10692. —— Cremation presented by the Odd fellows' cemetery association... S.F., Winterburn co., print. [1899] 56 p. illus. CHi

10693. Odd fellows' hall association. ...Annual report...1877/78, 1880/81–1881/82, 1883/84. S.F., 1878–84. 4 v. in 2. CU-B

10694. —— Constitution and by-laws... S.F., F. Eastman, print. 1858. 11 p. CLU

10695. Odd fellows, Independent order of. California. Fifty years of Odd-fellowship in California. Commemorating the founding of the Order by the instituting of the California Lodge no. 1, on Sept. ninth, eighteen hundred and forty-nine. [S.F.] Executive committee Golden jubilee celebration I.O.O.F. of Calif., 1899. 342 p. illus., ports. C CHi CSf CSmH CU-B

10696. —— San Francisco. Convention of delegates...convened, May 24th, 1884. Report of committee of investigation on the management of the trust. Submitted to convention, June 21, 1884. S.F., J. Winterburn, print., 1004. 51 p. CLU

10697. —— —— Cosmopolitan lodge, no. 194. Constitution, by-laws and rules of order...Instituted December 13th, 1871. S.F., J. Winterburn, print., 1872. 84 p. CLU

10698. —— —— Golden Gate lodge no. 204. Constitution, by-laws, order of business and rules of order ... S.F., Benjamin T. Conger, bk. and job print., 1872. 49 p. CHi

10699. —— —— Same. S.F., 1906. [97] p. CHi

10700. —— —— Harmonie lodge, no. 13. Constitution und neben-gesetze...Gegründet den 21sten Juni 1853. S.F., A.J. La Fontaine, 1860. 64 p. CU-B

10701. —— —— Same. S.F., 1873. 75 p. CHi

10702. —— —— Occidental lodge, no. 179.

Constitution, by-laws and rules of order... S.F., Winterburn & co., 1878. 76 p.   CHi

10703. Odd fellows, Independent order of. San Francisco. Occidental lodge, no. 179 (*cont'd*) Same. 1881. 100 p.   CHi

10704. —— —— **Pacific lodge no. 155.** Constitution, by-laws and rules of order...Instituted March 25, 1869. S.F., Winterburn & co., 1869. 91 p.   CHi

10705. —— —— **Templar lodge no. 17.** Constitution and by-laws...Instituted October 22, 1853. S.F., Agnew & Deffebach, 1858. 79 p.   CHi

10706. —— —— Same. S.F., Bacon & co., print., 1868. 126 p.   CLU

10707. —— —— **Wilden encampment no. 23.** Constitution, by-laws and rules of order... S.F., Hilton & Elkins, 1878. 42 p.   CHi

10708. —— —— **Yerba Buena lodge, no. 15.** Constitution, laws and regulations...instituted July 7th, 1853. S.F., Winterburn, print., 1862–1883.
CHi (1862, 1877)   CLU (1883)

10709. —— **Sovereign Grand lodge.** In the Sovereign Grand lodge, I.O.O.F. C. W. Dannals, P. G. R., and eleven others, appellants, vs. the Grand lodge of California, respondent. S. F., Winterburn & co., 1884. 55 p.   CHi

10710. —— —— Souvenir programme... San Francisco, Cal., September 20–25, 1915. S.F., Marshall press [1915] 80 p. illus., ports.   CHi

10711. Odd fellows' library association. Annual report... S.F., 1856– Printer varies.
CHi has 3d, 10th–11th, 13th–15th, 17th–18th, 20th, 23d, 26th–27th, 29th, 1858, 1865–66, 1868–70, 1873, 1875, 1878, 1881–82, 1884. CSmH has 3d, 1858. CU-B has 3d, 1858.

10712. Odd fellows' mutual aid association, San Francisco. ...Annual report...3d, 11th, 1870, 1878. S.F., 1871–79. 2 v.   CU-B

10713. —— By-laws... 1870, 1874, 1879, 1883–1884. S.F., 1870–84. 5 v. in 1.   CU-B

10714. Odd fellows' savings bank. By-laws... 1868–72. S.F., 1868–72.
CHi has 1870 CU-B has 1868, 1870–72.

10715. —— ...Semi-annual report...July 1867–1868, July 1870– June 1871, Jan.–June 1873, July–Dec. 1876. S.F., 1869–77. 5 v. in 1.   CU-B

10716. Odell, Robert S. History of Pacific states savings and loan company, 1932–1945. [S.F., 1945?] 16 p.   CHi

10717. O'Donnell, Charles Carroll. A life record of "Dr." C. C. O'Donnell... [S.F., 1884?] 7 p. Candidate for San Francisco coroner.   CLU

10718. Ohio society of San Francisco. San Francisco greets the President of the United States on the occasion of the launching of the battleship "Ohio". Illustrated souvenir containing the official programme. S.F., 1901. 64 p. illus.   CHi

10719. Ohlandt (N.) & co. [Catalog] fertilizers and fertilizing. S.F., Louis Roesch press [n.d.] 30 p.   CHi

10720. Ohlson, Robert Verner. The history of the San Francisco labor council, 1892–1939. [Berkeley, 1940] Thesis (M.A.)—Univ. of Calif., 1940.   CU

10721. Older, Cora Miranda (Baggerly) "Mrs. Fremont Older." San Francisco, magic city. N.Y., Longmans, 1961. 280 p. illus., ports.
CAla CHi CLSM CSfMI CSfU

10722. —— The story of a reformer's wife; an account of the kidnapping of Fremont Older, the shooting of Francis J. Heney, and the San Francisco dynamite plots... [N.Y., 1909] 17 p. illus., ports.
CSalCL CU-B

10723. —— William Randolph Hearst, American ...with a foreword by Fremont Older. N.Y., Appleton, 1936. 581 p.   CSfCW CSlu

10724. Older, Fremont. Fremont Older's story of the San Francisco bulletin... [S.F., S.F. Call-bulletin, 1929?] [4] p. illus., ports.   CU-B

10725. —— Growing up, by Fremont Older, editor, the San Francisco Call-bulletin; with an introduction by Annie Laurie. S.F., Call-bulletin, 1931. 168 p. illus., port.   CHi CLgA CSf CStclU

10726. —— The life of George Hearst, California pioneer, by Mr. and Mrs. Fremont Older... S.F., Print. for William Randolph Hearst by John Henry Nash, 1933. 238 p. port.   CHi CSfU CSjC

10727. —— My own story... S.F., Call pub. co., 1919. 197 p.
C CHi CL CLU CO CPom CSmH CU-B CV N TxU

10728. —— Same. Oakland, Post enquirer pub. co., 1925. 184 p. ports.   CHi CSfCW CSfU CU-B

10729. —— Same, revised. N.Y., Macmillan, 1926. 340 p.
Available in many California libraries and ODa

10730. —— The romance of San Francisco journalism. [S.F.? 1930?] 16 p. port.   CHi CU-B

10731. O'Leary, Mary of the Nativity, Sister. Hiram W. Johnson and California politics, 1910–1914. Wash., D.C., 1953. 107 p. Thesis (M.A.)—Catholic univ. of Am., 1953.   CSrD

10732. Olin, John Myers. Review of the Mooney case; its relations to the conduct in this country of anarchists, I. W. W. and Bolsheviki. Facts that every true American should know... [Madison, Wis.? 1920?] 104 p.   CL CLSU CO CSfCW CU-B

10733. Oliver, Bartley P. Monster combination auction sale of real estate...Wednesday and Thursday, December 12 and 13, 1900... [S.F., 1900] [8] p. maps.   CU-B

10734. [Oliver, Olive. Scrapbook of clippings about the theater in San Francisco and actors and actresses, kept by Olive Oliver during the period 188–?–1913?] 1 v. (unp.) ports.   CU-B

10735. Olmsted, Vaux and co., New York. Preliminary report in regard to a plan of public pleasure grounds for the city of San Francisco. By Olmsted, Vaux & co., landscape architects. N.Y., W.C. Bryant & co., 1866. [41] p.   CU-B

10736. Olney, James N., comp. [Scrap book of items about the San Francisco vigilance committee of 1856... S.F.? 1856?–57?] 167 p. of mounted clippings. illus., ports.   CU-B

10737. [Olney, Warren] [Hetch Hetchy valley; a letter to the members of the Sierra club] [S.F., 1909] 7 p.   CU-B

10738. —— The water question. Address of Mayor Warren Olney. [S.F.] Pub. by Bay cities water co. [1904?] 16 p.   CSmH

10739. Olney, Warren, jr. Proceedings before the Supreme court of the state of California, in tribute to the memory of Warren Olney, jr. Under the auspices of the bar association of San Francisco, April 4, 1939. [S.F.? 1939] 25 p. port.   CHi

10740. Olson, David Martin. City government and neighborhood organization: a case study of citizen participation and urban renewal [San Francisco] [Berkeley, 1958] Thesis (M.A.)— Univ. of Calif., 1958.   CU

10741. Olympic club of San Francisco. Annals of the Olympic club, San Francisco, 1914. Ed. by Theodore Bonnet under the direction of William F. Humphrey ... [S.F., 1914] 227 p. illus. (part. col.), ports.
C   CHi   CLU   CSf   CSfP   CSmH   CStclU   CU-B

10742. —— By-laws... [S.F., 1879?] 19 p.   CU-B

10743. —— By-laws and list of members...March 1, 1913. [S.F.] 1913. 104 p.   CSfCP   CU-B

10744. —— Constitution and by-laws... S.F., Alta Calif. bk. & job print. house, 1875. 12 p.   CU-B

10745. —— History of the Olympic club. S.F., Art pub. co., 1893. 81, 135 p. illus., ports.
     CLU   CSf   CSfCP   CSfP   CSmH

10746. —— New Olympic club building. S.F., 1930. 15 p.   CHi

10747. —— One hundred years ... centennial [1860–1960] S.F., J.H. Barry co., print., 1960. 160 p. illus., ports.   CHi

10748. O'Meara, James. Broderick and Gwin. The most extraordinary contest for a seat in the Senate of the United States ever known. A brief history of early politics in California... and an unbiased account of the fatal duel between Broderick and Judge Terry, together with the death of Senator Broderick. S.F., Bacon & co., 1881. 254 p.
CBb   CChi   CHi   CLO   CLSM   CP   CSd   CSf CSfCW   CSfWF-H   CSjC   CStbS   CSto   CStoC   OrU

10749. —— The Vigilance committee of 1856. By a pioneer California journalist. S.F., J.H. Barry, 1887. 57 p. Cover dated 1890.
Available in many California libraries and CaBViPA IHi   MiD-B   MoS   MoSHi   NHi   NN   OU

10750. Omnibus cable co. vs. Park and ocean railroad co., et al. In the Superior court of the city and county of San Francisco, state of California. The Omnibus cable company, plaintiff, vs. The Park and ocean railroad company, et al., defendants. Opening argument for plaintiff. Before Hon. E. R. Garber, judge. (February 9, 1892) Lloyd & Wood, attorneys for plaintiff. Wm. F. Herrin, of counsel. [S.F., 1892] 62 p.   CLU

10751. Omnibus railroad co. Articles of the association and by-laws of the Omnibus railroad company of the city and county of San Francisco. Adopted July 31st, 1861. S.F., B.F. Sterett, print., 1861. 15 p.   CU-B

10752. On the shores of the Pacific. Opening of the Panama Canal—1915. [n.p., 1915] [16] p. illus.
     C   CU-B

10753. 100 per cent club, San Francisco. A motion picture of the founding and development of San Francisco... S.F. [1922] [22] p. illus.   CU-B

10754. O'Neill, F. Gordon, comp. Ernest Reuben Lilienthal and his family. Prepared from family histories, documents, and interviews. [Stanford] 1949. 176 p. illus., ports.   CHi

10755. Ophir silver mining co. Annual report... 1875–1877. S.F., 1875–77.   CHi

10756. —— By-laws. S.F., Towne & Bacon, 1860. 13 p.   CU-B

10757. Oppenheim, Ramsey. San Francisco, world city; a market narrative of the capital of the western empire and her sister communities on San Francisco bay ... [S.F., Recorder print. & pub. co.] c1941. 31 p. illus., maps. "Appeared originally in *Western advertising*... July, 1941."   CO

10758. Orden der Hermannssöhne. San Francisco. Ernst van Bandel loge, no. 3. Neben–gesetze ... S.F., Druck von A.J. Lafontaine, 1878. 18 p.   CU-B

10759. —— **Grossloge.** Neuzehnhundertste jahresfeier der schlacht im Teutoburger walde. Gedenkblätter an das fest der deutschen von Californiens, San Francisco 1 und 8. August, 1909... [S.F., Hansen co., 1909] 136 p. illus., ports.   CHi

10760. Oregon railway and navigation co. Rules and regulations for the guidance of officers employed on the ... steamers. [S.F., 1881] 44 p.   CHi

10761. Oregon steamship co. Regulations for the ...steamers. [S.F., 1876] 26 p.   CHi

10762. Organized labor. Fifteenth anniversary and exposition souvenir edition, 1900–1915. [S.F., 1915] 80 p. (v.16, no. 7, Feb. 13, 1915)   CHi

10763. Oriental and Pacific steam navigation co. Memorial of the Oriental and Pacific steam navigation co., for a mail route between San Francisco and China, via the Sandwich islands. S.F., S.F. herald off., 1853.
     C   CSfCW   CSmH   WHi

10764. Orpheum theatre and realty co., New York. Orpheum circuit of theatres. This brochure published upon the occasion of the dedication of the New Orpheum theatre, San Francisco, April 19, 1909. [N.Y.? 1909?] 44 p. illus., ports.   CHi

10765. Orpheum theatre, 10th anniversary souvenir, June 30, 1887–June 30, 1897... [S.F.? 1897] [48] p. illus., ports.   CHi

10766. Osborn & Alexander, firm. The Shipman automatic coal oil steam engines...exclusive agents for the Pacific coast. Also, importers of and dealers in mechanics' tools, hardware and machinery... S.F., B.F. Sterett, print. [1890?] 46 p. illus.   CHi

10767. O'Shaughnessy, Michael Maurice. Hetch Hetchy; its origin and history. S.F., Recorder print. & pub. co., 1934. 133 p. illus.
C   CChiS   CHi   CL   CLO   CLS   CLU   CLgA CMerCL   CO   CRcS   CSf   CSfP   CSfSC   CSfU   CSmH CSrD   CU-B

10768. Osteyee, Leon C., pub. San Francisco before and after April 18, 1906; including the most interesting fire and earthquake scenes. [S.F., 1906] [56] p. illus.   CHi   CLgA   CSmH

10769. [O'Sullivan, William D.] Sermon by the Rev. J. Prendergast, V.G., at St. Mary's cathedral, at the obsequies of William D. O'Sullivan. S.F., 1885. 24 p.   CSfCW

10770. Otis, F. N. History of the Panama railroad, and of the Pacific mail steamship company. N.Y., Harper, 1867. 317 p. illus., maps, tables.   CStrJC

10771. Our Lady of Vladimir (convent) San Francisco. Russian orthodox convent of Our Lady of Vladimir. S.F. [1953?] 11 l. of mounted photos.   CSfCW

10772. Our society directory for San Francisco, Oakland and Alameda. S.F., J. Dewing co., 1888.   CHi

10773. Outside lands in the city and county of San Francisco. [n.p., n.d.] 8 p.   CHi

10774. Overland monthly. Thirtieth anniversary number. S.F., 1898. illus. (Second ser. v.32, no. 187)
CHi

10775. Overland telegraph co. Capital stock, $1,250,000. Officers: [etc.] Office of the company: No. 630 Montgomery street, San Francisco, California. [S.F.] Alta California off., 1861. 8 p.   CLU

10776. Pacific aero club, inc. Souvenir program, annual airship show. 2d, 1910. [S.F., 1910] 1 v. illus., ports.   CU-B

10777. Pacific and Atlantic telegraph line. [By-laws...] S.F., Alta job off., 1860. 8 p.   CSmH CU-B

10778. Pacific and Colorado steam navigation co. The Colorado river in its relation to the commerce of San Francisco. [S.F., D. Bruce, print., 1865?] [3] l.   CU-B

10779. Pacific art co., pub. San Francisco...The distributing point for both hemispheres... S.F., 1904–05. 182 p. illus., ports.
C CHi CLU CO CSf CSfWF-H

10780. Pacific bank, San Francisco. By-laws. S.F., 1866.   CSmH

10781. —— Pacific bank handbook of California, San Francisco, California, U.S.A. S.F., c1888. illus., ports., map.   CLU CStmo

10782. Pacific Bell telephone co. List of subscribers, July, 1888. [S.F., 1888] 139 p.   CHi

10783. Pacific bone coal and fertilizing material co. Circular...addressed to the farmers of the Pacific coast. S.F., G. Spaulding & co., print. [1880?] 16 p.
CU-B

10784. Pacific brass foundry. Pacific products. [S.F.? 1948?] 22 p. illus.   CHi

10785. Pacific bridge co. vs. Kirkham, Ralph W. In the Supreme court of state of California. Pacific bridge company, defendant, vs. R[alph] W. Kirkham, appellant. Appellant's points and authorities. C[harles] T[yler] Botts, attorney for appellant... S.F., Thomas' steam print. house, 1880. 10 p.   CHi

10786. —— ...Appellant's reply to respondent's supplemental brief... S.F., Thomas' steam print. house, 1880. 6 p.   CHi

10787. Pacific business college. Circular. 1884. S.F. [1884] 1 v. illus.   CU-B

10788. Pacific churchman. Centennial issue, February, 1954. S.F., 1954. 58 p. ports. (v.89, no. 2)
CHi

10789. Pacific club. Constitution and officers and members. 1880. S.F. [Alta California print] 1880. 30 p. Title changed in 1882 to Constitution and by-laws. Other editions followed: 1882, 1884, 1886, 1888.
CHi (1880, 1882, 1886, 1888) CSfCP (1884) CSfP (1884, 1886, 1888) CU-B (1882, 1886).

10790. Pacific coast aggregates, inc. Prospectus. 15,000 shares...cumulative preferred stock, convertible series... [n.p.] 1946. 40 p.   CHi

10791. Pacific coast association of fire chiefs. 23d annual convention...September twenty-seven to October first nineteen fifteen. Historical sketch of the fire department of San Francisco, commemorating the Congress of fire chiefs of the Pacific coast. [S.F., 1915] v.p. illus., ports.   CHi

10792. —— 29th convention...August 9–12, 1922 and golden anniversary congress of International association of fire engineers, August 15–18, 1922. 122 p. illus., ports., map.   CHi CO

10793. Pacific coast association of stationary engineers. California association no. 1, San Francisco. Constitution, by-laws and rules of order... organized Nov. 14, 1885. S.F., Brunt & Fisher, 1886. 32 p.
CHi

10794. Pacific coast electrical construction co. Dynamo-electric machines for light and power... S.F. [Bancroft, 188–?] 15 p. illus.   CU-B

10795. Pacific coast liberal Christian conference. Report of the proceedings of the meeting...held at San Francisco, November 1–4, 1885. S.F., 1886. 96 p. CHi

10796. Pacific coast loan association. Eighth annual report...for the year ending September 30, 1898. [S.F.? 1898?] [4] p.   CHi

10797. Pacific coast musical review. Panama-Pacific exposition souvenir and historical edition, Sept. 25, 1915. 82 p. illus., ports.   CHi

10798. Pacific coast stock exchange. Annual report... illus., ports. San Francisco stock exchange and Los Angeles stock exchange consolidated, Jan. 2, 1957.
CHi has 1957–58. CL has 1957–60.

10799. Pacific coast travelers' guide and San Francisco business directory...contains a complete list of the principal business firms of the city... S.F., Guide pub. co., 1869–70. 80 p. maps.
C CLU (July, Sept. 1869) CSmH (1870) CU-B (July 1869)

10800. Pacific commercial museum. The Pacific commercial museum; its history, purposes, officers, by-laws... October, 1900. S.F., Press of Payot, Upham & co. [1900] 32 p.   CU-B

10801. Pacific dispensary for women and children, San Francisco. ... Report... 1875/76–1882. S.F., 1876–83.
CU-B has 1875/76, 4th biennial, 1881–82.

10802. Pacific elastic sponge co. of California. [Catalog] 1868. S.F., 1868. 1 v.   CU-B

10803. Pacific fire rating bureau. ...Preliminary report. San Francisco earthquake of March 22, 1957... [n.p.] 1957. 7 p. illus., map.   CHi

10804. Pacific gas and electric co. Annual report. CHi has 1916–18, 1923, 1925–26, 1929, 1932–33, 1935–date. CL has 1926–50, 1952–60.

10805. —— Pacific gas and electric company and the Panama–Pacific international exposition, 1915. [S.F., 1915] 11 mounted col. pl.   CU-B

10806. —— Pacific gas and electric company; historical and descriptive... [S.F., Technical pub. co., 1910?] illus., ports. Reprint. from the *Jl. of electricity, power and gas.*   CSfCW

10807. —— Properties owned and operated, territory served, finances, history, statistics, California, U.S.A., 1911. [S.F.? 1912?] 268 p.   CHi

10808. —— Prospectus.
CHi has 1945, 1947, 1949, 1951–53.

10809. Pacific gas improvement co. vs. Ellert, L. R. et al. ...Pacific gas improvement co., complainant, vs. L. R. Ellert et al., defendants. Pacific gas improvement co., complainant, vs. James G. Fair et al., defendants... E. S. Pillsbury, John B. Mhoon, Robert Y. Hayne, of counsel for complainant. S.F., J. H. Barry, print. [1894] 2 v. in 1.   CU-B

10810. Pacific greyhound lines. ...50,000 shares, 4% cumulative preferred stock... [n.p.] 1945. 27 p. fold. map.   CHi

10811. Pacific hardware and steel co. [Catalog] General hardware. no. 12, 40. S.F. [19—?– 2 v. CHi has no. 40. CU-B has no. 12, 40.

10812. —— Pacific, where we live, move and have our being. [S.F., Sunset press, 1902?] [56] p. illus. CHi CU-B

10813. —— Stock list, June 1908. S.F. [1908] 1 v. illus. CU-B

10814. Pacific Hebrew orphan asylum and home society. ...Annual report... [187–?–] [S.F., 187–?–] illus. CHi (29th, 1899/1900, 34th, 1904/05) CU-B (35th–36th, 1905/06–1906/07)

10815. Pacific homeopathic dispensary association. Annual meeting. 1st, 1877– S.F., 1877– Organized Dec. 7, 1876. CHi has 2d, Jan. 17, 1878.

10816. Pacific insurance co. Annual statement... [3d] being from 30th June, 1865, to 1st July, 1866. [S.F.] Towne & Bacon, print. [1866] Broadside. CHi

10817. —— Are you insured? Read the within and patronize a home institution. S.F., Towne and Bacon, 1866. 32 p. CHi

10818. Pacific iron works. Catalogue, Dodd's sigmoidal water wheel... ed. 1891. S.F. [1891?] 40 p. illus. CHi

10819. —— Circular and pattern list. 1880. S.F. [1880] 1 v. CU-B

10820. Pacific kennel club. Catalog of the...annual bench show of the Pacific kennel club...2nd, 1889. S.F. [1889] 1 v. illus. CU-B

10821. Pacific laundry journal. National convention number, Pacific laundryman...1920. S.F., 1920. 192 p. illus., ports. CU-B

10822. Pacific lighting corp. Annual report. CHi has 1931–62. CL has 1952, 1954–60.

10823. —— The pipes of Prometheus, 75 years of service. [Incorporated in 1886] S.F., 1962. 16 p. illus. CHi

10824. Pacific loan association vs. Myers, John F., et als. In the Supreme court of the state of California. Pacific loan association, respondent, vs. John F. Myers and Matilda Myers, respondents, state of California, and city and county of San Francisco, appellants. Transcript on appeal [from Superior Court, San Francisco]. Walter M. Willett, attorney for appellants. Naphtaly, Friedenrich & Ackerman, attorneys for respondent, Pacific loan association. Wm. H. Jordan, attorney for respondents, John F. Myers and Matilda Myers. [S.F.] C.A. Murdock & co. [1899] 59 p. CHi

10825. Pacific mail steamship co. The memorial ...to the Senate and Assembly of the state of California. S.F. [Towne & Bacon, print.] 1866. 12 p. Requests a twenty year monopoly of all wharfing and other privileges connected with it of a part of San Francisco bay. Manuscript note on p. 12, "Written by HEH [Henry E. Highton]" CLU

10826. —— Same. 1868. 8 p. Asks for a change in the terms of a lease. CLU

10827. —— A sketch of the new route to China and Japan by the Pacific mail steamship co.'s through line of steamships between New York, Yokohama and Hong Kong, via the isthmus of Panama and San Francisco. S.F., Turnbull & Smith, print., 1867. 104 p. CSfCW

10828. Pacific mill and mine supply co. Me-chanical supplies and everything in belting. Catalogue, [19—?] S.F. [19—?] 1 v. illus. CU-B

10829. Pacific musical society. Biennial report 2d, 1913/15– [S.F.?] 1915. CHi

10830. Pacific novelty co. Miniature view book, Panama-Pacific international exposition. S.F. [1915] [32] p. of col. illus. (Beautiful views of the Jewel city ser.) CU-B

10831. —— Souvenir of San Francisco, California, the "Queen city." S.F., 1914. 30 col. illus. C CU-B NN

10832. —— Same. [1919?] 24 illus. C CO (1920)

10833. —— Souvenir of Uncle Sam's great fleet on the Pacific, May 1908. S.F., c1908. [50] p. illus., ports. CHi

10834. —— Souvenir views of the Panama-Pacific international exposition, San Francisco, California; opened by President Wilson, Feb. 20th, closes Dec. 4th, 1915. S.F. [1915] [36] p. of illus. (part col.) C CHi CRcS CSfU CSmH CStmo

10835. Pacific observatory association. Articles of incorporation, and constitution...San Francisco, California. Incorporated November, 1859. S.F., B.F. Sterett, 1859. 7 p. CU-B CtY

10836. The Pacific pneumatic gas co. Incorporated, 1869. S.F., A.L. Bancroft, 1870. 30 p. illus. CU-B

10837. Pacific Portland cement co. Golden Gate cement will give you perfect satisfaction. There's none better. S.F. [1909?] 60 p. illus., diagrs. CU-B

10838. Pacific public service co. Annual report... [192–?–1945] [n.p., 192–?–45] illus. CHi has 1939–45.

10839. Pacific pump & windmill co. Manufacturers and jobbers cyclone, monarch, tornado and steel star windmills... S.F., Brown & Bley co. [n.d.] 22 p. illus. CHi

10840. Pacific railroad convention. Memorial to the President of the United States, heads of departments, Senate and House of representatives [held in San Francisco, September A.D. 1859] S.F., Alta job off., 1859. 13 p. CHi CLU CU-B

10841. Pacific rolling mill co. Catalogue. [187–?]–1890. S.F. [187–?]–90. illus. (part fold.) CHi has 1885, 1890. CU-B has [187–?–80]

10842. Pacific rowing association, San Francisco. Constitution, by-laws and regatta rules... Organized Feb. 16, 1883. S.F., Bumm & Newhoff, 1884. 18 p. CHi

10843. Pacific rubber paint co. Best paint in the world. S.F. [1878?] 18 p. CU-B

10844. Pacific savings & homestead association. Indenture, by-laws, rules of order and certificate of incorporation... S.F., Towne & Bacon, 1862. CSmH

10845. Pacific saw manufacturing co. ... Price lists of the Pacific saw manufacturing co. and N. W. Spaulding... [S.F., 1876?] 93 p. illus., tables. CU-B

10846. Pacific shipbuilding association of the state of California. Certificate of incorporation and by-laws...December 3d, 1867. S.F., Turnbull & Smith, 1867. 20 p. CHi

10847. Pacific society of printing house craftsmen. The year book issued as a joint project...comprising these Pacific district clubs of the International association of printing house craftsmen. [S.F.] 1928. 136 p. illus. CHi

10848. Pacific states electric co. [Catalogue electrical supplies] no. 16–29. [S.F., 1911–29] illus.
CHi has no. 16–17, 22, 26, 29. CU-B has no. 16, 18.

10849. —— Same. Condensed. 6th–7th ed. N.Y., Howland pub. co., 1919. 480 p. illus.　　　　CHi

10850. —— Catalogue Mazda fixtures and brackets. no. 17–20. [n.p., n.d.] illus.　　　　　　　　CHi

10851. Pacific states savings, loan and building co. [Prospectus] S.F., Crocker [1889?] [8] p.　CHi

10852. Pacific states type foundry. Type, ornaments and brass rules. S.F. [n.d.] 94 p. illus.

10853. —— Type specimens. Illustrated price list and displayed designs. A reference book and catalogue of supplies for printers, etc. S.F. [n.d.] 200 p. illus.　CHi

10854. —— Same, with title: Specimen book and price list...S.F. [n.d.] [274] p.　　　　CHi

10855. Pacific steel and wire co. The Lamb cableway for log yarding and conveying, mining and quarrying, excavating and filling...Frank H. Lamb, patentee... S.F. [n.d.] 26 p. illus.　　　　　　　CHi

10856. —— Wire rope price list. [S.F., 1904] 19 p. illus.　　　　　　　　　　　　　　　CU-B

10857. Pacific stone co. Ransome's patent stone... Grindstones, water and acid filters. S.F. [187–?] 31 p.　CU-B

10858. Pacific tank & pipe co. Pacific wood stave pipe...catalogue number fourteen. S.F. [1921] 128 p. illus.　　　　　　　　　　　　　　　CHi

10859. Pacific telephone and telegraph co. Annual reports.
CHi has 1929–61.

10860. —— Chinatown telephone office, San Francisco. S.F. [1939?] [4] p. illus.　　　　CHi

10861. —— San Francisco and Oakland Chinese telephone directory, June 1945. [S.F., 1945]　CHi

10862. —— Telephone directory for the United Nations conference on international organizations. S.F., 1945. 3 v.
CHi has 1st, 2d, 3d issue, April 25, May 2, 17, 1945.

10863. Pacific typesetting and type foundry co. Specimen book of monotype faces. [S.F., n.d.] 19 p.　　　　　　　　　　　　　　　　CHi

10864. Pacific underwriters and bankers. Diamond jubilee edition. 1925.　　　　　C CU-B

10865. Pacific-union club. ...Constitution and by-laws...list of members...1889– S.F., 1889–
CHi has 1897, 1899, 1901, 1904–05, 1912, 1915, 1917, 1919, 1922, 1926, 1928, 1930, 1932, 1934, 1937, 1940, 1944, 1949. CLSU has 1937. CLU has 1919. CSf has 1944, 1947, 1949. CSfCP has 1901, 1912, 1915. CSfP has 1889, 1891, 1893, 1897–1899, 1901–02, 1904–06, 1912, 1915, 1917, 1919, 1922, 1924, 1926, 1928, 1930, 1932, 1934, 1937, 1940, 1944, 1947, 1949, 1951, 1953, 1955, 1957, 1960. CSfU has 1898. CSmH has 1893, 1898, 1912, 1926, 1928, 1930, 1932, 1934. CU-B has 1889, 1897, 1906, 1912, 1915, 1917, 1919, 1922, 1924, 1926, 1928, 1940.

10866. —— List of members of the Pacific-union club...April 1, 1893. [S.F., 1893?] 11 p.　CHi

10867. —— The Pacific union club, story of its first building. Being the hitherto unpublished report of [James W. Byrne] chairman of the building committee, April, 1906. Reprinted from old galley proofs recently recovered. S.F. [Bruce Brough press] 1928. 29 p. History of the Club building at Post and Stockton streets, completed in 1904, destroyed in the great fire of 1906.
　　　　　　　　　　　　　　　CHi CSfP

10868. Pacific wharf co. By-laws ... incorporated, June 1st, 1855. S.F., O'Meara & Painter, print., 1855. 20 p.　　　　　　　　　　　　CLU CU-B

10869. Pacific yacht club. Constitution, by-laws, sailing regulations, etc. S.F., 1889. 49 p. illus.
　　　　　　　　　　　　CHi CSfCW

10870. Pagano, Reinaldo. History of the Building service employees' international union in San Francisco, 1902–1939. [Berkeley, 1948] Thesis (M.A.)—Univ. of Calif., 1948.　　　　　　　　　CU

10871. [Page, Charles] A memorial to Charles Page [addresses in memory of Mr. Page delivered in the United States circuit court of appeals at San Francisco, on May 23, 1912] [S.F.? 1912] 47 p.　　　　　CHi

10872. Painter & Calvert, pharmaceutists. List of pharmaceutical preparations... S.F., Cubery & co., 1870. 20 p.　　　　　　　　　　　CHi

10873. Palace hotel. [Album of photographs of the Palace hotel, S.F. S.F., n.d.] 24 photos.　　CU-B

10874. —— [Descriptive brochure] S.F. [1921] [36] p. illus., map.　　　　　　　　CHi

10875. —— Facts on the Palace hotel. [n.p., n.d.] 6 p. Mimeo.　　　　　　　　　　CHi

10876. —— The Palace and Grand hotels, now under one management... [S.F., n.d.] 15 pl.　CU-B

10877. —— Palace hotel. S.F., Crocker, 1892. 57 p. illus., plans.　　　　　　　　　　CSf

10878. —— Same. [S.F., 1896] 1 v. pl.　CU-B

10879. —— [Prospectus] [S.F., Alta print., 187–?] [4] p.　　　　　　　　　　　CU-B

10880. —— Same. [1875?] [5] p.　　CU-B

10881. —— Souvenir of the Palace hotel, San Francisco, Cal. S.F., Crocker, 1891. 62 p. illus.　CU-B

10882. Palache, Gilbert vs. Pacific insurance co. In the Supreme court of the state of California. Gilbert Palache, appellant, vs. Pacific insurance company, respondent. Transcript on appeal. Wm. H. Rhodes, attorney for appellant. S. M. Wilson attorney for respondent. S.F., Co-operative print. co., 1871. 12 p.　　　CHi

10883. Palin, G. Herb. What the fairies found. [S.F., 1908] [8] p. illus. "Compliments of Sperry flour company, California."　　　　　　　CU-B

10884. Palmer, Emily Godfrey. A survey of the garment trades in San Francisco. [Berkeley, 1920] Thesis (M.A.)—Univ. of Calif., 1920.　　　CU

10885. Palmer, John Williamson. The new and the old; or, California and India in romantic aspects. N.Y., Rudd & Carleton, 1859. 433 p. illus. The author was a physician in San Francisco, 1849.
　　　　CBb CHi CLO CLSM CSf CSfCW

10886. Palmer, Olive (Holbrook), "Mrs. Silas H. Palmer," comp. Vignettes of early San Francisco homes and gardens...read...Dec. 1935 program of the San Francisco garden club. [S.F., c1935] [33] p.
　C CHi CSf CSfCP CSfCW CSfP CSmH CU-B

10887. Palmer, Phil. The cable cars of San Francisco; photographs by Phil Palmer, text by Mike Palmer. Berkeley, Howell-North, c1959. 64 p. illus.
　C CB CL CO CRb CRic CSd CSfSt CSto CU-B ODa

10888. —— Chinatown, San Francisco; photos, by Phil Palmer. Text by Jim Walls. [Berkeley] Howell-North [1960] 60 p. illus., map.
　　　　CAla CO CRb CSfU CU-B

10889. Palmer & Rey. ...Specimen book, second compact edition. S.F., 1884. [180] p. illus. CHi Other editions followed. CHi (1887, 1889)

10890. —— ...Specimen sheet of new and artistic types. S.F., 1882. 18 p. illus. CHi

10891. —— Specimens of electrotype cuts and ornaments. S.F., 1887. 224 p. illus. CHi

10892. Pan American league international. San Francisco branch. By-laws. [S.F.] 1949. 28 p. CHi

10893. Panama-Pacific international exposition co. The exposition; an elegant illustrated souvenir view book...S.F., R.A. Reid, 1915. [60] p. (chiefly illus.) CHi CRcS CU-B NHi

10894. —— The exposition in colors. S.F., R.A. Reid, 1915. 30 mounted col. pl. CSdS CSfCW

10895. —— Same. 62 mounted col. pl. CHi

10896. —— The great exposition. S.F., R.A. Reid, 1915. 88 p. of illus. (part col.) CU-B

10897. —— The jewel city in natural colours. S.F., R.A. Reid, 1915. 32 mounted col. pl. CHi CLgA CSdS

10898. —— Natural color studies of the Panama-Pacific international exposition. [S.F.] R.A. Reid [1915] 30 col. pl. CHi CLgA CU-B

10899. —— ...Official catalogue of exhibitors, Panama-Pacific international exposition, San Francisco, 1915. [Rev. ed.]... S.F., Wahlgreen co. [1915] v.p. CHi CO CSfCW CSfMI CU-B

10900. —— ...Official guide of the Panama-Pacific international exposition—1915, San Francisco, California ... S.F., Wahlgreen co., c1915. 160 p. illus. CBev CBu CHi CL CLU CO CSfMI CSfU CSfWF-H CStoC CU-B

10901. —— Official miniature view book. S.F., R.A. Reid, c1915. [64] p. (chiefly illus.) CHi CU-B

10902. —— Official souvenir view book... S.F., R. A. Reid, 1915. 40 p. illus. CAla CHi

10903. —— Official view book... S.F., Crocker, c1914. [32] p. of illus., ports. C CHi CSmH CU-B

10904. —— The red book of views of the Panama-Pacific international exposition... S.F, R.A. Reid, 1915. [96] p. of illus. C CHi CL CLU COHN CSmH CStrJC CU-B

10905. —— The splendors of the Panama-Pacific international exposition in hand coloured illustrations. Limited ed. [S.F., R.A. Reid, 1915] 134 p. mounted, col. pl. CHi CSfMI CSfP CU-B UHi

10906. Panoramic view of San Francisco. S.F., A. Rosenfield, 1862. fold. photo. CSmH CU-B

10907. Panoramic views of San Francisco, showing the "Golden Gate city" destroyed by earthquake and fire, April 18, 1906. S.F. & Oakland, S. Bieber [1906] CHi CU-B

10908. Pan-Pacific press association, ltd. History of the Panama-Pacific international exposition...at San Francisco, 1915...S.F. [1916?] 479 p. illus., ports. CHi CSf CU-B

10909. Paper world, pub. History of A. L. Bancroft & co., San Francisco, Cal. Holyoke, Mass., 1881. 6 p. illus. Reprint from *Paper world*, March 1881. CHi

10910. Paraffine paint co. P. & B. preservative paints. S.F. [1893?] 35 p. CHi

10911. —— P. & B. roofing... S.F. [1890?] 14 p. CHi

10912. Paris art co. Catalogue of ornaments and plaster cast reproductions from antique, medieval and modern art; subjects for art schools. [192–?] S.F. [192–?] 1 v. illus. CU-B

10913. Park, Andrew G. The city beautiful; San Francisco, past, present and future. Illustrated with photographs which were taken before, during, and after the earthquake and fire of April 18, '06, with a brief sketch of San Francisco's history and magnificent future. L.A., Houston & Harding, 1906. [52] p. illus. CHi CL CLU CSfCW CSfWF-H CU-B NN

10914. Parke & Lacy co. Hoisting, pumping and crushing machinery for mine prospecting and development...January 1, 1899. S.F. [1898?] 38 p. illus. CHi

10915. Parker, Alice Lee. Charles Fenderich, lithographer of American statesmen; a catalog of his work. Wash., D.C., Lib. of congress, 1959. 64 p. illus. CHi

10916. Parker, Frank. ...Anatomy of the San Francisco cable car... Stanford, Delkin [c1946] 62 p. illus., map. C CBb CHi CL CLU CLgA CMartC CO CSf CSfCP CSfP CSfWF-H CSj CSmat CSmH CStmo CU-B

10917. Parrott & co. A chronological history of the first hundred years, 1855–1955. S.F., 1955. 35 p. illus., ports., facsims. CHi CSf CU-B

10918. Parsons, E. T. A discussion of the Hetch Hetchy question. [S.F., 1910] 15 p. C

10919. Parsons, Edward Lambe. The diocese of California; a quarter century 1915–1940. Austin, Texas, Church hist. soc. [c1958] 165 p. CHi CSf

10920. Parsons, James Jerome. San Francisco. Garden City, N.Y., Doubleday [c1957] 64 p. illus. (part col.) CU-B

10921. Parsons, Brinckerhoff, Hall & MacDonald, New York. Regional rapid transit: a report to the San Francisco bay area rapid transit commission. N.Y. [1956] 106 p. col. maps, diagrs., tables. CHi CL CPa CSfSt

10922. —— [A statistical summary] Projected growth of the bay area, 1950 to 1970... S.F., S.F. bay area council, World trade center [c1957] 40 p. chiefly maps, tables. CSfSt CSfU

10923. Parton, Margaret. Laughter on the hill, a San Francisco interlude... N.Y., London, Whittlesey house, McGraw-Hill bk. co. [1945] 245 p. illus. Available in many California libraries and ODa.

10924. Patent earthquake and fire-proof chimney co. Prospectus... [S.F.? 1869?] 8 p. fold. plan. CU-B

10925. Patrick and co. Catalogue. Sept. 1913– S.F. [1913– illus. CHi ([1930?]) CU-B (1913)

10926. Patriotic pub. co. First to the front, 1st California U.S.V[olunteers]... [S.F., Stanley-Taylor co., print., 1898] [108] p. illus., ports. CHi CSf CSfCW CStclU

10927. Paul, Almarin B. The Americanized arrastra for working gold and silver ores. [S.F., 18—?] [4] p. illus. CU-B

10928. —— Paul's electro-chemical dry amalgamating barrel process. S.F., Spaulding & Barto print., 1872. 41 p. illus. CU-B

10929. Paulist fathers. Paulist fathers centennial year, 1958, for one hundred years, active with voice and with pen to crusade for the church of our land... S.F., Old St. Mary's church, 1958. 49 p. illus. CSf

10930. Payne's bolt works. [Catalog. 19—?] S.F. [19—?] 1 v. illus.   CU-B

10931. Payot, Upham & co. Catalogue of stationery, etc. S.F., 1892– illus.
CHi has 1892. CU-B has 1904.

10932. Payson, Albert Henry. In memoriam: Captain A. H. Payson. By Joseph A. Donohoe. [S.F., J. H. Nash, 1936] [10] p. port.   CHi

10933. The Peck-Judah co., inc. Summer trips, outings. 1911– S.F., 1911–
CHi has 1911, 1916.

10934. Peckham, Ignatius Martin. Alcaldes of San Francisco; a lecture. [n.p., 1956] 12 l.   CSt CU-B

10935. —— José Joaquín Moraga; address delivered by...before the friends of the Public library...June 30, 1953. S.F., 1953. 8 p. Mimeo.   CHi CSt CStclU

10936. —— Notes of vigilante days; a lecture... [S.F., 1939] 10 p.   CHi CU-B

10937. Peerless flash-light photograph co. [Brochure] S.F., Thomas print [1894] [12] p. illus.   CU-B

10938. Peixotto, Sidney Salzado. In memoriam: Sidney S. Peixotto, 1866–1925. [S.F., 1925] 7 p.   CHi

10939. [Pelton, John Cotter] ed. Origin of the free public schools of San Francisco; embracing the report of the committee appointed by the Board of education of the city and county of San Francisco. S.F., Vandall, Carr & co., print., 1865. 122 p.
C CHi CLU CSf CSmH CU-B

10940. Pelton water wheel co., inc. The Pelton water wheel [Catalog] 2d ed., 1889. S.F., Hicks-Judd co. [1889] 30 p.   CHi
Other editions followed. CHi (5th, 6th, 10th, 12th, 1892, 1895, 1919, 1920) CU-B (1890)

10941. Pennell, Joseph. San Francisco, the city of the Golden Gate...being twenty-five reproductions in photogravure from etchings and drawings. Bost., L. Phillips [c1912?] 25 l. xxiv pl.   CP CSmH

10942. —— Same. London & Edinburgh, T.N. Foulis [1913] 25 l. xxiv pl. (Cities ser.: Photogravure ed. II)
C CHi CoU TxU ViU

10943. —— Same. Bost., L. Phillips [1916] (Cities ser.)
CBb CBu CHi CL CLU CLgA CMartC CMerCL CO CRedl CRic CSf CSfWF-H CSmat CU-B

10944. Penny post company. Memorial of the Penny post company of California, praying indemnity for losses sustained in consequence of the unlawful detention of letters at the post office of San Francisco, by direction of the Postmaster-general. Wash., D.C., H. Polkington's steam press, 1856. 47 p.   CHi

10945. Peoples home savings bank. ...Ordinary deposit [book]... S.F. [1890?] [20] p. Contains rules and regulations, list of officers, shareholders, etc.   CHi

10946. Permanent free market committee. The Free public market of the San Francisco water front, its objects and the official history of the movement... S.F.? [1898] 16 p. incl. map.   CHi

10947. Perry, John, jr. and Turner, David S. vs. City and county of San Francisco. ...John Perry, jr., and David S. Turner, trustees of Lone Mountain cemetery, plaintiffs, vs. the city and county of San Francisco, the Board of supervisors of the city and county of San Francisco, P. H. Daly, R. P. Clement, W. B. Fairman... [and others] defendants. Answer of defendants. Horace M. Hastings, John B. Felton, Theodore H. Hittell, of

counsel for defendants. S.F., Wade & co., print., 1867. 18 p.   CU-B

10948. Perry, Manuel vs. United States. ...Manuel Perry, plaintiff in error, vs. United States of America, defendant in error. Brief for plaintiff in error. Edward A. O'Sea...attorney for plaintiff in error. S.F., Pernau-Walsh print. co. [1926] 73 p.   CU-B

10949. Perry, Stella George (Stern) The sculpture and mural decorations of the exposition; a pictorial survey of the art of the Panama-Pacific international exposition... S.F., Elder [c1915] 202 p. illus.
Available in many libraries.

10950. —— The sculpture and murals of the Panama-Pacific international exposition. The official handbook, giving the symbolism, meaning and location of all the works... S.F., The Wahlgreen co., c1915. 104 p. illus.   CHi CU-B

10951. Peters Wright school of dancing. A brief history... [S.F.? 194–?] 2 l. Mimeo.   CHi

10952. Petersen, Walter B. Braun-Knecht-Heimann co. and the chemical industry of California. Founded 1852. S.F., 1958. 35 l.   CU-B

10953. Pettijohn, Lucy. Development of the San Francisco water front. [Berkeley, 1927] Thesis (M.A.)— Univ. of Calif., 1927.   CU

10954. Petty, Claude Rowland. Gold rush intellectual: the California of John S. Hittell. [Berkeley, 1952] Thesis (Ph.D.)—Univ. of Calif., 1952.   CU

10955. Pfister, A. et al vs. Wade, Harry et al. In the Supreme court of the state of California. A. Pfister, et als, plaintiffs and respondents, vs. Harry Wade, et al, defendants, George D. Bliss, defendant and appellant. Points and authorities of appellant. M. Lynch, attorney for appellant... S.F., Francis, Valentine & co., 1881. 8 p.   CHi

10956. Pfister (J. J.) knitting co. Catalogue, knitted bathing suits... [1st– 188–?– S.F. [188–?]–1892. illus.
CHi has 4th, c1892. CU-B has 3d, 1888.

10957. —— Catalogue, no. 24, baseball and tennis goods. S.F., 1906. 1 no. illus.   CU-B

10958. [Phelan, James] In memoriam. Read at a meeting of the Society of California pioneers, San Francisco, April 3, 1893. [S.F., 1893] [15] p. illus., ports.
CHi CLU

10959. Phelan, James Duval. In memoriam. Meeting of the Board of supervisors of the city and county of San Francisco. Monday, August 11th, 1930, at 2 o'clock, p.m. [S.F., 1930] 17 p. mounted port.   CLgA

10960. Phelan building; an entirely new modern class "A" office building and a San Francisco landmark. [S.F., F.J. Cooper advertising agency, 1908?] [16] p.
CHi

10961. Phelps, Alonzo vs. Cogswell, Henry D. ... Alonzo Phelps, respondent, vs. Henry D. Cogswell, appellant...Henry E. Highton, attorney for appellant. Fox & Kellogg, attorneys for respondent... [S.F.] The C. White print. co. [1885] 2 v. in 1.   CU-B

10962. Phelps, Edwin vs. McGloan, James et al. ...Edwin Phelps (Charlotte A. Phelps, by substitution) plaintiff and appellant, vs. James McGloan et al., defendants and respondents...E. J. & J. H. Moore, attorneys for appellant. John B. Felton and Theodore H. Hittell, attorneys for respondents. S.F., E. Bosqui and co., print., 1870. 5 v. in 1.   CU-B

10963. —— ...Transcript on appeal... S.F., E. Bosqui and co., print., 1870. 79 p.   CHi

10964. Phelps' manufacturing co. Price list; machine and lag bolts, bolt ends, nuts and washers... S.F. [n.d.]   C-S

10965. Philadelphia and California mining co. Articles of association. Together with the by-laws, lease, map, &c. Phila., John C. Clark, print., 1852. 20 p. fold. chart.   CHi

10966. Philbrook, Horace Wiley. Appeal to the people. [S.F., 1898] 12 p. Caption title. Pamphlet in support of the author's candidacy for the office of judge of the Superior court of San Francisco.   CLU

10967. —— The corrupt judges of the Supreme court of the state of California. Memorial to the legislature of the state of California to remove from office W. H. Beatty, T. B. McFarland, W. C. Van Fleet, Ralph C. Harrison, C. H. Garoutte, Jackson Temple, F. W. Henshaw, justices of the Supreme court. For corrupt misconduct in office... S.F., 1897. 207 [35] p.   CHi

10968. The Philippine expedition 1898 and Camp Merritt, San Francisco. S.F., Pac. mutual life insurance co., 1898.   CStclU

10969. Phillips, Catherine (Coffin) Cornelius Cole; California pioneer and United States Senator... S.F., John Henry Nash, 1929. 379 p. illus., ports., facsims.
CAna CBb CChiS CHi COnC CP CSd CSfP
CSto CStoC CWhC CYcCL CStbS OrU TxU

10970. —— Portsmouth plaza, the cradle of San Francisco... S.F., Print. by J.H. Nash, 1932. 464 p. illus., ports., map. Bibliography: p. 439–446.
Available in many California libraries and IHi KHi
MoS NHi TxU ViW

10971. —— Through the Golden Gate: San Francisco, 1769–1937...L.A., Suttonhouse [c1938] 219 p. illus., port.
Available in many California libraries and CaBViPA
InI KU MiD MoS NHi NN ODa ViU

10972. Phleger, Herman. Pacific coast longshoremen's strike of 1934. Arbitration...argument...in behalf of waterfront employers... [S.F., Waterfront employers' union of S.F., 1934?] 71 p.   C CLU CO CU-B

10973. Phoenix photo co. Scenes of the San Francisco fire and earthquake, April 18, 1906. Series 1–4. [S.F., c1906]
C CHi CLgA CSmH (series 1–3) CU-B (series 4)

10974. The Photographers' association of California. Souvenir program second annual convention. S.F., Sunset press, 1904. 30 p. illus.   CHi

10975. Photographs of the relief camps for refugees from the San Francisco fire, 1906. 25 mounted photos.
CU-B

10976. Pickett, Charles Edward. Gwinism in California. [S.F., 1860] 8 p.   C CLU CSmH

10977. —— Land-gambling versus mining-gambling; an open letter to Squire P. Dewey, relative to his participation in land-gambling of San Francisco in early days, from one who knows. 2d ed., with additions. S.F., 1879. 24 p. Introductory note signed: C. E. Pickett.
C CHi CLU

10978. —— Repudiation, Supreme judges, and the newspapers. [S.F., 1857] 8 p.   CU-B NN

10979. Pictorial booklet of the ruined Catholic churches, San Francisco, April 18, 1906. [S.F., R.H. Corson & co., 1906?] fold. pl. containing 15 views and text. Cover title.   CLgA

10980. Pictorial photographic society of San Francisco. Third annual international exhibition...October 31 to December 7, 1924. [S.F., Taylor & Taylor, 1924] 17 p.   CHi

10981. A picture tour of San Francisco... S.F., Sunset press, 1929. 45 pl.   CHi CSd CSf

10982. Pierce (C. C.) and co., Los Angeles. The camera story of the San Francisco fire, Wednesday, April 18, 1906. [L.A., 1906?] [30] p. of illus.   CU-B

10983. Pike (A. W.) & co. Locksmiths' supplies... [S.F., Rosemont press, n.d.] 94 p. illus.   CHi

10984. A "Pile," or, a glance at the wealth of the monied men of San Francisco and Sacramento city. Also, an accurate list of the lawyers, their former places of residence, and date of their arrival in San Francisco. S.F., Cooke & LeCount, booksellers, 1851. 14 l.   CSmH
Photo copies held by: C CSf CSfCP CU-B

10985. Pillsbury, Arthur J. Republican policy and Pacific coast prosperity; being an impartial consideration of the "Sordid plea that it will pay" to acquire and Americanize the Philippine islands; what the Republican policy of territorial, commercial and industrial expansion has meant, and will mean to the city of San Francisco and its people. S.F. [1900?] [8] p. Prepared by direction of Republican state committee.   CHi

10986. Pillsbury, Madison & Sutro. The de Laveaga case. [S.F., 1913] 104 p.   CHi

10987. Pillsbury picture co., inc. San Francisco then and now... S.F., 1909. 14 p. of photos. CHi CSf

10988. Pim, Bedford. The gate of the Pacific. London, Lovell, Reeve & co., 1863. 432 p. illus., maps. CHi

10989. Pinney, Laura Young. A souvenir of San Francisco bay, within the Golden Gate. S.F., S.F. print co., 1893. 18 p. incl. illus.   CHi CSfCW

10990. Pioneer kindergarten society of San Francisco. Annual report...1887/88, 1894. S.F., C.A. Murdock & co., print., 1889–95. 2 v. in 1.   CU-B

10991. Pioneer rowing club. Constitution and by-laws. [S.F., 1891] 14 p.   CHi

10992. Pioneer white lead works. [Catalog] [187–?] S.F. [187–?] 1 v. illus.   CU-B

10993. Piper, Richard Upton. An examination of the "Marriage contract," and the "Dear wife letters," and other documents connected with the Sharon-Hill case in California. [S.F., Bosqui print. co., 1885] 130 p. illus., facsims.   CHi CSfCW

10994. Piper, Aden, Goodall co. To Mare island on the steamer *H. J. Corcoran.* [S.F., Sunset press, n.d.] [16] p. illus., map.   CHi

10995. Pitcher (E. C.) & co. [Catalog of...woodwork] [S.F., Edw. S. Knowles, print., 1904] 210 p. illus.
CHi

10996. Pixley, Frank Morrison. Speech of Hon. F. M. Pixley, at the ratification meeting held at Platt's hall, Tuesday evening, September 13th, 1864... [S.F., 1864] 8 p.   CHi CLU CSfCW

10997. Plan of Yerba Buena showing the location of town lots granted by Governor Alvarado to Jacob P. Leese and Salvador Vallejo May 21, 1839. Issued in facsimile by Thos. W. Norris as a memento of Christmas 1946. [S.F.] Grabhorn press [1946] [4] p. map, plan.
CHi CRcS

10998. Plant, Thomas G. The Pacific coast longshoremen's strike of 1934... [S.F., Waterfront employers' union of S.F., 1934] 43 p.   CLU CO CSf

10999. Plant rubber and asbestos works. General catalog. S.F. [19—?–] illus.
CHi has no. 6-A, no. 7, sec. 3, no. 9 (1931)

11000. Plate (A. J.) and co. Illustrated catalogue of revolvers. [187–?] S.F. [187–?] 1 v. illus.   CU-B

11001. Platt, Horace Garvin. Address against the municipal ownership of the Geary street railroad...at banquet of the Merchants' association, Palace hotel, November 12, 1902. [S.F.] Pernau press [1902?] 16 p.
CLU CU-B

11002. —— A short talk given by Horace G. Platt at a banquet given to Chauncey M. Depew by the Union league club, of San Francisco, April 4, 1896. [S.F.? 1896] [4] p.   CHi

11003. Playa Vicente rubber plantation and development co. Report to holders of acreage contracts ...by Harr Wagner. [S.F., 1905?] [16] p. illus.   CHi

11004. Plehn, Carl Copping. The San Francisco clearing house certificates of 1907–08... Berkeley, Univ. of Calif., 1909. 14 p. (*Pub. of the Acad. of Pac. coast history*, v.1, no. 1)
C CHi CRedl CSdS CSfP CSfWF-H CSj CSmH CU CU-B CViCL

11005. Ploeger, Louise Margaret. Trade unionism among women of San Francisco. [Berkeley, 1920] Thesis (M.A.)—Univ. of Calif., 1920.   CU

11006. [Plummer, John W.] The world's two greatest bridges. [S.F., Personal stationery co., c1936] 32 p. illus.   CHi CRcS CU-B

11007. Plummer (W. A.) manufacturing co. Catalog. no. 9-B. S.F. [191–?] illus.   CU-B

11008. Plunkett, William A. Our Supreme court. A remarkable opinion. [S.F., 1882] 8 p. Reprint. from *Daily evening bul.*, August 9, 1882. Review of opinion delivered by Chief Justice Morrison in case of Spring valley water works vs. Board of supervisors of San Francisco.
CHi

11009. Podesta Baldocchi, firm. Flowers are for everyone. [n.p., 1960] 9 p. illus.   CHi

11010. Point Lobos avenue homestead association. History of the title of...to a tract of land in the city and county of San Francisco... S.F., Waters, Newhoff & co., 1871. 8 p.   CHi

11011. Polack, Joel Samuel. In the matter of Yerba Buena island [bay of San Francisco, Cal.] Memorial of J. S. Polack...to the Senate and House of representatives of the United States of America... S.F., Francis & Valentine, 1870. 7 p.   N

11012. —— Yerba Buena, or Goat island; title by Mexican prescription. [S.F.? 18—?] 49 p.   CU-B

11013. [Polk, Willis] To remember Willis Polk, architect... S.F. [Printed for Spring valley water co. by John Henry Nash] 1926. [5] p. illus. No. 15 of 35 numbered copies.   CHi

11014. Pollack, Arnold, comp. and pub. Souvenir of the Tivoli opera house, Christmas 1894. S.F., J.E. Hoyle & co., print., 1894. [22] p. ports.   CHi

11015. Pollak, Victor F. 110 years of San Francisco; my memories. [S.F.] Pollak print., 1939. [19] p. illus., ports.   CSf CU-B

11016. —— Same. [1955?] 24 p.   C CL CO

11017. Pollock, Albin Jay. The underworld speaks; an insight to vice... S.F., Prevent crime bur. [c1935] [288] p. port.   CL CO CU-B

11018. Pomeroy, John Norton. The Hastings law department of the University of California. Inaugural address...August 8, 1878. S.F., A.L. Bancroft & co., 1878. 20 p.   CU-B

11019. Poodle dog restaurant. [Descriptive brochure] [S.F., Louis Roesch co., print., 1889?] 30 p. illus.
CSfP

11020. Pope, John F. Quarter centennial history of the First Baptist church, San Francisco, 1849 to 1874. S.F., John H. Carmany & co., 1874. 12 p.   CHi CSmH

11021. Popper, Max vs. Broderick, William. In the Supreme court of the state of California. Max Popper, plaintiff and appellant, vs. Wm. Broderick, defendant and respondent. Appellant's closing brief. Frank H. Gould and Wm. M. Cannon, attorneys for appellant. Filed... 1898...[S.F.] E.C. Hughes, print. [1898?] 20 p.   CHi

11022. Post, Louis F. The prophet of San Francisco; personal memories and reminiscences of Henry George. N.Y., Vanguard, 1930. 335 p.
C CBev CHi CL CLSU CLU CO CRcS CSf CSfCW CStmo CU-B CViCL

11023. Potrero and Bay view railroad co. By-laws ...Incorporated April 4th, 1866... S.F., F. Eastman, print., 1866. 18 p.   CLU

11024. Potter, C., comp. The mining directory: containing the names of mining companies and secretaries, in San Francisco: their locations and places of business... S.F., Dewey & co., pub. & print., 1864. 57 p.
CLU CSmH CU-B

11025. Potter, Elizabeth (Gray) Early Mexican ranchos in the San Francisco bay region... S.F., 1951. 37 p. illus., ports.   C CHi CL CSjC CU-B

11026. —— The San Francisco skyline... N.Y., Dodd, 1939. 284 p. illus., maps.
Available in many California libraries and NN ODa

11027. —— San Francisco under Spain and Mexico. [Berkeley] 1926. 199 l. Thesis (M.A.)—Univ. of Calif., 1926.   CU

11028. —— and Gray, Mabel Thayer. The lure of San Francisco; a romance amid old landmarks... S.F., Elder [1915] 96 p. illus.
Available in many California libraries and MiD MoS NN

11029. Potter, Roy Wilson. A case study of land use in San Francisco. [Berkeley, 1954] Thesis (M.A.)— Univ. of Calif., 1954.   CU

11030. Powell, Lawrence Clark. Philosopher Pickett, the life and writings of Charles Edward Pickett...including also unpublished letters written by him from Yerba Buena at the time of the conquest of California by the United States in 1846–47. Berkeley, Univ. of Calif. press, 1942. 178 p. front., facsims. Bibliography: p. 163–69.
Available in many California libraries and N TxU ViW

11031. Powell, Lyman Pierson, ed. Historic towns of the western states. N.Y. & London, Putnam, 1901. 702 p. illus., ports. (Am. historic towns) Contains: San Francisco, by Edwin Markham; Monterey, by Harold Bolce; and Los Angeles, by Florence C. Winslow.
C CBu CL CLSU CRedl CSf CSfP CSmH CStmo CU-B CViCL

11032. Powers, Carroll Morris. Methods of labor adjustment in the San Francisco bay region. [Berkeley, 1921] Thesis (M.A.)—Univ. of Calif., 1921.   CU

11033. Praslow, J. Der statt Californien in medicinisch-geographischer hinsicht. Göttingen, Vandenhoeck und Ruprecht, 1857. 66 p.
C CHi CL CLU CSfP CSmH CU-B

11034. —— Same, translated into English by Frederick C. Cordes. S.F., Ward Ritchie, 1939. 86 p. "Dr. Praslow practiced medicine in San Francisco from 1849 to 1856..."—Cowan.

C CBb CHi CL CLM CLSU CLU CO CSdU CSf CSmH CStmo CStrJC CU-B

11035. Presbyterian church in the U.S.A. Mission to the Chinese in California. Report... S.F., G. Spaulding & co., print., 1881. 16 p. CHi CU-B

11036. Prescott, Scott & co. [Catalogs] Builders of steam, air and hydraulic machinery... S.F., [1878—10 catalogs, titles vary. CHi

11037. Presentation order. Sacred Heart convent. Souvenir of the silver jubilee of the Sacred Heart presentation convent, San Francisco, California, 1869–1894. S.F., McCormick bros., 1894. 69 p. illus., ports. CHi CSfCW

11038. Presidio of San Francisco, 1776–1960; guide book and directory. [S.F., 1960] [40] p. illus., map. CHi

11039. Press club of San Francisco. Constitution ... S.F., J.K. Knarston, bk. & job print., 1888. 19 p. CSf CU-B

11040. —— Same. [S.F., Walter N. Brunt press, 1900?] 48 p. illus. CHi

11041. —— Four years after, Garrick theater, April 17, 1910. [S.F., 1910] [64] p. illus., ports. CHi CLU

11042. —— Scoop, victory edition, November 3, 1945. S.F., 1945. 188 p. illus., ports. CHi CRcS

11043. Price, J., comp. The buyers' manual and business guide; being a description of the leading business houses, manufactories, inventions, etc. of the Pacific coast... S.F., Francis & Valentine, steam bk. & job print. establishment, 1872. 192 p. illus. C CHi CL CLSU CLU CO CSf CSfP CSfWF-H CSmH CU-B

11044. Price, Rodman McCamley. Judicial proceedings against Rodman M. Price of New Jersey, on the charge of perjury. [n.p., 1880?] [8] p. Reprint. from the *Alta California*, June 15th and 20th, 1880. CHi

11045. —— [A series of legal actions between Rodman M. Price and Squire P. Dewey, Theodore Payne, Erasmus D. Keyes and Edmond Scott] N.Y., 1858– 6 v. plan, fold. table. The suits involve San Francisco real estate. CLU

11046. Price hay press co. Catalogue of baling presses, seed sowers and other agricultural implements... S.F., Baker and Hamilton, 1876–[1886?] illus. C-S has 1876. CU-B has [1886]

11047. Prieto, Guillermo. ...San Francisco in the seventies; the city as viewed by a Mexican political exile, translated and edited by Edwin S. Morby. S.F., Print. by J.H. Nash, 1938. 90 p. illus., port. Tr. of selections from the author's *Viaje a los Estados Unidos*, 1877–1878. cf. Introd.
Available in many California libraries and CaBViPA OrU TxU

11048. Prince and co. Catalogue of improved patent prize medal organs and melodeons. [1871] S.F., [1871] 1 v. illus. CU-B

11049. Principal productions corp., inc., Hollywood. Fisherman's wharf (production no. 334) Oct. 25, 1938. Final shooting script... Hollywood, 1938. Mimeo. CSf

11050. Proceedings on the occasion of the presentation of the gold medal to the city of San Francisco by the Republic of France at the hands of her ambassador his excellency Jean Jules Jusserand. S.F. [Stanley-Taylor co.] 1909. [13] p. Includes addresses by Jean Jules Jusserand and Mayor Edward R. Taylor. C CHi CLU CSmH

11051. Progressive novelty co., Oakland. The "Old Frisco" souvenir book. The saddest story ever told in pictures... San Jose, Melvin, Hillis & Black press [1906] [18] p. illus. CHi CStmo

11052. Protestant Episcopal church in the U.S.A. Domestic and foreign missionary society. The church in San Francisco; how it suffered from fire; what can be done to rebuild it. [n.p., n.d.] 15 p. illus. C

11053. —— General convention, 1901. California souvenir. The house of Bishops. General convention, San Francisco, October 1901. S.F., Pacific churchman, 1901. 63 p. illus. CHi

11054. —— —— For the use of the house of Bishops, delegates and deputies...San Francisco, Cal. October 1901. [S.F.? 1901] [12] p. CU-B

11055. Prudential insurance co. of America, Newark, N.J. San Francisco cancer survey... 1st–9th. Newark, N.J., 1924–1954. 9 v. ViU

11056. Public kindergarten society of San Francisco. Report...for the three years ending Sept. 1st, 1881. Containing a record of the Silver street school, the first free kindergarten west of the Rocky mountains. A history of the subsequent movement arising therefrom, throughout the city and state, and a plea for the better protection and education of our children. Organized, July 23, 1878. Kindergarten established Sept. 1, 1878. [S.F., C.A. Murdock print., 1881–1882] 2 v. CU-B

11057. Purcell, Charles Henry. Purcell pontifex, a tribute. S.F., Priv. printed by his friends, 1937. 79 p. illus., port. CHi CLU CSfU CSmat CU-B

11058. Purdy, Helen Throop. Portsmouth square. S.F., Calif. hist. soc., 1924. 16 p. C CHi CSf CSfU CSmat

11059. —— San Francisco as it was, as it is, and how to see it... S.F., Elder [c1912] 221 p. illus., map. Available in many California libraries and MiD MoS N NN NjR ODa UPB

11060. Purkitt, J. H. A letter on the water front improvement addressed to the Hon. James Van Ness, Mayor of San Francisco... S.F., Whitton, Towne & co., print., Excelsior job off., 1856. 32 p. C CLU CSfCW CSmH CU-B NvHi

11061. Quirot & co., pub. San Francisco, Upper California, in November, 1851. S.F., 1851. folded view. CSf

11062. Radin, Paul. ...The Italians of San Francisco, their adjustment and acculturation. Abstract from the SERA project 2-F2-98 (3-F2-145): [cultural anthropology project] Monograph no. 1. [S.F.] 1935. 2 pts. in 1 v. mimeo. No more published. C CChiS CHi CL CLSU CLU CO CRic CSd CSdS CSf CSfP CSmH CStclU CU-B NN

11063. Railroad terminus in San Francisco. [S.F., 187–?] [7] p. Caption title. CLU

11064. Rambai association of the Pacific coast. [Constitution] S.F. [1888?] 8 p. CHi

11065. Rand, McNally & co., pub. Rand McNally guide to San Francisco, Oakland, Berkeley, and environs of the bay cities... N.Y., S.F. [etc., c1925] 220 p. illus., maps. CHi CLSU CO CSdS CSf CU-B CViCL NN

11066. —— Same. Ed. of 1927. N.Y., S.F. [etc.] 1927. 189 p. illus., maps. CO CRcS CSdS CSmH NN

11067. —— San Francisco, Oakland and other bay cities; a visitor's guide. Chicago, N.Y., [1923] 85 [11] p. illus., map. "Prepared and printed by Rand McNally & company for the members of the N.E.A., 1923." "Round about the state": p. 57–82.
Available in many California libraries and CoU ViU

11068. Randall, Mary, comp. [Scrapbook of theater, concert and other programs, chiefly of San Francisco and Oakland, 1890–1903. "Collected by Mary Randall and Marion Randall Parsons."] 1 v. illus., ports.   CU-B

11069. Rankin, Ira P. vs. Newman, William J. et al. In the Supreme court of the state of California. Ira P. Rankin, special administrator of the estate of John Levinson, deceased, plaintiff and appellant, vs. Wm. J. Newman and Benjamin Newman, defendants and respondents. Argument of Horace W. Philbrook, attorney for the appellant. S.F., James H. Barry, print. [1894] 441 p.
CHi

11070. Ransome, Ernest Leslie. Ransome's patent concrete apparatus for moulding walls, patented March 24, 1885. No. 314398... [S.F., 1885?] 6 p.   CHi CU-B

11071. Raphael, Joseph. An exhibition of discovery, Joseph Raphael, 1872–1950 [held at the California historical society January 12 to February 6, 1960) [S.F.] Lawton Kennedy, print. [1960] 3 p.   CHi

11072. Rastall, B. M. San Francisco bay bridge studies and rapid transit problems. A report to the San Francisco chamber of commerce. [S.F., Phillips & Van Orden co., 193–?] 29 p. maps, charts.   CHi CU

11073. Rathbone, King & Seeley, firm. The RK&S story, 1849 and onward. [S.F., Schwabacher Frey, print., 195–?] 16 p. illus., ports.   CHi CU-B

11074. Ray, Milton S. The Farallones, The painted world, and other poems of California; with fifty-three illustrations and with a supplementary history and description of the Farallones, including notes on their plant, bird, and animal life... S.F., John Henry Nash, 1934. 2 v. "History and description ...": v.1, p. [49]–86. Plates with descriptive comment: v.2.
Available in many libraries.

11075. Raymond & Ely mining co. Annual report...1871/72– S.F., 1872–
CHi has 2d–5th, 1872/73–1875/76.

11076. Raynolds (C. T.) and co. Paints and oils, varnishes, artists' and decorators' materials, coach colors, brushes. Discount list, 1879. S.F. [1879] 1 v.   CU-B

11077. Read, Jay Marion. California's first medical historian, Victor Jean Fourgeaud, A.B., M.D. Reprint. from *Calif. and western medicine*, Feb., March 1931.
CHi

11078. —— A history of the California Academy of medicine, 1870 to 1930. S.F., Print. by Grabhorn for the Calif. acad. of medicine, 1930. 186 p. illus., ports., fold. facsim.   CBb CHi CLM CSf CStclU CU-B

11079. —— History of the San Francisco medical society. S.F., The Society, 1958– illus., ports. Contents.— v.1, 1850–1900.   CHi CLM

11080. Ready, Herbert V. ...The labor problem. [S.F.] Author, c1904. 96 p. illus. At head of title: "Let justice prevail".   CLU

11081. The Real estate associates. Constitution, by-laws and certificate of incorporation... S.F., Cubery and co., 1868. 30 p.   CHi

11082. Real estate research corp., Chicago. Summary of market analysis redevelopment area "E", San Francisco, Calif. ...[S.F.] 1956. 24 p.   CSt

11083. Realty directory co., comp. Realty directory of San Francisco, containing the names of the assessed owners of real estate...March 2, 1896 revised to Sept. 1, 1896. S.F., 1896.   CHi

11084. Reardon, P. H. Pacific coast price list. Sept. 1, 1920. S.F. [1920] 1 v. illus.   CU-B

11085. Reardon & Krebs. Typographers type book. S.F., c1955. 282 p. loose-leaf.   CHi

11086. Record, Jane Cassels. Ideologies and trade union leadership: the case of Harry Bridges and Harry Lundeberg. [Berkeley, 1954] Thesis (Ph.D.)— Univ. of Calif., 1954.   CU

11087. Recorder printing and publishing co. Bay counties legal directory, 1913–1914... S.F. [1913?] 162 p.   CHi

11088. Red cross. U.S. American national Red cross. California branch. Directory; organization of relief work in San Francisco, July 1, 1906. [S.F.? 1906?] 24 p.   C CHi

11089. —— —— **San Francisco chapter.** 50 years young! [S.F., 1948] [24] p. of illus.   CU-B

11090. —— —— —— History of the war activities of the San Francisco chapter... and a brief outline of its organization. [S.F.? 1919?] 33 p.   CU-B

11091. —— —— —— Telling the story... March, 1917. [n.p., n.d.] 46 p.   CHi

11092. —— —— —— The tenth birthday of new San Francisco, April 18th 1916. [n.p., n.d.] [16] p.   CHi

11093. Red men, Improved order of. California. Great council. Long talks of the chiefs of the great sun session. 16th, 18th, 1881–1882. [n.p.] 1881–82. 2 v. in 1.
CU-B

11094. —— —— —— Proceedings of the great council of California, from its organization to Cold Moon, G.S.D. 379. S.F., Clarke, 1869. 296 p.   CHi

11095. —— —— —— Proceedings of the great sun session... 9th–16th, 18th, 1874–1881, 1883. S.F., 1874–83. 9 v. in 6. illus., tables.   CU-B

11096. —— —— —— Reports of great chiefs of the general council of California... Thirteenth great sun session...July 8, 1878. [n.p., 1878] 19 p.   CHi

11097. —— —— —— Verhandlungen des grossstammes von Californien des unabhängigen ordens der Rothmänner. 1871–1872. S.F. [1871?–72] 2 v.   CU-B

11098. Red men's mutual aid association of San Francisco. Constitution des U.O.R.M. gegenseitige unterstützungs-gesellschaft zu San Francisco. [S.F.] U.J. Lafontaine [1869?] 18 p.   CU-B

11099. Redding, Benjamin B. ...In memoriam. Benjamin B. Redding, born January 17th, 1824, died August 21st, 1882... [S.F., Calif. acad. of sciences, 1882?] 18 p.   CLU

11100. Redington & co. Importers and wholesale druggists, and dealers in proprietary articles and druggists' sundries... S.F., J. Winterburn & co., 1891. 345 p. illus.   CHi

11101. —— Physicians' handbook. [188–?, 1883?] S.F. [1883?] 2 v. illus.   CU-B

11102. —— Revised glass prices current. [187–?] S.F. [187–?] 1 v.   CU-B

11103. —— Revised price list of pharmaceutical preparations. [188–?] S.F. [188–?] 1 v.   CU-B

11104. Redington, Hostetter and co. Precio corriente general de los principales efectos que se encuentran de venta en el almacen de drogas y medicinas, productos quimicos, etc. [187–?] S.F. [187–?] 1 v.　　CU-B

11105. Redwood association. Redwood in the San Francisco fire. [S.F., 1906] 3 l. 11 pl.　　CU-B

11106. Redwood manufacturers co. Catalogue. no. 2, 7, 10, 12, 23. S.F. [1905]–15. illus., tables.　　CU-B

11107. Reed, Charles Wesley. The comparative low standing of the public schools of San Francisco and their improvement. Delivered before the Commonwealth luncheon, Sept. 16, 1911. [S.F., 1911] 16 p.　　C CHi

11108. —— The law and the facts in relation to the fixing of water rates for the city and county of San Francisco. S.F. [n.d.] 47 p.　　C

11109. Reed, S. Albert. The San Francisco conflagration of April, 1906. Special report to the National board of fire underwriters, Committee of twenty... [N.Y.? 1906] 28 p. illus..
　　CHi CSfCP CSfWF-H CSmH CU-B

11110. Reedy, William Marion. 'Frisco the fallen ... pub. April 18, 1916, ten years after. S.F., L.S. Robinson, 1916. 15 p. illus.
　　CHi CLU CSmH CU-B

11111. —— Same, with title: The city that has fallen...Reprinted from Reedy's mirror, April 26, 1906. S.F., Bk. club of Calif., 1933. 13 p.
C CBb CHi CL CLO CLU CRic CSd CSf CSfCW CSfSt CSfU CSmH CStclU CU-B MoS

11112. Reid, Whitelaw. The story of San Francisco for English ears. London, Harrison and sons, 1908. 15 p. An address before the Luton (England) Chamber of commerce, annual dinner, Apr. 10, 1908.　　CLU CSfP

11113. Reid bros., inc. Catalogue of general hospital supplies. Edition "C". [c1924] 659 p. illus.　　CHi

11114. Remarks of the Chinese merchants of San Francisco upon Governor Bigler's message, and some common objections; with some explanations of the character of the Chinese companies, and the laboring class in California. S.F., Whitton, Towne & co., 1855. 16 p.
　　CHi CSmH CU-B NN PHi

11115. Rémond, Auguste. Report to the Rosario and Carmen mining company, San Francisco, with agreements, title deeds, certificate of incorporation, by-laws, etc. S.F., Charles F. Robbins & co., 1863.　　C

11116. Republic (steamship) The raising of the American steamship "Republic." S.F., Paul Elder, 1916.
　　CRcS

11117. Republican party. San Francisco. By-laws and list of members of the Republican committee of the county of San Francisco, adopted, Nov. 1858. S.F., Towne & Bacon, 1858. 8 p.　　CU-B

11118. Reul, Mary Cajetan, Sister. The congressional career of Sen. James Duval Phelan, 1861–1930. San Rafael, 1936. 108 p. Thesis (M.A.)— Catholic Univ. of America, 1936.　　CSrD

11119. Re-union of the pioneer *Panama* passengers on the fourth of June 1874, being the 25th anniversary of the arrival of the steamship *Panama* at San Francisco. S.F., Reprint. at the "Stock Report" off., 1874. 61 p.
　　CHi

11120. Review of the bulkhead, or water front question, and also of the several bulkhead bills now before the legislature. By a civil engineer. S.F., 1859. 22 p.
　　C CLU WHi

11121. Review of the tide land question. [S.F., 1866?] 29 p.　　CLU

11122. Revzan, David Allen. Trends in economic activity and transportation in San Francisco bay area.

Wash., D.C., National acad. of sciences—National research council, 1953. 161–321 p. maps, tables. (National research council. Highway research board. Parking as a factor in business, pt. 5)　　CSfSt

11123. Reynard press. Specimen book of types. 4th ed. S.F. [n.d.] 316 p.　　CHi

11124. Reynolds, R. J. ...The Negro and crime in San Francisco. Final report... [S.F.] 1947. 12 p. Mimeo.
　　CHi

11125. Reynolds, Rix & co. [Catalog] Dry air compressors. ...Miners' and builders' horse-power. S.F., Women's print. [1876?] 40 p. illus.　　CU-B

11126. Rhead, Bridget, vs. Mercantile trust co. of San Francisco. ...Bridget Rhead, plaintiff, vs. Mercantile trust company of San Francisco (a corporation), John J. Cartwell and Charles A. Ramm, as executors of the will of Patrick William Riordan, deceased; Mary's Help Hospital (a corporation) and P. E. Mulligan, as executor of the will of James Healy, deceased, defendants. Before Hon. George A. Sturtevant, judge. Plaintiff's brief in reply. W. H. Morrissey, Charles S. Wheeler, and John F. Bowie, attorneys for plaintiff. [S.F.] J.H. Barry co. [1916?] 358 p.　　CU-B

11127. Rhodes, William Henry. The political letters of Caxton, pseud. S.F., Alta Calif. presses, 1855. 18 p.
　　C CSmH CU-B

11128. Rice, George, & sons. The picture story of the San Francisco earthquake, Wednesday, April 18, 1906. L.A. [1906?] [30] p. of illus.
　　C CAla CHi CLU CO CSf CSmH CU-B

11129. Rice (Jerome) & co. ...Special commissioners' sale of Gronfier estate; peremptory sale portion of Powell estate...and other property, comprising a choice list of valuable real estate...on Wednesday, May 14th, 1862... [S.F.] Robbins & co., print. [1862] 25 p.
　　CLU

11130. Rice, Wilna Lucie (Edsen) Early German churches of San Francisco. [Berkeley, 1929] 198 l. Thesis (M.A.)— Univ. of Calif., 1929.　　CU-B

11131. Richards (C. F.) and co. Domestic receipt book. 1872. S.F. [1872] 1 v.　　CU-B

11132. Richards, George E. ...Official guide and maps of San Francisco street railways... S.F., c1894. 140 p.　　CLgA CSfCP CU-B

11133. Richards & Snow, firm. Post office equipment. ...agents for Yale lock manufacturing co. ...San Francisco. N.Y., The National print. co. [188–?] 42 p. illus.　　CU-B

11134. Richardson, Elmo R., comp. The papers of Cornelius Cole and the Cole family. Berkeley, Univ. of Calif. lib., 1956.　　CP

11135. Richardson, William Antonio. Testimony of William A. Richardson in the private land grant cases, 1852–1855. Testimony of Jeremiah E. Whitcher in the Limantour land grant case, January 18, 1856 [i.e. 1855] ... [Berkeley] 1941. 2 v. Typew.　　CU-B

11136. Richmond, Al. Native daughter; the story of Anita Whitney. S.F., A. Whitney 75th anniversary commission, 1942. 199 p. illus.　　CChiS CHi

11137. Ridgway, Charles. Through the Golden Gate, a story of remarkable adventures in California and along the west coast of America. Yokohama, Fukuin print. co., 1923. 79 p. port.　　CU-B

11138. Rieber laboratories. ...A statement of affairs, management, future. [S.F., Taylor & Taylor, 1916?] 22 p.　　CHi

11139. Rieder, Cardinell & co., pub. San Francisco and vicinity before and after the big fire, April 18th, 19th and 20th, 1906. L.A., c1906. 1 v. (chiefly illus., map)
C C-S CAla CHi CLU CO CSf CSfU CSmH CStclU CU-B NN

11140. —— San Francisco before and after the fire. L.A., c1906. folder (18 p.) illus.
CHi CSfSt CU-B OrU

11141. Riesenberg, Felix, jr. Golden Gate; the story of San Francisco harbor... N.Y. & London, Knopf, 1940. 347 p. illus., ports. Bibliography: p. 344–347.
Available in many California libraries and CaBViPA
CoD MiD MoS NHi NN ODa OU UPB

11142. Rigney, Francis Joseph. The real Bohemia. [1st ed.] N.Y., Basic books [1961] 250 p. illus.
CSfMI

11143. Riley, Bennet. Governor Bennett [sic] Riley's proclamation to the people of the district of San Francisco, June 4, 1849. L.A., Priv. print., 1956. 15 p. facsim.
CHi CLSM

11144. Riley, Cornelius J. A. [Manuscript account and notebooks. 1847–1874] 2 v. Cornelius Riley sailed from New York Feb. 20, 1854, and arrived in San Francisco Mar. 26. Engaged in the sailmaking and liquor business.
CSf

11145. Ringgold, Cadwalader. Correspondence to accompany maps and charts of California. [Wash., D.C.? 1851?] 15 p.
CHi CLU

11146. —— A series of charts, with sailing directions, embracing surveys of the Farallones, entrance to the bay of San Francisco, bays of San Francisco and San Pablo, straits of Carquines and Suisun bay, confluence and deltic branches of the Sacramento and San Joaquin rivers, and the Sacramento river (with the middle fork) to the American river, including the cities of Sacramento and Boston, state of California. Wash., D.C., Print. by J.T. Towers, 1851. 44 p. illus., maps.
C C-S CHi CL CLSM CLU (lacks charts) CSf CSfCP CSmH CU-B

11147. —— Same. 3d ed., with additions. 1852. 48 p. illus., maps.
CS CSd CU-B

11148. —— Same. 4th ed., with additions. Wash., D.C., 1852. 48 p. illus., maps.
C CHi CL CLSM CLSU CLU CSfCP CSfCW CSfP CSfU CSmH CU-B

11149. —— Same. 5th ed., with additions. 1852. 48 p.
MiD ViW

11150. Rinne, Rose Marie Shiely. The San Francisco–Oakland Bay bridge: its history and economic development. [Berkeley, 1936] Thesis (M.A.) — Univ. of Calif., 1936.
CU

11151. Riordan, Joseph W. The first half century of St. Ignatius church and college... S.F. [Crocker] 1905. 389 p. illus., ports.
C CHi CLU CLgA CO COHN CRcS CSf CSfCP CSfCW CSfP CSfU CSmH CU-B CaBViPA

11152. Riordan, Patrick William, Abp. In memoriam. [S.F., Abbott press, 1914] 69 p. illus., port.
CHi CSfCW

11153. Riots in San Francisco; a series of newspaper clippings. S.F., 1877.
CSS CSf CU-B

11154. Risdon iron and locomotive works. Catalogue. S.F., 1879–1906. illus.
CHi has 1879, 1884–85, 1895–97, 1901–02, 1906, no. 12 (n.d.) CU-B has no. 3, 5, 7, 15, 17, 1897–1901.

11155. Ritchie, Robert Welles. San Francisco. Sketches by Charles W. Simpson. S.F., S.F. committee,

National conference of social work, 1929. 12 p. col. illus. Reprint. from *The Ladies home jl.* of Feb. 1929.   CHi

11156. Ritz Old poodle dog. [Descriptive brochure] [n.p., n.d.] [8] p. illus.   CHi

11157. Rivors, [C.] A full and authentic account of the murders of James King of William, Dr. Randall, Dr. Baldwin, West and Marion. The execution of James P. Casey, Charles Cora, Philander Brace, and Joseph Heatherington by the Vigilance committee of San Francisco... Rochester, E. Darrow, 1857. 64 p. illus.   CHi CSmH

11158. Rix & Firth, Phoenix iron works. National air compressor and rock drills, manufactured by...S.F. [1888] 14 p. illus.   CHi

11159. Roach, Philip A. Address on the opening of the fair for the erection of the Roman catholic cathedral on Van Ness Avenue, Nov. 15, 1887, at the Mechanics pavilion. S.F., J.H. Barry, 1887. 24 p. pl.   CHi

11160. Roantree, James D. In memoriam, 1874–1924. [S.F., Print. by Taylor & Taylor, for Printers' bd. of trade] [3] l.   CHi

11161. Robbins, Charles F. & co. Guide to the telegraph fire alarm, for San Francisco, with a short history of the fire alarm telegraph... S.F. [1865] 32 p. illus.   CHi

11162. Robbins, Fred S. Facts and fancies of the tour thru Golden Gate park... S.F., Author, 1916.   C-S

11163. Robinson, James. Report upon the condition and requirements of the city front of San Francisco made to the San Francisco dock and wharf co., January 25, 1859... Sacramento, Crocker, 1859. 7 p. map.
C CHi CLU CSmH CU-B

11164. Robinson, John R. vs. the Central Pacific railroad co. of California. In the District court of the Fourth judicial district of the state of California, in and for the city and county of San Francisco. John R. Robinson, plaintiff, vs. the Central Pacific railroad company of California, et als., defendants. Complaint. Alfred A. Cohen, Delos Lake, attorneys for plaintiff. [S.F.?] 1876. 63 p.   CHi

11165. Robinson, Robert McClure. A history of the teamsters in the San Francisco bay area, 1850–1950. [Berkeley, 1951] Thesis (Ph.D.) — Univ. of Calif., Berkeley.   CU

11166. —— Maritime labor in San Francisco, 1933–37... [Berkeley, 1937] 182 l. Thesis (M.A.) — Univ. of Calif., 1937.   CU

11167. Robinson, T. B. Petition of T. B. Robinson, P. G. of Templar Lodge, no. 17, I.O.O.F., California, to re-open case... [S.F., 1889?] 63 p.   CHi

11168. Robinson, W. H., vs. Southern Pacific co. In the Supreme court of the state of California. W. H. Robinson, plaintiff and respondent, vs. Southern Pacific co. (corporation), defendant and appellant. Respondent's brief. C. M. Jennings, attorney for respondent. Filed... 1893. [n.p., 1893?] 79 p.   CHi

11169. Rodriguez, Marie Louise (Bine) The earthquake of 1906. S.F., Priv. print., 1951. 106 p.
C CHi CSf CSfSt CSt CSto CU-B

11170. Roebling (John A.) sons co. of California. Revised price list, Sept. 1, 1922. [n.p., 1922] 233 p.   CHi

11171. Rogers, Fred Blackburn. Montgomery and the Portsmouth. [S.F.] John Howell, 1958. 145 p. illus., ports., facsims. (The John Howell ser. on the U.S. Navy in old Calif.)

C CHi CL CLO CLSM CLgA CNF CRedl CRic
CSS CSd CSdS CSf CSfP CSfSt CSmat CStmo
CSto CaBViPA

11172. [Rogers, Robert Clay] My wife and I. Mementos for our children... S.F., For family circulation, 1871. 440 p. CHi

11173. Rollins, William, vs. Wright, John A. In the Supreme court of the state of California. William Rollins, respondent, vs. John A. Wright, appellant. Appellant's brief in reply. John A. Wright, Arthur Rodgers, attorneys for appellant. Filed August 1891... S.F., James H. Barry, print. [1891] 25 p. CHi

11174. Rolph, James, jr. A crisis in San Francisco ... [S.F., James H. Barry co., 1915?] 4 p. CHi

11175. Roney, Frank. Frank Roney, Irish rebel and California labor leader; an autobiography. Ed. by Ira B. Cross. Berkeley, Univ. of Calif. press, 1931. 573 p. illus., ports., facsims.
CAla CHi CL CLgA CSd CSf CSfCW CU-B

11176. Roos bros., inc. The story of Roos bros., outfitters since 1865. S.F., Priv. print., 1945. 39 p. illus., ports., facsims. CFS CHi CSf CU-B

11177. —— What do you know about the firm you work with. [S.F., Taylor & Taylor, 1919] [11] p. illus. CHi

11178. Roosevelt, Theodore. President Roosevelt's speech at Mechanics' pavilion, San Francisco, May 13, 1903. Compliments of Roos bros., outfitters for men and boys... [S.F., 1903] [8] p. ports. CHi

11179. Root, Henry. ...Personal history and reminiscences with personal opinions on contemporary events, 1845–1921. S.F., Print. for priv. circulation, 1921. 134 p. port.
C C-S CBb CHi CL CLU CLgA CMartC CO CSd CSf CSfCW CSjC CSmH CStclU CU-B

11180. Roquefeuil, Camille de. Camille de Roquefeuil in San Francisco, 1817–1818, by Charles N. Rudkin. L.A., Dawson, 1954. 83 p. (Early Calif. travels ser., 23) 200 copies printed by Greenwood press.
C CL CLO CLSM CLgA CO CSS CSf CSjC CStclU CSto CStoC CU-B CVtV CoD OU

11181. Rosen, Daniel Bernard. The history of the Presidio of San Francisco during the Spanish period. [Berkeley, 1957] Thesis (M.A.)— Univ. of Calif., 1957. CU

11182. Rosenberg bros. and co. Years mature... [S.F., c1943] 108 p. illus., ports., map.
CFS CHi CStmo CU-B CV

11183. Rosenthal, Marcus. In the Supreme court of the state of California. Ex parte Frank on habeas corpus. Petitioner's brief in reply. Marcus Rosenthal, counsel for petitioner. S.F., Francis & Valentine, 1878. 39 p. CHi

11184. [Rosenthal, Toby] Toby Rosenthal exhibition, San Francisco, Nov. 1884. Catalogue. S.F., Bosqui & co. print., 1884. 35 p. Includes biographical material. CHi

11185. Ross, Alex A. A study of the development and an evaluation of the San Francisco coordination council of youth welfare. [Berkeley, 1947] Thesis (M.A.)— Univ. of Calif., 1947. CU

11186. Ross, Arnold M. Twenty-five years of building the West, the story of Calaveras cement from 1925 to 1950. S.F., Calaveras cement co., 1950. [62] p. illus., ports. CHi CSfWF-H

11187. Ross, Eleanore Farrand. Beloved city... illus. by Julien Links. S.F., Press of Knight-Counihan, 1934. 58 p. illus. Little essays about San Francisco.
CHi CO CSf CSfU CSmH CSrD CU-B NN

11188. Rossi, Angelo J. In memoriam. S.F., A.J. Rossi memorial committee [1948] [12] p. port. "Address by Walter McGovern, City hall...April 7, 1948, upon the occasion of the public observance of the death of Angelo J. Rossi former mayor of San Francisco." p. [6]
CHi CLgA CRcS CSf

11189. Rosskam, Edwin. ...San Francisco, west coast metropolis...with an introduction by William Saroyan. N.Y., Toronto, Alliance book corp., Longmans [c1939] 136 p. illus.
Available in many California libraries and MiD NN ODa

11190. Rotary club, San Francisco. Roster... March, 1914. S.F., 1914. v.p. ports. CHi

11191. Rouleau, F. A. Abstract of title by F. A. Rouleau to the lands of the Flint tract homestead association. S.F., Cubery & co., 1874. 42 p. fold. map.
CHi CSf

11192. Rowell, Edward Joseph. The Union Labor party of San Francisco, 1901–1911... [Berkeley, 1938] 264 l. Thesis (Ph.D.)— Univ. of Calif., 1938. CU

11193. Roxburghe club of San Francisco. Chronology of twenty-five years, 1928–1953. [Ed. by Geo. E. Dawson. S.F., 1954] [82] p. illus. 26 pl.
C CHi CLU CU-B

11194. —— ...The first three years. S.F. [Johnck & Seeger] 1931. 38 p. CHi CLO CSf

11195. —— Seven pioneer San Francisco libraries. [S.F., Designed and print. by Lawton Kennedy] 1958. 41 p.
CHi CLO CLU CSd CSfCW CSfP CSfU CU-B

11196. Royce, Josiah. ...California, from the conquest in 1846 to the second Vigilance committee in San Francisco [1856] A study of American character... Bost. & N.Y., Houghton, 1886. 513 p. map. (Am. commonwealths. Ed. by H. E. Scudder. [v.7])
Other editions followed.
Available in many libraries.

11197. —— Same. [With an] introduction by Robert Glass Cleland. N.Y., Knopf, 1948. 394 p. (Western Americana, ed. by Robert Glass Cleland and Oscar Lewis)
Available in many California libraries and CaBViPA

11198. Roylance (J.) brass works. Catalogue no. 1. S.F. [J. Winterburn co., 1893] 144 p. illus. CHi

11199. Rucker-Fuller desk co. [Catalog, 191–?] S.F. [191–?] 1 v. illus. CU-B

11200. Ruef, Abraham. Freedom — for perjury; subordination of perjury persistently attempted by many months by the graft prosecution... Oakland [1908?] 51 p. CHi CLU CSf CU-B

11201. —— Letter of A. Ruef to the prison directors (dated July 14, 1911) S.F., Print. by the Calif. prison commission [1911] 15 p. CSmH

11202. —— Speech of A. Ruef. Full text of address delivered at Scottish hall on April 14, 1905. [S.F., 1905] CHi

11203. Russ building co. Annual report. [S.F., 1932–] illus.
CHi has 1932–34, 1952.

11204. —— [Descriptive brochure] S.F. [Taylor & Taylor] 1928. 30 p. illus. CHi

11205. —— [Pamphlets about the Russ Building. San Francisco, 1926–47] 7 pamphlets in 1 v.   CU-B

11206. —— Russ building tower. This booklet suggests the character of the present tenancy and the advantages to tenants afforded by the tallest office building in San Francisco. [S.F., Taylor & Taylor, 1934] [17] p. illus.   CHi

11207. —— Service directory, Russ building. S.F., 1927. [13] p.   CHi

11208. —— Thirty stories in San Francisco. [S.F., Taylor & Taylor, 1935] [16] p. illus.   CHi

11209. Russell, Matthew, *Father.* The life of Mother Mary Baptist Russell, Sister of Mercy, by her brother...N.Y., The Apostleship of prayer, 1901. 187 p. ports., pl. Biography of a pioneer Sister in San Francisco.   CHi CLgA CSfCW

11210. Russell, Thomas C., pub. Panoramic San Francisco, from California street hill, 1877. S.F., T.C. Russell [1911?] Panoramic view on continuous strip folded to form 11 leaves.
C CAla CHi CLSU CLU CO CSf CSfCW CSfMI CSfP CSfWF-H CSmH CStclU CU-B NN

11211. Rutan, Isaac M. vs. Wolters, Henry et al. In the Supreme court of the state of California. [San Francisco no. 567] Isaac M. Rutan, respondent, vs. Henry Wolters, et al., appellants. Respondent's brief. R. H. Countryman, attorney for respondent... [S.F.] D.S. Stanley & co. [1897] 12 p.   CHi

11212. Ryan, Frederick L. Industrial relations in the San Francisco building trades... Norman, Okla., Univ. of Okla. press, 1935. 341 p.
C CBu CChiS CL CLU CLgA CO CSdS CSf CSfCW CU (Thesis, 1930)

11213. Ryan, John J. Memoir of the life of Rev. Burchard Villiger of the Society of Jesus. Phila., Press of F. McManus, 1906. 324 p. illus., port. Biography of a pioneer priest who was president of St. Ignatius and Santa Clara college.   CLgA CSfCW

11214. [Ryan, Paul William] Big strike, by Mike Quin [pseud.] Postscript by Harry Bridges. Olema, Olema pub. co. [1949] 259 p. illus. Deals with San Francisco's general strike, 1934.   CHi CSto CU-B

11215. —— On the drumhead, a selection from the writing of Mike Quin [pseud.] A memorial volume. Ed., with a biographical sketch by Harry Carlisle. S.F., The Pac. pub. foundation, inc. [c1948] 244 p. illus.   CHi

11216. Rydell, Raymond A. Cape Horn to the Pacific; the rise and decline of an ocean highway. Berkeley, Univ. of Calif. press, 1952. 213 p. map. Bibliography: p. 183–98.
CBb CHi CLgA CLU CSf CSfP CU CUk

11217. Ryder, David Warren. A century of hardware and steel, being the story of Baker & Hamilton, a business institution which has helped to write the history of California and the Pacific coast... S.F., Hist. pub., 1949. 119 p. illus., ports., facsims.
CHi CLU CLgA CSf CSfP CSfWF-H CSto CU-B CV

11218. —— The first hundred years, being the highlighted history of the first & oldest wholesale drug house in the west, Coffin-Redington company, 1849–1949. [S.F.] Coffin-Redington co., 1949. 40 p. illus., ports., maps.   CHi CO CSf

11219. —— Men of rope, being the history of Tubbs cordage company...S.F., Hist. pub., 1954. 146 p. illus., ports., facsims.
C CBb CHi CRcS CSf CSfP CSfWF-H CU-B

11220. —— The Merrill story (being a record of the life and achievements of Charles Washington Merrill, and a history of the Merrill company and subsidiaries) [S.F., The Merrill co., 1958] 147 p. illus., ports., facsims.   CHi CSf CSfP

11221. —— San Francisco's Emperor Norton; the story of Norton I, emperor of America and protector of Mexico... [S.F., Alex. Dulfer print. & litho. co., c1939] 53 p.
C CHi CO CSd CSf CSfMI CSfWF-H CSluCL CSmH CU-B

11222. —— The story of Moss and the incredible west. [S.F., Keystone print. co.] c1945. [20] p. illus., ports. Deals with Moss stores, inc., operator of retail stores in California.   CHi

11223. —— Story of Sherman Clay and co., 1870–1947. [S.F., Sherman Clay, c1947] 54 p. illus., port.   C CHi

11224. —— Same, 1870–1952. [2d ed.] [S.F., Print. for Sherman Clay by Neal, Stratford & Kerr, 1952] 68 p. illus., ports.
C CHi CSf CSluCL CU-B

11225. —— The story of Telegraph hill... [S.F.?] L'Esperance, Silvertson & Beran [1948?]
C CO CSf CSfU CSfWF-H CSmH CStrJC

11226. —— They wouldn't take ashes for an answer...S.F., Fireman's fund insurance co. [1948] 41 p. illus.
C CHi CLU CO CSf CSfP CSfWF-H CSmH CU-B

11227. S&W fine foods inc. Annual report. CL has 1951–52, 1954–59.

11228. Sadler & co. [Descriptive catalogs of fireworks, flags, etc.]
CHi has 1884, 1905, 1912.

11229. Safarian, Joan Shivvers. Facilities for visually handicapped children in San Francisco. [Berkeley, 1950] Thesis (M.A.)—Univ. of Calif., 1950—Social welfare.   CU

11230. Safe deposit company of San Francisco. ...Incorporated 1874. Capital, $2,000,000; 20,000 shares, $100 each. [S.F., E. Bosqui & co., print., 1875?] 30 p. illus.   CHi CU-B

11231. Sailors' union of the Pacific. Sailors' union of the Pacific, 1885–1950. [S.F.? 1950?] [16] p. illus. Program of dedication ceremony of the Union hall in San Francisco, June 16, 1950.   C CHi

11232. —— Andrew Furuseth school of seamanship (S.S. Invader) Annual report... 1942/43. S.F. [1943–] 1 v. illus.   CU-B

11233. Saint, Alice Marion. Women in government, with special reference to San Francisco bay area. [Berkeley, 1930] Thesis (M.A.)— Univ. of Calif., 1930.   CU

11234. St. Andrew's society. By-laws, rules of order and list of members... Organized 21st September 1863. Incorporated, 4th Aug. 1865. Re-incorporated, January 9, 1877. S.F., John Wallace, 1877. 57 p.   CHi

11235. —— Historical report... S.F., J. Wallace, print., 1871. 48 p. "Revised list of members, 1871": p. 36–48.   CHi CLU

11236. St. Francis importation co. Price list... wines and liquors. S.F. [1915?] 22 p.   CHi

11237. St. Francis memorial hospital. 50 years... in the heart of San Francisco; report of the golden anniversary... [S.F.] 1955. 30 p. illus., ports.   CHi

11238. St. Joseph's hospital. Fifty golden years, 1889–1939. S.F., 1939. unp. illus.   CSfCW CSrD

11239. St. Joseph's union ... v.1–2, March 1887–Dec. 1888. S.F., Youths' directory, 1887–88. 2 v. in 1. illus., ports.   CU-B

11240. St. Luke's hospital. Mite society. Constitution and by-laws... Incorporated March 20, 1876. S.F., Cubery & co., 1876. 11 p.   CHi

11241. St. Mary's hospital. Annual report... [S.F., C.W. Gordon, print., 1905?–19]
CHi (1912, 1913/14)   CU-B (1905)

11242. St. Mary's hospital and the Sisters of mercy, 1903–1949...by Edward Topham. S.F., Priv. print., May 1950. 4 p. illus.   CSf

11243. St. Patrick's brotherhood. Anniversary celebration...San Francisco, California, March 17th, 1862. S.F., Waters bros. & co., bk. and job print., 1862. 12 p.   CU-B

11244. St. Patrick's shelter for men. Report. 6th. S.F., 1932. 1 v. illus., ports.   CU-B

11245. Sala (J. C.), firm. Catalogue and manual of civil engineers' and surveyors' instruments... S.F. [Upton bros., 1898] 167 p. illus.   CHi

11246. Salt Lake and Los Angeles railroad co. ...Statement. London, Southwood, Smith & co., 1889. 11 p. fold. map.   CHi

11247. The Salt river mare's nest. Thurs., Oct. 10, 1867. [S.F., 1867] Deals with Henry P. Coon.   CSmH

11248. Salvation army. Southern Pacific province. ...Re-construction days for the Salvation army, being a brief review of the Army's work in and about San Francisco, prior to April 18, 1906, and its re-establishment... S.F., Colonel Geo. French, 1906. [22] p. illus., port.   CU-B

11249. —— Territorial headquarters, San Francisco. The Salvation army reports, 1951. S.F., The army, 1951. 1 v.   CHi

11250. Sanborn, Vail & co. Catalogue of artist's materials... [1884, 190–? 192–? S.F., 1884–192–?] illus.   CHi (1884, 190–? 192–?)

11251. Sánchez, Nellie (Van de Grift) The life of Mrs. Robert Louis Stevenson. N.Y., Scribner's, 1920.   CHi

11252. Sanderson, J. An ocean cruise and deep water regatta of the Pacific yacht club, July, 1884. With illus. by G. J. Denny, S.F., H.S. Crocker, 1884. 55 p. illus.   CHi

11253. San Francisco vs. Bradbury, William B. ...The city and county of San Francisco, plaintiff, vs. William B. Bradbury and J. A. Magagnos and A. W. Stone, defendants... J. R. Brandon, attorney for appellant W. B. Bradbury. Craig & Meredith, attorney for city and county of San Francisco, respondent. Lloyd & Wood, attorneys for A. W. Stone, respondent... S.F., M. Weiss, Oriental print. and pub. house, 1888–91. 2 v. in 1.   CU-B

11254. San Francisco vs. Certain real estate. ... The city and county of San Francisco, appellant [i.e., respondent], vs. Certain real estate, respondent [i.e., appellant]... Daingerfield & Olney, attorneys for appellant. J. M. Nougues, counsel for respondent. S.F., 1872. 6 v. in 1.   CU-B

11255. San Francisco vs. Doe, Bartlett and Doe, J. S. et als. In the Supreme court of the state of California. People of the city and county of San Francisco, appellant, vs. Bartlett Doe and J. S. Doe et als., respond-

ents. Points of respondents. Theodore H. Hittell, attorney for respondents. S.F., Bacon & co. [1874] 6 p.   CHi

11256. San Francisco vs. Domett, Charles H. et. al. The Supreme court of the state of California. The Board of education of the city and county of San Francisco, trustees &c., plaintiffs respondents v. Charles H. Domett, James L. Fowler, and Wm. E. Domett, defendants appellants. Brief on behalf of plaintiffs, by Samuel W. Holladay. S.F., Spear, print., 1861. 16 p.   CHi

11257. San Francisco vs. Josselyn, G. M. et al. In the Supreme court of the state of California. People of the city and county of San Francisco, appellant, versus G. M. Josselyn, et als., respondents. Transcript on appeal ... S.F., W.M. Hinton & co., 1878. 17 p.   CHi

11258. San Francisco vs. Spring Valley water works. In the District court of the twenty-third judicial district of the state of California, in and for the city and county of San Francisco... Argument of John F. Swift, esq., special counsel for plaintiff. Jan. 10th, 1879. 56 p.   CHi

11259. San Francisco vs. the United States. Before the General land office of the United States. The city of San Francisco vs. the United States. Argument of John W. Dwinelle, special counsel for the city of San Francisco, against the Stratton survey of the four square leagues of pueblo lands confirmed to said city by the United States circuit court of California. [n.p., 1865?] 11, xx p.   CHi

11260. —— Before U.S. Board of land commissioners for California, no. 280. Brief of argument made by Horace Hawes, on behalf of United States. Delivered May 29, 30, 31, and June 2, 1854. S.F., Times and Transcript steam presses, 1854. 62 p.
C CHi CLU CP CSfCP CSfCW CSfP CSmH CU-B

11261. —— ...Brief of J. B. Crockett, of counsel for claimants. S.F., Herald steam presses, 1854. 27 p.
C CLU CSfCW CSmH CU-B KHi

11262. —— Documents, depositions, and brief of law points raised thereon on behalf of the United States, in case no. 280...S.F., Commercial power presses, 1854. 72 p. At end: J. H. McKune law agent. Horace Hawes, of counsel.   C CSfCW CSmH CU CU-B

11263. —— Points of fact and proofs in regard to land claim, no. 280, of the city of San Francisco...S.F., Whitton, Towne, & co., print., Excelsior job off., 1854. 19 p. Prepared by Isaac Thomas.   C CSfCW

11264. —— [Historical argument for the city, claiming it as a pueblo. n.p., 1862] 12 p.   CU-B

11265. —— In the Circuit court of the United States for the Tenth Circuit, in and for the Northern district of California. The city of San Francisco v. the United States. Transferred from the District court of the United States for the Northern district of California. On motion for rehearing. [S.F., 1865?] 101 p. Signed: John B. Williams, special counsel for U.S. "This was the famous case known as 'The pueblo case,' or land case no. 280, wherein San Francisco established her pueblo rights to the lands now within the boundaries of the city and county of San Francisco."—Cowan.   CLU CU-B

11266. —— In the U.S. District court, Northern district of California. San Francisco vs. the United States. Claim for the tract of land situated in the county of San Francisco, embracing the peninsula whereon the said city is situated. No. 280. [n.p., 1862] 12 p.   CU-B

11267. San Francisco. Bonded debt of the city and county of San Francisco...June 30, 1912. S.F. [1912?] 23 p.   C-S

11268. —— Excerpts from municipal reports, city and county of San Francisco, on lighting streets and public buildings... Comp., July, 1908, by San Francisco gas and electric company. [S.F., 1908?] [216] p.
CSf CU-B

11269. —— Old city hall buildings and list of public officers of the city and county of San Francisco, 1850–1895. [S.F., 1895?] [318]–382 p. illus.   CHi

11270. —— Remonstrance of the city of San Francisco, to the Legislature of the state of California, against the extension of the city of San Francisco. S.F., Commercial advertiser power presses, 1854. 8 p.
C CLU CSmH CU-B

11271. —— San Francisco town journal, 1847–1848, William A. Leidesdorff, treasurer. Oct. 7, 1847 to May 2, 1848. From the collection of Albert Dressler... [S.F., Albert Dressler] Print. by Crocker, 1926. [13] p. Facsimile reproduction from the original ms.
C CHi CLU CLgA CO CSf CSfP CSmH CU-B CWhC MoSHi

11272. —— (Archdiocese) Catholic directory... statistical handbook and telephone guide to all rectories, schools, institutions. Anno Domini 1936– S.F., The Monitor, 1936–
CHi has 1944, 1956. CSf has 1938, 1947, 1949, 1952, 1954. CSfCW has 1936, 1950, 1952, 1954, 1956, 1958–59.

11273. —— Synodus diocesana, santi francisci, habita mense Julii mdcclxii. S.F., Smyth et Shoaff, 1872. 19 p. Constitution and by-laws.   CHi

11274. —— Academy of Notre Dame. Prospectus... [S.F., Cosmopolitan print. [n.d.] 3 p. Manuscript note of visit 1870. Programme attached, dated 1878.   CHi

11275. —— African Methodist Episcopal church. Journal of the proceedings of the third annual convention of the ministers and lay delegates... Held in Bethel church, San Francisco, from September 4th to September 10th, 1863. S.F., B.F. Sterett, 1863. 43 p. Photocopy.   CHi

11276. —— [Alaska-Yukon Pacific exposition committee] San Francisco, California. [S.F., Designed & print. by Bolte & Braden co., 1909] 80 p.
C CL CSfCP CSmH CU-B

11277. —— Alcalde. Reports of the alcalde, comptroller, and treasurer of San Francisco. S.F., Print. at off. of Alta Calif., 1850. 36 p.
C CHi CU-B NHi (photostat)

11278. —— Baptist church. The emergency call of the stricken Baptist churches of San Francisco and vicinity to the Baptist brotherhood of America. [n.p., 1906] 8 p. illus. Covers appeals by the Baptist churches of San Francisco, Oakland, San Jose and Santa Rosa.
CHi

11279. —— Bethany Congregational church. Directory...1910. [n.p., n.d.] [6] p.   CHi

11280. —— Bible college. The Bible college message, March 1914. S.F. [1914] [16] p.   CU-B

11281. —— Board of city hall commissioners. History and report by A. T. Spotts, secretary of the Board of new city hall commissioners of [sic] the construction of the new city hall from April 4, 1870 to November, 1889. S.F., W.M. Hinton & co., 1889. 38 p. illus.   CHi

11282. —— —— Instructions and suggestions for the use of architects in preparing designs for the new City hall... S.F., Smyth & Shoaff, print., 1870. 14 p.
CHi CU-B

11283. —— —— Same, June 30, 1889 to November, 1890. S.F., 1890. 14 p. pl., tables.   CU-B

11284. —— —— New city hall, San Francisco, California. Specification for masonry, &c., in foundations. S.F., Smyth & Shoaff, print., 1871. 7 l.   CHi

11285. —— Board of education. An itemized statement of the San Francisco school construction fund as received by Alfred Roncovieri, Superintendent of schools, and distributed by the School reconstruction committee... [1907] 29 p.   C

11286. —— —— The public schools of San Francisco. John C. Pelton's course in regard to the same unmasked. Result of the investigation of the charges against John C. Pelton by the committee of the Board of education, June, 1865. S.F., 1865. 55 p.   CHi

11287. —— —— Report of special committee on examination of cosmopolitan schools... S.F., Edward Bosqui & co., print., 1867. 23 p.   C

11288. —— —— The school scandal of San Francisco. Being an account of the proceedings held before the investigating committee of the Board of education, and subsequently before the same body sitting jointly with the Finance committee of the Board of supervisors ... [S.F.] S.F. news co., 1878. 40 p.
C CSj CSmH CU-B

11289. —— A statement of the condition and wants of the Public school department of San Francisco, by a committee of the Board... S.F., Edward Bosqui & co., 1866. 93 p.   C CHi CLU CU-B

11290. —— —— Div. of publications. San Francisco, her story; written by a teachers' committee composed of Edith Cochran, Annette Schraft, Cecilia Papini, Zoa Meyer, Marguerite Lentz for class-room use in the San Francisco public schools. [S.F., Hooper print. co., press, c1932] 207 p. illus., maps.   CLgA

11291. —— Board of election commissioners. Extracts from the United States statutes, the constitution of the state of California, and the political and penal codes, relating to the elective franchise, registration of citizens and elections... S.F., 1878– Title varies.
CHi (1878, 1884, 1892) CSmH (1884)

11292. —— Board of engineers. Transbay bridge. Report...May, 1927. [S.F.] 1927. 90 p. fold. maps, pl. Signed: Robert Ridgway (chairman), Arthur N. Talbot, John D. Galloway.   CHi

11293. —— Board of fire underwriters. Rates revised and adopted, October, 1861. [S.F.? 1861] 11 p.
CU-B

11294. —— —— Same. March 1st, 1869. [S.F.? 1869] 28 p.   CU-B

11295. —— —— Same, 1878. Book of rates no. 3. S.F., 1878. 40 p.   CHi

11296. —— Board of fire wardens. Report of architects P. J. O'Connor and Augustus Laver on the construction of theatres, schools, churches, etc. ...1889.
C-S

11297. —— Board of health. In the matter of the investigation of the management of the almshouse of the city and county of San Francisco, under the superintendency of P. L. Weaver. S.F. [n.d.] 68 p.   C-S

11298. —— Board of park commissioners. The development of Golden Gate park and particularly the management and thinning of its forest tree plantations,

together with reports from Messrs. Wm. Ham. Hall...,
Fred. Law Olmsted...and John McLaren...S.F., Bacon
& co., 1886. 31 p.   CU-B

11299. —— —— Official guide to Golden Gate
park...S.F., F.F. Byington, 1893. 48 p. illus.
                                              CHi CU-B

11300. —— —— Same. S.F., F.F. Byington, 1894.
64 p. illus.   CU-B

11301. —— —— Souvenir programme...Decem-
ber 22nd, 1888. [S.F., 1888] [10] p. illus., ports.
                                                      CU-B

11302. —— **Board of police commissioners.** A
compilation of the laws regulating the organization and
control of the Police department... By Alfred Clarke.
S.F., 1878. 42 p.   CSf CSfU

11303. —— **Board of public works.** Consulting
architects. The proposed schemes for Civic center. S.F.,
1912. [3] l. pl.   CHi CSmH

11304. —— **Board of supervisors.** Book of franchises granted...including street and steam railroad, telephone, telegraph and miscellaneous franchises, pipe line,
spur track and miscellaneous permits. S.F., 1910. 412 p.
        CHi CL CSf CSfCP CSfMI CU-B

11305. —— —— Changes in names of streets
from January 1, 1909, to December 31, 1909. [S.F.] Rincon pub. co. [1910?] 12 p.   CU-B

11306. —— —— Description of public property
belonging to the city and county of San Francisco. S.F.,
J.H. Barry, print., 1893. 57 p.   CLU

11307. —— —— Description of public property,
including Channel St. and Mission creek lands, with table
of grades of the public streets, belonging to the city and
county of San Francisco. S.F., Geo. Spaulding & co., 1881.
140 p.   CU-B

11308. —— —— Give San Francisco control of
her harbor and promote industrial development... S.F.
[n.d.] 2 l.   C-S

11309. —— —— In the matter of the survey of
the pueblo of San Francisco. Appeal to the Hon. Secretary of the Interior from the decision of the Hon. Commissioner of the General land office of May 19, 1879.
[S.F.? 1879] 11 p.   CHi CU-B

11310. —— —— Proceedings had in Board of
supervisors and reports of engineer in the matter of
furnishing water supplies for the city and county of San
Francisco. [S.F.] Spaulding & Barto, steam bk. & job
print., 1875. 115 p. maps.
CHi C-S CLU CSf CSfCSM CSfMI CSfSC
CSfU   CU-B

11311. —— —— Progress report of the engineers
in charge to devise and provide a system of sewerage for
the city and county of San Francisco for the fiscal year
ending June 30, 1893 by Marsden Manson, and C. E.
Grunsky. S.F., Bosqui print. co., 1893. 104 p.   C CHi

11312. —— —— Same. Supplement. Official street
grades...S.F., Jas. H. Barry, print., 1894. 221 p.   CHi

11313. —— —— Public hearing on redevelopment of the western addition...on June 3, 1948... [S.F.?
1948] 69 l. Mimeo.   CO

11314. —— —— Real estate owned by the City
and county of San Francisco, and historical data relating
to the same... S.F., 1909. 208 p.   CHi CSf CSmH

11315. —— —— Regulation of water rates. Proceedings before the Board of supervisors. S.F. [Argonaut
job print.] 1880. 93 p.   CSf CU-B

11316. —— —— Report of Commission on change
of street names... appointed by the Mayor... S.F.,
Neal pub. co., 1909. 16 p.   C-S CHi

11317. —— —— Same, final report [supplement]
4 p.   CHi

11318. —— —— Report of the Special committee
of the Board...on the condition of the Chinese quarter
and the Chinese in San Francisco. July, 1885. [S.F.]
P.J. Thomas, 1885. 95 p.
        C CSf CSmH CStcrCL CU-B

11319. —— —— Report of the special committee
of the Board...together with communications of Gen. B.
S. Alexander...and Prof. George Davidson...on the
water supplies for the city of San Francisco. S.F., A.L.
Bancroft & co., print., 1872. 28 p.   CLU

11320. —— —— Report on city and county finances made pursuant to an order of the Board of supervisors by Edward Byrne. S.F., Monson, Valentine & co.,
1856. 21 p.   C CU-B NN

11321. —— —— Report on the condition of the
beach and water lots in the city of San Francisco. Made
in pursuance of an ordinance of the Common council of
said city, creating a commission to inquire into city property... S.F., Print. at the off. of the Evening picayune,
1850. 104 p. incl. tables.
                      C CLU CSmH CU-B ICN

11322. —— —— Report upon a system of sewer-
age for the city and county of San Francisco. Proposed by
C. E. Grunsky, civil engineer in charge, Marsden Manson,
C. S. Tilton, associate engineers. Aproved by Rudolph
Hering, consulting engineer. S.F., Hinton print. co.,
1899. 132 p.   CHi CSmH CU-B

11323. —— —— San Francisco municipal reports: 1859–60. [Seal] S.F., Towne & Bacon, 1860. 186 p.
        C CHi CSfMI CSfCP CSmH CSt CU CU-B
MoS NN

11324. —— —— Same, for the fiscal year 1861–
62... S.F., Eastman & Godfrey, print., 1862. 280 p. illus.
        C CHi CSmH CSt CStclU CU CU-B WHi

11325. —— —— Souvenir-Portolá. Public work
of San Francisco since 1906. Supplement to Municipal
reports 1908–09. [S.F., Neal pub. co., 1909] 64 p. illus.
                              CHi CSf CSfU CU-B

11326. —— —— Table of grades and description
of public property...and accepted streets in the city and
county of San Francisco. S.F., Spaulding & Barto print.,
1877. 96 p.   CHi CSfCW CU-B

11327. —— —— Table of streets, avenues, places,
etc. in the city and county of San Francisco...in accordance with orders nos. 1684 and 1606. S.F., G. Spaulding,
1882. 11 p. pl.   CHi

11328. —— —— Tables showing changes in
names of streets, also open, closed and accepted streets,
and width of streets, of the city and county of San Francisco. S.F., Hinton print. co., 1895. 185 p. tables.   CHi

11329. —— —— Same, January 1, 1909. S.F.,
1909. 107 p.   C-S CHi CSfMI

11330. —— —— **Special committee on pavements.** Report... S.F., A.L. Bancroft & co., 1870. 73 p.
illus., fold. pl.   CSfCW CU-B

11331. —— **Board of trade.** Annual report.
CHi has 1937–38, 1949–52, 1957–58.

11332. —— —— Constitution and by-laws of the
Merchants' protective association Board of trade of San
Francisco. Organized April 1877. S.F., B.F. Sterett, print.,
1878. 29 p.   CU-B

11333. San Francisco. Board of trade (*cont'd*)
Same. S.F., LeCount bros., print., 1885. 51 p.   CU-B

11334. —— Special committee on the inter-oceanic canal. Report. S.F., Dempster bros., 1880. 33 p.   CHi

11335. —— Board of water commissioners. Report on the various projects for the water supply of San Francisco, Cal. made to the Mayor...by G. H. Mendell... S.F., Spaulding, 1877. 223 p. maps.
CHi CLU CSf CU-B

11336. —— Boys' high school. Commencement exercises... S.F. [1880–92]
CHi has 1880, 1888–89, 1892.

11337. —— Bureau of architecture. Program of competition for the selection of an architect to prepare plans and specifications for a city hall... S.F., 1909. 21 p.   CHi

11338. —— Report of the City architect to the Board of public works upon buildings to be used for schools, hospitals, hall of justice and county jail for San Francisco in connection with the proposed bond issue submitted to the voters Monday, May 11, 1908 by Newton J. Tharp. [S.F.] Carlisle and co., print. [1908] 13 p.
CLU

11339. —— Bureau of engineering. The Hetch Hetchy project of the city and county of San Francisco, California, its progress, prospects and possibilities [by Michael M. O'Shaughnessy] S.F., 1920. 18 p. map.
CHi

11340. —— The Hetch Hetchy water and power project, the municipal railway, and other notable civic improvements of San Francisco, M. M. O'Shaughnessy, city engineer. Oct., 1922. S.F. 32 p. illus.
CHi CSf

11341. —— —— Hetch Hetchy water supply. S.F., 1925. 47 p. illus., fold. map.   CHi CSf

11342. —— —— The Hetch Hetchy water supply and power project of San Francisco. S.F., 1931. 64 p. illus., fold. map.   CHi CSf

11343. —— —— The Hetch Hetchy water supply of San Francisco; report...to the Mayor by Michael Maurice O'Shaughnessy March, 1916. S.F., Rincon pub. co. [1916] 44 p. illus., maps, fold. charts.   CHi CSf

11344. —— —— ... The municipal railway of San Francisco 1912–1921...S.F., J.A. Prud'homme composition co. [1921] 141 p. illus., ports.
CL CSf CSfMI CU-B

11345. —— Official grades of the public streets...comprising all grades established by March 20, 1909. Comp. by Marsden Manson. S.F., Bd. of supervisors. 310 p.   CSfU

11346. —— —— Same, December 31, 1912. Comp. by M. M. O'Shaughnessy. S.F., Phillips & Van Orden co. [n.d.] 340 p.   CSfP

11347. —— —— ... Report on rapid transit plans for the city of San Francisco with special consideration to a subway under Market street by Michael Maurice O'Shaughnessy... S.F. [Donaldson print. co.] 1931. 77 p. illus., fold. maps, charts.   CHi

11348. —— —— ...Report on the street railway transportation requirements of San Francisco with special consideration to the unification of existing facilities by Michael Maurice O'Shaughnessy. S.F. [Mercury press] 1929. 231, 24 p. fold. maps, charts.   CHi

11349. —— Reports on an auxiliary water supply system for fire protection for San Francisco, Cali-

fornia. Report[s] by Marsden Manson...H. D. H. Connick...T. W. Ransom...W. C. Robinson... S.F., Britton & Rey, 1908. 173 p. illus., fold. pl.   CHi

11350. —— Reports on the water supply of San Francisco, California, 1900 to 1908, inclusive. Pub. by authority of the Board of supervisors... S.F., Press of Britton & Rey, 1908. 230 p. illus., maps.
C-S CHi CLU CSf CSfCSM CSfMI CSfSC CU-B

11351. —— —— Streets accepted by the Board of supervisors... from Jan. 1, 1940 to Jan. 1, 1950. [S.F.] 1950. 43 p.   CHi

11352. —— Bureau of governmental research. The city; a publication devoted to the promotion and application of scientific principles of government. 1917– S.F., 1917– Suspended May 1918–Sept. 1921.
CLSU has v.27, no. 1, v.28, no. 1–2, v.29, no. 1, v.30, no. 1–2, v.33, no. 1. CO has v.6, no. 3 (May 1926)—date. CU-B has Feb. 21, Mar. 15, Apr. 4, 21, June 29, Nov., Dec. 24, 1917, Feb. 8, Apr. 2, 1918, Oct. 29–30, 1928, Feb. 27, 1930. CU-Bur. of pub. admin. has v.4, 1924–date.

11353. —— —— The San Francisco–San Mateo survey, 1928. Made for the San Francisco Chamber of commerce... [S.F., 1928] 196 p. illus., maps, diagrs., tables.   C CHi CStclU CU-B

11354. —— California collegiate institute for young ladies. Catalogue...9th, 11th, 14th session, 1862:2, 1864:1, 1865:2. S.F., 1862–65. 3 v.   CU-B

11355. —— California midwinter international exposition, 1894. A glimpse of the midwinter fair specially sketched and lithographed by Dickman-Jones company for the San Francisco morning call. S.F., 1894.
CAla CHi CLgA

11356. —— —— [California midwinter international exposition, San Francisco, January 1st to June 30th, 1894] [Portland, Me., Leighton & Frey souvenir view co., 1894] illus. sheet fold in 11 l., fold. map.
C CHi CL CLU CSf CSmH CU-B

11357. —— In remembrance of the Midwinter international exposition. S.F. [Hergert & Frey] 1894. Folder.
C CHi CLSU CLU CO COHN CSalCL CSf CSfCW CSfU CSmH CStclU CU-B

11358. —— —— Information for intending exhibitors... [S.F., 1893] 24 p.   CSmH

11359. —— The monarch souvenir of Sunset city and sunset scenes; being views of California midwinter fair and famous scenes in the golden state. A series of pictures taken by I. W. Taber...S.F., Crocker, 1894.
C CLU CSf CSfU CSjC CU-B NHi

11360. —— Official catalogue, Department of fine arts. John A. Stanton, chief. [S.F.] Harvey, Whitcher & Allen, 1894. 40 p.   CU-B

11361. —— —— Same, rev. ed. 69 l.
CHi CSmH

11362. —— The official catalogue... A reference book of exhibitors and exhibits, officers and members...[1st ed.] S.F., Harvey, Whitcher & Allen, 1894. 180 p. illus.   CLU CSmH

11363. —— —— Same. [2d ed.] S.F., 1894. 167 p.   CSmH

11364. —— Official guide to the California midwinter exposition in Golden Gate park, San Francisco ... S.F., G. Spaulding & co., c1894. 207 p. illus.
C CHi CLU CSmH CU-B

11365. —— Official history of the California midwinter international exposition...held in San Fran-

cisco from January to July, 1894. S.F., Crocker, 1894. 259 p. illus., ports.
C CHi CL CLU CLgA CSfMI NN

11366. —— ...Official portfolio of the California midwinter international exposition; illus. from water color drawings by C. Graham... S.F., Winters art litho. co. [1894?] 31 p. illus. CHi

11367. —— Official souvenir... S.F., R.A. Irving, 1894. 77 p. illus., ports. CHi CU-B

11368. —— —— Welcome to our California midwinter international exposition. Souvenir. Compliments of the city of Paris...S.F. [n.d.] 30 p. illus. CSmH

11369. —— **California palace of the Legion of honor.** Annual exhibition of American painting, 2d (i.e. 3d) November 19, 1947–January 4, 1948. S.F., 1947. 47 p. illus. CHi

11370. —— —— Catalogue, art collection of Alma de Bretteville Spreckels. S.F., 1926. [101] p. illus. CHi

11371. —— —— Catalogue, inaugural exposition of French art...1924–1925. [S.F., James H. Barry co. press, 1924?] [68] p. ports., pl. CIIi CU-B

11372. —— —— Diego Rivera, November 15, 1930–December 25, 1930. S.F. [Taylor & Taylor, 1930] [35] p. illus., port. CHi

11373. —— —— Exhibition of flower paintings from the seventeenth century to the present day. S.F. [Taylor & Taylor] 1931. 16 p. CHi

11374. —— —— Exhibition of French painting, from the fifteenth century to the present day, June 8th to July 8th, 1934...[S.F., Johnck & Seeger, print., 1934] 75 p. ports., pl. CHi CU-B

11375. —— —— Exhibition of Venetian painting, from the fifteenth century through the eighteenth century, June 25th to July 24th, 1938. S.F. [1938] [46] p. col. front., pl. CHi CU-B

11376. —— —— Foreign section of the twenty-sixth annual international exhibition of paintings from the Carnegie institute, April second–May thirteenth, MCMXXVIII... [S.F., 1928] 123 p. illus.
CHi CU-B

11377. —— —— The French in California; one hundred years of achievement, 1850–1950...November 11 through November 30, 1950. [S.F., Dela pub. co., 1950] [37] l. ports., pl., facsims. CHi CStclU CU-B

11378. —— —— ...Illustrated handbook of the collections. S.F., Lincoln park [1944] 119 p. illus.
CLSU CLU CSf CSmH

11379. —— —— Isadora Duncan, a memorial exhibition of drawings...sponsored by Mr. and Mrs. J. Harold Smith...under the auspices of the Artists guild of America. S.F., 1956. 20 p. illus. CHi

11380. —— —— Portraits by Savely Sorine... [S.F., Taylor & Taylor] 1932. [6] p. port. CHi

11381. —— —— Seven centuries of painting; a loan exhibition of old and modern masters...December 29, 1939 to January 28, 1940. [S.F., Recorder press, 1939] 63 p. pl. CHi CU-B

11382. —— **California school of fine arts.** Catalogue [1874?]– S.F., [1873?]– illus. Founded by the San Francisco art association in 1874 as California school of design. 1893–1906, Mark Hopkins school of art. 1908–1916, San Francisco institute of art.
CHi has 1901, 1920/21–1941/42. 1921–25, 1927–32. (Summer session) CU-B has 1920/21–1921/22.

11383. —— **California school of mechanical**

arts. Circular, 1901, 1910, 1930. S.F., 1901–1930. 3 v. California school of mechanical arts founded 1875 by James Lick. Wilmerding school of industrial arts founded in 1894. CHi

11384. —— **Calvary Presbyterian church.** Calvary through the years; compiled in commemoration of seventy five years of service in the city of San Francisco ...1854–1929 by Carol Green Wilson. [S.F., 1930?] 104 p. illus. CHi

11385. —— —— Christmas day, 1887. [S.F., 1887] 12 p. CHi CU-B

11386. —— —— Historical sketch of the Calvary Presbyterian church... S.F., J.H. Carmany & co., 1869. 39 p. C CHi CSmH CU-B

11387. —— —— Manual of Calvary Presbyterian church... S.F., 1863. 60 p. CU-B

11388. —— —— Same. 1867. 50 p.
C CLU CSf CU-B

11389. —— —— Provisionally organized July, 1854; house dedicated 14th January, 1855, and congregation fully organized. S.F., Stevens, print., 1860. 24 p.
CLU CU-B

11390. —— **Chamber of commerce.** Annals of the Chamber of commerce of San Francisco. S.F., Neal pub. co., 1909. 47 p.
C CLU CSf CSmH CU CU-B

11391. —— —— Annual report...1858/59–1913. S.F., 1859–[1914] Title varies: 1859–66. Abstract of proceedings.
C has [1858/59–1911]. C-S has 1858/59, 1864/65–1865/66. CHi has 1871/72, 1885, 1912, 1913. CLU has 1863/64, 1865/66, 1869/70, 1871/72, 1873/74, 1891/92, 1900/01, 1902/03, 1908/09. CO has 1889, 1906/07. CSf has 1858/59–[1914]. CSmH has 16th–18th, 20th, 34th, 40th, 49th, 52d–53d. CU has 1906–10. CU-B has 1858/59–[1914]. MoSHi has 1896/97. NvHi has 1858/59.

11392. —— —— Annual statistical report. 1st–10th, 1911–1921. [S.F., 1912, 1921] illus., map. No report for 1917.
C has 1911–14. CHi has 1911–12. CL has 1911–14, 1918–21. CLU has 1911–12, 1915. CSf has 1911–14, 1918–21. CSfCW has 1911. CSmat has 1911–14, 1918–21. CU-B has 1911–16, 1918–21.

11393. —— —— Articles of incorporation and by-laws. S.F., 1911–24. CHi (1916, 1924) CSf (1911)

11394. —— —— By-laws and rules... Instituted April, 1850. S.F., Pub. by order of the Chamber, 1857. 19 p. CU-B NvHi

11395. —— —— Certificate of incorporation and by-laws...adopted May 12, 1868... S.F., Winterburn & co., print, 1868. 54 p. CU

11396. —— —— ...The city and port of San Francisco... [S.F.] 1896. [24] p. illus. CU-B

11397. —— —— Constitution and by-laws... S.F., Print. Journal of commerce off., 1850. 8 p. CU-B

11398. —— —— Same. [Eureka job print. office, 1856] 18 p. CSmH CU-B

11399. —— —— ...Directory of foreign traders of San Francisco...1924. S.F. [1924]
CO CSf CU-B

11400. —— —— Same. 1926. CU-B

11401. —— —— ...Directory of manufacturers of San Francisco, California, comprising an alphabetically arranged list of manufacturers and a classified material section. 1920–1921. S.F. [c1920–22] maps.
C CSf CU-B

11402. San Francisco. Chamber of commerce (*cont'd*) Extracts from report of the committee appointed Nov. 11, 1873...to prepare bills for legislative action on the subject of fares and freights...S.F., 1874. 30 p.   CHi CU

11403. —— —— Facts about the Port of San Francisco... S.F., 1921. 142 p. illus., maps.
CSf CSfCP CSfU CSmH CU-B

11404. —— —— The Golden Gate, San Francisco; through these protecting headlands $473,793,940 worth of foreign commerce passed in during 1919. S.F., 1920. 16 p.   CHi CU-B

11405. —— —— Industrial San Francisco in word and picture. S.F., 1920. [20] p. illus., map.
C CHi CSf CU-B

11406. —— —— Law and order in San Francisco; a beginning...[S.F.] 1916. 41 p. illus.
C-S CHi CL CLSU CLU CO CRic CSd CSdS CSf CSfCP CSfCW CSfP CSmH CSmat CStmo CU CU-B MHi MoS MoSHi NHi

11407. —— —— List of members, May 1912. [S.F., Commercial news press, 1912?] 92 p.   CSf

11408. —— —— Port charges of the port of San Francisco. Report of a special committee to the Chamber of commerce, at an adjourned meeting, held November 22d, 1871... S.F., Alta Calif. print., 1871. 8 p.
CSmH CU-B

11409. —— —— Report of harbor and shipping commission of the Board of trustees of the Chamber of commerce of San Francisco upon utility of Panama route for freight transportation between San Francisco and the Atlantic states approved...November 16, 1907. S.F., Neal pub. co. [1907?] 16 p.   CSf CU-B

11410. —— —— Report of the committee appointed..."to report on the condition of our postal affairs and to consider the feasibility of improvements and reforms."... S.F., Waters bros. & co., 1864. 23 p.
CLU CU-B

11411. —— —— Report of the special committee of the Board of trustees...on insurance settlements incident to the San Francisco fire. Approved...November 13, 1906. [S.F., Spaulding-Graul co., 1906?] 56 p.
C CHi CSf CSfU CSmH CU CU-B

11412. —— —— Report to the U.S. Tariff commission by the committee on free port, appointed by the San Francisco chamber of commerce. [n.p.] 1918. 54 p.
CSf CU

11413. —— —— San Francisco... [S.F.] 1912. 47 p. illus., map.
C-S CHi CLU CSfU CU-B MoSHi NN
Other editions followed. CO (1915) CSmH (1915) CU-B (1913, 1915)

11414. —— —— San Francisco and the Canal. [n.p., n.d.]   C-S

11415. —— —— San Francisco and the Central empire. 2d ed. [S.F.] 1939. 19 p. illus.   CHi CU-B

11416. —— —— The San Francisco bay metropolitan area. Dec. 8, 1948. 43 p. maps.   CO

11417. —— —— San Francisco, hub of western industry. S.F., 1939. 22 p.   CU-B

11418. —— —— San Francisco, the financial, commercial and industrial metropolis of the Pacific coast: official records, statistics and encyclopedia...[S.F., Crocker, c1915] 134 p. illus.
C C-S CHi CLSU CLU CSf CSfCP CSfCW CSfMI CSfP CSmH CU CaBViPA NN

11419. —— —— The $10,000,000 Hetch Hetchy water bond issue. Report of the Committee on water and power of the municipal affairs committee of the San Francisco chamber of commerce. S.F., 1924. [16] p.
CU-B

11420. —— —— This is San Francisco, portrait of a city. S.F. [1947] 32 p. illus.   CRcS

11421. —— —— To the honorable the Congress of the United States. The Chamber of commerce of San Francisco respectfully ask the attention of your honorable body to that portion of the Tariff act of August, 1861. [S.F., 1861] 4 p.   CHi

11422. —— —— **Business and trade dept.** Large manufacturers directory; manufacturers in the 12 bay region counties employing 100 or more. S.F., 1948. 27 p.   CSdS CU

11423. —— —— —— Same. [S.F., 1951] 28 p.
CU CU-B

11424. —— —— —— Same. 13 bay region counties. [S.F., 1958] 26 p.   C CSfSO CU

11425. —— —— **Domestic trade dept.** San Francisco, "Golden Gate" to western business; directory of manufacturing, city and county of San Francisco. [S.F., 1957] 60 p.   C CSfSO CU-B

11426. —— —— —— ...San Francisco manufacturers... 1936–1949. S.F., 1936–49.
CSdS (1949/50) CSf (1936–37, 1940) CU (1938, 1945, 1946/48, 1949/50).

11427. —— —— **Industrial dept.** San Francisco bay region space age & electronic directory. [S.F., 1962] 24 p. 1959 ed. has title: Electronics directory.
CU

11428. —— —— —— Why manufacturers choose San Francisco. [S.F., 1928] 32 p. illus., maps, diagrs.   C CHi

11429. —— —— **Port promotion program committee.** A special report. Promotion and improvement of the port of San Francisco. S.F., 1950. 44 p.
CSfU

11430. —— —— **Publicity dept.** A trip to San Francisco. [S.F., 1919] 46 p. illus., fold. map.
CHi CO CSmH CU CU-B

11431. —— —— **Research dept.** Large employers in San Francisco. [S.F.] 1931. 19 l. Mimeo.   CU-B

11432. —— —— —— Organization list, military. [S.F.] 1938. 2 l. Mimeo.   CU-B

11433. —— —— —— Pioneer firms established in San Francisco prior to 1900 and still in existence... May, 1953. 5 l. Mimeo.   CHi

11434. —— —— —— San Francisco and the bay area; an economic survey and yearly review. 1933– [S.F., 1933– None published 1942. Title varies: 1933–44, San Francisco economic survey.
CHi has 1948. CSf has 1936 to date. CSfSt has 1949–54, 1956 to date. CU has 1933, 1937 to date. CU-B has 1937–40, 1944, 1946, 1951 to date.

11435. —— **Charters.** An act to charter the city of San Francisco, Upper California. [S.F.] Print. at the Alta California off., 1850. 4 p. The charter contains 28 articles prefixed with a resolution of the Town council of January 30, 1850.   CU-B NN

11436. —— —— The new city charter of the city of San Francisco. Published by authority. Adopted by the people of San Francisco at the general election held September 7th, 1853. S.F., Commercial advertiser, 1853. 24 p.   C CSmH CU-B NN

11437. —— —— [Other city charters...] [S.F., 1855–1931] C-S (1880, 1895, 1898, 1907–08, 1911, 1915, 1925) CHi (1883, 1887, 1895, 1897, 1900, 1907–08, 1911, 1925, 1929, 1931) CLU (1855, 1898) CSfMI (1883, 1887, 1895, 1898, 1900, 1911, 1915, 1931) CSfSt (1931) CSluCL (1898) MoSHi (1898) ViU (1931)

11438. —— **Charters, ordinances, etc.** Act of incorporation and ordinances of the city of San Francisco. S.F., Print. at the off. of the Evening picayune, 1850. 72 p.
C CSmH CU-B WHi

11439. —— —— Consolidation act of the city and county of San Francisco. [S.F.] Monson, Valentine, print. [1856] 48 p. The act was written by Horace Hawes and was passed by the Legislature, April 19, 1856.
C CLU CU-B

11440. —— —— The consolidation act, or charter of the city and county of San Francisco; with other acts specially relating to San Francisco...Comp. by T. Hart Hyatt, jr., attorney at law and published by order of the Board of supervisors. [S.F., T.B. Deffebach & co., print.] 1866. 439 p.
CHi

11441. —— —— Same. S.F., Cosmopolitan print. co., 1870. 309 p.
CHi

11442. —— —— Same. S.F., Spaulding & Barto, 1876. 319 p.
CSmH

11443. —— —— Same. Comp. by A. E. T. Worley. S.F., Print. by Wm. M. Hinton & co., 1887. 478 p.
C-S CHi CSf CSfMI CU-B

11444. —— —— Manual of the corporation of the city of San Francisco, containing a map of the city... S.F., G.K. Fitch & co., print., Times & transcript press, 1852. 261 p. maps. Other editions published.
C CHi CLU (and 1853 ed.) CSf CSfP CSfWF-H CSmH CU-B (and 1853 ed.) NN NvHi

11445. —— **Chinese chamber of commerce.** San Francisco's Chinatown; history, function and importance of social organizations. Reproduced by San Francisco Chinese chamber of commerce, 1953. 10 l.
CU-B

11446. —— **Church of the Advent.** Advent book, Christmas, 1901. S.F. [1901] 72 p. pl.
CHi

11447. —— **Church of the New Jerusalem.** "And they heard the voice of the Lord God walking in the garden"...S.F., 1939. [4] p.
CHi

11448. —— **Citizens.** An address from the workingmen of San Francisco to their brothers throughout the Pacific coast. [n.p.] 1888. 24 p.
CHi

11449. —— —— An appeal of the water-rate payers of San Francisco. Opinions of the press and of citizens upon the system of water rates. [S.F., 1880?] 36 p. Signed: H. Heynemann [and others]
CLU

11450. —— —— Appeal to the California delegation in Congress upon the Goat island grant to the Central Pacific R.R. co. ...S.F., Alta Calif. print. house, 1872. 59 p.
CHi CLU CSmH CU-B

11451. —— —— The Goat island grant...on the subject of the grant of Goat island to the Central Pacific R.R. co. S.F., Alta Calif. print. house, 1872. 15 p.
CU-B

11452. —— —— A memorial of citizens and taxpayers...protesting against the passage of a bill, introduced into the Assembly by Hon. Charles L. Wiggin. S.F., Towne & Bacon print., 1866. 8 p. Protests the grading of Rincon Hill.
CLU

11453. —— —— Memorial to congress from the citizens of San Francisco for the establishment of a branch mint at that place; and in relation to the United States assay office. Wash., Govt. print. off., 1851. 14 p.
CHi

11454. —— —— Memorial to His Excellency Andrew Johnson, president of the United States. Concerning Rincon point, San Francisco, California. S.F., E. Bosqui & co., print., 1865. 20 p.
CLU CU-B

11455. —— —— Same. Wash., D.C., Joseph L. Pearson [1865] 13 p.
CHi

11456. —— —— Memorial to the holders and owners of the floating debt of the city of San Francisco. S.F., Alta Calif. steam presses, 1857. 48 p. tables.
CLU CSf CU-B

11457. —— —— Mortgage tax. Partial list of signers to the mortgage pledge numbering more than 25,000 signatures from San Francisco. S.F., J.H. Carmany, 1875.
CSmH

11458. —— —— Petition of Citizens of San Francisco for the repeal of the mortgage tax law. [Sacramento, Gelwicks, state print., 1870]
CSmH

11459. —— —— Petition of unemployed laborers to the legislature of California. [Sacramento, Gelwicks, state print., 1870]
CSmH

11460. —— —— Proceedings in relation to the Mortara abduction: mass meeting at Musical hall, San Francisco, California, January, 1859... S.F., Towne & Bacon, 1859. 52 p.
C CHi CSmH CU-B

11461. —— —— Proceedings of the great mass meeting, in favor of the Union, held in the city of San Francisco, on...February 22d, 1861. S.F., Print. at the Alta Calif. job off., 1861. 32 p.
C CLU CSmH CU-B IHi NN WHi

11462. —— —— Proceedings of the meeting of the mechanics, merchants, traders, bankers, etc. ...in opposition to the license law. S.F., Calif. Courier print., 1854. 16 p.
C CSmH

11463. —— —— Reply to the report of the San Francisco delegation to the Senate, on Senate bill no. 163, an act concerning the rates of fare on street railroads in the city and county of San Francisco. Sacramento, 1864. 16 p.
CHi

11464. —— **Citizens' anti-bulkhead committee.** Address to the members of the state senate from the general committee, appointed by the citizens of San Francisco, in opposition to the Senate bill no. 167, commonly called "The Parsons' bulkhead bill." S.F., Alta Calif. job print., 1860. 14 p. Signed: H. F. Teschemacher, chairman. "Written by Henry E. Highton, 1860." ms. note p. [3]
CLU CU-B NvHi

11465. —— —— The antidote for the poison... Abstract of speeches and documents against the Parsons bulk-head bill... S.F., Towne & Bacon, 1860. 96 p.
C CLU CSmH CU-B

11466. —— **Citizens' committee.** Century of commerce celebration. 1835, 1935... San Francisco, California, October 14 to 19, 1935. [S.F., Recorder print. & pub. co., c1935] 63 p.
CHi CSf

11467. —— —— The golden banquet and other functions during reception of President Roosevelt. S.F. [Print. by the Stanley-Taylor co.] 1903. 100 p. mounted illus. (part col.), mounted ports.
CHi CSf CU-B

11468. —— —— Official souvenir program: San Francisco-Oakland bay bridge celebration Nov. 11–15, 1936... S.F., 1936. 15 p. illus.
CHi CLgA

11469. —— —— Souvenir of San Francisco's welcome home to Raphael Weill, July 11, 1919. [S.F., 1919] 7 p. port.
C-S CHi

11470. —— **Citizens committee for the study of teachers' salaries.** Salary schedules for San Francisco public schools. S.F., 1929. 102 p.
CHi

11471. San Francisco (*cont'd*) **Citizens committee to save the cable cars.** Why you should vote yes on "J". [S.F., 1954] 2 l.   CU-B

11472. —— **Citizens' health committee.** Eradicating plague from San Francisco; report...March 31, 1909. Prepared by Frank Morton Todd, historian for the Committee. [S.F., Press of C.A. Murdock & co., 1909] 313 p. illus.
C CHi CLM CLSU CLU COHN CSf CSfCW CSfP CSj CSmH CU-B MoS MoSHi ViU

11473. —— **Water front committee.** Insanitary conditions along the San Francisco water front; a report to the Citizens health committee of San Francisco by its Water front committee. S.F., 1908. 14 p.   C

11474. —— **City attorney.** Brief...by John J. O'Toole. Before the Secretary of the interior, United States of America, in the matter of the hearing on the legality of San Francisco's disposal of Hetch Hetchy hydroelectric power, called and held on May 6, 1935. S.F., Recorder print. and pub. co. [1935?] 70 p.   CHi

11475. —— ...In the matter of the application of James D. Phelan for rights of way in Hetch Hetchy Valley and Lake Eleanor, within the Yosemite national park. Petition [to the Secretary of the Interior] for review, by the city and county of San Francisco. [n.p., 1903?] 36 p. Submitted by Franklin K. Lane, city attorney.   CHi CU-B

11476. —— Report of city litigation, by S. W. Holladay, city and county attorney. S.F., Charles F. Robbins, 1861. 99 p.   C CHi CU-B

11477. —— **City college.** Catalogue...Apr. 1861, Nov. 1864, 1877/78. S.F., 1861–78. 3 v. fronts.   CU-B

11478. —— Circular... [S.F., 1868–1870?]
CHi (1870?) CSmH (1868)

11479. —— —— Prospectus, rules, regulations, &c. ... Established 1856. S.F., Sterett & co., print., 1856. 16 p.   C CU

11480. —— —— **University college and boarding school.** [Brochure. S.F.? 1871?] [3] p.   CHi

11481. —— **Civic federation.** Report on the assessor's office. 1896.   C-S NN

11482. —— **Civil service commission.** Two and a half years of civil service under the "new" charter Jan. 8, 1932 to July 8, 1934. Comp. by Wm. L. Henderson and L. A. Landreville. S.F., 1934. 39 p.   CHi

11483. —— **College of Notre Dame.** Prospectus and catalogue...for the academic year 1893/94. S.F., 1894. 1 v.   CU-B

11484. —— **College of physicians and surgeons.** Preliminary announcement... [n.p., 1896?] [4] p.   CHi

11485. —— **Commercial high school.** Catalogue. 1893. S.F., 1893. 1 v. illus.   CU-B

11486. —— **Commission for dedication of the Sutro monument.** The "Triumph of light." Dedication services at the Sutro monument on Mount Olympus, corner Ashbury and Sixteenth streets, San Francisco, Thanksgiving day, Thursday, Nov. 24th, A.D. 1887. S.F., Donald Bruce, 1888. 30 p. illus.   CHi

11487. —— **Commission to enquire into city property.** Report on the condition of the real estate within the city of San Francisco and the property beyond within the bounds of the old Mission Dolores... S.F., Print. off. Evening picayune, January, 1851. 156 p.
C CHi CLU CSmH CU-B ICN NN

11488. —— **Committee for major league base-**

ball. The city in your future. Play ball in San Francisco. [S.F., 1957] [32] p. illus., ports., maps, tables.   CU-B

11489. —— **Committee of tax-payers.** Tax-payer's review and objections to the Parsons bulkhead bill (Senate bill no. 40). ... S.F., S.F. Herald off., 1859. 13 p.   CLU CU CU-B WHi

11490. —— **Committee of vigilance, 1851.** ... Papers of the San Francisco Committee of vigilance of 1851. Ed. by Porter Garnett... Berkeley, Univ. of Calif., 1910–19. 3 v. illus., map. (Publications of the Acad. of Pac. coast history, v.1, no. 7, v.2, no. 2, v.4) v.3, ed. by Mary F. Williams.
Available in many California libraries and CaBViPA IHi KHi NHi NN

11491. —— **Committee of vigilance, 1856.** Constitution and address[!]... S.F., Morning globe print., 1856. 8 p.
CHi CLU CSfCP CSmH CU-B NN NHi

11492. —— —— [Pamphlets] 1856–1887. S.F., 1856–87.   CU-B

11493. —— —— Trial of David S. Terry... S.F., R.C. Moore & co., print., Alta Calif. newspaper off., 1856. 75 p.
C CCH CHi CLU COMC CSf CSfCP CSmH CU-B NvHi PHi WHi

11494. —— —— The Vigilance committee of 1856. [n.d.] 81 p. Typew.   C

11495. —— **Committee on reconstruction.** Plan of proposed street changes in the burned district and other sections of San Francisco... Submitted to the Board of supervisors, May, 1906. S.F., Hicks-Judd co., 1906. 187 p. maps.   C CHi CSfP CSmH CStclU CU-B MoS

11496. —— —— Report of the Sub-committee on statistics to the chairman and committee on reconstruction. S.F., 1907. 16 p.   C CHi

11497. —— —— Report of the Sub-committee on water supply and fire protection to the Committee on the reconstruction of San Francisco. [S.F., 1906] 8 p.
CSf CU-B

11498. —— —— Transcript of joint proceedings of sub-committees on: municipal departments (including police) ; special session of the legislature and state legislation; charter amendments; judiciary. May 1906. v.p.
CSf

11499. —— **Committee on the causes of municipal corruption.** Report on the causes of municipal corruption in San Francisco, as disclosed by the investigation of the Oliver grand jury... [S.F., Rincon pub. co., 1910] 54 p.
C-S CHi CLSU CLU CO CSf CSfP CSfU CSmH CStoC CU-B MoS NHi TxU ViU

11500. —— —— Same. "Reprinted with a preface and index of names and subjects by the California weekly, 26 Montgomery Street, San Francisco."   CHi

11501. —— **Congregation Beth Israel.** ...100th anniversary, 1860...1960. 48 p. illus., ports.   CHi

11502. —— **Congregational church.** [Records] S.F. [etc.] 1860–93. 13 v.   CU-B

11503. —— **Coordinating council.** Community resources, by coordinating council districts. S.F. [1941] 45 l. maps. Mimeo.   CSf

11504. —— **Dept. of city planning.** Daily trips in San Francisco; the daily vehicular passenger movements to work, to shop, to school, ... An analysis of survey data 1913, 1926, 1937, 1947 and 1954. [S.F.] 1955. 106 p.   CSf CSt

11505. —— —— The population of San Francisco; a half century of change. A presentation and analysis of facts, trends and changing relationships...between 1900 and 1950. S.F., 1954. 27 p. illus., maps.
CSf CSfSt CSt

11506. —— —— A subway and rapid transit system for San Francisco... S.F., 1950. CSt

11507. —— **Deutsches haus.** Das Deutsches haus. Polk & Turk Sts., San Francisco. [S.F., 1908?] [15] p. illus., plans. CU-B

11508. —— —— Gedenblätter zur eröffnungs feier des Deutschen hauses, 7ten bis 15ten Dezember 1912, San Francisco, Cal. [S.F., 1912] [40] p. illus., plans. CU-B

11509. —— **District attorney.** Survey of housing conditions in San Francisco as of May 1, 1947. Prepared by Edmund G. Brown. S.F., 1947. v.p. Mimeo. CSf

11510. —— **Engineer.** ...communication to the common council of San Francisco, in relation to street grades, May 22, 1854. S.F., Commercial advertiser power presses, 1854. 8 p. C CHi CSmH CU-B

11511. —— —— Grades of the public streets of the city and county of San Francisco. S.F., W.M. Hinton & co., 1889. 111 p. CSfCW

11512. —— —— Report of the Board of engineers upon the city grades. 1854. 27 p.
C CHi CSmH CU-B

11513. —— **Epworth Methodist Episcopal church.** Year book and directory, 1914... [n.p., n.d.] 44 p. illus. CHi

11514. —— **Exempt fire company.** By-laws... together with the Article of incorporation...and a numerical list of the members. S.F., J.M. Crane & co., 1872. 44 p.
CHi has 1881 ed. also.

11515. —— —— Code of laws. Adopted Dec. 8, 1862. Revised and adopted July 24, 1865. S.F., Agnew & Deffebach print., 1865. 30 p. CHi

11516. —— —— The exempt firemen of San Francisco: their unique and gallant record. Together with a resume of the San Francisco Fire department and its personnel; historical-biographical. S.F. [Harry C. Pendleton, pub.; Commercial pub. co., print.] 1900. 269 p. illus., ports. C CHi CLU CSf CSfP CSfWF-H CU-B

11517. —— —— Report of the receipts and disbursements...for charitable and other purposes, from 1852 to and including 1890. S.F., C.A. Murdock & co., 1891. 15 p. CHi

11518. —— —— Reports of the officers and auditing committee... [185-?-] S.F. [185-?-]
CHi has 1874, 1883, 1886.

11519. —— **Female institute.** ...A boarding school for young ladies, comprising a full course of English, French, classical and scientific studies for thorough instruction. The first school in California. Rev. J. Avery Shepherd, M.A., principal. Second catalogue, August 1857. S.F., Print. by A. Hamilton, 1857. 12 p. C CU

11520. —— **Fire dept.** Code of laws...of the Empire fire engine company, no. 1. S.F., Alta Calif. steam presses, 1850. 16 p. CU-B

11521. —— —— Constitution and by-laws of California engine co. no. 4. Firemen's journal bk. & job print. off., 1856. 24 p. CHi

11522. —— —— Constitution and by-laws of Knickerbocker engine company no. 5. ...adopted, October 17th, 1853. N.Y., Francis and Loutrel, 1853. 24 p. Lists officers from October 17, 1850 to January 1, 1853. CHi

11523. —— —— Same, rev., April 10, 1856. S.F., Monson, Valentine & co., print., 1856. 16 p. C CLU

11524. —— —— Constitution and by-laws of Monumental engine company no. 6. Organized September 10th, 1850. S.F., Commercial advertiser power presses, 1854. 10 p. CHi

11525. —— —— Same. S.F., Agnew & Deffebach, 1860. 26 p. CHi

11526. —— —— Constitution and by-laws of St. Francis fire company. Organized June 15th, 1850. S.F., C.A. Calhoun, 1857. 24 p. CU-B

11527. —— —— Constitution and by-laws of Sansome hook and ladder co., number three... S.F., Layden and O'Meara, job print., 1853. 32 p. CHi

11528. —— —— Constitution and by-laws of Volunteer engine co., no. 7. Amended, April 5th, 1859. S.F., C.F. Robbins, 1860. 18 p. CU-B

11529. —— —— Constitution, by-laws, and rules of order of Young America engine co. no. 13. S.F., Fireman's journal bk. and job print. off., 1856. 21 p. CU-B

11530. —— —— Quarterly report of F. E. R. Whitney, chief engineer...S.F., Fireman's journal off., 1857. 24 p. CHi

11531. —— —— Reports of the fire officers... on the fire of 1906...July, 1935. 71 l. Typew. CU-B

11532. —— —— Roll of certificate members... entitled to exemption from jury duty, under act of legislature approved March 25, 1853...S.F., Commercial advertiser power presses, 1853. 114 l. CSmH

11533. —— —— Same. S.F., Charles M. Chase and co., 1855. [36] p. [interleaved] CHi CSfCP

11534. —— —— The San Francisco fire department, 1893. [S.F., 1893] 64 p. illus. CSmH

11535. —— —— Second anniversary of the organization of the fire department of San Francisco, and celebration of the birth-day of Washington, Feb. 22d, 1853. S.F., 1853. 24 p. C CSmH CU-B

11536. —— —— Statement touching the "Charitable Fund" of the San Francisco fire department. [Caption-title] [S.F., 1866] 23 p. CSmH

11537. —— **First African Methodist Episcopal Zion church.** Souvenir program, ...dedication services ... S.F. [1960] [32] p. illus., ports. Contains short history of church, 1852-1960. CHi

11538. —— **First Baptist church.** By-laws... approved April 23d, 1902. [n.p., n.d.] 15 p. CHi

11539. —— —— 1849-1949...a history of the First Baptist church. S. F. [1905?] 89 p. illus., ports. CHi

11540. Not in use.

11541. Not in use.

11542. Not in use.

11543. —— **First church of Christ, Scientist.** By-laws and rules...organized Oct. 15, 1895, incorporated Feb. 4, 1899. Rev. Dec. 1960. S.F., 1961. 32 p. CHi

11544. —— **First Congregational church.** Annual directory. San Francisco.
CHi has 1899, 1905, 1909, 1922, 1924.

11545. —— —— 80th anniversary... S.F., 1929. 57 p. illus. CHi

11546. —— —— ...The golden jubilee, fiftieth

anniversary. First Congregational church, San Francisco, California...1899... [S.F., 1899] 34 p. illus., ports.
CHi CLU CSfP CSmH CU-B

11547. San Francisco. First Congregational church (*cont'd*) A hundred years of Congregationalism in San Francisco, 1849–1949, by Charles M. Bufford. Prepared for centennial meeting...held at Portsmouth plaza, July 31, 1949. [S.F., 1949] 47 p.   C CU-B

11548. —— —— Manual... Edward S. Lacy, pastor. Published by a vote of the church, March, 1857. 2d ed. S.F., Whitton, Towne & co., 1857. 35 p.
CHi WHi

11549. —— —— Same. 3d ed. S.F., Towne & Bacon, print., 1860. 42 p.   CBPac CSmH CU-B

11550. —— —— Same. ...with a list of members...by Charles Dana Barrows. S.F., 1884. 96 p. port. Brief history, 1849 to date.   C CHi CLU CU-B

11551. —— —— Same. 6th ed. 1893.   CU-B

11552. —— —— 100 anniversary directory, 1849–1949. [S.F., 1949] 61 p.   CHi

11553. —— —— Reports...1888. [S.F., 1888] 57 p.   CSmH

11554. —— —— Seventieth anniversary of the Gothic church. Anniversary dinner May 19, 1942. [S.F.] 1942. [12] p. illus. Gothic church at Post and Mason opened May 19, 1872.   CHi

11555. —— —— "Silver wedding," the twenty-fifth anniversary of the founding of the first Congregational church of San Francisco, celebrated Wednesday, July 29, 1874. [S.F.] Spaulding & Barto, 1874. 131 p. illus., ports.
C CCH CHi CL CLU CO CSfP CSfU CSmH CU-B NN

11556. —— **First English Evangelical Lutheran church.** Constitution... [n.p., n.d.] 8 p.   CHi

11557. —— **First Presbyterian church.** ...Anniversary [exercises]...40th–41st; 1889–1890. [S.F., 1889–90] 2 v.   CU-B

11558. —— —— History of...100 years in San Francisco, 1849–1949. By Louis Alfred Peterson. [S.F.? 1950?] 36 p. illus., ports.   C CHi CSmH

11559. —— —— Installation of the Rev. Thos. M. Cunningham as pastor...Wednesday evening, Oct. 20th, A.D. 1869. Published by request of the congregation. [S.F., C.W. Gordon, bk. and job print., 1869] 24 p.
CU-B

11560. —— **First Unitarian church.** Annual reports, 1951; 1959; 1960; 1962. S.F., 1951–1962. 4 v.
CHi

11561. —— —— Fifty years of the First Unitarian church of San Francisco, October 20, 1850–October 21, 1900, by Horace Davis. S.F., 1901. 109 p. illus., ports. Biographical sketches, p. 41–77.
CHi CLU CSfP CSfU CSj CSmH CU-B NN

11562. —— —— Same. [Sunday, Oct. 21, 1900] 15 p. illus., ports.   CU-B

11563. —— —— Foundation, historical sketch, and twenty years record. S.F., William & Alice Hinckley fund, 1910. 28 p.   CHi CLU

11564. —— —— An historical sketch... with annual reports for 1883–4. [S.F.? 1884?] 28 p. Founded Oct. 20th, 1850; incorporated Nov. 1855.   CHi

11565. —— —— One hundred years...1850–1950. [S.F., Grabhorn, 1950?] 48 p. illus.
C CHi CSfMI CSt

11566. —— —— Order of services at the dedication...July 17th, 1853 [and] Evening service, July 17th, 1853. [S.F.] Bartlett print. [1853] 2 l.   C-S CHi

11567. —— —— **Channing auxiliary.** [By-laws and list of members] S.F., 1926. 24 p. Founded 1887.
CHi

11568. —— —— **Dutton club.** Constitution. S.F., 1949. 9 l.   CHi

11569. —— —— **Pilgrim Sunday school.** Teachers' association. By-laws of the Teachers' association of the Pilgrim Sunday school, organized May 1854. S.F., Print. by R.B. Quayle & co., 1854. 4 p.
CHi CU-B

11570. —— —— **Society for Christian work.** Annual report, 1st, 1874– S.F., 1874– 1 v. Founded Oct. 1873.   CHi

11571. —— **First Universalist church.** Installation of Rev. E. L. Rexford, D.D., as pastor...Nov. 1st, 1874... S.F., Benj. Dore & co., bk. and job print. [1874] 24 p.   CHi

11572. —— **Girls' high school.** Annual commencement, May 28, 1867. [S.F.] Towne & Bacon, 1867. [4] p.
CHi has also 1871, 1873, 1880, 1884, 1888, 1895, 1897, 1898.

11573. —— **Golden gate bridge fiesta.** Gold book; official guide and directory, Golden gate bridge fiesta. S.F., W.L.Mackey and co., 1937. 128 p.   CSf

11574. —— —— Official souvenir program... celebrating the opening of the world's longest single span...May 27 to June 2, 1937. Sponsored by Golden gate bridge and highway district, Redwood empire association and the city and county of San Francisco. [S.F., 1937] 48 p. illus., ports.
CHi CLgA CSf CSfMI CU-B

11575. —— **Golden gate international exposition, 1939–1940.** Art. Official catalog, Palace of fine arts. S.F., Recorder print. co., Crocker-Schwabacher-Frey, 1940. 176 p. illus.   CHi

11576. —— —— Contemporary art of the United States; collection of the International business machines corporation... [n.p., c1940] [111] p. illus., ports.
CHi

11577. —— —— I saw that. Official camera album views, 1939 World's fair on San Francisco bay. S.F., Crocker, 1939. 30 p. illus.   CAla CHi CRcS

11578. —— —— [Miscellaneous pamphlets]
CHi CLSU CO CSf CSfCW CU-B

11579. —— —— Official guide book. [S.F., Crocker, 1939] 116 p. illus., map.
Available in many California libraries and MiD   UHi

11580. —— —— Same, 1940. [S.F., Crocker, 1940] 96 p. illus., maps.   CHi CO CU-B

11581. —— —— Pageant of the Pacific: Golden gate international exposition. Official de luxe views. World's fair on San Francisco bay. [S.F., 1939?] [24] p. illus.   CHi CRcS CU-B

11582. —— —— Treasure island and the world's greatest spans of steel; the Golden Gate international exposition celebrating completion of three great engineering feats: the San Francisco–Oakland bay bridge, the Golden Gate bridge and Treasure island. S.F., Crocker, c1940. 32 p.   CAla CHi CO

11583. —— —— **Dept. of fine arts.** Contemporary art; official catalog...Division of contemporary painting and sculpture. [S.F., S.F. bay exposition co., 1939] 82 p. illus. CHi CSfSt

11584. —— —— —— Decorative arts; official catalog...Division of decorative arts, Golden Gate international exposition, San Francisco, 1939. [S.F., S.F. bay exposition co., c1939] [105] p. illus.
CHi CMont CSfSt

11585. —— —— —— ...Masterworks of five centuries. S.F., 1939. [142] p. illus.
CChiS CHi CSfMI CU-B

11586. —— —— —— Pacific cultures [official catalog]...Division of Pacific cultures. S.F., 1939. 156 p. pl. CHi CSfSt

11587. —— **Grace cathedral.** Cathedral for the community. S.F., 1928. [12] p. CHi CRcS

11588. —— —— Grace cathedral. [S.F., Print. for Grace cathedral building fund by Taylor & Taylor, 1927] 18 p. illus. CHi CSfCW CSmH CU-B

11589. —— —— Same. [S.F., 1936?] [18] p.
C CHi CO

11590. —— **Grace church.** Jubilee...1849–1899. [n.p., 1899?] [32] p. pl., ports. C

11591. —— **Grace Methodist Episcopal church.** Commemorating the twenty-fifth anniversary of the erection of Grace Methodist Episcopal church, Oct. 22nd to 27th, inclusive, 1911. Souvenir program. S.F., 1911. 12 p. Organized 1865. CHi

11592. —— —— Year book and directory. [S.F.] 1894. 98 p. port. CU-B

11593. —— **Harbor master.** Reports for the years ending June 30, 1860–1917.
Also in: San Francisco municipal reports. 1859/60–1916/17. CSf CU-B

11594. —— **Hospital for children and training school for nurses.** Annual report... 1888– S.F., Walter N. Brunt press, 1888– illus.
C has 1888, 1891, 1901–04. CHi has 1897, 1906.

11595. —— **Howard Presbyterian society.** Annual report of the treasurer...
CHi has 21st, 22d, 1870/71–1871/72.

11596. —— **Howard street Methodist Episcopal church.** ...Dedication services...January twenty-eight, nineteen hundred and twelve. [S.F., Jas. T. Lynch, 1912] 11 p. illus. (ports.) At head of title: The church of the chimes. CHi

11597. —— —— "The retrospect." A glance at thirty years of the history of Howard street Methodist Episcopal church of San Francisco...S.F., A. Buswell & co., print., 1883. 212 p. ports.
C CCH CHi CO CSf CSfCW CSfP CSmH CU-B N NHi NN

11598. —— —— Year book and church directory, 1894–95. [S.F.] Bk. room print. [1894] 80 p. CU-B

11599. —— **Industrial school dept.** ...Annual report of the Board of managers... 1st–10th, 1859–[1869] S.F., 1859–[1869]
CHi has 1st–10th, 1859–[1869]. CSf has 1st–2d, 1859–60. CSfCW has 1st, 1859. CSmH has 1st–4th, 1859–62. CStclU has 1st, 1859. CU-B has 1st–3rd, 8th–10th, 1859–61, 1867–[1869]. NN has 1st, 1859.

11600. —— —— Specifications for the Industrial school building of San Francisco. [S.F., Sterett & Butler, print., 185–?] 15 p. CU-B

11601. —— **Infant shelter.** Infant shelter, home for San Francisco's dependent babies, founded 1874. [S.F., 1927] 13 p. illus. CLU CU-B

11602. —— **Italian chamber of commerce.** Hidden treasures of San Francisco. The Italian food shops... S.F., 1927. [24] p. illus. CU-B

11603. —— **Junior chamber of commerce. Marine committee.** San Francisco harbor, one of the nation's great assets and an important factor in western development; a harbor day picture story... [S.F.] 1951. 6 p. illus. CRcS

11604. —— **Ladies' seminary and gymnasium.** Ladies' seminary and gymnasium...under the direction of Miss J. Aldrich. S.F., Towne & Bacon, print. [186–?] 15 p. CU-B

11605. —— **Laguna de la Merced appraisal commission.** Testimony taken before... [S.F.?] S.W. Raveley, print. [1880?] 152 p. CHi CSmH

11606. —— **Laurel hill cemetery association vs. San Francisco.** In the Supreme court of the state of California, Laurel hill cemetery (an association), plaintiff and appellant, vs. city and county of San Francisco, et al., defendants and respondents. Appellant's points and authorities. Lloyd & Wood, and Haven & Haven, attorneys for the appellants... [S.F., 1905] 52 p. CHi

11607. —— ...Laurel hill cemetery, plaintiff in error, vs. city and county of San Francisco, Board of supervisors, et al., defendants in error. Brief on behalf of plaintiff in error. Thomas E. Haven, attorney for plaintiff in error. S.F., Recorder print. [1909] 130 p. CHi

11608. —— **Laurel hill cemetery association.** By-laws...Adopted 8th January 1917. Incorporated 16th December 1916. [S.F.] G.C. Smith, 1917. 12 p. CHi

11609. —— —— A plea for the continuance of Laurel hill cemetery... S.F., 1903. 40 p. CHi

11610. —— —— **Board of trustees.** Adress to the lot owners... [S.F., 1914] [8] p. CHi CU-B

11611. —— **Laurel hill memorial park.** Laurel hill... S.F., Paul Elder & co. [1937?] [30] p. illus.
CHi CSmH

11612. —— **Mariner's church.** Manual. S.F., Towne & Bacon, 1859. 17 p. C

11613. —— **Marshall's office.** Rules and regulations prescribed by the City marshall for the government of the Police department...approved Oct. 28th, 1853. Drawn up and compiled for the City marshall, B. Seguine, esq., by D. H. T. Moss, his assistant. S.F., George Kerr & co., Times and transcript power presses, 1853. 28 p.
CHi

11614. —— **May festival of 1878.** Souvenir, May festival, San Francisco 1878; edited by Sumner W. Bugbee, illustrated by Chas. Warren Stoddard, Jos. D. Strong, jr. S.F., S. Bugbee, pub., 1878. 14 p. illus.
CHi

11615. —— **Mayor (Selby)** Valedictory of Hon. Thos. H. Selby and inaugural address of Hon. Wm. Alvord. Published by order of the Board of supervisors of the city and county of San Francisco, Dec. 4th, 1871. S.F., Alta Calif. print. house, 1871. CSmH

11616. —— —— **(Alvord)** Valedictory of the Hon. Wm. Alvord and inaugural address of the Hon. James Otis. Pub. by order of the Board of supervisors of the city and county of San Francisco, Dec. 1st, 1873. S.F., Spaulding & Barto, steam bk. and job print., 1873. 23 p. CHi CSmH

11617. —— —— **(Hewston)** Valedictory of the Hon. Geo. Hewston, M.D., and inaugural address of the Hon. A.J. Bryant. ...Dec. 13, 1875. S.F., F. Eastman, print., 1875. 32 p. CSmH

11618. San Francisco (*cont'd*) **Mayor (Phelan)** Addresses, by Mayor James D. Phelan. S.F. [Cubery & co., print.] 1901. 78 p.   CLU

11619. —— Proceedings at the banquet given by Hon. James D. Phelan, mayor, to the officials of the city and county of San Francisco. Palace hotel, January 12th, 1901. [S.F., 1901] 56 p.   CLU

11620. —— Third inaugural message delivered to the Board of supervisors of the city of San Francisco, delivered January 8, 1900... S.F., Town talk press, 1900. 42 p.   C-S

11621. —— **(Rolph)** History of the San Francisco war memorial...at a special meeting of the Board of supervisors, Feb. 18, 1930, by Hon. James Rolph, jr. ... S.F., Recorder print. and pub. co. [1930] 193 p.   CHi CSfP NN

11622. —— —— Supplemental history of the San Francisco war memorial including copy of war memorial agreement between the regents of the University of California and the trustees, and amendments, and transcripts of proceedings of the Board of supervisors on February 25, February 26 and March 3, 1930 by Hon. James Rolph, jr. ... S.F. Recorder print. and pub. co. [1930] 112 p.   CHi NN

11623. —— **Mayor's unemployment committee.** Report... Winter of 1921–1922. [n.p., n.d.] 16 p.   CHi CSf

11624. —— **Mechanics' institute.** ...Annual report... 11th– 1866/67– S.F., 1867–
CSf has 1940/41. CSfMI has 11th–21st, 36th–, 1866/67–1876/77, 1890/91– CU-B has 12th, 14th, 17th, 36th–44th, 49th, 52d–94th, 1867/1868–1948/49.

11625. —— —— The building of a state: the Mechanics' institute, by J. H. Culver. Theory made practice...by Joseph M. Cumming. 17 p. illus. Extracts from *Overland monthly*, Sept. 1886, and *Sunset magazine*, May 1907.   CSfMI

11626. —— —— Catalogue of art department of the twelfth industrial exhibition, held under the auspices of the Mechanics' institute, Aug. 1877. S.F., A.L. Bancroft & co., 1877. 52 p.   CHi

11627. —— —— Catalogue of articles at the second industrial exhibition...held in the pavilion, September, 1858. S.F., Pub. by Hutchings & Rosenfield, Towne & Bacon, print., 1858. 44 p.   C CU-B

11628. —— —— Constitution... 1855–1908. S.F., 1855–1908.
CHi has 1895. CLU CSfMI has 1857, 1870, 1875–76, 1880, 1883, 1885–86, 1889, 1891, 1895, 1899, 1908. CSfU has 1878. CSmH has 1870, 1885. CU-B has 1855, 1870, 1875–76, 1883, 1886, 1891, 1895, 1908.

11629. —— —— 1883 souvenir of the Mechanics' fair containing the oration of Rev. Robert Mackenzie and a complete list of names of the exhibitors. Compliments of Pacific business college. [S.F.? 1883?] 11 p.   CHi

11630. —— —— ...Historical papers, comp. by Francis B. Graves, librarian; John H. Wood, secretary. [S.F.] 1916. 15 pamphlets in 1 v.   CSfMI

11631. —— —— 100 years of Mechanics' institute of San Francisco, 1855–1955. S.F. [1955] 50 p.
CBev CHi CLU CO CSfMI CSfP CSfU CSmH CSt CStmo CU-B

11632. —— —— Proceedings of the reception tendered to the workmen of the Union iron works... at the Mechanics' pavilion, Saturday evening, December 22, 1893. S.F., J.H. Barry, print. [1893?] 29 p.
CHi CLU

11633. —— —— Report of the...Industrial exhibition... 1st–29th, 1857/58–1896. S.F., 1858–1896.
C has 1st–2d, 1857/58–1858/59. CHi has 1st, 5th, 8th, 1857/58, 1865, 1872. CLU has 1st, 20th–26th, 1857/58, 1885–91. CSf has 20th–26th, 1885–91. CSfCSM has 1st, 17th, 24th–25th, 1857/58, 1883, 1889–90. CSmH has 2d, 20th, 22d–23d, 1858/59, 1885, 1887–88. CSt has 1st–2d, 1857/58–1858/59. CU-B has 1st–29th, 1857/58–1896. MoS has 24th, 1889. NvHi has 1st, 1857/58.

11634. —— —— Seventy-five years of history of the Mechanics' institute of San Francisco, comp. by John H. Wood. S.F., 1930. 48 p. illus.
C CHi CLSU CLU CO CSf CSfMI CSfP CSfWF-H CSmH CU-B

11635. —— **Medical college of the Pacific.** ... Annual announcement of the Medical department... 1859– S.F., Towne & Bacon, 1859–
CHi has 1873, 1879. CLU has 1879. CU-B has 1859–1860/61.

11636. —— **Mercantile library association.** Annual report...1st–41st, 1853/54–1893. S.F., 1855–1894.
CHi has 1st–2d, 4th, 6th–8th, 10th, 15th–19th, 23d, 32d, 37th–39th, 41st, 1853/54, 1857/58, 1859/60–1861/62, 1863, 1868–71, 1876, 1884, 1889–91, 1893. CSmH has 1st–9th, 1853/54–62. CU-B has 1st–9th, 1853/54–62. NN has 1st–7th, 1853/54–60. WHi has 4th, 1857/58.

11637. —— —— Constitution, by laws and list of members...S.F., Whitton, Towne & co., 1853. 18 p.
CU-B NN

11638. —— —— Constitution...with a brief history of the Association and a list of members. S.F., Daily evening news off., 1854. 46 p.   CSfMI NN

11639. —— —— Same...with statistics and list of officers from the commencement. S.F., Charles Robbins & co., 1862. 24 p.   CBPac CSmH CU-B

11640. —— —— Report of the committee... for the erection of an edifice for the use of this association... S.F., Towne & Bacon, print., 1859. 8 p.
CHi CLU CSfCP CSmH CU-B

11641. —— —— Special report of Robert B. Swain, president... Dec. 1, 1870. [S.F., Bacon & co., 1870] 20 p. front.   CHi

11642. —— **Municipal government survey advisory committee.** Report. [S.F.?] 1952. 15 l.
CSfSt

11643. —— **Museum of art.** Annual report by the president, 1st, 1921/22– S.F. [1922?]–   CHi

11644. —— —— ...Catalogue of the loan exhibition of paintings by old masters, in the Palace of fine arts...by J. Nilsen Laurvik, director. S.F., 1920. 69 p. pl., ports.   CHi CU-B

11645. —— —— ...Catalogue of the retrospective loan exhibition of European tapestries, by Phyllis Ackerman...S.F., 1922. 63 p. pl., map.   CHi CU-B

11646. —— —— Contemporary art. Paintings, watercolors and sculpture owned in the San Francisco bay region. Fifth anniversary exhibition Jan. 18 to Feb. 5, 1940. S.F., Borden print. co., c1940. 79 p. illus.   CHi

11647. —— —— Domestic architecture of the San Francisco bay region. [A catalog of an exhibition held]...Sept. 16, Oct. 30, 1949. [S.F., 1949] [28] p. pl.
C CArcHT CSfSt CSto CU-B

11648. —— —— Drawings by Maurice Sterne, accessions to Albert M. Bender collection, 1936–1937. S.F., 1937. 19 p. illus.   CHi

11649. —— —— Exhibitions. S.F. [1920?–] illus.

CHi has 1920–60 (incomplete) CU-B has 1952–58.

11650. —— —— First graphic arts exhibition of the San Francisco art association, Sept. 14 through Oct. 13, 1935. S.F., Taylor & Taylor, print. [1935] 26 p. illus.
CHi

11651. —— —— ...Fifty-fifth annual exhibition of the San Francisco art association; and loan exhibitions of modern French paintings, great prints of five centuries, Chinese art, tapestries, drawings... S.F., 1935. 48 p. pl.
CHi

11652. —— —— Two buildings, San Francisco, 1959. [S.F., 1959] 51 p. illus., map, plans. Catalogue of an exhibition of photographs of Crown Zellerbach and John Hancock buildings, Aug. 21–Sept. 20, 1959.
C CHi CSfU CSt

11653. —— **Navo shalom (home of peace) cemetery.** Rules and regulations...under the supervision of the congregation Emanu-El and Eureka benevolent society, 5620. S.F., Towne & Bacon, print., 1860. 10 p.
CU-B

11654. —— **Official committee for the reception of the fleet.** Report...and list of subscribers to the Entertainment fund. S.F., Johnston-Dienstag co., 1908. [28] p.
CHi CU-B

11655. —— —— [Scrap book presented to J. D. Phelan, chairman, by Harry Welsh, June, 1908] [23] p.
CU-B

11656. —— **Old St. Mary's church.** Cathedral on California street; the story of St. Mary's cathedral, San Francisco, 1854–1891, and of Old St. Mary's, a Paulist church, 1894–1951, by Thomas Denis McSweeney. Fresno, Acad. of Calif. church history, 1952. 95 p. illus., port.
Available in many libraries.

11657. —— —— Official program book...centennial, 1854–1954. [1954] 32 p. illus., col., pl., ports., facsims.
CLgA

11658. —— —— Old St. Mary's, A.D. 1854–1929, by John F. Carrere. S.F., Paulist fathers [1929?] [24] p. illus., ports.
CHi CSfP

11659. —— —— Old St. Mary's, A.D. 1854–1945. Old St. Mary's Chinese mission; Old St. Mary's service center; Paulist circulating library, by Paulist fathers. S.F. [1945?] 31 p. illus.
CSf CU-B

11660. —— —— Old Saint Mary's church, California street and Grant avenue. S.F., 1909. 27 p.
CHi CStclU

11661. —— —— Old St. Mary's, her story, by Marion McClintock. [S.F.] Old St. Mary's, c1954. [83] p. illus. (part col.) ports., plans.
CHi CLgA CNF CO COHN CStclU

11662. —— **Ordinances, etc.** An act concerning the city of San Francisco... [No. 1822, ordinance quieting land titles. No. 1845, ordinance designating public squares, etc.] (Approved March 11, 1858) [S.F., 1858] 8 p.
CLU

11663. —— —— The building law... for 1906. This book is filed for distribution from the Board of public works... [S.F., 1906] 112 p.
CSmH

11664. —— —— Building zone ordinance...approved October 3, 1921. [S.F., 1921?] [18] p. maps.
CHi

11665. —— —— Same. 1927. maps.
CSf

11666. —— —— Same, with amendments to March 1, 1935. S.F., Bd. of supervisors, 1935. 3 p. maps.
CSf

11667. —— —— City ordinances [relating to the organization and control of public schools] [S.F., 1856] 5 l.
CSmH

11668. —— —— The Clement ordinance, for settling the title to the outside lands... Approved Oct. 12th, 1866. S.F., Towne and Bacon, print., 1866. 7 p.
CHi CLU CSf CSmH

11669. —— —— Codified ordinances...comprised in general order no. 413, and subsequent orders to and including order no. 434. S.F., Towne & Bacon, print., 1861. 59 p.
CSmH CU-B

11670. —— —— A compilation of parts of the consolidation and other acts now in force, relating to the powers and duties of the Police department of San Francisco, January 1, 1870. S.F., Alta Calif. print. house, 1870. 13 p.
CU-B

11671. —— —— Comprehensive zoning ordinance. S.F., 1954. 76 l. Mimeo.
CSf

11672. —— —— General ordinances of the Board of supervisors. S.F. [1869?]–
CHi has 1888, 1904, 1910, 1915. CSfMI has 1869, 1894, 1896, 1907, 1910, 1915. CSfU has 1878. CSmH has 1904.

11673. —— —— Health and quarantine regulations for the city and harbor of San Francisco...general orders of the board of supervisors relating to the public health. S.F., E. Bosqui & co., print., 1876. 24 p. Report to the Mayor and Board of health of Cornelius Herz, M.D., and James Simpson, M.D., a committee appointed "to collect and arrange in convenient form the laws and ordinances..."
CHi

11674. —— —— Same. S.F., P.F. Thomas, 1878. 23 p.
CSfU

11675. —— —— Same. 1889. 47 p.
CSmH

11676. —— —— Laws of the fire department... S.F., John L. Sickler, bk. and job print., 1863. 60 p.
CHi

11677. —— —— The laws of the town of San Francisco. S.F., Print. at off. of Californian, 1847. 8 p. Dated at the end, Oct. 28, 1847. The enactments were: to prevent desertion of seamen, police regulations, licenses, town lots, improvements, etc., concerning constables.—Cowan.
C CSf CSmH CU-B

11678. —— —— Same. Reprinted, with an introduction by William W. Clary. San Marino, Friends of the Huntington lib., 1947. 16, 8 p.
CBb CHi CLSU CLU CLgA CO CPom CRedl CRic CSfWF-H CSmH CU-B CoD MHi TxU ViU

11679. —— —— Same. With a fragment by Nat Schmulowitz. S.F. [Greenwood press, Print. for the Roxburghe club] 1949. 7, 8 p. Facsimile of original edition.
C CHi CLU CLgA CO CSmH CU-B

11680. —— —— Ordinances and joint resolutions ...with a list of the officers of the city and county, and rules and orders of the Common council. Pub. by authority. S.F., Monson & Valentine, print., 1854. 525 p.
CLU COMC CSf CSfCP CSfMI CSfP CSmH CU-B NN NvHi WHi

11681. —— —— Ordinances of the Fire department of San Francisco, 1876. S.F., Kane & Cook's, print., 1876. 72 p.
CSmH

11682. —— **Panama-Pacific international exposition, 1915.** The blue book; a comprehensive official souvenir view book of the Panama-Pacific international

exposition at San Francisco, 1915... S.F., R.A. Reid, 1915. 327 p. illus.
C CChiS CEH CHi CL CLU CO CSf CSfMI CSfU CSfWF-H CStoC CStrJC CU-B CViCL

11683. San Francisco. Panama-Pacific international exposition (*cont'd*) Same. 2d ed. 1915. 328 p. illus.   CHi CChiS CSd CSfWF-H CSluCL MoS

11684. —— —— The lights go out; an account of the closing ceremonies...Dec. 4, 1915. [S.F., Blair-Murdock co. press, 1915] [13] p. front. (mounted facsim.)   CHi CLU CSfMI CSmH ViU

11685. —— —— Sculpture and mural paintings in the beautiful courts, colonnades and avenues...Text by Jessie Niles Burness. Official publication. S.F., R.A. Reid, 1915. [65] p. illus.
                              CHi CRcS CSfCW CU-B

11686. —— —— Souvenir of Pioneer and old settler's day, Panama-Pacific exposition, October 16, 1915. [S.F., 1915] 98 p. illus., ports.
          CHi CL CLU CO CSf CSfU CStclU CU-B

11687. —— **Dept. of fine arts.** Catalogue de luxe...ed. by John E. D. Trask and J. Nilsen Laurvik; illustrated with one hundred and ninety-two reproductions of paintings, sculpture, other exhibits and views of the Palace of fine arts. S.F., P. Elder and co. [c1915] 2 v. illus., plans.   CHi CO CSfMI CSfP CViCL

11688. —— **Planning commission.** The master plan...a brief summary of the master plan as adopted by the City planning commission on Dec. 20, 1945, with an outline of the task ahead. S.F., 1946. 16 p. maps.   CHi

11689. —— —— Report...with proposed zone plan for San Francisco. 1920. [S.F., 1920]   C-S

11690. —— —— Shoreline development; a portion of the master plan of San Francisco. (Preliminary report) [S.F.] 1943. 132 p. illus., maps, plans.
                              CHi CO CSfU

11691. —— **Plymouth church.** The church manual of the Second Congregational church...of San Francisco, California...April 1868. S.F., J.H. Carmany & co., print., 1868. 30 p.   CStclU CU-B

11692. —— —— The church manual of Plymouth church (formerly Second Congregational church)... October 1881. S.F., J. Winterburn & co., print., 1881. 43 p.
                                    CU-B

11693. —— **Police department.** Statement showing the detail and duty of each member...[S.F.] 1878. [7] p.   CSmH

11694. —— —— Summons to join Posse comitatus. [S.F., 1877] [2] p.   CSmH

11695. —— **Portolá festival, 1909.** Portolá festival, San Francisco, Oct. 19 to 23, 1909. Official souvenir program. [S.F., Print. by Stanley-Taylor co.] c1909. 128 p. illus., ports.
C CHi CL CLU CLgA CO CSf CSfCP CSmH CStclU CU-B

11696. —— ——, **1948.** Official souvenir program of Portola festival and Pageant, inc., San Francisco, Oct. 2 to Nov. 7, 1948. [S.F., 1948] [72] p. illus., ports.
                              CHi CU-B

11697. —— **Probate court.** ...In the matter of the last will and testament of David C. Broderick, deceased... S.F., Whitton, Waters & co., 1860. 121 p.
                                    CU-B

11698. —— **Produce exchange.** Annual report. 1st– , 1867– S.F., The Exchange, 1867– "Officers of the San Francisco produce exchange from 1867 to 1891, 24th annual report p. 7–16."

C (24th–34th) CHi (24th) CSf (20th–34th) CU-B (20th–34th)

11699. —— —— Articles of incorporation, by-laws and rules... S.F., C.A. Murdock & co., bk. and job print., 1877. 25 p.   CSmH CU-B

11700. —— —— Constitution and by-laws of the San Francisco produce exchange. S.F., Print. Wheeler & co., 1867. 12 p.   CU-B

11701. —— **Protestant Episcopal church. Order of St. John.** Eulexian lodge, Order of St. John; an account of its organization and activities. By W.C. Sharpsteen. [n.p., n.d.] 17 p. Mimeo. Founded January 1879 at Church of the Advent, San Francisco.   CHi

11702. —— **Public library.** Public Library building, erected nineteen hundred and sixteen. George W. Kelham, architect. Civic Center, San Francisco. [S.F., 19–?] [14] p.   CHi CO CSf CU-B

11703. —— **Public schools.** Closing exercises of the North Beach evening high school June 28, 1912; June 5, 1914. S.F., 1912–14. 2 v.   CHi

11704. —— —— Dedicatory exercises of the new building for the Boys' high school, Sutter street bet. Gough and Octavia, Nov. 15, 1875. S.F., Spaulding & Barto, 1875. 28 p. illus., plans. Includes text of addresses delivered at the exercises.   CHi

11705. —— —— Directory. 1911/12–13, 1920. S.F., 1911–20.   CHi

11706. —— —— Report of the Committee on the San Francisco high school...June 30, 1859. S.F., Towne & Bacon, print., Excelsior bk. and job off., 1859. 16 p.
                                    CHi

11707. —— —— San Francisco schools serve the community; a report to the community. S.F., 1947. 92 p. illus.   CSfU

11708. —— —— School progress report, 1947– 1955. [S.F., 1955] 138 l.   CSfSt

11709. —— —— Special report of the superintendent of public schools to the Board of supervisors; presented April 29, 1867. S.F., E. Bosqui & co., 1867.
                                    CSmH

11710. —— —— **Lowell high school. Students' association.** The red and white, centennial edition, 1856–1956. S.F., 1956. 285 p. illus. (Yearbooks, v.83)
                              CHi CSf CU-B

11711. —— —— **Lowell high school alumni association, pub.** Roster of graduates of the San Francisco high school, Boys' high school, Lowell high school, 1856–1930. S.F., 1930. [94] p.
                              CSf CSmH (June 1930)

11712. —— **Public utilities commission.** Lines and routes of municipal railway of San Francisco. S.F., 1950. 20 p. illus., maps.   CRcS

11713. —— —— A report on economic and organizational features of the Municipal railway... to the Honorable Board of supervisors... submitted by Arthur C. Jenkins... S.F., 1949. 202 l.   CSf CSt

11714. —— —— San Francisco water and power ... [S.F., Phillips & Van Orden co., inc.] 1935. 80 p. illus., maps.   CHi

11715. —— **Pueblo lands.** Memorial to the Congress of the United States against the confirmation of... the Stratton survey of the pueblo of S.F., 1880. 71 p.
                              CSf CSmH CU-B

11716. —— **Registrar of voters.** Street guide and list of hotels, apartments, etc., city and county of San

Francisco... issued by order of the Board of election commissioners. [S.F.] 1912–
C has 1915. CHi has 1923? CU-B has 1912, 1921?–23?

11717. —— **Roman Catholic orphan asylum.** Report of the trustees of the Roman Catholic orphan asylum and Free school association of the city of San Francisco. August 6th, 1854. S.F., O'Meara and Painter, 1854. 13 p. CU-B

11718. —— —— Same, Jan. 1st, 1857. S.F., O'Meara & Painter, print., 1857. 24 p. C

11719. —— —— Report of the Superioress... S.F., 1861. 2 p. CSmH WHi

11720. —— —— Same, December 31, 1861. [Sacramento, Benjamin P. Avery, state print., 1862] [6] p. WHi

11721. —— **St. Alban's Episcopal church.** Address to the churchmen of the diocese of California... [S.F., 1871] 19 p. CHi

11722. —— **St. Boniface church.** St. Anthony dining room, founded October fourth, nineteen hundred and fifty. S.F. [Golden Gate press, 1955] [28] p. illus. CHi CSf

11723. —— —— St. Boniface church diamond jubilee, 1860–1935. S.F., Chamber of commerce, 1912. [19] p. CHi CSf

11724. —— —— 100th anniversary...1860–1960. S.F., J.H. Barry co., 1960. 149 p. illus. CHi

11725. —— **St. Brigid's parish.** Golden jubilee souvenir, 1863–1913. S.F., 1913. 63 p. illus., ports. CSf

11726. —— **St. Cecilia's church.** The church of Saint Cecilia; dedicated by his Excellency, John J. Mitty, May 20, 1956. [S.F., 1956] 20 p. illus., ports. CLgA

11727. —— **St. Cecilia's parish.** Historical review...1917 to 1948, thirty-one years. [S.F., 1948?] CSf

11728. —— **St. David's Presbyterian church.** History of...1853–1953, one hundredth anniversary. 29 p. CHi

11729. —— **St. Francis of Assisi church.** ... The 100th anniversary...Sunday, Oct. 2, 1949. [S.F.? 1949?] 15 p. ports. CHi

11730. —— **St. Gabriel's church.** Commemorating the solemn blessing of...Sunday, May thirty-first, Nineteen hundred and forty-two. [S.F., 1942] [31] p. illus., ports. CU-B

11731. —— **St. Ignatius church.** Symbolism of the stained glass windows... [ed. by John C. Ward, S.J.] [S.F., 1944?] 64 p. illus. CLgA CSfU

11732. —— **St. John's Episcopal church.** Historical sketch. By Carol Richards Jossis. S.F., The Vestry, 1957. 4 p. illus. CHi

11733. —— **St. Luke's Episcopal church.** History and hand book of St. Luke's parish...1866–1891. S.F., Bacon & co., print., 1891. 29 p. CHi

11734. —— **St. Mark's Evangelical Lutheran church.** One hundred golden years in San Francisco, California; a history...1849–1949, by the Rev. J. George Dorn, pastor. [S.F., 1949?] 68 p. illus., ports. CU-B

11735. —— **St. Mary the Virgin.** Early beginnings of the Episcopal church of St. Mary the Virgin... By William W. Bolton. S.F. [Clark and McGettigan] 1949. 19 p. Mimeo. CHi

11736. —— —— Same. 3d ed. 1958. 17 p. CHi

11737. —— **St. Patrick's church.** Centennial souvenir...1851–1951. [S.F., The Charles L. Conlan print., 1951] [24] p. illus., ports. C CHi CLgA

11738. —— **St. Paul's parish.** Rules and regulations of the Chancel chapter [of the Woman's guild...] [S.F., Cubery & co., print., n.d.] 6 p. C

11739. —— **St. Paulus church.** A memorial of the golden jubilee... 1894–1944... S.F., 1944. 40 p. illus. CSf

11740. —— **St. Stephen's Episcopal church.** S. Stephen's book. In commemoration of the twenty-fifth anniversary of the founding of the parish of S. Stephen's. S.F., 1900. [35] p. ports. CU-B

11741. —— **School of the arts of the theatre.** ...Ellen Van Volkenburg [and] Maurice Browne, directors. [Prospectus. S.F., 1923] 11 p. CU-B

11742. —— **Seventh avenue Presbyterian church.** Seventh avenue Presbyterian church of San Francisco, California. An historical sketch...a victory celebration, December, 1939. [S.F., 1939] 21 p. illus., ports. CU-B

11743. —— **Simpson memorial Methodist Episcopal church.** Year book. S.F., Bk. room print., 1895. 72 p. front. (port.) At head of title: 1880, 1895. Preface: "This directory...giving a complete list of all names and addresses as they appear on the church records up to July 1, 1895..." CSfP

11744. —— **Sinai memorial chapel.** The perfect tribute, the story of a unique institution. [S.F., Chevra Kadisha, inc., 1949] [15] p. illus. CHi

11745. —— **Society of the New Jerusalem.** A brief account...together with the constitution and list of members... S.F., E. Bosqui & co., print., 1870. 17 p. CU-B

11746. —— **Stock and exchange board.** Constitution and by-laws... Organized September 11, 1862. S.F., Agnew & Deffebach, 1865. 20 p. CU-B

11747. —— —— Same. Revised Sept. 11th, 1867 ... S.F., Deffebach & co., print., 1867. 24 p.
CLU CU-B. Other editions followed. Publisher varies. C (1877, 1882) CHi (1907) CSfCSM (1876) CSmH (1877) CU-B (1870, 1874)

11748. —— **Stock exchange.** San Francisco stock exchange; history, organization, operation. [S.F., Public relations committee, 1930] 31 p. illus. CHi CSf
Other editions followed. C (1939) CHi (1939, 1947) CLU (1939) CU-B (1938)

11749. —— —— The San Francisco weekly stock report, and California street journal. v.3:17–v.11:4. Jan. 8, 1869–Dec. 22, 1871. [S.F.] 1869–71. 9 v. CU-B

11750. —— **Superintendent of streets.** List of public streets and street crossings, in the city and county of San Francisco... 1877... [S.F.] Kane & Cook [1877?] 72 p. C-S CU-B

11751. —— **Surveyor.** Report...April 7th, 1856. [S.F.] O'Meara & Painter, city print. [1856] 20 p. "John J. Hoff, city surveyor. In the Board of assistant aldermen, April 7th, 1856, received, and five hundred copies ordered published in pamphlet form. Robert C. Page, clerk." CHi CLU CSmH CU-B

11752. —— **Tax collector.** Delinquent tax list... 1869/70–1896. S.F., 1869–96. Issued as supplements to the following newspapers: 1869/70, The Examiner, 1887/88, San Francisco report.
C-S has 1869/70–1896. CSmH has 1869/70, 1887/88.

11753. —— **Third Congregational church.** Man-

ual... 3d ed. ... S.F., Press of Dempster bros., 1888.
58 p.   CU-B

11754. San Francisco (*cont'd*) **Town council. ...**
Proceedings of the Legislative assembly of the district of
San Francisco, from March 12th, 1849, to June 4th, 1849,
and a record of the proceedings of the ayuntamiento or
town council of San Francisco, from August 6th, 1849,
until May 3d, 1850... S.F., Towne & Bacon print., 1860.
296 p. port. Reprints the Proceedings of the town council of San Francisco. p. 47–219.
          C CHi CLU CSf CSmH CU-B

11755. —— Proceedings of the town council
of San Francisco, Upper California. S.F., Alta Calif.
press, 1849–50. 4 pts. in 1. 105 p. A record of meetings
held from August 6, 1849 to April 10, 1850.
    C CHi (lacks pt. 1) CLU (pt. 2 only) CSf (photo-
copy) CSmH CU-B (lacks pt. 1)

11756. —— **Traffic survey committee.** Report.
1st (1927)– S.F. [1927?]– 1 v.   CU-B

11757. —— **Transportation technical committee.** History of public transit in San Francisco, 1850–
1948 [by] the Transportation technical committee of the
Departments of public works, public utilities, police, and
city planning. [S.F.,] 1948. 69 l.
          CHi CO CSfWF-H CU-B

11758. —— **Trinity Episcopal church.** Memorials and historic objects... Research and compilation
by J. William Williams. [S.F.?] 1945. 49 p. illus., ports.
          CHi CU-B

11759. —— —— One hundred years a parish,
1849–1949. [S.F., The Vestry, 1949] 15 p. illus., ports.
          CHi

11760. —— —— The service for the laying of the
corner-stone...18 September, A.D. 1892, by the Rt. Rev.
W. F. Nichols... [S.F.? 1892?] 7 p.   C CHi

11761. —— —— 60th Easter anniversary, 1849–
1909. [S.F., 1909] [24] p. illus.   CHi

11762. —— —— Trinity church, San Francisco.
[S.F., 1939?] [12] p. illus., ports.   CHi CU-B

11763. —— —— Vital statistics from records in
Trinity Episcopal church of San Francisco. Copied and
arranged by Jessie Boudinot Flenner. 1936. 354 l. Typew.
          C C-S CL CLU CSf

11764. —— **Trinity Mission Sunday school.** Or-
der of exercises of... (formerly Episcopal Mission),
Wm. G. Badger, superintendent, at Platt's music hall,
Easter Sunday, April 20th, 1862... [S.F.] Towne &
Bacon, print. [1862] 12 p.   CU-B

11765. —— **Trinity Presbyterian church.** Ninety years in San Francisco's Mission district: a history...
1868–1958. [S.F.? 1958?] 24 p.   CHi CU-B

11766. —— **Union college.** Prospectus. S.F.,
Towne & Bacon, print. [186–?] 8 p.   CU-B

11767. —— —— Same, with a catalogue of the
pupils to the end of the year 1863. S.F., Towne & Bacon,
print. [1863] 12 p.   CU-B

11768. —— **Union square Baptist church.** Manual... S.F., Winterburn & co., print., 1866. 30 p.   CU-B

11769. —— **United community fund.** Group
work and recreation council. Research unit. Inventory of
leisure time resources...1958. [S.F., 1958] 110 p. illus.,
graphs, charts.   CSf

11770. —— **University.** ...Catalogue... 1860/
61– S.F., 1861–
    CHi has 1892/93, 1898/99. CSfCW has 1904/05.
CStclU has 1861/62. CU-B has 1860/61–1865–66.

11771. —— —— A report...submitted to the
Committee on accreditation of the State board of education. S.F., 1950. 76 p.   CSfU

11772. —— —— Appendix to same. S.F., 1950.
1 v. v.p.   CSfU

11773. —— —— San Francisco celebrates the
diamond jubilee of St. Ignatius college, 1855–1930. [S.F.,
1930] [48] p. illus.   CHi COHN

11774. —— —— University of San Francisco,
San Francisco, California. S.F. [1945?] [16] p. illus.
          COHN

11775. —— —— **Richard A. Gleeson library.**
[Scrapbook of photographs ...clippings, etc., concerning planning and building of the Gleeson library] [S.F.,
1948–196–?]   CSfU

11776. —— —— **The St. Ives law club.** The
first decade...1934–44. S.F. [1945?] 62 p. illus., ports.
          CLgA

11777. —— **University mound college.** [Cata-
logue] [n.p., n.d.]
    CHi has 1875/76.

11778. —— **Urban academy.** Circular of the Urban academy established in 1864 and situated on the
southwest corner of Mason and Geary streets, San Francisco, Cal. S.F., E. Bosqui & co., print., 1879. 23 p.
          CU-B

11779. —— —— Same. S.F., Dodge bros. &
Shreve, 1883. 48 p.   CHi

11780. —— **Veterinary college.** Prospectus.
[S.F.? 1904?] 1 v. Chartered 1899.   CHi

11781. —— **Washington grammar school.** A
brief history...by Frank Fischer. [S.F., 1933] 16 p.
illus.   CHi CSf CSfCW

11782. —— **Workingmen.** An address...to their
brothers throughout the Pacific coast. [S.F., 1888] 24 p.
          CHi CU-B

11783. [San Francisco after the earthquake and fire
of April 1906. S.F., 1906] 13 pl. in portfolio.   CU-B

11784. San Francisco almanac for the year 1859: containing a business directory of San Francisco, Sacramento, Marysville and Stockton, also public buildings
and engine houses in San Francisco, statistics, etc. S.F.,
W.F. Herrick & O. Hodge [1858] 176 p. illus., map.
          C CHi CLU CSmH CU CU-B

11785. San Francisco and bay cities Jewish blue book
... S.F., S.F. & bay cities Jewish blue bk. co., 1916.
          C C-S CSf CU-B

**11786. San Francisco and Great Salt Lake rail-
road co. Chief engineer.** Report of the chief engineer
of the proposed San Francisco and Great Salt Lake railroad on surveys made during 1892. [S.F., 1893] 50 p.   C

**11787. San Francisco and North Pacific railway
co.** [Brochure. S.F.? n.d.] [4] p. illus.   CU-B

11788. —— Third annual report... [S.F., 1892]
70 p. illus., map.   CHi

**11789. San Francisco and Ocean shore railroad
co., California.** Report upon the San Francisco and
Ocean shore railroad company, California... N.Y., E.
Wells Sackett & Rankin, stat. and print., 1881. 16 p.
front. 2 fold. maps. This line was to have run from San
Francisco along the coast southward to Santa Cruz.
          CLU

**11790. San Francisco and Port Costa seamen's
institutes.** Annual report. 1904 (12th).   CHi

11791. San Francisco & Sacramento railroad.
Report of the chief engineer upon the preliminary sur-

vey, revenue, and cost of construction, of the San Francisco and Sacramento railroad. S.F., Whitton, Towne & co., 1856. 40 p. fold. map.

Appendix of 8 pages consists of description of Solano county. Report by Theodore Judah. The railroad, projected to run from Sacramento to Benicia, was never built.   CU-B CtY

11792. San Francisco and San Joaquin valley railroad, San Francisco. Prospectus of... [S.F., 1893] 16 p.   CHi

11793. San Francisco and San Jose railroad co. The general railroad laws of California, and the bylaws of "The San Francisco and San Jose railroad company," with a list of the officers of the company. S.F., Alta Calif. bk. and job off., 1863. 44 p.   CLU

11794. San Francisco and the Bay area; an economic survey and yearly review, 1938–1958. illus.
C has 1949. CO has 1938–58.

11795. San Francisco and Tonopah mining exchange. Constitution and by-laws... S.F., Star press, J.H. Barry, 1903. 42 p.   CU-B

11796. San Francisco and vicinity before and after its destruction. Portland, Me., L.H. Nelson co. [c1906] [32] p. illus. Cover-title: Views of San Francisco and vicinity...   CU-B

11797. San Francisco architects', contractors' and builders' directory, 1889/90. S.F., Mather-Fitch pub. co., [1889?]   CSf CU-B

11798. San Francisco architectural club. Year book, 1913, 1915. S.F., 1913–1915. 2 v. illus., plans. Publisher varies. Fifth (1909), sixth (1913) and seventh (1915) exhibitions under the auspices of the Architectural league of the Pacific coast.   CHi

11799. San Francisco architectural society. Constitution and by-laws of... founded Jan., A.D. 1861. S.F., Agnew and Deffebach, 1861. 26 p.   CHi

11800. San Francisco art association. Annual exhibition, catalogue. S.F. [1871–?–
CHi has 43d–48th, 50th–58th, 79th, 1919–25, 1928–38, 1960. CSfCP has 4th, 1873. CU-B has 4th, 1873.

11801. —— Autumn exhibitions, catalogue. S.F., [187–?–
CHi has 1885, 1903.

11802. —— Catalogue of... Mark Hopkins institute of art. 1902, 1904. S.F., 1902–1904. 2 v. illus.
CU-B

11803. —— Catalogue [of] Mrs. Phoebe A. Hearst loan collection. Ed. by J. Nilsen Laurvik...The Palace of fine arts... S.F. [Taylor & Taylor] 1917. 253 p. illus., map.   CHi CU-B

11804. —— Catalogue of museum loan exhibition of work by the California group of contemporary American artists and Toby E. Rosenthal memorial exhibition... The Palace of fine arts...Jan. 24, 1919. [S.F., Taylor & Taylor, 1919] 67 p. illus.   CHi

11805. —— Catalogue [of the] exhibition [in the SFAA gallery, California school of fine arts] 1955/56–1956/57, no. 5. 1 v. illus., ports.   CU-B

11806. —— Certificate of incorporation, by-laws, list of officers, list of members. [S.F.] 1902. 47 p. front.
CU-B

11807. —— Constitution, by-laws, and list of members, organized March 28, 1871. S.F., E. Bosqui & co., print., 1873. 16 p.   CHi CLU CU-B

11808. —— Illustrated catalogue of the Post-exposition exhibition in the Department of fine arts, Panama-Pacific international exposition... [S.F., 1915?] 112 p. ports.
CBev CHi CSbr CSf CSfCW CSfMI CSmH CU-B

11809. —— Memorial exhibition, Rex Slinkard, 1887–1918. The Palace of fine arts...October third to twenty-seventh, nineteen nineteen. [n.p., n.d.] unp.
CHi

11810. —— Painting and sculpture... Berkeley, Univ. of Calif. press, 1952. [25] p. 96 pl.
CHi CPa CSt CU-B

11811. —— San Francisco art association... [brochure. S.F.? 1931?]   CHi

11812. —— Spring exhibition, catalogue. S.F., 1885–1905.
CHi has 1885, 1889, 1900, 1903. CU-B has 1905.

11813. San Francisco assaying and refining works. Tables of the value of gold and silver... S.F., Towne and Bacon, 1867. [56] p.
CHi CSfCW CSmH

11814. San Francisco association for the study and prevention of tuberculosis. Annual report.
CHi has 2d, 1909.

11815. San Francisco bacteriological society. Articles of incorporation. [1891] [13] p.   C

11816. [San Francisco baseball club] ...Souvenir program, opening of Ewing field, Saturday, May 16, 1914. [S.F., Chase & Roe, 1914] [16] p. illus., ports.
CHi

11817. San Francisco bay area council, inc. The Bay area, land of border incidence; text of the address made by the retiring chairman... Reginald H. Biggs at the 1958 annual dinner... [S.F., 1958] 10 p.   CHi

11818. —— Commerce and industry: directory of information, San Francisco bay area. S.F., 1947. 51 p. Statistical and directory information for the counties of San Francisco, Alameda, Contra Costa, Marin, Napa, San Mateo, Santa Clara, Solano, and Sonoma, and their principal cities.   C CHi

11819. —— Directory [of] federal and state agencies, San Francisco bay area. S.F., 1948– 2 v.   CSfSt

11820. —— Industrial location in the San Francisco bay area...for the manufacturer who seeks new plant location. [By Robert P. Danielson] S.F. [c1949] 58 p. col. maps (1 fold.), diagrs. Other editions followed.
C (1955) CSdS (1956) CSfSt (1949, 1958) CSt (1958)

11821. —— A voluntary program for air pollution control in the San Francisco bay area; initial report. [S.F.] 1953. 32 p. "Reference literature": p. 27–30.   C

11822. San Francisco bay cities club of printing house craftsmen. Craftsmanship in printing, its development and ideals, and how it may reach its highest expression in San Francisco. S.F., 1922. [20] p. front.
CHi

11823. San Francisco bay district agricultural society. Constitution and by-laws... S.F., Alameda herald print., 1860. 15 p.   CHi

11824. —— First annual exhibition, to be held in the city of San Francisco, October 4th...and 11th, 1860. S.F., Towne & Bacon, 1860. 35 p.
C CHi CLU CSmH NN

11825. San Francisco bay region. Special limited supplement. S.F., Am. hist. soc., 1924. 148 p. ports.
CSf CSmH CU-B

11826. San Francisco benevolent association.
The directory of the ...association. Organized in March,
1865... S.F., Towne & Bacon, print., 1865. 34 p.
CU-B

11827. [San Francisco block book] 100 v. blocks
317 to 420. [1868?–69?] [86] p. Ms.   CU-B

11828. —— Same. [1882?–1915] 9 v. Ms.
CSfCW CU-B

11829. —— Same. Showing size of lots and blocks
and names of property owners, comprising 50 varas, 100
varas, Western addition and Mission. 1894. S.F. [Hicks-
Judd] 1894. 431 l.   C-S CHi CLU CU-B

11830. —— Same. 2d ed. Comprising fifty vara
survey, one hundred vara survey Mission, Western addition, Richmond district, Sunset district, Flint tract and
Horner's addition. S.F., Hicks-Judd co. [1901] 736 p.
CHi CSmH

11831. —— Same. 3d ed. ...January, 1906. S.F.,
Hicks-Judd co., 1906. 897 p.   CHi

11832. —— Same. 4th ed. ...October, 1906. S.F.,
Hicks-Judd co. [1906] 897 p.
C CHi CO CSf CSfCP CSfMI CSfP CSmH
CU-B

11833. —— Same. ...1907. S.F., Hicks-Judd co.,
1907.   CHi

11834. —— Same. 5th ed. 1909–1910. S.F., Hicks-
Judd co.   CHi CSf

11835. —— Same, with title: Mery's block book
of San Francisco... S.F., 1909. 1048 p.   CHi

11836. San Francisco blue book...containing the
names, addresses... of the leading families of San Fran-
cisco-Oakland-Berkeley-Alameda... S.F., C.C. Hoag,
1879–1931. illus. Title varies: 1891–92, Our society blue
book... Publisher: To 1890/91, Bancroft co.; 1891/92,
Hoag & Irving; 1892/93–1931. C.C. Hoag; 1924, J.J. Hoag
& A.H. Page; 1925, A. Dulfer & J.J. Hoag; 1927, J.J.
Hoag. In 2 parts, separately paged. Pt. 1: San Francisco;
pt. 2: Southern Calif. Pt. 2 has title: The Blue book, and
in the 1925 ed. precedes pt. 1.
C has 1879, 1888/89–1889/90, 1891/92. C-S has 1888/
89–1889/90, 1892/93, 1894/95, 1896/97. CHi has 1879,
1884, 1888/89, 1891/92–1892/93, 1894/95–1897/98. CL
has 1889/90, 1892/93–1893/94. CLSU has 1891/92. CLU
has 1889/90, 1891/92, 1894/95. CO has 1889/90–1893/
94, 1896/97, 1899. CRcS has 1889/90, 1892/93. CSf has
1889/90, 1891/92, 1894/95. CSfCP has 1879, 1884, 1887/
88–1889/90, 1891/92–1892/93, 1894/95–1895/96, 1897/98–
1899. CSfMI has 1889/90–1892/93, 1899. CSfP has 1887/
88. CSmH has 1888/89–1893/94, 1899. CSrD has 1891/
92, 1899. CStrJC has 1887/88–1895/96. CU-B has 1888/
89–1895/96, 1897/98. After 1900 available in many California libraries and CoU has 1888/89, 1891/92–1892/93.
MoS has 1902, 1924.

11837. San Francisco breweries, ltd. Directors'
report and statement of accounts. 1907/08, 1914/15.
[S.F., 1908–15] 2 v.   CU-B

11838. —— The San Francisco breweries, limited, and the Debenture corporation, limited. Trust
deed to secure debenture stock, dated 27th Oct. 1899.
[London] Linklater, Addison, Brown & Jones [1899]
43 p.   CU-B

11839. San Francisco bridge co. San Francisco
bridge company and New York dredging company, civil
engineers and contractors for railway and highway
bridges, piers, ...structural iron and steel work. [N.Y.,
Chasmar-Winchell press, 1898] 56 p. illus.   CHi CU-B

11840. San Francisco bulletin. The Bulletin book,
a compilation of noteworthy articles by staff writers of
the San Francisco bulletin and others... [S.F., 1917]
112 p.   C CLU CSf CSmH

11841. —— Diamond jubilee, Sept. 8, 1925. [S.F.,
1925]   CHi

11842. —— Golden jubilee of the *Bulletin*, 1855–
1905. S.F., 1905. 44 p. illus.   C

11843. San Francisco business. Published weekly
by the San Francisco chamber of commerce. v.1–23, July
2, 1920–April 5, 1933. S.F., 1920–1933. 23 v. Successor to
San Francisco chamber of commerce activities.
C has [1922–1923] CSf has v.1–23. CU-B has v.1–11
(lack v.2 no. 26)

11844. San Francisco business register. Important
information for merchants and others visiting the city.
[S.F.] Towne & Bacon print. [1866?] 34 p. Consists of
advertising matter by San Francisco firms.   CU-B

**11845. San Francisco cadets, Company H. Sec-
ond regiment, N.G.C., Capt. C. E. S. McDonald,
com'g. Organized Aug. 7th, 1863.** Opinions of the
press and rules and regulations. [S.F., Francis & Valentine, print., 1873?] 27 p.   CU-B

11846. San Francisco, Cal. S.F., Hartwell & Mitchell,
1894. [29] l. illus.   CSf

11847. San Francisco call. Diamond jubilee, Sept.
5, 1925. [S.F., 1925]   CHi

11848. —— Earthquake and fire. San Francisco in
ruins. [Edition of] Thursday, April 19, 1906. S.F., 1906.
4 p. At head of title: The Call-Chronicle-Examiner.
CHi CU-B

11849. —— Fettered commerce. How the Pacific
mail and the railroads have bled San Francisco... S.F.,
Daily morning call co., 1892. 46 p.   CSf CU-B

11850. San Francisco call-bulletin. Call-bulletin
centennial; a century of progress, 1855–1955. [S.F., 1955]
[62] p. illus. (part col.) ports.
CHi CSf CSmat CU-B

11851. —— Centennial of gold discovery. Special
edition, January 24, 1948. S.F., 1948.   CHi

11852. —— Golden Gate bridge fiesta edition, May
26, 1937. S.F., 1937.   CRcS

11853. —— Pioneer edition, November 12, 1940.
S.F., 1940.   CHi

11854. San Francisco catastrophe; photographic reproductions of the great earthquake and fire of April 18,
1906... Engraved by H. A. Darms... St. Joseph, Mo.,
S.A. Moore, c1906.   C

**11855. San Francisco chamber of commerce ac-
tivities.** v.1–7, March 25, 1914–June 25, 1920. S.F.,
1914–1920. 7 v.   CSf CU CU-B (v.2, no. 4–v.7)

**11856. San Francisco chamber of commerce
journal.** Pub. monthly, by the Board of directors of the
San Francisco chamber of commerce. v.1–2. Nov. 1911–
March 1913. S.F., 1912–1913. 2 v. illus. Preceded by
Chamber of commerce journal, v.1, April 1911–Oct. 1911.
C CSf CU-B has v.1, no. 1–7, Apr.–Oct. 1911 [ser. 2]
v.1–2, no. [5] Nov. 1911–Mar. 1913.

11857. San Francisco Chinese directory...including
Oakland-East bay section 1949–1950. S.F., Jimmy Lum
advtg. service, c1949–50. 2 v.   CSf CU-B MiD

11858. San Francisco chronicle. California centennial edition... Sunday, Sept. 10, 1950. [S.F., 1950] 1 v.
illus., ports.   CHi CU-B

11859. —— California centennial (1848–1948). Portola celebration. Special edition. Monday, Oct. 18, 1948. S.F., 1948. v.p. illus. CHi CSf CU-B

11860. —— ... California centennial of gold discovery. Special edition, Jan. 24, 1948. S.F., 1948. 92 p. illus., ports., map. CHi

11861. —— California's diamond jubilee edition. Sept. 6, 1925. [S.F., 1925] CHi

11862. —— The city, San Francisco, in pictures... [S.F.] 1961. 85 p. illus. CSfMI

11863. —— ...Diamond jubilee, January 28, 1940. [S.F., 1940] 34 p. illus., ports. CU-B

11864. —— Golden jubilee and exposition edition, Jan. 16, 1915. [S.F., 1915] CHi

11865. —— Hills of San Francisco. Foreword by Herb Caen. [S.F., 1959] 87 p. illus. "Compiled from a series of articles which appeared in the *San Francisco chronicle*."
Available in many California libraries and MiD ODa.

11866. —— Markham's mistake. ... An incidental explanation of the origin of the Colonel's military title. [S.F.? 1890?] 16 p. Quotes the S.F. Chronicle's charges against Markham. CSmH

11867. —— The San Francisco chronicle and its history. The story of its foundation, the struggles of its early life, its well-earned successes. The new Chronicle building, the edifice and machinery described, comments of the press. S.F., 1879. 60 p. illus.
C CHi CL CLO CLU CO CPom CPs CSf CSfCP CSfCW CSfMI CSfU CSmH CU-B CaBViPA MHi MoS NN OU UHi

11868. —— [San Francisco earthquake and fire April 18, 1906– 50th anniversary; sections of the San Francisco chronicle and San Francisco examiner of Sunday, April 15, 1956. S.F., 1956] 1 v. v.p. illus., ports., facsims. CU-B

11869. San Francisco chronicle almanac and political and commercial statistician, 1898–1901. S.F., 1898–1901. 4 v.
C CHi (v.1) CL CO (v.4, no. 13) CSf (v.1–3) CU-B

11870. San Francisco churches and church institutions, destroyed April 18–20, 1906. [n.p., 1906?] 2 p. C

11871. San Francisco city-county record. The Portuguese in California. Cabrillo civic club first anniversary edition, Jan. 1935. S.F., 1935. 9 p. illus., ports. CHi

11872. San Francisco city lands. A collection of auction sale catalogs. S.F., 1854–67. CU-B

11873. [San Francisco city lots. A collection of auction sale catalogs, 1849–1850] CU-B

11874. San Francisco city missionary society. Annual reports, constitution... 1868–[1869] S.F., 1868–69. 2 v. C CU-B

11875. San Francisco college for women. ... Newspaper clippings about the first six years of the San Francisco college for women. The story of the valiant foundation band of nine religious of the Sacred Heart. ...Presented to the college by the collector, Monica Donovan. CSfCW

11876. San Francisco commercial association. Constitution and by-laws. S.F., Turnbull & Smith, 1868. 12 p. CU-B

11877. —— To the present and former members of the San Francisco commercial association. [S.F., 1870] 8 p. CU-B

11878. San Francisco commercial club. Birthday celebration of the new San Francisco Exposition auditorium, Tuesday, April 18, 1916. [Program] [S.F., 1916] 24 p. illus. CU-B

11879. —— By-laws, house rules, officers and members...1888– S.F., 1888–
C (1916) CHi (1950–54, 1957–59, 1961) CRcS (1950) CSf (1911, 1913, 1916) CSfCP (1888–?) CU-B (1888, 1913, 1916)

11880. —— History, by-laws, roster. S.F. [1950] 110 p. illus. "Written and produced by Leland Q. Svane." CHi CO CRcS

11881. [San Francisco commercial press] Clippings from California press in regard to steam across the Pacific, from March to November, 1860...S.F., Towne & Bacon, 1860. 104 p. C CHi CSmH CU-B NN

11882. San Francisco convention & tourist bureau. 28 years of visitor solicitation for San Francisco. S.F., 1937. 12 p. illus. Founded 1909. CHi

11883. —— You'll enjoy San Francisco. S.F. [1931?] 15 p. illus., map. CRcS

11884. San Francisco co-operative land and building association. Articles of association and certificate of incorporation... S.F., Waters, Newhoff & co., 1871. 64 p. CHi

11885. San Francisco county medical society. The new home of the San Francisco county medical society. [S.F., 1926] [3] p. illus. CHi

11886. San Francisco de Asís (mission). ...Restoration of Mission Dolores. Valencia theatre, Wed. eve., Oct. 25, 1916. [S.F.] Eureka press [1916] Cover-title [40] p. ports. Includes benefit program, advertising matter, a poem, and an article [2] p. by R. E. Cowan on San Francisco de Asís (Mission Dolores). CLU

11887. San Francisco destroyed. Milwaukee, Wis., C.N. Caspar co. [1906] illus., ports. CHi CLgA CRic

11888. The San Francisco dramatic review. September 9, 1899–March 3, 1906. CU-B

11889. ...San Francisco-East bay insurance phone directory. [S.F.] Underwriters' report [1933] 84 p. CU-B

11890. San Francisco, 1851, from Rincon hill, by Martin Behrman. c1910. Folded view. CHi CSf

11891. San Francisco; 1875—Early days. January, 1906—Pre-eminence, the great earthquake, April 18, 1906. ... L.A., Balloon route pub. co. [n.d.] unp. illus. CHi CMartC CO

11892. San Francisco employers' council. Articles of incorporation and by-laws. [S.F., n.d.] 12 p. CHi

11893. San Francisco evening post. San Francisco and its resources. A souvenir of the *Evening post.* [Denver, Carson, Hurst & Harper, art print., 1893] 82 p. illus., ports.
CHi CLU CSf CSfCW CSfWF-H CoD NN

11894. San Francisco examiner. Centennial of gold discovery. Special edition, Jan. 24, 1948. [S.F., 1948] CHi

11895. —— pub. Classified directory, 1919. Containing the name, the business and telephone number of business concerns, institutions and professional people of San Francisco, Oakland and bay cities. [S.F., 1919] 96 p. C-S

11896. —— Diamond jubilee edition. Sept. 5, 1925. [S.F., 1925] CHi

11897. —— Golden jubilee edition...Thursday, March 4, 1937. [S.F., 1937] [128] p. illus., ports.
CSf CU-B

11898. —— Panoramic views showing burned district of San Francisco after the earthquake and fire, April 1906. S.F., 1906. 2 v., 8 fold. mounted pl. Supplements to the San Francisco examiner, May–August 1906.
CAla (June 3, 1906 only) CHi CO

11899. —— Pictorial supplement, showing views of forthcoming Panama-Pacific international exposition, Sept. 7, 1912. 8 p.
CHi

11900. —— **Merchandising service bureau.** San Francisco and its sphere of advertising influence: a presentation of authentic data on the Northern and Central California market and its relation to the advertiser, together with a complete analysis of San Francisco newspapers, their lineage and advertising value. [S.F., 1926] 65 p. illus.
C

11901. —— **Want ad dept.** 50 years of progress in the Bay region... [S.F., 1935] 29 p. illus.
CU-B

11902. San Francisco federal business association. Directory of membership. ...Jan. 1933. [S.F., 1933] 1 v.
CU-B

11903. San Francisco federal savings and loan association. Date line—San Francisco. [S.F., 1960] 48 p. illus., ports.
CHi CSf CU-B

11904. San Francisco federation of women. Constitution and by-laws ... Organized June 10, 1891. S.F., Payot, Upham & co., 1893. 20 p.
CHi

11905. San Francisco female hospital. Report. S.F., E. Bosqui & co., 1874.
CHi

11906. San Francisco festival association. Century of commerce celebration, 1835–1935, San Francisco, California, October 14 to 19, 1935. [S.F., c1935] 63 p.
C CHi CLU CO CSfMI CSmH

11907. San Francisco fly casting club. [Membership roster, etc.] [S.F.] 1931. [12] p. illus.
CHi

11908. —— Official program, eighth international fly and bait casting tournament...S.F., 1915. [24] p. illus., ports. Contains history of club.
CHi

11909. San Francisco foundation. Report. S.F., [1928/51]–1962. illus., diagrs.
CHi has 1953/54, 1956/57–1959/60, 1961, 1962. CU-B has [1st]–10th, [1948/51]–1957/58.

11910. San Francisco free public market. The free public market on the S.F. water front... [1898?]
CU-B

11911. San Francisco fruit and flower mission for aiding the needy sick. Annual report. [S.F.?]
CHi has 1887–89, 1891, 1910/11, 1911/12.

11912. San Francisco garden club. The San Francisco garden club tour, 1939. [S.F., 1939] [11] p. map.
CHi

11913. San Francisco golf and country club. ... Club house and links, Ingleside, San Francisco, California. Club book for 1914. S.F., 1914. 45 p. front., fold. map.
CSf

11914. —— Constitution and by-laws with rules and list of members. [various titles]
CHi has 1914, 1925.

11915. San Francisco guide and souvenir. S.F., pub. by Palace hotel news stand [1901–06] illus., maps.
CSfCP has Apr. 1901, May 1902, Apr. 1903, Apr. 1904, July 1905, Apr. 1906. CU-B has Mar., Oct. 1902, Apr.–May 1904.

11916. San Francisco harbor. [S.F., Sacramento, etc. 1856–1926] 18 v. illus.
CU-B

11917. San Francisco high license association. ... Appeal...to mothers and fathers, ...for a high license ordinance in San Francisco. S.F., J.H. Barry, print. [189–?] 8 p.
CU-B

11918. San Francisco hotel association. Official hotel and shopping guide. S.F., 1939. 28 p. illus., map.
CRcS

11919. San Francisco hotel gazette and pocket time tables of the Southern Pacific company and other railroad lines. S.F., 1900. 96 p.
C-S

11920. San Francisco housing association. Holly Courts. [S.F., 1940] [8] p. illus.
CHi

11921. —— Report. 1st– 1911– [S.F.] 1911– illus., fold. map.
CU-B has 1911.

11922. San Francisco illustrated. S.F., Hirsch, Kahn & co. [18–?] 16 pl.
CU-B

11923. San Francisco in ruins; pictorial writing tablet... S.F., Advergraph press [1906] 36 pl.
CLU CSmH

11924. San Francisco kennel club. Official catalogue, annual dog show. 1st–14th, 1897–1912. S.F., 1897–1912. illus.
CHi has 1st, 8th, 1897, 1904. CU-B has 6th, 14th, 1902, 1912.

11925. San Francisco labor council. The new charter. Why it should be defeated... S.F. [1896?] 14 p.
CHi

11926. —— San Diego free speech controversy. Report...by special investigating committee, April 25th, 1912. [S.F., 1912] 12 p.
CHi CLU

11927. San Francisco ladies protection and relief society. Annual reports. 1st–90th [1854?]–1943. [S.F., 1854?]–1943.
C has 15th–16th, 25th–26th, 42d–43d. CHi has 5th, 23d–24th, 30th–31st, 42d–43d, 44th–46th, 48th–49th, 50th–51st, 52d–53d, 76th, 86th, 90th, 1858, 1876/77, 1883/84, 1885, 1897, 1900, 1903, 1905, 1907, 1929, 1939, 1943. CSmH has 10th, 44th–46th, 1862/63, 1900. CU-B has 12th–16th, 21st–22d, 34th, 48th–53d, 1864/65–1906. NN has 5th, 1858.

11928. —— Constitution and by-laws...with a list of members. S.F., 1853. 15 p.
CHi CU-B

11929. —— Report of the trustees...1860–1861... [Sacramento? 1860–61] 2 v.
CHi CSmH (1861) CU-B WHi (1861)

11930. San Francisco land association. Articles of association and agreement...with proceedings of the meetings of stockholders... Phila., Crissy & Markley, print., 1855. 30 p.
C CSmH CU-B

11931. —— Memorial, brief and affidavits of the San Francisco land association of Philadelphia... [Phila., 1876?] 24 p. A memorial to Congress concerning the Santillan grant.
CLU

11932. —— Report of the board of directors...to the stockholders. Phila., King and Baird, print. [1859] 10 p.
C

11933. San Francisco letter sheet price current and review of the market. v.1–2, 1849–1850. S.F. [Print. Pac. news off., 1849–50.]
CSfWF-H has v.1, no. 16, July 13, 1850. CU-B has v.1, no. 2, 17, Sept. 28, 1849, July 31, 1850.

11934. San Francisco lying-in hospital and foundling asylum. First [second] printed report of the secretary, attending physician and treasurer... 1869/71–1872/75. S.F., 1872–75. 2 v. in 1.   CU-B

11935. San Francisco market review. v.1. 1867–1874. S.F., 1867–74. 3 v. in 1.
CSmH has v.6, no. 216, 218–267, v.7, no. 268–9, 271–93, 295–319, v.8, no. 320–321, 323–372, Jan. 5, Jan. 19–Dec. 17, 1872, Jan. 3–10, Jan. 24–June 26, July 10–Dec. 25, 1873, Jan. 1–8, Jan. 22–Dec. 31, 1874. CU-B has v.1, no. 8, v.2, no. 41, Apr. 31, 1867, July 14, 1868.

11936. San Francisco maternity. ...Annual report ...S.F., 1904–14. Organized November 17, 1903, incorporated January 5, 1907.
CHi has 1906–07, 1910, 1914.

11937. [San Francisco medical benevolent society] Memorial of Dr. Francis B. Kane. [S.F., 1889] [4] p.   CHi

11938. San Francisco medical society. Constitution, by-laws and fee bill... Organized June 22, 1850. S.F., Calif. daily courier, print., 1850. 8 p.   CSmH

11939. —— Same [and] officers, standing committees and members... S.F., E. Bosqui & co., print., 1868. 36 p.   CU-B

11940. San Francisco mercantile union. ...Annual reference book...1902. S.F., 1902. 1 v.   CU-B

11941. The San Francisco merchant. Apr. 13, 1883–Aug. 30, 1890.   CU-B

11942. San Francisco merchants' exchange association. [By-laws] 1883.   CU-B

11943. San Francisco municipal journal. Progress edition...July 1, 1930. [S.F., 1930] 136 p. illus., ports.   CU-B

11944. San Francisco municipal record. Municipal record blue books. 1931–1932. illus.   CSf

11945. San Francisco municipal report. Our progressive government. S.F., Dolores press [1945] 64 p. illus.   CHi

11946. San Francisco municipal review. [Special number] Historical review devoted to...the Fire department. S.F., Dolores press [1943?] 56 p. illus.   CHi

11947. San Francisco music miscellany. [S.F., 1873–1914?] 91 v. in 2. illus.   CU-B

11948. San Francisco musical club. Fiftieth anniversary, 1890–1940. S.F., 1940. Formerly Abbey Cheney amateurs, 1890–1894.—The Chaminade club, 1894–1898.—San Francisco musical club, Oct. 6, 1898–   CHi

11949. —— San Francisco musical club... [founded 1809, incorporated 1952]...compiled by a committee, Mrs. Walter Alfred de Martini, chairman. S.F., 1953. 40 p.   CHi

11950. San Francisco musical fund society. Musical directory... January, 1873. 1st ed. S.F., Commercial steam print. house, 1873. 31 p.   CU-B

11951. The San Francisco news. Centennial review, edition of Saturday, Jan. 24, 1948. S.F., 1948. 28 p. illus., ports.   CHi

11952. —— Chinese New Year's edition. Sponsored by Chinese chamber of commerce, San Francisco. S.F., Feb. 12, 1959. 24 p. illus.   CSf

11953. —— Famous guide to San Francisco and the World's fair... S.F., c1939. 144 p. illus.   CHi

11954. —— Golden jubilee, celebrating 50th year. [S.F., 1953] 1a–16a, 1b–12b p. illus., ports.   CU-B

11955. San Francisco news letter and California advertiser. Artistic homes of California [chiefly San Francisco] [S.F.] Britton & Rey [1887–88] 69 pl.

C CHi CLU CO CSf CSfCW CSmH (52 pl.) CU-B

11956. —— Business blocks of San Francisco. [S.F.] Britton & Rey [1887–88] 12 pl.   CU-B

11957. —— ...City index and purchaser's guide. S.F., News letter off. [1872?] 185 p. illus., maps.
CHi CSf CU-B

11958. —— ...Diamond jubilee edition, Sept. 5, 1925. [S.F., 1925] 120 p. illus., pl.
CHi CLU CSf CSfP CSfWF-H CSrD CU-B

11959. —— ...Jubilee edition, 1856–1906. San Francisco news letter, 50th anniversary. Vigilante days and views of San Francisco 1851–1856 and 1906. [S.F., 1906] 64 p. illus., ports.   CHi CLU CSf CSfWF-H

11960. —— San Francisco news letter, 60th anniversary, 1856–July 20, 1916. [S.F., 1916] 82 p. illus., ports. Includes facsimile of the *San Francisco news letter.* A summary of events from the 20th of October to the 5th of November, 1856, mounted on p. 1.
C CLU CSf CSfWF-H

11961. San Francisco news letter and wasp. [75th anniversary number, Dec. 26, 1931] Colorful San Francisco... S.F., 1931. 98 p. illus.   CHi CSf

11962. San Francisco nursery for homeless children. Report... 10th, 12th–14th, 1899, 1901–1903. S.F., 1899–1903.   CHi

11963. San Francisco–Oakland bay bridge. [Scrapbooks of clippings showing the history of the San Francisco–Oakland bay bridge] Comp. by William Finley. 10 v. in portfolios. illus.   CU-B

11964. San Francisco–Oakland photo engravers union, no. 8. [50th anniversary, Diablo country club, Oct. 12, 1952] [S.F., Taylor & Taylor, 1952] [20] p.
CHi

11965. San Francisco office building and business directory. S.F., Ideal pub. co., 1904–05. 2 v.
CSmH CU-B (1905)

11966. ...San Francisco official guide [1906] and indexed map showing burned district... [S.F.] J.J. Hoag, c1906. 132 p. illus., map.   C

11967. ...San Francisco official guide and indexed map showing topography of city... [S.F.] J.J. Hoag. [1905] 120 p. illus., map.   CHi

11968. San Francisco; official memorial souvenir. [L.A., The Radial co., c1906] [40] p. illus.
C CLU CSmH

11969. San Francisco official street railway directory ... S.F., C.C. Hoag [&] J.J. Hoag, 1896.   CSfCW

11970. —— Same. c1902. 336 p. front. (fold. plan)
CU-B

11971. —— Same. 1903.
CLU CSfCP (1903, 1905?)

11972. San Francisco omnibus railroad co. Memorial to the legislature of California, on the subject of an increase on the rates of fare on horse railroads in San Francisco. S.F., Print. Towne & Bacon, 1864. 13 p.
CU-B

11973. San Francisco orphan asylum society. Annual reports... 1st– 1853 S.F., Print. by C. Bartlett, 1853– Printer varies.
CSf has 1st, 3d–4th, 6th–11th, 1853–55, 1857–62. CU-B has 10th, 1860. MHi has 8th, 1859.

11974. San Francisco package express co. By-laws...1869.   CU-B

11975. San Francisco patriotic liberty loan com-

mittee of one thousand. Golden roll of honor, third liberty loan... [n.p., n.d.] 158 p.　　　　　　CHi

11976. —— Personnel...[n.p., n.d.] 66 p.　　CHi

11977. San Francisco photographic salon. [Catalogue] S.F., Camera craft, 1901–1916. 4 v.
CHi has 1st, 2d, 3d, 5th.

11978. San Francisco; pictorial history of the fire and earthquake... N.Y., Elite art press, 1906.　C-S

11979. San Francisco; pictorial works. [n.p., 19—?] 24 p.　　　　　　　　　　　　　　　　　ViU

11980. San Francisco port of embarkation, transportation corps, Fort Mason, Camp Stoneman, Oakland army base. [S.F., n.d.] 25 p. illus., map.　　CHi

11981. San Francisco port society. Proceedings at the...anniversary...1st–47th. S.F., 1861–[1907] 45 v.
　C (3d, 14th) CSmH (28th) CSt (1862) CU-B

11982. San Francisco progress. California gold centennial, 1848–1948. Portola festival. Haight-Stanyan edition, Oct. 21–22, 1948. Special edition. S.F., 1948. 16, 24 p.　　　　　　　　　　　　　　　　　CSf

11983. San Francisco Protestant orphanage society. Edgewood; the San Francisco Protestant orphanage... [n.p., 1948?] folder 2 l.)　　　CHi

11984. —— Same. [n.p., 1958?] folder (5 l.) illus. List of members of Board of directors, 1958/59 inserted.
　　　　　　　　　　　　　　　　　　　　CHi

11985. —— The story of the San Francisco Protestant orphanage, a tale of seventy-three years (1851–1924) [S.F., 1924] 7 p.　　　　CHi CSf CU-B

11986. San Francisco public kindergarten society. Report for the three years ending Sept. 1st, 1881. Containing a record of...the first free kindergarten west of the Rocky Mountains. A history of the subsequent movement... [S.F., 1881] 31 p.　　CHi CLU

11987. San Francisco quarterly trades guide and merchants' directory. S.F., D.M. Bishop & co. [187–?]
　　　　　　　　　　　　　　　　CU-B (Dec. 1871)

11988. San Francisco real estate board. Constitution and by-laws and list of members... Organized Feb. 16, 1905. S.F., Shannon-Conmy print. co., 1909. 34 p.　　　　　　　　　　　　　　　　CHi

11989. San Francisco real estate circular. v.1–82, Dec. 1866–Dec. 1947. S.F., T. Magee & sons [etc.] 1866–1947.
C has v.2, no. 2, 41–82. CSf has v.2, no. 3–v.22, no. 3, v.30, no. 7–v.66, no. 7, Jan. 1868–Jan. 1887, May 1895–May 1932. CSmH has v.1, no. 3–v.3, no. 2, Jan. 1867–Dec. 1868. CU-B has v.1–14, no. 8, v.40, no. 6–v.75, 78–81, Dec., 1866–1946.

11990. —— San Francisco five years after the great fire of April 18, 1906; a review of the real estate market ... S.F., Thomas Magee & sons, 1911. 12 p. Supplement, April 1911.　　　　　　　　　　　　　C-S

11991. San Francisco real estate gazette. v.1, no. 1, May 29, 1869. S.F., Von Rhein, Levin & co., 1869.
　　　　　　　　　　　　　　　　　　　CU-B

11992. San Francisco real estate guide with partial list of real estate for sale...v.6, no. 1. Jan. 1891. S.F., O.D. Baldwin, Joost & Mertens, 1891.　CSf CU-B

11993. San Francisco real estate review. v.1, no. 1, 3–7. Oct. 31, 1868–Jan. 3, 1869. S.F., 1868–69.　CU-B

11994. San Francisco recorder. Historical and contemporary review of bench and bar in California. Issue of March 1926. S.F., 1926. 61 p.　　CV

11995. San Francisco relief and Red cross funds,

a corporation. ...Department reports as submitted to the Board of directors at the regular monthly meeting, Mar. 19th, 1907. [S.F., Starkweather, Latham & Emanuel, 1907] 30 p.　　C CHi CLU CSf CU-B

11996. —— ... Preliminary report concerning the financial operations of the Finance committee...and also of this corporation to Nov. 17th, 1906. [S.F., 1906] 45 p.
　　　　　　　　　　　　　　　　CHi CLU

11997. —— Report to the Massachusetts association for the relief of California, by Messrs. W. D. Sohier and Jacob Furth... S.F., 1906. 16 p.　　　　CLU

11998. San Francisco relief survey; the organization and methods of relief used after the earthquake and fire of April 18, 1906. Comp. from studies by Charles J. O'Connor, Francis H. McLean...N.Y., Survey associates, inc., 1913. 483 p. illus., map. (Russell Sage foundation pub.)
Available in many California libraries and OrU TxU UU ViU

11999. San Francisco retailers' council. Agreement between San Francisco department and specialty stores and Retail department store employees' union, local no. 1100 R.C.I.P.A., dated Nov. 1st, 1938. [S.F.? 1938?] 48 p.　　　　　　　　　　　　　　　CHi

12000. San Francisco, San Mateo and Santa Cruz railroad. Engineer's report... L. H. Shortt, engineer. S.F., Bacon & co. [1875?] 28 p.　　　　CLU

12001. San Francisco–San Mateo livestock exposition. Proposed International livestock exposition building to be erected by San Francisco–San Mateo counties and the state of California. S.F. [1932] [10] p. illus.
　　　　　　　　　　　　　　　　　　　CHi

12002. San Francisco savings union. [Half-yearly reports, 1863–
CHi has 1863–72, 1876, 1883–98.

12003. San Francisco schuetzen-verein, 1909. Golden jubilee, 1859–1909... [S.F., Louis Roesch co., 1909?] 24 p. illus., ports.　　　　　　　CHi

12004. San Francisco Scottish thistle club. Rules and regulations... Organized March 18, 1882. S.F., Frank Eastman & co., print., 1883. 52 p.　　CHi

12005. San Francisco settlement association. ... Annual report... 1st–11th, 1894/95–1904/05. S.F., 1895–1905.
CHi has 1894/95–1897/98, 1902/03. CLU has 1896/97, 1902/03–1904/05. CU-B has 1894/95, 1896/97–1898/99, 1902/03.

12006. San Francisco society for the prevention of cruelty to animals. ...Annual report... 1st– [186–?– S.F. [186–?–] illus., ports.
CU-B has 12th–13th, 34th, 39th, 1878/79–1879/80, 1901/02, 1906/07.

12007. —— By-laws...1868. S.F., 1868. 1 v.
　　　　　　　　　　　　　　　　　　　CU-B

12008. —— Our animals...75th anniversary of the San Francisco society...April 8, 1868–April 8, 1943. S.F., 1943. 47 p. illus.　　　　　　　　　　CHi

12009. San Francisco society of eye, ear, nose and throat surgeons. [Constitution and by-laws, fee-bill, list of members S.F., 1904] 23 p.　　CU-B

12010. San Francisco soldiers' and sailors' relief fund. Central committee. ...Relief fund of San Francisco, for the sick and wounded soldiers of the National army...circular to the counties and towns of the state. S.F., 1862. [4] p.　　　　　　　　　CHi

12011. San Francisco stamp society. Constitution and by-laws... S.F., 1918. 10 p. Founded 1915.　CHi

12012. San Francisco street railway guide...of all the city street railways... S.F., Bacon & co., c1892. 41 p.
C

12013. San Francisco symphony orchestra. ... Programme...1st season; 1911/12– S.F., 1911–
C has 5th–11th season. CHi has 1st–50th season, 1911/12–1962. CL has 1st, 3d, 5th–9th, 22d–26th season, 1911/12–1937/38. CSf has 1st–50th season, 1911/12–1962. CU-B has 1st–50th season, 1911/12–1962.

12014. San Francisco teachers. Musical festival of the fiftieth anniversary...of the public schools in San Francisco, April 30th to May 7th, 1905. [S.F., Tomoye press] 1905. unp. ports.
C

12015. San Francisco teachers' club. Chronological outline of the history of San Francisco. [n.p., n.d.]
C-S

12016. San Francisco teachers' mutual aid society. By-laws...Organized May 10, 1873; incorporated March 13, 1889. S.F., 1907. 36 p.
CHi

12017. San Francisco telegraph supply co. ... Telegraph instruments, machinery and supplies...electric burglar alarm...electric annunciators... [S.F., Excelsior press, 1880?] 14 p.
CHi

12018. San Francisco; the city of destruction... Portland, Me., L.H. Nelson co., c1906. [32] p. illus. Cover title: San Francisco; the story of the earthquake.
C CU-B

12019. San Francisco, the doomed city. Earthquake and fire... [L.A., M. Rieder, c1906] [22] p.
CHi CU-B

12020. San Francisco, the exposition city, 1915. [S.F., 1915] [10] p.
CU-B

12021. San Francisco, the exposition city, 1915, 'as I saw it': a descriptive view book in colors. L.A., H.H. Tammen, c1913. [28] p. illus.
C CHi

12022. San Francisco, the metropolis of the west. [S.F.] Western press assoc. [1910] [150] p. illus., ports., maps. "Men of today," by R. D. Thomas: p. [131–149]
CHi CLU CLgA CO CSfCW CSfU CSmH CU-B

12023. San Francisco tool co. [Catalogue of] irrigation and reclamation machinery... S.F., n.p., 1885. 42 p.
C-S

12024. —— Same. S.F., Mysell & Rollins, 1894. 72 p. illus.
CHi

12025. —— [Catalogue of wood-working machines] [S.F., 18—] 5 l. illus.
CU-B

12026. San Francisco tribune. Fourteen years of achievement; the record of San Francisco's progress... (Magazine supplement, March 1926) [S.F., 1926] 64 p. illus.
CHi

12027. San Francisco two years after; a series of pictures that tell the story of the city's marvelous renascence ... [S.F., 1908] 618 p. illus., ports.   CSmH CU-B

12028. San Francisco vereins. Constitution und neben-gesetze... [S.F.] 1870. 21 p.
CHi

12029. San Francisco water co. The charter, together with copies of the acts of the Legislature and ordinances of the city of San Francisco, from which are derived the incorporation, powers, and rights of said company... S.F., Towne & Bacon, 1860. 40 p.   CU-B

12030. —— Reports by engineers and others on a permanent supply of pure fresh water to the city of San Francisco. S.F., E. Bosqui & co., print., 1872. 80 p.
CHi CLU CSf CSmH CU-B

12031. —— Water rates, rules and regulations,

adopted by the directors, May 1, 1861. S.F., Agnew and Deffebach, 1861. 11 p. tables.   C CU-B

12032. San Francisco women artists. Constitution and by-laws. [S.F., 195–?] 19 p. Founded Feb. 12, 1925 as San Francisco society of women artists.   CHi

12033. —— San Francisco society of women artists, 1925–1929. [S.F., 1929?] 11 p.   CHi CU-B

12034. —— [Yearbook] 1928/29. S.F., 1928.
CHi

12035. San Francisco women's literary exhibit. Catalogue of California writers... Columbian exposition, 1893... [S.F., Co-operative print. co., 1892] 20 p.
C

12036. —— A list of books by California writers... S.F., Raveley print. co., 1893. 52 p.   CL

12037. San Francisco work-horse parade association. Catalogue, Annual parade. 1st–Sept. 1909. [S.F., 1909] 1 v. illus., ports.   CSf CU-B

12038. San Francisco yacht club. Annual regatta. 8th, Aug. 18, 1877. [S.F., 1877] 1 v.   CU-B

12039. —— Constitution and by-laws...also the sailing regulations, etc. S.F., Spaulding & Barto, 1877. 52 p. illus. (part col.) map, tables.   CSmH CU-B

12040. —— Same. 1904. 47 p.   CHi

12041. San Francisco's Chinatown, an aid to tourists and others in visiting Chinatown. October 1909. Portolá edition... S.F. [1909] 16 p. illus.   C C-S CLU

12042. San Joaquin valley canal co., San Francisco. Prospectus, engineer's report, certificate of incorporation and by-laws... S.F., M.D. Carr & co., 1866. 16 p. map.   CHi

12043. San Mateo city homestead association, San Francisco. Articles of incorporation and by-laws... S.F., E. Bosqui & co., 1869. 17 p.   CHi

12044. Sargent, Aaron Augustus. Remarks...in answer to Hon. D.C. McRuer upon the Goat island bill in its present aspects. ... before the Senate military committee, Jan. 31, 1873. [Wash., D.C., 1873] 13 p.
CLU

12045. Saunders, John H., vs. Clark, William S. In the Supreme court of the state of California. John H. Saunders and Clement Boyreau, plaintiffs and appellants, vs. William S. Clark, defendant and respondent. Petition for rehearing. John B. Felton and Saunders & Campbell, att'ys for plaintiffs and appellants. S.F., Towne & Bacon, 1865. 10 p. San Francisco land suit.
CLU

12046. Savage, John Lucian. Report on development of the San Francisco bay region... [S.F.?] 1951. 1 v. loose-leaf. 8 pl. (part. fold., incl. maps), tables.
C CSmat CSt

12047. Savage mining co. Annual reports. [186–?–187–?]
CHi has 1867/68–1870/71.

12048. Savelle, Max. This is my America; Pauline Dworzek and the Dworzek and Lorber families. Stanford [c1948] 43 p.   CHi

12049. Savings & loan society vs. Austin. In the Supreme court of the state of California. Savings & loan society, respondent, vs. Austin, tax collector, etc., appellant. Bartlett Doe, et al., respondents, vs. Austin, tax collector, etc., appellant. Argument on the unconstitutionality of the tax on solvent debts. John B. Felton, of counsel for respondents. [S.F.] Frank Eastman, print. [n.d.] 31 p.   CHi

12050. Savings and loan society. By-laws...incorporated July 23, 1857. With address to the members... S.F., Abel Whitton, print., 1860. 32 p.   CU-B
Other editions followed. CHi (1866, 1868) CSmH (1866) CU-B (1861)

12051. —— Seventh semi-annual report of the finance committee. Adopted January 31, 1861... S.F., Whitton, Waters & co., 1861. 16 p.   CU-B

12052. —— ...Conditions for depositors, and tables for loans. S.F., J.H. Carmany & co., 1871.   CSmH

12053. —— Real estate for sale. [189–?] S.F. [189–?] 1 v. maps.   CU-B

12054. Savings union bank and trust co. Fiftieth anniversary, 1862–1912. S.F. [The Furniture shop] 1912. [40] p. illus., ports.   CHi

12055. Sawyer, A. F. Mortuary tables of San Francisco...January 1st, 1862. S.F., Whitton, Waters & co., 1861. 18 p.   C CU-B

12056. Scanlan, Ralph J. The port of San Francisco and the Japanese-American trade. [Berkeley, 1926] Thesis (M.A.)—Univ. of Calif., 1926.   CU

12057. —— The potentialities of a foreign trade zone in the trade of the port of San Francisco. [Berkeley, 1930] Thesis (Ph.D.)—Univ. of Calif., 1930.   CU

12058. Scanlon, Lloyd Albert. Contests in the federal courts for possession of Yerba Buena Island. [Berkeley, 1962] Thesis (M.A.)— Univ. of Calif., 1962.   CU

12059. Schaeffer galleries. Paintings by Jane Berlandina at the residence of Le Roy M. Backus, Pacific coast director... [S.F., Taylor & Taylor] 1939. [3] l. illus.   CHi

12060. Schedler, C. W. Comments on the Reber plan prepared for Senator Downey at the hearing of Public works committee in San Francisco, California, Dec. 1949. [n.p., 1949] 24 p.   CU-B

12061. Scherer, James Augustin Brown. The first forty-niner and the story of the golden teacaddy. N.Y., Minton, Balch & co., 1925. 127 p. illus., port. The first forty-niner: Sam Brannan.
Available in many California libraries and CaBViPA OU TxU UHi UU ViU

12062. —— "The lion of the vigilantes," William T. Coleman and the life of old San Francisco... Indianapolis, N.Y., Bobbs [c1939] 335 p. illus., ports. "Sources": p. 320–324.
Available in many California libraries and CaBViPA IC MoS N ODa OU OrU TxU

12063. Schilling, A. & co. As others see us. S.F., 1910. 175 p. illus.   CHi

12064. —— The new way. S.F., 1908. 90 p.   CHi

12065. —— [Employees] To August Schilling & George F. Volkmann, 1881–1931. [S.F., Grabhorn, 1931] [23] p. pl. facsims. Cover title: Our golden jubilee.   CHi CU-B

12066. Schilling, August, comp. Inspiration. [Letters to August Schilling from those who received a copy of the book celebrating the golden jubilee of A. Schilling & company] [S.F., 1932] 1 v. unp. port., facsims.   CHi CU-B

12067. Schlage lock co. Schlage locks manufactured for residential, commercial, public, institutional and industrial buildings... S.F. [Strehl & Olivier, 1936] 182 p. illus.   CHi

12068. Schmolz, William. Schmolz's fan-wheel for drying... S.F., 1883. 24 p.   C-S

12069. Schroeder, Adolph, vs. Grady, John H. Adolph Schroeder vs. John H. Grady, Tax collector of the city and county of San Francisco. Brief for appellant. D. M. Delmas, att'y for appellant. J. P. Hoge, of counsel. [S.F.] Barry, Baird & co., print. [188–?] 9 p.   CU-B

12070. Schulz & Fischer, firm. ...Manufacturers of sterling silverware, and importers and dealers in silver plated ware, and fine table cutlery... [S.F.] T.J. Petit, print. [186–?] 7 pl.   CU-B

12071. Schussler, Hermann. Estimate of the value of the Spring Valley water works; cost of the proposed Calaveras water works... S.F., 1901. 53 p.   C CSfCW

12072. —— Report of H. Schussler, chief engineer of the Spring Valley water works on the various projects for supplying San Francisco with water. S.F., J.H. Carmany & co., print., 1876. 29 p.   CU-B

12073. —— The Twin Peaks tunnel problem. S.F., 1911. [4] p. fold. maps, fold. plans.   CHi CU-B

12074. —— The water supply of San Francisco... an address to the San Francisco section, American institute of electrical engineers, Nov. 19, 1909. S.F., 1909. 23 p. illus., 2 fold. pl. Reprint. from the *Jl. of electricity, power and gas*, Dec. 11, 1909.   C-S CHi

12075. —— The water supply of San Francisco, California, before and after the earthquake of April 18th, 1906... [N.Y., M.B. Brown press, 1906?] 103 p. illus., maps.
C CBu CHi CL CLU CO CSf CSfU CSfWF-H CSmH CU-B

12076. —— Same, with title...before, during and after the earthquake... 48 p.   C

12077. Schussler bros. Illustrated price catalogue. [188–?–189–?] S.F. [188–?–] 2 v. illus.   CU-B

12078. Scott, Florence Tarleton. An analysis of the board of directors of member agencies of the San Francisco Community chest. [Berkeley, 1947] Thesis (M.A.)— Univ. of Calif., 1947.   CU

12079. Scott, Mellier Goodin. New city: San Francisco redeveloped. Replanned and rebuilt under the Community development act of 1945, the blighted Western addition district would become one of San Francisco's most attractive residential areas. S.F., City planning commission, 1947. 23 p. illus.   CHi

12080. —— Progress in city planning. A report to the people of San Francisco; progress the last 100 years; action: 1940–1947; plans for 1948; organization; the next 100 years. S.F., Dept. of city planning [1948] 24 p. illus.   CHi

12081. —— The San Francisco bay area; a metropolis in perspective. Berkeley, Univ. of Calif. press, 1959. 333 p. illus., ports., maps.
Available in many California libraries.

12082. Scott, Reva Lucile (Holdaway) ...Samuel Brannan and the golden fleece, a biography. N.Y., Macmillan, 1944. 462 p. illus., ports. Bibliographical references included in "Notes" (p. 443–446) Bibliography: p. 447–450.
Available in many California libraries and UHi

12083. Scott, William Anderson. The Bible and politics; or, an humble plea for equal, perfect, absolute religious freedom, and against all sectarianism in our public schools. S.F., H.H. Bancroft & co., 1859. 146 p.   C CHi CSmH CSt CU-B CtY PHi

12084. —— A discourse for the times. By Rev. Dr. Scott, delivered in Calvary church, Sunday, July 27, 1856.

Education and not punishment, the true remedy for the wrong-doings and disorders of society. I Samuel, i, 24–28. S.F., 1856. 8 p. This was an attack upon the general principles of the activities of the Vigilance committee of San Francisco in 1856, making the author extremely unpopular among the supporters of that institution.— Cowan.

C CBPac CSaT CSmH CU-B N NN PHi

12085. —— A lecture delivered before the Merchantile library association of San Francisco, on the influence of great cities... June 16, 1854. S.F., Whitton, Towne & co., Excelsior job off., 1854. 33 p.

C CHi CSaT CSmH CU-B MWA NN

12086. —— My residence in and departure from California. Paris, E. Brière [1861] 31 p.

CHi CL CLU CO CSfCP CSmH CStbS CU-B

12087. —— The Pavilion palace of industry... S.F., Hutchings & Rosenfield, 1857. 24 p. illus. Description of the first industrial exhibition of the Mechanics' institute.

C CHi CLU CSaT CSfCW CSmH CU-B NN WHi

12088. —— Trade and letters; their journeyings round the world. Three discourses, delivered before the Mercantile library association of San Francisco... N.Y., Robert Carter & bros., 1856. 168 p.   CHi CSfCW

12089. —— The wedge of gold... S.F., Whitton, Towne & co., 1855. 183 p. Sermons in the Calvary Pres. church.

C CBPac CHi CL CLU CMary CO CSaT CSfCW CSmat CSmH CStr CU CU-B NN

12090. Scott mining and exploring co. By-laws... S.F., Alta California job print. off., 1864. 18 p.   CHi

12091. Scottish hall association of San Francisco. By-laws... S.F., D. Kerr, 1884. 15 p.   CHi

12092. —— Treasurer's report, 1887/1888. S.F., T.R. Tilley, print., 1888.   CHi

12093. [Scrapbooks about the theatre in San Francisco, covering the years 1895–1901, 1905–1914] 6 v. illus., ports.   CU-B

12094. [Scrapbooks of the San Francisco earthquake and fire, 1906] 3 v. illus.   CU-B

12095. Searight, Frank Thompson. The doomed city; a thrilling tale... Chicago, Laird & Lee [c1906] 186 p. illus.

C CHi CLgA CO CSd CSf CSfCW CSj CSmH CStoC CU-B MiD MoS NN

12096. Sears, Clark A., vs. Hathaway, E. V. Supreme court, state of California. Clark A. Sears, respondent, vs. E. V. Hathaway, et al., appellants. Appellant's brief. Pixley & Smith, attorneys for appellant. [S.F., 185–?] 35 p.   CHi

12097. Sears, Roebuck & co. The city of Saint Francis; a panoramic pageant of history. [S.F.? 1952?] [14] p. illus.   CHi

12098. Seawell, James Many. James M. Seawell, 1836–1917. [Honor blossoms on his grave...] [S.F., John Henry Nash, 1920] 9 p. port.   CHi

12099. The second sight mystery exposed. The secret out, a complete expose of the second sight mystery, as now being performed at the theatres. S.F., Winterburn & co., 1867. 16 p.   CHi

12100. Segal, Morley. James Rolph, Jr. and the Municipal railway, a study in political leadership. S.F., State college, 1959. 125 l. Thesis (M.A.)— San Francisco state college, 1959.   CSfSt

12101. Seiler (Paul) electrical works. Catalogue and price list for 1900. S.F., 1900. 43 p. illus.   CHi

12102. Selby (Thomas H.) & co. ...Catalogue and price list of plumbers' brass work... N.Y., Isaac J. Oliver [1859] 102 p. illus. In English and Spanish.   CHi

12103. Selby bros., Oakland. San Francisco earthquake and fire views, April 18th–21st, 1906. [24] p. illus.   CHi

12104. Selig, John Malcolm. The chief administrative officer in San Francisco. [Berkeley, 1939] Thesis (M.A.)— Univ. of Calif., 1939.   CU

12105. Selover, A. A., auctioneer. Catalogue of sale of lots in the city of San Francisco at public auction, on Monday, March 4, 1850... S.F., Alta California, 1850. 7 p.   CHi

12106. —— Same. April 20th... S.F., Jl. of commerce off., 1850. 8 p.   CHi

12107. Selover, Sinton & co. Abstract of sale of parts of the Folsom estate, consisting of lots, in the city of San Francisco... Jan. 10th and 11th, 1856... [S.F.] F. Eastman, print. [1856] 29 p.   CLU CU-B

12108. —— Catalogue. Executors sales of parts of the Folsom estate. Consisting of lots in the city of San Francisco, and in the town of Folsom, situated on the American river... S.F., Wm. W. Barnes [1855] 31 p.

CHi CLU CSfCP CSmH CU-B

12109. —— Same. ...Thursday, Nov. 13, 1856. S.F., Excelsior steam power presses [1856] [34] p.

C CSmH CU-B

12110. —— Sale...on Thursday, August 17th, 1854, at 12 o'clock, the interest of the state of California in water lot property in the city and county of San Francisco, by order of the California land commission. [S.F.] Times and Transcript power presses, 1854. 24 p.   CLU

12111. —— Same. ...Thursday, Oct. 26th, 1854. S.F., Whitton, Towne and co., print. [1854] 48 p.

CHi CU-B

12112. —— Same. ...Thursday, Jan. 18th, 1855 ... Sacramento, B.B. Redding, state print., 1855. 39 p.

CSfCP CSmH

12113. —— Same. ...Wednesday, Oct. 10, 1855. [S.F.] Times and transcript steam presses [1855] 56 p.

CLU CSfCP CU-B

12114. Selvin, David Frank. History of the San Francisco typographical union. [Berkeley, 1936] Thesis (M.A.)— Univ. of Calif., 1936.   CU

12115. Semenza, Laurence John. Some problems in installment selling in the San Francisco Bay region. [Berkeley, 1928] Thesis (M.A.)— Univ. of Calif., 1928.   CU

12116. Senate hotel. San Francisco, Hotel Senate, Turk Street at Larkin... [S.F., Olsen litho. co., n.d.] folder (6 p.) illus., map.   CHi

12117. Settler (in pro per) vs. San Francisco. The question of the title to the outside lands. Settler (in pro per) vs. the city of San Francisco. Argument of the plaintiff. S.F., Alta Calif. bk. & job print. off., 1866. 24 p. Signed: Eugene Liés, p. 13.

CL CLU CSf CU-B

12118. Settler Bill, *pseud.* ...Disposal of the pueblo lands, and startling developments. By Settler Bill, legislator of 1866... [n.p., 188–?] 14 p.   CU-B

12119. Settlers' protective union of tide land

titles. Report on title to tide lands, by a committee... appointed Mar. 14th, 1868... [S.F., 1868] 7 p.
CHi CU-B

12120. Seven arts club. [Brochure. S.F., 1923?] [16] p.
CHi

12121. Sewell, E. N. San Francisco; a few views showing progress in reconstruction two years after the great conflagration. [n.p.] 1908. 24 mounted photos.
C

12122. Sewell, Nelson Brown. Municipal ownership of street railways in San Francisco. [Berkeley, 1933] Thesis (M.A.)— Univ. of Calif., 1933.
CU

12123. Shafter, Oscar Lovell. Life, diary and letters of Oscar Lovell Shafter, Associate Justice, Supreme court of California, Jan. 1, 1864, to Dec. 31, 1868; ed. for Emma Shafter-Howard by Flora Haines Loughead... S.F., Blair-Murdock co., 1915. 323 p.
CBb CHi CSfCW

12124. —— Memorial...being words spoken at his burial by Rev. Dr. Stebbins, a sermon...by Rev. L. Hamilton, a sketch of his life and character...by Hon. John W. Dwinelle... S.F., 1874. 24 p.
CHi

12125. Sharon, William. [Series of legal actions, William Sharon vs. Sarah Althea Hill; and F. W. Sharon, his executor, vs. Sarah Althea Hill Terry, David S. Terry, and others. S.F., etc., 1884?–] 19 v. Suit in equity brought by William Sharon in the Circuit court of the United States for the district of California asking that an alleged marriage contract in Sarah Althea Hill's possession be adjudged a forgery. Suit brought by Sarah Althea Sharon in the Superior court of the city and county of San Francisco, state of California, asking that the alleged marriage contract be adjudged valid, that she be granted a divorce, and that a property settlement be made. Appeals, subsequent suits regarding the disposition of Sharon's estate after his death, etc. Arguments and pleas of counsel, opinions and decisions of courts.
CLU

12126. —— In the Circuit court of the United States ninth circuit, northern district of California. Frederick W. Sharon as executor, complainant, vs. David S. Terry and Sarah Althea Terry, his wife, defendants. No. 3138, Bill of revivor in equity. Francis G. Newlands, as trustee, et al., complainants, vs. David S. Terry...no. 6594, bill in equity... Argument of Wm. F. Herrin, for complainants, on demurrers to bills... S.F., Geo. Spaulding & co. [n.d.] 121 p.
CHi

12127. —— ...William Sharon, complainant, vs. Sarah Althea Hill, respondent, in equity. Closing argument for complainant by W. H. L. Barnes. S.F., Bosqui engraving and print. co. [n.d.] 224 p. illus.
CHi

12128. —— ... Oral argument for complainant by Wm. M. Stewart. [S.F., Bosqui engraving and print. co., n.d.] 106 p. facsims.
CHi

12129. —— In the Superior court of the state of California in and for the city and county of San Francisco, Department no. 2. Sarah A. Sharon, plaintiff, vs. William Sharon, defendant. Argument of Wm. M. Stewart. S.F., Geo. Spaulding & co. [n.d.] 14 p.
CHi

12130. —— In the Supreme court of the state of California (in banc). S. A. Sharon, plaintiff and respondent, vs. F. W. Sharon, executor of William Sharon. Argument of David S. Terry. Stockton, Mail steam bk. and job print., 1887. 94 p.
CSmH

12131. —— ...Argument of Samuel M. Wilson in the case of Sharon vs. Sharon upon the defendant's appeal from the order refusing a new trial...May 4th, 1889. 60 p.
CHi

12132. —— ... Brief for appellant on appeal from judgment declaring marriage... S.F., Geo. Spaulding & co. [1887] 39 p.
CHi

12133. —— ... Respondent's brief in reply, D. S. Terry, attorney for respondent. Stockton, Mail pub. house and bk. bindery, 1887. 50 p.
CHi CSmH

12134. Sharp, George F., vs. Baird, John, et al. ...George F. Sharp, plaintiff, vs. John H. Baird, Isaac N. Thorne, S. E. Thorne, Chas. J. Brenham, Sam'l J. Hensley, H. C. Wheeler, John Doe, and Richard Roe, whose real names are unknown to the plaintiff, defendants. Transcript on appeal. Wilson & Crittenden, attorneys for appellant; Geo. F. & Wm. H. Sharp, attorneys for respondent. S.F., Excelsior press, Bacon and co., print., 1869. 183 p. illus. (plan). Regarding land dispute in San Francisco.
CLU

12135. —— In the Supreme court of the state of California. George F. Sharp, plaintiff and respondent, vs. John H. Baird, et al., defendants and appellants. Brief of appellants in reply... S.F., Excelsior press, Bacon and co., print., 1870. 5 p.
CHi

12136. Sharpsteen, William Crittenden. History of Legal aid society of San Francisco. [S.F., 1944] 16 p.
CHi

12137. —— Record of the eighty-sixth company, California military reserve. [n.p., 1919?] 35 p. Formerly California old guard.
CHi

12138. Shasta water co. Annual report.
CL has 1954–59.

12139. Shaw, William James. An appeal to Californians to immediately undertake a peaceful revolution in 1876, and reorganize their state government; together with an address by the same author on the same subject, delivered in the Senate of California, Feb. 7th, 1856. S.F., print. for the author by A.L. Bancroft and co., 1875. 99 p.
CHi

12140. —— Speech...on the necessity of immediate constitutional reform, delivered in the Senate of California, Feb. 7, 1856. Sacramento, Democratic state jl., print., 1856. 36 p.
C CHi CSfCW CSmH CU-B NN NvHi

12141. Sheldon, Mark. An autobiographical sketch. S. F., Murdock press [191–?] 120 p. front.
CHi CSfCW

12142. Shelton, Edith. Let's have fun in San Francisco; a handbook to the city... [S.F., Author, Press of Knight-Counihan co., c1939] 147 p. illus.
C CHi CO CRcS CSf CU-B

12143. Shelton, Jack. How to enjoy 1 to 10 perfect days in San Francisco. [Larchmont, N.Y., Argonaut bks., 1961] 191 p. illus. (Argonaut "perfect travel" ser.)
CSfU

12144. Sherman, Isaac M. San Francisco. N.Y. [1852?] 1 v.
CSmH

12145. Sherman, William Tecumseh. Sherman and the San Francisco vigilantes. Unpublished letters of General W. T. Sherman. [N.Y., 1891] From *Century magazine*, Dec. 1891. p. 296–309.
C CHi CRedCL CU-B

12146. Sherman, Clay & co. Band instrument catalogue ... S.F., Schmidt label and litho. co. [189–?] 64 p. illus.
CHi

12147. —— Laudamus; portraits of notable musicians in and about San Francisco... [S.F., Taylor, Nash & Taylor, c1911] 238 p. ports.
CHi CSfCW

12148. Shiels, Edward E. S.F. no. 1223. In the Supreme court of the state of California. In the matter of the estate of Edward E. Shiels (deceased). Henry E. Monroe, appellant. George F. Shiels, respondent. Respondent's brief...Morrison, Foerster & Cope, attorneys for respondent. S.F., J.O. Jephson co., 1897. 32 p. CHi

12149. [Shimmons, J. H.] supposed author. The shame and scourge of San Francisco...the Rev. Isaac S. Kalloch...records of an evil life... [n.p., 1880?] 165 p.
C CLU CSmH CU-B

12150. Shloss, Morris, vs. creditors. In the Supreme court of the state of California. Morris Shloss, respondent, vs. his creditors, appellants. Brief for respondent. Theodore H. Hittell, attorney for respondent. S.F., Towne & Bacon, 1866. 19 p. CHi

12151. Shorb, Ethel R. Ethel R. Shorb, 1880–1959. By George Henry Cabaniss. [S.F., priv. print., 1959] [2] p. CHi

12152. Shreve & co. [Catalog] S.F., 1904– CHi (1904, 1914?) CU-B (1914?)

12153. —— ...Photographic souvenir. [S.F., Shirley Walker, 1906?] [24] p. illus. Photographs of San Francisco and the Shreve building before and after the fire. CHi CU-B

12154. Shuck, Oscar Tully. Historical abstract of San Francisco... In three volumes, v.1. S.F., Author, 1897. 104 p. illus., ports. No more published. Manuscript for v.2–3 lost in San Francisco fire of 1906. cf. Cowan, p. 213. Alphabetical arrangement: A–Funded.
C CHi CLU CO CSf CSfCP CSfCW CSmH CU-B CaBViPA NN

12155. —— Official roll of the city and county of San Francisco ab initio... S.F., Dempster bros., 1894. 128 p. Deals with consolidation of city and county.
CHi CLU CO CSf CSmH CU-B NN

12156. —— Sketches of leading and representative men of San Francisco...Ed. by eminent editors and authors of Calif. ...London, London & N.Y. pub. co. [etc., etc.] 1875. p. [703]–1097 [i.e. 1117] ports. Continuation of the author's *Representative and leading men of the Pacific.*
CHi CLSU CLU CSfCW CSmH CU-B NHi

12157. Shurtleff, George A. In memoriam, George A. Shurtleff, a member of the Society of California Pioneers. [S.F., 1902] [5] p. CHi

12158. Sierra club. The Sierra club, a handbook. Edited by David R. Brower. Editorial committee for the handbook: Ansel Adams [and others] S.F., c1947. 115 p. illus. CHi CSfSC
Other editions followed. CNF (1951) CRcS (1957) CSjC (1951)

12159. Signs of the times (periodical). Earthquake special, May 2, 1906. "What these things mean." Mountain View, Pac. press, 1906. CAla

12160. —— Souvenir edition...Earthquake and fire special. June 27, 1906. 24 p. CHi

12161. Sill, Daniel, jr., vs. Reese, Michael, et al. In the Supreme court of the state of California. Daniel Sill, jr., plaintiff and appellant, vs. Michael Reese, et al., defendants and respondents. Brief of respondents' counsel. S. M. Wilson [and] J. B. Felton, of counsel for respondents. S.F., Excelsior steam presses, Bacon & co., print., 1871. 60 p. Deals with de Haro suits. CLU

12162. Silver street kindergarten society. Annual statement...1882– S.F., C.A. Murdock & co., print., 1883–
CHi has 1886, 1888, 1891, 1893–97. CU-B has 1887, 1891, 1893.

12163. Silver terrace homestead association. Articles of association...incorporated Aug. 31, 1868. S.F., Democrat job off., 1868. 12 p. CHi

12164. Simon bros. The Simon brothers story! *Simon brothers news.* Diamond jubilee edition...May 8, 1950. [S.F., 1950] [4] p. CHi

12165. Simonds, William Day. Starr King in California... S.F., Elder [c1917] 105 p. front., port.
Available in many California libraries and IHi TxU

12166. Simonds saw co. Catalogue and price list. no. 7. S.F., 1901. illus. CU-B

12167. —— Same. S.F., Geo. L. Everett & co. [n.d.] 42 p. illus. CHi

12168. Simpson, Anna Pratt. Problems women solved, being the story of the Woman's board of the Panama–Pacific international exposition; what vision, enthusiasm, work and cooperation accomplished. S.F., The Woman's board, 1915. 191 p. mounted illus., ports.
CHi CLO CRcS CSdS CSf CSfCW CSfP CYcCL

12169. —— Story of the Associated charities since the fire of 1906. [S.F., 1909] C CCH CHi CU-B

12170. Simpson & Millar. Synopsis of the changes in the names of streets, etc., in the city and county of San Francisco... [S.F., 1895?] 34 p. CSf CU-B

12171. Sinclair, Fanny Wheeler. In memoriam, Fanny Wheeler Sinclair. [By William E. Ijams. S.F., 1882] 5 p. CHi

12172. Singer, Mort H., ed. Orpheum circuit [third of a century] [S.F.? 1920?] 152 p. illus., ports. CHi

12173. Sisters of mercy. Jubilee souvenir, 1854–1904. S.F. [The Moore-Hinds co., print., 1904] 85 p. illus., ports. C CHi CSfCW CSfMI CU-B

12174. —— Report of the Lady superior of the Sisters of mercy, San Francisco. [Sacramento, Chas. T. Botts, print., 1861] 2 p. CHi CSmH CU-B WHi

12175. Sisters of the Presentation. Golden jubilee ...1854–1904. S.F., Archdiocese [1904] [66] p. illus., ports. CHi

12176. 6:30 club, San Francisco. Ye booke of ye centurie: vvinne ye cvriovs will fynde a record of ye lst one hvndred meetinges of...ye sixe-thirtie clvbbe. S.F., C.A. Murdock & co., 1899. 19 p. CHi

12177. [Sketch book. Mechanics fair, 1878; letters describing the Industrial exhibition of the Mechanics institute... S.F., 1878] [32] p. illus. The last letter is signed: F.M.S. (for Frank Meriweather Smith?)
CU-B

12178. Skinner (H. E.) co. Catalog no. 1...fire arms, sporting goods. S.F. [Hicks-Judd co.] 1901. 78 p. illus. CHi

12179. Slattery, Catharine, vs. Hall, Henry, et al. In the Supreme court of the state of California. Catharine Slattery, Adm'x. of the estate of Michael Slattery, deceased, vs. Henry Hall, Andrew Mills, Edward C. Hinshaw, Orton Hubbell, Thomas McCune, and John Sharon. Transcript on appeal... S.F., Bacon and co., 1870. 80 p. maps. CHi

12180. Sly, L. H. Stanford court, San Francisco. S.F. [n.d.] 14 p. illus., plans. CHi

12181. Smith, Arthur. Art Smith's story; the autobiography of the boy aviator... Ed. by Rose Wilder Lane. S.F., The Bulletin [c1915] 94 p. port. CHi

12182. Smith (Barney) and co. Report on financial feasibility of the proposed southern crossing of San Francisco Bay, March 1958. N.Y., 1958. 22 l. CSt

12183. Smith, Bruce. Report of a survey of the San Francisco, California, Police Department. Westport, Conn., 1957. 143 l. tables.   C

12184. Smith, Charles vs. Cushing, Robert, et al. In the Supreme court of the state of California. Charles Smith, respondent, vs. Robert Cushing et al., appellants. Brief of respondent. Wilson & Crittenden, attorneys for respondent. S.F., Bacon and co., 1870. 14 p.   CHi

12185. Smith, Frank Meriweather, ed. San Francisco vigilance committee of '56, with some interesting sketches of events succeeding 1846... S.F., Barry, Baird & co., 1883. 83 p.
Available in many California libraries and CaBViPA IHi MHi MiD-B MoSHi N NN OU TxU ViU

12186. Smith, Peter, vs. Morse, P.A., et al. In the Supreme court of California. Peter Smith, respondent, vs. P. A. Morse and others, commissioners of the funded debt of San Francisco, appellants. Appellant's brief. October term, 1852. S.F., Monson, Haswell & co., print. [1852] 26 p.   CLU

12187. Smyth, Beatrice Bell. A cost of living study of the single business and professional woman in the San Francisco Bay district, 1930. [Berkeley, 1932] Thesis (M.A.)— Univ. of Calif., 1932.   CU

12188. Sneath, Richard G. History of the Merchants exchange bank of San Francisco, by R.G. Sneath, ex-president, addressed to its stockholders, March 12th, 1883. [S.F., 1883] 137 p.   CHi

12189. Snipper, Martin. A survey of art work in the city and county of San Francisco. Prepared for the Art commission. S.F., Art commission, c1953. [68] p. Mimeo.   CHi CSf

12190. Snow & May's art gallery. ...Catalogue of the collection of paintings and statuary...to be sold by auction at their store...Wednesday & Thursday, Dec. 19 & 20, '77... H. M. Newhall & co., auctioneers. S.F., Harrison, print. [1877] 26 p.   CU-B

12191. Snow & Roos' art gallery. Catalogue of pictures on exhibition...San Francisco. April, 1869. [S.F.] E. Bosqui & co., print. [1869] 7 p.   CU-B

12192. Social manual for San Francisco and Oakland, with addresses of people of society, membership of clubs [etc.]... S.F., City pub. co., 1884. 296 p. illus. CHi CLU CSf CSfCW CSfP CSfU CSfWF-H CSmH CU-B NHi

12193. Social register, San Francisco. N.Y., Social register assoc. [188–?]– Title varies: 1907–21, Social register, San Francisco, including Oakland.
C has 1927–28, 1930, 1932–33, 1935, 1942, 1946–47. CHi has 1907–08, 1911, 1913–17, 1919–20, 1922–1960. CO has 1945, 1950, 1952. CPa has 1940–41, 1943–46, 1956. CSf has 1907, 1922, 1924–36, 1941, 1947, 1951, 1953, 1955–60. CSfCW has 1924, 1926, 1929, 1937, 1940–42, 1944–45, 1949–50. CSfP has 1920, 1942, 1950–51, 1956. CSmH has 1918, 1929, 1957, 1960. CU-B has 1909–11, 1913–14, 1917, 1922, 1924, 1927, 1929, 1940, 1942, 1946. NHi has 1918–20, 1939, 1945, 1947, 1949, 1951–53.

12194. Socialist party (U.S.) California. San Francisco. Facts as to socialism, principles and candidates of the Socialist party, campaign of 1911. [S.F.] Gilmartin co. [1911?] 64 p. ports. Cover title. "Socialist party ticket, San Francisco."   CU-B

12195. Sociedad Hispano-Americana de benevolencia mutua, entra señoras, San Francisco. Constitucion y leyes...Organizada en el mes de abril de 1875. S.F., Impr. cosmopolitana, 1875. 18 p.   CHi

12196. Société française d'épargnes et de pré- voyance mutuelle. [By-laws.] S.F., Alta bk. and job off., 1861. 22 p.   CU-B

12197. —— Die französische gegebseitige spar- und leih- gesellschaft. Société française d'épargnes et de prévoyance mutuelle. Neben-gesetze. S.F., Demokrat job off., 1868. 22 p. tables.   CU-B

12198. Society events, season 1889. S.F., Wm. Wolf & co., 1890. 120 p. illus., advts.   C-S CHi

12199. —— Same. Season 1901–1902. [S.F., Edward H. Mitchell, 1902?] 171 p.   CHi

12200. Society for sanity in art, inc. San Francisco branch. Exhibition of painting and sculpture... California palace of the Legion of honor, San Francisco, Aug. 10th to Oct. 6th, 1940. [S.F.? 1940?] [41] p. illus.   CHi

12201. Society of American florists and ornamental horticulturists. Thirty-first annual convention, San Francisco, August 17, 18, 19, 20, 1915. [S.F.] Pac. coast horticultural soc. [1915?] 76 p. illus., ports.   CHi

12202. Society of California pioneers. Annual report of the officers... S.F., 1850–
C-S has 1906–07, 1910–22. CHi has 1895–96, 1898, 1903–10, 1913, 1918, 1921–27, 1931. CSf has 1891, 1893, 1895–96, 1901–02, 1904–05, 1908–09, 1910, 1913.

12203. —— Centennial roster, commemorative edition. Ed. by Walter C. Allen. S.F., 1948. 134 p. front.   CHi CSf

12204. —— Ceremonies at the laying of the cornerstone of the new Pioneer hall, July 7th, 1862... S.F., Charles A. Calhoun, 1862. 26 p.
C CHi CLU CSfCP CSmH CU-B NN

12205. —— Constitution and by-laws of the Society of California pioneers. S.F., 1850–
C-S has 1912, 1917, 1926. CHi has 1855, 1858, 1861, 1868–69, 1874, 1881, 1912, 1924, 1926, 1957. CLU has 1850. CPom has 1874. CRedl has 1912. CSf has 1874, 1881, 1894, 1908, 1912. CSfCP has 1850, 1861. CSjC has 1912. CSto has 1912. CU-B has 1850, 1853. MWA has 1853.

12206. —— Inaugural ceremonies at the opening of the new "Pioneer hall," eighth of January 1863. S.F., Alta Calif. bk. and job off., 1863. 27 p. Contents:—Inaugural address, by President O. P. Sutton. Oration, by Eugene Liés.   CHi CLO CSf

12207. —— Misrepresentations of early California history corrected. Proceedings of the Society of California pioneers in regard to certain misrepresentations of men and events in early California history, made in the works of Hubert Howe Bancroft, and commonly known as Bancroft's histories... S.F. [Sterett print. co.] 1894. 37 p.   C-S CHi CSf N

12208. —— Oration delivered...at their celebration of the... anniversary of the admission of the state of California into the union. S.F., 1853–1901. 1853 is in celebration of the third anniversary. First and second anniversary, 1851 and 1852, not published.
Scattered numbers found in many California libraries, principally in C CHi CSf CSfCP CSmH CU-B

12209. —— Report of the Committee of the Board of directors...on the financial condition of the society, March 1st, 1878. S.F., Women's co-operative print. union, 1878. 8 p. plus 24 p. of tables.   CHi CSf

12210. —— Report of the committee of the Board of directors...on the state of the society, Jan. 1, 1869... S.F., Frank Eastman, print., 1869. 15 p. Comprises records of the society for the years 1853–1868.
    CHi CLO CSf

12211. —— Report of the historical committee of the society...refuting certain slanderous and false statements made from time to time against the pioneer men and women of California by preachers of several religious denominations. S.F., 1901. 20 p.   C-S CHi CSf

12212. —— Souvenir program: The golden jubilee of aviation in California...Sept. 7, 1961. [S.F., 1961] [4] p. illus. Leaf inserted: radio program, aviation pioneers.   CHi

12213. —— Transactions of the society...Jan. 1st to May 7th, 1863. pt. 1, v.2. S.F., Calif. bk. and job off., 1863. 101 p. No others published.   CHi CLO CSf

12214. Society of decorative art. Catalogue of the Art loan exhibition, for the benefit of the Society of decorative art of California, at the rooms of the San Francisco art association...April 1881. [S.F.] C.A. Murdock & co., print. [1881] 87 p.   CHi CU-B

12215. Society of progressive spiritualists. By-laws... [S.F.? 1916?] 27 p. Incorporated March 17, 1884, re-incorporated May 18, 1916.   CHi

12216. Society of St. Vincent de Paul. San Francisco archdiocesan central council. Annual report. 97th, 99th, 1957, 1960. S.F., 1957–60. 2 v.   CHi

12217. Soetaert, Barbara Maynard. A history of education of the mentally retarded child in the San Francisco public schools. [S.F., San Francisco state college] 1955. 1 v. (v.p.) charts, forms. Graduate project—S.F. state college.   CSfSt

12218. Soldiers' relief fund committee. Reports ... S.F., S.H. Wade & co., print., 1865. 92 p.   C CHi CLU CSmH CU-B

12219. —— Subscribers to the Soldiers' relief fund. 1863–64. [S.F., 1863] 4 p.   CU-B

12220. Soleim, John Bernard. The export of fresh fruits from the port of San Francisco. [Berkeley, 1929] Thesis (M.A.)— Univ. of Calif., 1929.   CU

12221. Somers and co. vs. General relief committee et al. ...In the District court of appeal, state of California, First appellate district...Transcript on appeal from the judgment of the Superior court of the state of California, in and for the city and county of San Francisco, in favor of defendant San Francisco relief and Red cross funds, and from the order of said court denying plaintiff's motion for a new trial as to said defendant... [S.F.] Pernau pub. co., 1910. 88 p.   CU-B

12222. Sons of St. George. The coronation celebration, San Francisco and Alameda counties, California, U.S.A. Programme...on the day of the coronation of King George V, June twenty-second, nineteen hundred and eleven. [S.F., Wale print. co., 1911] [32] p. illus., ports.   CU-B

12223. Sons of the American revolution. California society. Addresses delivered before the California society of the Sons of the American revolution... S.F., 1909–17. Memorial sketches of all members who have died since April, 1906: v.1, p. 154–165. Biographical sketches: v.2, p. 91–117.
CHi has 1913, 1917. CSfCW has 1909, 1913. N has 1909.

12224. —— —— Genesis and revelations of the former "California society of sons of revolutionary sires" but now the California society of Sons of the American revolution. [S.F.? 1905?] 24 p. illus., ports.   CHi

12225. —— —— History, constitution, by-laws, membership... S.F., 1893. 29 p.   CHi
Other editions followed. CHi (1897, 1908?)

12226. —— —— Its origin, names of officers, constitution, by-laws, articles of incorporation, names of members and rules and regulations of auxiliaries... S.F., Alta print., 1876. 42 p. Instituted at San Francisco, California, October 22, 1875, as Sons of revolutionary sires.   CHi

12227. —— —— Register... S.F., 1901. cxxv, 197 p.   CSfCW

12228. Sorosis club. Constitution and by-laws, 1895–96. [S.F., Frank Eastman press, 1895?] 39 p.   CHi

12229. —— Same. Rev. ed. [S.F., 1907] 18 p.   CHi

12230. —— Same. Revision and reprint. [S.F.] 1921. 18 p.   CHi

12231. —— Year book. [S.F., 1903–
CHi has 1902–03; 1905–06; 1909–11; 1919–20; 1925–27.

12232. Sourdry, Amedee Martin. Development of public outdoor recreation facilities in the San Francisco Bay area. [Berkeley, 1949] Thesis (M.S.)—Univ. of Calif., 1949.   CU

12233. South of Market journal. v.1– Aug. 1925– [S.F. 1925–
C has [v.8–16], v.24, no. 4, Apr. 1948–1960. CSf has v.1–4, v.6–16 (incomplete), Aug. 1925–Oct. 1941. CU-B has v.7, no. 4–v.16, no. 7 [i.e. 9] May 1932–Oct. 1941 (incomplete)

12234. South Pacific coast railroad, San Francisco. [Descriptive pamphlet of territory served by S.P.C.R.R.] S.F. [188–?] 12 p.   CHi

12235. South San Francisco dock co. Certificate of incorporation, articles of association, by-laws...Incorporated Aug. 8, 1867. S.F., Alta Calif. print. house, 1867. 15 p.   CHi CU-B

12236. South San Francisco homestead and railroad association. Indenture, rules of order and certificates of incorporation. Adopted Nov. 13, 1862. S.F., Waters bros. & co., print., 1863. 19 p.   CHi CU-B

12237. Southern Pacific co. Bay memories; reprint of articles from the *Southern Pacific bulletin.* [1939] 15 p. On the passing of the ferries and their history.   CAla CO

12238. —— Circular 4, list of officers, agencies, stations, etc., issued July 1, 1960... S.F., 1960. 193, 54 p.   CHi

12239. —— Ferryboats on San Francisco bay; a general historical memorandum, Oct. 21, 1957. 20 p. Mimeo.   CHi

12240. —— Historical outline of Southern Pacific company...March, 1933. [113] p.   CHi CMartC

12241. —— Rules and regulations of the transportation department. Revised ed. [S.F.] 1907. 148 p.   CHi

12242. —— San Francisco imperishable. S.F. [n.d.] 1 sheet (fold.) in pocket, illus., map.   C CHi CSmH NHi

12243. —— Southern Pacific's first century. S.F., 1955. 107 p. illus., map.
"The text is a revision and expansion of what appeared in a previous booklet, '75 years of progress,'" verso t.-p.   CHi

12244. —— Statistical report. CL has 1943–59.

12245. —— Trips around San Francisco. [n.p.] 1917. 95 p. map.   C-S CHi

12246. —— **Passenger dept.** San Francisco hotels and reconstruction. Oct. 1906–Dec. 1907. S.F., 1906–07. illus.

CHi (Mar. 1907) CSf CSmH CU-B (Oct. 1906–Aug. 1907, Oct., Dec. 1907)

12247. Southworth, Philip T., vs. Moore, Ezekiel J., et al. In the District court of the 12th judicial district of the state of California, in and for the city and county of San Francisco. Philip T. Southworth, plaintiff, vs. Ezekiel J. Moore, David Wood, 2d, Charles Vandervoort, Joseph B. Hudson, William Hayes, Samuel W. Moore, and E. D. Kennedy, defendants. [Statement of complaint by Shafter, Park & Shafter, attorneys for plaintiff. S.F., 1857] [3] p.   CHi

12248. Souvenir. New city hall dome. July 12, 1897. Presented by the contractors and S.F. news letter. [n.p., 1897] [14] p. illus.   CHi

12249. Souvenir guide publishers. Souvenir guide [comprising] natural color views, half tones and descriptive text, portraying and interpreting the Exposition palaces, courts, art and symbolism. [S.F., c1915] 20 p. illus. (part col.)   CU-B

12250. Souvenir of San Francisco. [12 copyright photographs...from Philip Fry and co.'s art repository] [Phila., Janentzky & co., sole agents, 187–?] 14 l. of illus., fold. map. Cover title.   C

12251. Souvenir of San Francisco. Photogravures [by] the Albertype co., Brooklyn, N.Y. S.F., Denison news co. [190–?] 32 p.
CHi CLU CSfCW CSmH CU-B

12252. —— Same. Photo-gravures [by] the Albertype co., Brooklyn, N.Y. S.F., Cunningham, Curtiss & Welch, c1902. 33 pl.   CLU CoU

12253. —— Same. Photogravures [by] the Denison news co., Oakland pier, 1908. 32 pl.   CU-B MoSHi

12254. —— Same. [1904?] 32 pl.
CSf CStclU CStrJC

12255. Souvenir of the destruction of San Francisco by earthquake and fire...April 18, 19, 20 and 21, 1906, with introduction by Harrie Davis. N.Y., Illustrated press syndicate [c1906] [50] p. illus.   C MoS NN

12256. Spaulding (F. M.) and co. [Catalog] [188–?] S.F. [188–?] 1 v.   CU-B

12257. Spear, Edward S. & co. ...Catalogue of special and peremptory sale of oil paintings and statuary, by local artists, to be sold at auction...Aug. 17th & 18th, 1882... This collection comprises...paintings of...R. G. Holdredge, G. J. Denny, W. A. Coulter...[and others] ...S.F., Winterburn & co.'s print. [1882] [18] p.   CU-B

12258. Specifications for building the sea wall along the water front of San Francisco. [n.p., 1867?] 8 p. William J. Lewis, engineer.   CLU

12259. Speegle horizontal current wheel power co. Prospectus. [S.F., 1907?] 11 p. illus.   CU-B

12260. Speer, William. An answer to the common objections to Chinese testimony and an earnest appeal to the legislature of California for their protection by our law. S.F., B.F. Sterett, 1857. 16 p.
CHi CU-B PHi

12261. —— China and California; their relations, past and present. A lecture in conclusion of a series in relation to the Chinese people delivered in the Stockton street Presbyterian church, San Francisco, June 28, 1853 ...S.F., Marvin & Hitchcock, 1853. 28 p.
C CPac CHi CSmH CU-B

12262. —— An humble plea addressed to the legislature of California, in behalf of the immigrants from the empire of China to this state... S.F., Pub. at the off. of the Oriental...Print. by Sterett & co., 1856. 40 p.
C CHi CSmH CSt CU-B NN PHi

12263. Spelling, Thomas Carl. Iniquities of the new charter. Speech of T. Carl Spelling, esq., at Garibaldi hall, on Tuesday evening, Oct. 21st, 1896. [S.F., J.H. Barry, print., 1896] 16 p.   CHi CLU

12264. Spencer, Arthur Lloyd. Subdivision standards and design requirements in four counties in the San Francisco bay region. [Berkeley, 1951] Thesis (M.A. City planning)—Univ. of Calif., 1951.   CU

12265. Sprague, Francis William. Barnstable and Yarmouth sea captains and ship owners... List of sailings from New England to San Francisco, 1849–1856... [Bost., Priv. print., T.R. Marvin & son, print.] 1913. 52 p. illus., ports.   CLU CSf

12266. Spreckels (John D.) & bros. co. Gillingham London Portland cement. J. D. Spreckels & bros. co. ...San Francisco and Spreckels bros. commercial co., San Diego, sole importers. [S.F., 1893?] [4] p.   CU-B

12267. —— [Port of San Francisco. Glasgow, R. MacLehose, print. to the Univ., 1886] 20 p. illus., map.
CHi CSf CSmH

12268. —— Same, with title: Ports of San Francisco, San Diego, Puget Sound, Portland, and Honolulu. [S.F., print. by W.C. Brown, 1889] 54 p. illus., maps.
CSfU CSmH

12269. Spring valley campaign committee. The Spring valley purchase; facts, figures, arguments. Prepared for the information of the citizens of San Francisco under the direction of the Spring valley campaign committee. Feb. 1, 1921. S.F., Wilcox & co., 1921. 32 p. map.   CHi

12270. Spring valley water co. vs. San Francisco. In the Circuit court of the United States, ninth circuit, Northern district of California. Spring valley water company, complainant, vs. the city and county of San Francisco et al., defendants. Defendants' brief and argument on final hearing... S.F., James H. Barry co. [1906?] 791 p.   C-S CHi CLU CU-B

12271. —— ... Addenda to defendants' brief and argument on final hearing. [S.F.? 190–?] [37] p. of maps, tables.   CHi

12272. —— ... Complainant's opening brief and argument. A. E. Shaw [and] Heller, Powers & Ehrman, solicitors for complainant. S.F., The Murdock press [1908] 529 p. tables (part fold.)   CHi CU-B

12273. —— ... Oral argument of Edward J. McCutchen for complainant, on final hearing. [S.F.] Pernau pub. co. [1910?] 338 p. fold. table.   CU-B

12274. —— ... Oral argument of Thomas E. Haven on behalf of defendants on final hearing. Percy V. Long, city attorney, Thomas E. Haven, solicitors for defendants. [S.F.? 1910?] 308 p.   CHi CU-B

12275. —— The past, present and future water supply of San Francisco... as detailed in the report of Hermann Schussler, in affidavit of June 20, 1908, filed in the U.S. circuit court. S.F. [C.A. Murdock] 1908. 69 p. maps.   C CHi CL CLU CSf CSfU CU-B

12276. —— ... The Spring valley water works (a corporation), complainant, vs. the city and county of San Francisco (a municipal corporation) ... et al. ... defendants. No. 13,395 in equity. The Spring valley water company (a corporation), complainant, vs. the city and county of San Francisco (a municipal corporation) ... et al. ...defendants. Nos. 13,598 and 13,756 in equity.

Closing argument of Edward J. McCutchen for complainant, on final hearing. [S.F.] Pernau pub. co. [1910?] 249 p.   CU-B

12277. —— In the District court of the United States for the northern district of California, second division. Spring valley water company, complainant, vs. city and county of San Francisco, et al., defendants... in equity. Oral argument of Robert M. Searls for defendants on final hearing before Hon. H. M. Wright, standing master in chancery for said court. Aug. 24th–Sept. 1st, 1916... S.F., James H. Barry co. [1916] 593 p. map.   CHi

12278. —— In the Supreme court of the state of California. The Spring valley water works, petitioner, vs. the city and county of San Francisco et als., respondents. Motion, statement of case, and points and authorities, for petitioner. Charles N. Fox, attorney for petitioner. Lloyd & Newlands, and J. P. Hoge, of counsel. S.F., J. Winterburn & co., print., 1877. 36 p.   CLU

12279. —— Meaning and purpose of reservation in charters of corporations ... The Spring valley water works, plaintiff in error, vs. The Board of supervisors of ...San Francisco. Appeal from the Supreme court of California [to the U.S. Supreme court] [n.p., 188–?]   CSmH

12280. —— ...Spring valley water works, vs. Board of supervisors. Argument of F. G. Newlands...on the power of the Board of supervisors of the city and county of San Francisco to fix the rates which a private corporation shall charge for water supplied to the city and county and its inhabitants. [S.F.? 1881] 35 p.   CSmH CU-B

12281. Spring valley water co. vs. Schottler, Antoine. In the Supreme court of the state of California. Spring valley water works, appellant, vs. Antone [sic] Schottler et als. (Board of equalization), respondents. Argument of F. G. Newlands, of counsel for the Spring valley water works. Filed A.D. 1882... [n.p., 1882] 65 p.   CHi

12282. —— In the Supreme court of the United States. The Spring valley water works, plaintiff in error, vs. Antone Schottler, et als., defendants in error. Brief for plaintiff in error. Chas. N. Fox, attorney for plaintiff in error. [S.F.? 188–?] 38 p.   CLU

12283. —— ... San Francisco water rate case...; Spring valley water works vs. Antoine Schottler et al. ... Oral arguments on behalf of plaintiff by Charles N. Fox, Francis G. Newlands [and] George F. Edmunds. Wash., D.C., Thomas McGill, print. [1883?] [103] p. Arguments presented to the United States Supreme court, Nov. 20, 1883.   CHi

12284. Spring valley water co. By-laws, etc. . . . [S.F., Towne & Bacon print., 1862] 22 p.   C CSfCP

12285. —— Same, May 1, 1909. [S.F., 1909?] 19 p.   CU-B

12286. —— Deed, Spring valley water company to city and county of San Francisco; water system properties; dated as of March 3, 1910. [S.F., Gilmartin print., 1930] 125 p.   CHi

12287. —— The future water supply of San Francisco, a report to the Hon. Secretary of the interior and the Advisory board of engineers of the U.S. army, Oct. 31, 1912. [S.F., Rincon pub. co., 1912] 506 p. maps.
  C CHi CLU CSf CSfWF-H CSmH CStoC CU-B

12288. —— Laws, ordinances and acts of incorporation affecting the property and franchises of the Spring valley water works. S.F., Raveley print. co., 1893. 70 p.   CLU

12289. —— Letter from the Board of directors to the shareholders... March 17, 1919. 5 p.   CHi

12290. —— Letter from the president of Spring valley water company to the Mayor and to the Board of supervisors of the city and county of San Francisco, Nov. 28, 1910. [S.F., 1910] 8 p.   CU-B

12291. —— Letter from the president to the Special committee of the Board of supervisors on water supply. [S.F., 1908] 14 p.   CU-B

12292. —— Offer of the Spring valley water company to sell its works to the city and county of San Francisco Sept. 14, 1912. [S.F., 1912] 7 p.
                                          CHi CSmH CU-B

12293. —— Reports... S.F., 1875– Title varies.
  C has 1875–76, 1917. CHi has 1875, 1908, 1910, 1917–18, 1927–29, 1944–49, 1951. CLU has 1875. CSf has 1908. CSmH has 1875, 1907. CU-B has 1875, 1901–02, 1906–21, 1923–41, 1943–49.

12294. —— Resolutions upon the demise of Homer S. King. Adopted... the thirtieth day of December: MCMXIX. [S.F., Crocker, 1920?] [4] l.   CSmH

12295. —— Specifications for the construction of an iron pipe line for the Spring valley water works, July 12, 1887. [n.p., 1887?] 18 p.   C

12296. —— Statement to shareholders of the Spring valley water company in reference to decision of rate cases for 1903–4–5. [S.F., 1911] [3] p.   CU-B

12297. —— Typical views of San Francisco's water supply and surroundings, property of Spring valley water company. [n.p., 1910] [50] l.   CHi

12298. —— The water supply of San Francisco. [S.F., 1912?] [62] p. illus., fold. map.
                                          CHi CSmH CU-B

12299. Springer, Jason. Price current. [187–?] S.F. [187–?] 1 v. illus.   CU-B

12300. Stadtmuller, Edwin William. Those early years [in San Francisco. S.F., 1955] 94 p.
                          CHi CLU CSfMI CSmH CSt

12301. Stafford, William M. et al. vs. Lick, James et al. In the Supreme court, state of California. Appeal from the Twelfth district. Wm. M. Stafford, et al., appellants, v. James Lick, et al., respondents. January term, 1858. Brief for appellants. By Gregory Yale. [S.F.] O'Meara & Painter, print. [1858?] 27 p. A San Francisco land suit.   CLU CSmH CU-B

12302. —— ...William M. Stafford, Freeman S. McKinney, and Parker H. French, plaintiffs and respondents, vs. James Lick and Jean Ducau, defendants and appellants. Brief on behalf of appellants. Whitcomb, Pringle & Felton, attorneys for defendants. S.F., Towne & Bacon, print. [n.d.] 16 p.   CLU CSmH CU-B

12303. Stallard, J. H. The problem of municipal government of San Francisco... S.F., Overland mo. pub. co., 1897. 40 p. Reprint. from *Overland monthly*, Jan.–May, 1897.   CU-B

12304. Stanbery, Henry Van Beuren. Regional planning needs of the San Francisco bay area. [S.F.] San Francisco bay area council, 1954. 53 p. fold. map.
                                          C CSfSt CSt

12305. Standard gas engine co. Bulletin. no. 14, [190–?] S.F. [190–?] 1 no. illus., diagrs.   CU-B

12306. —— Catalogue. no. 2 [190–?] S.F. [190–?] 1 no. illus.   CU-B

12307. Standard oil company of California. Annual report. 1st, 1913– S.F., 1913–
  CHi has 1920, 1922, 1924–27, 1929, 1932–41, 1945–46,

1948–50, 1952–61. CL has 1943, 1946–60. CSfSO has 1913 to date.

12308. —— Articles of incorporation of Standard oil company (California). S.F., 1922. 231 p.   CSfSO

12309. Standard soap co. Price list. 1881. S.F. [1881] 1 v. illus.   CU-B

12310. Standart, Mary Colette, Sister. The early development of social and economic nativism in San Francisco and the mining regions of California. 1848–1856. [Wash., D.C., 1947] 85 p. Thesis (M.A.)—Catholic univ. of America, 1947.   CSrD

12311. Standwell's Pacific railroad guide and business directory. 4000 copies published monthly... Sacramento, 1869.

CSmH has Aug. 1869.

12312. Stanford university. Library. Lane medical library. ... Dedication of the Lane medical library, Leland Stanford jr. university, San Francisco, November 3, 1912... 1912. 31 p.   CHi CLU CSmH CU-B

12313. Stanich, John Robert. An architectural development of the panhandle area in San Francisco. [Berkeley, 1961] Thesis (M.A.)—Univ. of Calif., 1961.   CU

12314. Stanley-Taylor co. [Brochure] [S.F., 191–?] [7] p. illus.   CHi CU-B

12315. Star of Hope (ship). In the United States district court, northern district of California. Wm. C. Annan, et als, v. ship "Star of Hope," her tackle, &c. in admiralty; opinion of Hon. Ogden Hoffman, U.S. District judge, delivered April 12th, 1859. [S.F.? 1859?] 16 p.   CHi

12316. Starin, J. N., and Wand, T. L., pub. ... Souvenir of San Francisco... [S.F., 189–?] 44 pl. C (eds. with 41, 42, 48 pl.) CHi (ed. with 41 pl.) CLU CStclU

12317. Starr, Lando. Blue book of San Franciscans in public life... S.F., McLaughlin pub. co. [c1941] 308 p. illus., ports.   CL CO CSfU CU-B

12318. Starr, Walter A. In memoriam, 1903–1933 by Vincent Butler. [n.p., 1933?] [7] p. front.   CHi

12319. State of Maine association of California. Seventeenth annual re-union... held at Midwinter fair festival hall, San Francisco, Wednesday, June 6th, 1894. Oakland, 1894. 23 p.   CHi

12320. Stationery, drug, notion and music dealers board of trade. Constitution and by-laws. Adopted Aug. 17, 1878. S.F., A.L. Bancroft & co., print., 1878. 19 p.   CU-B

12321. Stebbins, Horatio. Anniversary sermon of the Rev. Horatio Stebbins, D.D., delivered Sept. 10, 1899 on the thirty-fifth anniversary of his ministry in the First Unitarian church, San Francisco, Cal. [S.F., Evening post, 1899] [6] p. port.   CHi

12322. —— Some reflections on the industrial troubles of the present time. [S.F., 1894] 16 p.   CHi

12323. —— A Thanksgiving discourse... S.F., Charles F. Robbins & co., 1864. 22 p.   CHi

12324. —— Thirty-one years of California; a secular discourse...on the occasion of the thirty-first anniversary of his ministry in San Francisco, Sept. 8, 1895... [S.F.] Channing auxiliary of the First Unitarian church of San Francisco, 1895. 22 p.   CSmH

12325. Stebbins, Lucy Ward. Julia George, an appreciation. Oakland, Eucalyptus press, 1945. 15 p. front. (mounted port.)   CHi

12326. Steele, Elder and co. [Catalog] 1882. S.F., 1882. 1 v. illus.   CU-B

12327. Steele, Rufus. The city that is; the story of the rebuilding of San Francisco in three years. S.F., Robertson, 1909. 101 p. illus.

Available in many California libraries and CaBViPA MoS NN OrU

12328. Steiger & Kerr stove and foundry co. Occidental stoves, ranges, heaters. [Catalog] no. 12. [S.F., 191–?] 65 p. illus.   CHi

12329. Steinbach, Rudolph, vs. Moore, Joseph H., et al. "Repartimiento" [In the] Supreme court of the state of California. Rudolph Steinbach, appellant, vs. Joseph H. Moore, et al., respondents. Brief on the part of the appellants... B. S. Brooks of counsel for appellants. [n.p., n.d.] 182 p.   CHi

12330. Stellman, Louis John. Port o'gold; a history-romance of the San Francisco Argonauts. Bost., R.G. Badger [c1922] 416 p. illus.

Available in many libraries.

12331. —— Sam Brannan, builder of San Francisco; a biography. N.Y., Exposition press [1954, c1953] 254 p. illus.

C CBb CChiS CHi CLO CLS CLSM CMon CMont CP CSS CSd CSf CSluCL CStcl CStoC UHi

12332. —— That was a dream worth building; the spirit of San Francisco's great fair portrayed in picture and words... S.F., Crocker, c1916. 42 p. illus.

C CHi CLO CLSU CLU CMerCL CMont CO COHN CRcS CSd CSfCW CSmH CU-B

12333. —— The vanished ruin era; San Francisco's classic artistry of ruin depicted in picture and song. S.F., Elder [c1910] 52 p. illus.

C C-S CBu CHi CL CLO CMerCL CO CSalCL CSf CSfCW CSfU CSmat CSmH CU-B CViCL NHi NN

12334. Stephen J. Field arrested for conspiracy and murder of the Hon. David S. Terry. Some of the reasons why he did not dare stand an investigation, but attempted to stigmatize the judge's wife in application to Governor Waterman of California begging to be released. Fresno, 1889. 21 p. "The above is compiled and published by the friends of the late Judge David S. Terry."   CHi

12335. Stephens-Adamson manufacturing co. Catalog 55. [S.F.] 1941. 624 p. illus.   CHi

12336. Sterling electric co. Everything electrical. [Catalog] [190–?] S.F. [190–?] 1 v. illus.   CU-B

12337. Stern, Rosalie Meyer. In memoriam. Rosalie Meyer Stern. 1869–1956. By Ansel and Virginia Adams. [S.F., Lawton Kennedy, print., 1956] 4 p. illus.   CHi

12338. Stetson, James Burgess. San Francisco during the eventful days of April, 1906; personal recollections. S.F., Murdock press [1906] 23 p.

C C-S CBu CHi CL CLU CLgA CO COHN CSf CSfCP CSfU CSfWF-H CSj CSmH NN

12339. —— Same. Rev. ed. S.F., Murdock press [1906] 41 p.   CHi CSfP

12340. Stevenson, Howard G. Ship Defiant; voyage from New York to San Francisco, 1875–1876, and subsequent voyages as the ship Amphitrite. S.F., Priv. print., 1937. 39 p. illus., map.   CHi

12341. Stevenson, Jonathan Drake. To the public. Geo. Barstow vs. J. D. Stevenson. [S.F., 1870?] 3 p. Signed at end: J. D. Stevenson, attorney at law. Land title, San Francisco.   CLU

12342. Stevenson, Robert Louis. The San Francisco of Robert Louis Stevenson... S.F., Priv. print. by Haywood H. Hunt, January 1923. 17 l. "This picture of San Francisco was written by Stevenson in 1882, as a contribution to the *London magazine of art*."—Cowan.
    C CHi CLSU CSjC CSmH CU-B

12343. Stewart, Earle K. Presidio history [by Earle K. Stewart and Kenneth S. Erwin] S.F., Priv. print., c1959. 100 p. illus. 72 pl.   CHi

12344. Stewart, George Rippey. Bret Harte, argonaut and exile... N.Y., Houghton, 1931. 384 p. illus., ports.   CHi CRcS

12345. Stewart, Robert E. Adolph Sutro, a biography. By Robert E. and Mary F. Stewart. Berkeley, Howell-North, 1962. 243 p. illus.   CHi

12346. Stewart, Watt, 1892– Henry Meiggs, Yankee Pizarro... Durham, N.C., Duke univ. press, 1946. 370 p. illus., port.   CHi

12347. Stock exchange club. By-laws, house rules, list of members. S.F., 1950. 53 p.   CHi

12348. ——— Supplement, list of members, Jan. 1954; April 1956; July 1957; April 1958. S.F., 1954–1958. 3 v.   CHi

12349. Stoddard, Charles Warren. A bit of old China... S.F., Robertson, 1912. 21 p. front. "This description of old San Francisco's Chinatown has been taken from Charles Warren Stoddard's book, entitled, *'In the footprints of the padres.'*"
    C CHi CL CLO CLSU CLU CMont CSdS CSf CSfCP CSfCW CSmH CU-B

12350. ——— Same. S.F., Crocker, 1925. 21 p. front.
    C CHi CLSU CLU CSf CSfCP CSmH

12351. ——— In the footprints of the padres. S.F., A.M. Robertson, 1902. 335 p.
    CHi CLU CLgA CMont CPom CSS CSd CSmH CStrCL CU-B ODa OrU ViU

12352. ——— Same. New and enl. ed. ... S.F., Robertson, 1912. 291 p. illus.
Available in many California libraries and OU

12353. Stoessel, Emil. San Francisco Jewish elite directory and society list. S.F., Bancroft co., 1892. 72 [7] p.   CLU CSmH CU-B

12354. Stoll and Van Bergen, firm. [Catalog] [189–?] S.F. [189–?] 1 v. illus.   CU-B

12355. Stone, Andrew Leete. The finger of God. A sermon preached in the First Congregational church, San Francisco, Cal., on the Sabbath morning after the great earthquake of October 21st, 1868. S.F., Excelsior press, Bacon & co., 1868. 18 p.   CHi CO CU-B

12356. ——— Leaves from a finished pastorage... N.Y., A.D.F. Randolph; S.F., S. Carson, 1882. 211 p.
    CSfCW

12357. Stone (L. D.) & co. ...Catalogue no. 1... harness, saddles, bridles... S.F., A.L. Bancroft & co., print. [1885] 272 p. illus.   CU-B

12358. Stoneberger, Alfred A. In memoriam. [S.F., Unity lodge A.O.U.W., 1897] 4 l.   CHi

12359. Story of the Montgomery block of San Francisco. [S.F.? 1948?] 12 p.   CHi

12360. Stout, Arthur B. Chinese immigration and the physiological causes of the decay of a nation... S.F., Agnew & Deffebach, 1862. 26 p.
    CHi CLU CSmH CSt CU-B

12361. ——— Report on medical education to the Medical society of the state of California, April 18th, 1877... S.F., Edward Bosqui & co., 1877. 11 p.   CHi

12362. Stow, Henry M. ...The Stow foundation pavement...Henry M. Stow, patentee... N.Y., Evening post steam presses [1870?] 26 p. illus.   CU-B

12363. Stow, Joseph W. Reply to the San Francisco gas co.'s circular about petroleum gas. [S.F., 1871] 13 p.   C

12364. Stow, *Mrs.* Joseph W. Probate chaff; or, Beautiful probate; or, Three years probating in San Francisco. A modern drama, showing the merry side of a dark picture... [n.p.] Author, 1879. 307 p. illus., port.
Relates to probate practice and women's rights.   CHi

12365. Stow, Nellie. Tower of strength in the city's building; a reminiscence, by Nellie Stow, secretary of the San Francisco Protestant orphanage. [1851–1941] [n.p., 1941] [15] p. illus.   CHi

12366. Strassburger & co., pub. Southern Pacific company; pioneers of western progress... S.F., Aug. 1929. 63 p. illus.   CHi CSfP

12367. Strauss, Joseph Baermann. Bridging "the Golden gate." [S.F.? 1921] 15 p. illus., diagrs.
    CHi CU-B

12368. ——— Rebuttal; Sunshine transbay boulevard bridge. [S.F., 1926] 84 p. Mimeo.   CHi

12369. Strauss (Levi) & co. Everyone knows his first name. [S.F., c1942] [28] p. illus., ports.   CHi

12370. Straut, W. E. Revised catalogue and price list. 1879. S.F. [1879] 1 v.   CU-B

12371. The Street repair association of San Francisco. Reports and recommendations...for the repairs and reconstructions of streets...urgently necessary in more than one thousand six hundred blocks. Based on... competent surveys extending through April, May and June, 1907. Compiled and prepared...by its Executive Committee. [n.p., n.d.] 233 l. typew. Includes "substantial reprint of the First report of its Executive committee on the fifteenth of July, 1907."   CSfP

12372. Stretch, Richard H. Report on Western avenue. [S.F., 1874] 10 p. maps.
    CHi CSfCSM CU-B

12373. Strother, French. The rebound of San Francisco...incidents by an eye witness... [N.Y., 1906] [10] p. illus.   CSf CU-B

12374. Studebaker bros. co. of California. Catalog. S.F. [etc.] [189–?]–1907. illus.
C-S has 1 catalog [n.d.] CHi has 2 catalogs [n.d.] CU-B has no. 19–20, 234, 236, 259–61 [189–?]–1907.

12375. ——— San Francisco (on the night of April 18th, 1906). [St. Louis, Woodward & Tiernan print. co., n.d.] [36] p. illus.   CHi

12376. Stuewe, A. A. San Francisco bay ports manual... S.F., Overland pub. co., c1924. 174 p. illus.
    CU-B

12377. Suermondt, Margaretha Pauline. Methods for the re-establishment of the mentally unfit in the community with special reference to the work of the San Francisco bay district of California. [Berkeley, 1925] Thesis (M.A.)—Univ. of Calif., 1925.   CU

12378. Sullivan, Frank J. The overhead trolley. [S.F., 1906?] 14 p.   CU-B

12379. Sullivan, James F. Diphtheria; epidemic of 1876–77. S.F., 1877. 17 p.   CLU

12380. Sullivan, Jeremiah F. [A book of newspaper clippings and other memorials of Judge J. F. Sullivan] [29] l. photos. tipped in.   CSfCW

12381. Sullivan, John. Story of a pioneer of pioneers, Mr. John Sullivan... [S.F., 1906?] 18 p. ports. "From the *Christmas leader*, Dec. 22, 1906."   CLU

12382. Sullivan, Reginald Noel. "Somewhere in France," personal letters of Reginald Noel Sullivan, S.S.U. 65 of the American ambulance field services. [S.F.] print. for priv. circulation, 1917. 53 p. front. (mounted port.)   CHi CSfCW

12383. Summit aircraft co. Seeing San Francisco and the Bay cities from the air. [S.F., 1928?] [4] p. illus.   CHi

12384. —— ...Taxiplane rates to all California points. [S.F., 1928?] [4] p.   CHi

12385. Sun tent and awning co. [Catalog. 1910? 1917] S.F. [1910? 1917] illus.
    CHi (1917) CU-B (1910?)

12386. Sunderstrom, Leonard Henry. A study of the factors affecting demand for ocean passenger transportation between California and Hawaii. [Berkeley, 1959] Thesis (M.A.)—Univ. of Calif., 1959.   CU

12387. Sunny Vale homestead association. Articles of association and by-laws... Also, the certificate of incorporation. S.F., Winterburn & co., print., 1869. 30 p.   CU-B

12388. Sunset bazaar photographic dept. Catalog of photographic apparatus, plates, papers and other photographic supplies, 1905. S.F., [Jalumstein print. co.] 1905. 94 p. illus.   CHi

12389. Sunset magazine, ed. ...San Francisco earthquake edition, 1906. (*Sunset mag.*, v.17 no. 2–3, June–July 1906)   CHi CSmat

12390. —— ...San Francisco one year after... illus. (*Sunset mag.*, April 1907)   CHi CSmat

12391. —— ...San Francisco two years after. A series of pictures that tell the story of the city's marvelous renascence, from photographs by H. C. Tibbitts... [1908] [32] pl. (*Sunset mag.*, v. 20, no. 6, April 1908)   CHi CSf CSmat

12392. —— ...San Francisco three years after the great fire... [1909] [16] p. illus. (*Sunset mag.*, v. 22, no. 4, April 1909)   CHi CSf CSmat CStmo

12393. Sunset photo supply co., inc. Confidential wholesale price list of photographic supplies and chemicals. 1911/12. S.F. [1911] 1 v.   CU-B

12394. Sunset seed and plant co. [Seed and general nursery stock catalogs]
CHi has 1894, 1897, [n.d.]

12395. Survey of business conditions in San Francisco... 1932–1943. [S.F., Chamber of commerce, 1932–43] Reproduced from typew. copy. January issue, 1932–1943 comprises a review of the preceeding year and has title: Annual survey of business conditions in San Francisco.   CU

12396. Sutherland, Monica (La Fontaine). The damndest finest ruins. [1st American ed.] N.Y., Coward-McCann [1959] 219 p. illus.
Available in many California libraries and MiD.

12397. —— Same, with title: The San Francisco disaster. London, Barrie and Rockliff [1959] 175 p. illus.   CSfU

12398. [Sutherland, *Mrs.* (Redding)] Five years within the Golden Gate. By Isabelle Saxon [pseud.]... London, Chapman & Hall, 1868. 315 p. Includes chapters on California, Nevada, and other parts of the West, and the Hawaiian Islands.
C-S   CHi   CLSU   CLU   CP   CSS   CSbr   CSf

CSfCSM   CSfCW   CSfP   CSmH   CU-B   CaBViPA CoU   MoS   NjR

12399. —— Same. Phila., Lippincott.   C

12400. Sutro, Adolph. The Bank of California against the Sutro tunnel... [Wash., D.C.? 1874?] 11 p.   CHi

12401. —— ...In the matter of the estate of Adolph Sutro, deceased. Points and authorities of appellants. Morrison & Cope, Bradley & McKinstry, J. C. McKinstry, attorneys for all appellants except people of the state of California. U. S. Webb, attorney-general of the state of California... [S.F.] James H. Barry co. [1907] 269 p.   CU-B

12402. —— Letter to the Regents of the University of California and to the Committee of affiliated colleges on the selection of a site for the affiliated colleges. S.F., 1895. 9 p.   C-S CHi

12403. —— The style of warfare as carried on by the California banking ring. Outrageous attacks on the honor and integrity of Mr. Sutro. What money will do! [Wash., 1874?] 5 p.   CHi

12404. Sutro, Oscar. Memorial tributes to Oscar Sutro. S.F., [Grabhorn] 1935. 73[1] p. port.   CHi

12405. Sutro & co. The Sutro story; 90 years in the West, 1858–1948. [S.F., 1948] [20] p. illus., ports.
    C CHi CLU CU-B

12406. Sutro baths. [A pictorial and descriptive journey to Sutro baths. S.F., Johnston-Ayres co. 1915?] 16 p. (chiefly illus.)   CHi CU-B

12407. Sutro baths, Cliff house, Sutro heights. Illus. by Taber. [S.F., 1895] 96 p. illus., port.   C CHi

12408. Sutro tunnel co. Certificate of incorporation and by-laws of the... S.F., Cosmopolitan print., 1869. 16 p.   CHi

12409. —— Same. S.F., Women's co-operative print. off., 1880. 16 p.   CHi

12410. Sutter street rail road co. Historical report of the management and financial condition...Sept. 22, 1865 to June 10, 1872... By H[enry] Casebolt, president. S.F., Cubery & co., 1873. 12 p.   CHi

12411. Swanberg, W. A. Citizen Hearst, a biography of William Randolph Hearst. N.Y., Scribner, c1961. 555 p. illus., ports.
Available in many California libraries.

12412. Swanson, Martin. Theodore Roosevelt and the Mooney case... the true facts in the San Francisco preparedness day bomb cases and the justness of Theodore Roosevelt's attitude in support of the prosecution of those cases. [S.F., 1921] 32 p.   CHi CSmH

12413. Swanstrom, Roy. Reform administration of James D. Phelan, mayor of San Francisco, 1897–1902... [Berkeley, 1948] 116 l. Typew. Thesis (M.A.)—Univ. of Calif., 1949.   CU CU-B

12414. Sweden. Official Swedish catalogue, Panama-Pacific international exposition, San Francisco, 1915. Stockholm, Centraltryckeriet, 1915. 287 p. illus., port., map, plan, pl.   CHi CSf

12415. Swedish society of San Francisco and Oakland. ...Constitution and by-laws... S.F., West coast pub. co., 1912. 47 p. In English and Swedish.   CHi

12416. Swett, John. History of the public school system of California. S.F., A.L. Bancroft & co., 1876. 246 p. illus. Some detailed account of schools in San Francisco.
C   CHi   CL   CLO   CLSU   CLU   CLgA   CMartC CO   CSS   CSf   CSfCW   CSfP   CSmH   CU-B

12417. —— Public education in California; its origin and development, with personal reminiscences of half a century. N.Y., Amer. bk. co., 1911. 320 p.
CHi CRedl CSf CSfCW CSfWF-H

12418. Swisher, Carl Brent. Stephen J. Field, craftsman of the law... Wash., D.C., Brookings, 1930. 473 p. front., ports., facsims.   CBb CHi CSfCW

12419. Symes, Lillian. Our American Dreyfus case; a challenge to California justice... Reprinted by permission, together with excerpts from substantiating documentary evidence... L.A., Inter-religious committee for justice for Thomas J. Mooney, 1935. 48 p. Reprint. from *Harper's mag.*, v. 162, May, 1931.
C-S CHi CL CLU CO CSf CSj CStrJC CU-B MoS

12420. T.P.S. publishing co. San Francisco; a city of ruins... Alameda, 1906. 60 photos.   CSf

12421. Taber, Isaiah West. ...Photographic album; principal business houses, residences and persons. Published by I. W. Taber, photographer. S.F., 1880. [108] p. chiefly mounted pl., ports.   CU-B

12422. —— View album and business guide of San Francisco, photographically illustrated... S.F. [1884] mounted pl. Photographs of San Francisco buildings.
CSfP

12423. Taber-Bigelow co. General catalog no. 1. [S.F.] 1911. 593 p. illus.   CHi

12424. Tait's cafe. [Descriptive brochure] [S.F., Schwabacher-Frey stationery co., n.d.] [12] p. illus.
CHi

12425. Talbert & Leet, auctioneers. Auction sale of salt marsh and tide lands belonging to the state of California. 128 full blocks and 71 fractional blocks, containing over three thousand lots. Sale to commence on Wednesday, Sept. 15, 1869, at 10 A.M. Sacramento, D.W. Gelwicks, state print., 1869. 23 p.   CHi

12426. [Talloires,   ] La ville chinoise de San Francisco. [n.p., 190–?] [136] p. illus.   CU-B

12427. Tarrant's academy. Tarrant's academy for boarding and day pupils... [S.F., 1889?] [8] p.   CHi

12428. Tax payers' protective union. Report of the Executive committee of the Tax payers' protective union, approved and adopted at a general meeting of members, held on the 14th August, 1861. S.F., Commercial bk. and job steam presses, 1861. 45 p. fold. tables.
CLU CSmH CSt CU-B

12429. Tay (George H.) co. ...Catalogue and price list of supplies for steam, gas and water fitters... S.F., 1905. 144 p. illus.   CHi

12430. —— [Catalogue]...brass and iron valves and cocks, cast and malleable fittings, pipe and tubular goods... [S.F., Hicks-Judd co.] 1911. 760 p. illus.
CU-B

12431. —— [Catalogue of] California hot air furnaces. [S.F., 1900?] 8 p. illus.   CU-B

12432. —— Special catalogue [of] Rumsey pumps, hand windmill power. [S.F., 19—?] 136 p. illus.
CU-B

12433. Tay-Holbrook, inc. General catalogue no. 31... wholesale distributors of sheet metals, plumbing supplies... furnaces, tools and machinery. [Chicago, R.R. Donnelley & sons, c1931] 494 p. illus.   CHi

12434. —— 100th anniversary, Tay-Holbrook inc., successors to George H. Tay company...and Holbrook, Merrill & Stetson... The story of a century of service. [S.F., 1948] 47 p. illus., ports.
C CHi CSf CSfWF-H CU-B

12435. Taylor, Beatrice V. Labor relations on the street railways of San Francisco. [Berkeley, 1928] Thesis (M.A.)—Univ. of Calif., 1928.   CU

12436. Taylor, Benjamin Franklin. Between the gates... Chicago, S.C. Griggs & co., 1878. 292 p. illus. Available in many libraries. Other editions followed.

12437. Taylor, Clementine E'damie Edmond. Record of her family and events of her life. Berkeley, Professional press, 1931. 15 p. port.   CHi

12438. Taylor, David Wooster. The life of James Rolph, jr. ... S.F., Committee for pub. of the life of James Rolph, jr., 1934. 126 p. illus., ports.
C CHi CL CLS CLU CLgA CO CSS CSf CSmH CU-B

12439. [Taylor, Edward DeWitt] This fortunate man, Edward DeWitt Taylor; remarks upon the occasion of a dinner given in his honor at the Hotel St. Francis, San Francisco, April 9, 1946, under the auspices of the Employing printers' association of San Francisco. [Stanford] 1948. 29 p.   CHi

12440. Taylor, Frank J. Uncle John McLaren... S.F., The St. Andrew's soc., 1939. 15 p. port. (Reprint. from *Saturday evening post*, July 29, 1939) On cover: Tribute to our oldest member on our seventy-sixth annual St. Andrew's day banquet, Dec. 6, 1939.   CHi

12441. Taylor, Katherine Ames. San Francisco, a trip book. S.F., Crocker, 1927. 70 p. illus., map.
C CHi CO CSf CSfWF-H CSmat CSmH CU-B

12442. —— Same. Stanford, 1929. 58 p. illus., map.
CU-B

12443. Taylor, Paul Schuster. Chapters from the early history of the seamen of the Pacific coast. [Berkeley, 1920] Thesis (M.A.)—Univ. of Calif., 1920.   CU

12444. —— The Sailors' union of the Pacific. [Berkeley, 1922] Thesis (Ph.D.)—Univ. of Calif., 1922.
CU

12445. Taylor, Ray W. Hetch Hetchy; the story of San Francisco's struggle to provide a water supply for her future needs... S.F., R.J. Orozco, 1926. 199 p. illus., ports., maps.
Available in many libraries.

12446. Taylor, William, bp. California life illustrated... N.Y., Carlton & Porter, 1858. 348 p. illus. Available in many libraries. Other editions followed. CCSC (rev. ed. n.d.) CLSM (1860, 1861) CPom (1881?) CU-B ([1867], 1882?) CViCL (1881?) IHi (1861) MoKU (1859)

12447. —— —— Index [for 1858 edition] Joseph Gaer, editor... [S.F., 1935] 22 l. (Index no. 9, SERA project 2-F2-132 (3-F2-197) Calif. literary research) Mimeo.   C-S CHi CLSM CRic CSf CStmo

12448. —— Seven years' street preaching in San Francisco, California; embracing incidents, triumphant death scenes, etc., by Rev. William Taylor... Ed. by W. P. Strickland. N.Y., Pub. for the author by Carlton & Porter, 1857. 394 p. port.
Available in many California libraries and CaBViPA NHi MoKU MoS OrU

12449. —— Same. N.Y., Phillips & Hunt; Cincinnati, Walden & Stowe [1857] 394 p. port.
CLSU CSfWF-H
Other editions followed. CHi (1867) CU-B (1858?, 1859, 1860?) MoS (1858) TxU (1858) ViU (1858) ViW (1858)

12450. —— Story of my life; an account of what I have thought and said and done in my ministry of more than fifty-three years... Edited by John Clark Ridpath

...with original engravings and sketches by Frank Beard. N.Y., Hunt & Eaton, 1895. 748 p. illus., port.
CBb CL CSfP

12451. —— Same, with title: William Taylor of California, Bishop of Africa; an autobiography... London, Hodder, 1897. 411 p. port.   CHi CL

12452. Taylor & Taylor, San Francisco. Types, borders and miscellany of Taylor & Taylor with historical brevities on their derivation and use. S.F., 1939. 563 p. illus.   CHi

12453. —— The work of Taylor & Taylor at the exhibition of American printing in New York City, 1920. [S.F., Taylor & Taylor, 1921] 11 p. illus.   CHi

12454. Tebbel, John William. The life and good times of William Randolph Hearst. N.Y., Dutton, 1952. 386 p.   CRedCL CSd CSlu

12455. Tehama street nurses. [Annual report] [S.F., The Twentieth century press, 1902?–1904?] CHi has 1903/04. CU-B has 1901/02.

12456. Teiser, Ruth. An account of Domingo Ghirardelli and the early years of the D. Ghirardelli company. S.F., D. Ghirardelli co., 1945. 30 p. illus., port.
CHi CLU CSmH

12457. —— Origin of Wells, Fargo & company, 1841–1852. [Cambridge, Mass.] Business hist. soc., 1948. 14 p. illus. Reprint. from its *Bulletin*, June 1948.   CHi

12458. —— Pioneer craftsmen in copper. S.F., C. W. Smith copper works [c1944] 16 p. illus., port.
CHi CU-B

12459. —— This sudden empire, California; the story of the Society of California pioneers, 1850 to 1950. S.F., Soc. of California pioneers, 1950. 76 p. illus.
CChiS   CHi   CLO   CMont   CNF   CRcS   CSf
CSfWF-H CSjC CSmat CStclU CSto CStoC CV
CaBViPA

12460. —— Wells, Fargo & company; the first half year. [n.p.] 1949. 11 p. map.   CHi

12461. Telegraph hill neighborhood association. Report. 1st [191–?– S.F., 191–?–] CHi has 9th, 1912. CU-B has 8th, Jan. 1911.

12462. Telesis. Regional planning, the next step for the bay area. S.F. [1940?] 9 l. (*Its* pub. no. 2)
CRcS

12463. Temperance legion. Constitution, by-laws and codes...organized Feb. 1st, 1866. S.F., F. Clarke, print., 1866. 32 p.   CHi

12464. Territorial pioneers of California. Constitution and by-laws of the association of Territorial pioneers of California. Adopted Nov. 10th, 1874. 44 p.
CHi

12465. —— First annual...Containing the history of the organization, constitution and by-laws, names of the officers...catalogue of all the members... S.F., W.M. Hinton & co., 1877. 171 p. map.   CHi CP N

12466. The Terry contempt. Order committing D. S. Terry for contempt. S.F., 1888. 49 p.   CHi

12467. Thiele, Theodore. Observations sur la situation de la Société Française de bienfaisance mutuelle, respectueusement offertes aux membres de cette institution... [Signed] Th. Thiele. S.F., 25 juin 1870. [S.F., 1870] Broadside.   CU-B

12468. Thirty-five companies. Committee of five. Report of the Committee of five to the "Thirty-five companies" on the San Francisco conflagration, April 18–21, 1906. [N.Y., Mail & express job print., 1907] 95 p. illus.
CHi CLU CSfCP CSfWF-H CU-B

12469. Thomas, Lately, *pseud.* A debonair scoundrel; an episode in the moral history of San Francisco. [1st ed.] N.Y., Holt [1962] 422 p. illus.   CHi CSfMI

12470. Thomas, Patrick J. Founding of the missions of California. History of the early days. San Francisco in 1876. S.F., Author, 1882. 192 p. map. 2d edition of his *Our centennial memoir*.
CLgA CSf CSmat CSmH

12471. —— Our centennial memoir... San Francisco de Assis in its hundredth year. The celebration of its foundation... S.F., Author, 1877. 192 p. illus., ports., map.
C CHi CL CLSU CLU CO CSf CSfCW CSfU
CSmat CSmH CSrD CStcrCL CU-B

12472. Thomas, Uriah B. Proposed plan for political organization... S.F., 1886. 24 p.   CHi

12473. [Thompson, Beach] Water supply for the city and county of San Francisco. Stanislaus river project. [S.F., 1906] 15 p. charts.   CHi

12474. Thompson, John. A historical statement of the work of the California bible society from October, 1849 to October, 1895... S.F., Bk. room print. [1895] [4] p.   CHi

12475. Thompson, Ralph M., comp. Handbook of California division, L[eague] of A[merican] W[heelmen], 1890. S.F., Hicks-Judd co., 1890. 92 p. illus., fold. map.   CHi

12476. Thompson, Ruth, and Hanges, Louis. Eating around San Francisco... N.Y., Suttonhouse, c1937. 296 p. illus.
C CBu CHi CL CMont CO CRcS CSal CSf
CSfMI CUk CV CViCL

12477. Thompson, William vs. Pioche, F. L. A. ... William Thompson, respondent, vs. F. L. A. Pioche et als., appellants... Haight & Temple, attorneys for respondent. John B. Felton, attorney for appellants. S.F., Waters, Newhoff & co., 1870. 2 v. in 1.   CU-B

12478. Thompson & co., comp. and pub. Historical and descriptive review of the industries of San Francisco, 1887... S.F. [1887] 204 p. illus.
C CU-B

12479. The Thomson & Orebaugh wholesale and manufactures' pocket business directory of San Francisco, Cal. for 1889–90. For the use...of out of town buyers. [S.F., 1889] 56 p.   CU-B

12480. Thrasher, Marion. The life of Dr. Carroll Thrasher [1876–1911] S.F., 1911. 69 p. port.   CHi

12481. Thunder powder co. Thunder powder... [S.F.] A. Carlisle & co. [1881] 16 p.   CU-B

12482. Thurman, Howard. Footprints of a dream; the story of the Church for the fellowship of all peoples. N.Y., Harper [c1959] 157 p. illus., ports.
C CL CSfMI CStcrCL CU-B NN

12483. Tibbets, S. M., vs. Newman, B. B. In the Supreme court of the state of California. S. M. Tibbets, respondent, vs. B. B. Newman, appellant. Brief for respondent. Theodore H. Hittell, attorneys for respondent. S.F., Towne & Bacon, 1867. 9 p.   CHi

12484. Tilden, Charles Lee. Notes on a talk...before the California historical society... Tuesday, Apr. 12, 1938, on the subject: "William C. Ralston and his times." [S.F., 1938] 15 l. Typew.   CHi CLU CU-B

12485. Tilford, Frank. Argument...on the subject of the San Francisco outside lands, delivered before the Judiciary committee of the Assembly, at Sacramento,

March 9, 1868. Sacramento, State capital reporter print., 1868. 17 p. CLU

12486. Tilton, Cecil Gage. William Chapman Ralston, courageous builder. Bost., Christopher pub. house [c1935] 474 p. illus., ports.
CBu CHi CL CLU CLgA CO CRcS CSd CSf CSfCW CSfP CSfWF-H CSjC CSmat CSmH CStrJC CU-B

12487. Tinnemann, Ethel Mary, Sister. Opposition to the San Francisco vigilance committee of 1856. [Berkeley, 1941] [188] l. Typew. Thesis (M.A.)—Univ. of Calif. 1941. CO COHN CU

12488. Title and document restoration co. vs. Kerrigan, Frank H. In the Superior court of the state of California, in and for the city and county of San Francisco. The Title and document restoration company (a corporation), petitioner, vs. Frank H. Kerrigan, judge of the Superior court of the state of California, in and for the city and county of San Francisco, department ten, respondent... Garret W. McEnerney, Walter Rothchild, Joseph H. Mayer, counsel for petitioner... [S.F.] Pernau pub. co. [1906] 2 v. in 1. CU-B

12489. Title insurance & guaranty co. A century of title service. [S.F., Recorder-Sunset press, 1948?] [24] p. illus., ports., map. CHi

12490. Tittel, Fred G. E. Memorial tribute to... by a friend. [S.F., 1877] 8 p. CHi CLU

12491. Tobin, Agnes. Letters, translations, poems, with some account of her life. S.F., Grabhorn, 1958. CSmat

12492. Tobisch, Othmar. The first one hundred years of the New Jerusalem society of San Francisco, California, 1852–1952. [S.F., 1952] 9 p. illus. CHi

12493. —— The Swedenborgian church of San Francisco, some historical recollections. S.F., Soc. of the New Jerusalem, 1950. 12 p. CHi

12494. Todd, Eleanor Adele. History of the Milk wagon drivers' union of San Francisco county, 1900–1933. [Berkeley, 1936] Thesis (M.A.)— Univ. of Calif., 1936. CU

12495. Todd, Frank Morton. The Chamber of commerce handbook for San Francisco, historical and descriptive; a guide for visitors... S.F., Chamber of commerce, 1914. 340 p. illus., map.
C CBu CHi CMartC CPom CRcS CSalCL CSd CSf CSfCP CSfP CSfU CSfWF-H CSmH CStmo CU-B CoD MiD MoS MoSHi NN

12496. —— How to see San Francisco by trolley and cable... [S.F., F.H. Abbott co.] c1912. 56 p. illus. CHi CSfCP CU-B NN

12497. —— A romance of insurance, being a history of the Fireman's fund insurance company of San Francisco. S.F., H.S. Crocker, c1929. 283 p. illus., ports., facsims. CHi CSf CSfP

12498. —— The story of the exposition, being the official history of the international celebration held at San Francisco in 1915 ... N.Y., Putnam, 1921. 5 v. illus., ports., maps.
Available in many California libraries and ODa

12499. Tolf, Albert. In old San Francisco; a cartoon history. [S.F., designed and pub. by Albert Tolf, 1959] unp. chiefly illus. "A selection of the historical cartoons which appeared in the San Francisco news during 1956, 1957 and 1958..." C CHi CSfMI CSfP

12500. Tom Mooney molders' defense committee. Governor Young "Pardon Tom Mooney he is inno-

cent." Judge Griffin...2d ed. ... S.F. [1929] 31 p. illus., ports. CU CU-B

12501. —— Justice raped in California; story of so-called bomb trials in San Francisco. 5th ed. S.F. [1917] 47 p. illus., ports., facsims. CHi CU-B

12502. —— Labor leaders betray Tom Mooney, member of the International molders union for 29 years ... 1st ed. [S.F., 1931] 50 p. ports. Letter from Tom Mooney inserted. CLU CO CU-B

12503. —— Same, with title: Tom Mooney, member of the International molders union for 29 years, betrayed by labor leaders...2d ed. ... 1931. 65 p. illus., ports. CU CU-B

12504. Topper (T. J.) co. Catalog of equipment for hotels, restaurants... S.F., 1927. 95 p. illus. CHi

12505. Tourist association of central California, pub. Central California, pleasure land for the tourist. Bulletin. S.F. [1915–191–?] illus., maps.
CHi (nos. 6, 11) CL (?) CO (1917) CSmH (no. 6) CU-B (nos. 6–8, 11, 13, 19–23, 26)

12506. Town and country club. By-laws and list of members... S.F., 1912. 49 p. CHi

12507. Town and stage. v. 1–2 (no. 1–204) Nov. 15, 1869–July 9, 1870. S.F. [J.F. Brown & co., etc.] 1869–1870. CU-B

12508. Towne & Bacon. Specimen pages of letter press printing from Towne & Bacon. [187–?] [S.F., 187–?] 1 v. CU-B

12509. A tract for the bulkhead, in the form of a dialogue between "A" and "B". [S.F., Whitton, Towne & co., print., 1856?] 8 p. Caption title. CLU

12510. Tracy engineering co. Catalogue no. 10, 12. ...Steam purifier. S.F., Nash & Taylor, 1915, 1919. illus. CHi

12511. Transamerica corp. Annual report.
CHi has 1930, 1932, 1937–41, 1943, 1947, 1951, 1957–58. CL has 1951–60.

12512. Transcript of records. No. 110–2561. Jan. 2, 1867–July 27, 1870; Dec. 29, 1871–Dec. 26, 1874. S.F., 1867–74. 14 v. Deeds, etc., continued by Edwards Abstract from records. San Francisco. CU-B

12513. Transportation club of San Francisco. Constitution, by-laws, house rules. S.F., 1954. 31 p. Founded 1904. CHi

12514. —— Officers, directors, list of members. S.F., 1956. CHi

12515. Trattner, Samuel, pub. San Francisco in miniature. Over 150 new views made exclusively for this publication. S.F. [191–?] [62] p. of illus. CU-B

12516. Trattner & Reese, pub. San Francisco before and after the fire; illustrated, and giving a brief description. Portland, Ore., c1906. 48 p. CHi

12517. Treadwell, J. W., realty co. Fillmore street, past, present and future. S.F. [c1913] [46] p. illus. CU-B

12518. Treadwell and co. Price list of hardware and farming tools, agricultural machinery...[1873?] S.F. [1873?] 1 v. illus. CU-B

12519. Treason and rebellion: being in part the legislation of Congress and of the state of California thereon, together with the recent charge by Judge Field, of the U.S. Supreme court, delivered to the grand jury in attendance at the U.S. Circuit court for the Northern district of California. With notes. S.F., Towne & Bacon, 1863. 47 p. Contains also: U.S. Circuit court of appeals

(9th circuit) In the matter of Ridgley Greathouse. [Opinion of J. Hoffman]   CHi CSfCW CSmH

12520. Treat, Archibald. A tribute to a man who built his fortune so that he could aid crippled children [Frederick Averill Robbins] S.F., E.L. Bosqui print. co., [1942] 18 p.   CHi

12521. Treutlein, Theodore Edward. Early explorations of San Francisco bay. [Berkeley, 1930] 93 l. maps. Thesis (M.A.)— Univ. of Calif., 1930.
CU CU-B

12522. Trinity school. [Catalog] 1st– 1876– S.F., 1876–1899.
CHi has 6th, 18th, 1881/82, 1894/95. CU-B has 7th, 14th–23d, 1882/83, 1890/91–1899/1900.

12523. Trollope, Anthony. A letter...describing a visit to California in 1875. S.F., Colt press, 1946. 32 p. front., illus.
Available in many libraries.

12524. Truman, Hooker & co. [Catalog of] mowers, plows, carriages, buggies, wagons, etc. no. 1– [1872?– S.F. [1871?–
C-S has 1890. CHi has no. 18 [1893?] CU-B has no. 15 [1889?]

12525. Truman, Isham & Hooker. [Catalog of] agricultural implements. S.F., 1887.   C-S

12526. Trumbo, Dalton. Harry Bridges; a discussion of the latest effort to deport civil liberties and the rights of American labor... [L.A., Plantin press, 1941] 28 p.   CHi

12527. Trumbull (R. J.) & co. [Catalogs of seeds, trees, plants]
CHi has 1879–80, 1884–86.

12528. Tubbs cordage co. Catalogue no. 7, 1915. S.F. [Taylor & Taylor, 1915] 40 p. illus.   CHi

12529. —— The story of rope... [S.F.?] c1939. 31 p. illus.   CHi

12530. Tule shooting club. By-laws, officers and members... S.F. [Backus print. co.] 1890. 16 p.   CHi

12531. Turner, David S. [Brief: Title to the Island of Yerba Buena, San Francisco] To the Senate and House of representatives of the United States. Wash., D.C., 1870. 11 p. Protest to Senate bill no. 332 for Western Pacific railroad.   CHi

12532. —— The following narrative, relating to the Island of Yerba Buena and the equitable claim upon the same by the present owners, who hold under the original settlers in July, 1849...on behalf of Benjamin S. Brooks, John Center and Egbert Judson. Wash., D.C., 1870. 8 p.
CHi

12533. Turner, Joseph. Poetical description of Golden Gate park, the city of San Francisco and its surroundings... S.F., J.R. Brodie & co., print., 1892. 40 p.
CLU

12534. Twelve years of teaching in the public schools of San Francisco, October, 1867. S.F., F. Eastman, print., 1867.   C

12535. Tyler, George E. [Catalogue of] sale of lots in the city of San Francisco at public auction...[on Monday the 19th day of November] S.F., Alta Calif. press, 1849. 8 p.   CHi CU-B

12536. —— Same, Wednesday, November 28, 1849 ... S.F., Alta Calif. press, 1849. 8 p.   CHi CU-B

12537. —— Same, Monday, December 10, 1849... S.F., Alta Calif. press [1849] 8 p.
CLU CSfCP CU-B

12538. —— Catalogue of sale of water lots in the city of San Francisco...on Thursday, January 3d, 1850... S.F., Alta Calif. press [1849] 12 p.   CHi

12539. Tyler, George W., vs. Pratt, Annie A. In the District court of the Fourth judicial district of the state of California, in and for the city and county of San Francisco. George W. Tyler, plaintiff, vs. Annie A. Pratt, defendant. S.F., Francis & Valentine, 1877. 61 p.
C-S CHi

12540. Tyler, Sydney. San Francisco's great disaster; a full account of the recent terrible destruction of life and property by earthquake, fire and volcano in California and at Vesuvius...With an interesting chapter on the causes of this and other earthquakes...by Ralph Stockman Tarr... Phila., P.W. Ziegler co. [c1906] 442 p. illus.
C CBev CHi CLgA CSd CSf CSfCP CSlu CSmH CU-B MiD-B NN NjR ODa ViU

12541. Tyler, William B. The festival of the great dragon. S.F., 1889. 12 photogravure pl.   CHi

12542. Typothetae of San Francisco. [Souvenir program] second annual outing, El Campo, May 25, 1901. [S.F., Murdock press, 1901?] 1 v. illus.   CHi CLU

12543. —— Tenth anniversary. June, 1898. 29 p. [S.F., 1898]   CHi

12544. Underwriters' fire patrol of San Francisco. Annual report. 1st– 1874– S.F., 1874–
CHi has 5th–32d, 35th–36th, 38th–66th, 1879–1906, 1909–10, 1912–1940. CU-B has 30th, 35th, 40th, 1904, 1909, 1914.

12545. Union club. By-laws, officers and members ... S.F., 1867–
CLU has 1867. CSfP has 1867, 1871, 1874, 1877, 1880, 1887.

12546. Union gas engine co. Catalogue no. 15... S.F. [Sunset press] 1902. [44] p. illus.   CHi

12547. Union gas machine co. The Union gas machine, runs by water... S.F., J.P. Tracy and co., print., 1878. 24 p. illus.   CU-B

12548. Union insurance co. Fire and marine insurance... S.F., E. Bosqui & co., print., 1866. 40 p.
CHi CU-B

12549. Union iron works. Blake and Dodge rock breakers. [S.F., 19—?] [16] p. illus.   CU-B

12550. —— The California stamp mill. [S.F., Murdock press, 18—?] 70 p. illus., diagrs.   CU-B

12551. —— Catalogue, no. 1–5. S.F., 1896–1898. illus., tables.
CHi has no. 1–4, 1896. CSf has no. 5, 1898. CU-B has no. 1, 3, 1896.

12552. —— Circular and pattern list. 1866–1880. S.F., 1866–80. 6 v. illus. diagrs.
CHi has 1866. CU-B has 1866, 1872–73, 1877, 1880–1880a.

12553. —— Folder no. 27, 35...description of French's patent automatic excavator... Oakland [1903?–1911] illus.
CHi has no. 27 [1903?] CU-B has no. 35, 1910/11.

12554. —— Specifications for a single screw steel steamer to carry oil in bulk and fitted for carrying general cargo for the Standard transportation company of Delaware... S.F. [Taylor & Taylor] 1915. 170, xxix p.
CHi

12555. Union league club. By-laws, rules, certificate of incorporation and list of officers and members of the Union league club. S.F., [Press of Sanborn Vail & co.] 1897. 56 p.   CLU

12556. —— Same. [S.F.] 1910. 80 p. pl.   CLU

12557. —— ...The Union league club has been incorporated, and is now fully organized and equipped... [S.F., 1889] [3] p.   CU-B

12558. Union oil co. of California. The Union oil company of California at the Panama-Pacific international exposition, 1915. [S.F.? 1915] [16] p.   CU-B

12559. Union Pacific railroad co. Diagrams, San Francisco theatres... [S.F., 1888] [24] p.
                                                      CSmH CU-B

12560. Union Pacific salt co. By-laws... Adopted March 25th, 1868. S.F., C.A. Calhoun, print., 1868. 15 p.
                                                           CU-B

12561. Union Pacific silk manufacturing co. Prospectus... S.F., Kane & Cook, 1875. 7 p.   CU-B

12562. Union party, California. Proceedings of the San Francisco Union ratification meeting held at Union hall, San Francisco, Tuesday evening, June 25, 1867. ...Reported in phonographic shorthand by Andrew J. Marsh. S.F., pub. by authority of Union state central committee, 1867. 24 p.   CHi

12563. Union photo-engraving co. Specimens from... [S.F., G. Spaulding & co., 189–?] 16 p. illus.
                                                           CU-B

12564. Union square garage, inc. Union square garage in the heart of San Francisco. [S.F., n.d.] 16 p.
                                                           CHi

12565. Union stone company of California. By-laws... (Sorel patent). ...With appendix of facts in relation to artificial stone... S.F., Winterburn & co., 1874. 27 p.   CU-B

12566. Union sugar co. 50 years in the field. S.F. [1947?] [16] p. illus., port.   CHi

12567. Unitarian club of California. Annual ladies' night, 1st– [1891?]– S.F. [1891?]– Organized Sept. 1890. 12th, reception to Booker T. Washington. CHi has 12th, 14th, 1903, 1905.

12568. —— [Annual report, membership list, by-laws]
CHi has 1900–1905.

12569. —— [Sixteen years' record, 1890–1906] [S.F., 1907] 21 p. Contains By-laws and list of members.
                                                           CHi

12570. United Americans, Order of. California. Washington chapter. By-laws of Washington chapter, no. 2. ...Instituted March 1, 1855. S.F., Hanna & co., print., 1855. 26 p.   CLU

12571. United daughters of the Confederacy. Jefferson Davis chapter no. 540, San Francisco. Constitution and by-laws, list of members, officers and committees. S.F. [1914?–1918] 2 v. Organized Nov. 20, 1901. Chartered Dec. 21, 1901.   CHi

12572. United employers, inc. Office workers salaries and personnel practices, San Francisco bay area, mid-year 1946-1957. Oakland [1946–57] 10 v. tables. United employers reports.   CSfSt

12573. United endowment associates. San Francisco. Grand lodge. Constitution and general laws of the Grand lodge...also constitution governing subordinate lodges, adopted Feb. 16, 1887. 3d ed. S.F., 1887. 119 p. Organized Aug. 23, 1884.   CHi

12574. —— —— The order of United endowment associates... S.F., C.W. Nevin & co. [1889?] fold. sheet   CHi

12575. United friends of the Pacific. San Francisco. Grand council. Constitution of the Grand council and laws... also, The Constitution of subordinate councils. 6th ed. S.F., Geo. Spaulding, 1886. 68 p.
                                                           CHi

12576. United land association, et al., vs. Abrahams, Lewis, et al. The Mission Creek case in the Supreme court of the United States, October term, 1907. United land association, et al., plaintiffs in error, vs. Lewis Abrahams, et al., defendants in error. Brief for plaintiffs in error. John G. Johnson [and] Charles A. Keigwin, attorneys for plaintiffs in error. S.F., Pac. print. and engraving co. [1907] 153 p.   CHi CLU

12577. —— ...Petition for rehearing. [S.F., 1908?] 33 p.   CLU CU-B

12578. United land association vs. Pacific improvement co. In the Supreme court of the state of California. United land assn. et al., appellants, vs. Pacific improvement co. et al., respondents. United land assn. et al., appellants, vs. Willows land assn. et al., respondents. Oral argument of W. B. Treadwell for respondents. S.F., Jan. 29, 1903. In bank. [S.F.] Pernau press [1903] 31 p.   CLU

12579. United nations conference on international organization, San Francisco. Program closing plenary session...June 26, 1945. [Wash., D.C., Govt. print. off., 1945] 19 p.   CHi

12580. United railroads of San Francisco. Seeing San Francisco aboard the sight-seeing car. S.F., M. Kollmann, c1905.   CSfWF-H CSmH

12581. United Republican league of San Francisco. Plan of organization of the United Republican league of San Francisco and constitution of assembly district clubs. S.F., F. Eastman & co., print. [n.d.] 15 p.
                                                           CU-B

12582. United society of Christian endeavor. Programme and music for the sixteenth international Christian endeavor convention. S.F., 1897. xlviii, 48 p.
                                                           CHi

12583. United States vs. Limantour, José Ybes. In the District court of the United States, for the Northern district of California. No. 429. The United States vs. José Y. Limantour. Transcript of record. Printed by order of P. Della Torre, esq., U.S. attorney. S.F., Whitton, Towne & co.'s print. [1857]–1858. 4 v. The above is the general title of the exhibits, etc., of the Limantour claim. v.1. U.S. land commission. Transcript of proceedings in case no. 549.–v.2. U.S. District court. Exhibits and depositions. 35a, 8B.–v.3. Archive exhibits. Appendix I, A-X, YY, and ZZ. Appendix, no. 2, Spanish exhibits, A–E, certificate.–v.4. Land commission exhibits, A-I, K-P.
C CLSM (v.1–2) CLU (v.3) CSd (v.1) CSmat (v.3 app. 1) CSmH CU-B

12584. United States vs. San Francisco. Supreme court of the United States. no. 287. The United States, appellants, vs. the city of San Francisco. And no. 288, the city of San Francisco, appellant, vs. the United States. Appeals from the Circuit court of the United States for the Northern district of California. Filed Oct. 4, 1866. [Wash., D.C.] Govt. print. off. [1866?] 435 p. San Francisco pueblo land cases.   CLU

12585. U.S. Army. General hospital, Presidio. The history of Letterman general hospital. S.F., The Listening post, 1919. 56 p. illus., ports.   CHi

12586. —— —— —— The United States Army general hospital, Presidio, California, during the years 1900 & 1901... [Wash., D.C., Govt. print. off., 1901] 101 p. port.   CSf CU-B MiD-B T

12587. U.S. Army. (*cont'd*) **Transportation terminal command, Pacific, information office.** The story of Fort Mason, historic U.S. Army post in San Francisco. S.F., 1960. 4 p. illus.   CHi

12588. —— **Circuit court (9th circuit)** Charges to the jury by judges Field and Hoffman of the United States Circuit court for the Northern district of California, in the [*J.M.*] *Chapman* [S.S.] treason case. S.F., Alta Calif. bk. and job off., 1863. 12 p.   CHi

12589. —— ...In re Tiburcio Parrott on habeas corpus. Rights of Chinese. Opinions of Hon. Lorenzo Sawyer, circuit judge, and Hon. Ogden Hoffman, district judge. [n.p., 1880] 40 p.   CHi

12590. —— ...[In the matter of Frederick W. Sharon as executor, complainant, vs. David S. Terry and Sarah Althea Terry, his wife, defendants. Francis G. Newlands, as trustee, et al., complainants, vs. David S. Terry and Sarah Althea Terry, his wife defendants] Opinion delivered at San Francisco, September 3, 1888, by Mr. Justice Field. 61 p.   CHi

12591. —— In the matter of Ridgley Greathouse. [Opinion of J. Hoffman] [S.F., 1863?] 18 p. Bound with Treason and rebellion...   CHi

12592. —— —— The invalidity of the "Queue ordinance" of the city and county of San Francisco; opinion of the Circuit court of the United States for the District court of the United States for the District of California in Ho Ah Kow v. Matthew Nunan, delivered July 7th, 1879. S.F., J.L. Rice & co., 1879. 43 p.
                                   C CHi CLU

12593. —— —— Opinion...in the matter of David Neagle upon habeas corpus. Delivered at San Francisco, Sept. 16, 1889, by Hon. Lorenzo Sawyer, U.S. Circuit judge. [n.p., 1889] 60 p.   CSfCW

12594. —— —— Opinions and decrees of the U.S. Circuit court, for the Northern district of California, in case of the city of San Francisco vs. the United States. The pueblo case. S.F., Towne & Bacon, print., 1865. 35 p.
                           CHi CLU CSmH CU-B

12595. —— —— Opinions of the United States Circuit court and the Supreme court of the state, as to the validity of certain large claims made against the city of San Francisco. S.F., Commercial steam presses, 1857. 21 p.   CHi CU-B

12596. —— —— Taxation of property of railroad companies in California...opinions of justice Field and judge Sawyer, delivered in the U.S. Circuit at San Francisco, September 17, 1883. [n.p., 1883] 96 p.
                                   CHi

12597. —— **Circuit court of appeals (9th circuit)** Decision holding Chinese crew insufficient and denying limitation of liability... In the matter of the petition of the Pacific mail steamship company, owner of the steamship "City of Rio de Janeiro" for limitation of liability. [S.F.] Recorder press [1904] 8 p.   CU-B

12598. —— —— ...Spring valley water company (a corporation), complainant, vs. The city and county of San Francisco... [et al.] defendants. Opinion of Hon. E. S. Farrington, United States district judge, District of Nevada, on application for a preliminary injunction... [n.p.] Recorder print. and pub. co. [1908?] 70 p.
                                   CU-B

12599. —— —— ...Opinion of Hon. E. S. Farrington, United States district judge, on final hearing. [S.F., 1910?] 108 p.   CHi CU-B

12600. —— **Coast and geodetic survey.** Report of the examination of the weights and balances of the

branch mint of the United States, San Francisco, California. By George Davidson. Wash., Govt. print. off., 1872. 30 p. tables.   CU-B

12601. —— **Congress. House. Committee on military affairs.** ... Jurisdiction of Alcatraz island. [Wash., D.C., Govt. print. off.,] 1914] 6 p. (63d Cong., 2d sess. H. report 897) Submitted by Julius Kahn, to accompany H. R. 9017.   CO CSf

12602. —— —— —— **Committee on private land claims.** ...The Bolton claim...Report to accompany bill H. R. 1302. [Wash., 1878] 20 p. (45th Cong. 2d sess. H. report. no. 243) Relates to the Santillan grant.   CLU

12603. —— —— —— **Committee on the judiciary.** Tom Mooney. Hearings...seventy-fifth Congress, third session on H. J. Res. 297 memorializing the Honorable Frank F. Merriam, Governor of the state of California, to grant to Thomas J. Mooney a full and complete pardon. 1938. 154 p.   CLU CO CU-B

12604. —— —— —— Testimony in the matter of the investigation of the charges preferred aginst Chief Justice Robert F. Morrison and Associate Justice John R. Sharpstein. [Wash., D.C.] 1886. 38 p.   CHi

12605. —— —— —— **Special committee of judiciary.** In the matter of District judge Harold Louderback—special hearing... S.F., Recorder print. & pub. co. [1932] 57 p.   CHi

12606. —— —— —— **Subcommittee on public buildings and grounds.** Rincon annex murals, San Francisco. Printed for the use of the Committee on public works. House joint resolution 211. Wash., D.C., Govt. print. off., 1953. 87 p. fold. pl.   CHi

12607. —— —— **Senate.** Letter from the Chief clerk of the War department, communicating...information in relation to the Presidio reservation at San Francisco. Wash., D.C., Govt. print. off., 1874. 7 p. (43d Cong. 1st sess. Ex. doc. no. 55) Contains also: Resolution of the Legislature of California in favor of the enactment of a law dedicating the Presidio reservation... for the purpose of a public park (41st Congress, 2d session, Senate. Misc. doc. no. 110) ; Presidio reservation, San Francisco. Resolution of the Legislature of California asking Congress to relinquish a portion of the Presidio reservation for a public park to the city and county of San Francisco. (43d Congress, 1st session, H.R. Misc. doc. no. 206. 1874. 1 p.) ; and Letter from the Secretary of war (with accompanying papers) relative to granting the Presidio reservation to the city of San Francisco for a public park... (41st Congress, 2d session. Senate. Misc. doc. no. 131. 1870. 7 p.)   CHi

12608. —— —— —— **Committee on military affairs.** Arguments before the Committee on military affairs of the Senate for and against the bill (H.R. 1553) to lease Goat Island for a railway terminus. [Wash., D.C., Govt. print off., 1873] 139 p. (42d Cong. 3d sess. Misc. doc. no. 75)   CLU CSfCW

12609. —— —— —— **Committee on the judiciary.** Thomas J. Mooney. Hearing...seventy-fifth Congress, second session on S. J. Res. 127, a joint resolution memorializing the Honorable Frank F. Merriam, Governor of the state of California, to grant to Thomas J. Mooney a full and complete pardon. 1938. 17 p.   CO

12610. —— **Dept. of the interior.** Decision of the Hon. Lucius Q. C. Lamar, Secretary of the interior, March 12, 1887, in the matter of the survey of the pueblo lands of San Francisco, denying application to recall the patent of the United States to the city of San Francisco issued June 20, 1884. Wash., D.C., 1887. 34 p.   CHi

12611. —— —— Decision of the Secretary of the interior in the matter of the survey of the pueblo lands of San Francisco. Wash., D.C., Govt. print. off., 1881. 13 p.   CLU CU-B

12612. —— —— ...In the matter of the pueblo lands of San Francisco. Brief on behalf of lot owners in support of appeal taken from the decision of the commissioner of the General land office approving the Stratton survey. Edward R. Taylor, Jarboe & Harrison, E. J. Pringle, for lot owners. S.F., Crocker [187–?] 42 p.   CLU CU-B

12613. —— —— ...In the matter of the survey of the pueblo lands of San Francisco. Arguments of counsel at the hearing before the Secretary of the interior on the 11th day of Dec. 1882. Wash., D.C., R.H. Darby, print. [1882?] 74 p.   CHi CLU

12614. —— **District court. California (Northern district)** ...Opinion delivered by his honor Ogden Hoffman, U.S. district judge, in the cases of José Y. Limantour, nos. 424 and 429 [Land Commission nos. 548 and 549], claiming four leagues of land in San Francisco county, and adjacent islands. ... S.F., Frank Eastman, print., 1858. 58 p.   CHi CLU CSmH CU-B NN

12615. —— —— —— Report of the trial of Luis Delvalle, consul for the Republic of Mexico, at the port of San Francisco, for a breach of the neutrality laws of the United States, in the District court of the United States for the Northern district of California. S.F., Whitton, Towne and co., 1854. 54 p.   CHi CSmH CU-B

12616. —— —— —— Spring valley water company, plaintiff, vs. City and county of San Francisco et al., defendants. Nos. 14275, 14735, 14892, 15131, 15344, 15569, 26, 96. Report of H. M. Wright, standing master in chancery, and supplemental report. E. J. McCutchen, Warren Olney, jr., A. Crawford Greene, attorneys for plaintiff. George Lull, Robert M. Searls, Jesse H. Steinhart, attorneys for defendants. [S.F., 1917?] 283 p. tables (1 fold.)   CU-B

12617. —— **Engineer dept.** Hetch Hetchy valley; report of Advisory board of army engineers to the Secretary of the interior on investigations relative to sources of water supply for San Francisco and bay communities, Feb. 19, 1913. Wash., D.C., Govt. print. off., 1913. 146 p. illus., fold. map, diagrs. (part fold.)   CHi CRcS CU-B

12618. —— —— ...Rocks in San Francisco harbor, California... [Wash., D.C., Govt. print. off., 1908] 13 p.   CU-B

12619. —— —— Yerba Buena island... in relation to the bill to quiet the title to Yerba Buena island. December 20, 1880... Wash., D.C., 1880. 27 p.   CU-B

12620. —— **General land office.** Before Commissioner of the General land office, Washington, D.C. In the matter of adjustment of the Congressional land grant of 150,000 acres to the state of California. Correspondence. Sacramento, State off., 1888. 15 p.   CHi

12621. —— **Joint army and navy board on a bridge from Hunter point to Bay farm island across San Francisco bay.** ...Report... [Wash., D.C., 1945] 1903–1927 p. illus.   CO

12622. —— **Mint.** Report of the commission on charges and allegations made by Hon. H. F. Page against H. L. Dodge, esq., Supt. of the mint. Aug. 31, 1881. 25 p.   C CU-B

12623. —— **National commission on law observance and enforcement. Section on lawless enforcement of law.** The Mooney-Billings report; suppressed by the Wickersham commission. N.Y., Gotham House, inc. [c1932] 243 p.
C CHi CL   CO CSf CSmH CU-B

12624. —— **Naval shipyard, San Francisco.** The shipyard with a future. S.F., S.F. naval shipyard employees' assoc. [1952?] [44] p.   CHi

12625. —— **Naval training and distribution center, Treasure island, San Francisco.** The naval history of Treasure island. ... Ed. by Lt. Cmdr. E. A. McDevitt, USNR. Treasure island, 1946. 269 p. illus. (part col.), ports., map, diagr.   CSf CU-B

12626. —— **Naval training station, San Francisco.** Souvenir... Christmas, 1914. S.F., 1914. [88] p. illus.   CHi

12627. —— —— U.S. Naval training station [established 1899] San Francisco, California. Captain Henry Glass, commandant. Oakland, Williford & Winchell, 1901. 38 p. illus.   CSF
Other editions followed. CHi (1902, [1916?]) CLU (1902) CSf (1904) CU-B (1902)

12628. —— **Post office, San Francisco.** Official San Francisco postal guide... S.F. [1891] 78 p. illus.   CU-B

12629. —— —— Same... [S.F.?] Souvenir pub. co. [1894] 40 p. illus., port.   CU-B

12630. —— —— ...Papers, documents, and correspondence in relation to the case of Charles L. Weller, deputy postmaster at San Francisco, Cal. ... Wash., D.C., W.A. Harris, print., 1859. 477 p. (35th i.e. 36th Cong., Special sess. S. Ex.)   CLU

12631. —— —— Post office manual...1871, 1878–1879. S.F., 1871–79. 3 v.
CHi (1878) CU-B (1871–79)

12632. —— —— Statement including correspondence and documents relating to allegations made against the San Francisco Post office and Charles L. Weller, post master. Sacramento, S.W. Raveley [1858?] 75 p.
C CHi CSmH CU-B

12633. —— **President, 1853–1857 (Pierce)** ...Message of the president of the United States, in compliance with a resolution of the Senate of the 28th ultimo, calling for information respecting any correspondence or proceedings in relation to the self-styled Vigilance committee in California... [Wash., D.C., 1856] 30 p. (34th Cong. 1st sess. S. Ex. doc. no. 101)
CHi CLU

12634. —— **Secretary of the interior.** Proceedings before the Secretary of the interior in re use of Hetch Hetchy reservoir site in the Yosemite national park by the city of San Francisco. Wash., D.C., Govt. print. off., 1910. 75 p.   CHi

12635. —— **Secretary of war.** Report...communicating, in compliance with a resolution of the Senate, of the 2d instant, correspondence in relation to the proceedings of the Vigilance committee in San Francisco, California. Feb. 10, 1857. 20 p. (34th Cong. 3d sess. S. Ex. doc. 43)   TxU

12636. —— **Supreme court.** The San Francisco pilotage case in the Supreme court of the United States. Opinion of the court by Mr. Justice Field: with notes on the law of pilotage, by Gregory Yale... S.F., Towne and Bacon, print., 1865. 54 p.   CLU

12637. U.S. (*cont'd*) **Work projects administration. California.** Inventory of the historical records of the Panama-Pacific international exposition... [n.p., n.d.] 245 l.   CU-B

12638. —— —— —— 1939 real property survey, San Francisco, California...WPA 665–08–3–173; sponsored by the Housing authority of the city and county of San Francisco, prepared by Wayne F. Daugherty. S.F. [1941] 3 v. illus., maps. Vol. 2 has title: Graphic presentation. Vol. 3 has title: San Francisco's housing, May 1941...a digest...text by Bernard Taper.
CLSU CLU (v.3) CO CSf CSfMI CSfU CU (v.1, 2)

12639. —— —— —— Report on progress of the works program in San Francisco. January, 1938... [S.F.? 1938] 170 l.   CHi CSfU CU-B

12640. —— —— **San Francisco.** History of journalism in San Francisco. 7 v. Mimeo. v.1–6 issued by the History of San Francisco journalism project; v.7 by the Writers' program of California.
C C-S (v.3, 4, 6, 7) CBb CHi CLSU CO CRedl CRic CSS CSf CSfCW CStmo CSto CU-B

12641. —— —— —— [History of music in San Francisco series]...Cornel Lengyel, editor... WPA 10377. History of music project. O.P. 665–08–3–80... sponsored by the city and county, San Francisco. S.F., 1939–1942. 7 v. illus. Mimeo. Includes bibliographies and music.
C C-S CBb CHi CLSU (v.4–7) CO CRedl CRic CSS (v.1, 4–7) CSd (v.2, 4–7) CSf CSfCW CSfMI (v.1–3) CSmat CSmH CStclU (v.4, 5) CStmo CSto CU-B

12642. —— —— —— The opportunity for pictorial art in modern medicine: an example in San Francisco. [S.F., 1938?] 16 p. illus.   CHi

12643. —— —— —— San Francisco theatre research... [First ser.]... S.F., 1938–42. v.1–17, 20. illus., ports. Mimeo. Includes bibliographies.
C C-S CBb CHi CL CLSU CO CRedl CRic CSS CSd (v.1) CSdS CSf CSfCW CSfMI (v.1–8, 10–14) CSmH CStmo CSto CU-B

12644. —— —— —— Same. 2d ed.
CLSU (v.1–4)   MoS (v.1, 3-8)

12645. —— —— —— Letters of appreciation and newspaper comment on monographs. Ed. by Lawrence Estavan. S.F., 1939. 36 p. Mimeo.   CSto

12646. United States steel corp. The San Francisco-Oakland bay bridge...superstructure constructed by American bridge company, Pittsburgh, Pa., for Columbia steel company... [Pittsburgh, Pa.] 1936. 93 p. illus.   C CHi CLSU CLU CSfMI CSfU CU-B

12647. United Swedish singers of the Pacific coast. Souvenir program of the fifth biennial musical festival and convention, held in San Francisco and Oakland, Cal. ...June 16th–24th, 1915, Panama-Pacific international exposition. [S.F., 1915] 67 p. illus., ports.   CU-B

12648. United workingmen's boot & shoe manufacturing co. Price list Sept. 16, 1912. S.F. [1912] 1 v.   CU-B

12649. United world federalists of California. Central chapter, San Francisco. Annual progress report toward world law, December 1951. 16 l.   CHi

12650. Universal cooler co. The universal cooler ... Refrigeration with ice, or chemicals, for breweries, distilleries, dairies, etc. ... S.F., 1880. 20 p. illus.
CU-B

12651. University club. By-laws, house rules and list of officers and members. [S.F., 1890–

CHi has 1890, 1898, 1903, 1910, 1916, 1924. CSf has 1890, 1910, 1916. CSfCW has 1890. CSmH has [1898?] 1903.

12652. University extension homestead association. Act of incorporation and articles of association... S.F., Mullin, Mahon & co., 1867. 22 p.   CHi

12653. University mound railroad. Circular to all owners of property interested in the building of the University mound railroad... [S.F., Waters, Newhoff & co., print., 1872] 10 p.   CLU

12654. University of San Francisco associates. The historical, economic and cultural interrelation of the city of San Francisco and the University of San Francisco... [S.F.? n.d.] v.p.   CHi

12655. Unna, Warren. The Coppa murals; a pageant of Bohemian life in San Francisco at the turn of the century. Introduction by Joseph Henry Jackson. [S.F.] Bk. club of Calif., 1952. 61 p. illus.
C CBb CHi CLU CO CSfU CSjC CSt CStclU CSto CStoC CU-B

12656. Upham, Samuel Curtis. Notes of a voyage to California via Cape Horn, together with scenes in El Dorado, in the year 1849–'50... Phila., Author, 1878. 594 p. illus., ports. Pages 214-357, and some parts of appendix, deal with California, chiefly San Francisco and Sacramento.
Available in many California libraries and CaBViPA IHi KyU

12657. Upper Fillmore merchants association. ...Directory of membership. January, 1957... [S.F.?, Barnett print., 1957?] [3] p.   CHi

12658. Upper Noe Valley neighborhood council. History committee. Report of the History committee, November 1959, Upper Noe Valley district in San Francisco. [S.F., 1959] 53 p. Mimeo.   CHi

12659. [Urban realty improvement co.] Character of improvements at Ingleside terraces. [n.p., n.d.] folder. illus.   CHi

12660. Urmy, Clarence Thomas. The day that I was born; being a story of old San Francisco. Saratoga, Troubadour press, 1924. 30 p. illus.   CHi CO

12661. Valencia, Candelario and Valencia, Paula, vs. Couch, John. Candelario Valencia and Paula Valencia, plaintiffs, vs. John Couch, defendant. Transcript on appeal. William W. Chipman, att'y. for plaintiffs, appellants, G. F. and W. H. Sharp, of counsel for defendant, respondent. S.F., Deffebach & co.'s. print. [1867] 24 p. map. At head of cover-title: No. 1206 from the County court of San Francisco, to the Supreme court of the state of California.   CHi

12662. Valencia theatre, San Francisco's newest and most beautiful playhouse, Valencia St. between 13th and 14th. [S.F.?] 1908. 14 p. illus., ports. Contains a description of the theater building and its theatrical company.
CHi

12663. Valentine, Alan Chester. Vigilante justice. N.Y., Reynal & co., 1956. 173 p.
Available in many California libraries and IC MiD MoHi MoS MoSU N NN ODa UPB ViU

12664. Valentine, Thomas B. vs. Jansen, Charles J. Thomas B. Valentine, plaintiff and respondent, vs. Charles J. Jansen, defendant and appellant. Transcript on appeal from the Fourth district court. Wilson & Crittenden, att'ys for appellant. B. S. Brooks, att'y for respondent. S.F., Turnbull & Smith, print., 1868. 114 p.
CLU

12665. Valentine, Thomas B. vs. Thompson, Andrew, et al. Thomas B. Valentine, appellant, vs. Andrew Thompson and Ellen Bolton Thompson, his wife, respondents. Transcript on appeal from the judgment of the Fourth district court in and for the city and county of San Francisco, and from the order denying the motion for new trial. B. S. Brooks, for appellant. Patterson, Wallace & Stow, for respondents. S.F., Francis & Valentine [1868] 94 p. A San Francisco lot suit.   CLU

12666. Vallejo brick and tile co., consolidated. Resolutions creating bonded indebtedness of one hundred thousand dollars passed at special meeting of Board of directors of Vallejo brick and tile company, consolidated (a corporation) held on November 18, 1912. [S.F., 1912] 55 p.   CU-B

12667. Van, Melvin. The big heart. Photography [by] Ruth Bernhard. [S.F., Fearon pub., c1957] 77 p. illus.
C CCoron CHi CNa CO CRedCL CRic CSd CSf CSfMI CSfSt CSluCL CSmat CSt CStmo CU-B CViCL

12668. Van Allmen, E. P. A study of the San Francisco district council of the Boy scouts of America made for the Council of social and health agencies of San Francisco. S.F., 1924. 88 p. Mimeo.   CHi

12669. Van der Naillen, Albert. The actual religious battle; or, Free religion vs. the old creeds. Lecture delivered at the Mercantile library hall, San Francisco, Cal., January 10, 1875... S.F., Off. of the "Pac. liberal," 1875. 25 p.   CHi

12670. Van Ness, James. Van Ness scrapbook... S.F. [n.d.]   CSmH

12671. Van Ness young ladies' seminary. Commencement exercises...1222 Pine street, Tuesday evening, May 22, 1894... [S.F.] 1894. 4 p.   CHi

12672. Van Wagenen, Richard Whitmore. Financial control in San Francisco: a case study. [Stanford] 1941. Thesis (Ph.D.)—Stanford univ., 1941.   CSt

12673. Van Winkle (I. S.) & co. Catalogue of ... importers of iron, steel, coal and blacksmiths' supplies. S.F. [1889] 72 p. illus.   CHi

12674. Varigny, Charles Victor Grosnier de. Los orijenes de San Francisco de California. (Traduccion especial de *La Revista de Ambos Mundos* para *La Patria*). Valparaiso, Chile, La Patria, 1887. 164 p.
CLO CSf CSmH

12675. —— San Francisco. I. Les origines. [Paris, 1886] From *Revue des deux mondes*, p. 168–192.   CU-B

12676. Vassault, Ferdinand, vs. Kirby, E. C. In the Supreme court of the state of California. Ferdinand Vassault vs. E. C. Kirby. Plaintiff's argument. M. M. Estee, for appellant. S.F., Francis & Valentine, print. [1869?] 14 p.   CHi

12677. Veatch, John A. Report of John A. Veatch to the Borax company of California. S.F., Whitton, Towne & co., 1857. 16 p.   C CLU CSfCSM CSmH CU

12678. Vest pocket guide and business directory of San Francisco. [S.F.? 1887?] 48 p. illus.   CHi

12679. —— Same. [S.F., E.C. Hughes, 1895] 47 p. illus., map.   CHi

12680. Veteran firemen's association of San Francisco, inc. Anniversary and annual fire book... 1st- , 1899?- [S.F.] 1899?- Title varies.
CHi has 24–25th, 31st, 33d–34th, 1923–24, 1930, 1932–33. CSf has 30th, 1929. CSmH has 33d, 1932.

12681. —— Constitution and by-laws... Organized Nov. 30, 1898, incorporated June 10, 1899. [S.F., U–W co., 1907?] 39 p. illus.   CHi CU-B (1930)

12682. Not in use.

12683. Not in use.

12684. Veteran volunteer firemen's association of California. Annual report of officers for the year 1895. S.F., 1895.   CHi

12685. Veterans of the Mexican war, San Francisco. Rules and regulations of Company A... S.F., Frank Eastman, 1871. 17 p.   CHi

12686. Views of San Francisco before and after earthquake. [S.F., E.P. Charlton & co., 1906?] [48] p. illus.   C-S CL CU-B

12687. Views of the church and college of St. Ignatius of the Society of Jesus, corner of Van Ness Ave. and Hayes St., San Francisco, California. Photographs by Watkins. [50 photos. c1905]   CL CLgA CSfU

12688. Vilas, Martin Samuel. The Barbary Coast of San Francisco... [n.p.] Author [1915] 6 l.
C CLU CSf CSmH

12689. —— Municipal railway of San Francisco ...September 1, 1915. [Burlington, Vt., Print. Free press assoc.] c1915. [31] p. illus.   CSf CSmH

12690. —— Water and power for San Francisco from Hetch-Hetchy valley and Yosemite national park... [Burlington, Vt., Print. Free press assoc.] c1915. 27 p. illus., ports.   C CO CSf CSmH CU-B

12691. Vincent (Sevin) & co. Catalogue of seeds and plants... S.F., Le Petit journal print., 1884. 80 p. illus.   CHi

12692. Vinson, Pauline. Hilltop Russians in San Francisco; pictures by Pauline Vinson, text by William Saroyan. [Stanford] Delkin, 1941. 7 p., 30 pl. "Five hundred copies printed at the Grabhorn press."
C CBb CBu CLSU CLU CRcS CRic CSf CSmH CSmat CStrJC CU-B CoD

12693. Visalia stock saddle co. Catalogue... S.F. [189–?–195–?] illus.
CHi has no. 17 (1911) 18, 19, 22 (1924) 24, 30 (1934) 31 (1938)

12694. Vivian, Imogen Holbrook. A biographical sketch of the life of Charles Algernon Sidney Vivian, founder of the Order of Elks. S.F., Whitaker & Ray co., 1904. 103 p. ports.   CHi

12695. Voget, Lamberta Margarette. The waterfront of San Francisco, 1863–1930: a history of its administration by the state of California... [Berkeley, 1943] 233 l. maps. Thesis (Ph.D.)— Univ. of Calif., 1943.   CU

12696. Volkmann, Daniel G. Sixty-five years of A. Schilling & company. S.F. [Lawton Kennedy, print.] 1959. 9 p. illus.   CHi

12697. Von Schmidt, Alexis Waldemar. Report to the Lake Tahoe and San Francisco water works company, on its source of supply; proposed line of works; estimated cost and income. ...October 1, 1871. S.F., Alta Calif. print house, 1871. 21 p.   C CHi CLU

12698. [Voorsanger, Jacob] The chronicles of Emanu-El. Being an account of the rise and progress of the Congregation Emanu-El, which was founded in July, 1850... S.F., 1900. 170 p. illus., ports., map.
C CHi CL CLU CSf CSfP CSfCW CSfU CSmH CU-B N

12699. Vulcan iron works. Aerial tramways. S.F. [190–?] 62 p. illus., diagrs.   CU-B

12700. Wagner, Henry Raup. Commercial printers of San Francisco from 1851 to 1880... Portland, Me., Southworth-Anthoensen press, c1939. 16 p. "Separate from the *Papers of the Bibliographical soc. of Am.*, volume thirty-three, 1939."
C CHi CLU CO CSf CSmH CU-B

12701. —— Recollections of Templeton Crocker, founder of the California historical society. [Oakland, Westgate press, 1950] [4] p.   CHi

12702. Wagoner, Luther, and Heuer, W. H. San Francisco harbor, its commerce and docks with a complete plan for development... report of the engineers of the Federated harbor improvement association. [S.F., Britton & Rey] 1908. 60 p. maps.
C CHi CL CLU CSf CSfU CSmH CU-B

12703. Wagstaff, Alexander E. Life of David S. Terry, presenting an authentic, impartial and vivid history of his eventful life and tragic death. S.F., Continental pub. co., 1892. 526 p.
CLO CMartC CP CSf CSfCW CSfP CSto

12704. Wainwright, James E. & co., auctioneers. Great sale of thoroughbred cattle!! Devons, Thursday, April 19, 1860...at Fish's stable, Pine St. ... S.F. [Towne & Bacon] 1860. [4] p. illus.   CHi

12705. —— Third great cargo sale of Japanese goods, ex schooner "Page," imported expressly for the holidays, will be held at Assembly hall, corner of Post and Kearny streets, Friday, December 23, '59... [S.F., 1859] 44 p.   CLU

12706. Wakeman, Edgar. The log of an ancient mariner... S.F., A.L. Bancroft & co., 1878. 378 p. illus., port. Includes account of Vigilance committee of 1851.
C CBb CHi CL CLSU CLU CMartC CMont CP CSf CSfCP CSfP CU-B

12707. Waldie, Helen B. Education in San Francisco, 1850–60: a study of frontier attitudes. [Stanford] 1954. Thesis (M.A.)— Stanford univ., 1954.   CSt

12708. Walker, David H. Pioneers of prosperity. S.F., 1895. 191 p.
C CBb CHi CL CLU CO CSd CSf CSfCSM CSfCW CSfP CSfSt CSfU CSj CStmo CU-B CaBViPA CoD MoS OrU

12709. Walker, Franklin Dickerson. Ambrose Bierce, the wickedest man in San Francisco. [S.F.] Colt press, 1941. 45 p. fold. facsim. Portrait on t.-p.
CChiS CHi CLO CLS CSd

12710. —— Frank Norris, a biography. Garden City, Doubleday, 1932. 317 p. port.   CHi

12711. —— San Francisco's literary frontier... N.Y., Knopf, 1939. 400 p. Bibliography: p. 363–370.
Available in many California libraries and CaBViPA MoS OU UHi ViU

12712. Walker, Fred Kaiser. James D. Phelan: democratic senator from California, 1915–1921. [Berkeley, 1947] Thesis (M.A.)— Univ. of Calif., 1947.   CU

12713. Wallace, Robert. Life and limb; an account of the career of Melvin M. Belli, personal-injury trial lawyer. Garden City, Doubleday, c1955. 250 p.
CMont CSalCL CSd

12714. Walsh, Alexander R., vs. Hill, George A. ...Alexander R. Walsh, respondent, vs. George A. Hill, et al., appellants. Transcript on appeal. Walter Van Dyke, att'y for appellants. J. McM. Shafter, att'y for respondent. S.F., M.D. Carr & co. [1869–70?] 3 v. in 1.
CLU CU-B

12715. Walsh's mail order house. [Catalog] S.F., Gilmartin co., [1905?] 88 p. illus.   CHi

12716. Walter (D. N. and E.) and co. [Catalog of] carpets, rugs, linoleums, mattings, curtains, shades, upholstery goods. [1906?] S.F. [1906?] 1 v. illus. (part col.)   CU-B

12717. Walter, Edgar. In memoriam: Edgar Walter, by San Francisco art association. [S.F., n.d.] 2 l.   CHi

12718. War memorial of San Francisco. Souvenir edition. [S.F., Pisani print. & pub. co., 1939?] 40 p. illus., ports.   CHi CU-B

12719. Ward, Mary A. Development of individual instruction at the San Francisco state normal school 1913–1917. Stanford, 1932. 262 l. Thesis (M.A.)— Stanford univ., 1932.   CSfSt (microfilm) CSt

12720. Ward bros. Album of San Francisco, Cal., 42 photo views. [Columbus, O., c1889] 13 pl. (2 double)   C CL

12721. Warner, Frank W., pub. Guide book and street manual of San Francisco, California. [S.F., Crocker, 1882] 174 p. illus., fold. map.
C CHi CSmH CU-B

12722. [Warshaw, Steven] The City of gold; the story of city planning in San Francisco. [S.F.] Crown Zellerbach corp., 1960. 48 p. illus.   CSfP

12723. Washington grammar school association of San Francisco. Constitution and by-laws adopted August 22, 1923. [S.F., 1923?] 15 p.   CHi

12724. Washington street wharf co. By-laws... Incorporated Aug. 24th, 1855. S.F., Monson & Valentine, 1855. 20 p.   CU-B

12725. Watchers, Anthony Lincoln. The development of civil service in San Francisco. [Berkeley, 1937] Thesis (M.A.)— Univ. of Calif., 1937.   CU

12726. Water-front building association. Officers, certificate of incorporation, by-laws and rules of order... S.F., Alta Calif. general print. house, 1869. 13 p. CU-B

12727. Waterfront employers association of San Francisco. April 21 agreement between Waterfront employers assn. of San Francisco and International longshoremen's assn. Dist. no. 38, local 38–79. With transcript of proceedings before Hon. M. C. Sloss, Federal arbitrator. Distributed by the San Francisco chamber of commerce. [S.F., 1936] 32 p.   CHi

12728. —— Maritime strikes on the Pacific coast; a factual account of events leading to the 1936 strike of marine and longshore unions. Statement of Gregory Harrison, Esq., on behalf of Coast committee for shipowners, before the United States maritime commission, at San Francisco, California, Nov. 2, 1936. [S.F.] 1936. 30 p.   CHi

12729. Waterfront employers union. "Full and by"; a message from the Waterfront employers union. S.F., Off. of the secretary, 1921. 22 p. illus.   CHi

12730. Waterhouse & Lester, firm. [Catalog] no. 8...hardwood, lumber, woodwork,... horse shoes, blacksmith tools and supplies... [S.F., Hicks-Judd co., 1900?] 543 p. illus., port.   CHi

12731. Waterman, Patricia Louise. Wartime manpower controls in the San Francisco bay area. [Berkeley, 1944] Thesis (M.A.)— Univ. of Calif., 1944.   CU

12732. Watkins, Eleanor Preston. The builders of San Francisco and some of their early homes, prepared for the National society of colonial dames of America in the state of California... S.F., 1935. 28 p. illus. Bibliography: p. 28.
C CHi CLU CO CSf CSfCP CSmH CU-B CViCL

12733. Watson, Douglas Sloane. An hour's walk through Yerba Buena, the town that existed for eleven years, seven months and five days and then became San Francisco. S.F. [Print. by Lawton R. Kennedy for the Yerba Buena chapter of E clampus vitus] Feb., 1937. 16 p. map.

CAla CBaB CBb CHi CL CO CSf CSfCP CSfU CSfWF-H CSjC CSmH CU-B

12734. —— Same. [2d ed. S.F.] 1957. 17 p. map, facsim. CHi CLU UPB

12735. —— Neighbors of yesterday. [S.F., Grabhorn, 1934] [11] p. illus. (Roxburghe club of S.F. Souvenirs) C CSmH

12736. —— San Francisco's first Christmas. [S.F.] Grabhorn, 1931. 10 p. Autographed presentation copy. CHi

12737. Watson, Mary. People I have met; ... S.F., Francis, Valentine & co., print., 1890. 91 p. ports. CHi CSfCW

12738. —— San Francisco society... S.F., Francis, Valentine & co., bk. & job print., & engravers, 1887. 42 p. C-S CU-B

12739. [Watson, Robert S.] San Francisco in 1849. Stray leaves by a pioneer. [18—?] [85] l. Photostat copy of manuscript. C

12740. Watt, Robert. Remarks of the Rev. Charles Reynolds Brown at the funeral of Robert Watt, July 13, 1907. [S.F., print. for C.O.G. Miller by Taylor & Taylor, 1946] 9 p. port. CHi

12741. Waugh, Evelyn Marguerite. The "Boston ships" in the Pacific, 1787–1840. [Berkeley, 1927] Thesis (M.A.) — Univ. of Calif., 1927. CU

12742. Waugh, Lorenzo. Constitution of the California youths' association. Organized November, 1859. Address to parents, citizens, and children. Odes, initiating formula, etc. Second and revised ed. S.F., Agnew & Deffebach, print., 1863. 40 p. port. CHi

12743. The Wave-power air compressing co. [Illustrated brochure] S.F. [Brown & Craddock] 1895. 14 p. illus. CHi

12744. [Weatherred, Edith Tozier] San Francisco (on the night of April 18th, 1906) [S.F., 1906] [4] p., 13 pl. C CHi CLgA CO CU-B NN

12745. Webb, Stephen Palfrey. A sketch of the causes, operations and results of the San Francisco vigilance committee in 1856, written by Stephen Palfrey Webb in 1874. [Salem, Mass.] 1948. 34 p. port. "Reprinted from *Essex inst. hist. collections*, v. 84, Apr. 1948. C CSf NHi

12746. Weber (C. F.) & co. Catalog of school equipment and school supplies... S.F. [Gilmartin co.] 1930. 176 p. illus. CHi

12747. —— General catalogue. no. 808, 912. S.F. [1907?–10?] illus. CU-B

12748. Webster, F. A. Souvenir album; fire and earthquake views of San Francisco...photos by F. A. Webster. Oakland, F. Worrall [1906] [16] p. illus. C CHi CSto

12749. Weed, Samuel Richards. My early experiences and recollections of the great fires and the first fire department in San Francisco... [S.F.] 1908. 26 p. CSmH CU-B

12750. Weeks-Howe-Emerson co. ...Catalogue [of]...ship chandlers... [S.F.?] illus.
CHi has no. 32, no. 4142 [1932?] 1941.

12751. Weidberg, Dorothy. The history of John Kentfield and company, 1854–1925, a lumber manufacturing and shipping firm of San Francisco... [Berkeley, 1940] 77 l. Typew. Thesis (M.A.)— Univ. of Calif., 1940. CU CU-B

12752. [Weil, Oscar] Oscar Weil; letters and papers. S.F., Bk. club of Calif., 1923. 117 p. port. CHi

12753. Weil and Woodleaf, firm. Catalogue. [187–?] S.F. [187–?] CU-B

12754. Weinstock-Nichols co. Catalogue...automobile accessories... S.F. [19—?] illus.
CHi has no. 5. CU-B has no. 6 [1915?]

12755. Weintraub, Hyman. Andrew Furuseth, emancipator of the seamen. Berkeley, Univ. of Calif. press, 1959. 267 p. port. CHi CRcS CU

12756. Welch, Frances Maude. Child dependency in San Francisco. [Berkeley, 1935] Thesis (M.A.)— Univ. of Calif., 1935. CU

12757. Wellman, Peck & co. Grocers catalogue and price book...Comp. by W.J. Tilley. S.F., Hicks-Judd co. [1896?] 162 p. illus. CHi

12758. —— Our first 100 years. [S.F., 1949] [24] p. illus., ports. CHi CU-B

12759. Wells, Evelyn. Champagne days of San Francisco... N.Y., London, Appleton-Century, 1939. 284 p. illus., ports.
Available in many California libraries and CaBViPA MoS NN NjR ODa TxU UPB

12760. —— Same. Garden City, N.Y., Doubleday, 1947. 284 p. illus., ports. CHi CLSU CU-B

12761. —— Fremont Older. N.Y., London, Appleton-Century, 1936. 407 p. illus., ports.
Available in many California libraries and TxU ViU

12762. Wells, Thomas Goodwin. Letters of an Argonaut. Extracts from the correspondence of the pioneer banker, Thomas Goodwin Wells. Edited by his son, Benjamin W. Wells. [L.A., Out West co., 1905?] 23 p. illus. "Reprint. from *Out West*." CLU CSf

12763. Wells, Fargo & co. Catalogue...historical exhibit, etc. at the 1893 world's Columbian exposition, Chicago... S.F., H.S. Crocker co. [1893?] 32 p. CHi

12764. —— ...Directory of Chinese merchants, San Francisco and Sacramento, in Chinese and English. [S.F.] Litho. Britton & Rey, 1873– Title varies.
CHi (1873, 1878, 1882) CSfP (1873) CSfWF-H (1878, 1882) CSmH (1882) CU-B (1873)

12765. —— Help for the afflicted. The Pacific slope to the rescue! To agents and employees of Wells, Fargo & co.'s express: in behalf of the yellow fever sufferers... [S.F., 1878] [4] p. CU-B

12766. —— List of officers, agents, and correspondents. S.F., N.Y., 1885–1912.
CHi has 1885–93, 1895–1910, 1912.

12767. —— San Francisco, 1915...for its patrons ...some brief general information to help them in their way about San Francisco. [S.F., c1915] 44 p. map. CHi CSf CU-B

12768. —— **Wells, Fargo & co.'s express. 1882.** Instructions. For the use of agents and employees only. S.F., Crocker, 1882. CSmH

12769. —— Wells, Fargo & co.'s express directory; list of principal points in territory occupied by Wells, Fargo & co. ... S.F. [Hicks & Judd] 1886. 160 p. CHi

12770. —— Wells, Fargo & co.'s express office directory, for 1856 containing a list of the offices, towns and counties in the state through which their lines extend... with general and special instructions... S.F., Whitton, Towne & co., 1856. 59 p.   C CSmH

12771. **Wells Fargo bank.** Annual report.
CL has 1956 to date.

12772. —— A brief history of Wells Fargo. S.F., [1941?] [12] p.   CHi
Other editions followed. CHi (1943?, 1955?, 1961) CRcS (1943?) CSmat (n.d.)

12773. —— Half an hour in Eldorado; a trip through the Wells Fargo bank historical collection of the old west. S.F., 1939. 29 p. illus.   CHi CRcS

12774. —— Since pony express days. [S.F.? c1930] [18] p. illus.   CHi

12775. **Wells Fargo library association.** Catalogue and by-laws... Organized: Aug. 1890. S.F., Dettner print. press, 1910. 104 p.   CHi

12776. —— Catalogues of the Wells-Fargo library association, 1898. [S.F., E.D. Taylor co., 1898?] 119 p. illus.   CU-B

12777. **[Welsh, William D.]** The years of paper; Isadore Zellerbach, 1866–1941. [n.p., Crown Zellerbach corp., 1941] 19 p. illus., ports.   CHi

12778. **Wendte, Charles William.** Thomas Starr King, patriot and preacher. Bost., Beacon press [c1921] 226 p. illus., port.
Available in many libraries.

12779. **Wenzel, Hermann.** Correct time. Pneumatic clock. S.F., B.F. Sterett, print. [187–?] [8] p. illus.   CU-B

12780. **Wertheimer co.** Illustrated catalogue [of] tobacco and cigars. 1892. S.F. [1892] 1 v. illus.
CU-B

12781. **West coast telephone co.** Annual report. 1954–60.   CL

12782. **West coast wire and iron works.** Illustrated catalogue. no. 2–3. S.F., [189–?–1899] illus.
CU-B

12783. **West end homestead association.** Articles of association, rules of order and certificate of incorporation... Adopted Nov. 15th, 1862. S.F., L. Albin, print., 1862. 20 p.   CU-B

12784. **[Western] amusement supply co.** Catalogue "B"...instruments, outfits and supplies for the motion picture theatre... [n.p., 1908?] 187 p. illus.
CHi

12785. **Western builders' supply co., inc.** Catalog of...art wood mouldings... S.F. [1927] [35] p. illus.
CHi

12786. **Western electric co.** General catalogue of electrical supplies. [n.p., c1901] 1073 p. illus. California electrical works, Pacific Coast agents, San Francisco, stamped on t.-p.   CHi

12787. **Western Pacific railroad co.** Annual report... [S.F., 1917]
CHi has 1st, 1916. CL has 1951–60.

12788. —— The Riviera of the golden west. S.F., Taylor, Nash & Taylor [c1913] 43 p.   CU-B

12789. **Western Pacific railroad co. of California.** Laws and documents showing the organization, powers, and rights... S.F., Towne & Bacon, 1865. 119 p.   CHi

12790. **Western pipe & steel co. of California.** [Illustrated brochure] [n.p., 1919] 104 p. illus., diagrs.
CHi

12791. —— Western corrugated culverts. Bulletin F. [S.F., Taylor, Nash & Taylor, 1912?] [12] p. illus.
CHi

12792. **Western world magazine.** v.1–2, May 1906– Oct. 5, 1907. [new series v. [1]–2 no. 2 Aug. 1908] S.F., 1906–08. illus., ports. Title varies: v.1–2, no. 2, New San Francisco magazine.
C (v.1 no. 1–3, v.2 no. 1, 4–26) C-S (v.1 no. 1–3) CHi (v.1 no. 1–4) CO (v.1 no. 1–2) CRedl (v.1 no. 1) CSS (v.1 no. 1, 2, 4) CSfCW (v.1 no. 1, 2, 4) CSmat (v.1 no. 1, 2, 4) CSmH (v.1 no. 1, 2, 4) CStclU (v.1 no. 1, 2, 4) CU-B (v. 1 no. 1, 2, 4, v.2 no. 3, 7–10, 12–16, [new ser.] v.2 no. 1–2)

12793. **West's (Miss) school for girls.** [Catalog] [S.F., 1889–1910]
CHi has 1897/98, 1910/11. CU-B has 1889/90, 1891/92, 1896/97, 1904/05.

12794. **Wetmore, Jesse L., vs. San Francisco.** ... Jesse L. Wetmore, appellant, vs. the city and county of San Francisco, respondent. Brief of respondent. W. C. Burnett, city and county attorney. John B. Felton, of counsel. S.F., Carr, Dunn & Newhoff, print., 1872. 45 p.
CU-B

12795. **Weule (Louis) co.** Chronometers, watches, sextants, sounding machines... S.F. [John Kitchen jr. co., n.d.] 46 p. illus.   CHi

12796. **Wharves of old San Francisco** as described by writers of the days of 1848–1850. 4 p. map. Typew.
CRcS

12797. **Wheelan, Fairfax Henry.** In memoriam, 1856–1915. S.F., The Harvard club [1915?] 6 p. port.
CHi

12798. —— The merchant the leavening force of civilization and the world's progress...address delivered ...before the Western retail lumbermen's association convention, Feb. 13–15, 1913. Reprint. from *Am. Lumberman*, March 1, 1913. 16 p.   CHi

12799. **Wheeler, Alfred.** Land titles in San Francisco and the laws affecting the same, with a synopsis of all grants and sales of land within the limits claimed by the city. S.F., Alta Calif. steam print. establishment, 1852. 127 p. map.
C CCH CHi CLU CSf CSfCP CSfMI CSfP CSmH CU-B CU-Law CStclU NHi NvHi

12800. **Wheeler, C. B.** ...Was the formation of the San Francisco Vigilance committee justifiable? [New Haven? 1857] 8 l. Photostat copy (positive). "Speech delivered at the Sophomore prize debate of the Brothers in unity of Yale college, January 14, 1857."   CLU CSf

12801. **Wheeler, Charles Stetson.** Memorial motions in court upon the death of Charles Stetson Wheeler. S.F., John Henry Nash, 1924. 75 p. port.   CHi

12802. **Whitall Tatum co.** Price list. 1908. S.F. [1908] 1 v. illus.   CU-B

12803. **White, Douglas, comp.** Selected bits of San Francisco architecture, prepared from designs originated by Edgar A. Mathews and Newton J. Tharp... S.F., Commercial art co., 1905. [72] p. illus.   CHi

12804. **White, Gerald T.** Formative years in the far west, a history of Standard oil company of California and predecessors through 1919. N.Y., Appleton-Century [c1962] 694 p. illus., ports., maps.
Available in many California libraries.

12805. **White and Bauer, pub.** The great earthquake in San Francisco. Estimated damages in detail. S.F. [1868] 16 p.   C CU-B

12806. White bros. Hardwood lumber, wagon stock, cabinet woods and veneers. [Catalog] 1880 [190–?] S.F., 1880–[190–?] 2 v. illus. CU-B

12807. White, Rogers & co. Catalogue...of the Wilfley concentrator... [S.F., 1897?] illus.
CHi has no. 1, no. 3.

12808. White House (department store) Catalogue no. 10, fall & winter, 1909–10. S.F., Raphael Weill & co., inc. [1909] 64 p. illus. CHi

12809. —— General directory, May 17, 1909. S.F. [1909] 1 v. CU-B

12810. Whited, Jesse M. California lodge no. 1 Free and accepted masons... [S.F., 1916] 31 p. CHi

12811. —— History of the Thirty-ninth triennial conclave, Grand encampment of Knights Templar of the United States of America...Held at San Francisco, California, July 7th to 13th, 1934. [S.F.? 1934?] 160 p. illus., ports. CHi

12812. Whitfield, Ruth Hall. Public opinion and the Chinese question in San Francisco, 1900–1947. [Berkeley, 1947] Thesis (M.A.)— Univ. of California, 1947. CU

12813. Whitman, Frederic Bennett. Western Pacific—its first forty years. A brief history (1910–1950). N.Y., Newcomen soc., in No. Am., 1950. 32 p. illus. CHi CL CSf

12814. Whittier, Charlotte Ann (Robinson) Charlotte Robinson Whittier, wife of William Franklin Whittier, San Francisco, May 21, 1831–Feb. 16, 1885. [S.F.] 1885. 71 p. port. A privately issued memorial volume. CHi

12815. Whittier, Coburn co. Catalogue. no. 4–5. [1908]–1909. S.F., [1908–09] 2 no. illus. CU-B

12816. Whittier, Fuller and co. Price list [of] paints, oils, varnishes, and brushes. [187–?] S.F. [187–?] 1 v. CU-B

12817. Who's who in San Francisco and bay area. 1940. [S.F.] S.F. Examiner [1940] 1 v. CU-B

12818. The wide West. ...Vigilance pictorial. 2 ed. [June 1856] [S.F.] W.W. Kurtz & co. [1856] [4] p. illus., port. Assassination of James King of Wm. CU-B

12819. Widows' and orphans' aid association of the police department of San Francisco. Constitution and by-laws...organized Jan. 13th, 1878. S.F., B.F. Sterett, print., 1878. 26 p. CHi

12820. [Wiegand, Conrad] Dr. Scott, the Vigilance committee and the church. A lecture...delivered in Musical hall, San Francisco, Oct. 12, 1856. S.F., Whitton, Towne & co., print., 1856. 52 p.
C CHi CLO CP CS CSaT CSfCW CSmH CU-B

12821. —— To the people of San Francisco and California, as citizens of the United States. [S.F., 1856] 8 p. Signed: Conrad Wiegand, late assayer of the U.S. branch mint. CSmH

12822. Wiens, Henry W. The career of Franklin K. Lane in California politics. [Berkeley, 1937] Thesis (M.A.)— Univ. of Calif., 1937. CU

12823. Wiester & co. ...catalogue of useful inventions...1877, 1880. [S.F., 1877–80] 2 v. illus. CU-B

12824. —— Price list of roller skates, 1883. S.F. [1883] 1 v. illus. CU-B

12825. Wight, Earl Hervie. Industrial physical education and recreation in factories of the San Francisco bay cities. [Berkeley, 1920] Thesis (M.A.)— Univ. of Calif., 1920. CU

12826. Wilbert (Fred V.) firm. [Catalog]... tool manufacturer. S.F. [193–?] loose-leaf. illus. CHi

12827. Wilcox, Delos Franklin. San Francisco's street railway problem; preliminary survey of franchise expirations and other matters... S.F., Pernau-Walsh print. co. [1927?] CHi CL

12828. Wilde's real estate review...v.1, no. 2–7, Oct. 1867–Feb. 1868. S.F., 1867–68. CU-B

12829. Wilkie (Andrew) co. [Catalog of store and office fixtures, interior wood decoration. S.F., Edw. S. Knowles, 1904] 210 p. illus. CHi

12830. [Will & Finck co.] [Catalog. S.F.?, 188–?] 156 p. illus. CHi CU-B

12831. Willey, Samuel Hopkins. Decade sermons. Two historical discourses occasioned by the close of the first ten years' ministry in California. S.F., Towne & Bacon, 1859. 46 p.
C CBPac CHi CSaT CSmH CU-B CtY MHi MWA MiD-B N PHi WHi

12832. —— Discourse at the closing exercises of the Howard Presbyterian church in their first house of worship, corner of Natoma and Jayne [i.e., Jane] streets, Sabbath morning, Jan. 6, 1867. By the Rev. Samuel H. Willey, first pastor of the church. S.F., Towne & Bacon, 1867. 20 p. CHi

12833. —— Farewell discourse delivered in the Howard st. Presbyterian church, on Sabbath morning, April 27th, 1862 . . . S.F., Towne & Bacon, 1862. 38 p.
CBPac CHi CSaT CU CU-B PHi

12834. —— The history of the first pastorate of the Howard Presbyterian church, San Francisco, Calif., 1850–1862. S.F., Whitaker & Ray, 1900. 171 p.
C CHi CLSU CLU CMont CO CSf CSmH CU-B CABViPA NHi NN

12835. Williams, Albert. A farewell discourse, delivered Sunday, October 8th, 1854, on the occasion of resigning the charge of the First Presbyterian church of San Francisco, California... S.F., B.F. Sterett, 1854. 22 p. CSmH CU CU-B MWA WHi

12836. —— A pioneer pastorate and times, embodying contemporary local transactions and events, by the...founder and first pastor of the First Presbyterian church, San Francisco. S.F., Wallace & Hassett, print., 1879. 255 p. port.
C CBb CHi CL CLU CMont CO CP CRedl CSdS CSf CSfCW CSfMI CSfP CSmH CU-B IHi N NHi NN

12837. —— Same. S.F., Bacon & co., 1882. 255 p. port. C CHi CL CLSU CU-B NHi

12838. Williams, Fred V. The hop-heads; personal experiences among the users of "dope" in the San Francisco underworld... S.F., W.N. Brunt, print., 1920. 133 p. C CLU CSmH CU-B

12839. Williams, Henry B. vs. Sutton, O. P. ... Henry B. Williams, administrator, etc., of the estate of Edward Mott Robinson, deceased, plaintiff, vs. O. P. Sutton, defendant. Transcript on appeal. J. G. McCullough, John T. Doyle, attorneys for appellant. W. H. Patterson, Winans & Belknap, attorneys for respondent. S.F., Turnbull & Smith, law print., 1869. 54 p. CU-B

12840. Williams, Henry F. Opening address, delivered at the inauguration of the fair of Mechanics' institute of San Francisco, Cal. ... S.F., Whitton, Towne & co., 1857. 24 p. C CSfCW CSmH CU-B

12841. —— Reprint of the address...Also, a list of

officers and directors of the Mechanics' institute from 1855 to 1861, inclusive. [n.p., n.d.] 6 p.   CU-B

12842. —— Street pavements; as viewed by G. K. Fitch, on one side, & H. F. Williams, on the other. S.F., 1877. 30 p. "Reprint. from the *San Francisco bul.*, Dec. 15th, 1876."   C

12843. **Williams, James.** Life and adventures of James Williams, a fugitive slave, with a full description of the underground railroad. Sacramento, 1873. 48 p. Life in San Francisco and Sacramento.   CHi

12844. **Williams, Mary Floyd.** History of the San Francisco Committee of vigilance of 1851... Berkeley, Univ. of Calif. press, 1921. 543 p. ports. (Univ. of Calif. pub. in history... vol. XII) Bibliography: p. 476–518.
Available in many California libraries and CaBViPA IHi N NN NjR OU UU ViU

12845. **Williams, Samuel.** City of the Golden Gate, a description of San Francisco in 1875... S.F., Bk. club of Calif., 1921. 44 p. illus. "Printed by Edwin E. Grabhorn." "The text and illustrations are from *Scribner's monthly,* July, 1875."
C CHi CLSU CLU CLgA CMont CO CSf CSfP CSfU CSmH CStclU CU-B NN

12846. **Williamson, Robert Stockton, and Heuer, W. H.** Report upon the removal of Blossom rock, in San Francisco harbor, California... 1870. Published by the authority of the Secretary of war. Wash., D.C., Govt. print. off., 1871. 40 p., 11 pl.
C-S CHi CSf CSfCSM CSfCW CSfU CSmH CU-B MoS

12847. **Willis, Parker B.** The Federal reserve bank of San Francisco; a study in American central banking... N.Y., Columbia univ. press, 1937. 277 p. diagrs.   CSf

12848. **Willmarth, Arthur F.** The San Francisco primer... S.F., G.A. Brown, c1903. [27] p. illus.   C

12849. **Wills, Helen.** Fifteen-thirty; the story of a tennis player. N.Y., Scribner's, 1937. 311 p. illus., ports.   CHi

12850. **Willson, Robert H., and Hodel, George and Emilia.** Foreign nationalities in San Francisco... 110 l. Typew. The Willson series of articles appeared in the *San Francisco examiner* during November and December of 1923. The Hodel series appeared in the *San Francisco chronicle* from February to May 1932.   CSf

12851. **Wilmerding school of industrial arts.** Circular. [1900–01–1905, 1930–31] S.F. 2 v. illus.   CU-B

12852. **Wilson, Adrian.** Printing for theater. S.F. [A. Wilson] 1957. 57 p. illus. (part mounted, part in pocket)   CSto CU-B

12853. **Wilson, Carol (Green).** Alice Eastwood's wonderland; the adventures of a botanist. S.F., Calif. acad. of sciences [1955] 222 p. illus.
CHi CMont CP CRedl CSalCL CSf CSfCW CSmat CStmo

12854. —— Borrowed babies; the story of the Babies aid, an agency of the Community chest of San Francisco. [S.F.] 1939. [13] p.   CHi

12855. —— Chinatown quest; the life and adventures of Donaldina Cameron. Stanford, 1931. 263 p. illus.
Available in many California libraries and ODa

12856. —— Same. Rev. ed. Stanford [1950] 197 p. illus.   CBaB CBb CHi CRedCL CSS CSfSt

12857. —— Gump's treasure trade; a story of San Francisco. N.Y., Crowell, 1949. 288 p. illus., port.
Available in many libraries.

12858. **Wilson, Charles L., vs. Brannan, Samuel.** In the Supreme court of the state of California. Charles L. Wilson, appellant, vs. Samuel Brannan, respondent. Brief for appellant. Cook and Hittell, attorneys for appellant. S.F., Towne & Bacon, 1864. 34 p.   CHi

12859. **[Wilson, James]** A pamphlet relating to the claim of Señor Don José Y. Limantour, to four leagues of land in the county adjoining and near the city of San Francisco, California. Published by order of the claimant. S.F., Whitton, Towne & co., print., 1853. 78 p. Signed: James Wilson, attorney to J. Y. Limantour.
C CHi CLU CSfCW CSmH CU-B

12860. **Wilson, James Russel.** San Francisco's horror of earthquake and fire...eye witnesses... Phila., National pub. co. [c1906] 416 p. illus., ports.
C CHi CL CLU CLgA CSbr CSmH CU-B CaBViPA MoS N NN

12861. **Wilson, Katherine.** Golden Gate, the park of a thousand vistas... Caldwell, Ida., Caxton, 1947. 143 p. illus., map.
Available in many California libraries and ODa

12862. **Wilson, Neill Compton.** Behind your sugar bowl, the story of sugar in words and pictures... [S.F., The Calif. and Hawaiian sugar refining corp., c1936] 30 p. illus.   CHi

12863. —— Deep roots; the history of Blake, Moffitt & Towne, pioneers in paper since 1855. S.F., Priv. print. [Taylor and Taylor] 1955. 112 p. illus.
CBb CHi CSd CSdS CSf CSfWF-H

12864. —— Here is the Golden gate: its history, its romance and its derring-do. N.Y., Morrow, 1962. 244 p. illus.   CAla

12865. —— Southern Pacific, the roaring story of a fighting railroad. By Neill Compton Wilson and Frank J. Taylor. N.Y., McGraw-Hill [1952] 256 p. illus., ports., map (on lining papers).
CChiS CHi CLgA CRedCL CSdS CSf CSfP CStclU

12866. —— Treasure express; epic days of the Wells Fargo. N.Y., Macmillan, 1936. 322 p. illus., ports.
CChiS CHi CRcS CRedCL CSal CSf CSfCW CSfP CStmo CSto

12867. **Wilson, Roderick J.** Scum on the top, with an introduction by Helene Wilson and a preface by Guy W. Finney. Wash., D.C., Expose pub. [c1954] 417 p. facsims.   CU-B

12868. **Wilson, T. E.** Statistics of the San Francisco fire... [n.p., n.d.] 4 p.   C

12869. **Wilson & bro., firm.** ...Doors, windows, blinds, etc. S.F. [1895] 80 p. illus.   CHi

12870. **Wiltsee, Ernest Abram.** Gold rush steamers of the Pacific. S.F., Grabhorn, 1938. 367 p. illus., ports. Ships to California from 1848 to 1869.
C CBb CHi CL CLSU CLU CLgA CO CRcS CSd CSf CSfP CSfWF-H CSjC CSmat CSmH CStbS CStrJC CU-B

12871. **Winkler, John Kennedy.** W. R. Hearst, an American phenomenon... N.Y., Simon and Schuster, 1928. 354 p. illus., ports.   CHi CSlu

12872. —— William Randolph Hearst, a new appraisal. N.Y., Hastings house [1955] 325 p. illus.
C CSlu

12873. **Winn, Albert Maver.** Address... delivered before the Council, the eight-hour associations, and United mechanics, by request of their joint committee at Platt's hall, San Francisco, Friday evening, June 3d, 1870. [S.F.? 1870?] 16 p.   CHi

12874. Wirt, Sherwood Eliot. Crusade at the Golden gate. Foreword and keynote sermon by Billy Graham. N.Y., Harper, c1959. 176 p. illus., ports. A report on Billy Graham's evangelistic campaign in San Francisco, April 27–June 22, 1958. CL

12875. Wittemann, Adolph. The California midwinter international exposition in photogravure... N.Y., A. Wittemann; S.F., Jos. A. Hofmann, c1894. 1 v. (chiefly illus.) C CHi CLU CO CSf CSfWF-H CU-B

12876. —— Photo-gravures from recent negatives by the Albertype company. S.F., J.A. Hofmann, c1892. 51 pl. On cover: Select San Francisco. CHi CLU

12877. —— San Francisco album, 69 photo-views of the city and surroundings. N.Y. [188–?] 11 p. 69 photos. on fold. sheet. CSd CSmH CU-B NN

12878. —— San Francisco illustrated. Indelible photographs. N.Y., The Albertype co., c1892. 1 v. of illus. CLU

12879. —— Seal rocks, Cliff house and Sutro heights, in photo-gravure from recent negatives. N.Y., c1892. 16 pl. CU-B

12880. Wolcott, N. A., pub. "San Francisco street & business directory, 1894." 147 p. CSfWF-H

12881. [Wolfe, Wellington C.] comp. San Francisco the metropolis of western America... S.F., Mercantile illustrating co. [1899] 212 p. illus., ports. CL CSf CU-B

12882. Wolff, Hugo F. Das Erdbeben in San Francisco; eine schilderung der schreckenstage vom 18. bis 21. April 1906. Bearbeitet und illustrirt nach authentischen berichten. N.Y. [1906?] 63 p. illus., plans. CLU CU-B

12883. [Wolfskill, Ney] Catalogue of Netsukè; Ney Wolfskill loan collection. S.F., Japanese section, Golden Gate Park museum, 1916. 58 p. CHi

12884. Woman citizen league. Official programme Chinatown carnival... Given under the auspices of the Woman citizen league...Endorsed by the Chinese Six companies, Chinese chamber of commerce and the Chinese N.S.G.W. Aug. 21st to 29th, 1915. [S.F., 1915] [16] p. CLU

12885. Woman's congress association of the Pacific coast. Annual meeting, 1st– [1894?]– S.F., 1894–98.
CHi has 2d, 5th, 1895, 1898.

12886. —— Constitution and by-laws. S.F., Thos. J. Davis, 1894. 12 p. Organized 1893. CHi

12887. Woman's congress of missions of the Panama-Pacific international exposition, San Francisco, 1915. The Woman's congress of missions of the Panama-Pacific international exposition, First Congregational church, San Francisco, June 6–13, 1915, under the auspices of the Council of women for home missions and the Federation of woman's boards of foreign missions of the United States. [S.F.? 1915] 162 p. illus., ports. CU-B

12888. Woman's union mission to Chinese women and children. Annual report...1880, 1883. S.F., G. Spaulding & co., print., 1880–83. CU-B

12889. Women's educational and industrial union of San Francisco. Annual report, 1st–13th, 1888/1889–1901. S.F., C.A. Murdock & co., 1889–1901. Founded Oct. 27th, 1888. CHi

12890. —— Souvenir program of the historical carnival given...Monday, Sept. 21, 1896, at Native son's hall. [S.F., 1896] [24] p. illus., ports. CHi

12891. Wong, Mrs. Clemens. ...Chinatown... [S.F.? c1915] 38 p. illus., ports. CHi

12892. Wong, Everett. The exclusion movement and the Chinese community in San Francisco. [Berkeley, 1954] Thesis (M.A.)— Univ. of Calif., 1954. CU

12893. Wong, Jade Snow. Fifth Chinese daughter. Autobiography. With illus. by Kathryn Uhl. 1st ed. N.Y., Harper, c1950. 246 p. illus. CHi CLgA CRcS CSf MiD

12894. [Wood, Charles Erskine Scott] Chinatown. S.F., Quong, Chun & co. [19—?] [3] p. CSmH

12895. Wood, Will C. A memorial tribute to Dr. Frederick Burk, president, State teachers college, San Francisco, 1899 to 1924, delivered at the Greek theatre, Berkeley, California, Sunday, June five, nineteen twenty-five, by Will C. Wood, Superintendent of public instruction. [3] p. port. CHi

12896. Wood-Crane co. [Catalog] [S.F., Blair Murdock co., n.d.] 82 p. illus. CHi

12897. Woodbridge, John Marshall. Buildings of the bay area, a guide to the architecture of the San Francisco bay region. Comp. by John Marshall Woodbridge and Sally Byrne Woodbridge, sketches by Rai Yukio Okamoto. N.Y., Grove press, c1960. nnp. illus., maps. CAla CHi CSfP

12898. Woodin & Little, firm. [Catalogs—pumps, windmills, brass goods] S.F.
CHi has no. 14, 16, 23, 31, 38. CU-B has no. 34, 35.

12899. Woodruff, Charles A. The work of the California volunteers as seen by an Eastern volunteer. An address...Oct. 25th, 1893. [S.F.? C.W. Gordon, print., 1893?] 12 p. (Soc. of Calif. volunteers. War papers, no. 1.) CHi

12900. Woodruff co., firm. The Woodruff company, constructing engineers... [S.F.] c1906. 40 p. illus. CU-B

12901. Woodward, Robert B. et al. vs. Raum, Mary C. et al. ...Statement on motion for a new trial. [division by the heirs of the Woodward's gardens] Superior court. City and county of San Francisco... [S.F., 1891] 2 v. CU-B

12902. Woodward's gardens. Catalogue of pictures & statuary in the art galleries at Woodward's gardens, on Mission and Valencia streets, between 13th and 14th streets. S.F., Jos. Winterburn & co., 1870. 11 p. CHi

12903. —— Catalogue of the great collection in natural history of the Woodward's gardens, San Francisco, Calif., at auction commencing Thursday, April 6th, 1893 ... S.F., 1893. 20 p. C

12904. —— Illustrated guide and catalogue of Woodward's gardens, located on Mission St., between 13th and 15th Sts. S.F., Francis & Valentine, 1873. 62 p. illus. CU-B

12905. —— Same. S.F., Alta Calif. book and job print. house, 1875. 84 p. illus. CHi CLU CO CSf CSmH CStrJC CU-B

12906. —— Same, comp. by F. Gruber. S.F., Francis, Valentine & co., 1879. 87 p. illus., port. CLSU CSf CU-B

12907. —— Same. 1880. 87 p. CHi

12908. Woolley, Lell Hawley. California, 1849–1913; or, The rambling sketches and experiences of sixty-four years' residence in that state. Oakland, DeWitt & Snelling, 1913. 48 p. port. CChiS CHi CLSM CSd CSf CSfCW CSfP CWhC

12909. Woolworth (F. W.) co. A pictorial travelog of San Francisco, pioneer city of the west. S.F., The Print. corp., c1938. 32 p. illus., map.   CHi

12910. —— A trip through Golden Gate park... S.F., The Print. corp., c1937. 32 p. illus.
    CHi CLU CRcS

12911. Woon, Basil Dillon. San Francisco and the golden empire. N.Y., H. Smith & R. Haas, 1935. 407 p. illus., maps.
Available in many California libraries and MiD NN ODa

12912. [Worden, Willard E.] The Exposition site: San Francisco, 1915. [Album of photographs, postcards, etc. S.F., 1911?] 1 v. chiefly mounted illus.   CU-B

12913. Working woman's homestead association. [Advertisement of sale of lots of homestead property in San Francisco through purchase of shares] [S.F., 1869] 2 l.   CU-B

12914. Workingmen's party of California. Anti-Chinese council. Investigating committee. Chinatown declared a nuisance! ... [S.F., 1880] 16 p.
    C CHi CLM CLU CO CSmH CU-B

12915. Works, John Downey. San Francisco water supply; speech...in the Senate of the United States, Dec. 2 and 3, 1913. Wash., D.C., 1913. 96 p.   CU-B

12916. The world's wonder bridges! Golden Gate and San Francisco-Oakland bay bridges. [S.F., Print. by Wobbers [193–?] [32] p. chiefly illus.   CU-B

12917. Worrilow, William H. James Lick (1796–1876); pioneer and adventurer; his role in California history. N.Y., Newcomen soc. of England, Am. branch [print. by Princeton univ. press] 1949. 36 p. illus.
    C CBev CChiS CHi CLSU CLU CLgA CRic CSdS CSf CSfCW CSfP CSmat CSmH CStmo CU-B CoD

12918. Wozencraft, Oliver M. Address delivered before the Mechanics' institute on the subject of the Atlantic and Pacific rail-road, the policy of our government in reference to internal improvements. S.F., Agnew & Deffebach job print., 1856. 25 p.   CSmH CU-B

12919. Wright, Benjamin Cooper. San Francisco's ocean trade, past and future; a story of the deep water service of San Francisco, 1848 to 1911. Effect the Panama canal will have upon it. S.F., A. Carlisle & co., 1911. 212 p. illus.
    C CBb CHi CL CLU CLgA CMartC CO CSf CSfCP CSfP CSmH CU-B CaBViPA

12920. Wright, Cary Thomas. Some problems in the foreign commerce of the port of San Francisco. [Berkeley, 1911] Thesis (M.S.) — Univ. of Calif., 1911.
    CU

12921. Wright, Mary Kathleen, *Sister*. Fifty years of the Sisters of mercy in San Francisco 1904–1954. Wash., D.C., 1955. 126 p. Thesis (Ph.D.) — Catholic Univ. of America, 1955.   CSrD

12922. Wright, Stephen A. vs. Ross, Ann S. In the Supreme court of the state of California. Stephen A. Wright, executor, appellant, vs. Ann S. Ross, executrix, et al., respondents. Transcript of record, on appeal from the twelfth District court, city and county of San Francisco. John Reynolds, attorney for appellant. W. W. Stow, attorney for respondents. [S.F.? 1864?] 76 p.   CHi

12923. Writers' program. California. San Francisco, the bay and its cities... Sponsored by the city and county of San Francisco. N.Y., Hastings house, 1940. 531 p. illus., maps. (Am. guide ser.) "A selected reading list": p. 501–504.

Available in many California libraries and CaBViPA MiD MoSHi NN ODa

12924. —— —— Same, 2d ed., rev. ...N.Y., Hastings house, 1947. 531 p. illus., maps. (Am. guide ser.)
Available in many California libraries and CoU MiD MoS OrU T TxU UPB UU

12925. [Yale, Gregory] Opinion...as to the effect of the act of Congress...entitled, "An act relating to pilots and pilot regulations" upon the state law of the 4th of April, 1864, relating to pilots and pilot regulations for this port and harbor. [S.F., 1866?] 21 p. Signed: Gregory Yale.   CLU

12926. —— Opinion upon the constitutionality of the law of pilotage of the state of California. For the Pilot association of San Francisco. S.F., F. Eastman, print., 1858. 13 p.   CLU

12927. —— Some of the objections to the Parsons' bulkhead bill... by a member of the San Francisco bar ... S.F., Valentine & co., print., 1859. 7 p.   CU-B

12928. —— Same. S.F., Alta Calif. job print., 1860. 8 p.   CLU CU-B

12929. Yeates, Fred. The gentle giant. S.F., Bank of America, 1954. 80 p. port. Biography of A. P. Giannini.
    CHi CNa CU

12930. Yellow cab co. Annual report.
CHi has 1946, 1947. CL has 1949.

12931. Yellow jacket silver mining co. Annual report...for the year ending June 30th, 1879. S.F., Daily exchange pub. co., 1879. 16 p. maps.   CHi

12932. Yick Wo vs. Hopkins. In the Supreme court of the United States. October term, 1885. Yick Wo, plaintiff in error, v. Hopkins, sheriff, in error, to the Supreme court of California; Wo Lee, appellant, v. Hopkins, sheriff, on appeal from Circuit court, ninth circuit, district of California: authorities and argument for defendant and respondent...[n.p., 1886] 112 p.   CHi

12933. Yorke, Peter Christopher, *Father*. America and Ireland; an open letter to Mr. Garret W. McEnerney. S.F., Text book pub. co. [1918] 62 p.   CHi

12934. The Yorke-Wendte controversy. Letters on the Papal primacy and relations of church and state. By the Rev. Chas. W. Wendte and Rev. Peter C. Yorke. S.F., Monitor pub. co., 1896. 327 p. "The letters published in this volume appeared in two S.F. papers during the months of January and February, 1896." A famous local controversy in San Francisco.   CLgA

12935. Young, John Philip. Journalism in California [and] Pacific coast and exposition biographies. S.F., Chronicle pub. co. [1915] 362 p. illus., ports.
Available in many California libraries and CaBViPA N UHi

12936. Young co. Marine hardware, boat equipment, 1946 catalog... S.F., 1946. 224 p. illus.   CHi

12937. Young ladies' institute. Grand institute. Constitution and by-laws of the Young ladies' institute governing the Grand and subordinate institutes. Adopted April, 1888. S.F., 1888. 56 p.   CU-B

12938. —— History of the Young ladies' institute. [S.F., 1956] 51 p. front.   CSfU

12939. Young men's Christian associations. San Francisco. ... Annual report. 1st, 1853/54– S.F., Whitton & co., print. [etc.] 1854– Printer varies.
C has 4th, 6th, 18th, 32d, 36th, 40th, 42d, 45th, 50th. CBPac has 1st, 1853/54. CHi has 1st, 7th–8th, 14th, 37th–38th, 1853/54, 1860–61, 1867, 1889–90. CLU has 1855/56, 1857/58–1858/59, 1861/62, 1865/66–1866/67, 1868/

69, 1881/82, 1892/93. CSaT has 2d, 1854/55. CSf has 1st, 1853/54. CSmH has 3d–4th, 1855/56–1856/57. CSt has 1st, 1853/54. CU-B has 1st–8th, 10th–15th, 18th, 21st–22d, 30th, 32d–35th, 37th–[43d]. NN has 2d, 5th, 1854/55, 1857/58.

12940. —— —— Dedicatory services, Young Men's Christian association building, San Francisco, May 12, 1903... [S.F.? 1903] [8] p.   CHi

12941. —— —— Five decades, MDCCCLIII–MCMIII; historical record... S.F., 1903. 121 p. illus., ports.   C CHi CLU CO CSmH CU-B

12942. —— —— Laying of the cornerstone of the new building... northwest corner Golden Gate Avenue and Leavenworth Street, Tuesday afternoon, the fifth of October, nineteen hundred nine... [S.F., 1909] [15] p. illus., port.   CHi CSf CU-B

12943. —— —— Man power in wartime. [S.F., 1918?] 15 p. mounted illus.   CU-B

12944. —— —— Miscellany. [S.F., 1869–1931] 20 v. in 1.   CU-B

12945. Young men's democratic club of San Francisco. Constitution, by-laws and rules of order... S.F., Herald off., 1856. 8 p.   C CLU CU-B

12946. Young men's democratic league. Pamphlet no. 1. January 1889. Corruption and bribery in elections, by James D. Phelan. Ballot reform, by F. I. Vassault. S.F., Bacon & co., 1889. 24 p.   CHi

12947. Young men's institute. Directory...containing a complete list of the officers and members, together with their residences and occupations. S.F., D. Geary, pub., 1889. 144 p.   CU-B

12948. Young women's Christian association. San Francisco. ... Annual report... 1st, 1878– S.F., Spaulding, Barto & co., print. [etc.] 1878–
C has 1878, 1890–94, 1897–99, 1904, 1914. CHi has 1898–1900. CU-B has 1878–1880/81, 1887, 1889, 1904.

12949. —— —— Historical sketch of the San Francisco association, 1878–1953. [S.F.? 1953?] [124] p. Mimeo.   CHi

12950. Yuba construction co. The Yuba ball tread tractor... [S.F., 192–?] 24 p. illus.   CHi

12951. Yuba manufacturing co. Yuba dredges. [1926? 193–?] S.F. [1926? 193–?] 2 v. illus.   CU-B

12952. —— Yuba, world leader, placer mining dredges... S.F. [1948] 27 p. illus.   CHi

12953. Zakheim, Bernard, and Wrightson, Phyllis. California's medical story in fresco. An illustrated account of the fresco decorations on the walls of Toland Hall, University of California medical center, San Francisco. S.F., Priv. print., 1939. 24 p. illus.   CHi

12954. Zane, John P. Reply of John P. Zane and B. W. Mudge, United States appraisers at San Francisco, Cal., to statements and charges concerning the appraisers' department contained in a pamphlet by C.D. Cushman, deputy collector, entitled, "Appeal to Hon. S.P. Chase, Secretary of the treasury." S.F., Towne & Bacon, 1862. 78 p.   CHi

12955. Zarchin, Michael Moses, 1893– Glimpses of Jewish life in San Francisco: history of San Francisco: Jewry. S.F., distributed by the author [1952] 221 p. Includes bibliography.
CHi CLgA CSf CSfMI CSfSt CSfU

12956. Zeigler, Wilbur Gleason. Story of the earthquake and fire; illus. with nearly 100 half-tone engravings from photographs... S.F., Murdock press, c1906. [110] p. illus.

C CAla CHi CLSU CLgA CO COHN CRcS CRic CSf CSfCW CSfP CSj CSmH CU-B CaBViPA

12957. —— Same. S.F., L.C. Osteyee, c1906. [112] p. illus.   MoS NN

12958. Zeitska institute. Graduating exercises, 1880, 1885, 1886, 1887. S.F., 1880–1887. 4 v.   CHi

12959. [Zellerbach, Isadore] In fond remembrances herein are set down the words spoken by Rabbi Irving F. Reichert at the memorial service for Isadore Zellerbach at Temple Emanu-El, San Francisco, Friday, Aug. 8, 1941. ... S.F., Grabhorn press, 1941. 15 p. port.   CSf

12960. Zellerbach paper co. History and description of paper making... [n.p., c1925] 32 p. illus.   CHi

12961. Zelver, Leslie. Non-investment theater in San Francisco, 1914–1954. [L.A.] 1956. Thesis (M.A.)—U.C.L.A., 1956.   CLU

12962. Zinn, William H. Portraits on installments or at reduced prices for cash. [Price list, etc.] S.F. [189–?] 22 p.   CU-B

SAN JOAQUIN COUNTY
(Created in 1850)

COUNTY HISTORIES

12963. Gilbert, Frank T. History of San Joaquin county, California... Oakland, Thompson & West [1879] 142 p. illus., maps.
C CBb CHi CLSU CLU CLod CO CS CSf CSfCP CSmH CSto CU-B NHi

12964. Guinn, James Miller. History of the state of California and biographical record of San Joaquin county ... State history by J. M. Guinn... History of San Joaquin county by George H. Tinkham... L.A., Historic record co., 1909. 2 v. ports. "History of San Joaquin county": v.1, p. 259–303. v.1, p. 1–242 is reprinted from author's *History of the state of California and biographical record of the San Joaquin valley* published in 1905, but remainder of text is different.
C CBaK CHanK CHi CL CLAC CLO CLSU CLob CMa CMont CO CSf CSfCP CSfU CSj CSmH CStclU CSto CStoC CU-B CV CViCL

12965. An illustrated history of San Joaquin county, California... Chicago, Lewis, 1890. 666 p. illus., port.
C CFS CHi CL CLSU CLod CO CP CS CSf CSjC CSmH CSt CSto CStoC CU-B CoD IC NHi NN WHi

12966. Stockton school district. Social science committee. History of San Joaquin county and Stockton. [n.d.] 25 l. illus., maps. Mimeo.   CSto

12967. Tinkham, George Henry. History of San Joaquin county, California, with biographical sketches of the leading men and women... L.A., Historic record co., 1923. 1640 p. illus., ports.
C CCH CHanK CHi CL CLU CLod CMS CO CSS CSf CSmH CSoCL CSto CStoC CU-B ICN MWA MiD-B NIC WHi

12968. U.S. Works progress administration. History of Stockton and San Joaquin county... Stockton, 1938. [385] l. Typew.   CSto

GREAT REGISTER

12969. San Joaquin county. Index to the Great register of the county of San Joaquin. 1866– Place of publication and title vary.

C has 1867–69, 1871–73, 1875–77, 1880, 1882, 1884, 1888 (biennially to)–1962. CL has 1867, 1869 (suppl.), 1870, 1873, 1876–77, 1879 (suppl.), 1880, 1882, 1886, 1888, 1890. CLU has 1875. CSto has 1914. CU-B has 1867–68 (suppl.), 1872–73, 1879–80.

DIRECTORIES

12970. 1871/72. County directory publishing co., pub. San Joaquin county directory. Sacramento, Crocker, 1871. 323 p.   CLU CSto

12971. 1878. Berdine, D. H., pub. Statistical county directory of San Joaquin county... Also embracing a directory of the city of Stockton... Stockton, 1878. 254 p.   C CHi CLU CSf CSmH CSto CU-B

12972. 1881–1884/85. McKenney, L. M. & co., pub. Stockton city, San Joaquin, Stanislaus, Calaveras, Tuolumne and Contra Costa counties, directory...Title varies: 1881 City and county directory of San Joaquin, Stanislaus, Merced and Tuolumne...Also, an historical sketch of the cities and towns...
C CHi (1884/85) CSto NHi

12973. 1883. Smith, J. W. & co., pub. City and county directory of Stockton city and San Joaquin county, for 1883–4... S.F. [n.d.] 282 p. illus.
C CSto CU-B

12974. 1887/88. California publishing co., pub. Stockton city and San Joaquin directory... S.F. 374 p.
C CSmH CSto CU-B

12975. 1888–1938. Polk, R. L. & co., pub. Polk's Stockton city and San Joaquin county directory. Publisher varies: 1891–1902 F. M. Husted & co.; 1904–06 A. Kingsbury; 1907–30 Polk-Husted directory co. Content varies: 1891 includes Stanislaus and Merced counties; 1893 includes Stanislaus, Tuolumne and Calaveras counties. Continued as Polk's Stockton city directory.
C has 1891, 1893, 1902, 1904, 1907/08–1911, 1913–33, 1935–38. C-S has 1912. CHi has 1908/09, 1913, 1927, 1929. CL has 1918, 1920–22, 1926–28, 1931. CLod has 1904, 1910, 1925–38. CSmH has 1888. CSto has 1888, 1891, 1893, 1895, 1902, 1904–28, 1930–33, 1935–38. CU-B has 1920, 1930–33, 1935–36.

12976. 1900. Pacific coast advertising and directory co., pub. Directory of Stockton city [and Lodi] and San Joaquin county, 1900... 280 p. [112] p.
C CSto

12977. 1928/29–1932. Matthews, Muldowney, Lucas, pub. ... Directory of San Joaquin county (including incorporated cities, municipalities and RFD patrons). Publisher varies: 1928/29–1930/31 Humphreys & Matthews, inc.   C (1928/29) CSto

Stockton

12978. 1852. The Stockton directory and emigrant's guide to the Southern mines. Published semi-annually. Stockton, "San Joaquin republican" off., 1852. 140 p. map.   CHi (Photocopy) CLU CSmH

12979. 1856. Harris, Joseph & co., pub. Stockton city directory, for the year 1856... Together with a historical sketch of Stockton, by J. P. Bogardus. S.F., Print. by Whitton, Towne & co., Excelsior job off., 1856. 96 p.   C CHi CSmH CSto CU-B

12980. 1870/71. Hopkins, C. M. & co. The Stockton city directory, for the years 1870–71, containing ...a sketch of the city of Stockton—its past and present ...First annual issue. 1870. 208 p.   CSmH CSto

12981. 1873/74. Root & co., pub. Stockton city directory, for 1873–4. First annual issue. 1873. 169 p.
C CSto NHi

12982. 1876/77. Bishop, D. M. & co., comp. Bishop's Stockton directory...Stockton, B. C. Vandall, 1876. 266 p.   CHi CLod CSfCW CSto CU-B

12983. 1896/97. Valley directory co., pub. The Valley directory company's Stockton city directory for 1896–97. Stockton, 1897. 392 p.   CSto CU-B

12984. 1898/99. Colnon & Nunan. The Mail's Stockton city directory... 394 p. map.   C CSto

12985. 1900/01. Stockton city directory for 1900–1901... 294 p. map.   CSto NHi

12986. 1939– Polk, R. L. & co., pub. Polk's Stockton city directory. L.A., 1939– Content varies: 1939–56 Stockton and Lodi. Preceded by Polk's Stockton city and San Joaquin county directory.
C has 1939–1942/43, 1945/46–1947/48. CHi has 1941, 1947/48, 1949/50, 1952–53, 1955–61. CL has 1939–1942/43, 1945/46, 1949/50, 1952–53, 1955–58, 1960. CSmat has 1958–59. CSto has 1939–1942/43, 1945/46–1947/48, 1957. CU-B has 1939–40, 1949/50, 1953, 1956, 1958–59.

Other Cities and Towns

12987. 1949. Fisher, C. H., pub. Lodi city and district directory. [Stockton] 102 p.   CSto

12988. 1957– Polk, R. L. & co., pub. Polk's Lodi city directory, including Acampo, Galt, Lockeford, Victor, Woodbridge... L.A., 1957–
CHi has 1957, 1959–60. CL has 1957. CSmat has 1958–59. CSto has 1959 to date.

12989. 1950. Fisher, C. H., pub. Tracy city and district directory. [Stockton, 1950] 63 p.   CSto

12990. 1956– Polk, R. L. & co., pub. Polk's Tracy city directory.
CHi has 1956, 1959. CSto has 1956, 1959.

GENERAL REFERENCES

12991. Alexander, Barton Stone. Letter of General B. S. Alexander (U.S. Engineer corps) on the reclamation of swamp and overflowed lands in San Joaquin county. San Jose, Mercury steam print, 1876. 10 p.
CHi

12992. Bahnsen, Robert Henry. A half-century of Lockeford, California; a survey of its history and the contribution of its founder, Dean Jewett Locke. Stockton, 1953. 173 p. maps. Thesis (M.A.)—College of the Pacific, 1953.   CStoC

12993. Banta, Henry Comes. Ups and dowens of a ole Calafornaen; a biographical sketch. Stockton, San Joaquin pioneer & hist. soc., 1954. [6] p.
CHi CSto CStoC

12994. California coast range coal mining co. Prospectus [and by-laws] ...incorporated January 7th, 1856. S.F. [Sun job off., print., 1856] 12 p. fold. map. Located at Corral hollow, San Joaquin county.
C CHi CLU CU

12995. Central California; San Joaquin county... Stockton, Atwood, print. [1887?] 42 p. illus.   CU-B

12996. Central Pacific railroad co. vs. Cohen, Alfred A. In the district court of the twelfth judicial district of the state of California, in and for the city and county of San Francisco. The Central Pacific railroad company vs. Alfred A. Cohen. Answer. Alfred A. Cohen, attorney pro se. [n.p., 1876] 31 p.   CHi

12997. —— ...Argument of defendant on motion of plaintiff to strike out portions of defendant's answer. [n.p., 1876] 20 p.   CHi

12998. The counties San Joaquin and Tuolumne in California. Stockton, Stockton mail [1903?] 32 p. illus.
CSto CU-B

12999. Ellis, Wilson R. ...The resources of San Joaquin county... S.F., Bacon & co., 1886. 64 p. illus.
C CU-B

13000. Escalon tribune. Escalon, San Joaquin county, California. Irrigation—prosperity. 1914. [18] p. illus.
CSto

13001. Finkbohner, Agnes Steiny. History and landmarks of San Joaquin county. 1924. 10 [i.e. 9] p. Typew.
CSto

13002. Fiscus, Richard Bruce. A study and comparison of a city home and a country home of the 1890's in San Joaquin county, California. [Berkeley, 1952] Thesis (M.A.)—Univ. of Calif., 1952.
CU

13003. Fisher, C. E. San Joaquin county... Sunset mag. homeseekers bur. for the Bd. of supervisors... [S.F.? 1913?] 64 p. illus.
CHi CLU CU-B NN

13004. Gateway; a magazine of central California...no. 1–6 [1902?–1909] [Stockton, Chamber of commerce, [1902?–09] illus. Superseded by Annual report.
CLU (no. 1) CSmH (no. 1) CU-B (no. 1) NN (no. 2–5, 1905–09)

13005. Guida generale italiana della contea di San Joaquin; Calestini's Italian commercial and residential directory, Stockton, 1916. [Stockton, L. Calestini, 1915] 136 p.
CU-B

13006. —— Same, with title: San Joaquin county Italian guide and directory, 1928–1929... Stockton, Italian guide and directory [1929?]
CSto

13007. Hutchinson, Myron, vs. Perley, Frederick A. Supreme court, state of California. April term, 1853. Myron Hutchinson, appellant, vs. Frederick A. Perley, respondent. Respondent's brief. [S.F.] Herald off. [1853?] 20 p.
CLU CSmH

13008. Immigration association of California. [County scrapbooks] [S.F., 188–?]
C

13009. Kneedler, H. S. San Joaquin county, California... S.F., Sunset mag. homeseekers' bur. [1909?] 31 p. illus., maps.
CHi CL CU-B

13010. Leonard, H. R. Report of H. R. Leonard, engineer of the Mokelumne City and Woodbridge railroad. Stockton, Conley and Patrick, 1862. 21 p. fold. map.
C CHi CSmH CU-B

13011. McKenzie, Annie. Our county: San Joaquin. Lodi, Author, 1935. 140 p. maps. Mimeo.
CLod

13012. Northern San Joaquin county board of trade, Lodi. Plain reasons why homeseekers should purchase homes in the northern portion of San Joaquin county... Stockton, Daily independent print., 1887. 31 p. illus.
CU-B

13013. [Orr, Nelson M.] San Joaquin county, California... Stockton, Ruggles & Robinson, 1888. 80 p. illus.
CL CU-B

13014. Reynolds, Henrietta. Pioneers of sandplains in San Joaquin county, California. [n.p.] 1953. 78 p.
C CSto

13015. Ripon. Board of trade. A booklet about Ripon. L.A., Neuner co., 1913?] 20 p. illus.
CSto

13016. Robertson (Walter J.), mining engineer, Stockton. Catalog no. 17, from prospectors' headquarters; everything for the prospector. [Stockton, n.d.] 16 p.
CHi

13017. Sanford, Louis Childs. California's back yard. [n.p., 1950?] 231 p. Mimeo. History of the Episcopal church in the San Joaquin valley.
CSto

13018. San Joaquin county vs. Central Pacific railroad co. et als. ...Amended complaint...No. 359 in the Superior court of the city and county of San Francisco, state of California, department no. 7. Alfred A. Cohen, attorney for plaintiff. D. S. Terry, C. T. Botts, of counsel. [S.F.] Bacon & co. [1880] 103 p.
CSto

13019. —— The county of San Joaquin, plaintiff and appellant vs. the Central Pacific railroad co. et al. ...Transcript on appeal... [S.F.] G. Spaulding & co. [1882] 197 p.
CU-B

13020. —— ... Appellant's reply to respondents ... S.F., G. Spaulding & co., 1883. 20 p.
CU-B

13021. —— ...Brief for appellant... S.F., G. Spaulding & co., 1883. 52 p.
CU-B

13022. San Joaquin county. Associated chambers of commerce. San Joaquin county, the diversified producer. Stockton, 1935. 18 p. illus.
CHi CRcS

13023. —— **Board of supervisors.** San Joaquin county, California: for the farmer. [Stockton?] Sunset mag. homeseekers' bur. for the Bd. of supervisors [1915?] 78 p. map.
CHi CL CLU CU-B

13024. —— **Citizens.** Petition of citizens of San Joaquin county relative to navigation of San Joaquin river. [Sacramento, Gelwicks, state print., 1870]
CSmH

13025. —— **School districts.** San Joaquin county school districts, 1911–12. Stockton, Atwood print. co. [1911?] [17] p.
CHi

13026. San Joaquin county, California. Its favorable location, rich soil [etc., etc.] City of Stockton, its industries, trade, commercial importance, and business advantages. Stockton, J. E. Ruggles, 1887. 130 p. illus., map.
CLod CSmH NHi NN

13027. San Joaquin county, the garden spot of central California, a farmer's paradise. [Stockton, Independent print., n.d.] 16 p.
CSto

13028. San Joaquin genealogical society, Stockton. 1850 census of San Joaquin county, California. Stockton, 1959. 70 l. Mimeo.
C CHi CLod CSto

13029. —— Gold rush days; vital statistics copied from early newspapers of Stockton, 1850–1855. Stockton, 1958. 103 l.
C CChiS CHi CL CLod CSd CSto

13030. —— Old cemeteries of San Joaquin county, California. Stockton, 1960–64. 3 v.
CHi

13031. San Joaquin society of California pioneers, Stockton. Constitution and by-laws... Organized December 7, 1868. Incorporated September 30, 1873. Stockton, Daily independent print., 1884. 40 p.
CSmH

13032. —— Same. Revised April 29, 1893. Stockton, T.W. Hummel co. print., 1893. 56 p.
C CU-B

13033. San Joaquin, the "Gateway" county of California. At the entrance to two of the greatest valleys in the world—the Sacramento and the San Joaquin... S.F., Bolte & Braden co. [1911?]
CHi CU-B

13034. San Joaquin valley college, Woodbridge. The eighth annual catalogue of the officers and students ... Stockton, T.W. Hummel & co., 1887. 34 p. illus.
C CU-B

13035. Shepard, William Peacey. Life and works of John J. Sippy. [Portland, Ore.? American public health assoc., Western branch, John J. Sippy memorial committee, 1950?] 22 p. port.
C

13036. **Stockton. Chamber of commerce.** General soil conditions and crops of San Joaquin county, California. Stockton [n.d.] 10 p. map. (Its Bul., no. 101)
CU-B

13037. **Stockton commercial association.** Stockton and San Joaquin county illustrated... S.F., Trade & commerce pub. co., 1895. 145 p. illus., ports.
CSmH CSto CU-B

13038. —— Same, with title: The city of Stockton and the county of San Joaquin, state of California, a field for factories. [Stockton] 1897. 34 p. illus., maps.
CHi CSto

13039. **Tracy. Chamber of commerce.** Tracy, San Joaquin county... [1922] [8] p. illus.
CU-B

13040. —— **Diamond jubilee, 1953.** Tracy diamond jubilee, 1878 to 1953. Tracy [1953] 80 p. illus.
C CP CSf CSto CU-B

13041. **Wells, Andrew Jackson.** California's Netherlands; delta lands of the Stockton colonies. [Sunset, 1904?] 33 p. illus., map. "Reprint. from *Sunset* for March and April, 1904."
C CHi

Lodi

13042. **Fisher, C. E.** ...Lodi, California... S.F., Sunset homeseekers' bur. [1913?] 32 p. illus.
CU-B

13043. **Hicks, Warren Brauckman.** A history of Lodi, California from early times to 1906. Seminar paper, June 1954. [Stockton, College of the Pacific, 1954] 81 p. illus., maps.
CLod

13044. **Lodi. Board of trade.** A few facts concerning us; illustrated with camera and pen. Lodi, Lemoin & Fish [1908?] folder (36 p.)
CHi

13045. —— **Chamber of commerce.** Lodi district, California. [Lodi, 1948] [23] p. illus.
CHi

13046. —— **First Congregational church.** Seventy-five years in Lodi; a history of the First Congregational church of Lodi, California. Lodi, c1947. 142 p. illus.
CLod

13047. —— **First Methodist church.** A record of the First Methodist church of Lodi, California, 1853–1958, including the early history of the church in the surrounding area. [Lodi, 1958] 42 p. illus.
C CHi CLod CSto

13048. **Lodi news-sentinel.** Special anniversary ed. September, 1956. 75 years faithfully serving the Lodi district. Lodi, 1956. 1 v. unp. illus., ports.
CU-B

13049. **Nesbit, Freda Jahant.** Lodi, the home of the Mokelkos. Lodi, Author, 1960. 14 p. map. Mimeo.
CLod

13050. **Palmer, Lillian Bechthold.** Background history of the Reimche and Bechthold families. Stockton, Author, 1957. 2 v. tables.
CLod

13051. —— Descendants of George Konrad Reimche, 1822–1957. Stockton, 1957. 6 p., 23 fold. p. ports.
CSto

13052. —— Descendants of Heinrich Bechthold, 1836–1957. Stockton, 1957. 6 p., 12 fold. p. ports. CSto

13053. **Public administration service, Chicago.** City government of Lodi, California. Chicago, 1947. 49 p.
CSto

13054. **Wetmore, Ralph Morton.** Historical study of the public schools of Lodi, from 1852 to 1938. Stockton, 1957. 146 p. maps, tables. Thesis (M.A.)—College of the Pacific, 1957.
CLod CStoC

Stockton

13055. **Alexander, Barton Stone.** Reports...of the preliminary surveys, cost of construction, etc., of the Stockton ship canal, Stockton, Calif. Stockton, Independent print., 1874. 29 p. map. On cover: Published by the citizens' Board of trade.
CHi CU-B

13056. **Allin, Benjamin Casey.** Reaching for the sea. Bost., Meador pub. co. [1956] 294 p. pl. Mr. Allin was the engineer for the port of Stockton.
CSto

13057. **The Arcade, firm.** [Catalog of] mail order department, M. S. Arndt & co., prop. [Stockton? 1895?] 36 p. illus.
CHi

13058. **Ashurst oil land and development co.** [Descriptive brochure] [n.p., 1902] 8 p.
CHi

13059. **Bannister, Edward.** True greatness: an address delivered during the late examination of the University of the Pacific, at Santa Clara, California, June 8th, 1857... S.F., Whitton, Towne & co., 1857. 16 p.
CU-B

13060. **Belding, Lyman.** Autobiography. 49 p. Typew. A California gold rush pioneer who settled in Stockton.
CSto

13061. **Burns, Robert Edward.** The first half-century of the College of the Pacific. Stockton, 1946. 105 p. Thesis (M.A.)—College of the Pacific, 1946.
CStoC

13062. **Business and professional women's club.** History... 1919–1946/47, 1952/53–1953/54. Stockton [1945?–1954] 2 v.
CSto

13063. **California. State agricultural society.** Official report of the...fourth annual fair, cattle show and industrial exhibition, held at Stockton, September 29th, 30th, Oct. 1st and 2nd, 1857. S.F., O'Meara & Painter, 1858. 186 p.
C CHi CLSM CU-B WHi

13064. **[California navigation and improvement co.]** The steamers of the C.N. & I. co. ...San Francisco, Stockton and way landings... [n.p., n.d.] [16] p. illus.
CHi

13065. **Crockwell, & Williams, comp.** Stockton illustrated in photogravure from recent photographs by J. Pitcher Spooner... N.Y., Albertype co., c1894. [41] l. illus., port.
CHi CSto

13066. **Ferguson, Robert.** Benjamin Holt and the Holt manufacturing company of Stockton. 1940. 15 p. Typew.
CHi CSto CStoC (also 1945. illus.)

13067. **Fisher, Leigh, & associates.** Stockton field: air trade study, airport master plan, terminal requirements, schematic plans, design comments for the city of Stockton, Calif. [South Bend, Ind., 1955] 155 p. diagrs.
CSto

13068. **Freemasons. Stockton. San Joaquin lodge, no. 19.** One hundred years, 1852–1952; a centennial story... [Stockton, 1952] 59 p. illus. CHi CSto

13069. Glimpses of Stockton, 1904, views used in local geography work. 1904. 2 v. Bound mounted pictures.
CSto

13070. **Glody, Robert.** A shepherd of the far north; the story of William Francis Walsh, 1900–1930. S.F., Harr Wagner, 1934. 237 p. ports. CHi CRcS

13071. **Gray, Vallena Gifford (Woodward)** The early history of Stockton. [Berkeley] 1925. 84 l. illus., port., maps. Thesis (M.A.)—Univ. of Calif., 1925. CU

13072. **Gridley, Reuel Colt.** Tribute to the memory of... Stockton, 1883. 40 p.
CSto

13073. **Grunsky, Carl Albert Leopold.** Dear family; the story of the lives of Charles and Clotilde Grunsky, 1823–1891, as revealed in diaries and in their letters... [n.p., n.d.] Mimeo.   CHi

13074. Grunsky, Carl Ewald. Stockton boyhood; being the reminiscences of Carl Ewald Grunsky which cover the years from 1855 to 1877. Ed. by Clotilde Grunsky Taylor. [Berkeley?] Friends of the Bancroft lib., 1959. 134 p. illus., port.   C CBb CHi CLSM CLU CO CSd CSf CSfWF-H CTurS CU-B

13075. Hardeman, Nicholas Perkins. The historical background of the deepwater port at Stockton, California, 1850–1927. [Berkeley, 1950] Thesis (M.A.)— Univ. of Calif., 1950.   CU

13076. —— History of the inland seaport of Stockton, California. [Berkeley, 1953] Thesis (Ph.D.)—Univ. of Calif., 1953.   CU

13077. Hickinbotham, J. T., Stockton. ... Price list...wagon and carriage woodwork and hard wood lumber... Stockton, D.H. Berdine, 1877. folder (10 p.)   CHi

13078. Hickinbotham bros., ltd. One hundred years, 1852–1952. [Stockton, Atwood print co., 1952] 1 v. (chiefly illus.)   C CSf CSto

13079. Holden, Erastus D. Sketch of E. S. Holden, by his son. [n.d.] unp. Typew.   C

13080. Hollembeak, Jessie Ryan. A history of the public schools of Stockton, California... [Stockton?] 1909. 173 p.
C CLU CSalCL CSdS CSmH CSto CStoC CU-B

13081. Holt manufacturing co. [Catalogs of harvesting equipment] CHi has 1910, 1912.

13082. —— Caterpillar...75 tractor...[catalog] [S.F., Taylor & Taylor] c1917. [38] p. illus.   CHi

13083. —— Same. c1918. [36] p. illus.   CHi

13084. Huffman, Robert Eugene. Newspaper art in Stockton, 1850–1892... [Cleveland] Western reserve univ., 1955. 407 l. Typew.   CSto

13085. Hunt, Rockwell Dennis. History of the College of the Pacific, 1851–1951, written in commemoration of the one hundredth anniversary of its founding. Stockton, College of the Pacific, 1951. 226 p. illus., ports., plan.
C CArcHT CHi CLU CLgA CLod CMartC CO CP CSdS CSfCW CSto CStoC CU-B OrU

13086. Laurence, Elisha R. vs. Kilgore, J. N. et al. ...E. R. Laurence, plaintiff and respondent, vs. J. N. Kilgore, J. P. Massie, the Stockton savings and loan society, a corporation, John Doe and Richard Roe, defendants and appellants. Transcript on appeal. Appeal from judgment of the Superior court of San Joaquin county, California... Stockton, Record print [1907] 182 p. Suit for recovery of damages for alleged fraud in a real estate transaction.   CLU

13087. Luke, Thomas H. History of Benjamin Holt, "Inventor"; California built combined harvesters. 1929. 19 p. Typew.
CHi CSto CStoC (also 1945. illus.)

13088. MacDonald, David Ferguson. Address delivered before the Independent order of Odd fellows, of the city of Stockton, Cal. ...February 14, 1860, on the occasion of the eighth anniversary of the organization of Charity lodge, no. 6. Stockton, Conley & Patrick, print. [1860] 15 p.   CLU CU-B

13089. Mann, Hattie M. Landmarks and reminiscences of Stockton's early days. Clippings from a Stockton paper of Feb. 14, 1903.   CSto

13090. Martin, V. Covert. Stockton album, through the years. R. Coke Wood [and] Leon Bush, collaborators in writing the manuscript. [1st ed.] Stockton [Simard print. co.] 1959. 237 p. illus., ports., maps, facsims.
C CChiS CHi CL CLod CRedCL CSdS CSfSt CSto CStcrCL CU-B

13091. Odd fellows, Independent order of. Stockton lodge, no. 11. Constitution, by-laws and rules of order... S.F., Winterburn and co., 1869. CSmH

13092. —— Proceedings at the celebration of the fortieth anniversary of the introduction of Odd fellowship in the United States, held in the city of Stockton, Tuesday, April 26, 1859, including an oration delivered by P. G. Rep. Nathan Porter, of San Francisco. Stockton, 1859. 48 p.   C CHi CU-B

13093. Pagliarulo, Carol Maris. Basques in Stockton, a study of assimilation. Stockton, 1948. 66 p. illus., map. Thesis (M.A.)—College of the Pacific, 1948.
CStoC

13094. Renison, William Thomas. Afterglow; memoirs of a happy ministry, by William T. Renison and Clara Shepherd Reid-Renison. N.Y., Exposition press [1953] 121 p.   CSto

13095. Rogers, Fred Blackburn. Soldiers of the overland; being some account of the services of General Patrick Edward Conner & his volunteers in the old west ... S.F., Grabhorn, 1938. 290 p. illus., ports., fold. maps, facsim.
CHi CLO CRcS CSdS CSf CSto CYcCL

13096. Saluting Shaw's centennial. 100th anniversary, 1854–1954. [n.p.] 1954. p. 35–66. illus. A Stockton firm.
CSto

13097. San Joaquin pioneer and historical society. A handbook to the contents of the Louis Terah Haggin memorial galleries and San Joaquin pioneer historical museum. [1st ed.] 1931. 32 p.   CHi

13098. —— The historical collections of the museum in Stockton, California; San Joaquin pioneer museum and Haggin galleries operated by the San Joaquin pioneer and historical society. Stockton [n.d.] unp. illus.
CL

13099. Shaw, J. R. Benjamin Holt and the Holt family. 1936. 7 p. Typew. From *Americana* [mag.] July 1936, no. 3.   CSto CStoC

13100. Sterling pump works, inc. Sterling deep well turbine pumps manufactured by...1924. [n.p.] 1924. 24 p. illus.   CHi

13101. Stockton. Board of trade. City of Stockton; its position, climate...etc., together with a brief sketch of the great San Joaquin basin of California... compiled by N. M. Orr, secretary. Stockton, "Independent" print., 1874. 58 p.   C CHi CLU CSmH CU-B

13102. —— —— City of Stockton and its surroundings [etc., etc.] The great San Joaquin basin and its wonderful resources... Comp. by N. M. Orr, secretary. Stockton, Daily independent, 1883. 91 p.
CLod CSmH CU-B NN

13103. —— —— Stockton, San Joaquin county, California. "The land of promise" [S.F., Crocker, 1898?] 44 p. illus.   CHi

13104. —— **Chamber of commerce.** Facts about the port of Stockton, California. Stockton [n.d.] 6 p. maps.   CRcS

13105. —— —— Open waterways regulate rates of transportation. [Stockton, 1907] [11] p. illus., map.
CSto

13106. —— —— [Petition of] Stockton Chamber of commerce...to the Senate and House of representatives of the United States...[Concerning] an examination and survey of the San Joaquin river. Stockton, 1906. unp. illus., map.   **C**

13107. —— —— Stockton, California, as a factory location. [1929?] 56 l. Mimeo.   **CU-B**

13108. —— —— Stockton, San Joaquin county, California. Stockton [1912] 48 p.   **CSto NN**

13109. —— —— Same. [1960] [22] p. illus.   **CHi**

13110. —— **Charters, ordinances, etc.** Charter and ordinances of the city of Stockton. Compiled and published by authority of the City council, May 1908. Stockton, Stockton mail, print. [1908?] 299 p.   **CStoC**

13111. —— **City council.** Recommendations for harbor improvement at Stockton, California. [Submitted to the Stockton city council by S. J. Jubb. 1920] 17 l. charts. Typew.   **CSto**

13112. —— **City planning commission.** Decade of city planning 1929–1939... [Stockton] 1939. Reprinted from the *Stockton daily record*.   **CSto CStoC**

13113. —— **Fire dept.** History of the Stockton fire department, 1850–1908... Stockton, Atwood print. co. [1908] 136 p. illus., ports.
              C CHi CLU CU-B CaBViPA

13114. —— **First Presbyterian church.** Ninetieth anniversary, March 17, 1940, First Presbyterian church, Stockton, California... Stockton, Simard print. co. [1940] 35 p. illus., ports.   **C CU-B**

13115. —— —— One hundred years, 1850–1950 ...[by Marguerite Smythe] [Stockton, Simard print. co., n.d.] 34 p. illus.   **C CHi CSto**

13116. —— **St. Gertrude's church.** Souvenir program. Dedication of St. Gertrude's school and convent, Sunday, October 16, 1949. [Stockton? 1949] [56] p. illus., ports. "History of St. Gertrude's parish": p. [7–8]
                                                      CLgA

13117. —— **St. John's Episcopal church.** Historical sketch commemorative of the 75th anniversary of the organization of St. John's parish, August 25th, 1850. [Stockton, 1925] 47 p. illus.   **C CSto**

13118. —— **St. Mary's parish.** History of St. Mary's parish; submitted for consideration in the Charles N. Kirkbride contest for local historical research by Charles F. Finney. [n.p.] 1939. 31 l. Typew.   **CSto**

13119. —— **Stockton high school.** Alumni association. Roll of graduates...1870–1902. [Stockton, n.d.] 30 p.   **CSto CU-B**

13120. —— **University of the Pacific.** Alumni directory. Sept. 1922. San Jose, 1922.   **CU-B**

13121. —— —— Catalogue... 1854/55– S.F. [etc.] 1854–
C has 1854/55, 1861/62, 1873–91, 1900–08. CHi has 1873/74, 1889/90. CU-B has 1854/55, 1856/57–1864/66, 1873/74–1876/77, 1878/79, 1883/84, 1889/90, 1901/02.

13122. —— —— The College of the Pacific; [a scenic inspiration to educational heights] [Stockton, Rosensteel print. co., 1936] [12] p. pl.   **C**

13123. —— —— [Picture and description of building] [Stockton, Rosensteel & Julius, print., 1924?] 14 p.   **C**

13124. —— **Young ladies' seminary.** Young ladies' seminary, Stockton, Cal. [Prospectus] Stockton, Independent bk. and job presses, 1868. [4] p.   **CU-B**

13125. Stockton and Copperopolis railroad co. Engineer's report of a preliminary survey...with estimates of the cost and traffic, October, 1862. Stockton, Armor & Clayes print., 1862. 46 p. Printed signature: H. P. Handy, engineer.   **CLU CSmH CU-B**

13126. Stockton independent. Classified directory
...
CSto has 1921, 1923, 1925, 1936/37.

13127. —— Illustrated supplement containing articles on industries, agriculture, climate, etc., of Stockton and San Joaquin county. Stockton [1903?] 40 p. illus.
                                                      CSto

13128. —— Optimist edition. Stockton [Nov. 21, 1915] v.p. illus.   **C**

13129. —— Souvenir of Stockton; Daily independent's camera glimpses of San Joaquin county scenes; homes and industries of the thriving people of California's richest valley... Stockton, J.L. Phelps & co., 1900. 4 p. pl.   **C CSto**

13130. Stockton mail. [Annual supplement] 1893, 1894. Stockton, Colnon and Nunan. 2 v. in 1. illus.   **C**

13131. Stockton mining exchange board. Compact and by-laws... Organized October 17, 1863. Stockton, Daily independent job off., 1863. 16 p.   **CU-B**

13132. Stockton park homestead association. Prospectus, certificate of incorporation, and articles of association and by-laws... S.F., Franklin print. house, 1869. 17 p.   **CU-B**

13133. Stockton port district. California lore. Port of Stockton. [Stockton, n.d.] 48 p. illus. From *"Tideways"*   **CSto**

13134. Stockton typographical union, no. 56. Scale of prices [1913] Stockton, The Mail pub. co. [1914] 8 p.   **CHi**

13135. Stuart, Reginald R. Tully Knoles of Pacific; horseman, teacher, minister, college president, traveler, and public speaker. A biography by Reginald R. Stuart and Grace D. Stuart. Stockton, College of the Pacific, 1956. 145 p. illus., ports.
                            CHi CLU CP CSf CSto

13136. Swenson, Bert Edward. A history of the Stockton recreation department, 1910–1947, including its early backgrounds and the development of its program and facilities. Stockton, 1950. 212 p. illus., ports. Thesis (M.A.)—College of the Pacific, 1950.   **CSto CStoC**

13137. Swenson, Stella Spillner. History of San Joaquin county chapter, American Red Cross, Stockton, California, 1898 to 1946. [Stockton] 1946. 102, 15 p. Mimeo.   **CSto**

13138. Tinkham, George Henry. A history of Stockton from its organization up to the present time, including a sketch of San Joaquin county... S.F., W.M. Hinton & co., print., 1880. 391 p. illus., ports.
C CHi CL CLSU CLU CLgA CLod CP CRic CSd CSf CSmH CStrJC CU-B NHi NN

13139. —— Story of the San Joaquin court house. A chronology for the information of the citizens of San Joaquin county. [n.p., 1950?] Mimeo.   **CSto**

13140. Watson, W. S. Report on the Stockton and Copperopolis railroad; its location, cost of construction, and resources. S.F., Towne & Bacon, 1866. 35 p.
                                                  C CSmH

13141. Western harvester co. Selling the Holt... combined harvester. Stockton [1926] 137 p. illus., tables, diagrs.   **CHi**

13142. —— Same. [c1927] 162 p. illus.   **CHi**

13143. Wheaton, Donald Whitney. The career of David S. Terry. [Berkeley, 1921] Thesis (M.A.)—Univ. of Calif., 1921.   CU CU-B

13144. Wise, Harold F., associates. Railroads and planning in metropolitan Stockton; a report to the City of Stockton. Menlo Park, 1955. 100 l. maps, tables. Processed.   C CSto

13145. —— Urban blight in Stockton, California: nature of urban blight; blight factors in Stockton; urban renewal legislation. A report to the city of Stockton, California. Menlo Park, 1954. 41 l. maps, tables.   CSto

13146. Wood, James Earl. Short history of the Stockton public library. 1929. Typew.   CSto

13147. York's practical school, normal academy and business institute, Stockton. [Descriptive brochure] [n.p., 1893?–96?] [3] p.
CHi has [1893? 1896?]

SAN LUIS OBISPO COUNTY
(*Created in 1850*)
COUNTY HISTORIES

13148. Angel, Myron. History of San Luis Obispo county, California, with illustrations and biographical sketches... Oakland, Thompson & West, 1883. 391 p. illus., port.
C CBb CCH CHi CL CLO CLSM CLU CO CSf CSfCP CSfCW CSlu CSluCL CSmH CSt CU-B CoD CoU CtY ICN KHi NN WHi

13149. Ballard, Helen M., and others. History of San Luis Obispo county, state of California; its people and its resources. Senator Chris N. Jespersen, editor-in-chief; Harold McLean Meier, publisher...Audrey V. Kell, biographical editor. [L.A.?] 1939. 318 p. illus., ports. "Miss Helen M. Ballard was author of the narrative or historical section of the [book]."—Note from H. M. Meier.   CL CLU CSlu CSluCL

13150. Historical records survey. California. San Luis Obispo county (San Luis Obispo) S.F., Northern Calif. hist. records survey project, 1939. 524 p. map. (Inventory of the county archives of Calif., no. 41) Mimeo.
C CBb CHi CLCo CLO CLSM CLSU CLU CMary CMont CO COMC CSS CSf CSfCSM CSjC CSlu CSluCL CSmH CSrCL CU-B ICN MoS N NN WHi

13151. Morrison, Annie L. (Stringfellow), and Haydon, John H. History of San Luis Obispo county and environs, California, with biographical sketches... L.A., Historic record co., 1917. 1038 p. illus., ports.
C CCH CFS CHi CL CLCo CLU CO CSf CSlu CSluCL CSmH CU-B

GREAT REGISTER

13152. San Luis Obispo county. Index to the Great register of the county of San Luis Obispo. 1866– Place of publication and title vary.
C has 1867–68, 1871–73, 1875, 1877, 1879–80, 1886, 1890, 1892, 1898 (biennially to)—1962. CL has 1867, 1868 (suppl.), 1872–73, 1877, 1879, 1880 (biennially to)— 1888. CLU has 1875. CSmH has 1880. CU-B has July 1867, 1868 (suppl.), Aug. 1871, 1872–73, 1879–80, 1884, 1892, 1940.

DIRECTORIES

13153. 1875. Paulson, L. L., comp. and pub. Hand-book and directory of San Luis Obispo, Santa Barbara, Ventura, Kern, San Bernardino, Los Angeles and San Diego counties, with a list of the post-offices of the Pacific coast; Wells, Fargo & co.'s offices... S.F., Francis & Valentine, commercial steam presses, 1875. 534 p.   C CHi CL CSlu CSmH CStb

13154. 1911–1914. Los Angeles city directory co., pub. San Luis Obispo city and county directory ... L.A., 1911–1914.
CSlu has 1912, 1914. CSluCL has 1914.

13155. 1931/32– A to Z directory publishers. San Luis Obispo city and county directory... San Luis Obispo [c1931?–c1933?]
CL has 1931/32, 1933/34. CSlu has 1931/32, 1933/34. CSluCL has 1931/32, 1933/34.

13156. 1938–1939. Leon, Fred S., comp. San Luis Obispo city and county directory... S.F., California directories. Publisher varies: 1938 General directories, L.A.   CSlu (1938–39) CSluCL (1939)

13157. 1946/47. Casey, J. E., pub. San Luis Obispo county directory and business guide... Ventura, 1946.   CSlu

San Luis Obispo

13158. 1904. Griffith, C. W., pub. San Luis Obispo city directory. 1904. 43 p.   CSlu
13159. 1942. Pacific directory co., pub. ...San Luis Obispo city directory. Covina, c1941.   CSlu

13160. 1942– Polk, R. L. & co., comp. Polk's San Luis Obispo–Paso Robles city directory, including Arroyo Grande, Atascadero, Morro Bay and Pismo Beach. L.A., 1942– Content varies: 1950–53 includes San Luis Obispo county.
CHi has 1950, 1953–54, 1956, 1958, 1960. CL has 1950, 1953–54, 1956–57. CSlu has 1942, 1950, 1953–54, 1956–58. CSluCL has 1942, 1946–47, 1950, 1953–54, 1956–58.

GENERAL REFERENCES

13161. Angel, Myron. Climate and wealth of San Luis Obispo county, California... San Luis Obispo, Reasoner pub. co., 1898. 12 p. illus.   CSlu

13162. —— La piedra pintada. The painted rock of California, a legend... L.A., Grafton pub. co. [c1910] 102 p. illus.
C CL CLU CO CPom CRedl CSf CSlu CSluCL CSmH CU-B

13163. Arroyo Grande, San Luis Obispo county, California. On the line of the Pacific coast railway. The garden of the county... [S.F.] E.C. Hughes, print. [1886?] 7 p.   CLU

13164. [Atascadero] colony holding corp. Bulletins. no. 1–11. 1913–23.
C has no. 1–11. CSluCL has no. 1–7.

13165. Atascadero press, comp. and pub. Atascadero, California, "The beautiful," the long life town. [Atascadero, 1923]   CSmH

13166. California. State polytechnic college, San Luis Obispo. Architectural engineering dept. A master plan for Cambria, by the Cambria Master plan group. San Luis Obispo, 1956. 96 p. illus., maps.
CSluCL

13167. —— —— —— Pismo Beach planning study. San Luis Obispo, 1959. 134 p. illus., maps.
CSluCL

13168. —— —— —— A planning study of Avila. San Luis Obispo, 1955. unp. illus., fold. maps, charts.   CSluCL

13169. —— —— —— Planning study of the southern coastal section of San Luis Obispo county. San Luis Obispo, 1955. 53 p. fold. maps, charts.   CSluCL

13170. —— —— —— San Luis Obispo county recreation. San Luis Obispo [1955] 74 p. illus., maps.   CSluCL

13171. —— —— —— South bay planning study. San Luis Obispo, 1957. 169 p. illus., maps.   CSluCL

13172. Carlson, Oliver. Hearst, lord of San Simeon, by Oliver Carlson and Ernest Sutherland Bates. N.Y., Viking, 1936. 332 p. illus., ports., map, facsim.
CHi CLU CRcS CRedCL CSd CSfU CSlu

13173. Cooper, De Guy, comp. Resources of San Luis Obispo county, California... S.F., Bacon & co., 1875. 63 p.   C CU-B

13174. Courter, John P., jr. History of the San Miguel mission. San Luis Obispo, Black, 1905. 44 p. illus.   C CSlu

13175. Dana, Juan Francisco. The blond ranchero; memories of Juan Francisco Dana as told to Rocky Dana and Marie Harrington. L.A., Dawson [1960] 133 p. illus., ports., facsims. 500 copies...printed... by Westernlore press.   CHi CLSM CLom CSf CU-B

13176. Engelhardt, Zephyrin, *Father.* ...San Miguel Arcangel, the mission on the highway... Santa Barbara, Mission Santa Barbara, 1929. 92 p. illus. Includes music.
Available in many libraries.

13177. Freemasons. California. Grand Encampment, Paso Robles, 1903. San Luis Obispo county and its resources; official program...Oct. 5–9, 1903. [n.p.] 1903. [28] p. illus.   CHi

13178. Hapgood, Norman. The changing years; reminiscences... Illustrated with photography. N.Y., Farrar [c1930] 321 p. illus. Contains material on William Randolph Hearst.   CSlu

13179. Heaton, Guy E. Atascadero... Paso Robles, Author, 1914. 24 p.   CSmH

13180. International appraisal association. Survey of San Luis Obispo county. L.A., 1930. v.p. illus., maps, diagrs.   CSluCL

13181. Irvine, Leigh Hadley. San Luis Obispo county: its climate, scenery... San Luis Obispo county chamber of commerce... San Luis Obispo [Tribune print.] 1915. 46 p. illus.   CAla CU-B

13182. Iverson, Eva C. Mission San Miguel Arcangel. San Miguel, Franciscan fathers, old mission [1940?] 31 p. illus.   CHi CStmo

13183. Knott, Rachel Thayer. A Morro miscellany. [n.p., c1933] 55 p.   CU-B

13184. Lewis, Oscar. Fabulous San Simeon; a history of the Hearst castle, a California state monument located on the scenic coast of California, together with a guide to the treasures on display. Photos. by Philip Negus Frasse. S.F., Calif. hist. soc. [1958] 86 p. illus. Available in many libraries.

13185. List of property for sale in San Luis Obispo county and elsewhere. San Luis Obispo, C.H. Phillips & co. [1882] 22 p.   CLU NN

13186. Mental hygiene society of San Luis Obispo county. Directory of community resources of San Luis Obispo county, California. [San Luis Obispo, Blake print.] 1954. 25 p.   CSlu

13187. On the road to romance. Caledonia, historical old land mark of San Luis Obispo county, California. Souvenir edition. [n.p., n.d.] [19] p.   CHi

13188. Pacific coast land bureau, pub. ...San Luis Obispo county and its offerings for settlement. List of property for sale in San Luis Obispo county and elsewhere, with maps of the county and ranchos. [S.F., 188–] 19 p. fold. maps.   CLU

13189. Pujol, Domingo, vs. McKinlay, James et al. In the Supreme court of the state of California. Domingo Pujol, plaintiff and respondent, vs. James McKinlay et al. defendants and appellants. Brief for appellant McKinlay et al. [Solomon] Heydenfeldt, of counsel. S.F., M.D. Carr & co. [1870?] 17 p. Claim to Rancho Moro y Cayucas.   CHi

13190. Roberts, Charles H., ed. San Luis Obispo county, California, 1920...Issued by the Board of supervisors... [San Luis Obispo, 1920?] 34 p. illus.   CL CU-B

13191. Robinson, William Wilcox. The story of San Luis Obispo county. San Luis Obispo, Title insurance and trust co. [c1957] 55 p. illus., fold. map.
C CAla CHi CL CLO CLSM CLU CO CP CSd CSlu CSluCL CStbS CU-B CoD

13192. San Luis Obispo, Paso Robles, Atascadero. Chambers of commerce, ed. San Luis Obispo county. [San Luis Obispo, 1922] 39 p. illus., map.   CHi CL CSlu CSmH

13193. San Luis Obispo county. Board of trade. The resources and attractions of San Luis Obispo county ... San Luis Obispo, Tribune print co., 1887. 38 p.
C CHi CL CLU CU-B NHi

13194. —— Ordinances, etc. San Luis Obispo county ordinance code. Published by order of the Board of supervisors... Adopted 1958. [n.p., 1958] loose-leaf.   CSlu

13195. —— Planning commission. Amended master plan of shoreline development for San Luis Obispo county, California. San Luis Obispo, 1955. 32 p. illus., fold. maps.   CSluCL

13196. —— —— A master plan for Cambria. San Luis Obispo, 1956. 7 p.   CSluCL

13197. —— —— The population of San Luis Obispo county by statistical areas. Rev. ed. San Luis Obispo, 1959. 26 p. fold. maps.   CSluCL

13198. —— —— Proposed plan of harbor development. San Luis Obispo, 1956. 48 p.   CSluCL

13199. San Luis Obispo county telegram-tribune. S. L. O. central coast playground ed. Hearst Castle-San Simeon special ed. May 30, 1958. [San Luis Obispo] 1958. 32 p. illus.   CU-B

13200. San Luis Obispo tribune, pub. ...Industrial review of San Luis Obispo county, California... [San Luis Obispo, 1903] 34 p. illus., ports.   CSlu

13201. San Miguel homestead association. Articles of association and by-laws... Adopted September 21, 1865. S.F., J.E. Damon & co., print., 1865. 20 p.   CU-B

13202. Shinn, Charles Howard. Study of San Luis Obispo county, Calif. ... [San Luis Obispo, Bd. of trade, 1901] 16 p. illus. Reprint. from *Sunset mag.*, Sept. 1901.   CLU CSmH CU-B NIC

13203. Silliman, Benjamin. ...Report upon the oil property of the Pacific coast petroleum company, of New-York, situated in San Luis Obispo county. To which is added *Notes of survey and exploration in 1850 and 1857*, by Col. J. Williamson... N.Y., W.A. Wheeler, 1865. 24 p.   C CU-B

13204. Smith, Margarita Griggs. The San Simeon story; the romantic story of San Simeon, 1827–1958. Sketches by George Avery. 1st ed. San Luis Obispo, Star-reporter pub. co. [1958] 56 p. illus.

C CHi CL CSalCL CSd CSlu CViCL

13205. Southern Pacific co. U.S. Army maneuvers. Camp Atascadero, near Paso Robles hot springs, California, Sept., Oct. 1910. [n.p., 1910] folder (54 p.) illus., maps. CU-B

13206. Stanley, Hartwell B. 1797–1897. A souvenir history of the mission of San Miguel…commemorating the one hundredth anniversary of the founding of the mission. Celebrated at San Miguel, Cal., September 28–30, 1897. [S.F., Crocker, 1897] [16] p. illus., ports.

CLU

13207. Templeton. First Presbyterian church. Brief history, First Presbyterian church, Templeton, California. Forteith [sic] anniversary of its dedication, November 11, 1928. [n.p., 1928] 15 p. illus. CHi

13208. Wadsworth, Thomas S. El Pizmo Beach for pleasure and profit. L.A., Author, 1908. CSmH

13209. Waltz, Marcus L., pub. Chronicles of Cambria's pioneers… [n.p.] 1946. unp. illus. CSluCL

13210. Weeks, George F., ed. The Santa Ysabel hot springs, San Luis Obispo county… S.F., Crocker, 1889. 16 l. C CHi CO CSmH CU-B

13211. Wells, Andrew Jackson. San Luis Obispo county… S.F., Sunset mag. homeseekers' bur. [1910] 31 p. illus. CHi CL CSalCL CSmH CU-B

13212. West coast land co., Templeton. …West coast land co. … Descriptive catalogue and prices of the Paso Robles, Santa Ysabel, and Eureka ranches… San Luis Obispo, Tribune print co., 1886. 23 p.

C CSmH

13213. —— Same. 1887. 43 p.

CL CLU CU-B

13214. Western publishers, Atascadero. Atascadero, a home community, most picturesque spot in California. [Atascadero] 1926. 32 p. illus. CU-B

13215. White, Emil, ed. Full color guide to the fabulous Hearst castle; California state monument, located on scenic highway one, the Cabrillo highway, at San Simeon, California. [Photos by George T. C. Smith, and others] [Big Sur, 1958] 40 p. illus.

C CHi CL CLU CMont CRcS CRic CSS CSd CSto CU-B

13216. Zimmermann, William. A short and complete history of the San Miguel mission. [n.p.] 1890. 12 p. CU-B

Paso Robles

13217. [Cress, Kate C.] Through "the pass of the oaks". S.F., Overland monthly pub. co., 1893. 15 p. illus. Signed: Kate C. Kress. CLU

13218. Le Count bros., pub. …The celebrated El Paso de Robles hot sulphur springs and world renowned mud baths… [S.F., 1890?] 33 p. CSmH

13219. [MacDonald, Donald] Paso Robles hot springs. [Paso Robles, 1902?] 23 p. illus. CU-B

13220. Morrow, W. C. Roads round Paso Robles. S.F., Southern Pac. co., 1904. 30 p. illus. C

13221. Morse, E. Malcolm. Hot springs…water of the Paso Robles hot springs and comparison with the analyses of some of the most celebrated springs of Germany and the United States… S.F., A. Roman & co., 1869. 14 p. C CU-B

13222. —— A treatise on the hot sulphur springs of Paso de Robles…S.F., Eaton & Edwards, 1874. 38 p.

CU-B

13223. Paso Robles hot springs. A health and pleasure resort of the highest class. [S.F., Sunset pub. house, n.d.] 4 l. 19 pl. CSmH

13224. [Sawyer, Frank W.] Paso Robles hot springs…Paso Robles, California. [S.F., Sunset pub. house, 1910?] 51 p. illus. C CHi CU-B

San Luis Obispo

13225. Angel, Myron, comp. History of the California polytechnic school at San Luis Obispo, California … San Luis Obispo, Tribune print., 1908. 126 p. illus., port. C CLSM CLU CSlu CU-B

13226. Blomquist, Leonard Rudolph. A regional study of the changes in life and institutions in the San Luis Obispo district, 1830 to 1850… [Berkeley, 1943] 211 l. Thesis (M.A.)—Univ. of Calif., 1943. CU-B

13227. California. State polytechnic college. Catalog. Formerly California polytechnic school. CL has 1930 to date.

13228. —— —— First annual catalogue…May 1903. Sacramento, W.W. Shannon, state print., 1903. 16 p. illus. CHi

13229. California polytechnic school. California's twentieth century school; agriculture, mechanics, household arts. [San Luis Obispo? 1913?] [14] p. illus. CHi

13230. California tourist bureau, Los Angeles. San Luis hot sulphur springs, San Luis Obispo, California. L.A. [n.d.] [16] p. illus. CLU

13231. Daniels, Mark. Vancouver's "enchanting dale." [n.p., n.d.] [11] p. CU-B

13232. Engelhardt, Zephyrin, Father. …Mission San Luis Obispo in the valley of the bears… Santa Barbara, Mission Santa Barbara, 1933. 213 p. illus., ports., maps.

Available in many libraries.

13233. Knights of Columbus. San Luis Obispo council no. 1271. Fiftieth anniversary, council 1271. [San Luis Obispo, 1957] 24 p. illus., ports., facsims.

CU-B

13234. McGowan, Edward. The strange eventful history of Parker H. French…with introduction, notes and comments by Kenneth M. Johnson. L.A., Dawson, 1958. 63 p. illus., facsim. (Early California travel series, no. 43)

CHi CL CLO CLS CLSM CLgA CRedl CSd CSf CStmo CU-B

13235. Mitchell, Grace Therese. The story of Mission San Luis Obispo de Tolosa in the valley of the bears. Written especially for Father John Harnett… [n.p., n.d.] 16 p. illus., ports. CU-B

13236. San Luis Obispo vs. Pacific-Southwest. Before the Civil aeronautics board, Washington, D.C. … Exhibits of the city of San Luis Obispo in the Pacific-Southwest case, docket no. 5645, et al. William M. Houser, jr., city attorney, San Luis Obispo, California. [n.p., 1959] unp. illus., maps, tables. Mimeo. CSlu

13237. San Luis Obispo. Board of education. Report of the survey, San Luis Obispo city schools, May, 1959. c1959. 514 p. maps, tables. Mimeo. CSlu

13238. —— **Board of trade.** San Luis Obispo. [San Luis Obispo? 1903?] [16] p. illus. CU-B

13239. —— **Chamber of commerce.** Only one; San Luis Obispo on the mission trail. San Luis Obispo, 1950. 14 p. illus. CRcS

13240. —— —— Souvenir of San Luis Obispo, California. [San Luis Obispo, 1908?] [45] p. illus. CHi

13241. —— **Charters, ordinances, etc.** Charter and ordinances of the city of San Luis Obispo under the re-organization of February 13, 1884. San Luis Obispo, Tribune print. co., 1886.
CSlu (also March 11, 1891)

13242. —— —— Charter of the city of San Luis Obispo, 1910. [n.p.] 1911. 45 p. Other editions: as amended July 1941 and July 1951. Charter effective May 18, 1955. CSlu

13243. —— —— History, laws, and ordinances of the town of San Luis Obispo... San Luis Obispo, "Democratic standard" print., 1870. 41 p. CU-B

13244. —— —— San Luis Obispo municipal code, as adopted June 27, 1955... San Luis Obispo, Blake print. [1955] loose-leaf. CSlu CSluCL

13245. San Luis Obispo county telegram-tribune. Centurama, 100 years of progress: San Luis Obispo, 1856–1956. [San Luis Obispo, 1956] v.p. illus., ports., maps, facsims. C CSluCL CU-B

13246. San Luis Obispo daily telegram. San Luis Obispo, California. [1925] 79 p. illus. CSluCL

13247. San Luis Obispo tribune. The holiday tribune. Special edition... [Jan. 1, 1882] San Luis Obispo, Tribune print. co., 1882. 24 p. CU-B

13248. —— Souvenir railroad edition, May 5th, 1894. San Luis Obispo, 1894. 104 p. illus., ports. C CL CSlu CSmH CU-B

13249. Smith, A. M. San Luis hot sulphur springs, San Luis Obispo... [San Luis Obispo? 1903?] 32 p. illus. CHi CU-B

13250. Stone and Youngberg, municipal financing consultants. Financing report, Whale rock water project, city of San Luis Obispo. 1957. 23 p. Mimeo. CSlu CSluCL

13251. Tigner, J. H. Souvenir, San Luis Obispo fire department. L.A., 1904. illus., ports. CL CSlu CU-B

SAN MATEO COUNTY
(Created in 1856 from portion of San Francisco county; annexed portion of Santa Cruz county in 1868)

COUNTY HISTORIES

13252. Alexander, Philip W., and Hamm, Charles P. History of San Mateo county... and the biographies of its representative men... Burlingame, 1916. 204 p. illus., ports.
C CBu CHi CL CLU CLgA CO CRcS CSf CSfCW CSmH CSmat CU-B ICN

13253. Cloud, Roy W. History of San Mateo county, California... Chicago, Clarke, 1928. 2 v. illus.
C CBu CCH CHi CO CRcS CSbr CSf CSmH (v.1) CSmat CSmatC CStclU MWA NN

13254. —— Index to the "Chronology of County events" (items from early newspapers) as reproduced in the *History*... compiled at San Mateo junior college under the direction of Frank M. Stanger. San Mateo, 1939. 17 l. Mimeo. CRcS

13255. Ebert, Eleanor. An outline of the history of San Mateo county. [Redwood City, Standard print., n.d.] 7 p. CRcS

13256. Historical records survey. California. San Mateo county... S.F., Hist. records survey, 1938. 184 p. illus., maps. (Inventory of the county archives of Calif., no. 42)
C CBb CHi CLCo CLO CLSM CLSU CLU CMary CMont COMC CRcS CSalCL CSf CSmH CU-B ICN WHi

13257. History of San Mateo county, California... including its geography, topography, geology, climatography, and description... biographical sketches of representative men; etc., etc. ... S.F., B.F. Alley, 1883. 322 p. ports.
C CBu CHi CLU CLgA CRcS CSf CSfCP CSfCW CSmH CSmat CSt CU-B

13258. Johnson, Mary B. A brief history of San Mateo county; historical records survey, a WPA project. [n.p., n.d.] 12 p. Typew. CRcS

13259. Moore & DePue's illustrated history of San Mateo county, California, 1878. S.F., G.T. Brown & co., 1878. 44 p. 46–109 pl. map.
C CHi CRc CRcS CSfWF-H CSmat CU-B WHi

13260. Stanger, Frank Merriman. History of San Mateo county...narrative and biographical. San Mateo, Cawston, 1938. 425 p. illus., ports.
C CBu CHi CL CLCo CPa CRc CRcS CSf CSfCP CSmH CSmat CSmatC

13261. —— Peninsula community book (San Mateo county, California) ... San Mateo, Cawston, 1946. 406 p. illus., ports., map.
C CBu CFS CHi CL CO CPa CRc CRcS CRic CSbr CSf CSfCP CSmat CSmatC CU-B CtY NN

GREAT REGISTER

13262. San Mateo county. Index to the Great register of the county of San Mateo. 1866– Place of publication and title vary.
C has 1867–69, 1871–72, 1875–77, 1879–80, 1882, 1884, 1886, 1890 (biennially to)–1962. CHi has 1894. CL has 1867, 1868–69 (suppl.), 1872–73, 1876–77, 1879 (suppl.), 1880, 1882, 1886, 1888, 1890. CLU has 1875. CRcS has 1910–30, 1938–56, 1958. CSmH has 1872, 1888, 1892, 1894. CU-B has July 1867, 1867–68 (suppl.), 1868–69 (suppl.), Oct. 1872, Aug. 1873, Apr. 1879, Aug. 1879 (suppl.)

DIRECTORIES

13263. 1956– Polk, R. L. & co., pub. Polk's Burlingame city directory. L.A., 1956– Content varies: 1956–59 Burlingame, Burlingame Hills and Hillsborough.
CHi has 1958, 1961. CSmat has 1956 to date.

13264. 1957– Polk, R. L. & co., pub. Polk's Menlo Park city directory. S.F., 1957–
CHi has 1957. CSmat has 1959.

13265. 1909. Directory publishing co., pub. Redwood city directory... S.F., 1909. 88 p. C CU-B

13266. 1916/17. Price, William A., pub. Redwood City directory... including Atherton, Menlo Park and San Carlos. Redwood City [1916] CHi

13267. 1946– Polk, R. L., pub. Polk's Redwood City directory. S.F., 1946– Content varies: 1946 Redwood City, including Atherton, Belmont, Emerald Lake, Menlo Park, San Carlos and Woodside; 1950–53 Redwood City, including Atherton, Belmont, Menlo Park, San Carlos, and Redwood City rural routes; 1954–55 excludes Menlo Park.
C has 1953. CHi has 1946, 1950, 1953–1956/57, 1958, 1960/61–1962. CL has 1958. CSmat has 1958. CU-B has 1953, 1956/57.

13268. 1942. Reinecke, W. O., comp. San Bruno and Lomita Park directory. History of San Bruno: p. 86–93. CSbr

13269. 1950– Polk, R. L. & co., pub. Polk's San Bruno city directory. Content varies: 1950 includes San Bruno, Millbrae, Lomita Park, Baden Tract, Brentwood, Buri Buri, Country Club Park, Francisco Terrace and Southwood.
CHi has 1950, 1953, 1955, 1959. CL has 1950, 1953. CSbr has 1950, 1953, 1955, 1959. CSmat has 1959. CU-B has 1953.

13270. 1958– Polk, R. L. & co., pub. Polk's San Carlos...city directory... L.A., 1958– 1960 includes Belmont. CHi has 1958, 1960.

13271. 1907/08– Polk, R. L. & co., pub. San Mateo city directory including Hillsborough. Monterey Park, 1907– Publisher varies: 1907/08–1910/11? Directory publishing co.; 1924–54 Coast directory co. Content varies: 1907/08 San Mateo, Burlingame and Homestead; 1909/10 San Mateo and Burlingame; 1910/11 San Mateo, Burlingame, Belmont, Easton, Hillsborough, Beresford and San Carlos; 1924–54 Burlingame, Hillsborough and San Mateo; 1955 San Mateo, Burlingame, Hillsborough and Burlingame Hills; 1956 San Mateo, Hillsborough and Burlingame Hills.
C has 1909/10, 1924. C-S has 1910/11. CHi has 1907/08, 1940–41, 1948/49, 1951, 1955–1961/62. CL has 1954–55, 1957–58. CSmat has 1907/08, 1909 to date.

13272. 1914–1922. Burlingame publishing co., pub. Directory of San Mateo, Burlingame and Hillsborough. Burlingame, 1914–22. 1914, 1918 comp. by B. W. Wall; 1920 comp. by Willis L. Hall. Published for the Merchants' association of San Mateo and Burlingame.
CHi (1920) CSfCW (1920) CSmat (1914, 1918, 1920, 1922)

13273. 1907/08. South San Francisco directory publishing co., pub. South San Francisco city directory ...containing complete directory of all residents... CSf

GENERAL REFERENCES

13274. Anthony, Mark, vs. Clark, James S. In the Supreme court of the state of California. Mark Anthony et al., appellants, vs. James S. Clark, respondent. Transcript on appeal. B. S. Brooks, attorney for appellants. Pringle & Pringle, attorneys for respondent. [S.F.] Women's co-operative union print. [1870] 30 p. San Mateo county land suit. CLU

13275. Armsby, Leonora (Wood) Musicians talk... N.Y., Dial press, inc., 1935. 242 p. Author's reminiscences as manager of the Philharmonic society of San Mateo county.
C CBev CBu CChiS CHi CL CLS CO COHN CRcS CRedl CSd CSdS CSf CSfCW CSmat CSmH CSrD CStmo CU-B

13276. [Baldwin & Howell, San Francisco] [Filoli, home of the late Mr. and Mrs. Wm. B. Bourn in Canada valley, San Mateo county... S.F., Recorder press, n.d.] [8] p. illus. CHi

13277. Belmont. College of Notre Dame. Prospectus... [1st– 1852?– S.F. [1852?–
CHi has 1857, 1886/87, 1930. CU-B has 1886/87, 1903/04.

13278. Belmont school. Belmont school, its home and school life. [S.F., Murdock press, 1903] [32] p. illus. CHi

13279. —— [Catalog] 1885/86 S.F. [1885–
CHi has 1896/97, 1902/03, 1914/15, 1917/18. CU-B has 1885/86–1886/87, 1888/89, 1890/91–1891/92, 1893/94–1895/96, 1898/99–1900/01.

13280. Beresford country club, San Mateo. List of members, June 1, 1912. [n.p., 1912] [4] p. CHi

13281. Bohannon (David D.), organization. Bohannon industrial park, San Mateo county, California. [San Mateo, 1954] folder. illus., maps. CRcS

13282. Bonestell, Cutler L. A Woodside reminiscence, as told by Grizzly Ryder. S.F., Priv. pub. & print. by Paul Elder and co., 1920. 16 p. illus. CHi

13283. Cady, Theron G. Tales of the San Francisco peninsula. San Carlos, C-T pub., 1948. 38 p. illus., ports.
C CAla CBu CHi CLgA CO CPa CRcS CRic CSf CSfWF-H CStclU CU-B

13284. California vs. San Francisco and San Jose railroad co. In the Supreme court of the state of California. People of the state of California, respondent, vs. the San Francisco and San Jose railroad company, appellant. Appeal from the twelfth district court, San Mateo county. Brief on the part of the appellant, including an argument on the unconstitutionality of the state revenue laws. Chas. N. Fox, counsel for appellant. S.F., Towne & Bacon print., 1865. 42 p. CHi

13285. California. Board of tide land commissioners. ...Auction sale of salt marsh and tide lands in San Mateo county, belonging to the state of California. Commencing on Tuesday, Sept. 26, A.D. 1871...at Platt's hall, San Francisco. John Middleton, auctioneer. [S.F., 1871] CSmH

13286. —— Dept. of highways. An address to the people of San Mateo county in relation to roads by the Department of highways, prepared by commissioner John R. Price. [n.p., 1898] 16 p. C CHi

13287. —— Laws, statutes, etc. The San Mateo county reform bill...passed at the fifteenth session of the California legislature. Sacramento, State print. off., 1864. 39 p. CU-B

13288. —— Legislature. Senate. Judiciary committee. Report...on special legislation. [Sacramento, D. W. Gelwicks, state print., 1868] 5 p. Deals with construction of turnpike roads in San Mateo, Santa Clara, Santa Cruz and Lake counties. CSmH

13289. Clark, James S. vs. Anthony, Mark. In the Supreme court of the state of California. James S. Clark, appellant, vs. Mark Anthony, respondent. Statement of facts. B. S. Brooks, for respondent. S.F., Women's co-operative print. union, 1875. 11, 6 p. Deals with San Mateo county land suit. CLU

13290. —— ... Transcript on appeal. Edward J. Pringle, attorney for appellant, B. S. Brooks, attorney for respondents. S.F., W.P. Harrison, law print. [1874] 94 p. illus., plans. CLU

13291. Cline bros., San Francisco, general agents. Rockaway Beach, the playground for San Francisco on Ocean shore railroad. 1 l. illus., fold. plan with map. CHi

13292. Cohen, William Irwin. Fiscal problems of urban growth in San Mateo county, California. [Berkeley, 1957] Thesis (M.A.)—Univ. of Calif., 1957. CU

13293. Colma nurseries, Colma. Spring, 1895, carnations, chrysanthemums, pelargoniums, cannas, roses etc., grown and offered for sale by Grallert & co. ... S.F., Upton bros. print., 1895. 14 p. CHi

13294. Crego & Bowley. Catalogue of pure bred short-horn dairy cows, heifers and bulls; graded short-horn cows and heifers, thoroughbred and trotting mares, together with all the farming stock & implements of the late Jno. Cumming, of Twelve-mile farm, Baden station, San Mateo county. To be sold at public sale by Messrs. Crego & Bowley, on Thursday, Aug. 30, 1877. S.F., Francis & Valentine, 1877. 12 p.   CHi

13295. [Denver, James William] Reply to Mr. Janin's second brief in the Pulgas rancho case, on the bill now before the committee on private land claims in the House of representatives. [n.p., 1872?] 4 p. Signed: J. W. Denver, attorney for petitioners.   CLU

13296. Dougal, William H. Off for California; the letters, log and sketches of William H. Dougal...Ed. by Frank M. Stanger, with a foreword by Joseph A. Sullivan. Oakland, Biobooks, 1949. 62 p. illus. (Calif. centennial ed. no. 22)
Available in many libraries.

13297. Doyle, John Thomas. Statement and abstract of the title of John T. Doyle to a parcel of land in San Mateo county... [n.p., 1889] 8 p.   CLU

13298. Drake, Fred Hugh. The history of San Carlos, California, from Portola to first American. [San Carlos?] c1953. [12] p. illus., ports., maps.
                                                              CAla CRcS

13299. Estep, Russell A. History of Belmont. [3d ed.] Belmont, Chamber of commerce [1955] 8 p.
                                                                    CRcS
Other editions followed. CHi (1961) CSmat (1959)

13300. Eyre, Florence (Atherton). ...Reminiscences of Peninsula gardens from 1860 to 1890...Reminiscences of East bay gardens from 1860 to 1890 by Bell Mhoon Magee. [S.F.? 1933] [14] p.   CHi CU-B

13301. The Flood estate; yesterday and today. Palo Alto, Skyline pub., 1952. illus. (*Skyline*, the peninsula at a glance, v.2, no. 2, Feb. 1952, p. 22–32)   CRcS

13302. Freeman, Eleanor. Stories of San Mateo county, written for boys and girls... S.F., Harr Wagner, 1938. 248 p. illus., map.
                                   CBu CRcS CSbr CSfWF-H CSmat

13303. Garden club of America. Annual meeting ...April 23 to 26, 1935... [S.F., Taylor & Taylor, 1935] 67 p. map. Includes short histories and descriptions of residences and gardens in Hillsborough, Woodside, Atherton, and Piedmont.   CHi

13304. Guido, Francis Anthony. Electric railways in San Mateo county. A history of the "Forty line." [San Francisco to San Mateo] 1938. 19 p. Ms.   CSmat

13305. Half Moon Bay. Chamber of commerce. Half Moon Bay, California. Woodcuts by Galen Wolf. Half Moon Bay [n.p.] 14 p. maps.   CRcS

13306. Half Moon Bay development co. [Descriptive brochure] Manhattan Beach, Half Moon Bay, California. [n.p., n.d.] [4] l. illus.   CHi

13307. Heath, Elinor G. A bibliographical guide to the study of the Indians of the San Mateo peninsula; compiled for the San Mateo county historical society. Ed. by F. M. Stanger. San Mateo, 1935. 15 p. Mimeo.
                                                                   CSmat

13308. Hensley-Smith co., San Francisco. San Pedro terrace by-the-sea. [S.F., Bolte & Braden co., print., 1908] 19 p. illus.   CHi

13309. Hobart (W. S.), farm. Synopsis of Hobart farm trotting stock at auction in the city of New York, December 20 and 21, 1892. [Peter C. Kellogg & co., auctioneers] [N.Y., John Polhemus print. co., 1892] 7 p.
                                                                    CHi

13310. Houston, Robert Chester. San Mateo county government... [L.A.? 1939?] 244 l. Thesis (M.A.) —Stanford univ., 1938.
                    C CBu CL CLU CRcS CSmat CSt

13311. ———— Same. [Palo Alto, 1939] Mimeo.
                                                                   CU-B

13312. Hubbard, Elbert. Little journey to San Mateo county, California. East Aurora, N.Y., Roycroft shop, c1915. 24 p. illus.
      C CAla CBu CHi CLO CRcS CSbr CSf CSmH
CSmat CU-B CYcCL

13313. Jibby, Willa Delores Kent. Peninsula activities; a review of progress 1948...of Atherton, Woodside and Menlo Park. San Mateo, Author, 1948. illus.
                                                                   CRcS

13314. ———— Same. 1948–49. 1949. 14 p. Ms. index.
                                                                   CRcS

13315. Kalenborn, Mrs. A. S. Early lumber industry in San Mateo county; a paper read at the meeting of the San Mateo county historical association in San Mateo, October 19, 1944. 10 p. Typew.   CRcS

13316. League of women voters of San Mateo, comp. Portrait of San Mateo county; local government at work. [n.p., 1954] 60 p. maps, charts.   CHi

13317. Luna, Miguel R. History of San Mateo county cemeteries. 1938. Typew.   CSmat

13318. [Lux, Charles] Argument of D. M. Delmas, counsel for petitioner, in the proceeding to have Jesse Sheldon Potter removed as executor of the will of Charles Lux, made before the Hon. George H. Buck, Superior judge of San Mateo county, on Wednesday, December 11, 1895. [S.F., 1895?] 73 p.   CHi

13319. [Maynard, J. C.] New revelation. The title to the San Mateo rancho explained. Plates showing the true boundaries as defined by the Mexican government, and the fabricated boundaries, as claimed by the grantees. [n.p., n.d.] 50 p. maps.
Memorial to the Congress of the U.S.   CLU

13320. Molther, Francis Averill. A study of the San Mateo county-wide-master-plan project. [Berkeley, 1958] Thesis (M.A.)—Univ. of Calif., 1958.   CU

13321. Newcomb, Robert M. Some contrasts in the features of the physical landscape of the southern San Francisco peninsula, California. [L.A.] 1951. Thesis (M.A.)—U.C.L.A., 1951.   CLU

13322. Newton, L. C., comp. San Mateo county today and yesterday; a pictorial review of interesting spots in San Mateo county, California. [Redwood City, The Times-Gazette, 1927] [31] p. (chiefly illus.)
                                                            CSmat CU-B

13323. Okubo, Miné. Citizen 13660; drawings and text by Miné Okubo. N.Y., Columbia univ. press, 1946. 209 p. illus. Tanforan assembly center, San Bruno, Calif.
                                                                    CSd

13324. Ortega de Argüello, Soledad et al vs. Greer, John et al. In the Supreme court of the state of California. Soledad Ortega de Argüello et al., respondents, vs. John Greer et al., appellants. Brief on behalf of respondents. Sidney L. Johnson, attorney for respondent. [S.F.] Francis, Valentine & co., print. [18—] 43 p. Deals with the Pulgas rancho in San Mateo county.
                                                                    CLU

13325. Pacific bone coal and fertilizing co. Catalog...Established 1878. Incorporated 1890... [S.F.? 1906?] 32 p. illus.   CHi

13326. Pacific coast jockey club. Inaugural meeting, 1923. Tanforan race course. San Bruno, Worthington Gates, 1923. [34] p. illus., ports.   CHi CRcS

13327. Panama-Pacific international exposition. San Mateo county commission. Illustrated road book of automobile tours in San Mateo county, California. [S.F., Abbott press] c1915. 12 p. illus.   CHi

13328. Peninsula development league. Plan for the development of the San Francisco-San Mateo peninsula. [n.p., 1922?] 8 p. map.   CHi

13329. Peninsula farms co., Pescadero. Farms to feed the multitude... [S.F., Abbott press, 1924] 19 p. illus., map.   CHi

13330. Raybould, D. A. Peninsula polo annual; an illustrated record of the season of 1912–13 in San Mateo, Hillsborough and Burlingame. San Mateo, Charles Glendower Ellicott [1913?] 78 p.   CHi

13331. Reid, Julia (Reed) Services at the funeral of Mrs. William T. Reid, with a brief sketch of her life. [S.F.] Priv. print., 1917. 11 p. illus.   CHi

13332. Repass, Merle Marion. The Hermit mine. [Stanford univ.] 1923. 76 l. map. Thesis (Engineer) — Stanford univ., 1923.   CSt CU

13333. Roads to roam. Historic sites with map and descriptions. [n.p., n.d.]   CSmat

13334. Roussel, Victoria, comp. "Nuggets" from San Mateo county history. San Mateo. History and landmarks section, San Mateo county federation of women's clubs [n.d.] 3 p. Typew.   CRcS

13335. San Bruno. Volunteer fire company, no. 1. Souvenir program September 9th, 1909. [So. S.F.] 1909. [20] p.   CHi

13336. San Carlos. Chamber of commerce. San Carlos, California, on the San Francisco peninsula. San Carlos [1948?] folder (5 p.)   CRcS

13337. San Carlos park syndicate. San Carlos park. [S.F., 1907] 49 p. illus., fold. pl., fold. maps.   C CHi CU-B

13338. Sanchez adobe centennial 1846–1946; program of a merienda to be held under the auspices of the San Mateo county historical association, Saturday, October 12, 1946. [San Mateo] 1946. [4] p. illus.   CHi CRcS

13339. San Francisco art gallery. The priceless treasures removed from "Filoli," the palatial residence of the late W. B. Bourn, esq., Woodside, Calif. At auction ... [S.F., 1937] 34 p. illus.   CHi

13340. San Francisco bay toll-bridge co., San Mateo. San Mateo bridge; the fast motor route... San Mateo, San Mateo times print, 1938?] [6] p. maps.   CHi

13341. San Francisco bureau of governmental research. San Mateo-San Francisco survey. 1928. 196 p.   CSmat

13342. San Francisco peninsula co. A little journey to Hillsdale at San Carlos. S.F. [1914?] 15 p. illus.   C CRcS

13343. San Mateo. College of San Mateo. Master plan for higher education in San Mateo county. San Mateo, 1959. 6 l. map. Mimeo.   CRcS

13344. San Mateo and Santa Clara county agricultural assoc., no. 5. Premium list of the exhibition. 4th, 1884. San Jose [1884]   CU-B

13345. San Mateo, Burlingame, Belmont, Menlo Park and Palo Alto; showing some of the beautiful homes... [n.p.] 1904. 37 pl.   C CRcS CU-B

13346. San Mateo, California. 16 p. illus. Reprint. from *Out West*, Feb., 1902.   CHi

13347. San Mateo county vs. Southern Pacific railroad. In the Circuit court of the United States, ninth circuit: District of California. County of San Mateo, plaintiff, vs. the Southern Pacific railroad company, defendant. Oral argument of T. B. Bishop, for defendant. Garber, Thornton & Bishop, of counsel for defendant. S.F., Crocker [188–?] 45 p.   CLU

13348. San Mateo county. Board of supervisors. A century of progress; San Mateo county. Redwood City, 1956. 91 p. illus., maps.   CRcS CSmat CSmatC

13349. —— —— Welcome to San Mateo county and California's most perfect climate. Redwood City [1958] illus., map.   CRcS

13350. —— **Centennials committee.** San Mateo county, 1856–1956; official souvenir book. [San Mateo, 1956] 31 p. illus., map.   CHi CRcS CSmat

13351. —— **Chamber of commerce.** San Mateo county; the greatest flower producing center in California. Redwood City [1927?] folder (6 p.) illus., map.   CRcS

13352. —— **Charters.** Charter of the county of San Mateo, state of California. Redwood City, Standard print. co., 1933.   CRcS

13353. —— —— Same. 1945 edition. [San Mateo, San Mateo times print.] 1945. 36 p.   CRcS

13354. —— **Civil service commission.** First five years of civil service in San Mateo county, California. Redwood City, 1948. 23 p.   CRcS

13355. —— **Dept. of public health and safety.** That you may know what goes on "behind the scenes" in this department...protecting your health...providing a helping hand to those in need... Redwood City, 1951. 24 p.   CRcS

13356. —— **Dept. of publicity.** Peninsula passport. [San Mateo, San Mateo times print., 194–?] 12 p. map.   CRcS

13357. —— **Park and recreation dept.** Park and recreation guidebook for San Mateo county, California, 1952. Redwood City, Courthouse [1952] 26 p. illus., map.   CRcS

13358. —— **Planning commission.** Shoreline and recreation...text and layout, Josephine C. Nestor. Redwood City, 1947. 31 p. illus., maps.   CRcS

13359. —— —— The subdivision of land in San Mateo county... [Redwood City] 1932. 78 p. illus.   CLSU CRcS CStclU CU-B

13360. San Mateo county development association. San Mateo county, California; a brief and uncolored statement. [S.F.? 1914?] 32 p. illus., map.   CRcS CU-B

13361. —— San Mateo county, California; a wealth of western living for your industry. San Mateo [1958] 16 p. illus., maps, charts.   CRcS

13362. —— San Mateo story. San Mateo [n.d.] folder (4 p.)   CRcS

13363. San Mateo county historical association. The historic San Francisco peninsula; San Mateo county, California. [San Mateo? San Mateo county centennials committee, 1948] [8] p. illus., map.   CHi CRcS CSmat

13364. San Mateo leader. The Peninsula edition. San Mateo, 1908. 16 p. illus.   C

13365. —— Souvenir magazine of San Mateo county. 1904. [San Mateo, 1904] illus., maps.
CSmat CU-B

13366. **San Mateo times.** Souvenir fiesta edition, 2d annual San Mateo county fiesta, October 8–11, 1936. San Mateo, 1936. 106 p. illus., ports. 80th anniversary of San Mateo county.   C

13367. [**Schilling, August**] Portola hall: a description of the country estate of August Schilling... S.F., Leighton press [n.d.] 34 p. illus., map.   CSf

13368. —— Portola hall-hills. [S.F., Print. for August Schilling by Foster & Short, inc., 1926. 1 v. (pl.)
CHi CRcS CSf CU-B

13369. **Schussler, Hermann.** The locality of the Broderick-Terry duel on Sept. 13, 1859... S.F., Print. for Historic landmarks committee of Native sons of the golden West, by John Henry Nash, 1916. 25 p. port., maps.   C CHi CLO CSf CSfCW CSmH CU-B

13370. **Selby, Rodgers & co.** Map of Lomita Park on line of San Mateo electric cars, San Mateo county, California; a new suburb of San Francisco outside the fog belt and only forty-five minutes from fifth and Market streets. S.F. [1904] 4 p. fold. map.   CHi

13371. **Shinn, Charles Howard.** Down the San Mateo peninsula. [n.p., n.d.] [16] p. illus. Reprint from *Sunset mag.*   CHi

13372. **South San Francisco. Chamber of commerce.** South San Francisco, the industrial city. [S.F., Bruce Brough, n.d.] unp. illus.   C

13373. **Stindt, Fred A.** Peninsula service; a story of Southern Pacific commuter trains. [San Mateo, 1957] 40 p. illus., map. (*Western railroader,* v.20, no. 9, issue no. 213)   CHi CRcS

13374. **Thomas bros.** Popular atlas, San Mateo county...Oakland, 1956– illus., maps (part col.)
CPa has 1956, 1958.

13375. Title to the San Mateo rancho explained. Plats showing the true boundaries... [n.p., n.d.] 50 p. fold. map.   CHi

13376. **U.S. Board of commissioners of California land claims.** Argument in the case of Argüello and others, claiming Rancho de las Pulgas. Made before the board, July 18, 1853. By William Carey Jones, of counsel for claimants. S.F., G. Kerr & co., 1853. 56 p. Deals with land in San Mateo county.   C CSfCW CU-B

13377. —— **Circuit court (9th district)** The railroad tax case. County of San Mateo vs. Southern Pacific railroad co. Opinions of Justice Field and Judge Sawyer delivered in the U.S. Circuit court at San Francisco, September 25th 1882. [Printed from a revised and official copy] [n.p., 1882?] 85 p.   CLU

13378. **Urban land institute, Washington, D.C.** Findings, recommendations and record of proceedings of the industrial development study for San Mateo county, California. Wash., D.C., 1953.   CRcS

13379. **Wells, Andrew Jackson.** San Mateo county, California. [S.F., Sunset mag. homeseekers' bur., 1909] 32 p. illus., maps.   CHi CRcS CSf CU-B

13380. **Williams, Robert Luther.** Eighty years of subdivision design; an historical evaluation of land planning techniques in San Mateo county, California. [Berkeley, 1951] Thesis (M.A.)—Univ. of Calif., 1951.   CU

13381. **Wolf, Galen.** Coastland, a short story telling of the vistas and the doings of a pleasant land. [n.p., n.d.] 3 p.   CRcS

13382. **Wyatt, Roscoe D.** Days of the Dons. [Redwood City, San Mateo county title co., 1949] 58 p. illus., port. "Ranchos on the San Francisco peninsula": p. 28–58.
C CBu CHi CL CLO CLSU CLU CLod CO CPom CRc CRcS CRedl CRic CSf CSfWF-H CSj CSjC CSmH CU-B CV

13383. —— Historic names and places in San Mateo county... Centennial ed. [San Mateo] Pub. for San Mateo county hist. assoc., c1947. 35 p. illus., map.
CHi CO CRcS CSbr CSfWF-H CU-B

13384. —— Names and places of interest in San Mateo county with pronunciation, history and traditions ... Redwood City, Pub. by the San Mateo county title co., for San Mateo county hist. assoc., c1936. 30 p. illus., map.
C CHi CL CLU CO CRc CRcS CSmat CSmatC CU-B

Burlingame

13385. **Burlingame. Chamber of commerce.** Burlingame, California; San Francisco's sunshine suburb... Burlingame, 1928. 24 p. illus.   C CU-B

13386. —— —— Same. [1938?] [1945?]
CRcS

13387. —— —— Who's who in business in Burlingame, containing a classified business and telephone directory of the members...1924–25. [Burlingame, 1924?] 1 v. illus.   CU-B

13388. —— **First Methodist church.** A prospectus of the proposed First Methodist church, Burlingame, California. [n.p., 1923?] [4] p. illus., plans.   CHi

13389. **Burlingame country club.** By-laws, officers and members... [S.F., 1893?–]
CHi has 1903, 1909, 1913, 1920, 1922, 1926, 1931, 1934, 1937, 1940, 1947.

13390. —— Notes and highlights, 1893–1943 [fiftieth anniversary] [n.p., 1943?] 15 p.   CHi

13391. **Burlingame land co., San Mateo.** 184 lots at Burlingame, San Mateo county. S.F., Lyon & Hoag [n.d.]   CSmH

13392. **Chapman, Constance (Lister) comp.** History of Burlingame... pub. in San Mateo times, September 7 thru October 21, 1934.   C CRcS CSmat

13393. **Davis & Clifton, real estate agents, Burlingame.** Beautiful Ray Park in the city of Burlingame. [n.p., 1941?] [5] p. map.   CHi

13394. **East Millsdale industrial park.** S.F., Coldwell, Banker and co. [n.d.] 4 p. map.   CRcS

13395. **General Pacific.** Annual report.
CL has 1954–59.

13396. **Lyon & Hoag, real estate, San Francisco.** Burlingame; why you should buy Burlingame lots. S.F. [1920?] [5] p. map.   CHi

13397. **St. Matthew's military school.** Album, souvenir of St. Matthew's school. [S.F.? 18—?] 18 mounted photos.   CU-B

13398. —— Announcement, St. Matthew's school ... [San Mateo, 1892] [8] p. illus.   CHi

13399. —— The athletic and military features of St. Matthew's military school...thirty-fifth year, 1900. [S.F., Louis Roesch co., 1900] [15] p. illus.   CHi

13400. —— Catalogue. 1873/74– S.F., 1873–
CHi has 1874/75, 1879/80–1881/82, 1884/85–1885/86, 1889/90, 1902/03–1904/05, 1909/10, 1911/12, 1914/15. CU-B has 1873/74–1874/75, 1877/78, 1879/80–1880/81, 1882/83, 1884/85, 1887/88–1893/94, 1896/97–1897/98, 1899/1900–1904/05, 1906/07, 1911/12.

13401. —— Classical and military school for boys, St. Matthews hall. S.F., M. Weiss, print. [18—] 4 p. CU-B

13402. San Mateo county historical association. From suburb to city; 50 years in Burlingame... [Burlingame] 1958. 30 p. illus., ports. "Special ed. of *La Peninsula*, jl. of the San Mateo county hist. assoc. May, 1958." CHi CO

Menlo Park

13403. Bath, Gerald Horton. The school that parents built: Peninsula school, Menlo Park, California. [Menlo Park? 191–?] 15 p. CHi

13404. —— The story of Peninsula school, Menlo Park, California. [S.F., Taylor & Taylor, c1936] 15 p. CHi

13405. Brotherton (R. H.), San Francisco. Pierce tract, Menlo Park, San Mateo county, California... [n.p., n.d.] folder (7 p.) illus., map. CHi

13406. Consolidated freightways. Annual report. CL has 1956–60.

13407. —— [Brochure]. [n.p., c1959] [32] p. illus., ports. CHi

13408. Hoag and Lansdale, San Francisco, pubs. Stanford Park, Ringwood Park, Baywood Field, subdivision of the town of Menlo. [S.F., Sierra color-type co., print., n.d.] [26] p. map. CHi

13409. Howard, Lowry S. Lowry S. Howard, 1891–1949. [Menlo Park? Menlo school and college, 1949?] 10 p. port. CHi

13410. —— The story of Menlo, past, present, future, by Lowry S. Howard, president, Menlo school and junior college. [Menlo Park?] The school, 1931. 22 p. illus., ports., map. CHi CU-B

13411. Menlo and peninsula land co. Menlo Park, the beautiful. [S.F., Bolte & Brader co., 1907?] [16] p. (chiefly illus.) fold. map. The Coleman tract offered for sale by real estate firm of Innes, McWilliams & company. CHi CU-B

13412. Menlo Park fire district. Matt Harris club. Annual business directory and fire prevention manual. [n.p., 1936] unp. CHi

13413. Muhall, Charles W. Sunset: the history of a successful regional magazine. [Stanford] 1955. Thesis (M.A.)—Stanford univ., 1955. CSt

13414. [O'Day, Edward Francis] Lindenwood. [S.F., Recorder press, 1937] [12] p. illus. Photographs by Gabriel Moulin. CHi

13415. Peninsula school, ltd. [Brochure] [Menlo Park, 1960] [12] p. CHi

13416. —— [Calendar] CHi has 1938/39.

13417. Saint Patrick's seminary. Golden jubilee, 1898–1948. 125 p. illus., ports. (The *Patrician*. Jubilee ed., v.18, no. 4) CLgA

13418. Sherwood hall nurseries. Catalogue... Menlo Park, San Mateo county, California, 1892. [n.p., 1892?] 29 p. illus. CHi

13419. Sunset (magazine) The Sunset story. Menlo Park, Lane pub. co. c1951. [34] p. illus. CHi CRcS CStclU CU-B

Redwood City

13420. American trust co. Redwood City office, 2529 Broadway, opens October 19. [Redwood City] [1936] 3 p. illus., map. CRcS

13421. Ampex corp. Annual report. CL has 1959–60.

13422. California homes. [Redwood City issue, July 1936] [S.F.] 1936. 39 p. CRcS

13423. Canyon sanatorium. [Brochure] [n.p., 1931?] 16 p. CHi

13424. Chemical process co., Redwood City. Annual report. CL has 1954–60.

13425. —— History. Redwood City [n.d.] CL

13426. O'Connell, Daniel, ed. Views in Wellesley Park. S.F., Crocker [c1889] 16 l. col. illus. CHi

13427. Redwood City. Chamber of commerce. Redwood City; the county seat of San Mateo county, California. Redwood City, 1922. 18 p. illus., map. Other editions followed. Title and imprint vary. CHi (1926) CRcS (1922, 1936)

13428. —— City council. Port of Redwood City, link in the commerce of the seven seas. [Redwood City, Harbor sponsor committee, 1936?] 7 p. illus. CRcS

13429. —— First Congregational church. Centennial celebration, 1862–1962. Comp. by Charles L. Huyck. [Redwood City? 1962?] 24 p. illus., ports. CHi

13430. —— St. Peter's Episcopal church. The faith of our fathers, a cavalcade of Redwood City organized by Esther Barnes, commemorating the 75th anniversary of St. Peter's church 1864–1939. Redwood City, 1939. 27 p. CRcS

13431. Redwood City democrat. Redwood City woman's club. Special issue, v.1, no. 1, July 4, 1910. Redwood City, 1910. 23 p. illus., ports. C

13432. Redwood City times-gazette. [Special edition] April 9, 1959. CHi

13433. Redwood City tribune. Centennial edition, Dec. 7, 1951. CHi

13434. Sequoia hospital. Dedication...by grand officers, Native sons of the golden west, Sunday, October 15, 1950. [Redwood City, Star advertiser, 1950] 4 p. CRcS

13435. —— The Sequoia hospital story. Redwood City, 1950. 7 p. illus., ports. CRcS

San Mateo

13436. Baldwin & Howell, San Francisco. The Hayward addition to San Mateo. 92 business and residence lots... S.F., Stanley-Taylor co. [1904] [4] p. illus., map. CHi

13437. —— Hayward park. Location, climate, transportation... [San Mateo, W. H. Bull, c1907] folder (8 p.) illus., map. CHi

13438. Baywood park co. Baywood; home lots of pleasant size on the famous Parrott estate in San Mateo. [n.d.] [16] p. CHi CSf

13439. —— Baywood, knolls and vales of loveliness, being the former Parrott estate at San Mateo. S.F. [J.H. Nash] 1927. [18] p. mounted photos. CL

13440. Burke, Winifred M. San Mateo city elementary schools, a 100 year history, 1854–1957. San Mateo, City school district, 1958. 43 p. illus., maps. CRcS CSmat

13441. East San Mateo land co. vs. Southern Pacific railroad co. ...East San Mateo land company (a corporation) plaintiff and appellant, vs. Southern Pacific railroad company (a corporation) defendant and respondent. Answer of plaintiff appellant to respondent's petition for a hearing by the Supreme court, after decision by the District court of appeal, state of California, first appellate district, and numbered therein civ. no. 1733. Henry Conlin...attorney for plaintiff and appellant. [n.p., 1916] 58 p.   CU-B

13442. —— ...Henry Conlin (substituted in the place of East San Mateo land co., a corporation, original plaintiff herein), plaintiff-appellant, vs. Southern Pacific railroad company (a corporation) defendant-respondent. Appellant's reply brief. Henry Conlin, Charles W. Cobb, Joseph J. Bullock, attorneys for appellant... S.F., Rincon pub. co. print [1917] 17 p.   CU-B

13443. Foss, Werner C. L. History of Ravenswood. San Mateo, San Mateo junior college, 1942. 21 p. Typew. Bibliography.   CRcS

13444. Hamilton, Jerome. First story of the old San Mateo adobe-hospice. 1938. Ms.   CSmat

13445. Holt, Robert B. C. B. Polhemus, builder of San Mateo. 1938. 5 p. Ms.   CSmat

13446. Home protective association, San Mateo. Smoke nuisance of the proposed Baden smelter. [San Mateo, 1907] 12 p. illus., map.   CHi

13447. Johnstone, E. McD. San Mateo, Burlingame and Belmont. [1896?] illus.   CSmat

13448. Killip & co., auctioneers. Catalogue of short horned cattle, Hambletonian trotting and thoroughbred horses, the property of Stephen B. Whipple, esq., to be sold at public auction, Wednesday, June 11, '73...San Mateo... S.F., Francis & Valentine, 1873. 39 p.   CHi

13449. Laurel hall college. Calendar and register ... 1870/76- S.F., Cubery & co., print., 1875-
CHi (1870/76) CU-B (1870/76, 1888/89)

13450. San Mateo. College of San Mateo. Special bulletin of San Mateo junior college, issued on the occasion of its twenty-fifth anniversary [1922-1947] San Mateo, 1947. 66 p.   CRcS

13451. —— —— A survey of San Mateo junior college, San Mateo, Calif., by James D. MacConnell and William R. Odell. Stanford, 1953. 144 p. illus., maps.
CChiS

13452. —— —— ...Your community college in review 1956-1959... San Mateo, 1959. 16 p. illus., maps.
CRcS

13453. —— **St. Matthew's Episcopal church.** [History] 1864-1958. [n.p., 1958] [12] p.   CHi CSmat

13454. San Mateo county. Board of trade. Promotion committee. San Mateo, California, the floral city. [S.F., Crocker, 1909?] [16] p. illus., map.   CHi

13455. San Mateo county historical association. A list of exhibits and sources of information in the museum and archives of the San Mateo county historical association on the campus of San Mateo junior college... [San Mateo?] 1942. 22 l. Mimeo.   C

13456. —— Museum of the San Mateo county historical association, in conjunction with the college of San Mateo. [San Mateo? 1955?] [6] p. illus.   CHi

13457. San Mateo institute. Circular and...catalogue...1864/66-1866/67. S.F., Mining and scientific press print: [etc.] 1865-67. 2 v. in 1.   CU-B

13458. —— Prospectus...1864. S.F., B.F. Sterett print., 1863.   CHi CU-B

13459. [San Mateo stock farm] ...Catalogue of trotting stock at the San Mateo stock farm, the property of Wm. Corbitt, San Mateo (San Mateo county), California. [n.p.] 1892. 216 p.   CHi

SANTA BARBARA COUNTY
(Created in 1850)

COUNTY HISTORIES

13460. Gidney, Charles Montville. History of Santa Barbara, San Luis Obispo and Ventura counties, California... Chicago, Lewis, 1917. 2 v. illus., ports. v.2 biographical.
C CHi CL CLAC CLCM CSf CSfMI CSlu CSmH CStb CStbS CVtCL CtY NN

13461. Historical records survey. California. Title-line inventory of the county archives of California. Santa Barbara county. L.A., So. Calif. hist. records survey, 1941. 187 l. Mimeo.   C

13462. [Mason, Jesse D.] History of Santa Barbara county, California, with illustrations and biographical sketches... Oakland, Thompson & West, 1883. 477 p. illus., ports. Contains also *A History of Ventura county, Calif.*, p. 349-463.
C CCH CHi CL CLO CLSU CLU CSf CSfCP CSfCW CSmH CStb CStbS CU-B CVtCL NN NcU

13463. —— Same. Reproduction...with introduction by Walker A. Tompkins. Berkeley, Howell-North, 1961. 477 p. illus., ports.   CAla CHi CLSM

13464. O'Neill, Owen Hugh, ed. History of Santa Barbara county, state of California...Biographical editor: James Clement Reid... Historian: Marian [i.e. Marion] Parks. Santa Barbara, H.M. Meier, 1939. 415, 496 p. illus., ports., map.
CF CHi CL CLCo CLU CLom CP CStb CStbS CU-B CVtCL

13465. Phillips, Michael James. History of Santa Barbara county... Chicago, Clarke, 1927. 2 v. illus., ports.
C CCH CHi CL CLAC CLCM CLU CO CSf CSjC CSmH CSt CSta CStb CStoC MWA NN WHi

13466. Storke, Yda (Addis) A memorial and biographical history of the counties of Santa Barbara, San Luis Obispo and Ventura, California... Chicago, Lewis, 1891. 677 p. illus., ports.
C C-S CBb CBev CHi CL CLAC CLCo CLSU CLU CLom CP CSalCL CSf CSfU CSlu CSluCL CSmH CSt CStb CVtCL CYcCL CoD KHi MiD-B N NN TxU

GREAT REGISTER

13467. Santa Barbara county. Index to the Great register of the county of Santa Barbara. 1866- Place of publication and title vary.
C has 1875, 1877, 1879, 1890 (biennially to) -1962. CL has 1869 (suppl. 1-2), 1872-73, 1877, 1879, 1882, 1886, 1888, 1890. CSmH has 1877, 1879 (suppl.), 1882, 1884 (suppl.), 1886, 1888 (suppl.), 1890. CStb has 1918, 1932, 1936, 1940. CU-B has July 1867, Oct. 1868 (suppl. 1-2), Sept. 1872, Oct. 1872 (suppl.), Aug. 1873, 1879, 1936. CVtCL has 1936.

DIRECTORIES

13468. 1922- A to Z directory publishers, pub. Northern Santa Barbara county directory and guide book of Santa Maria valley. Santa Maria, 1922- Title varies.
CHi has 1945/46, 1947/48. CL has 1922-23, 1945/46, 1951/52. CLom has 1945/46.

Santa Barbara

13469. 1886. Independent publishing co., pub. ...New directory of the city of Santa Barbara...together with a new map of the city streets... [n.p.] 1886. 82 p. fold. map. CU-B

13470. 1894– Polk, R. L. & co., pub. Polk's Santa Barbara city directory. L.A., 1894– Title varies: 1894 Business directory and pocket guide of Santa Barbara; 1897/98 Santa Barbara city and county business directory; 1904 Dana Burks' Santa Barbara city directory; 1908/09–1914/15 Santa Barbara city and county directory. Publisher varies: 1894–189–? Pacific directory co.; 1897/98 D. F. Hunt; 1904–51 Santa Barbara directory co.

C has 1923, 1927, 1929–30, 1934, 1937, 1938. CHi has 1908/09, 1915/16, 1917/18, 1927–1929/30, 1934–36, 1938–41, 1946, 1948–49, 1951, 1953–60. CL has 1897/98, 1911/12, 1912/13, 1915/16, 1917/18–1918/19, 1920–21, 1923, 1926–28, 1929/30, 1931–32, 1934, 1936–37, 1939, 1941–46, 1948–49, 1951, 1953–57, 1959–60. CLU has 1894, 1921. CStb has 1895–1959. CU-B has 1939, 1941, 1953.

13471. 1916/17. Pacific coast publishing co., pub. Santa Barbara, Lompoc and Santa Maria city directory, Santa Barbara county, 1916/17. Santa Barbara [1916] CLom

Santa Maria

13472. 1958– Polk, R. L. & co., pub. Polk's Santa Maria-Lompoc city directory...including Guadalupe, Orcutt and Vandenberg villages. Content varies: 1958–60 Santa Maria, Lompoc, Guadalupe and Orcutt. CHi has 1958, 1961. CLom has 1958–60.

GENERAL REFERENCES

13473. Abbott, Mamie (Goulet) Santa Ines hermosa; the journal of the padre's niece. Illus. by Nicholas S. Firfires. [1st ed.] Santa Barbara, Sunwise press, 1951. 262 p. illus.
Available in many libraries.

13474. Baer, Kurt. The treasures of Mission Santa Inés: a history and catalog of the paintings, sculpture, and craft works. Fresno, Acad. of Calif. church history, 1956. 323 p. illus. Includes bibliography.
Available in many California libraries and UPB

13475. Benefield, Hattie (Stone) For the good of the country; por el bien del país [the life story, a photo album and the family tree of William Benjamin Foxen] Illus. by Patricia Benefield Williams. L.A., Morrison, c1951. 138 p. illus., ports., maps.
C CBb CChiS CHi CL CLSM CLU CO CSalCL CSd CSf CSluCL

13476. Blick, James Donald. The Carpenteria area. [L.A.] 1950. Thesis (M.A.)—U.C.L.A., 1950. CLU

13477. Blockman, L. E. The Santa Maria oil fields ... [Berkeley, 1942] 4 l. Typew. CU-B

13478. Brown, Wilson & co. Palmer oil company, Old mission oil company; properties located in the Santa Maria oil field, Santa Barbara county, California. S.F. [1905?] [28] p. illus. CU-B

13479. California. Dept. of natural resources. Div. of beaches and parks. Final summary report of investigations at the Jalama winery by William M. Harrison... Goleta, 1960. 30 p. illus., fold. maps. Processed. C

13480. —— —— —— Final summary report of investigations at La Purisima mission state historical monument, by William M. Harrison, research associate, Department of social science, University of California. Goleta, 1960. 10 p. Processed. C

13481. —— University. Santa Barbara. [Catalog]
CL has 1916 to date.

13482. California taxpayers' association, inc. ... Santa Barbara county report. An analysis of governmental organization and expenditures...for the fiscal year ending June 30, 1927...general study of the fiscal system for the ten-year period 1918 to 1927... [L.A.] 1929. 154 p. illus. CLSU CSfSt CU-B

13483. Calkins, James W. vs. Steinbach, Rudolph et al. In the Supreme court of the state of California. James W. Calkins, plaintiff and respondent, vs. Rudolph Steinbach et al., defendants and appellants. Transcript on appeal (from Superior court, county of Santa Barbara). B. S. Brooks, atty. for appellant R. Steinbach. Estee & Boalt, Paul R. Wright attys. for respondents... [S.F.] B. H. Daly, print. [1883] 102 p. Santa Barbara land suit. CLU

13484. Carlson, Vada F. This is our valley, compiled by the Santa Maria valley historical society. L.A., Westernlore press, 1959. 286 p. illus., ports., facsims.
C CAla CHi CL CLO CLSM CP CSd CSlu CStb CU-B

13485. [Carpinteria realty co.] Carpinteria valley, Santa Barbara county, California. [Carpinteria? n.d.] [8] p. CLU

13486. Cate, Curtis Wolsey. School days in California; the story of Santa Barbara school, 1910–1950... The fifth decade, 1950–1960, by Oliver Curtis Crawford. [Carpinteria, Cate school, 1961?] 199 p. illus., ports. CHi

13487. [Chittenden, Newton H.] ...The watering places, health and pleasure resorts of the Pacific coast... Santa Barbara county ed. Santa Barbara, Daily press, 1881. [68] p. CU-B

13488. —— Same, 2d ed. rev. & enl. S.F., C.A. Murdock & co., 1884. 311 p. C-S CVtCL

13489. Citizens' committee for Cachuma water. A water history and the Cachuma project. Part one: General water history, 1782–1949; part two: Proceedings relating to, and features of the Cachuma project, 1939–1949. [Santa Barbara, 1949] 70 p. illus. CHi CLU

13490. Conrad, Francis W. Geography of Santa Barbara county, for the use of teachers, schools, families and tourists... Santa Barbara, Independent bk. and job print., 1889. CSmH

13491. County of Santa Barbara, California. [Santa Barbara, Press of C. L. Donohoe 1904?] 49 p. illus. "Prepared under direction of...Louisiana purchase exposition commissioners for Santa Barbara county." CHi CLU

13492. Dart, Marguerite Mildred. The history of the Lompoc valley, California. [Berkeley, 1954] 169 l. illus., maps. Thesis (M.A.)—Univ. of Calif., 1954. CLom CU CU-B

13493. Davison, Grace Lyons. Beans for breakfast. Solvang, Santa Ynez valley news, 1956. 97 p. CStb

13494. —— The gates of memory; recollections of early Santa Ynez valley. [Solvang, Santa Ynez valley news, c1955] 101 p. illus., ports.
C CAla CHi CL CLSM CLU CLob CO CP CRic CSd CSf CSfWF-H CStb CStmo CU-B NN

13495. De la Guerra, Pablo and de la Guerra, Francisco vs. Sullivan, Eugene L. ...Pablo de la Guerra and Francisco de la Guerro [!] (executors of José de la Guerra y Norriega [!] deceased) vs. Eugene

L. Sullivan. Defendant's argument and demurrer. Eugene Liés, counsel for defendant. S.F., Women's union print., 1872. 12 p.   CU-B

13496. Engelhardt, Zephyrin, *Father.* Mission La Concepcion Purisima de Maria Santisima. Santa Barbara, Mission Santa Barbara, 1932. 131 p. illus., maps. Bound with his *Mission Santa Inez.*
Available in many California libraries and CaBViPA

13497. —— ...Mission Santa Inés, virgen y martir, and its ecclesiastical seminary... Santa Barbara, Mission Santa Barbara, 1932. 194 p. illus., ports., map.
Available in many libraries.

13498. Fernald, Charles. A county judge in Arcady; selected private papers of Charles Fernald, pioneer California jurist. Glendale, A.H. Clark co., 1954. 268 p. ports., facsims.
C CBaB CBb CHi CLO CLom CRic CSalCL CSd CSfSt CSluCL CStb CStbS CStmo CWhC

13499. Franciscans. Province of Santa Barbara. Book of historical dates of the province of Santa Barbara. Santa Barbara, 1945. 366 p.   CStclU

13500. Gidney, Charles Montville. About Santa Barbara county... [S.F., 1910?] 15 p. illus. From *Overland monthly,* Aug., 1901.   CU-B KHi

13501. Green, John L. vs. Swift, Jarvis. In the Supreme court of the state of California. John L. Green, appellant, vs. Jarvis Swift, respondent. Transcript on appeal. B. S. Brooks [and] Wm. Leviston, for appellant. Chas. E. Huse, for respondent. [S.F., 1873–76?] 2 v. in 1. Santa Barbara county land suit.   CLU

13502. Halterman, J. Fred. The impact of population growth in the south coastal area of Santa Barbara county as it affects governmental services. [Goleta] 1957. 94 l. tables, diagrs. Mimeo. Includes bibliographical footnotes.   C CLU CSfSt CSt CStb

13503. Heath, Ethel Moor. Guide to rides and drives in Santa Barbara and vicinity... S.F., C.A. Murdock & co., print. [c1894] 43 p. map.
CHi CSmH CU-B

13504. —— Same. rev. by W. W. Osborne. Santa Barbara, c1904. 49 p. map.
C CL CLSU CLU CSf CSmat CSmH CU-B NN

13505. Hiscock, Ira V. A survey of health and welfare activities in Santa Barbara county, California... [Santa Barbara, 1930] 129 p. maps.   CLSU

13506. The history of Lompoc. 6 p. Typew.   CLom

13507. Huse, Charles E. Diary of "Judge" Charles E. Huse...from June 14, 1850 to January 8, 1852 (San Francisco); and October 17, 1853 to September 1857 (Santa Barbara). Ed. by W. H. Ellison. Santa Barbara. Univ. of Calif., 1953. 2 v. in 1.
CStb CStbS (microfilm copy)

13508. —— Sketch of the history and resources of Santa Barbara, city and county. Santa Barbara, Off. of Daily press, 1876. 49 p.
CHi CLSU CSmH CU-B NHi PHi

13509. Immigration association of California. [County scrapbooks] [S.F., 188–?]   C

13510. Jackson, Abraham Willard. Barbariana; or, Scenery, climate, soils and social conditions of Santa Barbara city and county, California. S.F., C.A. Murdock & co., print., 1888. 48 p.
C CHi CLU CSmH CStb CU-B

13511. Janssens, Victor Eugene August. The life and adventures in California of Don Agustín Janssens, 1834–1856. Ed. by William H. Ellison and Francis F.

Price. San Marino, Huntington lib., 1953. 165 p. illus., port., map. (Huntington lib. pub.) Bibliography: p. 155–160.
Available in many California libraries and CaBViPA OrU TxU ViU

13512. Le Berthon, J. L., pub. Naples. [L.A., 190–?] 8 l.   CSmH

13513. Levick, M. B. Santa Barbara county, California. S.F., Sunset mag. homeseekers' bur. [1911?]   CU-B

13514. Lockwood, Charles A. Tragedy at Honda; by Charles A. Lockwood and Hans Christian Adamson. Phila., Chilton co. [c1960] 243 p.   CHi CSf

13515. Lompoc. La Purisima church. La Purisima parish; 50th year souvenir booklet. [Lompoc, 1961] 20 p.   CHi

13516. Lompoc valley Chamber of commerce. Colorful Lompoc, the capital of missileland. 1960. unp. illus., map.   CLom

13517. —— Lompoc valley, Santa Barbara county, California. [Lompoc? 1904?] 31 p. illus.   CU-B

13518. —— Historic La Purisima, Lompoc, Santa Barbara county, California. [Lompoc, Lompoc record print, 1935?] [11] p. illus. (part col.), plan. "Acknowledgment is made to the Lompoc Chamber of commerce, who made possible the publication of this booklet, to Miss Marion Parks, who supplied much of the historical narrative, to J. Donald Adam, who edited this edition, and to the National park service." Foreword.
CHi CLU CSmH CU-B

13519. —— Same. [Lompoc, 1950?] folder (4 p.) illus.   CHi

13520. Lompoc valley land co. By-laws of the Lompoc valley land co. Location: Santa Barbara county. Incorporated August 22d, 1874. S.F., J. Winterburn & co., bk. & job print., 1874. 14 p.   CU-B

13521. [Mann, F. A.] La Purísima Concepción missions at Lompoc, California. A historical memorial. [Lompoc? 1912?] 54 p.   CSmH

13522. Mikesell, Marvin W. The Santa Barbara area, California: a study of changing culture patterns prior to 1865. [L.A.] 1953. Thesis (M.A.)—U.C.L.A., 1953.   CLU

13523. Mink, James V. The Santa Ynez valley. [L.A.] 1949. Thesis (M.A.)—U.C.L.A., 1949.   CLU

13524. Moller, George, comp. Mollers guide to Santa Barbara county. 1952. 38 p. maps.   CStb

13525. Murphy, the enemy of Santa Barbara. His attempts at dismemberment of our county—his past record — his future designs. — Official documents. [Santa Barbara? 1877?]   CSmH

13526. Murray, Walter. Narrative of a California volunteer. [Berkeley] Bancroft lib., 1878. 212 [i.e. 215] l.   CStbS

13527. Naples improvement co., pub. ...Naples! A poetic realm! The coming city by the sea!... Descriptive catalogue... S.F. [1887]   CSmH

13528. Odyssey of the Santa Barbara kingdoms and 138 miles north. Monterey, Pac. coast Odyssey pub., c1960. 90 p. illus., maps.   CU-B

13529. O'Neill, Owen Hugh. [Map of Santa Barbara county, California, comp. by O. H. O'Neill, county engineer. [Santa Barbara?] 1938. map. Accompanied by table of county land grants.   CLU

13530. Packard, Albert. To the commissioner of the General land office, and the United States surveyor general, for the state of California. In the matter of the survey of the Rancho of Los Prietos y Najalayegua, under the provisions of an act of Congress passed June 22d, 1866. [By Albert Packard, attorney for the town of Santa Barbara. Santa Barbara, 1867?] 5 p.   CLSM

13531. Periera and Luckman, architects. Santa Barbara college community study, Goleta, California. Project report vol. 926, 1958. loose-leaf. Processed.
                                                              CStb

13532. Perkins, Joseph J. Business man's estimate of Santa Barbara county, California. Its climate, soils and products... Santa Barbara, Press steam bk. & job print. house, 1881. 32 p.   CHi CLU NN

13533. —— Same. 2d ed. 1884. 33 p.
                                   C CLU CSmH CU-B NHi

13534. Purísima Concepción mission. Annual fiesta. 1st, 1958?– El Modena, 1958?–
CU-B has 2d, 1959.

13535. —— ...Biennial reports [17–?]–1834... Berkeley, 1938. Typew.   CSf CU-B

13536. The Rancho San Cárlos de Jonata in Santa Barbara county. Chain of title and affidavits, correspondence of R. T. Buell, owner, with creditors 1883. Santa Barbara, 1883. [4] 117 p.   CLSM

13537. Rhodes, *Mrs.* James M. Recollections of a great grandmother. Santa Barbara, 1925.   CSmH

13538. Rogers, David Banks. Prehistoric man of the Santa Barbara coast... [Santa Barbara] Santa Barbara museum of natural history, 1929. 452 p. illus., maps. Available in many libraries and CaBViPA MoS TxU

13539. Sands, Frank. A pastoral prince; the history and reminiscences of J. W. Cooper. Santa Barbara, Author, 1893. 190 p. illus. Reminiscences of Cooper, who came to California from Missouri in 1850. In 1863 settled in Lompoc valley, and became a raiser of sheep.
                                   CHi CLom CLSM

13540. Santa Barbara. Chamber of commerce. The city and county of Santa Barbara, California. [Santa Barbara 1902] 51 p. illus.   CU-B

13541. —— —— The city and valley of Santa Barbara... [Santa Barbara, Press of W.H. Arnc, 1904] 30 p. illus.   CHi CLU CU-B

13542. —— —— Same. [Santa Barbara, Donohoe print co., 1905?] 31 p. illus.   CHi CU-B

13543. —— —— Resources of Santa Barbara county, California... Santa Barbara, C.L. Donohoe, print., 1901. 119 p. illus.   CLU CSmH CU-B

13544. Santa Barbara county. Description of precincts of Santa Barbara county, California, 1936. [Santa Barbara] Schauer print. studio, inc. [1936?] 54 p.
                                                              CU-B

13545. —— **Board of forestry.** Santa Barbara county parks... [Santa Barbara, 1930] [30] p. illus.
                                                              CU-B

13546. —— **Board of supervisors.** The Santa Barbara county court house. [Santa Barbara, Schauer print. studio] 1929. [24] p. illus., plan.
                                   C CHi CStclU

13547. —— **Chamber of commerce.** Report of the special committee of the Chamber of commerce of Santa Barbara county in the matter of the Santa Barbara-Bakersfield railroad. [n.p.] July 16, 1909. 20 p.
                                                              CSmH

13548. —— —— Santa Barbara co., California. Santa Barbara, Pac. coast pub. co. [1907?] folder (32 p.) illus.   CU-B

13549. —— —— Santa Barbara: devoted to the attractions and advantages of the city and valley of Santa Barbara, California. Santa Barbara [1915?] 48 p.   NN

13550. —— **Planning commission.** The master plan of county roads and highways... Santa Barbara, 1938. 34 p. maps, charts.   CHi

13551. —— —— The master shoreline plan of Santa Barbara county, California. [n.d.] 27 p. Mimeo.
                                                              CStb

13552. Santa Barbara school. Santa Barbara school, Carpinteria, California. [n.p.] 1938. 31 p.   CHi

13553. Santa Maria. Chamber of commerce. Santa Maria valley; Santa Barbara county, California. Santa Maria [n.d.] unp. illus.   CSf

13554. Santa Maria kolonie. Prospectus...in sued Californien umfassend 7852 acker bohnen-, weizen-, zucker-rüben-, getreide, obst-und weide-land... [S.F., 1897] 8 l.   CSmH

13555. Santa Ynez land and improvement co. Santa Ynez valley, Santa Barbara county, California. S.F., Britton & Rey [188–?] 8 p.   C CHi CSmH CU-B

13556. Santa Ynez valley news. Santa Ynez valley, the geographical and agricultural center of Santa Barbara county. [Solvang, 1947?] [20] p. illus., map.
                                                              CU-B

13557. —— Solvang and the beautiful Santa Ynez valley, California. Solvang [n.d.] folder.   CRcS

13558. Selover, Frank M. Santa Barbara county... Published by the Santa Barbara county commission, Panama-Pacific international exposition, 1915. 32 p.
                                   CHi CU-B NN

13559. Silliman, Benjamin. ...Report upon the oil property of the Philadelphia and California petroleum company of Philadelphia, situated in Santa Barbara and Los Angeles counties...to which are added extracts from field notes...in 1850 and 1857 by Col. J. Williamson... Phila., E.C. Markley & son, 1865. 31 p.   CHi

13560. Spaulding, Edward Seldon. Adobe days along the channel. [Santa Barbara, Schauer print. studio] 1957. 124 p. illus. (part. col.) map.
C CHi CL CLSM CLU CLob CO CP CPom CSd CSfSt CSluCL CStb CStbS CStmo CU-B

13561. Stockton, Georgia. La Carpinteria. Carpinteria, Carpinteria hist. soc., 1960. 154 p. illus.
                                   CHi CLSM

13562. Stuart, James Ferguson. Appeal and argument in survey of Rancho Mission de la Purisima. James F. Stuart, attorney for settlers. S.F., Bacon & co., 1881. [51] p. 2 fold. maps.   CLU

13563. Tompkins, Walker A. Santa Barbara's royal rancho; the fabulous history of Los Dos Pueblos. Berkeley, Howell-North, 1960. 282 p. illus., ports., map (on lining papers).
CAla CHi CLSM CLom CSfMI CU-B

13564. United States vs. Covarrubias, J. M. et al. In the District court of the United States, Southern district of California. Mission lands of Santa Ynez. The United States, appellants, vs. J. M. Covarrubias et al., appellee. No. 369. Land commission, no. 538. Exhibits, from 1 to 42, inclusive filed in behalf of appellants. [S.F.] Daily herald print [1858?] 127 p.   CU-B

13565. United States vs. Yansens, Augustin. Supreme court of the United States no. 204; appeal from the District court U.S. for the Southern district of California [n.d.] 21 p. map (Ms.) Transcript of the proceedings in case no. 266, Augustin Yansens vs. the U.S. for the place named Lomas de la Purificacion.   C

13566. Wahab, Moneim Abdul. The Rincon oil field; a study in oil development and marketing. [L.A.] 1956. Thesis (M.A.)—U.C.L.A., 1956.   CLU

13567. Walsh, Marie T. "The mission of the passes," Santa Inés...L.A., Times-mirror press, 1930. 122 p. illus., ports.
C CBb CHi CL CLU CLgA CLob CO COHN CSd CSf CSlu CSmH CStmo CU-B

13568. Ward, Elizabeth Antoinette. La Carpinteria. Text by Elizabeth Antoinette Ward. Photographs by George Gilbert McLean. Foreword by Stewart Edward White. [Carpenteria, Carpenteria woman's club, c1910] 47 p. illus.   CLO

Santa Barbara

13569. All about Santa Barbara, Cal. ... Santa Barbara, Daily advertiser print. house, 1878. 96 p.
C CLU CSmH CU-B

13570. —— Same. 96 p. pl. "Two editions were printed, only one of which had five plates containing eight photographs."—Cowan.   CLU NHi UPB

13571. American autochrome co. Santa Barbara and its architecture. Chicago [1910?] 40 p. illus.   CHi

13572. Baer, Kurt. Painting and sculpture at Mission Santa Barbara. Wash., D.C., Acad. of Am. Franciscan history, 1955. 244 p. illus., port.
C CChiS CHi CLO CLSM CLU CLgA CO CSdS CSfMI CSt CStb CStclU CStoC CU-B

13573. Baptists. California. Santa Barbara association. Minutes of the...anniversary of the Sta. Barbara Baptist assoc'n...5th, 1881. Santa Barbara, Independent job print. house, 1881.   CSmH

13574. Bell, Katherine M. (Den) Swinging the censer; reminiscences of old Santa Barbara...comp. by Katherine Bell Cheney...Santa Barbara, 1931. 287 p. illus., ports.
C CBb CHi CL CLU CMartC CPa CSf CSfSt CSfU CSlu CSmH CStbS CStclU CStmo CU-B

13575. Bissell, Ervanna Bowen. Glimpses of Santa Barbara and Montecito gardens. [Santa Barbara, Schauer print. studio, c1926] 62 l. illus.
C CHi CLU CSf CSmH CU-B

13576. Borein, Edward. Ed Borein's West [leaves from the sketchbook of the last artist of the longhorn era] ed. by Edward S. Spaulding. [Santa Barbara, Schauer print. studio] c1952. 10 p. illus., port., 1 col. pl.
CBb CHi CL

13577. —— Etchings of the West... [Santa Barbara, 1950] [94] l. illus.   CHi

13578. Brunnier, H. J. Engineers' report, Santa Barbara earthquake, prepared by H. J. Brunnier, John G. Little [and] T. Ronneberg, for the research department of the California common brick manufacturers' association and allied interests. [S.F., Schwabacher-Frey stationery co., 1925] 7 p.   CU-B

13579. Burton, Elizabeth E. [Catalog of hand-wrought electric lamps and sconces] Santa Barbara [1920?] [32] p. illus.   CHi

13580. Caballeria y Collell, Juan. Historia de la ciudad de Santa Bárbara. Newspaper clippings.   CStb

13581. —— History of the city of Santa Barbara, California...tr. by Edmund Burke...F. de P. Gutierrez, print., 1892. 111 p. illus., port.
C CHi CL CLSU CLU CLgA CSmH CU-B CaBViPA MWA NN

13582. Carroll, Margaret A., comp. World war history of the Catholics of Santa Barbara, California. 1919. Typew.   CStb

13583. Citizens savings and loan association. 70 years in Santa Barbara, 1887–1957. Santa Barbara, 1957. 12 p. illus.   CHi

13584. Civic league. To the people of Santa Barbara and neighboring towns. [Programme and arrangements for the reception of the Atlantic squadron. Santa Barbara, 1908?] [4] p.   CU-B

13585. Classified boosters directory of Santa Barbara. CStb has 1937–52.

13586. Colligan, James Augustine. Some facts about Santa Barbara mission... [S.F.] Univ. of S.F. press, 1932. 45 p. illus.
CHi CL CLgA COHN CSfU CSmH CStclU CU-B

13587. Collison, Thomas F. El diario del viaje de los Rancheros visitadores (log of the R. V.)... [Santa Barbara, News-press print.] c1935. 154 p. illus., ports.
CL CLU CSf CSluCL

13588. Community arts association of Santa Barbara. Plans and planting committee. New Santa Barbara... Supplement, Santa Barbara's better-homes-in-America prize... [Santa Barbara, Schauer print. studio, inc.] 1926. 26 p. illus. Reprint. from *The Architect and engineer*, July, 1926.   C

13589. —— —— Old adobes of Santa Barbara, Spanish, Mexican and early American periods, 1782–1858. Santa Barbara, 1947. 15 l. illus., map. Mimeo.
C CHi CSmH CStb

13590. Conmy, Peter Thomas. Romualdo Pacheco, distinguished Californian of the Mexican and American periods. S.F., Grand parlor, Native sons of the golden West, 1947. 14 p.
CBev CHi CLU CP CSluCL CSmat CStmo CSto CoD

13591. Copeland's bookshop [and] The Ramona shop, pubs. Santa Barbara souvenir, with earthquake pictures... Santa Barbara [Schauer print. studio, 1925] [20] p. illus.   CHi

13592. Cullimore, Clarence C. Historic adobe houses of the Santa Barbara area. [n.d.] 179 p. illus. Typew. Bibliography: p. 176–79.   CBev CStb CStbS

13593. —— Same. Santa Barbara, Santa Barbara news-press, 1942. unp. Newspaper clippings.   CBaB

13594. —— Same. L.A., 1942. (Research report, Univ. of So. Calif., 1942)   CLSU

13595. —— Santa Barbara adobes. Santa Barbara, Santa Barbara bk. pub. co., c1948. 225 p. illus.
Available in many California libraries and CoD

13596. Curletti, Rosario Andrea. Pathways to pavements, the history and romance of Santa Barbara Spanish street names; illustrated by Peter Wolf. [1st ed.] [Santa Barbara, County national bank and trust co. of Santa Barbara, 1950] 87 p. illus.
C CBev CHi CLU CO CSd CSjC CSmH CSt CStclU CStoC CU-B MoS NN

13597. —— Same. Rev. ed. 1953. 92 p.
CHi CStb CStbS

13598. The de la Guerra house, City hall plaza, Santa Barbara, California. [Santa Barbara? n.d.] [8] p. illus.
CHi

13599. El Mirasol, Santa Barbara. Guests' guide and shopping list; where to go, what to see, where to shop in Santa Barbara... [Santa Barbara? Calif. directory co., n.d.] 32 p.   CHi

13600. —— [History and description] [Santa Barbara, Schauer print. studio, 1917?] [9] p. Reprint. from the *San Francisco news letter,* May 26, 1917.   CHi

13601. Engelhardt, Zephyrin, Father. ...Santa Barbara mission... S.F., James H. Barry co., 1923. 470 p. illus. Includes music.
Available in many libraries and CaBViPA.

13602. First national trust and savings bank of Santa Barbara. Facts behind the fame of Santa Barbara and Santa Barbara county, yesterday, today and tomorrow. Santa Barbara, 1946. illus., ports. Title varies.
                                                             CHi
Other editions followed. C (1949) CBev (1948) CHi (1948, 1950) CL (1950) CO (1950) CStb (1952) CStmo (1948) CU-B (1948)

13603. Foley, Edward T. Story of Foley farm. [L.A.] Ward Ritchie [c1961] 80 p.   CHi

13604. Franciscan college, Santa Barbara. Prospectus...with a catalogue of officers and students for the year 1873–74. Also, the exercises of the seventh annual exhibition and distribution of premiums. Santa Barbara, Russell & co., print., 1874. 24 p.   CSmH CU-B

13605. Garcia, J. S. vs. Jacques, Burkhill. In the District court of the first judicial district of the state of California, county of Santa Barbara. J. S. Garcia, ex. of will of P. P. Massini, deceased, plaintiff, vs. Burkhill Jacques, defendant. Before Murray, J. Defendant's brief. Messrs. Fernald & Richards, attorneys for defendant. Santa Barbara, Daily press steam print. house, 1874. 40 p. Suit over water-rights in Santa Barbara county.   CLU

13606. Garden club of America. "Arcady," Montecito, Santa Barbara, California. Garden club of America, April 15, 1926. [Santa Barbara, c1926] 76 p. 22 mounted pl. (1 fold.)   CSmH CU-B

13607. Geiger, Maynard J., Father. Calendar of documents in the Santa Barbara mission archives. Wash., D.C., Acad. of Am. Franciscan history, 1947. 291 p.
C CHi CL CLLoy CLS CLU CLgA CO CSdU CSf CSmH CStclU CU-B UU

13608. —— God's acre at Mission Santa Barbara; the history of the mission cemetery and its famous dead. [Santa Barbara, 1958] 32 p. illus., ports., plans.
                                              C CHi CU-B

13609. —— The history of California's Mission Santa Barbara from 1786 to the present. Santa Barbara, Franciscan fathers, old mission [1959?] 24 p. col. illus., map.   CHi CU-B

13610. —— Mission bells of Santa Barbara, their history and romance. [Santa Barbara? 1956?] 25 p. illus., ports.   CHi CLU CO CStbS CU-B

13611. A glimpse of El Montecito. [S.F., Norman Pierce co., c1905]   CSmH

13612. Halterman, John Frederick. An economic survey of Santa Barbara. Berkeley, Bur. of business and economic research, Univ. of Calif., 1947. 70 l.   CLU

13613. Hanson, Arthur N., comp. Santa Barbara. A compilation of facts for the information of the world at large. The city of roses... [L.A., B.R. Baumgardt, n.d.] 64 p. illus.   CLU CSmH CStb

13614. Hawley, Walter Augustus. The early days of Santa Barbara, California... N.Y., 1910. 105 p. illus.
CHi CL CLO CLU CP CPom CSfU CSfWF-H CSmH CStbS CStrJC CU-B CaBViPA KyU MiD-B MoSHi NHi NN TxU

13615. —— Same. Santa Barbara [Schauer print. studio] 1920. 103 p. illus.
Available in many California libraries and UPB

13616. Heininger, Charles P., pub. Souvenir of Santa Barbara, California. [S.F., c1888] 10 p. 13 pl. in folder.   CHi CSmH

13617. Higgins, Sarah Evelina Austin. La casa de Aguirre of Santa Barbara, 1841–1884. Santa Barbara, Press of El Barbareño, 1896. 29 p. illus.
          CHi CLSU CLU CLob CSmH CU-B

13618. Hill, Laurance Landreth, and Parks, Marion. Santa Barbara, tierra adorada; a community history ... L.A., Security first national bank of Los Angeles, c1930. 112 p. illus., ports.
C CHi CL CLO CLSU CLU CLom CMS CO CRcS CSmH CStbS CStmo CU-B CWhC MiD MoS NN OrU

13619. Hoffman, C. A. The earthquake of Santa Barbara, California, June 29, 1925; a photographic record. 1925.   CStb

13620. Huse, Charles E. et al. vs. Den, Richard A., et al. Argument of Oliver P. Evans for the heirs of Nicholas A. Den, in the case of Charles E. Huse, et al. vs. Richard A. [i.e. S.] Den, et al. [n.p., 1886?] 333 p.
                                                             CSmH

13621. Johnstone, E. McD. "By semi-tropic seas." Santa Barbara and surroundings. [Buffalo, N.Y., Matthews, Northrup & co., c1888] [48] p. illus., maps.
               CHi CLU CO CSmH CU-B NHi

13622. Langdon, Edgar. Sights and scenes of Santa Barbara and how to reach them. Santa Barbara, Daily news job [n.d.] [36] p.   CHi

13623. League of women voters, comp. The city government of Santa Barbara, California. Santa Barbara, 1957. 31 p. illus.   C CStb

13624. Lions international. Fourth district association. Roster of district officers and committeemen. Santa Barbara, 19—?–
CHi has 1950/51–1951/52.

13625. Lummis, Charles Fletcher. Stand fast Santa Barbara! Save the centuried romance of old California... Santa Barbara, Community arts assoc., 1923. 19 p. Reprint. from the *Santa Barbara morning press,* 1923.   C CLO CLU

13626. McGroarty, John Steven. Santa Barbara, California. Photographs by Samuel Adelstein. [n.p.] So. Pac. lines, 1925. 32 p. illus., map.
                             CHi CO CSf CSmH

13627. McIsaac, Colin H. Mission Santa Barbara; early days in Alta California... Classified business directory of Santa Barbara... Santa Barbara, c1917. 32 p.
                                                             CSmH

13628. —— Santa Barbara mission; early days in California...with revisions by Rev. Augustine Hobrecht, O.F.M. ... Santa Barbara, Schauer print. studio, inc., c1917. 35 p. illus.   CHi
Other editions followed. C (1926) CHi (1926, 1929) CLU (1923, 1926) CLSU (1929) CSf (1926) CSmH (1926) CStclU (1926) MiD (1923) MoS (1929)

13629. Maulsby, F. R. Santa Barbara, California. [S.F.? 19—?] 15 p. illus., map.   CU-B

13630. Miradero sanitarium. Miradero. Santa Barbara [n.d.] [7] p. 2 fold. pl.   CHi

13631. Montecito country club. By-laws, rules, officers, stockholders and members.
CHi has 1924.

13632. Moody, Charles Amadon. Santa Barbara. [L.A.? 1901] 16 p. illus. Reprint. from *Land of Sunshine*, November, 1901. CLU NN

13633. Morrison, Gouverneur Merion. The old mission bells will ring tonight. Santa Barbara, Santa Barbara daily news, 1931. unp. illus.
CSal CSd CSlu CStmo

13634. Morse, Ednah Anne (Rich) The story of the domestic science (1891)–domestic art (1895) and manual arts (1892) established by Miss Anna S. C. Blake in the Santa Barbara grade schools and of the applied arts and industrial arts equipped by friends as a memorial to school...N.Y., 1932. [143] p. loose-leaf. Contains also: Reminiscences.—Tribute to Lewis Kennedy Morse.—The letter (1860) from my pioneer father.—The letter (1863).—Tribute from a brother mason.
C CStbS

13635. Mount Calvary monastery. Mount Calvary monastery, the Order of the Holy Cross... [Santa Barbara, n.d.] [4] p. illus., map. CHi

13636. Nidever, George. The life and adventures of George Nidever (1802–1833) edited by William Henry Ellison. Berkeley, Univ. of Calif. press, 1937. 128 p. ports. Available in many California libraries and CaBViPA OrU

13637. Oetteking, Bruno. ...Skeletal remains from Santa Barbara, California... N.Y., Museum of the Am. Indian, Heye foundation, 1925. 168 p. illus. (Indian notes and monographs...misc. no. 39) C CHi

13638. O'Keefe, Joseph Jeremiah. Buildings and churches of the mission of Santa Barbara... Tr., written and comp. from the register, reports, and other documents in the archives of the mission... Santa Barbara, Independent job print. house, 1886. 40 p.
C CHi CL CLSU CLU CO CSmH CU-B CWhC

13639. The old mission of Santa Barbara. [n.p., n.d.] 6 pl. C

13640. Old mission restoration committee. [Description of the Santa Barbara mission after the Santa Barbara earthquake in 1925 and request for funds for restoring it. [Santa Barbara? c1926] [16] p. illus., facsim. CHi CU-B

13641. Old Spanish days in California. Official historical program, Old Spanish days [in] Santa Barbara ... Santa Barbara [192–?–] illus.
CHi has 1932, 1934, 1938, 1952. CU-B has 1927.

13642. —— Santa Barbara, la fiesta; being a series of twenty-five specially selected photographs portraying the romantic history of Spanish-California; and a series of sixteen specially selected photographs, depicting the scenic beauty of Santa Barbara and her colorful old Spanish days "la fiesta"... Santa Barbara, Schauer print. studio [n.d.] [48] p. illus., map. C

13643. Orr, Phil C. Excavations in Moaning cave. Santa Barbara, Santa Barbara museum of natural hist., 1952. 19 p. illus. (Dept. of anthropology. Bul. no. 1) CHi

13644. Pacific improvement co. Hope ranch; a story of two thousand acres of beautifully wooded land and a prophecy of its future. [S.F., Crocker, c1908] unp. illus., maps. C CHi CO CSmH

13645. Pictorial history of Santa Barbara earthquake, June 29, 1925...Santa Barbara, A.A. Lloyd, c1925. 30 pl.
CStbS

13646. Presbyterian church in the United States of America. Presbytery. Santa Barbara. Historical account of the presbytery of Santa Barbara and its individual churches. 1907. [Santa Barbara? 1907] 58 p.
CSmH

13647. Ramsey, Edith F. Santa Barbara from the days of the Indian. Pub. under the auspices of the Santa Barbara natural history soc. [n.p., 1919] [15] p.
CLU CLob

13648. Rancheros visitadores, Santa Barbara. Roster. [Santa Barbara, 19—?–] CLU has 1935–36.

13649. Red cross. U.S. American national Red cross. The earthquake disaster at Santa Barbara, California; an official report of the relief activities. Wash., D.C., June 1926. 19 p. C

13650. Rieder, M. Santa Barbara, the gem city of the western sea. L.A., Author [1907] [46] p. illus.
C CHi CO CU-B

13651. Roberts, Edwards. Santa Barbara and around there... Bost., Roberts bros., 1886. 191 p. illus.
C C-S CHi CL CLO CLSU CLU CO CP CSd CSfCW CSfMI CSmH CSmat CStbS CU-B CaBViPA ICN NHi NN

13652. —— A Santa Barbara holiday... [n.p.] c1887. [813]-835 p. illus. Reprint. from *Harper's mag.* for Nov., 1887. CHi CLU CSmH CU-B NHi

13653. Robinson, Charles Mulford. The report ...regarding the civic affairs of Santa Barbara... [Santa Barbara] Print. for the Civic league by the Independent, 1909. 36 p. CL CU-B

13654. [Roddy, Patrick, *Father*] Santa Barbara; queen of the missions. Sesquicentennial, 1786–1926. [Santa Barbara? G. Leslie Richards, c1936] [32] p. illus., ports. CBb CHi

13655. Rodríguez Ramón, Andrés. Alma y perfil de Santa Barbara. la. edicion. Santa Barbara, Schauer print. studio, 1956. 147 p. CStb CU-B

13656. Sanborn map co. Insurance maps of Santa Barbara, California. N.Y., 1907. 1 v. (col. maps) Maps kept up-to-date by printed slips pasted over sections of the maps. The "additional index" is dated January 1927.
CLU

13657. Sands, Frank, pub. Camera views of Santa Barbara, Cal. Santa Barbara [n.d.] 60 pl. in portfolio.
CHi CLU

13658. —— Santa Barbara at a glance. A compendium of reliable information for citizens, sojourners and strangers who may come in future... Santa Barbara, 1895. 54 p. illus. C CHi CU-B NN

13659. Santa Barbara. Board of trade. Santa Barbara, the ideal summer resort. Santa Barbara [1895] [20] p. CHi CLU CU-B

13660. —— **Botanic garden.** Annual reports. [Santa Barbara] 1939–
CHi has 1949. CStb has 1939–to date.

13661. —— —— ...Guide to the garden... Santa Barbara, 1944. 20 p. pl., double plan. C

13662. —— —— Same. 1957. 29 p. illus.
C CU-B

13663. —— **Chamber of commerce.** Community survey of Santa Barbara, California in cooperation with business development commission of the city of Santa Barbara, California. [Santa Barbara] 1954. 20 p.
CStb

13664. —— —— Facts about Santa Barbara, California. [Santa Barbara] 1960. CStb

13665. —— —— Official guide [to] Santa Barbara, California. [An official publication of the city of

Santa Barbara, California, Santa Barbara Chamber of commerce and convention bureau, Retail merchants association. 1st– ed., 1950– Santa Barbara, Rood associates, 1950– illus., maps.
CHi (5th, 1957) CStb (1st-3d, 1950, 1953, 1954) CStmo (6th, 1959) CU-B (6th, 1959)

13666. —— —— Santa Barbara, a midsummer paradise; the Newport of the Pacific. Santa Barbara, The Independent print. [190–?] unp. illus. CU-B

13667. —— —— Santa Barbara; the romantic charm of old California. Santa Barbara [n.d.] folder (6 p.) illus., map. CRcS

13668. —— —— Visitor's guide and sightseeing map, Santa Barbara and vicinity. Santa Barbara [n.d.] folder. CRcS

13669. —— —— Santa Barbara street names; their derivation and pronunciation. [Santa Barbara, 1945] [4] p. illus. CLU CU-B

13670. —— Justice's court. [Dockets of Justices Samuel Barney, A. F. Hinchman, J. A. Vidal and C. R. V. Lee, 1850–1855] 4 v. CU-B

13671. —— **Museum of art.** California pictorial, 1800–1900, an exhibition of two parts: the collection of Robert B. Honeyman, jr., and paintings by William Keith. [Santa Barbara, 1962] [28] p. illus. CHi

13672. —— —— The opening exhibition...painting today and yesterday in the United States... Santa Barbara, 1941. [115] p. illus. CHi

13673. —— **Museum of natural history.** Meeting in memory of Mary Pierrepont Bushnell Hazard... April 13, 1936: [addresses by Caroline Hazard, S. M. Ilsley, and P. M. Rea. Santa Barbara, 1936] [9] p. CHi

13674. —— **Ordinances, etc.** The code of the city of Santa Barbara, California, 1957; the general ordinances of the city published by orders of the mayor and city council. L.A., Mitchie city pub. co., 1957. 661 p. CStb

13675. —— **Teachers college.** [Catalog]
CL has 1921–28.

13676. Santa Barbara. A monthly magazine devoted to the interests of Santa Barbara Valley—the ideal homeland. v.1, no. 1–12, Jan.–Dec. 1906. Santa Barbara, Chamber of commerce [1906] illus. No more published?
C has Mission number, Jan. 1906, Floral number, May 1906. CSmH has Floral number, May 1906, Olive number, June 1906. CU-B has Mission number, Jan. 1906, School number, Mar. 1906, Water supply number, Oct. 1906, and Dec. 1906. NN has v.1 no. 1–12.

13677. Santa Barbara by the sea. [Santa Barbara, Daily news print., 18—?] [14] p. incl. illus. CHi CSmH

13678. Santa Barbara, California. S.F., Sunset pub. co., 1915. 15 p. CHi CL

13679. Santa Barbara college. ...Annual catalogue...4th, 1875/76. S.F., 1875. CU-B

13680. —— Register... S.F., Cubery & co., 1874. 24 p. illus. C

13681. Santa Barbara county. Chamber of commerce. Santa Barbara's old Spanish background; old mission, old adobes, county court house. [1941?] [12] p. illus. CO

13682. [Santa Barbara daily news] 86 views of Santa Barbara earthquake, June 29, 1925, with full description of quake. unp. CRedl

13683. Santa Barbara historical society. Report. no. 1, 1946. [Santa Barbara?] 1946. CHi CLU

13684. Santa Barbara hot sulphur springs co. Prospectus... Capital $50,000. S.F., F. Eastman, print., 1867. 13 p. mounted illus., form. CU-B

13685. Santa Barbara news press. Centennial edition. [Sections E, F, G, H] Sunday, April 25, 1954. Santa Barbara, 1954. 1 v. v.p. illus., ports., maps. C CHi CU-B

13686. —— ...Fiesta edition, July 31, 1949; Aug. 16, 1953. [Santa Barbara, 1949–] illus., ports., maps. CHi (1953) CU-B (1949)

13687. —— Old Mission marks end of huge restoration project. [Santa Barbara] 1958. B2–B8 p. illus., ports. CU-B

13688. Santa Barbara personnel association. Wage and salary administration committee. Santa Barbara wage and salary survey, November 1959. [Santa Barbara?] 1959. 36 p. CStb

13689. Santa Barbara pictorial. [Santa Barbara, Mission news agency, 1948?] [24] p. CHi

13690. Southern California acclimatizing association, Santa Barbara. Catalogs.
CHi has 1908, 1914.

13691. Southworth, John R. Los adobes antiguos de Santa Bárbara. Santa Barbara [Schauer print. studio, 1921] [14] p. illus. CU-B

13692. —— Historic adobes of Santa Barbara, Calif. Santa Barbara, News-press commercial print. [n.d.] 23 p. illus. C CHi CLO CO CStb

13693. —— Same. 3d ed. [1938] [28] p. illus. CSmH CU-B

13694. —— Santa Barbara & Montecito, past & present... Santa Barbara, Oreña studios, 1920. 267 p. illus.
C CBb CHi CL CLSU CLU CMerCL CO CRedl CRic CSd CSdU CSf CSfU CSmH CStbS CStmo CU-B NN

13695. —— Viva Santa Barbara. c1946. [n.p.] [48] p. illus., map. CHi

13696. Staats, Henry Philip. Californian architecture in Santa Barbara. N.Y., Architectural bk. pub. co. [c1929] 125 p. of illus. (incl. plans) C CLO CStmo

13697. Storke, Thomas More. California editor, by Thomas M. Storke in collaboration with Walker A. Tompkins. Foreword by Earl Warren. L.A., Westernlore press, 1959. 489 p. illus.
Available in many California libraries and CoD TxU

13698. Thomson, Virginia Winbourn. George Nidever: a pioneer of California. [Berkeley, 1952] Thesis (M.A.)—Univ. of Calif., 1952. CU CU-B

13699. Torrey, K. S. Sketches of the old Santa Barbara mission, where are gathered the Franciscan friars ... Troy, N.Y., Nims & Knight [1888] 18 l. incl. illus., pl. C CLO

13700. U.S. Dept. of the interior. Cahuma unit of the Santa Barbara county project, California. Letter transmitting a report and findings... Wash., D.C., Govt. print. off., 1948. 120 p. (80th Cong., 2d sess., 1948. H. doc. no. 587) CSdS

13701. Valley club of Montecito. By-laws, regulations, list of members. [n.p., n.d.]
CHi has 1931–32.

13702. Walter, Carrie (Stevens) Idyl of Santa Barbara... S.F., Golden era co., 1886. 54 p.
CLU CSmH CU-B

13703. Weber, Francis J. A biographical sketch of Right Reverend Francisco Garcia Diego y Moreno, first bishop of the Californias, 1785–1846. L.A., Borromeo guild, 1961. 50 p. illus., ports., map.
CHi CL CLSM

13704. Webster, Albert F. A sketch of Santa Barbara. Santa Barbara, Santa Barbara press, 1876. 13 p. tables. "From *Appleton's journal* for July [1876] Republished in the *Santa Barbara weekyy* [!] press, October 14, 1876, with editorial comments."
CLU

13705. Wells, Andrew Jackson. Santa Barbara, California...Homes—health and comfort. S.F., Sunset mag. homeseekers' bur., 1909. 30 p. illus., map.
CSf

13706. Wilson, Leila (Weekes) Monograph on the old Franciscan mission, Santa Barbara, California... [Santa Barbara] Pac. coast pub. co., 1913. [39] p. illus.
C CLU CU-B NN

13707. ——, ed. Santa Barbara, California... Santa Barbara, Pac. coast pub. co. [c1913] 104 p. illus., maps.
CHi CL CLU CP CSmH CU-B NN

13708. —— Same. 2d rev. ed. 1919. 96 p.
C CLSU

13709. Wilson, Neill Compton, comp. Rancheros visitadores: twenty-fifth anniversary, 1930–1955. [Limited ed. Santa Barbara, Rancheros visitadores, 1955] 142 p. illus. (part col.) ports., maps.
CBaK CL

13710. [Wood, Mary Camilla (Foster) Hall] Santa Barbara as it is... Santa Barbara, Independent pub. co. [1884] 101 p.
C CL CP CU-B NN

13711. Wright abstract co. Certificate of title made by the Wright abstract company. Santa Barbara, 1908–1915. 63 p. maps.
CSf

13712. Writers' program. California. Santa Barbara; a guide to the Channel city and its environs... Sponsored by Santa Barbara state college. N.Y., Hastings house, 1941. 206 p. illus. (Am. guide ser.) Bibliography: p. 194–197.
Available in many California libraries and CoU MiD MoS NHi NN NjR ODa TxU UPB

Santa Barbara Islands

13713. Hardacre, Emma (Chamberlain) Eighteen years alone, a tale of the Pacific. [Santa Barbara, Schauer print. studio] c1950. 22 p. port. Reprint. from *Scribner's monthly*, v.20, Sept. 1880.
CL CLU CU-B

13714. Heye, George Gustav. Certain artifacts from San Miguel island, California. N.Y., Museum of the Am. Indian, Heye foundation, 1921. 211 p. illus., maps. (Indian notes and monographs, v.7, no. 4)
CHi CLU CSd InI TxU ViU

13715. Hillinger, Charles. The Channel islands. With photographs by Howard Maxwell. L.A., Acad. pub. [c1958] 165 p. illus., maps (part. col.)
Available in many California libraries and NN.

13716. —— Channel islands. n.p. [1956] 26 p. illus., ports., map.
CL

13717. Holder, Charles Frederick. The Channel islands of California; a book for the angler, sportsman, and tourist... Chicago, McClurg, 1910. 397 p. illus., maps.
Available in many California libraries and MiD NHi

13718. McKern, Thomas Wilton. An anthropometric and morphological analysis of a prehistoric skeletal population from Santa Cruz island, California. [Berkeley, 1955] Thesis (Ph.D.)—Univ. of Calif., 1955.
CU

13719. Martin, Dorothy E. Bibliography of the Santa Barbara islands, California... [L.A., L.A. county museum] 1942. [34] l. Typew.
C

13720. Miller, Max Carlton. ...and bring all your folks; being a lighthearted examination of the southern California islands and some off Mexico, in case we get crowded off the mainland! [1st ed.] Garden City, N.Y., Doubleday, 1959. 238 p. illus.
Available in many California libraries and MiD NN

13721. Orr, Philip C. Radiocarbon dates from Santa Rosa island. Santa Barbara, Museum of natural history, 1956. 9 p. (Dept. of archeology, bul. no. 2)
CStb

13722. Putnam, Frederick Ward. ...Reports upon archaeological and ethnological collections from vicinity of Santa Barbara, California... [Wash., D.C., Govt. print. off., 1879] 497 p. illus., pl., map.
CSfSt

13723. Warren, Earl, jr. The agriculture of Santa Cruz island, with a survey of California's other coastal islands... [Davis? Bibliography: p. 49–50.
C

13724. Wheeler, Stanley A. California's little known Channel islands... Annapolis, Md., U.S. naval inst. [1944] p. 257–269. Reprint. from *U. S. naval inst. Proceedings*, Mar., 1944.
CL CO CU-B CVtCL

SANTA CLARA COUNTY
(*Created in 1850*)

COUNTY HISTORIES

13725. Daley, Edith. War history of Santa Clara county. [San Jose] Santa Clara county hist. soc. [1919] 77 p. ports. Contains names of men who entered U.S. service from county.
CHi CO CSj CSjC CSjCL CSmH CSt CStb CStclU CU-B IC

13726. Foote, Horace S., ed. Pen pictures from the garden of the world, or, Santa Clara county, California... Containing a history of the county of Santa Clara... and biographical mention of many of its pioneers and also of prominent citizens of to-day... Chicago, Lewis, 1888. 672 p. illus., ports.
C CAlaC CCH CHi CL CLSM CLSU CLU CLg CLgA CO CPa CRic CSf CSfMI CSfU CSfWF-H CSj CSjC CSjCL CSmH CSt CStclU CStoC CU-B CoD NHi NN UPB

13727. Historical atlas map of Santa Clara county, California... S.F., Thompson & West, 1876. 110 p. illus., maps.
C CCH CHi CL CLU CLgA CO CSf CSj CSjC CSjCL CSmH CSt CStclU CU-B CYcCL NN WHi

13728. Historical records survey. California. ...Santa Clara county (San Jose) S.F., Hist. records survey, 1939. 330 l. map. (Inventory of the county archives of Calif., no. 44) Reproduced from typew. copy. Bibliographical footnotes.
C CBb CHi CL CLCM CLCo CLO CLSM CLSU CLU CMont CO COMC CPa CSalCL CSf CSfCSM CSj CSjC CSjCL CSmH CSr CSrCL CStclU CU-B CYcCL ICN MoS N NN WHi

13729. [Munro-Fraser, J. P.] History of Santa Clara county, California... Also ...biographical sketches of early and prominent settlers and representative men ... S.F., Alley, Bowen & co., 1881. 798 p. illus., ports., map.

C CB CCH CHi CL CLCM CLCo CLSM CLU CLgA CO CP CPa CSd CSf CSfCP CSfMI CSfU CSfWF-H CSj CSjC CSjCL CSmH CSt CStclU CSto CStoC CStrJC CU-B CoD CtY ICN KHi MWA MiD-B N NHi NN WHi

13730. Patterson, Alma M. and McCabe, Bessie. Outline history of Santa Clara county, California. [San Jose, Melvin, Roberts and Horwarth] 1924. 11 p.   C

13731. Sawyer, Eugene Taylor. History of Santa Clara county, California, with biographical sketches... L.A., Historic record co., 1922. 1692 p. ports.

C CAla CBb CFS CHi CL CLSU CLU CLg CLgA CMS CO CPa CRcS CSd CSf CSj CSjC CSjCL CSmH CSt CStcl CStclU CStoC CU-B CtY ICN MWA MiD-B NN WHi

13732. U.S. Works projects administration. Santa Clara county, California; historical survey...sponsored by the Santa Clara county librarian. 1936. 2000 p. Typew.   CSjCL

GREAT REGISTER

13733. Santa Clara county. Index to the Great register of the county of Santa Clara. 1866– Place of publication and title vary.

C has 1867–69, 1871–73, 1875–76, 1879–80, 1882, 1884, 1888 (biennially to)– 1896, 1902 (biennially to)– 1962. CHi has 1877. CL has 1872–73, 1876–77, 1879 (suppl.), 1880, 1882 (suppl.), 1888, 1890. CLU has 1875. CSjCL has 1867 and suppl., 1867–68, 1873, 1877 and 1st, 2d, 3d suppl., 1878, 4th suppl., 1879 and 1st, 2d suppl., 1882 (biennially to)– 1896. CSmH has 1892. CU-B has 1867, Sept.–Oct. 1868 (suppl. 1–2), Nov. 1868, 1869 (wards 1-2), 1871, 1871 (suppl.), 1872, 1873, 1877, 1877 (suppl.), June 1878 (suppl.), 1879, 1879 (suppl. 1–2), Guadalupe precinct, 1884, 1886, 1886 (suppl.), 1890 (suppl.), Guadalupe precinct, 1890, Campbell precinct, 1910. CoD has 1888.

DIRECTORIES

13734. 1871/72. County directory publishing co., pub. Santa Clara county directory, including the cities and towns of San Jose, Santa Clara, Gilroy, Mayfield, ...for 1871–72. Together with a sketch of the cities and towns. Sacramento, 1871.

   CHi CL CSj CU-B

13735. 1875. Paulson, L. L., comp. & pub. Handbook and directory of Santa Clara, San Benito, Santa Cruz, Monterey, and San Mateo counties. S.F., Francis & Valentine commercial steam presses, 1875.

   C CHi CLU CSalCL CSf CSj CSmH CU-B

13736. 1881/82–1889. McKenney, L. M., & co., pub. San Jose city directory, including Santa Clara, San Mateo, Santa Cruz, San Benito and Monterey counties. S.F., 1880–89. Publisher varies: 1887/88, Uhlhorn & McKenney. Content varies: 1880, San Jose and Santa Clara county. 1884/85–1887/88, San Jose including Santa Clara, San Mateo and Santa Cruz counties.

C has 1881/82, 1884/85, 1889. CHi has 1884/85, 1887/88, 1889. CL has 1884/85, 1887/88. CStcrCL has 1887/88. NHi has 1889. UHi has 1884/85.

13737. 1890–1952. Polk, R. L. & co., pub. Polk's San Jose city and Santa Clara county directory. L.A., 1890–1952. Publisher varies: 1890–1905, F. M. Husted; 1906–27, Polk-Husted. Continued as Polk's San Jose city directory.

C has 1890, 1892–1900, 1902–1908/09, 1910/11–1917,

1922–23, 1925, 1927–30, 1932–33. C-S has 1906–1912/13. CHi has 1892, 1894, 1896, 1899, 1901–02, 1907/08, 1912/13, 1913/14, 1919, 1922, 1924, 1928–31, 1942, 1947, 1949/50, 1952. CL has 1911/12, 1913/14, 1915, 1917–20, 1923, 1928, 1932, 1940–44, 1949/50, 1952. CLg has 1919, 1934, 1936–41, 1943–45, 1947, 1949/50, 1952. CSfCW has 1920. CSjCL has 1906, 1907/08, 1911/12, 1915–17, 1923, 1926–45. CStcl has 1912/13, 1915–17, 1919, 1923–24, 1926–29, 1931–45, 1947–1949/50, 1952. CU-B has 1907/08, 1910/11, 1912/13–1915, 1922–30. MoS has 1898/99. NHi has 1896, 1899.

13738. 1937. Directory of Scandinavian people and those of Scandinavian descent residing in Santa Clara county, California. [San Jose, Union print. co.] 1937. 51 p.   CSjCL

San Jose

13739. 1870. Colahan, W. J., and Pomeroy, Julian, comp. San José city directory and business guide of Santa Clara co. for the year commencing January 1, 1870... First year of publication. S.F., Bacon & co., print., 1870. 242 p.

   C CHi CLU CSfWF-H CSmII CU-B WHi

13740. 1874. Hewson, John B., comp. Directory of the city of San José and guide to the business houses in Santa Clara co. for the year commencing Jan. 1, 1874 ... S.F., Bacon & co., print., 1874. 226 p. map.

   C CHi CLU CU-B

13741. 1876. Vandall, B. C., pub. Bishop's directory of the city of San Jose... Also a directory of Santa Clara... S.F., 1876.   CHi CSmH CU-B

13742. 1878. Cottle, Benjamin H., & Wright, Theodore F., pub. Directory of the city of San Jose for 1878 together with a historical sketch of the city... also a directory of Santa Clara. San Jose, 1878.   CHi

13743. 1882–1885. Southern California publishing co., pub. San Jose directory...to which is annexed a business directory of prominent San Francisco houses. S.F., 1882–85.   CSf CU-B (1882)

13744. 1954– Polk, R. L. & co., pub. Polk's San Jose city directory including Santa Clara. L.A., 1954– Title varies: 1954 Polk's San Jose and suburban directory. Preceded by Polk's San Jose directory including Santa Clara county.

CHi has 1954–62. CL has 1954–57. CLg has 1954–55. CSmat has 1958–59. CStCL has 1954–57, 1959–60.

Other Cities and Towns

13745. 1924. Coast directory co., pub. Los Gatos city directory. [Los Gatos] 1924. 90 p.   C

13746. 1956– Polk, R. L. & co., pub. Polk's Los Gatos city directory, including Monte Sereno, Campbell, and Saratoga. L.A., 1956– Content varies: 1956–60 Los Gatos, Campbell and Saratoga.

CHi has 1956, 1962. CLg has 1956, 1958, 1960, 1962. CSmat has 1958.

13747. 1895/96–1924. Times publishing co., pub. Directory of Palo Alto, Mayfield, Runnymede and Stanford university. Palo Alto [1895?]–1924. Publisher varies: 1895/96–18—H. S. Crocker co.; 1900/01–1901/02 Palo Alto times press. Content varies: 1895/96–18—Palo Alto and Stanford university; 1900/01–1901/02? Palo Alto; 1904 Palo Alto, Mayfield, Menlo Park, and Stanford university; 1910–1918/19 Palo Alto, Mayfield, and Stanford university.

C has 1900/01–1901/02, 1904, 1910–11, 1914/15, 1916/17, 1918/19, 1920/21–1924. CPa has 1895/96–1924. CSfCW has 1914/15–1922. CU-B has 1895/96.

13748. 1904–1906/07. Directory of Palo Alto and the campus...[1904–1907?] 2 v. Publisher varies: 1904 comp. and pub. by A. T. Griffin. 1906/07 includes directory of officers and students.   C

13749. 1926– Polk, R. L. & co., pub. Polk's Palo Alto directory including Stanford. None published in 1943, 1945. Content varies: 1926–32 Palo Alto, East Palo Alto, Ravenswood, Stanford and Menlo Park; 1946–55 Palo Alto including Stanford and Menlo Park.

C has 1926–42, 1944, 1946, 1953. CHi has 1927–29, 1946, 1948, 1950, 1953–62. CL has 1932, 1939–42, 1944, 1953–57. CPa has 1926–42, 1944, 1946–61. CSmat has 1958–59. CU-B has 1931–32.

GENERAL REFERENCES

13750. Ainsley (Gordon) rare bulbs and plants, Campbell. [Catalogs. n.p., n.d.]
CHi has 1929–33.

13751. Arnold brothers. ...Catalogue of fruit, vegetable, stock and grain farms, country homes, villas, residences, lots, blocks and timber lands, for the sale at the Pacific coast immigration association... San Jose, McNeil bros., print. [18–?] 58 p. illus.   CU-B

13752. Bateman, Herman Edward. History of the Santa Clara county (California) congressional district. [Berkeley, 1940] Thesis (M.A.)—Univ. of Calif., 1940.   CU

13753. Beach, Frank L. James Alexander Forbes, 1804–1881; British vice consul in California, 1842–1850. [S.F.] 1957. Thesis (M.A.)—Univ. of San Francisco.   CSfU

13754. Bell, John, ed. Bell's land register and Santa Clara county index... San Jose, Bell's land, loan and insurance agency, 1886.   CSjCL

13755. Bentel, Dwight E., and Freitas, Dolores. Stories of Santa Clara valley... San Jose, Rosicrucian press [c1942] 144 p. illus.
C CLgA CRcS CSalCL CSj CSjC CSjCL CSmH CStcl

13756. [Bingham, Earl S.] Santa Clara county, California. Souvenir, 16th international convention [Christian endeavor] San Francisco, July 7–12, 1897. [S.F., Crocker, 1897] 48 p. illus., ports.
                              CHi CStclU NN

13757. Blackford, Geo. W. vs. Whistler, Lydia et al. In the Supreme court of the state of California. Geo. W. Blackford, respondent, vs. Lydia Whistler, et als, appellants. Transcript on appeal. Black & Stephens, att'ys. for appellants. T. H. Laine, att'y for respondent. San Jose, Mercury steam print, 1879. 97 p.   CHi

13758. Boone, Lalla Rookh. The history of the Santa Clara valley: the Spanish period. [Berkeley] 1922. 185 l. illus., maps. Thesis (M.A.)—Univ. of Calif., 1922.
          CStclU (microfilm)   CU   CU-B

13759. Broek, Jan Otto Marius. The Santa Clara valley, California; a study in landscape changes. Utrecht, N.V.A. Oosthoek's uitgevers-mij, 1932. 184 p. illus., maps. Bibliography: p. [166]–177.
CLSU CSdS CSjC CSmH CStclU CU-B TxU ViU

13760. California vs. Cook, John. In the Supreme court of the state of California. The people of the state of California, ex rel., Peter Chrystal, applicant, vs. John Cook, et als., loan-commissioner of the county of Santa Clara. Brief of applicant. S.F., 1870. 7 p.   CHi

13761. California vs. Parks, et al. In the Supreme court of the state of California the people ex rel., Attor-

ney-general vs. Parks, et al. Argument of John Reynolds upon the validity of the debris tax. San Jose, Mercury steam print, 1881. 10 p.   CHi

13762. California. District court (20th district) Calendar of the twentieth District court, Santa Clara county. May term, 1876... Hon. David Belden, judge. San Jose, Mercury steam print, 1876. 47 p.   CHi

13763. —— Governor (John G. Downey) Governor's message relative to existing difficulties in Santa Clara county. [Sacramento, 1861] 13 p.   CSmH CU-B

13764. —— Legislature. Assembly. Committee on claims. Majority report...in relation to the petition of Thomas Thompson. [Sacramento, D.W. Gelwicks, state print., 1868] 4 p.
Land claims in Santa Clara county.   CSmH

13765. —— University. A brief account of the Lick observatory...prepared by Edward S[ingleton] Holden...2d ed. Sacramento, State print. off., 1895. 29 p., port.
CHi CLSU CSmH CU-B. Other editions followed: CHi (3d, 4th, 7th, 8th, 12th) CL (6th) CLU (6th) CO (4th, 7th) CSdS (7th) CSmat (5th) CU-B (6th)

13766. —— —— Hand-book of the Lick observatory of the University of California [by] Edward Singleton Holden. S.F., Bancroft co., c1888. 135 p. illus., ports.
                          C CHi CLU CU-B

13767. California development board. Santa Clara county, California, its climate, resources... [San Jose, 1915?] 59 p.   CHi CU-B

13768. California pioneers of Santa Clara county. By-laws and list of members... San Jose, 19—?–
C (1907) CHi (1946, 1957) CU-B (1907)

13769. —— California pioneers of Santa Clara county, organized June 22, 1875. [n.p., 1946?] 19 p.
                          C CHi CO CU-B

13770. —— Same. [n.p., 1958?] 24 p.   CHi

13771. —— Pioneer and old settlers' day...Panama-Pacific exposition. A souvenir. [San Jose? 1915]
                                              CSmH

13772. Campbell, James Henry vs. Santa Clara county. Board of supervisors et al. ...James H. Campbell, plaintiff and respondent, vs. the Board of supervisors of the county of Santa Clara and A. L. Hubbard, John Roll [and others]...defendants and appellants. Respondent's brief. James H. Campbell, attorney for self. John E. Richards of counsel... San Jose, Press of Melvin, Hillis & Black [1907] 29 p.   CU-B

13773. Campbell. Board of trade. Campbell, the orchard city, center of famous fruit district of Santa Clara valley, California... [Campbell, 1904?] [20] p. illus.   CU-B

13774. Carroll, Mary Bowden. Ten years in paradise. Leaves from a society reporter's note-book. [San Jose, Press of Popp & Hogan, 1903] 212 p. illus. A description of Santa Clara valley.
C C-S CHi CLgA CO CPa CRic CSd CSf CSfU CSfWF-H CSj CSjC CSjCL CSmH CStcl CStclU CU-B NN

13775. Clayton (James A.) & co. Desirable property for sale by Jas. A. Clayton, real estate agent... San Jose, Cottle & Brower, print. [1884] 42 p.   CSmH

13776. —— San Jose and Santa Clara county, California, the land of opportunity. San Jose [191–?] [28] p. illus., map.   CHi CSf CU-B

13777. Coates (Leonard) nursery co., Morgan Hill. [Catalog] 1916 and 1917. [S.F.? Taylor & Taylor, 1916] 33 p. illus.   CHi

13778. Coe, Charles W. Scenes of Santa Clara valley. San Jose, 1911. [50] p. of mounted photos. Photos by Andrew P. Hill, San Jose. "...The plates of these photographs were all destroyed by fire on the 18th of April 1906...Charles W. Coe." C

13779. Collins, Oriville E. vs. Scott, Angelia R. In the Supreme court of the State of California. Oriville E. Collins, et al., appellants, vs. Angelia R. Scott, et al., respondents. Points and authorities for respondents. Galpin & Zeigler, attorneys for respondents... S.F., W.A. Woodward & co. [1892] 22 p. CHi

13780. Cunningham, Florence R. New tales of old California. Our home town: the little sawmill on the shores of the Arroyo Quito. [Saratoga, 1942] 4 l. CHi CU-B

13781. Cutting, Theodore A. Historical sketch of Campbell. Campbell, Press of R.H. Knappen, 1929. [16] p. CLgA CO CSj CSmH

13782. —— Same, with title: History of Campbell. Campbell, T.A. Cutting & sons [c1947] 95 p. port. CU-B

13783. Daughters of the American revolution. California. Genealogical records committee. Early California wills, Santa Clara county, 1850–1864; Solano county, 1850–1873. Santa Clara records prepared by Santa Clara chapter... Solano records prepared by Solano chapter... [Santa Clara?] 1952. 49 l. Typew. C CL

13784. De Leuw, Cather & co. Trafficways plan for Santa Clara county, California. [S.F.] 1959. CSt

13785. Esberg, Alfred I. Rancho San Antonio, 1777– [n.p.] 1955. 5 l. Mimeo. CHi CU-B

13786. Foote, H. S. Hand book of political statistics of Santa Clara county, compiled from the public records and newspaper files, from the organization of the county. San Jose, Pioneer bk. and job print., 1878. 68 p. CHi

13787. Forbes, James Alexander. The battle of Santa Clara, an unpublished letter of James Alexander Forbes with a sketch by William H. Meyers of the battle of Santa Clara, 1847. S.F., Grabhorn, 1939. [4] p. illus. CHi CStclU

13788. Gates, Mary J. ...Rancho Pastoria de las Borregas. Mountain View, California. San Jose, Cottle & Murgotten, print., 1895. 27 p. Reprint. from the *Mountain View register*, Apr.-June, 1894. C CLU CSmH CU-B

13789. Gilroy. Chamber of commerce. Gilroy, the home of the prune, Santa Clara county, California. [n.p., 19–?] 20 p. illus., map. CSf CU-B

13790. —— **Charters.** Charter and municipal code. Published by authority of the Common council of the city of Gilroy, 1900. Gilroy, Gazette bk. and job print. [1900] CSmH

13791. Gilroy advocate. The Gilroy valley; its resources and home prospects. Gilroy, 1886. [8] p. CU-B

13792. Glover, Elma, ed. Santa Clara county... Pub. by the Bd. of trade of San Jose. [1888?] 64 p. illus. C CHi CSjCL

13793. Goold, Edmond L. ...In the matter of the survey of Las Animas. Objections on behalf of the owners of El Solis. (Patented in 1858) S.F., Francis and Valentine, law print., 1873. 27 p. CSmH

13794. Greenaway, Emerson. A metropolitan library system for Santa Clara county; studies on the organization of library services to meet new population demands. A report of a survey conducted for the county Board of supervisors upon the recommendation of the

county executive of the county of Santa Clara, California. San Jose [1958] 58 l. diagrs. CL CSjCL

13795. Griffin, Paul F. An industrial analysis of north Santa Clara county. San Jose, 1958. 43 p. CSt

13796. Guedici, Maria de Jesus vs. Boots, William. In the Supreme court of the state of California. Maria de Jesus Guedici, plaintiff and respondent, vs. William Boots, et als., defendants and appellants. Transcript on appeal. D. M. Delmas, for respondent. Frs. E. Spencer, for appellant. San Jose [1870] 44 p. Deals with Rancho Rincon de los Esteros in Santa Clara county. CLU

13797. Harrison, Edward Sanford. Central California, Santa Clara valley... San Jose, E.S. Harrison, C. Oberdeener [c1887] 142 p. illus., map. CHi CL CLU CO CSf CSfCSM CSj CSjC CSmH CStclU CU-B NN

13798. —— Gilroy, the most favored section of Santa Clara valley. Published for the Gilroy Board of trade by E. S. Harrison. [Gilroy, 1888?] 32 p. illus., map. CU-B

13799. Hearne bros., Detroit. Official Hearne brothers polyconic projection maps of all Santa Clara county. Constantly revised and kept up to date. [Detroit, 195–?] 1 v. (chiefly maps) C

13800. Herrington, D. W. vs. Santa Clara county. ...D. W. Herrington, appellant, vs. the county of Santa Clara, respondent. Petition for rehearing...Francis E. Spencer. [n.p., 186–?] 11 p. CU-B

13801. Herrington, D. W. vs. Sawyer, Ebenezer D. ...D. W. Herrington, district attorney, &c., vs. E. D. Sawyer, district judge... San Jose, 1868. 2 v. in 1. CU-B

13802. Herron, Laura Elizabeth. An educational history of Santa Clara county. [Berkeley, 1916] Thesis (M.A.)—Univ. of Calif., 1916. CU

13803. Immigration association of California. [County scrapbooks] [S.F., 188–?] C

13804. Industrial survey associates. Santa Clara county, its prospects of prosperity. Digest of a report for the Santa Clara county industrial survey advisory council and the San Jose chamber of commerce...with the assistance of the Area development division and the San Francisco regional office of the U.S. Department of commerce and the State office of planning and research. [S.F.?] 1948. 31 p. illus. C CSj

13805. Irvine, Leigh Hadley. ...Santa Clara county, California...produced under the direction of the Board of supervisors of Santa Clara county, California. [San Jose, Press of V.S. Hillis co., n.d.] 63 p. illus., maps. CHi CL CRcS CU-B

13806. —— Santa Clara county, Calif. Issued by San Jose Chamber of commerce. San Jose, Sunset pub. house, 1915. 64 p. CHi CO CStclU CU-B

13807. James, George Wharton. How we climb to the stars, and the Lick observatory, a lecture and guide book... S.F., Bancroft co., 1887. 39 p. illus. C CHi CL CLU CSmH CU-B

13808. League of women voters of San Jose. A citizen's guide to government in Santa Clara county, California. San Jose, 1958. unp. CLg

13809. Lessinger, Jack. The determination of land use in rural-urban transition areas; a case study in northern Santa Clara valley, California. [Berkeley, 1956] Thesis (Ph.D.)—Univ. of Calif., 1956. CU

13810. Lick, James vs. Alviso, Ignacio et al. ... James Lick, plaintiff vs. Ignacio Alviso et als., defendants.

Brief for defendants. Moore & Laine, att'ys for defendants. San Jose, W.A. January, print. [18–?] 16 p.
CU-B

13811. Los Altos co. Los Altos. [n.p., 1910?] 14 p. illus.   CHi

13812. McGlynn & Menton, San Francisco. Auction! auction! The Hale ranch, three and half miles from Mountain View, Santa Clara county. ...will be sold at auction on Saturday, March 22, 1902... S.F. [1902] double map. Part of Rancho San Antonio, Santa Clara county.   CHi

13813. Mader, George Goodrich. Planning the agriculture in urbanizing areas: a case study of Santa Clara county, California. [Berkeley, 1956] Thesis (M.A.) —Univ. of Calif., 1956.   CU

13814. Marcuse, Felix [owner and agent] Camp Wilderness, Lyndon station, located between Los Gatos and Alma; lots $20.00 and up... S.F., Janssen co. [n.d.] [12] p. illus.   CHi

13815. Mars, Amaury. Reminiscences of Santa Clara valley and San José, with the souvenir of the carnival of roses, held in honor of the visit of President McKinley, Santa Clara county, California, May 13-14-15, 1901. [S.F., Print. by Mysell-Rollins co., 1901] 276 p. illus., ports.
C CHi CL CLO CLgA CO CRic CSf CSj CSjC CSjCL CSmH CStclU CU-B KHi MoKU NN

13816. Martin, Richard Garland. Water conservation in the Santa Clara valley. [Berkeley, 1950] Thesis (M.A.)—Univ. of Calif., 1950.   CU

13817. Miller, Henry, et al. vs. Thomas, Massey, et al. In the Superior court of the state of California, in and for the county of Santa Clara. Henry Miller, et als., plaintiffs, vs. Massey, Thomas, et als., defendants. Report of referee. [n.p., 1885?] Rancho Las Animas.   CHi

13818. Miller, Myron Charles. A historical study of the development of Rancho Ojo de Agua de la Coche. [San Jose, 1952] Thesis (M.A.)—San Jose state college, 1952.   CSjC

13819. [Miller, Samuel] Lick observatory, Mount Hamilton. And Hotel Vendome, San Jose, California. [S.F., The Traveler, n.d.] 20 p. illus., port.   CU-B

13820. Moerenhaut, Jacob, et al. vs. Higuera, Valentin, et al. Supreme court of the state of California. Jacob A. Moerenhaut et al., appellants, v. Valentin Higuera et al., respondents. Brief for appellants... S.F., Commercial steam print. house [n.d.] 29 p.   CU-B

13821. Morgan Hill. Board of trade. Morgan Hill, Santa Clara county, California. [Morgan Hill, 1915] 16 p. illus., port.   CU-B

13822. Morrison, James vs. Mezes, S. M. et al. In the circuit court of the United States, for the districts of California. James Morrison vs. S. M. Mezes, and others, in equity. Motion for an injunction... S.F., Painter & co., 1861. 16 p.   CLU CU-B

13823. Mountain View. Board of trade. Mountain View, a region of health and prosperity... San Jose, Muirson & Wright [1903?] 31 p.   CU-B

13824. ——— ——— A region of health and prosperity, Mountain View... S.F., Print. by Stanley-Taylor co., under direction of "The Register" [1903?] 24 p.   CU-B

13825. New Chicago at port of Alviso...facts... showing location, present condition, future prospects... S.F., Woodward & co., print. [1890] 32 p.   CSf CU-B

13826. The new Pacific coast; a factual presentation of industrial development on the Pacific coast...with

particular reference to Santa Clara county, California. San Jose, Chamber of commerce [1946] 36 p. maps.
CHi

13827. Norberg, Leslie E. A history of the Santa Clara county office of education. [San Jose, 1951] 71 l. fold. map, charts. Thesis (M.A.)—San Jose state college, 1951.   CSjC

13828. Older, Cora Miranda (Baggerly) When Santa Clara was young. [Sixty-eight newspaper articles. S.F.? n.d.] [24] p.   CHi CSjCL CU-B

13829. Owen, J. J. Santa Clara valley: its resources, climate [etc.] with pen-sketches of prominent citizens. San Jose, Mercury steam print., 1873. 52 p. illus.
C CHi CSmH CStclU CU-B

13830. Parkhurst, W. A., and son, San Jose. San Jose and Santa Clara county...resources, attractions... profits of fruit raising... San Jose, Mercury steam bk. & job print. house, 1887. 43 p. illus.   CHi CU-B

13831. Perry, E. D., comp. Boundaries of the school districts of Santa Clara county... Watsonville, Print. by Pajaronian, 1894. 36 p.   CU-B

13832. [Pico, Antonio Maria] A los Californios. [S.F., Oficina del comite, 1860] folder (4 p.) An election circular written by Pico who was campaigning for his election as Senator from Santa Clara on the Republican ticket.—Cowan.   CSmH CU-B

13833. Picturesque San José and environments. An illustrated statement of the progress, prosperity and resources of Santa Clara county, California... San Jose, H.S. Foote & C.A. Woolfolk [c1893] [80] p. illus., maps.
CLU CSj CSjC CSjCL CSmH CU-B

13834. Reed, Edward P. vs. Allison, Robert and others. In the twentieth District court, state of California, Edward P. Reed vs. Robert Allison and others. Points and authorities for defendants, Hartman and Tyson. L.A., Mirror print. [187–?]   CHi

13835. Reeve, Lloyd Eric. Gift of the grape; based on Paul Masson vineyards, by Lloyd Eric Reeve and Alice Means Reeve. With a number of photos by Ansel Adams and Pirkle Jones. S.F., Filmer pub. co. [1959] 314 p. illus. (Lib. of Western industry)
C CHi CRcS

13836. Rice, Bertha Marguerite. Builders of our valley, a city of small farms. [n.p.] c1957. 1 v. illus., ports.   CHi CLg CLgA CSjC CSjCL CU-B

13837. ——— The women of our valley. [San Jose, The author] 1955–56. 2 v. illus., ports.
CHi (v.1) CLgA (v.2) CSjCL

13838. St. Joseph's college, Mountain View. Catalogue...for the academic year 1925–26. San Rafael, Hoey print. co., 1926. 61 p.   CHi

13839. Salmon, David William. Metropolitan area of Santa Clara county, California... Stanford univ., 1946. 281 l. Thesis (Ph.D.)—Stanford univ., 1946.
C CPa CSj CSjC CSjCL CStcl CU CU-B

13840. San Jose. Board of trade. Resources of Santa Clara valley, California; climate, productions, river & railroad systems... San Jose, Mercury steam print., 1875. 32 p. illus., map.   C CHi NHi

13841. ——— ——— Santa Clara county... San Jose, Smith & Wilcox, Mercury job rooms, 1890. 87 p.
CL CSf CSmH CU-B NN

13842. ——— Chamber of commerce. Cream of California... [n.p., 1911?] 10 p.   CHi

13843. ——— ——— Facts about the great Santa Clara valley... San Jose [1904?] 47 p.   CSmH CU-B

13844. —— —— The greatest land show in California is a trip through Santa Clara county. [San Jose, Melvin & Murgotten, 1913?] [16] p.   CHi

13845. —— —— Santa Clara county, California. [San Jose] Press of Muirson & Wright [1905] [19] p. illus. Compiled with the cooperation of the Santa Clara county Board of supervisors. Title varies. Many editions followed.

CHi (1905, 1913, 1935) CLU (1931?) CRcS (1926, 1931, 1938, 1939) CSf (1905) CSjCL (1931?) CStclU (1931?) CU-B (192–?, 1921?, 1931?, 1935)

13846. —— **Public library.** Authors of Santa Clara county. [San Jose, 1956] 110 p.   C CLg CSt

13847. San Jose Mercury, pub. Santa Clara county and its resources; historical, descriptive, statistical... [San Jose, c1895] 319 p. illus., ports., map.

CAlaC CHi CL CLg CLgA CO CP CPa CSf CSjC CSjCL CSmat CSt CStcrCL CU-B NHi

13848. —— Same. 2d ed. [c1896] 322 p. illus., ports., map.

CL CLU CSf CSj CSjC CSmH CSmat CStrCL CU-B MWA NN

13849. Santa Clara county. Board of supervisors. Santa Clara county, the sunny garden of California. Blossom time in the Santa Clara valley. San Jose, 1915. 16 p. illus.   CHi CL CU-B

13850. —— **Citizens.** Petition to the Legislature from citizens of Santa Clara county relative to mail service between the city of San Jose and the town of Almaden. [Sacramento, Gelwicks, state print., 1870] CSmH

13851. —— **Health dept.** Air pollution report: 1948–1955. San Jose, 1955. [16] p. illus.   CHi

13852. —— **Ordinances.** Ordinances of the county of Santa Clara, state of California... San Jose, Popp & Hogan print., 1913. 105 p.   CHi

13853. —— **Planning dept.** Milpitas; an arrested community meets the twentieth century [San Jose] 1954. 71 p. illus., maps.   CHi CRic CSjCL CSt

13854. —— —— Preliminary inventory of historical landmarks in Santa Clara county. San Jose, 1962. [15] p. tables.   CHi

13855. —— —— South Santa Clara county, a physical and economic survey. San Jose, 1957. 57 l.   CSt

13856. Santa Clara county, California. v.1, no. 1; Sept. 1887. [San Jose] Bd. of trade of San Jose, 1887. 96 p. illus., map. No more published.

C C-S CHi CLU CSj CSjCL CSmH CStclU CU-B

13857. Santa Clara county council on intergovernmental relations. A practical basis for developing better intergovernmental relations... San Jose [1947] 50 p. illus.   C CChiS CRcS

13858. Santa Clara county historical society. Papers read before the Santa Clara county historical society... [San Jose] 1911. 50 p.

C CHi CLO CLSU CSj CSjC CStclU

13859. Santa Clara county pioneers, San Jose. Constitution, by-laws and list of members of the Santa Clara pioneers, organized, June 22d, 1875... San Jose, Argus off. print., 1875. 19 p.   CHi CU-B

13860. Santa Clara valley agricultural society. ...Annual exhibition...to be held at San Jose... [ninth] 1868. San Jose, Owen & Cottle, print., 1868. 49 p. illus.   CU-B

13861. Santa Clara valley improvement club.

Santa Clara county, California. [San Jose, Muirson & Wright, 190–?] [20] p. illus.   CHi CU-B

13862. Stuart, Reginald R., ed. The Burrell letters; including excerpts from Birney Burrell's diary and *Reminiscences of an octogenarian*; a contribution to Santa Clara county history from the original manuscripts. Oakland, Westgate press, 1950.   CLg

13863. Swanson, Dorothea Louise (Schmitt) History of the Santa Clara valley: the American period, 1846–1865. [Berkeley, 1928] 241 l. port., maps. Thesis (M.A.)—Univ. of Calif., 1928.   CU CU-B

13864. Thomas bros. Popular atlas [of] Santa Clara county. Oakland, [195–?–]

CPa (1956, 1958) CSjCL (1952)

13865. Tibbetts, Fred H. Report on waste water salvage project to the board of directors, Santa Clara valley water conservation district... [San Jose, Wright-Eley print. co.] 1931. 78 p. illus., diagrs., tables.   CPa

13866. Treadwell, Edward Francis. The cattle king... N.Y., Macmillan, 1931. 367 p. ports. Biography of Henry Miller.

Available in many libraries.

13867. —— Same. rev. ed. Bost., Christopher pub. house [1950] 375 p. ports., map.

CHi CSS CSal CSf

13868. Tremayne, Frank Gilbert. History of the Santa Clara valley: the Mexican period. [Berkeley] 1923. 227 l. illus. Thesis (M.A.)—Univ. of Calif., 1923.

CU CU-B

13869. Tyler, William Harold. Trade union sponsorship of interracial housing: a case study [Milpitas, California] [Berkeley, 1957] Thesis (M.A.)—Univ. of Calif., 1957.   CU

13870. United States vs. Chaboya, Pedro. United States District court for the Northern district of California. United States v. Pedro Chaboya. Argument for claimant. Eugene Liés, of counsel. [S.F.?] Painter & co., print. [n.d.] 24 p.   CU-B

13871. United States vs. Higuera, José, heirs of. In the District court of the United States, for the Northern district of California. The United States vs. The heirs of José Higuera, no. 228. "Los Tularcitos."... S.F., Commercial steam presses [1861] 20 p.   CU-B

13872. U.S. District court. California (Northern district) ...No. 206. The United States vs. M. C. V. de Rodríguez et al. Opinion of the court. [S.F.? 1864] 31 p. Decision in the case of the claim of María Concepción Valencia de Rodríguez for the Rancho San Francisquito, in Santa Clara county.   CSmH

13873. —— **Work projects administration.** Visualore, Santa Clara county, California; a practical volume of visual, educational, commercial and industrial resources; prepared and pub. as a report on Official project 665-08-3-54...sponsored by Santa Clara county Board of supervisors. San Jose, Prepared under the direction of the Santa Clara county librarian, 1939. unp. Typew.

C CSjCL CU-B

13874. Walter, Carrie (Stevens) In California's garden, Santa Clara valley. [San Jose, A.C. Eaton] c1897. [32] p. illus.   CHi CSmH CU-B

13875. Wells, Harry Laurenz. In blossom land... San Jose and Santa Clara county... [San Jose, Santa Clara improvement club, 1901] unp. illus. Reprint from *Sunset mag.*   CHi CU-B

13876. Western land co., San Francisco. Partial list of Santa Clara lands for sale by Western land company. [S.F.? 189–?] 12 p.   C

13877. Whiteside, William A. An economic survey of the Milpitas area. Stanford, 1955. Thesis (M.A.)— Stanford univ., 1955.   CSt

13878. Wolf, E. Myron vs. Santa Clara county Board of supervisors. ...E. Myron Wolf, plaintiff and appellant, vs. the Board of supervisors of the county of Santa Clara, etc., et al., defendants and respondents. Transcript on appeal, from order of the Superior court of the county of Santa Clara. Honorable S. F. Leib, judge. E. Myron H. Campbell, district attorney, C. W. Cobb, attorneys for respondents... [S.F.] Pernau press [1904] 39 p.   CU-B

13879. Woman's club of Palo Alto, Palo Alto. Santa Clara valley; a promotion magazine... Palo Alto, 1911. 81 p. illus.   C CHi CPa CSmH CU-B

13880. Wooster, Whitton & Montgomery. California's richest realm. Santa Clara valley. Some views of the San Martin ranch subdivision... [San Jose, Muirson & Wright, print., 1901?] [32] p. illus.   CU-B

13881. Wright, William Hammond. The founding of the Lick observatory... Fifty years of research at the Lick observatory, by J. H. Moore. 30 p. illus. Reprint. from *Astronomical soc. of the Pacific.* Pub. v.50, nos. 295–96, June and August 1938.   CHi

13882. Wyatt, Roscoe D., and Arbuckle, Clyde. Historic names, persons and places in Santa Clara county. San Jose, San Jose chamber of commerce for the Calif. pioneers of Santa Clara county, 1948. 42 p. illus., ports.
C CHi CL CLU CLgA CO CSf CSfWF-H CSjC CSjCL CStcl CU-B CoU MWA

13883. Young, John V. Ghost towns of the Santa Cruz mountains. San Jose Mercury-herald, Sunday Apr. 22 to Sunday July 22, 1934. 14 issues, one each Sunday.
CLgA CSjC

Los Gatos

13884. Addicott, James Edwin. Grandad's pioneer stories; Santa Clara valley; "The cats" of Los Gatos. Los Gatos, Author, c1953. 78 p. illus.
CLg CSjC CSjCL CStclU CStcrCL

13885. —— Grandad's stunts. Los Gatos, Times press, c1951.   CAltu

13886. American trust co. A guide to historical photographs, Los Gatos, California, contained in a collection presented to the Los Gatos memorial library by the American trust company, March 1956. [Los Gatos? 1956] 24 p.   C

13887. California grape food co. The unfermented juice of the grape, its uses, value and forms as produced and bottled by the California grape food company. [n.p., 1893?] 24 p.   CHi

13888. First national bank of Los Gatos. Bank service. no. 1–100, October 1, 1913–1927.   CLg

13889. Hamsher, Clarence F. How Los Gatos got its name... [Los Gatos? Author, 1946] [4] p.   CHi

13890. League of women voters of Los Gatos. Los Gatos, 1958. unp.   CLg

13891. Los Gatos. Board of trade. Souvenir of Los Gatos, California; the city of homes. [Los Gatos, 1908?] 1 l. illus.   CHi

13892. ——— Chamber of commerce. Los Gatos, gem city of the foothills... [S.F.? Sunset mag. home-seekers' bur.? 1912?] 31 p. illus.   CHi CU-B

13893. ——— Same. [Los Gatos? 1916] 31 p. illus.   CU-B

13894. Montezuma school for boys, Los Gatos. [Brochure. n.p., 1952] [12]p. illus.   CHi

13895. ——— The Montezuma mountain school for boys. [S.F.? Schwabacher-Frey co., 1935?] 28 p. illus.   CHi

13896. ——— The Montezuma plan. Los Gatos, 1927. 18 p.   CU-B

13897. Walton, Effie. Two for the show. N.Y., Vantage, 1964. 116 p. illus. Autobiography of a Santa Clara valley real estate woman.   CLg

New Almaden

13898. Algunas declaraciones en al asunto de New Almaden en la Alta California. Mexico, Andrade y Escalante, 1859. 36 p.   C

13899. ——— Same, translated into English. Wash., D.C., G.S. Gideon, print., 1860. 41 p.   CLU

13900. Ascher, Leonard William. The economic history of the New Almaden quicksilver mine, 1845–1863. [Berkeley, 1934] Thesis (Ph.D.)—Univ. of Calif., 1934.
CU

13901. California. Legislature. Joint resolution of the Legislature of California relating to the New Almaden mine. Wash., D.C., Gideon [1860] 2 p.   CLU

13902. Castillero, Andrés vs. United States. In the United States District court, Northern district of California. Andrés Castillero vs. the United States, on appeal from the decree of the United States commissioners to ascertain and settle the private land claims in the state of California. Brief of Hall McAllister. [n.p., 1859?] 98 p.   CLU CSfCW CSmH CU-B CtY

13903. ——— ...Testimony of Antonio Suñol... San Francisco, July 27, 1860. [n.p., n.d.] 6 p.   CU-B

13904. ——— ...Testimony of E. W. F. Sloan...10 day August, A.D. 1860. [n.d., n.p.] 7 p.   CU-B

13905. ——— ...Testimony of W. F. Swasey... San Francisco, June 21, 1860. [n.p., n.d.] 8 p.   CU-B

13906. ——— ...Testimony of William S. Reese... San Francisco, July 18, 1860. [n.p., 1860] 3 p.   CU-B

13907. Castillero, Andrés. Registry and act of possession to the mine of New Almaden in 1845. [S.F.?] O'Meara & Painter [n.d.] 8 p.   C CSmH

13908. Castillero's mining right, or title. [n.p., 185–?] 140 p.   CLU

13909. Coignet. Rapport sur les mines de New Almaden (Californie) par m. Coignet, ingénieur, attaché à la mission scientifique du Mexique. Paris, Dunod, 1866. 47 p. fold. pl., fold. map. "Extrait des *Annales des mines,* tome IX, 1866."   C CLU

13910. [Eldredge, James] Private letters on the Fossatt-Almaden land claim, by James Eldredge. [n.p., 1862?] 12, 28, 16 p.   CHi

13911. [Goold, Edmond Louis] To the President of the United States: The undersigned, counsel in the suit entitled Maria Zernal de Berreyesa et als. versus the United States...respectfully represents... [n.p., 186–?] 8 p. Deals with the New Almaden mine.   CLU

13912. History of the mineral and allodial titles of the quicksilver mines in the Ranchos de los Capitancillos, Santa Clara county, California. [N.Y., 1858] 16 p. CLU

13913. Johnson, Kenneth M. The New Almaden quicksilver mine; with an account of the land claims involving the mine and its role in California history. Georgetown, Talisman, 1963. 115 p. illus., map.
CAla CHi

13914. Kuss, Henri. Memoir on the mines and works of Almaden... Tr. from the *Annales des mines.*

... S.F., Dewey & co., Mining and scientific press, 1879. 32 p. illus.   CLU

13915. [Mexico. Secretaría de relaciones exteriores] Report of Mexican plenipotentiaries. Translated from the Spanish. [n.p., 1859?] 8 p. Deals with the New Almaden mine.   CLU

13916. Muckler, Billie Phyllis. History of the Guadalupe quicksilver mine. [Berkeley, 1941] Thesis (M.A.)—Univ. of Calif., 1941.   CU CU-B

13917. New Almaden mines. Correspondence in relation to the New Almaden quicksilver mine of California, between the counsel for the proprietors and the government. S.F., Commercial steam presses [1859?] 65 p. Printed signatures at end: Reverdy Johnson, J. J. Crittenden, John A. Rockwell and J. P. Benjamin.
                                                      CLU CSmH CU-B

13918. —— Same. Wash., D.C., G.S. Gideon, print. [1859?] 77 p.   CLU

13919. —— Same, Tr. into Spanish. Mexico, Andrade y Escalante, 1860. 110 p.   C

13920. —— The discussion reviewed. S.F., Daily national off., 1859. 76 p. Written by Edmund Randolph, and signed "Burgher."   C CLU CSmH CU-B

13921. —— Same, as published December 31, 1858 and January 1, 1859. S.F., S.F. herald off., 1859. 11 p.
                                              C CLU CSmH CtY

13922. —— Further correspondence in relation to the New Almaden quicksilver mine of California, between the counsel for the proprietors and the government. S.F., Commercial steam presses [1859?] 43 p.
                                          C CHi CLU CSmH CU-B

13923. —— Same. Wash., D.C., G.S. Gideon, 1859. 42 p.   C

13924. —— A letter to the Attorney general on his report to the President on the resolution of the Legislature of California, from a California pioneer. N.Y., Baker & Godwin, print., 1860. 23 p.   C CLU CStclU

13925. —— Letters from the San Francisco daily herald, as published on the mornings of the 15th, 17th and 18th December, 1858. S.F., S.F. herald off., 1858. 8 p.
                                          CHi CLU CSmH CU-B

13926. Nowland, James A. Report of Jas. A. Nowland, Supt. of New Almaden mines, Jan. 1st, 1867. S.F., Edward Bosqui & co., 1867. 20 p.   C

13927. One statement of the Almaden case. A plea for the present possessors of the mine. [S.F.] O'Meara & Painter, print. [1858] 7 p. Signed at end: From the *Evening Bulletin* of 7th December, 1858.   CSmH CU-B

13928. Quicksilver mining co. Charter and by-laws; proceedings of the annual meeting of the stockholders, held at Philadelphia, Feb. 22, 1865. With reports and map. N.Y., R.C. Root, Anthony & co., 1865. 114 p. fold. map.   CHi

13929. Rauen, James J. A sociological history of New Almaden, California, 1800–1897. [San Jose] 1958.
                                                      CSjC

13930. Smart and cornered. How to get a mine without finding, opening or working one. By a quartz miner. S.F., Commercial bk. and job steam print. off., 1860. 31 p. Deals with the New Almaden mine.
                                  CLU CSmH CU CU-B NN (imp.)

13931. [Sullivan, Frank J.] A contested election in California. Frank J. Sullivan vs. Hon. C. N. Felton. Testimony of the qualified electors and legal voters of New Almaden... [n.p.] 1887. 163 p. illus. Reprint. from the *San Jose daily mercury,* Santa Clara county. Testi-

mony mostly concerning the management of the New Almaden quicksilver mines.   CLU CSfU

13932. Tobin, James vs. Walkinshaw, Robert et al. In the circuit court of the United States for the district of California. James Tobin vs. Robert Walkinshaw et als. Action of ejectment. M. Hall McAllister, circuit judge. Ogden Hoffman, district judge. S.F., Whitton, Towne & co.'s Excelsior steam presses [n.d.] 114 p. Suit involving the Justo Larios rancho.   CU-B

13933. —— ...James Tobin, trustee vs. Robert Walkinshaw, and others. In equity. Motion for injunction and appointment of receiver. Opinion of Judge McAllister. S.F., Whitton, Towne & co., 1856. 26 p.
                                          C CLU CSmH CU-B

13934. —— Supreme court of the United States, no. 227. James Tobin, pl'ff in error, vs. Robert Walkinshaw, James A. Forbes and William E. Barron. In error to the Circuit court U.S. for the Northern district of California. [Wash., D.C.] Gideon, print. [1858?] 116 p.
                                                      CLU

13935. United States vs. Castillero, Andrés. In the United States District court, Northern district of California. The United States vs. Andrés Castillero. "New Almaden" transcript of record. S.F., Whitton, Towne & co. print. [1858–1861] 4 v.
                     C CHi CL CLU CSj CSmH CStclU CU-B

13936. —— Various documents in the suit for the possession of the mine and lands of New Almaden, 1858–1863.
             C CHi CLU CSf CSfCW CSmH CtY ICN NN

13937. United States vs. Fossat, Charles. In the District court, Northern district of California. The United States vs. Charles Fossat. No. 132. "Los Capitancillos." Transcript of the record... [S.F.] Commercial steam presses [1861?] vii [5]–298 p. Documents in the suit for possession of the Rancho de los Capitancillos on which was located the New Almaden quicksilver mine.
                                                      CLU

13938. —— ...Testimony on boundaries. [S.F.] Commercial steam presses [1858] 178 p. fold. map.
                                              CHi CLU CSmH

13939. —— In the Supreme court of the United States. No. 242. December term, 1858. The United States vs. Charles Fossatt [!]: motion to dismiss appeal. Brief for appellants. [Wash., D.C., 1858] 16 p. Signed at end: J. S. Black, attorney general, Reverdy Johnson, for appellants. Deals with Rancho de los Capitancillos suit.
                                                      CLU

13940. United States vs. Parrott, John et al. In the Circuit court, Northern district of California. And the claim of Castillero, in the District court, for the New Almaden mine. Arguments of Mr. Peachy and Mr. Yale, in the District court, on the motion for a commission to take evidence in the city of Mexico, in support of the claim. [S.F.] O'Meara & Painter, print., 1859. 67 p.
                                          CHi CLU CSmH CU-B

13941. —— ...The United States of America v. John Parrott, Henry W. Halleck, James R. Bolton, William E. Barron, John Young and Robert Walkinshaw. In equity. [n.p., 185–?] 210 p.   CLU

13942. —— ...The United States of America, v. John Parrott, Henry W. Halleck, James R. Bolton [and others] in equity. [n.p., 1858] 27 p.   CLU

13943. U.S. Attorney General. New Almaden mine. Report of the Attorney General to the President on the resolutions of the legislature of California. S.F., Commercial steam bk. and job presses, 1860. 14 p.
                                                      CSmH

13944. —— **Circuit court (Ninth circuit)** ... James Tobin vs. Walkinshaw, et al. In ejectment. Opinion of the court delivered by Judge McAllister. September term, 1855. [n.p., 1855] 16 p.   CSmH CU-B

13945. —— —— ...The United States vs. John Parrott, et als. In equity. Opinions of Hon. M. H. McAllister and Hon. Ogden Hoffman, on motion for injunction and appointment of a receiver. S.F., Towne & Bacon, 1858. 7 p.   CSmH CU-B

13946. —— **Commission for settling private land claims in California.** ...Andres Castillero vs. the United States. No. 366. Claim for quicksilver mine of New Almaden. Brief for the United States. S.F., Herald off., 1855. 16 p.   CSmH

13947. —— —— ...Claim of Andres Castillero to the mine and land of New Almaden. [S.F.? 1855?] 70, 72 p.   CLU

13948. —— —— ...Opinion of commissioner R. Aug. Thompson, dissenting from the majority of the board. Delivered January 8, 1856. [S.F.] F.A. Bonnard print., Sun job off. [1856] 14 p.   CSmH

13949. —— **District court. California (Northern district)** ...The United States vs. Andres Castillero. No. 420, New Almaden. Opinion of his honor M. Hall McAllister, circuit judge, delivered January 16, 1861. S.F., Commercial steam bk. & job print., 1861. 72 p.   C CSmH CU-B

13950. —— —— —— ...Opinion of his Honor Ogden Hoffman, district judge, delivered January 17, 1861. S.F., Commercial steam bk. and job print., 1861. 158 p.   C CLU CSmH CU-B

13951. —— **Supreme court.** ...Andres Castillero, appellant, vs. the United States, and the United States, appellants, vs. Andres Castillero. Opinion of the court and dissenting opinions. Cross-appeals from the District court of the United States for the Northern district of California. [S.F.] Towne & Bacon, print. [1863?] 33, 3, 80 p. Cover title.   CLU

13952. Wells, William Vincent. A visit to the quicksilver mines of New Almaden. Belonging to the Quicksilver mining company. N.Y., Harper, 1863. 25–40 p. illus. Reprint. from *Harpers'* new monthly mag., June, 1863.   C CLSM CLU

13953. Yale, Gregory. Reply to a paper of E. L. Goold's relating to the New Almaden mine. Wash., D.C., G.S. Gideon, print., 1860. 15 p. Signed: Gregory Yales [!]   CLU

Palo Alto

13954. Abrams, Dolores M. A history of the Palo Alto community theatre, 1931–36. Stanford, 1957. Thesis (M.A.)—Stanford univ., 1957.   CSt

13955. The Business men of Palo Alto, pub. Palo Alto and its surroundings; the Leland Stanford junior university town. Palo Alto, 1894. 32 p. illus. CHi

13956. California. Dept. of education. ...Survey of the Palo Alto public schools, directed by Andrew P. Hill, jr. ... Sacramento, State print. off., 1931. 265 p. illus., maps.   CL CPa

13957. Castilleja school. Catalogue. 1892/93– Palo Alto [etc., 1892]–
CHi has 1907/08–1908/09, 1915/16, 1919/20, 1926/27, 1929/30. CU-B has 1892/93–1894/95, 1900/01, 1908/09–1909/10, 1911/12–1912/13, 1914/15, 1916/17, 1918/19, 1920/21, 1922/23–1926/27, 1929/30, 1931/32, 1934/35–1935/36.

13958. Dupuis, Victor. Victor Dupuis, French gardener and florist... [n.p., 1899?] [4] p.   CHi

13959. Fish, J. C. L. Typhoid fever epidemic at Palo Alto, California; a report made to the Palo Alto Board of health... Palo Alto, Board of health, 1905. 62 p. charts, maps.   CHi

13960. Harker's (Miss) school. Calendar. 1st– , 1902/03– Palo Alto, 1902–
CHi has 1906/07–1908/09, 1916/17. CU-B has 1909/10, 1920/21, 1927/28, 1939/40, 1941/42, 1950/51.

13961. —— Miss Harker's school, a home and day school for girls, Palo Alto, California. Palo Alto [1939] [43] p. illus.   CHi

13962. Hiller aircraft corp. Annual report. CHi has 1925. CL has 1954, 1958–59.

13963. —— Prospectus...May 15, 1951. [n.p.] 1951. 33 p.   CHi

13964. Johnson, Edith E. Leaves from a doctor's diary. Palo Alto, Pac. books, 1954. 279 p. port.   CSd

13965. Kirschner, Flora L. The post-war period of the Palo Alto community theatre, Fall, 1945–Fall 1955. Stanford, 1957. Thesis (M.A.)—Stanford univ., 1957.   CSt

13966. Layng, William G., auctioneer. Auction sale of standard bred horses from Palo Alto stock farm, Palo Alto, Cal. ... Thursday August 15th, 1901...721 Howard street, near Third, San Francisco. [S.F., Phillips, Smyth & Van Orden print., 1901?] 18 p.   CHi

13967. Not in use.

13968. Manzanita hall, Palo Alto. Catalogue. [19—?– Palo Alto [19—?–
CU-B has 1910/11, 1913/14, 1917/18.

13969. —— Manzanita hall, preparatory school for boys...1894/95. [Palo Alto? 1894] 24 p.   CU-B

13970. Mayfield, Santa Clara county. Carnival of roses, San Jose, May 1896. [San Jose? 1896?] [3] p. A review of the town of Mayfield, now part of Palo Alto.   CU-B

13971. Miller, Guy Chester, ed. Palo Alto community book. Guy C. Miller, editor-in-chief, Hugh Enochs, associate editor and compiler. Palo Alto, Arthur H. Cawston, 1952. 364 p. illus., ports.
C CHi CL CPa CSf CSmat CStoC CU-B

13972. Palo Alto. Chamber of commerce. Palo Alto. [192–?] 30 p. illus.   CSj

13973. —— —— Same. Palo Alto, Slonaker's print. house [1929] 15 p. illus., map.   CRcS

13974. —— —— Palo Alto, California, the home of President Hoover and of Stanford university. [Palo Alto? Sunset press, 1931] 20 p. illus., ports.   CRcS

13975. —— —— Palo Alto, California, where people like to live. [Palo Alto, 1960?] [8] p. illus.   CHi

13976. —— **Charters.** City of Palo Alto administrative code and charter. Effective July 1, 1950 as amended ... Palo Alto [1954] 83 p.   CPa

13977. —— **City planning commission.** Study for a regional plan of the district surrounding Palo Alto. Palo Alto, 1927. 13 p. fold. plan, diagrs.   CU-B

13978. —— **Ordinances, etc.** Fire prevention code. Palo Alto, 1954. 52 p.   CPa

13979. —— —— The ordinances of the town of Palo Alto; a municipal corporation of the sixth class. Rev. and codified...Comp. by Norman E. Malcolm... Palo Alto, Palo Altan print., 1905. 189 p.   CSfCW

13980. —— —— Zoning ordinance [and supplements] city of Palo Alto, April 1956. [Palo Alto? 1956?]
CPa

13981. —— **First Presbyterian church.** Thirty-fifth anniversary, 1893–1928. [n.p., Slonaker's print. house, 1928] [12] p.
CHi

13982. —— **Survey committee.** Community recreation survey of the city of Palo Alto, June, 1936. [Palo Alto, 1936] 68 p.
CPa

13983. Palo Alto, California, seat of Stanford university. [Palo Alto, Times pub. co., 1921] 30 p. illus., map.
CHi

13984. Palo Alto community players, inc. 1,001 first nights; the first quarter century of the Palo Alto community players, 1931–1956. [Palo Alto, 1955] 44 p. illus., ports.   C   CO   CPa   CRcS

13985. Palo Alto military academy. A school for junior boys. [S.F.] Kennedy-Ten Bosch co., 1928. 48 p. illus.
CHi

13986. Palo Alto news, comp. A.B.C. directory, classified business directory. Palo Alto, A.B.C. pub. co., 1932. Contains reverse telephone directory for Palo Alto, Atherton, Menlo Park, Mountain View and Sunnyvale.
CHi

13987. Palo Alto times. ...Memorial number... [Palo Alto, 1920] 96 p. illus., ports.   C   CHi   CPa

13988. Palo Alto tribune. First annual edition and rehabilitation number, April 19, 1907.
CHi

13989. Ramona street. Palo Alto [Merchants on Ramona street, n.d.] 14 p.   CHi   CRcS

13990. Russell, Frances Theresa (Peet) and Winters, Yvor. The case of David Lamson, a summary ... Introduction by Peter B. Kyne... S.F., Lamson defense committee, 1934. 103 p. port. History of Lamson murder trial.   C   CHi   CL   CO   CSj   CSmH   CU-B

13991. Seale academy. [Catalog] 1920/21–1922/ 23. Palo Alto. 1 v. illus., ports.
CU-B

13992. Stanford, Leland. Catalogue of trotting stock, the property of Leland Stanford, Palo Alto... 1882, 1884, 1886–1900. [S.F.? 1882–1900] Title varies. Publisher varies.
CHi

13993. Weymouth, Alice (Jenkins) The Palo Alto tree... Stanford [1930] 20 p. maps. "References": p. 19–20.
C   CHi   CO   CRcS   CSdS   CSf   CSfP   CSmat   CSmH   CStrJC   CU-B

13994. Wood, Dallas England, ed. History of Palo Alto... Palo Alto, Cawston, 1939. 347 p. illus., port.
C   CL   CLU   CO   CPa   CRcS   CSf   CSmH   CU-B   NN

San Jose

13995. Associated charities, San Jose. ...Annual report...1895, 1898–1904. San Jose, 1896–1905. 6 v.
CU-B

13996. Bacon's family shoe store. Catalogue. [189–?] San Jose [189–?] 1 v. illus.   CU-B

13997. Bleasdale, John I. The report of a jury of experts on brandy made by Gen. Henry M. Naglee, at San Jose... S.F., Spaulding, Barto & co., 1879. 48 p.
CHi

13998. Braly, John Hyde. Memory pictures; an autobiography. L.A., Neuner co., 1912. 263 p. illus.
CBb   CHi   CL   CSjC

13999. Brown, Edna May. A history of the Winchester mystery house. San Jose [Rosicrucian press, ltd., 194–?] 20 p. illus.
C

14000. Bruce's print & publishing house, San Francisco. Bruce's convention guide; Democratic state convention...Aug. 19, 1890, San Jose, California. [S.F., 1890] 13 p. ports.
CHi

14001. California vs. Worswick, George D. ... The people of the state of California, on the complaint of Charles J. Martin, plaintiff and appellant vs. George D. Worswick, defendant and respondent. Appellant's points and authorities. U. S. Webb, attorney general, and E. E. Cothran, attorneys for appellant... [n.p., 1903] 57 p.
CU-B

14002. California. Legislature. Assembly. Committee on claims. Report of the Committee on claims, with reference to the petitions of the city of San Jose for relief. [Sacramento] B.B. Redding, state print. [1885] 2 p.
CSmH

14003. —— **State agricultural society.** Official report of the...society's third annual agricultural fair, cattle show and industrial exhibition, annual meeting, etc., held at San Jose, October 7th, 8th, 9th and 10th, 1856. [S.F.] Calif. farmer off., 1856. 80 p. illus.
C   CHi   CLCM   CSfCP   CSmH   CU-B   NvHi

14004. —— **State college, San Jose.** After eighty years; San Jose state college. 1942.   CSjC

14005. —— —— Catalogue. 1870/71?– Sacramento [1870?–
CHi has 1873/74–1875/76, 1878/79, 1886/87, 1892/93. CL has 1924– to date. CSjC has 1870/71–1910. CU-B has 1870/71–1874/75, 1879/80, 1887/88, 1889/90–1893/94, 1895/96.

14006. —— —— Diamond jubilee, San Jose state college, 1862–1937. unp.   CSjC

14007. —— —— Diamond jubilee. Scrapbook.
CSjC

14008. —— —— Historical sketch of the State normal school at San Jose, California, with a catalogue of its graduates and record of their work for twenty-seven years. Sacramento, State print. off., 1889. 283 p. illus.
C   CChis   CHi   CL   CLO   CLSU   CO   COHN   CSdS   CSf   CSfCW   CSjC   CSmH   CU-B   NHi   ViU

14009. —— —— Pioneers for one hundred years, 1857–1957; San Jose state college. [San Jose, 1957] [26] p. illus., ports.   CSjC   CU-B

14010. —— —— President's convocation formally opening the centennial festival celebrating the one hundredth anniversary of the founding of San Jose state college. San Jose, 1957.   CSjC

14011. —— —— Record book, 1875/76–1902/03.
CSjC

14012. —— —— [Register, 1862–67]   CSjC

14013. California infantry. San Jose Zouaves (Militia) Constitution and by-laws of the San Jose Zouaves... [San Jose] Owen & Cottle, print., 1862. 11 p.
CU-B

14014. California state Sunday school convention. Journal of proceedings of the fourth annual... convention, held at San Jose...1871. S.F., Bacon & co., 1871. [114] p.
CHi

14015. California water service co. Annual report. San Jose, 19—?–
CHi has 1953, 1955. CL has 1954–60.

14016. —— Prospectus...December 3, 1946. [n.p.] 1946. 39 p. map.
CHi

14017. Cavanagh, C. R. Urban expansion and

physical planning in San Jose, California: a case study. [Berkeley, 1953] Thesis (M.A.)—Univ. of Calif., 1953.
CU

14018. Child, Stephen. A plan for the development of Alum Rock park (reservation) at San Jose... S.F., 1916. 2 v. Typew.   CSj CU-B

14019. Christman, Howard A., ed. First Methodist church, San Jose, California, a century of service, 1847–1947. [San Jose, 1947] [40] p. illus., ports.
CSj CSjCL CSmH CU-B

14020. Citizens' planning council of greater San Jose, 1943–1945. [San Jose, 1946] unp.   C

14021. Clark, Burton R. The open door college; a case study. N.Y., McGraw, 1960. 207 p. illus.
CChiS CLod

14022. Clark, Mary Margaret. Health in the Mexican-American culture; a community study of the Spanish speaking people of San Jose, California. Berkeley, Univ. of Calif. press, 1959. 253 p. map, diagrs., tables.
CChiS CLO CPa CSS CStmo CU-B CViCL

14023. Dailey, Morris Elmer. In memoriam, April 14, 1867–July 5, 1919... Sacramento, State bd. of educ. [1919]   CSjC

14024. —— Morris Elmer Dailey, 1867–1919. Arranged by the class of March 1921. San Jose, State normal school, 1921.   CSjC

14025. Davidson, Percy Erwin; Anderson, H. Dewey; and Shlaudeman, Karl. Occupational mobility in an American community [San Jose] Stanford, 1937. 203 p. Photoprinted.
C CChiS CL CO COnC CSdS CSf CSj CSjC CStmo CU-B CWhC

14026. Democratic party. California. Proceedings and the address and resolutions of the Democratic meeting, held at the capitol, at the city of San Jose, March 1851. To take measures for the organization of the Democratic party in California. San Jose, J. Winchester, print., 1851. 9 p.   C CU-B

14027. East San Jose homestead association. Good news for the homeless! East San Jose homestead association... [San Jose, 1869] [4] p.   CU-B

14028. Easton, Eldridge & co., San Francisco. ...Grand auction sale in, and excursion to San Jose, Saturday, August 20, 1887, where we will sell at auction ...the Sullivan tract... [n.p., 1887] [4] p. map.
CHi

14029. —— ...Second grand auction sale in, and excursion to San Jose, Saturday, August 27th, 1887, where we will sell at auction...300 choice residence lots... [n.p., 1887] [4] p. map.   CHi

14030. Empire engine co. no. 1. San Jose. Constitution and by-laws... San Jose. Owen & Cottle, print., 1863. 19 p.   CU-B

14031. Farwell, William. Housing a truth center; how it was accomplished. Kansas City, Mo., 1927. 16 p. illus., plan.   CU-B

14032. First national bank of San Jose. 75th anniversary, 1874–1949. [San Jose, 1949] [16] p. illus., ports., charts.   CHi

14033. Freemasons. San Jose. Royal Arch Masons. Howard chapter, no. 14. By-laws and roster of members, November 1, 1920. San Jose, 1920. [19] p.
CHi

14034. Gilbert, Benjamin Franklin. Pioneers for one hundred years, San Jose state college, 1857–1957. San Jose, San Jose state college, 1957. 243 p. illus., ports.

C CHi CL CLS CLgA CLod CP CRc CRcS CSdS CSjC CStoC CU-B CWhC

14035. Greathead, Sarah Estelle (Hammond) comp. The story of an inspiring past; historical sketch of the San Jose state teachers college, from 1862 to 1928, with an alphabetical list of matriculates and record of graduates by classes... San Jose, San Jose state teachers college, 1928. 506 p. illus., ports.
CChiS CHi CL CSjC CStoC CU-B

14036. Hall, Frederic. The history of San José and surroundings, with biographical sketches... S.F., A.L. Bancroft & co., 1871. 537 p. map. Appendix no. 6: Private land grants in the county of Santa Clara, p. 484–488.
Available in many libraries and CoU MiD-B MoSHi N NHi NN NjR OHi UPB

14037. Handel and Haydn musical society. Constitution and by-laws... San Jose, Advertiser print., 1875. [9] p.   CHi

14038. Hare, G. H. Guide to San Jose and vicinity; with a sketch of its early history and a...statement of resources, climate [etc.] San Jose, 1872. 85, 27 p. maps.
C CLU CSj CSmH NHi

14039. Heininger, Charles P., pub. A souvenir of San Jose, Cal. [S.F., 18—?] folder [17] p. of illus., map.
CU-B

14040. Hermann & Elliott, engineers, San Francisco. Report on the appraisement of properties of the San Jose water company...1913... [S.F.? 1914] 50 p.
CHi CU-B

14041. Howard's San Jose street directory and business house guide, 1902. [San Jose, 1902]   CU-B

14042. James, William F., and McMurry, George. History of San José, California. San Jose, Smith print. co., 1933. 170 p. illus.
CHi CL CLU CSf CSj CSjC CStclU CU-B

14043. —— History of San José, California, narrative and biographical... Paul Gordon Teal, biographical editor. San Jose, Cawston, 1933. 243 p. illus., ports.
C CL CO CSj CSjC CSjCL CSmH NN

14044. Jones, Herbert C. The first legislature of California; address by Senator Herbert C. Jones before California historical society, San Jose, December 10, 1949, presented to the Senate by Senator John F. Thompson. [Sacramento, Senate of the state of Calif., 1949] 18 p.
CLgA CO CStclU

14045. Jourcain, Esteban vs. San Jose. ...Esteban Jourcain, plaintiff, vs. the Mayor and common council of the city of San Jose and Joel C. Potter, defendants. Brief for plaintiff. J. M. Williams, Wm. Matthews, for plaintiff. San Jose, Daily evening courier print. off. [18—?] 12 p.   CU-B

14046. Larson ladder co. ...Catalog no. 10 and price list. [San Jose? 1929?] 36 p. illus.   CHi

14047. Luco, Juan M. et al. vs. Hare, Geo. H. et al. In the Circuit court of the United States, for the district of California. Juan M. Luco, et als., defendants. Brief in reply to defendant's brief. Irving & Brown, att'ys for plaintiffs. S.F., M.D. Carr & co., print., 1869. 47 p. A San Jose land suit.   CLU

14048. McKinstry, Elisha Williams. Jubilee celebration, San Jose, December 20, 1899; address of Elisha Williams McKinstry... [n.p., n.d.] 26 p.   C

14049. Mangold, George Benjamin, and Hardy, Sophie. Building a better San Jose; ...a survey conducted under the joint auspices of Board of supervisors of Santa Clara county [and] Community chest of Santa

Clara county. [San Jose, Wright-Eley print. co.] 1930. 163 p.

CHi CL CLSU CSj CSjC CSjCL CStclU CU-B

14050. Metropolitan publishing co. Commercial history of San Jose, California. [S.F.?] Pac. press for Metropolitan pub. co., 1892. 114 p. illus. CO CU-B

14051. Miller, Helen Cecilia, *Sister.* Myles Poore O'Connor, pioneer California philanthropist, 1823–1909. S.F., 1957. 174 l. photos., facsims. Thesis (M.A.)—Univ. of San Francisco, 1957. CSfU

14052. [Miller, Henry E.] The Sodom of this coast! San Jose worse than Philadelphia! Complete control of corrupt ring. "Boss" McKenzie's amazing work in Santa Clara county. [n.p., 1902] 8 p. CU-B

14053. Moody, Charles Amadon. San Jose. The garden city of the Santa Clara valley. [L.A.? 1910?] 24 p. illus. Reprint. from *Land of sunshine.* CLU

14054. National association of letter carriers. A manual of postal information, comp. and presented by the letter carriers of San Jose, California. 1893. [San Jose, J.B. Carey, 1893] CSmH

14055. —— Branch no. 193. San Jose postal guide; postal rates, registry and money order divisions, history of our post office and general information... San Jose, Hurlbert print. co., 1895. 79 p. illus., ports. CSmH CU-B

14056. Navlet, Charles C. Illustrated and descriptive catalogue of seeds, bulbs, plants... San Jose, Hurlbert bros. & co., print., 1893. 115 p. illus. CHi

14057. Northern California Indian association. [Letter of Mary Haven Edwards, president of the association to Col. R. H. Pratt, San Jose, Feb. 15, 1904] [n.p., 1904?] [4] p. CHi

14058. Norton, Henry Brace. Memorials... [San Jose] 1885. 110 p. CHi CSd CSfCW

14059. Pacific and Atlantic railroad co. Articles of association and by-laws...together with the general law of the state of California for incorporating railroad companies. San Jose, Damon, Emerson & Jones, print., 1851. 40 p. This railroad extended from San Jose to San Francisco, and was the first to be operated in California. CSmH CU-B

14060. —— The report of the chief engineer of the Pacific and Atlantic railroad company. William J. Lewis, chief engineer. [n.p.] 1852. 22 p. C CHi CSfCP CSmH CSt

14061. —— Same, January 1855. S.F., Whitton Towne and co., print., 1855. 23 p. C CSmH CU CU-B

14062. Republican congressional league of Santa Clara county, San Jose. Santa Clara county republicans to republicans of the eighth congressional district... [San Jose, 1918] [8] p. CHi

14063. [Rambo, W. T.] History of the Sainte Claire club. [San Jose, The Club, c1945] 229 p. illus., ports. CHi CStclU

14064. Robinson, Charles Mulford. The beautifying of San Jose; a report to the Outdoor art league. [San Jose? 1909] 39 p. illus., maps. C CHi NN

14065. Rock's nurseries. J. Rock's descriptive catalogue of fruit trees... S.F., P.E. Dougherty & co., 1882. 20 p. CHi

14066. —— J. Rock's descriptive catalogue of ornamental trees, shrubs, plants, roses, etc.... San Jose, Cottle & Brower, 1886. 78 p. illus. CHi

14067. Rosicrucian Egyptian, Oriental museum. The magnificent Trinity. [A catalogue of exhibits and a description of Rosicrucian park] [San Jose, Rosicrucian press, c1939] 28 p. illus., plan. CHi

14068. Ross, Frank H. Drives about San Jose and vicinity... [San Jose, A.C. Eaton print., 19–?] 11 p. illus. CHi CU-B

14069. Rucker, J. E., & son. ...Real estate catalogue with map and description of Santa Clara county... San Jose, Mercury bk. and job print. co., 1887. 59 p. illus., map. CHi

14070. —— Same. 1889. 59 p. CHi

14071. St. Joseph's benevolent society. Constitution and by-laws...established in San Jose, Cal., November, 1870. San Jose, Cottle & Brower, print., 1887. 43 p. CU-B

14072. San Jose vs. Reed, E. P. et al. ...The city of San Jose, plaintiff and respondent, vs. E. P. Reed et al., defendants and appellants. Appellants' points. Wm. Matthews, att'y for appellants... [n.p., 1883] 4 p. CU-B

14073. San Jose vs. Trimble, John. In the Supreme court of the state of California. The Mayor, etc. of San Jose, against John Trimble. Brief of John W. Dwinelle, as amicus curiae. On the application of the statutes of limitation of this state to Spanish and Mexican grants of land, as a political question. Upon re-argument. S.F., Excelsior steam presses, Bacon & co., print., 1871. 5 p. CHi

14074. —— ...Brief for respondent. H. P. Irving, of counsel for respondent. S.F., M.D. Carr & co., print. [n.d.] 25 p. CHi

14075. San Jose vs. United States. ...The Mayor and Common council of the city of San Jose vs. the United States. Brief on behalf of the United States. P. Della Torre, U.S. district attorney, for United States. Hepburn & Wilkins, of counsel. [S.F.] Commercial steam presses [1859] 39 p. CSmH

14076. San Jose. Board of education. Rules and regulations for the government of the public schools in the city of San Jose... [San Jose] San Jose Mercury off., 1869. 32 p. CU-B

14077. —— Chamber of commerce. San José (San Hosay)... [San Jose, 1904?] 32 p. illus. CHi CU-B
Other editions followed. CHi (19–?) CU-B (1912?, 1912, 1927?)

14078. —— —— Souvenir of the...annual Santa Clara valley Fiesta de las rosas... 1926–29. San Jose, Murgotten co., 1926–29. illus., ports. C (1926–27) CU-B (1926–27, 1929)

14079. —— —— Winchester mystery house, four miles west of San Jose. San Jose, 1937. 3 p. Typew. CRcS

14080. —— Charters, ordinances, etc. Charter and revised ordinances of the city of San Jose. 1882. San Jose, Cottle & Wright, newspaper and job print., 1882. 211 p. CHi

14081. —— —— Charter...prepared by a Board of fifteen freeholders, December, 1896. [San Jose?] 1896. 77 p. illus. CSmH

14082. —— —— Same. [1897] 48 p. CLU CLgA

14083. —— —— Charter...in effect July 1, 1916 ... CStclU

14084. —— —— General municipal ordinances of the city of San Jose, California. In effect [!] January

1, 1899. Compiled by authority of the Mayor and Common council. San Jose, Harris the print., 1899. 164 p.
CSmH

14085. —— —— Same. ...May 1st, 1904. Compiled by William B. Hardy. San Jose, G.F. Degelman, 1904. 218 p.
C

14086. —— —— The revised ordinances of the city of San Jose. Published by order of the common council. By A. C. Campbell, city attorney. San Jose, Owen & Cottle, print., 1862. 139 p.
CU-B

14087. —— Christian assembly. First Christian assembly in San Jose, California. [San Jose, 19–?] 24 p. illus.
CU-B

14088. —— —— Thirty years after; souvenir, thirtieth anniversary, founding of Christian assembly in San Jose, California. [San Jose, 1930] 38 p. illus.
CU-B

14089. —— City manager. San Jose shapes its future. [n.p., 1957] 44 p. illus., maps.
CO

14090. —— City planning commission. ...The master plan. [1958] 112 l. maps.
CO

14091. —— —— San Jose: design for tomorrow. [San Jose, 1960?] 57 p. illus., maps.
CHi

14092. —— City surveyor. Report upon a system of sewerage for the city of San Jose... San Jose, Yates & Spencer, print., 1871. 52 p.
CU-B

14093. —— Committee to prepare an address on construction of a railroad. Address of the committee appointed at a public meeting of the citizens of San Jose in relation to the feasibility and expediency of a railroad between San Francisco and San Jose, adopted, January 29, 1851. [San Jose, Argus off. print., 1851]
C

14094. —— First Congregational church. Constitution and by-laws of the first Congregational society. Membership rolls and statistics. San Jose, Cal. December 1, 1904. [San Jose] Cleveland print. co. [1904] 30 p.
CU-B

14095. —— First Methodist Episcopal church. Our golden jubilee, 1849–1899. First Methodist Episcopal church, San Jose, California. [San Jose, Brower & son print., 1899] 40 p. illus., ports.
CHi CU-B

14096. —— First Presbyterian church. Sixty years of history, 1849–1909. First Presbyterian church, San Jose, Calif. ... [San Jose, San Jose print. co., 1909] 36 p. illus., ports.
CLO CLU

14097. —— —— Ninety years of history, 1849–1939. [San Jose, 1939] 34 p. illus.
CHi CU-B

14098. —— Igreja Portuguesa das Cinco Chagas. Lembrança do dia da dedicaçao. [n.p.] Sousa print, 1919. [10] p. illus., ports.
CHi

14099. —— Italian Catholic church. Ricordo della posa della pietra angolare per la chiesa Cattolica nazionale Italiana in San Jose, California. [San Jose?] 1906. 46 p. illus.
CStclU

14100. —— Trinity parish. Diamond jubilee council. Seventy-five years in the life of Trinity Episcopal church, San Jose, California, 1861–1936. [San Jose, 1936] 71 p. illus., ports.
CHi CSjCL CU-B

14101. —— —— Trinity church, San Jose, California. Advent, 1860, to Easter, 1903. San Jose, Trinity parish guild, 1903. 92 p. illus., ports.
C CHi CLU CSj CSmH CU-B NN

14102. San Jose and Santa Clara railroad co. Alum Rock park, San Jose's beautiful resort... [San Jose? n.d.] [12] p. illus.
CU-B

14103. San Jose and Santa Clara valley... Comp. by Crockwell & Williams. S.F., 1894. 16 pl.
CHi

14104. San Jose conservatory of music. Art loan exhibition at California theatre for the benefit of... October 24th, 1887. San Jose, Mercury bk. & job print. co., 1887. 58 p.
CHi

14105. San Jose improvement club. San Jose, the new California. [San Jose, 19–?] 24 p. illus.
CU-B

14106. San Jose institute and commercial college. ...Biennial catalogue of officers and students... 1st– 1863/64– San Jose 1864–
CHi (1875/76)   CLU (1863/64)   CU-B (1863/64)

14107. San Jose library association. Constitution, by-laws, rules and regulations of the San Jose library association... San Jose, John H. Conmy, print., 1872. 48 p.
CU-B

14108. San Jose mercury. Grand army edition, Daily mercury...June, 1886. San Jose, 1886. 24 p. illus., tables.
CU-B

14109. San Jose mercury-herald. San Jose guide book...a numerical telephone & business directory. 1923. [San Jose, 1923] illus., maps.
CU-B

14110. San Jose mercury-news. Mercury centennial edition...June 17, 1951. [San Jose] 1951. 1 v. illus., ports.
CHi CU-B

14111. San Jose news. 75th anniversary, 1883–1958. A history of service to the people. San Jose, 1958. 56 p. illus., ports., facsims.
CO

14112. San Jose union society. Constitution and by-laws... Adopted November 26, 1866. San Jose, Owen & Cottle, print., 1867. 22 p.
CU-B

14113. San Jose water works. Annual report, 1951. San Jose [1952] 15 p.
CHi

14114. —— Prospectus. 30,000 shares...common stock... [n.p.] 1947. 31 p.
CHi

14115. —— A wealth of good water. San Jose [Rosicrucian press, 1919?] 26 p.
CRcS

14116. —— Same. [San Jose, 1940?] 26 p. illus.
CU-B

14117. Santa Clara county carnival of roses. Official souvenir of the carnival of roses held at San Jose, Santa Clara county, California, May 6, 7, and 9, 1896. San Jose, Abbott, Snow & co., pub., 1896. unp. illus., ports.
C CSmH

14118. Senter, William A. vs. Castro de Bernal, Blanda. In the Supreme court of the state of California William A. Senter et als., plaintiffs and respondents and appellants. Transcript on appeal. S. O. Houghton, for respondents. Frs. E. Spencer, J. A. Moultrie, C. T. Ryland, and Peckham & Payne, for appellants. San Jose, Owen & Cottle, print., Mercury off., 1869. 168 p.
CSfCW

14119. Sexton, Lucy Ann (Foster) ...The Foster family, California pioneers; first overland trip, 1849, second overland trip, 1852, third overland trip, 1853, fourth trip (via Panama) 1857. [Santa Barbara, Schauer print. studio, inc., c1925] 285 p. illus., ports.
CHi CSalCL CU-B

14120. Smith, Ruby K. The old family mansion. [n.p., Priv. pub., 1962] 19 p.
CHi

14121. Snell, George P. Hotel Vendome, San Jose ... [S.F., Press photo engraving, 1903?] [31] p. illus.
CSj CU-B

14122. Souvenir of San José, and vicinity. "The garden city." Comp. from recent negatives by Crockwell & Williams... [S.F.] c1894. 38 pl.

CHi CLSU CLU CSj CSjC CSmH CU-B NN

14123. Souvenir of your visit to the replica of the first capitol building, San Jose centennial celebration, December 15, 16, 17, 1949... [San Jose, 1949] [4] p.

CHi

14124. Spencer, A. J. Spencer vs. Spencer, or the skeleton exposed. Review of the proceedings in the twentieth district court, state of California, in and for Santa Clara county. January term. Hon. David Belden, judge. San Jose, 1875. 45 p.   CHi

14125. U.S. District court. California (Western district) Decree confirming Pueblo of San Jose, and letters in relation thereto. [n.p., n.d.] 10 p.   CU-B

14126. Vendome hotel, San Jose. Vendome hotel ... [n.p., 1920?] [10] p. illus.   CHi

14127. Views of San Jose and Santa Clara after the earthquake and fire, April 18th, 1906. San Jose, Eaton & co. [n.d.] photos.   CStclU

14128. Wahlquist, John Thomas. San Jose state college: nine decades of service. [Sacramento] 1954. 13 p. Reprint. from *California schools*, v.25, Feb. 1954.

CSjC

14129. Walter, Carrie (Stevens) Hotel Vendome, San Jose... S.F., Crocker, 1893. 64 p. illus., port.

CU-B

14130. —— Same. S.F., Crocker, 1894. 62 p. illus., port.   CSmH CU-B

14131. —— Same. 1897. 62 p.   CHi

14132. Washburn school. [Catalog] 1895/96, 1897/98–1901/02. San Jose. 1 v.   CU-B

14133. —— The Washburn school, university-preparatory work... [San Jose? n.d.] [3] p.   CU-B

14134. Wheeler, Osgood Church. Our ministerial destitution, and its supply. A discourse delivered at the dedication of the new Baptist meeting house in San Jose...May 8, 1859... Sacramento, Daily standard steam job presses, 1859. 8 p.   C CLU

14135. When San Jose was young; a series of interesting articles... [San Jose, 1917–1918] 163 p. of mounted clippings. Clippings from the *San Jose news*, Jan. 5, 1917 to Apr. 22, 1918.   CU-B

14136. White, Charles. Letter from San Jose, California, March 18, 1848. Introd. by Carey S. Bliss. L.A., Dawson, 1955. [10] p. (Early Calif. travels ser., 28) 200 copies printed.

CHi CL CLO CO CSS CSf CStoC CU-B CoD

14137. Winchester, Sarah L. Mrs. Winchester's extraordinary "Spook palace." American weekly, inc., c1928. 1 fold. sheet, 1 p. of mounted clippings, 1 map. Excerpts from *San Francisco examiner*, April 1, 1928.

C

14138. Winchester mystery house; the world's largest, oddest building. [San Jose? n.d.] [5] p. illus., map.   CHi

14139. Winther, Oscar Osburn. The story of San José, 1777–1869, California's first pueblo... S.F., Calif. hist. soc., 1935. 54 p. illus. (Histories of early Calif. towns. no. 2) Calif. hist. soc. Special pub. no. 11.

CHi CL CLU CLgA CO CSf CSfWF-H CSj CSjC CSmat CSmH CStclU CU-B OrU

14140. Wittemann, Adolph. Souvenir of San Jose, California and the Lick observatory (Mount Hamilton). In photo-gravure from recent negatives. N.Y., Albertype co., c1892. 16 pl.   CU-B

14141. Wolfe & McKenzie. Book of designs prepared from designs originated by Wolfe & McKenzie, architects... Containing 98 house plans...also halftone photographs... San Jose, c1907. 98 p. illus.   CHi

14142. Young men's Christian associations. San Jose. Constitution and by-laws of the Young men's Christian association of San Jose, Cal. ... San Jose, C.L. Yates, print., 1867. 13 p.   C CU-B

Santa Clara

14143. Briggs, George H. [Autograph letter, signed, from George H. Briggs to his brother Robert in Malden, Mass., describing his trip from San Francisco to San Jose and his stay in Santa Clara] [Mission of Santa Clara, July 29, 1850; n.p., 1946?] 1 l.

CL CStclU CU-B

14144. Colligan, James A. The life of Father Magin Catala... [San Jose? 1916?] 16 p. illus.

CHi CLgA CSf CSj CStclU CU-B

14145. —— The three churches of Santa Clara mission. S.F., 1921. 13 p.   CLgA CU-B

14146. Doyle, John Thomas. Address delivered by John T. Doyle...at the inauguration of the new hall of Santa Clara college, on Tuesday, August 9th, 1870. S.F., E. Bosqui & co., print., 1870. 18 p.

CLgA CSmH CU-B

14147. Engelhardt, Zephyrin, Father. The holy man of Santa Clara; or, Life, virtues and miracles of Fr. Magin Catala, O. F. M.... S.F., James H. Barry co., 1909. 199 p. illus., port.

C CBb CHi CL CLSU CLU CLgA CO COHN CSf CSj CSmH CSrD CStcl CStclU CU-B CaBViPA

14148. —— Same, with title: Un misionero santo ...[Tr. into Spanish by] P. Pedro Sanahuja, O. F. M. Barcelona, Casa editorial de arte catolico, Jose Vilamala, 1924. 320 p. illus.   CHi CStclU

14149. Hoskin, Beryl. A history of the Santa Clara mission library and an evaluation of the book collection of 1777–1851. San Jose, 1960. Thesis (M.A.)—San Jose state college, 1960.   CStclU

14150. —— Same. Oakland, Biobooks, 1961. 82 p.

CAla CHi CLg

14151. Mission Santa Clara; dedication ceremonies, site of first mission, January 12, 1777...January 12, 1953. [Santa Clara, Santa Clara Lions club, 1953] 16 p. illus.

CHi

14152. Nobili, John vs. Redman, J. W. The missions in California, and the right of the Catholic church to the property pertaining to them. Argument before the Supreme court of California, by Horace Hawes. S.F., Daily evening news off., 1856. 46 p. Suit in ejectment to recover a lot of land known as the Orchard of Santa Clara.–Cowan.   C CLCM CSmH CU-B ViU

14153. Santa Clara. Chamber of commerce. The city of Santa Clara, California; "the heart of the valley." Santa Clara [1936?] 17 p. illus.   CRcS

14154. —— —— Plan of Santa Clara, the heart of Santa Clara valley. Submitted to the citizens of Santa Clara by the Town plan committee, Russell Van Nest, consultant. Santa Clara, 1925.   CHi CStclU

14155. —— **Charters.** Charter of the city of Santa Clara, California. [n.p., n.d.] 24 p.   CStclU

14156. —— **Female collegiate institute.** Annual circular and catalogue...University of the Pacific, Santa Clara, California... 1860/61–1861/62. S.F., San Jose, 1861–62. 2 v. in 1.   CU-B

14157. —— —— [Order of exercises] June 8th, 1864. [Santa Clara] Owen & Cottle, print. [1864] 2 l.
CSmH

14158. —— **University.** ...Centennial celebration, May 1851–1951. Santa Clara [1952?] 6 p. illus.
CStclU

14159. —— —— Circular of information. Santa Clara, Collegium S.J. Sanctae Clarae in California, 1926. 13 p. illus. CStclU

14160. —— —— Descriptive catalogue of Santa Clara college. Santa Clara, 1854/55– Title varies: 1854–65 printed in San Francisco.

C has 1854/55–1899/1900, 1901/02–1904/05, 1906/07, 1924/25, 1933/34–1944/45. CHi has 1854/55, 1857/58, 1862/63, 1868/69–70, 1877/78, 1889/90, 1890/91, 1892/93, 1905/06. CL has 1892/93–1907/08, 1927/28–1961/62. CSmH has 1862/63, 1870/71, 1880/81–82, 1897/98. CStclU has 1854/55–1861/62. CU-B has 1854/55–1865/66, 1867/68–69, 1870/71, 1874/75, 1879/80–1881/82, 1885/86, 1895/96. MoSU has 1856/57, 1859/60–1861/62.

14161. —— —— ... Diamond jubilee volume, 1851–1926. [S.F., Print. by Cloister press, 1926] 106 p. illus., ports.
CHi CSd CSfU CSmH CStclU CStoC

14162. —— —— Echoes of the golden jubilee. [Santa Clara? 1901?] 75 p. Addresses delivered at Santa Clara college on the occasion of its golden jubilee, June 4–5, 1901. C CLgA

14163. —— —— Exposition catalogue of Santa Clara college. California midwinter [exposition?] Santa Clara, 1894. 40 p. illus. CStclU

14164. —— —— [History. n.p., 194–?] 1 v.
C

14165. —— —— Introducing the University of Santa Clara. Descriptive catalogue of Santa Clara college. Santa Clara [n.d.] 27 p. illus. CStclU

14166. —— —— ...Santa Clara college, Santa Clara, Cal. Fiftieth year. 1851–1901. Santa Clara, C.A. Nace, print. [1901] 41 p. illus. On cover: Golden jubilee.
C CLU CSfCW CSfU CSmH CStclU CU-B

14167. —— —— Santa Clara college, Santa Clara. Souvenir, golden jubilee...1851–1901. Santa Clara, Chas. A. Nace, print. [1901?] 64 p.

On cover: Souvenir of Santa Clara college, Santa Clara. C CHi CLgA CSmH CStclU

14168. —— —— Santa Clara, the mission university. [Palo Alto, National press, 1961?] 32 p. illus., map. CHi

14169. —— —— The servant of God, Father Magin Catalá who died in the odor of sanctity at Santa Clara, California, November 22, 1830. Santa Clara, 1937. 3 p. illus. CRcS CStmo

14170. —— —— Souvenir of Santa Clara college, Santa Clara, California. San Jose, Alfred C. Eaton, 1896. 29 l. 27 pl. CHi CStclU CU-B

14171. —— —— Same. 1906. 112 p. illus.
CLgA

14172. —— —— The University of Santa Clara builds for a second century. [Santa Clara, 1951] 17 p. illus., charts. CHi

14173. —— —— University of Santa Clara, 1851–1912. [n.p., n.d.] 31 p. Contains biographical sketches of former presidents and faculty members.
C CLgA

14174. —— —— ...University of Santa Clara; a history. From the founding of Santa Clara mission in 1777 to the beginning of the university in 1912. [Santa Clara] Univ. press, 1912. 122 p. illus., ports.
C CHi CLU CSf CSfCW CSfU CSmat CSmH CStclU CU-B NHi

14175. Santa Clara city homestead association. Map, prospectus, articles of association and certificate of incorporation... S.F., Spaulding & Barto, 1869. 20 p. map. CHi

14176. Santa Clara college and Santa Clara valley... Santa Clara, A.S. Allen, pub., Nace print co., 1911. illus. 63 p. CStclU

14177. Santa Clara mission centenary celebration, Santa Clara, California. 1822–1922. S.F., Recorder rotogravure [n.d.] 16 p. illus. CHi CStclU

14178. Santa Clara news. Progressive Santa Clara. Souvenir edition. Santa Clara, Nace print. co., 1904. illus., ports. [38] p. CHi CStclU

14179. Santa Clara woman's club. Santa Clara. [Santa Clara, 1906?] 16 p. illus. CHi

14180. Shipsey, Edward. Santa Clara, the small university... [n.p., 1931?] 19 p. illus. "Reprint of an essay published in the *Owl*, literary supplement of the '*Santa Clara*,' December 10, 1931." C CHi CStclU

14181. Stern, Aloysius S., *Father*, **comp.** Magin Catala, O. F. M., the holy man of Santa Clara. S.F., Univ. of San Francisco, 1955. [10] p. illus. Excerpt from *Sanctity in America* by most Reverend Amleto Giovanni Cicognani. CHi COHN CaBViPA

14182. —— Same. 3d ed. 1959. CStclU

14183. U.S. District court. California. (Northern district) Opinions delivered by his honor, Ogden Hoffman, district judge, in the cases of J. W. Redman and others, and Thomas O. Larkin, claiming the "Orchard of Santa Clara." P. Della Torre, esq., attorney for the United States. Thornton, Williams & Thornton, for Redman, et al. Whitcomb, Pringle & Felton, for T. O. Larkin. S.F., Whitton, Towne & co.'s print., 1858. 16 p. Case involving lands of mission Santa Clara. CSmH CU-B

14184. —— —— —— Opinions delivered by his honor Ogden Hoffman in mission cases. The United States, v. Andres Pico, et al., mission of San Jose. The United States, v. J. W. Redman, et al., "Orchard of Santa Clara." The United States, v. Thomas O. Larkin, "Orchard of Santa Clara." Opinion of Hon. M. H. McAllister, in Richard S. Den, v. Daniel A. Hill, et al., mission of Santa Barbara... S.F., National print., 1859. 50 p.
CU-B

14185. Walsh, Henry Louis Richard. The annals of Santa Clara, college and university, 1851–1951. Santa Clara, 1955. 3 v. in 2. CStclU

14186. —— History of University of Santa Clara. 2 v. Ms. CStclU

14187. —— Mission Santa Clara. [Guide book] [S.F.? 194–?] [30] p. col. illus.
CHi CO COHN CPa CSfU CStclU

14188. Woods, Henry Kingsmill, *Father*. Quod Faxit Deus. Reflections of a librarian. Varsi library, University of Santa Clara. S.F., John Henry Nash, print., 1932. 7 p. CStclU

Saratoga

14189. Coro foundation. Saratoga survey; a study of the feasibility of incorporating Saratoga, California. S.F., 1954. 13, A–10 l. map. C

14190. Garrod, R. V. Saratoga story. 1962. 191 p. illus. Reproduced from typew. copy. CLg

14191. Gordon, James E. Saratoga and its environs ... The natural home of the orange and lemon... [S.F., 189–?] 17 p. CSmH CU-B

14192. [McCrackin, Josephine (Wompner) Clifford] Villa Montalvo, Saratoga, Santa Clara county, California: country residence of James D. Phelan. [S.F.? 1915] 34 p. illus., ports. Reprint. from *Overland monthly*, Apr., 1915. CHi CSmH CU-B

14193. Paul Masson vineyards. The story of Paul Masson vineyards, established 1852... [n.p., 1959?] [6] p. illus. CHi

14194. —— The story of wine as depicted on Jose Moya del Pino's mosaic at the Paul Masson champagne cellars, Saratoga, California... [Saratoga, 1959] [16] p. illus. CHi

14195. Saratoga. Chamber of commerce. Saratoga, Santa Clara county, California. [Saratoga, n.d.] CStclU

14196. Saratoga blossom festival, 1915. Santa Clara county welcomes you to Saratoga's sixteenth annual blossom festival, March 27, 1915. [Programme] [San Jose, 1915] [20] p. illus. CHi

14197. Saratoga, the gateway to the Big Basin. San Jose, Wright-Eley co. [1916?] [12] p. illus., map. CHi

Stanford University

14198. Adams, Ephraim Douglass. The Hoover war collection at Stanford university, California; a report and an analysis... [Stanford, 1921] 82 p. CPa

14199. Albertype co., pub. The Leland Stanford junior university at Palo Alto, California. In photogravure from recent negatives. N.Y., c1893. 16 pl. CU-B

14200. Bancroft, Hubert Howe. History of the life of Leland Stanford, a character study. [1st Calif. ed.] Oakland, Biobooks, 1952. 235 p. ports. (Great American statesmen, no. 3; Calif. relations, 34) Available in many libraries.

14201. Berner, Bertha. Mrs. Leland Stanford; an intimate account. Stanford, 1935. 231 p. illus., ports. CPa CRcS CRedCL CSfCW CSfWF-H CStmo

14202. Burk, Frederic Lister. Second annual address before the alumni association of Leland Stanford junior university, May 29, 1894. [Palo Alto?] Alumni assoc., 1894. 12 p. CU-B

14203. Burns, Edward McNall. David Starr Jordan; prophet of freedom. Stanford, 1953. 243 p. illus. CBb CPa CRcS CRedCL CSf

14204. Carnall, N. C., & co., pub. Souvenir of the Leland Stanford junior university and description of Palo Alto, the university town. [S.F.] c1888. 15 p. illus., maps. C CSmH

14205. Clark, George T. Leland Stanford... Stanford, 1931. 490 p. illus., ports. Bibliography: p. 473–476. Available in many California libraries and MoS

14206. Cloud, Archibald Jeter. The Stanford axe. Illustrated by James H. Cheek. [Limited, autographed ed.] Palo Alto, Pac. bks. [1952] 46 p. illus. CHi CO CRcS CSf CSmat CU-B

14207. Not in use.

14208. Committee of economists. Report to the Committee of economists on the dismissal of Professor Ross from Leland Stanford junior university. [n.p., 1901] 15 p. CHi CU-B

14209. Conmy, Peter Thomas. The founding of Stanford university...1891–1941...by Peter T. Conmy, grand historian, N.S.G.W., July 1, 1941. [S.F., 1941] 5 p. CU-B

14210. Covey, Cyclone. Wow boys; the story of Stanford's historic 1940 football season, game by game. N.Y., Exposition press [1957] 277 p. illus., ports. C CPa CStmo

14211. Crothers, George Edward. The educational ideals of Jane Lathrop Stanford, co-founder of the Leland Stanford junior university... An address delivered before the 1933 California state conference of the Daughters of the American revolution. [San Jose, 1933] 32 p. CHi CPa

14212. —— Founding of the Leland Stanford junior university... S.F., A.M. Robertson, 1932. 44 p. illus. C CHi CO CPa

14213. —— Outline of the history of the founding of the Leland Stanford junior university. [15] p. Reprint. from *Stanford illustrated review*, v.33, no. 1. CHi CSal

14214. Davey, Frank. Leland Stanford, jr. university, Palo Alto, California, before and after the earthquake of April 18, 1906. Photographed by Frank Davey. San Jose, Melvin, Hillis & Black [1906] [6] p. [30] p. of illus. C CU-B

14215. Davis, Horace. The meaning of the University; an address at Leland Stanford junior university on Founder's day, March 9, 1894. S.F., 1895. 14 p. CU-B

14216. Elliott, Ellen Coit (Brown) It happened this way; American scene. Stanford, 1940. 332 p. illus. C CNF CO CPa CRcS

14217. Elliott, Orrin Leslie. Stanford university, the first twenty-five years... Stanford [c1937] 624 p. illus., ports. C CBaB CL CLS CLSU CLU CLgA CO COHN CPa CSdS CSf CSfCW CSj CSmH CStclU CStmo CU-B

14218. ——, and Eaton, O. V. Stanford university and thereabouts... S.F., C.A. Murdock & co., print., 1896. 79 p. illus., ports. C CHi CSf CSj

14219. Fisher, Harold Henry. A tower to peace; the story of the Hoover library on war, revolution and peace... Stanford, 1945. 31 p. illus. CSfCW

14220. Glimpses of Leland Stanford, jr., university, Palo Alto, California. Denver, J. Collier, 1902. [40] p. illus., plan. C CHi CU-B

14221. Grant, Joseph Donohoe. The Stanfords. Stanford, 1938. 14 p. CHi

14222. Grothe, Pete, ed. Great moments in Stanford sports [by] Herbert Hoover...[and others] Palo Alto, Pac. bks., 1952. 120 p. illus., ports. CU-B

14223. Hall, Willis Lincoln. Four notable mosaics of Stanford memorial church in color. Palo Alto, Willis L. Hall, 1927. 12 p. CPa

14224. —— Stanford memorial church... Palo Alto, Times pub. co., 1917. 45 p. illus., ports. C CRedl CSjCL

14225. —— Same. Palo Alto, Author, c1921. 64 p. illus., ports., map. C CL CO CRcS CSj CU-B Other editions followed: C (1922) CPa (1928) IHi (1928)

14226. Hayes, Doremus Almy. First annual address before the Alumni association of Leland Stanford junior university, May 30, 1893... [Palo Alto] Alumni assoc., 1893. 20 p. CU-B

14227. Hays, Alice N. David Starr Jordan, a bibliography of his writings, 1871–1931; with a personal appreciation by Robert E. Swain... Stanford, 1952. 195 p. (Univ. ser. Lib. studies, v.1)   CPa CSf

14228. Hoover, Mildred (Brooke) An unfinished manuscript of reminiscences and some extracts from her diary, with interpolations and epilogue. Casa del Oso [Santa Cruz county] 1940. 109 p. ports.   CHi CPa

14229. Howard, George Elliott. The American university and the American man; second commencement address, Leland Stanford junior university, May 31, 1893 ... Palo Alto, 1893. 22 p.   CU-B

14230. James, Norris E. Fifty years on the quad; a pictorial record of Stanford university and the 35,000 men and women who have spent a part of their lives on the campus, 1887–1937. Stanford, Alumni assoc. [c1938] 248 p. illus., ports.   CHi CPa

14231. Jordan, David Starr. The days of a man; being memories of a naturalist, teacher and minor prophet of democracy. Yonkers, World bk. co., 1922. 2 v. illus., ports.   CHi COnC CRcS CStmo

14232. —— ..."Lest we forget"; an address delivered before the graduating class of 1898, Leland Stanford jr. university, on May 25, 1898. Palo Alto, Pub. for the Univ. by the courtesy of J.J. Valentine, 1898. [5]–36 p.   CPa

14233. —— The story of a good woman; Jane Lathrop Stanford. Bost., Am. Unitarian assoc., 1912. 57 p.   CHi CPa CSfCW CSjC

14234. Kellogg, Vernon. Vernon Kellogg, 1867–1937. Wash., D.C., Anderson house, 1939. 160 p. illus.   CHi

14235. Lyman, George Dunlap. A friend to man: a tribute to William Wilson Carson. Stanford, Stanford associates [1937?] [14] p.   CHi

14236. McDonald, Emanuel B. Sam McDonald's farm; Stanford reminiscences... Stanford, 1954. 422 p. illus. (on lining-papers)
                           C CO CPa CRcS CSd CU-B

14237. Maritain, Jacques. Visit at St. Ann's chapel. [Palo Alto, Chi Rho press, 1955] 12 p. incl. illus. "The illustrations in this booklet are original serigraphs by André Girard, hand printed by Pied Piper press."
                                        C CSfCW

14238. Mirrielees, Edith Ronald. Stanford; the story of a university. N.Y., Putnam [1960, c1959] 255 p. illus., ports.
C CHi CLO CNF CRcS CSfP CStcl CStmo CU-B

14239. Mitchell, John Pearce. Stanford university, 1916–1941. [Stanford, 1958] 167 p. illus.
                                     C CO CPa

14240. O'Neil, Robert Grant, ed. The Stanford axe 1899–1930 [edited by] R. G. O'Neil...[and] J. F. Van der Kamp... [Stanford, c1930] 64 p. illus., ports.   CU-B

14241. Quelle, Mary Stewart. A visit to Stanford university. Stanford [c1903] 37 p. illus., ports., map.   CSfCW

14242. —— Same. 2d ed. 1905. 85 p. illus., ports., map.   C CSfCW CU-B

14243. Reid, Whitelaw. University tendencies in America; an address delivered at Leland Stanford junior university, April 19, 1901.   C

14244. Sears, Jesse Brundage. Cubberley of Stanford and his contribution to American education, by Jesse B. Sears and Adin D. Henderson. Stanford, 1957. 301 p. illus., ports., facsims.   CSd CStmo CU-B

14245. Shinn, Milicent Washburn. The Leland Stanford, junior, university. S.F. [1891] 19 p. illus. (Leland Stanford junior univ. miscellaneous papers, no. 2)   C CU-B

14246. Simkins, H. W., pub. Stanford university picture album... [Palo Alto, c1903] 22 p. of mounted photos.   CPa CSf

14247. —— Same. [c1905] [28] p., 45 pl.
                                       CHi CU-B

14248. Stanford, Jane (Lathrop) Address. Jane Lathrop Stanford to the Board of trustees of the Leland Stanford junior university. [S.F., 1902] 13 p.
                                       CHi CU-B

14249. —— Address of Jane Lathrop Stanford upon her inauguration as president of the Board of trustees of the Leland Stanford junior university. July 6th, 1903. [S.F., 1903] 22 p.   CHi CU-B

14250. —— Deed of grant, Jane Lathrop Stanford to the Board of trustees of the Leland Stanford junior university. [Dec. 9, 1901] [n.p., 1901?] [9] l.   CU-B

14251. —— The Leland Stanford junior university; address to the trustees, by Jane L. Stanford, surviving founder of the Leland Stanford junior university, February 11, 1897. Stanford, 1897. 12 p.   CHi CU-B

14252. Stanford, Leland. Catalogue of Leland Stanford's collection of pictures. S.F., 1882. 8 p.
                                          CU-B

14253. —— The great question. An interview with Senator Leland Stanford on money. [n.p., 189–?] 42 p.   CHi CU-B

14254. —— Inaugural address of Leland Stanford, governor of the state of California. Delivered January 10, 1862. [Sacramento, Benjamin P. Avery, state print., 1862] 7 p.   CU-B

14255. —— Memorial addresses on the life and character of Leland Stanford...delivered in the Senate and House of representatives, September 16, 1893, and February 12, 1894. Wash., Govt. print. off., 1894. 126 p. port.
CHi CLO CPa CSd CSfCW CSfP CSjC CStclU

14256. Stanford convalescent home. [Descriptive brochure] Stanford [1933] 35 p. illus.   CHi

14257. —— Same. [1950] 59 p. illus.   CHi

14258. Stanford, "from the foothills to the bay." [Palo Alto, Robinson & Crandall, 1915] [43] p. illus.
                                           CO

14259. —— Same. [1920?] 1 v. illus.   C

14260. Stanford memorial church. Stanford, 1905. 30 p.   CU-B

14261. —— Same. [S.F., H.S. Crocker co., c1918] [42] p. illus., pl.   C

14262. —— Same. [c1946] 31 p. illus.
                                    CLU CO CSf

14263. Stanford university. Addresses at the fourth annual commencement... May 29, 1895. Specialization in education [by] John Maxson Stillman... Address to the graduates [by] David Starr Jordan... Palo Alto, 1895. 29 p.   CU-B

14264. —— ...Annual commencement... Order of exercises... 1st, 1892– [Palo Alto?, 1892–   ]
CHi has 9th, 31st, 1900, 1922. CU-B has 3d–4th, 15th, 1894–95, 1906.

14265. —— Annual register. 1st, 1891/92– Palo Alto [etc.] 1892–
CHi has 3d–5th, 7th, 19th, 1893/94–1895/96, 1897/98, 1909/10. CL has 1933– to date. CPa has 1st, 1891/92– to date. CU-B has 1st, 3d–8th, 10th, 16th, 19th, 24th, 1891/92, 1893/94– 1898/99, 1900/01, 1906/07, 1909/10, 1914/15.

14266. —— Articles of organization of the faculty, with the by-laws of the Academic council and the by-laws and general resolutions of the Board of trustees. Stanford, 1937. p. 81–235. Reprint. from the *Trustees' manual*, 1937.   CHi

14267. —— Circular of information. no. 1–6. Palo Alto, 1891. 6 nos. in 1 v.
CHi has no. 1–5. CU-B has no. 1–6.

14268. —— Constitution and rules of the first congress of the Leland Stanford junior university, Palo Alto, California. S.F., Crocker, 1892. 16 p.   CU-B

14269. —— ...Exercises of the opening day of the Leland Stanford junior university, Thursday, October 1, 1891... Palo Alto, 1891. 28 p.   C CHi

14270. —— The first year at Leland Stanford junior university, Palo Alto, June 1892. [Stanford? 1892] [29] p. illus.   CHi CU-B

14271. —— The future program of Stanford. [Stanford, 1927?] [14] p. mounted illus.   CU-B

14272. —— General catalog. Stanford [19—?–
CL has 1917 to date.

14273. —— George Edward Crothers, a friend of Stanford university. Stanford, 1949. 82 p. illus., ports.
CHi CPa CU-B

14274. —— Inscriptions in the memorial church of Stanford university. [Stanford, c1905] 30 l.
CHi CO

14275. —— It is for us, the living... [Pub. for Stanford univ. by Stanford associates, 1944] [40] p. illus.   C CU-B

14276. —— Laying of the corner-stone of the Leland Stanford, junior, university. Prayer of Rev. Horatio Stebbins, D.D. Address of Judge Lorenzo Sawyer (president of the Board of trustees) May 14th, 1887. [Palo Alto? 1887] 16 p.   CU-B

14277. —— The Leland Stanford junior university, Palo Alto, Santa Clara county, California. [n.p., 1885?] 43 p. ports.   CPa CU-B

14278. —— Same. S.F., Bancroft, 1888. 64 p. illus., ports.   CHi CU-B

14279. —— Same. Palo Alto, 1892–93. [5]–48 p. illus.   CU-B

14280. —— ...List of officers and students... 1891–1892, 1894. [Palo Alto? 1891–1894] 3 v. in 1.
CU-B

14281. —— ...New building of the school of education and a history of the work in education, 1891–1938. [Stanford, 1938] 35 p. illus., diagrs.   CO

14282. —— [Pamphlets. S.F., etc., The Bancroft co., etc., 1888–1901] Contents: Tax exemption for Leland Stanford junior university: facts and figures, together with the constitution and methods of the Stanford university tax-exemption club.—The Leland Stanford university... Souvenir of the Leland Stanford jr. university.
C

14283. —— ...Schedule of lectures and recitations and directory... 1891/92–1893, 1894/95–1895/96. [Palo Alto? 1891–1895] 4 v. in 1.   CU-B

14284. —— Souvenir program fifteenth annual intercollegiate football game Stanford vs. California. [S.F.] Norman Pierce co., 1905. [23] p. illus.   CHi

14285. —— Stanford days. [Stanford, 1933?] [15] p. illus.   CO CRcS

14286. —— Alumni association. Alumni directory and ten-year book... 1st, 189–?– Stanford, 189–?–
C has 2d–4th, 1891–1910, 1891–1920, 1891–1931. CHi has 4th, 1891–1931. CPa has 3d–4th, 1891–1920, 1891–1931.

14287. —— —— Stanford alumni, 1891–1955. Stanford [1956] 2 v. pl., port.   C CHi CPa

14288. —— Dramatists' alliance. Stanford writers, 1891–1941. A book of reprints from undergraduate periodicals, showing the work of men now eminent in American letters... with brief biographical notes... Stanford, c1941. 118, xxv l.   CPa

14289. —— English club. The first year at Stanford; sketches of pioneer days at Leland Stanford junior university. Stanford, 1905. 159 p. front., 11 pl.
C CHi CPa CRcS

14290. —— —— Same. 2d ed. 1910, c1905. 159 p. front., 11 pl.   CHi CLU

14291. —— Graduate school of business. The Eugene B. Favre memorial in the library of the graduate school of business, Stanford university. Dedicated April 15, 1941. [Stanford? 1941] 23 p. illus.   CU-B

14292. —— Library. Degrees conferred by Stanford university June 1892–June 1924. Doctors of philosophy, masters of arts, engineers, with the titles of their theses. [Comp. by Alice N. Hays] Stanford [n.d.] 100 p.
CL

14293. —— —— New building of the Stanford university library and a history of the library, 1891–1919. 1919. 40 p. illus.
CHi CO CSjCL CSmH CU-B

14294. —— —— Hoover library on war, revolution and peace. Dedication... Stanford university, June 20, 1941. Stanford, c1941. 43 p. illus.   CL

14295. —— Museum. The Leland Stanford, jr., museum; origin and description. [n.p., n.d.] 29 p.
CHi

14296. —— School of medicine. [Catalog]
CL has 1920 to date.

14297. Stebbins, Horatio. Leland Stanford, jr., university, California. Sermon by Rev. Horatio Stebbins, D.D., delivered in the First Unitarian church, San Francisco, November 22, 1885. Sacramento, Crocker, 1885. 7 p.   CU-B

14298. Stillman, John Maxson. In memoriam. John Maxson Stillman. Stanford, 1924. [46] p. port.
CHi

14299. —— Story of Stanford. S.F., Crocker, 1935. 69 p.   CStclU

14300. Taylor, Katherine Ames. The romance of Stanford... S.F., Crocker, for Stanford alumni assoc., 1927. 49 p. illus.
C CChiS CHi CLSU CLU CO CSf CSmH CU-B

14301. Tresidder, Donald B. Stanford looks ahead ...an address at San Francisco, October 14, 1942. [n.p., 1942?] 12 p.   CHi

14302. Where the rolling foothills rise, comprising scenes in color and duotone, on and near the Stanford campus, with a poem by David Starr Jordan and a his-

torical sketch by Orrin Leslie Elliott. [Stanford] Stanford bk. store [c1919] [40] p. incl. mounted pl. (part col.)
C CPa

14303. Wilbur, Ray Lyman. Stanford horizons; "Where the red roofs rim the blue," selected addresses, 1916–1936. Stanford [c1936] 165 p.
CHi CPa CStmo

14304. [Wilson, Neill Compton] The launching of the S.S. *President Hoover*, sponsored by Mrs. Herbert Hoover. [S.F., Windsor press] 1930. 15 p. incl. illus. (mounted drawings)
CSfCW

14305. —— Saving just yesterday for tomorrow; the story of the great Hoover war library at Stanford university. Stanford, Stanford associates, 1935. 16 p. Reprint. from *Stanford illustrated review.*
CSdS

SANTA CRUZ COUNTY

(Created in 1850 as Branciforte county, but name changed before organization)

COUNTY HISTORIES

14306. Guinn, James Miller. History of the state of California and biographical record of Santa Cruz, San Benito, Monterey and San Luis Obispo counties... Chicago, Chapman pub. co., 1903 [c1902] 742 p. ports. The section on the counties is chiefly biographical.
C CBaK CHi CL CLLoy CLSU CLU CMont CO CSalCL CSt CSluCL CSmH CStclU CStcrCL CStoC CU-B CWhC ICN In

14307. Harrison, Edward Sanford. History of Santa Cruz county, California... S.F., Print. for the author by Pac. press, 1892. 379 p. illus., ports. Includes chapters contributed by various authors. "Part II. Biographies...": p. [225]–374.
C CHi CL CLCo CLU CLgA CO CPa CSf CSjC CSmH CStcrCL CU-B CoD CoU MWA N NHi NN WHi

14308. Martin, Edward. History of Santa Cruz county, California, with biographical sketches... L.A., Historic record co., 1911. 357 p. ports.
C CBaK CL CO CSfCP CSmH CStcrCL CStoC CU-B

14309. Rowland, Leon. Annals of Santa Cruz... Santa Cruz [Branson pub. co., c1947] 155 p. illus., port. Bibliography: p. [156]
C CAla CHi CL CLU CLgA CO CRic CSd CSf CSfU CSj CSluCL CSmH CSmat CStcrCL CStmo CStoC CU-B CVtV WHi

14310. Santa Cruz county, California. Illustrations descriptive of its scenery [etc., etc.] with historical sketch of the county. S.F., Elliott, 1879. 102 p. illus., ports., maps. Includes "A sketch of the general history of Santa Cruz, California," by S.H. Willey.
C CHi CL CLU CO CPa CSf CStcrCL CU-B CtY NN

GREAT REGISTER

14311. Santa Cruz county. Index to the Great register of the county of Santa Cruz. 1866– Place of publication and title vary.
C has 1868–69, 1871–73, 1880, 1890 (biennially to)– 1898, 1902, 1904, 1906, 1910 (biennially to)– 1962. CL has 1869, 1872–73, 1876, 1877 (addenda), 1886, 1888, 1890. CU-B has Aug.–Nov. 1868, 1872–73, 1879, Sept. 1938, Sept. 1904.

DIRECTORIES

14312. 1875–1884/85. McKenney, L. M. & co., pub. Coast county directory, including Santa Cruz, San Diego, Ventura, Monterey, San Benito, Santa Barbara, San Luis Obispo, and Los Angeles counties... S.F., 1875–84. 2 v.
C has 1884/85. CHi has 1884/85. CL has 1875, 1884/85.

14313. 1904/05–1923/24. Western directory co., pub. Santa Cruz county directory. Long Beach [1904?]–24. Title varies: 1904/05–1914/15 Santa Cruz county resident and classified business directory. Publisher varies: 1904/05 California directory co.; 1906/07–1907/08, 1916/17 Santa Cruz directory co.; 1910/11–1914/15 Albert G. Thurston.
C has 1907/08, 1916/17. CHi has 1910/11, 1921. CSmH has 1906/07, 1910/11, 1916/17, 1923/24. CStcrCL has 1904/05, 1910/11, 1912/13, 1914/15, 1916/17, 1918/19–1923/24.

14314. 1907. Pacific directory co., pub. Midget directory of the county of Santa Cruz... Santa Cruz, 1906. illus., maps.
CSmH

14315. 1925–1960. Polk, R. L. & co., pub. Polk's Santa Cruz city directory including Watsonville and Santa Cruz county. L.A., 1925–60. Continued as Polk's Santa Cruz city directory.
C has 1925, 1930, 1932, 1937, 1939–40. CHi has 1927–28, 1941, 1946, 1948, 1950, 1953–59. CL has 1932, 1941, 1954, 1956–58. CSmH has 1926, 1933, 1935, 1939. CSmat has 1958–59. CStcrCL has 1926–30, 1932–39, 1941, 1946, 1948, 1950, 1953–59. CU-B has 1946.

14316. 1938. Polk, R. L. & co., pub. Polk's Watsonville city directory, including Santa Cruz city and county. S.F., 1938. 618 p.
CHi

Santa Cruz

14317. 1897. Kramer, G. E., pub. Santa Cruz city directory. Santa Cruz [1897]
CU-B

14318. 1902. Irish, F. E., pub. Santa Cruz city directory... Santa Cruz [1902]
CStcrCL

14319. 1923. Imhoff, Scott L., pub. Santa Cruz city directory... published for Santa Cruz business men's association.
CStcrCL

14320. 1960– Polk, R. L. & co. Polk's Santa Cruz city directory including Watsonville, Aptos, Capitola, Freedom and Soquel. L.A., 1960– Preceded by Polk's Santa Cruz city directory including...Santa Cruz county.
CHi has 1960–62. CL has 1961.

GENERAL REFERENCES

14321. Atkinson, Fred William. 100 years in the Pajaro valley, from 1769 to 1868... [Watsonville, Register & Pajaronian press, print., Jan. 1935] 47 p. illus., port.
C CL CMont CSal CSf CSfP CSjC CSmH CStcrCL CU-B

14322. —— Same. Watsonville, Register & Pajaronian press [Ag. 1935] 73 p.
CLU

14323. Baylis, Charles D., ed. 250th coast artillery, army of the United States...Camp McQuaide, California, 1941. [Baton Rouge, La., Army and Navy pub. co., inc., c1941] 89 p. illus., ports.
CHi

14324. Ben Lomond health resort, comp. Ben Lomond, the gem of the Santa Cruz mountains, California. [San Jose, Melvin & Murgotten, inc., print., 191–?] 16 p. illus.
CHi

14325. Brooks, Elisha. A pioneer mother of California, written for his grandchildren to show them how the emigrants crossed the plains, and also what manner of person was their great grandmother. S.F., Harr Wagner, c1922. 61 p. ports.

CBb CChiS CHi CRcS CSfP CSjC CStcrCL CStmo CU-B CYcCL

14326. —— Same, with title: The life-story of a California pioneer. [S.F., Abbott-Brady print. corp., 1922] 62 p.   CHi CSf CSfP

14327. California. Dept. of natural resources. Division of beaches and parks. Santa Cruz beaches. Sacramento, State print. off., 1958.   CRcS

14328. —— **District court. (20th judicial district)** Law and trial calendar of the District court of the twentieth judicial district, of the state of California, in and for the county of Santa Cruz, for the October term, 1878. Hon. David Belden... [Santa Cruz, Sentinel print. co., 1878]   CSmH

14329. —— **Legislature. Assembly. Judiciary committee.** Reply of the Assembly judiciary committee in answer to the query: What officer will be tax collector on real estate and personal property in the county of Santa Cruz, after the first Monday in March, 1870? [Sacramento, Gelwicks, state print., 1870]   CSmH

14330. —— —— **Commissioners appointed to examine the harbor of Santa Cruz and Salinas slugh[!]** Report of the Commissioners appointed to examine the harbor of Santa Cruz and Salinas slugh, in the Bay of Monterey. [Sacramento, Gelwicks, state print., 1870]   CSmH

14331. —— **National Guard.** The National guardsman in camp. A summary of the duties of officers and soldiers. For use at Camp Stoneman, Santa Cruz, August 15 to August 23, 1885. Sacramento, J.J. Ayers, state print., 1885. 63 p.   CU-B

14332. [—— **Redwood park commission]** California redwood park; sometimes called Sempervirens park: an appreciation. Sacramento, State print. off., 1912. 128 p. illus.

C CChiS CHi CLLoy CLO CLSU CLU CPom CPs CRcS CSalCL CSd CSf CSfSC CSj CSmH CStclU CStoC CU-B CV

14333. —— **State board of forestry.** California redwood park, Santa Cruz County... Sacramento, 1907. 8 l. pl.   CHi

14334. Curtis, Mabel Rowe. The coachman was a lady; the story of the life of Charley Parkhurst. Watsonville, Pajaro Valley hist. assoc., 1959. 16 p. illus.
CHi CStcrCL

14335. Deleissegues, Rebecca, and Mylar, Lucretia. Early days in Corralitos and Soquel. Hollister, Evening free lance [1929] [16] p.
C CHi CLU CLgA CSmH CStcrCL CU-B

14336. Epworth League. California chapter. Mount Hermon Epworth league institute, held in connection with the fourth annual convention, California conference...June 20th to 26th, 1910. [Prospectus of the Institute] [Oakland, West coast print. co., 1910] [14] p. illus.   CHi

14337. Fehliman, Clinton E. Economic history of Santa Cruz county, California, 1850–1947. 44 p. Mimeo.
CStcrCL

14338. Forbes, Elizabeth M. C. Reminiscences of Seabright. Seabright, Author, 1915. 40 p.
CHi CLU CStcrCL

14339. Harding, James W. In the matter of the survey of the Rancho Arroyo de la Laguna. Appeal from the order of the surveyor-general rejecting the Freeman survey of said rancho. [S.F., 1879] 20 p. At head of title: In the U.S. Surveyor-general's office at San Francisco, Cal. Signed: J. W. Harding, att'y for contestants.
CLU

14340. —— ...Contestants' closing reply. [S.F., 1879] [4] p. At head of title: U.S. Land office department.   CLU

14341. —— ...Reply to claimant's appeal from the Hon. Commissioner's decision approving the Freeman survey. [S.F., 1880] 12 p. At head of title: Before the Hon. Secretary of the interior.   CLU

14342. Hertzog, Dorothy Allen. Isaac Graham, California pioneer. [Berkeley, 1941] Thesis (M.A.)— Univ. of Calif., 1941.   CU CU-B

14343. Hihn, Frederick A. vs. Peck, Henry W. and ux. and Brady & Nichols, et al. In the Supreme court of the state of California. Frederick A. Hihn, respondent, vs. Henry W. Peck and ux., also respondents, and Brady & Nichols, Porter and Bates' Adm'r., appellants, et als. Transcript on appeal from district court for Santa Cruz County. Sloan & Provines, for appellants. R. F. Peckham, for respondents. S.F., M.D. Carr & co., 1865. 164 p.   CHi

14344. Hill, Andrew J. [Photograph album of pictures taken in the Big Basin in May 1900 on the occasion of an initial exploration trip under the leadership of A. J. Hill. Compiled by W. W. Richards and presented to the Sempervirens Club of California in 1927. San Jose, 1955] 90 mounted photos., mounted facsim.   CU-B

14345. Hill, Frank E. The acquisition of California redwood park. Photographs by Andrew P. Hill. San Jose, Florence W. Hill, 1927. 26 p. illus., ports., maps.   C

14346. Immigration association of California. [County scrapbooks] [S.F., 188–?]   C

14347. Ingoldsby, John vs. Juan, Ricardo et al. In the Supreme court of the state of California. John Ingoldsby, respondent, vs. Ricardo Juan, et al., appellants. Statement of facts and proceedings on the trial, in the Seventh judicial district, county of Contra Costa, and argument for appellants. By R. F. Peckham. S.F., Herald print. [1858?] 40 p. A Soquel rancho suit.   CLU

14348. —— ...January term, 1858. John Ingoldsby, respondent, vs. Ricardo Juan, et al., appellants. Supplementary brief for appellant. [n.p., 1858?] 30 p. Signed: Halleck, Peachy & Billings, and Gregory Yale, for appellants.   CLU CSfCP CSmH

14349. Kroeger, Louis J., and associates. Library service in the city and county of Santa Cruz, California. S.F., 1953. 38 p.   C

14350. Logan, Mary E., comp. and pub. The loganberry... Oakland, c1955. 20 p. illus.
CHi CSto

14351. McHugh, Thomas L. Hazeldell Charivari, Christmas at Zayante, 1856, being the story of the wedding of Patty Reed to Frank Lewis; and a recount of the Donner party tragedy, 1846. Santa Cruz, Frontier gazette, 1959. 27 p.   CStcrCL

14352. Majors, Maria de los Angeles vs. Cowell, Henry et al. In the Supreme court of the state of California. Maria de los Angeles Majors, plaintiff and respondent, vs. Henry Cowell et al., defendants and appellants. The facts...[Respondent Majors' points and authorities ...C. B. Younger, for respondent Majors] [n.p., n.d.] Suit over the Refugio rancho.   CHi

14353. —— ... Transcript on appeal. Joseph H. Skirm, attorney for appellant. Logan, Hagan & Younger, attorney for respondent. Santa Cruz, Sentinel print. co., 1874. 82 p.   CLU

14354. Mitchell, George Dampier. The Santa Cruz earthquake of October, 1926. [Berkeley, 1928] Thesis (M.A.)—Univ. of Calif., 1928.   CU

14355. Mount Hermon association. ...The Mount Hermon association (incorporated) Mount Hermon, Calif. ... [n.p., 1907] [24] p. illus.   CHi CU-B

14356. Ord, James. The memoirs of James Ord of Ord rancho, California, ed. by Henry W. Shoemaker. Altoona, Pa., Altoona times tribune, 1920. 28 p. port.
                                    CHi CSf (Typew. copy)

14357. Peck, Henry W., and Peck, Maria Antonia vs. Hihn, Frederick A., et al. In the Supreme court of the state of California. Henry W. Peck and Maria Antonia Peck, plaintiffs and respondents, vs. Frederick A. Hihn, also respondent and Thomas Courtis [and others] appellants. Transcript on appeal from the Third district court, Santa Cruz County. John Wilson and Selden S. Wright, attorneys for appellants. R. F. Peckham, attorney for respondents. S.F., M.D. Carr & co., 1865. 157 p. A Soquel rancho suit.   CLU

14358. Peck, H[enry] W. and ux. vs. Hihn, F[rederick] A. and Vandenbergh, J. P. P. In the Supreme court of the state of California. H. W. Peck and ux., respondents, vs. F. A. Hihn, also respondent, and J. P. P. Vandenbergh, appellant, et als. Brief for appellant. Sloan & Provines, for appellant. S.F., M.D. Carr & co., 1865. 6 p. cover-title.   CHi

14359. Perry, E. D., comp. Boundaries of the school districts of Santa Cruz county... 1894... Watsonville, Print. by the Pajaronian, 1894. 36 p.   CU-B

14360. Raymond, Isabel Hummel. Mechanics' institute fair. A short descriptive sketch of Pajaro valley. Letter from Watsonville. [S.F.? 1887] [4] p.   CHi

14361. —— Santa Cruz county. Resources, advantages, objects of interest... Santa Cruz, Santa Cruz development assoc., 1877. 80 p. illus.
                    CHi CL CLU CSfCSM CSmH KHi

14362. —— Same. 1887.
                                    CHi CU-B NHi NN

14363. Robison, William Condit. The historical geography of the redwood forests of the Santa Cruz mountains. [Berkeley] 1949. Thesis (M.A.)—Univ. of Calif., 1949.   CU

14364. [Rowland, Leon] Santa Cruz sentinel-news eighty-nine years old. Brief history of newspapers of Santa Cruz county. [Santa Cruz, Santa Cruz sentinel news, 1944] [16] p.   CHi CSmH CU-B

14365. —— Story of old Soquel. Santa Cruz, Author, c1940. 32 p. illus.
C CHi CLU CSfWF-H CSmH CStclU CStcrCL CU-B

14366. Santa Cruz county. Board of supervisors. Live, work and play in beautiful Santa Cruz county, California. Santa Cruz [1939?] folder.   CRcS

14367. —— —— Santa Cruz county... [Santa Cruz, E.S. Harrison, c1890] 64 p. illus.   C

14368. —— —— Same. S.F., Schwabacher-Frey co. [1915] unp. illus.   CU-B

14369. —— Public schools. Public schools directory, 1941–1942. [Santa Cruz, 1941] 36 p.   CHi

14370. Santa Cruz county; a faithful reproduction in print and photography of its climate, capabilities and beauties. [S.F., Crocker] 1896. 200 p. illus., ports. By Phil Francis.
    C CHi CSf CStcrCL CU-B KHi NHi NN

14371. Santa Cruz improvement society. Views

of Santa Cruz city and county, California. The keystone county of the state. [Santa Cruz] 1893. [25] pl.   CLU

14372. Santa Cruz silver mining co., San Francisco. By-laws... Incorporated March 26th, 1863. S.F., Towne & Bacon, print., 1863. 16 p.   CU-B

14373. Smith, Harry R. Apart with him; fifty years of the Mount Hermon conference. Oakland, Western bk. & tract co., c1956. 137 p. illus.   CStcrCL

14374. Southern Pacific co. ...California resorts along the coast line and in the Santa Cruz mountains. S.F. [1903?] [12] p. illus.   CU-B

14375. Zayante Indian conference, Mount Hermon. [Proceedings, 5th, 1910. San Jose, 1910] 12 p. Held under the auspices of the No. Calif. Indian Assoc., San Jose.   CHi

Santa Cruz

14376. Anderson, C. L. Santa Cruz for homes. The climate, botany, geology and health of Santa Cruz and vicinity... S.F., W.W. Elliott & co., 1879. 7 p.   CSmH

14377. California Portland cement co., San Francisco. ...Cement works at Santa Cruz... S.F., E. Bosqui & co., 1880. 15 p.   CHi CSmH

14378. Heininger, Charles P., pub. Souvenir of Santa Cruz, Cal. [S.F., c1889] folder (12 p.) illus.
                                    CHi CU-B

14379. Hihn (F. A.) co. vs. Santa Cruz, and Union traction co. In the Supreme court of the state of California. F. A. Hihn company, plaintiff and appellant, vs. city of Santa Cruz, Union traction company, defendants and respondents. Brief in reply of respondent, City of Santa Cruz, by H. A. van C. Torchiana... Santa Cruz, Sentinel print., 1913. 181 p.   CSfCW

14380. Hobbs, W. H., pub. Album of Santa Cruz, Cal. [Santa Cruz, 18—?] folder (14 p. of illus.)
                                    CU-B

14381. Industrial survey associates. The industrial future of Santa Cruz, California: a report prepared for the Santa Cruz chamber of commerce. S.F., 1953. 76 p. illus., maps, diagrs., tables.   CSfSt

14382. James, J. King, pub. Vest pocket guide of Santa Cruz; a handy book of information and reference. Santa Cruz, 1902. [56] p. illus.   CHi

14383. Leask, Samuel. Some memories of an uprooted and transplanted Scot. [Santa Cruz, 1955] 253 p. illus. Reproduced from typew. copy.   C

14384. [Meyrick, Henry, comp.] Santa Cruz and Monterey illustrated hand-book. S.F., S.F. news pub. co., 1880. 50 p. illus.
    CL CSalCL CSfCSM CSmH CStcrCL CU-B

14385. Rowland, Leon. Old Santa Cruz mission. Santa Cruz, Author, c1941. 32 p. illus.
            C CHi CLU CO CSjC CStcrCL

14386. —— Santa Cruz was colony of Americanos in Mexican times... [Santa Cruz? n.d.] 3 p. of mounted clippings.   CU-B

14387. —— Villa de Branciforte, the village that vanished. [n.p.] c1941. 32 p. illus., map.
        C CHi CLU CRic CSmH CStcrCL CU-B

14388. Santa Cruz. Board of trade, pub. The city of Santa Cruz and vicinity, California... S.F., Murdock press, 1905. 40 p. illus.   CHi CLU CStcrCL CU-B

14389. —— Same. Santa Cruz, Sentinel press, 1908. 53 p. illus.
                    CHi CSmH CU-B CaBViPA

14390. —— Board of trustees. Resolutions presented from the trustees of the town of Santa Cruz. [Sacramento, Gelwicks, state print., 1870]   CSmH

14391. —— **Calvary church.** Golden jubilee, Calvary church, 1914; special souvenir magazine commemorating the semi-centennial anniversary of the laying of the cornerstone, June 29th, 1864. [Santa Cruz, 1914] [24] p. illus.   C

14392. —— **Chamber of Commerce.** Santa Cruz, California. [Santa Cruz, Sentinel print., 1914?] [16] p. illus., map.   CHi

14393. —— —— Same. [192–?] 10 p. illus., map.   CRcS

14394. —— **Charter.** Charter and general ordinances of the city of Santa Cruz. Santa Cruz, 1880. 104 p.   C

14395. —— **First Congregational church.** A manual of the First Congregational church and parish. Santa Cruz, Netherton & Bacon, print., [1897] 82 p. tables.   CU-B

14396. —— **High school.** World War II; service cardinal, 1948. Santa Cruz [1948] 295 p. illus., ports. Partial record of boys and girls of Santa Cruz high school who served in World War II.   C CU-B

14397. —— **Methodist Episcopal church.** Directory of the Methodist Episcopal church... Santa Cruz, Cal. ...Santa Cruz, Print. by "The Imperial" [1898] 57 p. port.   CHi CU-B

14398. —— —— Fifty-seventh anniversary historical sketch...Jubilee edition, July, 1905. Organized January, 1848. By Rev. Frank K. Baker. Santa Cruz, Sentinel print., 1905. 19 p. illus., ports.   C CSf CSmH CU-B

14399. —— —— ...Golden jubilee of the Santa Cruz Methodist Episcopal church. April 17th–21st, inclusive, 1898. [Santa Cruz, 1898] [6] p.   CU-B

14400. —— **Mission fiesta and pageant, 1935.** Santa Cruz fiesta and pageant...1935, official program. [Santa Cruz, 1935] 32 p. illus.   CU-B

14401. Santa Cruz art league. Annual art exhibition. Sixteenth exhibition, 1945. [Catalogue and list of prizes] [Santa Cruz, 1945?]   CHi

14402. Santa Cruz beach. "Never one dull moment"; the world's most famous play ground. [S.F., Britton & Rey, 1904] 23 p.   CSmH

14403. Santa Cruz riptide. Fiesta edition. Santa Cruz 180th birthday & centennial days. Santa Cruz, 1949. 19 p. illus., ports. (v.21, no. 41, Oct. 6, 1949)   C CHi CU-B

14404. —— Same. [181st] (v.22, no. 43, Oct. 19, 1950)   C CHi

14405. Santa Cruz sentinel. ...Special edition... [May, 1887] Santa Cruz, 1887. 22 p. illus., ports.   CU-B

14406. Sea Beach hotel, Santa Cruz, California. [S.F., Print. by Sunset, 1900?] 31 p.   CSmH

14407. Sempervirens club of California. [Views of California redwood park, Santa Cruz county, California] [Sacramento, State board of forestry, 1907] unp. pl.   C

14408. Simpson, Lesley Byrd. Early ghost town of California, Branciforte. S.F., Priv. print. for his friends by H.W. Porte, 1935. 12 p.
CHi CL CLU CSmH CU-B OrU

14409. Torchiana, Henry Albert Willem van Coenen. Story of the mission Santa Cruz... S.F., Elder, 1933. 460 p. illus., ports., maps.

Available in many California libraries and CoU OrU OU UU ViW

14410. The Traveler, San Francisco. Santa Cruz Venetian water carnival, June 11–12–13–14 and 15th, 1895. [S.F., 1895] [31] p. illus., port., map.   CHi CSmH CU-B

14411. Veerkamp, Narcissa Louise (Parrish) The early history of the Santa Cruz region. [Berkeley] 1925. 135 l. maps. Thesis (M.A.)—Univ. of Calif., 1925.   CU CU-B

14412. Willey, Samuel Hopkins. Historical paper relating to Santa Cruz, California, prepared in pursuance of the resolutions of Congress for the national centennial celebration, July 4, 1876. At the request of the Common council of Santa Cruz. S.F., A.L. Bancroft & co., 1876. 37 p.
C CHi CLSU CLU CSmH CU-B KHi NHi NN

14413. Wittemann, Adolph. Souvenir of Santa Cruz, Cal. In photo-gravure from recent negatives. N.Y., Albertype co., c1892. [16] pl.   CHi NN

14414. The Woman's aid society. Souvenir of a festival... Santa Cruz, Calif. ...May 14th–17th, 1890, given by the Woman's aid society... Santa Cruz, A.A. Taylor, "Surf" office, 1890. 64 p.   C

14415. Young ladies' seminary. [Prospectus] 1867. [S.F., 1866] 1 v.   CU-B

Watsonville

14416. Martin, Ed., comp. Directory of the town of Watsonville for 1873, together with a description of the Pajaro valley... Wastonville, C.O. Cummings, pub., 1873. 64, 24 p.
C CHi (facsim.) CLU CSmH CU-B NHi

14417. Pajaro Valley. Board of trade. Watsonville, Santa Cruz County, California, the apple and strawberry center west of the Missouri river. [Watsonville?] 1903. [16] p. illus., map.   CU-B

14418. [Robinson, Edward P., comp.] Watsonville, the first hundred years; incorporating the principal historical data as it appeared in the Centennial edition of the Watsonville Register-Pajaronian of July 2, 1952. Watsonville, Chamber of commerce, c1952. 82 p. illus., ports.
CBev CL CLU CP CRcS CSdS CStclU CStcrCL CStmo CU-B

14419. Watsonville. First Methodist church. The first hundred years; prologue to a second century of service [1852–1952] [Watsonville, 1952] 22 p. Mimeo.   CHi

14420. Watsonville register. The Pajaro valley progress edition, January, nineteen sixteen... [Watsonville, 1916] 32 p. illus., ports.   CU-B

14421. Watsonville register-Pajaronian. ...Centennial edition... July 2, 1952. Watsonville, 1952. [64] p. illus., ports.   CU-B

SHASTA COUNTY
(Created in 1850)

COUNTY HISTORIES

14422. Giles, Rosena A. Shasta county, California, a history. Foreword by Jos. A. Sullivan. Oakland, Biobooks, 1949. 301 p. illus., ports., map. (Calif. centennial ed., 19) Print. by Lederer, Street & Zeus co., inc.
C CAla CBb CBu CChiS CEH CFS CHi CL CLSU CLU CLgA CLob CMartC CMerCL CMl

CMon CO CPom CRb CRc CRcS CRedCL CRedl CRic CSS CSbr CSd CSdS CSf CSfCSM CSfSt CSfU CSj CSjC CSlu CSmH CSmat CSt CSto CStoC CStrJC CU-B CV CViCL CVtV CaBViPA CoD ICN In KyU MiD-B MoSHi NN OrU WHi

14423. Southern, May Hazel. Our stories [i.e. storied] landmarks, Shasta county, California... [S.F., P. Balakshin print. co., 1942] 100 p. illus.

C CAla CHi CLU CMary CO CRb CRic CS CSf CSfWF-H CSmH CSt CStcrCL CStoC CU-B CYcCL WHi

GREAT REGISTER

14424. Shasta county. Index to the Great register of the county of Shasta. 1866– Place of publication and title vary.

C has 1867–69, 1871–73, 1875–76, 1880, 1882, 1886 (biennially to)–1896, 1900 (biennially to)–1962. CHi has 1890. CL has 1867, 1868 (suppl.), 1872–73, 1876, 1879–80, 1882 (biennially to)–1890. CRedCL has 1894. CSmH has 1879, 1882. CU-B has 1867, 1868 (suppl.), 1872–73, 1879, 1934, 1936, 1938, 1940.

DIRECTORIES

14425. 1940– Polk, R. L. & co., pub. Polk's Redding city directory, including Central Valley, Enterprise, Project City and Summit City. L.A., 1940– Publisher varies: 1940?–42 Pacific directory co. Content varies: 1948?–51 Redding including Central Valley, Project City, Summit City and Toyon; 1953–56 Redding including Central Valley, Project City and Summit City.

CHi has 1949, 1951, 1953, 1955–56, 1958, 1960–61. CL has 1940, 1949, 1951, 1953, 1956. CRedCL has 1942, 1948, 1951, 1953, 1955–56, 1958–59. CU-B has 1951.

GENERAL REFERENCES

14426. Anderson valley news, Anderson. ...Historical number and fiftieth anniversary edition...1882–1932... June 30, 1932. Anderson, 1932. [4] p. illus., ports. CU-B

14427. [Audley, John] The legend of the Shasta spring of California... [S.F., Mt. Shasta mineral spring co., 1890?] 16 p. illus. CU-B

14428. Boggs, Mae Hélène (Bacon) Shasta dam. [n.p., 1937] 10 p. illus., ports. C CHi CU-B

14429. Buss, Shanahan & Abbott. Anderson, California. Resources of southern Shasta. [n.p., n.d.] [3] p. illus. CU-B

14430. California vs. Shepardson, M. In the Supreme court of California. The people of the state of California, plaintiffs and respondents, v. Milton Shepardson, defendant and appellant. Appellant's argument in reply. [Argument of Creed Haymond] Sacramento, H.A. Weaver, print., 1875. 188 p. CHi

14431. California. Dept. of public works. Division of water rights. ...Shasta river and adjudication proceedings... [Sacramento, State print. off., 1928] 236 p. CL CSf CU-B

14432. —— Legislature. Senate. Select committee on resolutions. Minority report...on resolutions of Miner's convention of Shasta county. Submitted March 17, 1855. 7 p. (S. doc. no. 16, sess. 1855) "Relates to Chinese miners."—Cowan. CHi CSmH

14433. —— —— —— —— ...Report of Mr. Flint, of the Select committee, to whom was referred the resolutions of Miner's convention at Shasta county. Submitted March 28, 1855. [Sacramento] State print. [1855] 13 p. (S. doc. no. 19, sess. 1855) CHi CLU

14434. —— State college, Chico. Lassen volcanic national park; a unit of work by the practicum class, spring 1947. [n.p., n.d.] unp. illus. CChiS

14435. Chapman's magazine, Berkeley. Shasta county. (In v.1, no. 1, p. 39–58 [1941?]) CO CRb CRedCL CU-B

14436. Chase, Don M. Pioneers; sketches of pioneer days in Shasta, Tehama, Trinity and Siskiyou counties, with emphasis on the beginnings of religious organizations. Redding, Author, c1945. [35] p. illus., ports., map.
CArcHT CChiS CHi CO CRedCL CSdS CSf

14437. Colburn, Frona Eunice Wait (Smith) The kingship of Mt. Lassen... [S.F., Nemo pub. co., c1922] 69 p. illus., port., map.
Available in many California libraries and MiD

14438. Collins & Lind, pub. "Lassen glimpses": the Lassen park guide book. Mineral, c1929. 32 p. illus. CHi CRedCL

14439. Courier-free press. Shasta county, California. Tourist guide...Redding [n.d.] 3 p. illus. CSf

14440. Day, Arthur Louis, and Allen, E. T. Volcanic activity and hot springs of Lassen peak. Wash., D.C., 1925. 190 p. illus., maps. (Carnegie inst. of Wash. Pub. no. 360)
C CChiS CL CLO CLSU CLU CRb CSf CSfCSM

14441. Dittmar, M. E. Shasta county. S.F., Sunset pub. co., 1913. 64 p. illus. CU-B NN

14442. —— Same. 1915. 64 p. illus.
CAla CChiS CHi CL CRedCL CU-B

14443. Fall River tidings, Fall River Mills. Fiftieth anniversary edition, 1893–1943... A history of the development of eastern Shasta county from pioneer days... [Fall River Mills, 1944] 40 p. illus., ports.
C CHi CRedCL CU-B

14444. Fink, Walter H. The old town of Shasta. [Souvenir Redding ceremonial Islam temple, A.A.O.N.-M.S., Redding, April 22–23, 1922] [n.p., 1922] 16 p. C

14445. Fort Crook historical society. ...centennial for benefit of museum, commemorating the establishment of Fort Crook, 1857. June 1st–2nd, 1957. [n.p., n.d.] 26 p. illus. CHi

14446. Frank, B. F., and Chappell, H. W., comp. The history and business directory of Shasta, comprising an accurate historical sketch of the county from its earliest settlement to the present time... Redding, Redding independent bk. & job print. house, 1881. 180 p.
C CHi CSmH

14447. Giles, Rosena A. History of Ball's ferry. [n.p., n.d.] 4 l. Typew. C

14448. Gray, Fred. Shasta cavalcade. Revised May 16, 1950. [n.p., 1950] 62 l. Typew. C

14449. Great Bear mining and developing co. Great Bear mining and developing company... S.F., J. Winterburn co., print., 1897. 8 p. CU-B

14450. The history of Anderson valley. [n.p., n.d.] [4] p. CHi

14451. Hogue, Helen Steadman. Peaceful now the trails. [Redding?] Shasta lake area news, c1948. [56] p. illus., ports. Indians of Shasta county.
C CHi CRedCL

14452. Honn, D. N. Shasta county, California... Endorsed by the Board of supervisors... Redding, Free press print. [1902] 1 fold. sheet. illus. CU-B

14453. Immigration association of California, pub. ...Shasta county. S.F. [n.d.] 2 p.   C CU-B

14454. Industrial planning associates. Economic potentials of Shasta county: an economic survey prepared for...Shasta county; with the cooperation of the Shasta county economic commission. [n.p.] 1957. 63 p.
CRedCL

14455. Kirov, George. Shasta dam. [S.F., P. Balakshin print. co.] 1941. 60 p. illus.   C CHi

14456. Kunze, C. E. The story of the magic pool. S.F., Pac. gas and electric co., 1921. 23 p. illus., port., plans.   C

14457. Kutras, George Christ. Redding, California: a survey of its economical, political and social growth. [n.p.] Author, 1952. 39 p. map.   CChiS

14458. —— Shasta, California: a history 1849–1888. [Chico] 1956. 115 l. Typew. Thesis (M.A.)—Chico state college, 1956.   CChiS CRedCL

14459. —— Sociological survey of Shasta dam communities. Chico state college course—Special problems 199. Chico, 1950. 17 l.   CChiS

14460. Lockley, Fred. To Oregon by ox-team in '47: the story of the coming of the Hunt family to the Oregon country and the experiences of G. W. Hunt in the gold diggings of California in 1849. Portland, Ore., Author [n.d.] 15 p.   CHi CSjC

14461. Loomis, Benjamin Franklin. Pictorial history of the Lassen volcano. Anderson, Anderson valley news press, c1926. 135 p. illus., maps.
C CFS CO COr CPom CRcS CRedCL CSfU CSmat CSmH CViCL MoHi

14462. —— Same. New ed. S.F., Calif. press, c1926. 141 p. illus., maps.
CChi CChiS CHi CLO CRb CRic CSf CSmH CU-B

14463. —— Same; rev. by Paul E. Schulz. 2d ed. Mineral, Loomis museum assoc., 1948. 124 p. illus., maps.
CArcHT CHi CL CLU CRb CSfCSM

14464. McNamar, Myrtle. Way back when. [Cottonwood?] c1952. 233 l. illus., maps. Foreword: "the civil, social and industrial history of a strip of territory ten to fifteen miles wide, along the Shasta-Tehama county line."
CChiS CHi CRb CRbCL CRedCL CStoC CU-B

14465. Merriam, Clinton Hart. Source of the name Shasta. Reprint. from *Jl. of the Wash. acad. of sciences*, Nov. 18, 1926, p. 522–25.   CHi

14466. Miller, Joaquin, i.e., Cincinnatus Hiner. The battle of Castle Crags. S.F., 1894. 20 p. Reprint. from *Leslie's monthly*, Mar., 1893.
CLU CO CP CU-B

14467. Neasham, Ernest R. Fall River valley; an examination of historical sources. [Chico, 1956] 177 l. illus. Thesis (M.A.)—Chico state college, 1956.
CChiS CRedCL

14468. Northern California counties association. Annual report. [Redding?, 1916?–1918] The Northern California counties association was organized in 1915 by the people of Lassen, Modoc, Shasta, Siskiyou and Trinity counties.
C has 2d, 4th, 1917, 1918.

14469. —— Northern California...Annual edition of Courier-free press. Ed. by Walter H. Fink. 1910–1920. Redding, 1919–20. illus., ports.   C CHi (1920) CU-B

14470. Osoffsky, Lottie. Pierson B. Reading, California pioneer. [Berkeley, 1937] 148 l. port., map. Thesis (M.A.)—Univ. of Calif., 1937.
CChiS (micro-film) CU CU-B

14471. Pacific constructors, inc. Shasta dam and its builders. [S.F.] 1945. 187 p. illus., ports., maps, diagrs.   CHi CRedCL

14472. [Redding. Chamber of commerce] Redding, California—Shasta county. [Redding?] Republic pub. [1957] 108 p. illus.   CRedCL

14473. —— —— Vacationing in and about Redding, California. [Redding, 1930] folder (5 p.) illus.
CHi CRcS

14474. Redding Record-searchlight. Centennial edition. June 10, 1950.   CHi

14475. Robinson, Clarence Cromwell. Ranching in the gay '90's. Marysville, Author, c1951. 199 p. illus. litho.   CRedCL CSto

14476. Schulz, Paul E. Stories of Lassen's place names; the origins and meanings of the place names in Lassen volcanic national park, with relevant annotations. Mineral, 1949. 62 p. map.
C CChiS CHi CL CLSU CLU CRb CRedCL CSf CSfCSM CSjC CSmH CU-B

14477. Shasta county. Board of supervisors. Shasta county California; agriculture, industry, mining, lumbering, scenic and historical. [Redding, 1939] 7 p. illus.   CHi CRcS

14478. —— **Water agency.** A feasibility report concerning the Trinity project as a source of domestic, commercial and industrial water for the Redding area, prepared by Clair A. Hill & associates. Redding, 1959. v.p. maps, charts.   CRedCL

14479. —— **World's fair committee.** Resources of Shasta county, California... [S.F., Estate of A.J. Leary, print., 1893] folder (10 p.)   CHi CSmH CU-B

14480. Shasta county illustrated and described, showing its advantages for homes. Oakland, Elliott, 1885. 70 p. illus., map.   CSmH

14481. Shasta county immigration association. Descriptive circular of Shasta county, California... Redding, Independent bk. & job off., 1882. 32 p.
CSmH CU-B CaBViPA

14482. —— Same. Redding, 1885. 32 p. illus.
C CL CU-B

14483. —— Shasta county, California...its resources, climate, growth and future... Redding, 1886. 31 l.   CSmH CU-B

14484. [Shasta county material presented by Mrs. Mae Hélène Bacon Boggs, August 9, 1934]   CU-B

14485. Shasta historical society. ...A concise Reading calendar. [n.p., 1943] 7 l. Biographical data on Pierson B. Reading.   CU-B

14486. —— The covered wagon. Annual.
CHi has 1951, 1954, 1956–60. CRedCL has 1946–50, 1952, 1954, 1957–58.

14487. —— Year book. 1943–1945. [Redding?] 1943–45.   CHi CRedCL CU-B

14488. Sinclair, William John. A preliminary account of the exploration of the Potter creek cave, Shasta county... [n.p., 1903?] 9 p.   CHi CStclU CU-B

14489. Southern Pacific co. Picturesque Shasta springs... [S.F.? n.d.] 8 col. pl.
C CRedCL CSjC CU-B

14490. —— Shasta route resorts. [n.p., 1899] folder (32 p.) illus., fold., map.   CU-B

14491. —— Same. [n.p., 1905] folder (40 p.) illus.   CHi CU-B

14492. Steger, Gertrude A. Place names of Shasta county. [Redding, Redding print. co., c1945] 75 p.
C   CChiS   CHi   CO   CRb   CRedCL   CSfWF-H
CU-B

14493. Tavern of Castle Crags, Castle Crag. Shasta and the Crags. [n.p., n.d.] [24] p. illus.   CU-B

14494. —— Tavern of Castle Crags. [S.F., Crocker, 18–?] [20] p. illus.   CU-B

14495. Treganza, Adan Eduardo. Salvage archaeology in the Whiskeytown reservoir area and the Wintu pumping plant, Shasta county, California. [S.F., State college, 1960] 49 p.   CSfSt

14496. Volkmann, Daniel G. Fifty years of the McCloud river club. S.F., Priv. print., 1951. [16] p. map.   CHi

14497. Walker, David H. Shasta county, California ... S.F., Sunset mag., Homeseekers' bur. [1908] 31 p. illus., map.   CHi

14498. Wiegel, Loraine (Heath) Memoirs of Buckeye and vicinity then and now. [Redding?] Shasta hist. soc., 1952. 31 p. illus., ports.   CO

14499. Woodward, Lois Ann. ...Old town of Shasta... Berkeley, 1937. 16 l. Typew.   CU-B

SIERRA COUNTY
(*Created in 1852 from portion of Yuba county*)

GREAT REGISTER

14500. Sierra county. Index to the Great register of the county of Sierra. 1872– Place of publication and title vary.
C has 1872–73, 1875–77, 1879–80, 1884, 1886, 1890 (biennially to)–1912, 1916 (biennially to)– 1926, 1930 (biennially to)–1962. CL has 1867 (1868–69 suppls.), 1872–73, 1876–77, 1879–80, 1882 (biennially to)– 1890. CLU has 1875. CSmH has 1882, 1896. CU-B has 1867–68 (suppl.), Oct. 1872, 1873, 1879, 1898 (suppl.), Nov. 1908, Nov. 1908 (Pike City), Nov. 1938, Nov. 1940.

GENERAL REFERENCES

14501. Ashburner, William. Report on the Sierra Buttes gold mine... S.F., E. Bosqui & co., print., 1870. 8 p.   CHi   CSmH

14502. Byington, Lewis Francis. Downieville and its historic past. [n.p., n.d.] 1 l. folded.   CHi

14503. —— Sierra county and its historic past, [n.p., n.d.] 1 l. folded.   CHi

14504. California vs. Phelan, Richard. In the Supreme court of the state of California. The people of the state of California, plaintiffs and respondents, vs. Richard Phelan, defendant and appellant. Petition for rehearing. S.F., 1899. 69 p.   CHi

14505. Chapman's magazine, Berkeley. Sierra county. (In v.1, no. 2, p. 7–11 [1941?])   CChiS   CO

14506. Cunningham, Patrick vs. Hawkins, Thomas H. In the Supreme court of the state of California. Patrick Cunningham, appellant, vs. Thomas H. Hawkins, respondent. Respondent's brief. An appeal from the Tenth district court. Creed Haymond, of counsel for respondent. Marysville, 1864. "An action of ejectment brought to recover the undivided one fourth of certain mining claims situated on Poverty Hill, in Sierra county, known as the 'Paddy Bull mining claims', and sometimes as the 'Bartlett, Craig & co.'s claims'."   CLU

14507. Downie, William. Hunting for gold... S.F.,

Calif. pub. co., 1893. 407 p. illus., port. Ed. by C. M. Waage.
Available in many California libraries and CaBViPA

14508. —— —— Index... Joseph Gaer, editor ... [S.F., 1935] 29 l. (Index no. 6, SERA project 2-F2-132 (3-F2-197) Calif. literary research) Mimeo.
CHi   CLSM   CP   CSdS   CSf

14509. Dressler, Albert, ed. California Chinese chatter. S.F., Author, 1927. illus. 120 telegrams exchanged among the Chinese to and from Downieville in the year 1874. An edition of 525 copies.
CChiS   CHi   CRcS   CRedCL   CRic   CSf   CSfP
CSfWF-H   CStmo   CV

14510. E clampus vitus. Ritual. Downieville, Sierra democrat print. [n.d.] 8 p.   CHi   CSmH

14511. Ferguson, Henry G., and Gannett, Roger W. Gold quartz veins of the Allegheny district, California. Wash., D.C., Govt. print. off., 1932. 139 p. illus., maps.   CChiS   CL   CLSU   CO   CSf   CU-B   CViCL

14512. Janin, Henry. Report upon the Sierra Buttes gold quartz mines, Sierra county, California. S.F., E. Bosqui & co., 1869. 15 p.   CHi   CSmH

14513. [Kirkpatrick mining and milling co.] The story of "Old Kirk." [n.p., n.d.] 14 p.   CHi

14514. McPherson, William Gregg. Diary of William McPherson, father of Clara McPherson Jones. [Orange, Orange daily news, 1937] 19 pts. Deals with mining in Downieville.   CSmH

14515. Moore, Adam Lee. No more gold slugs on bare bedrock. The life and adventures of Philo Havens, discoverer of gold on the forks of the North Yuba...as told by G. Ezra Dane. [n.p.] 1937. 4 p. port.   CSmH

14516. [The Mountain messenger] Downieville, in the heart of the Sierra county gold belt... [Downieville, 1924?] [4] p.   CHi

14517. Murphy, I. I. Life of Colonel Daniel E. Hungerford. Hartford, Conn., Case, Lockwood & Brainard co., 1891. 319 p. port.   CHi

14518. Odd fellows, Independent order of. Sierra co. Olive branch encampment no. 9. Constitution and by-laws...St. Louis, Sierra county, California. Constitution amended 1859. By-laws approved March 22d, A.D. 1859... S.F., Agnew & Deffebach, 1859. 36 p.   C

14519. —— Sierra lodge, no. 24. Constitution and by-laws... Instituted at Downieville, June 6, 1854. Sacramento, Crocker, 1866. 76 p.   C

14520. —— —— Table Rock lodge, no. 49. Constitution and by-laws... S.F., Eastman, 1858. 35 p.   C

14521. Perkins, Henry C. The Ruby drift gravel mine, Sierra county, Cal. Report of Henry C. Perkins, December 1, 1879. [S.F., 1879] 24 p.
CLU   CSmH   CU-B

14522. Pond, William Chauncey. Gospel pioneering: reminiscences of early Congregationalism in California, 1833–1920... [Oberlin, Ohio, News print. co.] 1921. 191 p. port. "The date 1833 on title-page is corrected to read 1853."—Cowan. Author was minister in Downieville from 1855 to 1865, following and preceding pastorates in San Francisco.
C   CBu   CChiS   CHi   CL   CLSU   CLU   CO   CSf
CSfU   CSmH   CStrJC   CU-B   CaBViPA

14523. —— Sermons, addresses, photographs, Bible with mss. notations, scrap-book of clippings, and other papers. 1850–[192–?]   CBPac

14524. Sierra citizen. v.1. Feb. 11, 1854–Feb. 3, 1855. Downieville, 1854–55. 1 v. illus.   CU-B

14525. Sierra county. Chamber of commerce. Sierra county, California; the playground of the Sierras. Downieville [n.d.] folder (12 p.) illus., map.
CHi CRcS

14526. West Fellows gold mining co. Prospectus ... N.Y., Francis Hart & co., print., 1866. 30 p. fold. chart.   CHi

14527. Wilson, Bourdon. Sierra county... S.F., Sunset mag. homeseekers' bur. [1910?] 31 p. illus.
CL CU-B

SISKIYOU COUNTY

(Created in 1852 from portions of Shasta, Trinity, and Klamath counties; annexed large part of Klamath in 1875; annexed section of Del Norte county in 1887)

COUNTY HISTORIES

14528. [Wells, Harry Laurenz] History of Siskiyou county, California...containing portraits and biographies of its leading citizens and pioneers. Oakland, D.J. Stewart & co., 1881. 218 p. ports., map.
C CCH CHi CSf CSfCP CSmH CStoC CU-B CYrS NHi

GREAT REGISTER

14529. Siskiyou county. Index to the Great register of the county of Siskiyou. 1866– Place of publication and title vary.
C has 1867–68, 1872, 1875, 1877, 1879–80, 1886, 1890 (biennially to)– 1904, 1908, 1910, 1912, 1914 (suppl.), 1916 (biennially to)– 1930, 1932 (suppl.), 1934 (suppl.), 1936 (biennially to)– 1962. CL has 1872–73, 1877, 1880 (biennially to)– 1890. CO has 1879. CU-B has 1867, 1868 (suppl.), 1872–73, 1875, 1877, 1879, 1882, 1886, 1938 (primary) suppl., 1938 (general), 1940 (primary) suppl., 1940 (general).

DIRECTORIES

14530. 1909. Directory publishing co., pub. Yreka, California directory... S.F., 1909. 66 p.   C

GENERAL REFERENCES

14531. Allen, James Michael. Wi-ne-ma, Modoc chieftainess, 1842–1932. [1st ed.] N.Y., Vantage press [1956] 116 p. illus.
C CAltu CRedCL CSS CViCL

14532. Arnold, Mary Ellicott. In the land of the grasshopper song; a story of two girls in Indian country in 1908–09, by Mary Ellicott Arnold and Mabel Reed. [1st ed.] N.Y., Vantage press [1957] 313 p. illus.
CArcHT CL CLU CSfSt CStmo CStoC CU-B

14533. Bland, T. A. Life of Alfred B. Meacham... together with his lecture. *The tragedy of the lava beds.* Wash., D.C., T.A. & M.C. Bland, 1883. 30, 48 p. illus., ports.   C CHi CLU CO CSf CSmH CU-B OrU

14534. Boyle, William H. Personal observations on the conduct of the Modoc war. Ed. Richard H. Dillon. L.A., Dawson's bk. shop [1959] 80 p. illus., port., map. Bibliography: p. 59–60.
C CAltu CChiS CLSM CLU CRb CSf CStmo CaBViPA

14535. Butte Valley irrigation district. Butte Valley, California; the valley of advantages. Macdoel [1927?] [9] p. illus., map.   CHi

14536. Chapman's magazine, Berkeley. Siskiyou county. (In v.1 no. 1, p. 67–80 [1941?])
CO CRb CU-B

14537. Cleghorn, John C. Historic water levels of Tule lake, California-Oregon and their relation to the petroglyphs. [Klamath Falls, Ore., Klamath county museum, 1959] 10 l. pl., map, diagrs. (Klamath county museum. Research papers, no. 1)   C CAltu

14538. Colonna, Benjamin Azariah. Nine days on the summit of Mt. Shasta... [New Market, Va., E.O. Henkel, 1923] 15 p.   CU-B

14539. Curtin, Jeremiah. Myths of the Modocs... London, S. Low, Marston & co., [c1912] 389 p.
CL CLSU CLU CRedCL CU-B CViCL

14540. —— Same. Bost., Little, 1912. 389 p.
C CO CRedl CSd CSf CViCL

14541. Edwards, Philip Leget. California in 1837, diary of Col. Philip L. Edwards containing an account of a trip to the Pacific coast, published in "Themis"... Sacramento, A.J. Johnston & co., print., 1890. 47 p.
C-S CHi CSd CSf

14542. —— Same, with title: The diary of Philip Leget Edwards... S.F., Grabhorn, 1932. 47 p. front. (Rare Americana ser., no. 4)
Available in many California libraries and OrU

14543. Eichorn, Arthur Francis. The Mt. Shasta story; being a concise history of the famous California mountain. [Mount Shasta, Mount Shasta herald, 1957] 112 p. illus.
C CArcHT CBev CChiS CL CLU CO CRedCL CSd CSfSC

14544. Foulke, Lewis M. The Big Ditch; a history of the old Big Ditch to Yreka, now known as the Edson-Foulke Yreka ditch company ditch. By L. M. Foulke, J. Farraher, E. L. Foulke. [Yreka, 1960] [6] p.   CHi

14545. Fox, John Samuel. Captain Jack's stronghold, registered landmark No. 9. Berkeley. Written under auspices of WPA, 1936. (Calif. hist. landmarks ser. ed. by Vernon Aubrey Neasham.)   CU-B

14546. French, Harold. Siskiyou county... Issued by the Board of supervisors and the Panama-Pacific international exposition commission of Siskiyou county... [n.p., 1915] 35 p. illus.
CChiS CHi CL CRedCL CU-B CaBViPA MWA

14547. Graves, Charles S. Before the white man came. Yreka, Siskiyou news, 1934. 99 p. illus.   CRb

14548. —— Lore and legends of the Klamath river Indians. Yreka, Press of the Times, 1929. 157 p. illus.
CArcHT CHi CRb CRedCL CUk

14549. Green, Harry H. Fort Jones semi-centenary, 1870–1921. N.Y., Author [1921] [123] p.   CHi

14550. Hagen, Olaf Theodore, comp. Modoc war; official correspondence and documents, 1865–1878... S.F., 1942. 2 v. Typew.   CU-B

14551. Heyman, Max L. Prudent soldier; a biography of Major General E. R. S. Canby, 1817–1873; his military service in the Indian campaigns, in the Mexican war, in California, New Mexico, Utah, and Oregon... Glendale, A.H. Clark co., 1959. 418 p. illus., ports., maps, facsims. (Frontier military ser., 3)   CSd CU-B

14552. Howard, Oliver Otis. My life and experiences among our hostile Indians. [Worthington] c1907. illus.   CAltu

14553. Immigration association of California. [County scrapbooks. S.F., 188–?]   C

14554. Isaacs, A. C. An ascent of Mount Shasta: 1856. Introd. by Francis P. Farquhar. L.A., Dawson,

1952. 22 p. (Early Calif. travels ser., 11) 250 copies printed by Feathered serpent press.

C CL CLO CLSM CLgA CO CSS CSf CSfSC CSjC CSto CStoC CU-B CVtV CaBViPA

14555. Johnstone, E. McD. Shasta, the keystone of California scenery... [Buffalo, N.Y., Art print. works of Matthews, Northrup & co., 1887] 46 p. illus.

C CHi CSf

14556. —— Same. [San Mateo, c1889] 46 p. illus.

CSmH CU-B NN

14557. Jones, J. Roy. Saddle bags in Siskiyou. ... Yreka, News-journal print shop, 1953. 419 p. illus., ports., fold. mounted map (on lining paper)

Available in many California libraries and CaBViPA

14558. Kidder, Leroy L. Story of a Siskiyou argonaut [with introduction by Edward L. Roberts]... c1920. 27 p. Reproduced from a scrap book loaned by Mr. Roberts. First published in the *Siskiyou news*, 1920.

C CArcHT

14559. Kober, George Martin. Reminiscences... Vol. I. Wash., D.C., Kober foundation of Georgetown univ., 1930. 403 p. illus., ports., maps. Includes account of the Modoc war and experiences with Chief Winnemucca and with Gen. Howard in campaign against Nez-Percés.

CSmH

14560. Lipps, Oscar Hiram. The case of the California Indians. Chemawa, Ore., U.S. Indian school print shop, 1932. 40 p. illus., map.

C CChiS CLSU CO CRedCL CSalCL CSd CSdS CSfCW

14561. [McKee, John] Second ascent of Mount Shasta. p. [373]–383. Detached copy (*Beadle's monthly*, v.2, no. 11)

CSmH CU-B

14562. Meacham, Alfred Benjamin. Wigwam and war-path; or, The royal chief in chains; illus. 2d and rev. ed. Boston, J.P. Dale & co., 1875. 700 p. illus., ports.

C CBb CL CLS CLSU CLU CO CRedl CSf CSj CSmH CU-B CaBViPA OrU

14563. —— Wi-Ne-Ma (the woman chief) and her people... Hartford, Conn., Am. pub. co., 1876. 168 p. illus., ports. Wi-Ne-Ma, Indian interpreter of Modoc war. By a survivor of lava beds massacre, in which Gen. Canby and Dr. Thomas were murdered.

C CL CLU CSf CSmH CU-B CaBViPA OrU

14564. Miller, Joaquin, i.e., Cincinnatus Hiner. Joaquin Miller, his California diary edited by John S. Richards. Seattle, Wash., F. McCaffery at Dogwood press, 1936. 106 p. illus.

CHi CLO

14565. —— Joaquin Miller's romantic life amongst the red Indians; an autobiography. London, Saxon & co. [1890] 253 p.

C

14566. —— Same. [1898] 253 p.

CU-B

14567. —— Life amongst the Modocs: unwritten history. London, Richard Bentley & son, 1873. 400 p.

C-S CBb CChiS CL CLSU CLU CLgA CO CRedCL CSbr CSfU CSj CSmH CSmat CStbS CU-B CaBViPA OrU

14568. —— Same. With title: Unwritten history: Life amongst the Modocs. American edition. Hartford, 1874.

CHi CRedl CSf OrU

14569. —— My life among the Indians... Chicago, Morrill, Higgins & co., 1892. 253 p.

CHi CU-B

14570. —— Shadows of Shasta... Chicago, Janson, McClurg & co., 1881. 184 p.

CSf

14571. Mt. Shasta register. [A register of people who ascended Mt. Shasta from 1868 to 1899] 398 p. Ms.

CU-B

14572. Muir, John. Steep trails; edited by William Frederic Badè, Bost., Houghton, 1918. 390 p. illus.

CBb CChiS CHi COnC CRcS CRedl CSfMI CSmat

14573. Mullan, John. Reports to Hon. George Stoneman, governor of California, on certain claims of the state of California against the United States. Nov. 1, 1878 to Nov. 1, 1886... Sacramento, State print. off., 1886. 580 p. Modoc war.

CSf CSmH CU-B

14574. Murray, Keith A. The Modocs and their war. Norman, Univ. of Okla. press [c1959] 346 p. illus., ports., map. (Civilization of the Am. Indian ser., no. 52)

Available in many California libraries and CaBViPA

14575. Nixon, Robert J. Modoc war, a brief and authentic history. 1938. Typew.

CAltu

14576. [Nolton, T. J.] comp. Siskiyou county, California. [Yreka, Siskiyou news power print., 1905]

CSmH

14577. Northern California Indian association. Field matron work in Siskiyou county. [San Jose? 1908?] [10] p.

CHi

14578. [Odeneal, T. B.] The Modoc war; statement of its origins and causes... Portland, Ore., "Bulletin" steam bk. & job print. off., 1873. 56 p.

CHi (facsim.) CSmH CU-B

14579. Oregon. Governor (Grover) Report of Governor Grover to General Schofield on the Modoc war, and reports of Maj. Gen. John F. Miller and General John E. Ross to the governor. Also, letter of the governor to the Secretary of the interior on the Wallowa valley Indian question. Salem, Ore., M.V. Brown, state print., 1874. 68 p.

C CSmH CU-B OrU

14580. Patterson, Stella Walthall. Dean Mad'm. N.Y., Norton, 1956. 261 p. illus. "The author, at eighty, spends a year alone in the Siskiyou mountains."

C CArcHT CL CRedCL CViCL

14581. Payne, Doris (Palmer) Captain Jack, Modoc renegade. Portland, Ore., Binfords, c1938. 259 p. illus., ports. Bibliography: p. 257–259.

C CArcHT CChiS CL CLSU CLU CO CRb CRedCL CSS CSalCL CSf CU-B KU OrU

14582. Riddle, Jeff C. Davis. The Indian history of the Modoc war and the causes that led to it. [S.F., Print. by Marnell & co., c1914] 295 p. illus., ports., map. Author son of Wi-Ne-Ma, Indian interpreter during Modoc war.

C CAla CArcHT CHi CL CLSU CLU CLgA CO CRedCL CSd CSf CSfMI CSmH CSrD CU-B OrU

14583. Simpson, William. Meeting the sun... London, Longmans, Green, Reader & Dyer, 1874. 413 p. illus. Includes a detailed history of the Modoc war.

CArcHT CLU CSf CSmH CU-B

14584. —— Same. 1877.

C

14585. Siskiyou chronicle. v.1–4. [1856?]–1859. Yreka, J.A. Glasscock & C.N. Thornbury [etc.] [1856?]–59.

C has Sept. 2, Oct. 21, 1858, July 9, 1859. CU-B has Sept. 2, Oct. 21, 1858, July 9, Aug. 27, 1859.

14586. Siskiyou county. Citizens. Petition of citizens of Siskiyou county in relation to the game laws of California. [Sacramento, F.P. Thompson, state print., 1878]

CSmH

14587. The Siskiyou pioneer in folklore, fact and fiction. v.1– 1946– Yreka, Siskiyou hist. soc., 1946– 1946–51 as the *Siskiyou pioneer, annual,* and *Yearbook* of the Society.

C has v.1–3 no. 3, 1946–60. C-S has v.1–3 no. 3, 1946–60. CChiS has 1947–51 (Annual). CHi has 1946–50, 1953–60. CLU has 1946–51 (Yearbook). CO has 1949–57. CRic has v.2 no. 2, Fall 1952. CSS has 1948 (Yearbook). CSf has v.1 no. 3–5, v.2 no. 1, 1948–51. CSfCSM has 1948–49, 1957. CSfWF-H has 1947–51. CU-B has v.1–2, 1947–57. CaBViPA has v.1, 1946–50. MWA has v.1–3 no. 2, 1946–59. NHi has v.1, 1946–50. NN has v.1–3 no. 2, 1946–59.

14588. Siskiyou news. Pioneer bridge dedication. Yreka, Aug. 22, 1931. 16 p. illus.   C

14589. Stewart, Charles Lockwood. The discovery and exploration of Mount Shasta. [Berkeley] 178 l. map. Thesis (M.A.)—Univ. of Calif., 1929.
    CChiS CU CU-B

14590. U.S. Adjutant general's office. General court martial, orders no. 32. [Charges against Captain Jack, Schonchis, Black Jim, Boston Charley, Barncho, alias one-eyed Jim, and Sloluck, alias Cok, Modoc Indian captives, and sentence to death] Wash., D.C., 1873. 5 p.
    CU-B

14591. —— Army. Dept. of the Columbia. Report of Colonel Alvan C. Gillem, 1st cavalry. Modoc war, 1873... To the Assistant adjutant general, headquarters Department of the Columbia... [n.p., 1874] 24 p.
    CHi (facsim.) CU-B

14592. —— War dept. ...Modoc war claims. Letter from the Secretary of war, transmitting the claims of the states of California and Oregon, and citizens thereof, on account of the Modoc war... [Wash., D.C.? 1874?]
    CU-B

14593. —— War relocation authority. Tule lake project, Newell, California. A Tule lake interlude. First anniversary Tule lake, W.R.A. project, May 27, 1942–43. Newell, The Tulean dispatch, War relocation authority [1943?] 109 p. illus., diagrs.   C

14594. Van Duzer, A. P. History of the operations of the Crystal creek sanitary association. Organized at Crystal creek, Scott Valley, Siskiyou county, Cal., Dec. 17, 1863. Yreka, Robert Nixon, jr., print., 1866. 16 p.
    CHi

14595. Wagner, Jack R. East of Shasta. [San Mateo, 1955] 40 p. illus., map.   CHi

14596. Wilson, Bourdon. Siskiyou county... S.F., Sunset mag. homeseekers' bur. [1910?] 64 p. illus.
    CChiS CHi CL CO CU-B NN

14597. Wilson, Hugh Robert. Causes and significance of the Modoc Indian war. Tulelake, Tulelake high school P.T.A., c1953. 28 p. illus.   C CAltu CArcHT

14598. Yreka. Chamber of commerce. Yreka, Siskiyou county, California. Yreka [1921?] folder (10 p.) illus., map.   CRcS

14599. —— Same. [1930?] [11] p. illus., map.
    CHi

SOLANO COUNTY
(*Created in 1850*)
COUNTY HISTORIES

14600. Gregory, Thomas Jefferson, and others. History of Solano and Napa counties, California, with biographical sketches... L.A., Historic record co., 1912. 1044 p. illus., port., maps.
    C CB CChiS CCH CF CFa CHi CL CLAC CLCM CLCo CLO CLSU CLU CLod CMartC CN CO CP CRic CS CSS CSf CSfCP CSfU CSj CSmH CStoC CU-A CU-B CV CViCL CoD ICN MWA MiD-B NN WHi

14601. Historical atlas map of Solano county, California. S.F., Thompson & West, 1878. 110 p. illus., maps.
    C CFa CHi CL CLU CSf CSmH CU-B CV CtY

14602. Hunt, Marguerite. History of Solano county, California by Marguerite Hunt and Napa county by Harry Lawrence Gunn... Chicago, Clarke, 1926. 2 v. ports. v.2: Biographical.
    C CBb CChiS CCH CFa CHi CLU CN CO COMC CSf CSlu CSmH CU-B CV IHi MWA NN WHi

14603. [Munro-Fraser, J. P.] History of Solano county... Illustrated. S.F., Wood, Alley & co., 1879. 503 p. ports. Includes biographical sketches.
    C C-S CAla CFa CHi CL CLAC CLU CO CSf CSfCP CSmH CSt CSto CStoC CU-B CV CYcCL NN

GREAT REGISTER

14604. Solano county. Index to the Great register of the county of Solano. 1866– Place of publication and title vary.
    C has 1867, 1872–73, 1875–80, 1882, 1886 (biennially to)– 1898, 1902 (biennially to)– 1962. CHi has 1880. CL has 1872–73, 1876–77, 1880 (suppl.), 1882 (suppl.), 1886, 1888, 1890. CSmH has 1866–? CU-B has 1866 (special election), 1867 (general), 1872–73, 1875, 1879–80, 1896, 1898, 1940.

DIRECTORIES

14605. Solano and Napa counties directory, including the cities and towns of Vallejo, Napa city, Benicia, Suisun, Fairfield, Dixon, Rio Vista, Batavia, Binghampton, Bridgeport, Vaca, Vacaville, St. Helena, Calistoga, Denverton, Maine Prairie, etc. for 1871–72. Sacramento, Crocker, 1871. 390 p.   C CU-B

Vallejo

14606. 1870. Kelley, John G., comp. The Vallejo directory for the year commencing March, 1870. Embracing a general directory of residents of the city of Vallejo and South Vallejo and business directory... Vallejo, Chronicle newspaper, bk. and job print., 1870. 309 p. History of Vallejo, p. 36–99.
    C CHi CSmH CSmat CV

14607. 1897. Vallejo directory co., pub. Vallejo directory for 1897, giving names of residents over 18 years of age, together with a business directory... [Vallejo, Vallejo news print., 1897] 154 p. illus., port.
    CHi CSmH

14608. 1901/02. Hartzell bros., pub. Directory of the city of Vallejo... Vallejo, Vallejo evening chronicle, 1901. 264 p.   C CHi CV

14609. 1904–1907/08. Kingsbury [firm] pub. Directory of Vallejo city and Benicia... 2 v. Title varies: 1904 Directory of Vallejo city and Solano county.   C-S

14610. 1911– Polk, R. L. & co., pub. Polk's Vallejo city directory. L.A., 1911– Publisher varies: 1911–25 Polk-Husted directory co. Content varies: 1911–25 Vallejo, Benicia, Fairfield and Suisun; 1942–57 Vallejo and Fairfield.
    C has 1926/27. C-S has 1911, 1912/13. CFa has 1915, 1918, 1920, 1923, 1925, 1926/27, 1928/29, 1930/31, 1933, 1935, 1937, 1939, 1942, 1950, 1953–58. CHi has 1942, 1947/48, 1950, 1953–58, 1960/61. CL has 1954, 1958. CSmat has 1958–59. CV has 1911, 1912/13, 1915, 1917–18, 1920, 1923, 1925, 1926/27, 1928/29, 1930/31, 1933, 1935, 1937, 1939, 1942, 1947/48, 1950, 1953–59.

Other Cities and Towns

14611. 1907. Directory publishing co., pub. Benicia city directory. S.F., 1907.   CHi

14612. [1947?] Fairfield-Suisun chamber of commerce. Directory: Fairfield, Suisun, Waterman Park.   CFa

14613. 1950. Smythe, pub. Smythe city and rural directory of Fairfield-Suisun. March 1, 1950.   CFa

14614. 1961. Polk, R. L. & co., pub. Polk's Fairfield-Suisun city directory. Monterey Park, 1961.
CHi CL

14615. 1950. Smythe, pub. Smythe city and rural directory of Vacaville, comp. May, 1950.   CFa

GENERAL REFERENCES

14616. Aspenall, William. Documents and testimony relating to the contested election case of Aspenall vs. Frisbie. [Sacramento, D.W. Gelwicks, state print., 1868] 91 p. Assemblyman for Solano co.   CSmH

14617. Breatt, Howard William. Robert Baylor Semple. [Berkeley, 1950] Thesis (History, M.A.)—Univ. of Calif., 1950.   CU

14618. Buck, L. W. ...L. W. Buck against J. M. Dudley, from the Nineteenth senatorial district, and E. C. Dozier against D. G. Barnes, for the Assembly from Solano county. Points and authorities of contestant. W. T. Baggett, A. C. Bradford, attorneys for contestants. Henry Edgerton, attorney for respondents. [n.p., 1883?] 14 p.
CU-B

14619. California taxpayers' association, inc. ...Report on Solano county. An analysis of the governmental organization and expenditures of the county for the fiscal year ending June 30, 1928, together with a general study of the fiscal system for the eight-year period, 1921–1928 ... L.A., 1929. 103 p.   C CU-B

14620. Cooper, Stephen, vs. Peña, Juan Felipe. In the Supreme court of the state of California. Stephen Cooper, plaintiff and appellant, vs. Juan Felipe Peña, defendant and respondent. Defendant's brief. John Currey, for defendant. [S.F.] B.F. Sterett, print. [1861?] 25 p. Suisun valley land case.   CLU

14621. Cordelia shooting club. California's first duck club. [S.F., 1880?] [1 l.] illus.   CHi

14622. District of Columbia. Supreme court. Opinion of Mr. Justice Wylie, of the Supreme court of the District of Columbia, as to the rights of pre-emptors on the "Soscol ranch" in California. Wash., D.C., Gibson bros., print., 1866. 16 p. Attached to cover is a sheet of manuscript notes by Gregory Yale.   CLU

14623. Dixon community council. Dixon, Solano county, nugget of the valley. Dixon [192–?] folder (6 p.) illus.   CHi

14624. Dunn, Arthur. Solano county, Calif. ... Issued by Sunset mag. service bur. for the Board of supervisors of Solano county. [S.F., 1915?] 63 p. illus., maps. Souvenir edition Panama-Pacific international exposition.
CHi CLU CSj CU-B CV

14625. Ewing, Thomas. Argument of Hon. Thomas Ewing, before the Secretary of the interior, in beaalf [!] of the pre-emptors on the Soscol ranch. Washington, Dec. 20, 1866. [Wash., D.C.?] Gibson bros., print., 1867. 15 p.   CLU

14626. Frisbie, John B., vs. Price, John R. In the Supreme court, state of California. John B. Frisbie, plaintiff and respondent, vs. John R. Price, et al., defendants and appellants. Transcript on appeal, from the

Seventh judicial district, county of Solano, Moore & Laine, attorneys for appellants. Whitney & Wells, attorneys for respondents. Sacramento, Crocker, 1864. 31 p. Soscol rancho land suit.   CLU

14627. [Frisbie, John B., & others] Memorial to ...The Senate & House of Representatives of the United States of America... [n.p., 1862?] 46 p. Petition of purchasers of the Rancho Soscol to confirm title to the Vallejo grant.   C CLU CSmH CU-B

14628. Hutton, Robert T. vs. Frisbie, John B. In the Supreme court of the state of California. Robert T. Hutton, appellant, vs. John B. Frisbie, et al., respondents. Brief for appellant. Thompson Campbell, John B. Felton, Theodore H. Hittell, attorneys for appellant. S.F., Deffebach & co., 1868. 106 p.   CHi

14629. Minahan, Eileen. The story of Chief Solano of the Suisun Indians. Fairfield, Solano county schools, 1955. 14 p. Mimeo.   CFa

14630. —— Same. Photography, Dr. J. Carol Conner. Fairfield, Solano county schools [1959] 16 p. illus.
CFa CHi

14631. Norton, George. ...Dixon, California, the dairy city... Homeseekers' bur. of Sunset... [S.F., 1912] 32 p. illus.   CL CU-B

14632. Palmer, Lyman L. Historical sketch of Rio Vista, Cal. and reminiscent sketches, forty years ago. Rio Vista, River news [1878] 32 p. port.   CU-B

14633. —— Same. 1914. 68 p. port.   CLU

14634. Peterson, Marcus Edmond. The career of Solano, chief of the Suisuns. [Berkeley, 1957] Thesis (M.A.)—Univ. of Calif., 1957.   CU

14635. [Price, John R.] Memorial concerning the settlers on the public lands in California, and particularly on the Soscol rancho. [n.p., 1862?] 8 p. Signed: John R. Price.   CLU CU-B

14636. Rio Vista. Centennial committee. This is our town; Rio Vista, California... [Rio Vista, 1958] [100] p. illus.   CFa CHi

14637. —— Chamber of commerce. Rio Vista, Solano county, California... Rio Vista [River news, 1927?] [6] p. illus.   CHi

14638. River news. The Eden of California, annual booster edition... 1923, 1925. Rio Vista [1923?–1925]
C CS

14639. Ryer, Mary Jane vs. Fletcher-Ryer company. In the Supreme court of the state of California. [Sacramento no. 520] Mary Jane Ryer, administratrix of the estate of William T. S. Ryer, deceased, respondent, vs. Fletcher-Ryer company, appellant. Appellant's opening points and authorities. R. H. Countryman, attorney for appellant... S.F., D.S. Stanley & co. [1898] 43 p.
CHi

14640. St. Gertrude's academy, Rio Vista. [Commencement programmes] 1st–4th, 1877–1880. Suisun, 1877–80.
CHi has 3d, 4th, 1879, 1880.

14641. Solano county. Election proclamation! Polling places and officers of election, Solano county... [Sacramento, 1872]   CSmH

14642. —— Board of supervisors. Solano county, California, the land of fruit, grain and money... [Vallejo, Press of Vallejo evening chronicle, 1905] 60 p. illus.
CHi CHi

14643. —— Board of trade. Solano county, California; its location, topography [etc., etc.] Oakland, Enquirer print. [1887?] 84 p. illus., map.
C CHi CLU CSf CSfCSM CU-B

14644. Solano county greets you. [Vallejo? 1939?] 17 p. illus., map. CRcS

14645. Solano county historical society. Membership roster. [1959?] [Vallejo? 1959?] unp. CU-B

14646. Stevenson, Jonathan Drake. ...Memorial and petition of Col. J. D. Stevenson of California, in relation to the survey of the bay of Suisun, Cal., in April, 1849. S.F., J.R. Brodie & co. [1886?] 5 p. CLU

14647. Suisun. Armijo union high school. [Courses of study, 1891] [n.p., 1891] 1 l. CHi

14648. U.S. District court. California (Northern district) ... Opinion delivered by Ogden Hoffman... in the case of Juan M. Luco, et al. no. 428, claiming "Ulpinas rancho"... S.F., Whitton, Towne & co., print., 1858. 33 p. CRb CSmH CU-B

14649. Waterman, R. H., et al., vs. Smith, Sampson. In the Supreme court of the state of California. R. H. Waterman, et al., appellants, vs. Sampson Smith, respondent. Appellants' points and argument. John Currey, attorney for appellants. [S.F.] Daily union job presses [18—] 66 p. "An action of ejectment...for the recovery of a tract of land in Suisun Valley." CLU

14650. Webster, Calvin R. Educational history of Solano county. S.F., Bancroft co., 1888. 170 p. CFa

14651. Weir, Andrew David. That fabulous Captain Waterman. N.Y., Comet press bks., 1957. 111 p. port. Waterman was founder of Fairfield and Cordelia was named after his wife. CFa CHi

14652. Wells, Andrew Jackson. Dixon, California, and its alfalfa lands... Sunset mag. homeseekers' bur. ... [S.F., 1911?] 32 p. illus. CHi CU-B

14653. —— Solano county, California. S.F., Sunset mag. homeseekers' bur. [n.d.] 63 p. illus., maps. CSf CV

14654. Whitney, Levi H., vs. Frisbie, John B. Supreme court of the United States. Levi H. Whitney, respondent, vs. John B. Frisbie, appellant. no. 298. [n.p., 18—] 17 p. Suit relating to the Soscol rancho. Signed: James A. Johnson, of counsel for respondent. CLU

14655. Wise, Harold F., associates. Report on the general plan for the Fairfield-Suisun planning area of Solano county, 1956. 150 p. illus., tables, map (in pocket) C

14656. Wiser, Harry David. A junior college program for Solano county. [Berkeley] 1956. Thesis (Ed.D.) —Univ. of Calif., 1956. CU

Benicia

14657. Atkins, Mary. The diary of Mary Atkins, a sabbatical in the eighteen sixties. Introduction by Aurelia Henry Reinhardt. Mills College, Eucalyptus press, 1937. 46 p. illus. CHi

14658. Benicia. Board of trustees. Official documents in relation to land titles in the city of Benicia... January, 1867... Suisun, Weekly Solano herald print. [1867] 15 p. C CU-B

14659. —— [Chamber of commerce] Historical Benicia. [Benicia, 1947] [4] p. CHi

14660. —— Charter. Charter of the city of Benicia. [Benicia] Benicia Sentinel print. [1851] CSmH

14661. —— College of Saint Augustine. Annual catalogue...1869–71. S.F., 1869–70. CHi has 1st, 1869. CU-B has 1869–71.

14662. —— —— Constitution and by-laws, together with the certificate of incorporation. S.F., Cubery & co., print., 1871. 14 p. CHi

14663. —— —— Official register. 1867–1889. S.F., 1867–90. Decennial edition 1878/79. 1888/89 edition lists all students from 1867–1889. C has 1872/73, 1880/81, 1888/89. CHi has 1871/72, 1873/74, 1875/76, 1877/78, 1878/79, 1887/88–1888/89. CStclU has 1867. CU-B has 1871/72, 1873/74, 1875/76, 1882/83, 1888/89.

14664. —— —— Regulations... S.F., Turnbull & Smith, 1869. 54 p. CHi CU-B

14665. —— —— St. Augustine's college, Benicia, Cal., the church school of the diocese of California. [Prospectus] [Benicia, 1872] [4] p. CU-B

14666. —— Collegiate institute. ...Circular, July, 1864. [S.F., Towne & Bacon, print., 1864] [3] p. illus. CU-B

14667. —— Young ladies' seminary. Catalogue ... 1st– [1852?–188–?] S.F. [1852?–188–?] C has 1868/69. CHi has 1860/61, 1861/62, 1869/70, 1872/73, 1883/84. COMC has 1856/57, 1860/61, 1861/62. CU has 1856/57, 1860/61, 1861/62. CU-B has 1855/56, 1863/64, 1867/68, 1869/70, 1871/72, 1874/75, 1876/77, 1879/80.

14668. Benicia agricultural works. ...Illustrated catalogue of agricultural implements and extras. Benicia, 1888. 178 p. CHi CU-B

14669. Benicia arsenal centennial, 1849–1949. [Benicia, Benicia welfare assoc., 1949] [44] l. illus., ports., facsims. CHi

14670. Benicia herald. Capitol rededication ed. March 15, 1958. [Benicia, 1958] 2A–24A, 1B–16B p. illus., ports. C CSf CU-B

14671. Benicia herald-new era, Benicia. Old timers special edition... Benicia, 1939. 16 p. illus., port. CU-B

14672. Benicia. Its resources and advantages for manufacture. Oakland, Tribune print. [1882?] 16 p. map. CLU CSmH CU-B

14673. Benicia. Synopsis of reasons why it should be made a port of entry. [Wash., D.C.] Gideon & co. [1850] 24 p. CHi CSmH

14674. California. Dept. of natural resources. Division of beaches and parks. Benicia Capitol state historical monument. [Sacramento, State print. off., 1957] [8] l. illus., port., map. CHi CRcS CStmo CU-B

14675. —— Dept. of public works. Division of architecture. Capitol of California, 1853, Benicia, restored 1957 by the Division... [Sacramento? 1958] [7] l. illus. CHi CU-B

14676. —— —— —— Restoration of the Benicia state capitol, Benicia, California. [Sacramento, 1958] [8] l. CU-B

14677. —— —— —— Restoration of the Benicia state capitol historical monument. Sacramento, 1956. [21] l. illus., plans. CU-B

14678. —— Legislature. An act to establish pilots and pilot regulations for the port and harbors of Benicia and Mare island. ...Benicia, Solano county herald off., 1856. 9 p. CHi

14679. Conmy, Peter Thomas. Benicia, intended metropolis. S.F., Grand parlor, Native sons of the golden West, 1958. 19 p. illus. Available in many California libraries and N

14680. Dalton, Alfred. A history of St. Paul's parish...Benicia... [Benicia? Herald print., 1905] [8] p. illus., port. CU-B

14681. Democratic party. California. Address of the majority of the Democratic members of both branches of the legislature of California, in public meeting assembled in convention at Benicia, Feb'y. 1854. S.F., Francis A. Bonnard, print., 1854. 16 p.
C CSmH CSt CU-B

14682. —— —— Convention, 1851. Report of the proceedings and address of the Democratic state convention assembled at Benicia, May 19, 20th and 21st, 1851. Stockton, San Joaquin republican, 1851. 16 p. NN

14683. Fisher, Frank B., Muller, Albert, and Andraieff, Florence. An historical background of the city of Benicia. Benicia, 1945. 20 p. illus., ports.
CO CU-B

14684. —— Same. 1946. 20 p. illus.
CHi CO CV

14685. [Imus, Clint] Benicia, California; industrial survey, 1923... [Benicia, 1923] 21 l. Typew.
C CSmH CU-B

14686. Johnston, Alva. The legendary Mizners. N.Y., Farrar, Straus [1953] 304 p. illus.   CSf CU

14687. Mizner, Addison. The many Mizners. N.Y., Sears pub. co., 1932.   CRcS

14688. Mizner, Lansing B. Memorial and accompanying papers in relation to the town of Benicia, on the Soscol rancho, Solano county, California. C. B. Houghton, Samuel C. Gray, Edwin Danforth, trustees of Benicia. Lansing B. Mizner, attorney for trustees. S.F., Francis, Valentine & co. [1865?] 23 p.   CHi

14689. Nichols, Elijah. Speech of Hon. Elijah Nichols, on the removal of the capital from Benicia, March 6, 1854. S.F., Golden era off., 1854. 8 p.   C CU-B

14690. Proceedings of a public meeting of the Democratic members of the legislature of California, opposed to the election of a United States senator at the present session of the legislature, held in the senate chamber at Benicia on Thursday evening, February 2, 1854. S.F., Placer times and transcript off., 1854. 8 p.   CU-B

14691. Saint Mary of the Pacific. ...Catalogue ...1872/73– S.F., 1873–
CHi has 1881–82. CU-B has 1872/73–1875/77.

14692. —— ...Prospectus of Saint Mary of the Pacific, a female boarding school, Benicia, California. S.F., Cubery & co., print., 1871. 12 p. front.   CU-B

14693. Solano county historical society. Benicia's early glory; California state capital, 1853–1854. Published for the dedication of the restored Old state capitol building, March 15, 1958. [Benicia? 1958] 111 p. illus. Includes bibliography.
C CFa CHi CO CSS CSt CSto CV

14694. Wingfield, John Henry. Higher education. A plea for St. Augustine college, Benicia, California... S.F., Cubery & co. steam bk. & job print., 1882. 22 p.
CLU CSmH CU-B

14695. Woodbridge, Sylvester. Funeral sermon of brother Edward F. Perkins, of the third California volunteers, preached before the Benicia lodge, no. 31 [Independent order of Odd fellows] October 26, 1862. S.F., Eastman & Godfrey, print., 1862. 12 p.
CLU CU CU-B

14696. —— Sermon, preached at the dedication of the First Presbyterian church, Benicia, California, March 9, 1851, by the pastor... Benicia, St. Clair, Pinkham & co., 1851. 14 p.
C CHi CLU CSmH CU-B NN (photostat) PHi

14697. Woodruff, Jacqueline McCart. Benicia, the promise of California, 1846–1889... [Vallejo, c1947] 84 p. illus.
C CHi CL CLU CMont CO CSf CSfWF-H CSmH CU (Thesis) CU-B CV

14698. Woolery, William Kirk. The educational resources of Benicia: a community survey. [Berkeley, 1915] Thesis (M.A.)—Univ. of Calif., 1915.   CU

Vacaville

14699. Crystal, Helen Dormody. The beginnings of Vacaville. [Berkeley, 1933] 321 l. illus., ports., maps. Typew. Thesis (M.A.)—Univ. of Calif., 1933.
CU CU-B

14700. [Livingston, Lawrence] Vacaville area general plan. Vacaville, Vacaville and county of Solano, 1958. 43 p.   CHi

14701. Nut tree restaurant. Nut tree history. [n.p., 1959?] folder (4 p.) map.   CHi

14702. Vacaville. Board of trustees. Vacaville, California... [Vacaville, Reporter pub. co., 1887?] [32] p. illus.   CU-B

14703. —— California college. Catalogue of the officers and students. 1874/75–1878/79. S.F., J.H. Carmany & co., bk. & job print., 1875–79. Publisher varies.
CHi has 1876/77, 1878/79. CU-B has 1874/75, 1878/79.

14704. —— —— Prospectus. 1871. [n.p., 1871] 12 p.   CU-B

14705. —— Chamber of commerce. Vacaville; an enterprising center occupying a position affording natural advantage and opportunity for the greater industrial and agricultural era of California. Vacaville, Reporter pub. co. [1947] 63 p. illus., map.   CHi CRic

14706. —— Union high school. American history class. Prunings from Vaca valley. [Vacaville] 1931. 20 p. illus.   CHi CU-B

14707. Wickson, Edward J. The Vacaville early fruit district of California. Second ed. S.F., Calif. view pub. co., 1888. 166 p. illus. (Calif. illustrated, no. 1)
C CO CSmH CU-B NHi

14708. Wilson, Luzena Stanley. Luzena Stanley Wilson, '49er; memories recalled years later for her daughter Correnah Wilson Wright; introduction by Francis P. Farquhar, illustrated by Kathryn Uhl. Mills College, Eucalyptus press, 1937. 61 p. illus.
CBb CFa CHi CLLoy CRcS CRic CSd CSto CStoC CU-A OrU

Vallejo

14709. Bouldin, D. W. vs. Calhoun, Edmund R. et al. D. W. Bouldin, plaintiff, vs. Edmund R. Calhoun, Philip C. Johnson and Chas. J. McDougal, U.S. naval officers in possession of Mare island, defendants. [S.F., 1878?] 212 p. Mare island land claim case.   CLU

14710. Browne, John A. Early days. Forty years of the Old town's early history. Illustrations by Gene Davis and Mary Bathe. Map by George Manyck. [Vallejo, 1943] 17 p. illus., map.   C

14711. California (battleship) U.S.S. California, built at Mare island navy yard, Mare island, California, keel laid October 25th, 1916, launched November 20th, 1919, commissioned August 10th, 1921. S.F., Pub. for the Ship's welfare fund, c1922. 30 p. illus., col. mount. front.
CHi

14712. California Pacific railroad co. By-laws... [Vallejo, Vallejo chronicle job print., 1870?] 22 p.
CHi

14713. Citizens' executive committee. Advantages, and solution of disadvantages, Mare island, in San Francisco bay, for naval base and navy yard; expert testimony to U.S. Commission on navy yards and naval stations from the Citizens' committee, Vallejo, California. [Vallejo] Vallejo chronicle [1916] 61 p. maps (part fold.)
CU-B

14714. Creedon, Elma May. Grandfather's diary [John Frey, city trustee] The problem of Vallejo's water supply. [n.p., Priv. print., n.d.] 70 p.   CV

14715. —— John Frey, city trustee. His part in solving Vallejo's water problem. [Vallejo? 194–?] 40 p. illus., ports.   CHi CU-B

14716. [Hittell, John Shertzer] The future of Vallejo by Solano. Vallejo, Vallejo recorder, 1868. 32 p.
C CU-B

14717. —— The prospects of Vallejo; or, Evidences that Vallejo will become a great city. Vallejo, Chronicle steam print. house, 1871. 56 p. map.
C CHi CLU CSmH CU-B

14718. —— The resources of Vallejo...reprinted from the *Solano county advertiser*, 1868–1869. 71 p. maps.   C CLU CSmH CU-B

14719. —— Vallejo in November, 1871, a sequel to *The prospects of Vallejo.* 51–62 p. map.   CSmH

14720. Lott, Arnold S. A long line of ships; Mare island's century of naval activity in California. Annapolis, Md., United States naval institute [1954] 268 p. illus., map.
C CAla CBb CHi CLgA CNa CP CSd CSf
CStmo CU-B CV

14721. Mare island. Centennial, 1954. Official souvenir program, celebrating the 100th anniversary of the West's oldest naval base, Sept. 16, 17, 18, 19, Vallejo, 1954. [Vallejo, 1954] 16 p.   CHi

14722. Mare-island-Vallejo, Solano county, California. [n.p.] 1921. 10 p. illus., ports., map. Special Mare island hospital no., *U.S. Naval medical bul.*   CSf

14723. Metcalfe, James B. Oration delivered at Vallejo, Cal. July 4th, 1881. [S.F.] Barry & Baird, print. [1881?] 14 p.   CHi

14724. [Mhoon, John B.] The Mare island case... Wash., D.C., J. L. Pearson, print. [1880?] 6 p.   CU-B

14725. Mrs. Jarley's wax works. [Descriptive pamphlet. n.p., n.d.] [4] p.   CHi

14726. Pacific homestead association of Vallejo. Act of incorporation, articles of association and by-laws of the Pacific homestead association of Vallejo. Incorporated February 17th, 1869... Sacramento, Russell and Winterburn, 1869. 24 p. maps.   C

14727. Red men, Improved order of. Vallejo. Samoset tribe no. 22. Constitution, by-laws and rules of order. Instituted 4th Sleep, Hot moon, G.S.D., 378. Vallejo, Chronicle print., 1898. 74 p.   CHi

14728. Shortridge, Samuel Morgan. Oration of Samuel M. Shortridge delivered at Farragut hall, Vallejo, Cal., July 5th, 1897... [Vallejo? 1897?] 32 p.
C CU-B

14729. Souvenir of Mare island navy yard and Vallejo, California, containing views of the principal points of interest. S.F., Polychrome co. [19—?] 17 l. chiefly illus.   CO

14730. Union homestead association, Vallejo. Articles of association and by-laws... Incorporated January 27, 1869... Vallejo, Print. by S.C. Baker, at Solano county advertiser off., 1869. 16 p.   CSmH CU-B

14731. U.S. Naval shipyard, Mare island. St. Peter's chapel... [n.p., 1951] [4] p.   CHi

14732. Vallejo. Chamber of commerce. Statistical facts, 1959. [Vallejo?] Solano county board of supervisors [1959?]   CV

14733. —— **Charter.** Adopted January 19–20, 1899. [n.p., n.d.]   CV

14734. —— —— Amendments. Adopted Feb. 16, 1907.   CV

14735. —— —— Same. July 24, 1946. [n.p., n.d.]   CV

14736. —— **First Baptist church.** Manual of the First Baptist church, Vallejo, California. Vallejo, Vallejo recorder print., 1868. 26 p.   CU-B

14737. —— **First Presbyterian church.** Seventy-fifth anniversary, First Presbyterian church, Vallejo, California, 1862–1937. [Vallejo, Times-herald, 1937] [12] p.
CU-B

14738. Vallejo central homestead association. Act of incorporation, articles of association and by-laws. Sacramento, Russell and Winterburn, 1868. 29 p.   C

14739. Vallejo city homestead association. Articles of association, acts of incorporation and by-laws... Incorporated February 24th, 1869... Sacramento, Crocker, 1869. 25 p.   C CU-B

14740. Vallejo library association. [Borrower's register of the Vallejo library association. Vallejo, 1862] [110] p. Ms.   C

14741. Vallejo realty co., San Francisco. Vallejo annex. [S.F., c1916] [7] p. illus., map.   CHi

14742. Vallejo times-herald. Mare island, 1854–1946; Pacific center for naval repair and construction, Vallejo, California. Supplement, March 9, 1947. [Vallejo, 1947] 60 p. illus.   C CHi

14743. —— ...Mare island navy yard centennial, 1854–1954. [Sept. 16, 1954. Vallejo, 1954] [1c]–140c p. illus., ports.   CHi CO CU-B

SONOMA COUNTY
(*Created in 1850*)

COUNTY HISTORIES

14744. Finley, Ernest Latimer, ed. ...History of Sonoma county, California... Santa Rosa, Press democrat pub. co., 1937. 453,384 p. ports. 2 pts. in 1. Part 1: Historical; Part 2: Biographical. "Golden Gate bridge ed." "Biographers: Byrd Weyler Kellogg, Helen Miller Lehman, Lucile Rood Kelley."
CHi CL CLU CO CPe CSfCP CSfCSM CStcrCL
CStr CStrCL CStrJC CU-B

14745. Gregory, Thomas Jefferson. History of Sonoma county, California, with biographical sketches... L.A., Historic record co., 1911. 1112 p. illus., ports., map. "Biographical": p. [257]–1112.
C CAla CCH CF CHi CL CLCo CLSU (1912)
CLU CN CO CPe CRic CSf CSfCP CSmH CStb
CStoC CStr CStrCL CStrJC CU-B CoD NN WHi

14746. —— Same [without biographical section] 251 p. illus., ports., map.   CLO

14747. Historical atlas map of Sonoma county, California... Oakland, Thomas Hinckley Thompson & co., 1877. 102 p. illus., maps.
C CCH CHi CLU CO CPe CSf CSmH CSt
CStr CStrCL CStrJC CU-B CYcCL CtY NN

14748. An illustrated history of Sonoma county, California. Chicago, Lewis, 1889. 737 p. illus., ports.

C CAla CCH CHi CL CLSM CLU CLod CPe
CSf CSmH CSmat CSr CSrCL CSt CStoC CStr
CStrJC CU-B CoD CtY NHi NN WHi

14749. [Munro-Fraser, J. P.] History of Sonoma
county [Cal.]... with a full and particular record of
the Spanish grants...S.F., Alley, Bowen & co., 1880.
717 p. port. Includes biographical sketches.
C CBb CCH CHi CL CLSM CLU CO COHN
CPe CSf CSfCP CSfCSM CSfU CSmH CStclU
CStr CStrCL CStrJC CU-B CoU CtY MWA N
NHi NN WHi

14750. Thompson, Robert A. Historical and de-
scriptive sketch of Sonoma county, California... Phila.,
L.H. Everts & co., 1877. 104 p. map.
C CHi CLCM CSfCSM CSmH CStr CStrCL
CStrJC CU-B CtY NHi WHi

14751. Tuomey, Honoria Rosalie Pamela. History of Sonoma county... Chicago, Clarke, 1926. 2 v.
illus., ports. v.2: Biographical.
C CHi CLob CN CO CPe CSf CSfU CSmH
CStoC CStr CStrCL CStrJC MWA NN WHi

GREAT REGISTER

14752. Sonoma county. Index to the Great register
of the county of Sonoma. 1866– Place of publication and
title vary.
C has 1867, 1871–73, 1875, 1879–80, 1884, 1888 (biennially to)– 1898 and (suppl.), 1900, 1902, 1906 (biennially to)– 1914, 1918 (biennially to)– 1962. CHi has
1898. CL has 1868 (suppl. 1869), 1872–73, 1877, 1880,
1882, 1886, 1888, 1890. CSmH has 1867, 1880. CStrJC.
CU-B has July, Sept. 1867, 1867 (suppl.), Nov. 1868,
1868 (suppl.), 1872–73, 1875, 1879, 1938 (primary), 1940
(general)

DIRECTORIES

14753. 1884/85. McKenney, L. M. & co., pub.
...8-county directory of Sonoma, Napa, Lake, Mendocino,
Humboldt, Yolo, Solano, and Marin counties... Oakland,
1883. 701 p.   CHi

14754. 1885. Disturnell & Harrington, pub. Sonoma county directory and gazetteer, containing the
names...of all adult persons in the towns of Santa Rosa,
Petaluma, Healdsburg and Cloverdale. Also, a gazetteer,
giving an exhibit of the resources of the county, and a
full and accurate description of the principal towns and
villages. S.F., 1885. 261 p.   C CLU CU-B

14755. 1896. Williams, G. M., pub. Santa Rosa
directory for 1896... To which is added the names of
all land owners of Sonoma county with the number acres
held by each; the number of acres planted in or value of
trees [etc.]... Santa Rosa, 1895. illus., ports.
                                              CStr CU-B
14756. 1899/1900. Oppenheimer, H. E., comp.
Sonoma county directory...arranged by towns alphabetically... S.F., Sonoma county directory pub. co.
[1899?] 245 p.   CStr

**14757. 1903/04– Press democrat publishing co.,
pub.** ...Directory of Santa Rosa, Petaluma and Sonoma
county. Santa Rosa, 1903– Publisher varies: 1903/04–
1905 A. Kingsbury. Content varies: 1903/04–1905 Santa
Rosa and Sonoma county.
C has 1915. CHi has 1913, 1915. CStr has 1903/04–
1905, 1913, 1915, 1924.

14758. 1908–1929/30. Polk, R. L. & co., pub.
Santa Rosa, Petaluma and Sonoma county directory. Publisher varies: 1908–11 Polk-Husted. Continued as Polk's
Santa Rosa city directory and Polk's Petaluma city directory.

C has 1908, 1911. C-S has 1908, 1909/10, 1911. CHi
has 1909/10, 1929/30. CPe has 1926, 1929/30. CStr has
1908, 1909/10, 1911, 1926, 1929/30. CU-B has 1909/10.

Santa Rosa

14759. 1935– Polk, R. L. & co., pub. Polk's
Santa Rosa city directory. L.A., 1935– Content varies:
1935–38 Santa Rosa, Healdsburg, Sebastopol and Cloverdale; 1947–53 Santa Rosa, Healdsburg and Sebastopol.
Preceded by Polk's Santa Rosa, Petaluma and Sonoma
county directory.
CHi has 1935, 1938, 1947, 1949, 1953–55, 1957–61. CL
has 1953–55, 1957–58. CStr has 1935, 1938, 1947, 1949,
1953–55, 1957–58.

14760. 1947. MacKay associates, pub. Santa
Rosa, California, city directory, 1947 [and] Sebastopol
city directory... San Jose, 1947. 319 p.   CStr

Other Cities and Towns

14761. 1895. Livernash & Peck, pub. A complete and concise business directory and descriptive
pamphlet of Healdsburg, Geyserville and Windsor; Russian river, Dry creek and Alexander vallies [sic]...
Healdsburg, Healdsburg enterprise print., 1895. 32 p.
                                                    CU-B
14762. 1895. Scudder, Noah W., pub. Petaluma
city directory, v.1, 1895. Petaluma, 1895.   CHi CPe

14763. 1907. Arthur, J. C., comp. Arthur's city
and rural directory of Petaluma, California. Illustrated
by the Petaluma chamber of commerce. Petaluma, Petaluma argus print., 1907. 184 p.   CHi

14764. 1939– Polk, R. L. & co., pub. Polk's
Petaluma city directory including Cotati and Penngrove.
L.A. [1939]– Preceded by Polk's Santa Rosa, Petaluma
and Sonoma county directory.
CHi has 1950, 1954, 1958. CL has 1939, 1950, 1954,
1956. CPe has 1947, 1950, 1954, 1956, 1958. CSmat has
1958. CU-B has 1950.

GENERAL REFERENCES

14765. Alexander, J. Russian river's only steamboat. [1856?] 4 p. Typew.   CStrCL

14766. Allen, Eugene Thomas. Steam wells and
other thermal activities at "The Geysers," California, by
E. T. Allen and Arthur L. Day. [Wash., D.C.] 1927. 106 p.
illus., fold. map. (Carnegie inst. of Wash. Pub. no. 378)
                                                   CSfCW

14767. Baer, George B. Cloverdale, the orange district of Sonoma county... Cloverdale, Cloverdale reveille
print., 1888. 32 [18] p.   CSmH CU-B

14768. —— Description of Cloverdale and vicinity
... Cloverdale, Cloverdale reveille print., 1887. 46 p.
                                                    CU-B

14769. Baldwin, Orville Raymond. Reminiscences. [Oakland, Author, c1941] 215 p. illus., ports.
                                                     CHi

14770. Bauer, Patricia McCollum. History of
lumbering and tanning in Sonoma county, California
since 1812. [Berkeley] 1951. Thesis (M.A. History)—
Univ. of Calif., 1951.   CU CU-B

14771. Borden, Stanley T. Petaluma & Santa Rosa
electric railroad. [San Mateo] 1960. 36 p. illus. (*Western railroader*, v.23 no. 4, Apr. 1960)   CHi

14772. Bowers, A. B. A history of "The Bowers
map bill," and of the map of Sonoma county. S.F., Frank
Eastman, 1869. 94 p. tables.   C

14773. Briggs, Fergusson & co., San Francisco.

Map of the town of El Verano and subdivisions of adjoining property of the Sonoma valley improvement co. ... S.F., Crocker [1888] [17] p. fold. map.   CHi

14774. Brown, Madie. California's Valley of the moon; historic places and people in the valley of Sonoma. Sonoma [1961] [20] p. illus., ports. Priv. print. by Lawton Kennedy.   CHi CStrJC

14775. [Browne, John Ross] The reclamation of salt marsh lands on Sonoma and Napa creeks. S.F., Alta Calif. print. house, 1872. 18 p. map.   CHi

14776. Burke sanitarium, Burke. [Brochure. Burke, 1912?] [24] p.   CHi

14777. Butterfield & Butterfield, auctioneers. The fabulous treasures of Fountaingrove; additions... S.F. [1948] [21] p.   CHi

14778. California. Dept. of natural resources. Div. of beaches and parks. Fort Ross. Sacramento, State print. off., 1955.   CRcS

14779. ——— ——— ——— Same. 1960. [3] p.   CHi

14780. California taxpayers' association, inc. Sonoma co., report... [L.A.] 1926. 16 p.
                                       C CLSU CU-B

14781. Camp Reverie in Russian river redwoods... [n.p., 1901?] 23 p. illus.   CU-B

14782. Caslamayomi rancho. [S.F.? 1865?]
                                                   CSmH

14783. Chapman, William S., vs. Polack, Mary and Forsyth, William. William S. Chapman, plaintiff and respondent, vs. Mary Polack and William Forsyth, defendants and appellants. James F. Stuart and H. A. Powell, attorneys for appellants. Filed A.D., 1885... [S.F.] S.W. Raveley, print. [1885] 43 p.   CSmH

14784. Chipman, William F. General Vallejo memorial association. [S.F.] General Vallejo memorial assoc. [1931] 26 p. illus., port.   CHi CSf

14785. Cloverdale. Congregational church. Historical booklet in commemoration of the seventy-fifth anniversary... Cloverdale [print. by Cloverdale reveille] 1944. 38 p.   CHi

14786. Cloverdale reveille. 75th anniversary edition. Cloverdale, 1954. 1 v. (v.p.) illus.   C

14787. [Coblentz, Edmond D.] The tale of Temelec hall. [n.p., c1953] 10 p. illus.   CHi CU-B

14788. Cole, W. Russell. ...Sonoma county, California. Issued by Sunset magazine homeseekers' bureau ...for the Sonoma county development association. S.F., 1914. 64 p. illus., map, tables.   CU-B

14789. The count found a valley. [Sonoma, Rancho Buena Vista, c1947] 12 p. illus., ports. Cover title. Printed by Idaho printcrafters, inc. The story of Buena Vista rancho and Count Agoston Haraszthy.   CHi CStrJC

14790. Daughters of the American revolution. California. Santa Rosa chapter. Sonoma county cemetery records from 1846 to 1921. Comp. by Edith W. (Mrs. Edson C.) Merritt and Pauline Whitney Olson. Santa Rosa, 1950.   CStr

14791. [Farafontoff, A. P.] Fort Ross; advanced military post which was the past glory of Russia in America [125-year jubilee] 1812–1937. [Shanghai, 1937] [40] l. illus. Russian and English.   CHi

14792. Ferguson, Ruby Alta. The historical development of the Russian river valley, 1579–1865. [Berkeley, 1931] 161 l. illus., maps. Thesis (M.A.)—Univ. of Calif., 1931. "Physiographically speaking, this thesis is confined to that portion of Sonoma co., Calif. ...commonly known as the Russian river valley..."—Preface.
                                       CU CU-B

14793. The Geysers, Sonoma county, California. [Oakland, R.S. Kitchener, print., 1905?] [14] p. illus.
                                                   CHi

14794. Gordon, Laura (De Force) The great geysers of California, and how to reach them... S.F., Bacon and co. [1877] 53 p. illus., map.
                             C CLU CSfCW CSmH

14795. Haase, Ynez. The Russian American company in California. [Berkeley] Thesis (M.A.)—Univ. of Calif., 1952.   CU

14796. Hammond, George Peter, ed. On the ambitious projects of Russia in regard to north west America, with particular reference to New Albion & new California, by an Englishman. S.F., Bk. club of Calif., 1955. 79 p. map.
CBb CL CLO CLSM CRedl CSalCL CSf CSjC

14797. Hansen, Harvey J. and Miller, Jeanne Thurlow. Wild oats in Eden: Sonoma county in the 19th century. [Also] Sonoma Indians, by David Wayne Peri. Photographs by Ansel Adams, John LeBaron and Beth Winter. Santa Rosa [n.p.] 1962. 147 p. illus.
                                       CAla CHi

14798. Haraszthy, Agoston. Grape culture, wines, and wine-making. N.Y., Harper, 1862. 420 p. illus.
                                       CStrJC CU-B

14799. ——— Same. With Notes upon agriculture and horticulture. N.Y., Harper, 1892. 420 p. illus.   CStrJC

14800. Harris, Thomas Lake. Brotherhood of the new life. Santa Rosa, Fountaingrove press, 1891. 15 p.
                                                   CStrJC

14801. ——— The new republic; a discourse of the prospects, dangers, duties and safeties of the times. Santa Rosa, Fountaingrove press, 1891. (Fountaingrove lib. Social ser., v.1, no. 1, March, 1891) 75 p.
                                       CHi CStrJC

14802. Hatch, Flora Faith. The Russian advance into California. [Berkeley] 1922. Thesis (M.A.)—Univ. of Calif., 1922.   CU CU-B

14803. Heald, W. T. History of the Heald family. Appearing in the Healdsburg tribune from July 15, 1954 to January 6, 1955 in twenty-four parts. [Healdsburg, 1954–55] 1 v. of newspaper clippings. illus., ports., map.
                                                   CU-B

14804. Healdsburg. Chamber of commerce. Healdsburg, California, and its surroundings. [Healdsburg?] 1909. 32 p. illus.   CU-B

14805. The Healdsburg tribune and enterprise, Healdsburg. ... Diamond jubilee souvenir edition, Aug. 26, 1940. [Healdsburg, 1940] 72 p. illus., ports.
                                       CHi CU-B

14806. Houseworth (Thomas) & co., San Francisco. Stereoscopic views of the great Geyser springs... also views of Calistoga and White sulphur springs... S.F. [1872?] [3] p.   CHi

14807. Hubbard, Harry D. Vallejo...ed. by Pauline C. Santoro. Boston, Meador pub. co., 1941. 374 p.
   C CBb CHi CL CLSU CMerCL CO CRcS
CSS CSd CSf CSjC CSmH CStbS CStr CU-B
CV CYcCL

14808. Immigration association of California. [County scrapbooks] [S.F., 188–?]   C

14809. Italian-Swiss agricultural colony, Sonoma county, California. Annual report [6th]...Incorporated March 12, 1881... S.F. [1887] 2 l.   CSmH

14810. —— [Brochure. n.p., 1898?] 30 p.   CHi

14811. —— Same. S.F., Gabriel-Meyerfeld co. [1911?] 28 p.   CHi

14812. —— L'Italian-Swiss colony...produttrice di eccellenti vini e acquaviti di California. [S.F., Britton & Rey, 1907?] 46 p.   CHi

14813. —— Receipt book of...[certificate of incorporation, officers, and by-laws] S.F., Alfred Chaigneau, print. [1885?] 35 p. In English and Italian.   CHi

14814. Johnck, Gabrielle. Bounty land, the story of Summer home park [by] Gabrielle Johnck, Bertram Johnck. S.F., Priv. print. the Tardy press, 1962. 70 p. illus., 2 fold. maps.   CAla CHi

14815. Kennedy, Mary Jean. Culture contact and acculturation of the southwestern Pomo. [Berkeley] 1955. Thesis (Ph.D.)—Univ. of Calif., 1955.   CU

14816. L., W. The great geysers of California; their wonderful appearance and surroundings. Exciting stage ride over the mountains. Foss! "The monarch of the coach box!" S.F., A.L. Bancroft & co., 1875. 25 p.   C CHi CSmH

14817. Lee, Charles H. Report on sanitary survey of Sonoma county, California, with recommendations for control of epidemics, February 1, 1944. For the Board of supervisors, county of Sonoma, and the Sonoma county department of public health. [S.F.? 1944] 94 p.   CHi

14818. Levick, M. B. Sonoma county, Calif. S.F., Sunset pub. co. 62 p.   CHi CStrCL CU-B

14819. —— Same. S.F., 1917. 63 p. maps.   CU-B

14820. Lothrop, Marian Lydia. Mariano Guadalupe Vallejo, defender of the northern frontier of California. [Berkeley, 1926] 253 l. Thesis (Ph.D.)—Univ. of Calif., 1926.   CU CU-B

14821. McGinty, Brian. Vintage time in the Valley of the moon. [Santa Maria, Allan Hancock, 1960] 20 p. illus., ports.   CHi

14822. McKenzie, John C. The chapel of Fort Ross. [n.p.] 1960. 11 p. illus. Mimeo. Includes bibliography.   CStrJC

14823. —— The restoration of Fort Ross, 1834 to 1961. [n.p., 1961?] [24] p. Mimeo.   CHi

14824. MacKenzie, Kenneth D. The Russians in California (prior to 1842) Stockton, 1926. 83 p. Thesis (M.A.)—College of the Pacific.   CStoC

14825. McKittrick, Myrtle Mason. Vallejo, son of California... Portland, Ore., Binfords [c1944] 377 p. Available in many California libraries and CaBViPA OrU

14826. Manning, Clarence A. Russian influence on early America. N.Y., Library pub., 1953. 216 p.   CLSM CSf

14827. Markov, Al. The Russians on the Pacific ocean (California, 1845). The Ivan Petroff translation, with a foreword by Arthur Woodward. L.A., Dawson, 1955. 65 p. (Early Calif. travels ser., 27) 300 copies printed by College press.
CBb CHi CL CLLoy CLO CLSM CLgA CP CRic CSd CSf CSjC CStbS CSto CStoC CU-B CVtV

14828. Milliken, James, comp. Sonoma county illustrated...an illustrated review of the resources and industries of the gem county of California...engravings by Geo. Rice & sons, Los Angeles, Cal., views by Wm. Shaw. Santa Rosa, Press-democrat pub. co., 1901. [21] p. 48 pl. incl. ports.   CHi CStrCL

14829. Moerenhout, Jacques Antoine et al. vs. Bell, Thomas A. In the Supreme court of the state of California. Jacob A. Moerenhout [!] et al., plaintiffs and appellants, vs. Thomas A. Bell, trustee, &c., defendant and respondent. Transcript on appeal, from Fourth district court. B. S. Brooks, att'y for appellants. Cope & Boyd, Wilson & Wilson, att'ys for respondent. [S.F.?] 1879. 271 p. Suit over La laguna de los gentiles rancho.   CLU

14830. Morrison, S. A., et al., vs. Bowman, James. In the Supreme court of the state of California. S. A. Morrison, et al., vs. James Bowman. Appellees' brief. D. O. Shattuck, attorney for appellees. S.F., Francis, Valentine & co. [n.d.] 31 p. Relates to the Blücher ranch, Sonoma county.   CHi

14831. Northwest coast of America & California: 1832. Letters from Fort Ross, Monterey, San Pedro and Santa Barbara, by an Intelligent Bostonian. L.A., Dawson, 1959. 19 p. (Early Calif. travels ser., 48) 180 copies printed by Plantin press.
CL CLSM CLgA CRedl CSS CU-B

14832. Okun', S[emen] B. The Russian-American company. Edited, with introduction, by B. D. Grekov. Tr. from the Russian by Carl Ginsburg; pref. by Robert J. Kerner. Cambridge, Harvard univ. press, 1951. 311 p. (Russian translation project ser. of the Am. council of learned soc., 9)   CHi CSf

14833. [Polack, J. S.] The great geyser springs of California. [S.F., Frank Eastman, 1863?] [3] p.   CHi

14834. Press democrat. Blueprint for progress, Sonoma county, land of golden opportunity: the Walsh report, new industries, industrial directory; special supplement of the Press democrat, Sunday, February 25, 1951. Santa Rosa, 1951. 24 p. illus., ports.   CU-B

14835. —— ...Guide book and classified directory of Sonoma county and Calistoga. 1949/50. [Santa Rosa, 1949] 94 p. illus. (part col.) maps.   CStrJC CU-B

14836. Reynolds & Brown. Healdsburg, California, and its environment...Descriptive pamphlet...presented by Reynolds & Brown, real estate agents and loan brokers... [Healdsburg, 18–?] 16 p.   CU-B

14837. Reynolds & Proctor, pub. Illustrated atlas of Sonoma county, California... Santa Rosa [1898] 80, 64 p. illus., ports., maps.
C CHi CPe CSf CSfU CSmH CStr CStrJC CU CU-B

14838. Russian river valley home seeker. Healdsburg and vicinity, a few facts about the resources and superior advantages of this section... Healdsburg, Healdsburg tribune print., 1901. 16 p. illus., map.   CStrJC

14839. Sage, Ralph A., pub. Agricultural, industrial and scenic resources of Sonoma county, California. ... Santa Rosa, 1919. 24 p. illus.   CStrJC

14840. San Francisco and North Pacific railway. Legend of Dah-nol-yo, Squaw Rock. [n.p., 1895?] [16] p. illus.   CHi

14841. Santa Rosa. Board of trade. The Santa Rosan; resources of Sonoma county... v.1, no. 1–2. July 1887–1888. Santa Rosa, 1887–88.   CU-B

14842. —— **Chamber of commerce.** Sonoma county; land of rich romance, historic lure. [Santa Rosa, c1930] 27 p. illus.   CHi

14843. Santa Rosa republican. The Sonoma county development edition; Santa Rosa republican supplement, February 22, 1911. unp. illus.   C

14844. Sonoma county. Board of education.

School districts of Sonoma county... 1911–1912. [Petaluma, Northern crown pub. co., print., 1911] 37 p.
CU-B

14845. —— **Board of supervisors.** Imperial Sonoma county in California's redwood empire. Sonoma [194–?] 4 p. illus., map.
CHi

14846. —— —— Sonoma county, California; its resources and advantages. [Santa Rosa? 1899?] [32] p. illus., fold. map.
CSmH CU-B

14847. —— **Board of trade.** Sonoma county, California, "on the Redwood highway." Santa Rosa [n.d.]
CL

14848. —— **Panama-Pacific exposition commission.** Sonoma county, California. [S.F., Union litho. co., 1915?] [18] p. col. illus., map.
CU-B

14849. —— **Planning commission.** A master plan of airports, Sonoma county, California. [Santa Rosa? 1947] 64 p. illus., map.
CU-B

14850. Sonoma county and Russian river valley... S.F., Bell & Heymans [1888] 86 p. illus., ports., map.
C CHi CLU CSd CSf CU-B

14851. **Sonoma county central land co.** ...Sonoma county land journal; devoted to useful information about Sonoma county... [Santa Rosa, C.M. Petersen, 1883–
CLU (v.1 no. 1) CSmH

14852. Sonoma county; her matchless resources... [n.p., 1894?] 27 p. illus.
CLU CU-B

14853. **Sonoma county land bureau.** Land register and Santa Rosa business directory. S.F., Wm. M. Hinton & co., 1884. 44 p.
CLU CU-B

14854. Sonoma county land register. Giving an accurate and detailed description, with price, of fruit farms, dairies, grain and hay farms... Santa Rosa, Press democrat, 1901. 24 p. map.
CHi CSmH CU-B

14855. Sonoma county land register and Santa Rosa business directory...v.1–6. S.F., 1881–86. Published quarterly by Guy E. Grosse and T.M. Peugh.
C-S has v.1–6, no. 22, Jan.–Mar. 1881–Apr. 1886. CHi has v.6 no. 22, Apr. 1886. CSmH has v.2 no. 5, v.3 no. 7, May 1882, Feb. 1883. NN has 1881.

14856. **Sonoma county taxpayers' association.** The Coyote valley dam; a report... [Santa Rosa] 1955. 20 p. illus., maps (part col., 1 fold.)
C

14857. **Sonoma county trail blazers.** SCTB [i.e., Sonoma county trail blazers] 1941 to 1951. Oakland, Anderson print. co., 1952. 119 p. illus., ports., maps.
CU-B

14858. **Sonoma democrat.** Admission day edition, September 9, 1885. Santa Rosa, 1885. 8 p.
CStrJC CU-B

14859. —— Democratic jubilee edition, November 19, 1892. Santa Rosa. 8 p.
CStrJC

14860. —— Historical edition of Santa Rosa, Calif. and Sonoma county. Jan. 2, 1875. Santa Rosa. 8 p.
CStrJC

14861. **Sonoma valley. Chamber of commerce.** Picturesque Sonoma county... Sonoma, Expositer print. [n.d.] unp. illus.
CSf

14862. —— —— Points of interest in and near Sonoma, "the cradle of California." Sonoma, Index-tribune print. [n.d.] folder (8 p.)
CHi CRcS

14863. **Southern Pacific co. Passenger department.** California resorts; Geysers, Napa and Lake mineral springs. S.F. [1901] [6] p.
CHi

14864. **Spelling, Carl.** Opportunities...of Sonoma county... [Santa Rosa, 1887?] 72 p. illus.
CU-B NN

14865. **Speth, Frank Anthony.** A history of agricultural labor in Sonoma county, California. [Berkeley] 1938. Thesis (M.A.)—Univ. of Calif., 1938.
CU

14866. **Stow, Nellie.** "The Russians in California." Prepared for the National society of colonial dames of America in the state of California... S.F., April, 1929. 14 p. illus.
CHi

14867. **Tays, George.** ...Armstrong redwoods state park... Berkeley, 1937. 4 l. Typew.
CU-B

14868. —— ...Sonoma coast park... Berkeley, 1937. 4 l. Typew.
CU-B

14869. **Tchitchinoff, Zakahar.** Adventures in California, 1818–1828. Introd. by Arthur Woodward. L.A., Dawson, 1956. 26 p. illus. (Early Calif. travels ser., 34) 225 copies printed by Mallette Dean.
C CL CLLoy CLO CLSM CLgA CSS CSd CSf CSjC CSto CStoC CU-B CVtV CaBViPA

14870. **Thomas bros.** Popular atlas of Sonoma county. Oakland, George Coupland Thomas, c1953. 48 numb. maps.
CStr

14871. **Thompson, Robert A.** The Russian settlement in California known as Fort Ross... Santa Rosa, Sonoma democrat pub. co., 1896. 34 p. illus.
C CHi CL CLS CLSU CLU CO CRcS CRedCL CRedl CSalCL CSdS CSf CSfP CSj CSjC CSmH CStr CStrJC CU-B CaBViPA

14872. —— Same. Oakland, Biobooks, 1951. 50 p. illus.
Available in many California libraries and CaBViPA

14873. **Titus, Llewellyn R., vs. Hatler, Alexander.** United States land office. Llewellyn R. Titus vs. Alexander Hatler. Brief. James F. Stuart, attorney for Hatler. S.F., Bacon & co., 1870. 13 p.
CHi

14874. **Treadwell, John B.** The Geysers, the most popular summer resort on the continent... Geyser springs, Sonoma county... [n.p., 1886?] 20 p.
CU-B

14875. **Treganza, Adan Eduardo.** Fort Ross; a study in historical archaeology. Report on archaeological investigations at Fort Ross state monument in the summer of 1953. [Berkeley, 1954] 26 l. illus. (Calif. Univ. Archaeological survey. Reports. no. 23) Contains bibliographies.
CL CU

14876. **Trussell, Margaret Edith.** Settlement of the Bodega bay region. [Berkeley] 1960. Thesis (M.A.) —Univ. of Calif., 1960.
CU

14877. **Vallejo.** Being a brief sketch of Don Mariano Guadaloupe Vallejo... S.F., Schwabacher-Frey stationery co., 1927. 4 l.
C CHi CLO CLU CSmH CU-B

14878. **Vallejo, Mariano Guadalupe, vs. the United States.** In the Court of Claims, no. 566. Mariano G. Vallejo vs. the United States. [n.p., 1858?] 105 p. A claim for occupation and use of Vallejo property by U.S. troops from July, 1846, to August, 1853.
CLU

14879. **Vallejo, Mariano Guadalupe.** Ecsposición que hace el comdanante [!] general interino de la Alta California al gobernador de la misma. [Sonoma, August 17, 1837] 21 p.
CSmH CSt CU-B

14880. —— M. G. Vallejo's release from Fort Sutter, August 2, 1846 [a facsimile of the Ms. signed by M. G. Vallejo in the collection of T. W. Norris] Livermore [n.d.] [2] l. pl., facsim.
CHi

14881. Wayside notes and days' doings at Blue Lick

springs and Camp Duchay. S.F., J. Winterburn & co., print., 1884. 34 p. CU-B

14882. Woodson, Rebecca Hildreth (Nutting) A sketch of the life of Rebecca Hildreth Nutting (Woodson) and her family. [Santa Rosa, 1909] 60 l. Ms. C CU-B

14883. Wright, Doris Marion. A guide to the Mariano Guadalupe Vallejo documentos para la historia de California, 1780–1875. Berkeley, Univ. of Calif. press, 1953. 264 p. CHi CSd CSjC

Petaluma

14884. [Ables, T. J.] Able's ranch near Petaluma, Sonoma co., Cal. October 12, 1857. [Letter...] [n.p.] 1857. folder. Typew. CSmH

14885. Britton & Rey, lithographers. [Views] Petaluma Sonoma cy., Cal., October 1855. L. W. Worth del. S.F. [1855] CSmH

14886. Kerrigan, H. W. Petaluma...Sonoma county, California. Petaluma, Chamber of commerce [1920?] 64 p. illus. CHi

14887. —— Petaluma "the world's egg basket." [Petaluma, Chamber of commerce, 192–?] [8] p. illus. CHi

14888. McNear (Geo. P.) grain and feed. Petaluma, the manufacturing and poultry center of California. [n.p., n.d.] folder with views, map, text on folded strip. CHi

14889. Mannion, Ed. Vallejo adobe, Petaluma; a souvenir. Yerba Buena chapter, E Clampus Vitus, April 12, 1958. Petaluma, Don Keller, 1958. [4] p. CHi CPe

14890. —— The Washoe house story. [Petaluma?] E Clampus Vitus, 1958. [4] p. illus. CHi CPe

14891. Petaluma. Board of trade. Petaluma: her advantages and resources...second edition. Petaluma, 1903. 16 p. illus. CHi

14892. —— —— Sonoma county, California. Its wonderful resources! Petaluma the trade center is situated on Petaluma creek, a navigable tide-water arm of the bay, and on the line of the San Francisco and North Pacific railroad... Petaluma [1887?] 7 p. CU-B

14893. —— **Chamber of commerce.** Make this city your headquarters and visit these points of interest in and around Petaluma. [Petaluma, 1940?] [4] p. map. CHi

14894. —— —— Petaluma, Sonoma county, California... Petaluma [1911?] 31 p. illus. CHi

14895. —— —— Petaluma: the Lowell of the West. Petaluma, 1906. 24 p. CHi CU-B

14896. —— **First Congregational church.** The centennial of the First Congregational church. [Petaluma, Petaluma print. co., 1954] 37 p. illus. CHi CSmH

14897. —— **Methodist church.** Dedication Sunday, January twenty-first, nineteen hundred forty-five... [Petaluma, Petaluma print., co., 1945] [19] p. illus., ports. CHi

14898. —— **St. Vincent de Paul parish.** Historical sketch... [Petaluma, 1962] 31 p. illus. CHi

14899. Petaluma argus-courier. Centennial edition, 1855–1955. [Aug. 18, 1955] Petaluma [1955] 1 v. (v.p.) illus., ports., maps. C CHi CU-B

14900. Petaluma centennial corp. Official souvenir program Petaluma centennial, August 24th to 30th, 1958. Petaluma, 1958. 48 p. illus. C

14901. Petaluma historical society. Bayard Taylor visits Petaluma. Petaluma, Petaluma print. co., 1959. 8 p. port. CStrJC

14902. Petaluma incubator co. Catalogue no. 42. [S.F., Mysell-Rollins co., 1901?] 63 p. illus., ports. CHi

14903. —— [Catalogue] [S.F., Geo. Spaulding & co., 1902?] 64 p. illus. CHi

14904. [Petaluma realty co.] Petaluma, California, at the top of San Francisco bay. [Yakima, Wash.] Republic press [1959?] 72 p. illus., ports., maps. CO CStrJC

14905. Petaluma society for the prevention of cruelty to animals. Report...to the Legislature of California, at its nineteenth session. [Sacramento, T.A. Springer, state print., 1872] 4 p. CSmH

14906. Protestant Episcopal church in the U.S.A. Northern California (Missionary district) Journal of the sixth convocation... held in St. John's church Petaluma, May 8th, 9th, and 10th, 1880. S.F., Bacon & co., 1880. 34 p. C

14907. Sonoma and Marin mutual beneficial association, Petaluma. Annual report...for 1868–69. [1 p.] CHi

14908. —— Rules and regulations... [S.F., Bacon & co., 1868?] 13 [6] p. CHi

14909. Treganza, Adan Eduardo. Archaeological investigation of the Vallejo adobe, Petaluma adobe state historical monument. [S.F.] S.F. state college [195–?] 18 p. CHi

14910. Vallejo, Mariano Guadalupe. The old adobe; a letter from General M. G. Vallejo. S.F. [printed by Duncan H. Olmsted] 1941. [6] p. mount. illus. The letter gives a description of Vallejo's home near Petaluma. C

14911. Waugh, Lorenzo. Autobiography of Lorenzo Waugh. Oakland, Pacific press, 1883. 311 p. front. (port.) Other editions followed.
CBb (4th, 1888) CHi (1883, 4th, 1888, 5th, 1896) CSf (4th, 1888) CSfCW (5th, 1896) CStrJC (1885) CUk (5th, 1896)

Santa Rosa

14912. Associated veterans of the Mexican war. Constitution and by-laws...of the Northern district of California. Santa Rosa, Sonoma democrat steam print., 1877. 7 p. CStrJC

14913. Bakewell, Thomas Vail. Municipal ownership in Santa Rosa... [n.p., 1900] 15 p.
CLU CSmH CU-B

14914. Baptists. California. State convention. Minutes of the first meeting...held at Santa Rosa, September 28, 1854. S.F., Whitton Towne & co., print., 1854. 8 p. CSmH

14915. Beeson, Emma (Burbank) The early life and letters of Luther Burbank, by his sister Emma Burbank Beeson...with introduction by David Starr Jordan. S.F., Harr Wagner [c1927] 155 p. illus., ports.
CHi CPa CSd CSf

14916. —— Stories of Luther Burbank and his plant school... N.Y., Chicago, etc., Scribner, 1920. 194 p. illus., col. plates, port. CSf

14917. Burbank, Luther. The harvest of the years. By Luther Burbank with Wilbur Hall. Bost., Houghton, c1926. 296 p. illus., ports. CHi CRedCL

14918. Burbank's experiment farms. [Descriptive catalogs of seeds, fruits, flowers, various economic plants] illus.

CHi has 1911–12, 1914–18, 1920–21, 1923.

14919. Candeub, Fleissig & associates. Feasibility report. S.F., 1961. 76 p.   CStrJC

14920. Carson, Charles F. The life of Luther Burbank. Santa Rosa, Press-democrat pub. co., 1949. 16 p. illus., ports.   CStrJC

14921. Clampett, Frederick William. Luther Burbank, "our beloved infidel," his religion of humanity ... N.Y., Macmillan, 1926. 144 p. front. (2 ports.) facsim.
                                                          CSfCW

14922. Denton, May (Ward) comp. The Crane family, from ox-team to tractor. [Santa Rosa] 1952. 32 p. Mimeo.   CStrJC

14923. Eagles, Fraternal order of. Santa Rosa. Aerie 210. Souvenir Aerie 210, F.O.E. ... Santa Rosa, Press-democrat pub. co., 1903. 18 p. illus.   CStrJC

14924. Finley, Ernest Latimer. Santa Rosans I have known. Santa Rosa, Press-democrat pub. co., 1942. 93 p. illus., ports.   C CHi CStr CStrJC

14925. Freemasons. Santa Rosa lodge, no. 57. One hundredth anniversary, Anno Lucis 5954, 1954. Santa Rosa, 1954. 58 p. illus., ports.   CHi

14926. Hayes, Everis A. Luther Burbank and his work, speech of Hon. Everis A. Hayes of California in the House of representatives, February 29, 1912. Wash., D.C. [Govt. print. off.] 1912. 15 p.   CHi

14927. Jordan, David Starr and Kellogg, Vernon L. The scientific aspects of Luther Burbank's work. S.F., A.M. Robertson, 1909. 115 p. illus., port.
                                                     CPa CSfCW

14928. The Luther Burbank society. [Prospectus] Mr. —— is respectfully invited to become a member of the Luther Burbank society, the plans and purposes of which are explained herein. [S.F., Taylor, Nash & Taylor, 1912?] 24 p. illus. (col.)   CHi

14929. Lynch, Ada Kyle. Luther Burbank, plant lover and citizen. S.F., Harr Wagner, 1924. 37 p. illus., ports.   CHi CStrJC

14930. Maxwell, Mary Ursula, *Sister*. Leadership of Mother Agatha Reynolds, Ursuline of the Roman union. [n.p., 1942] 176 p. illus.   CHi

14931. Native sons of the golden West. Admission day celebration, 1911, sixty-first anniversary of the admission of California as a state. Official souvenir program, Santa Rosa, Sept. 8, 9, 10... [Santa Rosa, Press-democrat, 1911] [40] p. illus.   CHi

14932. Portfolio of Santa Rosa and vicinity... Santa Rosa, H. A. Darms [c1909] 106 p. illus., maps. "A brief history of Sonoma county and Santa Rosa, compiled by Edward H. Brown...": p. 7–23.

   C CHi CL CO CSf CStr CStrJC CU-B

14933. Press democrat. Centennial edition [1856–1956, Oct. 1956. Santa Rosa, 1956] 1 v. (v.p.) illus., ports.   CHi CU-B

14934. —— ...A dreadful catastrophe visits Santa Rosa. Santa Rosa, 1906. [2] p.   CU-B

14935. —— Post earthquake editions. April 19, 20, 21, 23, 30, 1906. May 1, 2, 1906. Santa Rosa [Fountain-grove press?] 1906. single sheet.   CStrJC

14936. Republican printing house. Official program Labor day celebration... Santa Rosa, 1907. 20 p. illus.   CStrJC

14937. Santa Rosa. Chamber of commerce. The

City of Roses. Comp. by Edward H. Brown. Santa Rosa, Republican print., 1908. [40] p. illus., port.
                                                    CHi CStrJC

14938. —— —— Santa Rosa, California. Santa Rosa [1938] folder (7 p.) illus.   CRcS

14939. —— **Charter.** Adopted March 6, 1903. [Santa Rosa, 1903?]   CStrJC

14940. —— **The Christian church.** One hundredth anniversary, 1854–1954. By Lois Brewer Stiles. [Santa Rosa, 1954] 48 p. illus.   CHi CStrJC

14941. —— **Pacific Methodist college.** Catalogue. 1st–21st, 1861/62–1881/82. S.F., 1862–82. illus. Established 1861 in Vacaville, and continued its session there until May, 1870, when it was removed to Santa Rosa. The first regular session in Santa Rosa was opened August 1871.

CU-B has 2d–6th, 8th, 12th, 18th, 21st, 1862/63–1866/67, 1868/69, 1873/74, 1879/80, 1881/82.

14942. —— —— ...Faculty, and Board of trustees, course of study, rules and regulations, rates of tuition, board, etc. together with an address on education, by Rev. O. P. Fitzgerald. S.F., Towne & Bacon, print., 1861. 19 p.   CHi CU-B

14943. —— **Relief committee.** Report of Relief committee, April 20, 1906 to July 31, 1906. Prepared by order of the mayor and council of the city of Santa Rosa, California. [Santa Rosa, Press-democrat pub. co., 1906] 9 p.   CLU

14944. Santa Rosa, California. [Santa Rosa, Press-democrat, 1924?] [11] p. illus.   CHi

14945. Slater, Lillian Burger. Rose carnivals of Santa Rosa in review: 1894–1932. Santa Rosa, Press-democrat, 1932. 49 p. illus.   C CStrJC

14946. Smith, Temple. Views of Santa Rosa and vicinity before and after the disaster, April 18, 1906. L.A., Rieder, Cardinell & co. [1906] [32] p. of illus., ports.   C CHi CU-B

14947. Sonoma and Marin agricultural district fair. Souvenir program...Santa Rosa, Press-democrat print., 1913. 16 p. illus.   CStrJC

14948. Stevens, Will. The Santa Rosa story, condensed from three articles by Will Stevens in the San Francisco examiner. [Angwin, Litho. by Pac. union college press, 195–] 16 p. port.   CU-B

14949. Thompson, Robert A. Central Sonoma. A brief description of the township and town of Santa Rosa ... Santa Rosa [Wm. M. Hinton & co., print., S.F.] 1884. 164 p. p. [129]–164: "Proceedings at the laying of the cornerstone of the new court house."

   C CHi CLU CSf CSmH CStrJC (typew. copy) CU-B NHi

14950. —— A descriptive sketch of Santa Rosa, Sonoma county, Cal., and the surrounding country. Written for the Sonoma county land register... Santa Rosa, 1889. 20 p.   CSmH CU-B

14951. Wakeland, Weldon Lee. William A. Townes and the Santa Rosa press-democrat. [Berkeley, 1952] Thesis (M.A.)—Univ. of Calif., 1952.   CU

14952. Wright, C. A. & co., comp. Earthquake views of Santa Rosa, California, 1906. Santa Rosa, 1906. 26 p. illus.   CHi

14953. —— Santa Rosa and vicinity. [Santa Rosa, n.d.] unp. mounted photos.   C

Sonoma

14954. American institute of architects. Northern California chapter. East bay chapter. ... Historic

California; Sonoma-Benicia. [Inventories of historic buildings, Petaluma, Sonoma, Benicia, and Martinez] [n.p., n.d.] [20] l.   CHi

14955. Bennyhoff, James A. and Elsasser, Albert J. Sonoma mission; an historical and archaeological study of primary constructions, 1823–1913. Berkeley, Univ. of Calif. archaeological survey, 1954. 81 l. illus.
C CHi CStaC UU

14956. Cheever, Herbert Milton, comp. William Brown Ide and his descendants. Worcester, Mass., 1954. 53 p. Typew.   CHi (microfilm) CRb

14957. Cumberland college. Catalogue of Cumberland college, formerly Sonoma academy, for the collegiate year, ending May 1, 1861. Sonoma, Presbyterian print., [1861?] 15 p.   C

14958. Guthrie, Chester Lyle. ...Misión San Francisco Solano (Sonoma mission) 29 l. Typew.   CU-B

14959. Hussey, John Adam. The United States and the Bear flag revolt. [Berkeley, 1941] Thesis (Ph.D.)— Univ. of Calif., 1941.   CU CU-B

14960. [Ide, Simeon] A biographical sketch of William B. Ide...And what is claimed as the most authentic and reliable account of "the virtual conquest of California, in June, 1846 by the Bear flag party," as given by its leader, the late Hon. William Brown Ide...Claremont, N.H., 1880. 239 p.
C CHi CL CLSM CLSU CLU CP CSmH CStbS CU-B IHi

14961. —— Same with title: The conquest of California: a biography of William B. Ide...Oakland, Biobooks, 1944. 188 p. illus., map. (Calif. Centennial ed., no. 1) Printed at the Grabhorn press, San Francisco.
Available in many California libraries.

14962. Ide, William Brown. Who conquered California?... The most particular, the most authentic and the most reliable history of the conquest of California, in June, 1846, by the "Bear flag party"... Claremont, N.H., Print. & pub. by Simeon Ide, 1880. 137 p.
C (1882) CHi CL CLU CP CSmH

14963. Kirov, George. William B. Ide, the president of California. Sacramento, Senate of the state of California, 1935. 37 p. illus.
C CHi CL CLU CMartC CO CRb CRbCL CRic CSd CSf CSjC CSmH CU-B CViCL

14964. Murphy, Celeste G. The people of the pueblo; or, The story of Sonoma... Sonoma, W.L. & C.G. Murphy, 1935. 266 p. illus., ports.
C CBb CHi CL CLU CLod CO CRcS CRic CSf CSfU CSj CSjC CSmH CSmat CStrJC CU-B CV NN UPB

14965. —— Same. Centennial ed. Portland, Ore., Binfords, 1948. [c1937] 303 p. illus., ports.
C CChiS CHi CLU CLgA CN CO CRb CSbr CSd CSfSt CSmH CStcrCL CStr CV NHi

14966. Powell, Edward Alexander. Gentlemen rovers... N.Y., Scribner's, 1913. 245 p. illus.
CHi CU-B

14967. Price, T. M. An historic narrative of the Bear flag revolution. [n.p., n.d.] [23] p.   CHi

14968. Roberts, Helen M. Big chief Solano; a tale of Mission San Francisco Solano. [Stanford, c1948] 26 p. illus., map. (Ser. of mission tales. no. 21)   CHi

14969. Saint Mary's hall, Sonoma. Colejio de Santa María, Sonoma. Prospecto, catálogo, ejercisios finales, y distribución de premios. Sept. 28, 1855. S.F., Imp. de William Eastman, 1855. 19 p.
CSmH CU CU-B

14970. Sonoma centennial celebration; in commemoration of Mission Sonoma, June 30th to July 4th, 1923, Sonoma county, California. [Collected and arranged by Albert Dressler. S.F.] 1923. Collection of photographs and programs.   C

14971. Sonoma index-tribune. Centennial number. Sonoma, 1946. 60 p. illus., ports. (v.68, no. 46, June 1946) Commemorating the raising of the Bear flag, June 14, 1846.   C CFS CStrJC

14972. —— Mission centennial number, 1823–1923. Sonoma, 1923. [24] p. illus., ports., map. (June 30, 1923)
CU-B NN (Clippings mounted and bound)

14973. Sonoma valley historical society. Saga of Sonoma in the Valley of the moon; being the recollections of the richly historic spot and its environs, set down by old time residents. [Sonoma? 1954] 47 p.
C CHi CL CO CP CSto CStoC CStrCL CStrJC CU-B

14974. —— Sonoma sketches. Sonoma, 1950. 120 l. Reproduced from typew. copy.   C

14975. Thompson, Robert A. Conquest of California. Capture of Sonoma by Bear flag men June 14, 1846. Raising of the American flag in Monterey by Commodore John D. Sloat, July 7, 1846...Historical address delivered by R. A. Thompson in Sonoma, June 14, 1896... Santa Rosa, Sonoma democrat pub. co., 1896. 33 p. illus., port.
C CHi CLSU CLU CO CP CPom CSS CSd CSf CSmH CStr CStrJC CU-B

14976. Treganza, Adan Eduardo. Sonoma mission: an archaeological reconstruction of the Mission San Francisco de Solano quadrangle. [Reprint. Berkeley, Kroeber anthropological soc., 1956] 18 p. illus., maps.
CHi CL

14977. Tuomey, Honoria Rosalie Pamela, and Emparan, Louisa (Vallejo) History of the mission, presidio and pueblo of Sonoma... [Santa Rosa, Press-democrat pub. co.] 1923. 104 p. illus., ports.
C CHi CL CLSU CLU CMerCL CMont CRedl CRic CSS CSd CSf CSfP CSfU CSmH CStmo CStr CStrJC CU-B CaBViPA

14978. —— Same. 1934. 73 p. illus., ports.   CO

14979. Von Geldern, Otto. An address to the pioneer schoolboys and girls of Sonoma, made May 30, 1931 ... [n.p., 1931?] 7 p. Mimeo.   CHi

STANISLAUS COUNTY
(Created in 1854 from portion of Tuolumne county; annexed section of San Joaquin county in 1860)

COUNTY HISTORIES

14980. Annear, Margaret L., comp. ...A brief history of Stanislaus county; a source book for secondary schools, compiled by Margaret L. Annear, Herbert C. Florcken, Dr. Hugh Baker. [Modesto] County supt. of schools, 1950. unp. illus., ports., maps, facsims.
C CHi CMS CSfSt CTurS CU-B

14981. Elias, Solomon Philip. Stories of Stanislaus; a collection of stories on the history and achievements of Stanislaus county. Modesto, Author [1924] 344 p.
C CAla CB CBaB CBb CCH CFS CHi CL CLAC CLSU CLU CLgA CLob CMS CO CRiv CSS CSd CSf CSfP CSfU CSmH CSmat CStclU CStcrCL CStmo CStrJC CU-B CViCL CoD CtY NN UPB WHi

14982. History of Stanislaus county, California, with illustrations descriptive of its scenery, farms [etc., etc.]

With biographical sketches... S.F., Elliott & Moore, 1881. 254 p. illus., maps. Biographical sketches: p. [161]–224. "The local history of Stanislaus county was prepared by Hon. L. C. Branch."

C CHi CMS CSmH CU-B CtY

14983. McCabe, George T. Stanislaus county; its history... [Modesto] Stanislaus county bd. of trade, 1920. 64 p. illus., ports.   CMS

14984. Tinkham, George Henry. History of Stanislaus county, California, with biographical sketches... L.A., Historic record co., 1921. 1495 p. illus., ports.

C CCH CFS CHi CL CLSM CLSU CLU CMS CMerCL CO CSS CSf CSmH CSto CU-B CtY KHi MWA NN WHi

14985. Vasché, Joseph Burton. Our county, a story of Stanislaus. Modesto, Stanislaus county schools, 1941. 82 p. illus.   CHi

14986. —— Same, with title: The story of our county... 1942. 138 p. illus., maps. Reproduced from typew. copy.   CMS

14987. —— Same. [rev. ed.] 1950. 88 p. illus., maps.   C CChiS CU-B

GREAT REGISTER

14988. Stanislaus county. Index to the Great register of the county of Stanislaus. 1866– Place of publication and title vary.

C has 1867, 1869, 1871–72, 1875, 1886 (biennially to)–1962. CL has 1872–73, 1880, 1886, 1888, 1890. CSmH has 1880, 1898. CU-B has 1867, 1872–73, 1879, 1896, 1898, precinct index, general election, 1936, 1938, 1940.

DIRECTORIES

14989. 1884/85. McKenney, L. M., co., pub. 7-county directory of Stanislaus, Merced, Fresno, Kern, Tulare, San Bernardino, and Inyo counties. ... Oakland, 1884.   CHi CL

14990. 1910–1953. Polk, R. L. & co., pub. Polk's Modesto city directory including Turlock, Oakdale and Stanislaus county. Publisher varies: 1910–24 Polk-Husted directory co.

C has 1910–11, 1913–14, 1923, 1927, 1930–31, 1939–40. C-S has 1910–12. CHi has 1924, 1929, 1946, 1948, 1950, 1952–53. CL has 1939–42, 1950, 1952–53. CMS has 1910–11, 1912–22, 1925–29, 1930–39, 1950. CTurS has 1950.

Other Cities and Towns

14991. 1954– Polk, R. L. & co., pub. Polk's Modesto city directory, including Oakdale, Ceres, Hughson, Riverbank, and Salida. L.A., 1954– Content varies: 1954 Modesto, Turlock, Oakdale, Ceres, Keyes, Newman, Patterson, and Salida; 1956 includes Crows landing, Denair and Hughson; 1958 includes Riverbank; 1959 excludes Crows landing, Newman, and Patterson. Preceded by Polk's Modesto city directory including...Stanislaus county.

CHi has 1954, 1956–60, 1962. CL has 1954, 1956–58. CMS has 1954, 1956. CTur has 1964. CTurS has 1960.

14992. 1962– Polk, R. L. & co., pub. Polk's Turlock and Patterson city directory... L.A., 1962–

CMS has 1964. CTur has 1964. CTurS has 1962.

GENERAL REFERENCES

14993. Baldridge, Kenneth Wayne. A history of the Mormon settlement of central California with emphasis on New Hope and San Francisco, 1846–1847, and Modesto, 1920–1954. Stockton, 1956. 247 p. illus. Thesis (M.A.)—College of the Pacific, 1956.   CStoC

14994. Bell, Daisy. The history of Newman. Rev. ed. [Newman] 1962. 5 p.   CTur

14995. Beltrami, Albert Peter. The Modesto irrigation district; a study in local resources administration ... [Berkeley, 1955] 116 l. illus., map, tables. Thesis (M.A.)—Univ. of Calif., 1955.   CMS CTurS CU

14996. Bramhall, John T. The story of Stanislaus ... Modesto, Modesto herald, 1914. 61 p. illus.

CHi CL CMS CU-B

14997. Brennan, Florabel (McKenzie) Along the Stanislaus, 1806–1906. Compiled by Florabel McKenzie Brennan, president of Stanislaus pioneer and historical society, historian of Oakdale Chamber of commerce. [Oakdale] Oakdale leader, 1956. 32 p. illus., port., facsims.   C CHi CSto CTurS CU-B

14998. Cadwallader, E. J. History of Turlock, California. [Turlock, 1945] 25 l. Typew.

CMS CTur CTurS

14999. California vs. Modesto irrigation dist. In the Supreme court of the state of California. The people of the state of California, etc., plaintiffs and respondents, vs. Modesto irrigation district... Respondent's brief. [S.F., n.p.] 1901. 217 p.   CHi

15000. Λ California centennial souvenir, 1848–1948, Knights Ferry, May 29th and 30th. [Oakdale, 1948] 48 p. illus., ports.   CHi CTurS

15001. Cooperstown coal mining, petroleum and copper smelting co. Basis for the organization of the Cooperstown coal mining, petroleum and copper smelting company...Capital stock, $1,500,000. 15,000 shares. Par value, $100. S.F., Mining and scientific press bk. and job print., 1865. 12 p.   CLU

15002. Copley, Richard Eldridge. An historical geography of the dairy industry of Stanislaus county, California. [Berkeley, 1961] Thesis (M.A.)—Univ. of Calif., 1961.   CU

15003. Daughters of the American revolution. California. Genealogical records committee. Courthouse records, Stanislaus county, California: Marriages and wills. Comp. by Myrtle Dix. [n.p.] 1957. 303, 64 l. Contents: Pt. 1, Stanislaus county marriages, 1854–1906. – Pt. 2, Stanislaus county wills, 1872–1908.

C CHi CL CMS

15004. Downey historical society. Cemetery records of Stanislaus county, California, comp. by Downey historical society, Thomas Downey high school. Modesto, 1960. 125 l. map.   C CHi CMS

15005. Elliott, W. W., & co. Stanislaus county. [S.F., 1888] folder (24 p.) illus., map.   CU-B

15006. First Stanislaus county centennial celebration, La Grange, Calif., April 25th. [Modesto, Modesto litho., 1948] 36 p. illus., ports. "Program, under the direction of Catherine Ingalls, was prepared and edited by Jack Haugen."   CHi CTurS

15007. Fulkerth, L. W. Sunny Stanislaus. [Modesto, 1907?] [14] p. illus.   CU-B

15008. [Gallup, S. M.] A report of the freight and resources of the Southern mines and counties converging at Knight's Ferry... 1866. S.F., Towne & Bacon, 1866. 16 p.   CU-B

15009. History of Turlock, Turlock irrigation district and traffic rules. [Turlock, 1948] 50 p. illus.   CTurS

15010. Hocking, T. C. Sunny Stanislaus, the gateway to the great San Joaquin valley... Modesto, Stanislaus Bd. of trade [1902] 16 p. illus.

CHi CSmH CU-B

15011. Hohenthal, Helen Alma. A history of the Turlock district. [Berkeley, 1930] 316 l. illus., maps. Thesis (M.A.)—Univ. of Calif., 1930.
CMS CTur CTurS CU CU-B

15012. McKee, Irving. Red mountain, historic vineyard of Stanislaus county. [1] p. illus. Reprint. from *Calif., mag. of the Pac.*, Sept. 1949.
CHi

15013. Modesto. Board of trade. Stanislaus county... Advantages offered prospective settlers... Modesto, Daily & weekly news print., 1887. 48 p.
CSmH CU-B

15014. —— Chamber of commerce. Business and professional directory of Modesto and vicinity, July 1, 1947 to July 1, 1948. Modesto, Watts directory service [194–?] 79 p.
CMS

15015. Modesto journal. 100th anniversary, 1854–1954, Stanislaus county. Stanislaus centennial edition, Sept. 2, 1954.
CHi

15016. Modesto news. ...Annual progress edition; devoted to a comprehensive review of Stanislaus county's progress and possibilities. Modesto [1915, 1920] 2 v. illus.
C

15017. —— New era edition, Stanislaus county, California, Saturday, Sept. 12, 1908. [Modesto, 1908] [23] p. illus., ports.
CU-B

15018. Napier, Claude E. Knights Ferry; the story of the gateway to the Mother Lode. [1st ed.] Oakdale, Oakdale leader [c1949] 75 p. illus.
C CL CMS CMerCL CO CSto CU-B

15019. Newberry, Homer. A history of Hughson [1940] Ed. with an index by R. Dean Galloway. Turlock, Stanislaus state college library, 1964. 22 l. Typew.
CMS CTurS

15020. Newfield, Lou K. Turlock irrigation district, California. Turlock, Turlock board of trade [1919] 32 p. illus., tables.
CU-B

15021. Newman, Diamond Jubilee, 1888–1963. [Modesto, Belt print. and litho. co., 1963] 80 p. illus., ports.
CHi CMS CTurS

15022. Oakdale. Union high school. Circular of the Oakdale union high school, organized, May 1892... Term commences Monday, Sept. 12, 1892. Oakdale, Leader steam print, 1892. 13 p.
CU-B

15023. ...Ranchers directory: covering Stanislaus county, California. Modesto, Smith's print. shop [1926] 256 p.
CU-B

15024. —— Same: covering Stanislaus county and north part of Merced county... Modesto, Smith's print. shop [1928?] 189 p.
CU-B

15025. —— Same, compiled by Kelcie C. Grisham ...Modesto, Al G. Gowans, 1935. 149 p.
CMS

15026. Ray, Herndon Carroll, comp. Stanislaus county, 1854–1954, a century of growth... [Modesto?] Distributed by F.C. Beyer, county superintendent of schools, 1955. 55 p. illus.
C CHi CMS CO CTurS CU-B

15027. Reynolds, Charles D. [Account book of C. D. Reynolds, giving expenditures and receipts at the Black Hill ranch, Stanislaus county, 1871-1892] 318 p. Ms.
CU-B

15028. Reynolds, Mattie V. Knights Ferry, Stanislaus co. ... [Santa Cruz, 1939] 2 l. Typew. CU-B

15029. Rhea, James J. Stanislaus county, California. S.F., Sunset homeseekers' bur. for Stanislaus county bd. of trade [1912] 64 p. illus., maps. CHi CL CLU

15030. —— Same. [S.F., 1920] 64 p. illus., mount. fold. map.
CU-B

15031. —— The Turlock district, Stanislaus county, California. S.F., Sunset mag. homeseekers' bur. [1912] 32 p. illus., maps.
CHi CU-B

15032. Rhodes, Benjamin Franklin, jr. Thirsty land: the Modesto irrigation district, a case study of irrigation under the Wright law... [Berkeley, 1943] 166 l. maps. Thesis (Ph.D.)—Univ. of Calif., 1943.
CMS (microfilm) CU CU-B

15033. Riverbank news. The Riverbank story... Riverbank, 1952–1953. Clippings from the *Riverbank news*, Sept. 5, 1952–Feb. 27, 1953.
CMS

15034. Ruppel, Margaret Gaylord. El rancheria del rio Estanislaus; a history. [Pasadena, Castle press] c1946. 90 p. illus., ports., fold. map.
CL CSto

15035. Scarbrough, Lois M., comp. Stanislaus county agricultural statistics [1855–1957] [Modesto] 1957. unnumb. l. tables. Typew.
CMS

15036. Service, John. John Service, pioneer, prepared from his own words and records by Fred Field Goodsell, with the assistance of the children of John and Julia Service. [Waban? Mass.] 1945. 90 p. illus., group ports.
CHi CMS CSd CTurS CU-B

15037. Stanislaus county et al. vs. San Joaquin and Kings river canal and irrigation co., appellee. In the Supreme court of the United States. The county of Stanislaus, in the state of California; the Board of supervisors of said county... Geo. W. Toombs et al., appellants, vs. the San Joaquin and Kings river canal and irrigation company, appellee. Brief for appellants... [S.F.] Star press [1903] 148 p.
CHi

15038. Stanislaus county. [Resolutions adopted by citizens March 20, 1880, regarding action by Congress affecting title to Moquelemos and Roland grants] Broadside.
CU-B

15039. —— Board of supervisors. Stanislaus county, agriculture, industry, homes. [Modesto, 1937?] [24] p. illus.
CU-B

15040. —— —— Stanislaus county, founded 1854, dedicated to efficient, economical government. [Modesto, 195–?] 50 p. illus., ports.
CU-B

15041. —— —— Your Stanislaus county. [Modesto, 1959] 50 p. illus. Partial contents:—Your Stanislaus county's early history, by Ed Whitmore, p. 5–10.
CMS CTur CTurS

15042. —— Board of trade. Stanislaus county, California, where all the products of the semi-tropic and temperate zones grow... [Modesto, Modesto herald print., 1901] 15 p. illus.
CHi CU-B

15043. —— —— The story of Stanislaus county, California. Modesto, 1906. 26 p. illus., maps.
CU-B

15044. —— Chamber of commerce. The golden county of the great San Joaquin valley, California... [Modesto] 1907. unp. illus.
CSf

15045. —— —— Stanislaus county. The garden spot of the world...[Modesto] 1907. unp. illus.
CSf

15046. —— —— Stanislaus county blue book; a pictorial and descriptive portrayal of the growth and development of Stanislaus county...[Modesto, n.d.] 65 p. illus., port. Historical text condensed from *Stories of Stanislaus*, by Sol P. Elias.
CMS

15047. —— Development board. Stanislaus county, where the land owns the water and power. [Modesto, 1928?] [21] p. illus., map.
CHi CRcS

15048. Stanislaus county exhibit committee.
Stanislaus county, a story of fertility illustrated. [Modesto? 1902] [16] p. of illus.   CU-B

15049. Stanislaus county yearbook. [Modesto] 1939. 36 p. illus., ports.   CMS

15050. Turlock daily journal. Memory lane [historical section]. Tuesday, November 10, 1964. Turlock, 1964. 48 p. illus., ports.   CMS CTur CTurS

15051. —— ...Stanislaus fair and centennial edition. [Sections 2–3] Saturday, August 7, 1954. Turlock, 1954. 14,14 p. illus., ports.   CHi CU-B

15052. Turlock golden jubilee corp. Turlock golden jubilee, 1908–1958; May 25th to 30th, 1958. [Turlock, 1958] [n.p.] illus.   CMS CTurS

15053. Turlock irrigation dist. Report of the Turlock and Modesto irrigation districts, Stanislaus county, California, in reply to reports on the proposed use of Tuolumne river on behalf of San Francisco, Calif., and neighboring cities... Turlock, 1912.   C

**15054. Ward, Harriet (Williams) and Ulch, *Mrs. A. E.* [Scrapbooks on Stanislaus county, 1870–1930] 2 v. Newspaper clippings and typed excerpts from early-day Stanislaus county newspapers.   CMS

15055. Water users association of the Modesto and Turlock irrigation districts, California. Available sources of water supply for San Francisco and the Bay cities other than the Tuolumne river and the Hetch Hetchy valley. [n.p., 191–?] 8 p. illus., maps.   CU-B

15056. Waterford. Centennial planning committee. Waterford centennial, 1857–1957. Oct. 18–19. [Waterford, 1957] [32] p. illus., ports.
C CHi CL CMS CSf CTurS CU-B

Modesto

15057. Citizens act! Modesto, 1954. 76 p. illus.   C

15058. Creisler, Lillian. Little Oklahoma: a study of the social and economic adjustment of refugees in the Beard tract, Modesto, Stanislaus county, California. [Berkeley, 1940] Thesis (M.A.)—Univ. of Calif., 1940.   CU

15059. Davison, Gertie. Modesto garden club; club history from Feb. 1924 to May 1952. [Modesto, 1953] 35 p.   CMS

15060. McGrew, James Wilson. A study of the fringe areas of Modesto, California; an analysis and recommendations...by James Wilson McGrew and Arthur Bruce Winter. Denver, Univ. of Denver, Dept. of government management, 1948. 219 l. fold. col. maps.
C CLU ViU

15061. Meier, Harold M., comp. Modesto ABC classified business and numerical telephone directory, 1930. Modesto, Smith's print shop, 1930. 44 p.   CMS

15062. Modesto. Chamber of commerce. Modesto, California; the automobile gateway to Yosemite. Modesto, 1916. 30 p. illus., tables.   CMS

15063. —— —— Modesto, fastest growing city of the Pacific coast... Modesto, 1921. 34 p. col. illus.   CU-B

15064. —— —— ...A survey of facts, Modesto, California. Modesto [1923?] 60 p. tables. Mimeo.   CMS

15065. —— **City planning commission.** Modesto looks ahead; a study of the economy of Stanislaus county and its influence on the growth of Modesto. [Modesto] 1949. 56 l. Mimeo.   C CSt

15066. —— **First Methodist church.** A short history of the First Methodist church in Modesto, 1862–1962. By Herbert G. Florcken. Modesto, 1962. 62 p. illus., ports.   CHi CMS CTurS

15067. The Modesto bank. Forty-nine years in Stanislaus county, 1873–1922. [Modesto, 1922] [14] p.   CHi

15068. Newton, Lorenz Arthur. Annexation problems of the city of Modesto, California. [Berkeley, 1954] Thesis (M.A.)—Univ. of Calif., 1954.   CU

SUTTER COUNTY
(Created in 1850; later annexed portion of Butte county)

COUNTY HISTORIES

15069. [Chamberlain, William Henry and Wells, Harry Laurenz] History of Sutter county, California ... Oakland, Thompson & West, 1879. 127 p. illus., map.
C CHi CL CMary CO CSd CSf CSfCP CSmH CSt CU-B CYcCL NHi NN WHi

GREAT REGISTER

15070. Sutter county. Index to the Great register of the county of Sutter. 1867– Place of publication and title vary.
C has 1867–68, 1872–73, 1875–77, 1879–80, 1882, 1886 (biennially to)– 1904, 1908 (biennially to)– 1962. CL has 1872–73, 1876–77, 1880 (biennially to)– 1890. CSmH has 1873 [1880]. CU-B has July 1867, 1872–73, 1879–80. CYcCL has 1872–73, 1875, 1882, 1886, 1892, 1894, 1898– 1906, 1918, 1922, 1932, 1934, 1958.

GENERAL REFERENCES

15071. Butte Mountain rangers. Constitution and by-laws of the Butte Mountain rangers, Sutter county, California. Marysville, Daily appeal power press print, 1864. 15 p.   C

15072. Ginsburgh, Sylvan Jacob. The migrant camp program of the F.S.A. in California: a critical examination of operations at the Yuba City and Thornton camps. [Berkeley, 1943] Thesis (M.A.)—Univ. of Calif., 1943.   CU

15073. Guise, Clement. The Sutter basin controversy. A dissertation submitted in satisfaction of the requirements for History 101 in the Dept. of Social science of Sacramento state college. [Sacramento, 1959] 58 p. Typew.   CYcCL

15074. Immigration association of California, pub. ...Sutter county. S.F. [n.d.] 2 p.   CU-B

15075. Levick, M. B. Sutter county, California. S.F., Sunset mag. homeseekers' bur. [1911] 31 p. illus., maps.   CHi CU-B

15076. Moulton, L. F. The great water problem; also, results of a late survey from Knight's Landing to upper end of canal made by the old Swamp land commission. [Colusa, 1891] 16 p. map.   CLU

15077. Parkhurst, C. Yoell. Sutter county, California; a synopsis of the opportunities that await the prospective settler. S.F., Sunset mag. homeseekers' bur. [n.d.] 31 p. illus., maps.   C

15078. Sutter county. Board of education. School directory, Sutter county, California; 1925–1926. [Yuba City? 1925?] [19] p.   CHi

15079. —— **Chamber of commerce.** Sutter county, California's great opportunity. Yuba City [1926?] 19 p. illus., map.   CRcS

15080. Sutter-Yuba counties. Chamber of commerce. The Feather-Yuba region of California. Marysville [19—?] 22 p. illus.   CRcS

15081. U.S. Congress. House. 53d Congress, 3d session. Preliminary examination of Feather River, California, above Marysville. [Wash., D.C., 1894?] 4 p.
CHi

TEHAMA COUNTY
(Created in 1856 from portions of Shasta, Colusa, and Butte counties)

COUNTY HISTORIES

15082. Tehama county, California. Illustrations descriptive of its scenery, fine residences [etc., etc.] With historical sketch of the county. S.F., Elliott & Moore, 1880. 166 p. illus., ports., maps. "Historical reminiscences of Tehama county, California. By E. J. Lewis": p. 11–25.
C   CHi (microfilm)   CRb   CRbCL   CSmH   CU-B

GREAT REGISTER

15083. Tehama county. Index to the Great register of the county of Tehama, 1867– Place of publication and title vary.
C has 1875, 1877, 1880, 1884 (biennially to)– 1896, 1900 (biennially to)– 1962. CL has 1872–73, 1877 (suppl.), 1880, 1882 (suppl.), 1886, 1888, 1890. CRbCL has 1954, 1958. CU-B has 1867, 1872, 1873, 1879, 1936, 1940.

DIRECTORIES

15084. 1901. Cohen, M., comp. Red Bluff city directory, containing complete directory of all residents, classified business directory... Red Bluff, The people's cause, 1901. illus.   CRb

15085. 1938/39. Red Bluff city directory. Red Bluff, Times print. co., 1938.   CRb

15086. 1949. Red Bluff. Church of Jesus Christ of latter-day saints. Red Bluff city directory. Red Bluff, Hornbeck's print., 1949. 112 p.   CHi   CRb

15087. 1960. Mullin-Kille co., pub. The Mullin-Kille Red Bluff (including Antelope valley)...city directory, master edition. Chillicothe, Ohio, c1960. 450 p.
CHi

GENERAL REFERENCES

15088. Anderson, Robert A. Fighting the Mill Creeks. Being a personal account of campaigns against the Indians of the northern Sierras. Chico, Chico record press, 1909. 86 p. ports.
C   CChiS   CCorn   CHi   CL   CLU   CO   CRbCL   CRedCL   CRedl   CSf   CSmH   CU-B

15089. Booth, Newton. Address delivered before Red Bluff lodge, I.O.O.F. of the state of California, at a public celebration of the forty-first anniversary of the institution of the order in the United States, April 26th, 1860. S.F., Towne & Bacon, 1860.   C   WHi

15090. California. Dept. of natural resources. Division of beaches and parks. Ide adobe. Sacramento, State print. off., 1958.   CRcS

15091. —— —— —— Same. [1959] 4 p.
CHi

15092. Chapman's magazine, Berkeley. Tehama county. (In v.1, no. 1, p. 29–32 [1941?])
CO   CRb   CRic   CU-B

15093. Chrisman, G. H. Advantages and possibilities of Red Bluff and Tehama county. Red Bluff, Evening sentinel [1907?] unp. illus.   CRb   CRbCL   CSmH

15094. Coffman, P. H. Tehama county, California. Its soil, climate, and general resources... Red Bluff, Tehama county bd. of trade [1890?] 37 p.   CL   CU-B

15095. —— Same. [1887]   CSmH

15096. Corning. Chamber of commerce. Corning in the Sacramento valley. [Sacramento, J. M. Anderson co., 19—?] [20] p. illus.   CU-B

15097. Daughters of the American revolution. California. Genealogical records committee. Tehama county, California, wills from 1850 to 1900... notes taken by...Grace Mountain Keefer. Butte county, California, wills from 1850 to 1900...notes taken and compiled by...Laura Cline Patterson... Chico, 1951. 157 l. Typew.   C   CL

15098. Ellison, John F. Address delivered by... at the new era banquet, Redding, Calif., April 20, 1907.
CHi

15099. Ellison, Minnie Bell (Cason) Judge John F. Ellison, superior judge of Tehama county, California, 1890–1926. [Chico, Record press] 1929. 150 p. plates, ports.
C   CHi   CRb   CRbCL   CRcS   CRedCL   CSmH

15100. Foster & Woodson, Corning. When you purchase a piece of the earth for a home, it is not so much what you pay as what you get. The best is none too good. In Maywood colony, California, you get the best. [Corning, 1900] 106 p. illus., facsims.   CU-B

15101. Freemasons. Tehama. Molino lodge no. 150. One hundred years of masonry in Molino lodge no. 150. [Text and material compiled by Grover C. Davis, jr.] Red Bluff, Walker litho. co., 1961. 99 p. illus., ports.
CHi

15102. —— —— Tehama lodge no. 3. 75th anniversary and roll call of Tehama lodge...Masonic temple, January 8th, 1925. [n.p., 1925] [9] p.   CHi

15103. Hisken, Clara Hough. Tehama, little city of the big trees. N.Y., Exposition press [c1948] 51 p. illus., ports.
C   CChiS   CHi   CL   CLSU   CLU   CO   CRb   CRedCL   CSf   CSmH   CU-B   N   NN

15104. Immigration association of California. [County scrapbooks] [S.F., 188–?]   C

15105. Kimball, Gorham Gates. Trailing sheep from California to Idaho in 1865: The journal of Gorham Gates Kimball. Annotated by Edward N. Wentworth. 83 p. Reprint. from *Agricultural history*, v.28, p. 49–83, April 1954.   CHi

15106. Lassen lava. Official publication of Red Bluff rotary club no. 1786, Red Bluff, California, John G. Miller, editor. v.1, nos. 1–52, 1924–1925. illus., ports. Bibliographies.   CRb

15107. Los Molinos land co. Los Molinos, California. Spokane, Wash., American engraving co., Inland press [n.d.] unp.   CRbCL

15108. —— Los Molinos irrigated lands... Los Molinos [1910?] [16] p.   CSalCL   CU-B

15109. McAfee bros., land agents. Tehama county, California; geography, soil, climate, productions, etc. S.F. [1884?] 32 p. illus., maps, tables.   CSmH   CU-B

15110. McCoy, Leo Lewis. Land grants and other history of Tehama county. Interesting discussion of the early history—arrival of first American in the valley. Read at Red Bluff Rotary, June 18, 1926. Folded newspaper sheet in pamphlet binder. At head of title: The River rambler.   C

15111. —— Story of early days in Tehama county; Retired sheep man recalls snow storm fifty-four years ago as it cost him heavily; Career of Peter Lassen was one of great activity. [1927?] [6] l. Mounted newspaper clippings. Caption titles of three newspaper articles.   C

15112. The Maywood colony advocate, v. 1, nos. 10–15, 1899. N.Y., 1899. 1 v. illus.   C

15113. Mitchell, Edward H., pub. Red Bluff, Tehama county, California. [S.F., Red Bluff, pub. by E.H. Mitchell for C.H. Darrough, n.d.] 16 pl.   CU-B

15114. Moak, Sim. The last of the Mill Creeks and early life in northern California. Chico, Priv. print., 1923. 48 p. illus., ports.
C CArcHT CCorn CL CLU CO CRb CRbCL CSf CSmH CU-B

15115. Red Bluff. Chamber of commerce. History of Red Bluff. [Red Bluff, n.d.] [2] p. Mimeo.   CHi

15116. —— Tehama county...Written and compiled by W. C. Spann. S.F., Print. by Whitaker & Ray co. [1903?] 32 p. illus.   CHi CRbCL CU-B NHi

15117. —— —— The Iron Canyon irrigation project, Tehama county, California. [S.F., McNutt, Kahn & co., 1907] [19] p. illus., map.   CHi CU-B

15118. —— —— Red Bluff, California; county seat of Tehama county, natural distributing center of northern Sacramento valley. Red Bluff [n.d.] 5 p. maps. Mimeo.   CRcS

15119. —— —— Tehama county... Red Bluff [1910] [26] p. illus.   CU-B

15120. —— **First Presbyterian church.** 1860–1910. First Presbyterian church, Red Bluff, California. [Red Bluff, 1910]   CSmH

15121. Red Bluff news, Sept. 29, 1899. Special historical and biographical issue, illustrated.   CRbCL

15122. The Republican, Corning. Tehama county in picture and prose. Corning [1929?] unp. illus.   CRbCL

15123. Schoenfeld, Golda. Some landmarks and history of Tehama county, California. Manuscript read before Antelope women's club, December 1, 1922. 12 p. Typew.   CHi CRb CRbCL

15124. [Shackelford, H. B.] [Official] map [of the county of Tehama] Carefully compiled from actual surveys... [S.F., Britton & Rey, litho., 1887] [106] p.   CU-B

15125. Sierra flume and lumber co. The Sierra flume and lumber company of California. Illus. by Will L. Taylor. [1876–1877?] 29 pen and ink original drawings. 10 typew. p. of descriptive material by William Henry Hutchinson.
C CHi and CRb have photographed reproductions of the original and only known volume.

15126. Sierra lumber co. Red Bluff bridge and the Sierra lumber co. Its use granted by the Board of supervisors, July 10, 1876. History of the bridge and proceedings of the board. Red Bluff, "Sentinel" steam bk. and job print., 1884. 4 p.   CSmH

15127. Soderstrom, Paul. A study of consumer and retail buying and purchasing power in Red Bluff. [Berkeley, 1938] Thesis (M.A.)—Univ. of Calif., 1938.   CU

15128. Sweeney, John David, comp. History and geography of Tehama county. [Red Bluff] 1928. 14 mimeo. sheets. This material has been prepared for class use. It has been revised as far as possible down to 1928.   C

15129. —— Same. Red Bluff, Priv. print., 1930. 33 p. Adopted by County bd. of educ.
C CRb CRbCL CSmH CU-B

15130. —— The Lassen trail: its course, its hardships, its heroes...delivered at dedication of historic marker on the site of old Benton City, end of the Lassen trail, on Aug. 9, 1930. Gerber, Gerber star [1930?] 20 p.
C CRbCL

15131. —— Memories of Tehama school. [n.d.] 4 p. Typew.   CRbCL CWeT

15132. —— School days in Tehama county in days gone by. [n.d.] 33 p. Typew.   CRbCL

15133. —— Tehama county in the past. [n.d.] 21 p. Typew.   CBb CRbCL

15134. —— Thrilling crime chapter in early Tehama history when train robbers shot to kill, rode away in bicycles. [n.d.] 4 p. Typew.   CRbCL

15135. Tehama county. Charters. [Charter, 1917] California. Assembly concurrent resolution no. 6, with original signatures of those concerned. [n.p., n.d.]   CRb

15136. —— —— Freeholder's charter of the county of Tchama; including all amendments thereto, decisions of the courts affecting the same, and the constitutional provisions authorizing freeholder's charters. Comp. and annotated by Fred C. Pugh and Curtiss E. Wetter. Corning, Observer press, 1926.   CRb

15137. —— **Exposition commission.** Tehama, the county of diversified opportunity. [Red Bluff] Tehama county exposition commission and Board of supervisors [191–?] folder (15 p.) illus., col. map.
CHi CRcS CSf

15138. Not in use.

15139. [Tehama county history; miscellaneous sketches] 57 p. Typew. Partial contents: Education in Tehama county.— Barney Mayhew.— Joseph Spencer Cone.— History of Stanford-Vina ranch.— History of Tehama county post offices.— Nome Lackee Indian reservation (includes all the correspondence from the time of establishment in 1854 to its abandonment in 1861)— Peter Lassen.— Land grants of Tehama county.
CRb CRbCL

15140. Tehama county... Its advantages and disadvantages, as shown by a practical eastern farmer. Vol. I, no. 1. Red Bluff, Nov., 1886. [4] p.   CU-B

15141. Tehama county midwinter fair association. Tehama county, California: its climate, soil and resources... Red Bluff, [1893] 34 p.   CU-B

15142. U.S. Office of Indian affairs. Letter to L. L. McCoy about Nome Lackee Indians. May 29, 1930. 25 p. Typew. Contains letters and excerpts from Indian Office reports 1854 to 1867.   CCorn CRbCL

15143. Wells, Andrew Jackson. Tehama county, Sacramento valley, California. S.F., Sunset mag. homeseekers' bur. [1909] 31 p. illus., maps.   CSf CU-B

15144. Woodson, Warren N. Price list & description of a variety of desirable properties located in the Maywood colony, of which colony Corning is the residential and commercial center. Corning [n.d.] folder (12 p.)   CU-B

15145. —— Same. [1911] 64 p.   CHi CRbCL

15146. —— The trail of the trail blazers... Corning [Corning republican print., 1936?] 26 p. illus., port.
C CHi CRb CSfWF-H CSmH CU-B

TRINITY COUNTY

(Created in 1850, but attached to Shasta county until 1851; annexed portion of Klamath county in 1855)

COUNTY HISTORIES

15147. Bartlett, James W. Trinity county, California...a summary of its history, from May, 1845 to September, 1926. [Sacramento, News pub. co., 1926] 31 p.
C CArcHT CB CCH CHi CL CLU CMS CO CP CRb CRcS CSalCL CSf CSfCW CSfWF-H CYcCL CYrS

15148. Cox, Isaac. The annals of Trinity county, containing a history of the discovery, settlement and progress, together with a description of the resources and present condition of Trinity county... S.F., Commercial bk. & job steam print. establishment, 1858. 206 p.
C CF CHi CMa CSfCP CSfCW CSfU CSjC CStoC CU-B CWeT CYrS CtY

15149. —— Same. With annotations written by James W. Bartlett. [Weaverville] 1926. 283 l. Typew.
C CLSU CU-B

15150. —— —— Index. [1926?] 1 v. unp.　　C

15151. —— Same. Preface by Caroline Wenzel. Introduction by Owen C. Coy. The first California county history by George D. Lyman, M. D. Annotator's foreword by James W. Bartlett. Eugene, Ore., Print. for Harold C. Holmes by J. H. Nash, 1940. 265 p. illus. Includes facsimilies of cover and title-page from original edition. Annotations...by James W. Bartlett: p. 189–254.
C CAla CAlaC CArcHT CBb CChiS CHi CL CLAC CLCo CLSU CLU CLgA CO COMC CRcS CRedCL CRic CSf CSfCP CSfU CSjC CSmH CU-B CWeT MoSHi WHi

GREAT REGISTER

15152. Trinity county. Index to the Great register of the county of Trinity. 1866– Place of publication and title vary.
C has 1867–68, 1871–73, 1875, 1877, 1879, 1888 (biennially to)– 1896, 1900 (biennially to)– 1928, 1932 (biennially to)– 1962. CHi has Nov. 1862, Aug. 1879. CL has 1872–73, 1877, 1882 (suppl.), 1884 (biennially to)– 1890. CO has 1877. CSmH has 1868, 1873, 1879, 1880 (suppl.) CU-B has 1867, Nov. 1868, Sept. 1869, Oct. 1872, Sept. 1873, 1873 (suppl.), 1875, 1875 (suppl.), 1877, Aug. 1879, 1886, 1896–98, 1914–16, Aug., Nov. 1934, Nov. 1938, May, Aug., Nov. 1940.

GENERAL REFERENCES

15153. André, Alexander. A Frenchman at the California Trinity river mines in 1849. Introduction by Georges Joyaux. N.Y., Westerners New York posse, 1957. 25 p. map. Cover title: California Trinity river mines in 1849. "Three hundred copies printed."
C CArcHT CBaB CChiS CHi CL CLO CLSM CLU CRic CSd CSf CSfCSM CSto CStrCL CaBViPA

15154. Buck, Franklin Augustus. A Yankee trader in the gold rush; the letters of Franklin A. Buck, compiled by Katherine A. White. Bost. & N.Y., Houghton [c1930] 294 p. illus. Personal experiences of a young man in the gold rush days from Sacramento to Weaverville.
Available in many California libraries and ODa OrU ViU

15155. Burch, John Chilton. Speech...delivered at Weaverville, California, before a mass meeting of the Democracy and compromise union men of Trinity county, May 25, 1861. Sacramento, 1861. 8 p.　　CU CU-B

15156. California council for protection of roadside beauty. An historical landmark of pioneer California; an appeal for the preservation of Weaverville. [n.d.] 3 p. illus. Mimeo.　　CHi

15157. [Chapman's magazine, Berkeley] Trinity county, California. [1941?] 15 p. illus., map.
CO CRb CU-B

15158. Hotchkiss, Helen Evison. History of early Trinity county, California. [Berkeley, 1960] 162 l. plate, maps. Thesis (M.A.)—Univ. of Calif., 1960.
CU CU-B

15159. Immigration association of California. [County scrapbooks] [S.F., 188–?]　　　　C

15160. Integral quicksilver mining co. Prospectus of Integral mining company. [n.p., 1891] 8 p.
CU-B

15161. Jackson, J. J., comp. History of Weaverville volunteer fire department, on the occasion of the 11th annual firemen's ball, Feb. 25, 1950. [Weaverville, Trinity jl.] 1950. [8] p.　　CHi CU-B

15162. Jones, T. E. Report on the Red Hill hydraulic gold mines, Junction City mining district, Trinity county, California. By Hon. T. E. Jones [and others]... Bost., A. Mudge & sons, print., 1882. 21 p. fold. diagr.
CLU

15163. La Grange ditch and hydraulic mining company. By-laws... Incorporated June 28, 1871. S.F., A.L. Bancroft & co., 1871. 15 p.　　CHi CU-B

15164. Simmons, Paris B. Trinity Center now, and then. [Trinity Center, 1950] 64 p. illus., ports. "Trinity Center elementary school history project."
C CHi CO CRedCL CRic CSS CSf CU-B CWeT

15165. Trinity county, California. Official records. Trinity, the second largest producer of gold in California [in 1892] its minerals and 1000 of its mines, comp. from official records. [1892?] 24 l. Typew.　　C

15166. Trinity county historical society, Weaverville. Trinity; yearbook of the Trinity county historical society [founded Jan. 28, 1954] [Weaverville, 1955] illus., ports.
C has 1955–1958. CArcHT has 1955–1958. CHi has 1955–1959. CO has 1955. CWeT has 1955–1959.

15167. Trinity journal, Weaverville. Centennial, 1856–1956; 100 years of progress. Weaverville, 1956. 8, 2A–8A p. illus., ports., maps, facsim.　　CU-B

TULARE COUNTY

(Created in 1852 from portions of Mariposa and Los Angeles counties)

COUNTY HISTORIES

15168. History of Tulare county, California, with illustrations, descriptive of its scenery, farms [etc.] with biographical sketches. S.F., Elliott, 1883. 226 p. illus., ports., maps. "Organization of Kern county": p. 199–226.
C CBaK CCH CHan CHanK CHi CLU CU-B CViCL NN

15169. Menefee, Eugene L., and Dodge, Fred A. History of Tulare and Kings counties, California, with biographical sketches...L.A., Historic record co., 1913. 890 p.
C CF CHanK CHi CL CLCM CLCo CLO CLSU CLU CMont CO CRic CSd CSf CSmH CU-B CViCL In MWA NN WHi

15170. Small, Kathleen Edwards. History of Tulare county, California... Chicago, Clarke, 1926. 2 v. illus., ports., map. v.2: Biographical.

C CCH CHanK CHi CL CSf CSmH CStrCL CU-B CViCL CtY IHi MWA NN WHi

15171. Thompson, Thomas Hinckley. Official historical atlas map of Tulare county, California. Tulare, Author, 1892. 147 p. illus., maps.

C CBaB CBb CFS CHan CHanK CHi CL CLCM CLU CSf CSmH CSt CU-B CViCL NN WHi

GREAT REGISTER

15172. Tulare county. Index to the Great register of the county of Tulare. 1867– Place of publication and title vary.

C has 1869, 1872, 1877, 1879, 1880 (biennially to)– 1896, 1900, 1902, 1904, 1906, 1910 (biennially to)– 1962. CL has 1872, 1877, 1879 (suppl. 1–3), 1880, 1882, 1886, 1888, 1890. CU-B has 1867, 1868, Oct. 1872, 1873 (suppl. 1–2), 1879, 1879 (suppl. 1–3), 1880, 1882, Nov. 1940. CViCL has 1872–73, 1880, 1900, 1904, 1910*, 1915, 1916*, 1920, 1922, 1924, 1926, 1930 (biennially to)– 1962.

DIRECTORIES

15173. 1892. [Tulare register, pub.] Tulare county directory, with a classified directory of business of the county. 1892. 75 p.   CHan CViCL

15174. 1910–1958. Polk, R. L. & co., pub. Polk's Tulare county directory. L.A., 1910–58. Publisher varies: 1910–19 Tulare county directory co.

C has 1939. C-S has 1912–13. CFS has 1915, 1928/29, 1930/31, 1932/33, 1934, 1937, 1939, 1941, 1942/43, 1944, 1947/48, 1950, 1952, 1953/54. CHi has 1910, 1941, 1947/48, 1950, 1952, 1953/54, 1958. CL has 1912, 1926, 1928–29, 1937, 1941, 1942/43, 1950, 1952–57. CSmH has 1910. CViCL has 1912, 1926, 1930, 1932, 1934, 1936–37, 1939, 1941–44, 1950, 1952–58.

15175. 1925–1932/33. McNeel directory co., pub. Tulare county directory... Sacramento, 1925–32.

C has 1925, 1928/29, 1930/31, 1932/33.

15176. 1937. Driggers, Roy L., comp. Public directory for Tulare county, 1937. Visalia, Tulare county school dept., 1937. 30 p.   CViCL

Visalia

15177. 1900. Visalia delta, pub. Visalia city directory. Visalia, 1900. 104 p. illus.   CViCL

15178. 1913– Polk, R. L. & co., pub. Polk's Visalia city directory including Exeter, Farmersville, Ivanhoe and Woodlake.

C has 1913. CHi has 1959–62. CL has 1915. CSf has 1961. CU-B has 1947–48, 1950, 1955. CViCL has 1913, 1959.

15179. 1918– McNeel directory co., pub. Visalia city and rural directory. Stockton, 1918–

CViCL has 1918, 1920, 1922–23.

15180. 1949. Visalia. Church of Jesus Christ of latter-day saints. Visalia city directory. [Visalia] 1949. 172 p. map.   CViCL

Other Cities and Towns

15181. 1908. Pratt and Kunath, pub. First edition of the Porterville-Lindsay city directory... Porterville [1908?] 107 p.   C

15182. 1922. McNeel directory co., pub. Porterville city and rural directory. Stockton, 1922.   CFS

15183. 1958. City directory service co., pub. Official Porterville...city directory. Riverside [1958]

CFS

15184. 1959– Polk, R. L. & co., pub. Polk's Porterville city directory including Lindsay, Poplar, Strathmore, Terra Bella, Village gardens, and Woodville. L.A., 1959–

CHi has 1959, 1961. CViCL has 1959.

15185. 1959– Polk, R. L. & co., pub. Polk's Tulare city directory including Pixley, Tipton and Woodville. L.A., 1959–

CHi has 1959, 1961.

GENERAL REFERENCES

15186. Alexander, Charles. Battles and victories of Allen Allensworth... Bost., Sherman, French & co., 1914. 429 p. port.   CHi CViCL

15187. Alta irrigation dist. Annual report of the secretary, 1927– Dinuba, 1928–

CHi has 1927–28, 1936–39, 1941–49, 1952–58. CViCL

15188. Automobile club of southern California. Touring bureau, pub. Tulare county; general information... [L.A.? 19–?] 35 p. illus.   C CU-B

15189. Barry, George A. Tulare county... L.A., Out West co. [1902] 15 p. Reprint. from *Out West*, December 1902.   CHi CSmH CU-B

15190. Barton, Orlando. Early history of Tulare co. ... Visalia, 1905. 7 p.   CU-B

15191. Boone, W. P. Traver pioneers and incidents. [L.A.? Author, 1957?] 19 p. Mimeo.   CViCL

15192. Botsford & Hammond. Tulare county, California. A truthful description of its climate, soil, towns, and vast agricultural and other resources. Visalia [1885?] 50 p.   CViCL

15193. [Braly & Blythe] Tulare county, California. Its resources and advantages, its capabilities and its attractions to the home seekers. [Tulare, 1887?] 16 p. map.   NHi

15194. Brewer, Michael Fraser. Water pricing and allocation with particular reference to California irrigation districts. [Berkeley, 1959] Thesis (Ph.D.)— Univ. of Calif., 1959.   CU

15195. Britton & Gray, Washington, D.C. [Statement accompanying petition to the secretary of the interior from certain settlers of Tulare county, Calif. asking that the withdrawal of public lands in 1867 for the Southern Pacific railroad be rescinded.] Wash., D.C., 1869. 24 p.   CLU

15196. Business directory and historical and descriptive handbook of Tulare county, California. Tulare, Pillsbury & Ellsworth, 1888. 221 p. map.

CHi CSf CSmH CU-B CViCL

15197. California. Committee to survey the agricultural labor resources of the San Joaquin valley. Transcript of public hearing, August 2, 1950, Visalia, California. [Sacramento, State print. off., 1950] 99, 33 l. Mimeo.   CViCL

15198. California. District court. 13th district. [Case of Lovick P. Hall and Samuel J. Garrison, proprietor of the Equal rights expositor vs. County of Tulare, Calif. Abstract of decision, appeal, and judgment, District court, 13th judicial district, Tulare county, California, May 31, 1870–Nov. 15, 1872. Visalia, n.p., 1936] [8] l. Typew. Biographical data added.   CFS

15199. Dinuba. Chamber of commerce. Dinuba, a fine community of homes, farms, and business. [Dinuba, 1953?] 31 p. illus.   CFS

15200. —— **First Baptist church.** ...75 years of God's grace, 1882–1957 celebration, Feb. 9–10, 1957. Dinuba, 1957. 16 p. illus.   CHi CViCL

15201. Dinuba sentinel. Souvenir war album. Dinuba, 1943–44. 2 v. illus.   CViCL

15202. Drake, H. S. Exeter land development directory...Visalia, Times-delta [192–?] 240 p. maps.   CViCL

15203. —— Lindsay-Strathmore land development directory, Tulare county, California. Lindsay, Hall & Burr, c1929. 271 p. maps.   CU-B CViCL

15204. Elliott, W. W., and co., pub. A guide to the grand and sublime scenery of the Sierra Nevada in the region about Mount Whitney... S.F., 1883. 60 p. illus., map.   CL CU-B CViCL

15205. —— Same. 1886.   C

15206. Exeter. Board of trade. Exeter, Tulare county, California, the home of early oranges. California lands for wealth, California fruits for health. Exeter [1914?] [20] p. illus.   CU-B

15207. —— **First Presbyterian church.** Harold Cardwell Stadtmiller, the versatile schoolmaster. [Exeter, 1953?] 67 p.   CFS CHi

15208. Farquhar, Francis Peloubet. The story of Mount Whitney. S.F., 1929. [18] p. illus., ports. "Reprint. from *Sierra club bul.*, Feb. 1929."   C CHi

15209. Freemasons. Orosi. Orosi lodge no. 383. Golden anniversary...by Arthur Beckner. [Orosi?] 1956. 32 p. illus.   CViCL

15210. Frost, Arba W. Biographies of Tulare county judges. [n.d.] 50 l. ports. Typew. Contains chart of all Tulare county officials, 1852–1940.
In Tulare county law library.
CViCL has correspondence, 1936–38, in which information was gathered.

15211. —— Early government of Tulare county. [n.d.] 2 v. maps. Typew.   CViCL

15212. —— Tulare county court houses; brief history and excerpts from official records. 1943. 226 l. Typew.   CViCL

15213. —— Tulare county jail: excerpts from official records, 1854–1893. 1943. 98 l. Typew.   CViCL

15214. —— Visalia and Tulare railroad co. [Visalia, Author, 194–?] 41 l. Typew.   CViCL

15215. Glasscock, Carl Burgess. Bandits and the Southern Pacific. N.Y., Stokes, 1929. 294 p. ports.
Available in many California libraries.

15216. Griggs, Monroe Christopher. Wheelers, pointers and leaders. Ed. by Joseph E. Doctor and Annie R. Mitchell. Fresno, Acad. lib. guild, 1956. 60 p. illus., ports. "Published by the Tulare county historical society." Early teaming and transportation in Tulare county and San Joaquin valley.
C CFS CHi CLSM CLU CO CSfSC CSfU CSto CViCL

15217. Hall, Ansel Franklin. Guide to Giant forest, Sequoia national park...and the adjacent Sierra Nevada ... Yosemite, Author, 1921. 127 p.
      CLO CO CSfSC CU-B CViCL

15218. —— Same, with title: Sequoia and General Grant national parks... Berkeley, National parks pub. house [1930] 151 p.   CO CU-B

15219. Hopping, Kate (Redstone) Diary. [Kaweah?] 1902. unp. Ms.   CViCL

15220. Hurst, Harry. Alta pioneers. Dinuba, Alta advocate, Apr. 5, 1924. Apr. 10, 1925. 188 p. Alta irrigation district.   CFS CViCL

15221. Immigration association of California. [County scrapbooks] [S.F., 188–?]   C

15222. Jewell, Marion Nielsen. Agricultural development in Tulare county, 1870–1900... [L.A., 1950] 87 l. maps. Thesis (M.A.)—Univ. of So. Calif., 1950.   CViCL

15223. Jones, William Carey, jr. Kaweah experiment in co-operation. Reprint. from *Q. Jl. of economics*, Oct., 1891.   C

15224. Kalfayan, Garabed. The story of Yettem; in Armenian. Fresno, Kasparian, 1950. 308 p. illus. Yettem is a town in Tulare county.   CViCL

15225. Kaweah co-operative colony company, of California, ltd., a joint stock co. [Pamphlets relating to the Kaweah co-operative colony. S.F., 1886–89] 8 v. illus.   CLU

15226. —— Kaweah, a cooperative commonwealth located above Three Rivers P.O. on the Kaweah river, Tulare county... S.F., Burnette G. Haskell, 1887. 16 p.   CViCL

15227. —— A pen picture of the Kaweah co-operative colony co., limited, a joint stock company, located in Kaweah canyon, and the giant forest of Tulare co., Cal. ... S.F., Burnette G. Haskell, 1889. 32 p.
      C CSmH CU-B CViCL

15228. —— The persecution of Kaweah; story of a great injustice. Pub. by the eastern group of the Kaweah co-operative colony co. ...[N.Y.?] 1891. 44 p.
      CU-B

15229. —— Persecutions of the Kaweah colonists. Unimpeachable testimony as to their good faith and honest intentions... [n.p., 1893?] 7 p.   CU-B

15230. —— [Scrapbook of clippings of the Kaweah colony, 1890–1891] 34 p.   CViCL

15231. Keagle, Cora L. Pixley's history, 1886–1922; from *Pixley enterprise*, July 16–Aug. 12, 1939. Scrapbook.   CViCL

15232. Keller, C. F. To members of the Kaweah co-operative colony... [letters] by C. F. Keller, J. G. Wright, P. N. Kuss and W. J. Cuthbertson. [n.p., 189–?] 12 p.   CViCL

15233. Ketton, James M. Description and prospectus of oil lands, situated in Tulare co., Cal. N.Y., H. Spear, 1865. 11 p. fold. map.   C

15234. [Langdon, W. J.] Barcelona colony. [S.F., Crocker, 1891?] folder (24 p.) illus., map.   CHi

15235. League of women voters of California. Tulare county government, comp. by the League of women voters of California, and the Tulare county superintendent of schools. Visalia, Supt. of schools [1958] 54 p. illus.   CViCL

15236. Levick, M. B. Tulare county, Calif. S.F., Sunset mag. homeseekers' bur. for the Tulare county Bd. of trade. [S.F.? 1912?] 62 p. illus., map.
      CHi CL CSmH CU-B CViCL

15237. Lewis, Ruth Ronnie (Krandis) Kaweah: an experiment in cooperative colonization. Berkeley, Univ. of Calif. press, 1948. 13 p. Reprint. from *Pac. hist. review*, v.17, no. 4, Nov., 1948.   CViCL

15238. —— The rise and fall of Kaweah: an experiment in cooperative colonization, 1884–1892... [Berkeley, 1942] 97 l. Typew.   CU-B

15239. Lindsay gazette. Golden anniversary edition ...Oct. 19, 1951. Lindsay, 1951. unp. illus., ports., maps.
CHi CU-B

15240. Lower Kings river reclamation district vs. Phillips, P. C. In the Supreme court of the state of California. Lower Kings river reclamation district, no. 531, appellant, vs. P. C. Phillips, respondent. Transcript on appeal. S. C. Denson, Bradley & Farnsworth, attorneys for appellant. Daggett & Adams, attorneys for respondent... S.F., W.A. Woodward & co. [1894] 113 p. The suit concerns land in Tulare county. CHi

15241. Lucerne valley immigration association of Tulare county, California. ...The Lucerne valley of Tulare county...the banner wheat county in the state ... [S.F., Henderson & co., print., 1887?] 23 p. CU-B

15242. McCallum, William J. Camera studies, Sequoia-Kings Canyon national park. [Salinas, El Camino press, 1953] 1 v. (chiefly illus.) CU-B

15243. McCubbin, John Cameron. The Stockton-Los Angeles stage road; with emphasis upon that part which ran between the Kings and Kaweah rivers. [n.p., n.d.] 1 v. Typew. C

15244. ―――― Traver; the "ghost city" of the Golden state highway. [n.p., n.d.] 22 p. Typew. C

15245. McGee, Lizzie. Mills of the sequoias. Visalia, Tulare county hist. soc., 1952. 27 l. C CFS CHi CViCL

15246. [Martin, J. J.] The curse of capitalism... persecution of the Kaweah cooperative colony of California... [San Luis Obispo, 19–?] 164 l. Typew. CU-B

15247. Mather, Stephen Tyng. The bill to establish the Roosevelt-Sequoia national park. Buffalo, N.Y., Buffalo soc. of natural sciences, 1922. 16 p. illus., maps. "Reprint of *Hobbies*, Jan., 1922." C

15248. Maxwell, Hu. Evans and Sontag, the famous bandits of California. [S.F., S.F. print. co., 1893] 248 p. illus. CHi CU-B

15249. Mayfield, Thomas Jefferson. San Joaquin primeval, Uncle Jeff's story; a tale of a San Joaquin valley pioneer and his life with the Yokuts Indians, arranged by F. F. Latta... Tulare, Press of Tulare times, c1929. 88 p. C CBaB CFS CHi CLU CMerCL CSmH CU-B CViCL

15250. Medan, Caroline. Burnette Gregor Haskell: California radical. [Berkeley, 1958] Thesis (M.A.)— Univ. of Calif., 1958. CU

15251. [Miot, A. E.] Tulare county. Issued by Tulare county Board of trade. [S.F., 1915?] 31 p. illus. C CHi CL CLU CSfCSM CU-B CViCL

15252. ―――― Tulare county catechism...Issued by the Tulare county Board of trade. Visalia [1920?] 16 p. CHi CL CU-B CViCL

15253. ―――― Same. [1923] 16 p. illus. CHi

15254. ―――― Tulare county's wonderland highways and by-ways. Issued by Tulare county Board of trade. Visalia [19–?] 32 p. CHi CL CSfCSM CSmH CU-B CViCL

15255. Mitchell, Annie R. Golden memories, 1852–1952. [Visalia] Times-delta, 1952. [76] p. illus., ports., map. (In centennial ed. of the *Visalia times-delta*, Oct. 31, 1952) C CHi CViCL

15256. [Moore, A. R.] Scenes from Tulare county, California. [Porterville, 190–?] 48 pl. CLU CU-B

15257. Morrell, Ed. The twenty-fifth man; the strange story of Ed. Morrell, the hero of Jack London's "Star rover," lone survivor of the famous band of California feud outlaws. Montclair, N.J., New era pub. co. [c1924] 390 p. illus. CBb CSf CStmo CViCL

15258. Mt. Whitney club journal. v.1, nos. 1–3, 1902–1904. Visalia, 1902–04. No more published. C CSfSC CU-B CViCL

15259. National fruit growing co. Tulare county, the most prosperous and growing fruit center of California. S.F., [1893] 16 p. CFS

15260. ―――― Tulare county and California fruit lands... S.F., J.M. Torres, bk., law & commercial print. [1894?] 24 p. illus. CFS CL CU-B MWA

15261. Native daughters of the golden West. Tule Vista parlor, no. 305. Old cemeteries of southeastern Tulare county, California. Porterville, Farm tribune press, 1954. 18 p. illus. C CHi CL CLU CViCL

15262. Pogue, Grace Canan. The swift seasons. [Hollywood, Cloister press, c1957] 264 p. illus., ports. CFS CViCL

15263. ―――― Within the magic circle, a story of Woodlake valley, 1853–1943. [Visalia, Times-delta, 1943] 201 p. illus., ports. CFS CHi CViCL

15264. Presbyterian church in the U.S.A. Board of home missions. Dept. of church and country life. Rural survey of Tulare county, ... N.Y., Author, 1915. 115 p. illus., maps. CHi CLU CU-B CViCL

15265. Purdy, William George. Kaweah, a saga of the old colony... [n.p., n.d.] 15 l. Typew. CU-B

15266. ―――― Same. Visalia, Tulare county hist. soc. [1959] 15 l. CHi CU-B CViCL

15267. Rabe, Carl. The ascent of Mount Whitney ... Berkeley, 1888. 10 p. CU-B

15268. Robinson, William Wilcox. ...The story of Tulare county and Visalia, 1852–1952. [L.A.] Title insurance and trust co. [1952] 35 p.[1] p. illus., maps (1 fold.) C CB CFS CHi CL CLO CLSM CLU CO CPom CSfCSM CSfWF-H CStmo CU-B CViCL MoS

15269. ―――― Same. [2d ed.] [1955] 35 p. illus. CAla CHi CP CSluCL MWA MoHi

15270. Rudholm, Melvin P. A short history and survey of the Pixley union school district. [Fresno, 1956] 234 l. illus. Thesis (M.A.)—Fresno state college, 1956. CFS CViCL

15271. Smith, Wallace Paul Victor. Prodigal sons; the adventures of Christopher Evans and John Sontag. Bost., Christopher pub. house [1951] 434 p. illus. C CBb CFS CLU CRic CSf CSjC CStclU CStoC CViCL CU-B

15272. Smith, William Henry, jr. The organization of farms growing cotton in Tulare during the year 1940. [Berkeley, 1941] Thesis (M.S.)—Univ. of Calif., 1941. CU

15273. Stagner, Howard R. The giants of Sequoia and Kings canyon; one of the scenes and sketches series of publications... [Three Rivers] Sequoia natural hist. assoc., 1952. 31 p. illus. CViCL

15274. Steward, Julian Haynes. Indian tribes of Sequoia national park region... U.S. ...National park service. Field division of education, Berkeley, Calif. ... [Berkeley, 1935] 31 p. maps. Mimeo. CL CO CSd CSfSC CSmH CU-B

15275. Stewart, George William. History of the

Kaweah colony, 1885 to 1891. v.p. Copied from the *Weekly Visalia delta*, Nov. and Dec. 1891. CViCL

15276. —— Tulare county history scrapbook. [Visalia, Author, 1904–1930] 131 p. CViCL

15277. [Thew, Susan] Sequoia national park... [S.F., Thew, inc., c1926] 63 p. illus.
C CArcHT CFS CSfSC CSjC CU-B CViCL

15278. Trades magazine, devoted to California interests: immigrants land guide for Tulare county. v.1, 1881?– S.F.
C has v.3, no. 1, May 1885. 108 p. CU-B has v.1, no. 5, Jan. 1882. CViCL has v.3, no. 1, May 1885.

15279. Tulare county. Board of trade. Tulare county. [S.F., Press of Hicks-Judd co., 1904] 32 p. illus.
CU-B CViCL

15280. —— Same. Visalia, 1938. 11 p. illus., map. CRcS

15281. —— **Chamber of commerce.** A few facts about Tulare county, California "garden of the sun." Visalia, 1959. 80 p. illus., maps. CU-B CViCL

15282. —— Los Tulares [Tulare county, California centennial, 1852–1952. Visalia, 1952] [26] p. illus. CHi

15283. —— **Supt. of schools.** Public schools directory. 1st [1910/11?]–19— [Visalia, 1910?]–19—
CFS has 1948/49, 1956/57. CViCL has 1910/11, 1959/60.

15284. Tulare county employees association. Your Tulare county government... Visalia, 1958. [24] l. illus. CViCL

15285. Tulare county historical society. List of members, by-laws, minutes, etc. Visalia, 1920–21. 18 p. Kept in Minute book of the Visalia realty co. CViCL

15286. Tulare daily times and advance-register. Saluting today's war heroes and heroines: the Tulare community war album. [Tulare] 1945. 196 p. illus. CViCL

15287. Tulare irrigation dist. Reports on the projected works of the Tulare irrigation district, Tulare county, California, by the Board of directors and the engineers... Tulare, Daily evening register steam print., 1890. 47 p. port., diagrs., fold. map. C CLU CSmH

15288. Turnbull, Walter. Secure a 20-acre home in the Tulare colony for $250... [S.F.? Pac. coast land bur.? 1885?] 32 p. illus. CSmH CU-B

15289. —— ...Tulare county... [S.F.? Pac. coast land bur.? 1885?] 63 p. CL CSmH CU-B

15290. —— Same. [Tipton, Turnbull, 1892?] 46 p. CViCL

15291. Visalia. Chamber of commerce. Sequoia ...national park [Comp. by Walter Fry] [Visalia, 1935?] folder (9 p.) illus. CViCL

15292. Wells, Andrew Jackson. Kings and Kern canyons and the Giant forest of California. S.F., So. Pac. co., 1907. 32 p. CHi

15293. —— Lindsay, California... S.F., Sunset mag. homeseekers' bur. [1912?] 32 p. illus. CU-B

15294. Wheelock, Walt. Climbing Mount Whitney; by Walt Wheelock and Tom Condon. Glendale, La Siesta press, 1960. 36 p. illus., maps. CHi

15295. White, John R., and Pusateri, Samuel J. Sequoia and Kings canyon national parks. Stanford [1949] 212 p. illus., maps.
Available in many California libraries and MiD N

15296. —— Same. [rev. ed.] Stanford [1952] 104 p. illus. Includes bibliography.
C CArcHT CB CBaB CL CLU CO CPom CRedl CRic CSS CSfCSM CStmo CViCL MiD

15297. Wilson, Herbert Earl. The lore and lure of Sequoia. L.A., Wolfer print. co., 1928. 132 p. illus., ports. CFS CLO CMon CViCL

15298. Wood, Crispin Melton. A history of Mount Whitney. [Stockton, 1955] 131 p. illus. Thesis (M.A.)— College of the Pacific, 1955. CInI CStoC

15299. Wrought, Orlena (Barton) "The good old days," sawmills and home made dental tools. [Visalia, Tulare county hist. soc., 1951?] 2 l. CHi CU-B

Porterville

15300. Byron, William G. A geographic analysis of the Porterville area. [L.A., 1951] Thesis (M.A.)—Univ. of Calif., 1951. CLU

15301. Dockham, H. W. Porterville, Tulare county, California... [Porterville] Porterville enterprise, 1900. [28] p. illus. CViCL

15302. The Farm tribune. ...Progress edition, Thursday, Nov. 1, 1951. [Porterville, 1951] 1 v. (v.p.) illus., ports. CU-B

15303. Ford & Coffland. Porterville, the land of the golden fruit... [Porterville, 1894] 23 p. CU-B

15304. McAuley, James D. Polling parents about schools: a survey of parent attitudes toward the elementary schools of Porterville, California. [Fresno, 1955] 127 l. illus. Thesis (M.A.)—Fresno state college, 1955. CFS

15305. Milligan, John A. Fifty years of masonry in Porterville, California, 1890–1940. Porterville, The Lodge, 1940. 40 p. illus. CViCL

15306. [Moody, Charles Amadon] Porterville, California... [L.A.? 1901?] 16 p. illus. Reprint from *Land of sunshine*, v.14, p. 258–272, Mar. 1901.
CHi CSalCL CSmH CU-B KHi NN

15307. Porterville. Chamber of commerce. Porterville, California; Porterville people prosper... Porterville [190–?] 12 p. illus. CViCL

15308. —— —— Porterville, Tulare county, California. Metropolis of central California citrus belt; center of a district of diversified resources. [Porterville, 1914?] [32] p. illus. CU-B

15309. —— —— **Post war planning committee.** Post war and development plan for the Porterville district. [Porterville?] 1945. 32 p. fold. tables, fold. map. CU-B

15310. Putnam, Royal Porter. The journal of Royal Porter Putnam, Sept. 1857–July 1860. Porterville, The Farm tribune, 1961. 58 p. ports. CHi

15311. Stiner, Ina H. History of Porterville. [Porterville, 1934] 625 l. illus., maps, mounted photos., facsims. Typew. Half-title: t.-p. reads Some studies in local history, by the Library staff of the Porterville union high school and junior college. C

15312. —— Vandalia, Porterville, Plano: foundings on Tule river. Porterville, Author, 1945. 5 l. Mimeo. CViCL

15313. Williams, Hughe C., ed. and comp. Programme, Veterans' day and Porterville homecoming, 1957. [Porterville, 1957] [35] p. illus. Contains many old photographs of Porterville. CFS

Visalia

15314. Dawes, Thelma Elizabeth. The teaching load and school costs in the Visalia union high school district. [Stanford, 1947] 515 l. plates. Thesis (M.A.)—Stanford univ., 1947.   CViCL

15315. Delabar, Homer G. The rebels of Visalia, California, 1860–1865. Fresno, 1957. 122 l. illus. Thesis (M.A.)—Fresno state college, 1957.   CFS

15316. Drath, Ralph F. Visalia—metropolis of the cow country; a brief summary of the early history of Visalia and Tulare county. [L.A.] Author, 1940. 10 l. Mimeo.   CViCL

15317. Frost, Arba W. Early Masonic history, Visalia lodge, no. 128, F. & A. M. 1943. 73 l. Typew.
                                              CViCL

15318. —— Visalia scrapbook; copies of articles from the *Visalia delta*, June 25, 1859–June 11, 1863. 1941. 150 l. Typew.   CViCL

15319. —— "Vise" and Visalia: research and correspondence of A. W. Frost regarding Nathaniel Vise, his family and friends; the naming of Visalia, California, and Visalia, Kentucky. 1943. 151 l. Typew.   CViCL

15320. Hardy printing co., pub. Flood, December 1955. [Visalia, 1956] 66 p. chiefly illus., double map.
                                   CFS CU-B CViCL

15321. Lake, Earl Otto. News comes to a frontier town: Visalia, California, 1859–1900. [Berkeley, Author] 1939. 40 numb. l. illus. Typew. "Prepared as part of a course in journalism at the University of California."
                                              CViCL

15322. League of women voters of Visalia. Visalia, the biography of a town. Visalia, Visalia print. service, 1954. 20 p. illus.   CFS CP CViCL

15323. McClun, Richard. "The hole flood"; a humorous history of the January, 1956, flood in Visalia, California... Visalia, Commercial print. co., 1956. 21 p. illus.   CViCL

15324. Maddox, Ben Moyers. Ben M. Maddox; October 18, 1859–May 9, 1933. 16 p. port.   CHi

15325. Mary Thomas, *Sister* (Dorothy Hampton) Visalia, the mother parish of the San Joaquin Valley, and its first pastor, the Reverend Daniel Francis Dade. [Wash., D.C., 1944] 100 l. Thesis (M.A.)—Catholic univ. of Am., 1944.   CSrD

15326. Mitchell, Annie Rosalind and McEwen, Mary Walker. Visalia in early days. 1942. 4 l. Typew. (Copied from *The covered wagon*, Feb. 1942)   CViCL

15327. Parker, Basil G. Life and adventures; an autobiography. Plano, Reed, print., 1902. 88 p. port. Bound with: Recollections of the Mountain Meadow massacre.   CViCL

15328. Prestidge, George R. One hundredth anniversary, 1857–1957. Visalia lodge no. 128 F. and A. M. Visalia, Visalia lodge [1957] 43 p. illus.   CViCL

15329. Shippey, Mervyn G. A short history of the Visalia colored school...[n.p., n.d.] 19 l. illus., maps (2 fold., mounted), plans, facsims. Typew.   C

15330. —— Visalia normal school: a thirteen year history. 1935. 78 l. Typew.   C CViCL

15331. Van Norden, Rudolph W. Mt. Whitney power and electric company, southern San Joaquin valley, California. S.F., Technical pub. co., 1913. 81 p. illus., map. Reprint. from the *Jl. of electricity, power and gas,* Dec. 27, 1913.   CHi CViCL

15332. Visalia. Board of trade. Visalia, Tulare county. A brief description of the city, and its surrounding fruit and agricultural lands. [1st ed.] Visalia, Delta, 1890. 19 p.   C CViCL
Other editions followed. C (1892) CHi ([1902?]) CL (1892) CSmH (1892, 1912) CU-B (1892, [1902?]) CViCL (1895, [1902?, 1910] 1912)

15333. —— **Chamber of commerce.** Facts about the city of Visalia, and a classified business directory... 1943. 20 p.   CViCL

15334. —— —— There's something for everyone in versatile Visalia... Visalia [1956?] folder (11 p.) illus.   CFS

15335. —— **First Methodist Episcopal church.** Diamond jubilee, 1858–1933, souvenir... [Visalia, Times-delta, 1933] 29 p. illus.   CHi

15336. —— —— Golden jubilee souvenir...1858–1908; fiftieth anniversary celebration, Nov. 26–29, 1908. [Visalia, Dockham print. co., 1908] 35 p. illus.   CViCL

15337. —— **Methodist church.** Centennial souvenir...1852–1952. A brief history of the Methodist Episcopal church South, and the First Methodist Episcopal church from 1939 to 1952. [Visalia] 1952. [26] p. illus.
                                         CIIi CViCL

15338. —— **Methodist Episcopal church, South.** Brief history... By Arba W. Frost. 1938. 151 p. Typew. Membership roll: p. 48–151.   CU-B CViCL

15339. Visalia delta. Progress edition. Visalia. 1 v. illus.   C has 1913, 1915–16.

15340. Visalia times-delta, Visalia. ...Anniversaries edition; 80 years of service, Visalia times-delta, Visalia, California, 1859–1939... [Visalia, 1939] 104 p. illus., ports.   C CU-B CViCL

15341. —— Golden century ed., 1859–1959. Times-delta is 100 years old! Visalia, 1959. 1 v. (v.p.) illus., ports., facsims. Material for this edition comp. and written by Joseph E. Doctor.   CLU CU-B CViCL

TUOLUMNE COUNTY
(*Created in 1850*)

COUNTY HISTORIES

15342. Buckbee, Edna Bryan. The saga of old Tuolumne... N.Y., Press of the pioneers, 1935. 526 p. illus.
Available in many California libraries and CtY MWA NN NjN NvU WHi

15343. Greeley, O. F. Tuolumne county, California. [n.p.] c1901. 93 l. illus.   CSfWF-H

15344. Grigsby, Russell C. "From the backwoods of old Tuolumne"... Stockton, Author, 1943. 154 p. illus., ports.
C CBb CHi CL CLU CSalCL CSf CSfWF-H CSmH CSto CU-B CtY NN TxU

15345. A history of Tuolumne county, California. Comp. from the most authentic records. S.F., B.F. Alley, 1882. 509,48 p. ports. Preface signed: H.O.L. [i.e. Herbert O. Lang?]
C CHi CMS COHN CSf CU-B CtY NHi NN WHi

15346. —— Same. Berkeley, 1940. facsim.: 1 v. in 3 (509,48 l.) ports.
CAla CCH CLSM CLU CO CSmH CSoCL CU-B CYcCL

GREAT REGISTER

15347. Tuolumne county. Index to the Great register of the county of Tuolumne. 1866– Place of publication and title vary.
C has 1867, 1871, 1873, 1875, 1877, 1879, 1880 (bien-

nially to)– 1916 (and suppl.), 1918 (and suppl.), 1920, 1922 (and supply.), 1924 (biennially to)– 1962. CHi has 1898. CL has 1872–73, 1877, 1879–80, 1882 (suppl.), 1886, 1888, 1890. CLU has 1875. CSmH has 1867. CU-B has Aug. 1867, Oct. 1872, Aug. 1873, Aug. 1879, Oct. 1880, Nov. 1928, Aug. 1935, May, Aug. 1936, Nov. 1936 (suppl.), Aug. 1938, Nov. 1938 (suppl.), Nov. 1939, May, Aug., Nov. 1940, Aug. 31, 1943, May 1944, June 4, Nov. 5, 1946.

GENERAL REFERENCES

15348. Alta California, inc., comp. and pub. Tuolumne county... Sacramento [1938] 19 l.
                CSmH (microfilm) CU-B

15349. Ashburner, William. Report upon the "App" gold quartz mine... Tuolumne county... S.F., Towne & Bacon, print., 1866. 10 p.   CU-B

15350. Aucutt, Lucille. Life in California mining camps: a type study. [Berkeley, Univ. of Calif., 1931] 170 l. illus., ports., map. Thesis (M.A.)—Univ. of Calif., 1931. "Based primarily on the correspondence of the family of Pardon Smith...in the Southern mines..."— Preface.   CU CU-B

15351. Azevedo, M. Pictural Tuolumne. Made and pub. by M. Azevedo. Tuolumne [n.d.] [26] p. (chiefly illus.)   CU-B

15352. The Banner, Sonora. Centennial edition... Friday, July 15, 1949. Sonora, 1949. 16 p. illus., ports., map.   CU-B

15353. —— ...Fifty years of progress, 1885–1936, Tuolumne county... [Sonora, 1936] 32 p. illus., ports., map.   CHi CSmH CU-B

15354. —— Hetch Hetchy water supply ed. Mar. 19, 1920. Sonora, 1920. [8] p. illus., maps.   CU-B

15355. Booth, Edmund. Edmund Booth (1810–1905) forty-niner; the life story of a deaf pioneer, including portions of his autobiographical notes and gold rush diary, and selections from family letters and reminiscences. Stockton, San Joaquin pioneer and hist. soc., 1953. 72 p. mounted illus., ports.
  C CBb CHi CLod CMerCL CPom CRedCL CRic CSd CSjC CSt CSto CStoC CU-B

15356. Buckeye mining co., Sonora. Buckeye mining company, Sonora, Tuolumne county, California. [n.p.] Banner print. [1915?] [14 p.]   CHi

15357. Burden, Charles H. [Address] delivered Feb. 1, 1921, at Odd fellows banquet room at Chamber of commerce meeting. 9 p. Typew. Reminiscences of Tuolumne county.   C

15358. California. Laws, statutes, etc. Statutory acts for Tuolumne county...as set forth in the statutes of California during the sessions from 1850 to 1870... [Berkeley, 1935] Typew.   CU-B

15359. Chambers, Katherine Lee. Up the trail to Tuolumne. Pub. under the auspices of the Tuolumne county auxiliary to the Women's board of the P.P.I.E. by the Board of supervisors. Sonora, Independent print., c1915. [22] p. illus., map.   CU-B

15360. [Chinese camp mining district] The laws of Chinese camp, relating to the mines and mining claims, 1854. 23 p. Ms. Amended law of Chinese camp district (Nov. 17, 1855) on sheet pinned to leaf after the last manuscript page. Contains also: Mining laws of the Lone Star district of the Table Mountain.   C

15361. City of Sonora tunnel co. ...Organized April 5th, '53, under legislative act of April 14th, '53. Capital stock $200,000 in 2000 shares of one hundred

dollars each. [List of officers, articles of agreement, by-laws, etc.] Sonora, Herald off., 1853. 10 p.   CSmH

15362. Coates, Frank C. The early history of Tuolumne county, California... April 20, 1934. 133 p. photos., map. Thesis (M.A.)—College of the Pacific.   C

15363. [Curtin, J. B.] The mineral output of Tuolumne county since 1849. [Sonora, Independent job press] 1897. 8 p.   CSmH

15364. Davis, Sheldon. On the trail of Mark Twain and Bret Harte in the Mother Lode country. [From Stockton record, July 16, 23, 1921] Cameragraph copies of clippings and cuts from newspaper.   C

15365. Dedication of O'Shaughnessy dam, Hetch Hetchy project, built by the City and county of San Francisco; July seventh, 1923. [n.p., 1923] [4] p. illus.   CHi

15366. Dornberger, Suzette. The struggle for Hetch-Hetchy, 1900–1913. [Berkeley, 1934] 55 l. Thesis (M.A.)—Univ. of Calif., 1934.   CHi CU CU-B

15367. Dressler, Albert, ed. Letters to a pioneer senator; original extracts from the mail bag of a California statesman of the '50's. S.F., Crocker, 1925. 37 p. illus.
  CBb CHi CRic CSf CSfCW CSfWF-H CStmo CStoC

15368. Drummond, Frank J., and Martinez, Tyrrell. ...The popular and legal tribunals of Tuolumne county, 1849–1867...[written] for state of California, Department of natural resources, Division of parks... Berkeley, 1936. 75 l. (History of Calif. mining districts. Columbia ser.; H. E. Rensch, supervisor) Bibliography: leaf 74–75.   CHi CO CU-B

15369. Dunn, Arthur. Tuolumne county. S.F., Sunset mag. pub. co., 1915. 32 p.   CHi CU-B

15370. Gillis, William Robert. Gold rush days with Mark Twain... N.Y., Boni, 1930. 264 p. illus.
  Available in many California libraries and MoS ODa OrU ViU

15371. —— Memories of Mark Twain and Steve Gillis. Sonora, Banner print., c1924. 96 p. illus., ports.
  C CHi CLSU CLU CMerCL CO CRcS CSd CSdS (2d ed.) CSf CSfP CSfWF-H CSmH CU-B

15372. Golden rock co. Report of the engineer on the surveys of the Golden rock company's canal, Big Oak Flat, Tuolumne county. S.F., Agnew & Deffebach print., 1857. 44 p.   CSmH CU-B

15373. [Gray, Harriet (Helman)] A story of Jackass Hill. [Berkeley, 193–?] 73 l. Typew.   CU-B

15374. Hall, William Hammond. Before the Honorable Secretary of the interior of the United States of America, in the matter of the application (ex parte) of the Sierra ditch and water company... for approval of the map of Emigrant lake reservoir site, in Stanislaus forest reserve. Statement of facts...Nov. 22, 1905... Wash., D.C. [1905?] 20 p.   CHi

15375. —— The Eleanor-Cherry creeks. Water and reservoir rights and properties of the Sierra ditch and water co. [1909] 22 typew. sheets.   C

15376. —— In the matter of water storage and utilization on the Tuolumne river, California. To the Hon. James A. Garfield, Secretary of the interior. [S.F., Pernau pub. co., 1907] 11 p.   CHi

15377. Heckendorn, J. Miners' and business men's directory. For the year commencing January 1st, 1856. Embracing a general directory of the citizens of Tuolumne and portions of Calaveras, Stanislaus and San Joaquin

counties. Together with the mining laws of each district, a description of the different camps... By Heckendorn & Wilson. Columbia, Clipper off., 1856. 104 p. illus.
C CHi CSmH CU-B NN

15378. Hodge, Ernest Havilah. Centennial vignettes... [Tuolumne, 1950] 26 p.   CU-B

15379. Hunt, James E. Reminiscences of an old soldier. 183 l. Ms.   C

15380. Immigration association of California. [County scrapbooks] [S.F., 188–?]   C

15381. Jasper, Edward Maxwell. An economic survey of Tuolumne county. [Berkeley, 1933] Thesis (M.A.)—Univ. of Calif., 1933.   CU

15382. —— Tuolumne county, opportunity, recreation, romance. [Issued by order of Board of supervisors, Tuolumne county...photographs by Peter Taras... sketches by Harold Ralph... Sonora, The Banner, 1935] 28 p. illus.   CHi

15383. Kenny, William Robert. History of the Sonora mining region of California, 1848–1860. [Berkeley, 1955] 555 l. illus., maps, diagr. Thesis (Ph.D.)— Univ. of Calif., 1955.   CU CU-B

15384. Kreig, Allan. Last of the 3 foot loggers. San Marino [Pac. railway jl., 1962] 95 p. illus. (part col.) col. maps, facsims. (A Golden West book) Hetch Hetchy & Yosemite valleys railway co. Bibliography: p. [4]
CTurS

15385. McLaughlin, Roberta Evelyn (Holmes) Early development of the Sonora mining region. [Berkeley] 1925. 100 l. illus., maps. Thesis (M.A.)—Univ. of Calif., 1925.   CU CU-B

15386. —— The Southern mines of California; early development of the Sonora mining region. S.F., Grabhorn, 1930. 60 p. illus., maps. Bibliography: p. [57]–60.
C CBb CHi CLU CLgA COr CRc CRedCL CSal CSd CSfWF-H CSmH CStcl CStmo CU-B CViCL

15387. Mazeppa gold mining co. Mazeppa gold mining company of Tuolumne county, California. (Incorporated) Office: Examiner building, S.F., Cal. ... [S.F., n.d.] [4] p. illus., map.   CHi CU-B

15388. Morgan, Ora (Moss) Gold dust; a compilation of the writings of Ora Moss Morgan, Sonora, California, 1933–1950. [L.A.? Frank A. Morgan, 1959] 200 p.
C

15389. Muir, John. Let everyone help to save the famous Hetch-Hetchy Valley and stop the commercial destruction which threatens our national parks. [n.p.] 1909. 22 p. illus.   C

15390. O'Day, Edward Francis. An appreciation of James Wood Coffroth, written for his son James W. Coffroth... S.F., John Henry Nash, 1926. 65 p. port. Reminiscences of Tuolumne county.
C CBb CHi CSd

15391. Odd fellows, Independent order of. Sonora. Bold mountain encampment, no. 4. Constitution and by-laws...instituted March 1, 1855, at Sonora, Tuolumne co., Cal. S.F., C.F. Robbins & co., 1863. 25 p. illus.   C

15392. —— —— **Sonora lodge, no. 10.** Constitution, and rules of order...with an alphabetical list of members. Instituted June 7th, 1853. S.F., W.P. Harrison's print., 1865. 56 p. illus.   C

15393. —— —— —— Same. 1876. 26 p. illus.
C

15394. Perkins, William. Three years in California; William Perkins' journal of life at Sonora, 1849–1852. With an introduction and annotations by Dale L. Morgan and James R. Scobie. Berkeley, Univ. of Calif. press, 1964. 424 p. illus., port., maps, facsim. Published in Spanish in 1937 under title: El Campo de los sonoraenses; tres años de residencia en California, 1849–1851.
CAla CHi CTurS

15395. Pigné-Dupuytren, J. B. Rècit de l' expèdition en Sonore de M. de comte Gaston de Rausset-Boulbon, en 1854... S.F., L. Albin père, et fils, 1854. 16 p.   CSmH

15396. Progressive association, Sonora. Illustrated historical brochure of Tuolumne county, with map showing all patent mines and the mineral belts... S.F., Hicks-Judd co. print., c1901. 93 p. illus., map.
C CHi CLU CSS CSd CSfCSM CSmH CSoCL CU-B UPB

15397. San Joaquin genealogical society. Springfield trip; Round mountain area. 1958. 24 p. maps.
CChiS

15398. Sierra railway co. ...In old Tuolumne. [n.p., 1900?] [25] p.   CSmH CU-B

15399. Springfield tunnel and development co. [Prospectus] [n.p., 1905?] 2 p. fold. map.   CHi

15400. State resources. [Tuolumne county]... v.1, no. 6, April and May, 1890. Oakland, T. C. Howell, 1890. illus. A monthly publication devoted to the interests and development of the Pacific coast mines and mining.   CSf CSmH CSoCL

15401. [Sturz, J. H.] [Report on the Lucien hydraulic mine] [S.F.? 1878?] 12 p.   CL CU-B

15402. Taylor & Swerer, firm. Taylor & Swearer's [!] book, Tuttletown. 286 l. Ms. Account book covering period from March 21, 1853, to Nov. 1854.   C

15403. Thom, Robert. Mining report of Tuolumne county, California... Pub. under the direction of G. W. Price, county commissioner to the P.P.I.E. ... Sonora, Union democrat [1915?] 40 p. illus., map.   CHi

15404. [Thom, *Mrs.* Robert] comp. Memories of the days of old, days of gold, days of '49. [Sonora, Banner print., 1933?] [18] p. illus., map. Issued by the Tuolumne-Calaveras bi-county federation of women's clubs. "Bibliography of Tuolumne and Calaveras counties:" p. [18]
C CHi CLSU CLU CMont CPom CSfCP CSmH CU-B

15405. Tremain, Harry Clyde. The history of Tuolumne county during the gold rush...Stockton, 1947. 269 l. Typcw. Thesis (M.A.)—College of the Pacific, 1947.
CStoC

15406. Tuolumne county. Board of supervisors. Tuolumne county, California. Sonora [1929?] 23 p. illus., map.   CRcS
Other editions followed. CHi (1931, 194–?) CRcS (194–?)

15407. —— **Chamber of commerce.** Annual report. [Sonora]
CHi has 1950–51.

15408. —— —— Gold centennial, Tuolumne county. [Sonora, The Union democrat, 1949] 28 p. illus., maps (part col.) At head of title: 1848–50—1948–50.
CHi CLO CRic

15409. —— —— Tuolumne county, California. [Sonora, 1930] 21 p. illus.   CHi

15410. Tuolumne county water co. Constitution and by-laws... [Columbia, 1851] 1 l. Broadside. CHi

15411. —— Same. S.F., Towne & Bacon, print., 1864. 16 p.   CHi CSmH CU-B

15412. Tuolumne county's mineral wealth...official organ...Golden jubilee executive committee of Tuolumne county... Sonora, 1898. 17 p. illus., ports. On cover, v. 1, no. 1.   C CSto

15413. The Union democrat, Sonora. Tuolumne county, California...issued by the Union democrat under the auspices and direction of the supervisors of Tuolumne county. Sonora, J.A. Van Harlingen & co., c1909. 112 p. illus., map.
C CHi CL CLU CLod CO CRic CSf CSfCSM CSmH CU-B NN

15414. Vernon, James Y. Recreational and water supply in the upper basin of the Tuolumne river, California. [Los Angeles, 1951] Thesis (M.A.)—U.C.L.A., 1951.
CLU

15415. Walker, David H., jr. Tuolumne county... S.F., Sunset mag. homeseekers' bur. [1911] 31 p. illus.
CHi CSdS CU-B

15416. Whipple-Haslam, Mrs. Lee. Early days in California; scenes and events of the '50s as I remember them. Jamestown, Mother lode magnet [c1925] 34 p. illus. (port. group)   C CHi CSf

15417. Woods, Daniel B. Sixteen months at the gold diggings... London, Sampson Low; N.Y., Harper, 1851. 199 p.
Available in many California libraries and CaBViPA ViU

15418. —— —— Index...Joseph Gaer, ed. [S.F., 1935] 26 l. Index no. 18, SERA project 2-FS-132 (3-F2-197) (Calif. literary research) Reproduced from typew. copy.
C C-S CHi CLSU CLU CO CP CRic CSdS CSf CSfU CSmH CStmo CU-B

Columbia

15419. Britton & Rey, pub. [Views of] tremendous conflagration of Columbia, July 10th 1854. [S.F., 1854]
CSmH

15420. California. Dept. of natural resources. Division of beaches and parks. Master plan report for the development of Columbia historic state park, Tuolumne county, California. Prepared by Bliss & Hurt, Trudell & Berger, architects. S.F., 1950. 16 l. map, tables. Mimeo.   CHi CL CSdS CU-B

15421. —— —— —— Recommendations for the ultimate development of Columbia historic state park. S.F., 1950. l. 17–24. Mimeo.   CHi

15422. Columbia. First Presbyterian church. Centennial memories. "The church of the '49'ers" [n.p., 1955] 15 p.   CHi

15423. Columbia engine company, no. 2. Constitution and by-laws of Columbia engine company, no. 2. Adopted, Dec. 6th, 1859. Columbia, The Courier off., 1860. 8 p.   C CSmH

15424. Columbia gulch fluming co. Constitution and by-laws... Columbia, Print. at the Clipper off., 1856. 14 p.   CHi CSmH

15425. Columbia Hibernian benevolent society, no. 1. Constitution; by-laws and regulations... Established July 1857. S.F., O'Meara & Painter, 1858. 16 p.
C

15426. Columbia historical research project. ... Plans and elevations [of] buildings in Columbia, Calif.; [manuscript drawings] 48 plans.   CU-B

15427. Columbia mining district, California. Laws, statutes, etc. Columbia mining laws. [n.p., 1853?] Broadside.   CHi CSmH CU-B

15428. Columbia times, Columbia. The Columbia times carrier's address. For New Year's day, 1861... [Columbia, 1861. S.F.? 1945] Broadside. Facsim.
CHi CLU CSfWF-H CSmH CU-B

15429. Dane, George Ezra, and Dane, Beatrice J. Ghost town, wherein is told much that is wonderful, laughable, and tragic... about life during the gold rush and later in the town of Columbia on California's Mother Lode... N.Y., Knopf, 1941. 311 p. illus. Bibliography: p. 309-310.
Available in many California libraries and MiD MoSHi ODa OU UHi

15430. —— Same. N.Y., Tudor pub. co., 1948. 311 p. illus.   CBb CLgA CSS CStmo

15431. Early, Raymond. Columbia. S.F., Fearon pub. [1957] [80] p. illus., ports., maps.
Available in many California libraries and CoD NN

15432. Gray, Fred. California's fabulous century, an historical cavalcade. Revised as of August 19, 1950. [n.p., 1950] 61 l. Reproduced from typew. copy. Revised from working script "A golden century" (1948?) 56 l.   C

15433. Rensch, Hero Eugene. ...Columbia, a gold camp of old Tuolumne; her rise and decline... For state of California, Department of natural resources, Division of parks. Berkeley, 1936. 176 l. (History of mining districts of Calif. Columbia ser.) Mimeo.
C CHi CSfWF-H CSmH CU-B

15434. The Union democrat. Centennial edition ...honoring California's centennial celebration, 1849–1949, at Columbia state park, California, July 15, 16, 17, 1949; 100 years of progress... [Sonora] 1949. 24 p. illus., ports., map.   CU-B

15435. U.S. Work projects administration, California. Descriptive index to items referring to the mining town of Columbia, California, 1851–1870, in Tuolumne county newspapers... S.F., 1938. 157 l. Typew. CU-B

15436. [Weston, Otheto] Columbia, "gem of the southern mines"; a guide to the historic buildings, by Otheto [pseud.] [Coloma] Otheto's studios [n.d.] 16 p. illus.   CHi

15437. —— The story and sketches of Columbia, by Otheto [pseud.] [Columbia, Otheto's studios, c1945] [25] p. illus.   CHi CSfWF-H CTurS CU-B

15438. —— The story of Columbia; its rise and fall. [Columbia, Otheto's studios, 19—?] 17 p. illus.
CU-B

15439. Wilson, Francis W. ...A preliminary architectural study of the old mining town of Columbia... Berkeley, 1936. 52 l.   CSfWF-H CU-B

VENTURA COUNTY
(Organized in 1873 from portion of Santa Barbara county)

COUNTY HISTORIES

15440. Historical records survey. California. Ventura county (Ventura) ... L.A., So. Calif. hist. records survey project, 1940. 155 p. (Inventory of the county archives of California)   C CVtCL

15441. Ritter, Elizabeth Kreisher. History of Ventura county, state of California; its people and its resources. Edwin M. Sheridan, editor emeritus... Mary

Jane Windsor, biographical editor... [L.A.?] Harold McLean Meier, 1940. 403 p. illus., ports.
CLU CVtCL

15442. Sheridan, Solomon Neill. History of Ventura county, California. Chicago, Clarke, 1926. 2 v. illus., ports. v.2: Biographical.
C CL CLU CSf CSmH CVtCL CtY WHi

Great Register

15443. Ventura county. Index to the Great register of the county of Ventura. 1873– Place of publication and title vary.
C has 1875, 1877, 1879, 1880, 1882, 1886, 1888, 1890, 1898, 1902 (biennially to)– 1962. CL has 1873, 1877 (suppl.), 1879 (suppl.), 1880, 1882 (suppl.), 1884 (biennially to)– 1890. CLU has 1875. CSmH has 1879, 1880 (suppl.), 1882. CU-B has 1873, Apr. 1879, Apr. 1879 (suppl.), Aug. 1879 (suppl.), 1882, 1882 (suppl.), 1892, 1912, 1914.

Directories

15444. 1898/99. California directory co., pub. Homeseekers' and tourists' guide, and Ventura county directory. Comp. by Peter Milliken. Ventura, 1898. illus.
CHi

15445. 1908/09– Polk, R. L. & co., pub. Ventura county directory. L.A., 1908– Publisher varies: 1908/09–1951/52 Los Angeles directory co. Content varies.
C has 1918–19, 1926. CHi has 1912/13, 1916/17, 1934, 1946, 1948/49, 1951/52, 1956–61. CL has 1910/11, 1912/13, 1916/17, 1918/19, 1921/22, 1926, 1928, 1930/31, 1937, 1941/42, 1946, 1951/52, 1956, 1960. CLU has 1908/09.

Ventura

15446. 1953– Polk, R. L. & co., pub. Polk's Ventura city directory, including Ojai, Casitas Springs, Foster Park, Meiners Oaks, Montalvo, Oak View and Saticoy. Content varies: 1953 Ventura city, Oxnard and Port Hueneme. Preceded by Polk's Ventura county directory.
CHi has 1953, 1962. CL has 1953.

General References

15447. Alexander, W. E., comp. and pub. Historical atlas of Ventura county, California... [1918?] 14, 37 p. illus., maps. Includes *History of Ventura county*, by E. M. Sheridan.
CL CVtCL

15448. Bard oil and asphalt co. Bard oil and asphalt company, incorporated under the laws of California. [Official prospectus] L.A. [1900?] [5] p. illus., map.
CU-B

15449. Blanchard, Sarah Eliot. Memories of a child's early California days. [L.A., Ward Ritchie] 1961. 118 p. illus., ports.
CHi

15450. California petroleum co., New York. Report of the directors...to the stockholders, at the annual meeting held at Philadelphia, March 14, 1866. N.Y., Francis & Loutrel, print., 1866. 14 l. A reproduction of the original report.
CHi CLO

15451. California taxpayers' association, inc. ... Santa Paula city report... [L.A.] 1927. 49 p.
C CU-B

15452. Chittenden, Newton H. Homes, health and pleasure in southern California... Ventura county ed. ... San Buenaventura, 1883. 45 p.
CU-B

15453. Clarke, Robert M. Narrative of a native... L.A., Times-mirror co. [c1936] 160 p. illus. Deals with Santa Paula principally but touches on the other towns along the Santa Clara R.: Piru, Fillmore, Bardsdale & Ventura.
CBb CHi CL CLU CO CSfWF-H CSmH CU-B CVtCL

15454. Cleland, Robert Glass. The place called Sespe; the history of a California ranch... [Chicago] Priv. print., 1940. 120 p. map.
Available in many California libraries and NN

15455. —— Same. [Alhambra, Press of C.F. Braun, 1953] 120 p. map. facsim.
CHi CLO CLU CPom CStmo

15456. —— Same. San Marino, Huntington Lib., 1957. 120 p. map. facsim.
C CSdS CSf CSmat CStoC NHi NIC

15457. [Conckling, Harold] ...Ventura county investigation, 1933. Sacramento, State print. off., 1934. 244 p. illus.
CLSU CLU

15458. Daily, Wendell P. Album of memories... Camarillo, 1946. 254 p. illus., port.
CLU CSmH CVtCL

15459. Eldridge, George Homans, and Arnold, Ralph. ...Santa Clara valley, Puente Hills and Los Angeles oil districts, southern Calif. ... Wash., D.C., Govt. print. off., 1907. 266 p. illus., maps. (U.S. Geol. survey. Bul. no. 309)
CChiS CL CLS CLSU CLU CO CSdS CSfCSM CSmH CVtCL

15460. Gregor, Howard F. Changing agricultural patterns in the Oxnard area of southern California. [L.A.] 1950. Thesis (Ph.D.)—U.C.L.A., 1950. CLU

15461. Harrington, Robert E. Early days in Simi valley. Simi [Priv. print.] 1961. 119 p. illus., pl.
CHi CLSM

15462. Hufford, David Andrew. The real Ramona of Helen Hunt Jackson's famous novel. L.A., D.A. Hufford & co. [1900]
CStclU

15463. Immigration association of California. [County scrapbooks] [S.F., 188–?] C

15464. James, George Wharton. Through Ramona's country... Bost., Little [1908] 406 p. illus., ports.
Available in many California libraries and CaBViPA MiD OrU ViU

15465. —— Same. 1913. 406 p.   CHi CPs OU

15466. Kelly, John L. Description of a trip to St. Nicholas island in the year 1897. Typew.   CSd

15467. Lantz, Charles, vs. Broome, Thornhill Francis. Supreme court of the United States. October term, 1930. No. 992. Charles Lantz, petitioner, vs. Thornhill Francis Broome on petition for writ of certiorari to the Supreme court of the state of California. [Transcript of record] Filed May 21, 1931. (35,914) [Wash., D.C., Judd & Detweiler, print., 1931] 519 p. pl. (part fold.) maps (part fold.) Land suit, Rancho Guadalasca, Ventura county.   CLU

15468. LeResche, John Henry. The lower Ventura river valley. [L.A.] 1951. Thesis (M.A.)—U.C.L.A., 1951.   CLU

15469. Lonsdale, Richard E. Water problems of the Simi valley, Calif. [L.A.] 1953. Thesis (M.A.)— U.C.L.A., 1953.   CLU

15470. Lummis, Charles Fletcher. The home of Ramona. Photographs of Camulos, the fine old Spanish estate described by Mrs. Helen Hunt Jackson as the home of "Ramona." L.A., C.F. Lummis & co., c1887. [14] l. illus.
CHi CL CVtCL

15471. Lyon, Belle G. Early developments in Matilija canyon at Lyon's spring. 1st ed. [n.p., 1939] 59 l. Typew.   C

15472. Mott, Emma (Drown) ed. Legends and lore of the long ago (Ventura county, California) contributed by club women of Ventura county... L.A., Wetzel pub. co., 1929. 223 p. illus., ports.
C CBb CHi CL CLSU CLU CLob CO CSf CSmH CStmo CU-B CVtCL

15473. Ortega, E. C. Old Ortega adobe, history by a scion of the Ortega family. In letter dated Feb. 14, 1925, a copy of which is in Pioneer museum, Ventura.   CVtP

15474. Oxnard courier. Progress edition. [Oxnard]   C has 1912, 1915.

15475. Pen pictures of Ventura county, California. Its beauties, resources, and capacities. San Buenaventura, Free press print. off., 1880. 26 p.
CHi CLSM CU-B NN

15476. Robinson, William Wilcox. Story of Ventura county. [L.A.] Title insurance and trust co. [1955] 48 p. illus., map.
Available in many California libraries and MWA NbHi

15477. Russell, J. H. Cattle on the Conejo. [L.A.] W. Ritchie press, 1957. 135 p. illus., ports., map (on lining papers)
C CBb CBea CHi CL CLSM CLob CO CP CSd CStmo CU-B CVtCL CVtV CWhC UPB

15478. Santa Paula. First Presbyterian church. Sixty-fifth anniversary 1883–1948. [n.p., Brown & De-Haven] 1948. 33 p. illus., ports.   CHi

15479. Santa Paula chronicle. Greater Ventura county... Santa Paula, October, 1921. 64 p. illus.
C CU-B

15480. Security first national bank, Los Angeles. Research department. The growth and economic stature of Ventura county, 1960. [L.A.] 1960. 96 p.   CHi

15481. Sharp, James M. Brief account of the experiences of James Meikle Sharp. [n.p.] Author, 1931.
CHi CVtCL

15482. Sheridan, Edwin M. Historic spots of Ventura county. Ms. in Pioneer museum, Ventura.   CVtP

15483. —— Historical writings. [n.p., n.d.] 2 v.
CVtCL

15484. —— [Landmarks of Ventura county. n.p., 1925] 11 l. Typew.   C

15485. —— [Reminiscences of Ventura county. n.p., n.d.] 177 l. illus. Typew.   C

15486. —— Ventura county historic landmarks. clippings.   CVtCL

15487. Sheridan, Solomon Neill. Ventura county ... [S.F.? Sunset mag. homeseekers' bur. c1909?] 48 p. illus.   CHi CL CU-B

15488. Silliman, Benjamin. A description of the recently discovered petroleum region in California, with a report on the same. N.Y., Francis & Loutrel, 1864. 23 p. fold. chart. Deals with "the ranch of Ojai, near Buenaventura, in Santa Barbara county" now in Ventura county.
CHi CLU CVtCL (report only)

15489. —— Same. 1865. 24 p.
CHi CSfSO (photostat)

15490. Stuart, James Ferguson. Appeal and argument in survey of Rancho Sespe. S.F., Bacon & co., 1871. 44 p.   CLU

15491. —— Argument on the survey of the Rancho "Rio de Santa Clara"... Wash., D.C., McGill & With-erow, 1872. 30 p. Concerning the case of Valentine Cota et al. vs. the United States.   C CLU CStbS

15492. Teague, Charles Collins. Fifty years a rancher; the recollections of half a century devoted to the citrus and walnut industries of California and to furthering the cooperative movement in agriculture. L.A. [Ward Ritchie for the Calif. fruit growers exchange]
CBb CFS CHi CLO CLU CMon COnC CSd CVtCL CVtV

15493. Thille, Grace (Sharp) Day before yesterday. Santa Paula, 1952. 160 p. illus., ports.
CU-B CVtCL

15494. Thomas, William L. Geographical land classification in Las Posas valley, Ventura county, California. [L.A.] 1948. Thesis (M.A.)—U.C.L.A., 1948.
CLU

15495. Ventura county. Chamber of commerce. Ventura county, your opportunity in California. Ventura [1923?] 24 p. illus., map.   CRcS

15496. —— **Citizens.** To the Senate and House of representatives of the United States. Petition...for harbor improvement. January, 1888. [n.p., 1888] 8 p.
CSmH

15497. —— **Public schools.** Public school directory, 1906–7. [n.p., 1906] [15] p.   CHi

15498. Ventura county, California; all year. [n.p., 1930] [20] p. illus., map.   CHi

15499. Ventura county, California, its resources... San Buenaventura, Free press print. house, 1885. 39 p.
CL CLSM CSmH CU-B MWA

15500. Ventura county pioneer association. A tribute to the pioneers of Ventura county and to those who wish to do them honor. [Ventura, Art bronze products, 1936] [8] p. illus. On cover: "Society of Ventura county pioneers, Sept. 19, 1891."   C

15501. Ventura county star. Classified directory, containing the names, addresses and telephone numbers of representative manufacturing, business and professional interests, and institutions of Ventura and vicinity. [Ventura, 1926–1930]
C has 1926, 1930.

15502. Ventura county tourist & travel association. Ventura county California, historical and scenic points of interest on the mission trails U.S. highway 101 and the Roosevelt highway.   CVtV

15503. Ventura development association, pub. Ventura county... [S.F., Bancroft co., 1888?] 48 p.
CSmH CU-B

15504. —— ...Ventura county, resources... San Buenaventura [188–?] 11 p. illus., map.   CU-B

15505. Wilson, Wilma. "They call them camisoles." L.A., Lymanhouse [c1940] 271 p. illus.   C CSd

15506. Woolley, G. W. An exposition of facts connected with the survey and patent of the "Rio de Santa Clara" land grant, addressed to Congress... Wash., D.C., R.S. Bayne, 1876. 20 p. map.   NHi

Ojai Valley

15507. Bjelland, Earl G. The Ojai valley: a geographic study. [L.A.] 1951. Thesis (M.A.)—U.C.L.A., 1951.   CLU

15508. Boyle, Louis Morris. Orchid town is America's foremost Cymbidium orchid grower, El Rancho Rinconada, Ojai, California. Ojai, c1946. [101] p. illus. (part col.), maps.   C

15509. —— Out west: growing Cymbidium orchids and other flowers; the story of El Rancho Rinconada. [1st ed. L.A., Times-mirror press, 1952] 526 p. illus. (part col.), ports.   C CLU CSalCL

15510. Bristol, Walter W. Story of Ojai valley; an intimate account... Ojai, Ojai pub. co. [1946?] 158 p. front.   C CHi CLU CSf CSmH CVtCL

15511. Gerard, Frank R. J. The Ojai valley, Ventura county... Ojai, Ojai pub. co., 1927. 48 p. illus.   C CHi CL CSmH CU-B

15512. Gulliver, Harold G. Arbolada in the Ojai valley of southern California—the tale of a town reborn. [Garden City, N.Y., 1924] 20 p.   NN

15513. Makepeace, LeRoy McKim. Sherman Thacher and his school. Published for the Thacher school. New Haven, Yale univ. press, 1941. 205 p. illus., ports.   C CHi

15514. Ojai. Presbyterian church. Seventy-fifth anniversary, 1877–1952. [Programme] [Ojai, 1952] [4] p. illus.   CHi

15515. Ojai valley 50th anniversary invitational tennis tournament, April 28, 29, 30, 1949. [Ojai? 1949] [20] p. illus., map.   CHi

15516. The Thacher school. [Annual report] 1941–42.   CHi

15517. —— ...Directory. 1st– [1947?– n.p.] 1947–
CHi has 1947, 1954.

15518. —— New plans for the Thacher school. [Ojai? 1947] 16 p.   CHi

15519. —— [Scrapbook. Ojai? 1949?] [24] p. illus.   CHi

15520. —— The Thacher school semicentennial addresses... Ojai, 1939. 92 p.   CSmH

15521. —— Views, Thacher school and round about the Ojai valley, 1890 to 1912. [S.F., 1912] [32] p. illus.   CHi

15522. Woolman, Arthur Erwin. The Ojai valley, gateway to health and happiness. Sponsored by Marrone enterprises, Charles Marrone. Upper Ojai, Kuehl press, c1956. 77 p. illus.   CLom CLU CVtCL

Ventura

15523. Engelhardt, Zephyrin, *Father.* ...San Buenaventura, the mission by the sea... Santa Barbara, Mission Santa Barbara, 1930. 166 p. illus., ports., map.
Available in many California libraries and CaBViPA
NN

15524. Hobson, Edith May. The romantic history of San Buenaventura. [L.A., Press of J.F. McElheney, n.d.] 15 p. Contains also: Francis, Myrtle Shepherd. Reminiscences of old Ventura, p. 9–15.   C CHi

15525. Houston, Neil T. An economic study of the Ventura river municipal water district, by Neil T. Houston [and] William Bredo... SRI Project 1176. Menlo Park, Stanford research inst., 1955. 1 v. (v.p.) map, tables, plan.   C

15526. San Buenaventura mission. The celebration of the 175th anniversary of the founding of San Buenaventura mission and its restoration on March 31, 1957. [Ventura, Ventura print. and offset co., 1957] [20] p. illus., ports.   C CHi CP CU-B

15527. —— Sesquicentennial, 1782–1932. [8] p. illus., port., facsim.   C

15528. Security-first national bank. Early Ventura (San Buenaventura) a pictorial history of San Buenaventura from its early mission days to the turn of the century. 28 p. illus.   CHi CVtV

15529. Senán, José. The letters of José Senán, O. F. M., Mission San Buenaventura, 1796–1823. Trans. by Paul D. Nathan and ed. by Lesley Byrd Simpson. [S.F.] Pub. for The Ventura county hist. soc. by John Howell, 1962. 175 p. illus., fold. map.   CHi

15530. Sheridan, Edwin M. [History of Ventura and vicinity, n.p., 1924?] 15 l. Typew. "Read by E. M. Sheridan at a meeting of College women May 10, 1924."   C

15531. —— Old Olivas adobe, rare landmark of the early days; the building and the builder. [Ventura] Ventura daily post [1922] 14 l. illus.   CLSM

15532. Steinbach, Rudolph, vs. Norwood, Thomas, et al. In the Supreme court of the state of California. Rudolph Steinbach et als., plaintiffs and respondents, vs. Thomas Norwood et als., defendants and appellants ... [S.F., 1881] 3 pts. in 1 v. Ex-mission San Buenaventura land suit.   CLU

15533. Ventura. Charters, ordinances, etc. The town charter, acts, and ordinances in force (of a general nature) in the town of San Buenaventura. Compiled, codified and adopted by the Honorable, the Board of trustees on the 7th day of July, 1876. San Buenaventura, Shepherd & Sheridan, print., 1876. 26 p.   CLSM

YOLO COUNTY
(*Created in 1850*)

County Histories

15534. Amos, Vanna Mae. A historical account of people, resources and points of interest in early Yolo county for teacher use in enriching social studies. Sacramento [1957] 295 p. Project (M.A.) — Sacramento state college, 1957.   CSS

15535. [Coil, Nelle S.; McHugh, Tom; and others] History of Yolo county, California, its resources and its people... Woodland, 1940. 573 p. illus., ports. 2 pts. in 1. Part 1: Historical. Part 2: Biographical. "The biographical section of this volume was prepared by an independent staff of writers."—Nelle S. Coil in Foreword. William Ogburn Russell, editor in chief.
C CHi CL CLU CO CS CSt CU-A CU-B CWoY

15536. Gregory, Thomas Jefferson, and others. History of Yolo county, California, with biographical sketches... L.A., Historic record co., 1913. 889 p.
C CCH CF CL CLCM CLCo CLO CLU CS CSS CSf CSmH CSt CU-A CU-B CYcCL NN

15537. The illustrated atlas and history of Yolo county, Cal. containing a history of California from 1513 to 1850, a history of Yolo county from 1825 to 1880, with ...portraits of well-known citizens, and the official county map. S.F., De Pue & co., 1879. 105 p. illus., ports., maps. History of California by Frank T. Gilbert.
C CHi CO CSf CSmH CU-A CU-B CWoY CtY

Great Register

15538. Yolo county. Index to the Great register of the county of Yolo. 1866– Place of publication and title vary.
C has 1867, 1871–73, 1875, 1877–79, 1880, 1882, 1886 (biennially to)– 1962. CL has 1872–73, 1877, 1879 (suppl.), 1880, 1882, 1886, 1888, 1890. CLU has 1875. CSmH has 1867. CU-A has 2nd precinct, 1934–46. CU-B has 1867, 1872–73, 1879, 1879 (suppl.)

DIRECTORIES

15539. 1878/79. McKenney, L. M. & co., pub.
McKenney's district directory for 1878–9 of Yolo, Solano, Napa, Lake, Marin and Sonoma counties. With sketch of cities and towns. S.F., 1878–9.

                    C CSmH CU-B

15540. 1893/94. Rentschler, G. W., comp. Directory of Yolo, Solano, Sutter, Butte, Colusa, Glenn, Placer, Nevada, Yuba, Tehama [Sacramento] and Shasta counties. Supplemented by business directory of S.F., Oakland, Alameda and Berkeley. [S.F.] S.F. directory co., 1893. 629, 240 p.   C CS

15541. 1914. Harrison, L. W., comp. Yolo county residence and business directory... [Woodland, Mail press, 1914] 108 p.   C

15542. 1939– Polk, R. L. & co., pub. Polk's Woodland city directory. L.A., 1939–

C has 1939. CHi has 1939, 1948, 1951, 1953, 1957, 1960. CL has 1939, 1953, 1956–57.

GENERAL REFERENCES

15543. California. University. Davis campus. [Catalog] 1913– to date   CL

15544. Coward, W. M. Yolo county land review and business directory. Woodland, Democrat power press, 1888. 64 p.   CU-B

15545. Dunn, Arthur. Yolo county, California. Issued by Sunset mag. homeseekers' bur., San Francisco, Calif., for the Yolo county, California, Exposition commission, by order of the Yolo county Bd. of supervisors. [S.F., 1915?] 32 p. illus. "Souvenir edition. Panama-Pacific international exposition."
CAla CChiS CHi CLU CSj CSmH CU-A CU-B

15546. Durst, David M. Physiographic features of Cache creek in Yolo county. [Berkeley, 1915] Thesis (M.A.)—Univ. of Calif., 1915.   CU

15547. Edwards, Philip L. Speech of P. L. Edwards, esq., made before the Democratic state convention, on the 23d July, 1861. [Knights Landing, Knights Landing news print., 1861] 8 p.   CU-B

15548. [Ferris, John W.] Proposed reclamation of the "Yolo basin" in Yolo and Solano counties, California. [n.p., 190–?] 11[4] p. fold. map.   CU-B

15549. Haviland and Tibbetts, San Francisco. Report on Knight's Landing cut project to the Knight's Landing ridge committee. S.F., Haviland and Tibbetts, 1912. 111 p. tables, maps (part fold.), diagrs.   C

15550. Hesperian college, Woodland. ...Annual catalogue of the officers and students... 1860/61–63, 1866/69, 1873/74. Sacramento, 1862–74. 5 v.   CU-B

15551. [Kilgour, Byron] Country life in the city ...West Sacramento, California. [S.F., Print. by Taylor, Nash & Taylor, c1913] [38] p. illus.   CU-A CU-B

15552. The Mail of Woodland. Annual illustrated Mail. [Feb. 28, 1891] Woodland [1891] 16 p. illus., ports.   CU-B

15553. More, Rosemary MacDonald. The influence of water-rights litigation upon irrigation farming in Yolo county, California. [Berkeley, 1960] Thesis (M.A.)—Univ. of Calif., 1960.   CU

15554. Odd fellows, Independent order of California. Capay lodge, no. 230. Constitution, by-laws, rules of order, etc. ...instituted at Langville, Yolo county, March 18, 1875. S.F., New age, 1875. 50 p.   CHi

15555. Peck, W. Harold. California national guard;

brief history of Woodland unit, 1863–1951. [Woodland] The Record of Yolo county, 1951. 30 [3] p.   CHi

15556. Sacramento valley reclamation co. Tule lands of Sacramento valley in Yolo and Colusa counties, California. December, 1872. Louisville, Ky., John P. Morton & co., 1872. 24 p.   C CU-B

15557. Shields, Peter J. The birth of an institution, the agricultural college at Davis. [Sacramento? 1954] 38 p.   C CU-B

15558. Sinclair, R. D. Yolo county, California. [Woodland? Yolo county board of trade, 1913?] folder (30 p.) illus.   CHi CRcS CU-B

15559. Sprague, C. P., and Atwell, H. W., comp. & pub. The Western shore gazetteer and commercial directory...Yolo county... Woodland [1870] 602 p.
C CHi CL CLU CO CSfCSM CSmH CU-A NHi NN

15560. United Spanish war veterans. Woodland. Kenzie camp, no. 11. By-laws... [n.p.] Mail print. [1905] 7[1] p.   CHi

15561. [West Sacramento weekly reader] Eastern Yolo history: Broderick, West Sacramento, Bryte. [West Sacramento, 1941] 23 l. illus. Mimeo.   C

15562. Western co-operative colonization and improvement co. History and description of the Tancred colony. [n.p., n.d.] 16 p. illus.   CU-B

15563. Winters. Board of trade. Winters, California, a famous early fruit district. [Winters, 1902] 24 p. illus.   CHi CU-B

15564. Woodland. Chamber of commerce. Resources of Yolo county, California. [Woodland, Democrat press, 1910?] 52 p. illus.   CHi CU-B

15565. —— —— Same. [1938] 16 p.   CRcS

15566. —— —— Yolo county. [Woodland, 1940?] 16 p. Mimeo.   CHi

15567. —— Methodist church. History of the Methodist church, Second and North streets, Woodland, Calif. By W. Harold Peck. Centennial of Methodism in Yolo county... [Woodland?] c1952. 21 l. illus., ports. Reproduced from typew. copy.   C CHi

15568. Woodland community development study. Fields of flowers and forests of firs; a history of the Woodland community, 1850–1958. [Woodland, 1958] 238 p.   CHi

15569. Woodland daily democrat. Yolo county exposition number... Woodland, March 26, 1915. 40 p. illus.   C

15570. —— Yolo in word & picture. Woodland, 1920. 96 p. illus.   C CU-A CU-B CWoY

15571. Yolo county. Board of trade. Yolo, the safe county; "anything that grows anywhere, grows everywhere in —Yolo county." Woodland [1922] [7] p. illus., map.   CHi CRcS

15572. —— Board of trade and immigration association. Yolo county, California. Resources, advantages and prospects... Woodland, Main steam power print., 1887. 91 [4] p. illus., map. On cover: Edited by J. I. McConnell.   C CSmH CU-B

15573. Yolo county association opposed to secret societies. Record book, Dec. 12, 1878–1881. [Woodland, 1878–1892] 32 p. Ms.   C

15574. Yolo farmers' institute, Woodland. [Minutes of the meetings, Feb. 10, 1900–Mar. 24, 1906] 149 p. Ms.   CU-B

15575. —— Register. [Jan. 25, 1901–Mar. 24, 1906] 101 p. Ms.   CU-B

15576. Yolo water and power co. vs. Edmands, William O., et al. ...Yolo water and power company, a corporation, plaintiff and appellant, vs. William O. Edmands, Harriet Lee Hammond, as executrix of the last will and testament of Charles Mifflin Hammond, deceased, and Harriet Lee Hammond, defendants and respondents. Appellant's opening brief. Theodore A. Bell ...Arthur C. Huston, W. P. Thomas, attorneys for appellant... [n.p., 1919] 229 p.   CU-B

YUBA COUNTY
(*Created in 1850*)

COUNTY HISTORIES

15577. [Chamberlain, William Henry, and Wells, Harry Laurenz] History of Yuba county, California... Oakland, Thompson & West, 1879. 150 p. illus., maps.
C CCH CHi CL CLSU CLU CMary CO CSS CSf CSfCP CSfMI CSmH CU-B MiD-B MoSHi NN

15578. Delay, Peter Joseph. History of Yuba and Sutter counties, Calif., with biographical sketches... L.A., Historic record co., 1924. 1328 p. illus., ports.
C CBb CCH CHi CL CLO CLU CMary CO CS CSS CSf CSmH CSt CStoC CU-B CYcCL MWA

GREAT REGISTER

15579. Yuba county. Index to the Great register of the county of Yuba. 1866– Place of publication and title vary.
C has 1867–69, 1871–73, 1875–77, 1879–80, 1882, 1884, 1888 (biennially to)– 1896, 1900, 1902, 1904, 1908 (biennially to)– 1962. CL has 1867, 1868–69 (suppls.), 1872–73, 1876, 1877 (suppl.), 1879–80, 1882 (biennially to)– 1890. CLU has 1875. CSmH has 1880. CU-B has 1867, 1868 (suppl.), 1872–73, 1879–80, 1900–38, Aug., Nov. 1940.

DIRECTORIES

15580. 1881–1884/85. McKenney, L. M. & co., pub. County directory of Yuba, Sutter, Colusa, Butte and Tehama counties... Oakland, 1881–84.
C has 1881, 1884/85. CHi has 1884/85. CSmH has 1884/85. CYcCL has 1884/85.

15581. 1903/04. Appeal publishing co., pub. Yuba county directory and handy book of reference... Marysville, 1904.   C CU-B

Marysville

15582. 1853. Hale & Emory's Marysville city directory. August, 1853. First publication. Marysville, Marysville herald off., 1853. "The first ever published."
C CHi CMary CSmH CU-B NHi NN

15583. 1855. Colville, Samuel, comp. Colville's Marysville directory for the year commencing November 1, 1855...together with a historical sketch of Marysville. S.F., Monson & Valentine, 1855.
C CHi CLU CMary CSmH CU-B NHi

15584. 1856. Amy, George Sturtevant, and Amy, O., comp. G. and O. Amy's Marysville directory for the year commencing November 1, 1856...together with an historical sketch of Marysville... S.F., Commercial bk. & job steam print., 1856.
C CHi (photocopy) CMary CSmH CU-B

15585. 1858. Smith, Mix and Amy, G., comp. Amy's Marysville directory, for the year commencing June 1858 ...prefaced by a history of the county of Yuba... Marysville, Daily news bk. & job off., 1858.
C CHi (photocopy) CMary CSfCP CSmH CU-B

15586. 1861. Brown, W. C., pub. Brown's Marysville directory for the year commencing March, 1861... prefaced by historical sketches of industrial enterprises, benevolent and charitable associations, etc. Marysville, Daily Calif. express, 1861. CHi CMary CSmH CU-B

15587. 1870. Kelley, John G., comp. The Marysville, Yuba City and Colusa directory for the year commencing August 1, 1870... Also, sketches of Marysville and neighboring towns... First year of publication... [Sacramento, Crocker, 1870]   CHi CMary

15588. 1894/95. Corry, Trevor, comp. Marysville directory and handy book of reference... [Marysville] Appeal pub. co., 1895.   CMary

15589. 1897–98. Morrissey, J. M., comp. Directory of Marysville and Yuba City for 1897–98.   C

15590. 1910/11. Polk-Husted directory co., pub. City directory of Marysville and Yuba City. Marysville, 1911.   C CMary

15591. 1922–1932. McNeel directory co., pub. Marysville and Yuba City directory... Stockton, 1922–1932.
C has 1925, 1929, 1931–32. CHi has 1923. CMary has 1922–25, 1927, 1929, 1931–32. CYcCL has 1922–25, 1927, 1929.

15592. 1934– Polk, R. L. & co., pub. Polk's Marysville and Yuba City...directory including Yuba and Sutter counties. L.A., 1934–
C has 1950. CHi has 1940, 1946/47, 1950, 1954–55, 1957–58. CL has 1938, 1940, 1942, 1953–54, 1957–58. CMary has 1934, 1936, 1938, 1940, 1942, 1944, 1946, 1948, 1950, 1953–55, 1957–59. CSmH has 1938. CU-B has 1938, 1948–49, 1953–55, 1957–58. CYcCL has 1934, 1936, 1938, 1940, 1942, 1944, 1946–47, 1948–49, 1954–55, 1957–59.

GENERAL REFERENCES

15593. Adams, Dorothy Quincy. Life in the mining camps of the Yuba river valley... [Berkeley, 1931] 121 l. Thesis (M.A.)—Univ. of Calif., 1931.
CChiS (microfilm) CU CU-B

15594. Alta California, inc. Yuba county, California, "in the peach bowl of the world"; a general and historical summary... Sacramento [1938] 18 l.   CU-B

15595. Ashburner, William. Report on James O'Brien's mining property situated in Smartsville, Yuba co., Cal. S.F., E. Bosqui & co., print., 1868. 18 p.
CHi CSmH CU-B

15596. [California vs. Jefferds, William M.] In the Supreme court of the state of California. The people of the state of California, on the relation of C. E. Stone, plaintiff and appellant, vs. William M. Jefferds [et als.] defendants and respondents. Transcript on appeal. S.F., 1897. 78 p.   CHi

15597. Clyde, George Dewey. A detailed study of the water supply of the Yuba river. [Berkeley, 1923] Thesis (M.S.)—Univ. of Calif., 1923.   CU

15598. Conklin, Howard E., and Wertheimer, Ralph B. The possibilities of rural zoning in the Sierra Nevada foothills; a study in the livestock-forest area of Yuba county, California. Berkeley, Calif. agric. experiment station, 1942. 59 p. illus., maps.   CO

15599. De Long, Charles E. Diary of Charles E.

De Long, 1854– [1862] [384] l. Typew. Contains also typewritten copies of letters of Charles E. De Long.   C

15600. Ellis, William Turner. Memories, my seventy-two years in the romantic county of Yuba, California ... Eugene, Ore., Univ. of Oregon, Print. by J.H. Nash, 1939. 308 p. illus., ports.
CBb CBev CHi CL CLSU CLU CNF CO CRic CSS CSdS CSf CSjC CSmH CStcrCL CStrJC CU-B CYcCL OrU UPB

15601. —— The questionable ethics of power companies in general and of the Pacific gas & electric company in particular...an address... [Marysville? 1948] 27 p. illus.   CHi

15602. Excelsior water and mining co., Smarts-ville. Prospectus... With a report by Professor Price and Ashburner. [n.p.] Print. for the co., 1878. 27 p.
CSmH

15603. —— Report and prospectus. [S.F., 1878] 21 p.   CSmH

15604. Hahn, Campbell & associates. Industrial survey, Yuba county, California, 1948. 86 l. maps.
CMary CO

15605. Hanson, George Emmanuel. The early history of the Yuba river valley. [Berkeley] 1924. 163 l. Thesis (M.A.)—Univ. of Calif., 1924. "This region embraces much of Yuba, Nevada, and Sierra counties."–p. 8.
C CChiS (microfilm) CMary (microfilm) CU CU-B

15606. Hoblitzell, H. S. California. Early historical sketch of the city of Marysville and Yuba county...with an oration by Rev. W. W. McKaig delivered at the Centennial celebration held at Marysville theatre, July 4th, 1876. Marysville, Appeal office [1876] 15 p.   C

15607. Johnson, Samuel P. "Gold dredges," the part played by the Yuba manufacturing company in the great romance of dredging for placer gold, platinum and tin... S.F., Print. for the Yuba manufacturing co. by John Henry Nash [c1927] 44 p. illus.   CHi

15608. Levick, M. B. Yuba county, California... Issued by Sunset mag. homeseekers' bur. S.F. [1911] 29 p. illus., maps.   CHi CSd CU-B

15609. Manson, Marsden. ...Features and water rights of Yuba river, California... [Wash., D.C., Govt. print. off., 1901] 115–154 p. illus., map. Reprint. from U.S. Dept. of agric., Office of experiment stations Bul. 100, Report of irrigation investigations in Calif.
CO CSmH CU-B CViCL

15610. Marysville. Chamber of commerce. Lands and homes in Yuba county, Cal. Marysville [19—?] 12 p. illus.   CHi

15611. Marysville and Benicia national railroad co. Report of the engineers on the survey of the Marysville and Benicia national railroad. Marysville, Calif. express, 1853. 29 p.   C CLU CSmH CU-B

15612. Marysville appeal-democrat. Centennial edition. Jan. 23, 1960. [Sections B-E] Marysville, 1960. 1 v. (v.p.) illus., ports., facsim.   CHi CMary CU-B

15613. —— Yearbook section...Yuba, Sutter and southern Butte counties. 1928. 1 v. illus.   C

15614. Marysville democrat. Progress edition, 1913, Yuba county, California; agriculture, horticulture, dairying and mining. Marysville [1913] 48 p. illus. Supplement, April 12, 1913.   C CMary CO

15615. Meade, Agnes Weber. Public education in Yuba county. Centennial edition. Prepared and published

by Agnes Weber Meade, superintendent of schools, Yuba county, 1954. [Marysville] 1954. 50 p. illus., map.
CHi CMary

15616. Merriam, J. Chester. Bars on the Yuba river. Dobbins, 1951. 16 l. Mimeo. Distributed at Mt. Shasta district meeting of the Calif. lib. assoc., Chico state college, May 5, 1951.
C CChiS CHi CLU CO CRic

15617. Moraign, Ervin C. After the riot at Wheatland. [Sacramento] 1959. Typew. "A paper submitted in partial satisfaction of the requirements of History 199. Sacramento state college, Feb., 1959."   C

15618. Mueller, Kennith F. The development of the Yuba county water agency and an analysis of its project. Chico, 1960. 114 l. Thesis (M.A.)—Chico state college, 1960.   CChiS

15619. Olney, Caroline Rickey. Homes and happiness in Yuba county, California. [n.p., 1903?] 22 p. illus., map.   CHi

15620. Plotting to convict Wheatland hop pickers... Oakland, The Internat. press [1914?] 28 p.   CLU

15621. Probert, Frank H. History of the Yuba river district, California. 4 p. (Reprint. from *The Mining congress jl.*, Dec. 1924)

15622. Pumpelly, Raphael. Report on the properties of the Excelsior water and mining co., Smartsville, Cal. Bost., Print. by T.R. Marvin & son, 1878. 12 p.
CSmH CU-B

15623. Sherwood, T. J., comp. The resources of Yuba county, the garden spot of California...together with a short description of the cities, towns, manufactories and business houses... Marysville, Democrat pub. co., print., February, 1894. 56 p. illus., map.   CU-B

15624. Smith, A. S., pub. Three central semitropical counties, Yuba, Colusa and Butte; the land of oranges, lemons, peaches, apricots, etc. [Marysville? 1886?] 53 p. maps (1 fold.)   C CHi

15625. [Smith, Rollin Carrol] Postmarked Vermont and California, 1862–1864, ed. by Fannie Smith Spurling... Rutland, Vt., Tuttle pub. co., c1940. Letters of Rollin C. Smith written while he was living in California and letters written to him by his father, Orlin Smith of Pittsford, Vermont.
C CBb CIIi CL CRic CSS CSd CSf CSfWF-H CSmH CU-B MoHi

15626. Walker's manual, inc., pub. Story of Yuba. S.F., L.A. [c1938] 18 p. illus., map. "A study, largely historical in character...of Yuba consolidated gold fields."   CLU CRic

15627. Williams, C. E. Yuba and Sutter counties, California: their resources, advantages, and opportunities ... S.F., Bacon & co., 1887. 119 p. illus., maps.
C CL CLCM CLU CO CS CSdS CSfCSM CSmH CU-B KHi

15628. Yuba county. Election returns...for the precinct at Long Bar in Yuba county, for an election held on the 1st day of September, 1858.   CMary

15629. —— [Regulations regarding mining claims, also court record of civil cases. 1850–?] 349 [10] p. Ms.
C

15630. —— **Board of supervisors.** California: Yuba-Sutter counties; soil, water, climate, health and prosperity. [Marysville?] Bds. of supervisors of Yuba and Sutter counties [1915] 64 p. illus.
CChiS CHi CLU CMary CSmH CU-B

15631. —— —— Navigation of the Feather; various data compiled for presentation to the Board of engineers for rivers and harbors... upon the occasion of their visit to Yuba and Sutter counties, August 15, 1914. Marysville, 1914. 40 p. illus. Comp. by direction of the Supervisors of Yuba and Sutter counties and the Chambers of commerce.   CHi

15632. —— —— Yuba county, California, its resources and advantages, by Winfield J. Davis... Marysville, The Appeal co., 1908. 31 p.   CHi NN

15633. —— **Chamber of commerce.** Yuba county, California; home of the canning cling peach. [Marysville, 1927] [22] p. illus.   CHi

15634. —— **Water resources board.** Analysis of irrigation water needs for the future development of irrigated lands in Yuba county, California, 1955; estimated irrigation water requirement for eventual development of Yuba county farm lands. [Marysville, 1955] 22 p. maps.
CO

15635. Yuba county, the undeveloped empire of northern California. [Marysville, Democrat print. co., 1908?] 56 p. illus., ports.   CMary

15636. The Yuba levee. Built to protect the farming lands in Landa township, Yuba county, from the hydraulic tailings. S.F., 1877. 16 p. map.   CLU CSmH

Marysville

15637. Bergamini, Yolanda Carmen. The Marysville levee system. [Marysville, 1959?] 18 p. diagrs., maps (col.)   C CMary

15638. Brier, W. W. Letters of W. W. Brier, dated Marysville, California, January 11th, 1851—Rev. W. W. Brier was pastor of First Presbyterian church.   CMary

15639. Crockwell, J. H., comp. Souvenir of Marysville and Yuba City, in photogravure... N.Y., Albertype co. [1893?] 40 p. illus., port.   CSmH

15640. Davis, A. B., pub. A souvenir of the current events [for the] week commencing June third and ending June seventh, 1906. Marysville, 1906. [15] p. ports. Issued for a meeting of the Most worshipful sovereign grand lodge, F. & A. M., later known as Prince Hall grand lodge, Freemasons.   CHi

15641. Ellis, William Turner. The Marysville city levee. Marysville, Reifsnider's print. shop, 1943. 38 p. maps.   C CU-B

15642. Fireman's relief fund. Souvenir—Marysville fire department. Comp. by W. A. Gilmore. [Sacramento, Crocker] 1901. 39 p.   CMary

15643. Marysville. Record of deaths, Marysville, California [1870–1918] 698 p. [i.e., 696 p.] Ms.   C

15644. —— Reports of city officers, commencing with annual reports rendered April 3d, 1876. Scrapbook of newspaper clippings of city officers from April 3, 1876 to April 7, 1884.   CMary

15645. —— **Charters, ordinances, etc.** Charter and general municipal ordinances of the city of Marysville together with acts of the legislature relating to the city. Revised and compiled by F. E. Smith, city clerk, and W. H. Carlin, city attorney. Pub. by order of the Mayor and Common council. [Marysville, Appeal press] 1896. 141 p.   CHi CMary

15646. —— —— Codified ordinances. Marysville, Marysville herald off., 1854–56.   CMary

15647. —— —— Manual of the corporation of the city of Marysville. Containing the charter of the city. Marysville, California express off., 1854. 84 p.   CHi

15648. —— —— Same. Daily appeal off., 1865– CMary has 1865, 1870.

15649. —— **Union high school and Yuba county junior college districts.** Plan for the future; presented by W. R. Odell [and others] Stanford, 1957. 50 p. maps, charts.   CChiS

15650. —— **Vigilance committee.** Minutes... meeting of June 25 [1851] [Marysville, Marysville herald, July 3, 1851] Ms. book containing Constitution of the Marysville vigilance committee.   C CMary

15651. Marysville benevolent society. Petition... for an appropriation. [Sacramento, Gelwicks, state print., 1870]   CSmH

15652. [Marysville newspapers] Special editions: Diamond jubilee, 1860–1935; Yuba-Sutter fair, Sept. 17, 1947.   CMary

15653. Marysville pioneer society. Register... February 20, 1869. 19 p. Ms. Cameragraph reprod.   C

15654. Marysville savings bank. By-laws... S.F., Bacon & co., 1871. 12 p.   CHi

15655. Newlands, Francis G. Speech...at the Stockton convention on the Field resolutions. [S.F., 1884] 14 p.   CHi

15656. Ramey, Earl. The beginnings of Marysville. S.F., Calif. hist. soc., 1936. 105 p. illus., ports., maps. (Special pub. no. 12, Histories of early Calif. towns, no. 3)
C CHi CL CLSU CLU CLgA CO CSdS CSf CSmH CStrJC CU-B MoSHi N

15657. San Francisco and Marysville railroad co. Reports of the Board of directors and chief engineer... at the annual meeting of stockholders, Marysville, May 10th, 1860. Marysville, W.F. Hicks & co., 1860. 44 p. map. Third annual report.
C CMary CSmH CSt CU-B

15658. Statement of the controversy between Judge William R. Turner...and members of the Marysville Bar... [Marysville, 1878?] 33 p.   CSmH

15659. Taylor, George B. In the diocese of California. Report of the ecclesiastical trial of the Rev. Geo. B. Taylor, upon a presentment from the standing committee of the Protestant Episcopal church, of the diocese of California, for an alleged violation of the canons of the church. S.F., Gazlay's steam print., 1861.
CSmH CU-B

15660. Turner, William R., comp. Documents in relation to charges preferred by Stephen J. Field and others, before the House of assembly of the state of California, against William R. Turner, district judge of the Eighth judicial district of California...1851. S.F., Franklin bk. and job off., 1853. 29 p.
C CHi CLU CSmH CU-B

15661. —— Same. S.F., Whitton, 1856. 130 p. illus., port., fold. facsims. At head of title: Second edition, with an appendix.
C CHi CLCo CLU CSfCW CSmH CU-B

15662. U.S. Army. 13th Armored division. Pictorial history at Camp Beale, World war II.   CYcCL

15663. Walden, Albert. Man versus water. [n.p., 195-] 27 p. Typew. Bibliography: p. 27.   C

15664. Winkley, John W. Travel guide and community data, Marysville, California. Marysville district chamber of commerce [194-?] 8, 2 l. Ms.
CMary CO (photocopy)

REGIONAL WORKS

NORTHERN AND CENTRAL CALIFORNIA

15665. Adams, Ansel Easton. The pageant of history and the panorama of today in northern California, a photographic interpretation... with text by Nancy Newhall. S.F., 1954. [72] p. illus., port. A centenary publication of the Am. trust co., 1854–1954.
C CChiS CCoron CHi CLU CSf CSfP CSfWF-H CStbS CaBViPA

15666. Adams, James Capen. The hair-breadth escapes and adventures of "Grizzly Adams," in catching and conquering the wild animals included in his California menagerie. Written by himself. N.Y., 1860. 53 p.
CHi

15667. [Allsop, Thomas] California and its gold mines. Ed. by Robert Allsop. London, Groombridge and sons, 1853. 149 p.   CP CSfWF-H

15668. The Alta California Pacific coast and transcontinental railroad guide... S.F., F. MacCrellish & co. [c1871] 293 p. illus., fold. map.
CHi CL CLgA CSfCW

15669. Alverson, Rosana Margaret (Kroh) Sixty years of California song. [Oakland] Author, 1913. 275 p. illus., ports., col. coat of arms. Autobiography and reminiscences of musical events and personalities.
CHi CL CLod CRcS CRedl CSalCL CSfCW CSmat

15670. And high water! Pictorial review of northwestern California's disastrous Christmas flood, 1955. [Comp. ...by publishers of the Pacific logger] [Eureka, 1956?] 39 p. illus.   C CArcHT CEH CUk

15671. Andrews, Ralph Warren. Fish and ships, by Ralph W. Andrews and A. K. Larssen. [1st ed.] Seattle, Superior pub. co. [c1959] 173 p. illus.   CArcHT

15672. —— Glory days of logging. [1st ed.] Seattle, Superior pub. co. [1956] 176 p. illus.   CArcHT

15673. —— Redwood classic. Seattle, Superior pub. co. [c1958] 174 p. illus.
C CArcHT CChiS CLom

15674. —— This was logging! Selected photographs of Darius Kinsey. Text by Ralph W. Andrews. [1st ed.] Seattle, Superior pub. co. [1954] 157 p. illus.
CArcHT

15675. —— This was sawmilling. [Autographed ed.] Seattle, Superior pub. co. [1957] 176 p. illus.
CArcHT CHi

15676. Andrist, Ralph K. The California gold rush. By the editors of American Heritage, the magazine of history. Narrative by Ralph K. Andrist. N.Y., Am. heritage pub. co., 1961. 153 p. illus. (part col.)   CLSM

15677. Ansted, David Thomas. The gold-seeker's manual; being a practical and instructive guide to all persons emigrating to the newly-discovered gold regions of California. N.Y., D. Appleton; London, Van Voorst, 1849. 96 p.   CHi CSd CSf CSfP

15678. Atwell, Creede & Ebbets, pub. San Francisco and North Pacific sketch book. A brief description of the health and pleasure resorts along the line of the San Francisco & North Pacific R.R. ... [S.F.?] Henderson & co., print., 1888. 84 p. illus., maps.   C CU-B

15679. Auger, Edouard. Voyage en Californie... (1852–1853). Paris, L. Hachette et cie., 1854. 238 p.
CHi CSf CSfCW CStoC

15680. Automobile club of southern California. Mother Lode of California. L.A. [c1959] 42 p. illus.
CHi

15681. Awes, Addison, jr. Why a rich Yankee did not settle in California. Bost. and S.F., Cubery and co., 1900. 115 p. illus.   CCSC CHi CSrD CStoC

15682. Ayers, James J. Gold and sunshine, reminiscences of early California...Illustrations from the collection of Charles B. Turrill. Bost., R.G. Badger, The Gorham press [c1922] 359 p. illus., port.
CBb CHi CLO CLgA CLod CMartC COnC CRedl CSd CSf CSfCW CSfWF-H CSjC CStbS CStmo

15683. Bancroft's official railway guide of the San Francisco and North Pacific railway company. San Francisco to Ukiah, Cal., with all connections. no. 1– May, 1889– illus., tables.   CLU

15684. Bancroft's official railway guide of the Southern Pacific company's coast division, San Francisco to San Jose, Almaden, Gilroy, Tres Pinos, Santa Cruz, Castroville, Monterey, Salinas, Santa Margarita and intermediate points. S.F., Bancroft co., c1889– illus., tables.
CLU has v.1, no. 3.

15685. Barr, Louise Farrow. Presses of northern California and their books, 1900–1933... Berkeley, Book arts club, Univ. of Calif., 1934. 276 p.
CHi CL CLgA CSdS CSf CSfCW CSfP CU ViU

15686. Barry, William Jackson. Past and present, and men of the times... Wellington, New Zealand, McKee & Gamble, 1897. 253 p. ports. First edition had title: Up and down...   CU-B

15687. Bates, Mrs. D. B. Incidents on land and water; or, Four years on the Pacific coast. Bost., James French & co., 1857. 336 p. illus.   CHi CSfCW
Other editions followed. C-S (9th) CHi (3d, 4th, 7th–9th) CLO (4th) CP (4th) CSjC (5th) CStbS (5th) CStclU (4th) CStoC (5th) ViU (10th)

15688. Baylis, Douglas. California houses of Gordon Drake, by Douglas Baylis and Joan Parry. N.Y., Reinhold, 1956. 91 p. illus.   CChiS

15689. Becker, Howard I., ed. Letters; Gold rush days, '49. [Author, 1957] [58] p. Mimeo.   CHi

15690. Benjamin, Israel Joseph. Drei jahr in Amerika 1859–1862. Hannover, Selbstverlag des verfassers, 1862. 3 v. front. (port.) v.1. Die östlichen staaten der union and San Francisco. v.2. Reise im innern von Californien. v.3. Reise in den nordwestgegenden Nord-Amerika's.   CHi MoS

15691. —— Same, translated from the German by Charles Reznikoff, with an introd. by Oscar Handlin. [1st ed.] Phila., Jewish pub. soc. of America, 1956. 2 v. port. (The Jacob R. Schiff library of Jewish contributions to American democracy)   CBb CHi MoS

15692. Bennett, William P. The first baby in camp; a full account of the scenes and adventures during the pioneer days of '49...the pony express; some of the old-time drivers... Salt Lake City, Rancher pub. co., 1893. 68 p. fold. pl.
CHi CSf CStbS CStoC CoD MoHi UHi

15693. [Berry, Swift] Central overland pony express route and stations in California. Placerville, Central overland pony express trail assoc. [1956] 8 l.   C

15694. Bertram, Gordon W. Industrial relations in the construction industry: the northern California experience by Gordon W. Bertram and Sherman J. Maisel. Berkeley, Inst. of industrial relations, Univ. of Calif. [1955] 70 p. "Prepared in collaboration with the Real estate research program, Bureau of business and economic research, Univ. of Calif. It is listed in their publication series as Research report no. 7." Bibliographical footnotes.   CL CU

15695. —— Industrial relations in the northern California construction industry. [Berkeley, 1957] Thesis (Ph.D.)—Univ. of Calif., 1957.   CU

15696. Biggs, Donald C. The pony express; creation of the legend. S.F., Priv. print., 1956. 20 p. illus.   CHi

15697. Bigham, Robert W. California goldfield scenes. Introd. by A. G. Haywood... Nashville, So. Methodist pub. house, 1886. 283 p.   CHi CSf

15698. [Blenkle, Joe A.] Stories of the Sacramento river delta. [Rio Vista, Delta herald, 1952] 39 p. illus., ports., map.   C

15699. Bloss, Roy S. Pony express, the great gamble. Berkeley, Howell-North, 1959. 159 p. illus.
  CHi CRcS CSalCL CSd CSfP

15700. Boggs, Mae Hélène (Bacon) comp. My playhouse was a Concord coach; an anthology of newspaper clippings and documents relating to those who made California history during the years 1822–1888. Oakland, Howell-North press [c1942] 736 p. A potpourri of clippings and maps about the gold rush days—much about Shasta, Trinity, and northern California.
Available in many California libraries and GU MoSU OrU T TxU ViU. C has also typed copy of original manuscript and illustrative material gathered for compiling the published work. 7 v. ports., maps, facsims.

15701. Bolton, Herbert Eugene. Anza's California expeditions... Berkeley, Univ. of Calif. press, 1930. 5 v. illus., ports., maps. v.2–5 translated from original Spanish manuscripts and edited by H. E. Bolton. Contents: v.1. An outpost of empire, by H. E. Bolton.—v.2. Opening a land route to California; diaries of Anza, Díaz, Garcés, and Palóu.—v.3. The San Francisco colony; diaries of Anza, Font, and Eixarch, and narratives by Palóu and Moraga.—v.4. Font's complete diary of the Second Anza expedition.—v.5. Correspondence.
Available in many libraries.

15702. Bondinot, May Fidelia. The case of the *Mercury*, as typical of contraband trade on the California coast, 1790–1820. [Berkeley, 1916] Thesis (M.A.)—Univ. of Calif., 1916.   CU

15703. Bordeaux, Albert. Sibérie et Californie. Paris, Librairie Plon, 1903. 339 p.   CHi CSfCW

15704. Borden, Stanley T. The Albion branch, Northwestern Pacific. San Mateo, 1961. 32 p. Reprint. from *Western railroader*, v. 24, Dec. 1961.   CHi

15705. —— History and rosters of the Northwestern Pacific railroad and predecessor lines. San Mateo, 1949. 32 p. illus. Reprint. from *Western railroader*, v.12, no. 6, April 1949.   CHi

15706. Borthwick, J. D. Three years in California. Edinburgh & London, Wm. Blackwood & sons, 1857. 384 p. illus.
  C CAna CHi CL CLSU CLU CLgA CNF CP

CPom CSalCL CSd CSf CSfP CSfWF-H CSj CSmH CV CaBViPA

15707. —— —— Index. Prepared under the supervision of Joseph Gaer. Oakland, 1935. Mimeo.
  C C-S CHi CLSU CLU CO CP CSdS CSf CSfP CSmH CStbS CU-B

15708. —— Same, reprinted, with index and foreword by Joseph A. Sullivan. Oakland, Biobooks, 1948. 318 p. illus., map. (Calif. centennial ed., no. 17)
Available in many California libraries and OrU

15709. —— Same, with title: The gold hunters... ed. by Horace Kephart. N.Y., Outing pub. co., 1917. 361 p. "Reprint. in full with errors corrected."—Preface. Other editions followed.
Available in many California libraries and MiD ViU

15710. Bowe, Richard J., ed. A pictorial history of the Mother Lode and Sierra Nevada. [Tuolumne, Tuolumne prospector, 195–?] unp. illus., ports., map.
  C CFS CL

15711. Bradley, Glenn Danford. The story of the pony express;... the most remarkable mail service ever in existence and its place in history. Chicago, McClurg, 1913. 175 p. illus.   CSd CSfCW CSfCP CStbS

15712. —— Same. [2d ed.] Ed. by Waddell F. Smith. S.F., Hesperian house [1960] 195 p. illus., ports.
  C-S CHi CSfP

15713. Breck, Charles. Life of the Reverend James Lloyd Breck... N.Y., Young & co., 1886. 557 p.   CHi

15714. Brier, Howard M. Sawdust empire. N.Y., Knopf, 1957. 269 p.   CSmat

15715. Bristol, Sherlock. The pioneer preacher: an autobiography. N.Y., Chicago, Fleming H. Revell [c1887] 330 p.   CHi CSfP

15716. Brockman, Christian Frank. A guide to the Mother Lode country. Yosemite natural history assoc., 1948. 49 p. illus., maps. Special number of *Yosemite nature notes*, v.27, no. 1, Jan. 1948.
  C CHi CL CLgA CRic CSfSC CSfWF-H CSj CSjC

15717. Bronk, Mitchell. Discovering my fortyniner father... Phila., Judson press [c1942] 20 p.
  CHi CSd

15718. Brosch, W. L., ed. Travel trails. S.F., C. T. & T. bureau [c1932] 61 p. illus.   CHi CRic

15719. Brown, Joseph. Crossing the plains in 1849, by Jos. Brown, Marysville, California. [S.F., Upton bros. & Delzelle] 1916. 38 p.   CHi (photocopy) CMary

15720. Brown, Thomas P. Over the Sierra Nevada mountains via the Western Pacific railroad, the Feather river canyon route. S.F., Issued by Western Pacific news service [1940] 20 l. map, 2 fold. diagrs.   C CHi

15721. Browne, John Ross. The Coast rangers (a chronicle of adventures in California). Written and illustrated by John Ross Browne. [Introd. by Richard H. Dillon] Balboa Island, Paisano press, 1959. 86 p. illus. Reprint. from *Harper's new monthly mag.*, v.23–24, 1861–62.   C CAla CL

15722. —— A dangerous journey, California 1849. Palo Alto, A. Lites press, 1950. 93 p. col. illus. "First published...in *Harper's monthly* for May and June, 1862. Reissued in 1864 as [part of]...Crusoe's Island."
Available in many California libraries and CaBViPA MiD

15723. —— J. Ross Browne's illustrated mining adventures, California and Nevada, 1863–1865. Balboa

Island, Paisano press, 1961. 207 p. illus., maps incl. lining paper. [Selections from his writings]   CLSM

15724. Bruff, Joseph Goldsborough. Gold rush; the journals, drawings, and other papers of J. Goldsborough Bruff... N.Y., Columbia univ. press, 1944. 2 v. illus., maps.
Available in many California libraries and CaBViPA IHi MiD MoSU OrU UHi ViU

15725. ——— Same. Calif. centennial ed. N.Y., Columbia univ. press, 1949. 794 p. illus. "Without Bruff's earlier diaries and some other material which appeared in the two-volume 1944 edition now out of print."—*Pub. weekly.*
Available in many California libraries and CaBViPA MiD

15726. Buffum, Edward Gould. Six months in the gold mines: from a journal of three years residence in Upper and Lower California, 1847-8-9... Phila., Lea & Blanchard, 1850. 172 p.
CHi CLU CLgA CP CSf CSjC CSmH MoS ViW

15727. ——— Same. London, Richard Bentley, 1850. 244 p.   CHi CLU CSmH MiD

15728. ——— Same, edited and with an introduction by John W. Caughey. [L.A.] Ward Ritchie, 1959. 145 p.
C CAla CArcHT CBev CL CSd CaBViPA

15729. California vs. Gold run ditch and mining co. In the Superior court of the state of California, county of Sacramento. People of the state of California, plaintiff, vs. the Gold run ditch and mining company, defendant. Oral argument of Samuel M. Wilson, of counsel for defendant. March 1st and 2nd, 1882. [n.p., 1882] 183 p. A suit concerning hydraulic mining.   CHi

15730. ——— ...Argument of A. P. Catlin, esq., of counsel for defendant... Before Hon. Jackson Temple, superior judge, March 6, 1882. Sacramento, H.A. Weaver, print., 1882. 25 p.   CHi CLU

15731. California. Dept. of natural resources. Div. of beaches and parks. The golden chain of the Mother Lode. A report of a preliminary survey of the Mother Lode and adjacent areas leading to its preservation of the enjoyment and use of the general public as requested by ACR no. 128, 1959. By James S. Barrick... Sacramento, 1959. 81 p. illus.   CRcS CRic

15732. ——— ——— **Div. of mines.** De argento vivo; historic documents on quicksilver and its recovery in California prior to 1860, assembled by Elisabeth L. Egenhoff. [Sacramento] 1953. 144 p. illus., facsims. Supplement to *California jl. of mines and geology,* Oct. 1953.
Available in many California libraries.

15733. ——— ——— ——— The elephant as they saw it; a collection of contemporary pictures and statements on gold mining in California, assembled by Elisabeth L. Egenhoff. S.F. [1949] 128 p. illus. (part col.) Supplement to *California jl. of mines and geology,* Oct. 1949.
CBb CBev CHi CL CLO CLgA CRedCL CRic CSd CSdS CSf CSjC UHi

15734. ——— ——— ——— ...Geologic guidebook along Highway 49—Sierran gold belt: the Mother Lode country (centennial edition), prepared under the direction of Olaf P. Jenkins... [Sacramento, State print. off.] 1948. 164 p. illus., maps. (Its Bul. no. 141) "Survey of building structures of the Sierran gold belt—1848-70, by Robert F. Heizer and Franklin Fenenga": p. 91-164. "Publications consulted": p. 8.
Available in many libraries.

15735. ——— **Disaster office.** The big flood, California, 1955. Sacramento, 1956. 126 p. illus., map.
C CAla CArcHT CHi CRcS CSdS CSmat

15736. ——— **Legislature. Assembly.** Testimony taken by the committee on mining debris... [Sacramento, State print., 1878] 160 p.   CHi

15737. ——— **State water resources board.** Floods of California, 1955 (pictorial record). March 1956. [72] p.   C

15738. California Chinese mission. ...Annual report... 1st— 1875/76– S.F., 1876– A state-wide organization with auxiliaries and schools from Grass Valley to Santa Barbara.
CHi has 2d, 5th, 1876/77, 1879/80. CU-B has 4th, 8th, 11th, 17th, 20th, 1878/79, 1882/83, 1885/86, 1891/92, 1894/95.

15739. California gold regions, with a full account of their mineral resources; how to get there, and what to take; the expenses, the time, and the various routes. With sketches of California; an account of the life, manners, and customs of the inhabitants... N.Y., F.M. Pratt [1849?] 48 p.   CHi CL

15740. California historical society. Christmas in California. Part 1. Christmas at Sutter's fort in 1847, by John Bonner. Part 2. Christmas before the Americans came, by Jose Ramon Pico. S.F. [1956] 37 p. illus.
Available in many California libraries and CaBViPA

15741. California miners' association. Proceedings of the annual convention... S.F. [189–?–   ] Place of publication varies.
CHi has 11th, 1902. CLO has 10th, 1901. CSfP has 11th, 15th, 1902, 1906.

15742. California publishing co., comp. and pub. Central California illustrated. An illustrated review of the industries, resources, advantages, and improvements of the following central coast counties of California: Santa Clara, Monterey, Santa Cruz, San Mateo, Alameda. L.A. [1899?] 163 p. illus.   CSfCW CSmH

15742a. ——— La Californie. Documents officiels et renseignments recuellis et publies par J. Mithouard. 3d ed. Paris, Au comptoir des publications nationales, 1850. 4 l., 168 p. Official U.S. documents and other data on California resources, commerce, customs, navigation; information on gold regions and mining regulations.   CHi

15743. Carmany, John H. A review of the year 1866...resume of the mining operations of the entire Pacific coast ...summary of the financial and commercial interests of this city and state...comp. from the "Mercantile gazette and prices current" of Jan. 9th, 1867... S.F., H.H. Bancroft and co., 1867. 64 p.   CHi

15744. Carson, James H. Early recollections of the mines, and a description of the great Tulare valley... Stockton, Pub. to accompany the steamer edition of the "San Joaquin republican," 1852. 64 p. map. At head of cover-title: Second edition. Cover-title: ... Life in California, together with a description of the great Tulare valley. May has title: Map of the Southern mines. By C. D. Gibbes. 1852. "The first edition did not appear in book form, having been issued as a supplement to a number of the *San Joaquin republican.*"—Cowan.
CL CLU CNa CSS CSf CSjC CSmH CSto CU-B ICN

15745. ——— Same, reprinted. [Tarrytown, N.Y., W. Abbatt, 1931] 82 p. map. (*Mag. of history with notes and queries.* Extra number. no. 165...)
C CBu CLSM CLU CO CRiv CSmH CU-B MoS

15746. —— Same, with title: Recollections of the California mines...with a foreword by Joseph A. Sullivan. Oakland, Biobooks, 1950. 113 p. illus., maps. "Reprinted from the Stockton ed. of 1852."
Available in many California libraries and CoD KyU NvU

15747. Caughey, John Walton. Gold is the cornerstone; with vignettes by W. R. Cameron. Berkeley, Univ. of Calif. press, 1948. 321 p. illus.
Available in many California libraries and ODa OrU UHi

15748. —— Rushing for gold. Berkeley, Univ. of Calif. press, 1949. 111 p. (Am. hist. assoc., Pac. coast branch, special pub. no. 1) Reprint. from the *Pac. hist. review*, v.18, no. 1.
Available in many California libraries and OrU UHi

15749. Chalfant, Willie Arthur. Outposts of civilization. Bost., Christopher pub. house, 1928. 193 p.
CHi CInI CSf CSfCW CStbS

15750. Chambers, William. Gold and gold-diggers. [London, 1869] 32 p. CRedl

15751. Chapman, Arthur. The pony express; the record of a romantic adventure in business. Illus. with contemporary prints and photographs. N.Y. and London, Putnam, 1932. 319 p. illus., ports., facsims.
CHi CRcS CSd CSfCW

15752. Chevigny, Hector. Lost empire; the life and adventures of Nikolai Petrovich Rezanov. N.Y., Macmillan, 1937. 356 p. port. CRcS CSd CSf

15753. Child, Cyrus. Travel prospectus—dated Nevada City, Upper California, Dec. 10, 1850. 61 p. Ms.
CSfWF-H

15754. Chinard, Gilbert. Projet d'association agricole pour la Californie, 1851. 22 p. front. (facsim.), map. Reprint. from the *Bul. de L'Institut français de Washington.* Numéro douze. Décembre, 1939. CHi

15755. Christman, Enos. One man's gold; the letters & journals of a forty-niner. N.Y., Whittlesey house, McGraw-Hill, 1930. 278 p. illus., ports., facsims.
CBb CHi CLO COnC CRcS CRedl CRic CSd CSf CSfCW CStbS CStmo CYcCL ODa OrU

15756. Clark, Sterling B. F. How many miles from St. Jo? The log of Sterling B. F. Clark, a forty-niner, with comments by Ella Sterling Mighels; together with a brief autobiography of James Phelan, 1819–1892, pioneer merchant. S.F. [Taylor & Taylor] 1929. 56 p. illus., ports., facsim.
CBb CHi CLgA CRcS CSf CStbS CStclU

15757. Cohn, Henry. Jugenderinnerungen. Aus anlass der goldenen hochzeit meinen nachkommen zum gedächtnis. Stettin, den 24. Mai 1914. 55 p. port.
CHi

15758. Cole, Raymond Sterling. A historical study of the American military operations in the conquest of California. [Whittier, 1958] Thesis (M.A.)—Whittier college, 1958. CWhC

15759. Collier, William Lewis. Representative potters of northern California: their work and philosophy. [Berkeley, 1956] Thesis (M.A.)—Univ. of Calif., 1956.
CU

15760. [Committee of one hundred] Report of the California commissioners on the Atlantic and Pacific railroad... St. Louis, Industrial age print. co., 1872. 30 p. Commissioners appointed by the Committee of one hundred and other citizens. Signed: R. G. Sneath, C. T. Hopkins, John L. Hagen. CHi

15761. Cook, Elliott Wilkinson. Land ho! The original diary of a forty-niner...ed. by Jane James Cook. Baltimore, Remington-Putnam, 1935. 43 p.
CBb CHi CSd

15762. Cossley-Batt, Jill Lillie Emma. The last of the California rangers. N.Y. and London, Funk & Wagnalls, 1928. 299 p. illus., ports., facsims. "Account of the most stirring experiences in the long life of Captain William James Howard."—Introd.
Available in many California libraries.

15763. Coulter, Thomas. Notes on Upper California; a journey from Monterey to the Colorado river in 1832... L.A., Dawson, 1951. 39 p. col. front., fold. map. (Early Calif. travels ser., 1) 200 copies printed by Will Cheney. CL CLO CSd CSf CStclU CStoC

15764. Coy, Owen Cochran. In the diggings in 'forty-nine. L.A., Calif. state hist. assoc., 1948. 132 p. illus., port., maps. Bibliography: p. 117–121. Print. by Calif. state print. off.
Available in many California libraries and CaBViPA

15765. Crevelli, John P. Four hundred years of Indian affairs in the Northbay counties of California. [Berkeley, 1959] 148 p. Thesis (M.A.)—Univ. of Calif., 1959. CStrJC CU

15766. Crosby, Elisha Oscar. Memoirs of Elisha Crosby; reminiscences of California and Guatemala from 1849 to 1864, edited by Charles Albro Barker. San Marino, The Huntington lib., 1945. 119 p. illus., port. (Huntington lib. pub.)
CBb CChiS CHi CLO CLgA CSd CSdS CSf CSjC CStoC CU-B CWhC MoS N TxU ViU

15767. Crosley, Mary Edith. California's Mother Lode. Universal City, Crosley books [c1959] 46 p. illus.
C CHi

15768. Dahl, Albin Joachim. British investment in California mining, 1870–1890. [Berkeley, 1961] Thesis (Ph.D.)—Univ. of Calif., 1961. CU

15769. Damon, Samuel Chenery. A journey to lower Oregon & upper California, 1848–49. S.F., J.J. Newbegin, 1927. front. (port.)
CHi CSfCW CStclU IHHi

15770. Davis, Stephen Chapin. California gold rush merchant; the journal of Stephen Chapin Davis. Ed. by Benjamin B. Richards. San Marino, Huntington lib., 1956. 124 p. map.
Available in many California libraries and CaBViPA KyU MoSU N OrU ViU

15771. Davis, William J., comp. Northern California and builders. S.F. [Argonaut pub. co.] 1954. 108 p. illus., ports. C CSf CSt

15772. De Groot, Henry. Recollections of California mining life. Primitive placers and first important discovery of gold. The pioneers of the pioneers—their fortune and their fate. Written for the Mining and scientific press. S.F., Dewey & co., 1884. 16 p. illus.
CHi CLSM CSd CSf CSfCW CSfP

15773. [Delavan, James] Notes on California and the placers: how to get there, and what to do afterwards. By one who has been there. N.Y., H. Long & bro., 1850. 128 p. illus.
Available in many California libraries and ViU

15774. De Quincey, Thomas. California and the gold mania. Illustrated with sketches from Punch. S.F., Colt press, 1945. 63 p. col. pl. (Calif. classics, no. 3) This essay is reprinted from Ticknor, Reed and Fields ed. of *Letters to a young man...* 1854, p. 199–244.
CBb CChiS CHi CLSM CSd CV TxU ViU

15775. De Witt, Frederic M., pub. De Witt's guide to central California; an illustrated and descriptive handbook for tourists and strangers. S.F. [1902] 180 p. illus., fold. map, fold. plans.   CSf CSfCW

15776. Dexter, A. Hersey. Early days in California ... [Denver, Tribune-republican press] 1886. 214 p.
CoD

15777. Digby, George. Under the redwood trees. N.Y., Dutton, 1940. 285 p. An account of the author's life in northern California.
CArcHT CCoron CEH CMon CRcS CRic CSd CStcl CStmo CU-B CUk ODa

15778. Donohoe, Helen, Mother. The movement of population in and into California between June, 1848 and February, 1849, as occasioned by the discovery of gold. [Stanford, 1946] 111 p. illus., maps. Thesis (M.A.) —Stanford university, 1946.   CSfCW

15779. Dressler, Albert. California's pioneer artist, Ernest Narjot. A brief resume of the career of a versatile genius. S.F., Author, 1936. 12 p. illus.
CHi CSf CSfWF-H

15780. —— ed. California's pioneer circus; Joseph Andrew Rowe, founder; memoirs and personal correspondence relative to the circus business through the gold country in the 50's. S.F., Crocker, c1926. 98 p. illus.
CBb CChiS CHi CRedCL CRic CSS CSalCL CSd CSf CSfCW CSfWF-H CStmo CSto CStoC CViCL MoS

15781. Duhailly, Édouard. Campagnes et stations sur les côtes de l'Amérique du Nord. Paris, Leipsick, Jung-Treuttel, 1864. 294 p.   CHi CSfCW CU-B

15782. Dumas, Alexandre ...Un Gil Blas en Californie... Paris, Michel Levy frères, 1861. 323 p.   CSf

15783. —— Same. Tr. by Marguerite Eyer Wilbur. L.A., Primavera press, 1933. 166 p. fold. map.
Available in many California libraries and MoS ViU

15784. Dunbar, Edward E. The romance of the age; or, The discovery of gold in California... N.Y., Appleton, 1867. 134 p. illus., port.
CHi CLgA CLSM CSd CSf CSfCW CSfP CSmat CStoC UHi

15785. E clampus vitus. The enigmatical book of vitus. ... [S.F.] 1934. Contains a history of the order.
CHi

15786. —— The esoteric book... [L.A., Queen of the Cow counties, 1936] 119 p. illus.   CLO

15787. Ely, Edward. The wanderings of Edward Ely, a mid-19th century seafarer's diary; ed. by Anthony and Allison Sirna. N.Y., Hastings, c1954. 217 p.
CBb CHi CL

15788. Enochs, Elizabeth T. A study of place names in the American river drainage system, 1848–1854. [Sacramento, 1957] 89 p. Thesis (M.A.)—Sacramento state college, 1957.   CSS

15789. Erickson, Clarence Elmer. San Francisco bay and Delta area: Boating, fishing, hunting. [1st ed. Menlo Park, Lane pub. co., 1952] 32 p. col. maps. (Sunset sportsman's atlas)
C CLU CO CPa CRedl CSbr CSdS CSfMI CSjC CSluCL CSto CU-B

15790. —— Same. 2d ed. Menlo Park, c1955. 32 p. illus., maps.   CMont CSd CStcrCL CViCL

15791. Erskine, Gladys Shaw. Broncho Charlie, a saga of the saddle... The life story of Broncho Charlie Miller, the last of the Pony express riders. N.Y., Crowell [c1934] 316 p. illus., ports., maps, facsim.   CRic

15792. Essays for Henry R. Wagner, by Charles L. Camp [and others] S.F., Grabhorn press, 1947. 106 p. Pub. on the occasion of the 85th birthday of Henry R. Wagner, Sept. 27, 1947. Contents: The D. T. P. letters, by C. L. Camp.—The grizzly bear hunter of California, by F. P. Farquhar.—Balance vs. Balance, by G. L. Harding.—Place names from the Portola pilgrimage, by Dorothy H. Huggins.—Twenty-five California maps, by C. I. Wheat.   CBb CChiS CHi CLSM N TxU

15793. Evans, Albert S. À la California. Sketches of life in the golden state...With an introduction by Col. W. H. L. Barnes and illustrations from original drawings by Ernest Narjot. S.F., A.L. Bancroft & co., 1873. 379 p. illus.
CBb CHi CLgA CLom CLO CP CRcS CSalCL CSf CSfCW CSjC CSrD CSto CStoC

15794. —— Same, with title...also, an authentic account of the famous Yosemite valley. S.F., George H. Bancroft [1889] 404 p. illus.
CChiS CHi CRedl CSd CSfWF-H

15795. —— Same. S.F., Hartwell, Mitchell & Willis, 1897. 404 p. illus.   CFS CHi

15796. Evans, George W. B. Mexican gold trail; the journal of a forty-niner; ed. by Glenn S. Dumke, with a preface by Robert Glass Cleland. San Marino, The Huntington lib., 1945. 340 p. col. front., illus., pl. (Huntington lib. pub.) Bibliographical note, p. 329–31.
CBb CChiS CHi CLgA CRic CSd CSdS CSfCSM CStmo CTurS CVtV CWhC MoS OrU ViU

15797. Facts, by a woman. Oakland, Pac. press pub. house, 1881. 356 p. Experiences of an unidentified woman who made her living by traveling around selling books.
CSalCL

15798. [Falconer, Eric A.] Credo quia absurdum, being a compilation of historic documents and trivia pertinent to a full understanding of the meaning and purpose of the ancient and honorable order of E clampus vitus... Placerville, Old Hangtown, S.E.C.V., 1949. 77 p. illus.   CHi CLO CMont CO CSf

15799. —— The story of E clampus vitus, by Eric A Falconer Xnch [pseud.] [S.F.? 1960] 7 p.   CHi

15800. Fairchild, Lucius. ...California letters... edited with notes and introduction by Joseph Schafer... Madison, State hist. soc. of Wisconsin, 1931. 212 p. illus., ports. (Wisconsin hist. pub. Collection, v.31)
CBb CHi CLS CSd CSjC CStbS CStclU CStoC CWhC OrU ViU

15801. Farish, Thomas Edwin. The gold hunters of California. Chicago, M.A. Donohue & co., 1904. 246 p. illus., ports.   CBb CHi CLSM CP CSd CSf CStmo

15802. [Farquhar, Francis Peloubet] Accountant's guide to the gold regions. 1939. [S.F., Grabhorn, 1939] [4] p. fold. col. map. Issued by California soc. of certified public accountants.   CHi

15803. [Field, Charles Kellogg] The story of Cheerio. By himself. Garden City, N.Y., Garden City pub. co. [c1936] 382 p. illus. Limited edition.   CHi

15804. Fisher, William Arms. The narrative of 1853. [n.p., c1950] 35 p.   CHi

15805. Fitch, Henry S. Pacific railroad. An essay on the Pacific railway...embracing a new plan for the action of the government in aid of the enterprise, with suggestions concerning grants of land, & the influence which the construction of the Pacific railway will exert in behalf of the Republic, &c., &c. S.F., Frank Eastman, print., 1859. 19 p.   CSmH CU CU-B

15806. —— State policy. A plan by which the State can aid the construction of the Pacific railroad and secure a combination of beneficial finances sufficient to extend railway enterprises wherever the interests of the State require. S.F., Commercial bk. and job steam presses, 1859. 32 p.   CSmH CU-B CtY

15807. Fitzgerald, Oscar Penn. California sketches, new and old. Consolidated ed. [n.p., 1895] 336 p.   CHi

15808. Floyd, William H. Phantom riders of the pony express. Phila., Dorrance and co., inc., 1958. 142 p. illus.   CSf

15809. Folsom, Joseph Libbey. A letter of Captain J. L. Folsom reporting on conditions in California in 1848. From the original in the collection of Thos. W. Norris. Livermore, T. W. Norris, 1944. 22 p. map. "Two hundred and fifty copies printed at the Grabhorn press, San Francisco, December 1944."   CHi CRcS CSf CSjC CStclU

15810. Foster, George G., ed. The gold regions of California: being a succinct description of the geography, history, topography, and general features of California, including...the gold regions... N.Y., Dewitt & Davenport, 1848. 80 p. map. "A reproduction, under a new title, of his *The gold mines of California*; and also a geographical, topographical and historical view of that country."—Sabin.   C CHi CLO CP CSd CSmH

15811. —— Index... Joseph Gaer, ed. [n.p., 1935] 27 l. (Index no. 5, SERA project 2-F2-132 (3-F2-197) Calif. literary research) Mimeo.   C CHi CLSU CO CSalCL CSf CSmH CStmo

15812. Frangini, A. Colonie Italiche in California. Strenna nazionale. Cenni biografici. Vol. 65. S.F., M. Castagno & co., 1917. 150 p.   CHi

15813. Frederick, James Vincent. Ben Holladay, the stage-coach king. Glendale, A.H. Clark co., 1940. 334 p. illus., port., fold. map, facsims. (Western frontiersmen ser. 2)   CHi CSd CU-B

15814. Frémont, Jessie (Benton) A year of American travel. N.Y., Harper, 1878. 190 p.   CLSM CP

15815. —— Same. With an introduction by Patrice Manahan, and engravings by Ernest Freed. S.F., Bk. club of Calif., 1960. 121 p. illus. 450 copies printed at the Plantin press.   CLO CLSM

15816. Geiger, Vincent Eply. Trail to California; the overland journal of Vincent Geiger and Wakeman Bryarly; ed., with an introduction, by David Morris Potter... New Haven, Yale univ. press; London, H. Milford, Oxford univ. press, 1945. 266 p. front. (port.), fold. map.   C CBb CHi CU-B

15817. —— Same. New Haven, Yale univ. press [c1945, 1962] 266 p. fold. map. (A Yale Western Americana paperbound YW–1)   CU-B

15818. Gerstäcker, Friedrich Wilhelm Christian. Gerstäcker's travels...California and the gold fields. Tr. from the German. London & Edinburgh, T. Nelson & sons, 1854. 290 p.   C CLSU CLU CO CSf CSfP CSfWF-H CSmH

15819. —— Gold! Ein Californisches lebensbild. Jena, Herman Costenoble [n.d.] 580 p.   CLSM

15820. —— Narrative of a journey round the world. Comprising a winter-passage across the Andes to Chili; with a visit to the gold regions of California and Australia,

the South sea islands, Java, etc. N.Y., Harper, 1853. 624 p. Tr. from *Reisen* von F. Gerstäcker.   CHi (1854) CLSM CSfCW

15821. —— California gold mines; foreword by Joseph A. Sullivan. Oakland, Biobooks, 1946. 149 p. illus., map. (Calif. centennial ser. VI) The text used was selected from "the undated Harper edition" of *Travels round the world*, which is a translation of the author's *Reisen*. cf. Foreword.
Available in many California libraries and CaBViPA MiD OrU UHi

15822. —— Californische skizzen. Leipsig, Arnoldische buchhandlung, 1856. 379 p.   CHi

15823. —— Scènes de la vie Californienne. Traduites de l'allemand par Gustave Revilliod. Genève, Imprimerie de Jules-Gme. Fick, 1859. 260 p. illus.   CBb CHi CLU CSfWF-H CSmH CaBViPA

15824. —— Scenes of life in California, tr. from the French by George Cosgrave. S.F., J. Howell [1942] 188 p. illus. 500 copies printed at the Grabhorn press.
C CBb CHi CLO CLSU CLU CO CRcS CRic CSd CSdS CSf CSj CSmH CStmo CStrJC CViCL CaBViPA MiD

15825. —— The young gold-digger; or, A boy's adventures in the gold regions. London, N.Y., Routledge, Warne & Routledge, 1860.   CHi CYcCL

15826. Gibbs, James Atwood. Sentinels of the Pacific; the story of Pacific coast lighthouses and lightships. Portland, Ore., Binfords & Mort, 1955. 232 p. illus. Contains chapter on "Lighthouses — San Francisco bay to Crescent City" which gives historical and current information. Also has an account of the sinking of the *Emidio* on Dec. 20, 1941 by a Japanese submarine and the rescue which was performed from Humboldt bay.   CArcHT

15827. Gibson, Otis. Chinese in America. Cincinnati, Hitchcock and Walden, 1877. 403 p. Pertains chiefly to California.   CHi CSfCW CSto

15828. Gilbert, Benjamin Franklin. Confederate activity and propaganda in California. [Berkeley, 1940] Thesis (M.A.)—Univ. of Calif., 1940.   CU

15829. Gill, William. California letters of William Gill, written in 1850 to his wife, Harriet Tarleton, in Kentucky, ed. by Eva Turner Clark. N.Y., Down print. co., 1922. 43 p. port., map. 100 copies printed.   CBb CFS CHi CSf

15830. Gillihan, Allen F. A survey of the Indians of northeastern California, by Allen F. Gillihan and Alma B. Shaffer, for California state board of health, March 1921. [Sacramento] 83 p. typew. mounted photos.   CRedCL

15831. Gilpin, William. The central gold region... and observations on the Pacific railroad. Phila., Sower, Barnes & co.; St. Louis, E.K. Woodward, 1860. 194 p. 6 fold. maps.   CHi CSfCW

15832. Glasscock, Carl Burgess. Gold in them hills...the story of the West's last wild mining days. Indianapolis, Bobbs-Merrill, 1932. 330 p. illus., ports.   CHi CLod CSal CSf

15833. —— A golden highway: scenes of history's greatest gold rush yesterday and today. Indianapolis, Bobbs, 1934. 313 p. illus., ports. Record of a motor tour in California's mining region, incorporating the history of each place visited. Bibliography: p. [315]–21.
Available in many California libraries and CaBViPA MiD MoS ODa

15834. Goethe, Charles Matthias. "What's in a

name?" (Tales, historical or fictitious, about 111 California gold belt place names) Sacramento, Keystone press, c1949. 202 p. illus.

Available in many California libraries and GU MoS N ODa T ViU ViW

15835. Goodrich, B. F., firm, comp. Goodrich road sign, route book, central California. San Francisco to Santa Rosa, Yosemite valley and Saugus. [Akron, O., 19—?] 47 p.   CHi

15836. Goodwin, Charles Carroll. Steel rails on the old trails in the Western Pacific country... [S.F., Western Pac. railway, c1913] 31 p. map.   CHi

15837. Grabhorn, Jane Bissell. A California gold rush miscellany; comprising the original Journal of Alexander Barrington, nine unpublished letters from the gold mines, reproductions of early maps and towns from California lithographs; broadsides, etc. ... S.F., Grabhorn, 1934. 45 p. illus., fold. maps, facsims. (Rare Americana 2d ser., no. 4)

Available in many California libraries and ViU

15838. Gracey, E. William, comp. California and Nevada amateur directory for 1877. East Oakland, 1877. 39 p.   CHi

15839. Gramm, Walter Stanley. The development of electric power in northern California. [Berkeley, 1955] Thesis (Ph.D.)—Univ. of Calif., 1955.   CU

15840. Great western power co. of California. Great western power service. [S.F., Taylor & Taylor, 1928] [26] p. illus., maps.   CHi

15841. —— Proposal for power service... [S.F., Taylor & Taylor, 1928] [22] p. illus., maps.   CHi

15842. Guinn, James Miller. History of the state of California and biographical record of coast counties, California. An historical story of the state's marvelous growth from its earliest settlement to the present time...also containing biographies of well-known citizens of the past and present. Chicago, Chapman pub. co., 1904 [c1902] 1418 p. ports. Cover-title: Coast counties, California. Brief history of state and of San Francisco; no separate treatment of other coast counties.

Available in many libraries.

15843. Hale, Richard Lunt. The log of a forty-niner; journal of a voyage from Newbury-port to San Francisco in the brig *Genl. Worth*... [ed. by] Carolyn Hale Russ. Bost., B.J. Brimmer co., 1923. 183 p. illus., ports., facsims.
CBb CChiS CHi CLLoy CLSM CLgA CSd CSfCW CSjC CStcl CStmo CWhC MoS OrU ViU

15844. Hamilton & Brown, pub. Gazetteer of the California Pacific railroad and its branches. For the years 1871–72...a classified business directory of all the cities and towns on the line of the road, San Francisco inclusive. Together with the officers of the various municipalities, state and county officers...and a great variety of useful and statistical information... S.F., 1871.
C CHi CMary

15845. Harlan, Jacob Wright. California '46 to '88... S.F., Bancroft co., 1888. 242 p. front. (port.) The writer crossed the plains in 1846, part of the way with the Donner party.
CBb CHi CLSM CLgA CRic CSd CSf CSfCSM CSfCW CSfP CSjC CStbS CSto TxU

15846. Hartford union mining and trading co. Journal of...containing the name, residence and occupation of each member, with incidents of the voyage, &c., &c. Print. by J. L. Hall on board the *Henry Lee*, 1849. 88 p.

Authorship is attributed to John Linville Hall and to George Gideon Webster.
CSfCP CSmH CU-B CtY

15847. —— Same. With title: Around the Horn in '49; a journal... [Wethersfield, Conn., Reprint. by L. J. [!] 1898] 252 p. illus., ports.   CHi CSjC

15848. —— Same. With an introd. by Oscar Lewis. S.F., Bk. club of Calif., 1928. 250 copies printed by the Grabhorn press.   CBb CHi

15849. Hastings, Lansford Warren. ...The emigrants' guide to Oregon and California...reproduced in facsimile from the original edition of 1845, with historical note and bibliography by Charles Henry Carey. Princeton, Princeton univ. press, 1932. 157 p. front. (port.) (Narratives of the trans-Mississippi frontier)
CAna CBb CHi CLgA CSal CSdS CSfCW CStbS CStclU CSto AU MoS ViU ViW

15850. Haynor, Genevieve M. The history of gold dredging in California, 1848–1940. [Berkeley, 1941] Thesis (M.A.)—Univ. of Calif., 1941.   CU

15851. Hazelton, John Adams. The Hazelton letters; a contribution to western Americana. Ed. and annotated by Mary Geneva Bloom. Stockton, College of the Pac., c1958. 18 p. port.
CHi CL CRedCL CSd CSto

15852. Helper, Hinton Rowan. The land of gold. Reality versus fiction. Baltimore, Author, 1855. 300 p.
CHi CLgA CP CSd CSfCW CSjC CStbS ViU

15853. —— Same, with title: Dreadful California, being a true and scandalous account of the barbarous civilization...ed. by Lucius Beebe and Charles M. Clegg. Illus. by James Alexander. Indianapolis, Bobbs-Merrill, 1948. 162 p. illus.
CBaB CChiS CCoron CLLoy CLO CMon CNa CRc CSd CSf CSjC CSlu CWhC

15854. Hemphill, Vivia. Down the Mother Lode. Sacramento, Purnell's, 1922. 91 p.
CHi CLSM CRedCL CSto

15855. Hepburn, Andrew. Northern California. Bost., Houghton, 1959. 159 p. illus., maps.
CAla CChiS CCoron CLO CMon CNa CRic CSS CSd MiD

15856. Hinchliff, Thomas Woodbine. Over the sea and far away... London, Longmans, 1876. 416 p. illus.   CSfCW CU-B

15857. Hittell, John Shertzer. Mining in the Pacific states of North America. S.F., H.H. Bancroft & co., 1861. 224 p.
C CHi CLSM CLU CLgA CSfCP CSfCSM CSfCW CSfWF-H CSmH CSt CStclU CU CU-B CaBViPA MiD NN

15858. Hittell, Theodore Henry. The adventures of James Capen Adams, mountaineer and grizzly bear hunter of California. S.F., Towne & Bacon, 1860. 378 p. illus., port. Illustrations by Charles C. Nahl. Other editions followed: 1861, 1867, 1911, 1912.
C CHi CLSM CS CSd CSfCW CSfP CSmH CSt CU-B CtY ICN OrU

15859. Holbrook, John C. Recollections of a nonagenarian, of life in New England, the Middle West, and New York...together with scenes in California... Bost., Pilgrim press [c1897] 351 p. front. (port.), pl.
CHi CSfCW CU-B

15860. Hoppin, Charles Rossiter. Some of his letters home, 1849–1863, as written to his family in Niles, Michigan, following his immigration to California in 1849. Oakland, Priv. print., 1948. 30 p.   CHi

15861. Howe, Octavius Thorndike. Argonauts of '49; history and adventures of the emigrant companies from Massachusetts 1849–1850. Cambridge, Harvard univ. press, 1923. 221 p. front., plates. "List of mining companies from Massachusetts going to California in 1849, date of starting and arrival..."; Appendix, p. 187–213. Bibliography: p. 219–221.
Available in many California libraries and CoU MoS OrU ViW

15862. Hulbert, Archer Butler. Forty-niners; the chronicle of the California trail. Bost., Little, 1931. 340 p. illus. Bibliography: p. 323–333.
Available in many libraries.

15863. Hunter, George. Reminiscences of an old timer. S.F., Crocker, 1887. 454 p. illus., ports.
CBb CHi

15864. [Huntley, Henry Vere] California: its gold and its inhabitants. By the author of "Seven years on the slave coast of Africa"... London, Thomas Cautley Newby, 1856. 2 v.   CHi CP CSf

15865. Hussey, John Adam, ed. Voyage of the *Racoon*; a 'secret' journal of a visit to Oregon, California and Hawaii, 1813–1814...Drawings by Henry Rusk. S.F., Bk. club of Calif. [Print. by Taylor & Taylor] 1958. 36 p. illus.
CBb CHi CLgA CSalCL CSf CStmo CSto CaBViPA

15866. Hust, Stephen Grover. "This is my own, my native land." Yuba City, Independent press, 1956. 204 p.
Available in many California libraries.

15867. Hutchinson, William Henry. Another notebook of the old West; companion volume to A notebook of the old West. Chico, Hurst & Yount, 1954. 88 p.   CChiS CRb

15868. —— California heritage; a history of northern California lumbering. [Chico, Diamond Gardner corp., 1958?] [32] p. illus., map.
C CArcHT CChi CChiS CHi CLU CRb CSd CSto

15869. —— A notebook of the old West. Chico, Bob Hurst, 1947. 122 p. illus.   CHi

15870. —— One man's west. Companion volume to A notebook of the old West. Chico, Hurst & Yount [c1948] 127 p. illus.   CChiS CHi CRb CU-B

15871. Immigration society of Northern California. Northern California, a description of its soil, climate, productions, markets, occupied and unoccupied lands... Sacramento, Crocker, 1885. 72 p. illus., front. (map) Cover title: Homes in Northern California.   C

15872. Ingalls, John. California letters of the gold rush period; the correspondence of John Ingalls, 1849–1851, ed. by R. W. G. Vail. Worcester, 1938. 40 p. Reprint. from the proceedings of the Am. antiquarian soc. for April 1937.   CHi

15873. Isbell, F. A. Mining & hunting in the Far West, 1852–1870. With an introd. by Nathan van Patten. Burlingame, W.P. Wreden, 1948. 36 p. port. "Two hundred copies"...Greenwood press. A reprint of the ed. pub. ca. 1871.
CBb CHi CLgA CRic CSto

15874. Jackson, Joseph Henry. Anybody's gold; the story of California's mining towns... illustrated by E. H. Suydam. N.Y., London, Appleton-Century, 1941. 467 p. illus., maps. "Reading list": p. 447–453.
Available in many California libraries and CaBViPA GU MiD MoS N ODa

15875. —— Gold rush album. N.Y., Scribner, 1949. 239 p. illus.
Available in many California libraries and CaBViPA MiD MoS MoSU ODa OrU T UHi

15876. Jackson, William A. Jackson's map of the mining districts. N.Y., Lambert & Lane, 1849.   CHi

15877. —— Same. Appendix...bringing down all the discoveries since 1849... N.Y., 1851. 16 p.
CHi (2d ed. rev. & enl.) ViU

15878. Jewell, Harold Walter. The development of governmental restraints on hydraulic mining in California. Sacramento, 1955. 107 p. Thesis (M.A.)—Sacramento state college, 1955.   CSS

15879. Johnson, Humphrey Cyril. Scenic guide to northern California... [Susanville, Scenic guides] c1946. 112 p. illus., maps. C CL CLU CSj MiD

15880. —— Scenic guide to the Mother Lode; a special guide to California's gold camps of one hundred years ago. [n.p.] Author, c1948. 52 p. illus., maps.
C CLO CO CRedl CSj CSmH

15881. Johnson, Overton. Route across the Rocky mountains, with a description of Oregon and California ...by Overton Johnson and Wm. H. Winter, of the emigration of 1843. Lafayette, Ind., J.B. Semans, print., 1846. 152 p.   CHi

15882. —— Same. With preface and notes by Carl L. Cannon, from the edition of 1846. Princeton, Princeton univ. press, 1932. 199 p. pl., facsims. Narratives of the trans-Mississippi frontier.   CBb CHi CLgA

15883. Johnson, Theodore Taylor. Sights in the gold region, and scenes by the way. N.Y., Baker and Scribner, 1849. 278 p.
CHi CP CRedl CSd CSfCSM CSfCW CSfP CStbS CStoC GU

15884. —— Same, 2d ed., rev. and enl. 1850. 324 p. illus., fold. map.   CBb CHi CLSM CSf CSfCW

15885. —— Same, 3d ed., with title: California and Oregon; or, Sights in the gold region, and scenes by the way. Phila., Lippincott, Grambo & co., 1851. 348 p. illus., fold. map.   CLSM CLgA ViW
Other editions followed.   C-S (Dublin, 1850) CHi (1865) CLSM (1857) CSfCSM (1865) CSjC (1853) MoS (1865) ViW (1865)

15886. —— —— Index...Joseph Gaer, ed. [S.F., 1935] 29 l. (Calif. literary research project. Index no. 12) Mimeo. "SERA project 2-F2-132 (3-F2-197) Calif. literary research."   C-S CHi CSdS CSf CStmo

15887. Johnston, Philip. Lost and living cities of the California gold rush; California centennials guide. L.A., Touring bur., Automobile club of So. Calif., 1948. 61 p. maps.
C CHi CL CLO CLSU CLU CO CPom CSj CSmH GU MiD UHi

15888. Johnston, William Graham. Experiences of a forty-niner. A member of the wagon train first to enter California in the memorable year of 1849. Pittsburgh, Priv. print., 1892. 390 p. illus., ports., fold. map.   CHi

15889. —— Same, with title: Overland to California. Foreword by Jos. A. Sullivan. [1st Calif. ed.] Oakland, Biobooks, 1948. 272 p. illus., ports., maps. (Calif. centennial ed., 13)
CAna CBb CChiS CHi CLgA CRc CRic CSal CSd CSdS CSf CStclU CStmo CSto CStoC CYcCL OrU

15890. Johnstone, E. McD. Pacific coast souvenir.

Oakland, E.S. Denison [c1888] [12] p. 46 pl. Description of views by E. McD. Johnstone.

CHi CSfCW CU-B

15891. Justesen, Peter. Two years' adventures of a Dane in the California gold mines. By Peter Justesen (capt. in the Danish service) Tr. and print. for the author by John Bellows. Gloucester, Mass., 1865. CP

15892. Keller, George. A trip across the plains, and life in California; embracing a description of the overland route;...the gold mines of California; its climate, soil, productions, animals, &c., with sketches of Indian, Mexican and Californian character... [Massillon, Ohio, White's press, 1851] 58 p.

CHi (facsim.) CSmH

15893. —— Same. Foreword [by] J. A. Sullivan. [1st Calif. ed.] Oakland, Biobooks, 1955. 44 p. facsim. Includes reproduction of original t.p. "500 copies printed by Times-Star press, Alameda, Calif."

CBb CChiS CP CRic CSal CSalCL CSdS CSf CSjC CSto N

15894. Kelly, Thomas Smith, III. The marketing of redwood lumber through wholesale middlemen. [Berkeley, 1939] Thesis (M.A.)—Univ. of Calif., 1939. CU

15895. Kelly, William. An excursion to California ... With a stroll through the diggings and ranches of that country. London, Chapman & Hall, 1851. 2 v.

C CHi CLU CLgA CRedCL CSalCL CSf CSjC CSmH CStmo

15896. —— A stroll through the diggings of California. London, Simms and M'Intyre, 1852. 240 p.

CHi

15897. —— Same, with paintings by Charles Nahl and foreword by Joseph A. Sullivan. Oakland, Biobooks, 1950. 206 p. col. pl. Published in London, 1851, as v.2 of An excursion to California.

Available in many libraries.

15898. Keyes, Erasmus Darwin. From West Point to California. Foreword by Joseph A. Sullivan. [1st Calif. ed.] Oakland [1950] 90 p. ports. (Calif. relations, no. 24)

Available in many California libraries and N

15899. Kingsley, Nelson. Diary of...a California argonaut of 1849; ed. by Frederick J. Teggart. Berkeley, Univ. of Calif., 1914. 179 p. (Pub. of the Acad. of Pac. coast history, v.3, no. 3)

CBb CHi CRcS CSd CSdS CSfCW CU-B OrU

15900. Kinyon, Edmund. The Northern mines. Factual narratives of the counties of Nevada, Placer, Sierra, Yuba, and portions of Plumas and Butte. Grass Valley, Nevada City, Union pub. co. [1949] 167 p. illus., ports., map.

C CChiS CHi CO CSS CSf CSfCSM CSfWF-H CSmH

15901. Klappholz, Lowell. Gold! Gold! N.Y., McBride [c1959] 207 p. illus., map. CSf CSto

15902. Kneiss, Gilbert H. Redwood railways; a story of redwoods, picnics, and commuters. Berkeley, Howell-North, 1956. 165 p. illus., ports., maps (2 fold. in pocket), facsims.

Available in many California libraries and CaBViPA

15903. Koenig, George. Mother Lode, route no. 49; a practical automobile traveler's guide. S.F., Fearon [1957] 32 p. illus., maps.

C CP CRcS CRic CSd CSfSt CStmo

15904. Kotzebue, Otto von. Entdeckungs– reise in die Süd-see und nach der Berings-strasse zur erforschung einer nordöstlichen durchfahrt. Unternommen in den jahren 1815, 1816, 1817 und 1818... auf den...schiffe Rurick. Weimar, Gebrüder Hoffman, 1821. 3 v. in 1. illus., maps. CU-B

15905. —— Same, with title: A voyage of discovery, into the South Sea and Bering Straits... London, Longman, 1821. 3 v. illus., maps. CBb CHi CLgA CP

15906. —— Neue Reise um die welt, in den jahren 1823, 24, 25 und 26... Weimar, 1830: Verlag von Wilhelm Hoffman; St. Petersburg: bei I. Brief... 2 v. in 1. illus., maps. The second von Kotzebue expedition, in which "two months were passed in and around San Francisco Bay, September 27–November 25, 1824, with an overland trip to the Russian settlement at Fort Ross. The officers were entertained three days at Santa Clara Mission and made shorter calls at Dolores and San Rafael, which the captain calls San Gabriel."—Waters. Other editions were published in Russian, English, Dutch, etc.

CHi CL CLSU CLU CSfWF-H CSmH

15907. —— Same, with title: A new voyage around the world... tr. from the German edition. London, Henry Colburn and Richard Bentley, 1830. 2 v. illus., maps. CHi CLgA CSf

15908. Langsdorff, Georg Heinrich. Narrative of the Rezanov voyage to Nueva California in 1806; an English translation revised with the Teutonisms of the original Hispaniolized, Russianized, or anglicized by Thomas C. Russell. S.F., Priv. press of T.C. Russell, 1927. 158 p. illus., ports., map. 260 copies printed.

CChiS CHi CLM CLgA CSf CSfP CStclU CSto

15909. Latimer, Frances Ludowick. California and the Civil war. [Berkeley, 1929] Thesis (M.A.)— Univ. of Calif., 1929. CU CU-B

15910. Leach, Frank Aleamon. Recollections of a newspaper man; a record of life and events in California. S.F., S. Levinson, 1917. 416 p. illus., port.

Available in many California libraries and OrU

15911. Leader, Herman Alexander. The Hudson's Bay company in California. [Berkeley, 1928] Thesis (Ph.D.)—Univ. of Calif., 1928. CU CU-B

15912. Leeper, David Rohrer. The argonauts of 'forty-nine; some recollections of the plains and the diggings. South Bend, Ind., J.B. Stoll & co., 1894. 146 p. illus.

CBb CHi CLO CSd CSf CSfCW CStbS ViU

15913. —— Same. Reprinted by Long's college bk. co., Columbus, Ohio, 1950.

CArcHT CL CLSM COnC MiD

15914. Lemonnier, Leon. La ruée vers l'or en Californie... Paris, Gallimard, 1944. 467 p. maps. (La Suite des temps, 11) CSf

15915. [Letts, John M.] California illustrated: including a description of the Panama and Nicaragua routes. By a returned Californian. N.Y., William Holdredge, 1852. 224 p. illus. Plates drawn by George Victor Cooper.

CHi CLO CLgA CMartC CP CSfP CStoC

15916. —— Same. N.Y., R.T. Young, 1853. 224 p. illus. CHi CLSM CLod CRcS CSd CSf CSfCW

15917. —— Same, with title: A pictorial view of California; including a description of the Panama and Nicaragua routes... N.Y., Henry Bill, 1853. 224 p. 48 pl.

CSfCW CSfP CStbS

15918. —— —— Index... Joseph Gaer, ed. [S.F., 1935] 49 l. ([Calif. literary research project. Index no.] 13) Mimeo. "SERA project 2-F2-132 (3-F2-197) Calif. literary research."

C-S CHi CLSM CSdS CSf CSjC CStmo

15919. Levy, Herbert Morton. The northern California press and the Constitution of 1879. [Berkeley, 1952] Thesis (M.A.)—Univ. of Calif., 1952.　　CU

15920. Lewis, Oscar. The big four; the story of Huntington, Stanford, Hopkins, and Crocker, and of the building of the Central Pacific. N.Y., Knopf, 1938. 418 p. illus., ports., facsims.
Available in many California libraries.

15921. ——— ed. California in 1846; described in letters from Thomas O. Larkin, "The farthest West," E. M. Kern, and "Justice." Notes and introduction by Oscar Lewis. S.F., Grabhorn, 1934. 63 p. illus., ports., facsims. (Rare Americana, 2d ser. no. 5)
Available in many California libraries.

15922. Logan, Clarence A. Mother Lode gold belt of California. Sacramento, State print. off., 1935. 6 maps in pocket.　　CRcS

15923. Loofbourow, Leonides Latimer. In search of God's gold; a story of continued Christian pioneering in California. S.F., Historical soc. of the California-Nevada annual conference of the Methodist church and in cooperation with the College of the Pacific, Stockton, 1950. 313 p. illus., ports.　　CHi CL CP CSf

15924. Lorenz, Anthony J. Scurvy in the gold rush. Reprint. from *Jl. of the history of medicine and allied sciences* 1957, v.12, no. 4, p. 463–510.
　　CHi CSfWF-H

15925. Lucia, Ellis. The saga of Ben Holladay, giant of the old West... N.Y., Hastings house, 1959. 374 p. illus.　　CSf

15926. Lyman, Albert. Journal of a voyage to California, and life in the gold diggings, and also of a voyage from California to the Sandwich islands, by...a member of the Connecticut mining and trading company which sailed in the schooner *General Morgan* from New York, Feb. 22, 1849. Hartford, E.T. Pease; N.Y., Dexter & bro., 1852. 192 p.　　CHi HHi

15927. Lyman, Chester Smith. Around the Horn to the Sandwich islands and California, 1845–1850, being a personal record kept by Chester S. Lyman... Edited by Frederick J. Teggart...New Haven, Conn., Yale, 1924. 328 p. illus., ports.
Available in many California libraries and CaBViPA MoS ViU

15928. McCloskey, Joseph J. and Sharmann, Hermann J. Christmas in the gold fields, 1849. ...reminiscences...with illustrations taken from contemporary letter sheets. S.F., Calif. hist. soc., c1959. 33 p. illus. (Calif. hist. soc. Special pub. no. 31)
CAla CBb CHi CL CLSM CLgA CLod CNa CRedCL CSalCL CSd CStcl

15929. M'Collum, William. California as I saw it. Pencillings by the way of its gold and gold diggers. And incidents of travel by land and water. ... Buffalo, George H. Derby & co., 1850. 72 p.　　CHi

15930. ——— Same. Ed. by Dale L. Morgan. Los Gatos, Talisman press, c1960. 219 p. illus., maps (end papers)　　CHi CL CLSM

15931. McCue, Jim. Twenty-one years in California. Incidents in the life of a stage driver... S.F., Francis & Valentine [1878?] 30 p. port. on cover.　　CHi

15932. McGowan, Joseph Aloysius. Freighting to the mines in California, 1849–1859. [Berkeley, 1949] Thesis (Ph.D.)—Univ. of Calif., 1949.　　CU

15933. McIlhany, Edward Washington. Recollections of a '49er. A quaint and thrilling narrative of a trip across the plains, and life in the California gold fields during the stirring days following the discovery of gold in the far West... Kansas City, Mo., Hailman print. co., 1908. 212 p. illus., ports.
　　C CHi CLgA CMon MoS

15934. McKenney, L. & M. & co., pub. McKenney's...directory of the Central Pacific railroad and its branches...A guide and business directory...the names of business firms, their occupation and location. 1872–1883/84. S.F., 1872–1883.
CMary has 1872, 1882, 1883/84. CS has 1872.

15935. McNairn, Jack, and MacMullen, Jerry. Ships of the redwood coast. Stanford [1945] 156 p. illus. Bibliography: p. 149.
Available in many California libraries and CaBViPA

15936. McNeer, May Yonge. The California gold rush; illus. by Lynd Ward. N.Y., Random house [1950] 184 p. col. illus. (Landmark bks. [6])　　CLS CSdS

15937. McNeil, Samuel. McNeil's travels in 1849 to, through and from the gold regions in California. Columbus, Ohio, Scott & Bascom, print., 1850. 40 p. Facsim. ed. under the direction of the Yale univ. press, Christmas 1958. 300 copies printed for Frederick W. Beinecke.　　CHi

15938. McWilliams, John. Recollections of...his youth, experiences in California and the Civil war. Princeton, Princeton univ. press [n.d.] 186 p. front. (port.)　　CHi

15939. Makers of northern California; press reference. Sacramento, Sacramento union, 1917. 75 ports. Below each portrait is a short biographical sketch.
C CFa CHi CPom CSf CSmH CStoC CU-B MoS

15940. Maps of the Mother Lode showing connections from San Francisco. Placerville, Pony express courier, 1938. 30 p.　　CRcS

15941. Margo, Elisabeth. Taming the forty-niner. N.Y., Rinehart, 1955. 245 p. illus., port.
Available in many libraries.

15942. Margo, Joan. The food supply problem of the California gold mines, 1848–1855. [Berkeley, 1947] Thesis (M.A.)—Univ. of Calif., 1947.　　CU CU-B

15943. Marr, Paul Donald. Industrial geography of the San Francisco north bay area. [Berkeley, 1955] Thesis (M.A.)—Univ. of Calif., 1955.　　CU

15944. Marryat, Francis Samuel. Mountains and molehills, or, Recollections of a burnt journal... London, Longman, Brown, Green, & Longmans, 1855. 443 p. illus.
C CBaB CHi CL CLU CLgA CSfWF-H CSj CSmH CStbS CaBViPA

15945. ——— Same. N.Y., Harper, 1855. 393 p. illus.
C CHi CL CLO CLU CLgA CP CPom CRedl CSS CSd CSf CSfP CSfWF-H CSjC CSmH ViW

15946. ——— Same. Reprint. in facsimile from the 1st American ed. of 1855, with intro. and notes by Marguerite Eyer Wilbur. Stanford [1952] 393 p. illus.
CBaB CBb CChiS CHi CLLoy CMartC CMerCL CRedCL CRic CSS CSal CSf CSfCW CSfSt CSto CViCL MiD OrU UHi

15947. ——— ——— Index...Joseph Gaer editor... [S.F., 1935] 30 l. (Index no. 7, SERA project 2-F2-132 (3-F2-197) Calif. literary research) Mimeo.
　　CHi CLSM CLSU CP CSf CStmo

15948. Massett, Stephen C. Biobooks presents Stephen C. Massett in the first California troubadour. Prologue by Joseph A. Sullivan. Oakland, 1954. 96 p.

port., facsims. (Calif. relations, no. 37) Based on the author's autobiography published in 1863 under the title, Drifting about.

CBaB CBb CHi CL CLO CLgA CP CRedCL CRic CSalCL CSd CSdS CSf CSto CStoC

15949. —— "Drifting about," or what "Jeems Pipes of Pipesville" saw-and-did; an autobiography. N.Y., Carleton, 1863. 371 p. illus. Cowan: The author visited California with the gold rush... p. 112–144. p. 154–159 and p. 367–370 are given over to the author's second and third visits to the state.   CBb CHi CP CSfCW

15950. Matthews, Dave S. Lighter side of the Lode. Stockton, Muldowney print. co., 1950. 46 p.   CHi CSto

15951. Meads, Simeon P. Glimpses of the wet past in northern California... Berkeley, Sather gate bk. shop [n.d.] 110 p.   CHi

15952. A memorial and biographical history of northern California, illustrated. Containing a history of this important section of the Pacific coast from the earliest period of its occupancy...and biographical mention of many of its pioneers and also of prominent citizens of today... Chicago, Lewis, 1891. 834 p. illus., ports. Gives brief history of thirty-two northern California counties, including Klamath.

C CBb CChi CHi CL CLO CLU CMartC CMary CO CRb CRedCL CRic CSf CSfCSM CSjC CSmH CStbS CStclU CStoC CU-B CUk CaBViPA CtY IC ICN NHi TxU

15953. Same. Chicago, Lewis, 1891. 637 p. illus., ports.

C CFA CHi CLU COroB CRedCL CSf CSt CWeT CYcCL IC

15954. —— Same. Chicago, Lewis, 1891. 735 p. illus., ports. Contains additional biographical accounts.   CHi

15955. —— Same. Chicago, Lewis, 1891. 860 p. illus., ports. p. 834–860 comprise short biographies of Placer county residences.   C CAuP CSS CSf IC

15956. Merriam, Clinton Hart, ed. The dawn of the world; myths and weird tales told by the Mewan Indians of California. Cleveland, Arthur H. Clark co., 1910. 273 p. illus.

CBb CHi CMartC CRcS CSd CSrCL

15957. Merwin, Henry Childs. The life of Bret Harte, with some account of the California pioneers... Bost., Houghton, 1911. 362 p. illus., ports., pl.

CHi CL CSd CSf CYcCL ViU

15958. Methodist Episcopal church. Chinese and Japanese mission in the state of California. ...[Annual] report...

CHi has 1880/81, 1883/84.

15959. [Metlar, George W.] Northern California, Scott and Klamath rivers; their inhabitants and characteristics—its historical features—arrival of Scott and his friends—mining interests...together with a life-like picture of San Francisco... Yreka, Yreka union off., J. Tyson print., 1856. 24 p.   C CSmH CU-B

15960. Meyer, Carl. Nach dem Sacramento. Reisebilder eines heimgekehrten. Aarau [Switzerland] H.R. Sauerländer, 1855. 364 p.

C CHi CL CLSU CLU CSf CSfP CSmH CaBViPA MoKU NHi

15961. —— Same, translated with title: Bound for Sacramento; travel-pictures of a returned wanderer, translated from the German by Ruth Frey Axe. Claremont, Saunders studio press, 1938. 282 p.

C CBaB CChiS CHi CLO CLSU CLU CLgA CRcS CSS CSf CSmH CStmo CaBViPA OrU

15962. Mighels, Ella Sterling (Clark) Cummins. Life and letters of a forty-niner's daughter, by Aurora Esmeralda [pseud.] S.F., Harr Wagner, c1929. 371 p. illus.

CBb CChiS CHi CLod CLSM CRcS CRiC CSd CSf CSfCW CStmo

15963. Miller, Joaquin. Paquita, the Indian heroine. Hartford, Am. pub. co. [1881] 445 p. illus., port.   CHi CO

15964. The miners' companion and guide. A compendium of most valuable information for the prospector, miner, geologist, mineralogist and assayer; together with a comprehensive glossary of technical phrases used in the work. S.F., Pub. by J. Silversmith, "Mining and scientific press" off., 1861. 232 p. illus.

C CHi CLSM CLU CSmH

15965. The miners' own book, containing correct illustrations and descriptions of the various modes of California mining, including all the improvements introduced from the earliest day to the present time. S.F., Hutchings & Rosenfield, 1858. 32 p. Illustrations are by Charles Nahl.   CHi CSmH CU CU-B CtY NN

15966. —— Same. [N.Y., W. Abbatt, 1933] Reprint. in the *Mag. of history.* Extra number, no. 187, v.47, no. 3.   CRedl CSS CStmo CStoC

15967. —— Same. Reprint. from the original ed. of 1858. With introd. by Rodman W. Paul. S.F., Bk. club of Calif., 1949. 35 p. illus., port., facsims.

CBb CHi CLO CLgA CSalCL CSd CSf CSfCSM CSjC CSto

15968. [Mitchell, Samuel Augustus] Description of Oregon and California, embracing an account of the gold regions... Phila., Thomas, Cowperthwaite & co., 1849. 76 p. illus., fold. col. map.   OrU

15969. —— Texas, Oregon and California. Foreword by Joseph A. Sullivan. Oakland, Biobooks, c1948. (Calif. centennial ed. no.12) 46 p. col. ports., fold. col. map.

CBb CChiS CHi CLO CRcS CStmo CSto CV

15970. Moerenhout, Jacques Antoine. The inside story of the gold rush... tr. and ed. by Abraham P. Nasatir, in collaboration with George Ezra Dane who wrote the introduction and conclusion... S.F., Calif. hist. soc., 1935. 94 p. illus., port., fold. map (mining district of Calif., by William A. Jackson, 1849) (Calif. hist. soc. Special pub. no. 8)

CHi CLgA CSdS CSjC CSmat CStoC

15971. Moorman, Madison Berryman. The journal of...1850–1851, ed., with notes and an introd., by Irene D. Paden; together with a biographical sketch of the author by his granddaughter, Louise Parks Banes. S.F., Calif. hist. soc., 1948. 150 p. port., fold. map. (Calif. hist. soc. Special pub. no. 23)

CB CBb CChiS CHi CSd CStclU CStoC

15972. Morgan, Gene. Westward the course of empire; the story of the Pony express. Chicago, Lakeside press, 1945. 57 p. illus.   CLod

15973. Mossman, Isaac Van Dorsey. Pony expressman's recollections. With an introd. and notes by J. Heine Christ. [Portland, Ore.] Champoeg press, 1955. 55 p. illus.   CSto

15974. The Mother Lode magnet, ed. and pub. The lure of the Mark Twain–Bret Harte counties... Jamestown, 1931. 50 p. illus., fold. map.   C CHi

15975. Mother Lode towns, inc., pub. See the gold country; Mother Lode towns. S.F. [n.d.] folder (5 p.) illus., map.   CRcS

15976. Mulford, Prentice. Prentice Mulford's California sketches; ed. by Franklin Walker. S.F., Bk. club of Calif., print. by J.H. Nash, 1935. 105 p. The sketches, compiled from various periodicals, were published from 1865 to 1874.
CHi CRcS CSdS CSf CSfCW CStoC OrU

15977. ——— Prentice Mulford's story. Life by land and sea. N.Y., F.J. Needham, 1889. 299 p. Mulford spent sixteen years in California, beginning in 1856.
CBb CBev CHi CL CLSU CLU CLgA CPom CRcS CSS CSbr CSdS CSf CSjC CSmH CSmat CStbS CStrJC

15978. ——— Same. With a preface and conclusion by Arthur Edward Waite. London, W. Rider & son, 1913. 297 p.   CSalCL

15979. ——— Same. [1st California ed. Oakland, Biobooks, 1953] 145 p. illus.
Available in many California libraries.

15980. Myrick, David F. Railroads of Nevada and eastern California. Berkeley, Howell-North, 1962. v.1, The northern roads.   CAla CHi

15981. New York historical society. Gold fever; a catalogue of the California gold rush centennial exhibition, by R. W. G. Vail. N.Y., 1949. 40 p. illus., facsims. Reprint. from its *Quarterly,* Oct. 1949.
CHi CLO

15982. Newell, Gordon R. Pacific lumber ships... historic photos for salty savoring, by Gordon Newell and Joe Williamson. Seattle, Superior pub. co., 1960.   CSf

15983. ——— Paddlewheel pirate; the life and adventures of Captain Ned Wakeman. N.Y., Dutton, 1959. 248 p.   CMon CRcS CStcl CStmo CViCL

15984. Newton, John Marshall. Memoirs... (containing a narrative of my trip across the plains from Ohio to California; life and adventures at the "Diggins"; the French war at Moquelumne hill; etc.) Cambridge, N.Y., Washington county post, 1913. 91 p. port., pl.
CHi ViU

15985. Nordhoff, Charles. Northern California, Oregon, and the Sandwich islands. N.Y., Harpers, 1874. 256 p. illus., ports. Other editions, including London, Sampson Low.
Available in many California libraries and HHi ViU WM

15986. Northwestern Pacific railroad. Vacation 1904. [S.F.] 1904. 160 p. illus.   C-S
Other editions followed.   C (1908, 1909, 1915) CHi (1917, 1921, 1929)

15987. Norton, Lewis Adelbert. Life and adventures of Col. L. A. Norton: Written by himself. Oakland, Pac. press pub. house, 1887. 492 p. port.
CBb CHi CStoC

15988. O'Brien, Robert. California called them; a saga of golden days and roaring camps; illus. by Antonio Sotomayor. N.Y., McGraw-Hill, 1951. 251 p. illus.
Available in many California libraries.

15989. Ogden, Adele. The California sea-otter trade, 1784–1848. [Berkeley, 1938] Thesis (Ph.D.)— Univ. of Calif., 1938. Published in Univ. of Calif. Pub. in history, v.26, 1941. 251 p.
CU and CU-B have Thesis.

15990. O'Leary, A. A year in California and a contest with her quacks. [n.p.] 1888. 48 p.   CHi

15991. Olmsted, John. A trip to California in 1868. N.Y., Trow's print. and bookbinding co., 1880. 131 p.
CHi

15992. Owens, G., comp. A general directory and business guide of the principal towns in the upper country, embracing a portion of California... S.F., Pub. by A. Gensoul, Pacific map depot; Towne & Bacon, print., 1866. 170 p.   CHi

15993. Pancoast, Charles Edward. A Quaker forty-niner...ed. by Anna Paschall Hannum, with a foreword by John Bach McMaster. Phila., Univ. of Pennsylvania press, 1930. 402 p. illus., port., map, facsim.
CHi CLgA CRcS CRedCL CRedl CSal CSfCW CStaC CStbS CStmo CWhC ViU

15994. Parkinson, Jessie Heaton. Adventuring in California; yesterday, today, and day before yesterday; with memoirs of Bret Harte's "Tennessee." S.F., Harr Wagner, 1921. 120 p. illus.
CChiS CFS CHi CRcS CRic CSalCL CSf CStmo CSto

15995. Patterson, Lawson B. Twelve years in the mines of California; embracing a general view of the gold region... Cambridge [Mass.] Miles and Dillingham, 1862. 108 p.   CHi CSfCW CSfP CSjC

15996. Paul, Rodman Wilson. California gold; the beginnings of mining in the far west. Cambridge, Mass., Harvard, 1947. 380 p. illus., maps.
Available in many California libraries and CaBViPA GU MiD ODa OrU ViW

15997. [Payson, George] Golden dreams and leaden realities. By Ralph Raven [pseud.] With an introductory chapter by Francis Fogie, sen., esq. N.Y., Putnam, 1853. 344 p.   CSf

15998. Peacock, William. The Peacock letters, April 7, 1850 to January 4, 1852; fourteen letters written by William Peacock to his wife, Susan... Stockton, San Joaquin pioneer & hist. soc., 1950. 32 p. ports., facsim.
CHi CSS CSto CStoC CaBViPA

15999. Peale, Titian Ramsay. Diary...Oregon to California, overland journey, September and October, 1841, by Clifford Merrill Drury. Introd. and bibliography by Carl S. Dentzel. L.A., Dawson, 1957. 85 p. illus. (part col.) port. (Early Calif. travels ser., 36) 300 copies printed by College press.
CHi CL CLLoy CLO CLS CLSM CLgA CSd CSto CStoC CaBViPA

16000. Peck, George Washington. Aurifodina; or, Adventures in the gold fields. By Cantell A. Bigly [pseud.] N.Y., Baker & Scribner, 1849. 103 p.
CHi CP CSfCW MoKU ViU

16001. Peck, F. Taylor, jr. The life and letters of Albert Powell. [Mobile, Ala., n.d.] 75 l. Thesis (B.S.S.) —Spring Hill College, Mobile county, Ala.   C

16002. Pérez Rosales, Vicente. California adventure, tr. from the original Spanish, with an introd. by Edwin S. Morby and Arturo Torres-Ríoseco, with the 19th century Chilean classic Recuerdos del pasado. With decorations by Albert J. Camille. S.F., Bk. club of Calif., 1947. 96 p. port.   CHi CLgA CStoC

16003. Peters, Charles. The autobiography of... In 1915 the oldest pioneer living in California who mined in the "Days of old"... Sacramento, LaGrave co. [1915?] 231 p.
CHi CLSM CLgA CSf CSfP CSjC CSto

16004. Peterson, Harry C. The romance of California; birth of the golden empire, the thrilling days of '49; complete guide to the land of Bret Harte, Mark Twain. Sacramento, Chamber of commerce, c1938. 47 p. illus., map. "The tours through the Mother Lode were taken from a manuscript by F. A. Kazmarek."
C CChiS CHi CLgA CO CS CSfWF-H CSmH

16005. [Pfeiffer, Ida (Reyer)] A lady's visit to California, 1853. [1st Calif. printing] Oakland, Biobooks, 1950. 75 p. pl. (Calif. centennials no. 23) "Foreword" signed: Jos. A. Sullivan. Text from the author's second journey around the world (N.Y., Harper, 1856). Cf. Foreword.

Available in many California libraries and CaBViPA

16006. [Phelps, William D.] Fore and aft; or, Leaves from the life of an old sailor. By "Webfoot" [pseud.] With illustrations by Hammatt Billings. Bost., Nichols & Hall, 1871. 359 p. pl.   CBb CHi CLgA

16007. Phillips, Emmett, and Miller, John, comps. & eds. Sacramento valley and foothill counties of California... [Sacramento] Pub. under direction of the Sacramento valley expositions commission [by] Sacramento news pub. co., 1915. 96 p. illus.
          C CFa CHi CS CSCL CSd CSmH

16008. Pierce, Hiram Dwight. A forty-niner speaks. A chronological record of the observations and experiences of a New Yorker and his adventures in various mining localities in California... Introd. by Sarah Wiswall Meyer. Oakland, Keystone-Inglett print. co., 1930. 74 p. illus.   CHi CRedl CSfCSM

16009. Pioneer association of the counties of Marin, Sonoma, Napa, Lake, and Mendocino. Constitution and by-laws of... Petaluma, Petaluma jl. and Argus print., 1870. 32 p.   CStrJC

16010. Planer, Edward Thomas, jr. Spanish inland exploration in Alta California, 1790–1800. [Berkeley, 1934] Thesis (M.A.)—Univ. of Calif., 1934.
                                                      CU CU-B

16011. Player-Frowd, J. G. Six months in California. London, Longmans, Green, and co., 1872. 164 p.
                    CHi CLSM CP CSf CU-B

16012. Porter, Burton B. One of the people, his own story. Colton, Author, 1907. 382 p. front. (port.)
                              CBb CHi CLO CSfCW

16013. Powers, Alfred. Redwood country; the lava region and the redwoods. N.Y., Duell [c1949] 292 p. (Am. folkways)
Available in many California libraries and CaBViPA
IC InI MiD N NjN NvU ODa OrU OU TxU

16014. Prentice, Edwin Dwight. Letters...to his mother, sisters and friends, 1850 to 1856. S.F., Priv. print. [Philopolis press] 1916. 50 p.   CSfP

16015. Quaife, Milo Milton, ed. Pictures of gold rush California. Chicago, Lakeside press, 1949. 383 p. illus., maps. (The Lakeside classics, no. 47)
          CBb CLO CSf CVtV MoHi N ViU

16016. Rae, William Fraser. Westward by rail: the new route to the east. N.Y., D. Appleton, 1871. 391 p. front. (map)   CHi CSfCW

16017. —— Same. 2d ed. ... London, Longmans, Green, 1871.   CSto

16018. —— Same. Leipzig, B. Tauchnitz, 1874.
                                                    CSfCW

16019. Railway & locomotive historical society, inc. Pacific coast chapter. 25 years, a history of the Pacific coast chapter...1937–1962; issued by Pacific coast chapter news jointly with the Western railroader... San Mateo, 1962. 47 p. illus. (*Western railroader*, v.25, no. 6, June 1962)   CHi

16020. Raw gold, the lure of the Mother Lode. [Modesto, Bruce Anderson] 1934. 31 p. illus.   CFS

16021. Read, James A. Journey to the gold diggins, by Jeremiah Saddlebags. Illus. by J. A. and D. F. Read;

a collotype facsimile of the original edition of 1849. With an intro. by Joseph Henry Jackson. Burlingame, Print. for William P. Wreden by Grabhorn, 1950. 63 p. col. illus.   CBaB CBb CChiS CSd CSdS

16022. Redwood empire association. Brief history..."Builders of the Redwood empire." [Oct. 1926] 27 p. Typew.   CStrJC

16023. —— Golden gate bridge and highway district. Golden gate bridge redwood empire; all-year vacationland. S.F., 1948. folder, col. illus., map. CRcS

16024. Revere, Joseph Warren. Keel and saddle: a retrospect of forty years of military and naval service. Bost., J.R. Osgood and co., 1872. 360 p.
                    CBb CHi CSfCW CStoC

16025. Rezanov, Count Nikolai Petrovich. The Rezanov voyage to Nueva California in 1806; the report of...his voyage to that provincia of Nueva Espana from New Archangel; an English translation rev. and corrected with notes, etc., by Thomas C. Russell. S.F., Priv. press of T.C. Russell, 1926. 104 p. illus., port., facsim.
          CChiS CHi CLO CLgA CSfP CStclU CSto

16026. Richardson, Albert Deane. Beyond the Mississippi; from the great river to the great ocean. Life and adventure on the prairies, mountains, and Pacific coast, 1857–1867. Hartford, Am. pub. co., 1867. 572 p. illus., ports., fold. map.   CBb CHi

16027. Robbins, Fred Strong. Through forest and field with Fred S. Robbins, the Bulletin hike story writer; seventy-five walks in the counties bordering San Francisco bay... [S.F., Print. by H.M. Alexander] c1914. [20] p. illus.   C

16028. —— Same. 2d ed. [S.F.?] c1914. 39 p. illus.   CHi

16029. Robinson, Fayette. California and its gold regions; with a geographical and topographical view of the country, its mineral and agricultural resources... N.Y., Stringer & Townsend, 1849. 137 p. fold. map.
          CHi CLSM CP CSd CSdS CSf CSfCW

16030. —— —— Index...Joseph Gaer, ed. [S.F., 1935] 22 l. (Index no. 14, SERA project 2-F2-132 (3-F2-197) Calif. literary research) Mimeo.
                    CHi CLSM CSdS CSf

16031. Rock, Francis John. J. Ross Browne: a biography... Wash., D.C., 1929. 80 p. Thesis (Ph.D.)—Catholic univ. of Am., 1929.   CHi CLgA

16032. Rossi, Louis, *abbé*. Six ans en Amérique (Californie et Orégon) ... Paris [etc.] Librairie de Perisse frères, Règis Ruffet et cie., successeurs, 1863. 322 p. 2 fold. maps.   CU-B

16033. —— Same. 2d ed. Paris, E. Dentu, 1863.
                              CHi CSfCW CU-B

16034. —— Same, with title: Souvenirs d'un voyage en Orégon et en Californie... Paris, Martin-Beaupré frères, 1864.   CU-B

16035. Rühl, Karl. Californien... N.Y., E. Steiger, 1867. 283 p. 2 fold. maps.   CHi

16036. Russell, Mary Inez. Some of the brick and stone houses of the Mother Lode during the fifties and sixties. [Berkeley, 1939] Thesis (M.A.)—Univ. of Calif., 1939.   CU

16037. Ryan, William Redmond. Personal adventures in upper and lower California in 1848–49... London, William Shoberl, 1850. 2 v. illus.
          C-S CBb CHi CLSM CLgA CMont CP CSd
CSf CSfCW CSfP ViW

16038. —— —— Index...Joseph Gaer, ed. [S.F., 1935] 29 l. (Index no. 11, SERA project 2-F2-132 (3-F2-197) Calif. literary research)   C-S CHi CP CSdS CStmo

16039. [Sacramento region citizens council] This is California. [Sacramento, News pub. co., 1928] 32 p. illus.   CHi CU-B

16040. San Francisco chronicle, comp. Welcome to the West. S.F., 1961? 27 p.   CHi

16041. Sbarboro, Andrea. Fight for true temperance. [S.F., Hicks-Judd, 1908] 67 p.   CHi

16042. Schallenberger, Moses. The opening of the California trail; the story of the Stevens party from the reminiscences of Moses Schallenberger as set down for H. H. Bancroft about 1885, ed. and expanded by Horace S. Foote in 1888, and now ed. with intro., notes, maps, and illus. by George R. Stewart. Berkeley and L.A., Univ. of Calif. press, 1953. 115 p. illus., ports., maps. (Bancroft lib. pub., no. 4)
Available in many California libraries and CaBViPA

16043. Scheller, John Jacob. Extract from autobiography... (January 1, 1819–August 18, 1886). 1954. 10 l. Typew.   C

16044. Schlagintweit, Robert von. Californien. Land und leute... Cöln und Leipzig, E.H. Mayer; N.Y., E. Steiger; [etc., etc.] 1871. 380 p. illus.
C CHi CL CLU CSfCSM CSfU CSmH CU-B

16045. —— Same, with title: Californië en zijne bevolking. Tr. by W. ten Entel, jr. Deventer, A. ter Gunne, 1873. 243 p.   CHi CLU

16046. —— The Pacific-Eisenbahn in Nordamerika. Leipzig, 1870. 203 p.   C-S CHi

16047. Settle, Raymond W. Empire on wheels. By Raymond W. Settle and Mary Lund Settle. Stanford, 1949. 153 p. illus., ports., map (on lining papers), facsims.   CHi CSf

16048. —— Saddles and spurs; the Pony express saga; by Raymond W. Settle and Mary Lund Settle. Harrisburg, Pa., Stackpole, 1955.   CHi CRcS CSd

16049. Shaw, David Augustus. Eldorado; or, California as seen by a pioneer, 1850–1900. By Hon. D. A. Shaw. L.A., B.R. Baumgardt & co., 1900. 313 p. illus., port.
CBb CBea CHi CLSM CLgA CRic CSS CSd CSf CSfCW CSfP CSjC CStmo CStoC

16050. —— —— Index...Joseph Gaer, ed. [S.F., 1935] 13 l. (Index no.16, SERA project 2-F2-132 (3-F2-197) Calif. literary research) Mimeo.
C-S CHi CLSM CRic CSdS CSf CSfP CStmo

16051. Shaw, Pringle. Ramblings in California; containing a description of the country, life at the mines, state of society...being the five years' experience of a gold digger. Toronto, James Bain [1857] 239 p.
CHi CLSM

16052. Shaw, William. Golden dreams and waking realities; being the adventures of a gold-seeker in California and the Pacific islands. London, Smith Elder and co., 1851. 316 p.   CHi CSd CSfCW CSfP

16053. Shelford, Paul K. Protestant cooperation in northern California; the historical background of the federation and conciliar movement written in preparation for the golden anniversary of the founding, 1913–1963. Oakland, No. Calif.-Nevada council of churches, c1962. 115 p. ports.   CHi

16054. Sherman, Edwin A. The life of the late Rear-Admiral John Drake Sloat...compiled from the most authentic sources. Oakland, Carruth & Carruth, 1902. 258 p. illus., ports., genealogical tables, coat of arms.
CBb CHi CMont CP CSd CSf CSfCW CStbS CStoC CV MoS N

16055. Sherwood, J. Ely. California: her wealth and resources; with many interesting facts respecting the climate and people; the official and other correspondence of the day, relating to the gold region; Colonel Mason's report, and all that part of the President's message having reference to the country in which these vast discoveries have been made; also, a memorial offered in Congress, in relation to the proposed railroad to the Pacific ocean. N.Y., G.F. Nesbitt, print., 1848. 40 p.
CHi CP

16056. —— Same, reprinted. [Tarrytown, N.Y., W. Abbatt, 1929] 57 p.   CSfCW CSjC

16057. Shinn, Charles Howard. Land laws of mining districts. Baltimore, Johns Hopkins univ. press, 1884. 83 p.   CBb

16058. —— Mining camps. A study in American frontier government. N.Y., Scribner, 1885. 316 p.
CHi CRedl CSal CSd

16059. —— Same. Introd. by Joseph Henry Jackson. N.Y., Knopf, 1948. 291 p.
Available in many California libraries.

16060. Shumate, Charles Albert. E C V News from the miners, 1856–1860, extracted from several sources. [S.F., Designed and print. by Lawton Kennedy] 1960. [8] p. E C V: E clampus vitus. Presented on the occasion of the joint meeting of the Roxburghe club of San Francisco and the Zamorano club of Los Angeles, Sept. 17–18, 1960.   CHi

16061. Shutes, Milton Henry. Lincoln and California. Stanford [1943] 269 p. illus., ports.
Available in many California libraries.

16062. Simonin, L. ...Le mineur de Californie. Paris, L. Hachette, 1866. 52 p. (Conferences populaires ...)   CHi

16063. Simpson, Henry I. The emigrant's guide to the gold mines. Three weeks in the gold mines, or Adventures with the gold diggers of California in August 1848. ... By Henry I. Simpson, of the New York volunteers. N.Y., Joyce and co., 1848. 30 p. illus., fold. map.   CHi

16064. Sitton, Gordon Russell. California rice industry; a case study in the theory of the firm. Stanford, 1954. Thesis (Ph.D.)—Stanford univ., 1954.
CChiS (microfilm copy)   CSt

16065. Smith, Hugh Deming. History of the California press, 1834–1860. [Berkeley, 1940] Thesis (M.A.) —Univ. of Calif., 1940.   CU

16066. Sociedade União Portugueza do Estado da California. Concelho supremo. [Procedimentos] 1887–1898.   CHi

16067. South, Arethusa Aurelia. California inland navigation, 1839–1890. [Berkeley, 1939] Thesis (M.A.) —Univ. of Calif., 1939.   CU CU-B

16068. Southern Pacific co. The coast country, Santa Barbara to San Francisco. Ed. by Paul Shoup. S.F., 1905. 128 p. illus.   CAla

16069. —— Same. S.F. [1907] 95 p. illus., map.   CHi

16070. —— Redwood empire tour by train and motorcoach. [S.F., 1930] 13 p. illus., maps.   CRcS

16071. —— From the Crescent city to the Golden

gate via the Sunset route of the Southern Pacific company. 1886. [By Benjamin C. Truman] 99 p. illus., maps.
CL CP

16072. —— A souvenir of delightful journeys. [1914?] [40] p. illus., map.   CHi

16073. —— Wayside notes on the Sunset route, eastward from San Francisco. S.F., 1902. 79 p. illus.
CFS

16074. —— Same. S.F., 1911. 47 p. illus.   CHi

16075. **Sparks, Theresa A.** China gold. Fresno, Acad. lib. guild, 1954. 191 p. illus.
CBb CHi CSf CV

16076. **Spencer, Dorcas James.** A history of the Woman's Christian temperance union of northern and central California... Written by request of the state convention of 1911. Oakland, West coast print., 1913. 169 p. illus.   CHi CSf

16077. **State directory co., pub.** Northern California state directory...giving name, business and address of business and professional men... v.1, 1893/94. S.F. [1893?]   CSto

16078. **Steele, John.** In camp and cabin. Mining life and adventure in California during 1850 and later. By Rev. John Steele. Lodi, Wis., Author, 1901. 81 p.
CHi

16079. **Stellman, Louis John.** Mother Lode. The story of California's gold rush... S.F., Harr Wagner [c1934] 304 p. illus., ports.
Available in many California libraries and CaBViPA ODa

16080. **Stewart, George Rippey.** Take your Bible in one hand. The life of Wililam Henry Thomes... S.F., Colt press, c1939. 67 p.
CBb CHi CRcS CRedCL CSalCL CSf CSfP CStclU

16081. **Stillman, Jacob David Babcock.** Seeking the golden fleece; a record of pioneer life in California; ...footprints of early navigators, other than Spanish, in California, ...the voyage of the schooner *Dolphin.* S.F., A. Roman & co., 1877. 352 p. illus.
CBb CHi CLM CLSM CLgA CP CRedl CSd CSf CSfCW CSjC CSmat

16802. **Stockton. Chamber of commerce, pub.** Ghost towns and relics of '49. [Stockton, Associated print. co., 1936] [30] p. illus., ports., map. "The material and photographs...were prepared by Mr. F. A. Kazmarek."
C CLgA (carbon copy of the original typew. ms., lacking the photos.) CO CSmat CWhC

16083. —— Same. 1946. 31 p.
CHi CLSU CLgA CLod CMS CO CP CRic CSdS CSf CSfWF-H CSjC CSmH CSto CTurS

16084. —— Same. Centennial ed. 1948. 31 p. illus., ports., maps.   C CLU CStaC CSto

16085. **Strobridge, Idah (Meacham)** In miner's mirage-land. L.A., Baumgardt pub. co., 1904. 7 pl., 129 p. front.   CSf CU-B

16086. —— The land of purple shadows. L.A., Artemisia bindery, 1909. 133 p. illus.
CBb CHi CSd CU-B

16087. **Stong, Philip Duffield.** Gold in them hills ... 1st ed. Garden City, N.Y., Doubleday, 1957. 209 p.
Available in many California libraries and MiD N ODa

16088. Stories of the Sacramento river delta. [n.p., 1952?] 39 p. illus., ports., map.   CU-B

16089. **Strong, George H.** The cyclists' roadbook of California, containing maps of the principal districts, north, east, south from San Francisco, comp. for the No. Calif. div. of the League of American wheelmen...1893.
CStclU

16090. —— Same. 2d ed. [S.F., Hancock bros.] 1895. 47 p. fold. maps.   CSfCW

16091. **Sunset.** Gold rush country; guide to California's Mother Lode and northern mines, by the editors of Sunset books and Sunset magazine. Foreword by Oscar Lewis; endorsed by the Calif. hist. soc. [1st ed.] Menlo Park, Lane pub. co. [1957] 101 p. illus.
Available in many Calif. libraries and MiD MoS NN ODa OrU

16092. —— Northern California, by the editorial staffs of Sunset books and Sunset magazine. [1st ed.] Menlo Park, Lane pub. co. [1959] 127 p. illus.
Available in many California libraries and MiD ODa

16093. **Sutter.** Gold for digging in California. By Brigadier Sutter, U.S.A. London, G. Mansell [1850?] 16 p. map.   CHi

16094. **Sutton, Jack.** The pictorial history of southern Oregon and northern California. Grants pass, Ore., Grants pass bul., 1959. 100 p. illus.
C CArcHT CHi CSd CStmo

16095. **Swan, John Alfred.** A trip to the gold mines of California in 1848. Ed. by John A. Hussey. S.F., Bk. club of Calif., 1960. 51 p. illus., port.   CHi CLSM

16096. **Swift, Morrison I.** What a tramp learns in California. Social danger line. S.F., The Soc. of Am. socialists, 1896. 26 p.   CHi

16097. **Taber, Louise Eddy.** California gold rush days; stories from the radio series broadcast by Louise E. Taber. [S.F., Author, c1936–] 3 nos. illus., ports., map.
C CBu CHi CLO (v.1, no. 3) CLSU CLU CLgA CO CRcS CSf CSfCP CSfP CSfU CSfWF-H CSmH CSmat CU-B

16098. **Taylor, Bayard.** Eldorado; or, Adventures in the path of empire: comprising a voyage to California, via Panama; life in San Francisco and Monterey; pictures of the gold region, and experiences of Mexican travel... London, Richard Bentley, 1850. 2 v. illus. Other editions followed.
C-S CAna CHi CL CLU CRedl CSalCL CSdU CSf CSfCP CSfCW CSfP CSj CSmH CU-B

16099. —— Same. N.Y., Putnam, 1850. 2 v. Many other editions followed.
Available in many California libraries and HHi MoS UU ViU ViW

16100. —— Same...introd. by Robert Glass Cleland... N.Y., Knopf, 1949. 375 p. illus. (Western Americana...)
Available in many California libraries and MoS UHi

16101. —— —— Index for 8th ed., N.Y., Putnam, 1857. Joseph Gaer, ed. [S.F., 1935] 21 l. (Index no. 3, SERA project 2-F2-132 (3-F2-197) Calif. literary research) Mimeo.
C-S CHi CLSM CP CSdS CSf CStmo

16102. —— New pictures from California. Foreword by Joseph A. Sullivan. ... Oakland, Biobooks, 1951. 135 p. illus., map. (Calif. relations, no. 30) "Reprint. from text issued by Putnam, New York, 1894."
Available in many California libraries.

16103. **Taylor, Rinaldo Rinaldini.** Seeing the elephant; letters of R. R. Taylor, forty-niner, ed. by John Walton Caughey. [L.A.] Ward Ritchie, 1951.
Available in many California libraries and N OU

16104. Tegoborski, Louis de. Essai sur les conséquences éventuelles de la découverte des gîtes aurifères en Californie et en Australie. Paris, J. Renouard et cie., 1853. 199 p. CSfP

16105. —— Same. Weimar, Bernard Friedrich Voigt, 1853. 156 p. In German. CHi

16106. Tessan, Francois de. Promenades au Farwest. 3d ed. Paris, Plon-Nourrit, 1912. 337 p.
C-S CHi CSf

16107. Thornton, J. Quinn. Oregon and California in 1848: ...with an appendix including recent and authentic information on the subject of the gold mines of California... N.Y., Harper, 1849. 2 v. illus., fold. map. "This work is one of the best authorities of the period..." —Cowan. Reprint. in 1855 and 1864.
CHi CLgA CP CSalCL (v.1, 1864) CSfCW (v.1, 1855) MoS OrU ViU ViW (1855)

16108. Thurston, William. Guide to the gold regions of upper California. London, J. and D.A. Darling, 1849. 70 p. fold. map. CHi

16109. [Tide land reclamation co.] Fresh water tide lands of California. S.F., M.D. Carr & co., 1869. 47 p.
CHi

16110. Toll, George Bauer. Cooperative wholesaling efforts among retail grocers in northern California. [Berkeley, 1931] Thesis (M.S.)—Univ. of Calif., 1931.
CU

16111. Tourist association of the San Francisco bay and river counties. Seventeen trips by train, trolley, boat and motor. Authoritative and complete information compiled and circulated for the benefit of travelers in California. S.F. [n.d.] 40 p. map. C-S

16112. Tucker, Joseph Clarence. To the golden goal and other sketches. Dr. J. C. Tucker. S.F., William Doxey, 1895. 303 p. illus., port. CHi CSfP

16113. Turrill, Charles B. California notes... S.F., E. Bosqui, 1876. 232 p. map. At head of title: First volume. No more published.
C-S CHi CP CSf CSfCW CSjC CSmat CStclU CStoC CStrJC CViCL

16114. Tyson, James L. Diary of a physician in California; being the results of actual experience, including notes of the journey by land and water... N.Y., D. Appleton; Phila., G.S. Appleton, 1850. 92 p.
CHi CLM CLSM CSf

16115. —— Same. Index and forward (!) by Joseph A. Sullivan. Oakland, Biobooks, 1955. 124 p.
Available in many California libraries.

16116. —— Index [for 1850 ed.] Joseph Gaer, ed. [S.F., 1935] 24 l. (Index no. 15, SERA project 2-F2-132 (3-F2-197) Calif. literary research) Mimeo.
CHi CLSM CSf CStmo

16117. U.S. District court. California. Northern district. Reports of land cases determined in the United States district court for the Northern district of California. June term, 1853, to June term, 1858, inclusive by Ogden Hoffman. Vol. 1. S.F., Numa Hubert, 1862. 458, 146 p. No more printed. Appendix: Table of land claims.
C CHi CLSM CLSU CLU CLgA CSbCL CSfCW CSmH CU-B CtY MiD-B NIC NN

16118. —— Library of Congress. California: the centennial of the Gold Rush and the first state constitution [catalog of] an exhibit in the Library of Congress, Wash., D.C., Nov. 12, 1949 to Feb. 12, 1950. Wash., D.C., Govt. print. off., 1949. 97 p. illus., maps.
CChiS CHi CLM CLgA CSd CSdS CSfCSM CSfCW CSfP CSjC CStbS

16119. Upchurch, J. J. The life, labors and travels of Father J. J. Upchurch, founder of the Ancient order of united workmen, written by himself...Rev. and ed. by Sam. Booth. S.F., A.T. Dewey, 1887. 264 p. illus., port.
CHi

16120. Vance, Robert H. Catalogue of daguerreotype panoramic views in California...on exhibition at no. 349 Broadway (opposite the Carleton house). N.Y., Baker, Godwin & co., 1851. 8 p. CHi

16121. [Van Noy interstate co.] The Shasta route in all of its grandeur... [n.p., n.d.] C-S

16122. Vassar, John Guy. Twenty years around the world. 2d ed. N.Y., Rudd & Carleton, 1862. 598 p. front. (port.) CU-B
Other editions followed. CSfCW (1891)

16123. Visscher, William Lightfoot. A thrilling and truthful history of the Pony express; or, blazing the westward way, and other sketches and incidents of those stirring times. Chicago, Rand, McNally & co. [1908] 98 p. illus., ports.
CHi CLod CSd CSfCW CSfP

16124. [Vizetelly, Henry] Four months among the gold-finders in California; being the diary of an expedition from San Francisco to the gold districts by J. Tyrwhitt Brooks, M.D. [pseud.] N.Y., Appleton, 1849. 94 p. map. CHi CP

16125. —— Same. [2d ed.] London, David Bogue, 1849. 207 p. front. (map) Cowan notes editions in Dutch and German, 1849.
CHi (also Dutch and German ed.) CSd CSf CStoC (German ed.) MiD UHi

16126. —— Same, [and] What I saw in California ...by Edwin Bryant...to which is annexed an appendix ... Paris, A. and W. Galignani and co.; Baudry's European library, 1849. 136 p. map. CHi

16127. A volume of memoirs and genealogy of representative citizens of northern California, including biographies of many of those who have passed away... Chicago, Standard genealogical pub. co., 1901. 831 p. illus., ports. On spine: Genealogy and biography, California.
C CChiS CHi CLU CMS CO CSS CSf CSmH In MoS

16128. Wagner, Jack Russell. Short line junction; a collection of California-Nevada railroads. Fresno, Acad. lib. guild, 1956. 266 p. illus., ports., map.
C CBb CChiS CHi CL CLSM CNa CSd CSf CStmo CUk

16129. Walke, Thomas. ...letter from California (April 17, 1850) to his father, Anthony Walke, of Chillicothe, Ohio. Chillicothe, Priv. pub., D.K. Webb, 1950. [4] l. CHi CL MoS

16130. Walsh, Henry L. Hallowed were the gold dust trails; the story of the pioneer priests of northern California... [Santa Clara] Univ. of Santa Clara press, 1946. 559 p. illus., ports., maps. Bibliographical references included in "Notes to text" (p. 471–517). Chapters on Tuolumne, Calaveras, Amador, El Dorado, Placer, Mono, Alpine, Nevada, Sierra, Plumas, Lassen, Modoc, Siskiyou, Del Norte, Humboldt, Trinity, Shasta, Tehama, Glenn and Colusa, Butte, Sutter, Yuba, Yolo, and Sacramento counties.
Available in many California libraries and CaBViPA

16131. Walter, William Wilfred, comp. ... The great understander; ...true life story of the last of the Wells Fargo shotgun express messengers. Aurora, Ill., W.W. Walter, 1931. 315 p. illus. About Oliver Robert De La Fontaine, also known as Oliver Roberts. CInI CSf

16132. Walton, Daniel. The book needed for the times, containing the latest well-authenticated facts from the gold regions; also, a geographical and historical view of California... Bost., Stacy, Richardson and co., 1849. 32 p. Cover title: Wonderful facts from the gold regions; ...   CHi CL CP CSd

16133. Ward, Samuel. Sam Ward in the gold rush, ed. by Carvel Collins. Stanford, Stanford univ. press [1949] 189 p. illus., port., maps.
Available in many California libraries and MoS OrU

16134. Ware, Joseph E. The emigrants' guide to California. Reprint. from the 1849 ed., with introd. and notes by John Caughey. Princeton, Princeton univ. press, 1932. 63 p. illus., map, facsim.
    CChiS CLgA CMartC CNa SCf CVtV

16135. Warren, Herbert O. Journeys to the homes of famous Californians...Illus. by G. G. Patri. Originated and pub. by the Want ad dept., San Francisco examiner. S.F., 1927. 52 p. illus.   CHi CSf

16136. Way, Charles Caverno. A citrus survey of northern California. [Berkeley, 1917] Thesis (M.S.)—Univ. of Calif., 1917.   CU

16137. Weatherbe, D'Arcy. Dredging for gold in California. S.F., Mining and scientific press, 1907. 217 p. illus.   CHi CSf CSfCW

16138. Weber, Shirley H., ed. Schliemann's first visit to America 1850–1851. Cambridge, Mass., Harvard, 1942. 11 p.   CHi

16139. Webster, Kimball. The gold seekers of '49: a personal narrative of the overland trail and adventures in California and Oregon from 1849 to 1854. Manchester, N.H., Standard bk. co., 1917. 240 p. illus., port.
    CBb CHi CLSM CSf CSfCW CSfP UHi MoS

16140. Wellman, Paul Iselin. Gold in California. Illus. by Lorence Bjorklund. Bost., Houghton, 1958. 184 p. illus., map.   CL

16141. Wells, Evelyn, and Peterson, Harry C. The '49ers. Garden City, N.Y., Doubleday, 1949. 273 p. Based on articles in *Oakland tribune* between 1923 and 1926.
Available in many California libraries and CaBViPA MiD MoS ODa T TxU ViW

16142. Western directory co., pub. Northern California state directory. S.F., 1890.   CSf

16143. Western Pacific railroad co. Little stories along the line of the Western Pacific railroad. S.F., Western Pac. news service, n.d. 8 p. Mimeo.   CRcS

16144. —— [Pictures of the construction of the Western Pacific railroad. 1908?] 2 v.   C

16145. Weston, Otheto. Mother Lode album. Stanford [c1948] 177 p. illus., map.
Available in many California libraries and CaBViPA

16146. Weston, Silas. Life in the mountains: or, Four months in the mines of California. Providence, E.P. Weston, 1854. 34 p.   CHi

16147. —— Same. 2d ed., rev. Providence, Benjamin T. Albro, print., 1854. 46 p.   CHi

16148. Wheat, Carl Irving. The maps of the California gold region, 1848–1857; a biblio-cartography of an important decade... S.F., Grabhorn, 1942. 152 p. maps.
    C CHi CL CLU CLgA CLod CO CRcS CSd CSf CSfWF-H CSjC CSmH CStmo CStrJC ViU

16149. Whicher, John. Masonic beginnings in California and Hawaii. With a sketch of noted masonic personages... Pub. by order of the grand master. [n.p.] 1931. 91 p.   CHi CSf

16150. White, Stewart Edward. The forty-niners; a chronicle of the California trail and El Dorado. New Haven, Yale, 1918. 273 p. illus., ports. (Chronicles of Am. ser., 25) Reprint. 1921, 1926.
Available in many California libraries and AU MoS N TxU ViU

16151. [White, William F.] A picture of pioneer times in California, illustrated with anecdotes and stories taken from real life, by William Grey [pseud.]... S.F., W.M. Hinton, 1881. 677 p.
    CHi CLgA CSf CSfCW CSjC CStclU CStoC

16152. Whitney, Joel Parker. Fresh water tide lands of California... Cambridge, Mass., Riverside press, 1873. 38 p. map.   C CHi CSfCW

16153. Wierzbicki, Felix Paul. California, as it is, and as it may be; or, A guide to the gold region... S.F., Print. Washington Bartlett, 1849. 60 p. "This is the first descriptive work written and printed in California." —Cowan.   C CHi CMartC CSmH CU-B CtY ICN

16154. —— Same. 2d ed. 1849. 76 p.
    C CHi CLU CP CSf CU-B CtY MdHi

16155. —— Same...with an introd. by George D. Lyman... S.F., Grabhorn, c1933. illus.
Available in many libraries.

16156. Wilkes, Charles. Columbia river to the Sacramento. Oakland, Biobooks, 1958. 140 p. illus., 2 fold. maps. (Calif. relations, 46). Comprises chapters 4, 5 & 6 from v.5 of the author's Narrative of the United States exploring expedition during the years 1838, 1839, 1840, 1841, 1842. (Phila., Lea and Blanchard, 1845).
    CBb CChiS CHi CLO CP CSalCL CSd CSlu CSto CViCL CWhC

16157. —— Narrative of the United States exploring expedition. During the years 1838, 1839, 1840, 1841, 1842. By Charles Wilkes, U.S.N. commander of the expedition... Phila., Print. C. Sherman, 1844. 5 v. and atlas. illus., ports., maps. "After Wilkes' arrival at San Francisco in October [1841] he was entertained at San Rafael and Santa Clara missions, his experiences at the latter being described at some length. The overland party, under Lieutenant Emmons, made brief visits at Santa Clara, San Jose, and Dolores missions."—Waters.
Available in many California libraries.

16158. —— Same. Phila., Lea & Blanchard, 1845. 5 v. and atlas. illus., ports., maps.
    C CLSU CSmH CStbS

16159. —— Same. Phila., C. Sherman, 1849. 5 v. and atlas. illus., ports., maps.   CP CSmH

16160. —— Same. [London] Ingram, Cook & co., 1852. 2 v. illus., ports.   CHi

16161. —— Same. N.Y., Putnam, 1856. 5 v. and atlas. illus., ports., maps.   CHi

16162. —— Western America, including California and Oregon, with maps of those regions, and of "The Sacramento Valley." Phila., Lea and Blanchard, 1849. 130 p. 3 fold. maps.   CHi CLO CSfCSM

16163. Willcox, Robert N. Reminiscences of California life. Avery, Ohio, Willcox press, 1897. 290 p.
                    CHi

16164. Wilson, N. C. Pioneering in hydraulic dredging; the first half century of the industry, 1875–1925, and the romance of its founders. [n.p.] 1950. 89 p. Mimeo.   CHi

16165. Wiltsee, Ernest Abram. The franks of Hunter & co.'s express. 15 p. illus. Reprint. from the *Collector's club philatelist*, v.12, no. 3, July 1933. Hunter

& co.'s express served Amador, Eldorado, and Placer counties.   CHi CSfWF-H

16166. —— The franks of the Everts expresses. [n.p.] 1931. 16 p. illus. Reprint. from the *Collector's club philatelist*, v.10, no. 3, July 1931. The Everts expresses served Sierra and Plumas counties. CHi CSfWF-H

16167. —— The Joseph W. Gregory express 1850–1853... Federalsburg, Md., Stowell print. co., 1937. 29 p. illus. (Am. philatelist handbook, ser. 1937, no.1) Limited ed. Reproduced from the *American philatelist*, November 1936–March 1937.   CHi CSfWF-H

16168. —— The pioneer miner and the pack mule express. S.F., Calif. hist. soc., 1931. 112 p. illus., maps, facsims. (Half-title: Calif. hist. soc. Special pub. no. 5.)
CBb CHi CL CLgA COnC CRedCL CRedl CSfP CSfWF-H CSjC CStbS CStmo CStoC CYcCL

16169. —— The various expresses of the various Tracys. 16 p. illus., maps. Reprint. from the *Collector's club philatelist*, v.14, no. 3, July 1935. CHi CSfWF-H

16170. Wistar, Isaac Jones. Autobiography... 1827–1905... Phila., Wistar inst. of anatomy and biology, 1914. 2 v. 250 copies printed and distributed privately.
         CChiS CSfP

16171. —— Same. 1937. 528 p. illus., ports., fold. map.   CHi CRic

16172. —— Same. N.Y., Harper, 1937. 530 p. illus., ports., fold. map.
     CBb CHi CLgA CRcS CSf

16173. Work, John. Fur brigade to the Bonaventura; John Work's California expedition, 1832–1833, for the Hudson's bay company, ed. by Alice Bay Maloney... with a foreword by Herbert Eugene Bolton. S.F., Calif. hist. soc., 1945. 112 p. illus., ports., fold. map. (Calif. hist. soc. Special pub. no. 19)
CBb CChiS CFS CHi CLSM CRic CSdS CSto MoSU

16174. Wyld, James. A guide to the gold country of California... compiled from official despatches of Colonel Mason, Lieutenant-colonel Fremont, and other government authorities. London [1849] 62 p. map.
        CLU CSmH

16175. Wyman, Walker Demarquis, ed. California emigrant letters; illus. by Helen Bryant Wyman. N.Y., Bookman associates, 1952. 177 p. illus., map.
Available in many California libraries and MiD MoHi MoSU OrU UPB

16176. Zimmermann, W. F. A. Californien und das goldfieber; Reisen in dem wilden Westen Nord/Amerika's, leben und sitten der goldgräber, Mormonen und Indianer. Berlin, Thedor Thiele, 1863. 744 p. illus., 8 col. pl.   CHi

SOUTHERN CALIFORNIA

16177. Ainsworth, Edward Maddin. California jubilee; nuggets from many hidden veins. Culver City, Murray & Gee, 1948. 272 p.
CCoron CL CMon CPom CSf CStaC CStmo

16178. All year club of southern California. Southern California through the camera. L.A. [1929?] 47 p. illus.   CL

16179. Allen, Paul F. Tourists in southern California, 1875 to 1903. [Claremont, 1940] 149 l. Thesis (M.A.)—Claremont college, 1940. CCH

16180. Arrow research institute, West Los Angeles. Western lore and historical guide to southern California: ghost towns, ...historical landmarks, sites,

and monuments of the eleven southern California counties. [L.A., 1959?] 36 p. C CL CP CSd

16181. Arthur, Edward. Let's go prospecting. L.A., Author, 1954. 62 p. illus., maps. C CLU

16182. [Atchison, Topeka and Santa Fé railway] The beaches, Santa Fe route. [L.A., n.d.] [32] p. illus. Description and views of southern California beaches.
         CLU

16183. —— Summer in southern California... [Chicago, Rand McNally, 1895?] 54 p. illus., map.
         CP CSmH

16184. Atlas powder co., Wilmington, Delaware. On the aqueducts of the Pacific with Atlas giant powder. Wilmington, Del. [c1935] [66] p. The Colorado river aqueduct.   CHi

16185. Austin, Maude Mason. Annals of the desert; photographs by Gandara. Bost., Stratford, 1930. 101 p. illus.   CMon

16186. Bain, Joe S. War and postwar developments in the southern California petroleum industry. L.A., Haynes foundation, 1945. 49 p. CSfSO

16187. Bandel, Eugene. Frontier life in the army, 1854–1861. Tr. by Olga Bandel and Richard Jente. Ed. by Ralph P. Bieber. (Southwest hist. ser.) Glendale, Arthur H. Clark co., 1932. 330 p. illus., ports., fold. map.
    CHi CRcS CSd CU-B

16188. Bard, Cephas L. A contribution to the history of medicine in southern California. Annual address of the retiring president of the Southern California medical society, delivered at San Diego, Aug. 8, 1894. [n.p., 1894] 34 p.   CLM CLSM

16189. Baumgardt, B. R. & co., pub. Famous southern California scenes...a collection of 48 views... L.A., 1899. 49 l.   CHi

16190. —— Same. 1901. [47] l.   CHi

16191. Baur, John E. The health seekers of southern California, 1870–1900. San Marino, Huntington lib., 1959. 202 p. (Huntington lib. pub.)
C CChiS CLM CLO CLSM CLU CP CRedL CSd CSdS CSdU CSt CStclU

16192. Bennett, Bessie Price. The economic development of southern California with special reference to transportation, from 1870–1885. [Berkeley, 1927] 98 l. Typew. Thesis (M.A.)—Univ. of Calif., 1927.
        CU CU-B

16193. Benton, Frank Weber. Semi-tropic California, the garden of the world... L.A., Benton & co., 1914. 86 p. illus., col. pl., double map. On cover: San Diego exposition edition. C CHi CLO CSmH

16194. —— Same, President Wilson invitation edition, 1915. L.A., Benton & co. [1915?] 86 [24] p. illus., col. pl.   CLO CLSM

16195. —— Zig-zag sketches of semi-tropic California and Las Penasquitas. L.A., 1886. 29 p. CL

16196. Berton, Francis. A voyage on the Colorado, 1878; tr. and ed. by Charles N. Rudkin. L.A., G. Dawson, 1953. 103 p. illus., map. CBb CLLoy CVtV

16197. Bishop, William Henry. Old Mexico and her lost provinces; a journey in Mexico, southern California, and Arizona, by way of Cuba. N.Y., Harper, 1883. 509 p. illus.   CBb CHi OU ViU

16198. The Blue book; the standard society directory of southern California... 1894/95–1899. L.A., A.A. Thompson [c1894–99] Title varies.
CL (1894/95, 1897/98) CLO (1899) CLU (1899) CSd (1899) CSmH (1894/95, 1899) CStmo (1897/98, 1899) CU-B (1894/95)

16199. Bogardus, Emory Stephen. Southern California, a center of culture... L.A., Univ. of So. Calif. press, 1938. 84 p. illus., maps.
C CBaB CChiS CL CLO CLSU CLU CSdS CSjC CSta CStmo CWhC

16200. ———— Same. 2d ed. 1940. 100 p. illus., maps.
CLU

16201. Bogart, Ernest Ludlow. The water problem of southern California. [Urbana] Univ. of Ill., for Claremont college, 1934. 132 p. diagrs. (Claremont lib. ser., no. 2) C CHi CSd

16202. Boyd, Jessie Edna. Historical import of the orange industry in southern California. [Berkeley, 1923] Thesis (M.A.)—Univ. of Calif., 1923. CU CU-B

16203. Breeden, Marshall. The romantic southland of California... L.A., Kenmore pub. co., 1928. 207 p. illus., maps.
Available in many California libraries.

16204. Broomfield, Joan F. The fishery industry of southern California. [L.A., 1949] Thesis (M.A.)—U.C.L.A., 1949. CLU

16205. Burdick, Arthur J. The mystic mid-region, the deserts of the Southwest. N.Y., Putnam's, 1904. 237 p. illus. CHi CStmo

16206. Burns, L. L., comp. Scenic beauties of southern California. [n.p.] Benham co., 1909. CSmH

16207. Burton, George Ward. Burton's book on California and its sunlit skies of glory. L.A., Times-mirror print., 1909. 155 p. illus. C CSfCW CSd

16208. ———— Men of achievement in the great Southwest. A story of pioneer struggles during early days in Los Angeles and southern California. With biographies ... [L.A.] L.A. times, 1904. 149 p. illus., port.
CHi CL CLO CLSU CLU CSmH

16209. Caldwell, George Walter. Legends of southern California. S.F., Phillips & Van Orden co. [c1919] 101 p. illus. "The following stories are founded on legends of the Soboba Indians of southern California."—Introd. In verse form.
C CBu CHi CL CLSU CLU CMartC CO CPom CRedl CSd CSf CSmH CStmo CV MoS

16210. California. Colorado river board. California's stake in the Colorado river. 2d revision. Sacramento, 1952. 24 p. illus. CSdS

16211. ———— **Colorado river commission.** Colorado river and the Boulder canyon project; historical and physical facts in connection with the Colorado river and lower basin development. Sacramento, State print. off. [1931] 400 p. maps, charts, tables. Bibliography: p. 357–369. CStmo

16212. ———— **Commission of immigration and housing.** A report on large landholdings in southern California with recommendations. ... Sacramento, State print., 1919. 43 p. tables. CL

16213. ———— **Dept. of employment.** Directory of local unions, southern area. L.A., Southern area off. [195-?-] illus., maps.
CL has 1959.

16214. California federation of business and professional women's clubs. Southern district. Directory, constitution, by-laws. [L.A., 1924?–1932?]
CL has 1925/26–1927/28, 1930/31–1931/32.

16215. California state chamber of commerce. Southern California deserts. [1952] 30 p. illus., maps.
CLO CNa

16216. California teachers' association. Southern section. ...Handbook: a directory of school districts and teacher organizations in southern California with assessed valuation figures. 19— L.A., 19—
CL has 1960/61.

16217. Carrillo, Leo. The California I love. [Decorations by Don Perceval] Englewood Cliffs, N.J., Prentice-Hall, 1961. 280 p. illus. CAla CHi CL CLSM

16218. Carter, Charles Franklin. Some by-ways of California. N.Y., Grafton press, 1902. 189 p.
C CHi CLSM CNF CSalCL CSf CSfCW CSrD CStmo

16219. ———— Same. S.F., Whitaker & Ray-Wiggin co., 1911. 199 p.
CLSM CMon CRc CRcS CRic CStmo CV CViCL

16220. Chapin, Edward L. A selected bibliography of southern California maps. Berkeley, Univ. of Calif. press, 1953. 124 p. map.
C CHi CLU CSd CSdS CSf CSt TxU ViU

16221. ———— A selected cartobibliography of southern California. [L.A.] 1950. Thesis (M.A.)—U.C.L.A., 1950. CLU

16222. Chase, Joseph Smeaton. California desert trails... Bost., Houghton, 1919. 387 p. illus.
Available in many California libraries.

16223. Clark, Bruce Laurence. Topography of southern California. [Berkeley, 1909] Thesis (M.S.)—Univ. of California., 1909. CU

16224. Cleland, Robert Glass. The cattle on a thousand hills; southern California, 1850–1870. San Marino, Huntington lib., 1941. 327 p. illus. (Half-title: Huntington lib. pub.) "This book is an economic and social history of...southern California."
Available in many California libraries and IC NcU NjN NvU ODa OU OrU ViU

16225. ———— Same. ...1850–1880. [2d ed.] 1951. 365 p. illus., ports., maps. Bibliography: p. 339–349.
Available in many California libraries and GEU InI KyU MiD NjN NvU OU TxU UHi UPB

16226. Cole, Clifford A. The Christian churches (Disciples of Christ) of southern California; a history. [St. Louis, Christian bd. of pub.] 1959. 324 p. CL

16227. Connelley, William Elsey. Doniphan's expedition and the conquest of New Mexico and California. Topeka, Kans., Author, 1907. 670 p. illus., ports., maps. Includes a reprint of the work of Col. John T. Hughes [Doniphan's expedition] CHi CStmo

16228. Coons, Arthur Gardiner. Defense industry and southern California's economy. L.A., 1941. 12 p. (Pac. southwest acad. of political and social science. Pub. no. 20) CLU CSdS

16229. Corle, Edwin. Desert country. N.Y., Duell [c1941] 357 p. (Am. folkways, ed. by Ernest Caldwell)
CHi CLO CPs CSdS

16230. Cosgrave, George. Early California justice; the history of the United States district court for the Southern district of California, 1849–1944; ed. by Roy Vernon Sowers. S.F., Grabhorn, 1948. 97 p. facsims.
CBb CChiS CHi CLS CLSM CLU CLgA CRcS CRedCL CRic CSd CSdS CSf CSjC CStclU CSto CV

16231. Cossentine, Erwin Earl. A brief survey of Seventh-day Adventist work in southern California. [Claremont, 1933] 103 l. illus. Thesis (M.A.)—Claremont college, 1933. CCH

16232. Couts, Cave Johnson. Hepah, California. The journal of Cave Johnson Couts from Monterey, Nuevo Leon, Mexico to Los Angeles, California during the years 1848–1849. Ed. by Henry F. Dobyns. [Tucson] Arizona pioneers' hist. soc., 1961. 113 p. illus.
CAla   CHi

16233. Crahan, Marcus Esketh, comp. The wine and food society of southern California; a history with a bibliography of André L. Simon. [L.A.] Ward Ritchie, 1957. 60 p.
CLO

16234. Cromwell, Leslie. A study of the development of hydroelectric power in southern California. [L.A., 1951] Thesis (M.S.)—U.C.L.A., 1951.
CLU

16235. Crosfield, Gulielma. Two sunny winters in California. London, Headley, 1904.
CSd

16236. Davis, Cyrus M., comp. Southern California of today. L.A., Kingsley-Barnes & Neuner co. [1899]
CSd

16237. Dawson, Muir. History and bibliography of southern California newspapers, 1851–1876. L.A., Dawson's book shop, 1950. 86 p. facsims.
CHi   CL   CLO   CLU   CLgA   CP   CSd   CSf

16238. Dodge, Richard V. The California southern railroad, a drama of the southwest... [n.p., n.d.] 46 p. illus., 2 fold. tables. Reprint. from the *Railway and locomotive hist. soc. bul.* no. 80.
CLO   CSd

16239. Downey, Sheridan. Truth about the tidelands. S.F. [n.p.] 1948. 74 p.
CHi   CSfP

16240. DuBois, Constance Goddard. The condition of the Mission Indians of southern California. Phila., Off. of the Indian rights assoc., 1901. 16 p.
CChiS   CRedl

16241. Dumke, Glenn Schroeder. Boom of the eighties in southern California. San Marino, Huntington lib., 1944. 313 p. illus., ports. Bibliography: p. 279–293. Based upon the author's thesis (Ph.D.)—U.C.L.A., 1942. "Printed by Anderson and Ritchie: The Ward Ritchie press."
Available in many California libraries and T   UHi   ViU   WM

16242. —— The growth of the Pacific electric and its influence upon the development of southern California to 1911... [L.A., Occidental college, 1939] 131 l. maps. Thesis (M.A.)—Occidental college, 1939.
CLO

16243. Dunkle, John Robert. The tourist industry of southern California. [L.A., 1950] Thesis (M.A.)—U.C.L.A., 1950.
CLU

16244. Duvall, Fannie E. Old missions of southern California. Reproductions of pen and ink drawings by Fannie E. Duvall. L.A., Lang Bireley [1897] 15 p. illus.
CSfCW

16245. Earnest, Sue Wolfer. An historical study of the growth of the theater in southern California. [L.A., Univ. of So. Calif., n.d.]
CSd

16246. Eberhart, Harold Hal. Time makers in southern California archaeology. [L.A., 1957] Thesis (Ph.D.)—U.C.L.A., 1957.
CLU

16247. Edwards, Elza Ivan. Desert voices; a descriptive bibliography. With photographs and foreword by Harold O. Weight. L.A., Westernlore press, 1958. 215 p. illus., map, facsims.
Available in many California libraries and ViU

16248. —— Desert yarns. L.A., Ward Ritchie, 1946. 41 p. Ltd. ed. of 250 copies.
CBb   CLob   CSd

16249. Edwards, William A. and Harraden,

Beatrice. Two health seekers in southern California... Phila., Lippincott, 1897. 144 p.
C   CHi   CLU   CRedl   CSd   CSdS   CSf   ViU

16250. Ellerbe, Rose Lucile. History of the southern California woman's press club, 1894–1929. [L.A., Foster co., inc., n.d.] 68 p. port.
CHi   CL

16251. Elliott, Ana Mary. [San Jacinto mountain series. Clippings of the series of ten articles from *The Desert sun*, Apr. 14–June 16, 1959] Palm Springs, 1959. Includes information on the history, formation, and land use of the mountains.
CPs

16252. Emery, Kenneth Orris. The sea off southern California; a modern habitat of petroleum. N.Y., Wiley [1960] 366 p. illus.
C

16253. Empire publishing co. The Southern California blue book. Riverside, 1953.
CSd

16254. Erickson, Clarence E. Southern California coast: boating, fishing, beaches. [Menlo Park, Lane pub. co., 1953] 32 p. maps.
C   CSS

16255. Fages, Pedro. ...The Colorado river campaign, 1781–1782; diary of Pedro Fages, ed. by Herbert Ingram Priestley... Berkeley, Univ. of Calif., 1913. 101 p. front. (facsim.) (Pub. of the Acad. of Pac. coast history, v.3, no. 2) Spanish and English on opposite pages.
CHi   CU-B

16256. Fairbanks, Harold Wellman. Southern California, the land and its people; a reader for beginners in geography. S.F., Harr Wagner [c1929] 344 p. illus.
C   CChiS

16257. Federal art project. Southern California. Southern California creates. [n.p., 1939] 51 p. illus. Foreword by Stanton Macdonald-Wright.
CSd   CStmo

16258. Fera, Adolph Christian. Post cards of a tourist (Mr. "Skinny" East) cartoons of southern California. L.A., Henry J. Pauly co., 1910. [163] p. illus.
C

16259. Frampton, Jane. Fine printing in southern California. [n.p.] 1940. 120 l.
CL

16260. Garcés, Francisco Tomás Hermenegildo, Father. On the trail of a Spanish pioneer; the diary and itinerary of Francisco Garcés (missionary priest) in his travels through Sonora, Arizona, and California, 1775–1776; tr. ...and ed. ...by Elliott Coues... Harper, 1900. 2 v. illus., ports., maps.
C   CBb   CBev   CL   CLSU   CLU   CLgA   CO   CP   CRedl   CSS   CSd   CSf   CSfCP   CSmH   CStmo   CU-B   CaBViPA   MoS   TxU   UHi

16261. Goodwin, Jean. Block prints of the southland. Designed and cut in linoleum by Jean Goodwin with verse by Eleanor Hammack Northcross. Printed by Thomas Ellinsworth Williams, Arthur Ames. Santa Ana, Press of the Santa Ana junior college, 1931. unp.
CV

16262. [Granger, Lewis] Letters of Lewis Granger; reports of the journey from Salt Lake to Los Angeles in 1849, and of conditions in southern California in the early fifties. Introd. and notes by LeRoy R. Hafen. L.A., Dawson, 1959. 50 p. illus., port., facsims. (Early Calif. travels ser., 47) 250 copies printed by Ward Ritchie.
CBb   CHi   CL   CLLoy   CLO   CLSM   CLgA   CSS   CSd   CSdS   CSf   CStoC   CU-B   CVtV   N

16263. Greever, William S. Arid domain... Stanford, 1954. Deals with the Santa Fe Pacific railroad co.
CSd

16264. Griffin, John Strother. A doctor comes to California; the diary of John S. Griffin, assistant surgeon with Kearny's Dragoons, 1846–47. With an introd. and notes by George Walcott Ames, jr., and a foreword by

George D. Lyman. S.F., Calif. hist. soc., 1943. 97 p. port., maps. (Calif. hist. soc. Special pub. no. 18)
　　CBaB　CBb　CHi　CLM　CLS　CLgA　CNa　CNF CRedCL　CSalCL　CSjC　CStbS　CStoC

16265. Guinn, James Miller. Historical and biographical record of southern California; containing a history of southern California from its earliest settlement to the opening year of the twentieth century...Also containing biographies of well-known citizens of the past and present. Chicago, Chapman pub. co., 1902. 1019 p. ports. Includes counties of San Diego, Los Angeles, Santa Barbara, Ventura, Orange and Riverside.
　　C　CAna　CBb　CHi　CL　CLO　CLSM　CLSU　CLU CLgA　CLom　CO　CPom　CRiv　CSf　CSmH　CSta CStaCL　CStmo　CSuLas　CU-B　CUk　CoD　ICN　In MWA　NHi

16266. —— Same [with addition of San Bernardino county] 1295 p. illus., ports.
　　CBaK　CHi　CLO　CLU　CP　CSS　CSdS　CStbS CStmo　NbHi

16267. —— A history of California and an extended history of its southern coast counties, also containing biographies of well-known citizens of the past and present... L.A., Historic record co., 1907. 2 v. ports. Paged continuously. Includes counties of San Diego, Los Angeles, Santa Barbara, San Bernardino, Ventura, Orange, and Riverside.
　　C　CBb　CBu　CFS　CHi　CL　CLAC　CLO　CLS CLSM　CLSU　CLU　CLom　CO　COnC　CP　CPom CPs　CRedl　CSd　CSdCL　CSf　CSmH　CStmo　CU-B CWhC　CoD　CoU　CtY　MWA　N　OU　WHi

16268. —— Southern California, its history and its people... Illustrated. Complete in two volumes. [L.A.] Historic record co. [c1907] v.1: 574 p. illus., ports. Running title: *Historical and biographical record of southern California*, but contents vary considerably from those of author's work of this title published in 1902.
　　CLO has v.1 only.

16269. Hafen, Le Roy Reuben. Old Spanish trail: Santa Fe to Los Angeles, with extracts from contemporary records and including diaries of Antonio Armijo and Orville Pratt. Glendale, Arthur H. Clark, 1954. 377 p. illus., ports., fold. col. map.　　CBb　CHi　CSf

16270. Hall, William Hammond. Irrigation in California (southern)... Organization and operation in San Diego, San Bernardino, and Los Angeles counties. Second part of the Report of the State engineer of California on irrigation and the irrigation question... Sacramento, State print. off., 1888. 672 p. illus., maps.
　　C　CBb　CHi　CL　CLO　CLSU　CLU　CO　CRedl CSS　CSfCSM　CSj　CStmo　CViCL

16271. Hallenbeck, Cleve. Legends of the Spanish southwest by Cleve Hallenbeck...and Juanita H. Williams. Glendale, Arthur H. Clark, 1938. 341 p. illus.
　　　　　　　　　　　　　　CRcS　CSd　CSto

16272. —— Spanish missions of the old Southwest. Garden City, N.Y., Doubleday, 1926. 184 p. illus., maps.
　　　　CRcS　CRedl　CSalCL　CSd　CSjC　CStmo

16273. Halsey, Mina Deane. A tenderfoot in California, by M. D. Yeslah [pseud.] N.Y., Little & Ives co., 1908. 149 p. illus.　　CLO　CLSM　CLU　CSfCW　TxU
　　Other editions followed.　　CBb (1912)　CHi (1912, 1918)　CLU (1918)　CSd (1909)　CStcrCL (1912) CStmo (1921)　CWhC (1925)

16274. Hanna, Phil Townsend. The wheel and the bell; the story of the first fifty years of the Automobile club of southern California. L.A., Pac. press, 1950. 18 p. illus.　　　　　　　C　CHi　CLU　CNa　CP

16275. Hanson, John Wesley. The American Italy: ...southern California... Chicago, W. B. Conkey co. [1896] 296 p. illus. Agricultural resources and points of interest of the following counties: Santa Barbara, Ventura, Los Angeles, San Bernardino, Orange, Riverside, San Diego.
　　C　CL　CLO　CLSU　CLU　CP　CSj　CSmH　CU-B MiD

16276. Harris, Frank, ed. A guide to contemporary architecture in southern California, ed. by Frank Harris [and] Weston Bonenberger. [L.A.] Watling, 1951. 91 p. illus., maps, plans.　　　　C　CL　CLO

16277. Hepburn, Andrew. Southern California. [Rev. and enl.] Bost., Houghton, c1959. 160 p. illus., maps. (The Am. travel ser., no. 9)
　　C　CAla　CCoron　CHi　CLO　CLom　CMon　CNa CRb　CRic　CSalCL　CStmo

16278. Heston, Francis Eugene. The growth of urbanism on the southern California coast. [L.A., 1950] Thesis (M.A.)—U.C.L.A., 1950.　　　　　　CLU

16279. Hicks, Ratcliffe. Southern California; or, The land of the afternoon. Springfield, Mass., Springfield print. & bind. co., 1898. 88 p. illus., port.
　　C　CBb　CHi　CL　CLSU　CLU　CP　CSmH

16280. Hill, Harlan H. History of the Ridge route. [L.A., 1954] 90 l. Thesis (M.A.)—Occidental college, 1954.　　　　　　　　　　　　　　CLO

16281. Hogue, Harland Edwin. A history of religion in southern California, 1846–1880. Ann Arbor, Univ. microfilms [1958] 372 l. maps. Thesis (Ph.D.)— Columbia univ.　　　　　　　　　　　CCSC

16282. Holder, Charles Frederick. Life in the open; sport with rod, gun, horse, and hound in southern California. N.Y., Putnam, 1906. 401 p. illus., port.
　　　　　　　　　　　CHi　CStmo　WM

16283. —— Southern California: its climate, trails, mountains, canyons, watering places, fruits, flowers and game. A guidebook. L.A., Times-mirror, 1888. 187 p. illus.　　　　　　　　　　　　CHi　CLU

16284. Honnold, Douglas. Southern California architecture, 1769–1956. N.Y., Reinhold [1956] 96 p. illus.　　　　　　　　　　　C　CL　CStmo

16285. Hopmans, Walter Edward. A history of dentistry in southern California. [L.A., 1947] 205 l. Thesis (M.A.)—Occidental college, 1947.　　　　CLO

16286. Hunt, Aurora. Major general James Henry Carleton, 1814–1873. Glendale, A.H. Clark co., 1958. 390 p. illus., ports., maps, facsims.　　CSd　CU-B

16287. Jaeger, Edmund Carroll. The California deserts; a visitor's handbook, with chapters by S. Stillman Berry and Malcolm J. Rogers. Stanford; London, H. Milford, Oxford univ. press [c1933] 207 p. illus. "The area here treated embraces both the Mohave...and the Colorado desert of southeastern California and also certain contiguous portions of southern Nevada and western Arizona."—Introd.
　　Available in many California libraries and MiD　ODa ViW

16288. —— Same, revised. Stanford [c1938] 209 p. illus.
　　Available in many libraries.

16289. —— Same. 3d ed. Stanford [1955] 211 p. illus., maps.
　　CArcHT　CBb　CChiS　CCoron　CHi　CLS　CLU CO　CPs　CSS　CSbr　CSf　CSfCSM　CSt　CStmo MiD　TxU　ViW　WM

16290. James, George Wharton. B. R. Baumgardt & co's tourists' guide book to south California... L.A., B.R. Baumgardt & co. [1895] 457 p. illus.
C CHi CL CLU CP CSd CSmH

16291. —— Travelers' handbook to southern California... Pasadena, Author, 1904. 507 p. illus., port. Based on *B. R. Baumgardt & co's tourists' guide book to south California.*
C CHi CL CLO CLSU CLU CPom CPs CRedl CRic CSS CSj CSmH CStmo

16292. [Jamieson, J. Stewart] A pioneer in California. [n.p., 1949] 16 p.   CHi

16293. Japanese chamber of commerce of southern California. The history of the Japanese in southern California. L.A., 1956– illus., ports. Text in Japanese.
CL has v. 1.

16294. Jervey, Edward Drewry. The history of Methodism in southern California and Arizona. Nashville, Print. by Parthenon press for Hist. soc. of the so. Calif.-Arizona conference, 1960. 247 p. illus., ports.
CCSC CL

16295. Johnson, Humphrey Cyril. Scenic guide to southern California. Susanville, Scenic guides, 1946. 103 p. illus., maps.   C CStmo MiD

16296. Keeler, Charles Augustus. Southern California; illus. with drawings from nature and from photographs by Louise M. Keeler. L.A., Passenger department, Santa Fe [1898] 140 p. illus. Includes chapters on Riverside and San Diego counties, Los Angeles, Santa Barbara and the San Bernardino and San Gabriel valleys.
CBu CL CLU CMartC CP CSf CSj CSjC CSta CStcrCL NHi

16297. —— Same. 1899.   CHi CSd CSmH

16298. —— Same. 1901.   C CSmH MiD

16299. Kleinsorge, Paul L. The Boulder canyon project, historical and economic projects; with a foreword by Eliot Jones. Stanford, 1941. 330 p. illus.
CStmo

16300. Kress, George Henry. History of the medical profession of southern California, with an introd. by Walter Lindley. L.A., Times-mirror, 1910. 209 p. ports. First ed., one of the few copies distributed before the L.A. Times fire.   CLM

16301. —— Same. 2d ed. L.A., 1910. 209 p. ports. "Biographical [sketches]": p. [99]–209.
CHi CL CLM CLU

16302. Kubo, Shiro. Nanka no hiroshimajin [The Japanese from Hiroshima prefecture in southern California] L.A., 1914. v.p. In Japanese.   CHi

16303. Langsdorf, William Bell, jr. The real estate boom of 1887 in southern California... [L.A.] Occidental college, 1932. 109 l. Thesis (M.A.)—Occidental college, 1932. Appendix: "Los Angeles county towns founded in 1884–1888, according to county record": l. i–iv.   CLO

16304. "La Patria" di Los Angeles (Edizione speciale) Ricordo della colonia Italiana del Sud della California. [L.A.] 1915. 63 p. illus.   CLSM

16305. Lawrence, James William. A history of the significant factors contributing to the development of the Mojave desert (a source unit for teachers). [Whittier] 1959. 117 l. fold. map. Thesis (M.A.)—Whittier college, 1959.   CWhC

16306. Layne, Joseph Gregg. Western wayfaring; routes of exploration and trade in the American south-

west. With an introd. by Phil Townsend Hanna. L.A., Automobile club of So. Calif., 1954. 63 p. 28 maps.
CSd CStmo

16307. Lewis, James. Doorway to good living. Selected places: where to eat and where to stay, where to fish and where to play along the Pacific slope of the western wonderland. Beverly Hills, Lewis publicity serv., 1947. unp. illus., ports.   CSf

16308. —— Same, with title: Doorway to southern California... [1949] 95 p. illus., map.   C CL CLU

16309. Lindley, Walter, and Widney, Joseph Pomeroy. California of the south; its physical geography, climate...being a complete guide-book to southern California. N.Y., Appleton, 1888. 377 p. illus., ports., maps. Part II: Los Angeles, San Bernardino, Ventura, and Santa Barbara counties; included in Part III: comparative valuation of lands and products [etc.]
Available in many California libraries and CaBViPA MiD ViW WHi

16310. —— Same. 3d ed., rewritten and reprinted from new plates...1896. 335 p. illus., ports., map.
C CHi CL CLM CLO CLSU CLU CSf CSjC CSmH

16311. —— Same. L.A., c1944. unp. illus., map. Caption title: "Early life of Los Angeles." On cover: "Los Angeles is the damnest place."   CHi CL

16312. Lindsay, Cynthia (Hobart) The climate of lunacy; an unnatural history of southern California. London, H. Hamilton [c1960] 174 p.   CSfSt

16313. —— The natives are restless. Phila., Lippincott, 1960. 223 p.   CL

16314. Look. ...The Santa Fe trail, by the editors of Look. N.Y., Random house, 1946. 271 p. illus., ports., maps.   CSf

16315. Los Angeles. Chamber of commerce. Rack jobbers in southern California. L.A., 1956.   CL

16316. —— —— Sales manager's guide to southwestern bases: locations, personnel. L.A., 1959.   CL

16317. —— —— Southern California and national defense. [L.A., 1940] 4 pt. in 1 v. illus., map.
C CL CLSU CLU CSmH

16318. —— —— Uncle Sam's lands in southern California and how to acquire them. Rev. ed. [L.A., 1912] 8 p.   CSmH

16319. —— —— **Research dept.** Impact of future population growth on employment, retail sales, personal income, bank deposits, motor vehicles. Projections from 1960 by 5-year intervals. L.A. [1961] 24 p. illus., map.   CL

16320. —— —— —— Population 1940 in fourteen counties of southern California by communities. L.A., 1941. unp. "Based on the 1940 federal census and other recent estimates."   CL

16321. —— —— —— Population projections to 1980 by five year intervals, 14 southern California counties. L.A. [1958?] 36 p. illus.   CL

16322. Los Angeles examiner. A working sales control of the southern California market area. [L.A.] 1947. 151 p. illus. (part col.) maps (part fold.) Cover title: Sales operating in the southern California market.
CL

16323. Los Angeles herald. An illustrated souvenir directory of southern California... [L.A., Commercial print. house, 1903?] 141 p. illus., ports.
CLO CLSM CLSU CLU

16324. —— Same. De luxe edition. L.A. [n.d.] 144 p. illus.   C

16325. Los Angeles times. Southern California's standard guide book, 1910... L.A., Times-mirror print. & bind. house [1910] 231 p. maps. Chapters on the cities and towns of southern California.
C CL CLO CLU CP CSmH

16326. Loyer, Fernand, and Beaudreau, Charles, eds. ...Le guide français de Los Angeles et du sud de la Californie. A historical sketch of southern California with particular reference to the activities of people of French origin, as well as a portrayal of the educational, artistic, economic, and recreational aspects of life in present day southern California... [L.A., Franco Am. pub. co., c1932] 221 p. illus., ports. "English edition."
C CHi CL CLLoy CLO CLSU CLU CPom CSdU CSmH CStmo

16327. McGroarty, John Steven. California of the south; a history... Chicago, L.A. [etc.] Clarke, 1933–35. 5 v. illus., ports. v.2–5: Biographical.
Available in many California libraries and IHi (v.1–3 only) WHi

16328. McWilliams, Carey. ...Southern California country, an island on the land. N.Y., Duell [1946] 387 p. (Am. folkways, ed. by Erskine Caldwell) A history of southern California, mainly Los Angeles, from the social standpoint.
Available in many California libraries and CoU GEU IC MiD MoHi N ODa OU OrU TxU UHi ViU WM

16329. Madden, Jerome. Lands of the Southern Pacific railroad company of California, with general information on the resources of southern Calif. S.F. [1876?] 40 p. CHi
Other editions followed. C (1880) CL (1883) CLU (1880) CSf (1880) CSmH (1880)

16330. Mason, William. Where shall we go? A guide to the desert... L.A., Wolfer print. co. [1939] 65 p. maps. CU-B

16331. —— Same. [2d ed.] L.A., 1941. 62 p. illus., maps. C

16332. Mayo, Elton. Teamwork and labor turnover in the aircraft industry of southern California, by Elton Mayo...and George F. F. Lombard... Bost., Harvard univ., Grad. school of business admin., Bur. of business research [1944] 30 p. diagrs. CLU

16333. Methodist Episcopal church. Conferences. Minutes of the Southern California annual conference... L.A., Pub. by the Committee.
C has 3rd, 7th, 14th, 16th–26th, 1878, 1882, 1889, 1891–1901. CHi has 39th, 1914.

16334. Metropolitan transportation engineering board. Proposed freeway and expressway system for Los Angeles, Orange and Ventura counties. A report...recommended...to be the State highway district VII unit of the state-wide system of freeways...as contemplated under Senate concurrent resolution no. 26. L.A., 1958. 207 p. illus. CLU

16335. Metropolitan water district of southern California. Colorado river aqueduct. 2d ed. L.A., 1936. 65 p. illus., maps. Other editions followed.
CBev CLU COnC CStmo

16336. —— Final report of the Engineering board of review on the Colorado river aqueduct location...December 19, 1930. [L.A.? 1930] 45 p. map. CLU

16337. —— The great aqueduct. The story of the planning and building of the Colorado river aqueduct. L.A. [1941] 69 p. illus., ports., map, diagr.
CBb CLSM CSd CStmo

16338. —— History and first annual report for the period ending June 30, 1938. L.A., 1939. 353 p. illus., map. CRcS CStmo

16339. —— Water from the Colorado river. L.A., 1931. 31 p. illus. (part col.) maps. CLU

16340. Miller, Max Carlton. It must be the climate. N.Y., McBride, 1941.
CMon CNa CRb CRic CSd CSf CStmo

16341. —— Speak to the earth. N.Y., Appleton-Century, 1955. 310 p. illus. Deals with the petroleum industry. CHi CSd CU-B

16342. Milliman, Jerome Wilson. The history, organization and economic problems of the Metropolitan water district of southern California. [L.A., 1956] Thesis (Ph.D.)—U.C.L.A., 1956. CLU

16343. Miner, Frederick Roland. Outdoor southland of California, with illustrations from photographs and paintings by the author. L.A., Times-mirror press, 1923. 229 p. illus.
CBb CHi CL CLLoy CLU CRedl CSalCL CSd CSmH CStbS CStmo

16344. Mitchell, John Donald. Lost mines and buried treasure along the old frontier... Palm Desert, Desert magazine press [1953] 240 p. illus., maps.
CLO CU-B

16345. Montgomery, Clifford Marvin. Diary of the first Anza expedition to Calif. [Berkeley, 1919] Thesis (M.A.)—Univ. of Calif., 1919. CU

16346. Murdock, Glenn Evert. Earthquakes and southern California. Redlands, Fortnightly club, 1935. 25 p. Typew. CRedl

16347. Newmark, Marco Ross. Jottings in southern California history. L.A., Ward Ritchie [1955] 162 p. illus., ports.
Available in many California libraries and CaBViPA UHi

16348. [Nichols, C. S.] Prolific seven; where to find health, wealth, and pleasure. L.A., Grider & Dow, c1895. 100 p. illus., ports., map. "Descriptive and half-tone views of [the seven counties comprising] southern California." CL CLSU CLU CSmH

16349. O'Dell, Scott. Country of the sun: southern California: an informal history and guide. N.Y., Crowell [1957] 310 p.
Available in many California libraries and IC InI MiD MoS N UPB WM

16350. Olson, Reuel Leslie. The Colorado river compact. L.A., Author, 1926. 527 p. maps. Thesis (Ph.D.) —Harvard univ., 1926. CSd CStmo

16351. Padilla, Victoria. Southern California gardens; an illustrated history. Berkeley, Univ. of Calif. press, 1961. 359 p. illus. (part col.), ports. CHi CL

16352. Phillips, A. & co., pub. New facts and figures concerning southern California; including the actual experience of individual producers...from material furnished by the L.A. chamber of commerce. L.A., Evening express co., 1891. [15] p. Cover-title: Southern California: resources, progress and prospects.
CLU CoD

16353. Place, George E. & co., pub. Place's southern California guide book...of Los Angeles, San Bernardino and San Diego counties... L.A., 1886. 135 p.
C CL

16354. —— Same. [3d ed.] L.A., 1888–89. [113] p. illus. C CHi CL CLSU CLU CSmH

16355. Porter, Florence Collins, and Trask, Hel-

en Brown, eds. Maine men and women in southern California... L.A., Kingsley, Mason & Collins co., print., 1913. 144 p. illus., ports.   CL CSmH

16356. Powers, Stephen. Afoot and alone; a walk from sea to sea by the southern route. Adventures and observations in southern California, New Mexico, Arizona, Texas, etc. ... Hartford, Conn., Columbian bk. co., 1872. [c1871] 327 p. illus.
C CBb CHi CL CLO CLSU CLU CO CP CSfCW CSfP CSjC CSmH CStbS OU T TxU

16357. Press reference library (Southwest ed.) ... being the portraits and biographies of progressive men of the Southwest... L.A., L.A. examiner, 1912. 500 p. illus., ports.
C CHi CL CLO CLSU CLU CO CSdS CSf CSfU CSmH CStmo ViU

16358. Pythias, Knights of. California brigade, Third regiment. Souvenir of its organization and of southern California... [L.A., Kingsley, Moles & Collins, 1902] 127 p. illus.   C

16359. Remondino, Peter Charles. Climatic and other medical sketches. San Diego [n.p.] 1890.
   CLU CSd

16360. —— The Mediterranean shores of America. Southern California: its climate, physical, and meteorological conditions. Phila., F.A. Davis, 1892. 160 p. illus., map.
C CBb CLM CLO CLU CSS CSd CSdCL MiD NHi WM

16361. Rhoades, Elizabeth Roulette. Foreigners in southern California during the Mexican period. [Berkeley, 1925] Thesis (M.A.)—Univ. of Calif., 1925.
   CU CU-B

16362. Rice, George, pub. Southern California illustrated. L.A. [1883] 64 p. illus., map.
   CL CLU CSfCSM

16363. Rieder, Michael. Los Angeles and southern California. Denver, Williamson-Haffner engraving co., c1903. [19] l. of mounted illus.   C CLO CU-B

16364. Rindge, Frederick Hastings. Happy days in southern California. Cambridge, Mass., and L.A., Author [1898] 199 p.   C CHi CLU CPs CStmo

16365. Robinette, Vivien. We moved to California, a travel book. N.Y., Exposition press [1951] 103 p.
   C CL

16366. Robinson, William Wilcox. Panorama: a picture history of southern California, issued on the 60th anniversary of the Title insurance and trust company... L.A., Title insurance and trust co., 1953. unp. illus., ports., maps.
Available in many California libraries and CoD N NHi NbHi UHi ViU

16367. Rodman, Willoughby. History of the bench and bar of southern California... L.A., W.J. Porter, 1909. 267 p. illus., ports. Biographical sketches: p. 117–267.
C CHi CL CLO CLSU CLU CO CPom CSd CSf CSfP CSmH ViU

16368. Rolfe, Frank, comp. Commercial geography of southern California... [L.A., Biola press] c1915. 63 p. illus., maps. Chapters on agricultural, mineral, animal and manufacturing products, transportation and commerce of Los Angeles and environs, chief cities of southern California.   C CL CLSU CRedl CSd

16369. Ross, Robert Erskine. Wings over the marshes; shooting from an old log book. Introd. by W. H. T. Long. London, Batchworth press, 1948. 151 p. illus.
   C

16370. Ruess, Everett. On desert trails...introd. by Hugh Lacy, and foreword by Randall Henderson. Palm Desert, Desert magazine press, 1950. 80 p. illus., map.
   CLO CSd

16371. Sanborn, Katherine Abbott. A truthful woman in southern California. N.Y., Appleton, 1893. 192 p. Describes author's travels to San Diego, Los Angeles, Pasadena, Riverside, Santa Barbara.
C CHi CLO COHN CPom CRedl CSS CSmH MiD NHi OrU ViW WM

16372. —— Same. Reprint of 1893 ed. 1909. 192 p.
CBea CChiS CCoron CHi CLO CLU CO CSf CSmat CStmo

16373. Saunders, Charles Francis. Under the sky in California; illus. from photographs by C. F. and E. H. Saunders. N.Y., McBride, 1913. 299 p. illus.
Available in many California libraries and TMC ViU ViW

16374. Sayward, W. T. All about southern California... S.F., Woman's pub. co.'s print., 1875. 20 p.   CHi

16375. Security-first national bank, Los Angeles. Six collegiate decades; the growth of higher education in southern California...prepared under the direction of Laurance L. Hill... [L.A.] c1929. 111 p. illus., ports.
C CBev CHi CL CLO CLS CLSU CLU CLgA CSf CSmH CStmo

16376. Seymour, Charles Francis. Relations between the United States government and the Mission Indians of southern California. [Berkeley, 1906] Thesis (M.A.)—Univ. of Calif., 1906.   CU

16377. Shank, Theodore Junior. Garnet Holme: California pageant maker. [L.A., 1953] Thesis (M.A.)— U.C.L.A., 1953.   CLU CU-B

16378. Shinn, George Hazen. Shoshonean day; recollections of a residence of five years among the Indians of southern California, 1885–1889. Glendale, A.H. Clark, 1951. 183 p. 250 copies privately printed for the author.   C CChiS CLgA CRcS

16379. Simons, Ralph B. Boulder dam and the great southwest. L.A., Pac. pub., 1936.   CBb

16380. Sloane, Julia M. The smiling hill-top, and other California sketches...illus. by Carleton M. Winslow. N.Y., Scribner, c1919. 190 p. illus.
CLU CSd CSdS CSfCW CSjC CStmo CU-B MiD

16381. Social register, southern California, Los Angeles, Pasadena. N.Y., Social register assoc.
CL has 1916, 1925. CLU has 1921, 1924, 1927. NHi has 1918–1921.

16382. Southern California advertising co. Shriners' snap shots of southern California... L.A. [n.d.] unp. illus.   C

16383. Southern California bureau of information. Southern California; an authentic description of its natural features, resources, and prospects... L.A., 1892. 98 p. illus., map.   C C-S CLU CSd NHi

16384. —— Same, with title: The land of sunshine: southern California...comp. by Harry Ellington Brook for the Southern California world's fair association... L.A., 1893. 96 p. illus., map.
   CLSU CLU CSfCW CSmH

16385. Southern California labor press. Annual edition. L.A., Union labor pub. assoc. illus., ports.
CL has 1924–27.

16386. Southern California Panama expositions commission. Southern California, comprising the counties of Imperial, Los Angeles, Orange, Riverside, San Bernardino, San Diego, Ventura... [n.p., c1914] 263 p. illus.

Available in many California libraries and IC MiD WM

16387. Southern California railway co. A digest of southern California...Santa Fe route...[5th ed.] Chicago, 1894. 49 p. illus.   CL

16388. Southern Pacific co. California south of Tehachapi. S.F., 1908. 96 p. illus.   CHi OrU

16389. —— The inside track, the way to the wonderful fruit and flower garden of southern California. S.F., 1907. 24 p. illus., map.   CHi CU-B OrU

16390. —— Winter resorts; southern California desert winter resorts. [S.F.?] 1930. 7 p. illus.   CRcS

16391. Southwest blue book; a society directory of names, addresses, telephone numbers, names of clubs and their officers. [L.A.] Lenora H. King [19–?]–

C has 1926/27. CBev has 1942. CHi has 1932/33, 1935, 1939, 1942, 1944, 1947–48, 1950–52, 1954, 1960. CL has 1910, 1913–14, 1916–28, 1930–35, 1937–61. CLLoy has 1927, 1929/31, 1939. CLO has 1918, 1922/23–1924/25, 1926/27–1929/30, 1931/32, 1933/34, 1935–38, 1941, 1944, 1947, 1950, 1952–58. CLSU has 1908, 1914–16, 1919–35, 1937–49, 1951, 1955. CLU has 1920/21, 1929/30, 1932/33, 1943/44. CO has 1957. CP has 1923/24–1926/27, 1928/29–1938, 1940, 1942, 1944, 1946–47. CRedl has 1933/34. CSf has 1951. CSmH has 1913, 1918, 1919/20–40, 1942, 1944, 1946–52, 1954–52, 1957–8, 1960. CSta has 1910. CStmo has 1925/26. CU-B has 1922/23, 1935.

16392. Souvenir of the sister counties of southern California...embracing Los Angeles, San Diego, Orange, Riverside, San Bernardino, Ventura, Santa Barbara and Kern counties. L.A., Pac. souvenir pub. co. [1905?]
        CL CLO CLSU CPom CSf CSmH NN

16393. The standard blue book of California, 1913–14...An exclusive ed. de luxe of Los Angeles, San Diego and southern California. L.A., S.F. [etc.] A.J. Peeler & co. [c1912] 64 p. illus., ports.   CL CSf CSmH

16394. States publishing co., ltd., Los Angeles, comp. & pub. Southern California at a glance: history, romance, maps, facts, statistics... L.A. [c1930] 192 p. illus., maps. Bibliography included in the preface.
    C CLO CLSU CLU CPom CSd CSmH CStmo

16395. Steele, James. Old Californian days. Chicago, Belford-Clarke co., 1889. 227 p. illus. (The Household lib., v.6, no.3) Chiefly on the missions of southern California.   C CChi CHi

16396. —— Same. 1893. 227 p.   CHi

16397. —— Rand, McNally & co.'s guide to southern California direct... Chicago, Rand, McNally & co., 1886. 139 p. illus., fold. map.   C CHi NHi

16398. Storey, Samuel. To the golden land; sketches of a trip to southern California. London, Walter Scott, 1889. 101 p. illus., map.   C CHi NHi UHi

16399. Sunset. Southern California, by the editorial staffs of Sunset books and Sunset magazine. [1st ed.] Menlo Park, Lane pub. co. [1959] 127 p. illus.
    C CCoron CLom CLO CLU CNa CRb CRedCL CRic CSd CViCL WM

16400. Sunshine and grief in southern California, where good men go wrong and wise people lose their money, by an old promoter, forty years in the field of real estate. Detroit, Mich., St. Claire pub. co. [c1931] 206 p. illus., ports.   CL CSmH

16401. Swan, Howard. Music in the Southwest

1825–1950. San Marino, Huntington lib., 1952. 316 p. illus., port. (Huntington lib. pub.)
                    CHi CRedl CSd UHi

16402. Swift, John Cornish. The tuna fishery of southern California. [Berkeley, 1956] Thesis (M.A.)—Univ. of Calif., 1956.   CU

16403. Taft, Clinton J. Fifteen years on freedom's front. [L.A., Am. civil liberties union, So. Calif. branch, 1939] 46 p.   CLU

16404. Talbert, Thomas B. My sixty years in California; memoirs of pioneer days of Long Beach; drainage of Talbert district and the lower Santa Ana Valley; development of Orange county institutions; county farm and hospital, Irvine Park, highway system; Orange county coast; Bolsa Chica, Huntington Beach, and Newport harbor. Huntington Beach, Huntington Beach news press, 1952. 125 p. illus., ports.
    C CAna CBb CHi CL CLO CLSM CLU CLgA CLob COr CSd CSta CStaC CStaCL

16405. Taylor, Frank J. Black bonanza: how an oil hunt grew into the Union oil company of California. N.Y., Whittlesey house, c1950. 280 p. illus., ports., map (lining papers)
        CHi CLgA CP CSd CSfSO CStmo CV

16406. —— Same. 2d ed. rev. N.Y., McGraw-Hill, 1956. 255 p.   CSalCL CSd CSfSO

16407. Taylor, Raymond Griswold. Recollection of 60 years of medicine in southern California. L.A., Author, 1956. 4 v. illus. Reproduced from typew. copy.
                                    CLM

16408. Tileston, Laurence Lowndes. Some phases of the establishment of law and order in southern California, 1846–1875. [Berkeley, 1940] Thesis (M.A.)—Univ. of Calif., 1940.   CU

16409. The travelers and shippers guide; official organ of all modes of travel on the Pacific coast, v.1, no. 1, Sept. 5, 1886. L.A., W.W. Rodehauer, 1886.   C

16410. The tribune annual and southern California statistician... Historical, financial, commercial and agricultural facts of California and its southern counties... L.A., Tribune pub. co., 1889–90.
    CLU (1890) MiD (1889)

16411. Truman, Benjamin Cummings. The press of southern California, 1873. L.A. [Muir Dawson] 1951. 8 p.   CL CLO

16412. —— Southern California. L.A., M. Rieder, 1903. unp.   CSmH CStclU

16413. Underhill, Ruth Murray. The Indians of southern California. Illus. with photos and drawings by Velino Herrera. Ed. by Willard W. Beatty. [Wash., D.C.] U.S. Bur. of Indian affairs [1941] 73 p. illus., fold. col. map. (Sherman pamphlets no.2)
    CAla CLO CRcS CSalCL CSd CSdS CStmo

16414. U.S. Work projects administration, California. Check list of place names of southern California. Official project no. 65-1-07-2333, Work project no. 11857, Research and records division, Work projects admin. Sponsored by California state dept. of education, the Calif. state hist. assoc. L.A., 1941. 8 pts. in 1 v. Typew.
                                    CLU

16415. Van Dyke, Theodore Strong. Millionaires of a day: an inside history of the great southern California "boom"... N.Y., Fords, Howard & Hulbert, 1890. 208 p.
    C CBb CCoron CHi CL CLO CLSU CLU CLgA CO CP CPom CRedl CSS CSd CSf CSjC CSmH CStmo OrU

16416. —— Southern California: its valleys, hills and streams; its animals, birds, and fishes [etc.]... N.Y., Fords, Howard & Hulbert, 1886. 233 p.
Available in many California libraries and MiD NHi TxU WM

16417. Vaniman, Roscoe J. The southern California land boom of 1887 with special reference to Los Angeles county. [Claremont, 1940] 118 l. Thesis (M.A.)— Claremont college, 1940. CCH

16418. Venderink improvement co., Monrovia. Southern California. S.F., Crocker [1887?] [16] p. CU-B

16419. Walker, Franklin Dickerson. A literary history of southern California. Berkeley, Univ. of Calif. press, c1950. 282 p. illus., ports. (Chronicles of Calif.)
Available in many California libraries and UHi

16420. Walters, Madge (Hardin) Early days and Indian ways; the journal of Madge Hardin Walters. L.A., Westernlore press, 1956. 254 p. illus., ports. (Great West and Indian ser., 5) CChiS CU-B

16421. Warner, Charles Dudley. Our Italy... N.Y., Harper, 1891. 226 p. illus. Text contains an account of the industries (mainly agricultural) of the principal cities of southern California.
Available in many California libraries and OrU ViU ViW

16422. —— Same. London, 1892. CSfP

16423. [Washburn, Josephine M.] History and reminiscences of the Holiness church work in southern California and Arizona. South Pasadena, Record press [1911?] 463 p. ports. CHi CL

16424. Weeks, George F. California copy. Wash., D.C., Wash. college press, 1928. 346 p. illus., ports. CBb CHi CRedl CRic CSd CSf CSfP CStmo

16425. Weinland, Henry A. Now the harvest; memories of a county agricultural agent. N.Y., Exposition press, 1957. 96 p. CSd CU-B

16426. Welch, S. L., comp. Southern California illustrated; ...growth and industry of the three southern counties; prospects, climate, irrigation, resources and commercial prosperity of our semi-tropic land. L.A., Warner brothers, 1886/7. 152 p. illus. C CHi NHi

16427. When destruction walked abroad. [Oakland, E.M. De Lor, 1933?] [24] p. illus. Photographs of the southern California earthquake, Friday, March 10, 1933, with descriptive text. CLU

16428. Who's who in music and dance in southern California... 1933– Hollywood, Bur. of musical research, 1933– illus., ports. Includes essays and a biographical section. Editor: 1933– B. D. Ussher.
C CBev CL CLO CLU CSd CSmH have 1933. CLSU has 1933, 1940. CO has 1940.

16429. Who's who in the Pacific Southwest; a compilation of authentic biographical sketches of citizens of southern California and Arizona. L.A., Times-mirror, 1913. 410 p. ports. CLM CSdS CSfCW

16430. Wills, Mary H. A winter in California. Norristown, Pa., 1889. 150 p. C CHi CSalCL CSf

16431. Wilson, Benjamin Davis. The Indians of southern California in 1852; the B. D. Wilson report and a selection of contemporary comment. Ed. by John Walton Caughey. [1st ed.] San Marino, Huntington lib., 1952. 154 p. (Huntington lib. pub.) The report, prepared in 1852, was published serially in the *Los Angeles star*, July 18–September 19, 1868.
Available in many California libraries.

16432. Woods, Betty Jane. An historical survey of the Women's Christian temperance union of southern California. [L.A., 1950] 217 l. Typew. Thesis (M.A.)— Occidental college, 1950. CLO

16433. Xántus, János. Utazás Kalifornia déli részeiben, irta Xántus János...egy földképpel, nyolcz kö-és nyolcz fametszettel. Pesten, Kiadják Lauffer és Stolp, 1860. 191 p. illus., fold. map. CHi

16434. Youle, William E. Sixty-three years in the oilfields. [L.A.?] Fuller print. co. [1926?] unp. illus., ports. Priv. printed for his friends. Contains biographies of California oil men. CBb CHi CSfSO CSmH

16435. Zeitlin, Jacob Israel. Small renaissance: southern California style. [N.Y.] c1956. 17–27 p. Separate from the *Papers, Bibliographical soc. of Am.* v.50, 1st quarter, 1956. Read at the meeting of the Society at the Huntington library, San Marino, Calif., Aug. 27, 1955. Deals with book industries and trade. CHi

CENTRAL VALLEY

16436. Angel, Arthur Desko. Political and administrative aspects of the Central valley project of California. [L.A., 1944] Thesis (Ph.D.)—U.C.L.A., 1944. CLU

16437. Atchison, Topeka and Santa Fé railway co. The San Joaquin valley... L.A., 1902. 90 p. illus. CFS CHi CLU CViCL

16438. Austin, Mary Hunter. The flock...Illus. by E. Boyd Smith. London, A. Constable & co.; Bost. [etc.] Houghton, 1906. 266 p. illus.
C CAna CArcHT CBaB CHi CInI CLSM COr CSd CSdS CSf CSjC CStmo CU-B OU OrU TxU UPB

16439. Barr, James A. The development of the San Joaquin valley, address delivered in Merced at the annual meeting of the San Joaquin valley commercial association, Nov. 16, 1901. 15 p. CSto

16440. California. Committee to survey the agricultural labor resources of the San Joaquin valley. Agricultural labor in the San Joaquin valley; final report and recommendations. Sacramento, 1951. 405 p.
C CL CLO CLU CSdS CSfCW

16441. California artists and writers of the San Joaquin valley. Fruit of the valley. L.A., Ward Ritchie, 1942. 237 p. CChiS CHi

16442. A California pilgrimage; being an account of the observance of the sixty-fifth anniversary of Bishop Kip's first missionary journey through the San Joaquin valley together with Bishop Kip's own story of the event commemorated. Fresno, c1921 by Bp. Louis C. Sanford. 62 p. illus., ports. 250 copies printed by Bruce Brough, San Francisco, for private distribution.
CBb CHi CSto CStoC

16443. California state chamber of commerce. Travel committee. Visit the San Joaquin valley region, California, and the 1939 Golden gate international exposition. S.F., 1939. 6 p. illus. CRcS

16444. California state irrigation association. Tulare county unit. Save the back country! Only immediate state action can prevent a great tragedy. [Visalia? 1929] [11] p. illus., maps. CFS

16445. Carmichael co., Sacramento. The Sacramento valley of California. [Sacramento? 1911?] v.p. illus. Chiefly reprint. articles from the *Great west.* C

16446. Casey, Jack Tull. Legislative history of the Central valley project, 1933–1949. [Berkeley, 1949] Thesis (Ph.D.)—Univ. of Calif., 1949. CU

16447. Central California register. Annual review. [Fresno, Diocese of Monterey-Fresno]
CFS has 1935, 1940.

16448. Central valley highway association. Central valley highway. Hanford, 1948. unp. illus., maps.
C

16449. Central valley regional planning conference. Proceedings. 1st–2d, 1956–57. [Modesto?] 1956–57. 2 v. illus., maps.   C

16450. Choate, Mary Alberta. Aspirations, attitudes, and concepts of children of two contrasting socio-economic groups in the San Joaquin valley. [Berkeley, 1956] Thesis (Ed.D.)—Univ. of Calif., 1956.   CU

16451. Clark, Effie Elfreda (Marten) The development of wheat culture in the San Joaquin valley, 1846–1900. [Berkeley] 1924. 144 l. illus. Thesis (M.A.)—Univ. of Calif., 1924.   CU CU-B

16452. Clyde, Harry Schley. The regulation of the San Joaquin river for combined power and irrigation use. [Berkeley, 1924] Thesis (M.S.)—Univ. of Calif., 1924.
CU

16453. Connor, Forrest Pershing. The opposition to hydraulic mining in California. [Berkeley, 1950] Thesis (M.A.)—Univ. of Calif., 1950.   CU

16454. [Contant, George C.] A pardoned lifer; life of George Sontag [i.e., George Contant] former member notorious Evans-Sontag gang, train robbers. Written by Opie L. Warner. [San Bernardino, Index print., c1909] 211 p. front. (port.)   CBb CHi

16455. Cutter, Donald Colgett. Moraga of the military: his California service, 1784–1810. [Berkeley, 1947] Thesis (M.A.)—Univ. of Calif., 1947.   CU

16456. —— The Spanish exploration of California's Central valley. [Berkeley, 1950] Thesis (Ph.D.)—Univ. of Calif., 1950.   CU

16457. Derby, George Horatio ("John Phoenix") ...Report of the secretary of war, communicating...a report of the Tulare valley, made by Lieutenant Derby... [Wash., D.C., 1852] 17 p. map. (32d Cong., 1st sess. S. Ex. doc. no. 110) Reprint. in *Calif. hist. soc. Q.*, v.11, 1932, as part of *The topographical reports of Lieutenant G- H- D-, with intro. and notes by Francis P. Farquhar.*   CHi CL CSd CSf CSmH

16458. De Roos, Robert William. The thirsty land; the story of the Central valley project. Stanford [c1948] 265 p. illus., maps.
Available in many California libraries and ODa

16459. Dodge, John W. Electric railroading in central California. San Marino, 1956. 35 p. illus. Third anniversary special issue, *Pac. railroad jl.*, v.1, no. 12, Dec. 1956.   CSto

16460. Downey, Sheridan. They would rule the valley. S.F., 1947. 256 p. illus., map.
Available in many libraries.

16461. Driscoll, Jim. Land and power policies in the Central valley project. [Claremont, 1957] 103 l. Thesis (M.A.)—Claremont college, 1957.   CCH

16462. Durán, Narciso. ...Expedition on the Sacramento and San Joaquin rivers in 1817; diary of Fray Narciso Durán...[Berkeley, Univ. press, 1911] 21 p. Pub. of the Acad. of Pac. coast history, v.2, no. 5) Spanish and English.
C CBev CHi CL CLO CLSU CLgA CO CRedl CSS CSf CSfMI CSmH CStbS CU-B (also has original Spanish mss.) CViCL MoS OrU TxU

16463. Dyke, Dorothy Jeannette. Transportation

in the Sacramento valley, 1849–1860. [Berkeley, 1932] 107 l. illus., map. Thesis (M.A.)—Univ. of Calif., 1932.
CL CU CU-B

16464. Foote, Arthur De Wint. The redemption of the Great valley of California. [N.Y.] Am. soc. of civil engineers, 1909. 26 p. Reprint. from *A.S.C.E., Trans.*, Sept. 1909.   CFS CHi

16465. —— [Scrapbook of newspaper clippings on flood control and reclamation of land in the Sacramento valley, California. n.p., 1911–14] 1 v. mounted illus.
CU-B

16466. Fresno bee. The San Joaquin valley water story, as published in the Fresno bee. Fresno [1958] 26 p. illus.   CFS

16467. Frizzell, Alice Joy. Some economic and political aspects of water resource development in Central valley of California. [Berkeley, 1949] Thesis (M.A.)—Univ. of Calif., 1949.   CU

16468. Gama, Jose. A report on Putah Creek as a source of water supply for the irrigation of lands in the Sacramento valley. [Berkeley, 1923] Thesis (M.S.)—Univ. of Calif., 1923.   CU

16469. Garrod, Richard Milton. The Central valley project: a problem in regional planning. [Berkeley, 1952] Thesis (M.A.)—Univ. of Calif., 1952.   CU

16470. Gill, John Charles. The politics of the Central valley project. [Berkeley, 1950] Thesis (M.A.)—Univ. of Calif., 1950.   CU

16471. Gist, Brooks Dewitt. The years between. Tulare, Author, 1952. 224 p. illus., ports., map on lining papers. The story of the first one hundred years of the San Joaquin valley.
Available in many California libraries and NN

16472. Goldberg, Dan Shlomol. The development and utilization of groundwater in California. [Berkeley, 1939] Thesis (M.S.)—Univ. of Calif., 1939.   CU

16473. Goodall, Merrill Randall. Administration of the Central valley project. [Berkeley, 1942] Thesis (M.A.)—Univ. of Calif., 1942.   CU

16474. Graham, N. E. Irrigation water as a factor in a long-term mortgage loan policy in the upper San Joaquin valley. [Berkeley, 1951] Thesis (M.S.)—Univ. of Calif., 1951.   CU

16475. Grant, Ulysses S. Some problems of the Sacramento river; paper delivered at meeting called by River committee of Sacramento chamber of commerce, Nov. 20, 1923. [Sacramento] 1923. 11 l.   C

16476. Guinn, James Miller. History of the state of California and biographical record of the Sacramento valley, California, an historical story of the state's marvelous growth from its earliest settlement to the present time... Also containing biographies of well-known citizens of the past and present. Chicago, Chapman pub. co., 1906 [c1902] 1712 p. ports. Except for the biographical sketches, text of this work is same as that of the author's volume on coast counties.
C CAla CBb CChi CColu CCorn CHi CLSU CLU CMary CO CRb CS CSS CSdS CSf CSmH CStoC CU-B KHi MWA NHi NbHi

16477. —— History of the state of California and biographical record of the San Joaquin valley, California. An historical story of the state's marvelous growth from its earliest settlement to the present time... Also containing biographies of well-known citizens of the past and present. Chicago, Chapman pub. co., 1905. 1643 p. illus., ports. This has same general text as author's volume on coast counties, differing only in biographical sketches.

C CFS CHan CHi CL CLSU CLU CMS CO CSd CSmH CStoC CU-B CViCL MWA NN WHi

16478. Hall, J. E., comp. Abstract of newspaper accounts of flood damage, extent, duration, etc., in lower Sacramento and San Joaquin rivers, during the years of 1907, 1909, 1911 and 1914. 24 p. Typew.   C

16479. Hall, William Hammond. Central irrigation district, California: its physical, engineering and business problems and conditions. Its legal status [by] Wilson & Wilson. S.F., Bacon, 1891. 63 p. front. (fold. map), tables.   CHi CLU CSfCW NHi

16480. —— Sacramento valley river improvement, government policy and works... [S.F., 1905] 23 p.
          CHi

16481. Hansen, Hugh Groves. The Central valley project: federal or state? [Berkeley, 1955] Thesis (Ph.D.)—Univ. of Calif., 1955.   CU

16482. Hargrove, Robert L. The storage of flood waters; an argument...in support of a resolution passed by the legislature of the state of California requesting the federal government to construct a flood water canal from the San Joaquin river... [n.p., 1912?] 43 p.   CHi

16483. Hawk & Carly, Sacramento. Homes in the heart of California, Sacramento valley. Sacramento [n.d.] 40 p.   CHi

16484. Hubbard, Harry D. Building the heart of an empire, edited by James A. Metcalf; Spanish terms, phrases and translations edited by Marie Aldazabal. Bost., Meador pub. co., 1938. 318 p. illus., ports., maps. History of San Joaquin valley.
C CBb CHi CL CLU CLod CMerCL CRcS CRic CSS CSf CSj CSjC CSmH CStbS CV NN NvU

16485. Immigration association of California, comp. & pub. Resources of the Sacramento valley... S.F. [1883?] 40 p.   CU-B NN

16486. —— Same. [1886?]   CSmH

16487. —— Resources of the southern San Joaquin valley... S.F. [Bacon & co., print., 1885] 78 p.
          C CLU CSmH CU-B

16488. Irrigation in California. The San Joaquin and Tulare plains. Sacramento, Record steam bk. and job print. house, 1873. 22 p.   CSfCSM

16489. Johnson, William D. Inland steam navigation in California. [Stanford, 1952] 114 l. illus., maps. Thesis (M.A.)—Stanford univ., 1952.   CSt

16490. Kadir, Naji Abdul. Location and design of the Madera canal of the Central valley project, from the San Joaquin river to the Fresno river. [Berkeley, 1946] Thesis (M.S.)—Univ. of Calif., 1946.   CU

16491. Kelley, Robert L. Gold vs. grain, the hydraulic mining controversy in California's Sacramento valley; a chapter in the decline of the concept of laissez faire. Glendale, Arthur H. Clark co., 1959. 327 p. illus., fold. map. Based on the author's master's and doctoral theses—Stanford university.
CAla CChiS CHi CLO CLom CLSM CSd CSfCSM CSfSt CYcCL

16492. Kellogg, Charles. Charles Kellogg, the nature singer—his book. Morgan Hill, Pac. science press, 1929. 243 p. illus., ports., pl.   CHi CSd

16493. Kelton, Frank Caleb. Design of an irrigation distribution system for a project in the Sacramento valley. [Berkeley, 1916] Thesis (M.S.)—Univ. of Calif., 1916.   CU

16494. Kirov, George. Central valley project. [S.F., P. Balakshin print. co.] 1940. 40 p.   CHi

16495. Knoop, Anna Marie. The federal Indian policy in the Sacramento valley, 1846–1860. [Berkeley, 1941] Thesis (M.A.)—Univ. of Calif., 1941.
          CU CU-B

16496. Latta, Frank Forrest. Black gold in the Joaquin. Caldwell, Ida., Caxton, 1949. 344 p. illus., ports. Available in many California libraries and KU   TxU   UU

16497. —— California Indian folklore, as told to F. F. Latta by Wah-nom-kot [and others] Shafter, Author, 1936.   CBb

16498. —— Handbook of the Yokuts Indians. Bakersfield, Kern county museum, 1949. 287 p. illus., ports., map.
C CL CLO CLS CLU CMerCL CSS CSf CSmH

16499. —— Same, with title: Handbook of Yokuts Indians. Oildale, Bear state bks., 1949. 287 p. illus., ports., map.   C CBaB CBev CL CO CViCL

16500. Lawrence, William David. Henry Miller and the San Joaquin valley. [Berkeley, 1933] 180 l. illus., port., maps. Thesis (M.A.)—Univ. of Calif., 1933.
          CU CU-B

16501. Leonard, Charles Berdan. The federal Indian policy in the San Joaquin valley; its application and results. [Berkeley, 1928] Thesis (Ph.D.)—Univ. of Calif., 1928.   CU CU-B

16502. —— History of the San Joaquin valley. [Berkeley] 1922. 151 l. Thesis (M.A.)—Univ. of Calif., 1922.   CU

16503. Lippincott, Joseph B. Irrigation of the Sacramento valley. S.F., So. Pac. co., 1905. 24 p. illus.
          C

16504. McClain, Marcia Hall. The distribution of asparagus production in the Sacramento-San Joaquin delta. [Berkeley, 1954] Thesis (M.A.)—Univ. of Calif., 1954.   CU

16505. McDonald, Angus. One hundred and sixty acres of water; the story of the antimonopoly law. Wash., D.C., Public affairs inst., c1958. 37 p.   CFS

16506. McDonald, James R. Autobiography. Transcribed by Paul McDonald and presented by James R. McDonald, jr., in loving remembrance of our father. [Sacramento, 1956] 53 l. Photostat (negative) made by California state library from manuscript lent by Judge Sherrill Halbert, 1956.   C CHi (typescript)

16507. McGowan, Joseph A. History of the Sacramento valley. N.Y., Lewis hist. pub. co. [1961] 3 v. illus. Available in many California libraries.

16508. Magruder, Genevieve (Kratka) The upper San Joaquin valley, 1772–1870. [Bakersfield?] Published through cooperation of Kern county hist. soc. and the county of Kern through the county chamber of commerce, 1950. 84 p. illus., ports., maps. Thesis (M.A.)—Univ. of So. Calif., 1950.
CBaB CHi CLO CLob CLU CO CSjC CSto CStoC UPB

16509. Malaika, Jamil. Location and design of the Friant-Kern canal of the Central valley project. [Berkeley, 1946] Thesis (M.S.)—Univ. of Calif., 1946.   CU

16510. Mary Thomas, Sister (Dorothy Hampton) Apostle of the valley, the life of Daniel Francis Dade, pioneer priest of the San Joaquin valley. Fresno, Acad. of Calif. church history, 1947. 137 p. illus., ports., maps. Bibliography: p. 130–137.

C   CBb   CChiS   CHi   CL   CLO   CLSU   CLgA
CRcS   CSd   CSf   CSmH   CSrD   CViCL   CaBViPA

16511. Mezerik, Avrahm G. The pursuit of plenty: the story of man's expanding domain. N.Y., Harper, 1950. 209 p. The Central valley project.   CV

16512. Miller & Lux, inc. Fertile irrigated land in the San Joaquin valley, California. [S.F., n.d.] folder. illus.   CFS

16513. Mitchell, Annie Rosalind. Jim Savage and the Tulareño Indians. L.A., Westernlore press [1957] 118 p. illus. (Great West and Indian ser., 8)
Available in many California libraries and KU   MiD   N   TxU

16514. —— King of the Tulares, and other tales from the San Joaquin valley, 1772–1852. Visalia [Presses of Visalia times-delta] 1941. 251 p. illus. Bibliography: p. 243–245.
C   CBaB   CHi   CLU   CMerCL   CSjC   CStbS   CViCL

16515. Montgomery, Mary. History of legislation and policy formation of the Central valley project...by Mary Montgomery and Marion Clawson. Berkeley, U.S. Bur. of agric. econ., 1946. 276 p.
CChiS   CHi   CSfCW

16516. Moraga, Gabriel. The diary of Ensign Gabriel Moraga's expedition of discovery in the Sacramento valley, 1808. Tr. and ed. by Donald C. Cutter. [L.A.] Dawson 1957. 36 p. fold. map (Early Calif. travels ser., 41) 300 copies printed by Lawton Kennedy.
C   CHi   CLO   CLS   CLSM   CLgA   CO   CP   CRedl   CSS   CSd   CSf   CSfSt   CSfU   CStclU   CSto   CStoC   CU-B   CoD   NN   ViU

16517. O'Connell, Agnes Catherine. The historical development of the Sacramento valley before 1848. [Berkeley, 1930] 106 l. maps. Thesis (M.A.)—Univ. of Calif., 1930.   CU   CU-B

16518. Orcutt, W. W. Early days in the California fields. Taft, Midway driller pub. co., 1926.   CBb

16519. Palmer, Charles L. The story of the Kings river; a compilation of basic source material with bibliography... Fresno, P.G.&E. co. publicity and advertising dept., 1955. 62 l. maps (1 fold.)   C   CFS   CSfCSM

16520. Papen, Helen. Spanish explorations in the interior of California, 1804–1821. [Berkeley, 1920] Thesis (M.A.)—Univ. of Calif., 1920.   CU

16521. Pearson and company, pub. Brief description of the great San Joaquin valley, its extent and resources... S.F., 1868. 16 p.   CLU   CSmH

16522. Peterson, George Wilbur. American colonization of the upper San Joaquin valley, California, to 1860. [L.A., 1933] 173 l. Thesis (M.A.)—Univ. of So. Calif., 1933.   C   CViCL

16523. Porter, Rebecca N. Raisin valley. N.Y., Vantage press [c1953] 217 p.   C

16524. Raab, Norman Cecil. Total feasible development of the Calaveras river for irrigation purposes. [Berkeley, 1923] Thesis (M.S.)—Univ. of Calif., 1923.   CU

16525. Rojas, Arnold R. California vaquero... Fresno, Acad. lib. guild, 1953. 125 p. illus., ports.
Available in many California libraries and CaBViPA

16526. —— Last of the vaqueros. Fresno, Acad. lib. guild, 1960. 165 p. illus., ports.   CChiS   CL

16527. —— Lore of the California vaquero. Fresno, Acad. lib. guild, 1958. 162 p. illus.
Available in many California libraries.

16528. Sacramento valley and foothill counties, California. [Sacramento, News pub. co., 1915?] 95 p.
CHi

16529. Sacramento valley development association. ...Northern California and the Sacramento valley ...comp. by W. S. Green. [Sacramento, 1902] 20 p. illus.
CU-B

16530. —— Northern California: The Sacramento valley, its resources and industries...comp. by Norton Parker Chipman. [Colusa, 1901] 80 p. illus., map. "Reprint. from *Overland monthly*, April, 1901."
C   CHi   CSmH   NN

16531. —— Sacramento valley, California... S.F., Sunset mag. homeseekers' bur. [1911] 62 p. illus.
CHi   CS   CU-B   NN

16532. —— Sacramento valley, California; tour of Committees...of the Senate and House of representatives... Engineering data by Mr. J. B. Lippincott. ... [Sacramento, 1905?] [23] p. illus.   CHi   CSf

16533. San Joaquin valley agricultural society. ...Transactions and annual report...1st– , 1859/60– Stockton, 1861–
C has 1st–4th, 1859/60–1863. CLU has 2d, 1860/61. CU has 2d, 1860/61. CU-B has 2d–4th, 1860/61–1863. NN has 2d, 1860/61.

16534. San Joaquin valley counties association. San Joaquin valley, California. [Fresno, 19–?] 15 p. illus.
CHi   CLU   CSmH

16535. San Joaquin valley resources; devoted to the interests of the valley. v.1–3, no. 1; Mar. 1886– Apr. 1888. Visalia [E.H. Wilcomb, pub. and prop.] 1886– 88. 3 v. in 1. illus. Publisher varies. No more published.
C   CHi   CViCL

16536. San Joaquin valley tourist and travel association. Official San Joaquin valley-Sierra visitors guide. [Fresno, 1934?] [64] p. illus.   C   CFS

16537. Schmale, Freda Louise. Geographical study of a portion of the San Joaquin valley based upon the five foot contours map of the United States geological survey. [Berkeley, 1923] Thesis (M.A.)—Univ. of Calif., 1923.   CU

16538. Simpson, Richard P. The campaign for state purchase of the Central valley project, 1945–55. [Stanford, 1956] Thesis (M.A.)—Stanford univ., 1956.
CSt

16539. Smith, Wallace Paul Victor. The development of the San Joaquin valley, 1772–1882. [Berkeley, 1932] 238 l. illus., maps. Thesis (Ph.D.)—Univ. of Calif., 1932.   CU   CU-B

16540. —— Garden of the sun...A history of the San Joaquin valley, 1772–1939. L.A., Lymanhouse [c1939] 558 p. illus., ports., maps. Bibliographical references in "Notes": p. 541–49.
Available in many California libraries and N   NN

16541. —— Same. 3d ed. Fresno, M. Hardison, 1956. 567 p.
C   CL   CLSM   CPa   CSbr   CSd   CSdS   CSfSt   CSluCL   CU-B   CViCL   CoD   UPB

16542. —— Spanish exploration of the San Joaquin valley. [Berkeley] 1925. 74 l. map. Thesis (M.A.)— Univ. of Calif., 1925.   CU   CU-B

16543. Stockton mail. San Joaquin valley development edition, Saturday, July 22, 1911. Stockton, 1911. 64 p. illus. (*Stockton mail*, v.63, no.139)   C

16544. Thompson, John. The settlement geography of the Sacramento-San Joaquin delta, California.

[Stanford] 1957. 551 l. illus., maps. Thesis (Ph.D.)—Stanford univ., 1957.   C (microfilm copy) CSt

16545. Treat, O. J., pub. San Joaquin valley business and oil directory...embracing Fresno, Hanford, Visalia, Tulare, Selma, Merced, Madera, Modesto, Bakersfield, Porterville, Clovis, Sanger, Oil City. Fresno, c1900. 189 p.   CHan

16546. True, William. Some aspects of the conflict over Central valley project power. [Berkeley, 1950] Thesis (M.A.)—Univ. of Calif., 1950.   CU

16547. Tucker, E. H., comp. The Wright irrigation law... Selma, Daily irrigator print., 1889. 23 p.   CFS

16548. U. S. Bureau of agricultural economics. The effect of the Central valley project on the agricultural and industrial economy and on the social character of California. A report on Problem 24, Central valley project studies. Berkeley, 1945. 241 p.   CSdS

16549. —— Commission on the irrigation of the San Joaquin, Tulare, and Sacramento valleys. Report... Wash., D.C., Govt. print. off., 1874. 91 p. maps.   C CLU CSf CSmH CU-B TxU

16550. —— Congress. House. 62nd cong., 1st session. Doc. no. 76. Letter...transmitting...reports on examination of Sacramento river, Cal., from Sacramento to Red Bluff, and survey from Feather river to Chico landing. Text and maps. Wash., D.C. [Govt. print. off.] 1911. 19 p. maps.   CHi

16551. Vieths, Edward D. Demographic and economic effects of dam construction in the Central valley of California. [Stanford, 1953] Thesis (M.A.)—Stanford univ., 1953.   CSt

16552. Warkentin, Joel. A decade of migratory labor in the San Joaquin valley, 1940–1950. [Berkeley, 1952] Thesis (M.A.)—Univ. of Calif., 1952.   CU

16553. Wells, Andrew Jackson. The Sacramento valley of California... S.F., Passenger dept. of So. Pac. co., 1904. 112 p. illus.   CHi CSf CU-B NN
Other editions followed. C (1905) CHi (1908) CL (1908) CSS (1908) CSd (1905) CSmH (1906) CU-B (1908) CoU (1905) NN (1905, 1906)

16554. —— The San Joaquin valley of California ... S.F., Passenger dept., So. Pac. co., 1903. 96 p. illus.   C CViCL
Other editions followed. CHi (1908) CL (1908) CMS CMerCL (1908) CSmH (1908) CViCL (1906)

16555. [Wheeler, Arthur] The Valley road (illustrated) ; a history of the Traffic association of California, the League of progress, the North American navigation company, the Merchants' shipping association, and the San Francisco and San Joaquin valley railway... S.F., Wheeler pub. co., 1896. 224 p. illus., ports.   C CBb CHi CLSU CSd CSf CSfP CSfU CSmH CSto CV

16556. Not in use.

16557. Wildman, Esther Theresa. The settlement and resources of the Sacramento valley. [Berkeley] 1921. 118 l. Thesis (M.A.)—Univ. of Calif., 1921.   CU CU-B

16558. Wills, Harry W. Large scale farm operations in the upper San Joaquin valley, California. [L.A., 1953] Thesis (M.A.)—U.C.L.A., 1953.   CLU

16559. Wilson, Edwin E. Agricultural land ownership and operation in the southern San Joaquin valley. Berkeley, U.S. Bur. of agric. econ., 1945. 100 p.   CFS

16560. Wooldridge, Jesse Walton. History of the Sacramento valley, California... Chicago, Pioneer hist. pub. co., 1931. 3 v. illus., ports. v. 2–3; Biographical.
Available in many California libraries and CaBViPA IHi MWA WHi

16561. Writers' program. California. The Central valley project... Sacramento, Calif. state dept. of education, 1942. 165 p. illus., maps. Bibliography: p. 157–160. "Source material": p. [161]–165.
C CBb CChiS CHi CLSU CLU COHN CRc CRcS CSS CSdS CSfCW CSj CSjC CViCL T

SIERRA NEVADA

16562. Adams, Ansel Easton. Sierra Nevada; the John Muir trail... Berkeley, Archtype press, 1938. 49 mounted pl.
C CL CLU CLgA CSf CSfSC CSmH

16563. Andrews, Alice Lorraine. Sierra slopes and summits. S.F., Johnck & Seegar, print., 1931.   CSf

16564. —— Same. Berkeley, Brekas print., 1960. 46 p.   CHi

16565. Andrews, Ralph Warren. Redwood classic. 1st ed. Seattle, Superior pub. co., 1958. 174 p. illus., ports.
CB CBb CLgA CRic CSf CSfSC CSfSt CStrJC

16566. Badè, William Frederic. Life and letters of John Muir. Bost., Houghton, 1924. 2 v. illus., ports.   CHi CRcS CSfCW

16567. [Bishop, Francis A.] Report of the Chief engineer on the survey and cost of construction of the San Francisco & Washoe railroad of California, crossing the Sierra Nevada mountains from Placerville to the eastern boundary of California, on the line of business from San Francisco to the silver mines of Nevada. January 1865. S.F., Towne & Bacon, 1865. 20 p. Signed: Francis A. Bishop.   CLU

16568. California. Legislature. Senate. Committee on internal improvements. Report...with reference to a road across the Sierra Nevada. Senate doc. no. 22, session 1855. Sacramento, State print., 1855. 13 p.   CHi

16569. —— —— —— Fact-finding committee on commerce and economic development. Economic potentials of the Sierra Nevada mountain counties. Partial report. 1959. 31 p. tables.   CChiS

16570. —— Surveyor-general's office. Report of a survey of a portion of the eastern boundary of California, and of a reconnaissance of the Old Carson and Johnson immigrant roads over the Sierra Nevada. [Sacramento, 1856?] 334 p.   CSS

16571. Deane, Dorothy Newell. Sierra railway. Berkeley, Howell-North, 1960. 181 p. illus., map (on lining papers)
CLSM CSf CSfMI CSfU CSmH CTurS

16572. Erickson, Clarence E. The High Sierra; hiking, camping, fishing. Prepared in cooperation with the Sierra club. [Menlo Park, Lane pub. co., 1955] 40 p. illus., maps.   C CLO CSfSC CViCL

16573. Estes, Paul E. Recreational use of the High Sierra, California. [L.A., 1953] Thesis (M.A.)—U.C.L.A., 1953.   CLU

16574. Farquhar, Francis Peloubet. First ascents in the United States, 1642–1900. Berkeley [S.F., Grabhorn] 1948. 11 p.   CHi CSfCW

**16575. —— Jedediah Smith and the first crossing of the Sierra Nevada. [S.F., 1943?] [17] p. maps. Reprint. from *Sierra club bul.*, v. 28, no. 3, June 1943, p. 35–52.   CArcHT CHi CLSM

16576. ——, **comp.** Place names of the High Sierra. S.F., Sierra club, 1926. 128 p. Reprint. from *Sierra club bul.*, v.11: 380–407 and v.12: 47–63, 126–147, but omitting plates in original.
Available in many libraries.

16577. —— The Sierra Nevada of California. [London] Spottiswoode, Ballantyne & co., ltd., 1934. 14 p. illus. Selected references: p. 101–102. Reprint. from *Alpine jl.*, May 1934, p. 88–102.
               C CArcHT CHi CSf CStoC

16578. —— A souvenir of western summits. Berkeley, Grabhorn, 1947. 39 p. 100 copies printed.   CSfSC

16579. Gist, Brooks Dewitt. High Sierra adventure. Visalia, 1950. 108 p. illus., ports.
               C CLO CLU CP CViCL

16580. Goethe, Charles Matthias. Sierran cabin ...from skyscraper; a tale of the Sierran piedmont. [Sacramento] 1943. 185 p. illus.
CChiS CHi CLU CRcS CRedCL CRic CSS CSd CSf CStmo CUk CViCL ODa ViW

16581. Guinn, James Miller. History of the state of California and biographical record of the Sierras... Chicago, Chapman pub. co., 1906 [c1902] 781 p. Except for biographical sketches, text is same as in author's volume on coast counties.
    C CL CLU CO CQCL CSf CStoC CU-B

16582. [Hender, Arthur C.] A brief history of the Sierra railroad... [San Mateo, 1955] 38 p. illus. (*Western railroader*, v.18, no.6, April 1955) Oakdale to Jamestown.   CHi CSto

16583. Highway 50 association. Highway 50 wagon train caravan, Virginia City, Nevada to Placerville, California. [n.p.] 1958. [52] p. illus.   CHi

16584. —— Same, July 16 to July 23, 1961. [Placerville, Mountain democrat, 1961] 48 p. illus.   CHi

16585. Hildebrand, Joel H. A history of ski-ing in California. Reprint. from the 1939 issue of the British ski year book. Uxbridge, Eng., King and Hutchings [n.d.] 15 p.   CHi

16586. Hinkle, George, and Hinkle, Bliss (McGlashan) Sierra-Nevada lakes. Indianapolis, Bobbs [c1949] 383 p. illus., maps. (Am. lake ser., ed. by Milo M. Quaife) "The emphasis is historical rather than descriptive...The region under discussion [is that] between Honey lake and Mono."—Preface.
Available in many California libraries and MiD MoS N NjN UHi

16587. [Hurt, Bert] A sawmill history of the Sierra national forest, 1852–1940. U.S. Dept. of agriculture, Forest service [1941] [51] l. 60 mounted photos.   CFS

16588. Jordan, David Starr. Alps of King-Kern divide... S.F., A.M. Robertson, 1907. 22 p. illus. "This essay was first printed in *The Land of sunshine* (later *Out West*)."
C CBaB CHi CLU CRedl CSf CSfSC CSfU CSj CSmH CViCL

16589. —— California and the Californians. S.F., A.M. Robertson, c1907. 48 p. front.
     CBaB CBb CHi CSd CSjC CSmat CStmo

16590. —— California and the Californians and The Alps of King-Kern divide... S.F., Whitaker-Ray co., 1903. 63 p. illus., port.
C CBu CHi CLLoy CLU CO CRedl CRic CSd CSf CSjC CSmH CaBViPA N

16591. Josephson, Horace Richard. Factors affecting costs and returns of timber production in second-growth pine stands of the Sierra Nevada foothills. [Berkeley, 1940] Thesis (Ph.D.)—Univ. of Calif., 1940.   CU

16592. [King, Clarence] Clarence King memoirs; The helmet of Mambrino. N.Y., Pub. for the King memorial committee of the Century assoc., G.P. Putnam's sons, 1904. 427 p. ports. "Personal memoirs, contributed by some of his more intimate friends and associates."
                    CBb CHi

16593. —— Same. S.F., Bk. club of Calif., 1938.
                         CBb

16594. —— Mountaineering in the Sierra Nevada ... "Altiora petimus." Bost., James R. Osgood & co., 1872. 292 p. Farquhar lists two London editions in same year, followed by various editions in 1874, 1879, 1902, 1903, 1905.
Available in many California libraries and MiD NN OrU UHi ViW

16595. —— Same...edited and with a preface by Francis P. Farquhar. N.Y., Norton [c1935] 320 p. illus., port.
Available in many libraries.

16596. [Le Conte, Joseph] Journal of ramblings through the high Sierras of California by the "University excursion party." S.F., Francis & Valentine, 1875. 103 p. 9 photos. Priv. print. Also published in *Sierra club bul.*, 1900, v.3, no.1.
    C CHi CLU CSfSC CSjC CSmat CSmH CStbS

16597. —— Same, ed. by Francis P. Farquhar. S.F., Sierra club, 1930. 152 p. illus., port. With reproduction of original title-page, 1875. "Bibliographical notes": p. [149]–152.
C CBb CHi CLSU CLU CLgA CO CRedl CRic CSS CSf CSfMI CSfSC CSfU CSmH CStmo CV CViCL

16598. Le Conte, Joseph Nisbet. The High Sierra of California. Phila., Am. alpine club, 1907. 16 p. illus., fold. map. (Alpina Americana, no. 1)   CViCL

16599. —— Journal of a camping trip amongst the highest of the California Sierra, summer of 1890. 1890. 145 l. illus. Mimeo.   CHi CSfSC

16600. Lee, William Storrs. The Sierra. N.Y., Putnam [1962] 350 p. illus.
Available in many California libraries.

16601. Lewis, Dio. Gypsies; or, Why we went gypsying in the Sierras... Bost., Eastern bk. co., 1881. 416 p. illus., port.   C CL CLU CO CSf CSmH

16602. Lewis, Oscar. High Sierra country. [1st ed.] N.Y., Duell [1955] 291 p. map (on lining papers)
Available in many California libraries and MiD NHi ODa OrU

16603. Merriam, Robert Arnold. Effect of fire on streamflow from small watersheds in the Sierra Nevada foothills. [Berkeley, 1957] Thesis (M.S.)—Univ. of Calif., 1957.   CU

16604. Miller, Joaquin. First families of the Sierras. Chicago, Jansen, McClurg & co., 1876. 258 p.   CSf

16605. Muir, John. John of the mountains; the unpublished journals of John Muir. Ed. by Linnie Marsh Wolfe. Bost., Houghton, 1938. 459 p. illus., ports.
CBb CChiS COnC CRc CRcS CRedl CSd CSf CStcl CStoC CUk ODa

16606. —— Mountains of California. N.Y., Century [c1894] 381 p. illus., maps. Other editions followed in 1901, 1903, 1904, 1911, 1917, 1928.
Available in many libraries.

16607. —— My first summer in the Sierra... Bost., Houghton, 1911. 353 p. illus.
Available in many California libraries and MiD

16608. —— Same. Bost., Houghton, 1917. 271 p. illus. (Half-title: *His* Writings...Sierra ed. v.11)
CLSU CLU CLgA CMartC CO COnC CRedCL CSS CSfSC CUk

16609. —— Studies in the Sierra. With an introd. by William E. Colby, foreword by John P. Buwalda. S.F., Sierra club, 1950. 103 p. illus., port. "Originally appeared in 1874 and 1875 as a series of seven articles in the *Overland monthly*." "Glacial writings of John Muir."
CAla CChiS CLO CSf CSfCSM CSfSC CViCL

16610. —— The wilderness world of John Muir: with an introd. and interpretive comments by Edwin Way Teale; illus. by Henry B. Kane. Bost., Houghton, 1954. 332 p. illus.
CAna CHi CP CRcS CRedCL CSd CSf

16611. Oroville. Chamber of commerce. Feather river highway, scenic route through the Sierra Nevada mountains. Oroville, Feather river canyon council [n.d.] 2 p. illus., map.   CRcS

16612. Peattie, Roderick, ed. The Sierra Nevada: the range of light. N.Y., Vanguard [c1947] 398 p. illus., ports., map.
Available in many California libraries and MiD

16613. Power, Robert H. Pioneer skiing in California. Vacaville, Nut tree, 1960. 26 p. illus.
C CHi CSfSC

16614. Reynolds, Richard Dwan. Effect of natural fires and aboriginal burning upon the forests of central Sierra Nevada. [Berkeley, 1959] Thesis (M.A.)—Univ. of Calif., 1959.   CU

16615. Saunders, Charles Francis. The southern Sierras of California...illus. from photographs by the author. Bost., Houghton, 1923. 367 p.
Available in many California libraries and MiD WM

16616. —— Same. London, Hutchinson and co., 1924. 367 p.   UHi

16617. Seattle. John Muir school. The John Muir book. Seattle, Co-operative print. co., 1925.
CMartC COnC CRcS

16618. Sierra club, San Francisco. A climber's guide to the High Sierra. Ed. by David R. Brower. S.F., Sierra club, 1949. 6 pts. in 1 v. illus., maps. "Reprint. from the *Sierra club bul.*"   C CLU CSfSC

16619. —— Same. Ed. by Hervey Voge. S.F., Sierra club, 1954. 301 p. illus.
CAla CChiS CL CLU CLgA CRedl CRic CSd CSfCSM CSfSC CStmo CViCL MiD

16620. Sierra railway co. Yosemite valley via Big Oak Flat route... S.F. [1901] 23 p. illus.   CSmH

16621. —— Yosemite valley via line of Sierra railway company of California... [S.F.? 1898?] [12] p. illus.   CSfSC CU-B

16622. Southern Pacific co. Big trees of California. S.F., c1914. 32 p. illus.   CHi

16623. Starr, Walter Augustus, jr. Guide to the John Muir trail and the High Sierra region. S.F., Sierra club, 1934. 145 p. port., map. Other editions followed.
Available in many libraries.

16624. Stewart, George Rippey. Nomenclature of stream-forks on the west slope of the Sierra Nevada. [N.Y.] 1939. [8] p. illus. "Reprint. from *American speech*, Oct. 1939."   C

16625. Stoutenburg, Adrien. Snowshoe Thompson,

by Adrien Stoutenburg and Laura Nelson Baker. Illus. by Victor De Pauw. N.Y., Scribner [1957] 215 p. illus.
CRedCL CSto

16626. Thompson, Margaret Alice. Overland travel and the central Sierra Nevada, 1827–1849. [Berkeley, 1932] Thesis (M.A.)—Univ. of Calif., 1932.
CU CU-B

16627. Todd, Carolyn J. The Sierra Nevada. [L.A., 1949] Thesis (M.A.)—U.C.L.A., 1949.   CLU

16628. Wampler, Joseph Carson. High Sierra, mountain wonderland; an illustrated and informative book about the high country of the Sierra Nevada... Berkeley, 1960. 122 p. illus.   CChiS CSfSt CSfU

16629. [Watson, Douglas Sloane] West wind; the life story of Joseph Reddeford Walker, knight of the golden horseshoe. L.A., Priv. print. for his friends by Percy M. Booth, 1934. 109 p. illus., port., fold. map.
CBb CHi CLgA CSf

16630. Weed, Charles L. [Photographs of the Middle fork of the American river and Forest hill, the Yosemite valley and Mariposa big trees, Coloma and Placerville. Oct. 1858–July 1859] 47 mounted photos.
CU-B

16631. Weeks, David. ...Land utilization in the northern Sierra Nevada, by David Weeks, A. E. Wieslander, H. R. Josephson, C. L. Hill... Berkeley, Univ. of Calif., 1943. 127 p. illus., maps, tables, diagrs.   CLU

16632. White, Stewart Edward. The mountains... illustrated by Fernand Lungren. N.Y., McClure Phillips & co., 1904. 282 p. illus. Other editions followed.
Available in many libraries.

16633. —— The Pass... N.Y., Outing pub. co., 1906. 198 p. illus.
CHi CRc CRic CSd CSf CStcl ViU

16634. Whitney, Josiah Dwight. The auriferous gravels of the Sierra Nevada. Cambridge, Mass., Univ. press, 1879–80. 2 v. in 1. illus., maps. (*Memoirs* of the Museum of comparative zoology at Harvard college, v.6, no.1)   C CHi CLSU CRedl CSfCSM

16635. Wilkins, Thurman. Clarence King, a biography. N.Y., Macmillan, 1958. 441 p. port.
CBb CHi CRcS CRedCL CRedl CSd

16636. Wilson, Obed G. My adventures in the Sierras... Franklin, Ohio, Editor pub. co., 1902. 215 p. port.   C CHi CLU CSmH CU-B

16637. Winkley, John W. John Muir, naturalist. Nashville, Parthenon press [1959] 141 p. illus.   CHi

16638. Wolfe, Linnie Marsh. Son of the wilderness; the life of John Muir. N.Y., Knopf, 1945. 364 p. illus.   CChiS CHi CRcS CRedCL

16639. Wright, James William Abert. The cement hunters; lost gold mine of the High Sierra. Ed. by Richard E. Lingenfelter. L.A., Dawson, 1960. 52 p. illus., port.
CHi

16640. Wright, William. Snow-shoe Thompson, 1856–1876, by Dan De Quille [pseud.] L.A., Dawson, 1954. 63 p. (Early Calif. travels ser., 21) This biography of Snow-shoe Thompson, 'The Skiing mailman of the Sierra,' is reprinted from the *Overland monthly* of October, 1886. "Limited edition of 210 copies.—Preface."
CBb CLO CLSM CLgA CSS CSf CSfSC CSjC CSto CStoC CU-B CVtV

16641. Yeager, Dorr Graves. National parks in California. Menlo Park, Lane pub. co., 1959. 96 p. illus., maps.
Available in many California libraries.

CALIFORNIA STATEWIDE WORKS

16642. Abbott, Carlisle Stewart. Recollections of a California pioneer. N.Y., Neale pub. co., 1917. 235 p. front. (port.)

16643. Abbott, John Steven Cabot. Christopher Carson. N.Y., Dodd & Mead, 1873. 348 p.

CHi CL CP CSd

16644. Abdy, Rowena Meeks. Old California. S.F., J.H. Nash, 1924. 10 p. 10 mounted col. pl.

16645. Adams, Kenneth C., ed. From trails to freeways. Sacramento, Calif. highways and public works, 1950. 167 p. illus., maps.

16646. Ainsworth, Edward Maddin. California. L.A., House-Warven, 1951. 272 p.

16647. Ajisaka, Yoshisuke, etc. Picture albums of business families of the same lineage (i.e., Japanese) resident in America along the Pacific coast of the United States. Seattle, Ajisaka Orient tourist co., 1935. 500 p. illus., ports.

16648. Allen, Alice Mayhew. Early roads and trails in California; prep. for the National society of colonial dames of America, resident in the state of California. S.F., The society, 1942. 39 p. maps.

16649. Allen, Mary Moore. Origin of names of Army and Air corps posts, camps and stations in World War II in California. Goldsboro, N.C., Author, n.d. 67 p.

16650. Alta California: embracing notices of the climate, soil, and agricultural products of northern Mexico and the Pacific seaboard; also, a history of the military and naval operations of the United States directed against the territories of northern Mexico, in the year 1846–47... by a Captain of Volunteers. Phila., H. Packer & co., 1847. 64 p.   CHi

16651. Anderson, Winslow. Mineral springs and health resorts of California... S.F., Bancroft co., 1890. 384 p. illus.

16652. Anthony, Charles Volney. Fifty years of Methodism; a history of the Methodist Episcopal church within the bounds of the California annual conference from 1847 to 1897. S.F., Methodist bk. concern, 1901. 453 p. Many biographical sketches.

16653. Armenian directory of the state of California ...comp. by E. Harout. 1932–

16654. Armstrong, Leroy. Financial California. An historical review of the beginnings and progress of banking in the state. S.F., Coast banker pub. co., 1916. 191 p. illus., ports., facsims.

16655. Arnold, Robert K. The California economy, 1947–1980... Menlo Park, Stanford research inst., 1961. 456 p. illus., map.

16656. Art in California; a survey of American art with special reference to Californian painting, sculpture and architecture past and present, particularly as those arts were represented at the Panama-Pacific international exposition; being essays and articles by the following contributors: Bruce Porter, Everett Maxwell, Porter Garnett ... S.F., R.L. Bernier, 1916. 183 p. 332 plates.

16657. Associação portuguesa protectora e beneficente do Estado da California. Constituição do conselho supremo da... [Oakland, J. de Menezes & filhos, 1933] 164 p.

16658. Attivita' Italiane in California. Dato Aile stampe da G. M. Touni—G. Brogelli. [1929] 309 p. Historical and biographical materials about Italian pioneers.

16659. Audubon, John Woodhouse. Audubon's western journal: 1849–1850, being the Ms. record of a trip from New York to Texas, and an overland journey through Mexico and Arizona to the gold-fields of California. Cleveland, Arthur H. Clark co., 1906. illus., port., fold. map. 249 p.

16660. —— The drawings of John Woodhouse Audubon, illustrating his adventures through Mexico and California, 1849–1850. S.F., Bk. club of Calif., 1957.

16661. Austin, Mary Hunter. California, the land of the sun. Painted by Sutton Palmer, described by Mary Austin. N.Y., Macmillan [1914] 178 p. 32 col. illus.

16662. —— Same, with title, The lands of the sun. Bost., N.Y., Houghton Mifflin co., 1927. 214 p. illus.

16663. Ayers, James J. Gold and sunshine; reminiscences of early California; illustrations from the collection of Charles B. Turrill. Bost., Richard G. Badger, Gorham press, c1922. 359 p. illus.

16664. Baer, Kurt. Architecture of the California missions. Photos by Hugo Rudinger. Berkeley, Univ. of Calif. press, 1958. 196 p. illus.

16665. Bailey, Paul Dayton. Sam Brannan and the California Mormons. L.A., Westernlore press, 1943. 187 p. illus., ports., map.

16666. Balzer, Robert Lawrence. California's best wines. L.A., Ward Ritchie [1948] 153 p. map (on lining-papers)

16667. Bancroft, Hubert Howe. Chronicles of the builders of the commonwealth, historical character study. S.F., History co., 1891–1892. 7 v. and index. illus., ports., maps.

16668. —— History of California. S.F., History co., 1884–90. 7 v. (Works of Hubert Howe Bancroft, v.18–24)

16669. —— Pioneer register and index. (In his *History of California,* v.2–5) Alphabetical list of Californians from 1542 to 1848, with biographical notes. Reprinted. L.A., Dawson, 1964. Also, Baltimore, Regional pub. co., 1964.

16670. [Bancroft scraps] 113 v. in 121. Partial contents: v.1. California counties: Alameda to Los Angeles.– v.2. California counties: Los Angeles to Placer.– v.3. California counties: Placer to San Diego.– v.4. California counties: San Diego to Santa Cruz.– v.5. California counties: Santa Cruz to Yuba.– v.68. San Francisco legal affairs.– v.69. San Francisco charter.– v.70. San Francisco fire department.– v.71, 1–2. San Francisco miscellany.

CU-B

16671. Bangs, Edward Geoffrey. Portals West; a folio of late nineteenth century architecture in California. Pref. by Robert Gordon Sproul. [S.F.] Calif. hist. soc. [1960] 86 p. 36 illus. (Calif. hist. soc. Special pub. no. 35)

16672. Barns, George C. Denver, the man; the life, letters and public papers of the lawyer, soldier and statesman... Wilmington, Ohio, Author, 1949. 372 p. ports. Biography of James W. Denver who served in U.S. government as a Californian, 1850–57.

16673. Barrett, Edward L. The Tenney committee; legislative investigation of subversive activities in California. Ithaca, N.Y., Cornell univ. press, 1951. 400 p. (Cornell studies in civil liberty)

16674. Bashford, Herbert. A man unafraid; the story of John Charles Fremont. By Herbert Bashford and Harr Wagner. S.F., Harr Wagner pub. co., c1927. 406 p. illus., ports.

16675. Bates, Joseph Clement, ed. History of the bench and bar of California. S.F., Bench & bar pub. co., 1912. 572 p. ports.

16676. Bates, Lana Louise. The historical geography of California, 1542–1835. [Berkeley, 1928] Thesis (M.A.)—Univ. of Calif., 1928.

16677. [Bayard, Samuel John] A sketch of the life of Com. Robert F. Stockton; with an appendix, comprising his correspondence with the Navy department respecting his conquest of California; and extracts from the defence of Col. J. C. Fremont, in relation to the same subject; together with his speeches in the Senate of the United States, and his political letters. N.Y., Derby & Jackson, 1856. 210, 131 p. front. (port.)

16678. Beasley, Delilah Leontium. The negro trail blazers of California... L.A., Times-mirror print. & bind. house, 1919. 317 p. ports.

16679. Bekeart, Philip Baldwin. Flags that have flown over California. S.F., Author, 1929. 27 p. illus.

16680. Bernard du Hautcilly, Auguste. Voyage autour du monde, principalement à la Californie et aux Iles Sandwich, pendant les années 1826, 1827, 1828, et 1829: par A. Duhaut-Cilly... Paris: Chez Arthus Bertrand... Saint-Servan: Chez D. Lemarchand... 1834–35. 2 v. illus. "More than 300 pages of the work are devoted to California and its missions... Visits were made to ten missions: Dolores, Santa Cruz, San Carlos, Santa Barbara, Purisima Concepcion, Santa Inez, San Diego, San Luis Rey, Santa Clara, and San Francisco Solano."—Waters.

16681. Bigelow, John. Memoir of the life and public services of John Charles Fremont. N.Y., Derby & Jackson, 1856. 480 p. illus.

16682. Bird, Frederick Lucien and Ryan, Frances M. Public ownership on trial; a study of municipal light and power in California. N.Y., New republic inc., 1930. 186 p. diagrs.

16683. Björk, Kenneth. West of the Great Divide; Norwegian migration to the Pacific coast, 1847–1893. Northfield, Minn., Norwegian-Am. hist. assoc., 1958. 671 p. illus. (Pub. of the Norwegian-Am. hist. assoc.)

16684. Black Republican imposture exposed! Fraud upon the people. Fremont and his speculations... Washington, Polkinhorn's steam job off., 1856. 16 p.

CHi CStbS N ViU

16685. Bloom, Leonard. Removal and return. Berkeley, Univ. of Calif. press, 1949. 259 p. Evacuation of the Japanese in World War II.

16686. Blow, Ben. California highways; a descriptive record of road development by the state and such counties as have paved highways. S.F., Crocker, 1920. 308 p. illus., maps.

16687. Blum, George W., comp. and pub. The cyclers' guide and road book of California; containing map of California in relief with principal roads, seven sectional maps showing all available roads for cyclers from Chico to San Diego, and a map of Golden Gate park, 1896. S.F., 1895. 80 p. maps.

16688. Bogardus, John P., comp. Bogardus' illustrated California almanac...1857. S.F., Excelsior steam job print. off. [1857] 34 p.   C CHi CSmH

16689. Bollens, John Constantinus. Appointed executive local government; the California experience. L.A., Haynes foundation, 1952. 233 p. map.

16690. —— Local government in California, by John C. Bollens and Stanley Scott. Berkeley, Univ. of Calif. press, 1951. 154 p.

16691. —— Your California governments in action, by John C. Bollens and Winston Winford. Berkeley, Univ. of Calif. press, 1954. 296 p. illus., maps.

16692. Bolton, Herbert Eugene. Cross sword & gold pan: a group of notable full-cover paintings depicting outstanding episodes in the exploration and settlement of the West, by Carl Oscar Borg and Millard Sheets, with interpretative historical essays by Herbert E. Bolton ... L.A., Primavera press, 1936. [31] p. col. pl.

16693. Bolton, Ivy May. Father Junipero Serra; illustrated by Robert Burns. N.Y., Messner [1952] 160 p. illus.

16694. Book club of California. Keepsake series. 1– , 1933/34–S.F., 1934– Contents: no.1. The California mining town series.– no.2. The letters of western authors.– no.3. The California literary pamphlets.– no.4. Contemporary California short stories.– no.5. Coast and valley towns of early California.– no.6. Six California tales.– no.7. Pacific adventures.– no.8. California on canvas.– no.9. Guardians of the Pacific.– no.10. A camera in the gold rush.– no.11. The California poetry folios.– no.12. Letters of the gold discovery.– no.13. California clipper cards.– no.14. Bonanza banquets.– no.15. Pioneer western playbills.– no.16. Attention, pioneers!– no.17. Pictorial humor of the gold rush.– no.18. Early transportation in southern California.– no.19. The vine in early California.– no.20. Treasures of California collections.– no.21. Resorts of California.– no.22. Gold rush steamers.– no.23. California sheet music covers.– no.24. Early California mail bag.– no.25. Early California firehouses and equipment.– no.26. Portfolio of Book club printers, 1912–62.– no.27. California governmental seals.

16695. —— 13 California towns from the original drawings. S.F., 1947. [18] l. [13] pl. "Three hundred copies printed at the Grabhorn press of San Francisco..." "The drawings have been reproduced from the originals in the Bancroft library, University of California." Introd. and descriptive text by Edith M. Coulter and Eleanor A. Bancroft. Contents: Folsom.– Benicia.– Vallejo and Mare island.– Martinez.– Alviso.– Santa Cruz.– San Juan Bautista.– Monterey.– San Luis Obispo.– Santa Barbara.– San Bernardino.– Los Angeles.– San Diego.

16696. Botta, Paolo Emilio. Observations on the inhabitants of California, 1827–1828...Tr. by John Francis Bricca. L.A., Dawson, 1952. 20 p. (Early Calif. travels ser., 5) 140 copies printed by Wm. M. Cheney.

16697. Brace, Charles Loring. The new west; or, California in 1867–1868. N.Y., Putnam, 1869. 373 p.

16698. Brandon, William. The men and the mountain; Fremont's fourth expedition. N.Y., Morrow, 1955. 337 p. maps.

16699. Breeden, Marshall. Up, down and all around California, including fiction and facts about its fifty-eight counties, coast line and lighthouses. L.A., Times-mirror press, 1923. 115 p. Arranged by counties; brief and rather flippant descriptions.

16700. —— Same, revised, with title: California, all of it... L.A., Kenmore [c1925] 200 p. illus., pl.

16701. Brewer, William Henry. Up and down California in 1860–64... Edited by Francis P. Farquhar. New Haven, Conn., Yale; London, H. Milford, Oxford, 1930. 601 p. illus., ports., map.

16702. Brewster, Edwin Tenney. Life and letters of Josiah Dwight Whitney. With illustrations. Bost., Houghton, 1909. 411 p.

16703. Brown, William S. California rural land use and management; a history of the use and occupancy of rural lands in California, by Wm. S. Brown and S. B. Snow. U.S. Forest service. Calif. region, 1944. 639, 42 p.

16704. Bruner, Helen Marcia. California's old burying grounds... S.F. [Portal press] 1945. 24 p. illus. Bibliography: p. 24.

16705. Bryant, Edwin. What I saw in California, being the journal of a tour...through California in the years 1846, 1847... Second ed. N.Y., Appleton, 1848. 455 p. Cowan notes seven American editions in 1848 and others in foreign languages.

16706. —— —— Index...Joseph Gaer, ed. S.F.. 1935. 9 l. (Index no. 8, SERA project 2-F2-132 (3-F2-197) Calif. literary research) Mimeo.

16707. —— Same, reprinted, with notes, index and bibliography by Marguerite Eyer Wilbur. Santa Ana, Fine arts press, 1936. 481 p. illus., map. (Calafía ser. v.1) Bibliography: p. [441]–444.

16708. Bunje, Emil T. H. Pre-Marshall gold in California...by E. T. Bunje and James C. Kean. Produced on a Works progress administration project... sponsored by the Univ. of California, 1938. 2 v. maps. Typew.

16709. Burcham, Lee T. California range land; an historic-ecological study of the range resources of California. Sacramento, Calif. Div. of forestry, Dept. of natural resources, 1957. 261 p. illus., maps, charts, facsims., tables.

16710. Burdett, Charles. Life of Kit Carson, the great Western hunter and guide... Phila., Porter and Coates, 1865. 374 p. illus.

16711. Cahn, Frances. Welfare activities of federal, state, and local governments in California, 1850–1934... Berkeley, Univ. of Calif. press, 1936. 422 p.

16712. California. Adjutant general. History of the California state guard. [Sacramento, 1946] 232 p. illus., ports., maps.

16713. —— —— The muster rolls of the California volunteers in the "Spanish-American War of 1898"... Sacramento, 1899. 71 p.

16714. —— —— Records of California men in the War of the rebellion, 1861 to 1867. Rev. and comp. by Brig.-Gen. Richard H. Orton. Sacramento, State print. off., 1890. 887 p.

16715. —— **Board of state viticultural commissioners.** Directory of the grape growers and wine makers of California. Sacramento, Supt. of state print., 1888. 62 p.

16716. —— **Bureau of labor statistics.** History and description of each county in state. (In its *Second biennial rept.*, 1885/6, p. 153–324)

16717. —— **Bureau of livestock identification.** California brand book [192–?]– Sacramento, State print. off. [1920?]–

16718. —— **Dept. of natural resources.** [Reports on registered landmarks nos. 1–] The State department of natural resources and the State park commission in cooperation with the California state chamber of commerce. [Sacramento, 1932–] Mimeo. Index by counties, giving registration number, name, and location of each landmark.

16719. —— —— **Division of mines.** Fabricas;

a collection of pictures and statements on the mineral materials used in building in California prior to 1850. Assembled by Elisabeth L. Egenhoff as a supplement to the California journal of mines and geology for April 1952. [Sacramento, State print. off., 1952] 189 p. illus., port., maps.

16720. —— —— —— [Publications] S.F., 1880– Of these, most important are the *Report series* (followed by the quarterly *California journal of mines and geology* and now partially replaced by the *New series, county reports*), the *Bulletin series, Special reports*, and *Mineral information service*. See its list, *Publications*...to July 1, 1961.

16721. —— —— **Division of oil and gas.** Summary of operations, California oil fields, 4th– April, 1919– 1st and 3d issued as Annual reports of State oil and gas supervisor, 1915/16–1917/18.

16722. —— **Dept. of public works. Division of highways.** Inventory of urban planning for population areas of over 25,000 on the interstate system, 10,000–25,000 on the interstate system, over 25,000 not on the interstate system. [Sacramento, 1960] v.1–3. maps. Contents:– v.1. Los Angeles and vicinity.– v.2. San Francisco, Oakland, San Diego, San Jose, Sacramento, San Bernardino [and vicinities].– v.3. Concord and vicinity through Santa Rosa.

16723. —— **Governor (Markham)** The resources of California prepared in conformity with a law approved March 11, 1893. Sacramento, State print. off., 1893. 144 p. illus. Ed. by E. W. Maslin. Pages 5–98, "Description of the counties of the state"; is much like *California blue book*, but with longer articles on each county.

16724. —— **Highway advisory committee.** Report of a study of the state highway system of California. Sacramento, 1925. 111 p. illus., maps, diagrs.

16725. —— **Laws, statutes, etc.** The statutes of California and amendments to the codes... Sacramento, 1850 to date. Place and title vary. (e.g., 1850, San Jose, J. Winchester) Texts of city and county charters will be found here.

16726. —— **Legislature. Senate. Special committee to investigate Chinese immigration.** Chinese immigration. The social, moral, and political effect of Chinese immigration... Sacramento, State print., 1876. 302 p.

16727. —— **Mexican fact-finding committee.** Mexicans in California... Sacramento, State print. off., 1930. 214 p. maps, tables, diagrs. Will J. French, chairman.

16728. —— **Secretary of state.** California blue book and state roster. Sacramento, State print. off., 1891– [Published irregularly] "Origin and meaning of names of counties": 1907 and 1909. "Resources and production of counties": 1911, 1928, 1932. "Economic survey of California and its counties": 1942 and 1946. All issues contain lists of county and city officials.

16729. —— **State board of equalization.** Property tax assessment... [1949–] maps. Surveys for each county.

16730. —— **State geologist (John B. Trask)** [Reports of first State geological survey of California. S.F.] State print., 1853–56. 4 v. Reports on geology of northern and southern California and of the Sierra Nevada and the Coast range.

16731. —— **State geologist (Josiah Dwight Whitney)** ...Geology. 1865–1882. 2 v. (Geol. survey of

Calif.) v.1, pt.1 and v.2: Geology of the coast ranges.–v.2, pt.2: Geology of the Sierra Nevada.

16732. ——— **State library.** Complete list of members of the California legislature, senate and assembly, 1849–1900, arranged by district, comp. by Mrs. Alice Kirwan... [Sacramento] 1959. unp.

16733. ——— Descriptive list of the libraries of California, containing the names of all persons who are engaged in library work in the state. Sacramento, State print., 1904. 134 p. illus.

16734. ——— **Surveyor general's office.** Corrected report of Spanish and Mexican grants in California, complete to February 25, 1886... Published as supplement to official *Report*, 1883/84. [Sacramento, 1886] Issued also in *Report...1884/86–1886/88.*

16735. ——— **University. Heller committee for research in social economics.** Doors to jobs, a study of the organization of the labor market in California, by Emily H. Huntington... Berkeley and L.A., Univ. of Calif. press, 1942. 454 p. tables.

16736. ——— ——— **Los Angeles. Bureau of governmental research.** County government in California. 3d ed. Sacramento, County supervisors assoc. of Calif., 1958. 159 p.

16737. ——— **World's fair commission.** Final report...including a description of all exhibits from the state of California...at the World's Columbian exposition, Chicago, 1893. Sacramento, State print. off., 1894. 240 p. illus., fold. plan.

16738. "California as it is." Written by seventy of the leading editors and authors of the golden state for the *Weekly call*... S.F., S.F. call co. [1882] 175 p. front. Other editions followed.

16739. California federation of women's clubs. California federation of women's clubs organized at Los Angeles, Jan. 18th, 1900... L.A., Baumgardt, 1901. 31 p.

16740. ——— ...Official directory and register... officers and members... S.F. [190–?–] Publisher varies.

16741. ——— A record of twenty-five years...1900–1925. Comp. by Mary S. Gibson. S.F., 1927. 2 v. diagr.

16742. California; fifty years of progress. S.F., 1900. 300 p. illus., ports., map, tables.

16743. California information and almanac; a comprehensive study of past, present and future California. 1947/48– Lakewood, Calif. almanac co., c1947– illus., ports., pl., maps, tables. Title varies: 1947/48, 1953/54 *California almanac and state fact book.* Imprint varies.

16744. California: its past history; its present position; its future prospects: containing a history of the country from its colonization by the Spaniards to the present time; a sketch of its geographical and physical features; and a minute and authentic account of the discovery of the gold region, and the subsequent important proceedings. Including a history of the rise, progress, and present condition of the Mormon settlements. With an appendix, containing the official reports made to the government of the United States. London, The proprietors, 1850. 270 p. illus. (col.), map.

CHi CP CSfCW CSfP CSfWF-H N

16745. California manufacturers association... Annual register. 1st– 1948– L.A., Times-mirror press, 1948–

16746. California masonry; the written law, masonic beginnings in California and Hawaii, extinct masonic lodges of California, constitution, biographies, California masonry and Stanford university... L.A., Masonic history co., 1936. illus., ports. 3 v.

16747. California miners' association, pub. California mines and minerals. Published...under the direction of Edward H. Benjamin... S.F., 1899. 450 p. illus., ports., maps. "Individual chapters on the gold producing counties."

16748. California real estate association, pub. ...Official blue book roster of California real estate firms ... [L.A., 1928–] illus., ports., maps. Title varies: 1928–193–, Growth and progress of the golden west; 193–? –1938, State real estate blue book.

16749. California register and statistical reporter. S.F., Eureka office, 1856. 48 p. fold. map.   CU-B

16750. The California register, social blue book of California, v.1, 1954– Beverly Hills, Social blue book of Calif., inc., 1954– Published annually. Editor varies.

16751. California school directory. 1915/16– Berkeley, Calif. assoc. of secondary school administrators [1915?]– Title and publisher vary.

16752. California state almanac and annual register ...containing a complete list of the post offices of the state, names, places of residence and salaries of the executive department of the state government...1855–1856. Sacramento, Democratic state jl. off., print., 1855–56. 2 v.

C (1855–56) CHi (1855) CSmH (1855–56) CU-B (1855–56)

16753. California state business directory, a complete, classified and alphabetically arranged business directory of merchants, manufacturers, etc. of the state [1870?]–1875/76. S.F., D.M. Bishop & co. [1870–75]

16754. California state council of defense. Report of the Committee on petroleum. Sacramento, State print. off., 1917. 191 p. Report on California industry during World War I.

16755. California state gazetteer and business directory...1888–1898. S.F., R.L. Polk & co., 1888–98.

16756. California statistical abstract. 1958– [Sacramento, State print. off., 1958]– illus., maps.

16757. Californians "as we see 'em," a volume of cartoons and caricatures. [n.p., E.A. Thomson pub., 1906] 301 p.

16758. Camp, Charles Lewis. Earth song; a prologue to history. Berkeley, Univ. of Calif. press, 1952. 127 p. illus., maps. (Chronicles of Calif.)

16759. Capron, Elisha Smith. History of California, from its discovery to the present time; comprising also a full description of its climate, surface, soil, rivers, towns...agriculture, commerce, mines, mining, etc... Bost., John P. Jewett & co.; Cleveland, Ohio, Jewett, Proctor & Worthington, 1854. 356 p. map.

16760. Carosso, Vincent Phillip. The California wine industry, 1830–1895; a study of the formative years. Berkeley, Univ. of Calif. press, 1951. 241 p.

16761. [Carr, A.] Illustrated hand-book of California: her climate, trade, exports, etc., etc., agricultural and mineral wealth. London, S. Low, son, & Marston, 1870. 116 p. illus. (part col.) Preface signed: A. Carr.

16762. Carr, Ezra Slocum. The Patrons of husbandry on the Pacific coast. Being a complete history of ...agriculture in different parts of the world; of the origin and growth of the order of Patrons, with a... directory, and full list of charter members of the subordinate granges of California... S.F., A.L. Bancroft & co., 1875. 461 p.

16763. Carson, Christopher. Kit Carson's own story of his life as dictated to Col. and Mrs. D. C. Peters about 1856–57, and never before published; edited by Blanche C. Grant. Taos, N. Mex., B.C. Grant, 1926.

16764. Casas, Augusto. Fray Junípero Serra, el apóstol de California. Barcelona, L. Miracle [1949] 271 p. illus., ports., maps.

16765. Cass, Lewis. California claims. In Senate of the United States, February 23, 1848. Mr. Cass made the following report...the petition of John Charles Fremont... Wash., Govt. print. off., 1848. 83 p. (30th Cong. 1st sess. S. report no. 75)   CHi

16766. Cerruti, Enrique. Ramblings in California, the adventures of Henry Cerruti. Ed. by Margaret Mollins and Virginia E. Thickens. Berkeley, Friends of Bancroft library, 1954. 143 p. illus. "Five hundred copies designed and printed by the Gillick press, Berkeley, California."

16767. Chambers, Clarke A. California farm organizations; a historical study of the Grange, the Farm bureau and the Associated farmers: 1929–1941. Berkeley, Univ. of Calif. press, 1952. 277 p.

16768. Chapman, Charles Edward. The founding of Spanish California; the northwestward expansion of New Spain, 1687–1783. N.Y., Macmillan, 1916. 485 p. port., maps.

16769. Chase, Joseph Smeaton. California coast trails... Bost., Houghton, 1913. 326 p. illus.

16770. Childers, Laurence Murrell. Education in California under Spain and Mexico, and under American rule to 1851. [Berkeley, 1930] Thesis (M.A.)—Univ. of Calif., 1930.

16771. Clar, C. Raymond. California government and forestry, from Spanish days until the creation of the Department of natural resources in 1927. Sacramento, Calif. Div. of forestry, Dept. of natural resources, 1959. 623 p. illus., map.

16772. Clark, Francis D. The first regiment of New York volunteers, commanded by Col. Jonathan D. Stevenson in the Mexican war. Names of the members of the regiment... N.Y., Geo. S. Evans & co., 1882. 109 p. ports.

16773. Cloud, Roy Walter. Education in California; leaders, organizations and accomplishments of the first hundred years. Stanford [1952] 296 p. ports.

16774. Colburn, Frona Eunice Wait (Smith) ...Wines and vines of California...A treatise on the ethics of wine-drinking. Endorsed by the Board of state viticultural commissioners of California. S.F., Bancroft, 1889. 215 p. illus.

16775. [Cole, Cornelius] California three hundred and fifty years ago. Manuelo's narrative trans. from the Portuguese by a pioneer. S.F., Samuel Carson & co., 1888. 329 p. front.

16776. Cole, William L. California: its scenery, climate, productions and inhabitants... N.Y., Irish-American office, 1871. 103 p.

16777. Conference of California historical societies. Proceedings of the annual meeting. 1st– 1955– Stockton, College of the Pac., 1955–

16778. Congregational churches in California. General association... Constitution and by-laws, minutes and proceedings... 1st– 1857– Sacramento, S.F., 1857– Printer varies.

16779. Conkling, Roscoe Platt. The Butterfield overland mail, 1857–1869; its organization and operation over the southern route to 1861; subsequently over the central route to 1866; and under Wells, Fargo and Com-

pany in 1869. Glendale, Arthur H. Clark, 1947. 3 v. pl., maps. (Am. trail series, 3–5)

16780. Conmy, Peter Thomas. The historic Spanish origin of California's community property law and its development and adaptation to meet the needs of an American state. S.F., Native sons of the golden West, 1957. 25 p.

16781. —— The origin and purposes of the Native sons and daughters of the golden West. S.F., Dolores press, 1956. 24 p. port.

16782. Constructive Californians; men of outstanding ability who have added greatly to the Golden state's prestige. With a foreword by S. T. Clover. L.A., Saturday night pub. co., 1926. 214 p. ports.

16783. Cook, Sherburne Friend. The conflict between the California Indian and white civilization. Berkeley, Univ. of Calif. press, 1943. 4 v. (Half-title: Ibero-Americana: 21–24)

16784. Corle, Edwin. The royal highway (El camino real). Indianapolis, N.Y., Bobbs [c1949] 351 p. illus., ports., maps. "Past events are located in terms of present landmarks."—*Booklist.*

16785. Cowan, Robert Ernest, and Dunlap, Boutwell. Bibliography of the Chinese question in the United States... S.F., A.M. Robertson, 1909. 68 p.

16786. Cowan, Robert Granniss. Ranchos of California, a list of Spanish concessions, 1775–1822, and Mexican grants, 1822–1846. Fresno, Acad. lib., guild, 1956. 151 p. maps (on lining papers).

16787. Coy, Owen Cochran. California county boundaries: a study of the division of the state into counties and the subsequent changes in their boundaries. Sacramento, State print. off., 1923. 335 p. maps. (Pub. of Calif. hist. survey commission)

16788. —— California's constitution, by Owen C. Coy and Herbert C. Jones. L.A., Marjorie Tisdale Wolcott, c1930. 78 p.

16789. —— The genesis of California counties. Sacramento, State print. off., 1923. 92 p. maps. (Pub. of Calif. hist. survey commission)

16790. —— Guide to the county archives of California. Sacramento, State print. off., 1919. 622 p. maps. (Pub. of Calif. hist. survey commission)

16791. —— comp. & ed. Pictorial history of California. Berkeley, Univ. of Calif. Extension div. [c1925] 4 l., 261 pl.

16792. Crompton, Arnold. Unitarianism on the Pacific coast; the first sixty years. Bost., Beacon press [1957] 182 p.

16793. Cronise, Titus Fey. The natural wealth of California, comprising early history; geography, topography [etc.] together with a detailed description of each county; its topography, scenery, cities and towns [etc.] S.F., H.H. Bancroft, 1868. 696 p.

16794. Cross, Ira Brown. Financing an empire; history of banking in California. Chicago, S.F., L.A., Clarke, 1927. 4 v. illus., ports.

16795. —— A history of the labor movement in California... Berkeley, Univ. of Calif. press, 1935. 354 p. illus., ports., map.

16796. Cross, Ralph Herbert. Early inns of California, 1844–1869...1st ed. S.F., 1954. 302 p. illus., fold. map, facsims. Bibliography: p. 271–283. "500 copies designed and printed by Lawton Kennedy."

16797. Cross, William Thomas. Newcomers and

nomads in California, by William T. Cross and Dorothy E. Cross. Stanford, 1937. 149 p. illus., map, diagrs.

16798. Cunningham, William H. The log of the *Courier*, 1826–1827–1829...Illus. by Don Louis Perceval. L.A., Dawson, 1958. 75 p. illus. (Early Calif. travels ser., 44) 200 copies printed by Westernlore press.

16799. Cutts, James Madison. The conquest of California and New Mexico, by the forces of the United States, in the years 1846 and 1847. Phila., Carey & Hart, 1847. 264 p. port., maps, plans.

CHi CLSM CLgA CP CSf CSfCW MoS N

16800. Czarnowski, Lucille Katheryn. Dances of early California days. Palo Alto, Pacific books, 1950. 159 p. illus., diagrs.

16801. Dallas, Sherman Forbes. The hide and tallow trade in Alta California, 1822–1846. 329 p. Thesis (Ph.D.)—Indiana university, 1955.

16802. Dana, Richard Henry, jr. Two years before the mast... N.Y., Harper, 1840. 483 p.
Many editions followed.

16803. Daniells, T. G., ed. California, its products, resources, industries and attractions. What it offers the immigrant, homeseeker, investor and tourist. Pub. by the California Louisiana purchase exposition commission. Sacramento, Supt. state print., 1904. 208 p. illus.

16804. Daughters of the American revolution. California. History of California state society... 1891–1938. Comp. by Mrs. Walter S. Morley. [Berkeley, Lederer, Street & Zeus, 1938] 619 p. illus., ports.

16805. —— —— Honor roll; World war II service records, 1941–1945, of the husbands, sons, daughters, nephews, nieces, of the California members, Daughters of the American revolution. S.F., 1946– 11 v.

16806. —— —— War service records, 1914–1919. [1920] 1118 p. Typew.

16807. —— —— **Genealogical records committee.** Bible and family records. 1935–

16808. —— —— —— California census of 1852. 1934–35. 13 v. Typew.

16809. —— —— —— —— Index. 3 v. Typew.

16810. —— —— —— California pioneers. S.F., 1950. 245 l. "In 1930 the Standard Oil Company of California sponsored a weekly broadcast known as 'Romantic Forty-Niners' ...Excerpts from [the file of correspondence received in response to this broadcast]...relative to the arrival of pioneers in California...have been copied."—Preface. "Members of the Society of California pioneers of Santa Cruz county, California, 1887": l. 232–234. "San Bernardino Society of California pioneers": l. 236–[247]

16811. —— —— —— Court house and church records from California...Copied under the direction of the Genealogical records committee, 1936– Typew.

16812. —— —— —— ...Records of the families of California pioneers gathered by the various chapters from original sources in the years 1925–1926... [n.p., 1927–]

16813. —— —— —— Vital records from cemeteries in [California]... [n.p.] 1934– Reproduced from typew. copy.

16814. —— —— —— Wills and abstracts of wills from California counties. [S.F.?] 1957–

16815. Davidson, George. The origin and the meaning of the name California, Calafia the queen of the island of California, title page of Las Sergas. [S.F., F.F.

Partridge print.] 1910. 50 p. (Trans. and proceedings of the Geographical soc. of the Pac. Vol. VI, pt. I, ser. II)

16816. Davis, Winfield J. History of political conventions in California, 1849–1892... Sacramento, 1893. 711 p. (Pub. of the Calif. state library, no.1)

16817. Dellenbaugh, Frederick Samuel. Frémont and '49... N.Y. & London, Putnam, 1914. 547 p. col. front., pl., fold. maps.

16818. Denis, Alberta Johnston. Spanish Alta California. Decorations by Loren Barton. N.Y., Macmillan, 1927. 537 p. illus.

16819. Derby, George Horatio, "John Phoenix." The topographical reports of Lieutenant George H. Derby, with introduction and notes by Francis P. Farquhar. [S.F.] Calif. hist. soc., 1933. 81 p. illus., maps. (Calif. hist. soc. Special pub. no. 6)

16820. Dohrman, H. T. California cult; the story of Mankind united. Bost., Beacon press [1958] 163 p.

16821. Donnat, Léon. L'état de Californie, recueil de faits observés en 1877–1878... 1. partie: L'éducation publique, la presse, le mouvement intellectuel, suivie de renseignements sur l'état de l'instruction primaire aux États-Unis et en Europe. Paris, C. Delagrave, 1878. 325 p.

16822. Drake, Eugene B. Jimeno's and Hartnell's indexes of land concessions, from 1830 to 1846; also Toma de razon, or; Registry of titles, 1844–'45; approvals of land grants by the territorial deputation and departmental assembly of California, from 1835 to 1846, and a list of unclaimed grants. Compiled from the Spanish archives of the U.S. Surveyor-general's office. S.F., Kenny & Alexander, 1861. S.F., Kenny & Alexander, 1861. 17, 68 p.

C CHi CLSM CLU CSf CSfCW CSfMI CSmH CU CU-B NN WHi

16823. Druids, United ancient order. California. Proceedings of the Grand grove...from the organization to the close of the annual session of 1866, together with the annual reports, condition and progress of the Order. S.F., A.J. Lafontaine, 1866. 114 p.

16824. Drury, Wells and Drury, Aubrey. California tourist guide and hand book; authentic description of routes of travel and points of interest in California. Berkeley, Western guidebook co., 1913. 354 p. illus., maps.

16825. Duflot de Mofras, Eugène. Exploration du territoire de l'Oregon, des Californies et de la Mer Vermeille exécutée pendant les années 1840, 1841 et 1842... Paris, Arthus Bertrand, 1844. 2 v. in 4 and atlas. illus., maps. "Vol. 1 has a general history of the missions...and descriptions of the twenty-one individual missions."—Waters. C CLU CLgA CSmH

16826. —— Duflot de Mofras' travels on the Pacific coast... Tr., ed., and annotated by Marguerite Eyer Wilbur... Santa Ana, Fine arts press, 1937. 2 v. illus., maps. (Calafía ser. [no. 23])

16827. Durrenberger, Robert W. Patterns on the land; geographical, historical, and political maps of California. [Editors: Robert W. Durrenberger [and] William G. Byron; cartographer, John C. Kimura] L.A., Brewster pub. co. [1957] 59 p. maps (part col.)

16828. Eddy, Harriet G. County free library organizing in California, 1909–1918: personal recollections. Berkeley, Calif. lib. assoc., 1955. 113 p. ports., map.

16829. Ellis, George Merle. Trapper trails to California, 1826–1832: the narratives, journals, diaries, and letters of the mountain men who reached California over the southern routes. San Diego, 1954. 256 p. Thesis (M.A.)—San Diego state college, 1954.

16830. Ellison, William Henry. A self-governing dominion: California, 1849–1860. Berkeley, Univ. of Calif. press, 1950. 335 p. (Chronicles of Calif.)

16831. Englebert, Omer. The last of the conquistadors, Junipero Serra, 1713–1784. Tr. from the French by Katherine Woods. N.Y., Harcourt [1956] 368 p. illus.

16832. Evangelical Lutheran joint synod of Ohio and other states. California district; containing a short history of the congregations of the district, and the minutes of the conventions of the district for the years 1926 to 1930. [Columbus, O., 1930] 219 p. illus., port.

16833. Eyre, Alice. The famous Frémonts and their America. [Santa Ana] Fine arts press, 1948. 374 p. illus., ports., maps, facsims.

16834. Fahey, Herbert. Early printing in California. From its beginning in the Mexican territory to statehood, September 9, 1850. S.F., Book club of Calif., 1956. 142 p. illus., ports., facsims. "Printed at Grabhorn press."

16835. Farnham, Eliza Woodson (Burhans) California in-doors and out; or, How we farm, mine, and live generally in the Golden state. N.Y., Dix, Edwards & co., 1856. 508 p. "The Donner emigration of 1846": p. 380–457.

16836. Farnham, Thomas Jefferson. Travels in the Californias, and scenes in the Pacific ocean. N.Y., Saxton & Miles, 1844. 4 pts., 416 p. illus., fold. map. Published in many editions; some with title: Life and adventures in California and the early days of California.

16837. Federal art project. California art research [monographs] Gene Hailey, ed. 1st ser., v.1–20. S.F., 1937. 20 v. Mimeo. (Abstract from WPA project 2874, O.P. 65-3-3632)

16838. Federal writers' project. California. California; a guide to the golden state; ... N.Y., Hastings house, 1939. 713 p. (Am. guide ser.)

16839. Fenn, William Purviance. Ah Sin and his brethren in American literature... Peiping, China, College of Chinese studies cooperating with California college in China [1933] 131 p. Thesis (Ph.D.)—Univ. of Iowa, 1932.

16840. Fényes, Eva Scott. Thirty-two adobe houses of old California, reproduced from watercolor paintings by Eva Scott Fényes. Descriptive text by Isabel López de Fáges. L.A., Southwest museum, 1950. 76 p. 76 plates (1 col.)

16841. Ferrier, William Warren. Ninety years of education in California, 1846–1936. Berkeley [1937] 413 p.

16842. —— Pioneer church beginnings and educational movements in California. Berkeley, 1927. 89 p.

16843. Ferris, John Alexander. The financial economy of the United States illustrated, and some of the causes which retard the progress of California demonstrated; with a relevant appendix... S.F., Roman, 1867. 356 p.   CL

16844. Ferry, Hippolyte. Description de la nouvelle Californie; géographique, politique et morale... avec une grande carte de la nouvelle Californie. Des cartes particulières des baies de Monterey et de San Francisco ... Paris, L. Maison, 1850. 386 p. illus., maps (1 fold.)
                          CHi CLSM CLgA CP CSfCW

16845. Fisher, Walter Mulrea. The Californians. S.F., Bancroft; London, Macmillan, 1876. 236 p.

16846. Fitch, Abigail Hetzel. Junipero Serra, the

man and his work. Chicago, McClurg, 1914. 364 p. illus., port., map.

16847. Fleming, Sandford. God's gold; the story of Baptist beginnings in California, 1849–1860. Phila., Judson press [1949] 216 p. "Notes" (bibliographical): p. 207–216.

16848. Forbes, Alexander. California: a history of Upper and Lower California from their first discovery to the present time...A full view of the missionary establishments and condition of the free and domesticated Indians... London, Smith, Elder & co., 1839. 352 p. illus., port., map. Other editions followed.

16849. Forbes, James Alexander. The golden west; souvenir respectfully dedicated to the native sons and native daughters of the state. Primitive years in California... [L.A., Times-mirror print. co., c1919] 103 p. front. (port.)

16850. [Freeman, H. C., ed.] California's Grizzlies [144th field artillery] [S.F., 1918] 88 p. illus., ports.

16851. Freemasons. California. Grand lodge. Constitution...and minutes of the proceedings of the convention to constitute said lodge. S.F., Print. by Bartlett and Robb, Jl. of commerce off., 1850. 18 p. Proceedings at Sacramento city, April 17, 1850.   CSmH

16852. —— —— —— Same. Revised and adopted May 12, A. L. 5859... S.F., Frank Eastman, print., 1859. 37 p.   CU-B

16853. —— —— —— Same. Revised and adopted in May, A. L. 5859, and amended in May, A. L. 5861... S.F., Frank Eastman, print., 1861.   C CSmH

16854. —— —— —— Same. Revised and adopted in May, A. L. 5859, and amended to October, A. L. 5868, with general regulations now in force. S.F., Frank Eastman, print., 1869. 40 p.   CHi

16855. —— —— —— Same. ...October 1889 ... S.F., 1890. 44 p.

16856. —— —— —— Proceedings...1st, 1850– S.F., Frank Eastman, 1850–
1850–54 reprinted, 1857, as Transactions...from its organization in April, A. L. 5850 to and including its fifth annual communication in May, A. L. 5854, together with the proceedings of the convention assembled for its formation and the constitutions, standing resolutions, and by-laws of the Grand lodge.
C has 1st–5th (reprint), 6th–13th, 1850–62. CHi has 1st–5th (reprint), 6th–13th, 1850–62 and 1895, 1900. CLU has 6th, 1855. CMary has 10th, 1859. CSf has 1st–5th (reprint), 6th–25th, 1850–74. CSfP has 6th, 1855. CSmH has 1st–5th (reprint), 6th–13th, 1850–62. CU-B has 1st–5th (reprint), 6th–13th, 1850–62. WHi has 13th, 1862.

16857. —— —— —— Proceedings of the most worshipful Grand lodge, F. & A.M. of the jurisdiction of California at its celebration of the seventy-fifth annual communication...Los Angeles, October 14, A.D. 1924. L.A., 1925. 147 p. illus.   CHi

16858. —— —— **Knights templars. Grand commandery.** Proceedings of...August A.D. 1858... 1st–, 1858– S.F., Eastman, print., 1858– Issued separately but also paged continuously with: Proceedings of the Grand commandery of Knights templars, 1858–1871. Vol. 1.
C has 1st, 3d–5th, 1858, 1860–62. CSmH has 1st–5th, 1858–62.

16859. —— —— **Prince Hall grand lodge.** Centennial year book... S.F., 1955. 112 p. illus.   CHi

16860. —— —— —— 100 years of progress,

1855–1955...centennial at San Francisco, Calif., July 17–21, 1955. Oakland, Prince Hall Masonic digest, 1955. 19 p. illus. CHi

16861. —— —— —— Prince Hall Masonic directory. Most worshipful Prince Hall grand lodge free and accepted masons... [n.p., 1954] 56 p. CHi

16862. —— —— —— Souvenir program. 1855–100th anniversary–1955... S.F. [Color art press] 1955. 92 p. illus., ports., map. CHi

16863. —— —— **Royal Arch Masons. Grand chapter.** ...Proceedings...v.1– [A.I. 2384–88, i.e., 1854–1858]– S.F., Frank Eastman, 1861– Title varies: v.1, Transactions of the Grand chapter of Royal Arch Masons of the state of California, 1854–58. v.2, Journal of proceedings...1859–1864. Also issued separately, 1854– C has v.1 and separates, 2d, 4th, 6th, 7th, 9th, 1855, 1857, 1859, 1860, 1862. CHi has v.1–2 and separates, 2d, 6th, 1855, 1859, and 1866–67, 1870–71. CSmH has v.1–2 and separates, 2d, 3d, 9th, 1855, 1856, 1862. CU-B has v.2 and separates, 7th, 8th, 1860, 1861. WHi has separate, 8th, 1861.

16864. Frémont, Jessie Benton. Souvenirs of my time. Bost., D. Lathrop, 1887.

16865. Frémont, John Charles. Address to the people of California. San Jose, Argus print., 1850. 13 p. C

16866. —— Memoirs of my life, by John Charles Frémont. Including in the narrative five journeys of western exploration, during the years 1842, 1843–4, 1845–6–7, 1848–9, 1853–4... Chicago and N.Y., Belford, Clarke & co., 1887. 655 p. illus., port., maps. Narratives of journeys of exploration were previously published under various titles.

16867. Frickstead, Walter N., comp. A century of California post offices, 1848–1954. Oakland, Philatelic research soc., 1955. 395 p.

16868. Frignet, Ernest. La Californie; histoire, organisation politique et administrative, législation, description physique et géologique, agriculture, industrie, commerce. Paris, Schlesinger frères, 1866.

16869. Frost, John. History of the state of California, from the period of the conquest by Spain, to her occupation by the United States of America, containing an account of the discovery of the immense gold mines and placers... Auburn, Derby & Miller, 1850. (Frost's *Pictorial history of California*)

16870. Garrison, Myrtle. Romance and history of California ranchos... S.F., Harr Wagner [c1935] 206 p. illus.

16871. Gates, W. Francis, ed. Who's who in music in California. L.A., Colby and Pryibil, 1920. 151 p. illus.

16872. Gazlay, David M., ed. The California mercantile journal for 1860. A compilation of local and statistical information, general reading matter, &c., appertaining...to commercial, mercantile, mining, agricultural and manufacturing interests... v.1, S.F., George Elliott & co. [1860] 312 p. ports., illus. No other volumes published. CHi CLU CSfCP CSmH CU-B

16873. Geary, Gerald J. The secularization of the California missions (1810–1846) Wash., D.C., Catholic univ. of America press, 1934. 204 p. (Studies in Am. church history, v.17) Bibliography: p. 191–201.

16874. Geiger, Maynard J. The life and times of Fray Junípero Serra, O.F.M.; or, The man who never turned back, 1713–1784. Wash., D.C., Acad. of Am. Franciscan history, 1959. 2 v. illus., port., maps. (Pub. of the Acad. of Am. Franciscan history. Monograph ser., v.5–6) Bibliography: v.2, p. 405–484.

16875. Gente Italiana in California. L.A., "L'Italo-Americano," 1928. 256 p. illus., ports.

16876. Gibbs, James Atwood. Shipwrecks of the Pacific coast. [1st ed.] Portland, Ore., Binfords & Mort [1957] 312 p. illus.

16877. Giffen, Guy J. California expedition; Stevenson's regiment of first New York volunteers. Oakland, Biobooks, 1951. 109 p. illus. (Calif. relations, no. 26)

16878. Giffen, Helen Smith. Casas and courtyards: historic adobe houses of California. Foreword by W. W. Robinson; photos. by Guy J. Giffen. Oakland, Biobooks, 1955. 153 p. illus. (Calif. relations, no. 40)

16879. Glanz, Rudolf. Jews of California; from the discovery of gold until 1880. N.Y., Pub. with the help of the So. Calif. Jewish hist. soc., 1960. 188 p.

16880. Gleason, Joe Duncan. The islands and ports of California; a guide to coastal California. With illus. from paintings and drawings by the author. N.Y., Devin-Adair co., 1958. 200 p. illus.

16881. —— Islands of California: their history, romance and physical characteristics. With many illus. by the author. L.A., Sea publications, 1950. 104 p. illus., port., maps.

16882. Gleeson, William. History of the Catholic church in California... S.F., Print. for author by A.L. Bancroft & co., 1871–72. 2 v. illus., ports., map. Issued also in one-volume edition.

16883. Glover, William. The Mormons in California. Foreword, notes and a selected bibliography by Paul Bailey. L.A., Glen Dawson, 1954. 40 p. (Early Calif. travels ser., 19) 197 copies printed by Paul Bailey.

16884. Gold mines and mining in California, a new gold era dawning on the state, progress and improvements made in the business... S.F., G. Spaulding & co., 1885. 349 p. illus., ports.

16885. Goldmann, Jack Benjamin. A history of pioneer Jews in California, 1849–1870. [Berkeley, n.d.] 130 l. Typew.

16886. Good Templars, Independent order of. California. Constitution, by-laws and rules of order for Grand, subordinate, and district lodges... Sacramento, Crocker [1860?–19—] illus.

16887. —— —— **Grand lodge.** Address to the Grand and subordinate lodges of the Independent order of Good Templars of the state of California. First annual session held at Sacramento...May, 1860. Nevada [City] E.G. Waite & co., 1860. 7 p. CHi

16888. —— —— —— Proceedings...annual session...1st, 1860– Sacramento, 1860– C has 1st, 1860. CHi has 1st, 9th, 12th, 14th, 32d, 1860, 1868, 1871, 1875, 1891.

16889. Goodwin, Cardinal Leonidas. John Charles Frémont; an explanation of his career. Stanford, 1930. 285 p. map.

16890. Goodwin, Charles Carroll. As I remember them... Published by a special committee of the Salt Lake commercial club...Salt Lake City, Utah, 1913. 360 p. Reminiscences of California and Nevada pioneers.

16891. Gordon, Margaret S. Employment expansion and population growth, the California experience; 1900–1950. Berkeley, Univ. of Calif. press, 1954. 192 p. diagrs., tables. (Pub. of the Inst. of industrial relations, Univ. of Calif.)

16892. Gorter, Wytze and Hildebrand, George H. The Pacific coast maritime shipping industry, 1930–1948. Berkeley, Univ. of Calif. press, 1952–54. 2 v. diagrs., tables.

16893. Grand army of the republic. Dept. of California. Register...1886. S.F., Joseph L. Tharp, 1886. 278 p.

16894. ——— ——— Roster... S.F., Geo. Spaulding & co., 1883. 211 p.

16895. Grether, Ewald Theophilus. The steel and steel-using industries of California, prewar developments, wartime adjustments, and long-run outlook...Submitted by the Bur. of Business and economic research, Univ. of Calif. to the State reconstruction and reemployment commission. Sacramento, State print. off., 1946. 408 p.

16896. Griffenhagen, George. The story of California pharmacy. Madison, Wis., Am. inst. of the history of pharmacy, 1950. 58 p. illus.

16897. Gudde, Erwin Gustav. California place names; a geographical dictionary. Berkeley, Univ. of Calif. press, 1949. 431 p. "Glossary and bibliography": p. 401–429.

16898. ——— Same, 2d ed. with title: The origin and etymology of current geographical names. 1960. 383 p. maps.

16899. ——— ...German pioneers in early California ... Hoboken, N.J., 1927. 30 p. (Concord soc. Hist. bul. no. 6)

16900. Guzmán, José María. Breve noticia que da al Supremo Gobierno del actual estado del territorio de la Alta California, y medios que propone para la ilustracion & comercio en aquel pais, el guardian del Colegio Apostolico de San Fernando de Mexico. Año de 1833. México, Impr. de la Aguila, 1833. 8 p. table.

                                        CHi CSmH

16901. ——— Same. [Coyoacán, México, E. R. Goodridge and V. Ruiz Meza, 1949] 8 p. table. "Facsimile edition from plates engraved from the original, on watermarked paper of the period." With bio-bibliographical note by E. R. Goodridge and Victor Ruiz Meza.

16902. Hafen, LeRoy Reuben. The overland mail, 1849–1869; promoter of settlement, precursor of railroads. Cleveland, A.H. Clark co., 1926. 361 p. illus., ports., fold. map, facsims.

16903. Haiman, Miecislaus. ...Polish pioneers of California. Chicago, Polish R. C. union of Am., 1940. 83 p. illus., ports., map. (Annals of the Polish Roman Catholic union archives and museum. v.5)

16904. Hamilton, Wilson. The new empire and her representative men; or, The Pacific coast, its farms, mines ...etc. With interesting biographies and modes of travel. Oakland, Pac. press, 1886. 189 p. illus.

16905. Hanna, Phil Townsend. California through four centuries; a handbook of memorable historical dates ...with a foreword by Herbert Eugene Bolton; drawings by Raymond P. Winters. N.Y., Farrar & Rinehart [c1935]

16906. ——— The dictionary of California land names... L.A., Automobile club of So. Calif., 1946. 360 p.

16907. Hannaford, Donald R. Spanish colonial or adobe architecture of California, 1800–1850. N.Y., Architectural bk. pub. co., 1931. 4 p. l., 110 p. of illus.

16908. Harlow, Alvin Fay. Old waybills; the romance of the express companies... N.Y., Appleton-Century, 1934. 503 p. illus., ports., facsims.

16909. Harmon, Wendell E. A history of the prohibition movement in California. [L.A., 1955] Thesis (Ph.D.)—U.C.L.A., 1955.

16910. Harney, Paul John, Father. A history of Jesuit education in American California. 300 p. [Berkeley, 1944] Thesis (M.A.)—Univ. of Calif., 1944.

16911. Harris, Henry. California's medical story with an introduction by Charles Singer. S.F., Grabhorn press for J. W. Stacey, inc., 1932. 421 p. illus., ports. Bibliography: p. [397]–410.

16912. Hartwick, Sophus. Danske i California og California historie; beretninger om de Danskes og virke fra de tidligste pioner dage... S.F. [Bien's bogtrykkeri] 1939. 2 v. illus., ports., maps.

16913. Haskins, C. W. The argonauts of California ...N.Y., Pub. for author by Fords, Howard & Hulbert, 1890. 501 p. illus. Valuable for its *Pioneer index* (p. 360–501) containing names of 35,000 pioneers who arrived before Dec. 31, 1849.

16914. ——— Name index of the California pioneers, members of overland companies, and ship passenger lists given in the Argonauts of California... S.F., 1958. Typew.   CHi CU-B

16915. Hawthorne, Hildegarde. Romantic cities of California... illustrated by E. H. Suydam. N.Y., Appleton-Century, 1939. 456 p. illus.

16916. Heizer, Robert Fleming, ed. The California Indians; a source book, compiled and edited by R. F. Heizer and M. A. Whipple. Berkeley, Univ. of Calif. press, 1951. 487 p. illus., ports., maps.

16917. Helm, MacKinley. Fray Junípero Serra, the great walker. Stanford, 1956. 86 p. illus.

16918. Heustis, Daniel D. Narrative of the adventures and sufferings of Captain Daniel D. Heustis and his companions...with travels in California, and voyages at sea. Bost., Redding & co., 1847. 168 p. front.

16919. ——— Remarkable adventures, California, 1845. With an introduction by Carey S. Bliss. L.A., Dawson, 1957. 22 p. (Early Calif. travels ser., 40) 200 copies printed by W. M. Cheney.

16920. Higgins, Edwin. California's oil industry; an outline of its history, development, present importance and inherent hazards. [L.A.] Chamber of mines and oil, c1928. 39 p. illus., tables.

16921. Hilgard, Eugene Woldemar. Report on the physical and agricultural features of the state of California with a discussion of the present and future of cotton production in the state... S.F., Pac. rural press [1883] 138 p. charts, maps. A report submitted to the Supt. of the U.S. Census, June 1, 1883.

16922. Hine, Robert V. California's Utopian colonies. San Marino, Huntington library, 1953. 209 p. illus., ports., map (on lining papers) (Huntington lib. pub.) "Bibliographical note": p. 179–195.

16923. Historic spots in California... Stanford, 1932–1937. 3 v. maps. "Sources" at end of text on each county. Contents:—v.1. The southern counties, by Hero Eugene Rensch and Ethel Grace Rensch.—v.2. Valley and Sierra counties, by Hero Eugene Rensch and Ethel Grace Rensch and Mildred Brooke Hoover.—v.3. Counties of the coast range, by Mildred Brooke Hoover. Other editions followed.

16924. Hittell, John Shertzer. The commerce and industries of the Pacific coast of North America... S.F., A.L. Bancroft & co., 1882. 819 p. illus., maps.

16925. Hittell, Theodore Henry. History of California. S.F., Pac. press & Occidental pub. co., & N. J. Stone & co., 1885–1898. 4 v.

16926. —— The resources of California... S.F., A. Roman & co.; N.Y., W. J. Widdleton, 1863. 464 p. "Mining counties": p. 288–303. "Cities and towns": p. 397–421. Other editions followed.

16927. Hoick, John Edward. The fruitage of fifty years in California; a history of the Evangelical Lutheran synod of California, in connection with the United Lutheran church in America, 1891–1941...together with a brief sketch of each of the congregations of the synod, and a biography of the sons and daughters of the synod. [n.p., 1941] 179 p. illus., ports., maps.

16928. Holden, Erastus W., comp. Historic California: clippings. Alameda, Alameda free library, 1937. 5 v. v.1 & 2—Early California. Scrapbooks of clippings and photographs.

16929. Hopkins, Rufus C. Digest of Mexican laws, circulars and decrees, in the archives of Upper California. Compiled by R. C. Hopkins, keeper of the archives. S.F., O'Meara and Painter, bk. and job print., 1858. 112 p.
C CSmH

16930. Holdredge, Sterling M. State, territorial and ocean guide book of the Pacific, containing the time and distance tables, rates, fares and freight tariff, of all steamship, steamboat, railway, stage and express lines, on or connecting with the Pacific coast and the interior... S.F., 1866. 184 p. tables, maps.

16931. Hopkinson, Shirley Lois. An historical account of the evacuation, relocation and resettlement of the Japanese in the United States, 1941–1946. [Claremont, 1951] 264 l. Thesis (M.A.)—Claremont college, 1951.

16932. Hoppe, J[anus] Californiens, gegenwart und zukunft. Nebst beiträgen von A. Erman ueber die klimatalogie von Californien und ueber die geographische verbreitung des goldes. Berlin, G. Reimer, 1849. 151 p. 2 fold. maps. CHi CSfCW CStoC

16933. Hoyt, Hugh Myron. The wheat industry in California, 1850–1910. Sacramento, 1953. 163 p. Thesis (M.A.)—Sacramento state college.

16934. Hudson, James Jackson. The California national guard, 1903–1940. [Berkeley, 1952] Thesis (Ph.D.)—Univ. of Calif., 1952.

16935. Hughes, David. Welsh people of California, 1849–1906... S.F., 1923. 120 p.

16936. Hunt, Aurora. The army of the Pacific; its operations in California, Texas, Arizona, New Mexico, Utah, Nevada, Oregon, Washington, Plains region, Mexico, etc., 1860–1866. Glendale, Arthur H. Clark, 1951. 455 p. illus., ports., fold. map.

16937. Hunt, Rockwell Dennis, ed. California and Californians... The Spanish period, by Nellie Van de Grift Sanchez; the American period, by Rockwell D. Hunt; California biography, by a special staff of writers... Chicago, Lewis, 1926. 5 v. illus., ports., maps. v.2–5. Biographical.

16938. —— Same. 1932. 4 v. v.3–4: Biographical. Biographical contents of the two editions differ considerably.

16939. —— California firsts. Introd. by J. Wilson McKenney. S.F., Fearon pub. [1957] 314 p.

16940. —— California ghost towns live again... Stockton, College of the Pac., 1948. 69 p. illus. (Pub. of the Calif. history foundation, no.1)

16941. —— California's stately hall of fame. Stockton, College of the Pac., 1950. 675 p. ports. (Pub. of the Calif. history foundation, no.2) Bibliography: p. [601]–665.

16942. Hutton, William Rich. California, 1847–1852; drawings...reproduced from the originals in the Huntington library; with an introduction by Willard O. Waters. San Marino, Huntington lib., 1942. 56 pl. on 28 l., port. (Half-title: Huntington lib. pub.) "Hutton was a young surveyor who wrote descriptions and drew illustrations of the Gold Region, San Francisco, Monterey, San Luis Obispo, Santa Barbara, Los Angeles and San Bernardino."—Dawson, *West & Pacific.*

16943. —— Glances at California, 1847–1853; diaries and letters...with a brief memoir and notes by Willard O. Waters. San Marino, Huntington lib., 1942. 86 p. (Half-title: Huntington lib. pub.)

16944. Irvine, Leigh Hadley, ed. A history of new California, its resources and people... Chicago, 1887. 2 v. illus., ports. A second edition. Chicago, Lewis, 1905. 2 v. Largely biographical.

16945. Iyenaga, Toyokichi. Japan and the California problem, by T. Iyenaga...and K. Sato... N.Y., Putnam, 1921. 249 p. diagrs.

16946. Jackson, George Fred. The history of the Seventh-day Adventist education in California. [L.A., 1959] Thesis (Ed.D.)—U.C.L.A., 1959.

16947. Jackson, Helen Maria (Fiske) Hunt. A century of dishonor; a sketch of the United States government's dealings with some of the Indian tribes. New ed., enlarged by the addition of the report of the needs of the mission Indians of California. Bost., Roberts bros., 1885. 514 p.

16948. —— Glimpses of California and the missions...with illustrations by Henry Sandham. Bost., Little, 1902. 292 p. illus.

16949. Jackson, Joseph Henry. Bad company; the story of California's legendary and actual stage-robbers, bandits, highwaymen and outlaws from the fifties to the eighties. N.Y., Harcourt, 1949. 346 p. illus., ports.

16950. ——, **ed.** Continent's end; a collection of California writing. N.Y., McGraw-Hill, 1944. 415 p.

16951. James, George Wharton. Heroes of California... Bost., Little, 1910. 515 p. illus., ports.

16952. —— H.M.M.B.A. in California. Pasadena, Author, 1896. 338 p. illus., ports. Hotel men's mutual benefit association's trip.

16953. —— The 1910 trip of the H.M.M.B.A. to California and the Pacific coast. S.F., Bolte & Braden, 1911. 377 p. illus., ports.

16954. Japanese Presbyterian church. The history of the Japanese Presbyterian church on the Pacific coast. [S.F., 1911] [100] p. illus., ports. Text in Japanese and English.

16955. Jimeno Casarin, Manuel. Jimeno's index of land concessions from 1830 to 1845, and the "Toma de Razon," or registry of titles for 1844–45 in the archives of the office of the Surveyor General of the United States for California. S.F., Lee & Carl [1858] 32 p. CSmH

16956. Johnson, Herbert Buell. Discrimination against the Japanese in California; a review of the real situation... Berkeley, Courier pub. co., 1907. 133 p. fold. plan.

16957. Johnson, Kenneth M. Aerial California, an account of early flight in northern & southern California, 1849 to World War I. L.A., Dawson's, 1961. 91 p. illus.

16958. Jones, Idwal. Vines in the sun, a journey through the California vineyards. N.Y., Morrow, 1949. 253 p. illus.

16959. Jones, William Carey. Letters of William Carey Jones, in review of Attorney General Black's report to the President of the United States, on the subject of land titles in California. S.F., Commercial steam bk. and job print., 1860. 31 p.

16960. —— Report of the Secretary of the interior, communicating a copy of the report of William Carey Jones, special agent to examine the subject of land titles in California. Wash., D.C., 1851. 136 p. map. (31st Cong. 1st sess. Senate, Ex. doc. no. 18)

16961. —— Report on the subject of land titles in California...together with a translation of the principal laws on that subject, and some other papers relating thereto. Wash., D.C., Gideon & co., print., 1850. 60 p.

16962. Kanzaki, Kuchi. California and the Japanese. S.F., 1921. 98 p.

16963. Karperos, Andros. A geographic survey of the wine industry of California; its distribution and location. [Los Angeles, 1952] Thesis (M.A.)—U.C.L.A., 1952.

16964. Kelley, Douglas Ottinger. History of the Diocese of California from 1849 to 1914... Together with sketches of the dioceses of Sacramento and Los Angeles, and of the District of San Joaquin from their organization. S.F., Bur. of information & supply [1915] 471 p. illus., ports., map.

16965. Not in use.

16966. Kenneally, Finbar, *Father*. The seminaries of California as educational institutions, 1840–1950. [Toronto, 1956] 300 p. Thesis (Ph.D.) — Univ. of Toronto, 1956. Treats of Catholic seminaries, educational constitutions of first bishop, Francisco G. Diego, O.F.M., for college at Santa Ynez, and seminaries at San Francisco, 1851, Santa Clara, 1851.

16967. Kidner, Frank LeRoy. ...California business cycles... Berkeley, Univ. of Calif. press, 1946. 131 p. illus., tables, diagrs. (Pub. of the Bur. of business and economics research, Univ. of Calif.)

16968. King, Elmer R., comp. Handbook of historical landmarks of California. [L.A., Author, c1938] 150 p.

16969. King, Ernest Lamarr. Main line, fifty years of railroading with the Southern Pacific, by Ernest L. King, as told to Robert E. Mahaffay. Garden City, N.Y., Doubleday, 1948. 271 p.

16970. King, Thomas Butler. Report...on California. Wash., Gideon & co., 1850. 72 p. Report of special agent to California, addressed to the Secretary of state.
CLSM CP CSf CSfCW CSjC MoS

16971. Kip, William Ingraham. The early days of my episcopate. N.Y., Thomas Whittaker, 1892. 263 p. port.

16972. Kirker, Harold. California's architectural frontier; style and tradition in the nineteenth century. San Marino, Huntington lib., 1960. 224 p. illus.

16973. Kneiss, Gilbert H. Bonanza railroads. Stanford [c1941] 148 p. illus., map (on lining papers). Other editions followed.

16974. Knowland, Joseph Russell. California, a landmark history; story of the preservation and marking

of early day shrines; illustrated with photographs... [Oakland, Tribune press, c1941] 245 p. illus., ports.

16975. Kroeber, Alfred Louis. Handbook of the Indians of California. Wash., D.C., Govt. print off., 1925. 995 p. illus., maps. (U.S. Bur. of Am. ethnology. Bul. 78)

16976. Ladies of the Grand army of the republic. Dept. of California and Nevada. History of the Department of California, 1886–1914 [by Eva J. French. n.p., 1917, pref.] 89 p. ports.

16977. Lang, Walter Barnes. The first overland mail, Butterfield trail, St. Louis to San Francisco, 1858–1861. East Aurora, N.Y., Roycrofters, c1940. 163 p. illus.

16978. Lange, Fred W. History of baseball in California and Pacific coast leagues, 1847–1938... Memories and musings of an old time baseball player. Oakland, 1938. 231 p. ports.

16979. La Pérouse, Jean François de Galaup, comte de. Voyage de La Pérouse autour de monde... Paris, De l'imprimerie de la république. An V [1797] 4 v. and atlas. illus., port., maps.
C CLSU CLU CP CSf

16980. —— A voyage round the world, performed in the years 1785, 1786, 1787, and 1788... London, Print. for G. G. & J. Robinson [etc.] 1799. 2 v. and atlas. illus., port., maps. Translated from the French. Numerous other editions have appeared in various languages.
C CLSU CLU CLgA (in French) CP

16981. Latin American village studio. California centennial costume, 1845–1850. Santa Barbara, c1948. 16 col. plates.

16982. —— California's 14 historic flags, 1542–1851. Santa Barbara, 1958. 15 col. plates.

16983. —— California's heritage; 16 plates, text ed. by Margaret Campbell. Santa Barbara, 1949. Pictures and texts of main persons and events, chiefly between 1846–1849.

16984. —— California's state emblems, 1849–1957. [14 color prints] Santa Barbara, 1958.

16985. Lee, Edward Melvin. California gold—quarters—halves—dollars... L.A., Tower-Lee, 1932. 94 p. illus.

16986. Leggett, Herbert B. Early history of wine production in California. S.F., Wine inst., 1941. 124 p. Thesis (M.A.)—Univ. of Calif., 1939.

16987. Lelevier, Armando I. Historia del periodismo y la imprenta en el territorio norte de la Baja California. México [Talleres gráficos de la nación] 1943. 29 p. tables.

16988. Le Netrel, Edmond. Voyage of the *Héros*, around the world with Duhaut-Cilly in the years 1826, 1827, 1828 & 1829. Tr. by Blanche Collet Wagner. L.A., Dawson, 1951. 64 p. (Early Calif. travels ser., 3)

16989. Lévy, Daniel. Les Français en Californie. S.F., Grégoire, Tauzy et cie., 1884. 373 p.

16990. Lewis, Oscar. Here lived the Californians. N.Y., Rinehart, c1957. 265 p. illus., map.

16991. Longinos Martínez, José. California in 1792; the expedition of José Longinos Martínez. Tr. by Lesley Byrd Simpson. San Marino, Huntington lib., 1938. 111 p. illus., map. (Huntington lib. pub.)

16992. Los Angeles. Board of education. Pioneer and early public schools of California and of Los Angeles ...1948. 49 p. (Curriculum div. bul. 25)

16993. Loughead, Flora (Haines) Apponyi. The libraries of California; containing descriptions of the principal private and public libraries throughout the state. S.F., A.L. Bancroft co., 1878. 304 p. illus.

16994. Lucy-Fossarieu, Pierre Henri Richard de. Les langues indiennes de la Californie... Paris, Impr. nationale, 1881. 55 p.

16995. Lummis, Charles Fletcher. The Spanish pioneers and the California missions. New and enl. ed. Chicago, McClurg, 1929. 343 p. illus., ports., map. Revised edition of author's *The Spanish pioneers*, 1893.

16996. Lyman, George Dunlap. The scalpel under three flags in California. S.F., Calif. hist. soc., 1925. 67 p. illus., ports.

16997. [Lynch, James] With Stevenson to California, 1846. [n.p., 1896] 65 p. Privately printed, and dated from Tierra Redonda, San Luis Obispo county, July, 1896.

16998. —— Same. Oakland, Biobooks [1954] 56 p. illus., fold. map. (Calif. relations, no. 36) 500 copies designed and printed by Lawton Kennedy.

16999. McAllister, R. W. Lost mines of California and the southwest. S.F., Thomas bros., 1953. 97 p. illus., fold. map.

17000. McClatchy, V. S. Japanese immigration and colonization; brief prepared for consideration of the State department by V. S. McClatchy, representative of the Japanese exclusion league of California. Sacramento, Sacramento bee, 1921. 109 p.

17001. McClure, James D. California landmarks, a photographic guide to the state's historic spots... Stanford [c1948] 149 p. illus., ports., maps. A companion volume to *Historic spots in California*.

17002. McCoy, Esther. Five California architects. N.Y., Reinhold, c1960. 200 p. illus., ports., plans.

17003. McCumber, Harold Oliver. Pioneering the message in the golden West. Mountain View, Pac. press, 1946. 238 p. illus., maps. Based on author's doctoral dissertation (Univ. of Calif.) on beginnings of Seventh day Adventist church in California.

17004. McDow, Roberta Blakley. A study of the proposals to divide the state of California from 1860 to 1952. Stockton, 1952. 118 p. map. Thesis (M.A.)— College of the Pac., 1952.

17005. McEntire, Davis. The labor force in California; a study of characteristics and trends in labor force, employment, and occupations in California, 1900–1950. Berkeley, Univ. of Calif. press, 1952. 101 p. diagrs.

17006. McGroarty, John Steven, ed. The California Plutarch... L.A., J. R. Finnell, c1935. ports. v.1, 436 p.

17007. McKenney, L. M., pub. California state directory 1880–81, containing names, business and addresses of merchants, manufacturers and professional men... S.F., 1880. 1024 p.

17008. Mackey, Margaret Gilbert. Early California costumes, 1769–1850, and historic flags of California, by Margaret Gilbert Mackey and Louise Pinkney Sooy. [2d ed.] Stanford [1949] 138 p. illus., col. plate.

17009. MacMinn, George Rupert. The theater of the golden era in California. Caldwell, Ida., Caxton print., 1941. 529 p. illus., ports.

17010. McMurtrie, Douglas Crawford. An introduction and supplement to a History of California newspapers. S.F., Student press, Roosevelt junior high school, 1931. 12 p.

17011. —— The third historical record of printing in California. San Pedro, San Pedro high school print shop, 1935. 12 p.

17012. McNary, Laura K. California Spanish and Indian place names, their pronunciation, meaning and location. L.A., Wetzel pub. co., inc., 1931. 77 p.

17013. MacPhail, Archibald. Of men and fire, a story of fire insurance in the far west. S.F., Fire underwriters assoc. of the Pac., 1948. 148 p. illus.

17014. McWilliams, Carey. California, the great exception. N.Y., Current books, 1949. 377 p.

17015. —— Factories in the field; the story of migratory farm labor in California. Bost., Little, 1939. 334 p.

17016. —— Prejudice: Japanese-Americans: Symbol of racial intolerance. Bost., Little, 1944. 337 p.

17017. Marti, Werner H. Messenger of destiny: the California adventures 1846–1847 of Archibald H. Gillespie, U.S. Marine corps. S.F., Howell, 1960. 147 p. illus. The U.S. Navy in old California.

17018. Martin, Howard L. California insurance companies, 1850–1900. [S.F., 1960] Thesis (M.B.A.)— Golden gate college, 1960.

17019. Master hands in the affairs of the Pacific coast. Historical, biographical and descriptive. A résumé of the builders of our material progress. S.F., Western hist. & pub. co., 1892. 332 p. illus., ports.

17020. Meler, Vjekoslav, ed. The Slavonic pioneers of California... S.F., Slavonic pioneers of Calif. [1932] 101 p. illus., ports., maps.

17021. Men of California...1900 to 1902. S.F., Pac. art co. [c1901] 440 p. illus., ports. Edited by Wellington C. Wolfe. Portraits, with a line or two of information accompanying each. 1903 ed., *Men of the Pacific coast*.

17022. Men of California; western personalities and their affiliations, with club memberships and civic associations; illustrated record of men, with biographs of their activities. S.F., Western press reporter [c1925] 206 p. ports.

17023. Merriam, Clinton Hart. Studies of California Indians. Ed. by the staff of the Dept. of Anthropology of the University of California. Berkeley, Univ. of Calif. press, 1955. 233 p. illus., 48 pl., port., map, plans.

17024. Methodist Episcopal church. California. Minutes of the California annual conference... 1st– [1853?]– S.F. [1853?]– Printer varies.

C has 5th–7th, 10th, 1857–59, 1862. CBPac has 3d– 10th, 1855–62. CLU has 5th, 1857. CU-B has 4th–10th, 1856–62. NN has 9th, 1860. WHi has 6th, 1858.

17025. Mexico. Treaties, etc., 1848 (La Pena y Pena) The treaty of Guadalupe Hidalgo, February second 1848, ed. by George P. Hammond. Berkeley, Friends of the Bancroft lib. [1949] 79 p. map in folder.

17026. Meyers, William H. Journal of a cruise to California and the Sandwich islands in the United States sloop-of-war *Cyane*...1841–1844. Ed. by John Haskell Kemble. S.F., Bk. club of Calif., 1955. 68 p. col. illus., map. 400 copies printed by The Grabhorn press.

17027. Mighels, Ella Sterling (Clark) Cummins. The story of the files, a review of California writers and literature... [S.F., Co-operative print. co.] c1893. 460 p. illus., ports.

17028. Milliken, Ralph LeRoy. California dons. Fresno, Acad. lib. guild, 1956. 267 p. illus.

17029. Monnette, Orra Eugene. California chronology; a period of three hundred and fifty years, 1510–1860... L.A. [Standard print. co.] 1915. 52 p. pl.

17030. Moody, William Penn. The Civil war and reconstruction in California politics. [L.A., 1950] Thesis (Ph.D.)—U.C.L.A., 1950.

17031. Mora, Joseph Jacinto. Californios, the saga of the hard-riding vaqueros, America's first cowboys. Garden City, N.Y. Doubleday, 1949. 175 p. illus.

17032. Morley, Sylvanus Griswold. The covered bridges of California. Berkeley, Univ. of Calif. press, 1938. 92 p. illus.

17033. Morrow, William W. Spanish and Mexican private land grants. S.F., L.A., Bancroft-Whitney co., 1923. 27 p.

17034. Mott, Gertrude. A handbook for Californiacs; a key to meaning and pronunciation of Spanish and Indian place names... S.F., Harr Wagner, 1926. 104 p.

17035. Muir, Leo Joseph. A century of Mormon activities in California. Salt Lake City, Deseret news press, 1952. 2 v. illus., ports.

17036. Murbarger, Nell. Ghosts of the glory trail; intimate glimpses into the past and present of 275 western ghost-towns. Palm Desert, Desert magazine press, 1956. 291 p. illus.

17037. Murphy, William Hunt. A pictorial history of California. S.F., Fearon, 1958. 204 p. illus.

17038. Nadeau, Remi A. The ghost towns of California. [2d ed. L.A., Fortnight mag., 1954] 68 p. illus.

17039. Nasatir, Abraham Phineas. French activities in California; an archival calendar-guide. Stanford [c1945] 559 p. Bibliography: p. 38–59, 397–457.

17040. —— The French in the California gold rush. N.Y., Am. soc. of the French Legion of honor, 1934. 14 p.

17041. National society of the Colonial dames of America. California. Directory, 1914/15– [S.F.?] 1914–

17042. Negro Who's who in California, 1948 ed. [Ed. by Commodore Wynn] [L.A.? Negro Who's who in Calif. pub. co., 1948] 133 p. ports.

17043. Neuenburg, Evelyn. California lure; the Golden state in pictures. Prologue and epilogue by Oscar Lewis. Pasadena, Calif. lure pub., 1946. 311 p. illus. Other editions followed.

17044. Nevins, Allan. Frémont, the West's greatest adventurer... N.Y., Harper, 1928. 2 v. illus., ports., maps, facsims. Other editions followed.

17045. Newcomb, Rexford. The Franciscan mission architecture of Alta California. N.Y., Architectural bk. pub. co., 1916. xli pl., map. In portfolio.

17046. —— The old mission churches and historic houses of California; their history, architecture, art and lore...with 217 illustrations and measured drawings. Phila. & London, Lippincott, 1925. 379 p. illus.

17047. Newell, Gordon R. Pacific coastal liners, by Gordon Newell and Joe Williamson. Seattle, Superior pub. co. [c1959] 192 p. illus.

17048. Newsom, Joseph Cather, pub. Picturesque and artistic homes and buildings of California... S.F., c1890. 26, 112 p. illus., plans.

17049. Newsom, Samuel and Newsom, Joseph Cather, pub. ...Picturesque California homes no. 2. [S.F., Crocker, 1886] [20] l., 22 p. illus., plans.

17050. Nicosia, Francesco M. Italian pioneers of California. S.F., Italian-Am. chamber of commerce of the Pac. coast, 1960. 32 p.

17051. Nordhoff, Charles. California: for health, pleasure, and residence. A book for travellers and settlers. N.Y., Harper, 1872. 255 p. illus., maps.

17052. Obert, Karl. This is California: photographs. [1st ed.] Menlo Park, Lane pub. co. [1957] 239 p. illus., map.

17053. Odd fellows, Independent order of. California. Grand encampment. Constitution, by-laws and rules... Adopted May 7th, 1855. S.F., Sun off. print., 1855. 22 p.   CSmH CU-B

17054. —— —— —— Proceedings...from its organization, January 8th, 1855... 1st–8, 1855–1862. S.F., 1855–62. Printer varies. Proceedings 1 through 8 are continuously paged.

17055. —— —— Grand lodge. Proceedings... first session...May 17th, 1853. 1st– , 1853– S.F., 1853– Printer varies.

17056. —— —— —— Proceedings of the R. W. Grand lodge...from its organization May 17, 1853, to May 7, 1859, inclusive. Volume I. S.F., Frank Eastman, 1859. 582 p.

17057. Oil producers agency of California. The agency date book, 1900–1944. L.A., 1944. 33 p.

17058. —— Same. 2d ed. L.A., 1947. [216] p.

17059. Older, Cora Miranda (Baggerly) Love stories of old California; with a foreword by Gertrude Atherton. N.Y., Coward [1940] 306 p. illus., ports.

17060. Olmsted, Frederick Law. Report of state park survey of California. Prepared for the California state park commission. Sacramento, State print. off., 1929. 71 p. illus., fold. map.

17061. Opis Kalifornii pod wzgledem geograficznym, statystycznym. Cracow, Josef Czech, print., 1850. 31 p.
                                                                              CHi

17062. Ord, Maria de las Angustias (de la Guerra) Occurrences in hispanic California [related to Thomas Savage in Santa Barbara...1878]. Tr. and ed. by Francis Price and William H. Ellison. Wash., D.C., Acad. of Am. Franciscan history, 1956. 98 p. illus., ports.

17063. Ormsby, Waterman Lilly. The Butterfield overland mail... ed. by Lyle H. Wright and Josephine M. Bynum. San Marino, Huntington lib. [c1942] 1954. 179 p. col. illus.

17064. [Osborn, J. W.] The industrial interests of California: being a series of letters relating to our home manufactures, industrial labor, agricultural progress and material interests. By an old resident. S.F., Towne & Bacon, 1862. 94 p.

17065. Owen, Mrs. J. J. California, the empire beautiful; her great bays, harbors, mines, orchards and vineyards, olive, lemon and orange groves; her men and women, a prophecy of the coming race. S.F., Author, 1899. 243 p. illus. (part. col.), ports. Cover title: Sons and daughters of California.

17066. Pacific coast baseball league. Pacific coast baseball league records, 1903 to 1947. [L.A., 1947] 3 v.

17067. Pacific coast commerce builders. This volume contains descriptions and illustrations of the various commercial activities of the fifty-eight counties of California. Prepared by their several chambers of commerce. Pub. by the Commercial travelers congress building association... Ed. by M. B. Bergen and O. M. Preston. S.F. [Print. by Taylor, Nash & Taylor] 1914. 255 p. illus., ports., maps.

17068. Palm, Charles W., co., comp. California attorneys directory... L.A., 1897. 131 p.

17069. —— San Francisco oil exchange directory of the Pacific coast containing officers and members of San Francisco oil exchange, Los Angeles stock exchange, Fresno oil stock exchange, list of oil companies... L.A., 1901. 294 p.

17070. Palóu, Francisco. The founding of the first California missions...an historical account of the expeditions sent by land and sea in...1769, as told by Frey Francisco Palóu, and hitherto unpublished letters of Serra, Palóu and Gálvez...translated...with the aid of Thomas W. Temple II, by Douglas S. Watson... S.F., Print. Nueva Calif. press, 1934. 124 p. port., map.

17071. —— Noticias de la Nueva California... Mexico, Vicente Garcia Torres, 1857. Documentos para la historia de Méjico, ser. 4, v.6–7.   CU-B

17072. —— Same. S.F. [Calif. hist. soc.] Imprenta de Edouardo Bosqui y cia., 1874. 4 v. illus.
C C-S CHi CLU CLgA CSf CSmH

17073. —— Same, with title: Historical memoirs of New California...Tr. into English... Ed. by Herbert Eugene Bolton... Berkeley, Univ. of Calif. press, 1926. 4 v. illus., ports., maps.

17074. —— Relacion historica de la vida y apostolicas tareas del venerable padre Fray Junipero Serra, y de las misiones que fundó en la California Septentrional, y nuevos establecimientos de Monterey. México, en la imprenta de Don Felipe de Zúniga y Ontiveros, 1787. 344 p. pl., fold. map. Other editions in Spanish and English followed.
CHi CLSM CLSU CLgA CP CSd CU-B

17075. [Panattoni, Giovacchino V.] Professionisti Italiani e funzionari pubblici Italo-Americani in California. Sacramento [Author] 1935. 154 p. illus., map, ports.

17076. Parsons, Marian Randall. Old California houses: portraits and stories. Berkeley, Univ. of Calif. press, 1952. 143 p. illus.

17077. Patton, Annaleone Davis. California Mormons, by sail and trail. Salt Lake City, Deseret [c1961] 197 p. illus.

17078. Peattie, Roderick, ed. The Pacific coast ranges... N.Y., Vanguard press [c1946] 402 p. illus., map.

17079. Peixotto, Ernest Clifford. Romantic California; illus. by the author. N.Y., Scribner, 1910. 219 p. illus.

17080. Peninou, Ernest. Winemaking in California ...[by Ernest Peninou and Sidney Greenleaf] S.F., Peregrine press, 1954. 2 v. illus. v.1. How wine is made. —v.2. From the missions to 1894.

17081. Pennoyer, Albert Sheldon, comp. & ed. This was California: a collection of woodcuts and engravings reminiscent of historical events... N.Y., Putnam, 1938. 224 p. illus.

17082. Perlman, William J., comp. Music and dance in California. Ed. by Jose Rodriguez. Comp. by William J. Perlman, Bureau of musical research... [Hollywood, 1940] 467 p. illus., ports.

17083. Perret, Maurice Edmond. Les colonies Tessionoises en Californie. Préf. d'Enrico Celio. Lausanne, Librairie de l'université, 1950. 304 p. illus.
    CaBViPA

17084. —— The Italian Swiss colonies of California. [Berkeley] 1942. Thesis (M.A.)—Univ. of Calif., 1942.

17085. Perry, Mary Dorothea, *Sister*. A history of the educational work of the Sisters of the Holy Names of Jesus and Mary in California from 1868 to 1920. San Rafael, 1954. 178 p. Thesis (M.A.)—Catholic Univ. of Am., 1954.

17086. Peters, De Witt Clinton. Kit Carson's life and adventures... Together with a full and complete history of the Modoc Indians and the Modoc war... Hartford, Conn., Dustin, Gilman & co.; Cincinnati, Queen City pub. co. [etc. etc.] 1874 ['73] 604 p. illus.

17087. Peters, Harry Twyford, ed. California on stone...Garden City, N.Y., Doubleday, Doran & co., 1935. 227 p. 112 pl. ports., maps. Reproductions of lithographs of California with explanatory text.

17088. Petroleum world. California petroleum register. 1949– L.A., 1949–

17089. Pettis, George Henry. Frontier service during the rebellion; or, A history of Company K, First infantry, California volunteers... Providence, 1885. 60 p. Added t.–p.: Personal narratives of events in the war of the rebellion, being papers read before the Rhode Island soldiers and sailors historical society. 3d ser. no. 14.

17090. Phelps, Alonzo. Contemporary biography of California's representative men, with contributions from distinguished scholars and scientists. S.F., A.L. Bancroft & co., 1881–82. 2 v. ports.

17091. Phillips, A. & co. Annual and guide to California, issued by A. Phillips & co., managers of Boston and California excursions... [1887?] 112 p. illus.

17092. Phillips, Catherine (Coffin) Jessie Benton Frémont; a woman who made history. S.F., J.H. Nash, 1935. 361 p. illus., port., facsims.

17093. Phillips, D. L. Letters from California: its mountains, valleys, plains, lakes, rivers, climate and productions... Springfield, Ill., Illinois state jl. co., 1877. 171 p.

17094. Phillips, Henry DeWitt. Palou's noticias de la Nueva California. [Berkeley, 1921] Thesis (M.A.) —Univ. of Calif., 1921.

17095. Pierce, R. A. Lost mines and buried treasures of California; fact, folklore and fantasy concerning 110 sites of hidden wealth...with a map for the guidance of treasure seekers. [Rev. ed.] Berkeley, 1961. 28 p. map (fold.)

17096. Piette, Maximin. Evocation de Junípero Serra, fondateur de la Californie. Bruxelles, Lecture au foyer; Wash., D.C., Acad. of Am. Franciscan history [1946] 439 p. ports., maps, facsims.

17097. —— Le secret de Junípero Serra, fondateur de la Californie-Nouvelle, 1769–1784. 1st ed. Wash., D.C., Acad. of Am. Franciscan history [1949] 2 v. illus., port., maps, facsims.

17098. Pinkerton, Robert Eugene. The first overland mail. N.Y., Random house, 1953. 185 p.

17099. Pitt, Leonard M. The foreign miners' tax of 1850: a study of nativism and antinativism in gold rush California. [L.A., 1955] Thesis (M.A.)—U.C.L.A., 1955.

17100. Powell, H. M. T. The Santa Fe trail to California, 1849–1852; the journals and drawings of H. M. T. Powell, ed. by Douglas S. Watson. S.F., Bk. club of Calif. [Grabhorn press] 1931. 272 p. illus., fold. maps.

17101. Powell, John J. The golden state and its resources. S.F., Bacon & co., 1874. 219 p.

17102. Prendergast, Thomas F. Forgotten pioneers; Irish leaders in early California. S.F., Trade pressroom, 1942. 278 p. ports. Bibliography: p. 265–268.

17103. Press reference library (Western ed.) Notables of the West; being the portraits and biographies of the progressive men of the West... N.Y., Chicago [etc.] Internat. news service, 1913–15. 2 v. illus., ports. Largely devoted to California and the southwestern states.

17104. Preuss, Charles. Exploring with Frémont; the private diaries of Charles Preuss, cartographer for John C. Frémont on his first, second, and fourth expeditions to the far west. Tr. and ed. by Erwin G. and Elisabeth K. Gudde. 1st ed. Norman, Okla., Univ. of Okla. press, 1958. 162 p. illus. (Am. exploration and travel ser., no. 26)

17105. Priestley, Herbert Ingram. Franciscan explorations in California... edited by Lillian Estelle Fisher...with illustrations by Frederic W. Corson. Glendale, Arthur H. Clark co., 1946. 189 p. illus., map. (Half-title: Spain in the West. VI) Bibliography: p. [149]–159.

17106. Protestant Episcopal church in the U.S.A. California (Diocese) Journal of the proceedings of the annual conventions...To which is prefixed a list of the clergy and parishes of the diocese. 1st– [185–?–] Sacramento, S.F. [185–?–] Printer varies.

C has 7th–12th, 1857–62. CHi has 7th, 12th, 16th–18th, 22d–23d, 1857, 1862, 1866–68, 1872–73. CSaT has 8th–12th, 1858–62. CSmH has 8th–9th, 11th, 1858–59, 1861. CU-B has 7th–12th, 1857–62. NN has 7th–11th, 1857–61. WHi has 7th, 1857.

17107. —— —— Journal of the proceedings of the second adjourned meeting of the second triennial convention...May 1, 1855... S.F., Whitton, Towne and co., 1855. 36 p.   C CSmH CU-B NN

17108. —— —— Journal of the proceedings of the special convention...held in Grace church, Sacramento, Feb. 5, 1857, to which is prefixed a list of the clergy and parishes in the Diocese. Sacramento, James Anthony & co., print., Union bk. and job off., 1857. 16 p.
C CSaT CSmH NN WHi

17109. —— —— Journal of the proceedings of the triennial convention of the Protestant Episcopal church, in California. 1st–3d. [185–?–1856] S.F., C. Bartlett, bk. and job print. [185–?–56] Continued annually.—Cowan. Proceedings of the 3d convention printed by Whitton, Towne & co.

C has 3d, 1856. CHi has 2d, 1853. CSaT has 2d, 1852. CSmH has 2d–3d, 1853–56. CU-B has 2d–3d, 1853–56. NN has 2d–3d, 1853–56.

17110. —— —— Journal of the proceedings on an adjourned meeting of the second triennial convention ...May, 1854. S.F., Evening news, 1854. 16 p.
C CHi CSmH CU-B MHi NN

17111. Putnam, Ruth. California: the name. With the collaboration of Herbert I. Priestley. Berkeley, Univ. of Calif. press, 1917. p.[293]–365. fold. map. (Univ. of Calif. pub. in history. v.4, no. 4)

17112. Quigley, Hugh. The Irish race in California and on the Pacific coast... S.F., Roman & co., 1878. 548 p.

17113. Rand, McNally guide to California via the Santa Fe. Chicago [c1903] 242 p. illus., fold. map.

17114. Rea, Ellen Kate. The men who visited California first. [Berkeley, 1905] Thesis (M.L.)—Univ. of Calif., 1905.

17115. [Red cross. U.S. American national Red cross] A record of the Red cross work on the Pacific slope, including California, Nevada, Oregon, Washington, and Idaho with their auxiliaries;... Comp. and ed. by a committee appointed by the executive board of the California state Red cross... Oakland, Pac. press pub. co., 1902. 458 p. illus., ports.

17116. Redpath, Lionel V. Petroleum in California; a concise and reliable history of the oil industry of the state. L.A., Author, 1900. 158 p. illus., map.

17117. Reed, Merrill A. Historical statues and monuments in California. [Burlingame, Author, c1956] 176 p. illus.

17118. Rensch, Hero Eugene. Educational activities of the Protestant churches in California, 1849–1860. 1929. Thesis (M.A.)—Stanford univ., 1929.

17119. Repplier, Agnes. Junipero Serra, pioneer colonist of California. Garden City, N.Y., Doubleday, Doran & co., 1933. 312 p.

17120. Revere, Joseph Warren. A tour of duty in California...edited by Joseph N. Balestier... N.Y., C.S. Francis & co.; Bost., J.H. Francis, 1849. 305 p. illus., map. Reprinted with title: Naval duty in California. Biobooks, 1947.

17121. Robinson, Alfred. Life in California: during a residence of several years in that territory, comprising a description of the country and the missionary establishments...illus. with numerous engravings. By an American. To which is annexed a historical account of the origin, customs, and traditions of the Indians of Alta-California. Tr. from the original Spanish manuscript. N.Y., Wiley & Putnam, 1846. 341 p. illus. Other editions followed.

17122. —— —— Index [to first edition]... Joseph Gaer, editor. [S.F., 1935] 21 l. (Index no. 1, SERA projects 2-F2-132 [3-F2-197] Calif. literary research)

17123. Robinson, William Wilcox. Land in California, the story of mission lands, ranchos, squatters, mining claims, railroad grants, land scrip [and] homesteads. Berkeley, Univ. of Calif. press, 1948. 291 p. illus., maps. (Chronicles of Calif.)

17124. [Rodriguez de Montalvo, Garci] The Queen of California; the origin of the name of California, with a translation from the Sergas of Esplandian, by Edward Everett Hale. S.F., Colt press, 1945. 46 p. facsim., fold. col. map.

17125. Romero, John Bruno. Botanical lore of the California Indians, with side lights on historical incidents in California. N.Y., Vantage press [c1954] 82 p.

17126. Rose, Donald Harold. California's efforts to reduce juvenile delinquency, 1850–1925. [Berkeley, 1951] Thesis (M.A.)—Univ. of Calif., 1951.

17127. Rowland, Leon. Los fundadores. Herein are listed the first families of California and also all other persons with family names that were in California 1769–1785 except those who died at San Diego in 1769. Fresno, Acad. of Calif. church history, 1951. 46 p.

17128. Sabin, Edwin Legrand. Kit Carson days (1809–1868). Chicago, A.C. McClurg & co., 1914. 669 p. illus., ports., maps, facsims. Another edition: N.Y., The press of the pioneers, 1935. 2 v.

17129. Sacramento. C. K. McClatchy senior high school. Costumes of early California, comp. and written by students of C. K. McClatchy senior high school. Sacramento, Nugget press, 1958. 31 p. illus.

17130. Salinger, Jehanne Biétry, ed. Notre centenaire, le guide franco californien du centenaire. S.F., Pisani print. & pub. co., 1949. 279, 63 p. illus., ports.

17131. Sánchez, Nellie (Van de Grift) Spanish and Indian place names of California, their meaning and their romance. S.F., Robertson, 1914. 445 p. illus. Other editions followed.

17132. Sandmeyer, Elmer Clarence. The anti-Chinese movement in California. Urbana, Univ. of Illinois press, 1939. 127 p.

17133. Sanford, Louis Childs, *bp*. The province of the Pacific. Phila., Church hist. soc., c1949. 187 p. map. (Church hist. soc. pub. 28)

17134. Serra, Junípero, *Father*. Writings... Ed. by Antonine Tibesar. Wash., D.C., Acad. of Am. Franciscan hist., 1955– illus., port., maps. (Acad. of Am. Franciscan history. Documentary ser., v.4–6)

17135. Sestanovich, Stephen N., ed. Slavs in California... Oakland, 1937. 136 p.

17136. Seyd, Ernest. California and its resources. A work for the merchant, the capitalist, and the emigrant. London, Trübner and co., 1858. 168 p. illus. (part. col.), 2 fold. maps.
C-S CHi CLO CP CSf CSfCSM CSfCW CSfWF-H CStoC

17137. Shaw, Frederic Joseph. Oil lamps and iron ponies, a chronicle of the narrow gauges, by Frederic Shaw, Clement Fisher, jr. [and] George H. Harlan. S.F., Bay bks. ltd., 1949. 187 p. illus., ports., maps.

17138. Sherman, Edwin A., comp. Fifty years of masonry in California. S.F., Geo. Spaulding & co., 1897–1898. 2 v. illus.

17139. Sherman, William Tecumseh. Recollections of California. 1846–1861...foreword by Joseph A. Sullivan. Oakland, Biobooks, 1945. 147 p. facsims. (part fold., incl. map) (Calif. centennials no. 3)

17140. Shippey, Lee. It's an old California custom. N.Y., Vanguard press [1948] 292 p. (Am. customs ser.) With contemporary illustrations.

17141. Shuck, Oscar Tully, ed. Bench and bar in California... S.F., 1889. 543 p.

17142. —— The California scrap-book... S.F., H.H. Bancroft & co., 1869. 704 p. illus.

17143. —— History of the bench and bar of California; being biographies of many remarkable men... accounts of important legislation and extraordinary cases, comprehending the judicial history of the state... L.A., Commercial print. house, 1901. 1152 p. ports.

17144. —— Representative and leading men of the Pacific: being original sketches of the lives and characters of the principal men...of the Pacific states and territories ...to which are added their speeches, addresses, orations, eulogies, lectures, and poems... S.F., Bacon & co., 1870. 702 p. ports.

17145. Shuman, John. California medicine; a review... [L.A.?] A.R. Elliott pub. co., c1930. 183 p. illus. (ports.)

17146. [Silvis, Vito M.] California, la seconda Italia per gli italiani d'America. 1st ed. "Unico-originale." L.A., Italo-Am. bk. co. [c1934] v.p. illus., ports., maps.

17147. Simmons, J. C. The history of Southern Methodism on the Pacific coast... Nashville, Tenn., Southern Meth. pub. house, 1886. 454 p. port.

17148. Simpson, *Sir* George. Narrative of a journey round the world during the years 1841 and 1842...

London, Henry Colburn, 1847. 2 v. port., map. California in v.1, p. 253–411. Other editions followed.
C CLU CP CSalCL CSmH CaBViPA

17149. Sisters of Notre Dame. In harvest fields by sunset shores; the work of the Sisters of Notre Dame on the Pacific coast by a member of the congregation; Diamond jubilee edition, 1851–1926. S.F., Gilmartin co., 1926. 317 p. Includes early American history of San Jose and Santa Clara.

17150. —— Notre Dame in California, 1851–1951; a century of achievement. [n.p., n.d.] 32 p. illus., ports.

17151. Sisters of the Presentation. Souvenir brochure commemorating the one hundredth anniversary of the Sisters of the Presentation of the Blessed Virgin Mary in the United States, 1854–1954. [S.F.] 1954. [50] p. illus., ports.

17152. Skarstedt, Ernst Teofil. California och dess svenska befolkning... Seattle, Tryckt hos Washington print. co., 1910. 463 p. illus., ports., fold. col. map.

17153. Soares, Celestino. California and the Portuguese; how the Portuguese helped to build up California; a monograph written for the Golden Gate international exposition on San Francisco bay, 1939... Lisbon, S P N books, 1939. 69 p. illus., maps. Bibliography: p. 65–69.

17154. Society of Mayflower descendants. Register of the Society of Mayflower descendants in the state of California; a record of descent from passengers on the good ship "Mayflower," A.D. 1620, with an appendix. S.F., 1917.

17155. Sons of temperance. California. Grand division. Constitution of the order of the Sons of temperance of North America, together with the by-laws, rules of order, etc., of the Grand and sub-ordinate divisions of the state of California. S.F., B.F. Sterett, 1862. 48 p.
C CU-B

17156. —— —— —— Proceedings of... Organized September 9, 1851. S.F., 1853–61. Printer varies.
C (1855, 1861, semi-annual) CHi (1853) CU-B (1855, 1859)

17157. Southern Pacific co. California for the settler, the natural advantages of the Golden state for the present day farmer. By A. J. Wells. S.F., 1910. 98 p. illus., maps. Other editions followed.

17158. —— California for the tourist... S.F., 1910. 125 p. illus., maps. Other editions followed.

17159. —— A picture journey through California. Being a series of seventy-four photographs of California's principal spots of scenic, romantic and historic interest. [S.F., Sunset press, n.d.] illus.

17160. —— The road of a thousand wonders; the Coast line-Shasta route...S.F. [Sunset press, print.] 1905. 72 p. col. illus.

17161. Staff, Ruth. Settlement in Alta California before 1800. [Berkeley, 1932] Thesis (M.A.)—Univ. of Calif., 1932.

17162. Stalder, Walter. A contribution to California oil and gas history. L.A. 94 p. (Calif. oil world, Nov. 12, 1941, pt. II)

17163. Standard oil company of California. See your west... [S.F., 1946?] [52] p. mounted col. illus.

17164. Stanford research institute. Southern California laboratories, South Pasadena. The savings and loan industry in California, by C. Joseph Clawson, Frank W. Barsalou, and others. SRI project no. I-3065. Prepared for Savings and loan commissioner,

Div. of savings and loan, state of Calif. South Pasadena, 1960. v.p. illus.

17165. The state register and year book of facts: for 1857, 1859. S.F., Henry G. Langley and Samuel A. Mathews; Sacramento, James Queen, 1857–59. 2 v.

17166. Steele, Vincent Earl. The Society of Mary in California, 1884–1956. S.F., 1958. 172 l. photos. Thesis (M.A.)—Univ. of San Francisco.

17167. Stensrud, Edward Martinus. Lutheran church and California. S.F., Author, 1916. 282 p. illus., port., map.

17168. Streeter, William A. Recollections of historical events in California, 1843–1878. Ed. by William Henry Ellison. [S.F.? 1939?] 278 p. ports.

17169. Strong, Edward Kellogg. ...Japanese in California... Stanford, 1933. 188 p. diagrs. (Stanford univ. pub. Univ. ser. Education-psychology. v.1, no.2) "Data are presented regarding birthplace, age, sex, size of family, births and deaths, and also information concerning education, occupations, and religious affiliations." —Preface.

17170. Sullivan, G. W. Early days in California, the growth of the commonwealth under American rule, with biographical sketches of pioneers. v.1. S.F., Enterprise pub. co., 1888. illus., ports. No more published. Title on spine: Pioneer biographies.

17171. Sunset. Discovery trips in California; byways off the highways. 66 travel articles reprinted from *Sunset magazine*. [1st ed.] Menlo Park, Lane pub. co. [1955] 128 p. illus.

17172. Swasey, William F. The early days and men of California. Oakland, N.Y. [etc.] Pac. press [1891] 406 p. illus., port.

17173. Sweeny, Thomas W. Military occupation of California, 1849–1853... Reprint. from the *Jl. of the Military service institution*, 1909. 47 p. illus., ports., map.

17174. ...Syrian directory of the state of California, comp. ...by Rev. Elias Sady. [n.p., 1928?–   ]

17175. Taber, Cornelia. California and her Indian children... San Jose, No. Calif. Indian assoc., c1911. 74 p. illus., ports., fold. map.

17176. Tallack, William. The California overland express; the longest stage-ride in the world...introd. by Carl I. Wheat, and a check list of published material on the Butterfield overland mail by J. Gregg Lane. L.A., Hist. soc. of So. Calif., 1935. 85 p. front. (fold. map), illus.

17177. Taylor, Alexander Smith. Discovery of California and northwest America. The first voyage to the coasts of California; made in the years 1542 and 1543, by Juan Rodríguez Cabrillo and his pilot Bartolomé Ferrelo. S.F., Lecount and Strong, 1853. 19 p.

    CHi CSmH CStclU CU-B NN

17178. Taylor, Charles William, jr., pub. Bench and bar of California. Centennial edition, 1949. [Santa Rosa, Press democrat] 1949. 278 p. ports.

17179. —— Eminent Californians, 1953. Palo Alto [1953] 592 p. ports. Other editions followed.

17180. Tevis, A. H. Beyond the Sierras; or, Observations on the Pacific coast. Phila., J.B. Lippincott & co., 1877. 259 p. illus.

17181. Thomas, Dorothy Swaine (Thomas) Japanese American evacuation and resettlement. Berkeley, Univ. of Calif. press, 1946–1952. 2 v.

17182. Thomes, William Henry. On land and sea; or, California in the years 1843–44–45. Chicago, Laird & Lee, 1883. 351 p. illus., port.

17183. Thompson, Warren Simpson. Growth and changes in California's population. ... L.A., Haynes foundation, 1955. 377 p. illus. (Pub. of the John Randolph Haynes and Dora Haynes foundation: Monograph ser. no.38)

17184. Thurman, A. Odell. The Negro in California before 1890. Stockton, 1945. Thesis (M.A.)—College of the Pacific.

17185. Thurman, Sue Bailey. Pioneers of Negro origin in California. S.F., Acme pub. co. [1952] 70 p. illus., ports.

17186. Tibbitts, Grace Cilley. Rivers of California ... S.F., Colonial dames of Am. in Calif., 1938. 35 p. front. (map)

17187. Tinkham, George Henry. California men and events; time, 1769–1890... Stockton, Record pub. co., 1915. 330 p. illus., ports.

17188. —— The half century of California Odd Fellowship. Stockton, Record pub. co., 1906. 240 p. illus.

17189. Todd, John. The sunset land; or, The great Pacific slope. Bost., Lee and Shepard, 1870. 322 p.

17190. Torchiana, Henry Albert Willem van Coenen. California gringos. S.F., P. Elder and co., 1930. 281 p. illus.

17191. Torrens y Nicolau, Francisco. Bosquejo histórico del insigne Franciscano, V.P.F. Junípero Serra, fundador y apostol de la California septentrional. Felanitx, B. Reus, 1913. 227 p. pl., ports.

17192. Travers, James Wadsworth. California; romance of clipper ships and gold rush days. L.A., Wetzel [1950] 309 p. illus., ports., facsims.

17193. Trény. La Californie dévoilée; ou, Vérités irrécusables appuyés sur de nombreux témoignages sur cette partie du globe. 2d ed. Paris, 1850. 60 p. illus.

17194. Truman, Benjamin Cummings. Tourists' illustrated guide to the celebrated summer and winter resorts of California, adjacent to and upon the lines of the Central and Southern Pacific railroads... S.F., H.S. Crocker & co., 1883. 256 p. illus., map.

17195. Turner, Rose Andree. Palou—Noticias de la Nueva California: a translation of a part of the work, with historical introduction and critical notes. [Berkeley] 1923. 154 l. Thesis (M.A.)—Univ. of Calif., 1923.

17196. Turner, Ruth Elizabeth. Palou—Noticias de la Nueva California: a translation of a part of the work, with historical introduction and critical notes. [Berkeley] 1923. 140 l. Thesis (M.A.)—Univ. of Calif., 1923.

17197. United daughters of the Confederacy. California division. Year book, minutes of annual convention. [1901–] Organized October 1901.

17198. U.S. Bureau of land management. Patents insured pursuant to Spanish and Mexican land grants in the state of California. 1957. Microfilm.

    CChiS

17199. —— **Bureau of public roads.** Report of a study of the California highway system by the United States Bureau of public roads to the California highway commission and Highway engineer... [Wash., D.C.?] 1920. 277 p. illus., maps, charts.

17200. —— —— A report of traffic on state highways and county roads in California, 1922... Sacramento, State print. off., 1924. 147 p. tables, diagrs., charts.

17201. —— **Commission for settling private land claims in California.** Before the U.S. Commissioners for ascertaining private land claims etc. Case no. 609. Joseph S. Alemany, petitioner. Lands of the Catholic church. Opinion of the board confirming the claim, delivered by Commissioner Alpheus Felch, on December 18th, 1855. [S.F.] O'Meara & Painter, city print. [1855] 22 p. CU-B

17202. —— **Federal trade commission.** Report ...on the Pacific coast petroleum industry. Wash., Govt. print. off., 1921–1922. Pt. I, Production, ownership, and profits. Pt. II, Prices and competitive conditions.

17203. —— **Land commissioners for California.** Organization, acts and regulations of the U.S. Land commissioners for California, with the opinions of Commissioners Hall and Wilson on the regulation to allow adverse claimants to intervene in the original cases; and Commissioner Thornton's opinion, dissenting from that regulation, and a list of land titles prosecuted to date. S.F., Monson, Whitton & co., print., 1852. 43 p.
C CSfCW CSmH CU-B

17204. —— **President, 1849–1850 (Taylor)** ...California and New Mexico. Message from the President of the United States, transmitting information in answer to a resolution of the House of the 31st of December, 1849, on the subject of California and New Mexico. [Wash., 1850] 976 p. 7 maps (6 fold.) (31st Cong., 1st sess. House. Ex. doc. no. 17)

17205. —— **Resettlement administration.** Location and character of Indian lands in California. Prepared by Jesse Garcia, Philip J. Webster and staff. Wash., D.C., U.S. Dept. of agric., 1937. 164 p. illus. Mimeo.

17206. —— **War department. The Chief of staff.** Final report. Japanese evacuation from the west coast, 1942–1943. U.S. Army, Western defense command and 4th army, 1943.

17207. —— **War relocation authority.** Impounded people, Japanese Americans in the relocation centers. Wash., D.C., Govt. print. off. [1946] 239 p. "Prepared by E. H. Spicer, head, Community analysis section, and other members of the section."—p. 1.

17208. —— **Work projects administration. California.** ...Biographies of California authors and indexes of California literature...Editor, Edgar Joseph Hinkel. Pub. by the Alameda county library, Oakland, California, as a report of official project no. 65–1–08–2356 conducted under the auspices of the Work projects administration. Oakland, 1942. 2 v. Mimeo.

17209. Upham, Charles Wentworth. Life, explorations and public services of John Charles Fremont. Bost., Ticknor and Fields, 1856. 356 p. illus., port.

17210. Van Court, De Witt C. The making of champions in California. L.A., Premier print co. [1926] 160 p. illus., ports.

17211. Vancouver, George. A voyage of discovery to the North Pacific ocean and round the world... in the years 1790, 1791, 1792, 1793, 1794, and 1795... London, Print. for G. G. & J. Robinson & J. Edwards, 1798. 3 v. and atlas. illus., maps. Other editions: London, 1801, 6 v.; Paris, 1800, 3 v. and atlas; Paris, 1801–02, 6 v.

17212. Van Nostrand, Jeanne (Skinner) and Coulter, Edith Margaret. California pictorial; a history in contemporary pictures, 1786 to 1859... Berkeley, Univ. of Calif. press, 1948. 159 p. 69 pl. (Chronicles of Calif.)

17213. Van Noy interstate co., pub. Wonderful California. [Chicago, C.T. & co., n.d.] 80 pl.

17214. Vischer, Edward. Vischer's pictorial of California: landscape, trees and forest scenes...grand features of California scenery, life, traffic and customs. In five series of twelve numbers each, with a supplement, and contributions from reliable sources. S.F., J. Winterburn & co., 1870. 2 v. "The photographic reproductions of the superb drawings made by this talented artist, between 1858 and 1867, form the contents of the first volume. The second volume contains the descriptive text."—Cowan.

17215. Voorsanger, A. W. Western Jewry: an account of the achievement of the Jews and Judaism in California, including eulogies and biographies. The Jews in California by Martin A. Meyer. S.F., Emanu-El, 1916. 245 p. illus., ports.

17216. Wagner, Henry Raup. Juan Rodríguez Cabrillo, discoverer of the coast of California. S.F., Calif. hist. soc., 1941. 95 p. (Calif. hist. soc. Special pub. no. 17) 750 copies printed by Lawton Kennedy.

17217. —— Spanish voyages to the northwest coast of America in the sixteenth century... S.F., Calif. hist. soc., 1929. (Calif. hist. soc. Special pub. no. 4) 571 p. illus., maps.

17218. Ware, E. B. History of the Disciples of Christ in California... Healdsburg, 1916. 322 p. illus., ports.

17219. Warren, F. K., ed. California illustrated... Bost., De Wolfe, Fiske & co. [c1892] 142 p. illus.

17220. Watson, Douglas Sloane, ed. California in the fifties; fifty views of cities and mining towns in California and the West, originally drawn on stone by Küchel & Dresel and other early San Francisco lithographers. Introd. & explanatory text by Douglas S. Watson. S.F., John Howell, 1936. [113] p. 50 pl.

17221. Wecter, Dixon. Literary lodestone; one hundred years of California writing. Stanford, 1950. 31 p. illus.

17222. Weed, Joseph. A view of California as it is ...With a description of each county in California... S.F., Bynon & Wright, 1874. 192 p.

17223. Weik, Johann. Californien wie es ist; oder, Handbuch von Californien, mit besonderer berücksichtigung für auswanderer... Phila. und Leipzig, E. Schäfer, 1849. 107 p. CLSM

17224. Weintraub, Hyman. The I.W.W. in California: 1905–1931. [L.A., 1947] Typew. Thesis (M.A.)— U.C.L.A., 1947.

17225. Wells, Harry Laurenz. California names; over two thousand five hundred place names, individual names, words and phrases in common use in the Golden state, spelled, pronounced, defined and explained. L.A., Kellaway–Ide–Jones co., c1934. 94 p. map.

17226. Werth, John J. A dissertation on the resources and policy of California: mineral, agricultural and commercial, including a plan for the disposal of the mineral lands... Benicia, St. Clair & Pinkham, 1851. 87 p. C CHi CSmH CU-B CtY NN

17227. Weston, Charis (Wilson) California and the west, by Charis Wilson Weston and Edward Weston; a U.S. camera book with ninety-six photographs. N.Y., Duell, Sloan and Pearce [c1940] 127 p. illus., map, 96 pl. on 48 l.

17228. Wheeler, Osgood Church. The story of early Baptist history in California... [n.p., 1889] 40 p. port.

17229. Whicher, John. Extinct masonic lodges of California... [n.p.] pub. by order of the Grand master, 1933. 67 p.

17230. White, Michael Claringbud. California all the way back to 1828. Written by Thomas Savage for the Bancroft library, 1877. Introd. and notes by Glen Dawson. Illus. by Clarence Ellsworth. L.A., Dawson, 1956. 93 p. illus., port., map. (Early Calif. travels ser., 32) 300 copies printed by Westernlore press.

17231. White, Stewart Edward. Old California in picture and story; illustrated in color and black and white from contemporary prints. Garden City, N.Y., Doubleday, 1937. 122 p. illus.

17232. Whiting, J. S. Forts of the state of California, by J. S. Whiting and Richard J. Whiting. Seattle, Authors, 1960. 90 p. illus., maps.

17233. Whitsell, Leon O. One hundred years of Freemasonry in California. [S.F., Grand lodge, Free and accepted masons in California, c1950] 4 v.

17234. Who is who in California, 1958. L.A., John M. Moore, pub. and ed. [c1958] 829 p.

17235. Who's who among the women of California... Louis S. Lyons, ed., Josephine Wilson, acting ed. S.F., Security pub. co., c1922. 612 p. illus.

17236. Who's who in California; a biographical directory; being a history of California; ed. by J. B. Detwiler. 1928/29. S.F., c1929.

17237. Who's who in California, 1939/40. [L.A.] Who's who pub. co. [1939?] 224 p.

17238. Who's who in California, a biographical reference work of notable living men and women of California. v.1, 1942/43. L.A., Who's who pub. co., c1941. 1026 p.

17239. Who's who in California, 1955/56— L.A., Who's who hist. soc. 1955/56 ed. and pub. by Alice Catt Armstrong.

17240. Who's who in music in California. L.A., Pac. coast musician, 1920. 151 p. ports.

17241. Who's who in the west; a biographical dictionary of noteworthy men and women of the Pacific coast and the western states, v.1, 1949– Chicago, Marquis co., c1949–

17242. Who's who on the Pacific coast. A biographical dictionary of leading men and women of the Pacific coast states... v.1, 1947– Chicago, Marquis, 1947– v.1, pub. by Larkin, Roosevelt & Larkin, ltd.

17243. Wicher, Edward Arthur. The Presbyterian church in California, 1849–1927. N.Y., Frederick H. Hitchcock, Grafton press, 1927. 360 p. illus., ports.

17244. Wickson, Edward James. Rural California. N.Y., Macmillan, 1923. 399 p. illus., maps.

17245. Willard, Emma (Hart) Last leaves of American history: comprising histories of the Mexican war and California. N.Y., Putnam; London, Putnam's Am. agency, 1849. 230 p. front. (fold. map)

17246. Willey, Samuel Hopkins. Thirty years in California; a contribution to the history of the state from 1849 to 1879. S.F., A.L. Bancroft & co., 1879. 76 p.

17247. —— The transition period of California, from a province of Mexico in 1846 to a state of the American union in 1850. S.F., Whitaker and Ray co., 1901. 160 p.

17248. [Williston, H. C.] California characters, and mining scenes and sketches. By Whittlestick [pseud.] S.F., Bonestell & Williston, Wide west off., 1855. 24 p. illus.   C CHi CSf CSmH

17249. Wilson, Maud Eunice. Federal exploration in California, 1841–1855. [Berkeley, 1917] Thesis (M.A.)—Univ. of Calif., 1917.

17250. Wilson, Nichols Field. California business roll of honor. A salute for achievement to 711 California concerns who have served the public for half a century or more. [Buena Park] Ghost town news, c1943. 160 p. Supplement to *Ghost town news*, v.2, no. 10, April 1943.

17251. Wiltsee, Ernest Abram. The truth about Frémont; an inquiry... S.F., J.H. Nash, 1936. 54 p. front. (facsim.)

17252. Wimmel, Heinrich. Californien, sein minenbergbau, seine hülfsquellen und seine socialen verhältnisse, nach den Englischen frei bearbeitet. Cassel, Trömner & Dietrich, 1867. 200 p.   CHi

17253. Winkley, John W. The Methodist pioneers of California... Albany, Author, 1947. 41 p. illus.

17254. Winther, Oscar Osburn. Express and stagecoach days in California, from the gold rush to the civil war. Stanford, 1936. 197 p. illus., map (on lining papers), facsims.

17255. —— Via western express & stagecoach. Stanford [1945] 158 p. illus., ports., maps (on lining papers), facsims.

17256. Wood, Richard Coke. The California story, its history, problems, and government, by Richard Coke Wood and Leon George Bush. S.F., Fearon, 1957. 415 p. illus.

17257. Woods, James. Recollections of pioneer work in California... S.F., J. Winterburn & co., 1878. 260 p. "The writer was one of three ministers which formed the first Presbytery (O.S.) in California." Pref.

17258. Woods, James L. California pioneer decade of 1849; the Presbyterian church...Including Recollections of pioneer work in California by James Woods... combined with Annals and memories of pioneer times by James L. Woods, his son. S.F., Hansen co., press, c1922. 181 p.

17259. Wright, Benjamin Cooper. Banking in California: 1849–1910. S.F., H.S. Crocker co., 1910. 201 p. illus.

17260. —— The west the best, and California the best of the west... the business life of the golden state. S.F., A. Carlisle & co., 1913. 221 p.

17261. Yale, Charles G. List of working mines on the Pacific coast. S.F., Geo. Spaulding & co., 1882. 100 p.

COLLECTIONS

In this section, subject collections of pamphlets, maps, and photographs not individually listed, of local indexes, of old telephone directories, etc., are listed under "California Statewide" and the names of individual counties. A subject index follows the listing.

California Statewide

C–1. Agriculture and agricultural machinery: F. Hal Higgins collection, 175 vertical file drawers of fugitive material. CU-A

C–2. Automobile club of Southern California: History, 1900–50 (ms.); *Tour books*, 1908–50; photographs used in *Touring topics* and *Westways*, 1927–60. CLAC

C–3. Electric & steam railroads, bus, ferry & steamboat transportation in Napa valley & North bay: scrapbook of local newspaper clippings. CNF

C–4. Indian languages: collection of John Peabody Harrington. CSdS

C–5. Railroads: books, pamphlets, documents, decisions, speeches on Pacific railroads, including letters and pamphlets by John T. Doyle, Charles F. Adams, A. A. Cohen, C. P. Huntington, Leland Stanford, and Adolph Sutro. CSfCW

C–6. Railroads, San Francisco, Vallejo and Napa valley: San Francisco, Napa & Calistoga railroad; Northern electric railroad; San Francisco, Vallejo & Napa valley electric railroad; Napa valley electric lines. CNF

C–7. San Joaquin valley index: chiefly periodical articles not elsewhere indexed, relating to the seven counties of the San Joaquin valley south of Stanislaus county. CFS

Telephone directories. *Current collections of California telephone directories are found in many of the large city and university libraries. Public libraries usually hold current telephone directories of their own localities. These current collections are therefore not listed. Historical collections, however, are listed here under California or under the respective counties.*

C–8. Telephone directories: California, 1896–98. CHi has March 1896, March 1898.

C–9. Telephone directories: Fresno, Madera, Mariposa and Merced counties, 1905–to date.

CFS has 1905, 1916, 1923, 1955– (every 5th year after 1955) CL has 1935–50, 1952–54, 1956–to date.

C–10. Telephone directories: Pacific states, 1899. CHi CMary

C–11. Telephone directories: Sacramento, Amador, Butte, El Dorado, Nevada, Placer, Solano, Sutter, Yolo and Yuba counties, 1921–23. CHi has Nov., 1921, May 1923.

C–12. Telephone directories: San Francisco, Oakland, Alameda, Berkeley and counties of Alameda, Marin, San Mateo, 1907–08. CHi has Dec. 1907, May 1908.

C–13. Water problems of Southern California: over 1600 government documents, reports, etc. CCH

Alameda county

C–14. Alameda city: subject card index, made by Works progress administration workers, 1939. CAla

C–15. Alameda city newspapers (*Alameda encinal, Argus* and *Times-star*) index, 1869–1916. CAla

C–16. Oakland local history: subject card index, 1932–to date. CO

C–17. Telephone directories: Alameda and Contra Costa counties, 1900–06. CU-B

C–18. Telephone directories: Berkeley, 1904. CU-B

Fresno county

C–19. *Fresno bee*: clippings relating to Fresno state college and subject card index 1950–to date. CFS

Kern county

C–20. *Bakersfield Californian*, subject card index to local material, 1936–to date. CBaK

Los Angeles county

C–21. Claremont historical data, 1884–1938: scrapbooks of clippings, photographs. Also subject and name index. CCH

C–22. Los Angeles (city): water and electrical power development and distribution. CL CL-MR

C–23. Los Angeles county flood of 1938: scrapbooks of newspaper clippings and photographs. 13 v. CCH

C–24. Los Angeles map index: chronological listing of maps of Los Angeles (city and county). Holdings include photostats of early surveys such as Ord, 1849. CL

C–25. *Los Angeles star*: subject card index. CLU

C–26. *Los Angeles times*: subject card index 1881–1945. CLU

C–27. Majestic theater programs, 1908–11. CHi has 1908–09, 1916. CU-B has 1911.

C–28. Municipal government of Los Angeles: history with biographical data. CL CL-MR

C–29. Music, drama, dance events, including Los Angeles symphony orchestra, Los Angeles philharmonic orchestra, the People's orchestra, and Janssen symphony of Los Angeles and Los Angeles civic light opera: scrapbooks. CL CSd

C–30. Telephone directories: Alhambra, May 1909. CLU

C–31. Telephone directories: Los Angeles (city), 1882. CL CLU

C–32. Telephone directories: Los Angeles county, 1905–46.
CL has 1922, 1926–37, 1939–46. CLU has Apr., Sept. 1906. CSmH has Oct. 1905.

C–33. Telephone directories: Pasadena, South Pasadena, Lamanda Park, Altadena, California, June 1924. CHi

C–34. Theater programs: Los Angeles and Pasadena, 1857–to date.

C–35. World War II bond drives: Mills collection of materials. CCH

Mariposa county

C–36. Mariposa estate: papers relating to, 1863–73.
CSfCW

Monterey county

C–37. Telephone directories: Monterey and San Benito counties, Apr. 1914, Sept. 1930. CHi

C–38. Theater programs: the Wanderers, Salinas, California 1916/17 to 1928/29. C

Sacramento county

C–39. *Sacramento bee:* subject card index, 1912–37.
CS

C–40. Sacramento scenes: subject index on cards to all material in Sacramento picture file. CS

C–41. *Sacramento union:* subject card index, 1905–11. CS

San Bernardino county

C–42. Telephone directories: Redlands, 1904–
CRedl has 1904, 1906–16, 1927, 1929–32, 1937–to date.

San Diego county

C–43. *San Diego herald* (weekly): subject index, 1851–60. CSd

C–44. *San Diego union & daily bee:* subject index, v.1, March 20, 1871–to date. CSd

C–45. Telephone directories: San Diego county, 1887–
CLU has 1891. CSd has 1887, 1906, 1913, 1915, 1917, 1921, 1930– to date.

San Francisco county

C–46. Ballet, opera, play, artist, lecturer, vaudeville and variety shows: programs, 1850's to 1940's
CHi CU-B

C–47. Earthquake and fire, 1906.
C CHi CSf CSfCW CSfMI CU-B
C–48. Golden Gate international exposition, 1939–40.
CAla CHi CO CRcS CSf CSfSt CSmH CU-B

C–49. Menus: early San Francisco hotels and restaurants, chiefly 1850's. CU-B

C–50. Panama-Pacific international exposition, 1915.
C CAla CHi CLO CLU CO CRedl CSf CSfMI CSfP CSmH CU-B

C–51. Pious fund of the Californias: books, pamphlets, documents, 1833–1906.
C-S CHi CLgA CSfCW CStclU CU-B TxU

C–52. Telephone directories: San Francisco, 1897–1907.
C has Nov. 1897. CHi has 1900, 1902–07.

San Joaquin county

C–53. *San Joaquin republican:* subject card index, 1851–1854. CSto

C–54. Stockton: rainfall and floods, WPA manuscript materials, 1850–91. CSto

C–55. *Stockton record:* subject card index, 1946–to date. CSto

C–56. *Stockton times:* subject card index, 1850.
CSto

C–57. Stockton theaters: WPA manuscript materials, 1850–92. CSto

San Luis Obispo county

C–58. Hearst family and its properties at San Simeon. CSlu

Santa Clara county

C–59. Telephone directories: Santa Clara county and Redwood city, San Mateo county, 1903–21.
CHi has Jan. 1903, Oct. 1914, June 1915, Feb. 1916, Sept. 1918, Sept. 1921.

Tulare county

C–60. Stewart papers: correspondence of Col. George William Stewart and other materials relating to Sequoia national park and the military history of Tulare county. CViCL

SUBJECT INDEX TO COLLECTIONS

BIBLIOGRAPHICAL REFERENCES

Bepler, Doris West. Descriptive catalogue of materials for western history of California magazines, 1854–1890... [Berkeley, 1920] 299 l. Thesis (M.A.)—Univ. of Calif., May, 1920. "1029 items from *The Pioneer, Hutchings' California illustrated magazine, Overland monthly, Hesperian, Californian,* and *Golden Era,*" arranged by authors with subject index.

Bolton, Herbert Eugene. Guide to materials for the history of the United States in the principal archives of Mexico... Wash., D.C., Carnegie inst. of Wash., 1913. 553 p.

California. Dept. of natural resources. Div. of mines. ...Consolidated index of publications of the Division of mines and predecessor, State mining bureau, 1880–1943 inclusive. 1945. 872 p. (*Its* Bul. 131) An invaluable key to the history of mining counties, towns, and individual mines.

—— **University.** Catalogue, University of California press publications, 1893–1943. Berkeley, Univ. of Calif. press, 1944. 258 p. Contains serial publications of particular interest: Anthropological records, Publications in American archaeology and ethnology, and Publications in history.

—— —— Catalogue. University press publications. Berkeley and L.A., Univ. of Calif. press, 1948. 32 p. Contains books in print and all serial publications since 1943; kept up-to-date by annual publication *Books in print.*

—— —— **Bancroft library.** Catalog of printed books. Bost., G.K. Hall, 1964. 22 v.

—— —— —— A guide to the manuscript collections of the Bancroft library, ed. by Dale L. Morgan and George P. Hammond. Berkeley, Pub. for the Bancroft lib. by the Univ. of Calif. press, 1963– v.1: Pacific and western manuscripts (except California)

—— —— —— Index to printed maps. Bost., G.K. Hall, 1964. 521 p.

—— —— **Library.** List of printed maps of California. Comp. by J. C. Rowell. Berkeley, 1887. 33 p. (*Its* Lib. bul. no. 9)

—— —— **Reference division.** A union list of selected directories in the San Francisco bay region. Comp. by Carolyn L. Hale and Mary H. Lathe... Berkeley, 1942. 26 p. (*Its* Lib. bul. no. 19)

—— —— **Los Angeles.** Guide to special collections in the library... L.A., 1958. 76, [10] p. (*Its* Occasional paper no. 7)

California historical society. Index to California historical society quarterly. Volume one to forty, 1922–1961. S.F., 1965. 483 p.

California library association. 6th district. A union list of local documents in libraries of southern California, comp. under the direction of the Local documents committee. [L.A.] 1935. 166 l. (*Its* Pub., no. 1)

—— —— A union list of newspapers in offices of publishers and in libraries of southern California, comp. under the direction of the Newspaper section of the Coordinating committee for the union list of serials in the libraries of southern California. [L.A.] 1936. 201 l. (*Its* Pub., no. 2)

—— **Regional resources coordinating committee.** Finding list of special collections and special subject strengths of California libraries. Berkeley, 1956. 43 l.

California state publications. v.1– 1945/47– Sacramento, State lib., 1947–

Chandler, Katherine. List of California periodicals issued previous to the completion of the transcontinental telegraph (August 15, 1846–October 24, 1861) S.F., 1905. 20 p. (Pub. of the Lib. assoc. of Calif., no. 7)

Chapman, Charles Edward. Catalogue of materials in the Archivo general de Indias for the history of the Pacific coast and the American southwest... Berkeley, Univ. of Calif. press, 1919. 755 p.

Cowan, Robert Ernest. A bibliography of the history of California, 1510–1930...New ed. with an introduction by Henry R. Wagner and additional notes by Robert G. Cowan. Columbus, O., Long's college bk. co., 1952. 279 p.

—— A bibliography of the Spanish press of California, 1833–1845. S.F., 1919. 31 p.

Coy, Owen Cochran. A guide to California history. Dubuque, W.C. Brown co., 1951. 87 l. illus., maps.

Delmatier, Royce D. American newspaper files in 8 California libraries, 1900–1954; a listing of metropolitan newspapers having a circulation of over 50,000. Berkeley, Regional resources coordinating committee of the Calif. lib. assoc., 1954. 47 l.

Eberstadt, Edward Emory. The William Robertson Coe collection of western Americana. New Haven, Yale univ. lib., 1952. 110 p. pl., port., facsims.

Gaer, Joseph, ed. Bibliography of California literature; fiction of the gold-rush period, drama of the gold-rush period, poetry of the gold-rush period. [n.p., 1935] 123 l. illus. Mimeo. (Calif. literary research project. Monograph 8: Gc-d)

—— ...Bibliography of California literature, pre-gold rush period. [n.p., 1935] 69 l. Mimeo. (Calif. literary research project. Monograph 7: G-a)

Giffen, Helen (Smith) California mining town newspapers, 1850–1880; a bibliography. Van Nuys, J.E. Reynolds, 1954. 102 p. facsims.

Goodman, John Bartlett, III. An annotated bibliography of California county histories; the first one hundred-eleven years, 1855–1966, with intro., and the first California county history. L.A. [Priv. print.] 1966. 2 v.

Gould, Theodore F. The history of printing and publishing in California, 1833–1900; an annotated bibliography. (Calif. librarian, v.27, no. 2, April 1966, p. 97–106)

Greenwood, Robert, ed. California imprints, 1833–1862, a bibliography. Comp. by Seiko June Suzuki & Marjorie Pulliam and the Historical records survey. Los Gatos, Talisman press, 1961. 524 p.

Groves, Esther P. A checklist of California imprints for the years 1863 and 1864, with an historical introduction. Wash., D.C., 1960. 147 l. Thesis (M.S.)—Catholic univ. of America, 1960.

Hager, Anna Marie. The Historical society of southern California bibliography of all published works, 1884–1957, containing concise abstracts of all articles and an index by author and title. Comp. by Anna Marie Hager and Everett Gordon Hager. L.A., Hist. soc. of So. Calif., 1958. 183 p. (Hist. soc. of So. Calif. Special bk. pub. no. 2)

—— The Historical society of southern California topical index of all published works, 1884–1956 in the annual publications from 1884 through 1934, and the Quarterly publications from 1935 through 1957. L.A., Hist. soc. of So. Calif., 1959. 305 p. (Hist. soc. of So. Calif. Special bk. pub. no. 5)

—— Westways-Touring topics, cumulative index. 1909–1959. Comp. by Anna Marie and Everett Gordon Hager. [L.A.] Automobile club of So. Calif. [1961] 505 p.

Hanna, Phil Townsend. Libros Californianos; or, Five feet of books. Rev. and enl. by Lawrence Clark Powell. L.A., Zeitlin & Ver Brugge, 1958. 87 p.

Harding, George Laban. A census of California Spanish imprints, 1833–1845. (Calif. hist. soc. Q. v.12, no. 2, June 1933, p. 124–36)

Hasse, Adelaide Rosalia. Index of economic material in documents of the states of the United States; California 1840–1904. [Wash., D.C.] 1909. 316 p. (Carnegie inst. of Wash. Pub. no.85) Includes references under names of cities and counties.

Historical records survey. Inventory of federal archives in the states... [California, no.5. series 2–5, 8–9, 11] Oklahoma City, 1937–42. 7 v. in 13.

—— **California.** ...A checklist of California nondocumentary imprints, 1833–1855. Prepared by the Northern California historical records survey project from material furnished by the Historical records survey in all the states. S.F., 1942. 109 l. (Am. imprints inventory, no.31) Reproduced from typew. copy.

—— —— Guide to depositories of manuscript collections in the United States: California. Prepared by the Northern and Southern California historical records survey projects... L.A., So. Calif. hist. records survey, 1941. 76 l.

—— —— Guide to public vital statistics records in California...Prepared by the Northern California historical records survey, and the Southern California historical records survey... S.F., No. Calif. hist. records survey, 1941. 2 v.

—— —— Inventory of the state archives of California, Department of industrial relations, Division of immigration and housing. Prepared by the Northern California historical records survey project... S.F., No. Calif. hist. records survey, 1941. 45 l. map, diagrs.

Jensen, Esther Helen. A history of California periodical literature from 1891–1898 together with a descriptive catalogue of materials for western history in the most important magazines of the period. [Berkeley, 1923] Thesis (M.A.)—Univ. of Calif., 1923.

Kemble, Edward Cleveland. A history of California newspapers; being a contemporary chronicle of early printing and publishing of the Pacific coast; reprinted for the first time from the Sacramento daily union of December 25, 1858... Ed. with an introd. by Douglas C. McMurtrie. N.Y., Plandome press, 1927. 281 p. Another edition: Edited with a foreword by Helen Hard-ing Bretnor. Los Gatos, Talisman press, 1962. 398 p. Contains an index to newspapers and newspaper men.

Kennedy, Chester Barrett. Newspapers of the California northern mines, 1850–1860: a record of life, letters and culture. [Stanford] 1949. 641 l. Thesis (Ph.D.)—Stanford univ., 1949.

Layne, Joseph Gregg. Books of the Los Angeles district. L.A., Dawson's bk. shop, 1950. 61 p. facsims.

Norris, Thomas Wayne. A descriptive & priced catalogue of books, pamphlets, and maps relating...to the history, literature, and printing of California & the far West: formerly the collection of Thomas Wayne Norris, Livermore, California. Oakland, Holmes bk. co., 1948. 217 p. illus. Printed at Grabhorn press, S.F.

Pacific states newspaper directory, containing a carefully prepared list of all the newspapers and periodicals published in the Pacific states and territories...arranged alphabetically by town and also by counties...4th ed. S.F., Palmer & Rey, 1890. 320 p. illus.

Parish, John. California books and manuscripts in the Huntington library. [Cambridge, Harvard univ. press] 1935. 58 p.

Sacconaghi, Charles David. A checklist of California imprints for the years 1865 and 1866, with an historical introduction. Wash., D.C., 1963. 219 l. Thesis (M.S.)—Catholic univ. of America.

Smith, Olive Fay. A history of California periodical literature from 1899 to 1906; together with a descriptive catalogue of materials for western history in the most important magazines of the period. [Berkeley, 1924] Thesis (M.A.)—Univ. of Calif., 1924.

Tobin, Mary Helen. A history of California periodical literature from 1907 to 1914; together with a catalogue of materials for western history in the most important magazines of the period. [Berkeley, 1924] Thesis (M.A.)—Univ. of Calif., 1924.

U.S. Works progress administration. California. Bibliography of California fiction, poetry, drama in three volumes... project 165–03–7308, area serial 0803–1008, work project 6463, sponsored by the Alameda county library, Oakland, California prepared under the direction of Edgar J. Hinkel, editor. Oakland, 1938. 3 v.

Wagner, Henry Raup. California imprints, August 1846–June 1851. Berkeley, 1922. 97 p.

Wheat, Carl Irving. Books of the California gold rush. A centennial selection. S.F., Colt press, 1949. unp. facsims.

Yale university. Library. A catalogue of manuscripts in the collection of western Americana founded by William Robertson Coe, Yale university library. Comp. by Mary C. Withington. New Haven, Yale univ. press, 1952.

—— —— Collection of western Americana. Catalog. Bost., G. K. Hall, 1962. 4 v.

Index

Index

Numbers refer to entries, not pages.

[523]

Drobish, *Mrs.* Harry E.   1325
Drown, Emma, *see* Mott, Emma
  (Drown)
Druids, United ancient order of
  9228–29, 16823
Druids' hall soc. of the city & county
  of S.F.   9228
Drummond, Frank J.   15368
Drummond, Herbert William, jr.
  9230
Drury, Aubrey   5487, 9231, 16824
Drury, Clifford Merrill   9232, 15999
Drury, P. Shelden   9233
Drury, Wells   529, 1823, 16824
Duane, Charles P.   8164
Duarte, Andreas   2901
Duarte (city)   2938, 3226, 4555–57,
  4563
  Chamber of commerce   2901
  Directories   2725
DuBois, Constance Goddard   16240
DuBois, Philip   3900
DuBridge, Lee A.   4594
Ducau, Jean   12302
Ducommun metals & supply co.
  3794
Dudley, J. M.   14618
Due, John Fitzgerald   9234
Duffey bros.   9727
Duffus, Robert Luther   9235
Duffy, Clinton T.   4970, 5045
Duffy, Gladys (Carpenter)   4971
Duffy, Homer L.   7205
Duflot de Mofras, Eugène   16825–26
DuFour, Clarence John   6693
Duhailly, Édouard   15781
Duhaut-Cilly, Auguste, *see* Bernard
  du Hautcilly, Auguste
Duke, Donald   2902, 3795
Duke, Keith E.   6604
Duke, Vetelene (Williams)   5422
Dukesmith, Frank H.   571
Dulfer, Alex., print. & lithographic
  co.   11836
Dulin & co.   4546
Dulzura   7425
Dumas, Alexandre   9236, 15782–83
Dumke, Glenn Schroeder   15797,
  16241–42
Dunann, Charles Richard   9237
Dunbar, A. R., & co.   1851
Dunbar, Edward E.   15784
Dunbar, Horace   7699
Duncan, Blanton   3796–97
Duncan, Isadora   11379
Duncan, John   5102
Dunham, Carrigan & Hayden co.
  9238–40
Dunkerly, William J.   3085
Dunkle, John Robert   16243
Dunlap, Boutwell   16785
Dunlap, Florence McClure   9241
Dunlap, Marjorie Elise   9242
Dunlap, Nellie Story   6913
Dunn, Arthur   2022, 2399–400,
  5496, 14624, 15369, 15545
Dunn, Cecil Letts   2401
Dunn, Joseph Allan Elphinstone
  9243
Dunne, George Harold   3481
Dunne, William F.   9244
Dunning, B. F.   5115–16
Dunning, Duncan   5497
Dupetit-Thouars, Abel Aubert   5672
Dupont, Samuel Francis   9245
Duprè, Josephine A.   774
Dupuis, Victor   13958
Durán, Narciso   16462

Durant, Henry   788
Durham   1359
  Directories   1294
Durivage, John E.   8647
Durr tract   5612
Durrenberger, Robert W.   16827
Durst, David M.   15546
Durtain, Luc   9246
Duryea, Edwin, jr.   9247
Dustin, C. Mial   3798
Dusy, Frank   1943
Dutch Flat   6002, 6322
  Methodist church   6274
Dutch Flat blue gravel mining co.
  6321
Duvall, Fannie E.   16244
Duvall, Marius   5673
Dvorin, Eugene P.   4870
Dwinell, Israel Edson   823, 6694
Dwinelle, John Whipple   7013–14,
  7959–62, 11259, 12124, 14073
Dworzek family   12048
Dwyer, John T.   5982
Dwyer, Richard A.   2255
Dyas, W. G.   1481–82
Dyer, Ephraim   530
Dyke, Dorothy Jeannette   16463
Dyson, Robert   8444, 9248

E. B. Crocker art gallery, *see*
  Sacramento. Crocker art gallery
E clampus vitus   1824, 9249–50,
  12733–34, 14510, 15785–86, 15798–
  99, 16060
EPIC, *see under* Sinclair, Upton
Eagle Rock   3088
  Chamber of commerce   2903
Eagles, Fraternal order of   9251,
  14923
Eales, John Ray   3799
Earl, John O.   10225
Earle, Homer P.   4637
Earley, T.   4607
Earley, Thomas J.   5498
Earlimart Directories   2367
Early, H. Eugene   1575
Early, Raymond   15431
Earnest, Sue Wolfer   16245
Earnshaw, Teresa G.   270
East, Mr. "Skinny," *see* Fera,
  Adolph Christian
East bay cities sewage disposal
  survey Board of consulting en-
  gineers   142–43
East bay country club   144
East bay municipal utility dist.
  127, 145–50
East bay regional library committee
  151
East bay regional park dist.   152–53,
  237
East bay supporters for the southern
  crossing   154
East bay transit co.   155
East bay water co.   764
East Millsdale industrial park
  13394
East Oakland improvement assoc.
  775
East San Jose homestead assoc.
  14027
East San Mateo land co.   13441–42
Easterday (C. M.) firm   9253
Eastern Calif. museum   2240
Eastland, J. G.   9875
Eastman, Frank, & co.   896, 1251,
  1582, 6066, 7568, 8560, 9081, 9303,
  9440, 9455, 9586, 9595, 9601, 10032,

  10073, 10134, 10162, 10389, 10566,
  10634–37, 10694, 11023, 11617,
  12004, 12049, 12107, 12210, 12228,
  12534, 12614, 12685, 12926, 13684,
  14520, 14772, 14833, 15805
Eastman, William   14969
Eastman & Godfrey   6814, 6958–59,
  11324
Easton, Adeline (Mills)   9254
Easton, Ansel Ives   9254
Easton, Eldridge & co.   4743, 7497,
  9255–59, 14028–29
Easton, Wendell   1576
Eastwood, Alice   9052, 12853
Eaton, Alfred C.   13874, 14170
Eaton, Allen Hendershott   2241
Eaton, Hubert   3458
Eaton, O. V.   14218
Eaton & Edwards   13222
Eaton's restaurants   3255
Eaves, Edward Paul   9260
Eaves, Lucile   9261
Ebell soc.   776
Eberhart, Harold Hal   16246
Eberle economic service   3800
Eberly, Gordon Saul   2904
Eberstadt, Edward, & sons   5719
Ebert, Eleanor   13255
Eccleston, Robert   5103
Echo park evangelistic assoc.   4205
Echo pub. co.   2980
Eckenrod, Gervase Andrew   1982
Economical gas machine co.   9262
Economist pub. co.   400
Eddy, Elford   9263
Eddy, Harriet G.   16828
Eddy, John Mathewson   2074
Eden township
  Directories   30
Edgar, *Mrs.* W. A.   2173
Edgerly, Asa Sanborn   1880
Edgerton, Henry   6695, 8571
Edmands, William O.   15576
Edmonds, M. A.   8912
Edmunds, Charles Keyser   3423,
  7700
Edmunds, George F.   12283
Edsen, Wilna Lucie, *see* Rice,
  Wilna Lucie (Edsen)
Edson, Charles Farwell   3801
  Edson-Foulke-Yreka ditch co.
  14544
Edwards, Ben F.   777
Edwards (E. H.) co.   9264–65
Edwards, Elza Ivan   2298–300, 7366,
  16247–48
Edwards, F. E.   9863
Edwards, Gladys Brown   4774
Edwards, Hugh P.   1577
Edwards (James W.) dental depot
  9266
Edwards, Mary Haven   14057
Edwards, Philip Leget   14541–42,
  15547
Edwards, Vina Howland   9267
Edwards, W. F.   5983
Edwards, William Aloysius   7701–
  04, 16249
Edwards, William Grimm   9268
Edwards pub. co.   156, 9269, 12512
Edwards, Clarence Edgar   5874,
  9270
Eel river   1718, 10302
Eel river & Eureka railroad co.   2075
Egenhoff, Elisabeth L.   15732–33,
  16719
Eggert, Jerry   3802
Egl, Anthony   9271

Gordon, Dudley Chadwick 3851
Gordon, George 9581
Gordon, James E. 14191
Gordon (James E.) firm 9582
Gordon, Laura (De Force) 14794
Gordon, Margaret S. 16891
Gordon, Robert Matteson 4613
Gordon-Cummings, Constance
Frederica 5190–92
Gorham, George C. 8317, 9358–60,
9583
Gorham-Revere rubber co. 9584
Gorter, Wytze 16892
Goshorn, George S. 3455
Goss, Helen (Rocca) 546, 2593
Goss, Ila, see Barrett, Ila (Goss)
Goss, Mary Lathrop 7717
Gostick, Oda M. 6718
Gotchy, L. T. 2939
Goughenheim, Adelaide 9818
Goughenheim, Joey 9818
Gould & Curry silver mining co.
9585–86
Gould & Hutton 7307, 7374, 7378,
7766, 7831
Goulden & Jacobs 6278
Goulet, Mamie, see Abbott, Mamie
(Goulet)
Gourley, Gerald Douglas 3852
Government island 324–25
Gowans, Al G. 15025
Grabhorn, Edwin E. 8072
Grabhorn, Jane (Bissell) 6545,
15837
Grabhorn, Robert 8072
Grabhorn press 8087, 9587, 9766
Gracey, E. William 15838
Grady, Henry Francis 9588
Grady, John H. 8999, 12069
Graff, Hans 1998
Graham, Billy 12874
Graham, C. 9589, 11366
Graham, Donald M. 6404, 6409
Graham, Henry L. 7243
Graham, Howard Jay 9590–91
Graham, Isaac 14342
Graham (James) manufacturing co.
9592
Graham, Jerry B. 9593
Graham, John Charles 5383
Graham, Mary 9594
Graham, N. E. 16474
Graham photo co. 4614
Gramm, Walter Stanley 15839
Granada hills
Directories 2708
Grand army of the republic 798,
3853, 4687, 5832, 7006, 9595–97,
9832, 16893–94
Grand hotel 10876
Granger, Lewis 16262
Granstaff, Viola 9598
Grant, Blanche C. 16763
Grant, Joseph Donahoe 2084, 14221
Grant, Ulysses S. 16475
Grantville 7401
Graphic research service 9600
Grass Valley 6002, 6034–90, 9966
Chamber of commerce 5992, 6033,
6055–57
Church of Jesus Christ of latter-
day saints 6059
Directories 5962, 6101
Evening school 5993
First Methodist church 6060
Government 6058
Grass Valley exploration co. 6078,
6085

Grass Valley fire assoc. 6061
Grass Valley gold mining co.
6062–64
Grass Valley mining dist. 6065
Grass Valley silver mining co. 6066
Grass Valley telegraph 6052–53
Grass Valley union 5973, 5994
Graves, Alvin C. 5047
Graves, Charles S. 14547–48
Graves, Francis B. 339, 11630
Graves, Jackson Alpheus 3855–57
Graves, Samuel 9601
Gray, Blanche 2940
Gray, E. H. 1022
Gray, Elizabeth, see Potter,
Elizabeth (Gray)
Gray, Eunice T. 5592
Gray, Franklin C. 3409
Gray, Fred 14448, 15432
Gray, George D. 9602
Gray, Gertrude Mary, *Sister* 9603
Gray, Harriet (Helman) 15373
Gray, Henry M. 10014
Gray, James M. 317
Gray, John Alexander 7207
Gray, Mabel Thayer 11028
Gray, R. A. 1481
Gray, Robert D. 2830
Gray, Vallena Gifford (Woodward)
13071
Gray & DeMott 1314
Great American importing tea co.
9604
Great bear mining & developing co.
14449
Great Britain
Foreign office 3858
Great West (periodical) 1331–32,
16445
Great western financial corp. 3859
Great western power co. of Calif.
15840–41
Great western smelting & refining co.
9609
Greater America 7758
Greater L.A. citizens committee
2941
Greater north area chamber of
commerce 6570
Greater S.F. assoc. 8013, 9610
Greathead, Sarah Estelle
(Hammond) 14035
Greathouse, Ridgley 12591
Greaves, Jessie Hooper 9611
Greeley, O. F. 15343
Greely, Adolphus Washington 9612
Green, A. 9651
Green, Adam Treadwell 4615
Green, Alfred A. 10560
Green, Anna Walda 9613
Green, Buddy 799
Green, Carol, see Wilson, Carol
(Green)
Green, Earle M. 6480
Green, F. E. 7383
Green, Floride 9614
Green, Harry H. 14549
Green, John L. 13501
Green, Jonathan S. 9615
Green, Joseph L. 7718
Green, Will Semple 1454–55, 1472,
16529
Greenaway, Emerson 13794
Greenberg's (M.) sons 9616–18,
10673
Greenbie, Sydney 6279
Greene, A. Crawford 8941
Greene, Charles L. 6719

Greene, Charles Samuel 547
Greene, Clay M. 8342, 9619
Greene, Laurance 9620
Greene & Greene 4069
Greenebaum (Alfred) & co. 9621
Greenhood, Clarence David 9622
Greening, Catherine 2814
Greenleaf, Sidney 17080
Greenwade, John 6397
Greenwalt, Emmett Alwyn 7384
Greenwood, Robert 7003
Greer, Anne P. 9821
Greer, John 13324
Greer, Scott Allen 2943–44
Greeters guide of S.F. 9623
Greever, William S. 16263
Gregoire, L., & co. 8099
Gregor, Howard F. 15460
Gregory, Eugene J. 6795
Gregory (H. P.) & co. 9624
Gregory (Joseph W.) express 16167
Gregory, Platt 1588
Gregory, Thomas Jefferson 14600,
14745–46, 15536
Gregory, U. S. 1263
Gregory, Warren 9727
Grekov, B. D. 14832
Grey, Arthur Leslie 9625
Grey, William, see White, William
F.
Grider & Dow 16348
Gridley, Reuel Colt 13072
Gridley (city) 1316
Directories 1294
Griffenhagen, George 16896
Griffin, A. T. 13748
Griffin, Charles Francis 7972, 9069–
71
Griffin, Donald F. 3860
Griffin, Edna L. 4590
Griffin, George Butler 3861, 9626
Griffin, John Strother 3862, 16264
Griffin, Paul F. 13795
Griffin, William H. 9627
Griffin bros. 9628
Griffins, Evan 1667–68
Griffith, Beatrice Winston 3863
Griffith, C. W. 13158
Griffith, Enid S. 6280
Griffith, Griffith Jenkins 2945
Griffith, Howard F. 5764
Griffith, Richard 3489
Griffith observatory & planetarium,
see under Los Angeles
Griffith park 3874
Griffiths, Philip R. 9629
Griggs, Monroe Christopher 15216
Grigsby, Russell C. 15344
Grim, Fridolin 10550
Grimes, W. V. 5833
Grimshaw, Mary Alice 6149
Grisham, Kelcie C. 15025
Griswold, *Mrs.* A. H. 2176
Griswold, M. V. B. 1283
Griswold, W. N. 9630
Groeling, John Carman 2947
Grogan, Alexander B. 8534–35
Groh, R. S. 9631
Gronfier estate 11129
Gronowicz, Antoni 6216
Gross, Alexander 9632
Gross, Harold William 5700
Grosse, Guy E. 14855
Grosse, Marion A. 1911
Grossman, C. P. 4175
Grothe, Pete 14222
Gruber, F. 12906
Grugal, Donald Morris 7719

MacKay associates 14760
McKeand, G. W. 205
McKeany, Maurine 206
McKee, Irving 6040, 15012
McKee, John 14561
McKee (Samuel) & co. 10318
MacKellar, Christine Poole 2320
McKenna, Joseph 10461
McKenney, J. Wilson 7427
McKenney, L. M., & co. 17, 23, 1293,
  2043, 2615, 6530, 6532, 7995, 12972,
  13736, 14312, 14753, 14989, 15539,
  15580, 15934, 17007
McKenney directory co. 23, 6516
McKenzie, Annie 13011
McKenzie, "Boss" 14052
McKenzie, Florabel, see Brennan,
  Florabel (McKenzie)
Mackenzie, George G. 5232-33
McKenzie, John C. 14822-23
MacKenzie, Kenneth D. 14824
Mackenzie, Robert 11629
McKenzie, William 10319
Mackenzie & Harris 10320
McKeon, Owen F. 6337
McKern, Thomas Wilton 13718
Mackey, Margaret Gilbert 4199,
  17008
McKim, Paul N. 4200
McKinlay, James 13189
McKinley home for boys 4312
McKinney, Freeman S. 12302
McKinney, Mary Frances 10321
McKinney, William Clyde 2573
McKinnon, Mary Concepta, Sister
  4231
McKinstry, Elisha Williams 2388-
  89, 14048
McKisick, Lewis D. 8934
McKittrick, Myrtle Mason 5896,
  14825
MacKnight, Helen, see Doyle,
  Helen (MacKnight)
McLane, Charles Lourie 2001
McLane, Lucy Neely 5836-37
McLaren, John 10322, 11298,
  12440
McLaughlin, Roberta Evelyn
  (Holmes) 15385-86
McLean, Francis H. 11998
McLean, John Knox 726, 874
McLean, John T. 5113, 5234
McLean, Mildred 4808
McLean, Thomas David 7764
McLeod, Alexander 10323
McLeran, Thomas G. 10324-25
McMaster, John Bach 15993
Macmillan petroleum corp. 4202
McMiller, Harold Armin 10326
MacMinn, George Rupert 17009
MacMullan, C. S. 875
MacMullen, Jerry 10327, 15935
McMullen, Leon Russell 6427
McMullen, Mary Justine, Sister
  10328
McMurry, George 14042-43
McMurtrie, Douglas Crawford
  1820, 5736, 10329, 17010-11
McNab, John L. 10322
McNairn, Jack 15935
McNamar, Myrtle 14464
McNamara, J. B. 3654, 3693, 3773-
  74, 4374, 4462
McNamara, John 10325
McNamara, John J. 3654, 3693,
  3773-74, 4374, 4462
McNamee, Andrew 5529
McNary, Laura K. 17012

McNear (George P.) grain & feed
  14888
McNear, George Washington 4991
McNeel directory co. 1612, 6519,
  15175, 15179, 15182, 15591
McNeer, May Yonge 15936
McNeil, Samuel 15937
McNeil bros. 13751
McNutt, Susie L. 333
Macomber, Benjamin 10330
Macomber, Nancy 1607
Macondray & co. 8804, 10331
McOuat, H. W. 4203
MacPhail, Archibald 17013
McPhee, Douglas G. 10332-33
McPheeters, Julian C. 10334
McPherson, Aimee Semple 3634,
  4059-60, 4204-06, 4214, 4390-91,
  4447, 4521
Macpherson, Alexander W. 8537
McPherson, Clara, see Jones, Clara
  (McPherson)
McPherson, Daniel R. 1588
McPherson, Hallie Mae 10335
McPherson, William 3196-97, 7346
McPherson, William Gregg 14514
McPherson (city)
  Directories 6118
MacRae, A. W. 2424
McRae, Milton Alexander 7765
McRuer, Donald Campbell 10336
McSweeney, Thomas Denis 11656
McWilliams, Carey 578, 3806,
  10337, 16328, 17014-16
McWilliams, John 15938
Madden, Jerome 16329
Madden, Joseph Francis 6287
Maddox, Ben Moyers 15324
Maddox, C. Richard 3394
Maddux air lines 10338
Mader, George Goodrich 13813
Madera (city)
  Directories 4919, 5376
Madera canal 16490
Madera county 164, 4917-35
  Board of trade 4923
  Chamber of commerce 4925-28
  County histories 1843-44, 4917
  Government 4917, 4924
  Great register 4918
Madison, Henry 9233
Magagnos, J. A. 11253
Magazine of history 9280, 15745,
  15966
Magee, Bell Mhoon 13300
Magee, David 9728
Magee, David Bickersteth 10339-40
Magee, Dorothy 10339
Magee, T., & sons 11989
Magill, Harry Brown 5235-36
Magnolia Park
  Chamber of commerce 3404
Magruder, Genevieve (Kratka)
  2447, 16508
Mahakian, Charles 1938
Mahan, Terrance Leon 10341
Mahon, Timothy 4992
Mahon, Rapp, Thomas & co. 9054
Mahoney, David 10342, 10375
Mahood, Ruth Ione 4735
Mahr, August Carl 10343
Mahud, Tawfik Hassan 6428
Main & Winchester 10344
The Main sheet 10345
Maine, Charles 10346
Maine (state of) assoc., see State
  of Maine assoc.
Maisel, Sherman J. 10347, 15694

Major, Henry 3514
Majors, Alexander 10348
Majors, Maria de los Angeles
  14352-53
Makepeace, Le Roy McKim 15513
Malaika, Jamil 16509
Malaspina, Alessandro 5494, 5504
Malcolm, J. S. 876
Malcolm, Normal E. 13979
Malibu
  Chamber of commerce 4207
Mallett, Fowler 1608
Maloney, Alice Bay 16173
Mammoth lakes 5450, 5452
Manahan, Patrice 15815
Mandeville, Frank H. 7766
Mangold, George Benjamin 3590,
  4756, 4878, 7767, 14049
Manhattan Beach 2805
  Directories 2723, 2742
Mankind united 16820
Manley, Warren 10433
Manly, William Lewis 2321-25
Manly party 2343, 2350
Mann, F. A. 13521
Mann, Hattie M. 13089
Mann, Thomas 3507
Manning, Clarence A. 14826
Manning, James Francis 10349
Mannion, Ed 14889-90
Manoogian, Richard Jacob 2002
Mansbach (E.) & co. 10350
Mansfield, George Campbell 1289,
  1340-43
Mansfield, Nathan E. 1793
Mansfield, Richard 7733
Manson, Marsden 10351-57, 11311,
  11322, 11345, 11349, 15609
Manufacturers' assoc. of S.F. 9859,
  10358-59
Manufacturer's shoe & supply co.
  10360-61
Manufacturers' supply co. 8369
Manzanar 2230, 2241-42, 2258,
  2278-80
Manzanar commercial club 2256
Manzanita hall 13968-69
Mar Vista
  Directories 2700, 2724
Maraschi, A. 1583
Marberry, M. Marion 877, 10362
Marblehead land co. 3198
Marchant calculating machine co.
  879
Marchina, Fernando 9599
Marcosson, Isaac F. 4830
Marcrate, Arthur N. 4847
Marcum, Rosa Lee, see Baldwin,
  Rosa Lee (Marcum)
Marcus, William A. 10263
Marcuse, Felix 13814
Marcy, F. E. 7699
Marder, Luse & co. 10364-66
Mardikian, George Magar 10367
Mare Island 14678, 14709, 14713,
  14720-22, 14724
Marengo, Mary Ellen, Sister 10368
Marengo water co. 4208
Margo, Elisabeth 15941
Margo, Joan 15942
Margrave, Anne 2257
Maria Antonia, see Field, Maria
  Antonia
Maria Kip orphanage, see Kip
  (Maria) orphanage
Maricopa
  Directories 2369
Marin art & garden center 4993

Mitchell, Edward H.   583, 922, 6780,
  10479–80, 15113
Mitchell, George Dampier   14354
Mitchell, Grace Therese   13235
Mitchell, John Donald   16344
Mitchell, John Pearce   14239
Mitchell, Richard Gerald   1941
Mitchell, Samuel Augustus   15968–
  69
Mitchell, Stewart   6781
Mitchell, W. H.   6086
Mithouard, J.   15742a
Miwok Indians   5154
Mixon, *Mrs.* John L.   4227
Mizner, Addison   14687
Mizner, Lansing B.   14686, 14688
Mizony, Paul T.   7606, 7608–11
Moak, Sim   15114
Mobilized women's organizations of
  Berkeley   584
Mobley, Lawrence E.   10481
Modesto   14993, 15057–68
  Board of trade   15013
  Chamber of commerce   15014,
    15062–64
  Directories   14991
  First Methodist church   15066
  Government   15065
Modesto bank   15067
Modesto irrigation dist.   10354,
  14995, 14999, 15032, 15053
Modesto jl.   15015
Modesto news   15013, 15016–17
Modjeska, Helena   6216, 6220
Modoc county   5411–37, 14468–69
  County histories   5411, 15952–54
  Directories   5413
  Government   5431–32
  Great register   5412
Modoc county cattlemen's assoc.
  5433
Modoc county high school, *see* under
  Alturas
Modoc Indians   14539–40, 14563,
  14565–69, 17086
Modoc national forest   5419
Modoc war   14533–34, 14550, 14559,
  14562, 14573–75, 14578–79, 14582–
  84, 14590–92, 14597, 17086
Moeller, Earne W.   6163
Moerenhout, Jacques Antoine
  10484–85, 13820, 14829, 15970
Moerenhout, Jacob A., *see*
  Moerenhout, Jacques Antoine
Mohan, Hugh J.   6782
Mohr (R.) & sons   10486
Mohr Adams Plourde co.   7437
Moise (L. H.) firm   10487
Moise, Klinkner co.   10488
Moitoret, Anthony F.   212
Mojave desert   7096, 7118, 7124,
  7155, 7164, 16305
Mojave river   7095
Mokelkos Indians   13049
Mokelumne City & Woodbridge
  rail-road   13010
Mokelumne Hill   1259
Mokelumne river   146, 1441
Molander, Ruth Emilia   2466
Molera, Eusebius J.   5675
Moller, George   13524
Mollins, Margaret   16766
Molther, Francis Averill   13320
Monadnock building   10489
Moncrief, Frank M.   10490
Monday club of Oroville   1344
Moneta   2895
Money, William   4340

Monitor (newspaper)   1146, 10491–
  94, 12934
Monnette, Orra Eugene   4229–30,
  17029
Mono county   2235, 2237, 2243, 2253,
  2266, 3704–05, 5438–71
  County histories   5438–39
  Great register   5440
Monolith Portland cement co.   4231
Monotype composition co.   10495–96
Monroe, George Lynn   3406
Monroe, Henry E.   12148
Monrovia   4555–66
  Directories   2725
  First Presbyterian church   4561
  Government   4559, 4562
  Public schools   4560, 4563
Monroy, Florence Riley   10497
Monson & Valentine   1002, 6617,
  7985, 11680, 12724, 15583
Monson, Haswell & co.   7034, 7983,
  12186
Monson, Valentine & co.   9818,
  11320, 11439, 11523
Monson, Whitton & co.   7011
Montague (W. W.) & co.   10498–500
Montanya, *Mr.*   6296
Monte Sereno
  Directories   13746
Montebello   2856, 2915
  Directories   2683, 2726
Montebello Park   3257
Montebello tract   2856
Montecito   13575, 13606, 13611,
  13694, 13701
Montecito country club   16631
Monteith, John C.   7313
Monterey (city)   5484, 5594, 5601,
  5603, 5611–827, 6699, 6824, 7636,
  9080, 9210, 9615, 10624, 11031,
  14384, 14831, 16098–99
  Ayuntamiento   5743
  Chamber of commerce   5744
  Directories   5479–81, 14312
  Government   5747–49
  Library assoc.   5746
Monterey & Los Angeles (*Diocese*)
  3730, 6488
Monterey & Salinas valley R.R. co.
  5532
Monterey county   5472–844, 15742
  Chamber of commerce   5535–36
  County histories   5472–76, 14306
  Directories   17, 5478–81, 13735–36
  Government   5496, 5513, 5526,
    5533–34, 5537–42, 5555
  Great register   5477
Monterey county trust & savings bank
  5543
Monterey cypress   5631
Monterey democrat   7012
Monterey foundation   5752
Monterey history & art assoc.
  5753–54
Monterey new era   5750
Monterey oil co.   4232
Monterey Park   3368–69
  Directories   2686, 2727
Monterey peninsula country club
  5545–46
Monterey peninsula crime study
  committee   5547
Monterey peninsula herald
  5755–57
Monterey state capital committee
  5758
Montez, Lola   6034, 6038–39, 6054,
  6057, 6067, 6070, 6089–90

Montezuma school for boys   13894–
  96
Montgomery, A.   1480
Montgomery, Clifford Marvin
  16345
Montgomery, James M.   4643
Montgomery, Mary   16515
Montgomery, Zachariah   109, 923,
  10501–04
Montgomery & Brownson   5954
Montgomery block   10002, 12359
Montrose
  Directories   2728
Monumental engine co., no. 6
  11524–25
Mooar, George   10506
Mood, Fulmer   10507
Moody, Burdett   2203
Moody, Charles Amadon   3381,
  4188, 13632, 14053, 15306
Moody, Dan W.   7582
Moody, William Penn   17030
Mooney, Cornelius   8533
Mooney, Thomas J.   8565–66,
  10508–09, 10512, 12502–03
Mooney-Billings case   8796, 9106,
  9224, 9354, 9654, 9861, 9902, 10508–
  12, 10590, 10732, 12412, 12419,
  12500–01, 12603, 12609, 12623
Moore vs. Wilkinson   1315
Moore, A. R.   15256
Moore, Adam Lee   14515
Moore, Albert Alfonzo   924, 10513
Moore, Avery C.   10514
Moore, Bertram Bradt   7438, 10515
Moore, Charles C.   10187
Moore (Charles C.) & co.   10516
Moore, Charles Irwin Douglas   4233
Moore, E. B.   6391–92
Moore, E. J.   10962–63
Moore, E. S.   115–16
Moore, Edgar   2436
Moore, Ernest Carroll   3713, 4234
Moore, Ezekiel J.   12247
Moore, Frank M.   4630
Moore, Frank W.   2204
Moore, Gail Everett   1393
Moore (George P.) co.   10517
Moore, H. E.   7439
Moore, J. H.   10518, 10962–63,
  13881
Moore, John K.   10518–19
Moore, Joseph H.   12329
Moore, Marianne   4235
Moore, *Mrs.* Marion U.   6391–92
Moore, Paul W.   7072
Moore, R. C., & co.   11493
Moore, Samuel W.   12247
Moore, Thomas Morrell   10520
Moore & De Pue   13259
Moore & Laine   13810, 14626
Moore shipbuilding co.   925
Moore's Flat   5984
Moorman, Madison Berryman   15971
Moose, Loyal order of   10521
Moquelemos grant   15038
Mora, Joseph Jacinto   17031
Moraga, Gabriel   1575, 16455, 16516
Moraga, Joaquin   1531, 1575
Moraga, José Joaquin   10935
Moraga family   9350
Moraga land assoc.   1612
Moraga valley   1549, 1650
Moraign, Ervin C.   15617
Moran, Thomas   5189
Morbio, Patricia   10522
Morby, Edwin S.   11047, 16002
More, Rosemary MacDonald   15553

Murphys 1432, 1436–38, 1452
  St. Patrick church 1437
Murray, *judge* 13605
Murray, Eugene 10560
Murray, Justin 10561
Murray, Keith A. 14574
Murray, Philip 10562
Murray, Walter 13526
Murray, William H. 7968
Murray township 85, 162
Murrietta, Joaquin, *see* Murieta,
  Joaquin
Murrietta (city) 6448
Muse, Edward M. 6790
Musical center of Alameda associated
  studios 335
Musicians' union of S.F. 9613
Mussel Slough 2544, 2547, 2573,
  2578–79
Mussel Slough country, Settlers' com-
  mittee of, *see* Settlers' committee
  of the Mussel Slough country
Mutual aid & benevolent soc. of the
  employees of the S.F. gas-light co.
  10563
Muybridge, Eadweard J. 5250–51,
  10564
Myers, Jackson R. 1826
Myers, James Edward 10565
Myers, John F. 10824
Myers, Matilda 10824
Mylar, Isaac L. 7045
Mylar, Lucretia 14335
Myrick, David F. 15980
Myrick, T. S. 10566
Mysell & Rollins 8804, 12024
Mysell-Rollins bank note co. 10567

Naber, Alfs 10570
Naber, Brune 10570
Nadeau, Remi A. 4244–46, 17038
Nagel, Charles E. 6791
Naglee, Henry Morris 8030, 10125,
  10571–72, 13997
Nahl, Charles Christian 6043–48,
  15858, 15897, 15965
Nahl, Perham Wilhelm 10573
Napa (city) 5940–55
  Chamber of commerce 5945–46
  First Baptist church 5949
  Government 5947–48
  Public schools 5950, 5955
Napa city fire co. 2. 5951
Napa county 5845–955, 9769, 14863,
  16009
  Chamber of commerce 5905,
    5945–46
  County histories 5845–48, 14600,
    14602, 15952–54
  Directories 2043, 5850–53, 14605,
    14753, 15539
  Government 5901–04
  Great register 5849
Napa county abstract co. 5906
Napa county hist. soc. 5908–09
Napa county immigration assoc.
  5910
Napa ladies' seminary 5952
Napa register 5881, 5911, 5947
Napa reporter 5847, 5875, 5910,
  5954
Napa soda springs 5855, 5912
Naper, Joy H. 1789–90
Naphtaly, Friedenrich, & Ackerman
  10824
Napier, Claude E. 15018
Naples improvement co. 13527
Nares, L. A. 1861

Narjot, Ernest Etienne 15779,
  15793
Narod
  Directories 2740
Nasatir, Abraham Phineas 15970,
  17039–40
Nash, John Henry 5929, 9342,
  10684, 10689
Nash, Ray 2258
Nash, Ward B. 4725
Nast, Greenzweig y ca. 10574
Nathan, Paul D. 15529
Nathan, Dohrmann & co. 10575
Natick house 4170
National agricultural workers union
  2207
National air races 3032
National assoc. of credit men 10576
National assoc. of letter carriers
  14054–55
National assoc. of power engineers
  10577
National assoc. of stationary
  engineers 10577–78
National assoc. of stationers &
  manufacturers 10579
National bank of the Pac. 9273,
  10580–81
National bd. of fire underwriters
  587, 11109
National Catholic war council 4247
National City 7601–13, 7627
  Board of trade 7612
  Directories 7315
  First Methodist church 7608
National commission for the defense
  of democracy through education
  4646
National conference of social work
  11155
National democratic assoc. of S.F.
  10582
National education assoc. 743, 932,
  1084, 4248–50, 4306, 10583–86
National fireproofing co. 10587
National fruit growing co. 15259–60
National guard officers' assoc. of
  Calif. 10588
National home for disabled volunteer
  soldiers, Pac. branch 4251
National league of American pen
  women. Butte county branch 1290
National meter co. 10589
National Mooney-Billings committee
  9902, 10590
National Negro congress 3214
National orange show, *see* under San
  Bernardino
National printers 14184
National probation assoc. 3215,
  7780, 10591
National recreation assoc. 3216
National research council 11122
National sales managers' assoc. of
  Am. 10592
National shooting bund of the U.S.
  10593
National soc. for sanity in art 10594
National soc. of colonial dames of
  Am. 8437, 9105, 9852, 10595,
  12732, 14866, 17041
Native daughters of the golden West
  1284, 1345, 1613, 15261, 16781
Native sons of the golden West 217,
  933–34, 1285, 1345, 5548, 5648–49,
  6906, 6793–95, 7202, 8961, 10596–
  607, 13369, 13434, 13590, 14209,
  14679, 14931, 16781

Native sons' hall assoc. of Sacramento
  6792
Native sons of Vermont 10608
Natoma 6546
Natoma water & mining co. 6585
Natomas co., Sacramento 6796
Natomas co., S.F. 10609
Nature's herb co. 10610
Navlet, Charles C. 14056
Neagle, David 12593
Neal, Thomas Atwill 4252
Neale, Walter 10611
Neasham, Ernest R. 13754
Neasham, Vernon Aubrey 5549,
  5762–63, 14545
Neblo, Sandro 4253
Needles 7073, 7083, 7138
Neelly, Arthur E. 4110
Neff, J. H. 6285
Neff, Philip 2401, 3000–02, 4254–55
Negro Who's who in Calif. pub. co.
  17042
Nehrbas, H. F. 218
Neighborhood house 7793
Neil, Henry 10612
Neilson, William McCann 10613
Nelson (A. E.) co. 10614
Nelson, Eliza, *see* Fryer, Eliza
  (Nelson)
Nelson, Elmer S. 4831
Nelson, Herbert Joseph 7781
Nelson, Jack 6463
Nelson, Lawrence Emerson 4256,
  7251
Nelson, Ruth R. 7441
Nelson, Thomas, & sons 5252
Nenno, Faustina 6164
Nerac, Ellen 10615
Nerve print. co. 2075
Nesbit, Freda Jahant 13049
Nesbitt, Florence 4257
Nestor, Josephine C. 13358
Netherton & Bacon 14395
Netsuke 12883
Netz, Joseph 4258
Neuenburg, Evelyn 17043
Neuhaus, Eugen 7782, 10616–20
Neustadter bros. 10621
Neutra, Richard 1656, 4069
Nevada bank of S.F. 9020
Nevada City 6002, 6021, 6091–101
  Chamber of commerce 6098–99
  Directories 5962
  Government 6097
Nevada City daily gazette 5956,
  6082
Nevada City daily herald 6100
Nevada City morning union 6091
Nevada City nugget 6007–09
Nevada county 5956–6101, 6269,
  6313–14, 15605
  County histories 5956–57, 6256,
    15952–54
  Directories 1293, 5959–62, 6261,
    15540
  Government 6010–11
  Great register 5958
Nevada county development assoc.
  6012–13
Nevada county promotion committee
  6014
Nevada irrigation dist. 6075
Neve, Felipe de 4229, 5624
Neville, Amelia (Ransome) 10622
Neville & co. 10623
Nevin (C. W.) & co. 5461, 12574
Nevins, Allan 17044
Nevins, John A. 4259

New age 15554
New age pub. co. 2682
New Almaden 13850, 13898–953
New Chicago 13825
New Coso mining co. 2259–60
New England soc. of S.F. 9904
New Englander 8480
New Fillmore hotel 10625
New Haven, *see* Alvarado
New Hope 14993
New Idria mining & chemical co.
7020
New Idria mining co. 7001, 7015–16,
7018–19
New Jerusalem soc. of S.F. 12492
New Orleans true delta 6040
New Richmond land co. 1681
New San Francisco mag., see
Western world mag.
New Silver street kindergarten soc.
10626. *See also* Silver street
kindergarten soc.
New York hist. soc. 15981
New York Landing 1559
New York sun 250, 9950–51
New York times 10628
New York world 10629
Newberry, Homer 15019
Newcastle 6284, 6287
Newcastle building & loan assoc.
6289–92
Newcomb, Rexford 17045–46
Newcomb, Robert M. 13321
Newell, E. E., co. 10630
Newell, Gordon R. 4071, 15982–83,
17047
Newell-Murdoch co. 588, 10631–32
Newfield, Lou K. 15020
Newhall, Beaumont 4735
Newhall, G. A. 10633
Newhall, H. M. 10225
Newhall (H. M.) & co. 935, 10634–
37, 12190
Newhall, Nancy 2282, 5149, 15665
Newhall, Ruth Waldo 3217, 10638
Newhall (city) 2814
Newhall land & farming co. 3217
Newlands, Francis Griffith 10639,
12126, 12280–83, 12590, 15655
Newman, Bartell B. 10639–40,
12483
Newman, Ben Allah 3519
Newman, Benjamin 11069
Newman, T. 3218–20
Newman, William J. 11069
Newman (city) 14994, 15021
Directories 14991
Newman & Levinson 10641
Newman club, Berkeley 589–92
Newmans' Richelieu cafe 10642–43
Newmark, Harris 3221–23
Newmark, Marco Ross 16347
Newmark, Maurice M. 3194
Newport (F. P.) & co. 3224
Newport bay 6182, 6193, 16404
Newport Beach 6162, 6190
Directories 6132
News & recreation print. 3886
News pub. co. 6536
Newsom, Joseph Cather 17048–49
Newsom, Samuel 17049
Newson, Jerry 799
Newspaper artists league 10644
Newton, John Marshall 15984
Newton, L. C. 13322
Newton, Lorenz Arthur 15068
Newton, W. M. 7072
Neylan, John Francis 3673

Nicholas, B. C. 2208
Nichols, C. S. 16348
Nichols, Elijah 14689
Nichols, Ward M. 10645
Nichols, William Ford, *Bp.* 5013,
10646–47, 11760
Nickerson, George S. 10302
Nicosia, Francesco M. 17050
Nida, Richard Hale 7442
Nidever, George 13636, 13698
Niehaus bros. & co. 593
Nielson, Ernest J. 1943
Nieto, A. R. 1593
Nikolitch, Milan 3225
Niles
Chamber of commerce 219
Niles-Rentschler directory co. 8001
Nimitz, Chester William 5014
Nineteenth century round table
2548
Ning Kue Kung Wul dist. assoc.
10648
Nisbet, James 7970–72
Nixon, Raymond Thomas 9450
Nixon, Robert, jr. 14594
Nixon, Robert J. 14575
Nobili, John, *Father* 14152
Noble, John Wesley 15019
Nobles, Mary Ellen (Reeves) 2607
Nobles, William M. 2607
Noe, A. C. 2151
Noe, Catalina 8607
Noe, José de Jesus 10650–51
Noe, Maguel 8607
Noe, Vincente 8607
Noe ranch assoc. 10652
Noel, Joseph 936
Noe's college of osteopathy 10653
Nolan, Edward D. 10654
Nolen, John, & associates 7783–84
Nolte, G. S. 1944
Nolton, T. J. 14576
Nome Lackee Indian reservation
15139, 15142
"Non-pareil press" 2255, 2676
Norberg, Leslie E. 13827
Nordhoff, Charles 15985, 17051
Norman, Albert E. 937
Norman, Emmett B. 3226, 4555
Norman, *Mrs.* Emmett B. 4555
Norman, Robert T. 10655
Norman, Sidney 2328
Norman-Wilcox, Gregor 3227
Norris, Frank R. 6165, 10656,
12710
Norris, Kathleen (Thompson)
5039, 10657–59
Norris, Thomas Wayne 5724, 5816,
10997, 14880, 15809
North, John G. 6489
North, John W. 6481, 6503
North Am. aviation 3910, 4261–62
North Am. investment corp. 10660
North Am. navigation co. 16141
North Am. press assoc. 4263, 10661
North Beach & Mission railroad co.
10662
North end protective league
9669
North Hollywood
Directories 2729
North Ontario, *see* Upland
North Pacific coast railroad co.
4967, 5015
North Pasadena land & water co.
4647
North Richmond 1544, 1677
North San Juan 6002, 6031

North Sacramento 6570
Northcross, Eleanor Hammack
16261
Northcutt, John Orlando 3520
Northern & central Calif. 5022,
5103, 10080, 15665–16176
Northern Calif. counties assoc.
14468–69
Northern Calif. hist. records survey
project 5, 176, 1837, 2352, 5439,
5845, 6995, 7965, 9813–15, 13150
Northern Calif. Indian assoc. 14057,
14375, 14577
Northern Calif.-Nevada council of
churches 16053
Northern Calif.-western Nevada
council of churches 9206
Northern San Joaquin county bd. of
trade 13012
Northrop corp. 3395
Northrup, William Moulton 3368–
70
Northwestern national bank 4264
Northwestern Pac. railroad 5016,
15704–05, 15986
Northwestern realty co. 5017
Norton, Edwin Clarence 3229
Norton, George 14631
Norton, Henry Brace 14058
Norton, Joshua Abraham 8203,
9225, 10139, 11221
Norton, Lewis Adelbert 15987
Norton, Richard Henry 4265
Norton, W. A. 2737, 7069
Nortonville 1559, 1597
Norwalk
Directories 2730
Norwegian-Am. hist. soc. 16683
Norwood, Thomas 15532
Nougues, J. M. 11254
Nowland, James A. 13926
Noyo harbor 5342
Noyo river apple co. 5354
Nunan, Matthew 12592
Nunan, Thomas 10663
Nurses' settlement 10664
Nut tree restaurant 14701
Nutting, Rebecca Hildreth, *see*
Woodson, Rebecca Hildreth
(Nutting)
Nutting, W. R. 4929
Nye, Stephen Girard 220

Oak Mound school for boys & young
men 5953
Oakdale 16582
Directories 14991
Union high school 15022
Oakes, Charlotte 10665
Oakeshott, Gordon B. 10666
Oakey, Alexander F. 10667
Oakhurst
Chamber of commerce 4930
Oakland 44, 47, 94, 117, 169, 221,
577, 637, 688–1197, 3808, 8445,
8482, 8768, 8985, 9276–77, 10166,
10548, 10861, 11065–68, 11895,
12415
Anthony Chabot school 1063
Board of trade 132, 221, 842, 954,
1085
Brooklyn Presbyterian church
955
California college 956–59
California college of arts & crafts
960–62
California medical college 963
Chabot observatory 742

Oxnard 15460
  Directories 15446
Oxnard courier 15474
Oyster, Mary Agnes 5770

Pacheco, Romualdo 9222, 13590
Pacheco, Tomás 108
Pacheco (city) 1551, 1605
Pacific aero club 10776
Pacific airmotive corp. 3407
Pacific & Atlantic railroad co. 14059–61
Pacific & Atlantic telegraph line 10777
Pacific & Colorado steam navigation co. 10778
Pacific art co. 10779
Pacific bank 10780–81
Pacific Baptist assoc., *see* under Baptists. California.
Pacific Bell telephone co. 10782
Pacific bone & fertilizing material co. 10783
Pacific bone coal & fertilizing co. 13325
Pacific brass foundry 10784
Pacific bridge co. 10785–86
Pacific business college 10787
Pacific churchman (periodical) 10083, 10788
Pacific clay products 4283
Pacific club 10789
Pacific coast advertising directory co. 12976
Pacific coast aggregates 10790
Pacific coast architect (periodical) 4568
Pacific coast assoc. of fire chiefs 10791–92
Pacific coast assoc. of stationary engineers 10793
Pacific coast baseball league 17066
Pacific coast blue book co. 4284
Pacific coast borax co. 4535
Pacific coast club 3594, 4116
Pacific coast electrical construction co. 10794
Pacific coast immigration assoc. 13751
Pacific coast jockey club 13325
Pacific coast land bur. 1939, 13188, 15288–89
Pacific coast law print. & pub. co. 8972
Pacific coast liberal Christian conference 10795
Pacific coast loan assoc. 10796
Pacific coast merchants' protective assoc. 233
Pacific coast musical review 10797
Pacific coast musician 17240
Pacific coast petroleum co. 13203
Pacific coast pub. co. 13471
Pacific coast railway 13163
Pacific coast soc. of obstetrics & gynecology 9288
Pacific coast stock exchange 10798
Pacific coast wood & iron 1039
Pacific commercial museum 10800
Pacific constructors, firm 14471
Pacific directory co. 2690–91, 2697, 2702, 2718, 2744, 2746, 2752, 13158, 13470, 14314, 14425
Pacific discovery (periodical) 5014
Pacific dispensary for women & children 10801
Pacific elastic sponge co. of Calif. 10802

Pacific electric railway co. 2902, 3237, 3339–40, 3735, 3758, 4285, 4485, 16242
Pacific female college 1119
Pacific finance corp. 4286–87
Pacific fire rating bur. 10803
Pacific gas & electric co. 1441, 8439, 8925, 10190, 10804–08, 15601, 16519
Pacific gas improvement co. 10809
Pacific gold & motor 5667
Pacific greyhound lines 10810
Pacific Grove 5551, 5556, 5800, 5829–44
  Chamber of commerce 5523
  Directories 5479–81
  First Methodist church 5840
  Government 5838–39
  Public library 5844
Pacific Grove museum 5833
Pacific Grove review 5833, 5839, 5841
Pacific hardware & steel co. 10811–13
Pacific Hebrew orphan asylum & home soc. 10814
Pacific hist. review 6416, 8800, 15237, 15748
Pacific homeopathic dispensary assoc. 10815
Pacific homestead assoc. of Vallejo 14726
Pacific improvement co. 5497, 5551, 5674, 12578, 13644
Pacific insurance co. 10816–17, 10882
Pacific intermountain express co. 1120–21, 1162
Pacific iron works 10818–19
Pacific kennel club 10820
Pacific laundry jl. 10821
Pacific liberal 12669
Pacific lighting co. 10822–23
Pacific lighting corp. 4288
Pacific loan assoc. 10824
Pacific logger (periodical) 15670
Pacific lumber co. 2124
Pacific mail steamship co. 10051, 10770, 10825–27, 12597
Pacific medical & surgical jl. 10144
Pacific medical & surgical jl. & western lancet 8382
Pacific Methodist college, *see* under Santa Rosa
Pacific mill & mine supply co. 4289, 10828
Pacific mill & mining co. 8466
Pacific musical soc. 10829
Pacific mutual life insurance co. 4233, 4290, 10968
Pacific mutual news 4831
Pacific national guardsman 3931
Pacific news off. 11933
Pacific novelty co. 5256, 10830–34
Pacific observatory assoc. 10835
Pacific outdoor advertising co. 4291
Pacific Palisades 3238–39
  Directories 2731
Pacific planning & research 5771, 6364
Pacific pneumatic gas co. 10836
Pacific portable construction co. 4292
Pacific Portland cement co. 10837
Pacific press 396, 418, 736, 772, 843, 1096, 1122–23, 1468, 1474–75, 1809, 1913, 4743, 5206, 5370, 5514, 5880,

5961, 6534, 7239, 7572, 15797, 15987
Pacific print. co 7477, 12576
Pacific pub. co. 997
Pacific public service co. 10838
Pacific pump & windmill co. 10839
Pacific railroad convention 10840
Pacific railroad jl. 16459
Pacific railroad soc. 9234
Pacific railway commission 8955
Pacific railway co. 4264
Pacific railway jl. 2902, 3795, 15384
Pacific rolling mill co. 10841
Pacific rowing assoc. 10842
Pacific rubber paint co. 10843
Pacific savings & homestead assoc. 10844
Pacific saw manufacturing co. 10845
Pacific school of religion, *see* under Berkeley
Pacific shipbuilding assoc. of the state of Calif. 10846
Pacific soc. of print. house craftsmen 10847
Pacific southwest acad. of political & social science 3285, 4293, 16228
Pacific-Southwest case 13236
Pacific southwest exposition, *see* under Long Beach
Pacific souvenir pub. co. 16392
Pacific states electric co. 10848–50
Pacific states savings & loan co. 10716
Pacific states savings, loan & building co. 10667, 10851
Pacific states type foundry 10852–54
Pacific steel & wire co. 10855–56
Pacific stone co. 10857
Pacific sulphur chemical co. 1633
Pacific tank & pipe co. 10858
Pacific telephone & telegraph co. 208, 10397, 10859–62
Pacific theological seminary, *see* Berkeley. Pacific school of religion
Pacific tree & vine co. 2321
Pacific type foundry 10365
Pacific typesetting foundry co. 10863
Pacific typographical soc. 10329
Pacific underwriters & bankers 10864
Pacific-union club 10865–67
Pacific wharf co. 10868
Pacific yacht club 10869, 11252
Packard, Albert 13530
Packard, J. C. 7788
Packard, Walter Eugene 2576
Packard building 3873
Packman, Ana Begue 4294
Paddy Bull mining claims 14506
Paden, Irene (Dakin) 5257, 15971
Padick, Clement 4787
Padilla, Victoria 16351
Padua Hills 3427
Pagano, Reinaldo 10870
Page, A. H. 11836
Page, Charles 10871
Page, H. F. 12622
Page, James Rathwell 4295
Page (schooner) 12705
Pagliarulo, Carol Maris 13093
Painter, J. B. 7988
Painter, Jerome B., & co. 4979, 6911, 8425, 8810, 9800, 13822, 13870

Wood, L. K. 2141
Wood, Mary Camilla (Foster) Hall 13710
Wood, Myron W. 8
Wood, Nahum Trask 7560
Wood, Raymund Francis 203, 280, 2512, 5146
Wood, Richard Coke 1451–53, 4533, 13090, 17256
Wood, Will C. 12895
Wood, Alley & co. 14603
Wood-Crane co. 12896
Woodbridge, John Marshall 12897
Woodbridge, Sally Byrne 12897
Woodbridge, Sylvester 14695–96
Woodbridge (city) 13034
  Directories 13988
Woodbury, David Oakes 2225, 7625
Woodbury business college 4534
Woodhead, Martha Burton, see
  Williamson, Martha Burton
  (Woodhead)
Woodin & Little 12898
Woodlake
  Directories 15178
Woodlake valley 15263
Woodland, John E. 1402
Woodland (city) 15550, 15555
  Chamber of commerce 15564–66
  Methodist church 15567
Woodland community development
  study 15568
Woodland daily democrat 15544, 15569–70
Woodland mail 15541, 15552
Woodman, Ruth C. 4535
Woodruff, Charles A. 12899
Woodruff, Jacqueline McCart 14697
Woodruff co. 12900
Woods, Betty Jane 16432
Woods, Daniel B. 15417–18
Woods, Henry Kingsmill 14188
Woods, James 17257–58
Woods, James L. 17258
Woodside 13282
  Directories 13267
Woodson, Rebecca Hildreth
  (Nutting) 14882
Woodson, Warren N. 15144–46
Woodville
  Directories 15184–85
Woodward, Arthur 2226, 2325, 2407, 2415, 7561, 7942, 14827, 14869
Woodward, Lois Ann 4536–39, 4899, 6453, 7562, 14499
Woodward, Robert B. 12901
Woodward, Vallena Gifford, see
  Gray, Vallena Gifford (Woodward)
Woodward & Taggart 1195
Woodward's gardens 12901–07
Woodworth mines 6087
Woody, S. A. 2447
Wooldridge, Jesse Walton 16560
Woolery, William Kirk 14698
Wooley, H. M. 351
Woolfolk, C. A. 13833
Woollacott, H. J. 4540
Woolley, G. W. 15506
Woolley, H. S. 1753
Woolley, Lell Hawley 12908
Woolleyport harbor 1753
Woolman, Arthur Erwin 15522
Woolworth (F. W.) co. 12909–10
Woon, Basil Dillon 3544, 12911
Wooster, Whitton & Montgomery 13880
Wootten, Clarence B. 1975
Worden, Willard E. 668, 12912

Work, John 16173
Work projects admin., see under
  United States
Working woman's homestead assoc. 12913
Workingmen's party of Calif. 10321, 12914
Workman, Boyle 4541
Workman, William 2920, 7540
Works, John Downey 12915
Works, Lewis R. 3103
Works progress admin., see under
  United States
Worley, A. E. T. 11443
Wormser, Emilie, see Sussman,
  Emilie (Wormser)
Worrall, print. 1153
Worrilow, William H. 12917
Worswick, George D. 14001
Wozencraft, Oliver M. 12918
Wren, A. C. 281
Wride, Rosalie Reine 3604
Wright, Agnes Elodie 5825
Wright, Benjamin Cooper 12919, 17259–60
Wright, Benjamin Franklin 5826
Wright, C. A., & co. 14952–53
Wright, Cary Thomas 12920
Wright, Correnah Wilson 14708
Wright, Doris Marion 14883
Wright, Elizabeth Cyrus 5939
Wright, Flora Alice 5827
Wright, Frank Lloyd 4069
Wright, George F. 6512–13
Wright, H. M. 10243, 12616
Wright, Helen 7626
Wright, J. G. 15232
Wright, James William Abert 16639
Wright, John A. 11173
Wright, Louis B. 4839
Wright, Lyle H. 10081, 17063
Wright, Mary Kathleen, *Sister* 12921
Wright, Selden S. 8528, 14357
Wright, Stephen A. 12880
Wright, Theodore F. 13742
Wright, William 9293
Wright, William Hammond 13881
Wright, William Lawton 7563
Wright abstract co. 13711
Wright & Potter 6088
Wrightson, Phyllis 12953
Wrigley (Wm., jr.) enterprises 4859
Writers' program 669, 4542–43, 5579–81, 6986–87, 7202, 7954, 12640, 12923–24, 13712, 16561.
  See also Federal writers' project
Wrought, Orlena (Barton) 15299
Wulzen, Albert H. 1196
Wulzen realty co. 1713
Wurm, Theodore G. 5047
Wyandotte Directories 1294
Wyatt, Roscoe D. 13382–84, 13882
Wyld, James 16174
Wyman, J. E., & son 2085
Wyman, Walter Demarquis 16175
Wyman & co. 1714
Wyndham, Horace 6089–90
Wynn, Marcia Rittenhouse 2513–14

Xántus, János 16433

Yager, L. J. F., see Iaeger, Louis
  John Frederick
Yale, Charles G. 17261
Yale, Gregory 5020–21, 5089, 8528, 9665, 9731–32, 10438, 12301, 12636, 12925–28, 13953, 14348, 14622

Yale lock manufacturing co. 11133
Yansens, Augustin, see Janssens,
  Victor Eugene August
Yarnell, Caystile & Mathes 2788
Yates, C. L. 14142
Yates & Spencer 14092
Yavno, Max 8504
Yazdanmehr, Djahanguir 7038
Ybarra, Andres 7541
Yaeger, Dorr Graves 16641
Yeates, Fred 12929
Yeatman, Walter C. 4544
Yellow cab co. 12930
Yellow jacket silver mining co. 12931
Yerba Buena, see San Francisco
Yerba Buena island 8390, 8418, 9209, 9661, 9995, 10336, 11011–12, 11450–51, 12044, 12058, 12531–32, 12608, 12619
Yerdies, Maria Lebrado 5284
Yerger, Donald Price 5955
Yeslah, M. D., *pseud.*, see Halsey,
  Mina Deane
Yettem 15224
Ygnacio valley 1552
Yick Wo 12932
Yockey, Paul Milton 282
Yokuts Indians 16498–99
Yolo county 15534–37
  Board of trade 15558, 15571
  Board of trade & immigration
    assoc. 15572
  County histories 15534–37, 15952–54, 16507
  Directories 2043, 6516, 14753, 15539–42
  Exposition commission 15545
  Government 15545
  Great register 15538
Yolo county assoc. opposed to secret
  societies 15573
Yolo farmers' inst. 15574–75
Yolo water & power co. 15576
Yorba, Bernardo 6195
Yorba (city)
  Directories 6116
Yorke, Peter Christopher, *Father* 9024, 12933–34
York's practical school, normal acad.
  & business inst. 13147
Yosemite boys' camp 5308
Yosemite lodge 5313
Yosemite national park 5187, 5249, 10352, 15062
Yosemite national park co. 5309, 12690
Yosemite natural history assoc. 5154, 15716
Yosemite nature notes (periodical) 15716
Yosemite park & Curry co. 5312–15
Yosemite valley 1448, 4925, 5147–321, 8201, 9097, 10624, 12690, 15794, 15835, 16571, 16620–21, 16641
Yosemite valley railroad 5212
Yoshioka, Ben Tsutomu 4545
You Bet 6002
Youle, William E. 16434
Young, *Mrs.* C. W. 2903
Young, Clement Calhoun 6988
Young, Hugh A. 3605
Young, John 13940–42
Young, John F. 5321
Young, John Parke 4546
Young, John Philip 7973, 12935
Young, John V. 13883